In God's Image and Likeness

Ancient and Modern Perspectives on the Book of Moses

In God's Image and Likeness

Ancient and Modern Perspectives on the Book of Moses

Jeffrey M. Bradshaw

Eborn Publishing
Salt Lake City, 2010

imageandlikeness.net

2014 13 12 11 10   5   4   3   2   1

Eborn Publishing
3601 S. Constitution Blvd, Suite B120
West Valley City, Ut. 84119-3766
http://www.ebornbooks.com/

Printed in Hong Kong

Library of Congress Cataloging-in-Publication Data

Bradshaw, Jeffrey M.

In God's Image and Likeness: Ancient and Modern Perspectives
on the Book of Moses / Jeffrey M. Bradshaw.—1st ed.

For more information, see imageandlikeness.net

Includes bibliographical references and index.

ISBN-13: 978-1-890-71863-3 (Hardbound)
ISBN-13: 978-1-890-71864-0 (Leather)

To my parents,
Mark J. and Elma S. Bradshaw

In God's Image and Likeness
Ancient and Modern Perspectives on the Book of Moses

Table of Contents

Acknowledgments

I am grateful to Bret and Cindy Eborn for enabling this book to come to publication on a very challenging schedule. Their persistence and personal support are warmly appreciated and, I hope, will also be adequately rewarded. Joanne Bolton of Bolton Associates, introduced to us by Kathy Low and John Skinner of Press Check, Inc., was a literal answer to our prayers in helping us find a printer who could satisfy our difficult requirements. Joanne and her associates at Regal Printing attended to every detail with superb professionalism. I appreciate the kindness of the following individuals, who provided helpful comments, conversations, encouragement, and tangible support at various points along the way: Millie Anderson, David H. Bailey, Richard Barker, Kevin L. Barney, Michael H. Bourne, Matthew B. Brown, S. Kent Brown, Thomas Butler, James Carroll, Delton W. and Cherrie Clark, E. Douglas Clark, James E. Faulconer, Brant Gardner, Scott Gordon, Bill Hamblin, David K. Hart, Bryce Haymond, Daryl R. and Annie Hague, Ronan James Head, Matthew K. Heiss, Rich and Laura Hoffman, Richard J. Ingebretsen, Nicoletta Isar, Kent P. Jackson, Stephane and Agnès Janda, Robin S. Jensen, Bruno and Magali Kahne, David J. Larsen, Jeff Needle, Andrei Orlov, Virgil and Jackie Parker, Donald W. Parry, Daniel C. Peterson, Assaf Pinkus, George Potter, Glenn H. Robinson, Serge Ruzer, David R. Seely, Rudi and Sylvie Sordes, Trent D. Stephens, John Tvedtnes, John W. Welch, Kent White, and Diane E. Wirth.

Margaret Barker deserves a special thanks: first, for her courageous, careful, and broadminded scholarship that paved the way for many aspects of my own study; second, for numerous insightful comments on the manuscript; and third, for her exceptionally generous and encouraging manner—in itself, paramount evidence of her sincere Christian devotion.[1]

Chris Miasnik, a cherished friend since the days we were companions in the Belgium-Brussels mission, meticulously read through several drafts of the manuscript and offered many corrections, suggestions, and questions that greatly improved the finished result. Without the generous help of Chris and his wife Angie on many fronts, this book could not have appeared. A close friend and colleague at IHMC, Paul Feltovich, likewise reviewed the entire book and spent many hours with me in delightful conversations about it. Marcel Kahne, a pioneer of the Church in Belgium whose devotion and scholarship I have long admired, also spent many hours in correction of the manuscript.

Steve Whitlock generously allowed me to incorporate the results of his previous research into the annotated bibliography, and spent many hours in helping me to expand it, as well as in sharing his views, materials, and photographs. Steve also kindly accompanied me to Oxford in order to take high-quality photographs of the *Codex Sylvester*. Kerry Shirts kindly made the impossible-to-find 1995 edition of Eugene Seaich's *Ancient Texts and Mormonism* available to me,[2] and Todd Compton likewise graciously responded to a

---

1   For those not familiar with Barker's voluminous work, a helpful introduction may be found in two of her briefer volumes: *Temple Theology* and *The Hidden Tradition of the Kingdom of God*. Kevin Christensen has provided an overview of some of the many points of contact of Barker's writings with LDS doctrine and scripture (*Paradigms*; *Temple*). Barker herself has directly discussed the plausibility of the preexilic setting of 1 Nephi (*Joseph Smith and themes relating to Melchizedek in LDS scripture*) and sources relating to Melchizedek and the priesthood named for him (*Who was Melchizedek*).

2   J. E. Seaich, *Ancient Texts 1995*.

request for a copy of his 1985 *Epoché* article on mystery symbolism in Greek recognition drama.[3] Richard Livingston granted permission for me to excerpt from a recording on Truman G. Madsen's Claremont Mormon Studies Student Association inaugural lecture on *Mormonism and Philosophy*. Anne Feltovich identified and provided helpful background information on the *loutrophoros* of Plangon, and graciously shared her expertise as we spent many happy hours together in and around Athens. Edward L. Kimball graciously commented on the question of authenticity for an anecdote about his father, Spencer W. Kimball.

I owe thanks to Edward J. Brandt, who introduced me to the spare eloquence of biblical Hebrew during a beginners course at the University of Utah Institute of Religion many years ago.

Like so many LDS students of scripture, I am deeply indebted to the pioneering work of Hugh Nibley in Pearl of Great Price and temple studies.[4] It seemed that each time I began an examination of what I thought was a remote and unexplored corner of the research terrain, I soon discovered that Nibley—like Kilroy—had already been there first. This book would be significantly slimmer had not Hugh Nibley and Associates generously permitted the liberal use of quotations from his works throughout this book.

Among the many favorite works of art appearing in this book, I am honored to have received permission to include works from several contemporary LDS painters, illustrators, and photographers who deserve thanks by name: Wulf E. Barsch, Val Brinkerhoff, Jerry Harston, Brian Kershisnik, David Lindsley, David Linn, John M. Lundquist, Michael P. Lyon, J. Kirk Richards, Liz Lemon Swindle, Valeriano Ugolini, and Jay Bryant Ward.

Bobbie Reynolds and her colleagues at the Church Intellectual Property Office deserve a special thanks for their careful review of the manuscript and their willingness to allow me to include Church-copyrighted material. Robert O. Davis, curator of the LDS Museum of Church History and Art, promptly responded to requests for help in locating illustrations and pinpointing artists. Walter Rane also generously provided help in this regard. Dr. Bruce Barker-Benfield, Senior Assistant Librarian at the Department of Special Collections at the Bodleian Library in Oxford, and Carole Menzies and Jennifer Griffiths of the Taylor Bodleian Slavonic and Modern Greek Library were exceptionally helpful in coordinating requests for difficult-to-find sources. Pat Williams was patient and persistent in helping me obtain the permission to use the numerous quotations and illustrations that originally appeared in Deseret Book publications. Joany Pinegar, Richard Holzapfel, and Kent P. Jackson patiently worked with me to obtain permission for the use of material in the table describing the time sequence of the JST Old Testament translation. Alison Coutts and Don Brugger of the Neal A. Maxwell Institute for Religious Scholarship at Brigham Young University were exceptionally cordial, efficient, and generous in the process of obtaining necessary permissions for the use of materials from their publications. Alison Correnti of the Copyright Clearance Center assisted in the process of obtaining permission to use Steven Monte's masterful translation of Victor Hugo's *Conscience*. Acknowledgments for the help and generosity of organizations, library staff, and artists who provided permission and access to the many high-quality images used in this book are given in the *Figure Credits* section below.

---

3   T. M. Compton, *Token*.
4   For an assessment of Nibley's scholarship, especially his own use of sources, see S. S. Ricks, *Sure Foundation*.

I am grateful above all for the warm support of my immediate and extended family. Sakiusa and Seru Vakalala, Sr., providentially, put us in touch with Press Check, Inc. My sister Judi Morrell and her husband John have lent their loving, patient, and wise listening ear to me since I was very small. In quiet and important ways they have helped to mold me and this book. My younger brother Scott, my first and best childhood friend, and his wife Linn have been models of devotion in their service to God and family, and in their ever-ready welcome for me and for others in need. My sister Bonnie B. Robinson, who nurtured (and patiently endured) my budding "creativity" as a child, lovingly provided tangible support and was an important guiding voice to me as a novice to publishing for LDS readers. The wholehearted consecration of her talents in service to others has blessed many lives. Jonathan D. Bradshaw, an admired and admirable example of everything an older brother should be, designed the beautiful book cover and, along with his kind and perceptive wife An, have been friends to me in the highest sense of the word. My son Samuel H. Bradshaw spent countless hours of vacation time working on the book, and was responsible for many aspects of the overall book design as well as the definition of styles and templates.[5] Samuel and I also worked together on the layout, typesetting, and indexing of the book. The project could have not been completed without his generous, patient, and highly-skilled help. My other children and their spouses (Robert W. and Camille Bradshaw, M. Elizabeth and Sakiusa Vakalala, Jr., Thomas M. Bradshaw) offered their support and encouragement, and contributed helpful perspectives and feedback. Robert, Thomas, and Samuel also worked together to produce a Web site relating to the book. My wife Kathleen lovingly accommodated the many inconveniences of the writing process and was, as always, honest and insightful in her comments and unfailing in her support.

This book is lovingly dedicated to my parents, Mark John and Elma Singleton Bradshaw, students of scripture and disciples of Christ.

---

5   Typesetting was performed on an Apple Macintosh with Adobe InDesign CS4. Set in Adobe Minion Pro.

Figure Credits

Cover and Frontispiece: Jay Bryant Ward, http://www.jbwstudios.com/. Originally commissioned for the cover of the January 2006 *Ensign* magazine. *P-1.* Liz Lemon Swindle, with the assistance of Karalyn Fugal of Repartee Gallery and Pat Williams of Deseret Book. In L. L. Swindle, *et al., Joseph Smith*, p. 44; *P-2.* From D. Macaulay, *Moments*, plate xxvi. Copyright © 1978 by David Macaulay. Reprinted by permission of Houghton Mifflin Harcourt Publishing Company. All rights reserved.

0-1. Community of Christ, with the assistance of Robert Lewis. See S. H. Faulring, *et al., Original Manuscripts*, Plate 2, p. 406b; *0-2.* Brigham Young University Religious Studies Center, with the assistance of Joany Pinegar, Richard Holzapfel, and Kent P. Jackson. Adapted from S. H. Faulring *et al., Original Manuscripts*, pp. 57-59. See also R. J. Matthews, *Plainer*, p. 96; *0-3.* Liz Lemon Swindle; *0-4, 0-5.* Tate Gallery Picture Library, with the assistance of Cressida Kocienski; *0-6.* Jay Bryant Ward, http://www.jbwstudios.com/.

1-1. © Original at the chapel of the Frederiksborg Castle, Denmark. Used by permission of the Frederiksborgmuseum, with the assistance of Erik Westengaard. Thanks also to the LDS Church Visual Resources Library, and the assistance of Carrie Snow, Nancy Sargent, and Bruce Pearson; *1-2.* The British Museum Picture Library, with the assistance of Clive Coward and Axelle Russo; *1-3.* David Linn. In *All Things*, p. 57; *1-4.* Brian Kershisnik, http://www.kershisnik.com/, with the assistance of Lori Andersen. In L. Norris, *et al., Kershisnik*, p. 87; *1-5.* The M. C. Escher Company BV, with the assistance of Margareth Verbakel; *1-6.* Figure © Jeffrey M. Bradshaw; *1-7.* Photograph IMGP2175, 26 April 2009, Stephen T. Whitlock, with special thanks to Carole Menzies and Jennifer Griffiths of the Taylor Bodleian Slavonic and Modern Greek Library. From P. P. Novickij (Novitskii), *Otkrovenie Avraama*; *1-8.* Bibliothèque Nationale de France.

2-1. EMB-Service for Publishers, Adligenswil, Switzerland, with the assistance of Franz Gisler. Detail from the Sistine Chapel fresco; *2-2.* The M. C. Escher Company BV, with the assistance of Margareth Verbakel; *2-3.* EMB-Service for Publishers, Adligenswil, Switzerland, with the assistance of Franz Gisler. Detail from the Sistine Chapel fresco; *2-4, 2-5, 2-6.* The M. C. Escher Company BV, with the assistance of Margareth Verbakel; *2-7, 2-8.* EMB-Service for Publishers, Adligenswil, Switzerland, with the assistance of Franz Gisler. Detail from the Sistine Chapel fresco.

3-1. Picture Library, The Royal Collection, with the assistance of Karen Lawson © 2007 Her Majesty Queen Elizabeth II; *3-2.* Rome, Galleria nazionale d'arte moderna e contemporanea. With the permission of the Ministero per i Beni e le Attività Culturali, and assistance from Chiara Mutti; thanks also to Studio Fotografico, with the assistance of Giuseppe Schiavinotto; *3-3.* Tate Gallery Picture Library, with the assistance of Cressida Kocienski; *3-4.* Public Domain, http://en.wikipedia.org/wiki/Image:Great_Chain_of_Being_2.png. From D. Valades, *Rhetorica*; *3-5.* Public Domain, http:// en.wikipedia.org /wiki/ Image:Ein_sof.png; *3-6.* © David Lindsley, http://www.davidlindsley.com; *3-7.* Public Domain, from A-F. Prévost, *Voïages*, vol. 8. See http://www.columbiauniversity.org/itc/mealac/pritchett/00generallinks/prevost/southasia/zadamspeakceylon.jpg; *3-8.* Duncan Baird Publishers, with the assistance of Louise Glasson. From J. R. Porter, *Guide*, p. 28; *3-9.* The Neal A. Maxwell Institute for Religious Scholarship, Brigham Young University, with the assistance of Alison Coutts and Don Brugger. From D. W. Parry, *Garden*, pp. 134-135; *3-10.* John M. Lundquist. From J. M. Lundquist, *Meeting Place*, p. 45; *3-11.* Mary Evans Picture Library, from J. B. Villalpando, *Ezechielem*.

4-1. Photograph © 2007 Museum of Fine Arts, Boston, with the assistance of Erin Schleigh. The Art Object: Thomas Cole, American (born in England), 1801-1848, *Expulsion from the Garden of Eden*, 1828, Oil on canvas, 100.96 x 138.43 cm (39 ¾ x 54 ½ in.), Gift of Martha C. Karolik for the M. and M. Karolik Collection of American Paintings, 1815-1865, 47.1188; *4-2.* The William Blake Archive, with the assistance of William Shaw. Original in The British Museum; *4-3.* Museo Nacional del Prado, with the assistance of Concha Ocampos; *4-4.* Public Domain, http://iraq.iraq.ir/cpg/displayimage.php?album=5&pos=11; *4-5.* Photography and Rights Department, The Pierpont Morgan Library and Museum, RA 2001.76. Appreciation to Wayne Schrimsher for the digital scan; *4-6.* Tate Gallery Picture Library, with the assistance of Cressida Kocienski; *4-7.* Rachel Milstein. From R. Milstein, *et al.*, *Stories*. Original in Topkapi Saray Museum Library, H. 1227: Ms. T-7, Istanbul, Turkey; *4-8.* Art Resource, Inc., with the assistance of Jennifer Belt. Original at San Niccolo al Carmine, Siena (aka Santa Maria del Carmine), Pian de' Mantellini, Siena, Italy; *4-9.* Photographic Service, Royal Museum of Fine Arts of Belgium, Brussels, with the assistance of Nadia Ben Hamou; *4-10.* Bibliothèque Nationale de France, Add. 144.a. Fol., with the assistance of Mme Zerkane and Ingrid Appert, as well as the help of Elizabeth Witchell of the Warburg Institute. From R. Green, *et al.*, *Hortus*, Vol. 1, Original fol. HD 17r. (Figure 21); see also Vol. 2, p. 31, Figures 17-18, from the Bastard Calques plate 12, tracings of the original made ca. 1840; *4-11.* British Museum Images, with the assistance of Valentina Talian; *4-12.* David Wilder, The Jewish Community of Hebron, http://www.hebron.com; *4-13.* Alain Guilleux, alain.guilleux@free.fr; *4-14.* Photograph DSC00996, 28 June 2006, © Jeffrey M. Bradshaw; *4-15.* Department of Visual Services, National Gallery of Art, Washington, DC, 2000.3.1 (PA). Appreciation to Wayne Schrimsher for the digital scan; *4-16.* EMB-Service for Publishers, Adligenswil, Switzerland, with the assistance of Franz Gisler. Detail from the Sistine Chapel fresco; *4-17.* Kirk Richards, http://www.jkirkrichards.com; *4-18.* The British Library, with the assistance of Sandra Powlette; *4-19.* Figure © Jeffrey M. Bradshaw. Compare G. A. Anderson, *Perfection*, p. 80; *4-20.* Public Domain per http://www.archive.org/details/christianantiqui02smituoft. From W. Smith, *et al.*, *Dictionary*, 2:1307. See also M. B. Brown, *Girded*, p. 137; *4-21.* The Fitzwilliam Museum, University of Cambridge, PD 29-1949. Appreciation to Wayne Schrimsher for the digital scan.

5-1. Art Resource, Inc., with the assistance of Tricia Smith. Original in the Cathedral of St. Bavon at Ghent, Belgium; *5-2.* XIR24940 Credit: St. Michael Overwhelming the Demon, 1518 (oil on canvas) by Raphael (Raffaello Sanzio of Urbino) (1483-1520) ©Louvre, Paris, France/Giraudon/The Bridgeman Art Library, with the assistance of David Savage. Nationality/copyright status: Italian/out of copyright. Original in the Musée du Louvre, Paris, France; *5-3.* Österreichische Nationalbibliothek, Vienna, Bildarchiv, E 1546-C, with the assistance of Crista Müller and Silke Pirolt; *5-4.* Public Domain, from P. Henry, *Moldavie*, 2:246, with the assistance of Imaging Services, The British Library; *5-5.* Jerry Harston, with the assistance of Pat Williams of Deseret Book. From B. K. Packer, *Mediator 1978*, p. 9; *5-6.* Art Resource, Inc., with the assistance of Tricia Smith. Original in the Basilica di Santa Maria della Salute, Venice, Italy; *5-7.* Scala Archives, with the assistance of Michael Slade. Original in the Galleria Nazionale d'Arte Antica, Rome, Italy; *5-8.* Art Resource, Inc., with the assistance of Tricia Smith. Permission also granted from the Musée d'Orsay, Paris, France; *5-9.* Public Domain, http://catholic-resources.org/Dore/Images/OT-012.jpg. From J. J. Bourasse, *et al.*, *Vulgate*; *5-10.* Art Resource, Inc., with the assistance of Tricia Smith. In L. Ouspensky, *et al.*, *Icons*, p. 198. Original in the Tretyakov Gallery, Moscow, Russia; *5-11.* Figure © Jeffrey M. Bradshaw; *5-12.* Public Domain, per http://en.wikipedia.org/wiki/Image: Daniel_Webster_and_the_Devil_argue_in_court.jpg. From S. V. Benét, *Devil*, p. 12; *5-13.* The Warburg Institute, with assistance of Elizabeth Witchell. From R. Green, *et al.*, *Hortus*, Vol. 2, p. 352, Orig. Fol. HD 215v. (Plate 124). Photograph of C. M. Engelhardt, *Hortus*, Plate IX, located in the Metropolitan Museum of Art, New York City, New York, with the assistance of Eileen Sullivan.

6-1. Art Resource, Inc., with the assistance of Tricia Smith. Original in the Church of San Francesco, Arezzo, Italy; *6-2.* Adapted from D. H. Ludlow, *Encyclopedia of Mormonism*, 2:923, with the permission of the Brigham Young University Copyright Licensing Office and with the assistance of Nick Coakley and Carl Johnson; *6-3.* Assaf Pinkus. In A. Pinkus, *Impact*, p. 167 and A. Pinkus, *Workshops*, Illustration 63. Original located at the Heiligkreuz minster in Schwäbisch Gmünd, Germany, south-east portal; *6-4.* Basilica di S. Giovanni Battista in Monza, Italy; *6-5.* Photograph DSC00183, 14 September 2009, © Jeffrey M. Bradshaw; *6-6.* http://www.frankwesleyart.com, with the assistance of Athalie Wesley, Ralph Willis, and Naomi Wray. In N. Wray, *Wesley*, p. 45; *6-7.* Kunsthistorisches Museum, Vienna, with the assistance of Florian Kugler and Christa Hummel; *6-8.* The British Library, C. 188.a.17. In W. Tyndale, *New Testament 1526*; *6-9.* Wulf E. Barsch, http://webpac.lib.utah.edu/fa/UtahArtists/artists/barsch/index.html; *6-10, 6-11.* Courtesy of The Neal A. Maxwell Institute for Religious Scholarship, Brigham Young University, with the assistance of Alison Coutts and Don Brugger. In H. W. Nibley, *Message 2005*, p. 452; *6-12.* Art Resource, Inc., with the assistance of Tricia Smith. Original in Cappella Spagnuolo, Basilica di Santa Maria Novella, Florence, Italy; *6-13.* Photograph DSC03665, 23 September 2008, © Jeffrey M. Bradshaw; *6-14.* Bayerisches Nationalmuseum. In H. W. Nibley, *Message 2005*, p. 456.

E1-1. The British Museum, with the assistance of Clive Coward and Axelle Russo; *E2-1.* National Galleries of Scotland Picture Library, with the assistance of Rachel Travers; *E8-1.* Assaf Pinkus. Original at the Heilig-Kreuz-Münster (Holy Cross Minster) in Schwäbisch Gmünd, Germany, south portal of the choir; *E12-1.* Les Éditions Gallimard, with the assistance of Geneviève Fumeron. From Antoine de Saint Exupéry, *Dessins*, p. 461; *E12-2.* Laurent de Galembert. Figure translated from L. de Galembert, *Grandeur 2001*, p. 52.; *E19-1.* Public Domain, http://en.wikipedia.org/wiki/Image:WWPhelps.gif; *E19-2.* Lebrecht Music and Arts Photo Library, with the assistance of Katharine Ryall. Additional thanks to David Betts and Stephen Connock of the RVW Society, and to Hugh Cobbe; *E19-3.* Valeriano Ugolini, http://www.ugolinifineart.com/; *E20-1, E20-2.* Val Brinkerhoff, http://cfac.byu. edu/valbrinkerhoff/signs-2/; *E20-3.* Public Domain, from A. F. Kendrick, *Textiles 1*, Frontispiece; *E24-1.* Tate Gallery Picture Library, with the assistance of Cressida Kocienski; *E25-1.* Figure © Jeffrey M. Bradshaw; *E25-2.* Photographic Services and Permissions, New York Public Library, Spencer, Pers. Ms. 46. In R. Milstein, *et al, Stories*, Plate 13; *E36-1.* Copyright Clearance Center (www.copyright. com). From L. Ouspensky, *et al., Icons*, p. 148. *E36-2.* Photograph IMG_2770, 24 May 2008, Laura E. Hoffman; *E37-1.* Herzogin Anna Amalia Bibliothek in Weimar, Germany, with the assistance of Julia Glesner; *E41-1.* The Huntington Library, with the assistance of Donna Stromberg. For a facsimile of the entire Preface, see W. Blake, *Illuminated Blake*, p. 216; W. Blake, *Illuminated*, p. 295; W. Blake, *Milton*, p. 94; *E42-1.* Tate Gallery Picture Library, with the assistance of Cressida Kocienski; *E43-1.* Public Domain, http://commons.wikimedia.org/wiki/Image:Wolfgang-amadeus-mozart_1.jpg; *E44-1.* Public Domain, http://upload.wikimedia.org/wikipedia/commons/2/2d/Miranda_-_The_Tempest_JWW.jpg; *E50-1.* Imaging Services, The British Library, with the assistance of Graham Hutt; *E53-1.* Figure © Jeffrey M. Bradshaw; *E53-2.* Biblioteca Apostolica Vaticana. From a 12th century illuminated version of the *Homilies of James of Kokkinobaphos* from Byzantium (Vat. gr. 1162, fol. 35v.). See A. Eastmond, *Narratives*, plate 14; *E53-3.* Public Domain, http://upload.wikimedia. org/wikipedia/commons/3/32/AshburnPenatuchtFolio076rMosesReceivingLaw.jpg. Bibliothèque Nationale, nouv. acq. lat., no. 2334, folio 76 recto; *E53-4.* Copyright Clearance Center (www. copyright.com). From L. Ouspensky, *et al., Icons*, p. 166. *E53-5.* Val Brinkerhoff, http://cfac.byu.edu/valbrinkerhoff/signs-2/; *E53-6.* Photograph DSC03079, 24 May 2008, © Jeffrey M. Bradshaw; *E53-7.* Photograph Untitled-e1-2884x2471, 1977, Stephen T. Whitlock. Scanned from Kodachrome slide; *E53-8.* The Morgan Pierpont Library, from the Crusaders Bible, MS M.638, f. 40r. See http://www. themorgan.org/collections/swf/exhibOnline.asp?id=278 and G. R. Murphy, *Gemstone*, p. 34. *E53-9.* G. Ronald Murphy. Thanks also to Walter Milutzki, Director of the Dioezesanmuseum Bamberg, Bamberg, Germany. From G. R. Murphy, *Gemstone (excerpt)*, p. 10. *E53-10.* Photograph DSC02379, 8 March 2008, © Jeffrey M. Bradshaw; *E53-11.* University of California Press, with the assistance of Kim Hogeland. From P. H. Jolly, *Eve and Adam*, p. 25; *E53-12, E53-13.* Photographs IMGP2167 and IMGP2179, 26 April 2009, Stephen T. Whitlock, with special thanks to Carole Menzies and Jennifer Griffiths of the Taylor Bodleian Slavonic and Modern Greek Library. From P. P. Novickij (Novitskii), *Otkrovenie Avraama*; *E53-14.* Photograph DSC00198, 14 September 2009, © Jeffrey M. Bradshaw; *E53-15.* From E. R. Goodenough, *Dura Symbolism*, Photograph of the Cycle of Ezekiel, Vol. 11, Plate XXI. © Princeton University Press. Reprinted by permission of Princeton University Press, with the assistance of Watson Wang; *E54-1.* © Jeffrey M. Bradshaw; *E54-2.* Photograph IMGP1821 by Stephen T. Whitlock. Detail of Patriarchs Window, Holy Trinity Church, Stratford-upon-Avon, England, 24 April 2009; *E55-1.* By permission of The University of Oklahoma Press, from M. Graulich, *Myths*, p. 55; *E55-2.* Dr. Sandra Noble and FAMSI, the Foundation for the Advancement of Mesoamerican Studies, Inc. Detail of image at http://www.famsi.org/research/loubat/Telleriano-Remensis/page_19r.jpg. See also E. Q. Keber, *Telleriano-Remensis*, Folio 19r (misnumbered as 13r); *E55-3.* Dover Books, from restored rendering in G. Díaz, *et al., Codex Borgia*, Plate 66; *E55-4.* John E. Clark, on behalf of the New World Archaeological Foundation. From V. G. Norman, *Izapa Part 2*, p. 202 Figure 4.13, b; *E55-5.* John E. Clark, on behalf of the New World Archaeological Foundation. From V. G. Norman, *Izapa Part 2*, p. 202 Figure 4.13, c.

B-1. Public Domain, see http://en.wikipedia.org/wiki/Image:Mandean.jpg. From the frontispiece of E. S. Drower, *Water*. Thanks to Nick Wetton, representing the publisher John Murray.

FIGURE P-1. *Go with Me to Cumorah*, 1997. Liz Lemon Swindle, 1953-

PREFACE

> I took my stand halfway
>   between awe and love;
> a yearning for Paradise
>   invited me to explore it,
> but awe at its majesty
>   restrained me from my search…
> I revered what lay hidden
>   and meditated on what was revealed…
>
> Joyfully did I embark
>   on the tale of Paradise—
> a tale that is short to read
>   but rich to explore.
> My tongue read the story's
>   outward narrative,
> while my intellect took wing
>   and soared upward in awe
> as it perceived the splendor of Paradise—
>   not indeed as it really is,
> but insofar as humanity
>   is granted to comprehend it.[1]

This book was made possible by the unexpected blessing of a yearlong "sabbatical" in France. Though the book of Genesis has long been a favorite of mine, the project became possible only because our family's move to a new time zone afforded extra early morning study time before the day's e-mail messages began to arrive from across the Atlantic.

My original thought had been to focus on the poignant Jacob-Joseph story cycle, which has long attracted me. However, as I began the project in earnest, my thoughts were continually—and at first, I admit, reluctantly—led back to the book of Moses, a revelatory expansion of the first chapters of Genesis. My reluctance stemmed from a cognizance of my ignorance. Though the sobering demeanor of this marvelous book had become beautiful to me through long acquaintance,[2] I felt I had neither the time nor the expertise required to assimilate—let alone credibly contribute to—the mountain of prophetic writings and scholarship that had already addressed the many enigmas woven deeply into the fabric of this foundational work of scripture. In short, it seemed a story far too old for a green author.[3]

Despite my early misgivings, I found tangible reassurance and ongoing direction in the intimate dialogue of prayer, and friendly encouragement in the splendid scaffolding previously assembled by the patient labors of prior exegetes, to whom I acknowledge my

---

1   Ephrem the Syrian, *Paradise*, 1:2-3, p. 78.
2   See *Endnote P-1*, p. xxvii.
3   W. Shakespeare, *Venus*, 806, p. 1714. See *Endnote P-2*, p. xxvii.

deep indebtedness.[4] Looking back, I acknowledge with grateful surprise that the major ideas came together much more quickly than I had thought possible. A few months after our return from France, I had a reasonably complete draft of the commentary in hand. The bibliography and excursus sections followed.

While fellow Latter-day Saints will have little problem comprehending my still-growing attachment to Joseph Smith's translation of the early narratives of Genesis, many of my friends and colleagues will find it mystifying that I have devoted so much time and attention to a study of what may understandably seem to be no more than a fanciful collection of worn-out fables—one more shard among the dusty discards of the almost bygone religious passage of Western culture. In that regard, it must also be admitted that the central historical claims of Mormonism—and Christianity[5] itself, for that matter—hardly appear any less fantastic to the modern mind than the stories of Adam and Eve.[6] Even in the nineteenth century, Charles Dickens[7] approved as Hannay charged the Mormons with "the absurdity of seeing visions in the age of railways"—simultaneously commending our "immense practical industry" while decrying our "pitiable superstitious delusion." His conclusion at that time is one that would be met with understanding nods by many perplexed observers of Mormonism in our day: "What the Mormons do, seems to be excellent; what they say is mostly nonsense."[8]

In contrast to the predominantly polemical bent of apologetic and scholarly literature that appeared during the first century of Mormonism, recent decades have happily witnessed hundreds of broad studies of the founding stories and scriptures of the Latter-day Saints that can be appreciated by both members and non-members of the Church alike.[9] It is regrettable that serious studies of the Joseph Smith Translation (JST) of the Bible have been relatively late in coming, explorations of its textual foundations having begun in earnest only in the last forty years with the pioneering work of Richard P. Howard and Robert J. Matthews.[10]

Now, at last, as the book of Moses—and the related book of Abraham—are beginning to receive their due in the spotlight of scholarly scrutiny, they may well prove to be among the strongest witnesses of the prophetic mission of Joseph Smith.[11] For example, noted Yale critic of secular and sacred literature Harold Bloom, who classes these two books among the "more surprising" and "neglected" works of LDS scripture,[12] is intrigued by the fact that many of their themes are "strikingly akin to ancient suggestions"[13] that essentially restate "the archaic or original Jewish religion, a Judaism that preceded even the Yahwist." While expressing "no judgment, one way or the other, upon the authenticity" of LDS scripture, he finds "enormous validity" in the way these writings "recapture... crucial elements in the archaic Jewish religion.... that had ceased to be available either to normative Judaism or to

---

4   See *Endnote P-3*, p. xxvii.

5   See *Endnote P-4*, p. xxvii.

6   See *Endnote P-5*, p. xxvii.

7   See *Endnote P-6*, p. xxviii.

8   J. Hannay, *Smith*, p. 385, cited in R. J. Dunn, *Dickens*, p. 4. A non-LDS observer similarly wrote of the Mormons in 2009: "What would you do if you met people you admired greatly, who reminded you of the best examples of your fellow believers, yet whose faith rested on what you saw as patent absurdities" (W. Lobdell, *Losing*, pp. 121-122). He goes on to concede, however: "Yet what's so strange about Mormonism compared to traditional Christianity... The details of Mormonism are fresher, but not much more strange and mythical" (*ibid.*, pp. 126, 127). See *Endnote P-7*, p. xxix.

9   For broad perspectives from LDS and non-LDS scholars on the wide influence of Joseph Smith's life and work, see J. W. Welch, *Worlds* and R. L. Neilson, *et al.*, *Reappraisals*.

10   R. P. Howard, *Restoration 1969*; R. J. Matthews, *Plainer*.

11   See *Endnote P-8*, p. xxx.

12   H. Bloom, *Names Divine*, p. 25.

13   See *Endnote 2-28*, p. 130.

PREFACE

Christianity, and that survived only in esoteric traditions unlikely to have touched [Joseph] Smith directly."[14]

Having spent more than three years in focused study of the book of Moses, I have also been astonished with the extent to which its words reverberate with the echoes of antiquity—and, no less significantly, with the deepest truths of my personal experience. Indeed, I would not merely assert that the book of Moses holds up well under close examination, but rather that, like a fractal whose self-similar patterns become more wondrous upon ever closer inspection, the brilliance of its inspiration shines most impressively under bright light and high magnification: there is glory in the details.[15]

I owe my awakening to the literary beauty of scripture to a Brigham Young University (BYU) "Reading the Scriptures" course taught by Professor Arthur Henry King, or "Brother King" as he preferred to be called in class.[16] Converted to Mormonism in Britain during his later years, Brother King was a Shakespearian scholar and professional "stylistician"—in other words, an expert in how the nuances of linguistic expression reveal to their readers, both intentionally and unintentionally, not only the literary characters but also the authors themselves. Indeed, Brother King often mentioned how it was the very style of the First Vision account that convinced him that Joseph Smith was telling the truth.[17]

Brother King believed strongly in the virtues of reading the scriptures aloud.[18] He taught the members of our class how to experiment with different approaches to reading the same verse, how to listen to the wisdom of the spoken voice, and how the varying of emphasis and pauses for breath could highlight different shades of meaning in the text. Under his direction, we sang the scriptures as if they were music.

The Prophet Joseph Smith said that scripture should be "understood precisely as it reads."[19] Likewise, Brother King taught us to read slowly, and to persist in reading until the plain sense of the words became clear to us.[20] This approach differs from the facile skimming for rapid information ingestion that is the stuff of our daily business—the great Jewish scholar Martin Buber went so far as to term the application to scripture study of the modern unreflective method "the leprosy of fluency."[21]

Once having gained confidence in our grasp of the plain sense of the words of scripture, we must still decode its pervasive imagery. Our problem in that respect is that we live on the near side of a great divide that separates us from the religious, cultural, and philosophical perspectives of the ancients.[22] The Prophet Joseph Smith was far closer to this lost world than we are—not only because of his personal involvement with the recovery and revelatory expansion of ancient religion, but also because in his time many archaic traditions were still embedded in the language and daily experience of the surrounding culture.[23] Barker describes the challenges this situation presents to contemporary students of scripture:

---

14   H. Bloom, *American Religion*, pp. 98, 99, 101. See *Endnote P-9, p. xxx.*

15   See *Endnote P-10, p. xxx.*

16   See *Endnote P-11, p. xxxi.*

17   A. H. King, *Account*, pp. 42-43, 45; A. H. King, *Joseph*. See *Endnote P-12, p. xxxi.*

18   A. H. King, *Afterword*, pp. 233-236; A. H. King, *Rhetoric*, pp. 201-204; A. H. King, *Child*, pp. 101-102; A. H. King, *Education*, pp. 240-242; cf. D. Packard, *et al.*, *Feasting*, pp. 18-20, 199-203, 209-213.

19   J. Smith, Jr., *Words*, 29 January 1843, p. 161. See *Endnote P-13, p. xxxi.*

20   A. H. King, *Afterword*, pp. 233-234; D. Packard, *et al.*, *Feasting*, pp. 8-10.

21   See *Endnote P-14, p. xxxi.*

22   C. S. Lewis, *Descriptione*; G. d. Santillana, *et al.*, *Hamlet's Mill*, p. 10. See *Endnote P-21, p. xxxv.*

23   A. H. King, *Joseph*, pp. 287-288.

FIGURE P-2. *Inflatable Cathedral, 1978*
David Macaulay, 1946-

The things of God are of deep import; and time, and experience, and careful and ponderous and solemn thoughts can only find them out.[1] In vivid contrast to Joseph Smith's statement, David Macaulay's tongue-in-cheek simulation is "intended to create a distinguished setting at a moment's notice."[2] While the concept was just a gleam in Macaulay's eye when he created this drawing, inflatable churches are now available for rent or purchase. A Web site proudly proclaims: "The attention to detail is heavenly, complete with plastic 'stained glass' windows and airbrush artwork which replicates the traditional church. Inside it has an inflatable organ, altar, pulpit, pews, candles and a gold cross. Even the doors are flanked by air-filled angels. The church can be built in two hours and disassembled in less than one… It can be set up anywhere, from your garden to Malibu Beach, it's up to you. No problem with 'high heels.'"[3]

1	J. Smith, Jr., *Teachings*, 25 March 1839, p. 137.
2	D. Macaulay, *Moments*, caption for plate xxvi.
3	*Inflatable Church.*

Like the first Christians, we still pray "Thy kingdom come. Thy will be done in earth, as it is in heaven,"[24] but many of the complex system of symbols and stories that describe the Kingdom are not longer recognized for what they are.[25]

It used to be thought that putting the code into modern English would overcome the problem, and make everything clear to people who had no roots in a Christian community. This attempt has proved misguided, since so much of the code simply will not translate into modern English… The task, then, has had to alter. The need now is not just for modern English, or modern thought forms, but for an explanation of the images and pictures in which the ideas of the Bible are expressed.[26] These are specific to one culture, that of Israel and Judaism, and until they are fully understood in their original setting, little of what is done with the writings and ideas that came from that particular setting can be understood. Once we lose touch with the meaning of biblical imagery, we lose any way into the real meaning of the Bible. This has already begun to happen and a diluted "instant" Christianity has been offered as junk food for the mass market. The resultant malnutrition, even in churches, is all too obvious.[27]

24	Matthew 6:10.
25	M. Barker, *Hidden*, p. 128.
26	See *Endnote P-15*, p. xxxii.
27	M. Barker, *Earth*, pp. 1-2.

Consistent with Barker's observations, many observers have documented a worldwide trend toward a religious mind-set that prizes emotion[28] and entertainment[29] as major staples of worship. Even when undertaken with evident sincerity, religious gatherings of this sort scarcely rise above the level of a "weekly social rite, a boost to our morale,"[30] with perhaps a few exhortations on ethics thrown in. When the Bible is consulted at all, it is too often "solely for its piety or its inspiring adventures"[31] or its admittedly "memorable illustrations and contrasts" rather than its "deep memories" of spiritual understanding.[32] All this has resulted not only in a regrettable "secularization of religious symbolic language,"[33] but also in what Prothero calls a widespread "religious amnesia" that has dangerously weakened the foundations of faith.[34] Bloom concludes that since the current "American Jesus can be described without any recourse to theology" we have become, on the whole, a post-Christian nation.[35] Similarly, Herberg characterized our national "faith in faith" as a "strange brew of devotion to religion and insouciance as to its content."[36] Little wonder that the teaching of the central doctrines of the Gospel has been a significant focus of LDS Church leadership in recent years.[37] In this connection, Elder Neal A. Maxwell once remarked: "God is giving away the spiritual secrets of the universe," and then asked: "but are we listening?"[38]

I am fully conscious of the fact that an understanding of "the doctrine of the kingdom"[39] does not come by mere "study" alone, but "also by faith"[40] as we are asked to give loving and whole-hearted expression in our lives of what we feel and believe. I concur with Elder Marion G. Romney that: "One cannot fully learn the gospel without living it."[41] Indeed, as Elder Dallin H. Oaks has said about the most common way that we receive spiritual understanding: "revelation comes most often when we are on the move."[42] Such learning "by faith" is the supreme test—and among the sweetest rewards—of discipleship during this mortal "season of unanswered questions."[43] Thus, for each of us who love to study the scriptures, there is both encouragement and a warning in the wise words of the Danish Christian philosopher, Søren Kierkegaard:

> When you read God's word eruditely—we do not disparage erudition, far from it—but remember that when you read God's word eruditely, with a dictionary, etc., you are not reading God's Word... If you are a learned man, then take care lest with all your erudite reading (which is not reading God's Word) you forget perchance to read God's Word. If you are not learned—ah, envy the other man not, rejoice that you can at once get to the point of reading God's Word! And if there is a desire, a commandment, an order [that you read],... then be off at once

---

28 B. C. Hafen, *Anchored*, p. 3.
29 On the origins of today's "praise and worship" services, "patterned after the rock concert of secular culture," see F. Viola, *et al.*, *Pagan Christianity*, pp. 164-166.
30 P. Tillich, cited in R. Coles, *Secular Mind*, p. 5. See also *ibid.*, p. 18.
31 J. E. Seaich, *Ancient Texts* 1995, p. vii.
32 M. Barker, *Hidden*, p. 34.
33 J. H. Charlesworth, *Protestant View*, p. 84.
34 S. Prothero, *Literacy*, pp. 105-112.
35 H. Bloom, *Names Divine*, p. 104. See *Endnote P-16*, p. xxxiii.
36 Cited in S. Prothero, *Literacy*, p. 113. See *Endnote P-20*, p. xxxv.
37 See, e.g., H. B. Eyring, Jr., *Power*; S. D. Nadauld, *Principles*, pp. 88-89; B. K. Packer, *Plan of Happiness*; B. K. Packer, *Children*, p. 17; B. K. Packer, *Do Not Fear*, p. 79; B. K. Packer, *Errand*, pp. 307-312; M. K. Jensen, *Anchors*. LDS writers have often noted the fact that "God gave unto [men] commandments, *after* having made known unto them the plan of redemption" (Alma 12:32, emphasis mine). See *Endnote P-17*, p. xxxiii.
38 N. A. Maxwell, *Cosmos*, p. 2.
39 D&C 88:77.
40 D&C 88:118; cf. D. A. Bednar, *Seek*.
41 M. G. Romney, *Oath*, p. 19; M. K. Jensen, *Anchors*, p. 59. See *Endnote P-18*, p. xxxiv.
42 D. H. Oaks, *Sharing*, p. 7. See also B. C. Hafen, *Anchored*, pp. 3-5.
43 L. B. Wickman, *But If Not*, p. 30.

to do accordingly. "But," you perhaps would say, "there are so many obscure passages in the Holy Scriptures, whole books which are almost riddles." To this I would reply, "I see no need of considering this objection unless it comes from one whose life gives expression to the fact that he has punctually complied with all the passages which are easy to understand." Is this the case with you? [Thus a godly man must act:] if there were obscure passages, but also clearly expressed desires, he would say, "I must at once comply with the desire, then I will see what can be made of the obscure passages. Oh, but how could I sit down to puzzle over the obscure passages and leave the desire unfulfilled, the desire which I clearly understood?" That is to say: When you read God's Word, it is not the obscure passages which impose a duty upon you, but that which you understand and with that you must instantly comply. If there were only a single passage you did understand in Holy Scripture—well, the first thing is to do that; but you do not first have to sit down and puzzle over the obscure passages. God's Word is given in order that you shall act in accordance with it, not in order that you shall practice the art of interpreting obscure passages.[44]

---

44   Cited in S. Kierkegaard, *Parables*, p. 80; cf. S. Kierkegaard, *Self-Examination*, 12:318, pp. 28-29. See also J. E. Faulconer, *Dorrien*, pp. 433-435.

Endnotes

P-1   Said the Prophet Joseph Smith: "[H]e who reads [the sacred volume] oftenest will like it best, and he who is acquainted with it, will know the hand wherever he can see it."[45]

P-2   Coogan sums up the situation with respect to biblical studies as follows:

> The Bible is probably civilization's most over-studied book. Since academics have to publish to get jobs and keep them, and since there are fewer and fewer original things to say about the primary texts, biblical studies have often moved, understandably, to the fringes. Enormous amounts of time and energy are spent performing minute analyses of texts, themes and artifacts that more sensible historians regard as insignificant, or on studying studies of the Bible.[46]

P-3   Nibley reassuringly quipped that "It is better to be ignorant and interested than ignorant and not interested, and there's no third alternative here. We're ignorant in any case, so you might as well be ignorant and interested in these things."[47] Donald Knuth, a well-known computer scientist, wrote in the preface to his book of Bible commentary: "I can't say that my scientific background makes me a better Bible student, but I don't think it's a handicap either."[48] C. S. Lewis, in fact, observed that the perspective of an amateur may sometimes be helpful to other beginners: "The fellow-pupil can help more than the master because he knows less. The difficulty we want him to explain is one he has recently met." Thus, explained Lewis about his own venture into unfamiliar scholarly territory: "I write for the unlearned about things in which I am unlearned myself... I write as one amateur to another, talking about difficulties I have met, or lights I have gained... with the hope that this might at any rate interest, and sometimes even help, other inexpert readers. I am 'comparing notes', not presuming to instruct... The thoughts [this book] contains are those to which I found myself driven in reading the [scriptures], sometimes by my enjoyment of them, sometimes by meeting with what at first I could not enjoy"[49]

P-4   Thus Malcolm Muggeridge's poignant question, "Would something like the miracle of Bethlehem even be allowed to happen in our day?"

> In humanistic times like ours, a contemporary virgin... would regard a message from the Angel Gabriel that she might expect to give birth to a son to be called the Son of the Highest as ill-tidings of great sorrow... It is, in point of fact, extremely improbable, under existing conditions, that Jesus would have been permitted to be born at all. Mary's pregnancy, in poor circumstances, and with the father unknown, would have been an obvious case for an abortion; and her talk of having conceived as a result of the intervention of the Holy Ghost would have pointed to the need for psychiatric treatment, and made the case for terminating her pregnancy even stronger. Thus our generation, needing a Savior more, perhaps, than any that has ever existed, would be too humane to allow one to be born; too enlightened to permit the Light of the World to shine in a darkness that grows ever more oppressive.[50]

P-5   Already in 1905, Chesterton could write: "Atheism itself is too theological for us today."[51] Likewise, Taylor provides an eloquent discussion of the process and consequences of the loss of "immediate certainty" of the moral/spiritual in Western culture.[52] This point is illustrated by Peterson in his discussion of an essay by Jacob Weisberg that views "reliance upon religious faith in general, not merely Mormonism, 'as an alternative to rational understanding of complex issues'... Weisberg regards all religious doctrines as 'dogmatic, irrational, and absurd. By holding them, someone indicates a basic failure to think for himself or see the world as it is.'[53] More commonly held creeds have simply been granted an unmerited patina of respectability by the sheer passage of time. 'Perhaps Christianity and Judaism are merely more venerable and poetic versions of the same. But a few eons makes a big difference'"[54] Peterson also cites a critical review of Bushman's biography of Joseph Smith which implied that Bushman was overreaching himself in crafting a book that tries to make a place for "both inspiration and rational discourse." Peterson notes the "apparent assumption that rational discourse and inspiration are radically incompatible" and cites the

45   J. Smith, Jr., *Teachings*, 22 January 1834, p. 56.
46   M. D. Coogan, *Gulf*.
47   H. W. Nibley, *Apocryphal*, p. 266.
48   D. E. Knuth, *3:16*, p. 2.
49   C. S. Lewis, *Psalms*, pp. 1-2.
50   M. Muggeridge, *Jesus*, p. 19.
51   G. K. Chesterton, *Heretics*, p. 40.
52   C. Taylor, *Secular Age*—see, e.g., pp. 11ff. See also T. Asad, *Construction*, pp. 47-52.
53   See Asad for a view that "the reasons for a person's attachment to a given way of life, or conversion to another, cannot be reduced to an idealized model of scientific theory building" (T. Asad, *Criticism*, p. 235).
54   D. C. Peterson, *Reflections*, pp. xxiii-xxiv. See J. Weisberg, *Romney's Religion*.

reviewer's declaration "that, in order to earn a secular historian's acceptance, 'Smith's revelations would need to be explained materially as a product of his cultural or physical environment.'"[55]

Nonmember historian Jan Shipps' experiences in responding to media questions about Mormonism illustrate the kinds of issues that arise for believers of all faiths in our day:

> I remember very well how the voice of one reporter coming across the telephone wire expressed both exasperation and astonishment. "How," he wailed, "can perfectly sane people believe all this crazy stuff?" Because I had spent the first half of the 1980s writing a book designed to answer that very question, I had a ready reply... It usually began with my pointing out that the idea that Joseph Smith found golden plates and had revelations was not any more absurd than the idea that Moses and the Hebrews walked across the Red Sea without getting wet or that Jesus, who was dead, is now alive.[56]

That debates about the reality of Jesus' resurrection are not a new phenomenon of the age of science is emphasized by Wright, who reminds us: "We didn't need Galileo and Einstein to tell us that dead people don't come back to life."[57]

Getting to the nub of the problem, Neusner concludes that "among our colleagues are some who do not really like religion in its living forms, but find terribly interesting religion in its dead ones. That is why an old Christian text, one from the first century for example, is deemed a worthy subject of scholarship. But a fresh Christian expression (I think in this connection of the Book of Mormon) is available principally for ridicule, but never for study. Religious experience in the third century is fascinating. Religious experience in the twentieth century is frightening or absurd."[58]

While not accepting the historicity of the Book of Mormon, non-Mormon scholar O'Dea is one who at least took the book seriously "as a legitimate work of religious literature" and acknowledged that most of the theories of its origin advanced by its critics were unconvincing.[59] He observed with irony that "the Book of Mormon has not been universally considered by its critics as one of those books that must be read in order to have an opinion of it."[60]

P-6   Dickens later spoke admiringly of an uneducated but orderly group of Mormon emigrants he observed in Liverpool, concluding to his own surprise that if he hadn't have known who they were: "I should have said they were in their degree, the pick and flower of England."[61] "Dickens related his experience to Richard Monckton Milnes, Lord Houghton, who said that he had himself written on the topic of the Latter-day Saints in the *Edinburgh Review* in January 1862. In his article Milnes refers to a House of Commons inquiry in 1854...: 'The Select Committee of the House of Commons on emigrant ships for 1854 summoned the Mormon agent and passenger-broker before it, and came to the conclusion that no ships under the provisions of the 'Passengers Act' could be depended upon for comfort and security in the same degree as those under his administration.... [T]he Mormon ship is a Family under a strong and accepted discipline, with every provision for comfort, decorum and internal peace.'"[62]

Dickens' contemporaries John Stuart Mill and Thomas Carlyle also wrote sympathetically about the Mormons. In his 1859 essay *On Liberty*, Mill decried "the language of downright persecution which breaks out from the press of this country, whenever it feels called on to notice the remarkable phenomenon of Mormonism." While characterizing the religion as "the product of palpable imposture," all the more incredible because of its appearance "in the age of newspapers, railways, and the electric telegraph," Mill was not at all partial to the teachings of the Church. However, it deeply concerned him that "its prophet and founder was, for his teaching, put to death by a mob; that others of its adherents lost their lives by the same lawless violence; that they were forcibly expelled, in a body, from the country in which they first grew up; while, now that they have been chased into a solitary recess in the midst of a desert, many in this country openly declare that it would be right (only that it is not convenient) to send an expedition against them, and compel them by force to conform to the opinions of other people." That legitimate means of persuasion could be used to counter its teachings seemed acceptable. "But when the dissentients have conceded to the hostile sentiments of others, far more than could justly be demanded; when they have left the countries to which their doctrines were unacceptable, and established themselves in a remote corner of the earth, which they have been the first to render habitable to human beings; it is difficult to see on

55   D. C. Peterson, *Reflections*, p. xxx. See L. F. Maffly-Kipp, *Who's That*, p. 11.

56   J. Shipps, *Sojourner*, pp. 282-283; cf. R. L. Bushman, *Mormonism*, pp. 113-114.

57   N. T. Wright, *Surprised*, p. 294.

58   J. Neusner, *Vocation*, p. 117.

59   A. L. Mauss, *Near-Nation*, p. 307.

60   T. F. O'Dea, *Mormons*, p. 26.

61   C. Dickens, *Traveler*, 22, 4 July 1863, p. 262.

62   P. E. Kerry, *Carlyle*, pp. 266-267.

what principles but those of tyranny they can be prevented from living there under what laws they please, provided they commit no aggression on other nations, and allow perfect freedom of departure to those who are dissatisfied with their ways."[63]

In his 1854 draft of *Essay on the Mormons*, Carlyle described Mormonism as "a gross physical form of Calvinism… but in this one point incommensurably (transcendently) superior to all other forms of religion now extant. That it is believed, that it is practically acted upon from day to day and from hour to hour; taken as a very fact, the neglect or contradiction of which will vitiate and ruin all other facts of the day and of the hour. That is its immeasurable superiority."[64]

P-7   Elder Neal A. Maxwell expressed his "special appreciation for my friends who, though resolutely irreligious themselves, were not scoffers. Instead, though doubtless puzzled by me and their other religious friends, they were nevertheless respectful. I admire the day-to-day decency of such men and women. Though detached from theology, their decency is commendable."[65]

Among the many *religious* non-Mormon friends is historian Jan Shipps. She put her finger on part of the problem that people encounter in understanding LDS beliefs when she observed that "Mormonism is a really complex theological system… All its parts fit together beautifully. But if you just know a little bit about one of them, or part of them, it seems weird."[66] The well-known Vatican astronomer, Guy Consolmagno, found that two religions were universally dismissed by the subjectively-selected sample of scientists and engineers he interviewed as "obviously wrong": Scientology and Mormonism. However, he also notes a difference between the two: "… no scientist of my acquaintance has ever had something good to say about Scientology—rather ironic, given its name. But as it happens, I know a number of techies who are Mormons, including my thesis advisor at MIT."[67] As one who has experienced both the perplexity and the generosity of spirit of his non-LDS colleagues, prominent Mormon historian Richard L. Bushman shared the following:

> I have lived an academic life ever since I graduated from Harvard College in 1955 and then later received a Ph.D. in the history of American civilization from that same institution. Since then I have taught at Brigham Young University, Boston University, and the University of Delaware, been visiting professor at Brown and Harvard universities, and now am Gouverneur Morris Professor of History at Columbia University. In these many years as an academic, I have never been belittled for my religious beliefs or felt excluded. I have published books, contributed to conferences, entered into scholarly controversies, and had my share of honors without once feeling that my well-known faith raised a barrier.
>
> Only now and then have I caught a glimpse of the wonder my colleagues must feel that a rational, modern man believes the stories and doctrines of the Latter-day Saints. Soon after I was hired as professor of history and chair of the department at the University of Delaware, a member of the search committee invited me to lunch. While we were driving along, I mentioned my work on a biography of Joseph Smith, the founder of the Latter-day Saint Church. My colleague, doubtless to reassure me, turned quickly and said, "Dick, we took all that into account and decided it didn't matter." Apparently he was thinking of the peculiar tic in my intellectual makeup that allowed me to hold these strange beliefs. A similar reaction greeted me on coming to Columbia in 1989. Introduced to a member of the faculty, he said jovially, "Oh, you're the Mormon," an entirely amiable remark meant to make me feel at home. But one can imagine the repercussions if a new faculty member at Brigham Young University was greeted with "Oh, you're the Jew," or "Oh, you're the Catholic."
>
> The extravagant nature of the Latter-day Saint religion probably accounts for the perplexity of my colleagues. Christian and Jewish doctrines, weathered by time, no longer strike people as bizarre or unusual. One can hold to one of the moderate versions of these ancient religions without startling one's friends. But Joseph Smith saw the angel Moroni less than two hundred years ago and then brought home gold plates and translated the Book of Mormon. These miraculous events, happening so close to home, strain one's credulity. How can anyone in this day of science and skepticism believe that God sends angels to speak to humans and requires such unlikely acts as the translation of an ancient history with the aid of a Urim and Thummim? My sophomore tutor, the distinguished historian of science,

63   J. S. Mill, *Liberty*, pp. 163-166.
64   Cited in P. E. Kerry, *Carlyle*, p. 270.
65   N. A. Maxwell, *Inexhaustible*, p. 216.
66   M. Luo, *Test*. For an insightful essay charting the historical evolution of charges that Mormonism is not Christian, see J. Shipps, *Sojourner*, pp. 335-357. For general overviews of changes in public perceptions of the Mormons in America, see T. L. Givens, *Viper*; J. Shipps, *Sojourner*, pp. 51-123.
67   G. Consolmagno, *God's Mechanics*, p. 98. Consolmagno's masters thesis advisor was John S. Lewis, who joined the Church in Boston while teaching at MIT, and is currently an internationally-respected professor of planetary science at the University of Arizona.

I. B. Cohen, once coyly mentioned to me that many people thought LDS beliefs were pure garbage. He doubtless was trying gently to bring me to my senses after my sheltered upbringing as a member of the Church.[68]

While Mormons regard many of the doctrinal elaborations that occurred during the early centuries of Christianity as unwarranted intrusions of Greek philosophy into the straightforward historical truths of the Gospel, some non-Mormons see LDS theology merely as simplistic and naïve. For example Cahill writes that Mormonism resembles Manichaeism in its philosophical impoverishment, being "full of assertions, but [yielding] no intellectual system to nourish a great intellect."[69] While a strong rebuttal of Cahill's claim could be buttressed with arguments from a long line of scholars, both Mormon and non-Mormon, who have recognized the unique riches of the LDS tradition,[70] such an argument would distract attention from a more central point: Like all religious traditions with which I am personally acquainted, the primary interest of Mormonism is in developing a universal community of saints not an elite cadre of scholars.[71] In his essay on the *Difference between a Genius and an Apostle*, Kierkegaard eloquently captures this distinction between what he calls a "genius" and an "apostle":

> The genius, an aristocrat of the spirit, has had gifts lavished upon him by nature that distinguish him from his fellows. The apostle may be a commoner, a fisherman, a one-talent man by nature, or he may have ten talents—yet all that he has is dedicated to the service of the Eternal and as such is lifted up. The genius speaks with brilliance and charm. The apostle speaks with authority. The way of the genius is a way closed to all but a few. The way of the apostle is a way open to all as individuals—even to the genius himself if he can forsake the absorbing satisfactions of a brilliant self-sufficiency and be ready to will one thing.[72]

P-8   Several serious LDS studies of the book of Abraham are now available.[73]

P-9   Significantly, non-Mormon scholars W. D. Davies and Krister Stendahl separately noted their common view that "there is no other Christian community or community out of the Judeo-Christian tradition which has as positive and non-anti-Semitic ways of speaking about the Jews as have the Mormons."[74]

P-10   The way in which my "intellectual conversion" to the book of Moses was added to my spiritual witness recalled for me Elder B. H. Roberts' description of the greater appreciation he experienced of the Atonement as he finished the writing of a manual on that subject for the Seventy:

> [W]hile religion must appeal to and satisfy the emotional nature, it must also appeal to and satisfy the intellect… [T]his late inquiry into that subject has had a wonderful effect upon my own thought and state of mind… It has been a matter of faith with me and knowledge, by the testimony of the Spirit of God to my soul; but upon close inquiry, by deeper delving into the subject, my intellect also gives its full and complete assent… I account it for myself a new conversion, an intellectual conversion, … and I have been rejoicing in it of late exceedingly.[75]

I could also relate to the experience of Catherine Thomas, who found that needed episodes of spiritual illumination came "in context" through her work of teaching, and following an order and timing which only later became fully apparent:

> It was a time of germination. I had always been aware that thoughts came to me that illuminated life and the Gospel. Now I had an outlet for them. My writing began as I felt the need to explain some gospel principle or other to my students… I was always coming at a particular understanding in a way that needed context.[76]

68   R. L. Bushman, *R. L. Bushman*, pp. 79-80.

69   T. Cahill, *Irish*, p. 49.

70   See, e.g., C. L. Blomberg, *et al.*, *Divide*; H. Bloom, *American Religion*; R. Jospe *et al.*, *Covenant*; T. G. Madsen, *Reflections*; T. G. Madsen, *et al.*, *Human Nature*; T. G. Madsen, *Eternal Man*; S. M. McMurrin, *Theological*; R. L. Millet, *Different*; R. L. Millet, *Vision*; R. L. Millet, *et al.*, *Bridging*; R. L. Millet, *et al.*, *Claiming*; D. W. Musser, *et al.*, *Dialogue*; H. W. Nibley, *Temple and Cosmos*; B. T. Ostler, *Attributes*; B. T. Ostler, *Theism*; B. T. Ostler, *God*; S. J. Palmer, *Mormons and Muslims*; D. L. Paulsen, *Embodiment*; D. L. Paulsen, *Are Christians Mormon*; J. W. Welch, *Worlds*.

71   J. E. Faulconer, *Tracy*; J. Siebach, *Response*.

72   S. Kierkegaard, *Purity*, from Translator's Introduction, p. 21. For a similar point of view, see H. W. Nibley, *Prophets*. See also J. S. Tanner, *Men and Mantles*, pp. 159-160 and J. L. Kugel, *How to Read*, pp. 679-689.

73   See, e.g., E. D. Clark, *Blessings*; J. Gee *et al.*, *Astronomy*; H. W. Nibley, *Drama*; H. W. Nibley, *Message 2005*; H. W. Nibley, *Abraham 2000*; H. W. Nibley, *Teachings of the PGP*; M. D. Rhodes, *Hor*; J. A. Tvedtnes, *et al.*, *Traditions*.

74   K. Stendahl, *Third Nephi*, p. 151.

75   B. H. Roberts, *8 April 1911*, p. 59. Also quoted in T. G. Madsen, *Nine Reasons*, pp. 110-112.

76   M. C. Thomas, *Light*, p. 347.

The way in which the glory of God's work is ultimately revealed in the simple details of texts, events, and godly persons is brilliantly described by Chesterton:[77]

> The wise man will follow a star, low and large and fierce in the heavens; but the nearer he comes to it the smaller and smaller it will grow, till he finds it the humble lantern over some little inn or stable. Not till we know the high things shall we know how lowly they are. Meanwhile, the modern superior transcendentalist will find the facts of eternity incredible because they are so solid; he will not recognize heaven because it is so like the earth.

P-11 See Birch[78] for a vivid description of King's approach to scholarship and classroom style.

P-12 Wrote King:

> When I was first brought to read Joseph Smith's story, I was deeply impressed. I wasn't inclined to be impressed. As a stylistician, I have spent my life being disinclined to be impressed. So when I read his story, I thought to myself, this is an extraordinary thing. This is an astonishingly matter-of-fact and cool account. This man is not trying to persuade me of anything. He doesn't feel the need to. He is stating what happened to him, and he is stating it, not enthusiastically, but in quite a matter-of-fact way. He is not trying to make me cry or feel ecstatic. That struck me, and that began to build my testimony, for I could see that this man was telling the truth.[79]

P-13 By this, I do not think that the Prophet meant that a given passage of scripture can be understood in isolation, apart from the context in which it stands. Rather, for example, when he interpreted a parable, his "key" to "ascertain its meaning" was to "dig up the root," i.e., to "enquire [as to] the question which drew out the answer."[80] He was democratic in his desire to have the scriptures unfolded to all, decrying those who supposed that their plain truths were "mystery… and, therefore, are not to be understood." He declared that all the Saints could come to an understanding of such things "if [they] will but open [their] eyes, and read with candor."[81]

P-14 Buber described this as:

> … a disease of the spirit that can lead us to imagine that we already know what we are reading, causing us to blithely and triumphantly read past the text… The spiritual task of interpretation… is to affect or alter the pace of reading so that one's eye and ear can be addressed by the text's words and sounds—and thus reveal an expanded or new sense of life and its dynamics. The pace of technology and the patterns of modernity pervert this vital task. The rhythm of reading must, therefore, be restored to the rhythm of breathing, to the cadence of the cantillation marks of the sacred text. Only then will the individual absorb the texts with his or her life breath and begin to read liturgically, as a rite of passage to a different level of meaning. And only then may the contemporary idolization of technique and information be transformed, and the sacred text restored as a living teaching and instruction, for the constant renewal of the self.[82]

In an account of a personal incident from his university days, Faulconer describes his introduction to such an approach to reading scripture:

> Before studying [Genesis] with Professor Goldman, I memorized doctrines and scanned scriptures for evidence that would support the doctrines I believed. After studying with him I realized that although that kind of scripture study is essential, our learning is vastly improved if it is done against the background of close reading I learned from Professor Goldman…
>
> The heart of [this approach] is asking questions—asking questions of the scriptures and letting them answer, asking questions about details rather than about abstractions and generalities. What does "dominion" mean? Why does Adam say what he does in the way that he does? What does the form of his answer to God suggest? Why is the story told in this order rather than another? Often Professor Goldman's questions had no single, correct answer. Even when he had a plausible answer to one of his questions, he never assumed that he knew everything he needed to know. He might ask the same questions today that he asked a year ago and criticize his previous answers. He focused on questioning in a productive way rather than on merely answering, but asking those questions naturally led to ideas I had never considered. It surprised me how often such questions about details led to insights into my life.

77   G. K. Chesterton, *William Blake*, p. 210.
78   A. J. Birch, *King*.
79   A. H. King, *Joseph*, p. 288.
80   J. Smith, Jr., *Teachings*, 29 January 1843, pp. 276-277.
81   *Ibid.*, December 1835, p. 96.
82   Cited in M. Fishbane, *Spirituality*, p. 12.

As I imitated Professor Goldman, I began to wonder if my understanding of the Gospel was adequate. That too became a source for questions. To see whether the scriptures would refine my understanding. I began to ask questions like, I have always heard that such and such is true and I have always believed that this passage of scripture teaches that doctrine. Does it? Such questioning often showed me that my knowledge of the scriptures was shallow, that the verses I had used as supports for doctrines I believed not only supported those doctrines but also had a great deal to teach me.[83]

As a result of his experiences, Faulconer gives the following guidance to scripture readers:

Assume that the scriptures mean exactly what they say and, more important, assume that we do not already know what they say. If we assume that we already know what the scriptures say, then they cannot continue to teach us. If we assume that they mean something other than what they say, then we run the risk of substituting our own thoughts for what we read rather than learning what they have to teach us.... [A]ssume that each aspect of whatever passage we are looking at is significant and ask about that significance. To assume that some things are significant and others are not is to assume, from the beginning, that we already know what scripture means. Some things may turn out to be irrelevant, but we cannot know that until we are done.[84]

Similarly, Wright comments that if you read in this way:

… the Bible will not let you down. You will be paying attention to it; you won't be sitting in judgment over it. But you won't come with a preconceived notion of what this or that passage has to mean if it is to be true. You will discover that God is speaking new truth through it. I take it as a method in my biblical studies that if I turn a corner and find myself saying, "Well, in that case, that verse is wrong" that I must have turned a wrong corner somewhere. But that does not mean that I impose what I think is right on to that bit of the Bible. It means, instead, that I am forced to live with that text uncomfortably, sometimes literally for years (this is sober autobiography), until suddenly I come round a different corner and that verse makes a lot of sense; sense that I wouldn't have got if I had insisted on imposing my initial view on it from day one.[85]

By way of contrast, Kugel notes the "subtle shift in tone" that has come with "the emphasis on reading the Bible [solely] in human terms and in its historical context" without the counterbalance provided by traditional forms of scripture reading:

As modern biblical scholarship gained momentum, studying the Bible itself was joined with, and eventually overshadowed by, studying the historical reality behind the text (including how the text itself came to be). In the process, learning from the Bible gradually turned into learning about it. Such a shift might seem slight at first, but ultimately it changed a great deal. The person who seeks to learn from the Bible is smaller than the text; he crouches at its feet, waiting for its instruction or insights. Learning about the text generates the opposite posture. The text moves from subject to object; it no longer speaks but is spoken about, analyzed, and acted upon. The insights are now all the reader's, not the text's, and anyone can see the results. This difference in tone, as much as any specific insight or theory, is what has created the great gap between the Bible of ancient interpreters and that of modern scholars.[86]

P-15   About the abandonment of ancient modes of biblical interpretation, Kugel observes:

What [modern exegetes] generally share (although there are, of course, exceptions) is a profound discomfort with the actual interpretations that the ancients came up with—these have little or no place in the way Scripture is to be expounded today. Midrash, allegory, typology—what for? But the style of interpretation thus being rejected is precisely the one that characterizes the numerous interpretations of Old Testament texts by Jesus, Paul, and others in the New Testament, as well as by the succeeding generations of the founders of Christianity....

Ancient interpretive methods may sometimes appear artificial, but this hardly means that abandoning them guarantees unbiased interpretation... At times, [modern] interpretations are scarcely less forced than those of ancient midrashists (and usually far less clever).[87]

83   J. E. Faulconer, *Study*, pp. 6-7.

84   *Ibid.*, pp. 11-12.

85   N. T. Wright, *Authoritative*. See Berlin's seven principles of biblical hermeneutics for a detailed description of such an approach to scriptural understanding (A. Berlin, *Search*).

86   J. L. Kugel, *How to Read*, p. 666.

87   *Ibid.*, pp. 674, 676; cf. M. Barker, *Christmas*, pp. 29-30.

P-16 Since at least the time of Norman Vincent Peale's *The Power of Positive Thinking* (1952), a parade of quasi-religious books have, in the words of Prothero:

> … preached therapy more than theology, happiness rather than salvation. Then, as today, debating (or even discussing) religious doctrines was considered ill-mannered, a violation of the cherished civic ideal of tolerance, so it was difficult for children to learn or for adults to articulate what set their religious traditions apart from others.[88]

> Current interest in contemplative practice has caused "spiritual but not religious" folks to rediscover such neglected resources inside Christianity and Judaism as centering prayer and Kabbalah. But it has also led them to Buddhism, Hinduism, Taoism, and other Asian religions in search of various forms of meditation, yoga, and tai chi… Here too, however, the trend is toward religion stripped down to its "essentials"—essentials that in this case are confined almost entirely to the experiential or moral dimensions. This development is well advanced in the American Buddhist community, where some have argued that Buddhism can get along just fine without such staples as karma and reincarnation. "Buddhism Without Beliefs," as this movement has been called, aims to distill the Buddhist life down to nothing more than one's favorite sitting or chanting practice, and then to put that practice at the service of such American preoccupations as happiness.

> The tendency to shirk from doctrine is particularly pronounced in the "multi-religious America" camp. Here even the minimal monotheism of the Judeo-Christian-Islamic model must be sacrificed since many Buddhists don't believe in God and many Hindus believe in more than one. The only common ground here seems to be tolerance itself. When pluralists gather for interreligious dialogue, their discussions always seem to circle back to ethics… [without] a whisper of theology.[89]

P-17 Also of relevance is the significant effort currently being devoted to *The BYU New Testament Commentary*:

> Approved by the BYU administration and its Board of Trustees…, the project foresees the production of fifteen volumes of commentary on individual books of the New Testament.

The public announcement reads as follows:

> The Board of Trustees of Brigham Young University has recently approved the publication of a multi-volume commentary on the New Testament. A broad-based team of Latter-day Saint scholars have joined forces to produce the set. Planned to take about ten years to complete, this fifteen-volume series will combine the best ancient linguistic and historical evidence with Mormon interests and doctrinal perspectives…. This commentary will be the first to combine scholarly expertise and Mormon scripture. Each book in the New Testament will be examined word by word. In addition, relationships between the New Testament and the Book of Mormon and the Doctrine and Covenants will be carefully examined.

> The commentary will be not just another scholarly commentary, but particularly a Latter-day Saint Commentary. It will focus on passages of particular interest to Latter-day Saints; it will draw from all the LDS standard works; and we strive for it to be written with inspiration… [Part] of our purposes is to demonstrate the proper treatment of text transmission and translation—that is, to make use of what seems to be correct and offer alternate meaning for what seems to be incorrect. Each volume will contain substantial introductory and contextual material where questions of provenance, setting, authorship, intent and purpose will be addressed. Discussion of manuscript tradition and transcription will also be considered, as well as thematic or topical questions contained in the text being examined. The actual commentary will address the text as found in the King James Version. Pericopes, that is sections of the text divided into similarly-themed verses, generally no more than a dozen at a time, sometimes fewer, will be treated verse by verse, and word by word. Analytical commentary will be offered in terms of linguistic analysis, including alternative translation possibilities based on literal Greek meanings of words, historical background, and theological significance. Where issues of textual transmission arise, consultation will be made of Greek texts unavailable to the King James translators, some newly discovered and of early date, others the synthetic product of 400 years of additional research, textual comparison, and new discovery. Sources for linguistic considerations will include not only well known recent translations of the New Testament, but importantly the Joseph Smith Translation in what places

---

88   S. Prothero, *Literacy*, p. 113; cf. C. Lasch, *Revolt*, pp. 216ff.
89   S. Prothero, *Literacy*, p. 117

New Testament passages are addressed. Standard scholarly commentaries such as the *Anchor Bible Commentary* or *Sacra Pagina*, as well as many scholarly monographs and articles, will also be consulted. When Greek is cited it will be transliterated into the Roman alphabet used in English so as to be accessible to our readers. In this vein, both Greek and Latin references will be given in the original language and in a translated English form. For purposes of interpretation and comment, consideration will be given to writings spanning two thousand years from Apostolic Fathers and pre-Nicene Christian authors to the important truths revealed in latter-day scripture and the teachings of leaders of the Restoration from the time of Joseph Smith to the present day. Historical background, as it pertains to particular New Testament passages, will provide detailed discussion of the world at the time of Christ from cultural, political, and legal perspectives.

A Board of five editors, all senior and experienced BYU professors, directs the project.[90]

P-18 Elder Neal A. Maxwell wrote that:

… gaining knowledge and becoming more Christlike "are two aspects of a single process."[91] This process is part of being "valiant" in our testimony of Jesus. Thus, while we are saved no faster than we gain a certain type of knowledge,[92] it is also the case, as Richard Bushman has observed,[93] that we will gain knowledge no faster than we are saved… [B]ehaving and knowing are inseparably linked.[94]

P-19 Similarly, C. S. Lewis writes:

Most of us [should be] less urgently concerned with the Pauline question [of why it is theoretically impossible for us to perfectly obey the moral law] than with [the practical implications of] William Law's simple statement: "if you will here stop and ask yourselves why you are not as pious as the primitive Christians were, your own heart will tell you that it is neither through ignorance nor inability, but purely because you never thoroughly intended it."[95]

Kugel echoes the same spirit from a Jewish perspective:

In Judaism, Scripture is ultimately valued not as history, nor as theology, nor even as the great, self-sufficient corpus of divine utterances—all that God had ever wished to say to man. Judaism is not fundamentalism, nor even Protestantism. What Scripture is, and always has been, in Judaism is the beginning of a manual entitled *To Serve God*, a manual whose trajectory has always led from the prophet to the interpreter and from the divine to the merely human. To put the matter in, I admit, rather shocking terms: since in Judaism it is not the words of Scripture themselves that are ultimately supreme, but the service of God (the "standing up close") that they enjoin, then to suggest that everything hangs on Scripture might well be described as a form of fetishism or idolatry, that is, a mistaking of the message for its Sender and the turning of its words into idols of wood or stone… For Judaism, the crucial element has always been the imperative that Scripture's very existence embodies… the basic divine commandment reflected in Deuteronomy's exhortation "to serve the Lord your God with all your heart and all your soul"[96] and similar pronouncements. To flesh out this commandment was the purpose of all of Scripture and all later interpretation. With such a purpose foremost, the Bible's original component texts easily lent themselves to flexible reinterpretation…. The Bible, it seems to me, remains the most accessible… basic program for the service of God in daily life….

We have seen that, since ancient times, the trajectory of being God's servants inevitably led from words of God to merely human words, and that the latter have had a great deal to do with the essence of the Bible, turning all of it into a manual of "what to do." So, while I could not be involved

---

90 J. F. Hall, *Translated Correctly.*

91 C. T. Warner, *Truth*, p. 1490.

92 J. Smith, Jr., *Teachings*, 10 April 1842, p. 217; cf. Alma 12:30.

93 R. L. Bushman, *Faithful History*, p. 18.

94 N. A. Maxwell, *Inexhaustible*, pp. 212-213. See also A. S. Miller, *Atonement and Testimony.*

95 C. S. Lewis, *Pain*, p. 59. See W. Law, *Serious Call*, 2, p. 57. On the other hand, one might also admire those who, in an artless and unconscious manner, simply do good out of their very nature—or even out of a spontaneous burst of repentance, as in the delightful French Christmas story *La Pastorale des Santons de Provence*. There it was said of the miserly Roustido, following an sudden and uncharacteristic act of kindness inspired by the presence of the Christ child and His Mother: "Il venait de gagner le paradis sans le faire exprès" (= "He had just won a spot for himself in Paradise without knowing it.") (Y. Audouard, *Pastorale*, p. 76).

96 Deuteronomy 10:12.

in a religion that was entirely a human artifact, it would, in theory at least, be enough for me if God said what He is reported to have said in Exodus and Deuteronomy: "Do you want to come close to Me? Then do My bidding, become My employees." The fleshing out of that primal commandment takes place in Scripture and outside of Scripture, and it is all one sacred precinct; indeed, the divine presence suffuses every part of it.[97]

The idea of the primacy of service must, of course, be tempered by the knowledge that God's call to action "always comes through the filter of human understanding, and God asks for a creative, loving response on our part, not mere compliance." McLachlan compares it to the call one might see in the face of a loved one. "Whether and how I will respond" to such an encounter "is up to me."[98]

Augustine phrased his approach to this issue in terms of a balance:

> No man has a right to lead such a life of contemplation as to forget in his own case the service due to his neighbor; nor has any man a right to be so immersed in active life as to neglect the contemplation of God.[99]

However, I resonate more strongly with the view of Elder Bruce C. Hafen who argues that "a 'balanced' approach simply won't be enough when we encounter the most demanding experiences of our spiritual growth. When we find ourselves stretched to our extremities, we need a new level from which to draw more deeply on our Hebrew roots than our Greek roots."[100] To adopt such a perspective is not to devalue the life of the mind in religion, but rather, with C. S. Lewis, to reject the idea:

> … which lingers in the mind of some modern people that cultural activities are in their own right spiritual and meritorious—as though scholars and poets were intrinsically more pleasing to God than scavengers and bootblacks… The work of a Beethoven and the work of a charwoman become spiritual on precisely the same condition, that of being offered to God, of being done humbly "as to the Lord."[101]

P-20   As an example, Prothero cites a statement by Eisenhower to a Soviet official in a December 1952 meeting that "our form of government has no sense unless it is founded in a deeply felt religious faith, and I don't care what it is."[102] The same fierce loyalty to an abstract "idea" of God divorced from any particulars is expressed more prosaically in an off-the-street comment made to a sociologist by a high-school student in the Middle West, "Yeah, we smoke dope all over, in our cars, walking around before class, anytime, but that doesn't mean we don't believe in God or that we'll let anybody put God down."[103]

P-21   Efforts have been made to bridge this gap through books that explain the meaning of specific symbols used in scripture and temple worship. However, most of us not only struggle with the meaning of individual concepts and symbols, but also—and perhaps more crucially—in understanding how these concepts and symbols fit together as a whole. Scriptural and temple symbols and concepts are best understood, not in isolation, but within the full context of teachings to which they belong.

In this respect, Chesterton has compared our position to that of a "sailor who awakens from a deep sleep and discovers treasure strewn about, relics from a civilization he can barely remember. One by one he picks up the relics—gold coins, a compass, fine clothing—and tries to discern their meaning."[104] But the essential meaning is to be found not so much in the individual relics as in a grasp of the milieu that produced them.

---

97   J. L. Kugel, *How to Read*, pp. 685, 687, 689. The primacy of good deeds vs. *Torah* study was a matter of debate among the Jewish Sages. For example, according to one among them, the first question that will be addressed to man on Judgment Day is "Have you dealt honestly in the conduct of your business?" and the second question will be "Did you set fixed times for the study of *Torah*?" Another sage, however, stated: "Man's trial will begin with an examination of his study of *Torah*" (A. J. Heschel, *Heavenly Torah*, p. 206).

98   J. McLachlan, *Reply*, p. 209.

99   Augustine, *City*, 19:19, p. 413; cf. *Pirke Avot*: "Anyone whose wisdom exceeds his good deeds… [is like] a tree whose branches are numerous but whose roots are few; then the wind comes and uproots it and turns it upside down" (M. Lieber, *Pirkei Avos*, 3:22, p. 201).

100   B. C. Hafen, *Reason*, pp. 27-28. See S. Kierkegaard, *Fear*, pp. 20, 79-100, 189-192: "the teleological suspension of the ethical"; cf. discussion in R. Coles, *Secular Mind*, pp. 15-20.

101   C. S. Lewis, *Learning*, pp. 55-56.

102   S. Prothero, *Literacy*, p. 113.

103   P. Fussell, *Class*, p. 150.

104   P. Yancey, introduction to G. K. Chesterton, *Orthodoxy*, p. xiii.

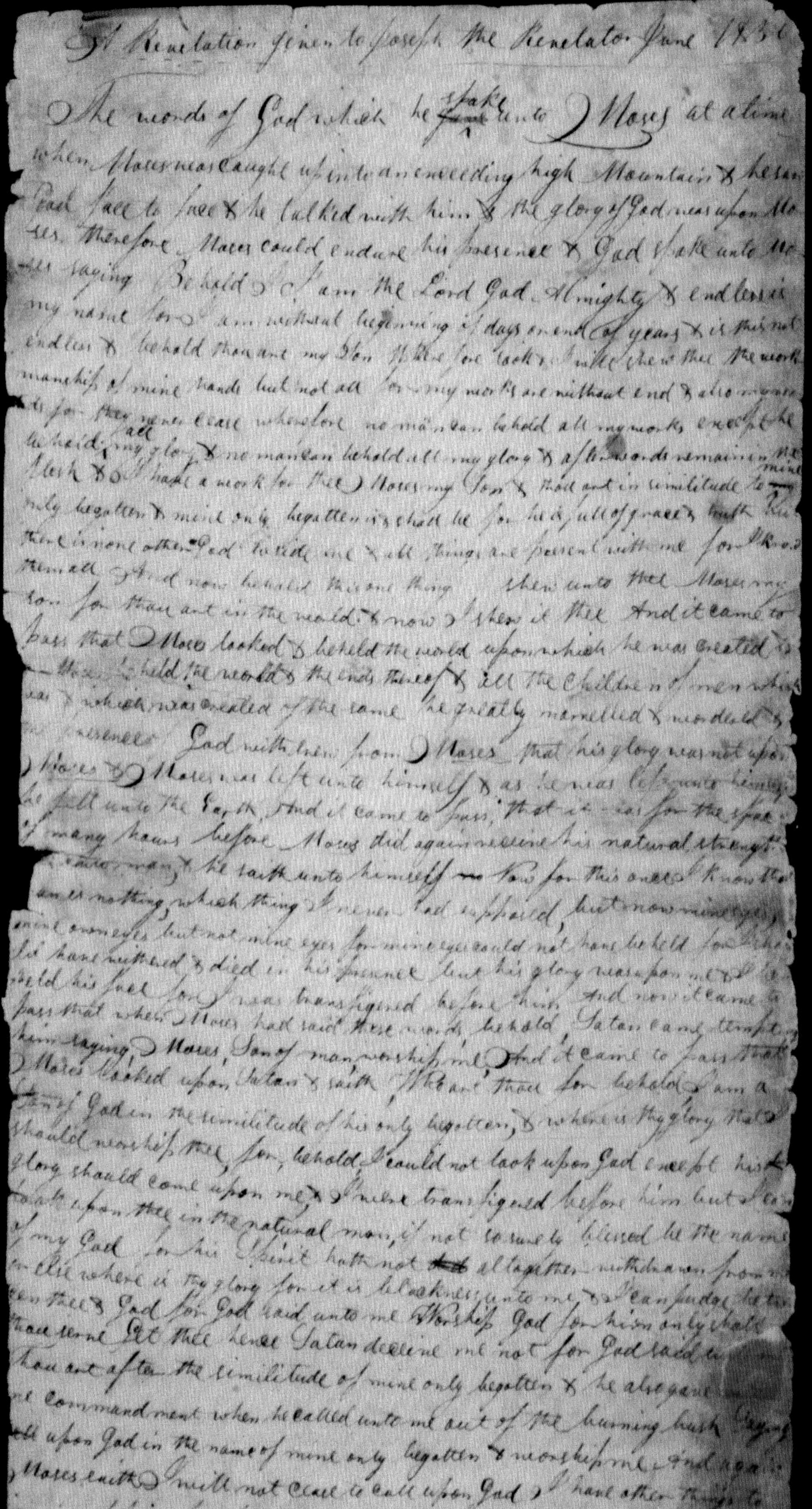

FIGURE 0-1. *Old Testament Manuscript 1, Page 1, 1830*

A revelation given to Joseph the Revelator, June 1830. This page, in Oliver Cowdery's handwriting, records the text of Moses 1:1-19. The account of this marvelous vision seems to have been dictated by the Prophet "without the slightest contemplation, hesitation, or uncertainty" (K. P. Jackson, *New Discoveries*, p. 154).

INTRODUCTION

The Joseph Smith Translation of the Bible

MANY new editions of the Bible appeared in America between 1777 and 1830. However, the Joseph Smith Translation (JST) was unique in that both the commission to translate and the means of performing the translation were the result of revelation from God.[1] Kent P. Jackson briefly relates the history as follows:

> Not long after the Church was organized in the spring of 1830, Joseph Smith began a careful reading of the Bible to revise and make corrections in accordance with the inspiration he would receive. From that labor came the revelation of much truth and the restoration of many of the "precious things" that Nephi had foretold would be taken from the Bible.[2] In June 1830, the first revealed addition to the Bible was set to writing. Over the next three years, the Prophet made inspired changes, additions, and corrections while he filled his calling to provide a more correct translation for the Church. Collectively, these are called the "Joseph Smith Translation."
>
> The first revelation of the Joseph Smith Translation is what we now have as Moses 1 in the Pearl of Great Price—the preface to the book of Genesis. Beginning with Genesis 1:1, the Prophet apparently had the Bible before him and read aloud from it until he felt impressed to dictate a change in the wording. If no change were required, he read the text as it stood. Thus dictating the text to his scribes, he progressed to Genesis 24, at which point he set aside the Old Testament as he was instructed in a revelation on March 7, 1831.[3] The following day, he began revising the New Testament.[4] When he completed John 5 in February 1832, he ceased dictating the text in full to his scribes and began using an abbreviated notation system. From that time on, it appears that he read the verses from the Bible, marked in it the words or passages that needed to be corrected, and dictated only the changes to his scribes, who recorded them on the manuscript.
>
> Following the completion of the New Testament in February 1833, Joseph Smith returned to his work on the Old Testament. He soon shifted to the abbreviated notation system for that manuscript also… [During this last phase of Old Testament translation] he dictated only the replacement words, as he had done earlier with the New Testament. At the end of the Old Testament manuscript, after the book of Malachi, the scribe wrote the following words:

---

1   P. L. Barlow, *Bible*, pp. 46-47.

2   1 Nephi 13:23-29.

3   See D&C 45:60-62. See *Endnote 0-1*, p. 19.

4   See *Endnote 0-2*, p. 19.

"Finished on the 2nd day of July 1833." That same day the Prophet and his counselors—Sidney Rigdon and Frederick G. Williams, both of whom had served as scribes for the new translation—wrote to Church members in Missouri and told them, "We this day finished the translating of the Scriptures, for which we returned gratitude to our Heavenly Father"[5]

Joseph and his scribes had been carrying many other responsibilities during this period of rapid Church expansion from New York to Ohio and Missouri. Therefore, one can easily imagine what relief they must have felt as they completed this phase of the work. Unfortunately, though the JST had progressed to the point where the Prophet was planning its publication, continual lack of time and means prevented it from appearing in its entirety during his lifetime.[6]

In August 1832, the first extract from JST Genesis, Moses 7, was published in the Church's newspaper, *The Evening and Morning Star*. Publication continued with additional extracts from the new translation[7] in March and April 1833.[8] Two years later, several verses from Moses 2-5 were used in the publication of the *Lectures on Faith* in the 1835 Doctrine and Covenants.[9] Finally, Moses 1 appeared in the January 16, 1843 edition of the *Times and Seasons*. Drawing on the earlier newspaper publications, Elder Franklin D. Richards included portions of Moses 1-8 in the first edition of the Pearl of Great Price, printed in England in 1851. However, subsequent editions of the Pearl of Great Price relied on the version of Moses 1-8 that had been published by the Reorganized Church of Jesus Christ of Latter Day Saints (RLDS, now officially named the Community of Christ).

The Prophet's wife, Emma, kept the original JST manuscripts until 1866, when they were given to the RLDS Church. Based on a review of original manuscripts by an RLDS publication committee, the "Inspired Version" (I.V.) of the Bible first appeared in 1867. In 1944, the RLDS Church brought out a carefully prepared "new corrected edition." However, because LDS scholars had not yet had an opportunity to compare the I.V. to the original manuscripts, its initial acceptance by Church members was limited.[10] An exhaustive study by Brigham Young University (BYU) religion professor Robert J. Matthews was published in 1975.[11] He established that the 1944 and subsequent editions of the "Inspired Version," notwithstanding their shortcomings, constituted a faithful rendering of the work of the Prophet Joseph Smith and his scribes—insofar as the manuscripts were then understood.[12]

With painstaking effort over a period of eight years, and with the generous cooperation of the Community of Christ, a facsimile transcription of all the original manuscripts of the JST was at last published in 2004.[13] A detailed study of the text of the portions of the JST relating to the book of Moses appeared in 2005.[14] Taken together, these studies allow us to see the process and results of translation with greater clarity than ever before.[15]

---

5   K. P. Jackson, *Cooperstown Bible*, pp. 59-60. See J. Smith, Jr., *Documentary History*, 2 July 1833, 1:368.
6   R. J. Matthews, *Plainer*, p. 391. See *Endnote 0-3*, p. 19.
7   Moses 6:43-68, 5:1-16, and 8:13-30.
8   K. P. Jackson, *Book of Moses*, p. 14.
9   See *Endnote 0-4*, p. 19.
10   T. E. Sherry, *Changing*.
11   For additional background on Matthews' work, see R. L. Huntington, *et al.*, *Robert J. Matthews*; B. M. Hauglid, *et al.*, *Community of Christ*.
12   R. J. Matthews, *Plainer*, pp. 200-201. See also K. P. Jackson, *Book of Moses*, pp. 20-33.
13   S. H. Faulring, *et al.*, *Original Manuscripts*. For additional background, see R. L. McConkie, *Miracle*.
14   K. P. Jackson, *Book of Moses*.
15   See *Endnote 0-5*, p. 19.

Scripture Reference	Date	Place	Scribe	Manuscript Reference
Moses 1; Community of Christ D&C 22	June 1830	Fayette, NY or Harmony, PA	Oliver Cowdery	OT1-1, line 1 to OT1-3, line 14
Moses 2:1-5:43; I.V. Genesis 1:1-5:28; Genesis 1:1-4:18	Between June and October 21, 1830	Harmony, PA and Fayette, NY	Oliver Cowdery	OT1-3, line 15 to OT1-10, line 5
Moses 5:43-5:51; I.V. Genesis 5:29-5:37; Genesis 4:18-24	October 21, 1830	Fayette, NY	John Whitmer	OT1-10, lines 6 to 23
Moses 5:52-6:18; I.V. Genesis 5:38-6:16; Genesis 4:25-5:11	November 30, 1830	Fayette, NY	John Whitmer	OT1-10, line 24 to OT1-11, line 40
Moses 6:19-6:52; I.V. Genesis 6:17-6:53; Genesis 5:12-21	December 1, 1830	Fayette, NY	Emma Smith	OT1-11, line 41 to OT1-14, line 1
Moses 6:52-7:1; I.V. Genesis 6:53-7:1	Between December 1 and December 10, 1830	Fayette, NY	John Whitmer	OT1-14, line 1 to OT1-15, line 16
Moses 7:2-7:69; I.V. Genesis 7:2-7:78	Ca. December 10 and 31, 1830	Fayette, NY	Sidney Rigdon	OT1-15, line 16 to OT1-19, line 34
Moses 8:1-8:30; I.V. Genesis 7:78-24:42; Genesis 5:22-24:41	Probably between February 1 and March 7, 1831	Probably in Kirtland, OH	Sidney Rigdon	OT1-19, line 35, OT1-61, line 5
I.V. Genesis 24:42-Nehemiah 10:30; Genesis 24:41-Nehemiah 10:30	July 20-31, 1832 to July 2, 1833	Hiram and Kirtland, OH	Frederick G. Williams	OT2-59, line 1 to OT2-81, line 20
Nehemiah 11-Psalm 10	Between late July 1832 and July 2, 1833	Kirtland, OH	Joseph Smith	OT2-81, line 21 to OT2-83, line 32
Psalm 11-Malachi	Between late July 1832 and July 2, 1833	Kirtland, OH	Frederick G. Williams	OT2-83, line 33 to OT2-119, line 5

Figure 0-2. *Time Sequence of the Joseph Smith Translation of the Old Testament*[16]

A Detailed Look at the JST Old Testament

A chart describing the circumstances of the JST additions and revisions to various portions of the Old Testament is shown above. It shows only the time of original translation. Subsequent Old Testament revisions were extensive but generally minor in substance.

Overall, 3,410 verses in the printed editions of JST differ in textual construction from the King James Version (KJV), using the numbering of the I.V. as the basis for comparison.[17] Of the total of 1,289 verses changed in the Old Testament, 25 correspond to the additions of Moses 1, and 662 occur in Genesis.[18] Hence, more than half of the changed verses in the JST Old Testament and 20% of those in the entire JST Bible are contained in Moses 1 and Genesis, with the most extensive modifications occurring in Genesis 1-24. As a proportion of page count, changes in Genesis occur four times more frequently than in the New Testament, and twenty-one times more frequently than in the rest of the Old Testament. The changes in Genesis are not only more numerous, but also more significant in the degree of doctrinal and historical expansion.

---

16   Excerpted from S. H. Faulring, *et al.*, *Original Manuscripts*, pp. 57-59; R. J. Matthews, *Plainer*, p. 96. From 8 March 1831 to sometime between 20-31 July 1832, the translation of the New Testament took place.

17   See *Endnote 0-6*, p. 19.

18   R. J. Matthews, *Plainer*, p. 424.

Certainly the importance of the early Genesis chapters justifies the proportionately greater time and attention they received. However, the JST translation schedule may also provide a clue to the reason why the first half of Genesis contained the overwhelming share of the Prophet's modifications. The original version of the translation of JST Genesis through chapter 24 was performed over the course of five to nine months.[19] These chapters contained very detailed revisions and rich prophetic additions to the original Genesis text. Work on the Old Testament was interrupted by first phase of New Testament translation, which began on 8 March 1831. By the time the Old Testament translation was resumed sixteen months later, the Prophet had stopped the practice of writing out the verses in full and instead adopted an abbreviated notation system he had developed for the New Testament. As Howard notes, this naturally led to fewer and briefer revisions.[20] Thus, it is no surprise that the first manuscript of the remainder of Genesis through the end of Malachi was completed at a much faster pace than the first half of Genesis.

None of this, however, ultimately changes the general conclusion that Genesis 1-24 was a priority in the overall translation process. Though we cannot know how much of Joseph Smith's daily schedule the translation occupied during each of its phases, it seems clear that Genesis 1-24—the first 1% of the Bible, corresponding to 24% of the overall three-year translation period—received a significantly more generous share of the Prophet's time and attention than did the remaining 99%.

What important things could Joseph Smith have learned from translating Genesis 1-24? To begin with, the story of Enoch and his righteous city would have had pressing relevance to the mission of the Church, as the Prophet worked to help the Saints understand the law of consecration and to establish Zion in Missouri. Thus, it is no coincidence that this account was first published in 1832 and 1833.[21] However, we should not allow the salience of these immediate events to overshadow the fact that the first JST Genesis chapters also relate the stories of other patriarchs, especially Adam, Noah, Melchizedek, and Abraham. In consideration of this fact, and other evidence from revelations and teachings of this period, I have been led to believe that a very significant aspect of the translation process as a whole was the early tutoring in temple-related doctrines received by Joseph Smith as he revised and expanded Genesis 1-24, in conjunction with his later translation of significant passages in the New Testament and, for example, the Old Testament stories of Moses and Elijah.[22] I believe that the book of Moses throws much more light on temple worship than has been previously supposed, and that it goes far beyond the obvious passages on the Creation, the Fall, and early events in the lives of Adam and Eve.

A corollary, in making this argument, is that a detailed understanding of the covenants and sequences of blessings associated with current forms of LDS temple worship were revealed to Joseph Smith several years before he began to teach them in plainness to the Saints in Nauvoo.[23] It has been generally supposed that in Kirtland the Prophet knew only a little about temple ordinances, and taught all of what he then knew to the Saints; and that when he got to Nauvoo the rest was revealed to him, and so he taught them something more. However, I think such a conclusion is mistaken. My study of the book of Moses and others of the initial revelations and teachings of Joseph Smith has convinced me that he knew early

---

19   Starting somewhere between June and October 1830 and ending 7 March 1831.
20   R. P. Howard, *Restoration 1969*, pp. 92-93. See also R. J. Matthews, *Plainer*, p. 80. See *Endnote 0-7*, p. 20.
21   K. Muhlestein, *Flow*, pp. 52-62.
22   J. M. Bradshaw, *Temple Themes*.
23   Cf. Matthew 17:9.

FIGURE 0-3. *Go With Me to Cumorah, 1997*
Liz Lemon Swindle, 1953-

Wherefore I give unto you that ye may now translate it, that ye may be prepared for the things to come.[1] The process of translating the Bible laid the foundation for many of the revelations of Joseph Smith.[2]

---

1   D&C 45:61.
2   R. J. Matthews, *Role of JST.*

on much more about these matters than he taught publicly, contradicting the view of those who consider the temple ordinances a late invention.[24] Indeed, in some cases, we know that the Prophet deliberately delayed the publication of early temple-related revelations connected with his work on the JST until the later Nauvoo period. For example, in Bachman's groundbreaking studies on the origins of D&C 132, which has not only to do with celestial marriage but also the whole context of temple work, he convincingly argued that nearly all of that section was revealed to the Prophet as he worked on the JST. This was more than a decade previous to 1843, when the revelation was first recorded.[25] Likewise, Joseph Smith waited until 1843 to publish the first chapter of the book of Moses. In that revelation, he had been specifically commanded not to show it "unto any except them that believe until I command you."[26] Some of what the Prophet learned as he worked on the JST and other translation projects[27] may have never been put to writing.[28] Brigham Young is remembered

---

24   See, e.g., the overviews of Moses 1 (p. 37) and Moses 5 (pp. 341-350) as well as *Excursus 3: Temple Blessings in the Oath and Covenant of the Priesthood*, p. 519. See *Endnote 0-8*, p. 20.
25   D. W. Bachman, *New Light.*
26   Moses 1:42.
27   See, e.g., Book of Abraham, Facsimile 2, explanations of figures 8-22.
28   See *Endnote 0-9*, p. 20.

FIGURES 0-4 AND 0-5.
Moses Indignant at the Golden Calf, ca. 1800
Rock Sculpted with Ark and Annunciation, 1827
William Blake, 1757-1827

SEE COLOR PLATES 0-4 AND 0-5.

And in a day when the children of men shall esteem my words as naught and take many of them from the book which thou shalt write, behold, I will raise up another like unto thee; and they shall be had again among the children of men.[1] The illustration on the left depicts Moses with the broken tablets from God at his feet in anger at the Israelites' idolatrous worship.[2] Note the contrast of "the magnificent angular figure of the indignant Moses with the graceful dancers on the left, behind whom stands Aaron" and the golden calf, upper left.[3]

Blake saw Moses as a symbol of the iron-hard rationality and repression of the Old Testament law that required redemption through "the power of the creative imagination and the worth of continual artistic labor." Figures of Moses, like other Blake protagonists, are "seen characteristically lifting their arms apart and breaking rocks or books into two, continually dividing material objects as they themselves are divided into various faculties."[4] In contrast, as shown in the second illustration prepared for Dante's *Divine Comedy,*[5] Blake compared the Ark of the Covenant to a "Dove of Peace" and a symbol of liberation. Dante had depicted purgatory as a high mountain with a narrow path leading up to the Garden of Eden, whose climb was necessary to overcome the effects of the Fall of Adam and partake of the Tree of Life. In canto 10, white marble carvings on the wall of the cliff offered examples of the virtue of humility—in this instance, the humility of Mary, the Lord's handmaiden, at the Annunciation, and that of David, the humble Psalmist who, in humble dress, dances before the Lord around the altar of the temple in celebration of the return of the Ark.[6]

Here, these two juxtaposed images are meant to symbolize loss and recovery of 'plain and precious things'[7] as recounted in the Joseph Smith Translation: On the one hand, JST Exodus 34:1-2 tells why the ordinances of the higher priesthood were generally withheld from the people following Israel's rebellion. On the other hand, JST Genesis affirms the lost truth that Moses and the Patriarchs took part in this holy order, and received the necessary understanding of the laws and ordinances of the Gospel that would allow them to ascend the mountain of the Lord and partake of the Tree of Life.[8]

---

1   Moses 1:41.
2   Exodus 32:19.
3   M. Butlin, *Blake,* p. 75.
4   P. Ackroyd, *Blake,* pp. 183. 184.
5   See *Endnote 0-12,* p. 21.
6   H. W. Nibley, *Drama,* p. 18., see D. Alighieri, *Commedia.*
7   1 Nephi 13:26-40.
8   See *Excursus 53: Comparative Explorations of the Mysteries,* p. 663.

as stating "that the Prophet before his death [spoke] about going through the translation of the scriptures again and perfecting it upon points of doctrine which the Lord had restrained him from giving in plainness and fulness at the time."[29]

The extensive nature of the restored prophecies concerning Joseph and his posterity in JST Genesis chapters 44 and 48 leads one to wonder what further revisions could have been made had the Prophet's schedule allowed for more time spent on the translation. For instance, consider the account in Genesis 49 of the patriarchal blessings that Jacob gave to his sons. From the perspective of the JST, this account is important both because of its doctrinal significance and also because the original texts are laden with difficulties for the translator. Yet, despite significant JST additions to the surrounding chapters 48 and 50, Genesis 49 was left disappointingly untouched.[30]

---

29   Cited in G. Q. Cannon, *Life,* pp. 147-148. See *Endnote 0-10,* p. 21.
30   See *Endnote 0-11,* p. 21.

Philip Barlow observes that Joseph Smith made six basic types of changes in the JST:

1. The first consists of the long revealed additions that have little or no biblical parallel, such as the visions of Moses and Enoch, and the passage on Melchizedek…[31]

2. A second type, which overlaps other categories, is a "common-sense" change [e.g., Genesis 6:6 "And it repented the Lord that he had made man…" is revised in Moses 8:25 to read: "And it repented Noah, and his heart was pained that the Lord had made man"[32]]… God, who is perfect, needs no repentance…

3. A third category is "interpretive additions," often signaled by the phrase "or in other words," which the Prophet appended to a passage he wished to clarify…[33]

4. "Harmonization" represents a fourth type of change… Smith reconciled passages that seemed to conflict with other passages…[34]

5. Many changes Smith made are not easily classified; one can observe only that frequently the meaning of a given text has been changed, often idiosyncratically…[35]

6. The final and by far most common type of change the Prophet made in the Bible includes grammatical improvements, technical clarifications, and modernization of terms…[36]

It should be noted that the 1828 Phinney Bible used by Joseph Smith often used more contemporary forms of King James words than other Bibles—in fact, Phinney was a more modern text than the one used in the current LDS Bible edition.[37] This has sometimes led to confusion in trying to sort out which changes were deliberately made by the Prophet and which simply arose from differences in the edition of the KJV he used.[38] Explains Jackson:

It is difficult to say whether the modernized spelling and usage of the Phinney Bible had an influence on the language of the Joseph Smith Translation. In sections of the new translation that have no counterpart in the Bible, both indefinite articles, "a" and "an," are used before words that begin with a pronounced letter "h." In passages on the manuscripts that are found in the King James translation, again both articles are found, despite the near-consistent use of "a" in the underlying Phinney Bible. The inconsistency in the manuscripts suggests that this particular modernization was not a high priority for Joseph Smith. But many other changes he made definitely had the effect of making the Bible more understandable for modern readers. The frequent changes to word order and modernizations in language, such as "wot" to "know"[—the manuscript at Exodus 32:1 revises "wot" to "know" with a note that "know" "should be in the place of 'wot' in all places"—]"saith" to "said," "that" and "which" to "who," and "ye" and "thee" to "you," show that the language of the Joseph Smith Translation was a more radical break with the tradition of the King James Version than were Phinney's limited efforts to update the spelling. Even so, those changes were applied inconsistently in the manuscripts, and the best suggestion is that even though the modernization of spelling and word usage was part of the new translation, other objectives were even more important.[39]

Regarding the completeness of the JST as we have it, Matthews has written:

---

31   Moses ch. 1, 7:20-67; and JST Genesis 14:25-40. See *Endnote 0-13*, p. 21.
32   Cf. Jeremiah 18:8.
33   E.g., JST Genesis 14:36, Luke 6:29.
34   E.g., Matthew 27:3-8 and Acts 1:18-19; John 1:18 and Exodus 33:11.
35   E.g., Proverbs 18:22; Matthew 2:13, 19; Matthew 8:10.
36   E.g., Matthew 3:4, "meat" changed to "food"; Matthew 6:4 "which: changed to "who"; 2 Corinthians 3:4 "to God-ward" changed to "toward God" (P. L. Barlow, *Bible*, pp. 51-53). See *Endnote 0-14*, p. 22.
37   K. P. Jackson, *Cooperstown Bible*, pp. 55-56.
38   R. J. Matthews, *Plainer*, pp. 174-175, 393.
39   K. P. Jackson, *Cooperstown Bible*, pp. 60, 62.

…the manuscript shows that the Prophet went all the way through the Bible from Genesis to Revelation. But it also shows that he did not make all the necessary corrections in one effort. This situation makes it impossible to give a statistical answer to questions about how much of the translation was completed or how much was not completed. What is evident, however, is that any part of the translation might have been further touched upon and improved by additional revelation and emendation by the Prophet.[40]

By 1833, we do know that Joseph felt it was sufficiently complete that preparations for publication could begin.[41]

JST Genesis and the Book of Moses

The material in the book of Moses was originally divided into six parts, titled as follows:

- A Revelation given to Joseph the Revelator June 1830 [= Moses 1][42]

- A Revelation given to the Elders of the Church of Christ on the first book of Moses ~~given to Joseph the Seer~~ Chapter first [= Moses 2-4][43]

- Chapter 2—A Revelation concerning Adam after he had been driven out of the garden of Eden [= Moses 5:1-5:59][44]

- Capter [sic] third <6th>[45] the genealogy from Adam to Enoch & plan of salvation &c [= Moses 6:1-6:52][46]

- Chapter IVth <7th> Enoch prophecy &c [= Moses 7:1-8:12][47]

- Chapter V <8>th Noahs prophecy of the deluge &c [= Moses 8:13-Genesis 6:22][48]

The portions of the book of Moses published by Elder Franklin D. Richards in the first version of the Pearl of Great Price were based on excerpts from Joseph Smith's earliest draft of JST Genesis. This was contained in a manuscript now called Old Testament 1 (OT1). Richards' excerpts had been taken from their first publication in the *Evening and Morning Star*[49] and the *Times and Seasons*[50] as well as from a no-longer-extant personal handwritten copy of some additional unpublished portions of these revelations. Taken together, these represented about three-fourths of the current content of the book of Moses. The bulk of Joseph Smith's work on a second manuscript (OT2) took place between March 1831 and July 1833, though the Prophet continued to make a few revisions and to prepare the manuscript for printing until his death in 1844. OT2 contained many minor revisions in wording over the earlier draft, though relatively little in the way of substantive prophetic additions.

---

40   R. J. Matthews, *Plainer*, p. 215.
41   See *Endnote 0-15*, p. 23.
42   S. H. Faulring, *et al.*, *Original Manuscripts*, p. 83; cf. p. 591.
43   *Ibid.*, p. 86; cf. p. 595. Muhlestein mistakenly states that this heading applied only to Moses 2-3 (K. Muhlestein, *Flow*, p. 43), whereas it actually encompasses Moses 4 as well.
44   S. H. Faulring, *et al.*, *Original Manuscripts*, p. 92; cf. p. 602. Muhlestein mistakenly states that this heading appeared just above Moses 4 (K. Muhlestein, *Flow*, p. 43), when it actually appears just prior to the start of Moses 5.
45   See *Endnote 0-16*, p. 23.
46   *Ibid.*, p. 608; cf. p. 101.
47   *Ibid.*, p. 615; cf. J. Smith, Jr., *Documentary History*, December 1830, 1:133.
48   S. H. Faulring, *et al.*, *Original Manuscripts*, p. 624; cf. p. 111.
49   August 1832 to April 1833.
50   January 1843.

When Elder Orson Pratt revised the Pearl of Great Price in 1878, he completely replaced the previously-used Moses material with a version based on the 1867 RLDS publication of the I.V. Unfortunately, the RLDS publication committee had inadvertently failed to incorporate changes made in the later OT2 manuscript. At the same time, they had included modifications made in the less-reliable versions printed in Church periodicals and had made some idiosyncratic changes of their own. While many of these problems have been corrected in the most recent editions of the I.V., some have unfortunately persisted in publications of the LDS book of Moses. Several other minor changes in text were also made in 1902 by Elder James E. Talmage, under the direction of the First Presidency, and in 1981 when an updated edition of the Pearl of Great Price was published by the Church.[51]

Official Status of the King James Version and the JST

The King James Version is the official Bible for English-speaking members of the LDS Church.[52] Granting that other Bible versions may be more accurate in some respects or easier to read, the KJV is preferred, if for no other reason, because of its lexical and stylistic correspondence to the Book of Mormon and modern-day revelation.[53]

In 1979 and 1981, the Church first published new editions of the scriptures which contained, along with various study aids, extracts of many (but not all) revisions from the JST.[54] Elder Boyd K. Packer heralded this publication event as "the most important thing that [the Church has] done in recent generations."[55] Although it is not the official Bible of the Church, the JST is seen as an invaluable aid in scripture study and a witness for the calling of the Prophet Joseph Smith.[56] The JST texts of Genesis 1-8[57] and Matthew 24[58] in particular hold a place of special importance in the LDS scriptural canon since they have been wholly incorporated within the Pearl of Great Price.

---

51   R. J. Matthews, *What Is*, pp. xxviii, 32, 33, 35, 36. See K. P. Jackson, *Book of Moses*, pp. 1-52 for details.
52   First Presidency of the Church of Jesus Christ of Latter-day Saints, *Statement*.
53   J. F. McConkie, *Revelation*, p. 126; D. Packard, *et al.*, *Feasting*, pp. ix-x. See also discussion in P. L. Barlow, *Bible*, pp. 176-177.
54   For more about the selection process for included excerpts and a useful collection of significant changes not contained in the LDS edition of the Bible, see T. E. Sherry, *et al.*, *Precious Truths*.
55   B. K. Packer, *Scriptures*, p. 53; cf. B. K. Packer, *Errand*, p. 160. See *Endnote 0-17*, p. 23.
56   *LDS Bible Dictionary*, s.v. Joseph Smith Translation.
57   I.e., Moses 1-8.
58   I. e., Joseph Smith-Matthew.

About This Book

A word of explanation is in order concerning the title of this book: *In God's Image and Likeness*, a phrase that has implications not only for human nature but also for the form and character of Divinity.[59] Three dimensions of resemblance between God and man stand out.

First, there is the idea of physical resemblance. While Church doctrine allows for wide differences of opinion regarding the origin of man,[60] LDS scripture is unequivocal in its teaching that Adam was created "in the image of his [God's] own body."[61] The Prophet spoke very plainly about the meaning of these words: "If the veil were rent today and… you would see [God] in all the person, image, fashion, and very form of a man, like yourselves. For Adam was a man formed in his likeness and created in the very fashion and image of God."[62]

Although, in our day, such a concept is rare outside of Mormonism, it was well attested in the ancient teachings of Judaism[63] and early Christianity.[64] For example, in an oft-cited story found in *Genesis Rabbah* 8:10, "Adam's likeness to God is so exact that Adam must be put to sleep so that the angels might worship the right person… In [*Yalqut Shimʻoni*] 1:20 on Genesis 2:9 the angels exclaim when they notice Adam's resemblance to God, 'Are there two powers in heaven?'"[65] Jewish scholar Jacob Neusner finds it "stunning" that the rabbinical commentators took this idea so literally, averring that even "the angels did not know man from God." "I cannot imagine," he says, "a more daring affirmation of humanity."[66]

Regarding the second dimension, Joseph Smith made it clear that the concepts of "image" and "likeness" applied not only to the physical appearance of Adam and Eve, but also to their spiritual nature which was, in the beginning, "innocent, harmless, and spotless." After the Fall, they were made to dwell in a mortal world where they could, in the process of time and through "the Atonement of Christ… and obedience in the Gospel," become sanctified and ultimately "attain to the [full] image, glory, and character of God."[67] This aspiration is echoed in ancient rabbinical teachings,[68] in New Testament passages,[69] in standard formulations in the Orthodox Church,[70] as well as among some in the Western tradition.[71] Though admittedly differing in their detailed understanding of such statements, early Christians would have agreed with Joseph Smith in affirming a "double movement" of image and likeness, whereby humans "begin like God and, at the same time, they come to be like Him."[72]

---

59   R. E. Friedman, *Commentary*, pp. 16-17. See also D. N. Freedman, *Humanity*, pp. 16-17, 22-25, quoted in Moses 2 *Gleanings*, pp. 122-124.

60   J. L. Sorenson, *Origin*, p. 1053.

61   Moses 6:9; cf. *Targum Yerushalmi*: "in the likeness of the presence of the Lord" (J. W. Etheridge, *Onkelos*).

62   J. Smith, Jr., 7 April 1844, in S. Larson, *King Follett*, p. 200. See *Endnote 2-28*, p. 130. Note, however: "The sense in which the Father's body is like a human body must be qualified" (B. Ostler, *Attributes*, p. 352). "Latter-day Saints affirm only that the Father has a body, not that His body has Him" (C. L. Blomberg, *et al.*, *Divide*, p. 88). See *Commentary* 1:6-g, p. 48 and *Excursus 7: Time and Eternity*, p. 537 for a discussion of philosophical and scientific issues.

63   See, e.g., M. S. Smith, *Monotheism*, pp. 86-93; E. J. Hamori, *Embodied God*.

64   See, e.g., D. L. Paulsen, *Embodiment*. One group of fourth-century desert monks became so incensed at Theophilus of Alexandria's assertions of God's incorporeality that they rioted and threatened to kill him. In response, he wrote a letter telling them to continue believing "a literal reading of Scripture, that God had bodily parts" (K. A. Shirts, *Resurrection*, citing E. A. Clark, *New Perspectives*, p. 147).

65   P. B. Munoa, *Four Powers*, p. 101.

66   J. Neusner, *Confronting*, p. 63. See also D. N. Freedman, *Humanity*, pp. 16-17. Note the "individual's close identification with God" in the rabbinical idea that He will "stroll with the righteous in the Garden of Eden in time to come. The righteous will be frightened in His presence, and the Holy and Blessed One will say, 'Why are you frightened of Me? I am just like you'" (*Sifra Behukotai* 111b, cited in A. J. Heschel, *Heavenly Torah*, p. 192).

67   J. Smith, Jr., *Words*, 9 July 1843, p. 231, punctuation modernized, bracketed word added for clarification; cf. T. G. Madsen, *LDS View*, p. 105; J. Smith, Jr., *Teachings 2007*, p. 52

68   See, e. g., A. J. Heschel, *Heavenly Torah*, pp. 192-193.

69   E.g., Romans 8:14-19; 2 Peter 1:3-4.

70   See *Endnote 0-18*, p. 23.

71   See *Endnote 0-19*, p. 23. See also *Figure E2-1*, p. 517.

72   J. E. Faulconer, *Adam and Eve*, 10; cf. Moses 4:28; Irenaeus, *Heresies*, 5:6:1, pp. 531-532. See *Endnote 0-20*, p. 23.

FIGURE 0-6. *First Parents, 2005*
Jay Bryant Ward, 1971-

SEE FIGURE P-1.

And Adam... begat a son in his own likeness, after his own image.[1] In deliberate parallel, this verse portrays the resemblance of a child to his mortal parents with the same words that described the relationship of Adam and Eve to God.

We are left to speculate about the identity of the child depicted in this illustration. Is it their firstborn son or daughter?[2] If so, what were the feelings of their heart, knowing as they did the opportunities and difficulties that would befall their posterity because of their choice in Eden? Is the baby Cain—or Abel?[3] What parent fully comprehends how fragile and unpredictable may be the life of a child? At such a moment of high hopes, who could have foreseen the sad fates of these two brothers?[4] Or perhaps the child is Seth, appointed to carry a righteous line forward, in contrast to the seemingly universal rebellion of their other children.[5]

Jay Bryant Ward is a native of Idaho Falls, Idaho. The painting was commissioned for the cover of the January 2006 *Ensign* magazine. Admitting that the subject was "a bit intimidating," he focused on "trying to convey the warmth and magic of... a new child."[6]

1 Moses 6:10.
2 Moses 5:2
3 Moses 5:16-17.
4 See Moses 5 *Gleanings*, p. 405.
5 Moses 6:1-2; cf. 5:13ff.
6 J. B. Ward, *News*.

Ancient and modern revelation describe a third dimension of resemblance between God and man: that of parenthood. Jesus repeatedly used terms "Father"[73] and "Abba"[74] as He taught and prayed. Paul declared that "we are the offspring of God,"[75] and other scriptures clearly affirm a likeness between the role of "human fathers" and that of God as "the Father of our spirits."[76] The parallel between the fatherhood of man and that of God is further reinforced when Seth is described as being "in [Adam's] own likeness, after his own image"[77] Although, admittedly, the process by which the spirits of mankind come into being has not been revealed—and moreover conceding that there is some aspect of the spirit's existence that is without beginning[78]—LDS doctrine affirms the fact that: "All men and women are in the similitude of the universal Father and Mother, and are literally the sons and daughters of Deity."[79]

"Be ye therefore perfect," we read in Matthew, "even as your Father which is in heaven is perfect."[80] The central message of the book of Moses is not revealed in its stories of the Creation and the Fall, as essential as these accounts may be, but rather in its invitation to conform our lives to the divine pattern whereby we may come to fully reflect God's image

73 Matthew 5:16-48; 6:1-32; 7:11-21; 10:20-33; 11:25-27; 15:13; 16:17-27; 18:10-35; 23:9; 26:29-53; Mark 11:25-26; Luke 6:36; 9:26; 10:21-22; 11:2-13; 12:30-32; 15:12-29; John 5:17-45; 6:27-65; 8:16-56; 10:15-38; 12:26-50; 14:2-31; 15:1-26; 16:3-32; 17:1-25; 20:17-21.
74 = Aramaic "father"—see Mark 14:36; cf. Romans 8:15; Galatians 4:6. Barney, *et al.* note: "The popular notion that this was a diminutive form with the intimate connotation of 'daddy' in our culture is not correct" (K. L. Barney. *et al., NT Footnotes*, 1:250).
75 Acts 17:29.
76 Hebrews 12:9. See K. L. Barker, *Zondervan*, Hebrews 12:9, p. 1913; cf. F. F. Bruce, *Hebrews*, Hebrews 12:9, p. 341. See *Endnote 0-21*, p. 24.
77 Moses 6:10; cf. Genesis 5:3.
78 D&C 93:23, 29-30, 33; K. W. Godfrey, *Intelligence*; P. N. Hyde, *Intelligences*; see *Excursus 8: The Origin and Premortal Existence of Human Spirits,* p. 540.
79 J. F. Smith, *et al., Origin*; see *Commentary 2:27-b*, p. 115. See *Endnote 0-22*, p. 24.
80 Matthew 5:48; cf. 3 Nephi 12:48. See *Endnote 0-23*, p. 24.

and likeness.[81] In the early chapters of the book of Moses, as in modern LDS temples, the story of events surrounding the Creation, the Fall, and the mortal life of Adam and Eve provides the context for the eventual unfolding of a progressive series of covenants intended to save and exalt mankind.[82] We read that, through faithfulness to each of these covenants, Enoch and his people became "of one heart and one mind,"[83] and were taken up to walk in the presence of God.[84] With similar intent, this wondrous work of scripture has been expressly written to "call [us] out of darkness into his marvelous light."[85]

Though I have written this book from the perspective of a believing and practicing member of the Church of Jesus Christ of Latter-day Saints,[86] I wish to make it clear that it is not an official publication of the Church, and that the views that are expressed are solely my own. Furthermore, I recognize that the nature of the subject matter has required my delving into many topics for which I claim no special expertise. Mistaken assertions, faulty matters of judgment, typographical errors, and editorial imperfections of many kinds have doubtless made their way into these pages. Thus I gratefully welcome any corrections or suggestions, in the hope that improvements may be made in future editions. It has been my prayer that this book, despite its insufficiencies, may be in its own way a worthy addition to the "great cloud of witnesses"[87] of the truthfulness of the restored gospel of Jesus Christ, and an encouragement to deeper study and appreciation of the book of Moses.

Arrangement of the Text and Illustrations

This volume contains the complete text of Moses 1-6:12—beginning with the account of the vision of Moses and continuing to the death of Adam. Each of the six chapters of commentary is prefaced by an *Overview* section discussing selected themes. A *Text and Commentary* section then follows. In this section, the text of the book of Moses is given at the top of each page, with accompanying commentary below. Bold-formatted words in the scriptural text point the eye to phrases that are the subject of commentary. Next, a *Gleanings* section appears, containing extended quotations. *Endnotes* are included at the end of each chapter.

Following the chapters on Moses 1-6, a separate *Excursus* section, containing extended discussions of selected subjects, can be found. An *Appendix* is dedicated to the topic of *The Origin of Man*. The *Annotated Bibliography of Ancient Texts* that follows provides descriptions of non-scriptural sources relevant to the book of Moses and the entire book of Genesis, grouped by the cultural or religious tradition that produced them. Where I thought it might be helpful to the reader, I also included general background information and summaries of pertinent beliefs of the cited groups. Throughout the entire book, abbreviated bibliographic information for each work consulted appears in the footnotes at the bottom of each page,[88] with additional source details available in the *References* section. Footnotes also document extensive cross-references to other sections of the book, preceded by an appropriate key word (e.g., *Commentary, Figure, Endnote,* overview). A set of *Color Plates* for selected figures

---

81   G. A. Anderson, *Perfection*, p. 8. See *Endnote 0-24*, p. 26.

82   See the overview of Moses 5, pp. 341-350.

83   Moses 7:18.

84   Moses 7:69.

85   1 Peter 2:9. Mercy Fielding Thompson recalls the Prophet specifically applying these words to the blessings of the endowment (M. F. Thompson, "Recollections of the Prophet Joseph Smith," *Juvenile Instructor*, 1 July 1892, p. 400, cited in J. Smith, Jr., *Teachings 2007*, p. 414).

86   See *Endnote 0-25*, p. 26.

87   Hebrews 12:1.

88   Due to an unfortunate glitch, citations with two authors appear with the first author's name, followed by "*et al.*," instead of adhering to the usual convention reserving this format for sources with three or more authors.

follows. For convenience, a set of *Indexes* appear at the very end of the book, including a *Thumbnail Index to Figures*.

Significant variants within the original JST manuscripts and the current edition of the Pearl of Great Price are described in the commentary. Although important JST modifications to the KJV text are signaled explicitly in the *Commentary* section, readers must consult their own Bibles for an exhaustive comparison of minor differences between the book of Moses and Genesis.

British spellings have been made consistent with American conventions. Transliterations of Greek and Hebrew terms have not been standardized but, when referenced by authors, are usually rendered in the same form as they appear in their original publication.

Unlike the book of Abraham, the book of Moses did not come to us with illuminating facsimiles. In selecting suitable illustrations to accompany the scriptural commentary, I have relied solely on personal taste and preference with respect to the choice of depictions and their place in the text—sometimes, in fact, I have associated meanings and settings that are quite foreign to the context of their first appearance. While considering the appropriateness of wresting these illustrations from their original surroundings and significations, I was interested to discover that such a practice may not be without ancient precedent: Kevin Barney argues that this approach could have been followed either by Abraham or an ancient Egyptian-Jewish redactor who may have adopted or adapted existing vignettes originally drawn to serve in an Egyptian religious context for use as illustrations to the text of the book of Abraham.[89] Whether or not this actually happened during the compilation of the book of Abraham, the idea served as welcome encouragement for the approach adopted here.

The prophetic books of the brilliant and eccentric visionary William Blake[90] also provided a model for the marriage of illustration and text in this commentary. Mitchell observed that Blake "tended to minimize the literal, denotative correspondences between the two forms,"[91] noting that "when Blake 'illustrates' a text, he expands and transforms it, and often provides a vision which can operate in complete separation from it."[92] In fact, Blake "often expands upon some point of only minor importance in the text, or even conveys an opposed or ironic vision."[93] Among the important functions of this technique is that "the disparity between poem and illustration entices the mind of the reader to supply the missing connections."[94] Also important for the illustration of a work of scripture featuring characters such as Adam and Eve, or Cain and Abel, in whose stories each one of us is intended to see ourselves, is the fact that Blake's "human figures have a kind of allegorical anonymity, and are clearly designed as types, not as subtly differentiated portraits."[95]

Sources and Citations

To aid the reader's own explorations, I have tried to provide complete documentation for the citations or ideas included in the commentary. Where references to third-party works are embedded within a given citation (e.g., ancient sources referred to by modern

---

89 See *Endnote 0-26*, p. 26.
90 See *Endnote 0-27*, p. 27.
91 W. J. T. Mitchell, *Blake's Art*, p. 139.
92 *Ibid.*, p. 138.
93 *Ibid.*, p. 144.
94 *Ibid.*, p. 141.
95 *Ibid.*, p. 145.

authors), I have attempted where possible to check the original sources by autopsy in order to verify accuracy and appropriateness, and have silently made corrections or updates where I thought it might be necessary or useful. Sometimes, when modern authors have not supplied references to clear allusions to scripture or other important sources, or where I have otherwise felt that it might be helpful to point out additional texts or cross-references within the book that relate to their assertions, I have inserted relevant citations to supporting documents or primary sources. In many cases I have also silently modernized or corrected punctuation and capitalization in quotations. Where actual changes in wording were made or in order to compensate for gaps due to ellipsis, I have documented the location of changes, expansions, or the insertion of alternate terms by square brackets.

Frequently, I associate multiple citations with the same passage of commentary. This practice is intended to signal consensus and differences of opinion among modern commentators, or to indicate concordance and divergence among ancient sources. More rarely, a citation may include references to multiple editions of a given source. It is hoped that these extensive links to pertinent references will encourage readers to check and improve upon my conclusions through their own study.

For the convenience of the reader, I have tried to substitute citations to more recent editions for older or less accessible ones (e.g., James Charlesworth's *Old Testament Pseudepigrapha* in place of R. H. Charles' *Apocrypha and Pseudepigrapha*) and English equivalents for non-English sources (e.g., *Mimekor Yisrael* for *Die Sagen der Juden*, Schaff for Migne). I have also substituted book of Moses chapter and verse numbers in the place of embedded references to the early chapters of Genesis occurring in works quoted in the text.

Unless otherwise noted, the translations of excerpts from non-English works are my own. Only rarely have I reproduced diacritical marks or vowel pointing in foreign terms that appear in the text.

Where multiple versions or editions of works containing a cited source may make it difficult for the reader to find a reference by page number alone, I have included dates (e.g., for statements of Joseph Smith) or chapter numbers (e.g., transcripts of courses taught by Hugh Nibley, pseudepigraphal or midrashic sources appearing in multiple editions) as part of the citation. In citing the words of Joseph Smith, I have generally used the readily available *Teachings of the Prophet Joseph Smith* or *Documentary History of the Church* in preference to more primary documents.[96] In some cases, however, I refer directly to manuscript sources when they seem to shed additional light on an interpretation.

I have not explicitly distinguished LDS from non-LDS authors, except when it concerned materials written by current or former General Authorities of the Church. In the latter case, I have prefaced the name of the author by the ecclesiastical title they held when the contribution was first made or published (e.g., "Elder," "President")—and frequently, in the case of Joseph Smith, the title of "Prophet."

On the Use of Ancient Texts

Ancient texts from Jewish, Islamic, early Christian, and other sources are quoted widely throughout this book. These present a special problem because in so many cases the age and provenance of these writings are uncertain. Moreover, the motivations of the (frequently

---

96   See *Endnote 0-28*, p. 27.

anonymous) authors, and the historical and prophetic basis of their compositions usually remain in doubt. Robinson, for one, has noted the difficulties in distinguishing between inspired literature (i.e., historical or revelatory writings akin to canonical scripture), inspired fiction (i.e., stories designed to teach doctrinal principles such as Elder Boyd K. Packer's parable *The Mediator*[97]), and outright "lying for the Lord" (i.e., pseudonymous forgeries that deceitfully present themselves as authoritative in order to promulgate self-serving interpretations).[98] With regard to the last category, R. H. Charles "maintained that the device of [deliberate] pseudonymity was a pious fraud adopted in a time that no longer believed in continuing revelation by authors who nevertheless wished to effect religious changes."[99]

Further complicating the evaluation of extracanonical texts is the multi-layered nature of the sources from which they were typically composed.[100] Such writings rarely if ever constitute *de novo* accounts of sacred events. Rather, they tend to incorporate diverse traditions of varying value and antiquity in ways that make it difficult to tease apart the contribution that each makes to the whole.[101] As a result, even relatively late documents rife with midrashic speculations unattested elsewhere,[102] unique Islamic assertions,[103] or seemingly fantastic Christian interpolations[104] may sometimes preserve fragments of authentically-inspired principles, history, or doctrine,[105] or may otherwise bear witness of legitimate exegetically-derived[106] or ritually-transmitted[107] actualities.

Nor are such truths confined to writings from Abrahamic lands and faiths.[108] As the Lord pointedly told Nephi: "I shall also speak unto *all* nations of the earth and they shall write it."[109] In light of this fact, it should not be at all surprising if genuinely revealed teachings, promulgated at one time but subsequently lost or distorted,[110] sometimes appear to have survived in heterodox strands of religious traditions the world over. Many of these teachings have served, in the words of the First Presidency, to "enlighten whole nations and to bring a higher level of understanding to individuals."[111] Nor, it seems, could the Lord's purposes have been achieved in any other way. As Elder Orson F. Whitney once said: "God is using more than one people for the accomplishment of his great and marvelous work. The Latter-day Saints cannot do it all. It is too vast, too arduous, for any one people."[112] Thus, in our search for truth, we must, as Charlesworth expressed, "be attuned critically to all possible sources of revelation," including "the word from God that has been heard by the great thinkers, inspired poets, and musicians."[113]

---

97 B. K. Packer, *Mediator 1977*; B. K. Packer, *Mediator 1978*; B. K. Packer, *Errand*, pp. 45-47.
98 S. E. Robinson, *Lying*, pp. 134-135.
99 Cited in *ibid.*, p. 142. See *Endnote 0-29*, p. 27.
100 S. K. Brown, *Nag Hammadi*, p. 257. See *Endnote 0-30*, p. 28.
101 See *Endnote 0-31*, p. 28.
102 See *Endnote 0-32*, p. 28.
103 See *Endnote 0-33*, p. 28.
104 See *Endnote 0-34*, p. 28.
105 See *Endnote 0-35*, p. 29.
106 See, e.g., J. L. Kugel, *Instances*, p. 156. See *Endnote 0-44*, p. 31.
107 See, e.g., H. W. Nibley, *Myths*, p. 42, quoted below.
108 See *Endnote 0-36*, p. 29.
109 2 Nephi 29:12, emphasis mine; cf. Alma 29:8, G. E. Jones, *Apocryphal*, pp. 28-29; cf. B. H. Roberts, *Defense*, 1:512; J. Smith, Jr., *Teachings*, 16 February 1832, pp. 10-11; 22 January 1834, p. 61.
110 See *Endnote 0-37*, p. 29.
111 S. W. Kimball, *et al.*, *God's Love*; S. J. Palmer, *Expanding*, p. v.
112 O. F. Whitney, *Discourse (April 1928)*, p. 59; see also *Respect for diversity of faiths, Diversity*.
113 J. H. Charlesworth, *Protestant View*, p. 84.

In evaluating evidence of antiquity for works of extracanonical literature, scholars must constantly maintain the careful balance articulated by Nickelsburg:

> One should not simply posit what is convenient with the claim that later texts reflected earlier tradition. At the same time, thoroughgoing skepticism is inconsonant with the facts as we know them and as new discoveries continue to reveal them: extant texts represent only a fragment of the written and oral tradition that once existed. Caution, honest scholarly tentativeness, and careful methodology remain the best approach to the data.[114]

By way of contrast, the comparative approach of Frazer[115] and others of the myth and ritual school of a century ago is largely discounted today,[116] its results having been compromised due to:

> (1) the looseness of the equations; (2) the reliance on suggestive and circumstantial detail; (3) the tendency to persuade by suggesting a large number of alternatives, all tending in the same direction, as if exhausting the possibilities, and cumulatively overdetermining the desired connection; (4) the disparate quality of the sources of evidence; and (5) the tendency to list all positive examples, but either no or few negative ones.[117]

An additional consideration complicating the evaluation of ancient sources is the fact that the line between historical and ritual aspects of some accounts is often purposely blurred for didactic reasons, as we see in the case of LDS temple texts.[118] In such situations, though the accuracy of an ancient account as a historical record or interpretation may be questionable, it may still be of interest because of the way it resonates with authentic doctrinal concepts and revealed ordinances. On this point, Nibley observes:[119]

> If we attempt to untangle the probably historical from the fanciful, we soon discover the common ground on which they meet and fuse: it is ritual. Myths arise at attempts to explain ritual doings, whose meaning has been forgotten—"What mean these stones?"[120] After much discussion back and forth, the consensus now emerges that it is the rites and ordinances that come first. This should have been clear from the outset, since myths and legends are innumerable while the rites and ordinances found throughout the world are surprisingly few and uniform, making it apparent that it is the stories that are invented—the rites are always there.[121]

> Such indeed has always been the Latter-day Saint position. Adam first performed an ordinance and when asked to give an explanation of it replied that he knew of none "save the Lord commanded me."[122] Then it was that the true explanation came forth from the mouth of a heavenly instructor.

Summarizing the LDS attitude toward ancient and modern revelation of religious truths, Truman G. Madsen writes:[123]

> To say that the gospel of Jesus Christ in its fulness is restored is to say that something has been lost and regained—but it is not to say that everything has. The Mormon believes that after every

---

114 G. W. E. Nickelsburg, *Judaism*, pp. 25-26.
115 J. G. Frazer, *Golden Bough*.
116 See *Endnote 0-38*, p. 30.
117 E. Csapo, *Mythology*, pp. 36-37. See *Endnote 0-39*, p. 30.
118 J. E. Faulconer, *Incarnation*.
119 H. W. Nibley, *Myths*, p. 42; cf. H. W. Nibley, *Sacred*, pp. 591-593; R. Guénon, *Symboles*, p. 210. See *Endnote 0-41*, p. 31.
120 See Joshua 4:6.
121 See *Endnote 0-40*, p. 30.
122 Moses 5:6.
123 T. G. Madsen, *Essay*, pp. xvi, xvii.

outpouring of divine light there is a record of degeneration and loss, the signs of which he thinks he can see in every generation. But Mormons have resisted from the outset the sectarian impulse: the isolation of a text or principle and the insistence that they alone possess and practice it. Exultant at a new revelatory downpour, the Mormon sees the implication: unless the same truths, authorities, and powers can be found in prior times and places; unless there have been genuine prophets, apostles and holy men who were, for all their individual traits, in touch with divine outpourings; unless there have been saints of former as well as of latter days—unless these things are so, Mormonism is without foundation. In other words, Mormonism has no claim to be a viable religion in the present unless it has been a viable religion in the past. And this is not just a halfhearted concession that there has been sort of, or part of, or a shadow of the fulness of the Gospel. It is to say that some, at least, among the ancients had it all. It is to match the thesis that from the early (and supposedly crude) beginnings things have become better; just as often they have, instead, become worse. Spiritual anabolism and catabolism have been at work in the religious life from the beginning....

If the outcome of hard archaeological, historical, and comparative discoveries in the past century is an embarrassment to exclusivistic readings of religion, that, to the Mormon, is a kind of confirmation and vindication. His faith assures him not only that Jesus anticipated his great predecessors (who were really successors) but that hardly a teaching or a practice is utterly distinct or peculiar or original in his earthly ministry. Jesus was not a plagiarist, unless that is the proper name for one who repeats himself. He was the original author. The gospel of Jesus Christ came with Christ in the meridian of time only because the gospel of Jesus Christ came from Christ in prior dispensations. He did not teach merely a new twist on a syncretic-Mediterranean tradition. His earthly ministry enacted what had been planned and anticipated "from before the foundations of the world,"[124] and from Adam down.

While recognizing the labors of generations of scholars that have begun to reveal the nature and sources of the voluminous canonical and extracanonical literature bearing on the themes of this book, there is much still to be learned. In particular, while many resemblances among ancient and modern sources have been exposed, it is a more difficult work to transform these parallels into "bridges" demonstrating how related ideas from widely-scattered cultures and diverse eras could have been shared and transmitted.[125] Though the teachings and revelations of Joseph Smith demonstrate to my own satisfaction that archaic concepts and stories can be recovered in exceptional circumstances through divine revelation, the diffusion of ideas by more ordinary means is clearly the rule in history.

Not only will future research continue to shed new light on the meaning of obscure scriptural concepts, it will also no doubt demonstrate that many of my readings have been the result of an inadequate grasp of ancient sources—while, on the other hand, countless illuminating sidelights have been missed entirely.[126] In selecting arguments and sources to be cited in this book, I have usually tried to err on the side of inclusion, thus making these texts more readily available to readers for study, discussion, and comparison of perspectives.[127] This approach has inevitably resulted in a work that resembles more an unevenly sifted and sometimes contradictory scrapbook of ideas and sources than a coherent and inerrant "guide for the perplexed." In this respect, perhaps, the sole subjective valuation of the worth of the book I am qualified to make is that it tries to be something like the kind of thing I should have liked to have had myself at the beginning of my own study—if only it had it been, in addition, written by someone with better credentials in the relevant fields

---

124 E.g., John 17:24; Ephesians 1:4; 1 Peter 1:20; Alma 22:13; D&C 130:20; Moses 5:57; Abraham 1:3.
125 Cf. E. R. Goodenough, *Introduction to Philo*, pp. ix-xi.
126 S. E. Robinson, *Lying*, pp. 147-148.
127 See *Endnote 0-42*, p. 31.

of scholarship than I can claim. Thus, it is with humble cognizance of such limitations that I proffer my mite of commentary, reflections, source translations, cross-references, footnotes, endnotes, bibliographic annotations, references, and indexes—all of which have been lovingly assembled in the hope of assisting readers with their own explorations of the book of Moses. Happily, I can be confident that future reflection and dialogue among fellow scripture lovers—augmented and confirmed by continuing revelation—will sooner or later identify those instances where limited knowledge and faulty judgment have led me to misinterpret sources or unwisely position the line of inclusion. In the meantime, as in any such endeavor, the guiding principle in determining the value of the sources and opinions in this book necessarily must be *caveat lector*—let the reader beware![128]

Elder Bruce R. McConkie has outlined the essential preconditions for any benefit to accrue from the use of extracanonical texts: "Obviously, to gain any real value from a study of apocryphal writings, the student must first have an extended background of gospel knowledge, a comprehensive understanding of the standard works of the Church, plus the guidance of the Spirit."[129] However, even when these preconditions are met, LDS readers may encounter additional pitfalls in their approach to extracanonical literature. For example, Gillum warns about extreme attitudes that lead people either to completely eschew such writings or to develop an unhealthy obsession with them.[130] While recognizing the ease with which any of us can be led astray when our enthusiasm outstrips our understanding, he also argues that "even as we should be prepared and open to personal revelation, so should we be ready and eager to learn from additional truths which may confirm our fundamental beliefs. Perhaps these apocryphal discoveries are mere preparations for more divine writings to be given us later." Revealing the principle governing his own stance, he writes that "whatever I read as apocrypha, in the very general sense, must not lead me farther afield, but back to the divine word of God."[131]

128   D&C 91:4-5; S. K. Brown, *Nag Hammadi*, pp. 257-258, 267-268.
129   B. R. McConkie, *Mormon Doctrine*, s.v., Apocrypha, p. 42; cf. D&C 91:4-6; E. J. Brandt, *Jasher*, pp. 308-309.
130   G. P. Gillum, *Bibliography*. See *Endnote 0-43*, p. 31.
131   *Ibid.*, p. 128.

Endnotes

0-1 Based on the results of their pioneering studies, Matthews[132] and Howard[133] had concluded that there was a period of overlap between March 8 and April 7, 1831—concurrent with the earliest phase of New Testament translation—during which OT1 Genesis 19:36-24:42a was completed and OT2 1:1-24:42a was recopied in slightly modified form. However, based on his later research, Jackson has concluded: "We understand the chronology better now. There was no overlap period."[134] For a review of other JST topics in recent research, see Jackson.[135]

0-2 It is both striking and characteristic of the Prophet that he so quickly followed the instructions given in the revelation by abruptly changing his translation priorities. Bushman observes: "Judging by his actions, Joseph believed in the revelations more than anyone.[136] From the beginning, he was his own best follower. Having the word of God at his back gave him enormous confidence."[137]

0-3 Jackson explains:

> Even though some of the… corrections [made after 1833] provide important clarifications and insights, the overwhelming majority of significant contributions of the Joseph Smith Translation were made during the original dictation… [Several] facts cast doubt on the common belief that he continued to revise the wording of the translation the rest of his life. From 2 July 1833 on, there are no references in his diaries and letters to his making additional changes. There are several statements regarding the preparation of the manuscript for publication, which probably refer not to changes in the translation but to the many insertions of punctuation, capitalization, and verse numbering. We cannot identify the handwritings or dates for these small changes, but most were probably made by clerks working under the Prophet's direction.[138]

In view of the many statements on record regarding the Prophet's efforts to bring the entire JST into publication, and its appearance in part in a series of Church publications, it is inaccurate to conclude that "he made no serious effort to publish the new translation."[139]

0-4 Additional translation work with direct relevance to Genesis had occupied the Prophet beginning in 1835, when Egyptian mummies and papyri first came into his hands.[140] By March 1842, Joseph Smith had begun publishing excerpts from his translation of the book of Abraham but, as with the JST, circumstances hindered his intention to publish the work in entirety.

Concerning the potential length of the completed translation of the book of Abraham, Oliver Cowdery stated that he could not say "how large volumes they will make; but judging from their size, and the comprehensiveness of the language, one might reasonably expect to see a sufficient [number] to develop much upon the mighty acts of the ancient men of God."[141] Scholars estimate that the current text of the book of Abraham constitutes perhaps about one-fourth of what was translated by Joseph Smith.[142] This somewhat conservative estimate of the size of the manuscript is based on Anson Call's recollection that a reading of the then-extant translation took two hours, compared to what would be about a half hour reading of the portions of the book of Abraham now contained in the Pearl of Great Price. Call wrote: "Joseph… said to us, 'Sit down and we will read to you from the translations of the book of Abraham.' Oliver Cowdery then read until he was tired when Thomas Marsh read making altogether about two hours."[143]

0-5 See Royal Skousen for a review of these recent studies of the original JST manuscripts.[144]

0-6 Of the fact that the need for these corrections was not seen to diminish the importance of the Bible for the early Saints, Givens perceptively writes:

---

132   R. J. Matthews, *Plainer*, pp. 67, 59, 73, 79.
133   R. P. Howard, *Restoration* 1995, pp. 66-68.
134   K. P. Jackson, *August 21 2006; July 6 2006*.
135   K. P. Jackson, *New Discoveries*.
136   See also R. L. Bushman, *Creation of the Sacred*, p. 98.
137   R. L. Bushman, *Rough Stone*, p. 173.
138   K. P. Jackson, *Genesis*, pp. 28-29.
139   R. L. Bushman, *Mormonism*, p. 68.
140   J. Gee, *Guide*, pp. 1-5.
141   O. Cowdery, *Mummies*, p. 236.
142   M. R. Ash, *ABCs*.
143   Anson Call, *Manuscript Journal*, Summer 1838, p. 9, cited in J. Gee, *Tragedy*, pp. 111-112.
144   R. Skousen, *Earliest*.

Joseph Smith's 1842 pronouncement that Latter-day Saints "believe the Book of Mormon to be the word of God,"[145] whereas they only accord the same credence to the Bible "as far as it is translated correctly,"[146] accords the former some kind of preeminence. The error would be to see, as one scholar has, a definitive "demotion of the Christian Bible by virtue of his claim that it had been improperly translated."[147] The matter isn't quite that simple. For one thing, as Philip Barlow has pointed out:

> Nothing… captures the evolving but enduring religious quintessence of Mormonism and its relationship to the balance of American religion better than a firm, comparative grasp of the Bible's place among the Latter-day Saints. This assertion applies even to Mormon theology and revelation, which… is inextricably enmeshed with and dependent on prior and often unconscious biblical perspectives.[148]

One historian even concludes, based on the relatively few changes Joseph made in his translation, that "what the effort demonstrated was not the distance, but the close parallels the early Saints and their first converts saw between the Bible and the Book of Mormon."[149] Apparently, Joseph was not speaking entirely tongue in cheek when he wrote, in response to the question of "wherein you differ from other sects" that "we believe the Bible."[150] As mentioned previously, early converts used the Bible as the standard against which they measured the Book of Mormon's teachings. Grant Underwood has shown that in early LDS publications the Bible was quoted anywhere from 19 to 40 times as often as the Book of Mormon.[151] Clearly this is hardly evidence of the Bible's demotion.[152]

0-7   Howard observes:

> One interesting insight comes to us when we see how much more extensive a revision of the … text was made, proportionately, in that part of the manuscripts written out in full.… [T]he natural tendency for the "translators" when writing out the text in full was to make many more revisions per verse and chapter of the King James text than was the case when they later adopted the brief notation system of transcribing their revisions.[153]

0-8   Of course, having an understanding of priesthood ordinances is not the same as being authorized to perform them. As Ehat, *et al.* have written about the "ordinances whereby men were ordained kings and priests": "These ordinances were not introduced in Kirtland because Elijah had not come to confer the fulness of the priesthood upon the Prophet before he administered the Kirtland Temple ordinances."[154]

0-9   This possibility should not be construed to imply that the Prophet did not make serious efforts to prepare the 1833 manuscript of the JST for publication during his lifetime, but only that he might not have been authorized at the beginning to teach everything he had learned during the translation process to others.

Another example of a revelation that was not published in Joseph Smith's lifetime is his revelation on war (D&C 87), received on December 25, 1832 and alluded to in D&C 130:12-13 (2 April 1843), and possibly never recorded in its completeness. Woodford[155] describes the extensive nature of the Prophet's visions on this subject as follows:

> Joseph later recorded in his history that he had seen in visions the end of this nation[156] and the breaking up of the government[157] if it continued to disregard the rights of the citizens. Elder Grant also recorded the extent of the visions by Joseph Smith concerning these matters. He wrote:

---

145   Article of Faith 8.
146   *Ibid.*
147   J. G. Gager, *Early*, p. 59.
148   P. L. Barlow, *Bible*, p. xi.
149   T. Smith, *Biblical Culture*, p. 21.
150   J. Smith, Jr., *Teachings*, 8 May 1838, p. 119.
151   G. Underwood, *Usage*, p. 53.
152   T. L. Givens, *Hand*, pp. 190-191.
153   R. P. Howard, *Restoration 1969*, pp. 92-93; cf. R. J. Matthews, *Plainer*, p. 80.
154   A. F. Ehat, *et al.*, cited in J. Smith, Jr., *Words*, p. 302 n. 9.
155   R. J. Woodford, *Historical Development*, 2:1094.
156   J. Smith, Jr., *Documentary History*, 4 March 1840, 4:89.
157   *Ibid.*, 16 December 1843, 6:116.

> The Prophet stood in his own house when he told several of us of the night the visions of heaven were opened to him, in which he saw the American continent drenched in blood, and he saw nations rising up against nation. He also saw the father shed the blood of the son, and the son the blood of the father; the mother put to death the daughter, and the daughter the mother; and natural affection forsook the hearts of the wicked; for he saw that the Spirit of God should be withdrawn from the inhabitants of the earth, in consequence of which there should be blood upon the face of the whole earth, except among the people of the Most High. The Prophet gazed upon the scene his vision presented, until his heart sickened, and he besought the Lord to close it up again.[158]

President Brigham Young was among those that felt that it "was not wisdom to publish it to the world" until many years after it was received.[159]

0-10　The accuracy of this statement, however, is questioned by Jackson: "This is a third-hand account that is hard to reconcile with known statements from Joseph Smith. It was published in 1888. I have serious doubts about it."[160] Though Jackson rightly raises questions about the provenance of the remembrance, I see nothing implausible or particularly difficult to reconcile in the statement itself.

0-11　Jackson sees such a scenario as very unlikely: "I think that Joseph Smith knew what he was doing. We don't have evidence of him complaining that he didn't have the time to work on it. When he felt it was finished, he announced that it was finished, and he quit working on it."[161] However, as a potential example of the difficulties posed by the rapid translation of the Old Testament, Royal Skousen notes that Isaiah 50 was "slavishly copied" from the 1830 edition of the Book of Mormon, "including all the errors that had entered the Book of Mormon text during its earlier transmission."[162] Skousen also sees the practice of marking entire books as correct near the end of the work on the JST[163] and the marking of other books as "virtually correct (with only a handful of changes)"[164] as evidence that "Joseph Smith definitely appear[ed] to be in a hurry to get this work done."[165]

0-12　"[J]ust like Mozart left his *Requiem* unfinished, so did Blake die before completing his illustrations of Dante's *Inferno*–the voyage into death. The commission for Dante's *Inferno* came to Blake in 1826, but his death in 1827 meant that only a handful of the watercolors were completed."[166]

0-13　Concerning the explicitly revelatory process by which Joseph Smith came to at least some of his new understandings of biblical texts, Flake writes:[167]

> Contemporaneous sources indicate that Smith made his more extensive changes to KJV Genesis by employing the same methods as when working from records purportedly written in ancient languages. Smith is quoted as saying: "After I got through translating the Book of Mormon, I took up the Bible to read with the Urim and Thummim. I read the first chapter of Genesis, and I saw the things as they were done, I turned over the next and the next, and the whole passed before me like a grand panorama; and so on chapter after chapter until I read the whole of it. I saw it all!"[168] A more authoritative account is provided by Smith himself in February 1832. "Upon my return from Amherst [Massachusetts] conference, I resumed the translation of the Scriptures.... While translating St. John's Gospel, myself and Elder Rigdon saw the following vision" of the resurrection of the dead.[169] Finally, in an 1843 funeral sermon, probably alluding to the account in Matt. 27:52 of graves opening at the death of Jesus, Smith spoke of "the visions that roll like an overflowing

---

158　J. M. Grant, *2 April 1854*, 2:147.

159　R. J. Woodford, *Historical Development*, 2:1105-1106. See B. Young, *20 May 1860*, p. 58.

160　K. P. Jackson, *August 21, 2006*; *July 6, 2006*.

161　K. P. Jackson, *July 6, 2006*; cf. K. P. Jackson, *Genesis*, p. 30.

162　R. Skousen, *Earliest*, p. 461.

163　Ruth, Ezra, Esther, Lamentations, Obadiah, Micah, Nahum, Habakkuk, Zephaniah, Haggai, Malachi.

164　Leviticus, Joshua, Judges, 2 Samuel, 1 Chronicles, Job.

165　R. Skousen, *Earliest*, p. 465.

166　P. Coppens, *Paintings of Visions*.

167　K. Flake, *Translating Time*, p. 506.

168　Lorenzo Brown in "Sayings of Joseph, by Those Who Heard Him at Different Times," Joseph Smith Jr. Papers, Church Archives, The Church of Jesus Christ of Latter-day Saints, Salt Lake City, UT, cited in K. Flake, *Translating Time*, p. 506 n. 31. Flake notes: "Brown's statement is based on his recollection in 1880 of a conversation that occurred in 1832. For questions concerning the reliability of this account, see R. J. Matthews, *Plainer Translation*, pp. 25-26, n. 12."

169　J. Smith, Jr., *Documentary History*, 16 February 1832, 1:245; cf. D&C 76 Section Heading. The scripture reference that inspired the vision was John 5:29.

surge, before my mind." More specifically, he said, "I saw the graves open & the saints as they arose took each other by the hand . . . while setting up."[170] Thus, although many emendations are editorial, the more radical of Smith's changes to the Bible were understood by him as a function of what he saw when reading it.

Once the understandings of these passages had been revealed, however, it remained to the Prophet to exercise considerable personal effort in rendering these experiences into words:[171]

At least with respect to the JST, it appears that when he read he saw events, not words. What he saw, he verbalized to a scribe. One of Smith's Book of Mormon scribes provided, in his own failed attempt to translate, the occasion for the most direct description of Smith's method. "You have not understood," God told Oliver Cowdery through Smith: "you have supposed that I would give it unto you, when you took no thought save it was to ask me. But… you must study it out in your mind; then you must ask me if it be right and… you shall feel that it is right. But if it is not right you shall have no such feelings, but you shall have a stupor of thought that shall cause you to forget that thing which is wrong; therefore you cannot write that which is sacred save it be given you from me."[172] Cowdery appears to have thought he could engage in the "inspired translation" of the Book of Mormon by parroting God's reading. In contrast, as implied by the above statement, Smith believed it necessary to determine independently how to represent what he read or saw. The appropriate question to God by the prophet-translator was whether his interpretation was correct, not what God's interpretation was.

Arguably, then, "translate" expressed Smith's experience of "study[ing] it out in [his] mind" or his sense of agency in front of the text. Smith did not think of himself as God's stenographer. Rather, he was an interpreting reader, and God the confirming authority. He did not experience revelation "as dictated, as something whispered in someone's ear" and, thus, provides a useful illustration of Ricoeur's argument that revelation is not propositional but "pluralistic, polysemic, and at most analogical in form."[173] Of equal significance, however, is the manner in which Smith's description of revelation communicates a sense of being limited by a text. It was possible to not "be right" in one's reading. Smith experienced revelation as an interpretive response to the text: not freely associated from, but bound by the "world of the text" in front of him, even if in an altered mental state or vision. In sum, Smith's use of "translate," for all its discursive weaknesses, conveyed his experience of creative agency before a text and, simultaneously, his sense of being bound by the text as an account of events or as history.

With respect to the English translation of the Book of Mormon, Royal Skousen argues that the actual choice of words chosen was given under "tight control."[174] However, in another place, Skousen discusses the question of whether one should assume that every change made in the JST constitutes revealed text.[175] Besides arguments that can be made from the actual text of the JST, there are questions regarding the reliability of and degree of supervision given to the scribes who were involved in transcribing, copying, and preparing the text for publication.[176] Differences are also apparent in the nature of the translation process that took place at different stages of the work. For example, while a significant proportion of the Genesis passages that have been canonized as the book of Moses "[look] like a word-for-word revealed text," evidence from a study of two sections in the New Testament that were translated twice indicates that the later "New Testament JST is not being revealed word-for-word, but largely depends upon Joseph Smith's varying responses to the same difficulties in the text."[177]

For an excellent discussion explaining why historicity neither requires inerrancy nor completeness, see Peterson[178] and Tanner.[179]

0-14   About such passages, Matthews concludes that: "Some… portions [of the JST] may be the result of

---

170   J. Smith, Jr., *Words*, 16 April 1843, pp. 196, 198.
171   K. Flake, *Translating Time*, pp. 507-508.
172   D&C 9:7-9.
173   P. Ricoeur, *Revelation*, pp. 76, 75.
174   R. Skousen, *Tight Control*.
175   R. Skousen, *Earliest*, pp. 456-470.
176   *Ibid.*, pp. 459-460.
177   *Ibid.*, pp. 461-462. For the original study, see K. P. Jackson, *et al.*, *Two Passages*.
178   D. C. Peterson, *Inerrancy*.
179   J. S. Tanner, *World and Word*.

the Prophet's analysis or minor corrections of a sort, and not necessarily the result of immediate revelation on the subject. There may be several kinds of material in the New Translation."[180]

0-15 In fact, in a few instances Joseph Smith specifically stated that terms that appeared later as part of the book of Abraham were better translations than the corresponding terms used in the earlier book of Moses.[181]

0-16 A new numbering for the chapter was inserted above the line of the text as shown here.

0-17 Similarly, Elder Bruce R. McConkie, who also served on the committee overseeing the new publication of the scriptures, counted this as one of three most significant developments in the Church in his lifetime—the other two being the revelation on the priesthood in 1978[182] and the reestablishment of the First Quorum of the Seventy.[183]

Underscoring the importance of this edition, the Church strongly recommends that English-speaking members use the LDS edition of the King James Bible, with excerpts from the Joseph Smith Translation and other extensive study helps.[184]

0-18 For example, as formulated by Lossky, "God became man in order that man might become god." He elaborates: "Fascinated by the *felix culpa,* we often forget that in breaking the tyranny of sin, our Savior opens to us anew the way of deification which is the final end of man."[185] This teaching, he asserts was "echoed by the Fathers and theologians of every age," citing as examples Irenaeus, Athanasius, Gregory Nazianzen, and Gregory of Nyssa.[186]

The *Orthodox Study Bible* interprets this view quite conservatively, however, saying:[187]

We do not become like God in His nature. That would not only be heresy, it would be impossible. For we are human, always have been human, and always will be human. We cannot take on the nature of God....[188]

Historically, deification has often been illustrated by the example of a sword in the fire. A steel sword is thrust into a hot fire until the sword takes on a red glow. The energy of the fire interpenetrates the sword. The sword never becomes fire, but it picks up the properties of fire.

0-19 For example: "The Son of God became a man to enable men to become sons of God."[189] Though it is impossible to "know what Lewis meant fully (and certainly what he understood and intended) by these statements"[190] his descriptions of mankind's potential is one resonates with the beliefs of Mormonism. For example, as he wrote in another place:

The command "Be ye perfect"[191] is not idealistic gas. Nor is it a command to do the impossible. He is going to make us into creatures that can obey that command. He said (in the Bible) that we were "gods"[192] and He is going to make good His words. If we let Him—for we can prevent Him, if we choose—He will make the feeblest and filthiest of us into a god or goddess, a dazzling, radiant, immortal creature, pulsating all through with such energy and joy and wisdom and love as we cannot now imagine, a bright stainless mirror which reflects back to God perfectly (though, of course on a smaller scale) His own boundless power and delight and goodness. The process will be long and in parts very painful; but that is what we are in for. Nothing less. He meant what He said.[193]

0-20 For example, Gregory of Nyssa wrote: "'Let us make man in our image, after our likeness.'[194] We

180 R. J. Matthews, *Plainer,* pp. 252-253.
181 J. Smith, Jr., *Teachings,* 5 January 1841, p. 181; 17 May 1843, p. 301.
182 Official Declaration 2.
183 B. R. McConkie, *Sermons,* p. 236.
184 First Presidency of the Church of Jesus Christ of Latter-day Saints, *Statement.*
185 V. Lossky, *Theology,* p. 134; cf. V. Lossky, *Image,* p. 97.
186 Irenaeus, *Heresies,* 5:Preface, p. 526; Athanasius, *Incarnation,* 54, p. 65; Gregory Nazianzen, *Apollinarius* 5-9, p. 81; Gregory of Nyssa, *Catechism* 25, p. 495. For comprehensive overviews of this topic, see N. Russell, *Deification*; J. Gross, *Divinization.* See also B. T. Ostler, *God,* pp. 391-426.
187 J. N. Sparks, *et al., Orthodox Study Bible,* p. 1692.
188 Cf. Gregory of Nyssa, cited in J. Gross, *Divinization,* p. 180. See also pp. 257, 272.
189 C. S. Lewis, *Mere,* 4:5, p. 155. See also the discussion of Emerson's views in R. H. Brodhead, *Prophets,* pp. 22-24.
190 R. L. Millet, *Transformation,* p. 152.
191 Matthew 5:48.
192 John 10:34-36.
193 C. S. Lewis, *Mere,* 4:9, p. 176.
194 Moses 2:26.

possess the one by creation; we acquire the other by free will."[195]

0-21   Although Bruce declines "to trace the metaphysical implications in the phrase,"[196] Attridge has no such hesitation, explaining: "These epithets were applied primarily to God's relationship to the angelic world, although references to God as father of human spirits are also found."[197]

0-22   The significance of the idea of God as first and foremost a "Father" is explained by Elder B. H. Roberts:

> There exists, I think, a real difference between the idea of "father" and "creator," …[though] each idea may include the other… The term "father" carries with it the notion of generation, begetting from one's own person, springing from one's own nature, and partaking of one's own physical and mental qualities and perhaps likeness, but the term "creator" does not necessarily convey that notion, since a created thing may be external to the nature of the being who created it; as, for example, when God created the heaven and the earth. In this case the heaven and the earth did not bear the image of God; nor was it made in his likeness, as the result was when God said, "Let us make man in our image, and after our likeness."[198]

Betz makes a similar point, though one might arguably differ with his extension of the epithet "Father" to describe God's role with respect to the whole of the Universe, rather than restricting it to his relationship with mankind as did Roberts:

> The address of God as "Father" names him as creator, sustainer, and protector of his entire creation, the universe. But the image of the father is more than a metaphor because it suggests that God has "fathered" his creation, his progeny. This terminology clearly differs from that of God as the divine "craftsman"…, "creator"…, or "master builder"… By comparison, the epithet "Father" suggests not only origin but also a permanent and personal kinship relationship between procreator and progeny. The Philonic epithet "the progenitor"… would come closest, but it does not occur in the New Testament."[199]

0-23   Commenting on the Savior's use of the word "perfect" in this context, Welch writes:[200]

> Although it is possible that the word "perfect" has only a straightforward ethical or religious meaning here,[201] reflecting perfect or "undivided obedience to God" and "unlimited love"[202] there is a stronger possibility that the word carries a ceremonial connotation in this particular text. It seems to me that in this verse, Jesus is expressing his desire that the disciples now advance from one level to a next level, to go on to become "perfect," "finished," or "completed" in their instruction and endowment.[203] In addition to the ritual context of the Sermon—the context usually determining the sense in which the intended "completeness" consists[204]—several reasons support this understanding.
>
> First, the Greek word translated into English as "perfect" in Matthew 5:48 is *teleios.* This important word is used in Greek religious literature to describe the person who has become fully initiated in the rituals of the religion.[205] *Teleios* is "a technical term of the mystery religions, which refers to one initiated into the mystic rites, the initiate."[206] The word is used in Hebrews 5:14-6:1 to distinguish between the initial teachings and the full instruction, and in Hebrews 9:11 it refers to the heavenly temple. Generally in the Epistle to the Hebrews, its usage follows a "special use" from

---

195   Gregory of Nyssa, *On the Origin of Man*, cited in A. Louth, *et al.*, *Genesis 1-11*, p. 33.

196   F. F. Bruce, *Hebrews*, p. 344.

197   H. W. Attridge, *Hebrews*, pp. 362-363.

198   B. H. Roberts, *Seventy's Fifth*, p. 47. See Moses 2:26.

199   H. D. Betz, *et al.*, *Sermon*, p. 387.

200   J. W. Welch, *Sermon*, pp. 57-62; cf. J. W. Welch, *Light*, pp. 116-120.

201   E.g., J. E. Talmage, *Jesus the Christ*, p. 232 n. 5; R. N. Holzapfel, *et al.*, *From Bethlehem*, pp. 337-338, 369-372; M. C. Thomas, *Sermon*, pp. 243-245.

202   G. Kittel, *et al.*, *Dictionary*, 8:73, 75, cited in J. W. Welch, *Sermon*, p. 58.

203   Commenting on the use of *teleios* in Matthew 5:48, Barclay notes that: "the Greek idea of perfection is *functional*. A thing is perfect if it fully realizes the purpose for which it was… made…. For what purpose was man created? …*Man was created to become like God*" (W. Barclay, *Matthew*, 1:177-178; cf. Moses 1:39). Compare Matthew 19:21, Hebrews 12:23, D&C 76:69. See also Ephesians 4:12, 14, where Paul defines the purpose of the "perfecting of the saints" as being that we might come "unto the measure of the stature of the fulness of Christ."

204   E. Yarnold, *Teleios*, p. 271, cited in J. W. Welch, *Sermon*, p. 58. See *Endnote E-258*, p. 769. See also H. W. Attridge, *Hebrews*, pp. 83-87, 161-164.

205   See *Excursus 53: Comparative Explorations: The Eleusinian Mysteries*, p. 675.

206   W. Bauer, *et al.*, *Lexicon*, p. 817, cited in J. W. Welch, *Sermon*, p. 58.

Hellenistic Judaism, where the word *teleioo* means "to put someone in the position in which he can come, or stand, before God."[207] Thus, in its ritual connotations, this word refers to preparing a person to be presented to come before God "in priestly action"[208] or "to qualify for the cultus"[209] Early Christians continued to use this word in this way in connection with their sacraments and ordinances[210]...

[The] so-called *Secret Gospel of Mark*, according to Clement, contained things "for the use of those who were being perfected (*teleioumenon*). Nevertheless, he [Mark] did not divulge the things not to be uttered, nor did he write down the hierophantic [priesthood] teaching [*hierophantiken didaskalian*] of the Lord, but... brought in certain sayings of which he knew the interpretation would, as a mystagogue, lead the hearers into the innermost sanctuary of that truth hidden by seven [veils]."[211]...The suggestion that the words of the Sermon, explicitly inviting its followers to become "perfected," may have stood in a similar tradition is, therefore, not without precedent in early Christianity.[212]

Moreover, the cultic use of the Hebrew term *shalom* may provide a concrete link between the Nephites and this Greek and Christian use of *teleios*. John Durham has explored in detail the fundamental meanings of *shalom*, especially in Numbers 6:26 and in certain of the Psalms, and concludes that it was used as a cultic term referring to a gift or endowment to or of God that "can be received only in his Presence,"[213] "a blessing specifically connected to theophany or the immanent Presence of God,"[214] specifically as appearing in the Temple of Solomon and represented "within the Israelite cult" and liturgy.[215] Baruch Levine similarly analyzes the function of the *shelamim* sacrifices as producing "complete," or perfect, "harmony with the deity, ... characteristic of the covenant relationship as well as the ritual experience of communion."[216]

Durham, along with several others, sees this Israelite concept in the word *teleios* in Matthew 5:48.[217] "Matthew does not use *teleios* in the Greek sense of the perfect ethical personality, but in the Old Testament sense of the wholeness of consecration to God."[218] It tends toward the meaning of "living up to an agreement without fault: as the Father keeps the covenants he makes with us.... *Teleioi* is a *locus technicus* from the Mysteries: the completely initiated who has both qualified for initiation and completed it is *teleios*, literally 'gone all the way,' fulfilling all requirements, every last provision of God's command. The hardest rules are what will decide the *teletios*, the final test—the Law of Consecration."[219] Thus, although we do not know what word Jesus used when he spoke to the Nephites that has been translated "perfect" in 3 Nephi 12:48, there is reason to believe that they would have known from their Israelite heritage a word like *shalom*, similar in cultic content to the Greek word *teleios*.

Accordingly, in commanding the people to "be perfect even as I, or your Father who is in heaven is perfect,"[220] it seems that Jesus had several things in mind besides "perfection" as we usually think of it. Whatever he meant, it involved the idea of becoming like God ("even as I or your Father who is in heaven"[221]), which occurs by seeing God[221] and knowing God.[222] These ultimate realities can be represented [ceremonially] in this world, for as Joseph Smith taught, it is through his ordinances that we are "instructed more perfectly."[223]

---

207 G. Kittel, *et al.*, *Dictionary*, 8:82, citing Hebrews 7:19, 10:1. Cited in J. W. Welch, *Sermon*, p. 59.

208 G. Kittel, *et al.*, *Dictionary*, 8:83, cited in J. W. Welch, *Sermon*, p. 59.

209 G. Kittel, *et al.*, *Dictionary*, 8:85, cited in J. W. Welch, *Sermon*, p. 59.

210 H. Stephanus, *Thesaurus*, 8:1961, cited in J. W. Welch, *Sermon*, p. 59.

211 M. Smith, *Secret Gospel*, p. 14.

212 "Tertullian, speaking of mediators of the divine (Moses among Jews, Jesus among Christians)," draws a parallel to Orpheus, Melampus, and Trophonius, who "'*initiationibus homines obligaverunt*' ('placed men in their service through initiations')" (P. Bonnechere, *Trophonius*, pp. 170-171. See Tertullian, *Apology*, 21, p. 36).

213 J. I. Durham, *Shalom*, p. 292, cited in J. W. Welch, *Sermon*, p. 60.

214 *Ibid.*, p. 281.

215 *Ibid.*, pp. 286-292.

216 B. A. Levine, *Presence*, pp. 35-36, cited in J. W. Welch, *Sermon*, p. 60.

217 J. I. Durham, *Shalom*, p. 293 n. 135.

218 G. Bornkamm, *et al.*, *Matthew*, p. 101, cited in J. W. Welch, *Sermon*, p. 61.

219 H. W. Nibley, *Matthew 5:48*, cited in J. W. Welch, *Sermon*, p. 61. See the overview of Moses 5, p. 350.

220 3 Nephi 12:48.

221 See 1 John 3:2.

222 See John 17:3.

223 J. Smith, Jr., *Documentary History*, 14 November 1835, 2:312. More to the point, the Prophet urged his

Finally, the style of the Sermon shifts into a different mode after this invitation to become perfect. The next section of the Sermon, contains no reference to the old law of Moses… [The] text has… moved on to a new stage of the experience,[224] thus accounting for the different world to which it seems to belong. In this higher level there will be greater emphasis on secret and inward righteousness, as well as controlling the needs of the flesh and of this world. Thus the text next presents a second set of requirements by discussing almsgiving, prayer, forgiveness, fasting, and total dedication of all that one has to God.

0-24   Thus, Anderson writes that the:

> … story of Adam and Eve was never narrated as a simple, objective account of human beginnings, as a story that could take its place alongside modern theories of the "big bang" or evolution. Instead, the story of Adam and Eve has always been subject to liturgical enactment. It derives its meaning from the world of penitence and restoration. A more pertinent parallel than Darwinian evolution is the parable of the Prodigal Son, a favorite Gospel reading in the Lenten season;[225]

0-25   This quote from President J. Reuben Clark, Jr. resonates with my own innate feelings:

> Years ago, I heard of a statement from a non-member banker of the city which has always impressed me. He is reported to have said, and of course this in jest, that Mormons have six senses: the five that ordinary mortals have and a sixth that enables him to believe Mormonism. I am more grateful than I can express for that sixth sense which enables me not only merely to believe, but to have a spiritual knowledge that all that I have said today is true.[226]

I realize from personal experience, however, that some people, lacking what is for me an instinctive and undeniable sense of the Infinite, find spiritual matters unreal and of no particular import:

> They do not deny them, but they live apart from them; they do not disbelieve them, but they are silent when they are stated. They do not question the existence of Kamtchatka,[227] but they have no call to busy themselves with Kamtchatka; they abstain from peculiar tenets. Nor in truth is this, though much aggravated by existing facts, a mere accident of this age—there are some people to whom such a course of conduct is always natural: there are certain persons who do not, as it would seem cannot, feel all that others feel; who have, so to say no ear for much of religion—are in some sort out of its reach.[228]

C. S. Lewis sympathetically portrayed such a character in his brilliant reworking of the myth of Cupid and Psyche.[229] From the perspective of her sister Psyche, the character Orual suffers from a sort of spiritual blindness: where Psyche sees a palace, Orual sees only rock and heather; when Psyche serves her wine, Orual tastes only spring water. By this means, Lewis compared the problem of Orual to that of "every nice, affectionate agnostic whose dearest one suddenly 'gets religion,' or even every lukewarm Christian whose dearest gets a Vocation." For such a one, the question ultimately becomes (if, indeed, it ever arises at all): "Is Psyche mad or am I blind?"[230]

0-26   Barney speculates as follows:

> … what if Abraham did not draw the facsimiles? What if they already existed and were either adopted or adapted by an Egyptian-Jewish redactor as illustrations of the attempt on Abraham's life and Abraham's teaching astronomy to the Egyptians? (For convenience, I shall refer to this hypothetical Jewish redactor as "J-red.") In this case, the facsimiles would have both an Egyptian context (reflecting the religious purpose for which they were originally created by the Egyptians) and a Semitic context (reflecting the religious purpose for which they were adopted or adapted by J-red). Thus the ultimate question would not be "What do the facsimiles mean to modern

---

followers to "go on to perfection, and search deeper and deeper into the mysteries of Godliness" (J. Smith, Jr., *Teachings*, 16 June 1844, p. 364). In this context, see also his frequent citations (and emendations) of Hebrews 5:1 (J. Smith, Jr., *Teachings*, 1 September 1835, p. 82; 15 October 1843, p. 328; 10 March 1844, p. 338; 8 April 1844, p. 360; J. Smith, Jr., *Documentary History*, 18 June 1840, 4:136).

224   Cf. H. W. Attridge, *Hebrews*, pp. 199-200, 204-205, 244-248, 269-272, 280-281. See also *Excursus 53: Comparative Explorations: The Mysteries of Aaron, Moses, and Melchizedek*, p. 663.

225   G. A. Anderson, *Perfection*, p. 187.

226   J. R. Clark, Jr., *Blessings*, pp. 878, 879.

227   A remote volcanic peninsula located in Siberia.

228   W. Bagehot, *Bagehot*, 1:42, cited in N. A. Maxwell, *Prove*, p. 88.

229   C. S. Lewis, *Faces*.

230   C. S. Lewis, *Letters 3*, letter to Katharine Farrer, 2 April 1955, p. 590.

Egyptologists?" nor "What would the facsimiles mean to an ancient Egyptian?" but rather "What would the facsimiles have meant to J-red?"[231]

0-27 Commenting on the death of Blake, William Wordsworth wrote: "There was no doubt that this poor man was mad, but there is something in the madness of this man which interests me more than the sanity of Lord Byron and Walter Scott."[232]

0-28 Despite heroic efforts to preserve an accurate record of the early history of the Church, a combination of factors—including regrettable lacunae in primary sources, scarcity of time and means, scribes varying in skill and commitment, and the less-stringent standards of nineteenth-century editorial practice—challenged the abilities of later editors to eliminate imperfections from the published accounts.[233] One result is that some statements included in the *Teachings of the Prophet Joseph Smith* (TPJS)[234] and the *Documentary History of the Church* (DHC)[235] have been erroneously attributed to the direct authorship of Joseph Smith or, in other instances, are the result of significant expansion of sketchy notes in the original sources (though often, it must be said, by intimates of the Prophet who were present to hear him). Although in some cases I have deliberately used primary accounts found in works such as *The Words of Joseph Smith*,[236] *The Personal Writings of Joseph Smith*,[237] and *The Papers of Joseph Smith*,[238] for the most part TPJS and DHC have proven to be reasonably reliable for my purposes.[239] The task of mapping citations in widely-available published sources to corresponding statements in primary ones will be made easier as progress continues on the authoritative *Joseph Smith Papers* project.[240] For a comprehensive guide to sources on Joseph Smith, see Whittaker.[241]

0-29 According to Robinson, the apocryphal literature "was employed in basically four ways: to fill in the gaps in the scriptural account, to attack opposing theologies, to defend against the attacks of others, and to bring about or to legitimize theological change."[242] With respect to scriptural gap-filling, he writes:

> It was noticed anciently that the scriptural narrative often omitted information it might have been nice to have. Moreover, these omissions were often the occasion for questions and doubts about the reliability of the scriptures. For example, where did Cain get his wife, and just which fruit was the forbidden one? Did Adam and Eve ever repent? (Genesis doesn't actually say so.) But if we turn to the *Testament of Adam* we learn that Cain married his sister Labuda, who incidentally was the real cause of the fight between Cain and Abel, and that the forbidden fruit was the fig. And if we have any doubts about the repentance of Adam and Eve, we can read all about it in the *Vita Adae et Evae*, in the *Conflict of Adam and Eve with Satan*, or in the *Penitence of Adam*. The *Book of Enoch* explains what Genesis (6:1-4) meant by the "sons of God" going in unto the "daughters of men," and the *Genesis Apocryphon* from Qumran can give us the details about the birth of Noah, or about Abraham and Sarah in Egypt. In fact, for the pseudepigrapher every question can have an answer.[243]

Our frequently unhealthy compulsion to fill in gaps in scripture stories and doctrinal understanding continues in modern times. The tendency is illustrated in a story recounted by Krister Stendahl: "You may have heard about the preacher who preached about the gnashing of teeth in hell. And one of the parishioners said, 'But what about us who have lost our teeth?' And the preacher answered, 'Teeth will be provided.'"[244]

Complicating the task for the researcher, however, is increasing evidence that what have been seen in the past as "gap-filling" elaborations in ancient narratives sometimes may be, in point of fact,

---

231 K. L. Barney, *Facsimiles*, p. 114.
232 M Butlin, *William Blake*. See *Endnote E-297*, p. 783.
233 D. C. Jessee, *JS History*; H. C. Searle, *History*.
234 J. Smith, Jr., *Teachings*.
235 J. Smith, Jr., *Documentary History*.
236 J. Smith, Jr., *Words*.
237 J. Smith, Jr., *Writings 2002*.
238 J. Smith, Jr., *Papers 1989-1992*.
239 J. Smith, Jr., *Teachings 2007*, prepared as a Priesthood and Relief Society manual for the Church, used a similar approach, relying on DHC whenever feasible.
240 J. Smith, Jr., *JS Papers Web Site*; J. Smith, Jr., *Papers 2008-*.
241 D. J. Whittaker, *Studying*.
242 S. E. Robinson, *Lying*, p. 143.
243 *Ibid.*, pp. 143-144.
244 K. Stendahl, *Third Nephi*, p. 152.

authentic ancient material. Explains Reeves:

> Under the old scheme of analyzing "gaps" in biblical narrative, one almost invariably viewed so-called "expansions" or "embellishments" gap-fillers, if you will—such as are found in rabbinic Midrash or the works belonging to the genre of "rewritten Bible" as post-textual responses to the interpretive problems posed by puzzling features of the biblical text. Under the new perspective I am advocating, we are no longer obligated to view these "gap-fillers" as interpretive responses to a base text. We can instead entertain the distinct possibility that Midrash, "rewritten Bible," and biblically-allied collections of traditions may preserve certain features or motifs or even in some cases provide more cohesive and thematically consistent presentations of stories than those eventually attested in what became the Bible.[245]

As an endorsement of this interpretive position, Reeves further cites Talmon, who argued that:

> "The new evidence proves convincingly that not all variants in Hebrew non-masoretic and translational witnesses resulted from scribal mistakes or the deliberate interference of emendators, revisers and copyists. Rather, variants in an ancient version preserve at times pristine readings which were accidentally lost in the course of time or were designedly suppressed by later tridents.[246] Accordingly, in tracing the transmission history of the biblical books and submitting them to critical analysis, the evidence of the ancient versions must be carefully weighed." He states further: "… it is my thesis that the presumably 're-told,' re-read,' 're-written,' etc. Bible-related works should mostly be viewed as crystallizations of 'living' literary traditions, which parallel presentations of these same traditions in the books of the Hebrew Bible, but do not necessarily spring from them."[247]

0-30   Wasserstrom aptly describes them as being "eclectically composed, internally differentiated, being comprised of heterogeneous narrative elements."[248]

0-31   For a discussion of the difficulties in teasing out Jewish from Christian contributions to the pseudepigrapha, see Kraft.[249]

0-32   For example, Schwartz asserts that "a great many rabbinic myths, as found in the Midrashim, are not new creations of the rabbis, as might appear to be the case. Rather they are simply the writing down of an oral tradition that was kept alive by the people, when there was no need to suppress it any longer."[250] Moreover, he points out that "the rabbinic texts themselves claim that these traditions are part of the Oral *Torah*, handed down by God to Moses at Mount Sinai, and are therefore considerably ancient."[251]

0-33   For example, Reeves has concluded "that the *Qur'an*, along with the interpretive traditions available in *Hadīth*, commentaries, antiquarian histories, and the collections of so-called 'prophetic legends' (*qiê aê al-anbiya'*), can shed a startling light on the structure and content of certain stories found in Bible and its associated literatures (such as Pseudepigrapha and Midrash). [Thus, the] *Qur'an* and other early Muslim biblically-allied traditions must be taken much more seriously as witnesses to 'versions of Bible' than has heretofore been the case."[252] Wasserstrom refers to "arguments to the effect that active reading of 'biblical' or 'extrabiblical' narratives by Muslims was an exercise which reflexively illuminates those 'original' sources'" and cites Halperin's argument that transmitters of these stories in the Islamic tradition "tended to make manifest what had been typically left latent in the Jewish version which they had received."[253] For a discussion of the complex two-way relationship between Jewish pseudepigrapha and Muslim literature, see Wasserstrom.[254]

0-34   For example, as Lipscomb observes, even some of the late medieval compositions that "do not derive directly from earliest Christianity" may be of "great importance… in the antiquity of some of the

---

245 J. C. Reeves, *Flowing Stream*.

246 I.e., bearers of the tradition to the next generation.

247 See Talmon's "Textual Criticism: The Ancient Versions," in *Text in Context: Essays by Members of the Society for Old Testament Study* [ed. A. D. H. Mayes; Oxford: Oxford University Press, 2000] 141-70, at pp. 149-50 and 157 respectively. Cited in J. C. Reeves, *Flowing Stream*.

248 S. M. Wasserstrom, *Muslim literature*, p. 95.

249 R. A. Kraft, *Pseudepigrapha*.

250 H. Schwartz, *Tree*, p. lxiv.

251 *Ibid.*, p. lxxxiv. See also E. J. Brandt, *Jasher*, pp. 305-306.

252 J. C. Reeves, *Flowing Stream*; see also T. Khalidi, *Muslim Jesus*, pp. 7-9, 16-17.

253 Cited in S. M. Wasserstrom, *Muslim literature*, p. 100.

254 *Ibid.*

traditions they contain, the uniqueness of some of their larger contribution to the development and understanding of Adam materials and of medieval Christianity."[255]

0-35   The issue of determining ground truth in determining the authenticity of ancient teachings is, of course, a thorny problem of its own. In making such judgments, LDS scholars are fortunate to be able to draw on the additional touchstone of modern revelation.

0-36   Of the intense efforts of the Egyptians to gain a toehold on certainty with respect to eternal truths, Edwards writes:

> The impression made on the modern mind is that of a people searching in the dark for the key to truth, and having found not one but many keys resembling the pattern of the lock, retaining all lest perchance the appropriate one should be discarded.[256]

Concerning the value of "pagan" religious traditions, Lewis wrote:

> Myths have been accepted as literally true, then as allegorically true (by the Stoics), as confused history (by Euhemerus), as priestly lies (by the philosophers of the Enlightenment), as imitative agricultural ritual mistaken for propositions (in the days of Frazer). If you start from a naturalistic philosophy, then something like the view of Euhemerus or the view of Frazer is likely to result. But I am not a naturalist. I believe that in the huge mass of mythology which has come down to us [in] a good many different sources are mixed—true history, allegory, ritual, the human delight in storytelling, etc. But among these sources I include the supernatural, both diabolical and divine. We need here concern ourselves only with the latter. If my religion is erroneous then occurrences of similar motifs in pagan stories are, of course, instances of the same, or a similar, error. But if my religion is true, then these stories may well be a *preparatio evangelica* [= preparatory gospel], divine hinting in poetic and ritual form at the same central truth which was later focused and (so to speak) historicized in the Incarnation… My conversion, very largely, depended on recognizing Christianity as the completion, the actualization, the *entelechy* [= guiding spirit], of something that had never been wholly absent from the mind of man. And I still think that the agnostic argument from similarities between Christianity and paganism works only if you know the answer. If you start by knowing on other grounds that Christianity is false, then the pagan stories may be another nail in its coffin: just as if you started by knowing that there were no such things as crocodiles then the various stories about dragons might help to confirm your disbelief.…
>
> The traditions conflict, yet the longer and more sympathetically we study about them the more we become aware of a common element in many of them: the theme of sacrifice, of mystical communion through the shed blood, of death and rebirth, of Redemption, is too clear to escape notice.[257]

Of course, the difference between LDS and Lewis' views is in our belief that the general trend of revelation from the beginning was not gradual and incremental, but rather that the fulness of the Gospel has been available to mankind at various times and places "from Adam down."[258]

0-37   Liberally citing Joseph Smith's teachings about the antiquity of temple rites, Nibley comments:[259]

> One can easily detect familiar echoes of the endowment in religious institutions and practices throughout the world. The phenomenon is readily explained by Joseph Smith, and students of comparative religion have now come around to the same conclusion—namely, that the real endowment has been on earth from time to time and has also been spread abroad in corrupted forms so that fragments from all parts of the world can be traced back to common beginnings. "It is reasonable to suppose," wrote Joseph Smith, "that man departed from the first teachings, or instructions which he received from heaven in the first age, and refused by his disobedience to be governed by them."[260] But… "man was not able himself to erect a system or plan with power sufficient to free him from a destruction which awaited him"; hence it was necessary to put him on the track again, as "from time to time these glad tidings were sounded in the ears of men in different ages of the world."[261] "Certainly God spoke to [Abel]: … and if He did, would He not… deliver to him the whole plan of the Gospel? … And if Abel was taught of the coming of the Son

255 W. L. Lipscomb, *Armenian*, pp. 1-6.
256 I. E. S. Edwards, *Pyramids*, pp. 27-28, cited in H. W. Nibley, *Greatness*, p. 310.
257 C. S. Lewis, *Without Dogma*, pp. 165-166, 175-176; cf. C. S. Lewis, *Miracles*, pp. 176-177 n. 1.
258 T. G. Madsen, *Essay*, p. xvii. See *Endnote 0-37*, p. 29.
259 H. W. Nibley, *Sacred*, pp. 575-576.
260 J. Smith, Jr., *Teachings*, 22 January 1834, p. 57.
261 *Ibid.*, p. 58.

of God, was he not taught also of His ordinances?"[262] ... "For our own part we cannot believe that the ancients in all ages were so ignorant of the system of heaven as many suppose."[263] He then went on to show how Abraham, too, had the endowment.[264]

Elder Neal A. Maxwell wrote:[265]

> Ideas taught in the restored gospel are often reflected in other cultures—in the literature, philosophy, folklore, and religion of peoples and places around the globe. Elder Joseph F. Smith at once explained this situation and underscored the uniqueness of Latter-day Saint understanding and of our position in the world of religion:
>
> > Undoubtedly the knowledge of this law [of sacrifice] and of other rites and ceremonies was carried by the posterity of Adam into all lands, and continued with them, more or less pure, to the flood, and through Noah, who was a "preacher of righteousness," to those who succeeded him, spreading out into all nations and countries, Adam and Noah being the first of their dispensations to receive them from God. What wonder, then that we should find relics of Christianity, so to speak, among the heathens and nations who know not Christ, and whose histories date back beyond the days of Moses, and even beyond the flood, independent of and apart from the records of the Bible.[266]
>
> It is clear that the dispersion, diffusion, and distortion of gospel truths has left fragments of the faith in various religions and cultures throughout the world. Many see in this an attempt by man to make his own god and religion in the absence of real ones. Rather than such similarities being evidence against the existence of God, however, these refracted truths bear witness of the initial wholeness which existed in the beginning with Adam.

See Barker[267] for a concise overview of the many factors that contributed to the loss of older traditions, especially those having to do with temple themes.

0-38   Nibley criticizes these early schools, as well as the more recent approach of Joseph Campbell.[268] Ackerman wryly observes that while the shortcomings of Frazer's approach were quickly discovered by his erstwhile followers, "to a remarkable degree, this news never reached the followers of the followers"[269]—a phenomenon that has continued to this day. Thus Burkert's cynical observation that "even when Frazer's position is destroyed it will rise again"[270]—as it has repeatedly done in several areas of scholarly study.

0-39   Comparative studies of this era tended to emphasize "the simple-minded error underlying religion, the barbarous practice underlying the story of Christ, and the savage origins behind Catholic and Anglican rituals." However, as Csapo observes, "[i]n a less polarized atmosphere, where religion and science have both receded from the fray, it is easier to see that everything Frazer discovered of the savage origins of Christian myth and ritual might be true without leaving much of a dent upon Christianity. Origins, after all, do not leave an indelible stamp on complex social institutions."[271] Origins are, of course, of great importance to LDS believers, who see the source of genuine ritual in divine revelation, beginning in primordial times. This belief allows for the alternative proposal that some parallels to LDS ordinances in ritual elements from other times are the cumulative results of corruptions of earlier-diffused pristine religious practices rather than formative catalysts that gradually led to the development of the forms in use today. Though such parallels do not by any means constitute proof, they may argue for possibility.

0-40   In the context of Greek ritual, Robertson likewise concludes:

> It is a general feature of Greek myths... that they are closely tied to ritual. A myth was told to explain a rite, and at the end of the telling the rite was held up as proof that the myth had happened so. In Greek literature the myths have of course moved away from their original setting, and the ritual counterpart goes unmentioned but for special cases, as at the conclusion of a few tragedies,

---

262   *Ibid.*, p. 59.
263   *Ibid.*
264   *Ibid.*, pp. 60-61.
265   N. A. Maxwell, *Flood*, p. 20.
266   J. F. Smith, *9 February 1873*, p. 325.
267   M. Barker, *Hidden*, pp. 7-10, 13-14.
268   H. W. Nibley, *What*, pp. 372-376.
269   R. Ackerman, *Myth and Ritual*, p. 188.
270   W. Burkert, cIted in G. A. Anderson, *Sacrifices*, p. 7.
271   E. Csapo, *Mythology*, p. 48.

or in later, learned prose and poetry. But the ritual always continued as before (that is the nature of ritual) and was familiar to everyone (similar festivals were celebrated in every city). It gave rise to new stories, or to variations of the old.[272]

0-41   Alter sees "the prose form of Hebrew narrative" as "chief evidence" of a "deliberate avoidance of epic" in the Bible: "Prose narration, affording writers a remarkable range and flexibility in the means of presentation, could be utilized to liberate fictional personages from the fixed choreography of timeless events and thus could transform storytelling from ritual rehearsal to the delineation of the wayward paths of human freedom."[273] In ironic contrast to the sentiment expressed by Alter, the recovery of the residual elements of authentic temple ritual in the early chapters of Genesis is often of great interest to Latter-day Saints.

0-42   "William James once remarked that there are two kinds of scholarly temperaments: those that dread above all the risk of possibly mistaking falsehoods for truths, and those that fear even more the risk of missing potentially valuable truths."[274] In my view, each of these temperaments has its place. While the discussion of new ideas to be examined in the light of reason and inspiration is integral to the burden of religious scholarship, this approach is, on the other hand, generally inimical to the responsibilities assumed by those who teach in official Church capacities, where only the settled doctrines of the Church are to be advanced, and these "so plainly that no one can misunderstand."[275]

Of course, the fact that the content of Church curriculum must be carefully considered is not necessarily inconsistent with the idea that class members should be expected to stretch their minds and hearts. Writes Nibley:

> Years ago when I wrote the 1957 priesthood manual, *An Approach to the Book of Mormon*,[276] the committee turned down every chapter. But President McKay overruled the committee on every chapter. He said that if it's over the brethren's heads, let them reach for it. He left every chapter just as I had it. The committee fumed at the mouth and protested, "We can't have it!" President McKay turned right around and said, "We jolly well *can* have it! Let them work at it a little." I was a good friend of Brother Richard L. Evans, who always used to tell me, "Always write as if you were writing to the tiredest farmer in Koosharem."[277] If you are writing to the tiredest farmer in Koosharem, what do you do to keep him awake? No attention span, no interest, or anything. He's just a tired, dead farmer. If he's the one you have to write for, you're certainly going to lose your other audience in a hurry. I never obeyed that command.[278]

0-43   Of the former group, categorized as "bibliolaters," Gillum writes:

> Some Latter-day Saints essentially take the position, "We have a Bible, a Book of Mormon, a Doctrine and Covenants, and a Pearl of Great Price; we need no more." Hugh Nibley was speaking to these people when he wrote: "An awesome outpouring of newly-discovered documents of direct bearing on the history and teachings of the Church is even now in full spate, amazing and confounding Jewish and Christian scholars, but bursting with good news for the Latter-day Saints—who ignore them completely."[279]

Addressing the latter group, Gillum warns:

> In my own opinion, apocryphal works can be so many jots and titillations, ultimately watering down our estimation of what true scripture really is. Before long a study of the apocrypha could lead us into believing that works like the Aquarian Gospel, Swedenborg's revelations, or Edgar Cayce's readings are as divine as our own Book of Mormon and the Bible. Indeed, with all of our added canonical scriptures, do we need to go into the scurrilous instead of the authentic?[280]

0-44   Kugel observes: "To make sense of these [brief and sometimes] offhand references—indeed, even to identify them as containing exegetical motifs—it is necessary to read the text in question against the background of the whole body of ancient interpretations."[281]

272   N. Robertson, *Orphic Mysteries*, p. 220; cf. H. W. Nibley, *Greatness*, pp. 294-295.
273   R. Alter, *Narrative*, pp. 25-26.
274   E. A. Beach, *Mysteries*. See W. James, *Will*, pp. 26, 94-95n.
275   H. B. Lee, *Teachings 1996*, 8 July 1966, p. 459.
276   H. W. Nibley, *Approach*.
277   A small town in southern Utah.
278   H. B. Nibley, *Nibliography*, p. 50.
279   G. P. Gillum, *Bibliography*, p. 128. See H. W. Nibley, *Educating*, p. 339.
280   *Ibid.*, p. 128.
281   J. L. Kugel, *Instances*, p. 156.

FIGURE 1-1. *Get Thee Hence, Satan, 1875*
Carl Heinrich Bloch, 1834-1890

And Moses received strength, and called upon God, saying: In the name of the Only Begotten, depart hence, Satan (**Moses 1:21**). Carl Bloch's dramatic painting of Jesus' temptation in the wilderness parallels Moses' encounter with Satan. The placement of the prostrate adversary at the feet of Christ recalls the prophecy that the head of the serpent would be crushed beneath the heel of the seed of the woman (Moses 4:21. See *Commentary* 4:21-d, p. 266.).

MOSES 1
The Vision of Moses[1]

Overview

COMPETING creation accounts from the Near East witness a variety of ancient beliefs concerning titanic struggles for preeminence among the gods. Apart from the possibility of a distant allusion in Genesis 1:2,[2] none of these concepts appear in the comparatively spare account of Creation in Genesis. The Pearl of Great Price, however, restores an authentic core of primeval traditions in its stories of Satan's rebellion in the premortal existence, and of his dramatic confrontation with Moses.[3] Counterbalancing these dark episodes, the Pearl of Great Price also gives us brief glimpses of the bright vistas of eternity experienced by Moses,[4] Enoch,[5] and Abraham.[6]

The most direct scriptural parallel to Moses' encounter with Satan is Jesus' temptation in the wilderness.[7] Just prior to the beginning of their formal ministries, the Devil finds each of them in a solitary place and launches a personal attack intended to undermine their confidence in who they are and what they have been called to do.[8] With astonishing presumption, he calls for their allegiance and worship. In each account, Satan is defeated in his clever questioning by an unshakable adversary and is forced to depart.

Historical Background: Alternations of Darkness and Light

The account of Moses' vision was no doubt reassuring to Joseph Smith as he faced his own trials during the period this revelation was received. Richard L. Bushman observes that Moses' test "echoed Joseph's struggle with darkness before his First Vision…[9] The book of Moses… conveys the sense of prophethood as an ordeal. Visions of light and truth alternate with evil and darkness."[10]

---

1   See *Endnote 1-1*, p. 75.
2   See *Endnote 1-2*, p. 75.
3   Moses 1:12-22, 4:1-4; Abraham 3:27-28.
4   Moses 1:8, 27ff.
5   Moses 7:23.
6   Abraham 3:21ff.
7   Matthew 4:1-11; Mark 1:12-13; Luke 4:1-13. See *Endnote 1-3*, p. 75.
8   See *Endnote 1-4*, p. 75.
9   Joseph Smith – History 1:15-16
10   R. L. Bushman, *Rough Stone*, pp. 135-136.

FIGURES 1-2 AND 1-3.
Jacob's Ladder, ca. 1800, William Blake, 1757-1827
Ascent, 1993, David Linn, 1959-

SEE COLOR PLATES 1-2 AND 1-3.

For behold, this is my work and my glory—to bring to pass the immortality and eternal life of man.[1] At left is William Blake's illustration of Jacob's vision of the ladder extending to heaven.[2] Blake eschews the traditional medieval portrayal of this event that required fifteen rungs to signify fifteen saving virtues. However, he does respect the convention that has ascending angels representing the active life, and descending ones the contemplative life.[3] Stars like the ones shown here are typically identified with angels or with the "angelic" status conferred upon mortals who had ascended to heaven.[4] The drawing shows "figures bearing scrolls, food and drink, and even the compasses that Blake normally associated with the unimaginative limit-setting of reason; here all the diverse attributes of the complete man are seen unified in the heavenly vision."[5]

In the second painting, the essentially collaborative nature of exaltation is addressed. Artist David Linn writes: "My intent was to address what is, for me, at the core of living the Gospel… I believe that living the Gospel requires us to lift one another out of darkness into light. This darkness or opposition can assume many forms, but is an essential element in this mortal probation, as father Lehi taught.[6] As we lift one another we form a living chain on this mountain of mortality and in the process learn those lessons that fit us for the presence of God."[7]

---

1   Moses 1:39.
2   Genesis 28:12.
3   R. Giorgi, *Anges*, pp. 140-143.
4   E.g., M. Barker, *Older*, pp. 92, 159 n. 65; M. Barker, *Timaeus*, pp. 274-275.
5   M. Butlin, *Blake*, pp. 86-87.
6   2 Nephi 2:11.
7   *All Things*, p. 57.

Moses 1 was given to Joseph Smith at such a time of alternation of darkness and light. Although he and Oliver Cowdery had purchased a large pulpit-style edition of the King James Bible in Palmyra in October 1829,[11] it was not until June 1830—during a period of jubilant expectation and intense persecution—that he was able to free himself to begin a new work of translation[12] that was intended to restore "many important points touching the salvation of men, [that] had been taken from the Bible, or lost before it was compiled."[13] Many wonderful events had recently transpired: the Book of Mormon had come from the press in March, the Church had been organized in April,[14] and the first conference had been held in early June. On the other hand, tremendous opposition began to mount during a visit of the Prophet to the saints in Colesville, New York later that month:

> On Saturday afternoon, June 26, they dammed a small stream to make a pond for baptisms and appointed a meeting for the Sabbath. That night the dam was torn out. The Mormons replaced the dam early Monday morning and held their baptism later that day… On their way back, a collection of the Knight's neighbors scoffed at the new Mormons as they passed by. Later about fifty men surrounded Joseph Knight's house, Joseph Smith said, "raging with anger, and apparently determined to commit violence upon us." When Joseph left…, the mob followed along, threatening physical attack…

> When village toughs failed to stop the baptisms, the law stepped in. Before the newly baptized members could be confirmed, a constable from South Bainbridge delivered a warrant

---

11   K. P. Jackson, *Cooperstown Bible*, pp. 56-57.
12   See *Endnote 1-5*, p. 75.
13   J. Smith, Jr., *Teachings*, 16 February 1832, pp. 10-11. See *Endnote 1-6*, p. 75.
14   See *Endnote 1-7*, p. 75.

FIGURE 1-4. *Dog Code, 1987*
Brian Kershisnik, 1962-

Here is wisdom and it remaineth in me.[1] The son of a petroleum geologist, artist Brian Kershisnik grew up in Angola, Thailand, West Texas, and Pakistan before going to Denmark as a missionary—learning much in the process about the inadequacy of language for communicating life's essential—and ultimately ineffable—realities.[2] About this painting, he writes: "This is… about communication that we do not, will not, or cannot understand. The written characters are borrowed from the writing of Joe Adams, a man with Down's syndrome with whom I have collaborated now for nearly ten years. His beautiful letters appear to mimic the act of writing as he has observed it. He can tell you what a block of his text is generally about because he knows that stories emerge in a mysterious way from characters just like his. I am fascinated by his unfathomable and beautiful symbols, and I borrowed several for this picture."[3]

Though we are of the same nature as God, and have the potential to eventually become like Him, the difference in our comprehension of the universe is far greater than the gap that divides animals from man.[4] Regrettably, we widen that gap when we refuse to speak to Him from the center of our souls.[5] Yet God continually endeavors to speak to us "in [our] weakness, after the manner of [our] language, that [we] might come to understanding,"[6] a concept that Stark calls "divine accommodation."[7]

In November 1832, Joseph Smith prayed fervently for a longer glimpse at the reality behind the "dark curtain," and a release from the limitations of human language: "Oh, Lord, deliver us in due time from the little, narrow prison, almost as it were, total darkness of paper, pen and ink; and a crooked, broken, scattered and imperfect language."[8] Our problem, of course, is not only one of language, but more importantly in the fact that, as Nibley observes, "You comprehend others only to the degree you are like them."[9]

---

1   Moses 1:31.
2   P. J. Schakel, *Reason*, p. 86; W. Shakespeare, *Hamlet*, 2:2:192, p. 1155.
3   L. Norris, *et al.*, *Kershisnik*, p. 87. See *Endnote 1-10*, p. 76.
4   See *Endnote 1-11*, p. 76.
5   C. S. Lewis, *Faces*, p. 294; P. J. Schakel, *Reason*, pp. 78-80, 85.
6   D&C 1:24. See *Endnote 1-12*, p. 76.
7   R. Stark, *Discovering*, pp. 5-8. See *Endnote 1-13*, p. 77.
8   J. Smith, Jr., *Documentary History*, 27 November 1832, 1:299. See *Excursus 1: Speech, Writing, and Revelation*, p. 512.
9   H. W. Nibley, *Unrolling*, p. 165; cf. *Commentary* 4:28-b, p. 276. See *Endnote 1-14*, p. 77.

for Joseph's arrest… On June 28, he was carried off to court in South Bainbridge by constable Ebenezer Hatch, trailed by a mob that Hatch thought planned to waylay them en route. When a wheel came off the constable's wagon, the mob nearly caught up, but, working fast, the two men replaced it in time and drove on. Hatch lodged Joseph in a tavern in South Bainbridge and slept all night with his feet against the door and a musket by his side.…

The hearing [the next day] dragged on until night, when Justice Chamberlain… acquitted Joseph. Joseph had no sooner heard the verdict than a constable from neighboring Broome County served a warrant for the same crimes. The constable hurried Joseph off on a fifteen-mile journey without a pause for a meal. When they stopped for the night, the constable offered no protection from the tavern-haunters' ridicule. After a dinner of crusts and water, Joseph was put next to the wall, and the constable lay close against him to prevent escape.

At ten the next morning, Joseph was in court again… [Joseph's lawyer John Reed] said witnesses were examined until 2 a.m., and the case argued for another two hours. The three justices again acquitted Joseph… The next day Joseph and Emma were safely home in Harmony.

Joseph and Cowdery tried to steal back to Colesville a few days later to complete the confirmations that the trials had interrupted, but their enemies were too alert. They had no sooner arrived at the Knights' than the mob began to gather. The Knights had suffered along with Joseph. On the night of the South Bainbridge trial, their wagons had been turned over

Figure 1-5. *Relativity, 1953*
M. C. Escher, 1898-1972

...all things are present with me, for I know them all.[1] Both scripture and prophetic statements imply that for the Lord "the past, the present, and the future were and are, with Him, one eternal 'now,'"[2] a condition that surpasses current scientific understanding.[3] Escher's representation invites viewers to contrast the limited point of view of each figure in the scene to such an all-encompassing perspective.

"This is perhaps Escher's best-known print on the theme of relativity. It also is a fine example of Escher's focus on unusual, and often conflicting, points of view. Here we have three forces of gravity working perpendicularly to one another. Three earth-planes cut across each other at right angles, and human beings are living on each of them. It is impossible for the inhabitants of different worlds to walk or sit or stand on the same floor, because they have differing perceptions of what is horizontal and what is vertical. Yet they may well share the use of the same staircase. On the top staircase illustrated here, two people are moving side by side and in the same direction, and yet one of them is going downstairs and the other upstairs. Contact between them is out of the question because they live in different worlds and therefore can have no knowledge of each other's existence."[4]

1   Moses 1:6.
2   J. Smith, Jr., *Teachings*, 15 April 1842, p. 220.
3   See *Commentary* 1:6-g, p. 48; *Commentary* 2:1-e, p. 94; and *Excursus 7: Time and Eternity*, p. 537.
4   M. C. Escher, *Graphic Work*. See *Endnote 1-8*, p. 75.

and sunk in the water. Mobbers piled rails against the doors and sank chains in the stream. On Joseph's and Cowdery's return to Colesville, there was no time for a meeting or even a meal before they had to flee. Joseph said they traveled all night, "except a short time, during which we were forced to rest ourselves[s] under a large tree by the way side, sleeping and watching alternately."[15]

Later, the Prophet coolly summarized these circumstances and described how the revelation of Moses 1 had provided needed encouragement:[16]

… amid all the trials and tribulations we had to wade through, the Lord, who well knew our infantile and delicate situation, vouchsafed for us a supply of strength, and granted us "line upon line" of knowledge—"here a little and there a little,"[17] of which the [vision of Moses] was a precious morsel.

The Setting and Genre of Moses 1[18]

The events described in Moses 1 apparently took place sometime after Jehovah called Moses out of the burning bush[19] but before Moses had returned to Egypt to deliver the children of Israel.[20] Extracanonical writings parallel the book of Moses account in affirming that the stories of the Creation and the Fall were revealed to this great prophet and leader of ancient Israel in vision. For example, the book of *Jubilees* prefaces a recital of the Creation and other events of Genesis with the Lord's instructions to Moses to record what he would see in vision.[21] Similarly, *4 Ezra* preserves a tradition that the Lord led Moses "up on Mount Sinai,

15   R. L. Bushman, *Rough Stone*, pp. 116-118.
16   J. Smith, Jr., *Documentary History*, June 1830, 1:98. See *Endnote 1-9*, p. 76.
17   Isaiah 28:10.
18   See *Endnote 1-15*, p. 78.
19   Moses 1:17.
20   Moses 1:25-26.
21   O.S. Wintermute, *Jubilees* 2:52, p. 54. See *Endnote 1-16*, p. 78.

where I kept him with me many days; and I told him many wondrous things, and showed him the secrets of the times and declared to him the end of times. Then I commanded him saying, These words you shall publish openly, and these you shall keep secret."[22]

The details of Moses' experience in chapter 1 place it squarely in the tradition of ancient "heavenly ascent" literature and its relationship to temple theology, rites, and ordinances.[23] Although the stories of such ascents are similar in many respects to temple initiation rites, they make the claim of being something more. While ancient temple rituals dramatically depict a figurative journey into the presence of God, the ascent literature portrays prophets who experience actual encounters with Deity within the *heavenly* temple—the "completion or fulfillment" of the "types and images" in the ordinances.[24] In such encounters, the prophet may experience a vision of eternity or the conferral of certain blessings that are "made sure"[25] by the voice of God Himself.

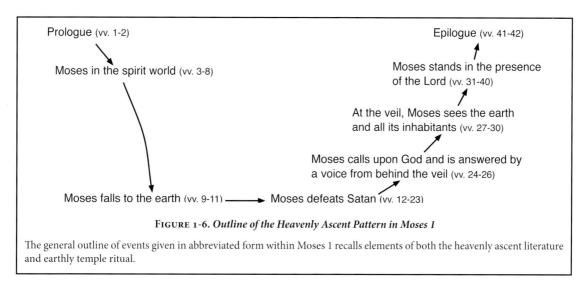

FIGURE 1-6. *Outline of the Heavenly Ascent Pattern in Moses 1*

The general outline of events given in abbreviated form within Moses 1 recalls elements of both the heavenly ascent literature and earthly temple ritual.

Though Moses 1 serves as a superb introduction to succeeding chapters describing the Creation and the Fall, its separate prologue[26] and epilogue[27] bracket the revelation, signaling its status as an independent narrative unit in its own right.[28] Verses 1-2 provide what Turner calls an "announcement of plot"[29]—a brief synopsis of the chapter describing how Moses was "caught up" to receive the glory of God and converse with Him face-to-face. The outline of events shown in the figure above details how Moses first leaves His heavenly home and then undertakes a step-by-step return to the Father.[30]

Following the prologue, Moses is given a description of God's majesty and a confirmation of the work to which he had previously been foreordained as a son of God in the similitude of the Only Begotten.[31] He is then shown the "world upon which he was created"—referring

---

22 B. M. Metzger, *Fourth Ezra,* 14:4-6, p. 553; cf. Moses 1:23, 1:42.
23 *Excursus 54: Table of Parallels with the Apocalypse of Abraham,* p. 694. See also e.g., E. Isaac, *1 Enoch,* 14:8-25, pp. 20-21; F. I. Andersen, *2 Enoch,* 1:8, pp. 114-117; H. C. Kee, *Testaments,* Levi 5, pp. 789-790; 2 Corinthians 12:1-3; Revelation 4:1; 1 Nephi 8-13; H. W. Nibley, *Teachings of the PGP,* 17, p. 205. See *Endnote 1-20,* p. 79.
24 H. W. Nibley, *Apocryphal,* p. 312; cf. pp. 310-311. See W. W. Isenberg, Philip, 85:14-16, p. 159.
25 2 Peter 1:10. See *Excursus 3: Temple Blessings in the Oath and Covenant of the Priesthood,* p. 519.
26 Moses 1:1-2.
27 Moses 1:42.
28 See *Endnote 1-17,* p. 78.
29 See *Endnote 1-18,* p. 78.
30 Moses 1:31. See *Endnote 1-19,* p. 78.
31 Moses 1:3-7. See *Endnote 1-21,* p. 79.

Figure 1-7. *Abraham and the Angel Yahoel Approach the Throne of God, ca. 1300.* Photo: Stephen T. Whitlock, 1951-

See Color Plate 1-7.

I saw… a throne [made] of fire and the many-eyed Wheels… And under the throne [I saw] four singing fiery Living Creatures… And a voice came to me… saying, …"Look at the levels which are under the expanse on which you are brought"… And while he was still speaking, … behold, the levels opened.[1] Striking parallels to Moses' experience are found in the *Apocalypse of Abraham.*[2] This illustration from a fourteenth-century Slavonic manuscript[3] shows Abraham and the Yahoel approaching the throne of God, or rather of Christ as the illustrator depicts the scene. Behind God sits a Metatron figure, whose identity may relate to the statement that "Michael is with me [God] in order to bless you forever."[4] Beneath the throne are two fiery seraphim and a many-eyed "wheel" praising God.

The throne is surrounded by a series of heavenly veils, representing different levels of the firmament separating the material world—signified by the outermost dark blue veil—from God. In both the *Apocalypse* and the book of Moses, the key phrase "as the voice was still speaking" marks the prophet's approach to the veil.[5] Like Moses, Abraham looks down upon the progressively opened veils to see the affairs of what is called in modern revelation the "kingdoms of a lower order,"[6] specifically, in this case, the events of the Creation and the Garden of Eden.[7]

1　A. Kulik, *Retroverting*, Apocalypse of Abraham 18:3, 19:1-4, pp. 24-25.
2　*Excursus 54: Table of Parallels with the Apocalypse of Abraham*, p. 694; cf. *Figure E53-12* and *Figure E53-13*, p. 684.
3　P. P. Novickij, *Otkrovenie Avraama.*
4　A. Kulik, *Retroverting*, Apocalypse of Abraham 10:17, p. 18.
5　See *Commentary* 1:27-a, p. 62.
6　D&C 130:9.
7　A. Kulik, *Retroverting*, Apocalypse of Abraham 21:1-23:13, pp. 26-28. See *Commentary* 1:27-b, p. 62.

to the preexistent spirit realm—and "all the children of men which are, and which were created"—paralleling the view of organized intelligences given to Abraham.[32] Then, having gone out the presence of the Father and no longer being clothed with His glory, Moses falls to the earth—meaning, first, that he collapsed in weakness, and, second, that he descended again to the relative darkness of the telestial world. He is then left to himself to be tested in a dramatic encounter with Satan.[33] Having banished Satan through the power of the Only Begotten (a motif linked to baptism[34]), Moses is "filled with the Holy Ghost."[35] Continuing to press forward, he "calls upon the name of God" in sacred prayer, and is answered by a voice from behind the veil enumerating specific blessings.[36] While "the voice is still speaking," Moses looks at the veil and beholds every particle of the earth and all of its inhabitants and then sees "many lands; and each land was called earth."[37]

The culminating sequence begins in verse 31 when Moses, having continued to inquire of the Lord,[38] comes to stand in His presence. God then speaks with Moses face to face,

32　Moses 1:8; cf. Abraham 3:22-23.
33　Moses 1:9-23.
34　See *Commentary* 1:20-a, p. 57.
35　Moses 1:24.
36　Moses 1:25-26. See *Endnote 1-22*, p. 79.
37　Moses 1: 27-28, 29. See *Endnote 1-23*, p. 79.
38　Moses 1:30.

FIGURE 1-8. *Guardians Part the Veils, Taking Muhammad by the Hand to See the Throne of God*

SEE COLOR PLATE 1-8.

When Gabriel took him up to each of the heavens and asked permission to enter, he had to say whom he had brought and whether he had received a mission [or: had been sent for] and they would say "God grant him life, brother and friend!" until they reached the seventh heaven and his Lord.[1] Doubting Meccans had asked that Muhammad "confirm the authenticity of his prophethood by ascending to heaven and there receiving a holy book... In this, he was to conform to a model illustrated by many still-extant legends... regarding Enoch, Moses, Daniel, Mani, and many other messengers who had risen to heaven, met God, and received from his right hand a book of scripture containing the revelation they were to proclaim."[2] During his "night journey" (*isra*), the angel Gabriel mounted him on Buraq, a winged steed, that "took him to the horizon" and then, in an instant, to the temple mount in Jerusalem.[3] At the Gate of the Guard, Ishmael "asks Muhammad's name and inquires whether he is indeed a true messenger."[4] After having given a satisfactory answer, Muhammad was permitted to gradually ascend from the depths of hell to the highest of the seven heavens on a golden ladder (*mi'raj*).[5] At the gates of the Celestial Temple, a guardian angel again "ask[ed] who he [was]. Gabriel introduce[d] Muhammad, who [was] then allowed to enter the gardens of Paradise."[6]

Commenting on the implications of this experience for later Muslims, Schimmel writes: "Islamic modernists..., when discussing the heavenly journey, have pointed out that Muhammad was able to speak to God in a true I-and-Thou relationship. This seemed to Iqbal a very important corrective of the widespread doctrine of the Unity of Being: the legend of the heavenly journey confirms that God is not a mute, remote *prima causa* but indeed a personal power who can be addressed, and thus proves that there is the possibility of a fruitful person-to-person dialogue between Creator and creature, a dialogue in prayer, out of which true religious activity can grow."[7]

1   M. Ibn Ishaq ibn Yasar, *Sirat Rasul Allàh* 270-271, p. 186.
2   D. C. Peterson, *Muhammad (2001)*, p. 527.
3   *Ibid.*, pp. 528-529.
4   A. Schimmel, *Messenger*, p. 160.
5   No relationship to the English word "mirage." See W. J. Hamblin, *et al., Temple*, p. 136; M. Ibn Ishaq ibn Yasar, *Sirat Rasul*, 263-271, pp. 181-187.
6   W. J. Hamblin, *et al., Temple*, p. 136 n. 134.
7   A. Schimmel, *Messenger*, p. 164.

describing His purposes for this earth and its inhabitants,[39] and outlining the Creation, the Fall, and how the Plan of Redemption was given to Adam and Eve.[40]

Moses' transforming experience prepared him for his the next stage of his mission.[41] Explaining the purpose of a vision of good and evil that was opened to the mind of Joseph Smith at Hill Cumorah in 1823, the angel Moroni said:

> "All this is shown, the good and the evil, the holy and the impure, the glory of God and the power of darkness, that ye may know hereafter the two powers and never be influenced or overcome by that wicked one. Behold, whatever entices and leads to good and to do good, is of God, and whatever does not is of that wicked one: it is he that fills the hearts of men with evil, to walk in darkness and blaspheme God; and you may learn from henceforth, that his ways are to destruction, but the way of holiness is peace and rest."[42]

39   Moses 1:35-40.
40   Moses chapters 2-5. See *Endnote 1-24*, p. 79.
41   See *Endnote 1-25*, p. 80.
42   *Messenger and Advocate,* 2:1, October 1835, p. 198, in F. W. Kirkham, *New Witness 1*, pp. 98-99 and J. Smith, Jr., *Papers 1989-1992*, 1:87; cf. D&C 88:6, 122:7-8.

MOSES 1

Moses 1: Text and Commentary

CHAPTER 1
(June 1830)

PROLOGUE (PP. 42-44)

THE *a*words of God, which he spake unto Moses at a time when Moses was *b*caught up into an *c*exceedingly high mountain,

2 And *a*he saw God face to face, and he talked with him, and the *b*glory of God was upon Moses; therefore Moses could endure his presence.

MOSES IN SPIRIT WORLD (PP. 44-50)

3 And *a*God spake unto Moses, saying: *b*Behold, I am the Lord God *c*Almighty, and *d*Endless is my name; for I am *e*without beginning of days or end of years; and is not this endless?

4 And, behold, thou art *a*my son; wherefore look, and I will show thee the workmanship of mine hands; but not all, for *b*my works are without end, and also my words, for they never cease.

5 Wherefore, no man can behold all my *a*works, except he behold all my glory; and *b*no man can behold all my glory, and afterwards remain *c*in the flesh on the earth.

6 And *a*I have a work for thee, Moses, my son; and thou art in the similitude of *b*mine Only Begotten; and mine Only Begotten *c*is and shall be *d*the Savior, for he is *e*full of grace and truth; but *f*there is no God beside me, and *g*all things are present with me, for I know them all.

7 And now, behold, *a*this one thing I show unto thee, Moses, my son, for *b*thou art in the world, and now I show it unto thee.

8 And it came to pass that *a*Moses looked, and *b*beheld the world upon which he was created; and Moses beheld the world and the ends thereof, and *c*all the children of men which are, and which were created; of the same he greatly marveled and wondered.

MOSES FALLS TO EARTH (PP. 51-52)

9 And the presence of God withdrew from Moses, that his glory was not upon Moses; and Moses was left unto himself. And *a*as he was left unto himself, he fell unto the earth.

10 And it came to pass that *a*it was for the space of many hours before Moses did again receive his natural strength like unto man; and he said unto himself: Now, *b*for this cause I know that *c*man is nothing, which thing I never had supposed.

11 But now *a*mine own eyes have beheld God; but not my natural, but my spiritual eyes, for my natural eyes could not have beheld; for I should have withered and died in his presence; but his glory was upon me; and I beheld his face, for I was transfigured before him.

MOSES DEFEATS SATAN (PP. 52-59)

12 And it came to pass that when Moses had said these words, behold, *a*Satan came *b*tempting him, saying: *c*Moses, son of man, *d*worship me.

13 *a*And it came to pass that *b*Moses looked upon Satan and said: Who art thou? For behold, *c*I am a son of God, in the similitude of his Only Begotten; and *d*where is thy glory, that I should worship thee?

14 For behold, I could not look upon God, except his glory should come upon me, and I were *a*transfigured before him. But *b*I can look upon thee in the natural man. *c*Is it not so, surely?

15 Blessed be the name of my God, for his Spirit hath not altogether withdrawn from me, or else *a*where is thy glory, for it is darkness unto me? And I can judge between thee and God; for *b*God said unto me: Worship God, for him only shalt thou serve.

16 *a*Get thee hence, Satan; deceive me not; for God said unto me: *b*Thou art after the similitude of mine Only Begotten.

17 And he also gave me *a*commandments when he called unto me out of the burning bush, saying: *b*Call upon God *c*in the name of mine Only Begotten, and worship me.

18 And again Moses said: I will not cease to call upon God, I have other things to inquire of him: for *a*his glory has been upon me, wherefore *b*I can judge between him and thee. Depart hence, Satan.

19 And now, when Moses had said these words, *a*Satan cried with a loud voice, and *b*ranted upon the earth, and *c*commanded, saying: *d*I am the Only Begotten, *e*worship me.

20 And it came to pass that *a*Moses began to fear exceedingly; and as he began to fear, he saw the bitterness of hell. Nevertheless, calling upon God, he received strength, and he commanded, saying: *b*Depart from me, Satan, for this one God only will I worship, which is the God of glory.

21 And now *a*Satan began to tremble, and the earth shook; and *b*Moses received strength, and called upon God, *c*saying: In the name of the Only Begotten, depart hence, Satan.

22 And it came to pass that *a*Satan cried with a loud voice, with weeping, and wailing, and gnashing of teeth; and *b*he departed hence, even from the presence of Moses, that he beheld him not.

23 And now *a*of this thing Moses bore record; but *b*because of wickedness it is not had among the children of men.

MOSES CALLS UPON GOD (PP. 59-61)

24 And it came to pass that *a*when Satan had departed from the presence of Moses, that *b*Moses lifted up his eyes unto heaven, *c*being filled with the Holy Ghost, *d*which beareth record of the Father and the Son;

25 And *a*calling upon the name of God, *b*he beheld his glory again, for it was upon him; and *c*he heard a voice, saying: *d*Blessed art thou, Moses, for I, the Almighty, have chosen thee, and *e*thou shalt be made stronger than many waters; for they shall obey thy command *f*as if thou wert God.

26 And lo, I am with thee, even unto the end of thy days; for *a*thou shalt deliver my people from bondage, even Israel my chosen.

VISION AT THE VEIL (PP. 62-64)

27 And it came to pass, *a*as the voice was still speaking, *b*Moses cast his eyes and beheld the earth, yea, *c*even all of it; and there was not a particle of it which he did not behold, discerning it *d*by the spirit of God.

28 And he beheld also the inhabitants thereof, and there was not a soul which he beheld not; and he discerned them by the Spirit of God; and their numbers were great, *a*even numberless as the sand upon the sea shore.

29 And he beheld many lands; and *a*each land was called earth, and there were inhabitants on the face thereof.

30 And it came to pass that Moses called upon God, saying: *a*Tell me, I pray thee, why these things are so, and by what thou madest them?

IN GOD'S PRESENCE (PP. 64-69)

31 And behold, the *a*glory of the Lord was upon Moses, so that *b*Moses stood in the presence of God, and talked with him face to face. And *c*the Lord God said unto Moses: For mine own purpose have I made these things. *d*Here is wisdom and it remaineth in me.

32 And *a*by the word of my power, have I created them, which is mine Only Begotten Son, who is *b*full of grace and truth.

33 And *a*worlds without number have I created; and I also created them for mine own purpose; and *b*by the Son I created them, which is mine Only Begotten.

34 And the first man of all men have I called [a]Adam, which is many.

35 But [a]only an account of this earth, and the inhabitants thereof, give I unto you. For behold, there are many worlds that have passed away by the word of my power. And there are many that now stand, and [b]innumerable are they unto man; but [c]all things are numbered unto me, for they are mine and I know them.

36 And it came to pass that Moses spake unto the Lord, saying: Be merciful unto thy servant, O God, and tell me concerning this earth, and the inhabitants thereof, and also the heavens, and then thy servant will be content.

37 And the Lord God spake unto Moses, [a]saying: The heavens, they are many, and they cannot be numbered unto man; but they are numbered unto me, for they are mine.

38 And as [a]one earth shall pass away, and the heavens thereof even so shall another come; and [b]there is no end to my works, neither to my words.

39 For behold, [a]this is my work and my glory—to bring to pass the immortality and eternal life of man.

40 And now, Moses, my son, I will speak unto thee concerning [a]this earth upon which thou standest; and thou shalt write the things which I shall speak.

EPILOGUE (PP. 69-71)

41 And in a day when the children of men shall esteem my words as naught and [a]take many of them from the book which thou shalt write, behold, [b]I will raise up another like unto thee; and they shall be had again among the children of men—among as many as shall believe.

42 (These words were spoken unto Moses in the mount, the name of which shall not be known among the children of men. And now they are spoken unto you. [a]Show them not unto any except them that believe. Even so. Amen.)

MOSES 1

MOSES 1

*1 The **words of God, which he spake unto Moses** at a time when Moses was **caught up** into an exceedingly high mountain,*

1   **a**   ***words of God, which he spake unto Moses.*** Verses 1 and 2 form a preface that should be read as an "announcement of plot" for what will occur in the rest of the chapter.[43] Nibley compares such remarks to "stage directions" written in red ink in Egyptian texts, intended for recital by the lectern priest.[44]

Allusions to a revelation on Sinai in which Moses saw the panorama of creation occur in several ancient sources[45]—this chapter gives an account of the dramatic context preceding that event.

b   ***caught up.*** The statement that Moses was "caught up" reveals that his ascent was accomplished by God's power and not his own. Such a grammatical construction is called the "divine passive," the unstated agent being God.[46]

Parallel descriptions occur elsewhere in scripture. 2 Corinthians 12:2 says that Paul was "caught up"—i.e., "snatched away"[47]—to the third heaven.[48] 1 Thessalonians 4:17 uses the same term to describe those who would be taken up from the earth to descend with Jesus Christ at his second coming.[49] Similarly, Enoch saw many who were "caught up by the powers of heaven into Zion" after his city had been taken up into heaven.[50] Such experiences may imply a context in which priesthood ordinances are received. For example, we are told elsewhere that Adam was "caught away by the Spirit of the Lord" into the water and baptized.[51]

Another close parallel to Moses' experience is found in 1 Nephi 11:1 where Nephi was "caught away in the Spirit of the Lord, yea, into an exceedingly high mountain, which [he] never had before seen."[52] Nephi later said that "upon the wings of his Spirit hath my body been carried away upon exceedingly high mountains,"[53] just as the *Apocalypse of Abraham* records that Abraham was raised up to heaven on the wings of a bird.[54]

Ephrem the Syrian portrays Eve in the Garden of Eden as a dove, and Satan appearing as a dove to deceive her.[55] However, the Prophet explained that: "The sign of the dove was instituted before the creation of the world, a witness for the Holy Ghost, and the Devil cannot come in the sign of a dove."[56] Nibley comments: "[T]he dove that takes one to heaven is the Holy Ghost, who also instructs and teaches 'through the heavens,' 'revealing… the grand Key-words… as, also, the sign'[57] by which alone supernal knowledge can be conveyed."[58] Whether representing the ascent to heaven of the souls of the living[59] or dead,[60] or else the

43   L. Turner, *Announcements*; cf. H. W. Nibley, *Teachings of the PGP*, 16, pp. 193-194.

44   H. W. Nibley, *Teachings of the PGP*, 16, pp. 193-194, 18, p. 220; cf. Moses 1:23, 42.

45   M. Barker, *Revelation*, pp. 24-25; E. D. Clark, *Prologue*.

46   K. L. Barney, *June 21 2006*.

47   Greek *harpazo*.

48   Cf. 3 Nephi 28:13.

49   Cf. D&C 88:96; 101:31; 109:75.

50   Moses 7:27.

51   Moses 6:64.

52   Cf. Exodus 19:3, Ezekiel 40:2; JST Matthew 4:8; Revelations 21:10; Moses 7:2. For other parallels between Nephi and Moses, see N. B. Reynolds, *Kingship*, pp. 172-177.

53   2 Nephi 4:25.

54   R. Rubinkiewicz, *Apocalypse of Abraham*, 12:10, p. 695; cf. H. W. Nibley, *Abraham 2000*, p. 18, Genesis 15:9ff. See *Figure E53-13*, p. 684 for an illustration from a Slavonic *Apocalypse of Abraham* that shows the patriarch and the angel Yahoel ascending on the wings of birds. See *Endnote 1-26*, p. 80.

55   Ephrem the Syrian, *Fall*, 4, p. 101. See *Commentary 3:9-g*, p. 163; 4:5-b, p. 246.

56   J. Smith, Jr., *Teachings*, 29 January 1843, p. 276; cf. B. R. McConkie, *Mortal Messiah*, 1:404; J. Smith, Jr., *Words*, 21 March 1841, p. 66.

57   Book of Abraham, Facsimile 2, explanation of Figure 7.

58   H. W. Nibley, *Abraham 2000*, pp. 56-57.

59   E.g., Nephi, Moses.

60   E.g., E. S. Drower, *Adam*, pp. 8, 32; H. W. Nibley, *New Look*, July 1969, p. 109; H. W. Nibley, *Approach to*

MOSES 1

*1 The words of God, which he spake unto Moses at a time when Moses was **caught up** into an **exceedingly high mountain,***

    descent of heavenly messengers to earth,[61] the common idea behind the symbol of a bird—and specifically in this context a dove—is that of sacred communication and communion between the spheres, "the certain tie between heaven and earth."[62]

c   *exceedingly high mountain.* The location of this mountain is assumed to be somewhere near the northwest edge of the Arabian Peninsula. Potter adduces evidence that identifies the site with a mountain in the vicinity of Midian named Jabel al-Lawz.[63] He argues that at this location, rather than at the traditional spot on St. Catherine's mountain in the Sinai Peninsula, Moses would have received his commission to free Israel from Egypt.[64] Later, it also would be the place where God would reveal the Law and the instructions for building the Tabernacle, and where the incident with the golden calf would take place.[65] Potter further conjectures that this may be the same "exceedingly high mountain" to which Nephi was "caught away" in vision,[66] since it is less than eighteen miles away from what some believe is the most plausible candidate for the valley of Lemuel, where he was camped at the time.[67]

    Note the similar wording that is associated with the mountain where God showed himself to the Brother of Jared: it was called Shelem "because of its exceeding height."[68] As Thomas observes, the essential thing is to suggest "a place that is suitably high for temple activity."[69] Thomas describes the spectrum of meanings associated with the three Hebrew consonants *slm*: "peace, tranquility, contentment, safety, completeness, being sound, finished, full, or perfect. Shelem (and Hebrew *shalom*) signify peace with God, especially in the covenant relationship. It also connotes submission to God, which we see in the Arabic words *muslim* and *islam*. In particular, *shelem* has reference to the peace offering of the law of sacrifice, which corresponds to the seeking of fellowship with God, and thereby has a relationship to the meanings of the *at-one-ment*; that is, *shelem*, fellowship, sealing, and *at-one-ment* have an obvious relationship."[70] Nibley further explains: "The original word of *Shelem, Shalom*, means 'peace,' but it originally meant 'safe' (safety, security) because it was a high place. The *Shelem* was a high place. It's still the word for ladder: *silma, selma,* a *sullam* in Arabic."[71] This connotation is significant because the ladder is a symbol often used to represent the process of exaltation.[72]

    Abraham, pp. 261-264; M. D. Rhodes, *Hor*, p. 20.

61   H. W. Nibley, *New Look*, July 1969, pp. 108-110, August 1969, pp. 75-77; H. W. Nibley, *Approach to Abraham*, pp. 258-265, 268-269; J. Smith, Jr., *Words*, before 8 August 1839, p. 10; J. Smith, Jr., *Teachings*, December 1835, p. 98.

62   H. W. Nibley, *New Look*, July 1969, p. 109; H. W. Nibley, *Approach to Abraham*, p. 263. See W. J. Hamblin, *et al.*, *Temple*, p. 156 for a Sufi allegory involving birds who fly to the Celestial Temple. See also E. A. S. Butterworth, *Tree*, pp. 82-83; B. Mika'el, *Mysteries*, pp. 18-20; *Figure 3-8*, p. 145; *Figure 6-14*, p. 473; *Commentary 2:2-c*, p. 97; *3:9-g*, p. 163; *4:5-b*, p. 246. See *Endnote E-204*, p. 754.

63   G. Potter, *Sinai*.

64   Exodus 3.

65   Exodus 19-32.

66   1 Nephi 11:1.

67   S. K. Brown, *Hunt*; G. Potter, *et al.*, *Lehi*, pp. 31-51; R. Wellington, *et al.*, *Lehi's Trail*, p. 29. For a differing view, see J. R. Chadwick, *Wrong Place*.

68   Ether 3:1. A change to "exceedingly" was made in the LDS 1921 edition (K. P. Jackson, *Book of Moses*, p. 57). Note that, like the Book of Mormon, OT1 and OT2 read "exceeding" rather than "exceedingly" (S. H. Faulring, *et al.*, *Original Manuscripts*, pp. 83, 591).

69   M. C. Thomas, *Brother of Jared*, p. 391. Regarding a plausible candidate for the mountain Shelem, Potter notes: "At nearly 6,000 feet, [Jabal Samham] is the highest mountain in southern Oman and is mentioned by name in Genesis 10:30, where it is known as 'Sephar, a mount of the east'" (G. Potter, *et al.*, *Lehi*, p. 130).

70   M. C. Thomas, *Brother of Jared*, p. 391.

71   H. W. Nibley, *Teachings of the PGP*, 16, p. 196.

72   R. Guénon, *Symboles*, pp. 336-339; cf. J. Smith, Jr., *Teachings*, 7 April 1844, p. 348—see pp. 346-348, 354. See also M. C. Thomas, *Hebrews*; M. C. Thomas, *Brother of Jared*; Genesis 28:12; overview of Moses 1, p. 34; *Figure*

*1 The words of God, which he spake unto Moses at a time when Moses was caught up into an **exceedingly high mountain**,*

*2 And **he saw God face to face,** and he talked with him, and the **glory of God was upon Moses;** therefore Moses could endure his presence.*

*3 And **God spake unto Moses,** saying: Behold, I am the Lord God Almighty, and Endless is my name; for I am without beginning of days or end of years; and is not this endless?*

In scripture, the term "mountain" is often used figuratively to describe temples.[73] When temples have not been available, mountains have often provided the same function.[74]

2   a   *he saw God face to face.* Moses' encounter with God was no mere dream or vague sense of presence, but rather an intimate and direct dialogue with a glorious visible and audible personage. The eyewitness quality of Moses' experience is emphasized by repeated references to its visual aspects.[75]

Thomas observes that "seeing" and "knowing" are often closely associated in scripture, the ultimate in knowledge being manifested when, like Moses or the Brother of Jared, one is permitted to see the Lord face to face.[76]

b   *glory of God was upon Moses.* The Hebrew word for the glory (*kabod*—heavy, weighty, burdensome) of God connotes the magnificence of His immediate presence. The sense in which this may also signal a real bodily presence is captured in the English phrase: "he was there in all his glory."[77]

The term "glory" is repeated twelve times within the chapter, serving to make the contrast between God's splendor and Satan's pale imitation blatantly apparent.[78] Moses 1 frequently reminds the reader that man can neither endure God's presence nor fully discern His works unless transfigured by His power.[79] The exposition of the theme of God's glory will culminate in v. 39.

3   a   *God spake unto Moses.* Although v. 6 seems to imply that God the Father is speaking directly to Moses, the voice is typically understood to be that of Jehovah, the premortal Jesus Christ.[80] Moses 5:9, in similar fashion, seems to be an example of the Holy Ghost speaking as the Father. Whereas such ambiguity in scripture sometimes may be due to historical complexities in textual transmission, in this context, it could be an example of *divine investiture.* This concept describes the situation where Christ is authorized to speak and act as if He were the Father.[81]

5-13, p. 351.

73   Isaiah 2:2; Psalm 48:2; R. J. Clifford, *Temple*; J. M. Lundquist, *Meeting Place*, pp. 6-10; J. M. Lundquist, *Typology*, pp. 84-86.

74   E.g., the Mount of Transfiguration (M. B. Brown, *Gate*, pp. 174-175, 195 n. 23), the mount where the Lord showed himself to the Brother of Jared (M. C. Thomas, *Brother of Jared*), and Ensign Peak in the Salt Lake Valley (M. B. Brown, *et al.*, *Symbols*, pp. 119, 159; B. H. Roberts, *Comprehensive History*, 3:386).

75   I.e., "see" (Moses 1:2, 20), "look" (vv. 4, 8, 13, 14), "behold" (vv. 5, 7, 8, 11, 22, 25, 27, 28, 29, 35, 39), "show" (v. 7), "eyes" (v. 11, 24), and "discern" (v. 28).

76   E.g., 1 Nephi 5:4; 3 Nephi 11:15; Alma 36:26; D&C 45:46; 50:45; 93:1. See also L. E. Dahl, *et al.*, *Lectures*, 7:16-18, pp. 101-103; J. Smith, Jr., *Words*, 27 June 1839, p. 5; 1 May 1842, p. 120; 14 May 1843, pp. 200-202; J. Smith, Jr., *Teachings*, 27 June 1839, pp. 149-150; M. C. Thomas, *Brother of Jared*, p. 395.

77   T. G. Madsen, *House*, p. 280.

78   Moses 1:13, 14, 15, 20.

79   Moses 1:1, 5, 9, 11, 14, 25, 31. See also vv. 27, 28; D&C 67:11-12; 84:22; D. C. Mouritsen, *Transfiguration*. Contrast *Commentary* 1:14-b, p. 54.

80   Cf. D&C 29:1, 42, 46; M. Barker, *Hidden*, p. 74; Irenaeus, *Proof*, 44-45, pp. 76-77; Novatian, *Trinity*, 18, pp. 627-629.

81   H. D. Peterson, *Commentary*, pp. 74-75. For the First Presidency's full statement on this and related topics, see J. R. Clark, *Messages*, 5:31-32. See also G. L. Burgon, *Name*; B. R. McConkie, *NT Commentary*, 1:73, 77, 85, 468; 2:183; 3:137, 138; B. R. McConkie, *Promised Messiah*, pp. 64, 349, 369, 370, 558, 601-602; B. R. McConkie,

*3 And **God spake unto Moses,** saying: **Behold, I am** the Lord God **Almighty,** and **Endless** is my name; for I am **without beginning of days or end of years;** and is not this endless?*

*4 And, behold, thou art **my** son; wherefore look, and I will show thee the workmanship of **mine** hands; but not all, for my works are without end, and also my words, for they never cease.*

Noting that "latter-day revelation gives us the fuller account and meaning of what actually took place on the Mount," Elder Alvin R. Dyer taught that both the Father and the Son were present on this occasion. He saw the event as "similar to that which was experienced by Joseph Smith in the Sacred Grove, wherein God the Father appeared and announced his Son who stood by him, by stating, 'This is my Beloved Son.'"[82] If such were indeed the case, it would allow for speech from both the Father and the Son on this occasion, and thus would obviate the need to interpret the words of God to Moses as an instance of divine investiture.

b   ***Behold I.*** The "I" is repeated in OT1: "Behold I I." The current text follows OT2.[83]

    I am. This phrase begins a typical *aretology,*[84] whereby God proclaims His particular virtues and offices.[85] By reinvoking at the start the divine title that was disclosed to Moses previously,[86] God both establishes His identity and sets the context for the later affirmations of His relationship with Moses.[87] Later, in Moses' dialogue with Satan, a similar interplay of divine titles and assertions of relationship recurs with different effect.[88]

c   ***Almighty.*** The title recalls the demonstration of God's power over the waters as the first act of creation.[89] Moses will in like manner "be made stronger than many waters."[90]

d   ***Endless.*** The term corresponds to the Hebrew *Ein Sof,* the name used for God in the Jewish Kabbalah.[91] "This name ties to God's characteristic of being 'without beginning of days or end of years' and His creation of 'innumerable' worlds.[92] It combines to form a single name with the term 'Eternal.'"[93] The endlessness of God, His works, and His words is stressed throughout the chapter: "without end," "numberless," "without number," "innumerable," "cannot be numbered," "no end."[94]

e   ***without beginning of days or end of years.*** In other places in scripture, this phrase is used to describe the Holy Priesthood.[95]

4   a   ***my... mine.*** The possessives "my" and "mine" are repeated by the Lord throughout His dialogue with Moses.[96] The recurrence of the pronouns "I" and "me" not only personalizes the account, but also throws into stark relief the almighty, endless, and eternal nature of

Mortal Messiah, 1:349; 2:81; H. D. Peterson, *Commentary,* pp. 74-75; D. R. Seely, *Jehovah;* J. E. Talmage, *Articles (1984),* pp. 424-425; J. A. Tvedtnes, *Metcalfe,* p. 18.

82   A. R. Dyer, *Meaning,* p. 12.

83   S. H. Faulring, *et al., Original Manuscripts,* pp. 83, 591.

84   Greek *arete* = virtue or quality.

85   H. W. Nibley, *Teachings of the PGP,* 17, pp. 213-214.

86   Exodus 3:13-14.

87   I.e., "thou art my son" (Moses 1:4), "my son, thou art in the similitude of mine Only Begotten" (Moses 1:6).

88   Moses 1:13, 19.

89   Moses 2:1-2.

90   Moses 1:25, R. D. Draper, *et al., Commentary,* p. 21.

91   H. W. Nibley, *Teachings of the PGP,* 17, p. 213.

92   Moses 1:3, 35.

93   R. D. Draper, *et al., Commentary,* p. 21. See Moses 7:35; D&C 19:11; D&C 132:20.

94   Moses 1:4, 28, 33, 35, 37, 38.

95   JST Hebrews 7:3.

96   I.e., "my name" (Moses 1:3), "my son" (vv. 4, 6, 7, 40), "the workmanship of mine hands" (v. 4), "my works"/ "my work" (vv. 4, 5, 38, 39), "my words" (vv. 4, 38, 41), "my glory" (vv. 5, 39), "mine Only Begotten" (vv. 6, 32, 33), "my chosen" (v. 26), "mine own purpose" (v. 31), "the word of my power" (vv. 32, 35), "they [i.e., all things, the heavens] are mine" (vv. 35, 37).

*4 And, behold, thou art **my** son; wherefore look, and I will show thee the workmanship of **mine** hands; but not all, for **my works are without end, and also my words,** for they never cease.*

*5 Wherefore, no man can behold all my **works**, except he behold all my glory; and **no man can behold all my glory**, and afterwards remain **in the flesh on the earth.***

*6 And **I have a work for thee, Moses, my son;** and thou art in the similitude of mine Only Begotten; and mine Only Begotten is and shall be the Savior, for he is full of grace and truth; but there is no God beside me, and all things are present with me, for I know them all.*

God in contrast to the subordinate status of Moses and the absurd pretensions of Satan. The frequent use of "I" continues in Moses 2, where the JST effects a transformation that collapses the distance of Genesis' third-person creation account into first-person narrative.

b   *my works are without end, and also my words.* See v. 32 and *Commentary* 1:38-b, p. 67.

5   **a**   *works.* This is given as "work" in OT2. OT1 and all publications read "works."[97]

    b   *no man can behold all my glory.* Clark cites a parallel talmudic source that says that: "God would not grant Moses' wish to behold all his glory."[98]

    c   *in the flesh on the earth.* No one can behold all God's glory before he has received God's fulness—thus Moses' vision must be limited at this time to "this one thing."[99] Note that the three Nephite disciples were "caught up into heaven" and "were changed from this body of flesh into an immortal state, that they could behold the things of God."[100]

Nibley remarks that "dire consequences" may result from transgression of divinely-set bounds: "*Pistis Sophia* went beyond her 'degree' and, becoming ambitious, 'looked behind the veil' [and] fell from glory."[101] Sounding a similar theme, a petitioner in the Islamic mystical text *The Mother of Books* is warned by God that if one were to move "the curtain and the veil the slightest bit [to] make the high king visible… their spirit would leave their body."[102]

The words "on the earth" were inserted in the hand of Sidney Rigdon above the relevant line of the passage in OT2, without punctuation.[103] RLDS D&C 22:3d adds a comma, resulting in the phrase "in the flesh, on the earth." If it correctly represents the intended sense, this alternate punctuation might imply that the two clauses are parallel and, perhaps, synonymous.

6   **a**   *I have a work for thee, Moses, my son.* Having sketched out the overwhelming extensiveness of His own works and glory,[104] God outlines the work that Moses is foreordained to perform, the nature of which will be further elaborated after his defeat of Satan.[105] The Prophet Joseph Smith spoke of Moses specifically as one of the "sons of God who exalt[ed] themselves to be Gods, even from before the foundation of the world."[106] In this verse, the Lord invokes Moses' status as a son of God in the similitude of [the] Only Begotten.[107] This suggests that Moses' vision must extend beyond any specific assignments to the realization that, in a general sense in this life, and more fully in the next, his work is to be patterned after God's

---

97   S. H. Faulring, *et al.*, *Original Manuscripts*, pp. 591 and 59.

98   E. D. Clark, *Prologue*, p. 140.

99   Moses 1:7. See also *Commentary* 4:28-b, p. 276.

100   3 Nephi 28:13, 15. See also 3 Nephi 28:36-40.

101   H. W. Nibley, *Message 2005*, p. 443. See C. Schmidt, *Pistis*, 1:29-30, pp. 83-91; G. R. S. Mead, *Pistis*, 1:29-30, pp. 33-36.

102   W. Barnstone, *et al.*, *Gnostic*, p. 672.

103   S. H. Faulring, *et al.*, *Original Manuscripts*, p. 591; K. P. Jackson, *Book of Moses*, p. 59. Contrast 2 Nephi 10:7.

104   Moses 1:4-5.

105   Moses 1:25-26.

106   J. Smith, Jr., *Teachings*, 16 June 1844, p. 375; cf. *Excursus 3: Temple Blessings in the Oath and Covenant of the Priesthood*, p. 519. See *Endnote E-4*, p. 703.

107   Cf. Moses 1:13, Deuteronomy 18:15.

*6 And **I have a work for thee, Moses, my son**; and thou art in the similitude of **mine Only Begotten**; and mine Only Begotten **is and shall be the Savior**, for he is **full of grace and truth**; but there is no God beside me, and all things are present with me, for I know them all.*

own as he assumes the role of lawgiver, savior, and mediator to his people.[108] Every person who has come to this earth similarly covenanted in premortal life to enter a partnership with the Lord to become saviors for the whole human family.[109]

b   *mine Only Begotten.* Although these words imply that this is the voice of God the Father, it could be instead Jesus Christ who is speaking as the Father by divine investiture of authority.[110]

Only Begotten. The expression "Only Begotten" appears five times in the KJV New Testament.[111] The term also appears nine times in the Book of Mormon, 13 times in the Doctrine and Covenants, and 25 times in the relatively brief book of Moses.[112]

Insofar as NT usage is concerned, Barney notes that "Only Begotten" derives from a mistranslation of a Greek term (*monogenes*) that means either "sole descent, only child" or "only, peerless, matchless, unique, of singular importance." "Although it is a mistranslation, it is not that far removed from the correct meaning, as the suggestion of being begotten is to some extent inherent in the designation 'son' (*huios*) itself."[113] However, it is clear that the Apostle "John did not refer to Jesus as God's 'only begotten' son, because he designated all who received Jesus as being spiritually begotten of God."[114] Moreover "in LDS thought we are all spiritually begotten sons and daughters of heavenly parents." In the case of the book of Moses and other modern scripture, Barney argues that the use of the term Only Begotten "is simply a reflection of the English translational tradition,… [though the phrase] works for us theologically with the qualifier 'in the flesh.'"[115]

c   *is and shall be.* This phrase serves to emphasize that Christ's work as the Savior was not limited to His earthly ministry, but had its beginning "from before the foundation of the world."[116] Moreover, being infinite and eternal, the Atonement can appropriately be referred to as if it had already taken place.[117]

d   *the Savior.* This title is not present in OT1,[118] but was added above the line in OT2 by an undetermined scribe.[119]

e   *full of grace and truth.* D&C 93 makes it clear that receiving the "fulness" is accomplished gradually by continuing from "grace to grace."[120] The same revelation invites us to follow Jesus Christ in the same way to the identical end.[121]

Comments Nibley, "How do you define grace? That's *charis*; that's everything good. *Charis* is your attitude toward others, toward everything else. It is an attitude of complete love. It is related to our word cheer and the Latin, *gratia* which means 'thanks, grace,' etc.…

---

108   Exodus 32:30ff.
109   Elder John A. Widtsoe, cited in A. F. Bennett, *Saviors*, pp. 11-12; B. K. Packer, *Holy Temple*, p. 216. See also *Commentary 1:39-*a, p. 68 and 1:41-b, p. 69.
110   See *Commentary* 1:3-a, p. 44.
111   Plus one JST addition in 1 Timothy 2:4.
112   Moses 1:6, 16, 17, 21, 32, 33; 2:1, 26, 27; 4:1, 3; 5:7, 9, 57; 6:52, 57, 59, 62; 7:50, 59, 62.
113   K. L. Barney, *Only.*
114   E.g., John 1:12-13; 1 John 3:9.
115   K. L. Barney, *Only.*
116   See *Commentary* 5:57-b, p. 399.
117   Cf. Jarom 1:11; Mosiah 3:13, 16:6.
118   See S. H. Faulring, *et al.*, *Original Manuscripts*, p. 83.
119   *Ibid.*, p. 591; K. P. Jackson, *Book of Moses*, p. 59.
120   Moses 1:12-16.
121   D&C 93:19-20. Cf. Moses 1:32, 5:7.

*6 And I have a work for thee, Moses, my son; and thou art in the similitude of mine Only Begotten; and mine Only Begotten is and shall be the Savior, for he is **full of grace and truth**; but **there is no God beside me**, and **all things are present with me**, for I know them all.*

Mephistopheles [is] all negative, all willing to destroy. This is the absolute opposite of that… nothing false, nothing deceiving, nothing phony."[122]

f ***there is no God beside me.*** Shortly, Moses will be required to refuse Satan's defiant command: "Moses, son of man, worship me."[123] Later, he will also face the overwhelming challenge of convincing the children of Israel that there is only one God that they should worship, in contrast to the numerous idolatrous deities to whom the Egyptians paid tribute.[124]

Joseph Smith taught that there is "but one God—that is, pertaining to us."[125] While clarifying the unique role of the Father with respect to mankind, neither this verse nor the statement of Joseph Smith denies existence to other perfected beings who, although not the subject of worship, may be rightfully called gods.[126]

Note that OT1 and OT2 read "none other God beside me."[127] The change to "no God" was first made by the RLDS I.V. publication committee.[128] The 1851 *Times and Seasons* publication had "besides" instead of "beside."[129]

g ***all things are present with me.*** Alma wrote: "all is as one day with God, and time only is measured unto men"[130] and D&C 130:7 states that "all things for [the angels'] glory are manifest, past, present, and future, and are continually before the Lord."[131] Moses seems to have temporarily had a similar experience as a mortal.[132] Elder Neal A. Maxwell concluded: "God does not live in the dimension of time as do we. We are not only hampered by our finiteness (experiential and intellectual), but also by being in the dimension of time. Moreover, God, since 'all things are present' with him, is not simply predicting based solely on the past. In ways that are not clear to us, he sees rather than foresees the future, because all things are at once present before him."[133]

A similar conception of God's experience of time was proposed in the sixth century by Boethius.[134] Current scientific theory also sees the concept of time as being less like a flowing river and more like "a giant block of ice with every moment forever frozen into place."[135] Though Einstein, for example, worried about the fact that science could not yet adequately account for the fact that the "experience of the 'now' means something special for man," he firmly resisted the temptation to concede to universal intuition.[136] A few weeks before his own death, he wrote to the grieving family of a lifelong friend who had just passed away: "Now he has departed from this strange world a little ahead of me. That means nothing. For us believing physicists, the distinction between past, present, and future is only a stubborn illusion."[137]

122   H. W. Nibley, *Teachings of the PGP*, 17, pp. 214-215.
123   Moses 1:12.
124   Exodus 20:2-5; 1 Corinthians 8:5-6. See statement of the First Presidency in J. R. Clark, *Messages*, 4:269-271.
125   J. Smith, Jr., *Teachings*, 16 June 1844, p. 370.
126   D&C 132:20. See also *Commentary* 2:26-a, p. 111; 4:11-b, p. 253; 4:28-a, p. 276.
127   S. H. Faulring, *et al.*, *Original Manuscripts*, pp. 83, 591.
128   K. P. Jackson, *Book of Moses*, p. 59.
129   *Ibid.*, p. 59.
130   Alma 40:8.
131   Cf. D&C 88:41, Isaiah 46:9-10, Acts 15:18, D&C 29:31-33.
132   See *Commentary* 1:27-b, p. 62.
133   N. A. Maxwell, *Things*, p. 29; cf. M. Barker, *Boundary*, pp. 215-217; C. S. Lewis, *Image*, pp. 88-89; C. S. Lewis, *Mere*, 4:3, p. 147; C. S. Lewis, *Providences*; J. E. Talmage, *Jesus the Christ*, p. 27 n. 1; *Hymns (1985)*, #133: "So may the world its future spread before Thee."
134   A. M. S. Boethius, *Consolation*, 5:3-6, pp. 100-114. For more on Boethius, see Moses 1 *Gleanings*, p. 73.
135   B. Greene, *Fabric*, p. 141.
136   *Ibid.*, p. 141.
137   Cited in W. Isaacson, *Einstein*, p. 540. See also D. Wilkinson, *Hawking*, pp. 119-121.

*6 And I have a work for thee, Moses, my son; and thou art in the similitude of mine Only Begotten; and mine Only Begotten is and shall be the Savior, for he is full of grace and truth; but there is no God beside me, and **all things are present with me**, for I know them all.*

*7 And now, behold, **this one thing** I show unto thee, Moses, my son, for **thou art in the world**, and now I show it unto thee.*

*8 And it came to pass that **Moses looked**, and beheld the world upon which he was created; and Moses beheld the world and the ends thereof, and all the children of men which are, and which were created; of the same he greatly marveled and wondered.*

The view that God "transcends" time in the above sense not only raises theological questions, but also entails dilemmas from philosophical and scientific perspectives, motivating Ostler's closely-reasoned arguments that an LDS theological position of this sort is untenable.[138] For example, if this picture of God's timelessness is accurate, it would seem that, in some manner, God must be able to stand outside of the universe while also being able to participate in it.[139] This idea stands in contrast to current scientific understanding embodied in the theory of relativity, which does not admit an observer from within to be "present to all actualities throughout the universe in a single frame of reference."[140] Moreover, though having appeared to prophets in glorified corporeal form, it seems reasonable to imply that God must somehow be capable of transcending fundamental limitations of human understanding deriving from the finite nature of physical senses and measures, the unimaginable scale of what would need to be known, and—if that were not enough—the fact that a perfect knowledge of the state of things seems precluded by the laws of quantum physics themselves.[141]

7 a **this one thing.** That is, the world upon which Moses was created.[142] The limited nature of Moses' vision is emphasized by reiteration: "this one thing," "the world," and "it."[143] So comprehensive is this limited view, however, that even it will prove overwhelming to Moses.[144]

Nibley comments: "'I'm going to limit you to this one thing because I have one assignment,' the Lord says. We focus on the thing we are supposed to do. '… for thou art in the world and now I show it unto thee.' I will show you the world you are in. [This is] the anthropic principle.[145] Where you are determines the way everything will appear to you and be to you because you have to act from that point. You don't see everything, you don't move in all directions, and you don't know what's behind you at this very moment."[146]

b **thou art in the world.** See *Commentary* 1:8-b, p. 50.

8 a **Moses looked.** When the Lord spoke with Abraham face to face, He first put His hand upon the latter's eyes to prepare him for his vision of the universe.[147] Joseph Smith was reportedly so touched at the beginning of the First Vision, and perhaps prior to receiving D&C 76.[148]

---

138 B. T. Ostler, *Attributes*; B. T. Ostler, *Theism*. See Sherlock for a useful summary and critique of Ostler's viewpoint (R. Sherlock, *Ostler*, pp. 292-299, 302-303).

139 B. K. Harrison, *Truth*, p. 166.

140 B. T. Ostler, *Attributes*, p. 354.

141 See *Excursus 7: Time and Eternity*, p. 537 for more discussion of these issues. Many sources contain extended discussions of God's foreknowledge and timelessness (e.g., B. M. Hauglid, *Time*; R. J. Ingebretsen, *Astronomy*, pp. 38-48; C. S. Lewis, *Miracles*, pp. 226-234; N. A. Maxwell, *Experience*, pp. 6-27; B. T. Ostler, *Theism*, pp. 25-75; D. L. Paulsen, *Response to Pinnock*, pp. 530-532; J. Smith, Jr., *Documentary History*, 6 February 1840, 4:78; J. Smith, Jr., *Teachings*, 15 April 1842, p. 220; W. V. Smith, *JS Commentary*, p. 81; J. E. Talmage, *Articles (1984)*, pp. 173-174). For an overview of Egyptian concepts, see H. W. Nibley, *Message* 2005, pp. 228-232.

142 Moses 1:8.

143 Cf. "but not all" (v. 4), "it remaineth in me" (v. 31), and "only an account of this earth" (v. 35).

144 Moses 1:8-10.

145 See *Commentary* 1:39-a, p. 68.

146 H. W. Nibley, *Teachings of the PGP*, 17, p. 215. See also H. W. Nibley, *Funeral*, pp. 298-299.

147 Abraham 3:11-12.

148 See *Endnote 1-27*, p. 80.

*8 And it came to pass that Moses looked, and **beheld the world upon which he was created**; and Moses beheld the world and the ends thereof, and **all the children of men which are, and which were created**; of the same he greatly marveled and wondered.*

b   ***beheld the world upon which he was created.*** "World" is used three times in this chapter—once in v. 7 and twice in v. 8. The related term "earth" is used in v. 5, and then afterwards is used exclusively until the end of the chapter.[149] "Earth" also appears throughout the account of creation in chapters 2-4.[150] Both terms appear in Moses chapters 5-7, with the term "earth" continuing to predominate.

This phrase arguably refers to the world of spirits rather than to the earth, paralleling Abraham's view of organized intelligences (spirits) that preceded his creation vision.[151] Clark cites a rabbinic source as saying that "'God did shew unto Adam every Generation,' meaning 'all the Souls, which were to come into the World,... so that Adam could perfectly distinguish them,' later 'thus it happened on Mount Sinai' with Moses, so that 'the Souls, which were not then born into the world, were present on Mount Sinai, in the same form in which they were to appear in the World.'"[152]

The statement about "the world upon which he was created" seems to be made in deliberate contradistinction to the later reference to "the earth upon which thou standest"[153]—the qualifications used in each case would be unnecessary if the "world" and the "earth" were one and the same place. Moreover, if the world Moses is shown in v. 8 were the same as the earth he beholds in vv. 27-28, why the need for two separate visions? Such puzzles are resolved if we take "world" in the book of Moses as most often referring to the realm of the human family in premortal life.[154] This also sets a context where the phrase "thou art in the world"[155] can be understood, not as an obvious truism, but as a comprehensible justification for why it was expedient to show Moses the world of spirits at that particular time. Finally, if we accept this interpretation, Moses 6:51 can function as a deliberate parallelism ("I made the world, and men before they were in the flesh") rather than as a pair of loosely related assertions.

OT2 reads "as Moses beheld the world."[156] The current text is from the *Times and Seasons*.[157]

c   ***all the children of men which are, and which were created.*** See *Commentary* 1:8-b, p. 50; and compare Moses 1:28, where Moses sees all the inhabitants of the earth. See also the similar experiences of Enoch,[158] the brother of Jared,[159] and Abraham.[160]

The OT1 phrase "which was and which was created"[161] was emended in the hand of Sidney Rigdon in OT2 to read "which are, and which were created."[162]

---

149   Moses 1:9, 19, 21, 27, 29, 35, 36, 38, and 40.
150   With the exceptions of Moses 1:33, 35; and 4:6.
151   Abraham 3:22-23; cf. Enoch's vision in Moses 6:36.
152   E. D. Clark, *Prologue*, p. 138; cf. *Qur'an* 7:172; 30:30; 33:7; 53:56; G. Weil, *Legends*, pp. 39-40; *Excursus 48: The Nature and Scope of Premortal Covenants*, p. 649.
153   Moses 1:40.
154   15 consistent occurrences; two possible exceptions in Moses 1:33, 35; two exceptions in 6:59; and one in 7:4.
155   Moses 1:7.
156   S. H. Faulring, *et al.*, *Original Manuscripts*, p. 591.
157   *History of JS 4:5*, p. 72. See K. P. Jackson, *Book of Moses*, p. 41.
158   Moses 7:23.
159   Ether 3:25.
160   Abraham 3:21-22.
161   S. H. Faulring, *et al.*, *Original Manuscripts*, p. 83.
162   K. P. Jackson, *Book of Moses*, pp. 59, 591.

9 And the presence of God withdrew from Moses, that his glory was not upon Moses; and Moses was left unto himself. And **as he was left unto himself, he fell unto the earth**.

10 And it came to pass that **it was for the space of many hours before Moses did again receive his natural strength like unto man**; *and he said unto himself: Now,* **for this cause I know** *that* **man is nothing**, *which thing I never had supposed.*

9 a *as he was left unto himself, he fell unto the earth.* Nibley describes this scene as "Moses, landing on earth as a natural man."[163] If we assume that this verse has a second meaning referring to Moses leaving his view of the spirit world[164] and returning to his vantage point on earth, this "fall" could be seen as a figurative recapitulation of Adam's Fall from the presence of God to the telestial state where Satan will be allowed to try him.

10 a *it was for the space of many hours before Moses did again receive his natural strength like unto man.* Moses was both spiritually and physically exhausted, recalling the aftermath of similar experiences by other prophets. Following one of his visions, Daniel reported that he "fainted, and was sick certain days,"[165] and of a second occasion he wrote: "I was left alone… and there remained no strength in me… and when I heard the voice of his words, then was I in a deep sleep on my face, and my face toward the ground."[166] Lehi "cast himself on his bed, being overcome with the Spirit."[167] Saul "fell to the earth" during his vision[168] and remained blind until healed by Ananias.[169] Similarly, Alma "fell to the earth; and it was for the space of three days and three nights that [he] could not open [his] mouth, neither had [he] the use of [his] limbs."[170] Of his weakness following the First Vision, Joseph Smith wrote: "When I came to myself again, I found myself lying on my back, looking up into heaven. When the light had departed, I had no strength…"[171] Concerning his experience of watching Joseph Smith and Sidney Rigdon as they received the vision of the three degrees of glory,[172] Philo Dibble wrote: "Joseph sat firmly and calmly all the time in the midst of a magnificent glory, but Sidney sat limp and pale, apparently as limber as a rag, observing which Joseph remarked, smilingly, 'Sidney is not used to it as I am.'"[173] Note also that when Jesus Christ was "led by the Spirit into the wilderness,"[174] it was at a point of physical weakness following a forty-day fast when Satan appeared to tempt Him.

b *for this cause I know.* OT1 and OT2 give this phrase as "for this once I know."[175] However, the current text follows the 1843 *Times and Seasons* publication.[176] Similar statements are common in ascension accounts, where they signify that one's eyes have been opened.[177]

c *man is nothing.* King Benjamin said: "Ye cannot say that we are even as much as the dust of the earth."[178] Elder Neal A. Maxwell wrote that Moses' statement "surely was not a reflection on man, 'God's greatest miracle,' but a placing of man in the vast perspective of God's creations and a realizing, even so, that we are God's exclusive work and his greatest glory."[179]

163 H. W. Nibley, *Assembly*, p. 128.
164 See *Commentary* 1:8-b, p. 50.
165 Daniel 8:26.
166 Daniel 10:8-9.
167 1 Nephi 1:7.
168 Acts 9:4.
169 Acts 9:17-18.
170 Alma 36:10; cf. Mosiah 27:12, 18-19.
171 JS-H 1:20.
172 D&C 76.
173 Cited in L. R. Flake, *Three Degrees*, p. 6.
174 JST Luke 4:1.
175 S. H. Faulring, *et al.*, *Original Manuscripts*, pp. 83, 592.
176 *History of JS* 4:5, p. 72. See K. P. Jackson, *Book of Moses*, p. 14.
177 Cf. *Commentary* 4:11-a, p. 253; 4:13-a, p. 258; 5:10-e, p. 363.
178 Mosiah 2:25; cf. Mosiah 4:5-7, 11; Alma 26:12; Helaman 12:7.
179 N. A. Maxwell, *Notwithstanding*, p. 75; cf. T. S. Monson, *Priesthood Trust*, p. 56. See also Moses 1:39.

MOSES 1

*10 And it came to pass that it was for the space of many hours before Moses did again receive his natural strength like unto man; and he said unto himself: Now, for this cause I know that **man is nothing**, which thing I never had supposed.*

*11 But now **mine own eyes have beheld God; but not my natural, but my spiritual eyes, for my natural eyes could not have beheld**; for I should have withered and died in his presence; but his glory was upon me; and I beheld his face, for I was transfigured before him.*

*12 And it came to pass that when Moses had said these words, behold, **Satan came tempting** him, saying: Moses, son of man, worship me.*

Moses has learned more than just the fact that man is nothing. The subsequent text pointedly demonstrates that, more generally, he has increased his capacity to discern good from evil.[180] Faulconer notes that it was only after that Moses saw that he was nothing that, "with extraordinary confidence, he is able to say to Satan, 'I am a son of God… where is thy glory, that I should worship thee?'[181]… Obviously, recognizing his own nothingness has nothing to do with having a bad self-image or groveling in his nothingness. It is instead coming to a full realization of his dependence upon God, of his inability to save himself and of God's merciful willingness to save him. That realization of his nothingness is also a realization of his relation to God as a child."[182]

11 a ***mine own eyes have beheld God; but not my natural, but my spiritual eyes, for my natural eyes could not have beheld.*** Joseph Smith explained that "All things… God… has seen fit… to reveal to us… are revealed to us in the abstract, and independent of affinity of this mortal tabernacle, but are revealed to our spirits precisely as though we had no bodies at all."[183] In vv. 13-15, Moses will recognize the difference between God's glory and Satan's darkness by the fact that he "must be protected to see Jehovah but could face this imposter with his natural eyes and without discomfort."[184]

OT1 reads "but now mine eyes, mine own eyes but not mine eyes for mine eyes could not have beheld."[185] The wording in all subsequent publications closely resembles changes made in the hand of Sidney Rigdon in OT2.[186]

12 a ***Satan came.*** Nibley comments: "Now the play begins because you have to have an antagonist and a protagonist in a play. Now Satan enters the scene. Notice, when the hero is at his lowest, when he is the most helpless, that is the time that Satan strikes… Faust is in the dark ready to commit suicide, and Satan appears to him there. It's the same thing with Job. The tempters, his companions, come to him then."[187] "The result is a *stichomythia*. Now we are going to get a combat… Before a duel between the heroes of the kings, there is a long preliminary exchange of insults that goes on.[188] This is a regular part of heroic literature."[189]

b ***tempting.*** The word "tempt" corresponds to Hebrew (*nsh*) and Greek (*peirazo*)—meaning to try, test, or prove. Such tests may be instigated by God,[190] by Satan,[191] or by others.[192]

180   See *Commentary* 1:11-18, pp. 52-56.
181   Moses 1:13.
182   J. E. Faulconer, *Self-Image*, p. 26.
183   J. Smith, Jr., *Teachings*, 7 April 1844, p. 355; cf. Job 19:25-26: "yet in my flesh shall I see God."
184   S. W. Kimball, *They Shall See God*; cf. H. D. Peterson, *Commentary*, p. 90; *Commentary* 1:12-d, p. 53; Moses 1:14; W. W. Isenberg, *Philip 57-58*, pp. 144-145. See also *Commentary* 1:2-b, p. 44 and Enoch's experience in Moses 6:36.
185   S. H. Faulring, *et al.*, *Original Manuscripts*, p. 84.
186   *Ibid.*, p. 592; K. P. Jackson, *Book of Moses*, p. 60.
187   H. W. Nibley, *Teachings of the PGP*, 17, p. 216.
188   See, e.g., 1 Samuel 17:8-10, 43-47.
189   H. W. Nibley, *Teachings of the PGP*, 18, p. 217; cf. S. D. Ricks, *et al.*, *King*, pp. 249-253.
190   E.g., Genesis 22:1.
191   E.g., Luke 4:2.
192   E.g., John 8:6.

12 And it came to pass that when Moses had said these words, behold, Satan came tempting him, saying: **Moses, son of man**, **worship me**.

13 **And it came to pass that Moses looked** *upon Satan and said: Who art thou? For behold,* **I am a son of God, in the similitude of his Only Begotten**; *and where is thy glory, that I should worship thee?*

c *Moses, son of man.* The scriptural epithet "son of man" can be interpreted in more than one way. The correct alternative can only be inferred by clues in the context of a given scriptural passage. In this verse and in translations of the Hebrew *ben 'adam*, the words refer to a descendant of Adam—in other words, "any mortal man."[193] However, when prefaced with the definite article ("*the* Son of Man"), they describe "an expected apocalyptic heavenly figure, identified with the Messiah."[194] In a related sense, Jesus is "the son of the archetypical Man, the perfect heavenly Man, the Eternal Father."[195] In the context of this verse, it should be remembered that Moses had just been told by the Lord that he was a "son of Man," in the similitude of the Only Begotten. Satan's words, referring to Moses as merely a "son of man," recall the tactic he later used to taunt Jesus Christ: "*If* thou be the Son of God…"[196]

d *worship me.* Prefiguring his encounter with Christ in the wilderness, Satan tempts Moses—in his physically weakened state—to worship him.[197] Moses, with a veil of forgetfulness obscuring the memory of his preexistent glory, and not yet having had his vision of the events of the Grand Councils, the Creation, and the Fall, was thought by Satan to have been easy prey. In this respect, Satan, "an unembodied spirit—he the disinherited, the rebellious and rejected son… [with] a remembrance of those primeval scenes"[198] was at a distinct advantage.

The Devil's recurrent demands for worship recall a story attested in several ancient sources that the premortal rebellion began when Satan refused God's request to bow down in homage to the newly-created Adam.[199]

13 a *And it came to pass that.* This OT1 phrase was changed to read "but it came to pass that" in OT2 by the hand of Sidney Rigdon.[200]

b *Moses looked.* OT2, in the handwriting of Sidney Rigdon, expands this phrase from OT1 to read "Moses lifted up his eyes and looked."[201]

c *I am a son of God, in the similitude of his Only Begotten.* His eyes having been opened, Moses confronts Satan with the same words that God spoke to him earlier.[202] These words constitute a "humiliating exposure of Satan"—an announcement that Moses "actually *is* what his adversary falsely *claims to be*."[203]

193 E.g., Daniel 8:17.
194 E.g., Daniel 7:13.
195 S. E. Robinson, *Names*, p. 740; cf. M. Barker, *Lost*, pp. 91-104. See Moses 6:57, 7:35.
196 Matthew 4:3, 6, emphasis mine. See the overview of Moses 5, p. 329, *Commentary* 2:26-c, p. 113, and *Excursus 30: Adam-God Theory and the Heavenly and Earthly Adam*, p. 603.
197 Cf. Matthew 4:8-9.
198 J. E. Talmage, *Jesus the Christ*, p. 124.
199 See the overview of Moses 4, p. 224, and *Excursus 23: The Roles of Christ, Adam, and Michael*, p. 582.
200 S. H. Faulring, *et al.*, *Original Manuscripts*, p. 592; K. P. Jackson, *Book of Moses*, p. 60.
201 S. H. Faulring, *et al.*, *Original Manuscripts*, p. 592; K. P. Jackson, *Book of Moses*, p. 60.
202 Moses 1:6; cf. *Commentary* 1:12-c, p. 53.
203 H. W. Nibley, *To Open*, p. 5, emphasis mine. See *Commentary* 1:10-c, p. 51 and Moses 1:16, 19.

13 And it came to pass that Moses looked upon Satan and said: Who art thou? For behold, I am a son of God, in the similitude of his Only Begotten; and **where is thy glory**, *that I should worship thee?*

14 For behold, I could not look upon God, except his glory should come upon me, and I were **transfigured before him**. *But* **I can look upon thee in the natural man**. **Is it not so, surely?**

15 Blessed be the name of my God, for his Spirit hath not altogether withdrawn from me, or else **where is thy glory, for it is darkness unto me?** *And I can judge between thee and God; for God said unto me: Worship God, for him only shalt thou serve.*

d *where is thy glory.* "The glory of God is intelligence, or, in other words, light and truth. Light and truth forsake that evil one."[204] The events of this vision show Satan to possess neither light[205] nor truth.[206]

14 a *transfigured before him.* The 1843 *Times and Seasons* publishers altered the text to read "strengthened before him."[207]

b *I can look upon thee in the natural man.* See *Commentary* 1:2-b, p. 44 and 1:11-a, p. 52.

c *Is it not so, surely? Blessed be.* OT1 reads "if not so surely blessed be."[208] OT2 crosses out part of the (erroneously copied?) phrase "is if not is" and reads simply "Surely blessed be."[209] The current wording first appeared in the 1843 *Times and Seasons* publication.[210]

15 a *where is thy glory, for it is darkness unto me?* Similarly, in the *Conflict of Adam and Eve with Satan*, God warns Adam and Eve about Satan, saying: "This is he who promised you majesty and divinity. Where, then, is the beauty that was on him? Where is his divinity? Where is his light? Where is the glory that rested on him?"[211]

Here, Satan no doubt appeared to Moses deceptively as an angel of light.[212] Elder Parley P. Pratt wrote that "although [spirits not worthy to be glorified] often attempt to pass as angels of light there is more or less of darkness about them. So it is with Satan and his hosts who have not been embodied."[213] Stone sees a passage in the Latin *Life of Adam and Eve* as implying "that all Satan lacked to look like a heavenly angel was the glory. He lost the glory when he fell, and he could take it on temporarily in order to deceive Adam and Eve."[214] Thus, Satan is sometimes depicted in early Christian art as angelic in form but differing in color—e.g., appearing with "false glory" in a blue tint rather than in a whiteness of glory.[215] One might alternatively interpret Satan's blue color as his appearing, deceptively, in a form corresponding to the blue robe of the high priest, a robe which represented being clothed in the likeness of the body—the blue-black "shadow"—of the incarnate Logos.[216] Comments Nibley: "Remember, glory cannot be faked… We try to do that with special effects, etc., but they always fall flat… Imitation glory is darkness; it's sad. The glory of a merry-go-round, or the glory of Las Vegas, all that light, all that neon glitter. Is that your idea of glory?"[217]

204   D&C 93:36-37.

205   E.g., Moses tells Satan that his purported glory "is darkness unto me" (Moses 1:15).

206   E.g., Satan's false claim: "I am the Only Begotten" (Moses 1:19). See *Commentary* 1:10-b, p. 51 and 1:12-d, p. 53.

207   *History of JS 4:5*, p. 72; see K. P. Jackson, *Book of Moses*, p. 14.

208   S. H. Faulring, *et al.*, *Original Manuscripts*, p. 84.

209   *Ibid.*, p. 592.

210   *History of JS 4:5*, p. 72. See K. P. Jackson, *Book of Moses*, p. 27.

211   S. C. Malan, *Adam and Eve*, 1:51, p. 56.

212   2 Corinthians 11:12-15; 2 Nephi 9:9; D&C 128:20, 129:4-7; J. Smith, Jr., *Teachings*, 1 April 1842, pp. 204-205.

213   P. P. Pratt, *Key*, p. 72.

214   M. E. Stone, *Adam's Contract*, pp. 18-19; cf. S. C. Malan, *Adam and Eve*, 1:27, pp. 27-29, 1:60, pp. 67-70, and 2:5, pp. 110-111.

215   M. E. Stone, *Adam's Contract*, pp. 18-19.

216   M. Barker, *Gate*, pp. 119-120; W. Williams, *Shadow*. See *Commentary* 4:5-a, p. 246.

217   H. W. Nibley, *Teachings of the PGP*, 18, p. 218; cf. H. W. Nibley, *House of Glory*, p. 334. For a listing of some of the Devil's purported disguises as given in ancient literature, see D. C. Allison, *Testament*, pp. 327-328. See

*15 Blessed be the name of my God, for his Spirit hath not altogether withdrawn from me, or else **where is thy glory, for it is darkness unto me?** And I can judge between thee and God; for **God said unto me: Worship God, for him only shalt thou serve**.*

*16 **Get thee hence, Satan**; deceive me not; for God said unto me: **Thou art after the similitude of mine Only Begotten**.*

*17 And he also gave me **commandments** when he called unto me out of the burning bush, saying: **Call upon God** in the name of mine Only Begotten, and worship me.*

Accounts of Satan's loss of glory are given in stories of his premortal rebellion[218] and of the penalties he received following his deception of Eve in the Garden of Eden.[219]

The current text of Moses follows OT1. The later OT2 reads instead "I say 'Where is thy glory?'"[220]

darkness. OT1 and OT2 read "blackness" in place of "darkness."[221] The change to "darkness" was first made in the 1843 *Times and Seasons* publication[222] and perpetuated in subsequent editions. The term "blackness" appears once in JST Genesis[223] and, likewise, the term "black" appears uniquely in Moses 7:22.[224]

b   ***God said unto me: Worship God, for him only shalt thou serve.*** In replying to Satan, the words of Moses fittingly parallel a saying of Jehovah, just as Christ, the embodied Jehovah, later cites the words of Moses during his temptation.[225]

16   a   ***Get thee hence, Satan.*** Moses will fail three times in his attempts to banish Satan,[226] succeeding at last only when he invokes the name of the Only Begotten.[227] Note that when Jesus banished Satan following his temptation in the wilderness, a single command from the Only Begotten Himself sufficed.[228]

b   ***Thou art after the similitude of mine Only Begotten.*** Cf. *Commentary* 1:13-c, p. 53.

17   a   ***commandments.*** OT1, OT2, and RLDS D&C 22:10 read "commandment."[229] The change to commandments, which had previously appeared in the 1851 *Times and Seasons* publication, stems from the 1902 LDS edition.[230]

b   ***Call upon God.*** This phrase recurs in verses 18, 20, and 25. Note that when Adam and Eve "called upon the name of the Lord,"[231] they were answered with commandments and angelic visitations revealing priesthood ordinances.[232] Discoursing on 2 Peter 1:10, the Prophet urged the Saints: "I would exhort you to go on and continue to call upon God until you make your calling and election sure."[233] Moses' perseverance in calling upon God illustrates this pattern, and eventually will be rewarded when he enters the Lord's presence.

Commentary 1:11-a, p. 52 and 1:13-d, p. 54.

218   *Commentary* 4:1-4, pp. 243-246 and the overview of Moses 4., pp. 223-227.
219   *Commentary* 4:20-21, pp. 264-267. See also *Commentary* 1:10-b, p. 51, 1:12-d, p. 53, 1:13-d, p. 54, and 3:25a, p. 185.
220   S. H. Faulring, *et al.*, *Original Manuscripts*, p. 592.
221   *Ibid.*, pp. 84, 592.
222   *History of JS* 4:5, p. 72.
223   Moses 7:8.
224   See *Commentary* 5:40-c, p. 386.
225   Deuteronomy 6:13; Matthew 4:10.
226   Moses 1:16, 18, 20.
227   Moses 1:21.
228   Matthew 4:11. See also *Commentary* 4:21-d, p. 266.
229   S. H. Faulring, *et al.*, *Original Manuscripts*, pp. 84, 592.
230   K. P. Jackson, *Book of Moses*, p. 61.
231   Moses 5:4.
232   See also *Commentary* 6:4-a, p. 477.
233   J. Smith, Jr., *Teachings*, 14 May 1843, p. 299.

*17 And he also gave me commandments when he called unto me out of the burning bush, saying: Call upon God **in the name of mine Only Begotten**, and worship me.*

*18 And again Moses said: I will not cease to call upon God, I have other things to inquire of him: for **his glory has been upon me**, wherefore **I can judge between him and thee**. Depart hence, Satan.*

*19 And now, when Moses had said these words, **Satan cried with a loud voice**, and **ranted upon the earth**, and **commanded**, saying: I am the Only Begotten, worship me.*

    c   ***in the name of mine Only Begotten.*** Although the commandment to pray "in the name of mine Only Begotten" does not appear explicitly in the Old Testament, the Bible does record that Moses learned the name of Jehovah at the time he saw the burning bush.[234] The book of Moses records that Adam received an identical commandment.[235]

18   a   ***his glory has been upon me.*** OT1 and OT2 add: "and it is glory unto me." However, the current text of the book of Moses follows the 1843 *Times and Seasons* publication.[236]

    b   ***I can judge between him and thee.*** This phrase confirms that Moses has, like Adam and Eve after the Fall, "learned to distinguish between good and evil."[237]

19   a   ***Satan cried with a loud voice.*** Moses' continued resistance calls for a dramatic change in tactics: "Satan… casts aside his celebrated but now useless subtlety and launches a frontal attack of satanic fury, a tremendous tantrum."[238]

       Blaming Adam for all his troubles, the Armenian version of the *Life of Adam and Eve* records that Satan "wept loudly" as he railed forth in self-pity, and the Latin version has him "groaning." The Georgian version highlights the manipulative intent of the Devil's theatrics, stating that he "began to cry with forced tears."[239]

    b   ***ranted upon the earth.*** The term "ranted" is a conjectural emendation of the term "wrent" in OT1 and OT2.[240] To rant is to speak in a violent, loud, extravagant, and vehement manner for maximal rhetorical effect.

       The JST manuscript has been emended differently in RLDS D&C 22:12 to read "*went* upon the earth." Although this reading is more natural from a grammatical perspective, it seems a poor fit to the context of the rest of the verse. Based on parallel spellings in the *Printer's Manuscript* of the Book of Mormon and the JST, Jackson rightfully concludes that the original manuscript term "wrent" "is likely a regional spelling of 'rent,' the past tense of 'rend,' 'to tear.'"[241] In other words, Satan "tore upon the earth."[242]

       This reading perfectly fits the character of the adversary: Satan's objective is to rend and destroy, while Christ's mission is to unite and atone.[243]

    c   ***commanded.*** Satan counters Moses' stubborn obedience to God's commandment[244] with a direct command of his own. In the end, it will be Satan who yields to Moses' command—a

---

234   Exodus 4:13-15.
235   Moses 5:8.
236   *History of JS 4:5*, p. 72. See K. P. Jackson, *Book of Moses*, p. 41.
237   H. W. Nibley, *To Open*, p. 18; cf. *Commentary* 1:10-b, p. 51; 4:11-a, p. 253; 4:13-a, p. 258; 5:10-e, p. 363.
238   H. W. Nibley, *To Open*, p. 5.
239   G. A. Anderson, *et al.*, *Synopsis*, 12:1, p. 15E.
240   S. H. Faulring, *et al.*, *Original Manuscripts*, pp. 84, 593.
241   K. P. Jackson, *Book of Moses*, p. 50.
242   Cf. *Commentary* 1:21-a, p. 57.
243   See the overview of Moses 6, pp. 467-469, and *Excursus 46: The Origin and Meaning of the Term "Atonement"*, p. 642.
244   Moses 1:17.

*19 And now, when Moses had said these words, Satan cried with a loud voice, and ranted upon the earth, and **commanded**, saying: **I am the Only Begotten**, **worship me**.*

*20 And it came to pass that **Moses began to fear exceedingly**; and as he began to fear, he saw the bitterness of hell. **Nevertheless, calling upon God, he received strength**, and he commanded, saying: **Depart from me, Satan**, for this one God only will I worship, which is the God of glory.*

*21 And now **Satan began to tremble, and the earth shook**; and Moses received strength, and called upon God, saying: In the name of the Only Begotten, depart hence, Satan.*

command executed in the authority and power of the priesthood after the order of the true Son of God.[245]

d ***I am the Only Begotten.*** Note that the truth of Moses' assertions[246] stands in direct contradiction to the false claims repeatedly advanced by Satan.[247]

e ***worship me.*** Islamic tradition includes a similar theme. Citing a commentary on *Qur'an* 21:29 ("I am a god besides Him"), the Islamic scholar al-Tabari takes the phrase to mean that Satan "calls to worship of himself."[248]

20 a ***Moses began to fear exceedingly... Nevertheless, calling upon God, he received strength.*** Nibley summarizes: "...true to the ancient pattern, the hero is momentarily bested, overcome by the powers of darkness... But with his last ounce of strength he calls upon God from the depths and is delivered: he has won the fight, he has prevailed against the power of him who 'sought to destroy the world, for he knew not the mind of God."[249] "This is the *de profundis*. That's the 130th Psalm... 'Out of the depths have I cried unto thee, O Lord."[250] Just as in the myth of Osiris, the "final test is the baptism... Moses is delivered from the waters and comes out."[251] In the typology of such tests, the righteous are raised in glory while the wicked drown and perish.[252]

b ***Depart from me, Satan.*** OT1 and OT2 read "Depart hence, Satan."[253] The current text of Moses follows the 1843 *Times and Seasons* publication.[254]

21 a ***Satan began to tremble, and the earth shook.*** The thunderous shaking of the ground echoes the emotional intensity of Satan's rage in terrifying reverberations. Writes Nibley: "[Satan is] the *gaieokhon*, the earthshaker. It means... both the earthshaker and the earthholder. If he holds it, he shakes it. So it goes back to the common thing, that he is of this earth, under the earth. And, of course, he is Pluto and he is wealth, too."[255]

Other scriptural references linking Satan and trembling include James 2:19 ("the devils also believe, and tremble"[256]) and Isaiah 14:4, 7, 16 ("How hath the oppressor ceased!... The

---

245 Moses 1:21-22; see also D&C 107:3.
246 See *Commentary* 1:13-c, p. 53 and Moses 1:16.
247 See *Commentary* 4:1-d, p. 243; 4:5-b, p. 246; 5:13-b, p. 365.
248 al-Tabari, *Creation*, 1:80, p. 251.
249 H. W. Nibley, *To Open*, p. 5. See Moses 4:6; cf. JS-H 1:15-17.
250 H. W. Nibley, *Teachings of the PGP*, 18, p. 219. See also H. W. Nibley, *Return*, p. 75.
251 H. W. Nibley, *Teachings of the PGP*, 10, p. 118; cf. *Figure 4-14*, p. 231. See *Endnote 4-50*, p. 312.
252 Exodus 14:27-30, 1 Peter 3:18-21; cf. *Commentary* 1:24-a, p. 59; 1:25-e, p. 60; 4:21-d, p. 266; 4:31-d, p. 280; 5:6-a, p. 360; *Figure 5-3*, p. 330; *Excursus 1: Speech, Writing, and Revelation*, p. 512. See *Endnote 5-23*, p. 435.
253 S. H. Faulring, *et al.*, *Original Manuscripts*, pp. 84, 593.
254 *History of JS 4:5*, p. 72. See K. P. Jackson, *Book of Moses*, p. 41.
255 H. W. Nibley, *Teachings of the PGP*, 17, pp. 212-213.
256 Greek *phrisso* = shudder or shiver. Cf. Matthew 8:29 where the trembling can be viewed as "indicating a cognizance of their appointed doom" (W. E. Vine, *et al.*, *Dictionary (1996)*, s.v. shudder, p. 573).

*21 And now **Satan began to tremble, and the earth shook**; and **Moses received strength, and called upon God**, saying: **In the name of the Only Begotten, depart hence, Satan**.*

*22 And it came to pass that **Satan cried with a loud voice**, with weeping, and wailing, and gnashing of teeth; and **he departed hence, even from the presence of Moses**, that he beheld him not.*

whole earth is at rest, and is quiet… Is this the man that made the earth to tremble,[257] that did shake[258] kingdoms").[259]

This verse is an interesting parallel to rabbinic commentary that also pictures Cain as someone who made the earth tremble.[260]

b ***Moses received strength, and called upon God.*** In the previous verse, Moses received strength after calling upon God—here, the order of these events is reversed.

c ***saying: In the name of the Only Begotten, depart hence, Satan.*** The dramatic turning point of this episode hinges on Satan's desperate false claim to be the Only Begotten, and Moses' final, successful dismissal of Satan, accomplished by invoking the name of the true Only Begotten.

A medieval Ethiopian text similarly witnesses a belief in the efficacy of the name of God in conquering Satan. In an account of the battle between Satan's rebellious armies and the hosts of heaven the angels twice charged Satan's ranks unsuccessfully. However, prior to their third attempt, they were given a cross of light inscribed "In the Name of the Father, and the Son, and the Holy Spirit," and "when Setna'el [Satan] saw that inscription he was vanquished."[261]

This verse has a complex history of revisions. OT1 reads: "And Moses receiving strength called upon God saying In the name of Jesus Christ depart hence Satan."[262] OT2 reads: "And Moses received strength and called upon God in the name of his Son, saying to Satan depart hence."[263] The 1866-67 RLDS Publication inexplicably substituted the title "Only Begotten" for "his Son." The book of Moses currently follows a combination of OT1 and OT2, while carrying over the term "Only Begotten" from the RLDS publication.[264]

22 a ***Satan cried with a loud voice.*** In an elegant parallel to verse 19, Satan cries out a second time with a loud voice. In this instance, however, the cry is not a flourish of rhetorical melodrama, but rather a despairing wail reflecting the misery and hopelessness of the damned.

b ***he departed hence, even from the presence of Moses.*** Silenced and vanquished, Satan disappears from the scene.

OT1 and OT2 read: "and departed hence; yea, from the presence of Moses."[265] The current text follows the 1843 *Times and Seasons* publication.[266]

---

257 Hebrew *ragaz* = to be agitated, angry, to quiver or quake (F. Brown, *et al., Lexicon*, p. 919b).
258 Hebrew *rash* = quake, shake (*ibid.*, p. 950b).
259 Cf. Moses 7:13, S. C. Malan, *Adam and Eve*, 1:48, p. 53; G. W. E. Nickelsburg, *1 Enoch*, 88:2, p. 364). See also *Commentary* 1:19-b, p. 56.
260 See *Commentary* 5:41-b, p. 388. See also Genesis 27:33 (Isaac) and Alma 11:46 (Zeezrom).
261 B. Mika'el, *Mysteries*, p. 17.
262 S. H. Faulring, *et al., Original Manuscripts*, p. 84.
263 *Ibid.*, p. 593.
264 K. P. Jackson, *Book of Moses*, p. 62; R. J. Matthews, *What Is*, pp. 35-36, 154.
265 S. H. Faulring, *et al., Original Manuscripts*, pp. 84, 593.
266 *History of JS* 4:5, p. 72. See K. P. Jackson, *Book of Moses*, pp. 17, 63.

*23 And now **of this thing Moses bore record**; but **because of wickedness it is not had among the children of men**.*

*24 And it came to pass that **when Satan had departed from the presence of Moses**, that **Moses lifted up his eyes unto heaven**, **being filled with the Holy Ghost**, **which beareth record of the Father and the Son**;*

*25 And **calling upon the name of God**, he beheld his glory again, for it was upon him; and he heard a voice, saying: Blessed art thou, Moses, for I, the Almighty, have chosen thee, and thou shalt be made stronger than many waters; for they shall obey thy command as if thou wert God.*

23 a ***of this thing Moses bore record.*** Johnson views this verse in company with v. 41 as a marker for a parallel panel structure comprising vv. 1-23 and 24-41.[267]

   b ***because of wickedness it is not had among the children of men.*** Turner wryly comments: "No doubt Satan was not anxious to have this demeaning episode publicized."[268]

24 a ***when Satan had departed from the presence of Moses.*** In some Christian traditions, the motif of the banishment of Satan is closely linked to the ordinance of baptism.[269] Note in this verse and the next the first explicit mention of the Father, the Son, and the Holy Ghost in close proximity, recalling the words of the baptismal prayer,[270] in conjunction with the subsequent statements that Moses "lifted his eyes unto heaven,"[271] was "filled with the Holy Ghost," and was "made stronger than many waters."[272] Such a reading would also be consistent with the book of Moses motif of calling upon God and being answered with additional commandments and ordinances, as noted previously.[273]

   b ***Moses lifted up his eyes unto heaven.*** Freed from transfixion on the vision of hell below, Moses looks up again to heaven. Similarly, "at the very moment when [he] was ready to sink into despair," Joseph Smith looked up to see "a pillar of light exactly over [his] head."[274]

   Nibley conjectured that this phrase signified that Moses was being "carried up to heaven… by the Holy Ghost."[275] However, it seems more likely that the event to which Nibley refers occurs a little later in the account.[276]

   c ***being filled with the Holy Ghost.*** The Holy Ghost has ministered to mankind since the time of Adam.[277]

   d ***which beareth record of the Father and the Son.*** Similar wording recurs three more times in the book of Moses.[278]

25 a ***calling upon the name of God.*** In his discussion of early Christian and Jewish rituals related to temple practices, Tvedtnes discusses the prayer circle, noting that "prayer opens the veil

267 M. J. Johnson, *Prologue*, pp. 12-13.
268 R. Turner, *Visions of Moses*, p. 55. See also *Commentary 1:42-a*, p. 69.
269 See *Commentary 1:20-a*, p. 57; 1:25-e, p. 60; 4:21-d, p. 266; 4:31-d, p. 280; 5:6-a, p. 360; *Figure 5-3*, p. 330; *Excursus 1: Speech, Writing, and Revelation*, p. 512. See *Endnote 5-23*, p. 435.
270 D&C 20:73.
271 Cf. Matthew 3:16; Mark 1:10; Luke 3:22; *Commentary 1:1-b*, p. 42.
272 Cf. *Commentary 5:9-b*, p. 362.
273 *Commentary 1:17-b*, p. 55.
274 JS-H 1:16. See *Commentary 1:27-b*, p. 62.
275 H. W. Nibley, *Teachings of the PGP*, 18, p. 220. See *Commentary 1:1-b*, p. 42.
276 See *Commentary 1:27-a*, p. 62.
277 See Moses 5:9; 6:52; 2 Peter 1:21; J. F. Smith, Jr., *Doctrines*, 1935, 1:46-47.
278 Moses 5:9; 6:66; 7:11.

*25 And **calling upon the name of God**, **he beheld his glory again, for it was upon him**; and **he heard a voice**, saying: **Blessed art thou, Moses**, for I, the Almighty, have chosen thee, and **thou shalt be made stronger than many waters**; for they shall obey thy command as if thou wert God.*

to allow one to enjoy the presence of God."[279] From this and subsequent verses, it can be concluded that Moses had learned so to pray.[280]

b *he beheld his glory again, for it was upon him.* The current text follow the 1843 *Times and Seasons* publication.[281] OT1 reads "was upon him." OT2, however, reads with a significant difference (in the handwriting of Sidney Rigdon): "he beheld again his glory, for it rested upon him."[282] If the altered wording was added under inspiration, perhaps it was intended to imply that the glory now conferred upon Moses was of a permanent rather than transient nature ("rested upon him" vs. "was upon him"[283])—his now having "put on the garment of glory,"[284] even "the robe of righteousness."[285]

c *he heard a voice.* Since the moment he "fell to the earth,"[286] Moses could no longer speak face to face with the Lord, having been "shut out from his presence."[287] However, when Satan was banished, the Lord began to minister to Moses through the intermediary of the Holy Ghost.[288] Now we are told that a voice speaks to Moses from beyond the heavenly veil, portending his return back into the Lord's presence.[289] Ancient ascent and temple texts affirm that in preparation for entry into the holy presence, the initiate exchanged words with a divine voice at the veil, sometimes depicted visually as the welcoming hand of God that is grasped by the initiate.[290] Once he has been thoroughly tested, the "last phrase" of welcome is extended to the successful candidate, "Let him come up!"[291]

The completion of this series of upward steps has required Moses' utmost tenacity. Comments Nibley: "Is this a return to heaven or is it halfway? Remember, [it's like climbing a] mountain. It's as high as you can go, I suppose[, then the Lord must take over]. But he sees the glory of God which was upon him. Then he heard a voice announcing he is the victor. He is recognized [as] the king."[292]

d *Blessed art thou, Moses.* The promise given to Moses concerning the work he was foreordained[293] to do is now reaffirmed. Here, at the heavenly veil, Moses receives blessings that foreshadow his role as deliverer to the children of Israel, in similitude of the Savior.

e *thou shalt be made stronger than many waters.* The most obvious reference here is to the power Moses will be given to divide the Red Sea.[294] However, we should also note the parallel

279   J. A. Tvedtnes, *Rituals*; B. K. Packer, *Personal Revelation*, p. 59; W. Clayton, *Chronicle*, 15 June 1844, p. 134.
280   Joseph Smith to Bathsheba W. Smith, *Juvenile Instructor*, 27, 1 June 1892, p. 345, cited in D. M. Quinn, *Prayer Circles*, p. 1.
281   *History of JS 4:5*, p. 72. See K. P. Jackson, *Book of Moses*, p. 41.
282   S. H. Faulring, *et al.*, *Original Manuscripts*, pp. 85, 593.
283   See Moses 1:2, 9, 11, 14, 18.
284   G. W. E. Nickelsburg, *et al.*, *1 Enoch*, 62:15-16, p. 81.
285   2 Nephi 9:14. See the overview of Moses 4, pp. 234-240.
286   Moses 1:9.
287   Cf. Moses 5:4.
288   Moses 1:24; cf. Moses 5:9.
289   Moses 1:31.
290   H. W. Nibley, *Message 2005*, pp. 449-457; P. Alexander, *3 Enoch*, p. 296 n. 45a; H. W. Nibley, *Atonement*, p. 562; *Figure 6-14*, p. 473; *Excursus 53: Comparative Explorations, Dexiosis*, p. 681; the *Mandaean Texts* and *Manichaean Texts* sections of *Annotated Bibliography*, pp. 870, 884; and *Figure B-1*, p. 872. See *Endnote 1-22*, p. 79.
291   M. E. Stone, *Fall of Satan*, p. 47; cf. Revelation 4:1: "Come up hither"; Matthew 25:21: "Enter thou into the joy of thy Lord."
292   H. W. Nibley, *Teachings of the PGP*, 18, p. 220.
293   Moses 1:6.
294   Exodus 14:21-22; Joshua 3:14-17.

*25 And calling upon the name of God, he beheld his glory again, for it was upon him; and he heard a voice, saying: Blessed art thou, Moses, for I, the Almighty, have chosen thee, and **thou shalt be made stronger than many waters**; for they shall obey thy command **as if thou wert God**.*

*26 And lo, I am with thee, even unto the end of thy days; for **thou shalt deliver my people from bondage**, even Israel my chosen.*

to God's subduing of the waters at creation,[295] particularly in light of the phrase that follows: "as if thou wert God." Recall also that God's voice is compared in scripture to the "rushing of great waters."[296] All this can be taken to mean that Moses is being promised the blessings of exaltation. Explains Nibley: "'In most versions of the year-drama [enacted in diverse cultures throughout the world and paralleling the experience of Moses],[297] the king wages combat with his dark adversary of the underworld, emerging victorious after a temporary defeat from his duel with death'... Moses is proclaimed king after he has overcome the waters of Meribah—death; therefore, God says, 'I shall make you king in my place, and you shall rule over my people as if you were God.' Moses is put in God's place."[298]

Also affirming the deification of Moses, Philo wrote: "For when [Moses] had left all mortal categories behind he was changed into the divine, so that such men become kin to God and truly divine."[299] With respect to Moses' command of the elements, Philo wrote that "... each of the elements was made subject to Moses as master and altered its inherent properties to become subject to his commands."[300] Philo realized that Moses' experience was not unique; rather, his exaltation exemplified a pattern that previously had been followed by Abraham and would continue to be emulated by all who belonged to true Israel.[301] According to Philo, Moses enters into God's presence and "abides there while he learns the secrets of the most holy mysteries. There he becomes not only one of the ... initiated, but also the hierophant[302] and teacher of divine rites, which he will impart to those whose ears are purified. He then has ever the divine spirit at his side, taking the lead in every journey of righteousness"[303] or, in other words, "to lead one along the 'whole road,' the entire way to perfection."[304]

f **as if thou wert God.** In the authority and power of the priesthood he has received, Moses soon will be fully enabled to speak and act on God's behalf.

The current text is consistent with OT1.[305] OT2 replaces these words with a new reading in the handwriting of Sidney Rigdon: "even as my commandments."[306]

26 a **thou shalt deliver my people from bondage.** God reiterates the commission He gave Moses at the time of his first call.[307]

---

295 See *Commentary* 2:2-b, p. 96; J. L. Kugel, *Instances*, pp. 156-157.––
296 D&C 110:3; cf. Ezekiel 1:24, 43:2; Revelation 1:15; D&C 133:22; cf. J. L. Kugel, *Instances*, pp. 156-157.
297 See *Commentary* 5:47-a, p. 395; *Excursus 35: Lamech's "Sword Song"*, p. 612; overviews of Moses 4 and 6, pp. 221, 458. See *Endnote 4-21*, p. 304. See *Endnote 4-4*, p. 298.
298 H. W. Nibley, *Circle*, p. 157. See H. W. Nibley, *Teachings of the PGP*, 10, p. 118; *Commentary* 1:20-a, p. 57. See also related discussion in N. Russell, *Deification*, p. 68.
299 Philo, *Exodus*, 2:29, p. 70; cf. R. S. Eccles, *Pilgrimage*, pp. 60-61. See *Endnote E-221*, p. 757.
300 See Philo, *Moses 1*, 1:155-156, p. 473.
301 M. Barker, *Hidden*, p. 7.
302 I.e., priestly revealer or guide.
303 Philo, *Giants*, 54-55, p. 473. See also E. R. Goodenough, *Introduction to Philo*, pp. 147-148; W. A. Meeks, *Moses*.
304 E. R. Goodenough, *Light*, p. 214 n. 105. See *Excursus 53: Comparative Explorations: The Mysteries*, p. 663ff.
305 S. H. Faulring, *et al.*, *Original Manuscripts*, p. 85.
306 *Ibid.*, p. 593; K. P. Jackson, *Book of Moses*, p. 63.
307 Exodus 3:7-10.

*27 And it came to pass, **as the voice was still speaking**, Moses cast his eyes and beheld the earth, yea, even all of it; and there was not a particle of it which he did not behold, discerning it by the spirit of God.*

27   **a**   ***as the voice was still speaking.*** Remarkably, a nearly identical phrase ("And while he [the angel] was still speaking") appears in the *Apocalypse of Abraham* immediately preceding Abraham's recitation of certain words taught to him by the angel in preparation for his ascent to receive a vision of the work of God.[308] In that account, Abraham's recitation ends with: "Accept my prayer and… sacrifice… Receive me favorably, teach me, show me, and make known to your servant what you have promised me."[309] The text relates that while Abraham "was still reciting the song" (i.e., a recitation of a fixed set of words he had been taught by the angel), he heard a voice "like the roaring of the sea"[310] and was brought into the presence of the fiery seraphim surrounding the heavenly throne.[311] Significantly, when Abraham passes back through the heavenly veil in the opposite direction on his return to the earth, the words "And while he was still speaking" recur.[312]

  b   ***Moses cast his eyes and beheld the earth.*** Previously, as he stood on the earth, Moses had "lifted up his eyes unto heaven."[313] Now, after ascending to heaven, he cast his eyes down to see the earth and all of its inhabitants.[314] He witnessed its entire history from beginning to end like Adam, Enoch, the Brother of Jared, John the Beloved, and others.[315] Moroni taught that those with perfect faith cannot be "kept from within the veil" (i.e., cannot be kept from passing through the veil[316])—meaning the heavenly veil behind which God dwells, whose earthly counterpart is the temple veil that divides the Holy Place from the Holy of Holies.[317]

The heavenly veil corresponding to the firmament of the Creation is sometimes represented as a shining pavement on which the Lord stands[318] or as the "sea of glass" where God resides.[319] Islamic and Jewish sources imply that the unenlightened might mistakenly confuse such a crystal pavement with water.[320] Such descriptions also relate to the white stone that will be given to the Saints "whereby things pertaining to a higher order of kingdoms will be made known."[321]

Extracanonical accounts speak of a "blueprint" of eternity that is worked out in advance and shown on the inside of the heavenly veil.[322] Writes Barker: "Those who passed beyond the veil found themselves outside time. When Rabbi Ishmael ascended and looked back he saw the curtain on which was depicted past, present and future. 'All generations to the end of time were printed on the curtain of the Omnipresent One. I saw them all with my own

---

308   R. Rubinkiewicz, *Apocalypse of Abraham*, 17:1, p. 696.

309   *Ibid.*, 17:20-21, p. 697.

310   Cf. "voice of many waters" (*ibid.*, 17:1, p. 696); *Commentary* 1:25-c, p. 60.

311   R. Rubinkiewicz, *Apocalypse of Abraham*, 18:1-14, p. 698.

312   *Ibid.*, 30:1, p. 704. For a discussion of parallels between the book of Abraham and the *Apocalypse of Abraham*, see J. W. Ludlow, *Visions*, pp. 62-65.

313   Moses 1:24.

314   Moses 1:28; cf. *Commentary* 1:8-b, c, p. 50.

315   D&C 107:56, Moses 7:4-67, Ether 3:25, M. C. Thomas, *Brother of Jared*, 1 Nephi 14:25, 1 Nephi 14:26; cf. Luke 4:5.

316   Ether 3:20; cf. Moses 3:26.

317   P. Alexander, *3 Enoch*, 45:1, p. 296 n. a.

318   E.g., Exodus 24:9-10; Daniel 10:6; D&C 110:2.

319   Revelation 4:6, 21:18, 21; D&C 130:8-9, 137:4; Ezekiel 1:22, 26.

320   A. al-Tha'labi, *Lives*, pp. 534-535; J. Dan, *Mysticism*, 1:276-279; W. J. Hamblin, *et al.*, *Temple*, pp. 131, 270; G. W. E. Nickelsburg, *1 Enoch*, 14:10, p. 257; B. M. Wheeler, *Prophets*, p. 270; *Qur'an* 27:38-44. See also 1 Kings 10:1-13; Ezekiel 1:22; Exodus 24:10; Revelation 21:18, 21.

321   D&C 130:4-11; cf. Revelation 2:17; *Commentary* 3:19-b, p. 177; *Figure 4-4*, p. 219. See *Endnote 4-9*, p. 299. See *Endnote 4-22*, p. 304. See *Excursus 53: Comparative Explorations: Jewish and Christian Analogues*, p. 679. See *Commentary* 1:6-g, p. 48 and 2:1-e, p. 94 regarding God's timelessness and the scope of divine knowledge.

322   H. W. Nibley, *Teachings of the PGP*, 10, p. 117.

27 And it came to pass, as the voice was still speaking, **Moses cast his eyes and beheld the earth***, yea,* **even all of it***; and there was not a particle of it which he did not behold, discerning it by the spirit of God.*

eyes'...[323] [Similarly,] Enoch was taken up by three angels and set up on a high place whence he saw all history, past, present and future."[324]

The *Apocalypse of Abraham* describes how the patriarch ascended, and then looked down to see the affairs of what is called in modern revelation the "kingdoms of a lower order."[325] The Lord's voice commanded him to look, and veils were opened beneath his feet: "And while he was still speaking the expanses under me, the heavens, opened and I saw on the seventh firmament upon which I stood fire spread out... And I looked... downward to the sixth firmament... [and] the sixth firmament... removed itself... [and] I saw... the fifth (firmament)."[326] Then, as did Moses, Abraham seems to have seen the heavenly plan for creation—"the creation that was depicted of old[327] on this expanse" (21:1[328]), its realization on the earth (21:3-5), the Garden of Eden (21:6), and the spirits of all men with certain ones "prepared to be born of you [i.e., Abraham] and to be called my people (21:7-22:5)"[329] When Abraham is told again to "Look... at the picture," he sees Satan inciting the Fall of Adam and Eve (23:1-14).[330]

Jesus Himself, when He was tempted in the desert saw "all the kingdoms of the world in a moment of time,"[331] an experience that Barker recognizes as "a characteristic of the temple mystics' overall view of history."[332] Islamic tradition preserves the same motif in the story of how "Adam took out the cloth and spread it out. Upon it were the forms of the prophets [= the pious] and the pharaohs [= the wicked], rank after rank."[333]

In November 1832, Joseph Smith used imagery related to the veil in a manner similar to all these accounts, as he and William W. Phelps prayed fervently for a longer glimpse at the reality behind the "dark curtain," and for a release from the limitations of human language: "Oh, Lord, when will the time come when Brother William, Thy servant, and myself, shall behold the day that we may stand together and gaze upon eternal wisdom engraven upon the heavens, while the majesty of our God holdeth up the dark curtain until we may read the round of eternity,[334] to the fulness and satisfaction of our immortal souls? Oh, Lord, deliver us in due time from the little, narrow prison, almost as it were, total darkness of paper, pen and ink; and a crooked, broken, scattered and imperfect language."[335]

c **even all of it.** OT1 and OT2 read "even all the face of it."[336] The change in the current text dates to the 1902 edition of the Pearl of Great Price.[337]

323 P. Alexander, *3 Enoch*, 45:6, p. 299.

324 M. Barker, *Temple Theology*, p. 28. See also M. Barker, *Boundary*, pp. 215-217.

325 D&C 130:9.

326 R. Rubinkiewicz, *Apocalypse of Abraham*, 19:1, 4-5, 9, pp. 698-699; cf. Abraham 3:1-18.

327 I.e., formerly shadowed, sketched, outlined, prefigured (R. Rubinkiewicz, *Apocalypse of Abraham*, p. 699 n. 21a).

328 Cf. Abraham 5:3-5.

329 Cf. Abraham 3:22-23.

330 R. Rubinkiewicz, *Apocalypse of Abraham*, pp. 699-701.

331 Luke 4:5.

332 M. Barker, *Hidden*, p. 95.

333 M. al-Kisa'i, *Tales*, p. 82.

334 Nibley discusses parallels between the picture shown to Moses, the "great round" of the hypocephalus, and imagery from Homer (H. W. Nibley, *Abraham 2000*, pp. 42ff.).

335 J. Smith, Jr., *Documentary History*, 27 November 1832, 1:299.

336 S. H. Faulring, *et al.*, *Original Manuscripts*, pp. 85, 593.

337 K. P. Jackson, *Book of Moses*, p. 45.

*27 And it came to pass, as the voice was still speaking, Moses cast his eyes and beheld the earth, yea, even all of it; and there was not a particle of it which he did not behold, discerning it **by the spirit of God**.*

*28 And he beheld also the inhabitants thereof, and there was not a soul which he beheld not; and he discerned them by the Spirit of God; and their numbers were great, **even numberless as the sand upon the sea shore**.*

*29 And he beheld many lands; and **each land was called earth**, and there were inhabitants on the face thereof.*

*30 And it came to pass that Moses called upon God, saying: **Tell me**, I pray thee, **why** these things are so, **and by what** thou madest them?*

*31 And behold, the **glory of the Lord** was upon Moses, so that **Moses stood in the presence of God, and talked with him face to face**. And the Lord God said unto Moses: **For** mine own purpose have I made these things. Here is wisdom and it remaineth in me.*

d   ***by the spirit of God.*** "This is not just God's ability to produce a comprehensive vision, but an ability to change Moses so that he could comprehend it."[338] The "spirit" by which Moses discerns is written in lower case in this verse; however, it inexplicably appears in upper case in a similar context in v. 28.

28 a   ***even numberless as the sand upon the sea shore.*** Here, the term numberless does not mean "infinite" but rather "too many to be counted."[339]

OT2 reads: "even as numberless."[340]

29 a   ***each land was called earth.*** Taken in the context of vv. 30-38, these words seem to imply that Moses saw many peopled planets, each one of which was called earth by its inhabitants. Alternatively, his view of "many lands" could be simply a part of "an account of this earth"[341] to which his vision was originally to be limited.

30 a   ***Tell me… why… and by what.*** The answers to these sacred questions will be given to Moses subsequently when he enters the presence of the Lord.[342]

In the hand of Sidney Rigdon, OT2 was changed to read "shew me,"[343] further emphasizing the visual nature of Moses' experience.[344] Consistent with the current text, OT1 reads "by what,"[345] while OT2 reads "by whom."[346]

31 a   ***glory of the Lord.*** OT1 and OT2 read "the glory of God"[347]—implying more clearly that Moses stood in the presence of the Father rather than the Son. The current text dates to the 1902 edition of the Pearl of Great Price.[348]

b   ***Moses stood in the presence of God, and talked with him face to face.*** This glorious event, anticipated by the chapter summary in v. 2, opens the culminating sequence of Moses' vision. In the final verses of this chapter, God will reveal something of His purposes and will introduce the vision of Creation, the Fall, and the Plan of Salvation recounted in chapters 2-5.

---

338   F. B. Salisbury, *Creation*, p. 65.
339   The same description is used in Genesis 22:17, Hebrews 11:12, D&C 132:30, and Abraham 3:14.
340   S. H. Faulring, *et al.*, *Original Manuscripts*, pp. 593-594.
341   Moses 1:35.
342   R. D. Draper, *et al.*, *Commentary*, p. 32. See Moses 1:31.
343   S. H. Faulring, *et al.*, *Original Manuscripts*, p. 594.
344   See *Commentary* 1:27-b, p. 62.
345   S. H. Faulring, *et al.*, *Original Manuscripts*, p. 85.
346   *Ibid.*, p. 594.
347   *Ibid.*, pp. 85, 594.
348   K. P. Jackson, *Book of Moses*, p. 45.

*31 And behold, the glory of the Lord was upon Moses, so that Moses stood in the presence of God, and talked with him face to face. And **the Lord God said unto Moses**: For mine own purpose have I made these things. **Here is wisdom and it remaineth in me.***

*32 And **by the word of my power, have I created them, which is mine Only Begotten Son,** who is **full of grace and truth.***

*33 And **worlds without number** have I created; and I also created them for mine own purpose; and **by the Son I created them,** which is mine Only Begotten.*

c   ***the Lord God said unto Moses.*** Speaking face to face, God now replies to the questions Moses raised in v. 30. Though God says here that He will not reveal the answer to Moses' first question ("why these things are so"), later He does give a limited explanation.[349] His answer to Moses' second question ("by what") is summarized in verse 32, and eventually elaborated in the account of the Creation in Moses 2-3.[350]

d   ***Here is wisdom and it remaineth in me.*** The phrase "it remaineth in me" subtly echoes scriptural passages that depict God and wisdom as inseparably associated since before the creation of the earth.[351] This exclusive relationship makes the mysteries of true wisdom inaccessible to man except as made known through God himself.[352] The Book of Mormon employs similar phraseology to describe how God's hidden intentions—in this case the preservation of Nephite records—are "wise purposes in him"—things that can only be known by direct revelation.[353] The term "wisdom" recurs once in the book of Moses, in an exposition on the gifts of the Comforter.[354]

In the mystical Islamic work *The Mother of Books*, a petitioner also prays with a "typical list of questions": "My Lord, how did the high king create all these spheres and palaces? From where did he make the spirits? What was the origin of his creation?" and receives an answer similar to the one given to Moses: "The creation of these realms is hard to fathom. Not everyone knows the way to knowledge, and its secret [is] well-concealed."[355] The *Gospel of Philip* specifies the mechanism of concealment in asserting that it is the "veil [that] at first concealed how God controlled the creation."[356]

32   a   ***by the word of my power, have I created them, which is my Only Begotten Son.*** See Moses 1:33; *Commentary* 2:1-d, p. 93; 2:5-c, p. 102.

b   ***full of grace and truth.*** See *Commentary* 1:6-e, p. 47 and Moses 5:7.

33   a   ***worlds without number.*** Clark[357] cites a passage in the *Zohar* which tells of "'a hidden region, so transcendent that it passes all understanding, the very source whence the worlds were designed and came into being'[358]... So also, according to the Syriac *Apocalypse of Baruch,* Moses was shown 'the worlds which have not yet come.'"[359]

b   ***by the Son I created them.***[360] That the worlds were not only created by the Son but also redeemed by him is made clear by the Prophet's poetic paraphrase of D&C 76:23-24:

349   Moses 1:39.

350   R. J. Matthews, *Moses*, p. 64.

351   E.g., Proverbs 8:22-30.

352   Job 28; 1 Corinthians 2:7-10; Alma 12:9-11; D&C 76:7, 10; 84:19; 107:18-19; see *Excursus 53: Comparative Explorations of the Mysteries,* p. 663.

353   1 Nephi 9:5. See also e.g., 1 Nephi 3:19; 5:22; 19:3; Words of Mormon 1:7; Alma 37:12, 14, 18.

354   Moses 6:61. See *Commentary* 4:11-a, b, c, p. 253, 4:12-c, p. 255, and *Excursus 2: Ancient Concepts of Wisdom,* p. 516.

355   W. Barnstone, *et al., Mother,* p. 685.

356   W. W. Isenberg, *Philip,* 84:23-25, p. 159.

357   E. D. Clark, *Prologue,* p. 139.

358   H. Sperling, *et al., Zohar,* Waera (Exodus 6:2-9:35), 22a, 3:75.

359   A. F. J. Klijn, *2 Baruch,* 59:9, p. 642. Cf. *Commentary* 1:35-b, p. 67.

360   See *Commentary* 1:32-a, p. 65.

*33 And worlds without number have I created; and I also created them for mine own purpose; and **by the Son I created them**, which is mine Only Begotten.*

*34 And the first man of all men have I called **Adam, which is many.***

> 19. And I heard a great voice, bearing record from heav'n,
> "He's the Savior, and only begotten of God—
> By him, of him, and through him, the worlds were all made,
> Even all that career in the heavens so broad,
>
> 20. Whose inhabitants, too, from the first to the last,
> Are sav'd by the very same Savior of ours;
> And, of course, are begotten God's daughters and sons,
> By the very same truths, and the very same pow'rs."[361]

by the Son. OT2 reads "by the same."[362] The change to "by the Son" was first made in the 1843 *Times and Seasons* publication.[363]

34 a *Adam, which is many.* Draper, *et al.*[364] conclude that the phrase "which is many" could mean one of three things: 1. that Adam is the first man of all men among all the worlds God has created; 2. that Adam is the name given to the first man on each of the many worlds God has created;[365] or, 3. that there are many descendants of Adam on this earth.[366]

The name "Adam" occurs in several Semitic languages. Westermann accepts a derivation from the Arab term *adim* meaning "skin" or "surface," thus simultaneously conveying the idea of the skin of the human being (*adam*) and the surface of the earth (*adamah*).[367] The motif associating Adam with the earth is found in several places in the book of Moses—for example, Adam is made from the dust of the ground,[368] it is later cursed because of him,[369] and he will return to it when he dies.[370] Whitlock also points out the association between the red earth and red blood (Hebrew *dam*)—blood being a condition of mortality.[371] He observes that there may be "something symbolic in the joining of the mortal/of-the-blood (Adam) with the living Eve (Hebrew *havvah* = "life") to produce living offspring, that transcends earthly life and is echoed in reverse in the Nativity."[372] Taking a cue from Moses 1:34, Nibley sees "many" as one connotation of the Egyptian name *Atum*, citing studies that define it to mean "both the creator ['the ancient one'] and 'the [collective] sum of all future beings'… 'all embracing,' 'the sum of everything'… or the uniting of many in one, combining all preexistent beings in a single archetype who thereby represents all beings thereafter."[373]

In Abraham 1:3, the word Adam is associated with the idea of his being a "first father."[374] The 1981 edition of the Pearl of Great Price corrected a portion of the text in this verse. It was given previously as "the first man, who is Adam, our first father," but in 1981 was amended to read "the first man, who is Adam, or first father." Note that Eve is similarly referred to in Moses 4:26 as the "first of all women," and that Nephi refers to Adam and Eve as our "first

361 J. Smith, Jr. (or W. W. Phelps), *A Vision*, 1 February 1843, stanzas 19-20, cited in L. E. Dahl, *Vision*, p. 298.
362 S. H. Faulring, *et al.*, *Original Manuscripts*, p. 594.
363 *History of JS 4:5*, p. 72. See K. P. Jackson, *Book of Moses*, p. 27.
364 R. D. Draper, *et al.*, *Commentary*, p. 33.
365 Brigham Young, 6 October 1854, cited in J. L. Robinson, *et al.*, *Robinson*, p. 172; E. W. Tullidge, *Women*, p. 180.
366 F. B. Salisbury, *Creation*, p. 66; J. Smith, Jr., *Teachings*, footnote by Elder Joseph Fielding Smith, Jr., p. 167.
367 C. Westermann, *Genesis 1-11*, p. 201; Suyuti in al-Tabari, *Creation*, 1:88, p. 260; B. M. Wheeler, *Prophets*, p. 17.
368 Moses 3:7.
369 Moses 4:23.
370 Moses 4:25. See D. N. Freedman, *et al.*, *Eerdmans*, p. 19.
371 Cf. J. Smith, Jr., 13 April 1843, "red earth" in E. England, *Laub*, p. 25.
372 S. T. Whitlock, *23 August 2006*.
373 H. W. Nibley, *Message 2005*, p. 217; cf. H. W. Nibley, *Abraham 2000*, p. 77; H. W. Nibley, *Teachings of the PGP*, 18, p. 222; 7, pp. 87-88.
374 B. R. McConkie, *Sermons*, p. 254; cf. W. Clayton, *Chronicle*, 28 December 1845, p. 238.

*34 And the first man of all men have I called **Adam, which is many**.*

*35 But **only an account of this earth**, and the inhabitants thereof, give I unto you. For behold, there are many worlds that have passed away by the word of my power. And there are many that now stand, and **innumerable are they unto man**; but **all things are numbered unto me, for they are mine and I know them**.*

36 And it came to pass that Moses spake unto the Lord, saying: Be merciful unto thy servant, O God, and tell me concerning this earth, and the inhabitants thereof, and also the heavens, and then thy servant will be content.

*37 And the Lord God spake unto Moses, **saying: The heavens**, they are many, and they cannot be numbered unto man; but they are numbered unto me, for they are mine.*

*38 And as **one earth shall pass away, and the heavens thereof** even so shall another come; and **there is no end to my works, neither to my words**.*

parents."[375] President Brigham Young taught that Adam "signifies first man, and Eve signifies first woman." "Every world has an Adam, and an Eve: named so, simply because the first man is always called Adam, and the first woman Eve."[376] By implication, Munoa connects "the motif of… being the first" with that of being "the oldest"—hence, the use of "'Ancient of Days' as a title for Adam."[377]

35 a *only an account of this earth.* See *Commentary* 1:5-b, p. 46, 1:5-c, p. 46, and 1:7-a, p. 49.

b *innumerable they are unto man.* President Brigham Young said: "How many earths are there? I observed this morning that you may take the particles of matter composing this earth, and if they could be enumerated they would only be a beginning to the number of the creations of God; and they are continually coming into existence, and undergoing changes and passing through the same experience that we are passing through."[378]

OT1 and OT2 read "numberless";[379] the current text follows the 1843 *Times and Seasons*.[380]

c *all things are numbered unto me, for they are mine and I know them.* Cf. Moses 1:37; Matthew 10:30: "But the very hairs of your head are all numbered."

37 a *saying: The heavens.* The text follows OT1.[381] OT2 reads "of the heavens, saying, These."[382]

38 a *one earth shall pass away, and the heavens thereof.* Though this could be taken as referring to the natural winding down of our particular part of the universe, it seems more likely that this passing away signifies the undoing of the first act of Creation—not a destruction, but rather a reunification of the formerly divided heaven and earth. At that time, said the Lord, "the veil of the covering of my temple, in my tabernacle, which hideth the earth, shall be taken off, and all flesh shall see me together."[383]

b *there is no end to my works, neither to my words.*[384] The endlessness of God's works and His words are inseparably linked. Jesus Christ, as the "word of my power,"[385] is the one by

375 1 Nephi 5:11; cf. *Wisdom of Solomon*, where Adam is also called the "first father" (S. Sandmel, *et al.*, *Solomon*, 10:1-2, p. 104; see also Isaiah 43:27).
376 B. Young, *8 October 1854*, pp. 100, 93.
377 P. B. Munoa, *Four Powers*, pp. 108-109. See also Joseph Smith, Jr. in D. M. Quinn, *Prayer Circles*, p. 83; overview of Moses 5, p. 325.
378 B. Young, *10 July 1870*, p. 71; cf. *Commentary* 1:33-a, p. 65. See Moses 1:35-38.
379 S. H. Faulring, *et al.*, *Original Manuscripts*, pp. 85, 594.
380 *History of JS* 4:5, p. 72. See K. P. Jackson, *Book of Moses*, p. 17.
381 S. H. Faulring, *et al.*, *Original Manuscripts*, p. 85.
382 *Ibid.*, p. 594.
383 D&C 101:23; cf. Isaiah 25:6-9; 3 Nephi 26:3-5; H. W. Nibley, *Treasures*, pp. 185-186; *Commentary* 2:3-a, p. 99.
384 Cf. Moses 1:4.
385 See *Commentary* 1:32-a, p. 65; cf. D&C 29:30; John 1:1-3.

38 And as one earth shall pass away, and the heavens thereof even so shall another come; and **there is no end to my works, neither to my words.**

39 For behold, **this is my work and my glory—to bring to pass the immortality and eternal life of man.**

whom these works were created. Likewise, Egyptian creation texts link the divine word with creative power,[386] a theme also taken up in Jacob 4:9. Explains Nibley: "It is the Egyptian *sia*, 'intelligence,' awareness, that comes first. But it is lost without *hu*, 'authoritative utterance,'[387] 'communication'... The one is incomplete without the other, and this is made very clear in the oldest Egyptian creation drama,[388] where God 'conceives in his mind' and then 'utters with his mouth,' communicating his intention to the council of the gods at each step of the creation. This is the very modern doctrine of anthropism.[389] Without *sia*—intelligence, awareness—what would exist? And if it were confined to one mind only, what would be accomplished?"[390]

39 a *this is my work and my glory—to bring to pass the immortality and eternal life of man.*
Flake writes: "With this reply, [Joseph] Smith rejected 1,500 years of Christian theological anthropology by making God ontologically related to creation. God is both defined as Father and glorified as God by the capacity and purpose to engender the divine life in humans. To Smith, 'Father God' is not only a metaphor for expressing divine love, but is definitive of God and indicative of human possibility, even human capacity to receive the divine nature."[391]

"Immortality is to live forever in the resurrected state with body and spirit inseparably connected."[392] This is a blessing that will be given to each one of God's children.[393] On the other hand, eternal life "is to gain exaltation in the highest heaven,"[394] which means having "the kind of life that God has. All those who become sons and daughters of God will have the additional gift of eternal life, which is the greatest gift of God."[395] Comments Nibley: "[God's] whole concern... is to pass on to others what he has. 'The glory of God is intelligence,'[396] which he wishes to share with all others. Glory is shared intelligence. Hence his works always go along with his words."[397]

God's work and glory must by inference become man's work and glory.[398] Elder John A. Widtsoe has written: "Under the gospel what is man's highest ideal? Under the gospel it must be to become like the Father. If the Lord's concern is chiefly to bring happiness and joy, salvation, to the whole human family, we cannot become like the Father unless we too engage in that work."[399]

The earlier version of this verse in OT1 reads: "this is my work to my glory to the immortality and the eternal life of man."[400]

386   E.g., J. B. Pritchard, *ANET*, pp. 5-6.
387   A. H. Gardiner, *Grammar*, pp. 588, 580.
388   See *Excursus 1: Speech, Writing, and Revelation*, p. 512.
389   See *Commentary* 1:39-a, p. 68.
390   H. W. Nibley, *Drama*, p. 26.
391   K. Flake, *Translating Time*, p. 519.
392   B. R. McConkie, *Mormon Doctrine*, p. 376.
393   1 Corinthians 15:22.
394   S. W. Kimball, *Eternal Hope*, p. 72. See also J. Smith, Jr., *Teachings*, 7 April 1844, pp. 346-347.
395   J. F. Smith, Jr., *Doctrines*, 22 April 1939, 2:8. See D&C 14:7.
396   D&C 93:36.
397   H. W. Nibley, *Return*, p. 60. See *Commentary* 1;38-b, p. 67.
398   See *Commentary* 1:6-a, p. 46.
399   Cited in A. F. Bennett, *Saviors*, pp. 11-12; B. K. Packer, *Holy Temple*, p. 216. See G. B. Hinckley, *Sunday AM, 2 April 1995*, pp. 17-18, 20; M. G. Romney, *Living*, p. 93. See also *Excursus 4: Chance and Purpose in Creation*, p. 524.
400   S. H. Faulring, *et al.*, *Original Manuscripts*, p. 86; R. J. Matthews, *What Is*, p. 31.

*40 And now, Moses, my son, I will speak unto thee concerning **this earth upon which thou standest; and thou shalt write** the things which I shall speak.*

*41 And in a day when the children of men shall esteem my words as naught and **take many of them from the book which thou shalt write**, behold, **I will raise up another like unto thee; and they shall be had again among the children of men**—among as many as shall believe.*

*42 (These words were spoken unto Moses in the mount, the name of which shall not be known among the children of men. And now they are spoken unto you. **Show them not unto any except them that believe**. Even so. Amen.)*

40   a   *this earth upon which thou standest; and thou shalt write.* As this verse makes clear, Moses authored an original version of the creation account by specific assignment.[401]

Johnson sees a small chiasm stretching from Moses 1:40 through 2:1 pivoting around the prophecy of another one like Moses being raised up, with v. 42 being treated as parenthetical.[402]

OT2 refers to Moses in the second person plural form—or perhaps it should be regarded simply as a modernization of the archaic "thou": "this earth upon which you stand; and you shall write."[403]

41   a   *take many of them from the book which thou shalt write.*[404] In this connection, note that the overwhelming bulk of JST Genesis revisions consist of additions rather than omissions of material. Barker has written extensively about conscious omissions and alterations of scriptures relating to key doctrines in the Old Testament.[405] A specific example of material presumably removed from a later chapter of Genesis is the prophecy of Joseph recorded in JST Genesis 50:24-37 and 2 Nephi 3:5-22.

    b   *I will raise up another like unto thee; and they shall be had again among the children of men.* Compare *2 Enoch*: "And… another generation will arise, the last of many… And I shall raise up for that generation someone who will reveal to them the books in your handwriting and those of your fathers. And he will have to point out to… truthful men, and those who carry out my will."[406]

Moses uses similar words in his prophecy of the coming of the Savior.[407] However, the current passage clearly refers to Joseph Smith, who is specifically compared to Moses in other scriptures.[408]

42   a   *Show them not unto any except them that believe. 4 Ezra* records that the Lord commanded Moses to openly reveal only part of his visions on Mt. Sinai; the rest was to be kept secret. Similarly, Ezra is reported to have been told that certain books were to be read by the "worthy and unworthy" whereas others were to be only given "to the wise."[409] The *Mishnah* contained a "rule that certain texts could not be read in public, or could be read but not explained.[410] Ezekiel's vision of the throne was one such passage; it could not be discussed

401   Cf. O. S. Wintermute, *Jubilees*, 2:1, p. 55.
402   M. J. Johnson, *Prologue*, pp. 15-16.
403   S. H. Faulring, *et al.*, *Original Manuscripts*, p. 594.
404   Cf. Moses 1:23; 1 Nephi 13:4, 24-28.
405   E.g., M. Barker, *Older*; M. Barker, *Joseph Smith*, pp. 77-78.
406   F. I. Andersen, *2 Enoch*, 35:1-2, p. 158. Cf. Luke 2:14.
407   Deuteronomy 18:15; Acts 3:19-26; 1 Nephi 22:20-21; 3 Nephi 20:23; JS-Hist 1:40.
408   2 Nephi 3:9; D&C 28:2, 103:16; cf. D&C 107:9. See K. Muhlestein, *Flow*, pp. 48-49.
409   B. M. Metzger, *Fourth Ezra*, 14:6, 45-47, pp. 553, 555. Rabbinical arguments to this effect are summarized in A. J. Heschel, *Heavenly Torah*, pp. 656-657. See also H. W. Nibley, *Teachings of the PGP*, 18, pp. 223-224. For examples of other scriptural passages that speak of restrictions on making revelations known, see 2 Corinthians 12:4; 3 Nephi 17:16-17; 28:13-16; Ether 3:21-4:7; Moses 4:32. See also *Commentary* 1:23-b, p. 59.
410   J. Neusner, *Mishnah*, Hagigah 2:1, p. 330.

42 (These words were spoken unto Moses in the mount, the name of which shall not be known among the children of men. And now they are spoken unto you. **Show them not unto any except them that believe.** *Even so. Amen.)*

unless the other person already understood it 'of his own knowledge.' Nor could the blessing of the priests—'May the Lord make his face shine upon you'[411] be explained."[412]

The current text follows OT1, except that the archaic "shew" has been changed to "show."[413] In OT2, a slightly different phrase ("And now they are also spoken unto you. Shew them not unto any except them that believe until I command you. Amen") is crossed out and the phrase "Even so" is omitted, so that the chapter ends with the phrase "children of men."[414].

---

411   Numbers 6:24-26.
412   M. Barker, *Christmas*, pp. 91-92.
413   S. H. Faulring, *et al.*, *Original Manuscripts*, p. 86.
414   *Ibid.*, p. 595.

Gleanings

Table of Contents

MOSES 1

Hugh W. Nibley: A Chapter of "Most Boundless Wonder and Esteem"[415]

[Joseph Smith] brought out three formidable volumes of scripture. One need look no farther than the opening chapter of each of these to realize that a new dispensation is indeed upon us, with all the visions and blessings of old. The first section of the Doctrine and Covenants… takes up all the main themes of the gospel that had been the burden of every former dispensation, and had been lost in all the dark intervals between them, and weaves them together into one strong texture in which warning and deliverance are equally balanced… At the same time, the opening chapter of the Book of Mormon emerges as the perfect model and type of those more specialized apocalypses or testaments attributed to individuals that are now taking up their position in the growing procession of early Jewish and Christian Apocrypha…

But it is the first chapter of the book of Moses that commands the most boundless wonder and esteem… What other prelude could there be to the history of the race, what other prologue could ever give it such depth of meaning and such gratifying consistency? First, we find Moses in the presence of God and the bosom of eternity, being apprised of a special calling to which he has been appointed as co-worker with the Savior.[416] A preliminary test is indicated—suddenly the lights go out and Moses is found lying unconscious and helpless upon the earth; as he slowly comes to himself, he recognizes the misery and the glory of fallen man: "Now… I know that man is nothing, which thing I never had supposed." And then, in the same breath: "But now mine own eyes have beheld God… his glory was upon me… I was transfigured before him."[417] Weakness is his present condition, glory his everlasting birthright.

It is in this moment of man's greatest helplessness and vulnerability that Satan chooses to strike, attempting first by persuasion and then by intimidation to get Moses to worship him as the god of this world. But Moses has not wholly forgotten who he is, "a son of God, in the similitude of the Only Begotten,"[418] and denounces Satan as a sham, while professing himself awaiting further light and knowledge: "I will not cease to call upon God, I have other things to inquire of him."[419] The humiliating exposure of Satan becomes unendurable when Moses announces that he actually *is* what his adversary falsely *claims to be*, "a son of God, in the similitude of his Only Begotten; and where is thy glory that I should worship thee?"[420] This is too much for Satan, who casts aside his celebrated but now useless subtlety and launches a frontal attack of satanic fury, a tremendous tantrum, as he "cried with a

---

415 H. W. Nibley, *To Open*, pp. 4-6. emphasis throughout is mine.
416 Moses 1:3-9.
417 Moses 1:10-11.
418 Moses 1:13
419 Moses 1:18.
420 Moses 1:13.

loud voice, and [ranted] upon the earth, and commanded, saying: I am the Only Begotten, worship me."[421] The whole scene is presented in dramatic form as a ritual combat, a *sticho-mythia*, and true to the ancient pattern, the hero is momentarily bested, overcome by the *powers* of darkness, as he "began to fear," and "saw the bitterness of hell."[422] But with his last ounce of strength he calls upon God from the depths and is delivered: he has won the fight, he has prevailed against the power of him who "sought to destroy the world," "for he knew not the mind of God."[423]

And now the scene changes (verses 23 and 24 read like stage directions); the lights go up, the music soars and Moses, though remaining on earth, is again invested with glory and hears the voice of God proclaiming him victor, worthy and chosen to lead God's people "as if thou wert God"[424]—the type and model of the ancient Year King proclaimed after his victory over death as God's ruler on earth. He is specifically told that he shall "be made stronger than many waters"[425]—for he has just passed through the waters of death and rebirth, *de profundis*; and shown himself capable and worthy of the mission which is now entrusted to him.

After this royal acclamation, reminiscent of combat and coronation episodes dramatized in the earliest year rites throughout the ancient world, after the coronation, the scene again changes, as Moses and the reader view the field of labor in which the prophet is to work; he receives a thorough briefing, an intimate knowledge of the earth in its cosmic setting, its physical makeup ("every particle" of it), and everything that lives upon it.[426] Naturally, he wants to know what is behind the behind and beyond the beyond, but God assures him that such knowledge is not for now: "But only an account of this earth, and the inhabitants thereof, give I unto you,"[427] with which knowledge Moses is finally "content."[428] Nevertheless, quite fundamental to a correct understanding of this world is its relationship to the wider structure of things, to heavens without end and worlds without number, constantly coming into existence and passing away in an endless processing; "… and there is no end to my works, neither to my words."[429] And this cosmic discourse is summed up and concluded in the most comforting proclamation of all: "For behold, this is my work and my glory—to bring to pass the immortality and eternal life of man."[430] All this becoming and passing away, the endless processing of the same elements, would offer only the overpowering and depressing prospect of science fiction, were it not for that ultimate assurance: man is going somewhere after all; in the course of nature he is doomed[431] but the course of nature does not have the last word—God is on top of the problem and he is working for us.

The three concluding verses of the chapter place upon it an undeniable seal of authenticity. Of careful concern in each of the records handed down through the Prophet Joseph is the establishing of the exact manner in which the work has been preserved. This is another mark of the newly-discovered pseudepigrapha: these verses of Moses might have been taken

---

421   Moses 1:19.
422   Moses 1:20.
423   Moses 4:6.
424   Moses 1:25.
425   Moses 1:25.
426   Moses 1:27-28.
427   Moses 1:35.
428   Moses 1:36.
429   Moses 1:38.
430   Moses 1:39.
431   2 Nephi 9:7.

out of any number of Jewish or Christian Apocrypha; especially those writings from the "Forty-day Literature" in which the Coptic records are so rich: "And now Moses, my son… thou shalt write the things which I shall speak. And in a day when the children of men shall esteem my words as naught and take many of them from the book which thou shalt write, behold, I will raise up another like unto thee; and they shall be had again among the children of men—among as many as shall believe."[432] And so the present dispensation gets them: "And now they are spoken unto you. Show them not unto any except them that believe."[433] Such is the standard formula for the preservation and transmission of apocalyptic writings.

Joseph Smith, Jr.: To Foreknow Is Not the Same as to Foreordain[434]

I believe that God foreknew everything, but did not foreordain everything; I deny that foreordain and foreknow is the same thing.[435]

C. S. Lewis: The Nature of God's Foreknowledge[436]

Lewis, summarizing 5:3-6 of Boethius' *De Consolatione Philosophiae*[437] writes:

… the question never was whether foreknowledge necessitates the act but whether it is not evidence that the act must have been necessary. Can there, then, be foreknowledge of the indeterminate? In a sense, yes. The character of knowledge depends not on the nature of the object known but on that of the knowing faculty. Thus in ourselves sensation, imagination, and *ratio* all in their several ways "know" man. Sensation knows him as a corporeal shape; imagination, as a shape without matter; *ratio*, as a concept, a species. None of these faculties by itself gives us the least hint of the mode of knowledge enjoyed by its superior. But above *ratio* or reason there is a higher faculty *intelligentia* or understanding… And Reason cannot conceive the future being known except as it would have to be known, if at all, by her; that is, as determinate. But it is just possible even for us to climb up to the intelligential level and get a glimpse of the knowledge which does not involve determinism.

Eternity is quite distinct from perpetuity, from mere endless continuance in time. Perpetuity is only the attainment of an endless series of moments, each lost as soon as it is attained. Eternity is the actual and timeless fruition of illimitable life. Time, even endless time, is only an image, almost a parody, of that plenitude; a hopeless attempt to compensate for the transitoriness of its "presents" by infinitely multiplying them… And God is eternal, not perpetual. Strictly speaking, He never foresees; He simply sees. Your "future" is only an area, and only for us a special area of His infinite Now. He sees (not remembers) your yesterdays acts because yesterday is still 'there' for Him; he sees (not foresees) your tomorrow's acts because He is already in tomorrow. As a human spectator, by watching my present act,

---

432   Moses 1:40-41.
433   Moses 1:42.
434   J. Smith, Jr., *Documentary History*, 6 February 1840, 4:78.
435   Cf. "Everything is foreseen, and free choice is given" (J. Neusner, *Mishnah*, Abot 3:15, p. 680). See the related discussion in A. J. Heschel, *Heavenly Torah*, pp. 216-219.
436   C. S. Lewis, *Image*, pp. 88-89; cf. C. S. Lewis, *Mere*, 4:3, p. 147; C. S. Lewis, *Miracles*, On Special Providences, pp. 226-234.
437   A. M. S. Boethius, *Consolation*, pp. 100-114. See L. T. Zagzebski, *Dilemma*, for a formal treatment of Boethius' proposal (pp. 36-65), and various alternatives to it. G. E. Ganssle, *God and Time* provides additional useful philosophical perspectives on these and related questions. C. H. Pinnock, *et al.*, *Openness* includes chapters from a variety of theological and philosophical perspectives that, among other things, question the idea of extent of God's foreknowledge. For a brief sampling of scientific perspectives, see *Excursus 7: Time and Eternity*, p. 537.

does not at all infringe its freedom, so I am nonetheless free to act as I choose in the future because God, in that future (His present) watches me acting.

David L. Paulsen: God's Foreknowledge and Man's Freedom[438]

Latter-day Saints differ among themselves in their understandings of the extent of God's foreknowledge. Some, including Presidents Brigham Young and Wilford Woodruff, have thought that God increases endlessly in knowledge and, hence, presumably, at every time lacks exhaustive foreknowledge.... Other Latter-day Saints hold to a more traditional view that God's knowledge, including the foreknowledge of future free contingencies, is exhaustively complete.... Despite these differing views within the LDS tradition, there is accord on three fundamental points: (1) man is an agent with power to choose other than what he, in fact, chooses; (2) Whatever the extent and nature of God's foreknowledge, it is not inconsistent with man's freedom—God's knowledge does not causally determine human choices; and (3) God's knowledge, like God's power, is maximally efficacious. No event occurs that he has not anticipated at least *qua* possibility or has not taken into account in his planning.

Richard L. Bushman: A God Who Is Approachable and Friendly[439]

The vision of Moses… depicts a Creator whose power and might exceeded all human comprehension. Moses is given a glimpse of God's glory while on a high mountain[440] and then Moses abruptly drops back to earth.[441] Decimated by the experience, Moses exclaims in wonder: "Now for this cause I know that man is nothing, which thing I never had supposed."[442] He recognizes that he cannot even look upon God without the protection of His Spirit when he says, "Now mine own eyes have beheld God; but not my natural, but my spiritual eyes, for my natural eyes could not have beheld; for I should have withered and died in his presence; but his glory was upon me; and I beheld his face."[443] Even so, Moses is not entirely intimidated by the God of his visions. Moses asks God why he created the worlds and persists when God rebuffs him.[444] Finally the great God yields to Moses' entreaties and explains that the divine purpose is "to bring to pass the immortality and eternal life of man."[445] This God was willing to converse about His purposes…[E]mergent Mormonism portrayed a God who was approachable and friendly.

---

438   D. L. Paulsen, *Response to Pinnock*, pp. 530-532.
439   R. L. Bushman, *Creation of the Sacred*, p. 95.
440   Moses 1:1-2.
441   Moses 1:9.
442   Moses 1:10.
443   Moses 1:11.
444   Moses 1:30-36.
445   Moses 1:39.

Endnotes

1-1 This account of Moses' visions, constituting section 22 of the Community of Christ editions of the Doctrine and Covenants, was reprinted in the prefatory material of their Inspired Version of the Bible until the 1991 edition, when it was omitted "because of space considerations only."[446]

1-2 Some scholars find traces of such beliefs in the subduing of the powers of watery chaos prior to creation.[447]

1-3 See Barker for a summary of parallels between Jesus' experience in the wilderness, His baptism, and the ascension literature.[448]

1-4 Noting parallels in the experiences of Adam, Enoch, Moses, Jesus Christ, and Joseph Smith in confronting the power of the Devil, Elder Alvin R. Dyer observed that Satan "has exerted his greatest influence of evil when a dispensation of the Gospel has been given in an effort to prevent it."[449] In answer to Heber C. Kimball's concern that "there might be something wrong in him" because of the vision of evil spirits he had had while opening missionary work in England, the Prophet is reported by Kimball's daughter Helen Mar Whitney to have said: "'When I heard of it, it gave me great joy, for I then knew the work of God had taken root in that land. It was this that caused the Devil to make a struggle to kill you.' Joseph then said the nearer a person approached to the Lord, the greater power would be manifest by the Devil to prevent the accomplishment of the purposes of God."[450]

1-5 Matthews comments: "Oliver Cowdery and Joseph Smith... did not state their purpose in purchasing the Bible at that time, but in view of the instructions and experiences they had received, it is possible that they were thinking of a new translation of the Bible even at that early date."[451] Moses 1 was recorded on the first three pages of a fifty-two page folio that continued without a break into the translation of the first chapters of Genesis, and was similarly positioned in later JST manuscripts. It seems reasonable to conclude that Moses 1 was not merely "an independent revelation that evolved into a retranslation of the Bible,"[452] but rather was preconceived as an integral part of the translation project from its inception.

1-6 As was later explained, "[f]rom what we can draw from the Scriptures relative to the teaching of heaven, we are induced to think that much instruction has been given to man since the beginning which we do not possess now."[453] Joseph Smith also wrote: "I believe the Bible as it read when it came from the pen of the original writers. Ignorant translators, careless transcribers, or designing and corrupt priests have committed many errors."[454] See Matthews for an overview of this topic.[455]

Flake summarizes how scholarly views of the Bible have changed since the time of Joseph Smith:

> Today, the Bible itself is believed to be largely the product of periodic manipulation of foundational texts. "Redaction" has become the preferred term for an invasive revision of a source that seamlessly inserts new material in an authoritative text in order to meet new exigencies. Though only a gleam in the eye of the academy at the time Smith was writing and still a source of concern for literalist readers, redaction has become the regnant explanation for the construction of the Bible as having "experienced change, accretions, and reinterpretations as it was being transmitted through centuries."[456]

1-7 Joseph's continuing role as a seer and a translator had been affirmed by a revelation received at that organizational meeting.[457]

1-8 Describing the artist's frustration with his own limited capacities for expression, Callaghan writes:

---

446   J. Smith, Jr., *Holy Scriptures.*
447   *Commentary* 2:2-c, p. 96.
448   M. Barker, *Risen,* pp. 49-50; M. Barker, *Hidden,* pp. 91-95.
449   A. R. Dyer, *Meaning,* p. 11.
450   *Women's Exponent,* 15 December 1885, cited in H. L. Andrus, *et al., They Knew,* p. 176; J. Smith, Jr., *Encyclopedia,* p. 190.
451   R. J. Matthews, *Plainer,* p. 26.
452   R. L. Bushman, *Mormonism,* p. 64
453   J. Smith, Jr., *Teachings,* 22 January 1834, p. 61.
454   *Ibid.,* 15 October 1843, p. 327.
455   R. J. Matthews, *Role of JST.*
456   K. Flake, *Translating Time,* p. 509.
457   D&C 21:1-68.

"Escher… could not bear to look at his prints after he had finished them and did not hang any of them in his studio. He considered them failures because none fully captured the visions of his mind's eye."[458]

1-9   For Joseph Smith, as Bushman insightfully observes, knowledge was not only a source of power and salvation[459] but also of comfort.[460] Said the Prophet on one occasion, "I am glad I have the privilege of communicating to you some things which if grasped closely will be a help to you when the clouds are gathering and the storms are ready to burst upon you like peals of thunder. Lay hold of these things and let not your knees tremble, nor hearts faint."[461]

1-10   About the spiritual nature of his art, Kershisnik wrote:

Spiritual art is by no means limited to so-called religious subject matter, nor is art with religious subject matter necessarily the fruit of the Spirit. Spiritual art is the result of honest and goodly efforts to reach for an understanding that is beyond our own, hopefully enabling us to better see God. Additional results of this effort, such as increased understanding of ourselves and others, are incidental, even if they are significant.

I rarely paint scriptural imagery. I hope (God is my critic) that I always paint spiritual art, even if it is not obviously so.[462]

1-11   About this gap between human actuality and potential, President Spencer W. Kimball wrote: "… from the worm to the god is the potential of man.[463] When he was created, there were put into him the seeds of godhood, the power to think and to reason, the power to lift himself from beasthood to godhood."[464]

The idea of Christ as the good shepherd[465] is not only an apt description of His role in relation to us, but also of our relationship to Him. In other words, it is meant to show not only that He cares for us individually as a shepherd cares for each one of his sheep, but also that we are at present, in comparison to Him, an ignorant, helpless, and wayward lot.[466] This realization gives a new appreciation for the depth of the "condescension of God."[467]

In scripture, the vastness of God's wisdom is frequently contrasted to the pretended wisdom of man.[468] This is personified in the book of Proverbs as the pursuit of the "foolish woman,"[469] or in apocalyptic literature as the image of "the whore of all the earth."[470] The consequences of such "foolishness"[471] might be confined in scope or, as in the account of the Watchers, the unlawful use of wisdom could lead to a virtually unredeemable corruption of the entire earth.[472]

1-12   Notwithstanding all this, Madsen argues that the distinction between God and man is not unbridgeable:

Sören Kierkegaard's widely influential phrase, "the infinite qualitative distinction between God and man," is misleading and debasing. The distinction is neither infinite nor qualitative. Vast though it is, it is a distinction of degree. To deny our divine origins—and likewise our divine potential—is blasphemous humility. Even when we see ourselves as "less than the dust of the earth,"[473] we are of the same species as the gods. The ultimate intent and meaning of Christ's life and death is *theosis*: the universal transformation of the whole of human nature and the whole of the human family.[474]

---

458   C. A. Callaghan, *Other Worlds,* p. 10.

459   D&C 130:18-19; 131:5-6; J. Smith, Jr., *Teachings,* 8 April 1843, pp. 287-288; 14 May 1843, p. 297.

460   R. L. Bushman, *Rough Stone,* pp. 487-488.

461   J. Smith, Jr., *Words,* 16 April 1843, p. 196.

462   *All Things,* p. 54.

463   Psalm 22:6; 8:4-6.

464   S. W. Kimball, *Perfect.*

465   E.g., John 10:1-18.

466   Isaiah 53:6.

467   1 Nephi 11:16, 11:26.

468   E.g., 1 Corinthians 1:24-2:16; 2 Nephi 9:28, 9:42, 9:43; 15:21; 27:26; 28:15; Alma 37:7.

469   E.g., Proverbs 7:4-27; 9:13-18.

470   Revelation 17:1-18; 1 Nephi 14:10; 22:13; 2 Nephi 10:16; D&C 29:21; 86:3.

471   1 Corinthians 1:20.

472   M. Barker, *Older,* pp. 94-95. See Moses 8:13 and *Excursus 24: The Watchers,* p. 585.

473   Mosiah 4:2; Helaman 12:7.

474   T. G. Madsen, *et al., Human Nature,* p. 107.

1-13 Stark defines the concept of "divine accommodation," which "holds that *God's revelations are always limited to the current capacity of humans to comprehend*—that in order to communicate with humans, God is forced to accommodate their incomprehension by resorting to the equivalent of 'baby talk.'" Moreover, "all revelations are subject to misunderstanding, exaggeration, and faulty transmission."[475]

Further elaborating this concept, McLachlan writes: "Latter-day Saints do not attribute infallibility to the scriptures because the scriptures are filtered through human understanding—whether by the prophets who received and wrote the message or we who are attempting to understand it."[476]

1-14 Nibley observes:

You comprehend what you are like, don't you? In other words, you identify. We are told time and again that when Jesus came down to earth he took flesh so that we could comprehend him. He became like us. "Among the angels he was an angel. Among men he was a man." He descends to the level of the people whom he must teach, because he must do it in order to teach them… You comprehend others only to the degree that you are like them… By comprehending something, you embrace it, literally; it is part of you; you identify with it completely. This means that life will look very different hereafter, when we can identify with, for example, animals. It wouldn't be unfair to lower creatures to compare them with ourselves—they would lose nothing by it. Can they not have joy in the sphere in which they were created without having our particular type of glory? They aren't missing anything at all, because we're sharing a common existence. The man comprehends a great deal more in the love of his dog, and the other way around. If there is a good feeling between the man and his dog, neither feels cheated; neither feels that he is being left out of anything, because they are actually sharing in each other's worlds. You can say that a man has a very intelligent dog of which he is very fond and that the dog is very fond of the man. They actually share a very real experience, so that neither has to envy the other at all.[477]

The philosopher Wittgenstein famously wrote: "If a lion could talk, we could not understand him" (*Wenn ein Löwe sprechen könnte, wir könnten ihn nicht verstehen*).[478] This does not mean that a lion cannot have a language that in principle could be "translated" to our own, but rather that his whole experience of life is so different from ours that the meaning of the words would be lost. In Wittgenstein's terms, this is due to the fact that we cannot enter into the lion's "form of life" (*Lebensform*). Similarly, "when we come into a strange country with entirely strange traditions; and, what is more, even given a mastery of the country's language[, we] do not *understand* the people. (And not because of not knowing what they are saying to themselves.) We cannot find our feet with them."[479]

By way of contrast, Jesus' divinity coupled with his full experience of humanity endows him with the capacity to "[bear] our griefs and [carry] our sorrows,"[480] knowing "according to the flesh how to succor his people."[481] Jesus Christ "ascended up on high, as also he descended below all things, in that he comprehended all things, that he might be in all and through all things, the light of truth."[482] Because He understands us, He can help us. As William James wrote:

In this real world of sweat and dirt, it seems to me that when a view of things is "noble," that ought to count as a presumption against its truth, and as a philosophic disqualification. The prince of darkness may be a gentleman, as we are told he is, but whatever the God of earth and heaven is, he can surely be no gentleman. His menial services are needed in the dust of our human trails, even more than his dignity is needed in the empyrean.[483]

Hustwit observes that "[God] has not remained an abstraction apart from human life and suffering… [On the other hand,] Aristotle's unmoved mover has nothing to say to a human being, but if it did, like Wittgenstein's lion, no one would understand it. Neither would it have the moral authority to speak."[484]

475 R. Stark, *Discovering,* pp. 6, 52

476 J. McLachlan, *Reply,* p. 209.

477 H. W. Nibley, *Unrolling,* pp. 165-166.

478 L. Wittgenstein, *Investigations,* II:xi, pp. 190c, 190.

479 *Ibid.,* p. 190c.

480 Isaiah 53:4.

481 Alma 7:12.

482 D&C 88:6; cf. 1 Nephi 11:16; 11:26; D&C 122:8.

483 W. James, *What Pragmatism Means,* p. 72. See also P. M. Van Buren, *Lions,* p. 228.

484 R. Hustwit, *Kierkegaard.*

1-15   See Johnson[485] for the application of methods of biblical criticism to the text of Moses 1.

1-16   Clark summarizes parallels between Moses 1, the book of *Jubilees,* and various Jewish traditions about the ascension of Moses. Summarizing significant passages in *Jubilees,* he writes that:

> … in contrast to Genesis, the creation account is preceded by an entire chapter of prologue that describes the setting for the subsequent divine revelation to Moses. Moses is divinely summoned to a mountain where he experiences God's glory and is instructed to record what he would be told. He is then apprised of the future apostasy of the children of Israel after they are settled in the promised land and how they would kill the prophets and go into captivity. He learns that eventually, however, the children of Israel would repent and be transplanted back as a righteous plant. Following Moses' intercessory prayer, in which he pleads with the Lord to show mercy and salvation to the people, Moses is again instructed to write everything that should be made known to him, and the "angel of the presence" is told to dictate to Moses the whole account of the creation and the division of years until all creation would be renewed by the powers of heaven."[486]

1-17   Of this chapter's relationship to the later work on Genesis, Matthews wrote: "The Prophet did not say what connection this revelation has with the actual Translation of the Bible or whether it was received while he was engaged in the translation. However the fact that it was included in each of the three of the Old Testament manuscripts of the New Translation suggests that there is a close historical connection."[487]

1-18   Writes Turner:

> Narratives in general have several ways of alerting readers to what is likely to transpire in the story as it unfolds, or how to make sense out of what they have just read, and Genesis itself uses several such conventions. For example, it prefaces some individual stories with headlines which give advance warning about the significance or meaning of the ensuing narrative, as in 22:1: "After these things God tested Abraham." This headline does not tell us why God wanted to test Abraham, but it informs us that if we are to read 22:2ff. correctly, we must view it from this perspective.… [Though] the reader is [frequently] left on his or her own with the text,… [there] are important exceptions to this,… for Genesis does employ what might be termed *Announcements of Plot.* Each of the four narrative blocks which comprise the book (i.e., the primeval history and the stories of Abraham, Jacob, and Jacob's family) is prefaced by statements which either explicitly state what will happen, or which suggest to the reader what the major elements of the plot are likely to be… and it is a natural question for the reader to ask whether in fact what is expected to happen actually does happen.[488]

> Indeed, as Alter expresses, while the purpose of the whole of biblical narrative is to "reveal the enactment of God's purposes in historical events," this enactment "is continuously complicated by a perception of two, approximately parallel, dialectical tensions. One is a tension between the divine plan and the disorderly character of actual historical events, or, to translate this opposition into specifically biblical terms, between the divine promise and its ostensible failure to be fulfilled; the other is a tension between God's will, His providential guidance, and human freedom, the refractory nature of man."[489]

1-19   Apart from the specifics of what is actually said, an important purpose of the chapter's prologue—as similarly in the function of Moses 1 as a whole to the story of creation, and, for that matter, the story of creation to the entire book of Genesis—is, as Lewis aptly described the opening paragraph of *Paradise Lost,* to give us "the sensation *that some great thing is now about to begin.*"[490] No doubt this purpose accounts in part for the style and structure of the tightly-packed narrative and dialogues of Moses 1 as well as, perhaps, the solemn and grand repetitions of God's near soliloquy in Moses 2. To get a proper sense for the intended effect of the whole, it is useful to read the first four chapters of Moses at one sitting. At such times, advises Lewis, we should permit ourselves to be swept along "as though we were attending an actual recitation and nowhere [allowed] to settle down and luxuriate on any one line or paragraph." Though the focus of the story changes from chapter to chapter, these transitions should

---

485   M. J. Johnson, *Prologue.*
486   E. D. Clark, *Prologue,* p. 135. See also H. W. Nibley, *To Open,* pp. 7-19.
487   R. J. Matthews, *Plainer,* p. 27.
488   L. Turner, *Announcements,* pp. 13-14.
489   R. Alter, *Narrative,* p. 33.
490   C. S. Lewis, *Preface,* VII, p. 41.

be "felt as we feel the pause in a piece of music, where the silence is part of the music, and not as we feel the pause between one item of a concert and the next."[491]

1-20　　Rabbi Nathan says that on Sinai, Moses "was sanctified and became like the ministering angels."[492] Going further, "Philo is so carried away by the exalted Moses that he frequently speaks of him as having been deified, or being God. 'For when he had left all mortal categories behind he was changed into the divine, so that he might be made akin to God and truly divine.'[493] Philo vacillates on this point, but the fact that he could make such a statement is highly significant."[494] Fletcher-Louis summarizes similar teachings from the Dead Sea Scrolls.[495]

Ginzberg reports traditions of "several ascensions of Moses": a first "at the beginning of his career," a second "at the revelation of the *Torah*," and the third "shortly before his death."[496] For a brief overview of accounts that interpreted Moses' ascent to Sinai as an ascent to the Holy of Holies, see Barker.[497] For useful general summaries of ascent literature, see Barker, Hamblin, and McConkie.[498] For an interpretation of the Islamic *hajj* pilgrimage as a form of ascent, see Ashraf,[499] and for the Islamic story of Habib, who "entered [Paradise] alive," see Yasar.[500] For a discussion of Moses' vision on Sinai as an ascent and rebirth, see Borgen.[501] See also *Excursus 2: Ancient Concepts of Wisdom,* p. 516.

1-21　　For a discussion of "prologues in heaven" in scripture, literature, and ancient sources see Nibley[502] and the overviews of Moses 3 and 4.[503]

1-22　　"In a stock presentation found in early Jewish synagogues as well as on very early Christian murals, 'the hand of God is represented, but could not be called that explicitly, and instead of the heavenly utterance, the *bath-kol* [echo, distant voice, whisper] is given.' …In early Christian representations the hand of God reaching through the veil is grasped by the initiate or human spirit who is being caught up into the presence of the Lord."[504] Discussions of the sacred handclasp are available in several sources.[505]

1-23　　In extracanonical writings, accounts of similar visions speak of a "blueprint" of eternity that is worked out in advance and shown on the inside of the heavenly veil.[506]

1-24　　This tentative interpretation of the structure and sequence of the events of Moses 1 resulted from an effort to understand several puzzling questions raised by a close reading of the text. For instance, why do we find similar wording in verses 2 and 31? Answer: Verse 2 anticipatorily summarizes verse 31, the most important event of the chapter where Moses sees God face to face. Why are there two seemingly similar visions of the world/earth and the children of men/inhabitants?[507] Answer: The first is a vision of the spirit world and its organized intelligences,[508] and the second is of the earth and its inhabitants. Why does the text specify "the world upon which he was created" instead of simply "the world"?[509] Answer: Moses' spirit was created at or near the residence of God (the place of "first

491　*Ibid.,* pp. 41, 45.

492　J. Goldin, *Fathers,* 1, p. 3.

493　Philo, *Exodus, 2:29,* p. 70.

494　E. R. Goodenough, *Introduction to Philo,* pp. 148-149; cf. R. S. Eccles, *Pilgrimage,* pp. 60-61. See E. R. Goodenough, *Light,* pp. 223-229. See *Endnote E-221,* p. 757.

495　C. H. T. Fletcher-Louis, *Glory,* pp. 136-149.

496　L. Ginzberg, *Legends,* 5:417.

497　M. Barker, *Great High Priest,* pp. 218-219.

498　M. Barker, *Risen;* M. Barker, *Temple Theology;* W. J. Hamblin, *Temple Motifs;* J. F. McConkie, *Premortal.*

499　S. A. Ashraf, *Inner,* p. 125.

500　M. Ibn Ishaq ibn Yasar, *Making,* pp. 227-228.

501　P. Borgen, *John and Philo,* pp. 60-65.

502　H. W. Nibley, *Teachings of the PGP,* 17, pp. 205-216.

503　See the oveviews of Moses 3, pp. 134-139 and Moses 4, pp. 216-227.

504　H. W. Nibley, *Atonement,* p. 562.

505　T. M. Compton, *Token;* T. M. Compton, *Handclasp;* S. D. Ricks, *Dexiosis.* See also *Commentary* 1:25-c, p. 60; *Figure* 5-13, p. 351; *Figure* 6-14, p. 473; *Excursus 53: Comparative Explorations, Dexiosis,* p. 681; *Figure* B-1, p. 872.

506　See *Commentary* 1:27-b, p. 62.

507　Moses 1:7-8, 1:27-28.

508　Cf. Abraham 3:22-23.

509　Moses 1:8.

creation"[510]), however subsequent events of his vision take place after he "fell unto the earth."[511] Why does Moses hear only a "voice" in verses 25-27? Answer: During his experiences on the telestial earth, the Holy Ghost ministers to him[512] while he is temporarily separated from the Lord's presence. The divine voice comes from behind the heavenly veil, preparing him to speak with God face to face.[513]

1-25   An *endowment* may be a prerequisite for the carrying out of certain divine assignments, especially missionary work.[514] In a meeting with the Twelve where the gathering of volunteers for expeditions to explore the West for future colonization was discussed, Joseph Smith said, "I want every man that goes to be a king and a priest. When he gets on the mountains, he may want to talk with his God."[515]

1-26   The mention of the descent of the dove at Jesus' baptism in all four Gospels and in the Doctrine and Covenants suggests the importance of this event. It is striking, however, that none of these scriptural accounts offer any explanation of the dove's appearance, apparently assuming that its significance will be apparent to the careful reader. A connection between the experiences of Moses and that of Jesus at his baptism can be made if one regards the event, as does Barker, as a heavenly "ascent experience."[516] Such an experience would be consistent with the idea of baptism as a figurative death and resurrection.[517] This interpretation also sheds light on the Evangelists' description of the opening of the heavens, the proclamation of Divine Sonship by the Father,[518] and the presence of the dove as a symbol of the renewing of creation and the subduing of Satan.[519] Schroer emphasizes the connection between the symbolism of the dove, the Holy Spirit, and the ancient figure of Wisdom: "Like heavenly Sophia, the Son is the sole mediator of divine revelation, and the content of that heavenly revealed knowledge is Wisdom or the Son her/himself.… The baptismal event reveals that Jesus is the person in whom/upon whom Wisdom/Spirit finds rest," and the dove serves as a tangible messenger of Divine love and approval.[520] "[T]he dove always symbolized the love of God for man and the love of man for God, love in which the hope of immortality was found and realized."[521]

1-27   Walker recorded the following concerning the First Vision:

> Br. John Alger said while speaking of the Prophet Joseph, that when he, John, was a small boy he heard the Prophet Joseph relate his vision of seeing the Father and the Son. [He said t]hat God touched his eyes with his finger and said "Joseph, this is my beloved Son hear him." As soon as the Lord had touched his eyes with his finger, he immediately saw the Savior. After meeting, a few of us questioned him about the matter and he told us at the bottom of the meeting house steps that he was in the house of Father Smith in Kirtland when Joseph made this declaration, and that Joseph while speaking of it put his finger to his right eye, suiting the action with the words so as to illustrate and at the same time impress the occurrence on the minds of those unto whom he was speaking. We enjoyed the conversation very much, as it was something that we had never seen in church history or heard of before.[522]

---

510   See the book of Abraham, Facsimile 2, figures 1-2.

511   Moses 1:9; cf. B. Young, *10 July 1874*, p. 143.

512   Moses 1:24.

513   Cf. Moses 5:4, 5:9.

514   E.g., Luke 24:49; D&C 105:11-13; Brigham Young in W. Clayton, *Chronicle*, 26 December 1845, p. 234. See *Excursus 15: Description of the LDS Temple Endowment*, p. 557.

515   J. Smith, Jr., *Teachings*, 23 February 1844, p. 333; cf. 12 November 1835, p. 91.

516   M. Barker, *Risen*; cf. M. Barker, *Hidden*, pp. 91-94; G. Lettieri, *Ambiguity*, pp. 26-29; *Commentary 5:6-a*, p. 360.

517   Romans 6:4-6.

518   Matthew 3:16; Mark 1:10; Luke 3:22; John 1:32; D&C 93:15; M. Barker, *Risen*, pp. 46-49; cf. *Commentary 1:24-a*, p. 59. Barker notes that the oldest surviving versions of Luke's gospel quote the royal birth texts of the temple: "You are my son. Today I have begotten you" (Luke 3:22, quoting Psalm 2:7)—"this was the high priest's experience when he was born as the Son before being sent out into the world: he stood before the throne" (compare Galatians 4:4). "In his description of Jesus' departure, he also used high priestly imagery: Jesus blessed the disciples (Luke 24:50) and 'a cloud took him out of their sight' (Acts 1:9)" (M. Barker, *Christmas*, pp. 50, 52).

519   M. Barker, *Risen*, p. 36 n. 21; Genesis 8:6-12; *Commentary 2:2-c*, p. 96; 4:21-d, p. 266; 4:31-d, p. 280.

520   S. Schroer, *Dove*, pp. 144, 145, 137-138; cf. Isaiah 11:2; Matthew 11:19; 1 Corinthians 1:24; M. Barker, *Hidden*, p. 93; E. R. Goodenough, *Pagan Symbols*, 8:27-46.

521   E. R. Goodenough, *Pagan Symbols*, 8:41.

522   J. Smith, Jr., n. d., as reported in C. L. Walker, *Diary*, 2 February 1893, 2:755-756, punctuation and capitalization modernized.

Whether literally or figuratively, Joseph said that his eyes were also touched prior to his receiving D&C 76:

> … the Lord touched the eyes of our understandings, and they were opened, and the glory of the Lord shone round about.
>
> And we beheld the glory of the Son, on the right hand of the Father, and received of his fulness.[523]

As in the First Vision, the initial result of the "touch" that opened Joseph Smith's eyes was that he beheld the Savior in His glory. The statement that they "received of his fulness" is also remarkable. Here are the corresponding verses in the Prophet's poetic rendition of D&C 76:

> 15. I marvel'd at these resurrections, indeed!
> For it came unto me by the spirit direct:—
> And while I did meditate what it all meant,
> *The Lord touch'd the eyes of my own intellect:—*
>
> 16. Hosanna forever! *they open'd anon,*
> And the glory of God shone around where I was;
> And there was the Son, at the Father's right hand,
> In a fulness of glory, and holy applause.[524]

1-28   Joseph Smith used the ladder to represent the process of exaltation: "When you climb up a ladder, you must begin at the bottom, and ascend step by step, until you arrive at the top; and so it is with the principles of the Gospel—you must begin with the first, and go on until you learn all the principles of exaltation."[525] For an in-depth discussion of the symbolism of the ladder, see Guénon.[526]

1-29   Similar patterns between the *Merkabah* literature and Islamic *mi'raj* accounts are described by Schimmel, "for instance, the wayfarer's examination at the gate; the 'staying upright'; the idea that the angels, contrary to the perfected seeker, are not allowed into the Divine Presence; and the symbolism of the Divine Throne, which appears so prominently in poetical descriptions of the *mi'raj*, especially in the Persianate tradition."[527] See Schimmel[528] for an extensive discussion of Muhammad's experience and its significance in ancient and modern Islamic traditions.

---

523   D&C 76:19-20.
524   J. Smith, Jr. (or W. W. Phelps), *A Vision,* 1 February 1843, stanzas 15-16, p. 82, reprinted in L. E. Dahl, *Vision,* p. 297; emphasis added. Thanks to Bryce Haymond for pointing out this reference.
525   J. Smith, Jr., *Teachings,* 7 April 1844, p. 348; cf. 7 April 1844, pp. 346-348, 354.
526   R. Guénon, *Symboles,* pp. 336-339. See also *Commentary* 1:1-c, p. 43 and *Figure* 5-13, p. 351.
527   A. Schimmel, *Messenger,* p. 298 n. 8.
528   *Ibid.,* pp. 159-175.

FIGURE 2-1. *Creation of Sun, Moon, and Planets, 1511*
Michelangelo Buonarroti, 1475-1564

And I, God, said: Let there be lights in the firmament of the heaven, to divide the day from the night (Moses 2:14). Distinction and separation are the central themes of the creation account. Here, God dramatically extends his arms in opposite directions, majestically assigning the golden ball of the sun to rule the day, and the gray moon to rule the night. To achieve a "special otherworldly effect," the moon was "painted without paint"—in other words, it is the actual color of the bare plaster surface beneath the fresco itself (B. Blech, *et al.*, *Secrets*, p. 195).

Although, from an LDS perspective, it is hard to imagine a more "traditional" depiction of creation, Michelangelo's portrait is thoroughly unacceptable to rabbinic Judaism. For one thing, Ellis observes, the anthropomorphic portrayal violates both the second commandment and also the idea that God is "unknowable, unimaginable" and "visually unportrayable." Additionally, God is shown as effecting creation through action rather than by the sole means of "potent speech-acts that enact the creative power of language." Thus, he explains, Michelangelo's God is both inexplicably busy and "un-Jewishly mute" (R. S. Ellis, *Images*). "For the Jew," writes Susan Handelman, "God's presence is inscribed or traced within a text, not a body. Divinity is located in language, not person" (*ibid.*).

MOSES 2

The Creation

MOSES 2

Overview

AFTER the period of arrests and mob threats that accompanied the transcription of Moses 1 in June 1830, Joseph Smith and Oliver Cowdery divided their time between "the studying of the scriptures," "preaching," "confirming the church at Colesville," and performing their "labors on the land."[1] Oliver was scribe not only for the first manuscript version of Moses 1, but also for Moses 2-5:43 which is known to have been completed sometime before 21 October 1830.[2] The heading to OT1 Moses 2-4 specifically indicates that this portion of the translation was "given to the Elders of the Church of Christ," likely at the second conference of the Church that was held on September 26-28, 1830.[3]

Contributions of the Books of Moses and Abraham

While it is true that some significant details were added to Genesis in the translation of Moses 2, it is perhaps more noteworthy that the effort resulted in no major reshaping of the creation story.[4] A brief prologue affirming that the account derives from the words of the Lord directly to Moses is added in verse 1. The repetition of the phrase "I, God" throughout the chapter also emphasizes its firsthand nature. The fact that all things were created "by mine Only Begotten"[5] is made clear, as is the Son's identity as the co-creator at the time when God said "Let us make man."[6] Consistent with the words of Christ to the Brother of Jared,[7] we learn that man was created in the image of the Only Begotten, which is equated to being created in God's own image.[8] Apart from these important points, the structure and basic premises of the Genesis account of the Creation were left intact.

While following generally similar schemas, the two later versions of the creation story given in the book of Abraham and in modern temples are replete with additional changes—some subtle and others stunning—that give new perspectives on the events portrayed. Nielsen and Ricks provide a useful summary of these differences:

---

1   D&C 26:1.

2   S. H. Faulring, *et al.*, *Original Manuscripts*, p. 57.

3   K. Muhlestein, *Flow*, p. 43. See *Endnote 2-1*, p. 125.

4   See *Endnote 2-2*, p. 125.

5   Moses 2:1.

6   Moses 2:26.

7   Ether 3:15.

8   Moses 2:27.

By the time Joseph Smith published [the book of Abraham] "translation" in 1842, he had gained a much deeper understanding—both through additional revelation and through some study of Hebrew.[9] In light of the doctrine of the Council in Heaven, Joseph Smith had pointed out that the Hebrew term Elohim, a plural form, should be rendered the "Gods" in the creation account, not as the traditional "God."[10] It is so rendered throughout Abraham's account.[11] In light of the doctrine of the eternal nature of matter, the word traditionally translated as "created" becomes "organized." The phrase "without form and void" (Hebrew *tohu wa-bohu*) is rendered, quite properly, "empty and desolate" and describes the condition of the earth after it was organized, not before.[12]

FIGURE 2-2. *The First Day of Creation, 1925*
M. C. Escher, 1898-1972

And the earth was without form and void; and I caused darkness to come up upon the face of the deep; and my Spirit moved upon the face of the water; for I am God.[1] The Hebrew term here translated "moved" is used in Deuteronomy 32:11 to describe an eagle hovering attentively over its young.[2] Consistent with such a picture, the book of Abraham employs the term "brooding."[3]

1   Moses 2:2.
2   U. Cassuto, *Adam to Noah*, p. 25.
3   Abraham 4:2. See *Commentary* 2:2-a, p. 97.

The term "day" (Hebrew *yom*) for the seven "days" of Creation is given as "time," a permissible alternative in both Hebrew and English; and it is explicitly pointed out that the "time" in which Adam should die if he partook of the forbidden fruit "was after the Lord's time, which was after the time of Kolob[, a great star that Abraham had seen nearest to the throne of God, whose revolution, one thousand years by our reckoning, is a day unto the Lord]; "for as yet the Gods had not appointed unto Adam his reckoning."[13]

On the basis of the above passage, which clearly excludes the possibility of earthly twenty-four-hour days being the "days" or "times" of Creation, some Latter-day Saint commentators have argued for one-thousand-year periods as the "times" of Creation as well as the "time" of Adam's earthly life after the fall; others have argued for indefinite periods of time, as long as it would take to accomplish the work involved.[14] Abraham's account does contain the interesting passage, in connection with the "organizing" of the lights in the "expanse" of heaven, "The Gods watched those things which they had ordered until they obeyed."[15] Abraham's account actually includes twelve different "labors" of the Gods, divided up among the "days" in the manner of Genesis. The later temple account of Creation gives an abbreviated version of those

9   See *Endnote 2-3*, p. 125.
10   J. Smith, Jr., *Words*, 16 June 1844, p. 379.
11   See *Endnote 2-4*, p. 125.
12   Abraham 4:2.
13   Abraham 5:13, 3:2-4 and *Excursus 18: Kolob*, p. 565. See *Endnote 2-5*, p. 125.
14   See *Endnote 2-6*, p. 125.
15   Abraham 4:14-18.

labors, divided up differently among the seven days while retaining the same order, suggesting that it may not be significant which labor is assigned to which day.[16]

Abraham connects the seemingly differing accounts of Genesis 1 and 2 within the context of the Council in Heaven. Abraham's seven-day account proceeds through the work of the first five creative times and part of the sixth as the physical creation of the earth and its preparation to support life before life was actually placed upon it. Thus, during the third time, "the Gods organized the earth to *bring forth* grass and the earth to bring forth the tree from its own seed."[17] And during the fifth time, the Gods "prepared the waters that they might bring forth great whales, and every living creature, and every winged fowl after their kind."[18] Similarly, on the sixth time "the Gods prepared the earth to bring forth the living creature after his kind. And the Gods saw they would obey."[19] Then upon the sixth time, the Gods again took counsel among themselves and determined to form man, and to give them dominion over the plants and animals that should come upon the earth.[20] "And the Gods said among themselves: On the seventh time we will end our work, which we have counseled; and we will rest. And thus were their decisions at the time that they counseled among themselves."[21] The account paralleling Genesis 2 then follows smoothly as an account of the actual placing of life upon the earth: "And the Gods came down and formed these the generations of the heavens and of the earth, when they were formed in the day that the Gods formed the earth and the heavens, according to all that which they had said concerning every plant of the field before it was in the earth."[22]

The different creation accounts were necessarily prepared so that they could be appreciated despite the limits of human comprehension—"in [our] weakness, after the manner of [our] language, that [we] might come to understanding."[23] Though it might be tempting to label one version of the story as more "accurate" or "complete" in some sense than another, differences, and even seeming inconsistencies, sometimes may be due to the unique perspective from which each account is being given. For example, while some of the events of Genesis are clearly told from a divine point of view, others are phrased in "phenomenal language," i.e., "wording that represents things as they appear to a casual human observer on the face of the earth."[24] Access to multiple accounts also leads us to consider why certain details in a story are present in one version and not in another[25]—especially when it would have seemed natural to include them.[26] Different versions of the same events may be recorded for disparate sets of readers, or may deliberately serve different pedagogical purposes,[27] a possibility to be discerned through careful examination of the material.[28]

Creation as Progressive Distinction and Separation

Consider that the first action of Creation in Moses 2 is the appearance of light and its separation from darkness.[29] Griffith-Jones eloquently presents some of the many possible insights that could be gleaned from this fact:

---

16   See *Endnote 2-7*, p. 125.
17   Abraham 4:12, emphasis added.
18   Abraham 4:21.
19   Abraham 4:24-25.
20   Abraham 4:26-29.
21   Abraham 5:2-3.
22   F. K. Nielsen, *et al.*, *Creation Accounts*, pp. 340-342. See Abraham 5:4-5.
23   D&C 1:24. See *Endnote 2-8*, p. 126.
24   W. Bradley, *Why*, p. 164. See *Endnote 2-9*, p. 126.
25   See *Endnote 2-10*, p. 126.
26   D. Packard, *et al.*, *Feasting*, pp. 23-24.
27   See *Endnote 2-11*, p. 126.
28   See *Excursus 6: The Authority and Power of Scripture*, p. 531.
29   See *Endnote 2-12*, p. 126.

MOSES 2

How do we recognize… order in the world outside? We might answer in the Old [Testament's] terms: God imposed, at Creation's start, the first of all further distinctions—the separation that brought the first form to chaos—and met the first condition for its sight… There was darkness over the deep: There were no distinctions to be known and no light to know "them" by. For before all else, we need light. It is this that makes all subsequent distinctions "visible," accessible to our eyes or minds. It is not surprising, in turn, that for the proper process and result of right thinking we speak of light. The sun casts light on the world; our reasoning and imagination cast light on its working. The first source is a daily symbol of God's creative work; the second is our finite, fallible copy of that activity. We make distinctions by the sun's light and our mind's together. When are these distinctions of our own secure? Our poet might have answered, when they conform to the distinctions made and illumined together by that first creative blaze.

Light makes it possible to discern differences. To discern differences brings light. To speak of judging, the Greeks used a more general word than ours: They would "distinguish" or "discern" between two things or opinions. It is no accident that [the first chapters of both Genesis and the Gospel of John link] light and the judgment that it makes possible and that brings light in its turn. Judgment and discrimination: of physical objects, of relations, and of the moral world…[30]

FIGURE 2-3. *Separation of Light from Darkness, 1511*
Michelangelo Buonarotti, 1475-1564

In the beginning I created the heaven and the earth…. And I, God said, Let there be light; and there was light. And I, God, saw the light; and that light was good. And I, God, divided the light from the darkness.[1] In Michelangelo's sublime depiction of the first act of Creation, "the Almighty is twisted around in serpentine manner, much like the contorted position the artist himself was assuming to create the fresco."[2] God runs his fingers through indistinct chaos, separating the brownish obscurity of darkness from the white cloudlike billows of light. While Michelangelo linked the scene typologically to the Last Judgment,[3] this masterful imagery is an even more fitting portrayal of the symbolism of the "First Judgment," effected at the moment when Satan's rebellious hosts were cast out of heaven.[4]

In support of arguments for a typological interpretation of the Sistine Chapel ceiling, Anderson writes: "Michelangelo, unlike many of his contemporaries, was not a simple, uneducated artisan. Rather, he was a deeply religious man who frequently attended Mass, pored over scriptural texts and commentaries, and, in his early years, was deeply moved by the infamous religious reformer in Florence, Savonarola. Like many in pre-Reformation Rome, Michelangelo was also deeply impressed with how the beginnings of Creation were not only a witness to the glory of the Creator but also pointed, however mysteriously, to our end or *telos* within the cosmos."[5]

Though depicting the very beginnings of Creation, the panel was ironically painted "near the end of Buonarotti's sufferings up on the ceiling. He was in a desperate rush to finish, both for his personal health and because there was concern that the pope, who had been very ill, might not live to see the project completed. If Julius had died before it was done, the next pontiff might have cancelled the artist's contract, and perhaps have changed or abandoned the work as well. In creating this panel, Michelangelo worked without… his assistants who would prepare the full-size cartoons to transfer the outlines of the figures to be painted into the wet plaster *intonaco*.[6] In fact, this sculptor who had said of himself 'I am no painter' painted this entire panel *in one day—totally freehand,* something few highly experienced fresco artists would ever dare attempt."[7]

1   Moses 2:1, 3-4.
2   B. Blech, *et al.*, *Secrets*, p. 193. See *Endnote 2-13*, p. 126.
3   P. De Vecchi, *et al.*, *Michelangelo*, pp. 171, 205.
4   See *Commentary* 2:4-c, p. 101 and Moses 4:3-4.
5   G. A. Anderson, *Perfection*, p. 111. See *Endnote 2-14*, p. 127.
6   I.e., the thin layer of plaster on which the fresco was painted.
7   B. Blech, *et al.*, *Secrets*, pp. 194-195.

30   R. Griffith-Jones, *Witnesses*, pp. 296-297.

The effects of the creation of light and its division from darkness cascade through the rest of the chapter as each of its episodes recounts the successive generation of new and finer-grained distinctions that define created elements through the principle of separation.[31] We sense important lessons to be grasped in the very way the story is presented to us. For example, Leo Strauss reflects on the beauty and order revealed by the fractal self-similarity in each stage of the account:

> [F]rom the principle of separation, light [which allows discernment and distinction]; via something which separates, heaven;[32] to something which is separated, earth and sea; to things which are productive of separated things, trees, for example; then things which can separate themselves from their courses, brutes; and finally a being which can separate itself from its way, the right way...[33]

Up to the point where Adam is formed, the order of Creation is decidedly hierarchic.[34] However, the final creative act, where a rib is separated out from the man to make the woman,[35] is portrayed to demonstrate the relationship of Adam and Eve as "equal partners."[36] Other textual clues also set this creative act apart from all the rest. For one thing, we know that the man and the woman are created in the image of God—in other words, that they are both "after his kind."[37] And, just as important, we learn that since the man and the woman are not only of the same kind, but also bone of the same bone and flesh of the same flesh, they are not to separate from one other, but are to become "one" in a perfect unity that approaches identity.[38] With the creation of Adam and Eve completed, God can declare His work to be "very good."[39]

FIGURES 2-4 TO 2-6. *The Second, Third, and Fourth Days of Creation, 1925-1926*
M. C. Escher, 1898-1972

31   See *Endnote 2-15*, p. 127.
32   See *Endnote 2-16*, p. 127.
33   Cited in L. R. Kass, *Wisdom*, p. 33. See *Endnote 2-17*, p. 127.
34   See *Endnote 2-18*, p. 128.
35   Moses 3:21-22.
36   G. B. Hinckley, *et al.*, *Proclamation*; cf. S. W. Kimball, *Teachings 1982*, 26 February 1977, p. 315; B. Blech, *et al.*, *Secrets*, p. 202. See *Endnote 2-19*, p. 128.
37   Moses 2:26-27.
38   Moses 3:23-24, *Commentary* 2:27-a, p. 115; J. R. Holland, *Souls*, pp. 17-18; cf. H. W. Nibley, *Atonement*, p. 568; R. M. Zlotowitz, *et al.*, *Bereishis*, p. 111.
39   Moses 2:31. See *Endnote 2-20*, p. 128.

FIGURE 2-7. *The Creation of Adam, 1510*
Michelangelo Buonarotti, 1475-1564

SEE COLOR PLATE 2-7.

And I, God, created man in mine own image, in the image of mine Only Begotten created I him; male and female created I them.[1] Of this scene, De Vecchi eloquently writes: "Perhaps the best-known of the scenes in the Sistine Chapel, the Creation of Adam must also have aroused particular admiration among the artist's contemporaries, who discerned in it the materialization of one of the highest ideals of Renaissance culture: the 'dignity' of man, created by God 'in his own image'… [T]he exaltation of the spiritual faculties of man was never separated from that of the beauty of the human body, 'the mirror of God' and the culmination of the Creation… Vasari describes Adam as 'a figure whose beauty, pose, and contours are of such a quality that he seems newly created by his Supreme and First Creator rather [than] by the brush and design of a mere mortal.' Seen against an indistinct natural background that is only just hinted at, as if it were the dawn of the world, the youthful, athletic figure reclining on a grassy slope, almost on the edge of an abyss, seems as if he is about to rise from the ground. He holds out his arm toward that of the Lord, who, borne aloft amidst a flight of angels,[2] stands out brightly against the shell of shadow of his huge purple mantle.[3] The remarkable invention of the outstretched arm and the forefingers about to meet becomes a metaphor for the vital energy that passes from the Creator to the creature fashioned in his image, awakening his heroic vigor… [Adam's] adolescent face, seen in profile, still lacking a definite expression, contrasts with the mature, intensely energetic one of the Lord, with his gray hair and long beard streaming in the air."[4]

Although Adam and the Father are the central figures of this panel, much attention has been given to the beautiful and enigmatic female figure who is intently regarding the creation of the first man while wrapped in the loving embrace of God's left arm. Her identity has variously been given as the immortal Sophia (Wisdom),[5] or as the premortal Eve. Relying on the analysis of the structure of the three Sistine Chapel Adam and Eve panels by art historian Leo Steinberg,[6] Anderson notes: "Just to the right of Eve sits an infant[7] who is also held by God the Father, though this time with just the thumb and index finger. The extension of his fingers corresponds exactly to the way a priest would grasp the Eucharistic wafer. In other words, this child is Mary's boy, the Christ child. Strikingly, he is the only figure on the entire ceiling who looks directly down into the gaze of the viewer. And so our question as we ponder the women in these three panels: Are they Eve, the first woman and spouse of Adam, or Mary, the Mother of Jesus and symbol of the Church? Or perhaps more accurately, are these women in truth both Eve and Mary?"[8] Anderson concludes that just as Christ is portrayed in scripture as the second Adam,[9] Mary is being depicted here as the second Eve.

---

1   Moses 2:27.
2   Or the premortal spirits of humanity (B. Blech, *et al., Secrets,* p. 200). See *Endnote 2-21,* p. 128.
3   See *Endnote 2-21,* p. 128.
4   P. De Vecchi, *et al., Michelangelo,* p. 163.
5   B. Blech, *et al., Secrets,* pp. 197, 199.
6   L. Steinberg, *Who's Who.*
7   See *Endnote 2-22,* p. 129.
8   G. A. Anderson, *Perfection,* p. 4.
9   1 Corinthians 15:22, 45-47.

FIGURE 2-8. *The Creation of Eve, 1510*
Michelangelo Buonarotti, 1475-1564

SEE COLOR PLATE 2-8.

And I, the Lord God, caused a deep sleep to fall upon Adam… And the rib which I, the Lord God, had taken from man, made I a woman.[1] Vasari describes the overall scene by contrasting the poses of Adam and Eve: "One [is] almost dead from being imprisoned by sleep, while the other comes alive completely reawakened by the benediction of God. The brush of this most ingenious artisan reveals the true difference between sleep and awakening, as well as how stable and firm His Divine Majesty may appear when speaking in human terms."[2] In his analysis of the painting, Anderson notes some details that are "highly unusual. Adam lies slumped around a dead tree, an odd sight for a luxuriant garden where death was, as of yet, unknown. The only way to understand this tired figure is to see him as a prefiguration of Christ, the second Adam,' who was destined to hang on a barren piece of wood. 'The sleep of [Adam],' the fourth-century theologian St. Augustine observed, 'clearly stood for the death of Christ'…[3] If this is how we are to read this image of Adam, perhaps a similar interpretation holds for Eve. To get our bearings on this we must bear in mind two facts. First, Mary as the 'second Eve' is she who gives birth to Christ. Second, Mary as the 'symbol of the church' is she who emerges from the rib of Christ on the Cross[, symbolized by the blood and water that issued from His side]. In this central panel of the Sistine ceiling, we see both the first and second Eve emerging from the ribs of Adam… Further support for this comes from the history of the chapel itself. It was built on the model of Solomon's Temple and was dedicated on August 15, 1483, the feast day of the Assumption and Coronation of the Virgin Mary in Heaven. A favored image of Mary in Christian devotional practice was Mary as the ark or tabernacle of God. Like the Ark of the Covenant in the Old Testament, the throne upon which God almighty took his seat, Mary was the seat in which God took human form. Like the Temple itself, she housed the *verum corpus* or the 'true body' of God."[4] Significantly, this image is the center point of the entire chapel ceiling.

---

1   Moses 3:21-22.
2   P. De Vecchi, *et al.*, *Michelangelo*, p. 151.
3   See Augustine, *City*, 22:17, p. 496.
4   G. A. Anderson, *Perfection*, pp. 5-8.

The Order and Perfection of Creation

The goodness of the completed Creation is beautifully expressed in literary form through the symbolism of numbers, the *heptad*, representing divine perfection.[40] "[T]he narrative's seven literary units feature seven times the formula for the effectuation of the divine will and the statement of divine approval; and the six days of Creation culminate in the climactic seventh."[41] Other details of the Hebrew text highlight the same theme:[42]:

The first sentence has seven words in Hebrew	7
The second sentence has fourteen words in Hebrew	7 x 2
The account of Creation is given in 56 verses	7 x 8
The name of God (*Elohim*) appears 35 times	7 x 5
Earth (*erets*) appears 21 times	7 x 3
Heavens (*shamayim, raqia*) appears 21 times	7 x 3
Good (*tov*) seven times	7
The seventh paragraph in Hebrew corresponds to the 7th day[43]	7

In order to emphasize the central focus of the chapter, the length of the description of each period of Creation grows longer as the story progresses: "The first two days are briefly recounted (with 31 and 38 words respectively). The next three days (days 3, 4, and 5) are approximately double that length (69, 69, and 57 words, respectively); and the account of the final creative day (day 6) is doubled again (149 words)."[44]

	Group I The Resource		Group II The Utilizer
Day	*Creative Act*	*Day*	*Creative Act*
1	Light	4	The luminaries
2	Sky, leaving terrestrial waters	5	Fish and fowl
3	Dry land including plants (makers of fruits) (Lowest form of organic life)	6	Land animals including humankind (Highest form of organic life)

Figure 2-9. *Schema of the Days of Creation*

In the beginning, the earth was "formless and empty"[45]—hence, in apparent consistency with the logic of the KJV translators (though probably not with the original Hebrew), it is fitting that God's first three creative acts should supply form, and that His final three acts should fill the resultant void.

The order and perfection of Creation is also shown through the division of its steps into "two parallel groups, each of which comprises the four creative acts performed in three days. The third day in each group is distinguished by two productions. In each group the movement is from heaven to terrestrial water to dry land. Moreover, the arrangement is such that each creation in the first group furnishes the resource that is to be utilized by the corresponding creature in the second group."[46] Only the Sabbath day remained unpaired. For this reason, the Jewish sages quoted her complaint—to which God's answer was, "The community of Israel, lo, that is your mate."[47] And so it was that when "Israel stood before Mount Sinai, the Holy One, blessed be He, said to them, 'Remember what I said to the Sabbath: 'The community of Israel is your mate.' Now therefore: 'Remember the Sabbath

---

40   See *Endnote 2-23*, p. 129.
41   N. M. Sarna, *Genesis*, p. 4.
42   M. Kahne, *Symbolique*. See also U. Cassuto, *Adam to Noah*, pp. 14-15.
43   See *Endnote 2-24*, p. 129.
44   D. A. Dorsey, *Structure*, p. 48.
45   Moses 2:2; J. H. Sailhamer, *Genesis*, pp. 24-25, 27-28; cf. "unarranged [disorganized] and unadorned" (Shelemon, *Book of the Bee*, 3, p. 7).
46   N. M. Sarna, *Genesis*, p. 4. See *Endnote 2-25*, p. 130.
47   J. Neusner, *Genesis Rabbah 1*, 11:8, p. 117. See *Endnote 2-26*, p. 130.

day to keep it holy.'"[48] To "keep it holy" is to be the lover or partner of the Sabbath, since the Hebrew term for marriage (*kiddushin*), comes from the same root as "holy."[49]

Having prepared a perfect environment in which life and learning could flourish, God blesses the man and the woman, commands them to be "fruitful and multiply, and replenish the earth," and gives them dominion "over every living thing."[50] Foreshadowing the additional commandment they will receive in the Garden of Eden,[51] He gives them instructions about what they should and should not eat, and the chapter ends with the close of the sixth day.[52]

---

48   *Ibid*. See Exodus 20:8.
49   See A. J. Heschel, *Heavenly Torah*, p. 216 and p. 216 n. 26.
50   Moses 2:28.
51   Moses 3:16-17.
52   Moses 2:29-31.

Moses 2: Text and Commentary

CHAPTER 2
(June–October 1830)

PROLOGUE (PP. 93-99)

AND it came to pass that ⁽ᵃ⁾the Lord spake unto Moses, saying: Behold, ⁽ᵇ⁾I reveal unto you concerning this heaven, and this earth; write the words which I speak. ⁽ᶜ⁾I am the Beginning and the End, the Almighty God; ⁽ᵈ⁾by mine Only Begotten I created these things; yea, ⁽ᵉ⁾in the beginning ⁽ᶠ⁾I created the heaven, and the earth upon which thou standest.

2 And the ⁽ᵃ⁾earth was without form, and void; and ⁽ᵇ⁾I caused darkness to come up upon the face of the deep; and ⁽ᶜ⁾my Spirit moved upon the face of the water; for I am God.

THE FIRST DAY (PP. 99-104)

3 And I, God, said: ⁽ᵃ⁾Let there be light; and ⁽ᵇ⁾there was light.

4 And ⁽ᵃ⁾I, God, saw the light; and ⁽ᵇ⁾that light was good. And ⁽ᶜ⁾I, God, divided the light from the darkness.

5 And ⁽ᵃ⁾I, God, called the light Day; and the darkness, I called ⁽ᵇ⁾Night; and ⁽ᶜ⁾this I did by the word of my power, and ⁽ᵈ⁾it was done as I spake; and the ⁽ᵉ⁾evening and the morning were the first day.

THE SECOND DAY (PP. 104-105)

6 And again, I, God, said: ⁽ᵃ⁾Let there be a firmament in the midst of the water, and it was so, even as I spake; and I said: Let it divide the waters from the waters; and ⁽ᵇ⁾it was done;

7 And ⁽ᵃ⁾I, God, made the firmament and divided the waters, yea, the great waters under the firmament from the waters which were above the firmament, and it was so even as I spake.

8 And I, God, called the firmament Heaven; and the evening and the morning were the second day.

THE THIRD DAY (PP. 105-107)

9 And I, God, said: Let the waters under the heaven be gathered together unto one place, and it was so; and I, God, said: ⁽ᵃ⁾Let there be dry land; and it was so.

10 And I, God, called the dry land Earth; and the gathering together of the waters, called I the ⁽ᵃ⁾Sea; and ⁽ᵇ⁾I, God, saw that all things which I had made were good.

11 And I, God, said: ⁽ᵃ⁾Let the earth bring forth grass, the herb yielding ⁽ᵇ⁾seed, the fruit tree yielding fruit, ⁽ᶜ⁾after his kind, and the tree yielding fruit, whose seed should be in itself upon the earth, and it was so even as I spake.

12 And the earth brought forth grass, every herb yielding seed after his kind, and the tree yielding fruit, whose seed should be in itself, after his kind; and I, God, saw that all things which I had made were good;

13 And the evening and the morning were the ⁽ᵃ⁾third day.

THE FOURTH DAY (PP. 107-109)

14 And I, God, said: ⁽ᵃ⁾Let there be lights in the firmament of the heaven, ⁽ᵇ⁾to divide the day from the night, and ⁽ᶜ⁾let them be for signs, and for seasons, and for days, and for years;

15 And let them be for lights in the firmament of the heaven ⁽ᵃ⁾to give light upon the earth; and it was so.

16 And I, God, made two great lights; the greater light to rule the day, and the lesser light to rule the night, and the greater light was the sun, and the ⁽ᵃ⁾lesser light was the moon; and the stars also were made even according to my word.

17 And I, God, set them in the firmament of the heaven to give light upon the earth,

18 And the sun to rule over the day, and the moon to rule over the night, and to divide the light from the darkness; and I, God, saw that all things which I had made were good.

19 And the evening and the morning were the fourth day.

THE FIFTH DAY (PP. 109-110)

20 And I, God, said: ⁽ᵃ⁾Let the waters bring forth abundantly the moving creature that hath life, and fowl which may fly above the earth in the open firmament of heaven.

21 And I, God, created ⁽ᵃ⁾great whales, and every living creature that moveth, which the ⁽ᵇ⁾waters brought forth abundantly, after their kind, and every winged fowl after his kind; and I, God, saw that all things which I had created were good.

22 And ⁽ᵃ⁾I, God, blessed them, saying: Be fruitful, and multiply, and fill the waters in the ⁽ᵇ⁾sea; and let fowl multiply in the earth;

23 And the evening and the morn-ing were the fifth day.

THE SIXTH DAY (PP. 110-118)

24 And I, God, said: ⁽ᵃ⁾Let the earth bring forth the living creature after his kind, cattle, and creeping things, and beasts of the earth after their kind, and it was so;

25 And I, God, made the beasts of the earth after their kind, and cattle after their kind, and everything which creepeth upon the earth after his kind; and I, God, saw that all these things were good.

26 And I, God, said unto mine Only Begotten, which was with me from the beginning: ⁽ᵃ⁾Let us make ⁽ᵇ⁾man ⁽ᶜ⁾in our image, after our likeness; and it was so. And I, God, said: ⁽ᵃ⁾Let them have dominion over the fishes of the sea, and over the fowl of the air, and over the cattle, and over all the earth, and over every creeping thing that creepeth upon the earth.

27 And I, God, created man in mine own image, in the image of mine Only Begotten ⁽ᵃ⁾created I him; ⁽ᵇ⁾male and female created I them.

28 And I, God, blessed them, and said unto them: ⁽ᵃ⁾Be fruitful, and multiply, and replenish the earth, and ⁽ᵇ⁾subdue it, and have dominion over the fish of the sea, and over the fowl of the air, and over every living thing that moveth upon the earth.

29 And I, God, said unto man: Behold, I have given you every ⁽ᵃ⁾herb bearing seed, which is upon the face of all the earth, and every tree in the which shall be the fruit of a tree yielding seed; ⁽ᵇ⁾to you it shall be for meat.

30 And to every beast of the earth, and to every fowl of the air, and to everything that creepeth upon the earth, wherein I grant life, there shall be given every ⁽ᵃ⁾clean herb for meat; and it was so, even as I spake.

31 And I, God, saw everything that I had made, and, behold, ⁽ᵃ⁾all things which I had made were very good; and the evening and the morning were the sixth day.

*1 And it came to pass that **the Lord spake unto Moses**, saying: Behold, **I reveal unto you concerning this heaven, and this earth**; write the words which I speak. **I am the Beginning** and the End, the Almighty God; **by mine Only Begotten I created these things**; yea, in the beginning I created the heaven, and the earth upon which thou standest.*

1 a ***the Lord spake unto Moses.*** Johnson notes that the JST revisions have produced a parallel between the opening of Genesis and the first verses of Leviticus, Numbers, and Deuteronomy: "All these verses begin with the words of God to Moses, then these words are related to the people. There is a progression to the verses as well. Moses, Leviticus and Numbers have the words of God spoken unto Moses, while Deuteronomy 1, the word has passed from God and now resides with Moses and is given to all Israel… The first two events take place in a temple-type surrounding, the high mountain and the Tabernacle. The next time the word is presented, it is down to earth, in the wilderness. This seems to be symbolic of the spiritual attitudes of Israel for the years to come."[53]

   b ***I reveal unto you concerning this heaven and this earth.*** In other words, the account given to Moses is not all-encompassing in scope. Note that the KJV plural "heavens" is changed to the singular "heaven" in Moses 2:1, 4, presumably "because every earth has its heaven."[54]

   c ***I am the Beginning.*** While the Gospel of John begins its Christological exposition of the opening verses of Genesis with its bold assertion: "In the beginning was the Word,"[55] the alternative gloss of Genesis 1:1 provided by the Midrash is bibliocentric: "By means of 'the beginning' [that is to say, the *Torah*] did God create."[56] In another variation on this theme, the *Targum Yerushalmi* explicitly connects these words to the Old Testament Wisdom tradition: "In wisdom the Lord created."[57] The book of Moses adds its unique voice to the long history of exegesis for this verse, taking the term "Beginning" to refer to the Father, who created all things by His Only Begotten, the living and personal "Word of [His] power."[58]

   d ***by mine Only Begotten I created these things.*** This statement reiterates the central role of the Son in Creation.[59] The book of Abraham goes even further to describe a plurality of Gods who participated in Creation.[60] These included Michael (the premortal Adam), as well as others.[61] President Brigham Young said that "the earth was organized by three distinct characters, namely, Elohim, [Je]hovah, and Michael, these three forming a quorum, as in all heavenly bodies, and in organizing element."[62]

   References to heavenly councils in the Old Testament are sometimes obscured by the KJV translation. For example, Tvedtnes observes that "congregation of the mighty"[63] is better rendered "council of God," and the term "secret"[64] should be read "council."[65] The term is also sometimes translated as "assembly"[66] or "counsel."[67] Nibley likewise saw an allusion to

53 M. J. Johnson, *Prologue*, pp. 25-26.
54 H. W. Nibley, *Teachings of the PGP*, 18, p. 224. See *Commentary* 2:1-e, p. 94.
55 John 1:1.
56 J. Neusner, *Genesis Rabbah 1*, 1:1, p. 2.
57 J. W. Etheridge, *Onkelos*, cf. A. B. S. Ed-Din, *Sufism*, p. 231. See also P. Borgen, *John and Philo*, pp. 48-50; J. H. Charlesworth, *Lady Wisdom*; H. N. Ridderbos, *John*, pp. 31-36.
58 OT1 Moses 2:5 in S. H. Faulring, *et al.*, *Original Manuscripts*, p. 86; Moses 1:32; *Commentary* 1:38-b, p. 67; 2:1-d, p. 93; *Excursus 49: The People of the Book*, p. 651; N. Birch, *Hellenization*; J. A. Tvedtnes, *Follett*.
59 Cf. Moses 1:32-33, Hebrews 1:2.
60 Abraham 4:1ff.
61 J. F. Smith, Jr., *Doctrines*, 1954, 1:74-75.
62 B. Young, *9 April 1852*, p. 51.
63 Psalm 82:1.
64 Job 15:8, 29:4; Psalm 25:14; Proverbs 3:32.
65 J. A. Tvedtnes, *Follett*.
66 E.g., Psalm 111:1.
67 E.g., Psalm 55:14.

1 And it came to pass that the Lord spake unto Moses, saying: Behold, I reveal unto you concerning this heaven, and this earth; write the words which I speak. I am the Beginning and the End, the Almighty God; **by mine Only Begotten I created these things***; yea,* **in the beginning I created the heaven, and the earth** *upon which thou standest.*

a heavenly council in John 1:1: "In the beginning was the Word"—taking Word[68] to connote discussion, council, word, or reason.[69]

Basing his remarks on an emendation of the Hebrew, Joseph Smith offered the following translation of the first verse of Genesis: "In the beginning, the head of the Gods called a council of the Gods; and they came together and concocted a plan to create the world and people it."[70] Two months later, he varied the wording: "'In the beginning the head of the Gods brought forth the Gods,' or as others have translated it, 'The head of the Gods called the Gods together.'"[71] Barney argues that the Hebrew behind "the head one of the Gods" could be equated to the term "God Most High" (*El Elyon*), the God Melchizedek worshipped.[72] Compare Nibley's translation of John 1:1: "In the ruling council was a spokesman and the spokesman was in the godhead, that is among the gods, and the spokesman was himself a god."[73]

e   ***in the beginning.*** Sailhamer reasons, based on the grammar of this verse and on parallels in other locations in the Bible, that the phrase in the beginning marks, not an absolute origin for the thing described, but rather "the starting point of a period of time" which the ancient reader would expect to be paired with a corresponding end. Hence, by starting the account with these words, "the author has not only commenced a history of God and his people, he has also prepared the way for the consummation of that history at 'the end of time'" when God will create "a new heaven and a new earth."[74]

f   ***I created the heaven, and the earth.*** This phrase constitutes the "announcement of plot" for Moses 2,[75] a "title or superscription for the entire chapter"[76] and, in fact, in a measure for the entire Old Testament.[77] Sailhamer moreover detects a polemic against idolatry in this verse, citing textual parallels and a similar spirit in the message of Jeremiah 10:10-11 that invites the nations to compare "the true God… the living God" to the "gods who have *not* made the heavens and the earth."[78]

Whereas the idea of God organizing the world from preexisting matter was a part of many ancient cosmologies, Jewish scholars began to articulate the alternative doctrine of *creatio ex nihilo*[79] by the later part of the second temple period.[80] *Ex nihilo* Creation subsequently became the prevalent interpretation in the Christian tradition.[81] By way of contrast, Joseph Smith stated that the word "created" should be rendered "formed, or organized."[82] This is

---

68   Greek *logos*.

69   H. W. Nibley, *Teachings of the PGP*, 9, p. 110.

70   J. Smith, Jr., *Teachings*, 7 April 1844, p. 349.

71   *Ibid.*, 16 June 1844, p. 371. See also D&C 121:32.

72   K. L. Barney, *Six*, p. 114. See K. L. Barney, *Emendation* and *Six* for in-depth discussions of the linguistic details and discussions of key concepts relating to the Prophet's commentary on this verse. See also J. A. Tvedtnes, *Follett*; *Commentary* 1:33-b, p. 65; *Commentary* 2:26-a, p. 111.

73   Cited in J. F. Hall, *Translated Correctly*.

74   J. H. Sailhamer, *Genesis*, pp. 20-23. See Revelation 21:1; Isaiah 65:17. See also *Commentary* 1:6-g, p. 48; 2:1-c, p. 93; *Excursus 7: Time and Eternity*, p. 537.

75   L. Turner, *Announcements*.

76   B. T. Arnold, *Genesis*, p. 25.

77   J. H. Sailhamer, *Genesis*, p. 20.

78   Emphasis added. See also Psalm 96:5.

79   I.e., creation from nothing, erroneously inferred from Psalm 33:6, 9 and 2 Esdras 6:38.

80   S. Sandmel, *et al.*, *2 Maccabees*, 7:28, p. 243.

81   N. M. Sarna, *Genesis*, p. 5.

82   J. Smith, Jr., *Teachings*, 5 January 1841, p. 181, consistent with Abraham 4:1.

*1 And it came to pass that the Lord spake unto Moses, saying: Behold, I reveal unto you concerning this heaven, and this earth; write the words which I speak. I am the Beginning and the End, the Almighty God; by mine Only Begotten I created these things; yea, in the beginning **I created the heaven, and the earth** upon which thou standest.*

*2 And the **earth was without form, and void**; and I caused darkness to come up upon the face of the deep; and my Spirit moved upon the face of the water; for I am God.*

because, said he, the term "does not mean to create out of nothing; it means to organize—the same as a man would organize materials and build a ship. Hence we infer that God had materials to organize the world out of... chaotic matter."[83] Barney concludes that historical and scientific evidence "strongly favors Joseph Smith's rejection of *creatio ex nihilo*."[84]

the heaven and the earth. The use of the definite article in such phrases typically signifies a *merism*, two opposing words that, taken together, are meant to denote a whole—in this case the entirety of the created universe.[85] The same terms used separately in later verses are taken to refer "to the sky and the dry land in the more restricted and concrete sense."[86] Opposing the interpretation of this phrase as a merism, Cassuto argues that the "ancient Hebrew conceived God alone as a unity; what we designate 'the universe,' they regarded as two separate entities: the heavens are the Lord's heavens, but the earth He has given to the sons of men."[87] Both an earlier phrase ("this heaven and this earth") and a subsequent elaboration ("the earth upon which thou standest") in the book of Moses version of this verse argue in favor of Cassuto's reading.

2   a   *earth was without form, and void.* Choice of an appropriate translation of the Hebrew corresponding to this phrase depends on the grammatical interpretation of the verb "to be":

- Friedman finds evidence for its rendering in the past perfect form ("the earth had been shapeless and formless"), with the resulting implication that the earth "had already existed in this shapeless condition *prior to the [period of] Creation* [described in scripture]" as "an undifferentiated, shapeless fluid"[88] corresponding to unorganized matter.

- Tvedtnes, interpreting this phrase as describing a condition existing *at the moment of the Creation*, translated it as "the earth then being [or having become] uninhabited and desolate," implying "that Elohim's work with the earth was begun because it was (or had become) unpopulated, covered with the waters of a flood." He notes that in Moses 2:2 that "God says he caused the darkness to appear;"[89] and

- Both Abraham 4:2 and direct statements by Joseph Smith[90] describe the "empty and desolate" state of the earth *after its initial creation*. The phrase "they had not formed anything but the earth"[91] should not be taken in its absolute sense that nothing else in the universe had yet been made, but rather that no feature of the newly-organized earth had yet appeared.

without form, and void. The term does not imply an "ominous chaos" but rather an "unproductive 'emptiness.'"[92] The difficult Hebrew phrase *tohu wa-bohu*, corresponding to the book

83   *Ibid.*, 7 April 1844, pp. 350-351.

84   K. L. Barney, *Six*, pp. 108-112. See also H. R. Johnson, *Big Bang*; K. E. Norman, *Ex Nihilo*; B. T. Ostler, *Nothing*; S. D. Ricks, *Ex Nihilo*. "The primary transition is not from nothingness to being but from chaos to order" (T. L. Brodie, *Dialogue*, p. 133). See also *Commentary* 2:2-a, p. 95.

85   C. Westermann, *Genesis 1-11*, p. 101.

86   N. M. Sarna, *Genesis*, p. 5.

87   U. Cassuto, *Adam to Noah*, p. 20. See Psalm 115:16. Sacks rightly observes that the phrase "does not present itself with the same unity expressed by the [Greek] word *kosmos*" (cited in T. L. Brodie, *Dialogue*, p. 133).

88   R. E. Friedman, *Commentary*, p. 6, emphasis mine.

89   J. A. Tvedtnes, *Science and Genesis*, p. 42. See discussion in V. P. Hamilton, *Genesis*, pp. 115-116.

90   J. Smith, Jr., *Teachings*, 5 January 1841, p. 181.

91   Abraham 4:2.

92   B. T. Arnold, *Genesis 2009*, p. 37; cf. T. L. Brodie, *Dialogue*, p. 133.

*2 And the **earth was without form, and void**; and **I caused darkness to come up upon the face of the deep**; and my Spirit moved upon the face of the water; for I am God.*

of Abraham's "empty and desolate," is used two other places in scripture: once, as part of Jeremiah's vision of the return of primal desolation as the result of his people's wickedness,[93] and again in a similar allusion by Isaiah.[94] *Tohu* by itself is likely related to the Ugaritic term for desert. *Bohu* does not have a Semitic cognate and thus seems to be a nonce term coined specifically to reinforce and rhyme with it—as in the English expressions "hodge-podge" and "helter-skelter."[95] Alter suggests the translation "welter and waste" in order to partially capture the rhyming effect of the original through alliteration.[96]

b   ***I caused darkness to come up upon the face of the deep.*** The meaning of darkness in this context is not obvious. The idea of its role as an active element in the events of Creation is strengthened by the causative added in this verse, and also by the corresponding statement in Abraham that the "darkness reigned." These prophetic readings recall ancient creation accounts that portray darkness not merely as the absence of light, but as an entity in its own right.[97] Starting with the Philo's idea of the Logos as the "shadow of God"[98] and drawing on a version of the creation story that passed through the hands of the Gnostics,[99] it is possible to imagine the darkness representing "the Lord himself who passed through veil to… create the world" and who was then enthroned to reign over the waters of chaos.[100]

Another way of interpreting the passage is to take the phrases "darkness… upon… the deep" and "Spirit upon the… waters" as being opposive and temporally successive. A sense consistent with this reading is that God allowed His presence to be withdrawn for a time, bringing darkness (disorder, disorganization) upon the deep, as a precursor to the subsequent moving of His Spirit upon the waters, and the appearance of light (order, organization).

Some commentators see traces of Near Eastern mythology in the description of the subduing of the adversarial powers of watery chaos prior to creation.[101] Scattered in fragmentary form throughout the prophetic, poetic, apocalyptic, and wisdom literature of the Bible are other possible allusions to primordial combat scenes.[102] Parallels have also been noted to Jesus' stilling of the storm[103] and walking on the water,[104] symbolically crushing it beneath his heel.[105] A related idea is found in Orthodox tradition, which holds that the serpent's head was crushed in the River Jordan at the time that Jesus was baptized.[106] D&C 61:17-19 speaks of the cursing of the waters in the last days, and warns that "the destroyer rideth upon the face thereof."[107] Lending credence to an association between this passage in Hebrew and the Babylonian creation account are arguments for an etymological relationship between the term for the god *Tiamat* in *Enuma Elish* and the Hebrew *tehom*, which is translated as "deep" in this verse.[108] On the other hand, in contrast to the view that there is a thematic connection

---

93   Jeremiah 4:23-27.
94   Isaiah 34:11.
95   V. P. Hamilton, *Genesis*, p. 108.
96   R. Alter, *Five Books*, p. 17.
97   Cf. Isaiah 45:7 and N. M. Sarna, *Genesis*, p. 6.
98   Philo, *Interpretation*, 3, 96, p. 61.
99   R. A. Bullard, *et al.*, *Archons*, 95, p. 168.
100   M. Barker, *Gate*, p. 120.
101   N. M. Sarna, *Genesis*, pp. 3, 6; cf. *Commentary* 1:25-e, p. 60. See *Endnote 2-27*, p. 130.
102   E.g., Exodus 15; Job 26:13, 38-41; Psalms 18, 19, 24, 33, 68; 74:12-15; 93, 104; Proverbs 8:22-33; Isaiah 27:1, 40-42; Habakkuk 3:8; Revelation 12:1-12. See M. Fishbane, *Myth*, pp. 37-92.
103   Mark 4:35-41.
104   Mark 6:45-51.
105   N. Wyatt, *Space*, pp. 95-120. See *Commentary* 4:21-d, p. 266.
106   V. Nersessian, *Treasures*, p. 71. See *Commentary* 1:1-b, p. 42 and 4:31-d, p. 280.
107   Cf. R. M. Zlotowitz, *et al.*, *Bereishis*, p. 230, fn. 1.
108   See also Genesis 49:25; Deuteronomy 33:13; Habakkuk 3:10; Isaiah 51:10. Note that English translations typically add a definite article to *tehom* (i.e., "*the* deep") which does not appear in Hebrew, thus masking its

*2 And the earth was without form, and void; and **I caused darkness to come up upon the face of the deep**; and **my Spirit moved upon the face of the water**; for I am God.*

with Babylonian accounts, some have interpreted this verse as a polemic deliberately intended to rule out any such affinities[109]—though this view is now in decline.[110] Regardless of one's opinion on these possible correspondences, Wenham rightly points out that the "uniqueness and sovereignty of God in Genesis give reports of his deeds quite a different quality from the myths of ancient polytheism."[111]

c **my Spirit moved upon the face of the water.** In Deuteronomy 32:11, the Hebrew term behind moved (*rachaph*) is used to describe an eagle hovering attentively over its young.[112] *Genesis Rabbah* captures the spirit of this interpretation: "The spirit of God hovered like a bird which is flying about and flapping its wings, and the wings barely touch [the nest]."[113] "The basic idea of the [verb] stem is vibration, movement.[114] Hitherto all is static, lifeless, immobile. Motion, which is the essential element in change, originates with God's dynamic presence."[115]

The book of Abraham employs the term "brooding" rather than "moving." This change is consistent with Seixas' book of *Hebrew Grammar* studied by Joseph Smith in Kirtland. Milton interpreted the passage similarly in *Paradise Lost*, drawing from images such as the dove sent out by Noah,[116] the dove at Jesus' baptism[117] and a hen protectively covering her young with her wing:[118] "[T]hou from the first Wast present, and with mighty wings outspread Dovelike satst brooding on the vast abyss And mad'st it pregnant."[119] "Brooding" enjoys rich connotations, including, as Nibley observes, not only "to sit or incubate [eggs] for the purpose of hatching" but also "'to dwell continuously on a subject.' Brooding is just the right word—a quite long quiet period of preparation in which apparently nothing was happening. Something was to come out of the water, incubating, waiting—a long, long time."[120]

Some commentators emphatically deny any connection of the Hebrew term with the concept of brooding.[121] However, the "brooding" interpretation is not only attested by a Syriac cognate[122] but also has a venerable history, going back at least to Rashi who spoke specifically of the relationship between the dove and its nest. In doing so, he referred to the Old French term *acoveter*,[123] related both to the modern French *couver*[124] and *couvrir*.[124] Intriguingly, this latter sense is related to the Hebrew term for the atonement, *kippur*.[125]

---

character as a proper noun and obscuring the possible allusion to *Enuma Elish*. "In the New Jerusalem, where evil is vanquished, there is no sea (Revelation 21:1)" (T. L. Brodie, *Dialogue*, p. 133).

109 For summaries of these arguments, see V. P. Hamilton, *Genesis*, pp. 110-111; C. Westermann, *Genesis 1-11*, pp. 104-106.
110 B. T. Arnold, *Genesis 2009*, p. 38.
111 G. J. Wenham, *Genesis 1-15*, p. 52; cf. B. T. Arnold, *Genesis 2009*, pp. 31-32.
112 F. Brown, *et al.*, *Lexicon*, 7363, p. 934b; U. Cassuto, *Adam to Noah*, p. 25.
113 J. Neusner, *Genesis Rabbah 1*, 2:4, p. 25.
114 See its use in, e.g., Jeremiah 23:9.
115 N. M. Sarna, *Genesis*, p. 7.
116 Genesis 8:6-12. See *Commentary* 1:1-b, p. 42; 3:9-g, p. 136.
117 John 1:32. See Moses 5 *Gleanings*, p. 403.
118 Luke 13:34.
119 J. Milton, *Paradise Lost*, 1:19-22, p. 16; cf. Augustine, *Literal*, 18:36; E. A. W. Budge, *Cave*, p. 44.
120 H. W. Nibley, *Before Adam*, p. 69.
121 E.g., U. Cassuto, *Adam to Noah*, pp. 24-25.
122 F. Brown, *et al.*, *Lexicon*, 7363, p. 934b.
123 From Latin *cubare*—to brood and protect.
124 From Latin *cooperire*—to cover completely.
125 M. Barker, *Atonement*; A. Rey, *Dictionnaire*, 1:555.

*2 And the earth was without form, and void; and I caused darkness to come up upon the face of the deep; and **my Spirit moved upon the face of the water**; for I am God.*

Barker admits the possibility of a subtle wordplay in examining the reversal of consonantal sounds between "brood/hover" and "atone": "The verb for 'hover' is *rchp*, the middle letter is *cheth*, and the verb for 'atone' is *kpr*, the initial letter being a *kaph*, which had a similar sound. The same three consonantal sounds could have been word play, *rchp/kpr*. Such things did happen."[126] "There is sound play like this in the temple style.[127] The best known example is Isaiah 5:7, where justice and righteousness sound like bloodshed and cry."[128] In this admittedly speculative interpretation, one might see an image of God figuratively "hovering/ atoning" over the singularity of the inchoate universe, prior to the dividing and separating process that was initiated by the first acts of Creation.[129]

my Spirit. The Hebrew term for Spirit (*ruach*) has the root meanings of 'wind' or 'breath.' This brings to mind the role of wind as the agent by which water is separated in two other places in the Bible—at the conclusion of the Flood[130] and at the crossing of the Red Sea.[131] In a poetic sense, the Spirit can be seen as the light-bearing, life-giving breath of God, blowing away the darkness of the deep.

water. The singular rather than the plural term for "water" appears in OT2.[132] However "waters,"[133] the original term in Genesis, is used in OT1 as well as in the later translation of the book of Abraham. This raises the possibility that the change in OT2 was made erroneously or on John Whitmer's initiative rather than the Prophet's.[134]

The most obvious implication of Abraham 4:2 is that the waters corresponded to the terrestrial seas that covered the earth following its initial creation. Some commentators, however, have associated the term "water" in its singular form with unorganized matter— the unexplained unity that existed prior to the creation process of demarcation, distinction, separation, and naming.[135] Summarizing the opinion of Jewish sages, Zlotowitz writes: "The 'water' mentioned in this verse is not the water that is in the 'seas.'[136] It is clear that there was a certain common matter which was called 'water.' Afterwards, it was divided into three forms; a part of it became 'seas,' another part of it became 'firmament'; a third part became that which is above the 'firmament'—entirely beyond the earth.[137] Perhaps this is why… water is invariably in the plural form—suggestive of this pluralistic division."[138] *Genesis Rabbah* suggests that a watery origin of all things is behind the etymology of the plural term "heavens": "And God called the firmament heaven (*sha*)."[139] Rav said: *Shamayim* is a composite of *esh* ('fire') and *mayim* ('water'). The Holy One took fire and water, and worked them into each other, and out of the two, heaven was made.[140]"

Although no explicit blessing of the waters is mentioned in Moses' account, D&C 61:14 records: "Behold, I, the Lord, in the beginning blessed the waters; but in the last days, by

---

126   M. Barker, *11 June 2007.*
127   See M. Barker, *Hidden*, pp. 15-17.
128   M. Barker, *11 June 2007.*
129   See H. J. Hodges, *Dove* for a cogent analysis of Milton's sources and of general Hebrew-to-English translation issues. See also *Commentary* 1:1-b, p. 42 and 4:5-b, p. 246.
130   JST Genesis 8:47.
131   N. M. Sarna, *Genesis*, p. 6. See Exodus 14:21.
132   S. H. Faulring, *et al., Original Manuscripts*, p. 595.
133   Hebrew *mayim.*
134   K. P. Jackson, *Book of Moses*, p. 10; cf. *Commentary* 2:6-a, p. 104 and 2:21-a, p. 110.
135   C. Roy, *Liquide.*
136   Moses 2:10.
137   See M. Maimonides, *Guide*, 2:30, 2:352-353.
138   R. M. Zlotowitz, *et al., Bereishis*, p. 38. See D. Kimhi's commentary on Genesis, excerpted in E. Monk, *Hachut.*
139   Moses 2:8.
140   H. N. Bialik, *et al., Legends*, 18, p. 9; J. Neusner, *Genesis Rabbah 1*, 4:7, p. 43; cf. J. Hirschman, *Baraita*, p. 6.

3 And I, God, said: **Let there be light***; and* **there was light***.*

the mouth of my servant John, I cursed the waters." The mention of John's cursing may have reference to the events of Revelation 8:8-11 and Revelation 13.[141]

3 **a** ***Let there be light.*** God's words heralding the coming of light constitute His first creative act.[142] This utterance introduces the theme of a God who works in Creation and in history through commands "whose execution must necessarily follow."[143] Execution is assured as the result of a pattern including not only speech,[144] but also action,[145] inspection,[146] and evaluation[147]—a sequence repeated seven times in this chapter.

The formula "Let there be" is expressed three times in the Creation account, each time for celestial phenomena: for light,[148] for the firmament,[149] and for the sun and moon.[150] In the case of the firmament and the sun and moon, the "Let there be" formula is followed with the statement that God "made" them,[151] the underlying Hebrew describing a process of formation from preexisting materials rather than through God's utterance alone.[152]

b ***there was light.*** The nature of the light referred to in this verse is not explained. Several possibilities have been suggested. Some interpreters see this event as consonant with the prevailing scientific view that describes the birth of our universe as a sudden burst of light and energy of unimaginable scale. Others see this phrase as referring to a "local" event whereby the natural light of the sun was created.[153] It is, of course, a given that the sun was created prior to the fourth day, though from the vantage point of earth no light will "appear in the firmament" until that later time.[154]

In contrast to such naturalistic readings, Nibley's interpretation seems more consistent with related scriptural passages—namely, that the light referred to was the result of God's presence: "All this time the Gods had been dwelling in light and glory, but the earth was dark… This was not the first creation of light. Wherever light comes into darkness, 'there is light.'"[155] Consistent with this view, President John Taylor wrote that God "caused light to shine upon [the earth] before the sun appeared in the firmament; for God is light, and in him there is no darkness.[156] He is the light of the sun and the power thereof by which it was made; he is also the light of the moon and the power by which it was made; he is the light of the stars and the power by which they are made."[157] D&C 88:12-13 continues this description to make it clear that this light is something over and above mere physical light as generally conceived, since it not only "enlighteneth your eyes" but also "quickeneth your understandings," governs and "giveth life to all things," and "proceedeth forth from the presence of God to fill the immensity of space."[158] As Isaac Watts expressed: "In vain the bright, the burning sun / Scatters his feeble light; / 'Tis Thy sweet beams create my noon; / If Thou withdraw, 'tis night."[159]

---

141   See *Commentary* 2:22-a, p. 110.
142   C. Westermann, *Genesis 1-11*, p. 110.
143   *Ibid.*, p. 111.
144   On God's creation through speech, see Jacob 4:9.
145   Moses 2:4, 7, 12, 16, 21, 25, 27.
146   Moses 2:3, 7, 9, 11, 15, 24, 30.
147   Moses 2:4, 10, 12, 18, 21, 25, 31.
148   Moses 2:3.
149   Moses 2:6.
150   Moses 2:14. See N. M. Sarna, *Genesis*, p. 7.
151   Moses 2:7, 16.
152   R. E. Friedman, *Commentary*, pp. 6-7.
153   R. D. Draper, *et al.*, *Commentary*, p. 193.
154   Moses 2:14-19. See F. B. Salisbury, *Creation*, p. 71.
155   H. W. Nibley, *Before Adam*, p. 69.
156   See 1 John 1:5; cf. Psalm 104:2.
157   J. Taylor, *31 December 1876*, p. 327. See D&C 88:7-9.
158   Cf. Psalm 36:9. See *Commentary* 2:1-e, p. 94 and *Excursus 7: Time and Eternity*, p. 537.
159   I. Watts, *Hymns*, God, my only Happiness (Psalm 73:25), 2:94, p. 432.

MOSES 2

*3 And I, God, said: Let there be light; and **there was light**.*

*4 And **I, God, saw the light**; and that light was good. And I, God, divided the light from the darkness.*

The idea of God Himself as the source of this special light is consistent with many ancient sources.[160] For example, rabbinical commentators saw the light at the beginning of Creation as the splendor of God Himself, who "cloaked himself in it as a cloak" and it "shone forth from one end of the world to the other."[161] Rabbinic tradition further explained that the wicked are not worthy to enjoy this light of God's presence, therefore it was stored away after the seventh day of Creation to be enjoyed later by the righteous in the Messianic Age.[162] A corresponding light was said to fill the place of God's presence in the temple: "The brightness of the Holy of Holies was the light of Day One, before the visible world had been created... Those who entered the Holy of Holies entered this place of light, beyond time and matter, which was the presence of 'the King of kings and Lord of lords who alone has immortality and dwells in unapproachable light.'[163] This was the place of glory to which Jesus knew he would return after the crucifixion, 'the glory which I had with thee before the world was made.'[164] In the *Gospel of Thomas*, Christians are described as the new high priesthood who enter the light, and Jesus instructed his disciples to say to the guardians (the cherub guardians of Eden?) 'We came from the light, the place where the light came into being on its own accord and established [itself]...'"[165]

Related to these concepts is the idea that the heavenly hosts—variously described as including the angels, the sons of God, and the souls of humanity—were part of the light on Day One of Creation.[166] Although a more limited version of this idea is often associated with the fathers of the early Christian church, its origin actually goes back centuries earlier to strands of Jewish tradition. For example, *Jubilees* reports that on the first day God created various ranks of angels along with "all of the spirits of his creatures which are in heaven and on earth."[167] Zoroastrian texts also speak of a spiritual creation of all mankind (and also of the spirits who chose to follow the evil *Angra Mainyu*) prior to the physical creation.[168] In contrast to later Christian thought that characterized the angels as a different race of beings than man, Joseph Smith taught that "there are no angels who minister to this earth but those who do belong or have belonged to it"—i.e., as human mortals.[169] Note that in Hebrew, the same word (*malak*) is used for "angel" and "messenger."[170]

4   a   I, God, saw the light. This phrase recalls the idea from quantum theory that certain properties at the atomic scale cannot be said to "be there" until they are revealed to an experimental observer—a notion that can be interpreted as blurring the distinction between reality and information. Nibley muses: "[L]ight itself is relative, a part of the energy spectrum seen by some being with the capacity to be aware of it... Basic chemicals react to light, but are they aware of it—do they comprehend it?"[171]

---

160   See, e.g., J. L. Kugel, *Instances*, pp. 157-160.

161   J. Neusner, *Genesis Rabbah 1*, 3:4, p. 29; cf. Psalm 104:2, J. ben Solomon, *Chronicles*, 1:4-5, p. 6.

162   D. C. Matt, *Zohar 1*, Be-Reshit 1:31b, p. 192; J. Neusner, *Genesis Rabbah 1*, 3:6, p. 30; Rashi, *Genesis Commentary*, 1:4, pp. 5-6. See *Excursus 14: The Garden of Eden as a Prototype for the Temple*, p. 555.

163   1 Timothy 6:16.

164   John 17:5.

165   M. Barker, *Revelation*, p. 22; cf. H. W. Nibley, *Message 2005*, pp. 440-441. See H. Koester, *et al.*, *Thomas*, 50, p. 132.

166   M. Barker, *Angels*, p. 29. See the overview of Moses 3, p. 136. For more on this topic, see *Commentary 2:4-c*, p. 101; *3:1-b*, p. 151; *Excursus 8: The Origin and Premortal Existence of Human Spirits*, p. 540.

167   O. S. Wintermute, *Jubilees*, 2:2, p. 55.

168   E.g., F. M. Müller, *Bundahis*, 1:1-14, pp. 3-6.

169   D&C 130:5.

170   See discussion in M. Barker, *Hidden*, pp. 61-62; M. Barker, *Angel Priesthood*, pp. 124-126.

171   H. W. Nibley, *Before Adam*, p. 69.

*4 And **I, God, saw the light**; and **that light was good**. And **I, God, divided the light from the darkness**.*

John 1:5 and D&C 88:6 could be seen as stressing related themes. Whereas "the light shineth in darkness; and the darkness comprehended it not," Jesus Christ, by way of contrast, "ascended up on high, as also he descended below all things, in that he comprehended all things, that he might be in all and through all things, the light of truth."

C. S. Lewis beautifully expressed the fact that it is possible to learn to distinguish between good and evil without partaking of sin, when in *Perelandra* he has the King say to Ransom: "We have learned of evil, though not as the Evil One wished us to learn. We have learned better than that, and know it more, for it is waking that understands sleep and not sleep that understands waking."[172]

b *that light was good.* Light makes it possible to discern differences and, in turn, to discern differences brings light.[173] Both the Hebrew text of Genesis and the English text of the book of Abraham describe an event involving perception, evaluation, and understanding, not passive visual examination: e.g., "that light was good,"[174] "They… comprehended the light, for it was bright."[175]

Note that this judgment of the light's goodness precedes the separation of light and darkness. Even though the formula expressing God's approval, repeated seven times in this account, affirms His unqualified acceptance of all the results of Creation,[176] most commentators see this order of events as "an indication of the divine 'preference' for the light."[177]

OT1 reads "the light was good."[178]

c *I, God, divided the light from the darkness.* The process of Creation involves the making and naming of distinctions. In the beginning, all is unorganized matter; later God divides the light from the darkness, the water above from that below the firmament, and the dry land from the sea. He then differentiates among the different species of plants and animals "after their kind," between man and the animal kingdom, between man and woman, and finally between the seventh day and the other six days of Creation.[179]

The Hebrew root *bdl*—divide or separate—occurs explicitly five times in the first chapter,[180] and the expression "after his kind" occurs ten more times,[181] describing the separation into different kinds of species. Significantly, the same Hebrew root appears in Exodus within temple contexts describing the need for a veil to divide "between the Holy Place and the Most Holy"—the place of light where God dwells.[182]

divided the light from the darkness. If the light mentioned previously includes the glory and presence of God, the angels, and the spirits of men and all other creatures, what does it mean to say that this light was divided from the darkness? Assuming that the events of the first day of Creation took place in the spirit world,[183] it is possible to see an allusion to the premortal separation of the spirits who rebelled ("the darkness") and were cast out of the

---

172   C. S. Lewis, *Perelandra*, p. 179.

173   R. Griffith-Jones, *Witnesses*, pp. 296-297.

174   Moses 2:4.

175   Abraham 4:4. See N. M. Sarna, *Genesis*, p. 7.

176   N. M. Sarna, *Genesis*, p. 7.

177   C. Westermann, *Genesis 1-11*, p. 113.

178   S. H. Faulring, *et al.*, *Original Manuscripts*, p. 86.

179   See R. E. Friedman, *Commentary*, p. 7.

180   Moses 2:4, 6, 7, 14, 18.

181   Moses 2:11, 12 (twice), 21 (twice), 24 (twice), 25 (three times).

182   Exodus 26:33; cf. Psalm 104:2; Isaiah 40:22; Jeremiah 10:12; Ezekiel 42:20; 2 Nephi 8:13; D&C 104:14; overview of Moses 3, p. 148.

183   M. Barker, *Revelation*, p. 22.

*4 And I, God, saw the light; and that light was good. And **I, God, divided the light from the darkness**.*

*5 And **I, God, called the light Day**; and the darkness, I called **Night**; and **this I did by the word of my power**, and it was done as I spake; and the evening and the morning were the first day.*

presence of God ("the light").[184] The tenor aria of the archangel Uriel from Haydn's 1798 *Die Schöpfung* ("The Creation") beautifully expresses the idea: "Now vanish before the holy beams / The gloomy shades of ancient night; / The first day appears. / Now chaos ends, and order fair prevails. / Affrighted fly hell's spirits black in throngs: / Down they sink in the deep abyss / To endless night."[185] A parallel to this event can be seen in the book of Enoch where rebel angels (in this case, the Watchers,[186] rather than the premortal hosts of Satan) are sent to dwell forever in the abyss.[187]

Allusions to similar themes can be traced to Jewish sources. For example, addressing a question about the division of light and darkness on the first day, Rabbi Yannai said that it referred to the day of judgment.[188]

Joseph Smith observed that: "wherever light shone, it stirred up darkness. Truth and error, good and evil, cannot be reconciled."[189]

5   a   ***I, God, called the light Day.*** God's absolute sovereignty over His creations is shown through His naming of Day and Night, the firmament, the sea, and the earth.[190] In similar fashion, having been granted dominion by God,[191] man's sovereignty over all other creatures will be affirmed when he is assigned the task of naming the animals.[192]

  b   ***Night.*** The phenomenon of darkness at nightfall is not a given everywhere in our galaxy. Our "solar system is located far enough from the galactic center so that there is a phenomenon for us called 'night'.... If we could be transported to a planet orbiting one of the stars in the central regions of the galaxy we would find ourselves overwhelmed with light from all directions. The sky—both day and night—would be packed with a million times more stars than our earthly night sky, and each star would be brighter than the brightest star in our present night sky."[193] To look at this another way, the fact that the sky is dark at night in our part of the galaxy tells us that the beginning of the universe was recent enough that "the light from very distant stars has not had time to reach us yet. That [explains] why the sky at night isn't glowing in every direction."[194]

  c   ***this I did by the word of my power.*** Two interpretations are possible. On the one hand, this phrase, added in the book of Moses, can be seen as a more or less synonymous parallel to the expression that "it was done as I spake." On the other hand, it could be taken to indicate that the light and darkness were "made" in a different fashion than the entities created on subsequent days. A similar phrase, "even according to my word,"[195] recurs in the description of the appearance of the sun, moon, and stars.

184   Moses 4:3-4; cf., e.g., D. Maclagan, *Myths*, p. 11.
185   1:2 — *Nun schwanden vor dem heiligen Strahle*.
186   See *Excursus 24: The Watchers*, p. 585.
187   G. W. E. Nickelsburg, *1 Enoch*, 21:7-10, p. 297; cf. D&C 29:38.
188   J. Neusner, *Genesis Rabbah 1*, 3:8, p. 34; cf. Moses' comment to Satan: "I can judge between thee and God" (Moses 1:15; cf. 1:18) and *Commentary 2:5-f*, p. 104. See also *Commentary 2:3-b*, p. 99; 3:1-a, p. 151; *Excursus 8: The Origin and Premortal Existence of Human Spirits*, p. 540; *Excursus 24: The Watchers*, p. 585.
189   J. Smith, Jr., *Minutes*, 6 October 1843, p. 331.
190   N. M. Sarna, *Genesis*, pp. 7-8.
191   Moses 2:28.
192   Moses 3:19-20. See N. M. Sarna, *Genesis*, p. 22 and *Commentary 3:19-b*, p. 177.
193   E. N. Skousen, *Earth*, pp. 245-246.
194   S. Hawking, *Nutshell*, p. 72.
195   Moses 2:16.

*5 And I, God, called the light Day; and the darkness, I called Night; and **this I did by the word of my power**, and **it was done as I spake**; and the **evening and the morning were the first day**.*

An important clue to the interpretation of this passage can be found in JST John 1:1-19, which invokes the language of Genesis to affirm that the Son, by whom "all things were made," is "the true light, which lighteth every man who cometh into the world."[196] Moses 1:32 specifically equates "the word of my power" with "my Only Begotten Son," a reading that is strengthened by the fact that "Word" is capitalized in OT1.[197]

d   *it was done as I spake.* This formula, and its variants ("and it was done," "and it was so," and "even as I spake"), have been liberally added throughout the book of Moses. The term "ordered" is used in place of "spake" in the book of Abraham—possibly to avoid the assertion that the Creation was accomplished solely by God's speech. Rather, the book of Abraham phrase could be seen as expressing the idea that all of the resultant Creation was accomplished in perfect conformance to His will.[198]

e   *evening and the morning were the first day.* A first notion of "time" appears only after the primeval unity was first divided. Note that evening and morning signify respectively, not the earth's daily sunset and dawning, but rather the suspension and resumption of distinct "times" of divine creativity, corresponding to groups of works performed.[199]

The Hebrew term for day, *yom*, is not only used to refer to a fixed twenty-four-hour period but also to a period of indeterminate length, as in the expression the "day of the Lord"[200] or in Moses 3:4 where it is used to signify the entire period of Creation.[201] Thus we are not limited to supposing that the Creation was accomplished in six solar days or six thousand years but rather can view the 'week' of Creation as part of seemingly overlapping periods of potentially long and varying length.[202]

Note that like the Egyptian practice (and unlike the system that governs the current Jewish religious calendar) each "day" of Creation begins with the dawn.[203] Thus Cassuto translates: "And there was evening and there was morning, one day," and then comments: "When day-time had passed, the period allotted to darkness returned (and there was evening), and when night-time came to an end, the light held sway a second time (and there was morning), and this completed the first calendar day (one day), which had begun with the creation of light."[204] Abraham's account of the Creation follows the same scheme, though with a difference in how it is formulated.

first day. The Hebrew expression means "Day One," differing from subsequent periods of Creation that are described using cardinal numbers (e.g., second, third). According to Barker, some Jewish sages "remembered this as the Day (or the State) in which the Holy One was one with his universe. Day One was thus the state of unity underlying (rather than preceding) all the visible creation… Those who entered the Holy of Holies[, the place in the temple representing both the state before Creation and the state of oneness that would eventually prevail again,[205]] understood how that original unity had become the diversity of the visible creation… [where] everything was created distinct, according to its kind."[206]

196   JST John 1:3, 9; cf. D&C 88:12-13.
197   S. H. Faulring, *et al.*, *Original Manuscripts*, p. 86.
198   See also *Commentary* 2:10-b, p. 105.
199   Cf. Abraham 4:5, 8, 13, ff.
200   E.g., Isaiah 2:12; 13:5, 9; Jeremiah 46:10; Ezekiel 13:5; Amos 5:18, 20.
201   See W. Bradley, *Why*, p. 168.
202   Alma 40:8; B. R. McConkie, *Christ and the Creation*, p. 11; B. Young, *17 September 1876*, p. 231.
203   U. Cassuto, *Adam to Noah*, pp. 28-30; N. M. Sarna, *Genesis*, p. 8.
204   U. Cassuto, *Adam to Noah*, p. 28.
205   Ephesians 1:10; D&C 27:13; 128:18.
206   M. Barker, *Temple Theology*, pp. 24-25. See also P. H. Reardon, *Reflections*, pp. 32-33.

MOSES 2

6 And again, I, God, said: **Let there be a firmament in the midst of the water**, *and it was so, even as I spake; and I said: Let it divide the waters from the waters; and* **it was done**;

7 And **I, God, made the firmament and divided the waters**, *yea, the great waters under the firmament from the waters which were above the firmament, and it was so even as I spake.*

Genesis Rabbah explains the meaning of Day One: "…for the Holy One, blessed be he, gave him one day, and what is that day? It is the Day of Atonement."[207]

6   a   ***Let there be a firmament in the midst of the water.*** From the point of view of the Creation, this verse seems to be describing how the waters were "'divided' between the surface of the earth and the atmospheric heavens that surround it."[208] Figuratively, however, it alludes to the veil that divided off the Holy of Holies in the temple.[209]

The Prophet's translation of Abraham 4:6 may have been informed by his study of Hebrew in Kirtland, where a more precise rendering of Genesis into English would be: "And Elohim said, Let there be an expanse in the midst of the waters and let it divide the waters and the waters."[210] Joshua Seixas' *Grammar*, which was the basis of Joseph Smith's study, notes "expanse" as the meaning of the corresponding Hebrew term for the KJV "firmament." "The verbal form is often used for hammering out metal or flattening out earth, which suggests a basic meaning of 'extending.'"[211]

As in v. 2, the singular rather than the plural term for "water" appears in OT2,[212] though "waters,"[213] the original term in Genesis, is used in OT1 as well as in the later translation of the book of Abraham—raising the possibility that this change was made on John Whitmer's own initiative.[214]

b   ***it was done.*** The fact that the phrase "that it was good" is missing in this instance has been variously accounted for in rabbinical writings. One explanation for the omission is that "rain has no value unless there is dry land to be fructified; [and since] the creative acts relating to water are not completed until the third day, [that] account… appropriately records the formula twice."[215]

A simpler explanation for the omission is that the eyes of a scribe copying the manuscript might have inadvertently jumped from the identical letters that would have appeared on this line and the one following.[216] This argument is supported by the Greek *Septuagint* text, which includes the missing phrase.[217]

7   a   ***I, God, made the firmament and divided the waters.*** Bradley comments: "The formation of a perfectly balanced water cycle is crucial to life on planet Earth. If there were too much carbon dioxide… or water in the atmosphere, then the temperature of the surface of the earth would rise monotonically, giving off more evaporation and causing a greater increase in temperature by trapping more heat and further increasing the temperature until the oceans were boiled dry. On the other hand, if the earth had insufficient greenhouse gases (e.g., water vapor and carbon dioxide), then the residual water might have condensed out of the atmosphere in the form of ice and snow. Since ice and snow have a high luminescence,

207   J. Neusner, *Genesis Rabbah 1*, 2:3, p. 23; cf. *Commentary* 2:4-c, p. 102. For differing explanations of the use of the Hebrew expression "one day" in this context, see J. H. Sailhamer, *Genesis*, p. 28.

208   B. R. McConkie, *Christ and the Creation*, p. 11.

209   L. Ginzberg, *Legends*, 1:51. See the overview of Moses 3, p. 148.

210   P. L. Barlow, *Bible*, p. 70.

211   N. M. Sarna, *Genesis*, p. 8.

212   S. H. Faulring, *et al.*, *Original Manuscripts*, p. 595.

213   Hebrew *mayim*.

214   K. P. Jackson, *Book of Moses*, p. 10. Cf. *Commentary* 2:21-a, p. 110.

215   N. M. Sarna, *Genesis*, p. 8.

216   R. E. Friedman, *Commentary*, p. 10.

217   C. Dogniez, *et al.*, *Pentateuque*, p. 135; R. J. V. Hiebert, *Septuagint*, p. 1.

*7 And **I, God, made the firmament and divided the waters**, yea, the great waters under the firmament from the waters which were above the firmament, and it was so even as I spake.*

8 And I, God, called the firmament Heaven; and the evening and the morning were the second day.

*9 And I, God, said: Let the waters under the heaven be gathered together unto one place, and it was so; and I, God, said: **Let there be dry land**; and it was so.*

*10 And I, God, called the dry land Earth; and the gathering together of the waters, called I the **Sea**; and **I, God, saw that all things which I had made were good**.*

the greater reflectivity of the radiant energy from the earth's surface combined with the lower energy-trapping efficiency of the dry atmosphere would have caused all the water on the surface of the earth to be converted to ice and snow. Thus the final product of an earth with just the right balance of water and carbon dioxide in the atmosphere and water in the oceans to maintain a moderate temperature over much of the earth (2°C-40°C) is quite remarkable."[218]

9 a *Let there be dry land.* Creation stories in many ancient cultures begin with the appearance of the "primeval hill"—the first land mass rising out of the receding waters. In ancient Israel, the holiest spot on earth was the Foundation Stone in front of the Ark within the temple at Jerusalem: "it was the first solid material to emerge from the waters of Creation,[219] and it was upon this stone that the Deity effected Creation."[220] This is one reason why temples are nearly always built upon a high elevation, consistent with the idea of the temple as a sacred mountain.

A rabbinical midrash says that at the time when the dry land was formed, "mountains and hills were lifted up everywhere… and valleys were formed and the waters flowed and collected in them."[221] Bradley concludes that the picture of the formation of dry land is "consistent with known earth history. The dry land mass increased monotonically from 0 percent to the current 29 percent in the first four billion years of earth's history through volcanic activity and plate tectonics. During the past five hundred million years, the forces of erosion seem to have been balanced by the dry land-generating forces of volcanic activity and plate tectonics, giving us a relatively constant land mass. Particularly interesting is the recent scientific evidence that the percentage of land mass appears to be crucial to making earth a suitable habitat for life, and we now have just the optimal amount."[222]

10 a *Sea.* The current text renders this term in the singular with the definite article. However, Genesis has "Seas," and OT1 has "the Seas."[223] A post-1845 change to OT2 gives the reading as the plural "Seas," omitting the definite article.[224]

b *I, God, saw that all things which I had made were good.* Sailhamer comments: "Throughout the opening chapter, God is depicted as the one who both knows what is 'good' for man and is intent on providing the good for him. In this way the author has prepared the reader for the [story of the Fall]."[225] While mankind's limited ability to discern "good from evil" is the inevitable consequence of his lack of experience, he alone is responsible for his arrogance in the face of this ignorance whereby he exercises his agency to "set… aside" the "counsel of God."[226] It is in light of mankind's propensity to suppose that they know good from evil "of

218 W. Bradley, *Why*, pp. 172-173.
219 Psalm 104:7-9.
220 J. M. Lundquist, *Meeting Place*, p. 7. See *Figure* 3-10, p. 147.
221 M.-A. Ouaknin, *et al.*, *Rabbi Éliézer*, 5, p.39.
222 W. Bradley, *Why*, p. 173.
223 S. H. Faulring, *et al.*, *Original Manuscripts*, p. 87.
224 *Ibid.*, p. 595; K. P. Jackson, *Book of Moses*, p. 68.
225 J. H. Sailhamer, *Genesis*, p. 27.
226 2 Nephi 9:28.

*10 And I, God, called the dry land Earth; and the gathering together of the waters, called I the Sea; and **I, God, saw that all things which I had made were good**.*

*11 And I, God, said: **Let the earth bring forth grass**, the herb yielding seed, the fruit tree yielding fruit, after his kind, and the tree yielding fruit, whose seed should be in itself upon the earth, and it was so even as I spake.*

themselves" that scripture portrays mankind's ongoing rebellion "not merely as… sin, but also as the work of fools."[227]

With this in mind, it is interesting to note that in the fourth chapter of Abraham, God's evaluative appraisals of the goodness of His work are actually replaced by repeated variations of a phrase that describes the unbroken thread of perfect obedience running through the entire process of Creation: "and the Gods saw that they were obeyed."[228] This theme appears in the account of the creation of the earth and the waters,[229] the plants,[230] the lights in the heavens,[231] and the animals.[232] To the rule of obedience that governs the universe, man is portrayed as the sole sad exception.[233]

Nibley sees God's unfailing respect for the exercise of agency as enabling what he calls "the principle of maximum participation": "'They obeyed'[234] is the active voice, introducing a teaching that, in my opinion, is by far the most significant and distinct aspect of Mormonism. It is the principle of 'maximum participation,' of the active cooperation of all of God's creatures in the working out of his plans, which, in fact, are devised for their benefit: "This is my work and my glory…'[235] Everybody gets into the act. Every creature, to the limit of its competence, is given the supreme compliment of being left on its own, so that the word 'obey' is correctly applied. 'We will go down, for there is space there, and we will take of these materials, and we will make an earth whereon these may dwell.'[236] Why? 'And we will prove them herewith, to see if they will do all things whatsoever the Lord their God shall command them.'[237] What he commands is what will best fulfill the measure of their existence, but they are not forced to do it—they are not automata. Adam was advised not to eat the fruit but was told at the same time that he was permitted to do it.[238] It was up to him whether he would obey or not. If he did obey, he would qualify for a higher trust."[239]

11   a   *Let the earth bring forth grass.* Nibley notes that the corresponding phrase in Abraham: "Let us prepare the earth to bring forth grass" makes it clear that "what they ordered was not the completed product, but the process to bring it about, providing a scheme under which life might expand… Note the future tense: the [earth is] so treated that [it] will have the capacity. The Gods did not make [grass] on the spot but arranged it so that in time they might appear. They created the potential."[240]

grass. Though the English text seems to imply four kinds of plant life (grass, herb, two kinds of trees), the underlying Hebrew word rendered grass (*deshe'*) is actually a generic term

227   J. H. Sailhamer, *Genesis*, p. 27.

228   See M. Fishbane, *Myth*, pp. 101-102 for a parallel from the Midrash.

229   Abraham 4:10.

230   Abraham 4:12.

231   Abraham 4:18.

232   Abraham 4:21, 25; cf. P. Alexander, *3 Enoch*, 19:9, p. 699.

233   Helaman 12:4-26; Jeremiah 5:22-24; G. W. E. Nickelsburg, *1 Enoch*, 2:1-5:4, p. 150; *Commentary* 2:31-a, p. 118.

234   Abraham 4:18.

235   Moses 1:39.

236   Abraham 3:24.

237   Abraham 3:25.

238   Moses 3:17.

239   H. W. Nibley, *Before Adam*, p. 71. See *Commentary* 4:11-c, p. 254. and the discussion of agency in K. E. Robson, *Response*, pp. 415-418.

240   H. W. Nibley, *Before Adam*, p. 70.

*11 And I, God, said: Let the earth bring forth grass, the herb yielding **seed**, the fruit **tree** yielding **fruit**, **after his kind**, and the tree yielding fruit, whose seed should be in itself upon the earth, and it was so even as I spake.*

12 And the earth brought forth grass, every herb yielding seed after his kind, and the tree yielding fruit, whose seed should be in itself, after his kind; and I, God, saw that all things which I had made were good;

*13 And the evening and the morning were the **third day**.*

*14 And I, God, said: **Let there be lights in the firmament of the heaven**, to divide the day from the night, and let them be for signs, and for seasons, and for days, and for years;*

for vegetation which is subdivided into plants (herbs) and fruit trees in the last part of the verse.[241] Thus, a plainer translation might read: "Let the earth bring forth vegetation: both the herb yielding seed, and the fruit tree yielding fruit."

b   ***seed… tree… fruit.*** "[T]he Hebrew words *zera, es,* and *peri* mean, respectively, 'semen or embryos of any plant species,' 'any large plant containing woody fiber,' and 'the food and/or embryos produced by any living thing.'"[242]

c   ***after his kind.*** Elder Boyd K. Packer has written: "No lesson is more manifest in nature than that all living things do as the Lord commanded in the Creation. They reproduce 'after their own kind.'[243] They follow the pattern of their parentage."[244] The Prophet Joseph Smith said that it is a "fixed and unalterable… decree of the Lord that every tree, fruit, or herb bearing seed should bring forth after its kind, and cannot come forth after any other law or principle."[245] This "decree" is expressed within the elegant economy of the laws of genetics.

13   a   ***third day.*** Starting with this verse, Abraham's account uses the term "time" rather than "day."

14   a   ***Let there be lights in the firmament of the heaven.*** Unlike the Genesis account, which describes the appearance of plant life before the sun and moon lighted the earth, the Creation sequence presented in the temple endowment follows a different ordering and division of events.[246] Joseph Smith's teachings support the fact that these heavenly bodies were created prior to the earth: "… the starry hosts were worlds and suns and universes, some of which had being millions of ages before this earth had physical form."[247] Hence, it is clear that vv. 14-15 do not describe the *creation* of the sun, moon, and stars but rather "the appearance of the sun through the darkness, much the way the sunrise is described in Genesis 44:3, Exodus 10:23, and Nehemiah 8:3."[248] As in several other places in Genesis, the event is phrased in "phenomenal language," i.e., "wording that represents things as they appear to a casual human observer on the face of the earth."[249] For example, commenting on the term lights as it is used in this verse, Nibley observes that: "From our position that is just what they are—lights, nothing more."[250]

Bradley comments: "For God to cause the sun and moon to appear to observers on earth, dust and debris had to first be removed from the atmosphere, then the atmosphere itself had to be "transformed from translucent (light-diffusing) to transparent (light-transmitting). It is generally accepted that the earth's early atmosphere was rich in carbon dioxide, which

241   N. M. Sarna, *Genesis*, p. 9; cf. Leviticus 27:30.

242   W. Bradley, *Why*, p. 173.

243   Moses 2:12, 24.

244   B. K. Packer, *Pattern*, p. 289.

245   J. Smith, Jr., *Words*, 20 March 1842, p. 107.

246   R. D. Draper, *et al.*, *Commentary*, p. 189; B. R. McConkie, *Christ and the Creation*, p. 11; F. B. Salisbury, *Creation*, p. 108.

247   E. W. Tullidge, *Women*, p. 178.

248   J. H. Sailhamer, *Genesis*, p. 26; cf. p. 34.

249   W. Bradley, *Why*, p. 164; cf. H. W. Nibley, *Before Adam*, pp. 65-68.

250   H. W. Nibley, *Before Adam*, p. 74.

14 And I, God, said: **Let there be lights in the firmament of the heaven, to divide the day from the night,** *and* **let them be for signs, and for seasons, and for days, and for years;**

15 And let them be for lights in the firmament of the heaven **to give light upon the earth;** *and it was so.*

would have created a greenhouse effect. This greenhouse effect of 'days' one through three would have created a more uniform climate over the entire earth (which is consistent with fossil evidence of lush vegetation covering the entire earth in the past), and would have muted seasonal variations in weather. This greenhouse effect was probably the consequence of a high concentration of carbon dioxide. The creation of plant life in 'day' three would result in the gradual conversion of the atmosphere from one that was carbon dioxide rich to one that is oxygen rich, since plants consume carbon dioxide and give off oxygen. Beginning with a carbon-dioxide-rich atmosphere would benefit the development of flora, while the transformation to an oxygen-rich atmosphere would help to stimulate the development of more complex animal life."[251]

The relatively lengthy chiastic description of the sun, moon, and stars as creations of God, taken with the fact that these celestial bodies are not described by name, has the effect of discrediting the idea of their worship as familiar deities of the ancient world.[252] Stars, however, sometimes retain their status as symbols representing the "sons of God" and "angels" elsewhere in the Old Testament and the Book of Mormon.[253]

b   *to divide the day from the night.* Nibley wrote: "Such a division had already taken place at the beginning, but this was a new time-system for this earth."[254]

c   *let them be for signs, and for seasons, and for days, and for years.* "A 'sign' is a symbol, a mark, an arbitrary indicator, a means of measuring. It is only a sign relative to a particular observer. These lights were not originally created as markers of time, but [now that they were visible to earth] they could be used as such, they could be 'organized for' such."[255] This period of Creation marks "the first appearance of the seasons and the first opportunity to be able to use the celestial bodies to make a calendar."[256] The word "seasons" probably is meant to include the functions of the sun and moon within the calendar of religious festivals.[257]

15 a   *to give light upon the earth.* It is the earth, not the heavens, that require the illumination provided by God's light.[258] Likewise, modern temples are made to brilliantly shine so as to light up their nighttime surroundings, while at the same time being furnished with opaque windows that restrict outside illumination.[259] Thus, the temple's function is symbolically portrayed as *giving* light, not receiving it from elsewhere.[260] "The ancients said: 'Whoever builds windows in his house, makes them wide outside and narrow inside, that they should bring in the light. Not so in the Temple; because there the light was within, and shone forth onto the whole world.' 'As oil gives light—so the Temple gives light to the world.'"[261]

Elder John A. Widtsoe wrote: "Spiritual power is generated within temple walls, and sent out to bless the world. Light from the house of the Lord illumines every home within the Church

---

251   W. Bradley, *Why*, p. 165; cf. D. N. Brems, *Divine Engineering*, pp. 37-39. Contrast the alternative explanations given in M. D. Rhodes, *et al.*, *Astronomy*, pp. 31, 33.

252   C. Westermann, *Genesis 1-11*, pp. 126-132; cf. Basil, *Hexaemeron*, 5:1, p. 76; D. Wilkinson, *Hawking*, pp. 175-176; *Commentary* 2:21-b, p. 109.

253   E.g., Job 38:7 and 1 Nephi 1:10.

254   H. W. Nibley, *Before Adam*, p. 74.

255   *Ibid.*, p. 74; Abraham 4:14; cf. D&C 88:42-45.

256   W. Bradley, *Why*, p. 165.

257   The Hebrew term is translated "holy convocations" in Leviticus 23:2ff. (B. T. Arnold, *Genesis 2009*, p. 42).

258   Cf. N. M. Sarna, *Genesis*, p. 10; S. Shokek, *Yashar*, p. 41.

259   See D&C 43:15-16; J. E. Talmage, *Parables*, p. 5.

260   J. Neusner, *Genesis Rabbah 1*, 3:4, p. 29; cf. Porch of Wisdom, *Faith and Reason*, p. 70.

261   Z. Vilnay, *Sacred Land*, p. 82. See 1 Kings 6:4, Jeremiah 11:16.

15 And let them be for lights in the firmament of the heaven **to give light upon the earth**; *and it was so.*

16 And I, God, made two great lights; the greater light to rule the day, and the lesser light to rule the night, and the greater light was the sun, and the **lesser light was the moon**; *and the stars also were made even according to my word.*

17 And I, God, set them in the firmament of the heaven to give light upon the earth,

18 And the sun to rule over the day, and the moon to rule over the night, and to divide the light from the darkness; and I, God, saw that all things which I had made were good;

19 And the evening and the morning were the fourth day.

20 And I, God, said: **Let the waters bring forth abundantly the moving creature that hath life, and fowl** *which may fly above the earth in the open firmament of heaven.*

21 And I, God, created **great whales**, *and every living creature that moveth, which the waters brought forth abundantly, after their kind, and every winged fowl after his kind; and I, God, saw that all things which I had created were good.*

fitted for its reception by participation in temple privileges. The path from the temple to the home of man is divinely brilliant. Every home penetrated by the temple spirit enlightens, cheers, and comforts every member of the household. The peace we covet is found in such homes. Indeed, when temples are on earth, the whole world shares measurably in the issuing light; when absent, the hearts of men become heavy, as if they said, with the people of Enoch's day, 'Zion is fled.'"[262]

16 a *lesser light was the moon.* Writes Nibley: "[F]rom where I stand, [the moon] can be made to serve a number of special purposes. Aside from measuring time, those heavenly bodies do 'give light upon the earth'[263]… An astronomer… recently calculated the probability of a planet in the solar system having a moon (just one moon, at that) that subtended exactly the same arc in the sky as does the sun from the surface of some planet. The chances are astronomically remote, so remote, indeed, that there seems to be something deliberate about what is otherwise a stunning coincidence."[264]

20 a *Let the waters bring forth abundantly the moving creature that hath life, and fowl.* Sea animals and birds are introduced on the fifth day, while animals who live on land will appear on the sixth.

that hath life. The Hebrew "animate life" is used to distinguish between animals and plants.[265] "In Hebrew, as in many other languages, the words for 'life' (*chay*) and 'animal' (*chayah*) are cognate."[266]

The recurrence of the special Hebrew creation term *bara* in v. 21 suggests to Sailhamer "the beginning of a new stage in the Creation, namely, the creation of 'living beings'…. The choice of the verb… here is also related to the development of the theme of the 'blessing' since there is an alliteration between 'to create' (*bara*) and 'to bless' (*barak*) throughout the account."[267]

21 a *great whales.* The Hebrew term *tannin*, which appears in Canaanite myths to describe an opponent to Baal, refers to a kind of giant sea creature, later associated in the Bible with the monsters Rahab[268] and Leviathan.[269] When Moses and Aaron come to the Egyptian court,

262 Cited in N. P. Olsen, *Logan Temple*, p. vii; cf. A. K. Parrish, *Widtsoe*, p. 44. See Moses 7:69.
263 Abraham 4:15.
264 H. W. Nibley, *Before Adam*, pp. 74-75.
265 J. W. Wevers, *Notes*, p. 10; R. M. Zlotowitz, *et al.*, *Bereishis*, p. 60.
266 L. R. Kass, *Wisdom*, p. 35; cf. Latin *anima*, "soul" or "life," and *animalia*, "animals." See also *Endnote* 3-9, p. 199.
267 J. H. Sailhamer, *Genesis*, p. 35.
268 Isaiah 51:9.
269 Isaiah 27:1.

*21 And I, God, created **great whales**, and every living creature that moveth, which the **waters** brought forth abundantly, after their kind, and every winged fowl after his kind; and I, God, saw that all things which I had created were good.*

*22 And **I**, God, **blessed them**, saying: Be fruitful, and multiply, and fill the waters in the **sea**; and let fowl multiply in the earth;*

23 And the evening and the morning were the fifth day.

*24 And I, God, said: **Let the earth bring forth the living creature after his kind**, cattle, and creeping things, and beasts of the earth after their kind, and it was so;*

25 And I, God, made the beasts of the earth after their kind, and cattle after their kind, and everything which creepeth upon the earth after his kind; and I, God, saw that all these things were good.

the same term is used to describe the creatures into which their staffs (and those of the magicians) were transformed.[270]

In Mesopotamian creation stories, "in order to create, the Creator has first to subdue sea monsters. [Moses 2] is criticizing this false theological view and asserting that God created everything."[271]

    b   *waters.* OT1 and all published versions have the plural "waters."[272] OT2 shows a correction from "water" to "waters."[273]

22 **a**   *I... blessed them.* Following inspection and approval comes benediction. God blesses the fish and fowl to "be fruitful, and multiply." Neither the plants nor the land animals receive a comparable blessing—the plants because they are not "living creatures" and, according to Rashi, the land animals because of the serpent "which was destined to be cursed."[274] Note that "the divine blessing is reserved for the three most critical junctures in the narrative: the introductory statement;[275] the creation of organic life;[276] and the creation of human life."[277]

    b   *sea.* Genesis and OT1 have "Seas."[278] A change in Sidney Rigdon's hand in OT2 crosses out the plural indicator "s."[279]

24 **a**   *Let the earth bring forth the living creature after his kind.* Three kinds of animals are listed: cattle (i.e., livestock), creeping things (i.e., reptiles, insects, and very small animals whose bodies appear to move close to the ground,[280] and beasts of the earth (i.e., wild animals).

Though v. 24 states that the animals were brought forth from the earth, v. 25 clarifies that they were made by God. Sailhamer comments: "Apparently the author wanted to show that though the command was the same for the creation of both the vegetation and the living creatures on land, there was a distinction between the origin of the two forms of life. Vegetation was produced from the land, but the living creatures were made by God himself. Life stems from God and is to be distinguished from the rest of the physical world."[281]

---

270   Exodus 7:9-12 and R. E. Friedman, *Commentary*, p. 11.
271   D. Wilkinson, *Hawking*, p. 175. See *Commentary* 2:14-a, p. 107.
272   S. H. Faulring, *et al.*, *Original Manuscripts*, p. 87; K. P. Jackson, *Book of Moses*, p. 69.
273   S. H. Faulring, *et al.*, *Original Manuscripts*, p. 596; K. P. Jackson, *Book of Moses*, p. 69.
274   Rashi, *Genesis Commentary*, p. 13.
275   Moses 2:1.
276   Moses 2:20.
277   Moses 2:26. See V. P. Hamilton, *Genesis*, p. 132 and *Commentary* 2:2-b, p. 98.
278   S. H. Faulring, *et al.*, *Original Manuscripts*, p. 87.
279   *Ibid.*, p. 596.
280   N. M. Sarna, *Genesis*, p. 11.
281   J. H. Sailhamer, *Genesis*, p. 37.

26 And I, God, said unto mine Only Begotten, which was with me from the beginning: **Let us make** *man in our image, after our likeness; and it was so. And I, God, said: Let them have dominion over the fishes of the sea, and over the fowl of the air, and over the cattle, and over all the earth, and over every creeping thing that creepeth upon the earth.*

26 a *Let us make.* Notably, both other instances of the use of this plural formula in Genesis involve important decisions about the fate of humanity: the expulsion from Eden[282] and the dispersal after the destruction of Babel.[283]

Despite the fact that Seixas's *Grammar*, which Joseph Smith studied in Kirtland, describes the Hebrew term *Elohim* as 'a singular noun with a plural form,'[284] the Prophet came to interpret the term as a plural.[285]

The plural form of this expression has long been an interpretive problem for commentators that look at the Old Testament through the lens of strict monotheism. The phrase is often explained by way of analogy to 'the royal we' used by a king or queen in self-reference, however this does not explain why it occurs only in the early chapters of Genesis and nowhere else.[286] Moreover, the point of the verse at hand is to show "the unique correspondence between God and man, not the majesty of God."[287]

A view consistent with LDS scripture[288] is to imagine the setting for the verse as God addressing a heavenly council.[289] It is significant, observes Faulconer, that: "Human creation is not a simple act of God's *fiat*; rather, creation is a subject of consideration and discussion... God creates humanity in response to others, rather than as a mere act of self-will. Even in the beginning there is already relation: there is no absolute beginning, not even in the beginning."[290] Describing this scene, the Prophet stated: "The head God called together the Gods and sat in grand council to bring forth the world."[291] Friedman likewise writes: "In pagan myth, the chief god, when formally speaking for the council of the gods, speaks in the plural."[292] Since, for most Christian and Jewish commentators, the idea of a plurality of gods is unacceptable, a court of angels is often imagined in place of a polytheistic council—though one is forced to admit that the concept of many gods is hinted at elsewhere in the Old Testament.[293] Further describing the composition of a council of gods, Barker argues that the ancient religion of Israel, prior to alterations by reforming Deuteronomists, clearly distinguished between the "Most High God" and several Sons of God, the chief of which was *Yahweh* (Jehovah).[294] She marshals evidence to show that the early Jewish converts to Christianity who retained shreds of the ancient belief naturally saw Jesus Christ as the bodily manifestation of *Yahweh*, the Holy One of Israel.[295]

The abrupt change of style between the description of the creation of animals ("Let the earth bring forth...") and that of man ("Let us make...") signals the unique status of the man and the woman, created in God's image and likeness as the pinnacle of the "manifestly ascending

282 Moses 4:28; cf. Genesis 3:22.
283 Genesis 11:7; cf. JST Genesis 11:5. See N. M. Sarna, *Genesis*, p. 12.
284 Cited in P. L. Barlow, *Bible*, p. 70.
285 J. Smith, Jr., *Teachings*, 16 June 1844, pp. 371-372.
286 R. E. Friedman, *Commentary*, p. 12.
287 K. A. Mathews, *New American*, p. 161.
288 E.g., D&C 121:32; Abraham 4:26.
289 D. N. Freedman, *Humanity*, pp. 18-21. See also *Commentary* 2:27-b, p. 115.
290 J. E. Faulconer, *Adam and Eve*, 5; cf. Gregory of Nyssa, *On the Origin of Man* and Chrysostom, *Sermons on Genesis* 2:1, cited in A. Louth, *et al.*, *Genesis 1-11*, p. 28.
291 J. Smith, Jr., *Teachings*, 7 April 1844, p. 348.
292 R. E. Friedman, *Commentary*, p. 12.
293 See M. S. Heiser, *et al.*, *Exchange*; M. S. Smith, *Monotheism*; *Commentary* 1:6-f, p. 48; 4:11-b, p. 253; 4:28-a, p. 276.
294 E.g., M. Barker, *Older*, pp. 174-176.
295 E.g., M. Barker, *Angel*, pp. 190-212.

*26 And I, God, said unto mine Only Begotten, which was with me from the beginning: **Let us make man** in our image, after our likeness; and it was so. And I, God, said: Let them have dominion over the fishes of the sea, and over the fowl of the air, and over the cattle, and over all the earth, and over every creeping thing that creepeth upon the earth.*

gradational order" of Creation.[296] Moreover, the phrasing of Abraham's account ("Let us go down and form man.... So the Gods went down to organize man"[297]), together with the additional detail about the creation of Adam and Eve provided in Moses 3, make strikingly clear the increased personal and direct involvement of God in the creation of man. The idea in and of itself does not necessarily conflict with scientific evidence that seems to rule out the concept of a "special creation" for the human body, however, as Jackson comments: "Whatever the process for creating humans may have been, the scriptures are clear in differentiating between that process and the process by which other life was made."[298]

Though more often seen as referring to the physical creation, these verses have sometimes been associated with the creation of the spirits of all mankind.[299] Some support for these readings has been found in D&C 77:12,[300] Abraham 5:2ff., and a statement reportedly made by Joseph Smith that Adam received the First Presidency and its keys[301] "before the world was formed as in Genesis 1:26-28."[302] The latter statement seems coherent only in light of the Prophet's interpretation of the term "world" as meaning the spirits of all mankind: "The world and earth are not synonymous terms. The world is the human family."[303]

As for the central message of the set of verses that introduce the creation of mankind, Sarna comments: "The divine intent and purpose are solemnly declared in advance, and the stereotyped formula 'and it was so' gives way to a thrice-repeated avowal that God created the man, using the significant verb *b-r-*: Human beings are to enjoy a unique relationship to God, who communicates with them alone and who shares with them the custody and administration of the world.[304] At the same time, the pairing of the creation of man... with that of land animals, and their sharing in common a vegetarian diet, focuses attention on the dual nature of mankind, the creatureliness and earthiness as well as the Godlike qualities."[305]

b   ***man.*** Man, as used in this context, is "sex neutral, like 'animal.'"[306] Sarna elaborates: "Hebrew *'adam* is a generic term for humankind; it never appears in Hebrew in the feminine or plural. In the first five chapters of Genesis it is only rarely a proper name, "Adam." The term encompasses both man and woman, as shown in verses 27-28 and Genesis 5:1-2,[307] where it is construed with plural verbs and terminations."[308] President Spencer W. Kimball further explained that man, as used here, was not meant to describe "a separate man, but a complete man, which is husband and wife."[309] By way of contrast, the use of the Hebrew term *'ish* to mean "man" in the everyday sense is eventually introduced only after the woman (*'ishah*) is created.[310]

---

296   N. M. Sarna, *Genesis*, p. 11.
297   Abraham 4:26-27.
298   K. P. Jackson, *Genesis*, p. 82. See *Commentary 3:7-a*, p. 157.
299   J. F. Smith, Jr., *Origin*, p. 99; B. Young, *18 June 1865*, p. 122.
300   See *Commentary 3:2-a*, p. 151.
301   Meaning the keys to administer all the affairs of the Kingdom of God on the earth.
302   J. Smith, Jr., *Words*, before 8 August 1839, p. 8.
303   J. Smith, Jr., *Words*, 5 January 1841, p. 60. For more on spiritual creation of mankind, see the overview of Moses 3, pp. 134-139.
304   Cf. Psalm 8:4-7.
305   N. M. Sarna, *Genesis*, p. 11.
306   L. R. Kass, *Wisdom*, p. 36.
307   Cf. Moses 6:9.
308   N. M. Sarna, *Genesis*, p. 12.
309   S. W. Kimball, *Blessings*, p. 71.
310   See also *Commentary 2:27-a, b*, p. 115; *3:23-c*, p. 183.

MOSES 2

*26 And I, God, said unto mine Only Begotten, which was with me from the beginning: Let us make man **in our image, after our likeness**; and it was so. And I, God, said: Let them have dominion over the fishes of the sea, and over the fowl of the air, and over the cattle, and over all the earth, and over every creeping thing that creepeth upon the earth.*

c   ***in our image, after our likeness.*** Unlike the earlier creatures who were each made "after his kind,"[311] man and woman were made in God's image and likeness.[312] The Prophet Joseph Smith made it clear that this phrase applied not only to the physical appearance of Adam and Eve, but also to their spiritual nature which was, in the beginning, "innocent, harmless, and spotless, bearing the same image as the Gods. And when man fell he did not lose His image, but [only] His character, still retaining the image of his Maker… And through the atonement of Christ, and the resurrection and obedience in the Gospel, we shall again be conformed to the [full] image of… Jesus Christ,[313] then we shall have attained to the [full] image, glory, and character of God."[314] About this "double movement" of image and likeness, Faulconer observes: "humans begin like God and, at the same time, they come to be like him."[315] Notice that these phrases are reversed when the birth of Seth is described: "in his [Adam's] own likeness, after his own image."[316]

Moses 6:9 is more specific than 2:26 in saying that man was created "in the image of his [God's] own body."[317] Joseph Smith spoke very plainly about the meaning of these words: "God Himself who sits enthroned in yonder heavens is a Man like unto one of yourselves—that is the great secret! If the veil were rent today and… you would see Him in all the person, image, fashion, and very form of a man, like yourselves. For Adam was a man formed in his likeness and created in the very fashion and image of God."[318] Munoa concurs, citing Levison who concluded that "The image itself consists of physical similarity to God."[319] He then recalls the tradition in *Genesis Rabbah* 8:10 that "Adam's likeness to God is so exact that Adam must be put to sleep so that the angels might worship the right person… In [*Yalqut Shimʾoni*] 1:20 on Genesis 2:9 the angels exclaim, when they notice Adam's resemblance to God, 'Are there two powers in heaven?'"[320] Neusner finds it "stunning" that the rabbinical commentators took this idea so literally, affirming that even "the angels did not know man from God," stating, "I cannot imagine a more daring affirmation of humanity."[321]

Moses 2:27 equates the image of God to the image of the Only Begotten: "in mine own image, in the image of mine Only Begotten."[322] This recalls similar teachings in Philo and the Gnostics that "the *Logos* is the Shadow/Image of God,[323] [while] the man of [Moses 2:26-7] is the shadow/image of the *Logos*, a shadow of a shadow, as it were."[324]

311   See *Commentary* 2:11-c, p. 107.

312   J. H. Sailhamer, *Genesis*, p. 37.

313   Romans 8:29.

314   J. Smith, Jr., *Words*, 9 July 1843, p. 231, punctuation modernized, bracketed words added for clarification; J. Smith, Jr., *Teachings 2007*, p. 52 interprets and punctuates the citation differently, and changes "retaining" to "retained" (cf. T. G. Madsen, *LDS View*, p. 105).

315   J. E. Faulconer, *Adam and Eve*, 10; cf. Irenaeus, *Heresies*, 5:6:1, pp. 531-532; Moses 4:28. See also Origen, *On first principles* 3:6:1, Diadochus of Photice, *On spiritual perfection* 4, Gregory of Nyssa, *On the Origin of Man*—all three cited in A. Louth, *et al.*, *Genesis 1-11*, pp. 29-30, 33.

316   Moses 6:10.

317   Cf. *Targum Yerushalmi*: "in the likeness of the presence of the Lord" (J. W. Etheridge, *Onkelos*).

318   J. Smith, Jr., 7 April 1844, cited in S. Larson, *King Follett*, p. 200.

319   See also D. N. Freedman, *Humanity*, pp. 16-17, cited in Moses 2 *Gleanings*, pp. 123-124.

320   P. B. Munoa, *Four Powers*, p. 101.

321   J. Neusner, *Confronting*, p. 63. See E. J. Hamori, *Embodied God* and D. L. Paulsen, *Embodiment* for historical overviews of the doctrine of divine embodiment. See also D. N. Freedman, *Humanity*, pp. 16-17; *Introduction*, p. 10; *Commentary* 1:6-g, p. 48; 1:12-c, p. 53; *Excursus 7: Time and Eternity*, p. 537; *Excursus 30: Adam-God Theory and the Heavenly and Earthly Adam*, p. 603.

322   Cf. John 14:7-10.

323   E.g., Philo, *Interpretation*, 3, 96, p. 61.

324   W. Williams, *Shadow*, citing Philo, De opificio mundi 25 (1:6). Philo, however, did not have in mind a physical

*26 And I, God, said unto mine Only Begotten, which was with me from the beginning: Let us make man **in our image, after our likeness**; and it was so. And I, God, said: **Let them have dominion** over the fishes of the sea, and over the fowl of the air, and over the cattle, and over all the earth, and over every creeping thing that creepeth upon the earth.*

> Sarna comments: "The words used here to convey these ideas can be better understood in the light of a phenomenon registered in both Mesopotamia and Egypt where the ruling monarch is described as 'the image' or 'the likeness' of a god… Without doubt, the terminology employed in [Moses] 2:26 is derived from regal vocabulary, which serves to elevate the king above the ordinary run of men. In the Bible this idea has become democratized. All human beings are created 'in the image of God'; each person bears the stamp of royalty."[325]

d   ***Let them have dominion.*** The *Cave of Treasures* has God speaking the following words to Adam: "Adam, behold; I have made thee king, and priest, and prophet, and lord, and head, and governor of everything which hath been made and created; and they shall be in subjection unto thee, and they shall be thine, and I have given unto thee power over everything which I have created."[326]

Nibley comments: "A favorite theme of Brigham Young was that the dominion God gives man is designed to test him, to enable him to show to himself, his fellows, and all the heavens just how he would act if entrusted with God's own power; if he does not act in a godlike manner, he will never be entrusted with a Creation of his own, worlds without end."[327] Similarly, Faulconer observes that "in ruling over the world, humans are its gods, those through whom Creation is either condemned or destroyed. In this, humans are like God: we and the world are judged through our dominion; God and the world are justified by His."[328]

Nibley writes that the word "dominion" comes from the Latin *dominus* ("lord"), "specifically 'the lord of the household,' in his capacity of generous host… [responsible as] master for the comfort and well-being of his dependents and guests."[329] The word expresses "the coercive power of the monarch, consonant with the explanation just given for 'the image of God.' This power, however, cannot include the license to exploit nature banefully, for the following reasons: the human race is not inherently sovereign, but enjoys its dominion solely by the grace of God. Furthermore, the model of kingship here presupposed is Israelite, according to which… the limits of [the rule of the monarch] are carefully defined and circumscribed by divine law, so that kingship is to be exercised with responsibility and is subject to accountability. Moreover, man, the sovereign of nature, is conceived at this stage to be functioning within the context of a 'very good' world in which the interrelationships of organisms with their environment and with each other are entirely harmonious and mutually beneficial, an idyllic situation that is clearly illustrated in Isaiah's vision of the ideal future king.[330] Thus, despite the power given him, man still requires special divine sanction to partake of the earth's vegetation, and although he 'rules' the animal world, he is not here permitted to eat flesh."[331] To have "dominion" in the priesthood sense means to have responsibility,[332] specifically as God's representative on earth.[333] As Nibley succinctly puts it: "Man's dominion is a call to service, not a license to exterminate."[334]

---

resemblance (see J. Gross, *Divinization*, p. 76, citing De opificio mundi 69 (1:18)). See also Ether 3:15-16.
325   N. M. Sarna, *Genesis*, p. 12. See also N. M. Sarna, *Mists*, p. 51; *Commentary* 6:10-a, p. 482.
326   E. A. W. Budge, *Cave*, p. 53.
327   H. W. Nibley, *Dominion*, p. 10.
328   J. E. Faulconer, *Adam and Eve*, 7. For LDS-authored collections of statements from secular and religious sources on man's stewardship for animals and for the earth, see G. E. Jones, *Animals*; R. D. Stratton, *Kindness*.
329   H. W. Nibley, *Dominion*, p. 7.
330   Isaiah 11:1-9.
331   N. M. Sarna, *Genesis*, pp. 12-13. See Moses 2:29-30; cf. Genesis 9:3-4.
332   J. F. Smith, Jr., *Way 1945*, 1931, p. 221.
333   G. J. Wenham, *Genesis 1-15*, pp. 30-31; Hirsch, cited in R. M. Zlotowitz, *et al.*, *Bereishis*, p. 70.
334   H. W. Nibley, *Dominion*, p. 18; cf. T. L. Brodie, *Dialogue*, p. 136.

*27 And I, God, created man in mine own image, in the image of mine Only Begotten **created I him**; **male and female created I them**.*

27 a *created I him… created I them.* In light of the interplay between "him" and "them" in this verse, one strand of rabbinic tradition proposes that "man was originally created male and female in one." In the creation of woman, it was suggested that "God… separated the one (female) side,"[335] in a fashion that recalls Greek traditions telling of originally androgynous humans who were split because of their rebellion, older Egyptian texts where the male earth god (*Geb*) and the female heaven (*Nut*) were separated in the beginning of Creation,[336] and Zoroastrian texts that describe the couple as having been at first "connected together and both alike."[337] More conventionally, however, we might rather suppose that the three lines of this stately poetic diction are structured as they are in order to successively draw our attention to three things: first, to the creation of man in the Divine image; second, to the fact that this resemblance exactly parallels the one that exists between the Father and the Son; and third, to the essential distinction of gender.[338]

With respect to the oneness of man and woman, Elder Erastus Snow expressed that "there can be no God except he is composed of the man and woman united, and there is not in all the eternities that exist, nor ever will be, a God in any other way. There never was a God, and there never will be in all eternities, except they are made of these two component parts: a man and a woman, the male and the female."[339] Similarly, the *Talmud* comments that "a man without a wife is not a man, for it is said, 'male and female He created them… and called their name Man'[340] [i.e., only together, as man and wife, is he called 'Man']."[341]

b *male and female.* Both men and women are created in the divine image and likeness, which has implications not only for human nature but also for the character of God.[342] The 1909 and 1925 First Presidency statements commenting on the origin of man both include the assertion that: "All men and women are in the similitude of the universal Father and Mother, and are literally the sons and daughters of Deity."[343]

Though masculine verbs and adjectives are used with God's name (also masculine), evidence exists that the Ugaritic goddess Asherah was sometimes worshipped as a female consort to Jehovah in preexilic times.[344] Allusions to a female deity are also seen by some in biblical references to Wisdom[345] and in the texts of mystic Judaism referring to the *Shekhinah*.[346] Jeremiah spoke out against the worship of the "queen of heaven,"[347] though, as Peterson points out, such prophetic opposition does not seem to appear before the eighth century BCE.[348] From his study of this verse, Freedman concludes: "Just as the male God is the model

---

335   A. Cohen, *Chumash*, Genesis 2:21, p. 11. See J. Neusner, *Genesis Rabbah 1*, 8:1, p. 73.

336   H. W. Nibley, *Teachings of the PGP*, 7, pp. 88-89.

337   F. M. Müller, *Bundahis*, 15:2, p. 53. See references to related concepts in additional cultures in J. E. Seaich, *Ancient Texts 1995*, pp. 916-918.

338   Cf. U. Cassuto, *Adam to Noah*, pp. 57-58. See D. N. Freedman, *Humanity*, p. 23; *Commentary* 2:27-b, p. 115.

339   E. Snow, *3 March 1878*, p. 270.

340   See Moses 6:10.

341   Yevamos 63a, cited in R. M. Zlotowitz, *et al.*, *Bereishis*, p. 167; cf. 1 Corinthians 11:11. See *Endnote 2-19*, p. 128.

342   R. E. Friedman, *Commentary*, pp. 16-17.

343   H. J. Grant, *et al.*, *Evolution*, p. 244; J. F. Smith, *et al.*, *Origin*, p. 203. Additional information relating to the LDS concept of a "Mother in Heaven" can be found in K. L. Barney, *Mother in Heaven*; E. A. Cannon, *Mother in Heaven*; J. M. Derr, *et al.*, *Relief Society*, pp. 57-58, 449 nn. 129, 131; G. B. Hinckley, *Daughters*; D. L. Paulsen, *Are Christians Mormon*, pp. 96-107. See also M. Barker, *Christmas*, pp. 39-44.

344   D. C. Peterson, *Asherah 1998*, pp. 202-209. See also e.g., Deuteronomy 16:21; 1 Kings 14:15, 23; 2 Kings 17:15-16.

345   *Hokhmah* in Hebrew, *Sophia* in Greek—see, e.g., Proverbs 8:1-31.

346   H. Schwartz, *Tree*, pp. 45-59.

347   Jeremiah 44:17ff.

348   D. C. Peterson, *Asherah 1998*, p. 201. See also M. Barker, *Wisdom*; M. Barker, *Revelation*, pp. 204-206; M. Barker, *Queen*; M. Barker, *Temple Theology*, pp. 75-93; D. N. Freedman, *Humanity*, pp. 22-25 (cited in Moses

27 And I, God, created man in mine own image, in the image of mine Only Begotten created I him; **male and female** *created I them.*

28 And I, God, blessed them, and said unto them: **Be fruitful, and multiply, and replenish the earth,** *and* **subdue it, and have dominion** *over the fish of the sea, and over the fowl of the air, and* **over every living thing** *that moveth upon the earth.*

and image for the first man, so some divine or heavenly female figure serves as the model and likeness for the human female, the first woman."[349]

The First Presidency's *Proclamation on the Family* affirms that gender is an eternal aspect of the spiritual identity of each individual.[350] The terms "male and female" used for Adam and Eve "emphasize their sexuality in a way 'man and woman' would not."[351] Sarna observes: "No... sexual differentiation is noted in regard to animals... The next verse shows [human sexuality] to be a blessed gift of God woven into the fabric of life. As such, it cannot of itself be other than wholesome. By the same token, its abuse is treated in the Bible with particular severity. Its proper regulation is subsumed under the category of the holy, whereas sexual perversion is viewed with abhorrence as an affront to human dignity and as a desecration of the divine image of man."[352]

28 a ***Be fruitful, and multiply, and replenish the earth.*** The Hebrew phrase for "be fruitful and multiply" (*peru urebu*) may be a deliberate play on the "without form and void" (*tohu va-bohu*) of v. 2: "In this case, the living creatures of God's Creation are hereby empowered to perpetuate God's life-giving creativity by bringing still more life into the world, by filling up and inhabiting that which was previously empty and uninhabitable."[353] "The difference between the formulation here and God's blessing to the fish and fowl in verse 22 is subtle and meaningful. Here God directly addresses man and woman."[354]

The word "replenish" can be misleading to modern English speakers. The corresponding Hebrew term *male* does not mean to "refill" but simply to "fill" or "make full." Thus, Sarna renders the command in this verse as "Be fertile and increase, fill the earth."[355]

Turner observes that although keeping this commandment will not be easy in light of the pain of childbirth,[356] the murderous dispositions of some men,[357] the threat of famine and floods,[358] and the failure of mankind to disperse and "fill the earth" as they were commanded to do,[359] the book of Genesis demonstrates that "God intervenes to make sure it is obeyed, willingly or not."[360]

Keller notes that the commandment anticipates the departure of Adam and Eve from Eden, since they "were commanded to multiply and replenish the earth, not the Garden."[361]

b ***subdue it, and have dominion... over every living thing.*** The commandment to "subdue" the earth conveys the idea of settlement and agriculture, as described in Moses 3:5, 15.[362]

2 *Gleanings*, pp. 122-123). For a discussion of related themes in the Book of Mormon, see K. Christensen, *et al.*, *Nephite Feminism*. For a brief summary of the role of female deities in Israelite worship, see, e.g., W. J. Hamblin, *et al.*, *Temple*, pp. 60-63.

349 D. N. Freedman, *Humanity*, p. 24. Some rabbinical sources see the female figure of Wisdom as assisting God in Creation, while others argue vehemently that God had no help of any kind (J. L. Kugel, *Instances*, pp. 160-162).

350 G. B. Hinckley, *et al.*, *Proclamation.*

351 B. T. Arnold, *Genesis*, p. 35.

352 N. M. Sarna, *Genesis*, p. 13. See also *Commentary* 2:26-b, p. 112, 3:23-c, p. 183.

353 B. T. Arnold, *Genesis 2009*, p. 42.

354 N. M. Sarna, *Genesis*, p. 13.

355 *Ibid.*, p. 13.

356 Moses 4:22.

357 Moses 5:31-32, 47; 6:15; 8:18.

358 Moses 8:4, 30.

359 Genesis 11:1-9.

360 L. Turner, *Announcements*, p. 49.

361 R. R. Keller, *Teaching*, p. 103. Cf. D. H. Oaks, *Plan*, p. 73; 2 Nephi 2:23.

362 V. P. Hamilton, *Genesis*, p. 140; cf. D&C 26:1. On dominion, see *Commentary* 2:26-d, p. 114.

*28 And I, God, blessed them, and said unto them: Be fruitful, and multiply, and replenish the earth, and **subdue it, and have dominion** over the fish of the sea, and over the fowl of the air, and **over every living thing** that moveth upon the earth.*

*29 And I, God, said unto man: Behold, I have given you every **herb bearing seed**, which is upon the face of all the earth, and every tree in the which shall be the fruit of a tree yielding seed; **to you it shall be for meat**.*

In light of subsequent events in Genesis, Turner concludes: "Although humans increasingly dominate the animal creation and eventually rule despotically (an intensification of the original command), there is an ironic sense in which animals, through the serpent, exercise an ongoing dominion over the humans (a reversal of the original command)… Also, the earth becomes increasingly difficult to dominate. It overwhelms most of humanity in the Flood, and all of humanity in death."[363]

29 a *herb bearing seed… fruit of a tree.* In the Garden of Eden, man is to eat fruits from the trees and grain sown by seed, whereas the wild green grasses of the field are given for the food of animals.[364]

b *to you it shall be for meat.* For modern English speakers, the term "meat" would be better translated as "food." Vegetarianism is given as the rule in the Garden of Eden; man's use of animals for food will not be explicitly sanctioned until after the Flood.[365] Isaiah's vision of the earth in its paradisiacal glory during the Millennium appears to foresee carnivores and omnivores again becoming herbivorous.[366]

Stephens, *et al.* summarize the kinds of questions that verses 29-30 pose for science:

> If all animals ate plants, the anatomy and physiology of some animals must have changed drastically afterwards. For example, a lion's intestinal tract is only about ten feet long and is well-suited for digesting and absorbing the high-protein nutrients of meat. By contrast, a cow's intestinal tract is nearly sixty feet long and is well-suited for the long, slow process of fermenting and digesting the relatively low levels of nutrients in grasses and hay. A lion fed only grass and hay will soon die of starvation.[367]

That man himself is to some degree responsible for the enmity between humankind and wild beasts is evidenced by a statement from Joseph Smith: "Men must become harmless before the brute creation, and when men lose their vicious dispositions and cease to destroy the animal race, the lion and the lamb can dwell together, and the sucking child can play with the serpent in safety."[368] *2 Enoch* teaches that men will be held accountable for their treatment of animals in this life, asserting that "the Lord will not judge a single animal soul for the sake of man but human souls he will judge for the sake of the souls of their animals" and that at the time of the "great judgment… every kind of animal soul will accuse the human beings who have fed them badly."[369]

363   L. Turner, *Announcements*, pp. 48-49.
364   Moses 2:30. See *Commentary* 3:5-a, p. 154 and 4:24-b, p. 271.
365   JST Genesis 9:10-11.
366   Isaiah 11:7; 65:25. See N. M. Sarna, *Genesis*, pp. 13-14.
367   T. D. Stephens, *et al.*, *Evolution*, p. 173. See the overview of Moses 3, pp. 139-144 for a discussion of different perspectives that bear on this issue.
368   J. Smith, Jr., *Teachings*, 26 May 1834, p. 71.
369   F. I. Andersen, *2 Enoch* 58:4, 6, p. 184.

*30 And to every beast of the earth, and to every fowl of the air, and to everything that creepeth upon the earth, wherein I grant life, there shall be given every **clean herb** for meat; and it was so, even as I spake.*

*31 And I, God, saw everything that I had made, and, behold **all things** which I had made **were very good**; and the evening and the morning were the sixth day.*

30   a   *clean herb.* In Genesis and Abraham, the term "green herb" is used. The term "clean" in the Old Testament sense meant what was allowed or permitted by God's law.[370] Salisbury creatively interprets this change as perhaps allowing for the eating of non-green edible things (e.g., mushrooms) as well as the avoidance of green plants that are "poisonous or otherwise unsuited for certain animals."[371]

31   a   *all things… were very good.* Unlike other living things, God did not pronounce mankind good at the time of its creation. Now that man and woman are both created and blessed, God can pronounce the entirety of His Creation very good—meaning beautiful, appropriate, and "that the all or the whole was now complete, lacking in nothing."[372] Mankind is not yet in itself good in the moral sense—being free to choose, it "remains to be seen whether man will become good, whether he will be able to complete himself (or to be completed)."[373] "Always keep in view," said Brigham Young, "that the animal, vegetable, and mineral kingdoms—the earth and its fulness—will all, except the children of man, abide their creation—the law by which they were made, and will receive their exaltation."[374]

Soon after the Fall, Satan exercised dominion over "his" kingdom[375] and "the wickedness of men [became] great in the earth."[376] Indeed, as Hendel observes, the story of the Flood eventually inverted the perception of God in Moses 2:31 with the statement that: "God looked upon the earth, and, behold, it was corrupt."[377] By way of contrast, the stories of Adam, Enoch, Noah, and others of the righteous throughout in Genesis also establish a pattern of hope, showing that God does not forget the obedient but rather sends them messengers who teach them the gospel and give them additional instructions pertinent to their situation.[378] "As many commentators have noted, the process begun with the Creation in [Moses 2] concludes only with God's covenant with Moses and Israel at Sinai, and in particular with the last action at Sinai: the completion of the Tabernacle in Exodus 40, when Yahweh's divine presence (His *kabod*) enters the Tabernacle to dwell among the Israelites."[379]

---

370   E.g., Genesis 7:2.
371   F. B. Salisbury, *Creation*, p. 73. See *Commentary* 2:29-a, p. 117.
372   L. R. Kass, *Wisdom*, p. 37; cf. C. Westermann, *Genesis 1-11*, pp. 166-167; R. M. Zlotowitz, *et al.*, *Bereishis*, pp. 78-79, 103.
373   L. R. Kass, *Wisdom*, p. 39.
374   B. Young, *30 September 1860*, p. 191; cf. H. W. Nibley, *Dominion*, p. 11. See also *Commentary* 2:10-b, p. 105.
375   Moses 6:15.
376   Moses 8:22.
377   Moses 8:29. See R. S. Hendel, *Poetics of Myth*, pp. 162-163.
378   Moses 5:4-8; Alma 12:28-35.
379   R. S. Hendel, *Poetics of Myth*, p. 163.

Gleanings

Table of Contents

Steven Marx: Eternity Unfolding into Time[380]

In the Bible's last book, where chronicle dissolves into vision, time folds up into eternity. In the Bible's first book, eternity unfolds into time as its stories progress from the opening demarcation of day and night to the Creation…

Terryl L. Givens: All We Have is Historical Time[381]

[Wrote] the religious scholar Wilfred Cantwell Smith, "With the relatively recent rise in Western consciousness… of the new sense of history… and the (consequent?) careful and rigorous distinction between history and myth… what happened by and large was that the West opted for history and rejected myth." Regarding a scriptural event like the earth's creation, for example, he writes, "We may recognize now that the problem… [is] the notion that one is dealing here with historical time, rather than mythical time." But with Joseph [Smith], all we have is historical time—but it is transformed into a dimension that extends infinitely in both directions.

Hugh W. Nibley: The Creation as an Open-Ended and Ongoing Process[382]

The Creation process as described in the Pearl of Great Price is open ended and ongoing, entailing careful planning based on vast experience, long consultations, models, tests, and even trial runs for a complicated system requiring a vast scale of participation by the creatures concerned. The whole operation is dominated by the overriding principle of love.

Hugh W. Nibley: The Organization of the Universe[383]

"And the Gods organized the lights in the expanse of the heaven"[384]… The key word is "organized." That means everything arranged from subatomic particles to molecules, to

380   S. Marx, *Shakespeare*, p. 21.

381   T. L. Givens, *Joseph Smith*, p. 61.

382   H. W. Nibley, *Before Adam*, p. 69.

383   H. W. Nibley, *Drama*, pp. 31-32.

384   Abraham 4:14.

organizing the family, an army, a church, or a galaxy. Here we see the mazy motion of the dancers' chorus and semichorus, as they divide the day from the night and organize themselves into groups to take position, "To be for signs and for seasons, and for days and for years."[385] Again it says not "to be signs," but to be for signs, and for days, and for seasons and for years; they are taking their places for the benefit of man. "And the Gods organized the two great lights, the greater light to rule the day, and the lesser light to rule the night; with the lesser light they set the stars also; And the Gods set them in the expanse of the heavens, to give light upon the earth, and to rule over the day and over the night, and to cause to divide the light from the darkness."[386] Is all that repetition necessary? This is not a laborious tale for the simpleminded, but the unfolding of a splendid pageant, the Dance of Life, the ever-popular torch dance.

Not long ago we used to laugh our heads off at the idea that God created the stars and their motions for the benefit of puny man. Today the shoe is on the other foot. Now we are asked to believe how the unimaginable raging forces of the universe, completely uncontrolled and undirected, should zero in on this little planet with nothing but the most benevolent results, adjusting a score of fine-tuned constants to each other with unerring accuracy in defiance of entropy. Not long ago it was believed that such a coincidence was so rare that it could have happened only once in the universe, that is, that this could be the only possible habitable world. But today it seems that the main concern of astronomers is life on other worlds.

Hugh W. Nibley: The Focus of the Creation Story[387]

Human history is not primarily concerned with the creatures of other ages or of other planets; its proper beginning is placed at that momentous period of transition between the Cretaceous and the Tertiary when the first angiosperms appeared as grass, flowers, shrubs, and trees, supplying sustenance for the elephant, the lion, and other large mammals. The mammoths were the first to appear of those herds of grazing animals, the herd which emerged as soon as the grass was provided—a very sudden event in the course of nature, "an explosion," Loren Eisley calls it. They supplied a livelihood for the predators—the lion, the tiger, and the bear, which preyed upon the herd. All these were in preparation for man.

Times and Seasons: Each Creature to Fulfill the Measure of Its Creation[388]

The world was not made to be annihilated nor the creatures that He has formed; all of them were intended to fulfill the measure of His Creation. The sun, the moon, the stars, the earth, man, beast, bird and fish, all occupy their several spheres, all were made for the glory of God, and all were intended to fill up the measure of their creation, and to bring about His purposes and the beast of the forest, the fish of the sea, or the fowl of the air, all are necessary in the vast works of creation and the chirping sparrow upon the house top fulfills the measure of his creation, in his own sphere, as much as an archangel does in his.... It is true that they move in different spheres and occupy a different glory; but although we cannot now see these various connecting links, the time will come, when we shall hear "every creature in heaven, every creature on the earth, and every creature under the earth, say blessing,

---

385   *Ibid.*
386   Abraham 4:16–17.
387   H. W. Nibley, *Return*, p. 73. See also H. W. Nibley, *Sacred*, pp. 546-547.
388   *The Gathering*, p. 408.

and glory, and honour, and might, and majesty, and dominion, be ascribed unto Him that sitteth upon the throne, and unto the Lamb forever."[389]

Albert Schweitzer: "Father, Bless All Things That Have Breath"[390]

As far back as I can remember I was saddened by the amount of misery I saw in the world around me…

One thing that specially saddened me was that the unfortunate animals had to suffer so much pain and misery. The sight of an old limping horse, tugged forward by one man while another kept beating it with a stick to get it to the knacker's yard at Colmar, haunted me for weeks.

It was quite incomprehensible to me—this was before I began going to school—why in my evening prayers I should pray for human beings only. So when my mother had prayed with me and had kissed me goodnight, I used to add silently a prayer that I had composed myself for all living creatures. It ran thus: "O, heavenly Father, protect and bless all things that have breath; guard them from all evil, and let them sleep in peace."…

From experiences like these, which moved my heart and often made me feel ashamed, there slowly grew up in me an unshakable conviction that we have no right to inflict suffering and death on another living creature unless there is some unavoidable necessity for it, and that we ought all of us to feel what a horrible thing it is to cause suffering and death out of mere thoughtlessness. And this conviction has influenced me only more and more strongly with time. I have grown more and more certain that at the bottom of our heart we all think this, and that we fail to acknowledge it and to carry our belief into practice chiefly because we are afraid of being laughed at by other people as sentimentalists, though partly also because we allow our best feelings to get blunted. But I vowed that I would never let my feelings get blunted, and that I would never be afraid of the reproach of sentimentalism.

Hugh W. Nibley: All Nature Becomes an Enemy to Fallen Man[391]

One of the best-known teachings of the Jews is that when man (Israel in particular) falls away from God, all nature becomes his enemy.[392] Modern revelation confirms this: when all the people became wicked in Enoch's day, "the earth trembled, and the mountains fled… and the rivers of water were turned out of their course; and the roar of lions was heard out of the wilderness."[393] Just so, in the last days "all the growing things will be blighted by the… great lawlessness, and plagues will come over all creatures of all the earth."[394] Where people refuse the gospel, according to Brigham Young, "that land will eventually… become desolate, forlorn, and forsaken"[395] as nature refuses her bounties.

The explanation of this all-out hostility is simple. "The animal, vegetable, and mineral kingdoms abide the law of their Creator; the whole earth and all things pertaining to it, except man, abide the law of their creation," while "man, who is the offspring of the Gods, will not

---

389   See Revelation 5:13.
390   A. Schweitzer, *Light*, pp. 11-13.
391   H. W. Nibley, *Dominion*, pp. 16-17.
392   See, e.g., G. A. Anderson, *et al.*, *Synopsis*, 37(10):3-38(11):1, pp. 42E-43E; 44(24):4, p. 66E.
393   Moses 7:13.
394   See R. Rubinkiewicz, *Apocalypse of Abraham*, 29:14-15, p. 704.
395   B. Young, *28 June 1873*, p. 69.

become subject to the most sensible and self-exalting principles."[396] With all things going in one direction, men, stubbornly going in the opposite direction, naturally find themselves in the position of one going the wrong way on the freeway during rush hour; the struggle to live becomes a fight against nature. Having made himself allergic to almost everything by the Fall, man is given the choice of changing his nature so that the animal and vegetable creation will cease to afflict and torment him,[397] or else of waging a truceless war of extermination against all that annoys him until he renders the earth completely uninhabitable.

David Noel Freedman: God, Man, and Gender in the Hebrew Bible[398]

Even if we cannot entirely probe the mind of *P*,[399] the presumed author of [Moses 2:26-28], we can speak with less hesitation about the editor *R* (for Redactor) who consciously and deliberately associated these passages as part of a larger corpus and a more detailed picture of the Godhead.

God is speaking to others[400] when he says, "Let us make man (*'adam*) in our image, according to our likeness." God will do the making, as is confirmed in verse 27… Humans of both genders are created in the image of God, but that is an image that he already has shared with others, chiefly the *bene 'elohim*,[401] who constitute his associates in the heavenly realm. These are presumably the same ones who are addressed in [Moses 4:28], and who share with God in the knowledge of good and evil, and also in eternal life.

Another very important distinction emerges from our text. Speaking generically, God creates humanity (*'adam*) in his image, but humanity includes both male and female. The specific human being actually created first is "the man" (*ha'adam*), that is, "male," and shares that maleness with God, in the latter's image. While it is often said that the God of the Bible is beyond gender, and that may be true in philosophical or theological terms and categories of thought, that is hardly the case with either biblical language or biblical thinking. In the Hebrew Scriptures, he is always clearly male, even patriarchal. Occasionally, he is described as having qualities and emotions associated with women, especially mothers in childbirth or those bereaved, but these are poetic and metaphoric descriptions which are also applied to human males and do not affect their basic and essential masculinity. As can be shown in numerous ways, the God of the Hebrew Bible is undeniably male and masculine. And so is the first human: *ha'adam*.

It has also been suggested that the God of the Bible is androgynous, having both male and female characteristics, and that the same was the case with the first human being. Later the first man and the first woman were created by dividing the first androgyne into male and female counterparts, which is, to say the least, a very curious and forced reading of the story in [Moses 3]. While the idea continues to have appeal in certain quarters and may find some echoes and evidence in the myths and traditions of various peoples, the Bible shows little awareness of any such possibility, and on any reasonable reading of the Genesis texts such a conclusion cannot be reached or sustained. There is nothing androgynous about the God of the Bible or about the first man.

---

396 B. Young, *23 March 1862*, p. 246.
397 B. Young, *6 April 1852*, p. 203.
398 D. N. Freedman, *Humanity*, pp. 22-25.
399 = the hypothesized Priestly-source behind many portions of the Genesis text.
400 I.e., an assembly of heavenly beings.
401 Hebrew "sons of God."

What about the first woman? I think the clause "male and female he created them" is to be correlated literally with the phrase "in our image, after our likeness." Just as the male God is the model and image for the first man, so some divine or heavenly female figure serves as the model and likeness for the human female, the first woman. We know that goddesses figured notably in the religion of historic Israel and Judah, although ultimately they were banished from the official cult. We have convincing if not conclusive evidence for the association of specific goddesses with different shrines and cult centers in Israel and Judah during the monarchic period, and we can identify them as consorts of Yahweh…

If it is objected that by the time that *P* wrote [Moses 2], the goddesses had been put away and banished from the official religion, which I doubt, then it would still not be difficult to find a divine or heavenly female model or image for female humanity. Such a figure is to be located in a perfectly orthodox biblical context, usually dated in the early post-exilic period, but having roots in the same mythology from which the stories of Creation have their origin. Consider the remarkable passage in Proverbs 8:22-31 in which the status and role of Lady Wisdom (in Hebrew *hokmah*) are described… According to this and other passages, Lady Wisdom was begotten or created before the general Creation, and in fact served Yahweh as co-worker or agent in the process of creation. Further, she was his close and intimate companion in the heavenly home…

[I]t is quite legitimate to imagine the conversation recorded in [Moses 2:26-28]… as being addressed to a person like Lady Wisdom: "Let us make humanity in our image, according to our likeness…" The man was made in the image of the male God Yahweh, and the woman after the likeness of the female companion of God, Lady Wisdom (*hokmah*).[402]

David Noel Freedman: The Basic Likeness Is in Physical Appearance[403]

[W]e note that humanity occupies a unique status in contrast with all of the other created beings on the earth: being made in the image and according to the likeness of God. The basic likeness is in physical appearance, as study of the etymology and usage of both terms shows: *selem* [= image] and *demut* [= likeness]. These terms are used in cognate languages of statues representing gods and humans in contemporary inscriptions, and certainly the intention is to say that God and man share a common physical appearance. If or when God makes himself visible to human beings, they will recognize their own features, and vice versa. The image is the same, and the basic features are comparable. While God is not human and humans are not divine, they share a common appearance, or physique. Whenever God is described in the Hebrew Bible, he has features that human beings also have.[404] The correspondence is by no means limited to body parts, but extends to the whole makeup of God and humans, including mind and spirit, thoughts and words. We must not press the resemblances too far, as there are constant admonitions that God is different in profound respects,[405] but these would hardly be necessary if not for the basic similarities. Only human beings, of all earthly creatures, share image and likeness with the Deity.

---

402 In contrast to Freedman's view, note that God the Father is specifically said to be speaking to His Only Begotten in Moses 2:26.

403 D. N. Freedman, *Humanity*, pp. 16-17. See *Endnote 2-28*, p. 130.

404 Cf. Ezekiel 1:26-28.

405 Cf. Isaiah 55:6-11.

Leon R. Kass: The Most Godlike and Most Questionable of Creatures[406]

The Hebrew word translated "image" is *tselem*, from a root meaning "to cut off," "to chisel"; *tselem*, something cut or chiseled out—in the first instance, a statue—becomes, derivatively, any image or likeness or resemblance. Any image, insofar as it is an image, has a most peculiar manner of being: it both is and is not what it resembles. The image of my granddaughter that smiles at me out of the picture frame on my desk is my granddaughter—not yours. But it is not really she—just a mere image. Although being merely a likeness, an image not only resembles but also points to, and is dependent for its very being on, that of which it is an image. Man, like any other creature, is simply what he is. But according to the text, he is—in addition—also something more insofar as he resembles the divine.… But the text does not exaggerate our standing. Man may be, of all the creatures, the most intelligent, resourceful, conscious, and free—and in these respects the most godlike—but he is also the most questionable. In fact, Genesis 1, read with an eye for the fine print, provides this teaching as well. Man may have powers that resemble divinity, but he is also at most merely an image; man, who quite on his own is prone to think of himself as a god on earth and to lord it over the animals, is reminded by the biblical text that he is, like the other creatures, not divine. Though brought into being by a special creative act, man appears on the same day as the terrestrial animals; though in some respects godlike, man belongs emphatically to the world of animals, whose protective ruler he is told to be. As the later verses about food remind us, we are, like the animals, needy and vulnerable. Man is the ambiguous being, in between, more than an animal, less than a god.[407] This fact—and it is a fact—makes man a problem, as the Bible, even in this celebratory chapter, subtly teaches.

Gregory of Nyssa: We Acquire the Likeness By Free Will[408]

"Let us make man in our image, after our likeness."[409] We possess the one by creation; we acquire the other by free will. In the first structure it is given us to be born in the image of God; by free will there is formed in us the being in the likeness of God.… "Let us make man in our image": Let him possess by creation what is in the image, but let him also become according to the likeness. God has given the power for this. If he had created you also in the likeness, where would your privilege be? Why have you been crowned? And if the Creator had given you everything, how would the kingdom of heaven have opened for you? But it is proper that one part is given you, while the other has been left incomplete: this is so that you might complete it yourself and might be worthy of the reward which comes from God.

Diadochus of Photice: The False Glitter of This Life[410]

All men are made in God's image; but to be in his likeness is granted only to those who through great love have brought their own freedom into subjection to God. For only when we do not belong to ourselves do we become like him who through love has reconciled us to himself. No one achieves this unless he persuades his soul not to be distracted by the false glitter of this life.

406   L. R. Kass, *Wisdom*, pp. 37-39.
407   See Psalm 8:5.
408   Gregory of Nyssa, *On the Origin of Man*, cited in A. Louth, *et al.*, Genesis 1-11, p. 33.
409   Moses 2:26.
410   Diadochus of Photice, *On Spiritual Perfection* 4, cited in A. Louth, *et al.*, *Genesis 1-11*, p. 30.

Endnotes

2-1   See K. Muhlestein, *Flow*, pp. 43-44 for a discussion of the dating of Moses 2-5:43 in conjunction with the conference of the Church.

The transcription of Moses 1-5:43 was to be Oliver Cowdery's only direct contribution to the development of the JST manuscript. In August, he went to live with the Whitmers in Fayette, New York. A few weeks later, with Emma's father Isaac Hale now convinced that Joseph was an imposter and with persecution in the area mounting, the Smiths also moved into the Whitmer home. Shortly after moving in with the Whitmers, Oliver wrote a letter criticizing in strong terms the wording of one of the revelations[411] and, a little while later, also joined the Whitmer family in giving credence to the purported revelations of Hiram Page. After reconciliation with Joseph, Cowdery was instructed to leave on a mission to Ohio and Missouri at the September 26-27 conference.[412] The work of transcribing and copying the translation then fell exclusively to John Whitmer, Emma Smith, and Sidney Rigdon.

2-2   With respect to "certain generalizations shared by Roman, Orthodox, and Protestant Christians," Flake notes two major differences with LDS doctrine: "(1) the world was created from nothing and constituted an expression of God's absolute goodness; hence, (2) humans, as created beings, are ontologically unrelated to God and brought evil into being by their action.... In Smith's redaction of Genesis, people—as uncreated children of God—come first, and the world later."[413] Flake observes that in LDS thought "God's goodness and sovereignty is measured by the power to redeem human agents *in extremis*, not the power to create them *ex nihilo*."[414]

2-3   In fact, in a few instances Joseph Smith specifically stated that terms used in Abraham, but not in Moses, were better translations.[415] However, it should be remembered that the Prophet's understanding of scripture came by inspiration as well as study. For this reason, Shirts rightly observes that we should be cautious not to overestimate the degree to which his limited instruction in Hebrew may have influenced specific word choices in the book of Abraham.[416]

2-4   Not only did the Prophet render Elohim as the singular "God" throughout the book of Moses, he also modified the KJV version of Exodus 22:18 to read "God" instead of "gods."[417].

2-5   Note that Kolob "is not the center of the universe but governs only one class of stars."[418]

2-6   See Brems[419] and Draper, *et al.*[420] for LDS attempts to map the biblical days of Creation to current scientific understanding of periods of geological and biological development. See also *Excursus 5: Science and Mormonism*, p. 526.

2-7   See also Salisbury and Stokes.[421] Among the most puzzling aspects of Moses' Creation account to moderns is that light and plants appear in the story before the creation of the sun, moon, and stars. One partial response is to note the obvious contrast between this account and the Babylonian recital that portrays these bodies as gods rather than creations—the delayed appearance of heavenly bodies in Genesis emphasizes their demotion in importance. And once the sun, moon, and stars finally make their appearance, the point is made clearly that they are mere luminaries—set in their places to mark the days and seasons as they shine on the earth—while the more significant light of God is that which appeared on the first day "to fill the immensity of space."[422] It is also possible, as discussed in the overview of Moses 3, pp. 146-148, that "the apparently temporal order could be an image for the ontological order; the temporal sequence of comings into being could be a vivid literary vehicle for conveying the intelligible and hierarchic order of the beings that have come to be and are."[423] The

411   J. Smith, Jr., *Documentary History*, August 1830, 1:104-105.
412   R. L. Anderson, *Ohio*, pp. 195-198; S. R. Gunn, *Cowdery*, pp. 71-77; P. R. Legg, *Cowdery*, pp. 49-53; J. Smith, Jr., *Documentary History*, August, 26-27 September 1830, 1:109-111.
413   K. Flake, *Translating Time*, pp. 510, 511-512.
414   *Ibid.*, p. 514.
415   J. Smith, Jr., *Teachings*, 5 January 1841, p. 181; 17 May 1843, p. 301.
416   K. A. Shirts, *Hebrew*.
417   L. C. Zucker, *Hebrew*, p. 51.
418   H. W. Nibley, *Before Adam*, p. 67.
419   D. N. Brems, *Divine Engineering*, p. 93.
420   R. D. Draper, *et al.*, *Commentary*, pp. 194-195, 197-198, 201-202, 205, 207-208, 210, 216-217.
421   F. B. Salisbury, *Creation*, p. 106; W. L. Stokes, *Creation Scriptures*, pp. 129-130.
422   D&C 88:12.
423   L. R. Kass, *Wisdom*, pp. 30-31.

thrust of Moses' account in particular seems intended to establish a parallel between the process of Creation and the building of the Israelite temple, a likeness that may have motivated some of the differences in presentation and in the order of events between Moses' account of Creation and the one given in modern temples.[424] This is one of many examples of the unique perspective that Genesis offers on the story of beginnings.

2-8   If the past portends the future, the fundamental properties of the universe will eventually turn out to be even stranger than we now imagine. Quantum mechanics has already shown us how spectacularly wrong our common-sense intuitions about the properties of particles have been. As the eminent physicist Richard Feynman said: "I think I can safely say that nobody understands quantum mechanics… Do not keep saying to yourself, if you can possibly avoid it, 'But how can it be like that?' because you will get 'down the drain,' into a blind alley from which nobody has yet escaped. Nobody knows how it can be like that."[425]

2-9   On the importance of perspective in scriptural interpretation, Nibley wrote:

> The Latter-day Saints have four basic [Creation] stories, those found in the Bible, the book of Moses, the book of Abraham, and the temple—each seen from a different angle, like the four Gospels, but not conflicting if each is put into its proper context. And what is that context? One vitally important principle that everyone seems to have ignored until now is the consideration that everything is presented to us in these accounts through the eyes or from the point of view of the individual observers who tell the story. Historians long ago came to realize that the boast of German *Geschichtswissenschaft*—to report what happened at all times "*wie es eigentlich geschah*," the whole truth, the complete event in holistic perfection as it would be seen by God—is a philosopher's pipe dream.… The rainbow, like the sunrise, is strictly the product of a point of view, for which the beholder must stand in a particular place while it is raining in another particular place and the sun is in a third particular place, if he is to see it at all. It is a lesson in relativity.…[426]

2-10   For example, it is possible that some or all of the detailed description of the Garden of Eden found in the book of Moses may have been left out of the book of Abraham because it was a later interpolation.[427]

2-11   For example, each of the four New Testament gospels seems to have been composed to appeal to different audiences.[428] Since no single account or rendering of a complex scriptural event or concept will suit every situation, the translator or compositor must determine pragmatically, as Joseph Smith expressed it, whether a particular version "is sufficiently plain to suit [the] purpose as it stands."[429] The same principle applies to temple architecture. Though all temples have the same basic layout and function, each may have "a slightly different design, because it performs a different purpose."[430]

With respect to the careful selection and shaping of the Nativity account, Barker comments:

> A basic story was told but not with the mundane detail that modern writers might choose to include. There was no mention of, for example, nappies or whatever was used at the time, although the infant Jesus doubtless needed them. But there was mention of the manger, and so we ask, Why was that detail included? Those elements in the story that could be linked to prophecy, and illuminated by it, were naturally the most emphasized. This is not to say that the story of Jesus' life was simply compiled from prophecies, as some have suggested. Rather, the incidents seen to be significant were emphasized, and the material of interest to modern biographers was not.[431]

2-12   The Hebrew term *bara´* may have as a primary meaning the idea of separation or cutting.[432] "God masterfully divides the cosmos by a series of 'cuts' and differentiates its components into 'kinds.'"[433]

2-13   The "magnificent torso" of God also imitates the central figure of the Greek masterpiece *Laocöon*,

424   See the overview of Moses 3, p. 146.
425   R. Feynman, *Law*, p. 123.
426   H. W. Nibley, *Before Adam*, pp. 64, 66.
427   See *Commentary* 3:10-a, p. 170.
428   B. R. McConkie, *NT Commentary*, 1:65.
429   D&C 128:18.
430   H. W. Nibley, *Meaning of Temple*, p, 35. See *Excursus 16: The Role of Revelation in Temple Building*, p. 561.
431   M. Barker, *Christmas*, p. 18.
432   F. Brown, *et al.*, *Lexicon*, p. 155; C. Westermann, *Genesis 1-11*, p. 99.
433   B. T. Arnold, *Genesis 2009*, p. 37.

discovered just two years prior to the start of the Sistine Chapel project.[434]

2-14   Michelangelo was not only steeped in Christian theology, but also seems to have been very familiar with the texts of Jewish Midrash and medieval mysticism.[435]

2-15   In fact, upon reflection one might easily conclude that "there is a kind of 'proto-fall' implicit in the principle of divisiveness that characterizes the Bible's view of the Creation."[436] The process of division and separation began even before the Creation, when those who kept their first estate were separated from those who did not.[437] The theme continues as the focus of the narrative moves from the actions of God to those of Adam and Eve. Exercising the agency that has been granted them, they partake of the forbidden fruit, and are cast out of the Garden, experiencing an immediate separation from the presence of God, and eventually a separation of body and spirit at death. Jewish kabbalists taught that the:

> … Tree of Life and the Tree of Knowledge were bound together in perfect harmony until Adam came and separated them, thereby giving substance to evil, which had been contained within the Tree of Knowledge of Good and Evil and was now materialized in the evil instinct (*yezer ha-ra*). It was Adam therefore who activated the potential evil concealed within the Tree of Knowledge by separating the two trees and also by separating the Tree of Knowledge from its fruit, which was now detached from its source. The event is called metaphorically 'the cutting of the shoots' (*kizzuz ha-neti'ot*) and is the archetype of all the great sins mentioned in the Bible, whose common denominator was the introduction of division into the divine unity. The essence of Adam's sin was that it introduced 'separation above and below' into what should have been united, a separation of which every sin is fundamentally a repetition—apart, that is, from sins involving magic and sorcery, which according to the kabbalists joins together what should have remained separate. In actual fact, this view, too, tends to stress the separation of the power of judgment contained within the Tree of Knowledge from the power of lovingkindness contained within the Tree of Life. The latter pours out its influx unstintingly, while the former is a restrictive force with a tendency to become autonomous.[438]

One way of interpreting the stories of Enoch, Noah, the Tower of Babel, and Abraham and his posterity is as a continuation of the theme of separation. Moreover, as Lieber observes: "Throughout the *Torah*, we find this emphasis on distinction and separation: sacred and ordinary time, permitted and forbidden foods, ritually pure and impure persons, no mixing of diverse seeds or cross-breeding animal species."[439]

2-16   "The Midrash[440] pictures the lower waters weeping at being separated from the upper waters, suggesting that there is something poignant in the creative process when things once united are separated."[441]

2-17   Drawing on a long philosophical tradition beginning with Plato, the idea of distinction as a foundational concept in perception and reality was taken up in a diversity of ways by mathematics and psychology in the twentieth century. Three examples will be mentioned here:

1. Personal construct theory originated in the 1950's from the research of George Kelly, a clinical psychologist who emphasized the psychological role of certain sorts of distinctions (constructs) underlying the processes of perception and reasoning.[442] Anticipating later versions of constructivism, Kelly held that "reality" does not reveal itself to us directly, but rather is subject to as many different constructions as we are able to invent.[443]

2. The concept of distinction is also fundamental to an understanding of the classical formulation of information theory.[444] Our subjective experiences of uncertainty and astonishment with respect

---

434   B. Blech, *et al.*, *Secrets*, p. 193; cf. pp. 110-112.

435   *Ibid.*, pp. 46-73.

436   K. Burke, *Governance*, p. 16.

437   Abraham 3:26-28.

438   G. Scholem, *Kabbalah*, p. 124.

439   D. L. Lieber, *Etz Hayim*, p. 5.

440   See J. Neusner, *Genesis Rabbah 1*, 5:4, p. 48.

441   D. L. Lieber, *Etz Hayim*, p. 5; cf. H. N. Bialik, *et al.*, *Legends*, 26 and note 5, p. 10; B. Blech, *et al.*, *Secrets*, p. 193; A. J. Heschel, *Heavenly Torah*, pp. 124-126. See also Moses 7:28.

442   G. A. Kelly, *Personal Constructs*; G. A. Kelly, *Mathematical*; G. A. Kelly, *Introduction*.

443   N. M. Agnew, *et al., Construing reality*; N. M. Agnew, *et al., Fallible but functional*.

444   C. E. Shannon, *et al., Communication*.

to events in the world (essentially amounting to prospective and retrospective ignorance) can be formulated quantitatively in three related concepts: probability, information, and surprise. These concepts can be most easily understood in terms of a fourth concept, entropy, a term borrowed from thermodynamics. In a physical system, entropy can be interpreted as uncertainty about which quantum state a system is in. In an information theoretic context, entropy can be defined as the uncertainty of an event, the average amount of information yielded by an event, or the average surprise evoked by that event. Entropy is a measure of disorder; hence information (*negentropy*) is a measure of order or of organization, since the latter, compared to distribution at random, is an improbable state. Entropy is maximized when all outcomes for an event are equally probable (e.g., for a 'fair' coin, p(head) = p(tail) = .5). Useful distinctions "create" information (or in other words, they reduce entropy) in that they provide a way of grouping events into categories of unequal probability.

3. Another well-known example comes from the work of G. Spencer Brown, a brilliant and controversial philosopher and mathematician who introduced an elegant idiosyncratic calculus based on the idea that "a universe comes into being when a space is severed or taken apart. The skin of a living organism cuts off an outside from an inside. So does the circumference of a circle in a plane. By tracing the way we represent such a severance, we can begin to reconstruct, with an accuracy and coverage that appear almost uncanny, the basic forms underlying linguistic, mathematical, physical, and biological science, and can begin to see how the familiar laws of our own experience follow inexorably from the original act of severance. The act is itself already remembered, even if unconsciously, as our first attempt to distinguish different things in a world where, in the first place, the boundaries can be drawn anywhere we please."[445]

2-18   *Genesis Rabbah* constructs an argument from the order of creation to justify the conclusion that: "Whatever is created in sequence after its fellow rules over its fellow."[446]

Gregory of Nyssa commented that "nature makes an ascent as it were by steps… from the lower to the perfect form.[447] Elsewhere he writes that "the Deity proceeds by a sort of graduated and ordered advance to the creation of man."[448]

2-19   Hirsch comments: "Unlike man, the material for woman's body was not taken from the earth. God built one side of man into woman—so that the single human being now became two. Thereby, the complete equality of man and woman was irrefutably demonstrated."[449] The Jewish sages recognized "that man is incomplete without woman, as much as woman without man."[450] "In this sense," concludes Neusner, "they see the two as complementary and essential, so they do not maintain that one gender takes priority over another."[451]

In the *Conflict of Adam and Eve with Satan*, Satan appears as an angel of light and falsely asserts that Adam was created out of *his* side.[452]

2-20   Matthew Henry saw woman as the crown of all Creation: "Yet man being made last of the creatures, as the best and most excellent of all, Eve's being made after Adam, and out of him, puts an honor upon that sex, as the glory of the man.[453] If man is the head, she is the crown, a crown to her husband, the crown of the visible creation. The man was dust refined, but the woman was dust double-refined, one remove further from the earth."[454] The First Presidency of Heber J. Grant, J. Reuben Clark, and David O. McKay likewise expressed a related sentiment: "The true spirit of the Church of Jesus Christ of Latter-day Saints gives to woman the highest place of honor in human life."[455]

2-21   Blech and Doliner comment:

> In 1975, a Jewish surgeon, Dr. Frank Mershberger became fascinated with the "distinct shape of the cape and the dangling scrap of cloth. He mentally found himself picturing the diagrams he had

445   G. S. Brown, *Laws*, p. xxix.
446   J. Neusner, *Genesis Rabbah 1*, 19:4, p. 202.
447   Gregory of Nyssa, *On the Creation of Man 8:7*, cited in A. Louth, *et al., Genesis1-11*, p. 28.
448   Gregory of Nyssa, *On the Soul and the Resurrection*, cited in A. Louth, *et al., Genesis 1-11*, pp. 28-29.
449   Cited in R. M. Zlotowitz, *et al., Bereishis*, 1:108-109.
450   Cf. 1 Corinthians 11:11.
451   J. Neusner, *Confronting*, p. 74. See *Commentary* 2:27-a, p. 115 and 3:22-a, p. 181.
452   S. C. Malan, *Adam and Eve*, 1:60, p. 68.
453   1 Corinthians 11:7.
454   M. Henry, *Commentary*, 2:21-25, p. 10; cf. G. B. Hinckley, *Teachings 1997*, November 1991, p. 695.
455   J. R. Clark, *Messages*, 6:5.

studied in his Anatomy 101 textbook back in medical school. The cerebrum, the cerebellum, the occipital lobe, the cortex, the brain stem… of course. They were all there. What Michelangelo had hidden in the painting was a perfect cross-section of the human brain. But—why?

Again, he was showing to others "in the know" what he had learned surreptitiously through illegal dissections. The only people who might have recognized the hidden internal organs in the ceiling would have been other seekers of knowledge who had pursued the same forbidden activities…

Michelangelo concealed this forbidden evidence of anatomical studies to convey the concept of creation rooted in wisdom; the 'brain' of God, so to speak, is the source of humankind's appearance on the earth. It is yet another illustration of an idea stressed in the Kabbalah—the brain is the organ mystically linked to the *s'firah* of *Chochmah*/Wisdom.[456] Incredibly, Michelangelo was aware of an even deeper truth, noted long ago in kabbalistic thought: it is not the entire brain that is linked to *Chochmah*/Wisdom but only its right hemisphere, exactly the part that Michelangelo painted in this panel. The artist found a way to echo visually the ancient Jewish prayer proclaiming that God created Adam with *Chochmah*, the right side of the divine brain.

Some experts think that the extra interlocking figures surrounding God are the major brain centers and the ganglia (intersections of the 'highway' of the nervous system). However, there is also a far more fascinating mystical explanation. According to *Talmud*, Midrash, and Kabbalah, the drop of semen that impregnates the womb of the woman does not originate in the male reproductive system but comes from within the man's brain instead.[457] According to this interpretation, all those figures surrounding the Creator are us, the future descendants of Adam and Eve, waiting to be conceived. That makes all of us direct descendants of God, awaiting birth from his brain—a powerful universalistic concept….

[Moreover, consistent with the Kabbalah's concept of *Mochah Stima'ah*, the hidden brain that inspires the creative will in humans, Michelangelo] painted Wisdom/*Chochmah* in the female guise of Sophia, flanked by the now-classic figure of the white-bearded God representing *Yisrael Saba*, and the infant representing *Yisrael Zuta*, all enclosed inside the right hemisphere of the human brain, blessing the Man's left hand with the talent and the will to create. Seen in this way, hidden inside this world-famous scene is nothing less than a forbidden anatomy lesson, a journey into the depths of Kabbalah, and a secret self-portrait of Michelangelo as Adam—not by way of the artist's physical appearance but rather of his very soul."[458]

2-22 Blech and Doliner raise the intriguing possibility that the child is "the soul of Adam, about to be transmitted into Adam. Notice that the infant's body position is imitating that of Adam. It is about to be infused into Adam through Adam's left hand. According to tradition, the left hand is the one through which we receive blessings and benedictions, since its blood vessels lead directly to the heart. Even today, countless people around the world wear the red string of the matriarch Rachel's blessing—on their left wrist. Michelangelo knew that his talents, too, were a blessing received from God. Is it only a coincidence that the artist, who depicted Adam receiving his soul from the Creator through his left hand, was also himself left-handed?"[459]

2-23 See Freedman for a discussion of the role of the number eight as an additional "symbol of totality and perfection" in the story of the Creation.[460]

2-24 Kahne observes that the story of the Garden of Eden is also characterized by frequent use of the number seven: a. The words for man (*ish, adam*) appear 28 times; b. The woman, 21 times (*isha, ezer, tsela*); c. Words from the stem *akhal* ("to eat"), 21 times; d. Words from the stem *laqah* ("to take") ,seven times; e. *Qedem* ("east"), seven times; f. Eden, seven times; g. In Hebrew, the section on Eden is seven paragraphs long.

Kahne sees the "same preoccupation with the number seven… in the gospel of John. In chapter 1, John begins his gospel by a kind of Genesis where he takes up the theme of creation again: 'In the beginning was the Word' [cf. the 'God said' of Genesis]… all things were made by him [cf. In the beginning, God created the heavens and the earth]… In him was… the light of men [cf. Moses 2:3: 'Let there be light']." John 1:1-28 comprises the first day. The second, third, and fourth days are introduced by

456   See, e.g., L. Schaya, *Meaning*, p. 35; A. Kaplan, *Sefer Yetzirah* 1:4, pp. 38-40.

457   See, e.g., A. Green, *Guide*, p. 115; A. Kalan, *Bahir* 1:155, pp. 56-57.

458   B. Blech, *et al.*, *Secrets*, pp. 199-201.

459   *Ibid.*, p. 199.

460   D. N. Freedman, *Humanity*, pp. 13-14.

"the next day."[461] Then, there are three days,[462] which makes seven days in all. The three days may symbolize the time between his death and resurrection and the marriage of Cana, the marriage of the son of God with mankind."[463]

2-25   It should be noted that, in contrast to current scholarship, the prevailing custom at that time was to divide the three pairs differently as: 1-2, 3-4, 5-6.[464]

The Church Fathers analyzed the Creation in three parts: the work of creation, the work of separation, and the work of adornment.[465]

2-26   "In both the linear and parallel structures, the Sabbath day stands in the position of emphasis: it culminates the linear arrangement; and it stands unique and unmatched (and thus highlighted) in the parallel scheme. Its highlighting foreshadows its future importance."[466]

2-27   Currid calls the relationship between the Hebrew creation story and Egyptian cosmogony "striking" in at least three aspects: "(1) the nature and character of the creator-god; (2) the manner in which the creator-god fashioned the universe; and (3) the sequence and constitution of creation":[467]

Actually, the biblical account has greater affinity with the Egyptian texts than with the Mesopotamian. For the main Mesopotamian creation myth (*Enuma Elish*) is oriented toward conflict and violence. The universe came into existence because of a battle between the gods; it was a mere consequence of a war aimed at determining who would be the lord of the gods.... There is no conflict, on the other hand, in either the biblical or Memphite cosmology. Creation did not occur as a result of a contest or a struggle. Thus, while much has been written about the Mesopotamian influences upon or parallels with the biblical text, the Egyptian parallels regarding the means of creation are more substantial.[468]

2-28   Truman G. Madsen gave the following anecdote regarding Freedman's views on man's being in the "image and likeness" of God:

We are close friends with David Noel Freedman... [He] said to me one day, ..."All my life I've been looking for a religion that combined... normative Judaism and first-century Christianity... I think I've found it." I said, "Where?" "You." He has in mind hard textual analysis ...and when it says in Genesis about "image and likeness" he points out, "That means that, as I can say to you, 'Here is a statue of you. It has been carved in every detail with your likeness and image. The only difference between the statue and you is that you're alive.' But when it says 'image and likeness' it means exact similitude."[469]

Born into a Jewish family and later becoming an ordained Presbyterian clergyman, David Noel Freedman "was a legend among Bible scholars. After all, he had managed to graduate from UCLA when he was only 17 and then went on to get a degree in Hebrew Bible from Princeton Theological Seminary and a doctorate from Johns Hopkins University (a colleague reports that he wrote two dissertations, both of which were later published as books). He was a former president of the *Society of Biblical Literature* and editor in chief of the massive *Anchor Bible Project*, which consists of dozens of volumes of commentary and explanation."[470]

William Blake was also a vigorous advocate of the idea of man's literal resemblance to God, as related by Chesterton:[471]

Let the ordinary modern man, who is, generally speaking, not a materialist and not a mystic, read first these two lines from the poem falsely called ""The Auguries of Innocence":

God appears and God is light
To those poor souls that dwell in night.

---

461   John 1:29, 35, 43.

462   John 2:1.

463   M. Kahne, *Symbolique*.

464   U. Cassuto, *Adam to Noah*, p. 13.

465   E.g., T. Aquinas, *Summa*, First Part, Question 74, repl. 1.

466   D. A. Dorsey, *Structure*, p. 49.

467   J. D. Currid, *Egypt*, pp. 54-55.

468   *Ibid.*, pp. 63-64.

469   T. G. Madsen, *Philosophy and Mormonism*.

470   S. Dolbee, *Freedman*.

471   G. K. Chesterton, *William Blake*, pp. 147-148, 209-210.

He will not find anything objectionable in that, at any rate; probably he will bow his head slightly to a truism, as if he were in a church. Then he will read the next two lines:

> But does a human form display
> To those that dwell in realms of day.

And there the modern man will sit down suddenly on the sofa and come finally to the conclusion that William Blake was mad and nothing else. But …[this] is the point about Blake that must be understood if nothing else is understood. God for him was not more and more vague and diaphonous as one came near to Him. God was more and more solid as one came near. When one was far off one might fancy Him to be impersonal. When one came into personal relation one knew that He was a person… God is merely light to the merely unenlightened. God is a man to the enlightened.…

It was a mark of the old eastern initiations… that as a man climbs higher and higher, God becomes to him more and more formless, ethereal, and even thin. And in man of these temples, both ancient and modern, the final reward of serving the god through vigils and purifications, is that one is at last worthy to be told that the god doesn't exist.

Against all this emasculate mysticism Blake like a Titan rears his colossal figure and his earthquake voice. Through all the cloud and chaos of his stubborn symbolism and his perverse theories, through the tempest of exaggeration and the full midnight of madness, he reiterates with passionate precision that only that which is lovable can be adorable, that deity is either a person or a puff of wind, that the more we know of higher things the more palpable and incarnate we shall find them; that the form filling the heavens is the likeness and appearance of a man.

See also *Introduction*, p. 10 and *Figure* E2-1, p. 517.

FIGURE 3-1. *The Garden of Eden, 1612*
Jan Breughel, the Elder, ca. 1568-1625

And I, the Lord God, planted a garden eastward in Eden, and there I put the man whom I had formed (Moses 3:8). Brueghel masterfully fills the foreground of the scene with the abundance, happiness, and beauty of newly-created life, and then from there skillfully draws our eyes toward the two tiny figures in the background ominously reaching for the fruit of the Tree of Knowledge.

MOSES 3
The Garden of Eden

Overview

MOSES 3:4 begins a second creation narrative that differs from Moses 2 in vocabulary, style, and use of the divine name (i.e., God vs. Lord God). Repetitions and seeming contradictions with elements of the previous recital of creation events are also apparent. These observations are long-recognized issues in biblical study and can be seen as providing support for the argument that multiple sources have been incorporated into the scriptural text as we now have it.[1] An impressive array of evidences for the seeming heterogeneity of sources within the first five books of the Bible have converged to form the basis of the Documentary Hypothesis, a broad scholarly consensus whose most able current popular expositor has been Richard Friedman.[2]

However, even those who find the Documentary Hypothesis compelling have good reason to admire the resulting literary product on its own terms. For example, in the case of the two Creation chapters, Friedman himself writes that in the scriptural version of Genesis we have a text "that is greater than the sum of its parts… [T]he combination of the from-the-sky-down and the from-the-earth-up accounts produces a much richer and much more whole conception of Creation than we would have if there were only one account. Also, placing the cosmic conception first creates the impression of the wide camera view narrowing in. This feeling of narrowing in will continue through the coming stories, contributing to the rich-in-background feeling."[3]

A central point made obvious by the juxtaposition of the two creation narratives is that, "in contrast to Mesopotamian thought, … the emergence of evil [on earth] is subsequent to Creation and not part of the creative process itself… What the… author [of the second account] sets out to explain, using familiar mythic *topoi* in the manner of the sages, is how evil could be generated in a Creation declared (seven times) to be good. In this sense, therefore, one may say that the [second] narrative contains the reflection generated by the [first] Creation recital."[4] Taken together, the accounts preserved in Moses 2-4 describe the

---

1   See *Endnote 3-1*, p. 197. See also A. J. Heschel, *Heavenly Torah*, pp. 650-657 for relevant rabbinical arguments.
2   R. E. Friedman, *Hidden*; R. E. Friedman, *Sources*; R. E. Friedman, *Who*. See *Endnote 3-2*, p. 197.
3   R. E. Friedman, *Commentary*, p. 16; cf. T. L. Brodie, *Dialogue*, pp. 123-132. See *Endnote 3-3*, p. 197.
4   J. Blenkinsopp, *P and J*, p. 7.

transition of Adam and Eve from a divinely established state of order and sovereignty to a world of inevitable decay and unrighteous dominion.[5]

Following a description of the sanctification of the seventh day[6]—in essence the creation of sacred time—we are given an account of the forming of man's body from the earth,[7] the creation of sacred space in the Garden of Eden,[8] a summary of the commandments concerning its care and use,[9] the naming episode as a fulfillment of previous instructions relating to man's dominion,[10] and a culminating lesson about the binding oneness that is meant to characterize the relationship of Adam and Eve.[11] A final verse reminds us of the couple's state of innocence, preparing us for the story of the Fall in Moses 4.[12]

Spiritual Creation

Between the end of the first Creation account and the beginning of the second one is a brief statement meriting special attention: "I, the Lord God, created all things… spiritually, before they were naturally upon the face of the earth."[13] Notwithstanding the help provided by the clarifying additions given in the JST, this passage has raised many difficulties in interpretation. Joseph Smith must have had his own questions about these verses—which we can infer from the fact that he received a revelation containing further explanation[14] at about the same time the relevant portions of the book of Moses were given:[15]

> 30 But remember that all my judgments are not given unto men; and as the words have gone forth out of my mouth even so shall they be fulfilled, that the first shall be last, and that the last shall be first in all things whatsoever I have created by the word of my power, which is the power of my Spirit.
>
> 31 For by the power of my Spirit created I them; yea, all things both spiritual and temporal—
>
> 32 First spiritual, secondly temporal, which is the beginning of my work; and again, first temporal, and secondly spiritual, which is the last of my work—[16]
>
> 33 Speaking unto you that you may naturally understand; but unto myself my works have no end, neither beginning; but it is given unto you that ye may understand, because ye have asked it of me and are agreed.[17]
>
> 34 Wherefore, verily I say unto you that all things unto me are spiritual,[18] and not at any time have I given unto you a law which was temporal; neither any man, nor the children of men; neither Adam, your father, whom I created.
>
> 35 Behold, I gave unto him that he should be an agent unto himself; and I gave unto him commandment, but no temporal commandment gave I unto him, for my commandments are spiritual; they are not natural nor temporal, neither carnal nor sensual.[19]

---

5   K. Burke, *Governance*, p. 17.
6   Moses 3:1-3.
7   Moses 3:6-7.
8   Moses 3:8-14.
9   Moses 3:15-17.
10   Moses 3:18-20.
11   Moses 3:21-24.
12   Moses 3:25.
13   Moses 3:5.
14   See *Endnote 3-4*, p. 197.
15   See K. Muhlestein, *Flow*, pp. 49-52.
16   See *Endnote 3-5*, p. 197.
17   See *Endnote 3-6*, p. 198.
18   See *Endnote 3-7*, p. 198.
19   D&C 29:30-35.

To a degree, these verses seem a paraphrase and clarifying expansion of ideas and phrases in 1 Corinthians 15:45-48, with "temporal" replacing "natural" in order to better emphasize the contrast the Lord is making between His "time" and ours. In other words, while it is logical from *our* perspective to speak of the "beginning" and "last" phases of God's work,[20] from His *eternal* perspective the "works have no end, neither beginning"[21] but are "one eternal round."[22] The verses make it clear that this applies not only to God's works, but also to His commandments.[23]

By spiritual creation is meant the premortal creation of "all things" in their spiritual state, including the creation of Eden, and everything in it.[24] This is consistent with the view of Elder Bruce R. McConkie, who "conceded that the word 'spiritual'" in Moses 3 has "a dual meaning and applies to both the premortal life and the paradisiacal creation."[25]

The statements in the book of Moses tell us much about the universal *scope* of spiritual creation ("all things," "all things which I prepared for the use of man"[26]), but say nothing directly about the *process*. Later revelation and teachings of Church leaders have made it clear that both humans and animals[27] possess individual spirits that predated their physical bodies.[28] A First Presidency statement in 1909 on the *Origin of Man* further stated that "man, as a spirit, was begotten and born of heavenly parents, and reared to maturity in the eternal mansions of the Father… Man is the child of God."[29] Note also Joseph Smith's teachings affirming that there is some aspect of the spirit's existence which was not created, although the exact nature of this eternal part of man has not been authoritatively settled.[30]

Scriptural descriptions of the Garden of Eden not only seem to imply that something about its "time," but also its "state," and "sphere," differed from the postlapsarian environment of Adam and Eve. Lehi explained that had it not been for the Fall, "All things which were created must have remained in the same state in which they were after they were created; and they must have remained forever, and had no end."[31] Expressing a related idea, Moses 3:9 says that "all things which I prepared for the use of man" were "spiritual" when they were created, for they remained "in the sphere in which I, God, created [them]."

Everything placed in the Garden of Eden was, of course, also considered "spiritual." We are told in Moses 3 that man, the trees, and the animals became "living souls" when they were formed from a combination of spiritual and natural elements.[32] All these things were considered "spiritual" in the sense that they were in a state of relative perfection before the Fall.[33]

Below, we discuss the spiritual creation of mankind and of Eden in more detail.

---

20   D&C 29:32.
21   D&C 29:33.
22   See, e.g., 1 Nephi 10:19.
23   D&C 29:35.
24   See *Endnote 3-8,* p. 198.
25   Cited in C. R. Harrell, *Preexistence,* p. 20. See *Endnote 3-9,* p. 198.
26   D&C 29:5, 9.
27   See *Endnote 3-10,* p. 199.
28   J. F. Smith, Jr., *Doctrines,* 15 February 1941, 1:62.
29   J. F. Smith, *et al., Origin.*
30   K. W. Godfrey, *Intelligence;* P. N. Hyde, *Intelligences;* see *Excursus 8: The Origin and Premortal Existence of Human Spirits,* p. 540.
31   2 Nephi 2:22. See *Endnote 3-11,* p. 199.
32   Moses 3:7, 9, 19. See *Endnote 3-12,* p. 200.
33   J. F. Smith, Jr., *Doctrines,* 1954, 1:76.

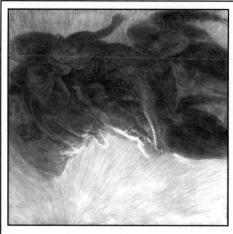

Figure 3-2. *The Creation of Light, 1913*
Gaetano Previati, 1852-1920

See Color Plate 3-2.

And I, God, said: Let there be light; and there was light.[1] Some ancient sources assert that the heavenly hosts—variously described as including the angels, the sons of God, and/or the souls of humanity—were part of the light on Day One of creation.[2] Williams explains: "The *pneumatikos* or spiritual first Adam, born on the first day, is associated both with the Spirit of God that hovered over the pre-mundane waters[3] and, more commonly, the light of [Moses 2:3]. The latter reading is based on a pun on the Greek word *phōs*, used in the [*Septuagint*] translation of Genesis 1:3 meaning both 'light' and 'man.' Thus, the product of God's command, 'Let there be light (*phōs*),' was a divine Light-Man, an *anthropos* enveloped within and consisting of light. This interpretation is Jewish and can be found as early as the second century BCE."[4]

Though the idea is not widely known or appreciated today, the visual depiction of this event has a venerable history, stretching from medieval times to our own, as seen in this magnificent painting by Previati.[5]

---

1   Moses 2:3.
2   M. Barker, *Angels*, p. 29.
3   Moses 2:2.
4   W. Williams, *Shadow*.
5   See *Commentary* 2:2-b, p. 99; 2:4-c, p. 101; 3:1-b, p. 151; *Excursus 8: The Origin and Premortal Existence of Human Spirits,* p. 540

The Spiritual Creation of Mankind

We are told very little in the book of Moses about the premortal creation of human spirits and the physical creation of the human body. The fact that all mankind existed as spirits in "heaven" before they came to earth is stated in simple terms.[34] The formation of man's physical body from the "dust of the earth" and woman's from the "rib" of the man are described in figurative terms.[35] Additionally, the book of Abraham makes it clear that when God breathed the "breath of life" into man, it meant that He took Adam's spirit and placed it into his body.[36]

With respect to the premortal life of man's spirit, the phrase "and all the host of them" that follows the statement that "the heaven and the earth were finished" has long been a subject of discussion and speculation. The belief that "angels," "sons of God," and/or "the souls of humanity" were part of that "host" and that they were created prior to everything else appears in the book of Job,[37] in extracanonical books such as *Jubilees*,[38] and in the teachings of Elder Joseph Fielding Smith.[39] Barker argues that a similar story was once part of Genesis, but was expurgated during or after the Jewish exile.[40]

---

34   Moses 3:5. See *Endnote 3-14,* p. 200.
35   Moses 3:6. See *Appendix*, pp. 785-802 for a collection of statements on the origin of man.
36   Abraham 5:7; cf. J. Smith, Jr., *Teachings*, 17 May 1843, p. 301.
37   Job 38:4, 7.
38   O. S. Wintermute, *Jubilees*, 2:2, p. 55.
39   J. F. Smith, Jr., *Answers*, 1966, 5:182-184; cf. J. Smith, Jr., *Teachings*, 2 May 1844, p. 365. See also *Commentary* 2:2-b, p. 99; 2:4-c, p. 101; 3:1-b, p. 151; *Excursus 8: The Origin and Premortal Existence of Human Spirits,* p. 540. See *Endnote 3-15,* p. 200.
40   M. Barker, *Beyond*, pp. 196-198; M. Barker, *Timaeus*, pp. 283-285; M. Barker, *Temple Roots*, pp. 80-81; M. Barker, *Hidden*, pp. 20-21. See *Endnote 3-16,* p. 200.

FIGURE 3-3. *The Four and Twenty Elders, ca. 1805*
William Blake, 1757-1827

SEE COLOR PLATE 3-3.

Now the Lord had shown unto me, Abraham, the intelligences that were organized before the world was… And God… stood in the midst of them, and he said: These I will make my rulers.[1] Though the image is used here to evoke the premortal scene described by Abraham, Blake's pencil and watercolor drawing was originally meant to illustrate John's vision of the heavenly throne: "and one sat upon the throne… and round about the throne were… four and twenty elders sitting, clothed in white raiment… And before the throne there was a sea of glass like unto crystal… and round about… were four beasts full of eyes… The four and twenty elders fall down before him… and worship him that liveth for ever and ever, and cast their crowns before the throne saying, Thou art worthy, O Lord, to receive glory and honour and power: for thou hast created all things."[2]

1   Abraham 3:22-23.
2   Revelation 4:2, 4, 6, 10-11.

In contrast to the spare account of the spiritual creation of mankind, much more detail is given about relationships and events that subsequently took place in the premortal life.[41] Couched in a revelation about cosmology,[42] the book of Abraham gives an extended lesson about the relationships that prevailed among "the intelligences that were organized before the world was."[43] Summarizes Bushman:

> Abraham's astronomy envisioned an ascending order of planetary rule based on slowness of time. Wherever there was one planet or star, "there shall be another planet whose reckoning of time shall be longer still; and thus there shall be the reckoning of the time of one planet above another, until thou come nigh unto Kolob, which Kolob is after the reckoning of the Lord's time; which Kolob is set nigh unto the throne of God, to govern all those planets which belong to the same order of that upon which thou standest."[44] The series moved from the earth's "order" of planets upward through ever-slowing planets, moons, suns, and stars to Kolob.…[45]
>
> This fundamental cosmic order was mirrored in humans' relationship with God. Midway through the text, the Lord compares humans to the stars. The ranking of the planets and stars, the Lord said, carries over to the ranking of spirits: "The Lord said unto me, these two facts do exist, that there are two spirits, one being more intelligent than the other, there shall be another more intelligent than they; I am the Lord thy God, I am more intelligent than they all."[46] Like the stars, the spirits rise in ascending order to God, echoing the traditional idea of the Great Chain of Being.[47] The verse suggests that the source of God's authority comes from his being the highest and greatest of the intelligences, "more intelligent than they all." Years earlier, Joseph had written that "the glory of God is intelligence, or, in other words, light and truth."[48] Now he showed a universe filled with individual intelligences ruled by a God who was "more intelligent than they all." God's power grew out of his glory and intelligence rather than [the erroneous idea of] his having created everything out of nothing.[49]

41   See *Endnote 3-17*, p. 200.
42   See *Endnote 3-18*, p. 201.
43   Abraham 3:22. See *Excursus 9: The Premortal Organization of the Human Family*, p. 544.
44   Abraham 3:9. See *Excursus 18: Kolob*, p. 565 and *Excursus 19: "If You Could Hie to Kolob"*, p. 566.
45   See *Endnote 3-19*, p. 201.
46   Abraham 3:19. See *Endnote 3-20*, p. 201.
47   A. O. Lovejoy, *Great Chain*; cf. R. L. Bushman, *Mormonism*, p. 72. See *Excursus 10: The Great Chain of Being*, p. 546. See also F. M. Huchel, *Cosmic*, pp. 10-11.
48   D&C 93:36.
49   R. L. Bushman, *Rough Stone*, pp. 455-456.

 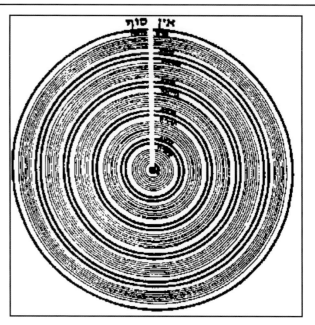

Figure 3-4. *The Great Chain of Being, in Rhetorica Christiana, 1579,* **Didacus Valades**
Figure 3-5. *A Depiction of Ein Sof and the Encircling Angelic Hierarchies*

These two facts do exist, that there are two spirits, one more intelligent than the other; there shall be another more intelligent than they; I am the Lord thy God, I am more intelligent than they all.[1] The hierarchical structure of the cosmos represented by the depiction of the Great Chain of Being at left starts from the most foundational element (i.e., rock, which merely exists), up through plants and various classes of animals. Man, being composed of both body and spirit, occupies a transitional level "a little lower than the angels."[2] God, here conceived as a purely spiritual Prime Mover, reigns supreme over all, while the Devil and his angels languish in the flames of hell below, cut off forever in their exile from the rest of Creation.

Jewish kabbalists refer to the fundamental aspect or absolute essence of God represented in the center of the figure at right as *Ein Sof,* meaning "without end," "that which is beyond all limits," boundless or infinite.[3] The concept defies description, embodying "absolute perfection in which there are no distinctions and no differentiations."[4] Encircling *Ein Sof* are a succession of angelic hierarchies (*olamot*—universes). The pictorial image associated with the inner "rung of being" of the Kabbalah is the crown: *Keter*—but, writes Matt, "we should also recall that the more primary meaning of the word *keter* is 'circle'; it is from this that the notion of the crown is derived. In *Sefer Yetsirah* we are told that the *sefirot* are a great circle, 'their end embedded in their beginning, and their beginning in their end,'"[5] recalling scriptural passages that speak of God's course as being "one eternal round."[6]

---

1   Abraham 3:19.
2   Psalm 8:5. See *Endnote 3-21,* p. 202.
3   A. Green, *Guide,* pp. 34-35; H. W. Nibley, *Teachings of the PGP,* 17, p. 213; cf. *Commentary* 1:3-d, p. 45. See *Endnote 3-22,* p. 202.
4   G. Scholem, *Kabbalah,* p. 89. See *Endnote 3-23,* p. 202.
5   D. C. Matt, *Zohar 1,* p. xlvii; cf. A. Green, *Guide,* p. 39. See D. Blumenthal, *Merkabah,* 1:7, p. 17; P. Mordell, *Sefer Yetsirah,* 3:15, p. 44.
6   E.g., 1 Nephi 10:19.

The Prophet summarized: "The organization of the spiritual and heavenly worlds, and of spiritual and heavenly beings, was agreeable to the most perfect order and harmony: their limits and bounds were fixed irrevocably, and voluntarily subscribed to in their heavenly estate by themselves, and were by our first parents subscribed to upon the earth."[50] Thus, "Father Adam, the Ancient of Days and father of all, and our glorious Mother Eve," among the "noble and great ones" who excelled in intelligence in their premortal life, were foreordained to their mortal roles.[51] Having received perfect physical bodies, Adam and

---

50   J. Smith, Jr., *Teachings,* 9 October 1843, p. 325.
51   D&C 138:38-39; Abraham 3:22-23; S. W. Kimball, *Righteous Women,* p. 102; J. Smith, Jr., *Words,* 12 May 1844,

FIGURE 3-6. *Behold Your Little Ones, 1983*
David Lindsley, 1954-

SEE COLOR PLATE 3-6.

So they brought their little children and set them down upon the ground round about him, and Jesus stood in the midst... And he spake unto the multitude, and said unto them: Behold your little ones... and... angels... came down and encircled those little ones about, and they were encircled about with fire.[1] Consistent with imagery elsewhere in scripture and rabbinical tradition, this scene from the Book of Mormon is described as a series of concentric circles surrounding the spot where the Savior stood.[2] Jesus' placement of the children so that they immediately surrounded Him—their proximity exceeding even that of the encircling angels and accompanying fire—conveyed a powerful visual message about their holiness: namely, that "whosoever... shall humble himself as this little child, the same is greatest in the kingdom of heaven."[3]

---

1   3 Nephi 17:12, 23-24.
2   See *Figure 4-4*, p. 219 and *Excursus 11: The Sacred Circle*, p. 547.
3   Matthew 18:4.

Eve were placed in a specially-prepared proving ground where, until the time of their transgression, they would live in a spiritual state.[52]

The Spiritual Creation of Eden

What was the nature of the initial proving ground created for Adam and Eve? In the space of a few verses, scripture recounts that God "planted a garden eastward in Eden" containing a river and a variety of beautiful fruit trees—including the Tree of Life and the Tree of Knowledge of Good and Evil.[53] In a single brief enigmatic reference, Moses 3:9 elaborates on the spiritual state of existence that applied to all things in the Garden: "... it was spiritual in the day that I created it; for it remaineth in the sphere in which I, God, created it." The use of "for" to introduce the dependent clause of this verse seems to imply that the spiritual state of the Garden was due to the fact that it had remained in a particular "sphere." This raises the question as to what is meant by the term "sphere."

The first thing to notice is that the Prophet Joseph Smith never used "sphere" in the contemporary English sense of a "globe" or a "celestial body," preferring the terms "world" or "planet" when that meaning was intended. In his revelations and teachings, "sphere" always refers to one of three things:

1. the orbit or order of a heavenly body;[54]
2. a domain of thought;[55]
3. a realm of activity, power, or influence.[56]

---

p. 371; J. Smith, Jr., *Teachings*, 12 May 1844, p. 365.
52   2 Nephi 2:22-23.
53   Moses 3:8-14.
54   See *Endnote 3-24*, p. 202.
55   See *Endnote 3-25*, p. 202.
56   See *Endnote 3-26*, p. 202.

In the context of Moses 3:9, only the first and third of the senses could reasonably apply. However, since the book of Abraham[57] strongly correlates increases in proximity of orbit with higher orders of celestial governance, these two senses, in fact, converge. Taken together with Abraham 5:13 and D&C 130:4—which imply that the "reckoning" of time of the Garden in its spiritual state was "after the Lord's time, which was after the time of Kolob"[58]—the implication seems to be that the prelapsarian Garden of Eden was "nigh unto Kolob,"[59] with events *after* the Fall occurring in another sphere—and hence in a different state.[60]

This interpretation immediately raises serious issues. For one thing, a view that the earth was physically transported from one position in space to another is impossible to harmonize with current planetary science unless one makes the very doubtful assumption, as does Andrus,[61] that under the special conditions prevailing at the time of Creation "it may have been possible to move the earth in space at a great speed without the disruption that might otherwise accompany such a move." For such a view to be plausible, not only would the movement of Earth itself have to be considered, but also the fact that "the solar system is a multiple body system with many complex interactions taking place."[62] Equally problematic is the fact that all lines of scientific evidence support the conclusion that both the sun and the earth were created at about the same time from the same source, and that the earth was part of our solar system from its beginning.

A second problem in understanding the spiritual creation of Eden relates to the scriptural account of how death entered the world.[63] President Harold B. Lee gave the following description of the effects of Adam and Eve's transgression on the rest of creation:

> Besides the Fall having had to do with Adam and Eve, causing a change to come over them, that change affected all human nature, all of the natural creations, all of the creation of animals, plants—all kinds of life were changed. The earth itself became subject to death.... How it took place no one can explain, and anyone who would attempt to make an explanation would be going far beyond anything the Lord has told us. But a change was wrought over the whole face of the creation, which up to that time had not been subject to death. From that time henceforth all in nature was in a state of gradual dissolution until mortal death was to come, after which there would be required a restoration in a resurrected state.[64]

President Lee's clear statement about the effects of the Fall is difficult to reconcile with the presence of ancient fossils predating man's arrival, arranged in progressive complexity in the earth's strata. Elder James E. Talmage of the Quorum of the Twelve, a geologist by training, expressed the following observations in 1931:

> The oldest... rocks thus far identified in land masses reveal the fossilized remains of once living organisms, plant and animal... These lived and died, age after age, while the earth was yet unfit for human habitation.

> From the fossilized remains of plants and animals found in the rocks, the scientist points to a very definite order in the sequence of life embodiment, for older rocks, the earlier formations,

57   Abraham 3:9, 16.
58   See also J. Smith, Jr., *Words*, 9 March 1841, pp. 64-65.
59   See *Excursus 18: Kolob*, p. 565 and *Excursus 19: "If You Could Hie to Kolob"*, p. 566.
60   See *Endnote 3-27*, p. 203.
61   H. L. Andrus, *God*, pp. 314-315.
62   H. K. Hansen, *Astronomy*, p. 188.
63   See *Endnote 3-28*, p. 203.
64   H. B. Lee, *Teachings 2000*, 23 June 1954, p. 20.

reveal to us organisms of simplest structure only, whether of plants or animals. These primitive species were aquatic; land forms were of later development.[65]

Those who, like President Lee, have made statements strongly expressing the view that no death existed on earth before the Fall should not be portrayed as intrinsically unsympathetic to science, but more fundamentally as resisting any views that compromise authoritatively-expressed doctrines relating to the Creation, the Fall, and the Atonement. Likewise, scientifically-minded people of faith such as Elder Talmage are not seeking to subordinate the claims of faith to the program of science, but naturally desire to circumscribe their understanding of truth—the results of learning by "study and also by faith"[66]—into "one great whole."[67]

In 1910, the First Presidency affirmed that to the extent that demonstrated scientific findings can be harmonized with "divine revelation [and] good common sense," they are accepted "with joy."[68] In this regard, Elder Lee spoke approvingly of a story recounted by LDS scientist Harvey Fletcher about President Joseph F. Smith's reply to questions posed to him at BYU about the topic of evolution:

> After listening patiently he replied: "Brethren, I don't know very much about science. It has not been my privilege to study... deeply... any of the sciences, but this I do know, that God lives, and that His Son instituted this church here upon the earth for the salvation of men. Now Brethren, you have that testimony, and I've heard you bear it. It's your job to try and see how these seeming difficulties can be overcome."[69]

While it would be presumptuous to speak of any final solution to the problem of reconciling science and scripture on specifics relating to the Garden of Eden and the nature of life before the Fall, three groups of general possibilities are briefly considered below.[70]

1. Eden located on the earth as a place where special conditions prevailed. This scenario, advocated by Draper, *et al.*, posits that Eden existed at a specific location on the earth, and that "spiritual" conditions governed life in the Garden before the Fall while, at the same time, "natural" conditions prevailed elsewhere on the earth.[71] Such a proposal accords well with a common LDS view that attributes a continuous identity of the physical earth from its creation in a spiritual state, to its "Fall" to a telestial one, to its eventual transformation to a paradisiacal millennial state, and ultimately to a glorified celestial status.[72] It also provides an explanation for ancient fossil remains by allowing for death and disease to have taken place for an indefinite period of time outside the Garden, while deathless conditions are seen as having prevailed before the Fall for Adam and Eve and all else within Eden's precincts.[73] On the other hand, nothing in the scriptural description of the Garden's four rivers springing from one head seems to correlate easily with the geography of Missouri (or anywhere else on the earth, for that matter), either present or past. Moreover, it seems awkward to speak of a single earth existing in a hybrid state—partly spiritual and partly natural.[74]

---

65 J. E. Talmage, *Earth and Man*, p. 242. See *Endnote 3-29*, p. 203.
66 D&C 88:118.
67 H. W. Hunter, *Teachings 1997*, 30 August 1984, p. 182.
68 J. F. Smith, *et al.*, *Words in Season*.
69 H. B. Lee, *Teachings 1996*, 6 June 1953, p. 340. See also H. B. Lee, *Place*.
70 Cf. *Commentary 3:8-b*, p. 160. See *Endnote 3-30*, p. 203.
71 R. D. Draper, *et al.*, *Commentary*, p. 227.
72 E.g., J. F. Smith, Jr., *Doctrines*, October 1928, 1:73-74.
73 See *Endnote 3-31*, p. 203.
74 See *Endnote 3-32*, p. 203.

Finally, this proposal offers no guidance about how to reconcile current scientific thinking with statements from scripture and early Church leaders that seem to imply that the earth was moved from one location in the universe to another.

2. Eden situated in a different place or "state" than the earth as we know it. A second possibility is that the events of the Fall did not take place on the earth as we know it. For example, the bodies of Adam and Eve could have been prepared in some manner beforehand on the earth[75] and afterward the couple could have been temporarily placed in a terrestrial environment to experience the events of the Garden of Eden.[76] As with the first possibility discussed above, this interpretation of the story would be consistent with the implication of Moses 3:8 that the bodies of Adam and Eve were created outside the Garden (i.e., on the earth?[77]) and only later placed in Paradise ("there I put the man whom I had formed"[78]). Special conditions, perhaps paralleling those that characterize worlds where translated beings dwell,[79] would be required as part of the design of the Garden of Eden.[80] An important consequence of this view is that the subsequent Fall would not have required the movement of an entire planet from one place to another, but only the removal of Adam and Eve from the state or place of Eden to the telestial earth (a form of "reverse translation")—an earth where natural conditions (including death and "time") had already prevailed from the beginning of its creation.[81] A strong point of this proposal is that it allows for an earth consistent with scientific findings of a long and continuous biological, geographical, and planetary history.

Several ancient parallels can be taken as suggesting the idea that the Garden was not on the earth but rather in a place of a higher order or "sphere" to which Adam and Eve were "transplanted" from the earth.[82] For example, in *4 Ezra* God speaks of Eden as "the garden which our right hand had planted *before* the earth appeared."[83] *2 Enoch* gives an interesting variation of the phrase in Moses 4:25 "for dust thou wast, and unto dust shalt thou return": "You are earth, and into the earth once again you will go, out of which I took you. And I will not destroy you, but I will send you away to what I took you from."[84] This can be read as implying that Adam, his body formed out of earthly materials and afterwards placed in the Garden, was sent back again from Eden to Earth to live after the Fall.[85] Similarly, Anderson reads the *Life of Adam and Eve* as asserting that "Adam and Eve do not inhabit the earth until after they are cast out of the Garden"[86] and "fall down to the world."[87] Islamic scripture and commentary record a parallel view in the teaching that, although it was the "divine plan" that Adam and Eve (representing all mankind)[88] should come to the earth to live,[89]

75   See *Endnote 3-33*, p. 204.

76   Cf. S. D. Ricks, *Adam's Fall*, pp. 598-599; S. E. Robinson, *Book of Adam*, p. 141; O. S. Wintermute, *Jubilees*, 3:9, p. 59.

77   The fifteenth-century *Creation and Fall* speaks of Adam having been created from the "common earth" rather than the "earth of Paradise" where he was later placed (M. Herbert, *Irish Apocrypha*, p. 3).

78   Cf. R. M. Zlotowitz, *et al.*, *Bereishis*, p. 94.

79   J. Taylor, *Mediation*, 1882, pp. 75-78.

80   H. L. Andrus, *God*, p. 381 n. 88. See *Endnote 3-34*, p. 204.

81   See *Endnote 3-35*, p. 204.

82   D. C. Matt, *Zohar 1*, Be-Reshit 1:35b, pp. 221-222. See *Endnote 3-36*, p. 204.

83   B. M. Metzger, *Fourth Ezra*, 3:6, p. 528, emphasis added; cf. Jerahmeel ben Solomon, *Chronicles*, 1:2, p. 5; M.-A. Ouaknin, *et al.*, *Rabbi Éliézer*, 3, p. 30; H. Sperling, *et al.*, *Zohar*, Leviticus 34b, 4:391.

84   F. I. Andersen, *2 Enoch*, 32:1, p. 154.

85   *Ibid.*, p. 155 n. 32b.

86   G. A. Anderson, *Ezekiel*, p. 142.

87   M. E. Stone, *Fall of Adam*, 19, p. 7; cf. W. L. Lipscomb, *Expulsion*, 1, p. 135.

88   See *Endnote 3-37*, p. 205.

89   See *Endnote 3-38*, p. 205.

FIGURE 3-7. *Adam's Peak, 1780*
Antoine-François Prévost

We said: Get down… And there is for you in the earth an abode and a provision for a time.[1] The widespread tradition that Adam and Eve descended to the earth after the Fall is associated with several geographical spots. One example is the mountain of Sri Pada[2] or Adam's Peak in Sri Lanka whose top bears an indentation resembling a five-foot-long footprint on a boulder at the summit.

To reach the holy site, pilgrims cross a 30-mile-long chain of limestone shoals[3] from India to Sri Lanka and, once arrived, ascend, as shown in this illustration, by pulling themselves up with chains to the top.[4] Describing his own ascent by this means, the English politician Sir James Emerson Tennent (1804-1869), whose meticulously-researched book on Ceylon remained the standard history of the island until well into the 20th century,[5] wrote: "As the pillar-like crag rounds away at either side, the eye, if turned downwards, peers into a chasm of unseen depth; and so dizzy is the elevation, that the guides discourage a pause, lest a sudden gust of wind should sweep the adventurous climber from his giddy footing, into the unfathomable gulfs below."[6]

1   *Qur'an* 2:3, as translated in A.at-Tabataba'i, *Al-Mizan*, 2:36, 1:177.
2   = sacred footprint.
3   Rama's/Nala's/Adam's bridge.
4   H. W. Nibley, *Teachings of the PGP*, 16, p. 195. See also *Figure 6-14*, p. 473.
5   K. M. de Silva, *Tennent*, pp. 24, 25; R. Jones, *Tennent*.
6   J. E. Tennent, *Ceylon*, 2:138-139.

they "begin in a garden not of this world."[90] According to the *Qur'an*, they did not stay in this other-worldly Garden forever because:

> Satan made them both slip[91] from it, and drove them out of what they were in; and We said: Get down,[92] some of you being the enemies of others.[93] And there is for you in the earth an abode and a provision for a time.[94]

One Islamic tradition records that at the time of their removal from Eden to the earth, Adam and Eve descended respectively upon the Saudi Arabian hills of al-Safä and

90   F. I. Andersen, *2 Enoch*, p. 155 n. 32b. See *Endnote 3-39*, p. 206.
91   See *Endnote 3-40*, p. 206.
92   See *Endnote 3-41*, p. 206.
93   See *Endnote 3-42*, p. 206.
94   A.at-Tabataba'i, *Al-Mizan*, 2:36, 1:177. See *Endnote 3-43*, p. 206.

al-Marwah[95] where Adam is said to have "remained in prostration for forty days, weeping for the Garden."[96] Other commentators have written that it was not a mountain but rather a valley called *Saràndib*[97] wherein "Adam descended from… heaven."[98]

3. Eden as a place whose description includes figurative elements. The blend of figurative elements in the stories of the Creation, the Fall, and the Garden of Eden provides a powerful means to teach complex ideas that would be difficult to comprehend and recall if presented in purely abstract terms. Though affirming the identity of Adam and Eve as historical figures, the reality of the Fall, and the tangible nature of the "sacred space" of Eden, Joseph Fielding McConkie is not troubled by the presence of symbols and metaphors in scriptural accounts:

> What, then, do we conclude of the Eden story? Was it figurative or literal? We answer by way of comparison. It, like the temple ceremony, combines a rich blend of both. Our temples are real, the priesthood is real, the covenants we enter into are real, and the blessings we are promised by obedience are real; yet the teaching device may be metaphorical. We are as actors on a stage. We role-play and imagine. We do not actually advance from one world to another in the temple, but rather are taught with figurative representations of what can and will be.… In the story of man's earthly origin we find the rich blend of figurative and literal that is so typical of the Bible, of the teachings of Christ, and of our daily experience—this that the story might unfold according to the faith and wisdom that we bring to it. Like all scriptural texts, its interpretation becomes a measure of our maturity and our spiritual integrity.[99]

In support of this view, which is not necessarily incompatible with the other interpretations discussed above, it can be easily admitted that the scriptural details of locations and specific events in Moses 3-4 are obscure, and that there is a strong symbolic component of many of the descriptions of the places, characters, props, and events of Eden. In fact, Faulconer explains that reading scripture "typologically, figurally, anagogically, or allegorically" is not what a premodern would have done:

> … instead of or in addition to reading literally. Such readings are part and parcel of a literal reading. Premodern understanding does not reduce the biblical story to a reference to or representation of something else, though it also does not deny that there may be an important representative element in scripture.[100] Instead, premoderns believe that to understand the story of Israel is essentially to understand history—actual history, the real events of the world—as incarnation, a continuing incarnation, as types and shadows…[101]

---

95   See *Endnote 3-45*, p. 207.

96   al-Qummi in A. at-Tabataba'i, *Al-Mizan*, 1:197. See also M. al-Kisa'i, *Tales*, pp. 55-57, 65-66; A. al-Tha'labi, *Lives*, p. 59; G. Weil, *Legends*, pp. 34-36; *Commentary 5:4-c*, p. 357; 5:6-a, p. 360.

97   The term is probably derived from Ceylon (Sri Lanka).

98   A. at-Tabataba'i, *Al-Mizan*, 1:213; cf. A. al-Tha'labi, *Lives*, p. 58; J. C. Reeves, *al-Yaqubi*; G. Weil, *Legends*, p. 33. See *Endnote 3-46*, p. 208.

99   J. F. McConkie, *Eden*, pp. 29, 35.

100   Cf. H. W. Nibley, *Treasures*, pp. 179-180; H. W. Nibley, *Teachings of the PGP*, 16, p. 203; *Excursus 13: Some Perspectives on Historicity*, p. 552.

101   J. E. Faulconer, *Incarnation*, p. 48. See also J. S. Tanner, *World and Word*, pp. 226-230; M. Barker, *Christmas*, pp. 29-30. Regarding types and shadows, see, e.g., Mosiah 3:15. See *Endnote 3-47*, p. 208.

FIGURE 3-8. *Court of the Palms Mural at Mari (Tel Hariri), Syria, ca. 1750 BCE*

And I, the Lord God, planted a garden eastward in Eden, and there I put the man whom I had formed… And I… planted the tree of life also in the midst of the garden, and also the tree of knowledge of good and evil. And I… caused a river to go out of Eden… and from thence it… became into four heads.[1] Writes Porter: "Some of [the mural's] features strikingly recall details of the Genesis description of the Garden of Eden. In particular, the mural depicts two types of tree,[2] guarded by mythical winged animals or cherubim.[3] The lower half of the central panel shows figures holding jars from which flow four streams[, with a seedling growing out of the middle,[4] in a basement room that might be seen as providing an ideal setting for ritual washings].[5] The upper scene may depict a king being invested by the Mesopotamian fertility goddess Ishtar: Eve has been associated with such divine figures."[6] Note the king's right hand raised, perhaps in an oath-related gesture.[7] His outstretched left hand receives the crown and staff of his office.[8] In the symmetrical side panels at the far left and right of the mural, two naked men climb each of the two date palms;[9] the one on the right can clearly be seen as harboring a dove.[10] Like the two goddesses witnessing the investiture, the figures near the trees raise their hands in worship and supplication,[11] suggesting a parallel between the tree and the king himself. Like the tree, the king is an "archetypal receiver and distributor of divine blessing."[12]

---

1   Moses 3:8-10.
2   Cf. Moses 3:9.
3   Cf. Moses 4:31. See *Commentary* 4:31-c, p. 280.
4   Alma 32:41-42.
5   Cf. Moses 3:10, 1 Nephi 11:25.
6   J. R. Porter, *Guide*, p. 28.
7   S. D. Ricks, *Oaths*, pp. 49-50.
8   Cf. R. Giorgi, *Anges*, p. 281. See *Figure 4-6*, p. 224.
9   Associated in some cultures with the idea of heavenly ascent and the attainment of divine vision. See, e.g., E. A. S. Butterworth, *Tree*, p. 213.
10   See *Commentary* 1:1-b, p. 42; 3:9-g, p. 166; 4:5-b, p. 246; *Figure 6-14*, p. 473; *Excursus 50: Fu Xi and Nü Gua*, p. 654. See *Endnote 3-48*, p. 209.
11   Y. M. al-Khalesi, *Palms*, pp. 45, 54, 56; L. M. Hilton, *Hand*; S. D. Ricks, *Oaths*, pp. 49-50; D. R. Seely, *Raised Hand*; cf. *Commentary* 5:4-a, p. 355. See *Endnote 5-65*, p. 449. See *Endnote 6-30*, p. 499.
12   T. Stordalen, *Echoes*, p. 101.

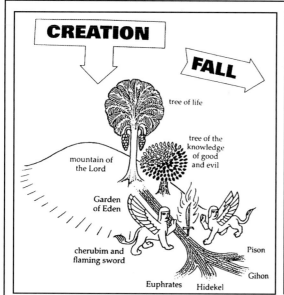 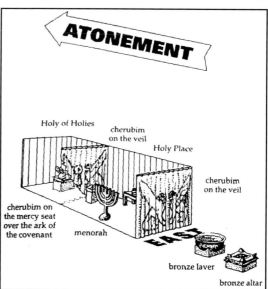

FIGURE 3-9. *Sacred Topography of Eden and the Temple, 1994*
Michael P. Lyon, 1952-

Thus shall Aaron come into the holy place: with a young bullock for a sin offering, and a ram for a burnt offering. He shall put on the holy linen coat, and he shall have the linen breeches upon his flesh, and shall be girded with a linen girdle, and with the linen mitre shall be attired... [he] shall wash his flesh in water, and so put them on... Then shall he kill the goat of the sin offering... and bring his blood within the vail... and sprinkle it upon the mercy seat: And he shall make an atonement for the holy place... because of their transgressions.[1] The Garden of Eden served as a prototype for Israelite temples where atonement was made for the sins of the people. About the journey made within the temple, Nibley comments: "Properly speaking, one did not go 'through' the temple—in one door and out another—for one enters and leaves by the same door, but by moving in opposite directions... The Two Ways of Light and Darkness are but one way after all, as the wise Heraclitus said: 'The up-road and the down-road are one'; which one depends on the way we are facing."[2]

---

1   Leviticus 16:3-4, 15-16.
2   H. W. Nibley, *Message 2005*, pp. 442-443.

The Garden of Eden and the Creation as Models for the Temple

As additional evidence for mutual dependence between the creation accounts of Moses 2 and of Moses 3, it should be noted that the stories of the Creation and the Garden of Eden are united in the architecture and the ritual of both ancient and modern temples.[102] Indeed, the Garden itself can be seen as a natural "temple," where Adam and Eve lived in God's presence for a time, and mirroring the configuration of the heavenly temple intended as their ultimate destination.[103] Moses 4 tells of how Adam and Eve were cast out from God's presence after the Fall and, in modern temples, the posterity of Adam and Eve trace the footsteps of their first parents both away from Eden and then in reverse direction.[104] First, they witness the events that led to the expulsion of the man and the woman. Then, starting from the setting of the telestial world in which we now live, they are returned to the paradisiacal glory of the Garden, and ultimately to the presence of God.[105] In conformance with the law of Moses:

---

102   M. B. Brown, *Gate*, pp. 26-33, 113-117; D. W. Parry, *Garden*, pp. 126-127.
103   J. M. Lundquist, *Reality*; J. A. Parry, *et al.*, *Temple in Heaven*; T. Stordalen, *Echoes*, pp. 112-116, 308-309. See *Excursus 14: The Garden of Eden as a Prototype for the Temple*, p. 555.
104   Cf. John 16:28.
105   G. M. Leonard, *Nauvoo*, pp. 258-259; J. E. Talmage, *House of the Lord*, 4, pp. 54, 55; B. Young, *6 April 1853 - B*, p. 31. See *Excursus 15: Description of the LDS Temple Endowment*, p. 557.

FIGURE 3-10. *Sacred Stones Emerging from the Waters*
John M. Lundquist

And I, God, said: Let the waters under the heaven be gathered together unto one place, and it was so; and I, God, said: Let there be dry land; and it was so.[1] In ancient Israel, the holiest spot on earth was believed to be the Foundation Stone in front of the Ark within the temple at Jerusalem: "it was the first solid material to emerge from the waters of Creation,[2] and it was upon this stone that the Deity effected Creation."[3] Lundquist cites a famous passage in the *Midrash Tanhuma* to this effect: "Just as the navel is found at the centre of a human being, so the land of Israel is found at the center of the world. Jerusalem is at the center of the land of Israel, and the temple is at the center of Jerusalem, the Holy of Holies is at the center of the temple, the Ark is at the center of the Holy of Holies, and the Foundation Stone is in front of the Ark, which spot is the foundation of the world."[4] Ancient temples found in other cultures throughout the world also represent—and are often built upon—elevations that emulate the holy mountain at the starting point of Creation.[5] Nibley writes that the temple is "the 'hierocentric point,' the place where all time, space, and humanity come together. The word *templum* not only designates the template, the point of cutting between the *cardo* and *decumanus* from which the observer of the heavens makes his viewing, it is also the diminutive of the word *tempus*, denoting that it measures the divisions of time and space in a single pattern. There, all the records of the past are kept and all of the prophecies for the future are divined."[6] To the temple are owed the beginnings of culture and civilization.[7]

Often symbolized as a cosmic tree, the temple "originates in the underworld, stands on the earth as a 'meeting place,' and yet towers (architecturally) into the heavens and gives access to the heavens through its ritual."[8] In this beautiful photograph by Lundquist, a structure of sacred stones emerging from the surrounding waters evokes "tranquility charged with divine force."[9]

1 Moses 2:9.
2 Psalm 104:7-9.
3 J. M. Lundquist, *Meeting Place*, p. 7.
4 *Ibid.*, p. 7; cf. E. A. S. Butterworth, *Tree*, pp. 88-89; J. M. Lundquist, *Temple of Jerusalem*, p. 26; Z. Vilnay, *Sacred Land*, pp. 5-6; O. S. Wintermute, *Jubilees*, 8:19, p. 73; 3:9-14, 27, pp. 59-60; 4:26, p. 63. See *Endnote 3-51*, p. 209.
5 See E. A. S. Butterworth, *Tree*.
6 H. W. Nibley, *Return*, p. 47.
7 H. W. Nibley, *What*, pp. 379-381.
8 J. M. Lundquist, *Fundamentals*, p. 675. See *Excursus 50: Fu Xi and Nü Gua*, p. 654.
9 J. M. Lundquist, *Meeting Place*, p. 45.

Anciently, once a year on *Yom Kippur*, the Day of Atonement, Adam's eastward expulsion from the garden was reversed when the high priest traveled west past the consuming fire of sacrifice and the purifying water of the laver, through the veil woven with images of cherubim. Thus, he returned to the original point of Creation, where he poured out the atoning blood of the sacrifice, reestablishing the covenant relationship with God.[106]

The process of Creation has frequently provided a second model for temple building and ritual.[107] For example, Nibley's unique reading of the first lines of *Enuma Elish* associates the Babylonian creation story with temple themes:

At once above when the heavens had not yet received their name and the earth below was not yet named, the Holy of Holies, the most inner sanctuary of the temple... had not yet been built.[108]

106 D. W. Parry, *Garden*, p. 135. See also R. N. Holzapfel, *et al.*, *Father's House*, pp. 17-19.
107 H. W. Nibley, *Return*, pp. 71-73.
108 H. W. Nibley, *Teachings of the PGP*, 10, p. 122; cf. E. A. Speiser, *Creation Epic*, 1:1ff., pp. 60-61.

Later, explained Nibley:

> Marduk progressed through the heavens inspecting their places of various worlds, and there he established a new world, an exact replica of the Apsu, the dwelling of Ea. Remember "like unto the other worlds we have hitherto created." Same thing here—following the heavenly pattern. As President Joseph F. Smith said, this earth in its natural state is exactly like the world that came from the hand of God, and it's a duplicate of his own.[109] "The Lord Marduk took its measurements. [They are extremely important here.] He built the famous Midok. He built his own palace, the Eshar, the temple of Eridu, the first temple on earth, representing the earth itself at creation [notice the name of Eridu, *eretz*, earth…] after its pattern. The palace of Eshar which he built was thus the [model of] heaven itself… He caused Anu, Enlil, and Ea [the three degrees of glory] to come and occupy the temple for its dedication."[110]

Likewise, as Barker describes, "the [Israelite] temple represented the Creation and the Creation was the true temple. The Holy of Holies with the divine throne and the angels behind the veil were the invisible creation; the great hall of the temple was the Garden of Eden, the visible creation."[111] Nibley called the temple as a "scale-model of the universe," a place for taking bearings on the cosmos and finding one's place within it.[112]

There is evidence that the creation account of Genesis 1:1-2:4 was used in Israel's temple liturgy before the Babylonian exile, paralleling the use of other creation accounts in New Year's rites throughout the Near East.[113] In fact, the very architecture of the Tabernacle and the temple of ancient Israel seems to have been a similitude based on Moses' vision of the Creation.[114] The requirement for such a likeness may have motivated differences between Moses' creation account and those given in the book of Abraham and in modern temples,[115] the form of the Genesis description having been shaped to advantage for teaching the pattern of temple building. Note the following reconstruction by Ginzberg:

> God told the angels: On the first day of Creation, I shall make the heavens and stretch them out; so will Israel raise up the Tabernacle as the dwelling place of my Glory.[116] On the second day I shall put a division between the terrestrial waters and the heavenly waters, so will [Moses] hang up a veil in the Tabernacle to divide the Holy Place and the Most Holy.[117] On the third day I shall make the earth to put forth grass and herbs; so will he, in obedience to my commands, eat herbs on the first night of Passover and prepare shewbread before me.[118] On the fourth day I shall make the luminaries; so he will stretch out a golden candlestick before me.[119] On the fifth day I shall create the birds; so he will fashion the cherubim with outstretched wings.[120] On the sixth day I shall create man; so will Israel set aside a man from the sons of Aaron as high priest for my service.[121]

109   No source given.

110   H. W. Nibley, *Teachings of the PGP*, 10, p. 126; cf. E. A. Speiser, *Creation Epic*, 4, pp. 66-67.

111   M. Barker, *Hidden*, p. 18; cf. M. Barker, *Christmas*, pp. 3-4. See *Excursus 25: The Tree of Life as the Hidden Throne of God*, p. 591.

112   H. W. Nibley, *Meaning of Temple*, pp. 14-15; cf. H. W. Nibley, *Greatness*, p. 301.

113   M. Barker, *Hidden*, pp. 17-18; S. D. Ricks, *Liturgy*.

114   M. Barker, *Revelation*, pp. 24-25. See *Excursus 16: The Role of Revelation in Temple Building*, p. 561.

115   See *Endnote 2-7*, p. 125.

116   Exodus 40:17-19.

117   Exodus 40:20-21. See *Excursus 17: The Veil of the Temple*, p. 564.

118   Exodus 12:8, 25:30.

119   Exodus 25:31-40, 37:17-24. See *Endnote 3-49*, p. 209.

120   Exodus 25:18-22, 37:6-9.

121   L. Ginzberg, *Legends*, 1:51; cf. W. Williams, *Shadow*; A. LaCocque, *Trial*, p. 54 n. 18, pp. 65-66 n. 57; Exodus 40:12-15. See *Endnote 3-50*, p. 209.

THE ARK OF THE COVENANT
SHEWING Y BARRS ON Y SIDE
ACCORDING TO I KINGS VIII 8
THE CHERUBIMS ABOVE ON
THE COVERING, EACH WITH
TWO WINGS WITHOUT HANDS

AND A CLOUD ABOVE BE-
TWIN Y CHERUBIMS WHICH
SEEMS TO SHINE AND, AS
IT WERE EMBRACED BY
WINGS OF Y CHERUBIMS
according to Schatover & others

FIGURE 3-11. *Holy of Holies in Solomon's Temple*
Juan Bautista Villalpando, 1594-1605

From the ground unto above the door were cherubims and palm trees made, and on the wall of the temple.[1] The palm trees and pillars in the Holy of Holies in Solomon's temple can be seen as representing "a kind of stylized forest."[2] The angels on the walls may have represented God's heavenly council,[3] or perhaps more generally the promise to the saints of communion with the "general assembly and church of the Firstborn,"[4] whose presence in heaven is mirrored on earth by those who have attained "angelic" status through being admitted to the presence of the Lord. The same kind of imagery in a Christian setting is suggested by the Chapter House in Worcester Cathedral, England, with "traces of painted drapery and angels in the bays and remains of a Tree of Jesse curling around the central pillar."[5] Writes Barker: "The outer part of the temple was 'the Holy Place,' meaning that it had been made holy, and it represented the visible world of ordinary human life. The sanctuary behind the curtain, however, was the invisible world of the angels[,] the 'Most Holy Place.'"[6]

Barker further explains: "The Hebrew words translated 'Most Holy' or 'Holy of Holies' do not mean simply a greater degree of holiness. They mean 'actively holy, imparting holiness.' 'The [tabernacle furnishings] shall be most holy' we read in Exodus, 'whatsoever touches them will become holy.'[7] 'Most holy' was the transforming, consecrating state, the source of power; and 'holiness' was the transformed, consecrated state."[8] "Most Holy Place" meant "that it was the source of the holiness that made the rest of creation holy. It was the presence of God."[9]

1   Ezekiel 41:20.
2   T. Stordalen, *Echoes*, p. 122.
3   M. B. Brown, *Gate*, p. 113.
4   D&C 107:19.
5   R. Rosewell, *Paintings*, p. 37, caption to Figure 39. See *Endnote E-212*, p. 755.
6   M. Barker, *Angels*, p. 13.
7   Exodus 30:29.
8   M. Barker, *Hidden*, pp. 21-22.
9   M. Barker, *Angels*, p. 13.

Exodus 40:33 describes how Moses completed the Tabernacle. The Hebrew text exactly parallels the account of how God finished Creation.[122] *Genesis Rabbah* comments: "It is as if, on that day [i.e., the day the Tabernacle was raised in the wilderness], I actually created the world."[123]

Fittingly, just as the first book of the Bible, Genesis, recounts the story of Adam and Eve being cast out from the Garden, its last book, Revelation, prophesies a permanent return to Eden for the sanctified.[124] In Eden, "there was no need for a temple—because Adam and Eve enjoyed the continual presence of God"—likewise, in John's vision "there was no temple in the Holy City, 'for its temple is the Lord God.'"[125] To reenter the Garden is to return to the original spiritual state of immortality and innocence through the atonement, and to know the oneness that existed at the dawn of Creation in an even more perfect manner.[126]

122   Moses 3:1. See *Endnote 3-52*, p. 209. See also R. S. Hendel, *Poetics of Myth*, p. 163.
123   J. Neusner, *Genesis Rabbah* 1, 3:9, p. 35.
124   Revelation 22:1-5. See M. Barker, *Revelation*, pp. 327-333; R. D. Draper, *et al.*, *Promises*.
125   W. J. Hamblin, *et al.*, *Temple*, pp. 14-15. See Revelation 21:22.
126   See the overview of Moses 6, pp. 463-472. See *Endnote 3-53*, p. 209.

MOSES 3

150

Moses 3: Text and Commentary

CHAPTER 3
(June–October 1830)

THE SEVENTH DAY (PP. 151-153)

THUS the *a*heaven and the earth were finished, and *b*all the host of them.

2 And *a*on the seventh day I, God, ended my work, and all things which I had made; and *b*I rested on the seventh day from all my work, and all things which I had made were finished, and I, God, saw that they were good;

3 And I, God, *a*blessed the seventh day, and *b*sanctified it; because that in it I had *c*rested from all my work which I, God, had created and made.

CREATED SPIRITUALLY (PP. 153-156)

4 *a*And now, behold, I say unto you, that *b*these are the generations of the heaven and of the earth, when they were created, *c*in the day that I, the *d*Lord God, made the heaven and the earth,

5 And *a*every plant of the field before it was in the earth, and every herb of the field before it grew. For I, the Lord God, *b*created all things, of which I have spoken, spiritually, before they were naturally upon the face of the earth. For I, the Lord God, *c*had not caused it to rain upon the face of the earth. And I, the Lord God, had created all the children of men; and not yet a man to till the ground; for *d*in heaven created I them; and *e*there was not yet flesh upon the earth, neither in the water, neither in the air;

CREATION OF ADAM (PP. 156-159)

6 But I, the Lord God, spake, and *a*there went up a mist from the earth, and watered the whole face of the ground;

7 And I, *a*the Lord God, formed man *b*from the dust of the ground, and *c*breathed into his nostrils the breath of life; and man became a *d*living soul, the *e*first flesh upon the earth, the *f*first man also; nevertheless, all things were before created; but spiri-

tually were they created and made according to my word.

THE GARDEN OF EDEN (PP. 159-172)

8 And I, the Lord God, *a*planted a garden *b*eastward in *c*Eden, and there *d*I put the man whom I had formed.

9 And out of the ground *a*made I, the Lord God, to grow every tree, naturally, that is *b*pleasant to the sight of man; and man could behold it. And *c*it became also a living soul. For *d*it was spiritual in the day that I created it; for *e*it remaineth in the sphere in which I, God, created it, yea, even all things which I prepared for the use of man; and man saw that it was good for food. And I, the Lord God, *f*planted the *g*tree of life also *h*in the midst of the garden, and also the *i*tree of knowledge of good and evil.

10 And I, the Lord God, *a*caused a river to go out of Eden to water the garden; and from thence it was parted, and became into four heads.

11 And I, the Lord God, called the name of the first *a*Pison, and it compasseth the whole land of Havilah, *b*where I, the Lord God, created much gold;

12 And the gold of that land was good, and there was *a*bdellium and the *b*onyx stone.

13 And the name of the second river was called *a*Gihon; the same that compasseth the whole land of Ethiopia.

14 And the name of the third river was *a*Hiddekel; that which goeth toward the east of *b*Assyria. And the fourth river was the *c*Euphrates.

ONE TREE FORBIDDEN (PP. 173-176)

15 And I, the Lord God, *a*took the man, and put him into the Garden of Eden, *b*to dress it, and to keep it.

16 And I, the Lord God, commanded the man, saying: Of every tree of the garden thou mayest freely eat,

17 But of the tree of the knowledge of good and evil, *a*thou shalt not eat of it, nevertheless, *b*thou mayest choose for thyself, for it is given unto

thee; but, remember that I forbid it, for *c*in the day thou eatest thereof thou shalt surely die.

ADAM NAMES ANIMALS (PP. 176-180)

18 And I, the Lord God, said unto mine Only Begotten, that *a*it was not good that the man should be alone; wherefore, *b*I will make *c*an help meet for him.

19 And *a*out of the ground I, the Lord God, formed every beast of the field, and every fowl of the air; and *b*commanded that they should come unto Adam, to see what he would call them; and they were also *c*living souls; for I, God, *d*breathed into them the breath of life, and commanded that whatsoever Adam called every living creature, that should be the name thereof.

20 And *a*Adam gave names to all cattle, and to the fowl of the air, and to every beast of the field; but as for Adam, *b*there was not found an help meet for him.

CREATION OF EVE (PP. 180-186)

21 And I, the Lord God, caused a *a*deep sleep to fall upon Adam; and he slept, and I *b*took one of his ribs and closed up the flesh in the stead thereof;

22 And *a*the rib which I, the Lord God, had taken from man, *b*made I a woman, and *c*brought her unto the man.

23 And *a*Adam said: This I know now is *b*bone of my bones, and flesh of my flesh; she shall be called *c*Woman, because she was *d*taken out of man.

24 Therefore shall a man leave his father and his mother, and shall *a*cleave unto his wife; and they shall be one flesh.

25 And *a*they were both naked, the man and his wife, and *b*were not ashamed.

*1 Thus the **heaven** and the earth were finished, and **all the host of them**.*

*2 And **on the seventh day I, God, ended my work**, and all things which I had made; and I rested on the seventh day from all my work, and all things which I had made were finished, and I, God, saw that they were good;*

1 a ***heaven.*** Note the change from the KJV plural "heavens" here and in v. 4.[127]

   b ***all the host of them.*** The idea is that the whole of creation is now organized and poised for action—all the actors and props are now in readiness for what will follow. Note the plural "hosts" in Abraham 5:1.

      In modern English, the phrase is typically translated "all their array." This reading preserves the sense of orderly, disciplined, and regimented arrangement conveyed by the underlying Hebrew.[128] Unfortunately, however, it obscures the military connotations associated with its use in most other Old Testament contexts.[129] This latter sense is usually still preserved in the KJV and, for example, in modern French and Spanish translations.[130]

      Zlotowitz explains that the common Old Testament phrase "host of the heavens" typically "refers to the celestial bodies, and occasionally refers to the angels."[131] Barker likewise sees an oblique reference in the term "host" to an account of the creation of "angels" or "sons of God" that appears to have been expurgated from some manuscripts of the Creation story during or after the Jewish exile.[132] The Jewish sage Ramban goes further to specifically include "the souls of humanity" as part of the host of heaven.[133] Jolly has documented nine Umbrian-Roman Creation cycles, all suggesting that "Adam and Eve's souls were made on Day One and stored away until later joined with their bodies in [Moses 3]." In these depictions, "Adam's and Eve's souls are shown as nude males and females, red and blue respectively, and in most they are surrounded by red and blue *mandorlas* [aureoles]."[134] Elder Joseph Fielding Smith similarly saw the host as including the organization and foreordination of spirits in premortal life.[135]

2 a ***on the seventh day I, God, ended my work.*** Sarna notes that this phrase does not necessarily imply any divine action on the seventh day; thus the phrase could alternatively be given as: "by the seventh day I, God, had ended my work" or "on the seventh day I, God, declared my work ended."[136] He further observes that: "The human institution of the Sabbath does not appear in the narrative. Indeed, the Hebrew noun *Shabbat* is absent, and we have only the verbal forms of the root… Nevertheless, there cannot be any doubt that the text provides the unspoken foundation for the future institution of the Sabbath. Not only is vocabulary of the present passage interwoven with other Pentateuchal references to the Sabbath,[137] but the connection with Creation is made explicit in the first version of the Ten Commandments, given in Exodus 20:8-11.… Through his weekly suspension of normal human activity, man

127 See *Commentary* 2:1-e, p. 95.
128   J. W. Wevers, *Notes*, p. 20.
129 F. Brown, *et al.*, *Lexicon*, pp. 838 d-839 a-c.
130 E.g., in French: "armée" = army (R. De Vaux, *Bible*, p. 18; L. Segond, *Bible*, p. 10); "milice" = militia (A. Chouraqui, *Bible*, p. 20). Likewise in Spanish: "huestes" = hosts (LDS book of Moses, 1993 edition).
131 R. M. Zlotowitz, *et al.*, *Bereishis*, p. 80. For an example of the former sense, see Deuteronomy 4:19; for the latter, see 1 Kings 22:19.
132 M. Barker, *Beyond*, pp. 196-198; M. Barker, *Timaeus*, pp. 283-285; M. Barker, *Temple Roots*, pp. 80-81. See also M. Barker, *Angel*, pp. 4ff; K. Christensen, *Paradigms*, pp. 23-24; W. L. Lipscomb, *Creation*, 1, p. 118; *LXX* Deuteronomy 32:8 (C. Dogniez, *et al.*, *Pentateuque*, p. 844 and n;; M. K. H. Peters, *Deuteronomy*, p. 37).
133 D. Blumenthal, *Reading*.
134 P. H. Jolly, *Eve and Adam*, p. 38.
135 J. F. Smith, Jr., *Answers*, 1966, 5:182-184. See also J. Smith, Jr., *Teachings*, 2 May 1844, p. 365; *Commentary* 2:2-b, p. 99, 2:4-c, p. 101; *Excursus 8: The Origin and Premortal Existence of Human Spirits*, p. 540; overview of Moses 3, p. 136.
136 N. M. Sarna, *Genesis*, p. 15.
137 Exodus 16:5, 22, 26; 23:12; 31:13-17; 34:21; 35:2; Leviticus 23:3.

*2 And **on the seventh day I, God, ended my work**, and all things which I had made; and I rested on the seventh day from all my work, and all things which I had made were finished, and I, God, saw that they were good;*

*3 And I, God, **blessed the seventh day**, and sanctified it; because that in it I had rested from all my work which I, God, had created and made.*

imitates the divine pattern."[138] Moreover, like other events in the story of Genesis, the scriptural account portrays the past as harbinger of the future. Writes Sailhamer: "At important points along the way, the author will return to the theme of God's 'rest' as a reminder of what yet lies ahead.[139] Later biblical writers continued to see a parallel between God's 'rest' in Creation and the future 'rest' that awaits the faithful."[140]

In the book of Hebrews, readers are urged to enter into the "Lord's rest."[141] Writes Thomas: "They had tarried too long in the foothills of spiritual experience. Having 'tasted of the heavenly gift,… the good word of God, and the powers of the world to come,'[142] they could no longer delay resuming the climb lest they lose the promise…. The promise that Paul refers to repeatedly is that same promise explained in Doctrine and Covenants 88:68-69: 'Therefore, sanctify yourselves… and the days will come that you shall see [God]; for he will unveil his face unto you.'"[143]

D&C 77:12 seems to imply that it was God's work thus far, rather than the seventh day itself, that was sanctified. Additionally, the verse can be taken to say that the creation of man's physical body took place at the beginning of the seventh day rather than the end of the sixth: "… as God made the world in six days, and on the seventh day he finished his work, and sanctified it, and also formed man out of the dust of the earth." Because the verse seems to contradict the standard interpretation of Moses 2:26-27 as being an account of the physical creation of mankind, some have concluded that there is either a semantic or "grammatical ambiguity" in the revelation,[144] or perhaps some error of transcription, since "early manuscript copies of section 77 have not survived."[145] Yet others argue for the view that Moses 2:26-27 is an account of the creation of the spirits of mankind.[146]

b *I rested.* The theme of God's rest recurs three times in this verse. Rather than speaking and working, here He blesses and sanctifies. Moreover, Sailhamer observes: "Unlike the other days of Creation,… the seventh day stands apart from the other six days in not having an account of its conclusion. It is this feature of the narrative that has suggested a picture of an eternal, divine 'Sabbath'.… Consequently, immediately after the narrative of the Fall,[147] …the verb *asah* points to an interruption of God's 'Sabbath'" when, as a final act of Creation, He made coats of skin for Adam and Eve."[148]

3 a *blessed the seventh day.* The culmination of the week of divine activity is not an act of creation, but rather the blessing and sanctification of the day when Creation had ceased. Unlike the specific blessings to man and the animals given in Moses 2:22, 28, this blessing "is undefined and pertains to time itself… God, through His creativity, has already established His sovereignty over space; the idea here is that He is sovereign over time as well."[149]

---

138   N. M. Sarna, *Genesis*, pp. 14, 15.
139   Moses 3:15; 8:9; Genesis 8:4; Exodus 20:11; Deuteronomy 5:14; 12:10; 25:19.
140   J. H. Sailhamer, *Genesis*, p. 39. See Psalm 95:11; Hebrews 3:11.
141   Hebrews 4:3, 10.
142   Hebrews 6:4-6.
143   M. C. Thomas, *Hebrews*, pp. 479-480.
144   S. E. Robinson, *et al.*, *D&C Commentary*, 2:347—e.g., perhaps "finished" should be taken as meaning "ended."
145   L. W. Cook, *Revelations*, p. 312.
146   See *Commentary* 2:26-a, p. 111.
147   Moses 4:27.
148   J. H. Sailhamer, *Genesis*, pp. 38-39.
149   N. M. Sarna, *Genesis*, p. 15.

3 And I, God, blessed the seventh day, and **sanctified it***; because that in it I had* **rested from all my work** *which I, God, had created and made.*

4 ***And now, behold, I say unto you,*** *that* **these are the generations of the heaven and of the earth***, when they were created, in the day that I, the Lord God, made the heaven and the earth,*

b *sanctified it.* To "sanctify" something is to declare it not merely *good* (as was done for the products of the six days of Creation) but rather to make it *holy.* From this perspective, Madsen explains, "far from [it] being a day of strict injunctions, which are joyless duties imposed on duties of the prior day, the Sabbath is the reward for, the outcome of, indeed the climax of all other preparatory creations. It is not an imposed stoppage. It is what all the preparation was designed for, and therefore it has great value. It was, indeed, made for man."[150]

c *rested from all my work.* The term translated as "rested" fundamentally means "cessation," "and implies… the celebration and completion of an accomplishment."[151]

4 a *And now, behold, I say unto you.* This introductory phrase in Moses reinforces the interruption of narrative flow already apparent in KJV Genesis. Though typically seen as a clumsily exposed stitch in a narrative seam joining two separate accounts of Creation, there may be more editorial subtlety and skill shown here than what is immediately apparent. For example, Nibley has explained the apparent discontinuity between the previous narrative and the verses that follow as a purposive shift, regarding the Creation account as stage directions composed to accompany a ritual drama.[152] In such a reading, as the previous verse closes the curtain on the drama's prologue outlining the seven days of Creation, the narrator pauses to explain that all things were created spiritually prior to their natural appearance on the earth.[153] Following this interlude, the curtain reopens and we witness a change of scene: we are now viewing the details of the story of the creation of man not from the vantage point of heaven, but instead as it is seen from the Garden.[154]

Sarna comments: "This change in perspective is signaled by the inversion [in Genesis and Abraham (though not in Moses)] of the regular sequence 'heaven and earth' in the opening sentence. The almost unique expression 'earth and heaven' suggests pride of place [in the account that follows] for terrestrial affairs."[155] Thus, the account of Moses 3, which presupposes a knowledge of the preceding events of Creation, reiterates many of the themes in Moses 2 albeit with a terrestrial perspective—one that sets the context for the crucial events in Eden that will so radically alter the human condition.[156]

b *these are the generations of the heaven and of the earth.* As in its other occurrences, this formula is meant to introduce the story that follows, not to summarize the preceding account.[157] Moreover, the phrase "And the Gods came down" in Abraham 5:4[158] also seems to signal the beginning of a new narrative unit rather than the end of the former one. Thus, we might alternately punctuate this passage as follows: "… these are the generations of the heaven and the earth, when they were created: At the time that I, the Lord God, made the heaven and the earth…"[159]

MOSES 3

150 T. G. Madsen, *Sabbath*, p. 332; cf. R. M. Zlotowitz, *et al., Bereishis*, p. 82; Mark 2:27.
151 B. T. Arnold, *Genesis*, p. 24.
152 H. W. Nibley, *Myths*, p. 42; cf. H. W. Nibley, *Drama*, p. 36.
153 Moses 3:4-5.
154 H. W. Nibley, *Message 2005*, p. 284; H. W. Nibley, *Before Adam*, p. 72.
155 N. M. Sarna, *Genesis*, p. 16.
156 *Ibid.*, p. 16.
157 *Ibid.*, pp. 48-49; V. P. Hamilton, *Genesis*, pp. 4-5, 151.
158 Paralleling the wording of Abraham 4:26-27.
159 Cf. R. E. Friedman, *Commentary*, p. 16.

*4 And now, behold, I say unto you, that **these are the generations of the heaven and of the earth**, when they were created, **in the day** that I, the **Lord God**, made the heaven and the earth,*

*5 And **every plant of the field before it was in the earth, and every herb of the field before it grew**. For I, the Lord God, created all things, of which I have spoken, spiritually, before they were naturally upon the face of the earth. For I, the Lord God, had not caused it to rain upon the face of the earth. And I, the Lord God, had created all the children of men; and not yet a man to till the ground; for in heaven created I them; and there was not yet flesh upon the earth, neither in the water, neither in the air;*

MOSES 3

Wenham observes that this introductory statement "not only links this cycle of narratives with those which follow,[160] but implies that the characters who appear in [Moses 3 and 4] are as real as the patriarchs."[161]

generations. Friedman suggests that the term generations, which recurs ten additional times in Genesis as part of the phrase "these are the generations," is more adequately translated as records: "The word is used both to introduce records of births[162] and to introduce stories of events within a family[163]… It thus means historical records, and usually family records."[164]

Using the same technique of "pearling" that is repeated throughout the Hexateuch,[165] the topic of mankind at the end of Moses 2 becomes the focus of the new unit.[166]

c   **in the day.** This expression should not be taken as implying that everything was created in one day, but rather in the sense of "At the time that He made."[167]

d   **Lord God.** The consensus of most scholars is that the use of the divine name "Lord God" (as opposed to "God" in Moses 2) signals a different source for the text that follows.[168] However, this does not explain why a compound form of the name is used so frequently in this part of Moses/Genesis when all other portions of the book associated with the same source simply use "Lord." One conjecture is that the two names have been conjoined in order to emphasize "the concept of a God whose sovereign control extends to both the material[169] and the moral[170] world."[171] Similarly, the compound name seems to simultaneously express the conviction that God was both the Creator of the world and the covenant partner of Israel.[172] "YHWH reflects the divine as engaged with humankind."[173]

The compound name is notably missing in the dialogue between Eve and the serpent, who refers to Deity exclusively as Elohim (God).[174]

5   a   **every plant of the field before it was in the earth, and every herb of the field before it grew.** The passage beginning with this verse might be paraphrased as follows: "Before there were any troublesome weeds, before the cultivated grain was grown, before God caused the rain

160   E.g., Moses 6:8 or Genesis 11:27.
161   G. J. Wenham, *Genesis 1-15*, p. 54.
162   As in Moses 6:8; cf. 6:5, 22 where the term "genealogy" is used.
163   As in Genesis 37:2.
164   R. E. Friedman, *Commentary*, p. 16.
165   See, e.g., Moses 4:29, 5:1.
166   D. A. Dorsey, *Structure*, p. 49.
167   U. Cassuto, *Documentary*, p. 73. See Moses 2:5-e, p. 103.
168   R. E. Friedman, *Who*, pp. 81-83.
169   Moses 2.
170   Moses 3.
171   V. P. Hamilton, *Genesis*, p. 153. See also U. Cassuto, *Documentary*, pp. 15-41; R. M. Zlotowitz, *et al.*, *Bereishis*, pp. 87-89.
172   G. J. Wenham, *Genesis 1-15*, p. 57.
173   T. L. Brodie, *Dialogue*, p. 126; cf. pp. 143-144.
174   See *Commentary* 4:7-a, p. 251.

*5 And **every plant of the field before it was in the earth, and every herb of the field before it grew**. For I, the Lord God, **created all things**, of which I have spoken, **spiritually, before they were naturally upon the face of the earth**. For I, the Lord God, **had not caused it to rain upon the face of the earth**. And I, the Lord God, had created all the children of men; **and not yet a man to till the ground**; for in heaven created I them; and there was not yet flesh upon the earth, neither in the water, neither in the air;*

to fall, before man was commanded to till the ground, God made all things spiritually. He made man from the ground, planted a Garden for him, and put him there." The details of the arrangement of the Garden will be described in the next few verses,[175] highlighting the careful design and planning involved. Once all this has been explained, the story will resume by repeating and elaborating God's act in placing man in the Garden.[176]

It appears that this passage is intended to do more than affirm the spiritual creation of plant life. While the "as not yet" pattern is a common opening to ancient creation accounts,[177] the Genesis/Moses version is unique in that it seems to indicate that the Fall, rather than the first act of Creation, is the principal transforming event with which the account is concerned. Consistent with this suggestion, Cassuto concludes that the primary function of the formula "every... before" is to foreshadow the requirement for human cultivation of the earth after the Fall. In support of this reading, Cassuto cites a connection between the initial absence of the plants (*siah* = shrub) of the field and herb ('*eshebh* = grain) of the field mentioned here, and the later introduction of the thorns and thistles (interpreted as a particularization of *siah*) and herb of the field as a consequence of transgression in Moses 4:24.[178] From this perspective, the phrase could be seen as part of the opening bracket to the account that ends in 4:29,[179] serving to highlight the fact that neither the troublesome weeds (that depend on rain) nor the life-sustaining grains (that depend upon human cultivation) were to appear until after the Fall, when Adam and Eve were bereft of the fruit provided by the trees of the Garden.[180] From that point on, they would be obliged to till the ground by their own efforts and to call upon God to provide the rain on which the productivity of their fields would depend.[181]

b   ***created all things... spiritually, before they were naturally upon the face of the earth.*** This statement affirms that a spiritual creation preceded the natural (physical) creation. By spiritual creation is meant the premortal creation of all things in their spiritual state, including the creation of Eden, and everything in it.[182]

c   ***had not caused it to rain upon the face of the earth... and not yet a man to till the ground.*** Water in the Garden was to be provided by natural irrigation and not by rain (v. 6). After the Fall, rain was provided to water the grain tilled by Adam and Eve.

Sailhamer senses an allusion to the coming flood narratives in this statement about the withholding of rain.[183] In Genesis 7:4, God reverses the words of Moses 3:5 when He says: "I will cause it to rain upon the earth."

Active labor will be required of man within Eden, though not the same kind of labor that will be required when he begins to till the ground after the Fall.[184]

---

175   Moses 3:8-14.
176   Moses 3:15ff.; cf. J. H. Sailhamer, *Genesis*, p. 44.
177   E.g., E. A. Speiser, *Creation Epic*, 1:1-2, pp. 60-61. See discussion in C. Westermann, *Genesis 1-11*, pp. 43-47.
178   U. Cassuto, *Adam to Noah*, pp. 101-103.
179   See *Commentary* 4:29-c, p. 279l; cf. Moses 5:1, 2 Nephi 2:19
180   Moses 3:9.
181   R. M. Zlotowitz, *et al.*, *Bereishis*, pp. 88-90. See also *Commentary* 3:5-c, p. 155 and 4:24-b, p. 271.
182   See the overview of Moses 3, pp. 134-135, 139-144; *Commentary* 3:9-a, p. 162; 3:9-e, p. 162.
183   J. H. Sailhamer, *Genesis*, p. 40.
184   See *Commentary* 4:29-c, p. 279 and Moses 5:1. See also Moses 3:15-b, p. 173.

*5 And every plant of the field before it was in the earth, and every herb of the field before it grew. For I, the Lord God, created all things, of which I have spoken, spiritually, before they were naturally upon the face of the earth. For I, the Lord God, **had not caused it to rain upon the face of the earth**. And I, the Lord God, had created all the children of men; **and not yet a man to till the ground**; for **in heaven created I them**; and **there was not yet flesh upon the earth, neither in the water, neither in the air**;*

*6 But I, the Lord God, spake, and **there went up a mist from the earth**, and watered the whole face of the ground.*

Gaon sees a distinction between "ground" (*adamah*) and "earth" (*eretz*) in that the former "has an agricultural connotation implying 'soil,' while… 'earth' is a geographical term meaning the world in general or specifically the land of Israel."[185] Thus, in our verse: "had not caused it to rain upon… the earth" refers to the "world in general" while "not yet a man to till the ground" is speaking of the "cultivatable soil" that will become the responsibility of Adam to work after he and Eve are forced to leave the Garden.

d   ***in heaven created I them.*** Though some see Moses 2:26-27 as a reference to the creation of the spirits of mankind,[186] Elder Joseph Fielding Smith has commented: "There is no account of the creation of man or other forms of life when they were created as spirits. There is just the simple statement that they were so created before the physical creation. The statements in Moses 3:5 and Genesis 2:4 are interpolations thrown into the account of the physical creation, explaining that all things were first created in the spirit existence in heaven before they were placed upon this earth."[187]

e   ***there was not yet flesh upon the earth, neither in the water, neither in the air.*** See *Commentary 3:7-f, p. 159.*

6   **a**   ***there went up a mist from the earth.*** The English term "mist" seems out of place here, however evidence exists for a connection between the obscure Hebrew *'ed* and the Akkadian *edu*, "flood, waves, swell."[188] Thus one might translate this phrase alternately as: "a flow [or 'spring'[189]] would well up from the ground and water the whole surface of the earth."[190] This is consistent with being told later that "the Lord God caused a river to go out of Eden to water the garden."[191] Unlike the uncertain flows of the desert *wadi* which swelled when God provided rain and dried up when rain was withheld, the continuous flow of water from the deep assured the garden of unfailing fertility.[192] Moreover, in connection with the account of man's creation in v. 7, some commentators conclude that the resulting mixture of soil and water figuratively provided "the raw material with the proper consistency for being molded into man."[193]

---

185   R. M. Zlotowitz, *et al.*, *Bereishis*, p. 90.

186   See *Commentary* 2:26-a, p. 111.

187   J. F. Smith, Jr., *Doctrines*, 1954, 1:75-76. For summaries of teachings about premortal life and the origin of the human spirit in early LDS thought, see V. Hale, *Spirit*; C. R. Harrell, *Preexistence*; B. T. Ostler, *Preexistence*; B. L. Top, *Life Before*. See also *Excursus 8: The Origin and Premortal Existence of Human Spirits*, p. 540.

188   V. P. Hamilton, *Genesis*, p. 155.

189   R. J. V. Hiebert, *Septuagint*, p. 2.

190   N. M. Sarna, *Genesis*, p. 17.

191   *Commentary* 3:10-a, p. 170.

192   Cf. JST Genesis 13:10; U. Cassuto, *Documentary*, p. 104.

193   N. M. Sarna, *Genesis*, p. 17; contrast C. Westermann, *Genesis 1-11*, pp. 203-207. See also *Commentary 3:7-c, p. 157.*

MOSES 3

*7 And I, **the Lord God, formed man from the dust of the ground**, and breathed into his nostrils the breath of life; and man became a living soul, the first flesh upon the earth, the first man also; nevertheless, all things were before created; but spiritually were they created and made according to my word.*

7   **a**   ***the Lord God, formed man.*** The point being made here is that God provided a body made of earthly elements for the preexistent spirits of Adam and Eve.[194] The process by which this was done is left obscure. As Elder Packer wrote: "We are told that [the account of the Creation] is figurative insofar as the man and the woman are concerned."[195]

The wording of the scriptural account implies that God was involved in a more personal way in the forming of man than He was in the rest of the creation.[196] Accordingly, scriptures and statements of Church leaders have frequently been adduced to argue that Adam was born of divine parentage in a very literal sense.[197] However, the scriptures are not consistent on this point. For example, in 1830 the Prophet translated Moses 6:22, which referred to a "genealogy of the sons of Adam, who was the son of God." However, a little over a year later he modified a similar KJV New Testament genealogical account ("Adam, who was the son of God") to read "Adam, who was formed of God."[198] Moreover, Moses 6:8 and 6:68 could be taken as support of the view that 6:22 is meant to describe a covenant relationship rather than only a physical descent. Regarding the manner in which the bodies of Adam and Eve were created, President Spencer W. Kimball said, "We don't know exactly how their coming into this world happened, and when we're able to understand it the Lord will tell us."[199] As Draper concludes: "Genesis, Moses, and Abraham preserve the 'official' account of humankind's entrance into the world as revealed by God. He has not seen fit to reveal more."[200]

Like Genesis, the Mandaean *Ginza* implies that the supreme deity, Manda d-Hiia, was personally required to cast the spirit into Adam, as the seven creators assisting him were unable to do this.[201]

man. See *Commentary* 2:26-b, p. 112.

b   ***from the dust of the ground.*** In simple terms, Elder McConkie took this to mean that "the physical body which [Adam] received was created from the elements of the earth."[202] Moses 6:59 elaborates by saying that man was "born into the world by water, and blood, and the spirit, which I have made, and so became of dust a living soul."

The term "dust" reappears in vv. 20 ("dust shalt thou eat") and 25 ("dust thou wast, and unto dust shalt thou return"), connoting in all cases weakness and mortality. However, several passages in the Old Testament all "speak of an exaltation from the dust, with the dust representing either pre-royal status,[203] poverty,[204] or death."[205]

Note the word play here in the sequence of three Hebrew words: "mist/flow" (*'ed*), "man" (*'adam*) and "ground" (*'adamah*).[206] "The verb 'formed' (Hebrew *va-yitser*) is frequently used of the action of a potter (*yotser*), so that man's creation is portrayed in terms of God molding

---

194   H. J. Grant, *et al., Evolution*; J. F. Smith, *et al., Origin.*
195   B. K. Packer, *Law and Light*, p. 11.
196   See *Commentary* 2:26-a, p. 111.
197   E.g., H. L. Andrus, *Doctrinal (Rev.)*, pp. 144-147; R. D. Draper, *et al., Commentary*, pp. 214-216.
198   JST Luke 3:45. See also discussion in R. D. Draper, *Allegory*, p. 27.
199   S. W. Kimball, *Blessings*, p. 72.
200   R. D. Draper, *Allegory*, p. 82. See *Appendix* for statements regarding the origin of man.
201   GR 3:1. See W. Barnstone, *et al., Gnostic*, pp. 543-548; W. Barnstone, *Other*, pp. 134-138; W. Foerster, *Gnosis*, 187-192; E. Lupieri, *Mandaeans*, pp. 187-191.
202   B. R. McConkie, *Mormon Doctrine*, p. 209.
203   1 Kings 16:2.
204   1 Samuel 2:8; Psalm 113:7.
205   Isaiah 26:19; Daniel 12:2. See V. P. Hamilton, *Genesis*, p. 158.
206   R. E. Friedman, *Commentary*, p. 17.

*7 And I, the Lord God, formed man **from the dust of the ground**, and **breathed into his nostrils the breath of life**; and man became a **living soul**, the first flesh upon the earth, the first man also; nevertheless, all things were before created; but spiritually were they created and made according to my word.*

the clayey soil into shape and then animating it. This image is widespread in the ancient world [and is explicit in Job 4:19; 33:6].… [It] simultaneously expresses both the glory and the insignificance of man. Man occupies a special place in the hierarchy of Creation and enjoys a unique relationship with God by virtue of being the work of God's own hands and being directly animated by God's own breath. At the same time, he is but dust taken from the earth, mere clay in the hands of the divine Potter, who exercises absolute mastery over His Creation."[207] Jewish sages also saw a parallel between the making of man and the making of dough offering (*hallàh*).[208]

c   ***breathed into his nostrils the breath of life.*** Biblical and Egyptian sources associate the receiving of divine breath not merely with an infusion of life, but also with royal status.[209] Williams cites texts that compare this action with the process by which idols were "'incarnated' by the divine spirit, the so-called *mīs pî* (= Washing-of-the-mouth) or *pit pî* (= Opening-of-the-mouth) ritual."[210]

It is significant that the book of Moses adds a similar phrase to describe the creation of animals.[211] However, man and beast differ in that the former is created in the image of God and is given dominion over the animals.

The Prophet Joseph Smith said that: "The 7th verse of 2nd chapter of Genesis ought to read—God breathed into Adam his spirit [i.e., Adam's spirit] or breath of life; but when the word '*ruach*' applies to Eve, it should be translated lives."[212] The year previous, a related statement about Adam had been incorporated into the translation of Abraham 5:7: "And the Gods formed man from the dust of the ground, and took his spirit (that is, the man's spirit), and put it into him; and breathed into his nostrils the breath of life, and man became a living soul."

In Genesis, two Hebrew words *nishma*[213] and *ruach*[214] are associated with the "breath of life," although the argument that these terms imply the concept of a distinct spirit entity is by no means universally accepted in Judaism.[215] While *ruach* is applied to God, man, and animals, the use of *nishma* is reserved for God and man alone.[216] Curiously, "the word *ruach* does not appear in [Genesis 2:7] nor in Genesis 3:20, where the name Eve (*Chavvah*, meaning life-giving) appears. It is clear why Joseph Smith used the word *ruach* in connection with Genesis 2:7, but his use of this word in connection with Genesis 3:20 is not so clear. Possibly he wanted to emphasize Eve's role as lives-giver, which coincides with the usage of lives [that would]… appear in the revelation on eternal marriage."[217]

d   ***living soul.*** D&C 88:15 explains that "the spirit and the body are the soul of man." The book of Moses explains that man, the trees,[218] and the animals[219] in the Garden became "living

207   N. M. Sarna, *Genesis*, p. 17.
208   Numbers 15:20. See J. Neusner, *Confronting*, 14:1, pp. 70-72.
209   E.g., Lamentations 4:20. See V. P. Hamilton, *Genesis*, pp. 158-159.
210   W. Williams, *Shadow*.
211   Moses 3:19.
212   J. Smith, Jr., *Teachings*, 17 May 1843, p. 301.
213   E.g., Genesis 2:7; 7:22.
214   E.g., Genesis 6:17; 7:15, 22.
215   N. Gillman, *Death*, pp. 75-78.
216   V. P. Hamilton, *Genesis*, p. 159.
217   J. Smith, Jr., *Words*, p. 281 n. 4. See D&C 132:22-24.
218   Moses 3:9.
219   Moses 3:19.

*7 And I, the Lord God, formed man from the dust of the ground, and breathed into his nostrils the breath of life; and man became a **living soul**, the **first flesh upon the earth**, the **first man also**; nevertheless, all things were before created; but spiritually were they created and made according to my word.*

*8 And I, the Lord God, **planted a garden** eastward in Eden, and there I put the man whom I had formed.*

MOSES 3

souls" once the result of their prior spiritual creation was combined with natural elements. However, the fact that the trees of the garden became "living souls" does not necessarily imply that each tree possessed an *individual* spirit in the same sense that man and animals do.[220]

Consistent with LDS teachings about the resurrection of animals, the Armenian *Life of Adam and Eve* reports that just as Adam will live again and will be anointed with the "oil of joy," so "it shall happen in the same fashion to all the wild beasts of the earth, who will arise in resurrection and be worthy of entering the Garden. [God] shall anoint them with that oil."[221]

e   *first flesh upon the earth.* This verse has long been an interpretive problem for LDS readers, since at face value the phrase seems to be saying that man's appearance on earth preceded that of the animals—and thus implying that man's body was formed through "special creation."[222] However, adopting the most common way this verse has been understood in recent times, Draper, *et al.*, comment: "'Flesh' here, of course, refers to mortality—Adam was the first mortal human being on the earth."[223] This interpretation is consistent with the majority of scriptural references to the term "flesh."[224] Elder Joseph Fielding Smith agreed, arguing that the phrase should not be interpreted to mean that animal life was not present on earth prior to Adam's coming to live there.[225]

f   *first man also.* The First Presidency stated in 1909: "Adam, our progenitor, 'the first man,' was, like Christ, a preexistent spirit, and like Christ he took upon him an appropriate body, the body of a man, and so became a 'living soul'... The word of the Lord declares that Adam was the 'first man of all men,'[226] and we are therefore in duty bound to regard him as the primal parent of our race. It was shown to the brother of Jared that all men were created in the beginning after the image of God;[227] and whether we take this to mean the spirit or the body, or both, it commits us to the same conclusion: Man began life as a human being, in the likeness of our heavenly Father."[228]

8   a   *planted a garden.* This verse should not be read as a second version of the account of the creation of vegetation found in Moses 2. Westermann explains that this verse "is not a narrative about the creation of plants, but about the provision of nourishment for the human creatures"—specifically, the fruit trees of the Garden of Eden.[229]

---

220   D&C 77:2; cf. *Commentary* 3:5-b, p. 155. See *Endnote 3-10*, p. 199.

221   G. A. Anderson, *et al.*, *Synopsis*, 42:4, p. 45E.

222   E.g., O. Pratt, *12 November 1879*, pp. 200-201.

223   R. D. Draper, *et al.*, *Commentary*, p. 223; cf. Moses 3:5. See *Endnote 3-56*, p. 210.

224   E.g., 2 Nephi 4:34; 28:31; Jeremiah 17:5; Isaiah 40:6; 1 Nephi 22:23; Galatians 5:19; 1 John 2:16. A notable exception is a mention of the resurrected body of Christ in Luke 24:39. See R. J. Matthews, *Fall*, pp. 47-48.

225   J. F. Smith, Jr., *Origin*, p. 328.

226   Moses 1:34.

227   Ether 3:15.

228   J. F. Smith, *et al.*, *Origin*, p. 205. For the full statement, along with other statements of Presidents of the Church and accompanying background information, see *Appendix*, pp. 785-802.

229   C. Westermann, *Genesis 1-11*, p. 208.

*8 And I, the Lord God, **planted a garden eastward** in Eden, and there I put the man whom I had formed.*

> **garden.** The Garden of Eden is a prototype for the temple,[230] and appears to be patterned after a heavenly predecessor.[231] Thus, scriptural references to "the Garden of the Lord"[232] and "the Garden of God"[233] may apply in most cases equally well to both Eden and to its heavenly counterpart—a situation that leads to confusion in some sources.[234] As to the Garden of Eden, Hamilton concludes that: "[God] is its planter, but not its occupant."[235] It was created specifically for Adam and Eve.[236]
>
> b **eastward.** To an ancient reader in the Mesopotamian milieu, the phrase "eastward in Eden" could be taken as meaning that the garden sits at the dawn horizon—the meeting place of heaven and earth. The pseudepigraphal *Conflict of Adam and Eve with Satan* skillfully paints such a picture: "On the third day, God planted the Garden in the east of the earth, on the border of the world eastward, beyond which, towards the sun-rising, one finds nothing but water, that encompasses the whole world, and reaches unto the borders of heaven."[237] This idea corresponds to the Egyptian *akhet*, the specific place where the sun god rose every morning and returned every evening, and also to the Mandaean "ideal world" which was held to hang "between heaven and earth."[238] The Chinese *K'un-lun* also "appears as a place not located on the earth, but poised between heaven and earth."[239] The gardens of *Gilgamesh* and the Ugaritic *Baal* and *Mot* were liminally located at the "edges of the world" or, in other words, "at the borders between the divine and the human world."[240] Similarly, *2 Enoch* locates paradise "between the corruptible [earth] and the incorruptible [heaven]."[241]

By its very nature, the horizon is not a final end point, but rather a portal, a place of two-way transition between the heavens and the earth. Writes Nibley: "'Egyptians… never… speak of [the land beyond the grave] as an earthly paradise; it is only to be reached by the dead.' … [It] is neither heaven nor earth but lies between them… In a Hebrew Enoch apocryphon, the Lord, in visiting the earth, rests in the Garden of Eden and, moving in the reverse direction, passes through 'the Garden to the firmament'[242]… Every transition must be provided with such a setting, not only from here to heaven, but in the reverse direction in the beginning."[243] "The passage from world to world and from horizon to horizon is dramatized in the ordinances of the temple, which itself is called the horizon."[244] Situating this concept with respect to the story of Adam and Eve, the idea is that the Garden "was placed between heaven and earth, below the firmament [i.e., the celestial world] and above the earth [i.e., the telestial world], and that God placed it there… so that, if [Adam] kept [God's] commands He might lift him up to heaven, but if he transgressed them, He might cast him down to this earth."[245] Suggestions for physically locating Eden include: "a region [on Earth] where an immortal, paradisiacal condition prevailed in contrast to the rest of the mortal earth,"[246] a separate

230 D. W. Parry, *Garden*,
231 T. Stordalen, *Echoes*, pp. 65-66; J. H. Walton, *Ancient*, pp. 124-125; J. F. Smith, *18 June 1882*, p. 175.
232 Genesis 13:10; Isaiah 51:3.
233 Ezekiel 28:13, 31:9.
234 E.g., J. Tromp, *Literary*, pp. 30, 34abe.
235 V. P. Hamilton, *Genesis*, p. 161; cf. T. Stordalen, *Echoes*, p. 298.
236 For more on Eden, see the overview of Moses 3, pp. 139-144.
237 S. C. Malan, *Adam and Eve*, 1:1, p. 1.
238 E. S. Drower, *Mandaeans*, p. 56; E. Lupieri, *Mandaeans*, p. 128.
239 J. S. Major, *Heaven*, p. 156.
240 T. Stordalen, *Echoes*, pp. 285-286.
241 F. I. Andersen, *2 Enoch*, 8:5, p. 116; cf. p. 116 n. l.
242 See P. Alexander, *3 Enoch*, 5:5, p. 260. See *Endnote 3-57*, p. 210.
243 H. W. Nibley, *Message 2005*, pp. 294-295. See also H. W. Nibley, *Teachings of the PGP*, 16, pp. 198-199.
244 Siegfried Schott, cited in H. W. Nibley, *Teachings of the PGP*, 16, p. 199.
245 Shelemon, *Book of the Bee*, 15, p. 20.
246 R. D. Draper, *et al.*, *Commentary*, p. 227.

*8 And I, the Lord God, planted a garden **eastward** in **Eden**, and there I put the man whom I had formed.*

place of a higher (terrestrial) order, realm or "sphere," and/or a setting of an indefinite nature blending figurative and physical elements.[247]

Eastward orientation is not only associated with the rising sun, but also with its passage from east to west as a metaphor for time.[248] The Hebrew phrase *mi-kedem* ('in the east') in the Genesis account could also be translated "in the beginning" or "in primeval times."[249] Likewise, for the Egyptians, the West, the direction of sunset, was the land of the dead—hence the many tombs built on the west bank of the Nile.

Eastward may also refer to the Garden of Eden's position relative to the Creator. The initial separation of Adam and Eve from God occurs when they are removed from His presence to be placed in the Garden "eastward in Eden"[250]—that is, east of the "mountain" where, in some representations of the sacred geography of Paradise, He is said to dwell. Such an interpretation also seems to be borne out in later events, as eastward movement is repeatedly associated with increasing distance from God.[251] For example, after God's voice of judgment visits them "from the west,"[252] Adam and Eve experience an additional degree of separation when they are expelled through the Garden's eastern gate.[253] Cain was "shut out from the presence of the Lord" as he resumed the journey eastward to dwell "in the land of Nod, on the east of Eden,"[254] a journey that eventually continued "from the east" to the "land of Shinar" where the Tower of Babel was constructed.[255] Finally, Lot traveled east toward Sodom and Gomorrah when he separated himself from Abraham.[256] On the other hand, Abraham's subsequent "return from the east is [a] return to the Promised Land and… the city of 'Salem,"[257] being "directed toward blessing."[258] The Magi of the Nativity likewise came "from the east" to Bethlehem.[259]

c **Eden.** "The name [Eden] has been derived from the Sumerian *edinu*, 'a plain,' but an Aramaic-Akkadian bilingual inscription suggests that the real meaning is 'luxuriance,'"[260] or "abundance," more specifically an abundance of life-enriching water.[261] "The idea is that man's food was ever ready at hand. The attractive, nutritious, and delectable qualities of the fruit are stressed with the next episode in mind. The human couple will not be able to plead deprivation as the excuse for eating the forbidden fruit."[262]

The ideas of luxuriance and plenty bring to mind the prominent place-name "Bountiful" in the Book of Mormon[263]—in fact, the probable site of the Old World Bountiful was reputed to be a place of such great abundance that its inhabitants were denounced by Islamic Hud traditions for their "attempt to create an earthly replica of paradise."[264] Similarly, the word

---

247 See the overview of Moses 3, pp. 139-144.

248 N. Wyatt, *Space*, pp. 35-52; cf. Philo, *Questions on Genesis*, 1:7, p. 5.

249 T. Stordalen, *Echoes*, pp. 261-270; cf. Habakkuk 1:12.

250 Moses 3:8.

251 J. H. Sailhamer, *Genesis*, pp. 41-42; T. Stordalen, *Echoes*, pp. 267-268.

252 See *Commentary* 4:14-c, p. 259.

253 Moses 4:31.

254 Moses 5:41.

255 Genesis 11:2.

256 Genesis 13:11.

257 J. H. Sailhamer, *Genesis*, p. 59 and Genesis 14:17-20. For statements attributed to the Prophet Joseph Smith regarding Adam and Eve's location and movements after the Fall, see *Figure 6-2*, p. 457.

258 T. L. Brodie, *Dialogue*, p. 117.

259 Matthew 2:1. See *Figure E53-5*, p. 673 and *Excursus 53: The Cave of Treasures*, p. 674.

260 N. M. Sarna, *Genesis*, p. 18.

261 T. Stordalen, *Echoes*, pp. 257-261.

262 N. M. Sarna, *Genesis*, p. 18.

263 E.g., 1 Nephi 17:5; Alma 22:29-31.

264 W. J. Hamblin, *Prophets*, pp. 137, 146-147, 155 n. 52; G. Potter, *et al.*, *Lehi*, p. 126; Qur'an 2:25, 26:128, 134, 46:21.

8 And I, the Lord God, planted a garden eastward in **Eden,** *and there* **I put the man** *whom I had formed.*

9 And out of the ground **made I, the Lord God, to grow every tree, naturally, that is pleasant to the sight of man; and** *man could behold it. And* **it became also a living soul.** *For it was* **spiritual in the day that I created it***; for* **it remaineth in the sphere in which I, God, created it***, yea, even all things which I prepared for the use of man; and man saw that it was* **good for food***. And I, the Lord God, planted the tree of life also in the midst of the garden, and also the tree of knowledge of good and evil.*

"Nauvoo," which appeared in Seixas' Hebrew textbook in a Sephardic transliteration as one form of the verb *naʾah*, means "to be comely."[265]

d   *I put the man.* The phrase implies that Adam's creation had taken place somewhere other than the Garden of Eden itself. The location of the temple mount is often mentioned.[266] The *Pirkei de Rabbi Eliezer* explains the symbolism: "The Holy One, blessed be He, showed to the first man a surfeit of love by creating him at a pure place—the location of the Temple—and in introducing him into His palace [i.e., the Garden of Eden]."[267] A targum likewise records that "the Lord God took Adam from the mountain of worship, the place whence he had been created, and made him dwell in the Garden of Eden to labor in the law, and to keep its commandments."[268] *Jubilees* says that Adam and Eve were introduced into the Garden forty (Adam) and eighty (Eve) days after their creation, consistent with temple laws of purity.[269]

9   **a**   *made... to grow every tree, naturally.* The sense of the additions made by Joseph Smith might be paraphrased as follows: "All the beautiful trees were made to grow naturally so that man could see them and enjoy their fruit. Because they were spiritual at the time they were created and remained in that 'sphere,' they also became 'living souls.' Similarly, everything else that had been prepared for man's use originally was spiritual."[270]

     b   *pleasant to the sight of man; and... good for food.* These words anticipate the later temptation of Eve.[271] Elder B. H. Roberts argued that this statement meant to include the Tree of Knowledge among the trees that were good for food.[272] However, so far as I have been able to ascertain, he is alone in this view.

     c   *it became also a living soul.* OT1 reads "they became also a living soul."[273] A substitution of "it" for "they" appears in the hand of Sidney Rigdon in OT2.[274]

     d   *it was spiritual in the day that I created it.* See the overview of Moses 3, pp. 134-135, 139-144 and *Commentary 3:9-e*, p. 162.

     e   *it remaineth in the sphere in which I, God, created it.* Lehi explained in similar words that had it not been for the Fall, "All things which were created must have remained in the state in which they were after they were created; and they must have remained forever, and had no end."[275] However, in the book of Moses, the use of the term "sphere" introduces an additional nuance of meaning to this idea. Inferring the meaning from Joseph Smith's usage

265   Isaiah 52:7; Song of Solomon 1:10; K. L. Barney, *Nauvoo*. See also H. W. Nibley, *Teachings of the PGP*, 16, pp. 200-201. Ezekiel 28:13, 31 further describe the beauty of Paradise.

266   R. M. Zlotowitz, *et al.*, *Bereishis*, p. 94; *Commentary 4:25-c*, p. 273.

267   M.-A. Ouaknin, *et al.*, *Rabbi Éliézer*, 12, p. 82.

268   M. Maher, *Pseudo-Jonathan*, 2:15, p. 23. See also *Commentary 3:15-a*, p. 173.

269   O. S. Wintermute, *Jubilees*, 3:8-12, p. 59. See Leviticus 12:1-6, where the purity laws are applied only to the mother. See M. Barker, *Christmas*, p. 37.

270   See *Commentary 3:5-b*, p. 155, *3:7-e*, p. 158, and the overview of Moses 3, pp. 134-135.

271   See *Commentary 4:12-a*, p. 255; cf. D&C 59:18.

272   B. H. Roberts, *The Truth*, p. 341.

273   S. H. Faulring, *et al.*, *Original Manuscripts*, p. 89.

274   *Ibid.*, p. 598; K. P. Jackson, *Book of Moses*, p. 74. See *Commentary 3:7-e*, p. 158.

275   2 Nephi 2:22. See *Endnote 3-11*, p. 199.

*9 And out of the ground made I, the Lord God, to grow every tree, naturally, that is pleasant to the sight of man; and man could behold it. And it became also a living soul. For it was spiritual in the day that I created it; for **it remaineth in the sphere in which I, God, created it**, yea, even all things which I prepared for the use of man; and man saw that it was good for food. And I, the Lord God, **planted** the **tree of life** also in the midst of the garden, and also the tree of knowledge of good and evil.*

elsewhere,[276] the term refers either to an orbit of a heavenly body or an area of activity, power, or influence—connotations that may be seen as near synonyms given the cosmology of Abraham 3.[277] Taken together with other references in the book of Abraham, an implication of the text seems to be that the location of where the Fall took place was somewhere in the vicinity of Kolob, which signifies, according to the book of Abraham, "the first creation, nearest to the celestial, or the residence of God."[278]

f *planted.* OT1 reads "placed,"[279] a closer parallel to the term put used to describe how Adam came into the Garden.[280] The change to "planted" is in the script of Sidney Rigdon.[281]

g *tree of life.* Elder Bruce R. McConkie wrote that the Tree of Life "figuratively refers to eternal life"[282]—in whatever degree, of course, those who partake are qualified to receive it.[283] Nephi referred to the Tree of Life as a manifestation of the "love of God," which is "the most desirable above all things," to which the angel rejoined, "Yea, and the most joyous to the soul."[284] Regarding the idea of a tree as a representation of life, earth, and heaven, Stordalen writes: "Every green tree would symbolize life, and a large tree—rooted in deep soil and stretching towards the sky—potentially makes a cosmic symbol."[285]

It should be emphasized that the Tree of Life does not represent eternal life merely in an abstract sense, but rather as a symbol of embodied deity. Thomas explains that "most often in scripture… the tree is an anthropomorphic symbol. A tree serves well as such a symbol because it has, after all, limbs, a circulatory system, the bearing of fruit, and so forth. Specifically, scriptural trees stand for Christ and his attributes."[286] Wyatt concurs, noting that: "The trees are… messianic symbols. The Menorah is probably what Moses is understood to have seen as the burning bush in Exodus 3."[287] Thus, Jehovah, the premortal Jesus Christ, was represented to Moses as one who dwells in the midst of the burning glory of the Tree of Life.[288]

Going further, there is a sense that such trees can represent not only Deity but also humans who have, through temple rites of investiture,[289] become kings.[290] The same concept applies

276 See the overview of Moses 3, p. 139.
277 See especially Abraham 3:9, 16.
278 Book of Abraham Facsimile 2, explanation for Figure 1; cf. *Kirtland Egyptian Papers*, KEPE 1, Grammar and Alphabet, pp. 27-28—see also pp. 30, 32, 34). See *Excursus 18: Kolob*, p. 565.
279 S. H. Faulring, *et al.*, *Original Manuscripts*, p. 89.
280 Moses 2:8.
281 S. H. Faulring, *et al.*, *Original Manuscripts*, p. 598; K. P. Jackson, *Book of Moses*, p. 74.
282 B. R. McConkie, *New Witness*, p. 86; cf. A. Gileadi, *Studies*, p. 10; B. C. Hafen, *Broken*, p. 30; Vos, cited in V. P. Hamilton, *Genesis*, p. 209 n. 6.
283 See D&C 88:28-32; R. J. Matthews, *Probationary Nature*, p. 56.
284 1 Nephi 11:22-23.
285 T. Stordalen, *Echoes*, pp. 288-289.
286 M. C. Thomas, *Jacob's Allegory*, p. 13. See also J. W. Miller, *Tree*.
287 N. Wyatt, *Space*, p. 169. Wyatt also makes the intriguing (but seemingly far-fetched) suggestion that the duality of the two trees "fits the late Jewish idea of two messiahs" (*ibid.*, p. 167).
288 See *Endnote 3-54*, p. 210. Related tree symbology appears in many other cultures. See, e.g., E. A. S. Butterworth, *Tree*; B. Gardner, *Second Witness*, 1:153-169; J. O. Ryen, *Mandaean Vine*, pp. 204-221; T. Stordalen, *Echoes*, pp. 230ff., 291-294, 429ff., 459ff. for in-depth discussions.
289 See, e.g., the discussion of Psalm 110 in M. Barker, *Who was Melchizedek*.
290 Cf. Daniel 4:20, 22: "The tree… is thou, O king." See also *Commentary 4:13-b*, p. 258; Judges 9:7-21; E. D.

9 And out of the ground made I, the Lord God, to grow every tree, naturally, that is pleasant to the sight of man; and man could behold it. And it became also a living soul. For it was spiritual in the day that I created it; for it remaineth in the sphere in which I, God, created it, yea, even all things which I prepared for the use of man; and man saw that it was good for food. And I, the Lord God, planted the **tree of life** *also in the midst of the garden, and also the tree of knowledge of good and evil.*

in a more general way to all the righteous who are ultimately destined to share the same status.[291] Wyatt writes that "the tree is... a royal symbol... An essential element in royal ideology is the secret knowledge to which the king becomes privy during the royal ascent at his enthronement. The importance of the tree in symbolic geography is particularly clear in this passage: this is a huge structure holding up the sky, as the *axis mundi*... The king is represented as himself the *axis mundi*. Although the figure is probably based primarily on biblical conceptions, it also corresponds remarkably closely to Assyrian ones, undoubtedly held in common with Babylonian ideology. An important iconographic motif in Assyria shows the king tending the Tree of Life. The royal palace at Nineveh had panels with reliefs of the cult of the tree surrounding the throne room. The king was thus represented precisely as Adam, who walked in the garden."[292]

The Tree of Life has often been specifically "associated or identified with [the Ugaritic goddess] Asherah, the divine mother of the king" as well as Mary, the mother of Jesus[293]—perhaps symbolizing both the mother herself and also, more generally, the "act of divine supply."[294] The figure of the dove, also associated with mother-goddess figures in the ancient Near East,[295] is connected to symbol of the date-palm as a Tree of Life (see below). In the *Genesis Apocryphon*, Abraham dreams of a cedar and a date-palm, respectively symbolizing himself and his wife.[296] The Mandaean *Book of John the Baptist* identifies Mary with a vine or tree which stands at the mouth of the life-giving waters.[297] The symbolic association of the Tree of Life with the divine mother may help explain the terminology of Christian traditions that stressed the responsibility of Joseph—the husband of Mary, the mother of Jesus—to "guard/keep" her.[298] In this connection, Gallez observes that: "The word virgin, *'almah*, derives from a stem originally meaning 'guard, keep.'"[299]

Ancient commentators often identify the Tree of Life with the olive tree.[300] Its extremely long life makes it a fitting symbol for eternal life, and the everyday use of the oil as a source of both nourishment for man and fuel for light evokes natural associations when used in

---

Clark, *Cedars*; T. Stordalen, *Echoes*, pp. 89-92, 100-101, 291. Cf. Adam and Eve as "saplings" destined to become "cedars of Lebanon" in D. C. Matt, *Zohar 1*, Be-Reshit, 1:35a-b, pp. 220-222.

291 E.g., Psalm 1:1-3, 92:11-12; Matthew 7:17; D&C 97:9; J. H. Charlesworth, *Odes*, 11:16-19, p. 745. See also J. H. Charlesworth, *Concept of Resurrection*, p. 4, commenting on a Qumran text (F. G. Martinez, *Hymns*, 16:5-6, p. 345).

292 N. Wyatt, *Space*, p. 170. See also E. A. S. Butterworth, *Tree*, passim.

293 *Ibid.*, p. 170; cf. 1 Nephi 11:8-22; M. Barker, *Joseph Smith*, p. 76; M. Cazenave, *Encyclopédie*, p. 44; D. C. Peterson, *Asherah 1998*; D. C. Peterson, *Asherah 2000*; H. Schwartz, *Tree*, p. 50; cf. *Qur'an* 19:23-26; A. at-Tabataba'i, *Al-Mizan*, 6:146.

294 T. Stordalen, *Echoes*, p. 289; cf. Egyptian tree imagery connected with Hathor, Nut, and Isis (see, e.g., J. O. Ryen, *Mandaean Vine*, pp. 205-206; A. Roberts, *My Heart*, pp. 26-27 and *passim*).

295 K. van der Toorn, *et al.*, *Dictionary*, p. 263.

296 F. G. Martinez, *Genesis Apocryphon*, p. 232; cf. Psalm 92:12.

297 Here the Euphrates, in other places such vines are placed near the Jordan, evoking the imagery of baptism associated with the latter site (G. R. S. Mead, *Mandaean John*-Book, 35, pp. 65-67; see also J. J. Buckley, *Mandaeans*, pp. 50-53; J. O. Ryen, *Mandaean Vine*, pp. 58-61, 221).

298 See T. Stordalen, *Echoes*, pp. 290-291; M. Barker, *Infancy Gospel of James* 1:13, p. 156. Cf. the cult of *Diana Nemorensis* (see, e.g., J. T. Dyson, *King*).

299 É.-M. Gallez, *Le Messie*, p. 206; cf. *Commentary* 3:15-b, p. 173. For more on the symbolism of the Tree of Life, see *Figure 3-10*, p. 147; overview of Moses 4, pp. 227ff; *Excursus 25: The Tree of Life as the Hidden Throne of God*, p. 591.

300 C. W. Griggs, *Tree of Life*; S. D. Ricks, *Olive*, pp. 464-466; J. A. Tvedtnes, *Olive Oil*, pp. 429-430.

9 And out of the ground made I, the Lord God, to grow every tree, naturally, that is pleasant to the sight of man; and man could behold it. And it became also a living soul. For it was spiritual in the day that I created it; for it remaineth in the sphere in which I, God, created it, yea, even all things which I prepared for the use of man; and man saw that it was good for food. And I, the Lord God, planted the **tree of life** *also in the midst of the garden, and also the tree of knowledge of good and evil.*

conjunction with the ritual anointing of priests and kings, and the blessing of the sick.[301] Egyptian texts sometimes describe the *ished-tree* from which Osiris was freed[302] as being an olive tree. According to Nibley: "In early times Ptah, Horus, Seth, and Thoth all enjoyed the epithet, "he who possesses life beneath his olive tree."[303] Extracanonical literature recounts that on his sickbed Adam requested Eve and Seth to return to the Garden to retrieve oil from the "tree of his mercy."[304] Recalling the story of the dove that returned to Noah's ark with the olive branch in its mouth, one rabbinical opinion gives it that the "gates of the Garden of Eden opened for the dove, and from there she brought it."[305] Nibley cites a relevant passage from Cyril's lectures on the mysteries: "Having [like Adam] been cut off from the wild olive tree, you are driven (goaded) toward the good olive tree, that you might become sharers in the fatness of the true olive."[306] Two days after a revelation telling how war was to be "poured out upon all nations," Joseph Smith designated D&C 88, by way of contrast, as the "olive leaf… plucked from the Tree of Paradise, the Lord's message of peace to us."[307]

Of course, the Tree of Life has been identified with other trees as well.[308] For instance, a tall tree with leaves like the carob or the cypress and bearing clusters of fruit like white grapes is sometimes mentioned.[309] White grapes seen in a dream (as opposed to black ones) are seen in the *Zohar* as a "good omen," signifying "that Judgment has already been softened by compassionate care and tending."[310] The "almond tree is the first tree of spring in the Near East, sometimes waking as early as mid-December, when it decks itself in radiant white… an ideal image of life [and] resurrection… whose fruit… has been described as 'perfect.'"[311] Joseph Smith, Sr. had a vision in which he saw a tree that was "exceedingly handsome," with "beautiful branches [that] spread themselves somewhat like an umbrella, and [which] bore a kind of fruit, in shape much like a chestnut bur, and as white as snow, or, if possible whiter."[312]

The date palm is the sacred tree in Assyrian mythology, and its longevity was a fitting symbol for long life to the Egyptians, being "called *ba*, like the immortal part of the soul," which could also be represented by a bird.[313] The Old Testament Deborah rendered judgment as she dwelt under a palm tree,[314] and the temples of Solomon and of Ezekiel's vision were decorated with palms.[315] As a sign of victory and kingship, palm fronds were a central

301 T. G. Madsen, *Gethsemane*; T. G. Madsen, *Sacrament*, p. 97; J. A. Tvedtnes, *Olive Oil*, p. 429.

302 Cf. *Figure 4-13*, p. 231; *Commentary 4:14-d*, p. 260; *Excursus 42: Nebuchadnezzar's "Fall,"* p. 632; *Excursus 53: Comparative Explorations of the Mysteries*, p. 663. See *Endnote 4-50*, p. 312.

303 H. W. Nibley, *Message 2005*, p. 291. The *ished* is usually identified as the Persea (R. H. Wilkinson, *Art*, p. 117).

304 Cf. G. A. Anderson, *et al.*, *Synopsis*, Latin 36:2, p. 40E; M. D. Johnson, *Life*, 36:2, p. 272 & 9:3, p. 273; S. C. Malan, *Adam and Eve*, 36:1-3, pp. 39-40; overview of Moses 6, p. 462.

305 J. Neusner, *Genesis Rabbah 1*, 33:6, p. 351; cf *Commentary 1:1-b*, p. 42, 2:2-c, p. 97; 4:5-b, p. 246. See *Endnote E-204*, p. 754.

306 H. W. Nibley, *Message 2005*, 2.3, p. 519; cf. Cyril of Jerusalem, *Five*, 2:3, p. 147.

307 J. Smith, Jr., *Teachings*, 14 January 1833, p. 18.

308 M. E. Stone, *Fall of Satan*, p. 50.

309 M. Barker, *Joseph Smith*, p. 76; cf. H.-G. Bethge, *et al.*, *Origin*, 110:15-16, p. 179; R. Milstein, *Stories and Illustrations*, p. 107; G. W. E. Nickelsburg, *1 Enoch*, 32:4, p. 320. See *Endnote E-113*, p. 729.

310 D. C. Matt, *Zohar 3*, Va-Yeshev 1:192a, p. 173 and p. 173n. 555.

311 Yarden, cited in M. B. Brown, *et al.*, *Symbols*, pp. 87-88 n. 141.

312 L. M. Smith, *Lucy's Book*, pp. 297-298; cf. 1 Nephi 8:11: "white, to exceed all the whiteness that I had ever seen."

313 J. O. Ryen, *Mandaean Vine*, p. 205; cf. *Commentary 1:1-b*, p. 42; 4:5-b, p. 246. See *Endnote 3-58*, p. 212.

314 Judges 4:5.

315 1 Kings 6:29, 32, 35; 7:36; 2 Chronicles 3:5; Ezekiel 40:16, 22, 26, 31, 34, 37; 41:18-20, 25-26; *Figure 3-11*, p. 149.

9 And out of the ground made I, the Lord God, to grow every tree, naturally, that is pleasant to the sight of man; and man could behold it. And it became also a living soul. For it was spiritual in the day that I created it; for it remaineth in the sphere in which I, God, created it, yea, even all things which I prepared for the use of man; and man saw that it was good for food. And I, the Lord God, planted the **tree of life** *also in the midst of the garden, and also the tree of knowledge of good and evil.*

part of the celebration of Christ's triumphal entry into Jerusalem.[316] In Islamic tradition, Muhammad built his home from the palm, it being a symbol of rest and hospitality in the Middle East.[317] The *Qur'an* also describes the palm as providing shelter and nourishment for Mary, who was said to have borne Jesus in the wilderness beneath such a tree.[318] The earliest Mandaean sources also see the primeval Tree of Life as a date palm, whose "fertile union with the wellspring" emanates vines that will themselves become Trees of Life.[319] A single one of these important date palm trees "often yielded more than one hundred pounds of fruit per year over a productive lifetime of one hundred years or more. Akkadian synonyms for date palm included 'tree of abundance' (*isu masru*) and 'tree of riches' (*isu rasu*)—appropriate names for the vehicle of agricultural success and richness."[320] Also of relevance is Visotzky's collation of ancient sources that refer to the "conversation of palm trees" by which the pious obtained wisdom and warning.[321] In favor of the date palm as a representation of the Tree of Life depicted in Lehi and Nephi's visions, Potter cites sources associating this tree specifically with the motifs of kingship, wisdom, the mother of a divine child, and the cosmos mentioned above.[322] Moreover, Nephi contrasts the fruit of the Tree of Life to the forbidden fruit: "the one being sweet and the other bitter."[323] The date palm's fruit—often described as "white" in its most desirable varieties, well-known to Lehi's family, and likely available in the Valley of Lemuel where the family was camped at the time—would have provided a more fitting analogue than the olive to the love of God that was "sweet above all that is sweet."[324]

Reconciling the competing symbolism of a Tree of Life that bears sweet fruit like the date as opposed to oil-producing fruit like the olive is a Gnostic suggestion that the Garden story was concerned with *three* special trees rather than two. In addition to the original Tree of Life and Tree of Knowledge, the third tree, an olive tree, is said to have sprouted up only *after* the transgression of Adam,[325] when a Savior was mercifully provided for him. In Christian imagery a related idea was often visually represented by a cruciform tree flanked by two small identical trees from Paradise.[326] The centrally-depicted "Tree of Mercy," said in other sources to have been planted by Seth over the grave of Adam, would be destined to bear "the fruit of the crucified Christ."[327] Thus, in a sense, there were thought to be two "Trees of Life": the original Edenic eschatological tree with its sweet fruit, and the subsequently-sprouted

---

316   John 12:12-13; cf. Revelation 7:9, 14.

317   Cf. Leviticus 23:40-43; Nehemiah 8:13-17.

318   *Qur'an* 19:23-26. See also A. at-Tabataba'i, *Al-Mizan*, 6:146; M. Barker, *Christmas*, pp. 125, 140, 144-145, 164. See a depiction of this event in D. Jackson, *Marvellous*, p. 29 Figure 25.

319   J. O. Ryen, *Mandaean Vine*, pp. 203-204, 246-247. See also E. S. Drower, *Thousand*, pp. 110, 111, 120, 267. Compare NT and Egyptian imagery described in A. Roberts, *Anointing*, pp. 90-91, 94.

320   T. Stordalen, *Echoes*, p. 82. See also S. Fine, *Date Palm*.

321   B. L. Visotzky, *Conversation*; cf. H. W. Nibley, *Message 2005*, p. 288; *Figure* 3-8, p. 145; *Figure* 3-10, p. 147; *Excursus 50: Fu Xi and Nü Gua*, p. 654. See *Endnote 3-48*, p. 209.

322   G. Potter, et al., *Lehi*, pp. 43-45.

323   2 Nephi 2:15.

324   Alma 32:42.

325   H.-G. Bethge, et al., *Origin*, 111:1-7, p. 179. For the text, see *Gleanings*, p. 189. See *Endnote 3-55*, p. 210.

326   J. O'Reilly, *Iconography*, pp. 176, 178, 186, 188, 192-193. The flanking trees depicted on the Holy Crown of Hungary surrounding an enthroned Christ are identified as heavenly cypresses (E. Tóth, *Holy Crown*, pp. 23, 28). In imagery going back to pre-Christian times, the paired trees represent "the cypress-tree and life-giving water, the pattern of the two ways, to left or to right" (E. A. S. Butterworth, *Tree*, p. 216). The depiction also recalls the two Menorot that flank the scroll shrine in Palestinian synagogue mosaics (N. Wyatt, *Space*, p. 169).

327   R. W. Baldwin, *Legend*. See also W. W. Isenberg, *Philip*, 73:15-19, p. 153; J. O. Ryen, *Mandaean Vine*, pp. 214-215, 221.

9 And out of the ground made I, the Lord God, to grow every tree, naturally, that is pleasant to the sight of man; and man could behold it. And it became also a living soul. For it was spiritual in the day that I created it; for it remaineth in the sphere in which I, God, created it, yea, even all things which I prepared for the use of man; and man saw that it was good for food. And I, the Lord God, planted the **tree of life** *also* **in the midst of the garden***, and also the tree of knowledge of good and evil.*

oil-bearing Tree of Mercy, the latter being a symbol of the Savior, His Atonement, and the Gospel that would be explained to Adam and Eve after the Fall. In a larger sense, the olive tree also was used as a symbol of the whole house of Israel,[328] whose mission it is to help carry out the Savior's work of blessing all the nations of the earth[329]—part of the "Messianic calling [appointed to all] those who receive the Messiah."[330] It was from the olive tree that the oil for an atoning anointing of healing and sanctification was procured, serving the role of a secondary "Tree of Life" in the sense that the Savior's power could reverse the blows of death to which Adam and Eve previously had been subjected.[331]

While admittedly speculative, this view is attractively coherent. Since every mortal has, like Adam and Eve, taken of the Tree of Knowledge "after the similitude of Adam's transgression,"[332] Jesus Christ, our salvific "Tree of Mercy," supplies the requisite "oil of gladness"[333] to all who accept Him as their Redeemer. As the only true "keeper of the gate,"[334] He lovingly welcomes the faithful back into the presence of the Father, where the paradisiacal Tree of Life, bearing the sweet fruit of eternal life and the fulness of the love of God, is found.[335]

h   ***in the midst of the garden.*** The Hebrew of the phrase "in the midst" literally means "in the center," and derives from a root with the meaning "inner."[336] The phrase serves to emphasize the prominent position of the tree—there would have been no need to add it if it was meant to be read "in the garden generally" as with all the other trees.[337] Likewise, in the *Zohar*, the Tree of Life is said to have been "precisely in the middle of the garden,"[338] where it is the source of the "river of emanation" which "proceeds from the highest *sefirot*[339] to the *Shekhinah*,[340] the garden. Below Her, the unity of the divine yields multiplicity."[341]

Although the phrase "in the midst" is specifically applied only to the Tree of Life,[342] the Tree of Knowledge is later said by Eve to be located there, too.[343] (The *Zohar* implausibly resolves this contradiction simply by saying that the Tree of Knowledge was "not precisely in the middle."[344]) The subtle conflation of the location of two trees seems intentional, preparing readers for the confusion that later ensues in the dialogue with the serpent.[345] The dramatic irony of the story is heightened by the fact that while the reader is informed about both trees, Adam and Eve are only specifically told about the Tree of Knowledge. Satan will exploit their ignorance to his advantage.

328   E.g., Jacob 5; Isaiah 5:1-7; Romans 11:16, 24. See also B. Gardner, *Second Witness*, 2:520-556.

329   See Genesis 22:18.

330   T. G. Madsen, *Chosenness*, p. 142.

331   Cf. the overviews of Moses 4, p. 236 and Moses 6, p. 460. See also *Commentary* 5:47-b, p. 396.

332   Romans 5:14; cf. D&C 93:38; B. L. Top, *Life Before*, p. 95.

333   Hebrews 1:9.

334   2 Nephi 9:41.

335   See *Commentary* 4:31-e, p. 282.

336   S. K. Brown, *Voices*, p. 175.

337   U. Cassuto, *Adam to Noah*, p. 110.

338   D. C. Matt, *Zohar 1*, Be-Reshit 1:35a, p. 220.

339   I. e., the highest of the ten attributes of God.

340   I. e., the divine presence of God in the world, seen as the feminine aspect of Deity.

341   D. C. Matt, *Zohar 1*, Be-Reshit 1:35b, p. 224. See *Commentary* 3:10-a, p. 170.

342   Rashi, *Genesis Commentary*, 1:25.

343   Moses 4:9. See U. Cassuto, *Adam to Noah*, p. 111.

344   D. C. Matt, *Zohar 1*, Be-Reshit 1:35a, p. 220n. 921.

345   See *Commentary* 4:9-a, p. 252 and 4:14-e, p. 260. For a full and supportive analysis of this view, see T. N. D. Mettinger, *Eden*, especially pp. 34-41.

*9 And out of the ground made I, the Lord God, to grow every tree, naturally, that is pleasant to the sight of man; and man could behold it. And it became also a living soul. For it was spiritual in the day that I created it; for it remaineth in the sphere in which I, God, created it, yea, even all things which I prepared for the use of man; and man saw that it was good for food. And I, the Lord God, planted the tree of life also **in the midst of the garden**, and also the **tree of knowledge of good and evil**.*

Elaborate explanations have been advanced as attempts to describe how both the Tree of Life and the Tree of Knowledge could share the center of the Garden.[346] For example, it has been suggested that these two trees were in reality different aspects of a single tree,[347] that they shared a common trunk,[348] or else that they had branches that were intertwined.[349] One of the most interesting strands of Jewish tradition holds that the branches of the Tree of Knowledge hid the Tree of Life from direct view, and that "God did not specifically prohibit eating from the Tree of Life because the Tree of Knowledge formed a hedge around it; only after one had partaken of the latter and cleared a path for himself could one come close to the Tree of Life."[350] In this same sense, Ephrem the Syrian calls the Tree of Knowledge "the veil for the sanctuary"[351]—the Tree of Life having been planted in an inner place so holy that Adam and Eve would court mortal danger if they entered unprepared. Though God could minister to them in the Garden, they could not safely enter His world.[352] An object lesson reported in a Gnostic story tells of how "*Pistis Sophia* went beyond her 'degree' and, becoming ambitious, 'looked behind the veil' [and] fell from glory.'"[353] Elder Bruce C. Hafen has explained: "God placed cherubim and a flaming sword to guard the way of the tree of life until Adam and Eve completed, and we, their posterity, complete [the] preparatory schooling [of mortality. God] cannot fully receive us and give us the gift of celestial life—partaking of [His] very nature—until we have learned by our own experience to distinguish good and evil."[354]

i   *tree of knowledge of good and evil.* Much has been written about this tree.[355] The idea of a second special tree in the Garden of Eden is generally seen by scholars as unique to the biblical account, though a case can be made for two trees with analogous descriptions in the *Qur'an*[356] and in the Zoroastrian *Bundahishn*.[357] If only a single tree is mentioned in ancient accounts, it is usually an analogue to the Tree of Life,[358] though the theme of the protagonist's search for knowledge or wisdom often appears in such stories in one form or another.[359]

The Hebrew expression "knowledge of good and evil" can mean knowledge of what is good and bad, or of happiness and misery—or else knowledge of "everything" if "good and evil"

---

346 R. M. Zlotowitz, *et al.*, *Bereishis*, p. 96.

347 R. Guénon, *Symboles*, p. 325.

348 L. Ginzberg, *Legends*, 5:91 n. 50.

349 See *Figure 5-3*, p. 330; *Excursus 25: The Tree of Life as the Hidden Throne of God*, p. 591; *Excursus 50: Fu Xi and Nü Gua*, p. 654.

350 R. M. Zlotowitz, *et al.*, *Bereishis*, p. 101; cf. p. 96. See also L. Ginzberg, *Legends*, 1:70, 5:91 n. 50.

351 Ephrem the Syrian, *Paradise*, 3:5, p. 92.

352 D&C 76:87, 112; Ephrem the Syrian, *Paradise*, 3:13-17, pp. 95-96; *Excursus 25: The Tree of Life as the Hidden Throne of God*, p. 591; *Excursus 50: Fu Xi and Nü Gua*, p. 654.

353 H. W. Nibley, *Message 2005*, p. 443; cf. C. Schmidt, *Pistis*, 1:29-30, pp. 83-91; G. R. S. Mead, *Pistis*, 1:29-30, pp. 33-36; *Excursus 25: The Tree of Life as the Hidden Throne of God*, p. 591ff.

354 B. C. Hafen, *Broken*, p. 30; cf. L. Schaya, *Meaning*, p. 16. See *Commentary 3:17-c*, p. 175; *4:28-b*, 276; overview of Moses 4, pp. 227-234.

355 For more on the symbolism of the tree, see the overview of Moses 4, pp. 227-234. See also *Commentary 4:11-c*, p. 254 and *4:28-a*, p. 276.

356 *Qur'an* 2:35, 7:19ff. vs. 53:14; cf. J. O. Ryen, *Mandaean Vine*, p. 220 and *Excursus 25: The Tree of Life as the Hidden Throne of God*, p. 591—see especially *Figure E25-2*, p. 593. See also A. al-Tha'labi, *Lives*, p. 49.

357 F. M. Müller, *Bundahis*, 9:5-6; 18:1, 9; 27:2-4, pp. 31, 65, 66, 99-100.

358 M. Barker, *Creation Theology*, p. 8.

359 C. Westermann, *Genesis 1-11*, pp. 245-248. See T. Stordalen, *Echoes*, pp. 294-296, 462-465 for a useful survey of literature on the Tree of Knowledge.

*9 And out of the ground made I, the Lord God, to grow every tree, naturally, that is pleas-
ant to the sight of man; and man could behold it. And it became also a living soul. For it was
spiritual in the day that I created it; for it remaineth in the sphere in which I, God, created it,
yea, even all things which I prepared for the use of man; and man saw that it was good for food.
And I, the Lord God, planted the tree of life also in the midst of the garden, and also the* **tree
of knowledge of good and evil**.

is taken as a merism. Perhaps the most relevant hint on the meaning of the phrase comes
from Deuteronomy 1:39, which speaks of little children "who… have no knowledge of good
and evil," suggesting "that they are not legally responsible for their actions."[360] In this sense,
the term aptly refers not to abstract conceptual knowledge but rather to the kind of "knowledge which infancy lacks and experience acquires."[361] Thus, Solomon fittingly prayed for the
ability "to discern between good and evil" so that he would be able to function in his royal
role.[362] Consistent with this interpretation, other scriptures refer to the ability to know good
from evil,[363] which presupposes "man's power to choose the sweet even when it is harmful
and reject the bitter even when beneficial."[364] What is common to both scriptural and extracanonical references is that they are "concerned with knowledge (or wisdom) in the general,
comprehensive sense. Any limitation of the meaning of 'the knowledge of good and evil' is
thereby excluded. It can mean neither moral nor sexual nor any other partial knowledge, but
only that knowledge which includes and determines human existence as a whole[, the ability
to master]… one's own existence."[365]

A final conjecture on the meaning of the phrase comes from Tvedtnes, who sees in the underlying Hebrew the possibility that "good" refers to the Tree of Life and "evil" referred to
the Tree of Knowledge. Thus, one might read: "tree of life… tree of knowledge—good and
evil."[366] In context, however, the reading is unconvincing.

Jewish and Christian traditions often identify the Tree of Knowledge of good and evil as a
fig tree, thus heightening the irony later on when Adam and Eve attempt to cover themselves
with its leaves.[367] The fruit of the fig tree is known for its abundance of seeds, thus an apron
of green fig leaves is an appropriate symbol for Adam and Eve's ability to "be fruitful and
multiply"[368] after the Fall. Similarly, in the Zoroastrian *Bundahishn*, the special tree standing
near to the Tree of Life is called the "tree of many seeds."[369] A Coptic text says that the leaves
of the Tree of Knowledge "are like fig leaves. Its fruit is like a good appetizing date."[370] The
fig tree also is prominent as a symbol in the New Testament, and at a crucial point in Jesus'
ministry became the subject of a curse,[371] which Ephrem speculates was done "in order to
show that there was no longer any need of fig leaves to serve as Adam's garment."[372] Most
likely because "the word for wheat in Hebrew is a homonym with the word for sin," some
rabbinical and Islamic sources identify the tree with a special variety of wheat, with a "fruit…
like the kidneys of the cow, softer than butter and sweeter than honey."[373] Others, seeing a

360 V. P. Hamilton, *Genesis*, p. 166.
361 J. H. Hertz, *Pentateuch*, p. 8; cf. J. E. Faulconer, *Adam and Eve*, 19-20.
362 1 Kings 3:9; cf. *Targum Yerushalmi*: "the Tree of Knowledge, of which any one who ate would distinguish
   between good and evil" (cited in J. W. Etheridge, *Onkelos*).
363 2 Nephi 2:5, 26; Alma 12:31, 29:5; Helaman 14:31; Moroni 7:15-16, 19; Moses 6:56.
364 A. Cohen, *Chumash*, p. 10.
365 C. Westermann, *Genesis 1-11*, pp. 247-248; cf. T. N. D. Mettinger, *Eden*, pp. 61-63; A. LaCocque, *Trial*, pp. 77-
   79.
366 J. A. Tvedtnes, *September 26, 2006*.
367 E.g., D. C. Matt, *Zohar 1*, Be-Reshit 1:36b, p. 229. See Moses 4:13; *Commentary 4*:14-d, p. 260.
368 Moses 2:28.
369 F. M. Müller, *Bundahis*, 9:5, 18:9, 27:2, pp. 31, 66, 99-100.
370 H.-G. Bethge, *et al.*, *Origin*, 110:22-23, p. 179.
371 Matthew 21:18-20; 24:32; Luke 13:6-9; John 1:48; James 3:12; cf. Joel 2:22.
372 Ephrem the Syrian, *Diatessaron*, cited in M. Barker, *Hidden*, p. 34.
373 M. Ibn Ishaq ibn Yasar, *Making*, pp. 34, 37; cf. A. al-Tha'labi, *Lives*, p. 49; G. Weil, *Legends*, pp. 31, 45; B. M.

*9 And out of the ground made I, the Lord God, to grow every tree, naturally, that is pleas-ant to the sight of man; and man could behold it. And it became also a living soul. For it was spiritual in the day that I created it; for it remaineth in the sphere in which I, God, created it, yea, even all things which I prepared for the use of man; and man saw that it was good for food. And I, the Lord God, planted the tree of life also in the midst of the garden, and also the **tree of knowledge of good and evil**.*

*10 And I, the Lord God, **caused a river to go out of Eden** to water the garden; and from thence it was parted, and became into four heads.*

parallel in the story of Noah's drunkenness after the Flood, suggest that the forbidden fruit was the grape[374]—though the possibility of polemical motivations for this tradition cannot be ignored.[375] The pomegranate and the apple (based on the correspondence between the Latin *malus* = evil and *malum* = apple)[376] have also been proposed. One rabbinic source asserts that God deliberately "did not reveal the nature of the tree that it might not be said, 'Through this tree Adam brought death into the world.'"[377]

10 a *caused a river to go out of Eden.* Sarna comments: "The story of man is abruptly interrupted by a description of the geographical setting of the Garden. This pause functions as a ten-sion-building device, for the reader is left wondering about the role of the two special trees [referred to in verse 9]. The identical literary stratagem is employed in the story of Joseph, where the digression of Genesis 38 heightens the reader's suspense at a critical moment in the development of the plot."[378]

The major burden of the passage is to assert that "the 'life-arteries' of all lands of the earth have their source in the river that watered paradise."[379] The water is said to originate "oppo-site the throne of glory."[380] Springing up from the ground,[381] it flows down the mountain of God.[382] Similarly, in Nephi's dream he saw the "fountain of living waters" originating at the "Tree of Life"—both the tree and the waters being a "representation of the love of God."[383] Outside the Garden (or, less plausibly, within the Garden[384]), the river "separates into four branches that probably represent the four quarters of the inhabited world.[385] In other words, the river of Eden also nourishes the whole earth with its life-giving waters."[386] The mention of the fact that the river leaves Eden to go out to the rest of the world subtly prepares the reader for Adam and Eve's later departure.[387]

The bronze sea in Solomon's temple has sometimes been regarded as a representation of the river's subterranean source of water "'from which the ancients believed all life and fertility were derived.' If so,… the four sets of oxen facing the four cardinal directions [might symbolize] the four rivers of Eden that watered the courtyard of the earth,"[388] corresponding to the water that gushed out from underneath the east threshold of Ezekiel's vision of a

---

Wheeler, *Prophets*, pp. 27-28; cf. E. A. W. Budge, *Cave*, pp. 18-19 n. 1; B. Mika'el, *Mysteries*, p. 26

374   See JST Genesis 9:24; A. al-Tha'labi, *Lives*, p. 49; H. E. Gaylord, Jr., *3 Baruch*, 6:15-17, p. 669; H. W. Nibley, *Sacred*, pp. 577-579; H. W. Nibley, *Message 2005*, p. 308; cf. M. Ibn Ishaq ibn Yasar, *Making*, p. 37.

375   N. Koltun-Fromm, *Aphrahat*. See *Endnote E-113*, p. 729.

376   Or perhaps: Latin *pomum* (fruit) = French *pomme* (apple) (A. LaCocque, *Trial*, p. 95 n. 47).

377   J. Neusner, *Genesis Rabbah 1*, 15:7, p. 168.

378   N. M. Sarna, *Genesis*, p. 19.

379   C. Westermann, *Genesis 1-11*, p. 216.

380   P. Alexander, *3 Enoch*, 18:19, p. 273; cf. D. W. Parry, *Garden*, p. 130.

381   See *Commentary* 3:6-a, p. 156.

382   D. W. Parry, *Garden*, p. 131.

383   1 Nephi 11:25.

384   R. Giorgi, *Anges*, p. 25.

385   Cf. T. Stordalen, *Echoes*, pp. 275-276.

386   N. M. Sarna, *Genesis*, p. 19; cf. T. Stordalen, *Echoes*, p. 111.

387   E. Kastler, *Commentaire*.

388   M. B. Brown, *Gate*, p. 121.

*10 And I, the Lord God, **caused a river to go out of Eden** to water the garden; and from thence it was parted, and became into four heads.*

*11 And I, the Lord God, called the name of the first **Pison**, and it compasseth the whole land of **Havilah**, where I, the Lord God, created much **gold**;*

millennial temple.[389] Medieval religious iconography sometimes featured a basin containing the waters of life as a representation of the Tree of Life.[390]

Verses 10-14 (or, alternatively, 11-14) have long been suspected of being either a late interpolation or at least having come from a different source than the rest of the chapter.[391] Perhaps this explains why verses 11-14 are omitted from the book of Abraham. Through the inclusion of these verses, the editor seems to be insisting on a specific Near Eastern setting. However, discouraged by the seeming lack of geographical consistency in the description of the four rivers going out from Eden, later commentators have had difficulty finding consensus.[392] Because of the nature of the Garden of Eden itself,[393] "neither biblical records nor secular history and archaeological research" are likely to ever "identify the dimensions or the location of the garden [of Eden] in terms of the present-day surface of the earth."[394] On the other hand, statements attributed to the Prophet Joseph Smith may be taken as providing an indication of Adam and Eve's migration *after* the Fall.[395]

OT1 reads in the passive voice ("And a river went out of Eden").[396] The current text follows OT2, recorded in the hand of Sidney Rigdon.[397]

11 a *Pison… Havilah… gold.* The name Pison, with a possible meaning of something like "Gusher,"[398] appears nowhere else in the Old Testament. Havilah, perhaps signifying "sandy land,"[399] is mentioned elsewhere as a personal name[400] and as a region apparently in Arabia.[401] Jewish sages identified the river with the Nile or the Ganges.[402] After careful analysis, Stordalen concludes that "no river fits the description… unless the Red Sea and the Arabian Ocean are taken together to form a mighty 'river'"—a view that he thinks conceivable "in the eye of an ancient cosmographer… [looking] from the shores of Southern Arabia."[403]

While Eden is described as a place of luxurious growth and abundance of water and fruit, Hamilton notes that gold and other precious metals are associated only with the territories outside of it.[404] The mines or rivers of Nubia, a region south of Egypt "corresponding roughly to present-day Nilotic Sudan,"[405] would be a possible source of gold corresponding to a place name for Havilah located in the Egyptian sphere, while in Genesis 10:29, Havilah is stated to be a 'brother' of Ophir, a country famous for gold. Note also the mention of gold and precious stones, recalling scriptural descriptions of the temple.[406]

---

389 See Ezekiel 47:1; cf. Joel 3:18; Zechariah 14:8; 1 Kings 7:39; 2 Chronicles 4:10; Revelation 21:6, 22:1. See also A. LaCocque, *Trial*, pp. 80-81.
390 R. Giorgi, *Anges*, pp. 20-22.
391 T. Stordalen, *Echoes*, pp. 270-271; C. Westermann, *Genesis 1-11*, pp. 215-216.
392 See *Endnote 3-59*, p. 212.
393 See the overview of Moses 3, pp. 139-144.
394 G. W. Doxey, *Eden*, p. 534.
395 See *Figure 6-2*, p. 457 and *Excursus 39: The Location of Adam-ondi-Ahman*, p. 623.
396 S. H. Faulring, *et al.*, *Original Manuscripts*, p. 89.
397 *Ibid.*, p. 598; K. P. Jackson, *Book of Moses*, p. 74; cf. Moses 3:11-a, p. 172.
398 V. P. Hamilton, *Genesis*, p. 169.
399 N. M. Sarna, *Genesis*, p. 19.
400 Genesis 10:7, 29.
401 Genesis 25:18.
402 R. M. Zlotowitz, *et al.*, *Bereishis*, pp. 96-97.
403 T. Stordalen, *Echoes*, p. 279.
404 V. P. Hamilton, *Genesis*, p. 169.
405 N. M. Sarna, *Genesis*, p. 20.
406 E.g., Haggai 2:7-8; Revelation 21:18; 2 Nephi 5:15-16.

MOSES 3

11 And I, the Lord God, called the name of the first Pison, and it compasseth the whole land of Havilah, **where I, the Lord God, created** *much gold;*

12 And the gold of that land was good, and there was **bdellium** *and the* **onyx stone.**

13 And the name of the second river was called **Gihon;** *the same that compasseth the whole land of Ethiopia.*

14 And the name of the third river was **Hiddekel;** *that which goeth toward the east of* **Assyria.** *And the fourth river was the* **Euphrates.**

    b   *where I, the Lord God, created.* OT1 reads in the passive voice ("where there were created").[407] OT2 reads "where I, the Lord, created."[408] The current text dates to the 1902 edition of the Pearl of Great Price.[409]

12 **a**   *bdellium.* Sarna writes: "Bdellium is mentioned again only in Numbers 11:7, where it is assumed to be a well-known substance. From ancient times, opinion has been divided as to whether it was a precious stone or a much-valued aromatic resin called *bdellion* by the Greeks."[410]

    b   *onyx stone.* Writes Sarna: "Hebrew *shoham* is an oft-mentioned precious stone; its exact identity is uncertain."[411] In Exodus, it is mentioned as one of the stones for the priestly breastplate.[412] An alternative translation might be *lapis lazuli.*[413]

13 **a**   *Gihon.* Gihon may be connected with a Hebrew verb that means "to break loose."[414] In a valley at the foot of the Mount of Olives just outside of Jerusalem is a spring by this name.[415] The mention of the "land of Ethiopia" (or Cush) makes identification of the river difficult because there are several candidates for its location.[416] Stordalen resurrects an ancient opinion, generally rejected by modern commentators, that the river was meant to be identified with the Nile.[417]

14 **a**   *Hiddekel.* Called the Tigris in Greek and the Dijlah in Arabic. "Hebrew 'hiddekel' is mentioned again only in Daniel 10:4."[418]

    b   *Assyria.* "'Asshur' may be either the city of Ashur, which lay west of the Tigris, or the larger region of Assyria, to which it gave its name."[419]

    c   *Euphrates.* The river was so well-known that no further topographical description was required.[420] In many places in the Bible it is called simply "the River." Speaking of the land that was purposed for Abraham's posterity, God said in one of many references that it would extend from "the river, the river Euphrates, even unto the uttermost sea."[421]

In Psalms, it is prophesied that Solomon would "have dominion… from the river unto the ends of the earth."[422] Though the wording in Psalms is clearly related to descriptions of the promised land found in the Old Testament, the phrase "ends of the earth" always refers in

407   S. H. Faulring, *et al.*, *Original Manuscripts*, p. 89.
408   *Ibid.*, p. 598.
409   K. P. Jackson, *Book of Moses*, p. 47.
410   N. M. Sarna, *Genesis*, p. 20.
411   *Ibid.*, p. 20.
412   Exodus 28:13-20; 39:10-13.
413   N. M. Sarna, *Genesis*, p. 20.
414   See Job 38:8; 40:23; V. P. Hamilton, *Genesis*, p. 169.
415   1 Kings 1:33, 38, 45; 2 Chronicles 32:30; 33:14.
416   N. M. Sarna, *Genesis*, p. 20.
417   T. Stordalen, *Echoes*, pp. 279-281.
418   N. M. Sarna, *Genesis*, p. 20.
419   *Ibid.* p. 20. See T. Stordalen, *Echoes*, pp. 282-283.
420   N. M. Sarna, *Genesis*, p. 20.
421   Deuteronomy 11:24.
422   Psalm 72:8.

*14 And the name of the third river was Hiddekel; that which goeth toward the east of Assyria. And the fourth river was the **Euphrates**.*

*15 And I, the Lord God, **took the man, and put him into the Garden of Eden, to dress it, and to keep it**.*

> scripture to the whole world, rather than just to Palestine. Thus, in this larger sense, the passage in Psalms could be seen as a prophecy alluding to the eventual Davidic reign over the whole earth, starting at the place where the world began—namely at the source of the river of Eden (or alternately "rivers," as seen from a vantage point outside of the Garden)—and extending from thence to the four corners of the earth.

15 a *took the man, and put him into the Garden of Eden.* After the digressive description of the rivers, the action of verse 8 is repeated so as to take up the story where it left off.[423] But there is a subtle difference. Instead of merely reiterating the idea of v. 8 that the man was put in the Garden, as one might do with an inanimate object, it is additionally said here that the Lord "took" him. In biblical tradition this implies that the man is now called and given something to do.[424]

Moreover, Sailhamer sees special significance in the difference between the term underlying the word "put" in v. 8[425] and the one behind "put" in v. 15.[426] The latter is a term "elsewhere… reserved for two special uses: God's 'rest' or 'safety', which he gives to man in the land,[427] and the 'dedication' of something in the presence of the Lord[428] …Man was 'put' into the garden where he could 'rest' and be 'safe', and man was 'put' into the garden 'in God's presence' where he could have fellowship with God."[429]

b *to dress it, and to keep it.* The Hebrew terms for "to dress" (*abad*) and "to keep" (*shamar*) respectively connote to "work, serve, till"[430] and "keep, watch (guard), preserve."[431] Significantly, these are the very words that are used to describe the tabernacle duties of the Levites.[432] For example, Numbers 3:8 says that the Levites "shall keep (*shamar*) all the instruments of the Tabernacle of the congregation, and the charge of the children of Israel, to do the service (*abad*) of the Tabernacle." Thus, Wenham's remark that "if Eden is seen then as an ideal sanctuary, then perhaps Adam should be described as an archetypal Levite."[433] Sailhamer similarly comments: "Man's life in the garden was to be characterized by worship and obedience; he was a priest, not merely a worker and keeper of the Garden…. Throughout [Moses 3] the author has consistently and consciously developed the idea of man's 'likeness' to God along the same lines as the major themes of the Pentateuch as a whole, namely, the theme of worship and Sabbath rest. A further confirmation [of this reading] is the fact that in v. 16 we read for the first time that 'God commanded'… the man whom he had created. Just as in the remainder of the *Torah*, enjoyment of God's good land is made contingent on 'keeping'… God's commandments."[434] Barker observes: "The sixth day represented the era of human history, in which Adam had to work for the Creator until the Sabbath rest when God saw that everything was very good.[435] Jesus alluded to this belief when he healed on the

---

423 N. M. Sarna, *Genesis*, p. 20. For parallel constructions, see Genesis 39:1 = 37:36; 43:24 = 43:17.
424 E. Kastler, *Commentaire*; cf. 2 Samuel 7:8.
425 Hebrew *wayyasem*.
426 Hebrew *wayyannihehu*.
427 E.g., Genesis 19:6; Deuteronomy 3:20; 12:10; 25:19.
428 Exodus 16:33-34; Leviticus 16:23; Numbers 17:4; Deuteronomy 26:4, 10.
429 J. H. Sailhamer, *Genesis*, pp. 44-45.
430 F. Brown, *et al.*, *Lexicon*, pp. 712b-713c.
431 *Ibid.*, p. 1036b.
432 G. J. Wenham, *Genesis 1-15*, p. 67; cf. U. Cassuto, *Adam to Noah*, pp. 122-123; D. W. Parry, *Service*, p. 45.
433 Cited in M. B. Brown, *Gate*, p. 33.
434 J. H. Sailhamer, *Genesis*, p. 45; cf. Deuteronomy 30:16, 1 Nephi 2:20.
435 Moses 2:31.

*15 And I, the Lord God, took the man, and put him into the Garden of Eden, **to dress it, and to keep it**.*

16 And I, the Lord God, commanded the man, saying: Of every tree of the garden thou mayest freely eat,

*17 But of the tree of the knowledge of good and evil, **thou shalt not eat of it**, nevertheless, **thou mayest choose for thyself**, for it is given unto thee; but, remember that I forbid it, for in the day thou eatest thereof thou shalt surely die.*

Sabbath and, when criticized, reminded the Jews that he and his father were still working,[436] in other words, that the creation was not yet 'very good.'"[437]

Consistent with a general tendency to downplay or omit temple imagery, Islamic sources do not mention the duty of Adam and Eve to care for the Garden.[438]

17   a   *thou shalt not eat of it.* Whereas the Hebrew text uses the singular "thou," implying that the commandment was given to Adam alone, the Greek *Septuagint* uses the plural "you."[439] The idea that both Adam and Eve were both present to hear this command from God was not uncommon in Jewish and early Christian tradition.[440] Later commentators apportioned blame to Adam and Eve differently, depending on whether they assumed that Adam was alone or that both of them were present to hear the original commandment.

This is the first negative commandment. It requires man to "exercise restraint and self-discipline in the gratification of his appetite,"[441] prefiguring the later dietary instructions given to Noah,[442] Moses,[443] and as part of the modern-day Word of Wisdom.[444] In a larger sense, the commandment represents the bounds that man must keep on all desires and passions.

In the version of this verse published in the 1835 edition of the *Lectures on Faith* 2:10, the words "neither shall you touch it" follows this phrase.[445]

b   *thou mayest choose for thyself.* This added phrase to the book of Moses makes it clear that Adam and Eve are to be placed in a situation where they must exercise their freedom to choose. Elder Joseph Fielding Smith offers the following paraphrase of the command: "The Lord said to Adam, here is the tree of the knowledge of good and evil. If you want to stay here then you cannot eat of that fruit. If you want to stay here, then I forbid you to eat it. But you may act for yourself and you may eat of it if you want to. And if you eat of it you will die."[446] Continues Elder Smith: "In no other commandment the Lord ever gave to man, did he say: 'But of the tree of the knowledge of good and evil, thou shalt not eat of it, nevertheless, thou mayest choose for thyself.'"[447]

The Prophet Joseph Smith emphasized that "Adam did not commit sin in eating the fruits, for God had decreed that he should eat and fall. But in compliance with the decree he should

---

436   John 5:17.

437   M. Barker, *Hidden*, p. 19. See *Commentary* 3:9-g, p. 164; 4:31-e, p. 282; 5:34-c, p. 382.

438   D. C. Peterson, *Qur'anic Tree of Life*.

439   L. C. L. Brenton, *Septuagint*, Genesis 2:17, p. 3; C. Dogniez, *et al.*, *Pentateuque*, Genesis 2:17, pp. 140-141.

440   G. A. Anderson, *et al.*, *Synopsis*, 32:1, p. 36E; G. A. Anderson, *Perfection*, pp. 81-84. See also *Figure* 4-10, p. 228 and *Commentary* 4:9-b, p. 252.

441   N. M. Sarna, *Genesis*, p. 21.

442   JST Genesis 9:9-11.

443   Leviticus 11.

444   D&C 89.

445   K. P. Jackson, *Book of Moses*, p. 75. See *Commentary* 4:9-b, p. 252. Note that this variation is specifically omitted from the enumeration of changes given in the 1990 edition of the *Lectures on Faith* (L. E. Dahl, *et al.*, *Lectures*, pp. 40, 109).

446   J. F. Smith, Jr., *Fall*, reprinted in Church Educational System, *Charge*, p. 124. See also J. F. Smith, Jr., *Answers*, 1963, 4:81.

447   J. F. Smith, Jr., *Doctrines*, 22 April 1939, 1:114. See Moses 3:17.

MOSES 3

17 But of the tree of the knowledge of good and evil, thou shalt not eat of it, nevertheless, **thou mayest choose for thyself,** *for it is given unto thee; but, remember that I forbid it, for* **in the day thou eatest thereof thou shalt surely die.**

die. Only he should die was the saying of the Lord; therefore the Lord appointed us to fall and also redeemed us."[448]

c ***in the day thou eatest thereof thou shalt surely die.*** The form of the expression "thou shalt surely die" is "characteristic of divine or royal threats" demonstrating "God's seriousness in prohibiting access to the tree."[449]

Spiritual death after the eating of the fruit would be swift, since transgression would require Adam and Eve to be separated from God's presence.[450] Physical death would be just as sure, but not so immediate—as seen later, the lives of Adam and Eve will be mercifully "prolonged" so that they can experience a "state of probation."[451]

Mettinger argues that the phrase "in the day" is not necessarily temporal and may, as in some other biblical instances, carry a conditional sense ("for *if* thou eatest…"): "The exact point of time for death is not the issue."[452] However, if we do take the phrase as temporal, it seems clear from the context of the corresponding verse in the book of Abraham that the term "day" would have to be interpreted "after the Lord's time" (i.e., 1,000 years), for "at the time the Lord said this to Adam, there was no mode of counting time by man, as man now counts time."[453] Moses 6:12 records that Adam died at 930 years of age.[454]

Since the Tree of Life is not specifically included in the prohibition, commentators have speculated as to whether Adam and Eve may have eaten from it to prolong their lives so long as they remained in the Garden. For example, Stephens argues that Adam and Eve were inherently mortal at the time they were created but remained immortal in the Garden because they had continual access to the Tree of Life.[455] If they had hair and skin like ours, he reasons, then their bodies must have contained dead cells, and to a biologist, there is little difference between cell death and organismal death. However, this is a different matter if death is defined as the separation of an individual spirit from the body. Regarding this question, the Prophet Joseph Smith taught: "When God breathed into man's nostrils he became a living soul, before that he did not live, and when that was taken away his body died."[456]

In contrast to Stephens' interpretation, Elder Bruce R. McConkie maintained that the chief idea represented by worthily partaking of the fruit of the Tree of Life was not immortality but rather eternal life[457]—bestowed in the appropriate degree to those who partake of the fruits of Christ's atonement.[458] Therefore, in this view, Adam and Eve's only approach to the Tree of Life will be by way of first taking the fruit of the Tree of Knowledge, then leaving the Garden to pass into mortality, and returning at last to take of the sweet fruit only if and when they are fully qualified—and authoritatively invited—to do so.[459]

Regarding the question of death before the Fall for non-human forms of life, Matthews' article in the *Encyclopedia of Mormonism* is careful not to overstate what can be said authori-

---

448 J. Smith, Jr., *Words*, 9 February 1841, p. 63, spelling and punctuation modernized.
449 G. J. Wenham, *Genesis 1-15*, p. 67.
450 Cf. G. A. Anderson, *Perfection*, pp. 128-129.
451 2 Nephi 2:21.
452 T. N. D. Mettinger, *Eden*, pp. 22-23; cf. A. LaCocque, *Trial*, p. 75.
453 J. Smith, Jr., *Words*, 9 March 1841, pp. 64-65, spelling and capitalization modernized.
454 See *Commentary* 6:11-a, p. 482 and 6:12-a, p. 483.
455 T. D. Stephens, *et al.*, *Evolution*, pp. 181-185; T. D. Stephens, *Tree of Life*.
456 J. Smith, Jr., *Spirits*, p. 746.
457 B. R. McConkie, *New Witness*, p. 86; cf. A. Gileadi, *Studies*, p. 10; B. C. Hafen, *Broken*, p. 30.
458 D&C 88:28-32; R. J. Matthews, *Probationary Nature*, p. 56.
459 See *Commentary* 3:9-h, p. 167; 3:9-g, p. 163. See also *Commentary* 4:28-b, p. 276 and *Excursus 25: The Tree of Life as the Hidden Throne of God*, p. 591.

*17 But of the tree of the knowledge of good and evil, thou shalt not eat of it, nevertheless, thou mayest choose for thyself, for it is given unto thee; but, remember that I forbid it, for **in the day thou eatest thereof thou shalt surely die.***

*18 And I, the Lord God, said unto mine Only Begotten, that **it was not good that the man should be alone***; wherefore, **I will make an help meet for him***.*

tatively: "Various interpretations have been suggested concerning the nature of life on the earth before the Fall and how the Fall physically affected the world, but these go beyond the clearly stated doctrine of the Church. The Church and the scriptures are emphatic, however, that the Fall brought two kinds of death to Adam and his posterity" (i.e., spiritual and physical death).[460]

18   **a**   ***it was not good that the man should be alone.*** This was the first declaration by God that some aspect of creation was *not* good.[461] Recall that in Moses 2, God did not declare His handiwork "very good" until after He had created woman.[462] In the narrative of the creation of Eve, writes Sailhamer, the author "put the final touches on his account of what it means for man to be 'in God's image and likeness'" by making it clear that "man's creation 'in God's image' also entails a 'partnership'… with his wife."[463]

    b   ***I will make.*** The book of Abraham and the *Septuagint* emphasize a connection with Moses 2:26 by their use of the phrase "I will make/Let us make" in the statement of God's intention and in the subsequent use of the special verb *bara* to describe the creative act itself.[464]

    c   ***an help meet for him.*** The Hebrew means "a helper or strength corresponding to him"—or, in other words, a completing counterpart. "This term cannot be taken as demeaning because Hebrew *'ezer*, employed here to describe the intended role of the woman, is often used of God in His relation to man."[465] President Howard W. Hunter said: "The Lord intended that the wife be… a companion equal and necessary in full partnership."[466] Thus, in Moses 2, both man and woman are created in the image of God, and in Moses 3, they are described as corresponding strengths.[467]

Westermann concludes that there is more intended here than merely "help at work" or "the begetting of descendants": "The man is created by God in such a way that he needs the help of a partner; hence mutual help is an essential part of human existence."[468] *Targum Yerushalmi* captures this sense when it refers to the woman as the man's "yoke-fellow."[469]

Note that the book of Abraham, unlike the book of Moses, places the creation of woman before the naming of the animals.[470] Nibley summarizes this altered sequence: "The man becomes 'the man Adam' in the fullest sense only when he opens his eyes in a new world and, having forgotten what went before, 'sees' and 'knows' as his intellect awakens. But the most important thing he sees and knows is his wife, after which God makes him aware of the rest of the Creation, which he proceeds to investigate and name."[471]

---

460   R. J. Matthews, *Fall*, p. 486; cf. R. D. Draper, *et al.*, *Commentary*, p. 186; M. D. Rhodes, *et al.*, *Astronomy*, p. 27.
461   V. P. Hamilton, *Genesis*, p. 175.
462   Moses 2:27, 31. See G. B. Hinckley, *Women*, p. 67.
463   J. H. Sailhamer, *Genesis*, p. 46.
464   U. Cassuto, *Adam to Noah*, p. 92.
465   N. M. Sarna, *Genesis*, p. 21.
466   H. W. Hunter, *Teachings 1997*, November 1994, p. 152.
467   R. E. Friedman, *Commentary*, p. 19. Brodie contrasts the positive picture of Woman at her creation with the highly negative Greek account of Hesiod (T. L. Brodie, *Dialogue*, p. 141).
468   C. Westermann, *Genesis 1-11*, p. 227; cf. Ecclesiastes 4:10.
469   J. W. Etheridge, *Onkelos*.
470   Cf. 2 Nephi 2:15.
471   H. W. Nibley, *Message 2005*, p. 284.

MOSES 3

*19 And **out of the ground I**, the Lord God, **formed every beast of the field**, and every fowl of the air; and **commanded that they should come unto Adam**, to see what he would call them; and they were also living souls; for I, God, breathed into them the breath of life, and commanded that whatsoever Adam called every living creature, that should be the name thereof.*

19 a ***out of the ground, I... formed every beast of the field.*** A beast of the field is a wild animal.[472] The Hebrew admits a translation of the term behind "formed" as "had formed." This would allow for a creation sequence consistent with Moses 2, where the animals appeared before man's creation.[473] Sarna and Bradley both argue that the reference to the creation of the animals is incidental, and should not be taken to indicate that Adam was created before they were[474]—unless, perhaps, one takes the animals created in the Garden as being distinct from the ones previously created on Earth.[475] In any case, here we are made to know that the bodies of the animals were made of the "dust of the earth," as was the body of Adam.

Westermann notes that the descriptions of the animals are not formulaic, since the narrator is not "concerned with the creation of animals in general... [but rather] is thinking of the animals from the viewpoint of human beings. Can animals be their helpers or companions? And so the fish do not come into consideration."[476] In this connection, Cassuto also notes the omission of cattle (an antonym to beasts of the field) which, unlike the "classes of creatures that man can catch only by hunting," "were already with him in the Garden of Eden."[477]

b ***commanded that they should come unto Adam.*** Sarna comments: "In [Moses 2] God bestows names only on the cosmic phenomena connected with time and space. Here He assigns to man the role of naming terrestrial animates, which... is another way of expressing the bestowal of authority and dominion over them, the idea contained in [2:28]."[478] Naming the animals is a way of incorporating them into his world and his life.[479]

Whereas Jewish tradition records that the animals subsequently bowed to Adam,[480] pseudepigraphic and Islamic accounts instead have angels paying homage to him.[481] Recalling Barker's contention that Genesis passages relating to angels were subject to tampering by second temple scribes,[482] a substitution of "beasts" for "angels" in the biblical account becomes possible to imagine. Note also that the book of Revelation closely associates beasts and angels who worship together at God's throne in heaven.[483] Moreover the serpent, an accomplice of Satan, is specifically identified as a "beast of the field."[484]

With these considerations in mind, a parallel tradition from Islamic sources that appears in place of the episode of the naming of animals should be considered.[485] The story tells of how Adam, before the Fall and after having been given instruction by God, was directed to recite a series of secret names to the angels in order to convince them that he was worthy of the elevated status that had been bestowed upon him.[486] Zilio-Grandi comments: "While in the

472   R. E. Friedman, *Commentary*, p. 19.
473   V. P. Hamilton, *Genesis*, p. 176. But see also the discussion in J. H. Sailhamer, *Genesis*, p. 48.
474   W. Bradley, *Why*, p. 175; N. M. Sarna, *Genesis*, p. 21.
475   See discussion in the overview of Moses 3, pp. 139-144.
476   C. Westermann, *Genesis 1-11*, pp. 227-228.
477   U. Cassuto, *Adam to Noah*, pp. 129, 131.
478   N. M. Sarna, *Genesis*, p. 2.
479   C. Westermann, *Genesis 1-11*, pp. 228-229.
480   G. A. Anderson, *et al.*, *Synopsis*, 44 16:2b, p. 49E; M.-A. Ouaknin, *et al.*, *Rabbi Éliézer*, 11, p. 78.
481   See the overview of Moses 4, p. 225.
482   M. Barker, *Beyond*, pp. 195-196; M. Barker, *Great High Priest*, p. 157.
483   Revelation 4:6-9, 19:4; D&C 77:2-4.
484   See *Commentary* 4:5-a, p. 246 and 4:6-a, p. 249.
485   J.-L. Monneret, *Grands*, p. 481 n. 12; cf. M. al-Kisa'i, *Tales*, p. 28; al-Tabari, *Creation*, 1:94-97, pp. 266-269; G. Weil, *Legends*, p. 22.
486   *Qur'an* 2:30-33; cf. the idea of the naming as a test for Adam (vs. Satan) in al-Tabari, *Creation*, 1:97, p. 269; M. J. B. bin Gorion, *et al.*, *Mimekor*, 3, 1:6-7; L. Ginzberg, *Legends*, 1:62-64, 5:84-86 n. 35; E. G. Mathews, Jr., *Armenian*, p. 148 and n. 35; J. Neusner, *Genesis Rabbah 1*, 17:4:2, p. 183; M.-A. Ouaknin, *et al.*, *Rabbi Éliézer*,

*19 And out of the ground I, the Lord God, formed every beast of the field, and every fowl of the air; and **commanded that they should come unto Adam**, to see what he would call them; and they were also living souls; for I, God, breathed into them the breath of life, and commanded that whatsoever Adam called every living creature, that should be the name thereof.*

Bible God lets Adam choose the names of things, in the *Qur'an* it is God who teaches—who reveals therefore—the names to Adam.... Extremely high value is attributed to knowledge... Indeed, it is not by obedience that the ability to represent God in the governance of the world is measured, but by knowledge."[487]

With respect to this account of Adam's premortal accomplishment, *Qur'an* commentators themselves "dispute which particular names were involved; various theories [taking the position that] they were the names of all things animate and inanimate, the names of the angels, the names of his own descendants, or the names of God."[488] *Al-Mizan* asserts that this was not a simple dictionary recital showing off the power of Adam's memory, but rather "something totally different from what we understand from the knowledge of names."[489] Alusi concludes that Adam's saying of these names is "in the end, like saying the names of God, for power concerns God Himself in His ruling of the world."[490]

Later, in a separate incident that was said to have occurred *after* the Fall, Islamic writings recount that "Adam received (some) words from his Lord" that enabled him to repent and return to good standing with God,[491] so he could eventually go back to the Garden of Eden.[492] Ayoub writes: "Much disagreement has arisen among commentators regarding the words that Adam received from his Lord... Ibn 'Arabi says that these were 'lights and states [*ahwal*] or stations [*maqamat*] of the realm of dominion and power and the realm of the subtle [*mujarradah*] spirits... It may also be that Adam received from God *gnoses*, sciences, and truths.'"[493] *Al-Mizan* declines speculation about what specific words were revealed but rather elaborates on their function: "It was this learning of the words that paved the way for the repentance of Adam... Probably, the words received at the time of repentance were related to the names taught to him in the beginning.... There must have been something in those names to wipe out every injustice, to erase every sin and to cure every spiritual and moral disease;... those names were sublime creations hidden from the heavens and the earth; they were intermediaries to convey the grace and bounties of Allàh to His creation; and no creature would be able to attain to its perfection without their assistance."[494]

In deceptive counterpoint, Islamic legend portrays Satan as persuading his accomplices, the peacock and the serpent,[495] to help him tempt Adam and Eve by promising them that he would reveal to them "three mysterious words, which shall preserve thee from sickness, age,

---

13, pp. 87-88; *Commentary 3:23-c*, p. 183; *Excursus 24: The Watchers*, p. 585.,

487   I. Zilio-Grandi, *Paradise*, pp. 84, 87; cf. D&C 107:18-19; 130:18-19; 131:5-6. This is a theme often mentioned in the teachings of Joseph Smith, e.g., J. Smith, Jr., *Teachings*, 5 October 1840, pp. 166-167; 10 April 1842, p. 217; 8 April 1843, p. 288; 14 May 1843, p. 297; 21 May 1843, pp. 305-306; 11 June 1843, p. 309; 9 October 1843, pp. 324-326; 21 January 1844, pp. 329-331; 7 April 1844, pp. 344-350, 354, 357; 16 June 1844, p. 371; J. Smith, Jr., *Documentary History*, 17 May 1843, 5:392; 27 August 1843, 5:555.

488   *Adam and Eve.*

489   A. at-Tabataba'i, *Al-Mizan*, 1:163.

490   Cited in I. Zilio-Grandi, *Paradise*, pp. 86-87. See *Endnote E-11*, p. 706.

491   *Qur'an* 2:37.

492   A. al-Tha'labi, *Lives*, p. 59; cf. M. al-Kisa'i, *Tales*, p. 60.

493   M. M. Ayoub, *Qur'an (Vol. 1)*, pp. 84-85.

494   A. at-Tabataba'i, *Al-Mizan*, 1:188-189, 211.

495   The peacock was a representative "fowl of the air"—and Satan's "favorite." On the other hand, the cock was "the most hateful to him" (M. al-Kisa'i, *Tales*, p. 71). The serpent was a representative "beast of the field."

*19 And out of the ground I, the Lord God, formed every beast of the field, and every fowl of the air; and **commanded that they should come unto Adam**, to see what he would call them; and they were also living souls; for I, God, breathed into them the breath of life, and commanded that whatsoever Adam called every living creature, that should be the name thereof.*

and death."[496] The account recalls an incident in the *Gospel of Thomas* where "Jesus reveals three words" to Thomas "which must have been the three words of the secret Name."[497]

Among other ancient documents from around the world, the Egyptian *Book of the Dead* takes up a similar theme as it describes the manner in which initiates were to advance past a series of gatekeepers through his knowledge of certain names.[498] Writes Nibley: "The importance of knowing the names of things and giving those names when challenged is more than the mere idea of the password; it is, according to Derchain, nothing less than the logical source of 'the entire mechanism of Egyptian mythology and liturgy'—namely, 'the law which makes of the name a veritable attribute of the thing named.'"[499] Hence, the frequent theme of danger for any possessor of the name who revealed it to an unauthorized party.[500] The Coptic *Discourse on Abbaton*, which may have been influenced by texts of the same nature, explicitly associates "absolute authority" over the angels with a knowledge of their names,[501] and, elsewhere, Josephus records that the Essenes were under a vow to preserve the names of the angels.[502] Madsen proposes that the idea that the "proper use of the name YHWH constitutes a covenant between Israel and her God" may be the reason behind the third commandment.[503] According to Schimmel, a scholar of Islamic mysticism: "The Hope of discovering the Greatest Name of God has inspired many a Sufi who dreamed of reaching the highest bliss in this world and the next by means of this blessed name."[504] The dedicatory prayer for Solomon's temple stressed that it was not meant to be a residence for God, since He "lived in his 'dwelling place in heaven' but that the 'name of God' dwelt in the Temple."[505] The shout of the people at Christ's triumphal entry becomes more understandable when translated as "Blessed is he who comes *with* the Name of the Lord."[506]

Is it possible that Adam himself received a name as part of this episode? The fact that the first reference to Adam as a proper name is given in v. 20 seems to lend support to such a conjecture. It also seems significant that the final instance of naming in the story of the Garden and the Fall—Adam's bestowal of a permanent proper name on Eve—occurs in immediate proximity of the account of God's making coats of skin for the couple.[507]

While Genesis reads, "and brought them,"[508] OT1 reads "and commanded that they should be brought."[509] A change in the handwriting of Sidney Rigdon in OT2 was the source of

496 G. Weil, *Legends*, p. 26. See *Commentary* 3:9-h, p. 167; 4:5-b, p. 246; 4:9-a, p. 252; 4:14-e, p. 260; *Excursus 25: The Tree of Life as the Hidden Throne of God*, p. 591; cf. A. al-Tha'labi, *Lives*, pp. 50-51.

497 H. Koester, *et al.*, *Thomas*, 13, pp. 127-128; M. Barker, *Hidden*, p. 42.

498 B. T. Ostler, *Clothed*, pp. 8-10. See *Commentary* 4:31-c, p. 280.

499 H. W. Nibley, *Message 2005*, p. 451; cf. B. H. Porter, *et al.*, *Names*, pp. 501-504; *Commentary* 5:31-a, p. 379; J. Assman, *Search*, pp. 83-110.

500 J. B. Pritchard, *Unknown Name*; cf. Judges 16:4-20; B. H. Porter, *et al.*, *Names*, pp. 508-513.

501 E. A. W. Budge, *Cave*, pp. 58-59; cf. Judges 13:17-18.

502 F. Josephus, *Wars*, 2:8:7, p. 477.

503 T. G. Madsen, *Putting*, p. 459.

504 A. Schimmel, *Mystical*, p. 25; cf. B. H. Porter, *et al.*, *Names*, pp. 510-512.

505 W. J. Hamblin, *et al.*, *Temple*, p. 27; cf. p. 182. See also 1 Kings 8:27-30; D&C 110:7.

506 "With" = "in'" in Hebrew (M. Barker, *Hidden*, p. 44; cf. Matthew 21:9). The meaning of being "willing to take upon [us] the name of Jesus Christ" in the sacrament is clear in light of temple ordinances (D. H. Oaks, *Taking Upon Us*; D. A. Bednar, *Name*, p. 98; D&C 20:77; 109:22, 26, 79; *Excursus 17: The Veil of the Temple*, p. 564).

507 Moses 4:26-27; cf. T. G. Madsen, *Putting*, pp. 458-459; B. H. Porter, *et al.*, *Names*, pp. 504-507; J. E. Seaich, *Ancient Texts 1995*, p. 668. See D&C 130:11; *Commentary* 1:27-b, p. 62; 3:23-c, p. 183; 4:26-a, p. 273; overview of Moses 4, p. 238; *Excursus 53: Comparative Explorations: Jewish and Christian Analogues*, p. 679.

508 Genesis 2:19.

509 S. H. Faulring, *et al.*, *Original Manuscripts*, p. 90.

MOSES 3

*19 And out of the ground I, the Lord God, formed every beast of the field, and every fowl of the air; and **commanded that they should come unto Adam,** to see what he would call them; and they were also **living souls**; for I, God, **breathed** into them the breath of life, and commanded that whatsoever Adam called every living creature, that should be the name thereof.*

*20 And **Adam** gave names to all cattle, and to the fowl of the air, and to every beast of the field; but as for Adam, **there was not found an help meet for him**.*

*21 And I, the Lord God, caused a **deep sleep** to fall upon Adam; and he slept, and I took one of his ribs and closed up the flesh in the stead thereof;*

the current text.[510] In both versions, the JST reading that, unlike Eve, the animals were not brought personally by God to Adam, has the effect of highlighting the special nature of the introduction of the man and the woman in v. 22.[511]

c *living souls.* See *Commentary* 3:7-e, p. 158.

d *breathed.* See *Commentary* 3:7-d, 158.

20 a *Adam.* This is the first reference in Hebrew to Adam as a proper name, "probably because the narrative now speaks of the man as a personality rather than an archetypal human."[512] For conjectures on the meaning of the name Adam, see *Commentary* 1:34-a, p. 66.

b *There was not found an help meet for him.* The account of Adam's search for "an help meet" assures the reader "that man was not like the other creatures."[513] Through the process of naming the animals, Adam observes the universal pairing of male and female in the animal world and becomes aware of his exceptional solitary state.[514] Now, not only God, but also Adam, recognized fully that it was not good to be alone, and he is now ready "to appreciate and cherish the gift that the Lord God was to give him."[515]

Anticipating Moses 4:18, Rashi further comments: "Because God foresaw that [Adam] will complain against her, [Eve] was not given him until he expressly asked God for her."[516]

21 a *deep sleep.* "Hebrew *tardemah* is used of abnormally heavy sleep, divinely induced."[517] The image is one of transition from a former state into a new one, a "sleep and a forgetting,"[518] which, in Egyptian rites, preceded the bestowal of instructions and power, and the appearance of the great wife and mother-goddess.[519] An Islamic legend says that Adam slept after having eaten grapes from Paradise given him by Gabriel.[520] In the Gnostic *Apocryphon of John,* Adam's sleep is induced by drinking the waters of forgetfulness, recalling the Greek conception of the water of the River Lethe in the underworld that made the souls who drank of it forget their previous lives.[521] Without remembrance of all that came before, Adam "was simple as a new-born child."[522]

When the sleeping Adam lost the memory of his past, he also became ignorant of other things. The *Apocalypse of Adam* records Adam saying that "the first knowledge that breathed

---

510 *Ibid.,* p. 599; K. P. Jackson, *Book of Moses,* p. 76.

511 See *Commentary* 3:22-c, p. 182.

512 N. M. Sarna, *Genesis,* p. 22. See *Commentary* 3:19-b, p. 177.

513 J. H. Sailhamer, *Genesis,* p. 47.

514 N. M. Sarna, *Genesis,* p. 22.

515 U. Cassuto, *Adam to Noah,* p. 128.

516 R. M. Zlotowitz, *et al., Bereishis,* p. 107; cf. p. 105. See *Commentary* 4:18-a, p. 263.

517 N. M. Sarna, *Genesis,* p. 22.

518 William Wordsworth in L. Richards, *Marvelous,* p. 290.

519 H. W. Nibley, *Message 2005,* pp. 245-256; cf. the sleep of Jacob at Beth-El (H. W. Nibley, *Sacred,* p. 581).

520 G. Weil, *Legends,* p. 23.

521 W. Barnstone, *et al., Gnostic,* p. 160; cf. C. Schmidt, *Pistis,* 4:144, pp. 749-753; G. R. S. Mead, *Pistis,* 6, 144, 380, p. 315; H. W. Nibley, *Apocryphal,* p. 309; F. Wisse, *Apocryphon of John,* 22:20-26, p. 117.

522 U. Cassuto, *Adam to Noah,* p. 113. See also *Commentary* 3:23-c, p. 183.

*21 And I, the Lord God, caused a **deep sleep** to fall upon Adam; and he slept, and I **took one of his ribs** and closed up the flesh in the stead thereof;*

*22 And **the rib** which I, the Lord God, had taken from man, made I a woman, and brought her unto the man.*

within us" left them and that "the eternal knowledge of the God of truth withdrew from me and your mother Eve."[523] Likewise, we read in the Gnostic *Hypostasis of the Archons*: "Now the 'deep sleep that they caused to fall upon [Adam], and he slept' is Ignorance."[524] The awakening of Adam represents the beginning of his recovery from his state of ignorance and mortality.[525] In the *Hypostasis*, it is Eve, "the spirit-endowed woman," who says to the sleeping Adam, "Arise,"[526] however, in the *Apocalypse of Adam* this same role is played instead by "three men" of surpassing "glory." Although in Adam's new state of ignorance he was at first "unable to recognize" them, they proceeded to reveal knowledge to him about his Creator. This same knowledge is said to have later been revealed to Adam's son Seth.[527] Note that sleep also preceded the establishment of God's covenants with Abraham[528] and Jacob.[529]

In a related but wider sense, the Book of Mormon speaks of wicked mortals as being captivated by the "deep sleep... of hell"[530] wherein one is "encircled about by the bands of death, and the chains of hell,"[531] and of being "redeemed from hell" by the Lord whereby one is "encircled about eternally in the arms of his love."[532]

   b   ***took one of his ribs.*** Note that the verb "took" is used for the second time in this chapter.[533]

22 a   ***the rib.*** President Spencer W. Kimball taught that: "The story of the rib, of course, is figurative."[534] As Sarna describes: "The mystery of the intimacy between husband and wife and the indispensable role that the woman ideally plays in the life of man are symbolically described in terms of her creation out of his body. The rib taken from man's side thus connotes physical union and signifies that she is his companion and partner, ever at his side."[535]

In Mesopotamian literature, *Ea*, the god of wisdom, is "described as 'the ear of [the god] Ninurta' because the ear was regarded as the seat of intelligence. In Greek mythology, Athena, the goddess of wisdom, sprang from the forehead of Zeus, the seat of the brain."[536] In the Bible, by way of contrast, the use of the word rib "expresses the ultimate in proximity, intimacy, and identity."[537] Writes Nibley: "The rib in Arabic is the *urka* or *silka*. It is the expression for anything as close to you as a thing can possibly be."[538] Note that in the Sumerian myth of *Enki and Ninhusag*, Ninti is the name of a deity who cures Enki's rib—her name meaning both "the lady of the rib" and "the lady who makes life."[539]

---

523 G. W. MacRae, *et al.*, *Adam 1990*, 64:24-29, 65:10-11, p. 279; cf. S. E. Robinson, *Apocalypse of Adam*, pp. 10-11.

524 R. A. Bullard, *et al.*, *Archons*, 89:7, p. 164; cf. F. Wisse, *Apocryphon of John*, 22:20-28, p. 117.

525 Cf. *Commentary* 5:4-c, p. 357. See also Isaiah 60:1; 1 Corinthians 15:34; Moroni 10:31.

526 R. A. Bullard, *et al.*, *Archons*, 89:11-13, p. 164.

527 See G. W. MacRae, *et al.*, *Adam 1990*, 65:26-67:28, pp. 279-280; S. E. Robinson, *Apocalypse of Adam*, 65:26-67:28, pp. 11-13. For more on the theme of three heavenly messengers sent to instruct Adam, see *Figure 5-9*, p. 339 and *Figure 5-10*, p. 340.

528 Genesis 15:12.

529 Genesis 28:11. See J. H. Sailhamer, *Genesis*, p. 46.

530 2 Nephi 1:13.

531 Alma 5:7.

532 2 Nephi 1:15; cf. Romans 13:11-12; 2 Nephi 4:27-28; Jacob 3:11. See also 1 Thessalonians 5:4-8.

533 See *Commentary* 3:15-a, p. 173.

534 S. W. Kimball, *Blessings*, p. 71.

535 N. M. Sarna, *Genesis*, p. 22.

536 *Ibid.*, p. 22.

537 H. W. Nibley, *Patriarchy*, p. 87.

538 H. W. Nibley, *Teachings of the PGP*, 18, pp. 229-230.

539 G. Greenberg, *Myths*, p. 55. See *Commentary* 4:26-a, p. 273.

*22 And **the rib** which I, the Lord God, had taken from man, **made I a woman**, and **brought her unto the man**.*

Cassuto suggests that God "did not take the bone alone, as the exegetes usually understand the verse… [T]he Creator took together with the bone also the flesh attached to it, and from the flesh He formed the woman's flesh, and from the bone her bones."[540] Such a reading anticipates Adam's later declaration that Eve was "bone of my bones, and flesh of my flesh"[541]—the Hebrew words for ribs and bones exploiting a reversal of consonants in conscious wordplay.[542]

The eighteenth-century non-conformist preacher Matthew Henry is a frequent source of the oft-quoted but rarely-attributed sentiment that "the woman was made of a rib out of the side of Adam; not made out of his head to rule over him, nor out of his feet to be trampled upon by him, but out of his side to be equal with him, under his arm to be protected, and near his heart to be beloved."[543] Poetic versions of the idea found their way into nineteenth-century American ballads such as *Wedlock*[544] and *Adam and Eve's Wedding Song*,[545] and also frequently appeared in LDS and non-LDS contexts throughout the 20th century.[546] The general tenor of this theme, however, had been formulated long before Henry's time in the patristic literature—notably by Hugh of St. Victor (ca. 1134),[547] Martin of Leon (d. 1203),[548] the Armenian Nestorian Bishop Shelemon (ca. 1222),[549] and, most famously, St. Thomas Aquinas (1274).[550] In the fourteenth century, Chaucer drew on these patristic sources in composing a version of the statement for *The Parson's Tale*.[551] *Genesis Rabbah* had developed a similar idea much earlier, though in a derogatory vein.[552]

b   ***made I a woman.*** The Hebrew term for "made" in this verse, which has the sense of "built," is used only this once in the Creation narratives. Sarna notes: "In a word play, *Genesis Rabbah* 18:1 connects the present use of *b-n-h*, 'to build,' with *b-y-n*, 'to discern,' indicating that 'woman was endowed with intelligence surpassing that of man.'"[553]

c   ***brought her unto the man.*** "As noted in a midrash, the image may well be that of God playing the role of the attendant who leads the bride to the groom. Without doubt, the verse conveys the idea that the institution of marriage is established by God Himself."[554] In one source Eve describes her appearance by saying: "I was decked out like a bride, And I reclined in a wedding-chamber of light."[555] This is consistent with the Prophet's teaching that Adam and Eve were sealed as one by God within an eternal covenant of marriage.[556] Nibley

540   U. Cassuto, *Adam to Noah*, p. 134.

541   See *Commentary* 3:23-b, p. 183.

542   J. H. Sailhamer, *Genesis*, p. 47.

543   M. Henry, *Commentary*, 2:21-25, p. 10.

544   J. A. Lomax, *et al.*, *Ballads*, pp. 567-569.

545   The lyrics are traditionally attributed to Abraham Lincoln. However, this is doubtful since closely-related versions of the song had already appeared in England as early as 1740 (J. Lair, *Songs*, pp. 23-25).

546   E.g., V. M. Adams, *Eve*, p. 97; H. L. Andrus, *God*, p. 354; T. M. Burton, *Marriage*, pp. 12-13; J. R. Holland, *et al.*, *Some Things*, p. 107; J. F. McConkie, *Eden*, p. 26; J. F. McConkie, *et al.*, *Revelations*, pp. 216-217; R. M. Nelson, *Lessons*, p. 86; E. G. White, *Faith I Live By*, p. 251. See also S. Mariella, *Head*; S. Mariella, *Parson's Tale*.

547   Hugh of Saint Victor, *De Sacramentis*, 1:6:35, p. 117.

548   In J. P. Migne, *Patrologiae Latina*, Sermo 7 in Septuagesima 2, 208:583.

549   Shelemon, *Book of the Bee*, 14, pp. 18-19.

550   T. Aquinas, *Summa Theologica* 1:1, q. 92 a. 3. See R. R. Keller, *Adam*, p. 161; M. R. Makarewicz, *Patristic*, p. 61.

551   G. Chaucer, *Canterbury*, 927-930, pp. 303-304. See M. R. Makarewicz, *Patristic*, pp. 61-63, 147-184; S. Mariella, *Head*; S. Mariella, *Parson's Tale*.

552   J. Neusner, *Genesis Rabbah 1*, 18:2:1, p. 191.

553   N. M. Sarna, *Genesis*, pp. 22-23. See *Commentary* 4:12-e, p. 256 and 5:11-a, p. 364.

554   N. M. Sarna, *Genesis*, p. 23.

555   M. E. Stone, *Adamgirk*, 3:1:7, p. 48.

556   J. Smith, Jr., *Papers 1989-1992*, 24 November 1835, 1:146; J. Smith, Jr., *Documentary History*, 24 November 1835, 2:320; cf. H. L. Andrus, *God*, p. 354; J. F. Smith, Jr., *Doctrines*, 26 March 1932, 2:71; O. Pratt, *29 August 1852*, pp. 58-59.

MOSES 3

22 And the rib which I, the Lord God, had taken from man, made I a woman, and **brought her unto the man***.*

23 And **Adam said***: This I know now is* **bone of my bones, and flesh of my flesh***; she shall be called* **Woman***, because she was taken out of* **man***.*

elaborates: "[W]e learn in the *Gospel of Philip* and the *Apocalypse of Adam* how Adam and Eve were united in celestial union before the creation of the world but, upon descending to the earth, became separated, with death entering into the scene.[557] Christ came to earth, says the *Gospel of Philip*, 'for the express purpose of bringing them together in eternal life. Thanks to him those who are united in the Bridal Chamber will never more be separated.'[558] The ordinances here are symbolic, but the images are important models to be followed."[559] Note also that a sacred marriage (*hieros gamos*) of a royal pair was replayed for millennia all over the world as part of yearly solstice or equinox rituals.[560]

23   a   *Adam said.* "Man's first recorded speech is a cry of ecstatic elation at seeing the woman."[561] At last, he had found his own likeness, a companion whose strength corresponded to his own.[562]

b   *bone of my bones, and flesh of my flesh.* In the Old Testament, this phrase has not only the obvious meaning, but also is used to signify that two people belong to each other.[563] Going further, Hamilton sees in this statement not merely a statement of relationship, but a pledge of covenantal loyalty, serving "as the biblical counterpart to the modern marriage ceremony, 'in weakness [i.e., flesh] and in strength [i.e., bone]'… Both the man and the woman share the entire spectrum of human characteristics, from strong to weak."[564]

c   *Woman… man.* "Hebrew '*ishah*… '*ish*, though actually derived from distinct and unrelated stems, are here associated through folk etymology by virtue of assonance."[565] Westermann, following Speiser,[566] observes that the English "woman, derived from 'wife of man,' [offers an even] better linguistic foil than the Hebrew noun."[567]

The book of Moses and Genesis accounts tell the story of the naming of the woman in two parts. In the first part, described in this verse, "the man gives her a generic, not a personal, name, and that designation is understood to be derived from his own, which means he acknowledges woman to be his equal. Moreover, in naming her '*ishah*, he simultaneously names himself. Hitherto he is consistently called '*adam*; he now calls himself '*ish* for the first time. Thus he discovers his own manhood and fulfillment only when he faces the woman, the human being who is to be his partner in life."[568]

Later, in 4:26, after the couple has partaken of the fruit of the Tree of Knowledge, is the second part of the story, where Adam will give her the permanent proper name of Eve.[569] "Just as the episode reported in 3:19 was considered by Islamic commentators to be a test of Adam's knowledge of certain names as a measure of worthiness for his exalted role,[570] so

557   W. W. Isenberg, *Philip*, 70:10-20, pp. 150-151; G. W. MacRae, *Adam 1983*, 1:2-5, p. 712; G. W. MacRae, *et al.*, *Adam 1990*, 65:5-28, p. 279.
558   See W. W. Isenberg, *Philip*, 70:19-20, p. 151; H. W. Nibley, *Message 2005*, p. 528.
559   H. W. Nibley, *Patriarchy*, p. 104.
560   H. W. Nibley, *Message 2005*, pp. 305-307. See M. Nissinen, *Sacred Marriages*.
561   N. M. Sarna, *Genesis*, p. 23.
562   J. H. Sailhamer, *Genesis*, p. 47. See *Commentary* 3:18-c, p. 176.
563   Genesis 29:14; Judges 9:2; 2 Samuel 5:1; 19:12-13; 1 Chronicles 11:1; R. E. Friedman, *Commentary*, p. 20.
564   V. P. Hamilton, *Genesis*, p. 180. See also *Commentary* 3:22-a, p. 181.
565   N. M. Sarna, *Genesis*, p. 23.
566   E. A. Speiser, *Genesis*, p. 18.
567   C. Westermann, *Genesis 1-11*, p. 232.
568   N. M. Sarna, *Genesis*, p. 23. See *Commentary* 2:26-b, p. 112 and 2:27-b, p. 115.
569   See *Commentary* 4:26-a, p. 273.
570   See *Commentary* 3:19-b, p. 177.

*23 And Adam said: This I know now is bone of my bones, and flesh of my flesh; she shall be called **Woman**, because she was **taken out of man**.*

*24 Therefore shall a man leave his father and his mother, and shall **cleave unto his wife**; and they shall be **one flesh**.*

also was the story of the naming of Eve seen in the same way. Notice the words al-Tha'labi uses to describe the incident: "When Adam awoke from his sleep he saw [Eve] sitting at his head. The angels said to Adam, testing his knowledge: 'What is this, Adam?' He answered: 'A woman.' They asked: 'And what is her name?' he replied: 'Eve (hawwa).'"[571]

The presence of what seemed to be two separate accounts of the creation of woman in Moses 2 and 3 led some medieval Jewish commentators to propose that the stories concerned two different women, thus prompting extravagant speculation about the supposed first wife of Adam, known as the sinister Lilith in midrashic literature.[572]

d ***taken out of man.*** Recalling similar expressions relating man to the "ground from whence he was taken,"[573] Cassuto argues that "analogy of expression points to analogy of thought. The man who was taken from the ground must associate with it in his lifetime through his work, and return to it at his demise; similarly, the woman who was taken from the man and brought forth from his body must return to the man and associate with him constantly."[574]

man. The word man is capitalized in the KJV but not in Moses. This is probably because of the fact that in other places in modern scripture "Man" is used exclusively to refer to God the Father.[575]

24 **a** ***cleave unto his wife... one flesh.*** This verse contains the central message of the portion of the Creation account contained in this chapter: that man and woman are to learn to live together in oneness, "united by sympathy in their griefs and joys."[576] Writes Faulconer: "The seemingly parenthetical note of [Moses 3:24] not only shows us that human being is communal, it also prefigures the expulsion of Man and Woman from the garden... Man and Woman will be forced to leave their father and mother—in this case God—and cleave to each other... It is not simply that Man and Woman have the option of remaining immortally in the Garden in ignorance or leaving with knowledge to die. But—if their lives are to be meaningful, if they are to be bound to one another, if they are to be fruitful, if they are to escape the emphatic negative with which God has judged the situation of one alone, in other words, if they are to be human—they must live in community and they must do so estranged from God."[577]

Wenham observes that one flesh "does not denote merely the sexual union that follows marriage, or the children conceived in marriage, or even the spiritual and emotional relationship that it involves, though all are involved in becoming one flesh. Rather it affirms that just as blood relations are one's flesh and bone..., so marriage creates a similar relation between man and wife... The kinships established by marriage are... not terminated by death or divorce."[578] Likewise, Elder Jeffrey R. Holland writes: "[P]hysical union ordained of God for a married couple, deals with a symbol that demands special sanctity. Such an act of love between a man and a woman is—or certainly was ordained to be—a symbol of total union: union of their hearts, their hopes, their lives, their love, their family, their future, their

571 A. al-Tha'labi, *Lives*, pp. 48; cf. p. 54; See also al-Tabari, *Creation*, 1:120, p. 291 and the question and response passages in Egyptian temple ritual (H. W. Nibley, *Message 2005*, pp. 449-452). See *Endnote 3-45*, p. 207.

572 E.g., R. Graves, *et al.*, *Myths*, pp. 65-69; H. W. Nibley, *Teachings of the PGP*, 18, p. 229; R. Patai, *Goddess*, pp. 221-254; cf. M. al-Kisa'i, *Tales*, pp. 86-87; S. C. Malan, *Adam and Eve*, 2:3, pp. 106-108.

573 See Moses 4:25, 29.

574 U. Cassuto, *Adam to Noah*, p. 136.

575 E.g., JST Matthew 9:6; D&C 49:22; Moses 6:57, 7:35. See *Commentary* 1:12-c, p. 53.

576 Philo, *Fragments*, Extracts from the *Parallels of John of Damascus* 748:B, p. 883.

577 J. E. Faulconer, *Adam and Eve*, 30.

578 G. J. Wenham, *Genesis 1-15*, p. 71.

*24 Therefore shall a man leave his father and his mother, and shall **cleave unto his wife**; and they shall be **one flesh**.*

*25 And **they were both naked**, the man and his wife, and were not ashamed.*

everything. It is a symbol that we try to suggest in the temple with a word like 'seal'… But such a total, virtually unbreakable union, such an unyielding commitment between a man and a woman, can only come with the proximity and permanence afforded in a marriage covenant, with the union of all that they possess—their very hearts and minds, all their days and all their dreams… And the external symbol of that union, the physical manifestation of what is a far deeper spiritual and metaphysical bonding, is the physical blending that is part of—indeed, a most beautiful and gratifying expression of—that larger, more complete union of eternal purpose and promise."[579]

"The underlying meaning of the [idea of two distinct entities becoming attached to one another while preserving their separate identities] becomes clear, if it is noted that the verb *d-v-k* [cleave, cling] is often used to describe human yearning for and devotion to God.[580] Sexual relations between husband and wife do not rise above the level of animality unless they be informed by and imbued with spiritual, emotional, and mental affinity."[581] "'Cleave'… usually means to unite with, whether speaking of cleaving to one's wife as above, to the Lord (as R. Akiva insists in the *Babylonian Talmud*: 'Cleaving unto the Lord your God—literally cleaving'), or in other contexts[582]—though the meaning seems to have shifted from 'union' to 'obedience' after the demise of the ancient temple."[583] Likewise "forsake" is often used in a biblical context to describe Israel's departure from her covenant with the Lord.[584] The apostle Paul conferred an allegorical meaning on this verse when, while citing it, he wrote to the members of the church in Ephesus that "we are members of [Christ's] body, of his flesh, and of his bones… This is a great mystery: but I speak concerning Christ and the church."[585]

Sailhamer notes the frequent pattern of "using a poetic speech and a short epilogue to conclude a narrative" throughout the Old Testament, but at a "much higher level within the entire Pentateuch, suggesting that the technique was extended as a part of the structure embracing the whole of the book."[586] We find this pattern, for example, not only after the end of the account of the Creation,[587] but also at the close of the story of the Fall[588] and the end of the narrative about Cain.[589]

his wife. In Hebrew, "his woman." That the term does not imply possession or domination by the man is evidenced by the reference to "her man" in 3:12.[590]

25 a ***they were both naked.*** In the Garden, Adam and Eve were no longer "clothed" with the memory and glory of their their earlier state.[591] The verse attests to the couple's innocence, their lack of awareness of the change that had come over them—and the greater change that was yet to come.

579   J. R. Holland, *Souls*, pp. 17-18.

580   A. J. Heschel, *Heavenly Torah*, pp. 190-193.

581   N. M. Sarna, *Genesis*, p. 23.

582   2 Kings 5:27; Psalm 102:5, 137:6.

583   M. Barker, *Temple Theology*, p. 37. See the overview of Moses 6, pp. 463-469; *Figure* 5-11, p. 343; *Excursus 2: Ancient Concepts of Wisdom*, p. 516; *Excursus 46: The Origin and Meaning of the Term "Atonement"*, p. 642.

584   E.g., Jeremiah 1:16. See V. P. Hamilton, *Genesis*, p. 181.

585   Ephesians 5:30, 32. See Augustine, *The City of God* 22:17; Jerome, *Homilies* 66; Quodvultdeus, *Book of promises and predictions of God*, 1:3, cited in A. Louth, *et al.*, *Genesis 1-11*, pp. 70-71.

586   J. H. Sailhamer, *Genesis*, pp. 6-7.

587   Moses 3:23, 24.

588   Moses 4:20-25, 26-31.

589   Moses 5:47-48, 49-59.

590   R. E. Friedman, *Commentary*, p. 20. See also *Commentary* 4:22-c, p. 268.

591   See *Commentary* 3:21-a, p. 180; 4:16-b, p. 262; overview of Moses 4, p. 236.

MOSES 3

25 And **they were both naked***, the man and his wife, and* **were not ashamed***.*

> The verse is meant to prepare us for Moses 4:13.[592] It "forms the transition to the next episode by means of a word play on 'naked' (Hebrew *'arom*, pl. *'arummim*) and 'shrewd' (Hebrew *'arum*).[593] It also conveys an anticipatory hint at [how the two concepts are going to be related]."[594] Approximating the Hebrew word-play in English, we might say (with Wenham) that the couple aspired to be "shrewd," and they ended up "nude."[595]
>
> While the shame of Adam and Eve's transgression will be mercifully covered,[596] the serpent—initially vaunted as the most shrewd of all animals—will become instead the most naked and lowly of creatures—its loss of glory exposed humiliatingly by God.[597]

b   ***were not ashamed.*** That the ancient reader would not have regarded the account of the Fall merely as a lesson in naturalistic anthropology is convincingly argued by Anderson: "When the eyes of Adam and Eve were opened [after their transgression], there was indeed something new to see. That newness was not a movement from a prepubescent naïveté to a more mature sense of self. Rather that newness was a state of estrangement from self and from God, an estrangement marked by the loss of a supernatural covering."[598] While the couple were as yet free from transgression they could stand "naked" in God's presence without shame,[599] being "clothed with purity"[600] in what early commentators called "garments of light."[601]

---

592   C. Westermann, *Genesis 1-11*, p. 234.
593   See *Commentary* 4:5-b, p. 246.
594   N. M. Sarna, *Genesis*, p. 23.
595   G. J. Wenham, *Genesis 1-15*, p. 72; cf. B. T. Arnold, *Genesis 2009*, p. 63,
596   *Commentary* 4:27-a, p. 274.
597   *Commentary* 4:20a-g, pp. 264-265 and 4:21-a-d, pp. 265-267; cf. *Commentary* 1:15-d, p. 54; M. Gadd, *Naked*.
598   G. A. Anderson, *Garments*, p. 106-107.
599   D&C 121:45.
600   2 Nephi 9:14.
601   G. A. Anderson, *Perfection*, p. 215. See the overview of Moses 4, p. 236.

Gleanings

Table of Contents

Stefano Levi Della Torre: The Refraction of Heaven Falls on Eden[602]

The Garden has a center and two trees are planted in it, of life and knowledge respectively [Moses 3:9]. As in the case of man, the Garden is the place where the refraction of heaven falls on the earth: vertically, pathways towards the divine prerogatives, immortality and knowledge, like trees growing upwards; horizontally, "a river flows out of Eden to irrigate the garden and from there splits to form four streams"[603] to irrigate the world's regions. The four rivers are the link between Eden and the earth which will be populated by the generations of human beings. Eden is immanent in the history and geography of civilizations: it is the hydraulic heart of the world.

Margaret Barker: The Creator at the Heart of Creation

The Bible begins with the story of Creation. This is the biblical word for environment… But environment can imply that we humans are at the center, and everything happens around us. The biblical idea of the Creation constantly reminds us of the Creator, and in the Bible, the act of Creation is something unique to God. The special verb used in the biblical stories, *bara*, is never used of human activity. God creates.

Later tradition recorded that both the temple in Jerusalem and the Tabernacle which Moses had built in the desert represented Creation. The Tabernacle had been erected in obedience to the Lord's command to Moses: "Build me a holy place so that I may 'dwell' (in the Greek translation this is 'be seen') in your midst."[604] In their place of worship, then, they acknowledged that it was the Creator who was at the heart of the Creation, not the human… Adam was the first high priest of the temple, and care of the Creation was his liturgy. The word "liturgy" originally meant a public service performed for a master, or for the state, but in

---

602   S. L. Della Torre, *Anxiety*, p. 12.

603   See Moses 3:10.

604   Exodus 25:8.

the case of priests, it meant their service for God. The temple was the Creation and, as later interpreters taught, the Creation was the temple.[605]

What the temple structure depicted was the hidden glory of God at the heart of the material world, the eternal within the temporal. Thus Paul, thinking in his temple framework, could write: "God sent *forth* his Son."[606] The Son coming into the world was envisaged as One emerging from the glory into our material world, passing from eternity into time.[607]

C. S. Lewis: Tending the Garden of Our Natures[608]

It is no disparagement to a garden to say that it will not fence and weed itself, nor prune its own fruit trees, nor roll and cut its own lawns. A garden is a good thing, but that is not the sort of goodness it has. It will remain a garden, as distinct from a wilderness, only if someone does all these things to it. Its real glory is of quite a different kind. The very fact that it needs constant weeding and pruning bears witness to that glory. It teems with life. It glows with color and smells like heaven and puts forward at every hour of a summer day beauties which man could never have created and could not even, on his own resources, have imagined. If you want to see the difference between its contribution and the gardener's, put the commonest weed it grows side by side with his hoes, rakes, shears, and packet of weed killer; you have put beauty, energy and fecundity beside dead, sterile things. Just so, our "decency and common sense" show gray and deathlike beside the geniality of love. And when the garden is in its full glory the gardener's contributions to that glory will still have been in a sense paltry compared with those of nature. Without life springing from the earth, without rain, light and heat descending from the sky, he could do nothing. When he has done all, he has merely encouraged here and discouraged there, powers and beauties that have a different source. But his share, though small, is indispensable and laborious.

When God planted a garden He set a man over it and set the man under Himself. When He planted the garden of our nature and caused the flowering, fruiting loves to grow there, He set our will to "dress" them. Compared with them it is dry and cold. And unless His grace comes down, like the rain and the sunshine, we shall use this tool to little purpose. But its laborious—and largely negative—services are indispensable. If they were needed when the garden was Paradisiacal, how much more now when the soil has gone sour and the worst weeds seem to thrive on it best?… To liberate that splendor, to let it become fully what it is trying to be, to have tall trees instead of scrubby tangles, and sweet apples instead of crabs, is part of our purpose.

Jerome: The Tree of Life Represents Wisdom, Christ, and the Righteous[609]

Now if wisdom is the Tree of Life, Wisdom itself indeed is Christ. You understand now that the man who is blessed and holy is compared to this tree—that is, he is compared to Wisdom. Consequently, you see too that the just man, that blessed man who has not followed the counsel of the wicked—who has not done that but has done this—is like the tree that is planted near running water.[610] He is, in other words, like Christ, inasmuch as he "raised us

---

605   M. Barker, *Paradise*, p. 1.

606   Galatians 4:4; cf. *Commentary* 4:29-a, p. 278 and 4:30-a, p. 279.

607   M. Barker, *Christmas*, pp. 3-4.

608   C. S. Lewis, *Loves*, Charity, pp. 163-165.

609   Jerome, *Homilies 1*, cited in A. Louth, *et al.*, *Genesis 1-11*, p. 55.

610   Psalm 1:3.

up together and seated us together in heaven."[611] You see then that we shall reign together with Christ in heaven. You see too that because this Tree has been planted in the Garden of Eden, we have all been planted there together with him.

On the Origin of the World: The Olive Tree as a Third Special Tree[612]

Then justice created Paradise. Paradise is beautiful and is outside the circuit of the moon and the circuit of the sun in the land of pleasure,[613] which is in the east in the rocky region.[614] Desire dwells in the middle of the beautiful, stately trees. The Tree of Life eternal, as it appeared by the will of god, is in the north[615] of paradise to give immortality to the souls of holy people[616] who will leave their poor modeled bodies at the end of the age. The Tree of Life looks like the sun, and its branches are lovely. Its leaves are like the leaves of the cypress, its fruit is like a cluster of white grapes and its height reaches the sky.[617]

Next to it is the Tree of Knowledge,[618] which is endowed with the power of God. It is glorious as the moon shining brightly, and its branches are lovely. Its leaves are like fig leaves and its fruit is like a bunch of good, delicious dates. The Tree of Knowledge is in the north of Paradise to arouse the souls from demonic stupor, so that they might come to the Tree of Life, eat its fruit, and condemn the authorities and their angels…[619]

After this the olive tree sprouted, and it was to purify kings and high priests of justice[620] who were to come in the last days. The olive tree appeared through the light of the first Adam[621] for the sake of the oil of anointing that kings and high priests would receive.[622]

Hugh W. Nibley: The Temple as the Origin of Culture and Civilization[623]

The "spin-offs" are things not essential to the temple's form and function, but the inevitable products of its existence. To begin with, there was an urgent need of accommodations for all those pilgrims from far away; hence those booths, memorialized in the Hebrew Festival of Booths, remains or records of which we find in many parts of the world. Our words "hotel" and "hospital" go back to those charitable organizations which took care of sick and weary pilgrims to the holy places—the Hospitalers of the Crusades offered hospitality also under the name of Templars, for it was travelers to the temple that they were aiding and protecting. Since all who came had to bring food for the festival as well as animals for offerings and sacrifice, those who lived a great distance (more than three days away in Israel[624]), finding the transport of such items of great difficulty, could instead bring the money value of those offerings to the Temple, which thus became a place of exchange and banking—our word

---

611 Ephesians 2:6.
612 M. Meyer, *Origin*, 110:2-111:8, pp. 210-211. See also J. O. Ryen, *Mandaean Vine*, pp. 214-215, 221.
613 I.e., Eden = "luxuriance" (N. M. Sarna, *Genesis*, p. 18) or "abundance" (T. Stordalen, *Echoes*, pp. 257-261); cf. "Bountiful" (e.g., 1 Nephi 17:5, Alma 22:29-31).
614 Literally, "in the midst of the stones" (H-G. Bethge, *Origin*, 110:15-16, p. 178).
615 On the significance of "north," see A. S-M. Ri, *Commentaire de la Caverne*, pp. 120-121.
616 Literally, "to make eternal the souls of the pure" (*ibid.*, 110:10-11, p. 178).
617 Cf. M. Barker, *Joseph Smith*, p. 76; R. Milstein, *Stories and Illustrations*, p. 107; G. W. E. Nickelsburg, *1 Enoch*, 32:4, p. 320. See also L. M. Smith, *Lucy's Book*, pp. 297-298; 1 Nephi 8:11.
618 I.e., *gnosis*.
619 I.e., the divine forces who had, in the Gnostic view of things, wickedly forbidden this fruit to Adam and Eve out of envy.
620 I.e., righteousness. See Hebrews 7:2.
621 I.e., the highest God, seen by Gnostics as benevolent.
622 See *Endnote 3-55,* p. 210. See also *Commentary 3:9-g,* p. 163.
623 H. W. Nibley, *What*, pp. 379-381.
624 See Deuteronomy 14:22-27; 26:12-14.

money comes from the temple of Juno Moneta, the holy center of the Roman world. Along with that, the bringing of a variety of different goods and products from widely separated places inevitably gave rise to a lively barter and exchange of goods, and everywhere a fixture of the great year rites was the yearly fair, the market-booths of the merchants added to those of the visiting pilgrims, with artisans, performers, and mountebanks also displaying their wares.

The main action at the temple was the *actio*, for which the Greek word is *drama*, with parts played by priestly temple actors and royalty. Creation was celebrated with the Creation Hymn or *poema*—the word "poem" means, in fact, Creation—sung by a *chorus* which, as the name shows, formed a circle and danced as they sang. Since nothing goes unchallenged in this world, a central theme of the temple rites was the dramatization (often athletic) of the combat between the powers of life and death which could take many forms—wrestling, boxing, dueling, foot or chariot races, beauty contests to choose a queen, competitions in song and dance. The temple was the original center of learning, beginning with the heavenly instructions received there. It was the *Museon* or home of the Muses, each representing a branch of study, and the scene of learned discussions among the wise men who from the earliest recorded times would travel from shrine to shrine exchanging wisdom with the wise, as Abraham did in Egypt. For the all-important setting of times and seasons, careful astronomical observations were taken and recorded at the place with mathematical precision, while the measurements of fields and buildings called for sophisticated geometry followed by great architectural and engineering skill that commands the highest respect to this day. The Garden-of-Eden or Golden-Age motif was essential to this ritual paradise, and the temple grounds contained all manner of trees and animals, often collected with great botanical and zoological zeal from distant places. Central to the temple school for the training of priests and nobles was the great library containing both the holy books revealed from on high, whether as divine revelation or as star readings (both declared the glory of God), and the records of human history including the "Books of Life," the names of all the living and the dead—genealogy. Aside from memorials kept in writing (the art, as we have seen, originating in the economy of the temple) were the ancestral pictures—statues, busts, and paintings giving inspiration to the fine arts. The purpose of the rites being to establish and acknowledge the rule of God on earth through his agent and offspring the King, who represented both the first man and everyman, the temple was the ultimate seat and sanction of government. Our government buildings with their massive columns, domes, marble and bronze, and so forth are copies of classic Greek and Roman temples. The meeting of the people at the holy place made the New Year the time for contracts and covenants, and all of these were recorded and stored in the temple, which was of course the seat of law, both for the handing down of new laws and ordinances by divine authority and for the settling of disputes between mortals. The king was a Solomon sitting as Judge on the occasion, as one who had been tested to the limit and, after calling upon God from the depths, had emerged triumphant, worthy to lead the army of the Lord to spread his rule over the as yet unconquered realms of darkness beyond the holy influence of the temple.

Joseph Smith, Jr.: We Are Ready to Embrace All True Principles

[T]he first and fundamental principle of our holy religion is that we believe we have a right to embrace all and every item of truth, without limitation or without being circumscribed or prohibited by the creeds or superstitious notions of men.[625]

---

625   J. Smith, Jr., *Writings 2002*, 22 March 1839, p. 458.

[T]he Latter-day Saints have no creed, but are ready to believe all true principles that exist, as they are made manifest from time to time.[626]

The inquiry is frequently made of me. "Wherein do you differ from others in your religious views?" In reality and essence we do not differ so far in our religious views, but that we could all drink into one principle of love. One of the grand fundamental principles of "Mormonism" is to receive truth, let it come from whence it may.…

If I esteem mankind to be in error, shall I bear them down? No. I will lift them up, and in their own way too, if I cannot persuade them my way is better; and I will not seek to compel any man to believe as I do, only by the force of reasoning, for truth will cut its own way. Do you believe in Jesus Christ and the Gospel of salvation which He revealed? So do I. Christians should cease wrangling and contending with each other, and cultivate the principles of union and friendship in their midst; and they will do it before the Millennium can be ushered in and Christ takes possession of His kingdom.[627]

Have the Presbyterians any truth? Yes. Have the Baptists, Methodists, etc. any truth? Yes. They all have a little truth mixed with error. We should gather up all the good and true principles in the world and treasure them up, or we shall not come out true "Mormons."[628]

President Brigham Young: Mormonism Includes All Truth[629]

"Mormonism"… embraces every principle pertaining to life and salvation… no matter who has it. If the [unbeliever] has got truth it belongs to "Mormonism." The truth and sound doctrine possessed by [other churches], and they have a great deal, all belong to this Church… All that is good, lovely, and praiseworthy belongs to this Church… "Mormonism" includes all truth. There is no truth but what belongs to the Gospel.

Elder John Taylor: I Believe in Every True Principle[630]

I am a [Universalist], and I am also a Presbyterian, and a Roman Catholic, and a Methodist. In short, I believe in every true principle that is embodied in any person or sect, and reject the false. If there is any truth in heaven, earth, or hell, I want to embrace it, I care not what shape it comes to me, who brings it, or who believes in it, whether it is popular or unpopular. Truth, eternal truth, I wish to float in and enjoy… I believe we have many great and true principles revealed from the heavens… If any man under the heavens can show me one principle of error that I have entertained, I will lay it aside forthwith and be thankful for the information. On the other hand, if any man has any principle of truth, whether moral, religious, philosophical, or of any other kind that is calculated to benefit mankind, I promise him I will embrace it…

C. Terry Warner: Two Aspects of a Single Process[631]

For Latter-day Saints, salvation is a matter of growing in truth, and particularly in knowledge of the gospel of Jesus Christ. Joseph Smith taught that "a man is saved no faster than

---

626 J. Smith, Jr., *Documentary History*, 1 January 1843, 5:215.
627 J. Smith, Jr., *Teachings*, 9 July 1843, pp. 313-314.
628 *Ibid.*, 23 July 1843, p. 316.
629 B. Young, *8 April 1867*, p. 375; B. Young, *Discourses*, p. 3.
630 J. Taylor, *Gospel Kingdom*, 12 June 1853, pp. 49-50; J. Taylor, *12 June 1853*, p. 155.
631 C. T. Warner, *Truth*, p. 1490.

he gets knowledge"[632] and that "it is impossible for a man to be saved in ignorance."[633] In context these statements mean that one cannot be saved in ignorance of the Gospel of Jesus Christ. Latter-day Saints who recognize that truth is not merely a property of language but is central to a life of obedience to the Savior do not interpret these passages to mean that the learned—the scholars and scientists—have a better chance of being saved. Gaining knowledge and becoming more godlike are two aspects of a single process, which helps explain the Latter-day Saint emphasis on education and personal scripture mastery as well as on righteous living.

Juanita Brooks: Nothing But the Truth Is Good Enough[634]

I feel sure that nothing but the truth can be good enough for the church to which I belong.

Henry Eyring: In This Church You Only Need to Believe the Truth

I once had the privilege of attending a youth conference and responding to questions of the assembled young people. A young man asked, "In high school we are taught such things as pre-Adamic men, but we hear another thing in Church. What should I do about it?"[635]

I think I gave the right answer. I said, "In this Church, you only have to believe the truth. Find out what the truth is!"

The Church is not worried about that question or other similar questions because the Church is committed only to the truth. I do not mean to say that individuals in the Church always know the whole truth, but we have the humility sometimes to say we do not know all the answers about these things.

Some have asked me, "Is there any conflict between science and religion?" There is no conflict in the mind of God, but often there is conflict in the minds of men. Through the eternities, we are going to get closer and closer to understanding the mind of God; then the conflicts will disappear....

I have one caution about scholarship as it relates to the Church... We need to be continually reminded that however interesting some... topic might be, it has no relevance to religious faith, one way or the other. You can't intellectualize your way to a testimony. There will always be another question beyond the one you have just answered. Incidentally, the same is true of science. None of its findings are final. Still, some people seem to stumble when they run into a contradiction...

... I... understand that people who think they have to be as smart as the Lord, understand everything, and have no contradictions in their minds may have trouble. There are all kinds of contradictions I don't understand, but I find the same kinds of contradictions in science, and I haven't decided to apostatize from science.

In the long run, the truth is its own most powerful advocate....[636]

---

632   J. Smith, Jr., *Teachings*, 10 April 1842, p. 217.
633   D&C 131:6.
634   J. Brooks, *Mountain*, p. xx.
635   See *Endnote 3-60*, p. 212.
636   H. Eyring, *Reflections*, pp. 7, 8, 47.

Do we understand everything about science? Of course we don't. A substantial part of what we teach is baloney. But it is part of our religion that we do not understand things completely. The Lord gives us here a little and there a little, and as time goes on, it is going to get better. So I am not going to spend two minutes to try and prove that everybody in the Church always says things exactly correctly because it would not be true, and I am not here to provide any half-baked argument to support the scriptures. They do not need it. If they did, my support would not help much anyway. I think that my religion is on a basis of just looking at how this thing works, of being humble enough to pray and trying to live up to the spirit of the Gospel and actually feeling the Spirit of the Holy Ghost. I think anybody can feel the Spirit of the Holy Ghost if he is humble… So I do not worry in the least about problems like which one of my ancestors was a monkey, if any of them. However the Lord did things suits me just fine. There is nothing I can do about it anyway. It is all over, and I am just exactly like I am however He did it. And so for the life of me I am never able to worry along with the people who think science is a threat to religion. It just is not. It could not be, and if it is, you had better fix your religion or your science, or both.[637]

I do not know just how soon or when we will know more. I am sure the Lord is not particularly frightened at his clever children. I am sure that He thinks they are pretty dumb. So people who think He is jealous have quite different ideas of how great He is than I do. I think that all of the things that we think are clever, that we might do, must be so trivial to Him that I am sure that He is not jealous. Do not worry about it. I mean, do not hold off on any bright ideas that you have for fear the Lord will be worried about you overtaking Him. I think it will be safe.[638]

Just how [God] runs the world I'm obliged to leave up to Him. All I can do is to find out how He does it by every means available.[639]

President Brigham Young: Whether the Bible Is Correct or Not[640]

How long [the earth] has been organized is not for me to say, and I do not care anything about it. As for the Bible account of Creation we may say that the Lord gave it to Moses, or rather Moses obtained the history and traditions of the fathers, and from them picked out what he considered necessary, and that account has been handed down from age to age, and we have got it, no matter whether it is correct or not, and whether the Lord found the earth empty or void, whether he made it out of nothing or out of rude elements; whether he made it in six days or in as many millions of years, is and will remain a matter of speculation in the minds of men unless He gives revelation on the subject.

Henry Eyring: The Scriptures Are As Accurate As God Requires[641]

The scriptures record God's dealing with his prophets, and they are as accurate as God, in his wisdom, requires.… God has told us that the scriptures are incomplete. We are promised that we will receive more when we have mastered the lessons of what we have.[642] Hence, teaching us how to live and treat others and how to obey the rules and laws of the Gospel is the primary purpose of the scriptures; they are spiritual guides to religious questions.

637   H. J. Eyring, *Mormon Scientist*, pp. 169-170.
638   *Ibid.*, p. 180.
639   *Ibid.*, p. 125.
640   B. Young, *14 May 1871*, p. 116.
641   H. Eyring, *Reflections*, pp. 49, 51.
642   See *Endnote 3-61*, p. 212.

Of course, the scriptures do treat incidentally scientific, historical, and other nonreligious questions. In these areas they should be supplemented by all relevant information. Viewed in this light, most problems disappear. I am obliged, as a Latter-day Saint, to believe whatever is true, regardless of the source. Questions involving the age of the earth, pre-Adamic man, or organic evolution may seem to us to be interesting and important. However, I doubt that God thinks they matter enough to have provided definitive explanations in our current scriptures. They will all receive adequate answers in due course.[643] Whatever the ultimate answers are, the Gospel will remain, and new questions will take the place of those we solve. For me, the truth of the Gospel does not hinge on such questions, interesting as they are.

James E. Faulconer: On the Hazards of Using Secular Conceptions[644]

It is common to understand religious Creation accounts as reflections on the origins of the cosmos, answers to the question "why?" that are in some sense parallel to the scientific question "why?" That is a mistake. There may be cases in which myth functions as a kind of primitive science, but the biblical story of Creation is not one of them.[645] Of course, secularists are not the only ones to assume that the Bible story of Creation is a case of primitive science. Some religious people also make the assumption, especially those who consider themselves literalists. Ironically, when people argue for Creation science or for what is usually called a literal reading of the Bible, they are agreeing with the secular understanding of things. They use conceptual structures taken from secularism, such as the necessity that explanation have a scientific form, to try to understand the Bible. Some give up or metaphorize the Bible when faced with the project of making the Bible and science answer the same questions, but some keep the Bible and insist that its account can be brought within the secular myth, though of course they would not say that is what they are doing. But both those who metaphorize and those who would make the Bible scientific both do essentially the same thing: they begin from a secular understanding of the Bible… Both assume that secularism gives us the basic structure of understanding and that all accounts must be hung on that structure. They disagree about what conclusions that leads one to, but they agree that the secular myth is the one that must be used for understanding.

However, when the Bible tells us how the world was created, it does so with interests, goals, and basic assumptions so different from those of science that we ought to be suspicious of claims that both the Bible and science are answering the same question, "How did the world come to be?" Such claims equivocate, for the question does not mean the same thing in a biblical context that it means in a scientific one. The great temptation is to assume that mythic accounts of Creation are cases of primitive science. Perhaps some are. Surely we do not want to claim that all myth has the same goals. However, it is far from obvious that all creation myths are primitive science. In fact, in the case of the Bible, those who take it to be a scientific or quasi-scientific account have the considerable burden of proof. The interest of the biblical origin stories is much more on things like how the human condition came to be what it is, how evil came into the world, and why the covenant applies to each person than it is on the physical processes involved in Creation. It is not clear that Genesis has any interest in the latter at all.

---

643   D&C 101:32-34.
644   J. E. Faulconer, *Dorrien*, pp. 426-427.
645   See, e.g., N. Frye, *Great Code*.

Hugh W. Nibley: What About Creatures Who Lived Before Adam?[646]

The philosopher Arthur Schopenhauer, in his *Essay on the Christian System*, said that the two fatal flaws of Christianity were (1) denying spirit and mind to any other creatures but ourselves and (2) allowing life on no other world but our own.…[647]

This… should be no concern [for us].…

The fifth chapter of Genesis begins with a very important episode—the formal establishment of Adam's family organization. It begins with a book, a book of remembrance or genealogy, entitled "The Book of the Generations of Adam." It begins, "In the day the Gods set apart [*bara*—we are being very literal here] Adam in the likeness of the Gods [*bi-dmuth elohim*] he made him. Male and female he set them apart, and gave them a blessing, and gave them their names as Adam, in the day he set them apart."[648] Next comes Seth in the proper line of Adam, and the patriarchal line follows. The preceding chapter tells of the division into Cainites and Sethites, and it is significant that the line of Cain is omitted from the genealogy of Adam. The book of Moses tells of multitudes of Adam's children born before Cain and Abel.[649] They had followed Satan by choice and were disqualified as sons of God…[650] Those who accepted the covenant were called sons of God and also the sons of Adam: "And this is the genealogy of the sons of Adam, who was the son of God."[651] Only those qualify as *bene-Adam* [sons of Adam] who are still in the covenant.…

So we might well ask:[652] What about those people who lived before Cain and Abel?[653] What about those who disappeared from sight?[654] What about those who were not even warned of the Flood?[655] What about those many, many who visited the earth as resurrected beings?[656] What about the Watchers?[657] What about the sons of God who should not marry the daughters of men, and vice versa?[658] And what about the giants they begot when they did marry?[659] What about the comings and goings of Enoch's day between the worlds?[660] What about his own status as "a wild man,… a strange thing in the land."[661] Who were his people, living in a distant land of righteousness, who never appear on the scene?[662] What about the Three Nephites, whose condition so puzzles Moroni, until he is told that they are neither mortal nor immortal?[663] What about the creatures we do not see around us? What about the Cainites?[664] What about the nations among whom Noah will have surviving progeny?[665]

646   H. W. Nibley, *Before Adam*, pp. 50, 51, 78, 79, 82, 83.
647   See *Endnote 3-62*, p. 212.
648   See Genesis 5:1-3.
649   Moses 5:12, 16.
650   Moses 7:33, 37.
651   Moses 6:22.
652   See *Endnote 3-63*, p. 212.
653   Moses 5:12.
654   Moses 7:21.
655   Moses 7:12, 22.
656   E.g., Genesis 18:2, 19:1, 32:24.
657   J. L. Kugel, *Traditions*, pp. 179-185, 194-216; H. Schwartz, *Tree*, pp. 457-458. See *Excursus 24: The Watchers*, p. 585.
658   Moses 8:13-22.
659   Moses 8:18.
660   Moses 7:27.
661   Moses 6:38.
662   Moses 6:41.
663   Mormon 8:10-11.
664   Moses 8:41-42.
665   Moses 7:51-53.

Speaking of Noah, God promised Enoch "that he [God] would call upon the children of Noah; and he sent forth an unalterable decree, that a remnant of his seed [Enoch's through Noah] should always be found among all nations, while the earth should stand;[666] and the Lord said: Blessed is he through whose seed Messiah shall come."[667] Methuselah boasted about his line as something special.[668] Why special if it included the whole human race? These blessings have no meaning if all the people of the earth and all the nations are the seed of Noah and Enoch. What other line could the Messiah come through? Well, there were humans who were not invited by Enoch's preaching—not included among the residue of the people not entering Enoch's city. They were "the residue of the people which were the sons of Adam; and they were a mixture of all the seed of Adam save it was the seed of Cain, for the seed of Cain... had not place among them"....[669]

Do not begrudge existence to creatures that looked like men long, long ago, nor deny them a place in God's affection or even a right to exaltation—for our scriptures allow them such. Nor am I overly concerned as to just when they might have lived, for their world is not our world. They have all gone away long before our people ever appeared. God assigned them their proper times and functions, as He has given me mine—a full-time job that admonishes me to remember His words to the overly eager Moses: "For mine own purpose have I made these things. Here is wisdom and it remaineth in me."[670] It is Adam as my own parent who concerns me. When he walks onto the stage, then and only then the play begins. He opens a book and starts calling out names. They are the sons of Adam, who also qualify as the sons of God, Adam himself being a son of God. This is the book of remembrance from which many have been blotted out. They have fallen away, refused to choose God as their father, and by so doing were registered in Satan's camp. "Satan shall be their father, and misery shall be their doom."[671] Can we call them sons of Adam, *bene-Adam*, human beings proper? The representative Egyptians, Babylonians, Greeks, and Romans, to name only the classic civilizations of old, each fancied themselves to be beings of a higher nature, nearer to gods than others who inhabited the land with them (and before them) or who dwelt in other lands. And yet they did not deny humanity to them.

Adam becomes Adam, a hominid becomes a man, when he starts keeping a record. What kind of record? A record of his ancestors—the family line that sets him off from all other creatures... Whether the former speculation about life on other worlds is now to be upgraded to life from other worlds remains to be seen, but Adam is wonderful enough without that. That gap between the record keeper and all the other creatures we know anything about is so unimaginably enormous and yet so neat and abrupt that we can only be dealing with another sort of being, a quantum leap from one world to another. Here is something not derivative from anything that has gone before on the local scene, even though they all share the same atoms.

666 See *Endnote 3-64*, p. 212.
667 Moses 7:51-53.
668 Moses 8:2-3.
669 Moses 7:22.
670 Moses 1:31.
671 Moses 7:37.

Endnotes

3-1   Sailhamer aptly summarizes the situation when he writes that "Genesis is characterized by both an easily discernible unity and a noticeable lack of uniformity... The unity of the Book of Genesis... should be seen in its compositional strategy as a whole rather than in an absolutely smooth and uniform narrative... The picture of the narratives of Genesis that emerges... is that of a carefully wrought account of Israel's history fashioned from the narratives and genealogical tables of Israel's own ancestral archives."[672] Such an idea should not be foreign to readers of the Book of Mormon, where inspired editors have explicitly revealed their weaving of separate overlapping records into the finished scriptural narrative.[673] In contrast to the carefully controlled prophetic redaction of the Book of Mormon, however, we do not know how much of the subsequent editing of the Old Testament may have taken place "with less inspiration and authority."[674]

3-2   The best summary of the diverse range of views and major issues from an LDS point of view is K. L. Barney, *Reflections*. Other LDS perspectives include P. L. Barlow, *Bible*, pp. 103-147; S. K. Brown, *Approaches*; R. D. Draper *et al.*, *Commentary*, pp. 413-419; A. A. Hutchinson, *Midrash*; G. Potter, *Bible Scholarship*; J. L. Sorenson, *Brass Plates*. See, e.g., T. L. Brodie, *Dialogue*, pp. 495-501 for a critique of the Documentary Hypothesis.

3-3   Apart from source considerations, arguments from literary analysis have been made to explain the seeming duplication and reversal of Creation events in Moses 3. For example, Rashi insists that such repetition is consistent with the rules of expounding *Torah*: "In the case of a general statement that is followed by a narrative, [the narrative] is a detailed account of the first, broad statement... One... is under the impression that [the second account of the creation of man] is a different incident than the earlier mention of his creation, yet it is nothing but a detailed account of the first mention."[675] Faulconer concludes:

> There may be contradictions within the text, but the more obvious those contradictions are, the less likely it is that they are contradictions that undo the text. It is too much to assume that the redaction of Genesis was a product of blindness. A considerable amount of "cut and paste" work was surely involved in the creation of the Genesis story, but unless we can come to no other reasonable conclusion, we should assume that the text is cut and pasted in this way rather than some other for a reason. Thus, it would be a mistake to think that the elements of the narrative merely contradict each other. The story we have before us is one text that calls to be read as such...[676]

For more detailed analyses of literary arguments for the unity of the final form of the records that make up the book of Genesis, see U. Cassuto, *Documentary*; U. Cassuto, *Adam to Noah*, pp. 84-94; and I. M. Kikawada, *et al.*, *Before Abraham*.

3-4   The Prophet's revelations usually came as a result of wrestling with problems or the need for answers to specific inquiries.[677]

3-5   Robinson and Garrett provide an explanatory summary of this verse:

> In the beginning, God spiritually created man—Adam and Eve. This means, on the one hand, that He created their spirits, but it also refers to their physical creation in Paradise or Eden, where they were not yet mortal, and where they were governed by and in communion with Him. With the Fall, humanity became mortal and temporal—physical, or "of the flesh," in the full sense. Being "in the flesh," or in mortality, they could also have children, and the great plan was set in motion. Thus, bringing humanity from its celestial, spiritual home down to a telestial, mortal world was the beginning of Christ's work.
>
> At the end of his work, however, Christ will take fallen and temporal humanity and raise it back up again to glory in the Resurrection. The resurrected body is a spiritual body (not a spirit body) in the sense that it is immortal and is permanently infused with the spirit that governs it. This differs from our mortal condition in which our spirit is only a temporary tenant of our body and is often ignored. The beginning of Christ's work—Creation—is to get us here, to bring us from the

672   J. H. Sailhamer, *Genesis*, p. 5.
673   K. P. Jackson, *Genesis*, pp. 58-61. For a summary of Jewish sources documenting the idea that Moses used previously extant records in composing Genesis, see A. J. Heschel, *Heavenly Torah*, pp. 650-653.
674   *Ibid.*, p. 63.
675   Rashi, *Genesis Commentary*, p. 24. See also U. Cassuto, *Documentary*, pp. 91-92.
676   J. E. Faulconer, *Adam and Eve*, 3.
677   See, e.g., M. V. Backman, Jr., *et al.*, *JS and D&C*.

spiritual realm to the temporal; the end of Christ's work—Redemption—is to get us home again, from the temporal realm back to the spiritual. So in this instance, as in many others, the first will be last and the last will be first.[678]

3-6   Jason Lundquist observes that the "paradoxical construction" of D&C 29:32 "is a necessary misrepresentation, since God himself does not think of the creation in temporal terms: 'Unto myself my works have no end, neither beginning.'[679] He describes his deliberate choice of an inaccurate representation as an effort to '[speak] to you that you may naturally understand.'"[680]

3-7   Nibley observes:

It's perfectly true that in this world there is the temporal and the spiritual, and yet there is no distinction between them. There is no system that is not spiritual, and there is none that is not material. The spirit itself is composed of matter. We fuse the two in the Gospel; only there can it be done.[681]

3-8   Some see the planning process for the formation of the heavens and the earth as resulting in a "blueprint" that can be taken as constituting a sort of spiritual creation.[682] Though advance planning doubtless took place, such a process is never referred to in scripture as a form of spiritual creation.

Note also that some LDS commentators have interpreted the account of Moses 2 as referring to the creation of all things in spirit form.[683] In a more limited way, others have associated Moses 2:26-27 with the creation of the spirits of all mankind.[684] Such ideas, however, have fallen into general disfavor. In any case, LDS teachings seem to be in agreement that the account given in Moses 3:6-7 describes, though in a figurative manner, the creation of a perfect physical body for Adam. Following the creation of his body, Adam was placed in the Garden of Eden, a "spiritual" realm of the terrestrial order.

For additional discussion of approaches to interpreting the term "spiritual creation" as described in the early revelations of Joseph Smith, see Harrell.[685]

3-9   The degree to which the premortal, mortal, and postmortal phases of the story of Adam and Eve parallel the experience of every one of God's children raises the question about whether, before taking upon themselves mortality, there would have been an opportunity for these spirits to have disobeyed God's commandment "after the similitude of Adam's transgression."[686]

The rebellion of Satan and his hosts clearly demonstrates that sin was possible in the premortal life. However, it is a matter of conjecture whether sin and repentance were part of the general experience of all who lived in the spirit world. D&C 93:38 reads: "Every spirit of man was innocent in the beginning; and God, having redeemed man from the fall, men become again, in their infant state, innocent before God." Top interprets the verse as follows: "The key word is "again." This seems to indicate that men had lost innocence in the premortal world through sin and disobedience, but were once again, through the great plan of Redemption, made innocent before God upon entering mortality 'in their infant state.'"[687]

Regarding this issue, Skinner writes:

Elder Orson Pratt, writing about the nature of sin in our premortal existence, said that "among the two-third [of God's spirit children] who remained, it is highly probably that, there were many who were not valiant…, but whose sins were of such a nature that they could be forgiven through faith in the future sufferings of the Only Begotten of the Father, and through their sincere repentance and reformation. We see no impropriety in Jesus offering Himself as an acceptable offering and

---

678   S. E. Robinson, *et al.*, *D&C Commentary*, 1:205. See also J. F. McConkie, *et al.*, *Revelations*, p. 239.

679   D&C 29:33.

680   J. H. Lundquist, *Keywords*, pp. 3-4 n. 3; cf. 2 Nephi 31:3, Ether 12:25.

681   H. W. Nibley, *Conversation*, p. 64.

682   See *Excursus 8: The Origin and Premortal Existence of Human Spirits,* p. 540.

683   E.g., R. O. Cowan, *Answers*, p. 94; O. Pratt, *12 November 1879,* p. 200; B. H. Roberts, *The Truth*, pp. 289-296; E. N. Skousen, *Earth*, pp. 298-302.

684   See *Commentary* 2:26-a, p. 111.

685   C. R. Harrell, *Preexistence*, pp. 5-7.

686   Romans 5:14.

687   B. L. Top, *Life Before*, p. 95; cf. Moses 6:53. See also *Excursus 3: Temple Blessings in the Oath and Covenant of the Priesthood*, p. 519.

sacrifice before the Father to atone for the sins of His brethren, committed not only in the second, but also in the first estate."[688]

Is it possible that the reason one-third of the Father's children were cast out of his presence for rebellion is that they ultimately and finally refused to accept not just the role of Jesus as our Redeemer but also the means by which their rebellion could have been forgiven, namely the Atonement of Jesus Christ, which was operative in our premortal existence? Perhaps.[689]

3-10   D&C 77:2 states that "the spirit of man [is] in the likeness of his person, as also the spirit of the beast, and every other creature which God has created."[690] The Gnostic *Secret Book of John* similarly records the initial creation of a "psychical man… his body composed entirely of animating soul" that contains every feature of the physical body that was subsequently formed.[691] On these matters, there can be little disagreement. However, what constitutes a "creature" in the context of D&C 77:2 has sometimes been debated. For example, Stephens, *et al.* ask whether the fact that everything was created spiritually in the beginning necessarily implies that every form of microscopic life possesses an individual spirit.[692] Moreover, though some early Church leaders believed that there was a sense in which there is life in all matter "independent of the spirit given of God to undergo this probation,"[693] the question of whether each instance of plant life possesses an individual spirit in the likeness of their physical form has not been authoritatively settled.[694]

It should be noted in this connection that while the current meaning of "creature" encompasses animals and people, the archaic sense derived from the Latin is more general, signifying "anything that has been created." However, with one exception, every usage in the Book of Mormon and Doctrine and Covenants refers to people (e.g., "preach the gospel to every creature," "justice claims the creature"). Significantly, the sole exception uses the word in the archaic sense: "that the church may stand independent above all other creatures," the context implying that the Church itself is a "creature" (i.e., a creation) since it was created by God.[695] Notably, in Moses and Abraham, the compound term "living creature" is reserved for animals.[696]

3-11   Some readers take this verse as an argument that death did not occur before the Fall. However, in this connection, Stephens and Meldrum ask:

What does the term "all things" refer to? Verse 23 appears to refer to Adam and Eve only, and verse 24 uses the term "all things" twice to refer to concepts. Can we be certain that "all things" in verse 22 means Adam, Eve, all the animals, and all the plants? Could the term "things" simply mean *conditions*? …If Adam had not transgressed, his condition of immortality in the Garden would have continued indefinitely.[697]

Perhaps more plausibly, Clayton observes:[698]

The meaning of [2 Nephi 2:22-23] must be carefully evaluated. "The state in which they were after they were created" (for plants and animals) is not defined anywhere in scripture. "And had no end" does not necessarily mean eternal life, just a continuation of state. It could mean the creations were mortal and would have continued mortal forever, with no hope of eternal continuance. The word "they" refers to Adam and Eve throughout the chapter, but the meaning of "they" is grammatically unclear in verse 22. Verse 23 picks right back up with "they" referring to Adam and Eve, suggesting that it is Adam and Eve in verse 22 who would have "remained forever and had no end."

I would punctuate the verses this way:

22 And now, behold, if Adam had not transgressed he would not have fallen, but he would have remained in the garden of Eden, and all things which were created must have remained in the same state in which they were after they were created.

---

688   O. Pratt, *The Seer*, 1:4, p. 54, punctuation standardized.
689   A. C. Skinner, *Temple Worship*, pp. 51-52. Thanks to Bryce Haymond for pointing out this reference.
690   Cf. J. F. Smith, *et al.*, *Origin*, 4:203-205.
691   W. Barnstone, *et al.*, *Gnostic*, p. 150.
692   T. D. Stephens, *et al.*, *Evolution*, p. 124.
693   B. Young, *23 March 1856*, p. 277.
694   See also *Commentary* 2:20-a, p. 109; 3:7-e, p. 158; Moses 7:48.
695   D&C 78:14.
696   Moses 2:20-25, 3:19; Abraham 4:24-25, 5:20.
697   T. D. Stephens, *et al.*, *Evolution*, p. 135. See D. Boyce, *On Science*, pp. 200-203 for a rebuttal of this view.
698   R. W. Clayton, *Questions*.

23 And they must have remained forever, and had no end, and they would have had no children; wherefore they would have remained in a state of innocence.

3-12   Consistent with what is found elsewhere in scripture, "natural" has to do with the kinds of things that humans can see[699] and understand[700] by means of their physical faculties, without the additional teaching and transforming power of the Spirit.[701]

The terms "natural" and "spiritual" are also used by Paul to compare the earthly state of the human body with the glory it will receive in the resurrection.[702] In modern scripture, the resurrected body is explained to be the result of the process of inseparably connecting a spirit with the elements of a glorified natural body.[703]

3-13   This is consistent with the view of Elder McConkie, who "conceded that the word spiritual in these passages [within Moses 3] has 'a dual meaning and applies to both the premortal life and the paradisiacal creation,' …[while emphasizing] that the 'more pointed and important meaning' is that of a 'paradisiacal creation.'"[704]

3-14   Note that Moses 2:26-27 has sometimes been seen as referring to the creation of the spirits of all mankind.[705]

3-15   *Jubilees* reports the creation on the first day of various ranks of angels along with "all of the spirits of his creatures which are in heaven and on earth."[706] Barker writes that this belief "seems to have been a controversial matter since later scholars taught that the angels were created on the second day… or on the fifth… This was to emphasize that no angel had been the co-creator"[707]—thus contradicting earlier teachings that God counseled with others in the execution of the Creation.[708]

3-16   Summarizes Barker:

The sequence in *Jubilees* is the same as in Genesis 1, except that *Jubilees* gives far more detail about Day One, the secrets of the Holy of Holies. There are seven works on Day One: heaven, earth, the waters, the abyss, darkness and light—all of which can be deduced from Genesis—and then the ministering angels [and "all of the spirits of his creatures"], who are not mentioned in Genesis…

It has long been accepted that Genesis 1 is a reworking of older material and is related to other accounts of creation known in the Ancient Near East. One of the main elements to have been removed is any account of the birth of the gods, even though Genesis 2:1-4 retains traces of the older account: 'Thus the heavens and the earth were finished and all the host of them. These are the generations of the heavens and the earth.' In Job 38:7, however, we still read of the sons of God who shouted for joy on the first day of creation when the foundations of the earth were laid, and "sons of God" implies that they were begotten, not created. The rest of Job 38 describes the works of Day One: the boundary for the waters, the gates of deep darkness, the storehouses of snow and hail, wind, rain and ice, the pattern of the stars. And the point of all this is to ask Job: "Where were you when all this was done?" a strange question for the Lord to ask Job unless there was a known tradition of someone who witnessed the work of Creation and thus became wise.[709]

3-17   For more detail on the events surrounding the grand councils in heaven, see the overview of Moses 4, pp. 220-223.

699   Moses 1:10, 11; 3:9; 6:36.
700   Moses 3:33; Alma 26:21.
701   1 Corinthians 2:14; Mosiah 3:16, 19; Alma 41:11, 12; 42:10; D&C 67:10-12; Moses 1:14.
702   1 Corinthians 15:44: "it is sown a natural body; it is raised a spiritual body."
703   E.g., Alma 41:4; D&C 88:28; 93:33-34.
704   C. R. Harrell, *Preexistence*, p. 20.
705   See *Commentary* 2:26-a, p. 111.
706   O. S. Wintermute, *Jubilees*, 2:2, p. 55.
707   M. Barker, *Great High Priest*, p. 157. See J. Neusner, *Genesis Rabbah 1*, 3:8, p. 1:34.
708   See *Commentary* 2:26-a, p. 111.
709   M. Barker, *Beyond*, pp. 195-196.

3-18 Although such an idea seems foreign to the modern mind, science, astronomy, and religion were inseparable fields of study in ancient times.[710] Abraham's study of the "movement of the stars, considering the quality of the affixed time" is mentioned in conjunction with "all appointed souls" in the *Chronicle* of Symeon Logothetes .[711] The relative length of movement of heavenly bodies is also treated extensively, for example, in *1 Enoch*.[712] A continued connection between these subjects can also be inferred from modern revelation.[713]

3-19 For discussions of parallels and divergences between these ideas and the 19th century theology of Thomas Dick, see Jones[714] and Smith.[715] Rhodes and Moody make the point that Abraham is not describing a heliocentric or a geocentric system of cosmology: "If anything, it would be a Kolob-centric system."[716]

Ultimately, however, the account of Abraham reveals that the point of the discussion is not to enlighten the reader about astrophysics, but to describe the orderly hierarchy of intelligences in the universe, moving in "one eternal round":[717]

> For Lucian, choral movement was primordial since it was of divine origin; the exemplary model of choral dance was the movement in cosmic harmonic concord of the stars and the planets:
>
> > With the Creation of the universe, the dance, too, came into being, which signifies the union of the elements. The round dance (*choros*) of the stars, the constellation of planets in relation to the fixed stars, the beautiful order and harmony in all its movements, is a mirror of the original dance at the time of creation. The dance is the richest gift of the Muses… Because of its divine origin, it has a place in the mysteries and is beloved by the gods and carried out by human beings in their honor.[718]

3-20 Nibley expands on this topic:

> This brings up a theological question to which only the book of Abraham offers a clear solution, namely the problem of hierarchy. This was the secret of Egypt's strength and stability, a strict hierarchical order of everything, which everyone respected. It was hard for Satan to subject himself to any other being,[719] it is still hard for the individual human to recognize his inferiority to another. Again and again, we are reminded of the strangely obvious principle that one thing can be above another. According to Miriam Lichtheim, who supplies us with over seven hundred gems of Egyptian wisdom, every man's ego is constantly threatened by other egos, and none is secure—the weakest can damage the strongest.[720] Again and again, Abraham takes the trouble to remind us of what should be obvious…[721] Why is he so insistent on anything so obvious? And so society throughout history has been locked in a paralyzing round of Thorstein Veblen's 'invidious comparison.'[722] We have to live with it; why can't we admit it cheerfully? I have children who can run circles around me brainwise—should that depress me?… Does the Son envy the Father, or is the Father jealous of him?… Abraham removes the mean, invidious element and makes the order of things accessible to all…[723] One cannot plead that he is a latecomer, that others came early and got the jump on him…[724] Who is responsible then? It is all in my own hands. Intelligence was not created—it unfolds; no matter how backward I may be I can rejoice in my ignorance, knowing that wonderful things are awaiting my discovery. When I am honest, that is, intelligent enough to search out and dwell upon the things I do not know or in which I have been mistaken, rather than

710 M. Barker, *Lost*, p. 25; H. W. Nibley, *Teachings of the PGP*, 5, pp. 53-65; G. de Santillana, *et al.*, *Hamlet's Mill*.

711 Cited in J. A. Tvedtnes, *et al.*, *Traditions*, p. 250.

712 G. W. E. Nickelsburg, *et al.*, *1 Enoch* 72-82, pp. 96-116.

713 E.g., D&C 88:5-61; 121:26-32. For an overview of the doctrine of other worlds from pseudepigraphal sources, see H. W. Nibley, *Apocryphal*, pp. 285-295.

714 E. T. Jones, *Thomas Dick*.

715 W. V. Smith, *JS Commentary*, pp. 102-104.

716 M. D. Rhodes, *et al.*, *Astronomy*, p. 22.

717 1 Nephi 10:19; Alma 7:20; 37:12; D&C 3:2, 35:1.

718 N. Isar, *Dance of Adam*, p. 183, citing Lucian, *The Dance*.

719 See Moses 4:3; Abraham 3:28; N. J. Dawood, *Koran*, 2:34, 7:11, 15:30-31, 17:61, 18:50, 20:116, 38:73-74; J. Milton, *Paradise Lost*, 1:261, p. 22.

720 M. Lichtheim, *Wisdom*, pp. 16-18.

721 See Abraham 3:6, 8, 16.

722 T. Veblen, *Leisure*, pp. 21-22. See *Endnote 5-71*, p. 451.

723 See Abraham 3:18-19.

724 See D&C 93:23, 29.

preening myself on the little I do know, surveying such latent discoveries is like a child waiting to open packages on Christmas morning.[725]

Elsewhere, Nibley observes:

Pharaoh was the top of the pyramid, Wilson notes in a useful insight, "the only point of contact with the gods."[726] But where does the top, the *pyramidion*, end and the pyramid begin? They are all one, every level indispensable to the next to make the solidest of structures and to take us all up to heaven along the same celestial ramp and broadening sunbeam.[727]

3-21   In the original, "a little lower than the gods" (Hebrew *elohim*).

3-22   Contrast Christian views of the spheres of the heavens, "with earth at the center and the Prime Mover at the outer edge."[728]

3-23   Like the complex Christian formulations of the Trinity resulting from post-apostolic church councils, the tortuous descriptions of the emanations of God in medieval Jewish mysticism are due in part to difficulties in reconciling the conception of an absolutely transcendent Deity with His evident participation in the business of mankind and His "readiness to communicate (prophecy and revelation) and be communicated with (prayer and piety)." In this vein, Blumenthal faults Lovejoy's history of the rise and fall of the idea of the "Great Chain of Being" for overlooking "the dialectic tension between God's transcendence and God's accessibility… [and how it] varied from one cultural context to another."[729]

3-24   For example, the Prophet said on one occasion that the sun, moon, and stars "all move in perfect harmony in their sphere and order,"[730] and on another he spoke of "the great God who holds this world in its sphere or its orbit—the planets."[731] Eliza R. Snow is thought to have drawn on teachings she received directly from Joseph Smith when she wrote: "For a wise and glorious purpose / Thou has placed me here on earth / And withheld the recollection / Of my former friends and birth. / Yet ofttimes a secret something / Whispered, 'You're a stranger here'; / And I felt that I had wandered / From a more exalted sphere."[732] D&C 77:2 (March 1832) says that the four beasts of Revelation 4:6 represented "the glory of the classes of being in their destined order or sphere of creation." In a discourse about the four beasts in Revelation, the Prophet is similarly quoted as saying that they "were perfect: they were like angels in their sphere,"[733] although it should be noted that there is no mention of the word "sphere" in the extant source manuscripts for this discourse.[734]

3-25   Preparing the minds of the hearers of the King Follett discourse, the Prophet said that he wanted to "get you into a more lofty sphere than what the human being generally understands"[735] or, as given in Larson's amalgamated version of the text, to "lift your minds into a more lofty sphere and exalted standing."[736]

3-26   D&C 93:30 states that: "All truth is independent in that sphere in which God has placed it, to act for itself, as all intelligence also" (6 May 1833). On another occasion, the Prophet gave "instructions respecting the different offices, and the necessity of every individual acting in the sphere allotted to him or her."[737] He also stated that "the spirits of men… are governed by the same priesthood that Abraham, Melchizedek, and the apostles were, that they are organized according to that priesthood which is everlasting—'without beginning of days or end of years'[738]—that they all move in their respective spheres and are governed by the law of God, that when they appear upon the earth they are in a probationary state and are preparing, if righteous, for a future and a greater glory."[739] Finally, in

725   H. W. Nibley, *Drama*, pp. 27-29.

726   J. A. Wilson, *Culture*, p. 73.

727   H. W. Nibley, *Greatness*, p. 280.

728   E. Edson, *et al.*, *Cosmos*, p. 10.

729   D. Blumenthal, *Great Chain*. For an excellent overview of LDS and non-LDS literature on the personal and passible nature of God, see D. L. Paulsen, *Are Christians Mormon*, pp. 52-62.

730   J. Smith, Jr., *Words*, 20 March 1842, p. 107.

731   *Ibid.*, 7 April 1844, p. 357.

732   *Hymns (1985)*, #292. For more about the background of this hymn, see J. M. Derr, *Personal Journey*.

733   J. Smith, Jr., *Teachings*, 8 April 1843, p. 292.

734   J. Smith, Jr., *Words*, 8 April 1843, pp. 182-190.

735   J. Smith, Jr., *Words*, 7 April 1844, p. 349.

736   J. Smith, Jr., 7 April 1844, in S. Larson, *King Follett*, p. 199.

737   J. Smith, Jr., *Words*, 28 April 1842, p. 115.

738   Hebrews 7:3.

739   J. Smith, Jr., *Spirits*, p. 745.

the conclusion of a letter to presidential candidate John C. Calhoun, he asserted that the power of Congress "is as almighty in its sphere as Jehovah is in his."[740]

3-27 This statement is corroborated by several other statements made by early members and leaders of the Church.[741] For example, Brigham Young "gave it as his opinion that the Earth did not dwell in the sphere in which it did when it was created, but that it was banished from its more glorious state or orbit of revolution for man's sake."[742] Joseph Smith himself is remembered as having taught that when the earth is ready to be "crowned with celestial glory" it "will be rolled back into the presence of God."[743] Even if the Prophet's statement is taken to be both accurately reported and prophetically inspired, it is possible that the "movement" of the earth implied was not a physical movement in the ordinary sense, but rather some other kind of change in "sphere" or "state."[744]

3-28 While members of the Church have always been free to express diverse opinions on such questions, they are likewise counseled to avoid overstating what can be said authoritatively. As a model of this kind of restraint, Matthews' article in the *Encyclopedia of Mormonism* gives the following conclusion about the issue at hand: "Various interpretations have been suggested concerning the nature of life on the earth before the Fall and how the Fall physically affected the world, but these go beyond the clearly stated doctrine of the Church. The Church and the scriptures are emphatic, however, that the Fall brought two kinds of death to Adam and his posterity."[745]

3-29 Draper, *et al.* summarize the insurmountable difficulties with past efforts to explain these fossilized remains as byproducts of the earth's purported creation out of other planets.[746] However, fossils aside, Rhodes and Moody do make the point that McIntire's account of the sermon of Joseph Smith that is the source of the idea that the earth was composed of disorganized fragments from elsewhere in the universe uses the word "'globes' rather than 'planets,' which could refer to any celestial body: planet, comet, asteroid, or star. All the elements out of which this earth is formed (with the exception of hydrogen and some helium) were formed inside stars. The elements up to iron are formed in the various stages of fusion a star goes through during its lifetime. Elements heavier than iron are formed primarily in supernova explosions and are then dispersed throughout the galaxy by that same explosion. Thus the elements of this earth did indeed come from other 'globes' that were disorganized—a supernova is a fairly substantial disorganization."[747]

3-30 See Stordalen[748] for a brief summary of the history of non-LDS scholarship regarding the location of Eden.

3-31 Jackson has proposed another alternative—namely, that:

> … during the time the earth was being created, there was death on Earth… [W]hen the Creation had progressed to the point the earth was ready for Adam and Eve, a… dramatic transformation took place that glorified it and transformed it from its developing condition into a state or paradise in which there was no death… Later, the fall of our first parents caused the fall of the earth and of all that was in it. The Fall brought death into our world, and the condition of paradise was withdrawn. Since geological evidence records only death, not life, no trace of Eden would remain once it had ceased to exist, no matter how long it lasted.[749]

3-32 Arguing against such a possibility, Joseph Fielding McConkie writes:

> Some have argued that the paradisiacal glory of which we speak was confined to the Garden of Eden while evolutionary processes were taking place through the rest of the earth. The great difficulty with this idea is that it confines the effects of the Atonement to forty acres (or whatever

---

740 J. Smith, Jr., *Documentary History*, 2 January 1844, 6:160.

741 J. Taylor, *29 August 1857*; J. Smith, Jr., n. d., as reported in C. L. Walker, *Diary*, 2:505; B. Young, *13 July 1862*, p. 317; B. Young, *10 July 1874*, p. 143.

742 "Record of Acts of the Apostles," *1849 Record Book*, p. 41, Church Archives, cited in J. Smith, Jr., *Words*, p. 84 n. 12.

743 J. Smith, Jr., *Words*, 5 January 1841, pp. 60, 84.

744 See H. L. Andrus, *God*, pp. 312-314 for a discussion of these and similar citations. For different interpretations of the effects of the Fall, see the overview of Moses 3, pp. 140-144.

745 R. J. Matthews, *Fall*, p. 486; cf. R. D. Draper, *et al.*, *Commentary*, p. 186; M. D. Rhodes, *et al.*, *Astronomy*, p. 27. For more on this question, see *Commentary* 3:17-c, p. 175.

746 R. D. Draper, *et al.*, *Commentary*, pp. 186-187.

747 M. D. Rhodes, *et al.*, *Astronomy*, p. 28.

748 T. Stordalen, *Echoes*, pp. 250-254.

749 K. P. Jackson, *Genesis*, p. 77.

MOSES 3

the size the Garden of Eden was). The plain testimony of scripture is that the entire earth and all created things were affected by the Fall, and thus recipients of the blessings of the Atonement.[750]

3-33 For relevant statements concerning the origin of man, see *Appendix*, pp. 785-803.

3-34 Such a view presumes that the bodies of Adam and Eve, having been prepared on earth and later placed in the Garden, were perfect physical bodies, maintained in a state of immortality because of the unique conditions of a terrestrial world that prevailed in the Garden. Likewise, the animals and plants in the Garden would have to be either of special kinds indigenous to Eden or, if of earthly origin, somehow maintained in an immortal (and presumably vegetarian) state until the time of the Fall.[751]

Regarding the state of Adam's body at his creation, Robinson summarizes the views of ancient Jewish scholars:

> The rabbis were divided on whether Adam was created mortal or immortal. It seems that there were three basic viewpoints. The first was that Adam was created immortal in the Garden but was punished with death, which was hereditary in his posterity. The second view was that Adam was created immortal but that his punishment was personal, not hereditary. That is, men die because of their own sins and not because of Adam's sin. Thus if a man were to live without sin, he would still be immortal. In fact, the rabbis pointed to Enoch and other translated individuals as examples of this kind of man. The third view was that Adam was created mortal and that his eventual death was inevitable; his sin, however, brought about violent, painful, and premature death. Had he not sinned, death would have been, after a long and happy life, a beautiful transition from this life to the next. More recent theologians have pointed out that Adam cannot be considered to have been "immortal" at his creation, at least not in the strict sense, since he had the ability to die in the event of his sinning. In this sense, the state of the first Adam parallels the state of the second Adam, Christ. For in their respective gardens, Eden and Gethsemane, each had the ability to die if they so chose, but neither was under the necessity of dying.[752]

3-35 This view must, of course, allow for the eventual renewal and sanctification of the earth that is now the home of mankind.[753] It should be noted that neither D&C 88:26 nor Article of Faith 10 refer unambiguously to a Fall as a past event involving the physical earth itself. Article of Faith 10 simply asserts that: 1) the earth will be made new again (i.e., brought back again to whatever the earth's original state was—whether that state was telestial or terrestrial) and 2) that additionally it will "receive its paradisiacal glory," which seems most straightforwardly to imply that the earth will attain this status for the first time in the Millennium—the text does not say "again receive." Similarly, although D&C 88:26 speaks of the history and the future of the earth in terms that parallel human death and resurrection, both are referred to as being future rather than past events:[754] "notwithstanding it shall die, it shall be quickened again… and the righteous shall inherit it."

3-36 Cryptic statements by some of early church leaders also spoke of a process of transplantation to describe Adam and Eve's coming to earth.[755] However, the adoption of such a view does not necessarily entail acceptance of Brigham Young's enigmatic teaching that Adam (the premortal Michael) came to earth as an already-resurrected being.[756]

Summarizing teachings from a variety of gnostic sources, Nibley describes the cosmos as:

> … an infinity of dwelling-places (*topoi*), either occupied or awaiting tenants.[757] These are colonized by migrants from previously established toposes or worlds, all going back ultimately to a single original center.[758] The colonizing process is called "planting," and those spirits that bring their treasures to a new world are called "Plants," more rarely "seeds," of their father or "planter" in another world.[759] Every planting goes out from a Treasure House, either as the essential material

---

750   J. F. McConkie, *Answers*, p. 161.
751   See also *Commentary* 2:29-b, p. 117.
752   S. E. Robinson, *Book of Adam*, pp. 138-139.
753   E.g., Revelation 21:1; D&C 63:21, 88:18-19, 130:9.
754   J. F. Smith, Jr., *Way 1945*, 1931, pp. 349-350.
755   E.g., B. Young, *28 August 1852*, p. 275; B. Young, *20 April 1856*, p. 319; B. Young, *9 October 1859*, pp. 285-286. See also J. F. Smith, Jr., *Origin*, pp. 276-277; J. F. Smith, Jr., *Doctrines*, 1920, 1:139-140.
756   See *Excursus 30: Adam-God Theory and the Heavenly and Earthly Adam,* p. 603.
757   See, e.g., F. I. Andersen, *2 Enoch*, 49:2, p. 176-177.
758   See, e.g., D. M. Parrott, *Eugnostos*, 113:14-19, p. 239.
759   See, e.g., E. S. Drower, *Prayerbook*, 378, p. 283, 286; M. Lidzbarski, *Johannesbuch*, 14, 2:60 n. 6; cf. H. W. Nibley,

elements or as the colonizers themselves, who come from a sort of mustering-area called the "Treasure-house of Souls."[760]

With its "planting" completed, a new world is in business, a new Treasury has been established from which new Sparks [life-giving emanations from God] may go forth in all directions to start the process anew in ever new spaces;[761] God wants every man to "plant a planting," nay, "he has promised that those who keep his Law may also become creators of worlds":[762] "... and ye shall create for yourselves aeons, worlds, and heavens, so that the intelligible spirits may come and dwell in them. And ye shall be gods, and ye shall know that ye come from God, and ye shall see that He is God in you, and He shall dwell in your aeon."[763] But keeping the law requires following the divine pattern in every point; in taking the Treasure to a new world, the Sent One (who follows hard on the heels of the colonists) seeks nothing so much as complete identity with the One who sent him; hence, from first to last one mind alone dominates the whole boundless complex. Because each planting is completely dependent on its Treasure House or home base, the system never breaks up into independent systems; in this patriarchal order all remains forever identified with the Father from whom all ultimately comes forth.[764]

3-37   Comments *Al-Mizan*: "The story of Adam may have been used by Allàh to represent the rise, fall and rise again of [all] mankind. Adam was the first representative of humanity, and his life was a symbol, a miniature, of the human beings' life-span in this world."[765]

3-38   Monneret comments: "The sanction will be death, following a temporary stay on the earth. Man is condemned to descend from Paradise where he lived; returning there will become henceforth the goal he will strive to attain through his good works on earth."[766] *Al-Mizan* concurs, explaining:

> The context... clearly show[s] that it was for the earth that Adam was created; it was the original plan that he should live and die in the earth. Allàh had temporarily placed the couple in the Garden to test them... so that on eating from [a particular tree] they should become aware of their nakedness and then be sent down to the earth... If their eating of the tree, the uncovering of their private parts and the life of this world were not a confirmed divine plan, an irrevocable predetermined decree, they would have been returned to their place in the Garden as soon as they were forgiven their mistake. In short, it was the divine plan that they should spend some time in the Garden to get them prepared for the life in this world; and their removal from the Garden, according to the causal [relationship] decreed by Allàh, depended on their eating from the tree and becoming aware of their nakedness, and it happened because they listened to the whispering of the Satan.[767]

In another Islamic text, Adam replies to the two angels Harut and Marut[768] who berated him for his part in the Fall: "Have pity and stop your scolding, for that which has happened to me was fixed and determined by my Lord!"[769] In another Islamic text, Adam replies to a similar charge by Moses by saying, "Do you rebuke me for something God made incumbent upon me forty years before I was created?"[770] In this sense, Al-Tha'labi reasons that "God expelled Adam from the Garden before He brought him into it, for that is what He says: 'I am about to place a viceroy on the earth,'[771] and He did

Sparsiones, pp. 151-164. See also E. S. Drower, *Thousand*, pp. 110, 111, 120, 267; J. O. Ryen, *Mandaean Vine*, pp. 203-204, 246-247.

760   See, e.g., M. Lidzbarski, *Johannesbuch*, 63, 2:218; 59, 2:207; 57, 2:203-205. See also H. Schwartz, *Tree*, 199, p. 165 and *Figure 4-10*, p. 228.

761   See, e.g., M. Lidzbarski, *Ginza*, GR 10:1, p. 240; C. Schmidt, *Bruce Codex*, 1 Jeu 5-7, pp. 21-33; C. O'Brien, *1 Jeu*, 5-7, pp. 234-238.

762   See C. Schmidt, *et al.*, *Altgnostisches Werk*, 19:30-35, p. 360.

763   Cf. R. Haardt, *Gnosis*, GR 3:1, pp. 354-355.

764   H. W. Nibley, *Treasures*, p. 185. See, e.g., M. Lidzbarski, *Ginza*, 10:1, p. 241; See H. W. Nibley, *Treasures*, pp. 208-211 n. 96-102 for a more complete set of references to the ancient literature.

765   A. at-Tabataba'i, *Al-Mizan*, 2:36, 1:187-188.

766   J.-L. Monneret, *Grands*, p. 482 n. 21,

767   A. at-Tabataba'i, *Al-Mizan*, 2:35, 1:179-181.

768   Corresponding to Harvotat and Amurtat of the Zoroastrian *Avesta*; cf. Shemhazi and Azael in Jewish legend. See M. al-Kisa'i, *Tales*, p. 342 n. 32.

769   J. C. Reeves, *Harut wa-Marut*.

770   Abu Hurayrah in B. M. Wheeler, *Prophets*, p. 30.

771   *Qur'an* 2:30.

not say: 'in the Garden.'"[772]

3-39   There are "contradictory hadiths" in Islam about whether the Garden of Eden was earthly, heavenly, or something in between.[773] *Al-Mizan* gives one view of Islamic teachings in this regard: "It follows that Adam had lived a heavenly — and not earthly life in the Garden. This observation gives us a certainty that the Garden of Adam was in the heaven, although it was not the Garden of eternal abode from which one is never turned out."[774] "The phrase, 'a garden of this world,' has been used in contrast to the Garden of everlasting abode. It indicates a state between this world and the hereafter... The said Garden may be called a Garden of *al-Barzakh*."[775] The Arabic *barzakh* means a limit or boundary separating two things. Besides being used here to describe the place of the Garden, the term is also employed in the name of the "intermediate realm" constituting the state, place and time between one's death and the Day of Resurrection.[776] "The sentences, 'Adam descended on the (hill of) *as-Safa*', and 'Hawwa' [Eve] descended on the (hill of) *al-Marwah*', indicate that, before it, they were somewhere above this world... Apart from that, many traditions of *Ahlu 'l-bayt* (a.s.) show that the Garden of Adam was in the heaven, and that he and his wife descended from the heaven."[777]

3-40   The Arabic seems to simultaneously convey both the idea of a transgression and a fall to a new state: "*Azalla* (translated as "made them slip") is derived from *zall*, to slip (foot or tongue) unintentionally. The result was that they were made to depart from the happy condition in which they were."[778]

3-41   According to the *Qur'an*, Adam and Eve were twice told to go down:[779] thus, they "were removed first from the Garden to its courtyard and then from the courtyard to the earth."[780] "*Habt* sometimes means going down a declivity, or descending from a high place to a low one, but its more frequent use in literature is simply in the sense of removing from one place to another... It also signifies simply change in condition. According to LL, *habata* means he came forth from it and also he became lowered or degraded. And *habt* further signifies falling into evil; or becoming low or abject; or suffering loss or diminution. This loss or suffering is brought about by means of indulgence in evil."[781]

3-42   Dahood translates this as: "be enemies to each other."[782] The syntax denotes at least three persons, hence *al-Mizan* concludes that the statement was addressed to Adam, Eve, and Satan.[783] To these three, ibn Ishaq adds the serpent.[784] It is impossible not to hear in this phrase an echo of the prediction of enmity between the serpent and the seed of the woman in Moses 4:21. Writes al-Tha'labi: "Man is an enemy of the serpent, smashing her head whenever he sees her. The peacock is his enemy and the serpent is his enemy, biting her whenever she can. And Iblis [the Devil] is the enemy of all of them."[785]

3-43   In other words, the change in conditions will not be permanent, but is only a temporary state of probation: "The words 'an abode and a provision for a time' refer to man's span of life on earth, which is limited as compared with the eternal life of the next world."[786]

3-44   For a photo of one of the chains, said to go back to the time of a visit by Alexander the Great in 330 BCE[787] but probably first put there by an early Sinhalese king,[788] see M. Akslund, *Footprint*, plate 25. Nibley writes:

---

772   A. al-Tha'labi, *Lives*, p. 53.

773   Porch of Wisdom Cultural Institution, *Faith and Reason*, p. 161. See *Excursus 53: Comparative Explorations of the Mysteries*, p. 663.

774   A. at-Tabataba'i, *Al-Mizan*, 2:36, 1:192.

775   *Ibid.*, 1:197.

776   M. M. Ali, *Qur'an*, 23:100, p. 675.

777   A. at-Tabataba'i, *Al-Mizan*, 1:197-198.

778   M. M. Ali, *Qur'an*, n. 63, p. 20.

779   *Ibid.*, 2:36, 38, pp. 20-21.

780   A. at-Tabataba'i, *Al-Mizan*, 1:209. See *Commentary* 4:31-a, p. 280.

781   M. M. Ali, *Qur'an*, p. 21 n. 64.

782   N. J. Dawood, *Koran*, p. 13.

783   A. at-Tabataba'i, *Al-Mizan*, 2:36, 1:187; cf. 7:24; 20:123.

784   M. Ibn Ishaq ibn Yasar, *Making*, p. 37; cf. A. al-Tha'labi, *Lives*, p. 53.

785   A. al-Tha'labi, *Lives*, p. 54.

786   M. M. Ali, *Qur'an*, p. 21 n. 65.

787   See the accounts of the 14th-century Persian voyager Abu Abdullah Muhammad Ibn Battuta and the 15th-century Persian poet Ashraff's Zaffer Namah Skendari, cited in J. E. Tennent, *Ceylon*, 1:606, 2:139,

788   V. S. Dhammika, *Sri Pada*; S. S. M. Nanayakkara, *Sri Pada*.

This idea of footprints on the mountains is very common... Remember Adam's mountain in Ceylon (Sri Lanka)? In the center of the island is this vast sort of Monadnock with a footprint on it, the place where Adam landed when he came to this earth. It's the oldest pilgrimage there. Pilgrims come from all over. They cross Adam's bridge, which was formerly a land bridge from India to Ceylon. Then the idea is to climb and pull yourself up the mountain... You can still see pictures in the *National Geographic* with chains, ropes and everything else. Originally, there was a handrail that rotted away. They pulled themselves up....

Anyway, we have... Adam's mountain where Adam came to earth and Adam fell... The [*Qur'an*] tells us the story...[789]

In recent years, parts of Adam's/Rama's bridge have been threatened by a proposed canal project.[790]

3-45   The name *Safā* is said to have come because Adam was "known as the Chosen [*safwa*] of God" and the names of *Marwa* because "womankind [*mar'a*] sat there."[791] After his descent to earth, Adam was commanded to make a pilgrimage to Mecca and to build a house for God there.[792] Contemporary *hajj* pilgrims pass through a stage of prayer in the field of '*Arafat*, said to be where Adam and Eve "met after their expulsion from heaven, and it was on the Mount of Mercy (*Jabal al-rahman*) in this plain that their prayer for forgiveness was accepted."[793] Al-Tha'labi precises that when Adam and Eve were rejoined "they recognized each other by questioning on a day of questioning. So the place was named '*Arafat* (questions) and the day, '*Irfah*."[794] Here also, all the souls of mankind emerged from Adam and covenanted with God[795]—thus: "To come to 'Arafat is to become fully conscious of that covenant and to remember that 'He' alone is all in all."[796]

The two knolls near Mecca are also important in Islamic tradition for their association with Hagar's frantic search for water to quench the thirst of Ishmael.[797] Often, pilgrims performing the *hajj* also follow it by completing the *sa'ee* (meaning 'running') in commemoration of that event. Women walk and men jog or run the three-kilometer distance back and forth between the hills seven times, starting at *al-Safā* and ending at *al-Marwah*. Tradition says that Adam had also been commanded to run in that place, after which "the earth, with God's permission, burst forth with a spring filled with water that was colder than ice, sweeter than honey and more redolent than musk."[798]

Traditions about Adam's descent are also associated with *Sri Pada* (literally "Sacred Footprint," also known as "Adam's Peak") in Sri Lanka (Ceylon), which rises dramatically from the surrounding plain to a height of 7360 feet. This location is understood throughout the East as being, for Adam and Eve, "the best of all possible worlds after being thrown out of Paradise."[799] A boulder at the peak containing an indentation resembling a five-foot-long footprint is said by Buddhists to be that of the left foot of the departing Buddha,[800] and of Shiva by Tamil Hindus.[801] Further tying the location to descriptions of the Garden of Eden, the place is also seen by Buddhists and Hindus as origin of three or four of the most important rivers.[802] A legend of more recent origin attributes the footprint to the Apostle Thomas, missionary to India or to the Eunuch of Candace, Queen of Ethiopia,[803] while a 15th-century Chinese work attributes the footprint to Pan Gu (P'an Ku), the primordial man in some versions of Chinese mythology.[804] Moreover, there are Muslim, Mandaean, Gnostic and Christian traditions that

---

789   H. W. Nibley, *Teachings of the PGP*, 16, pp. 195-196.

790   *Hindu groups oppose canal project (September 12).*

791   M. al-Kisa'i, *Tales*, p. 65.

792   *Ibid.*, p. 61; cf. 62, 65-66. See also al-Tabari, *Creation*, 1:123-124, pp. 294-295; *Figure 4-4, p. 219.*

793   See *Excursus 47: Islamic Perspectives Relating to Redemption*, p. 645.

794   A. al-Tha'labi, *Lives*, p. 54; cf. al-Tabari, *Creation*, 1:120, p. 291. See *Commentary 3:23-c, p. 183.*

795   *Qur'an* 7:172, 30:30, 33:7, 53:56; M. al-Kisa'i, *Tales*, pp. 63-64; G. Weil, *Legends*, pp. 39-40; B. M. Wheeler, *Prophets*, p. 32-33; *Excursus 48: The Nature and Scope of Premortal Covenants*, p. 649.

796   S. A. Ashraf, *Inner*, p. 122.

797   Genesis 21:12-21.

798   M. al-Kisa'i, *Tales*, p. 67. For a geographical perspective of *hajj* events, see R. C. Martin, *Encyclopedia*, 2:531-532. Other purported locations for the descent of Adam and Eve to earth are given in al-Tabari, *Creation*, 1:120-121, pp. 290-292 and A. al-Tha'labi, *Lives*, p. 53.

799   E. Lupieri, *Mandaeans*, p. 143.

800   M. Akslund, *Footprint*, pp. 16-55; S. C. Malan, *Adam and Eve*, p. 215 n. 22; J. E. Tennent, *Ceylon*, 1:327.

801   M. Akslund, *Footprint*, pp. 135-139; J. E. Tennent, *Ceylon*, 2:132.

802   M. Akslund, *Footprint*, pp. 136-137.

803   *Ibid.*, p. 139; J. E. Tennent, *Ceylon*, 2:133. On Candace, see Acts 8:27.

804   V. S. Dhammika, *Sri Pada*; J. E. Tennent, *Ceylon*, 1:609.

claim it as "the place where Adam landed when he came to this earth."[805] Alluvial deposits at the mountain's foot are rich in gems which, according to one Muslim tradition, were formed from the tears that Adam and Eve shed after they were made to leave Eden. Other traditions about the place tell of "trees whose leaves when eaten, restore old age to youth" and "that some of the fig-leaves with which Adam was girt about, having been scattered by the wind in his fall from Paradise, those leaves became the sweet spices for which [Sri Lanka] is celebrated."[806]

"[E]xtending [its] past religious and political glories two hundred years into the future," famed science fiction writer Arthur C. Clarke included Adam's Peak in his 1979 book, *The Fountains of Paradise*. Here, the author transforms the mountain where Adam is said to have descended from heaven "into the only place on earth where an orbital space tower might be constructed. Through Adam's Peak, Sri Lanka is made a port for the entire solar system."[807] Of note is the fact that Clarke had made Sri Lanka his home in 1956, and died there in 2008.[808]

3-46   "Hyde… refutes the etymology of 'Taprobana' from *Div* (= isle) *Rohan*—the name for Adam's Peak in the *Qur'an*, and proposes to bring 'Serandib,' from *Selen*, or 'Seilan-dib,' island of Seylan [Ceylon = Sri Lanka]—Singhala."[809]

3-47   Elaborating more fully on the distinction between premodern and modern concepts of literal truth, Faulconer writes:

> … we [moderns] take the literal truth to be the truth that most accurately describes or refers to what happened, independent of any symbolic ordering, and we take the "spiritual sense" to be something beyond the literal, to what we call "merely symbolic." Premoderns, however, do not disjoin the literal and the spiritual. For them, it means, "what the letters, i.e., the words say," rather than, "what an objective report would say." "What *x* says" and what *x* describes accurately" do not mean the same, even if the first is a description. Even a careless reading of medieval discussions of scriptural exegesis will show that the medievals' interest was not in deciding what the scriptures portray, but in what they say. They do not take the scriptures to be picturing something for us, but to be telling us the truth of the world, of its things, its events, and its people, a truth that cannot be told apart from its situation in a divine, symbolic ordering.[810]

> Of course, that is not to deny that the scriptures tell about events that actually happened… However, premodern interpreters do not think it sufficient (or possible) to portray the real events of real history without letting us see them in the light of that which gives them their significance—their reality, the enactment of which they are a part—as history, namely the symbolic order that they incarnate. Without that light, portrayals cannot be accurate. A bare description of the physical movements of certain persons at a certain time is not history (assuming that such bare descriptions are even possible). "Person A raised his left hand, turning it clockwise so that .03 milliliters of a liquid poured from a vial in that hand into a receptacle situated midway between A and B" does not mean the same as "Henry poured poison in to Richard's cup." Only the latter could be a historical claim (and even the former is no bare description).[811]

Faulconer moreover makes it clear that what some people take to be "literal" interpretations of scripture results in "rob[bing] it of its status as a way of understanding the world."[812] William Blake makes the same point poetically:[813]

> This life's dim Windows of the Soul
> Distorts the Heavens from Pole to Pole

805   H. W. Nibley, *Teachings of the PGP*, 16, p. 195; cf. E. S. Drower, *Mandaeans*, pp. 10, 259; M. Ibn Ishaq ibn Yasar, *Making*, pp. 33, 38; E. Lupieri, *Mandaeans*, pp. 142-144; J. E. Tennent, *Ceylon*, 1:583-584; 2:133-136; B. M. Wheeler, *Prophets*, pp. 25-26.

806   S. C. Malan, *Adam and Eve*, p. 214 n. 20; cf. al-Tabari, *Creation*, 1:124-126, pp. 296-297. Hymn lovers will recognize this theme, found in "From Greenland's Icy Mountains": "What though the spicy breezes blow soft o'er Ceylon's isle" (*Hymns (1948)*, #40). These words are omitted in *Hymns (1985)*, #268.

807   C. S. Campbell, *Images*, p. 296.

808   For another example of where this theme has been absorbed into modern literature, see *Excursus 12: Saint Exupéry and Genesis*, p. 549.

809   S. C. Malan, *Adam and Eve*, p. 215 n. 22.

810   Cf. A. G. Zornberg, *Genesis*, pp 31-32.

811   J. E. Faulconer, *Incarnation*, pp. 44-45; cf. J. E. Faulconer, *Study*, pp. 124-128.

812   J. E. Faulconer, *Dorrien*, p. 426. See the quotation by Faulconer in Moses 3 *Gleanings*, p. 194.

813   W. Blake, *The Everlasting Gospel*, section 5, l, cited in M. Muggeridge, *Jesus*, p. 25

> And leads you to believe a Lie
> When you see with, not thro', the Eye.

"Thus," says Muggeridge, "Blake distinguishes between the fantasy that is seen with the eye and the truth that is seen through it. They are two clearly demarcated kingdoms; and passing from one to the other, from the kingdom of fantasy to the kingdom of reality, gives inexpressible delight."[814]

3-48 In the Sumerian myth of *Enki and Ninbursag*, Enki was cursed because he ate the carefully nurtured plants of Ninhursag, the mother-goddess.[815] Date palms, however, were not only depicted as a source of sweet fruit but also, according to texts from many centuries later, they sometimes were climbed to obtain access to a source of wisdom or warning. Notes Visotzky: "For a period of close to five hundred years, stories from Semitic religious communities preserved (in Palestinian Aramaic, koine Greek, and rabbinic Hebrew) snatches of the conversation of palm trees. The palms speak in dreams to one another and in broad daylight to those who would transgress against them. What seems to bind the dialogues together is that in every case, the ultimate hearer is a towering religious figure."[816]

An example of the theme of warning is illustrated in the *Genesis Apocryphon*, where we find Abram dreaming of a cedar and a date-palm, representing himself and his wife Sarai. It is only through the pleadings of the palm tree that the cedar is spared from the axes of the woodcutters.[817] A similar theme is found in the biography of Mani, where Elchasai the Baptist climbs a date palm and is apparently warned that he should not cut it down for wood.[818] On the other hand, the function of the trees as a source of wisdom is shown in the *Pistis Sophia*, which reports that God spoke "mysteries" to Enoch "out of the Tree of *Gnosis* [Knowledge] and out of the Tree of Life in the paradise of Adam."[819]

See the Persian *Shahnama* epic,[820] where a talking tree rebukes Alexander the Great "for his lust of conquest and prophesies his death in a distant land."[821]

3-49 There is evidence that, in the first temple, the Menorah was placed in the Holy of Holies to represent the tree of life.[822]

3-50 Rabbinic tradition also saw the human body as a microcosm of creation and of the temple, e.g., "The Temple corresponds to the whole world and to the creation of man who is a small world."[823]

3-51 In Muslim tradition, the primordial mound was located at the site of Mecca rather than Jerusalem: "The first part of the Earth to appear on the face of the water was Mecca, and God spread out the Earth below it. Therefore it was called *Umm al-Qura*, namely the 'model (= mother) of all towns.'"[824]

3-52 Currid discusses the fact that Exodus 1-15 "owes much of its structure, language, and theology to the Genesis creation account," providing a fitting prelude to the crowning creation of the temple in subsequent chapters:

> The scriptural writer understood and described the exodus as a second creation. It was a new conquest of chaos, another prevailing over the waters of the deep, and a redemptive creation of the people of Israel. This view has found its way into the literature of biblical studies. What has not often been recognized is that the preceding plague account is an ironic undoing or destruction of the creation order in the land of Egypt. God took the creation order of Genesis 1 and reversed it in Exodus 7-12 for the purposes of reducing order to chaos and bringing judgment upon Egypt."[825]

3-53 Writes Barker:

> On Day One there was light, separated from darkness, and this corresponded to the Holy of Holies. This light was the presence of God and the state of the angels, who were both in the light and

---

814 M. Muggeridge, *Jesus*, p. 25.
815 J. B. Pritchard, *ANET*, 197-219, p. 40.
816 B. L. Visotzky, *Conversation*, p. 212; cf. H. W. Nibley, *Message 2005*, p. 288; E. A. S. Butterworth, *Tree*, p. 213. See *Commentary 3:9-g*, p. 163.
817 F. G. Martinez, *Genesis Apocryphon*, 19:14-17, p. 232.
818 R. Cameron, *et al.*, *CMC*, pp. 11, 13.
819 C. Schmidt, *Pistis*, 2:99, p. 495; G. R. S. Mead, *Pistis*, 2:246, p. 205.
820 A. Ferdowsi, *Shahnama*, pp. 517-519.
821 E. Edson, *et al.*, *Cosmos*, p. 55, caption to Figure 29.
822 See *Excursus 51: The Five Lost Things of the Temple*, p. 658,
823 *Midrash Tanhuma-Yelammedenu* 3, cited in W. Williams, *Shadow*.
824 A. al-Tha'labi, *Lives*, p. 6.
825 J. D. Currid, *Egypt*, p. 115.

MOSES 3

of the light. Just as light cannot be divided into distinct parts, but is all one, so, too, the angels of Day One are in some sense one.[825]

3-54   For depictions of Christ appearing in the midst of the burning bush, see D. Jackson, *Marvellous*, p. 104 Figure 85; p. 105 Figure 86.

Recall also the description in Orson Pratt's remembrance of Joseph Smith's First Vision where, as the light drew nearer:

> … it increased in brightness, and magnitude, so that, by the time that it reached the tops of the trees, the whole wilderness, for some distance around, was illuminated in a most glorious and brilliant manner. He expected to have seen the leaves and boughs of the trees consumed, as soon as the light came in contact with them.[826]

3-55   The *Gospel of Philip* seems to paint a similar picture of the olive tree as a secondary Tree of Life, separate from the original Tree of Life: "… the Tree of Life is in the middle of the garden. However, it is from the olive tree that we get the chrism, and from the chrism, the resurrection."[827] While Tvedtnes favors an interpretation that sees only one tree in this passage,[828] Ryen's view of two distinct trees seems more consistent with the text, since "it is not… said that the oil comes from the Tree of Life, but from the olive tree."[829] Nevertheless, because the olive tree is seen as the source of resurrection, it "may therefore be correct to say that the olive tree is a Tree of Life as well."[830]

3-56   See Jones[831] for the view that "the bodies for man and other living things were indeed created or organized from the dust of the earth over eons of time before Adam, but that independent spirits were not placed into the bodies until Adam." In this sense, according to Jones, Adam then became the "first flesh."

3-57   Corresponding to the imagery of the Garden of Eden as a "way station," the temple is, as Nibley argues:[832]

> … best thought of in terms of a tent, …until the time comes when the saints "will no longer have to use a movable tent,"[833] according to the early Fathers, who get the idea from the New Testament…[834] It is now fairly certain, moreover, that the great temples of the ancients were not designed to be dwelling-houses of deity but rather stations or landing-places, fitted with inclined ramps, stairways, passageways, waiting-rooms, elaborate systems of gates, and so forth, for the convenience of traveling divinities, whose sacred boats and wagons stood ever ready to take them on their endless junkets from shrine to shrine and from festival to festival through the cosmic spaces. The Great Pyramid itself, we are now assured, is the symbol not of immovable stability but of constant migration and movement between the worlds; and the ziggurats of Mesopotamia, far from being immovable, are reproduced in the seven-stepped throne of the thundering sky-wagon.

Scripture makes a clear distinction between the fixed heavenly temple and its "portable" counterparts. For example, in Psalm 18[835] and D&C 121:1, the "pavilion" (i.e., booth or canopy; Hebrew *sukkah*) of "God's hiding place" should not be equated with the celestial "temple" (i.e., palace; Hebrew *hekal*) to which the prayers of the oppressed ascend,[836] but rather as a representation of a movable

---

825   M. Barker, *Angels*, p. 13.

826   D. C. Jessee, *First Vision*, p. 21; cf. D. Jones, *History*, p. 15; William Smith, 1883, in D. Vogel, *Early*, 1:495.

827   W. W. Isenberg, *Philip*, 73:15-19, p. 153.

828   J. A. Tvedtnes, *Olive Oil*, p. 429.

829   J. O. Ryen, *Mandaean Vine*, p. 214.

830   *Ibid.*, p. 214.

831   S. E. Jones, *Death*.

832   H. W. Nibley, *Tenting*, pp. 42-43.

833   See Origen, *John*, 10:23, p. 404. "The pitching of the tent outside the camp represents God's remoteness from the impure world" (H. W. Nibley, *Tenting*, p. 79 n. 40).

834   E.g., "John 1:14 reads literally, 'the logos was made flesh and pitched his tent [*eskenosen*] among us'; and after the Resurrection the Lord 'camps' with his disciples, Acts 1:4. At the Transfiguration Peter prematurely proposed setting up three tents for taking possession (Matthew 17:4; Mark 9:5; Luke 9:33)" (H. W. Nibley, *Tenting*, p. 80 n. 41).

835   Cf. 2 Samuel 22.

836   Psalm 18:6; D&C 121:2. J. F. McConkie, *et al.*, *Revelations*, p. 945 mistakenly identifies the "pavilion" of D&C 121:1 as God's heavenly residence, while S. E. Robinson, *et al.*, *D&C Commentary*, 4:151 correctly identifies the "pavilion" as a "movable tent."

"conveyance,"[837] here veiled by dark rain clouds, in which God could swiftly descend to rescue His people from mortal danger.[838] The sense of the action is succinctly captured by Alter: "The outcry of the beleaguered warrior ascends all the way to the highest heavens, thus launching a downward vertical movement."[839]

Both Noah's ark and the Tabernacle of Moses were portable sanctuaries of rescue that paralleled in function God's heavenly chariot.[840] Significantly, the word used in Genesis for ark (*tevah*) reappears for the only time in the Bible in the story of the infant Moses, who was placed in a basket in the Nile and saved by Pharaoh's daughter.[841] Describing the similar chest-like construction of the ark, Westermann writes that it was "a huge, rectangular box with a roof, divided into rooms."[842] The account thus makes it clear that the ark "was not shaped like a ship and it had no oars,"[843] "accentuating the fact that Noah's deliverance was not dependent on navigating skills, [but rather happened] entirely by God's will."[844]

The ark and the Tabernacle are the only two structures mentioned in the Bible whose designs were directly revealed by God.[845] The ark's three decks suggest the divisions of the Tabernacle. Indeed, each deck of the ark "was the same height as the Tabernacle and three times the area of the Tabernacle court."[846] Further strengthening the association between the ark and the Tabernacle is the fact that Mishnaic Hebrew used the Hebrew term *tevah* for the Ark of the Covenant.[847] In addition, the Greek term for Noah's ark "later becomes the standard word" for the Ark of the Covenant.[848] Westermann concludes: "The place where God allows his glory to appear is the place whence the life of the people is preserved. The ark corresponds to this in the primeval event where the concern is for the preservation of humanity and what is saved is natural creation… The parallel between the ark and the Tabernacle has a profound meaning."[849]

The sense of the term "gopher wood"—unique to Genesis 6:14—is uncertain. The possibility of conscious wordplay in the juxtaposition of *gpr* with *kpr* ("pitch") cannot be ruled out. Intriguingly, the form and imagery of the latter (i.e., smearing, covering, wiping) suggest the Hebrew word for atonement.[850]

Many modern exegetes envisage a resinous timber and take the term "gopher" to mean cypress wood.[851] Because it is resistant to rot, the wood of the cypress tree was used in ancient times for the building of ships and the construction of coffins. There is an extensive mythology on the cypress tree in cultures throughout the world. It is known for its fragrance and longevity[852]—qualities that naturally link it with the Garden of Eden. Consistent with this idea, cypress trees were often used to make temple doors—gateways to Paradise.

837   Appropriately translated from the Greek as "Tabernacle" (J. N. Sparks, *et al.*, *Orthodox Study Bible*, Psalm 17(18):12, p. 691). See *Endnote E-116*, p. 731.

838   K. L. Barker, *Zondervan*, p. 803 n. 18:7-15. Some Christians also came to view this Psalm as foreshadowing the Incarnation (J. N. Sparks, *et al.*, *Orthodox Study Bible*, p. 691 n. 17). Noah's ark was sometimes seen in a similar fashion: "The ark was a type of the Mother of God with Christ and the Church in her womb (Akath). The floodwaters were a type of baptism, in which we are saved (1 Peter 3:18-22)" (*ibid.*, Genesis 6:14-21, p. 12).

839   R. Alter, *Psalms*, p. 53 n. 8.

840   See *Excursus 25: The Tree of Life as the Hidden Throne of God*, p. 591.

841   Exodus 2:3, 5. See U. Cassuto, *Noah to Abraham*, p. 59.

842   C. Westermann, *Genesis 1-11*, p. 418.

843   By way of contrast, the flood vessel of the *Epic of Gilgamesh,* was explicitly called a "boat" (A. George, *Gilgamesh*, 11:24, p. 89). Despite several such differences, significant parallels to Noah's ark and flood can be made (C. Westermann, *Genesis 1-11*, pp. 418-421).

844   R. M. Zlotowitz, *et al.*, *Bereishis*, p. 230; cf. U. Cassuto, *Noah to Abraham*, pp. 60-61. Certain features of the ark's construction, including its single opening, recall the Jaredite barges (H. W. Nibley, *Lehi 1988*, pp. 359-379)—and, for that matter, Adam's Cave of Treasures (see *Excursus 53: Comparative Explorations, The Cave of Treasures*, p. 669).

845   See *Figure E54-2*, p. 696. See also *Excursus 16: The Role of Revelation in Temple Building*, p. 561.

846   J. Dunn, *et al.*, *Commentary*, p. 44.

847   V. P. Hamilton, *Genesis*, p. 280.

848   J. W. Wevers, *Notes*, Genesis 6:14, p. 83.

849   C. Westermann, *Genesis 1-11*, p. 421.

850   See *Endnote 6-36*, p. 502.

851   R. Alter, *Five Books*, Genesis 6:14, p. 41; K. L. Barker, *Zondervan*, Genesis 6:14, p. 14.

852   A 4500-year-old Cypress tree stands on the grounds of the Grand Mosque of Abarqu, near the village Shiraz in Iran's southeastern province of Yazd. This was formerly the site of a Zoroastrian temple. Indeed, Zoroaster himself is said to have planted a cypress at the temple of Khorasan (M. Boyce, *Zoroastrians*, p. 158).

3-58   Compare the Mandaean *masiqta* (death rite), where a dove (called *bai* or *ba*) is sacrificed and a fragment of its flesh is used to signify the ascent of the departing spirit.[853]

3-59   For example, frustrated by the lack of geographical consistency in the description of the four rivers of vv. 11-14, Stordalen adopts a contrarian view with respect to the direction of flow of the rivers. He adopts a map resembling the Babylonian world map where the rivers are seen as running out of the Garden, into the "Cosmic Sea" surrounding the circular disk of presumed biblical cosmography, and "from the four cosmic corners [of the disk] towards the terrestrial center" of the earth.[854]

3-60   Though he consciously avoided giving the impression that his was his final point of view, Eyring favored prevailing scientific opinions about the origin of man. In 1971, he wrote to a correspondent: "… the evidence seems to me to point to the existence of pre-Adamic man… Our scriptural accounts are brief and don't seem to me to rule out these possibilities."[855] Elsewhere, Eyring stated, albeit with characteristic tentativeness: "Some people object to the slightest hint of being related to the rest of the animal kingdom, particularly the hairy apes… I've never had that particular aversion. In fact, I've kind of enjoyed what little I've seen of them…. I'd be content to discover that I share a common heritage with them, so long as God is at the controls."[856]

Regarding Eyring's "unequivocally equivocal position on evolution," one person recalled discussing the problems of early man with him in his office: "I then asked, 'How do you believe it was?' You replied, 'I believe whichever way it turns out to have actually been.'"[857]

3-61   An excellent discussion of this line-upon-line process can be found in D. B. Parkinson, *Received*, pp. 262-270.

3-62   Henry Eyring recalled a conversation with Albert Einstein relating to this topic: "On another occasion, Professor Hugh S. Taylor and I were taking Professor Einstein and an Israeli chemistry professor to Professor Einstein's home in a car. The subject turned to religion and I explained to Professor Einstein our LDS belief in a preexistence. He immediately asked about the preexistence of animals. I explained our belief that everything was created spiritually before its temporal existence. This interested him, but the conversation was terminated at the end of the journey."[858]

3-63   Results of DNA studies seem to indicate that both the most recent common male and female ancestors of mankind each lived long before the Fall of Adam and Eve[859]—or, for that matter, at a more distant period than Noah, whose sons traditionally have been understood to be the sole male survivors of the Flood.[860] The series of questions Nibley raises here are with an eye to finding scriptural support for surviving non-Noachian lineages that would help explain such scientific findings. These would be neither descendants of Noah nor of Adam but rather contemporaries whose descendants presumably mixed with the Adamic lineage. Of relevance is the argument by Parr that promised blessings from patriarchs such as Abraham, Isaac, and Jacob are of necessity driven by covenant and lineal descent, not by genetics, since specific "nuclear DNA finding its way from any one of these progenitors to any descendent of today is extremely unlikely from a biological perspective."[861] Happily, the promises made to the faithful covenant posterity are not about inheriting fragments of Abrahamic DNA, but rather about receiving a fulness of Abrahamic blessings, assured through faithfulness.

3-64   Note that OT2 reads "from a remnant of his seed should come all nations."[862] It is not known whether this change was made under the direction of the Prophet or made by one of his associates as the record was being prepared for publication.

---

853   E. S. Drower, *Adam*, pp. 8, 32.

854   T. Stordalen, *Echoes*, pp. 284-285, 299. For yet another perspective, see J. S. Major, *Heaven*, pp. 156-158 for a description of the four cosmic rivers in early Chinese Han thought.

855   H. J. Eyring, *Mormon Scientist*, p. 125.

856   H. Eyring, *Reflections*, p. 60.

857   H. J. Eyring, *Mormon Scientist*, p. 228.

858   H. Eyring, *Faith*, p. 178. See H. J. Eyring, *Mormon Scientist*, p. 263 for an alternative account of what must have been the same incident.

859   E.g., D. N. Brems, *Divine Engineering*, pp. 128-129; F. S. Collins, *Language*, p. 126.

860   See D. E. Jeffery, *Noah's Flood* and C. M. White, *et al.*, *Noachian Flood Story* for considered LDS perspectives on reconciling current scientific findings with the Genesis flood story. See also J. A. Widtsoe, *Flood*; Morris S. Petersen, *Earth*, p. 432.

861   R. Parr, *Missing*, pp. 94-97. See also D. J. Meldrum, *Children* 2003; D. J. Meldrum *et al.*, *Children JBMS*; D. J. Meldrum, *et al.*, *Children 2007*; T. D. Stephens, *Tree of Life*.

862   S. H. Faulring, *et al.*, *Original Manuscripts*, p. 621.

FIGURE 4-1. *Expulsion from the Garden of Eden, 1828*
Thomas Cole, 1801-1848

So I drove out the man, and I placed at the east of the Garden of Eden, cherubim and a flaming sword, which turned every way to keep the way of the tree of life (Moses 4:31). In his characteristic epic style, Thomas Cole depicted Adam and Eve being expelled from the lush garden to live in the relative wilderness of the mortal world. The image of the tiny couple is almost lost in the wide expanse of the landscape, emphasizing the greatness of the power of God and the grandeur of His Creation as compared with the forced humility of fallen mankind. The light emanating from the Garden contrasts with the darkness of the way ahead for Adam and Eve.

MOSES 4

The Fall

Overview

FOLLOWING a rapid sweep across the vast panorama of the Creation and the Garden of Eden in Moses 1-3, the narrative slows to a more measured pace at the beginning of Moses 4—and with good reason, for it is at this point that the whole purpose of Creation begins to unfold. A statement attributed to Cardinal John Henry Newman sums up a message that can be taken from the juxtaposition of the accounts of the Creation and the Fall: "It is better that the whole universe disappear than that one little, little lie be spoken."[1] In other words, the moral significance of the choice made in Eden—and of similar choices we make on a daily basis—outweighs in importance the entire amoral universe.

The pivotal nature of Adam and Eve's choice is made clear in the structure of Moses 4 itself. Wenham sees the corresponding chapter in Genesis as a "masterpiece of palistrophic writing, the mirror-image [chiastic] style, whereby the first scene matches the last, the second the penultimate and so on: ABCDC'B'A'... Not only does the literary structure move in and out in this fashion, but so does the action: it commences outside the Garden, the dialogues are conducted within the Garden, and the decisive act of disobedience takes place at its very center."[2] In this way, the focal theme of "opposition in all things"[3] reveals itself in both the content and the structure of the account.

A modified version of Wenham's schema, as applied to the book of Moses, follows:

    A. 3:5-17: Adam and Eve are placed in the Garden and are given a commandment
        B. 3:18-25: The spiritual order of relationships before the Fall
        (4:1-4: Digression on Satan's fall)
            C. 4:5-11: The dialogue between Eve and the serpent
                D. 4:12-14: Adam and Eve transgress the commandment
            C.' 4:15-19: The dialogue between Adam, Eve, and God
        B.' 4:20-27: The temporal order of relationships after the Fall
    A.' 4:28-31: Adam and Eve are driven out of the Garden

---

1   J. M. Bradshaw, *AHK Notes*.

2   G. J. Wenham, *Genesis 1-15*, p. 51. See *Endnote 4-1*, p. 298.

3   2 Nephi 2:11.

Scenes A and A' feature God as the only actor and feature a vocabulary that is unique to this part of Genesis—"in the east" "tree of life" "garden of Eden" "till" and "guard." "In scene [A] man is made from 'the dust of the [ground] and placed in the garden,[4] whereas in the final scene man is driven from the Garden, by implication back to the dust of the [ground] from which he was taken."[5] In scenes B and B', God is the principal actor and the scenes are both "concerned with relationships between man and the rest of Creation"—first the ideal situation, then, by way of contrast, the situation after the Fall. "Finally both scenes end with statements about woman's role as wife and mother[6] and about clothing."[7] Scenes C and C' are dialogues about the eating of the fruit and its consequences that both take place in the center of the Garden. The three comments about the tree made by the serpent match the three questions God poses to Adam and Eve.[8] Scene D stands apart—Adam and Eve "are alone: neither God nor the serpent is mentioned… The "crucial words 'and he ate' are… sandwiched between a twofold mention of the desired effects of the fruit: its ability to open eyes and to give knowledge."[9]

The Everlasting Covenant

Similar in function to the digression of Moses 3:5, the narrative aside of Moses 4:1-4 temporarily interrupts the flow of events in order to provide the interpretive framework for the story that follows.[10] We learn that the real beginning of things was not in the first moment of Creation, but rather in a series of preparatory events with a premortal covenant at its crux. The Prophet Joseph Smith explained: "Everlasting covenant was made between three personages before the organization of this earth, and relates to their dispensation of things to men on the earth; these personages, according to Abraham's record, are called God the first, the Creator, God the second, the Redeemer, and God the third, the witness or Testator."[11]

Textual traces alluding to an everlasting covenant with universal scope have been explored by scholars. According to Murray, the central feature of this "cosmic covenant" was: "… a belief which ancient Israel shared with neighboring cultures… in a divinely willed order harmoniously linking heaven and earth. In Israelite tradition this was established at Creation, when the cosmic elements were fixed and bound to maintain the order… Human collaboration in this task was effected by maintaining justice with mercy and by ritual actions, in which kings played the leading part."[12]

Barker conjectures that a clue to the relationship between "creation" and "covenant" can be found in the etymology of the two terms:

> The word *bara´* is similar in sound and form to the word for covenant, *berith*, and the Hebrew dictionary suggests that the root meaning of "covenant" is "to bind." This similarity of the words for covenant-and-binding and the uniquely divine creative activity leads me to suspect that is the key to the older Creation story, that the words had been related. [The first or "invisible" creation] was a process of binding into bonds, engraving limits and definitions, and then using them to order the visible creation. When the Lord spoke to Job from the whirlwind and

---

4   Moses 3:7-8.
5   G. J. Wenham, *Genesis 1-15*, p. 50. See Moses 4:31; cf. 4:25.
6   Moses 3:24; 4:26.
7   G. J. Wenham, *Genesis 1-15*, p. 50. See Moses 3:25; 4:27.
8   G. J. Wenham, *Genesis 1-15*, p. 51.
9   *Ibid.*, p. 51.
10   See *Endnote 4-2*, p. 298.
11   J. Smith, Jr., *Teachings*, 16 May 1841, p. 190. See *Endnote 4-3*, p. 298.
12   R. Murray, *Cosmic*, p. xx. See *Endnote 4-4*, p. 298.

reminded him that he did not have the wisdom of those who had witnessed the Creation, He said: "Who… shut in the sea… and prescribed bounds [my "engraved thing"] for it… and said, 'Thus far shall you come, and no farther…'?"[13] "Can you bind the chains of the Pleiades, or loose the cords of Orion?"[14] "Do you know the ordinances ["engraved things"] of the heavens? Can you establish their rule [*mstr*] on the earth?",[15] a word which does not appear elsewhere in the Hebrew Scriptures. This is significant as it clearly refers to the correspondence between earth and heaven…"[16]

FIGURE 4-2. *God Creating the Universe, ca. 1794/1824*
William Blake, 1757-1827

SEE COLOR PLATE 4-2.

When he prepared the heavens, I was there: when he engraved a circle upon the face of the deep:… when he set for the sea its engraved mark… when he engraved the foundations of the earth.[1] Joseph Smith anticipated with great longing the day when he, like the author of Proverbs, would be able to "gaze upon eternal wisdom engraven upon the heavens."[2] Themes relating to these primordial "bounds" also appear in the Doctrine and Covenants[3] and in other statements by Joseph Smith.[4]

Perhaps the best-known illustration by Blake, this picture often appears with the inaccurate title of "The Ancient of Days." The solitary posture of the form seems to have been prescribed by Milton, who wrote of the moment when the Almighty "took the golden Compasses prepar'd… to circumscribe This Universe, and all created things: One foot he centred, and the other turn'd Round through the vast profunditie obscure."[5]

Although the tools of an architect are frequently used in medieval depictions of the Creation to portray the geometry of the heavens, seas, and earth, Blake also may have been attracted to this symbol because of his acquaintance with Freemasonry while he was an apprentice engraver.[6] An associate of Blake said that the artist saw the vision of this image hovering "at the top of his staircase; and he [was] frequently… heard to say, that it made a more powerful impression upon his mind than all he had ever been visited by."[7] He worked and reworked this image continually, reportedly returning to it for a final effort in the last hours before his death.[8]

In the *Preludium* of Blake's *Europe*, for which a version of this image forms the frontispiece, he asks, "And who shall bind the infinite with an eternal band? To compass it with swaddling bands?"[9] In Blake's mythology, Urizen—representing the "horizon" or "your reason," with the emblem of the Eye—was identified with his view of Jehovah as a wrathful, law-giving creator-God. In another one of Blake's prints, he pictures Isaac Newton using "the compasses in the same sense as a symbol of a defining, limiting creation by the reason unenlightened by the imagination."[10] Similarly, Urizen was portrayed as "a being who began in light, even though he ended in restriction, privation and dread. He may be able to cast off those States in which he has resided, and thus reclaim his true self, his true glory."[11]

---

1   Proverbs 8:27-29, following the translation of M. Barker, *Temple Theology*, p. 39; cf. Job 26:10.
2   J. Smith, Jr., *Documentary History*, 27 November 1832, 1:299.
3   E.g., D&C 88:34-38, 42-45; 121:30-32; 132:5, 11.
4   J. Smith, Jr., *Words*, 9 October 1843, p. 253; J. Smith, Jr., *Teachings*, 20 March 1842, pp. 197-198.
5   J. Milton, *Paradise Lost*, 7:224-228, p. 145; compare Blake's *Urizen* (1794), where he: "… formed golden compasses / And began to explore the Abyss" (W. Blake, *Illuminated*, 7:8, p. 428); Chesterton called the figure "a monstrously muscular old man, with hair and beard like a snowstorm, but with limbs like young trees" (*William Blake*, p. 55).
6   P. Ackroyd, *Blake*, p. 377.
7   *Ibid.*, p. 378.
8   See *Endnote 4-82*, p. 321.
9   W. Blake, *Illuminated*, 2:13-14, p. 422.
10   M. Butlin, *Blake*, pp. 52-53; cf. W. Blake, *Illuminated Blake*, pp. 155-156.
11   P. Ackroyd, *Blake*, p. 379. See *Excursus 20: The Circle and the Square*, p. 571 and *Excursus 50: Fu Xi and Nü Gua*, p. 654.

---

13   Job 38:8-11.
14   Job 38:31.
15   Job 38:33. See also G. W. E. Nickelsburg, *et al.*, *1 Enoch*, 69:16-25, pp. 90-91.
16   M. Barker, *Temple Theology*, p. 44. See Matthew 6:10.

FIGURE 4-3. *The Third Day of Creation, ca. 1504*
Hieronymus Bosch, ca. 1450-1516

SEE COLOR PLATE 4-3.

… the worlds were framed by the word of God.[1] Since ancient times, the circle and the square have been ubiquitous symbols of creation, the cosmos, and the covenants that relate them.[2] Though not a thoroughly accurate translation of the underlying Greek, the KJV reading of Hebrews 11:3 aptly evokes an image of a square enclosing a circle, as in the work by Bosch at left. Moreover, the KJV rendering of the Greek term *katartizo* as "framing" resonates in the modern ear as the sort of creation act that relies on the tools of the architect and the carpenter to circumscribe and bound the thing framed. The Greek term translated worlds is *aiones*—literally "eons" or "ages," but here signifying the whole universe of space and time.[3]

"In Bosch's image… the Creator [upper left] is outside the terrestrial sphere, with the inscription 'He said and it was done; he commanded and they were created,' and in a deliberate ambiguity the world is portrayed both as it was originally and as it was restored after the Flood (the two events being typologically connected)."[4]

---

1   Hebrews 11:3.
2   See *Excursus 20: The Circle and the Square,* p. 571.
3   F. F. Bruce, *Hebrews,* pp. 47-279.
4   D. Maclagan, *Myths,* pp. 34-35.

It is significant that this premortal engraving of bounds, limits, and ordinances not only pervades all of Creation, but also is said to be traced on the very garment of God: "And it is every part engraved from within and from without JHWH JHWH."[17]

Related themes appear in the Doctrine and Covenants[18] and in statements by Joseph Smith. For example, in 1842 the Prophet stated that "God set the sun, the moon, and the stars in the heavens, and gave them their laws, conditions, and bounds, which they cannot pass, except by His commandments; they all move in perfect harmony in their sphere and order; and are as lights, wonders and signs unto us. The sea also has its bounds which it cannot pass."[19] He also said that knowledge about "the organization of the spiritual and heavenly worlds, and of spiritual and heavenly beings" and the "limits and bounds" that were irrevocably and "voluntarily subscribed to by themselves… can, and may be known, through the revelations of God in the way of his ordinances, and in answer to prayer."[20]

Just as the limits and bounds prepared prior to the physical creation were irrevocable, so also these "[o]rdinances instituted in the heavens before the foundation of the world, in the priesthood, for the salvation of men, are not to be altered or changed."[21] God said, respecting the obligations that He takes upon Himself conditional on our obedience to covenants: "I… am bound when ye do what I say; but when ye do not what I say, ye have no promise."[22]

---

17   *Hekhalot Rabbati* 3:4, cited in *Testament of Job,* p. 866 n. 48h; cf. Isaiah 49:16, Zechariah 13:6. See *Endnote 4-6,* p. 298.
18   E.g., D&C 88:34-38, 42-45; 121:30-32; 132:5, 11.
19   J. Smith, Jr., *Teachings,* 20 March 1842, pp. 197-198.
20   J. Smith, Jr., *Words,* 9 October 1843, p. 253.
21   J. Smith, Jr., *Teachings,* 11 June 1843, p. 308; cf. D&C 124:33, 40-41; 132:5, 11, 28; J. Smith, Jr., *Words,* 22 January 1843, p. 159; 11 June 1843, pp. 213, 215; 9 October 1843, p. 254; 12 May 1844, p. 368; B. Young, *8 October 1854,* p. 89.
22   D&C 82:10.

FIGURE 4-4. *Masjid al-Haram at Night*

The photo shows the sacred mosque of Mecca during the Islamic month of *Dhu al-Hijjah*, the peak period of *hajj* (= pilgrimage).[1] As part of the ritual of *tawaf*, hajj pilgrims enact the symbolism of the circle and the square as they form concentric rings around the rectangular *Ka'bah* (= cube). Their counterclockwise circumambulation is performed seven times to demonstrate "the unity of the believers in the worship of the One God," and to commemorate similar events in the lives of Muhammad and earlier prophets. Islamic tradition says that near this location Adam had been shown *al-Baytu l-Ma'mur* (the worship place of angels, sometimes called the "Visited House"), which was directly above the *Ka'bah* in heaven,[2] and that he was commanded to build a house for God in Mecca where he could, in likeness of the angels, "circumambulate... and offer prayer...[3] There [God] would offer him Iblis [= the Devil[4]] to stone as the angels had done when [Iblis had] refused to prostrate himself" before Adam.[5] Tradition recounts that the first house of God had been built by the angels 2,000 years before Adam,[6] and that since the time of Adam it was destroyed and rebuilt many times by prophets and other notables,[7] including Ibrahim (Abraham) and Ishmael. A "diamond of paradise"[8] that was "whiter than snow"[9] was said to have been given to Adam after the Fall. Later, however, it turned black because of the misdeeds of mankind.[10] The Black Stone (*al-hajar al-aswad*) associated with Adam, representing the primordial covenant between God and mankind,[11] is now located on the southeast corner of the *Ka'bah*, thus identifying the instrument of seership with both the foundation stone of creation and of the sacred structure.[12] The sacred rock beneath the Muslim Dome of the Rock (*Qubbat al-Sakhra*), built on the Temple Mount in Jerusalem, plays a similar role for that monument.[13]

---

1   See R. C. Martin, *Encyclopedia*, 2:529-533; G. D. Newby, *Encyclopedia*, pp. 71-72.
2   G. Weil, *Legends*, p. 83.
3   S. A. Ashraf, *Inner*, p. 125. See *Endnote 4-7*, p. 299.
4   From Greek *diabolos* (A. al-Tha'labi, *Lives*, p. 8 n. 12; cf. p. 56 and p. 56 n. 17).
5   M. al-Kisa'i, *Tales*, p. 61; cf. al-Tabari, *Creation*, I:123-124, pp. 294-295; A. al-Tha'labi, *Lives*, p. 60; M. Ibn Ishaq ibn Yasar, *Making*, p. 38; I. Ibn Kathir, *Stories*, pp. 23-27; B. M. Wheeler, *Prophets*, pp. 30-32. See *Excursus 8: The Origin and Premortal Existence of Human Spirits*, p. 540. See *Endnote 4-8*, p. 299.
6   M. al-Kisa'i, *Tales*, pp. 61, 62, 66.
7   G. Weil, *Legends*, p. 42; cf. H. W. Nibley, *Drama*, p. 8. See also B. M. Wheeler, *Mecca*, pp. 45-46.
8   G. Weil, *Legends*, p. 83.
9   al-Tabari, *Creation*, 1:132-133, p. 303; A. al-Tha'labi, *Lives*, p. 61.
10   al-Tabari in G. D. Newby, *Encyclopedia*, al-hajar al-aswad, p. 71; B. M. Wheeler, *Prophets*, p. 27; cf. H. W. Nibley, *Message 2005*, p. 196; G. Weil, *Legends*, pp. 41-42; al-Tabari, *Creation*, 1:122, p. 293; 1:131, pp. 301-302; Revelation 2:17; D&C 130:10-11; *Commentary* 1:27-b, p. 62; and 3:19-b, p. 177. See *Endnote 4-9*, p. 299. See *Excursus 53: Comparative Explorations: Jewish and Christian Analogues*, p. 679.
11   M. Chebel, *Symboles*, p. 60.
12   H. W. Nibley, *Message 2005*, pp. 195-196. See Matthew 16:16-19, JST John 1:42, and *Figure 3-10*, p. 146.
13   W. J. Hamblin, *et al.*, *Temple*, pp. 140-145. See also G. Strathearn, *et al.*, *Great Mosque*.

The annual Day of Atonement was given to ancient Israel in order to renew the everlasting covenant that has been repeatedly broken by man.[23] The power to repair, bind, or seal

---

23   Isaiah 24:4-6; D&C 1:11-16; G. W. E. Nickelsburg, *et al.*, *1 Enoch*, 65:10-11, 69:1-25, pp. 85, 90-91. See *Endnote 4-10*, p. 301.

was vested in the high priest, whose role was to secure the bonds of the covenant. The high priest himself represented the seal or bond which held the covenant in place, the one who wore the Name with power to bind or loose the covenant bond on earth and in heaven.[24] The temple rites of the Old Testament anticipated fulfillment in the Atonement of Jesus Christ, the "mediator of the new covenant."[25]

The great premortal covenant had as its central purpose to provide the possibility of exaltation to the spirits that then lived in God's presence. Wrote the Prophet Joseph Smith: "God himself, finding he was in the midst of spirits and glory, because he was more intelligent, saw proper to institute laws whereby the rest could have a privilege to advance like himself. The relationship we have with God places us in a situation to advance in knowledge. He has power to institute laws to instruct the weaker intelligences, that they may be exalted with himself."[26] Bushman comments with the observation that "God did not present himself as sovereign but as teacher and father, offering to help the intelligences grow."[27]

Mankind is invited to join in the great collaborative process of salvation and exaltation through what is known in our day as the "New and Everlasting Covenant."[28] In fact, writes Barker: "The great oath, the cosmic covenant and the eternal [i.e., new and everlasting] covenant are all the same thing…"[29]

The Grand Councils

An unsigned editorial in the *Times and Seasons* explained that a "council of heaven[30] was had among the gods in the eternal world pertaining to… Creation, before ever [God's creatures] were formed… and by him who comprehends the end from the beginning and before whom, and with whom, the present, the past, and the future are one eternal now."[31] Even at that time, God "fully understood… their organization, habits, propensities, the object of their creation, the position they would take in the order of that creation, and how, and by what means they would be made happy, and increase his glory."[32]

As part of the deliberations of the councils, the work to be performed was explained and the premortal spirits were organized and foreordained to help carry it out.[33] "Though the plan from first to last is entirely God's own," explains Nibley, "he discusses it with others, 'consulting the souls of the righteous before deciding to create the world,'[34] not because he needs their advice, but because the plan concerns them and requires their maximum participation in it."[35] As part of the proceedings of these councils, God "agree[d] to form them tabernacles"[36]—i.e., physical bodies, and also to effect a physical creation resulting in

---

24   M. Barker, *Temple Theology*, p. 50; cf. Matthew 16:19. See *Endnote 4-11*, p. 302.

25   Hebrews 12:24, D&C 107:19. See also M. Barker, *Atonement*; M. Barker, *Revelation*; M. Barker, *Great High Priest*.

26   J. Smith, Jr., *Teachings*, 7 April 1844, p. 354.

27   R. L. Bushman, *Mormonism*, p. 73.

28   See the overview of Moses 5, pp. 340-344 and *Excursus 48: The Nature and Scope of Premortal Covenants*, p. 649.

29   M. Barker, *Lost*, pp. 80-81. See *Endnote 4-12*, p. 302.

30   See *Endnote 4-13*, p. 302.

31   See *Endnote 4-14,* p. 302.

32   *The Gathering*, pp. 407-408; cf. J. Smith, Jr., *Teachings*, 15 April 1842, p. 220.

33   Abraham 3:22-23; D&C 138:38-39; see the overview of Moses 3, pp. 136-139 and *Excursus 9: The Premortal Organization of the Human Family*, p. 544.

34   See J. Neusner, *Genesis Rabbah 1*, 8:7:1, p. 80.

35   H. W. Nibley, *Treasures*, p. 174.

36   J. Smith, Jr., *Words*, 28 March 1841, p. 68. See *Endnote 4-15,* p. 303.

an earth where these embodied spirits could live as mortal beings. The book of Abraham records that "one among them that was like unto God… said unto those who were with him: We will go down, for there is space there, and we will make of these materials, and we will make an earth whereon these may dwell;[37] And we will prove them herewith, to see if they will do all things whatsoever the Lord their God shall command them."[38]

It was known in advance not only that Adam and Eve would take the forbidden fruit, but also that each member of the family of man—Jesus Christ excepted—would yield to sin "in similitude of Adam's transgression."[39] Thus, a Savior was required to bear the weight of an "infinite and eternal" atonement.[40] Jesus Christ, already known by all to be God's "Beloved and Chosen from the beginning"[41] and having the "right by inheritance,"[42] was the only One who could adequately respond to God's question: "Whom shall I send?" Indeed, Brent Top rightly observes that this question was intended as "an invitation for Jesus to publicly and voluntarily accept the calling and appointment that was his birthright as the Firstborn, the Preeminent One.[43] It was a call for our commitment and common consent rather than a request for résumés."[44]

Both the nature of the premortal councils and their themes of discussion are witnessed in extracanonical sources. For example, according to Nibley, a major message of *Jubilees* was to show that the annual assemblies of Israel for great festivals were "the ritual repetition, not merely of the gathering at the foot of Sinai when Moses brought them together to counsel them, but specifically of the great assembly that met above at the Creation of the world."[45] Citing the Jewish wisdom writings of *Ben Sirach*, he argued that while Noah and others participated in a *renewal* of the eternal covenant, its first establishment was a universal event to which all mankind were eyewitnesses in the beginning, when God "endowed them [i.e., the human race to-be] with the life-giving law. He established a perpetual covenant with them and revealed to them his decrees. Their eyes saw his glorious majesty, and their ears heard the glory of his voice."[46]

Additional Jewish texts broaden the concept of participation in these premortal councils to include others beyond the more commonly discussed "angels" or "sons of God." For example, *Genesis Rabbah* records that God "took counsel with the souls of the righteous before creating the world"[47] and, again, that it was with the participation of the "souls of the righteous" who dwelt with God that He "decided to create the world."[48] "Specifically named as being present are Adam, Noah, Abraham, and Moses."[49] Likewise, the Gnostic *Second Treatise of the Great Seth* represents Christ as speaking about how "the whole multitude of

---

37   See *Endnote 4-16*, p. 303.

38   Abraham 3:24-25. See *Excursus 23: The Roles of Christ, Adam, and Michael*, p. 582. See *Endnote 4-17*, p. 303.

39   Romans 5:14.

40   Alma 34:10-16, 2 Nephi 9:5-26.

41   Moses 4:2.

42   J. Smith, Jr., 6 April 1843, as reported in E. England, *Laub*, p. 22. See *Endnote 4-18*, p. 303.

43   Psalm 89:27; Colossians 1:15; Romans 8:29; Hebrews 1:6; D&C 93:21.

44   B. L. Top, *Life Before*, p. 109.

45   H. W. Nibley, *Expanding 1992*, p. 192; H. W. Nibley, *Teachings of the PGP*, 6, p. 72; cf. H. W. Nibley, *Expanding 1992*, p. 186. *Commentary* 1:25-e, p. 60. On the year-rite, see *Commentary* 1:25-e, p. 60; 5:47-a, p. 395; *Excursus 35: Lamech's "Sword Song"*, p. 612; and the overview of Moses 6, p. 458. See *Endnote 4-21*, p. 304.

46   S Sandmel, *et al.*, *Ecclesiasticus*, 17:11-13, p. 133.

47   J. Neusner, *Genesis Rabbah 1*, 8:7:1, p. 80.

48   H. Freedman, *et al.*, *Midrash*, Ruth 2:3, 7:28. See *Endnote 4-19*, p. 303.

49   J. F. McConkie, *Premortal*, p. 180, citing a study by Wernick.

the Assembly came together" "before the foundation of the world."[50] In an earlier passage, the text has Christ saying:

> "Let us gather an assembly together. Let us visit that creation of his. Let us send someone forth in it, just as he visited [the] Ennoias, the regions below. And I said these things to the whole multitude of the multitudinous assembly of the rejoicing Majesty. The whole house of the Father of Truth rejoiced that I am the one who is from them. I produced thought about the Ennoias which came out of the undefiled Spirit, about the descent upon the water, that is, the regions below. And they all had a single mind, since it is out of one. They charged me since I was willing. I came forth to reveal the glory to my kindred and my fellow spirits."[51]

A significant passage relating to the Savior's voluntary decision to redeem mankind is found in the early Christian *Discourse on Abbaton* where He describes the creation of Adam:

> [The Father] took the clay from the hand of the angel, and made Adam in Our image and likeness, and He left him lying for forty days and forty nights without putting breath into him. And He sighed over him, saying, "If I put breath into this man he will suffer many pains." "Put breath into him; and I will be his advocate." And My Father said to me, "If I put breath into him, Thou must go down into the world and to suffer many pains for him, before Thou shalt have redeemed him and brought him back to his primal state." And I said: "Put breath into him, and I will be his advocate, and I will go down into the world, and will fulfill Thy Covenant."[52]

A similar theme is attested in the Jewish *Pesikta Rabbati*, where God tells the Messiah what will befall him if he chooses to suffer for the sins of mankind:

> "There are souls that have been put away with thee under My throne, and it is their sins which will bend thee down under a yoke of iron and make thee like a calf whose eyes grow dim with suffering, and will choke thy spirit as with a yoke; because of the sins of these souls thy tongue will cleave to the roof of my mouth. Art thou willing to endure such things?…"

> The Messiah will say: "Master of the universe, with joy in my soul and gladness in my heart I take this suffering upon myself, provided that not one person in Israel perish;[53] that not only those who are alive be saved in my days, but that also those who are dead, who died from the days of Adam up to the time of redemption; and that not only these be saved in my days, but also those who died as abortions [i.e., stillborns, miscarriages, and deliberately aborted fetuses]; and that not only these be saved in my days, but all those whom Thou thoughtest to create [i.e., evidently as mortals] but were not created. Such are the things I desire, and for these I am ready to take upon myself [whatsoever Thou decreest]."[54]

The Plan of Salvation formulated in the premortal councils required voluntary acceptance by all those who would participate in it. The Prophet Joseph Smith stated that: "At the first organization in heaven we were all present and saw the Savior chosen and appointed, and the plan of salvation made, and we sanctioned it."[55] Our sanction of the plan seems to have included covenants of obedience and sacrifice relating to its conditions and consequences.[56]

The Savior's willingness to undergo all that the atonement required evoked great awe and profound gratitude. "When the plan was announced to the assembled hosts, and the full

50   J. A. Gibbons *et al.*, *Great Seth*, 65:33-36, p. 369.

51   *Ibid.*

52   Timothy of Alexandria, *Abbaton*, p. 198. See also E. A. W. Budge, *Cave*, p. 55; R. M. Nelson, *Creation*, p. 84; cf. al-Tabari, *Creation*, 1:91, p. 26.

53   Cf. John 17:12.

54   W. G. Braude, *Rabbati*, 36:1, 2:678-679.

55   J. Smith, Jr., *Words*, 5 January 1841, p. 60.

56   See *Excursus 48: The Nature and Scope of Premortal Covenants*, p. 649.

MOSES 4

Figure 4-5. *When the Morning Stars Sang Together, 1820*
William Blake, 1757-1827

See Color Plate 4-5.

Where wast thou when I laid the foundations of the earth?... When the morning stars sang together, and all the sons of God shouted for joy?[1] Upheld by God's outstretched arms, the stars and angels loudly voice their praises.[2] Beneath His arms, the sun-god Helios (or, alternatively, Logos, the horseman[3]) and Selene (or, alternatively, Wisdom, leading away *Leviathan*) represent day and night[4]— one of the many oppositions to which mankind is constantly subjected.[5] Shut out from the glorious scenes on high, "Job, his wife and his friends kneel in a distinct, cave-like Earth below."[6]

The black and white etching of this illustration adds "small sketches of the first six days of creation in the margin (up to but not including the creation of man) and in the center, above God, [Blake] drew the angels which embody seventh-day consciousness."[7] In the top margin of this version "is a quotation from Job 38:31: 'Canst thou bind the sweet influences of Pleiades or loose the bands of Orion?': the two constellations are represented by the angels accompanying the stars in the upper corners. St. Gregory, commenting on this passage, had equated the Pleiades with the Gospel and Orion with the Law. Blake is therefore asking if one can bind the Gospels, [as he saw Job as having] attempted by following the rigid tenets of orthodox religions, or loose the Mosaic Law, as Jesus did to achieve Man's salvation."[8]

1   Job 38:4, 7.
2   In praise of this depiction, Chesterton writes: "When [Blake] gets the thing right he gets it suddenly and perfectly right... We feel that the sons of God might really shout for joy at the excellence of their own portrait" (G. K. Chesterton, *William Blake*, p. 21).
3   M. Barker, *Temple Theology*, pp. 76, 78.
4   M. Barker, *Angels*, p. 174; M. Butlin, *Blake*, p. 100.
5   2 Nephi 2:11.
6   M. Butlin, *Blake*, p. 100. See *Excursus 53: Comparative Explorations of the Mysteries*, p. 663.
7   S. Mitchell, *Job*, p. xxi.
8   M. Butlin, *Blake*, p. 102.

scope and magnanimity of it dawned upon them, they burst into spontaneous shouts of joy and joined in a hymn of praise and thanksgiving, the Morning-song of Creation, which remains to this day the archetype of hymns, the great *acclamatio*, the primordial nucleus of all liturgy."[57]

Rebellion in Heaven

The Father's plan was not accepted by all. Lucifer, "an angel of God who was in authority in the presence of God" and "a son of the morning," "rebelled against God, and sought to take the kingdom of our God and his Christ."[58] The Prophet explained: "The contention in heaven was—Jesus said there would be certain souls that would not be saved; and the Devil said he could save them all, and laid his plans before the grand council, who gave their vote in favor of Jesus Christ. So the Devil rose up in rebellion against God, and was cast down, with all who put up their heads for him."[59] Elder Joseph Fielding Smith explained that as a result of this rebellion a third part of the premortal spirits were "denied the privilege of

57   H. W. Nibley, *Treasures*, p. 173; cf. H. W. Nibley, *Expanding 1992*, pp. 191-192. See *Endnote 4-20*, p. 303.
58   D&C 76:25-26, 28. See also Isaiah 14:4-23, Revelation 12:3-9, D&C 29:36-45, Abraham 3:27-28; cf. Daniel 8:10-12, Ezekiel 28:11-19, Luke 10:18, F. I. Andersen, *2 Enoch*, 29:4-5, p. 148; L. Ginzberg, *Legends*, 1:62-64, 5:84-86 n. 35; and *Excursus 21: The Power and Premortal Status of Satan*, p. 575. See *Endnote 4-23*, p. 305.
59   J. Smith, Jr., *Teachings*, 7 April 1844, p. 357. See *Endnote 4-24*, p. 305.

FIGURE 4-6. *Satan in His Original Glory, ca. 1805*
William Blake, 1757-1827

SEE COLOR PLATE 4-6.

Thou wast perfect in thy ways from the day that thou was created, till iniquity was found in thee.[1] The fall of the king of Tyre in Ezekiel's lamentation is frequently interpreted as having been typed on the rebellion of Satan.[2] Blake's rendition is derived from a reading of v. 14 of the Latin *Vulgate* that sees him as the "cherub with extensive wingspan."[3] The orb and scepter symbolize the power and authority from God given before his fall from heaven.[4] He stands on the heavenly mountain, surrounded by "tiny, joyous figures embody[ing] the precious stones and beautifully crafted musical instruments mentioned in the Biblical text."[5]

To highlight Lucifer's perversity, Blake has conspicuously reversed the hands in which the emblems of monarchy are normally held. For example, in British coronation ceremonies, the sword[6] is held in the right hand so that it may be used "to stop the growth of iniquity, protect the Holy Church of God and defend widows and orphans." The Orb is meant to be held in the left hand in order to signify "the domination of Christ over the whole world."[7] In another part of the coronation ceremony, the new monarch will hold the Scepter with the Cross in the right hand as an "ensign of power and justice" and the Rod with the Dove in the left as a "symbol of equity and mercy." Prior to all these ceremonies, the monarch is "divested of... robes" and "screened from the general view" in order to be "imbued with grace" through the Archbishop's anointing with holy oil "on hand, breast and forehead."[8]

---

1   Ezekiel 28:15.
2   G. A. Anderson, *Ezekiel*, pp. 133-147; cf. Isaiah 14. In some ways, of course, the imagery is typed on Adam also.
3   Latin *cherub extentus* (R. Weber, *Vulgata*, Ezechiel 28:14, p. 1306), recalling the stretched out wings of the cherubim above the Ark (Exodus 25:20). See M. Greenberg, *Ezekiel 21-37*, pp. 583-584; D. I Block, *Ezekiel 25-48*, pp. 112-113.
4   Cf. E. A. W. Budge, *Rebellion*, pp. 294-295.
5   *Gothic*.
6   "The association of swords with royal symbolism is found in many different cultural traditions. Swords are used in various cultures as symbols of investiture. The sword and the rod, for which it is a substitute, is also used as a mark of religious authority" (B. M. Wheeler, *Mecca*, p. 43).
7   B. Nichols, *Coronation*, p. 15; contrast L. M. Hilton, *Hand*; M. von Wellnitz, *Liturgy*, p. 32, and *Figure 3-8*, p. 145.
8   B. Nichols, *Coronation*, pp. 18, 14. About ablutions and anointing of kings in other cultures, see S. D. Ricks, *et al.*, *King*, pp. 241-244, 254-255. See also *Excursus 52: Washing, Anointing, and Clothing Among Early Christians*, p. 661.

---

being born into this world and receiving mortal bodies....[60] The Lord cast them out into the earth, where they became the tempters of mankind."[61]

Satan's plan for universal salvation was rejected for two reasons. First, he "sought to destroy the agency of man";[62] and second, being jealous,[63] "selfish, ambitious, and striving to excel,"[64] he sought that God should give him His "own power."[65]

The heavenly conflict initiated by the Devil and his angels and their resultant expulsion from heaven is described in several extracanonical texts.[66] Although no direct mention is made of Satan's counterproposal to the Father's plan nor of his jealousy of the One who was chosen to redeem mankind, a vast assortment of references describe an ongoing rivalry

---

60   See *Endnote 4-25*, p. 306.
61   J. F. Smith, Jr., *Doctrines*, 1916, 1:65. See *Endnote 4-26*, p. 306.
62   Moses 4:3. See *Endnote 4-27*, p. 307.
63   B. Young, 29 December 1844, reported in E. England, *Laub*, p. 28.
64   J. Smith, Jr., *Words*, 14 May 1843, p. 201.
65   Moses 4:3. See *Endnote 4-28*, p. 307.
66   See *Endnote 4-29*, p. 307.

FIGURE 4-7. *Adam Enthroned, the Angels Prostrating Themselves before Him, 1576*

And when We said to the angels: "Prostrate yourselves before Adam," they all prostrated themselves except Satan, who in his pride refused and became an unbeliever.[1] A large Jewish, Islamic, and Christian literature describes an ongoing rivalry between the Devil and Adam. This rivalry is said to have begun at the time the newly-created Adam was presented to the hosts of heaven, when Satan refused to pay him homage. One Islamic version of the story "says that seven days after Adam's creation God sent from Paradise a throne of red gold studded with pearls, silk cloths, and a crown. Seven hundred angels who were with Iblis [the Devil, who at that time was their leader,] arranged themselves in rows, a circle within a circle around Adam."[2] His throne was placed where the *Ka'bah* is now,"[3] immediately adjacent to the Tree of Life.[4] Adam is here depicted as a "young man, richly dressed and crowned, seated on a royal throne with legs… kneeling in respect and modesty."[5] "The central theme in Islam pertaining to Adam is the gift of prophecy bestowed on him immediately after his creation, and referred to by the theologians as 'light'… The concept of light, used to symbolize God and his message through prophecy, eventually gave rise to the flame-shaped halo as the prophetic attribute. Iblis … feels endangered by the introduction of light into the material world. He refuses to submit to the newly created man, thus proclaiming the continuation of the war between Darkness and Light."[6]

1   N. J. Dawood, *Koran* 2:34, p. 13; cf. 7:11-18, 15:26-44, 17:61-65, 18:50-51, 38:67-88.
2   See *Figure* 3-6, p. 139 and *Excursus 11: The Sacred Circle*, p. 547.
3   R. Milstein, *Stories and Illustrations*, pp. 106-107.
4   See *Excursus 25: The Tree of Life as the Hidden Throne of God*, p. 591.
5   R. Milstein, *Stories and Illustrations*, p. 107.
6   *Ibid.*, p. 106; cf. *Commentary* 2:4-c, p. 101.

between Satan and Adam.[67] This rivalry is said to have begun at the time the newly-created Adam was presented to the hosts of heaven, and to have continued in a series of attempted deceptions by Satan after the couple had been evicted from Eden.[68] When Adam asked Satan why he had become his adversary, the Devil replied:

> "I came to this measure because of you, on the day on which you were created, for I went forth [i.e., was expelled from heaven] on that day. When God breathed his spirit into you, you received the likeness of his image… Then Michael [or God, in some other texts] summoned all the angels, and God said to them, 'Come bow down to god whom I made [sic].' Michael bowed first. He called me and said, 'You, too, bow down to Adam.' I said 'Go away, Michael! I shall not bow [down] to him who is posterior [younger, junior] to me, for I am former [older, senior]!'"[69]

In an early Christian text, the Savior discusses the results of Lucifer's intransigence:

> And when My Father saw [Satan's] pride and arrogance, and knew that his wickedness and evil-doing were as great as his pride, He commanded the hosts of heaven, saying: "Take away the writing from the hand of this arrogant one,[70] strip off his armor,[71] and cast him down to

67   See *Excursus 23: The Roles of Christ, Adam, and Michael*, p. 582. See *Endnote 4-30*, p. 307.
68   See the overview of Moses 5, pp. 329-338.
69   G. A. Anderson, *et al.*, *Synopsis*, Armenian recension, 12:1-14:3, pp. 15-17. See *Excursus 8: The Origin and Pre-mortal Existence of Human Spirits*, p. 540 for a discussion of Satan's claim that he is "former." See also *Excursus 23: The Roles of Christ, Adam, and Michael*, p. 582 for further discussion of this story.
70   See *Endnote 4-32*, p. 308.
71   See *Endnote 4-33*, p. 308.

FIGURE 4-8. *The Fall of the Rebel Angels, ca. 1528*
Domenico Beccafumi, ca. 1486-1551

SEE COLOR PLATE 4-8.

How art thou fallen from heaven, O Lucifer, son of the morning! How art thou cut down to the ground, which didst weaken the nations![1] This painting, Beccafumi's second version of a work commissioned by the Carmelite friars of San Niccolo al Carmine, features God presiding, with right arm raised, over the expulsion of Lucifer and his angels from heaven. God "appears as a monumental figure, seated in judgment. The bright red of his voluminous mantle and the golden hemisphere behind him ensure that this figure dominates the composition as a whole. The angelic company is organized into an orderly choir of seated figures surrounding God, with only a few of their companions engaged in expelling the rebel angels. Saint Michael has been placed much lower in the composition and acts as the principal agent between heaven and hell… [H]olding a sword above his head, he… appears in a pale pink and golden yellow tunic, tied across the chest with pale blue ribbons. Beneath him, the fallen angels recline in a series of subterranean vaults lit by sulphurous light. The Devil has been transformed into a snarling monstrous beast that has the appearance of a classical chimaera."[2]

1   Isaiah 14:12.
2   *Beccafumi.*

the earth, for his time has come. He is chief of the rebels and is like a king to them, and he commands them as a captain commands his troops; and the names of the rebels are written in the list which is in his hand." And the angels gathered themselves together, but they hesitated to take the list from the rebel's hand. Then My Father commanded them to bring a sharp reaping knife, and to thrust it into his sides and through his body, and to sever the bones of his back and shoulders; and he was unable to stand.[72] Then My Father commanded a mighty angel to smite him and to cast him out of heaven, because of his pride; and the angel crushed in his ribs, and broke his wings,[73] and he and those angels who were with him became devils.[74]

1 Enoch, a text highly regarded in the primitive church[75] and quoted verbatim in Jude 1:14-15, represents the "first rebel angel" who was responsible for "all sins"[76] as a star that fell from heaven.[77] When Enoch looked again, he saw "many stars descend and cast themselves from heaven to that first star."[78] In *1 Enoch*, however, these "many stars" are not the angels that fell in primordial rebellion with Lucifer—though they recapitulate in many ways the same pattern. They are, instead, the Watchers—described variously as angels or mortals[79] who were given a mission to look after the inhabitants of the earth.[80] Though they were originally commissioned to "teach the sons of man, and perform judgment and uprightness upon the earth,"[81] they were seduced instead by the beauty of the "daughters of men."[82] Stories recount how they "corrupted their way and their ordinances… And injustice grew upon the earth

72   See *Endnote 4-34*, p. 308.
73   See *Endnote 4-35*, p. 309.
74   Timothy of Alexandria, *Abbaton*, p. 199. See also E. A. W. Budge, *Cave*, pp. 58-59; E. A. W. Budge, *Rebellion*, p. 294; H. W. Nibley, *Sacred*, p. 557.
75   See *Endnote 4-36*, p. 310.
76   G. W. E. Nickelsburg, *et al.*, *1 Enoch*, 10:8, pp. 28, 372.
77   *Ibid.*, 86:1, p. 364. See *Endnote 4-37*, p. 310.
78   *Ibid.*, 86:3, p. 364; cf. Moses 7:26.
79   I.e., covenantal "sons of God" in the patriarchal line of Seth and Noah.
80   J. L. Kugel, *Traditions*, pp. 179-185, 194-216; H. Schwartz, *Tree*, pp. 457-458. See *Commentary* 5:41-b, p. 388, Moses 8:13, and *Excursus 24: The Watchers,* p. 585.
81   O. S. Wintermute, *Jubilees*, 4:15, p. 62.
82   M.-A. Ouaknin, *et al.*, *Rabbi Éliézer*, 22, pp. 134-137; cf. Moses 8:13-22.

FIGURE 4-9. *The Fall of the Rebel Angels, 1562*
Pieter Bruegel, the Elder, ca. 1525-1569

SEE COLOR PLATE 4-9.

And there was a war in heaven: Michael and his angels fought against the dragon... and his angels... And the great dragon was cast out, that old serpent, called the Devil, and Satan, which deceiveth the whole world: he was cast out into the earth, and his angels were cast out with him.[1] The violence and fierceness of the battle of the rebel angels as they fall "with hideous ruin and combustion down"[2] leaps out from Bruegel's canvas to engulf the viewer in its chaos and confusion.

Lewis notes the steady deterioration in the artistic portrayal of angels over the centuries: "Fra Angelico's angels carry in their face and gesture the peace and authority of Heaven. Later come the chubby infantile nudes of Raphael; finally the soft, slim, girlish, and consolatory angels of nineteenth-century art, shapes so feminine that they avoid being voluptuous only by their total insipidity... They are a pernicious symbol. In Scripture the visitation of an angel is always alarming; it has to begin by saying 'Fear not.' The Victorian angel looks as if it were going to say, 'There, there.'"[3]

---

1   Revelation 12:6, 9.
2   J. Milton, *Paradise Lost*, 1:46, p. 17.
3   C. S. Lewis, *Screwtape*, 1961 Preface, p. 7.

and every imagination of the thoughts of all mankind was thus continually evil."[83] From unions between these fallen ones and the women are said to have come a progeny of wicked giants.[84] In the likeness of Prometheus,[85] the Watchers were ultimately condemned to eternal punishment for having spread forbidden knowledge among all mankind.[86] The resultant depravity was a precursor to the Flood from which Noah and his family were saved.[87]

Transgression in Eden

In the premortal world, Satan had sought to achieve the "salvation" of all mankind through the destruction of their agency.[88] This course of action is entirely consistent with his efforts on earth to encourage the tantalizingly addictive use of coercion among fallen mankind. D&C 121 makes it plain that it is the tendency of "almost all men" to "exercise unrighteous dominion" whereby we undertake "to cover our sins, or to gratify our pride, our vain ambition, or to exercise control or dominion or compulsion... in... unrighteousness."[89] However, the principle of agency was so essential to the Father's Plan of Salvation[90] that it was necessary from the beginning to establish strict limits on the power of the adversary to compel men to do evil.[91] Joseph Smith explained that "God would not exert any compulsory means, and the Devil could not,"[92] the conditions of mortality having been set up on the basis of "three

---

83   O. S. Wintermute, *Jubilees*, 5:2, p. 62. See *Endnote 4-38,* p. 310.
84   Cf. Moses 7:15, 8:18.
85   G. W. E. Nickelsburg, *1 Enoch*, pp. 191-193; A. T. Wright, *Evil Spirits*, pp. 115-117.
86   E.g., D. C. Olson, *1 Enoch*, pp. 908-911; cf. Moses 5:51-56.
87   See 1 Peter 3:20, 2 Peter 2:5, Moses 8:30. Significantly, the ark itself "was designed as a temple" (C. H. T. Fletcher-Louis, *Glory*, p. 41).
88   For an extended discussion of Satan's adversarial role, see J. M. Bradshaw, *et al.*, *Satan*.
89   D&C 121:39, 37.
90   Alma 42:5.
91   See *Endnote 4-39,* p. 310.
92   J. Smith, Jr., *Teachings*, 16 May 1841, p. 187.

FIGURE 4-10. *God Creating Eve, God Instructing Adam and Eve, late twelfth century*

Of every tree of the garden thou mayest freely eat, But of the tree of the knowledge of good and evil, thou shalt not eat of it.[1] Herrad of Hohenbourg was a twelfth-century abbess under whose direction a comprehensive and copiously illustrated compendium of knowledge and salvation history, called *Hortus Deliciarum* (Garden of Delights), was assembled. Preserved for centuries at the Augustinian monastery of St. Odile at Hohenbourg, it was placed in the municipal library of Strasbourg about the time of the French Revolution. Though it was tragically destroyed during the siege of Strasbourg in 1870, portions of the text and illustrations had been previously copied, enabling the later partial reconstruction and publication of the work.

Anderson points out an interesting divergence between Genesis story and the drawing featured here: "Whereas Genesis 2 recounts that Adam was created first,[2] given a commandment,[3] and only then received a spouse,[4] the *Hortus Deliciarum* has it that Adam was created, then Eve was drawn from his rib, and finally both were given a commandment."[5] At right, God gestures toward the Tree of Knowledge in warning as He takes Adam by the wrist.[6] At the same time, Eve raises her arm in what seems a gesture of consent to God's commandment.[7]

In the middle of the drawing, a Tree of Life has sprouted human faces resembling Adam and Eve, attesting to ancient Jewish and Christian traditions about individual premortal existence.[8] This "Tree of Souls"[9] which, in Jewish legend, represented the heavenly Tree of Life, was thought to produce "new souls, which ripen, and then fall from the tree into the *Guf*, the Treasury of Souls in Paradise. There the soul is stored until the angel Gabriel reaches into the treasury and takes out the first soul that comes into his hand" so it can be born into mortality.[10]

---

1   Moses 3:16-17.
2   Genesis 2:4-7.
3   Genesis 2:16-17.
4   Genesis 2:19-24.
5   G. A. Anderson, *Perfection*, p. 83; cf. G. A. Anderson, *Original Form*, n. 6, pp. 216-217; *Commentary* 4:9-b, p. 252.
6   See *Excursus 53: Dexiosis*, p. 681.
7   S. D. Ricks, *Oaths*, pp. 49-50; see *Figure 5-3*, p. 330.
8   See the overview of Moses 3, pp. 136-139.
9   In support of this idea, Jewish tradition cites Hosea 14:9: "I am like a cypress tree in bloom; your fruit issues forth from Me" (H. Schwartz, *Tree*, 199, p. 165).
10   See H. Schwartz, *Tree*, 199, p. 165 and the overview of Moses 3. For a description of similar Gnostic and Mandaean concepts, see J. O. Ryen, *Mandaean Vine*, pp. 217, 223-224. In the New World, Mayans had a similar teaching (A. J. Christenson, *Sacred Tree*, p. 11). As to the Tree of Life as a symbol of divine motherhood, see *Commentary* 3:9-g, p. 163; R. Green, *et al.*, *Hortus*, vol. 1, fig. 21, see also 2:31.

independent principles—the Spirit of God, the spirit of man, and the spirit of the Devil."[93] He further observed that "Satan was generally blamed for the evils which we did, but if he was the cause of all our wickedness, men could not be condemned. The Devil could not compel mankind to do evil, all was voluntary."[94] Since "[a]ll beings who have bodies have power over those who have not," the Adversary has "power over us only as we permit him."[95] Thus, "[a]ll men have power to resist the Devil."[96]

Under these conditions, the battle begun by Satan in the premortal councils was waged again in the Garden of Eden. "The serpent's invitation to rebellion is simply Lucifer pursuing his earlier, failed agenda. This point is impressed upon the reader by the fact that the JST story of the council is inserted into the traditional Genesis narrative immediately after the command to humans not to eat of the fruit and before the serpent makes his entrance."[97] The tactics for Satan's renewed effort to "destroy the agency of man" in the Garden of Eden are laid out clearly in the "announcement of plot" of verse 4.[98] There, the reader is informed that Lucifer, after his revolt in heaven, became "the father of all lies, to deceive and to blind men, and to lead them captive at his will, even as many as would not hearken unto [the Lord's] voice." Although Adam and Eve's subsequent faith in Jesus Christ and obedience to their covenants ultimately will enable them to "escape from the grasp of… death and hell,"[99] Satan will enjoy temporary success as he carries out his familiar script of lies, deception, blindness, and captivity to the letter in the Garden of Eden.[100]

It should be remembered, however, that while the conditions in Paradise were expressly designed to provide a test of obedience, the actual prize at stake was knowledge—the knowledge required for Adam and Eve to be saved and, ultimately, to be exalted. The Prophet taught that the "principle of knowledge is the principle of salvation,"[101] therefore "anyone that cannot get knowledge to be saved will be damned."[102] Since "It is impossible for a man to be saved in ignorance,"[103] one of the Adversary's chief activities is to take "away light and knowledge through disobedience,"[104] resulting in "captivity and death… for [the Devil] seeketh that all men might be miserable like unto himself."[105]

This raises a conundrum: Since salvation was to come through knowledge, why did Satan encourage rather than prevent the eating of the forbidden fruit by Adam and Eve? It is evident that their transgression must have been as much an important part of the Devil's strategy as it was a central feature of the Father's plan. The difference in intention between God and Satan was only made apparent, however, when it came time for Adam and Eve to take the *next* step.[106] In this regard, the scriptures seem to suggest that the Adversary wanted Adam and Eve to eat of the fruit of the Tree of Life directly after they took of the

---

93   J. Smith, Jr., *Teachings*, 16 May 1841, p. 189. See *Endnote 4-40*, p. 310.
94   *Ibid.*, 16 May 1841, p. 187.
95   *Ibid.*, 5 January 1841, p. 181.
96   *Ibid.*, 16 May 1841, p. 189.
97   K. Flake, *Translating Time*, p. 513.
98   L. Turner, *Announcements*; cf. *Commentary* 1:1-a, p. 42.
99   2 Nephi 9:10.
100   *Commentary 4:4-b*, p. 246. See *Endnote 4-41*, p. 310.
101   J. Smith, Jr., *Teachings*, 14 May 1843, p. 331; cf. D&C 130:18-19; *Excursus 47: Islamic Perspectives Relating to Redemption*, p. 645
102   J. Smith, Jr., *Words*, 14 May 1843, p. 200, spelling and punctuation standardized.
103   D&C 131:6. See *Endnote 4-42*, p. 310.
104   D&C 93:39.
105   2 Nephi 2:26-27; cf. Moses 2:18. See *Endnote 4-43*, p. 310.
106   Cf. T. Stordalen, *Echoes*, p. 231.

FIGURE 4-11. *Anubis Leads Nakht Towards the Entrance to the Other World, ca. 1350-1300 BCE*
FIGURE 4-12. *Palm Tree Growing over "Adam's Grave" at the Tomb of the Patriarchs in Hebron*

May I be like one of you, a friend of the Lord of Eternity, may I walk like you walk, may I stand like you stand, may I sit like you sit, may I speak like you speak before the great God, Lord of the West.[1] The figure at left[2] is from the hieroglyphic funerary papyrus of the Royal Scribe and Chief Military Officer, Nakht.[3] Anubis, the "guardian of the gateway,"[4] is frequently shown as "leading the deceased into the presence of Osiris and assisting in the ceremony of the weighing of the heart"[5] in afterlife judgment. Here, they approach a tree that stands before the "false door," representing the entrance to the "Other World."[6] To reach that door, they must pass by the tree, a symbol that is frequently associated, like the door itself, with the "horizon."[7]

Traditions about Adam's burial in the cave of Machpela in Hebron are preserved in Jewish sources.[8] At right above is a palm tree marking the spot of "Adam's Grave" within the edifice built by Herod the Great to commemorate the burial of Abraham and Sarah, Isaac and Rebekah, and Jacob and Leah.[9] In contrast to the liminal symbolism of the tree in the Egyptian figure above, the funerary "Tree of Life" may have represented victory over death and the final reward of the righteous deceased.

---

1   R. O. Faulkner, *et al.*, *Book of the Dead*, Spell 117, p. 113.
2   BM 10471, in *ibid.*, p. 112.
3   *Ibid.*, p. 9.
4   J. Assman, *Death*, p. 335.
5   R. H. Wilkinson, *Art*, p. 65.
6   See *Endnote 4-47*, p. 311.
7   See *Commentary 4:14-e*, p. 260 and *Excursus 53: Comparative Explorations of the Mysteries*, p. 663. See also D. E. Wirth, *Parallels*, p. 154. See *Endnote 4-48*, p. 312. See also *Commentary 3:8-b*, p. 160.
8   E.g., M. McNamara, *Targum Neofiti*, 23:2, p. 120 and p. 120 n. 1; J. Neusner, *Genesis Rabbah 2*, 58:4, p. 297; M.-A. Ouaknin, *et al.*, *Rabbi Éliézer*, 20, pp. 127-128; 36, p. 224; H. Schwartz, *Tree*, 445, pp. 343-344, 639, pp. 504-506; see *Excursus 53: Comparative Explorations of the Mysteries*, p. 663.
9   N. Arnon, *Machpela*, p. 13. The "Tomb of the Patriarchs" is called *Ma'arat HaMachpela* in Hebrew, and *Haram al-Khalil* in Arabic. See *Endnote 4-50*, p. 312.

Tree of Knowledge—a danger which moved God to take immediate preventive action.[107] For had Adam and Eve eaten of the fruit of the Tree of Life at that time, said Alma, "there would have been no death" and no "space granted unto man in which he might repent"—in other words no "probationary state" to prepare for a final judgment and resurrection.[108] Reiterating the same point in similar words, Alma later explained that had Adam and Eve been allowed to "take also of the tree of life, and eat and live forever" he would have had no "time granted… to repent… and serve God," and "no space for repentance… and the great plan of salvation would have been frustrated."[109]

---

107   Moses 4:28-31; Alma 12:23, 42:2-3.
108   Alma 12:23-24.
109   Alma 42:3-5. See *Endnote 4-45*, p. 311.

FIGURE 4-13. *Rameses II in the Ished-tree 13th Century BCE.* **Photo: Alain Guilleux, 1966-**

Adam and his wife hid themselves from the presence of the Lord God in the center of the tree of the garden.[1] In contrast to Chouraqui's carefully rendered translation quoted here, the KJV reads "*amongst* the trees of the garden." However, as the alternate translation demonstrates, the Hebrew for "tree," *etz,* also may be read as singular—an important subtlety glossed over in nearly every vernacular edition of the Bible. As Kastler observes, "they are not merely touching the [Tree of Knowledge] but they have for all intents and purposes merged with it… The tree has become their refuge—or perhaps their prison."[2] They have experienced a kind of death.

The image of the guilty parties, Adam and Eve, being figuratively shut up in a tree recalls Egyptian motifs, such as the one evoked by the portrayal of Ramesses II as Osiris shown here.[3] Nibley also mentions "*Book of the Dead* vignettes showing the Lady incorporated—all but her upper part, and in many cases all but her arms only—in the fruit-bearing tree [suggesting] that the woman in the tree must actually have been eaten by it; she is the first victim, so to speak, and now invites her male companion to share her condition."[4] In ancient year-rites in Egypt, the splitting of the tree "both terminates life and liberates it" allowing the captive initiate to be reborn.[5] The splitting of the tree also is also said to represent, "among other things, the 'splitting of 'good' and 'evil,'" or the law of opposites."[6]

An Islamic tradition relates that: "Adam went inside of the tree to hide,"[7] recalling al-Tha'labi's version of the story of the martyrdom of Isaiah.[8] As in Egyptian texts, pseudepigraphal accounts report that Isaiah's death in a split tree was immediately followed by his rebirth and ascension to heaven.[9] A similar motif has been found in the New World.[10]

---

1 Genesis 3:8, after A. Chouraqui, *Bible*, p. 22; cf. R. M. Zlotowitz, *et al.*, *Bereishis*, p. 123.
2 E. Kastler, *Commentaire.*
3 A. Guilleux, *Temple de Derr.* See *Endnote 4-49*, p. 312.
4 H. W. Nibley, *Message 2005*, p. 309; cf. *Commentary 4:14-e*, p. 260, *Excursus 42: Nebuchadnezzar's "Fall"*, p. 632, and *Excursus 53: Comparative Explorations of the Mysteries*, p. 663. See *Endnote 4-50*, p. 312.
5 H. W. Nibley, *Message 2005*, p. 289. See also pp. 288-293.
6 *Ibid.*, p. 290.
7 Wahab b. Munabbih in B. M. Wheeler, *Prophets*, p. 25.
8 A. al-Tha'labi, *Lives*, p. 557 and p. 557 n. 15; cf. M. A. Knibb, *Isaiah*, 5:1-14, pp. 163-164. See also pp. 146-147.
9 M. A. Knibb, *Isaiah*, 6:1-11:43, pp. 164-176.
10 V. G. Norman, *Izapa Part 2*, p. 202. Also cited in B. Gardner, *Second Witness*, 1:168. See *Commentary 4:14-e*, p. 260 and *Excursus 55: Mesoamerican Stories of Creation and the Original Transgression*, p. 697.

MOSES 4

The reason why this is so is lucidly explained by Skousen, and is relevant regardless of whether one sees Adam's action of eating as being literal or metaphorical:

> There appears to be a very specific reason why it was necessary to have humanity pass through the portals of death so that their spirits could be separated temporarily from their bodies.

> First of all, the Lord tells us that man cannot be exalted "in the flesh." "Neither can any natural man abide the presence of God," explained the Lord.[110] There is something inherently mundane about the mortal clay which prevents it from being elevated to a celestial glory in and of itself. It can only be elevated by combining it with glorified spirit matter. In other words, a temporal body can only be exalted by becoming "inseparably connected"[111] with spirit matter after the spirit matter has been glorified or celestialized…

---

110 D&C 67:12; Moses 1:5.
111 D&C 93:33.

FIGURE 4-14. *Eve, After the Transgression, 1869*
Eugène Delaplanche, 1836-1890
Photo: Jeffrey M. Bradshaw, 1956-

The serpent beguiled me, and I did eat.[1] The vacant, tearless eyes and agonized posture of the solitary slumped figure bespeak the depth of Eve's utter hopelessness immediately following her transgression.

1   Moses 4:19.

FIGURE 4-15. *The Rebuke of Adam and Eve, 1626*
Domenico Zampieri (Domenichino), 1581-1641

SEE COLOR PLATE 4-15.

And the man said: The woman thou gavest me, and commandest that she should remain with me, she gave me of the fruit of the tree and I did eat.[1] Of this painting, Conisbee writes: "*The Rebuke of Adam and Eve* perfectly illustrates Domenichino's classical style at the peak of his career… The group of God and the angels is derived directly from Michelangelo's *Creation of Adam*… and should be read as an homage by the seventeenth-century painter to his great predecessor… Following Italian tradition, Domenichino shows the Tree of Knowledge as a fig tree, rather than the apple tree which was more usual in northern European art. In a clear narrative sequence, God the Father, borne by cherubim and angels, descends to rebuke Adam, who blames Eve, who in turn points to the serpent as the cause of their fall from grace. Animals still roam freely in their earthly paradise, but the lion at the right is already metamorphosing from a friendly feline to an aggressive beast."[2]

1   Moses 4:18.
2   P. Conisbee, *Art*.

Speaking of the process wherein the temporal body is fused with the spirit body at the time of the resurrection, the Lord said: "They who are of celestial spirit shall receive the same body which was a natural body… and your glory [which obviously would have to be the glory of one's spirit] shall be the glory by which your bodies are quickened."[112]

In other words, the Lord has to have the opportunity of redeeming and glorifying the spirit first[113]—then the glorified spirit is used as the quickening medium to refine the physical body.

From this it becomes obvious why it would have been disastrous for Adam and Eve to have partaken of the fruit of the Tree of Life so that they could not die! Their spirits would have been imprisoned within their temporal bodies forever—incapable of Redemption, incapable of exaltation. The entire plan of salvation would have been annihilated by this single act….

112   D&C 88:28.
113   See *Endnote 4-46*, p. 311.

FIGURE 4-16. *Expulsion of Adam and Eve, 1510*
Michelangelo Buonarrotti, 1475-1564

SEE COLOR PLATE 4-16.

So I drove out the man.[1] With drawn sword, the angel drives Adam and Eve out of the Garden. In striking contrast to their noble, vigorous, and handsome bearing before the Fall, they appear pained, cowering, and much older. With his hands raised and the sword poised at the back of his neck, Adam appears "to be warding off the angel, surrendering, [or] saying that he is going. Could it also be that he is...[depicted as] pushing God away"?[2]

1   Moses 4:31.
2   R. J. Smith, *Sistine.*

FIGURE 4-17. *Cherubim and the Flaming Sword, 2000*
J. Kirk Richards, 1977-

SEE COLOR PLATE 4-17.

I placed at the east of the Garden of Eden, cherubim and a flaming sword, which turned every way to keep the way of the tree of life.[1] In temple contexts, the essential function of the cherubim was analogous to their role at the entrance of the Garden of Eden: they were to be as sentinels guarding the portals of the temple against unauthorized entry, governing subsequent access to secure compartments, and ultimately assisting in the determination of the fitness of temple worshipers to enter God's presence.[2] The sword is described by Sarna as a "separate, protective instrument, not said to be in the hands of the cherubim."[3] While the function of the cherubim is to selectively admit those authorized to enter, Nibley argues that the fire and steel combined in the sword are specifically meant to repulse the serpent, forever preventing its return to the Garden.[4]

J. Kirk Richards was born "near Brigham Young University, the fourth of eight musical children. He attributes much of his love for the arts to an early emphasis on musical training in the home."[5] "Richards studied with nationally acclaimed artists James Christenson, Wulf Barsch, Bruce Smith, and Swiss born symbolist painter, Patrick Denovas." In addition to crediting the influence of these artists on his painting, he admires the work of masters such as Rembrandt and Michelangelo who "have both abstract and realist figures in their paintings" and who "combine the two extremes in an amazing way." His own work is noted for its "expressive realism, elegant composition, and brilliant representation of light in primarily Judeo-Christian themes."[6]

1   Moses 4:31.
2   D&C 132:19; D. W. Parry, *Garden*, p. 139; B. Young, *6 April 1853 - B*, p. 31.
3   N. M. Sarna, *Genesis*, p. 30.
4   H. W. Nibley, *Message 2005*, pp. 319-320.
5   J. K. Richards, *Bio.*
6   S. Lemon, *Richards.*

Alma points out that "living forever" or conquering temporal death was not important at this time: "Now behold, it was not expedient that man should be redeemed from this temporal death, for that would destroy the great plan of happiness."[114] It was first "expedient that mankind should be reclaimed from this spiritual death,"[115] which means to return to the presence of God. And since the physical body cannot endure the presence of God in its mundane state it was necessary to permit the spirit to be released from the body. When the spirit had been

114   Alma 42:8.
115   Alma 42:9.

"reclaimed from the spiritual death" and, as the Lord says made into a "celestial spirit,"[116] then it could be used as a refining element to exalt the elements of the temporal body.[117]

It is easy to see a parallel between Satan's initial proposal in the spirit world and his later strategy to "frustrate" the plan of salvation through his actions in Eden. Just as his defeated premortal plan had proposed to provide a limited measure of "salvation" for all by precluding the opportunity for exaltation, so it seems plausible that his unsuccessful scheme in the Garden was intended to impose an inferior form of immortality that would forestall the possibility of eternal life.[118] However, because the Devil "knew not the mind of God," his efforts "to destroy the world"[119] were in vain: the result of his deceitful manipulations to get Adam and Eve to eat the forbidden fruit was co-opted by God, and the risk of their partaking immediately of the fruit of the Tree of Life was averted. Elder Bruce C. Hafen explained: "God placed cherubim and a flaming sword to guard the way of the Tree of Life until Adam and Eve completed, and we, their posterity, complete [the] preparatory schooling [of mortality]. Our tutorial is the gospel, a schoolmaster that brings us to Christ.[120] But He cannot fully receive us and give us the gift of celestial life—partaking of God's very nature—until we have learned by our own experience to distinguish good and evil."[121]

FIGURE 4-18. *The Expulsion of Adam and Eve, 1646*

SEE COLOR PLATE 4-18.

I beheld that I was naked, and I hid myself.[1] In Orthodox tradition, Adam and Eve are frequently portrayed in regal robes before the Fall, and as naked afterward. Here, the top panel shows God seated in the heavenly council surrounded by angels and the four beasts of the book of Revelation. The second panel depicts, from left to right: Adam and Eve clothed in heavenly robes following their creation; then stripped of their glorious garments and "clothed" only in mortal skin after eating the forbidden fruit; and finally both clad in fig leaf aprons as Eve converses with God. The third panel shows Adam conversing with God, the couple's expulsion from the walled Garden through a door showing images of cherubim, and their subsequent hardship in the fallen world. Orthodox tradition generally leaves Adam and Eve in their aprons after the Fall and expulsion, seeing them as already having received their "coats of skin" at the time they were clothed in mortal flesh.

1   Moses 4:16.

The Nakedness and the Clothing of Adam and Eve

Moses' account depicts Adam and Eve as naked and without shame in the Garden,[122] and clothed by God in coats of skin only later, after the Fall.[123] However, many of the earliest artistic depictions of the story show a surprising reversal of the situation, portraying Adam

116   D&C 88:28.
117   W. C. Skousen, *First 2,000*, pp. 66-68.
118   See *Excursus 22: The Nature of Satan's Premortal Proposal*, p. 577.
119   Moses 4:6.
120   See Galatians 3:24.
121   B. C. Hafen, *Broken*, p. 30; cf. L. Schaya, *Meaning*, p. 16.
122   Moses 3:25.
123   Moses 4:27.

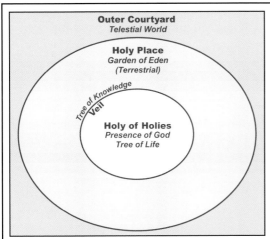

FIGURE 4-19.
Zones of Sacredness Within Eden

Jewish, Christian, and Muslim sources sometimes speak of a "wall" surrounding whole of the Garden,[1] and of an inner "hedge" or "veil" that separated the Garden from the Tree of Life.[2] In his caption to a similar figure, Anderson writes: "According to Ephrem, Adam and Eve have access to most of Eden. The animals[3] live just outside the sacred confines, and Adam and Eve have to go to the edge of Eden to tend them. It is here, at Eden's border, that Eve converses with the snake. The Tree of Knowledge guards the entry point to the Inner Sanctum, the Holy of Holies, wherein the Tree of Life is found. Adam and Eve were not sufficiently holy at creation to enter this room… [S]ince they tried to enter prematurely, they were driven out of Eden altogether."[4]

In at least one version of the story, Eve's violation of the boundary God had set that barred the way to the "midst of the Garden"[5] had been preceded by her deliberate opening of the gate to let the serpent enter the Garden's outer wall.[6]

1   E.g., G. A. Anderson, *et al.*, *Synopsis*, 19:1a-19:1d, pp. 56E-57E; M. Herbert, *Irish Apocrypha*, p. 2 ("wall of red gold");
     G. Weil, *Legends*, p. 53.
2   E.g., R. M. Zlotowitz, *et al.*, *Bereishis*, pp. 96, 101; Ephrem the Syrian, *Paradise*, 3:5, p. 92.
3   The distinction between "animals" and "men" may have a symbolic significance here. See *Endnote E-95*, p. 725.
4   G. A. Anderson, *Perfection*, p. 80.
5   See *Commentary 3:9-h*, p. 167; *Excursus 25: The Tree of Life as the Hidden Throne of God*, p. 591.
6   G. A. Anderson, *et al.*, *Synopsis*, 19:1a-19:1d, pp. 56E-57E. See *Commentary 4:6-b*, p. 249.

and Eve clothed in regal glory within Eden, and naked after their expulsion.[124] How can this be?

Recalling the parallels between the Garden of Eden and Israelite Houses of God, Anderson points out that "the vestments of the priest matched exactly those particular areas of the Temple to which he had access… Each time the high priest moved from one gradient of holiness to another, he had to remove one set of clothes and put on another to mark the change":[125]

> (a) Outside the Tabernacle priests wear ordinary clothes. (b) When on duty in the Tabernacle, they wear four pieces of clothing whose material and quality of workmanship match that of the fabrics found on the outer walls of the courtyard.[126] (c) The High Priest wears those four pieces plus four additional ones—these added garments match the fabric of the Holy Chamber where he must go daily to tend the incense altar.

> In Eden a similar set of vestments is found, again each set suited to its particular space. (a) Adam and Eve were, at creation, vested like priests and granted access to most of Eden. (b) Had they been found worthy, an even more glorious set of garments would have been theirs (and according to St. Ephrem, they would have entered even holier ground). (c) But having [transgressed], they were stripped of their angelic garments and put on mortal flesh. Thus, when their feet met ordinary earth—the realm of the animals—their constitution had become "fleshly," or mortal.[127]

Consistent with this schema, each stage in the sequence of changes in Adam and Eve's status in the book of Moses is marked by a change in their appearance.[128] The imagery of cloth-

124   G. A. Anderson, *Perfection*, p. 119; see a Muslim parallel in R. Milstein, *et al.*, *Stories*, B&W plate 2.
125   G. A. Anderson, *Perfection*, p. 122. See *Endnote 4-51*, p. 312.
126   Exodus 28.
127   G. A. Anderson, *Perfection*, p. 123. See *Endnote 4-52*, p. 312.
128   See *Endnote 4-53*, p. 313.

ing is "a means of linking together in a dynamic fashion the whole of salvation history; it is a means of indicating the interrelatedness between every stage in this continuing working out of divine Providence," including "the place of each individual Christian's [ordinances[129]] within the divine economy as a whole."[130] Note the chiastic structure of the sequence, which begins and ends in glory:[131]

> *1. From glory to nakedness.*[132] Though "naked" because their knowledge of their premortal state had been taken away by a veil of forgetfulness,[133] Adam and Eve had come to Eden nonetheless "trailing clouds of glory."[134] While the couple, as yet, were free from transgression, they could stand "naked" in God's presence without shame,[135] being "clothed with purity"[136] in what early commentators called "garments of light"[137] or "garments of contentment."[138] In one source, Eve describes her appearance by saying: "I was decked out like a bride, And I reclined in a wedding-chamber of light."[139]

> In the context of rituals and ordinances based on the experiences of Adam and Eve, Nibley explained: "The garment [of light] represents the preexistent glory of the candidate... When he leaves on his earthly mission, it is laid up for him in heaven to await his return. It thus serves as security and lends urgency and weight to the need for following righteous ways on earth. For if one fails here, one loses not only one's glorious future in the eternities to come, but also the whole accumulation of past deeds and accomplishments in the long ages of preexistence."[140]

> *2. From innocence to transgression.*[141] Rabbinical tradition taught that, following his transgression, "Adam... lost his [heavenly] clothing—God stripped it off him..."[142] and similarly that Eve "was stripped of the righteousness in which [she] had been clothed."[143] Likewise, the *Discourse on Abbaton* records that both Adam and Eve "became naked" upon eating the forbidden fruit.[144] According to the *Life of Adam and Eve*, God then "sent seventy plagues upon us, to our eyes, and to our ears and as far as our feet, plagues and portents laid up in his treasuries."[145] Anderson takes this to mean that "Adam has exchanged an angelic constitution for a mortal one," in other words that he has been "clothed with flesh."[146] Shamed by their loss of glory, Adam and Eve covered their earthly bodies with fig leaf aprons.[147]

> Rabbinical writings describe how, in likeness of Adam and Eve, each soul descending to earth "divests itself of its heavenly garment, and is clothed in a garment of flesh and blood,"[148] the prior

---

129   The original reads "Baptism" here.

130   Brock in Ephrem the Syrian, *Paradise*, pp. 66-67.

131   See *Endnote 4-54*, p. 313.

132   Moses 3:25.

133   R. A. Bullard, *et al.*, *Archons*, 89:3-7, p. 164; G. W. MacRae, *et al.*, *Adam 1990*, 64:24-29, 65:10-13, p. 279; C. Schmidt, *Pistis*, 4:144, pp. 749-753; G. R. S. Mead, *Pistis*, 6, 144, 380, p. 315; cf. *Commentary* 3:21-a, p. 180.

134   W. Wordsworth in L. Richards, *Marvelous*, p. 290. See *Endnote 4-56*, p. 313.

135   Moses 3:25; cf. D&C 121:45.

136   2 Nephi 9:14; cf. Chrysostom, *Homilies on Genesis*, 15:14, in A. Louth, *et al.*, *Genesis 1-11*, p. 72. See *Endnote 4-57*, p. 314.

137   G. A. Anderson, *Perfection*, p. 215; cf. D. C. Matt, *Zohar 1*, Be-Reshit 1:36b, pp. 229, 230. For an in-depth discussion of this topic, see G. A. Anderson, *Garments*.

138   M. al-Kisa'i, *Tales*, p. 61. See *Endnote 4-58*, p. 314.

139   M. E. Stone, *Adamgirk*, 3:1:7, p. 48.

140   H. W. Nibley, *Message 2005*, p. 489. See also E. Hennecke, *et al.*, *Acts of Thomas*, 108.9-15, pp. 498-499; B. T. Ostler, *Clothed*, p. 4. See *Endnote 4-59*, p. 314.

141   Moses 4:16.

142   L. Ginzberg, *Legends*, 1:79; cf. D. C. Matt, *Zohar 1*, Be-Reshit 1:36b, p. 229.

143   L. Ginzberg, *Legends*, 1:96; cf. M. E. Stone, *Adamgirk*, 3:1:9, p. 48 and 3:1:17, p. 50. See *Endnote 4-60*, p. 314.

144   Timothy of Alexandria, *Abbaton*, p. 200. See *Endnote 4-61*, p. 315.

145   G. A. Anderson, *Perfection*, p. 127; cf. G. A. Anderson, *et al.*, *Synopsis*, Georgian version, 34(8):2, p. 38. See *Endnote 4-62*, p. 315.

146   G. A. Anderson, *Perfection*, p. 127. See *Endnote 4-63*, p. 315.

147   See *Commentary* 4:13-b, p. 258.

148   H. Schwartz, *Tree*, 200, p. 166.

FIGURE 4-20.
Sacred Tree on the Apron of Charlemagne, eighth century

And they sewed fig-leaves together and made themselves aprons.[1]
While Adam and Eve's original fig-leaf aprons were made without divine authorization, a similar article has been used in ritual contexts to represent true power and authority. For example, a sacred tree was symbolically represented on an apron worn by the eighth-century Christian king Charlemagne.[2] Kings in the Middle East were often represented as various sorts of trees. In Egypt and Mesoamerica,[3] foliated aprons were used as a sign of authority.

1   Moses 4:13.
2   W. Smith, *et al.*, *Dictionary*, 2:1307. Also included in M. B. Brown, *Girded*, p. 137. See *Commentary* 4:13-b, p. 258.
3   See, e.g., D. E. Wirth, *Parallels*, p. 106 and pp. 109-110, Figures 6.23, 6.24.

glory being, as it were, "veiled… in flesh."[149] The various "afflictions" of mortality initially given to Adam and now bestowed upon "all… generations"[150] frequently number seven rather than the seventy mentioned above: "They are against the 'seven natures: the flesh for hearing, the eyes for seeing, the breath to smell, the veins to touch, the blood for taste, and bones for endurance, and the intelligence for joy';[151] or against life, sight, hearing, smell, speech, taste, procreation."[152] Though Adam and Eve were protected from fatal harm at the time of extremity, ancient texts recount that Satan had been allowed to hurt them, and the "wounds," foreshadowing the later wounds received by Christ at His crucifixion,[153] "remained on their bodies."[154] Nibley sees the wounds of nature and of Satan to various parts of the body as figuratively corresponding to the "blows of death" taught by Satan to Cain.[155] He describes their enactment in Jewish ritual as follows: "The wages of sin is death, and the dead body is chided at an old-fashioned Jewish funeral because its members no longer function, and each one is struck an impatient and accusing blow. This is the *chibut ha-keber*: 'On the third day the departed is treated with increased rigor. Blows are struck on his eyes because he would not see, on his ears because he would not hear, on his lips because they uttered profanities, on his tongue because it bore false testimony against his neighbor, on his feet because they ran toward evil doing.'"[156]

3. From transgression to blamelessness.[157] Except through his eventual death, Adam was powerless to rid himself of the mortal flesh he had now put on. However, while still in this life, he was enabled to "[put] off the natural man and [become] a saint through the atonement of Christ" so that he could be found "blameless in the sight of God."[158] The book of Moses account is consistent with this sort of symbolism. When Adam asked why "men must repent and be baptized," the Lord replied: "Behold I have forgiven thee thy transgression in the

149   *Hymns (1985)*, #175. See *Endnote 4-64*, p. 315.
150   G. A. Anderson, *et al.*, *Synopsis*, Latin 34:2, p. 38E.
151   Cf. F. I. Andersen, *2 Enoch*, 30:8-9, p. 150.
152   H. W. Nibley, *Message 2005*, p. 178. See H. C. Kee, *Testaments*, Reuben 2:1-9, p. 782.
153   H. W. Nibley, *Prayer Circle*, p. 60. See S. C. Malan, *Adam and Eve*, 1:23, 69, pp. 23, 83-84; cf. J. Cooper, *et al.*, *Testament*, 1:23, pp. 73, 75; M. E. Stone, *Legend*, p. 160.
154   S. C. Malan, *Adam and Eve*, 1:46, p. 50. See also 1:59, p. 66.
155   H. W. Nibley, *Teachings of the PGP*, 19, p. 253. See also *Commentary* 5:29-b, p. 377, 5:47-b, p. 396.
156   H. W. Nibley, *Message 2005*, pp. 173-174.
157   Moses 4:27, 6:50-53.
158   Mosiah 3:19, 21; cf. Moses 5:5-8.

FIGURE 4-21. *The Clothing of Adam and Eve, 1803*
William Blake, 1757-1827

SEE COLOR PLATE 4-21.

Unto Adam, and also unto his wife, did I, the Lord God, make coats of skins, and clothed them.[1] Blake depicts the exit scene at the gates of Eden as a tender moment of forgiveness and farewell. In childlike submission and gratitude, Adam and Eve bow their heads and, clothed with garments of animal skin made by the Father as a protection and a reminder, prepare to leave God's embrace and prove themselves by overcoming the dangers of the mortal world.

1   Moses 4:27.

Garden of Eden."[159] The coats of animal skins given to Adam and Eve were a visible sign of God's forgiveness, constituting a tangible witness of the couple's acceptance of the Atonement that would reverse the "blows of death," cover the shame of nakedness they experienced following their transgression, and "replace sin… with light and healing."[160] The "second skin" provided by the Lord figuratively replaced their covering of mortal skin with the flesh of Jesus Christ, the "second Adam,"[161] through whose power they would experience a "renewing of their bodies."[162] Indeed, the Hebrew term for atonement exactly fits this situation, meaning "to cover or recover, cover again, to repair a hole, cure a sickness, mend a rift, make good a torn or broken covering."[163] Though the leather garment given to Adam and handed down through the patriarchs was foremost a sign of repentance,[164] it was also a sign of authority,[165] and a symbol of "royal rebirth and rejuvenation."[166] It provided protection,[167] afforded modesty, reminded Adam and Eve of their covenants, and served as an earnest of the glorious celestial robes that awaited them through their faithfulness.[168] It appears that once Adam and Eve had successfully completed their probation on earth, the garment of skins was no longer needed.[169]

The putting off of the "natural man" so as to be made a "new creature" in Christ[170] is figuratively enacted in the rites of some Christian traditions relating to the renunciation of Satan and the acceptance of Christ through baptism. In these rites, the candidate "is stripped of the garments inherited from Adam and vested with the token of those garments he or she shall enjoy at the resurrection."[171] In some early Christian traditions, the idea of "reversing the blows of death"

---

159   Moses 6:53; cf. *Commentary* 4:24-b, p. 271 and 4:25-a, b, p. 272, See *Endnote 4-65,* p. 316.

160   T. G. Madsen, *Foundations*, p. 2.

161   Romans 5:12-21; 1 Corinthians 15:20-22, 45-50.

162   D&C 84:33. See *Excursus 3: Temple Blessings in the Oath and Covenant of the Priesthood*, p. 519 and *Excursus 52: Washing, Anointing, and Clothing Among Early Christians*, p. 661.

163   M. Barker, *Atonement*; cf. T. G. Madsen, *Sacrament*, p. 13. See *Endnote 6-36*, p. 502.

164   H. W. Nibley, *Evangelium*, p. 38 n. 78.

165   H. W. Nibley, *Vestments*, p. 124.

166   H. W. Nibley, *Message 2005*, p. 425.

167   See *Endnote 4-66*, p. 316.

168   C. E. Asay, *Garment*, p. 37; E. T. Marshall, *Garments*; H. W. Nibley, *Vestments*, p. 124. See also *Commentary* 3:25-a, p. 185 and 4:27-a, p. 274.

169   JS-H 1:31; cf. Ephrem the Syrian, *Diatessaron*, cited in M. Barker, *Hidden*, p. 34; M. Lidzbarski, *Ginza*, GL 2:19, p. 488; H. W. Nibley, *Apocryphal*, p. 299.

170   Mosiah 3:19, 2 Corinthians 5:17.

171   G. A. Anderson, *Perfection*, p. 130. See also M. Barker, *Gate*, pp. 113-114; B. T. Ostler, *Clothed*, p. 3; S. D. Ricks, *Garment*, p. 709; M. von Wellnitz, *Liturgy*, pp. 11-12; Romans 6:3-4; 1 Corinthians 15:53; and *Commentary* 4:21-d, p. 266. See *Endnote 4-67*, p. 317.

was also represented by a special anointing with the "oil of mercy" prior to (or sometimes after) baptism or washing, as the candidate is signed upon the brow, the nostrils, the breast, the ears, and so forth.[172] This anointing recalls an incident in the *Life of Adam and Eve* where Adam, as he lay on his deathbed, requested Eve and Seth to fetch him oil from the Tree of Life in the Garden of Eden.[173] One may also see these symbols of the Atonement in Christ's miracles of healing and forgiveness.[174]

4. From blamelessness to celestial glory.[175] While the coats of skins "covered" the direct effects of Adam and Eve's transgression (corresponding to the idea of justification), additional clothing worn over the first garment represented their being endowed with glory, holiness, and godliness (i.e., sanctification).[176] In connection with the doctrines and ordinances of the gospel that promise "eternal life... unto all the obedient,"[177] Adam and Eve would, in the resurrection, be "clothed with honour and majesty... [and] covered... with light as with a garment,"[178] in perfect similitude of God's own glory.[179] Rabbinical writings recount that: "When the time comes for the soul to leave this world, the Angel of Death strips off the worldly garment, and at the same instant the soul is clothed in the holy garment that was stripped away when it descended to this world. Then the soul delights in having been stripped of its worldly body and in having its original garment restored."[180] Similarly, Nephi describes the worthy dead as "being clothed with purity, yea, even with the robe of righteousness."[181] *1 Enoch* says that the "righteous and the chosen will have arisen from the earth... and have put on the garment of glory... the garment of life from the Lord of Spirits; and your garment will not wear out, and your glory will not fade in the presence of the Lord of Spirits."[182] "For these are those selected by God for an everlasting covenant and to them shall belong the glory of Adam."[183]

In ancient Israel, the temple clothing of priests symbolized the heavenly clothing that would someday supersede it.[184] Nibley explains that "the white undergarment is the proper preexistent glory of the wearer, while the [outer garment of the high priest] is the priesthood later added to it."[185] Anderson describes God's concerted attempt at Sinai to figuratively reverse the effects of the Fall of mankind and then to cover him with glory "by ordaining that Israel wash and then put on new clothes. 'When you have already been washed and purified through the Law of God,' Origen declared, 'then Moses will dress you with a garment of incorruptibility so

MOSES 4

---

172   H. W. Nibley, *Message 2005*, p. 174; B. T. Ostler, *Clothed*, p. 2; cf. Cyril of Jerusalem, *Five*, 21:1-6, 7:149-150; H. W. Nibley, *Message 2005*, 3:1-6, pp. 516-517; M. von Wellnitz, *Liturgy*, pp. 10-11, 13, 28-29; and *Commentary 3:9-g*, p. 165. See *Endnote 4-68*, p. 317.

173   G. A. Anderson, *et al.*, *Synopsis*, pp. 33E-45E; cf. M. Herbert, *Irish Apocrypha*, p. 16. See the overview of Moses 6, pp. 460-462. See *Endnote 4-69*, p. 317.

174   E.g., His driving out of evil spirits and His use of oil in blessing the sick (Mark 6:13), the gesture of touching of the eyes of the blind (Matthew 9:29; Mark 8:23-25)) and in His story of the Good Samaritan, where the "half dead" victim was administered to by having oil and wine poured in his wounds (Luke 10:30, 34). See H. W. Nibley, *Message 2005*, pp. 175-77; J. W. Welch, *Samaritan (1999)*; J. W. Welch, *Samaritan (2007)*.

175   Moses 4:27.

176   See *Excursus 26: Justification and Sanctification*, p. 596. See *Endnote 4-70*, p. 317. In this connection, Elder Joseph Fielding Smith wrote that temples are "places for sanctification" ("The Los Angeles Temple," *Improvement Era*, November 1951, p. 798, cited in T. G. Madsen, *Purposes*, p. 93).

177   Moses 5:11.

178   Psalm 104:1-2.

179   1 John 3:1-3. See *Endnote 4-71*, p. 317.

180   H. Schwartz, *Tree*, 200, p. 166. See also E. Hennecke, *et al.*, *Acts of Thomas*, 111-112:72-80, p. 502; H. W. Nibley, *Message 2005*, p. 496; B. T. Ostler, *Clothed*, pp. 4-5.

181   2 Nephi 9:14; cf. Revelation 3:4-5, 4:4, 6:11, 7:9, 13-15; *2 Esdras* 2:45; *Commentary* 1:25-b, p. 60.

182   G. W. E. Nickelsburg, *et al.*, *1 Enoch* 62:15-16, p. 81.

183   Rule of the Community 4:22-23 in F. G. Martinez, *DSS Translated*, p. 7; H. W. Nibley, *Message 2005*, p. 467.

184   J. A. Tvedtnes, *Clothing*, pp. 662-695.

185   H. W. Nibley, *Message 2005*, pp. 489-490, citing Hoffman; cf. M. von Wellnitz, *Liturgy*, pp. 17, 19-20; Abraham 3:26: "added upon."

that 'your shame may never appear'[186] and 'this mortality may be absorbed by life.'[187] And what was done to Israel in this general way was done to the priesthood in a much more dramatic way. Priests' clothing anticipated the resurrection body that all would receive at the end of time. There is a Jewish tradition that the high priest was exempted from the power of the angel of death while he wore those robes."[188]

In his *Hymns on Paradise*, Ephrem the Syrian summarizes the blessings that come to the posterity of Adam and Eve through their faithfulness:

> Among the saints none is naked,
>   for they have put on glory,
> nor is any clad in those leaves,
>   or standing in shame,
> for they have found, through our Lord,
>   the robe that belonged to Adam and Eve.[189]

The contrast between authentic robes of righteousness and the deceptive trappings of earthly "glory" is so obvious that no one should be fooled; however, history shows that the humans are perennial dupes for vanity's sake. Kierkegaard warns that we must always remember that the temporary "distinctions of earthly existence are only like an actor's costume" and that "every individual should watchfully and carefully keep the fastening cords of this outer garment"—our earthly status and distinctions— "loosely tied," not tightly laced about us, "so that in the moment of transformation" when our true selves are again revealed "the garment can easily be cast off… and the inner glory… [shine] through…"[190]

---

186 Exodus 20:26.
187 Origen, *Leviticus 1-16*, 6:7, cited in G. A. Anderson, *Perfection*, pp. 122, 124. See 2 Corinthians 5:4.
188 G. A. Anderson, *Perfection*, pp. 122, 124. See *Endnote 4-72*, p. 317.
189 Ephrem the Syrian, *Paradise*, 6:9, p. 112. See *Endnote 4-73*, p. 318.
190 S. Kierkegaard, *Parables*, pp. 47-48. See *Endnote 4-74*, p. 318.

Moses 4: Text and Commentary

CHAPTER 4
(June–October 1830)

REBELLION OF SATAN (PP. 243-246)

AND *ᵃ*I, the Lord God, spake unto Moses, saying: *ᵇ*That Satan, whom thou hast commanded in the name of mine Only Begotten, is the same which was from the beginning, and he came before me, saying—Behold, *ᶜ*here am I, send me, *ᵈ*I will be thy son, and *ᵉ*I will redeem *ᶠ*all mankind, that one soul shall not be lost, and *ᵍ*surely I will do it; wherefore *ʰ*give me thine honor.

2 But, behold, *ᵃ*my Beloved Son, *ᵇ*which was my Beloved and Chosen from the beginning, said unto me—*ᶜ*Father, thy will be done, and the *ᵈ*glory be thine forever.

3 Wherefore, because that *ᵃ*Satan rebelled against me, and sought to destroy the agency of man, which I, the Lord God, had given him, and also, *ᵇ*that I should give unto him mine own power; *ᶜ*by the power of mine Only Begotten, *ᵈ*I caused that he should be cast down;

4 And he *ᵃ*became Satan, yea, even the devil, the *ᵇ*father of all lies, to deceive and to blind men, and to lead them captive at his will, even as many as would not hearken unto my voice.

TRANSGRESSION (PP. 246-257)

5 And now the *ᵃ*serpent was more *ᵇ*subtle than any beast of the field which I, the Lord God, had made.

6 And Satan put it into the heart of the serpent, (for he *ᵃ*had drawn away many after him,) and he *ᵇ*sought also to beguile Eve, for he *ᶜ*knew not the mind of God, wherefore he *ᵈ*sought to destroy the world.

7 And he said unto the woman: Yea, *ᵃ*hath God said—Ye shall not eat of every tree of the garden? (And he *ᵇ*spake by the mouth of the serpent.)

8 *ᵃ*And the woman said unto the serpent: We may eat of the fruit of the trees of the garden;

9 But of the fruit of the *ᵃ*tree which thou beholdest in the midst of the garden, God hath said—Ye shall not eat of it, *ᵇ*neither shall ye touch it, lest ye die.

10 And the serpent said unto the woman: *ᵃ*Ye shall not surely die;

11 For God doth know that in the day ye eat thereof, then *ᵃ*your eyes shall be opened, and *ᵇ*ye shall be as gods, *ᶜ*knowing good and evil.

12 And when the *ᵃ*woman saw that the tree was good for food, and that *ᵇ*it became pleasant to the eyes, and a tree to be desired *ᶜ*to make her wise, *ᵈ*she took of the fruit thereof, and did eat, and also *ᵉ*gave unto her husband with her, and he did eat.

APRONS AND HIDING (PP. 258-261)

13 And the *ᵃ*eyes of them both were opened, and they knew that they had been naked. And they sewed *ᵇ*fig-leaves together and made themselves aprons.

14 And *ᵃ*they heard the voice of the Lord God, *ᵇ*as they were walking in the garden, *ᶜ*in the cool of the day; and Adam and his wife went to *ᵈ*hide themselves from the presence of the Lord God *ᵉ*amongst the trees of the garden.

CONFESSION (PP. 261-263)

15 And *ᵃ*I, the Lord God, called unto Adam, and said unto him: *ᵇ*Where goest thou?

16 And he said: *ᵃ*I heard thy voice in the garden, and *ᵇ*I was afraid, because I beheld that I was naked, and I hid myself.

17 And I, the Lord God, said unto Adam: *ᵃ*Who told thee thou wast naked? *ᵇ*Hast thou eaten of the tree whereof I commanded thee that thou shouldst not eat, if so thou shouldst surely die?

18 And the man said: The *ᵃ*woman thou gavest me, and *ᵇ*commandest that she should remain with me, she gave me of the fruit of the tree and I did eat.

19 And I, the Lord God, said unto the woman: What is this thing which thou hast done? And the woman said: The *ᵃ*serpent beguiled me, and I did eat.

CONSEQUENCES (PP. 264-273)

20 And *ᵃ*I, the Lord God, said unto the serpent: *ᵇ*Because thou hast done this *ᶜ*thou shalt be cursed above *ᵈ*all cattle, and above every beast of the field; *ᵉ*upon thy belly shalt thou go, and *ᶠ*dust shalt thou eat all the days of thy life;

21 And *ᵃ*I will put enmity between thee and the woman, between *ᵇ*thy seed and *ᶜ*her seed; and *ᵈ*he shall bruise thy head, and thou shalt bruise his heel.

22 Unto the woman, I, the Lord God, said: *ᵃ*I will greatly multiply thy sorrow and thy conception. *ᵇ*In sorrow thou shalt bring forth children, and *ᶜ*thy desire shall be to thy husband, and he shall rule over thee.

23 And unto Adam, I, the Lord God, said: *ᵃ*Because thou hast hearkened unto the voice of thy wife, and hast eaten of the fruit of the tree of which I commanded thee, saying—Thou shalt not eat of it, *ᵇ*cursed shall be the ground *ᶜ*for thy sake; *ᵈ*in sorrow shalt thou eat of it all the days of thy life.

24 *ᵃ*Thorns also, and thistles shall it bring forth to thee, and *ᵇ*thou shalt eat the herb of the field.

25 *ᵃ*By the sweat of thy face shalt thou eat bread, *ᵇ*until thou shalt return unto the ground—for thou shalt surely die—for out of it wast thou taken: for *ᶜ*dust thou wast, and unto dust shalt thou return.

ADAM NAMES EVE (PP. 273-276)

26 And *ᵃ*Adam called his wife's name Eve, because she was the *ᵇ*mother of all living; for thus have I, the Lord God, called the *ᶜ*first of all women, which are many.

27 Unto Adam, and also unto his wife, did I, the Lord God, make *ᵃ*coats of skins, and *ᵇ*clothed them.

EXPULSION FROM EDEN (PP. 276-282)

28 And I, the Lord God, said unto mine Only Begotten: Behold, the *ᵃ*man is become as one of us to know good and evil; and now *ᵇ*lest he put forth his hand and partake also of the tree of life, and *ᶜ*eat and live forever,

29 Therefore I, the Lord God, *ᵃ*will send him forth from the Garden of Eden, *ᵇ*to till the ground from whence he was taken;

30 For as I, the Lord God, liveth, even so *ᵃ*my words cannot return void, for as they go forth out of my mouth they must be fulfilled.

31 So *ᵃ*I drove out the man, and I placed *ᵇ*at the east of the Garden of Eden, *ᶜ*cherubim and a *ᵈ*flaming sword, which turned every way *ᵉ*to keep the way of the tree of life.

EPILOGUE (PP. 282-282)

32 (And these are the words which I spake unto my servant Moses, and they are true even as I will; and I have spoken them unto you. *ᵃ*See thou show them unto no man, until I command you, except to them that believe. Amen.)

*1 And **I, the Lord God, spake unto Moses**, saying: **That Satan, whom thou hast command-ed** in the name of mine Only Begotten, **is the same which was from the beginning**, and he came before me, saying—Behold **here am I, send me**, I will be thy son, and **I will redeem** all mankind, that one soul shall not be lost, and surely I will do it; wherefore give me thine honor.*

1 **a** ***I, the Lord God, spake unto Moses.*** The JST transforms the narrative into a direct, first-person form, as it did in the Creation account of Moses 2-3.

b ***That Satan, whom thou hast commanded… is the same which was from the beginning.*** "Satan" is a word of Hebrew origin, meaning an accuser or adversary. The qualifier ("whom thou hast commanded") refers to 1:21, where Moses commanded Satan "in the name of the Only Begotten" to depart. Here, in verses 1-4, the Lord digresses from the story of the Fall in order to give the background needed to understand the roles of Satan and the Savior.

In the *Qur'an* and in the book of Moses—in contrast to Genesis—the corresponding accounts of Satan's rebellion and Adam and Eve's Fall form "a single, continuous story."[191]

c ***here am I, send me.*** Draper, *et al.* note that this statement carries the intrinsic claim "that the speaker is in the right path, ready to do the Lord's bidding."[192] Likewise, Auerbach observes that the phrase is meant to indicate "a moral position in respect to God."[193] The fact that Satan's intentions were already in direct opposition to God's plan falsifies his claim of moral readiness, substantiating the scriptural assertion that the Devil is "a liar from the beginning."[194]

Since Jesus Christ was already known by all to be God's "Beloved and Chosen from the beginning,"[195] the very fact that Satan sought to answer the call was in itself a direct affront to the Father. Top correctly concludes that there was only One who could rightly reply to God, observing: "In light of the premortal stature of Christ, it appears more likely that the Father's question 'Whom shall I send?' was an invitation for Jesus to publicly and voluntarily accept the calling and appointment that was his birthright as the Firstborn, the Preeminent One. It was a call for our commitment and common consent rather than a request for résumés."[196]

Satan's self-centeredness is fittingly reflected in the wording of his proposal. With passionate rapid-fire delivery, he narcissistically repeats the terms "I" and "me" six times in the short span of half a verse. OT1 and OT2 reinforce the stylistic egoism of the phrase "Behold, here am I" with their briefer reading: "Behold I"[197]—the latter rendering in all likelihood being closer to the phrase would have been worded by an ancient speaker.[198] The current wording first appeared in the 1902 edition of the Pearl of Great Price.[199]

d ***I will be thy son.*** Compare Moses 1:19 where, in a rage, Satan claimed the role he was here denied—namely, the right to become the Only Begotten of the Father in the flesh.[200]

e ***I will redeem.*** Whatever Satan exactly meant by his proposal to become the "redeemer" of all mankind, it was doubtless very different from what the Savior offered. Elder Spencer J. Condie observed: "Because [the Devil's] plan… required no Atonement for sin, … he could save his own satanic skin from any suffering."[201]

191 A. at-Tabataba'i, *Al-Mizan*, 2:35, 1:179.
192 R. D. Draper, *et al.*, *Commentary*, p. 38; cf. Genesis 22:1; Isaiah 6:8; Acts 9:10; Abraham 3:27.
193 E. Auerbach, *Mimesis*, p. 8; cf. H. Fisch, *Presence*, p. 307.
194 D&C 93:25.
195 Moses 4:2.
196 B. L. Top, *Life Before*, p. 109. See *Excursus 23: The Roles of Christ, Adam, and Michael*, p. 582.
197 S. H. Faulring, *et al.*, *Original Manuscripts*, pp. 90, 599.
198 E. Auerbach, *Mimesis*, p. 8.
199 K. P. Jackson, *Book of Moses*, p. 79.
200 See also *Commentary* 1:13-c, p. 53; Moses 5:13.
201 S. J. Condie, *Agency*, p. 6.

*1 And I, the Lord God, spake unto Moses, saying: That Satan, whom thou hast commanded in the name of mine Only Begotten, is the same which was from the beginning, and he came before me, saying—Behold, here am I, send me, I will be thy son, and I will redeem **all mankind, that one soul shall not be lost**, and **surely I will do it**; wherefore **give me thine honor**.*

*2 But, behold, **my Beloved Son, which was my Beloved and Chosen from the beginning**, said unto me—**Father, thy will be done**, and the glory be thine forever.*

f   ***all mankind, that one soul shall not be lost.*** Joseph Smith summarized the competing claims and the result of Satan's rebellion: "The contention in heaven was—Jesus said there would be certain souls that would not be saved; and the Devil said he could save them all, and laid his plans before the grand council, who gave their vote in favor of Jesus Christ. So the Devil rose up in rebellion against God, and was cast down, with all who put up their heads for him."[202] George Laub's retrospective summary of what appears to be the same discourse more specifically indicates that the only ones that Jesus said he could not save (i.e., save in one of the three kingdoms of glory) were those who sinned against the Holy Ghost—in other words, the sons of perdition.[203] President Brigham Young affirmed: "None are condemned except those who have the privilege of receiving the words of eternal life and refuse to receive them."[204] "God will save all who are determined to be saved."[205]

Ironically, Satan, the one who proposed a plan whereby no soul would be lost, became himself a soul who Jesus could not save. Indeed, upon him was conferred the name of "perdition"—loss itself.[206] In poignant parallel, Satan became a type for Judas Iscariot, of whom Jesus Christ said in his prayer at the Last Supper: "those that thou gavest me I have kept, and none of them is lost, but the son of perdition."[207]

g   ***surely I will do it.*** Satan seems not merely to be claiming that he will surely redeem all mankind, but also that he alone can do it and—even more arrogantly—that he can do it alone.

h   ***give me thine honor.*** Note that D&C 29:36 equates God's power with His honor.

2   **a**   ***my Beloved Son.*** The phrase "my Beloved" is repeated twice in the verse, emphasizing the deep and personal regard of the Father for his Son. Contrast this with the distancing third-person reference that introduces the Adversary in verse 1: "That Satan…"

b   ***which was my Beloved and Chosen from the beginning.*** Elder Neal A. Maxwell eloquently enumerated the reasons why Jesus was so uniquely honored: He was "utterly incomparable in what He is, what He knows, what He has accomplished, and what He has experienced.… In intelligence and performance, He far surpasses the individual and composite capacities and achievements of all who have lived, live now, and will yet live!… He rejoices in our genuine goodness and achievement, but any assessment of where we stand in relation to Him tells us that we do not stand at all! We kneel!"[208]

c   ***Father, thy will be done.*** Elder Maxwell described the nature of the premortal council, affirming that it "was not an unstructured meeting, nor was it a discussion between plans, nor an idea-producing session, as to how to formulate the plan for salvation and carry it out. Our Father's plan was known, and the actual question put was who the Father should send to carry out the plan."[209] Abraham 3:27 makes it clear that it was actually Jesus Christ who was the first to answer the Father's request.

---

202   J. Smith, Jr., *Teachings*, 7 April 1844, p. 357.
203   J. Smith, Jr., 7 April 1844, as reported in E. England, *Laub*, p. 22. See D&C 76:43-44, the overview of Moses 4, p. 223, and *Excursus 22: The Nature of Satan's Premortal Proposal*, p. 577.
204   B. Young, *12 June 1860-b*, p. 294.
205   B. Young, *9 November 1856*, p. 111; cf. B. Young, *17 February 1861*, p. 125; C. S. Lewis, *Divorce*, p. 72.
206   J. F. McConkie, *et al.*, *Revelations*, p. 217. See D&C 76:37-39.
207   John 17:12. See *Commentary 5:24-b*, p. 375.
208   N. A. Maxwell, *Redeemer*, p. 8.
209   N. A. Maxwell, *Deposition*, p. 11.

*2 But, behold, my Beloved Son, which was my Beloved and Chosen from the beginning, said unto me—**Father, thy will be done**, and the **glory be thine forever**.*

*3 Wherefore, because that **Satan rebelled against me, and sought to destroy the agency of man**, which I, the Lord God, had given him, and also, **that I should give unto him mine own power**; **by the power of mine Only Begotten, I caused that he should be cast down**;*

In stark contrast to Satan's speech, the Redeemer never once mentions the words "I" or "me," being wholly focused on the will and the glory of the Father.

d ***glory be thine forever.*** Jesus later contrasted His position to the one adopted by Satan: "He that speaketh of himself seeketh his own glory: but he that seeketh his glory that sent him, the same is true, and no unrighteousness is in him."[210]

3 a ***Satan rebelled against me, and sought to destroy the agency of man.*** D&C 29:36 underscores the irony of Satan's efforts to destroy man's agency by pointing out that it was "because of their agency" that a "third part of the hosts of heaven" were permitted to follow him in rebellion.

Although the exercise of agency was surely a condition of the premortal existence, Moses 7:32 seems to imply, erroneously, that it did not exist until Adam and Eve came into the Garden: "I gave unto them their knowledge, in the day I created them; and in the Garden of Eden, gave I unto man his agency." OT2, however, renders this verse differently: "I gave unto them their intelligence and in the Garden of Eden man had agency."[211] Whether this emendation took place at the initiative of a scribe or under the direction of the Prophet, its purpose is obvious: to make it clear that agency was not something "given" for the first time to mankind in the Garden, but rather that it was something they already had. The modification also forestalls a possible implication that Adam and Eve had already been given "knowledge" at the time of their creation. Significantly, OT2 states that they were given "intelligence" rather than "knowledge" at that time. Thus, the change leads us to infer that Adam and Eve began to obtain the "knowledge" they lacked only later, after their transgression.

b ***that I should give unto him mine own power.*** Commented Elder Maxwell: "[Satan] wanted glory, not growth; control, not salvation. His ascendancy meant more to him than our agency. The Devil is a despot."[212]

c ***by the power of mine Only Begotten.*** Moses had seen the power of the Only Begotten used in a similar way when, in His name, he commanded Satan to depart.[213]

d ***I caused that he should be cast down.*** Lehi records that an "angel of God... had fallen from heaven; wherefore he became a devil, having sought that which was evil before God."[214] Although Moses 4:6 and Abraham 3:28 say only that "many" followed Satan, the Doctrine and Covenants is more specific. The Lord, speaking of Satan's rebellion said that it was "a third part of the hosts of heaven" that he "turned... away from me because of their agency."[215]

It is possible to see an allusion to this event in the separation of light and darkness in Day One of creation.[216] A parallel can also be seen in the account of how God "drove out the man" from the Garden[217]—though, in Adam's case, God held out the joyous possibility for his return.

210 John 7:18.
211 S. H. Faulring, *et al.*, *Original Manuscripts*, p. 618; K. P. Jackson, *Book of Moses*, p. 25. See *Excursus 47: Islamic Perspectives Relating to Redemption, p. 645*
212 N. A. Maxwell, *Deposition*, p. 81. See *Commentary* 4:1g, p. 244.
213 *Commentary* 1:21-c, p. 58.
214 2 Nephi 2:17; cf. Revelation 12:7-9; 2 Peter 2:4: Jude 1:6; Isaiah 14:12-17; D&C 29:36-38; Abraham 3:28.
215 D&C 29:36; cf. Revelation 12:14.
216 See *Commentary* 2:4-c, p. 101.
217 See *Commentary* 4:31-a, p. 280.

*4 And he **became Satan**, yea, even the devil, the **father of all lies, to deceive and to blind men, and to lead them captive at his will, even as many as would not hearken unto my voice**.*

*5 And now the **serpent** was more **subtle** than any beast of the field which I, the Lord God, had made.*

4   a   ***became Satan.*** From this moment, Satan is no more a mere rebel but rather a hostile and perpetual adversary.[218] Only little children[219] and the righteous[220] fully escape some measure of his power. "During the millennium he will be bound, and then loosed at the end of that period…[221] At the end, he will be vanquished… and banished to his hell."[222]

     b   ***father of all lies, to deceive and to blind men, and to lead them captive at his will, even as many as would not hearken unto my voice.*** Verse 4, and especially this phrase, should be read as an "announcement of plot" for what will follow in the rest of Moses 4.[223] Satan will lie to Eve in order to *deceive* her; her eyes will not suddenly be opened with the wisdom he promised, but rather she will become *blind* with regard to her true situation, and she and Adam will be figuratively *led captive* into the tree in a vain effort to hide their transgression from God. All this came as a consequence of the fact that they *did not hearken* to the voice of the Lord.[224] Later, after having violated the "first commandments" and entered mortality, God "made known unto them the plan of redemption" and "gave unto them [other] commandments"[225] so that through their faith and obedience they could "escape from the grasp of… death and hell."[226]

5   a   ***serpent.*** Nephi and John both identify Satan by referring to him figuratively as "that old serpent."[227] However, the latter part of this verse leads the reader to a literal interpretation when it refers to the serpent as a simple "beast of the field."[228] The portrayal of the serpent as a "beast of the field" rather than as one of the "creeping things"[229] is consistent with the ancient imagery that portrays the serpent as a legged animal before the Fall.[230]

     b   ***subtle.*** The Hebrew term behind "subtle" depicts the serpent as shrewd, cunning, and crafty, but not as wise.[231] "Subtle," in this context, also has to do with the ability to make something appear one way when it is actually another.[232] Thus, it will not be in the least out of character later for Satan or his accomplices to disguise their identity in order to deceive.[233]

     In explaining how Satan deceived Eve through the serpent, the *Cave of Treasures* cites the example of teaching parrots to speak through the use of a mirror. Their trainer "bringeth a large mirror and placeth between himself and the bird. He then beginneth to talk to the bird, and immediately the parrot heareth the voice of the man, it turneth round, and when it seeth its own form reflected in the mirror; it becometh pleased straightway, because it imagineth that a fellow parrot is talking to it… In this manner… did Satan enter in and dwell in the

---

218   See *Commentary* 4:1-b, p. 243.
219   D&C 29:47; Moroni 8:8.
220   1 Nephi 22:26; J. Smith, Jr., *Words*, 5 January 1841, p. 60; G. Weil, *Legends*, p. 38.
221   See Revelation 20:2-3, 7. See also D&C 43:31; 45:55; 88:110-111.
222   R. D. Draper, *et al.*, *Commentary*, p. 40. See D&C 88:110-115.
223   L. Turner, *Announcements*.
224   See *Commentary* 4:16-a, p. 262; Moses 4:23; 2 Nephi 9:28-29.
225   Alma 12:31-32.
226   2 Nephi 9:10. See *Commentary* 5:24-a, p. 375.
227   2 Nephi 2:18; Revelation 12:9.
228   See *Commentary* 3:19-a, p. 177 and 4:6-a, p. 249.
229   Moses 2:24.
230   See *Commentary* 4:20-e, p. 265.
231   V. P. Hamilton, *Genesis*, pp. 187-188; R. W. L. Moberly, *Serpent*, p. 25. See *Commentary* 3:25-a, p. 185.
232   See *Commentary* 4:13-b, p. 258.
233   See below. Also Moses 1:19; D&C 50:2-3; 52:14; 128:20; 129:8; G. A. Anderson, *et al.*, *Synopsis*, 44:1-2a, p. 51E; R. Giorgi, *Anges*, pp. 85-88.

*5 And now the serpent was more **subtle** than any beast of the field which I, the Lord God, had made.*

serpent, … and when he saw Eve by herself, he called her by her name. And when she turned round towards him, she saw her own form reflected in him, and she talked to him."[234] Hence, the common visual portrayal of a serpent with features of a human female was not designed to assert that the woman was devilish, but rather to depict the Devil as trying to allay Eve's fears, deceptively appealing to her by appearing in a form that resembled her own.[235] Compare Ephrem the Syrian's *On the Fall*,[236] where Satan makes himself a dove to resemble Eve, who is also portrayed as a dove.[237]

Of significance here is the idea of the serpent as a symbol of Christ and his life-giving power.[238] In the Garden of Eden, Satan appears in the form of a serpent, yet deceptively brings death. In other OT references, the serpent also has "a strangely ambivalent significance… As it was by a serpent that the children of Israel were smitten in the desert, so it was by a serpent that they were healed.[239] It is the serpent who defeats the serpent… The *Caduceus*, the sign of the two interlaced serpents [which is used today as a symbol of the medical profession], was the sign of *Aesculapius*, who healed the dead, one signifying death, the other life…"[240] More generally, the *Caduceus* signifies "that all things have their opposites."[241]

The serpent is not only a symbol of life, but also of revealed wisdom. Jesus instructed his disciples to be "wise as serpents, and harmless as doves"[242] and there is archaeological evidence from iron age temples that these two motifs had been associated for centuries.[243] Biblical or mythological trees of immortality[244] are not infrequently depicted with a serpent or dragon at the bottom and one or two birds at the top. Sometimes the bird is a dove,[245] but often it is a hawk, falcon, or eagle—occasionally described as the serpent's adversary.[246] As mentioned above, Ephrem the Syrian portrays Eve in the Garden of Eden as a dove that is deceived by Satan's appearance as a dove.[247] In the Gnostic *Apocryphon of John*, Christ-Sophia, "the other side of the serpent, personified in an eagle," is made to say: "I appeared in the form of an eagle on the Tree of Knowledge… that I might teach them and awaken them out of the depth of sleep."[248] In connection with a portrait of an eagle—the symbol of Zeus—positioned behind a head of Orpheus in the Jewish synagogue at Dura Europos, Goodenough gives the bird the same meaning "that it frequently had in the east, when it symbolized divine inspiration, just as it continues to do in Christianity when connected with John the Evangelist, and when used on the lectern for the Bible in Christian Churches."[249] In Joseph Smith-Matthew 1:27 the gathered elect are likened to eagles, and in the parable of the mustard seed, birds are portrayed as lodging in the branches of the full grown tree of the

---

234 E. A. W. Budge, *Cave*, pp. 63-64.
235 J. O'Reilly, *Iconography*, p. 168.
236 Ephrem the Syrian, *Fall*, 4, p. 101.
237 See below and *Commentary 1:1-a*, p. 42.
238 Numbers 21:8-9; John 3:14-15; 2 Nephi 25:20; Alma 33:19; Helaman 8:14-15.
239 Numbers 21:4-9; cf. Exodus 7:8-12; John 3:14-15. See *Endnote 4-75*, p. 319. For a comprehensive study of the ambivalent symbolism of the serpent, see J. H. Charlesworth, *Serpent*.
240 H. W. Nibley, *Message 2005*, p. 314. See also A. C. Skinner, *Serpent*.
241 H. W. Nibley, *Prayer Circle*, p. 74. See *Endnote E-107*, p. 727.
242 Matthew 10:16. See also Alma 18:22, D&C 111:11, J. Smith, Jr., *Teachings*, 29 January 1843, p. 276.
243 A. C. Skinner, *Serpent*, pp. 381-382.
244 See, e.g., D. E. Wirth, *Decoding*, pp. 80-83.
245 See *Figure* 3-8, p. 145 and *Figure* 6-14, p. 473.
246 See, e.g., P. Alexander, *3 Enoch*, 2:1, p. 257; E. R. Goodenough, *Dura Symbolism*, 9:91-92; E. Isaac, *1 Enoch*, 96:2, p. 76; G. R. S. Mead, *Mandaean John-Book*, 35, pp. 65-67; J. Priest, *Moses*, 10:8-10, p. 932; M. D. Rhodes, *Hor*, p. 20; E. A. Speiser, *Etana*; F. Wisse, *Apocryphon of John*, 20:26-35, p. 118; book of Abraham Facsimile 2, figure 7; Deuteronomy 32:11; Isaiah 40:31; Revelation 4:7, 8:13, 12:14.
247 Ephrem the Syrian, *Fall*, 4, p. 101.
248 F. Wisse, *Apocryphon of John*, 23:26-31, p. 118. See G. Lettieri, *Ambiguity*, p. 47.
249 E. R. Goodenough, *Dura Symbolism*, 9:92.

*5 And now the serpent was more **subtle** than any beast of the field which I, the Lord God, had made.*

kingdom of God.[250] Significantly, Daniel 4:20-22 makes it clear that such a tree can represent, not only the kingdom of God, but also an individual who has grown to full perfection.[251] The birds, representing "powers, gifts and angels,"[252] mediate access to divine knowledge and healing power by such a person, either bringing it down from heaven or carrying the visionary upward on their wings.[253] Just as Noah was informed by the dove who brought an olive branch from "beyond the gates of the Garden of Eden" to the ark,[254] so the Prophet Joseph Smith compared one of his revelations to an "olive leaf... plucked from the Tree of Paradise."[255]

In the context of this verse, Draper, *et al.* conclude that Satan "has effectively come as the Messiah, offering a promise that only the Messiah can offer, for it is the Messiah who will control the powers of life and death and can promise life, not Satan."[256] Not only has the Devil come in guise of the Holy One, he seems to have deliberately appeared, without authorization, in a most sacred place.[257] If it is true, as Ephrem the Syrian believed, that the Tree of Knowledge was, among other things, a figure for "the veil for the sanctuary,"[258] then Satan has positioned himself, in an extreme of sacrilegious effrontery, as the very "keeper of the gate."[259] This, then, becomes a type for the scene to which Paul alludes in his description of events that were to precede the second coming of Christ: "for that day shall not come, except there come a falling away first, and that man of sin be revealed, the son of perdition; Who opposeth and exalteth himself above all that is called God, or that is worshipped; so that he as God sitteth in the temple of God, *showing himself that he is God.*"[260]

What was the nature of the forbidden fruit? Recalling an Egyptian version of the story, which revolves around the presumption of the hero, Setne, "in taking the book of Knowledge, which was guarded by the endless serpent,"[261] Nibley comments that "a book of knowledge is certainly more logical" as the object of temptation than would be a piece of actual fruit.[262] In this vein, Islamic legend insists on the idea that Satan was condemned for his claims that he would reveal a knowledge of certain things to Adam and Eve. He is portrayed as recruiting his accomplices (the "vain" peacock and the "fair and prudent" serpent, "the queen of all beasts... [who] was created a thousand years before Adam"[263]) by deceptively promising them that he would reveal to them "three mysterious words" which would "preserve [them] from sickness, age, and death."[264] Having by this means won over the serpent, Satan then directly equates the effect of knowing these secret words with the eating of the forbidden fruit by promising the same protection from death to Eve if she will but partake.[265] Nibley elaborates: "Satan disobeyed orders when he revealed certain secrets to Adam and Eve, not

250   Matthew 13:32; Mark 4:32; Luke 13:19; H. Koester, *et al., Thomas,* 20, p. 128.

251   Cf. G. R. S. Mead, *Mandaean John-Book,* 35, pp. 65-67; *Commentary 3:9-g,* p. 163.

252   J. Smith, Jr., *Teachings,* December 1835, p. 98.

253   Cf. *Commentary 1:1-b,* p. 42; *Figure 3-8,* p. 145; *Figure 6-14,* p. 473; *Figure E53-13,* p. 684; M. E. Lewis, *Early,* pp. 191-192; G. R. S. Mead, *Mandaean John-Book,* 35, pp. 65-67. See *Endnote E-204,* p. 754.

254   J. Neusner, *Genesis Rabbah 1,* 33:6, p. 351, Genesis 8:11.

255   J. Smith, Jr., *Teachings,* 14 January 1833, p. 18; cf. *Commentary 3:9-g,* p. 165.

256   R. D. Draper, *et al., Commentary,* p. 43; see John 5:25-26; 2 Nephi 9:3-26

257   *Ibid.,* pp. 42, 150-151.

258   Ephrem the Syrian, *Paradise,* 3:5, p. 92.

259   2 Nephi 9:41.

260   2 Thessalonians 2:3-4, emphasis added. See also *Commentary 1:15-d,* p. 54.

261   H. W. Nibley, *Message 2005,* p. 310.

262   *Ibid.,* p. 311. For a Jewish story of a book of knowledge given to Adam in Eden, see S. Savedow, *Rezial,* pp. 2-4.

263   See the overview of Moses 4, pp. 224-225 and *Excursus 8: The Origin and Premortal Existence of Human Spirits,* p. 540.

264   G. Weil, *Legends,* p. 26.

265   *Ibid.,* p. 30. For a similar theme in the story of the Watchers, see *Excursus 24: The Watchers,* p. 585.

*5 And now the serpent was more **subtle** than any beast of the field which I, the Lord God, had made.*

*6 And Satan put it into the heart of the serpent, (for he **had drawn away many after him**,) and he **sought also to beguile Eve**, for he knew not the mind of God, wherefore he sought to destroy the world.*

because they were not known and done in other worlds, but because he was not authorized in that time and place to convey them."[266] Although Satan had "given the fruit to Adam and Eve, it was not his prerogative to do so—regardless of what had been done in other worlds. (When the time comes for such fruit, it will be given us legitimately.)"[267]

6   a   *had drawn away many after him.* This JST change reemphasizes the point that the serpent is not to be identified with Satan himself, but is rather a subsequently-recruited accomplice. Verse 5 mentioned it simply as a "beast of the field which I, the Lord God, had made."[268] The phrase in v. 7, "And he [Satan] spake by the mouth of the serpent," further reinforces this same idea. Such an interpretation, however, should be considered in light of what is presented in the LDS temple endowment.

In an effort to explain the role of the serpent, the Fathers of the Ethiopian Church stressed the idea that Satan "could not carry out his plan... if he entered Paradise in his own form."[269] The *Cave of Treasures* says that "he knew his appearance was foul, and that if Eve saw his form, she would betake herself to fly straightway before him."[270] Having failed to enlist any of the other animals as his helper,[271] the Devil "covered himself with the serpent" or, in other words, "he took the serpent as a garment."[272]

The Greek, Armenian, and Georgian versions of the *Life of Adam and Eve* attempt to explain how the serpent was "drawn away" by Satan. The accounts imply that the serpent received food inferior to that given to the other animals (i.e., the thistles growing outside the Garden rather than the paradisiacal fruit found within it) and, inexplicably, that the serpent had been previously expelled from the Garden, just as Satan had been.[273] Moreover, Satan argued that the serpent should not allow himself to bow down to Adam: "You came into being before him: why is it that you, who are the former one, worship the later? Rather should the younger worship the older."[274] Explains Stone, "These oddities may be taken to be the result of words of the great Deceiver. Satan lies... for the purpose of inciting the serpent to rebellion. One way he does this is rhetorical, by likening the serpent to himself. He implies that, like him, the serpent has been expelled; like him, the serpent has been deprived of the benefits of paradise." Whether or not this assertion is true of the serpent, "all of this clearly implies that Satan was expelled and Satan was deprived of benefits."[275]

b   *sought also to beguile Eve.* Nibley explains: "The perfect and beautiful union of Adam and Eve excited the envy and jealousy of the Evil One, who made it his prime objective to break it up... His first step (or wedge) [was] to get one of them to make an important decision without consulting the other. He approached Adam in the absence of Eve with a proposition

266   H. W. Nibley, *Return*, p. 63.
267   H. W. Nibley, *Gifts*, p. 92. See also *Commentary* 3:9-h, p. 167; 3:19-b, p. 177; 4:9-a, p. 252; 4:14-e, p. 260. See *Excursus 25: The Tree of Life as the Hidden Throne of God*, p. 591. See *Endnote 4-76*, p. 319.
268   See the discussion in U. Cassuto, *Adam to Noah*, pp. 139-142. See also *Commentary* 3:19-a, p. 177.
269   E. A. W. Budge, *Cave*, p. 65. See also W. L. Lipscomb, *Creation*, 10-11, pp. 120, 262.
270   E. A. W. Budge, *Cave*, p. 63.
271   B. Mika'el, *Mysteries*, pp. 24-25.
272   H. E. Gaylord, Jr., *3 Baruch*, 9:7, pp. 672-673.
273   G. A. Anderson, *et al.*, *Synopsis*, 44(16):2-3, pp. 18E, 49E-50E; cf. Timothy of Alexandria, *Abbaton*, p. 200 and *Commentary* 4:6-b, p. 249.
274   G. A. Anderson, *et al.*, *Synopsis*, Armenian, 44(16):2b, p. 49E; cf. M. Herbert, *Irish Apocrypha*, pp. 3-4. See *Commentary* 6:2-d, p. 476 and *Excursus 21: The Power and Premortal Status of Satan*, p. 575.
275   M. E. Stone, *Fall of Satan*, p. 56.

*6 And Satan put it into the heart of the serpent, (for he had drawn away many after him,) and he **sought also to beguile Eve**, for he **knew not the mind of God**, wherefore he **sought to destroy the world**.*

to make him wise, and being turned down he sought out the woman to find her alone and thus undermine her resistance more easily. It is important that he was able to find them both alone."[276]

Christian traditions recount that Adam and Eve were each given responsibilities to care for different areas of the Garden and to feed particular kinds of animals.[277] Eve was said to have been approached by the Tempter at an hour when the angels charged to guard her were called away to prayer.[278] According to the *Discourse on Abbaton*, when she "came forth, and passing northwards through Paradise, she came to the wall to fetch food for the beasts [according to the Father's command]... Now the Devil lived nigh unto Paradise, and he lay in wait for Adam and Eve by day and by night. And when he saw Eve by herself he entered into the serpent, saying: I will whisper in her ear, I will make her to eat of the tree, and I will cause them to be turned out from Paradise, for I myself was turned out."[279] Although most traditions say that Satan recruited the serpent because he could find no way to personally enter the Garden, the Greek version of the *Life of Adam and Eve* implies that Satan entered Paradise by means of Eve, who expressly let him through its gate: "And I [i.e., Eve] opened [it for him] and he entered the Garden and went before me. He walked a little way, then turned and said to me: 'I have changed my mind, and I will not give you [something] to eat.' [These things he said wishing to trap me in the end. And he said to me: I will not give you something to eat] unless you swear to me that you will give also to your husband."[280]

c ***knew not the mind of God.*** Similarly, Satan lacks the power to directly discern the mind of man. D&C 6:16 states that "there is none else save God that knowest thy thoughts and the intents of thy heart." President Joseph F. Smith explained: "There is a difference between knowledge and pure intelligence. Satan possesses knowledge, far more than we have, but he has not intelligence or he would render obedience to the principles of truth and right."[281] Indeed, disobedience of itself leads to increased darkness and ignorance.[282]

Nibley calls Moses 4:6 "the most encouraging verse in all the scriptures. Satan seems to be getting the upper hand all the time, but he doesn't know the mind of God. There are a lot of things he doesn't know." "Mephistopheles[, the "Satan" character in *Faust*,] is the one... who always wants to do evil and only succeeds in doing good. Of course, it drives him wild. He can't win."[283]

d ***sought to destroy the world.*** The statement makes more sense if "the world" is interpreted to signify not the material earth, but more specifically its inhabitants.[284] In support of this reading, Joseph Smith said: "The world and earth are not synonymous terms. The world is the human family."[285] In a similar vein, he equated "the end of the world" not with the physical calamities that the earth would undergo, but rather with "the destruction of the wicked."[286]

---

276 H. W. Nibley, *Patriarchy*, p. 88; cf. Moses 3:18; G. A. Anderson, *et al.*, *Synopsis*, 33:2, p. 37E; D. C. Matt, *Zohar 1*, 1:36a, pp. 226-227.

277 See, e.g., G. A. Anderson, *et al.*, *Synopsis*, 32:2-3, p. 36E.

278 G. A. Anderson, *Original Form*, n. 7, p. 217. Compare M. Barker, *Infancy Gospel of James* 1:13, p. 156.

279 Timothy of Alexandria, *Abbaton*, pp. 199-200; cf. G. A. Anderson, *et al.*, *Synopsis*, 15:3-17:2, pp. 49E-51E; Commentary 4:6-a, p. 249.

280 G. A. Anderson, *et al.*, *Synopsis*, 19:1a-19:1d, pp. 56E-57E. On the gate, see M. Herbert, *Irish Apocrypha*, p. 5.

281 J. F. Smith, *Gospel Doctrine*, 1919, p. 58.

282 Alma 12:11; J. Smith, Jr., *Teachings*, 22 January 1834, p. 67.

283 H. W. Nibley, *Teachings of the PGP*, 17, p. 208.

284 See 2 Nephi 2:18; 9:8-9.

285 J. Smith, Jr., *Words*, 5 January 1841, p. 60.

286 *Ibid.*, before 8 August 1839, p. 13, see also p. 25.

*6 And Satan put it into the heart of the serpent, (for he had drawn away many after him,) and he sought also to beguile Eve, for he knew not the mind of God, wherefore he **sought to destroy the world**.*

*7 And he said unto the woman: Yea, **hath God said**—Ye shall not eat of every tree of the garden? (And he **spake by the mouth of the serpent**.)*

OT1 reads "he thought to destroy."[287] The term "sought" first appeared in OT2.[288]

7   a   ***hath God said.*** Hamilton views this difficult Hebrew phrase as a "feigned expression of surprise" and indignation: "Indeed! To think that God said you are not to eat of any tree of the Garden!"[289] "The serpent's obvious inaccuracy in his rendition of God's prohibition sounds like… lack of subtlety" but is actually a "well-known trick of the con-man to appear stupid to put others in a position of sham superiority."[290] The serpent "grossly exaggerates God's prohibition" and attempts to move Eve's perception of God "from beneficent provider to cruel oppressor."[291] Moreover, the "serpent subtly softens the severity of the prohibition by using [the word 'said'] in place of the original 'command.' Then it deliberately misquotes God so that the woman cannot give a one-word reply but is drawn into conversation that forces her to focus upon the forbidden tree that he had not mentioned."[292] A similar tactic to misrepresent God's commandments as deliberately repressive was used by Korihor in the Book of Mormon.[293]

In contrast to the name used by others in the rest of this chapter, Satan uses the term "God" rather than "Lord God."[294] Explains Wenham: "The god they are talking about is malevolent, secretive, and concerned to restrict man: his character is so different from that of Yahweh Elohim that the narrative pointedly avoids the name."[295] Alternatively, the narrator may simply be reflecting the idea that the name of the Lord is so sacred that it cannot be uttered by the serpent.

    b   ***spake by the mouth of the serpent.*** An Islamic tradition imagines that Satan seated himself "in the hollow part of [the serpent's] front teeth, poisoned them to all eternity," and spoke to Eve from the mouth of the beast itself.[296]

The serpent consistently uses plural verbs in his dialogue with Eve. Some commentators take this fact, in connection with the implication that her companion was "with her."[297] to indicate that Adam was within earshot of the whole conversation. However, given the specific mention that the serpent "sought… to beguile Eve"[298] and the fact of Adam's silence throughout the episode, it seems more likely that Eve was alone, and that Satan's speech was meant to include Adam only indirectly. Note, however, a tradition preserved in a twelfth-century Christian source that has the scene beginning "with an unsuccessful attempt to lead Adam astray" before Satan approaches Eve.[299]

---

287   S. H. Faulring, *et al.*, *Original Manuscripts*, p. 90.

288   *Ibid.*, p. 600.

289   V. P. Hamilton, *Genesis*, p. 186. Compare U. Cassuto, *Adam to Noah*, p. 144. See also 4QGen[k] 3:1: ["Has God] *really* [said, 'You shall not eat of any tree of] the garden'?" (M. Abegg, Jr., *et al.*, *Scrolls Bible*, p. 7 n. 8, emphasis mine. See also 1QGen 3:11-14). The interrogative particle translated "really" is neither found in the Masoretic text nor the *Septuagint*.

290   A. LaCocque, *Trial*, p. 145.

291   V. P. Hamilton, *Genesis*, pp. 188-189.

292   N. M. Sarna, *Genesis*, p. 24.

293   Alma 30:13, 23-27.

294   See *Commentary* 3:4-e, p. 154.

295   G. J. Wenham, *Genesis 1-15*, p. 57.

296   G. Weil, *Legends*, pp. 25-29; cf. A. al-Tha'labi, *Lives*, p. 51.

297   Moses 4:12.

298   Moses 4:6.

299   E. Auerbach, *Mimesis*, p. 146; cf. al-Tabari, *Creation*, 1:104, p. 275. See *Commentary* 4:6-a, p. 249.

*8 **And the woman** said unto the serpent: We may eat of the fruit of the trees of the **garden**;*

*9 But of the fruit of the **tree** which thou beholdest **in the midst of the garden**, God hath said—Ye shall not eat of it, **neither shall ye touch it, lest ye die**.*

*10 And the serpent said unto the woman: **Ye shall not surely die**;*

8   a   ***And the woman… garden.*** This entire verse was omitted, no doubt inadvertently, in OT1.[300] A note in OT2 in the handwriting of Sidney Rigdon restored the missing text.[301]

9   a   ***tree… in the midst of the garden.*** The indefinite reference to "the tree" paves the way for later confusion about its identity and purpose.[302] Whereas the previous narrative explicitly disclosed to the reader only that the Tree of Life was in the middle of the Garden,[303] Eve's statement now makes it clear that the Tree of Knowledge must have been located there as well—or at least in the same general direction.[304] Satan will exploit the ambiguity to further his purpose.[305] Explains Barker: "When the serpent tempted Eve, he made the two trees seem identical: the Tree of the Knowledge of Good and Evil would open her eyes, and she would be like God, knowing both good and evil. Almost the same was true of the Tree of Life, for Wisdom opened the eyes of those who ate her fruit, and as they became wise, they became divine."[306]

The plausibility of the theme of confusion between the two trees in the record of Moses is strengthened by its appearance in related non-Biblical accounts. For example, in the *Qur'an* Satan does more than simply say that Eve will not suffer death if she eats the forbidden fruit. Instead, he goes beyond mere denial to make the false claim that it is "the tree of immortality."[307] However, in reality the tree was just the opposite of what the Devil stated it to be: "It was the tree of death, the spiritual death of man."[308]

   b   ***neither shall ye touch it, lest ye die.*** Some interpreters have concluded that Eve is herself "[exaggerating] the stringency of the divine prohibition, [thus introducing] into her own mind the suggestion of an unreasonably strict God."[309] Rabbinical commentators used this story to draw a lesson about the principle of not adding to the commandments of God.[310]

However, pointing to parallels that evidence "a graver connotation than mere touching,"[311] Cassuto sees the clause *neither shall ye touch it* as "simply synonymous with the preceding clause": "Ye shall not eat of it."[312] Thus, it is possible that Eve was simply relating details of what she had been told, consistent with the *Qur'an* which says the tree was not even to be approached.[313] Also supporting this view is an 1835 LDS publication of the verse which added the words "neither shall you touch it" to the Lord's original commandment.[314]

10   a   ***Ye shall not surely die.*** A tone of sarcasm and derision can be discerned in the serpent's contradiction of God's words, doubtless intended to make Eve appear foolish and naïve in her

---

300   S. H. Faulring, *et al.*, *Original Manuscripts*, pp. 90-91.
301   *Ibid.*, p. 600.
302   See *Commentary* 3:9-h, p. 167 and 4:14-e, p. 260.
303   Moses 3:9.
304   E. Kastler, *Commentaire*.
305   Moses 4:9-11.
306   M. Barker, *Wisdom*, p. 2.
307   M. M. Ali, *Qur'an*, 20:120, p. 624; cf. A. al-Tha'labi, *Lives*, pp. 50-51.
308   M. M. Ali, *Qur'an*, p. 20 n. 62. See also *Commentary* 4:5-b, p. 246.
309   N. M. Sarna, *Genesis*, p. 24.
310   Deuteronomy 4:2, 13:1. See G. A. Anderson, *Perfection*, pp. 77-78; J. Goldin, *Fathers*, 1, pp. 8-10; *Commentary* 3:17-a, p. 174.
311   E.g., Genesis 20:6, 26:11.
312   U. Cassuto, *Adam to Noah*, p. 145.
313   M. M. Ali, *Qur'an*, 2:35, p. 19.
314   K. P. Jackson, *Book of Moses*, p. 75.

10 And the serpent said unto the woman: **Ye shall not surely die***;*

11 For God doth know that in the day ye eat thereof, then **your eyes shall be opened***, and ye* **shall be as gods***, knowing good and evil.*

credulity. A similar tone can be heard in the words of Nehor, who "testified unto the people that… they need not fear nor tremble."[315] The *Zohar* has Satan saying, "Look, I touched this tree and did not die. You, too, come and touch it with your hand; you won't die."[316]

The serpent had now successfully initiated the first part of a threefold attack, subtly mixing truth with deception. He first sought to eliminate Eve's fears through emphatically contradicting the very words God spoke in 3:17. Next, the serpent attempted to undermine God's credibility by ascribing self-serving motives to Him.[317] Finally, it appealed to "an attractive standard of utility"[318] in promising that eating of the fruit would bring knowledge.[319]

One Christian account gives Satan as the one who "picked the apple, and gave it to Eve."[320] Another source imagines the Tempter's words: "How sweet does it smell! How good does it taste! How beautiful is its color!" Eve, in turn, later uses these words to persuade Adam.[321]

This entire verse was omitted, no doubt inadvertently, in OT1.[322]

11 a ***your eyes shall be opened.*** This biblical expression is used to describe a sudden vision of something that was previously hidden.[323] Here, however, the serpent's statement is but a half-truth. It is true that Adam and Eve's eyes will be opened to a glimpse of the divine, but what will they know? At first, only that they are naked.[324] Later, they will begin to further exercise their capacity for discernment—for example, in recognizing Satan for who he is.[325]

b ***ye shall be as gods.*** Elder Brigham Young said that Satan told Eve "many truths and some lies."[326] The truths include Satan's statement that through the fruit Adam and Eve would begin to acquire an attribute of discernment possessed by God Himself.[327] However, the Devil's claim also misleads because it implies that the couple would attain to godhood through the mere act of eating.[328] "Partaking of the forbidden fruit is only the beginning of [the learning] process."[329] Ultimately, "deification comes through obedience to God, not through disobedience."[330]

Shakespeare's *Macbeth* parallels the drama of this verse when Lady Macbeth expresses hope that their ungodly act "shall to all our nights and days to come / Give solely sovereign sway and masterdom."[331] Thus, she sets aside the warning of Banquo: "And oftentimes, to win us to our harm, / The instruments of darkness tell us truths, / Win us with honest trifles, to betray 's / In deepest consequence."[332]

---

315 Alma 1:4.
316 D. C. Matt, *Zohar 1*, Be-Reshit 1:36a, p. 227; cf. M. A. Ouaknin, *et al.*, *Rabbi Eliézer*, 13, p. 90; J. Goldin, *Fathers*, 1, pp. 8-9.
317 See *Commentary* 4:11-b, p. 253.
318 N. M. Sarna, *Genesis*, p. 25.
319 See *Commentary* 4:11-c, p. 254.
320 M. Herbert, *Irish Apocrypha*, p. 5.
321 Wahb bin Munabbi, cited in al-Tabari, *Creation*, 1:106, p. 277.
322 S. H. Faulring. *et al.*, *Original Manuscripts*, p. 91. The missing text was inserted into OT2 (*ibid.*, p. 600).
323 See *Commentary* 4:13-a, p. 258; cf. *Commentary* 1:10-b, p. 51.
324 Moses 4:13. See *Commentary* 3:25-a, p. 185.
325 Cf. *Commentary* 1:18-b, p. 56, 5:10-e, p. 363.
326 B. Young, December 1844, reported in E. England, *Laub*, p. 28.
327 B. Young, *23 June 1867*, p. 70. See also J. L. Kugel, *Instances*, pp. 163-165.
328 See *Commentary* 4:28-a, p. 276.
329 B. C. Hafen, *Broken*, p. 30.
330 J. N. Sparks, *et al.*, *Orthodox Study Bible*, p. 6 n. 3:1-7.
331 W. Shakespeare, *Macbeth*, 1:5:69-70, p. 1317.
332 *Ibid.*, 1:3:123-126, p. 1315. See L. A. Cormican, *Idiom*, pp. 25-26.

*11 For God doth know that in the day ye eat thereof, then your eyes shall be opened, and **ye shall be as gods**, **knowing good and evil**.*

The serpent's statement presupposes the possibility of many gods.[333] Sarna points out that "any possible ambiguity inherent in the use of the same word for 'God' and for ['gods'] is here removed by the plural form of the verb 'know' (*yode'ei*) and by verse [28] ('one of us')."[334]

In an Armenian text, the serpent implies that God obtained the knowledge that made Him Divine by the same means being proffered to Eve: "'God was a man like you, when He ate of this fruit He became God of all. Because of this matter He said, 'Do not eat!' Lest you become god.'"[335] This exaggeration contains the cunning insinuation that God forbade the eating of the fruit out of jealousy: "The serpent's deception is… his equation of godliness with defiance… The serpent implies that God… wishes them to be without likeness to Him, that He does not want them to become as He is."[336] This sense is also well captured in a midrash: "The snake began to slander his Creator, saying, 'From this tree did God eat, and then He created the world. Then He told you, 'You shall not eat of it,'[337] so that you should not create other worlds. For everyone hates the competition."[338] The serpent intended to shake Eve's confidence in God's generosity and goodness by making Him out to be a selfish rival.[339]

A Zoroastrian text has Satan proposing that both he and Eve partake of the fruit together: "Let us eat of the gathering from this tree, and let us give it to Adam."[340] An Islamic story implies that Satan sought to persuade Eve by attributing his own immortality to the effects of eating the fruit. When Eve saw Satan near the tree and inquired who he was, he is said to have replied: "'I was man, but have become an angel.' 'By what means?' 'By eating of this blessed fruit, which an envious God had forbidden me to taste on pain of death. I long submitted to His command, until I became old and frail… I then longed for death, and expecting to meet it by eating of this fruit, I stretched out my hands and took of it; but lo! it had scarcely touched my lips, when I became strong and beautiful as at first; and though many thousand years have since elapsed, I am not sensible of the slightest change either in my appearance or in my energies.'"[341] "If you eat from this tree," al-Qummi cites Satan as saying to Adam and Eve, "you shall be two angels and dwell in the Garden forever."[342]

c   ***knowing good and evil.*** In the *Discourse on Abbaton*, Satan says: "ye shall know the good and the evil, and ye shall [be able] to separate the sweet from the bitter."[343] D&C 29:39 affirms that "if they never should have bitter they could not know the sweet," implying that the "forbidden tree offers an experience that is both pleasant and painful; it awakens those who partake of it to the higher knowledge and to the pain that both come with moral choice."[344]

---

333   See *Commentary* 1:6-f, p. 48 and 2:26-a, p. 111.

334   N. M. Sarna, *Genesis*, p. 25. For historical and LDS views on deification, see Brock's comments in Ephrem the Syrian, *Paradise*, pp. 72-74; M. Barker, *Hidden*, pp. 23-24; M. Barker, *et al.*, *Seeking*; E. Benz, *Imago Dei (1978)*; E. Benz, *Imago Dei (1969)*; B. R. Bickmore, *Restoring*, pp. 149-159; C. L. Blomberg, *et al.*, *Divide*, pp. 77-110; M. J. Christensen, *et al.*, *Partakers*; J. Gross, *Divinization*; J. B. Haws, *Deification*; F. Luz, *Orthodoxie*, pp. 82-91; J. F. McConkie, *Sons*; S. Nes, *Uncreated Light*; K. E. Norman, *Deification*; K. E. Norman, *Deification*; B. T. Ostler, *God*, pp. 321-426; D. L. Paulsen, *Are Christians Mormon*, pp. 73-96; D. C. Peterson, *et al.*, *Offenders*, pp. 75-92; D. C. Peterson, *Ye Are Gods*; S. E. Robinson, *Are Mormons Christians?*, pp. 60-70; N. Russell, *Deification*; J. Vajda, *Partakers*.

335   Or, in another recension, "become a god, his equal." M. E. Stone, *Armenian Apocrypha 1996*, 4, p. 25. See also W. L. Lipscomb, *Creation*, 16-17, pp. 120-121, 262.

336   J. E. Faulconer, *Adam and Eve*, 34.

337   Moses 3:17.

338   J. Neusner, *Genesis Rabbah 1*, 19:4, p. 202; cf. M. Maher, *Pseudo-Jonathan*, 3:24-25, pp. 25-26; D. C. Matt, *Zohar 1*, Be-Reshit, 1:36a, p. 225.

339   E. Kastler, *Commentaire*. See *Excursus 10: The Great Chain of Being*, p. 546.

340   F. M. Müller, *Sikand-Gumanik Vigar*, 13, p. 210.

341   G. Weil, *Legends*, pp. 30-31.

342   M. M. Ayoub, *Qur'an (Vol. 1)*, p. 88; cf. al-Tabari, *Creation*, 1:108-109, pp. 279-280; A. al-Tha'labi, *Lives*, p. 51.

343   Timothy of Alexandria, *Discourse*, p. 485. This phrase is omitted in Timothy of Alexandria, *Abbaton*, p. 200.

344   A. Berlin, *et al.*, *Jewish*, p. 16.

*11 For God doth know that in the day ye eat thereof, then your eyes shall be opened, and ye shall be as gods, **knowing good and evil**.*

*12 And when the **woman saw that the tree was good for food**, and that **it became pleasant to the eyes**, and a tree to be desired **to make her wise**, she took of the fruit thereof, and did eat, and also gave unto her husband with her, and he did eat.*

Sarna expands the serpent's words as follows: "You will be endowed with new mental powers, with the capacity for reflection that allows one to make decisions independently of God."[345] In other words, the choice will be open to Adam and Eve to exercise moral autonomy, to walk solely in the light of their own limited reason and experience without reference to divine instruction.[346] Dauber calls this as a "substitution of knowledge for relationship"—what LaCocque describes as a "perverted knowledge that ponders the pro and con, the positive and the negative, the advantage and the disadvantage, outside of and as a shield against commitment... [thus] objectifying partnership and partner alike."[347] Describing the situation of those who are similarly deceived, Jacob lamented: "wo unto him that has the law given... and that transgresseth... for awful is his state! O that cunning plan of the evil one! O the vainness, and the frailties, and the foolishness of men! When they are learned, they think they are wise, and they hearken not unto the counsel of God."[348] By way of contrast, knowledge leads to wisdom for those who "hearken unto the counsels of God."[349]

12 a ***woman saw that the tree was good for food.*** While Eve makes no reply, the narrator makes it clear that the tree has become the exclusive object in her imagination's view.[350] Note the "undertone of irony in the formulation that she 'saw that it was good,' for it echoes God's recurring judgment about His creation in [Moses 2]. Now, however, good has become debased in the woman's mind. Its definition is no longer God's verdict but is rooted in the appeal to the senses and in utilitarian value."[351]

b ***it became pleasant to the eyes.*** The Hebrew expresses a strong intensity of desire fueled by appetite—which Alter renders in his translation as "lust to the eyes."[352] Significantly, while the KJV says that "it *was* pleasant," the JST says "it *became* pleasant." It seems that the more Eve looked, the more attractive the fruit appeared. Origen comments: "The eyes of sense were... opened, which they had done well to keep shut, that they might not be distracted and hindered from seeing with the eyes of the mind."[353]

c ***to make her wise.*** The Hebrew term "*le-haskil* is the capacity for making decisions that lead to success. The targums as well as the *Septuagint*, Latin, and Syriac versions all derive the verb from the stem *s-k-l*,' to see, contemplate'" which accords with the visual nature of the temptation.[354] The desire to obtain the clear vision promised by wisdom is a good thing, but Eve's choice is mistakenly founded on a base of confusions and half-truths, and will not achieve the desired result.[355] Though eating the forbidden fruit will bring Adam and Eve to the threshold of knowledge, it will not automatically confer wisdom.[356]

345   N. M. Sarna, *Genesis*, p. 25; cf. B. C. Hafen, *Broken*, pp. 38-39.
346   D&C 1:16, 88:35; J. D. G. Dunn, *et al.*, *Commentary*, p. 40; L. R. Kass, *Wisdom*, p. 44; G. J. Wenham, *Genesis 1-15*, pp. 63-64; R. W. L. Moberly, *Serpent*, p. 24. "Man... is always distressed to feel that what is good seems bitter to him and what is evil seems delightful." The commandments of God are designed "precisely to overcome man's inclination to decree what [is] good or bad for him according to his desires and tastes," helping him learn "from experience to recognize... authentic good and evil" (R. Barthélemy, *God*, p. 24).
347   A. LaCocque, *Trial*, p. 143.
348   2 Nephi 9:27-28; cf. Mosiah 3:19. Jeremiah describes such individuals as those who "walk... after the imagination of their evil heart" (Jeremiah 3:17; cf. Deuteronomy 29:19). See also *Commentary* 4:28-a, p. 276.
349   2 Nephi 9:29. See *Excursus 27: Diligence, Obedience, and Friendship*, p. 597.
350   E. Kastler, *Commentaire*; cf. U. Cassuto, *Documentary*, p. 147.
351   N. M. Sarna, *Genesis*, p. 25; cf. J. H. Sailhamer, *Genesis*, pp. 26-27.
352   R. Alter, *Five Books*, p. 24.
353   Origen, *Against Celsus* 7:39, cited in A. Louth, *et al.*, *Genesis 1-11*, pp. 80-81. See John 5:39.
354   N. M. Sarna, *Genesis*, p. 25.
355   E. Kastler, *Commentaire*.
356   See also *Commentary* 1:31-d, p. 65, 4:11-b, p. 253, and *Excursus 2: Ancient Concepts of Wisdom*, p. 516.

MOSES 4

12 And when the woman saw that the tree was good for food, and that it became pleasant to the eyes, and a tree to be desired **to make her wise, she** *took of the fruit thereof, and* **did eat,** *and also* **gave unto her husband with her, and he did eat.**

The threefold description of Eve's temptation corresponds to the three parts of Satan's argument: 1. The fruit will not bring death, but rather is "good for food"; 2. It will open their eyes to "pleasant" things; and 3. It will bring knowledge of good and evil, thus making her "wise." Moreover, the temptation involves three aspects of mankind's powers of sense and discernment: "the mouth for food, the eyes for sight, and the heart... for understanding."[357] Finally, as Hendel observes: "In this ascending scale of sensation—from bodily appetite to visual aesthetics to intellectual desire—we follow an internal, subjective progression of desire... In this turning moment the woman's desire ascends from the belly to the eyes to the mind, coloring her desire as at once animal, human, and quasi-divine (or at least drawn towards it)."[358]

d   she... did eat. The Hebrew contains six instances of doubled consonants, the "extremely difficult pronunciation... [forcing] a merciless concentration on each word"[359] that amounts to a chewing of the phrase. Thus, the difficulties of diction simulate the excruciation of transgression.

Elder Talmage describes Eve's action as "indulgence in food unsuited to [her] nature."[360] However, Elder McConkie leaves the door open for a figurative interpretation: "What is meant by partaking of the fruit of the Tree of Knowledge of good and evil is that our first parents complied with whatever laws were involved so that their bodies would change from their state of paradisiacal immortality to a state of natural mortality."[361]

Whatever else we might infer about the nature of the event, the text does seem to justify the rejection of at least one popular idea about the specifics of the transgression. "Against the interpretation that [the fruit represented carnal knowledge] is the fact... that sexual differentiation is made by God Himself,[362] that the institution of marriage is looked upon... as part of the divinely ordained order,[363] and that... 'knowledge of good and bad' is a divine characteristic."[364] Butterworth observes: "Adam does not say 'I was ashamed *before* Eve, because I was naked.'"[365] Westermann concurs, concluding that the opening of the eyes experienced by Adam and Eve in v. 13 "does not mean that they become conscious of sexuality."[366] It is later, immediately following the account of their expulsion from Eden, that we are given the significant detail that "Adam knew his wife, and she bare unto him sons and daughters."[367]

Through the Fall, "death [came] upon mankind... which is the temporal death."[368]

e   gave unto her husband with her, and he did eat. Whereas Eve was beguiled by the serpent,[369] having mistakenly taken the forbidden fruit "from the wrong hand,"[370] "there was

357   J. W. Wevers, *Notes*, p. 39.
358   R. S. Hendel, *Poetics of Myth*, p. 160; cf. R. S. Hendel, *Tangled Plots*, p. 40.
359   V. P. Hamilton, *Genesis*, p. 190.
360   J. E. Talmage, *Jesus the Christ*, 3, p. 18.
361   B. R. McConkie, *Sermons*, p. 189.
362   Moses 2:27.
363   Moses 2:25.
364   N. M. Sarna, *Genesis*, p. 19; see Moses 4:11, 28.
365   E. A. S. Butterworth, *Tree*, p. 73, emphasis added.
366   C. Westermann, *Genesis 1-11*, p. 251.
367   Moses 5:2. See J. E. Talmage, *Jesus the Christ*, p. 30.
368   Alma 12:24. On the relationship between death and the Fall, see the overview of Moses 3, pp. 140-144.
369   J. E. Talmage, *Articles (1984)*, p. 63.
370   M. C. Thomas, *Women*, p. 53.

MOSES 4

12 And when the woman saw that the tree was good for food, and that it became pleasant to the eyes, and a tree to be desired to make her wise, she took of the fruit thereof, and did eat, and also **gave unto her husband with her, and he did eat**.

no deception involved when Adam partook… It appears that Adam purposely fell that he might remain with Eve, according to the commandment of the Lord."[371] Note, however, that the scriptures usually refer to the incident generically as *Adam's* transgression.[372]

Nibley elaborates on the scene and its implications. He observes that while Eve was the one deceived, she also became the first to correctly understand what must be done as a result of her transgression: "After Eve had eaten the fruit and Satan had won his round, the two were now drastically separated, for they were of different natures. But Eve, who in ancient lore is the one who outwits the serpent and trips him up with his own smartness, defeated this trick by a clever argument. First, she asked Adam if he intended to keep all of God's commandments. Of course he did! All of them? Naturally! And what, pray, was the first and foremost of those commandments? Was it not to multiply and replenish the earth, the universal commandment given to all God's creatures? And how could they keep that commandment if they were separated? It had undeniable priority over the commandment not to eat the fruit. So Adam could only admit that she was right and go along: 'I see that it must be so,' he said, but it was she who made him see it. This is much more than a smart way of winning her point, however. It is the clear declaration that man and woman were put on the earth to stay together and have a family—that is their first obligation and must supersede everything else."[373] Eve's perspicacity, augmented by the experience she has gained in the taking of the fruit, is recognized by a diversity of traditions that associate her with Wisdom (*Sophia*). The wisdom she had begun to acquire was later demonstrated through her insightful psalm of gratitude.[374]

The Greek *Life* recounts that Satan had refused to give Eve the fruit unless she swore an oath that she would also give it to her husband.[375] Tvedtnes[376] cites an Armenian text that has Eve trying to persuade Adam as follows: "'This fruit is extremely sweet and tasty…' Adam said, 'I cannot taste it and become like you….' But Eve cried and begged him and said, 'Eat and do not separate me from you. If we live, let us live together, and if we die, let us die together.'"[377]

her husband. In Hebrew, "her man." See *Commentary* 3:24-a, p. 184.

he did eat. Whether one takes the nature of the fruit to be literal or figurative, the insightful comments of Kass on the aptness of the "metaphor that lets prohibited eating stand for prohibited knowing" are pertinent: "Eating is the incorporation of 'other' and its transformation into 'same.' Eating the proper food maintains oneself and one's own wholeness. But eating improper food, food that cannot be assimilated, means taking in material that remains indigestible, that remains separate and alien. Taking in wrong food thus produces a certain duality and negativity within; it invites self-attention and judgmental self-consciousness, precisely the result (in our story) of the act of transgressive eating."[378]

371 J. F. McConkie, *et al.*, *Revelations*, p. 221 and Moses 4:18; cf. 1 Timothy 2:14; V. P. Hamilton, *Genesis*, pp. 182-184; B. R. McConkie, *New Witness*, p. 86; S. E. Robinson, *Book of Adam*, p. 133; J. E. Talmage, *Articles (1984)*, pp. 59, 63; O. Pratt, *18 July 1880*, pp. 288-289; O. F. Whitney, *Thoughts*, 12, pp. 284-285. See *Excursus 25: The Tree of Life as the Hidden Throne of God*, p. 591.
372 Moses 6:9; Alma 12:22; D&C 29:36, 40; Article of Faith 2.
373 H. W. Nibley, *Patriarchy*, pp. 88-89.
374 Moses 5:10-11; cf. *Commentary* 3:22-b, p. 182 and 5:11-a, p. 364.
375 G. A. Anderson, *et al.*, *Synopsis*, 19:1d, p. 57E.
376 J. A. Tvedtnes, *Follett*.
377 W. L. Lipscomb, *Creation*, 20, 23, 26, pp. 121-122, 263. See also M. Roper, *Adam*; M. E. Stone, *Armenian Apocrypha* 1996, 6-9, pp. 27-33.
378 L. R. Kass, *Wisdom*, pp. 65-66.

*13 And the **eyes of them both were opened**, and they knew that they had been naked. And they sewed **fig-leaves** together and made themselves **aprons**.*

13 a *eyes of them both were opened.* In other Old Testament instances, this phrase connotes a sudden vision of hidden things.[379] By this they know that they are naked.[380] Jacob equates a "perfect knowledge" of "nakedness" with "guilt" and "uncleanness" while associating the perfect knowledge of the "righteous" with "enjoyment" and "being clothed with purity, yea, even with the robe of righteousness."[381] Partaking of the fruit of the tree allowed Adam and Eve to begin to experience and distinguish good from evil—the "opposition in all things" described in 2 Nephi 2:11. In demonstration of her new capacity for discernment, Eve immediately "sees through Satan's disguise of clever hypocrisy, identifies him, and exposes him for what he is."[382]

Unlike the richly-described, finely-nuanced account of the temptation dialogue, the tightly-coupled chain of verbs that follow it ("took," "eat," "gave," "eat") "indicate rapid, single-minded action"—nothing more is said, seen, or felt until this verse, when the eyes of Adam and Eve are opened.[383] Then, at once, the action starts again ("sewed," "made")—all the frantic movements proclaiming loudly, by their silent execution, the anguished undertone of shame and fear—"the physical act… as an expression of an inner state of an alarm."[384] The desired effect of this economical yet artful mode of narrative construction is to help the perceptive reader understand that the Lord God, Adam and Eve's benevolent provider who has been absent from their minds throughout the previous episode, has now reentered their thoughts with painful effect.

b *fig-leaves… aprons.* The derivation of the Hebrew term for apron (ʾagorah), sometimes translated as "girdle," confirms that this was an article of clothing intended to "enclose and cover the area of [the] lap or loins."[385] "The fig tree has unusually large and strong leaves. Incidentally, it is indigenous to the Land of Israel, where it was cultivated very early, but it was not known in Babylon; hence this detail reflects a West Semitic, not a Mesopotamian, cultural background."[386] The fruit of the fig tree is known for its abundance of seeds, thus an apron of green fig leaves is an appropriate symbol for Adam and Eve's ability to procreate, to "be fruitful and multiply"[387] after the Fall.

In v. 27, God Himself will be the One to clothe Adam and Eve, whereas in v. 13 we were told that Adam and Eve "made themselves aprons."[388] Like their tasting of the forbidden fruit, the endeavor of Nimrod to build a tower to "reach unto heaven,"[389] Sarah's essay to realize the blessing of posterity through her handmaiden Hagar,[390] and Rebekah's disguising of Jacob to assure that he would receive the birthright blessing,[391] this action exemplifies the "recurring theme… of the attempt and failure of human effort in obtaining a blessing that only God can give."[392]

It is perfectly in character for Satan to have planted the suggestion of making aprons, since he often appropriates false signs of power and authority for himself in order to deceive.[393] In this

---

379 E. A. S. Butterworth, *Tree*, pp. 74-75; cf. Genesis 21:19; Numbers 24:3-4; 2 Kings 6:17-20. See *Endnote 1-27*, p. 80. See also Butterworth's discussion of 1 Samuel 14:24-30 in *ibid.*, p. 78 where the honey is compared to the "secret knowledge" of the seer.

380 See *Commentary 3:25-a*, p. 185, *4:11-a*, p. 253, and *4:16-b*, p. 262.

381 2 Nephi 9:14; cf. Mormon 9:4-5. See also D. E. Bokovoy *et al.*, *Testaments*, pp. 61-65; J. R. Holland, *Christ*, pp. 244-245; and the overview of Moses. 4, pp. 236-240.

382 H. W. Nibley, *Patriarchy*, pp. 92-93; cf. *Commentary 1:10-b*, p. 51, *1:18-b*, p. 56; and *5:10-e*, p. 363.

383 R. Alter, *David*, p. 251; cf. G. J. Wenham, *Genesis 1-15*, p. 75.

384 R. Coles, *Secular Mind*, p. 12.

385 M. B. Brown, *Girded*, p. 130.

386 N. M. Sarna, *Genesis*, p. 26. See *Excursus 28: Ritual Aprons in Ancient Times*, p. 600.

387 Moses 2:28.

388 Moses 4:12.

389 Genesis 11:1-9.

390 Genesis 16:1-4.

391 Genesis 27:1-40.

392 J. H. Sailhamer, *Genesis*, p. 61.

393 2 Corinthians 11:12-15; 2 Nephi 9:9; D&C 128:20, 129:4-7; R. Giorgi, *Anges*, pp. 85-88, see also p. 234; B. T. Ostler,

*13 And the eyes of them both were opened, and they knew that they had been naked. And they sewed **fig-leaves** together and made themselves **aprons**.*

*14 And **they heard the voice** of the Lord God, **as they were walking** in the garden, **in the cool of the day**; and Adam and his wife went to hide themselves from the presence of the Lord God amongst the trees of the garden.*

sense, perhaps, there is an affinity with the *Zohar*'s association of Adam and Eve's fig leaves with a knowledge of "sorcery and magic," false forms of "protection" and counterfeits of the true priesthood.[394] Moreover, it is consistent with the plan of the Adversary to encourage sinners to flee from the presence of God rather than to reconcile and return to Him.[395] In this instance, the contrast between the false clothing made from leaves and the true clothing made from the skins of animals seems paralleled in the story of Cain and Abel, where the former makes an unacceptable offering from the fruits of the ground while the latter follows the God-given pattern of animal sacrifice.[396] Citing another scriptural passage, Brown discusses the lambskin aprons of the warring Lamanites in the Book of Mormon, bringing to mind the Lord's warning about "false prophets which come to you in sheep's clothing."[397]

Note that this is Satan's third attempt to mislead Adam and Eve by false appearances. First, he appeared as a serpent, deceptively employing a symbol of Christ.[398] Second, he made claims that confused the identities of Tree of Knowledge and the Tree of Life.[399] Finally, in the episode of the fig-leaf aprons, he suggested a course of action to Adam and Eve that substituted a self-made emblem of power and authority for the true article.

14 a ***they heard the voice.*** The last time God had spoken to the couple was when He gave them instructions about the trees. The account of the Lord's dramatic reappearance makes it clear that Adam and Eve had been left to themselves during their temptation, allowing them to make their choice without feeling that God was constantly looking over their shoulder.[400]

There is irony in the fact that the narrative of judgment opens "with a subtle but painful reminder of the single requirement for obtaining God's blessing: 'to hear/obey the voice of the Lord God.'"[401] This scene in Eden foreshadows the coming of the Lord to Sinai[402] and the frightened response of the people: "Let not God speak with us, lest we die."[403] As we hear the verdict pronounced, we recognize that the actors "are not depicted [merely] as individuals involved in a personal crisis; rather they are representatives. We are left with the impression that this is not their story so much as it is our story, the story of mankind."[404]

b ***as they were walking.*** In contrast to the Genesis account of this incident, the book of Moses makes it clear that it was Adam and Eve that were walking, not the Lord.[405] The change in OT1 from "as *he* was" to "as *they* were" appears to be in the hand of Joseph Smith.[406]

c ***in the cool of the day.*** The phrase can be translated as "in the wind, breeze, spirit, or direction" of the day—in other words, the voice is coming from the west, the place where the sun sinks.[407] Since the voice is coming from the west, some commentators infer that Adam and Eve were then located on the east side—the end of the Garden furthest removed

Clothed, p. 6; J. Smith, Jr., *Teachings*, 1 April 1842, pp. 204-205.

394 D. C. Matt, *Zohar 1*, Be-Reshit 1:36b, p. 229; 1:53b, pp. 296-297, p. 229 nn. 990-991; and p. 297 n. 1433.

395 Cf. 2 Nephi 32:8.

396 *Commentary* 5:19-b, p. 371.

397 M. B. Brown, *Girded*, p. 145. See Matthew 7:15; 3 Nephi 14:15; cf. Zechariah 13:4.

398 *Commentary* 4:5-b, p. 246.

399 *Commentary* 4:9-a, p. 252.

400 See *Endnote 4-77*, p. 320.

401 J. H. Sailhamer, *Genesis*, p. 52.

402 Exodus 20:18-21; Deuteronomy 5:25, 18:16.

403 Exodus 20:18-19.

404 J. H. Sailhamer, *Genesis*, pp. 52, 54-55.

405 Cf. Abravanel, cited in U. Cassuto, *Adam to Noah*, p. 152.

406 S. H. Faulring, *et al.*, *Original Manuscripts*, p. 91; K. P. Jackson, *Book of Moses*, pp. 80-81.

407 R. M. Zlotowitz, *et al.*, *Bereishis*, pp. 122-123.

14 And they heard the voice of the Lord God, as they were walking in the garden, **in the cool of the day;** *and Adam and his wife went to* **hide themselves from the presence of the Lord God amongst the trees of the garden.**

from the presence of the Lord—and possibly related to what Islamic commentary calls "the courtyard."[408] In other words, they seem to have one foot outside the Garden already.[409] Thus, God's question to Adam in the Genesis account—"Where art thou?"—might be taken as deeply ironic. In the view of Didymus, it is really not a question but rather "a statement of judgment as to what Adam has lost."[410]

The idea of Adam and Eve being in the "courtyard" of Eden is an appropriate fit to the function of the outermost of the three divisions of the Israelite temple, a place of confession as the first step of reconciliation.[411]

d   ***hide themselves from the presence of the Lord God.*** Hearing the Lord's voice, Adam and Eve quickly return from the place of their wandering at the edge of the Garden. Their flimsy covering of fig leaves, coupled with their choice of hiding place "by the tree of which [they] had eaten," trumpets the nature of their transgression.[412]

e   ***amongst the trees of the garden.*** The Hebrew for tree, *etz*, can be read as singular or plural. Though translators typically avoid a difficult interpretive problem by understanding the word in this context to have a collective sense, Chouraqui intensifies the irony of the situation by his careful rendering of the key phrase describing Adam and Eve's place of concealment: "in the center of [i.e., within] the tree of the garden."[413] A similar Islamic tradition relates that: "Adam went inside of the tree to hide,"[414] recalling al-Tha'labi's version of the story of the martyrdom of Isaiah: "When their prophet Isaiah finished his speech, they came after him to kill him and he fled from them. A tree met him and split itself open for him and he entered it. The Devil came upon him and seized a fringe of his garment and showed it to them, so they took saws in its middle and sawed it until they cut it and cut him while he was in the midst."[415] Isaiah's death in the split tree was immediately followed by his rebirth and ascension to heaven.[416]

Regarding the appearance of this motif in the New World, Norman notes the "'broken tree trunk' symbol" connected with the explanation of the origin of some tribes, including the Mixtecas. This idea can be seen in a "Tamoanchan pictograph or hieroglyph depicting a man emerging from a split tree trunk in symbolic birth." The "tree of the Mixtec codices is a Tree of Life or World Tree extending above and below this earth, but principally a 'tree of the heavens' in Omeyocan guarded by the creator couple where it gives birth to humanity. It can be stated simply that in ancient Mexico the broken tree represents a birth, death, or migratory transition for man."[417]

---

408   A. at-Tabataba'i, *Al-Mizan*, 1:209; cf. *Commentary 3:8-b*, p. 160. See *Endnote 3-41*, p. 206.

409   See *Commentary* 4:15-b, p. 261 and 4:31-b, p. 280.

410   Cited in G. A. Anderson, *Perfection*, pp. 215-216.

411   J. L. Carroll, *Reconciliation*, pp. 96-99. See *Commentary* 4:15-b, p. 261.

412   G. A. Anderson, *et al.*, *Synopsis*, 44:5a, p. 58E. See U. Cassuto, *Adam to Noah*, pp. 154-155; S. C. Malan, *Adam and Eve*, 1:36, p. 40 and 1:38, p. 42.

413   = "au milieu de l'arbre du jardin" (A. Chouraqui, *Bible*, Genesis 3:8, p. 22); "within the tree in the middle of the garden" (J. N. Sparks, *et al.*, *Orthodox Study Bible*, Genesis 3:8, p. 8). Cf. R. M. Zlotowitz, *et al.*, *Bereishis*, p. 123.

414   Wahab b. Munabbih in B. M. Wheeler, *Prophets*, p. 25.

415   A. al-Tha'labi, *Lives*, p. 557 and p. 557 n. 15; cf. M. A. Knibb, *Isaiah*, 5:1-14, pp. 163-164 and pp. 146-147.

416   M. A. Knibb, *Isaiah*, 6:1-11:43, pp. 164-176. See also the story of Nebuchadnezzar (Daniel 4:10-28). For literary parallels to the motif of a soul being shut up in a tree, see, e.g., Ariel in *The Tempest* (W. Shakespeare, *Tempest*, 1:2:275-293, p. 1615), Fradubio in *The Faerie Queene* (E. Spenser, *Faerie Queene*, 1:2:42, see n. to Stanza 42, 8-9, p. 52), Polydorus in the *Aeneid* (Virgil, *Aeneid*, 3, pp. 70-71), and Pier delle Vigne in the forest of suicides in the *Divine Comedy* (D. Alighieri, *Commedia*, 13). Similar themes appear in stories about Osiris, Adonis, Attis, and Dionysus—see convenient summaries in e.g., J. G. Frazer, *Golden Bough*, though Frazer's inferences are not always to be trusted. See also D. E. Wirth, *Parallels*, p. 105.

417   V. G. Norman, *Izapa Part 2*, p. 202; also cited in B. Gardner, *Second Witness*, 1:168. See also *Excursus 55:*

*14 And they heard the voice of the Lord God, as they were walking in the garden, in the cool of the day; and Adam and his wife went to hide themselves from the presence of the Lord God **amongst the trees of the garden**.*

*15 And **I, the Lord God, called unto Adam**, and said unto him: **Where goest thou?***

The image of the guilty parties, Adam and Eve, being figuratively shut up in a tree recalls Egyptian motifs, as in the legend of Osiris, who was "shut up in the cedar tree[418] and had to be liberated from it in order to be resurrected."[419] Nibley mentions *"Book of the Dead* vignettes showing the Lady incorporated—all but her upper part, and in many cases all but her arms only—in the fruit-bearing tree [suggesting] that the woman in the tree must actually have been eaten by it; she is the first victim, so to speak, and now invites her male companion to share her condition."[420] Thus, in ancient year-rites in Egypt, the splitting of the tree "both terminates life and liberates it" allowing the captive initiate to be reborn.[421] The splitting of the tree also is also said to represent, "among other things, the 'splitting of 'good' and 'evil,'" or the law of opposites set forth in the *Shabaka* creation text."[422] Perhaps the symbolism of death and rebirth is behind an enigmatic assertion in the *Sepher Rezial*. After stating that "Adam and his wife are concealed in the middle of the tree in the garden," the text adds: "It is not a cemetery."[423]

Comments Kastler: "[N]ow they are not merely touching the tree but they have for all intents and purposes merged with it… The tree has become their refuge—or perhaps their prison… Despite it all, the Lord God will not abandon them."[424]

15　a　***I, the Lord God, called unto Adam.*** Though Adam makes the Tree of Knowledge his hiding place, Jewish pseudepigraphal sources tell how, when the moment of judgment arrived, God's "chariot throne [descends and] rests at the Tree of Life and all the flowers come into bloom."[425] An Islamic source likewise reports that God's voice of judgment came "from the tree," meaning the Tree of Life.[426] Cassuto points out examples from elsewhere in the Bible where the verb "call" "is used in the sense of to summon a person to give an account of his actions."[427]

　　b　***Where goest thou?*** The change from the KJV "Where *art* thou?" to the JST "Where *goest* thou?" emphasizes the fact that the Lord is not assessing Adam's location but rather requesting him to reflect openly on his intentions—in view of the fact that his feet are now pointed toward the exit of the Garden.[428] Rasmussen observes: "From man God does not need information. Man's response must be man's own self."[429] Cassuto further explains: "The commentators who consider the question to be aimed at discovering where the man was hiding have overlooked the words '[and said unto] him'… The query… resembles the question the Lord God asks Cain,[430] 'Where is Abel your brother?,' when Abel's body is lying on the ground beneath the open sky, and no attempt is made to conceal it… We may

Mesoamerican Stories of Creation and the Original Transgression, p. 697.
418　Others usually identify the tree with the willow (e.g., R. H. Wilkinson, *Art,* p. 117).
419　H. W. Nibley, *Message 2005,* p. 290; cf. *Figure 4-13,* p. 231, *Excursus 42: Nebuchadnezzar's "Fall",* p. 632, and *Excursus 53: Comparative Explorations of the Mysteries,* p. 663. See *Endnote 4-50,* p. 312.
420　H. W. Nibley, *Message 2005,* p. 309. For the standard symbolism of the Lady, see R. H. Wilkinson, *Art,* p. 117.
421　*Ibid.,* p. 289; cf. pp. 288-293. See *Commentary 4:21-d,* p. 266, *Figure 4-11,* p. 230, and *Figure 4-13,* p. 231.
422　H. W. Nibley, *Message 2005,* p. 290.
423　S. Savedow, *Rezial,* In the beginning, para. 7, p. 63.
424　E. Kastler, *Commentaire.*
425　M. Barker, *Temple Theology,* p. 89 and G. A. Anderson, *et al., Synopsis,* 44(22):3-4, p. 62E. See also *Excursus 25: The Tree of Life as the Hidden Throne of God,* p. 591.
426　G. Weil, *Legends,* p. 32.
427　U. Cassuto, *Adam to Noah,* p. 155 and, e.g., Genesis 12:18, 20:9, 26:9-10; Deuteronomy 25:8.
428　See *Commentary 4:14-c,* p. 259.
429　D. Rasmussen, *Question,* p. 7.
430　Moses 5:34.

15 And I, the Lord God, called unto Adam, and said unto him: **Where goest thou?**

16 And he said: **I heard thy voice** *in the garden, and* **I was afraid, because I beheld that I was naked**, *and I hid myself.*

17 And I, the Lord God, said unto Adam: **Who told thee thou wast naked?** *Hast thou eaten of the tree whereof I commanded thee that thou shouldst not eat, if so thou shouldst surely die?*

compare the case to that of a man who comes to chide his little son who misbehaved himself and then hid himself behind the door in order to avoid looking at his father's angry face; the father who is well aware of the child's hiding-place, calls out to him, 'Where are you?,' meaning: Why are you there? Is that where you should be? Come out and face me! The man's answer is in keeping with this interpretation; he does not reply, 'I am in such-and-such a place,' but he explains why he is concealing himself."[431] Rashi draws additional parallels to the Lord's dialogues with Hagar,[432] Balaam,[433] and Hezekiah.[434]

God's call, of course, is not issued as an angry threat, but rather as an invitation for Adam to return and report on his stewardship of the Garden.[435] To accomplish His objective, God seeks to "draw rather than drive him out of hiding."[436] Elder David A. Bednar comments: "There was no one-way lecture to a disobedient child, as perhaps many of us might be inclined to deliver. Rather, the Father helped Adam as a learner to act as an agent and appropriately exercise his agency."[437] By this act, God "demonstrate[s] his own loving kindness, and… invites them to make admission of their faults."[438]

16 a   *I heard thy voice.* These words can also be translated "I hearkened to thy voice"—the irony of the reply, of course, is evidenced in the fact that this is precisely what Adam did not do previously.[439] Instead, both of them had hearkened to the voice of the serpent in making fig-leaf aprons and going into hiding.

  b   *I was afraid, because I beheld that I was naked.* The JST rendering ("because *I beheld that I was naked*" vs. "because *I was naked*") poignantly underscores Adam's heightened self-awareness after his eyes had been opened. Note that while Adam speaks of his fear of appearing naked, he says nothing about his transgression. However, it was, of course, a recognition of his fallen state that caused Adam, like Isaiah, to fear in the presence of the Lord.[440]

  Of relevance to this incident is Sarna's observation that, in contrast to the practice of priests in some Near East cultures, the Israelite ethos specified that it was improper for a man to appear naked before God; indeed the law described in great detail the particular dress that was suitable for the act of worship.[441]

17 a   *Who told thee thou wast naked?* Though Adam and Eve had discovered their own nakedness after their eyes were opened, God knew that it was Satan who had drawn attention to their shame, and who had incited them to make aprons and hide.[442] Hence Rashi's reading: "From where are you to know what shame there is in standing naked?"[443]

---

431   U. Cassuto, *Adam to Noah*, pp. 155-156.

432   Genesis 16:8.

433   Numbers 22:9.

434   Rashi, *Genesis Commentary*, 1:34; Isaiah 39. See also *Commentary* 5:34-a, p. 382; Ether 3:7: "Arise, why hast thou fallen?"

435   E. Kastler, *Commentaire*.

436   V. P. Hamilton, *Genesis*, p. 193.

437   D. A. Bednar, *Seek*, p. 63.

438   Chrysostom, *Homilies on Genesis*, 17:22, cited in A. Louth, *et al.*, *Genesis 1-11*, p. 85.

439   N. M. Sarna, *Genesis*, p. 26.

440   Isaiah 6:5; contrast Ether 3:6-8.

441   N. M. Sarna, *Genesis*, p. 26; Exodus 20:26; 28:42-43. See also *Commentary* 3:25-a, p. 185; 4:27-a, p. 274; and the overview of Moses 4, p. 234.

442   See *Commentary* 4:13-b, p. 258 and T. Stordalen, *Echoes*, p. 463.

443   Rashi, *Genesis Commentary*, 1:34; cf. Mizrachi "Who told you of the implication of your nakedness?"

17 And I, the Lord God, said unto Adam: **Who told thee thou wast naked? Hast thou eaten** *of the tree whereof I commanded thee that thou shouldst not eat, if so thou shouldst surely die?*

18 And the man said: The **woman thou gavest me,** *and* **commandest that she should** **remain with me,** *she gave me of the fruit of the tree and I did eat.*

19 And I, the Lord God, said unto the woman: What is this thing which thou hast done? And the woman said: The **serpent beguiled me, and I did eat.**

b   ***Hast thou eaten of the tree... ?*** God poses a third interrogative to Adam. Again, the "question urges confession rather than condemnation."[444]

According to Anderson, the reason Satan is not interrogated is because he "was not and never will be afforded any chance at repentance," having committed the unpardonable sin.[445] "Human beings, on the other hand," continues Anderson, "are offered the opportunity to mend their ways from the age of majority until the close of their lives. For men and women, God's mercy has no bounds."[446]

18   a   ***woman thou gavest me.*** Summarizing Adam's reply in the book of Genesis, Stordalen writes: "Out of ten Hebrew words, three are designed to censure YHWH God, six to put the blame on the woman, and only one admits that he has in fact done what YHWH God accuses him of."[447]

Regarding Adam's reference to Eve, midrash says that Adam "hurled against God the very kindness which God had shown him, the gift of Eve, by implying that God had caused him to sin by giving him that woman."[448] The irony of Adam's reply is even more evident in light of the tradition that God deferred creating the woman until Adam felt compelled to ask for her.[449] Observes Faulconer: "Though they must... cleave to one another, we do not see Man and Woman cleaving to anyone yet... Instead we see them denying their community with each other, just as, in their defiance, they denied their community with God."[450]

b   ***commandest that she should remain with me.*** This phrase, added to Adam's reply in the book of Moses, provides a defensible rationale for his transgression: he took the forbidden fruit in order to remain with Eve, thus breaking one commandment in order to keep a prior and more important one.[451]

OT1 employs the past tense of the verb, i.e., "commanded." Beginning with the 1878 edition of the Pearl of Great Price, it was changed to read "commandedst." In the 1981 edition, another change was made: "commandest." Jackson observes that the "deletion of the second letter 'd' avoids a difficult consonant cluster, yet it changes the tense of the clause from the past to the present."[452] Non-English translations of this verse, however, retain the past tense.

19   a   ***serpent beguiled me, and I did eat.*** While Eve, like Adam, points blame elsewhere, Hamilton observes that "her answer lacks some of the less attractive parts of her spouse's... She does not say 'the serpent whom you made.' Nor does she say 'the man to whom you gave me.'"[453] Wordplay in Eve's statement is evident with the juxtaposition of the Hebrew words for serpent (= *nachash*) and "beguiled" (= *nasha*).

444   V. P. Hamilton, *Genesis*, p. 194.
445   Cf. *Jubilees*: "the Lord cursed the serpent and he was angry with it forever" (O. S. Wintermute, *Jubilees*, 3:23, p. 60).
446   G. A. Anderson, *Perfection*, p. 138. See *Commentary* 4:15-b, p. 261.
447   T. Stordalen, *Echoes*, p. 237.
448   Cited in R. M. Zlotowitz, *et al.*, *Bereishis*, p. 125.
449   *Commentary* 3:20-b, p. 180.
450   J. E. Faulconer, *Adam and Eve*, 40.
451   See *Commentary* 4:12-e, p. 256,
452   K. P. Jackson, *Book of Moses*, p. 52.
453   V. P. Hamilton, *Genesis*, p. 194.

*19 And I, the Lord God, said unto the woman: What is this thing which thou hast done? And the woman said: The **serpent beguiled me, and I did eat**.*

*20 And **I, the Lord God, said unto the serpent: Because thou hast done this thou shalt be cursed above all cattle, and above every beast of the field**; upon thy belly shalt thou go, and dust shalt thou eat all the days of thy life;*

20   **a**   ***I, the Lord God, said unto the serpent.*** "Of the three parties to the transgression, the serpent alone is summarily sentenced without prior interrogation—a token of God's withering disdain for it.… In each [of the three cases], the judgment is of a twofold nature: it affects what is of central concern in the life of each entity, and it regulates a basic relationship."[454] As for the serpent, it is henceforth restricted to a humiliating diet and form of locomotion, and will be crushed under the heel of the seed of the woman; the woman will suffer in childbearing and in the challenges of a marriage relationship undertaken in the conditions of a fallen world;[455] and the man is consigned to hard labor and to strict obedience to the commandments of the Lord.[456]

          In the case of the man and the woman, Cassuto notes that what may seem solely as punishments should be regarded instead as "measures taken for the good of the human species in its new situation."[457] Exposed in nakedness, God will clothe them;[458] subject to temporal and spiritual death, God will bless them with posterity and the eventual possibility of eternal life;[459] and bereft of the food of the Garden, God will provide Adam and Eve with the seeds of life-sustaining grains.[460]

   b   ***Because thou hast done this.*** This phrase, repeated with variation as part of the sentence of Adam in v. 23, indicates that the repercussions mentioned are the natural consequences of transgression, rather than arbitrary penalties imposed by God.[461] No similar phrase appears in the words spoken to Eve.

   c   ***thou shalt be cursed above.*** That is, "thou shalt be cursed more than." "Hebrew *'arur mi-kol* evokes the description in verse [5], …*'arum mi-kol*, 'more shrewd than,' in a kind of literary framework expressing the idea of measure for measure."[462]

          The serpent, whose blessing seems to have been anticipatorily omitted at Creation, is now cursed.[463] However, the man and the woman, previously blessed,[464] receive no curse.

   d   ***all cattle, and above every beast of the field.*** This penalty, placed upon the serpent, symbolizes the curse placed upon those that followed Lucifer in the premortal life: "Throughout eternity [those who followed Lucifer in premortal life] will remain lower than the cattle or the beasts of the field, for even the beasts have bodies of flesh and bone and enjoy the privilege of resurrection, whereas the Devil and his angels remain unembodied spirits forever."[465] Even in the millennial day, when all the rest of Creation will enjoy peace and plenty, "dust [still] shall be the serpent's meat."[466] In cultures where the serpent was worshipped, this curse

454   N. M. Sarna, *Genesis*, pp. 24, 27.
455   See *Commentary* 4:22-c, p. 268.
456   See *Commentary* 5:5-c, p. 359.
457   U. Cassuto, *Adam to Noah*, p. 163.
458   Moses 4:27.
459   Moses 4:22 and *Commentary* 4:31-e, p. 282.
460   Moses 4:25.
461   E. Kastler, *Commentaire*.
462   N. M. Sarna, *Genesis*, p. 27.
463   See *Commentary* 2:22-a, p. 110.
464   Moses 2:28.
465   J. F. McConkie, *et al.*, *Revelations*, p. 271.
466   Isaiah 65:25.

MOSES 4

*20 And I, the Lord God, said unto the serpent: Because thou hast done this thou shalt be cursed above **all cattle, and above every beast of the field**; **upon thy belly shalt thou go**, and **dust shalt thou eat all the days of thy life**;*

*21 And **I will put enmity between thee and the woman**, between thy seed and her seed; and he shall bruise thy head, and thou shalt bruise his heel.*

also proclaimed the eventual humiliation of all false gods, and the firm requirement of submission to the Lord as the only object of worship.[467]

e   ***upon thy belly shalt thou go.*** In the art of the ancient Near East, the serpent is often shown as originally walking erect, sometimes with legs.[468] For example, a legged serpent appears in illustrated form in the *Joseph Smith Papyrus V*.[469] Several Middle Eastern traditions speak of the serpent's magnificent "camel-like" appearance before its cursing.[470] Nibley elucidates the symbolic meaning of the figurative indignity imposed on the serpent: "The loss of limbs and organs guarantees that the rebel will never rise anew in his full powers, which he will never possess again… He may never more progress, being bound forever in one place."[471]

Correspondingly, the Mosaic law will declare that what goes along on its belly is an abomination to Israel.[472]

f   ***dust shalt thou eat all the days of thy life.*** "The idea of eating dust, in a metaphorical sense of course, occurs several times in Scripture with reference to the plight of conquered foes."[473] Here, this constitutes an apt punishment, since the transgression itself had involved eating.[474] Corresponding words are found in the judgment against the man in v. 23 ("in sorrow shalt thou eat of it [i.e., the ground] all the days of thy life") but not in that of the woman.[475]

21 a   ***I will put enmity between thee and the woman.*** The serpent appeared to Eve in the guise of friendship; now that her eyes have been opened, she will recognize him as an enemy to be regarded with revulsion.[476] The theme of "opposition in all things"[477] now has been introduced in a broader sense.

The *Qur'an* records a passionate exchange of words following Lucifer's expulsion from heaven. Here Satan unleashes a tirade of threats, followed by a summary dismissal by God: "'Because… [Thou hast adjudged me to be erring],' [the Devil] declared, 'I will waylay Your servants as they walk on Your straight path, then spring upon them from the front and the rear, from their right and from their left…' 'Begone!' [God] said."[478]

Nibley elaborates on the scene: "[Satan,] nettled by this rebuke and the curse, …flares up in his pride and announces what his program for the economic and political order of the new world is going to be. He will take the resources of the earth, and with precious metals as a medium of exchange he will buy up military and naval might,[479] or rather those who control it, and so will govern the earth—for he is the prince of this world. He does rule: he is king. Here at the outset is the clearest possible statement of a military-industrial complex

467   Cf. T. Stordalen, *Echoes*, p. 470.
468   N. M. Sarna, *Genesis*, p. 27.
469   H. L. Andrus, *God*, p. 371; H. W. Nibley, *Message 2005*, p. 318; J. M. Todd, *Fragment*, p. 40E.
470   E.g., al-Tabari, *Creation*, 1:104-110, pp. 275-281; S. C. Malan, *Adam and Eve*, p. 214 n. 20; p. 217 nn. 27-29.
471   H. W. Nibley, *Abraham 1981*, p. 180. See also H. W. Nibley, *Message 2005*, pp. 315-318.
472   Leviticus 11:42.
473   U. Cassuto, *Adam to Noah*, p. 160. See e.g., Psalm 72:9; Isaiah 49:23, 65:25; Micah 7:17.
474   N. M. Sarna, *Genesis*, p. 27.
475   See also *Commentary* 4:23-d, p. 270.
476   N. M. Sarna, *Genesis*, p. 27.
477   See 2 Nephi 2:11.
478   N. J. Dawood, *Koran*, 7:11-18, pp. 109-110; cf. 15:32-44; 17:61-63; 38:74-85. See also M. Herbert, *Irish Apocrypha*, p. 11.
479   See S. C. Malan, *Adam and Eve*, 1:57, p. 65.

*21 And **I will put enmity between thee and the woman**, between **thy seed** and **her seed**; and **he shall bruise thy head, and thou shalt bruise his heel**.*

ruling the earth with violence and ruin. But as we are told, this cannot lead to anything but war, because it has been programmed to do that. It was conceived in the mind of Satan in his determination 'to destroy the world.'[480] The whole purpose of the program is to produce blood and horror on this earth."[481]

b   ***thy seed.*** This phrase no doubt is meant to include both a reference to Cain, who later virtually shared identity with Satan[482] and became a hated fugitive,[483] and also to his unrighteous descendants, who lived out their generations in a state of "enmity" with the posterity of Seth.[484] More generally, the "seed" of the serpent comprises all the wicked, of whom the Lord said: "Satan shall be their father, and misery shall be their doom."[485]

c   ***her seed.*** It is significant that the statement refers not to the couple, but to Eve alone. Elder James E. Talmage explains this as a reference is to Jesus Christ, who is the "only instance of offspring from woman dissociated from mortal fatherhood."[486]

d   ***he shall bruise thy head, and thou shalt bruise his heel.*** The change from the KJV "it" to the book of Moses "he"[487] emphasizes the Messianic implication of the verse: although the serpent (Satan), in its weakened condition, may afflict and torment man, his power will ultimately be destroyed by the seed of the woman (Christ). The *Targum Yerushalmi* preserves a unique reading when it has God saying: "For them [i.e., the posterity of Adam and Eve]… there will be a remedy, but for you [i.e., the serpent] there will be no remedy; and they are to make peace in the end, in the days of the King Messiah."[488]

The first occurrence of "bruise" is better rendered as "crush," since the Savior's blow to the serpent will be fatal.[489] Indeed, the Redeemer "shall crush the head of the serpent (Satan and his kingdom) with the very heel that was bruised (the [heel of Christ, who performed the] atoning sacrifice)."[490] Historically, Christians have called this prophecy the *protoevangelium*, the first explicit Biblical allusion to the good news of the Gospel. A related theme also appears in the Egyptian *Book of the Dead*, where "the cat who split the *ished-tree* and released the god also beheads the god's mortal enemy, the *Apophis* serpent, beneath the same *ished-tree*," its paw resting heavily on the head of the serpent in accompanying illustrations.[491]

Just as Jesus Christ will put all enemies beneath his feet,[492] so the Prophet Joseph Smith taught that each person who would be saved must also, with His help, gain the power needed to "triumph over all [their] enemies and put them under [their] feet,"[493] possessing the "glory, authority, majesty, power and dominion which Jehovah possesses."[494]

In Orthodox tradition, the prophecy about the trampling of the serpent's head was fulfilled when Jesus was baptized: "the first Adam, deceived by the serpent, was expelled from

---

480   Moses 4:6.
481   H. W. Nibley, *Gifts*, p. 92.
482   See *Commentary* 5:24-a, p. 375 and 5:24-b, p. 375.
483   Moses 5:39.
484   See *Commentary* 5:41-b, p. 388.
485   Moses 7:37; cf. John 8:44; Acts 13:10; 1 John 3:10-12; Alma 30:60.
486   J. E. Talmage, *Jesus the Christ*, p. 41.
487   "He" first appeared in OT2 (S. H. Faulring, *et al.*, *Original Manuscripts*, p. 601; K. P. Jackson, *Book of Moses*, p. 83).
488   M. Maher, *Pseudo-Jonathan*, 3:15, pp. 27-28; cf. the *Targum Yerushalmi* (J. W. Etheridge, *Onkelos*).
489   U. Cassuto, *Adam to Noah*, p. 161. See also B. T. Arnold, *Genesis 2009*, pp. 68-69.
490   *Old Testament Student Manual, Religion 301*, p. 41.
491   H. W. Nibley, *Message 2005*, pp. 311-312. See *Commentary* 4:14-e, p. 260.
492   1 Corinthians 15:25-26.
493   J. Smith, Jr., *Teachings*, 14 May 1843, p. 297. See also 17 May 1843, p. 301; 21 May 1843, p. 305.
494   L. E. Dahl, *et al.*, *Lectures*, 7:9, p. 98. See also 7:16, p. 101. Note that authorship of the *Lectures* is uncertain.

21 And I will put enmity between thee and the woman, between thy seed and her seed; and **he shall bruise thy head, and thou shalt bruise his heel***.*

Paradise, and by providence the second Adam crushed the head of the dragon in the river Jordan."[495] During liturgical enactment of the rite of baptism, the following words are recited in an allusion to Psalm 74:13-14: "Thou also didst hallow the Jordan's currents, sending from Heaven the Holy Spirit. And thou didst bruise the head of the serpent that lurketh therein."[496] Moreover, in the Jordan, "the Divine Word who 'put on the body,' deposits humanity's lost Robe of Glory…, and at each Christian baptism it is received in potential from the Font (often described both as the Jordan and as a womb…); finally, at the Last Judgment, it becomes the clothing of the Righteous in reality."[497] Of the "drama of baptism," Anderson writes: "When Satan hears of the pending enrollment of the *catechumen*,[498] he shows the same hostility he had formerly shown towards the exaltation of Adam and the resurrection of Christ… [Theodore writes that Satan ']tries and endeavors to bring us to the judgment hall as if we had no right to be outside his ownership. He pleads that from ancient times and from the creation of the head of our race we belong to him by right[…' Having pledged to resist Satan, the candidates were urged to 'stand with outstretched arms in the posture of one who prays, and look downwards and remain in that state in order to move the judge to mercy.'"[499] In some contexts, the candidates "stood [barefoot] on animal skins while they prayed, symbolizing the taking off of the garments of skin they had inherited from Adam"[500] as well as figuratively enacting the putting off the serpent, the representative of death and sin, under one's heel.[501] Thus the serpent, his head crushed by the heel of the penitent relying on the mercies of Christ's atonement, is by a single act renounced, defeated, and banished.[502]

The *Midrash ha Ne'elam* records the valuable instruction that "the serpent can slay a man only through the heel when he transgresses and tramples God's commandments under his heel… The Evil Inclination slays man by inducing him to trample the commandments."[503] Thus, using the same Hebrew term, Cain's downfall is portrayed as his failure to quickly crush Satan, who craves to wound him.[504] Similarly, the same imagery is employed in Genesis 25:26, where Jacob's seizing of the ineffectual Esau's heel is a portent that he will ultimately prevail in his ongoing rivalry with his elder brother.[505]

---

495   V. Nersessian, *Treasures*, p. 71. See *Commentary* 1:1-b, p. 42.

496   V. Nersessian, *Treasures*, p. 71. See *Commentary* 2:2-c, p. 96.

497   Ephrem the Syrian, *Poems*, p. 51 n. 3.

498   = candidate for baptism.

499   G. A. Anderson, *Perfection*, pp. 183-184.

500   *Ibid.*, p. 184.

501   *Ibid.*, p. 131. See *Commentary* 1:20-a, p. 57; 1:24-a, p. 59; 4:31-a, p. 280; 5:23-c, p. 374,

502   For additional discussion, see V. P. Hamilton, *Genesis*, pp. 197-200. See also *Commentary* 2:2-c, p. 96 and *Excursus 52: Washing, Anointing, and Clothing Among Early Christians*, p. 661.

503   Cited in R. M. Zlotowitz, *et al.*, *Bereishis*, p. 129; cf. Matthew 7:6; 1 Nephi 19:7; Mosiah 29:21-22; Alma 5:53, 60:33; Helaman 4:21-22, 6:31, 12:2; 3 Nephi 14:6, 28:35; D&C 3:15.

504   See *Commentary* 5:23-c, p. 374 and 4:22-c, p. 268.

505   "Since Esau was drawn after that serpent, Jacob dealt with him tortuously like a serpent… laying his hand on that heel to subdue it" (D. C. Matt, *Zohar 2*, Toledot 1:138a, p. 269; cf. H. Sperling, *et al.*, *Zohar*, Mishpatim, Saba (The Old Sage), 3:309-316).

MOSES 4

22 Unto the woman, I, the Lord God, said: **I will greatly multiply thy sorrow and thy conception. In sorrow thou shalt bring forth children,** *and* **thy desire shall be to thy husband, and he shall rule over thee.**

22   a   *I will greatly multiply thy sorrow and thy conception.* Before the Fall, Adam and Eve could not bear children.[506] Now Eve is told that as part of the repeated blessings of motherhood she must also undergo the recurrent pain incident to each childbirth.[507] Sailhamer reminds us, however, that these birth pangs "are not merely a reminder of the… Fall; they are as well a sign of impending joy: 'We know that the whole creation has been groaning as in the pains of childbirth right up to the present time. Not only so, but we ourselves, who have the firstfruits of the Spirit, groan inwardly as we wait eagerly for our adoption as sons, the redemption of our bodies. For in this hope we were saved.'"[508] These blessings of Redemption will come through the "seed of the woman," namely Jesus Christ.[509]

     b   *In sorrow thou shalt bring forth children.* President Spencer W. Kimball wrote: "I wonder if those who translated the Bible might have used the term 'distress' instead of 'sorrow.' It would mean much the same, except I think there is great gladness in most Latter-day Saint homes when there is to be a child there."[510] In fact, the Hebrew verb used here and in verse 23 "means pain or hurt rather than grief."[511] According to Sarna: "Intense pain in childbearing is unique to the human species and generally unknown to other female mammals."[512] Faulconer observes: "Knowledge, the knowledge of good and evil, the knowledge that brings mortality, makes pain possible. Pain naturally accompanies all creation and is at least possible in all relation."[513]

         Of the terms chosen to represent Adam and Eve's suffering, Cassuto further observes: "Apparently we have here a play upon words with reference to *es* [= tree]: it was with respect to *es* that the man and woman sinned, and it was with *esebb* [= pain] and *issabbon* [= toil, suffering] that they were punished… The very fact that Scripture does not employ here the usual phrases found in connection with the suffering of childbirth… proves that it was some specific intention… that these words were selected."[514] The same term for sorrow recurs when Noah is "pained that the Lord had made man on the earth, and it grieved him at the heart."[515]

         Unlike the consequences described for the serpent and the man, no "curse" is mentioned in connection with what is said to the woman.

     c   *thy desire shall be to thy husband, and he shall rule over thee.* In interpreting this verse, it is important to realize that the Hebrew term translated here as "desire" does not denote physical attraction, but rather a wish to "overcome or defeat another."[516] This sense is captured in a Christian phrasing of Adam's punishment: "your family will be forever contending against you."[517] Comments Sarna: "It is quite clear from the description of woman…[518] that the ideal situation, which hitherto existed, was the absolute equality of the sexes. The new state of male dominance is regarded as an aspect of the deterioration in the human condition

506   Moses 5:11; 2 Nephi 2:23.
507   See *Commentary* 4:23-d, p. 270.
508   J. H. Sailhamer, *Genesis*, p. 26. See Romans 8:22; cf. Matthew 24:8.
509   See *Commentary* 4:21-d, p. 266.
510   S. W. Kimball, *Blessings*, p. 72.
511   R. D. Draper, *et al.*, *Commentary*, p. 48.
512   N. M. Sarna, *Genesis*, p. 28.
513   J. E. Faulconer, *Adam and Eve*, 44.
514   U. Cassuto, *Adam to Noah*, p. 165.
515   Moses 8:25.
516   J. H. Sailhamer, *Genesis*, p. 58; cf. B. T. Arnold, *Genesis 2009*, pp. 70-71. See *Commentary* 4:21-d, p. 266, 5:23-c, p. 374, and 5:23-e, p. 374.
517   M. Herbert, *Irish Apocrypha*, p. 6.
518   Moses 3:18, 23.

22 Unto the woman, I, the Lord God, said: I will greatly multiply thy sorrow and thy conception. In sorrow thou shalt bring forth children, and **thy desire shall be to thy husband, and he shall rule over thee**.

that resulted from the defiance of divine will."[519] Hamilton sees here a desire of sin "to break the relationship of equality and turn it into a relationship of servitude and domination... Far from being a reign of co-equals over the remainder of God's creation, the relationship now becomes a fierce dispute, with each party trying to rule the other. The two who once reigned as one attempt to rule each other."[520] Summarizing the unfortunate new state of affairs described in this verse, McKinlay observed that "the Fall of man and the continual source of degeneration in this world have resulted in the estrangement of parents from God, from each other, and from their children." On the other hand, "the healing of this broken harmony is the essence of eternal life."[521]

Martin Luther aptly describes God's design of marriage as a "school of love."[522] As couples and families learn to live together in intimacy, affection, and oneness, they experience the finest kind of preparation for eternal life that mortality can provide.[523] President Spencer W. Kimball emphasized that in celestial marriage the "man and the wife are equals" and that the designation of "authority" to man "does not mean that he is superior."[524] He explained that the role of the husband is to "preside" rather than to "rule"[525] and stressed the need for women to be "contributing and full" partners in marriage.[526] As Nibley points out: "There is no patriarchy or matriarchy in the Garden; the two supervise each other. Adam is given no arbitrary power; Eve is to heed him only insofar as he obeys their Father—and who decides that? She must keep check on him as much as he does on her. It is, if you will, a system of checks and balances in which each party is as distinct and independent in its sphere as are the departments of government under the Constitution—and just as dependent on each other."[527] In fact, Thomas observes, a primary objective of mortality seems to have been precisely "to foster the conditions in which the man and the woman may achieve interdependence," thus affording us an opportunity to rise to "the challenge of not only perfecting ourselves individually but also perfecting ourselves in relationships.... Relationships were given to us to develop us in love."[528]

Like the blessing of childbirth, the experience of married love holds out a promise of happiness, yet its practice, in a fallen world, will be frequently mixed with sorrow "till God make men of some other mettle than earth."[529] Unfortunately, "[t]here has been no change in the constitution of man since he fell."[530] "Sad experience" has shown "that it is the nature and disposition of almost all men, as soon as they get a little authority, as they suppose, [to] immediately exercise unrighteous dominion,"[531] a tendency which modern prophets have repeatedly condemned.[532] Of the great blessings that await all generations of women who

---

519   N. M. Sarna, *Genesis*, p. 28; R. M. Zlotowitz, *et al.*, *Bereishis*, p. 131. See also J. E. Talmage, *Jesus the Christ*, 27, pp. 441-442, 450 n. 5.

520   V. P. Hamilton, *Genesis*, p. 202; cf. H. W. Nibley, *Patriarchy*; G. J. Wenham, *Genesis 1-15*, pp. 81-82. Contrast the implausible suggestion that "rule over" be translated "rule with" (V. M. Hudson, *et al.*, *Response*, p. 332 n. 62).

521   L. A. McKinlay, *Patriarchal Order*.

522   Cited in E. England, *Church*, p. 4.

523   J. R. Holland, *Souls*.

524   S. W. Kimball, *Teachings 1982*, 26 February 1977, p. 315.

525   S. W. Kimball, *Blessings*, p. 72.

526   S. W. Kimball, *Teachings 1982*, May 1976, p. 315.

527   H. W. Nibley, *Patriarchy*, p. 93.

528   M. C. Thomas, *Women*, pp. 54, 55, 56.

529   W. Shakespeare, *Much Ado*, 2:1:59, p. 338.

530   J. Smith, Jr., *Teachings*, 22 January 1834, p. 60.

531   D&C 121:39.

532   E.g., G. B. Hinckley, *Teachings 1997*, November 1991 and 29 January 1984, pp. 1-2, 322-323, 326; G. B. Hinckley, *6 October 1996*, pp. 100-101; G. B. Hinckley, *4 October 1998*, pp. 211-212; G. B. Hinckley, *6 April*

*22 Unto the woman, I, the Lord God, said: I will greatly multiply thy sorrow and thy conception. In sorrow thou shalt bring forth children, and **thy desire shall be to thy husband, and he shall rule over thee**.*

*23 And unto Adam, I, the Lord God, said: **Because thou hast hearkened unto the voice of thy wife**, and hast eaten of the fruit of the tree of which I commanded thee, saying—Thou shalt not eat of it, **cursed shall be the ground for thy sake; in sorrow shalt thou eat of it all the days of thy life**.*

have thus suffered, Elder James E. Talmage has written: "When the frailties and imperfections of mortality are left behind, in the glorified state of the blessed hereafter, husband and wife will administer in their respective stations, seeing and understanding alike, and cooperating to the full in the government of their family kingdom. Then shall woman be recompensed in rich measure for all the injustice that womanhood has endured in mortality. Then shall woman reign by Divine right, a queen in the resplendent realm of her glorified state, even as exalted man shall stand, priest and king unto the Most High God."[533]

23 a *Because thou hast hearkened unto the voice of thy wife.* The phrase "hearkened unto the voice of" is an idiom meaning "obeyed."[534]

b *cursed shall be the ground.* In contrast to the personal nature of the judgment pronounced on the serpent, Adam himself is not cursed. Instead it is the soil, from which his own body was formed, that will now oppose him, disturbing the original harmony between man and nature. Barker notes: "This notion of moral ecology is a major biblical theme; it is explicitly formulated in Leviticus 18:24-28 and 20:22, and it underlies the great exhortations of Leviticus 26 and Deuteronomy 28."[535]

D&C 61:17 implies that the curse has been reversed "in the last days": "And, as I, the Lord, in the beginning cursed the land, even so in the last days have I blessed it, in its time, for the use of my saints, that they may partake the fatness thereof."

c *for thy sake.* In contemporary commonsense interpretation, this phrase is often taken to mean that the cursing of the ground was done for the personal benefit or advantage of Adam. However, a more accurate rendering in modern English of "for thy sake" is simply "because of thee."[536] In other words, the Lord is merely saying that the cursing of the ground is an inevitable consequence of Adam's transgression.

d *in sorrow shalt thou eat of it all the days of thy life.* Sailhamer reminds us that this phrase should be associated with the theme of "eating" throughout the scriptures: e.g., "the *Torah's* teaching regarding clean and unclean food[537] and the regulations for annual 'feasts' to celebrate God's gift of the 'good land' in the covenant.[538] To this could be added the larger context of the role of 'feasts' and 'eating' in the biblical *eschaton*."[539]

The judgments on the serpent and on the man are linked by the theme of eating of the dust or ground all the days of their life.[540] Similarly, through the repetition of the term "sorrow,"[541] there is a deliberate correspondence implied between a woman's labor of childbearing and

---

2002, pp. 127-131; G. B. Hinckley, *3 October 2004*, pp. 260-263.

533 J. E. Talmage, *Eternity of Sex*.

534 G. J. Wenham, *Genesis 1-15*, p. 82. See *Commentary* 4:16-a, p. 262.

535 N. M. Sarna, *Genesis*, p. 28. See also *Commentary* 5:37-a, p. 384 and Moses 5:56.

536 N. M. Sarna, *Genesis*, p. 28. The Greek reads "in your labors" (J. W. Wevers, *Notes*, p. 46).

537 Leviticus 11; Deuteronomy 14.

538 Leviticus 23.

539 I.e., accounts of the end of the world. See J. H. Sailhamer, *Genesis*, p. 57; Revelation 19:9; D&C 27:5-14, 59:13-21.

540 See *Commentary* 4:20-f, p. 265.

541 Hebrew *'itsavon*.

23 And unto Adam, I, the Lord God, said: Because thou hast hearkened unto the voice of thy wife, and hast eaten of the fruit of the tree of which I commanded thee, saying—Thou shalt not eat of it, cursed shall be the ground for thy sake; **in sorrow shalt thou eat of it all the days of thy life.**

24 **Thorns also, and thistles** *shall it bring forth to thee, and* **thou shalt eat the herb of the field.**

the male equivalent of arduous physical labor.[542] Thus, as Hamilton notes, both divine consequences "are directed to a point of highest fulfillment in the life of the female and the male."[543] Sarna concludes that the phrase "all the days of your life" is missing from the judgment of the woman "because childbearing does not occur all the days of a woman's life."[544]

24　a　***Thorns also, and thistles.*** Adam's first source of sorrow will come from the troublesome weeds that the earth will bring forth in abundance. "Says the Lord: As you have eaten the fruit, thus knowing good and evil, likewise you will have to distinguish good in what you eat (gramineous plants) from evil (thorns)."[545]

　　b　***thou shalt eat the herb of the field.*** A second source of sorrow is the loss of the fruit trees of Eden as the source of man's food. Rabbinical and early Christian literature and commentary formulated a reading of vv. 24-25 that saw in this phrase the consignment of Adam and Eve to a period of humiliating penance, to a degree in the likeness of Nebuchadnezzar's abasement to a beastlike state.[546] The *Gospel of Philip* says: "There are two trees growing in Paradise. The one bears [animals], the other bears men. Adam [ate] from the tree which bore animals. [He] became an animal."[547] *Philip* uses, as Barker points out, "the usual apocalyptists' code of mortal = animal and angel = man. The text is broken, but the sense is clear enough."[548] Ephrem the Syrian reasoned that since Adam "went astray through [an animal] he became like the [animals]: He ate, together with them as a result of the curse, grass and roots."[549] Playing on the double meaning of *veirdu* in 2:28, Rashi comments that instead of "having dominion" over the beasts he now would "fall down" below with them.[550] His nature would become that of "animal flesh."[551]

The *Targum Yerushalmi* says that after hearing the consequences of his transgression, Adam pleaded that he might be spared: "I beseech by the mercy before you, O Lord, let me not be reckoned before you as cattle, that I should eat the grass of the surface of the field. I will arise and labor… and I will eat the food of the earth; and thus let there be a distinction before you between the children of men and the offspring of cattle."[552] Tradition records that God answered his prayer, making it clear that this curse was not meant as an arbitrary "punishment" but rather as a temporary ascetic "discipline for spiritual renewal."[553] To a group of spurned penitents in the Book of Mormon, Alma said: "… it is well that ye are cast out, that ye may be humble, and that ye may learn wisdom."[554]

542　N. M. Sarna, *Genesis*, p. 28.
543　V. P. Hamilton, *Genesis*, p. 203.
544　N. M. Sarna, *Genesis*, p. 28.
545　S. L. Della Torre, *Anxiety*, p. 7. See *Commentary 3:5-a*, p. 154.
546　Daniel 4. See H. W. Nibley, *Message 2005*, p. 289 and *Excursus 42: Nebuchadnezzar's "Fall,"* p. 632,.
547　W. W. Isenberg, *Philip*, 71:21-72:4, p. 152.
548　M. Barker, *June 11 2007*. See M. Barker, *Hidden*, pp. 45-47; C. H. T. Fletcher-Lewis, *Glory*, p. 33.
549　Ephrem the Syrian, *Paradise*, 13:5, p. 170. See *Commentary 2:29-a*, p. 117; cf. G. A. Anderson, *et al.*, *Synopsis*, 4:2, p. 5E; G. A. Anderson, *Penitence*, pp. 13-19; G. A. Anderson, *Perfection*, pp. 141-147; W. W. Isenberg, *Philip*, 55:10-11, p. 143; M. Herbert, *Irish Apocrypha*, pp. 8, 11.
550　S. L. Della Torre, *Anxiety*, p. 7.
551　S. C. Malan, *Adam and Eve*, 1:55, p. 61.
552　M. Maher, *Pseudo-Jonathan*, 3:18, p. 28.
553　G. A. Anderson, *Original Form*, p. 229. See also *Excursus 53: Comparative Explorations of the Mysteries*, p. 663.
554　Alma 32:12.

*25 **By the sweat of thy face shalt thou eat bread**, until thou shalt return unto the ground—
for thou shalt surely die—for out of it wast thou taken: for dust thou wast, and unto dust shalt
thou return.*

25 a   *By the sweat of thy face shalt thou eat bread.* Unlike his life before the Fall, Adam was
consigned to work hard for his food. The importance of this labor is underscored when
the language about tilling of the earth[555] and eating of bread by the sweat of his brow[556]
is repeated in Moses 5. "The curse lies not in the work itself, which is decreed for man
even in Eden,[557] but in the uncooperative nature of the soil, so that henceforth the wresting
of subsistence from it entails unremitting drudgery."[558] In this regard, temporal death will
contribute "something positive here" to man, since it ultimately provides "the term of his
toilsome work."[559] Despite such hardships, the subsequent news of the coming Redeemer
will enable Adam to exclaim: "… in this life I shall have joy."[560]

As part of the reading noted in v. 24, this phrase was seen by some early interpreters as
God's promise to provide a less humiliating form of sustenance once Adam's penance was
complete. At its conclusion, "God rescinds [His] initial decree and offers [him] seed-bearing
grain from which he can make bread… [thus fulfilling] a prophecy made at the end of the
sixth day of creation."[561] A Coptic Christian tradition specifically mentions wheat (along
with instructions for sowing and reaping) as having been divinely provided in answer
to Adam's cries of hunger, and recounts that "his descendants have lived on wheat ever
since."[562] Similar themes are found in Islamic sources.[563] In addition, the Sumerian text *Ewe
and Wheat* recounts how wool and wheat were divinely provided in primeval times: "The
people in those distant days, They knew not bread to eat; They knew not cloth to wear; They
went about with naked limbs in the Land, And like sheep they ate grass with their mouth…
Then Enki spoke to Enlil: 'Father Enlil, Ewe and Wheat… Let us now send them down from
the Holy Hill.'"[564]

Linking the situations of Adam and Nebuchadnezzar to that of each penitent Christian,
Ephrem the Syrian wrote that "only when [Nebuchadnezzar] repented did he return to his
former abode and kingship. Blessed is He who has thus taught us to repent so that we too
may return to Paradise."[565] The bread promised to Adam on conditions of repentance and
baptism by water can be seen as a type of Christ, the "bread of life."[566] Christ's advent was,
of course, preceded by John, dressed in the rough clothes of a penitent, eating what he could
find in the wild, and baptizing "unto repentance."[567]

The change from "In" to "By" reflects the text of OT1 rather than OT2.[568]

---

555   Moses 5:1, 3.
556   Moses 5:1.
557   Moses 3:15.
558   N. M. Sarna, *Genesis*, p. 28.
559   C. Westermann, *Genesis 1-11*, p. 267.
560   Moses 5:10.
561   G. A. Anderson, *Penitence*, p. 19. See Moses 2:29.
562   *Coptic Apocrypha*, cited in E. A. W. Budge, *Cave*, pp. 18-19 n. 1. See also M. al-Kisa'i, *Tales*, pp. 68-70; al-Tabari,
        Creation, 1:127-130, pp. 298-300; S. C. Malan, *Adam and Eve*, 1:66-68, pp.78-83; D&C 89:17; and the overview
        of Moses 5, p. 341.
563   G. Weil, *Legends*, pp. 31, 45. See also M. Ibn Ishaq ibn Yasar, *Making*, pp. 34, 37; cf. A. al-Tha'labi, *Lives*, p. 63-
        65; G. Weil, *Legends*, pp. 31, 45; B. M. Wheeler, *Prophets*, pp. 27-28.
564   R. J. Clifford, *Ewe*, 20-24, 37-38, 40, pp. 45-46. See also *Commentary* 3:9-g, p. 163; 3:9-i, p. 168; and 5:2-a, p.
        354.
565   Ephrem the Syrian, *Paradise*, 13:6, p. 171. See *Excursus 43: Adam and Eve in Mozart's "Magic Flute"*, p. 634.
566   John 6:35.
567   Matthew 3:11. See T. G. Madsen, *Sacrament*, p. 85.
568   S. H. Faulring, *et al.*, *Original Manuscripts*, pp. 92, 601; K. P. Jackson, *Book of Moses*, p. 84.

*25 By the sweat of thy face shalt thou eat bread, **until thou shalt return unto the ground**— for thou shalt surely die—for out of it wast thou taken: for **dust thou wast, and unto dust shalt thou return**.*

*26 And **Adam called his wife's name Eve**, because she was the **mother of all living**; for thus have I, the Lord God, called the first of all women, which are many.*

b ***until thou shalt return unto the ground.*** Adam is sharply reminded of his new mortal condition. He and Eve have not yet fully become "as gods," but instead have become subject to temporal and spiritual death.

Later, the conditions for Redemption and an eventual return to God's presence will be given to Adam and Eve, with an emphasis on the need for obedience and sacrifice as the first steps on the way back to Paradise.[569] Evidence of God's intent to reverse this curse can also be seen in the blessing brought to "all the families of the earth"[570] through the Abrahamic covenant, which "was once more to unite the divided families, and change the curse, pronounced on the ground on account of sin, into a blessing for the whole human race."[571]

c ***dust thou wast, and unto dust shalt thou return.*** *2 Enoch* gives a unique reading of this verse: "You are earth, and into the earth once again you will go, out of which I took you. And I will not destroy you, but I will send you away to what I took you from. Then I can take you once again at my second coming."[572] This reading implies that Adam, his body created out of earthly materials and then placed in Eden, was sent back from Eden to Earth to live after the Fall. At the second coming, he would again be "taken" from the earth to live with God.[573]

26 a ***Adam called his wife's name Eve.*** The previous name given to Eve ['ishah = woman] was provisional,[574] Adam's full understanding having been obscured by his deep sleep during the creation of his companion.[575] The eating of the fruit of the Tree of Knowledge had increased their understanding and had also enabled the possibility of childbirth. Now, in connection with God's making of coats of skins for the couple,[576] Adam could at last bestow a fitting personal name on Eve, one "that expresses her nature and destiny positively and sympathetically."[577] "Her first name pointed to her origin ('out of man'), whereas her second name pointed to her destiny ('the mother of all living')."[578] Writes Hirsch: "Though through her sin, death first came upon mankind, she became "the dispenser of life… She is not only the physical but the spiritual and intellectual perpetrator of mankind's higher calling."[579]

b ***mother of all living.*** Adam rejoiced in the promise of motherhood given to Eve.[580] Though they were now subject to death, human life would continue afterwards through the fulfillment of God's command to multiply and replenish the earth.[581] Since she had not yet given birth, Hamilton takes the form of the statement as being a "prophetic perfect," emphasizing that the event foretold is as good as done.[582]

569 *Commentary* 5:4-b, p. 357.
570 *ha'admah*, Genesis 12:3.
571 Keil and Delitsch, *Commentary on the Old Testament*, 1:193, cited in J. E. Seaich, *Ancient Texts 1995*, pp. 665-668 n. 65; cf. Galatians 3:28-29.
572 F. I. Andersen, *2 Enoch*, 32:1, p. 154.
573 Cf. F. I. Andersen, *2 Enoch*, p. 155 n. 32b. Compare this with the rendering from the *Samaritan Pentateuch*: "To *your* dust you shall return" (M. Barker, *11 June 2007*, emphasis mine). See also *Commentary* 3:8-d, p. 162, and the overview of Moses 3, pp. 141-144.
574 *Commentary* 3:23-c, p. 183.
575 *Commentary* 3:21-a, p. 180.
576 Moses 4:27.
577 N. M. Sarna, *Genesis*, p. 29; cf. R. M. Zlotowitz, *et al.*, *Bereishis*, p. 135. See also *Commentary* 3:19-b, p. 177.
578 J. H. Sailhamer, *Genesis*, p. 57.
579 Cited in R. M. Zlotowitz, *et al.*, *Bereishis*, p. 136.
580 Moses 4:22.
581 V. P. Hamilton, *Genesis*, pp. 206-207.
582 *Ibid.*, p. 205. See also D. W. Parry, *et al.*, *Isaiah*, pp. 601-602.

*26 And Adam called his wife's name Eve, because she was the **mother of all living**; for thus have I, the Lord God, called the **first of all women, which are many**.*

*27 Unto Adam, and also unto his wife, did I, the Lord God, make **coats of skins**, and clothed them.*

The name "Eve" corresponds to the Hebrew *havvah*, whose vocalization suggests the possible meaning of "propagator of life."[583] Faulconer comments: "Eve is the mother of all living. Through her, life has come to the world—to her, to Man, to everything. In that sense, though Eve is created from the flesh of Man, she is also the creator of Man as fully human. To ask who was created from whom would be pointless. Standing 'across from' one another, they each create the other, and through their labor together they create the world."[584]

In early Christian tradition, Eve and Mary are often associated with the imagery of weaving, since it is due to the former that garments of flesh are "woven" for each child, and through the birth of Christ from the latter that the effects of the Fall were undone—thus eventually enabling mankind's garments of flesh to be replaced with robes of glory. Anderson notes that newly-married women in thirteenth-century Venice were given gifts of distaffs and spindles, their wombs being compared to that of the Mother of God: "The children they were to bear were none other than the 'image and likeness' God had intended at the very inception of the world. It would be hard to give a higher valuation of connubial love."[585]

    c   ***first of all women, which are many.*** Cf. *Commentary* 1:34-a, p. 66. See also Moses 6:9.

27 **a** ***coats of skins.*** Because of their transgression, Adam and Eve are no longer "naked… and not ashamed,"[586] thus God will mercifully clothe them with coats of animal skins. As a replacement for their flimsy apron of fig leaves[587] and in partial compensation for the loss of their "garment of light," the Lord's "garments of skin"[588] are intended to protect Adam and Eve in their exposed and fallen state, to remind them of their covenants, and to serve as a token of the glorious celestial robes that awaited them through their faithfulness.[589] Thus, *Targum Pseudo-Jonathan* translates "coats of skin" as "garments of glory."[590] Writes Nibley: "…a garment is a sign of protection, of dignity, of modesty; it is not just a sign of those things, it actually does impart them."[591]

Faulconer points out that "clothing is the only cultural artifact whose creation is ascribed to God. All other artifactual creations are attributed to human beings[—specifically to the descendants of Cain].[592] God's creation of clothing for Man and Woman stands out from the text, perhaps to show that they are unable to remove their shame themselves, to show that their exposure can be covered only by the Divine."[593]

Later echoes of this event in scripture, tradition, and ordinances leave no doubt that the account of the clothing of Adam and Eve, immediately following the mention of the naming of Eve, was meant to be understood in a ritual context. For example, Brown sees

---

583 V. P. Hamilton, *Genesis*, pp. 205-206; J. H. Hertz, *Pentateuch*, p. 12; N. M. Sarna, *Genesis*, p. 29.

584 J. E. Faulconer, *Adam and Eve*, 47.

585 G. A. Anderson, *Perfection*, p. 89. See also *Commentary* 4:27-a, p. 274; A. al-Tha'labi, *Lives*, pp. 62-63; P. H. Jolly, *Eve and Adam*, p. 60-61; and the *Protoevangelium of James*, where Mary is described as weaving the temple veil at the time of the annunciation (E. Hennecke, *et al.*, *Protoevangelium*, 10-12, pp. 379-380. See M. Barker, *Christmas*, pp. 142-143).

586 Moses 3:25.

587 Moses 4:13.

588 J. H. Sailhamer, *Genesis*, p. 58.

589 L. Ginzberg, *Legends*, 1:79, 96; H. W. Nibley, *Vestments*, p. 124. See also *Commentary* 3:25-a, p. 185 and the overview of Moses 4, pp. 237-239.

590 M. Maher, *Pseudo-Jonathan*, 3:21, p. 29 and p. 29 n. 43.

591 H. W. Nibley, *Vestments*, p. 116. "This is no fig-leaf Band-Aid. This is genuine protection" (T. L. Brodie, *Dialogue*, p. 152).

592 Cf. Moses 5:42-46.

593 J. E. Faulconer, *Adam and Eve*, 48, n. 24.

*27 Unto Adam, and also unto his wife, did I, the Lord God, make **coats of skins**, and clothed them.*

Jacob's manner of dress in receiving his birthright blessing as an "investiture with sacrificial goatskins" and mentions Hebrew traditions that "on this occasion Jacob was dressed in the priestly robes of Adam."[594] The Hebrew term for coats is the same one used to describe the knee- or ankle-length garment Jacob made for Joseph,[595] as well as one of the garments worn by priests that was intended "to cover their nakedness."[596] Tradition recounts both how the garment of Adam was preserved and passed down through the line of righteous patriarchs, and also how various intrigues were undertaken to steal and copy them.[597]

The *Conflict of Adam and Eve with Satan* tells how an angel made the garments with palm thorns: "And the angel said to Adam, 'Go forth, and bring some palm thorns.' Then Adam went out, and brought some, as the angel had commanded him. Then the angel began before them to work out the skins, after the manner of one who prepares a shirt. And he took the thorns and stuck them into the skins, before their eyes. Then the angel again stood up and prayed to God that the thorns in those skins should be hidden, so as to be, as it were, sewn with one thread.[598] And so it was by God's order; they became garments for Adam and Eve, and He clothed them withal."[599] Moreover, Islamic tradition records that "Eve spun and wove under the angel's direction, making a veil for herself and a garment for Adam, and both Adam and Eve imparted the information which they had received from Gabriel to their grandchildren and great-grandchildren."[600]

The *Targum Pseudo-Jonathan* says that God made the clothing "from the skin which the serpent had cast off."[601] At least one tradition speaks of the clothing as being made from tree bark.[602] Islamic texts speak of Adam as being commanded to sacrifice a ram, and Eve spinning and weaving its wool to provide the clothing that they would wear on their journey to build the House of Allàh in Mecca.[603] More plausible ancient traditions hold that Adam and Eve's coats of skin were made of sheepskin,[604] God Himself having shown Adam and Eve how animal sacrifice was to be performed.[605] As a reminder of the ritual significance of the clothing, al Tha'labi cites the idea that "You must wear wool, for then you will be recognized in the Hereafter."[606] McConkie notes a symbolism in the selection of a lamb whose death by the shedding of blood was required by the law of sacrifice, and whose skins were presumably used to provide the garments: "The garments constituted a constant reminder of the protection they would enjoy (through the blood of the Lamb, even the Son of God) from all the effects of the Fall."[607] Thus, the skin garments embody both "a token of death"[608] and a promise of life.

V. 27 is missing from OT1, but was inserted in OT2.[609] The OT2 term "skin" was changed to "skins."[610]

594   M. B. Brown, *Girded*, p. 145.
595   Genesis 37:3.
596   Exodus 28:42; V. P. Hamilton, *Genesis*, p. 207.
597   H. W. Nibley, *Lehi 1988*, pp. 168-170; H. W. Nibley, *Vestments*, pp. 128-131; H. Schwartz, *Tree*, pp. 437-438. See L. Wilson, *Joseph Wise*, pp. 231-232 for an overview of parallels between Joseph and Adam.
598   Cf. the garment worn by the high priest and by Jesus (J. A. Tvedtnes, *Clothing*, p. 692; D. Wilson, *Conflict*, p. 40).
599   S. C. Malan, *Adam and Eve*, 52, p. 57.
600   G. Weil, *Legends*, p. 46.
601   M. Maher, *Pseudo-Jonathan*, 3:21, p. 29.
602   Shelemon, *Book of the Bee*, 17, p. 24.
603   M.al-Kisa'i, *Tales*, p. 68; al-Tabari, *Creation*, 1:123, p. 294; B. M. Wheeler, *Prophets*, p. 31.
604   M. B. Brown, *Girded*, pp. 143-144; S. C. Malan, *Adam and Eve*, 1:50, p. 55.
605   Cf. J. H. Sailhamer, *Genesis*, p. 58; G. Weil, *Legends*, pp. 45-46. See *Commentary 5:5-b*, p. 359.
606   A. al-Tha'labi, *Lives*, p. 63.
607   J. F. McConkie, *et al.*, *Revelations*, p. 223.
608   S. C. Malan, *Adam and Eve*, 1:52, p. 57.
609   S. H. Faulring, *et al.*, *Original Manuscripts*, pp. 92, 602.
610   K. P. Jackson, *Book of Moses*, p. 84.

*27 Unto Adam, and also unto his wife, did I, the Lord God, make coats of skins, and **clothed them**.*

*28 And I, the Lord God, said unto mine Only Begotten: Behold, the **man is become as one of us to know good and evil**; and now **lest he** put forth his hand and **partake also of the tree of life**, and eat and live forever,*

b   ***clothed them.*** The Genesis mosaics in San Marco, Venice shows God helping Eve put on a garment,[611] thus emphasizing that He did not merely provide the coats of skin for them but also actually performed the act of clothing them personally.

28 **a**   ***man is become as one of us to know good and evil.*** Verses 28-31 provide God's summary about what has just happened and give a rationale for His removal of Adam and Eve from the Garden of Eden. While the serpent had painted a picture of wrathful punishment by a jealous God, the Lord's actions will instead further bless the couple. Through partaking of the forbidden fruit, Adam and Eve have begun to know good and evil—in that respect becoming "as gods."[612] Now that the couple has made their free choice of mortality as the way forward, God will enable them to gain further experience by sending them out of the Garden under conditions that He had expressly designed to meet that purpose.[613] He will provide a Savior for them, and will make the Gospel with its covenants and ordinances available so that, through their faithfulness, they might be sanctified and return to His presence.[614]

In contrast to the Bible, which exclusively employs the term "good *and* evil,"[615] the Book of Mormon and the book of Moses contain nine instances of the similar phrase "good *from* evil."[616] Though, admittedly, the difference in connotation between these terms is not entirely consistent across all scriptural references to them,[617] one might still argue for a distinction between the knowledge Adam and Eve initially acquired when they determined to eat the forbidden fruit, and that which they gained later through the experience of repeated choice in a fallen world. Unlike the former knowledge that had come in response to Satan's deception and as the result of moral autonomy exercised in *transgression* of divine instruction,[618] the essential knowledge attained gradually by Adam and Eve during their later period of mortal probation would depend on their *hearkening* to the "Spirit of Christ,"[619] mercifully made available to them through the power of Redemption,[620] and enabling them to "know good from evil… with a perfect knowledge, as the daylight is from the dark night."[621]

b   ***lest he… partake also of the tree of life.*** Though no explicit prohibition occurs prior to this verse, several lines of evidence converge to suggest that Adam and Eve had never taken of the fruit of the Tree of Life while they lived in Eden. For example, a unique Samaritan exegesis of Moses 3:16 excludes the Tree of Life from the original permission given to Adam and Eve to eat from the trees of the Garden.[622] Here, in addition, the use of the term "also" (Hebrew *gam*) suggests that Adam and Eve had not yet partaken of its fruit at the time these

---

611 P. H. Jolly, *Eve and Adam*, p. 56

612 *Commentary* 4:11-b, p. 253.

613 Moses 4:22-25; D&C 122:7.

614 E.g., Moses 4:27; 5:5-9; 6:64-65. See also Hafen in Moses 4 *Gleanings*, pp. 294-296.

615 Genesis 2:9, 17; Genesis 3:5, 22; Deuteronomy 1:39; 2 Samuel 19:35; Proverbs 31:12; Isaiah 5:20; Jeremiah 24:3; Amos 5:14; Matthew 12:35; Luke 6:45; Hebrews 5:14. The phrase is also used in the Book of Mormon and the Pearl of Great Price: 2 Nephi 2:18, 15:20; Alma 29:5, 42:3; Moses 3:9, 17; Moses 4:11, 28; Moses 5:11; Abraham 5:9, 13; JS-H 1:33.

616 2 Nephi 2:5, 26; Alma 12:31, 29:5; Helaman 14:31; Moroni 7:15-16, 19; Moses 6:56.

617 E.g., The reference to "good from evil" in Alma 12:31 equates to the use of the term "good and evil" in Genesis 3:22 and Moses 4:28.

618 D&C 1:16; J. D. G. Dunn, *et al.*, *Commentary*, p. 40; L. R. Kass, *Wisdom*, p. 44; G. J. Wenham, *Genesis 1-15*, pp. 63-64. See *Commentary* 4:11-c, p. 254.

619 Moroni 7:16, 19.

620 2 Nephi 2:26.

621 Moroni 7:15.

622 S. Lowy, *Principles*, p. 403.

*28 And I, the Lord God, said unto mine Only Begotten: Behold, the man is become as one of us to know good and evil; and now **lest he** put forth his hand and **partake also of the tree of life**, and **eat and live forever**,*

words were spoken. Evidence for the use of *gam* in the sense of "new and additional activity" is provided in 4:12 ("and *also* gave to her husband").[623] Moreover, Barr studied 131 cases of "lest" (Hebrew *pen*) in the Bible "and found none which means 'lest someone continue to do what they are already doing.'"[624] Finally, the case for such a reading is strengthened conclusively if eating of the fruit of the Tree of Life is taken not merely as the means of ensuring immortality, but as representing the "gift of eternal life"[625]—bestowed in the appropriate degree to those who partake of the fruits of Christ's atonement.[626] Vos concurs with this reading, concluding that "the tree was associated with the higher, the unchangeable, the eternal life to be secured by obedience throughout the probation."[627] According to this view, Adam and Eve never would have been permitted to partake of the fruit of the Tree of Life at their own discretion. Rather, their only approach to the Tree of Life will be by way of leaving the Garden to pass into mortality, and then returning at last to take of the sweet fruit only when they have completed their probation and are authoritatively invited to do so.[628] In this way, their lives, their knowledge, and their exercise of divine power would be wisely limited until they have completed the process of sanctification.[629]

C. S. Lewis succinctly expressed the reason for this essential prerequisite of sanctification by a question: "How can [God] meet us face to face till we have faces?"[630]—meaning that before we can expect to really know God we must become "clean mirrors filled with the image of a face that is not ours."[631] In other words, we must become new creatures in Christ, having cast off all pretense and competing personae. Only then will God become "wholly beautiful" to us—or we at last will be shown how beautiful He always was—and that same beauty will be in some smaller measure ours.[632] In the words of John: "Beloved, now are we the sons of God, and it doth not yet appear what we shall be: but we know that when he shall appear, we shall be like him: for we shall see him as he is. And every man that hath this hope in him purifieth himself, even as he is pure."[633]

c   ***eat and live forever.*** During their sojourn in the Garden of Eden, Adam and Eve had enjoyed immortality, but their partaking of the forbidden fruit now made them subject to death. As a result of their choice, "the new situation to be avoided is... the eating from the [Tree of Life] after having taken from the Tree of Knowledge."[634] The *Targum Pseudo-Jonathan* summarizes the situation, asserting that if Adam had kept the commandments: "he would have lived and endured like the Tree of Life forever. But now, since he has not observed what I commanded him, ... let us banish him from the Garden of Eden, before he puts forth his hand and takes (also) of the fruit from the Tree of Life, ...and endure forever."[635]

---

623   V. P. Hamilton, *Genesis*, p. 209. See also T. N. D. Mettinger, *Eden*, p. 20.

624   T. Stordalen, *Echoes*, pp. 230-231. However, contrary to Barr, see exceptions in Exodus 1:9; 2 Samuel 12:27.

625   D&C 14:7.

626   D&C 88:28-32; R. J. Matthews, *Probationary Nature*, p. 56. See *Commentary* 3:17-c, p. 175. Note, however, that in the vision of Lehi there is not the same sense of ultimacy in the taking of the fruit, since some, "after they had tasted of the fruit... were ashamed... and... fell away" (1 Nephi 8:28). "If the Tree of Life in Lehi's vision represented the love of God, then the Tree of Life in the Garden represents a fulness of that love" (M. A. Shields, *Your Endowment*, p. 45).

627   Cited in V. P. Hamilton, *Genesis*, p. 209 n. 6.

628   D&C 88:68.

629   See C. C. Riddle, *New*, p. 228; *Commentary* 1:5-c, p. 46, 4:11-c, p. 254; the overview of Moses 5, pp. 338-350.

630   C. S. Lewis, *Faces*, p. 294.

631   C. S. Lewis, *Literature*, p. 416; cf. Alma 5:14-19: "having the image of God engraven upon your countenances." Note accounts in Second Temple Jewish pseudepigrapha where visionaries are transformed and "encounter their heavenly counterparts and... behold the divine Face like their own reflection in a mirror" (A. A. Orlov, *Mirror*, p. 151).

632   C. S. Lewis, *Faces*, pp. 304-308. See also C. S. Lewis, *Malcolm*, pp. 20-22; P. J. Schakel, *Reason*, pp. 78-86, and C. S. Lewis to Rose Macaulay, cited in W. Hooper, *Lewis Companion*, p. 252.

633   1 John 3:2-3; cf. Moroni 7:48; D&C 130:1-3.

634   T. Stordalen, *Echoes*, p. 231; cf. H. W. Nibley, *Atonement*, p. 555.

635   M. Maher, *Pseudo-Jonathan*, 3:22, p. 30.

*28 And I, the Lord God, said unto mine Only Begotten: Behold, the man is become as one of us to know good and evil; and now lest he put forth his hand and partake also of the tree of life, and **eat and live forever**,*

*29 Therefore I, the Lord God, **will send him forth** from the Garden of Eden, to till the ground from whence he was taken;*

Death is an essential part of the plan of salvation. In preparation for eternal life, mankind must have their days "prolonged" and undergo a "state of probation."[636] Otherwise "the great plan of salvation would be frustrated" because there would be "no space for repentance"[637] or, in other words, "no probationary time"[638] before the spirits of Adam and Eve would be forever united with an immortal resurrected body.[639] Only they "who are of a celestial spirit" can receive a body quickened with celestial glory,[640] thus it is essential that each person be given sufficient opportunity to "repent while in the flesh"[641]—and also, possibly with more difficulty,[642] for a limited time in the spirit world[643]—before the final judgment and resurrection. If Adam and Eve had taken the fruit of the Tree of Life immediately after having eaten from the Tree of Knowledge, they would have been "forever miserable,"[644] having become "immortal in their fallen state,"[645] living forever in their sins.[646]

Applying the lesson that was taught by the Levitical laws of rigorous purity for those who served in ancient temples to the situation of Adam and Eve, Anderson observes: "Exile [from the Garden] was not simply punishment; it was a form of protection. For to remain before God in Eden, while defiled by sin, was to court unnecessary danger, perhaps even death."[647] To prevent such catastrophe, concludes Anderson, the Lord immediately restricted their access to the Tree of Life.[648]

29   a   *will send him forth.* The phrase in Hebrew reads "put him forth,"[649] paralleling the language of verse 28. Thus, the sense is that rather than allow man to "put forth" his hand,[650] man is "put forth" from the Garden.[651]

Exegetes have long puzzled over the significance of the double reference to Adam and Eve's expulsion in vv. 29 and 31. A change from the Genesis and OT1 "sent" to "will send" in OT2 was made in the handwriting of Sidney Rigdon.[652] This rendering allows this description of the "first" expulsion of Adam and Eve to be seen simply as an anticipatory statement of the Lord's intention, corresponding to the actual event later described in v. 31. By way of contrast, some traditions see the couple's exit from the Garden of Eden as having occurred in two stages. For example, the *Qur'an* explicitly records that Adam and Eve were twice told to go down,[653] explaining that they "were removed first from the Garden to its courtyard and

636   2 Nephi 2:21.

637   Alma 42:5. See also Alma 34:33.

638   Alma 42:4.

639   See also Alma 12:21-27; D&C 132:19; W. C. Skousen, *First 2,000*, pp. 42-44, 66-68.

640   D&C 88:28.

641   2 Nephi 2:21.

642   M. J. Ballard, *Three Degrees 1949*, p. 241.

643   1 Peter 4:6; Alma 42:10.

644   Alma 12:26.

645   W. C. Skousen, *First 2,000*, p. 68.

646   Cf. Alma 42:3-5; Helaman 5:10-11. See also *Commentary* 3:9-h, p. 167 and the overview of Moses 4, pp. 227-234.

647   G. A. Anderson, *Perfection*, p. 129.

648   See *Commentary* 3:17-c, p. 175.

649   Hebrew *shillah*.

650   Moses 4:28.

651   R. E. Friedman, *Commentary*, p. 25. See *Commentary* 4:31-a, p. 280.

652   S. H. Faulring, *et al.*, *Original Manuscripts*, p. 602; K. P. Jackson, *Book of Moses*, p. 85.

653   M. M. Ali, *Qur'an*, 2:36, 38, pp. 20-21.

*29 Therefore I, the Lord God, **will send him forth** from the Garden of Eden, **to till the ground** from whence he was taken;*

*30 For as I, the Lord God, liveth, even so **my words** cannot return void, for as they **go forth** out of my mouth they **must be fulfilled**.*

then from the courtyard to the earth."[654] A somewhat different view of a two-stage removal would be consistent with Ephrem's idea of an attempted intrusion into the celestial regions of the Garden, followed by an expulsion from the terrestrial paradise to the telestial earth.[655]

b *to till the ground.* The fact that man is now required to till the ground is "to be seen as an ironic reversal of man's original purpose" to worship and to obey in the spirit of rest originally ordained for the unending paradisiacal Sabbath.[656] A Hebrew wordplay underscores the change of situation for Adam and Eve: instead of worship (*le-obdah*) they will till the ground (*la-abod*); and their failure of obedience (*le-somrah*) has caused them to be kept (*lismor*) from the Tree of Life.[657]

Earlier, Moses 3:5 had recorded that the earth and the heavens and the plants had been made, but there was not yet "a man to till the ground."[658] However, now that knowledge of good and evil has been given to mankind, that Eve has become capable of bearing children, and that labor has been introduced into the world, the *moral* creation of Adam and Eve is underway.[659]

A scriptural theme associated with Jesus Christ is that of His role as Lord of the vineyard.[660] "The fifth Similitude of the *Shepherd of Hermas*[661] figures the mission of Jesus in the world through a symbolism of the vineyard, an enclosed place of delights and of testing, an image of the Garden of Eden. God entrusts his vineyard to a servant (the man Jesus) so that he may guard it and surround it with a fence; the servant surrounds the vineyard with a palisade (of angels). He cultivates it (pulling up weeds until he is weary and sorrowful[662]) and makes it bring forth fruit… [I]n this similitude there seems to be the suggestion of the identification of Jesus with the new and pious Adam."[663]

30 a *my words… go forth… must be fulfilled.* In other words, Adam and Eve were "sent forth" in order to fulfill the words of the Lord that had previously "gone forth." The unstated implication is that because God's words will not return "void," so in the end Adam and Eve will not return without having accomplished all that they had been commanded to do. Thus, writes Anderson: "The work that God has begun in creation he will bring to completion."[664] Faulconer further explains: "Common Christian exegesis… notwithstanding, … this is no unfortunate Fall… If we see that the introduction of death is also a birth (into the human world and the possibility of genuine human and, thus, godly existence among humans), then we see that [Moses 2-4] is an account of Creation, not of Creation and Fall."[665]

OT1 reads "word" not "words."[666] The current text follows a change made to OT2.[667]

654   A. at-Tabataba'i, *Al-Mizan*, 1:209.
655   Ephrem the Syrian, *Paradise*, 3:5, p. 92; 3:13-15, pp. 95-96.
656   J. H. Sailhamer, *Genesis*, pp. 45, 47-48. See *Commentary* 3:15-b, p. 173.
657   Moses 4:31. See J. H. Sailhamer, *Genesis*, p. 59.
658   See *Commentary* 3:5-a, p. 154.
659   J. E. Faulconer, *Adam and Eve*, 46.
660   Jacob 5; Matthew 21:33-44; Mark 12:1-11; Luke 13:6-10.
661   C. Osiek, *Shepherd*, 5:2 [55], 5:4 [57], pp. 170-172, 175-181.
662   See Genesis 3:17-18.
663   G. Lettieri, *Ambiguity*, p. 33 n. 22.
664   G. A. Anderson, *Perfection*, p. 8. Cf. *Gleanings*, p. 188; Galatians 4:4: "God sent forth his Son."
665   J. E. Faulconer, *Adam and Eve*, 51.
666   S. H. Faulring, *et al.*, *Original Manuscripts*, p. 92.
667   *Ibid.*, p. 602.

*31 So **I drove out the man**, and I placed **at the east of the Garden** of Eden, **cherubim** and a **flaming sword**, which turned every way to keep the way of the tree of life.*

31 a *I drove out the man.* The Hebrew word *geresh* ("drove out") is harsher than the term *shillah* ("send him forth") in verse 29. Significantly, the same two terms are used in the same order by the Lord to describe how Pharaoh would expel Israel from Egypt.[668]

Adam and Eve's new condition is one of spiritual death.[669] Sailhamer points out: "The penalty is identical to that established by the Mosaic law: to 'be put to death'... is to be 'cut off from his people.'"[670] Their transgression has cut them off from the immediate "protective presence" of God they had experienced in the Garden,[671] and their "removal from His presence suggests a process of death."[672]

b *at the east of the Garden.* The entrance to the Garden—and presumably the only means of access—is on the east side, at the end farthest away from the mountain of God's presence.[673]

c *cherubim.* The term, which is left untranslated, may be related to the Akkadian *karibu* (intercessor) or *karibi* (gatekeepers).[674] In Hebrew, the definite article is used (i.e., *the* cherubim), presupposing the reader's familiarity with these beings.[675] In ancient texts, cherubim appear "as guarding sacred vegetation, as carrying (or being) the throne of YHWH and as carrying YHWH in celestial transport."[676] Consistent with the concept of the temple as a representation of the Garden of Eden, cherubim also figured prominently in the layout of the Tabernacle and permanent structures subsequently built for worship. "Two golden cherubim with outstretched wings overshadowed the cover of the Ark in the Tabernacle in the wilderness,[677] and from the space between them issued the divine Voice that spoke to Moses.[678] Pictorial representations of the cherubim were also worked into the cloth curtains of the Tabernacle.[679] The same cherubic motif decorated Solomon's Temple,[680] was envisaged by Ezekiel in his restored temple,"[681] and was used to decorate medieval cathedrals. Hansen suggests that statues of Joseph and Hyrum Smith that once flanked the east entrance to the Salt Lake Temple also symbolized the role of the cherubim.[682] In our day, such symbolic protectors are used to guard entrances to banks and government buildings.

In each of the temple contexts mentioned above, the essential function of the cherubim placed at crucial locations was analogous to their role in the Garden; they were to be as sentinels guarding the portals of the temple against unauthorized entry, governing subsequent access to secure compartments, and ultimately assisting in the determination of the fitness of temple worshipers to enter God's presence.[683]

d *flaming sword.* Translated by Sarna as "the fiery ever-turning sword," this is a "separate, protective instrument, not said to be in the hands of the cherubim." Like the cherubim, the Hebrew "carries the definite article and so was also something well known to the Israelite imagination, even though it is not again mentioned in the Bible precisely in this form."[684]

---

668 Exodus 6:1. See N. M. Sarna, *Genesis*, p. 30.
669 D&C 29:41.
670 J. H. Sailhamer, *Genesis*, p. 59. See Exodus 31:14.
671 Cf. Moses 5:39. See *Commentary* 4:3-d, p. 245.
672 R. W. L. Moberly, *Serpent*, p. 18.
673 See *Commentary* 4:14-c, p. 259.
674 D. N. Freedman, *et al.*, *Eerdmans*, p. 233.
675 N. M. Sarna, *Genesis*, p. 30.
676 T. Stordalen, *Echoes*, p. 293. See *Excursus 25: The Tree of Life as the Hidden Throne of God*, p. 591.
677 Exodus 25:18-22.
678 Numbers 7:8-9.
679 Exodus 26:31; 36:8, 35; 37:7-9.
680 I Kings 6:23-35; 7:36; 8:6-7. See *Figure 3-9*, p. 146 and *Figure 3-11*, p. 149.
681 N. M. Sarna, *Genesis*, p. 375; Ezekiel 41:18-20, 25.
682 G. E. Hansen, Jr., *et al.*, *Sacred Walls*, p. 79.
683 D&C 132:19; D. W. Parry, *Garden*, p. 139; H. Schwartz, *Tree*, 518, p. 404; B. Young, *6 April 1853 - B*, p. 31. See also *Commentary* 3:19-b, p. 177; R. Guénon, *Symboles*, pp. 105-113; J. A. Tvedtnes, *Rituals*.
684 N. M. Sarna, *Genesis*, p. 30. See also H. Schwartz, *Tree*, 518, p. 404.

31 So I drove out the man, and I placed at the east of the Garden of Eden, cherubim and a **flaming sword**, *which turned every way to keep the way of the tree of life.*

Parry[685] describes each of the three elements mentioned in more detail:

1. *Sword*. In this context, the weapon of war anticipates the sword of the Lord that delivers judgment. It blesses the righteous and slays the wicked: "I kill and I make alive; I wound, and I heal: neither is there any that can deliver out of my hand."[686]

2. *Flame of fire*. The flames enable the sword to scorch and devour, as it slashes and penetrates. The combined imagery of fire and the sword recalls Isaiah 66:15-16: "For by fire and by his sword will the Lord plead with all flesh";

3. *Turned every way*. The scene is one of continual whirling, perhaps in a zig-zag way to protect the path.

Indirect references to the cherubim and flaming sword can be found in Ezekiel[687] and in Isaiah's vision of the seraphim protecting the throne of God.[688] Moreover, the angel that turned Balaam's ass aside was said to have had a sword in his hand.[689] Cassuto also notes a more subtle association between flames and angels in Psalm 104:4.[690]

Swords symbolize discernment and that which separates."[691] While the function of the cherubim is to selectively admit those authorized to enter, Nibley argues that the fire and steel combined in the sword are specifically meant to repulse the serpent, forever preventing its return to the Garden.[692] "This symbolism has been retained in some religious traditions through rites enacting the banishment of Satan prior to the baptism of a new Christian.[693] Just as the flaming sword at the gates of the Garden of Eden represents God's resolve to prevent the return of the serpent, the renunciation rite signifies the baptismal candidates' definitive rejection of the Devil prior to their passing through the gateway to eternal life. Celestial law prohibits dual citizenship in the kingdoms of God and Satan.[694] Thus, as Elder Maxwell taught, the disciple of Christ "has his citizenship in the kingdom, but carries his passport into the… world—not the other way around."[695]

Barker cites the writings of the Church Fathers that associate the symbolism of the fiery sword with the purifying "baptism by fire" that was seen to constitute the final test of the candidate's worthiness to enter the kingdom of God: "[At his baptism,] Jesus himself stood in the river of fire, next to the flaming sword which barred the way to the presence of God… The river of fire, then, was the boundary between earth and heaven… which the 'seed' must pass if it is to reach the *Pleroma*.[696] The veil of the temple shielded 'things' from its brightness and Jesus, the high priest, stood behind the veil in the Holy of Holies to assist those who passed through. The *hylikon*, the material, was burned away 'in its passage through the fire'."[697]

---

685 D. W. Parry, *Cherubim.*

686 Deuteronomy 32:29-41.

687 Ezekiel 1:4-28.

688 Isaiah 6:1-8.

689 Numbers 22:23.

690 U. Cassuto, *Adam to Noah*, p. 176.

691 A. L. Gaskill, *Lost*, p. 299.

692 H. W. Nibley, *Message 2005*, pp. 319-320.

693 Cf. Moses' experience in Moses 1:16-22. See also *Commentary* 1:1-b, p. 42; 4:21-d, p. 266.

694 See Matthew 6:24; H. W. Nibley, *Gifts*, p. 104.

695 N. A. Maxwell, *Some Thoughts*, p. 589.

696 = the dwelling place of God. J. P. Migne, *Patrologiae Graeca*, Excerpts 38, 9:677 and *ibid.*, Excerpts 52, 9:683; cf. the "awful gulf, which separated the wicked from the tree of life" in Nephi's vision (1 Nephi 15:28; cf. 1 Nephi 12:18).

697 M. Barker, *Risen*, pp. 42-43. See also Gregory Nazianzen, *Oration 39*, 16, p. 358; Origen, *Luke*, Homily 24 Luke 3:15-16, p. 103, 1 Corinthians 3:13, and *Excursus 11: The Sacred Circle*, p. 547.

*31 So I drove out the man, and I placed at the east of the Garden of Eden, cherubim and a flaming sword, which turned every way **to keep the way of the tree of life**.*

*32 (And these are the words which I spake unto my servant Moses, and they are true even as I will; and I have spoken them unto you. **See thou show them unto no man**, until I command you, except to them that believe. Amen.)*

e   **to keep the way of the tree of life.** The mention of a *via sacra* leading from the place of Adam's exile back to the Garden ends the story on a note of hope.[698] The cherubim will open the way for man once he is prepared to enter the Celestial Paradise and eat of the Tree of Life.[699] Hirsch comments that the scriptural phrase "can mean to protect and preserve the way so that it shall not be lost for mankind, so that he will be able to find it again and ultimately go back on it… He finds support for this in the fact that this task was entrusted to Cherubim, using the same word to describe the golden protectors of the Holy Ark in the Tabernacle and Temple."[700] A rabbinic tradition has it that the last divine word that rang in the ears of Adam and Eve as they left the Garden of Eden was *tashub*, meaning "You shall return!"[701]

Note that the Hebrew term for "to keep" (*shamar* = keep, watch, guard, preserve) is identical to the earlier term describing one of the two duties given to Adam when he was originally placed in the Garden.[702] Adam's former function "to keep the Garden"—which, of course, equates to the task of keeping "the way to the tree of life"—will henceforth be assumed by the cherubim.[703] However, since no one is now appointed to fulfill the duty to "dress" the Garden (*abad* = work, serve within it as the archetypical Levite), it must remain unoccupied and unworked until man, prepared with "intelligence and knowledge" gained through "diligence and obedience," is ready to enter its sacred precincts,[704] fully prepared to "stand in holy places and be not moved."[705]

Of the Tree of Life that awaits the returning exiles, *1 Enoch* says that "its fruit will be as food for the chosen [elect]," its "fragrances will be in their bones" ("it is possible that the author is thinking of resurrection to the body," comments Nickelsburg), and "they will live a long life upon the earth."[706] As a fitting sequel to this narrative sequence, Moses 5-7 will describe the unfolding revelation of the "plan of redemption" to Adam and Eve and their posterity that will make possible their return to Paradise and to the presence of God.[707]

32   **a**   **See thou show them unto no man.** See *Commentary* 1:42-a, p. 69.

---

698   R. M. Zlotowitz *et al.*, *Bereishis*, p. 140.

699   Revelation 2:7, 22:14; G. A. Anderson *et al.*, *Synopsis*, 44:4, p. 71E; M. D. Johnson, *Life*, 28:4, p. 285; S. C. Malan, *Adam and Eve*, 38:2, p. 41; H. W. Nibley, *Message 2005*, p. 320; M. E. Stone, *Fall of Satan*, pp. 49-53; G. Weil, *Legends*, p. 36; B. M. Wheeler, *Prophets*, p. 29; cf. T. Stordalen, *Echoes*, pp. 416-417.

700   Cited in R. M. Zlotowitz, *et al.*, *Bereishis*, pp. 140-141. See *Commentary* 5:4-b, p. 357.

701   A. LaCocque, *Trial*, 31.

702   *Commentary* 3:15-b, p. 173.

703   Cf. U. Cassuto, *Adam to Noah*, p. 174. See also D. I. Block, *Ezekiel 25-48*, p. 113.

704   D&C 130:18-19; see *Excursus 27: Diligence, Obedience, and Friendship*, p. 597.

705   D&C 87:8; cf. D&C 45:32; A. G. Zornberg, *Genesis*, pp. 8, 16, 20-22, 27-28, 32-33.

706   G. W. E. Nickelsburg, *1 Enoch*, 24:4-6, p. 312, 315.

707   Alma 12:23-34.

Gleanings

Table of Contents

Terryl L. Givens: The Fall Is Situated in the Context of Human Agency[707]

If mortality is not man's original condition, a view of human nature based on scriptural descriptions of an embodied state is at one remove from the truth of the matter. The Book of Mormon is emphatic in its insistence that the detritus of the fall—sin and death especially—is a dark middle passage, not a point of origin, in humanity's spiritual odyssey. That is why, as regards Adam's transgression, the Book of Mormon weighs in with an unqualified endorsement of the "fortunate Fall"…[708]

In fact, the expulsion from the Garden was not wrathful punishment of a primal wickedness but merciful forestalling of premature immortality, in accordance with a plan that anticipated a temporary spiritual isolation from God…[709]

---

707 T. L. Givens, *Hand*, pp. 203-205.

708 2 Nephi 2:22-25.

709 Alma 12:24-26. See *Endnote 4-78*, p. 320.

The Fall of man was fortunate, the Book of Mormon explains, not because in some Miltonic sense it called forth a triumphal act of supernal grace,[710] but because its actuality in the world is the sign—and price—of the moral freedom that precedes it. Freedom, in turn, is the precondition for human happiness…[711]

Thus the Book of Mormon view of the human condition emphasizes what was validated by the Fall—moral freedom—not what was temporarily assumed—sinfulness. In characterizing sin itself as an essential precondition for the very possibility of human happiness, the scripture emphasizes freedom rather than depravity…

Against this backdrop, then, the Book of Mormon develops a doctrine of the atonement in such a way as to reclaim the principle of justice from a kind of Platonic abstraction or equivalence with God himself and to situate it in the context of human agency. This may well be one of its greatest theological contributions.

Richard L. Bushman: A Profoundly Voluntaristic Universe[712]

The story of the beginning envisions a profoundly voluntaristic universe. Human beings are not the creatures of God, because He did not create their inner essence. They are radically free intelligences, as eternal as God Himself. Nor did He impose His will on these lesser intelligences through an exercise of power. He offered them laws by which they could advance with the option of accepting or not. The books of Abraham and Moses incorporate this choice into a story. They tell about a time when Lucifer, a brilliant spirit in the heavenly reams, offered "to redeem all mankind, that one soul shall not be lost."[713] The drawback of this guaranteed salvation was that Lucifer would destroy human agency… Following God and Christ entailed the huge risk of sin and suffering. By allowing spirits their freedom, God left room for some to fall out of His presence into the realms of darkness and chaos… All the spirits who came to earth chose to take the risk.

C. S. Lewis: The Effects of the Fall in Daily Life[714]

According to [the doctrine of the Fall], man is… a creature ill-adapted to the universe not because God made him so but because he has made himself so by the abuse of his free will… [The doctrine] exists to guard against two sub-Christian theories of the origin of evil—Monism, according to which God Himself, being "above good and evil," produces impartially the effects to which we give these two names, and Dualism, according to which God produces good, while some equal and independent Power produces evil. Against both these views Christianity asserts that God is good; that He made all things good and for the sake of their goodness; that one of the good things He made, namely, the free will of rational creatures, by its very nature included the possibility of evil; and that creatures, availing themselves of this possibility, have become evil.…

From the moment a creature becomes aware of God as God and of itself as self, the terrible alternative of choosing God or self for the center is opened to it. This sin is committed daily by young children and ignorant peasants as well as by sophisticated persons, by solitaries no less than by those who live in society: it is the fall in every individual life, and in each day

---

710   J. Milton, *Paradise Lost*, 12:469-478, p. 253. See p. 291 below.
711   2 Nephi 2:13.
712   R. L. Bushman, *Mormonism*, p. 73.
713   Moses 4:1.
714   C. S. Lewis, *Pain*, pp. 61, 66-68, 71, 74-75, 76-77.

of each individual life, the basic sin behind all particular sins: at this moment you and I are either committing it, or about to commit it, or repenting it. We try, when we wake, to lay the new day at God's feet; before we have finished shaving, it becomes our day and God's share in it is felt as a tribute which we must pay out of "our own" pocket, a deduction from the time which ought, we feel, to be "our own." A man starts a new job with a sense of vocation and, perhaps, for the first week still keeps the discharge of the vocation as his end, taking the pleasures and pains from God's hand, as they come, as "accidents." But in the second week he is beginning to "know the ropes": by the third, he has quarried out of the total job his own plan for himself within that job, and when he can pursue this he feels that he is getting no more than his rights, and, when he cannot, that he is being interfered with. A lover, in obedience to a quite uncalculating impulse, which may be full of good will as well as of desire and need not be forgetful of God, embraces his beloved, and then, quite innocently, experiences a thrill of sexual pleasures; but the second embrace may have that pleasure in view, may be a means to an end, may be the first downward step towards the state of regarding a fellow creature as a thing, as a machine to be used for his pleasure. Thus the bloom of innocence, the element of obedience and the readiness to take what comes is rubbed off every activity. Thoughts undertaken for God's sake—like that on which we are engaged at the moment—are continued as if they were an end in themselves, and then as if our pleasure in thinking were the end, and finally as if our pride or celebrity were the end. Thus all day long, and all the days of our life, we are sliding, slipping, falling away—as if God were, to our present consciousness, a smooth inclined plane on which there is no resting. And indeed we are now of such a nature that we must slip off, and the sin, because it is unavoidable, may be venial. But God cannot have made us so. The gravitation away from God, "the journey homeward to habitual self," must, we think, be a product of the Fall....

As a young man wants a regular allowance from his father which he can count on as his own, within which he makes his own plans (and rightly, for his father is after all a fellow creature) so [fallen mankind] desired to be on their own, to take care for their own future, to plan for pleasure and for security, to have a *meum*[715] from which, no doubt, they would pay some reasonable tribute to God in the way of time, attention, and love, but which nevertheless was theirs not His. They wanted, as we say, to "call their souls their own." But that means to live a lie, for our souls are not, in fact, our own.[716] They wanted some corner in the universe of which they could say to God, "This is our business, not yours." But there is no such corner....

God might have arrested this process by miracle: but this—to speak in somewhat irreverent metaphor—would have been to decline the problem which He had set Himself when He created the world, the problem of expressing His goodness through the total drama of a world containing free agents, in spite of, and by means of, their rebellion against Him... God saw the crucifixion in the act of creating the first nebula. The world is a dance in which good, descending from God, is disturbed by evil arising from the creatures, and the resulting conflict is resolved by God's own assumption of the suffering nature which evil produces....

With this I have said all that can be said on the level at which alone I feel able to treat the subject of the Fall. But I warn my readers… that this level is a shallow one. We have said nothing about Trees of Life and of Knowledge which doubtless conceal some great mystery:

---

715   I.e., a thing of one's very own. See *Endnote 4-79*, p. 320.
716   See 1 Corinthians 6:19-20.

and we have said nothing about the Pauline statement that "as in Adam all die, so in Christ shall all be made alive"...[717] We have recently been told by scientists that we have no right to expect that the real universe should be picturable, and that if we make mental pictures to illustrate quantum physics we are moving further away from reality, not nearer to it. We have clearly even less right to demand that the highest spiritual realities should be picturable, or even explicable in terms of our abstract thought.

Elder Boyd K. Packer: Moral Agency[718]

The agency the Lord has given us is not a "free" agency. The term "free" agency is not found in the revelations. It is a moral agency. The Lord has given us freedom of choice:

> That every man may act in doctrine and principle pertaining to futurity, according to the moral agency which I have given unto him, that every man may be accountable for his own sins in the day of judgment.[719]

There is no agency without choice; there is no choice without freedom; there is no freedom without risk; nor true freedom without responsibility.

C. Terry Warner: Agency and Accountability[720]

In LDS doctrine, to be "accountable" means that one must answer to God for one's conduct. Answering for the deeds done in mortality is not simply an administrative requirement but an aspect of human nature itself: to be a child of God is to possess agency, which is both the power to choose between obedience and rebellion and the accountability for how that power is used.

Henry Eyring: God's Respect for Agency[721]

Lucifer promised to bring salvation to every soul, whether the person to be saved desired it or not. Dictators have been operating in the same way from time immemorial... God's non-intervention in human affairs is not a sign of His absence or His disinterest. Rather, it exemplifies one of His greatest gifts—... agency, which enables us to work out our individual salvation. If Lucifer were ruling the world, no one could doubt his presence....

God rules from heaven. He does it with such silken threads that some think He has lost the reins. Some people do not even know that He exists. Others wonder whether He exists. I have often thought that a condition like this could never have come about if a dictator such as Hitler or Stalin were ruling.

God is so gentle, so dedicated to the principle that men should be taught correct principles and then govern themselves, that they should take responsibility for their own mistakes, that His children can actually question whether He exists. I cannot think of anything which more wonderfully typifies His mercy, His kindness, His consideration for us, His concern for us, than that He does it all with bonds that are like strongest steel but are so gentle that you cannot see them.

---

717   1 Corinthians 15:22.
718   B. K. Packer, *Govern Themselves*; B. K. Packer, *Errand*, p. 179; see also pp. 176-183.
719   D&C 101:78.
720   C. T. Warner, *Accountability*.
721   H. Eyring, *Faith*, pp. 104, 106.

Marden J. Clark: Heaven and Hell[722]

"[X. J. Kennedy's] poem is brief:

> Nothing in Heaven functions as it ought:
>> Peter's bifocals, blindly sat on, crack;
> His gates lurch wide with the cackle of a cock,
>> Not with a hush of gold as Milton had thought;
> Gangs of the slaughtered innocents keep huffing
>> The nimbus off the Venerable Bede[723]
> Like that of an old dandelion gone to seed;
>> The beatific choir keeps breaking up, coughing.
> But Hell, sleek Hell hath no freewheeling part:
>> None takes his own sweet time, none quickens pace,
> Ask anyone, How come you here, poor heart?—
>> And he will slot a quarter through his face,
> You'll hear an instant click, a tear will start
>> Imprinted with an abstract of his case.

It's a simple enough poem, at least on the surface. Most readers will recognize it as a sonnet… It has a rhyme scheme students of literature "scan" as *abba abba cdcdcd*. The rhyme scheme divides the poem neatly into two parts: the octet (eight lines) and the sestet (six lines). The octet traditionally sets up some kind of problem or question or situation, the sestet somehow answers or responds to or plays against the octet. In this poem the picture of hell in the sestet plays against that of heaven in the octet. We may be struck by the unusual qualities of heaven and hell and the images used to make us see each.…

The sonnet is one of the most restrictive of forms… And yet some of the most lovely, most "spontaneous," most energetic poems in the language are written in sonnet form… The poem gets most of its energy from what the poet does with its form: from the way it works within or strains against or plays with the conventions of its form.

One might begin to test such a statement simply by making a prose paraphrase of the poem: "Neither heaven nor hell is what we think it is; people make mistakes in heaven, but nothing goes wrong in hell." But where is our energy?… [Something has gone wrong with the meter], even with the first line: "Nóthing/in heáv/en fúnc/tions ás/it ought." The first [iambic] foot is reversed. And except to emphasize the meter most of us would not stress "as." Or look at line eight: "The bé/atíf/ic choir/keeps break/ing úp,/coughing." Almost regular—until it coughs at the end, in an extra inverted foot! The rime doesn't quite work either: crack, cock; huffing, coughing. Other sounds jar: bifocals against crack, cackle against cock. And cocks don't "cackle" anyway. Nothing in this octet functions as it ought. And that, of course, is the point.

But Hell, sweet Hell! The meter is perfectly regular—and perfectly mechanical. "And hé/will slot/a quart/er through/his face." The rhymes are also perfect—and mechanical. And that, again, is the point. In this mechanical hell a soul is a piece of mechanism, a slot machine or coin-operated computer which uses even his tears as something on which to "print an abstract of his case."

---

722   M. J. Clark, *Liberating*, pp. 2-3, 5-7.
723   See *Endnote 4-80, p. 321.

The major energy of the poem, though, comes from the way the two parts play against each other. Our first reaction to this heaven may be negative. But we look back from the perfect but mechanical hell, where no man takes his own sweet time nor quickens his pace, to that imperfectly functioning heaven, where even St. Peter, the dispenser of judgments, has to have bifocals and is both forgetful and blind enough to sit on and crack them. And suddenly one's own sweet time becomes very sweet and precious indeed. The imperfections of heaven are humorous enough, but they too become precious because we recognize that they result from the fact of freedom. Even the slaughtered innocent children are free, free to form gangs and to blow the seedy halo off one of the venerable saints. That, I presume, is mostly what the poem is "about": the meaning of freedom in religious terms. It is easy enough to make a prose statement of that meaning: the price of freedom is a certain amount of inefficiency, in heaven or in earth; lack of freedom may be efficient enough but its price is infinitely greater: the soul becomes a mechanism. That is a meaningful statement and it has its own kind of energy. But contrasted with the poem it is insipid.

Hugh W. Nibley: Satan Bribes Us to Sin[724]

Satan cannot force us to sin, in which case we would be helpless ([i.e.,] innocent—no contest!); but he can bribe us to sin, in which case we are guilty and follow him on our own free will. We make covenants with the understanding that we mean to keep them, and the alternative is to place ourselves in Satan's power.[725] We are placed here expressly to be proven herewith whether we will be true and faithful to our understanding with God, while Satan is allowed to try us and to tempt us, to invite and to entice, to see how far he can shake us.

Louis Ginzberg: Satan's Method of Compromises[726]

The serpent pushed Eve against the tree, and [then] said: "Thou seest that touching the tree has not caused thy death. As little will it hurt thee to eat the fruit of the tree…." To give due weight to these words, the serpent began to shake the tree violently and bring down its fruit. He [then] ate thereof, saying: "As I do not die of eating the fruit, so wilt thou not die".… [Eve then] made a compromise with her conscience. First she ate only the outside skin of the fruit, and then, seeing that death did not fell her, she ate the fruit itself.

President Joseph Smith, Jr.: Nature of Adam and Eve's Transgression[727]

Adam did not commit sin in eating the fruits, for God had decreed that he should eat and fall. But in compliance with the decree, he should die. Only [that] he should die was the saying of the Lord; therefore the Lord appointed us to fall and also redeemed us. For "where sin abounded, grace did much more abound."[728]

Elder Dallin H. Oaks: The Difference Between Transgression and Sin[729]

It was Eve who first transgressed the limits of Eden in order to initiate the conditions of mortality. Her act, whatever its nature, was formally a transgression but eternally a glorious

---

724   H. W. Nibley, *Return*, p. 75.

725   Moses 4:4; 5:23.

726   L. Ginzberg, *Legends*, 1:72-74; cf. D. C. Matt, *Zohar 1*, Be-Reshit 1:36a, p. 227; cf. M. A. Ouaknin, *et al.*, *Rabbi Eliézer*, 13, p. 90; J. Goldin, *Fathers*, 1, pp. 8-9.

727   J. Smith, Jr., *Words*, 9 February 1841, p. 63, spelling, capitalization, and punctuation standardized.

728   Romans 5:20.

729   D. H. Oaks, *Plan*, p. 73; cf. R. D. Draper, *et al.*, *Commentary*, p. 231.

necessity to open the doorway toward eternal life. Adam showed his wisdom by doing the same.…

We celebrate Eve's act and honor her wisdom and courage in the great episode called the Fall.… Elder Joseph Fielding Smith said: "I never speak of the part Eve took in this Fall as a sin, nor do I accuse Adam of a sin.… This was a transgression of the law, but not a sin"…[730]

This suggested contrast between a sin and a transgression reminds us of the careful wording in the second Article of Faith: "We believe that men will be punished for their own *sins*, and not for Adam's *transgression*."[731] It also echoes a familiar distinction in the law. Some acts, like murder, are crimes because they are inherently wrong. Other acts, like operating without a license, are crimes only because they are legally prohibited. Under these distinctions, the act that produced the Fall was not a sin—inherently wrong—but a transgression—wrong because it was formally prohibited. These words are not always used to denote something different, but this distinction seems meaningful in the circumstances of the Fall.

Allamah at-Tabataba'i: The Prohibition Was of an Advisory Nature[732]

If the prohibition against eating from the tree had the force of an authoritative command, an ordained law, Adam and his wife should have been returned to their place in the Garden as soon as their repentance was accepted. But they were not. It decisively proves that the prohibition was of advisory nature like telling someone not to put his hand in a fire; if he does not listen to the advice, his hand would certainly burn, and the subsequent apology would not unburn it, even if the apology was accepted. Likewise, Adam and his wife disregarded the advice, and as a result of eating from the tree, had to go out of the Garden and live in the earth a life of trial and hardship. Their repentance could not take them back to the Garden as their coming to the earth was the natural and inevitable result of that action. The prohibition, in short, was not a law ordained by the Master—like the announcement that a man who neglects to pray would enter the Fire; or the one who disobeys the rules of the *shari'ah*[733] would be punished. If it were like such a command, the repentance would have rubbed out the effect of disobedience and they would have been sent back to the Garden straightaway.

The *Zohar*: Adam Committed Only One Sin[734]

When a man dies, he is presented to Adam whom he accuses of being the cause of all mankind's death. But Adam repudiates this, saying: "True, I committed one sin. But is there even one among you—even the most pious, who has not been guilty of more than one?"[735]

Elder Brigham Young: The Fall Was Necessary[736]

God first introduced sin into the world that man might be exalted and bring about the great purpose of God. For this was foreordained from before the foundation of the world, that men might be exalted, and first to descend below all things that he or they might rise above

---

730 J. F. Smith, Jr., *Doctrines*, 22 April 1939, 1:114-115.
731 Emphasis mine.
732 A. at-Tabataba'i, *Al-Mizan*, 1:193-194.
733 = Islamic law.
734 R. M. Zlotowitz, *et al.*, *Bereishis*, p. 171; cf. D. C. Matt, *Zohar 1*, Be-Reshit 1:57b, 1:327.
735 Cf. John 8:7.
736 B. Young, December 1844, reported in E. England, *Laub*, p. 28, spelling and punctuation standardized. See also B. Young, *3 June 1855*, p. 302.

all things as the Father did before us, and be able to create worlds, and go from one world to another.

In my fullest belief, it was the design of the Lord that Adam should partake of the forbidden fruit, and I believe that Adam knew all about it before he came to this earth. I believe there was no other way leading to thrones and dominions only for him to transgress, or take that position which transgression alone could place man in, to descend below all things, that they might ascend to thrones, principalities, and powers; for they could not ascend to that eminence without first descending, nor upon any other principle.

Richard D. Draper, *et al.*: Adam and Eve Had to Make the Choice[737]

God, being perfect, could not place Adam and Eve into such an imperfect, fallen world. They had to make that choice for themselves. By means of this qualifying statement, "Thou mayest choose for thyself," God is making it clear to Adam and Eve that this is a necessary step they must take for themselves, and He explains the consequences of this choice—death.

Truman G. Madsen: God's Trust in Women[738]

A woman was the first to taste death and the first to witness resurrected life. That is no co-incidence. It is a lasting testimony of God's trust in women.

Truman G. Madsen: The Nature of the Fall[739]

In major Jewish and Christian traditions, the Fall has often been treated as catastrophic. Associated traditions, as those of Augustine and Calvin, maintain that an omnipotent God Himself elected the Fall and its entire train of dire consequences. Moreover, with absolute foreknowledge, He decreed that the stain of Adam be transmitted to all of his descendants. This is the dogma of original sin.[740] It is equally perplexing that He preordained his Son to reverse and heal these corruptions that He Himself had initiated.

In LDS parlance, Adam and Eve made a momentous decision both to leave their celestial home and then to embrace mortality by partaking of the forbidden fruit which led to their expulsion. However they did not fall from "dreaming innocence," but from their prior condition as preeminent spirit-children of God. In the Garden, one law was broken: "Partake not."[741] But Adam joined Eve to fulfill another law and commandment: "Multiply and replenish the earth." Whatever culpability Scripture assigns to Adam and Eve, it is not transmitted. An LDS Article of Faith based on Doctrine and Covenants 93 and Moses 6:59 states, "Men will be punished for their own sins and not for Adam's transgression."[742]

The *locus classicus* in LDS scripture for the overarching outcome of the Fall seems on the face of it a cruel juxtaposition. "Adam fell that men might be [in mortal life]. And men are that they might have joy."[743] The context of this statement expounds the indispensability of human experience, including the mortal experience as the backdrop of joy…

---

737   R. D. Draper, *et al.*, *Commentary*, p. 230.
738   T. G. Madsen, *House of Love*, p. 50.
739   T. G. Madsen, *LDS View*, pp. 99-100.
740   See *Endnote 4-81*, p. 321.
741   See Moses 3:16-17.
742   Article of Faith 2.
743   2 Nephi 2:25.

Physical embodiment and mortality can be a step forward in the eternal journey. The Fall was in this and other ways purposive. It was descent essential to a higher ascent. By their opening the way for other spirits to enter embodiment and mortality, Adam and Eve fulfilled both a parental role and a sacrificial role. For this they are to be honored.

This is not to minimize the harsh and even tragic consequences that have come in the wake of the Fall. The Fall brought a partial separation from the presence of God. It brought exposure to our inhumanity towards one another, and to natural disasters in an environment often hostile to human endurance and felicity. And it brought death.

But the Fall did not destroy individual freedom, initiative, or accountability. It did not impose sinfulness—or absolute depravity—upon Adam or upon any or all of his children.

Gary A. Anderson: *Felix Culpa*[744]

The Latin phrase *felix culpa* "occurs in the famous song of the Easter Vigil, the *exultet*, a song sung over the paschal candle at the beginning of the liturgy. In recounting the history of salvation that will culminate in the death and resurrection of Jesus Christ, the song stops midway to exclaim, 'O necessary sin of Adam, that Christ has blotted out by his death; O happy fault [*felix culpa*] which has earned for us such a great Redeemer.'"

John Milton: Over Wrath, Grace Shall Abound[745]

O goodness infinite, goodness immense!
That all this good of evil shall produce,
And evil turn to good; more wonderful
Than that by which creation first brought forth
Light out of darkness! Full of doubt I stand,
Whether I should repent me now of sin
By me done and occasioned, or rejoice
Much more, that much more good thereof shall spring,
To God more glory, more good will to Men
From God, and over wrath, grace shall abound.

W. Cleon Skousen: Why a Time of Probation Is Needed[746]

[God] wanted us to come in direct contact with sin and rebellion but under circumstances where we would not become permanently scarred by the experience.…

This was not possible "in heaven." There celestial law prevails which means that perfection is maintained and any sin or rebellion is not tolerated with even the "least degree of allowance."[747] Of course, like our brothers and sisters of the preexistence we could have rebelled, but not without suffering the immediate consequences. In heaven there is no opportunity to "learn" about rebellion, for those who indulge in it feel the immediate impact of judgment.

In order to learn what sin and rebellion are like we had to be removed from the celestial kingdom of the Father into an environment where good and evil exist side by side. It had

---

744   G. A. Anderson, *Perfection*, p. 192.
745   J. Milton, *Paradise Lost*, 12:469-478, p. 253, spelling modernized.
746   W. C. Skousen, *First 2,000*, pp. 42-44.
747   D&C 1:31.

to be a place where we could "taste" and have time to decide which we would choose.[748] It had to be a place where judgment was temporarily suspended so that in case we became enmeshed in grievous error during our learning process we would still have time to turn back before a judgment was pronounced or a final penalty imposed. In other words, provision had to be made so that there was "a space granted unto man in which he might repent,"[749] a time in which to turn back and, insofar as possible, regain the lost ground…

As Alma says: "This life is the time to prepare to meet God; yea, behold the day of this life is the day for men to perform their labors!"[750]

The Khoja Shia Ithna-Asheri Muslim Community: Why Are We Tested?[751]

Allàh wishes that mankind, by obeying the divine law (shari'ah) and struggling through the various circumstances that he encounters in life, will blossom from potentiality to actuality, and will thereby attain the level of perfection that has been intended for him… The mettle of man is gold ore that is purified in the crucible of Divine tests and guidance…

The second purpose that these tests serve is to awaken man from his sleep of heedlessness. The Qur'an explains that one of the purposes of tragedy and disaster is to test man and thereby jar him from his stupor of heedlessness. In a way, tragedy in man's life serves the same purpose as the ridges that are embossed on some modern motorways and highways that are meant to wake drivers during the monotony of highway driving so they do not fall asleep at the wheel.…

[T]he purpose for which man was created is only met if man achieves perfection through his freely chosen actions. Although the disbelievers and sinners who do not reach perfection certainly do not achieve the true goal of their creation (i.e., acting according to Allàh's decree and wishes) they nonetheless do not go against the existential goal of man's creation. This is because Allàh wanted with His existential will that man be able to choose between truth and falsehood.

Hugh W. Nibley: Adam and Eve Received Similar Consequences[752]

Now a curse was placed on Eve, and it looked as if she would have to pay a high price for taking the initiative in the search for knowledge. To our surprise, the identical curse was placed on Adam also. For Eve, God "will greatly multiply thy sorrow and thy conception. In sorrow shalt thou bring forth children."[753] The key is the word for sorrow, atsav, meaning to labor, to toil, to sweat, to do something very hard. To multiply does not mean to add or increase but to repeat over and over again; the word in the Septuagint is plethynomai, as in the multiplying of words in the repetitious prayers of the ancients. Both the conception and the labor of Eve will be multiple; she will have many children. Then the Lord says to Adam, "In sorrow shalt thou eat of it all the days of thy life"[754] (that is, the bread that his labor must bring forth from the earth). The identical word is used in both cases; the root meaning is to work hard at cutting or digging; both the man and the woman must sorrow and both must

---

748   D&C 29:39.
749   Alma 12:24; cf. 42:4.
750   Alma 34:32.
751   Porch of Wisdom Cultural Institution, *Faith and Reason*, pp. 77-78, 174.
752   H. W. Nibley, *Patriarchy*, pp. 89-90.
753   Moses 4:22.
754   Moses 4:23.

labor. (The *Septuagint* word is *lype*, meaning bodily or mental strain, discomfort, or affliction. It means not to be sorry, but to have a hard time)… The thing to notice is that Adam is not let off lightly as a privileged character; he is as bound to Mother Eve as she is to the law of her husband. And why not? If he was willing to follow her, he was also willing to suffer with her, for this affliction was imposed on Adam expressly "because thou hast hearkened unto… thy wife, and hast eaten of the fruit."[755]

Hugh W. Nibley: No Patriarchy or Matriarchy in the Garden[756]

There is no patriarchy or matriarchy in the Garden; the two supervise each other. Adam is given no arbitrary power; Eve is to heed him only insofar as he obeys their Father—and who decides that? She must keep a check on him as much as he does on her. It is, if you will, a system of checks and balances in which each party is as distinct and independent in its sphere as are the departments of government under the Constitution—and just as dependent on each other.

Abu Ishaq al-Tha'labi: God's Gifts to Satan[757]

"Lord," said Iblis,[758]… Where… is my dwelling to be?"
"When you descend to the earth," said God, "your dwelling place will be places of filth!"
"What shall I read?" asked Iblis.
"Poetry and song!"[759]
"What will call me to prayer?"
"Musical instruments!"[760]
"What will be my food?"
"That over which my name is not pronounced!"
"What will my drink be?"
"Wine!"
"Where will I dwell?"
"Public baths!"
"Where will be my gathering place?"
"Markets!"
"What is my battle-cry to be?"
"My curse!"
"What is my garment to be?"
"My wrath!"
"What is my prey?"
"Women!"

---

755   Moses 4:23.
756   H. W. Nibley, *Patriarchy*, p. 93.
757   M.al-Kisa'i, *Tales*, p. 51; cf. A. al-Tha'labi, *Lives*, p. 70 and the list of blessings given to mankind in M. al-Kisa'i, *Tales*, pp. 49-50.
758   = the Devil.
759   "Reflecting Muhammad's reputed dislike of poetry and poets" (A. al-Tha'labi, *Lives*, p. 70).
760   "The *muezzin* calls the faithful to prayer, while the reed-pipe in the early days of Islam was considered anathema because most players were women of questionable behavior" (*ibid.*, p. 70).

President Ezra Taft Benson: An Understanding of the Fall Is Necessary[761]

The plan of Redemption must start with the account of the Fall of Adam. In the words of Moroni, "By Adam came the fall of man. And because of the fall of man came Jesus Christ,… and because of Jesus Christ came the redemption of man."[762] Just as a man does not really desire food until he his hungry, so he does not desire the salvation of Christ until he knows why he needs Christ. No one adequately and properly knows why he needs Christ until he understands and accepts the doctrine of the Fall and its effect upon all mankind.

Elder Bruce C. Hafen: The Two Trees and the Purpose of Mortality[763]

Life is a school, a place for us to learn and grow. Our Teacher and Headmaster has placed us on the earth in a risk-filled environment called mortality. Here we may learn what we must know and become what we must be, not only to live with him someday, but to be like him.

To learn these profound lessons of life, we must undergo many experiences that subject us to the sorrow and contamination of a lone and dreary world. These experiences may include sin, but they also include undeserved pain, disappointment, and adversity. Every one of us will taste some bitter mixture of these forces. We must taste a measure of the bitter in order to prize the sweet.

But how, then, can we overcome the ill effects and consequences of this necessary contamination? The blessed news of the gospel is that the Atonement of Jesus Christ can purify us from all uncleanness and sweeten all the bitterness we taste. The Atonement not only pays for our sins, it heals our wounds—the self-inflicted ones and those inflicted from sources beyond our control. The Atonement also completes the process of our learning by perfecting our nature and making us whole. In this way, Christ's atonement makes us as he is. It is the ultimate source of our forgiveness, our perfection, and our peace of mind.

In the beginning, the Lord God taught this vision of life's nature and purpose to Adam and Eve. To symbolize these teachings, he placed two trees in the Garden of Eden: the Tree of Knowledge and the Tree of Life. The fruit of the first tree seemed desirable, but it became bitter as it led to the knowledge of good and evil. The second tree was sweet, and it led to a fulness of Godlike life. We, like Adam and Eve, taste the bitter fruit of the first tree that we may know to prize the sweet fruit of the second tree.

The Tree of Knowledge (learning through mortal, sometimes bitter, experience) and the Tree of Life (the Father's sweet bestowal of forgiveness and a divine character) are both necessary for us to find fulfillment and meaning. Neither tree—neither force—is sufficient unless completed by the other.

The mortal learning experience, represented by the Tree of Knowledge, is so necessary that God placed cherubim and a flaming sword to guard the way of the Tree of Life until Adam and Eve completed, and we, their posterity, complete this preparatory schooling. Our tutorial is the gospel, a schoolmaster that brings us to Christ.[764] But he cannot fully receive us and give us the gift of celestial life—partaking of God's very nature—until we have learned by our own experience to distinguish good from evil. In multiplied sorrow we must bring

---

761   E. T. Benson, *Book*, p. 85.
762   Mormon 9:12.
763   B. C. Hafen, *Broken*, pp. 29-31.
764   See Galatians 3:24.

forth children.[765] We must walk the earth through sharp thorns and poison thistles.[766] The ground is cursed for our sakes.[767] By the sweat of our faces we must eat bread until we return to the ground from whence we were taken.[768]

This treacherous path led Adam and Eve through the valley of death and pain. It weighed them down with the toil of earthly experience, until they knelt before God in the depths of humility. Through faithful obedience and sacrifice, they learned, they repented, and they reached out to God through the veil of mortality with all the energy of their hearts.

Thus the Tree of Knowledge symbolizes the entire process by which Adam and Eve—and we—learn through the dreary loneliness of earthly experience. Partaking of the forbidden fruit was only the beginning of that process.[769]

Over time Adam and Eve endured faithfully, until one day they began to grasp the joy of their Redemption. This was the day when the Savior began to lift them up in reverent humility. By then their hearts were broken and their spirits contrite in two ways: first, their sorrow for their sins, and second, their courageous response to the natural adversity of the lone and dreary world. Then at last the Good Shepherd placed them on his shoulder and carried them homeward to the fruits of his love through the power of his precious Atonement, cleansed and perfected from the ill effects of all mortal bitterness.

Our Savior's sanctifying power is represented by the Tree of Life. Without that power, there is no life, only death and timeless despair. Had they never partaken of this second tree, Adam and Eve would have wandered in their quest for knowledge into a path of endless misery. This result would have fulfilled what Satan intended when he tempted them in the Garden to seek knowledge without obedience, for he seeks "that all might be miserable like unto himself."[770]

Adam and Eve began the lifelong process of seeking after the fruit of the Tree of Life when, once their eyes were opened, they refused to worship Satan and chose, rather, to plant the seed of faith in the Lord Jesus Christ.[771] They then nourished their small seedling with much care, so that it would not wither in the scorching heat of opposition.[772] When finally, after great patience and diligence, they plucked and tasted the fruit of the Tree of Life, it was sweet above all that is sweet and pure above all that is pure;[773] for it represents the pure love of God, the most desirable of all things,[774] made possible through the infinite Atonement of him who died of a broken heart.

He, too, knew of toil, and sweat, and sorrow, for Man of Sorrows was his name.[775] In the days of his flesh, he prayed with strong crying and tears unto him that was able to save him from death.[776] He was despised and rejected of men.[777] He was acquainted with grief and

---

765   See Moses 4:22.
766   See Moses 4:24.
767   See *ibid.*
768   See Moses 4:25.
769   See *Commentary* 4:28-a, p. 276 about knowledge of "good *and* evil" vs. "good *from* evil."
770   2 Nephi 2:27.
771   See Alma 32:28.
772   See Alma 32:37.
773   See Alma 32:42.
774   See 1 Nephi 11:22.
775   See Isaiah 53:3.
776   See Hebrews 5:7.
777   See Isaiah 53:3.

bruised for our iniquities.[778] Having himself suffered temptation, he can succor those who are tempted.[779] For his followers, the sweetest moment of his life was when he drank the bitter cup.[780]

Hugh W. Nibley: The False Finery of Academic Caps and Gowns[781]

Twenty-three years ago today, if you will cast your minds back, on the same occasion [of BYU Commencement] I gave the opening prayer in which I said, "we have met here today clothed in the black robes of a false priesthood." Now many have asked me since then if I really said such a thing, but nobody has ever asked what I meant by it. Why not? Well, some knew the answer already; and as for the rest, we do not question things at "the BYU"! But for my own relief, I welcome this opportunity to explain.

First, why a priesthood? Because these robes originally denoted those who had taken clerical orders; and a college was a "mystery," with all the rites, secrets, oaths, degrees, tests, feasts, and solemnities that go with initiation into higher knowledge.

But why false? Because it is borrowed finery, coming down to us through a long line of unauthorized imitators. It wasn't till 1893 that "an intercollegiate commission was formed… to draft a uniform code for caps, gowns, and hoods" in the United States. Before that there were no rules. You could design your own!; and that liberty goes back as far as these fixings can be traced. The late Roman emperors, as we learn from the infallible DuCange, mark each step in the decline of their power and glory by the addition of some new ornament to the resplendent vestments that proclaim their sacred office and dominion. Branching off from them, the kings of the tribes, who inherited the lands and claims of the empire vied with each other in imitating the Roman masters, determined to surpass even them in the theatrical variety and richness of caps and gowns.…

And down through the centuries the robes have never failed to keep the public at a respectful distance, inspire a decent awe for the professions, and impart an air of solemnity and mystery that has been as good as money in the bank.

Hugh W. Nibley: The Hymn of the Pearl[782]

In coming to earth each man leaves his particular treasure, or his share of the Treasure, behind him in heaven, safely kept in trust ("under God's throne") awaiting his return.[783] One has here below the opportunity of enhancing one's treasure in heaven by meritorious actions, and also the risk of losing it entirely by neglecting it in his search for earthly treasure.[784] Hence the passionate appeals to men to remember their tremendous stake on the other side and "not to defraud themselves of the glory that awaits them" by seeking the things of the world.[785] To make the "treasure" test a fair one, the two treasures are placed before

---

778   See Isaiah 53:3, 5.

779   See Hebrews 2:18.

780   See D&C 19:18.

781   H. W. Nibley, *Leaders*, pp. 491-492, 495.

782   H. W. Nibley, *Treasures*, pp. 177-178. For a more detailed translation and summary, see H. W. Nibley, *Message 2005*, pp. 487-501.

783   E.g., A. F. J. Klijn, *2 Baruch*, 54:13, p. 640: "you have prepared under your throne the treasures of wisdom"; M. Lidzbarski, *Ginza*, GR 12:7, p. 381:21: "the living water below the throne"; M. Lichtheim, *Memphite*, 61, 1:55: "The Great Throne… is the granary of Ta-tenen."

784   E.g., Matthew 25:14-29.

785   E.g., A. F. J. Klijn, *2 Baruch*, 52:7, p. 639: "Prepare your souls for that which is kept for you, and make ready your souls for the reward which is preserved for you"; E. Hennecke, *et al.*, *Apocalypse of Paul*, 20, pp. 771-772:

us on an equal footing (the doctrine of the Two Ways), their two natures being mingled in exactly equal portions in every human being.[786] To neutralize what would otherwise be the overpowering appeal of the heavenly treasure, the memory of its former glories has been erased from the mind of man, which is thus in a state of equilibrium, enjoying by "the ancient law of liberty" complete freedom to choose whatever it will.[787] In this state, whatever choice is made represents the true heart and mind of the one who makes it. What conditions the Elect to make the right choice is no unfair advantage of instruction—for all men are aware of the issues involved—but a besetting nostalgia, a constant vague yearning for one's distant treasure and happy heavenly home. This theme, akin to the Platonic doctrine of *anamnesis*,[788] runs through all the apocrypha and scriptures; it is beautifully expressed in the *Hymn of the Pearl* from the *Acts of Thomas*.[789]

In this classic tale, a king's son has come down to earth to find a pearl which he is to return to its heavenly depository; here below he becomes defiled with the things of the world until a letter from heaven, signed by all the Great and Mighty Ones, recalls to him his true heritage and his purpose in coming to earth, whereupon he casts off his earthly garments and with the pearl returns to the waiting arms of his loved ones in the royal courts on high and to his robe of glory that has been carefully kept for him in the Treasury. Our various "treasure" texts consistently refer to going to heaven as a return, a joyful homecoming, in which one follows the steps of Adam "back to the Treasury of Life from which he came forth."[790] A great deal is said about a garment that one changes in passing from one stage to another, the final garment of glory being often equated to the Treasure itself.[791] This garment introduces us to the very important ritual aspect of the treasure story, for it is generally understood that one can return to one's heavenly treasure only by the careful observance of certain rites and ordinances, which provide the means both of receiving instruction and demonstrating obedience. In the Mandaean economy the ordinances are the Treasure, the knowledge of the proper procedures being the very knowledge by which the elements are controlled and the spirit of man exalted.[792]

"there are many good things which the Lord has prepared and his promise is great… Paul, may you receive the reward."

786   E.g., F. G. Martinez, *DSS Translated*, 1QS 4:16-17, p. 7: "For God has sorted them into equal parts until the last day."

787   E.g., Pseudo-Clement, *Recognitions*, 3:26, p. 121.

788   = the idea of things having been remembered from a former existence.

789   E. Hennecke, *et al.*, *Pearl*; M. R. James, *Soul*.

790   E.g., W. Barnstone, *et al.*, *Songs of Thomas*, 1:49, p. 620.

791   E.g., M. Lidzbarski, *Ginza*, GR 1:64-65, 72, p. 13; GR 10:1, p. 243:35-36.

792   E.g., E. S. Drower, *Thousand*, pp. 212, 241, 245.

Endnotes

4-1 Westermann concurs with this basic division of structure, concluding that there are "two main parts, the prohibition and its transgression, and the punishment. Every single sentence takes on meaning according to its position in these parts. It is clear what the whole is about: it is a story of the breaking of a law and punishment."[793]

4-2 The placement of these verses just prior to the story of the transgression in the Garden, rather than in chronological sequence preceding the Creation, serves to highlight thematic links between Satan's rebellion and Adam's Fall. It also sets the stage for the similar parting of the two ways on earth in the next chapter.[794]

4-3 Tvedtnes notes that this "covenant between the three members of the Godhead is confirmed in an early Ethiopic Christian document, the *Kebra Nagast*":[795] "For the Father, and the Son, and the Holy Spirit with good fellowship and right good will and cordial agreement together made the Heavenly Zion to be the place of habitation of their Glory. And then the Father and the Son, and the Holy Spirit said, 'Let Us make man in Our similitude and likeness,' and with ready agreement and good will They were all of this opinion. And the Son said, 'I will put on the body of Adam,' and the Holy Spirit said, 'I will dwell in the heart[s] of the Prophets and the Righteous'; and this common agreement and covenant was [fulfilled] in Zion, the City of their Glory."[796]

4-4 Hugh Nibley pioneered early explorations of themes relating to creation rituals and associated covenants from the time of his dissertation[797] and early writings on hierocentric civilizations[798] to his increasing focus on temple topics from the 1970s onward.[799] Ricks provides a brief summary of this vast literature.[800] In 1992, Murray devoted a monograph to the subject of the "cosmic covenant," arguing that it is an important "theme in its own right… [with] roots in near eastern religious culture distinct from the origins of the covenants associated with Moses, Abraham, and the House of David."[801] Margaret Barker has picked up and extended many of the threads explored by Murray.[802]

4-5 Ryan notes that the "Divine Architect employs a compass to draw his lines and boundaries, [while] he himself is confined within a circle."[803] In an ironically fitting sense, such a view is consistent with LDS theology that sees God's power as "circumscribed" in important respects.[804]

4-6 The *Testament of Job* attests that garments inscribed with the sacred name may also be worn by mortals. After Job's daughter "wrapped herself just as her father said… she received another heart, so that she no longer thought about earthly things. And she chanted verses in the angelic language, and ascribed a hymn to God in accord with the hymnic style of the angels.[805] And as she chanted the hymns, she permitted 'the Spirit' to be inscribed on her garment."[806]

Of the relationship between the name and the covenant, Barker writes: "Closely linked to this oath is the 'name' or the 'secret name,' which was the means of enforcing and maintaining the covenant/oath. The name had been named before the creation, presumably to make the Creation possible."[807] Note the similar close association of a unique name for the Savior with the covenant that King Benjamin administers to his people.[808]

---

793 C. Westermann, *Genesis 1-11*, p. 193.

794 See the overview of Moses 5, pp. 343-350.

795 J. A. Tvedtnes, *Follett*.

796 E. A. W. Budge, *Kebra*, 1, p. 1.

797 H. W. Nibley, *Roman Games*.

798 H. W. Nibley, *Hierocentric*; cf. H. W. Nibley, *Assembly*, pp. 121-126 and *Excursus 35: Lamech's "Sword Song"*, p. 612.

799 B. J. Petersen, *Nibley*, pp. 354ff.

800 S. D. Ricks, *Liturgy*.

801 R. Murray, *Cosmic*, p. xvii.

802 See *Commentary* 1:25-e, p. 60, 4:14-e, p. 260; 5:47-a, p. 395.

803 R. Ryan, *Companion to Blake*, p. 156.

804 See, e.g., B. T. Ostler, *Attributes*, pp. 105-135.

805 Cf. 2 Nephi 31:13, 32:2-3.

806 R. A. Kraft, *Job*, 48:1-4, p. 83. The *Conflict of Adam and Eve with Satan* gives a description of how the name representing the covenant was woven into such a garment (see *Commentary* 4:27-a, p. 274).

807 M. Barker, *Lost*, p. 78.

808 Mosiah 5:6-12.

4-7   A second circumambulation is performed near the end of the pilgrimage in order to complete the figurative ritual ascent:

> If a man's pilgrimage has been completed both externally and internally and his realizations are depicted above, then he must once again go seven times around the *Ka'bah*, feeling this time as if he is going around the Throne of God. He is then entitled by God to enter into the station of nearness to the Almighty, Whose vision he achieves. It is to this achievement of direct vision of the Lord that God refers when He says, "And he made them drink the purest of drinks."[809] This is symbolized externally by the drinking of the water of the holy well Zamzam after the completion of the circumambulation. When a person attains to this stage of consciousness, all veils are removed and he talks to the Lord without any veil between them… This *tawaf* symbolizes man's detachment from the lowest region and his journey to that region which is the highest of the high, his real homeland.[810]

Note that an upraised veil (*kiswa*) hangs from the gate of the *Ka'bah*. "Such veils are used allegorically by Muslim mystics to stand for ignorance masking the true nature of God."[811]

Those who participate in the *hajj* are washed, dressed in white, and given a "'new name,' one that they must not reveal—for it is theirs to use in the next life when they approach Allàh… Muslims are urged to return to Mecca again…, but these pilgrimages are for or in behalf of other people, preferably relatives, who did not have the chance to go. Apparently, they may get the 'new name' for them as well."[812]

The ritual of circumambulation is also practiced within the Dome of the Rock in Jerusalem: "The sacred Rock, focus of so many beliefs and traditions, is surrounded by marble piers and columns. Encircling the structure is a corridor, which Muslims use to circumambulate the Rock as they do the *Ka'bah* in Mecca."[813]

4-8   "The stoning of the Devil (*rajm al-shaytan*) [still] forms part of the [modern] pilgrimage ritual. Pilgrims gather stones at Arafat and bring them to Mina where pillars set up to represent Satan are pelted. From this comes Satan's epithet *al-Rajim* (= the stoned one)."[814]

4-9   A similar stone, with a new name written on it, is to be given "to each of those who come into the celestial kingdom."[815] The close association between this stone, the "hidden manna," and the "new name" in Revelation 2:17 implies that such a stone was given to others besides Adam in the preexistence. In the poem *My Old White Stone*, W. W. Phelps writes:[816]

> O keep my old "white stone," Father,
> O keep it till I come;
> The stone I had of thee at home,
> Before this world was known;
>
> For Lo! in it is my "new name"—
> The name thou gavest me,
> When I was wash'd and set apart
> For the glory yet to be.
>
> Eternity is thine, Father,
> Age after age has gone,
> And yet, among thy sons, as one,
> My spirit moves divine

809   *Qur'an* 76:21.
810   S. A. Ashraf, *Inner*, p. 125.
811   W. J. Hamblin, *et al.*, *Temple*, p. 155.
812   D. Rona, *Revealed*, p. 190.
813   W. J. Hamblin *et al.*, *Temple*, p. 141 n. 140.
814   M. al-Kisa'i, *Tales*, p. 344 n. 48.
815   D&C 130:4-11. See *Endnote E-11*, p. 706. See also *Commentary 1:27-b*, p. 62 and *Figure 4-4*, p. 219. See *Endnote 4-22*, p. 304. See *Excursus 3: Temple Blessings in the Oath and Covenant of the Priesthood*, p. 519 and *Excursus 53: Comparative Explorations: Jewish and Christian Analogues*, p. 679.
816   *Deseret News*, 6, 416, cited in T. G. Hatch, *Visions*, pp. 230-231. The poem was set to the music of "The Indian Student's Lament," better known as the tune of "O Give Me Back My Prophet Dear" (M. Hicks, *Music*, p. 68 and p. 73 n. 65).

With light and life, and sense and love,
Through realms where wisdom's known,
To find, by faith, my path back home,
To my gem—my old "white stone."

The sweetest joy that seems, Father,
Is now and than a view,
Of that eternal world and you,
That flashes through my dreams

In some blest spot that's still and pure,
Where virtue's bliss is known,
And where my spirit eyes can see,
For themselves, my old "white stone."

Commenting on the passage of the *Hymn of the Pearl* where the protagonist says that he brought "precious stones from India and Kushan and gold and silver, and they girt me with a diamond" (= Greek *adamas*), Nibley writes:

> There's an interesting footnote on *adamas*, on the diamond, here. You see, the word Adam was associated with diamond.[817] *Adamantis* means that which cannot be damaged, that which is immortal. There's a long story behind that. Diamond is the urim and thummim, the sacred stone that was given to Adam when he came down. So the name *Adamantis* was given to him—the prince of stones.[818]

In another place, Nibley elaborates further:[819]

> We associated Adam's diamond with the Stone of Truth in the *Book of Breathings*.[820] In this context the diamond identifies the speaker with Adam… the prevailing of the diamond over steel signifies that the true nature of the spirit can never be completely destroyed by earthly elements. This is confirmed by Klijn's rendering, "they furnished me with adamant which can crush iron,"[821] the coincidence of the words Adam, diamond, and adamant being intentional. We have shown elsewhere that the diamond in the girdle is the stone of life (sometimes the plant of life) which, in the Alexander period, the hero bears with him, having fetched it from the underworld, the hero leaves the girdle and its precious stone on the bank as he bathes in a deep pool, and the serpent steals them, thus robbing him of the hope of immortality. The story is told not only of Alexander but also of the very ancient Gilgamesh, taking it back to the beginning of history.

Moreover:[822]

> According to Rabbi Eliezer, each of the twelve tribes was represented by a stone on the breastplate of the high priest, and it was said that Joshua could tell which tribe had sinned when their tribe's stone was dim…[823] J. Massingberd Ford calls the stone of Peter and Abraham "the Jewel of Discernment,"[824] thus lending belated support to Joseph Smith's interpretation of John 1:42 JST: "Thou shalt be called *Cephas*, which is, by interpretation, a seer, or a stone"… The image of Peter the Rock, now viewed as an old and authentic Hebrew concept[825] throws a new light on a remarkable account of the setting apart of Peter found in one of the oldest of Christian writings, the *Gospel of the Twelve Apostles*, in which the Lord says to Peter, "Come to me on this stone, that I might give thee a blessing and a name in all the world." Peter then sits on the stone; the Lord proceeds to pronounce over him something like the Opening of the Mouth formula: "Thy head shall never pain thee, neither shall thine eyes fail thee, nor thy fingers falter, etc."[826] And the name he gives him is Peter—Seer-stone, Stone of Truth. He gave him that name in return for Peter's

---

817   H. W. Nibley, *Message 2005*, p. 196.
818   H. W. Nibley, *Teachings of the PGP*, 4, p. 48.
819   H. W. Nibley, *Message 2005*, p. 489; cf. H. W. Nibley, *Approach*, pp. 351-358.
820   H. W. Nibley, *Message 2005*, pp. 190-202.
821   Cf. E. Hennecke, *et al.*, *Acts of Thomas*, 108:8, p. 498; M. R. James, *Thomas*, p. 411.
822   H. W. Nibley, *Message 2005*, pp. 192-193.
823   M.-A. Ouaknin, *et al.*, *Rabbi Éliézer*, 38, pp. 238-239.
824   J. M. Ford, *Jewel*, p. 109, cited in H. W. Nibley, *Message 2005*, p. 192.
825   D. Flusser, *Qumran*, pp. 138-43, cited in H. W. Nibley, *Message 2005*, p. 192.
826   E. Revillout, *Évangile des Douze*, p. 147 2ᵉ fragment.

recognition "that Jesus was Anointed,"[827] while the talk of gates and keys[828] refers to the "much desired admission to… the Temple," with special "contrast between the inescapable mass of the dead and the community of the living."[829] There is much evidence that all important Matthew 16:18ff refers to temple work as understood by the Latter-day Saints. The Coptic *Apocryphon of Adam* says that in the last days the Righteous will be found "upon a high mountain, upon a Stone of Truth (*hijn ou-petra nteme*), and be accordingly named (or the mountain and stone will be named) "the Words of Immortality and Truth."[830]

A related tradition in a Coptic source reports that a girdle of sapphire was taken from Satan and given to Michael when he replaced the fallen archangel as "General-in-Chief of all the hosts of the heavens." God is portrayed as telling him: "Gird this girdle of sapphire about thy loins, so that when those who are waging war against thy Lord see thee they may be quickly overcome."[831] The stone was an appropriate sign of divine authority, since God's throne was said by Ezekiel to be made of sapphire.[832] This same idea was used to explain the color of the fringes in Jewish prayer shawls: "The thread of blue in the *tzitzit* resembles the hue of the sea, and the sea mirrors the azure of the sky, and the sky reflects the radiance from the throne of God's glory, concerning which it is written: 'Under His feet… a sapphire stone.'"[833] The sapphire may have also been a symbol of incarnation, the dark-blue of the jewel corresponding to the color of the robe of the high priest which represented the glorious physical body denied to Satan but given to Adam.[834] In later accounts connected with Solomon's building of the temple, the stone was symbolized by a signet ring with a sacred seal.[835]

Nibley identifies the Stone of Truth in its role of "foundation stone, as the cornerstone of the Hebrew scriptures was a *pyramidion* or sun-stone, Egyptian style, the headstone of the corner" of the temple. However, it must be understood that the true temple was not to be built of ordinary dead stones, but rather of "lively [i.e., living] stones… a spiritual house, an holy priesthood,"[836] "Jesus Christ himself being the chief corner stone… [growing] unto an holy temple in the Lord."[837] This same idea could be applied to the patriarchs: "… as the Tabernacle is a miniature replica of the cosmos, Adam/Aaron is a microcosmic replica of the sanctuary."[838] Similarly, Nibley cites a tradition that "the foundation-stone upon which God founded the True Temple—the *hagion kosmikon*, [i.e.,] the world itself—… was the 'living Rock'—the patriarch Abraham."[839] The identification of a living seer as the cornerstone of the temple undergirds the image painted by Christ of the foundational role of revelation in the establishment of the Church: "Thou art Peter, and upon this rock I will build my church."[840] In the words of Elder James E. Talmage, "Revelation from God to His servants invested with the Holy Priesthood through authorized ordination as was Peter is the impregnable 'rock' upon which the Church is built."[841]

4-10   Writes Barker:

> This bonding together of the Creation is the key to understanding the Day of Atonement, the great ritual performed exclusively by the high priest at the New Year. The eternal covenant, or the covenant of eternity, was also described as the covenant of peace or wholeness. It bound all creation together in its bonds, but these bonds could be broken by human sin. Isaiah has a vivid picture of how the Creation collapses under the weight of human sin: "The earth mourns and withers, the world languishes and withers, the heavens languish together with the earth. The earth lies polluted under its inhabitants, for they have transgressed the laws, violated the statutes, broken the eternal

827   R. W. Riddle, *Cephas-Peter*, p. 178, cited in H. W. Nibley, *Message 2005*, p. 193. See Matthew 16:16.
828   Matthew 16:18-19.
829   V. Burch, *Stone*, pp. 148-149, cited in H. W. Nibley, *Message 2005*, p. 193.
830   Cf. G. W. MacRae, *et al.*, *Adam 1990*, 85:10-14, p. 286.
831   E. A. W. Budge, *Rebellion*, pp. 294-295.
832   Ezekiel 1:26. See M. Barker, *Gate*, pp. 152-153.
833   Second-century Rabbi Meir, cited in K. Boren, *Winepress*, p. 82.
834   W. Williams, *Shadow*.
835   W. J. Hamblin, *et al.*, *Temple*, pp. 149-150.
836   1 Peter 2:5; cf. D&C 92:2. See also D. B. McKinlay, *Peter*, pp. 497-498.
837   Ephesians 2:20-21.
838   W. Williams, Shadow.
839   H. W. Nibley, *Message 2005*, p. 195.
840   Matthew 16:18.
841   J. E. Talmage, *Jesus the Christ*, 22, p. 342 n. 7.

covenant."[842] The Creation was fragmented and collapsing because it had lost its union with the Creator. The bonds of the covenant were restored by the Atonement, and thus the Creation was reunited with the Creator and renewed at the start of the year.[843]

Significantly, as part of the reforms of the Deuteronomists, the Day of Atonement "was simply dropped from the… calendar,[844] but its original significance was remembered and repeated in the later targums and became the great proclamation of Christianity."[845]

4-11   Based on her study of *1 Enoch* 48:2-3, Barker concluded that the Son of Man, represented on earth as the great high priest:

> … was part of the created order of things, and that the means of restoring the Creation was provided in the original plan which was outside time and therefore not strictly "before" anything. Knowing this name added force and strength to the oath.[846] The climax of the last vision of judgment in the Similitudes is the revealing of the "name" of the Son of Man. This… is… likely to mean the revelation of an especially powerful name with which to bind the oath, and thus restore the Creation to its original state, as it had been before the incursion of evil. The vision ends with the Son of Man passing judgment on all those who had corrupted the earth, binding them so that evil passes away.[847]

4-12   Barker observes:

> Of all the major covenants, we tend to emphasize the one at Sinai, but this covenant did not become important for the people of Israel until quite late in their history… But older than the Mosaic covenant was the royal covenant, which promised stability to the royal house… This older royal covenant was very similar to the cosmic or eternal covenant which we find in the *Similitudes of Enoch*.[848] In the Old Testament the royal covenant was associated with the "anointed one," and with kings who were called the "sons of God." This makes it very likely that the cosmic/royal covenant was the background to some parts of the New Testament (e.g., Romans 8:19: "creation waits with eager longing for the revealing of the sons of God").[849]

Reynolds argues that the emphasis on covenant was lost in the early centuries of the Christian era.[850]

4-13   Though the singular term "Grand Council" is often used in scripture and in statements by Joseph Smith and others, it seems evident that there must have been a series of councils that took place in the premortal life.

As to the location of these councils, Joseph Smith's poetic rendition of D&C 76 speaks of "the council in Kolob."[851] Note that Abraham 3:21 specifies that God "came down" when He organized the premortal intelligences. Thus, strictly speaking, these councils do not take place in heaven, if we mean by the term the place where God lives, though Kolob is said to be "nearest to" that place.[852]

4-14   The *Apocalypse of Abraham* seems to allude to the grand councils in heaven and the foreordination of the premortal posterity of Abraham in the following words:

> And I saw there a great crowd of men and women and children… and he [God] said to me: "This is my will with regard to what is in the light [or council] and it was good before my face. And then, afterward, I gave them a command by my word and they came into existence. Whatever I had decreed was to exist had already been outlined in this and all the previously created (things) you have seen stood [or took position] before me… these are the ones I have prepared to be born of you and to be called my people."[853]

---

842   Isaiah 24:4-5.

843   M. Barker, *Great High Priest*, pp. 74-75; cf. D&C 1:15ff.; Moses 7:25ff.

844   Deuteronomy 16.

845   M. Barker, *Hidden*, p. 36.

846   Cf. Mosiah 5:7-12.

847   M. Barker, *Lost*, p. 79. See also T. G. Madsen, *Putting*.

848   E. Isaac, *1 Enoch*, 69:13-26, pp. 48-49; G. W. E. Nickelsburg *et al.*, *1 Enoch*, 69:13-26, pp. 90-91.

849   M. Barker, *Lost*, pp. 80-81.

850   N. B. Reynolds, *Decline of Covenant*.

851   J. Smith, Jr. (or W. W. Phelps), *A Vision*, 1 February 1843, stanza 7, p. 82, reprinted in L. E. Dahl, *Vision*, p. 296.

852   Abraham, Facsimile 2, Fig. 1.

853   P. Alexander, *3 Enoch*, 21:7, 22:2, 5, pp. 699-700.

4-15   Matthew Brown succinctly summarizes the teachings of Joseph Smith on the importance of a physical body:[854]

> "All beings who have bodies have power over those who have not," said the Prophet Joseph Smith.[855] The "spirits of the eternal world" are as diverse from each other in their dispositions as mortals are on the earth. Some of them are aspiring, ambitious, and even desire to bring other spirits into subjection to them. "As man is liable to [have] enemies [in the spirit world] as well as [on the earth] it is necessary for him to be placed beyond their power in order to be saved. This is done by our taking bodies ([having kept] our first estate) and having the power of the resurrection pass upon us whereby we are enabled to gain the ascendancy over the disembodied spirits."[856] It might be said, therefore, that "the express purpose of God in giving [His spirit children] a tabernacle was to arm [them] against the power of darkness."[857]

In a footnote relating to this passage, Brown includes additional relevant citations from the Prophet:[858]

> "The design of God before the foundation of the world," said Joseph Smith, "was that we should overcome and thereby obtain a resurrection from the dead, [and] in this wise obtain glory, honor, power, and dominion." Receiving a physical body was "needful, inasmuch as [some] spirits in the eternal world glory in bringing other spirits in[to] subjection unto them, striving continually for the mastery."[859] "God is good and all His acts [are] for the benefit of inferior intelligences. God saw that those intelligences had not power to defend themselves against those that had a tabernacle. Therefore, the Lord call[ed] them together in Council and agree[d] to form them tabernacles that He might [en]gender the spirit and the tabernacle together so as to create sympathy for their fellowman.… [I]t is a natural thing with those spirits that [have] the most power to [bear] down on those of lesser power."[860]

Nephi taught that if disembodied spirits who had lost their bodies through death did not regain a physical body in the resurrection, the Devil would have all power over them:

> 8 O the wisdom of God, his mercy and grace! For behold, if the flesh should rise no more our spirits must become subject to that angel who fell from before the presence of the Eternal God, and became the devil, to rise no more.

> 9 And our spirits must have become like unto him, and we become devils, angels to a devil, to be shut out from the presence of our God, and to remain with the father of lies, in misery, like unto himself…[861]

4-16   Nibley cites a parallel in the Mandaean *Ginza* where, after having been embraced and received secret names, Ptah-Uthra, the Creator god, was told, "Go down to that place where there is no occupied place, where there is no world, and create for us another world after the fashion of the Sons of Salvation."[862]

4-17   A near echo of Abraham 3:25 can be heard in *Kebra Nagast*, where angels, jealous of God's special treatment of Adam despite his transgression, beg Him to create physical bodies for them and allow their fidelity to be proven: "And now try us well, and put us to the test so that Thou mayest know whether we are able to keep Thy word."[863]

4-18   This statement is from a recollection of a discourse by Joseph Smith likely given on 7 April 1844.[864]

4-19   These and some of the following quotations were previously noted by Tvedtnes.[865]

4-20   Continues Nibley: "This is an unfailing part of the picture; the Hallelujah chorus with its refrain of

---

854   M. B. Brown, *Plan*, p. 33.

855   J. Smith, Jr., *Words*, 5 January 1841, p. 60.

856   *Ibid.*, 21 May 1843, p. 208.

857   *Ibid.*, 19 January 1841, p. 62.

858   M. B. Brown, *Plan*, p. 47.

859   J. Smith, Jr., *Words*, 21 May 1843, p. 207.

860   *Ibid.*, 28 March 1841, p. 68.

861   2 Nephi 9:8-9.

862   H. W. Nibley, *Apocryphal*, p. 283; cf. K. Rudolph, *Coptic*, GR 3:1, p. 171.

863   E. A. W. Budge, *Kebra*, 100, p. 186.

864   J. Smith, Jr., 7 April 1844. See E. England, *Laub*, pp. 2, 32n. 24; cf. *Excursus 22: The Nature of Satan's Premortal Proposal*, p. 577.

865   J. A. Tvedtnes, *Follett*.

'Forever and ever!' is the closing section of almost any ritual text."[866]

Speaking of the angel singing witnessed by the shepherd's on the night of Christ's birth, Barker writes:[867]

> The song of the heavenly host was a sign of the new creation, the restoration of the covenant that meant the renewal of the earth. Whenever the angels or the heavens sing in the Old Testament, it is a sign of the new creation. At the beginning of Creation, "the morning stars sang together and all the sons of God shouted for joy."[868] When the Lord called the Servant and announced a new beginning, there was a new song, or possibly a "renewing" song.[869] Praise renewed the earth. When Isaiah heard the angels singing "Holy, holy, holy is the Lord of hosts," he knew that the whole earth was full of his Glory.[870] Gregory of Nyssa… said that sin had silenced the voice of praise on earth… With the coming of the Savior…heaven and earth formed one choir again, and harmony was restored. Peace on earth among men.[871]

4-21   The ancient annual celebration of the new year,[872] the *hilaria*, "was the occasion on which all the world joined in the great creation hymn, as they burst into a spontaneous song of praise recalling the first creation." Nibley notes that the Greek term for the "mercy seat" is *hilasterion*—the place of the *hilaria*—and sees parallels both with Alma's "song of redeeming love"[873] and also with the "new song" sung by the hundred and forty-four thousand redeemed before the throne of God.[874]

4-22   Nibley, citing Neusner,[875] recalls how sacrifices were performed in the Jerusalem temple: "the priest, gird up with his robe, 'slaughtered with his right hand, and received in his left.' 'The sprinkling of the blood… [thus] accomplishes atonement, or *kapporah*.' The hand is held in such a manner as to hold the blood, as it holds the oil in the anointing."[876]

Hilton elaborates on the temple-related origin of the priestly practice of cupping the hand, whether to hold an offering or to receive a divine gift:

> After the children of Israel left Egypt, Moses called for contributions to build the Tabernacle. The Lord had shown Moses on the mount the pattern of the Tabernacle, with its furnishings, vessels, and rituals. One commandment Moses received from the Lord was, "thou shalt make the… spoons… of pure gold."[877] In due course, each leader of the 12 tribes donated a golden spoon of 10 shekels weight, filled to overflowing with frankincense.[878]

> The spoon was termed *kaph* in hebrew, which means literally "hollow of the hand," or the hand in cupping shape.…

> Once a year, on the Day of Atonement, the High Priest of the Aaronic line entered the Holy of Holies of Moses' Tabernacle or, later, of Solomon's temple, by passing through the veil. He carried the frankincense and the spoon, a hand in cupping shape, as he passed through…[879]

> It was considered especially important for the priest to take up the raw incense in the hollow of his hand, not with his fingers, without dropping one small grain, and to pour it onto the fire.…[880]

> Incense spoons, or hands in cupping shape, are seen not only in the ancient art of Palestine and Syria, but also in Yemen and Mexico.…

---

866   H. W. Nibley, *Treasures*, p. 191 n. 13.

867   M. Barker, *Christmas*, pp. 81-82.

868   Job 38:7.

869   Isaiah 42:10.

870   Isaiah 6:3.

871   Barker cites Gregory of Nyssa, *Oratio in Diem Natalem Christi*, in J. P. Migne, *Patrologiae Graeca*, 46:1128-1137.

872   *Commentary* 1:25-e, p. 60, 5:47-a, p. 395, *Excursus 35: Lamech's "Sword Song"*, p. 612, and the overviews of Moses 4 and 6, pp. 221, 458. See *Endnote 4-4*, p. 298.

873   Alma 5:26.

874   H. W. Nibley, *Atonement*, pp. 564-566; cf. H. W. Nibley, *Teachings of the Book of Mormon*, 2:228-230; Revelation 14:3. See also E. R. Goodenough, *Dura Symbolism*, 9:89-104.

875   J. Neusner, *Without Myth*.

876   H. W. Nibley, *Sacred*, p. 593. See also M. Barker, *Revelation*, p. 28.

877   Exodus 25:29.

878   Numbers 7:84-86.

879   Leviticus 16:12-13; cf. Revelation 8:4.

880   Leviticus 16:12.

In Egypt literally dozens of reliefs of such spoons are constructed in the form of a bowl held in the hollow of a carved hand....

... John A. Tvetdnes... [pointed] out that the Hebrew original of the word "consecrate," referring to the ordination of priests in Old Testament times, literally means "to fill the hand"....[881]

... Tvedtnes notes that "there are some hints that the open hand is to be filled with sacrificial items (meat, etc.)...[882] In the Temple, the priest evidently stood with hand in cupping shape, ready to receive something which was given to him. It was probably incense, though in the last days,[883] it will evidently be the white stone or urim and thummim, with the new name written in it."[884]

Though European kings, whose garments and emblems of kingship resembled those of the Israelite high priest until the fashion of military dress eventually became the style,[885] are often pictured with an orb in their cupped hand, "no such ensign as an orb existed until the 11th century," previous depictions having been "symbolic."[886]

4-23 Luke 10:18, which one could easily believe was a quotation from a lost ancient source, seems in context not only to refer to a past event, but also to prophesy of the diminishing of Satan's remaining power on earth at the time when all power will be given to Christ on Heaven and on Earth.[887]

4-24 Four accounts of the discourse are given below. The first three were used to create the amalgamated statement quoted on p. 223 above. It is significant that the statement about the premortal rebellion was given in the context of a discussion of the unpardonable sin.[888]

Report of Wilford Woodruff: All will suffer until they obey Christ himself. Even the Devil said, I am a savior and can save all. He rose up in rebellion against God and was cast down. Jesus Christ will save all except the sons of perdition. What must a man do to commit the unpardonable sin? They must receive the Holy Ghost, have the heavens opened unto them, and know God, and then sin against him. This is the case with many apostates in this Church: they never cease to try to hurt me, they have got the same spirit the Devil had, [and] you cannot save them. They make open war like the Devil.[889]

Report of Thomas Bullock: No man can commit the unpardonable sin after the dissolution of the body, but they must do it in this world. Hence the salvation of Jesus Christ was wrought out for all men to triumph over the Devil. For he stood up for a Savior. Jesus contended that there would be certain souls that would be condemned and the Devil said he could save them all. As the Grand Council gave in for Jesus Christ, so the Devil fell, and all who put up their heads for him. All sin shall be forgiven except the sin against the Holy Ghost.[890]

Report of William Clayton: I said no man could commit the unpardonable sin after the dissolution of the body. Hence the salvation that the Savior wrought out for the salvation of man—if it did not [indecipherable, TPJS says "catch"] him in one place it would another. The contention in heaven was Jesus said there were certain men [who] would not be saved, [and] the Devil said he could save them. He rebelled against God and was thrust down.[891]

Report of George Laub: Jesus Christ, being the greater light or of more intelligence, for he loved righteousness and hated iniquity, He, being the elder brother, presented himself for to come and redeem this world, as it was his right by inheritance. He stated [that] He could save all those who

---

881 Exodus 28:9, 29, 41; Exodus 29:33, 32:29; Leviticus 8:33, 16:32, 21:10; Numbers 3:3; Judges 17:5, 12; 1 Kings 13:33; 1 Chronicles 29:5; 2 Chronicles 29:31; Jeremiah 44:25; Ezekiel 43:26. See also H. W. Attridge, *Hebrews*, p. 85.

882 See Leviticus 8:26-28 and Exodus 29:24. See also 2 Chronicles 13:9, which should read "to fill his hand with a young bullock" (KJV: "to consecrate himself with a young bullock").

883 See Revelation 2:17; D&C 130:4-11; cf. *Commentary 1:27-b*, p. 62 and *Figure 4-4*, p. 219. See *Endnote 4-9*, p. 299. See *Excursus 53: Comparative Explorations: Jewish and Christian Analogues*, p. 679.

884 L. M. Hilton, *Hand*, pp. 171-176. See also J. L. Carroll, *et al.*, *Incense*; Cyril of Jerusalem, *Five*, 5:21, p. 156; H. W. Nibley, *Sacred*, Figure 48, p. 592; H. W. Nibley, *Vestments*, Figure 22, p. 106.

885 E. Tóth, *Holy Crown*, p. 63.

886 *Ibid.*, p. 57.

887 See Matthew 28:17-18; H. A. Kelly, *Satan*, pp. 97-100.

888 See *Commentary 4:1-e*, p. 244.

889 J. Smith, Jr., *Words*, 7 April 1844, p. 347, spelling and punctuation standardized.

890 *Ibid.*, 7 April 1844, p. 353, spelling and punctuation standardized.

891 *Ibid.*, 7 April 1844, p. 361, spelling and punctuation standardized.

did not sin against the Holy Ghost and they would obey the code of laws that was given. But their circumstances were that all who would sin against the Holy Ghost should have no forgiveness neither in the world nor in the world to come. For they strove against light and knowledge after they had tasted of the good things of the world to come. They should not have any pardon in the world to come. because they had a knowledge of the world to come and were not willing to abide the law. Therefore they can have no forgiveness there, but must be most miserable of all, and never can be renewed again.[892] But Satan or Lucifer, being the next heir…, had allotted to him great power and authority, even Prince of the air. He spake immediately and boasted of himself saying, "Send me, I can save all, even those who sinned against the Holy Ghost." And he accused his brethren[893] and was hurled from the Council for striving to break the law immediately. And there was a warfare with Satan and the Gods. And they hurled Satan out of his place and all them that would not keep the law of the Council. But he himself being one of the Council would not keep his or their first estate, for he was one of the sons of perdition and consequently all the sons of perdition became devils, etc.[894]

Note that Laub's report, taken from his journal, is a retrospective summary. The value of Laub's summary is in that it contains details not recorded elsewhere, however, it is certainly less reliable overall than the three contemporaneous accounts,[895] having probably been reconstructed in 1845 "from notes of actual speeches heard but not accurately dated and from memory of those speeches and other teachings he had heard."[896]

4-25   The Prophet Joseph Smith stated that:

… the greatness of [Satan's] punishment is that he shall not have a tabernacle… So the Devil, thinking to thwart the decree of God, by going up and down in the earth, seeking whom he may destroy—any person that he can find that will yield to him, he will bind him, and take possession of the body and reign there, glorying in it mightily, not caring that he had got merely a stolen body; and by-and-by some one having authority will come along and cast him out and restore the tabernacle to its rightful owner. The Devil steals a tabernacle because he has not one of his own; but if he steals one, he is always likely to be turned out of doors.[897]

4-26   Milton's classic words in *Paradise Lost* eloquently capture the scene of Satan's fall:

… cast… out from Heav'n, with all his Host
Of Revel[898] Angels, by whose aid aspiring
To set himself in Glory above his Peers,
He trusted to have equal'd the most High,
If he oppos'd; and with ambitious aim
Against the Throne and Monarchy of God
Rais'd impious War in Heav'n and Battel proud
With vain attempt. Him the Almighty Power
Hurld headlong flaming from th'Etherial Skie
With hideous ruine and combustion down
To bottomless perdition, there to dwell
In Adamantine Chains and penal Fire,
Who durst defie th'Omnipotent to Arms.[899]

The *Conflict of Adam and Eve with Satan* contains the following account of Satan's rebellion, as recounted by the angels:

"But now, O Adam, we will make known to thee, what came upon us through him, before his fall from heaven.

892   See Hebrews 6:4-8.

893   See Revelation 12:10.

894   J. Smith, Jr., 7 April 1844, reported in E. England, *Laub*, p. 22, spelling and punctuation standardized.

895   A. Ehat, *et al.*, in J. Smith, Jr., *Words*, pp. xvi-xvii.

896   E. England, *Laub*, p. 32 n. 24. On the issue of finding the correct date for the discourse referenced by this journal entry, see E. England, *Laub*, pp. 2, 32 n. 24.

897   J. Smith, Jr., *Words*, 14 May 1843, pp. 200-201; J. Smith, Jr., *Encyclopedia*, 14 May 1843, pp. 187-188.

898   I.e., rebel.

899   J. Milton, *Paradise Lost*, 1:37-49, p. 17.

He gathered together his hosts, and deceived them, promising them to give them a great kingdom, a divine nature; and other promises he made them.

His hosts believed that his word was true, so they yielded to him, and renounced the glory of God.

He then sent for us—according to the orders [i.e., ranks or dignities] in which we were—to come under his command, and to hearken to his vain promise. But we would not, and we took not his advice.

Then, after he had fought with God, and had dealt frowardly with Him, he gathered together his hosts, and made war with us. And if it had not been for God's strength that was with us, we could not have prevailed against him to hurl him from heaven.

But when he fell from among us, there was great joy in heaven, because of his going down from us. For had he continued in heaven, nothing, not even one angel would have remained in it.

But God in his mercy, drove him from among us to this dark earth; for he had become darkness itself and a worker of unrighteousness.

And he has continued, O Adam, to make war against thee…"[900]

See the section on *Zoroastrian Texts* below for an account of the origin of the "evil principle" in consequence of the free choice of some of the spirit children of the supreme deity, Ahura Mazda.[901]

4-27 In this context, agency does not describe the everyday sense of making arbitrary decisions, but rather the possibility of moral choices between right and wrong according to the light one is given[902] while being subject to the enticings of God and Satan.[903] In recent years, Elder Boyd K. Packer, among others, has also repeatedly stressed the importance of accountability in such choices.[904] Thus, Warner has appropriately defined agency in the scriptural sense as "both the power to choose between obedience and rebellion and the accountability for how that power is used."[905]

4-28 Note that D&C 29:36 equates power with "honor"—presumably this is related to the glory that the Devil sought in conjunction with his proposal to save all mankind.[906]

4-29 For discussions of the Judaic use of the Hebrew term for Satan as a description of a generic adversarial role rather than as a specific individual of cosmic stature, see Kelly and Pagels.[907] For a collection of essays that treat the role of Satan within secular literature, see Bloom.[908] On the waning of the idea of a personal Devil in modern times, see Kelly.[909]

4-30 There is perhaps an echo of the conflict between Satan and Jehovah in Egyptian accounts of "the council in heaven and the controversy over the right to dominion with Horus winning over Seth—being recognized as the firstborn, the sole heir and the opener of the ways."[910]

4-31 Sources are unanimous in characterizing this prostration of the angels as one of "honor and greeting, not one of prayer and worship."[911]

Al-Tabari's *Tarikh* includes several versions of this story.[912] Note, however, the contrast to the Christian view of Satan as a rebellious angel:

The Islamic view of angels holds that they possess no will of their own but, according to the doctrine of angelic impeccability, are able merely to execute God's bidding; they are, therefore, incapable of such a willful act of disobedience to God's command as that of Iblis. By maintaining his absolute but mistaken fidelity to God alone [i.e., under the assumption that the reason Iblis would not bow

900 S. C. Malan, *Adam and Eve*, 1:55, pp. 61-62.
901 *Annotated Bibliography*, pp. 858, 859.
902 D&C 93:31.
903 Moroni 7:12-13.
904 E.g., B. K. Packer, *Covenants*; B. K. Packer, *Errand*, pp. 176-183; cf. D&C 101:78.
905 C. T. Warner, *Accountability*. See *Excursus 22: The Nature of Satan's Premortal Proposal*, p. 577.
906 Moses 4:1.
907 H. A. Kelly, *Satan*, pp. 13-30; E. Pagels, *Satan*, pp. 38-48.
908 H. Bloom, *Satan*.
909 H. A. Kelly, *Satan*, pp. 308-322.
910 H. W. Nibley, *Teachings of the PGP*, 6, p. 77. See also H. W. Nibley, *Message 2005*, pp. 396-401 and *Excursus 1: Speech, Writing, and Revelation*, p. 512.
911 A. al-Tha'labi, *Lives*, p. 48.
912 al-Tabari, *Creation*, 1:91-94, pp. 263-266; cf. I. Ibn Kathir, *Stories*, pp. 23-27.

down to Adam was that he reserved that action of devotion exclusively to God], Iblis refused to obey God's command, although, as his act has been interpreted, he was involuntarily obedient to God's eternal will and knowledge, inasmuch as He had willed before all time that Iblis not bow down to Adam, in contradistinction to His command that he do obeisance. "God can command a thing and yet will that it not be, and He can will a thing to be and command it not to be: He commanded Iblis to bow down to Adam but willed that he not bow down; had He willed it, he would have necessarily obeyed. He forbade Adam to eat of the tree but willed that he eat; had He willed that he not eat, he would not have eaten."[913] As expressed by the martyr-mystic Husayn ibn Mansur al-Hallaj, executed in Baghdad in 922, Iblis was like a man bound hand and foot and cast into the sea while being admonished not to get wet! Because Iblis was incapable of recognizing the divine part of man to which he was bade prostrate himself, the later mystics dubbed him "the absolute monotheist" and "the one-eyed."[914]

4-32   Elsewhere, Budge translates this as "the written authority that was in his hand" in which was written "the names of all the angels under his command. Knowing their names, his authority over them was absolute."[915] Nibley translates the term "writing" as token, mark, document, or authorization,[916] which is consistent with a story in a late Ethiopian text of the attempt of the penitent thief who was crucified with Christ to enter Paradise. He succeeds at last only when he shows the Cherubim "the writing which was in his hand, [that] was written in the blood… of our Lord Jesus Christ."[917] Likewise, the Mandaean *Ginza* says that the ascending one will be greeted by "the one who holds the nails of glory and the signs in the hands, and the key of the *kushta* of both arms."[918]

4-33   Presumably, the armor refers to his "garment of glory."[919] The *Gospel of the Secret Supper* likewise describes the rebellious Satan and his followers being deprived of their glorious apparel: "Then the father ordered his angels, 'Rip off their robes!' The angels stripped all those angels who had listened to Satan of their robes, their thrones, and their crowns… My father transformed him because of his pride, and he withdrew the light from him.[920] His face became like red fire and was fully like that of a man."[921] Similarly, *The Cave of Treasures* says that Satan "lost the apparel of his glory. And behold, from that time until the present day, he and all his hosts have been stripped of their apparel, and they go naked and have horrible faces."[922]

4-34   Having broken the oath and covenant of the priesthood and altogether turned from it,[923] Satan is portrayed as having been stabbed and cut from shoulder to shoulder with a knife in ritual fashion. He has committed the unpardonable sin and cannot be redeemed.[924] Other traditions mention a specific angel or cherub whose wing becomes the weapon by which Satan is smitten and rendered helpless.[925] Al-Kisa'i's *Qisas Al-Anbiya* recounts that when Lucifer's "countenance was transformed into that of the Devil[, t]he angels, gazing upon his evil appearance and smelling his abominable stench, fell on him with their spears, cursing him and saying, 'Accursed! Accursed! Damned! Damned!'"[926]

Nibley relates the following general information concerning the symbolic enactment of curses as part of temple ritual:

> The ritual performance of a curse was anciently an imitation sacrifice. The priest shed his own blood either for the king, whom he originally represented, or for the people, whom the king also

---

913   Kulayni, *al-Usul*, 1, 151, cited in M. al-Kisa'i, *Tales*, pp. 341-342 n. 23.

914   M. al-Kisa'i, *Tales*, pp. 341-342 n. 23.

915   E. A. W. Budge, *Cave*, p. 59; cf. *Commentary* 3:19-b, p. 177. See also Milik's translation in an account of the Watchers: "in one (hand) the authorization (?) of the Giants" (QG5 (4QEnGib 3) cited in J. C. Reeves, *Jewish Lore*, p. 64, see also p. 103 n. 3.

916   H. W. Nibley, *Sacred*, p. 557.

917   I. Mika'el, son of Bakhayla, *Godhead*, p. 136. See also N. Isar, *Dance of Adam*, pp. 180-181.

918   M. Lidzbarski, *Ginza*, GL 1:1, p. 429, cited in H. W. Nibley, *Apocryphal*, p. 300; cf. Isaiah 49:16; Zechariah 13:6; Cyril of Jerusalem, *Five*, 2:5, p. 148. See *Commentary* 5:4-a, p. 355; 5:5-b, p. 359; and *Excursus 37: Traditions About the Role of Abel*, p. 617.

919   G. W. E. Nickelsburg ,et al., *1 Enoch*, 62:15, p. 81.

920   Note that Satan was also Lucifer, bearer of the light.

921   W. Barnstone, *et al.*, *Secret Supper*, pp. 743-744.

922   E. A. W. Budge, *Cave*, p. 56.

923   D&C 84:41.

924   See *Commentary* 4:1-e, p. 244; 4:17-b, p. 263; and 4:20-c, p. 264.

925   G. A. Anderson, *Ezekiel*, pp. 142-143.

926   M. al-Kisa'i, *Tales*, p. 28.

represented.[927] But as he can represent them by proxy, so he too may shed his blood by proxy by the sacrificial beast. All of this, of course, is "a similitude of the sacrifice of the Only Begotten,"[928] which atoned for the sins of all, and thus redeems or saves from death.

In the old covenant, when the leper is declared clean and his life restored, two birds are taken: one is killed and the other is drenched with its blood,[929] and then allowed to fly away free, taking the leper's sins with it, while the patient is sprinkled with the same blood.[930] Being thus delivered from death, he washes his clothes, shaves his hair, and bathes. Then he brings two lambs, one for trespass, the price of sin;[931] its blood is placed upon the right ear of the one to be cleansed and upon the thumb of his right hand.[932] Then the priest takes the oil held in his left hand,[933] and after sprinkling it puts it on the right ear and right thumb of the healed person, where the blood had been, pouring the rest of the oil on his head[934]—it is the oil of healing. This is a private version of the public rite in which Aaron and his sons lay their hands on the head of a ram, transferring their guilt to it, slay it, and then put the blood on their own thumbs and ears.[935] The ram is burnt for a sin-offering as an atonement.[936] It is clear when one thinks back to the ram that was sacrificed in the place of Isaac, Abraham's offering of his only son, that this all looks forward to the great atoning sacrifice, the whole idea being to celebrate our redemption from death.[937] We are told that a covenant must be made by the shedding of one's own blood unless a substitute can be found to redeem one.[938] In ancient times, all the sacrifices were symbolic,[939] and Maimonides says that in the entire history of Israel only nine heifers were really sacrificed.[940] Certainly one of the striking things about the newly discovered Temple Scroll is the avoidance of bloody sacrifice, which takes place only at a discreet distance from the temple.

The ear has a significance in ancient Israel. When a servant in Israel, out of pure love, wished to be sealed to a master for the rest of his life, even though free to go his own way, his bond was made sure by fixing his ear to the door with a nail driven through it.[941] It was a relatively painless operation, since there are only three nerves in the lobe of the ear. But it would be hard to find a more convincing symbol of anything fixed in a sure place.[942]

A medieval Ethiopian Christian text portrays Adam as enacting similar covenantal gestures as part of his exaltation by God before the angels in the Garden of Eden:[943]

> Then God said unto his angels, "This is My image. I have given unto him everything which is lower than Myself [in rank]. Thus saying I have appointed him to be governor [thereof]. Take four sheep which are in the Garden (i.e., Paradise), and slay them, and smear thy hand with the blood, and thy right ear, and the fingers of thy right hand, and [the toes of] the right foot. And this shall be a memorial for thy children, and thou shalt become associated with the *Surafel* (i.e., the Seraphim) in the mysteries."[944]

4-35   Nibley explains: "This cost him a third of his strength and rendered him forever incapable of prevailing by force. Henceforth, he gains his ends by deception and trickery, which makes him all the more dangerous."[945]

---

927   See 1 Samuel 13:8-14.
928   Moses 5:7.
929   See Leviticus 14:1-6.
930   See Leviticus 14:7.
931   See Leviticus 14:8-12.
932   See Leviticus 14:14.
933   See Leviticus 14:15.
934   See Leviticus 14:17-18.
935   See Leviticus 8:22-24.
936   See Leviticus 9:2-7.
937   See Exodus 13:8-10.
938   See Numbers 8:13-15.
939   See Leviticus 5.
940   *Commentary on the Mishnah*, Laws of the Red Heifer 3:4, cited in J. Neusner, *Without Myth*, p. 99. See also J. Neusner, *Mishnah*, 6 (Purities), Parah, 3:5, p. 1016.
941   See Deuteronomy 15:16-17.
942   H. W. Nibley, *Sacred*, pp. 554-557; cf. Isaiah 22:23. See also S. D. Ricks, *Oaths*, pp. 46-48.
943   See *Endnote 4-58,* p. 314.
944   B. Mika'el, *Book*, p. 21.
945   H. W. Nibley, *Sacred*, p. 557. See *Commentary 4:20-f*, p. 265.

4-36   Indeed, noting the high regard among the LDS for this pseudepigraphal book, Nickelsburg falsely assumes that it is part of the Mormon canon: "Among twentieth-century Christians, only the Ethiopian Church and the Church of Jesus Christ of Latter-day Saints consider the Enoch writings to be authoritative."[946]

4-37   Note that in early Christian texts (e.g., the *Life of Adam and Eve*), Satan is always portrayed as being cast down "to the earth (and not to Hades as one might have expected)."[947]

4-38   Christensen also argues for a Book of Mormon parallel to the story of the Watchers:

> … the account of Amulon's wicked priests shows the use of allusions to the fallen angel myth to interpret that story. The arch sin of the fallen angels in the Enoch accounts was pride, and in consequence of their fall, they spread a corrupt form of wisdom. In the Enoch accounts, the fallen angels intermarried with human women, and their offspring were destroyed in the time of Noah. In the Book of Mormon, Amulon's priests are described from the beginning as proud;[948] they also pervert sacred knowledge for gain[949] and take wives they should not have.[950] Amulon's priests teach the Lamanites to be cunning and wise "as to the wisdom of the world."[951] Finally, their descendants from the union with the stolen wives become "hardened" and meet with destruction.[952]

4-39   Said Elder Boyd K. Packer:

> Lucifer in clever ways manipulates our choices, deceiving us about sin and consequences. He, and his angels with him, tempt us to be unworthy, even wicked. But he cannot, in all eternity he cannot, with all his power he cannot completely destroy us; not without our own consent. Had agency come to man without the Atonement, it would have been a fatal gift.[953]

4-40   Barker similarly concludes that, at least during the intertestamental period, one would expect to find evidence for a combination of influences to account for mankind's disobedience:

> It is clear that there was a whole spectrum of ideas as to the nature of sin and evil… At one end, sin was disobedience, an individual's transgression of one of the laws, and at the other sin was also disobedience, but the disobedience of angels who misused their divine knowledge and brought calamity to the earth as a result. Somewhere between these two extremes, we can place the two spirits at work to influence man's actions, a position which seems to be a compromise between the "external influences" view of *1 Enoch*, and the "intentional disobedience" view of later Judaism.[954]

4-41   The motif of the divergence of the two ways for those who hearken[955] and for those who do not hearken to the voice of the Lord[956] will dominate the remainder of the book of Moses, culminating in the sanctification of Enoch's Zion on the one hand[957] and the destruction of the Noachian flood on the other.[958]

4-42   Indeed, knowledge is one of the preconditions to the full exercise of agency in this life: "Behold, here is the agency of man, and here is the condemnation of man; because that which was from the beginning is plainly manifest unto them, and they receive not the light."[959] "And it is given unto them to know good from evil; wherefore they are agents unto themselves."[960]

4-43   Satan's misery is no doubt due in large measure to his being deprived of a body. 2 Nephi 9:9 says that if there were no resurrection we would continue our existence only as spirits, "to remain with the father of lies, in misery, like unto himself." Recall also the Prophet Joseph Smith's statement that "the

946   G. W. E. Nickelsburg, *1 Enoch*, p. 82.
947   G. A. Anderson, *Ezekiel*, p. 142.
948   Mosiah 11:5-13.
949   Mosiah 11:5-6; 12:28-29.
950   Mosiah 20:1-5.
951   Mosiah 24:7; cf. 23:31-35; 24:1-7.
952   K. Christensen, *Temple*, pp. 465-466; cf. Alma 25:4, 7-9. See the overview of Moses 5, p. 349.
953   B. K. Packer, *Who Is Jesus Christ*, p. 18.
954   M. Barker, *Older*, pp. 233-234.
955   Moses 5:17.
956   Moses 5:16.
957   Moses 7:69.
958   Moses 8:30. See the overview of Moses 5, pp. 344-350.
959   D&C 93:31.
960   Moses 6:56.

greatness of [Satan's] punishment is that he shall not have a tabernacle."[961] D&C 138:50 says that "the dead [look] upon the long absence of their spirits from their bodies as a bondage,"[962] and, on the other hand, D&C 93:33-34 reads that: "spirit and element, inseparably connected, receive a fulness of joy; And when separated, man cannot receive a fulness of joy." Therefore, when Lehi teaches that "Adam fell that men might be; and men are, that they might have joy,"[963] it is no error to take the scripture in context as meaning to equate "a fulness of joy" with the blessing of a glorified resurrected body.

Truman G. Madsen has written:

> In LDS theology, the physical body is not the muffling and imprisoning of the spirit. The body is the spirit's enhancement. It is an instrument of redemption; and the instrument itself is to be redeemed. Indeed, in it s most inclusive sense, "soul" is honorifically defined in Doctrine and Covenants 88:15-17 as spirit and body combined, "inseparably connected," or fused. So, as the *Teachings* informs us, 'The great principle of happiness consists in having a body"...[964]

> This may be the inversion—some would say the misreading—of the classical reading of Plato that insists every sublimely true and good and beautiful thing is absolutely separate from the material world and even from particularity. Instead, apparently, even ideational realms of the most profound subtlety and nuance are beyond full apprehension and comprehension when we are not embodied. Further, what we see, hear, smell, taste, and touch on earth only foreshadows the expansion of sensate awareness in the world to come—hence the criticality of Christ's resurrection, and through Him, our own.[965]

4-44 In a scene that recalls elements of the *protoevangelion*, Nibley notes that "the cat who split the *ished-tree* and released the god also beheads the god's mortal enemy, the *Apophis* serpent, beneath the same *ished-tree*."[966] The cat's paw rests heavily on the head of the serpent in accompanying illustrations.

4-45 Rasmussen gives an alternative explanation for Satan's actions: "Apparently [the Devil] did not know the divine plan of Redemption as we know it.[967] For his own purposes, therefore, Satan sought to persuade the ancestors of the family of humankind to do a deed that would separate them from the presence of God in spiritual death and later separate their spirits from their bodies in physical death; then they would be like his unembodied spirit followers and be subject to him."[968]

4-46 An example of preparatory redemption is given in Ether 3:13, where the brother of Jared is told in conjunction with his vision of the premortal Jesus Christ: "Because thou knowest these things, ye are redeemed from the fall; therefore ye are brought back into my presence; therefore I show myself unto you."

4-47 The door represents the entrance to the "road to Rosetjau,"[969] the path through the Underworld or Netherworld that must be traversed by the dead. The nature of the journey is described by Assman:

> The body of water that the deceased must cross in order to attain eternal life separates the two aspects of the netherworld as a place of death and a place of life. The idea of distancing from death is here turned into a mater of spaces, while the idea of the Judgment of the Dead turns it into a matter of ethics and law. In the conceptual horizon of the Judgment of the Dead, the deceased was obliged to distance himself from this guilt so as not to fall victim to the Devouress. Here, mortal danger threatened him from the guardians and "policemen" in the netherworld, whom Osiris had bidden to ward off evil. In the horizon of overcoming space, he was threatened by bird catchers

961 J. Smith, Jr., *Words*, 14 May 1843, p. 201; J. Smith, Jr., *Encyclopedia*, 14 May 1843, p. 187.

962 See also D&C 45:17; cf. the Mandaean idea of reunification of a spirit and body, exactly resembling one another, which is seen "as if [one] had come out of prison" (E. S. Drower, *Mandaeans*, p. 55).

963 2 Nephi 2:25.

964 J. Smith, Jr., *Teachings*, 5 January 1841, p. 181. *Ch-d-h*, one of the Hebrew roots for "joy" (as in e.g., Nehemiah 8:10: "the joy of the Lord") has three meanings: "gladness; ... togetherness or being joined one with another; and ...something about the temple" (T. G. Madsen, *Joy*; F. Brown, *et al.*, *Lexicon*, p. 292 d). No doubt related to these meanings is the Book of Mormon dictum: "Man is that he might have joy" (2 Nephi 2:25; cf. D&C 42:61), and, in the Greek NT: "Enter thou into the joy of thy Lord" (Matthew 25:21; cf. *Commentary* 1:25-c, p. 60). See also 1 Chronicles 16:27; Y. Buxbaum, *Mystic Joy*, pp. 2, 249 n. 1, 250 n. 17.

965 T. G. Madsen, *LDS View*, p. 101.

966 H. W. Nibley, *Message 2005*, pp. 311-312. See *Commentary*, 4:21-d, p. 266.

967 2 Nephi 9:5-10.

968 E. T. Rasmussen, *OT Commentary*, p. 14; cf. 2 Nephi 9:8.

969 R. O. Faulkner, *Book of the Dead*, heading to Spell 117, p. 113.

who had spread a giant net over this body of water. He escapes this danger, for he is able to name all the individual elements of this net in a mysterious spirit language, which proves him to be an initiated member of the divine realm, a transfigured ancestral spirit.[970]

4-48   On the false door as a "horizon," Assman writes:

[The] false door was not only an interface between the inaccessible and the accessible portions of the tomb, and between this realm and the next one, but also a symbol of the celestial gateway… that led to the sky… We must therefore picture this gate as located in that liminal area between sky and earth that… we conventionally render as "horizon." This translation is not entirely correct, for a horizon depends on the standpoint of the beholder, and it shifts as he moves along, so that it can never be reached. As the Egyptians conceived it, however, the [horizon] could indeed by reached. It was the zone at the edge of the world, where the sun rose and set… The false door was therefore also such a symbol, that is, "sacramentally explainable."[971]

4-49   Assman properly characterizes the function of the Egyptian myth of Osiris as follows: "The myth is not theology, *it does not inquire after the essence of the gods; rather, it surrounds human actions with a story that invests them with meaning.*"[972]

4-50   The more standard interpretation of the symbolism of the "Lady of the Tree" is closer to a Tree of Life motif than to a Tree of Knowledge figure as Nibley seems to suggest here. According to Assman:

The goddess of the West appears in the role of provisioner of the deceased. In all its variations, this is the principal motif of the idea of transition: the deceased's journey into the afterlife always leads to a place where he is forever provided with food and drink. Along with the goddess of the West, Nut and Hathor also play the role of the goddess of provisions; the three goddesses are indistinguishable in this role. There is also the tree goddess, who is usually a manifestation of Nut, but who can also be Hathor. This is a goddess in the form of a tree that dispenses eternal nourishment to the deceased.… In all [her] welcoming and embracing forms, she promises the deceased security, eternal renewal, air, water, and nourishment. As nurse and nourisher, she manifests herself as a sycamore, the Tree of Life, who dispenses eternal nourishment to the deceased.[973]

WIth respect to the tree, Nibley writes:[974]

At least from the beginning of the New Kingdom, every major city in Egypt had a tomb of Osiris that was sheltered by a tree, which was represented as the cedar of Byblos sheltering the coffin of Osiris in that city… From the long *Book of Breathings*, we learn that there was a cave beneath the *ished-tree*. According to the well-known legend, Osiris was actually shut up in the cedar tree and had to be liberated from it in order to be resurrected.[975] Joseph's grave was an *Urhügel* at Shechem, sheltered by a tree, in Egyptian fashion.

In a decoration on a twelfth-century altar, such a tree is stands above the tomb of Christ.[976]

4-51   The teaching that mortal life is just one of a series of temporary transitions recalls an inscription at a mosque at Fatehpur Sikri, India, and also attested in the *Clerical Instruction* of Petrus Alphonsi, where Jesus is quoted as saying: "This world is a bridge. Pass over it, but do not build your dwelling there."[977] Barnstone notes that the spirit of this statement closely resembles *Gospel of Thomas* 42: "Be passersby" or, in a less literal reading, "Come into being as you pass away."[978]

4-52   Many early Christians adopted this rabbinical teaching. For example, Origen taught that Adam and Eve were "wonderfully adorned in Eden. Like the high priest Aaron, [Adam's] life before God was marked by glorious apparel. After his transgression, [he] was stripped of his glory…"[979]

---

970   J. Assman, *Death*, p. 131.

971   J. Assman, *Death*, p. 335.

972   J. Assman, *Search*, p. 129, emphasis in original.

973   J. Assman, *Death*, p. 153, 171. See also, e.g., R. H. Wilkinson, *Art*, p. 117.

974   H. W. Nibley, *Message 2005*, p. 290; cf. the palm tree over "Adam's grave" at Machpelah (N. Arnon, *Machpela*, p. 13). See also *Figure 4-12*, p. 231; *Commentary 4:14-e*, p. 260; *Excursus 42: Nebuchadnezzar's "Fall"*, p. 632; and *Excursus 53: Comparative Explorations of the Mysteries*, p. 663.

975   See *Commentary 4:14-e*, p. 260 and *Excursus 53: Comparative Explorations of the Mysteries*, p. 663—especially p. 669ff.

976   G. R. Murphy, *Gemstone*, p. 25.

977   W. Barnstone, *et al.*, *Gnostic*, p. 662.

978   *Ibid.*, p. 54.

979   *Homilies on Leviticus* 6:7, cited in G. A. Anderson, *Perfection*, p. 122.

Several early Christian texts likewise agree that "Adam and Eve had been created in an intermediate state; whether or not they would be raised to a higher state God leaves to the outcome of the exercise of their free will."[980]

4-53   The close relationship between ritual clothing actions and temple ordinances is summarized by Ostler:

> The ritual action of putting on a sacred garment is properly termed an "endowment." The word garment is, in fact, representative of ordinances found in ancient texts. The Greek word… that means "garment," or… "to clothe upon," was used to represent sacramental, baptismal, and sealing ordinances in the *Clementine Recognitions*,[981] an extremely important and ancient Christian (Ebionite) work. The Latin *induere*, meaning "to clothe," and *inducere*, "to lead or initiate," are the roots for our English word "endowment." All connote temple ordinances.[982]

Although generally in agreement with the points made in Ostler's article, specific meanings associated with the sequence of changes in garments outlined in this chapter differ from his presentation in various details.[983]

4-54   The same pattern typified the life of Christ, except that He lived without sin.[984] Anderson summarizes:

> Prior to his incarnation, Christ resided in heaven clothed in glory. He descended to earth, assuming the garments of flesh bequeathed by Adam at his fall. There, he persevered all temptation and was obedient even to the point of death. As a result God the Father raised him from the dead and reclothed him with a glorious body on Easter morning.[985]

4-55   Though the rebellion of Satan and his hosts clearly demonstrates that sin was possible in the premortal life, it is a matter of conjecture whether sin and repentance were part of the general experience of all who lived in the spirit world. D&C 93:38 reads: "Every spirit of man was innocent in the beginning; and God, having redeemed man from the fall, men become again, in their infant state, innocent before God." Top interprets the verse as follows: "The key word is 'again.' This seems to indicate that men had lost innocence in the premortal world through sin and disobedience, but were once again, through the great plan of Redemption, made innocent before God upon entering mortality 'in their infant state.'"[986] Another possibility is that the comma between "again" and "in" was inserted erroneously. Without this comma, the scripture would simply imply that the Redemption of Christ (accomplished through the ordinances) brings men again to an infant state, in other words, innocent before God.

4-56   An Islamic legend states that before the soul of Adam entered his body, it was first commanded to bathe "in the sea of glory which proceedeth from [God]."[987] Jewish and Islamic sources sometimes describe Adam and Eve's original glory as "a garment of translucent skin"[988] which, when "he yielded to sin, …was exchanged for the (present) skin, but a remnant of it has been left in his fingertips to remind him of his original condition."[989]

About his own belief in a preexistence, Wordsworth stated:

> It is far too shadowy a notion to be recommended to faith, as more than an element in our instincts of immortality. But let us bear in mind that, though the idea is not advanced in revelation, there is nothing there to contradict it, and the Fall of Man presents an analogy in its favor. Accordingly, a preexistent state has entered into the popular creeds of many nations; and, among all persons acquainted with classic literature, is known as an ingredient in Platonic philosophy.… Having to wield some of its elements when I was impelled to write this poem on the "Immortality of the

980   Brock in Ephrem the Syrian, *Paradise*, p. 90.
981   Pseudo-Clement, *Recognitions*, 4:36, pp. 142-143. See also Pseudo-Clement, *Homilies*, 8:22-23, pp. 274-275.
982   B. T. Ostler, *Clothed*, p. 1.
983   Cf. B. T. Ostler, *Clothed*, p. 10.
984   Hebrews 4:15.
985   G. A. Anderson, *Perfection*, p. 130.
986   B. L. Top, *Life Before*, p. 95; cf. Moses 6:53. See *Excursus 3: Temple Blessings in the Oath and Covenant of the Priesthood*, p. 519.
987   G. Weil, *Legends*, p. 20.
988   Arabic *zifr* vs. *jild*.
989   A. al-Tha'labi, *Lives*, p. 47, cf. p. 53. See also al-Tabari, *Creation*, 1:105, p. 276; p. 276 n. 677; and 1:128, p. 299.

Soul," I took hold of the notion of preexistence as having sufficient foundation in humanity for authorizing me to make for my purpose the best use of it I could as a poet.[990]

4-57   Cf. the statement from the *Qur'an*: "Righteousness is the best kind of garment."[991]

4-58   The Prophet Joseph Smith taught that Adam received the First Presidency and its keys (i.e., the keys necessary to direct the Kingdom of God on the earth) "before the world was formed."[992] Similarly, the book of the *Cave of Treasures* records that immediately following his creation, "Adam was arrayed in the apparel of sovereignty, and there was the crown of glory set upon his head, there was he made king, and priest, and prophet, there did God make him to sit upon his honorable throne, and there did God give him dominion over all creatures and things."[993]

A medieval Ethiopian Christian text similarly portrays Adam in the Garden of Eden being commanded by God to enact a series of covenantal gestures in order to "become associated with the *Surafel* (i.e., the Seraphim) in the mysteries."[994] Afterward, God gloriously clothed him:

> … He arrayed Adam in apparel of light which resembled the flower of the rose, and He bound on his head a magnificent crown one part of which resembled a flame and the other the sun. And he made for him a tunic of light and girded it about his body: and he made a helmet of iron for his skull (or, forehead). And God had an elephant brought and He mounted Adam thereon, and He gave him a spear in his hand, and He made sandals of gold for his feet.[995]

In this manner, Adam and Eve, "though naked, [were] still clothed."[996]

Islamic tradition also records Adam's enthronement, recording that in "the midst of Paradise there stood a green silken tent, supported on golden pillars, and in the midst of it there was a throne, on which Adam seated himself with Eve."[997] Zilio-Grandi observes that, according to the *Qur'an*, "the reason why [Adam] was created and placed in the universe… [was] to be a viceregent (*halifa* = caliph). On this question the *Qur'an* states at verse 2:30: '… thy Lord announced to the angels: I am about to place a viceregent in the earth.'" Alusi explains that:

> The meaning of the word *halifa* here referred to is that Adam is successor to God on His earth, just as every prophet is a caliph of God on the earth, insofar as he takes the place of God in maintaining ('*imara*) the earth, in governing (*siyasa*) men and perfecting their souls, transmitting the Decree of the most High… Adam was the first prophet, the first to whom revelation was given…[998]

4-59   This theme is beautifully developed in the early Christian *Hymn of the Pearl*, summarized by Nibley[999] in Moses 4 *Gleanings*, p. 296.

4-60   The *Targum Pseudo-Jonathan* says that Adam and Eve were "divested of the purple robe in which they had been created.[1000] An Islamic source recounts the event as follows:

> Scarcely had Adam received the fruit when his crown rose toward heaven, his rings fell from his fingers, and his silken robe dropped from him. Eve, too, stood spoiled of her ornaments and naked before him, and they heard how all these things cried to them with one voice, "Woe unto you! your calamity is great, and your mourning will be long: we were created for the obedient only: farewell until the resurrection!" The throne which had been erected for them in the tent thrust them away and cried, "Rebels, depart!" The horse Meimun, upon which Adam attempted to fly, would not suffer him to mount, and said, "Hast thou thus kept the covenant of Allàh?"

> All the creatures of Paradise then turned from them, and besought Allàh to remove the human pair from that hallowed spot. Allàh himself addressed Adam in a voice of thunder, and said, "Wast thou not commanded to abstain from this fruit, and forewarned of the cunning of Iblis [Satan],

---

990   Cited in B. L. Top, *Life Before*, p. 7.

991   J.-L. Monneret, *Grands*, 7:26, p. 217.

992   J. Smith, Jr., *Words*, before 8 August 1839, p. 8.

993   E. A. W. Budge, *Cave*, p. 53; cf. Timothy of Alexandria, *Abbaton*, pp. 198-199.

994   See *Endnote 4-34*, p. 308.

995   B. Mika'el, *Book*, pp. 21-22; cf. M.al-Kisa'i, *Tales*, pp. 28-29.

996   Ephrem the Syrian, *Paradise*, Hymns on Faith (The Pearl), 133:2, p. 71.

997   G. Weil, *Legends*, p. 25.

998   I. Zilio-Grandi, *Paradise*, pp. 82-83.

999   H. W. Nibley, *Message 2005*, pp. 487-501. See also H. W. Nibley, *Treasures*, pp. 177-178.

1000   J. W. Etheridge, *Onkelos*; cf. "stripped of the clothing of fingernails" or "garments of splendor" (M. Maher, *Pseudo-Jonathan*, 3:7, p. 26 and p. 26 n. 12).

thy foe?" Adam attempted to flee from these upbraidings, and Eve would have followed him, but he was held fast by the branches of the tree Talh, and Eve was entangled in her own disheveled hair.[1001]

As discussed earlier in this overview, Satan had been similarly deprived of his garments of glory at the time of his rebellion, becoming a type, in that respect, for Adam and Eve. The couple's transgression in Eden in turn became a type for the rebellion of Israel at Sinai: "In rabbinic sources… was the tradition that Israel put on crowns when they accepted the *Torah*. These crowns kept the angel of death at bay. When Israel venerated the golden calf, the crowns were stripped away and Israel returned to a mortal state. A classic proof text of this was Psalm 82:6:

I say, "You are gods,
        children of the Most High, all of you;
nevertheless, you shall die like mortals,
        and fall like any prince."

This verse was paraphrased 'When you accepted the *Torah* you shined like the angels; but now, having worshipped the calf, you shall die like Adam.'"[1002] In a broader sense, Anderson argues that "In the story of the Fall,… we have a presentation of Israel's central story in miniature."[1003]

4-61 Sailhamer highlights the distinction between the use of the Hebrew *arom* for "naked" in 3:25 and the similar *erom* in 4:13: "Whereas both terms are infrequently used in the Pentateuch, *erom* is distinguished by its use in Deuteronomy 28:48, where it depicts the state of Israel's exiles who have been punished for their failure to trust and obey God's word… [Thus, the] effect of the Fall was not simply that the man and the woman come to know that they were 'naked' (*arom*). The effect is rather that they come to know that they were 'naked' (*erom*) in the sense of being 'under God's judgment,' as in Deuteronomy 28:48."[1004]

4-62 Anderson notes that the "reference to seventy afflictions is certainly a sign that the afflictions have covered every inch of Adam's body, seventy being a number of wholeness in the biblical tradition."[1005]

4-63 Thus, Adam and Eve could be seen as having received two "garments" of skin: the first when they were clothed with mortal flesh, and the second when they were clothed by God in coats of animal skin. Confusion in many commentaries may have resulted from the conflation of these two events. Moreover, rabbinical wordplay equated the coats of skin (*cor*) with garments of light ('*ur*),[1006] which, notes Nibley, has also led to "a great deal of controversy."[1007]

The *Book of the Rolls* describes Adam and Eve being "clothed with flesh" as follows: "After the clothing of fig-leaves they put on clothing of skins, and that is the skin of which our bodies are made, being of the family of man, and it is a clothing of pain."[1008]

4-64 In theologically-laden verses neither included in the LDS *Hymnbook*[1009] nor the current British Methodist book of hymns,[1010] Charles Wesley's magnificent Christmas anthem "Hark! the Herald Angels Sing"[1011] also includes the concept of Jesus, the "second Adam," being "veiled in flesh."[1012] Wesley presents this idea in a manner consistent with Paul's teaching that "in him dwelleth all the fullness of the Godhead bodily,"[1013] though LDS reject a Trinitarian interpretation of that scriptural passage.[1014] Note also the entreaty for Christ to join each person "in mystic union" so that Father "Adam's likeness" in them may be replaced by the image of Christ, the "Second Adam":

1001 G. Weil, *Legends*, p. 32.
1002 G. A. Anderson, *Perfection*, p. 125.
1003 *Ibid.*, p. 121. See also J. A. Tvedtnes, *Laws*, pp. 387-391.
1004 J. H. Sailhamer, *Genesis*, p. 49; cf. Ezekiel 16:39; 23:29.
1005 G. A. Anderson, *Perfection*, p. 127.
1006 J. Neusner, *Genesis Rabbah 1*, 20:12, p. 227.
1007 H. W. Nibley, *Vestments*, p. 124. See also S. D. Ricks, *Garment*, pp. 706-708; J. A. Tvedtnes, *Clothing*, pp. 651-654.
1008 M. D. Gibson, *Rolls 1901*, p. 113.
1009 *Hymns (1985)*, #209.
1010 British Methodist Conference, *Hymns*, #106.
1011 Originally entitled "Hymn for Christmas-Day," with the first line of "Hark how all the Welkin [= sky, heaven] rings" (J. Wesley, *et al.*, *Hymns*, p. 142).
1012 See also W. Williams, *Shadow*.
1013 Colossians 2:9.
1014 B. W. Ricks, *Godhead.*, pp. 79-87, 97-101.

…

Christ, by highest heav'n adored,
Christ, the everlasting Lord,
Late in time behold him come,
Offspring of a virgin's womb;

Veiled in flesh the Godhead see!
Hail th' incarnate Deity!
Pleased as man with men to dwell,
Jesus, our Immanuel.[1015]

…

Come, Desire of nations, come,
Fix us in Thy humble home.
Rise, the Woman's conqu'ring Seed,
Bruise in us the Serpent's head.

Now display thy saving power,
Ruined nature now restore;
Now in mystic union join
Thine to ours, and ours to Thine.

Adam's likeness, Lord, efface,
Stamp Thy Image in its place.
Second Adam from above,
Reinstate us in Thy love.

Let us Thee, though lost, regain,
Thee, the Life, the Heav'nly Man:
O, to all Thyself impart,
Formed in each believing heart.[1016]

4-65   Nibley asks:

Why do we have to be baptized with water? The answer is: "I've forgiven the cause. Now, you have to get rid of the effect. The cause was the Fall. It made you dirty, but you have to wash off now. You have to take advantage in good faith of the sacrifice that has been made for you. Here's the chance. It's a very simple thing to do, but you have to do it." Why is it that man must repent and be baptized? "Not because you are damned but because I have forgiven you," he says… "I have taken care of the transgression in the Garden of Eden." That's the *Erbsunde*, the primal sin. To think we are not responsible for that and, therefore, we are not to blame for our sins is ridiculous. That sin has been forgiven, so if you want to go on what you do then is wash off and get started again. He says here, "The Son of God hath atoned for original guilt, wherein the sins of the parents cannot be answered upon the heads of the children, for they are whole from the foundation of the world."[1017] But "when they begin to grow up, sin conceiveth in their hearts."[1018]

Note that OT2 and current book of Moses use the singular "transgression," while OT1 uses the plural term "transgressions."[1019]

4-66   In describing the ascent of chosen souls upward, the Mandaean *Ginza* uses the image of the vine as "a symbol of the soul's equipment or clothing on her journey to the light. The equipment or clothing can mean both protection … and help for the soul. With the vine's assistance, she can ascend and see the place of light."[1020] In another passage, Ryen again sees "the vine as a clothing for the soul… The vine is qua 'garment' a protection for the soul. The uprising soul is according to Mandaean tradition in need of protection against the evil planets and other demonized beings. The soul's clothing is here identified with a vine, which in its turn is said to have been established in the house of the 'Great, First Life.' The vine is according to this statement related in a special way to Life, and this gives the

---

1015 Originally, "Please as man with men t'appear, Jesus our Immanuel here" (J. Wesley, *et al.*, *Hymns*, p. 142).

1016 J. Wesley, *et al.*, *Hymns*, pp. 142-143, spelling, capitalization, and punctuation modernized.

1017 Moses 6:54.

1018 H. W. Nibley, *Teachings of the PGP*, p. 278. See Moses 6:55.

1019 S. H. Faulring, *et al.*, *Original Manuscripts*, pp. 101, 613.

1020 J. O. Ryen, *Mandaean Vine*, p. 109. See M. Lidzbarski, *Ginza*, GL 3:26, p. 551:16-19.

garment of the soul even greater importance… [T]he vine is here clearly a metaphor for the soul's protective clothing on her journey up to the Lightworld."[1021] It is also significant that in several texts the Mandaean liturgical equipment (wreath, staff, vestment, and possibly the myrtle) were said to have originated from mythic vines.[1022] Heavenly equipment of this sort was also bestowed on the dead at the culmination of their ascent.

The protection provided by the garment was accompanied by a promise of heavenly assistance. In this connection, Nibley cites the following passage from *Ginza*: "… when Adam stood praying for light and knowledge a helper came to him, gave him a garment, and told him, 'Those men who gave you the garment will assist you throughout your life until you are ready to leave earth.'"[1023]

4-67   The function of the skin garment was subsumed by the linen coat and breeches worn next to the skin by priests in the Tabernacle precincts at the time of Moses,[1024] purportedly in order "to avoid the shedding of animal blood."[1025] Moreover, as Brown observes, "The fine linen worn by heavenly beings is described as 'clean and white' or 'pure and white' and is therefore an appropriate symbol of worthiness or righteousness.[1026] Since linen is not the product of an animal that is subject unto death,[1027] or 'corruption' as it is called, it is also a fitting symbol of immortality, which is also called 'incorruption.'"[1028]

4-68   A related pattern is still preserved among Armenian Christians—first, the anointing with olive oil "in the different parts of the body," then baptism, then the dressing of the "new Adam," then, following prayer, an anointing with perfumed oil representing "the seal of the covenant."[1029]

Similar anointings are performed today by the Roman Catholic Church in the sacrament of Extreme Unction, more recently given the preferred name of the "Anointing of the Sick." The rite includes anointing of "the organs of the five external senses (eyes, ears, nostrils, lips, hands), of the feet, and, for men (where the custom exists and the condition of the patient permits of his being moved), of the loins or reins." In the Eastern Church, the "parts usually anointed are the forehead, chin, cheeks, hands, nostrils, and breast."[1030]

4-69   In fact, the title "Christ" is explained in Pseudo-Clement's *Recognitions* 1:45:2 as an anointing of oil from the Tree of Life: "Although indeed He was the Son of God, and the beginning of all things, He became man; Him first God anointed with oil which was taken from the wood of the Tree of Life: from that anointing therefore He is called Christ."[1031]

4-70   Cf. Ephrem the Syrian: "Adam put off his glory in a moment; ye have been clothed with glory in a moment."[1032]

4-71   The *Life of Adam and Eve* attests that at death Christians were to be dressed according to specific instructions in anticipation of this glorious resurrection.[1033]

4-72   Roper discusses the successive putting on of clothing as a metaphor for the accrual of glory by candidates for initiation in the Mandaean tradition. The action of clothing is associated with a testing process that includes a series of ritual handclasps:

1021 J. O. Ryen, *Mandaean Vine*, p. 85. See M. Lidzbarski, *Ginza*, GR 15:6, p. 317:32-36.

1022 J. O. Ryen, *Mandaean Vine*, pp. 250-252.

1023 H. W. Nibley, *Apocryphal*, p. 299. The German reads: "*Wie Adam dasteht und sich aufzuklären sucht, kam der Mann, sein Helfer. Der hohe Helfer kam zu ihm, der ihn in ein Stück reichen Glanzes hineintrug. Er sprach zu ihm: 'Ziehe dein Gewand an… Die Männer, die dein Gewand geschaffen, dienen dir, bis du abscheidest'*" (M. Lidzbarski, *Ginza*, GL 2:19, p. 488).

1024 See Exodus 39:27-28.

1025 R. Eisler, *Ièsous Basileus ou Basileusas*, 2:34, cited in H. W. Nibley, *Dominion*, p. 18.

1026 See Revelation 3:4-5; 15:6; 19:8.

1027 Philo, *Specialibus 1*, 84, p. 542.

1028 M. B. Brown, *Gate*, pp. 81-82. See 1 Corinthians 15:52-54.

1029 M. E. Stone, *Angelic Prediction*, p. 125. See also Stone's discussion of *2 Enoch* 22:8-9 (M. E. Stone, *Angelic Prediction*, pp. 126-127; cf. F. I. Andersen, *2 Enoch*, 22:8-9, pp. 138-139) and Nibley's discussion of the Egyptian rite of the Opening of the Mouth (H. W. Nibley, *Message 2005*, pp. 164-182). For a comprehensive survey of early and medieval baptismal liturgies, see B. D. Spinks, *Baptism*.

1030 P. J. Toner, *Extreme Unction*, p. 716. See also A. Villien, *Sacraments*, pp. 202-234.

1031 Pseudo-Clement, *Recognitions*, p. 89; cf. F. S. Jones, *Recognitions*, pp. 76-77.

1032 Ephrem the Syrian, *Epiphany*, 6:9, p. 274; cf. 13:1-22, p. 283.

1033 See *Commentary* 6:12-b, p. 483.

Both the *Ginza…* and the *Canonical Prayer-Book of the Mandaeans* describe how, upon death, the soul, leaving behind her mortal body, will ascend to the heavenly world of Light from which she originally came. As she ascends through the heavenly spheres, the soul must pass through a series of gates or "watch-houses" where the soul is detained and questioned and where the souls of the wicked and unprepared are punished. As it successfully passes each watch-house the soul dons a series of sacred vestments at each successful passage. "Garment on garment she putteth on, she arrayed herself in robe after robe…. She laugheth, rejoiceth, leapeth for joy, danceth, exulteth, and is overjoyed about the glorious splendor resting [upon her] and the glory that accrueth to her."[1034] This text continues, "And on she went and reached Abathur's house of detention, (Abathur), the Ancient, Lofty, Holy and Guarded one." Abathur is a powerful angel who guards the entrance into paradise. "There his scales are set up and spirits and souls are questioned before him as to their names, their signs, their blessing, their baptism and everything that is therewith."[1035]

4-73   In one of the *Hymns on Virginity*, Ephrem describes "the whole purpose of the Incarnation… as the restoration of Adam's original garment":[1036]

> Blessed are you whom they told among the trees,
> "We have found Him Who finds all,
> Who came to find Adam who was lost,
> and in the garment of light to return him to Eden."[1037]

Parallels between the Fall and the Atonement are brought out in one of Ephrem's *Hymns on the Nativity*:[1038]

> All these changes did the Merciful One make,
> stripping off glory and putting on a body;
> for He had devised a way to reclothe Adam
> in that glory which he had stripped off.
> He was wrapped in swaddling clothes,
> corresponding to Adam's leaves,
> He put on clothes
> in place of Adam's skins;
> He was baptized for Adam's sin,
> He was embalmed for Adam's death,
> He rose and raised Adam up in His glory.
> Blessed is He who descended,
> put Adam on and ascended.

4-74   The full words of Kierkegaard read:

> To love one's neighbor means, while remaining within the earthly distinctions allotted to one, essentially to will to exist equally for every human being without exception…. Consider for a moment the world which lies before you in all its variegated multiplicity; it is like looking at a play, only the plot is vastly more complicated. Every individual in this innumerable throng is by his differences a particular something; he exhibits a definiteness but essentially he is something other than this—but this we do not get to see here in life. Here we see only what role the individual plays and how he does it. It is like a play. But when the curtain falls, the one who played the king, and the one who played the beggar, and all the others—they are all quite alike, all one and the same: actors. And when in death the curtain falls on the stage of actuality (for it is a confused use of language if one speaks about the curtain being rolled up on the stage of the eternal at the time of death, because the eternal is no stage—it is truth), then they also are all one; they are human beings. All are that which they essentially were, something we did not see because of the difference

---

1034 E. S. Drower, *Prayerbook*, p. 44, cf. p. 45.

1035 M. Roper, *Adam*. See E. S. Drower, *Prayerbook*, p. 45. See also *Excursus 51: The Five Lost Things of the Temple*, p. 658. For discussions of sacred clothing in LDS, Jewish, Christian, and Muslim tradition, see C. E. Asay, *Garment*; M. B. Brown, *Girded*; M. B. Brown, *Gate*, pp. 80-88; E. R. Goodenough, *Light*, pp. 265-267, 326-329, 351, 366-367; E. R. Goodenough, *Dura Symbolism*, 9:126-128, 162-164; C. W. Griggs, *Evidences*; E. T. Marshall, *Garments*; H. W. Nibley, *Vestments*; B. T. Ostler, *Clothed*; S. D. Ricks, *Garment*; J. A. Tvedtnes, *Clothing*; J. W. Welch, et al., *Gammadia*; W. Williams, *Shadow*. See also the overview of Moses 4, pp. 234-240.

1036 S. Brock, in Ephrem the Syrian, *Paradise*, p. 68.

1037 Ephrem the Syrian, *Virginity*, 46:9, p. 331.

1038 23:13. See Ephrem the Syrian, *Paradise*, p. 69.

we see; they are human beings. The stage of art is like an enchanted world. But just suppose that some evening a common absent-mindedness confused all the actors so they thought they really were what they were representing. Would this not be, in contrast to the enchantment of art, what one might call the enchantment of an evil spirit, a bewitchment? And likewise suppose that in the enchantment of actuality (for we are, indeed, all enchanted, each one bewitched by his own distinctions) our fundamental ideas became confused so that we thought ourselves essentially to be the roles we play. Alas, but is this not the case? It seems to be forgotten that the distinctions of earthly existence are only like an actor's costume or like a travelling cloak and that every individual should watchfully and carefully keep the fastening cords of this outer garment loosely tied, never in obstinate knots, so that in the moment of transformation the garment can easily be cast off, and yet we all have enough knowledge of art to be offended if an actor, when he is supposed to cast off his disguise in the moment of transformation, runs out on the stage before getting the cords loose. But, alas, in actual life one laces the outer garment of distinction so tightly that it completely conceals the external character of this garment of distinction, and the inner glory of equality never, or very rarely, shines through, something it should do and ought to do constantly.[1039]

4-75   Currid discusses the ambivalence of the serpent motive in connection with the Egyptian context of the construction of the bronze serpent by Moses, which "signified blessing and curse. Those Hebrews who were bitten by the fiery serpents needed only to look to the bronze serpent and they would be healed. That was the blessing. However, the brass image also symbolized the destruction of Egypt (which had occurred during the Exodus plagues) and of those who wished to return to Egypt and her ways. That was the curse."[1040]

4-76   The fifteenth-century *Adamgirk* asks: "… if a good secret [or mystery[1041]] was in [the evil fruit], Why did [God] say not to draw near?"[1042] and then answers its own question implicitly. Simply put, the gift by which Adam and Eve would "become divine,"[1043] and for which the Tree of Knowledge constituted a part of the approach, was, as yet, "an unattainable thing [t]hat was not in its time."[1044] Though God intended Adam and Eve to advance in knowledge, Satan was condemned because he had acted unilaterally and preemptively, in the realization that introducing the fruit of the Tree of Knowledge to Adam and Eve under circumstances of disobedience would bring the consequences of the Fall upon them, putting them in a position of vulnerability and danger. Note that the knowledge itself was good—indeed it was absolutely necessary for their salvation—however, some kinds of knowledge are reserved to be revealed by God Himself "in his own time, and in his own way, and according to his own will." [1045] As Joseph Smith taught: "That which is wrong under one circumstance, may be, and often is, right under another."[1046] By way of analogy to the situation of Adam and Eve, recall that service in temples under conditions of worthiness is intended to bestow glory upon the participants, but, as taught in Levitical laws of purity, doing the same "while defiled by sin, was to court unnecessary danger, perhaps even death."[1047]

The message about the results of eating of one or the other tree is clear. In both cases, those who eat become "partakers of the divine nature"[1048]—the Tree of Life symbolizing the means by which eternal life is granted to the faithful, while the Tree of Knowledge enables those who ingest its fruit to become

---

1039 *Works of Love*, pp. 92-96 (SV XLL 86-91), cited in S. Kierkegaard, *Parables*, pp. 47-48.

1040 J. D. Currid, *Egypt*, p. 149.

1041 M. E. Stone, *Adamgirk*, p. 53 n. 108.

1042 *Ibid.*, 3:2:5, p. 53.

1043 *Ibid.*, 1:3:71, p. 101. Note, however, that this promise actually would be fulfilled through taking of the Tree of Life, not of the Tree of Knowledge as deceptively asserted here by Satan.

1044 *Ibid.*, 1:3:27, p. 96.

1045 D&C 88:68.

1046 J. Smith, Jr., *Documentary History*, 11 April 1842, 5:135. Continuing, the Prophet wrote: "A parent may whip a child, and justly, too, because he stole an apple; whereas if the child had asked for the apple, and the parent had given it, the child would have eaten it with a better appetite; there would have been no stripes; all the pleasure of the apple would have been secured, all the misery of stealing lost. This principle will justly apply to all of God's dealings with His children. Everything that God gives us is lawful and right; and it is proper that we should enjoy His gifts and blessings whenever and wherever He is disposed to bestow; but if we should seize upon those same blessings and enjoyments without law, without revelation, without commandment, those blessings and enjoyments would prove cursings and vexations" (*ibid.*).

1047 G. A. Anderson, *Perfection*, p. 129.

1048 2 Peter 1:4.

"as gods, knowing good and evil."[1049] The story of the Fall teaches, however, that eating of either tree in an unprepared state may bring disastrous consequences that can be reversed only through a divine plan of mercy that will enable them to overcome spiritual and physical death.

See Mettinger[1050] for a discussion of how, in Job 15:7-8, we are made to understand that the "wisdom of the first human being is the quality that was seized by the first man in the divine council. The situation is not one of eavesdropping. Rather, the first man supposedly had access to the divine assembly... [and] this wisdom was attained without divine authorization."

Though Satan seems to have been aware of what had been "done in *other* worlds,"[1051] Moses 4:6 makes it clear that he "knew not the mind of God" with respect to *this* one. Indeed, we might say that it was his very ignorance of God's designs that paved the way of knowledge for Adam and Eve. The Adversary intended to thwart God's plan by inducing their transgression, but instead unknowingly served as the required catalyst for the divinely-ordained exercise of human choice. In this set up for Satan, God had beat the Devil at his own game; in fact, we might say that He had out-tempted the great Tempter.

If, then, there was, as it seems we must assume, something different about this world as compared to the others Satan had known, what was it? Intriguingly, scripture mentions only one single respect in which this earth is unique, in contrast to all the other worlds belonging to the order of those created by Jesus Christ, namely that it was here, and here alone, that He wrought out His Atonement. Though LDS teachings affirm that all these many worlds shared the same Savior,[1052] they are also clear in asserting that it took place, once and for all, here on the Earth. Moreover, scripture tells us why this planet was singled out: it was the only one among His creations that would be wicked enough to crucify their own Savior.[1053]

Building on this line of thought, is it possible, as C. S. Lewis tried to imagine,[1054] that there are at least some other worlds, more enlightened than our own, on which the fruit of the Tree of Knowledge was not forbidden at the outset and on which there was no corresponding Fall? Certainly, Joseph Smith's teachings about "translated" beings who live on more glorious worlds in such a blessed state give hints of such ideas.[1055] Though any further speculation seems unwarranted, one conclusion, at least, seems compelling: Satan's shortsighted strategy can only be explained in terms of an effort to opportunistically exploit his discovery of certain differences between this world and the "other worlds" of which he had cognizance; and God's success in co-opting the Devil's strategy depended on Satan's ignorance of the ultimate purpose for these differences.

4-77   Judaism developed the principle of *hester panim* (= the hiding of the face) to describe the idea of a "temporary suspension of God's surveillance."[1056]

4-78   Flake elaborates:

> In the JST narrative, humans are by nature separate, not evil. "The Fall" is not a fall into evil, but into alienation. Adam and Eve's legacy is not to change human nature but, rather, to change the conditions under which that nature will be developed, that is, out of God's presence and in a world where "God gave unto man that he should act for himself. Wherefore, man could not act for himself save it should be that he was enticed by the one or the other,"[1057] according to the Book of Mormon.[1058]

4-79   Lewis expanded on this theme in *Perelandra*, the second work in his science fiction trilogy.[1059] As Downing explained:

1049 Moses 4:11; cf. Moses 4:28.
1050 T. N. D. Mettinger, *Eden*, pp. 90-92.
1051 H. W. Nibley, *Return*, p. 63, emphasis mine; cf. H. W. Nibley, *Gifts*, p. 92.
1052 See, e.g., D&C 76:41-42; J. Smith, Jr. (or W. W. Phelps), *A Vision*, 1 February 1843, stanzas 19-20, cited in L. E. Dahl, *Vision*, p. 298; D&C 88:51-61; J. Taylor, *Government*, 1852, pp. 76-77
1053 2 Nephi 10:3; Moses 7:36-37; J. F. Smith, Jr., *Signs*, 14 October 1942, p. 5.
1054 C. S. Lewis, *Perelandra*.
1055 J. Smith, Jr. *Teachings*, 5 October 1840, pp. 170-171.
1056 A. LaCocque, *Trial*, p. 84 n. 5.
1057 2 Nephi 2:16.
1058 K. Flake, *Translating Time*, p. 517.
1059 C. S. Lewis, *Perelandra*.

Maleldil [God] has decreed the floating islands to be the proper home of the king and queen of Perelandra, and he has forbidden them to dwell on the fixed land. At first thought, one would tend to associate a fixed land with absolutes, eternal truths, anchoring oneself in unchanging realities. And floating islands would connote the opposite—relativism, instability, being driven by the caprices of the moment. In the Epistle of James the doubter is described as being "like a wave of the sea driven with the wind and tossed"…[1060] But for Lewis the emphasis is not upon stability vs. instability but upon relinquishing control and accepting what is given. When Ransom[,the hero of the story,] wonders if Maleldil had told the king how the queen's temptation would turn out, the king answers, "He gave me no assurance. No fixed land. Always one must throw oneself into the wave."[1061]

4-80   "The Venerable Bede (672-735 CE) was an English monk most noted for his ecclesiastical history of England. He wrote a number of works in Latin, mostly Bible commentaries that were highly valued throughout the Middle Ages."[1062]

4-81   Though many Christians disparage the doctrine of original sin, "G. K. Chesterton affirmed it with equal insistence, adding the sardonic note that it is the only doctrine of the Christian faith that is empirically provable."[1063] See S. Taylor, *Broken-Mirror*, for a thoughtful discussion of original sin in LDS theology, and its relationship to Augustinian and Pelagian ideas.

4-82   Chesterton gives the following account of Blake's final hours:[1064]

His last sickness fell upon him very slowly, and he does not seem to have taken much notice of it. He continued perpetually his pictorial design; and as long as they were growing stronger he seems to have cared very little for the fact that he was growing weaker himself. One of the last designs he made was one of the strongest he ever made—the tremendous image of the Almighty bending forward, foreshortened in colossal perspective, to trace out the heavens with a compass. Nowhere else has he so well expressed his primary theistic ideas—that God, though infinitely gigantic, should be as solid as a giant. He had often drawn men form the life; not infrequently he had drawn his dead men from the life. Here, according to his own conception, he may be said to have drawn God from the life. When he had finished the portrait (which he made sitting up in his sick-bed) he called out cheerfully, "What shall I draw after that?" Doubtless he racked his brain for some superlative spirit or archangel which would not be a mere bathos after the other. His rolling eyes (those round lustrous eyes which one can always see roll in his painted portraits) fell on the old frail and somewhat ugly woman who had been his companion so long, and he called out, "Catherine, you have been an angel to me; I will draw you next." Throwing aside the sketch of God measuring the universe, he began industriously to draw a portrait of his wife, a portrait which is unfortunately lost, but which must have substantially resembled the remarkable sketch which a friend drew some months afterwards; the portrait of a woman at once plain and distinguished, with a face that is supremely humorous and at once harsh and kind. Long before that portrait was drawn, long before those months had elapsed, William Blake was dead.

Whatever be the explanation, it is quite certain that Blake had more positive joy on his death-bed than any other of the sons of Adam. One has heard of men singing hymns on their death-beds, in low plaintive voices. Blake was not at all like that on his death-bed: the room shook with his singing. All his songs were in praise of God, and apparently new: all his songs were songs of innocence. Every now and then he would stop and cry out to his wife, "Not mine! Not mine!" in a sort of ecstatic explanation. He truly seemed to wait for the opening of the door of death as a child waits for the opening of the cupboard on his birthday. He genuinely and solemnly seemed to hear the hoofs of the horses of death as a baby hears on Christmas Eve the reindeer hooves of Santa Claus. He was in his last moments in that wonderful world of whiteness in which white is still a color. He would have clapped his hands at a white snowflake and sung as at the white wings of an angel at the moment when he himself turned suddenly white with death.

A little later, George Richmond included the following in a letter:

He died on Sunday night at 6 o'clock in a most glorious manner. He said he was going to that Country he had all his life wished to see and expressed himself happy, hoping for salvation through Jesus Christ. Just before he died his countenance became fair. His eyes brightened and he burst out into singing of the things he saw in heaven.[1065]

1060 James 1:6.
1061 D. C. Downing, *Planets*, p. 91. See C. S. Lewis, *Perelandra*, p. 181.
1062 J. A. Tvedtnes, *et al.*, *Traditions*, p. 213. See *Bibliography*, p. 843.
1063 Cited in A. Jacobs, *Original Sin*, p. x.
1064 G. K. Chesterton, *William Blake*, pp. 66, 69-70.
1065 Cited in P. Ackroyd, *Blake*, p. 389.

FIGURE 5-1. *The Offering of Abel and Cain, 1425-1429*
Jan van Eyck, ca. 1395-1441

And the Lord had respect unto Abel, and to his offering; But unto Cain, and to his offering, he had not respect (Moses 5:20-21). This carefully conceived scene, executed in grisaille to decorate the top of a niche containing a portrait of Adam, is part of a set of large altarpiece panel paintings in the *Joost Vijdt* chapel in the Cathedral of St. Bavon at Ghent, Belgium. The portrayal of Abel lifting up the lamb "prefigures both the sacrifice of Christ and the Eucharist" (E. Kren, *et al.*, *Ghent*). The contrasting choices of Cain and Abel with respect to their covenantal obligations typify the parting of the ways of righteousness and wickedness that begins in Moses 5. Of those who followed the latter, Jude wrote: "Woe unto them! For they have gone in the way of Cain" (Jude 1:11).

MOSES 5

The Two Ways

Overview

NOT long after the departure of Oliver Cowdery for Fayette, New York in early August 1830, Joseph Smith wrote: "I began to arrange and copy the revelations which we had received from time to time; in which I was assisted by John Whitmer,[1] who now resided with me."[2] The heading that prefaces the section of the JST corresponding to Moses 5:1-6:52 reads "Chapter Second—A Revelation concerning Adam after he had been driven out of the Garden of Eden."[3]

While the importance of the account of the Creation and the Fall in Moses 1-4 cannot be overstated, a careful reading of Moses 5-8 is required to see the prior material in its overall context.[4] Reeves observes:

> Most modern students of Bible fail to discern the pivotal significance which [the tale of Cain and Abel] plays in the present narrative structure of Genesis because of the enormous religious significance with which ancient, medieval, and modern Christian interpreters have invested the immediately preceding story of Adam and Eve in the Garden. The subsequent Cain and Abel affair is homiletically reduced to an afterthought cast under the dark shadow of human hubris and disobedience to God. But I would like to suggest that while admittedly the episode of disobedience in the Garden was not a good thing, the story of Cain and Abel introduces something far worse into the created order; namely, the "corruption" and "bloodshed" of which the Qur'anic angels speak.[5] It represents a critical turning point in antediluvian history, and is (from the point of view of the final redactor of Genesis) the key crime which leads ineluctably to the Flood.[6]

Happily, however, the story of Adam and Eve and their family found in Moses 5 "is not an account of sin alone but the beginning of a drama about becoming a being who fully

---

1   See *Endnote 5-1,* p. 432.

2   J. Smith, Jr., *Documentary History,* July 1830, 1:104. Whitmer transcribed the remainder of Moses 5 and portions of Moses 6 on two occasions: October 21 (Moses 5:43-51) and November 30 (Moses 5:52-6:18). See S. H. Faulring, *et al., Original Manuscripts,* p. 57.

3   S. H. Faulring, *et al., Original Manuscripts,* p. 92.

4   C. Westermann, *Genesis 1-11,* pp. 2-3.

5   See M. M. Ali, *Qur'an,* 2:30, p. 17; cf. Moses 6:15, 8:28.

6   J. C. Reeves, *Flowing Stream.* See *Endnote 5-2,* p. 432.

reflects God's very own image. Genesis is not only about the origins of sin; it is also about the foundations of human perfection. The work that God has begun in Creation He will bring to completion.... [E]arly Jewish and Christian readers [were] aware of this while most of their modern counterparts have not been."[7] The clarity with which the fundamental doctrines, laws, and ordinances of the Gospel begin to unfold in Moses 5 fully justifies Nibley in calling it "the greatest of all chapters" in scripture.[8]

Consistent with the overall developmental themes of perfection and corruption throughout the remainder of the book of Moses, chapter 5 is structured into a series of stories highlighting the contrast between those who would and would not hearken to the voice of God.[9] We read the record of Adam and Eve's obedience to the "second commandments"[10] given after the Fall and of the angel's explanation of the law of sacrifice.[11] We also are provided with an extended account of how, with the tragedy of Cain and Abel,[12] "the rebellion in the heavens was transmitted to a rebellion on the earth."[13] Following the brief genealogies of the posterity of Cain,[14] we encounter the story of Lamech's rise to the pinnacle of wickedness through the murder of his rivals,[15] an account that foreshadows the sad notice of the complete parting of the ways between the righteous and the wicked.[16]

Moses 5 fills in many details that are missing from Genesis, such as the reason why Cain's offering was rejected,[17] and the fact that there were descendants born to Adam and Eve prior to Cain and Abel.[18] It was from among these descendants that Cain chose a wife[19]— and, later, it was from among these same family members he had reason to fear vengeance for his crime against Abel.[20] Sarna argues that many details of this sort were no doubt originally contained in an independent narrative, of which the traditional text of Genesis preserves only the "bare bones of the story."[21] Thus, it is not surprising that valuable text and commentary relating to themes missing in Genesis but found in the book of Moses have survived in fragmentary form within Jewish, Islamic, early Christian, and other sources— though, not unexpectedly, seemingly genuine ancient material is mixed with material of more dubious provenance.[22] Robinson summarizes some of the significant parallels between such literature and the prophetic additions to Genesis provided in the book of Moses:

> Among the extracanonical themes found in the writings of Joseph Smith—themes confirmed to be ancient ones in light of the literature discovered only after his death—are the heavenly messengers, the raising of Adam, Adam's detection of Satan disguised as an angel of light (a false messenger), the promise to Adam of a coming Savior, the gathering of Adam's righteous posterity to receive his final blessing or testament, and Adam's prediction of future world history. In addition, the doctrine of the two Adams—the divine, heavenly Adam and the

---

7   G. A. Anderson, *Perfection*, p. 8. See *Endnote 5-3*, p. 432.

8   H. W. Nibley, *Teachings of the PGP*, 19, p. 231.

9   See Moses 5:16, 17, 23, 57.

10   Alma 12:37. See also Alma 12:29-35.

11   Moses 5:1-12.

12   Moses 5:13-41.

13   J. Taylor, *Mediation*, 1882, p. 68; J. Taylor, *Gospel Kingdom*, 1882, p. 101.

14   Moses 5:42-46.

15   Moses 5:47-54.

16   Moses 5:55-59.

17   Moses 5:18-26.

18   Moses 5:2.

19   Moses 5:28.

20   Moses 5:39.

21   N. M. Sarna, *Genesis*, p. 31. See *Endnote 5-4*, p. 432.

22   S. E. Robinson, *Lying*. See *Excursus 29: The Development of Extracanonical Literature on Adam and Eve*, p. 601.

created, earthly Adam—found in many of the ancient traditions but mostly unknown to scholars until around the turn of the century, may have some application to certain cryptic remarks of Brigham Young on the subject of our primal ancestor....[23]

It is… remarkable that Joseph Smith could reconstruct the main outlines of the ancient extra-canonical Adam literature without benefit of acquaintance with the pseudepigrapha known to us in the twentieth century.[24]

The Many Roles of Adam

Though surprisingly little is said about Adam and Eve[25] in the Old Testament outside of the first chapters of Genesis,[26] other works of scripture further describe their crucial roles in helping to carry out the Plan of Salvation.[27] We also have accounts of two discourses by Joseph Smith where he focused on the figure of Adam, with particular emphasis on his responsibilities with respect to certain priesthood keys and his "standing as head of the human family." Teachings from these discourses, given 2 July 1839 and 5 October 1840, illuminate some of Adam's many roles and assignments:

- *Adam is Michael the Archangel.* "He is Michael the Archangel, spoken of in the Scriptures."[28]

- *Adam was placed at the head of the organization of premortal spirits.* "The Father called all his spirits before Him at the creation of man, and organized them. He (Adam) is the head, and was told to multiply."[29]

- *Adam held the keys of the Presidency from generation to generation.* "The Priesthood was first given to Adam: he obtained the First Presidency, and held the keys of it from generation to generation. He obtained it in the Creation, before the world was formed, as in Genesis 1:26, 27, 28. He had dominion given him over every living creature."[30]

- *Adam is the "Ancient of Days," and the first to whom priesthood ordinances were revealed.* "Adam, who was the first man,… [or] 'Ancient of Days,'[31] or in other words, the first and oldest of all, the great, grand progenitor of whom it is said in another place he is Michael, because he was the first and father of all, not only by progeny, but the first to hold the spiritual blessings, to whom was made known the plan of ordinances for the salvation of his posterity unto the end, and to whom Christ was first revealed, and through whom Christ has been revealed from heaven, and will continue to be revealed from henceforth."[32] "That he received revelations, commandments and ordinances at the beginning is beyond the power of controversy; else how did they begin to offer sacrifices to God in an acceptable manner? And if they offered sacrifices they must be authorized by ordination."[33]

- *Adam blessed his posterity in Adam-ondi-Ahman.* "I saw Adam in the valley of Adam-ondi-Ahman. He called together his children and blessed them with a patriarchal blessing. The Lord appeared in their midst, and he (Adam) blessed them all and foretold what should

---

23   See *Excursus 30: Adam-God Theory and the Heavenly and Earthly Adam,* p. 603.
24   S. E. Robinson, *Book of Adam,* p. 147. See *Endnote 5-5,* p. 433.
25   See *Endnote 5-6,* p. 433.
26   See *Endnote 5-7,* p. 433.
27   E.g. Romans 5:14; 1 Corinthians 15:22; Jude 1:9; Revelation 12:7; 2 Nephi 2; Alma 12, 42; D&C 27:11, 29:26, 78:16, 84:16, 88:112, 107:54, 116:1, 117:8, 128:21, 137:5, 138:38. See also *Excursus 23: The Roles of Christ, Adam, and Michael,* p. 582.
28   J. Smith, Jr., *Teachings,* 2 July 1839, p. 157. See *Endnote 5-8,* p. 433.
29   *Ibid.,* p. 157. See *Endnote 5-9,* p. 433.
30   See *Endnote 5-10,* p. 433.
31   See *Endnote 5-11,* p. 434.
32   J. Smith, Jr., *Teachings,* 5 October 1840, p. 167.
33   *Ibid.,* 5 October 1840, pp. 168-169

FIGURE 5-2. *The Archangel Michael Subduing Satan, 1518*
Raffaello Sanzi (Raphael), 1483-1520

SEE COLOR PLATE 5-2.

For Michael shall fight their battles, and shall overcome him who seeketh the throne of him who sitteth upon the throne, even the Lamb.[1] To the story of Michael as a triumphant warrior in the premortal war in heaven, the Doctrine and Covenants adds a prophecy that he will lead angelic armies against the host of Satan in a final battle following the Millennium.[2]

As a symbol of the temporarily renewed relationship between France and the Church—and of the pontiff's campaign for a joint expedition against the Turks—Pope Leo X commissioned this painting for the French king Francis I, the grandmaster of the *Order of St. Michael*.[3] Middleton writes: "Raphael… 'the prince of painters' is considered by many, and with some justification, to be the greatest painter who ever lived… One of Raphael's last works, the present painting anticipates the high baroque in its turbulent movement and vivid coloration, and set the standard pattern for depictions of this celestial event for the next four hundred years."[4]

---

1   D&C 88:15.
2   D&C 88:110-116.
3   Musée du Louvre, *Saint Michel*.
4   J. Middleton, *Michael*.

befall them to the latest generation. This is why Adam blessed his posterity: he wanted to bring them into the presence of God. They looked for a city, etc., 'whose builder and maker is God.'"[34]

- *By Adam's authority, the priesthood keys are revealed.* "The keys [of the Priesthood] have to be brought from heaven whenever the Gospel is sent. When they are revealed from heaven, it is by Adam's authority."[35] "[God] set the ordinances to be the same forever and ever, and set Adam to watch over them, to reveal them from heaven to man, or to send angels to reveal them. 'Are they not all ministering spirits, sent forth to minister for them who shall be heirs of salvation?'[36] These angels are under the direction of Michael or Adam, who acts under the direction of the Lord."[37]

- *Others will give account of their stewardship to Adam, and Adam will give account to Christ.* "Christ is the Great High Priest; Adam next."[38] "The keys were… given… by him to others. He will have to give an account of his stewardship, and they to him."[39] "This, then, is the nature of the Priesthood; every man holding the Presidency of his dispensation, and one man holding the Presidency of them all, even Adam; and Adam receiving his Presidency and authority from the Lord, but cannot receive a fulness until Christ shall present the Kingdom to the Father, which shall be at the end of the last dispensation."[40]

---

34   J. Smith, Jr., *Teachings*, 2 July 1839, pp. 158-159; Hebrews 11:10; cf. J. Smith, Jr., *Teachings*, 18 December 1833, pp. 38-39; *Excursus 38: The Meaning of "Adam-ondi-Ahman"*, p. 622; *Excursus 39: The Location of Adam-ondi-Ahman*, p. 623; and *Excursus 40: Dating Joseph Smith's Vision of Adam-ondi-Ahman*, p. 625. See *Endnote 5-12*, p. 434.
35   J. Smith, Jr., *Teachings*, 2 July 1839, p. 157; cf. K. Rudolph, *Coptic*, GL 3:43, p. 270.
36   Hebrews 1:14.
37   J. Smith, Jr., *Teachings*, 5 October 1840, p. 168.
38   *Ibid.*, 2 July 1839, p. 158.
39   *Ibid.*
40   *Ibid.*, 5 October 1840, p. 169.

- *Adam will hold a council to prepare his posterity for the second coming of Christ.* "Father Adam, Michael… will call his children together and hold a council with them to prepare them for the coming of the Son of Man. He (Adam) is the father of the human family, and presides over the spirits of all men, and all that have had the keys must stand before him in this grand council. This may take place before some of us leave this stage of action. The Son of Man stands before him, and there is given him glory and dominion. Adam delivers up his stewardship to Christ, that which was delivered to him as holding the keys of the universe, but retains his standing as head of the human family."[41]

As a supplement to the wealth of extrabiblical material available in LDS scripture, Robinson notes that the "figure of Adam was long a favorite with the authors of both Jewish and Christian apocryphal and pseudepigraphal literature."[42] He writes:

There was a rich tradition of Adam literature in ancient Judaism and early Christianity.[43] The interest in Adam and the focus on his experiences both before and after the Fall were much more intense during those earlier periods of history than in the modern world generally, where the figure of the primal ancestor has lost its normative character. Perhaps as a result of that loss of interest, many of the ancient books attributed to or associated with Adam have not survived, among them the *Book of Adam*, the *Book of the Generations of Adam*, the *Testament of the Protoplasts*, the other *Apocalypse(s) of Adam*, and the *Book of the Daughters of Adam*.

Among the Latter-day Saints, however, the figure of Adam largely retains its normative character. In this sense, the Latter-day Saints are closer to the ancient world and to the early Church than are most of our contemporaries. Indeed, the Latter-day Saint temple endowment may be said in some sense to be our own "Book of Adam and Eve," and functions in the Latter-day Church in precisely the same way that extracanonical Adam literature functioned in ancient Judaism and early Christianity.[44]

Robinson summarizes some of the reasons why the life of Adam has been the natural focus for temple ritual, both inside and outside of LDS tradition:

As the first created one, the protoplast, Adam served as a revelator of the mysteries of Creation and of the natural order of the universe. As the first human being, he stood as the archetypical exemplar of the human condition and of man in his quest for and relationship with God. As the… common ancestor, all human experience was conveniently subsumed under the experience of Adam in the beginning.[45]

Commenting on the function served by dramatic presentations of the Fall in medieval mystery plays, Auerbach makes a distinction that bears on the experience of LDS temple worship: "In contrast to the feudal literature of the courtly romance, which leads away from the reality of the life of its class into a world of heroic fable and adventure, here there is a movement in the opposite direction, from distant legend and its figural interpretation into everyday contemporary reality."[46] Of the relationship between Adam's experiences and our own, Nibley writes:

Let us consider our Adam. What kind of being is he? The same kind as ourselves—but what is that? He plays a surprising number of roles, each with a different persona, a different name, a different environment, a different office and calling: (1) he was a member of the presidency

---

41 *Ibid.*, 2 July 1839, p. 157.
42 S. E. Robinson, *Testament of Adam*, p. 3.
43 See *Endnote 5-13*, p. 434.
44 S. E. Robinson, *Book of Adam*, pp. 146-147.
45 S. E. Robinson, *Testament of Adam*, p. 3.
46 E. Auerbach, *Mimesis*, pp. 158-159. See *Endnote 5-14*, p. 434.

when the earth project was being discussed; (2) he was on the committee of inspection that came down from time to time to check up on the operation; (3) then he changed his name and nature to live upon the earth, but it was a very different earth from any we know; it had to be a garden place specifically prepared for him. (4) When he left that paradise, he changed his nature again and for the first time began to reckon the passing of time by our measurements, becoming a short-lived creature subject to death. (5) In this condition, he began to receive instructions from heavenly mentors on how to go about changing his condition and status, entering into a covenant that completely changed his mentality and way of life... The man Adam passes from one state of being to another, and so do we: "as we have borne the image of the earthly, we shall also bear the image of the heavenly."[47] (6) In time he died and became a spirit being, the head of all his spirit children in the waiting place, according to common Christian tradition as well as our own. (7) Then he became, after Christ, the firstfruits of the resurrection and returned triumphantly to his first and second estates (8) to go on to glory and eternal lives. In these seven or eight Adams, we have another fundamental teaching that sets Mormonism off... [Rather than a one-act drama, we] see an ongoing epic of many episodes, each one a play in itself—a dispensation.[48]

The Doctrine of the Two Ways

Relating the themes of opposition and agency that are portrayed in the life of Adam and Eve and enacted in our own, Nibley frequently wrote about "the inescapable choice between Two Ways."[49] Although this theme is Jewish,[50] says Allison, "it is also Greek; the motif indeed belongs to world-wide moral tradition."[51] Nibley explains:

> No teaching is more frequently met with nor more emphatically brought home in the earliest Christian literature than the famous doctrine of the "Two Ways," which proclaims that there lie before every human being and before the church itself two roads between which a choice must be made. The one is the road of darkness, the way of evil; the other, the way of light. Every man must choose between the two every day of his life; that choosing is the most important thing he does, and the two ways, good and evil are absolutely essential to God's plan. There is nothing weak or vicious in the arrangement, for every man is clearly given to understand that as he chooses so he will be judged. He will be judged by God in the proper time and place. Meantime he must be free, perfectly free, to choose his own way.[52]

> None may commit his decision to the judgment of a faction, a party, a leader, or a nation; none can delegate his free agency to another. "Thou shalt not follow a multitude to do evil."[53] We cannot protest innocence on the grounds of having been given bad advice, doing what we did for the best interests of the country, doing only what others were doing, or being forced to do it by the need to check and frustrate a nefarious enemy....

> It is easy to imagine absolutes, and to think and argue in terms of absolutes, as the theologians have always done: Good and evil, light and darkness, hot and cold, black and white—we know exactly what they are; but in the real world we rarely experience the pure thing—our own experience lies between. Yet standing on that middle ground, we are faced with absolute decisions. It is not where we stand, says Ezekiel,[54] that makes us good or evil in God's eyes—no

---

47   1 Corinthians 15:49.
48   H. W. Nibley, *Before Adam*, p. 77.
49   H. W. Nibley, *Prophetic*, p. 462. See also J. W. Welch, *Sermon*, pp. 47, 75; J. W. Welch, *Light*, pp. 173-174, 187, 218. See *Endnote 5-15*, p. 434.
50   See, e.g., Deuteronomy 30:19. An early Christian dictum held that "there is no third term" (*tertium non datur*) or, we might say, "there is no other way" (A. LaCocque, *Trial*, p. 71).
51   D. C. Allison, *Testament*, p. 242.
52   H. W. Nibley, *Liberty*, pp. 184-185; cf. H. W. Nibley, *Consecration*, p. 435.
53   Exodus 23:2.
54   Ezekiel 18:19-28.

one has reached the top or bottom in this short life—but the direction in which we are facing. There we have only two choices. The road up and the road down are the same, says Heracleitus. It all depends on the way you are facing. You are taking either the up-road or the down-road; there is no third way, for if you try to compromise and go off at an angle, you will never reach either goal. You are either repenting or not repenting, and that is, according to the scriptures, the whole difference between being righteous or being wicked.[55]

By means of this "doctrine of probation," it is continually demonstrated "that the embattled hosts on earth [are] but a local version of the war in heaven."[56] The most astonishing aspect of it is that although "'[t]he devil is an enemy unto God, and fighteth against him continually,'[57]... God permits it! He has expressly allowed Satan, the common enemy, to try men and to tempt them—that is the whole point of the thing; men must be exposed to both influences so each can make his own choice."[58] "'To these two ways all the children of men are born,'" says the *Rule of the Community* (*Manual of Discipline*) from Qumran, "'and to these two divisions they are heirs; every one of them each in his generation, and in his time every man shares more or less in both of them.'[59] The whole human race, 'all kinds of their spirits and their natures'[60] are put to the same test, each in his own dispensation, 'until the final appointed end-time.'"[61]

The Way of Satan

As an illustration of the pull of the downward way, Nibley succinctly summarizes the stock story of Satan's efforts to supplant God's plan of dominion with his own—a sequence of scenes that has been replayed countless times since Adam and Eve left the Garden of Eden:

> The story is told not only of Adam but of the other great patriarchs as well. Noah was confronted by the same party with the same proposition while he was working in his garden after the Flood.[62] Abraham too had an Eden and an altar, and while he was once calling upon God in prayer, Satan suddenly showed up with an insolent, "Here I am!" and proceeded with his sales pitch.[63] Moses like Christ was tempted on a mountain, by the same person and with the same proposal: "If thou wilt worship me, all shall be thine."[64] Adam is thus only the first; the elements of the story that follow are found in various combinations among the many texts of the growing Adam literature that is coming to light in our generation. The texts often take dramatic form indicative of ritual origin.[65]

> As Adam was praying one day, runs the story, a distinguished gentleman appeared on the scene and engaged him in conversation... [H]e was well-dressed, and came to Adam with "cunning and smooth talk, as a true friend genuinely concerned for his welfare."[66] He began with some harmless generalities — the weather and the scenery: it was, he observed, a most

---

55   H. W. Nibley, *Prophetic*, pp. 462-463. See *Endnote 5-16*, p. 434.
56   H. W. Nibley, *Expanding 1992*, p. 195.
57   Moroni 7:12.
58   H. W. Nibley, *Prophetic*, p. 461. See *Endnote 5-17*, p. 435.
59   *1QS 4:15-16.*
60   *1QS 3:13-14.*
61   *1QS 4:25.* H. W. Nibley, *Expanding 1992*, pp. 197-198. See *Instruction on the Two Spirits, Rule of the Community, 1QS 3:13-4:25* in F. G. Martinez, *DSS Translated*, pp. 6-8; H. W. Nibley, *Message 2005*, pp. 465-467; G. Vermes, *Complete*, pp. 101-103. See also *The Two Ways, 4Q473* in G. Vermes, *Complete*, p. 443
62   M. J. B. bin Gorion, *et al., Mimekor*, 13, 1:24; J. Neusner, *Genesis Rabbah 2*, 36:3, p. 29.
63   D. C. Allison, *Testament*, 16:6-10, pp. 319, 328-331; L. Ginzberg, *Legends*, 1:270-272; E. P. Sanders, *Testament of Abraham*, 16:6-10, p. 892; cf. M. J. B. bin Gorion, *et al., Mimekor*, 22, 1:58-59
64   Moses 1:12-19; Luke 4:9.
65   See *Endnote 5-18*, p. 435.
66   K. Kohler, *Jewish Quarterly Review* 7, 1895, p. 589. See also D. C. Allison, *Testament*, 16:5, pp. 319, 328; E. P. Sanders, *Testament of Abraham*, 16:5, p. 892.

FIGURE 5-3. *How the Devil Deceived Eve, early 14th century*
Lutwin

When eighteen days of their weeping were completed, then Satan took on the form of a Cherub with splendid attire, and went to the Tigris river to deceive Eve.[1] The illustration comes from the only existing copy of *Eva und Adam*, a mid-15th-century manuscript in the National Library in Vienna, whose original by the otherwise unknown Lutwin was probably written in the early 14th century. The Middle High German text was composed in the form of poetry, and is thought to be based on an unidentified Latin source incorporating elements "not included in any of the known versions of the *Vita Adae et Evae*."[2] In the drawing, the raised earth next to the water represents the Garden of Eden (often described in similar texts as being "high above the earth"[3]) from which Adam and Eve have been expelled. The Tree of Life and the Tree of Knowledge both stand in the center of the Garden with their branches intertwined.[4]

According to Lutwin: "Eve stood in the water for eighteen days doing her penance without a word (to anybody) while fasting with pitiful lamentation. Then Satan roused himself, for he was sorry to see anything good being achieved, for that was not in accordance with his false counsel. He had transformed his horrible appearance into that of an angel of light and, on seeing her weeping in the water, asked:[5] 'Eve, why are you crying? Now you must no longer lament, for God has taken heed of your penance. This very moment I am to return you to the place where you were banished, and all will be well with you as it was before. You need no longer do penance, for we angels have requested this of God…' With that the Devil offered her his hand and then helped her out of the water and onto the bank."[6] The text just above the illustration rubric comments: "*Dis was ir ander myssetat*" ("This was her second[7] mistake"[8]). Lutwin continues: "[T]he Devil in angel's clothing led Eve by the hand (to the place) where she found Adam, who with heartfelt contrition was standing in the Jordan as a penance. The same wicked spirit, the sum of all that is evil, had thought that with his false lies he could betray Adam as he had Eve. Adam, however, was so wise that… he recognized his dissimulation… at once."[9]

In response to Adam's query to Satan as to why he was so intent on troubling them, the Devil replied with the story of his refusal to bow down with the other angels in homage to the first created man as the "image of God."[10] Then "Adam, sighing, turned to heaven. He prayed: 'Creator, sweet God, everything that heaven and earth contain is under your command; in your mercy drive from me this evil spirit who alienates me from you. Give me the joy and the status which he lost in heaven.[11] This I ask of you, Lord, grant me this through your goodness and in your honour.' After these words the Devil vanished."[12] Adam's upraised arm is "a gesture of both speech and action"[13] that could be taken as an oath-, covenant-, or prayer-related movement,[14] a warning for Eve,[15] and/or an attempt to repel Satan.[16]

1   G. A. Anderson, *et al.*, *Synopsis*, Armenian 9:1, p. 11E.
2   Latin *Life of Adam and Eve*; M.-B. Halford, *Eva und Adam*, p. 37; cf. p. 95.
3   M. E. Stone, *Selections*, p. 188. See also M. D. Gibson, *Rolls 1901*, p. 112.
4   See *Commentary* 3:9-h, p. 167; *Excursus 25: The Tree of Life as the Hidden Throne of God*, p. 591; and *Excursus 50: Fu Xi and Nü Gua*, p. 654. Cf. Wahb bin Munabbih in al-Tabari, *Creation*, 1:106, p. 277; B. M. Wheeler, *Prophets*, p. 23.
5   The *Life of Adam and Eve* says this was done with "weeping and… false tears dripping down on his garment and from his garment down to the ground" (G. A. Anderson, *et al.*, *Synopsis*, Georgian 9:2, p. 11E; cf. S. C. Malan, *Adam and Eve*, 1:60, p. 70).
6   M.-B. Halford, *Eva und Adam*, pp. 255-256; cf. M. Herbert, *Irish Apocrypha*, pp. 9-10.
7   Or "other."
8   Line 1310, M.-B. Halford, *Eva und Adam*, pp. 146, 260.
9   *Ibid.*, p. 259; cf. M. Herbert, *Irish Apocrypha*, p. 10; D&C 128:20, 129:4-7; *Commentary* 1:12-d, p. 53.
10   See the overview of Moses 4, p. 224 and *Excursus 23: The Roles of Christ, Adam, and Michael*, p. 582.
11   See the overview of Moses 4, p. 225 and *Excursus 21: The Power and Premortal Status of Satan*, p. 575.
12   M.-B. Halford, *Eva und Adam*, p. 262.
13   P. H. Jolly, *Eve and Adam*, p. 14.
14   S. D. Ricks, *Oaths*, pp. 49-50; J. W. Wevers, *Notes*, p. 200. Note that in one source, before her penance, Eve is instructed by Adam: "Raise your hand toward the Lord" (M. Herbert, *Irish Apocrypha*, p. 9).
15   S. E. Robinson, *Book of Adam*, p. 142.
16   Cyril of Jerusalem, *Five*, 19:2, 4, pp. 144-145; H. W. Nibley, *Message 2005*, 1:2, 4, p. 516. See *Commentary* 5:29-a, p. 377 and *Excursus 21: The Power and Premortal Status of Satan*, p. 575.

glorious and beautiful world. This, however, by way of leading up to his next point, which was that he happened to be the owner and proprietor of it all.[67] Yes sir, as far as the eye could see it was all his, and he tolerated no nonsense in it: nobody dared make trouble where he was in charge. This was all hokum, of course; "Satan never owned the earth; he never made a particle of it," said Brigham Young, "his labor is not to create, but to destroy."[68] But to demonstrate his authority, when three strangers (usually described as angels)[69] appeared on the scene at this moment, he at once challenged them as trespassers, asking them if they had any money. He explained to Adam that everything in his world could be had for money,[70] and then got down to business. For the fellow was all business, a person of integrity, ready to keep his part of an agreement (the agreement always turns out to be a trap for the other party), pious and God-fearing,[71] dedicated to hard work — he works, in fact, "like a demon." He was there to offer Adam the chance of a lifetime to buy in on a scheme that would give him anything he wanted in this world. It was an ingenious and simple self-financing operation in which one would buy power with wealth and then more wealth with the power, until one might end up owning and controlling everything. The initial capital? It was right under their feet! You begin by taking the treasures of the earth, and by exchanging them for the services of important people in key positions; you end up running everything your way. What if your rule is one of blood and terror? Better to rule in hell, as Milton's Satan puts it, than to be ruled in heaven![72]

The most widely-known extracanonical account of Adam and Eve's experiences after they leave the Garden of Eden is the *Life of Adam and Eve* (hereafter *Life*), which exists in Greek, Latin, Armenian, and Georgian recensions[73] as well as in several later texts derived in part from it.[74] A major theme of this series of stories concerns the unsuccessful attempts of Satan to deceive Adam and Eve, who become increasingly immune to his wiles through the knowledge and protective power provided by angelic teachings, covenants, and ordinances.

For example, the *Life* tells of how Adam, following his transgression and expulsion from Eden, spent forty days of penance standing in the Jordan River[75]—the same river that Christ would be baptized in, and the same period of time that Catholics (including candidates for baptism) traditionally spend in prayer and fasting during Lent.[76] Likewise, Eve is said to have agreed to spend thirty-seven days in the Tigris River. During Eve's penance, Satan appears as an angel of light to persuade her to leave the river prematurely. Robinson notes the significant warning that Adam had previously given her: "'Take great care of thyself. Except thou seest me and all my tokens,[77] depart not out of the water, nor trust in the words, which are said to thee, lest thou fall again into the snare.' Thus, properly equipped, Eve does not succumb to Satan the second time, according to the Slavonic version."[78]

67   G. A. Anderson, *et al.*, *Synopsis*, 33/34.1-35/37.1, p. 6E.

68   B. Young, *31 July 1864*, p. 320.

69   See references in H. W. Nibley, *Since*, pp. 460-461. See *Endnote 5-19*, p. 435.

70   Cf. R. A. Kraft, *Job*, 23:3b, p. 45: "Pay the price and take what you want." See also R. A. Kraft, *Job*, 6-7, pp. 27-29; H. W. Nibley, *Prayer Circle*, p. 63; H. W. Nibley, *Consecration*, p. 439. See *Endnote 5-20*, p. 435.

71   See *Endnote 5-21*, p. 435.

72   H. W. Nibley, *Dominion*, pp. 13-14; cf. J. Milton, *Paradise Lost*, 1:261, p. 22. See *Endnote 5-22*, p. 435.

73   G. A. Anderson, *et al.*, *Synopsis*.

74   E.g., E. A. W. Budge, *Cave*; S. C. Malan, *Adam and Eve*.

75   See *Endnote 5-23*, p. 435.

76   G. A. Anderson, *et al.*, *Synopsis*, pp. 8-9; M. D. Johnson, *Life*, 6:1-8:3, pp. 258, 260; cf. Moses 6:52-68 and *Commentary 5:6-a*, p. 360. See *Endnote 5-24*, p. 436.

77   In another version of the story, Adam implies that Eve was to wait in the water until "an angel of God" came to bring her out (M. Herbert, *Irish Apocrypha*, p. 10).

78   S. E. Robinson, *Book of Adam*, p. 142. See also B. T. Ostler, *Clothed*, p. 6.

FIGURE 5-4. *The Bond of Adam, after a Church Mural in Voronet, Moldavia, 1547*

The Devil said, 'I will not permit you to till the earth, unless you sign a cheirograph, pledging that you belong to me'[1] The story of the *Cheirograph* begins when the Devil claims ownership of the earth and accuses Adam of trespassing. "In this remarkable image," part of the unique iconographical programme of four churches in North Moldavia, the robed Adam kneels before the naked Satan and "dutifully signs a bond of indebtedness that deeds over to [the 'Lord of the Earth' himself and] all his offspring."[2] Satan's plan fails, of course, because—as Adam knows—God is the true "Lord of the earth." The title at the top of this picture reads: "Here Adam is writing his *Cheirograph*."[3]

1   G. A. Anderson, *et al.*, *Synopsis*, Slavonic 33-34.6, p. 6E.
2   G. A. Anderson, *Perfection*, p. 163.
3   P. Henry, *Moldavie*, 2:246, republished in G. A. Anderson, *Perfection*, p. 163. See also M. E. Stone, *Adam's Contract*, pp. 57-59.

Another account of Satan's deception is found in the story of Adam's *cheirograph*, from the Slavonic *Life*. A *cheirograph* is literally a "note of hand,"[79] but in this context it means more specifically a "contract":[80]

> Adam took the oxen and began to till, that he might obtain nourishment.
>
> Then the Devil appeared and stood steadfastly in front of the oxen and wouldn't allow Adam to till the earth. And the Devil said to Adam, "the earth is mine,[81] God owns Heaven (and the Garden). If you want to become mine, then, by all means, till the earth. If, however, you want to belong to God then go only into Paradise."
>
> Adam said, "God owns Heaven and Paradise, but God also owns the earth and the sea and the entire world."
>
> The Devil said, "I will not permit you to till the earth, unless you sign a *cheirograph*, pledging that you belong to me."
>
> Adam said, "Whoever is Lord of the earth, to him both I and my children belong."[82] Adam knew of course that the Lord would come down to the earth and take on himself the form of a man and trample down the Devil.

79   Greek *kheir* = hand, *graph* = writing.
80   M. E. Stone, *Legend*, pp. 152-153. See also *Excursus 37: Traditions About the Role of Abel*, p. 617.
81   See *Endnote 5-26*, p. 436.
82   See *Endnote 5-27*, p. 437.

The Devil said, "Write for me your *cheirograph*."

And Adam wrote and said, "Whoever is Lord of the earth, both I and my children belong to him."

The Devil took the *cheirograph* for himself.[83]

Satan's plan fails, of course, because—as Adam knows—God is the true "Lord of the earth." Related accounts describe how the *cheirograph* is destroyed by Christ at His baptism or, according to some versions, at the time of His visit to "proclaim liberty to the captives" in spirit prison following His crucifixion.[84]

In contrast to stories that emphasize the role of Satan as a deceiver and tempter, we find him elsewhere employed not as "a figure of complete evil" but rather as a means to represent "the principle of justice."[85] For example, a ninth-century midrash reads:

> Satan [comes] on the Day of Atonement to accuse Israel and he specifies the iniquities of Israel, saying: Master of the universe, as there are adulterers among the nations of the earth; so, too, among Israel. There are thieves among the nations of the earth; so, too, among Israel. But the Holy One, blessed be He, specifies the just deeds of Israel. Then what does He do? He suspends the beam of the scales and looks to see what the balance or imbalance is between the iniquities and the just deeds. And as they are weighed—the iniquities against the just deeds, these against those—the two pans of the scale balance exactly. Thereupon Satan goes out to fetch more iniquities to put in the pan of iniquities and bring it down.
>
> What does the Holy One, blessed be He, do? Even while Satan is going about seeking iniquities, the Holy One, blessed be He, takes the iniquities out of the pan and hides them under His royal purple.[86] Then Satan comes and finds no iniquity on the scales, as is said "The iniquity of Israel shall be sought for, and there shall be none."[87] When Satan sees there is no iniquity, he cries out before the Holy One, blessed be He: Master of the universe, "Thou hast carried away the iniquity of Thy people."[88] When David realized what God does, he said: "…Happy is he whose transgression is carried away, whose sin is hidden."[89]

"In this midrash," Peter Schäfer argues, "the principles of justice and mercy are evenly balanced—the one personified in Satan, the other concretized in the robe of God—and justice was overtaken by mercy."[90] Anderson further observes that: "Mercy would have no value unless it was calibrated against a strict measure of justice.[91] But a world that is just, through and through, would allow no room for humans."[92]

In the well-known parable by Elder Boyd K. Packer entitled *The Mediator*, a theme similar to the story of the *cheirograph* is concerned, not with a tale about Satan's fraud in claiming ownership of the earth, but rather with the dilemma of trying to reconcile the strict demands

---

83   G. A. Anderson, *et al.*, *Synopsis*, 33-34.1-35-37.1, p. 6E.
84   Isaiah 61:1; cf. *Excursus 37: Traditions About the Role of Abel*, p. 617 and *Figure* 6-12, p. 471. See *Endnote 5-28*, p. 437.
85   G. A. Anderson, *Perfection*, pp. 167-168.
86   See *Endnote 5-29*, p. 437.
87   Jeremiah 50:20.
88   Psalm 85:3.
89   W. G. Braude, *Rabbati*, 45:2, pp. 783-784. See Psalm 32:1.
90   G. A. Anderson, *Perfection*, pp. 167-168; cf. Alma 34:15: "the bowels of mercy… overpowereth justice." See *Endnote 5-30*, p. 437.
91   Cf. Alma 42:22-25.
92   G. A. Anderson, *Perfection*, p. 168. As Joseph Smith said: "God does not look on sin with allowance, but when men have sinned there must be allowance made for them (J. Smith, Jr., *Teachings*, 9 June 1842, p. 240; cf. D&C 1:31-32). See *Endnote 5-31*, p. 437.

Figure 5-5. *The Foolish Man and the Creditor, 1978*
Jerry Harston, 1943-

And thus we see that all mankind were fallen, and they were in the grasp of justice.[1] In the parable of Elder Boyd K. Packer, the theme of the *cheirograph* is combined, not with a tale about fraud and deception, but about the dilemma of trying to reconcile a creditor's strict demands for justice with his client's pleas for mercy. Elder Packer writes that the debtor "had been warned about going into that much debt, and particularly about his creditor. But… he was sure he could pay for it later. So he signed a contract."[2]

The later intercession of Christ as the Mediator recalls Shakespeare's words describing the accusation of the unyielding Angelo and the moving reply of Isabella on behalf of her guilty brother Claudio:

Angelo: Your brother is a forfeit of the law,
And you but waste your words.

Isabella: Alas! Alas!
Why, all the souls that were were forfeit once;
And He that might the vantage best have took
Found out the remedy. How would you be,
If He, which is the top of judgment, should
But judge you as you are? Oh, think on that;
And mercy then will breathe within your lips
Like man new made.[3]

---

1   Alma 42:14.
2   B. K. Packer, *Mediator 1977*, p. 54; B. K. Packer, *Errand*, p. 44.
3   W. Shakespeare, *Measure*, 2:2:70-79, p. 560.

of justice with mankind's need for mercy. Though the subject of the story represents, like Adam, an "Everyman," his antagonist is not the Devil but rather an unyielding creditor who demands that the terms of the contract for repayment of a loan be fully satisfied, despite the entreaties of his client for mercy. Rejoins the creditor:

> Mercy is always so one-sided. It would serve only you. If I show mercy to you, it will leave me unpaid. It is justice I demand. Do you believe in justice?" "I believed in justice when I signed the contract," the debtor said. "It was on my side then, for I thought it would protect me. I did not need mercy then, nor think I should need it ever. Justice, I thought, would serve both of us equally as well." "It is justice that demands that you pay the contract or suffer the penalty," the creditor replied. "That is the law. You have agreed to it and that is the way it must be. Mercy cannot rob justice."

> There they were: One meting out justice, the other pleading for mercy. Neither could prevail except at the expense of the other. "If you do not forgive the debt there will be no mercy," the debtor pleaded. "If I do, there will be no justice," was the reply.

> Both laws, it seemed, could not be served. They are two eternal ideals that appear to contradict one another. Is there no way for justice to be fully served, and mercy also?

> There is a way! The law of justice can be fully satisfied and mercy can be fully extended—but it takes someone else. And so it happened this time.

> The debtor had a friend. He came to help. He knew the debtor well. He knew him to be short-sighted. He thought him foolish to have gotten himself into such a predicament. Nevertheless, he wanted to help because he loved him. He stepped between them, faced the creditor, and made this offer. "I will pay the debt if you will free the debtor from his contract so that he may keep his possessions and not go to prison."

As the creditor was pondering the offer, the mediator added, "You demanded justice. Though he cannot pay you, I will do so. You will have been justly dealt with and can ask no more. It would not be just."

And so the creditor agreed.

The mediator turned then to the debtor. "If I pay your debt, will you accept me as your creditor?" "Oh yes, yes," cried the debtor. "You saved me from prison and showed mercy to me." "Then," said the benefactor, "you will pay the debt to me and I will set the terms. It will not be easy, but it will be possible. I will provide a way. You need not go to prison."

And so it was that the creditor was paid in full. He had been justly dealt with. No contract had been broken.

The debtor, in turn, had been extended mercy. Both laws stood fulfilled. Because there was a mediator, justice had claimed its full share, and mercy was satisfied.[93]

The Mediator, of course, represents Jesus Christ, who "atoneth for the sins of the world, to bring about the plan of mercy, to appease the demands of justice, that God might be a perfect, just God, and a merciful God also."[94]

Since the Atonement will cover the offenses of the innocent and unwittingly deceived, as well as temporarily shortsighted individuals who repent and prepare themselves to receive the gift of the Savior's great sacrifice, there is a happy ending for each of the stories thus far recounted. However, Moses 5 has a different message about the fate of those who unrepentantly "love darkness rather than light, because their deeds are evil."[95] Of such was Cain who, had he "fulfilled the law of righteousness as did Enoch… could have walked with God all the days of his life and never failed of a blessing."[96] Instead, he "sinned with his eyes open,"[97] "was cursed,"[98] and became known not merely as one of the "sons of perdition"[99] but rather, in similitude of Satan, as "Perdition" itself, it having been prophesied that Cain, if he did not repent, would be so preeminent in evil that he would "rule over" Satan.[100]

Nibley describes the approach by which Satan "plans to put the world under his bloody and horrible misrule." He appeals to anyone willing to consecrate their time and efforts to adopt his agenda—namely to "murder and get gain"[101]—as their own:

He will control the world economy by claiming possession of the earth's resources; and by manipulation of its currency—gold and silver—he will buy up the political, military, and ecclesiastical complex and run everything his way. We see him putting his plan into operation when he lays legal claim to the whole earth as his estate, accusing others of trespass, but putting everything up for sale to anyone who has the money. And how will they get the money? By going to work for him. He not only offers employment but a course of instruction in how the whole thing works, teaching the ultimate secret: "That great secret"[102] of converting life into property. Cain got the degree of *Master Mahan*,[103] tried the system out on his brother, and

---

93   B. K. Packer, *Mediator 1977*, p. 55; B. K. Packer, *Errand*, pp. 44-46. See *Endnote 5-32*, p. 437.
94   Alma 42:15.
95   D&C 10:21.
96   J. Smith, Jr., *Words*, 5 October 1840, p. 41.
97   J. F. Smith, Jr., *Doctrines*, 30 March 1935, 2:280. See *Endnote 5-33*, p. 437.
98   J. Smith, Jr., *Words*, 5 October 1840, p. 40.
99   D&C 76:32-35.
100 See D&C 76:26; Moses 5:23-24.
101 Moses 5:31.
102 Moses 5:49-50.
103 See *Commentary 5:31-a*, p. 379.

FIGURE 5-6. *Cain and Abel, ca. 1540*
Tiziano Vecellio (Titian), 1490-1576

SEE COLOR PLATE 5-6.

And it came to pass that while they were in the field, Cain rose up against Abel, his brother, and slew him.[1] The scriptures are silent on the details of Abel's murder, however one tradition has it that Abel, at the invitation of Cain, "came to a lonely place… Then Cain… walking a little behind him… hastened, and smote him with [a] staff, blow upon blow, until he was stunned."[2] Inflicting wounds on "all parts of his body," in the manner of the "blows of death" taught by Satan himself, Cain was said to have finally "killed him by striking him on the neck."[3]

Of this painting by Titian, Brenson writes that "the sharply delineated, muscular, animated figures… seem to jump off the ceiling… When Cain lifts up his club, about to slam it down on his brother, helplessly teetering on the edge of a rock, it seems as if the club will come down on us."[4]

1   Moses 5:32.
2   S. C. Malan, *Adam and Eve*, 1:74, pp. 100-101. Some sources describe the weapon as the "jaw-bone of a camel" (M. Herbert, *Irish Apocrypha*, p. 18).
3   *Talmud*, Sanhedrin 37b, cited in R. M. Zlotowitz, *et al.*, *Bereishis*, p. 151. See the overview of Moses 4, p. 236; *Commentary 5:29-b*, p. 377; 5:47-b, p. 396.
4   M. Brenson, *Titian*. See *Endnote 5-34*, p. 437.

FIGURE 5-7. *Cain and Abel*
Pietro Novelli (Il Monrealese), 1603-1647

SEE COLOR PLATE 5-7.

And the Lord said unto Cain: Where is Abel thy brother? And he said: I know not. Am I my brother's keeper?[1] In this unsettling scene, we see God speaking from a cloud to the fleeing Cain as he runs past the still-burning altar. Abel's lifeless body, dominating the foreground, loudly proclaims the falsity of Cain's profession of ignorance. The contrast of the skin color to the gray monochrome of the background highlights the link between the three actors.

1   Moses 5:34.

FIGURE 5-8. *Cain, Based on Victor Hugo's Poem, 1880*
Fernand-Anne Piestre (Cormon), 1845-1924

SEE COLOR PLATE 5-8.

And Cain said… I shall be a fugitive and a vagabond in the earth.[1] Cormon's tableau depicts the furtive wanderings of the dispossessed son of Adam: "When Cain, dishevelled, angry, in the middle of a storm, / Fleeing with his children wrapped in hides to keep warm, / Was running from Jehovah, he arrived at the base / Of a solitary mountain in the middle of a waste"[2] In Victor Hugo's poem, Cain anxiously marches his family from place to place to escape the lidless gaze of the eye of his conscience "entirely open, in the depths of the sky, / which stared at him fixedly from out of the night"—a torment he could not evade, even in the final darkness of the tomb. Of the role of light and shadow in Cormon's painting, Rosenblum writes: "To convey the sense of dread before the weight of Jehovah's moral law, Cormon has exaggerated the length of the shadows cast before the fleeing procession of man, woman, and child, as if the oppressive light of truth were pursuing the guilty tribe across the barren plain."[3]

---

1   Moses 5:38-39.
2   V. Hugo, *Poetry*, p. 215. For the full poem, see *Gleanings*, p. 407.
3   R. Rosenblum, *Paintings*, p. 388.

gloried in its brilliant success, declaring that at last he could be free, as only property makes free, and that Abel had been a loser in a free competition.[104]

Sarna summarizes the thematic progression between chapters 4 and 5 of the book of Moses: "The transgression in the Garden was an offense against God; now it is man against his brother, which is also an offense against God. It was the 'fruit of the tree' that led to the downfall of Adam and Eve; it is the 'fruit of the soil' that leads to Cain's undoing. The first human was worried about death; now the experience of death becomes a reality."[105] Though Cain disavowed knowledge of Abel's fate, the crime was not hid from the Lord, who lamented: "The voice of thy brother's blood cries unto me from the ground."[106]

In consequence of Cain's murderous act, he was told: "the ground shall not henceforth yield unto thee her strength. A fugitive and a vagabond shalt thou be in the earth."[107] He was "driven… out… from the face of the Lord" and a "mark" was set upon him "lest any finding

---

104   H. W. Nibley, *Foundation*, pp. 165-166.
105   N. M. Sarna, *Genesis*, p. 31.
106   Moses 5:35.
107   Moses 5:37. See *Endnote 5-35*, p. 438.

him should kill him."[108] Being "shut out" from the presence of the Lord, he and his family dwelt "in the land of Nod, on the east of Eden"[109]—a place even further removed from the presence of God than the land where his parents had settled after the Fall.[110] Of his fate, Nibley writes:

> Cain began as a farmer; but when following Satan's instructions, he made use of that great secret of how to murder and get gain, the earth refused him her strength, and he became a wanderer. Since time immemorial that homeless tribe (the land of Nod means land of unsettled nomad) is designated throughout the East by the name Qayin, meaning a wandering metal-worker, the mark of his trade and his tribe being the face blackened at the forge; he is a skillful maker and peddler of weapons and jewels, the twin destroyers and corrupters of mankind.[111]

The Way Back

Moses 5 not only describes the path that leads to spiritual death, but also the way to eternal life.[112] Jacob explained that this "way is prepared from the fall of man... And men are instructed sufficiently that they know good from evil." He specifically mentions instruction because a knowledge of good from evil is not obtained as the result of mere blind experience in a fallen world. On the contrary, it requires that a "law [be] given unto men." However, because even those who are struggling to do right will inevitably violate that law, "no flesh is justified," and all mankind is thus "cut off" "by the temporal law... and also, by the spiritual law." Hence the need for "redemption... in and through the Holy Messiah."[113]

D&C 29:42 affirms that Adam and Eve received knowledge of all these things through specially appointed messengers:

> But, behold, I say unto you that I, the Lord God, gave unto Adam and unto his seed, that they should not die as to the temporal death, until I, the Lord God, should send forth angels to declare unto them repentance and redemption, through faith on the name of mine Only Begotten Son.[114]

God's motivation in instituting laws was not arbitrary—His purpose is, as the Prophet Joseph Smith explained, "to instruct the weaker intelligences," allowing fallen humanity to gradually "advance in knowledge" so that eventually they "may be exalted with [God] himself."[115] The Syriac version of the *Testament of Adam* expresses the similar belief of early Christians who taught that the plan of salvation was revealed to Adam in order to bring the eventual possibility of godhood within the reach of fallen mankind:

> And on this account [God] taught me in the midst of Paradise when I picked the fruit in which death was hiding. And He said to me, "Adam, do not fear. A god you desired to be; a god I will make you. However, not right now but after a space of (many) years. Right now I am going to drive you from Paradise, and I will bring you down into the earth of thorns. Your back I will bend (and) your knees will quake from old age overtaking you. I am delivering you up to death. The maggot and worm will devour your body.

---

108   Moses 5:39-40.
109   Moses 5:41.
110   See *Commentary* 3:8-b, p. 161 and *Commentary* 5:41-c, p. 390.
111   H. W. Nibley, *Stewardship*, p. 60.
112   2 Nephi 21:30-31.
113   2 Nephi 2:4-6.
114   See *Endnote 5-36*, p. 438.
115   J. Smith, Jr., *Teachings*, 7 April 1844, p. 354.

FIGURE 5-9.
Abraham Entertains Three Strangers, 1866
Paul Gustave Doré, 1832-1883

And I saw before me three men whose appearance I could not recognize... saying to me, "Rise up, Adam, from the sleep of death, and hear about the aeon [i.e., the manifestation of God] and the seed of that man to whom life has come."[1] Extracanonical texts speak of three messengers who appeared to warn, protect, and instruct Adam and Eve, and of how their efforts were resented and opposed by the Evil One.[2] Similar accounts are also given concerning other prominent Old Testament figures, including Abraham. About the identity of these envoys, Nibley writes: "The Mandaean literature will tell you that the messengers that came to instruct Adam and Eve were the apostles who later became the pillars of the Church (Peter, James and John)."[3] In modern times, Peter, James, and John were again sent to restore the Melchizedek Priesthood.[4]

In the case of Abraham, rabbinical commentary takes great care to depict the extraordinary nature of Abraham's hospitality to all travelers which, in his hundredth year, was rewarded by the visit of these three messengers from God.[5] As in many other such accounts, his blessings came only after a period of intense trial: "On the third day after his circumcision,[6] when Abraham was suffering dire pain, God spoke to the angels, saying, 'Go to, let us pay a visit to the sick'...."[7] The day whereon God visited him was exceedingly hot,[8] for He had bored a hole in hell, so that its heat might reach as far as the earth, and no wayfarer venture abroad on the highways, and Abraham be left undisturbed in his pain. But the absence of strangers caused Abraham great vexation, and he sent his servant Eliezer forth to keep a lookout for travelers. When the servant returned from his fruitless search, Abraham himself, in spite of his illness and the scorching heat, prepared to go forth on the highway..."[9] Taken from his groundbreaking illustrated Bible,[10] Doré's woodcut shows Abraham at this very moment, just as he began to set off alone for the desert and was dramatically brought to his knees by this sudden encounter[11] with the three divine messengers.[12]

Hugh Nibley, who was deeply moved by this story,[13] said of Abraham: "He seemed to be generous to the point of lacking common sense," citing a rabbinic account of his welcoming words to the messengers: "'Lord of the Universe,' he cried, recognizing one of them, 'is it the order of the Cosmos that I sit while you remain standing?'[14] The scene, as... André Parrot... remarks, 'is as magnificent as it is strange.'"[15]

---

1   G. W. MacRae, *Adam 1983*, 2:1-2, p. 712.
2   E.g., M. Lidzbarski, *Ginza*, GR 3:1, pp. 197-198; 11:1, pp. 263-264. See also *Bibliography, Mandaean Texts*, p. 869.
3   H. W. Nibley, *Teachings of the PGP*, 19, p. 233. See *Endnote 5-37*, p. 438.
4   D&C 128:20.
5   See *Excursus 31: The Hospitality of Abraham*, p. 606.
6   Genesis 17:23-27.
7   See *Endnote 5-38*, p. 439.
8   See *Endnote 5-39*, p. 440.
9   L. Ginzberg, *Legends*, 1:240-241; cf. *Babylonian Talmud*, Baba Metsi'a 86b, cited in H. N. Bialik, *et al.*, *Legends*, 26, p. 35; A. Elkaïm-Sartre, *Ein Yaakov*, 52, pp. 909-910. See also E. D. Clark, *Blessings*, pp. 171-179; M.-A. Ouaknin, *et al.*, *Rabbi Éliézer*, 29, p. 170. See *Endnote 5-40*, p. 440.
10 J. J. Bourasse, *et al.*, *Vulgate*.
11 See *Endnote 5-41*, p. 440.
12 Genesis 18:3; R. M. Zlotowitz, *et al.*, *Bereishis*, 18:2, p. 628. See *Endnote 5-42*, p. 441.
13 B. J. Petersen, *Nibley*, pp. 332-333.
14 Cf. *Tanhuma*, cited in R. M. Zlotowitz, *et al.*, *Bereishis*, 18:2, p. 626.
15 H. W. Nibley, *Drama*, p. 3.

FIGURE 5-10.
The Holy Trinity, ca. 1408-1425
Andrei Rublev, ca. 1360-70-ca. 1427-30

SEE COLOR PLATE 5-10.

That they all may be one; as thou, Father, art in me, and I in thee, that they also may be one in us.[1] In the Orthodox Church, the icon of the three divine messengers who appeared to Abraham is used as a symbol of the oneness of the Godhead, and the "beginning of the promise of Redemption" which reached "its fulfillment on the day of the Pentecost," binding together the Old Testament and New Testament Churches.[2] In LDS doctrine, the oneness of purpose and holiness attained by the Godhead is a blessing held out for all faithful disciples of Christ, as expressed in the high priestly prayer of the Lord at the Last Supper cited above. To both the head and the body of the Church, the Lord said in 1831: "...be one; and if ye are not one ye are not mine."[3]

With reference to accounts of visits of divine messengers to Adam and Eve, Gaskill observes that: "Peter, James, and John, whether appearing to Adam and Eve or serving as the head of the post-resurrection Church in the meridian of time, are symbols of something much greater than themselves, namely, the Godhead.... as [are] all subsequent First Presidencies. Whether these three brethren, or any set of tripartite messengers had physical contact with Adam and Eve (or any other Old Testament figure) makes no difference. What is of importance is what they brought and whom they represented."[4]

"Many scholars consider Rublev's *Trinity* the most perfect of all Russian icons and perhaps the most perfect of all the icons ever painted."[5] The basic form of the icon is a circle: "Passing through the upper part of the nimbus of the central Angel and partly cutting off the bottom of the pedestals, this circle embraces all three figures, showing very faintly through their outlines... In this way the central Angel, though taller than the others, does not overwhelm or dominate them... The icon... has action, expressed in gestures, communion, expressed in the inclining of the heads and the postures of the figures, and a silent, motionless peace... [T]he gestures of the hands are directed towards the eucharistic chalice, with the head of a sacrificial animal, which stands on the white table as on an altar. Symbolizing the voluntary sacrifice of the Son of God, it draws together the gestures of the Angels, indicating the unity of will and action of the Holy Trinity, Who entered into a covenant with Abraham." The Father, represented at left, is dressed differently than the other two. He wears "a pale pink cloak with brown and blue-green lights" of "sober and indefinite hue" that covers both shoulders. The Son, depicted in the middle, "has the customary colors of... a purple *chiton* [= a draped, belted tunic] and a blue cloak" draped over His left shoulder, the color of the cloak symbolizing incarnation.[6] Behind Him grows a Tree of Life, born of His sacrificial death. The "principal color" of the Holy Spirit is green, represented in the cloak draped over His right shoulder. Here, the color green "signifies 'youth, fullness of powers.' This specifically indicates the properties of... renewing all things and giving them life."[7] The symbolism recalls the promise made to those who are to be "sanctified by the Spirit unto the renewing of their bodies."[8]

---

1   John 17:21.
2   L. Ouspensky, *et al.*, *Icons*, p. 200. See also G. Bunge, *Rublev Trinity*, pp. 45-57.
3   D&C 38:27.
4   A. L. Gaskill, *Lost*, p. 302. See also *ibid.*, pp. 303-306. Cf. Nibley: "When Peter spoke to Adam, which Peter was it? The Peter of Adam's day? No, the timeless Peter" (H. W. Nibley, *Consecration*, p. 439).
5   *The Holy Trinity*.
6   W. Williams, *Shadow*.
7   L. Ouspensky, *et al.*, *Icons*, p. 202.
8   D&C 84:33.

And after a short time my mercy (will be) revealed to you: I will go down to you... For your sake, Adam, I become an infant... For your sake, Adam, I ascend the cross... For your sake, Adam, I open the tomb."[116].

The set of laws and ordinances that were given to Adam and Eve is known collectively as "The New and Everlasting Covenant."[117] This comprehensive covenant includes the

---

116   S. E. Robinson, *Testament of Adam*, 3:2-3, pp. 97, 99; cf. M. D. Gibson, *Rolls 1901*, p. 117; E. P. Sanders, *Testament of Adam 1983*, 3:2-3, p. 994.
117   H. C. Kimball, *6 January 1861*, p. 330; Book of Abraham, Facsimile 2, Figure 3.

baptismal and temple covenants as well as covenants made at other times.[118] Because God is everlasting, the Covenant is also "everlasting": it was first given to Adam, and later to all subsequent prophets.[119] Because it is given anew each time the Gospel is restored, the Lord also describes it as "new."[120] Riddle summarizes the two basic parts of the Covenant:

> Part one is the covenant of baptism, being born of water and of the Spirit. The covenant of baptism is our pledge to seek after good and to eliminate all choosing and doing of evil in our lives, and it is also our receiving the power to keep that promise.[121] Part two of the New and Everlasting Covenant is to receive the power and authority of God and to become perfect in using that power and authority to minister to other beings to bring about their happiness.[122]

Elder Bruce R. McConkie's name for the first part of the New and Everlasting Covenant is the "Covenant of Salvation." It is "accepted by men in the waters of baptism"[123] and is confirmed by the laying on of hands. Adam and Eve were the first mortals to receive this covenant, as Enoch recounts.[124] As an element of the process of repentance, sacrifice is both a necessary precursor to baptism and a requirement for renewal of that covenant.[125] The ordinance of sacrifice given to Adam and Eve[126] corresponds in our day to the sacrament.[127] Thus, as Elder McConkie explained, three ordinances (baptism, sacrifice, sacrament) are associated with one and the same covenant.[128] Throwing light on the symbols of the sacrament, Alma equates the eating and drinking of the "bread and the waters of life" with "partaking of the fruit of the tree of life."[129] By this means, we literally become "partakers of the divine nature."[130] Thus also, Coptic Christian writings saw in a grain of wheat, mercifully granted to Adam and Eve after their exile from Eden, the flesh of God Himself.[131]

Jesus taught Nicodemus that "Except a man be born of water and of the Spirit, he cannot enter into the kingdom of God."[132] Although in a narrow sense this commandment is fulfilled through baptism and confirmation, in reality these first ordinances are only the "gate" through which we begin our journey down the "strait and narrow path which leads to eternal life."[133] Additional ordinances—along with the development of perfect faith, hope, and charity—are a necessary part of the process of spiritual rebirth that ultimately results in sanctification:[134] "And now... after ye have gotten into this strait and narrow path, I would ask if all is done? Behold, I say unto you, Nay... Wherefore, ye must press forward... and if ye press forward, feasting upon the word of Christ, and endure to the end, behold, thus saith the Father: Ye shall have eternal life."[135] Speaking plainly on this topic, the Prophet

---

118 *Gospel Principles*, p. 98.
119 E.g., JST Genesis 9:21-23, 13:13; JST Deuteronomy 10:2; cf. D&C 49:9, 66:2, 88:133.
120 *Gospel Principles*, p. 98. See Jeremiah 31:31-34; Ezekiel 37:26; H. C. Kimball, *6 January 1861*, p. 330.
121 D. A. Bednar, *Strength*, p. 77.
122 C. C. Riddle, *New*, p. 228.
123 B. R. McConkie, *New Witness*, p. 293.
124 Moses 6:64-65. See *Endnote 5-43*, p. 441.
125 D&C 20:37, 59:9-12.
126 Moses 5:5-9.
127 D&C 59:8-14.
128 B. R. McConkie, *New Witness*, p. 293.
129 Alma 5:34.
130 2 Peter 1:4.
131 E. A. W. Budge, *Cave*, pp. 18-19 n. 1; cf. S. C. Malan, *Adam and Eve*, 1:68, p. 81; B. Mika'el, *Apocalypse*, pp. 102, 131; John 6:25-58. See *Endnote 5-44*, p. 441.
132 John 3:5.
133 2 Nephi 31:17-18.
134 E. T. Benson, *Teachings 1988*, 28 September 1982, p. 337; B. C. Hafen, *Disciple's Journey*, pp. 292-301.
135 2 Nephi 31:19-20; cf. Jacob 6:11. See *Endnote 5-45*, p. 442.

declared that being "born again comes by the Spirit of God through ordinances"[136]—with the understanding that the bestowal of these ordinances and keys will continue even in the next life.[137] Joseph Smith explicitly linked the manner in which higher ordinances were given to the Saints to the figure of Adam, calling it the "order pertaining to the Ancient of Days."[138]

Elder McConkie calls the second part of the New and Everlasting Covenant "The Covenant of Exaltation." He explains how it is related to the oath and covenant of the Priesthood:[139]

> When we receive the Melchizedek Priesthood, we enter into a covenant with the Lord. It is the covenant of exaltation. In it, we promise to magnify our callings in the priesthood, to keep the commandments, "to give diligent heed to the words of eternal life,"[140] to "live by every word that proceedeth forth from the mouth of God,"[141] and to enter the patriarchal order, which leads to a continuation of the family unit in the realms ahead.[142]

Eventually, those who keep this oath and covenant are promised "all that [the] Father hath."[143] When they are fully prepared, greater light and knowledge about the covenant will be given them through personal communion with the Father:

> 47 And every one that hearkeneth to the voice of the Spirit cometh unto God, even the Father.
> 48 And the Father teacheth him of the covenant which he has renewed and confirmed upon you…[144]

Specific teachings about the New and Everlasting Covenant are to be had in the temple.[145] Elder Ezra Taft Benson elaborated on this subject: "Celestial laws, embodied in certain ordinances belonging to the Church of Jesus Christ, are complied with by voluntary covenants. The laws are spiritual. Thus, our Father in Heaven has ordained certain holy sanctuaries, called temples, in which these laws may be fully explained, the laws include the law of obedience and sacrifice, the law of the gospel, the law of chastity, and the law of consecration."[146] In the temple, the story of events surrounding the Creation and the Fall provide a context for the presentation of covenants that are made as part of the endowment.[147] Thus, it would not be surprising to find that a similar pattern of interleaving history and covenant-making themes may have also helped dictate both the structure and the content of the material selected for inclusion in the book of Moses. Writes Johnson:[148]

> Throughout the text [of the early chapters of the book of Moses], the author stops the historic portions of the story and weaves into the narrative framework ritual acts such as sacrifice and sacrament; ordinances such as baptism, washings and the gift of the Holy Ghost; and oaths and covenants, such as obedience to marital obligations and oaths of property consecration.... [If

136   J. Smith, Jr., *Teachings*, 2 July 1839, p. 162; cf. D&C 84:19-22. See *Endnote 5-46*, p. 442.
137   S. W. Kimball, *Potential*; B. Young, *14 August 1872*, pp. 136-139.
138   J. Smith, Jr., *Teachings*, 4 May 1842, p. 237. See *Endnote 5-47*, p. 442.
139   D&C 84:33-48.
140   D&C 84:43.
141   D&C 84:44.
142   B. R. McConkie, *New Witness*, pp. 312-313. See D&C 132:19-24 and *Excursus 3: Temple Blessings in the Oath and Covenant of the Priesthood*, p. 519.
143   D&C 84:38. This verse corrects a common misinterpretation of Luke 15:31 which falsely concludes that when the Father gives all He has to one of his children it somehow diminishes what He can give to the others (D. Packard *et al.*, *Feasting*, p. 49).
144   D&C 88:47-48; cf. John 14:16, 23; D&C 88:3-4, 130:3; J. Smith, Jr., *Teachings*, 27 June 1839, p. 151.
145   See *Endnote 5-48*, p. 442.
146   E. T. Benson, *Vision*. See *Excursus 51: The Five Lost Things of the Temple*, p. 658.
147   J. E. Talmage, *House of the Lord*, p. 54.
148   See *Endnote 5-49*, p. 443.

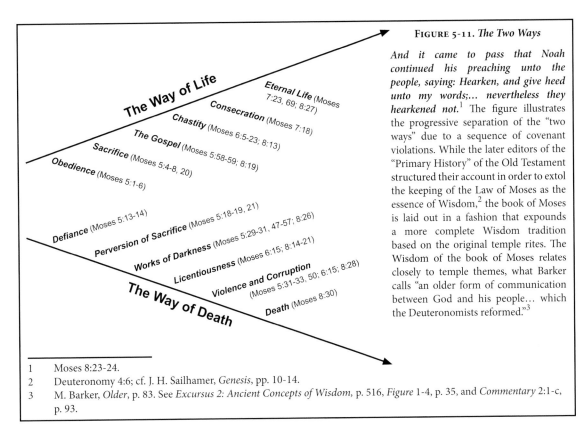

FIGURE 5-11. *The Two Ways*

And it came to pass that Noah continued his preaching unto the people, saying: Hearken, and give heed unto my words;... nevertheless they hearkened not.[1] The figure illustrates the progressive separation of the "two ways" due to a sequence of covenant violations. While the later editors of the "Primary History" of the Old Testament structured their account in order to extol the keeping of the Law of Moses as the essence of Wisdom,[2] the book of Moses is laid out in a fashion that expounds a more complete Wisdom tradition based on the original temple rites. The Wisdom of the book of Moses relates closely to temple themes, what Barker calls "an older form of communication between God and his people... which the Deuteronomists reformed."[3]

1   Moses 8:23-24.
2   Deuteronomy 4:6; cf. J. H. Sailhamer, *Genesis*, pp. 10-14.
3   M. Barker, *Older*, p. 83. See *Excursus 2: Ancient Concepts of Wisdom*, p. 516, *Figure 1-4*, p. 35, and *Commentary* 2:1-c, p. 93.

we assume that material similar to Moses 1-8 might have served as a temple text,[149] it would be expected that as] this history was recited, acts, ordinances and ceremonies would have been performed during this reading. For instance, during the story of Enoch and his city of Zion, members of the attending congregation would be put under oath to be a chosen, covenant people and to keep all things in common, with all their property belonging to the Lord.[150]

A precedent for the idea of structuring key scriptural accounts to be consistent with a series of temple-related covenants can be found in Welch's analysis of the Sermon on the Mount[151] and the Sermon at the Temple,[152] where he found that:

> The commandments issued... are not only the same as the main commandments always issued at the temple, but they appear largely in the same order: obedience and sacrifice,[153] evil speaking of the brethren,[154] chastity and a higher understanding of marriage and divorce,[155] love for one's enemies and obedience to the law of love or the law of the Gospel,[156] and alms to the poor and consecration of one's life to the worship and service of God.[157]

In a similar vein, David Noel Freedman has found evidence for an opposite pattern of covenant-*breaking* in the "Primary History" of the Old Testament. He argues that the books of the Bible from Exodus through Kings were deliberately edited to reveal:

149   See *Endnote 5-50*, p. 443.
150   M. J. Johnson, *Prologue*, pp. 23-24, See *Endnote 5-51*, p. 443.
151   Matthew 5-7.
152   3 Nephi 11-18.
153   See 3 Nephi 12:19.
154   See 3 Nephi 12:22.
155   See 3 Nephi 12:28-32.
156   See 3 Nephi 12:39, 41-45.
157   J. W. Welch, *Temple in the Book of Mormon*, p. 373; 3 Nephi 13:1, 20, 24. For a more complete account see J. W. Welch, *Sermon* and J. W. Welch, *Light*. See *Endnote 5-52*, p. 443.

MOSES 5

… a pattern of defiance of the Covenant with God that inexorably leads to the downfall of the nation of Israel, the destruction of the Temple, and the banishment of survivors from the Promised Land. Book by book… the violation of the first nine [of the Ten C]ommandments are charted one by one. Because covetousness lies behind all the acts committed, each act implicitly breaks the Tenth Commandment as well. This hidden trail of sin betrays the hand of a master editor, who skillfully has woven into Israel's history a message to a community in their Babylonian exile that their fate is not the result of God's abandoning them, but a consequence of their abandonment of God.[158]

An interesting result of looking carefully at the history of Adam through Enoch and Noah as a temple text is the realization that—like both of Christ's great Sermons and the biblical text of the "Primary History"—the series of covenant-related themes unfolds in what appears to be a definite order of progression. Also remarkable is the fact that both the ultimate consequences of covenant-keeping as well as those of covenant-breaking are fully illustrated at the conclusion of the sequence: in the final two chapters of the book of Moses, Enoch and his people are taken up to walk in the presence of God[159] while the wicked are destroyed in the great Flood.[160]

Obedience vs. Defiance. Elder Bruce R. McConkie stated that: "Obedience is the first law of heaven, the cornerstone upon which all righteousness and progression rest."[161] The reason why this is so is explained by Nibley: "If every choice I make expresses a preference, if the world I build up is the world I really love and want, then with every choice I am judging myself, proclaiming all the day long to God, angels, and my fellowmen where my real values lie, where my treasure is, the things to which I give supreme importance. Hence, in this life every moment provides a perfect and foolproof test of your real character, making this life a time of testing and probation."[162]

A Christian account relates that Adam made his first covenant with God—a covenant of obedience—"ere he came out of the Garden, [when he was by the tree] whereof Eve took the fruit and gave it him to eat."[163] It seems reasonable to suppose that the law of sacrifice, a companion to the law of obedience, was also given to Adam and Eve at this time, before they came to live in the mortal world.[164] Moses 5:1-6 highlights the subsequent obedience of Adam and Eve by enumerating their faithfulness to each of the commandments they had been given. Adam, with his fellow-laborer Eve, began to "till the earth, and to have dominion over all the beasts of the field, and to eat his bread by the sweat of his brow."[165] Likewise Eve fulfilled the commission she had received in the Garden of Eden and "bare… sons and daughters, and they began to replenish the earth."[166] Moreover, "Adam was obedient to the commandments of the Lord" in obeying the law of sacrifice and offering "the firstlings of their flocks" for "many days," despite the fact that he did not yet fully understand the reason why he had been thus commanded.[167]

---

158   D. N. Freedman, *Nine 2001*, p. 1. For a full exposition of Freedman's arguments, see D. N. Freedman, *Nine 2000*. See also *Excursus 32: Freedman's Analysis of the Primary History*, p. 607.
159   Moses 7:69.
160   Moses 8:30. See *Endnote 5-53*, p. 444.
161   B. R. McConkie, *Mormon Doctrine*, p. 539. See also H. B. Eyring, Jr., *Be One*, pp. 67-68.
162   H. W. Nibley, *Zeal*, p. 66.
163   S. C. Malan, *Adam and Eve*, 1:3:7, p. 4. See *Figure* 4-10, p. 228.
164   Cf. *Excursus 48: The Nature and Scope of Premortal Covenants*, p. 649. See *Endnote 5-54*, p. 444.
165   Moses 5:1; cf. Mosiah 6:6-7.
166   Moses 5:2.
167   Moses 5:5-6.

Later, in defiant counterpoint, Satan also came among the children of Adam and Eve, demanding their obedience, "and he commanded them, saying: Believe it not; and they believed it not." From that point on, many of them openly demonstrated that they "loved Satan more than God," becoming "carnal, sensual, and devilish."[168]

Sacrifice vs. Perversion of Sacrifice. President David O. McKay described the essence of the law of sacrifice as follows: "The first law of mortal life, self-preservation, would claim the most luscious fruit, the most tender meat, the softest down on which to lie. Selfishness, the law of nature would say, 'I want the best; that is mine.' But God said: 'Take of the firstlings of your herds and of your flocks.'[169] The best shall be given to God... Thus should God become the center of our being."[170] The *Lectures on Faith* further explain that: "When a man has offered in sacrifice all that he has for the truth's sake, not even withholding his life, and believing before God that he has been called to make this sacrifice because he seeks to do His will, he does know, most assuredly, that God does and will accept his sacrifice and offering, and that he has not, nor will not seek his face in vain. Under these circumstances, then, he can obtain the faith necessary for him to lay hold on eternal life."[171]

Once Adam and Eve had passed their initial test of obedience to the new commandments they had been given in the Garden after their transgression, God, seeing that it was "expedient that man should know concerning the things whereof he had appointed unto them... sent angels to converse with them... and made known unto them the plan of redemption."[172] To Adam was explained that the law of sacrifice "is a similitude of the sacrifice of the Only Begotten of the Father, which is full of grace and truth."[173]

Abel followed the pattern of his father in perfect obedience to God and offered a lamb in sacrifice. By way of contrast, Cain, at the command of Satan, "offered the fruit of the ground as a sacrifice, which was not symbolic of Christ's great act of Redemption... Instead of purchasing a lamb or another animal that would serve as an appropriate sacrifice, he offered what he produced."[174] Speaking of the reason Cain's sacrifice was rejected, the Prophet Joseph Smith explained that "ordinances must be kept in the very way God has appointed,"[175] in this case by "the shedding of blood... [as] a type, by which man was to discern the great Sacrifice which God had prepared."[176] Not only must the form of the ordinance comply with the divine pattern, but also the heart must be filled with the spirit of sincere repentance, since "the shedding of the blood of a beast could be beneficial to no man, except it was ... done with an eye looking forward in faith on the power of that great Sacrifice for a remission of sins."[177] Following the "great and last sacrifice"[178] of Jesus Christ, no further shedding of blood was required, but rather the sacrifice of "a broken heart and a contrite spirit."[179]

---

168 Moses 5:13.
169 Deuteronomy 12:6.
170 D. O. McKay, *Cherished*, 25 September 1941, p. 19. See also D. O. McKay, *Treasures*, 20 December 1920, pp. 275-278.
171 L. E. Dahl, *et al.*, *Lectures*, 6:7, p. 93.
172 Alma 12:28-30.
173 Moses 5:7. See *Excursus 33: The Restoration of Sacrifice*, p. 609.
174 H. L. Andrus, *Doctrinal*, p. 387.
175 J. Smith, Jr., *Teachings*, 5 October 1840, p. 169.
176 *Ibid.*, 22 January 1834, p. 58.
177 *Ibid.*, p. 58.
178 Alma 34:14.
179 D&C 59:8. See also *Excursus 33: The Restoration of Sacrifice*, p. 609.

FIGURE 5-12. *The Devil Approaches Jabez Stone, 1937*
Harold Denison, 1870-1943

And Satan said unto Cain: Swear unto me by thy throat… And Satan sware unto Cain that he would do according to his commands.[1] Ever ready to make a deal, Satan eagerly exchanged deadly oaths with Cain. At the beginning, such an arrangement is always congenial —"the Devil serves his client, gratifies his slightest whim, pampers his appetites, and is at his beck and call throughout his earthly life, putting unlimited power and influence at his disposal through his command of the treasures of the earth, gold and silver. But in exchange the victim must keep his part of the agreement, following Satan's instructions on earth and remaining in his power thereafter. That is the classic bargain, the pact with the Devil, by which a Faust, Don Juan, Macbeth, or Jabez Stone achieve the pinnacle of earthly success and the depths of eternal damnation."[2]

This illustration is taken from Stephen Vincent Benét's 1936 story *The Devil and Daniel Webster*, made into a popular film in 1941. Piazza characterizes the latter as "a fascinating allegory, filmed on the eve of World War II, of a society gone mad with materialism, a premonition of the opportunities and dangers awaiting the United States as it recovered from the Great Depression." Old Scratch is portrayed as polite, refined, and soft-spoken—and as usual, he "gets the best lines" as he preaches his gospel of cold cash to a down-on-his-luck New Hampshire farmer, making it clear at the end of the film that there is nothing he wants more than to have each viewer in his power.[3] Warned Benét "[I]f a smooth-spoken and businesslike stranger should appear at your door and offer you all that money can buy in exchange for your freedom of soul, it might be well to look him over rather carefully. I seem to have heard that there are such people abroad in the world, even today."[4]

---

1   Moses 5:29-30.
2   H. W. Nibley, *Enoch*, pp. 174-175.
3   T. Piazza, *Devil*.
4   S. V. Benét, *Author*.

The Gospel vs. Works of Darkness. Although in a general sense, "the law of the Gospel embraces all laws, principles, and ordinances necessary for our exaltation,"[180] the interpretive context of the temple specifically brings to mind pointed instructions relating to Christlike behavior toward one's fellow man. These instructions parallel some of the items prohibited in the community that produced the *Dead Sea Scrolls*, "such as laughing too loudly, gossiping, and immodest dress."[181] D&C 20:54, also bearing on this theme, instructs teachers in the Church that they should watch over members, assuring that there is "neither hardness with each other, neither lying, backbiting, nor evil speaking." Likewise, members of the Kirtland School of the Prophets were told: "cease from all your light speeches, from all laughter, from all your lustful desires, from all your pride and light-mindedness, and from all your wicked doings."[182] Thus, as Nibley summarizes, "the law of the Gospel requires self-control in everyday situations,"[183] putting "restraints on personal behavior" while "it mandates deportment… to make oneself agreeable to all."[184] Elaborating on these qualities, he wrote:

> As to light-mindedness, humor is not light-minded; it is insight into human foibles… What is light-minded is *kitsch*, delight in shallow trivia; and the viewing of serious or tragic events with complacency or indifference. It is light-minded, as Brigham Young often observed, to

---

180   E. T. Benson, *Teachings 1988*, 28 September 1982, p. 337.
181   H. W. Nibley, *Sacred*, p. 34.
182   D&C 88:121.
183   H. W. Nibley, *Sacred*, p. 34.
184   H. W. Nibley, *Drama*, p. 36.

take seriously and devote one's interest to modes, styles, fads, and manners of speech and deportment that are passing and trivial, without solid worth or intellectual appeal. As to laughter, Joseph Smith had a hearty laugh that shook his whole frame; but it was a meaningful laugh, a good-humored laugh.[185] Loud laughter is the hollow laugh, the bray, the meaningless laugh of the soundtrack or the audience responding to prompting cards, or routinely laughing at every remark made, no matter how banal, in a situation comedy. Note that "idle thoughts and... excess of laughter" go together in D&C 88:69.

As to light speech and speaking evil, my policy is to criticize only when asked to: nothing can be gained otherwise. But politicians are fair game—the Prophet Nathan soundly denounced David though he was "the Lord's anointed,"[186] but it was for his private and military hanky-panky, thinking only of his own appetites and interests.[187] Since nearly all gossip is outside the constructive frame, it qualifies as speaking evil.

As to lustful desires and unholy practices, such need no definition, one would think. Yet historically, the issue is a real one that arises from aberrations and perversions of the endowment among various "Hermetic" societies which, professing higher knowledge from above, resort to witchcraft, necromancy, and divination, with a strong leaning toward sexual license, as sanctioned and even required by their distorted mysteries...[188]

Conforming to the sequence of revealed laws found in other temple texts, the term "Gospel" occurs in the book of Moses as part of two passages—and in neither case does the order of its appearance defy our expectation of consistency with the sequence of temple covenants.[189] We read that Adam and Eve were tutored by holy messengers,[190] and that he and Eve in turn "made all things known unto their sons and daughters."[191] The mention of the Holy Ghost falling upon Adam[192] carries with it the implication that he had at that point already received the ordinance of baptism,[193] something that might have logically occurred soon after the angel's explanation of the meaning of the law of sacrifice.[194] The ordinance of baptism was followed by additional instruction concerning the plan of salvation given "by holy angels,... and by [God's] own voice, and by the gift of the Holy Ghost."[195] Bestowals of divine knowledge, the making of additional covenants, and the conferral of priesthood power must have surely accompanied these teachings.[196] "And thus all things were confirmed unto Adam, by an holy ordinance, and the Gospel [was] preached, and a decree [was] sent forth, that it should be in the world, until the end thereof."[197]

Sadly, scripture records that, despite Adam's efforts to the contrary, "works of darkness began to prevail among the sons of men."[198] Rejecting the covenants, the ordinances, and the universal scope of the brotherhood of the Gospel, they reveled in the exclusive nature of

MOSES 5

---

185   See R. L. Bushman, *Rough Stone*, pp. 483-485.
186   See, e.g., David's characterization of Saul in 1 Samuel 24:6.
187   See 2 Samuel 12.
188   H. W. Nibley, *Sacred*, pp. 553-554. See *Endnote 5-56*, p. 445.
189   Moses 5:58-59 and 8:19.
190   D&C 29:42; Moses 5:7-8, 58.
191   Moses 5:12.
192   Moses 5:9.
193   Moses 6:64.
194   Moses 5:6-8.
195   Moses 5:58; cf. 6:52-64.
196   Moses 6:67-68.
197   Moses 5:59.
198   Moses 5:55.

their "secret combination" by whose dark arts "they knew every man his brother,"[199] and they engaged in "wars and bloodshed… seeking for power."[200]

Chastity vs. Licentiousness. Nibley writes that this covenant of "self-control"[201] places a "restraint on uncontrolled appetites, desires, and passions, for what could be more crippling on the path of eternal progression than those carnal obsessions which completely take over the mind and body?"[202] Both chastity outside of marriage and fidelity within marriage are required by this covenant,[203] as Welch explains in the context of Jesus' Sermon at the Temple:

> The new law [in 3 Nephi 12:27-30] imposes a strict prohibition against sexual intercourse outside of marriage and, intensifying the rules that prevailed under the old law, requires purity of heart and denial of these things… [204]

> In connection with the law of chastity, Jesus teaches the importance of marriage by superseding the old law of divorcement with the new law of marriage: "It hath been written, that whosoever shall put away his wife, let him give her a writing of divorcement. Verily, verily, I say unto you, that whosoever shall put away his wife, saving for the cause of fornication, causeth her to commit adultery; and whoso shall marry her who is divorced committeth adultery"[205]… The context of the Sermon at the Temple suggests that this very demanding restriction applies only to husbands and wives who are bound by the eternal covenant relationship involved here. This explains the strictness of the rule completely, for eternal marriages can be dissolved only by proper authority and on justifiable grounds. Until they are so divorced, a couple remains covenantally married.[206]

Moses 6:5-23 describes the ideal family order established by Adam and Eve. Such an order is also implied in 8:13, where Noah and his righteous sons are mentioned. The patriarchal order of the priesthood "which was in the beginning" and "shall be in the end of the world also"[207] is depicted as presiding over a worthy succession of generations in the likeness and image of Adam,[208] just as Adam and Eve were made in the image and likeness of God.[209]

However, in contrast to these "preachers of righteousness,"[210] extracanonical traditions speak of "fornication… spread from the sons of Cain" that "flamed up," and moreover tell how, "in the fashion of beasts, they would perform sodomy indiscriminately."[211] Various sources describe how these practices then spread to Seth's male descendants as "the Malicious One increased his struggle to bring close the sons of Seth to the daughters of Cain."[212] The apogee of this wickedness was reached in the days of Noah,[213] when the "sons of God" who "hearkened not" to Noah broke their covenants and illicitly took to themselves[214] "the daughters of men."[215] Wholly consumed in consuming, according to the

---

199   Moses 5:51.
200   Moses 6:15.
201   H. W. Nibley, *Sacred,* p. 34.
202   H. W. Nibley, *Drama,* pp. 36-37.
203   Cf. D&C 42:22-24.
204   See *Endnote 5-57,* p. 445.
205   3 Nephi 12:31-32.
206   J. W. Welch, *Sermon,* pp. 52-53; cf. J. W. Welch, *Light,* pp. 91-92.
207   Moses 6:7; see also D&C 107:40-41, Abraham 1:26.
208   Moses 6:10.
209   Moses 6:9, 22.
210   Moses 6:23.
211   M. E. Stone, *Question,* 5, 8, pp. 119, 121.
212   *Ibid.,* 9, p. 121. See *Endnote 5-58,* p. 446.
213   Moses 8:13, 21.
214   See *Endnote 5-59,* p. 447.
215   See Moses 5:41-b, p. 388; the overview of Moses 4, p. 226; and *Excursus 24: The Watchers,* p. 585.

dictates of their appetites and passions, they are described as being wantonly absorbed in "eating and drinking, and marrying and giving in marriage."[216] Christensen sees a parallel to these events in the Book of Mormon story of the priests of Noah who abandoned their wives and then kidnapped and took to themselves daughters of the Lamanites.[217] As with those who lived in the days of Noah, the hardened "descendants from the union with the stolen wives" ultimately met with destruction.[218]

Consecration vs. Corruption and Violence. President Ezra Taft Benson has described the law of consecration as being "that we consecrate our time, talents, strength, property, and money for the upbuilding of the kingdom of God on this earth and the establishment of Zion."[219] He notes that all the covenants made up to this point are preparatory, explaining that: "Until one abides by the laws of obedience, sacrifice, the gospel, and chastity, he cannot abide the law of consecration, which is the law pertaining to the celestial kingdom."[220] Nibley similarly affirms that this law is "the consummation of the laws of obedience and sacrifice, is the threshold of the celestial kingdom, the last and hardest requirement made of men in this life"[221] and "can only be faced against sore temptation."[222] In compensation for this supreme effort, President Harold B. Lee avers that to the "individual who thus is willing to consecrate himself, [will come] the greatest joy that can come to the human soul."[223] Consecration is, as Welch affirms, the step that precedes perfection.[224]

Moses 7 describes how Enoch succeeded in bringing a whole people to be sufficiently "pure in heart"[225] to fully live the law of consecration.[226] In Zion, the "City of Holiness,"[227] the people "were of one heart and one mind, and dwelt in righteousness; and there was no poor among them."[228] Moreover, it can be safely presumed that, as with the Nephites following the visit of Christ: "There were no contentions and disputations among them, and every man did deal justly one with another. And they had all things in common among them; therefore, there were no rich and poor, bond and free, but they were all made free, and partakers of the heavenly gift."[229] Note that this ideal of economic reform is not based merely on the idea of fair division of property,[230] but rather on the higher principle "that everything we have belongs to the Lord; therefore, the Lord may call upon us for any and all of the property which we have, because it belongs to Him."[231]

Just as the life of Enoch can be regarded as a type of the spirit of consecration, so Lamech, who also lived in the seventh generation from Adam, serves as a scriptural example of its anti-type. While Enoch and his people covenanted with the Lord to ensure that there would

---

216 Moses 8:20-21.

217 Mosiah 20:4-5.

218 K. Christensen, *Temple*, p. 466 and Alma 25:4, 7-9. See *Endnote 4-38*, p. 310.

219 E. T. Benson, *Teachings 1988*, 28 September 1982, p. 121; cf. G. B. Hinckley, *Teachings 1997*, 10 April 1996, p. 147; H. B. Lee, *Teachings 1996*, 6 October 1973, p. 318.

220 E. T. Benson, *Teachings 1988*, 28 September 1982, p. 121 and D&C 78:7.

221 H. W. Nibley, *Foundation*, p. 168.

222 H. W. Nibley, *Sacred*, p. 34.

223 H. B. Lee, *Teachings 1996*, 4 April 1947, p. 318. See *Excursus 34: The Law of Consecration*, p. 611.

224 J. W. Welch, *Sermon*, pp. 60-61; cf. Matthew 19:21. See *Endnote 0-23*, p. 24.

225 D&C 97:21. Being "pure in heart" qualifies one to "see God" (Matthew 5:8, 3 Nephi 12:8, D&C 97:16).

226 See *Endnote 5-60*, p. 447.

227 Moses 7:19.

228 Moses 7:18.

229 4 Nephi 1:3-4; cf. H. W. Nibley, *Weep*, p. 372.

230 See *Endnote 5-61*, p. 447.

231 J. R. Clark, Jr., *Evening*, p. 55.

be "no poor among them,"[232] Lamech "entered into a covenant with Satan"[233] to see to it that he would never find himself as one of the poor. Lamech's "secret works" contributed to the rapid erosion of the unity of the human family, culminating in a terrifying chaos where "a man's hand was against his own brother, in administering death" and "seeking for power."[234]

In the same measure that the righteousness of the people of Enoch was unprecedented, so the "corruption and violence" of the people that reached a climax at the time of Noah was beyond anything heretofore witnessed.[235] In a striking echo of Moses 7:48, we are told that "[e]ven the earth complained and uttered lamentations."[236] To Enoch, the Lord sorrowed: "Behold these thy brethren; they are the workmanship of mine own hands… And… I [have] said… that they should love one another, and that they should choose me, their Father; but behold, they are without affection, and they hate their own blood… and among all the workmanship of my hands there has not been so great wickedness as among thy brethren… wherefore should not the heavens weep, seeing these shall suffer?"[237] Like the inhabitants of Sodom and Gomorrah, the wicked at last "were destroyed, because it was better for them to die, and thus be deprived of their agency, which they abused, than entail so much misery on their posterity, and bring ruin upon millions of unborn persons."[238]

The promise of being "received… into [God's] own bosom"[239] like Enoch and his people is extended to all those who, through the cleansing power of the Atonement "after all [they] can do,"[240] prepare themselves to receive it.[241] "Therefore, sanctify yourselves that your minds become single to God, and the days will come that you shall see him; for he will unveil his face unto you, and it shall be in his own time, and in his own way, and according to his own will. Remember the great and last promise which I have made unto you."[242]

The supreme qualification signaling readiness for this crowning blessing is charity, what Nibley calls the "essence of the law of consecration…, without which, as Paul and Moroni tell us, all the other laws and observances become null and void.[243] Love is not selective, and charity knows no bounds."[244] Thus, "if I expect anything in return for charity except the happiness of the recipient, then it is not charity."[245] For in charity, Nibley continues, "there is no bookkeeping, no *quid pro quo*, no deals, interests, bargaining, or ulterior motives; charity gives to those who do not deserve and expects nothing in return; it is the love God has for us, and the love we have for little children, of whom we expect nothing but for whom we would give everything."[246]

---

232   Moses 7:18.

233   Moses 5:49.

234   Moses 6:15. See *Excursus 35: Lamech's "Sword Song"*, p. 612.

235   Moses 8:28.

236   A. B. Mika'el, *Mysteries*, p. 29; cf. G. W. E. Nickelsburg, *1 Enoch*, 7:6, 9:2, 87:1, pp. 182, 202, 364; M. Wise, *et al.*, *DSS*, 4Q203 Frag. 8:9, p. 294. See also D. C. Peterson, *Weeping God*; A. C. Skinner, *Vindicated*.

237   Moses 7:32-33, 36-37. See *Endnote 5-62*, p. 447.

238   J. Taylor, *Government*, 1852, p. 53; cf. P. P. Pratt, *10 April 1853*, p. 259.

239   Moses 7:69.

240   2 Nephi 25:23.

241   D. H. Oaks, *To Become*.

242   D&C 88:68-69; cf. J. Smith, Jr., *Teachings*, 7 April 1844, p. 350.

243   See 1 Corinthians 13:1-3; Moroni 7:44.

244   H. W. Nibley, *Foundation*, p. 172.

245   H. W. Nibley, *Perspectives*, p. 495.

246   H. W. Nibley, *Since*, p. 347.

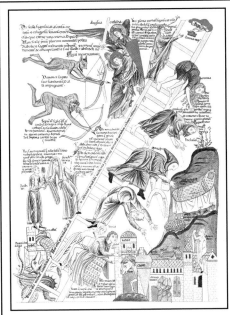

FIGURE 5-13. *The Ladder of Virtues, late twelfth century*
Herrad of Hohenbourg

SEE COLOR PLATE 5-13.

And now abideth faith, hope, charity, these three; but the greatest of these is charity.[1] This twelfth-century illustration shows the ladder of virtues, an ancient symbol of the process of spiritual progression.[2] Speaking of Jacob's dream of the heavenly ladder in Genesis 28, Elder Marion G. Romney said: "Jacob realized that the covenants he made with the Lord were the rungs on the ladder that he himself would have to climb in order to obtain the promised blessings—blessings that would entitle him to enter heaven and associate with the Lord."[3] Thus, the Prophet Joseph Smith correlated the "three principal rounds of Jacob's ladder" with "the telestial, the terrestrial, and the celestial glories or kingdoms."[4]

Faith, hope, and charity are portrayed as the three major rungs of the ladder in many ancient Christian sources. It is through *faith* that men are *called* to enter the gateway to the kingdom through baptism and confirmation. Those who subsequently prove themselves ready through their faithfulness to the Gospel are *chosen* or *elected* to inherit the kingdom "according to a preparatory redemption"[5] and they obtain a first *hope* of attaining it through the "earnest of the Spirit in [their] hearts."[6] Finally, having served God and their fellow man "at all hazards" in similitude of the Son of God,[7] and being filled with a *"perfect brightness* of hope"[8]

through *charity*, the "pure love of Christ,"[9] they are prepared to have their election *made sure* and they are eventually *sealed up* to eternal life and exaltation.[10] "There are many called, but few are chosen" in this ultimate sense of the word.[11] "And why are they not chosen? Because their hearts are set so much upon the things of this world, and aspire to the honors of men."[12] Their "bowels are not filled with charity"[13] which is, as Nibley affirms, the "essence of the law of consecration."[14]

In this drawing, the figure of Charity, representing those who have had their election "made sure," is depicted as having reached the summit of the ladder. Her hand is extended toward the hand of the Lord, shown emerging from a cloud and holding the crown of Life.[15] Other personages below her fall short as they are attracted by one thing or another. The hermit is too busy cultivating his garden and neglects his prayers; the reclusive monk longs for sleep; the alms-seeking monk falls for a large basket filled with pieces of silver—what his heart treasures most; the priest's attention is not occupied by his church but rather by friends, good food and drink, lusts of the flesh, and simony (i.e., the selling of ecclesiastical privileges for money); the nun chatting with the priest is seduced by the pleasures of the world and by family wealth; while the lay woman (attracted to jewels and beautiful lodgings) and the soldier (tempted by horses, arms, and other soldiers to command) have hardly begun the climb. At the bottom of the ladder, the Devil, whose temptations have ensnared all except Charity herself, appears in the form of a dragon, while his minions take steady aim at their victims with bow and arrow. The Prophet Joseph Smith taught: "Until we have perfect love we are liable to fall, and when we have a testimony that our names are sealed in the Lamb's Book of Life we have perfect love, and then it is impossible for false Christs to deceive us."[16] The caption on the ladder bears a message of encouragement, proclaiming that all those who have fallen will have the opportunity, through sincere penitence, to begin their climb anew.[17]

1   1 Corinthians 13:13.
2   R. Guénon, *Symboles*, pp. 336-339; J. Smith, Jr., *Teachings*, 7 April 1844, pp. 346-348, 354; M. C. Thomas, *Hebrews*; M. C. Thomas, *Brother of Jared*; N. M. Sarna, *Mists*, p. 82. See *Figures* 1-2 and 1-3, p. 34 and *Commentary* 1:1-c, p. 43.
3   M. G. Romney, *Temples*, pp. 239-240. See H. W. Nibley, *Sacred*, pp. 579-581.
4   J. L. Carroll, *Reconciliation*, p. 95 n. 18; J. Smith, Jr., *Teachings*, 21 May 1843, p. 305.
5   Alma 13:3.
6   2 Corinthians 1:22, 5:5; cf. Ephesians 1:14.
7   J. Smith, Jr., *Teachings*, 27 June 1839, p. 150.
8   2 Nephi 31:20; cf. Ether 12:28: "a *more excellent* hope."
9   Moroni 7:47; cf. D&C 121:45.
10 See *Endnote 5-63*, p. 448.
11 D&C 121:34; cf. Matthew 20:16, 22:14; D&C 95:5-6, and *Excursus 3: Temple Blessings in the Oath and Covenant of the Priesthood*, p. 519.
12 D&C 121:34-35.
13 D&C 121:44.
14 H. W. Nibley, *Foundation*, p. 172. See *Endnote 5-64*, p. 448.
15 Cf. *Commentary* 1:25-c, p. 60. See *Endnote 1-22*, p. 79.
16 D. Q. Cannon, *et al.*, *Far West*, 25 October 1831, p. 23; J. Smith, Jr., *Teachings*, 25 October 1831, p. 9; cf. 2 Peter 1:5-11, Moroni 8:25-26.
17 R. Green, *et al.*, *Hortus*, 2:352-353.

Moses 5: Text and Commentary

CHAPTER 5
(June–October 1830)

OBEDIENCE SHOWN (PP. 354-359)

AND [a]it came to pass that after I, the Lord God, had driven them out, that Adam began to till the earth, and to have dominion over all the beasts of the field, and to eat his [b]bread by the sweat of his brow, [c]as I the Lord had commanded him. And Eve, also, his wife, did labor with him.

2 And [a]Adam knew his wife, and she bare unto him sons and daughters, and they began to multiply and to replenish the earth.

3 And from that time forth, the [a]sons and daughters of Adam began to divide [b]two and two in the land, and to [c]till the land, and to tend flocks, and they also begat sons and daughters.

4 And [a]Adam and Eve, his wife, called upon the name of the Lord, and [b]they heard the voice of the Lord from the way toward the Garden of Eden, speaking unto them, and they saw him not; [c]for they were shut out from his presence.

5 And [a]he gave unto them commandments, that they should worship the Lord their God, and should [b]offer the firstlings of their flocks, for an offering unto the Lord. And [c]Adam was obedient unto the commandments of the Lord.

SACRIFICE EXPLAINED (PP. 360-362)

6 And [a]after many days [b]an angel of the Lord appeared unto Adam, saying: Why dost thou offer sacrifices unto the Lord? And Adam said unto him: [c]I know not, save the Lord commanded me.

7 And then the angel spake, saying: [a]This thing is a similitude of the sacrifice of the Only Begotten of the Father, which is [b]full of grace and truth.

8 Wherefore, thou shalt [a]do all that thou doest in the name of the Son, and [b]thou shalt repent and [c]call upon God in the name of the Son forevermore.

ADAM AND EVE REJOICE (PP. 362-364)

9 And [a]in that day the [b]Holy Ghost fell upon Adam, which [c]beareth record of the Father and the Son, saying: [d]I am the Only Begotten of the Father from the beginning, henceforth and forever, that [e]as thou hast fallen thou mayest be redeemed, and all mankind, even as many as will.

10 And in that day [a]Adam blessed God and was [b]filled, and [c]began to prophesy concerning all the families of the earth, saying: [d]Blessed be the name of God, for [e]because of my transgression my eyes are opened, and in this life I shall have joy, and [f]again in the flesh I shall see God.

11 And [a]Eve, his wife, heard all these things and was glad, saying: Were it not for our transgression [b]we never should have had seed, and never should have known good and evil, and the joy of our redemption, and the eternal life which God giveth unto all the obedient.

12 And Adam and Eve blessed the name of God, and they [a]made all things known unto their sons and their daughters.

THE TWO WAYS (PP. 364-367)

13 And [a]Satan came among them, saying: [b]I am also a son of God; and he commanded them, saying: Believe it not; and they believed it not, and they loved Satan more than God. And [c]men began from that time forth to be [d]carnal, sensual, and devilish.

14 And [a]the Lord God called upon men by the Holy Ghost everywhere and commanded them that they should repent;

15 [a]And as many as believed in the Son, and repented of their sins, should be saved; and as many as believed not and repented not, should be damned; and the words went forth out of the mouth of God in [b]a firm decree; wherefore they must be fulfilled.

CAIN'S SACRIFICE (PP. 367-373)

16 And [a]Adam and Eve, his wife, ceased not to call upon God. And [b]Adam knew Eve his wife, and she conceived and bare [c]Cain, and said: I have gotten [d]a man [e]from the Lord; [f]wherefore he may not reject his words. But behold, [g]Cain hearkened not, saying: [h]Who is the Lord that I should know him?

17 And she again conceived and bare his brother [a]Abel. And [b]Abel hearkened unto the voice of the Lord. And Abel was a [c]keeper of sheep, but [d]Cain was a tiller of the ground.

18 And Cain loved Satan more than God. And Satan commanded him, saying: [a]Make an offering unto the Lord.

19 And [b]in process of time it came to pass that [c]Cain brought of the fruit of the ground an offering unto the Lord.

20 And [a]Abel, he also brought of the firstlings of his flock, and of the fat thereof. And the Lord had respect unto Abel, and to his offering;

21 But unto Cain, and to his offering, he had not respect. Now [a]Satan knew this, and it pleased him. And [b]Cain was very wroth, and [c]his countenance fell.

CAIN REJECTS THE LORD (PP. 373-376)

22 And [a]the Lord said unto Cain: [b]Why art thou wroth? Why is thy countenance fallen?

23 [a]If thou doest well, thou shalt be accepted. And if thou doest not well, [b]sin lieth at the door, and [c]Satan desireth to have thee; and except thou shalt hearken unto my commandments, [d]I will deliver thee up, and it shall be unto thee according to his desire. And [e]thou shalt rule over him;

24 For from this time forth [a]thou shalt be the father of his lies; thou shalt be called [b]Perdition; for [c]thou wast also before the world.

25 And it shall be said in time to come—That these abominations were had from Cain; for he rejected the greater counsel which was had from God; and this is a cursing which I will put upon thee, [a]except thou repent.

26 And [a]Cain was wroth, and [b]listened not any more to the voice of the Lord, neither to [c]Abel, his brother, who walked in holiness before the Lord.

27 [a]And Adam and his wife [b]mourned before the Lord, because of Cain and his brethren.

CAIN SLAYS ABEL (PP. 376-382)

28 And it came to pass that [a]Cain took one of his brothers' daughters to wife, and they loved Satan more than God.

29 And [a]Satan said unto Cain: [b]Swear unto me by thy throat, and if thou tell it thou shalt die; and swear thy brethren by their heads, and [c]by the living God, that they tell it not; for [d]if they tell it, they shall surely die; and this [e]that thy father may not know it; and [f]this day I will deliver thy brother Abel into thine hands.

30 And [a]Satan sware unto Cain that he would do according to his commands. And all these things were done in secret.

31 And Cain said: [a]Truly I am Mahan, the master of this great secret, [b]that I may murder and get gain. Wherefore Cain was called Master Mahan, and [c]he gloried in his wickedness.

32 And [a]Cain went [b]into the field, and [c]Cain talked with Abel, his brother. And it came to pass that while they were in the field, Cain rose up against [d]Abel, his brother, and [e]slew him.

33 And *a*Cain gloried in that which he had done, saying: *b*I am free; *c*surely the flocks of my brother falleth into my hands.

CONSEQUENCES (PP. 382-390)

34 And the Lord said unto Cain: *a*Where is Abel, thy brother? And he said: *b*I know not. *c*Am I my brother's keeper?

35 And the Lord said: *a*What hast thou done? The *b*voice of thy brother's blood cries unto me *c*from the ground.

36 And now *a*thou shalt be cursed *b*from the earth which hath opened her mouth to receive thy brother's blood from thy hand.

37 When thou tillest the *a*ground it shall not henceforth yield unto thee her strength. A *b*fugitive and a vagabond shalt thou be in the earth.

38 And Cain said unto the Lord: Satan tempted me *a*because of my brother's flocks. And I was wroth also; for his offering thou didst accept and not mine; *b*my punishment is greater than I can bear.

39 Behold *a*thou hast driven me out this day from the face of the Lord, and from thy face shall I be hid; and I shall be a fugitive and a vagabond in the earth; and it shall come to pass, that *b*he that findeth me will slay me, because of mine iniquities, for these things are not hid from the Lord.

40 And I the Lord said unto him: *a*Whosoever slayeth thee, vengeance shall be taken on him *b*sevenfold. And *c*I the Lord set a mark upon Cain, lest any finding him should kill him.

41 And Cain *a*was shut out from the presence of the Lord, and with his wife and many of his brethren dwelt *b*in the land of Nod, *c*on the east of Eden.

POSTERITY OF CAIN (PP. 390-395)

42 And Cain knew his wife, and she conceived and bare *a*Enoch, and he also begat many sons and daughters. And *b*he builded a city, and *c*he called the name of the city after the name of his son, Enoch.

43 And *a*unto Enoch was born Irad, and other sons and daughters. And Irad begat Mahujael, and other sons and daughters. And *b*Mahujael begat Methusael, and other sons and daughters. And *c*Methusael begat Lamech.

44 And Lamech *a*took unto himself *b*two wives; the name of one being *c*Adah, and the name of the other, Zillah.

45 And Adah bare *a*Jabal; he was the father of *b*such as dwell in tents, and they were keepers of *c*cattle; and his brother's name was Jubal, who was the father of all such as handle the *d*harp and organ.

46 And Zillah, she also bare *a*Tubal Cain, an instructor of every *b*artificer in brass and iron. And *c*the sister of Tubal Cain was called Naamah.

WORKS OF DARKNESS (PP. 395-399)

47 And *a*Lamech said unto his wives, Adah and Zillah: Hear my voice, ye wives of Lamech, hearken unto my speech; for I have slain a man to my *b*wounding, and *c*a young man to my hurt.

48 If Cain shall be avenged *a*sevenfold, truly Lamech shall be seventy and seven fold;

49 For Lamech having entered into a covenant with Satan, after the manner of Cain, wherein he became *a*Master Mahan, master of that great secret which was administered unto Cain by Satan; and *b*Irad, the son of Enoch, having known their secret, began to reveal it unto the *c*sons of Adam;

50 Wherefore Lamech, being angry, slew him, not like unto Cain, his brother Abel, for the sake of getting gain, but *a*he slew him for the oath's sake.

51 For, from the days of Cain, there was a *a*secret combination, and their works were in the dark, and they knew every man his brother.

52 Wherefore the Lord cursed Lamech, and *a*his house, and *b*all them that had covenanted with Satan; for they kept not the commandments of God, and it displeased God, and he ministered not unto them, and their works were abominations, and began to spread among all the *c*sons of men. And it was among the sons of men.

53 And among the daughters of men these things were not spoken, because that *a*Lamech had spoken the secret unto his wives, and they rebelled against him, and declared these things abroad, and had not compassion;

54 *a*Wherefore *b*Lamech was despised, and cast out, and came not among the sons of men, *c*lest he should die.

55 And thus the works of darkness began to prevail among all the sons of men.

56 And *a*God cursed the earth with a sore curse, and was angry with the wicked, with all the *b*sons of men whom he had made;

57 For *a*they would not hearken unto his voice, nor believe on his Only Begotten Son, even him whom he declared should come in the meridian of time, who was *b*prepared from before the foundation of the world.

THE GOSPEL PREACHED (PP. 400-401)

58 *a*And thus the *b*Gospel began to be preached, from the beginning, *c*being declared by holy angels sent forth from the presence of God, and by his own voice, and by the gift of the Holy Ghost.

59 *a*And thus *b*all things were confirmed unto Adam, by an holy ordinance, and the Gospel preached, and *d*a decree sent forth, that it should be in the world, until the end thereof; and thus it was. Amen.

MOSES 5

*1 And **it came to pass that after I, the Lord God, had driven them out, that Adam began to till the earth,** and to have dominion over all the beasts of the field, and to eat his **bread by the sweat of his brow, as I the Lord had commanded him. And Eve, also, his wife, did labor with him.***

*2 And **Adam knew his wife,** and she bare unto him sons and daughters, and they began to multiply and to replenish the earth.*

1   a   *it came to pass that after I, the Lord God, had driven them out, that Adam began to till the earth.* The structure and symmetry of vv. 1-3 help paint a scene of pastoral tranquility. Adam, Eve, and all Creation, as yet untroubled by Satan (v. 13), carry out their labors in perfect obedience to the instructions God gave in the Garden of Eden.[247]

OT1 reads "for after that he had been driven out he began to till the Earth."[248]

to till the earth. "Adam was a ploughman when ploughing first begun," English farmers once sang with pride.[249] "Here, in the place of the 'subdue' of the King James version, we have explicitly the word 'till' applied to the earth alone, while 'dominion' is reserved for the animal kingdom."[250] The tilling reported here was previously anticipated in Moses 3:5 and 4:29.[251]

"Tilling the earth" is a frequent theme in the Book of Mormon. Indeed, 2 Nephi 2:19 and Alma 42:2 specifically state that Adam and Eve were driven out of the Garden of Eden to till the earth. The linking of the themes of obedience and the tilling of the earth is found in Mosiah 6:6-7, and tilling is followed by a mention of children in 2 Nephi 2:19-20 and Ether 6:13-16. Tilling as part of settling a new land can be seen in 1 Nephi 18:24, Enos 1:21, and Ether 6:13, and the making of tools to till the earth is mentioned in Ether 10:25.

b   *bread by the sweat of his brow.* God rewarded the labor of Adam and Eve with a harvest of life-sustaining grain. Bread relieved them from the diet of wild plants and roots they had presumably followed immediately after their expulsion from Eden.[252]

OT1 and OT2 read "by the sweat of the brow"[253]—"his" was substituted by the 1866-67 RLDS Publication Committee.[254]

c   *as I the Lord had commanded him. And Eve, also, his wife, did labor with him.* Vv. 1-6 highlight the obedience of Adam and Eve by enumerating their faithfulness to each of the commandments they had been given. Adam, with his fellow-laborer Eve, began to "till the earth, and to have dominion over all the beasts of the field, and to eat his bread by the sweat of his brow."[255] Likewise Eve fulfilled the commission she had received in the Garden of Eden and "bare… sons and daughters, and they began to replenish the earth."[256] Moreover "Adam was obedient to the commandments of the Lord" to "offer the firstlings of their flocks" for "many days," despite the fact that he did not yet fully understand the reason why he had been thus commanded.[257]

2   a   *Adam knew his wife.* The book of Moses expresses this event in the simple past, rather than in the pluperfect (i.e., "Adam had already known his wife") preferred by some interpreters.[258]

247   Moses 4:22, 25.
248   S. H. Faulring *et al., Original Manuscripts,* p. 92.
249   R. Palmer, *Painful Plough,* p. 54.
250   H. W. Nibley, *Dominion,* p. 6.
251   See *Commentary* 3:5-a, p. 154; 4:24-b, p. 271; 4:25-a, p. 272; and 5:2-a, p. 354.
252   See *Commentary* 4:24-b, p. 271 and 4:25-a, p. 272. See also 3:9-g, p. 163; 3:9-i, p. 168; the overview of Moses 5, p. 341; and *Excursus 42: Nebuchadnezzar's "Fall."* p. 632.
253   S. H. Faulring, *et al., Original Manuscripts,* pp. 92, 602.
254   K. P. Jackson, *Book of Moses,* p. 22.
255   Moses 5:1; cf. Mosiah 6:6-7.
256   Moses 5:2.
257   Moses 5:5-6.
258   G. A. Anderson, *Perfection,* p. 217.

*2 And **Adam knew his wife**, and she bare unto him sons and daughters, and they began to multiply and to replenish the earth.*

*3 And from that time forth, the **sons and daughters** of Adam began to divide **two and two** in the land, and to **till the land**, and to tend flocks, and they also begat **sons and daughters**.*

*4 And **Adam and Eve, his wife, called upon the name of the Lord**, and they heard the voice of the Lord from the way toward the Garden of Eden, speaking unto them, and they saw him not; for they were shut out from his presence.*

An Armenian text explicitly states: "When Adam and Eve left the Garden, they were still virgins."[259]

"Ancient writers often mentioned sexual relations as an indication that a period of penitence or mourning had come to its natural termination."[260] For example, one text says that Adam "having abandoned the sad mourning, at the command of God and the instruction of an angel... came to his wife Eve to beget a child."[261] The same pattern of mourning followed by an explicit mention of sexual relations is implied in Moses 6:2, which follows the narrative of the rebellion of Cain and the death of Abel.[262]

3   a   ***sons and daughters.*** In contrast to Genesis, the book of Moses specifically mentions children who were born prior to Cain and Abel. Al-Kisa'i recounts that Eve had twenty births prior to Cain and Abel—each of the births producing a set of twins, male and female.[263]

     b   ***two and two.*** The monogamous pairing described here can be contrasted with the presumably unauthorized polygamous marriage of the wicked Lamech[264] and the general licentiousness of the people in the days of Noah.[265]

     c   ***till the land... sons and daughters.*** The wording of this verse parallels the description of Adam and Eve's faithfulness to God's commandments.[266] We are meant to understand that the sons and daughters of Adam and Eve were as thoroughly obedient as their parents.

4   a   ***Adam and Eve, his wife, called upon the name of the Lord.*** Here, we are told that Adam and Eve "called upon the name of the *Lord*"—meaning Jehovah. Later, they will receive the more specific instruction that they should "call upon God in the name of the *Son*."[267]

William Clayton wrote that the "first word Adam spoke" was "a word of supplication."[268] Ancient sources purport to give details about the form of prayer used by Adam and Eve. For example, the practice of prayer with uplifted hands is frequently mentioned, e.g., "Adam was then offering on the altar, and had begun to pray, with his hands spread unto God."[269] This classical *orans* (= Latin "praying") posture is a traditional priestly gesture that Christians have long associated with the Crucifixion.[270] Brown explains the practice of praying with upraised hands by reference to Isaiah 1:15-16, where it is evident "that the Lord's eyes are drawn to those who lift up clean (or innocent) hands to Him, while He hides His eyes, or

259   M. E. Stone, *Sethites*, 1, p. 203; cf. Shelemon, *Book of the Bee*, 18, p. 24; M. E. Stone, *Question, 1*, p. 118; B. M. Wheeler, *Prophets*, p. 29. For a discussion of early Christian view on the consummation of Adam and Eve's marriage and its implications for celibacy in early Christian thought, see G. A. Anderson, *Perfection*, pp. 43-73.
260   G. A. Anderson, *Penitence*, pp. 30-31.
261   M. E. Stone, *Forefathers*, 27, p. 193; cf. M. E. Stone, *Adam and Grandsons*, 1, p. 92.
262   See *Commentary* 5:16-a, p. 367 and 5:16-b, p. 367.
263   M. al-Kisa'i, *Tales*, p. 73; cf. al-Tabari, *Creation*, 1:137-147, pp. 308-317.
264   Moses 5:44.
265   Moses 8:21.
266   Moses 5:1-2.
267   Moses 5:8. See *Commentary* 5:8-a, p. 361 and 6:4-a, p. 477.
268   W. Clayton, *Chronicle*, 15 June 1844, p. 134.
269   S. C. Malan, *Adam and Eve*, 1:59, p. 83. See also Moses 7:41; H. W. Nibley, *Prayer Circle*, pp. 56-60; J. A. Tvedtnes, *Temple Prayer*, pp. 81-88; M. von Wellnitz, *Liturgy*, p. 31; *Figure 3-8*, p. 145; and *Figure 6-14*, p. 473.
270   See *Endnote 5-65*, p. 449.

*4 And **Adam and Eve, his wife, called upon the name of the Lord**, and they heard the voice of the Lord from the way toward the Garden of Eden, speaking unto them, and they saw him not; for they were shut out from his presence.*

glances away, from those whose hands are unclean… Notice also that raising the hands essentially exposes the heart to the Lord. Hence we find the directive in Job 11:13 to 'prepare thine heart, and stretch out thine hands toward him' and the admonition of Lamentations 3:41: 'Let us lift up our heart with our hands unto God in the heavens.' These two concepts are combined in the well-known temple scripture: 'Who shall ascend into the hill of the Lord? Or who shall stand in his holy place? He that hath clean hands, and a pure heart.'[271]

Parry sees in Psalm 24 a possible reference to a prayer circle, noting that "prayer with upraised arms was an essential feature of holy petitions put up to God in the temple of Solomon."[272] "Clean hands" can be thought of as a symbol of the justificatory remission of sins while a "pure heart" can be considered as the result of the process of sanctification.[273] The one whose "palms are innocent, and whose heart is pure" will have the "privilege of appearing before God in his temple,"[274] that he "may know him, and the power of his resurrection, and the fellowship of his sufferings, being made conformable unto his death."[275] Hence a Christian text that has the penitent thief being welcomed into Paradise only after he shows to the Cherubim "the writing [token, mark, authorization[276]] which was in his hand, [that] was written in the blood… of our Lord Jesus Christ."[277] The symbolism relates to sacrifice "after the order of the Melchizedek Priesthood"[278]—not the Levitical offering of animal sacrifice but an ongoing dedication of one's own life in a spirit of consecration.[279] Elder Neal A. Maxwell explained that "real, personal sacrifice never was placing an animal on the altar. Instead, it is a willingness to put the animal in us upon the altar and letting it be consumed!"[280]

Accounts purporting to record the words of Adam and Eve's prayer have long puzzled interpreters. For example, Nibley cites *The Conflict of Adam and Eve with Satan*, which says that Adam and Eve "stood with upstretched hands calling upon the Lord, as 'Adam began to pray in a language which is unintelligible to us.'"[281] The *Gospel of Bartholomew* 2:13 likewise has Mary, the mother of Jesus, and the apostles praying with outspread hands. Her prayer begins with words that James reports as being "hopelessly corrupted," and that Hennecke simply omits.[282] While James justifies abandoning any attempt at decipherment by saying "the matter is not of importance,"[283] Nibley correctly explains that her "speaking in an unknown language" is actually "the usual code introducing [such a] prayer."[284]

Repetition is another hallmark of solemn prayer. For example, at the dedication of the Kirtland temple the Prophet prayed following the pattern of "Adam's prayer"[285] with threefold

271 M. B. Brown, *Gate*, p. 125 and Psalm 24:3-4; cf. 1 Timothy 2:8; D&C 109:19; S. A. Ashraf, *Inner*, p. 125.

272 D. W. Parry, *Psalm 24*, p. 61 n. 9.

273 D. A. Bednar, *Clean Hands*, pp. 82-83.

274 D. W. Parry, *Psalm 24*, p. 60.

275 Philippians 3:10.

276 H. W. Nibley, *Sacred*, p. 557.

277 I. Mika'el, son of Bakhayla, *Godhead*, p. 136; cf. *Commentary 5:5-b*, p. 359; *Excursus 37: Traditions About the Role of Abel*, p. 617; M. Lidzbarski, *Ginza*, GL 1:1, p. 429; S. C. Malan, *Adam and Eve*, 1:69, pp. 83-84. See *Endnote 4-32*, p. 308. See *Endnote E-146*, p. 736.

278 J. Smith, Jr., *Words*, p. 55 n. 29. See Mosiah 13:27-35.

279 See *Excursus 33: The Restoration of Sacrifice*, p. 609. See also H. W. Nibley, *Prayer Circle*, pp. 59-60.

280 N. A. Maxwell, *Deny*.

281 H. W. Nibley, *Prayer Circle*, pp. 57-58. See S. C. Malan, *Adam and Eve*, 1:5, p. 6.

282 E. Hennecke, *et al.*, *NT Apocrypha*, 2:493 n. 2; cf. G. Scholem, *Trends*, p. 62: "original and… bizarre phrases and word combinations.… regarded as the original language of the creature addressing its Creator."

283 M. R. James, *Bartholomew*, p. 171.

284 H. W. Nibley, *Unrolling*, p. 164. See also C. Schmidt, *Pistis*, 4:136, p. 707; G. R. S. Mead, *Pistis*, 5:136, pp. 295-296; H. W. Nibley, *Apocryphal*, pp. 306-307, 313-314; H. W. Nibley, *Prayer Circle*, pp. 56-58.

285 H. W. Nibley, *House of Glory*, p. 339.

*4 And **Adam and Eve, his wife, called upon the name of the Lord**, and **they heard the voice of the Lord from the way toward the Garden of Eden**, speaking unto them, and they saw him not; **for they were shut out from his presence**.*

repetition: "O hear, O hear, O hear us, O Lord! …that we may mingle our voices with those bright, shining seraphs around thy throne."[286] Similarly, Abraham, having "rebuilt the altar of Adam" at the command of an angel,[287] is reported as having repeatedly raised his voice to God, saying: "El, El, El, El, Iaoel…[288] Accept my prayer."[289] Abraham's prayer was also in imitation of Adam, who was reported in one account to have supplicated: "May the words of my mouth be acceptable."[290] The threefold repetition in some versions of the story may represent the tradition that it was on the third day when Adam's urgent and persistent request for additional knowledge from the Lord was at last answered with instruction by an angel. The angel is said to have borne a book that "teaches [those who are wise and God-fearing] how to call upon the angels and make them appear before men, and answer all their questions."[291] Likewise, the Prophet Joseph Smith was anxious to teach the Saints the manner by which they could "pray and have [their] prayers answered."[292]

b ***they heard the voice of the Lord from the way toward the Garden of Eden.*** In response to their obedience and prayers, Adam and Eve heard the Lord's voice calling them back from their place of exile. Later, He gave them additional commandments (and covenants) to in order to set their feet back on the way toward the Garden of Eden which is, of course, the path that terminates in "the way of the Tree of Life."[293]

In a passage from the *Midrash Tehillim*,[294] the Hebrew term *teshuvah*, which denotes "return" but scripturally means "repentance" or "conversion," is used to describe the way back to the Garden, signifying "the movement that brings every thing and every being back to its supernal origin," the "return to the celestial abode."[295] The spiritual movement of turning away from the world and back toward mankind's heavenly origins is mirrored in the layout of ordinance rooms in some modern temples.[296]

3 Enoch relates that the "first man and his generation dwelt at the gate of the Garden of Eden so that they might gaze at the bright image of the *Shekhinah*."[297] "The entrance to the Garden therefore symbolizes the human possibility of reaching a privileged vantage point from which a higher knowledge may be obtained."[298]

c ***for they were shut out from his presence.*** Lacking knowledge of the conditions by which they could receive the blessings of the Atonement, Adam and Eve experienced a temporary state of spiritual death—the "first death, even that same death which is the last death" for the wicked.[299]

Nibley comments: "They could hear his voice speaking from the Garden, but they saw him not. They were shut out from his presence, but the link was there. This is what the rabbis call the

---

286 D&C 109:78-79.

287 H. W. Nibley, *Prayer Circle*, p. 57.

288 I.e., Yahweh-El = Jehovah (M. Barker, *Gate*, p. 153; H. W. Nibley, *Prayer Circle*, p. 57).

289 R. Rubinkiewicz, *Apocalypse of Abraham*, 17:13, 20, p. 697.

290 L. Ginzberg, *Legends*, 1:91; cf. Psalm 54:2: "Hear my prayer, O God; give ear to the words of my mouth."

291 L. Ginzberg, *Legends*, 1:92; cf. S. Savedow, *Rezial*, p. 6. Early Christians, when they gathered to "lift up [their] hearts to heaven," were reminded that God Himself (with the angels) would be an "onlooker" to their proceedings (J. Cooper, *et al.*, *Testament*, 1:23, p. 71).

292 To Bathsheba W. Smith, *Juvenile Instructor*, 27, 1 June 1892, p. 345, cited in T. G. Madsen, *Joseph Smith*, p. 99. Cf. J. Smith, Jr., *Teachings*, 28 April 1842, p. 226.

293 Moses 4:31.

294 W. G. Braude, *Midrash on Psalms*, 90:12, 2:94.

295 G. B. Eden, *Mystical Architecture*, pp. 16, 17 n. 7.

296 See, e.g., J. E. Talmage, *House of the Lord*, pp. 118-134.

297 P. Alexander, *3 Enoch*, 5:3, p. 259.

298 G. B. Eden, *Mystical Architecture*, p. 18.

299 D&C 29:41.

*4 And Adam and Eve, his wife, called upon the name of the Lord, and they heard the voice of the Lord from the way toward the Garden of Eden, speaking unto them, and they saw him not; **for they were shut out from his presence**.*

*5 And **he gave unto them commandments**, that they should worship the Lord their God, and should offer the firstlings of their flocks, for an offering unto the Lord. And Adam was obedient unto the commandments of the Lord.*

bath-kol. The *bath-kol* is the 'echo.' Literally, it means the 'daughter of the voice.' After the last prophets, the rabbis didn't get inspiration, but they did have the *bath-kol*. They could hear the voice. They could hear the echo. You could have inspiration, intuition, etc. (not face-to-face anymore, but the *bath-kol*)."[300]

Despite significant differences, initiation rites in Greco-Roman mystery religions and traditions of early Christian mysticism shared the idea of an upward physical movement symbolizing an ascent from darkness to increasingly greater light. For example, some Greek rites required the initiate to sleep in the darkness of an underground room or cave before their period of instruction began, simulating the process of rebirth.[301] Likewise, some traditions have Adam and Eve living in the darkness of a cave after their expulsion from Eden.[302] Armenian texts, though without in this case specifically mentioning a cave, describe an intermediate place of darkness where Adam and Eve spent time after they left the Garden: "And they [the angels] took Adam and Eve away from the Garden. And they went outside to a dark and gloomy place, [and] they remained there [six days] without eating, weeping inconsolably, and bemoaning themselves. But after six days the Lord took pity on them, and he sent his angel to take them out of the darkness, and he guided and brought them into this bright world."[303] Likewise, Islamic scholar al-Qummi describes a period of misery for Adam and Eve after the Fall, recording the story that upon their descent to earth they were placed on two mountain peaks where Adam remained weeping for forty days.[304]

Nibley comments: "They had been cast out into another world, into another Life. Life became short and miserable, and Adam didn't know whether he would ever get out of it again. The lights went out. When he saw the sun go down, he had no assurance the sun would ever rise again. He was utterly depressed. Then he comes and receives the instruction from the angel that tells him he doesn't have to remain there… Remember, we had that light-dark-light business (preexistence, existence, and hereafter; past, present, and future). You get a religion which is light all the way. There was light in the preexistence. They are going to have light now, and light hereafter, rather than darkness in all three."[305]

5   a   ***he gave unto them commandments.*** "What was the reward for diligence in prayer?" asks Draper, *et al.* "The answer is more commandments."[306] These were among what Alma termed the "second commandments," given because of Adam and Eve had transgressed the "first commandments."[307] Nibley continues: "Now he gives them commandments. He gives them the law of God. He gives them the law of obedience. He gives them the law of sacrifice,

---

300   H. W. Nibley, *Teachings of the PGP*, 19, p. 233.

301   D. Ulansey, *Mithraic*, pp. 35-36; cf. *Commentary 3:21-a*, p. 180. See *Excursus 53: Comparative Explorations, The Mysteries*, p. 663.

302   E. A. W. Budge, *Cave*, p. 69; S. C. Malan, *Adam and Eve*, 1:3:16, p. 5; H. Schwartz, *Tree*, p. 344. See *Excursus 53: Comparative Explorations, The Cave of Treasures*, p. 669.

303   W. L. Lipscomb, *Creation*, 46-47, p. 126; cf. W. L. Lipscomb, *Creation*, 50-51, pp. 265-266, S. C. Malan, *Adam and Eve*, 1:4-16, pp. 5-18 and *Excursus 53: Comparative Explorations, Cave of Treasures*, p. 669.

304   A. at-Tabataba'i, *Al-Mizan*, 1:197; cf. A. al-Tha'labi, *Lives*, pp. 58-59. See *Commentary 5:6-a*, p. 360, and the overview of Moses 3, p. 143.

305   H. W. Nibley, *Teachings of the PGP*, 19, pp. 231, 234.

306   R. D. Draper, *et al.*, *Commentary*, p. 58. See D&C 88:13 (light = law). Compare M. Lieber, *Pirkei Avos*, 4:2, pp. 219-221: "one *mitzvah* leads to another *mitzvah*, and one sin leads to another sin; the consequence of a *mitzvah* is a *mitzvah*, and the consequence of a sin is a sin."

307   Alma 12:31-37.

*5 And **he gave unto them commandments**, that they should worship the Lord their God, and should **offer the firstlings of their flocks**, for an offering unto the Lord. And **Adam was obedient** unto the commandments of the Lord.*

and he gives them the law of the Gospel…, which they follow. They are starting on the way back now."[308]

OT1 and OT2 have the singular term "commandment."[309] The use of the plural in the current text perpetuates a change introduced by the 1866-67 RLDS Publication Committee.[310]

b **offer the firstlings of their flocks.** As an element of the process of repentance, sacrifice is both a necessary precursor to baptism and confirmation, and a requirement for renewal of that covenant.[311] The ordinance of animal sacrifice given to Adam and Eve[312] corresponds in our day to the sacrament.[313] Thus, as Elder Bruce R. McConkie explained, three ordinances (baptism, sacrifice, sacrament) are associated with one and the same covenant.[314]

Rabbi Nathan says that at the dawning of the first day after their expulsion, Adam "arose and built altars… and he offered [an ox] up as a burnt offering."[315] In another text, Adam and Eve make a first sacrifice of their own blood: "Adam and Eve stood on their feet; and Adam said to Eve, 'Gird thyself, and I will also gird myself'… Then Adam and Eve took stones and [made] an altar; and they took leaves… with which they wiped, from the face of the rock, the blood they had spilled.[316] But that which had dropped on the sand, they took… and offered it upon the altar… Then Adam and Eve… wept, thus entreating God, 'Forgive us our trespass and our sin, and look upon us with Thine eye of mercy.'"[317] Nibley cites an account where Satan smites Adam with a sacrificial weapon as he made his offering: "Adam fell on the altar and would have died were it not that God intervened and healed him on the spot, declaring that what Adam had suffered so far was acceptable to him as a true sacrifice, being in the similitude of his own offering: 'Even so will I be wounded!'"[318]

An Islamic tradition records that "the angel Gabriel brought a lamb, and taught Adam to kill it in the name of Allàh."[319] In addition to the coming of the angel, Islamic sources also associate a deceitful appearance of Satan with the act of sacrifice. As part of the *hajj*, pilgrims go to Mina "to throw stones at Satan and to sacrifice some animal in the Name of God."[320] The explanation of this ritual is that "Satan tried to deceive Abraham and Ishmael, but they realized who he was and threw stones at him."[321]

c **Adam was obedient.** Though both Adam and Eve are commanded, only Adam is specifically mentioned as being obedient. Maybe this is because, as a priest, he is the one who actually carried out the performance of the offering. In any case, there is no implication that Eve was *not* obedient.[322]

---

308 H. W. Nibley, *Teachings of the PGP*, 19, p. 233.
309 S. H. Faulring, *et al.*, *Original Manuscripts*, pp. 93, 603.
310 K. P. Jackson, *Book of Moses*, p. 29.
311 D&C 20:37, 59:9-12.
312 Moses 5:5-9.
313 D&C 59:8-14.
314 B. R. McConkie, *New Witness*, p. 293.
315 J. Goldin, *Fathers*, 1, p. 14.
316 See *Commentary 5:4-a*, p. 355 and *Excursus 37: Traditions About the Role of Abel*, p. 617.
317 S. C. Malan, *Adam and Eve*, 1:23, p. 23.
318 H. W. Nibley, *Prayer Circle*, p. 60. See S. C. Malan, *Adam and Eve* 1:69, pp. 83-84; cf. J. Cooper, *et al.*, *Testament*, 1:23, pp. 73, 75 and I. E. Rahmani, II, *Testamentum*, 1: De Oblatione Sacrificii, pp. 40-41, 44-45.
319 G. Weil, *Legends*, p. 45; cf. A. al-Tha'labi, *Lives*, p. 62; J. H. Sailhamer, *Genesis*, p. 58; *Commentary 4:27-a*, p. 274.
320 See *Excursus 47: Islamic Perspectives Relating to Redemption*, p. 645.
321 S. A. Ashraf, *Inner*, p. 122. Note that Muslims generally see Ishmael rather than Isaac as the son who Abraham was commanded to sacrifice (see Genesis 22 and *Qur'an* 37:102).
322 Cf. *Commentary 5:1-d*, p. 354 and 6:1-a, p. 475.

MOSES 5

*6 And **after many days an angel** of the Lord appeared unto Adam, saying: Why dost thou offer sacrifices unto the Lord? And Adam said unto him: **I know not, save the Lord commanded me.***

6   **a**   ***after many days.*** The law of sacrifice was given as "a test of being faithful while not perceiving (fully) the reason behind an instruction."[323] Here we are specifically told that the additional light and knowledge that Adam sought did not come immediately. However, writes Nibley: "[The Lord] doesn't keep you waiting forever. Give your test sufficient time, enough to show your integrity, and you will get your answer."[324]

Jubilees 3:9 records that Adam had previously spent forty days, presumably representing some kind of preparatory experience, "in the land where he was created" prior to being placed into the Garden of Eden.[325] Likewise, in direct correspondence to the idea of the period of testing for Adam involving "many days" mentioned here, the *Life of Adam and Eve* tells of how Adam, following his transgression and expulsion from Eden, spent forty days of penance standing in the Jordan River—the same river that Christ would be baptized in, and the same period of time that Catholics (including candidates for baptism) traditionally spend in prayer and fasting during Lent.[326] Also relevant in this connection is Peter's association of Noah's ark, which protected the righteous during a cleansing renewal of the earth lasting "forty days and forty nights,"[327] with Christ's preaching to the disobedient and the saving effect of baptism.[328] Stone notes that a period of forty days also evokes "Moses' ascent to Mount Sinai, during which period the Israelites sinned with the golden calf.[329] It is also the duration of Christ's withdrawal to the desert and his successful repulse of Satan.[330] In that period Adam fasted…, as Moses did on the mountain[331] and Elijah did on Mount Horeb.[332] In the biblical incidents, there is an element of testing: the Israelites failed where Moses succeeded; Elijah recognized God in the small, still voice; and Christ succeeded against Satan. It is very likely that this biblical pattern, including a testing, influenced the formulation in *Life of Adam and Eve*."[333]

b   ***an angel.*** Nibley argues on the basis of scriptural parallels and pseudepigraphal accounts that there were three messengers rather than one: "The… *Apocryphon of John*… will tell you that it was three messengers that were sent to instruct them. [334]The Mandaean literature will tell you that the messengers that came to instruct Adam and Eve were the apostles who later became the pillars of the Church (Peter, James and John).[335] They came and instructed Adam and Eve in the Garden."[336]

Alma 12:28-35 implies that Alma was aware of the material in this account, either through direct revelation or through his study of the brass plates.

c   ***I know not, save the Lord commanded me.*** Comments Nibley: "I doubt not that when we know the reasons for some of the things we do now on faith, the practical value of the actions

---

323   T. Stordalen, *Echoes*, p. 226.

324   H. W. Nibley, *Teachings of the PGP*, 19, p. 234.

325   O. S. Wintermute, *Jubilees*, 3:9, p. 59; cf. Timothy of Alexandria, *Abbaton*, p. 198.

326   G. A. Anderson, *et al.*, *Synopsis*, pp. 8-9; M. D. Johnson, *Life*, 6:1-8:3, pp. 259-260; cf. *Commentary* 1:1-b, p. 42; Moses 6:52-68.

327   Genesis 7:12.

328   1 Peter 3:18-21.

329   Exodus 32.

330   Matthew 4:1-11.

331   Exodus 34:28.

332   1 Kings 19:8.

333   M. E. Stone, *Adam's Contract*, pp. 13-14.

334   F. Wisse, *Apocryphon of John*, II 1 2:5-9, p. 105.

335   See H. W. Nibley, *Since*, pp. 460-461 n. 47.

336   H. W. Nibley, *Teachings of the PGP*, 19, p. 233. See *Figure 5-9*, p. 339 and *Figure 5-10*, p. 340.

6 And after many days an angel of the Lord appeared unto Adam, saying: Why dost thou offer sacrifices unto the Lord? And Adam said unto him: **I know not, save the Lord commanded me**.

7 And then the angel spake, saying: **This thing is a similitude of the sacrifice of the Only Begotten of the Father,** *which is* **full of grace and truth**.

8 Wherefore, thou shalt **do all that thou doest in the name of the Son,** *and* **thou shalt repent** *and call upon God in the name of the Son forevermore.*

will be so plain that we will wonder how we could have missed it, and then we shall be heartily glad that we did what we were told to do."[337]

7 a **This thing is a similitude of the sacrifice of the Only Begotten of the Father.** In this connection, Joseph Smith taught: "Certainly, the shedding of the blood of a beast could be beneficial to no man, except it was done in imitation or as a type, or explanation of what was to be offered through the gift of God Himself, and this performance done with an eye looking forward in faith on the power of that great Sacrifice for a remission of sins… [W]henever the Lord… commanded [men] to offer sacrifices to Him,… it was done that they might look forward in faith to the time of his coming and rely upon the power of that Atonement for a remission of their sins."[338]

The *Conflict of Adam and Eve* gives an account of how Adam and Eve's prayer at the altar was answered: "Then came the Word of God to Adam, and said unto him, 'O Adam, as thou hast shed thy blood, so will I shed My own blood when I become flesh of thy seed; and as thou didst die, O Adam, so also will I die. And as thou didst build an altar, so also will I make for thee an altar on the earth; and as thou didst offer thy blood upon it, so also will I offer My blood upon an altar on the earth. And as thou didst sue for forgiveness through that blood, so also will I make My blood forgiveness of sins, and blot out transgressions in it. And now, behold, I have accepted thy offering, O Adam, but the days of the covenant, wherein I have bound thee, are not fulfilled. When they are fulfilled, then will I bring thee back into the Garden. Now, therefore, strengthen thy heart; and when sorrow comes upon thee, make Me an offering, and I will be favorable to thee.' This, then, was the first offering Adam made unto God; and so it became his custom to do."[339]

b *full of grace and truth.* See *Commentary* 1:6-e, p. 47.

8 a *do all that thou doest in the name of the Son.* Nephi teaches similarly: "But behold, I say unto you that ye must pray always, and not faint; that ye must not perform any thing unto the Lord save in the first place ye shall pray unto the Father in the name of Christ, that he will consecrate thy performance unto thee, that thy performance may be for the welfare of thy soul."[340]

The mention of "the Son" without further explanation implies that Adam had previously received knowledge about the mission of the Only Begotten. An account of such instruction being given to Adam can be found in Moses 6:51-63. Note also the correspondence in the mention of repentance made here and in 6:50.[341]

b *thou shalt repent.* Nibley remarks: "This perpetual repentance is a very interesting thing. Of course, we do that all the time. We can only call upon God correctly if we repent. We must repent and call upon him forevermore. You can see why. To repent means putting yourself in the condition of repentance, of recognition of your unworthiness. How long are you unworthy? How long do you need to repent? We are told until you are full of grace and truth.

337 H. W. Nibley, *Ritual*, p. 149.
338 J. Smith, Jr., *The Elders*, p. 143. See also H. W. Nibley, *Teachings of the PGP*, 19, p. 233.
339 S. C. Malan, *Adam and Eve*, 24/25, pp. 24, 25; cf. H. W. Nibley, *Prayer Circle*, p. 60.
340 2 Nephi 32:9.
341 See *Commentary* 5:4-a, p. 355 and 5:9-b, p. 362.

8 Wherefore, thou shalt do all that thou doest in the name of the Son, and **thou shalt repent** *and* **call upon God in the name of the Son forevermore.**

9 And **in that day** *the* **Holy Ghost fell upon Adam,** *which* **beareth record of the Father and the Son,** *saying:* **I am the Only Begotten of the Father** *from the beginning, henceforth and forever, that* **as thou hast fallen thou mayest be redeemed,** *and all mankind, even as many as will.*

When you are full of grace and truth, then maybe you might not need to repent anymore. But I think that's quite a while before any of us will be full of grace and truth. One person needs it just as badly as another. If we repent, we are approaching him honestly. If we don't, we're not approaching him honestly."[342]

c   **call upon God in the name of the Son forevermore.** Cf. *Commentary* 1:17-b, p. 55.

9   a   *in that day.* The phrase emphasizes the connection between what Adam has just learned and the joy he expressed in the promise of Redemption.

     b   *Holy Ghost fell upon Adam.* The explanation of the meaning of the law of sacrifice in vv. 6-8 sets the stage for the baptism of Adam. Though, contrary to expectation, an explicit account of this event is reserved for the sermon of Enoch,[343] Adam's baptism plausibly can be inferred from the explicit mention of the Father, the Son, and the Holy Ghost in this verse.[344]

         With no human administrator available to perform Adam's baptism, it was accomplished in an exceptional manner by his being "caught away by the Spirit of the Lord, and… carried down into the water."[345] Similarly, in the Mandaean account of Adam's baptism, the ordinance was completed by *Hibil Ziua,* who is often identified with *Manda d-Hiia,* the Mandaean Redeemer figure.[346]

         After giving the account of Adam's baptism, Enoch affirms that he also received the Melchizedek Priesthood.[347] No doubt additional priesthood ordinances were given to Adam at the same time or soon thereafter.[348]

     c   *beareth record of the Father and the Son.* The Holy Ghost here speaks on behalf of the Father by divine investiture of authority.[349] In Moses 6:61 He is given the title of "the record of heaven," and in 6:66 He is called "the record of the Father."[350]

     d   *I am the Only Begotten of the Father.* OT1 reads "I am Jesus Christ."[351] The current text is consistent with a change made in OT2.[352]

     e   *as thou hast fallen thou mayest be redeemed.* Helaman 8:18 also affirms that a knowledge of the Redemption was given to mankind "a great many thousand years before his [Christ's] coming."

342   H. W. Nibley, *Teachings of the PGP,* 19, p. 234.
343   Moses 6:51-64.
344   Cf. *Commentary* 1:24-a, p. 59, 1:24-c, p. 59, Moses 7:11.
345   Moses 6:64.
346   E. S. Drower, *Prayerbook,* p. 30. A Manichaean text similarly speaks of Adam being baptized by Jesus. See *Endnote B-16,* p. 907.
347   Moses 6:67-68.
348   See *Commentary* 5:59-c, p. 400.
349   See *Commentary* 1:3-a, p. 44.
350   R. D. Draper, *et al., Commentary,* p. 59.
351   S. H. Faulring, *et al., Original Manuscripts,* p. 93.
352   *Ibid.,* p. 603.

*10 And in that day **Adam blessed God** and was **filled**, and **began to prophesy concerning all the families of the earth**, saying: **Blessed be the name of God**, for **because of my transgression my eyes are opened**, and **in this life I shall have joy**, and **again in the flesh I shall see God**.*

10 a *Adam blessed God.* Nibley asks: "How can you bless God? Does he need blessing?... A blessing can go in both ways. A blessing is full approval and full acceptance of another... Bless has a double etymology. One says it's from the Old English word, *blotsian*, connected with our word 'blood.' To make a blood sacrifice; to bless in that sense. But bless is also connected with the word 'bliss,' a complete approval..., a complete acceptance when you bless God. So people can bless each other. You can bless your father or your mother as well as they can bless you."[353]

b *filled.* That is, filled with the Holy Ghost.[354] The phrase "with the Holy Ghost" was inserted into OT2 by an unknown scribe, then crossed out.[355]

c *began to prophesy concerning all the families of the earth.* Similarly, in D&C 107:56 we are told that at a great gathering preceding his death Adam prophesied about "whatsoever should befall his posterity unto the latest generation." Though the details of his prophecies are not given in extant scripture, we are told that Adam's words are recorded "in the book of Enoch" and will "be testified of in due time."[356]

d *Blessed be the name of God... in this life I shall have joy.* Adam's words are phrased in elegant parallel. Moreover, in vv. 10-11, Adam and Eve's individual expressions of newfound understanding and joy meld to form a harmonious dual psalm of gratitude.

OT1 omits a part of the expression, and reads instead: "blessed be the name of God for my transgression for in this life I shall have joy."[357]

e *because of my transgression my eyes are opened... again in the flesh I shall see God.* The second part of Adam's parallel expresses a significant insight: the crowning moment and the supernal reward of the opening of Adam's eyes is that again one day he shall see God.

Nibley comments: "What were his eyes opened to? All sorts of things. They have eaten the fruit already and their eyes were opened. They became what the Old Testament calls *piqeakh*. A *piqeakh* is a person whose eyes are open, and he sees things that other people don't see. Laman and Lemuel accused their father of being a visionary man. That's the way it is nearly always rendered in the Bible. A visionary man is a *piqeakh*. Like the attendants of Elisha who see the horses there when other people can't see them,[358] you see things that really are there but others can't see them. There is such a condition. But this is not what he refers to... Here because of his transgression, his eyes are open to his vulnerability. His eyes are open to his condition now. He knew he was in a bad condition, but his eyes were opened to the real situation. There is a whole series of eye openings here. Moses said, '...Now for this cause I know that man is nothing which thing I never had supposed.'[359] He had come down to this earth. His eyes were opened, and he realized how low he could get. That had never occurred to him. His eyes were opened again. Then it says, 'he lifted up his eyes' and again he saw God on his throne.[360] So we see different things that are there or that aren't. '...Because of my transgression my eyes are opened...'[361] [The creation of a hologram was once thought to be]

353   H. W. Nibley, *Teachings of the PGP*, 19, pp. 235-236.
354   Cf. 3 Nephi 12:6.
355   S. H. Faulring, *et al.*, *Original Manuscripts*, p. 603; K. P. Jackson, *Book of Moses*, p. 49.
356   D&C 107:57. See the overview of Moses 6, p. 457.
357   S. H. Faulring, *et al.*, *Original Manuscripts*, p. 93.
358   2 Kings 6:15-18.
359   Moses 1:10.
360   See Moses 1:24ff.
361   Moses 5:10.

*10 And in that day Adam blessed God and was filled, and began to prophesy concerning all the families of the earth, saying: Blessed be the name of God, for **because of my transgression my eyes are opened**, and in this life I shall have joy, and **again in the flesh I shall see God**.*

*11 And **Eve**, his wife, heard all these things and **was glad, saying**: Were it not for our transgression **we never should have had seed**, and never should have known good and evil, and the joy of our redemption, and the eternal life which God giveth unto all the obedient.*

*12 And Adam and Eve blessed the name of God, and they **made all things known unto their sons and their daughters**.*

*13 And **Satan came among them**, saying: I am also a son of God; and he commanded them, saying: Believe it not; and they believed it not, and they loved Satan more than God. And men began from that time forth to be carnal, sensual, and devilish.*

impossible on a two dimensional surface… But you can do it. When you go into some new phase, your eyes are opened. So be ready for all sorts of surprises."[362]

transgression. As in Article of Faith 2, the term "transgression" is deliberately used rather than the more common word "sin." Elder Dallin H. Oaks sees a parallel with "a familiar distinction in the law. Some acts, like murder, are crimes because they are inherently wrong. Other acts, like operating without a license, are crimes only because they are legally prohibited. Under these distinctions, the act that produced the Fall was not a sin—inherently wrong—but a transgression—wrong because it was formally prohibited."[363]

    f   ***again in the flesh I shall see God.*** The Hebrew text of the corresponding words in Job 19:26 is notoriously corrupt. If we assume that the author of Job was deliberately citing an ancient source such as this one, the parallel phrasing of the book of Moses would be a valuable witness of the authentic reading. A rabbinic source makes the point about resurrection "in the flesh" even more dramatically, saying that the dead will rise "in their own clothes."[364]

11 **a** ***Eve… was glad, saying.*** Comments Nibley: "It is [Eve] who perceives and points out to Adam that they have done the right thing after all. Sorrow, yes, but she is willing to pass through it for the sake of knowledge—knowledge of good and evil that will provide the test and the victory for working out their salvation as God intends… She discovers the principle of opposites by which the world is governed and views it with high-spirited optimism: it is not wrong that there is opposition in everything, it is a constructive principle making it possible for people to be intelligently happy. It is better to know the score than not to know it."[365]

    b ***we never should have had seed.*** While absent from Adam's psalm of praise, the theme of childbearing is the focus of Eve's first expression of gratitude. Draper, *et al.* further observe that "Eve's use of the plural [in this verse] contrasts with Adam's singular pronouns in Moses 5:10 and divulge her broad and instinctive concern for her family members."[366]

12 **a** ***made all things known unto their sons and their daughters.*** Again stressing the obedience of Adam and Eve, the text tells us that they taught the Gospel to their children.[367] An Islamic tradition also says that Adam and Eve "imparted the information which they had received from Gabriel to their grandchildren and great-grandchildren."[368]

13 **a** ***Satan came among them.*** As soon as Adam and Eve began to teach the gospel to their children, Satan moved in to blunt their influence. The Prophet Joseph Smith said: "In

362   H. W. Nibley, *Teachings of the PGP*, 19, p. 236; cf. *Commentary* 1:10-b, p. 51, 4:13-a, p. 258.

363   D. H. Oaks, *Plan*, p. 73.

364   R. Hiyya ben Joseph, *Bybylonian Talmud*, Kethuboth 111b, cited in D. H. Akenson, *Surpassing Wonder*, p. 384.

365   H. W. Nibley, *Patriarchy*, pp. 92-93; cf. *Commentary* 4:12-e, p. 256.

366   R. D. Draper, *et al.*, *Commentary*, p. 60.

367   Cf. *Commentary* 5:59-c, p. 400, Moses 6:1.

368   G. Weil, *Legends*, p. 46.

MOSES 5

*13 And **Satan came among them**, saying: **I am also a son of God**; and he commanded them, saying: Believe it not; and they believed it not, and they loved Satan more than God. And **men began from that time forth** to be **carnal, sensual, and devilish**.*

relation to the kingdom of God, the Devil always sets up his kingdom at the very same time in opposition to God."[369]

In contrast to the eloquent expressions of Adam and Eve, Satan's preaching is painted in brash and abrupt terms. From the fact that so many were so easily persuaded (he simply said: "Believe it not" and "they believed it not"), it seems that the people were predisposed to reject the word of the Lord. As Nibley observes: "All it took was somebody to say 'don't believe it.' They want that to happen. They are triggered to receive that because of the amount of discipline that's required if you accept it… [The law of obedience is] a strenuous thing. It requires some concentration. You can't keep a celestial order on earth without working at it all the time… In Fourth Nephi you see how the people got tired of it. They thought it was just not worth the trouble. It was easier going back to the old way and becoming competitive and teaching their children to hold the Lamanite children in contempt, etc. This was the easy thing to do."[370]

b   *I am also a son of God.* Being a "son of God" is more than being a spirit child of God. Hence, this statement is a bald lie. At one time, Lucifer had been a son of God,[371] but no more. His title is now Perdition.[372]

Satan has no qualms about assuming the garb of piety to further his purposes. An Islamic scholar relates: "The old man who was the first to pledge his allegiance to Abu Bakr and whose forehead was calloused from extensive prostrations, was the accursed Satan.… He was the first to ascend to the pulpit. He expressed with tears running down his cheeks, 'Praise be to the Allàh.'"[373]

Nibley comments on this verse as follows: "Notice, that… [Satan's] appeal [is] that he is a son of God… He's all for the Gospel. He is all for saving people. In the Council in Heaven he wanted them saved. too, and he wanted to do the saving. There are lots of people that way, that want to do the right thing as long as they are in charge. But if they are not in charge, all government is then just an evil. When they are in charge, they run everything… When he appeared, his first step was to make a command, speak outright. He wants to be worshipped. That's what he wanted in the first place. ('Give me thine honor.'[374]) So he commands them."[375]

c   *men began from that time forth.* Contrast Moses 6:4.

d   *carnal, sensual, and devilish.* Though, in a general sense, the Fall was the cause of all mankind becoming carnal, sensual, and devilish "by nature,"[376] this passage makes it clear that it was only "from that time" when men individually chose to reject the Gospel, demonstrating that they "loved Satan more than God," that they fully suffered the effects of alienation from God. Such individuals remain "as though there was no redemption made," "knowing evil from good, subjecting themselves to the devil."[377] On the other hand, those who accept the Atonement of Christ become "free forever, knowing good from evil, to act for themselves and not be acted upon."[378]

369   J. Smith, Jr., *Teachings*, 2 May 1844, p. 365.
370   H. W. Nibley, *Teachings of the PGP*, 19, p. 237.
371   See Job 1:6.
372   *Commentary* 1:13-c, p. 53; 4:1-d, p. 243; 4:1-e, p. 244; 4:5-b, p. 246; 5:24-a, p. 375; 5:24-b, p. 375.
373   al-Kafi, vol. 8, cited in Porch of Wisdom Cultural Institution, *Faith and Reason*, pp. 115, 118.
374   Moses 4:1.
375   H. W. Nibley, *Teachings of the PGP*, 19, p. 237.
376   Mosiah 16:3; Alma 42:10.
377   Mosiah 16:5, 3.
378   2 Nephi 2:26.

*13 And Satan came among them, saying: I am also a son of God; and he commanded them, saying: Believe it not; and they believed it not, and they loved Satan more than God. And men began from that time forth to be **carnal, sensual, and devilish**.*

*14 And **the Lord God called upon men by the Holy Ghost everywhere and commanded them that they should repent**;*

The word "carnal," from a Latin root meaning "flesh," is closely associated in scripture with the terms "natural,"[379] "temporal,"[380] and "earthly."[381] It represents the condition of estrangement from spiritual things experienced by individuals in their fallen, mortal, and corrupt state before they are born again.[382] The "sensual" man or woman is one who privileges the satisfaction of bodily appetites and passions. Such a person becomes "devilish" when "he… persists in his own carnal nature, and goes on in the ways of sin and rebellion against God, remaineth in his fallen state and the devil hath all power over him… being an enemy to God; [as] the devil [is] an enemy to God."[383] Nibley alternately renders the phrase as "lecherous, pampered, and vicious."[384]

This oft-cited triplet appears to be one of the many stock, fixed distinctive combinations of words "which belonged to the literary tradition of Israel and Canaan, and poets [and prophets], specially trained in their craft, drew on this stock to aid in the… composition of parallel lines…. [These combinations were, figuratively speaking, part of] the poets' dictionary, as it has been called."[385] Though its equivalent appears only once in the Bible,[386] a combination of these terms in pairs or triplets occurs several times in LDS scripture.[387]

14   a   *the Lord God called upon men by the Holy Ghost everywhere and commanded them that they should repent.* The Holy Ghost, an invisible yet powerful opponent to Satan's preaching, provided a witness to the things that Adam and Eve taught.[388] But: "There's the rub… Who wants to be told to repent? You are not going to get votes by telling people to repent, but by telling them that everything is wonderful."[389]

Elsewhere Nibley writes: "The test for this life is not for knowledge; it is not for intelligence, or for courage, or for anything like that. That would be a huge joke. None of us knows very much, none of us is very brave, none of us is very strong, none of us is very smart. We would flunk those tests terribly… [There are] two things and the only two things we are good at: we can forgive and we can repent."[390] Humbly feeling his limitations in so many things, it was a consoling thought to Elder George Albert Smith that life offers an absolutely level playing field with regard to the personal qualities that matter most: "As I have looked at other men both in the Church and out of the Church,… seeing many who are my superiors in education and in experience, perhaps also in intelligence and in other characteristics, I have taken satisfaction in knowing that I am the moral equal of any man alive."[391]

---

379   E.g. D&C 29:35.

380   E.g., Alma 36:4.

381   E.g., James 3:15.

382   E.g., Romans 8:6; 2 Nephi 9:39; Mosiah 3:19, 7:24-25; Alma 22:13, 41:13; D&C 67:10-13; B. R. McConkie, *Mormon Doctrine*, pp. 113, 195, 267-268, 702.

383   Mosiah 16:5; cf. Mosiah 3:19.

384   H. W. Nibley, *Assembly*, p. 129.

385   Berlin, cited in J. T. Duke, *Pairs*, p. 33. See also K. L. Barney, *Poetic*; J. A. Tvedtnes, *Word Groups*.

386   James 3:15.

387   Mosiah 16:3; Alma 41:13, 42:10; D&C 20:20, 29:35; Moses 5:13, 6:49.

388   Moses 5:12. See 5:58-c, p. 400.

389   H. W. Nibley, *Teachings of the PGP*, 19, p. 237. See also J. B. MacDonald, *Holiness*, p. 83.

390   H. W. Nibley, *Funeral*, p. 301.

391   G. A. Smith, n. d., reported by G. A. Smith, Jr. and cited in M. J. Pusey, *Builders*, p. 226.

*15 And **as many as believed in the Son, and repented of their sins, should be saved; and as many as believed not and repented not, should be damned**; and the words went forth out of the mouth of God in **a firm decree**; wherefore they must be fulfilled.*

*16 And **Adam and Eve, his wife, ceased not to call upon God**. And **Adam knew Eve his wife**, and she conceived and bare **Cain**, and said: I have gotten **a man** from the Lord; wherefore he may not reject his words. But behold, Cain hearkened not, saying: Who is the Lord that I should know him?*

15 a ***And as many as believed in the Son, and repented of their sins, should be saved; and as many as believed not and repented not, should be damned.*** Draper, *et al.* characterize this decree as "a legal declaration from the divine world." They note that "Jesus virtually quoted these terms as He instructed His apostles for the last time; then He gave these instructions to His New World disciples."[392]

 b *a firm decree.* See *Commentary* 5:59-d, p. 401.

16 a *Adam and Eve, his wife, ceased not to call upon God.* There is an implied connection between the prayers of Adam and Eve and the arrival of Cain, who Eve acknowledged as having come "from the Lord."[393] Childbirth as a blessing from God in answer to prayer is also highlighted in the stories of Abraham and Sarah[394] and Hannah and Elkanah.[395]

OT1 reads: "And Adam ceased not to call upon God; and Eve also his wife."[396]

 b *Adam knew Eve his wife.* Sarna comments: "'Knowing' in the Bible is not essentially intellectual activity… Rather, it is experiential, emotional, and, above all, relational… For that reason, the Hebrew stem *y-d-'* can encompass a range of meanings that includes involvement, interaction, loyalty, and obligation. It can be used of the most intimate and most hallowed relationships between man and wife, and between man and God. Significantly, the verb is never employed for animal copulation."[397]

Cassuto points out that the Hebrew term for "know/knew," found at several key points throughout this chapter,[398] "contains a link with the previous section, whose essential theme is centered on the Tree of Knowledge."[399]

 c *Cain.* The Hebrew stem *k-n-h* typically means "to own or acquire"[400] but there is evidence for a secondary stem meaning "to produce or create."[401] Interestingly, this latter stem also appears in the name of Elkanah, a father whose name mockingly highlighted his inability to produce children.[402] The name is also related to the stem *k-y-n* which means "to form, fashion, or forge," and the name *kayn* denotes a "smith" in Aramaic and Arabic.[403]

 d *a man.* The Hebrew term for man, *'ish*, is striking in this context because it is never used elsewhere to refer to a newborn. By way of explanation, Sarna hears an echo of Adam's cry

---

392 R. D. Draper, *et al.*, *Commentary*, p. 63. See Mark 16:16; Mormon 9:23; Ether 4:18.

393 *Commentary* 5:16-e, p. 368.

394 Genesis 17:16.

395 1 Samuel 1:11, 20. See *Commentary* 5:2-a, p. 354; Moses 5:4. Parallels between the births of Cain and Abel and those of Jacob and Esau are noted in C. Westermann, *Genesis 1-11*, pp. 292-293.

396 S. H. Faulring, *et al.*, *Original Manuscripts*, p. 93.

397 N. M. Sarna, *Genesis*, p. 31.

398 Vv. 2, 6, 16 (twice), 21, 29, 34, 42, 51.

399 U. Cassuto, *Adam to Noah*, p. 197. See also pp. 178-248 *passim*.

400 Cf. "possession" in J. Smith, Jr., 13 April 1843, as reported in E. England, *Laub*, p. 25.

401 E.g., Genesis 14:19; Deuteronomy 32:6; Psalm 115:19, 139:13; U. Cassuto, *Adam to Noah*, pp. 199-202; N. M. Sarna, *Genesis*, p. 32.

402 1 Samuel 1:11.

403 N. M. Sarna, *Genesis*, p. 32. See *Commentary* 5:24-b, p. 375.

*16 And Adam and Eve, his wife, ceased not to call upon God. And Adam knew Eve his wife, and she conceived and bare Cain, and said: I have gotten **a man from the Lord**; wherefore he may not reject his words. But behold, Cain hearkened not, saying: Who is the Lord that I should know him?*

in 3:23: in effect Eve now can be seen as saying, "I, woman (*'ish(sh)ah*), was produced from man (*'ish*); now I, woman, have in turn produced a man."[404]

e   *from the Lord.* This phrase has long been a problem for interpreters.[405] Sarna sees the Hebrew *'et YHVH* as better rendered "together with" or "with the help of" the Lord.[406] In the talmudic literature, *Niddah* 31a states: "There are three copartners in the production of a human being: God, father, and mother."[407] The use of "Lord" rather than God is explained in Jewish sources as an emphasis on His attributes of mercy rather than of justice.[408] Note that Eve "is the first person to pronounce the name of God [i.e., Jehovah] in the Bible."[409]

Hamilton, following earlier exegetes, observes that there is no reason to rule out the argument that *'et* is, in this verse, simply intended to function in its typical role as the marker of the direct object of the verb. For example, we read in Luther's revised translation of 1546: "I have gotten the man, [namely or even] the Lord."[410] "This rendering suggests," according to Hamilton, "that in the birth of Cain Eve thought, mistakenly, that the divinely promised seed of [Moses 4:21] had now come in Cain. The child, whose birth is so welcomed, could be looked on as God himself."[411] Also concluding that "she thought the deliverer had been sent by God," Boice renders Eve's exclamation as "Here he is" or "I've gotten him."[412] That Eve could have been so deceived in thinking the promised Redeemer had already come in the person of Cain is highly doubtful. However, in a wider sense, her words may be taken as foreshadowing her hope that, in contrast to her wayward progeny,[413] Cain would "not reject [the Lord's] words" and would become the progenitor of the righteous branch of her family through whom the promise of 4:21 would eventually be fulfilled. As in subsequent patriarchal tradition, "a representative child continued to be God's visible guarantee for the present and a pledge for the future. Also, he was representative of the interests and spiritual and material fortunes of the whole lot who were joined to him."[414]

The *Qur'an* tells of how Adam, seeing Eve's hardships in the final stages of pregnancy, promised God that he would always remember Him, if He would grant them a righteous (*siddiq*) child—a "testifier of truth."[415] This is the same term used to describe Enoch (= Idris[416]), Abraham,[417] and Joseph.[418] Thus, it was natural that the parents had high hopes for Cain. Writes Nibley: "You think of Cain as a very blessed and special person. They thought he was. They expected great things of him. They expected that he would turn the tide. Everything had gone against Adam and Eve. Many of their posterity were not repenting…

---

404   N. M. Sarna, *Genesis*, p. 32; cf. L. R. Kass, *Wisdom*, p. 126.
405   V. P. Hamilton, *Genesis*, p. 221; C. Westermann, *Genesis 1-11*, pp. 289-292.
406   N. M. Sarna, *Genesis*, p. 32.
407   Cited in N. M. Sarna, *Genesis*, p. 32; R. M. Zlotowitz, *et al.*, *Bereishis*, p. 142.
408   R. M. Zlotowitz, *et al.*, *Bereishis*, p. 142.
409   R. E. Friedman, *Commentary*, p. 26.
410   T. Gallus, *Der Nachkomme 1*, p. 124; cf. *Targum Pseudo-Jonathan*: "I have acquired a man, the Angel of the Lord," where "the Angel of" is clearly a gloss to explain away the literal meaning (M. Maher, *Pseudo-Jonathan*, p. 31 n. 2). See also *Excursus 37: Traditions About the Role of Abel*, p. 617.
411   V. P. Hamilton, *Genesis*, p. 221. See also *Commentary 4:21-d*, p. 266; T. Gallus, *Der Nachkomme 1*, pp. 116-132; W. C. J. Kaiser, *Toward*, p. 37; G. J. Wenham, *Genesis 1-15*, p. 102.
412   J. M. Boice, *Genesis 1-11*, p. 250.
413   Moses 4:13.
414   W. C. J. Kaiser, *Toward*, p. 37.
415   M. Ibn Ishaq ibn Yasar, *Sirat Rasul*, p. 183 n. 1.
416   M. M. Ali, *Qur'an*, 19:56, p. 603.
417   *Ibid.*, 19:41, p. 601.
418   *Ibid.*, 12:46, p. 46; Genesis 41:38-39. See J.-L. Monneret, *Grands*, n. 24, p. 483.

*16 And Adam and Eve, his wife, ceased not to call upon God. And Adam knew Eve his wife, and she conceived and bare Cain, and said: I have gotten a man **from the Lord**; **wherefore he may not reject his words**. But behold, **Cain hearkened not**, saying: **Who is the Lord that I should know him?***

*17 And she again conceived and bare his brother **Abel**. And Abel hearkened unto the voice of the Lord. And Abel was a keeper of sheep, but Cain was a tiller of the ground.*

There was hope that Cain would be the right one, that he wouldn't reject the words. He would put things back on the track. But he didn't."[419]

Further supporting the idea of Cain's special potential are traditions of unusual circumstances surrounding his birth. In some accounts, the newborn Cain is described as "a glorious person"[420] being "like the color of stars,"[421] "a designation which associates Cain with the angels."[422] This description can be compared to that of the newborn Noah[423]—or, on the other hand, to "Satan himself."[424]

f ***wherefore he may not reject his words.*** The theme of obedience—which formed both the hinge of the plot of Moses 4 and the central motif of the story of Adam and Eve after their expulsion in Moses 5—is once again highlighted by the hopeful words of Eve. Sadly, Eve's children had already begun to reject God's words.[425]

g ***Cain hearkened not.*** Contrast *Commentary* 5:17-d, p. 370.

OT1 reads: "But, behold, also Cain hearkened not."[426]

h ***Who is the Lord that I should know him?*** Draper, *et al.*[427] note that "Cain's arrogant question will be mirrored later by that of Pharaoh,[428] as well as that of King Noah" in the Book of Mormon.[429] The recurrence of the word "know"[430] fittingly recalls the covenant relationship between Adam, Eve, and God that resulted in Cain's birth—the type of "covenant relationship that Cain refuses to enter."[431]

17 a ***Abel.*** The announcement of a second birth cues the reader to one of the many occurrences of the OT pattern of sibling rivalry, where the younger son is the one favored of God.[432]

For reasons that are not stated, Eve gives an explanation for Cain's name but not for Abel's. The Hebrew term for Abel's name does appears in Ecclesiastes 1:2 and 12:8 in the well-known phrase "vanity of vanities" (*hevel hevelim*, i.e., the greatest vanity or "vanity of vanities" as it is rendered in the KJV).[433] It can also be translated as "breath" or "nothingness."[434] Sarna comments: "The name may augur his destiny… *Hevel* is often used to express the fleeting nature of life. The name may alternatively, or perhaps simultaneously, contain a reference to his vocation in that Syriac *hablâ* means a 'herdsman.'"[435]

419 H. W. Nibley, *Teachings of the PGP*, 19, p. 238.
420 *Ibid.*, 19, p. 241.
421 G. A. Anderson *et al.*, *Synopsis*, Armenian 21:3a, p. 24E.
422 J. Tromp, *Cain*, pp. 290-291.
423 G. W. E. Nickelsburg, *1 Enoch*, 106:2-6, p. 536.
424 H. W. Nibley, *Teachings of the PGP*, 19, p. 241.
425 Moses 5:13.
426 S. H. Faulring *et al.*, *Original Manuscripts*, p. 93.
427 R. D. Draper *et al.*, *Commentary*, p. 65.
428 See Exodus 5:2.
429 Mosiah 11:27.
430 Moses 5:16.
431 See *Commentary* 5:34-b, p. 382.
432 See *Commentary* 6:2-d, p. 476.
433 V. P. Hamilton, *Genesis*, p. 222.
434 Cf. "sorrow," J. Smith, Jr., 13 April 1843, as reported in E. England, *Laub*, p. 25.
435 N. M. Sarna, *Genesis*, p. 32.

*17 And she again conceived and bare his brother Abel. And **Abel hearkened** unto the voice of the Lord. And Abel was a **keeper of sheep**, but **Cain was a tiller of the ground**.*

b   ***Abel hearkened.*** The fundamental contrast between Cain and Abel is succinctly stated.[436]

c   ***keeper of sheep.*** Hamilton points out that Abel "is followed in that vocation by such notables as Jacob,[437] Joseph,[438] Moses,[439] and David."[440] "Since, in the biblical view, mankind was vegetarian until after the Flood, the function of animal husbandry at this point was to supply milk, hides, and wool."[441]

Kass expresses an ancient view that exalted the life of the shepherd over that of the farmer: "The shepherd… lives a simple and by and large artless life. His work is mild and gentle; his rule requires no violence. The sheep graze as they roam and produce wool and milk out of their own substance, the shepherd contributing nothing but also harming nothing. Though he wanders the earth as he pleases, the shepherd has no illusions of self-sufficiency; indeed he is likely to feel acutely the dependence of his entire life on powers not under his control and processes not of his own creation. The settled farmer seeks to design his life, the wandering shepherd allows his life to be designed by the world.… When it finally comes, the shepherd may be more open to the edifying and elevating call of the Lord."[442]

d   ***Cain was a tiller of the ground.*** Kass summarizes the view that the very nature of Cain's profession had spiritual risks requiring special vigilance: "Rather than serving God, farmers are in danger of serving the earth as if it were a divinity; they are at risk of becoming slaves to the earth. It is not just that they are at the mercy of the elements… The farmer is bound to his plot, rooted in place just like his crops, not free to leave, not free to escape the grip of necessity by which the cursed ground holds him fast, as it were, by the throat."[443]

Tromp comments: "Cain's role in the Armenian/Georgian version [of the *Life of Adam and Eve*] may be seen to symbolize the destructive forces in humanity: whereas Adam had been taught agriculture, so that he and his posterity might live,[444] Cain plucks up the grass, his mother's inferior, but only sustenance.[445] Tradition holds Cain to be a farmer, but here he not merely shows himself an ill-omened pupil of his father. He is even the one 'who first, when [the earth] was giving birth to every kind of animals and plants and was bright with all the products of its fruitfulness, set a bar to that fruitfulness.'"[446] The angel-midwife who delivered Cain is reported to have said to him: "… you are Cain, the perverse one, killer of the good, for you are the one who plucks up the fruit-bearing tree, and not he who plants it."[447]

Of Cain's farming practices, Josephus reports the tradition that: "Cain was not only very wicked in other respects, but was wholly intent upon getting; and he first contrived to plough the ground."[448] Franxman sees this as a condemnation of those who dishonor God by offering him "products forced from nature by the ingenuity of grasping man,"[449] and Feldman notes that Josephus' statement "connects Cain's name, which means 'acquisition,' …with this quality in his character."[450]

---

436   See Moses 5:16.

437   Genesis 30:36.

438   Genesis 37:2.

439   Exodus 3:1.

440   1 Samuel 16:11; 17:34. See V. P. Hamilton, *Genesis*, p. 222.

441   N. M. Sarna, *Genesis*, p. 32.

442   L. R. Kass, *Wisdom*, pp. 131, 132. This is, of course, a generalization of an ancient view—not a condemnation of modern farming methods, nor an endorsement of current animal raising practices.

443   *Ibid.*, p. 131.

444   G. A. Anderson, *et al.*, *Synopsis*, Armenian 21:3a, p. 24E.

445   *Ibid.*, Latin 22:2, p. 26E.

446   J. Tromp, *Cain*, p. 289. See Philo, *Rewards*, 68, p. 670.

447   G. A. Anderson, *et al.*, *Synopsis*, Georgian 21:3c, p. 25E.

448   F. Josephus, *Antiquities*, 1:2:1, p. 26.

449   T. W. Franxman, *Genesis*, p. 67. See also p. 66 and n. 5.

450   L. H. Feldman, *Hellenization*, p. 346. See *Commentary* 5:37-a, p. 384.

17 And she again conceived and bare his brother Abel. And Abel hearkened unto the voice of the Lord. And Abel was a keeper of sheep, but **Cain was a tiller of the ground**.

18 And Cain loved Satan more than God. And Satan commanded him, saying: **Make an offering unto the Lord**.

19 And **in process of time** *it came to pass that* **Cain brought of the fruit of the ground** *an offering unto the Lord.*

> The overall description recalls D&C 59:18, 20, which warns that the "things which come of the earth" are "made to be used, with judgment, not to excess, neither by extortion." The term "extortion" has the sense of forcible extraction or wresting out, as when money is obtained through coercion or threats. Explains Nibley: "From the wine and olive presses we get the word 'extortion,' meaning to squeeze out the last drop, another way to make a margin of profit—putting the squeeze on, wringing out the last drop."[451] Robinson and Garrett write: "There is a difference between use and exploitation. Humans did not 'use' the passenger pigeon very wisely; they are now extinct. The resources of nature are given to man to manage, not to pillage. Wholesale destruction of natural resources violates God's command that they be used 'with judgment, not to excess, neither by extortion.' Perhaps 'extortion,' which literally means to 'twist out,' here refers to forcing more from a resource than it can bear."[452]

18 a *Make an offering unto the Lord.* Comments Nibley: "Notice [that Satan] says, 'Make an offering unto the Lord.' He doesn't say, make an offering unto me, or make an offering unto devils… He claims to be running the Gospel on earth… Cain is being obedient… but not following the law of God. He is following the law of Satan… He's being obedient to Satan."[453]

19 a *in process of time.* Westermann notes that this phrase in Genesis "presumes that something has already happened beforehand… We cannot reconstruct it."[454] Verse 18 in the book of Moses, however, appropriately provides the missing event.

b *Cain brought of the fruit of the ground.* Cain, at the command of Satan, "offered the fruit of the ground as a sacrifice, which was not symbolic of Christ's great act of Redemption… Instead of purchasing a lamb or another animal that would serve as an appropriate sacrifice, he offered what he produced, even as Abel offered that which he produced."[455] Echoing the account of the Fall, an Islamic source says that the offering was of figs.[456] Speaking of the reason Cain's sacrifice was rejected, the Prophet Joseph Smith explained that "ordinances must be kept in the very way God has appointed,"[457] in this case by "the shedding of blood… [as] a type, by which man was to discern the great Sacrifice which God had prepared."[458] Not only must the form of the ordinance comply with the heavenly pattern, but also the heart must be filled with the spirit of sincere repentance, since "the shedding of the blood of a beast could be beneficial to no man, except it was … done with an eye looking forward in faith on the power of that great Sacrifice for a remission of sins."[459] Thus, Cain's sin was not merely that he failed to comply to the outward requirements of the law of sacrifice, but also that he did not offer it in righteousness with a "broken heart and a contrite spirit."[460]

451 H. W. Nibley, *Work*, pp. 216-217.
452 S. E. Robinson, *et al.*, *D&C Commentary*, 2:167.
453 H. W. Nibley, *Teachings of the PGP*, 19, pp. 238-239; cf. *Commentary* 5:29-c, p. 378.
454 C. Westermann, *Genesis 1-11*, p. 294; cf. G. J. Wenham, *Genesis 1-15*, p. 103.
455 H. L. Andrus, *Doctrinal*, p. 387.
456 J. C. Reeves, *al-Yaqubi*.
457 J. Smith, Jr., *Teachings*, 5 October 1840, p. 169.
458 *Ibid.*, 22 January 1834, p. 58.
459 *Ibid.*, 22 January 1834, p. 58.
460 See 1 Samuel 15:22-23; Psalm 51:17-18; Proverbs 15:8-9, 21:3, 27; Isaiah 1:10-20; Hosea 14:2; Micah 6:6-8; 3 Nephi 9:19-20; D&C 64:34; J. R. Holland, *Amazed*, p. 204.

MOSES 5

*19 And in process of time it came to pass that **Cain brought of the fruit of the ground** an offering unto the Lord.*

*20 And **Abel**, he also **brought of the firstlings of his flock, and of the fat thereof**. And the Lord had respect unto Abel, and to his offering;*

*21 But unto Cain, and to his offering, he had not respect. Now **Satan knew this**, and it pleased him. And **Cain was very wroth**, and his countenance fell.*

Some interpreters have argued that Cain's offering of "the fruit of the ground" should have been perfectly acceptable according to subsequent Old Testament practice. However, with reference to the idea of a cereal offering in Mosaic worship, Andrus notes:[461] "Israel was later commanded to bring the first fruits of the field to the priests as an offering to the Lord. But these offerings were, in the main, to be given to the poor, the widows, and the fatherless.[462] In some instances they were also used in conjunction with the sacrifice of lambs, but not as a substitute for the shedding of blood."[463]

20   a   *Abel… brought of the firstlings of his flock, and of the fat thereof.* In the book of Hebrews, "Abel's (pre-levitical) sacrifice [is *not*] contrasted with that of Christ. In this respect, there is an implied analogy between Abel… and Melchizedek" in the righteous nature of their actions.[464] We are meant to notice a difference from Cain in the care with which Abel selected his offering. About the offering of Abel, Cassuto comments: "This twofold emphasis—on the firstlings, which are the best of the flock, and on the fat portions, which are their best parts… underlines… Abel's desire to gratify his Creator, and to honor him to the best of his ability; his oblation is accompanied by good intent."[465]

In later Old Testament cultic practice, the desirable fatty portions of the sacrifice were seen as belonging to God and forbidden for human consumption.[466] By way of contrast, the Armenian *Abel and Cain* describes Cain's offering as coming from grain which had been exposed, beaten down by the wind, and injured as it was trampled underfoot.[467]

21   a   *Satan knew this.* What knowledge the Devil has, he uses manipulatively. In this case, Satan not only knew of Cain's anger after the rejection of his sacrifice, but also certainly knew beforehand that a sacrifice of the sort he commanded Cain to make would be rejected.

      b   *Cain was very wroth.* The Hebrew term, often used in the Bible as a "prelude to homicidal acts,"[468] can express either anger or grief.[469] What is clear in any event is that Cain's brooding twisted his self-pity and resentment into violent passion,[470] which soon ignited an explosion of murderous aggression. Wrote Elder Spencer W. Kimball: "It is doubtful if Cain had murder in his heart when his first jealous thought crossed his mind, when the first hate began to develop; but ounce by ounce, moment by moment, the little parasite developed to rob him of his strength, his balance, and his peace. The evil took over, and Cain… changed his appearance, his attitudes, his life, and became a world wanderer, vicious and desolate."[471]

Following Rousseau, Kass concludes that the source of Cain's anger is perceived injury born of self-regard (= French *considération*): "Once there is self-regard, there will be perceived insult experienced as injustice. Once there is perceived injustice, there will be anger and

---

461   H. L. Andrus, *Doctrinal*, p. 388.
462   See Deuteronomy 26.
463   See Leviticus 23:10, 17-18.
464   P. Ellingworth, *Greek Hebrews*, p. 571.
465   U. Cassuto, *Adam to Noah*, p. 206.
466   E.g., Leviticus 3:3-5, 9-11, 14-16.
467   W. L. Lipscomb, *Abel*, 7, pp. 258, 258 n. 5, 270.
468   G. J. Wenham, *Genesis 1-15*, p. 106; Genesis 34:7, Numbers 16:15, 1 Samuel 18:8, 2 Samuel 3:8, Nehemiah 4:1.
469   U. Cassuto, *Adam to Noah*, p. 207; V. P. Hamilton, *Genesis*, pp. 224-225; N. M. Sarna, *Genesis*, p. 33.
470   Cf. *Commentary* 5:26-a, p. 376.
471   S. W. Kimball, *Mistletoe*, p. 229.

21 But unto Cain, and to his offering, he had not respect. Now Satan knew this, and it pleased him. And **Cain was very wroth, and** **his countenance fell**.

22 And **the Lord said unto Cain**: **Why art thou wroth?** *Why is thy countenance fallen?*

23 **If thou doest well, thou shalt be accepted**. *And if thou doest not well, sin lieth at the door, and Satan desireth to have thee; and except thou shalt hearken unto my commandments, I will deliver thee up, and it shall be unto thee according to his desire. And thou shalt rule over him;*

the desire for revenge. And the larger the self-regard, the greater the exacted vengeance."[472] Warner has argued convincingly that the self-absorbed perspective that nurtures such feelings is rooted in moral choice, essentially a betrayal of what we know to be right.[473]

c   *his countenance fell.* The Hebrew phrase roughly corresponds to the idea of being "crestfallen"[474] or "downcast."[475]

22   a   *the Lord said unto Cain.* Just as Jeremiah pleaded with his people to "amend [their] ways" and refrain from "shed[ding] innocent blood" so that they could "dwell in… the land that [God] gave to [their] fathers,"[476] so the Lord lovingly persuades Cain to turn to Him, lest it "be unto [him] according to [Satan's] desire."[477] Sadly, despite the Lord's entreaties to Cain and his spiritual successors "that they should love one another, and that they should choose me, their Father;… they [were] without affection, and they [hated] their own blood."[478]

Comments Nibley: "The Lord counsels [Cain] and speaks with him very kindly, very gently, with much long-suffering, you will notice… [H]e doesn't say, now you will be damned on the spot and wiped out because you didn't do right, but He says, you are running a risk. You're at risk if you start doing that sort of thing. 'Sin lieth at the door [it's not far away].' If you are going to keep up with this sort of thing, you are in real trouble… You hearken to God's voice or you are in Satan's power: 'All who do not live up to their covenants will be in my power.' That's the provision that has been made. You have the one choice or the other."[479]

b   *Why art thou wroth?* "The narrative… focuses our attention to Cain's response. It is there that the narrative seeks to make its point. Cain's response was twofold: (1) anger against God[480] and (2) anger against his brother."[481]

23   a   *If thou doest well, thou shalt be accepted.* The Hebrew text of this verse in Genesis is so riddled with difficulties for the interpreter that "every attempt to extract a meaning from the verse is more or less of a *tour de force*."[482] The book of Moses agrees in substance with the traditional rendering of the first part of the verse, but then extends the text to make it clear that it is not "sin" *per se* but rather Satan who has made Cain the object of his desire. Again it is also Satan, not sin, who will in the end be ruled over (i.e., mastered) by Cain.

thou shalt be accepted. The phrase in literal Hebrew refers to a "lifting up," perhaps a sort of contrast with the "crouching down" (= lieth) in the phrase that follows.[483] The wording of this phrase in OT1 ("shalt thou not be accepted"[484]) is identical to that of Genesis.

472   L. R. Kass, *Wisdom*, p. 139.
473   C. T. Warner, *Bonds*, pp. 19-38.
474   V. P. Hamilton, *Genesis*, p. 224.
475   M. Maher, *Pseudo-Jonathan*, 4:5, p. 32.
476   Jeremiah 7:5-7.
477   J. H. Sailhamer, *Genesis*, p. 62.
478   Moses 7:33.
479   H. W. Nibley, *Teachings of the PGP*, 19, pp. 239-240.
480   Moses 5:26.
481   J. H. Sailhamer, *Genesis*, p. 61. See Moses 5:32.
482   Skinner, cited in V. P. Hamilton, *Genesis*, p. 225.
483   U. Cassuto, *Adam to Noah*, pp. 210-212.
484   S. H. Faulring, *et al.*, *Original Manuscripts*, p. 94.

*23 If thou doest well, thou shalt be accepted. And if thou doest not well, **sin lieth at the door**, and **Satan desireth to have thee**; and except thou shalt hearken unto my commandments, **I will deliver thee up**, and it shall be unto thee according to his desire. And **thou shalt rule over him**;*

b   ***sin lieth at the door.*** "Sin" makes its first appearance in the Bible here. Hamilton explains: "Because [Cain's] offering has been rejected by God he is seething with anger. In such an emotional state he is easy prey for sin which crouches lionlike and waits to jump on him."[485]

c   ***Satan desireth to have thee.*** The words for "desireth" and "rule" in the Hebrew text parallel the terms used earlier to describe the tendency for marriage relationships in a fallen world to deteriorate into a state of competition and rancor.[486] Unwilling to escape the bands of wickedness, Satan and Cain will be eternally locked together in the utterly destructive embrace of unrighteous dominion.[487]

Cassuto notes as well that the Hebrew term used for the verb in "bruise his heel"[488] comes from a stem that is cognate with "desire" as it is used in this verse,[489] thus evoking the mortal danger Cain is courting in giving in to Satan's craving to wound him, and also perhaps suggesting that he must quickly act to crush his opponent.[490]

d   ***I will deliver thee up.*** If Cain persists in wickedness, God's protective power will be withdrawn from him.

e   ***thou shalt rule over him.*** In every respect, Cain will become more of a devil than the Devil himself. In v. 24, Satan's own ignominious titles, "Perdition"[491] and "the father of lies,"[492] are ultimately conferred upon him.

Elder Joseph Fielding Smith made the following comment relating to Cain's subsequent "ascendancy" over Satan: "Now as to whether or not those who in mortal life rebel and become sons of perdition will be able to exercise greater dominion than those who followed Lucifer, who became the Devil and arch-enemy of Jesus Christ, might be a moot question. However, the Lord has made it definitely clear that Cain will hold that ascendancy in the realm of wickedness; that Satan desired to have him, and the implication is clear that the reason was because Cain had a body of flesh and bones.… As far as Cain is concerned, the information given is definite that he became Perdition, and that Lucifer who is Satan, became subject to him. It appears that the reason Satan desired to have him was due to the fact that Cain had obtained a body of flesh and bones and therefore had superior power, and Satan was willing to accept and be obedient to him because of that condition. The natural conclusion is, therefore, that a devil with a body of flesh and bones has some power greater than one who was denied the physical body."[493]

Note that Cain's ultimate ascendancy over Satan is foreshadowed in v. 30, where Satan takes an oath to "do according to [Cain's] commands."

---

485   V. P. Hamilton, *Genesis*, pp. 201-202.
486   See *Commentary* 4:22-c, p. 268.
487   See D&C 121:39; 2 Nephi 4:18; and Alma 5:7, 10.
488   See *Commentary* 4:21-d, p. 266.
489   U. Cassuto, *Adam to Noah*, p. 161.
490   Cf. Hamilton's translation of the last clause of v. 23 "you, you are to master it!" (V. P. Hamilton, *Genesis*, p. 228).
491   D&C 76:26.
492   2 Nephi 9:9, Moses 4:4.
493   J. F. Smith, Jr., *Answers*, 1958, 2:170-171. The teachings of Joseph Smith relating to the fact that "beings who have bodies have power over those who have not" (J. Smith, Jr., *Words*, 5 January 1841, p. 60) are summarized elsewhere. See *Endnote 4-15*, p. 303. See also *Excursus 21: The Power and Premortal Status of Satan*, p. 575.

MOSES 5

24 For from this time forth **thou shalt be the father of his lies**; *thou shalt be called* **Perdition**; *for* **thou wast also before the world.**

24 **a** ***thou shalt be the father of his lies.*** The scripture portrays Cain's wickedness as even greater than that of Satan. Though Satan continues to be the "father of lies,"[494] it will be as if Cain were the "grandfather." Elder Bruce R. McConkie comments: "Both Satan and Cain... have been liars from the beginning.[495] The name signifies authorship and sponsorship of all that is dishonest and which leads away from the truth. In a similar sense Satan is the 'master of sin'[496] and the father of secret combinations and every evil thing."[497]

b ***Perdition.*** Emphasizing Cain's accountability, Elder Joseph Fielding Smith writes: "Cain sinned with his eyes open, so he became Perdition."[498] Whereas Judas Iscariot was called the "son of perdition" by Jesus Christ,[499] Cain is the only scriptural personage referred to as "Perdition" itself.

The title "Perdition"—from a Latin root meaning "to destroy, to ruin"—is an ironic reversal of one of the derivations of the name Cain: "to produce, to create."[500] Nibley further explains: "'Perdition' means... one fallen from high estate... Nine days[, as Milton says,] he fell in 'hideous ruin and combustion down,' down, down'...[501] He was among the highest in heaven up there, and down he fell."[502]

Writes Andrus: "To become Perdition, Cain would have to commit the unpardonable sin. 'No one can commit the unpardonable sin,' Joseph Smith explained, '... until he receives the Holy Ghost.'[503] Having received the Holy Ghost, one must then commit murder, wherein he sheds innocent blood. Said the Prophet: 'The unpardonable sin is to shed innocent blood, or be accessory thereto.'[504] Innocent blood is the blood of the righteous. It is sanctified blood. And to shed innocent blood, one must come out in open opposition to the kingdom of God so as to assent unto the death of Christ."[505] At that point, when one is "fully ripe," the Spirit utterly ceases to "strive with man" and he is "cut off from the presence of the Lord."[506] In rejecting the law of sacrifice, trampling the Savior under his feet, and shedding the innocent blood of his brother, Cain put himself beyond the reach of the Atonement.

c ***thou wast also before the world.*** From this verse, Elder Bruce R. McConkie concludes that Cain was a friend of Lucifer in premortality, and at that time had already charted his future course.[507]

Comments Nibley: 'This refers back to the time in the Council in Heaven, in glory. Satan is not going to say, you brought me into this world and put me in this terrible jam, and I had nothing to say about it. Oh no, you were in the preexistence, too. You were high up there because you are Perdition now. '...for thou wast also before the world.' You had your preexistence and your chance."[508]

---

494 2 Nephi 9:9, Moses 4:4.

495 2 Nephi 9:9; Moses 5:18-27; D&C 93:25; cf. Alma 5:25. See *Commentary* 4:1-c, p. 243.

496 Mosiah 4:14.

497 B. R. McConkie, *Mormon Doctrine*, p. 278; cf. 2 Nephi 26:22; Helaman 6:26; Moroni 7:12. See *Commentary* 4:4-b, p. 246.

498 J. F. Smith, Jr., *Doctrines*, 30 March 1935, 2:280. Other scriptural passages that refer to the title "perdition" and "sons of perdition" include John 17:12; 2 Thessalonians 2:3; 3 Nephi 27:32, 29:7; D&C 75:26, 32, 43.

499 John 17:12; 3 Nephi 27:32, 29:7.

500 See *Commentary* 4:1-f, p. 244; 5:16-c, p. 367.

501 See J. Milton, *Paradise Lost*, 1:46, p. 17.

502 H. W. Nibley, *Teachings of the PGP*, 19, p. 240.

503 J. Smith, Jr., *Teachings*, 7 April 1844, p. 357.

504 *Ibid.*, 16 May 1843, p. 300; D&C 132:27.

505 H. L. Andrus, *Doctrinal (Rev.)*, p. 335. See also J. Smith, Jr., *Teachings*, 7 April 1844, p. 358.

506 Ether 2:15; cf. Moses 8:17.

507 B. R. McConkie, *NT Commentary*, 1:715; cf. John 8:44; 1 John 3:11-12; J. A. Widtsoe, *Evidences*, p. 212.

508 H. W. Nibley, *Teachings of the PGP*, 19, p. 240.

*25 And it shall be said in time to come—That these abominations were had from Cain; for he rejected the greater counsel which was had from God; and this is a cursing which I will put upon thee, **except thou repent.***

*26 And **Cain was wroth**, and **listened not any more** to the voice of the Lord, neither to **Abel**, his brother, who **walked in holiness** before the Lord.*

*27 **And Adam and his wife mourned before the Lord**, because of Cain and his brethren.*

*28 And it came to pass that **Cain took one of his brothers' daughters to wife, and they loved Satan more than God.***

25 a   ***except thou repent.*** God tenders a loving plea to Cain, as the tragic son of Adam nears the final crossroads. Nibley observes: "It's still not too late. This is the gospel of repentance. As long as you are in this earth, you can still repent. As long as we are in this earth, there is no one who doesn't need to repent… The door is open to everyone here… As Ezekiel[509] says… However wicked the bad guys have been all their days, they can still repent and become righteous. And however righteous the good guys have been all their days, they can still fall and become the wicked. The door is open right to the end. Never, never claim that you are saved. No one is saved here[—no one is] beyond sinning… And again, no one is damned. You are not damned on this earth. You are damned in the judgment in the hereafter. And you are not saved on this earth. You are in between and you are being tested. Therefore, this life became, as [Lehi] says, a time of probation."[510]

26 a   ***Cain was wroth.*** Cain does not answer the Lord, but inwardly fans his smoldering resentment into a flame of murderous passion.[511]

    b   ***listened not any more.*** Writes Nibley: ""The… door of repentance is held open right to the last moment, when it is Cain himself who breaks off the conversation and angrily stamps out, refusing to listen 'any more to the voice of the Lord' or to his brother's remonstrances."[512] Arnold observes: "Eve had been talked into her sin. Cain could not be talked out of his, even by God himself."[513]

    c   ***Abel… walked in holiness.*** Joseph Smith explained that Abel "magnified the Priesthood which was conferred upon him, and died a righteous man, and therefore has become an angel of God by receiving his body from the dead, holding still the keys of his dispensation; and was sent down from heaven unto Paul to minister consoling words, and to commit unto him a knowledge of the mysteries of godliness."[514]

27 a   ***Adam and his wife.*** OT1 reads: "And Adam also, and his wife."[515]

    b   ***mourned before the Lord.*** This expression may indicate the practice of bringing one's concern for loved ones to the altar as the subject of special prayer.[516]

28 a   ***Cain took one of his brothers' daughters to wife, and they loved Satan more than God.*** The mention of Cain's brothers in v. 27, coupled with the statement that they loved Satan more than God,[517] makes it seem reasonable to suppose that Cain's wife was the daughter

509   Ezekiel 18:26-27.

510   H. W. Nibley, Teachings of the PGP, 19, p. 241; see 2 Nephi 2:21.

511   Cf. *Commentary* 5:21-b, p. 372.

512   H. W. Nibley, *Enoch*, pp. 175-176.

513   B. T. Arnold, *Genesis*, p. 40.

514   J. Smith, Jr., *Teachings*, 5 October 1840, p. 169 and Hebrews 11:4; see also D&C 84:16. For an LDS perspective on the authorship of Hebrews, see T. L. Szink, *Authorship*. See *Excursus 37: Traditions About the Role of Abel*, p. 617.

515   S. H. Faulring *et al.*, *Original Manuscripts*, p. 94.

516   R. D. Draper *et al.*, *Commentary*, p. 67; H. W. Nibley, *Prayer Circle*, pp. 75-79. See also M. B. Brown, *Gate*, pp. 124-126; D. W. Parry, *Psalm 24*; D. M. Quinn, *Prayer Circles*; J. A. Tvedtnes, *Temple Prayer*; M. von Wellnitz, *Liturgy*, pp. 32-33.

517   Cf. Moses 5:13.

28 And it came to pass that **Cain took one of his brothers' daughters to wife, and they loved Satan more than God.**

29 And **Satan said unto Cain: Swear unto me by thy throat,** *and if thou tell it thou shalt die; and swear thy brethren by their heads, and by the living God, that they tell it not; for if they tell it, they shall surely die; and this that thy father may not know it; and this day I will deliver thy brother Abel into thine hands.*

of one of the unbelieving sons of Adam rather than of the righteous Abel. Note the later Old Testament custom "for men to marry a niece, as did Nahor, brother of Abraham."[518] Falk writes: "During the tribal period, marriage was contracted within the kinship group. Originally the rule, perhaps, applied even to close relatives, requiring marriage with a man's paternal sister. Later, the same tendency took the form of a preference for one's niece or cousin."[519]

According to Jewish, Christian, and Islamic sources, Cain's wife had not been the first object of his desire. Accounts tell of the twin sisters of Cain and Abel, and relate that Adam appointed which of the sisters each brother was to marry. Angry because the sister promised to Abel was more beautiful, Cain was said to have killed his brother "out of passion for [his] sister."[520] A Manichaean version of the story goes further in claiming that Abel's wife was unfaithful, and when Abel learned about her involvement with Cain, his complaints to her and to his mother Eve provoked Cain's murderous anger.[521] President Spencer W. Kimball concurred with the plausibility of such a scenario: "If we had the record, we would probably find that Cain was promiscuous, for seldom do great crimes travel in single file."[522]

29 **a** *Satan said unto Cain.* Remarks Nibley: "God discusses things with men 'in all humility' for the sake of our enlightenment. Satan too loves to 'discuss,' but what a different type of discussion! He is not teaching but laying traps; his whole line is a sales pitch with his own advantage as the end. He is not enlightening but manipulating. He does not reason, but bargains."[523] The *Apocalypse of Abraham* counsels: "Answer [Satan] not, lest his will affect you."[524]

b *Swear unto me by thy throat.* Nibley observes: "The throat is one of the most vulnerable parts of the body to an ancient weapon such as a knife or a spear. Hence, it is vital to the continuation of life. In addition, cutting the throat of an sacrificial animal began the process of a sacred offering. It seems plain that Satan's oaths gain credibility not through his name but only through repeating the divine name ["swear… by the living God"] and, possibly, mimicking genuinely sacred covenants made in God's name."[525]

Anciently, discretion in the revealing of sacred religious knowledge was solemnly enjoined by the symbolic enactment of self-cursing. For example, a hint of such may be seen in the following is statement attributed to Abu Hurayrah, who is said to have received secret knowledge from Muhammad during the Islamic Prophet's final years in Medina: "I have memorized two kinds of knowledge from Allàh's Apostle… I have transmitted one of them

518 R. D. Draper, *et al.*, *Commentary*, p. 67. See Genesis 11:27-29.

519 Z. W. Falk, *Law*, p. 129. See Genesis 11:29; 20:12; 24; 28.

520 M. al-Kisa'i, *Tales*, pp. 346-347 n. 60; al-Tabari, *Creation*, 1:137-147, pp. 308-317; A. al-Tha'labi, *Lives*, pp. 73-76; E. A. W. Budge, *Cave*, pp. 69-70; L. Ginzberg, *Legends*, 5:138; M. Ibn Ishaq ibn Yasar, *Making*, pp. 38-39; J. L. Kugel, *Traditions*, pp. 147-148; S. C. Malan, *Adam and Eve*, 1:76-79, pp. 95-103; J. C. Reeves, *al-Yaqubi*; S. E. Robinson, *Testament of Adam 1983*, 3:5, p. 994; H. Schwartz, *Tree*, 575, pp. 449-450; Shelemon, *Book of the Bee*, 18, pp. 25-26; M. E. Stone, *Question*, 1-2, pp. 118-119; M. E. Stone, *Sethites*, 1-3, pp. 203-204; G. Weil, *Legends*, pp. 42-43. See also *Excursus 50: Fu Xi and Nü Gua*, p. 654.

521 J. C. Reeves, *Heralds*, p. 80.

522 S. W. Kimball, *Teachings 1982*, 26 September 1971, p. 268.

523 H. W. Nibley, *Beyond Politics*, p. 291.

524 P. Alexander, *3 Enoch*, 14:12, p. 696. See n. 14 l.

525 R. D. Draper, *et al.*, *Commentary*, pp. 67-68; cf. J. E. Seaich, *Ancient Texts 1995*, p. 669.

29 And Satan said unto Cain: **Swear unto me by thy throat,** *and if thou tell it thou shalt die; and swear thy brethren by their heads, and* **by the living God,** *that they tell it not; for* **if they tell it, they shall surely die;** *and this* **that thy father may not know it;** *and* **this day I will deliver thy brother Abel into thine hands.**

to you, and if I spread the second, then my throat would be cut."[526] In the performance of sacred covenants in ancient times, writes Westermann, "Words and actions are part of the oath. There can be the raising of the hand or some other action(s). A standard form which is very common is the conditional self-cursing…[527] The one who passes between the divided halves of the slain animals invokes death upon himself should he break the word by which he has bound himself in the oath."[528] Sarna also cites an example in the Aramaic *Sefire Treaty* from northern Syria: "As this calf is cut up, thus Matti'el… shall be cut up."[529] In Arabic, the "original meaning [of the word for oath] is the right hand. As they strike by, raise, or give, the right hand when taking an oath, showing allegiance or concluding a deal, the word was metaphorically used for the oath."[530]

As a parallel to this passage about the oath Cain made to Satan in seeming imitation of genuine ancient religious practices, Nibley cites a Greek fragment of *1 Enoch* (*Gizeh*) describing the events surrounding the marriage of the Sons of Heaven and the Daughters of Men, where their leader Semiazus [= Satan] says: "'I am afraid you will not be willing to go through with this thing… And they answered him all saying, We will all swear with an oath, and bind each other by a mortal curse [literally, anathemize each other], that we will not go back on this agreement [*gnome*] until we have carried it out; … Then they all swore together and pronounced the doom of death on each other."[531] In the same spirit, the oath between Cain and Satan is appropriately described in the Doctrine and Covenants as a "conspiracy."[532]

c   ***by the living God.*** Nibley comments: "Notice…, who do they swear by? By the living God. They don't swear by anybody else."[533] Similarly, we read in *1 Enoch*: "Kasbeel, the chief of the oath… when he dwelt high above in glory… requested Michael to show him the hidden name, that he might enunciate it in the oath, so that those might quake before that name and oath who revealed all that was in secret to the children of men."[534]

d   ***if they tell it, they shall surely die.*** Draper, *et al.* explain: "The stakes for turning against one's oath were deadly. Here death can result from mere spoken words."[535] This verse foreshadows vv. 49-50, where Lamech slays Irad "for the oath's sake" because he had begun to reveal "their secret."

e   ***that thy father may not know it.*** Satan is particularly concerned that the oath be kept secret from Adam.

f   ***this day I will deliver thy brother Abel into thine hands.*** Comments Nibley: "God and Satan both presented plans of dominion to Adam and then to his son Cain. [Adam] chose one plan, [Cain] the other."[536] Satan's hatred of Jehovah mirrored Cain's animosity toward Abel

---

526   M. I. I. Bukhari, *Sahih*, 3:43:120, 1:113. See also A. B. S. Ed-Din, *Sufism*, p. 236.

527   E.g., Genesis 15:9ff.

528   C. Westermann, *Genesis 1-11*, p. 225; cf., e.g., V. P. Hamilton, *Genesis*, pp. 430-433.

529   N. M. Sarna, *Genesis*, pp. 114-115; cf., e.g., Alma 46:20-21; D. R. Seely, *Genesis 15*, pp. 356-358.

530   A. at-Tabataba'i, *Al-Mizan*, 2:224, 4:4; cf. D. R. Seely, *Raised Hand*. See *Endnote 4-34*, p. 308.

531   H. W. Nibley, *Enoch*, p. 182; cf. R. H. Charles, *Enoch*, 6:2-5, p. 278; H. W. Nibley, *Enoch*, p. 10; G. W. E. Nickelsburg, *1 Enoch*, 6:3-5, p. 174; Moses 6:29.

532   D&C 84:16; cf. *Commentary 5:47-b*, p. 396.

533   H. W. Nibley, *Teachings of the PGP*; cf. *Commentary 5:18-a*, p. 371.

534   H. W. Nibley, *Enoch*, p. 182; cf. G. W. E. Nickelsburg, *et al.*, *1 Enoch*, 69:13-14, p. 90.

535   R. D. Draper, *et al.*, *Commentary*, p. 68.

536   H. W. Nibley, *Dominion*, p. 13.

29 And Satan said unto Cain: Swear unto me by thy throat, and if thou tell it thou shalt die; and swear thy brethren by their heads, and by the living God, that they tell it not; for if they tell it, they shall surely die; and this that thy father may not know it; and **this day I will deliver thy brother Abel into thine hands**.

30 And **Satan sware unto Cain** *that he would do according to his commands. And all these things were done in secret.*

31 And Cain said: **Truly I am Mahan,** *the master of this great secret,* **that I may murder and get gain.** *Wherefore Cain was called Master Mahan, and he gloried in his wickedness.*

as, in the words of President John Taylor, "the rebellion in the heavens was transmitted to a rebellion on the earth."[537]

30 a *Satan sware unto Cain.* Nibley points out the illusory nature of Satan's seeming subservience: "Cain rule over Satan? Yes, that is the arrangement—the Devil serves his client, gratifies his slightest whim, pampers his appetites, and is at his beck and call throughout his earthly life, putting unlimited power and influence at his disposal through his command of the treasures of the earth, gold and silver. But in exchange the victim must keep his part of the agreement, following Satan's instructions on earth and remaining in his power thereafter. That is the classic bargain, the pact with the Devil, by which a Faust, Don Juan, Macbeth, or Jabez Stone achieve the pinnacle of earthly success and the depths of eternal damnation."[538]

31 a *Truly I am Mahan.* Draper, *et al.* comment: "Cain takes a new name as an indicator of his new status, also a later characteristic of righteous persons (Abram becomes Abraham;[539] and so on)."[540] Nibley discusses a possible etymology of the name: "The word 'secret' is *sirra* in Arabic; the eighth form of the verb, *mustirra*, means 'to hold a secret, to keep a secret.' It's the same as the Greek word *sathra* for secret. The Egyptian word is *seshet*; *mesehet* is 'to hold a secret.' *Sether* is the Hebrew word for keeping a secret (the master of the secret). So this word 'master' may not be our word 'master' at all, but 'master' means 'keeper of secret,' and 'Mahan' means 'great.' In any language, *maha* means 'great.' Words like *magnus*, mighty, might, many, *maharaja*; anything that's big is *ma*. So this could mean Master Mahan, the 'great secret keeper.' (It could be; this is just a suggestion here.)"[541]

Note that in OT1, "Mahan" is consistently spelled "Mahon," which suggests how the Prophet might have pronounced the name while dictating the manuscript.[542] The spelling was changed to "Mahan" in OT2.[543]

b *that I may murder and get gain.* The essence of the great secret of Cain is what Nibley calls "converting life into property. Cain got the degree of Master Mahan, tried the system out on his brother, and gloried in its brilliant success, declaring that at last he could be free, as only property makes free, and that Abel had been a loser in a free competition."[544]

President Spencer W. Kimball warned that "we must eliminate the individual tendency to selfishness that snares the soul, shrinks the heart, and darkens the mind. President [Marion G.] Romney recently referred to the tragic cycle of civilization, a cycle propelled by anyone who seeks for power and gain. Was it not this that led Cain to commit the first murder 'for the sake of getting gain'?[545] Is not this the spirit of the anti-Christ in which 'every man prospered according to his genius, and … every man conquered according to his strength;

537 J. Taylor, *Mediation*, 1882, p. 68; J. Taylor, *Gospel Kingdom*, 1882, p. 101.
538 H. W. Nibley, *Enoch*, p. 175. See *Commentary* 5:23-e, p. 374.
539 See Genesis 17:5.
540 R. D. Draper, *et al.*, *Commentary*, p. 68; cf. Moses 5:49; *Commentary* 3:19-b, p. 177.
541 H. W. Nibley, *Teachings of the PGP*, 19, p. 242.
542 S. H. Faulring, *et al.*, *Original Manuscripts*, pp. 94-95.
543 *Ibid.*, pp. 605, 607.
544 H. W. Nibley, *Foundation*, p. 166. See *Commentary* 5:38-a, p. 384.
545 Moses 5:50,

31 And Cain said: Truly I am Mahan, the master of this great secret, **that I may murder and get gain***. Wherefore Cain was called Master Mahan, and* **he gloried in his wickedness***.*

32 And **Cain went into the field***, and* **Cain talked with Abel, his brother***. And it came to pass that while they were in the field, Cain rose up against Abel, his brother, and slew him.*

and whatsoever a man did was no crime'?[546] Did not Nephi single this out as the spirit which led his generation to destruction?"[547]

   c   ***he gloried in his wickedness.*** See *Commentary* 5:33-a, p. 381.

32 **a**   ***Cain went.*** Wenham writes: "The awfulness of the deed is accentuated by the stark brevity of the description… [T]he terseness conveys the feel of the story hastening to its climax."[548]

   b   ***into the field.*** Sarna notes: "Hebrew *sadeh* refers to the open, uninhabited country away from the settled areas. It was often the scene of crime."[549] Later in the OT, the word "field" will appear in several other stories of sibling rivalry and fratricide: the story of Jacob and Esau,[550] Joseph and his brothers,[551] Abimelech, who killed seventy of his brothers,[552] and the war between the tribe of Benjamin and those of his brothers.[553]

   c   ***Cain talked with Abel, his brother.*** The Hebrew indicates that the phrase has been truncated (i.e., "Cain said to his brother Abel…"). Friedman conjectures that Cain's words were "skipped in the Masoretic text by a scribe whose eye jumped from the first phrase containing the word 'field' to the second."[554] Sarna notes that the "Aramaic targums, like the Greek, Syriac, and Latin versions of the text, add: 'Come let us go into the field'… Others took Hebrew *va-yo'mer* to mean 'He had words with him.'"[555] Cassuto renders the phrase as "Cain appointed a place where to meet Abel his brother," commenting: "first he arranged the meeting and then he turned the meeting into an assault."[556]

In addition to the general themes of Cain's jealousy and wickedness mentioned previously, ancient sources cite other immediate pretexts for Cain's argument with Abel. One version of the story has it that Cain coveted a twin sister who had been appointed by Adam to be Abel's wife.[557] Al-Tabari, on the other hand, recounts that "Adam singled Abel out for [receiving God's] knowledge" and that "Cain… killed Abel out of envy."[558] Implausibly, Jewish midrash[559] envisions an argument over property as the catalyst for Cain's fatal quarrel with Abel: "[W]hen they divided the world, one took the land and the other took the movables. The former said, 'You are standing on my land,' while the other said 'What you are wearing is mine!' One said 'Strip,' while the other retorted 'Fly [off my land].'"[560] The dispute recalls the Sumerian myth of *Dumuzi and Enkimdu,* whose plot is based on, Kramer asserts, "what may not inaptly be described as the 'Cain-Abel' motif."[561]

---

546   Alma 30:17.

547   S. W. Kimball, *Pure,* p. 79. See 2 Nephi 26:10-11.

548   G. J. Wenham, *Genesis 1-15,* p. 106.

549   N. M. Sarna, *Genesis,* p. 33. See N. M. Sarna, *Mists,* p. 69 for a photograph of a Druze shrine purporting to be the tomb of Abel.

550   Genesis 25-27. See 25:27, 29.

551   Genesis 37. See 37:7, 15.

552   Judges 9. See 9:27, 32, 44.

553   R. E. Friedman, *Commentary,* p. 27; Judges 20:31. See also Deuteronomy 22:25.

554   R. E. Friedman, *Commentary,* p. 26.

555   N. M. Sarna, *Genesis,* p. 33.

556   U. Cassuto, *Adam to Noah,* pp. 213, 215. An Islamic account of the dialogue between Cain and Abel can be found in *Qur'an* 5:27-29.

557   See *Commentary* 5:28-a, p. 376 and *Excursus 50: Fu Xi and Nü Gua,* p. 654.

558   al-Tabari, *Creation,* 1:159-160, p. 331.

559   J. Neusner, *Genesis Rabbah 1,* 22:7, p. 247.

560   Cited in R. M. Zlotowitz, *et al., Bereishis,* p. 149.

561   S. N. Kramer, *Dumuzi,* p. 41.

*32 And Cain went into the field, and **Cain talked with Abel, his brother**. And it came to pass that while they were in the field, Cain rose up against **Abel, his brother**, and **slew him**.*

*33 And **Cain gloried** in that which he had done, saying: **I am free; surely the flocks of my brother falleth into my hands**.*

> **Abel, his brother.** The word "brother" is repeated seven times in verses 32-36, mercilessly highlighting the grim perfidy of Cain's crime.

> d **slew him.** The Hebrew term is *harag*, signifying intentional murder, in contrast to the sixth commandment's *rasah*, a term that includes manslaughter.[562] Sarna comments: "The transgression in the Garden was an offense against God; "now it is man against his brother, which is also an offense against God. It was the 'fruit of the tree' that led to the downfall of Adam and Eve; it is the 'fruit of the soil' that leads to Cain's undoing. The first human was worried about death; now the experience of death becomes a reality."[563]

> 33 a **Cain gloried.** The mood of Cain was previously described as "very wroth" and of a fallen countenance.[564] Then, according to an Armenian text, after he "killed his brother he went away cheerfully."[565] In ironic counterpoint to Moses 1:39, Cain has now made the work of death the object of his glorying.[566]

> b **I am free.** Elder Bruce C. Hafen writes: "Cain was never more in bondage than when he said he was free."[567] Observes Elder Neal A. Maxwell: "A confused Cain, a vain Cain, not only murdered his brother while they conversed together in the field, but also gloried in the murder of Abel, when Cain said (probably shouted), 'I am free.' So often violence creates the illusion of freedom or possession. So often sin creates a momentary illusion which those involved are taken in by... [It seems] that the raucousness and the shouting of sin, the Cain-like glorying in it, is also the sound of pain trying to erase itself."[568]

> Nibley comments: "Recently this gospel was proclaimed by one of the richest Americans addressing the student body of Ohio State University...: 'There is nothing that gives freedom,' he said, 'like bucks in the bank.' This seems to be the policy we are following today, and there is no doubt whose policy it is."[569] "What is the market?" former French prime minister Édouard Balladur disparagingly asked, "It is the law of the jungle."[570] This much-maligned statement was actually put to a test by Piccione and Rubenstein, who found that "the notion of a jungle equilibrium" demonstrates "a number of standard results of competitive markets." They observed that "the virtue of the market system is that it utilizes people's natural desire to acquire wealth," while "the jungle uses people's natural willingness to exercise power and to dominate without employing central government."[571]

> c **surely the flocks of my brother falleth into my hands.** Nibley points out that "all the oldest words for money simply mean flocks."[572] "Satan promised Cain what he had promised Adam before: You can have anything in this world for money... The words for money we have here are, remember, '...surely his flocks fall into my hands.' So we have flocks, fee, Old English *feoh*, and German *Vieh*, meaning cattle or flocks of all kinds. The Arabic word for flocks is

562 V. P. Hamilton, *Genesis*, p. 230.

563 N. M. Sarna, *Genesis*, p. 31.

564 Moses 5:21-22, 26.

565 W. L. Lipscomb, *Abel*, 34, p. 165.

566 See also Moses 5:31. Cf. *Commentary* 5:47-a, p. 395.

567 B. C. Hafen, *et al.*, *Belonging*, p. 276; cf. N. A. Maxwell, *Deposition*, p. 85; N. A. Maxwell, *Praise*, p. 72. See also 2 Peter 2:19; 2 Nephi 2:26-30.

568 N. A. Maxwell, *Insights*, p. 50. See also N. A. Maxwell, *Enemy*, p. 76; N. A. Maxwell, *Seventh*, p. 78; Proverbs 14:13.

569 H. W. Nibley, *Work*, p. 230.

570 Cited in A. Greenspan, *Turbulence*, p. 277.

571 M. Piccione, *et al.*, *Equilibrium*, pp. 883, 894.

572 H. W. Nibley, *Consecration*, p. 436. See Moses 5:38.

MOSES 5

33 And Cain gloried in that which he had done, saying: I am free; **surely the flocks of my brother falleth into my hands.**

34 And the Lord said unto Cain: **Where is Abel, thy brother?** *And he said:* **I know not. Am I my brother's keeper?**

ghanam, which is our word "gain"... *Ghaniy* is "to be rich." The land Ghana means 'rich land.' A *ghaniuun* is a rich person (plural *aghniyau*). That's the way you measured it."[573]

34 a   Where is Abel, thy brother? "[T]he question is a means of opening the conversation, perhaps eliciting confession and contrition."[574] Sarna notes that this verse "virtually reproduces" the Lord's question to the fleeing Adam in the Garden of Eden: "the divine question to the culprit in each case— 'Where?' — receives an evasive reply in both chapters."[575] The wording of the curse is similar, too—"the son, like his parents in the previous chapter, is 'banished' and settles to the east of Eden."[576] Unlike his parents, however, he will not repent and begin a return to the presence of God. Like Satan and the fallen angels, Cain and those who persist in follow his ways are cast out of Paradise forever.[577]

b   I know not. Once more the term "know" recurs in the story of Cain.[578] His renewed effort at self-deception recalls the confession of Amulek, "I did harden my heart, for I was called many times and I would not hear; therefore I knew concerning these things, yet I would not know."[579]

Though Cain disavowed knowledge of his brother's fate, the crime was not hid from the Lord, who lamented: "The voice of thy brother's blood cries unto me from the ground."[580] Elder Spencer W. Kimball wrote: "When Cain's great sin was conceived in his heart and the propitious moment had arrived for the foul deed, undoubtedly he looked to the right and to the left and behind him and was certain there was no eye and no ear; he perpetrated his heinous crime and left his righteous brother lying in his blood. The Lord perceived it all—the sights and sounds and thinking and malice and intents and desires and urges."[581]

c   Am I my brother's keeper? It is no coincidence that the Hebrew stem for "keeper" is the same one used in the Lord's commandment to Adam and Eve that they should "dress and keep" the Garden of Eden.[582] Following Daube, Hamilton notes that keeper is "a legal term for a person entrusted with the custody and care of an object."[583] Though, apart from this verse, it is never used in scripture in connection with a responsibility of one person for another, the verbal form of "keep" "often appears in the OT to describe God's relationship to Israel."[584] Israel is His peculiar treasure. "He is its keeper and as such he never slumbers or sleeps.[585] Moses' prayer for the people of Israel is that the Lord bless them and keep them."[586] Abraham's blessings are confirmed upon him because he "obeyed my voice, and kept my charge" (= "kept my keeping"[587]—repeating the Hebrew root twice for emphasis).[588]

573   H. W. Nibley, *Teachings of the PGP*, 19, p. 243. See *Commentary* 5:31-c, p. 379.
574   N. M. Sarna, *Genesis*, p. 34; cf. W. L. Lipscomb, *Abel*, 36, p. 165.
575   See *Commentary* 4:15-b, p. 261.
576   N. M. Sarna, *Genesis*, p. 31; see also J. H. Sailhamer, *Genesis*, p. 65.
577   Moses 5:41.
578   See *Commentary* 5:16-b, p. 367 and 5:16-h, p. 369.
579   Alma 10:6.
580   Moses 5:35.
581   S. W. Kimball, *Temptation*, p. 243.
582   See *Commentary* 3:15-b, p. 173.
583   V. P. Hamilton, *Genesis*, p. 230.
584   *Ibid.*, p. 231.
585   Psalm 121:4-8, where five times God is called the one who "keeps" Israel.
586   V. P. Hamilton, *Genesis*, p. 231. See Numbers 6:24.
587   Genesis 26:5.
588   R. E. Friedman, *Commentary*, p. 28.

34 And the Lord said unto Cain: Where is Abel, thy brother? And he said: I know not. **Am I my brother's keeper?**

35 And the Lord said: **What hast thou done?** *The* **voice of thy brother's blood cries unto me from the ground.**

Though the English translation we have here is more or less accurate, Royal Skousen notes that it fails to fully convey the haughty impudence of Cain's reply:[589] "Couldn't Abel take care of himself? Did he have to have someone look after him? The Hebrew word for 'keeper,' *shomer*, refers to a watchman, a guard, or anyone who has charge, care or oversight of something. Typically, we have keepers of sheep, baggage, wardrobes, altars, doors, houses, gates, city walls, forests, fields, and the king's women. Although *shomer* does not apply to children, the modern reader might get a better feel for Cain's answer if we paraphrased it as: 'How should I know? Am I my brother's baby-sitter?'"[590] Chauncey Riddle suggests an answer to Cain's question: "No, Cain, you are not expected to be your brother's keeper. But you are expected to be your brother's brother."[591]

35   **a**   ***What hast thou done?*** This would be better punctuated with an exclamation mark ("What has thou done!")—it is "[n]ot a question, but a cry of horror."[592]

      b   ***voice of thy brother's blood cries unto me.*** Draper, *et al.* point out that "in a legal sense spilt blood stands as a witness that a crime may have been committed."[593] The Hebrew stem of "cries out" "connotes a plea for help or redress on the part of the victim of some great injustice."[594] For example, we read elsewhere in the OT about the cries of "the afflicted in Sodom and Gomorrah,[595] the overworked and exhausted Israelites in Egypt,[596] or the afflicted stranger, widow, or orphan."[597]

        blood. The Hebrew plural for blood used here (*damim*) usually indicates "a context of bloodshed or bloodguilt."[598] Sarna notes that the "*Mishnah Sanhedrin* 4:5, so the targums, takes the plural to include, apart from the blood of the victim, also that of the potential offspring now doomed never to be born: 'Whoever takes a single life destroys thereby an entire world.'"[599]

      c   ***from the ground.*** "The earth itself demands from God that He should execute justice on one who destroys a man."[600] Explains Nibley: "Every creature is supposed to have its time, but the purpose of the earth is to sustain and support life. Anything that destroys life prematurely is against the purposes for which it was constructed, and the earth is offended. That negates its whole purpose."[601]

        Gelander observes that "while in the story of Eden the earth is alienated from Man, in the story of Cain it is the sinner who is alienated from the earth, since the disruption of harmony had already been caused by Adam and Eve in the preceding stage. Now the alienation is made personal."[602]

---

589   W. L. Lipscomb, *Abel*, 35, p. 165.
590   R. Skousen, *Darkly*, p. 9; cf. Wenham's "Am I the shepherd's shepherd?" (G. J. Wenham, *Genesis 1-15*, p. 106).
591   Cited in J. R. Holland, *Rudder*, p. 142; cf. N. A. Maxwell, *Wherefore*, p. 88.
592   N. M. Sarna, *Genesis*, p. 34.
593   R. D. Draper, *et al.*, *Commentary*, p. 70.
594   N. M. Sarna, *Genesis*, p. 34, cf. p. 132. See G. W. E. Nickelsburg, *1 Enoch*, 22:5-7, p. 300; 9:2, 10, p. 202. See also pp. 305-306 n. 5-7.
595   Genesis 18:13.
596   Exodus 3:7.
597   V. P. Hamilton, *Genesis*, p. 231 and Exodus 22:21-24. See *Excursus 37: Traditions About the Role of Abel*, p. 617.
598   N. M. Sarna, *Genesis*, p. 34.
599   N. M. Sarna, *Genesis*, p. 34; cf. J. Goldin, *Fathers*, 31, p. 136.
600   Hirsch, cited in R. M. Zlotowitz, *et al.*, *Bereishis*, p. 152.
601   H. W. Nibley, *Teachings of the PGP*, 20, p. 245.
602   S. Gelander, *Creator*, p. 6.

*36 And now **thou shalt be cursed from the earth** which hath opened her mouth to receive thy brother's blood from thy hand.*

*37 When thou tillest the **ground** it **shall not henceforth yield unto thee her strength**. A **fugitive and a vagabond** shalt thou be in the earth.*

*38 And Cain said unto the Lord: Satan tempted me **because of my brother's flocks**. And I was wroth also; for his offering thou didst accept and not mine; **my punishment is greater than I can bear**.*

36   a   ***thou shalt be cursed.*** Westermann points out: "In [Moses 4] neither the man nor the woman are cursed but only the serpent. In [Moses 5], however, the man Cain is cursed."[603]

        Cain's curse resembles the warning of exile given to Israel in Deuteronomy: "Cursed shalt thou be in the city, and cursed shalt thou be in the field. Cursed shall be thy basket and thy store. Cursed shall be the fruit of thy body [i.e., thy posterity], and the fruit of thy land, the increase of thy kine, and the flocks of thy sheep."[604]

   b   ***from the earth.*** Kass points out that the "preposition here translated 'from' could also be translated 'by' or 'of' or even 'more than'; Rashi reads that Cain is now cursed more than the ground, the ground having been cursed for man's sake at the end of the Eden story."[605] Just as the serpent who was "more subtle" than any beast of the field[606] became "more cursed" than all cattle and beasts,[607] so the one who loved Satan "more than" God[608] will be cursed "more than" the earth from which he wrested his living.[609]

37   a   ***ground… shall not henceforth yield unto thee her strength.*** From now on, the soil will be unproductive for Cain. Writes Hirsch: "When the man tears asunder the bond between himself and God, then God tears asunder the bond between man and the earth."[610] Comments Nibley: "What Cain has done by murder is… to curtail life… As a result the earth is not going to give you anything. You have taken life from it; now it will not return life to you."[611]

   b   ***fugitive and a vagabond.*** Hamilton treats these two words as a hendiadys (i.e., two words expressing a single idea), thus a signifying a "wandering fugitive."[612] Not only the unfruitfulness of the ground, but also Cain's new lifestyle would make it impossible for him to continue as a successful tiller of the soil. Yet more devastating is the fact that, like Ishmael and Esau, Cain "is now ousted from civilization… Rootlessness is the punishment and the wilderness is the refuge of the sinner."[613]

38   a   ***because of my brother's flocks.*** See *Commentary* 5:33-c, p. 381.

   b   ***my punishment is greater than I can bear.*** The Hebrew *awon* can be understood as either "punishment" or "sin," while the verb *nasa* can mean "to bear" or "to be forgiven."[614] By way of analogy to Leviticus 5:1, Anderson reads: "The weight of my sin is too great for me to bear."[615]

603   C. Westermann, *Genesis 1-11*, p. 306.
604   J. H. Sailhamer, *Genesis*, pp. 64-65. See Deuteronomy 28:16-18; cf. Isaiah 26:21, ch. 27.
605   L. R. Kass, *Wisdom*, p. 143 n. 27. See Moses 4:23.
606   Moses 4:5.
607   Moses 4:20.
608   Moses 5:18; cf. vv. 13, 28.
609   See Moses 4:23 and *Commentary* 5:17-c, p. 370.
610   Hirsch, cited in R. M. Zlotowitz, *et al.*, *Bereishis*, p. 153.
611   H. W. Nibley, *Teachings of the PGP*, 20, p. 245. See *Commentary* 4:23-b, p. 270; 5:17-c, p. 370; Moses 5:56.
612   V. P. Hamilton, *Genesis*, p. 232.
613   *Ibid.*, p. 232.
614   G. A. Anderson, *Sin*, p. 24. See also N. M. Sarna, *Genesis*, p. 34; U. Cassuto, *Adam to Noah*, p. 222; M. Ibn Ishaq ibn Yasar, *Making*, p. 40.
615   G. A. Anderson, *Sin*, p. 24.

39 Behold **thou hast driven me out this day from the face of the Lord, and from thy face shall I be hid**; *and I shall be a fugitive and a vagabond in the earth; and it shall come to pass, that* **he that findeth me will slay me, because of mine iniquities**, *for these things are not hid from the Lord.*

40 And I the Lord said unto him: **Whosoever slayeth thee**, *vengeance shall be taken on him sevenfold. And I the Lord set a mark upon Cain, lest any finding him should kill him.*

39 a *thou has driven me out this day from the face of the Lord, and from thy face shall I be hid.* Andrus observes that: "To be shut out from the presence of the Lord means that Cain was deprived of the blessings of the priesthood. In their fall from their state of paradisiacal glory, Adam and Eve had been shut out from the presence of the Lord. But the Holy Priesthood which Adam received gave him 'the privilege of receiving the mysteries of the kingdom of heaven.'[616] Those who are ordained to that priesthood may 'have the heavens opened unto them… and… enjoy the communion and presence of God the Father, and Jesus the mediator of the new covenant.'"[617]

Explains Nibley: "The worst penalty you can possibly have is to be driven from the face of the Lord. You will no longer be facing in that direction. You will no longer have much to look forward to if you are driven from the face of the Lord. God will be an alien to him. He has alienated himself. He has cut himself off. Remember that verse where [Cain] turns on his heel and walks out. "And Cain was wroth, and listened not any more to the voice of the [Lord;[618]]… He carries that all the way through… He has become an outlaw now… A person who was outlawed had no law to protect him, so anyone who found him was perfectly free to kill him. He had no protection. To whom could he flee? Who was his protector? He had no lord to champion him. He couldn't go to the courts because he was outlawed. He had [no] protection. He had nothing."[619]

The current edition of the book of Moses is consistent with OT2.[620] OT1 reads: "thou hast driven me out this day from the face of the Earth."[621]

b *he that findeth me will slay me, because of mine iniquities.* "He who turned on one of his relatives now must watch out for any of his relatives,"[622] lest a family member "feel free to exact blood vengeance."[623]

The text here follows OT2.[624] OT1 reads: "everyone that finds me will slay me because of mine oath,"[625] presumably referring to the pact he had made with Satan.

40 a *Whosoever slayeth thee.* Sarna is impressed with this phrase as a solemn legal declaration by the Lord, declaring that even a murderer such as Cain will still be under God's protection: "I promise, if anyone kills Cain."[626] The Lord's promise of protection for Cain makes it clear that "blood-revenge is not pleasing in the sight of the Lord."[627] As Nibley notes: "In making an example of Cain, God absolutely forbade the use of Cain's own methods against him."[628]

---

616 D&C 107:19.
617 H. L. Andrus, *Doctrinal*, pp. 391-392 and D&C 107:19.
618 Moses 5:26.
619 H. W. Nibley, *Teachings of the PGP*, 20, p. 246.
620 S. H. Faulring, *et al.*, *Original Manuscripts*, p. 606.
621 *Ibid.*, p. 95.
622 V. P. Hamilton, *Genesis*, p. 233.
623 N. M. Sarna, *Genesis*, p. 35.
624 S. H. Faulring, *et al.*, *Original Manuscripts*, p. 606.
625 *Ibid.*, p. 95.
626 N. M. Sarna, *Genesis*, p. 35.
627 U. Cassuto, *Adam to Noah*, p. 185.
628 H. W. Nibley, *Dominion*, p. 16.

40 And I the Lord said unto him: **Whosoever slayeth thee**, *vengeance shall be taken on him* **sevenfold**. *And* **I the Lord set a mark upon Cain**, *lest any finding him should kill him.*

Kass concludes: "As a result of this solicitous speech, Cain may at this moment glimpse the difference between a god to whom one sacrifices vegetables and the God who takes notice of, and who is outraged by, bloodshed (and who, at least for now, provides even for murderers)."[629]

b *sevenfold.* Cassuto argues that a penalty based on a commonsense reading of this verse would not be in accord with justice. Rather, observing that seven is the number of perfection, he argues that seven times "connotes in perfect measure, with the full stringency of the law…[630] He who slays Cain will… be guilty of a dual offence: the crime of shedding blood, and the sin of contemning[631] the Lord's judgment by augmenting the Divine punishment."[632]

In an alternate interpretation with a long rabbinic history, Zlotowitz follows Rashi and Ibn Ezra in translating the phrase as; "Therefore, whoever slays Cain before seven generations have passed will be punished."[633] This idea was connected with the tradition that Cain was later killed by his descendant Lamech[634]—and perhaps also with the eventual destruction of the Flood. The *Conflict of Adam and Eve with Satan* sees God granting a temporary reprieve of seven generations of life to Cain to enable him the possibility of repentance.[635]

c *I the Lord set a mark upon Cain.* Draper, *et al.* note that: "The mark is not the same as the curse, which carried multiple penalties,"[636] the most serious being "shut out from the presence of the Lord."[637] Indeed, in the case of Cain, the mark was a sign of divine protection[638] and also, as Nibley observes, "a warning to all the rest of us—hands off! If Cain must be punished, God does not solicit our services for the job: 'Behold, the judgments of God will overtake the wicked; and it is by the wicked that the wicked are punished.'"[639]

Hamilton notes that the function of the mark or sign is paralleled in "Exodus 12:13 (the blood on the doors at Passover which identifies the occupants); Genesis 1:14 (the heavenly lights which identify time periods); Numbers 2:2 (the banners in the Israelite camp which identify the various families); Joshua 2:12 (the sign which identifies Rahab's house)."[640] As Adam and Eve are clothed with coats of skins before being driven from the Garden[641] and as God "announces the post-Flood covenant even before the Flood commences,"[642] so "Cain is marked before he is exiled."[643] However, while Adam and Eve's clothing provided a comforting sign of God's unfailing solicitude, Cain's mark will serve "as a constant reminder of [his] banishment, his isolation from other people."[644]

629   L. R. Kass, *Wisdom*, p. 144.
630   Cf. Psalm 12:6, 129:12.
631   I.e., treating with contempt.
632   U. Cassuto, *Adam to Noah*, p. 226.
633   R. M. Zlotowitz, *et al.*, *Bereishis*, p. 155.
634   See *Commentary* 5:48-a, p. 396 and 5:50-a, p. 397.
635   S. C. Malan, *Adam and Eve*, 1:79, pp. 102-103.
636   R. D. Draper, *et al.*, *Commentary*, p. 73. See Moses 5:36-37, 41.
637   Moses 5:41; cf. 2 Nephi 5:20.
638   N. M. Sarna, *Genesis*, p. 35.
639   H. W. Nibley, *Test*, pp. 537-538 and Mormon 4:5. See also H. W. Nibley, *Since*, pp. 352-353; T. L. Brodie, *Dialogue*, p. 154.
640   V. P. Hamilton, *Genesis*, p. 235.
641   Moses 4:27.
642   JST Genesis 8:23.
643   V. P. Hamilton, *Genesis*, p. 207.
644   G. J. Wenham, *Genesis 1-15*, p. 110.

MOSES 5

*40 And I the Lord said unto him: Whosoever slayeth thee, vengeance shall be taken on him sevenfold. And **I the Lord set a mark upon Cain**, lest any finding him should kill him.*

Though readers have often assumed that the mark was a dark skin, the text of the verse itself fails to give warrant for any particular conclusion about the nature of the mark given to Cain. Nor is the verse explicit about whether the mark was passed on to his descendants.[645] Of possible relevance to this question is Moses 7:22 which states that "the seed of Cain were black."[646] Allred, however, finds even this statement inconclusive, arguing that it could be a figurative expression referring to "those who followed Cain in his wicked practices," referring to them "in the same manner that the Jews were called the children of the Devil."[647] Similarly, Goldenberg has argued that, as with the four horsemen of Revelation 6:1-8, the blackness of individuals depicted in *1 Enoch* and in other ancient Near Eastern sources is used in a purely symbolic fashion to represent evil and exclusion from the covenant community.[648] He conjectures that beliefs about Cain's skin becoming black were the result of textual misunderstandings.[649]

Consistent with this view is Al-Kisa'i's report of a tradition that Lamech (the son of the Sethite Methuselah—not to be confused with the Cainite Lamech of Moses 5:43-54) married Methuselcha, a descendant of Cain. Though mentioning the fact that there was "enmity that existed between the children of Seth and the children of Cain," the story implies that there was nothing in their outward appearance that would identify them as being of different lineages, since Lamech had to tell her his parentage explicitly. Described in wholly positive terms, Methuselcha was said in this tradition to have become the mother of Noah.[650]

Ancient sources give a variety of alternative conjectures about the "distinctive mark on the body" of Cain, including a mark[651] on the hand, arm, or brow or a horn on the forehead.[652] Some traditions say that Abel's dog, member of a species "outstanding in its loyalty to a master who has done it a good turn," was assigned to go with Cain on his travels to forever remind him of his own evil deed to his brother.[653] Of relevance to the argument by some that the mark may have been voluntarily perpetuated after the time of Cain for purposes of tribal identification is the Book of Mormon precedent for a self-imposed "mark of red" upon the forehead adopted by a group of Nephites who aligned themselves with the Lamanites.[654] Moreover, Speiser discusses several Old Testament examples of a mark on the forehead.[655] These examples can be compared to the contrasting idea of a protective sign of holiness on the forehead.[656]

645 For arguments to the that it was not passed on, see, e.g., U. Cassuto, *Adam to Noah*, pp. 227-228; C. Westermann, *Genesis 1-11*, pp. 312-313.

646 Cf. J. Smith, Jr., *Documentary History*, 25 January 1842, 4:501. Note also the statement that a "blackness came upon all the children of Canaan," seemingly in direct consequence of a notable act of genocide (Moses 7:7-8; M. H. Martins, *Blacks*, pp. 10-11).

647 A. Allred, *Traditions*, p. 49. See John 8:44.

648 D. M. Goldenberg, *Curse*, pp. 152-154; cf. G. W. E. Nickelsburg, *1 Enoch*, 85:3-88:3, p. 364. See also manuscript versions of Moses 1:15, as well as *Commentary* 1:15-a, p. 55.

649 D. M. Goldenberg, *Curse*, pp. 178-182. For similar conclusions relating to the mark imposed upon the Lamanites in the Book of Mormon (e.g., 1 Nephi 12:23, 2 Nephi 5:21-24, Alma 3:6-19, 3 Nephi 2:14-16), see B. Gardner, *Second Witness*, 2:108-123; J. L. Sorenson, *Ancient*, p. 90.

650 See M. al-Kisa'i, *Tales*, pp. 91-93.

651 E.g., God's name (M. Maher, *Pseudo-Jonathan*, 4:15, p. 34).

652 See H. W. Nibley, *Abraham 2000*, pp. 584-585; cf. J. Neusner, *Genesis Rabbah 1*, 22:12, p. 253; C. Westermann, *Genesis 1-11*, pp. 312-314.

653 R. M. Zlotowitz, *et al.*, *Bereishis*, p. 156.

654 Alma 3:13-19.

655 E. A. Speiser, *Genesis*, p. 31. See Exodus 13:16; Deuteronomy 6:8, 11:18; and Ezekiel 9:4, 6.

656 Exodus 28:36-38; Revelation 7:3, 9:4, 14:1, 22:4; D&C 77:9, 133:18. See also *Commentary* 5:47-b, p. 396 and Revelation 13:16, 14:9, 20:4.

MOSES 5

*40 And I the Lord said unto him: Whosoever slayeth thee, vengeance shall be taken on him sevenfold. And **I the Lord set a mark upon Cain**, lest any finding him should kill him.*

*41 And Cain **was shut out** from the presence of the Lord, and with his wife and many of his brethren dwelt **in the land of Nod**, on the east of Eden.*

Regardless of the exact nature of the mark imposed upon Cain, it seems reasonable to suppose that the separation between the Sethites and the Cainites paralleled the situation of the Nephites and the Lamanites where, even though the original distinction was lineage-based, it is known that each group eventually came to include like-minded associates in addition to actual descendants.[657]

Adopting an entirely different perspective, Sailhamer proposes yet another alternative regarding the nature of the mark. He argues that this narrative should be "read in light of the Deuteronomic legislation of the 'cities of refuge'... The purpose of the cities of refuge was to insure that 'innocent blood will not be shed in your land'...[658] The narrative may be suggesting not only that Cain's offense was punishable by death but also that the city Cain built[659] was an early 'prototype' of the cities of refuge"[660]—though, of course, later cities afforded asylum only for cases of unpremeditated killing.[661] For these and other reasons, Sailhamer conjectures that "Cain's city may have been intended as the 'sign' that gave divine protection to Cain."[662]

41   a   *was shut out.* See *Commentary* 5:4-c, p. 357 and 5:34-a, p. 382.

The text is consistent with OT2.[663] OT1 reads "went out."[664]

b   *in the land of Nod.* The Hebrew term *nod* means "wandering"—thus "He who had been sentenced to be a *nad* settles in the land of *nod*. The wanderer ends up in the land of wandering."[665] Rashi gave an alternative interpretation of Nod as "trembling": "Anywhere that [Cain] would go, the earth would tremble beneath him, and the people would say, 'Keep away from him! This is the one who killed his brother!'"[666] This reading has an interesting parallel in Moses' encounter with Satan[667] and the *Septuagint* reading of Genesis 4:14 where Cain complains: "I shall be groaning and trembling upon the earth."[668]

Of the later life of Cain and his posterity, one tradition records that Cain came, after many wanderings, "to a certain place called Cainan, where he committed all manner of crimes, laying wait for wayfaring men and putting them to death, and heaping up wealth untold from his spoils of them."[669] In an account that Franxman characterizes as "no brief attack,"[670] Josephus elaborates: "And when Cain had travelled over many countries, (after God's sentence upon him) he, with his wife, built a city named Nod, which is a place so called,

---

657   Cf. Jacob 1:13-14; Alma 3:13-19, 24:29, 43:13, 47:35; Helaman 11:24; 4 Nephi 1:35-38. See *Commentary* 5:41-b, p. 388.
658   Deuteronomy 19:10.
659   Moses 5:42.
660   J. H. Sailhamer, *Genesis*, pp. 62, 64.
661   Z. W. Falk, *Law*, p. 72.
662   J. H. Sailhamer, *Genesis*, p. 67. See also G. J. Wenham, *Genesis 1-15*, pp. 108-109, *Commentary* 5:41-b, p. 388; 5:42-c, p. 391.
663   S. H. Faulring, *et al.*, *Original Manuscripts*, p. 606.
664   *Ibid.*, p. 95.
665   V. P. Hamilton, *Genesis*, p. 235.
666   Rashi, *Genesis Commentary*, 4:16, p. 47; cf. *Midrash Tanhuma*, Bereshit 9, cited in H. N. Bialik, *et al.*, *Legends*, 101, p. 24.
667   See *Commentary* 1:21-a, p. 57.
668   R. J. V. Hiebert, *Septuagint*, p. 4; cf. D. J. Harrington, *Pseudo-Philo*, 2:1, p. 305; S. C. Malan, *Adam and Eve*, 1:79, pp. 102-103; M. E. Stone, *Abel*, 5:3, pp. 153, 153 n. 5:3; M. E. Stone, *Forefathers*, 15, pp. 187-188. For additional discussion and parallels, see W. L. Lipscomb, *Armenian*, pp. 90-91.
669   S. C. Malan, *Adam and Eve*, p. 227.
670   T. W. Franxman, *Genesis*, p. 71.

*41 And Cain was shut out from the presence of the Lord, and with his wife and many of his brethren dwelt **in the land of Nod**, on the east of Eden.*

and there he settled his abode; where also he had children. However, he did not accept of his punishment in order to amendment, but to increase his wickedness; for he only aimed to procure everything that was for his own bodily pleasure, though it obliged him to be injurious to his neighbors. He augmented his household substance with much wealth, by rapine and violence; he excited his acquaintance to procure pleasure and spoils by robbery, and became a great leader of men into wicked courses. He also introduced a change in that way of simplicity wherein men lived before; and was the author of measures and weights; and whereas they lived innocently and generously while they knew nothing of such arts, he changed the world into cunning craftiness.... Even while Adam was alive, it came to pass, that the posterity of Cain became exceeding wicked, every one successively dying, one after another, more wicked than the former. They were intolerable in war, and vehement in robberies; and if any one were slow to murder people, yet was he bold in his profligate behavior, in acting unjustly, and doing injuries for gain."[671]

Pirkei Eliezer stresses how the posterity of Cain descended into an animal-like existence: "The generations of Cain walked around in utter nakedness, both men and women, like animals, and they corrupted themselves with all manner of debauchery, a man with his mother or his daughter, or with the wife of his brother or of his neighbor, in public and on the streets, the evil inclination in their thoughts and in their hearts."[672]

The book of Moses, texts preserved by the early Christians, and older traditions of exegesis[673] all speak of a divinely-mandated separation of the Sethites from the Cainites. For example, Enoch saw a vision of the "residue of the people which were the sons of Adam" and specifically noted that "the seed of Cain... had not place among them."[674] In an Armenian text, Seth and his descendants are said to have lived "in the mountains close to the Garden,[675] while Cain with his race (dwelt) on the plain, where Cain killed Abel."[676] Later, however, having been seduced by the Cainite women, the sons of Seth and Enosh came down from the mountain and "mingled them with themselves promiscuously."[677]

Comments Nibley: "In every dispensation of the Gospel, the Lord has insisted on segregating his covenant people from the rest of the world: if they were not ready to 'come out of her, [O] my people'[678] willingly, he saw to it that the world was more than willing to persecute and expel them."[679] "Enoch establishes the first walled city and the first army. And down the line we go. It's the two civilizations. The pastorals are up in the highlands, out in the mountains. Those are the Sethians. It says they live in the holy places. Their main center is called the Mountain of the Cave of Treasures, being [their equivalent of] the Hill Cumorah where they keep all their records and also their sacred things. When Adam died, he was buried in the cave. When they had to leave, they took him with them.[680] They separated then, and the holy ones were left on the mountain and lived after the manner of the righteous with their flocks.

---

671   F. Josephus, *Antiquities*, 1:2:2, p. 27. For parallel accounts of the decline of man in Greek and Roman literature, see L. H. Feldman, *Hellenization*, pp. 347-350.

672   M.-A. Ouaknin, *et al.*, *Rabbi Éliézer*, 22, pp. 134-135.

673   See examples in, e.g., C. Westermann, *Genesis 1-11*, p. 338.

674   Moses 7:22.

675   Cf. Moses 7:17.

676   M. E. Stone, *Sethites*, 9, p. 205; cf. Eutychus in S. C. Malan, *Adam and Eve*, p. 227; 2:8, p. 115.

677   M. E. Stone, *Sermon Concerning Flood*, 4-6, pp. 177-178; cf. M. al-Kisa'i, *Tales*, p. 88; Ephrem the Syrian, *Paradise*, 1:11, pp. 81-82; Ether 7:4. See *Endnote 5-58*, p. 446.

678   Revelation 18:4.

679   H. W. Nibley, *Weep*, p. 341.

680   See *Excursus 45: Impact of the "Black Death" on Art and Literature*, p. 640.

*41 And Cain was shut out from the presence of the Lord, and with his wife and many of his brethren dwelt **in the land of Nod, on the east of Eden.***

*42 And Cain knew his wife, and she conceived and bare **Enoch**, and he also begat many sons and daughters. And he builded a city, and he called the name of the city after the name of his son, Enoch.*

They gathered fruit it says in 'the manner of Paradise.' They still gathered any fruit of the Garden they chose to take, and they didn't toil to acquire."[681]

Though the people of the covenant have sometimes been drawn out from the world, either to reduce the risk of apostasy or to gather a number in one place sufficient to enable temple-building,[682] such separation was, of course, unnecessary in times where righteousness prevailed among all peoples.[683] Moreover, in our time, Church members have been specifically counseled against gathering to a central location, so that the kingdom of God can be built up in every land.[684] Living during a period when the apostolic commission to "teach all nations"[685] is at last nearing fulfillment, President Howard W. Hunter specifically warned that there is "no room" in the Gospel "for a contracted, narrow, or prejudicial view" and that our message must strike "squarely against all stifling traditions based on race, language, economic or political standing, educational rank, or cultural background."[686]

   c   ***on the east of Eden.*** By the phrase on the east of Eden, we are meant to understand that the place where Cain came to live was even further removed from the presence of God than was the land where his Adam and Eve and their righteous descendants lived after the Fall.[687] For example, tradition reports that "Cain went off by himself and lived in the land of Nod, a place lower still than that of Sheth and Enosh."[688] In the Old Testament, "the eastern region always forms a place of refuge for murderers, for the cities of refuge that Moses later set aside were also to the east 'the place of the sun-rise.'"[689]

42 a   ***Enoch.*** According to Sarna, the basic meaning "has to do with initiation, dedication, and education. Thus the name may be symbolic, signifying the regeneration of life."[690]

A linear succession of descendants of Cain—seven first-born sons—is given here, after which the genealogy branches. Sarna observes: "The lineage of Cain is not mentioned again in the Bible. No details are given of his span of life, and even the fact of his death is not noted. The same is true of the list of his descendants. The entire line passes into oblivion."[691] Some traditions record that he continued his ceaseless wandering until he drowned in the great Flood;[692] others that he was slain by Lamech.[693] Yet another set of accounts frame his death in a context of poetic justice, saying that he "was killed when his house, made of stones, fell upon him, stoning him to death. Thus was Cain killed in the same way he had killed his brother, confirming that a man shall be killed with the weapons with which he kills his fellow man."[694] Figuratively comparing the collapse of Cain's house to the fall of the "great and

681   H. W. Nibley, *Teachings of the PGP*, 21, p. 259 and S. C. Malan, *Adam and Eve*, 2:11, pp. 118-119. See *Commentary* 5:40-c, p. 386 and Moses 5 *Gleanings*, p. 415.

682   J. Smith, Jr., *Teachings*, 11 June 1843, pp. 307-308.

683   E.g., 4 Nephi 1:17.

684   H. B. Lee, *Strengthen*; B. R. McConkie, *New Witness*, p. 595.

685   Matthew 28:19.

686   H. W. Hunter, *Teachings 1997*, 5 October 1991, p. 101. See also J. E. Faust, *Heirs*.

687   G. J. Wenham, *Genesis 1-15*, p. 110. See also *Commentary* 3:8-b, p. 161.

688   Ephrem the Syrian, *Paradise*, 1:11, pp. 81-82.

689   R. M. Zlotowitz, *et al.*, *Bereishis*, p. 158 and Deuteronomy 4:41. See *Commentary* 5:40-c, p. 386.

690   N. M. Sarna, *Genesis*, p. 36. See *Commentary* 6:3-b, p. 477.

691   N. M. Sarna, *Genesis*, p. 36.

692   G. W. E. Nickelsburg, *1 Enoch*, 22:12, p. 253.

693   See *Commentary* 5:50-a, p. 397.

694   H. Schwartz, *Tree*, p. 451. See O. S. Wintermute, *Jubilees*, 4:31-32, p. 64; Exodus 21:24; Leviticus 24:19;

MOSES 5

*42 And Cain knew his wife, and she conceived and bare **Enoch**, and he also begat many sons and daughters. And **he builded a city**, and **he called the name of the city** after the name of his son, **Enoch**.*

spacious building" of Lehi's vision,[695] Nibley suggests an implied moral of this story: "Cain built the first great house of vanity, and it fell upon him and killed him."[696]

b **he builded a city.** Given the Lord's prophecy that Cain will become "a fugitive and a vagabond,"[697] we do not expect to find him building a city. Hamilton suggests: "Perhaps Cain's act is one of defiance. He has had enough of the life of the nomad. He refuses any longer to abide under God's terms. The only other reference to building a city in Genesis 1-11 is the incident at Babel: 'Come, let us build ourselves a city...'[698] Here the whole city-building, tower-erecting project is one that God condemns...[699] We suggest that Cain's act of city building is an attempt to provide security for himself, a security he is not sure God's mark guarantees. In the words of J. Ellul, Cain 'wants to find alone the remedy for a situation he created, but which he cannot himself repair because it is a situation dependent on God's grace.'[700] It is as if "Cain said in his heart, 'If it is decreed upon me to be a wanderer on the earth, the decree shall not apply to my offspring.'"[701]

Pseudo-Philo records that Cain founded seven cities.[702] "The mention of Abel's murder thus serves primarily to characterize the first city-builder, hinting that this key element of human civilization was tainted from the start,"[703] and anticipating a general "antipathy toward cities"[704] throughout the rest of Genesis.

c **he called the name of the city... Enoch.** Hamilton notes that "Hebrew syntax would permit, if not suggest, that the subject of 'he was a city builder' and 'he named the city' was Enoch...[705] To name a city after oneself or after another probably implies that the named individual assumes ownership over and responsibility for the city that bears his name."[706]

This wicked city of Enoch "was almost certainly founded... in fear of violent death, but first, in fratricide."[707] It stands in ironic parallel to the later story of the prophet Enoch who founded a city of righteousness and brotherly love that has become associated with his name.[708] Indeed, it is no coincidence that the descendants of the Sethites "run in seven lines with almost the same names [as the descendants of Cain]. But," claims Nibley, "they are read differently as if you were punning on them, like twin names. This is a typical trick. The Egyptians do it all the time."[709]

Deuteronomy 19:21.
695 1 Nephi 11:36.
696 H. W. Nibley, *Rediscovery*, p. 223.
697 Moses 5:37.
698 Genesis 11:4.
699 Cf. Helaman 6:28.
700 V. P. Hamilton, *Genesis*, p. 238.
701 Nachamanides, cited in J. H. Hertz, *Pentateuch*, p. 15. See *Commentary* 5:40-c, p. 386.
702 D. J. Harrington, *Pseudo-Philo*, 2:3, p. 305.
703 F. J. Murphy, *Pseudo-Philo*, pp. 31-32.
704 T. L. Brodie, *Dialogue*, p. 116.
705 Cf. G. J. Wenham, *Genesis 1-15*, p. 111. For examples of calling a city after one's own name, see Deuteronomy 3:14; 2 Samuel 5:9, 12:28; Alma 6:7.
706 V. P. Hamilton, Genesis, p. 237. See, e.g., 1 Kings 16:24.
707 L. R. Kass, *Wisdom*, p. 145.
708 Moses 7:19, 69.
709 H. W. Nibley, *Teachings of the PGP*, 20, p. 249; cf. H. W. Nibley, *Enoch*, p. 178; G. J. Wenham, *Genesis 1-15*, pp. 123-124.

*43 And **unto Enoch was born Irad**, and other sons and daughters. And Irad begat Mahujael, and other sons and daughters. And **Mahujael begat Methusael**, and other sons and daughters. And **Methusael begat Lamech**.*

*44 And Lamech **took unto himself** two wives; the name of one being Adah, and the name of the other, Zillah.*

43   a   unto Enoch was born Irad. Nibley conjectures that the name Irad "means the 'shy person,' the person who holds back and is withdrawn, who is unsure of himself."[710]

Of interest is a suggestion by Sarna of a possible connection between Irad and the ancient world: "Curiously, in Sumerian tradition, the first city was Eridu, now Tell abu Shahrain, in southern Mesopotamia, which excavations have revealed to be the oldest site in that part of the world. It has been suggested, therefore, that the statement in verse 17, 'He founded a city, and named the city after his son,' really belongs here, so that Enoch, not Cain, built the first city and named it Irad (= Eridu) after his son."[711]

b   Mahujael begat Methusael. Note that both names include the ending *-el*, thus bearing a title of God.[712] Diverse conjectures have been made about the meaning of the name Mehujael: "God makes live," "blotted out by God," and "seer of God."[713] Sarna conjectures that Methusael could mean "'the man of Shael,' with the latter element originally being *she'ol*, 'the underworld.'"[714] Nibley suggests: that "Mahijael and Mehujael both mean the same thing. They mean a person who has been smitten by God with a disease of some sort. The basic root *meha* means to have a chronic disease… That means you have had divine smiting… Uncomplimentary names… Methusael… means 'the one who has been prayed for' [or 'one who prays,' one who supplicates']. This is a more complimentary name."[715]

c   Methusael begat Lamech. Many suggestions have been given for the meaning of the name Lamech. It may be related to a similar Arabic word that means "strong young man."[716] Alternatively, Cassuto argues that the name Lamech may be related to "the Mesopotamian word *lumakku*, which signifies a certain class of priests."[717] In a different direction, Nibley concludes that, consistent with his place in the story as one who recapitulates and multiplies the sins of Cain, "Lamech means destruction, loss, perdition. His name shall be perdition."[718]

Several traditions speaks of Lamech as being blind.[719]

44   a   took unto himself. The wording "took unto himself" is paralleled in the description of the illicit relationships of the wicked husbands in the days of Noah.[720] Wright observes that "there is no indication… that a marriage actually took place, but rather [the phrase] could be translated and understood as 'Lamech took to himself two women.'"[721]

An Armenian tradition says that Adah and Zillah were taken by Lamech after he killed their husbands, "the two brothers of Enoch." The text says that he also "wished to kill Enoch, but God transferred [i.e., translated] him."[722] While this account identifies the prophet Enoch as the intended victim, it is also plausible (apart from the reference to translation) that the Enoch mentioned might have been meant, in an earlier version of the text, to refer to Lamech's second-great-grandfather, for whom the city of Cain was named.[723]

---

710   H. W. Nibley, *Teachings of the PGP*, 20, p. 248.
711   N. M. Sarna, *Genesis*, p. 36. See *Commentary* 5:49-b, p. 397.
712   R. D. Draper, *et al.*, *Commentary*, p. 74.
713   N. M. Sarna, *Genesis*, p. 36.
714   *Ibid.*, p. 36.
715   H. W. Nibley, *Teachings of the PGP*, 20, p. 248.
716   N. M. Sarna, *Genesis*, p. 36.
717   U. Cassuto, *Adam to Noah*, p. 233.
718   H. W. Nibley, *Teachings of the PGP*, 20, p. 249.
719   E.g., M. E. Stone, *Sethites*, 10, p. 205. See *Commentary* 5:50-a, p. 397.
720   Moses 8:14, 21. See the overview of Moses 5, p. 349.
721   A. T. Wright, *Evil Spirits*, pp. 135-136.
722   M. E. Stone, *Abel*, 5:4, pp. 153-154.
723   Moses 5:42-43.

*44 And Lamech **took unto himself two wives**; the name of one being **Adah, and** the name of the other, **Zillah**.*

*45 And Adah bare **Jabal**; he was the father of such as dwell in tents, and they were keepers of cattle; and his brother's name was Jubal, who was the father of all such as handle the harp and organ.*

Josephus paints a picture of Lamech as having been "skilful in matters of divine revelation."[724]

b *two wives.* This mention of Lamech's wives may constitute a "tacit condemnation" of unauthorized polygamy.[725] Citing the troubles of even the righteous patriarchs Abraham and Jacob, Hamilton observes that "nearly every polygamous household in the OT suffers most unpleasant and shattering experiences... The domestic struggles that ensue are devastating."[726]

c *Adah, and... Zillah.* Sarna writes that these "names may respectively mean 'dawn' and 'dusk.'"[727] Nibley concurs: "There is always the light one and dark one here," as in the stories of Sarah ("a raving [i.e., ravishing] blonde") and Hagar ("a dark Egyptian woman"),[728] Miriam and Zipporah (Miriam was smitten with leprosy for having mocked the Ethiopian Zipporah[729]), and the Song of Solomon ("I am black but comely").[730]

Adah's descendants are the herdsmen and musicians, whereas Zillah's branch produces the pioneers in technology.[731]

45 a *Jabal.* Of the name, Nibley writes: "Our word 'jubilee' comes from it. It means 'to sing, to rejoice, to jubilate' and the like."[732]

"Verses [45-47] describe several components of city life: "animal husbandry (Jabal[733]), arts (Jubal[734]), craftsmanship (Tubal-Cain[735]), and, it appears, law"[736]—all in concert with the rise of "secret combinations" (Lamech[737]).

The similar-sounding names of the three brothers "suggests a closeness of relationship between the pastoral, musical, and metalworking arts... [A] wall painting from the rock tomb of Khnumhotep at Beni Hasan, about 160 miles (257 km.) south of Cairo and dating to ca. 1900 BCE.... portrays the arrival of a caravan of Asiatics, and prominently featured among their baggage are livestock, a lyre, and bellows."[738] Cassuto also points out that in the story of each of the three sons is "some allusion to the name of their ancestor, Cain [*Qayin*]... Of Jabal it is said that he was the father of those who dwell in tents and have cattle [*miqne*]... Jubal is called the father of all those who play the lyre and the pipe, a description that suggests the idea of *qina* [dirge]... [A]s for... Tubal-cain, Cain actually forms a part of his name."[739]

724   F. Josephus, *Genuine Works*, 1:2:2, p. 27.

725   N. M. Sarna, *Genesis*, p. 37; A. T. Wright, *Evil Spirits*, p. 136 n. 178; M. Herbert, *Irish Apocrypha*, p. 18. See also Jacob 2:27-30; *Commentary* 5:3-b, p. 355.

726   V. P. Hamilton, *Genesis*, p. 238.

727   N. M. Sarna, *Genesis*, p. 37.

728   Genesis 16.

729   Numbers 12:1, 10.

730   H. W. Nibley, *Teachings of the PGP*, 20, pp. 252-253 and Song of Solomon 1:5. See *Commentary* 5:47-a, p. 395 and *Excursus 35: Lamech's "Sword Song"*, p. 612.

731   C. Westermann, *Genesis 1-11*, p. 332.

732   H. W. Nibley, *Teachings of the PGP*, 20, p. 251.

733   Moses 5:45.

734   *Ibid.*

735   Moses 5:46.

736   J. H. Sailhamer, *Genesis*, p. 67.

737   Moses 5:47-55, *Commentary* 5:47-a, p. 395.

738   N. M. Sarna, *Genesis*, p. 37. For a reproduction of the image, see A. Feyerick, *et al.*, *Genesis*, p. 68.

739   U. Cassuto, *Adam to Noah*, p. 235.

MOSES 5

*45 And Adah bare Jabal; he was the father of **such as dwell in tents**, and they were keepers of **cattle**; and his brother's name was Jubal, who was the father of all such as handle the **harp and organ**.*

*46 And Zillah, she also bare **Tubal Cain**, an instructor of every **artificer in brass and iron**. And **the sister** of Tubal Cain **was called Naamah**.*

b   ***such as dwell in tents.*** The statement draws a contrast to Adam and Abel, who were not nomadic. "Such people are noted in the later story of Enoch, son of Jared.[740] This account assigns the origins of nomadic peoples to Cain's posterity."[741]

c   ***cattle.*** All kinds of livestock, including sheep.[742]

d   ***harp and organ.*** Sarna gives this as "the lyre and the pipe," representing stringed and wind instruments generically.[743] The lyre has "a history traceable to ca. 3000 BCE." Nibley comments: "One thing about the nomads is that they practiced the nomadic arts which are portable. Not architecture or sculpture or painting or even pottery, but what is it? It's weaving, singing, and musical instruments."[744]

Extracanonical sources often describe the musical developments reported here in negative terms. For example, *The Sethites and the Cainites* speaks of these innovators as "evil and disorderly" men who, at the direction of the "Malicious One," discovered "false music and dances and musical instruments."[745] The music which "led them into confusion" is seen to have had a "prominent role… in the seduction of the Sethite men by the Cainite women."[746] Rashi cites midrash to argue that Jubal used these instruments "to play music for idolatry."[747]

46 a   ***Tubal Cain.*** Tubal means "metalworker" and Cain means a "smith." "Accordingly, the two elements of the name given to the son of Zillah both mean the same thing, and both designate his profession. The second element really explains the first, the meaning of which was probably lost to the Israelite audience."[748]

Rashi takes the name as "indicating that he 'improved upon' [*tuval*] Cain's work by preparing the weapons for bloodshed,"[749] thus making it easier to continue Cain's murderous precedent.

b   ***artificer in brass and iron.*** Pseudo-Philo sees metalwork as having promoted the spread of idolatry: "This is the Tubal who showed men techniques in using lead and tin and iron and bronze and silver and gold. And then those inhabiting the earth began to make statues and to adore them.[750]

c   ***the sister… was called Naamah.*** "This expression… ties to nothing else in the narratives," suggesting that a story about her might have been lost in the account. "In Hebrew, her name derives from the root meaning 'to be pleasant'"[751] or "to sing."[752] The latter signification, in conjunction with the weapon-making of Tubal Cain and the musical instruments of Jubal, perhaps suggests a tie between this verse and the poem introduced in the next one.

---

740   See Moses 6:38; 7:5.
741   R. D. Draper, *et al.*, *Commentary*, p. 74.
742   N. M. Sarna, *Genesis*, p. 37.
743   *Ibid.*, p. 37. See Job 21:12, 30:31.
744   H. W. Nibley, *Teachings of the PGP*, 20, p. 251.
745   M. E. Stone, *Sethites*, 10, p. 205.
746   M. E. Stone, *Armenian Apocrypha 1996*, p. 120 n. 7; cf. M. al-Kisa'i, *Tales*, p. 88; A. Gileadi, *Diatribes*, pp. 368-371; D. J. Harrington, *Pseudo-Philo*, 2:7-8, p. 305; F. J. Murphy, *Pseudo-Philo*, p. 32.
747   Rashi, *Genesis Commentary*, 4:21, p. 50.
748   N. M. Sarna, *Genesis*, p. 38.
749   Cited in R. M. Zlotowitz, *et al.*, *Bereishis*, p. 161.
750   D. J. Harrington, *Pseudo-Philo*, 2:9, p. 305.
751   R. D. Draper, *et al.*, *Commentary*, p. 75. See F. Brown, *et al.*, *Lexicon*, p. 653.
752   N. M. Sarna, *Genesis*, p. 38.

*46 And Zillah, she also bare Tubal Cain, an instructor of every artificer in brass and iron. And **the sister** of Tubal Cain **was called Naamah**.*

*47 And **Lamech said unto his wives**, Adah and Zillah: Hear my voice, ye wives of Lamech, hearken unto my speech; for I have slain a man to my wounding, and a young man to my hurt.*

Some traditions hold that Naamah became the wife of Noah.[753]

47 a *Lamech said unto his wives.* Lamech's poetic declaration in verses 47-48 could be taken in one of two ways: either as a protestation of his innocence ("If Cain, who killed his brother with malice, merited a sevenfold degree of protection from vengeance, I, who killed after deliberate provocation, deserve that same protection to a seventy-sevenfold extent") or as an admission of his personal guilt ("If Cain suffered seven times, I, who am guiltier, will suffer seventy-seven times").[754] The former interpretation clearly is a better fit to context.

The purpose of Lamech's argument, then, was to show his wives that "he had not shed innocent blood... He did not 'hate his neighbor, lie in wait for him, rise up against him, and kill him'[755] as Cain had done, but rather he based his appeal on a plea of self-defense"—his act of murder having been performed because he had been previously wounded and injured by the one slain. Thus, Sailhamer's translation: "a man for wounding me, a young man for injuring me." In this case the "wound" inflicted by Irad would have been figurative rather than physical—the primary "injury" given to Lamech being the betrayal of the oath.[756] As Rousseau observed, the consequences of vengeful attitudes spread rapidly through corrupt societies: "[E]veryone punishing the contempt shown him in a manner proportionate to the stock he set by himself, vengeance became terrible, and men bloodthirsty and cruel."[757]

Proud and cynical, Lamech's so-called "sword song"[758] was not only a statement of self-justification, but also a paean to his own prowess, the sort of "taunts, threats, and boastings, which are of the kind customarily uttered in ancient times by those about to engage in combat"[759]—evil words that compound ill deeds.[760] One is reminded of Korihor who proudly proclaimed that "every man prospered according to his genius, and that every man conquered according to his strength; and whatsoever a man did was no crime."[761] Songs such as these were regularly sung in bloody contests as part of the new-year rites performed in virtually all ancient cultures.[762] As in all such hero tales, the skilled poet exercises his craft in order to glorify actions "which, were it not for his poetry, would appear as merely violent."[763]

Cassuto senses "a kind of antithetic parallelism to the statement at the beginning of the section: "Eve gloried in the fact that she had formed and given birth to a man;[764] here Lamech prides himself on having cut off the life of a man.[765] The earlier vaunt was *with* the Lord; the later, *against* the Lord."[766]

753 J. H. Hertz, *Pentateuch*, p. 16. See discussion in D. Fohrman, *Beast*, pp. 195-196.

754 T. W. Franxman, *Genesis*, pp. 75-76; cf. J. H. Sailhamer, *Genesis*, p. 67.

755 Cf. Deuteronomy 19:11.

756 See *Commentary* 5:50-a, p. 397.

757 J.-J. Rousseau, *Inequality*, 2:16, p. 176. See discussion in L. R. Kass, *Wisdom*, p. 146; cf. pp. 138-139.

758 U. Cassuto, *Adam to Noah*, p. 240.

759 N. M. Sarna, *Genesis*, p. 39. See also C. Westermann, *Genesis 1-11*, pp. 336-337; 1 Samuel 17:10, 36, 43-46.

760 See W. Shakespeare, *Errors*, 3:2:20, p. 92.

761 Alma 30:17.

762 See *Commentary* 1:25-e, p. 60; *Excursus 35: Lamech's "Sword Song"*, p. 612; and the overviews of Moses 4 and 6, pp. 221, 458. See *Endnote 4-21,* p. 304.

763 Robert Sacks, cited in L. R. Kass, *Wisdom*, p. 146 n. 32.

764 Moses 5:16.

765 Cf. *Commentary* 5:33-a, p. 381.

766 U. Cassuto, *Adam to Noah*, pp. 242-243.

*47 And **Lamech said unto his wives**, Adah and Zillah: Hear my voice, ye wives of Lamech, hearken unto my speech; for I have slain a man to my **wounding**, and **a young man** to my **hurt**.*

*48 If Cain shall be avenged **sevenfold**, truly Lamech shall be **seventy and seven fold**;*

The song is constructed as a series of parallel clauses addressed to Adah and Zillah. Nibley points out a similarity with poetic forms typically sung by an antiphonal chorus of competing women in connection with year-rites:[767]

Adah and Zillah	ye wives of Lamech
Hear	hearken
my voice	my speech
a man	a young man
to my wounding	to my hurt
Cain	Lamech
sevenfold	seventy and seven fold

b   *wounding… hurt.* Nibley comments: "If we look up these words that are used here for killing and slaying, we will find what they mean. This *patza* for 'wounding me'… doesn't mean wound. It means 'to place a cut or mark upon, to put a ritual mark.' The other, *khabura*, we are told, is the mark or stroke of a wound on the skin. There's a conflict in which ritual wounds are inflicted. We are told that Satan showed Cain the blows of death… He taught them to him before he could have his showdown with Abel."[768] The idea of Cain's having administered the "blows of death" in the manner of Satan may lie behind the rabbinic tradition that "Cain pelted all parts of Abel's body, inflicting many blows and wounds, until he killed him by striking him on the neck."[769] Just as Cain is said to have placed gruesome ritual marks on Abel at his death, so the record has the Lord setting a mark upon Cain to preserve his life—suggesting, perhaps, a sobering instance of "measure for measure."

c   *a young man.* Modern commentators typically see "man" and "young man" as referring to a single victim. The problem is that, since Irad was Lamech's great-grandfather,[770] he would not have been a young man. The term, however, might be "understood as derogatory: 'This man, my antagonist, is but a mere child in combat!'"[771]

48   **a**   *sevenfold… seventy and seven fold.* Lamech was in effect declaring that the justification for his act of murder was far more compelling than that of Cain's—as seventy-seven compares to seven in order of degree.[772] Note that Lamech is of the seventh generation from Cain.

Some Jewish, Christian, and Gnostic interpreters saw the first part of this phrase as meaning that "seven times vengeance has been exacted from Cain." The related phrase in Moses 5:40 also was sometimes interpreted by readers of the *Septuagint* as "he who kills Cain will loose seven punishments." This led to a proliferation of lists describing what the seven punishments were.[773] An idea that Cain's punishment was suspended for seven generations was also connected with the tradition that Lamech—a descendant of the seventh generation—killed Cain.[774]

767   See *Excursus 35: Lamech's "Sword Song"*, p. 612.

768   H. W. Nibley, *Teachings of the PGP*, 20, p. 253. See also H. W. Nibley, *Teachings of the PGP*, 19, p. 253 and the overview of Moses 4, p. 236.

769   *Talmud*, Sanhedrin 37b, cited in R. M. Zlotowitz, *et al.*, *Bereishis*, p. 151, emphasis added; cf. *Midrash Tanhuma*, Bereshit 9, cited in H. N. Bialik, *et al.*, *Legends*, 101, p. 23; J. L. Kugel, *Traditions*, p. 153; *Commentary 5:29-b*, p. 377.

770   Moses 5:43.

771   N. M. Sarna, *Genesis*, p. 39.

772   Moses 5:40; U. Cassuto, *Adam to Noah*, p. 243. See *Commentary 5:47-a*, p. 395.

773   W. L. Lipscomb, *Armenian*, pp. 42-51, 86-91.

774   See *Commentary 5:40-b*, p. 386 and 5:50-a, p. 397.

*49 For Lamech having entered into a covenant with Satan, after the manner of Cain, wherein he became **Master Mahan**, master of that great secret which was administered unto Cain by Satan; and **Irad**, the son of Enoch, having known their secret, **began to reveal it** unto **the sons of Adam**;*

*50 Wherefore Lamech, being angry, slew him, not like unto Cain, his brother Abel, for the sake of getting gain, but **he slew him for the oath's sake**.*

49 a *Master Mahan.* See *Commentary* 5:31-a, p. 379.

b *Irad... began to reveal it.* Apparently Irad betrayed the oath he had made not to reveal the "great secret... administered to Cain by Satan."[775]

c *sons of Adam.* This might be the same Cainite group later referred to as the "sons of men," since the Hebrew is virtually identical in both cases.[776] However, more plausibly, Draper, *et al.* see this verse as describing the spread of secret combinations from the posterity of Cain to the covenant sons of Adam,[777] who are elsewhere referred to as the "sons of God."[778]

50 a *he slew him for the oath's sake.* This phrase confirms that the "wounding" and "hurt" that Lamech used to justify his act of murder were not merely the result of a chance brawl with Irad or a scheme to acquire his possessions. The fact that the victim was slain "for the oath's sake" evidences a carefully calculated assassination to protect the interests of the secret combination to which Lamech had pledged his allegiance.[779]

Schwartz sees the song in vv. 47-48 as a "perplexing passage [that] is almost certainly a fragment of a lost myth about Lamech."[780] Lacking the details about the name of the victim supplied by the book of Moses, Jewish and early Christian texts often connect the song to a story about accidental killings by Lamech: "According to this legend, Lamech, who was blind, went hunting with his son. Lamech's son saw Cain with a horn growing out of his forehead [the horn is here taken to be the mark of Cain], mistook him for a beast, and directed Lamech to kill him."[781] After he discovered what had happened, Lamech, clapping his hands in grief, "struck his son and caused his death."[782] Thus, Lamech says: "By a wound of mine [i.e., by my blindness] I slew a man [Cain]"—and "by a blow of mine [i.e., by clapping my hands] a child [either Tubal-Cain (Cain's grandson) or Enoch (Cain's son)]."[783] Stone translated a variant of the story where the killing of Cain and his son with a stone was done deliberately "in order to lift the ignominy from their own race."[784] Nibley calls all these accounts of Lamech something "they made up to explain this garbled thing in which we only have two lines in the whole Old Testament to explain what's going on," in contrast to the book of Moses where "we get a pretty good picture."[785]

As a result of the killing, the wives of Lamech are said to have "hated him from that day" and, having "separated from him," "sought to kill him." This is taken as the reason that Lamech tried to convince them by his words that he "did this thing unknowingly."[786]

775   See *Commentary* 5:49-b, p. 397.
776   See *Commentary* 5:52-c, p. 398.
777   R. D. Draper, *et al.*, *Commentary*, p. 76.
778   Moses 8:13-14. See the overview of Moses 5, p. 348.
779   See Moses 5:29 and *Commentary* 5:47-b, p. 396.
780   H. Schwartz, *Tree*, p. 452.
781   W. L. Lipscomb, *Armenian*, p. 91. See *Commentary* 5:42-q, p. 390; 5:48-a, p. 396; A.al-Tha'labi, *Lives*, p. 80; W. L. Lipscomb, *Abel*, 47-51, pp. 167-169; Shelemon, *Book of the Bee*, 19, pp. 29-30; B. M. Wheeler, *Prophets*, p. 41.
782   H. Schwartz, *Tree*, p. 451.
783   H. N. Bialik, *et al.*, *Legends*, pp. 24-25.
784   M. E. Stone, *Forefathers*, 16, p. 188; cf. al-Tabari, *Creation*, 1:144, pp. 314-315; M. E. Stone, *Abel*, 5:3, p. 153.
785   H. W. Nibley, *Teachings of the PGP*, 20, p. 255.
786   M. M. Noah, *et al.*, *Jasher*, 2:32-36, p. 4.

*51 For, from the days of Cain, there was a **secret combination**, and their works were in the dark, and they knew every man his brother.*

*52 Wherefore the Lord cursed Lamech, and **his house**, and **all them that had covenanted** with Satan; for they kept not the commandments of God, and it displeased God, and he ministered not unto them, and their works were abominations, and began to spread among all the **sons of men**. And it was among the sons of men.*

*53 And among the daughters of men these things were not spoken, because that **Lamech had spoken the secret unto his wives**, and they rebelled against him, and declared these things abroad, and had not compassion;*

51 a *secret combination.* In the Book of Mormon, the oaths that were later administered to those who formed secret combinations among the Jaredites were said to have been "handed down even from Cain, who was a murderer from the beginning… And… they are had among all people."[787]

52 a *his house.* That is, his family.

   b *all them that had covenanted.* OT1 reads: "all they that had covenanted."[788]

   c *sons of men.* In the book of Moses, this term is always used to designate those who reject the Gospel and follow Satan. In this verse, it most likely refers to the male descendants of Cain and his associates.[789]

53 a *Lamech had spoken the secret unto his wives.* The damaging results of Lamech's wives having "rebelled against him, and declared these things abroad" triggered an absolute clamp-down among the rest of the "sons of men" on speaking to their wives (i.e., "the daughters of men") about their secret affairs.

   Comments Nibley: "Lamech became an outcast like Cain, not because of the murder but because his wives started spreading his secrets—the very ones he had murdered Irad for divulging."[790] Elaborating on ancient parallels, he writes: "One of the most widespread themes of myth and legend is the tragedy of the hero who yields up to the charms of a fair maiden or *femme fatale* and ends up revealing to her hidden mysteries. The story meets us in the oldest Egyptian epic (where the lady Isis wheedles out of Re the fatal knowledge of his true name) and in tales of Samson and Delilah, the daughter of Jared, Lohengrin, and so on, in which the woman is Pandora who must know what is in the box.[791] On this theme the Gizeh fragments of *1 Enoch* offer a significant parallel to the Joseph Smith version, in which the common background of the text and the confusion of the later scribes are equally apparent: … 'And now concerning the Watchers, [say to them,] You were in heaven and there you knew every *mysterion* which had not been made known to you as well as that mystery which God allowed; and that you disclosed to your wives in the hardness of your heart, and it was through this mystery that women and men caused iniquities to abound

---

787   Ether 8:15, 20. On the history and nature of secret combinations, see M. B. Brown, *Girded*; B. Gardner, *Gadianton*; P. Mouritsen, *Combinations*; H. W. Nibley, *Approach*, pp. 378-399; H. W. Nibley, *Since*, pp. 363-372; H. W. Nibley, *Freemen*, pp. 358-369; H. W. Nibley, *Forty Years After*, pp. 551-563; H. W. Nibley, *Teachings of the Book of Mormon*, 74, 3:213-215; 76, 3:238-248; 77, 3:249-255; N. B. Oman, *Combinations*; D. C. Peterson, *Gadianton Masonry*; D. C. Peterson, *Gadianton Robbers*; D. C. Peterson, *Secret Combinations*; B. W. Warren, *Secret Combinations*. See also *Excursus 24: The Watchers*, p. 585.

788   S. H. Faulring, *et al.*, *Original Manuscripts*, p. 96.

789   See *Commentary* 5:49-c, p. 398; Moses 5:56, 8:19-21.

790   H. W. Nibley, *Enoch*, p. 177.

791   Cf. H. Schwartz, *Tree*, pp. 455-457.

*53 And among the daughters of men these things were not spoken, because that **Lamech had spoken the secret unto his wives**, and they rebelled against him, and declared these things abroad, and had not compassion;*

*54 **Wherefore Lamech was despised, and cast out**, and came not among the sons of men, **lest he should die**.*

55 And thus the works of darkness began to prevail among all the sons of men.

*56 And **God cursed the earth with a sore curse**, and was angry with the wicked, with all the **sons of men** whom he had made;*

*57 For **they would not hearken unto his voice**, nor believe on his Only Begotten Son, even him whom he declared should come in the meridian of time, who was **prepared from before the foundation of the world**.*

upon the earth.[792] Similarly, the *Combat of Adam and Eve*[793]… tells you here how Lamech was betrayed by his two wives."[794] "Lamech's wives… 'had not compassion' and spread the secret things abroad."[795]

Besides the secrecy enjoined among the wicked members of the conspiracy, the spread of knowledge of these evil practices was a perennial concern to the righteous, as in the case of Moroni, who declined to reveal specifics when discussing the secret combinations of the Jaredites.[796]

54 a *Wherefore.* OT1 has an "X" mark inserted above the beginning of v. 54, and OT2 has a crossed-out heading "Chapter third."[797] The mistakenly-placed heading appears again in its rightful place just prior to the portion of the manuscript corresponding to Moses 6:1.[798]

b *Lamech was despised, and cast out.* Lamech's associates did not immediately slay him, as the penalty of the oath allowed, though he was despised and cast out. He went into exile to avoid any future retribution.

c *lest he should die.* Lamech's expectation of immunity from blood vengeance, as expressed in his song, were not fulfilled.

56 a *God cursed the earth with a sore curse.* See *Commentary* 4:23-b, p. 270 and 5:37-a, p. 384.

b *sons of men.* See *Commentary* 5:52-c, p. 398.

57 a *they would not hearken unto his voice.* Contrast Adam's obedient hearkening in 6:1.

b *prepared from before the foundation of the world.* This refers to the fact that the atoning mission of Jesus Christ was anticipated and planned for in the premortal life before the creation of the world.[799] The Prophet Joseph Smith said: "I believe that God foreknew everything, but did not foreordain everything; I deny that foreordain and foreknow is the same thing. He foreordained the fall of man; but all merciful as He is, He foreordained at the same time, a plan of Redemption for all mankind. I believe in the Divinity of Jesus Christ, and that He died for the sins of all men, who in Adam had fallen."[800]

792 H. W. Nibley, *Enoch*, p. 183; cf. R. H. Charles, *Enoch*, 16:2-3, p. 294; G. W. E. Nickelsburg, *1 Enoch*, 16:2-3, p. 267; H. W. Nibley, *Teachings of the PGP*, 20, p. 256. See also *Excursus 24: The Watchers*, p. 585.
793 S. C. Malan, *Adam and Eve*, 2:13, p. 122.
794 H. W. Nibley, *Teachings of the PGP*, 21, pp. 258-259.
795 H. W. Nibley, *Return*, p. 63 and Moses 5:47-48, 53. See *Excursus 24: The Watchers*, p. 585.
796 Ether 8:20-26.
797 S. H. Faulring, *et al.*, *Original Manuscripts*, pp. 96, 607.
798 *Ibid.*, p. 608.
799 Alma 13:3; 1 Peter 1:20; Revelation 13:8; Ether 3:14; Moses 4:2.
800 J. Smith, Jr., *Documentary History*, 6 February 1840, 4:78; cf. J. Smith, Jr., *Teachings*, 22 January 1834, pp. 57-58.

*58 **And thus** the **Gospel began to be preached, from the beginning, being declared by holy angels** sent forth from the presence of God, **and by his own voice, and by the gift of the Holy Ghost**.*

*59 **And thus all things were confirmed unto Adam, by an holy ordinance**, and the Gospel preached, and a decree sent forth, that it should be in the world, until the end thereof; and thus it was. Amen.*

58 a *And thus.* In a manner with which readers of the Book of Mormon are well-acquainted, this phrase signals the beginning of the solemn summary contained in the final two verses of Moses 5. The importance of the events of this chapter and the promise that the fulness of the Gospel given to Adam will "be in the world until the end thereof" is highlighted by the threefold repetition of "and thus," terminating in the concluding phrase: "and thus it was. Amen.

b *Gospel began to be preached, from the beginning.* Compare, e.g., John 8:56; Hebrews 1:1-2, 11:13; Jacob 4:4-5, 7:10-11; D&C 29:41-42; Eusebius, *Ecclesiastical*, 1.2, pp. 15-21.

c *being declared by holy angels…, and by his own voice, and by the gift of the Holy Ghost.* Mormon taught that the "office of [the] ministry [of angels] is to call men unto repentance, and to fulfill and to do the work of the covenants of the Father, which he hath made unto the children of men, to prepare the way among the children of men, by declaring the word of Christ unto the chosen vessels of the Lord, that they may bear testimony of him."[801]

Because of their perfect "heed and diligence" Adam and Eve had learned the "mysteries of God"[802] from "holy angels sent forth from the presence of God, and by his own voice, and by the gift of the Holy Ghost."[803] They, in turn, "made all things known unto their sons and daughters."[804] Those who "believed it not"[805] could not be granted additional light and knowledge, though the Lord continued to plead with them to repent through the power of the Holy Ghost.[806]

59 a *And thus.* The term thus in this verse is subordinate to its prior usage in v. 59. Here it signifies "in this manner" or "by this means," referring to the fact that it was through the medium of angels,[807] and of God's own voice,[808] and of the gift of the Holy Ghost[809] that "all things were confirmed unto Adam, by an holy ordinance."[810]

b *all things were confirmed unto Adam, by an holy ordinance.* A contrast is implied between Adam's having had all things confirmed by an holy ordinance from God, and Cain and Lamech's having sworn their allegiance to Satan. Details about the holy ordinance referred to are not given,[811] though it is probably no coincidence that Moses 6 will focus on Adam's role as the "first father" in the order of the patriarchal priesthood.[812]

801 Moroni 7:31.
802 Alma 12:9.
803 Moses 5:58.
804 Moses 5:12.
805 Moses 5:13.
806 Moses 5:14. See Moroni 7:32; Alma 12:10-11, Moses 7:27.
807 E.g., Moses 5:6.
808 E.g., Moses 5:4.
809 E.g., Moses 5:9.
810 Moses 5:59.
811 See *Commentary* 5:9-b, p. 362.
812 See *Commentary* 6:7-a, p. 480.

59 And thus **all things were confirmed unto Adam, by an holy ordinance,** *and the Gospel preached, and* **a decree sent forth, that it should be in the world, until the end thereof; and thus it was. Amen.**

The text is consistent with OT2.[813] OT1 does not include the phrase "unto Adam, by an holy ordinance."[814]

all things. Cf. *Commentary* 5:12-a, p. 364.

d ***a decree sent forth, that it should be in the world, until the end thereof; and thus it was. Amen.*** Just as the decree in v. 15 parallels a passage near the end of the gospel of Mark, so this declaration is echoed by the final words of the Savior in Matthew: "and, lo, I am with you always, even unto the end of the world. Amen."[815]

MOSES 5

---

813 S. H. Faulring, *et al.*, *Original Manuscripts*, p. 607.
814 *Ibid.*, p. 96.
815 Matthew 28:20.

Gleanings

Table of Contents

Gaetano Lettieri: Genesis Parallels in Christ's Baptism and Temptation[816]

There seem to be systematic analogies between the proto-history of the Genesis Adam and the baptism of Jesus as the origin of the new creation.[817] First, the re-emergence of Jesus… from the waters of life reactualizes the waters of Eden, above all the descent of the Spirit (the same vital breath of [Moses 3:7]) on the waters.[818] The waters of Genesis also figure the symbol of the *chrism*,[819] the messianic spirit[820] and the new alliance between God and man represented by the dove of Noah.[821] The… re-opening of the heavens and the divine voice which reaffirms the reacquired perfect offspring, the glorious "being in [His] image" of the man Jesus in whom God is pleased recalls Isaiah 42:1 and 63:11-19 and above all Psalm 2:7, where a reference to the creation of Adam seems to be possible, as fulfilling the "it was very good" of [Moses 2:31].

If at first sight these analogies may appear forced or dubious, they gain strength from the analogies, a good deal more evident, concerning the episode of the temptation of Jesus. The temptation is the other inseparable side of the baptism for the synoptic tradition: Jesus is pulled away violently from the Spirit (an analogous and contrary movement to that of the expulsion from Paradise) and placed for forty days in the closed-in and lonely place of Satan's temptation (the desert is the image of Eden turned upside down, the place fit for the punishment capable of taking away the sin of Adam).[822] Jesus lives in the peaceful company of the wild animals where the original harmony of creation is recovered, together with Adam's lordship over the beasts.[823] In the desert Jesus is served by (receives nourishment from?) the angels, which corresponds to the information we have in some Judaic apocrypha of the angels as servants and dispensers of food to the prelapsarian[824] Adam.[825]

The paradisal symbolism and eschatological significance of the scene of the messianic baptism, and of the temptation in the desert, are definitely proved by references to certain passages in Isaiah:[826]

> 15 Until the spirit be poured upon us from on high, and the wilderness be a fruitful field, and the fruitful field be counted for a forest.

> 16 Then judgment shall dwell in the wilderness, and righteousness remain in the fruitful field.

> 17 And the work of righteousness shall be peace; and the effect of righteousness quietness and assurance for ever.

> 18 And my people shall dwell in a peaceable habitation, and in sure dwellings, and in quiet resting places;

> 3 For the Lord shall comfort Zion: he will comfort all her waste places; and he will make her wilderness like Eden, and her desert like the garden of the Lord…

---

816   G. Lettieri, *Ambiguity*, pp. 26-28.
817   See *Commentary* 2:2-c, p. 97.
818   See Moses 2:2 and the river of Paradise in Moses 3:10.
819   = anointing.
820   See Isaiah 61:1-2.
821   See Genesis 8:11: the dove returns with an olive branch.
822   D. H. Akenson, *Surpassing Wonder*, p. 265 sees here the imagery of the wanderings of the children of Israel in the desert for forty years.
823   See Moses 2:26 and, in an eschatological perspective, Isaiah 11:6-8 and 65:25.
824   = before the Fall.
825   See G. A. Anderson, *et al.*, *Synopsis*, 4:2, p. 5E.
826   Isaiah 32:15-18 and 51:3.

Hugh W. Nibley: Rites and Ordinances Begin As Acts of Faith[827]

Divinely instituted rites and ordinances have to do in the first instance with things which men do for no other reason than that God has commanded them. They are, first of all, acts of faith and are meritorious as such. They must be hard enough and demanding enough not to become mere acts of dull, automatic repetition, and their immediate practical value may not be so obviously apparent that there is no room left in their performance for a real test of faith. When one goes to train with a master, not merely with the object of serving time for a certificate as in our modern "character factories," but in order to learn all the master has to teach and to become as far as possible perfect in an art, a science, or a craft, the first and all-important step is to establish a condition of complete trust between the master and the disciple. The candidate must by sure tests show his implicit faith and unhesitating obedience to every command in every situation. Soon enough he will understand why he must take a seemingly absurd position or perform some apparently meaningless operation; but unless and until he does the thing, and does it entirely on faith, and does it with a will, he will never come to that understanding, worlds without end.

There are many things that can only be explained after they are done, and then the explanation of what seemed so arbitrary and mysterious usually turns out to be extremely obvious and natural. We are required, for example, to use oil in some of the ordinances of the Church, and water in others. If you ask me why, I will answer, "I know not, save that the Lord hath commanded."[828] That is reason enough. It does not follow that these things have no real purpose aside from the symbolic and disciplinary: A small child uses soap on faith—a mere act of obedience, we might say, with the soap as a symbol of cleanliness, but actually it goes much further than that; the soap performs a real function which the child does not understand. I doubt not that when we know the reason for some of the things we do now on faith, the practical value of the actions will be so plain that we will wonder how we could have missed it, and then we shall be heartily glad that we did what we were told to do. Meantime the Lord advises us in these things, and it is up to us to trust his judgment. If the primary purpose of our being on earth is to be tested, and the first thing to be tested is our faith and obedience, it is foolish to ask for a full explanation before we will move a muscle. There are many operations in mathematics and the arts that can only be understood after they have been carried out....

One of the most remarkable features of Latter-day Saint ordinances is that they are, or claim to be, pristine. They are the same ordinances that were given in the beginning. That is the way God wants it, and that is the way it must be. The whole validity of such ordinances depends on their having been revealed directly from heaven. No effort is made to give practical or rational explanation of these ordinances; they are not interpreted symbolically, nor are they justified by their aesthetic appeal, which is extremely limited. We do these things on faith for no other reason save that the Lord has commanded us to do them. The importance of a living prophet in such a ritual scheme of things will be at once apparent. Granted that the real business of life is to do what God wants us to, the whole problem is then to determine what that is. Only a prophet can tell us.

827   H. W. Nibley, *Ritual*, pp. 148-149, 151.
828   Moses 5:6.

Arta R. Ballif: *Lamentation* (Comments by Elder Bruce C. Hafen)[829]

Arta Romney Ballif once wrote a poem called "Lamentation," in which she imagined Eve's experience as a mother and a wife—her questions, her cries for understanding, her quest to know God… :[830]

> And God said, "BE FRUITFUL, AND MULTIPLY—"
> Multiply, multiply—echoes multiply
> God said, "I WILL GREATLY MULTIPLY THY SORROW—"
> Thy sorrow, sorrow, sorrow—
>
> I have gotten a man from the Lord
> I have traded the fruit of the garden for fruit of my body
> For a laughing bundle of humanity.
>
> And now another one who looks like Adam
> We shall call this one "Abel."
> It is a lovely name, "Abel."
>
> Cain, Abel, the world is yours.
> God set the sun in the heavens to light your days
> To warm the flocks, to kernel the grain
> He illuminated your nights with stars
> He made the trees and the fruit thereof yielding seed
> He made every living thing, the wheat, the sheep, the cattle
> For your enjoyment
> And, behold, it is very good.
> …
>
> Adam? Adam
> Where art thou?
> Where are the boys?
> The sky darkens with clouds.
> Adam, is that you?
> Where is Abel?
> He is long caring for his flocks.
> The sky is black and the rain hammers.
> Are the ewes lambing
> In this storm?
>
> Why your troubled face, Adam?
> Are you ill?
> Why so pale, so agitated?
> The wind will pass
> The lambs will birth
> With Abel's help.
>
> Dead?
> What is dead?
>
> Merciful God!
> Hurry, bring warm water
> I'll bathe his wounds

829   B. C. Hafen, *et al.*, *Belonging*, pp. 86-90.
830   See *Endnote 5-66*, p. 449.

Bring clean clothes
Bring herbs.
I'll heal him.

I am trying to understand.
You said, "Abel is dead."
But I am skilled with herbs
Remember when he was seven
The fever? Remember how—
Herbs will not heal? Dead?

And Cain? Where is Cain?
Listen to that thunder.

Cain cursed?
What has happened to him?
God said, "A fugitive and a vagabond?"

But God can't do that.
They are my sons, too.
I gave them birth
In the valley of pain.

Adam, try to understand
In the valley of pain

I bore them
fugitive?
vagabond?

This is his home
This the soil he loved
Where he toiled for golden wheat
For tasseled corn.

To the hill country?
There are rocks in the hill country
Cain can't work in the hill country
The nights are cold
Cold and lonely, and the wind gales.

Quick, we must find him
A basket of bread and his coat
I worry, thinking of him wandering
With no place to lay his head.
Cain cursed?
A wanderer, a roamer?
Who will bake his bread and mend his coat?

Abel, my son dead?
And Cain, my son, a fugitive?
Two sons
Adam, we had two sons
Both—Oh, Adam—
multiply
sorrow

Dear God, why?
Tell me again about the fruit
Why?
Please, tell me again
Why?

This poem movingly depicts Eve's anguish—yet it does not tell us why she and Adam lost their sons. They may not have known why. They must have wondered if those losses were their own fault. Had they failed as parents? The poem imagines that in her very uncertainty, Eve felt estranged from God, cut off, not at all "at one" with him. And it is fair to assume that Adam's and Eve's questions and fears in losing Abel and Cain were literally "multiplied" on other dark days throughout their lives. Like Eve, sometimes we do not know—perhaps cannot know—how fully we are at fault for the bitterness we taste. When we taste the bitter, we, like Eve, can only keep trying, and wondering, and asking for understanding. We might then cry out as Joseph Smith did: "O God, where art thou? And where is the pavilion that covereth thy hiding place?"[831] Does the Atonement speak to such questions? We testify that it does.

Elder Howard W. Hunter: A Successful Parent Is One Who Has Loved[832]

A successful parent is one who has loved, one who has sacrificed, and one who has cared for, taught, and ministered to the needs of a child. If you have done all of these and your child is still wayward or worldly, it could well be that you are, nevertheless, a successful parent. Perhaps there are children who have come into the world that would challenge any set of parents under any set of circumstances. Likewise, perhaps there are others who would bless the lives of, and be a joy to, almost any father or mother.

Victor Hugo: Conscience[833]

When Cain, dishevelled, angry, in the middle of a storm,
Fleeing with his children wrapped in hides to keep warm,
Was running from Jehovah, he arrived at the base
Of a solitary mountain in the middle of a waste
As night came down and darkness gave the shadows depth.
His wife, exhausted, and his children, out of breath,
Said to him, 'Let's lie down here and go to sleep.'
Cain dreamed at the mountain's foot, unable to sleep.
Lifting his head, he looked up and saw an eye
Entirely open, in the depths of the sky,
Which stared at him fixedly from out of the night.
"I am too close," he said, shuddering at the sight.
And so he woke his sleeping sons along with his wife
And set out again, as if fleeing for his life.
He marched for thirty nights; he marched for thirty days.
He traveled, silent, pale, afraid of noises, in a daze,
Furtively, without looking back or stopping once,
Without rest, without sleep, until he came after months

---

831   D&C 121:1. See *Endnote 3-57*, p. 210.
832   H. W. Hunter, *Concern*, November 1983, p. 115.
833   V. Hugo, *Poetry*, pp. 215, 217. See *Endnote 5-67*, p. 449.

MOSES 5

To the coast which would be the Assyrian shore.
"Let us stop here," he said, "This refuge is secure.
We've reached the world's limits. Let us rest—or try to."
But as he went to sit, he glanced across the sky's blue
And saw the eye hanging in the last place he had looked.
Fear sent him into convulsions. As he shook
He shouted "Cover me!" With their fingers on their mouths,
All of his children watched their father's trembling hands.
Cain said to Jab, whose sons would later move about
As nomads under tasseled tents across the sands,
"Spread out the canvas of your tent over here."
And so they put together a floating barrier.
In order to secure it, leaden weights were fastened on
"You can see nothing now?" asked Zillah, sweet as dawn,
The blond child, daughter of his daughters and his sons.
"I still see that eye!" was Cain's terrified response.
Then Jubal, father of those men who travel from
Market towns blowing horns and banging on their drums,
Said, "I know how to build a wall." So he designed it,
Had it made from bronze, and put Cain behind it.
But Cain said, "The eye is still out there, hovering."
Enoch said, "Let's build a score of towers in a ring
So terrifying no one will dare to come close.
Let's build a city with a large gate we can close.
Let's build a city and we'll seal him inside."
And so the forefather of blacksmiths, Tubalcain,
Constructed an inhuman city, tall and wide.
While he was building it, his brothers on the plain
Were hunting down the children of Enosh and Seth.
They ripped out the eyes of every person they met.
And every night they fired their arrows at the stars.
Granite replaced the canvas walls. And iron bars
Were used to join the huge blocks of this citadel.
The city looked as if it were a city from hell:
Its towers caused a night to fall on outlying fields.
Its walls were like mountains. For they built them not to yield
To anything. They scrawled above its gate: "No Gods allowed."
And when they had finished walling in and walling out
They put Cain in the towers' most secure and guarded wing.
But he remained listless, and only seemed to stare.
"Has the eye disappeared?" asked Zillah, trembling.
Cain answered back to her, "No. It's still there."
And then he said to them, "I want to live underground
Like a hermit in his tomb—in some place without sound
Where no one will see me, and I won't see them as well."
And so they dug a ditch, and Cain replied, "You've done well."
Then he went down into the black crypt alone.
And when he was sitting in the darkness on his throne,

And they had sealed the vault in which he would remain,
The eye was in the tomb there and looked straight at Cain.

Leon R. Kass: The Maxim of a Would-Be Murderer[834]

Though an analytic philosopher or White House lawyer might try to argue that Cain's speech was true—for where indeed is the soul of Abel now?—Cain, to protect himself, lies to God… Indeed, to keep the inquisitive voice from forcing him to fully confront the meaning of his deed, he answers the question with a question no doubt tinged with indignation and even mocking: Why are you asking me? Am I supposed to be his guardian? You, you who liked his sacrifice, you who made him prosper—aren't you his keeper? Why don't you know where he is? And (implicitly) what kind of a guardian are you?

God… is not deceived. On the contrary, He treats Cain's question, with its blatant disregard for brother Abel's whereabouts, as tantamount to a confession. Fully understood, "Am I my brother's keeper?" turns out, in fact, to be the maxim of a would-be murderer, an expression of fratricidal intent. For to deny responsibility for your brother is, tacitly, to profess indifference to his fate. To care not at all about his existence and welfare is to be tacitly guilty of all harm that befalls him: in short, to say yes even to his death and disappearance.

Hugh W. Nibley: Knowledge Is Not for Power and Gain[835]

"Knowledge is power" is the slogan of a rascally world. Why else love truth? "Is it because you can discover a beauty in it, because it is congenial to you, or because you think it will make you a ruler or a lord? If you conceive that you will attain to power, upon such a motive, you are much mistaken," says Brigham. "It is a trick of the unseen power that is abroad amongst the inhabitants of the earth, that leads them astray, binds their minds, and subverts their understanding." Then he goes all out: "Suppose that our Father in heaven, our elder brother, the risen Redeemer, the Savior of the world, or any of the Gods of eternity should act on this principle, to love truth, knowledge, and wisdom, because they are all powerful, and by the aid of this power they could send devils to hell, torment the people of the earth, exercise sovereignty over them, and make them miserable at their pleasure; they would cease to be Gods,… the extension of their kingdom would cease, and their God-head come to an end."[836] Yet this is the realm we seek and the direction we work toward: Leave the motives out and let the purpose in. Especially there are some things we should never look for—power and gain.

Hugh W. Nibley: Satan's Great Secret of "Success"

The cynical conclusion is that no one can resist Satan's bargain, and in the history of the world very few people have. The first to accept was Cain, who "loved Satan more than God," though at the latter's advice he continued to make offerings to the Lord.[837] The "great secret" of success that he learned from his new teacher was that he could get anything in this world by the calculated use of force, with no need to be ashamed since it could all be done in the sacred name of freedom; instead of being appalled at the blood on his hands, "Cain gloried in that which he had done, saying: I am free; surely the flocks [wealth, *pecus*, *Vieh*] of my

---

834   L. R. Kass, *Wisdom*, p. 142.
835   H. W. Nibley, *Funeral*, p. 294.
836   B. Young, *27 February 1853*, p. 117.
837   Moses 5:18, 21.

brother falleth into my hands."[838] Cain slew Abel not, as we like to think, in a fit of passion but with cold calculation, "for the sake of getting gain."[839] He was all business. As for the victim, he was quite able to take care of himself, and if he failed, that, by the rules of the new game, it was his hard luck: "Am I my brother's keeper?"[840] Significantly enough, when this forthright, no-nonsense economy, unencumbered by enervating sentimentality, worked against Cain, he straightway became a bleeding heart in his own behalf, and appealed for the mercy he would not give. "My punishment is greater than I can bear!"[841] In making an example of Cain, God absolutely forbade the use of Cain's own methods against him: "Whoever slayeth thee, vengeance shall be taken on him sevenfold."[842]

Because of the Fall, man has become the enemy of his own environment, at odds with the whole creation, allergic to all manner of things good in themselves that afflict and torment him: "The animal, vegetable, and mineral kingdoms abide the law of their Creator; the whole earth and all things pertaining to it, except man, abide the law of their creation."[843] Conflict is inevitable, with man stubbornly refusing to become subject to the most sensible and self-exalting principles, determined to subdue the earth in his way. "We see all the world trying to lord it over God's heritage. It is in the spirit that the evil principle and power is trying to overcome and rule over the divine principle planted there. This constantly leads the children of men astray."[844] So there is a fundamental conflict here, and it goes back to the beginning. It is said that Satan approached Adam with certain propositions that he later presented to Cain, Noah, Abraham, and Job, in which he set forth his plan for running things: (1) He claimed all of God's earth, "most glorious and beautiful" from end to end for his own; (2) then he put up everything in it for sale to anyone who had the money; (3) and finally he revealed the source of power and dominion under his system: it all rested on possession of the treasures of the earth, with which one can buy any military and political power necessary to rule, or rather misrule, among the children of men.[845]

In 1540 when Pedro de Tovar came up to Bear Chief, who was standing to greet him on the rise at Old Oraibi, the chief reached out his hand to establish the visitor's identity by offering him the sacred handclasp, the *nachwach*—was he really the promised White Brother? Naturally, the Spaniard, who had come looking for gold and nothing else, thought he was asking for money and placed a gold coin in his hand. "Have you any signs or tokens?" asked the chief. "Yes, I have money," replied the visitor. From that moment the Hopis knew it was not the one they were looking for, and to this day they have never been converted to Christianity. We are most fortunate in possessing Satan's game-plan, which he gave away in a fit of temper in the Garden of Eden. The perennial source of wealth, the treasures of the earth, are to be controlled by the convenient symbols of a money economy, gold and silver; these are used to buy up kings and presidents, armies and navies, popes and priests. They are controlled by "secret combinations, to get power and gain,"[846] and the result is rule by violence. Adam rejected the plan, but Cain bought into it, and so became "master of this

---

838   Moses 5:31-33.
839   Moses 5:50, 38.
840   Moses 5:34.
841   Moses 5:38.
842   H. W. Nibley, *Dominion*, pp. 15-16. See Moses 5:40.
843   B. Young, *23 March 1864*, p. 246.
844   B. Young, *5 January 1860*, p. 107.
845   H. W. Nibley, *Environment*, p. 45.
846   Ether 8:22; cf. Ether 8:18-19.

great secret, that I may murder and get gain"[847]—the great design which at last is nearing fulfillment in our day of converting all living things into marketable commodities.[848]

Leon R. Kass: The Self-Deception of Self-Sufficiency[849]

Concerned with his position as number one, eager to establish himself as lord and master of his domain, Cain (like Romulus, the mythic founder of Rome) commits the paradigmatic crime of the political founder: fratricide. For the aspiration to supremacy and rule entails necessarily the denial and destruction of radical human equality, epitomized in the relationship of brotherhood. To wish to rule, to dominate, to be in command, means—by its very nature—the wish not only to remove all rivals but also to destroy the brotherly relation with those under one's dominion. The ruler, as ruler, has no brothers.

The more that rude and ambitious men have to do with one another, the more they both need to fear and seek to outdo one another. For both reasons—safety and pride—they cultivate prowess in fighting.[850] They build city walls to protect them from their enemies; but the existence of walls creates new enmities and invites attack. The city begun in fear proudly begets one of heroic ambition. There is a direct line from the plowshare to the sword.[851]

As we will see even more clearly later on, when we come to the city and tower of Babel, the Bible in its beginning takes sides in an ancient quarrel about the origin and goodness of the city and civilization. According to the more optimistic view, the city is rooted in need and comes to be by a process of natural growth, beginning with the household, then the tribe, then the village, then the merging of several villages to form the city. According to Aristotle, the city is the first truly self-sufficient community; it comes into being for the sake of life, but it exists for the sake of living well. According to the more pessimistic view, shared by the Bible, the city is rooted in fear, greed, pride, violence, and the desire for domination. These questionable beginnings continue to infect civilization as such. In addition, the city's aspiration to self-sufficiency is highly problematic.[852] This, too, our story makes plain.

But the context of the story of Cain is not simply political. Cain was jealous over a matter of divine favor… This prototypical human being begets a line leading to civilization, the arts, and the heroes—all manifestations of an impulse toward self-sufficiency… Lamech, the hero, acts as if he has succeeded; but we, readers prepared by what has come before, know that he is self-deceived.

President Spencer W. Kimball: The False Gods We Worship[853]

[Many] have submitted themselves in one degree or another to the enticings of Satan and his servants and joined with those of "the world" in lives of ever-deepening idolatry….

Few men have ever knowingly and deliberately chosen to reject God and his blessings. Rather, we learn from the scriptures that because the exercise of faith has always appeared to be more difficult than relying on things more immediately at hand, carnal man has tended to transfer his trust in God to material things. Therefore, in all ages when men have

---

847 Moses 5:31.
848 H. W. Nibley, *Promised lands*, pp. 98-99.
849 L. R. Kass, *Wisdom*, p. 147.
850 See *Commentary 5:47-a*, p. 395.
851 See Isaiah 2:4; Joel 3:10; Micah 4:3.
852 See *Endnote 5-68*, p. 450.
853 S. W. Kimball, *False Gods*, pp. 4-6.

fallen under the power of Satan and lost the faith, they have put in its place a hope in the "arm of flesh" and in "gods of silver, and gold, of brass, iron, wood, and stone, which see not, nor hear, nor know"[854]—that is, in idols. This I find to be a dominant theme in the Old Testament. Whatever thing a man sets his heart and his trust in most is his god; and if his god doesn't also happen to be the true and living God of Israel, that man is laboring in idolatry....

The Lord has blessed us as a people with a prosperity unequaled in times past. The resources that have been placed in our power are good, and necessary to our work here on the earth. But I am afraid that many of us have been surfeited with flocks and herds and acres and barns and wealth and have begun to worship them as false gods, and they have power over us. Do we have more of these good things than our faith can stand? Many people spend most of their time working in the service of a self-image that includes sufficient money, stocks, bonds, investment portfolios, property, credit cards, furnishings, automobiles, and the like to guarantee carnal security throughout, it is hoped, a long and happy life. Forgotten is the fact that our assignment is to use these many resources in our families and quorums to build up the kingdom of God—to further the missionary effort and the genealogical and temple work; to raise our children up as fruitful servants unto the Lord; to bless others in every way, that they may also be fruitful. Instead, we expend these blessings on our own desires, and as Moroni said, "Ye adorn yourselves with that which hath no life, and yet suffer the hungry, and the needy, and the naked, and the sick and the afflicted to pass by you, and notice them not"....[855]

In spite of our delight in defining ourselves as modern, and our tendency to think we possess a sophistication that no people in the past ever had—in spite of these things, we are, on the whole, an idolatrous people—a condition most repugnant to the Lord.

We are a warlike people, easily distracted from our assignment of preparing for the coming of the Lord. When enemies rise up, we commit vast resources to the fabrication of gods of stone and steel—ships, planes, missiles, fortifications—and depend on them for protection and deliverance. When threatened, we become anti-enemy instead of pro-kingdom of God; we train a man in the art of war and call him a patriot, thus, in the manner of Satan's counterfeit of true patriotism, perverting the Savior's teaching:

> Love your enemies, bless them that curse you, do good to them that hate you, and pray for them which despitefully use you, and persecute you; That ye may be the children of your Father which is in heaven.[856]

Elder Neal A. Maxwell: The Painful Sound of Cain-like Glorying

A confused Cain, a vain Cain, not only murdered his brother while they conversed together in the field, but also gloried in the murder of Abel, when Cain said (probably shouted), "I am free."

So often violence creates the illusion of freedom or possession. So often sin creates a momentary illusion which those involved are taken in by. I've never been able to erase from my mind the boasting words of army buddies following their night of adultery, which I heard while trying to go back to sleep on an army cot no farther away from here than Camp

---

854   Daniel 5:23.
855   Mormon 8:39.
856   Matthew 5:44-45.

Williams. I saw the shame of several of those same men in the days and weeks that followed. It seemed to me then, as it does now, that the raucousness and the shouting of sin, the Cain-like glorying in it, is also the sound of pain trying to erase itself.[857]

Cain's… erroneous thinking about freedom evokes Peter's warning words: "Of whom a man is overcome, of the same is he brought in bondage."[858] True, strident souls may even fake laughter amid bondage and sin, but another proverb applies: "Even in laughter the heart is sorrowful; and the end of that mirth is heaviness."[859]

Gross sin not only dulls the feelings, it also impairs the intellect. After murdering Abel, Cain ironically boasted, "I am free"![860] Did the herd of Gadarene swine similarly console themselves, thinking that they were actually rugged individualists as they raced down the hill to their destruction?[861]

Illustrative of poor perspective of another type is the fact that, after jealously slaying Abel, Cain cried out in a pathetic outburst of self-deception, "I am free,"[862] but he was never less so! Like Pilate's trying to wash his hands in vain, and like Hitler's careful efforts to keep his name off certain Holocaust documents, so today many do not really want the consequences of what they want. But in God's inexorable ecology consequences do come, accompanied by severe individual accountability.[863]

Hugh W. Nibley: The Two Ways vs. The Two Parties

When the early church began to grow in power and influence and worldliness, the ancient doctrine of the Two Ways[864] was quickly replaced by that of the Two Parties. The former specified that there lies before every mortal, at every moment of his life, a choice between the Way of Light and the Way of Darkness; but the latter doctrine taught that righteousness consisted in belonging to one party (ours), and wickedness in belonging to the other (theirs)…. [W]hen the two ways were identified with the two parties by the churchmen—ours and yours—the doctrine was exploited with inexorable logic: Since there are only two sides, one totally evil and the other absolutely good, and I am not totally evil, I must be on God's side, and that puts you on the other side… With withering contempt, Isaiah denounces the comfortable logic: It is not for you to say who is on the Lord's side, says the Lord; that is for me to say, and those who most loudly offer me their support and cry "Lord! Lord!" are those in whom I most disapprove.[865] "See the foe in countless numbers, marshaled in the ranks of sin,"[866] we sing, as if we have already chosen sides and know who the bad people are, because we are on the Lord's side. "Fight for Zion, down with error, flash the sword above the foe, every stroke disarms a foeman,"[867] and so on. No error on our side? The point of all such hymns is that it is sin and error that we are fighting, not people guilty of sin and error—for we are all such people, and each one can only confront and overcome sin and error in himself. You cannot tell the righteous from the wicked, the Lord told Joseph Smith,

---

857 N. A. Maxwell, *Insights*, p. 50.
858 2 Peter 2:19; see also 2 Nephi 2:26-30.
859 N. A. Maxwell, *Seventh*, p. 78; see Proverbs 14:13.
860 Moses 5:33.
861 N. A. Maxwell, *Enemy*, p. 76.
862 Moses 5:33.
863 N. A. Maxwell, *Praise*, p. 72.
864 See overview of Moses 5, p. 328.
865 See Matthew 7:21.
866 *Hymns (1985)*, #259.
867 *Ibid.* The hymn actually reads "*Strike* for Zion" instead of "*Fight* for Zion."

you cannot tell your friends from your enemies. Be still and let me decide the issue!....[868] Mormon died fighting the Lamanites, who were not as wicked as his own people![869]

[Fortunately, the] gospel of repentance is a constant reminder that the most righteous are still being tested and may yet fall, and that the most wicked are not yet beyond redemption and may still be saved. And that is what God wants: "Have I any pleasure at all that the wicked should die?"[870] There are poles for all to see, but in this life no one has reached and few have ever approached either pole, and no one has any idea at what point between his neighbor stands. Only God knows that.[871]

As I listen to our Elders' quorums [ringing] out [with] militant hymns every Sunday morning, slashing their swords above the foe, conquering at every step, scattering the hosts of darkness, reveling in the victory of the right[872]— one question keeps recurring to my mind, "Where is the battle?".... The Devil is using diversionary tactics to get us on the wrong battlefield.[873]

Satan's masterpiece of counterfeiting is the doctrine that there are only two choices, and he will show us what they are. It is true that there are only two ways, but by pointing us the way he wants us to take and then showing us a fork in that road, he convinces us that we are making the vital choice, when actually we are choosing between branches in his road. Which one we take makes little difference to him, for both lead to destruction. This is the polarization we find in our world today. Thus we have the choice between Shiz and Coriantumr—which all Jaredites were obliged to make.[874] We have the choice between the wicked Lamanites (and they were that) and the equally wicked (Mormon says "more wicked"[875]) Nephites. Or between the fleshpots of Egypt[876] and the stews of Babylon,[877] or between the land pirates and the sea pirates of World War I, or between white supremacy and black supremacy, or between Vietnam and Cambodia, or between Bushwhackers and Jayhawkers, or between China and Russia, or between Catholic and Protestant, or between fundamentalist and atheist, or between right and left—all of which are true rivals, who hate each other. A very clever move of Satan! …It should be apparent that you take no sides [when you are presented with the Devil's dilemma].[878]

On the last night of a play the whole cast and stage crew stay in theater until the small or not-so-small hours of the morning striking the old set. If there is to be a new opening soon, as the economy of the theater requires, it is important that the new set should be in place and ready for the opening night; all the while the old set was finishing its usefulness and then being taken down, the new set was rising in splendor to be ready for the drama that would immediately follow. So it is with this world. It is not our business to tear down the old set—the agencies that do that are already hard at work and very efficient—the set is coming down all around us with spectacular effect. Our business is to see to it that the new set is well on the way for what is to come—and that means a different kind of politics, beyond the

868   D&C 10:37.
869   H. W. Nibley, *Prophetic*, 462-464.
870   Ezekiel 18:23.
871   H. W. Nibley, *Prophetic*, pp. 461-462.
872   See *Hymns (1985)*, #259.
873   H. W. Nibley, *Battle*.
874   Ether 14:20.
875   Alma 47:36; cf. Helaman 6:31-38.
876   Exodus 16:3.
877   Daniel 1:5.
878   H. W. Nibley, *Gifts*, pp. 113-114.

scope of the tragedy that is now playing its closing night. We are preparing for the establishment of Zion.[879]

Alexander Solzhenitsyn: The Line Between Good and Evil[880]

If only it were all so simple! If only there were evil people somewhere insidiously committing evil deeds, and it were necessary only to separate them from the rest of us and destroy them. But the line dividing good and evil cuts through the heart of every human being. And who is willing to destroy a piece of his own heart? During the life of any heart this line keeps changing place; sometimes it is squeezed one way by exuberant evil and sometimes it shifts to allow enough space for good to flourish. One and the same human being is, at various ages, under various circumstances, a totally different human being. At times he is close to being a devil, at times to sainthood. But his name doesn't change, and to that name we ascribe the whole lot, good and evil.[881]

Giulio Busi Eden: The Distance Between Gehenna and Eden[882]

"Gehenna and Eden. What's the distance between them? A hand's breadth…"[883] Gehenna and Eden are as close as the distinction between good and evil, which is often so subtle as to be almost imperceptible.[884]

Hugh W. Nibley: The Cainites and the Sethites

From [Seth] comes that line of successors in the priesthood, duly registered in the Book of Life, from which the wicked were excluded.[885] After Seth came Enos, who decided to make an important move. Since "in those days Satan had great dominion among men, and raged in their hearts," causing "wars and bloodshed… in administering death, because of secret works, seeing for power"[886]—exactly as in the modern world—Enos gathered "the residue of the people of God" and with them migrated out of the country "and dwelt in a land of promise," named Cainan after his son…[887]

In *The Combat of Adam and Eve*,[888] as Migne observes, "the author depicts the descendants of Adam as divided into two separate and distinct branches: the Cainites dedicated to following Satan, who lived in a fertile country but very far distant from Eden, and who devoted themselves to all the pleasures of the flesh and all manner of immorality," and the Sethites who "dwelt in the mountains near the Garden,[889] were faithful to the divine law, and bore the names of the Sons of God."[890]

This is the story they tell between the [Sethites] and the Cainites… Their cultures have different traditions, but the Cainites win hands down [in popularity]… The plains had great attraction for the more simple-living people of the high places. They naturally were enticed. Satan took charge

879   H. W. Nibley, *Beyond Politics*, p. 302.
880   Cited in A. J. Colton, *Solzhenitsyn*, p. 11.
881   See *Endnote 5-74*, p. 452.
882   G. B. Eden, *Mystical Architecture*, p. 19.
883   H. Freedman, *et al.*, *Midrash*, Ecclesiastes, VII.14.3, 8:197.
884   Almost imperceptible, that is, to the natural eye. If the natural eye is the only means by which we can see, we will perceive very little indeed (cf. B. K. Packer, cited in D. A. Bednar, *Quick*, p. 36; see also Moroni 7:14-16).
885   Moses 6:5-8.
886   Moses 6:15.
887   Moses 6:17.
888   S. C. Malan, *Adam and Eve*, 2:11, pp. 118-119.
889   Cf. Moses 7:17. Ri cites several sources that locate the Sethites on Mount Hermon (see A. S-M. Ri, *Commentaire de la Caverne*, pp. 74, 207).
890   H. W. Nibley, *Enoch*, pp. 177-178.

down below. He made a covenant. They talk a lot about the covenant, how he directed them and gave them the jewelry and the beautiful clothes and loud instruments. He specialized in brass bands. This would attract the attention of the young people up on the heights. They'd come and look down with some envy at all the fun that was going on down there in the plain—all the lights, the dancing, the carousing, etc. Then we come down the list here. After Cainan and Mahalaleel, then comes Jared. His name means "going down," because that was the day when they went down from the mountain; they left it. Jared told his sons, if you ever go down there, you'll never get back. At first they didn't know the way down, so Satan had to teach them. Satan actually came with a delegation of very important-looking people. He came up and invited Jared, "Come down, Brother Jared, and visit us in the city down below. You'll see what a nice society we have and you will love to stay with us. You'll see what it's like." He was curious, so he went down with them. They dressed up like angels, and they fooled him. He actually was fooled until he got back home, and the angel came and told him, "Look, this is terrible. You've been led astray. Don't let your people do this." Satan showed them a way down. There was a gully where a stream went down, and you could get down that way. They started drifting down and joining in the fun. Incidentally, when Jared went there, he was introduced into all the delights of the place. Immediately, they started giving him a real show. It was a session—a real orgy with obscene goings-on, etc. He was horrified because the men who came to get him had convinced him....

They won Jared over, but he saw where it was going. Well, his kids started going down and joining in the fun. They couldn't find their way back, and they didn't want to come back either. But they were warned ("if you do"). Pretty soon there was only a small community left up on the hill, the righteous and holy ones.[891]

President Joseph Smith, Jr.: Sacrifice As a Type of the Redeemer[892]

It is reasonable to suppose that man departed from the first teachings, or instructions which he received from heaven in the first age, and refused by his disobedience to be governed by them.

Consequently, he formed such laws as best suited his own mind, or as he supposed, were best adapted to his situation. But that God has influenced man more or less since that time in the formation of law for His benefit we have no hesitancy in believing; for, as before remarked, being the source of all good, every just and equitable law was in a greater or less degree influenced by Him. And though man in his own wisdom would not admit the influence of a power superior to his own, yet for wise and great purposes, for the good and happiness of His creatures, God has instructed man to form wise and wholesome laws, since he had departed from Him and refused to be governed by those laws which God had given by His own voice from on high in the beginning. But notwithstanding the transgression, by which man had cut himself off from an immediate intercourse with his Maker without a Mediator, it appears that the great and glorious plan of His Redemption was previously provided; the sacrifice prepared; the Atonement wrought out in the mind and purpose of God, even in the person of the Son, through whom man was now to look for acceptance and through whose merits he was now taught that he alone could find redemption, since the word had been pronounced, "Unto dust [thou shalt] return."[893]

---

891   H. W. Nibley, *Teachings of the PGP*, p. 261; cf. S. C. Malan, *Adam and Eve*, 2:17, pp. 125-130; 2:20-21, pp. 133-140.
892   J. Smith, Jr., *Teachings*, 22 January 1834, pp. 58-59.
893   Moses 4:25.

But that man was not able himself to erect a system, or plan with power sufficient to free him from a destruction which awaited him is evident from the fact that God, as before remarked, prepared a sacrifice in the gift of His own Son who should be sent in due time, to prepare a way, or open a door through which man might enter into the Lord's presence, whence he had been cast out for disobedience. From time to time these glad tidings were sounded in the ears of men in different ages of the world down to the time of Messiah's coming. By faith in this Atonement or plan of Redemption, Abel offered to God a sacrifice that was accepted, which was the firstlings of the flock. Cain offered of the fruit of the ground, and was not accepted, because he could not do it in faith, he could have no faith, or could not exercise faith contrary to the plan of heaven. It must be shedding the blood of the Only Begotten to atone for man; for this was the plan of Redemption; and "without [the] shedding of blood [was] no remission";[894] and as the sacrifice was instituted for a type, by which man was to discern the great Sacrifice which God had prepared; to offer a sacrifice contrary to that, no faith could be exercised, because Redemption was not purchased in that way, nor the power of the Atonement instituted after that order; consequently Cain could have no faith; and whatsoever is not of faith, is sin. But Abel offered an acceptable sacrifice, by which he obtained witness that he was righteous, God Himself testifying of his gifts. Certainly, the shedding of the blood of a beast could be beneficial to no man, except it was done in imitation, or as a type, or explanation of what was to be offered through the gift of God Himself; and this performance done with an eye looking forward in faith on the power of that great Sacrifice for a remission of sins. But however various may have been, and may be at the present time, the opinions of men respecting the conduct of Abel, and the knowledge which he had on the subject of Atonement, it is evident in our minds, that he was instructed more fully in the plan than what the Bible speaks of, for how could he offer a sacrifice in faith, looking to God for a remission of his sins in the power of the great Atonement, without having been previously instructed in that plan? And further, if he was accepted of God, what were the ordinances performed further than the offering of the firstlings of the flock?

Elder Joseph Fielding Smith: Sacrifice Is to Place All upon the Altar[895]

Sacrifice does not mean that we are to inflict punishment upon ourselves. It does not mean that we are to be persecuted, or to deprive ourselves of comforts and blessings of mortal life, not in the least, but that we are willing to place upon the altar all things, even our lives, for the kingdom of God, and that we will accept in fulness all the principles of the gospel and put them into practice. Sacrifice of the world? Yes, if you want to call it such, and the things of the world, to a concentration of the mind and action upon the things of the kingdom of God.

Elder Lorenzo Snow: Through Sacrifice You Are Proven[896]

The priesthood was bestowed upon you, as upon the Son of God Himself, for no other purpose than that, through sacrifice, you might be proven, that, peradventure, at the last day, you might stand approved before God, and before perfect and holy beings;… it [is] necessary to forget self, and individual aggrandizement, and seek the interest of your brethren.

---

894   Hebrews 9:22.
895   J. F. Smith, Jr., *Discourse (1925)*, p. 76.
896   L. Snow, *5 April 1877*, p. 376.

Elder Neal A. Maxwell: Real Sacrifice[897]

… [R]eal, personal sacrifice never was placing an animal on the altar. Instead, it is a willingness to put the animal in us upon the altar and letting it be consumed! Such is the "sacrifice unto the Lord… of a broken heart and a contrite spirit,"[898] a prerequisite to taking up the cross, while giving "away all [our] sins" in order to "know God,"[899] for the denial of self precedes the full acceptance of Him.

Elder Bruce C. Hafen: Sacrifice of a Broken Heart and a Contrite Spirit[900]

To lay claim to the Savior's sacrifice, we, like Adam and Eve, must also obey and sacrifice. We must bring an offering that in some way approximates his own suffering—the sacrifice of a broken heart and a contrite spirit.[901]

The Savior's completion of His Atonement changed the nature of the law of sacrifice in a way that requires that our hearts be broken. Formerly, the Old Testament's law of sacrifice required literal animal sacrifices and burnt offerings. But after the Atonement fulfilled the law of Moses, Jesus explained to the Nephites that they should do away with animal sacrifices. Henceforth, He taught that whoever would come unto him with a broken heart and a contrite spirit, He would baptize with fire and with the Holy Ghost.[902]

Elder James E. Talmage believed that the physiological cause of Christ's death was, literally, a broken heart.[903] This element in our Lord's sacrifice suggests two differences between animal sacrifices and the sacrifice of a broken heart. First is the difference between offering one of our possessions, such as an animal, and offering our own hearts. Second, one who offers an unblemished animal, the firstling of a flock, acts in similitude of the Father's sacrifice of his unblemished, firstborn Son. By contrast, one who offers his own broken heart acts in similitude of the Son's terribly personal sacrifice of Himself. Thus, the figurative breaking of our own hearts, represented by our repentance and our faithful endurance of the mortal crucible—our own taste of a bitter cup—is a self-sacrifice that mirrors the Savior's own self-sacrifice. He is the Father's, and we are His. The Father is in Him, and He is in us.[904] Perhaps, in this sense only, those whose sacrificial attitude resembles His, even if only slightly, are prepared to be endowed with his grace.

In this sacrificial spirit, the righteous Saints who belong to the Holy One of Israel are those who have endured the crosses of the world and despised the shame of it.[905] These are the who shall inherit the kingdom of God and whose joy shall be full forever.[906]

---

897   N. A. Maxwell, *Deny*, p. 68.
898   D&C 59:8.
899   Alma 22:18.
900   B. C. Hafen, *Broken*, p. 32.
901   See, e.g., D&C 59:8.
902   3 Nephi 9:19-20.
903   J. E. Talmage, *Jesus the Christ*, ch. 35 n. 8, pp. 620-621. See also W. R. Litchfield, *Search*.
904   See John 17:21.
905   See Hebrews 12:2, 2 Nephi 9:18.
906   See 2 Nephi 9:18.

Truman G. Madsen: "Partakers of the Divine Nature"[907]

We are taught that by partaking of "things unfit,"[908] our first parents passed through the doors of mortality and in a measure lost touch with the divine realm. Can we reverse the process by taking of things fit?....

Such progression toward the divine is brought to pass in part through eating—specifically, eating sacramental elements.

One guide to this transformation is clear in Peter's writings. He speaks of the exceedingly great and precious promises of Christ and says that through the ordinances, we are "partakers of the divine nature"....[909]

Death came to Adam and Eve by eating, we can reverse the blows of death and attain a higher and higher resurrection. Food is not the enemy: food is what we not only need but what we are ("we are what we eat"). And what the Spirit is making of us.

C. S. Lewis: Three Kinds of People[910]

There are three kinds of people in the world. The first class is of those who live simply for their own sake and pleasure, regarding Man and Nature as so much raw material to be cut up into whatever shape may serve them... In the second class are those who acknowledge some other claim upon them—the will of God,... or the good of society—and honestly try to pursue their own interests no further than this claim will allow. They try to surrender to the higher claim as much as it demands, like men paying a tax, but hope, like other tax-payers, that what is left over will be enough for them to live on. Their life is divided, like a soldier's or a schoolboy's life, into time "on parade" and "off parade," "in school" and "out of school." But the third class is of those who can say like St. Paul that for them "to live is Christ."[911] These people have gotten rid of the tiresome business of adjusting the rival claims of Self and God by the simple expedient of rejecting the claims of Self altogether... The will of Christ no longer limits theirs; it is theirs. All their time, in belonging to Him, belongs also to them, for they are His.

C. S. Lewis: No Soul That Constantly Desires Joy Will Miss It[912]

There are only two kinds of people in the end: those who say to God, "Thy will be done,"[913] and those to whom God says, in the end, "Thy will be done." All that are in Hell, choose it. Without that self-choice there could be no Hell. No soul that seriously and constantly desires joy will ever miss it. Those who seek find. To those who knock it is opened.[914]

Kathleen Flake: Bound for Glory[915]

Where I come from, Jesus saves all but those who make a fully-informed choice not to be saved. These few naysayers—so far only one on the record, namely, Judas, who knew

---

907   T. G. Madsen, *Sacrament*, p. 147.
908   Cf. J. E. Talmage, *Jesus the Christ*, 3, p. 18.
909   2 Peter 1:4.
910   C. S. Lewis, *Three Kinds*, p. 315.
911   Philippians 1:21.
912   C. S. Lewis, *Divorce*, p. 72; cf. B. Young, *9 November 1856*, p. 111; B. Young, *17 February 1861*, p. 125.
913   Matthew 6:10, 26:42.
914   See Matthew 7:7.
915   K. Flake, *Bound for Glory*.

and rejected Jesus[916]—go to a place of "outer darkness,"[917] or a habitation without God and, hence, without glory. Everybody else is resurrected to various degrees of glory; their differences measured by the Pauline comparison of sun to moon to stars and all stages of light between.[918] The assignment of a habitation is based not directly on what we've done, but on what we want.[919] Or, more accurately, final judgment is based on what we have become through the choices we have made.[920] At the moment of judgment, we will have no choice but to be what we most genuinely are.[921] But, again, the worst that can happen to us in this schema is that we get what we are capable of wanting, though that may not always feel so good, as we know from our earthly experience.

Once one admits a belief in a divine judgment, the question of fairness necessarily arises. Millions never hear of the Christian gospel or are subject to circumstances that give them limited opportunity for moral development. Latter-day Saints believe the playing field is leveled by provision of a two-stage process in the afterlife: the first, called the "spirit world," allows for further preparation for the second (the degrees of glory), and the demarcation between the two is God's judgment.[922] Those who did not, in mortality, hear of Christ will be taught, and will have the choice of whether to be baptized.[923] In the next world, too, faith is an act of will and is not required for resurrection.[924] Once all have had the chance to make an informed decision, they are judged by God and inhabit the degree of glory commensurate with their choice.[925]

… Final judgment is based on that which humans can never know: the truest desires of the heart as crafted by choice and circumstance, susceptible to healing after death, and always bound for glory.

C. S. Lewis: Turning our Natural Loves into Charity[926]

The invitation to turn our natural loves into Charity is never lacking. It is provided by those frictions and frustrations that meet us in all of them; unmistakable evidence that (natural) love is not going to be "enough"—unmistakable, unless we are blinded by egotism. When we are, we use them absurdly. "If only I had been more fortunate in my children (that boy gets more like his father every day) I could have loved them perfectly." But every child is sometimes infuriating; most children are not infrequently odious. "If only my husband were more considerate, less lazy, less extravagant"… "If only my wife had fewer moods and more sense"… "If my father wasn't so infernally prosy and close-fisted." But in everyone, and of course in ourselves, there is that which requires forbearance, tolerance, forgiveness. The necessity of practicing these virtues first sets us, forces us, upon the attempt to turn—more strictly, to let God turn—our love into Charity. These frets and rubs are beneficial. It may even be that where there are fewest of them the conversion of natural love is most difficult. When they are plentiful the necessity is as fully satisfied and as little impeded as earthly conditions allow—to see that we must rise when all seems so well already—this may require

---

916   John 13:21-27, 17:12.
917   Matthew 22:13; D&C 76:43-48; 101:91; 133:76.
918   1 Corinthians 15:40-42; cf. D&C 76:96-98.
919   Alma 41:3; D&C 88:32-33; 137:9.
920   D. H. Oaks, *To Become*.
921   Alma 12:12-15.
922   Alma 40:11-26.
923   1 Corinthians 15:29; D&C 137:7-10; 138.
924   1 Corinthians 15:22.
925   D&C 88:27-32.
926   C. S. Lewis, *Loves*, Charity, pp. 186-187.

a subtler conversion and more delicate insight. In this way also it may be hard for "the rich" to enter the Kingdom.

Francis M. Gibbons: President Harold B. Lee and Pure Love[927]

It was… in Mexico City, at the Sunday morning session, that President Harold B. Lee was first sustained as the president of the Church in a public meeting.… [At] the concluding address of the conference at the end of the Sunday afternoon session…[928] he bore a fervent testimony and shared with the audience a sweet experience he had the day after he was ordained as the president of the Church. "As my wife and I kneeled in humble prayer," he said, "suddenly it seemed as though my mind and heart went out to all three million members throughout the world. I seemed to love every one of them, regardless of their nationality or their color, whether rich or poor or educated or not. I suddenly felt as though they all belonged to me, as though they were all my own brothers and sisters." In the spirit, the prophet extended his love and blessings to the audience, invoking the Spirit of the Lord to abide with them always.

The depth of feeling this experience and these words evoked are reminiscent of the spirit induced by the remarkable dream President Lee had shortly before the dedication of the Los Angeles Temple. And the overflowing love he felt for all members of the Church, as he kneeled with Sister Lee the morning following his ordination as the president of the Church, seems to have fulfilled the condition for prophetic worthiness defined by President David O. McKay in his prayer dedicating the Los Angeles Temple, which was echoed in President Lee's vivid dream.[929] What [President Lee] did or accomplished during his remarkable career does not define or explain that greatness. It is rather what he was or what he became that does so. That he spearheaded the welfare program, nurtured and shepherded the correlation program, and was the moving force behind the restructuring of the headquarters organizations, are extraordinary achievements, not to be disparaged. But they pale in comparison to the quality of genuine, universal love that at last found lodgement in the mind and heart of this prophet… This quality of love was evident in every aspect of his short tenure as the president of the Church. Those who associated with him, or who heard him speak, were conscious of it and felt its influence.

George F. Gibbs: True Wealth[930]

How well and truly has it been said, in defining true wealth, that it consisted in the number of things a man loved and blessed, and the number of things that love and bless him… How well it describes the wealth of the Patriarch, the man chosen and ordained of heaven to stand at the head of a numerous family! It was the kind of wealth, because it was the very choicest, that was promised to Abraham after he had been tried and proven. It is the heritage of all good and great men.

Hugh W. Nibley: The Dramatic and the Pragmatic in the Temple[931]

There are two parts to the temple ceremony, the dramatic and the pragmatic… The play is ended by the appearance of heavenly messengers who now bid farewell to the artifice of

---

927 F. M. Gibbons, *Harold B. Lee*, pp. 461-463.
928 H. B. Lee, 27 August 1972.
929 See *Endnote 5-69*, p. 450.
930 E. R. Snow, *Lorenzo Snow*, p. 473.
931 H. W. Nibley, *Drama*, pp. 36-37.

the antique theater and engage us in a new type of learning. Everything up to this point has been by way of explaining our position in this world…

But now comes the serious business of our temple. The antique temple drama ends in nothing. The stage lights go out and the house lights go up. Now we must be introduced to the rites and principles that will carry us far beyond this world. We are introduced to special messengers, teachers, and guides and told to pay heed to their counsel, which will continue to lead us on the path of life and salvation. Significantly, those instructions are all in the nature of restrictions and limitations to be set on what could be the exercise of unlimited power through unlimited time. Satan wanted power all for himself: "because that Satan… sought… that I should give unto him mine own power; by the power of mine Only Begotten, I caused that he should be cast down."[932] And so like the Ten Commandments the promises and covenants of the temple seem strangely negative to the vanity and arrogance of men. The first is obedience, the restraint on the individual's power. The second is restraint on possession of things; the eternal spirit cannot be attached to them—one must be willing to sacrifice. The third puts restraints on personal behavior, it mandates deportment, self-control to make oneself agreeable to all. The fourth is restraint on uncontrolled appetites, desires, and passions, for what could be more crippling on the path of eternal progression than those carnal obsessions which completely take over the mind and body? Finally, the fifth covenant is a limitation on the innate selfishness of the other four—everything you have must be set apart to the everlasting benefit of all.

But we cannot leave it here. Everything about the temple calls for conclusion and a decision; we cannot remain in limbo suspended between the two worlds. Whether we catch a glimpse of the inside of the temple as we approach it from without, or of the outside world once we are inside, they are worlds apart. Latter-day Saint temples have always provided a soothing transition to soften the culture shock, the passing from one existence to another. Gardens of almost unearthly beauty offer an easy and credible passage by sharing the essential qualities of both worlds, "most glorious and beautiful."

But the wonder is that everything about this experience is real. For seventy-two years I have gone to the temple and listened carefully to everything, and at no time could I say, "There is something wrong here; this is not the way it is!" On the contrary, the lesson is brought home with irresistible force that we do not know everything. There is wonder upon wonder awaiting. What the temple teaches is as real as the temple itself.

Hugh W. Nibley: What Does the Temple Teach Me?[933]

When I ask what the temple teaches me, the answer is loud and clear: to control my actions. That is self-discipline and that is what I promise to exercise with every covenant. The law of sacrifice requires me to do things I could more easily not do; the law of the gospel requires self-control in everyday situations, avoiding the same unseemly acts as are condemned in the instructions of the *Dead Sea Scrolls*, such as laughing too loudly, gossiping, and immodest dress. That chastity is nothing but self-control needs no argument. And the hardest of all, the law of consecration, can only be faced against sore temptation, and still confronts us with unresolved dilemmas. What I promise to do with every covenant is to order my life and, specifically, as it is fully laid out in the book of Moses for all the world to see, to do all that I do in the name of the Son, to "repent and call upon God in the name of the Son

---

932 Moses 4:3.
933 H. W. Nibley, *Sacred*, p. 34.

forevermore."[934] Note that the covenant is between me and the Father. I am to order my life, and no one else is to do it for me; the only judge of my behavior is the Father. Only the two of us know how I really qualify in this. We establish our agreement in the temple because it is a house of God. He takes over completely. It is in no sense an ordinary house. This should be borne in mind at all times, even to the forgetting of time and place.

Truman G. Madsen: The Temple Enables Blending of Spirit with Flesh[935]

The privilege of attending the house of God is in effect to have our physical beings brought into harmony with our spirit personalities… [A] testimony of President Lorenzo Snow [is] to the effect that participating in the temple ceremonies is the only way that the knowledge locked in one's spirit can become part of this flesh;[936] thus occurs that inseparable union, that blending, which makes possible a celestial resurrection. It is as if, if I may mix the figure, we are given in the house of God a patriarchal blessing to every organ and attribute and power of our being, a blessing that is to be fulfilled in this world and the next, keys and insights that can enable us to live a godly life in a very worldly world, protected—yes, even insulated—from the poisons and distortions that are everywhere.

Merlin G. Myers: The Efficacy of the Ordinances[937]

The efficacy of the ordinances mentioned in [D&C 1:15-23] springs from the fact that they represent eternal realities—the order of heaven. It is in them that the knowledge and power of godliness are manifest to men on earth. They facilitate for man access to these realities and thereby provide divine and sacred paradigms around which man can pattern his life. In the temple there is scarcely a relationship for which a model is not provided—relationships with God, with the earth and its whole web of life, between husband and wife, between parents and children, between siblings, and among men generally. These models or patterns allow us to see the earth, ourselves, and our bodies, with their marvelous creative capacities, as part of a divine order of things transcending the arbitrariness and transience of human arrangements. They allow man to become discretionary about his experiences and to mobilize his capacities with genuine conviction. They also facilitate a sense of community not available otherwise.

Hugh W. Nibley: The Law of Consecration

God has announced that He has a plan to prepare for himself special people and to make His church "independent above all other creatures beneath the celestial world."[938] We get as far as the word "independent" and, without reading another syllable farther, declare our resolution to get rich and thereby achieve the independence God wants us all to have.

But if God has a plan, why not let Him tell us what it is, instead of cutting Him off in the middle of a sentence the way Cain did when he saw that God's plan would interfere with his own plans for getting rich?[939]

---

934   Moses 5:8.
935   T. G. Madsen, *House*, pp. 280-281.
936   See *Endnote 5-70*, p. 451.
937   M. G. Myers, *Kinship*, p. 94.
938   D&C 78:14.
939   Moses 5:23-33.

MOSES 5

The Lord speaks of the Church's being "independent"—nothing about the individual; and of independence, but only of the powers here below "beneath the celestial world," not of orders from above. He makes it all very clear: It is my plan—not yours![940] "It is my purpose to provide for my saints, for all things are mine. But it must needs be done in mine own way,… that I, the Lord, have decreed to provide for my saints."[941] The plan is a heavenly one, given as a special blessing to the elect, God's own people, to set them apart from the rest of the world—there is no human invention about it. But that one word, "independent," is enough to set us off after the way of the world, interposing our own plan right in the middle of the sentence, so that it will look like his, not even bothering to consider what the Lord has in mind. And what do we come up with? Nothing in the world but the old familiar run-of-the-mill capitalism—the world's way after all. Is this what the Lord has been holding in reserve for his people?

"It must needs be done in mine own way," says the Lord, and in the very same sentence gives us as the essence of that plan, "that the poor shall be exalted, in that the rich are made low"[942]—all brought to the same economic level—so that we all have "sufficient for our needs," which is quite enough for anyone. The idea is "that you may be equal in the bonds of heavenly things, yea, and earthly things also.… For if ye are not equal in earthly things ye cannot be equal in obtaining heavenly things."[943] It is nothing more nor less than a redistribution of the wealth, for "it is not given that one man should possess that which is above another."[944] As Brigham Young put it, "the underlying principle… was that there should be no rich and no poor."[945]

Our difficulty with the law of consecration is a cultural one; since the days of Cain and Abel men have been pulled in two opposite directions, given a choice between two ways, representing what some have called "the mad force of the sun and the wise force of the earth."[946] The two contrasting cultures may be characterized as stable or stationary on the one hand, and acquisitive or expansive on the other hand—eternal vs. temporary, agrarian vs. hunting, cooperative vs. competitive, contemplative vs. execrated, seeking either wisdom or riches, and so on.[947] The law of consecration is that of a stable society; the law of the marketplace is that of an expansive, acquisitive, brittle, untrustworthy, predatory society.…

But where… is the progress [in stable societies], then? Do they progress? It is exciting and marvelous to see progress in the learning experience of each generation. As an unceasing stream of children enter the scene, they must learn it all from the beginning, and for them it is as fresh and new as the world in the Creation, and nothing is more delightful to their elders than to teach them and watch them learn and grow, while the teachers themselves discover wonder upon wonder, more than a lifetime can contain, both in the world around them and in the contemplative depths of their own minds. For these people, who seem to us to be stuck in a rut, the world is always changing, for they move with the miracle of the year and the revolutions of the heavens from one ambience to another. And beauty swallows them up all the time. They revel in it. They have to express themselves in prayer as they go out to their fields or come back. And this is common to all the great civilizations

---

940   D&C 78:14.
941   D&C 104:15-16.
942   D&C 104:16.
943   D&C 78:5-6.
944   D&C 49:20.
945   H. W. Nibley, *Weep*, pp. 371-372. I have been unable to find the source for the citation by Brigham Young.
946   See J. Brunhes, *Human Geography*, p. 7.
947   D&C 6:7.

of the past. To endure long enough to make a contribution, a culture had to be stable. In bad times of world crisis caused by major climatic changes, many were forced to become marauding nomads, the hordes of the steppes, the expansive warriors who made their final camp the capital of the world and sought to spread their empires over all people as their divine calling. Of course, that is the Roman heritage, and our heritage too....

What does every civilization leave behind? What is going to be the net product of our civilization? It's garbage, it's junk. You can see that, and it's mounting. It sounds rhetorical: we have to produce things (expand in producing); then we have to increase consumption, so we have to increase desire for things with advertising flimflam; then we have to consume very fast and discard a great deal, because there is available a new and improved version. So discarding goes on, as Congressman Wright pointed out recently: "The principal exports of the United States today are used packages and scraps." We are impatient of the slow ways of nature. We have to go faster and faster, and the biggest question has become the dumps.

In the last phase of World War II, I was in Heidelberg in the Sixth Army Group, writing up the daily intelligences. I had been there on my mission, and nobody had ever heard of such a thing as a garbage dump in Europe; yet here was a huge garbage dump. You knew the Americans had arrived—the Army. And everywhere the Americans were in occupation were the giant garbage dumps. Since then there have been garbage dumps everywhere; what our civilization leaves behind is garbage. Which is what happens everywhere. Rubble is all we have of any ancient civilization, as far as that goes; it's more sanitary now because it's been oxidized....

What do the other civilizations leave behind, the ones I call the stable ones? The ones after the manner of the old people. They leave themselves behind. Their next generation takes over and carries on. Time means nothing to them. It's an eternal order of the law. The law of consecration is an eternal order. We will just leave ourselves, the culture, behind, without any loss of product. People will have plenty to do and plenty to think of...

Great civilizations like the Egyptian or Greek left magnificent garbage, sometimes great stuff to look at. When Salt Lake City is leveled by a nuclear bomb, what will be left behind? What will future civilizations dig up? What will be worth even looking at or digging up? What will survive? The Lord says, "There is no end to my works or my words."[948] The civilization survives only on its words. That's what we have from the Greeks, the Egyptians, and the Hebrews. We have the scriptures. We have the Testaments. We have the Book of Mormon. What has survived is a voice from the dust speaking to us; that's all that has survived. We wouldn't even know that that civilization ever existed without the voice from the dust. That which survived is the word.[949]

C. S. Lewis: We Live in an Age of Campaigns[950]

In all previous ages that I can think of, the principal aim of rulers, except at rare and short intervals, was to keep their subjects quiet, to forestall or extinguish widespread excitement and persuade people to attend quietly to their several occupations. And on the whole their subjects agreed with them. They even prayed (in words that sound curiously old-fashioned) to be able to live "a peaceable life in all godliness and honesty" and "pass their time in rest

---

948   Moses 1:4.
949   H. W. Nibley, *Consecration*, pp. 448, 451-452, 483-484.
950   C. S. Lewis, *Descriptione*, pp. 8, 10-11.

and quietness." But now the organization of mass excitement seems to be almost the normal organ of political power. We live in an age of "appeals," "drives," and "campaigns"....

[The birth of the machines] lifts us at once into a region of change far above all that we have hitherto considered. For this is parallel to the great changes by which we divide epochs of pre-history. This is on a level with the change from stone to bronze, or from a pastoral to an agricultural economy. It alters Man's place in nature. The theme has been celebrated till we are all sick of it, so I will here say nothing about its economic and social consequences, immeasurable though they are. What concerns us more is its psychological effect. How has it come about that we use the highly emotive word "stagnation," with all its malodorous and malarial overtones, for what other ages would have called "permanence"? Why does the word "primitive" at once suggest to us clumsiness, inefficiency, barbarity? When our ancestors talked of the primitive church or the primitive purity of our constitution they meant nothing of that sort... Why does "latest" in advertisements mean "best"? ...I submit that what has imposed this climate of opinion so firmly on the human mind is a new archetypal image. It is the image of old machines being superseded by new and better ones. For in the world of machines the new most often really is better and the primitive really is the clumsy. And this image, potent in all our minds, reigns almost without rival in the minds of the uneducated. For to them, after their marriage and the births of their children, the very milestones of life are technical advances. From the old push-bike to the motor-bike and thence to the little car; from gramophone to radio and from radio to television; from the range to the stove; these are the very stages of their pilgrimage. But whether from this cause or from some other, assuredly that approach to life which has left these footprints on our language is the thing that separates us most sharply from our ancestors and whose absence would strike us as most alien if we could return to their world. Conversely, our assumption that everything is provisional and soon to be superseded, that the attainment of goods we have never yet had, rather than the defense and conservation of those we have already, is the cardinal business of life, would most shock and bewilder them if they could visit ours.[951]

Hugh W. Nibley: The Lesson of the Sixth Century BCE[952]

It is not without significance that Lehi counted among his contemporaries not only the greatest first names in science, and art, and politics, and even business—for Croesus belonged to his generation—but the most illustrious religious founders in history. Others are lost in the midst of history, but consider all these: Gautama Buddha, Confucius, Lao Tse, Vardhamana Mahavira (the founder of Jainism), Zarathustra, Pythagoras—all of Lehi's day... The only question has been about Zarathustra...[953]

... [A]ll these founders and religious men were seekers for light, and whatever degree of success they may have enjoyed, their lives are an eloquent commentary on the unparalleled display of physical, mental, and spiritual energy that renders the century of Lehi unique among all others. It was an unsettled age of big ideas and big projects, and time of individual enterprise and great private fortunes, flourishing precariously under the protection of great rival world powers, everlastingly intriguing and competing for markets and bases. A strange, tense, exciting, and very brief moment of history when everything was with the future. No other moment of history was more favorable for the transplanting of civilizations, so heavily burdened with the heritage of the past, or so rich in promise....

---

951   See *Endnote 5-71*, p. 451.
952   H. W. Nibley, *Lesson*.
953   See *Zoroastrian Texts*, p. 856.

MOSES 5

Here is a lesson for our own times: What would one have said of the future… success [of these efforts]? With so many great men, with such scientific and philosophical brains around, man will have learned all the secrets of nature and brought the Millennium. But let us visit the earth three hundred years later, and what do we find? There have been no great natural calamities, the vast majority of the race have enjoyed almost unbroken peace and security, wars are now being fought by small professional armies, things are pretty safe for other people—but where are the signs of progress we expected? Only in the accumulation of gadgets. There's a marvelous technical development, but it's already showing signs of decline… Gadgets have accumulated but brains have not. The world swarms with PhD's, bright, ambitious men, but there are no great men. For degrees are gadgets, and can be turned-out in any desired amount. Administration has become a fine art by the third century, but thinking has become a lost art. The third century B.C.E. was a world of technicians and educators, but as the educators made their courses easier and easier, the number of competent new technicians being turned-out became less and less. The slogans of "education for living" and "education for success" completely stifled research within two generations of Aristotle, and soon applied research followed suit. Even the modest minimum quota of technicians failed to reproduce itself, and so the amazingly advanced and sophisticated techniques of the ancients, useful and appreciated as they were, were all completely lost. Let that be a lesson for us.

Truman G. Madsen: The Meaning and Power of the Endowment[954]

When I was a graduate student in Los Angeles, California, I attended a meeting presided over by President McKay… [He] gave what I consider one of the greatest discourses ever given on the temple. In shorthand I took down one paragraph that I have quoted over and over. It changed me. This is the summation:

> Brothers and sisters, I believe there are few, even temple workers, who comprehend the full meaning and power of the temple endowment. Seen for what it is, it is the step-by-step ascent into the Eternal Presence. If our young people could but glimpse it, it would be the most powerful spiritual motivation of their lives.

I was staying at a cabin a distance away with an aunt who had abandoned the Church. In an earlier conversation, when I asked her how she felt about her previous temple experience, she was disparaging and even hostile.

I approached her with this question, "What do you think of David O. McKay?"

She replied, "I think he's one of the most Christlike men I've ever known of."

I then asked, "Would you be interested in what he said about the temple today?"

She said, "Yes."

And then I quoted the statement… above. After looking at the stars for a while she said to me, "Well maybe if I had listened reverently I might feel the same way."

When people have disparaged the temple ceremony in my hearing, I have often thought of that comment and of President McKay's impressive stature, and I have said to myself, How can anybody believe there is anything evil about temple ordinances when he looks at the

---

954   T. G. Madsen, *Presidents*, David O. McKay, pp. 269-270; cf. T. G. Madsen, *House*, p. 282.

prophet? President McKay was a man who had been in the temple every week for fifty years. And it showed.

Truman G. Madsen: Giving Our All in Covenant-Making[955]

The temple is a house of covenant-making. I recall in my own earlier days, just before my mission, when I began to understand how deep-reaching and far-reaching these covenants are; I remember shrinking in a way, inwardly, and saying, "I'm not ready… to make that kind of promise." I am now convinced… that the earlier you can give your whole heart to covenant-making, the greater can be your expectations of the Lord's blessings. I believe that as long as we say, sometimes dishonestly, "Well, I don't want to make a promise like that; I'm afraid I couldn't keep it," that's only beginning to get ready to think about anticipating, and it does not bring any strength. It's when you make a covenant in the presence of witnesses and even in the sense of the presence of God that the heavens begin "to shake for your good"[956]—when you mean it—[that] He promises with absolute conviction and trust in you, "I make the same covenant with you, and I will never break it."[957] Ultimately, He asks us to give our all in covenant-making, with the promise that then, and only then, He will give His all in our behalf.[958] Every blessing that is possible to receive will remain with us and [will continually increase] down the road in greater and greater fulfillment as we live. The… New and Everlasting Covenant centers in His sanctuary, the temple.

Truman G. Madsen: Begotten Through Christ[959]

Today the religious world often speaks of the "twice-born person," or of being a "born again Christian," not fully comprehending how complete is His promise to those who come to Him. It is one thing to have faith, and another to have repentance, but in the House of the Lord, His House, He requires of his children an outgoing covenant-making from the heart, and then makes promises, even more inclusive than those that come with the first principles and ordinances. When the Prophet Joseph Smith sent the first Twelve abroad to Britain, one of the instructions he gave is summed up in one sentence. He said, Brethren, "being born again, comes by the Spirit of God through ordinances."[960] And all ordinances, therefore, are channels of his Spirit. But the crowning ordinances are those of the Holy Temple. "Being born again, comes by the Spirit of God through ordinances"….

You have all been born as spirit children, and as such have a divine nature. You have now been born of mortal parents, and have been privileged, then, with a body, which is a step forward in your progression, not a step back… We are… to proceed to watch and pray, that it may be developed into the very likeness of our spirits, which are divine, and ultimately, then, to become, as it were, a product of another birth, which is the birth we call Jesus, who becomes, in the process of ordinances, our father. That's a proper use of the word "father" for Jesus, for he says in [D&C] 93:22, "all those who are begotten through me (through the ordinances) are partakers of the glory of the same (meaning his role as first-born), and are the Church of the Firstborn." Imagine. He has sacrificed for us in order that we can inherit what He alone could have claimed to be, the first-born. He's saying, "It will be as if you were [the first-born]; all of the blessings and powers that have been bestowed upon Me are now

---

955   T. G. Madsen, *Foundations*, pp. 2-3.
956   D&C 21:6.
957   See D&C 84:40.
958   See D&C 84:38.
959   T. G. Madsen, *Foundations*, pp. 2, 5-6.
960   J. Smith, Jr., *Teachings*, 2 July 1839, p. 162; cf. D&C 84:19-22.

transmitted to you, if you are willing to come to Me." They are "begotten through me" and are "partakers of the glory of the same."

…[T]here will be another birth ahead of us, and that's called the resurrection. And then the promise that we can be like him will be literal and complete.

Elder Bruce C. Hafen: A Disciple's Journey[961]

A disciple moves from darkness into light, which increases from the dim light of the stars to the moon and then to the brightness of the sun. Joseph Smith compared these heavenly bodies with the telestial, terrestrial, and celestial kingdoms. As the temple teaches, we can and should move toward that celestial light during mortality. We need not be of the world, even if we must live in the world.

Imagine that two vertical lines separate the stars, moon, and sun into three sections. Each line suggests a major transition as we move from one stage to the next. However, our journey is not rigidly sequential. Our experiences may move us back and forth.

Envision also two circles, each with a center point, located in stage one and in stage three. These circles represent the gravitational pull from the opposing poles of our journey. In the darkness of stage one, he who claims to be the god of this world exerts a constant force to hold us back from moving toward the light. As we cross the first barrier, we will leave the strongest satanic tugging—though he will always try to ensnare us wherever we are in the journey.

Reaching out from the center of light in stage three, Jesus also "entices"[962] us with a spiritual gravitational pull toward Him. Think of the father of the prodigal son, praying his son home. When the father saw his son coming from afar, the father "had compassion, and ran" to the boy "and fell on his neck, and kissed him."[963]

I compare that father to Christ, who is so eager for our return that He comes to meet and strengthen us all along our way. Nephi wrote, "It is by grace that we are saved, after all we can do."[964] Christ's running to us is a vivid symbol of that grace. We talk often in the Church about coming to Christ. Perhaps we should talk more about how Christ also comes to us. No matter where we are on that path, we are never lost to Him. We often sing "Who's on the Lord's side? Who?"[965] Let us also sing "Be still, my soul: The Lord is on *thy side*."[966] We never have more value in the Lord's sight than when we are feeling completely worthless.

Various terms describe this process. Mormon called a disciple a "true follower" of Christ[967]— one who follows the Son to return to the Father. Moroni said, "Come unto Christ, and be perfected in him."[968] Jesus asked, "What manner of men ought ye to be? . . . Even as I am."[969]

---

961 B. C. Hafen, *Disciple's Journey*, pp. 292-293, 297, 299, 301; cf. B. C. Hafen, *Anchored*, pp. 10-12, 16-17, 19, 22-23, 30-31.

962 See 2 Nephi 2:16, 9:31; Mosiah 3:19; Helaman 6:26, 7:16; Moroni 7:12-13.

963 Luke 15:20.

964 2 Nephi 25:23.

965 *Hymns (1985)*, #260.

966 *Hymns (1985)*, #124; emphasis added.

967 See Moroni 7:48.

968 Moroni 10:32; cf. v. 33.

969 3 Nephi 27:27.

Our Primary children sing "I'm trying to be like Jesus."[970] Whatever we call it, this journey is the gospel's central concern.

Some non-LDS observers of our Church think we haven't made this concept very clear. One of them said that while Mormons emphasize "Christ's dying for humanity," they don't go on and "link the Atonement to that part of the [LDS] 'plan of salvation' that involves progression toward godhood."[971] In other words, she thinks we haven't explained what the Atonement has to do with becoming like Jesus.

Another prominent observer recently chided us for not explaining in a public way what he called our "doctrine of the perfectibility of mankind into divine form."[972] In fact, however, the Restoration answers these questions with stunning clarity....

Let's clarify a point here that we sometimes miss. Some describe the entire spiritual growth process as faith, repentance, baptism, and the Holy Ghost—as if once we've received the Holy Ghost, the hard work is done and our exaltation is assured, so long as we don't do something seriously wrong. "Endure to the end," we say, as if that means relaxing in some eternal rocking chair.[973] God will just reel us in, like a fish hooked on a line. but it's not quite that simple.

On the contrary, receiving the Holy Ghost marks the *beginning* of our real spiritual growth, not the *end* of it.[974] Baptism and the Holy Ghost only let us enter "in by the gate."[975] Then the Holy Ghost leads us along the "strait and narrow path"[976] of becoming sanctified disciples—not as narrow spectators but by our straining every spiritual muscle, drinking in the power of temple ordinances, and feasting actively on Christ's words to nourish us in becoming ever more holy.[977] And the long-term goal of that journey is to become like Him.

Does the Atonement have anything to do with this higher, developmental part of the journey or is it limited to the forgiveness part? Moroni taught that Christ's grace helps us move well beyond forgiveness toward becoming like Him, or sanctified. He wrote, "Come unto Christ, and be perfected in him."[978]

So, after weeding out our worldly ways, Christ's perfecting grace helps us replace those weeds with the divine flowers of Christlike attributes. You might say He wants to plant a garden in us. But we must satisfy certain conditions for this growth to occur, just as we had to satisfy the condition of repentance in order to receive forgiveness....

As we approach the second barrier of sacrifice, we move symbolically from the moon to the sun. All of the moon's light is reflected from the sun—it is borrowed light.[979] Heber C. Kimball used to say that when life's greatest tests come, those who are living on borrowed light—the testimonies of others—will not be able to stand.[980] We need our own access to the light of the Son.

---

970   *New Songbook*, pp. 78-79.
971   J. Shipps, *Sojourner*, p. 112.
972   N. Feldman, *Mormonism*.
973   See *Endnote 5-72*, p. 451.
974   See *Endnote 5-73*, p. 452.
975   2 Nephi 31:18.
976   2 Nephi 31:19.
977   See 2 Nephi 32:3-6.
978   Moroni 10:32; see also v. 33.
979   See book of Abraham, Facsimile 2, figure 5.
980   O. F. Whitney, *Kimball*, pp. 446, 450.

Baptism represents the first sacrifice. The temple endowment represents the second sacrifice. The first sacrifice was about breaking out of Satan's orbit. The second one is about breaking fully into Christ's orbit, pulled by His gravitational power. The first sacrifice was mostly about giving up temporal things. The second one is about consecrating ourselves spiritually, holding back nothing. As Elder Maxwell said, the only thing we can give the Lord that He didn't already give us is our own will.[981] Seeking to be meek and lowly, disciples gladly offer God their will. As our children sing, "I feel my Savior's love…. / He knows I will follow him, / Give all my life to him."[982] And then what happens? In President Benson's words, "When obedience ceases to be an irritant and becomes our quest, in that moment God will endow us with power."[983]

….[S]anctification is the stage where we are not only with God, but like God—for only those who have become like Him can be with Him. Jesus said, "It is enough for the disciple that he *be* as his master."[984] This state of being is the hope, the vision, and the heart of a disciple's journey. Our deepest desire is, in the words of both John and Mormon, that "when he shall appear, we shall be like him."[985]

Being like Him means we possess His divine attributes, such as charity. Do we develop charity by our own power, or is it a gift from God? It is both. In the current BYU vernacular, we must be "fully invested" in Him—as he is fully invested in us. Only then will God "bestow" charity "upon all who are true followers of his Son."[986] We can't develop a Christlike love by ourselves, but we can do all in our power to become a "true follower"—meek, lowly of heart, and submissive to correction and affliction. Then the Comforter, the Holy Ghost, "filleth" us "with hope and perfect love, which… endureth [forever], when all the saints shall dwell with God."[987]

George Herbert: The Call[988]

Come, my Way, my Truth, my Life:
    Such a Way, as gives us breath:
Such a Truth, as ends all strife:
    Such a Life, as killeth death.

Come, my Light, my Feast, my Strength:
    Such a Light, as shows a feast:
Such a Feast, as mends in length:
    Such a Strength, as makes his guest.

Come, my Joy, my Love, my Heart:
    Such a Joy, as none can move:
Such a Love, as none can part:
    Such a Heart, as joys in love.

---

981 N. A. Maxwell, *Mentor*, p. 17.
982 *New Songbook*, pp. 74-75.
983 Cited in D. L. Staheli, *Obedience*, p. 82.
984 Matthew 10:25; emphasis added.
985 1 John 3:2; cf. v. 3. See also Moroni 7:48.
986 Moroni 7:48.
987 Moroni 8:26. Elder Hafen's full article includes an extended overview of doctrines relating to man's progress toward perfection.
988 G. Herbert, *Temple*, 125, p. 163. See *Endnote 6-48*, p. 507.

Endnotes

5-1   Whitmer had been previously called to assist with the work of translation.[989]

5-2   Reeves elaborates:

> Evidence supporting this point can be gathered from both the structural and exegetical scrutiny of the Masoretic text of Genesis. A structural examination swiftly reveals that the stories of Adam and Eve in the Garden and of Cain and Abel form almost perfect mirror-images:

Gen 2:4b-3:24	*Genesis 4:1-16*
Adam: 'worker'	Cain: 'worker'
within Eden	outside of Eden
admonished to avoid a type of action	admonished to avoid a type of action
does the action anyway	does the action anyway
in association with a woman	possibly over a woman[990]
question/response sequence	question/response sequence
result: death (mortality)	result: death (murder)
plus curses (including…)	plus curses (more than…)
expulsion	expulsion

> While both stories result in the manifestation of death, the deaths depicted are in no way equivalent. The death which results from Adam's disobedience may be a misfortune, but it is presented as a universal, natural, and even inevitable event which will eventually lay claim to all organic life… By contrast, the death introduced by Cain's homicide is a qualitatively different type of demise: it is individually plotted and targeted, and it represents an premature termination of a divinely-ordained determination of lifespan.[991]

> Gage analyzes parallels between the stories of Adam and Noah and their descendants, seeing "the record of postdiluvian history [being] stylized so as to be essentially a reduplicative chronicle of antediluvian history," with prophetic implications for "general apostasy and cosmic judgment" in the last days.[992]

5-3   Anderson further explains:

> The final editor of the Bible… [links] his account of Creation's beginnings with the end toward which Creation points, although the links are only apparent after the whole story has unfolded. Our own conceptions of Creation are far more scientific in outlook, and we expect Creation stories merely to disclose the rudiments of nature's origins. Not so the ancients. They told Creation stories with the primary purpose of providing a cosmic foundation for the meaning and purpose of human life. Creation of human life could not be understood fully without relating Creation to its appropriate *telos* or end…[993]

> In between the opening narratives about the creation of human beings and the end toward which this points—the election of Israel at Mt. Sinai—we find a lengthy set of stories about Israel's pre-Sinaitic ancestors. Unlike… myths of origin [from other cultures], the biblical story takes a long time before it discloses its ultimate aim. No doubt this delay is intentional; it allows Israel's appearance in the story—like her election itself—to emerge as a surprise, a completely unexpected event from the perspective of Genesis 1-11.…

> As scholars have long noted, the building of [the Tabernacle] parallels the creation of the world.… But the point is more profound than that of mere literary parallel. The construction of the Tabernacle is the climax of Creation. At Sinai, God descended to earth and drew Israel to himself. Creation remained unfinished until the day the Tabernacle was completed.[994]

5-4   Sarna notes the recurrence of the heptad as a prominent feature of this chapter: "Tying together these apparently discrete units are notices about the developments in civilization that each contains. These developments number seven in all: agriculture, sheep-breeding, urbanism, pastoralism, music, metallurgy, religion. The symbolic number seven is featured repeatedly: sevenfold vengeance is

---

989   D&C 26.

990   Ginzburg, accumulates references to this motif in rabbinic, Christian, and Muslim sources (L. Ginzberg, *Legends*, 5:138-139 n. 17; cf., e.g., E. Isaac, *1 Enoch*, 85:3, p. 63; G. W. E. Nickelsburg, *1 Enoch*, 85:3, p. 364; O. S. Wintermute, *Jubilees*, 4:1-9, p. 61).

991   J. C. Reeves, *Flowing Stream*.

992   W. A. Gage, *Gospel*, pp. 9, 14.

993   Cf. J. E. Faulconer, *Incarnation*.

994   G. A. Anderson, *Perfection*, pp. 200-202.

invoked;[995] Lamech is the seventh generation from Adam; his song refers to 'sevenfold' and 'seventy-seven'; the number of souls mentioned in all, from Adam to Lamech's offspring, is twice seven; and the name Abel appears seven times, as do also the word 'brother' and 'name.'"[996] See also Cassuto's discussion of numerical symmetries in this chapter which, in addition to other textual arguments, give credence to his view of a "decisive proof of the unity of the section and the completeness of its structure."[997]

5-5   A description of Adam and Eve was given by Zebedee Coltrin who, in company with the Prophet Joseph Smith and others, saw them in vision:

> The heavens gradually opened, and they saw a golden throne, on a circular foundation, something like a lighthouse, and on the throne were two aged personages, having white hair, and clothed in white garments. They were the two most beautiful and perfect specimens of mankind he ever saw. Joseph said, "They are our first parents, Adam and Eve." Adam was a broad-shouldered man, and Eve as a woman, was large in proportion.[998]

In the *Apocalypse of Paul*, the apostle ascends to heaven where he is introduced to a series of prophets and saints. He also uses the term "beautiful" to describe Adam: "And I looked and saw another who surpassed them all, very beautiful. And I said to the angel: Who is this, my lord? He said to me: This is Adam, the father of you all."[999]

5-6   For summaries of LDS and ancient teachings about Adam, see Bailey, Palmer, and Turner.[1000] McConkie and Millet have also published a collection of LDS readings relating to Adam.[1001]

5-7   Concerning Genesis 2-3, Brueggemann writes: "It has been assumed that this is a decisive text for the Bible and that it states the premise for all that follows. In fact, this is an exceedingly marginal text. No clear subsequent reference to it is made in the Old Testament, though there are perhaps links in Ezekiel 28."[1002] However, Stordalen rebuts the some of the "common scholarly presumptions" that have led to such a view, observing that: "For the unprepared reader…, the apprehension of Genesis 2-3 as a marginal story is bound to be a surprise."[1003] He cites the many well-documented Old Testament references to themes in these chapters.[1004] In addition, he notes long-standing arguments that "motives from the Eden story appear in so-called eschatological passages in prophetic books."[1005] Overall, Stordalen's exhaustive study provides an impressive refutation of Brueggemann's thesis.

See Pritchett[1006] for a discussion of biblical passages[1007] that seem to fit well with Lehi's preexilic understanding of the Fall. Significantly, three of these four scriptures (Hosea being the exception) "mention the Fall of Adam in close connection with the fall of Satan," just as 2 Nephi 2, Moses 4, and the Islamic literature do. Pritchett concludes that although "the Old Testament never refers to Adam's sin by using the word 'Fall,' it does teach or reflect the following basic elements of this doctrine in various scriptures: (1) that Adam's sin resulted in a metamorphosis from immortality to mortality, (2) that mankind inherited its mortal state from Adam, (3) that all mankind has fallen into sin, and (4) that evil and suffering in the world could be for man's benefit as well as his punishment."[1008]

5-8   A Coptic text asserts that Satan formerly held this office.[1009]

5-9   Callender cites Job 15:7-9 and 38:4-7 as evidence that Adam was seen anciently as a son of God and a member of the premortal council.[1010]

5-10   Roper cites the *Book of the Rolls*, which "explains that before his fall, 'Adam was king, priest, and

995 Moses 5:40, 48.
996 N. M. Sarna, *Genesis*, p. 31.
997 See U. Cassuto, *Adam to Noah*, pp. 190-195.
998 *Salt Lake School*, p. 45.
999 *Apocalypse of Paul*, 51, in E. Hennecke, *et al.*, *NT Apocrypha*, 2:795. See descriptions of Seth as "beautiful" in *Commentary* 6:10-a, p. 482.
1000 A. A. Bailey, *LDS Adam*; M. J. Palmer, *Ancient Adam*; R. Turner, *Adam*.
1001 J. F. McConkie, *et al.*, *Adam*.
1002 W. Brueggemann, *Genesis*, p. 41.
1003 T. Stordalen, *Echoes*, p. 21.
1004 Genesis 13:10; Isaiah 51:3; Ezekiel 28:11-19, 31:1-18, 36:35; Joel 2:3, Proverbs 3:18, 11:30, 13:12, 15:4; and LXX Isaiah 65:22.
1005 T. Stordalen, *Echoes*, p. 22.
1006 B. M. Pritchett, Jr., *Lehi's Theology*. See 2 Nephi 2.
1007 E.g., Psalm 82:7; Hosea 6:7; Job 31:33; Ezekiel 28:11–19.
1008 B. M. Pritchett, Jr., *Lehi's Theology*, p. 77.
1009 See *Excursus 21: The Power and Premortal Status of Satan,* p. 575.
1010 D. E. Callender, *Adam*, pp. 137-160.

MOSES 5

prophet.' After his Fall he is told, 'Adam! Do not grieve, for I will restore thee to thine inheritance, out of which thy rebellion has brought thee.' That is, he will be restored as a king and a priest."[1011] The Clementine *Recognitions* says that this status was conferred upon Adam through an anointing "from the Tree of Life."[1012]

5-11 Roper cites a study where "Munoa demonstrates that the enthroned figures of Abel and Adam portrayed in this text are influenced by the descriptions in Daniel chapter 7 and that Adam in the *Testament of Abraham* should be understood to represent the ancient of days, agreeing with Joseph Smith's teaching that Adam was the 'Ancient of Days.'"[1013] In addition, Roper notes that Munoa cites "texts which prove that the [exalted] status granted to a figure like Adam could be held by others."[1014]

5-12 See Seaich for an argument that the term "Hebrew" was used as a "code expression" idea of a wanderer on a spiritual journey of "cultic migration" in some strains of Judaism and early Christianity.[1015]

5-13 An excellent, though somewhat dated, overview of the extracanonical Adam literature for LDS readers can be found in Robinson.[1016]

5-14 Similarly, Stordalen observes:

Within the story world, what happened to Adam and Eve took effect for all their descendants. Not only are these two the ancestors of humankind. They are also typical figures, acting and speaking in ways which disclose human predispositions and character. The Eden story would indeed seem preoccupied with present human existence.[1017]

Speaking more generally about the "timeless unity" of such accounts, Klauck observes that the fact that they are "in principle not bound to any unique historical event makes it easier to conceive of a continual recapitulation of the sequence of events, thereby giving the initiand the possibility of entering into this cyclical sequence."[1018]

5-15 The doctrine of the "Two Ways," which goes back in its current form at least to the time of the early Christian *Didache* (ca. 60-150 CE),[1019] should be distinguished from the metaphysical dualism espoused by, for example, the followers of Mani.[1020]

5-16 Nibley writes elsewhere:

The test for this life is not for knowledge; it is not for intelligence, or for courage, or for anything like that. That would be a huge joke. None of us knows very much, none of us is very brave, none of us is very strong, none of us is very smart. We would flunk those tests terribly… [There are] two things and the only two things we are good at: we can forgive and we can repent. These are the two things the angels envy us for, as the church fathers said… Of course, that is the whole thing in the Gospel. "Wherefore [the first word to Adam],… thou shalt repent and call upon God in the name of the Son forevermore."[1021] When the Lord came to the Nephites, among his first words to them were these: "This is the gospel, that the Father commandeth all men, everywhere, to repent."[1022] This is not a popular doctrine. In my thirty-five years at BYU, I have heard only one sermon (given by Stephen L Richards, incidentally) on repentance. And it was not well-received. "Don't tell us to repent. Repentance is for the bad guys." But [all] must repent constantly, each for himself. You can't repent another person. Ezekiel 38:18-19 defines a righteous man. Who is righteous? Anyone who is repenting. No matter how bad he has been, if he is repenting he is a righteous man. There is hope for him. And no matter how good he has been all his life, if he is not repenting, he is a wicked man. The difference is which way you are facing. The man on the top of the stairs facing down is

1011 M. Roper, *Adam*; cf. E. A. W. Budge, *Cave*, p. 53; Timothy of Alexandria, *Abbaton*, pp. 198-199.
1012 F. S. Jones, *Recognitions*, 1.46.1-1.47.1, pp. 77-79.
1013 M. Roper, *Adam*; cf. P. B. Munoa, *Four Powers*, ch. 3, pp. 43-81; D&C 27:11, 116:1. See also *Commentary* 1:34-a, p. 66.
1014 P. B. Munoa, *Four Powers*, p. 82. See also J. E. Seaich, *Ancient Texts 1995*, pp. 206-207.
1015 J. E. Seaich, *Ancient Texts 1995*, pp. 812-817, 870-875.
1016 S. E. Robinson, *Book of Adam*.
1017 T. Stordalen, *Echoes*, p. 301.
1018 H.-J. Klauck, *Context*, p. 89.
1019 B. D. Ehrman, *Didache*, 1-6, pp. 314-315.
1020 I. Gardner, *et al.*, *Manichaean*, pp. 182-187; A. Welburn, *Mani*, pp. 159-168.
1021 Moses 5:8.
1022 3 Nephi 11:32.

much worse off than the man on the bottom step who is facing up. The direction we are facing, that is repentance; and that is what determines whether we are good or bad.[1023]

5-17   "All have fallen," affirms Nibley, "but how far we fall depends on us."[1024]

5-18   Seaich summarizes literature alluding to the possibility of a temple drama having been presented in the Jerusalem temple.[1025]

5-19   Nibley writes elsewhere:

> And when Abraham prayed at his altar, "Have mercy, show me, teach me, give to thy servant light and knowledge thou hast promised to send him!" Satan promptly appears on the scene with an insolent "Here I am!" And as he began to teach Abraham, a true messenger from God arrived and cast Satan out and proceeded with the proper instructions.[1026]

In Egyptian literature, this same character appears as the "false Horus" "preserved in Spell 312 of the *Coffin Texts*[1027] and the 78th chapter of the *Book of the Dead*"[1028]:

> The scene opens with the King as Osiris lying helpless on the lion couch, calling upon the Most High God to deliver him from his plight; in reply to his prayer a Messenger (angel) appears in the form of a hawk[1029] and offers to save him; but the messenger has neither the power nor the authority—he must go up to heaven to get the proper authorization from the Lord of All. While he is away a false Horus—a comic character according to some—appears and boasts of his power and glory, offering to deliver the victim on the couch. A few questions dealing with the mysteries of the veil soon expose him as an ignoramus and a fraud, and the real Horus appears, while a voice from heaven attests his *bona fides*, and the hero on the bed is delivered.[1030]

5-20   Elsewhere Nibley gives the fitting name of "Satan's Golden Question"[1031] to the Devil's taunting query ("Have you any money?").

5-21   Nibley notes: "To Moses, [Satan] even claims to be the Son of God;[1032] he speaks only with reverence of the Father as his father."[1033]

5-22   C. S. Lewis observes:

> Milton was right... The choice of every lost soul can be expressed in the words "Better to reign in Hell than serve in Heaven."[1034] There is always something they insist on keeping, even at the price of misery. There is always something they prefer to joy — that is, to reality. [You] see it easily enough in a spoiled child that would sooner miss its play and its supper than say it was sorry and be friends.[1035]

5-23   Of Adam's baptism, Ephrem the Syrian wrote: "In baptism Adam found again / that glory that was among the trees of Eden. / He went down, and received it out of the water; / he put it on, and went up and was adorned therein... Man fell in the midst of Paradise, / and in baptism compassion restored him.... They clothed themselves with leaves of necessity; / but the Merciful had pity on their beauty, / and instead of leaves of trees, / He clothed them with glory in the water."[1036]

Roper cites Mandaean accounts:

1023 H. W. Nibley, *Funeral*, p. 301.
1024 H. W. Nibley, *Patriarchy*, p. 93.
1025 J. E. Seaich, *Ancient Texts 1995*, pp. 809-812.
1026 H. W. Nibley, *Prayer Circle*, p. 64; see P. Alexander, *3 Enoch*, 14:9-14, p. 696. About the three messengers, see *Figure* 5-9, p. 339 and *Figure* 5-10, p. 340.
1027 R. O. Faulkner, *Coffin*, Spell 312, pp. 229-233.
1028 R. O. Faulkner, *et al.*, *Book of the Dead*, Spell 78, pp. 74-78.
1029 Cf. book of Abraham Facsimile 1.
1030 H. W. Nibley, *The Three Facsimiles from the Book of Abraham*, p. 4. See also H. W. Nibley, *New Look*, August 1969, pp. 76-80; H. W. Nibley, *Approach to Abraham*, pp. 279-287.
1031 H. W. Nibley, *Autobiography*, p. xxi.
1032 Moses 1:19.
1033 H. W. Nibley, *Dominion*, n. 41, p. 21.
1034 Cf. J. Milton, *Paradise Lost*, 1:261, p. 22.
1035 C. S. Lewis, *Divorce*, p. 69.
1036 Ephrem the Syrian, *Epiphany*, 12:1, 4, p. 282.

MOSES 5

In Mandaean teaching an Hibil-Ziua,[1037] an *uthra* or angel was sent from God to teach Adam and baptize him. "This is the baptism wherewith Adam the first man was baptized by Hibil-Ziua…. Any man who has strength thereto and who loveth his soul, let him come and go down into the Jordan, be baptized, receive the pure sign, put on robes of radiant light and set a fresh wreath upon his head.' And Adam descended into the Jordan and submerged himself thrice." When Adam came up out of the water the heavenly messenger took him by the right hand. "And he grasped his hand in *kushta*[1038] and seated him before him and recited the sealing prayers…. This is the limit (end) of the baptism which came into this world, the (baptism) wherewith Hibil-Ziua baptized Adam and first man, and it was preserved in the ages for the elect righteous for it was written down in the scroll."[1039] In Mandaean Book of Adam, called the *Ginza*, an angel teaches Adam the way back to his heavenly home, "When he [Adam] heard this from him he was overjoyed. He himself had brought him hither and (now) he became his guide to the other world. He undressed him (and) clothed him with his garment, he escorted him, made him ascend, and set him up in the House of the Mighty (Life). He took him by the right hand and put him in charge of his own treasurers."[1040]

5-24   The *Conflict of Adam and Eve with Satan* recounts the baptisms of Adam and Eve in more specific detail.[1041] Like earlier accounts, Satan tempts them to leave the water before the required number of days has been accomplished, however the primary thrust of the larger story is that Adam and Eve must stay in the "Cave of Treasures" for forty days.[1042]

5-25   In other versions of this story, "the difficulty was darkness: they lost the Paradisiacal light. Outside the Garden, the sun set and when it grew dark, they became afraid. Satan came and promised them that, if they signed a contract… with him, he would bring the light."[1043]

In the Armenian *Expulsion of Adam from the Garden* text, Adam promises to Satan: "Until the unbegotten is born and the immortal dies, we and all our offspring will be your servants."[1044] These seemingly impossible conditions are, of course, fulfilled in Christ who, in the most common versions of the story, is portrayed at his baptism as treading underfoot the serpents guarding the contract in the Jordan River.[1045] In other versions, the *cheirograph* is torn during Christ's descent into Hades/ Limbo—depictions of the event sometimes show one half of it remaining in Christ's hand and the other in Satan's. (Sometimes a scroll is shown in Christ's hand as he descends—this object perhaps representing a conflation of the *cheirograph* with the idea of a written gospel that He was to preach to the dead.[1046]) Not infrequently, the accounts of the Christ's baptism and his descent into the realm of the dead are combined in some fashion.[1047]

5-26   The Devil's assertion that he owns the earth echoes Luke's account of Satan's promise to give Jesus the power and kingdoms of the world "for that is delivered unto me; and to whomsoever I will I give it."[1048] In turn, as Kelly observes,[1049] these words seem to be a mocking imitation of the Lord's statement to Jeremiah about His right to give the Earth to King Nebuchadnezzar: "I have made the earth… by my great power… and have given it unto whom it seemed meet unto me."[1050]

Kass cites Rousseau on the inherently "audacious and self-assertive" nature of any man who presumes ownership of the land:

> The first man who, having enclosed a piece of ground, to whom it occurred to say this is mine and found people sufficiently simple to believe him, was the true founder of civil society. How many crimes, wars, murders, how many miseries and horrors Mankind would have been spared by him

---

1037 Literally, Abel Splendor

1038 I.e., truth—an exchange of right hands in a truthful oath.

1039 E. S. Drower, *Prayerbook*, pp. 28-32.

1040 M. Roper, *Adam*. See W. Foerster, *Gnosis*, GL 18:1, pp. 201-202.

1041 S. C. Malan, *Adam and Eve*, 1:1, pp. 1-2; 1:32-33, pp. 34-36.

1042 *Ibid.*, 1:59, pp. 66-67. For an Islamic account of the baptism of Adam and Eve, see M. al-Kisa'i, *Tales*, p. 61.

1043 M. E. Stone, *Legend*, p. 150; cf. J. Goldin, *Fathers*, 1, p. 14; S. C. Malan, *Adam and Eve*, 1:11-16, pp. 12-18. See *Commentary 5:4-c*, p. 357.

1044 W. L. Lipscomb, *Expulsion*, 19, p. 139.

1045 M. E. Stone, *Adam's Contract*, pp. 22-24, 54-57.

1046 1 Peter 4:6.

1047 M. E. Stone, *Adam's Contract*, pp. 59-62. See *Excursus 37: Traditions About the Role of Abel*, p. 617.

1048 Luke 4:6.

1049 H. A. Kelly, *Satan*, pp. 96-97.

1050 Jeremiah 27:5; cf. L. C. L. Brenton, *Septuagint*, Jeremiah 34:5, p. 947.

who, pulling up the stakes or filling in the ditch, had cried out to his kind: Beware of listening to this imposter; you are lost if you forget that the fruits are everyone's and the Earth's no one's…[1051]

See also Rousseau's discussions of the mental prerequisites for agriculture, the connection of farming and metallurgy, and the link between landed property and the first rules of justice, as well as the contributions of property to vanity, inequality, domination, and war.[1052]

5-27 For a summary of a variant on the legend of the *cheirograph* where the agreement takes a somewhat different form, see *Excursus 37: Traditions About the Role of Abel*, p. 617.

5-28 The two events, of course, paralleled each other: Christ's death, descent into the world of spirits, and resurrection were prefigured by His going down into and coming up from the water at His baptism.[1053]

5-29 The translator comments that the royal purple constitutes "His attribute of mercy. The purple is said to be the place in which the names of martyrs are inscribed."[1054]

5-30 Elder Hafen sees the doctrines of justice and mercy as offering:

> … an analogy for the coming together of the masculine and the feminine. In his great discourse on justice and mercy, Alma describes justice as masculine and mercy as feminine: "Justice exerciseth all *his* demands, and also mercy claimeth all which is *her* own; and thus, none but the truly penitent are saved."[1055] This does not mean that women are not just, nor that men are not merciful. But in the masculine sense of justice and the feminine sense of mercy, we see interdependent principles that are reconciled by the higher unifying power of the Atonement. Here is perhaps a type of the way a husband and wife are unified by the combined male and female elements of a higher divine nature.[1056]

5-31 An old Jewish parable about justice and mercy deftly addresses the dilemma of how to simultaneously combine the attributes of Justice and Mercy:

> [A] king had two cups, and pondered that if he poured hot liquid into them they would crack, whereas if he poured cold liquid into them they would contract. Neither solution was just right, and so he determined to mix the two fluids, "and (the cups) stood (firm)." The implication of this parable is then drawn for the case at hand, and a mythic narrative is presented whereby the Holy One ponders at the problem of Creation. "If I create the world with the Attribute of Mercy, sins will multiply; (whereas if I do so) with the Attribute of Judgment, the world will not last. The only thing is for Me to create it with both attributes—and would that it might stand fast!"[1057]

5-32 Widely-varying conceptions of the Atonement have been formulated over the past centuries. However, this parable should not be interpreted as an effort to advance theological arguments about its doctrinal specifics.

5-33 For one to become a son of perdition, taught the Prophet Joseph Smith: "He has got to say that the sun does not shine while he sees it; he has got to deny Jesus Christ when the heavens have been opened unto him."[1058]

Said President Brigham Young: "Cain conversed with his God every day, and knew all about the plan of creating this earth, for his father told him. But, for the want of humility, and through jealousy, and an anxiety to possess the kingdom, and to have the whole of it under his own control, and not allow anybody else the right to say one word, what did he do? He killed his brother. Then the Lord put a mark on him."[1059]

5-34 Of Titian, one source asserts that:

1051 J.-J. Rousseau, *Inequality*, 2:1, p. 170.

1052 *Ibid.*, 1:22, pp. 151-152; 2:19-29, pp. 177-182; cf. L. R. Kass, *Wisdom*, p. 130 n. 10; *Commentary* 5:17-c, p. 370.

1053 See *Commentary* 1:1-b, p. 42 and 1:24-a, p. 59.

1054 W. G. Braude, *Rabbati*, p. 784n. 5.

1055 Alma 42:24, emphasis is Elder Hafen's.

1056 B. C. Hafen, *Covenant*, p. 177.

1057 M. Fishbane, *Myth*, pp. 100-101; cf. J. Neusner, *Genesis Rabbah 1*, 12:15, pp. 136-137; 13:3, pp. 133-134.

1058 J. Smith, Jr., *Teachings*, 7 April 1844, p. 358. See M. B. Brown, *Plan*, pp. 38, 50-51 for additional discussion.

1059 B. Young, *3 December 1854*, pp. 142-143.

... the general verdict has been that he is the greatest of painters, considered technically... [He] may properly be regarded as the greatest manipulator of paint in relation to color, tone, luminosity, richness, texture, surface and harmony, and with a view to the production of a pictorial whole conveying to the eye a true, dignified and beautiful impression of its general subject matter and of the objects of sense which form its constituent parts. In this sense Titian has never been deposed from his sovereignty in painting, nor can one forecast the time in which he will be deposed... Titian is a painter who by wondrous magic of genius and of art satisfies the eye, and through the eye the feelings — sometimes the mind.[1060]

5-35   In the spring of 1836, Elder David W. Patten is said to have encountered Cain as a wanderer in rural Tennessee.[1061] Reported secondhand several decades after the fact in a letter by Abraham O. Smoot to President Joseph F. Smith, there are several reasons to question the reliability of the account.[1062]

5-36   Like the book of Moses—and unlike Genesis—the *Qur'an* specifically highlights the need for revelation to guide mankind after the Fall. Seeing "the sending of Divine Revelation" as an "act of Divine mercy,"[1063] *Qur'an* 2:38 reads:

> "Get you down hence, all," We said. "When my guidance is revealed to you, those that follow My guidance shall have nothing to fear or to regret."[1064]

Of the closing words of this section, Ali comments that this statement is:

> ... a general law that Divine Revelation will be granted to the whole of humanity and prophets will appear everywhere from time to time, and that it would be by following the Guidance sent by God through His prophets that men will attain to perfection. This state of perfection is described as a state in which "no fear shall come upon them, nor shall they grieve." The man who truly follows the Divine Revelation shall have no fear of the Devil misleading him, for he has subjugated his devil, nor shall he grieve that he wasted the opportunity given him in this life, for he turned it to the best use.[1065]

5-37   Nibley discusses the theme of the "three men in white" elsewhere.[1066] His endnote cites Widengren[1067] and al-Tha'labi.[1068] Then he writes: "According to one Mandaean text, these men later lived on the earth as apostles"[1069]—regrettably without giving details on the Mandaean text to which he is referring. Nibley further alludes to the same theme elsewhere, though the footnotes in some instances are also insufficient:

> We read of another team of three men: "When Adam called upon God, the Great Spirit sent them from the land of brightness, those who would belong to the twelve."[1070] So at one time three of the apostles were sent down. These were the three, the pillars of the Church as described later in the New Testament in Galatians 2:9—Peter, James, and John.[1071] Whenever that expression is used—"The three who belonged to the twelve"—it means Peter, James, and John, who were hidden within the veil of light (Goodenough shows who they were[1072]). The three Sent Ones in another account are Michael, Raphael, and Gabriel.[1073] But if you go to the same account in the earlier Greek version, they are the Father, Michael, and the angels, when Jesus says, "I will come, and my Father, and Michael." So it's Elohim, Jehovah, and Michael (and all the angels); this is the highest committee.[1074]

1060 *Titian.*

1061 L. A. W. Wilson, *Patten*, p. 50.

1062 A. Allred, *Traditions*, pp. 38-39.

1063 M. M. Ali, *Qur'an*, fn. 57, p. 19.

1064 N. J. Dawood, *Koran*, 2:38, pp. 13-14.

1065 M. M. Ali, *Qur'an*, p. 21 n. 66a.

1066 E.g., H. W. Nibley, *Since*, pp. 155-156.

1067 G. Widengren, *Mandäer*, p. 86.

1068 Perhaps corresponding to the reference to three angels accompanying Adam in A. al-Tha'labi, *Lives*, p. 47.

1069 H. W. Nibley, *Since*, pp. 460-461 n. 47.

1070 Presumably the same Mandaean text referred to above (*Ginza Rba*?), but again no details allowing an identification of the source are given; cf. p. 308.

1071 Cf. Matthew 17:1.

1072 See, presumably, E. R. Goodenough, *Dura Symbolism*, 9:165-174, 10:95-97, 11:334.

1073 S. C. Malan, *Adam and Eve*, 29-31, pp. 31-33.

1074 H. W. Nibley, *Apocryphal*, p. 303; cf. H. W. Nibley, *Rediscovery*, fig. 47, p. 239 which was originally published in E. R. Goodenough, *Dura Symbolism*, 11:334.

Roper,[1075] summarizing the frequently cited Mandaean idea that identifies these messengers with Abel, Seth, and Enos/Enosh, writes as follows:

> … three angels are… found in the Mandaean Adam and Eve stories, where Manda d-Hiia, a kind of angelic Redeemer figure, sends three kingly angelic messengers, called *uthras* to teach Adam and Eve the rituals which are necessary for this life and which will help them to ascend back to the place where God the "Great Life" dwells. Kurt Rudolph notes that the fundamental mission of these messengers of light [is] to "instruct the faithful and redeem their souls."[1076] The leader Manda d-Hiia, whose name means the "Son of the Life" and who personifies redemptive knowledge, oversees the activities of the three, who in Mandaean traditions are called Hibil, Sitil, and Anos.[1077] These three function under his direction and are said to have appeared to Adam and other notable prophet figures of the past to reveal saving knowledge and sacred Mandaean rituals. ["[W]ith a single exception we find no cases in which the messengers of light appear in a historical setting."] "They are," to quote [Rudolph] "mythological figures who appear in particular generations and merely repeat the 'primeval revelation' made to Adam."[1078] They reveal to each generation, what was first and originally revealed to Adam in the beginning.

In the *Conflict of Adam and Eve with Satan*, the Lord sends three angels, Michael, Gabriel, and Raphael to Adam and bestow upon him gifts of gold, frankincense and myrrh, which Christ taught them were symbolic of God's kingship, suffering and death.[1079] Later, in one of his many attempts to deceive Adam, Satan and two other devils disguise themselves as angels of God in imitation of the three holy angels who had previously brought Adam these gifts. On this occasion Adam incorrectly believed that these three were the same angels who visited him before. "Because, when they came to Adam the first time, there came upon him from them, peace and joy, through their bringing him good tokens; so Adam thought that they were come a second time to give him other tokens for him to rejoice withal…. So when Adam heard these words he believed them, and said to these angels, 'Speak the word of God, that I may receive it.' And Satan said unto him, 'Swear, and promise me that thou wilt receive it.' Then Adam said, 'I know not how to swear and promise.' And Satan said to him, 'Hold out thy hand, and put it inside my hand.'" Then Adam held out his hand, and put it into Satan's hand. In this story, Adam and Eve are not married yet. So when Satan commands Adam to have sexual relations with Eve, Adam realizes that these are not angels from God and says, "'But God never spoke the words thou hast told me; and ye are not God's angels, nor yet sent from Him. But ye are devils, come to me under the false appearance of angels. Away from me; ye cursed of God!' And those devils fled from before Adam."[1080]

On several occasions, Wilford Woodruff described three unnamed angelic messengers dressed in white who protected him from the power of the Adversary.[1081]

5-38 Zlotowitz summarizes the teachings of the sages on this point:[1082]

> Rav Chama[1083] taught that it was the third day after Abraham's circumcision [the third day after an operation being the most painful for adults…] and God came and inquired after his welfare….[1084]

1075 M. Roper, *Adam.*

1076 K. Rudolph, *Coptic*, p. 136.

1077 Abel, Seth, and Enos/Enosh.

1078 W. Foerster, *Gnosis*, p. 137.

1079 S. C. Malan, *Adam and Eve*, 29-31, pp. 31-33. See *Excursus 53: Comparative Explorations: The Cave of Treasures*, p. 669.

1080 S. C. Malan, *Adam and Eve*, 70-71, pp. 84-87. See also *ibid.*, p. 211 n. 13: "… three pure Genii—Aebel, Anush, and Shetel [Abel, Enos/Enosh, Seth] were given [Adam] for companions…"

1081 W. Woodruff, *Journal*, 18 October 1840, 1:532; W. Woodruff, *Angels 1889*, p. 218; W. Woodruff, *Angels 1896*, p. 236; W. Woodruff, *Moses Thatcher*, p. 199; W. Woodruff, *Life*, 18 October 1840, p. 130. For other discussions of such messengers, see S. K. Brown, *Nag Hammadi*, p. 260; A. L. Gaskill, *Lost*, pp. 300-306; G. W. MacRae, *Adam 1983*, 2:1-2, p. 712; H. W. Nibley, *Since*, pp. 155-156; H. W. Nibley, *Teachings of the PGP*, 19, p. 233; S. E. Robinson, *Apocalypse of Adam*, 65:24-32, pp. 7-8. 11. See also *Commentary* 3:21-a, p. 180, and 5:6-b, p. 360.

1082 R. M. Zlotowitz *et al.*, *Bereishis*, 18:1-2, p. 624.

1083 *Bava Metzia*, 86b, cited in R. M. Zlotowitz *et al.*, *Bereishis*, 18:1-2, p. 624.

1084 "The general practice is not to visit the sick until the third day of their illness" (Nachalas Yaakov in Rashi, *Genesis Commentary*, 18:1, 2:174).

Rashi states in general terms "to visit the sick" rather than more specifically "to visit him," because…, God meant to establish a general precedent for man to emulate. Had Rashi stated that it was specifically to visit Abraham in his sickness, then people might be misled to construe that only the righteous ill are to be visited.

… God visited the convalescing Abraham to signify Divine approval of his compliance with God's command; the revelation itself constituting the reward for his obedience.

5-39 On the purported significations of the heat of the sun that day, see Matt and Zlotowitz.[1085]

5-40 Mizrachi notes: "The sick normally stay indoors. Abraham went outdoors so that he could offer hospitality to passing travelers."[1086]

5-41 Zlotowitz cites Ramban's observation: "In the literal sense, the *Torah* mentions that Abraham was sitting by the door of his tent to inform us that Abraham had not expected a prophetic vision. He had neither 'fallen on his face' [to make himself fit to receive prophecy,] nor was he engaged in prayer; it came upon him unexpectedly as a sign of favor…"[1087]

Legend further recounts that Abraham was sitting under the paradisiacal oak of Mamre when he received the visit of the three strangers. Sometimes identified with the Tree of Life, the oak was reputed to possess healing properties and powers that ultimately enabled Abraham to "rectify the world" in his day.[1088] Traditions speak of a nearby altar where ritual meals, offerings, and the receipt of divine oracles and revelations could take place.[1089] Religious devotions performed in such settings were an approved necessity in nomadic times, but were later condemned when they became a distorted substitute for temple worship.[1090]

Three sites in the vicinity of Hebron have been associated with the location of Abraham's tree. One of these locations, venerated since the beginning of the Middle Ages and located near the site the church of the Holy Trinity Monastery (Moskabia) built in 1871, is kept by the Russian Orthodox Church. Located about 1 km. west of the bypass road, it was subect of contention among the Palestinians and two different factions of the Russian Orthodox Church from 1997-2007.[1091] Israel Abrahams gave the following description of the site in 1912:

Abraham's Oak[1092] is still shown at Hebron, and one can well imagine how it was thought that this magnificent terebinth dated from Bible times. A few years ago it was a fresh, vigorous giant, but now it is quite decayed. The ruin began in 1853, when a large branch was broken off by the weight of the snow. Twelve years ago the Russian Archimandrite of Jerusalem purchased the land on which the tree stands, and naturally he took much care of the relic. In fact, he took too much care, for some people think that the low wall which the Russians erected as a safeguard round the Oak, has been the cause of the rapid decay that has since set in. Year by year the branches have dropped off, the snow and the lightning have had their victims. It is said that only two or three years ago one branch towards the East was still living, but when I saw it, the trunk was bare and bark-less, full of little worm-holes, and quite without a spark of vitality…

Abrahams' description still fits what I found in a visit to the site in May 2008.

Sites identified with the oak of Mamre at an earlier date include Jebel er-Rumeide and Ramet el-Khalil.[1093] At the latter location, poorly preserved Herodian, Roman, and Byzantine ruins can be seen, as well as signs of towers and walls from the Davidic kingdom and the early monarchy.[1094] About the site, Wilkinson writes:

1085 D. C. Matt, *Zohar 1*, Be-Reshit 1:21b, p. 162; R. M. Zlotowitz *et al.*, *Bereishis*, 18:1, pp. 126-127.

1086 *Sifsei Chachomim*, cited in Rashi, *Genesis Commentary*, 18:1, 2:174.

1087 Cited in R. M. Zlotowitz *et al.*, *Bereishis*, 18:1, p. 626.

1088 D. E. Callender, *Adam*, pp. 43ff; L. Ginzberg, *Legends*, 5:235 n. 137; H. Schwartz, *Tree*, 519, pp. 404-405. See also *Excursus 45: Impact of the "Black Death" on Art and Literature*, p. 640.

1089 T. Stordalen, *Echoes*, pp. 125-126.

1090 *Ibid.*, pp. 122-136. See, e.g., Deuteronomy 12:2; Isaiah 1:29; Hosea 4:13; cf. D&C 124:30. Other OT mentions of oaks possibly associated with a cultic function include Genesis 35:4; Judges 9:6, 37; 1 Samuel 10:3.

1091 *Russian Orthodox Church Outside Russia.*

1092 *Balut es-Sebat* = Oak of Rest.

1093 = Arabic "the high place of the Friend," i.e., Abraham; cf. Hebrew "Hebron" from *haver* = friend.

1094 C. Umhau Wolf, cited in Eusebius, *Onomasticon*, Section A, n. 5; *Mamre*.

The terebinth was reported by Josephus, to be very large, and to have been planted at the Creation of the world.[1095] Eusebius, while saying that it was still to be seen, told how the Gentiles worshipped it, and tells how Eutropia in reaction persuaded her son-in-law Constantine to build a Christian basilica there.[1096] The emperor said it was suitable for Christians to honor the place where Abraham entertained "two angels and the Savior." The existing site was a courtyard and a well, and Constantine added a small church at the eastern end.[1097]

See a drawing of the general plan of the church in the writings of Egeria.[1098] The account of the Bordeaux Pilgrim's visit is included in Egeria, *Travels*, 599, pp. 33-34. The site is located about 400 meters from the Glass Junction.[1099]

5-42 Clark adduces evidence that the senior one of these translated beings was Melchizedek, "who now resided in Enoch's translated city of Zion."[1100]

5-43 It would be impossible to keep the covenant made at baptism without divine help. Thus, as part of confirmation, the newly-baptized are given the Gift of the Holy Ghost. Explains Riddle: "The immediate reward to the covenanter [following baptism]… is that hands are then laid upon the person's head, he is blessed with the right to the constant companionship of the Holy Spirit, and he is commanded to receive that companionship unto himself. Only with the help received through that constant companionship can any individual keep the promises made in the waters of baptism."[1101] The purpose of the process of sanctification is to gradually endow the individual with the strength needed to fully resist temptation and to embrace holiness.[1102]

In his analysis of the use of the word "confirm" in the early days of the Restoration, Underwood reminds us that:

> … other translations of the Greek word *episterizo*, rendered "confirming" in the King James Version, include "strengthening," "establishing," and "consolidating." This hints at a richer understanding of the term "confirm" in the 1830s. To confirm someone was more than to ceremonially affirm their membership in the church. The link with an NT-based Christian discourse suggests that the 1830s usage retained the rich original connotation of confirmation as a means of spiritually strengthening and establishing the Saints through the conferral of the Holy Ghost. What happened when hands were laid on the head of a newly baptized convert was not the bestowal of two separate gifts (formal membership status and the gift of the Holy Ghost), but rather a single gift, which was expected to open the door to spiritual strength and stability.[1103]

5-44 Seeing the "pangs of hunger" of Adam and Eve, the Father is recorded in a Coptic text as saying to the Son:

> "If Thou art moved with compassion for the man whom We have created, and who has rejected My commandment, go Thou and give him Thine own flesh and let him eat thereof, for it is Thou Who has made Thyself his advocate." Then our Lord took a little piece of the flesh of His divine side, and rubbed it down into small pieces, and showed them to His Father. When God saw them He said to His Son, "Wait and I will give Thee some of My own flesh, which is invisible." Then God took a portion of His own body, and made it into a grain of wheat, and He sealed the grain in the middle with the seal wherewith He sealed the worlds of light, and then gave it to our Lord and told Him to give it to Michael, the archangel,[1104] who was to give it to Adam and teach him how to sow and reap it. Michael found Adam by the Jordan, who as he had eaten nothing for eight days was crying to God for food, and as soon as Adam received the grain of wheat, he ceased to cry out, and became strong, and his descendants have lived on wheat ever since. Water, wheat and the throne of God "are the equals of the Son of God."[1105]

1095 F. Josephus, *Wars*, 4:9:7, p. 542.

1096 Eusebius, *Onomasticon*, s.v., Arbo and s.v. Drus; Eusebius, *Constantine (1890)*, 3:51-53, pp. 533-534.

1097 J. Wilkinson, in Egeria, *Travels*, p. 22.

1098 Egeria, *Travels*, p. 23.

1099 *Hebron: Historical background*.

1100 E. D. Clark, *Blessings*, p. 173.

1101 C. C. Riddle, *New*, p. 231.

1102 See *Excursus 26: Justification and Sanctification*, p. 596.

1103 G. Underwood, *Discourse*, p. 33.

1104 Note the theme of delegation from the Father to the Son, then to Michael, and, finally, to His representative on earth.

1105 E. A. W. Budge, *Coptic Apocrypha*, cited in E. A. W. Budge, *Cave*, pp. 18-19 n. 1. See also *Commentary 3:9-i*, p.

MOSES 5

An Ethiopian source asserts that the Tree of Life "is the Body of Christ which none of the Seraphim touch without reverent awe."[1106] Note that the Egyptian Osiris was thought to have introduced wheat and the vine to mankind, and also saw wheat grains as having been formed from his body.

5-45   The book of Moses draws comparisons between natural birth and spiritual rebirth in the context of Enoch's sermon describing the forgiveness and baptism of Adam. However the later reference to "the words of eternal life"[1107] implies that additional ordinances were necessary to complete the process of sanctification: "inasmuch as ye were born into the world by water, and blood, and the spirit, which I have made, and so became of dust a living soul, even so ye must be born again into the kingdom of heaven of water, and of the Spirit, and be cleansed by blood, even the blood of mine Only Begotten; that ye might be sanctified from all sin, and enjoy the words of eternal life in this world, and eternal life in the world to come, even immortal glory."[1108]

5-46   Vladimir Lossky, an Orthodox theologian, expressed a similar thought when he wrote: "In effect, the revealed truth is not a dead letter but a living Word; it can be attained only in the church, through initiation by the 'mysteries' or sacraments into the 'mystery which hath been hid from ages and from generations, but now is made manifest to his saints.'"[1109]

5-47   The Prophet Joseph Smith made this remark in the context of his description of giving the fulness of temple ordinances for the first time to a select few in Nauvoo:

> … instructing them in the principles and order of the Priesthood, attending to washings, anointings, endowments, and the communication of keys pertaining to the Aaronic Priesthood, and so on to the highest order of the Melchizedek Priesthood, setting forth the order pertaining to the Ancient of Days, and all those plans and principles by which any one is enabled to secure the fulness of those blessings which have been prepared for the Church of the First Born, and come up and abide in the presence of the Elohim in the eternal worlds. In this council was instituted the ancient order of things for the first time in these last days. And the communications I made to this council were of things spiritual, and to be received only by the spiritual minded: and there was nothing made known to these men but what will be made known to all the Saints of the last days, so soon as they are prepared to receive, and a proper place is prepared to communicate them…[1110]

5-48   An Islamic source describes how the earthly temple, in direct communication with the throne of God, was given to Adam and Eve to restore the access to the presence of God that they had lost upon their expulsion from Eden:

> And when Allàh was now about to withdraw his presence for the whole of this life from Adam, the latter uttered so loud a cry, that the whole earth shook to its foundations: the All-merciful thereupon extended his clemency, and said, "Follow yonder cloud; it shall lead thee to the place which lies directly opposite my heavenly throne; build me a temple there, and when thou walkest around it, I shall be as near to thee as to the angels which encompass my throne!"[1111]

Lundquist explains "the intimate relationship" between "the role of covenant and law in ancient Israel" and the temple:

> [O]rder cannot exist, the earth cannot be made cosmic, society cannot function properly, law cannot be decreed, except in a temple established on earth that is the authentic and divinely revealed counterpart of a heavenly prototype.[1112] As J. Z. Smith has written so cogently for the *Enuma Elish*, it is "not so much a cosmogony as it is the myth of the creation of a temple." It is the creation of the temple, with its cosmic overtones, that founds and legitimizes the state or the society, which, in turn, makes possible the promulgation of law. Once promulgated in the ritual manner described, the law serves as the text of a covenant process carried out in front of the temple's pillars [representing "the ubiquitous trees of life that flank temple entrances and that border scenes of temple ritual,"[1113]] accompanied by animal sacrifice and a communal meal. All these features,

168, 4:25-a, p. 272, 5:2-a, p. 354, and *Excursus 42: Nebuchadnezzar's "Fall,"* p. 632. Cf. D&C 89:17.

1106   B. Mika'el, *Book*, p. 26.

1107   Cf. John 6:68, 17:8. See also book of Abraham, Facsimile 2, Figure 7.

1108   Moses 6:59.

1109   L. Ouspensky, *et al.*, *Icons*, p. 13; see Colossians 1:26.

1110   J. Smith, Jr., *Teachings*, 4 May 1842, p. 237.

1111   G. Weil, *Legends*, pp. 40-41.

1112   E.g., Isaiah 2:3.

1113   J. M. Lundquist, *Temple, Covenant, and Law*, p. 300; cf. T. Stordalen, *Echoes*, pp. 120-122.

so characteristic of ancient Near Eastern temple practice from earliest times, are embedded within the earliest traditions of Late Bronze Age community formation in biblical Israel.[1114]

5-49   Brown sees traces of ritual instruction in some of the *Nag Hammadi* texts: "For instance, one notes the strictly dialogue character of the *Gospel of Thomas*. It is a rather simple step to suggest that the dialogue may well have been memorized by one or more participants and then recited in front of a live audience as a means of teaching. Examples could be multiplied."[1115]

5-50   Welch defines as a "temple text":

> … one that contains the most sacred teachings of the plan of salvation that are not to be shared indiscriminately, and that ordains or otherwise conveys divine powers through ceremonial or symbolic means, together with commandments received by sacred oaths that allow the recipient to stand ritually in the presence of God. Several such texts are found in the Book of Mormon. In addition to the text of Ether 1-4 regarding the brother of Jared, the most notable are Jacob's speech in 2 Nephi 6-10, Benjamin's speech in Mosiah 1-6, Alma's words in Alma 12-13, and Jesus' teachings in 3 Nephi 11-18.[1116]

Nibley also analyzed a portion of the Joseph Smith Papyri as a temple text.[1117]

5-51   The recurrent thread of stories in these chapters of those who "hearkened not" could, of course, serve as a fitting counterpoint to the examples of those who kept their covenants.[1118]

5-52   Welch sees similar themes:

> … in the book of Leviticus, regarded by Jews as the most sacred of the five books of Moses. Its main concerns are implementing the law of sacrifice,[1119] bestowing the priesthood,[1120] assuring purity,[1121] holy living and loving one's neighbor,[1122] defining chastity,[1123] hallowing the sabbath days,[1124] eschewing blasphemy,[1125] and caring for the poor and consecrating property to the Lord.[1126] Not being steeped in the ethical and spiritual dimensions of the law of Moses, modern LDS readers tend to overlook the profound religious legacy of these underlying purposes of the law that have enduring relevance to the temple.[1127]

Nibley describes the sequence of rites and covenants as follows:

> To organize a race of priests in ancient as in modern days, God processed all volunteers by a series of preparatory steps. First, there is an initiatory stage in which one is physically set apart from the world: actually washed, anointed, given a protective garment, and clothed in sanctified robes. This is merely preliminary and qualifies one to proceed, in earnest not of what one has become, but of what one may and wishes to become.

> After the initiatory, the candidates are assembled and asked (and this we find in the *Dead Sea Scrolls* as well as in many other ancient works): "Do you agree and are you resolved to do things His way rather than your way—to follow the law of God?" The candidate is not told at this time what the law of God requires, only whether he is willing to trust God's judgment and accept it no matter what it is. After that, all argument is out of the question.

> Next the candidate is asked, "If so, will you be obedient to him no matter what he asks of you?"—a commitment to obedience before the demand is made.

1114 J. M. Lundquist, *Temple, Covenant, and Law*, pp. 302-303. See also H. W. Nibley, *Hierocentric*.

1115 S. K. Brown, *Nag Hammadi*, pp. 260, 275.

1116 J. W. Welch, *Temple in the Book of Mormon*, p. 301.

1117 H. W. Nibley, *Message 2005*.

1118 For references to the theme of hearkening, see Moses 4:4, 23; 5:16, 17, 23, 27, 57; 6:1, 52; 8:13, 15, 20, 21, 23, 24; JST Genesis 11:6; cf. 2 Nephi 9:28-29; Mosiah 3:19.

1119 Leviticus chs. 1-7, 17.

1120 Leviticus chs. 8-10.

1121 Leviticus chs. 11-16.

1122 Leviticus ch. 19.

1123 Leviticus ch. 20.

1124 Leviticus ch. 23.

1125 Leviticus ch. 24.

1126 Leviticus chs. 25-27.

1127 J. W. Welch, *Temple in the Book of Mormon*, pp. 374-375.

The next step is more specific and more serious: "Will you willingly sacrifice anything he asks for, including your own life?"

Whoever accepts this in the solemnity of the occasion may easily relax his resolve in days that follow, and so the next question is, "Will you at all times behave morally and soberly?"—that is, take all this very seriously, not just now but every day throughout your life. Thus a pattern of life is set to implement this. Your determination must be confirmed by your deportment at all times. This is the law of the gospel.

Finally God says, "Very well, this is what I want you to do."[1128] The next verse begins to describe the Ten Commandments, implemented by a strict and specific regime. It begins with general orders, to be observed all the times. The Ten Commandments are standing orders. What follows are the necessary steps to implement the law and put it into operation. The Book of Moses [i.e., the Pentateuch] is the law, the *Torah*. The prophets that follow don't add to the law; they but appeal to the people to observe it, to return to it, because the people, again and again, haven't been observing it. Whether Isaiah, Jeremiah, or the minor prophets, they decry the conditions of the people. They promise destruction. Why? Because the people have not kept the law. All the prophets promised that things would be wonderful if the people would only keep the law. That's the message of the prophets: Keep the law. It will be wonderful if you do, and terrible if you don't. This is the message. This is the one law that Moses gave.[1129]

5-53   Though differing in detail from the schema here described, a number of Jewish sources describe the similar process of the removal of the *Shekhinah*—representing God's presence—in seven stages:

> … as a result of the sins of subsequent generations. Thus the *Shekhinah* withdrew to the first heaven when Adam sinned, and withdrew further from this world following the sin of Cain, the generations of Enosh, the generation of the Flood, that of the Dispersion, that of the Sodomites, and that of the Egyptians in the days of Abraham… In *Pesikta de-Rav Kahana* 1:1, a process of return is also described.[1130] Thus, when Abraham arose, the *Shekhinah* came back from the seventh heaven to the sixth; likewise, the merits of Isaac, Jacob, Levi, Kehat, Amram, and Moses each brought the *Shekhinah* closer to the earth. So the erection of the Tabernacle was the final stage in a process of return that had begun in the time of Abraham.[1131]

Gileadi likewise finds a governing literary structure for the whole of the Book of Isaiah based on a view of Israel's past and future in relation to "the law of opposites, how one course of action leads to exaltation and another leads to damnation":[1132]

> Humiliation and exaltation are… represented as two alternative conditions that humanity may attain, the other categories of the Bifid Structure being incidental to or supportive of these two. The antithetical nature of each pair of themes reflects the principle of opposites or of "the two ways"— a kind of dualism found commonly in apocalyptic literature. These opposite human conditions originate as cursings and blessings promised by God in his covenant with his people Israel: the Lord's people may experience either benediction (exaltation, etc.) or malediction (humiliation, etc.), depending on their observance or transgression of the laws of the covenant.[1133]

> Although people throughout the earth's history have always chosen one path or the other, in the last days all peoples, Israelite and non-Israelite, will divide into these two categories… Thus, in the end, a separation occurs so that the righteous may be delivered when the wicked are destroyed.[1134]

5-54   Note that Adam and Eve were provided with coats of skin *before* they left the Garden of Eden.[1135]

5-55   In this connection, Nibley elsewhere cites the literature of the Greeks and Romans:

> A transitional figure between the ritual and the literary is Pluto of Hades, the god of wealth: "All the riches of gems and precious metals hidden beneath the earth are his, but he owns no property above ground." So he brutally kidnaps the fair Proserpine, who represents all the beauty and

---

1128 See Deuteronomy 5:6.
1129 H. W. Nibley, *Consecration*, pp. 424-425.
1130 W. G. Braude, *et al.*, *Kahana*, pp. 5-8.
1131 H. Schwartz, *Tree*, p. 51; cf. pp. 55-56.
1132 A. Gileadi, *Literary*, p. 32.
1133 *Ibid.*, pp. 38-39
1134 *Ibid.*, p. 250.
1135 Moses 4:27.

harmony of nature, to establish his claim over the earth; but the marriage is barren—Pluto can intimate and coerce, but like his Egyptian counterpart Seth he can neither beget nor create; what he buys with the treasures of the earth is nothing but a rule of blood and horror. But Greek comedy and Roman satire depict with agonizing frankness the irresistible success of Pluto's program in a decadent world. In Aristophanes' last play, *The Pluto*,[1136] Hermes the messenger of Zeus comes to earth as a prophet to denounce mankind for having turned from the worship of heaven to the worship of wealth or Pluto: "You have all committed a great sin," he says, "and must be destroyed." But seeing how well the people are living, he soon decides to change sides and asks for a job with the establishment.[1137] Next, the high priest of Zeus, finding himself unemployed, is forced to apply to Pluto for a job; what is his surprise when he finds none other than Zeus himself now working in the front office of Pluto, Inc. The cynical conclusion is that no one can resist Satan's bargain, and in the history of the world very few people have.[1138]

5-56 In writing about the Savior's Sermon at the Temple in 3 Nephi, Welch discusses similar prohibitions "against anger, ill-speaking, and ridicule of brethren":

… Jesus upgraded the old law against murder into a higher prohibition against becoming angry or speaking derisively or critically about one's brother: "Ye have heard that it hath been said by them of old time, and it is also written before you, that thou shalt not kill, and whosoever shall kill shall be in danger of the judgment of God; but I say unto you, that whosoever is angry with his brother shall be in danger of his judgment. And whosoever shall say to his brother, Raca, shall be in danger of the council; and whosoever shall say, Thou fool, shall be in danger of hell fire."[1139]

In the brotherhood of a priesthood setting, I interpret this as amounting especially to a prohibition against speaking evil against any other priesthood brother, let alone against God. In effect, it prohibits all manner of evil or unholy speaking against any brother, and thus all the more so against the Lord's anointed leaders. According to the Sermon at the Temple, anyone who is angry with a brother is said to be in danger of his judgment (the implication is that the offended person is a "brother" who has power to render judgment). Anyone who calls his brother "Raca" is in danger of being brought before "the council," that is, the elders in charge of administering the kingdom. Those who persist in such misconduct are in danger of hell fire. Since the word "Raca" means "empty-head," the thrust of this injunction is that laughing at a brother's foolishness (that is, what to a lay member may seem to be foolishness) is prohibited.

Such provisions and disciplinary procedures are especially pertinent to a community of covenanters, as the evidence that Manfred Weise and others have marshalled regarding rules of discipline at Qumran and in the earliest Christian community tends to show. According to one of the rules of the Dead Sea community found in the *Manual of Discipline* 7:8, "anger against a fellow-member of the society could not be tolerated under any circumstances" and they applied a punishment "in any case of a member harbouring angry feelings."[1140] Indeed, the *Manual of Discipline* 1:16-2:18 concludes its covenant-making ceremony by subjecting those who enter into the covenant unworthily to judgments of the community council and to punishments similar to those mentioned in Matthew 5:21-22.[1141] Weise argues that comparable councils were also convened in the early Church, as evidenced in 1 Corinthians 5:4-5, 1 Timothy 1:20, and the writings of Ignatius, specifically for the purpose of disciplining those who affronted Christ by insulting those people in whom Christ's spirit dwelt. Such deprecations are "not merely chidings in a banal sense, rather they insult to the core the community of God, viz., the covenant-community (*Verbundenheit*) of God. Therein lies their seriousness."[1142]

5-57 Welch further elaborates on the penalty for violation of this covenant:[1143]

1136 Aristophanes, *Plutus*.
1137 Cf. *Excursus 24: The Watchers*, p. 585.
1138 H. W. Nibley, *Dominion*, pp. 14-15.
1139 3 Nephi 12:21-22.
1140 See F. G. Martinez, *DSS Translated*, p. 11; G. Vermes, *Complete*, p. 107.
1141 see F. G. Martinez, *DSS Translated*, pp. 3-5; G. Vermes, *Complete*, pp. 99-100.
1142 J. W. Welch, *Sermon*, p. 49; cf. J. W. Welch, *Light*, pp. 83-86.
1143 J. W. Welch, *Sermon*, p. 52; cf. J. W. Welch, *Light*, pp. 96-98.

In committing to live by this law, the righteous bear a heavy responsibility and are symbolically crucified themselves—"wherein ye will take up your cross"...[1144] All references to plucking out the eye or to cutting off the hand that offends are absent in the Book of Mormon text, suggesting that this problematic verse in the Sermon on the Mount, on its face, does not fully reflect Jesus' original intent. Instead, the Sermon at the Temple speaks at this point of a total commitment—of the disciple taking up a symbolic cross, a symbol of capital punishment. This demands that the righteous strictly exercise the virtue of self-control, and it also reflects a warning that, if a person violates the law of chastity, the penalty will involve serious consequences. In particular, the disciple must be willing to deny himself these things and, in so doing, "cross" himself[1145] or, in Jesus' words, "take up your cross."[1146] The image this may bring to mind is that of a covenanter taking this obligation very seriously, for hanging or exposing a body on a tree or on a cross was part of the standard punishment under the law of Moses for any person who committed a sin worthy of death. This form of punishment was apparently known to the Nephites through the Brass Plates and the writings of the prophet Zenos.[1147] Deuteronomy 21:22 speaks of exposing the body of the culprit "on a tree," a practice observed by the Nephites,[1148] which Peter connected with the death of Jesus on the cross.[1149] Thus, with this teaching in the Sermon at the Temple, one possibly confronts the idea that the disciple must be willing to take upon himself the very form of mortal punishment that Jesus himself suffered. As a practical matter in early Christianity, the punishment of those violating this covenant of chastity probably took the form of excommunication, understanding being "cut off" in Matthew 5:30 as "a communal parable."

5-58   An Armenian text reports:

Satan's goal was to destroy humankind. When he saw that Adam did not die on account of the sin and that God did not get angry and destroy everybody because of Cain's deed, then he turned to other means. By means of the fault [of] lust[ing] after women, he inflamed the sons of Seth, and twenty men would die over one woman, killing one another.[1150]

Another source emphasizes the lures that the daughters of Cain invented in order to seduce the Sethites:

The daughters of Cain made sinful inventions, braids, coiffures, antimony and rouge. And they made various sorts of musical instruments, and they adorned themselves and their daughters, and they went to Mount Ahermon [where the sons of Seth and Enosh dwelled]. And after two hundred years of their ascesis [strict self-discipline], they (i.e., the Cainite women), having seduced them, caused them to descend from the mountain, and they mingled them with themselves promiscuously.[1151]

An Islamic account blames the musical innovations of Jubal and Tubal-Cain:

After five hundred years of the life of Yarad [Jared] had passed, the descendants of Shīth [Seth] violated the oaths and covenants which they had taken upon themselves, and they began to descend to the land wherein the descendants of Qābīl [Cain] dwelt. Their initial fall was occasioned by Satan taking the form of two "human Satans": the name of one was Yūbal [Jubal], and the other was named Tūbal-qīn [Tubal-Cain]. He taught them different sorts of melodies and music. Yūbal made flutes, mandolins, lutes, and horns, while Tūbal-qīn made drums, tambourines, and cymbals. The progeny of Qābīl had no work with which to busy themselves or to talk about except for (what) Satan (wanted). They began practicing forbidden acts and committing sins, and they would gather together to engage collectively in acts of moral depravity. Those of their men and women who were older were worse offenders in this than their younger ones. They would assemble together, play their instruments, beat the drums and tambourines, (strum) the lutes, (strike) the cymbals, shout, and laugh. (This ruckus continued) until a few of the descendants of Shīth [Seth]—the people of the mountain—heard their voices. One hundred men from among them came together for the purpose of descending to the progeny of Qābīl and determining the reason for the noise. When

1144 3 Nephi 12:30.
1145 Alma 39:9.
1146 3 Nephi 12:30.
1147 See 1 Nephi 19:13.
1148 See 3 Nephi 4:28.
1149 See Acts 10:39.
1150 M. E. Stone, *Abel*, 6:1-6:2, pp. 154-155.
1151 M. E. Stone, *Sermon Concerning Flood*, 4-6, pp. 177-178.

this news reached Yarad [Jared], he came to them and implored them—invoking God—to recall the injunction of their forefathers; he (also) adjured them by the blood of Hābīl [Abel]. Akhnūkh bin Yarad [Enoch, son of Jared] then stood up before them and said, "Know that those of you who defy our father Yarad and violate the oath of our ancestors by descending from our mountain will never again re-ascend (it)!" But they insisted on descending, and after they had descended, they consorted with the daughters of Qābīl and as a result committed shameless perversions.[1152]

5-59   With respect to the passage that says that the wicked husbands "took themselves wives,"[1153] Wright observes: "The idea that the *bene elohim* married the daughters of humanity… has been the consensus of scholarship for some time, but an examination of early Jewish sources seems to leave room for a different interpretation of the verse, one that reveals relationships outside the boundaries of matrimony."[1154]

5-60   Bushman sees the story of Enoch as being important to Joseph Smith because:

… like the vision of Moses, it bears on [his] prophetic identity. Later, when Joseph disguised his identity to elude his enemies, he took the name of Enoch as a pseudonym.[1155] As he was a modern Moses, so was he a modern Enoch. Enoch's call comes not on a high mountain like Moses', but in a voice from heaven… In a response that echoes Smith's unease about his own prophethood, Enoch protests, 'Why is it that I have found favour in thy Sight, and Am but a lad, & all the people hate me, for I am slow of speech: Wherefore am I thy Servent?'[1156] Joseph had been a boy, with no desire to preach, when he received his call.…

The Enoch narrative created a deep history for the young church. The revelation came while Oliver Cowdery and the missionaries to the Lamanites headed west to find a site for the City of Zion. The writings gave the little flock a pattern for their own city-building. Enoch's people dwelt in a city called Zion "because they were of one heart and of one mind, and dwelt in righteousness; and there was no poor among them," a city so righteous, it "was taken up into heaven."[1157] Though modeled after Enoch's Zion, Joseph's New Jerusalem was not to follow Enoch's "City of Holiness"[1158] into heaven. Quite the reverse. In Enoch's vision, latter-day people gather from all over the earth into a holy city, "called Zion, a New Jerusalem."[1159] Rather than rising, this city stays put, and Enoch's city descends from heaven to meet the people of the New Jerusalem on earth…[1160] The Millennium begins in a happy union of two holy peoples on a cleansed earth.[1161]

5-61   Elder Orson Pratt stated that: "No equality can be brought about by dividing property; the Lord never intended such an order of things. It is not a division of property that is going to bring about a oneness among the Latter-day Saints in temporal things, but it is a union of property, that all the property may be united, and considered belonging to the Lord, and to every individual in the whole Church, as joint heirs with Him, or as His stewards."[1162]

5-62   The weeping of the heavens parallels an earlier mention of God's weeping,[1163] a motif that has been explored elsewhere.[1164] Note, however, that in contrast to what has been concluded in previous LDS analyses of the passage, the text of OT2 depicts Enoch, rather than God, as the one who wept.[1165] In

1152 J. C. Reeves, *al-Yaqubi*. See also W. L. Lipscomb, *Seth*, 18-23, pp. 193-196. Cf. *Excursus 24: The Watchers*, p. 585.
1153 Moses 8:14; cf. 8:21.
1154 See A. T. Wright, *Evil Spirits*, pp. 133-136). See also *Commentary 5:44-a*, p. 392.
1155 D. J. Whittaker, *Substituted Names*.
1156 Moses 6:31, original spelling and punctuation retained.
1157 Moses 7:18, 21.
1158 Moses 7:19.
1159 Moses 7:62.
1160 Moses 7:63.
1161 R. L. Bushman, *Rough Stone*, pp. 138-139, 141.
1162 O. Pratt, *10 September 1854*, p. 100.
1163 Moses 7:28.
1164 E.g., E. England, *Weeping*; D. C. Peterson, *Weeping God*.
1165 "Enoch looked upon the residue of the people and wept. And he beheld and lo the heavens wept also and shed forth their tears as the rain upon the mountains. And Enoch said to the heavens…" (S. H. Faulring, *et al.*, *Original Manuscripts*, p. 618; K. P. Jackson, *Book of Moses*, p. 25) vs. "the God of heaven looked upon the residue of the people, and he wept; and Enoch bore record of it, saying: How is it that the heavens weep, and shed forth their tears as rain upon the mountains. And Enoch said unto the Lord…" (Moses 7:28). Moses 7:28 follows OT1 except in the following instance: "And Enoch said unto the heavens" (S. H. Faulring, *et al.*, *Original Manuscripts*, p. 106).

both versions, it is God who replies to *Enoch's* lament.[1166]

Corroborating the OT2 manuscript, a Manichaean text also describes a weeping Enoch:

> "I am Enoch the righteous. My sorrow was great, and a torrent of tears [streamed] from my eyes because I heard the insult which the wicked ones uttered."[1167]

We find such insulting words, of course, in the mouths of the antediluvians in Moses 8:21. Elsewhere, Enoch himself prophesied a future judgment upon the "ungodly sinners" who have "uttered hard speeches… against [the Lord]."[1168] Perhaps the most telling reference, however, is an ancient exegetical tradition cited by Reeves[1169] that associates the speech of Job in 21:7-15 "to events transpiring during the final years of the antediluvian era."[1170] Indeed, in one source these verses are directly linked to Enoch himself.[1171] In defiance of the Lord's entreaty to ""love one another, and… choose me, their Father,"[1172] the wicked are depicted as "say[ing] unto God":

> 14 … Depart from us: for we desire not the knowledge of thy ways.

> 15 What is the Almighty, that we should serve him? And what profit should we have if we pray unto him?[1173]

5-63   Robinson and Garrett elaborate:

> One's call is merely God's invitation to serve in his kingdom, however, one's election, or being chosen, is God's confirmation that one has responded worthily to that calling, has magnified it and used its power correctly, and is therefore worthy to continue exercising its powers and prerogatives in time and in eternity.

> It will be seen, then, that the time between one's calling and one's finally being chosen or elected is one's time of probation, or testing. In the furnace of persecution, many who have once been called to be Saints and even to help lead the Church have not endured. They had been called, but they "washed out" and so were not ultimately chosen. Without subsequent repentance… they could not be the Lord's elect or part of his chosen people. It will also be seen that one's election by God being made as sure and certain as one's calling amounts to the effective end of that person's individual probation, though it may not be the end of some pains and sorrows of mortality. For most Saints, this occurs after a lifetime of faithful endurance, though some receive this blessing while still in the flesh.[1174]

In his carefully-worded paraphrase of Paul's description of charity[1175] within the thirteenth Article of Faith,[1176] Joseph Smith pointedly distinguished between the Saints' previous attainments with respect to faith ("We believe all things") and hope ("we hope all things"), and their as yet unfulfilled aspirations with respect to charity. In their current state, their strivings for charity could accurately be characterized only in terms of a partial attainment and a yearning for the necessary strength to realize its perfection: "we have endured many things, and hope to be able to endure all things."

5-64   Speaking of the supreme virtues and temptations, Nibley writes:[1177]

> If the law of consecration is the supreme test of virtue—the final one—money is to be the supreme temptation to vice; sex runs a poor second, but on both counts, this is the time and place for us to meet the challenge of the flesh. It is the weakness of the flesh in both cases to prove our spirits stronger than the pull of matter, to assert our command over the new medium of physical bodies before proceeding onward to another state of existence. As Brigham Young often repeats,

1166 Moses 7:32.
1167 *Cologne Mani Codex* 58:6f., cited in J. C. Reeves, *Heralds*, p. 183.
1168 Jude 1:15; cf. E. Isaac, *1 Enoch*, 1:9, pp. 13-14. See also 2 Peter 2:5, which also labels this generation as "ungodly."
1169 E.g., M.-A. Ouaknin, *et al.*, *Rabbi Éliézer*, 22, pp. 134, 136. See J. C. Reeves, *Heralds*, p. 200 n. 17.
1170 J. C. Reeves, *Heralds*, p. 187.
1171 P. Alexander, *3 Enoch*, 4:3, p. 258.
1172 Moses 7:33.
1173 Cf. Exodus 5:2, Malachi 3:13-15, Mosiah 11:27, Moses 5:16.
1174 S. E. Robinson, *et al.*, *D&C Commentary*, 4:160; see 2 Peter 1:10, 18-19.
1175 1 Corinthians 13:7.
1176 Articles of Faith 1:13.
1177 H. W. Nibley, *Consecration*, pp. 434-435.

"God has given us the things of this world to see what we will do with them."[1178] The test will be whether we will set our hearts on the four things that lead to destruction. Whoever seeks for (1) wealth, (2) power, (3) popularity, and (4) the pleasures of the flesh—anyone who seeks those will be destroyed, says the Book of Mormon.[1179] Need we point out that those four things compose the whole substance of success in the present-day world. They are the things that money will get you.

5-65   Commenting on the *orans* gesture, Emminghaus writes:

> From the point of view of religious history, the lifting of the hands… is an expressive gesture of prayer to the "gods above"[1180]… General anthropology has… shown us that among all peoples, the offering and showing of the open palms, which therefore cannot hold weapons or anything dangerous, is a sign of peaceful intent… Thus open hands uplifted are a universal gesture of peace, confidence, and petition; in contrast, a clenched fist means threat and challenge to battle. In the Old Testament, lifting the hands to God,[1181] or toward the Temple[1182] was a universal custom.
>
> This Jewish gesture of prayer was apparently adopted by Christians for private as well as communal prayer. Tertullian refers to it:[1183] The Jews, because of their feelings of guilt, do not dare to lift their hands to Christ. "But we not only lift them, but even extend them, imitating the Lord's passion, as we also confess Christ in prayer." The oldest depiction of the crucifixion of Christ (still very muted, because otherwise so scandalous to Romans), on the wooden portals of Santa Sabina on the Aventine in Rome (6th c.) shows the crucified Lord with slightly bent arms and open, nailed hands, but without an express depiction of the cross—almost as if he were standing in front of the framework of a house. This is precisely the form of the *orans* posture as Tertullian pictures it: In the Christians who are praying in this way, the Father also sees the dying son on the cross. Naturally, this interpretation of the *orans* posture is secondary and allegorizing, but it is still interesting and revealing.[1184]

In the art of the catacombs, the *orans* gesture was specifically associated with prayer offered by or in behalf of deceased souls. Explains Hassett:

> Numerous biblical figures, for instance, depicted in the catacombs — Noah, Abraham, Isaac, the Three Children in the Fiery Furnace, Daniel in the lions' den—are pictured asking the Lord to deliver the soul of the person on whose tombs they are depicted as He once delivered the particular personage represented. But besides these biblical *Orans* figures there exist in the catacombs many ideal figures (153 in all) in the ancient attitude of prayer, which, according to Wilpert, are to be regarded as symbols of the deceased's soul in heaven, praying for its friends on earth. This symbolic meaning accounts for the fact that the great majority of the figures are female, even when depicted on the tombs of men. One of the most convincing proofs that the *Orans* was regarded as a symbol of the soul is an ancient lead medal in the Vatican Museum showing the martyr, St. Lawrence, under torture, while his soul, in the form of a female *Orans*, is just leaving the body.[1185]

5-66   *1 Enoch* says that when Abel disappeared, Eve "lamented bitterly… and searched for [him]."[1186]

5-67   The only recorded encounter between Victor Hugo and Mormonism is that of a visit by the indefatigable French missionary Louis Bertrand, during the period that Hugo and other refugees were living in exile in Jersey. Likely, Bertrand, who had been highly involved in political and social reform movements in France before joining the Church, "was closely connected to Hugo or some other revolutionary then on the island, and it was because of this association that the group [was willing to listen to him]."[1187] Elder John Oakley, a missionary familiar with Bertrand's work, wrote a letter to Brigham Young saying that they "granted [Bertrand] a hearing; they listened with attention at the time, but their

---

1178 No source given.

1179 1 Nephi 22:23; 3 Nephi 6:15.

1180 See R. H. Wilkinson, *Art*, pp. 28-29 for a discussion of the gesture in Egyptian worship; cf. *Figure 3-8*, p. 145. See *Endnote 6-30*, p. 499.

1181 E.g., Exodus 9:29, 33: Psalm 28:2, 63:5, 88:10.

1182 E.g., 1 Kings 8:38.

1183 See Tertullian, *Prayer*, 14, p. 685.

1184 J. H. Emminghaus, *Eucharist*, p. 133.

1185 M. M. Hassett, *Orans*, p. 269.

1186 G. W. E. Nickelsburg, *1 Enoch*, 85:6, p. 364.

1187 R. D. McClellan, *Bertrand*, p. 11.

heads were too full of revolution to think much about the gospel of Jesus Christ."[1188] Brief references to Mormonism appear in two places in Hugo's later writings. In one of the religious poems collected in his *Contemplations, La Fin de Satan et Dieu* (= The End of Satan and God), his "contact with the Mormons left a trace, specifically in his poem on God where, listing the conceptions of God that he finds unacceptable, he writes: '... Is it the God that one sees at Versailles... Or do you speak of the judging God?... Is it the Mormon God that you must have? Or the God that tortured Labarre?'"[1189] Later, in a passage describing some of the reasons he was so little loved by the inhabitants of Jersey, he writes: "For the English, I am shocking, eccentric, improper. I do not adjust my tie correctly. I get my shaves at the barber shop on the corner, which... brands me as a workman (something most despised in England); I offend their prudery; I attack the death penalty, which is unrespectable. I say 'Sir' to a lord, which is impious; I am neither Catholic, nor Anglican, nor Lutheran, nor Calvinist, nor Jewish, nor Methodist, nor Wesleyan, nor Mormon: therefore atheist. Moreover, I am French, which is odious; republican, which is abominable; outlawed, which is repulsive; vanquished, which is disgraceful—and, as the crowning dishonor, a poet. Because of all that, not very popular."[1190]

A remembrance of a letter that Victor Hugo wrote to a French Swiss convert is also preserved. Having been impressed with *Les Misérables*, Josephine de la Harpe Suder wrote to Hugo "and gave him the first principles of the restored gospel of Jesus Christ in its fulness as a panacea" to the problems outlined in his novel. Hugo "promptly answered, not by the hand of his secretary, but under his own veritable hand," saying: "Madame: You are a very noble woman, but, permit me to say, I think you are in error. I herewith send you another of my works, and I lay my portrait at your feet. Very respectfully yours, Victor Hugo." The author of the account, Hannah T. King, observing that "both these great, grand spirits have passed away," pictures "the nobly enthusiastic Latter-day Saint Josephine," if permitted, seeking Hugo out and again "laying the gospel before his enfranchised soul; enfranchised from the trammels of earth life, and the light of immortality beaming around him, and a small still voice whispers to me he will gladly embrace it."[1191]

5-68   In contrast to the idea of self-*sufficiency*, modern Church leaders have stressed the principle of self-*reliance*, acknowledging the hand of God as the giver of all, and retaining the principle of generosity and service to others.[1192]

5-69   Gibbons describes this experience as follows:

> Toward the end of summer [of 1955], Elder Lee was assigned by President McKay to lead out in making and executing final plans for the dedication of the Los Angeles Temple. This brought them into frequent contact as the arrangements were finalized. In late February 1956, Elder Lee had a vivid dream about President McKay in which the prophet gave instructions about the love of God and its relationship to the command that we love our neighbors as ourselves. When President McKay offered the prayer dedicating the Los Angeles Temple on March 11, 1956, Elder Lee was startled that the prayer's ending essentially repeated what he had seen and heard in the dream. "I was deeply moved as the dedicatory prayer was read," he explained in his diary under that date,[1193] "because of a dream I had two weeks ago, in which President McKay was impressing me with the meaning of the love of God, as it relates to the love of our fellowmen and of His service. The dedicatory prayer closed with similar instructions to those I had heard in my dream two weeks before." The impact of this dream upon Elder Lee, and the dedicatory prayer that followed it, seems to have been profound and lasting.[1194]

Elder Lee seems to have been referring to thoughts inspired by the last paragraph of the dedicatory prayer, which makes a reference linking love of God and of fellow men: "Now, dear Lord, our Eternal Father, through love for thee and their fellow men, faithful members of thy Church and others who believe in thee, by tithes and other generous contributions, have made possible the erection and

---

1188 *Manuscript History of Brigham Young (1853)*, p. 133, cited in R. D. McClellan, *Bertrand*, p. 10. See also J. Oakley, *2 February 1854*, cited in C. Euvrard, *Bertrand*, p. 197.

1189 C. Euvrard, *Bertrand*, p. 199.

1190 Cited in C. Euvrard, *Bertrand*, p. 200. For more on the religious views of Victor Hugo during this period, see C. Euvrard, *Bertrand*, pp. 197-203.

1191 H. T. King, *Victor Hugo*.

1192 B. K. Packer, *Self-Reliance*; B. K. Packer, *Emotional Problems*; M. G. Romney, *Self-Reliance*; M. R. Ballard, *Self-Reliant*.

1193 H. B. Lee, 11 March 1956.

1194 F. M. Gibbons, *Harold B. Lee*, p. 331. See also L. B. Goates, *Harold B. Lee*, p. 324.

completion of this holy house."[1195]

5-70   I have been unable to find the source for the statement of President Snow. However, he is remembered in one place to have said:

> We were selected, ordained, and set apart there [i.e., in premortal life] according to our worthiness and preparation and training to come forth when our preparation fitted clearly into the great plan of our Father. And as we live worthy the Holy Spirit brings this knowledge to this body, and that is the only way we become acquainted with the knowledge of our spiritual understanding. This body must get acquainted with former pre-existent experiences through being revealed to, and made a part of, this flesh.[1196]

President Joseph Fielding Smith has written the following:

> The Spirit of God speaking to the spirit of man has power to impart truth with greater effect and understanding than the truth can be imparted by personal contact even with heavenly beings. Through the Holy Ghost the truth is woven into the very fiber and sinews of the body so that it cannot be forgotten. So positive and powerful are the teachings of the Spirit that when a man receives this knowledge and partakes of this power of God, which can only come after receiving the covenants and obligations belonging to the New and Everlasting Covenant, and he then turns away from this knowledge and these covenants, he sins knowingly.[1197]

5-71   The idea of "planned obsolescence," industrial designer Brooks Stevens' "major lasting contribution to design theory" sparked the popular imagination following a talk he gave to a local advertising club in Minneapolis, Minnesota. His definition of the concept was "instilling in the buyer the desire to own something a little newer, a little better, a little sooner than is necessary."[1198] The practical effect of this concept is magnified by the fact that in American culture, as recent research and everyday experience confirms, "happiness is a relative state… determined mainly by how we view our lives and accomplishments relative to those of our peers"[1199]—Veblen's "invidious comparison."[1200] Hence, the successful appeal of advertisers to the companion idea of "conspicuous consumption," i.e., the "consumption of valuable goods [as] a means of reputability to the gentleman of leisure."[1201] In order to secure its intended effect, not only should such consumption be very obvious, but "it must be wasteful" as well.[1202]

Revelation 3:17 well describes the illusory nature of such wealth when viewed from the Lord's perspective: "… thou sayest, I am rich, and increased with goods, and have need of nothing; and knowest not that thou art wretched, and miserable, and poor, and blind, and naked."

5-72   President Hugh B. Brown said the following:[1203]

> [S]ometimes …some of us seem to indicate that having been baptized, received the Holy Ghost, having done the things preliminary thereto such as having faith and repentance, and then having gone to church, and the men having received the priesthood, that we've done all that we ever need to do, that we've "arrived." Then the older ones among us rest our hands comfortably on the shelf that nature gradually prepares for us, and we lean back and enjoy the ecstasy of thinking we're going to be transported into heaven immediately. It is to me something like a man who learned of electricity, that is, learned that there was such a thing, and he paid the necessary price and made the necessary preparations and had a conduit wire connected to his house. And he bought him a little ten-watt bulb and installed it in the back room of his house and then sat down, put on his slippers, and took his pipe, and sat in the rocking chair and, "I've got electricity. I'm the happiest man in the world. Nobody else can boast of more than I, because they too have electricity. And I

1195   D. O. McKay, 11 March 1956. See *Improvement Era*, April 1956, p. 227; reprinted in C. A. Orton, *Faith*, p. 195.

1196   L. Snow, 6 April 1894, as reported in *Journal of John Whitaker* (1884-1912), cited in T. G. Madsen, *How We Know*, p. 25.

1197   J. F. Smith, Jr., *Doctrines*, 1935, 1:47-48. See also J. F. Smith, Jr., *Seek Ye*, 18 June 1958, pp. 213-214.

1198   *Industrial Strength Design*; cf. Greenspan's related idea of "creative destruction" (A. Greenspan, *Turbulence*, pp. 48-51).

1199   A. Greenspan, *Turbulence*, p. 269. For a rich characterization of the many ways that the class system reveals itself in American culture, see P. Fussell, *Class*.

1200   T. Veblen, *Leisure*, pp. 21-22.

1201   *Ibid.*, p. 47.

1202   *Ibid.*, p. 60.

1203   H. B. Brown, *Education*.

have electricity." Not knowing, not realizing that what he had was a little ten-watt bulb and that he was in semi-darkness. Not realizing that if he would he could have had ten-thousand times that illumination. He could have had a bulb in every room, and one over the reading lamp, and on the piano, and all around him and then he could have been utilizing the power of electricity by installing those gadgets which are so expensive, and yet seemingly in this age so necessary. He could have done all his work with electricity. But there he sits, placidly rocking, "Thank God I've got electricity."

Sometimes Latter-day Saints say, "Thank God I've got the Gospel. I've joined the Church. I'm going to heaven as soon as I die." There's an awful shock coming to some people because "the glory of God is intelligence."[1204] And there are some Latter-day Saints who have only a ten-watt bulb of spiritual insight and knowledge. And that ten-watt bulb will take them only where they use ten-watt bulbs. And they wouldn't be able to endure the glory of anything brighter. And that's the reason men can't enjoy the glory of God and endure it: they're not prepared for it.

5-73   Describing the affirmative nature of the process of sanctification, Chesterton writes:[1205]

[T]hose who are acquainted with all the philosophy (nay, religion) which is typified in the art of drawing on brown paper, know that white is positive and essential. I cannot avoid remarking here upon a moral significance. One of the wise and awful truths which this brown-paper art reveals is this: that white is a color. It is not a mere absence of color; it is a shining and affirmative thing, as fierce as red, as definite as black. When, so to speak, your pencil grows red-hot, it draws roses; when it grows white-hot, it draws stars. And one of the two or three defiant verities of the best religious morality—of real Christianity, for example—is exactly this same thing. The chief assertion of religious morality is that white is a color. Virtue is not the absence of vices or the avoidance of moral dangers; virtue is a vivid and separate thing, like pain or a particular smell. Mercy does not mean not being cruel or sparing people revenge or punishment: it means a plain and positive thing like the sun, which one has either seen or not seen. Chastity does not mean abstention from sexual wrong; it means something flaming like Joan of Arc. In a word, God paints in many colors, but He never paints so gorgeously—I had almost said so gaudily—as when He paints in white.

5-74   Taking this idea a step further, Chesterton writes:[1206]

When Diogenes went about with a lantern looking for an honest man, I am afraid he had very little time to be honest himself… The error of Diogenes lay in the fact that he omitted to notice that every man is both an honest man and a dishonest man. Diogenes looked for his honest man inside every crypt and cavern, but he never thought of looking inside the thief. And that is where the Founder of Christianity found the honest man; He found him on a gibbet and promised him Paradise. Just as Christianity looked for the honest man inside the thief, democracy looked for the wise man inside the fool. It encouraged the fool to be wise. We can call this thing sometimes optimism, sometimes equality; the nearest name for it is encouragement. It had its exaggeration—failure to understand original sin, notions that education would make all men good, the childlike yet pedantic philosophies of human perfectibility. But the whole was full of faith in the infinity of human souls, which is in itself not only Christian but orthodox; and this we have lost amid the limitations of pessimistic science. Christianity said that any man could be a saint if he chose; democracy, that every man could be a citizen if he chose.

1204 D&C 93:36.
1205 G. K. Chesterton, *Piece of Chalk*, pp. 17-18.
1206 G. K. Chesterton, *Charles Dickens*, pp. 45-46.

FIGURE 6-1. *Adam and His Children, ca. 1447-1466*
Piero della Francesca, ca. 1420-1492

And a book of remembrance was kept… in the language of Adam… and… their children were taught (Moses 6:5-6). Pictured on his deathbed, Adam is supported by Eve and surrounded by a daughter and two sons. In the background, Seth converses with an angel. The scene of the *Death of Adam* is part of a cycle of frescoes in the church of San Francesco in Arezzo, Italy illustrating the *Legend of the True Cross.* In this cycle, the classical forms of the *quattrocento* appear against a "sparse, often surrealist landscape—the pictorial equivalent of silence. To the modern eye, Piero's paintings show a subdued emotion, where rational theory appears to have overwhelmed naturalism" (*Piero della Francesca*). For a more detailed description of the scenes depicted in the series of frescoes, see *Excursus 36: The Legend of the True Cross,* p. 614 and *Excursus 45: Impact of the "Black Death" on Art and Literature,* p. 640.

MOSES 6:1-12
Adam the Patriarch

Overview

FOLLOWING a hiatus on the work of Bible translation of a little more than a month, John Whitmer served as scribe for Moses 5:52-6:18 on November 30, 1830.[1] By December 10, with the assistance of Emma Smith and John Whitmer, the Prophet had completed the manuscript through the end of Moses 6.

From the story of Lamech in Moses 5, Cassuto draws the lesson:

> … that material progress did not go hand in hand with moral advancement. Not only did violence prevail in the world, but it was precisely in deeds of violence that these generations gloried. The very qualities that are ethically reprehensible, and are hateful in the sight of the Lord, were esteemed in the eyes of men. In such circumstances, the Judge of the whole earth could not but execute judgment. All the achievements of material civilization are not worth anything without moral virtues, and cannot protect man from retribution. We have here a kind of prelude to the decree of the Flood.[2]

Mercifully postponing judgment, however, God first launched successive waves of what Nibley calls a "crash program" to gather any that would hearken to the call of repentance—first to Adam-ondi-Ahman, and later to Enoch's city.[3] The absolute failure of the final ministry of the long-suffering Noah definitively confirmed that there were none but his immediate family who would listen, and demonstrated the inevitability of the sweeping destruction of the Flood.

The first twelve verses of Moses 6 describe the final events in the life of Adam as a patriarch to the righteous branch of his posterity.[4] The focus of the account is on the birth of the righteous Seth and the beginning of the patriarchal line that will culminate, in the seventh generation from Adam, with the call of Enoch.

MOSES 6

---

1   S. H. Faulring, *et al.*, *Original Manuscripts*, p. 57.
2   U. Cassuto, *Adam to Noah*, p. 244.
3   H. W. Nibley, *Teachings of the PGP*, 21, pp. 262, 263.
4   Cf. Abraham 1:26.

The Patriarchal Priesthood and the Line of Seth

Verse 2 announces the first theme of the chapter: despite the death of Abel, a righteous posterity to Adam will be raised up through Seth, ensuring the continuity of a covenant people. Joseph Fielding McConkie writes:

> Seth means "the appointed" or "substitute," he being effectually the second Abel. As such he becomes a natural type for Christ, who like Abel was first a martyr, and then like the second Abel, Seth, ruled in glory with his father.[5]

In the Greek *Life of Adam and Eve*, as Tromp notes, Seth not only "continues humanity" but is also the one who "hands on the primeval mysteries."[6] Similarly, D&C 107 records that the "evangelical [or patriarchal[7]] order of the priesthood was confirmed to be handed down from father to son, and rightly belongs to the literal descendants of the chosen seed, to whom the promises were made."[8] The revelation goes on to say that Seth was "ordained by Adam at the age of sixty-nine years, and was blessed by him three years previous to his (Adam's) death, and received the promise of God by his father, that his posterity should be the chosen of the Lord, and that they should be preserved unto the end of the earth."[9] Regarding the description of Seth's role in Gnostic texts, S. Kent Brown writes:

> While Adam was the founder of the covenant race, it was Seth and his successors who perpetuated the covenant people and who came to be known as "the seed of the great Seth" or "the great, incorruptible, immovable race of the great, mighty men of the great Seth"[10]… In his earthly function, …Seth came to reveal secrets about the heavens and the future which he had learned both from his father and from revelation…[11] In fact, he authored a book which was hidden in order to come forth in the latter days, a work reportedly containing the secrets of the universe which Seth and the covenant people had known and revered from the beginning.[12]

Just as the Book of Mormon, as a history of those who were Nephites by lineage or "adoption," does not record the story of the Lamanites and their associates,[13] so the book of Moses story tells us very little about the history of the Cainites or of the children of Adam that were born before Cain and Abel[14] who "followed Satan by choice and were disqualified as sons of God."[15] The account instead focuses on the inauguration of temple ordinances among the righteous, which began, as Nibley indicates, "when God set them apart, gave them a blessing, gave them a new name, [and] registered them in the new Book of the Generations of Adam."[16]

5   J. F. McConkie, *Symbolism*, p. 181 and Moses 6:3-4. See *Excursus 37: Traditions About the Role of Abel*, p. 617.

6   J. Tromp, *Cain*, p. 295.

7   J. Smith, Jr., *Teachings*, 27 June 1839, p. 151.

8   D&C 107:39-40.

9   D&C 107:42. See *Endnote 6-1*, p. 491.

10   A. Böhlig, *et al.*, *Egyptians*, III, 51.19-20, 54.9-10, 59.13-15, 60.25-61.1, pp. 212-213, 215.

11   Cf. G. W. MacRae, *et al.*, *Adam 1990*, 85.19-31, p. 286.

12   S. K. Brown, *Nag Hammadi*, pp. 262-263 and A. Böhlig, *et al.*, *Egyptians*, III, 68.1-69.5, p. 218. See *Endnote 6-2*, p. 491.

13   J. L. Sorenson, *Ancient*, pp. 50-56.

14   Moses 5:12, 16.

15   H. W. Nibley, *Before Adam*, p. 78 and Moses 7:33, 37. See also D. J. Meldrum, *et al.*, *Children JBMS*; D. J. Meldrum, *et al.*, *Children 2007*, pp. 7-13; T. D. Stephens, *Tree of Life*; *Commentary 6:8-c*, p. 480.

16   H. W. Nibley, *Return*, pp. 62-63 and Moses 5:5-9; cf. Revelation 20:12.

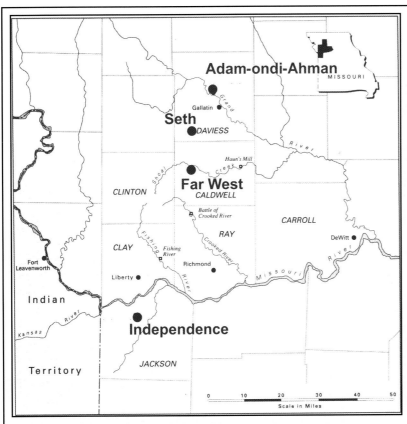

FIGURE 6-2. *Church History Sites in Western Missouri, 1831-1839*

This earth was once a garden place, With all her glories common; And men did live a holy race, And worship Jesus face to face, In Adam-ondi-Ahman.[1] Although "neither biblical records nor secular history and archaeological research" are likely to ever "identify the dimensions or the location of the Garden [of Eden] in terms of the present-day surface of the earth,"[2] statements attributed to the Prophet Joseph Smith might be read as implying indications of Adam and Eve's step-by-step migration *after* the Fall, paralleling the general direction of the movement of the Saints in Missouri after their expulsion from Jackson County.[3] North of Independence, in Caldwell County, is an area that the Saints named Far West. It was near that place, according to the Prophet, that Cain killed Abel.[4] Continuing about twelve miles further in that same general direction is a location where the Prophet proposed building a stake and city that was to be named Seth, in memory of the son who consoled Adam and Eve after their loss of Abel.[5] About 13 miles north of Seth and 70 miles north of Independence is Adam-ondi-Ahman, where Adam gave a final blessing to his posterity.[6]

1   *Hymns (1985),* #49.
2   G. W. Doxey, *Eden,* p. 534. See the overview of Moses 3, p. 141.
3   See *Excursus 39: The Location of Adam-ondi-Ahman,* p. 623.
4   See statements and discussion in L. C. Berrett, *et al., Missouri,* pp. 322-323. See also Moses 5:32.
5   *Ibid.,* p. 371-372; J. Smith, Jr. *Papers 2008-,* Journals 1:392. See Moses 6:2.
6   D&C 107:53-56

The Great Council at Adam-ondi-Ahman

Joseph Smith revealed the name of the location where Adam gave his final blessing to be *Adam-ondi-Ahman,* which Nibley takes as meaning "Adam (or "man") in the presence of God."[17] In this place, Adam gathered his posterity three years prior to his death, and "predicted whatsoever should befall his posterity unto the latest generation."[18]

The Prophet said that the purpose of Adam's blessing was to "bring [his posterity] into the presence of God."[19] Andrus explained that "Adam… realized his desire to a degree, for 'the Lord appeared unto them.'[20] But even this blessing was short of the ultimate purpose of the Gospel, which was to bring all those of Adam's descendants who would obey its divine truths back into the presence of God and to endow them with celestial glory."[21]

17   *Excursus 38: The Meaning of "Adam-ondi-Ahman",* p. 622. See *Endnote 6-3,* p. 491.
18   L. C. Berrett, *et al., Missouri,* pp. 377-456, D&C 107:53-56. See *Endnote 6-4,* p. 492.
19   J. Smith, Jr., *Teachings,* 2 July 1839, p. 159.
20   D&C 107:54. See also E. A. Whitney, *Leaf,* 'He [Adam] sealed them for eternal life."
21   H. L. Andrus, *Perfection,* p. 411.

MOSES 6

A description of a gathering like the one described in D&C 107 is given in the *Life of Adam and Eve*. Descriptions of the number present vary widely: while most versions of the tradition mention thirty sons and thirty daughters, the Latin recension uniquely pictures a surprisingly large assembly of "15,000 men, not counting women and children."[22] The Georgian version recounts the story as follows:

> For all the years of Adam were 930 years. And [those who were descended] from him multiplied over the earth and settled it. And when the 930 years were completed, Adam fell ill and cried out in a loud voice and said, "Gather to me all my descendants and I will see them before my death."
>
> And all his progeny gathered to him who had settled, and he divided the three parts of the earth among his descendants. And all Adam's descendants assembled by him, for they had taken a position before his doors, in the place which Adam had made, and into which he would enter and address his prayers to God.[23]

Another extrabiblical source purporting to give an account of this event is the *Apocalypse of Adam*, which Robinson describes as:

> … an account of Adam's final instructions to his son Seth. Since the 700th year[24] should be understood as the 700th year of Seth's life, it is also, according to the *Septuagint* chronology, the last year of Adam's life. This would indicate that the document is not an apocalypse, but rather a testament in the pattern of the *Testaments of the Twelve Patriarchs*,[25] where the fathers also call their sons together just before their deaths for a last word of instruction and exhortation.[26]

The *Conflict of Adam and Eve* with Satan recounts that "Adam let his blessing descend upon Seth, and upon his children, and upon all his children's children."[27] Nibley argues that this "great assembly" was "the original model" for the widespread tradition of annual year-rites thereafter performed throughout the world.[28]

Beyond their obvious value as part of the scriptural record, revelations about the council at Adam-ondi-Ahman seem to have provided the Prophet with a prototype for church governance,[29] a model whose importance persists to the present time.[30] His revelation appears to have been based on a vision, since he speaks of *seeing* the event.[31] Connections between this vision, the translation of the early chapters of the book of Moses, and the organization of church councils are seen by Matthews to be "reasonable and possible—even probable."[32] Moreover, Dahl cites close affinities with D&C "sections 68, 84, 88, 102, and 107, which speak of priesthood matters in terms of ancient councils, priesthood genealogies, keys and powers."[33]

---

22 G. A. Anderson, *et al.*, *Synopsis*, 30:3, p. 34E. See *Endnote 6-6*, p. 493.

23 G. A. Anderson, *et al.*, *Synopsis*, 30(5):1-30(5):3, pp. 33E-34E; cf. E. A. W. Budge, *Cave*, pp. 71-73; M. D. Gibson, *Rolls 1901*, pp. 115-118; S. C. Malan, *Adam and Eve*, 2:8, pp. 114-116. See *Endnote 6-7*, p. 493. See A. S-M. Ri, *Commentaire de la Caverne*, pp. 179 for a discussion of Adam's "house of prayer" as a temple.

24 G. W. MacRae, *Adam 1983*, 64, 1:1, p. 712; G. W. MacRae, *et al.*, *Adam 1990*, Pl. 64:4, p. 279; S. E. Robinson, *Apocalypse of Adam*, Pl. 64:4, p. 10.

25 H. C. Kee, *Testaments*.

26 S. E. Robinson, *Apocalypse of Adam*, p. 6.

27 S. C. Malan, *Adam and Eve*, 2:8, p. 115. See *Endnote 6-8*, p. 493.

28 H. W. Nibley, *Eternal Round*, p. 383. See *Commentary 1:25-e*, p. 60; *5:47-a*, p. 395; *Excursus 35: Lamech's "Sword Song"*, p. 612; the overview of Moses 4, pp. 221. See *Endnote 4-21*, p. 304.

29 R. L. Bushman, *Councils*; R. L. Bushman, *Rough Stone*, pp. 251-269.

30 M. R. Ballard, *Counseling*. See *Endnote 6-9*, p. 493.

31 J. Smith, Jr., *Teachings*, before 8 August 1839, p. 158. See *Excursus 40: Dating Joseph Smith's Vision of Adam-ondi-Ahman*, p. 625.

32 R. J. Matthews, *Plainer*, p. 260.

33 L. E. Dahl, *Plain*, p. 126. See *Endnote 6-10*, p. 493.

The Prophet Joseph Smith was concerned about maintaining a proper spirit in the meetings of the early Church. He had seen by revelation the manner in which ancient assemblies were conducted, and was pained by the offensive behavior that he had sometimes witnessed:

> How vain and trifling have been our spirits, our conferences, our councils, our meetings, our private as well as public conversations—too low, too mean, too vulgar, too condescending for the dignified characters of the called and chosen of God.[34]

Having spoken for the first time about the correct order of councils in the Church at a conference in Hiram, Ohio, on October 11, 1831, the Prophet reported: "The Elders were instructed in the ancient manner of conducting meetings, of which knowledge most of them were ignorant."[35] Beginning on that day, the Prophet called and set apart six brethren to visit the several branches of the Church and teach them "the ancient manner of conducting meetings as they were led by the Holy Ghost."[36] The minutes do not give additional detail about the specifics that they were to teach,[37] however one week after the final selection of brethren for this assignment had been completed, Orson Hyde, one of the six called to teach the branches, requested a revelation from the Prophet. The Lord's response reads in part:[38]

> 1 My servant, Orson Hyde, was called by his ordination to proclaim the everlasting gospel, by the Spirit of the living God, from people to people, and from land to land, in the congregations of the wicked, in their synagogues, reasoning with and expounding all scriptures unto them.

> 2 And, behold, and lo, this is an ensample unto all those who were ordained unto this priesthood, whose mission is appointed unto them to go forth—

> 3 And this is the ensample unto them, that they shall speak as they are moved upon by the Holy Ghost.

> 4 And whatsoever they shall speak when moved upon by the Holy Ghost shall be scripture, shall be the will of the Lord, shall be the mind of the Lord, shall be the word of the Lord, shall be the voice of the Lord, and the power of God unto salvation.

> 5 Behold, this is the promise of the Lord unto you, O ye my servants.

Although the passage certainly can be applied more generally, Elder Hyde no doubt saw its relevance to his recent assignment to teach the branches to conduct meetings "as they were led by the Holy Ghost."[39] While it was the duty of the presiding authority to provide adequate opportunity for discussion of all matters laid before a council, all present at the meeting had an equally binding responsibility to refrain from speaking impetuously.[40] On the contrary, each council member was charged to "speak [only] as they are moved upon by the Holy Ghost,"[41] thus following the example of Adam's posterity, who "rose up and blessed Adam,"[42] and of the patriarch himself, who prophesied "being full of the Holy Ghost."[43] Joseph Smith explained: "Each should speak in his turn and in his place, and in his time and

---

34 J. Smith, Jr., *Teachings*, 25 March 1839, p. 137. See *Endnote 6-11*, p. 493.

35 J. Smith, Jr., *Documentary History*, 11 October 1831, 1:219.

36 D. Q. Cannon, *et al.*, *Far West*, p. 17, spelling, grammar, and punctuation modernized; cf. Moroni 6:9; D&C 46:2. See *Endnote 6-12*, p. 493.

37 See *Endnote 6-13*, p. 494.

38 D&C 68. See J. Smith, Jr., *Documentary History*, 1 November 1831, 1:227-229.

39 D. Q. Cannon, *et al.*, *Far West*, p. 17, spelling, grammar, and punctuation modernized; cf. D&C 46:2.

40 See *Endnote 6-14*, p. 494.

41 D&C 68:3. See *Endnote 6-15*, p. 494.

42 D&C 107:54.

43 D&C 107:56.

MOSES 6

season, that there may be perfect order in all things; and that every man, before he makes an objection to any item that is brought before a council for consideration, should be sure that he can throw light upon the subject rather than spread darkness, and that his objection be founded in righteousness."[44]

That the Saints will have ample opportunity in the future to experience firsthand "the ancient manner of conducting meetings" is attested by Elder Joseph Fielding Smith, who wrote:[45]

> Not many years hence there shall be another gathering of high priests and righteous souls in this same valley of Adam-ondi-Ahman. At this gathering Adam, the Ancient of Days, will again be present. At this time the vision which Daniel saw will be enacted.[46] The Ancient of Days will sit. There will stand before him those who have held the keys of all dispensations, who shall render up their stewardships to the first Patriarch of the race, who holds the keys of salvation....[47] This council in the valley of Adam-ondi-Ahman is to be of the greatest importance to the world. At that time there will be a transfer of authority from the usurper and imposter, Lucifer, to the rightful King, Jesus Christ... Our Lord will then assume the reins of government; directions will be given to the Priesthood; and He, whose right it is to rule, will be installed officially by the voice of the Priesthood there assembled. This grand council of Priesthood will be composed, not only of those who are faithful who now dwell on this earth, but also of the prophets and apostles of old, who have had directing authority. Others may also be there, but if so they will be there by appointment, for this is to be an official council called to attend to the most momentous matters concerning the destiny of the earth.
>
> When this gathering is held, the world will not know of it; the members of the Church at large will not know of it, yet it shall be preparatory to the coming in the clouds of glory of our Savior Jesus Christ as the Prophet Joseph Smith has said.

Seth's Quest for the Oil of Mercy

Tradition records that after recounting the story of the Fall to his posterity at the gathering before his death, Adam asked Eve and Seth to retrieve oil from the Tree of Life so he could receive a healing ordinance of anointing.[48] Nibley summarizes:

> [W]hen at the end of his life Adam felt the accumulating effect of these mortal blows upon him and sensed the approach of death, he implored Eve, "Go with my son Seth near to Paradise... and pray God to... send his angel to Paradise, and give me of the tree out of which the oil floweth, and bring it me, and I shall anoint myself and shall have rest from my complaint."[49] He was asking for the "oil of mercy," which alone could reverse the seven "blows of death" inflicted as a result of the Fall.[50] For the ultimate healing of the oil of mercy was not to be given to men until the coming of the Messiah, as Eve and Seth were informed by an angel who met them on the way back to the Garden to fetch the oil for Adam.[51] When the Messiah did come, according to the *Clementine Recognitions*,[52] he provided that all who come to his kingdom should be anointed with the oil of the Tree of Life, the very oil with which the Father had anointed him

---

44 J. Smith, Jr., *Teachings*, 15 January 1836, pp. 93-94. See *Endnote 6-16*, p. 494.

45 J. F. Smith, Jr., *Way 1945*, 1931, pp. 289, 291. See also B. R. McConkie, *Millennial Messiah*, pp. 578-588.

46 Daniel 7:9-14; cf. D&C 116.

47 J. Smith, Jr., *Teachings*, 2 July 1839, pp. 157-159.

48 G. A. Anderson, *et al.*, *Synopsis*, pp. 34E-45E; cf. M. Herbert, *Irish Apocrypha*, p. 16. See also *Commentary 3:9-g*, p. 163 and the overview of Moses 4, p. 239. For Islamic versions of this story, see M.al-Kisa'i, *Tales*, pp. 78, 82-83; A. al-Tha'labi, *Lives*, pp. 60-62; B. M. Wheeler, *Prophets*, p. 33. See also J. E. Hanauer, *Folklore*, pp. 39-41.

49 See G. A. Anderson, *et al.*, *Synopsis*, Greek 9:3-9:4, pp. 39E-40E. See *Endnote 6-17*, p. 495.

50 G. A. Anderson, *et al.*, *Synopsis*, Greek 40:1, p. 44E. See the overview of Moses 4, p. 237; *Commentary 5:29-b*, p. 377; 5:47-b, p. 396.

51 G. A. Anderson, *et al.*, *Synopsis*, Greek 40:1-43:3, pp. 44E-46E.

52 Pseudo-Clement, *Recognitions*, 1:45:5, p. 89; cf. F. S. Jones, *Recognitions 1995*, 1:45:5, p. 77.

FIGURE 6-3. *The Quest of Seth for the Oil of Mercy, 1351-1360.* **Photo: Assaf Pinkus.**

And Adam told Eve, "Arise and go with Seth, my son, to the Garden… And (God) will send his angel to the Garden where the Tree of Life is, from which the oil flows out, so that he may give you a little of that oil… and I will anoint myself and I will be healed of my sufferings.[1] Echoing the themes of this story, Revelation 22:2 speaks of "the leaves of the tree [that] were for the healing of the nations" and early Christians wrote of being anointed with oil from the Tree of Life in imitation of Adam.

In this sculpture preserved at the *Heilig-Kreuz-Münster* (Holy Cross Minster) in Schwäbisch Gmünd, Germany, "Adam lies on the ground, on his sickbed, supporting his head in his hands. Eve sits behind him. Her right hand grasps his shoulder while her left is held to her breast, exhibiting her storm of emotions. Behind them one can see a sprouting tree. To their right Seth receives a branch from an angel standing at the entrance to a Gothic structure symbolizing Paradise. Inside the canopy is a tree. Seth points toward his parents. The scenes depict Eve's mourning over the death of Adam and Seth's journey to Paradise, prefigurations of the Pieta and Crucifixion."[2]

---

1   G. A. Anderson, *et al.*, *Synopsis*, Georgian 36(9):3-4, p. 39E, 40E.
2   A. Pinkus, *Impact*, pp. 167-168. For more on the background of these sculptures, see *Excursus 45: Impact of the "Black Death" on Art and Literature*, p. 640.

to be the *initium omnium*.[53] The final culmination of the whole plan of salvation, according to a very old Judeo-Christian writing, will be when Michael opens the gates and bestows the healing oil on the righteous as "the hundred-fold reward of those who have worked and toiled diligently."[54]

The story of Adam's quest to have the gates of Paradise reopened and to obtain the healing oil of the Tree of Life once again underscores the fact that:

> … this story of Adam and Eve was never narrated as a simple, objective account of human beginnings, as a story that could take its place alongside modern theories of the "big bang" or evolution. Instead, the story of Adam and Eve has always been subject to liturgical enactment.

---

53   I.e., the first of all. See Pseudo-Clement, *Recognitions*, 1:45:4-5, p. 89; cf. F. S. Jones, *Recognitions 1995*, 1:45:4-5, pp. 76-77.
54   H. W. Nibley, *Message 2005*, p. 174 and H. E. Gaylord, *3 Baruch*, 15:1-2, p. 676. See *Endnote 6-18*, p. 495.

FIGURE 6-4. *Ampulla 11, with inscription "Oil from the Tree of Life," 5th-6th century*

To him that overcometh will I give to eat of the tree of life, which is in the midst of the paradise of God.[1] In the early church, oil from *ampullae* (flasks) of this sort was used in rites of anointing accompanying baptism. The Armenian liturgy includes two anointings—"one with unperfumed oil before the baptism and the other, after it, with the myron or perfumed oil."[2] Likewise, in the *Life of Adam and Eve*, Adam asked Seth to retrieve oil from the Tree of Life to heal him from the effects of the Fall, with clear allusions to washing and anointing.[3]

Filled with holy oil, *ampullae* such as this one from a collection in the treasury of the Basilica di S. Giovanni Battista in Monza, Italy, were carried home as relics of the True Cross by Byzantine pilgrims to the Holy Land.[4] One such pilgrim wrote: "The Cross is brought out of this small room for veneration… and they offer oil to be blessed in little flasks. When the mouth of one of the little flasks touches the Wood of the Cross, the oil instantly bubbles over, and unless it is closed very quickly it all spills out."[5] About the image on the *ampulla*, Anderson writes: "Notice that Christ is crucified on a cross that looks like a tree[6]—the actions of the first Adam are undone by the second. And those who benefit are the recently baptized, who enjoy the healing oils that were denied Adam once he was evicted from Paradise."[7] The two crucified thieves flank the Savior, and two kneeling suppliants, representing the pilgrims themselves, reach out to touch the cross in veneration.[8] Careful inspection also reveals that waters representing the rivers of paradise are flowing from the base of the cross/Tree of Life: "from these rivers, as from the side of Christ, flowed life for men and for angels."[9]

---

1   Revelation 2:7. On the themes of the Book of Life and the Tree of Life in the book of Revelation, see K. L. Barney, *A Book or a Tree*.
2   M. E. Stone, *Angelic Prediction*, p. 125.
3   G. A. Anderson, *et al.*, *Synopsis*, p. 40; G. A. Anderson, *Penitence*, pp. 49-53.
4   See *Excursus 36: The Legend of the True Cross*, p. 614.
5   Cited in G. Vikan, *Byzantine*, p. 22.
6   Cf. H. Maguire, *Paradise*, p. 30.
7   G. A. Anderson, *Perfection*, p. 133.
8   G. Vikan, *Byzantine*, pp. 23-24.
9   *Ibid.*, p. 22; cf. H. Maguire, *Paradise*, p. 29. See also *Excursus 45: Impact of the "Black Death" on Art and Literature*, p. 640.

It derives its meaning from the world of penitence and restoration. A more pertinent parallel than Darwinian evolution is the parable of the Prodigal Son,[55] a favorite Gospel reading in the Lenten season.

The story of the Fall had value in the early church because every Christian was called to situate his or her life in between the contours of Adam and Christ as well as Eve and Mary. The arc that extends from Adam to Christ defines a horizon of mercy.[56]

---

55   Luke 15:11-32.
56   G. A. Anderson, *Perfection*, p. 187.

FIGURE 6-5. *Toward Immortality and Eternal Youth, 1907*
Albert-Dominique Roze, 1861-1952
Photo: Jeffrey M. Bradshaw, 1956-

SEE COLOR PLATE 6-5.

O death, where is thy sting? O grave, where is thy victory?[1] The quest for immortality has been a part of countless myths and stories, including one from 1889 entitled *In the Year 2889.* Published under Jules Verne's name but written by his son Michel,[2] it contains an account of a Dr. Faithburn, "a firm believer in human hibernation," who had his vital functions "suspended" and was carefully placed in a coffin, with instructions about the proper way for him to be awakened one hundred years to the day later. As the whole world awaited the news, the casket was opened. Dr. Faithburn, "a veritable mummy," was taken out, and efforts were made to revive him. "'Dead!' proclaims Dr. Wilkins. 'And how long has he been dead?' Dr. Wilkins makes another examination. 'A hundred years,' he replies."[3]

More than a century after his death, Jules Verne (1828-1905) is still reputed by some to be "the most read, the most published, and the most translated" author on earth.[4]

Fittingly, it was Michel Verne who commissioned Albert Roze, a pupil of Rodin, to create this unusual tomb in the Cimitière de la Madeleine, Amiens, France, attesting his father's hope in the resurrection—an unattainable feat for the science of 2889 but certainly not impossible to God.[5] The monument, entitled "Vers l'Immortalité et l'Éternelle Jeunesse" (Toward Immortality and Eternal Youth), features a sculpture of Jules Verne raising the broken tombstone. With his right arm extended, he looks steadily upward at the heavens. The head is modeled on Verne's death mask. In 1984, the Czech astronomer, Zdenek Kopal, then at the University of Manchester, England, visited the grave and there buried a pinch of moon dust he had obtained from NASA in tribute to the man who had famously imagined such a voyage.[6]

---

1   1 Corinthians 15:55.
2   W. Butcher, *Verne,* p. 250.
3   J. Verne, *2889 (English);* cf. J. Verne, *2889 (French),* pp. 38, 44.
4   W. Butcher, *Verne,* p. 331 n. 1.
5   See *Endnote 6-19,* p. 495.
6   *Letter to Professor Miroslav Šťastný.*

MOSES 6

"The Whole Meaning of the Law"

The story of Adam and Eve's expulsion from and return to the Garden parallels a common three-part literary pattern in ancient Near Eastern literature: trouble at home, exile abroad, and happy homecoming.[57] The pattern is as old as the Egyptian story of Sinuhe from 1800 BCE[58] and is replicated in scriptural accounts of Israel's apostasy and return[59] as well as in the lives of biblical characters such as Jacob.[60] The theme is as ubiquitous in modern literature as it was in those times.[61]

To the ancients, however, this pattern was more than a mere storytelling convention, since it reflected a sequence of events common in widespread ritual practices for priests and kings.[62] Barker describes how the thinking of early Christians applied this pattern to the story of Adam and Eve, and how it may have reflected their own hopes for a return to the original faith, the authentic priesthood, and the true temple:

> The Christian vision reverses the story in Genesis 1-3, and has humans restored to Eden… Adam was remembered as the first high priest, and Jesus was described as the new Adam. The

---

57   A. Gileadi, *Literary,* p. 12. See *Endnote 6-20,* p. 496.
58   J. B. Pritchard, *ANET,* pp. 18-22. The pattern of "return" in this story is discussed in J. Assman, *Death,* pp. 164-185.
59   J. E. Coleson, *Life Cycle;* A. Gileadi, *Literary;* A. Gileadi, *Decoded;* S. D. Ricks, *Prophetic.*
60   Genesis 27-33.
61   N. Frye, *Secular Scripture.* See *Endnote 6-21,* p. 496.
62   See, e.g., D. E. Callender, *Adam,* pp. 211-218.

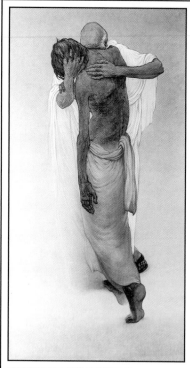

Figure 6-6. *The Forgiving Father, ca. 1954-1958*
Frank Wesley, 1923-2002

SEE COLOR PLATE 6-6.

But when he was yet a great way off, his father saw him, and had compassion, and ran, and fell on his neck, and kissed him.[1] Raised a Methodist in North India, Frank Wesley expressed familiar biblical themes in art using the vernacular of his native land. This famous picture shows a "Brahmin father, pale skinned and pure, embracing his exhausted, sun-scorched son who would so obviously fall to the ground from exhaustion without his father's supportive embrace."[2] "The color contrast is very strong at the top to emphasize the difference between purity and sin. But the loving embrace of the father, with the son's face covered against his chest, begins to merge at the base of the two figures until their clothing is blended."[3] During the springtime *Holi* (= fire) festival, celebrated most enthusiastically in North India, revelers throw colored powders and liquids on each other to celebrate the triumph of good over evil—yellow, blue, and pink being among the most popular colors. As the father sustains his faltering son, the fabric of the son's robe becomes imbued with these colors, symbols of divine purity.

The picture was originally painted for the Chapel of a Social Center in Japan. Sadly, the Center was destroyed by the bombing of Hiroshima, however it was later rebuilt "to serve a former outcast group." "[O]ne of the most powerful effects of the painting is that neither face is shown. One can move quite readily—or perhaps with some hesitancy—to either figure. After all, it is not easy to repent, or in many instances, to forgive."[4]

1   Luke 15:20.
2   G. Wheeler, *et al.*, *Wesley.*
3   N. Wray, *Wesley*, p. 44.
4   N. Wray, *Background.*

Christians remembered and hoped for the earlier Eden—the true temple—and saw themselves returning to the place and the priesthood from which they had been driven. This was their world view.… [T]he "Moses" religion with the Ten Commandments and the Aaron priesthood did not finally replace the Abrahamic faith and the Melchizedek priesthood [as the dominant strain of Judaism] until just before the first temple was destroyed.[63]

True to the archetype of Adam and Eve, the parable of the Prodigal Son also concerns the outbound journey of the transgressor, his "coming to himself"[64] in the remembrance of the bounty of his former home, and his return to the embrace of a loving father.[65] "However large his family a father cannot spare [even] one."[66] He watches and waits until his lost child returns,[67] and when he sees him, "he disregards the deference due him,"[68] throws aside any notion of propriety,[69] and runs to greet his wayward son. "There is no holding back on the father's part, no waiting for his [son] to make the first move."[70] The father reaches out eagerly in tender embrace, bestows a kiss as a token of pardon,[71] and joyfully prepares the emblems of investiture: a robe, a ring, a pair of shoes, and a fatted calf.[72]

63   M. Barker, *Temple Theology*, pp. 4, 7. See also M. Barker, *Revelation*, pp. 20, 327.
64   Luke 15:17. See *Endnote 6-22*, p. 496.
65   Luke 15:11-32. See W. Barclay, *Parables*, p. 187; A. J. Hultgren, *Parables*, p. 72; R. L. Millet, *Lost*. See *Endnote 6-23*, p. 496.
66   W. Barclay, *Parables*, p. 183.
67   See *Endnote 6-24*, p. 496.
68   See *Endnote 6-25*, p. 496.
69   See *Endnote 6-26*, p. 497.
70   D. Packard, *et al.*, *Feasting*, p. 47.
71   J. Jeremias, *Parables*, p. 102.
72   See *Endnote 6-27*, p. 497.

FIGURE 6-7. *The Return of the Prodigal Son, 1773*
Pompeo Batoni, 1708-1787

SEE COLOR PLATE 6-7.

O Lord, wilt thou encircle me around in the robe of thy righteousness![1]
In the words of his plea for deliverance, Nephi draws on the culture of
the desert. Fleeing to the tent of a sheikh who will defend him against his
enemies, the weary fugitive humbly kneels and says, "I am your suppliant."
Honor impels the sheikh to put the hem of his great hooded robe over the
suppliant's shoulder with a comforting promise of protection, "This is your
tent, this is your family. We'll make a place for you."[2]

1   2 Nephi 4:33.
2   H. W. Nibley, *Teachings of the Book of Mormon*, 16, 1:199.

With equal poignancy, Nephi explores this theme in an anguished psalm of danger and
deliverance.[73] Packard describes the setting:

> This passage occurs at a crucial point in the Book of Mormon. Lehi has just died, leaving his
> sons without his guidance. Under Lehi's authority, Nephi had become his brothers' "ruler" and
> "teacher."[74] But with Lehi gone, Laman and Lemuel are angry with Nephi, saying, "We will not
> have him to be our ruler; for it belongs unto us, who are the elder brethren, to rule over this
> people."[75] Just after Nephi's psalm, we find Laman and Lemuel becoming increasingly angry
> with Nephi, "insomuch that they did seek to take away [his] life."[76] The Lord warns Nephi to
> flee for his life into the wilderness, just as He earlier warned Lehi to escape from those who
> sought his life.[77]

Nibley explains the significance of the words of Nephi's psalm for the people of the desert:

> When [an Arab is trying to escape his enemies], he runs to the tent of any great sheikh he
> can find. He goes in and kneels down before the sheikh and says, "I am your suppliant."[78] The
> sheikh is then obligated to put his *caftan* [—his great hooded robe—] over [the suppliant's]
> *katef* which is the same word as shoulder—to put the hem of his garment over his shoulder and
> say, "*Ahlan wa-sahlan wa-marhaban.* This is your tent, this is your family." The Hebrew word
> *ohel* for tent is the same as the Arabic word *ahl* for family.[79] He says, "We'll make a place for
> you."[80] Then the lord or the chief is under obligation to defend you against the enemies that are
> chasing you. You are now under his protection, and he will protect you.[81]

73   2 Nephi 4:15-35.
74   2 Nephi 5:19.
75   2 Nephi 5:3.
76   2 Nephi 5:2.
77   D. Packard, *et al.*, *Feasting*, p. 92; see 2 Nephi 2:1-2.
78   Arabic *Ana dakhiluka.*
79   "When he says *ahlan*, that means both family and tent" (H. W. Nibley, *Teachings of the Book of Mormon*, 18,
      1:225).
80   In Arabic, "*marhaban* means 'have place'" (*ibid.*).
81   H. W. Nibley, *Teachings of the Book of Mormon*, 16, 1:199; cf. Psalm 27:5, H. W. Nibley, *Approach*, pp. 74-75,

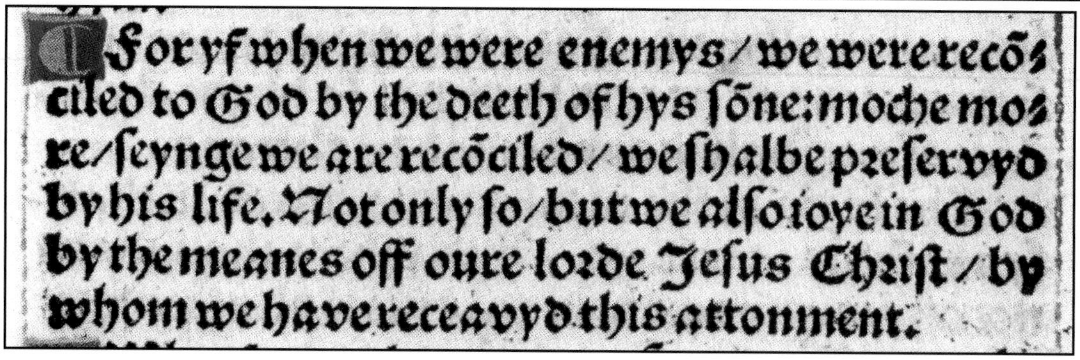
For yf when we were enemys / we were recõ-
ciled to God by the deeth of hys ſõne: moche more / ſeynge we are recõciled / we ſhalbe preſervyd
by his life. Not only ſo / but we alſo ioye in God
by the meanes off oure lorde Jeſus Chriſt / by
whom we have receavyd this attonment.

FIGURE 6-8. *Romans 5:10-11 in William Tyndale's English Translation of the New Testament, 1526*

For if when we were enemies, we were reconciled to God by the death of his Son: much more, seeing we are reconciled, we shall be preserved by his life. Not only so, but we also joy in God by the means of our Lord Jesus Christ, by whom we have received this atonement.[1] Like many others of Tyndale's memorable translations of scriptural phrases, this version became the basis for the historically dominant rendering of the text into English. In the English Bible, "atonement" is "the single word of Anglo-Saxon origin that describes a theological doctrine; other doctrinal words come from Latin, Hebrew, or Greek."[2]

Harold Bloom not only considers William Tyndale "the greatest of [English] Bible translators," but also "the only true rival of Shakespeare, Chaucer, and Walt Whitman as the richest author in the English language," and an "authentic inventor of an English prose style austerely sublime."[3] In a paper delivered at the opening reception of a Library of Congress exhibition on Tyndale and the Bible, David Daniell, chair of the Tyndale Society and curator of the event for the British Library, said: "I was recently in the state of Utah [at Brigham Young University], where a student who is a clever man with a computer gave me at last the definitive figure for how dependent the King James [New Testament] is on Tyndale, and I am happy to announce tonight that the definitive figure is 83 percent. Eighty-three percent of the King James Bible is Tyndale exactly."[4]

Elder John A. Widtsoe considered the King James Bible unsurpassed in its "beauty of language and spiritual connotation."[5] The fact that the Book of Mormon and the Doctrine and Covenants are both "consistent with the King James tradition"[6] allows phrases from any one of these books of scripture to more easily suggest associations with like passages in the other two works.[7] But, questions of literary aesthetics and stylistic consistency aside, how faithful is the KJV translation to the voice of the original? With respect to the Old Testament, Robert Alter, a contemporary expert in the analysis of biblical narrative as literature, has given his opinion as follows: "The language of biblical narrative in its own time was stylized, decorous, dignified, and readily identified by its audiences as a language of literature, in certain ways distinct from the language of quotidian reality. The tricky complication however, is that in most respects it also was not a lofty style, and was certainly neither ornate nor euphemistic.... a plain spoken one, and, moreover one that evinces a strong commitment to using a limited set of terms again and again, making an aesthetic virtue out of repetition... The right direction [for a modern English equivalent to ancient Hebrew style] I think was hit on by the King James Version... There is no good reason to render biblical Hebrew as contemporary English, either lexically or syntactically. This is not to suggest that the Bible should be represented as fussily old-fashioned English, but a limited degree of archaizing coloration is entirely appropriate..."[8] Summarizing the limitations of current translations of the Bible, Alter concludes that "in the case of the modern versions, the problem is a shaky sense of English, and in the case of the King James Version, a shaky sense of Hebrew.... [That being said] the KJV, as Gerald Hammond, an eminent British authority on Bible translations has convincingly argued,[9] remains the closest approach for the English reader to the original—despite its frequent and at times embarrassing inaccuracies, despite its archaisms, and despite its insistent substitution of Renaissance English tonalities and rhythms for biblical ones."[10]

---

1 Tyndale's translation of Romans 5:10-11, spelling modernized.
2 S. M. Wilcox, *Tyndale*, p. 81; but see discussion of Latin precedents in *Excursus 46: The Origin and Meaning of the Term "Atonement"*, p. 642.
3 H. Bloom, *Names Divine*, pp. 28, 47, 31; cf. D. Daniell, *Mind*, pp. 7-8; J. Pelikan, *Whose Bible*, p. 174; N. Shaheen, *References*, pp. 18-19.
4 G. Fineberg, *Let There Be*. See also Y. French, *Courage*.
5 J. A. Widtsoe, *Evidences*, p. 120.
6 D. Packard, *et al.*, *Feasting*, pp. ix-x.
7 J. F. McConkie, *Revelation*, p. 126. See also discussion in P. L. Barlow, *Bible*, pp. 176-177.
8 R. Alter, *Genesis*, p. xxv. See also G. Hammond, *Translations*, pp. 664-665. Note, however, that this statement does not apply equally well in the case of the KJV New Testament. See *Endnote 6-35*, p. 502.
9 G. Hammond, *Translations*.
10 R. Alter, *Genesis*, pp. ix-x. Attempting to correct the deficiencies of the KJV while retaining appropriate elements of its style, Alter has produced masterful translations of the Pentateuch, the story of David, and the Psalms (R. Alter, *Five Books*: R. Alter, *David*; R. Alter, *Psalms*).

Nephi relies on the Lord Himself as his Protector. The scriptural imagery has him running toward the place of safety with upraised arms, a sign of distress that can be seen clearly from a distance, from beyond the point where the sound of the voice could be heard.[82] Above all else, Nephi wants to be encircled with the Lord's robe of righteousness, to be one with Him, to have his sins covered over with the Lord's glory, and to have that glory be eternally upon him. Yet he knows that his deliverance from sin and death will not be a cheap affair that might be effected by a mere declaration of reassuring words. Instead, his Redemption is a possibility that carries a dreadful cost.[83] This truth is no mere footnote to the Gospel but rather, as Alma explains: "the whole meaning of the law, every whit pointing to that great and last sacrifice; and that great and last sacrifice will be the Son of God, yea, infinite and eternal."[84]

The results of this "great and last sacrifice" have been described in many different ways. For example, there is the term "expiate" which means "to completely satisfy or appease; to make propitious"[85] and the term "redeem" which can mean to "pay a ransom to deliver a captive"[86] These two terms address the idea of *justification*, the aspect of the sacrifice of Christ that enables forgiveness and release from the bondage of sin. But they do not adequately express the concept of *sanctification*, the complementary process by which we may be "spiritually… born of God," having received a "mighty change in [our] hearts" and "his image" in our countenances.[87] For, in the end, it is not enough for us to be cleansed from all sin: we must also acquire the divine attributes that qualify us for the society of celestial beings. As Elder Dallin H. Oaks explained: "… the Final Judgment is not just an evaluation of a sum total of good and evil acts—what we have done. It is an acknowledgment of the final effect of our acts and thoughts—what we have become."[88]

Embracing the meaning of each of the more limited descriptions, the term "atonement" describes both the process and the ultimate result of the sacrifice of Jesus Christ.[89] It focuses attention on the most central and important concept of that sacrifice—namely, the idea of "taking two things that have become separated, estranged, or incompatible… and bringing them together again, thus making the two be 'at one.'"[90]

The significance of the Atonement is both intimately personal on the one hand, and a matter of cosmic scale on the other. The cosmic dimension of the Atonement includes the plan of the Father to bring all of creation into perfect harmony, that His "kingdom come. [His] will be done in earth, as it is in heaven."[91] Just as Creation began with subjecting the unity of unorganized matter to successive stages of division and separation, so, in the end of God's work on this earth, all things are to be brought together in one again.[92] For example, in Ephesians 1:10, we read that the Lord intends to "gather together in one all things in Christ, both which are in heaven, and which are on earth."[93] Similarly, in D&C 128:18, the Lord says that "it is necessary in the ushering in of the dispensation of the fulness of times… that a whole and complete union, and

MOSES 6

---

82   See *Endnote 6-30*, p. 499.

83   D. Bonhoeffer, *Cost*, pp. 45-48. "Surely it is a lighter labor to make a world than to save one. Scripture will call the heavens the work of God's finger (Psalm 8:3), but redemption will be called the labor of His arm (Psalm 77:15) and the travail of His soul (Isaiah 53:11)" (W. A. Gage, *Gospel*, pp. 83-84).

84   Alma 34:14.

85   See *Endnote 6-31*, p. 499.

86   See A. Rey, *Dictionnaire*, s.v. "acheter," 1:15-16; "expier," 1:817. See *Endnote 6-32*, p. 499.

87   Alma 5:14. See *Excursus 26: Justification and Sanctification*, p. 596

88   D. H. Oaks, *To Become*, p. 32. See also J. E. Faulconer, *Self-Image*. See *Endnote 6-33*, p. 501. See also *Excursus 22: The Nature of Satan's Premortal Proposal*, p. 577.

89   H. W. Nibley, *Teachings of the Book of Mormon*, 16, 1:199.

90   S. E. Robinson, *Believing*, p. 7. See *Excursus 46: The Origin and Meaning of the Term "Atonement"*, p. 642.

91   Matthew 6:10; cf. 3 Nephi 13:10; D&C 65:5-6; M. Barker, *Earth*, pp. 8-9; H. W. Nibley, *Teachings of the PGP*, 10, p. 126.

92   See *Endnote 6-34*, p. 501.

93   See also 1 Corinthians 15:28; Colossians 1:15-17; D&C 27:13.

Figure 6-9. *Gate to Paradise*
Wulf E. Barsch, 1943-

See Color Plate 6-9.

Adam, do not fear. A god you desired to be; a god I will make you... And after a short time my mercy (will be) revealed to you.[1] Wulf Barsch's depiction of the Gate to Paradise shows the way back to the Garden of Eden. " [T]he palm evokes the wandering tribes of Israel… for it is their hope and succor in the desert."[2]

Born in Reudnitz, Bohemia, Barsch was a student of printmaking and painting in Hanover and Hamburg. His paintings, typically depicting ideal "landscapes of the mind," are replete with abstract symbols of color and form, yet evidence the sensibilities of the old masters.[3] Appraising Barsch's work, Nibley wrote: "there is a sense of deep concern, an ominous and brooding feeling of admonition and warning… The pictures do not tell a story—there is nothing trivial, contrived, clever or cute about them; they seem more like a solemn summing-up, with something of both suspense and finality about them."[4] In his work, Barsch often relates the Gospel to themes of cosmology, astronomy, and ancient Jewish, Christian, and Egyptian tradition. He said: "I've never gotten over the idea that somehow Egypt is our schoolmaster. Joseph Smith knew that the Egyptians had real archaic wisdom. The ancient order, as he called it, and our temples are full of references to eternal life and its connected cosmology. While everyone else throughout the ages threw up their hands in hopelessness at the terrible questions surrounding the cosmos, the ancient Egyptians never gave up asking and praying for answers."[5]

1   S. E. Robinson, *Testament of Adam 1983*, 3:2, p. 994.
2   H. W. Nibley, *From the Earth*, p. 554.
3   R. G. Oman, *et al.*, *Images*, pp. 152-153.
4   H. W. Nibley, *From the Earth*, pp. 552, 554.
5   *All Things*, p. 10.

welding together of dispensations, and keys, and powers, and glories should take place, and be revealed from the days of Adam even to the present time."

The intimate personal dimension of the Atonement was described by Jesus Christ in His "High Priestly Prayer" on behalf of His disciples. He pleaded that they, and those they later would teach, would be "made perfect in one":

> 20 Neither pray I for these alone, but for them also which shall believe on me through their word;
>
> 21 That they all may be one; as thou, Father, art in me, and I in thee, that they also may be one in us: that the world may believe that thou hast sent me.
>
> 22 And the glory which thou gavest me I have given them; that they may be one, even as we are one:
>
> 23 I in them, and thou in me, that they may be made perfect in one[94]

At a first level of understanding, the Hebrew term for atonement, *kippur*, can be thought of as roughly approximating the English word "cover."[95] In the Mosaic temple, the idea of *kippur* related to the *kapporet* that formed the lid of the ark of the temple where Jehovah stood to forgive—or cover—the sins of the people. The veil of the temple, also a *kapporet*, covered the entry of the Holy of Holies. Besides the notion of "covering of sin" implied by the term *kippur*, however, there appears to have been the additional concept of "union,"

94   John 17:20-23; cf. D&C 38 :27. See B. T. Ostler, *God*, pp. 420-423.
95   See *Endnote 6-36*, p. 502.

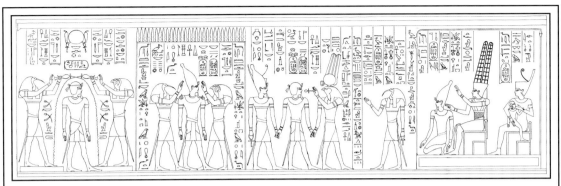

FIGURE 6-10. *Drawing of a Barque Shrine, Karnak, ca. 320 BCE*
Michael P. Lyon, 1952-

I have come into thy presence, Wennefer. I have brought to thee the Osiris Ani, his heart having been found faithful…, having come forth from the testing (balance) devoid of offense to any god or goddess.[1] "This sequence from a temple at Karnak shows how the royal initiation culminated in ritual embraces. In each scene the words of instruction are written over the heads of the speakers. First comes the washing or baptism, then (in another room) the bestowal of crown and throne; then the candidate is conducted by ministers of 'life, health, strength, and joy' to Thoth the [Master of Ceremonies], who introduces him at the last shrine, where he receives the paternal embrace that confirms his 'appearing in glory on the throne of his father Re.' Finally the maternal embrace of Innt, who says, 'I nurse thee with my milk.' Thus the rites end in the intimate embrace of the primordial family."[2]

---

1   *Book of the Dead*: Papyrus of Ani 2:374; 3 pl. 4, as cited in H. W. Nibley, *Message 2005*, p. 448.
2   H. W. Nibley, *Message 2005*, p. 445; cf. H. W. Nibley, *Teachings of the Book of Mormon*, 16, 1:201.

a "covering with glory," in the ancient temple cult.[96] After the priest and the people had completed all the rituals and ordinances of the atonement, the veil was opened so that the Lord could tell the people that their sins had been forgiven, symbolically welcoming them into His presence.[97] Following his study of the term *kippur*, Nibley concluded that:

> … the literal meaning of *kaphar* and *kippurim* is a close and intimate embrace, which took place at the *kapporeth* or the front cover or flap of the Tabernacle or tent.[98] The Book of Mormon instances are quite clear, for example, "Behold, he sendeth an invitation unto all men, for the arms of mercy are extended towards them, and he saith: Repent, and I will receive you."[99] "But behold the Lord hath redeemed my soul from hell; I have beheld his glory, and I am encircled eternally in the arms of his love"[100]… From this it should be clear what kind of oneness is meant by the Atonement—it is being received in a close embrace of the prodigal son, expressing not only forgiveness but oneness of heart and mind that amounts to identity.[101]

Those who, like Adam and Eve, receive the Gospel become "partakers of the divine nature"[102] and by virtue of this fact participate in Christ's sufferings as well as His glory.[103] Nowhere is this fact more apparent than in the temple where, as Madsen points out, "a full-scale covenant relationship, the Atonement of Christ may be written, as it were, in our

---

96   M. Barker, *Temple Theology*, p. 37. Barker associates such ritual imagery with the concept of "cleaving" to God (see A. J. Heschel, *Heavenly Torah*, pp. 190-193). She notes, however, that "the meaning seems to have shifted from 'union' to 'obedience' after the demise of the ancient temple." See *Commentary* 3:24-a, p. 184 and *Excursus 2: Ancient Concepts of Wisdom*, p. 516.
97   H. W. Nibley, *Teachings of the Book of Mormon*, 16, 1:198.
98   See *Endnote 6-37*, p. 503.
99   Alma 5:33.
100   2 Nephi 1:15.
101   H. W. Nibley, *Atonement*, pp. 567-568; cf. the ritual embrace in Egyptian temple rites (H. W. Nibley, *Message 2005*, pp. 445-449). See *Endnote 6-38*, p. 504.
102   2 Peter 1:4. For more on this verse, see J. Starr, *Partakers* and B. T. Ostler, *God*, pp. 392-395.
103   Romans 8:17. See *Endnote 6-39*, p. 504.

FIGURE 6-11. *Drawing from the Stela of Tantamani, Karnak, ca. 660 BCE*
Michael P. Lyon, 1952-

I have received thee in an embrace of gold; I enfold thee with permanence, stability, and satisfaction; I endow thee with health and joy of heart, I immerse thee in rejoicing, joy, gladness of heart and delight forever.[1] "The last king of the 25th Dynasty receives the royal embrace from Amun-Re… The characters on the right are various symbols of embracing."[2] "The two arms [of the *selkit* ideogram here] are embracing, and they are embracing the *djed* symbol, which represents the marrow in the bones.[3] This is called 'health and strength.' He says here, 'I give thee all life and power.' This is a picture of the symbol for life—actually the umbilical cord, the navel. The other is [the] *was* [scepter], which is always rendered as 'power in the priesthood, authority to speak for the priesthood, etc.' Also, when he went forth, according to Moet, they embraced him on either side. The kings always had those two fans called the *shuit* or the *khaibit*. This is the counterweight which hangs on the breast to impart breath and life."[4]

---

1   Ptah the creator to Rameses III, cited in H. W. Nibley, *Message 2005*, p. 452.
2   H. W. Nibley, *Message 2005*, p. 452.
3   In the *Book of the Dead*, the symbol specifically denotes the spine of Osiris (I. Shaw, *et al.*, *Dictionary*, p. 98).
4   H. W. Nibley, *Teachings of the Book of Mormon*, 16, 1:201.

very flesh."[104] "One is… obliged," writes Seaich, to become not only "'one flesh' with Christ, but [also] one life, one sacrifice, thus participating actively in the eternal act of love which began in the heavens."[105] Continues Madsen:

> Anticipating Christ's coming, Nephi exhorted the righteous to "[endure] the crosses of the world."[106] Following his ordeal and resurrection, Christ declared that we must all "take up [our] cross" and "deny [ourselves] of all ungodliness."[107] For the Master, the cross preceded the crown.[108] So also in our lives. Our afflictions may ultimately be swallowed up in the joy of Christ, but we will have had to have come up through our own afflictions to share His throne.[109]

As one who held fast to the promises throughout his own trials, the Prophet Joseph Smith boldly assured the Saints: "All your losses will be made up to you in the resurrection provided you continue faithful [to Christ]. By the vision of the Almighty I have seen it."[110] For all those who, in the footsteps of Adam and Eve, strive to serve God to the best of their understanding, the day will come when both the sufferings of life and the pain of death "shall be sweet unto them"[111] whereas, for the unrepentant, not only the inevitable

---

104   T. G. Madsen, *Suffering*, p. 234. See Romans 8:17; 2 Corinthians 4:10; Galatians 2:20, 6:17; S. C. Malan, *Adam and Eve*, 1:69, pp. 83-84; I. Mika'el, son of Bakhayla, *Godhead*, p. 136, *Commentary* 5:4-a, p. 355, and *Excursus 37: Traditions About the Role of Abel*, p. 617.

105   J. E. Seaich, *Ancient Texts 1995*, p. 550 and Revelation 13:8. Gross notes that "to imitate the 'passion' of a hero-savior in order to ensure salvation" is the heart of the mysteries (J. Gross, *Divinization*, p. 87). Cf. P. E. S. Thompson's observation that the story of God's choosing of Abraham—and later of Israel—"was to demonstrate that it was not an election to privilege… but to responsibility for all mankind" (cited in A. LaCocque, *Trial*, p. 19).

106   2 Nephi 9:18.
107   Moroni 10:32.
108   Cf. C. S. Lewis, *Weight*, p. 105.
109   T. G. Madsen, *Suffering*, pp. 240-241. For William Blake's vision of the struggle to establish the heavenly kingdom on earth, see *Excursus 41: William Blake's "Jerusalem": A Vision of the Kingdom*, p. 627. For Shakespeare's appropriation of Genesis themes relating to Creation and Redemption, see *Excursus 44: Shakespeare Creates a World: "The Tempest"*, p. 635.

110   J. Smith, Jr., *Teachings*, 16 April 1843, p. 296.
111   D&C 42:46.

FIGURE 6-12.
Descent of Christ into Limbo, 1368
Andrea da Firenze, active 1343-1377

SEE COLOR PLATE 6-12.

Remember that… the keeper of the gate is the Holy One of Israel; and he employeth no servant there; and there is none other way save it be by the gate.[1] This painting illustrates the descent of Jesus Christ, after His death and before His resurrection, into what is called in Roman Catholic tradition "Limbo."[2] Limbo was described as a place reserved for the just who died before Jesus Christ came to earth (Limbo of the Patriarchs) and also, in the Augustinian tradition at least, for infants who died before they could receive baptism and be freed from "original sin" (Limbo of Infants).[3] Here, in a depiction of an event called "The Harrowing of Hell,"[4] Jesus Christ is shown carrying a Crusader's flag into the dominion of Death and Hell, whose broken gates are gaping wide.[5] Satan, grasping a useless key, peers out from beneath the feet of the advancing Christ. Adam (recognizable here by his long white hair and beard) and Eve (at his arm) are shown as the first ones to be reclaimed by Christ, followed by Abel (carrying a lamb), and other notables including Abraham, David, and Solomon. As they are brought forth, Adam, Eve, and the other just souls are typically shown in depictions of this scene as being taken by the "right hands of fellowship"[6] or pulled by the wrist from their graves,[7] emphasizing their utter dependence on the sure and steady strength of the Savior for their escape.[8] Nibley paraphrases the teaching of the *Pistis Sophia*, which emphasizes that "[u]ntil Christ came… no soul had gone through the ordinances in their completeness. It was He who opened the gates and the way of life."[9]

Of the significance of this scene for temple worship, Madsen writes: "As the 'keeper of the gate,'[10] Jesus the Christ summons us, 'Come unto me in my holy sanctuary,'[11] and he promises, 'Whoso knocketh, to him will [I] open.'[12] He is in His sanctuary; 'he employeth no servant there.'[13] We who put off our shoes to walk on holy ground need not be put off by the fact that mere mortals administer these divine ordinances. They may be familiar and ordinary persons from just around the corner. Yet they represent the Lord Himself. Christ Himself is blessing us, reaching down to us through those ordinances. The Lord Himself is waiting for us beyond the veil. It is He who voices and magnifies and endows the temples with a summation of human experience that is a step-by-step ascent into His presence."[14]

1　2 Nephi 9:41.
2　From Latin *limbus*, referring to the edge or boundary of hell.
3　R. Giorgi, *Anges*, pp. 46-49; cf. 1 Peter 3:18-21, 4:6 and Ephesians 4:8-10—paraphrasing Psalm 68:18.
4　*Harrowing.*
5　The jaws and teeth of the gates shown here are vestiges from imagery connecting the abyss of hell to the stomach of Leviathan or the great fish that swallowed Jonah. In the Harrowing of Hell, "Christ shoves the cross into death's gullet and forces it to vomit up souls" (C. W. Bynum, *Resurrection*, p. 148n. 102; cf. *ibid.*, pp. 192-199).
6　Galatians 2:9; M. R. James, *Apocryphal*, p. 140.
7　R. Giorgi, *Anges*, pp. 46-48.
8　G. A. Anderson, *Perfection*, pp. 158, 175. See also T. M. Compton, *Handclasp*, pp. 620-621; S. D. Ricks, *Dexiosis*, Mosiah 22:22, *Commentary* 1:25-c, p. 60., *Figure* 5-13, p. 351; *Figure 6-14*, p. 473, *Excursus 53: Comparative Explorations, Dexiosis*, p. 681; and *Figure B-1*, p. 872. See *Endnote 1-22*, p. 79.
9　H. W. Nibley, *Apocryphal*, p. 310. See C. Schmidt, *Pistis*, 3:135, pp. 701-705; G. R. S. Mead, *Pistis*, 4:135, pp. 293-294.
10　2 Nephi 9:41.
11　Matthew 11:28. See 2 Chronicles 30:8; D&C 110:7-9.
12　2 Nephi 9:42.
13　2 Nephi 9:41.
14　T. G. Madsen, *Temple and Atonement*, pp. 77-78.

---

encounter with death but also all memory of their illusory pleasures will be tainted with deep sorrow and bitterness.[112] C. S. Lewis observed profoundly that:

> … both good and evil, when they are full grown, become retrospective. Not only [the Heavenly] valley but all [their] earthly past will have been Heaven to those who are saved. Not only the twilight in [the spirit prison], but all their life on earth too, will then be seen by the damned to have been Hell. That is what mortals misunderstand. They say of some temporal suffering, "No future bliss can make up

---

112　D&C 42:47; cf. Luke 16:25.

for it," not knowing that Heaven, once attained, will work backwards and turn even that agony into a glory. And of some sinful pleasure they say "Let me but have this and I'll take the consequences": little dreaming how damnation will spread back and back into their past and contaminate the pleasure of the sin. Both processes begin even before death. The good man's past begins to change so that his forgiven sins and remembered sorrows take on the quality of Heaven: the bad man's past already conforms to his badness and is filled only with dreariness.[113] And that is why, at the end of all things, when the sun rises [in the place of God's glory] and the twilight turns to blackness down [where Satan reigns], the Blessed will say, 'We have never lived anywhere except in Heaven,' and the Lost, 'We were always in Hell.' And both will speak truly.[114]

Figure 6-13. *Charity with an Anchor, 1876.*
Photo: Jeffrey M. Bradshaw, 1956-

Here, then, are two irrevocable acts …to give powerful encouragement to us, who have claimed his protection by grasping the hope set before us. That hope we hold. It is like an anchor for our lives, an anchor safe and sure. It enters in through the veil, whose Jesus has entered on our behalf as a forerunner, having become a high priest forever after the order of Melchizedek.[1] Alluding to the blessings of the Oath and Covenant of the Priesthood,[2] the author of Hebrews assures the Saints of the firmness and unchangeableness of God's promises. The "two irrevocable acts" are "God's promise and the oath by which He guarantees that promise."[3]

By this scripture, we are meant to understand that so long as the we hold fast to the Redeemer, who has entered "through the veil on our behalf… as a forerunner," we will remain firmly anchored to our heavenly home, and the eventual realization of the promise "that where I am, there ye may be also."[4] There is also undoubtedly the sense that "Jesus, the high priest, [stands] behind the veil in the Holy of Holies to assist those who [pass] through."[5] "The anchor would thus constitute the link that 'extends' or 'reaches' to the safe harbor of the divine realms… providing a means of access by its entry into God's presence."[6] Comparing the symbol of the anchor to an image in Virgil, Witherington concludes that he was "thinking no doubt of an iron anchor with two wings rather than an ancient stone anchor."[7] The shape of the anchor recalls both the covenant and the oath by which the former is "made sure."[8]

The symbol of the anchor can be related to the tradition of pounding nails into the Western Wall of the Jerusalem Temple. Rona writes: "Older texts reveal a now-forgotten custom of the 'sure nails.' This was the practice of bringing one's sins, grief, or the tragedies of life to the remains of the temple wall and 'nailing' them in a sure place. The nails are a reminder of Isaiah's prophecy that man's burden will be removed when the nail in the sure place is taken down."[9]

Christian use of anchor imagery goes back to "the first century cemetery of St. Domitilla, the second and third century epitaphs of the catacombs."[10] Although the anchor is frequently depicted in connection with a figure representing the Hope afforded by Jesus Christ, it is, from the perspective of those who aspire to a place in God's presence, an even more appropriate companion to the crowning blessings associated with the requirement of Charity,[11] as shown in this stained glass panel by Ward and Hughes from the cathedral in Lichfield, England.

1   S. Sandmel, *et al., New English Bible*, Hebrews 6:18-20. See also Ether 12:4.
2   D&C 84:33-48. See also M. G. Romney, *Oath*, p. 17 and *Excursus 3: Temple Blessings in the Oath and Covenant of the Priesthood*, p. 519.
3   K. L. Barney, *NT Footnotes*, 3:82 n. *d.* See also M. G. Romney, *Oath*, p. 17; J. Smith, Jr., *Words*, 27 June 1839, p. 5; J. Smith, Jr., *Documentary History*, 1 May 1842, 4:608; 2 Nephi 31:20; Enos 1:27.
4   John 14:3. See also Hebrews 4:14; H. W. Attridge, *et al., Hebrews*, pp. 118-119.
5   M. Barker, *Risen*, pp. 42-43. See also Gregory Nazianzen, *Oration 39*, 16, p. 358; Origen, *Luke*, Homily 24 on Luke 3:15-16, p. 103; 1 Corinthians 3:13; *Excursus 11: The Sacred Circle*, p. 547.
6   H. W. Attridge, *et al., Hebrews*, p. 184; cf. pp. 185, 222-224. See also L. T. Johnson, *Hebrews*, pp. 172-173.
7   B. Witherington, III, *Letters*, p. 225.
8   2 Peter 1:10,
9   D. Rona, *Revealed*, p. 194. See Isaiah 22:23-25.
10   *Christian Symbols*.
11   See *Figure 5-13*, p. 351. In 2 Nephi 31:20, Nephi associates this "love of God and of all men" with the ultimate attainment of both a *"perfect brightness* of hope" and the sure promise of the Father ("Ye shall have eternal life").

113   See *Endnote 6-41*, p. 505.
114   C. S. Lewis, *Divorce*, pp. 67-68.

FIGURE 6-14.
The Woman at the Tomb and the Ascension, ca. 400

Here, then, are two irrevocable acts …to give powerful encouragement to us, who have claimed his protection by grasping the hope set before us. That hope we hold. It is like an anchor for our lives, an anchor safe and sure. It enters in through the veil, whose Jesus has entered on our behalf as a forerunner, having become a high priest forever after the order of Melchizedek.[1] A fitting metaphor for the mortal lives of Adam and Eve is given in Lehi's dream of the Tree of Life, which included a "rod of iron" to which his sons were urged to cling or hold fast as they advanced on the pathway to eternal life.[2] It is easy to imagine the perilous journey of Lehi's vision as paralleling accounts of ritual ascent by ropes, handrails, and chains to God's presence at the top of sacred mountains.[3] The Islamic mystical text *The Mother of Books* describes such a scene: "Then all the seven palaces and heavenly far spheres are joined… by chains of light as by a rope or cable. The spirit of speech now commands the human spirits, 'Grasp this holy cord, and by this heavenly journey rise higher.' So God's word is fulfilled: 'He holds on to the firm handhold.'"[4] Though such an ascent in ancient times required a combination both of man's efforts and the safety provided by the help of the handholds generously provided, the final step into God's presence has always been made only through the grace of the condescending Lord, whose eternally-binding gesture of welcome, fellowship, and safety was required to assure the initiate a permanent place beyond the veil.[5] Note that the "great and spacious building" of Lehi's vision was, like the mountain of Paradise, also "high above the earth."[6] Erected in the same spirit as was the Tower of Babel,[7] it represents all man-made rivals to the sacred Mountain of the Lord.

About this illustration, Nibley comments: "This ancient Christian diptych combines Resurrection and Ascension motifs in a way that recalls Egyptian parallels… Note especially the stretched-forth hand that receives the ascending one[8] and the document that he holds."[9] Though most sources see the hand as belonging to God, the Mandaean *Ginza* describes a scene where the worthy deceased one, interred in his sacral garment, is raised by the hand of Adam.[10] The building is the original form of the Holy Sepulchre or "Edicule," rebuilt in the 19th century within the larger church of the same name.[11] "An angel sits in front of the tomb (flanked by sleeping Roman guards) and speaks to the three Marys of the Resurrection."[12] Near the entrance to the heavenly sanctuary are two apostles, most likely Peter and James,[13] one covering his face and the other praying with uplifted hands.[14] Beside them and immediately adjacent to the sepulchre stands a Tree of Life. Two birds perch in its branches, though only one of them can be said to be definitely eating of its fruit.[15]

---

1   S. Sandmel, *et al.*, *New English Bible*, Hebrews 6:18-20; cf. p. 246. See also Isaiah 42:6, Philippians 3:10-14.

2   1 Nephi 8:20-24, 30; 15:23-24.

3   H. W. Nibley, *Teachings of the PGP*, 16, p. 195; cf. *Figure 3-7*, p. 143. See *Endnote 6-44*, p. 505.

4   W. Barnstone, *et al.*, *Mother*, p. 683 and *Qur'an* 2:2:256, 31:22. See *Endnote 6-45*, p. 506.

5   John 14:2-23; D&C 98:18.

6   1 Nephi 8:26; cf. 11:35-36, 12:18.

7   Genesis 11:1-9.

8   Here, of course, the figure represents Jesus Christ (W. J. Hamblin, *Temple Motifs*, p. 473 n. 99).

9   H. W. Nibley, *Message 2005*, p. 456.

10   K. Rudolph, *Coptic*, GL 3:43, p. 270; cf. J. Smith, Jr., *Teachings*, 2 July 1839, p. 157; 5 October 1840, p. 168. See *Endnote 6-46*, p. 506.

11   A. Parrot, *Golgotha*, p. 82; Z. Vilnay, *et al.*, *Vilnay Guide*, pp. 102-103.

12   W. J. Hamblin, *et al.*, *Temple*, p. 105.

13   In an apocryphal account, only these two, rather than the full set of apostles, receive special instructions from Jesus Christ and witness His Ascension (F. E. Williams, *Apocryphon of James*, 15:5-16:2, pp. 36-37). See also D. R. Cartlidge, *et al.*, *Art*, p. 133.

14   See *Commentary 5:4-a*, p. 355.

15   J. O'Reilly, *Iconography*, p. 176; cf *Commentary 1:1-b*, p. 42; *3:9-g*, p. 165; *4:5-b*, p. 246; *Figure 3-8*, p. 145; *Excursus 50: Fu Xi and Nü Gua*, p. 654. See *Endnote 6-47*, p. 506.

MOSES 6

Moses 6:1-12: Text and Commentary

CHAPTER 6
(November–December 1830)

RIGHTEOUS LINE OF SETH (PP. 475-478)

AND *a*Adam hearkened unto the voice of God, and *b*called upon his sons to repent.

2 And *a*Adam knew his wife again, and she bare a son, and he called his name *b*Seth. And *c*Adam glorified the name of God; for he said: *d*God hath appointed me another seed, instead of Abel, whom Cain slew.

3 And God revealed himself unto Seth, and *a*he rebelled not, but offered an acceptable sacrifice, like unto his brother Abel. And to him also was born a son, and he called his name *b*Enos.

4 And *a*then began these men to call upon the name of the Lord, and the Lord blessed them;

BOOK OF REMEMBRANCE (PP. 478-483)

5 And a *a*book of remembrance was kept, in the which was recorded, *b*in the language of Adam, for it was giv-en unto as many as called upon God *c*to write by the spirit of inspiration;

6 And by them their *a*children were taught to read and write, having a *b*language which was pure and undefiled.

7 Now *a*this same Priesthood, *b*which was in the beginning, shall be in the end of the world also.

8 Now *a*this prophecy Adam spake, as he was moved upon *b*by the Holy Ghost, and a *c*genealogy was kept of the children of God. And *d*this was the book of the generations of Adam, saying: In the day that God created man, in the likeness of God made he him;

9 *a*In the image of his own body, male and female, created he them, and blessed them, and *b*called their name Adam, in the day when they were created and became living souls in the land upon the *c*footstool of God.

10 And Adam lived one hundred and thirty years, and begat a son *a*in his own likeness, after his own image, and called his name Seth.

11 And the days of Adam, after he had begotten Seth, were *a*eight hundred years, and he *b*begat many sons and daughters;

12 And all the days that Adam lived were *a*nine hundred and thirty years, and *b*he died.

(Moses 6:13-8:30 follows in the Pearl of Great Price)

*1 And **Adam hearkened unto the voice of God**, and **called upon his sons to repent**.*

*2 And **Adam knew his wife again**, and she bare a son, and he called his name **Seth**. And Adam glorified the name of God; for he said: God hath appointed me another seed, instead of Abel, whom Cain slew.*

1   **a**   ***Adam hearkened unto the voice of God.*** This statement about Adam contrasts with 5:57, where we are told that the sons of men "would not hearken unto [God's] voice." Consistent with the declaration[115] and decree[116] of the Lord, Adam preached repentance to his posterity.

          As in Moses 5:5, note that only Adam's name is mentioned, and not Eve's.[117] This omission should not be taken as implying that Eve did *not* hearken.

   b   ***called upon his sons to repent.*** Cf. *Commentary* 5:12-a, p. 364.

2   **a**   ***Adam knew his wife again.*** Because of his grief at the loss of Abel, some traditions record that Adam "knew his wife again" to conceive Seth only when he was finally commanded to do so by an angel.[118]

          Verse 2 constitutes both a summing up of the previous chapter and an anticipation of the next several verses of this one, consistent with Cassuto's two principles of biblical exposition: 1. that the "conclusion of a narrative should reflect the opening," and 2. "that the stories should have happy endings."[119] In both sections, "Adam knew his wife," the child is named with reference to the Lord/God, Cain and Abel are mentioned, and two births are recorded.[120] Moreover, just as Adam and Eve "ceased not to call upon God,"[121] Seth and Enos will "call upon the name of the Lord."[122]

          Despite the death of Abel, a righteous posterity to Adam will be raised up through Seth, ensuring the continuity of a covenant people. Parallels between Abel and Seth are made explicit in vv. 2-3. The shedding of the blood of the righteous and innocent Abel— the beloved son of the Ancient of Days whose story has always been linked with the idea of proper sacrifice[123]—seems to have given rise to a curious ordinance of sprinkling with blood and "washing" (or "baptism") for little children that was denounced by the Lord in JST Genesis 17:4-7.[124]

   b   ***Seth.*** Sarna connects the name Seth "with the stem *sh-y-t,* 'to place, put, set'… Since the noun *shat* means 'foundation,' as in Isaiah 19:10 and Psalm 11:3, there may lie behind the name the notion that, as *Numbers Rabbah* 14:20 has it, 'With him the world was founded [anew].'"[125] In this sense, there also may be an allusion to temple-building and seership.[126]

          Nibley conjectures that "Seth means 'second or substitute or equal.' *Shetaa* means the same thing as two, double, [or] twin because it tells us in the scriptures that he will take the place of Abel."[127] Islamic tradition reports that, in contrast to stories about Adam and Eve's previous

---

115   Moses 5:14-15.
116   Moses 5:58-59.
117   See *Commentary* 5:5-c, p. 359; cf. 5:1-d, p. 354.
118   W. L. Lipscomb, *Seth,* 1-4, pp. 189-190; cf. Ibn Kathir in B. M. Wheeler, *Prophets,* p. 29. See also *Commentary* 5:2-a, p. 354.
119   U. Cassuto, *Adam to Noah,* p. 190.
120   *Ibid.,* p. 243. See Moses 5:16-17, 6:2-3.
121   Moses 5:16.
122   Moses 6:4.
123   J. Smith, Jr., *Teachings,* 22 January 1834, pp. 58-59.
124   Cf. Moroni 8. See also *Excursus 37: Traditions About the Role of Abel,* p. 617.
125   N. M. Sarna, *Genesis,* p. 39; cf. H. Freedman, *et al., Midrash,* 6:618.
126   See *Figure* 3:10, p. 147 and *Commentary* 2:9-a, p. 105. See *Endnote 4-9,* p. 299.
127   H. W. Nibley, *Teachings of the PGP,* 21, p. 260.

2 And Adam knew his wife again, and she bare a son, and he called his name **Seth**. *And* **Adam glorified the name of God; for he said: God hath appointed me another seed, instead of Abel, whom Cain slew.**

children, "Seth was born without a twin,"[128] perhaps suggesting that he was a "replacement" for Abel.[129]

Gardner suggests a derivation of the name from the Babylonian word for "six," "as a description, not only evocative of the Babylonian numerical system's base 60…, but suggestive also of new creation in view of Adam's being created on the sixth day…[130] Seth's name is theologically evocative of new beginnings:[131] there are six years between sabbath years."[132]

c   ***Adam glorified the name of God; for he said.*** Notably, the book of Moses has Adam rather than Eve giving the child a name. The phrase "for he said" implies that Adam "glorified the name of God" in the very act of naming. Indeed, whereas in the naming of Cain, Eve said "*I* have gotten,"[133] Adam said of Seth "*God* hath appointed."[134] For a discussion of the "two different systems of naming children"—namely, either by the father or by the mother—see Cassuto.[135]

d   ***God hath appointed me another seed, instead of Abel, whom Cain slew.*** Joseph Fielding McConkie observes that Seth is "effectually the second Abel. As such he becomes a natural type for Christ, who like Abel was first a martyr, and then like the second Abel, Seth, ruled in glory with his father."[136] An Armenian text explains: "Seth was given to Adam as a son of consolation, in place of Abel. God pronounced him and his sons, 'Sons of God.' And this is the reason that he made writing. He was first called 'God.'… And [his posterity] were called true 'sons of God' because God loved them, before they fornicated"[137]—i.e., when later Sethites began to follow the wicked practices of the Cainites.[138]

The story of the families of Cain and Seth introduces a larger theme that will continue throughout the OT: "Though Cain's sons have prospered and become the founders of the new world after the Fall, the focus of the narrative turns from the line of Cain to that of the new son born 'in place of Abel.'… In such narratives as these, the author clearly betrays his interest in the 'seed'[139] (*zera*) of the woman. The focus is on the 'seed' and the one who will crush the head of the snake. A pattern is established in chapter [5] that will remain the thematic center of the book. The one through whom the promised seed will come is not the heir apparent, that is, the eldest son, but the one whom God chooses[140][—a motif first introduced in the story of Satan's jealousy of Michael's preeminent position in premortality[141]]. Abel, the younger of the two sons, received God's favor,[142] Seth, still the younger son, replaced Abel."[143] This pattern is repeated in the stories of Isaac[144] (replacing

---

128   al-Tabari, *Creation*, 1:152, p. 324.
129   See *Commentary* 6:2-d, p. 476.
130   Moses 2:26-31.
131   Moses 6:2-3.
132   B. K. Gardner, *Calendar*, p. 195 n. 577.
133   Moses 5:16.
134   Cf. V. P. Hamilton, *Genesis*, p. 242; R. M. Zlotowitz, *et al.*, *Bereishis*, p. 164.
135   U. Cassuto, *Documentary*, pp. 65-66.
136   J. F. McConkie, *Symbolism*, p. 181. See Moses 6:3-4.
137   M. E. Stone, *Abel*, 4:2, 4:5, pp. 150, 151.
138   See Moses 5 *Gleanings*, p. 415.
139   Moses 4:21.
140   H. W. Nibley, *Teachings of the PGP*, p. 238.
141   See *Excursus 21: The Power and Premortal Status of Satan*, p. 575; cf. *Commentary* 4:6-a, p. 249.
142   Moses 5:17.
143   J. H. Sailhamer, *Genesis*, p. 69.
144   Genesis 17:19,

2 And Adam knew his wife again, and she bare a son, and he called his name Seth. And Adam glorified the name of God; for he said: **God hath appointed me another seed, instead of Abel, whom Cain slew***.*

3 And God revealed himself unto Seth, and **he rebelled not, but offered an acceptable sacrifice, like unto his brother Abel***. And to him also was born a son, and he called his name* **Enos***.*

4 And **then began these men to call upon the name of the Lord***, and the Lord blessed them;*

Ishmael), Jacob[145] ("supplanting" Esau), Ephraim and Manasseh[146] (replacing Reuben and Simeon), and Jacob and Joseph[147] ("first-born… in tribulation" as replacements for Laman and Lemuel)."[148] In contrast, "Cain takes his place in the narrative as one who was not to become part of the line of the 'seed,' With him throughout the remainder of the Book of Genesis are Japheth,[149] Ham,[150] Nahor,[151] Ishmael,[152] Lot,[153] and Esau."[154]

3   a   *he rebelled not, but offered an acceptable sacrifice, like unto his brother Abel.* Seth's obedience to the law of sacrifice confirms that he is indeed a fitting replacement for the righteous Abel.[155]

b   *Enos.* Like the name "Adam," Enos (or Enosh) means "man."[156] While the choice of Cain's name had revealed Eve's hope for a child that could be looked on as God himself,[157] the name of Seth's son "puts the emphasis on the basic frailty of man because the stem '-*n-sh* means 'to be weak.'"[158]

Cassuto notes a second parallel between Adam and Enos: "This son would be the founder of the human race belonging to the line of Seth, which was destined to survive upon earth, just as [the Cainite] Enoch was the inaugurator of the branch of mankind descended from Cain, whose days were not prolonged."[159]

4   a   *then began these men to call upon the name of the Lord.* Cassuto points out the "parallelism of both language and theme here: a human being is called by a name suited to him—Enosh; and God is called by a name befitting Him—Lord [YHWH]."[160] Perhaps a stronger parallel is to be found with v. 1: Adam "called upon his sons to repent," and they in turn "began… to call upon the name of the Lord." Previously, when Adam and Eve "called upon the name of the Lord,"[161] they were answered with commandments and angelic visitations revealing priesthood ordinances. Likely, we are meant to infer that the prayers of Seth and Enos were answered similarly.[162]

MOSES 6

145   Genesis 27:36,

146   Genesis 48:5,

147   2 Nephi 2:1-2,

148   J. A. Tvedtnes, *First-Born*, p. 208.

149   Genesis 10:2-5.

150   Genesis 10:6-20.

151   Genesis 11:29; 22:20-24.

152   Genesis 17:20.

153   Genesis 19:19-38.

154   J. H. Sailhamer, *Genesis*, p. 69. On Esau, see Genesis 36.

155   *Commentary* 6:2-b, p. 475.

156   U. Cassuto, *Adam to Noah*, p. 246.

157   See *Commentary* 5:16-e, p. 368.

158   N. M. Sarna, *Genesis*, p. 39.

159   U. Cassuto, *Adam to Noah*, p. 246, cf. p. 229. See *Commentary* 5:42-a, p. 390.

160   U. Cassuto, *Adam to Noah*, p. 246.

161   Moses 5:4.

162   cf. Moses' experiences—see *Commentary* 1:17-b, p. 55; 1:18, 20, 25

*4 And **then began these men to call upon the name of the Lord**, and the Lord blessed them;*

*5 And a **book of remembrance was kept**, in the which was recorded, in the language of Adam, for it was given unto as many as called upon God to write by the spirit of inspiration;*

A contrasting parallel should also be noted: "And men began from that time forth to be carnal, sensual, and devilish."[163] This parallel may account for the idea in the targums that idol worship commenced at this time.[164]

While this verse contains the fourth instance in four verses of "call" and "name," it contains the only instance of "Lord" (= Jehovah, instead of "God"). Cassuto notes the key position that the mention of the name of Jehovah plays with respect to the Genesis account, observing that the corresponding verse occurs "precisely at the seventieth reference" to the Divine name, and that "with these words the section comes to an end. It is inconceivable that all this should be pure coincidence."[165]

5   a   ***book of remembrance was kept.*** Nibley infers from this scripture that "the written records should be as old as the human race itself... According to [the ancients], the king had access to that divine book which was consulted at the time of the creation of the world... A later... Pharaoh recalls, 'My heart yearned to behold the most ancient books of Atum. Open them before me for diligent searching, that I may know god as he really is!'... In Egypt every step of the founding of a new temple had to follow the prescriptions given in the heavenly book, since such a founding represented and dramatized the creation of the earth itself."[166]

The theme of writing is associated with Adam in the story of the *cheirograph*[167] and in various traditions concerning the testament of Adam.[168] The *Zohar* also has a tradition of an esoteric Book of Adam that was transmitted to him "after his departure from the Garden of Eden" by the angel Rezial and "three envoys" who accompanied him. The same book was also said to have been given to the righteous Enoch and to the "sons of Elohim, who contemplate and know it."[169] The book was intended to preserve "the primordial wisdom of paradise for Adam and his generations" and also "the genealogy of the entire human race." A pseudepigraphal *Sefer Rezial* was compiled in its present form in the seventeenth century "comprising ancient magical, mystical, and cosmological teachings."[170]

Al-Kis'ai recounts that "on the first night of Ramadan... God revealed to Adam twenty-two leaves, on which were several chapters written in disjointed letters, none of which were joined together. This was the first book God revealed to Adam. It contained a thousand words, comprising duties, traditions, legislation, the foreboding threat, and accounts of the world. In it God showed him the actions of the people of every age... Adam looked upon all of that and knew what his children would do after him. And Adam read it to his children. Then God commanded him to write... with the pen the twenty-eight letters which are in the *Torah*, the Gospels, the Psalms, and the *Qur'an*.... When these letters had been revealed, Adam learned them and taught them to his son Seth... until God sent Enoch... to whom He revealed fifty pages... And they passed down the Books of Seth and Enoch and the Book of Adam until the time of Noah and Abraham."[171]

163   Moses 5:13.

164   See J. W. Etheridge, *Onkelos*; M. Maher, *Pseudo-Jonathan*, 4:26, p. 35.

165   U. Cassuto, *Adam to Noah*, p. 192.

166   H. W. Nibley, *Written Word*, p. 104. See *Excursus 16: The Role of Revelation in Temple Building*, p. 561.

167   See the overview of Moses 5, p. 332 and *Excursus 37: Traditions About the Role of Abel*, p. 617.

168   E.g., S. E. Robinson, *Testament of Adam*.

169   D. C. Matt, *Zohar 1*, Be-Reshit 1:37b, pp. 237-238; cf. Be-Reshit 1:55b, pp. 310-313.

170   D. C. Matt, *Zohar 1*, p. 237 n. 1041.

171   M. al-Kisa'i, *Tales*, pp. 75-76; cf. al-Tabari, *Creation*, 1:151, p. 322.

*5 And a **book of remembrance was kept**, in the which was recorded, **in the language of Adam**, for it was given unto as many as called upon God to write by the spirit of inspiration;*

Consistent with an emphasis on the central role of language and writing in the story of Adam, some Islamic traditions assert that the first thing created by God was a divine pen.[172] No doubt inspired by a relevant verse in the *Qur'an*,[173] this story might also "reflect an extension of the Christian notion that the pen is an extension of the Logos or Word."[174] After having given instructions to his posterity, Adam was said to have written his "will" (= testament) which was then prominently "placed on a ladder (like that used for the ascent and descent of angels and souls),"[175] thus providing a hint as to its contents. The divine pen was also associated with "prophethood," as in the case of Enoch who, in order to emphasize the nature of this gift, specifically was said to have written with "the pen."[176]

b **in the language of Adam.** In similar words, Nephi writes that his record was made "in the language of [his] father."[177] Verse 6, however, says that the language used by Adam and his children "was pure and undefiled." Of relevance, as Robertson acknowledges, is the "widely held Mormon belief that the founding members of the Jaredite civilization preserved the Adamic language at their immigration to the New World.[178] Thus the description by the brother of Jared of his apocalyptic vision was rendered linguistically inaccessible without divine interpretive help, since 'the language which ye shall write I [God] have confounded.'"[179] Robertson wisely cautions, however, that the "concept of the Adamic language grew among Latter-day Saints out of statements from scripture, comments of early Church leaders, and subsequent tradition. It does not play a central doctrinal role, and there is no official Church position delineating its nature or status."[180]

Widespread Jewish tradition has it that "Hebrew was the original language of mankind until the time of the confusion of languages, and that Eber was the only one who retained it."[181] *Jubilees* 12:25-27 sees Hebrew as the "tongue of creation," which had to be revealed anew to Abraham "because it ceased from the mouth of all of the sons of men from the day of the Fall."[182] Islam includes a "belief in the singular qualities of Arabic,"[183] however it was not Adam but Ishmael who was said to have been "the first to speak in proper and correct Arabic."[184]

Eco has written an engrossing survey from ancient to modern times of the quest either to recover or to invent the perfect language.[185] McWhorter and Ostler have written accessible "natural histories" of language,[186] and Pennock has argued against both old creationism and "intelligent design," using linguistic evolution as a test case.[187] Ruhlen attempts to demonstrate widespread underappreciated connections between the world's language families.[188]

172   M. al-Kisa'i, *Tales*, 1, p. 5; al-Tabari, *Creation*, pp. 198-203.
173   *Qur'an* 96:4.
174   M. Ibn Ishaq ibn Yasar, *Making*, p. 33.
175   al-Tabari, *Creation*, 1:161, p. 332; cf. M. Ibn Ishaq ibn Yasar, *Making*, p. 41. See *Figures* 1-2 and 1-3, p. 34, and *Figure* 5-13, p. 351.
176   M. Ibn Ishaq ibn Yasar, *Making*, p. 42.
177   1 Nephi 1:2.
178   Ether 1:33-43; 3:24-28.
179   Ether 3:21-28.
180   J. S. Robertson, *Adamic Language*, p. 18.
181   L. Ginzberg, *Legends*, 5:205 n. 91.
182   O. S. Wintermute, *Jubilees*, p. 82.
183   F. Leemhuis, *Interpretation*, p. 155.
184   Ibn Kathir, cited in B. M. Wheeler, *Prophets*, p. 109; cf. Abu Ja'far al-Baqir: "clear Arabic" (cited in B. M. Wheeler, *Prophets*, p. 110; cf. *Qur'an* 16:103, 26:195).
185   U. Eco, *Search*.
186   J. McWhorter, *Power of Babel*; N. Ostler, *Empires*.
187   R. T. Pennock, *Tower*, esp. pp. 117-179. See G. Deutscher, *Unfolding* for an account of linguistic evolution.
188   M. Ruhlen, *Origin*.

MOSES 6

*5 And a book of remembrance was kept, in the which was recorded, in the language of Adam, for it was given unto as many as called upon God **to write by the spirit of inspiration**;*

*6 And by them **their children were taught to read and write**, having a **language which was pure and undefiled**.*

*7 Now **this same Priesthood, which was in the beginning, shall be in the end of the world also**.*

*8 **Now this prophecy Adam spake**, as he was moved upon **by the Holy Ghost**, and a **genealogy was kept of the children of God**. And this was the book of the generations of Adam, saying: In the day that God created man, in the likeness of God made he him;*

    c   **to write by the spirit of inspiration.** OT1 renders this phrase as: "to write with the finger of inspiration."[189]

6   **a**   **their children were taught to read and write.** See *Commentary* 6:5-a, p. 478.

    b   **language which was pure and undefiled.** See *Commentary* 6:5-b, p. 479.

7   **a**   **this same Priesthood.** That is, the patriarchal order of the priesthood.[190]

      OT1 reads with a slight difference: "Now this was in the beginning that shall be at the end of the world."[191]

    b   **which was in the beginning, shall be in the end of the world also.** In D&C 29:30, the Lord declared that "the first shall be last, and that the last shall be first in all things whatsoever I have created by the word of my power." In the beginning, God established the same patriarchal order on earth that had been known in heaven. "It was a perfect theocratic, patriarchal system with father Adam at the head. This system prevailed among the righteous from Adam to the time of Abraham and beyond."[192] In the last dispensation God has restored the higher priesthood and associated ordinances of the Abrahamic covenant that had been generally withheld from Israel.[193] "Today dedicated husbands and wives enter this order in the temple in a covenant with God. The blessings of this priesthood [are] given only to husbands and wives together."[194]

      This restored order is "the Melchizedek Priesthood organized according to an eternal family order, rather than according to offices, quorums, and councils that comprised the Church as an instrument to build up the divine patriarchal order."[195] During the Millennium, it will be gradually put into full operation. Elder Joseph Fielding Smith wrote that the celestial family organization will be "one that is complete—an organization linked from father and mother and children of one generation, to the father and mother and children of the next generation, thus expanding and spreading out down to the end of time."[196]

8   **a**   **Now this prophecy Adam spake.** Evidently referring to the statement recorded in v. 7.

    b   **by the Holy Ghost.** This phrase is present in OT2 but not in OT1.[197]

    c   **genealogy was kept of the children of God.** The scriptures are mainly a record of the patriarchs and their descendants—the fate of other lines remains more or less a mystery. Highlighting

---

189   S. H. Faulring, *et al.*, *Original Manuscripts*, p. 97.

190   H. L. Andrus, *Perfection*, pp. 299-330.

191   S. H. Faulring, *et al.*, *Original Manuscripts*, p. 97.

192   R. L. Millet, *et al.*, *Destiny*, p. 39.

193   D&C 84:23-25; JST Exodus 34:1-2. See also B. R. McConkie, *NT Commentary*, 2:503-504.

194   L. A. McKinlay, *Patriarchal Order*.

195   H. L. Andrus, *Doctrines*, pp. 159-160.

196   J. F. Smith, Jr., *Doctrines*, 4 April 1942, 2:175. See *Excursus 9: The Premortal Organization of the Human Family*, p. 544.

197   S. H. Faulring, *et al.*, *Original Manuscripts*, pp. 97, 608.

*8 Now this prophecy Adam spake, as he was moved upon by the Holy Ghost, and a **geneal-ogy was kept of the children of God**. And **this was the book of the generations of Adam**, saying: In the day that God created man, in the likeness of God made he him;*

*9 **In the image of his own body**, male and female, created he them, and blessed them, and **called their name Adam**, in the day when they were created and became living souls in the land upon the footstool of God.*

our ignorance of these peoples, Nibley asks: "What about those people who lived before Cain and Abel?[198] What about those who disappeared from sight?[199] What about those who were not even warned of the Flood?[200] What about those many, many who visited the earth as resurrected beings?[201] What about the Watchers?[202] What about the sons of God who should not marry the daughters of men, and vice versa?[203] And what about the giants they begot when they did marry?[204] What about the comings and goings of Enoch's day between the worlds?…[205] What about the Cainites?[206] What about the nations among whom Noah will have surviving progeny?…[207] Methuselah boasted about his line as something special.[208] Why special if it included the whole human race? These blessings have no meaning if all the people of the earth and all the nations are the seed of Noah and Enoch."[209]

d ***this was the book of the generations of Adam.*** Sarna comments: "This is most likely the title of an ancient genealogical work that served as the source for the data provided in the present chapter, in [Genesis] 11:10-27, and possibly in other genealogical lists as well. Hebrew *sefer*, here rendered ['book'], specifically denotes a written document, not an oral composition."[210] Interrupted by restored extracts from the lost book of Enoch,[211] the account contained in this record is seemingly resumed again in Moses 8:1.[212]

Comments Nibley: "Adam becomes Adam, a hominid becomes a man, when he starts keeping a record. What kind of record? A record of his ancestors—the family line that sets him off from all other creatures… That gap between the record keeper and all the other creatures we know anything about is so unimaginably enormous and yet so neat and abrupt that we can only be dealing with another sort of being, a quantum leap from one world to another. Here is something not derivative from anything that has gone before on the local scene, even though they all share the same atoms."[213]

9 a ***In the image of his own body.*** See *Commentary* 2:26-c, p. 113.

b ***called their name Adam.*** Here "Adam" is used as a name for all mankind, men and women, rather than as the proper name of the first father.[214]

MOSES 6

198 Moses 5:12.
199 Moses 7:21.
200 Moses 7:12, 22.
201 E.g., Genesis 18:2, 19:1, 32:24.
202 J. L. Kugel, *Traditions*, pp. 179-185, 194-216; H. Schwartz, *Tree*, pp. 457-458; *Excursus 24: The Watchers*, p. 585.
203 Moses 8:13-22.
204 Moses 8:18.
205 Moses 7:27.
206 Moses 8:41-42.
207 Moses 7:51-53.
208 Moses 8:2-3.
209 H. W. Nibley, *Before Adam*, p. 79. For a longer version of this statement by Nibley, see Moses 3 *Gleanings*, p. 195.
210 N. M. Sarna, *Genesis*, p. 41.
211 Moses 6:26-7:69.
212 See *Commentary* 6:5-a, p. 478.
213 H. W. Nibley, *Before Adam*, pp. 82, 83.
214 See *Commentary* 2:27-a, p. 115.

9 In the image of his own body, male and female, created he them, and blessed them, and called their name Adam, in the day when they were created and became living souls in the land upon the **footstool of God.**

10 And Adam lived one hundred and thirty years, and begat a son **in his own likeness, after his own image**, *and called his name Seth.*

11 And the days of Adam, after he had begotten Seth, were **eight hundred years**, *and he begat many sons and daughters;*

c   **footstool of God.** Draper, *et al.* note that this "is the earliest reference to the earth as God's footstool. On one level, it links him closely with the earth. On another, it demonstrates that the created or terrestrial order [before the Fall stood] below the celestial order."[215]

10   a   **in his own likeness, after his own image.** Writes Friedman: "The first man's similarity to his son is described with the same two nouns that are used to describe the first two humans' similarity to God.[216] It certainly sounds as if it means something physical here… In any case, the significance of this verse is to establish that whatever it is that the first humans acquire from God, it is something that passes by heredity. It is not only the first two humans but the entire species that bears God's image."[217] Sarna concurs: "Each act of procreation is an imitation of God's original creation of man."[218]

With respect to Seth, Stone notes that in the scriptural account he "is said to have been created in the image of Adam,[219] while various accounts in the Adam literature call him the 'image of God.'"[220] By way of contrast, "Cain… was *not* similar to Adam."[221] The *Cave of Treasures* records that Seth was called "the Beautiful" and was "a man mighty and perfect like unto Adam."[222] Similarly, in a statement about his brother Alvin, the Prophet said that he "was a very handsome man, surpassed by none but Adam and Seth, and of great strength."[223] D&C 107:43 records that Seth "was a perfect man, and his likeness was the express likeness of his father, insomuch that he seemed to be like unto his father in all things, and could be distinguished from him only by his age." Adam has also been described as "beautiful" in both ancient and modern sources.[224]

Hamilton observes that all of this is a fulfillment of a promised blessing: "That Adam reproduces himself through Seth, and Seth through Enosh, etc., demonstrates that God's blessing has become effective. They are not only created by God but blessed by God. Such blessing is manifested in multiplication. It is appropriate that the creation of man be prefaced to Adam's descendants through Seth rather than through Cain."[225]

11   a   **eight hundred years.** A change to OT1 in Oliver Cowdery's handwriting reads "870." This change was made sometime after his return from his mission to the Lamanites in August 1831 and before July 1832.[226] He also made several other changes to the ages of the patriarchs in OT1, but they do not appear in OT2, which had been transcribed previously. It cannot be definitively confirmed whether these changes were made under the direction of the Prophet,

---

215   R. D. Draper, *et al.*, *Commentary*, p. 87.
216   Moses 2:26-27.
217   R. E. Friedman, *Commentary*, p. 30.
218   N. M. Sarna, *Genesis*, p. 41. See *Commentary* 2:26-c, p. 113.
219   Moses 6:10.
220   See, e.g., M. E. Stone, *Armenian Apocrypha* 1996, p. 150 n. 4.2.
221   *Targum Jonathan*, cited in R. M. Zlotowitz, *et al.*, *Bereishis*, p. 168.
222   E. A. W. Budge, *Cave*, p. 71; cf. S. C. Malan, *Adam and Eve*, 2:2, pp. 105-106; Shelemon, *Book of the Bee*, 18, p. 27.
223   J. Smith, Jr., *Documentary History*, 9 January 1843, 5:247.
224   See *Endnote 5-5*, p. 433.
225   V. P. Hamilton, *Genesis*, p. 255.
226   S. H. Faulring, *et al.*, *Original Manuscripts*, p. 97; K. P. Jackson, *Book of Moses*, p. 102. See also *Excursus 40: Dating Joseph Smith's Vision of Adam-ondi-Ahman*, p. 625.

*11 And the days of Adam, after he had begotten Seth, were **eight hundred years**, and he **begat many sons and daughters**;*

*12 And all the days that Adam lived were **nine hundred and thirty years**, and **he died**.*

however there is a parallel in one instance between the revised age of the prophet Enoch in Moses 8:1 and his age in D&C 107:49, which was recorded in 1835.[227]

About these changes, Jackson and Swift observe: "As we study the ages of the Patriarchs, we find there is always internal consistency for each man. There is never an instance in which the age has been changed for how long a Patriarch lived after the birth of his son without the same number of years being add to the Patriarch's life.... Although there is internal consistency for each Patriarch, there is no such consistency throughout the changes. No two men have the same number of years added to their lives... Also, there is no discernible pattern among the changes."[228] Moreover, none of these changes are reflected in the numerous variations found in ancient manuscripts of the Bible.

Although no explanation is provided for the puzzlingly long lives of the patriarchs, the careful attention given to their ages by the Prophet here, in D&C 107:42-53, and in the *Lectures on Faith* argues for the conclusion that their ages were interpreted literally by him. Note that in view of the "exaggerated traditions current in the ancient East," Cassuto concludes that the ancient reader would find these numbers "low and modest"![229] Writes Friedman: "It is clear that this author thought of a year as a normal solar year because that is how long the Flood lasts. The point to note is: life spans are pictured as growing shorter. The ten generations from Adam to Noah approach ages of 1,000. But the last one to live more than 900 years is Noah. The next ten generations start with Shem, who lives 600 years, and life spans decline after him. The last person to live more than 200 years is Terah. Abraham (175), Isaac (180), and Jacob (147) live long lives, but not as long as their ancestors. And Moses lives to be 120, which is understood to have become, at some point, the maximum for human life."[230]

b **begat many sons and daughters.** *1 Enoch* describes the children born to Adam and Eve after Seth as being wicked, in the likeness of Cain.[231]

12 a **nine hundred and thirty years.** A change to OT1 in Oliver Cowdery's handwriting reads "1000."[232] Edward Stevenson reported a statement by Joseph Smith that Adam "was within six months of a thousand years old, which is one day with the Lord's time, thus fulfilling the Lord's decree: In the day thou eatest of the fruit of that tree thou shalt surely die—and he did, six months before the day was out."[233] The figure of 1000 years for the death of Adam can be found in Islamic traditions.[234]

b **he died.** Three years prior to his death, Adam gathered his descendants to Adam-ondi-Ahman and "predicted whatsoever should befall his posterity unto the latest generation."[235] Other gatherings of a similar nature are mentioned elsewhere in scripture.[236]

MOSES 6

---

227 There are complex dating issues relating to Moses 6 and D&C 107. See *Endnote 6-3*, p. 491.

228 K. P. Jackson, *et al.*, *Patriarchs*, p. 7.

229 U. Cassuto, *Adam to Noah*, p. 264.

230 R. E. Friedman, *Commentary*, p. 31. See Moses 8:17.

231 G. W. E. Nickelsburg, *1 Enoch*, 85:8, p. 364.

232 S. H. Faulring, *et al.*, *Original Manuscripts*, p. 97. See *Commentary 3:17-c*, p. 175; 6:11-a, p. 482.

233 Edward Stevenson, *Life*, p. 64, spelling and punctuation modernized. See also p. 49. Cited in K. P. Jackson,*et al.*, *Patriarchs*, p. 8.

234 M. al-Kisa'i, *Tales*, p. 80; A. al-Tha'labi, *Lives*, p. 81; al-Tabari, *Creation*, 1:160, p. 331; Ibn Kathir, cited in B. M. Wheeler, *Prophets*, p. 34.

235 L. C. Berrett, *et al.*, *Missouri*, pp. 377-456; D&C 107:53-56; the overview of Moses 6, p. 457.

236 E.g., Genesis 49:1ff.; 2 Nephi 1:1ff.; Ether 6:19ff.

*12 And all the days that Adam lived were nine hundred and thirty years, and **he died**.*

The *Life of Adam and Eve* recounts God's instructions for the dressing of Adam and Eve in preparation for their burial and in anticipation of the resurrection:[237] "God spoke to Michael and said, 'Go to the Garden of the [third] heaven and bring [me] three linen cloths'... and cover Adam's body."[238] Later, "Michael, the archangel, came and spoke to Seth and taught him how to dress [Eve following her death]... and said 'Thus shall you dress every human being who dies, until the day of the end, through the resurrection.'"[239]

237　See the overview of Moses 4, p. 239.

238　G. A. Anderson, *et al.*, *Synopsis*, 48:1-2, pp. 86E-87E; cf. M. Herbert, *Irish Apocrypha*, p. 16; A. al-Tha'labi, *Lives*, p. 81.

239　G. A. Anderson, *et al.*, *Synopsis*, 51:1-2, p. 94E; cf. M. al-Kisa'i, *Tales*, p. 82; M. Ibn Ishaq ibn Yasar, *Making*, p. 41. See also al-Tabari, *Creation*, 1:161-162, pp. 332-333: "separate layers of shrouds."

Gleanings

Table of Contents

Elder Neal A. Maxwell: The Future Reunion at Adam-ondi-Ahman[240]

The valley of Adam-ondi-Ahman will ring again—this time with the sounds of dispensational reunion, as it glows with gathering![241] Those of Enoch's utterly unique city of "one heart" will greet those of the New Zion with holy embraces and holy kisses amid the sounds of sweet sobbing![242] The "hills shall tremble" at the presence of the lost tribes, and hearts, as well as ice, will melt, as they come "filled with songs of everlasting joy."[243]

Elder Bruce R. McConkie: All Things Center in the Family[244]

All things center in the family, and the family is the center of all things. Salvation itself is a family affair and consists of the continuation of the family unit in eternity. God himself is exalted and omnipotent because he is a Father, and his kingdoms and dominions are composed of his children over whom he rules in equity and justice forever. The whole system of salvation, of revelation, of religion, of worship — all that comes from Deity for the benefit of man — is tied into a divine patriarchal system. If any of us gain the fulness of reward in our Father's kingdom, it will be because we enter into family relationships that are eternal in nature; it will be because we have perfected our own patriarchal family units. These concepts are part of the very foundation upon which true religion rests.

Hugh W. Nibley: The Efficacy of the Atonement[245]

But how could a few hours on the cross be effective through infinite time? Even in our limited sphere of action, one can never know how one's actions affect the lives of others for good or ill. One deed can go on reverberating through the ages; such were certain actions of Adam, Abraham, or Cain. The Atonement was one such act, the greatest, performed only once, Paul tells us. The Catholics think they repeat it literally in the mass. We call it to remembrance in the sacrament. The Atonement is universal and eternal.[246] The fifth-century rhetorician Isocrates once observed that if every man in Greece could lift twice as

---

240   N. A. Maxwell, *Yet Reveal*, p. 52.

241   See Daniel 7:13-14; D&C 107:53-57; D&C 116:1.

242   See Moses 7:62-63.

243   See D&C 133:26-33.

244   B. R. McConkie, *Mortal Messiah*, 1:214.

245   H. W. Nibley, *Atonement*, p. 598.

246   2 Nephi 9:7.

much, run twice as fast, jump twice as far, and so on, the world would be little better off—animals and machinery do the fast and heavy work anyway. But if just one man could think twice as clearly as anyone does now, the whole world could be blessed forever after. Here is a kind of action that has infinite leverage, and what gives it that leverage is faith.

M. Catherine Thomas: The Atonement and the Sealing Power[247]

The temple is the narrow channel through which one must pass to reenter the Lord's presence. A mighty power pulls us through that channel, and it is the sealing power of the *at-one-ment* of the Lord Jesus Christ. The Savior's *at-one-ment* is another word for the sealing power. By the power of the *at-one-ment*, the Lord draws and seals his children to himself in the holy temples.

Truman G. Madsen: The Fulness of the Atonement[248]

The Atonement saves us *from* death, sin, hopeless ignorance, and lasting estrangement from those we have the capacity to love, but it also saves us *for* an abundance of life, blessings that the scriptures call "the fulness." He who was described as having an "infinity of fulness"[249] promises his fulness to those who come to him. Thus, for example, these fulnesses are associated with temple worship and temple covenants:

- *a fulness of the earth.*[250] This earth is to become heaven, a celestial orb. And worship is defined as coming "unto the Father in my name, and in due time receiv[ing] of his fulness."[251] Each time we dedicate a temple, we remove part of the curse on the earth.

- *a fulness of truth.*[252] The principles of intelligence—of light and truth such that one may be "glorified in truth"—are latent and manifest in the temple. All the functions of intellect are there to be mined: memory, imagination, lucid and coherent reasoning powers, and anticipatory knowledge. Of course, learning can be had from many sources. But the light and truth that "groweth brighter and brighter until the perfect day"[253] are in the House of the Lord.

- *a fulness of the Holy Ghost.*[254]

- *a fulness of the priesthood.*[255]

- *a fulness of the glory of the Father*, "which glory shall be a fulness and a continuation of the seeds forever."[256] In the temple the powers of godliness are called down, and we are told they are otherwise not manifest unto men in the flesh.[257] Joseph Smith commanded, "Go to and finish the temple, and God will fill it with power, and you will then receive more knowledge concerning this priesthood."[258] Further he said that the Melchizedek Priesthood was "not the power of a Prophet nor Apostle nor Patriarch only but of King and Priest to God, to open the windows of Heaven and pour out the peace and law of endless

---

247   M. C. Thomas, *Brother of Jared*, p. 388.
248   T. G. Madsen, *Temple and Atonement*, pp. 72-74.
249   D&C 109:77.
250   See D&C 59:16.
251   D&C 93:19.
252   See D&C 93:26.
253   D&C 50:24.
254   See D&C 109:15.
255   See D&C 124:28.
256   D&C 132:19; see Abraham 2:9-11.
257   See D&C 84:20-21.
258   J. Smith, Jr., *Teachings*, 27 August 1843, p. 323.

life to man."[259] This is the vital reenactment of the promises to Abraham, Isaac, and Jacob, a posterity not only numerous but radiant like unto the stars.

- *a fulness of joy that is related to all of these.*[260] Joseph Smith said, "the mighty anchor holds the storm, so let these truths sink down in our hearts, that we may even here begin to enjoy that which shall be in full hereafter."[261] In the midst of a multitude filled with celestial wholeness at the temple in Bountiful, Jesus said, "Now behold, my joy is full. And when he had said these words he wept."[262] There, heaven came so close even the children spoke with the tongue of angels. It was an ineffable outpouring. In Hebrew the root word for "joy" is tied to ʿabodah, works, specifically temple service. The word originates with feasting, partaking of the sacrificial meal, in the temple. Here is the foreshadowing of the Messianic feast, the "marriage supper of the Lamb," the future sacramental partaking of new wine in his kingdom.[263] It is the glorious foundation of the reminding, enlivening, and covenant-making process we call the sacrament.

Hugh W. Nibley: That They May Grow[264]

[D&C 109:15] is the classic statement of the purpose of education: "And that they may *grow.*" But here it is a special kind of growth: To "grow up in thee, and receive a fulness of the Holy Ghost, and be organized according to thy laws, and be prepared to obtain every needful thing"—growth, fulness, organization, not organization for organization's sake, but to expedite "obtain[ing] every needful thing." To do this we are instructed to stay alert, to pay attention, and to come [to the temple] often. We are not to sit like bags of sand but to receive a fulness—nothing left out, "every needful thing," in short, all that one is able to receive. The Lord has much to say about fulness. If I could do more than I am doing, or carry more than I am carrying, or learn more than I am learning, etc., I am quite literally rejecting the fulness.

Arthur Henry King: Atonement—the Healing of the Soul[265]

We have in our own church the ability to understand the particular etymology of atonement better than any other branch of Christianity. That is because we believe in the soul as a central concept. And the soul is not, to us, an alternative word for spirit, as with so many people. The soul is, for us, the union of spirit and body in this world so that the spirit may become flesh (incarnate) in order to gain experience and go a great step forward in eternal progression. Entering the flesh is not a way down and away as with Eastern religions; rather, it is a way on, a way up, because it provides experiences of varying sensation in many directions.

The word "sensation" may, in its turn, be refined into "sensibility," a word not readily understood because many people think it means "being sensible" in the sense of "common sensibility." Sensibility, however, is the culture of the soul; this meaning appears clearly in the French *sensibilité*. (This is a meaning of sensibility that is gradually growing in English. We might substitute it for sensitiveness, but sensitiveness has not the European connotation

---

259   J. Smith, Jr., *Words*, 27 August 1843, p. 245, spelling, capitalization, and punctuation modernized.
260   See D&C 93:33-34.
261   J. Smith, Jr., *Words*, 16 April 1843, p. 196.
262   3 Nephi 17:20-21.
263   See D&C 27:5-14; 133:10.
264   H. W. Nibley, *House of Glory*, p. 330.
265   A. H. King, *Wholeness*, pp. 333-334.

of sensibility.) Soul, then is the union, the fusion of spirit (finer matter) with body (coarser matter). We are not to think of the spirit as living in the body like a squirrel in a cage...

Furthermore, once we realize that healing has to do with spirit and body together as soul—healing is healing of the soul—we cannot separate the processes of being healed in the body and being healed in the spirit; they belong together. And that is one of the significances, perhaps the great significance, of the Lord's miracles. We understand the inseparability of these healing processes more intensely when we know how the Doctrine and Covenants speaks of "soul" and "matter."

Dietrich Bonhoeffer: The Cost of Discipleship[266]

Cheap grace is the deadly enemy of our Church. We are fighting today for costly grace.

Cheap grace means grace sold on the market like cheapjacks' wares. The sacraments, the forgiveness of sin, and the consolations of religion are thrown away at cut prices... Grace without price; grace without cost! The essence of grace, we suppose, is that the account has been paid in advance; and, because it has been paid, everything can be had for nothing. Since the cost was infinite, the possibilities of using and spending it are infinite. What would grace be if it were not cheap?

Cheap grace means grace as a doctrine, a principle, a system. It means forgiveness of sins proclaimed as a general truth, the love of God taught as the Christian "conception" of God. An intellectual assent to that idea is held to be of itself sufficient to secure remission of sins...

Cheap grace means the justification of sin without the justification of the sinner. Grace alone does everything, they say, and so everything can remain as it was before... Let the Christian rest content with his worldliness and with this renunciation of any higher standard than the world... Let him be comforted and rest assured in his possession of this grace—for grace alone does everything. Instead of following Christ, let the Christian enjoy the consolations of his grace!...

Cheap grace is the preaching of forgiveness without requiring repentance, baptism without church discipline, Communion without confession, absolution without personal confession. Cheap grace is grace without discipleship, grace without the cross, grace without Jesus Christ, living and incarnate.

Costly grace is the treasure hidden in the field; for the sake of it a man will gladly go and sell all that he has.[267] It is the pearl of great price which to buy the merchant will sell all his goods.[268] It is the kingly rule of Christ, for whose sake a man will pluck out the eye which causes him to stumble,[269] it is the call of Jesus Christ at which the disciple leaves his nets and follows him.[270]

Costly grace is the gospel which must be sought again and again, the gift which must be asked for, the door at which a man must knock.[271]

266   D. Bonhoeffer, *Cost*, pp. 45-48.
267   See Matthew 13:44.
268   See Matthew 13:46.
269   See Matthew 5:29.
270   See Matthew 4:19-20.
271   See Matthew 7:7.

Such grace is costly because it calls us to follow, and it is grace because it calls us to follow Jesus Christ. It is costly because it costs a man his life, and it is grace because it gives a man the only true life. It is costly because it condemns sin, and grace because it justifies the sinner. Above all, it is costly because it cost God the life of his Son: "ye were bought [with] a price,"[272] and what has cost God much cannot be cheap for us. Above all, it is grace because God did not reckon his Son too dear a price to pay for our life, but delivered him up for us.

Elder Jeffrey R. Holland: "Clothed with Purity"[273]

In the imagery of the gospel of Jesus Christ, it is always better to be clothed than unclothed, to be robed rather than naked. Jacob taught that the wicked will have a knowledge of guilt and uncleanness that leads them to feel naked before God, whereas the righteous shall have a perfect knowledge of their enjoyment and their righteousness, "being clothed with purity, yea, even with the robe of righteousness."[274]

As a universal gift flowing from the Atonement of Christ, the Resurrection will clothe with a permanent, perfected, restored body every spirit ever born into mortality. Furthermore, for every person who accepts the principles and ordinances of the gospel, that person's body will be something of a robe of righteousness. Therein is the Redemption of the soul, and therein is a fulness of joy throughout all eternity, including, in its highest order, "a fulness and a continuation of the seeds forever and ever."[275]

The royal role and priestly power of celestial kings and queens, including the restored and perfected bodies commensurate with such a station, are among the highest and holiest gifts of the Atonement of Jesus Christ. When we consider that the alternative was to see our bodies decayed and lifeless in the grave while our spirits became "devils, angels to a devil, to be shut out from the presence of our God, and to remain with the Father of lies, in misery, like unto himself,"[276] little wonder we say of the Savior of the world, "O the greatness of the mercy of our God, the Holy One of Israel! For he delivereth his saints from that awful monster the devil, and death, and hell."[277] Little wonder that one stands "all amazed at the love Jesus offers me, confused at the grace that so fully he proffers me.... Oh, it is wonderful, wonderful to me!"[278]

MOSES 6

---

272 1 Corinthians 6:20; 7:23.
273 J. R. Holland, *Christ*, pp. 244-245.
274 2 Nephi 9:14.
275 D&C 132:19.
276 2 Nephi 9:9.
277 2 Nephi 9:19.
278 *Hymns (1985)*, #193.

George Herbert: Love[279]

Love bade me welcome: yet my soul drew back,
    Guilty of dust and sin.
But quick-eyed Love, observing me grow slack
    From my first entrance in,
Drew nearer to me, sweetly questioning,
    If I lack'd anything.

A guest, I answer'd, worthy to be here:
    Love said, you shall be he.
I the unkind, ungrateful? Ah my dear,
    I cannot look on thee.
Love took my hand, and smilingly did reply,
    Who made the eyes but I?

Truth Lord, but I have marr'd them: let my shame
    Go where it doth deserve.
And know you not, says Love, who bore the blame?
    My dear, then I will serve.
You must sit down, says Love, and taste my meat:
    So I did sit and eat.

---

279   G. Herbert, *Temple*, 162, p. 200. See *Endnote 6-48*, p. 507.

Endnotes

6-1 Note, however, that while the descent of the patriarchal priesthood is from Adam through Seth, the line of the "Holy Priesthood" is traced from Adam through Abel.[280] Elder Alvin R. Dyer explains:

> [D&C 84 cites a] particular record of the holy priesthood... with the priesthood lineage of Moses, the great law-giver of ancient Israel. It designates those who held and conferred the priesthood, even to Abraham who received it from Melchizedek, and through the lineage of the fathers to Enoch, and from Enoch to Abel, whom Cain killed seeking to attain the priesthood birthright. Abel was ordained under the hands of his father Adam, the first man. The patriarchal line of priesthood, however, descended from Adam who was the first man through his son Seth.[281]

> It is to be noted from [D&C 107:39-42], that the patriarchal priesthood descent is from Adam through Seth; whereas the line of authority in the "holy priesthood" is from Adam through Abel who was slain by the conspiracy of his brother Cain, but who received the priesthood by the commandments of God, by the hand of his father Adam, who was the first man.[282] From Noah back to Adam both the "holy priesthood," and the "patriarchal priesthood" have the same line except for the positions held by Seth in the "patriarchal" and Abel in the "holy" priesthoods. No doubt both priesthoods, as here designated, which are separate to some extent as to office and purpose, are integral in the order of priesthood after the order of the Son of God which is after the holiest order of God the Father.[283]

6-2 In one of the most well-known of these texts (*The Second Treatise of the Great Seth*): "Apart from the title, the name Seth never occurs in the text, though perhaps Jesus Christ is meant to be identified with Seth."[284]

Emphasizing the importance of Seth as a prophet, Islamic tradition records that "50 scrolls were revealed to him."[285]

6-3 Regarding the dating of D&C 107, Marquardt writes:

> These instructions are a composite of several documents originally written on different dates... The April date is based on the journal of William E. McLellin who recorded that Joseph Smith and others of the twelve apostles left Kirtland and went to nearby Huntsburg, Ohio, being there on 26-30 March 1835.[286] There is no record of Smith or the apostles returning to Kirtland. The traditional date of 28 March 1835 is based on a letter dated 28 March 1836 [sic], recorded in the *Kirtland Council Minute Book*, LDS archives (198).[287] It appears that the March date is in error and that the meeting where the Twelve "had a time of general confession" was held on the afternoon of 28 April 1835.[288]

Recalling Oliver Cowdery's role as scribe at the meeting where D&C 107:1-58 was received, Brigham Young later remarked: "You read that Oliver Cowdery was the Second Elder and you remember the Rev[elation] on the Priesthood; and Joseph was two hours laboring with O. C. to get him to write the Rev. in humility."[289]

Significantly, the date that D&C 107 was recorded corresponds to a period where Joseph Smith was reviewing the JST manuscript prior to its intended publication.[290] An insertion written above the line in OT1, giving a revised age of Enoch at the time of his translation, parallels the end of D&C

280 See D&C 84:16.
281 A. R. Dyer, *Who Am I*, p. 276.
282 D&C 84:16.
283 A. R. Dyer, *Who Am I*, pp. 409-410. See also J. F. Smith, Jr., *Answers*, 1958, 2:174.
284 J. A. Gibbons, *et al.*, *Great Seth*, p. 362.
285 B. M. Wheeler, *Prophets*, p. 43.
286 W. E. McLellin, *McLellin*, IV, p. 153.
287 See F. C. Collier, *et al.*, *Council*, p. 111.
288 H. M. Marquardt, *Revelations*, p. 267; cf. "A record of the transactions of the Twelve apostles," 1835, in *Patriarchal Blessing Book 1*, LDS Archives. See also the earlier discussion in W. E. McLellin, *McLellin*, pp. 167-168 n. 70. Through work on the *Joseph Smith Papers Project*, it has been determined that verses 59-100 *passim* of section 107 were received on November 11, 1831 (R. J. Woodford, *Discoveries*, p. 31).
289 *Minutes of the School of the Prophets*, 15 April 1868, Provo, Utah, copy at the Utah State Historical Society, Salt Lake City, UT, cited in L. W. Cook, *Revelations*, p. 328 n. 5.
290 L. E. Dahl, *Plain*, p. 126; H. M. Marquardt, *Revelations*, p. 270. See also R. P. Howard, *Restoration 1995*, pp. 106-109; R. J. Matthews, *Plainer*, p. 41.

107:49.[291] Other revisions to the ages of the patriarchs were also made during this period.[292]

A seemingly pre-1835 mention of the term "Adam-ondi-Ahman" occurs in D&C 78:15. However, though the revelation is dated March 1832, vv. 15-16 contain significant additions that were probably made in 1835, as the Doctrine and Covenants was being prepared for publication. [293]Likewise, in the *Teachings of the Prophet Joseph Smith*, the name "Adam-ondi-Ahman" is used as part of an account of a blessing given on 18 December 1833.[294] The blessing incorporates phrasing identical to D&C 107:53-55. However, as Matthews reports:

> … the source for the quotation in *Teachings* is not clear. It is given as the *Manuscript History of the Church*, but the *Manuscript History* in the Library of the Historical Department of the LDS Church in Salt Lake City does not contain the passage under consideration. An account of the blessing was also printed in *History of Joseph Smith*,[295] but this publication does not contain the information in question. It is possible that the account in the *Teachings* is an edited version containing information that was not actually given at the time of the 1833 blessing.[296]

6-4　The *Talmud*, Avodah Zarah 5a records a tradition that Adam saw all that would happen in future generations:

> What is the meaning of the verse "this is the book of the generations of Adam"? Did Adam have a book?—What it implies is that God showed to Adam every generation with its expositors, every generation with its Sages, every generation with its leaders."[297]

Frequently mentioned (with variation in detail) in ancient Jewish and Christian literature is prophecy of Adam that the world would be destroyed once by water and once by fire.[298] Most of the accounts tell about a record (i.e., this prophecy, astronomical information, or music) that was inscribed either on two pillars or else on tablets. To assure the survival of the record, the two pillars were made of different materials, one of which would be preserved in case of flood and the other of which would be impervious to fire. These two modes of destruction are illustrated in the Old Testament accounts of Noah's flood[299] and of the fiery end of Sodom and Gomorrah,[300] as well as in non-biblical stories concerning periodic cycles of destruction and renewal of the earth.[301]

Some sources relate the themes of the pillars or stelae and the Flood to the construction of the Tower of Babel. As related by Schwartz:

> Why did they build the tower? Some say they believed that the firmament was in danger of tottering, and the tower they built was to be one of four pillars to support the heavens.[302] That was the eastern pillar, and others were to be built in the north, in the south, and in the west.

> Other say that they built the tower out of fear of another Flood. They hoped to avoid the waters of the Flood by inhabiting the heights of the tower, and they took axes with them to cleave the heavens, so that all the waters stored there would run out before God could cause them to Flood.[303]

6-5　Of this parallel, Campbell writes:

> Adam and Eve were forced out of Paradise… and moved seventy miles to the north into the dreary workaday world. The Saints, perceiving themselves as God's chosen people, had the opportunity

291　S. H. Faulring, *et al.*, *Original Manuscripts*, p. 110; cf. Moses 8:1.

292　*Ibid.*, pp. 97-98; cf. D&C 107:41-52.

293　H. M. Marquardt, *Revelations*, pp. 197-198.

294　J. Smith, Jr., *Teachings*, pp. 38-39.

295　*History of JS 6:12*, p. 947.

296　R. J. Matthews, *Adam-ondi-Ahman*, p. 29.

297　Cited in R. M. Zlotowitz, *et al.*, *Bereishis*, p. 166.

298　See relevant passages in G. A. Anderson, *et al.*, *Synopsis*, Latin 49:1-50:3, p. 91E; Addendum, p. 96E; L. Ginzberg, *Legends*, 1:121-122; Jerahmeel ben Solomon, *Chronicles*, 24:7, 26:16, pp. 51, 56; F. Josephus, *Genuine Works*, 1:2:3, p. 27; S. C. Malan, *Adam and Eve*, 2:8, p. 115; M. M. Noah, *Jasher*, 2:12-13, p. 4; S. E. Robinson, *Testament of Adam*, Greek 3:5-6, pp. 99, 101; H. Schwartz, *Tree*, 567, p. 444; Shelemon, *Book of the Bee*, 18, p. 28; O. S. Wintermute, *Jubilees*, 8:3, p. 71.

299　Genesis 6:5-9:17.

300　Genesis 19:24-28.

301　J. C. Reeves, *Jewish Lore*, pp. 87-90.

302　See *Excursus 50: Fu Xi and Nü Gua*, p. 654.

303　H. Schwartz, *Tree*, 590, p. 464. See Commentary 1:8-b, p. 50 and *Excursus 48: The Nature and Scope of Premortal Covenants*, p. 649.

to re-experience these sacred places and even the expulsion process. Their view was that they were necessarily forced out of Jackson County by disobedience, as was Adam, into other historic biblical sites as God directed them. Just as there was purpose in Adam's expulsion—to begin the endless generation of humanity—the Saints also saw purpose in their travails—to prepare themselves and the land for the second return of Christ.[304]

6-6 Islamic sources also vary widely in their estimates of Adam's living posterity, some asserting that they were "in number forty, or, according to others, seventy thousand."[305]

6-7 Joseph Smith is said to have identified the location of Adam's altar at Adam-ondi-Ahman.[306]

6-8 Al-Tabari implies that sacred knowledge was contained in the *Testament of Adam*: "[Adam] made his son Seth his legatee and wrote his last will. Then he handed the document containing his last will to Seth and commanded him to keep it concealed from Cain and his children, because Cain had killed Abel out of envy. That was when Adam singled Abel out for [receiving God's] knowledge. Seth and his children kept concealed the knowledge they possessed, and Cain and his children did not have any knowledge they could use."[307]

6-9 Initial similarities, as well as the growing differences with modes of governance in other religious denominations, are discussed in Flake.[308] An intriguing aspect to this study is the observation that the priesthood council organization evidently was not seen as superseding the patriarchal order of fathers and sons, but rather was something that existed side by side with it.[309]

6-10 For discussions of the concept of heavenly councils from an LDS point of view, see Peterson[310] and Ostler.[311]

6-11 These words were penned by the Prophet as part of a letter from the Liberty Jail in 1839. Just prior to the comment quoted above, the Prophet spoke of the spirit that must animate the minds and hearts of ministers of God:

> A fanciful and flowery and heated imagination beware of; because the things of God are of deep import; and time, and experience, and careful and ponderous and solemn thought can only find them out. Thy mind, O man! If thou wilt lead a soul unto salvation, must stretch as high as the utmost heavens, and search into and contemplate the darkest abyss, and the broad expanse of eternity—thou must commune with God. How much more dignified and noble are the thoughts of God, than the vain imaginations of the human heart! None but fools will trifle with the souls of men…. [L]et honesty, and sobriety, and candor, and solemnity, and virtue, and pureness, and meekness, and simplicity crown our heads in every place; and in fine, become as little children, without malice, guile or hypocrisy.[312]

6-12 The entry of the official minutes of the conference held on October 11, 1831 reads:

> Certain points were discussed by Brother Joseph Smith, Jr., who said that the Elders present were to tarry until the morrow and hold a meeting so that the members might understand the ancient manner of conducting meetings as they were led by the Holy Ghost. He also said that this was not perfectly known by many of the Elders of this Church… Brother Oliver Cowdery then made a move that this conference take into consideration the propriety of appointing six Elders to visit the several branches of this church setting them in order… And accordingly Brothers David Whitmer and Reynolds Cahoon were chosen and appointed, the other four remain to be chosen hereafter.[313]

The four additional brethren chosen were Simeon Carter, Orson Hyde, Hyrum Smith, and Emer Harris. They were set apart for this calling two weeks later on October 25, 1831.[314]

---

304 C. S. Campbell, *Images*, p. 79.

305 G. Weil, *Legends*, p. 46.

306 L. C. Berrett, *et al.*, *Missouri*, pp. 384-389.

307 al-Tabari, *Creation*, 1:159-160, p. 331.

308 K. Flake, *Councils*.

309 *Ibid.*, pp. 6-7.

310 D. C. Peterson, *Ye Are Gods*, pp. 506-508.

311 B. T. Ostler, *God*, pp. 41-82, 395-408.

312 J. Smith, Jr., *Teachings*, 25 March 1839, p. 137.

313 D. Q. Cannon, *et al.*, *Far West*, p. 17, spelling, grammar, and punctuation modernized.

314 *Ibid.*, pp. 24-25; J. Smith, Jr., *Documentary History*, 25 October 1831, 1:219.

6-13   The minutes of the meeting of October 25, 1831 are preserved, however, and one imagines in reading them that the Prophet Joseph and the other brethren were doing their best in that meeting to emulate the ancient pattern. At that meeting, in addition to prayer, singing, instruction from Sidney Rigdon and the Prophet, and conducting of a few items of Church business, each of the brethren had an opportunity to express their feelings and testimony about the work in which they were engaged.[315]

6-14   Elder Neal A. Maxwell once cited an example of this quality of mind:

> It was said of one able, but comparatively meek, member of a nineteenth-century British cabinet, serving in Parliament: "If it was his duty to speak, he spoke, but he did not want to speak when it was not his duty—silence was no pain and oratory no pleasure to him."[316]

6-15   The Lord was explicit in saying to Hyrum Smith that before he could "declare" His word he must first "obtain" it—only then would he merit the blessing "to have [His] Spirit and [His] word, yea, the power of God unto the convincing of men."[317] The prophet Jacob perfectly expressed this principle when he wrote: "Wherefore I, Jacob, gave unto them these words as I taught them in the temple, *having first obtained* mine errand from the Lord."[318] The *American Heritage Dictionary* clarifies the older meaning of the word "errand" as being "a mission or an embassy" or, more specifically related to this context, "an oral message that has been entrusted to one."[319]

6-16   On 12 February 1834, at a meeting held at the home of the Prophet in Kirtland, the Prophet gave further instructions on the order by which ancient councils were conducted, as they had been shown him in vision. The members of the first High Council were about to be called out of the number of those brethren then present, and the Prophet wanted them to understand the order by which they were to conduct their business so they could obtain the voice of the Lord by revelation on each matter laid before them:

> I remarked that I should endeavor to set before the council the dignity of the office which had been conferred on me by the ministering of the angel of God, by his own voice, and by the voice of the Church; that I had never set before any council in all the order in which it ought to be conducted, which, perhaps, has deprived the councils of some or many blessings… In ancient days, councils were conducted with such strict propriety that no one was allowed to whisper, be weary, leave the room, or get uneasy in the least, until the voice of the Lord, by revelation, or the voice of the council by the Spirit, was obtained, which has not been observed in this Church to the present time. It was understood in ancient days, that if one man could stay in council, another could; and if the president could spend his time, the members could also; but in our councils, generally, one will be uneasy, another asleep; one praying, another not; one's mind on the business of the council, and another thinking on something else.[320]

To complete the organization of the first High Council, the Prophet writes:

> … I laid my hands upon the twelve Councilors, and commanded a blessing to rest upon them, that they might have wisdom and power to counsel in righteousness, upon all subjects that might be laid before them. I also prayed that they might be delivered from those evils to which they were most exposed, and that their lives might be prolonged on the earth… I then gave the assistant Presidents a solemn charge to do their duty in righteousness, and in the fear of God; I also charged the twelve Councilors in a similar manner, all in the name of Jesus Christ. We all raised our hands to heaven in token of the everlasting covenant, and the Lord blessed us with His Spirit. I then declared the council organized according to the ancient order, and also according to the mind of the Lord.[321]

Andrus has summarized additional instructions of Joseph Smith to his brethren on these matters:

> "The way to get along in any important matter is to gather unto yourselves wise men, experienced and aged men, to assist in council," he said. "Handsome men are not apt to be wise and strong-minded men; but the strength of a strong-minded man will generally create coarse features, like

315   D. Q. Cannon, *et al.*, *Far West*, pp. 19-24.

316   W. Bagehot, *Bagehot*, cited in N. A. Maxwell, *Meekly Drenched*, pp. 129-130.

317   D&C 11:21; cf., e.g., D&C 50:13-22.

318   Jacob 1:17, emphasis mine.

319   *American Heritage Dictionary*, s.v. "errand."

320   J. Smith, Jr., *Teachings*, 12 February 1834, p. 69.

321   J. Smith, Jr., *Documentary History*, 19 February 1834, 2:32-33.

the rough, strong bough of the oak."[322] But more than a strong mind was necessary. Having organized the first High Council at Kirtland, the Prophet said: "I urge the necessity of prayer, that the Spirit might be given, that the things of the Spirit might be judged thereby, because the carnal mind cannot discern the things of God."[323] A man had also to purify his heart. "No man is capable of judging a matter, in council, unless his own heart is pure," he declared on another occasion; "… we are frequently so filled with prejudice, or have a beam in our own eye, that we are not capable of passing right decisions."[324]

6-17 Stories of healing power brought from Paradise have been preserved in Islamic tradition. For example, the special coat made for Joseph was said to have been "woven in Paradise, and it had the smell of Paradise. When it only touched an afflicted or ailing man, that man would be restored to health and be cured… It was that shirt… that had belonged to Abraham." When the shirt was brought to Joseph's ailing and blind father, Jacob, he "put it over his face and his eyesight was restored."[325] Jewish tradition traces this garment through the patriarchs back to Adam.[326] The smell of Jacob's garment mentioned by Isaac as he pronounced the birthright blessing is understood by some to be the fragrance of the Garden of Eden, and (perhaps synonymously) by others as the "aroma of the fragrant incense which would one day be offered in the temple."[327]

6-18 While Seth sought to bring the oil of the Tree of Life from Paradise to Earth, a Mandaean rite for the dying involves the placement of a vial of specially-prepared oil in the pocket of the sacred burial clothing so that it can be conveyed at death from Earth to Heaven. In this context, the oil is seen to represent a "letter" or message.[328]

6-19 Though Verne remained a devout (though in some respects unorthodox) Catholic throughout his life, it is only with subtlety that religious themes in his works can be detected, apart from the occasional pious insertions required by his publisher.[329] Brandon explains this anomaly as follows:

> … the Verne-style of scientific fiction was developed in great measure as a reaction to [Edgar Allan] Poe's explicitly materialistic scientific romances. Verne liked Poe's work, but disliked Poe's tendency to make up science—and what he disliked most about it was that Poe made up the science in order to avoid supernatural explanations. So Verne wrote a different kind of scientific romance, one that respected the natural and moral order established by Providence. The curious resulting paradox, which has often been noted, is that Poe, the materialist, is famous for his stories about the supernatural; and Verne, the Catholic, is famous for stories that have no explicit supernatural intervention at all.[330]

See Butcher[331] for a discussion of the role of "Providence" in Verne's writings. Unfortunately, like other frequently mischaracterized aspects of the life of "one of the most widely distorted, censored, and mistranslated authors of all time,"[332] the applying of labels such as "skeptic," "wishy-washy" and "vaguely Catholic" to describe Verne's faith in his "definitive" biography seems highly inappropriate in light of contemporary documentation.

In Verne's chapter about the Mormons in *Around the World in 80 Days*,[333] we are given a small window on his views of this unusual "sect," though his comic lens was directed here less for the education, and more for the entertainment, of his readers. The story "takes advantage of the opportunity to enliven the crossing of Utah with two comical Mormon elements—the introduction of Elder William Hitch, who tries to convert Passepartout, and the barely successful flight of a Mormon who, even with one

MOSES 6

322 J. Smith, Jr., *Teachings*, 14 May 1843, p. 299.
323 J. Smith, Jr., *Documentary History*, 19 February 1834, 2:31.
324 H. L. Andrus, *Doctrines*, p. 201. See J. Smith, Jr., *Teachings*, 12 February 1834, p. 69.
325 A. al-Tha'labi, *Lives*, pp. 228, 229. See Hauglid for a discussion of previous mistakes in the translation of this verse (B. M. Hauglid, *Garment of Joseph*).
326 E.g., R. M. Zlotowitz, *et al.*, *Bereishis*, p. 1063 n. 1 and pp. 1136-1137 n. 27. See H. W. Nibley, *Lehi 1988*, pp. 168-170; H. W. Nibley, *What*, p. 366; H. W. Nibley, *Vestments*, pp. 128-131; H. W. Nibley, *Message 2005*, p. 309.
327 R. M. Zlotowitz, *et al.*, *Bereishis*, p. 1136 n. 27.
328 E. S. Drower, *Prayerbook*, 73, pp. 61-63; E. Lupieri, *Mandaeans*, p. 29.
329 W. Butcher, *Verne*, p. 282.
330 Brandon, *Master*.
331 W. Butcher, *Verne*, pp. 281-282.
332 *Ibid.*, p. xv.
333 J. Verne, *Around*, 27, pp. 167-173.

wife, had more than he could handle."[334] No doubt relying on his habit of voracious reading and notetaking in preparation for his writing,[335] Verne proves to be better informed than many of his contemporaries in his whirlwind tour of Mormon history and Utah geography. He shows, however, no knowledge of any Mormon activity in his native France. This is understandable since, due to meager results and political troubles, the French mission had closed for the second time in 1864.[336]

6-20   Campbell, somewhat controversially, expands this idea to the level of a universal "monomyth." He characterizes the "adventure of the hero" in general stages of departure, initiation, and return.[337] From a ritual perspective, these three parts correspond to van Gennep's classic stages of separation (*préliminaire*), transition (*liminaire*), and reintegration (*postliminaire*).[338] Turner generalized and elaborated Van Gennep's three stages and applied them to the phenomenon of religious pilgrimage.[339]

6-21   Somewhat controversially, Northrop Frye asserted the virtual universality of this theme, writing that there are "four primary narrative movements in literature. These are, first, the descent from a higher world; second, the descent to a lower world; third, the ascent from a lower world; and fourth, the ascent to a higher world. All stories in literature are complications of, or metaphorical derivations from, these four narrative radicals… Explicitly for the first eighteen centuries of the Christian era, and implicitly after and long before that, these patterns of ascent and descent have been spread over a mythological universe consisting of four main levels, two above our own, and one below it. The highest level is in heaven, the place of the presence of God… Level two is the earthly paradise or Garden of Eden, where man lived before the fall… Level three is the world of ordinary experience we now live in… Level four is the demonic world or hell, in Christianity not part of the order of nature but an autonomous growth, usually placed below ground."[340]

6-22   About the significance of this phrase, Snodgrass writes:

> Although some, on the basis of Semitic evidence, think "when he came to himself" (*eis heauton de elthon*) means repentance, all it really means is "he came to his senses." The repentance itself is expressed in the confession in vv. 17b-19 and 21. On the other hand, "came to his senses" must be taken seriously, for it is the prerequisite to or first step of repentance. The parable does not mention repentance:; it speaks only of the prodigal's coming to his senses, his confession, and his return. No doubt for any Jew those were valid aspects of repentance, even if they do not cover everything involved.[341]

6-23   The life of Jesus Christ followed a similar pattern, though He was without sin: "I came forth from the Father, and am come into the world: again, I leave the world, and go to the Father."[342]

6-24   The parable teaches that "God goes out to seek the sinner, or, that He is actually waiting and watching for the sinner to come home. [Jesus' contemporaries might in their] gentler moments agree that God would accept a penitent sinner; but [they] never dreamed of a God who went out to look for sinners. The shepherd searched for the sheep; the woman searched for the coin; God searches for men."[343]

6-25   "We would expect the father, being the patriarch, to have summoned his son to him. It seems a great concession for him to go out to the elder son, even more of a concession than his going out to meet the younger one, which occurred under exceptional circumstances".[344]

"Verse 21 = 18f., except for the final words 'treat… servants,' which the father does not allow his son to utter; instead he changes the unspoken words to their opposite, and treats the returning one, not as a wage-earner, but as an honored guest."[345]

334   W. Decoo, *Image*, p. 10. See W. Butcher, *Verne*, p. 173.

335   W. Butcher, *Verne*, pp. 248, 285, 287, 349 n. 9.

336   C. Euvrard, *Bertrand*, p. 285. See also R. D. McClellan, *Bertrand*, pp. 16-17.

337   J. Campbell, *Hero*, pp. 49-251.

338   A. van Gennep, *Rites*, pp. 11. V. Turner, *Ritual Process*, contributed much to the bringing of van Gennep's neglected work into greater prominence.

339   V. Turner, *et al.*, *Pilgrimage*, esp. pp. 1-17, 34-39. For a brief summary of later critiques of Turner's model, especially his notion of *communitas*, see J. Eade, *et al.*, *Contesting the Sacred*, pp. x-xxiii, 4-5.

340   N. Frye, *Secular Scripture*, pp. 97-98.

341   K. R. Snodgrass, *Stories*, p. 138.

342   John 16:28.

343   W. Barclay, *Parables*, p. 183.

344   D. Packard, *et al.*, *Feasting*, p. 47.

345   J. Jeremias, *Parables*, p. 102.

6-26 "'Ran'—a most unusual and undignified procedure for an aged oriental, even though he is in the greatest haste":[346]

> However inwardly glad he may have been to see his son again, no older, self-respecting Middle Eastern male head of an estate would have disgraced himself by the undignified action of running to greet his son (v. 20). Nor would he have interrupted the son's speech before a full display of repentance (cf. v. 21 with vv. 18-19) or instantly commanded such a luxurious outpouring of affection for him (vv. 22-23). All of these details strongly suggest that Jesus wanted to present his audience with more than a simple, realistic picture of family life. Rather he used an extraordinary story to illustrate God's amazing patience and love for his ungrateful children.[347]

> Even though the father has compassion on his son, a proper response for him would be to let the young man arrive home, fall on his knees, and ask for forgiveness. Then in the best of all circumstances, the father would respond with words of forgiveness and a review of expectations. The son would, in effect, be on probation around home for a time; perhaps he could remain there until he could earn enough to leave as an independent person once again.

> But those measures of decorum are not what happen. The father runs to meet the son—an outlandish behavior, as emphasized by many interpreters. According to tradition, the "way" a man walks "shows what he is,"[348] and therefore a dignified man does not run. We must imagine here a prominent person wearing a long robe. In order to run, he must pull up the robe, exposing his legs, which would have been considered shameful in a Semitic culture. Even in a gentile Greco-Roman context, a "proud man" makes slow steps."[349]

A *hadith qudsi* of Muhammad portrays God as saying: "And if [my servant] draws nearer to Me by a handsbreadth, I draw nearer to him by an armslength; and if he draws nearer to Me by an armslength, I draw nearer to him by a fathom; and if he comes to Me walking, I come to him running."[350]

In *Pesiqta Rabbati*[351] is found the following:

> Consider the parable of a prince who was far away from his father—a hundred days' journey away. His friends said to him: "Return to your father." He replied: "I cannot: I have not the strength." Thereupon his father sent word, saying to him: "Come back as far as you can according to your strength, and I will go the rest of the way to meet you." So the Holy One, blessed be He, says to Israel: *Return unto Me, and I will return unto you.*[352]

6-27 "The robe stands for honor; it was the first or the best robe; it was not to disgrace but to honor that the son came home. The ring stands for mastery. The ring would be a signet ring; and when a master gave his ring to a servant or a father to his son, it meant that he was handing into his control all his possessions. The shoes stand for the status of a son. Slaves went barefoot but the children of the family went shod."[353]

Jeremias compares the father's orders with Genesis 41:42:[354]

> … when Joseph was appointed chief vizier, he received from Pharaoh a ring, a robe of fine linen, and a golden chain: (1) First comes the ceremonial robe, which in the East is a mark of high distinction. There is no bestowal of orders, but when a king wants to honor a deserving official, he presents him with a costly robe; investiture with a new garment is therefore a symbol of the new age. In other words, the son is treated as a guest of honor. (2) The ring and the shoes: excavations have shown that the ring is to be regarded as a signet ring; the gift of a ring signified the bestowal of authority.[355] Shoes are a luxury, worn by free men; here they mean that the son is no longer to go about barefoot like a slave. (3) As a rule, meat is rarely eaten. For special occasions a fatted calf is prepared. Its killing means a feast for the family and the servants and the festal reception of the

346 *Ibid.*, p. 102; cf. K. R. Snodgrass, *Stories*, p. 126.
347 C. L. Blomberg, *Parables*, p. 176.
348 S. Sandmel, *et al.*, *Ecclesiasticus*, 19:30, p. 136.
349 A. J. Hultgren, *Parables*, p. 78.
350 W. A. Graham, *Divine*, p. 127.
351 W. G. Braude, *Rabbati*, 44:9, 2:779.
352 Malachi 3:7; cf. 2 Nephi 25:23.
353 W. Barclay, *Parables*, pp. 181-182.
354 J. Jeremias, *Parables*, pp. 102-103.
355 Cf. S. Sandmel, *et al.*, *1 Maccabees*, 6:15, p. 208.

returning son to the family table.[356] The three orders given by the father are the manifest tokens of forgiveness and reinstatement, evident to all.

The phrase "all that I have is thine," uttered to the older son, "reminds us of a part of the oath and covenant of the priesthood, in which the Lord says, 'And he that receiveth my Father receiveth my Father's kingdom; therefore all that my Father hath shall be given unto him.'[357] Apparently, in the heavenly scheme, all can be given to each, without diminishing what each receives."[358]

6-28   Similarly: "The great [Arab writer] Abu Zaid said there was one prayer that he had learned in a dream which alone was his guarantee of safety in the desert: 'Preserve me, O God; … guard me in my person and my property.… Cover me with the curtain of grace.'"[359] Nibley also explains the inverse of this picture:[360]

> And the opposite of that you will find in Alma 5:7…: "Behold, he changed their hearts. Behold, they were in the midst of darkness; nevertheless, their souls were illuminated by the light of the everlasting word; yea, they were encircled about by the bands of death [that's the other encircling; Satan can encircle you too], and the chains of hell, and an everlasting destruction did await them." You get this same negative idea right here in verse 10: "And now I ask of you on what conditions are they saved? Yea, what grounds had they to hope for salvation? What is the cause of their being loosed from the bands of death, yea, and also the chains of hell?"
>
> In the one you are bound tight to one person; in the other you are bound tight to another. And there is nothing ever mentioned about anything in between the two… The opposite of oneness is in Alma 5:25. This is the alternative to being embraced, to being taken into the family. "I say unto you, Nay; except ye make our Creator a liar from the beginning, or suppose that he is a liar from the beginning, ye cannot suppose that such can have place (remember, Nephi said to Zoram, 'You come down to our father's tent in the desert and you can have place with us';[361] *marhaban* means 'have a place with us,' and here he uses that term again) in the kingdom of heaven; but they shall be cast out for they are the children of the kingdom of the devil." The opposite is to be cast out or not included—thrown out of the house. Then notice verse 57 in the same chapter… "Come ye out from the wicked, and be ye separate, and touch not their unclean things. The names of the wicked shall not be mingled with the names of my people." The idea is being cast out and cut off completely, and that's what we are talking about here.

In the *Zohar* is found the following: "if a person comes to purify himself, he is assisted from above; his Lord's assistance encircles him, and he is protected, called 'holy.' If a person comes to defile himself, numerous bands of dazzling demons lie in wait for him; they all hover over him, surrounding him, defiling him, and he is called 'impure.'"[362]

6-29   A relevant picture is painted in the Muslim *Hadith al-Kisa* (Tradition of the Cloak or Mantle), where Muhammad was said to have thrown his cloak over certain members of his family (Hasan, Husain, Fatima) to affirm their purity,[363] and to assert his love for those of his own household (*ahl al-bayt*).[364] Though the general intent of the story is clear, its specific interpretation has long been a matter of deep division among Islamic groups. While Shi'ites take this incident as conferring a special status for the blood relatives of Muhammad and his wives (identified with the *imams*), the Sunnis see the story as symbolizing the unity of all pious Muslims as part of *ahl al-bayt*.[365]

Peterson further comments on the differences between these groups: "Several nineteenth-century Orientalists saw a similarity between the Shi'ites and the Reorganized Church of Jesus Christ of Latter Day Saints [now renamed the Community of Christ]. Both groups expected the succession to the founding prophet to remain in the prophet's family. But the Shi'ites have the more radical theology

---

356   "Hultgren estimates that the price of a goat was one-tenth that of a cow" (cited in K. R. Snodgrass *Stories*, p. 126).

357   D&C 84:38.

358   D. Packard, *et al.*, *Feasting*, p. 49.

359   H. W. Nibley, *Approach*, p. 253.

360   H. W. Nibley, *Teachings of the Book of Mormon*, 16, 1:200-201.

361   See 1 Nephi 4:34.

362   D. C. Matt, *Zohar 2*, Hayyei Sarah 1:125b, p. 215.

363   See Qur'an 33:33.

364   I. Muslim, *Sahih*, 1001:5955, 4:1293-1294; cf. 996:5915, 5920, 5923, 4:1285, 1286-1287.

365   I. Muslim, *Sahih*, 4:1294 n. 2714; Porch of Wisdom Cultural Institution, *Faith and Reason*, pp. 313-318; cf. Matthew 12:46-50.

in Islam, whereas the Reorganized Church is far closer to mainstream Protestantism than are the Mormons and is now abandoning the notion of family succession."[366]

6-30   Writes Nibley:[367]

> As you approach the camp surrounding the temple, you signify your intent with a reassuring sign, a *signum*, visible from a distance, calling attention to yourself as Adam does in his prayer and demonstrating your peaceful intent. Upon reaching the gate, you present your token, a tangible object (compare touch, digit, *dactyl*, or a solid handclasp). All these serve as a *tessera hospitalis*, admitting one to a closed group or a party, or a club, guild meeting, etc. It is presented to the doorkeeper, a herald trained in such matters: "The Holy One of Israel is the Keeper of the Gate, and he employs no servant there!" Most important, "he cannot be deceived."[368] The token recognized, you pronounce your name to the doorkeeper in a low voice, a whisper, for it is a special name agreed on between you and your host and should not be picked up and used by anyone else.

6-31   "Christ's sacrifice [may be] understood in terms of expiation,[369] the canceling of guilt and cleansing of sin."[370] The term is derived "from L. *expiatus*, pp. of *expiare* 'make amends,' from *ex-* 'completely' + *piare* 'propitiate, appease,' from *pius* 'faithful, loyal, devout.'"[371] Unfortunately, the meaning of the term "expiation" in English and Romance languages has shifted quite a distance from its roots, leading French translators of the *Septuagint* to replace it by *apaisement* (= English "appeasement").[372]

6-32   King writes: "We find, for example, in Leviticus 1:4 the sense "expiation" (appeasement by sacrifice); in Romans 3:24, "redemption" (which means "buying back"); and in 1 John 2:2, the word "propitiation" (meaning "making gracious")."[373]

Seaich writes:[374]

> Scripture and popular writings have long been filled with assorted attempts to understand what really took place on Calvary, variously describing the crucified Jesus as a "ransom" for captive men,[375] an "advocate" taking man's case before the Father,[376] a sacrificial "victim" whose blood "deterges"[377] the wicked from sin,[378] a 'propitiation' satisfying God's demand for justice,[379] a "Paschal Lamb,"[380] a "penal substitute" who is punished in place of the gulty (Luther, Calvin), or even a "commercial transaction" made to "buy" humanity from Satan's grasp (Ambrose, Gregory of Nyssa).[381]

> The idea of "redeeming" men from the grasp of Satan was probably based on Acts 26:17-18, which depects man in the Devil's power, and in need of deliverance. The idea of "ransom" corresponds to the OT *koper*, the price paid to free someone from bondage.[382] The "advocate" (*parakletos*, 1 John 2:1) was the OT *go'el*, a family member who assumed the responsibility for the welfare of his relatives, i.e., who "took their part."[383] The "deterging" of the Holy of Holies with a victim's blood is detailed in Leviticus 16-17; thus Paul's "propitiation" is actually the Mercy Seat (*kapporet*) where the blood of the victim was sprinkled on the Day of Atonement,[384] and where God agreed to

366   D. C. Peterson, *Abraham*, p. 110 n. 84.

367   H. W. Nibley, *Temples Everywhere*, p. 14.

368   2 Nephi 9:41.

369   Greek *hiastérion*; Romans 3:25.

370   D. N. Freedman, *et al.*, *Eerdmans*, s.v., Atonement, p. 128.

371   D. Harper, *Dictionary*, s.v., expiation.

372   C. Dogniez, *et al.*, *Pentateuque*, Glossaire, s.v. apaisement, pp. 868-870. See *Excursus 46: The Origin and Meaning of the Term "Atonement"*, p. 642 and *Excursus 47: Islamic Perspectives Relating to Redemption*, p. 645.

373   A. H. King, *Atonement*, p. 318.

374   J. E. Seaich, *Ancient Texts 1995*, p. 554 n. 175.

375   Matthew 20:28; 1 Timothy 2:6.

376   1 John 2:1.

377   I.e., cleanses, from Latin *de-* "off, away" + *tergere* "to rub, polish, wipe" (D. Harper, *Dictionary*).

378   Hebrews 9:13-14.

379   Romans 3:25.

380   John 1:29.

381   J. E. Seaich, *Ancient Texts 1995*, pp. 553-554.

382   E.g., Exodus 21:30; Job 33:24, 36:18; Psalm 49:17.

383   Job 19:25; Ruth 2:20, 4:1; Jeremiah 32:6-12.

384   Leviticus 16.

meet with man;[385] the Apostle now makes Jesus the Church's new "Mercy Seat" or Mediator. The "Paschal (Passover) Lamb" refers to the sacrificial animal whose blood was scattered on the door posts of the Israelites to protect them from the Destroying Angel.[386] All of these ideas... from the old Jewish cult... were retained... to identify Christ's new work with the traditional expectations of Judaism.

Note that Seaich overreachingly saw the metaphors for the Atonement relating to the OT sacrificial rites solely as attempts to relate Christ's mission to Jewish expectation. Hence, for example, his unconvincing and mistaken interpretation of D&C 19:16-17 as not meaning "that his sacrifice was a substitute for our sacrifices, but simply that his suffering on the cross makes it possible for us to escape an 'eternal punishment for sin'[387] which would one day be as painful as his."[388]

Regarding "redemption," Hugh Nibley explains:[389]

> The monetary metaphor is by far the commonest, being the simplest and easiest to understand. Hence, frequently the word "redemption" literally means to buy back, that is, to reacquire something you owned previously. Thus Moses: "But because the Lord loved you, and because he would keep the oath which he had sworn unto your fathers, hath the Lord brought you out with a mighty hand, and redeemed you out of the house of bondmen, from the hand of Pharaoh."[390] Redemption, or Atonement, restores one to a former, happier condition. "And what one nation in the earth is like thy people, even like Israel, whom God went to redeem for a people to himself, and to make him a name, and to do for you great things and terrible, for thy land, before thy people, which thou redeemest to thee from Egypt, from the nations and their gods?"[391] By redemption, someone has paid a price to get you off, but the frequent use of the commercial analogy is not out of reverence for trade and commerce but the opposite. The redeemed are bought to clear them of all worldly obligation by paying off the world in its own currency, after which it has no further claim on the redeemed: "And the child of eight days shall be circumcised for you, every male through your generations, born of a house or a purchase of silver of any outsider who is not of thy seed. He must certainly be circumcised, born of your house, or bought with your silver; and it shall be my covenant in [among or with] thy flesh for an everlasting covenant."[392] All the newborn are taken into the family, which is united by an eternal covenant by the token shedding of blood (circumcision) to become the seed of Abraham—this is a real at-one-ment.
>
> The Greek equivalent is *lytrosis*, a ransoming. Paul tells the saints to prepare for the salvation that has been made available by disengaging from this world—"denying ungodliness and worldly lusts, we should live soberly, righteously, and godly, in this present world"[393]—so that God "might redeem us from all iniquity, and purify unto himself a peculiar people."[394]

Elsewhere, Nibley explains redemption as meaning that a:[395]

> ... price is paid... and it's got you off, but you don't even have to know the person who paid the price, let alone be one with him. The idea of being one goes beyond having the price paid.

The term "reconciliation," used frequently in the New Testament to translate this concept and deriving from a root that means "to be seated again with someone," is a step closer to the meaning of "atonement" but does not go far enough in conveying the idea of perfect unity.[396] About the terms "reconciliation," "return," and "repentance," Nibley writes:

> [Just prior to Romans 5:11,] Paul has... told us that the Lord "sat down at the right hand of the Majesty on High," so "reconciliation" is a very good word for atonement there, since it means literally to be seated again with someone (*re-con-silio*)—so that atonement is to be reunited with

385   Exodus 25:22; Numbers 7:89.
386   Exodus 12:3.
387   D&C 19:11-12.
388   J. E. Seaich, *Ancient Texts 1995*, p. 562; D&C 19:15.
389   H. W. Nibley, *Atonement*, pp. 556-557.
390   Deuteronomy 7:8.
391   2 Samuel 7:23.
392   Genesis 17:12-13.
393   Titus 2:12.
394   Titus 2:14.
395   H. W. Nibley, *Teachings of the Book of Mormon*, 16, 1:198.
396   Cf. John 17:23.

God. The Greek word translated as "reconciliation" is *katallagein*. That is a business term which the Greek-English Lexicon tells us means "exchange, esp. of money; … change from enmity to friendship, reconciliation; … reconciliation of sinners with God." It is the return to the *status ante quo*, whether as a making of peace or a settlement of debt.[397]

[*Katallagein*] means "changing back again to where you were." It's the same thing as *teshûvah* in Hebrew. *Teshuvah* is the Hebrew term for "returning, repentance." But where is the oneness [you find in the term "atonement"]?[398]

[*Teshuvah*] means "a return"—you return to where you were.[399] But you can never come back; you can't go home again after you have sinned. That has to be washed away, so there is baptism. The idea is to return, but how can you return to a place if you never were there before? All throughout the doctrine of atonement, a pre-existence is assumed—returning to the presence of the Father, coming home again. *The Pearl*, the earliest Christian hymn, is beautiful on that particular subject…[400] In [the term] reconciliation you have a settlement or an understanding, but that doesn't make you one…[401]

6-33 John the Apostle wrote: "Beloved, now are we the sons of God, and it doth not yet appear what we shall be: but we know that, when he shall appear, we shall be like him; for we shall see him as he is."[402]

6-34 The need for this reunification is not only due to the physical division and separation of creation, but also in order to restore the order of the everlasting covenant that has been continually and repeatedly broken by man.[403] Barker comments:

Those who entered the Holy of Holies understood how that original unity had become the diversity of the visible creation… The Holy of Holies was the Kingdom, which explains why the heavenly city in the book of Revelation is a giant cube: it was the Holy of Holies. Those who experienced only the visible creation knew that it was divided and separated. Genesis 1 described the process: the firmament separated the waters, the lights of heaven separated light from darkness, and everything was created distinct, according to its kind. Only those who had access to the secrets knew of the underlying unity.[404]

The Holy of Holies, Day One[, as opposed to the cardinal term "the first day"], was the state of unity outside time and matter, before the world was created by dividing and separating according to their kinds (the theme of Genesis 1), and so all angels must have been in some sense a Unity….

This important concept illuminates the great high priestly prayer of Jesus in John 17. At first He prays to be glorified with the Father in His presence, "With the glory I had with thee before the world was made,"[405] and He speaks of "my glory which thou has given me… before the foundation of the world,"[406] clear references to the Holy of Holies/Day One. The major theme of the prayer is unity, "that they may be one even as we are one."[407] The perfect unity is a sign of divinity, and proof of Jesus" origin.[408] He has come from the One, He is part of the One, and He makes his disciples One. The theme is repeated at the end of the Book of Revelation, where the servants of God-and-the-Lamb (a unity) worship Him in the place where the Lord God is their Light, and they have His Name on their foreheads. In other words, they have been admitted to the Holy of Holies/Day One, and they bear on their foreheads the mark of high priesthood, the Name….

The unity-and-plurality of the angels underlies even familiar texts. The Hebrew word usually translated "God" is a plural form, *elohim*, and the sense of a passage sometimes demands that the English be "God" and sometimes "angels." Thus Psalm 82 begins: "*elohim* has taken his stand in the council of *El*, in the midst of the *elohim* he gives judgment." This is understood to mean "God

397   H. W. Nibley, *Atonement*, p. 556.
398   H. W. Nibley, *Teachings of the Book of Mormon*, 16, 1:198.
399   See *Commentary* 5:4-b, p. 357.
400   J. K. Elliott, *Pearl*; H. W. Nibley, *Message 2005*, pp. 487-501.
401   H. W. Nibley, *Teachings of the Book of Mormon*, 16, 1:198.
402   1 John 3:2; cf. Moroni 7:48. See B. T. Ostler, *God*, pp. 408-419.
403   Isaiah 24:4-6; D&C 1:11-16; G. W. E. Nickelsburg, *et al.*, *1 Enoch*, 1 Enoch 69:16-25, pp. 90-91.
404   M. Barker, *Temple Theology*, p. 25.
405   John 17:5.
406   John 17:24.
407   John 17:22. See B. T. Ostler, *God*, pp. 420-423.
408   John 17:23.

MOSES 6

[thus too in the *LXX*] has taken His place [singular because of the singular verb] in the council of *El* [but the *LXX* has "gods"], in the midst of the gods/angels [where a singular would make no sense] he gives judgment." The very familiarity of this ambiguity should not allow us to overlook the fact that it is there. The great statement of monotheism is literally a statement that "our *elohim*" are/is a unity: "The Lord our God/gods is One Lord."[409] Origen knew that the angels fell when they broke their unity with God.[410]

John's concept for the unity of the divine good is exactly counter-balanced by his depiction of the unity of demonic evil;[411] one monster with many heads and horns, permitted to rule but not to triumph.[412]

6-35   What is true of the appropriateness of King James English for rendering the Old Testament does not automatically extend to the text of the New Testament, which was written in common everyday Greek. "As one eminent authority put it, 'an elaborate, elegant style is unsuited to' [New Testament] translation, 'and in proportion as it is rendered in a conscious literary style, it is misrepresented to the modern reader.'[413]"[414]

For a controversial and thought-provoking discussion of differences between Hebrew and Greek thought, see Boman.[415]

6-36   Of the meaning of *kpr*, Margaret Barker writes:

> Atonement translates the Hebrew *kpr*, but the meaning of *kpr* in a ritual context is not known. Investigations have uncovered only what actions were used in the rites of atonement, not what that action was believed to effect. The possibilities for its meaning are "cover" or "smear" or "wipe," but these reveal no more than the exact meaning of "breaking bread" reveals about the Christian Eucharist....
>
> I should like to quote here from an article by Mary Douglas published... in *Jewish Studies Quarterly*:[416]
>
>> Terms derived from cleansing, washing and purging have imported into biblical scholarship distractions which have occluded Leviticus' own very specific and clear description of atonement. According to the illustrative cases from Leviticus, to atone means to cover or recover, cover again, to repair a hole, cure a sickness, mend a rift, make good a torn or broken covering. As a noun, what is translated atonement, expiation or purgation means integument made good; conversely, the examples in the book indicate that defilement means integument torn. Atonement does not mean covering a sin so as to hide it from the sight of God; it means making good an outer layer which has rotted or been pierced.
>
> This sounds very like the cosmic covenant with its system of bonds maintaining the created order, broken by sin and repaired by "atonement."[417]

Nibley gives the following analysis:

> The word... *kpr, kippur*... [is] cognate with our word cover; it's pronounced *kfr*. So we have cover, but that is just the beginning of this very interesting word. It's the same in Aramaic; it's "to cover over your sins." This is the way Jastrow's big two-volume lexicon explains it: It means "to arch over; to bend over; to cover; to pass over with the hand, especially the palm of the hand." The word for palm of the hand in all Semitic languages is *kap*. It means "to cover, hence to grasp by the hand; to wipe over, hence to cleanse, to expiate, to forgive, to renounce, to deny, to be found, to encircle." All these in one word.[418]

---

409   Deuteronomy 5:4.

410   M. Barker, *Angel Priesthood*, pp. 108-110. See Origen, *De Principiis*, 1:8, pp. 264-267.

411   Revelation 12:3, 13:1, and 17:3.

412   M. Barker, *Revelation*, p. 229.

413   Cited in J. R. Clark, Jr., *Why the KJV*, p. 355.

414   P. L. Barlow, *Bible*, p. 170.

415   T. Boman, *Hebrew Thought*.

416   M. Douglas, *Atonement*, p. 117. See also M. Douglas, *Leviticus*, p. 234: "Leviticus actually says less about the need to wash or purge than it says about 'covering.'"

417   M. Barker, *Atonement*.

418   H. W. Nibley, *Teachings of the Book of Mormon*, 16, p. 198.

6-37 The importance of this symbol of the atonement was also emphasized in Egyptian temple rites:

> The normal sequence of ordinances as depicted in temple reliefs is, according to Barguet, washing, laying on of hands, leading by the hand, entering the gate, embracing, and crowning. In Egyptian rites, gates or doorways are symbolic of passage and arrival, of the completion of one phase of the operation and the beginning of another; not only is the gate the normal place for the embrace of greeting and farewell, but, as the symbols and inscriptions engraved on the door frames of tombs and temples make clear, the portal itself typifies the performing of such an embrace. A spontaneous and natural gesture, embracing is not only a sign of affection but also one of acceptance, recognition, and reception at every level, from the formal and hypocritical embrace of the diplomat to the "mystical union" of the initiate. The ritual embrace is the "culminating rite of the initiation"; it is "an initiatory gesture weighted with meaning…, the goal of all consecration."[419]

Seaich notes the following parallels in Jewish and Christian sources:[420]

> The embrace itself goes back at least to the Old Testament legends of Elijah and Elisha, who raised widows' sons by "stretching" themselves upon their dead bodies and placing mouth upon mouth, eyes upon eyes, and hands upon hands.[421]

> The same embrace reappeared in the early Christian *Gospel of Thomas*, where Jesus tells the disciples that they must "become one" with him by placing eyes in the place of an eye, and a hand in the place of a hand, and a foot in the place of a foot, and an image in the place of an image.[422]

> That this was remembered even during the Middle Ages is shown by the fact that the *Seder Eliyahu Rabbah* (eighth century) also explains how God will resuscitate the dead by lifting them out of the dust, setting them on their feet, and placing them between his knees to embrace them and press them to him.…

> Compare Acts 20:10, where Paul raises a man from the dead with a sacred embrace. Also the Jewish apocryphon, *Joseph and Aseneth*, where Joseph gives his bride eternal life with an embrace and a kiss.[423] The *Seder Eliyahu Rabbah* adds specifically that the Messiah will be the very "Son of the Widow" whom Elijah raised from the dead.…[424]

> The concomitant expression, "fellowship," which has remained so closely associated with this embrace in Masonic lore, likewise had an ancient origin, being identical to the Greek word, *koinonia*, used to describe the union of Christ and his disciples, who must suffer what the Savior suffered in order to obtain eternal life:

>> As ye are sharers (*koinonoi*) of the sufferings (of Christ), so shall you also be of the consolation.[425]

>> That I might know him and the power of his resurrection, and the fellowship of his sufferings (*koinonian tes pathematon autou*), being conformed to his death, that if possible I may obtain the resurrection from the dead.[426]

>> He has given us precious and very great promises that you might become sharers (*koinonoi*) of the Divine Nature, having escaped the corruption that is in the world.[427]

> Additional embraces depicting this saving "fellowship" have been preserved in the early Jewish-Christian *Odes of Solomon*:[428]

>> Thou hast given us thy fellowship.[429]

419   H. W. Nibley, *Message 2005*, p. 427.
420   J. E. Seaich, *Freemasonry*. See also J. E. Seaich, *Ancient Texts 1995*, pp. 826-828.
421   1 Kings 17:21; 2 Kings 4:34.
422   H. Koester, *et al.*, *Thomas*, 22, p. 129.
423   C. Burchard, *Joseph*, 15:5-6, p. 226; 19:10-11, p. 233.
424   See G. Kittel, *et al.*, *Dictionary*, 9:527, cited in J. E. Seaich, *Freemasonry*.
425   2 Corinthians 1:5-7.
426   Philemon 3:10-11.
427   2 Peter 1:4.
428   J. H. Charlesworth, *Odes*.
429   *Ibid.*, 4.

MOSES 6

I have been united to Him... Indeed, he who is joined to Him who is immortal Truly shall become immortal.[430]

And Immortal Life embraced me And kissed me. And from that is the Spirit which is within me. And it cannot die because it is life.[431]

And I put off darkness, And put on light.

And even I myself acquired members... And his everlasting fellowship.[432]

Like the arm of the bridegroom over the bride So is my yoke over those who know me.[433]

The Coptic *Gospel of Philip* similarly retains the Greek word, *koinonia*, to describe Mary Magdalene's redemptive relationship with Christ,[434] a relationship which apocryphal writers understood to be that of "consort" or "wife."[435] This again reflects the wide-spread tradition in the Western Church that Mary was the "fallen" human counterpart of the Church, whom Jesus had come to redeem, even as Hosea's wife, Gomer, had been the counterpart of Yahweh's fallen "Bride," the spiritually "dead" Israel.[436] By such fellowship, "the holy united itself to the unholy in order to make it holy,"[437] i.e. shared its Divine Nature with its defunct "partner" (*koinonos*) in order to bring her back to life.

The tradition of the embrace and ceremonial entry into the church and the altar within Catholic liturgy are discussed by von Wellnitz.[438]

6-38   In support of his conclusions, Nibley cites cognates from both Arabic and Egyptian:

The Arabic *kafara* puts the emphasis on a tight squeeze, such as tucking in the skirts, drawing a thing close to one's self. Closely related are Aramaic and Arabic *kafat*, meaning a close embrace, which are certainly related to the Egyptian *hpet*, the common ritual embrace written with the ideogram of embracing arms.[439] This... ritual embrace... consummates the final escape from death in the Egyptian funerary texts and reliefs, where the son Horus is received into the arms of his father Osiris.[440]

The Egyptian word [*hpet*] may be cognate with the Latin *capto*, and from it comes the Persian *kaftan*, a monk's robe and hood completely embracing the body.[441]

6-39   The Gnostic *Apocryphon of James* has Christ saying to his Apostles: "If you consider how long the world existed [before] you, and how long it will exist after you, you will find that your life is one single day and your sufferings one single hour... Scorn death, therefore, and take thought for life! Remember my cross and my death, and you will live!"[442]

6-40   Citing Elder Neal A. Maxwell, Elder Bruce C. Hafen writes:[443]

"The very act of choosing to be a disciple... can bring to us a certain special suffering," because affliction and chastening are "a form of learning as it is administered at the hands of a loving Father."[444] He also said, "If we are serious about our discipleship, Jesus will eventually request each of us to do those things which are most difficult for us to do."[445] And so, he said, "sometimes the best people... have the worst experiences...because they are the most ready to learn."[446]

---

430   *Ibid.*, 3:7-8.

431   *Ibid.*, 28:7-8.

432   *Ibid.*, 21:3-5.

433   *Ibid.*, 42:8.

434   W. W. Isenberg, *Philip*, 59:8-9, p. 145; 63:33, p. 148.

435   Cf. R. M. Wilson, *Philip*, p. 115.

436   Hosea 1-3.

437   F. I. Andersen, *et al.*, *Hosea*, p. 165; cf. 1 Corinthians 7:14; D&C 74.

438   M. von Wellnitz, *Liturgy*, pp. 33-34.

439   See R. H. Wilkinson, *Art*, pp. 50-51.

440   H. W. Nibley, *Atonement*, p. 559; cf. D. R. Seely, *Hand of God in the Book of Mormon*, pp. 147-149.

441   H. W. Nibley, *Atonement*, pp. 558-559.

442   F. E. Williams, *Apocryphon of James*, 5:23-35, p. 32.

443   B. C. Hafen, *Disciple's Journey*, p. 300.

444   N. A. Maxwell, *Experience*, pp. 32, 39.

445   N. A. Maxwell, *Choose*, p. 46.

446   N. A. Maxwell, remarks at Joseph S. Clark funeral, 23 February 1996, cited in B. C. Hafen, *Disciple's Life*, p. 20.

6-41 In a similar vein, Faulconer has written:

> The notion of repentance makes sense on a view that allows for backwards causation, but not on the usual view of time. If the past is indeed absolutely past and not to be changed, then repentance is a sham. It is no more than feeling sorry for what happened and it is probably an exercise in bad-faith to take it as more than that. God's promise to remember our sins no more is only a rhetorical flourish and I have difficulty understanding why an atonement is needed or what it could possibly do.
>
> Assume, however, that repentance is meaningfully described as Christianity describes it, as a change of one's personal history. One might make sense of such a view by thinking that repentance has to do with events rather than points of time. To repent is to change the meaning of a past event. But if the existence of the past is a function of its meaning in the present (something I believe but cannot argue for here), then the existence of the past is altered when I change its present meaning by repenting.[447]

6-42 In recent years, the concept of Limbo for unbaptized children has increasingly fallen into disfavor in the Roman Catholic Church.[448]

6-43 The Savior not only is the "keeper of the gate," He is the very gate itself. Writes Ostler:

> The quasi-canonical *Pastor of Hermas* is a good illustration of the necessity of both the garment and the name [to pass through the last barrier to the presence of God]:
>
> No man shall enter into the kingdom of heaven except he shall take upon him the name of the "Son of God".... The gate is the Son of God, who is the only way of coming to God.... No man can enter into the kingdom of God except these [virgins] clothe him with their garment.[449] It availeth nothing to take up the name of the "Son of God" unless thou shalt receive the garment.... A man shall in vain bear his name unless he is endowed with his powers.[450]
>
> Christ is also represented as the door to the kingdom of heaven in the *Odes of Solomon*. "He gave me the way of His precepts and I opened the doors that were closed.... Nothing appeared closed to me: Because I am the door of everything."[451] Since the gate is Christ, the scene at the gate is often one of intimate union with Christ, as in the *Apocryphon of James*. After the spirit is clothed again with its garment, Christ tells the Apostle,
>
> > Behold, I shall reveal everything to you, my beloved. Know that you came forth just as I am. Behold, I shall reveal to you Him who is hidden. Now stretch out your hand. Now take hold of me.... Those who wish to enter and seek to walk in the way that is before the door, open the door through you.[452]

6-44 Note al-Tabari's mention of "an iron rod growing on the mountain," which he implausibly explains in terms of the origin of toolmaking by Adam.[453]

After mentioning the pilgrimage by handrail, ropes, and chains to the top of Adam's Peak in Sri Lanka, Nibley writes:

> There is an account of the iron rod from Jerusalem that led to the temple... Remember, before the top of the mountain was leveled off for the temple, it was much higher, and it was risky. When it was rainy and stormy (it was Spring when people would have to go), it was hard to get up there, to follow the sacred trail up.
>
> They still do that in Athens, going up to the Acropolis the same way—the sacred trail going to the top of the mountain. So they had the handrail going up to help people. It was iron, but it rusted away. It was supplanted by wood, brass, and other things. But they always used the expression, for old or weak people or when it was dangerous and slippery, to get to the temple you had to hang

447   J. E. Faulconer, *Hebrew Time*. See also J. E. Faulconer, *Study*, pp. 148-149; M. C. Thomas, *Light*, pp. 349-350.

448   International Theological Commission, *Hope*.

449   Cf. Matthew 22:1-14; J. E. Talmage, *Jesus the Christ*, pp. 501-502, 504.

450   Cf. C. Osiek, *Shepherd*, 9:12 [89]:4, 6, p. 230; 9:13 [90]:2, p. 230.

451   Cf. J. H. Charlesworth, *Odes*, 17:9, 11, pp. 750, 751.

452   B. T. Ostler, *Clothed*, p. 9; cf. C. W. Hedrick, *et al.*, *James*, 57:4-11, 55:6-11, pp. 274, 273. See also J. H. Charlesworth, *Odes*, 37:1-4, p. 766; 42:14, p. 771; J. K. Elliott, *Pearl*, 98-102, p. 327; H. W. Nibley, *Message 2005*, 98-102, pp. 499-501.

453   al-Tabari, *Creation*, 1:126-127, p. 297.

onto the railing, "grasp the iron rod." This emerges in the Book of Mormon in a context which Joseph Smith couldn't have discovered or anybody else in his time.[454]

Lehi's dream does not contain any explicit description of a mountain, but only a reference to a "strait and narrow path, which came along by the rod of iron, even to the tree by which [Lehi] stood; and it also led by the head of the fountain, unto a large and spacious field."[455] However the fact that the waters are described as originating at the Tree of Life[456] implies at the very least that the tree sits on higher ground than the surrounding area.

6-45   Islamic commentary on this verse describes a handhold as "something which the hands can grasp for safety in a moment of danger. It may be a loop or a handle, or anchor. It is without flaw, so that there is no danger of breaking; our safety is absolutely assured so long as we hold fast to it. Our safety then depends on our own will and faith…"[457] Another commentator further elucidates: "When one wants to lay one's hold on a thing, one has to discard all other things before that. In other words, one has first to leave unwanted things, then comes the stage of holding fast to the desired thing… Its root meaning is attachment; it is said 'arahu and i'tarahu both of which mean 'was attached to him'… You cannot be sure of your hold unless you keep the handle in your grip…"[458]

6-46   The document in the hand of the ascending one can be profitably discussed in light of the Mandaean consecrating rituals for a *ganzibra* (= treasurer), the name for the office probably being derived from the idea that the individual would have a stewardship for sacred religious texts (e.g., *Ginza*). (Drower learned that this rite was originally intended to be performed for all dying persons, but is rarer now due to the shortage of priests.[459]) In this ceremony, a worthy person who is soon to die bears a message or "letter" of the new *ganzibra* to the World of Light. The "letter" takes the physical form of a vial of specially-prepared oil made from sesame and dates which is sealed with the priest's ring and the imprint of one of his fingernails, and then placed in the pocket of the overshirt or smock of the dying one's sacred burial clothing.[460] In the liturgy that accompanies the sealing of the flask of oil we read of the journey of the soul to the House of Life, proceeding by a series of ritual stages marked by handclasps:

> A sealed letter which leaveth the world
> —A letter written in good-faith (*kushta*)
> And sealed with the seal of the Mighty [Life]—
> … The spirits of Purgatory abased their heads
> And the soul passed the purgatory-spirits by.
> … As she reached the waters of death
> There came forth towards her
> A great Beam of radiance [and] of life, [who]
> Grasped her by the palm of her right hand
> And brought her over the waters of death
> The soul flieth and goeth
> Until she reacheth the House of Life,
> And when He heard her call, the Life
> Sent a messenger towards her,
> [Who] grasped her by the palm of her hand,
> Conducted her, [came] to support her [embrace her?]
> In the likeness of the Life to the place
> Of radiance, light and beams of effulgence;
> To unite her to [the company of] '*uthras*.[461]

6-47   Similar themes are found in sources from many different traditions. For example, the image of two birds, one eating and one watching, recalls the famous scene from the Hindu scriptures: "Two birds, inseparable friends, cling to the same tree. One of them eats the sweet fruit, the other looks on without eating. On the same tree a man sits grieving, immersed, bewildered, by his own impotence

---

454   H. W. Nibley, *Teachings of the PGP*, 16, pp. 195-196.

455   1 Nephi 8:20.

456   1 Nephi 11:25.

457   A. Ali, *Qur'an*, 2:256, p. 106 n. 301; cf. Hebrews 3:14. See H. W. Attridge, *et al.*, *Hebrews*, pp. 118-119.

458   A. at-Tabataba'i, *Al-Mizan*, 2:256; 4:173-174.

459   E. S. Drower, *Adam*, pp. 73-74.

460   E. Lupieri, *Mandaeans*, p. 29.

461   E. S. Drower, *Prayerbook*, 73, pp. 61-63. See also E. S. Drower, *Prayerbook*, 49, pp. 43-46; 63, p. 52.

(*an-îsâ*). But when he sees the other lord (*isa*) contented, and knows his glory, then his grief passes away."[462] The tree in question is the sacred *Bodhi* (fig, pippala). Christian texts also mention birds who sometimes lodged in the Tree of Life to eat "the berries of the tree. These were large berries, sweeter than all honey, and more intoxicating than every wine."[463] In a relief relating to the Mithraic mysteries, "Mithra and Sol clasp hands over an altar, while a spit of meat pecked at by a raven is directly above the union of the hands. Vermaseren interprets this as a treaty before 'the divine meal which itself took place before their ascent to heaven in the chariot of the sun.'"[464]

The idea of two convergent doves at the top of the Tree of Life recalls a Roman design with two doves that may have a Greek antecedent. Butterworth relates the "legend that two eagles (or swans or crows) were dispatched by Zeus from the opposite ends of the earth and that they met at the Pythian oracle, which had its seat at the Delphic omphalos."[465] He also notes that "imperial coins show a bird on either side of the Paphian omphalos" (*ibid.*).

Of the symbolism of the dove in pagan, Jewish, and Christian iconography, Goodenough writes:

> The bird, especially the dove, has come in many situations to suggest an association with soul, immortality, and love, three conceptions which are really one since the first two mean life directly, and since also love is life. The dove properly, as soul or divine love, takes its place in the vine, and feeds on the grapes, whence, as from the cup, it gets, or gives divine life. The logic of symbolism is highly circuitous. Association which returns by a circle to its point of origin only enhances the value of the symbol. It is absurd to say that the cupid and dove, if they represent divine love given to man, cannot at the same time be the souls of the departed getting their eternal life from the juice; that they cannot simultaneously be the saved and saviors. This is utterly to misunderstand symbolism and religion alike. The analogy seems to me quite perfect with the Christian lamb, which can interchangeably be Christ himself, Christ's loving sacrifice of himself, or a member of Christ's flock. A religious aspirant who craves to assimilate divine life into himself through the god's love and to achieve mystical union here and immortality hereafter, sees the process at the same time to be the exaltation of the believer into identity with the savior, so that the symbol of the savior represents the one who is saved. In all the mysteries, as in Christianity, the believer became identified with the person of the saving god by identifying himself with the god's experiences.[466]

6-48   *Wikipedia* gives the following about the life of Herbert:[467]

> George Herbert (3 April 1593 – 1 March 1633) was a Welsh poet, orator and priest. Being born into an artistic and wealthy family, he received a good education which led to his holding prominent positions at Cambridge University and Parliament. As a student at Trinity College, Cambridge, England, George Herbert excelled in languages and music. He went to college with the intention of becoming a priest, but his scholarship attracted the attention of King James I. Herbert served in parliament for two years. After the death of King James and at the urging of a friend, Herbert's interest in ordained ministry was renewed. In 1630, in his late thirties he gave up his secular ambitions and took holy orders in the Church of England, spending the rest of his life as a rector of the little parish of St. Andrew Bemerton, near Salisbury. He was noted for unfailing care for his parishioners, bringing the sacraments to them when they were ill, and providing food and clothing for those in need. Throughout his life he wrote religious poems characterized by a precision of language, a metrical versatility, and an ingenious use of imagery or conceits that was favoured by the metaphysical school of poets. He is best remembered as a writer of poems and the hymn "Come, My Way, My Truth, My Life."

Many of Herbert's poems were included in the posthumously-published volume entitled *The Temple*. It is reported that the author, on his death-bed, delivered the book to his executor, with the following instructions:[468]

> Sir, I pray deliver this little book to my dear brother Ferrar, and tell him, he shall find in it a picture of the many spiritual conflicts that have passed betwixt God and my soul, before I could subject

462   F. M. Müller, *Upanishads 2*, Mundaka 3:1-2, p. 38; cf. R. T. H. Griffith, *Rig Veda*, 1:164:22, p. 111; F. M. Müller, *Upanishads 2*, Svetasvatara 4:6-7, pp. 234-235; Katha 3:1, p. 12.

463   M. Herbert, *Irish Apocrypha*, p. 19; cf. p. 17.

464   M. J. Veraseren, *Mithras*, p. 98, cited in T. M. Compton, *Handclasp*, pp. 619-620.

465   E. A. S. Butterworth, *Tree*, p. 36.

466   E. R. Goodenough, *Pagan Symbols*, 8:36-37.

467   *George Herbert.*

468   From the preface of G. Herbert, *Temple*, p. vi.

mine to the will of Jesus my master, in whose service I have now found perfect freedom; desire him to read it, and then if he can think it may turn to the advantage of any dejected poor soul, let it be made public; if not, let him burn it, for I and it are less than the least of God's mercies.

The English composer Ralph Vaughan Williams set music to a carefully selected set of Herbert's poems in his 1911 *Five Mystical Songs*. Palmer writes:[469]

> Both what Herbert said… and the way he said it appealed to the Christian agnostic (or "disappointed theist") in Vaughan Williams… "Love bade me welcome" looks both more inward and… far further forward than the other songs. The rapt stillness at its center—the Act, at which point, in the traditionally Edenic key of *E*, wordless voices intone the *O sacrum convivium*,[470] is one of the great moments in Vaughan Williams.

As a fitting coincidence, the Harvard University library copy used to create a digital version of this book is signed, "Amy Lothrop, December 25, 1889." Amy Lothrop was the pen name of Anna Bartlett Warner (1827-1915), who is best known for having written the children's prayer song, "Jesus Loves Me, This I Know."

---

469 C Palmer, *Vaughan Williams*, p. 4.

470 *O sacrum convivium* is a liturgical reflection on the Sacrament of the Lord's Supper: "O sacred banquet! / in which Christ is received, / the memory of his Passion is renewed, / the mind is filled with grace, / and a pledge of future glory to us is given. / Alleluia." As the words make it clear, however, the sacrament is only a foretaste of the celestial feast. Thus, in the musical setting for Herbert's dialogue with Deity, one might further imagine the culminating encounter of Divine acceptance, the wordless refrain in the crucial instant at once expressing both the ineffable joy of the penitent soul and the magnitude of the love freely offered through the sufferings of our Lord.

Excursus

EXCURSUS

Excursus 1
Speech, Writing, and Revelation

SPEECH and writing are so commonplace that their almost miraculous nature is easily forgotten. Far from being mechanical processes, both their encoding and their decipherment relies on a complex creative act that is amazing to consider:

> Michael Reddy[1] points out the predominance of what he calls the "conduit metaphor," the fallacious belief that when we talk, we talk about the world directly, and send our thoughts felicitously over to other individuals through the conduit of language. Linguistic communication is typically viewed as the cloaking of ideas in words, as if words as packages somehow contain reports on the world they represent.

> Reddy observes that none of this really happens. When one person talks to another, words do not come out of the speaker's mouth as packages full of direct report on facts, which the hearer then opens up to discover the fully packed meaning inside. On the contrary, the speaker forces air out of the lungs and shapes the molecules with the vocal apparatus; these molecules vibrate on the hearer's eardrums, sending neurochemical impulses to the brain. The hearer then constructs a model of what the speaker is thought to have said. People understand each other and communicate not by direct conveyance at all, but by broadcasting signals, which themselves evoke mental models… We do not speak about the extensional world, but about the model of the world we make up in our heads.[2]

Writing allows a similar process to take place among people separated by time or distance. Nibley comments:

> Writing is as marvelous and subtle a thing in its operation and in its effects as television. Here we have a means of transmitting not only the deeds but also the very thoughts of men through unlimited expanses of space and time—and this amazingly economical and efficient device has been in the possession of the human race from its very beginning. Writing was not devised by men as a tool to help them in their everyday affairs: successful businessmen have been illiterates, and there is ample evidence that writing was adapted to commercial uses only after such uses were found for it. If you bring together all the written records of man's past, you will discover that the overwhelming mass of material is religious in nature, and that the primary purpose to which writing has been put through the ages has not been for business records and correspondence, in which writing is employed awkwardly and without enthusiasm, but for keeping a remembrance of God's dealings with men. The specific purpose of writing, as the Egyptians put it, is to record the *mdw ntr*, the divine words.[3]

Different theories on the origins of writing raise "contentious" questions,[4] however it is widely agreed that the first "continuous texts" of Old Egyptian date to the third millennium BCE.[5] Nibley explains both "the popularity and the variety of ancient writing… by its religious nature," noting that "new scripts invariably appear as the vehicles of new religions" and that "all of man's greatest inventions and discoveries seem to have the primary purpose of putting him into communication with the other world."[6] Whoever reads the scriptures today "has before him the words of God to men from the beginning, in witness of which

EXCURSUS

---

1   M. Reddy, *Conduit.*
2   W. Frawley, *Semantics*, pp. 23-24.
3   H. W. Nibley, *Gnostics*, p. 207.
4   J. T. Hooker, *Reading*, p. 6. For a readable history of world languages, see N. Ostler, *Empires.*
5   W. V. Davies, *Hieroglyphs*, p. 81.
6   H. W. Nibley, *Written Word*, p. 109.

the very letters on the page are but slightly conventionalized forms of the original symbols in which the message was conveyed," thus these writings "are the nearest approach and the best clue thus far discovered to the genesis of the written word."[7]

Despite the crucial role of the written word in conveying knowledge of God, Brigham Young was emphatic that: "Language to convey all the truth, does not exist. Even in the Bible, and all books that have been revealed from heaven unto men, the language fails to convey all the truth as it is."[8] That is because an understanding of truth, especially spiritual truth, does not come through language itself, but through a process of revelation. After having been filled with the Holy Ghost following his baptism, Joseph Smith wrote: "Our minds being now enlightened, we began to have the scriptures laid open to our understandings, and the true meaning and intention of their more mysterious passages revealed unto us in a manner which we never could attain to previously, nor ever before had thought of."[9] He also said that: "...we never can comprehend the things of God and of heaven, but by revelation. We may spiritualize and express opinions to all eternity; but that is no authority."[10]

The Prophet taught that gospel ordinances were given for the express purpose of giving us a direct experience of spiritual matters:

> Could we read and comprehend all that has been written from the days of Adam, on the relation of man to God and angels in a future state, we should know very little about it. Reading the experience of others, or the revelation given to them, can never give us a comprehensive view of our condition and true relation to God. Knowledge of these things can only be obtained by experience through the ordinances of God set forth for that purpose. Could you gaze into heaven five minutes, you would know more than you would by reading all that ever was written on the subject.[11]

Oliver Cowdery observed that "one touch with the finger of his love, yes, one ray of glory from the upper world, or one word from the mouth of the Saviour, from the bosom of eternity, strikes [fiction and falsehood] into insignificance and blots it forever from the mind!"[12]

7   *Ibid.*, p. 122.
8   B. Young, *27 February 1853*, p. 117.
9   JS-H 1:74.
10 J. Smith, Jr., *Teachings*, 8 April 1843, p. 292.
11 J. Smith, Jr., *Teachings*, 9 October 1843, p. 324; cf. 8 April 1843, p. 292.
12 O. Cowdery, *Phelps*, p. 16.

EXCURSUS

Figure E1-1. *Shabaka Stone, ca. 710 BCE*

According to Nibley's unique exegesis,[1] the drama recounted on the Shabaka stone "begins with Ptah [the creator god] in his glory, and he wishes to transmit the powers of heaven (the powers he possesses) to the earth, the same celestial order.... The whole purpose of this is to show that the king at Memphis (Shabaka in this case) holds the same authority that was held by God and was handed down to man through Atum and through the heavenly council to the spirits and brought down to earth [1-6]....[2] [Geb, lord of the gods,] calls the council of the gods and they discuss a division between Seth and Horus [7]... Seth is our Satan, of course... [T]he land is divided between them... He sends each one to his part of the hall and says, 'Let there be no more argument between you' [8-9]. And each one takes his place [10a-b, 11a-12b]. But then he does a strange thing. He decides to give the whole inheritance to Horus [10c, 13a-16b]. Why is that?.... [Because] the division of the land is not the question of who is to be priest and king, and there can only be one...[3] [Geb] speaks again to the council of the gods and says, 'This is my son who is born, who is Horus, and who is born at the new year' [17a-b, 18a-b]. So [the text] celebrates the new year. It's the beginning of a new age... This is the end of Act One.... So we get to Act Two, and the trouble begins.... All of a sudden the Osiris theme is introduced.... Osiris is overcome and either thrown into the water or drowned... by the wicked Seth [17c, 19; cf. 62].... And Horus gave an order and cried out to [Isis and Nephthys], 'Ladies, go rescue him and take him from the water and prevent his drowning' [18c, 19, 20a, 21a; cf. 62]. [J]ust in time they catch him and bring him up again upon the land [20b, 21b; cf. 63]... 'He now enters through the gate [it also means initiation] of the glory of the land of the holy ones, the lords of eternity' [21b; cf. 63-64]. The final test is the baptism. He emerges from the waters of life [cf. Moses 1:20].... 'When you reach the great throne, there he shall be united in salvation and safety'.... Notice the two brother signs, *sensen*, with the nose there for sniff: 'And they shall kiss one another and fall upon each other's shoulders [cf. Moses 7:63]... And he shall be entered into the brotherhood of the gods' [22; cf. 64]... Osiris doesn't stay in the grave. He comes and introduces the ordinances for redemption for the dead on earth. So he enters into his temple. Here is the house of the great old man [21b; cf. 64]. It is often rendered 'the house of the Ancient of Days,' in other words God's representative on earth."[4]

In addition to the themes discussed above, Nibley describes the Shabaka Creation account [48-61] which is, in Sparks' words "reminiscent of Genesis" in its use of verbal commands.[5] Nibley also sees in this account an "Opening of the Mouth."[6] "All hail the plan of the Most High God presented to the Council; he plans and executes as he conceives in his heart and utters with his tongue his plan to be approved by the assembled hosts of the gods and preexistent spirits [53-54, 57]. Every living thing is invested with his divine power, shared by 'gods, mortals, beasts, all creeping things and other forms of life' [54]. Man is spiritually begotten and physically formed, the future ruler of the earth, endowed with eyes to see, ears to hear, a nose to smell, etc. [56]. The earth being prepared with all good things to receive him, a law is given to implement and explain the purpose of the earth as a place of probation: 'All who do good will be for eternal life, and all those who do evil for eternal bondage. This law is to be the measure of all things'—it is the purpose of all man's actions on earth [57]. 'And God finished his work... and was pleased with it' [59]. The heavenly plan was then implemented and carried out on earth, ... as fields and cities sprang up around these holy centers [59-61]."[7]

Regarding the influence of this text, Nibley reports that it is, "in the opinion of Sethe, Junker, Breasted, and others 'the most instructive which we possess for the inner content of Egyptian religion.'"[8] Nibley also cites Zabkar, who concluded that the Memphite Theology "'traveled from century to century, from one theological system to another; its theme resounds from the first line of Genesis, and from there on through the Old Testament and the latest period of Hebrew literature'... More than that, 'the Memphite Theology, through the Old Testament, prepared... the consciousness of the religious world for John's *Logos* doctrine about the manifestations and creative power of the Word of God, so the Amarna Theology sounded some themes which in the New Testament and especially in John's Gospel represent the fundamental features of the relation between the Father and the Son.'"[9]

The Shabaka stone purports to have been inscribed as a faithful and permanent reproduction of an ancient deteriorating document containing the Memphite theology, with worm holes in the original represented as intentional gaps in the text. However, most scholars have concluded that various archaisms and features of the layout were purposely added to give the stela an air of antiquity. While earlier studies placed the origin of the text in the Old Kingdom, prior to the Pyramid texts, more recent research posits a date no earlier than the 13th century BCE, and possibly as late as 710 BCE. Twenty-three of the sixty-four columns have been worn away. Unfortunately, much of the damage was done to the inscriptions in Roman times when this artifact was appropriated for use as a stationary lower millstone—the radial grooves having been deliberately made so as to let the flour come out—"like using the Great Seal of England to crack nuts," complained Nibley.[10]

1   See *Endnote E-1*, p. 702.

2   Cf. M. Lichtheim, *Memphite*, p. 56 n. 2.

3   Cf. *ibid.*, p. 56 n. 3. On the contest of Horus and Seth, and the triumph of Horus, see J. Assman, *Search*, pp. 134-147.

4   H. W. Nibley, *Teachings of the PGP*, 8-10, pp. 99-100, 105-106, 103, 107, 117-119; cf. H. W. Nibley, *Expanding 1992*, pp. 182-184. For a standard translation, see M. Lichtheim, *Memphite*.

5   M. Lichtheim, *Memphite*, p. 56 n. 10; K. L. Sparks, *Ancient Texts*, p. 324.

6   H. W. Nibley, *Teachings of the PGP*, 9, pp. 108-115.

7   H. W. Nibley, *Sacred*, pp. 589-590.

8   K. Koch, *Wort*, cited in H. W. Nibley, *Greatness*, p. 303. See also A. Roberts, *Anointing*, p. 93.

9   L. V. Zabkar, *Theocracy*, p. 87, cited in H. W. Nibley, *Greatness*, pp. 303-304.

10   H. W. Nibley, *Expanding 1992*, p. 181. See H. W. Nibley, *Expanding 1992*, pp. 180-181 for a "readable" drawing.

Excursus 2
Ancient Concepts of Wisdom

ANCIENT concepts of Wisdom found in the book of Job are far removed from the secular and pietistic sayings in most of the rest of the wisdom literature of the Bible, much of which can be described as "a hotchpotch of trivia, some witty, others just banal."[13] Knowing he could not quench his thirst from these "broken cisterns," Job sought "the fountain of living waters,"[14] placing "emphasis on seeing God after so much mere hearsay."[15] Barker reminds us that this "hankering after divine wisdom… is exactly the theme of Job, where Job is challenged and eventually condemned on the grounds of his claim to knowledge. The book is not just about suffering but also about Job's claim to know":[16]

> In Job 38:7… we… read of the sons of God who shouted for joy on the first day of Creation when the foundations of the earth were laid… The rest of Job 38 describes the works of Day One… And the point of all this is to ask Job: "Where were you when all this was done?" a strange question for the Lord to ask Job unless there was a known tradition of someone who witnessed the work of Creation and thus became wise.[17]

Extracanonical sources not only reinforce the priority of theophany over theodicy in the story of Job, but also introduce the theme of apotheosis. These traditions associate Job with key elements of temple ritual and apocalyptic accounts of heavenly ascents, some of which find parallels in the LDS understanding of the career of Adam and Eve. For example, Job's ascent not only included a visit to a heavenly throne, but also descriptions of sacred clothing ("And as she chanted the hymns, she permitted 'the Spirit' to be inscribed on her garment"[18]), prayer circles ("And they lifted me up, supporting my arms on each side"[19]), ritual oaths ("Behold my sign!"[20]), and tests for knowledge ("Arise, gird your loins like a man. I shall ask you certain questions, and you shall give me certain answers!"[21]). Like both the biblical story and the temple tradition, the pseudepigraphal account includes a series of tests provided by Satan himself who, for example, at one point cruelly declares to the penniless Job that he "can have anything in this world for money."[22] Indeed, throughout all the Job traditions[23]—as in the stories of the Fall of Adam and Eve, the heavenly ascent of Moses, and Jesus' temptation in the wilderness—the Adversary provides an essential element, "helping" the hero meet the requirement to prove himself worthy of a continued journey toward divine light and knowledge.[24]

Barker argues that important elements of the wisdom traditions in Israel, including Wisdom traditions specifically associated with Adam,[25] have been obscured or lost through exclusion from the canon and deliberate alteration of what remained, and must be reconstructed from extracanonical sources that often blend wisdom with the apocalyptic.[26] In such literature:

---

13 M. Barker, *Older*, p. 84.

14 Jeremiah 2:13.

15 R. Murphy, *Wisdom*, p. 16; cf. J. L. Crenshaw, *Love*, pp. 62-63; Job 19:26-27, 42:5; Abraham 1:2.

16 M. Barker, *Older*, p. 238.

17 M. Barker, *Beyond*, pp. 195-196.

18 R. A. Kraft, *Job*, 48:4, p. 83.

19 R. P. Spittler, *Testament of Job*, 40:2, p. 859. See also H. W. Nibley, *Prayer Circle*, p. 63.

20 See discussion of Job 31:35 in B. Haymond, *Job's Covenant*. Cf. R. J. Clifford, *Wisdom*, p. 86; S. D. Ricks, *Oaths*.

21 H. W. Nibley, *Prayer Circle*, p. 63; cf. Job 38:3; R. P. Spittler, *Testament of Job*, 47:5, p. 865: "Arise, gird your loins like a man. I shall question you, and you answer me."

22 H. W. Nibley, *Prayer Circle*, p. 63; df. H. W. Nibley, *Consecration*, p. 439; R. P. Spittler, *Testament of Job*, 23:3, p. 848: "Pay the price and take what you like."

23 On the theme of divine testing in Job, and the book's affinities with the story of the Fall, see T. N. D. Mettinger, *Eden*, pp. 54-58.

24 See Moses 4:5ff., 1:12-22; Matthew 4:1-11; Luke 4:1-13. For more on this topic, see J. M. Bradshaw, *et al.*, *Satan*.

25 D. E. Callender, *Adam*, pp. 2-4, 13-14, 67-84. Contrast A. G. Zornberg, *Genesis*, pp. 25, 27 regarding *Torah* at Creation.

26 See Endnote E-2, p. 702.

FIGURE E2-1. *The Lord Answers Job from the Whirlwind, 1826*
William Blake, 1757-1827

SEE COLOR PLATE E2-1.

And behold, the glory of the Lord was upon Moses, so that Moses stood in the presence of God, and talked with him face to face.[1] Like Job, each of us must eventually "see the face of God" and, seeing, either "live" or "die."[2] As C. S. Lewis wrote: "In the twinkling of an eye, in a time too small to be measured, and in any place, all that seems to divide us from God can flee away, leaving us naked before Him, like the first man, like the only man, as if nothing but He and I existed. And since that contact cannot be avoided for long, and since it means either bliss or horror, the business of life is to learn to like it. That is the first and great commandment."[3]

Blake's depiction shows God surrounded by a concourse of angels. To Chrysostom, the cloud and whirlwind that came down on the mountain suggested that He "wanted to place heaven over Job as though setting His very throne near him."[4] Job looks up to converse with God face to face, while his friends lie prostrate in terror.[5] In other versions of this drawing, Job is caught up with God in the circle, their identical faces mirroring one other in serene mutual regard. According to Fisch, the key to understanding the illustration is that "Man is about to take on the nature of God... For according to Blake's radical reading of the Gospel, ...Man himself—not merely Jesus, but every man and woman—is potentially endowed with divine glory and even divine power! ...This is what Blake termed the religion of the Divine Humanity."[6] He expressed this thought in the couplet: "God becomes as we are, that we may be as he is."[7] Both William Blake and Joseph Smith, according to Harold Bloom, "sought to end the distinction between the human and the divine."[8]

---

1   Moses 1:31.
2   Cf. Exodus 33:11/D&C 84:22 vs. JST Exodus 33:20. See P. J. Schakel, *Reason*, pp. 125-126, 197 n. 27.
3   C. S. Lewis, *Dogma*, p. 126.
4   J. Chrysostom, *Job*, 38:1, p. 186.
5   Job 38:1.
6   H. Fisch, *Presence*, pp. 310-312. "The ordinary educated modern person staring at these 'Job' designs can only say that God is a mere elderly twin brother of Job. Blake would have at once retorted that Job is an image of God" (G. K. Chesterton, *William Blake*, p. 149).
7   W. Blake, *Natural Religion*, p. 41; cf. G. B. Hinckley, *Don't Drop*, p. 46; P. B. Munoa, *Four Powers*, p. 102; L. Snow, *Teachings 1984*, 15 June 1901, p. 1. See *Endnote 2-28*, p. 130. See also *Introduction*, pp. 10-11.
8   H. Bloom, *Genius*, p. 699.

... the exaltation of the wise man is a common motif... The wise man has knowledge of God, is a child/servant of the Lord, has God as his Father and, as God's son, will receive help.[27] At the great judgment he will be exalted and take his place with the sons of God, the Holy Ones.[28] In *1 Enoch* this pattern is applied to the Son of Man, the Elect One, or to the community of the righteous elect ones....[29] Wisdom was the secrets of creation, learned in heaven and brought to earth, the recurring theme of the apocalypses. There must have been some way in which the king, and the wise men, "went" to heaven like the prophets in order to learn these secrets by listening in the council of God[30] which compares the commandments favorably to something else, unspecified, which had to be brought from heaven by someone else.[31]

By piecing together the ancient sources,[32] it can be surmised that the knowledge revealed to those made wise included an understanding of premortal life, the order of creation, and the eternal covenant[33]—and it "provided a clue to the pattern and future destiny of the universe"[34] that "gave power over creation when used in conjunction with supernatural forces."[35]

---

27   S. Sandmel, *et al., Solomon*, 2:12ff., pp. 98-99.
28   *Ibid.*, 5:1ff., p. 100.
29   G. W. E. Nickelsburg, *et al., 1 Enoch*, 46, 62-63, 104, pp. 59-60, 79-83, 161-163.
30   Job 15:8; Proverbs 30:1-4; cf. Deuteronomy 30:11-14.
31   M. Barker, *Older*, pp. 92, 95; cf. M. Barker, *Great High Priest: Temple Roots*, p. 343, n. 23.
32   See *Endnote E-3*, p. 702. See also, e.g., J. M. Bradshaw, *Ezekiel*.
33   M. Barker, *Older*, p. 82.
34   A. E. Harvey, *Companion 2004*, p. 533.
35   M. Barker, *Older*, p. 82; cf. JST Genesis 14:30-31.

Barker notes that the Messiah (= the anointed one) and the high priests who represented him in the temple figuratively received Wisdom as they were anointed with oil from the Tree of Life.[36] This Wisdom was brought:

> … from heaven to earth, and the people knelt before him to receive it. This must underlie the now opaque lines in Proverbs 30:1-4, which have been reconstructed as [follows]:
>
> > For I surpass all men and have the discernment of Adam. God has surely given me Wisdom and I know the knowledge of the holy ones. Who has ascended to the clouds and come down, and who has gathered the wind in his fists? Who has caught up the waters in his garment and established the ends of the earth? What is his name and what is the name of his son? Surely, you know.
>
> However the finer detail is reconstructed, the meaning is clear enough, as is the disordered state of the text. Given the tendencies of the second temple editors, the one undoubtedly explains the other. The messianic prophecy in Isaiah 11 must have had a similar setting: "The Spirit of the Lord shall rest upon him, the spirit of wisdom and understanding, the spirit of counsel and might, the spirit of knowledge and the fear of the Lord."[37]

Eventually, the *Torah* was substituted for the ancient concept of Wisdom:

> [W]e have to ask what was meant by Deuteronomy 4:6, which seems to be saying that the Law was to function as the wisdom of the chosen people. Does this mean the central role of the *Torah* was formerly the role of wisdom? Deuteronomy, which is not noted for its toleration of foreign ways, is here finding a central place for something which we assume to have been foreign. Perhaps [the] *Torah* was being offered as a substitute for something in the older cult whose legitimacy they could not deny. Wisdom was an older form of communication between God and his people. Wisdom was something which the Deuteronomists reformed.[38]

In his valuable chapter, Schäfer documents how the gift of prophecy was replaced during the Jewish exile by the concept of the *Torah* as Wisdom. Though the exact chronology varies, the "common denominator" for the set of dates given by the later rabbis is "guided by the conception that the cessation of prophecy was connected with the destruction of the First Temple."[39] This transformation constituted "the replacement of the unpredictable voice of prophecy with the more manageable one of scholarship and bureaucratic precedent":[40]

> The Written and Oral *Torah* are dependent on each other…; the Wisdom of the book pours itself into an abundance of teaching [epitomized by midrash] and has finally replaced prophecy. The rabbis of classical rabbinic Judaism have not only brought this idea to a grandiose fruition, they also have put themselves on top of it. They are the ones who in the end guarantee that the abundance of teaching is directed into the right channels, so to speak; that it does not flood—and destroy—everything.[41]

Ancient concepts of Wisdom find parallels elsewhere in the ancient Near East. For example, Egyptian ritual, once thought of as only intended for the dead, has increasingly been studied in terms of its use as an initiation of transfiguration for the living.[42]

---

36   M. Barker, *Angel Priesthood*, p. 130.
37   *Ibid.*, pp. 130-131.
38   M. Barker, *Older*, p. 83. See *Figure 1-4*, p. 35, *Figure 5-11*, p. 343 and *Commentary 2:1-c*, p. 93.
39   P. Schäfer, *Torah as Wisdom*, p. 28.
40   D. C. Peterson, *Muhammad (2001)*, p. 598
41   P. Schäfer, *Torah as Wisdom*, p. 34.
42   B. J. Petersen, *Nibley*, p. 369. See *Endnote E-1*, p. 702. J. D. G. Dunn, *et al.*, *Commentary*, p. 358 cites parallels between Egyptian ritual and Job 31. *Excursus 6: The Authority and Power of Scripture*, p. 531 further explores the relationship between the wisdom revealed through continuing revelation and its embodiment in scripture.

Excursus 3
Temple Blessings in the Oath and Covenant of the Priesthood

CONTRARY to a common belief that the highest temple ordinances were not anticipated until the last few years of Joseph Smith's ministry, several references to temple-related concepts occur in his early revelations. Many of these ideas were not publicly explained by the Prophet until long after the time they were given to him. For example, three verses from the revelation on priesthood received on 22-23 September 1832 succinctly describe a definite sequence of promised blessings that were not fully bestowed upon the Saints until more than ten years later in Nauvoo:

> And the sons of Moses and of Aaron shall be filled with the glory of the Lord, upon Mount Zion in the Lord's house, whose sons are ye; and also many whom I have called and sent forth to build up my church.
>
> For whoso is faithful unto the obtaining these two priesthoods of which I have spoken, and the magnifying their calling, are sanctified by the Spirit unto the renewing of their bodies.
>
> They become the sons of Moses and of Aaron and the seed of Abraham, and the church and kingdom, and the elect of God.[43]

And the sons of Moses and of Aaron shall be filled with the glory of the Lord; …in the Lord's house, whose sons are ye. The temple is the place where the Lord will bestow His glory upon the saints.

whoso is faithful unto the obtaining these two priesthoods and the magnifying their calling. The higher ordinances of the temple are to be given only when the prerequisites of faithfulness here described have been met. The two priesthoods referred to, Aaronic and Melchizedek, are described in D&C 84:6-32.[44] Worthy women may, of course, receive temple blessings without priesthood ordination.

To magnify a calling means to faithfully perform the duties pertaining to it "with all diligence" and "by laboring with our might."[45] "When [a person] has proved himself by a worthy life, having been faithful in all things required of him, then it is his privilege to receive other covenants and to take upon himself other obligations."[46] This process continues until eventually, having received step-by-step all required ordinances and covenants, and having continued in faithfulness, that person will "receive of the Father's fulness and of his glory."[47]

sanctified by the Spirit unto the renewing of their bodies. Since celestial personages are beings of both "spirit and element, inseparably connected,"[48] the promise of sanctification necessarily encompasses a renewal of the physical body. Explained Truman G. Madsen:

EXCURSUS

Excursus 53: Comparative Explorations of the Mysteries, p. 663 discusses the relationship between Wisdom and ancient rites pertaining to the "mysteries of the kingdom." For additional discussion of the relationship between the law of Moses and the older Wisdom tradition, see R. Murphy, *Wisdom*, p. 21; P. Schäfer, *Torah as Wisdom*. For an in-depth survey of connections between the wisdom literature and the Book of Mormon, see K. Christensen, *Temple*, pp. 488-504. See also *Commentary* 1:31-d, p. 65; 2:1-c, p. 93; *Figure 1-4*, p. 35; *Figure 5-11*, p. 343.

43   D&C 84:33-34. Another example can be found in D&C 93:1.
44   See S. B. Farley, *Oath*, pp. 221-222; J. F. Smith, Jr., *Oath*, p. 92.
45   Jacob 1:19; cf. *Doctrine and Covenants Student Manual*, p. 183.
46   J. F. Smith, Jr., *Way 1945*, 1931, p. 208.
47   *Ibid.*
48   D&C 93:33.

"As spirits, we are born of heavenly parentage. In the quickening processes of the temple we become Christ's—in mind, spirit, and body. Thus, when Joseph Smith first sent the Twelve to England he instructed them to teach: 'Being born again, comes by the Spirit of God through ordinances.'"[49] Speaking of Christ as the prototype for all those who receive these ordinances, the *Gospel of Philip* expresses the same concept: "He who…[was begotten] before everything was begotten anew. He [who was] once [anointed] was anointed anew. He who was redeemed in turn redeemed (others)."[50]

Anciently, this renewal was both symbolized and actualized when Aaron was "wash[ed]," "anoint[ed]," and clothed in "holy garments… so that he [might] minister unto [the Lord] in the priest's office,"[51] thus recapitulating his foreordination to this calling.[52] In premortal life, faithful women were also "given certain assignments" to be carried out later on earth.[53]

As the Prophet Joseph Smith prayed for his friend Joseph Knight, Sr. that his "trembling, tortured, and broken body [might] be renewed" and restored to "the vigor of health,"[54] so one who has received the blessing of these temple rites might also hope in faith to be physically "quickened, renewed, and strengthened."[55] The ultimate renewal of the body is, of course, the change that will take place for those found worthy to enter the celestial kingdom at the time of their resurrection.[56] However, there are also blessings of physical renewal that can be claimed in the here and now.[57] Sometimes, taught Joseph Smith, the receipt of these ordinances may produce a "visible effect"[58] on the individual.

sons of Moses and of Aaron. The promise of the renewing of the body mentioned in verse 33 includes being counted as part of God's chosen lineage, either literally or through "adoption."[59] "Sonship denotes belonging to a family and having certain rights as a member and as an heir."[60] Thus, as sons of Moses and Aaron, faithful priesthood holders have become rightful heirs to the blessings of the greater and the lesser priesthoods respectively.[61] In similitude of Moses and Aaron, priesthood holders assist in gathering latter-day Israel and establishing them as a people of the Lord.[62] They perform temple work wherein they "offer an acceptable offering and sacrifice in the house of the Lord."[63]

The lesser priesthood, which was "confirmed… upon Aaron and his seed,"[64] "holdeth the key of the ministering of angels and the preparatory gospel."[65] The greater or Holy Priesthood

49   T. G. Madsen, *et al.*, *House of Love*, p. 48. See J. Smith, Jr., *Teachings*, 2 July 1839, p. 162.

50   W. W. Isenberg, *Philip*, 70:36-71:3, p. 152. See *Endnote E-4*, p. 703.

51   Exodus 40:12-13. See *Excursus 52: Washing, Anointing, and Clothing Among Early Christians*, p. 661.

52   A poem by W. W. Phelps asserts that "[b]efore this world was known," certain spirits "were wash'd and set apart for the glory yet to be." He says they were also given a "white stone" with a "new name" (*Deseret News*, 6, 416, cited in T. G. Hatch, *Visions*, p. 230). See *Endnote 4-9*, p. 299. See also J. Smith, Jr., *Words*, 12 May 1844, p. 371; J. Smith, Jr., *Teachings*, 12 May 1844, p. 365; Alma 13:1-8; cf. Moses 1:6; Abraham 3:23. See *Endnote E-5*, p. 704.

53   S. W. Kimball, *Righteous Women*, p. 102. See Emma Smith's blessing request, where she asked that she might live to "perform all the work that [she] covenanted to perform in the spirit-world" (G. N. Jones, *Emma*, p. 295).

54   J. Smith, Jr., *Documentary History*, 2 August 1842, 5:124.

55   O. Pratt, *9 March 1873*, p. 365.

56   D&C 88:29. See the account of L. Snow, June 1846, cited in M. U. Beecher, *Iowa*, pp. 268-269.

57   See, e.g., D&C 84:80; B. K. Packer, *Holy Temple*, p. 154; H. B. Brown, *Participation*, p. 507; H. B. Eyring, Jr., *Oath*, p. 62; T. G. Madsen, *Man Illumined*, p. 311; M. G. Romney, *Covenant*, p. 98; B. Young, *29 June 1873*, p. 123.

58   J. Smith, Jr., *Words*, 27 June 1839, p. 4.

59   See *Endnote E-6*, p. 704.

60   S. B. Farley, *Oath*, p. 223.

61   D&C 84:6, 18; Abraham 1:2.

62   D&C 84:2.

63   D&C 84:31-32.

64   D&C 84:18.

65   D&C 84:26.

"administereth the gospel and holdeth the key of the mysteries of the kingdom, even the key of the knowledge of God."[66] Moses sought unsuccessfully to prepare the children of Israel to receive the greater priesthood "that they might behold the face of God."[67] Joseph Smith further explained: "All priesthood is Melchizedek; but there are different portions or degrees of it. That portion [i.e., the greater priesthood] which brought Moses to speak with God face to face was taken away [after the children of Israel rebelled in the wilderness;][68] but that [lesser priesthood] which brought the ministry of angels remained."[69]

As a consequence of the greater priesthood being withheld from the children of Israel, His "holy order, and the ordinances thereof" that would have allowed them to have His "presence... in their midst"[70] were generally unavailable.[71] Later, when the Mosaic Tabernacle was constructed, the high priest alone was authorized to pass through the veil and enter into the Lord's presence in the Holy of Holies, and that only once a year. However, in New Testament times, and again in the latter days, the ordinances of the high priesthood have been made available to all who qualify themselves to receive them.[72]

seed of Abraham. Those who have become sons of Moses and of Aaron are eligible to receive the blessings of Abraham, as they are given in patriarchal marriage ordinances in the temple.[73]

"Abraham received promises concerning his seed, and of the fruit of his loins... [that] both in the world and out of the world should they continue as innumerable as the stars... This promise is yours also, because ye are of Abraham..."[74] Of course, being a literal descendant of Abraham does not guarantee the fulfillment of these promises, as they are conditioned upon personal faithfulness to the covenants received: "they are not all Israel, which are of Israel: Neither, because they are all children of Abraham, are they the seed.... But the children of the promise are counted for the seed."[75]

"Elder McConkie noted that 'what we say for Abraham, Isaac, and Jacob we say also for Sarah, Rebekah, and Rachel, the wives... who with them were true and faithful in all things,'[76] for, as President Joseph Fielding Smith taught, 'the Lord offers to his daughters every spiritual gift and blessing that can be obtained by his sons.'"[77]

the church and kingdom. The phrase "the church and kingdom" refers to the blessings belonging to one who is made a "king and a priest unto God, bearing rule, authority, and dominion under the Father."[78] Correspondingly, women may likewise receive the

---

66   D&C 84:19. See discussion by Clark of how Abraham received the blessings of the priesthood, including the Patriarchal Priesthood (E. D. Clark, *Blessings*, pp. 81-85).

67   D&C 84:23.

68   JST Exodus 34:1-2.

69   J. Smith, Jr., *Words*, 5 January 1841, p. 59.

70   JST Exodus 34:1-2; cf. D&C 107:19.

71   See *Excursus 53: Comparative Explorations of the Mysteries*, p. 663.

72   J. Smith, Jr., *Words*, p. 305 n. 28.

73   J. Smith, Jr., *Teachings*, 27 August 1843, pp. 321-323.

74   D&C 132:30-31. For Goodenough's relevant discussion of Philo's allegorical views regarding Abraham, Isaac, and Jacob, see E. R. Goodenough, *Light*, pp. 136-179 and E. R. Goodenough, *Introduction to Philo*, pp. 140-145.

75   JST Romans 9:6-8.

76   B. R. McConkie, *Mothers*, p. 37.

77   S. B. Farley, *Oath*, p. 225. See J. F. Smith, Jr., *Magnifying*, p. 66.

78   O. Hyde, *Diagram*, p. 23. See also D&C 76:56-59.

"confirmation of promises" that they "could become queens and priestesses in the eternal worlds."[79]

"Not all members of The Church of Jesus Christ of Latter-day Saints are members of the Church of the Firstborn[80] …for, as Elder McConkie explained, 'the Church of the Firstborn is made up of… those who are destined to be joint-heirs with Christ in receiving all that the Father hath.'"[81] To merit these blessings, faithful priesthood holders must continue in righteousness until, in this life or the next, they are invited to receive additional ordinances, including the fulness of the Melchizedek Priesthood (or the "Holy Priesthood, after the order of the Son of God"[82]), sometimes called the "second anointing."[83]

Differentiating the blessings of the fulness of the priesthood from the ones associated with Moses and Abraham, Ehat and Cook wrote that Abraham's "Patriarchal Priesthood (the ordinances of the endowment and patriarchal marriage for time and eternity)… [is] not the same as the crowning ordinances of the Melchizedek Priesthood."[84] The Prophet Joseph Smith explained that "Melchizedek… had still greater power… which was not the power of a Prophet nor Apostle nor Patriarch only, but of King and Priest to God.… No man can attain to the joint heirship with Jesus Christ without being administered to by one having the same power and authority of Melchizedek."[85]

The blessings of the fulness of the Melchizedek Priesthood, along with the keys to every other gospel ordinance, are confirmed upon the faithful through the power of Elijah, sealing in heaven what is sealed on earth.[86] Contrasting the role of the blessings of the Melchizedek Priesthood given through the "spirit of Elijah" to those of the Aaronic Priesthood bestowed through the preparatory "spirit of Elias,"[87] Joseph Smith said:

> This power of Elijah is to that of Elias what, in the architecture of the temple of God, those who seal or cement the stone to their places are to those who cut or hew the stones—the one preparing the way for the other to accomplish the work. By this we are sealed with the Holy Spirit of Promise (i.e., Elijah).
>
> To obtain this sealing is to make our calling and election sure, which we ought to give all diligence to accomplish.[88]

the elect of God. The "elect" are those who not only have been "called"[89] but also—through their faithfulness—have been "chosen."[90] They have had their calling and election made "sure"[91] or, in other words, as a result of enduring to the end in faithfulness they have received the "more sure word of prophecy"[92] from God Himself,[93] the assurance that they

---

79   G. M. Leonard, *Nauvoo*, pp. 260-261.
80   D&C 76:54, 67, 71, 94. Contrast D&C 76:102.
81   S. B. Farley, *Oath*, p. 226. See B. R. McConkie, *Mormon Doctrine*, p. 139.
82   D&C 107:3.
83   J. F. Smith, Jr., *Magnifying*, pp. 65-66.
84   See J. Smith, Jr., *Words*, p. 303 n. 21.
85   J. Smith, Jr., *Words*, 27 August 1843, p. 245. See *Endnote E-7*, p. 704.
86   J. Smith, Jr., *Teachings*, 5 October 1840, p. 172; 10 March 1844, p. 338. See *Endnote E-8*, p. 705.
87   See *Endnote E-9*, p. 705.
88   J. Smith, Jr., *Words*, 10 March 1844, p. 335, modernized. The parenthetical "(i.e., Elijah)" is in the original.
89   D&C 84:33.
90   See *Figure* 5-13, p. 351.
91   2 Peter 1:10. See also D&C 53:1; B. M. Hauglid, *Calling and Election*.
92   2 Peter 1:17-19; D&C 131:5-6; cf. D&C 84:43; Moses 6:59.
93   D&C 84:47-48, 88:68, 132:49; J. Smith, Jr., *Teachings*, 27 June 1839, pp. 150-151.

will receive the full blessings of the celestial kingdom forever and ever.[94] To each one will eventually be given a "white stone, whereon is a new name written, which no man knoweth save he that receiveth it. The new name is the key word."[95]

The assurance of the "more sure word of prophecy" comes only to those who have proven their determination to serve God "at all hazards."[96] As Ehat and Cook explained: "Perhaps Abraham received the 'anointing and sealing' (the priesthood ordination of king and priest) under the hands of Melchizedek,[97] but the 'election sure'—the absolute assurance of power in the priesthood—came directly from God only after Abraham indicated his willingness to sacrifice Isaac."[98] Regarding the timing of this assurance for others besides Abraham, Robinson and Garrett write:[99]

> For most of the Saints, the fulfillment of God's covenant promises will take place at the second coming of the Savior in the resurrection of the just. Some Saints [e.g., Abraham], however, are privileged to receive the unconditional promise of exaltation from the Lord's own mouth[100] while they are still in mortality. Joseph Smith stated publicly that "to obtain a promise from God for myself that I shall have eternal life… is the more sure word of prophecy."[101] These individuals, such as the brother of Jared,[102] have faith no longer (in the usual sense), for after receiving such a guarantee from the Lord, they subsequently know of themselves, nothing doubting.

The eventual fulfillment that follows the divine promise of election described above is called the "spirit of Messiah," whereby the Savior was given "all power in heaven and in earth" and "enthroned in the heavens as King of kings and Lord of lords."[103] That this blessing has already been extended to others besides Jesus Christ, who have also "kept their second estate,"[104] is attested by D&C 132:29, where the Lord told the Prophet Joseph Smith that "Abraham received all things… and hath entered into his exaltation and sitteth upon his throne." Likewise, all men and women worthy of exaltation, those who are called "just men made perfect through Jesus,"[105] after they have finished their probationary labors, receive the "Father's kingdom," therefore "all that the Father hath" is given to them:[106] "Then shall they be gods, because they have no end; therefore shall they be from everlasting to everlasting, because they continue; then shall they be above all, because all things are subject unto them. Then shall they be gods, because they have all power, and the angels are subject unto them."[107] This is the complete fulfillment of the promise of being "endowed with power from on high."[108]

---

94   D&C 132:26. See B. R. McConkie, *Mormon Doctrine*, pp. 109-110. See *Endnote E-10*, p. 705.

95   D&C 130:11; cf. Revelation 2:17. See *Endnote E-11*, p. 706. See also *Commentary* 1:27-b, p. 62; 3:19-b, p. 177; *Figure 4-4*, p. 219. See *Endnote 4-9*, p. 299. See *Endnote 4-22*, p. 304. See *Excursus 53: Comparative Explorations, Cista Mystica*, p. 679.

96   J. Smith, Jr., *Teachings*, 27 June 1839, p. 150.

97   Genesis 14:17-24 and JST Genesis 14:25-40. See E. D. Clark, *Blessings*, pp. 135-139.

98   J. Smith, Jr., *Words*, p. 305 n. 29. See also J. Lane, *Redemption*; J. Smith, Jr., *Words*, p. 302 n. 8.

99   S.E. Robinson, *et al.*, *D&C Commentary*, 4:238.

100 J. Smith, Jr., *Words*, 27 June 1839, p. 5. See also J. Smith, Jr., *Documentary History*, 1 May 1842, 4:608; cf. Luke 24:36-40; 2 Nephi 31:20; Enos 1:27; *Hymns (1985)*, #134: "His voice is heard: 'Ye shall obtain." See *Endnote E-11*, p. 706.

101 J. Smith, Jr., *Words*, 21 May 1843, p. 209.

102 Ether 3:19.

103 J. Smith, Jr., *Words*, 10 March 1844, p. 336. See Matthew 28:18; Revelation 17:14, 19:16. Hauglid mistakenly identifies the "spirit of Messiah" as the divine promise of election rather than as its eventual fulfillment (see B. M. Hauglid, *Calling and Election*, p. 214). The distinction is made more clear in the account of Joseph Smith's discourse in *Words* cited here than in the version in *Teachings* that he references.

104 See Abraham 3:26.

105 D&C 76:69; cf. Hebrews 12:23. See H. W. Attridge, *Hebrews*, p. 376; S. E. Robinson, *et al.*, *D&C Commentary*, 2:310-311. See *Endnote 0-23*, p. 24.

106 D&C 84:38.

107 D&C 132:20; cf. J. Smith, Jr., *Words*, 10 March 1844, p. 336.

108 D&C 38:32; R. L. Bushman, *Rough Stone*, pp. 156-157, 175, 204-205, 216-217, 308-321, 387-388, 450-452.

Excursus 4

Chance and Purpose in Creation

TO what extent does our study of the universe make it evident that the requirements for human habitation figured in God's plans for the creation of the physical universe? Reflections by scientists and philosophers over the past several decades have led to widespread acknowledgment of the "anthropic principle" which, roughly stated, says that "we see the universe the way it is, at least in part, because we exist."[109] In other words, our existence as human beings would be impossible if the universe were different in certain key ways.

In its most common forms, the anthropic principle should not be confounded with the more specific and controversial claims of the "intelligent design" movement.[110] However, the principle does suggest to believers that some basic features of the universe required for our existence were anticipated by the Creator from the beginning.[111] Davies, who accepts a relatively strong version of the anthropic principle but not a personal God, writes: "Far from exposing human beings as incidental products of blind physical forces, science suggests that the existence of conscious organisms is a fundamental feature of the universe. We have been written into the laws of nature in a deep and, I believe, meaningful way."[112] With characteristic hyperbole, Nibley rhapsodizes: "Not long ago we used to laugh our heads off at the idea that God created the stars and their motions for the benefit of puny man. Today the shoe is on the other foot. Now we are asked to believe how the unimaginable raging forces of the universe, completely uncontrolled and undirected, should zero in on this little planet with nothing but the most benevolent results, adjusting a score of fine-tuned constants to each other with unerring accuracy."[113]

Can similar arguments be made with respect to biological development? Scientists who accept the standard view that the structural features of living things arise through the mechanisms of random mutation followed by natural selection typically see no role for divine direction in the process of common descent. However, some believing advocates of evolution who want to leave room for participation by God in the process (as well as some nonbelievers) seek ways to explain how certain events that seem randomly determined could nonetheless be controlled in some fashion to produce predictable results, resulting in a world where natural selection is not the "exclusive driving force" for biological development.[114] For example, Stephens points to research results indicating that evolutionary development is not exclusively "the result of genetic control but of genes interacting with material or design constraints," allowing "plenty of room for God to operate with predictability within evolution's bounded variation."[115] In other words, there may be yet undiscovered laws of nature that constrain development to the extent that the mortal human form is inevitable—complete with seemingly imperfect adaptations such as blind spots, wisdom teeth, and the

---

109 S. Hawking, *Nutshell*, p. 86.

110 See *Excursus 5: Science and Mormonism*, p. 526.

111 See *Endnote E-12*, p. 706.

112 P. Davies, *Mind*, p. 21. For a very readable exposition of these ideas, see P. Davies, *Goldilocks*.

113 H. W. Nibley, *Drama*, p. 32.

114 O. Gingerich, *Universe*, p. 98. See E. Jablonka, *et al.*, *Evolution* for a discussion of new findings in molecular biology that point to mechanisms of adaptation that go beyond natural selection of chance DNA variations. See J. B. Cobb, Jr., *Back to Darwin*, especially pp. 311-411, for a respectful and well-reasoned discussion about various approaches for integrating evolution and religious thinking.

115 T. D. Stephens, *et al.*, *Evolution*, p. 200. See also S. C. Morris, *Solution*; T. D. Stephens, *Tree of Life*.

appendix. However, the jury is still out on whether such constraints in and of themselves are sufficient to completely specify the outcome of evolution.[116]

Others are exploring ways in which evidence for quantum chance as a fundamental property of the universe (e.g., Bell's Theorem, which seems to have provided a refutation of Einstein's famous conviction that "God does not play dice with the universe"[117]) could still allow for the possibility of Divine intervention,[118] whether it be "preferred pathways for random chance to follow"[119] or direct guidance of some of the seemingly random events "without requiring a locality-violating physical signal."[120] This being said, Gingerich argues that evidence for Divine intervention of this sort seems inevitably beyond the ken of science— though fortunately, however, such assumptions are ultimately irrelevant to the way science is conducted:

> One can believe that some of the evolutionary pathways are so intricate and so complex as to be hopelessly improbable by the rules of random chance, but if you do not believe in divine action, then you will simply have to say that random chance was extremely lucky, because the outcome is there to see. Either way, the scientist with theistic metaphysics will approach laboratory problems in much the same way as will his atheistic colleague across the hall. And probably both will approach some of the astonishing adaptations seen in nature with a sense of surprise, wonder, and mystery.[121]

116   T. Butler, *2 October 2006.*
117   See W. Isaacson, *Einstein,* pp. 326, 335.
118   T. Butler, *2 October 2006*; K. W. Giberson, *Saving Darwin,* p. 220; F. B. Salisbury, *Divine Design.*
119   O. Gingerich, *Universe,* p. 119.
120   P. Dowe, *Galileo,* p. 186.
121   O. Gingerich, *Universe,* pp. 101-102. See *Endnote E-13,* p. 707. For a brief and highly readable summary of the debate surrounding various views concerning the anthropic principle and its implications for the nature and existence of God, see P. Dowe, *Galileo,* pp. 148-169.

EXCURSUS

Excursus 5

Science and Mormonism

SCIENCE and Mormonism have nearly always been on very friendly terms, with Church members sharing the deep conviction that, as expressed by former scientist and apostle Elder James E. Talmage, "within the gospel of Jesus Christ there is room and place for every truth thus far learned by man, or yet to be made known."[122] With respect to the idea that the Church is required to welcome religious and moral truth from all sources, President Brigham Young stated:

> "Mormonism"… embraces every principle pertaining to life and salvation… no matter who has it. If the [unbeliever] has got truth, it belongs to "Mormonism." The truth and sound doctrine possessed by [other churches], and they have a great deal, all belong to this Church… All that is good, lovely, and praiseworthy belongs to this Church… "Mormonism" includes all truth. There is no truth but what belongs to the Gospel.[123]

With specific regard to scientific truth, President Young's approach was no less open and all-embracing. As Barlow summarizes:

> Brigham Young's position was in one sense more "liberal" even than that of [many contemporaries]. Not a scholar himself and easily put off by what he saw as scholars'… pretentious ways, Young still wished to distance the Mormon response to science from what he took to be the common Christian reaction. Widespread infidelity in the world did not surprise him, he said, because religious teachers often advanced notions "in opposition to… facts demonstrated by science," making it difficult for honest, informed people to embrace the claims of religion. Geology, to take a specific instance, "is a true science; not that I would say for a moment that all the conclusions and deductions of its professors are true, but its leading principles are; they are facts…." "[Our] geologists… tell us that this earth has been in existence for thousands and millions of years… [and Mormonism] differ[s] from the Christian world, for our religion will not clash with the facts of science."[124]

Moreover, President Young said:

> The idea that the religion of Christ is one thing, and science is another, is a mistaken idea, for there is no true religion without true science, and consequently there is no true science without true religion.[125]

Subsequent Presidents and General Authorities of the Church have advanced similar views about the ultimate compatibility of religious and scientific truths and, with notably few exceptions, have maintained markedly positive attitudes toward both the methods and conclusions of mainstream science and the advance of modern technology. A barometer for the positive attitude toward science among the membership of the Church has been a series of studies over the last several decades documenting numbers of scientists with backgrounds in different faith groups. For example, LDS historian of science Erich Paul noted:

> … a 1974 article appearing in *Science*—published by the largest scientific society in America, the *American Association for the Advancement of Science*, and, along with the British journal *Nature*, certainly the most influential science magazine—reported that Mormonism had

---

122 J. E. Talmage, *Earth and Man*, p. 252.
123 B. Young, *8 April 1867*, p. 375; B. Young, *Discourses*, p. 3.
124 P. L. Barlow, *Bible*, pp. 90-91. See B. Young, *14 May 1871*, pp. 115-117.
125 B. Young, *3 May 1874*, p. 52.

produced more scientists per capita than virtually all religious movements in twentieth-century America.[126] Although there are social, religious, and theological reasons for this mostly supportive relationship, the facts strongly indicate that Mormonism and at least science as philosophy are basically non-combative.[127]

A more recent study reported that in the 1990 listing of 120,000 American Men and Women of Science, "Utah stood 21 percent above the second place state, which was Delaware."[128] This was despite the fact that there were more Mormon scientists outside of Utah and Idaho than inside, that practicing Mormons no longer constitute the majority population in Utah, and that there has been an increase in the overall orthodoxy of Mormon scientists.[129]

Such findings about LDS scientists are consistent with other studies affirming an exceptional proportion of Mormons in American university faculties across all disciplines. A major survey published in 2007 reported that while non-LDS "Christians are underrepresented among faculty," Mormons are "overrepresented compared to the general public."[130]

Although the reasons for the attraction of science and academia for members of the Church have not been adequately studied, BYU professor and administrator Noel B. Reynolds offers one opinion:

> In spite of occasional eruptions of anti-intellectualism in the LDS community, the long-term reality has been that Mormons, perhaps more than any other religious group, seek and respect learning.[131] Joseph Smith set the example himself, establishing schools for adults and studying biblical languages. The LDS community has always produced far more than its share of highly educated people.... [and in the LDS community] the more educated a person is, the more likely he or she is to be fully observant and faithful.[132]
>
> There may be good reasons for this surprising characteristic of the Latter-day Saints. Mormonism is a religion of both the spirit and the intellect. Mormon missionaries tell their investigators that they have answers to the great human questions. Conversion stories are always stories of learning and inspiration… Mormonism is not a religion that tells its members they have no right to know the divine mysteries.[133] Rather, it tells them to seek knowledge of all things. There is nothing that God is not willing to reveal to his children, even to the point of showing himself to them on special occasions.
>
> Nor are Mormons taught to be irrational or to despise logic in their understanding of the divine. From Joseph Smith to the present prophets, the Saints have always been urged to grasp a grand and coherent vision of themselves and their relationship to God. They are urged to acknowledge contradictions in their own lives and beliefs and to reconcile themselves to the full set of gospel truths. Latter-day Saints learn early that the Spirit can be their most valuable asset in this great quest, and that there is no true opposition between mind and spirit. The two must function harmoniously together to reach fully satisfying truth.
>
> It would be fair to say that Latter-day Saints see themselves as both prophets and intellectuals. They depend daily on spiritual guidance, and they treasure deeply the understanding of God and his world that they have been given. They feel responsible to search the scriptures as a means of strengthening their spirits and their understandings simultaneously. They are

126   K. R. Hardy, *Origins*.
127   E. R. Paul, *Science*, pp. 6–7.
128   R. T. Wooton, *Saints*, p. 58.
129   See *Endnote E-14*, p. 707.
130   G. A. Tobin, *et al.*, *Religious Beliefs*, p. 20. See *Endnote E-15*, p. 707.
131   See *Endnote E-16*, p. 708.
132   See *Endnote E-17*, p. 708.
133   See *Endnote E-18*, p. 708.

EXCURSUS

suspicious of people who seem to emphasize one of these sources of knowledge to the neglect of the other.[134] Both are God-given, and both are necessary for a fulness of life.

The testimony that individual Latter-day Saints bear of the truthfulness of the Church and the Book of Mormon, as well as the other revelations of Joseph Smith is highly personal. The mind and spirit of a man or woman are finally quite private in their innermost workings. Each person must come to that mix of understanding and spiritual assurance that he or she finds adequate. There is nothing that others can hand out off a shelf that will do the job. It requires personal inquiry, reflection, prayer, and openness to God's revelations.[135]

With respect to the creation account in Genesis, the Latter-day Saints have avoided some of the serious clashes with science that have troubled other religious traditions. For example, they have no serious quarrel with the concept of a very old earth whose "days" of creation seem to have been of very long, overlapping, and varying duration.[136] With respect to beliefs about the origin of man, Sorenson emphasizes the point that acceptance of essential doctrinal claims rather than belief in a particular *modus operandi* for the creation of man is ultimately the determinant of Mormon orthodoxy:

> While the current state of revealed truth on the LDS doctrine of man's origin may permit some differences of opinion concerning the relationship of science and religion, it clearly affirms that God created man, that the Fall of Adam was foreknown of God and was real and significant, and that the Atonement of Christ was foreordained and necessary to reverse the effects of the Fall. Perhaps because these claims embrace the main doctrinal issues relevant to the condition of man, the description of the actual creation process does not receive much attention from the general membership of the Church or from the authorities.[137]

There are other indicators of LDS moderation on these potentially divisive issues. For example, while the issue of how school teachers should handle questions about the origin of man has occasionally surfaced in public discussion, Utah and other states with large LDS populations have wisely refrained from embracing creationist agendas in their science curricula. Consistent with this stance, LDS scientist David Bailey has very competently summarized scientific inadequacies and theological incompatibilities of the creationist movement in both its "young earth" and "intelligent design" forms.[138] No matter how well-intentioned, Gingerich insightfully observes that intelligent design is "misguided when presented as an alternative to the naturalistic explanations offered by science, which do not explicitly require the hand of God... This does not mean that the universe is actually godless, just that science within its own framework has no other way of working."[139] He characterizes the universe in which we live as one "... where God can play an interactive role unnoticed by science, but not excluded by science."[140] Similarly, BYU Philosophy Professor James Faulconer argues that although scientists need not take a strictly scientific attitude except when they are explicitly doing science, the "scientific region, the region in which one investigates bodies using the assumptions, methods, and background of science, is necessarily godless. Scientific objects, themselves 'impoverished' or abstracted objects,

---

134   See, e.g., D&C 88:118.
135   N. B. Reynolds, *Preface*, p. xi.
136   See the overview of Moses 2, p. 84 and *Commentary* 2:5-e, p. 103.
137   J. L. Sorenson, *Origin*, p. 1053. See *Endnote E-19*, p. 709.
138   D. H. Bailey, *Mormonism*; D. H. Bailey, *Deceiver*; D. H. Bailey, *Latter-day*; D. H. Bailey, *Church and Evolution*; D. H. Bailey, *What's Wrong*. See *Endnote E-20*, p. 709.
139   O. Gingerich, *Universe*, p. x.
140   *Ibid.*, p. 111.

incarnate the work and understanding of that region. Other objects incarnate other regions and orderings."[141] Continuing, he explains:

> This is not to criticize scientists for that attitude or to suggest that God ought to be part of science. A great many other important things also do not exist in a world inhabited scientifically, things such as morality and value or, of less consequence, good taste in food or clothing. That absence is the consequence of the specialized incarnation required of science and is only a problem if scientists (or more often those who idolize science because they know too little of it) forget that such a specialized incarnation is not the only one, the best one, or the final one.[142]

Even some of the most doubting of scientists have stated their willingness to keep their mind open to the possibility of a God—so long as it is a God "worthy of [the] grandeur"[143] of the Universe. For example, the well-known skeptic Richard Dawkins stated: "If there is a God, it's going to be a whole lot bigger and a whole lot more incomprehensible than anything that any theologian of any religion has ever proposed."[144] Similarly, Elder Neal A. Maxwell approvingly quoted the unbelieving scientist Carl Sagan, noting that he:

> ... perceptively observed that "in some respects, science has far surpassed religion in delivering awe. How is it that hardly any major religion has looked at science and concluded, 'This is better than we thought! The Universe is much bigger than our prophets said—grander, more subtle, more elegant. God must be even greater than we dreamed'? Instead, they say, 'No, no, no! My god is a little god, and I want him to stay that way.' A religion, old or new, that stressed the magnificence of the Universe as revealed by modern science might be able to draw forth reserves of reverence and awe hardly tapped by the conventional faiths. Sooner or later, such a religion will emerge."[145]

The characteristic of awe mentioned by Sagan—so vital to the pursuit of knowledge in both science and religion—has been equated by Elder Maxwell with the scriptural term "meekness."[146] Among other things, an attitude of meekness requires moving forward according to the best of our knowledge while simultaneously recognizing the provisional nature of our current understanding.[147] Indeed, it is because of the limits of our knowledge that we court danger when we try to effect a premature reconciliation of scientific and religious issues. BYU emeritus Professor of Physics and Astronomy B. Kent Harrison wisely wrote:

> Some disagreements [between science and religion] are inevitable because our knowledge is incomplete. But we believe in a unified truth and so we eventually expect agreement. It is tempting to seek agreement now. *However, it is inappropriate, and often dangerous, to attempt a premature reconciliation or conflicting ideas where there is a lack of complete knowledge.*[148] If a scientist concludes that there is no God—based on inadequate evidence!—and thereby casts doubt on those who believe in God, he does them a disservice. For example, it is inappropriate for a scientist who accepts organic evolution to claim that there is no God. (However, many scientists do indeed take the position that they cannot comment on religious truth because they have little or no information on it.)

---

141 J. E. Faulconer, *Incarnation*, p. 41.
142 *Ibid.*, p. 59. See also F. J. Ayala, *Darwin's Gift*, pp. 171-202; M. Heidegger, *Technology*, pp. 115-182.
143 R. Dawkins in D. Van Biema, *God vs. Science*, p. 55.
144 In *ibid*. See *Endnote E-21*, p. 710.
145 Cited in N. A. Maxwell, *Cosmos*, p. 1. See *Endnote E-22*, p. 710.
146 N. A. Maxwell, *Disciple-Scholar*, pp. 14-18. See *Endnote E-23*, p. 710.
147 See *Endnote E-24*, p. 710.
148 See *Endnote E-25*, p. 710.

Similarly, if an ecclesiastic states that such and such a scientific idea is not true—based on inadequate evidence!—then he does a disservice to the scientist who has carefully explored that idea. As a hypothetical example, it would be inappropriate for a church authority to make a flat statement that special relativity is invalid because it limits information transmission such as prayer to the very slow (!) speed of electromagnetic waves. It may later turn out to be invalid in some sense, but current experimental and other considerations support it strongly.[149]

The proper stance, it seems, is to withhold judgment on such questions until we have more information[150]—but also to take advantage of what knowledge we do have.[151]

Some take the fact that science reverses its positions from time to time as a disturbing thing. On the contrary, I feel that we should take such events as encouraging news. In this regard, I side with those who locate the rationality of science not in the assertion that its theories are erected upon a consistent foundation of undeniable facts, but rather in the idea that it is at heart a self-correcting enterprise that can put any of its claims in jeopardy—though, of course, not all at once.[152]

The most effective scientists move forward by adopting a given way of understanding their domain of interest, not simply because they might feel "justified" by the best available evidence in doing so, but more fundamentally because in actual practice the most effective means of investigation available is to commit oneself to a position and then, from that vantage point, to explore its consequences thoroughly.[153] We put on our chosen perspectives like a pair of glasses, and then try them out for a while to see if our capacities both for navigation and for additional discovery have increased.[154] In this way, scientific theory becomes useful not merely as a picture of reality but, more importantly for the ongoing process, as "a device for the attainment or formulation of greater knowledge about it."[155] This requires one to embrace not only the question "How do we know our hypotheses are correct?" but also "How can we, to the greatest possible degree, expose our hypotheses to the light of experience in order to evaluate and refine them as thoroughly as possible?" Relative to this point, Hugh Nibley has written that the aim of honest scholarly discussion should be "to talk about the material at hand, hoping that in the course of the discussion every participant will privately and inwardly form, reform, change, or abandon his opinions… and thereby move in the direction of greater light and knowledge."[156] Speaking about religious matters, the Apostle Paul succinctly expressed a similar idea: "Prove [i.e., examine, put to the test] all things; hold fast that which is good."[157]

---

149   See *Endnote E-26*, p. 711.
150   See *Endnote E-27*, p. 711.
151   B. K. Harrison, *Truth*, pp. 153-154.
152   G. Bateson, *Mind*, p. 216; G. Bateson, *et al.*, *Angels*, pp. 36-49; W. Weimer, *Notes*, pp. 47-49.
153   W. Weimer, *Notes*, p. 49.
154   *Ibid.*, pp. 72-74.
155   A. Kaplan, *Inquiry*, p. 286. See *Endnote E-28*, p. 711.
156   H. W. Nibley, *Since*, p. xiv; cf. W. Weimer, *Notes*, pp. 78-86. See also M. J. Mahoney, *Scientist*, pp. 195-220.
157   1 Thessalonians 5:21. Representative works for understanding the broader history and the wide-ranging and complex sets of assumptions involved in recent debates about religion and science include D. N. Brems, *Divine Engineering*; A. R. Buskirk, *Science*; F. S. Collins, *Language*; G. Consolmagno, *God's Mechanics*; P. Dowe, *Galileo*; A. Flew, *There Is*; K. W. Giberson, *Saving Darwin*; O. Gingerich, *Universe*; K. R. Miller, *Darwin's God*; J. P. Moreland, *et al.*, *Views*; R. L. Numbers, *Creationists*; M. Ruse, *Evolution-Creation*. Walker provides a discussion of prominent works by proponents of scientific atheism from an LDS point of view (S. C. Walker, *Selling*).

Excursus 6
The Authority and Power of Scripture

THERE are few other branches of Christianity that revere Holy Scripture as do the Latter-day Saints. Yet, paradoxically, there is no other Christian faith that has felt such liberty—or rather such *necessity*—to continually add to and even revise it.[158] This is because Latter-day Saints are not fundamentally a "People of the Book" but instead a "People of Continuing Revelation."[159] In other words, not only do they subscribe to the idea of an expanded canon through the acceptance of three additional books of scripture besides the Bible, but also to the concept of an open and unended one,[160] regarding efforts to "harden on the all-sufficiency or only-sufficiency of any part of scripture" as tantamount "to prais[ing] the cup and reject[ing] the fountain."[161] Thus, members of the Church hold that sacred texts are not only always open to the rendering of a "plainer translation,"[162] but also to the possibility of significant expansion and elaboration by the current President of the Church.[163] The priority of prophetic prerogative over the authority of any written text is expressed by Elder Orson F. Whitney as follows:

> No book presides over this Church and no book lies at its foundation. You cannot pile up books enough to take the place of God's priesthood inspired by the power of the Holy Ghost.... No man ought to contend for what is in the books, in the face of God's mouthpiece, who speaks for him and interprets his word. To so contend is to defer to the dead letter in preference to the living oracles, which is always a false position.[164]

Of course this understanding does not presume a contest between scripture, on the one hand, and the direction of the leaders of the Church, on the other, for when living prophets speak under inspiration, their words become a part of scripture itself. Thus, in former times, wrote the Apostle Peter, scripture was the result of a process whereby "holy men of God spake as they were moved by the Holy Ghost"[165] and, as long as the Holy Ghost can so operate, scripture will continue to come forth by the same means.[166] Elaborating on this principle, a revelation to Joseph Smith in 1831 stated:

> 2 And, behold, and lo, this is an ensample unto all those who were ordained unto this priesthood, whose mission is appointed unto them to go forth—
>
> 3 ... that they shall speak as they are moved upon by the Holy Ghost.
>
> 4 And whatsoever they shall speak when moved upon by the Holy Ghost shall be scripture, shall be the will of the Lord, shall be the mind of the Lord, shall be the word of the Lord, shall be the voice of the Lord, and the power of God unto salvation.[167]

Hence, to Latter-day Saints, a closed and immutable canon is inconsistent with the idea of God's continuing revelation, as expressed in the ninth *Article of Faith*: "We believe in all that

---

158   See *Endnote E-29*, p. 711.
159   D. H. Oaks, *Scripture Reading*, p. 7. See *Excursus 49: The People of the Book*, p. 651.
160   2 Nephi 29:3-14; A. B. Morrison, *Canon*, pp. 3-4.
161   T. G. Madsen, *Essay*, p. xf. See *Endnote E-30*, p. 712.
162   D&C 128:18.
163   J. F. Smith, *Gospel Doctrine*, 1902, pp. 36-37.
164   O. F. Whitney, *7 October 1916*, pp. 55-56. See *Endnote E-31*, p. 712.
165   2 Peter 1:20.
166   See *Endnote E-32*, p. 712.
167   D&C 68:2-4. See *Endnote E-33*, p. 712.

God has revealed, all that he does now reveal, and we believe that he will yet reveal many great and important things pertaining to the kingdom of God."[168] Thus, President Spencer W. Kimball affirmed that "revelation continues and that the vaults and files of the Church contain these revelations which come month to month and day to day."[169]

To Richard Bushman, this principle of continuing revelation constitutes "Joseph Smith's significance for our time":

> He stood on the contested ground where the Enlightenment and Christianity confronted one another, and his life posed the question, Do you believe God speaks? Joseph was swept aside, of course, in the rush of ensuing intellectual battles and was disregarded by the champions of both great systems, but his mission was to hold out for the reality of divine revelation and establish one small outpost where that principle survived. Joseph's revelatory principle is not a single revelation serving for all time, as the Christians of his time believed regarding the incarnation of Christ, nor a mild sort of inspiration seeping into the minds of all good people, but specific, ongoing directions from God to his people. At a time when the origins of Christianity were under assault by the forces of Enlightenment rationality, Joseph Smith returned modern Christianity to its origins in revelation.[170]

Ellis Rivkin, speaking from the tradition of Reformed Judaism, eloquently expressed his inability to accept the versions of Christianity that he had encountered precisely because of their rejection of the idea that revelation continues. Though his characterization of the term "revelation" is very broad, his words echo themes to which the hearts of believing Latter-day Saints could enthusiastically warm:

> I did not become a Christian because to have done so would have deprived me of the revelations that preceded the rise of Christianity and the revelations that were to follow. I would have cut myself off from a divine odyssey that reaches back to the Patriarchs and reaches forward to the Messianic Age, an odyssey of a people ever searching for the fullness of God... For what we find spread before us is a record of continuous revelation to and through the Jews—revelations through prophets, through books, through Scribes-Pharisees, through philosophers, through Christ-Jesus, through rationalists, through kabbalists, through charismatics, through Reformers, and even through Jewish secularists and nationalists....
>
> The Jewish people [are] thus very much alive today for, it seems to me, their divine odyssey is not yet at an end. Humankind has still not recognized that God is One, that His Universe is a good one, and that every individual is created in His image and after His likeness. The end of days, which the prophets preached, is still far off. The meaning of the Jewish odyssey has yet to be assimilated. Paradise has not yet been regained. A re-genesis still eludes us. The need of Israel for multiple revelations is still manifest to those Jews, like myself, who see and feel this need. This, then, explains how I, a Jew, can look at the New Testament and read it as a record of a revelation-mutation and yet not become a Christian. For whereas a true Christian is totally fulfilled in Christ and needs no other revelation, I cannot be so fulfilled. I cannot be so fulfilled because I have become convinced that so long as God reveals himself through human instruments, every revelation is partial.[171] I therefore feel the need for all the revelations that were given to Israel in the past, all the revelations that are being given to Israel in the present, and all the revelations that may be given to Israel in the future until the ushering in of the Messianic Age gives us, at long last, the fulness of God.[172] Convinced that until the end of days the divine light will always be refracted through human prisms and convinced at the same time

---

168 See *Endnote E-34*, p. 713.
169 S. W. Kimball, *Revelation*, p. 78.
170 R. L. Bushman, *Twenty-First Century*, p. 274.
171 Cf. 1 Corinthians 13:9-10, 12; D&C 1:24.
172 Cf. Articles of Faith 1:9.

that the divine light will always be straining to break through, I do not wish to have the light streaming toward me and yet see it not.[173]

While the gift of prophecy is to be coveted by every follower of Christ,[174] the living Prophet and, to a more limited degree, the General Authorities of the Church ultimately bear the responsibility of speaking for the Church as a whole.[175] "That is not to say, of course," clarifies Elder Alexander B. Morrison, "that every word the Brethren speak is scripture."[176] President J. Reuben Clark taught that all Church members and officers, including the General Authorities:

> … must act and teach subject to the overall power and authority of the President of the Church… Sometimes in the past they have spoken "out of turn," so to speak… [Even] the President of the Church, himself, may not always be "moved upon by the Holy Ghost," when he addresses the people.[177] This has happened about matters of doctrine (usually of a highly speculative character) where subsequent Presidents of the Church and the people themselves have felt that in declaring the doctrine, the announcer was not "moved upon by the Holy Ghost." How shall the Church know…? The Church will know by the testimony of the Holy Ghost in the body of the members,… and in due time that knowledge will be made manifest.[178]

"In a way," said President Clark, "this completely shifts the responsibility from them to us to determine when they so speak."[179]

Of course, the prerogative to speak by the power of the Holy Ghost is not reserved for a select few. In fact, Mormons would readily assent to Moses' response to the complaint that some in the camp of Israel were seen prophesying: "… would God that all the Lord's people were prophets, and that the Lord would put his spirit upon them!"[180] As non-Mormon anthropologist Mark P. Leone observes, this fact runs counter to public stereotype:

> Mormonism is almost always characterized as hierarchical, authoritarian, and literalistic; frequently it is likened in organization and dogmatic rigidity to the Roman Catholic church. But these represent the surface, not the core, of contemporary Mormonism. At the heart of Mormonism is a continuous revision of meaning by the individual believer, a process facilitated by the immediacy and availability of revelation and the freedom to discuss all religious topics in the conviction that all can be equally well understood…. Mormonism has evolved a do-it-yourself theology which makes the growth of professional theologians impossible as well as unnecessary. A group of professional theologians would be a disadvantage to Mormonism: they would clash with a population of the faithful charged with the same tasks. Even more fundamental, a formal theology would centralize the creed and rigidify the doctrinal base of faith…. Mormonism publicly proclaims the duty of every member of the church to flesh out the bones of the faith for himself.[181]

The "do-it-yourself" tradition observed by Leone was encouraged by Joseph Smith, who intensely disliked being "bound up by… creeds,"[182] saying:

---

173 E. Rivkin, *Jesus*, pp. 148, 150-151. See also J. Pelikan, *Whose Bible*, pp. 69-86. For a valuable study on the indispensability of continuing revelation, see H. W. Nibley, *Prophets*.

174 See, e.g., Numbers 11:29; Revelation 19:10.

175 A. B. Morrison, *Canon*, pp. 8-10.

176 *Ibid.*, p. 4.

177 See *Endnote E-35*, p. 713.

178 J. R. Clark, Jr., *Writings*, pp. 101-102.

179 *Ibid.*, p. 96.

180 Numbers 11:29. See D. H. Oaks, *Revelation*; D. H. Oaks, *Personal World*.

181 M. P. Leone, *Roots*, pp. 171-172. See *Endnote E-36*, p. 713.

182 J. Smith, Jr., *Teachings*, September 1835, p. 100.

I cannot believe in any of the creeds of the different denominations, because they all have some things in them I cannot subscribe to, though all of them have some truth. I want to come up into the presence of God, and learn all things; but the creeds set up stakes, and say, "Hitherto shalt thou come, and no further"; which I cannot subscribe to.[183]

Once, when a member of the Church was criticized for his sermon, the Prophet Joseph responded:

I did not like the old man being called up for erring in doctrine. It looks too much like the Methodists,[184] and not like the Latter-day Saints. Methodists have creeds which a man must believe or be asked out of their church. I want the liberty of thinking and believing as I please. It feels so good not to be trammeled. It does not prove that a man is not a good man because he errs in doctrine.[185]

Brigham Young likewise saw dangers in the extremes of conformity: "There is too much of a sameness in this community.... I am not a stereotyped Latter-day Saint and do not believe in the doctrine... away with stereotyped Mormons."[186]

Today, the Church continues to resist "the replacement of the unpredictable voice of prophecy with the more manageable one of scholarship and bureaucratic precedent,"[187] and eschews the notion that credentials in professional theology are necessary for Church leaders. "'Theology,' writes F. E. Peters, 'discourse about God according to the principles of reason, was the invention of a people without benefit of revelation.'... [Theology] tames prophecy, manages it, and most often, worships at its tomb.'"[188]

The incremental process by which revelation is received accounts for the way the body of scripture has been collected into the canonical works. For a subject matter of such vital importance, one might have expected that it would have been organized into a comprehensive and orderly presentation of topics that would aid the believer to come to a firm grasp of the most vital truths inhering in the extensive corpus of God's Word.[189] However, that is not what we have been given. Instead, stories and revelations grounded in the circumstances of particular individuals at specific times have been passed down, and we are expected to learn from them not as intellectual abstractions, but as we "liken [them] unto us."[190] In this spirit, Givens observes that we are not to regard these texts as "a freestanding source of religious doctrine, authority, and inspiration, whose meaning could be grasped without too much reference to original or later contexts"[191] but rather we are to enter into a particular relation with these texts.[192] King expressed how the very language of religion invites us to enter such a relation:

183   *Ibid.*, 15 October 1843, p. 327.

184   The Prophet's criticism of the Methodists was confined to their creeds. He recognized that they possessed many truths (e.g., J. Smith, Jr., *Teachings*, 23 July 1843, p. 316), and in fact as a youth had become at one point "partial" to their teachings (JS-H 1:8).

185   J. Smith, Jr., *Documentary History*, 8 April 1843, 5:340.

186   B. Young, *23 September 1860*, p. 185, cited in H. W. Nibley, *Leaders*, p. 498. See also B. Young, *14 November 1869*, pp. 153, 155.

187   D. C. Peterson, *Muhammad (2001)*, p. 598.

188   *Ibid.*, p. 598. See *Endnote E-37*, p. 714. That is not to say that there are no serious scholars of theology among the Mormons. See, e.g., *The Society for Mormon Theology and Philosophy*.

189   B. K. Packer, *Plan of Happiness*, pp. 1-2. See *Endnote E-38*, p. 714.

190   1 Nephi 19:23. See *Endnote E-39*, p. 714.

191   M. Levering, *Rethinking*, p. 3.

192   T. L. Givens, *Hand*, p. 191.

The language of religion has from the beginning been the language of the total soul, the most profound and widespread rhetorical language with the maximum amount of effect. The truths we find in the scriptures are not couched in the prose appropriate to a scientist announcing a discovery to the world for the first time and trying to persuade other people to believe it. The language of the scriptures is the language of and to the whole individual; by that, I mean language that appeals to the whole individual—language that is there not simply to give us plain sense (and there is plenty of plain sense in the scriptures), but to back up that plain sense with an appeal couched in emotive language that enables us to feel the truth and exhorts us to follow the truth. The scriptures ask us to be different, not [merely] to think different....[193]

[But w]hat do we do with [the scriptures]? We abstract principles from them... We abstract ideas. We abstract "concepts"... [However,] I do not find the word ["concept"] in the Bible or the Book of Mormon. It is not "concepts" with which we are concerned in scriptural writings. When the Lord uttered his Beatitudes, he did not say, "Blessed is peace," but "Blessed are the peacemakers"...[194] Reality is not peace, but peacemakers, and peace exists only in peacemakers... The ultimate reality is not love, but a loving person: God is a person, not an abstract. We must not lose the great traditions of our forefathers, who knew how to handle and respond to the language of scripture but would have raised their eyebrows at "concepts."

It is not helpful to think that all there is in the scriptures is a plain message that we can dig out and reformulate for ourselves. There are people who are willing (at the low emotive level at which they choose to live) to take the scriptures as a number of messages of plain sense that can be encapsulated, that can be learned, that can be called principles, and that one then lives by. But that is not living by every word that cometh out of the mouth of the living God.[195]

When Jupiter and Mercury left the hospitable cottage of Baucis and Philemon, they gave the old couple the gift of an inexhaustible pitcher; however much was poured out of it, the pitcher remained full.[196] The scriptures are like that pitcher; however much they have given us, they have more to give. We drink them for life; we shall drink them forever.[197]

Similar thoughts have been expressed by C. S. Lewis, who commends us to receive "the Word of God" from scripture:

> ... not by using it as an encyclopedia or an encyclical but by steeping ourselves in its tone or temper and so learning its overall message.

> To a human mind this working-up (in a sense imperfectly), this sublimation (incomplete) of human material, seems, no doubt, an untidy and leaky vehicle. We might have expected, we may think we should have preferred, an unrefracted light giving us ultimate truth in systematic form—something we could have tabulated and memorized and relied on like the multiplication table...

> We may observe that the teaching of Our Lord Himself, in which there is no imperfection, is not given us in that cut-and-dried, fool-proof, systematic fashion we might have expected or desired. He wrote no book. We have only reported sayings, most of them uttered in answer to questions, shaped in some degree by their context. And when we have collected them all we cannot reduce them to a system. He preaches but He does not lecture. He uses paradox, proverb, exaggeration, parable, irony; even (I mean no irreverence) the "wisecrack." He utters maxims which, like popular proverbs, if rigorously taken, may seem to contradict one another.

193   Cf. J. S. Tanner, *World and Word*, pp. 231-234. See *Endnote E-40*, p. 715.
194   Matthew 5:9.
195   A. H. King, *Total*, pp. 186-187. See Matthew 4:4. Cf. D. Packard, *et al.*, *Feasting*, pp. 236-237. See *Endnote E-41*, p. 715.
196   N. Hawthorne, *Pitcher*.
197   A. H. King, *Afterword*, p. 237.

EXCURSUS

His teaching therefore cannot be grasped by the intellect alone, cannot be "got up" as if it were a "subject." If we try to do that with it, we shall find Him the most elusive of teachers. He hardly ever gave a straight answer to a straight question. He will not be, in the way we want, "pinned down." The attempt is (again, I mean no irreverence) like trying to bottle a sunbeam....

... It may be that what we should have liked would have been fatal to us if granted. It may be indispensable that Our Lord's teaching, by that elusiveness (to our systematizing intellect), should demand a response from the whole man, should make it so clear that there is no question of learning a subject, but of steeping ourselves in a Personality, acquiring a new outlook and temper, breathing a new atmosphere, suffering Him, in His own way, to rebuild in us the defaced image of Himself... And in the same way, the value of the Old Testament may be dependent on what seems its imperfection. It may repel one use in order that we may be forced to use it in another way[:] ...to feel the very contentions between the Word and the human material through which it works. For here again, it is our total response that has to be elicited.[198]

---

198   C. S. Lewis, *Psalms*, 11, pp. 112-114.

Excursus 7
Time and Eternity

ALTHOUGH big bang cosmology now predominates in both scientific thought and popular imagination, the concept of an expanding universe with a definite beginning is a fairly recent development.[199] Such a view has implications not only about the process of Creation, but also about the nature of the Creator Himself. For example, if it is true, as according to most contemporary cosmologists, that time as well as space in our universe began with the big bang, then because "our entire universe was created by God, … one naturally assumes that he existed prior to that creation, outside our perceived universe, implying that his time is different from our time. Alma 40:8—'all is as one day with God, and time only is measured unto men'—makes the dichotomy clear, although it does not help us understand God's time."[200] An understanding of a God "prior to" and "outside of" our universe goes beyond "current theories of fundamental physics and cosmology [which] forbid any communication with or intervention by inhabitants of universes beyond the one created in the big bang."[201] In some way that we do not now understand, God seems able both to transcend and to fully participate in our universe.[202] Indeed, the incarnation of the Son of God—not to mention our own status both as eternal identities and, simultaneously, as travelers within a particular instance of space-time—appears to provide a tangible witness to that idea.

Current scientific conceptions of time require "abandoning the idea that there is a universal quantity called time that all clocks would measure. Instead, everyone would have his or her own personal time. The times of two people would [almost] agree if the people were at rest with respect to each other, but not if they were moving."[203] Though the book of Abraham is silent regarding questions relating to the relativity of time in this sense, it does include substantial passages describing differences in the "reckoning" of time on different planets due to the length of their rotations.[204] Nibley notes that: "Time is not reckoned in absolutes but is limited to Abraham's system; 'the reckoning of the Lord's time' is not reckoned absolutely but 'according to the reckoning of Kolob'—an in-between element to gear Abraham's time to a larger but not necessarily the largest system. There is also reckoning by sun and moon, relative to 'the earth upon which thou standest.'[205] In verse 6 the expression 'set time' is used four times, reminding us that there is more than one frame of time reference."[206] The key point being made by this section of the book of Abraham is that: "There is, in fact, no absolute reference frame for reckoning time—it depends on one's location."[207]

Some physicists have begun to imagine ways in which "time" could be conceived as existing independently of the "space-time" associated with the big bang, a quest that might ultimately help us understand in some small degree the eternal nature of God.[208] For

---

199 D. H. Bailey, *Foundations*; W. Bradley, *Why*, p. 171; S. Hawking, *Nutshell*, p. 71; D. Wilkinson, *Hawking*, pp. 102-121.

200 B. K. Harrison, *Truth*, p. 166, cf. R. T. Pack, *Quantum Cosmology*. See also *Commentary* 1:6-g, p. 48.

201 D. H. Bailey, *Foundations*, p. 74.

202 J. E. Faulconer, *Embodiment*; H. R. Johnson, *Big Bang*, pp. 309-311.

203 S. Hawking, *Nutshell*, p. 9.

204 M. D. Rhodes, *et al.*, *Astronomy*, pp. 21-22.

205 Abraham 3:4-5.

206 H. W. Nibley, *Before Adam*, p. 68.

207 M. D. Rhodes, *et al.*, *Astronomy*, p. 22.

208 See *Commentary* 1:6-g, p. 48 and 2:1-e, p. 94.

example, the "most popular version" of current scientific ideas regarding vacuum energies and inflationary theories of the universe "does not require a singularity"—a state of infinite density where the laws of physics are assumed to break down—at the beginning of the universe.[209] As physicist Fred Adams states: "The big bang does not represent creation *ex nihilo*... Energy is the currency of the cosmos, so this incorrect assumption would imply that an extraordinarily large violation of energy conservation took place at the beginning of time."[210]

Hartle and Hawking's elegant "no boundary" proposal—with a model of "imaginary time" (i.e., a more basic form of time that has no beginning or end) running at right angles to the model of ordinary time (i.e., the "real" time that began with the big bang) and with rules that determine the history in each model of time in terms of the history of the other model—is one attempt to reconcile theorems that the universe is finite and had a definite beginning (in ordinary time) with a desire to do away with the need for any such boundary conditions (in imaginary time).[211] Just as Antarctic explorers seamlessly change their direction from south to north once they pass the pole, so someone traveling back in imaginary time would, when he "passed" the big bang, would simply start moving forward in time again.[212] The attractiveness of this model to some scientists is that it implies a universe that began in a way that is consistent with the laws of physics rather than created in some unknowable fashion. While this proposal might be taken as an argument against the concept of a God who created all things *ex nihilo*,[213] it does not seem however, on the face of it, to raise any obstacles for LDS doctrine, which does not preclude the possibility of time as "a dimension that extends infinitely in both directions."[214]

Since God and man are, as expressed by Elder B. H. Roberts, "co-eternal,"[215] many of these questions about the relationship of time and eternity also relate to our own nature—and the nature of matter itself. For example, the relationship of spirits possessing qualities that are infinite and eternal with bodies that are finite and physical is not yet understood. D&C 93:29 states that "man was also in the beginning with God. Intelligence, or the light of truth, was not created or made, neither indeed can be."[216] Joseph Smith also taught: "Element had an existence from the time [God] had. The pure principles of element are principles that never can be destroyed. They may be organized and reorganized, but not destroyed. Nothing can be destroyed. They never can have a beginning or an ending; they exist eternally."[217] Though quantum fluctuations seem to occur and there are still other mysteries to be solved with respect to the nature of our expanding universe, this statement is consistent with current scientific views, so long as one takes the term "pure principles of element" to refer to whatever mass-energy primitives are ultimately found to exist.[218] The Prophet taught that "spirit matter" was composed of the same primitives that we are currently able to apprehend in the universe, but in "purer" form: "There is no such thing as immaterial matter. All spirit

209   H. R. Johnson, *Big Bang*, p. 284; cf. pp. 288, 292-293.
210   Cited in *ibid.*, pp. 290-291.
211   S. Hawking, *Nutshell*, p. 82; cf. D. Wilkinson, *Hawking*, pp. 102-108. See *Endnote E-42*, p. 715.
212   P. Halpern, *et al.*, *Brave*, pp. 174-175.
213   P. Dowe, *Galileo*, pp. 46-48. See *Endnote E-43*, p. 716.
214   T. L. Givens, *Joseph Smith*, p. 61.
215   In J. Smith, Jr., *Teachings*, p. 353 n. 8. See *Excursus 8: The Origin and Premortal Existence of Human Spirits*, p. 540.
216   See *Excursus 8: The Origin and Premortal Existence of Human Spirits*, p. 540.
217   J. Smith, Jr., 7 April 1844, in S. Larson, *King Follett*, p. 203; cf. D&C 93:33; *Hymns (1985)*, #284.
218   R. W. Bradshaw, *9 October 2006*; T. Butler, *9 October 2006*; H. Eyring, *Faith*, p. 78.

is matter but is more fine or pure and can only be discerned by purer eyes; We cannot see it; but when our bodies are purified we shall see that it is all matter."[219]

Some emerging cosmological theories speak of a "multiverse" where "[t]iny universes continually pop into existence, both from extant universes and from the multiverse. Most of these baby universes quickly vanish again into the vast reservoir, but some inflate to enormous sizes… [Guth conjectures that:] 'A fractal pattern is created, meaning that the sequence of false vacuum, pocket universe, and false vacuum is replicated on smaller and smaller scales. Thus, a region of false vacuum does not produce merely one universe, but instead produces an infinite number of universes!'"[220] Barrow sees the "self-reproducing eternal inflationary universe [as] almost certainly [having] no beginning. It can be continued indefinitely into the past."[221]

As to the current scientific view of the future of our universe, it "seems grim" from "a human perspective." "Over billions of years,… the stars will eventually burn out. As the acceleration of the universe continues, distant galaxies will disappear from view, communication will be lost, and a dark, cold acceleration death or heat death will occur."[222] Long before then, we would face unimaginable peril from the increasing brightness, followed by the death, of our own sun. The fact that the existence of God transcends the birth and death of universes attests to the truth that our own identities, being possessed of a similar eternal nature, will also survive the presumed winding-down of this universe. From his survey of scientific evidence, Johnson concludes: "While it is difficult to imagine any direct evidence for anything outside our universe, good theoretical reasons support a belief in such an overarching entity," including "an endless background of energy for whatever else exists," "a multitude of other bubble universes," "God… [and] the spirits of mankind," and—possibly— "dimensions, natural laws, mass-energy, and wave functions." Since our understanding of these points, of course, is "rather primitive," Johnson cautions that "these possibilities are only suggestions meant to stir thinking."[223]

As a final issue to consider, if it turns out that the scriptural term "light" subsumes the scientific concept of mass-energy in some meaningful way, then the composite picture is of a cosmos consistent with the idea that "light proceedeth forth from the presence of God to fill the immensity of space."[224] Indeed, current scientific theories regarding the plenitude of pervasive energy seem to directly contradict any notion of absolute "emptiness" even in the most remote corner our universe. Writes Johnson: "In quantum mechanics a certain amount of energy is always present… An imaginary region containing nothing at all would collapse to zero size.… One must therefore discard old and seemingly obvious ideas about nothing or empty space, which do not exist in our universe. In reality empty space is filled with particles and waves, many of which we do not currently understand, and the mass-energy of empty space dominates our universe."[225]

---

219 D&C 131:7-8. See J. Smith, Jr., *Words*, 17 May 1843, p. 203. See also J. Smith, Jr., *Spirits*, p. 745 where the "substance" of "spirit" is described as being "more pure, elastic, and refined matter than the body."

220 H. R. Johnson, *Big Bang*, pp. 202-203. See also K. D. Hagen, *Multiverse*; M. E. McDonald, *Cosmology*; cf. D&C 88:37. Note that the idea of a multiverse, with its related theoretical underpinnings, is controversial—in part because of the seeming impossibility of any direct empirical confirmation.

221 Cited in H. R. Johnson, *Big Bang*, p. 298. See *Endnote E-44*, p. 716.

222 H. R. Johnson, *Big Bang*, p. 301. See *Endnote E-45*, p. 716.

223 *Ibid.*, pp. 305-306.

224 D&C 88:12. See *Commentary 2:3-b*, p. 99; M. D. Rhodes, *et al.*, *Astronomy*, p. 23.

225 H. R. Johnson, *Big Bang*, pp. 295-296. Diverse views on the philosophical and scientific problems relating to the nature of God and of the universe can be found in, e.g., D. H. Bailey, *Foundations*; D. H. Bailey, *Science*; D. H. Bailey, *Omnis*; P. Davies, *About Time*; P. Davies, *Goldilocks*; P. Dowe, *Galileo*; J. E. Faulconer, *Embodiment*;

Excursus 8
The Origin and Premortal Existence of Human Spirits

CONVINCED that the doctrine of a "real" (vs. "ideal") preexistence of the spirits of mankind is absent in early LDS scripture, Ostler concludes that relevant passages in the book of Moses either referred to "a conceptual or intellectual blueprint"[226] or else, as he argues more strongly, the creation of all things in the Garden of Eden in their spiritual state at the time they were placed there.[227] In support of the idea that scripture also does not allow a premortal existence for Adam's spirit, he cites D&C 29:36: "the devil was before Adam." Granting Ostler's assumption that Joseph Smith may have had only an incipient understanding of the doctrine of preexistence in the early 1830s, Ostler's interpretation nonetheless overreaches by dismissing the plain sense of Moses 3:5 as referring to a "real" premortal creation ("I… had created all the children of men… in heaven created I them").[228]

It should also be noted that a reading of D&C 29:36 different from that of Ostler's is possible. For instance, the intention of the statement that "the devil was before Adam" may not be to preclude the idea of some kind of premortal existence for all mankind, but simply to indicate that the Devil's spirit, like that of Jesus Christ, was senior to that of the premortal Adam's. Moreover, it is also true that Adam—i.e., the embodied man who, with the memory of his premortal existence obliterated, was tempted by the Devil in the Garden—had not yet been formed with a physical body at the time of Lucifer's rebellion. Finally, note the Lord's statement to Cain in Moses 5:24: "For from this time forth thou shalt be the father of [Satan's] lies; thou shalt be called Perdition; for thou wast also before the world." It seems reasonable to assume that if Cain, like Satan, was "before the world," that Adam also enjoyed a premortal existence in spirit form.

Stories in early Christian literature and in the *Qur'an* specifically connect Satan's rebellion with the concept that "the devil was before Adam." For example, one text reports that Adam, having learned of Satan's success in tempting Eve, demands to know why he has done such a thing, and it is precisely the fact of his own seniority that the Devil uses to buttress his claim of superiority:[229]

> I came to this measure because of you, on the day on which you were created, for I went forth on that day. When God breathed his spirit into you, you received the likeness of his image… Then Michael [or rather God, in some of the other texts[230]] summoned all the angels, and God said to them, 'Come bow down to god whom I made.' Michael bowed first. He called me and said, 'You too, bow down to Adam.' I said 'Go away, Michael! I shall not bow [down] to him who is posterior to [i.e., was born after] me, for I am former!"[231]

G. E. Ganssle, *God and Time*; O. Gingerich, *Universe*; B. Greene, *Fabric*; H. R. Johnson, *Big Bang*; H. Küng, *Beginning*; S. M. McMurrin, *Theological*; B. T. Ostler, *Attributes*; B. T. Ostler, *Theism*; B. T. Ostler, *God*; E. R. Paul, *Science*; C. H. Pinnock, *et al.*, *Openness*; R. D. Potter, *Paradoxes of Providence*; K. E. Robson, *Time*; D. Wilkinson, *Hawking*; E. O. Wilson, *Creation*; L. T. Zagzebski, *Dilemma*. See also Moses 1 *Gleanings*, p. 73.

226 See *Endnote E-46*, p. 716.

227 B. T. Ostler, *Preexistence*, p. 130. Givens mistakenly follows Ostler in this reading (T. L. Givens, *When Souls*, p. 214).

228 See *ibid.*, p. 142, n. 9. Other relevant early statements that also support a "real" premortal creation include Moses 1:8, 5:24, 6:51; D&C 49:17, 77:2. See *Commentary* 1:8-b, p. 50.

229 See *Excursus 10: The Great Chain of Being*, p. 546.

230 *Excursus 23: The Roles of Christ, Adam, and Michael*, p. 582.

231 G. A. Anderson, *et al.*, *Synopsis*, Armenian recension, 12:1-14:3, pp. 15-17; cf. M. al-Kisa'i, *Tales*, pp. 27-28; al-Tabari, *Creation*, 1:54, p. 224; A. al-Tha'labi, *Lives*, p. 45; G. A. Anderson, *et al.*, *Synopsis*, 16:2, p. 49E; E. A. W. Budge, *Cave*, pp. 55-59; N. J. Dawood, *Koran*, p. 13; M. Herbert, *Irish Apocrypha*, pp. 2, 10-11; L. Ginzberg, *Legends*, 1:62-64, 5:84-86 n. 35; H. W. Nibley, *Sacred*, p. 557; M.-A. Ouaknin, *et al.*, *Rabbi Éliézer*, 13, pp. 87-88;

In this connection, recall also Satan's angry claim to priority of worship in the temptation of Moses: "Satan cried with a loud voice, and ranted upon the earth, and commanded, saying: I am the Only Begotten, worship me."[232] It is also significant that the theme of the "elder [serving] the younger"[233] is prominent throughout the rest of Genesis.[234] The motive carries through in Exodus as well with the idea that Israel, arriving long after the great civilizations of Egypt, Sumer, and Babylon, was nonetheless to be considered the first-born child of God.[235] Barker also notes a "dark parody of the story when John describes the reign of the beast.[236] The second beast, the agent of the first beast, deceived those on the earth with an image of the beast that could breathe and speak. All those who would not worship the image of the beast were killed."[237]

D&C 93 is one of the earliest revelations on the origin and premortal existence of human spirits outside of the book of Moses. Received on 6 May 1833, the Lord states that:

> Ye were also in the beginning with the Father; that which is Spirit, even the Spirit of truth.... Man was also in the beginning with God. Intelligence, or the light of truth, was not created or made, neither indeed can be. All truth is independent in that sphere in which God has placed it, to act for itself, as all intelligence also, otherwise there is no existence... For man is spirit. The elements are eternal, and spirit and element inseparably connected, receive a fulness of joy.[238]

During the Nauvoo period, the Prophet greatly elaborated on the origin and nature of spirits. For example, in 1839, Willard Richards recorded Joseph Smith as saying: "The spirit of man is not a created being; it existed from eternity and will exist to eternity. Anything created cannot be eternal. And earth, water, etc.—all these had their existence in an elementary state from eternity. The Father called all spirits before him at the creation of man and organized them. He (Adam) is the head, and was told to multiply."[239] On 6 February 1840 he said: "I believe that the soul is eternal; and had no beginning; it can have no end.... the soul of man, the spirit, had existed from eternity in the bosom of Divinity."[240] On 28 March 1841, he remarked to the school at Nauvoo that "the spirit or the intelligence of men are self-existent principles before the foundation [of] this earth... God saw that those intelligences had not power to defend themselves against those that had a tabernacle [i.e., a body], therefore the Lord called them together in council and agreed to form them tabernacles."[241] The King Follett discourse, given on 7 April 1844, contains the most extensive statement of these teachings, again emphasizing "that spirit has no beginning—it was not created; ...and that God, being greater than the other spirits, instituted laws so that the spirits could advance like himself."[242]

Timothy of Alexandria, *Abbaton*, p. 199; Hebrews 1:6; *Qur'an* 2:34, 7:11, 15:30-31, 17:61, 18:50, 20:116, 38:73-74. See also *Commentary* 1:12-d, p. 53 and 4:6-a, p. 249. See *Endnote E-48*, p. 716.

232   Moses 1:19. See *Endnote E-49*, p. 716.

233   Genesis 25:23.

234   I.e., Cain/Abel, Ishmael/Isaac, Esau/Jacob, Leah/Rachel, Reuben/Joseph, Manasseh/Ephraim; cf. Laman/Nephi; cf. *Commentary* 6:2-d, p. 476. See *Endnote E-50*, p. 716.

235   G. A. Anderson, *Perfection*, pp. 27-28 and Exodus 4:22. See *Excursus 23: The Roles of Christ, Adam, and Michael*, p. 582. For more on Satan's premortal rebellion see the overview of Moses 4, p. 223; *Excursus 21: The Power and Premortal Status of Satan*, p. 575; *Excursus 22: The Nature of Satan's Premortal Proposal*, p. 577.

236   Revelation 13:11-15.

237   M. Barker, *Christmas*, p. 38.

238   D&C 93:23, 29-30, 33.

239   J. Smith, Jr., *Words*, before 8 August 1839, p. 9, spelling and punctuation modernized.

240   *Ibid.*, 6 February 1840, pp. 33, 46-47. See also 5 January 1841, p. 60.

241   *Ibid.*, 28 March 1841, p. 68, spelling and punctuation modernized. See also E. England, *Laub*, pp. 22-23, 28

242   V. Hale, *Spirit*, pp. 118-119. For the complete discourse, see J. Smith, Jr., 7 April 1844, in S. Larson, *King Follett*.

Figure E8-1. *Creation Sequence, 1351-1360*

The pseudepigraphal *Jubilees* described the creation on the first day of various ranks of angels along with "all of the spirits of his creatures which are in heaven and on earth."[1] A more limited version of this idea, one that excluded the spirits of humans and animals, was later propagated in theological writings of the early Christian church. These writings, however, continued to advance the argument that the creation of the angels took place "in the beginning." For example, St. Basil spoke of "a spiritual light" "even before this world" consisting of "intellectual and invisible natures, all the orderly arrangement of pure intelligences, who are beyond the reach of our mind and of whom we cannot even discover the names."[2] Through the influential writings of St. Augustine,[3] the idea that the angels were among the things created "in the beginning" became further entrenched in Christian belief. The argument was further developed in a treatise called *De coelesti hierarchia* (The Celestial Hierarchy),[4] traditionally ascribed to Dionysius the Areopagite[5] but actually dating to some centuries later. Here, the author elaborates tenuous allusions in Ephesians 1:21, 6:12 and Colossians 1:16, 2:15 to describe in great detail three angelic hierarchies, each consisting of three choirs or orders—nine choirs of angels in all.[6]

Accordingly, following the description of Pinkus,[7] the opening depiction in the sequence of Creation in the great minster at Schwäbisch Gmünd illustrates the nine choirs of angels worshiping the Creator (top). The next image (bottom) actually mingles two distinct episodes into one: the division of light from darkness (sometimes taken to signify the casting down of Satan and his angels[8]), and the division of heaven and earth. A close look at the globe will reveal that the band across the Cosmos is the firmament with the signs of the zodiac. Moreover, in an arrangement entitled *thema mundi*, the figure functions as a liturgical calendar, in which the arrangement of the zodiacs in relation to the sun indicates a specific feast or biblical event.[9]

---

1   O. S. Wintermute, *Jubilees*, 2:2, p. 255. For a broad survey of the history of the idea of premortal existence in Western thought, see T. L. Given, *When Souls*.

2   Basil, *Hexaemeron*, 1:5, p. 54.

3   Augustine, *Literal*, I:1:3, I:17:32, VII:5:7, pp. 1:20, 1:38, 2:7.

4   Pseudo-Dionysius, *Hierarchy*; cf., e.g., the later Shelemon, *Book of the Bee*, 5, pp. 9-11.

5   Acts 17:34.

6   See *Endnote E-47*, p. 716.

7   A. Pinkus, *20 January 2007*.

8   See *Commentary* 2:4-c, p. 101.

9   For more on this topic, see A. Pinkus, *Patrons*.

One of the most challenging problems in sorting out the meaning of these statements is the variety of terms used to describe the same or similar concepts. In the past, LDS authors have frequently tried to draw a distinction between an "intelligence" (taken to be the eternal, uncreated part of each individual) and a "spirit" (taken to be the result of subsequent "organization" of an "intelligence" by God). However, these terms are conflated in Webster's 1828 dictionary, which defines an "intelligence" as a spirit being.[243] Moreover, the King Follett discourse uses the terms "spirit," "mind," "soul," and "intelligence" more or less synonymously.[244]

Another potential source of misunderstanding is Joseph Smith's statement that "the mind of man—the intelligent part—is as immortal as, and coequal with, God Himself."[245] However, later editors amended "coequal" to read "co-eternal," consistent with the *Oxford English Dictionary* definition of the Latin original ("of equal age, companion in age") and the seventeenth century meaning of the term ("of the same age, coeval").[246]

Some of the Nauvoo saints were also perplexed by the Prophet's teachings relating to the eternal nature of spirits. For example, Joseph Lee Robinson wrote:

> [T]he question arose then, 'How is God the father of our spirits?' I wondered, studied and prayed over it for I did want to know how it could be. I inquired of several of the brethren how that could be—a father and son and the son as old as the father. There was not a person that could, or that would even try to explain that matter. But it came to pass that in time a vision was opened, the voice of the Spirit came to me saying that all matter was eternal, that it never had a beginning, and that it should never have an end, and that the spirits of all men were organized of a pure material or matter upon the principle of male and female, so that there was a time when my immortal spirit, as well as every other man's spirit that was ever born into the world—that is to say, there was a moment when the spirit was organized or begotten or born so that the spirit has a [F]ather, and the material or matter that our tabernacles are composed of is eternal and, as we understand, are organized upon the principles of male and female.[247]

With respect to the official position of the Church, in 1974, a question was raised to Elder Bruce R. McConkie as to whether it could be authoritatively said "that we had no identity, that we were not individual intelligent entities before we were born into the spirit world?" While not speaking officially for the Church, Elder McConkie answered with his personal opinion:

> As to official Church pronouncements on doctrinal points, they are almost nonexistent.... As far as I know there is no official pronouncement on the subject at hand.... In my judgment, spirit element exists and it was organized into spirit beings, or in other words intelligence exists and it became the intelligences that were organized. In my judgment there was no agency prior to spirit birth and we did not exist as (individual) entities until that time... [When the subject has come up] in reading and approving priesthood and auxiliary lessons... [in] each of these instances, the matter was deleted from the lesson. In each case it was expressly stated that we have no knowledge of any existence earlier than our existence as the spirit children of God.[248]

243   N. Webster, *Dictionary*; cf. B. H. Roberts, *The Truth*, p. 77.

244   V. Hale, *Spirit*, pp. 118-119. See J. Smith, Jr., 7 April 1844, in S. Larson, *King Follett*.

245   J. Smith, Jr., 7 April 1844, S. Larson, *King Follett*, p. 196.

246   See T. L. Givens, *When Souls*, pp. 219-220.

247   J. L. Robinson, *Journal*, 21, cited in C. R. Harrell, *Preexistence*, p. 87. For a reasoned argument in defense of this perspective, see M. B. Brown, *Plan*, pp. 15-16, 25-28. See also T. L. Givens, *When Souls*, p. 217.

248   Cited in B. L. Top, *Life Before*, pp. 44-45. For historical overviews of LDS views on the origin of human spirits, see V. Hale, *Spirit*; C. R. Harrell, *Preexistence*; B. T. Ostler, *Preexistence*. A collection of statements from Church leaders on these and related topics can be found in B. L. Top, *Life Before*, pp. 39-88. A description of differences between the LDS concept of a premortal life and views with affinities to Hermeticism (such as those cited by J. L. Brooke, *Refiner's Fire*) can be found in D. C. Lindquist, *Devils*. Winston surveys the concept of preexistence in Hellenic, Judaic and Mormon sources (D. Winston, *Preexistence*). See Nibley for an interpretation of the Egyptian Shabaka stone as implying that man's creation is a twofold process: begetting and formation (H. W. Nibley, *Teachings of the PGP*, pp. 110-111, 113). See also *Commentary* 2:3-b, p. 99; 2:4-c, p. 101; 3:1-b, p. 151; and the overview of Moses 3, p. 136.

Excursus 9
The Premortal Organization of the Human Family

OSTLER rightly observes that the term "organization" mentioned in Abraham 3:22 does not refer to "organization of the spirit body through spiritual birth, but social organization of spirits into a heavenly council of preexisting entities."[249] This interpretation is consistent with the terminology of Joseph Smith, who stated that:

> Spirits are eternal. At the first organization in heaven, we were all present and saw the Savior chosen and appointed, and the plan of salvation made, and we sanctioned it.[250]

In another place, he uses the term "organization" in a similar sense:

> The design of God before the foundation of the world was that we should take tabernacles… inasmuch as [a portion of] the spirits of the eternal world glory in bringing other spirits in subjection to them, striving continually for the mastery. He who rules the heavens when He has a certain work to do calls the spirits before him to organize them. They present themselves and offer their services.[251]

Scriptures then available to the newly-restored Church[252] also describe the premortal foreordination of individuals to priesthood callings,[253] though at first the Saints did not seem to infer the doctrine of mankind's preexistence from them.[254] It is evident, however, that the Prophet sometimes knew more about such doctrines than he felt at liberty to teach at the time.[255] Elder Neal A. Maxwell wrote: "Whether [the delay in Joseph's speaking publicly about the doctrines of premortal existence] reflected imperfect record-keeping, the Lord's timing, Joseph's degree of readiness, or the people's readiness to receive, or all such factors, we do not know."[256]

With respect to premortal foreordination to priesthood callings, the Prophet Joseph Smith later said: "Every man who has a calling to minister to the inhabitants of the world was ordained to that very purpose in the Grand Council of heaven before this world was. I suppose that I was ordained to this very office in that Grand Council."[257] The Prophet also spoke of Moses and other prophets who were "sons of God who exalt[ed] themselves to be Gods, even from before the foundation of the world."[258] "[A]ll those to whom a dispensation was to be committed were set apart and ordained at that time, to that calling."[259]

Regarding corresponding premortal assignments for women, President Spencer W. Kimball said:

---

249 B. T. Ostler, *Preexistence*, p. 133. See also R. E. Cooper, *Promises*, pp. 102-104; C. R. Harrell, *Preexistence*, p. 12; S. W. Kimball, *Righteous Women*, p. 102.

250 J. Smith, Jr., *Words*, 5 January 1841, p. 60.

251 J. Smith, Jr., *Words*, 21 May 1843, p. 207, spelling, capitalization, and grammar modernized. See also J. Smith, Jr., *Words*, before 8 August 1839, p. 9; 19 January 1841, p. 62; 28 March 1841, p. 68; 9 October 1843, p. 253; J. Smith, Jr., *Documentary History*, 1 April 1842, 4:575; J. Smith, Jr., *Teachings*, 2 May 1844, p. 365.

252 E.g., 1 Peter 1:2; Alma 13:1, 3; Jeremiah 1:5.

253 See also Abraham 3:22-23; D&C 138:38-39.

254 C. R. Harrell, *Preexistence*, pp. 3-5; B. T. Ostler, *Preexistence*, p. 128.

255 E.g., G. Q. Cannon, *Life*, pp. 147-148; J. Smith, Jr., *Teachings*, 7 April 1844, p. 361.

256 N. A. Maxwell, *Small Moment*, p. 85.

257 J. Smith, Jr., *Teachings*, 12 May 1844, p. 365.

258 *Ibid.*, 16 June 1844, p. 375; cf. Moses 1:3-7.

259 J. Smith, Jr., *Words*, 12 May 1844, p. 371.

Remember, in the world before we came here, faithful women were given certain assignments while faithful men were foreordained to certain priesthood tasks. While we do not now remember the particulars, this does not alter the glorious reality of what we once agreed to. You are accountable for those things which long ago were expected of you just as are those we sustain as prophets and apostles![260]

Church leaders have not only taught of premortal callings and assignments, but also have discussed the perfect organization of the human family in the eternal world.[261] For example, on 17 February 1847, Brigham Young had a dream in which he saw the Prophet:

> Joseph stepped toward me, and looking very earnestly, yet pleasantly said, "…Be sure to tell the people to keep the Spirit of the Lord; and if they will, they will find themselves just as they were organized by our Father in Heaven before they came into the world. Our Father in Heaven organized the human family, but they are all disorganized and in great confusion." Joseph then showed me the pattern, how they were in the beginning. This I cannot describe, but I saw it, and saw where the Priesthood had been taken from the earth and how it must be joined together, so that there would be a perfect chain from Father Adam to his latest posterity. Joseph again said, "Tell the people to be sure to keep the spirit of the Lord and follow it, and it will lead them just right."[262]

In Hosea Stout's report of the dream, Brigham quoted Joseph as saying:

> "When the small still voice speaks, always receive it, and if the people will do these things, when they come up to the Father, all will be as in the beginning, and every person stand as at the first." I saw how we were organized before we took tabernacles and every man will be restored to that which he had then, and all will be satisfied.[263]

In a passage that sheds further light on this eventual reorganization of the human family, President Young said:

> I want to tell you a thing with regard to parents, wives, brothers and sisters, etc. The time will come when it will be told you where this man, and that woman shall be placed. The real blood of Joseph will be selected out from among the tribes of Israel, and every man, and woman will be put in their places, and stand in their order where the Lord designs them to be.[264]

Then, explaining that the highest blessings can come to all "who have behaved themselves, and proved faithful to their calling," he taught that those of the true blood of Israel will be known by their fruits:[265] "What does gentile signify? Disobedience. What does Israel signify? Obedience."[266]

The now discontinued practice of priesthood adoption (i.e., the sealing of living Church members into the families of prominent Church leaders) seems to have been meant, at least in part, to anticipate such a reorganization of the human family as it was then understood. Today, however, children are sealed only to their biological or legally adoptive parents.[267]

EXCURSUS

---

260   S. W. Kimball, *Righteous Women*, p. 102.
261   H. C. Kimball, *4 December 1856*, pp. 135-136; J. F. Smith, Jr., *Way 1945*, 1931, pp. 50-51; B. Young, *6 April 1862.*
262   B. Young, *History 1847-1850*, 23 February 1847, pp. 35-36.
263   J. Brooks, *Stout*, 1:238.
264   B. Young, *8 October 1854*, p. 100.
265   Matthew 7:16.
266   B. Young, *8 October 1854*, p. 100. See *Endnote E-6*, p. 704.
267   L. J. Arrington, *Brigham Young*, p. 102; R. E. Bennett, *Missouri*, pp. 186-194; R. E. Bennett, *Line*; D. B. Horne, *Cannon*, 5 April 1894, pp. 311-314; G. Irving, *Adoption*; B. K. Packer, *Holy Temple*, p. 194; W. Woodruff, *Adoption*. For more on the general topic, see H. L. Andrus, *Perfection*, pp. 299-330; H. L. Andrus, *Doctrines*, pp. 159-160, 490-567; R. E. Cooper, *Promises*, pp. 100-131; L. A. McKinlay, *Patriarchal Order*; L. A. McKinlay,

Excursus 10
The Great Chain of Being

THE Great Chain of Being was a prominent feature of the worldview of the majority of educated people from antiquity until relatively recent times.[268] The essence of its classic form is succinctly captured by Lewis:

> According to this conception degrees of value are objectively present in the universe. Everything except God has some natural superior; everything except unformed matter has some natural inferior. The goodness, happiness, and dignity of every being consists in obeying its natural superior and ruling its natural inferiors. Hierarchy is destroyed either by ruling or obeying natural equals or by failing to obey a natural superior or to rule a natural inferior.[269]

Extracanonical sources attest to the fascination of the ancients with the names and ranks of angels present at the dawn of Creation,[270] strikingly yet imperfectly paralleling the book of Abraham's descriptions of the gradations of intelligence among preexistent spirits.[271] From this perspective, Satan's premortal rebellion pits his thirst for purloined glory against the very economy of a world where superior intelligence—in the divine sense of the word[272]—determines the natural order of things. His appeal to Eve that the forbidden fruit would make her and Adam as the gods plays to similar effect on human vanity. We see this process at work in the writings of Milton, in whose time the idea of natural hierarchies was less foreign than it is to our own. Thus, as described in Lewis' preface to *Paradise Lost*, Satan's rebellion:

> … begins with talk about liberty, but very soon proceeds to "what we more affect, Honour, Dominion, glorie, and renoune" (VI, 421). The same process is at work in Eve. Hardly has she swallowed the fruit before she wants to be "more equal" to Adam; and hardly has she said the word "equal" before she emends it to "superior" (IX, 824).[273]

To Milton, the natural order of heaven is a buttress against the tyranny of evil. Paradoxically, it:

> … exists for the sake of what seems its very opposite—for freedom, almost for extravagance. The pattern deep hidden in the dance, hidden so deep that shallow spectators cannot see it, alone gives beauty to the wild, free gestures that fill it, just as the decasyllabic norm gives beauty to all the licenses and variations of the poet's verse.[274]

Life Eternal, pp. 268-297. For additional discussion on the scope and limitations of foreordination, see H. L. Andrus, *God*, pp. 286-296; M. B. Brown, *Plan*, pp. 40-46.

268   See *Endnote E-51*, p. 716.

269   C. S. Lewis, *Preface*, XI, p. 73. See, e.g., W. Shakespeare, *Troilus*, 1:3:85-110, p. 455.

270   E.g., Pseudo-Dionysius, *Hierarchy*; O. S. Wintermute, *Jubilees*, 2:2, p. 255.

271   Abraham 3:16-19.

272   D&C 93:36.

273   C. S. Lewis, *Preface*, XI, p. 78.

274   *Ibid.* XI, p. 81. See also *Commentary 4:11-b*, p. 253 and *Excursus 8: The Origin and Premortal Existence of Human Spirits*, p. 540.

Excursus 11
The Sacred Circle

THE symbol of the sacred circle appears in a large number of ancient sources. Sometimes such references are very subtle and can be easily overlooked. For instance, in Abraham 3:23, God is described as standing "in the midst" (i.e., "in the center") of the premortal souls.[275] Nibley clarifies this description by observing that: "He's surrounded on all sides."[276] Likewise, Lehi describes God upon his throne "surrounded with numberless concourses of angels in the attitude of singing and praising their God,"[277] a pattern that was reenacted in ancient prayer circles. Nibley again points out: "A concourse is a circle. Of course [numberless] concourses means circles within circles and reminds you of dancing. And what were they doing? Surrounded means 'all around'... It was a choral dance."[278]

Note that the center of the sacred circle does not represent some abstract epitome of goodness, nor merely a ceremonial altar or throne, but God Himself. The Gnostic *Acts of John* records that a prayer circle was formed by the apostles, with Jesus at the center: "So he told us to form a circle, holding one another's hands, and himself stood in the middle."[279] Brown likewise observes how, at Jesus' first appearance to the Nephites, He "stood in the midst of them,"[280] and cites other Book of Mormon passages associating the presence of the Lord "in the midst" to the placement of the temple and its altar.[281]

The center is the holiest place, and the degree of holiness decreases in proportion to the distance from it.[282] Brown noted such a configuration when Jesus blessed the Nephite children:

> As the most Holy One, [the Savior] was standing "in the midst," at the sacred center.[283] The children sat "upon the ground round about him."[284] When the angels "came down," they "encircled those little ones about." In their place next to the children, the angels themselves "were encircled about with fire."[285] On the edge stood the adults. And beyond them was what we might term profane space which stretched away from this holy scene... Was there not a visual message to the adults about the special status of children in Jesus' eyes?[286]

Hence, Jesus' instructions: "Behold your little ones."[287] C. S. Lewis observes: "From Christianity itself we learn that there is a level—in the long run the only level of importance—on which the learned and the adult have no advantage at all over the simple and the child."[288]

275 Cf. *Commentary* 3:9-h, p. 167; 4:9-a, p. 252; 4:14-e, p. 260. See also D&C 88:13, 41.

276 H. W. Nibley, *Teachings of the PGP*, 17, p. 213.

277 1 Nephi 1:8.

278 H. W. Nibley, *Teachings of the PGP*, 17, p. 211; cf. B. R. Bickmore, *Restoring*, pp. 304-306; F. M. Huchel, *Cosmic*, pp. 6-9, F. M. Huchel, *Cosmic (Book)*. See *Endnote E-52*, p. 717.

279 E. Hennecke, *et al.*, *Acts of John*, 94, p. 227.

280 3 Nephi 11:8.

281 E.g., 2 Nephi 22:6; 3 Nephi 11:8, 21:17-18; cf. Isaiah 12:6; Jeremiah 14:9; Hosea 11:9; Joel 2:27; Micah 5:13-14; Moses 7:69; Zechariah 3:5, 15, 17. See S. K. Brown, *Voices*, pp. 150-151; R. D. Draper, *et al.*, *Commentary*, pp. 150-151.

282 Such symbolism illuminates the cosmology of the book of Abraham, where the planet Kolob is "set night unto the throne of God" (Abraham 3:9) with other planets in increasing distance from the center. Indeed, the term Kolob may be related to the idea of "center" or "heart"—see *Excursus 18: Kolob*, p. 565. See also F. M. Huchel, *Cosmic*, pp. 10-11.

283 3 Nephi 17:12, 13.

284 3 Nephi 17:12.

285 3 Nephi 17:24; cf. D&C 137:2; Ezekiel 1:4.

286 S. K. Brown, *Voices*, pp. 147-148.

287 3 Nephi 17:23.

288 C. S. Lewis, *Pain*, p. 70. See *Figure 3-6*, p. 139.

The flames encircling the angels, the children, and the Lord recall the imagery of the "empyrean heaven,"[289] where the highest heaven is represented as a circular realm of pure fire.[290] The concept of heaven as a series of concentric circles can be contrasted to the figure of the intersecting circle and square—the latter symbolizing the coming together of heaven and earth in both the temple and in the soul of the seeker of Wisdom.[291]

When associated with the forward movement of time, the symbol of the circle is often represented as a spoked wheel rotating around a fixed center point or axis.[292] In this sense, early LDS writings speak of the "great wheel of the kingdom" that represented the rolling forward of the work of God,[293] the "great wheel of fortune" that will soon reverse the situations of favored and unfavored peoples,[294] and the "great wheel of nature" that demonstrates the march of time and the "over-ruling hand" of God in the course of events.[295] "It's the wheel that goes round and round but never moves," Nibley explains, corresponding to the Roman *quadrata*, which "represents the four corners of the earth, and the center of everything."[296]

Nibley also observes that the:

> … central pole of the tent… is often identified with the pole (the polestar) of the heavens.[297] "The tent itself is the *Weltenmantel*, the expanse of the firmament. Other tent poles sometimes represent the four cardinal points or the two turning points of the sun in the summer and winter solstice." The tent pole theme is carried over into the pillars of the temples and palaces, even into the columns of medieval churches and the stately facades of our own public buildings.[298]

Humphrey and Vitebsky further explain:

> In vertical space the center is the point of opening from one level to another and is often represented in architecture as a pillar, *stupa*, mountain or ladder to heaven. Altars similarly constitute a center, as the point at which a sacrifice can move between the plane of the earth and that of the gods. A center can also lead downward. As well as reaching up to heaven, the Rock in Jerusalem holds down the chaotic waters in the abyss under the earth.…
>
> Many traditions make it clear that the center is not so much an absolute concept as a relational one, the point toward which a community's life, thought, and activity are oriented. In these cultures there can be multiple centers, with each city, temple, and house having its own pillars, altars, and shrines.[299]

---

289   Greek *empyros* = fiery, derived from *pyr*= fire—and not to be confused with the unrelated term "imperial." See, e.g., R. Giorgi, *Anges*, pp. 63-65.

290   See M. Barker, *Holy of Holies*, p. 185, *Commentary 4:31-d*, p. 280.

291   See *Excursus 20: The Circle and the Square*, p. 571. See R. Guénon, *Symboles*, pp. 83-93, 110-111 for additional discussion of the symbolism of the center and surrounding circumferences.

292   R. Guénon, *Symboles*, pp. 86-92.

293   J. M. Grant, *13 July 1855*, p. 60; Orson Hyde, *24 October 1841*, p. 459; B. Young, *17 April 1845*, p. 401; *Times and Seasons*, April 1840, 1:91; 15 December 1840, 2:249; 1 March 1841, 2:340; 22 November 1841, 3:741.

294   W. B. Pace, *Autobiography*; J. Smith, Jr., *Documentary History*, 16 December 1838, 3:233; cf. T. G. Madsen, *Sacrament*, p. 132; *Wheel of Fortune*; A. J. Heschel, *Heavenly Torah*, pp. 209-210.

295   E Snow, *13 March 1878*, p. 268; B. H. Roberts, *God Glorified*, p. 18; *Times and Seasons*, 13 December 1841, 3:758. See *Endnote E-53*, p. 717.

296   H. W. Nibley, *Circle*, p. 144.

297   Cf. the imagery of Zion as a tent expanding outward from a center stake (Isaiah 53:2; D&C 57:3; 101:21).

298   H. W. Nibley, *Circle*, p. 145. See also N. Isar, *Dance of Adam*, pp. 196-199.

299   C. Humphrey, *et al.*, *Sacred Architecture*, p. 140.

FIGURE E12-1. *The Flight of the Little Prince, 1943*
Antoine de Saint Exupéry, 1900-1944

"'What! So you fell from the sky?... Which planet are you from?'"[1]
Saint Exupéry's drawing of the flight of the Little Prince is a fitting
companion to ancient accounts of the descent of Adam to Earth.[2]
The drawing, which was not included in the published book, bears
"the marks of having been crumpled into a ball by the author."[3]

1   A. de Saint Exupéry, *Prince*, p. 12.
2   *Aux Sources*, p. 55; A. de Saint Exupéry, *Dessins*, p. 461.
3   S. Schiff, *Saint-Exupéry*, inserted between pp. 180-181.

Excursus 12
Saint Exupéry and Genesis

SAINT Exupéry's drawing of the flight of the Little Prince is a fitting companion to ancient accounts of the descent of Adam to Earth.[300] It is without question that the important elements of his most famous book can be traced to sources in his own life and experience.[301] Although Saint Exupéry would have already been familiar with the story of Adam and Eve from his Catholic upbringing, it is not out of the question that he may have also drawn consciously or unconsciously from Islamic traditions about Adam learned through his contacts with Bedouins in North Africa.

The Little Prince—reputed to be the fourth best-selling book in the world after the Bible, the *Qur'an*, and *Das Kapital*, and translated into more than a hundred languages—describes *un petit bonhomme tout à fait extraordinaire* who fell to earth after leaving his "Eden" on another planet. Described as a prince, the context of the story makes it clear that, like Adam, he plays the role of an Everyman—unnamed, of uncertain age, and seemingly having always existed. Abandoning his role as the sole gardener for his unique rose, and having failed upon six other planets to find a suitable occupation, he lands in the dreary desert and is first initiated into knowledge of the earth by a serpent, who also eventually becomes the means of his returning as an immortal to his home planet. Though often seen exclusively as a fairy tale, de Galembert argues that it is better described as a semi-autobiographical myth that strives to recapture a lost sense of the sacred:

---

300   *Aux Sources*, p. 55; A. de Saint Exupéry, *Dessins*, p. 461.
301   J. Dupuis, *et al.*, *Saint-Ex*; M. Quesnel, *Naissance*

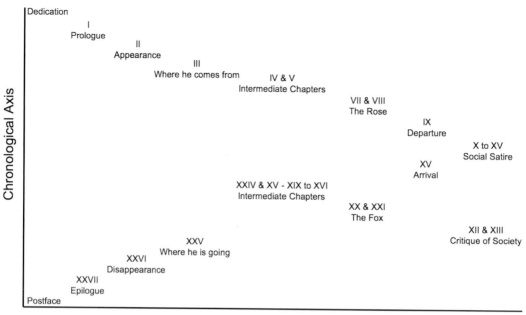

FIGURE E12-2. *Chiastic Structure of The Little Prince, 2001*[302]
Laurent de Bodin de Galembert, 1977-

Fairy tales are degenerate myths, myths profane and desacralized. They describe a world of disillusionment, where magic and marvels have replaced the sacred. Myths, on the other hand, elevate stories to a level of transcendence in an effort to understand great mysteries and revelations of highest import... In a world that has lost its feel for the sacred, in a world intellectualized and dehumanized to the point of barbarism, Saint Exupéry's work seeks to counter the movement of the prevailing current that leads to the degeneration of myth into fairy tale. Because an environment rationalized to the point of absurdity leaves no place for wonder and childish innocence, Saint Exupéry seeks to rediscover the sense of the sacred in a return to a myth-form that better suits its direction and purpose.[303]

In the book, Saint Exupéry's series of parables illustrating the complexities of human love reveal mankind's universal and poignant longing for deep and enduring relationships, "a dream of things as they might have been lived had not reality prematurely destroyed them."[304] However, in *The Little Prince*, "[e]very religious symbol, especially those having to do with eternity, immortality, and the survival of love, becomes nothing more than nostalgic memories of lost hope... too weak to call forth the reality they evoke."[305] Like *Citadelle*, a posthumously published work, the text of *The Little Prince* "represents a piece of spiritual ground marked out by a weary man with a vestigial sense of Catholicism and an innate sense of responsibility who has lived a life thirsting for the values but free of the bounds of both... What is surprising... [in reviewing Saint Exupéry's literary output throughout his life is] that his themes could remain constant throughout a novel of aviation, a book of personal essays, a children's allegory, and a succession of philosophical dialogues spoken at the desert court of an imaginary ruler."[306]

---

302   Translated from L. de Galembert, *Grandeur 2001*, p. 52.
303   L. de Galembert, *Grandeur 2001*, p. 46; L. de Galembert, *Grandeur 2003*, p. 70.
304   E. Drewermann, *Parabole*, p. 283.
305   *Ibid.*
306   S. Schiff, *Saint-Exupéry*, p. 444.

The effortless journey through the air of the Little Prince to and from his home planet can be contrasted with the mechanically-aided flight of the adult pilot, whose predicament in the story parallels Saint Exupéry's 1935 plane crash in the Sahara Desert.[307] Matheme observes that sometimes Saint Exupéry himself "flew without his flying machine… when, lying on his back in the Saharan night, he felt himself falling upward."[308] Of such an experience, Saint Exupéry wrote:

> When I opened my eyes I saw nothing but the pool of nocturnal sky, for I was lying on my back with outstretched arms, face-to-face with that hatchery of stars. Only half awake, still unaware that those depths were sky, having no roof between those depths and me, no branches to screen them, no root to cling to, I was seized with vertigo and felt myself as if flung forth and plunging downward like a diver.[309]

He interpreted this experience figuratively as the realization that even the canopy of heaven itself must not be seen as absolute protection nor as an invitation to enjoy the sedentary comfort induced by gravity and inertia, but rather should serve to reinforce in each of us the human imperative to fly onward toward the stars, despite our fears. Of the surprise and discomfort brought on by this realization, he wrote: "I have pity for the soul… who awakes in the great patriarchal night believing itself sheltered under the stars of God, and suddenly realizes that he is in the midst of a journey."[310]

The closing sentence of Saint Exupéry's *Wind, Sand, and Stars*, a book that poignantly describes the adventures and dangers of early aviation, illuminates the metaphor of transcendent longing hidden in its simple title. Matheme comments: "Saint Exupéry conjures up the creation story of God breathing life into Adam. It has the power to remind us that this story is played out whenever a human spirit, an emigré, searching for its homeland, enters a physical body at birth: 'Only the Spirit, if it breathe upon the clay, can create Man.'"[311] In his works, Saint Exupéry repeatedly "directs our eyes to the stars—we are souls carried on the wind in bodies of sand, and we look up longingly to the stars, our homeland."[312]

---

307   J. Dupuis, *et al.*, *Saint-Ex*, p. 30; M. Quesnel, *Naissance*, p. 8.
308   B. Matheme, *Wind*.
309   A. de Saint Exupéry, *Terre*. 4:4, pp. 62-63.
310   A. de Saint Exupéry, *Citadelle*.
311   A. de Saint Exupéry, *Terre*, 8:4, p. 182.
312   B. Matheme, *Wind*.

Excursus 13
Some Perspectives on Historicity

NON-MORMONS are often initially attracted to (or repelled from!) the Church because of the distinctive lifestyle of its active members. For many, the promise of health and happiness for individuals, families, and communities is a welcome antidote to the angst and alienation of the age. Yet, perhaps counterintuitively at first glance, these aspects of personal and social well-being do not constitute the central nor usually the first message of the missionaries. Instead, they typically begin their series of lessons by reciting the historical events of the Restoration. The case for obedience to the doctrines and practices of the Church explained in subsequent lessons is thus made, not as an appeal to the common sense of the investigator or to some body of empirical evidence, but primarily on the basis that these commandments were given by divine revelation. In other words, potential converts are not asked to consider whether their lives will be happier as a result of accepting the Gospel (though, of course, this is implied), but rather to find out for themselves whether the historical events of the Restoration and the teachings revealed by modern prophets are *true*.[313]

Summarizing this perspective, Richard L. Bushman has observed that:

> …stories of sacred occurrences formed the substance of Mormon belief as early as 1830. What distinguished Mormonism was not so much the Gospel Mormons taught, which in many respects resembled other Christians' teachings, but what they believed had happened—to Joseph Smith, to Book of Mormon characters, and to Moses and Enoch.[314] Mormons ever afterward were unable to take much interest in formal theology or systematizing treatises like [Alexander] Campbell's. No such attempts achieved the place in Mormon faith that creeds assumed in other churches. The core of Mormon belief was a conviction about actual events. The test of faith was not adherence to a certain confession of faith, but belief that Christ was resurrected, that Joseph Smith saw God, that the Book of Mormon was true history, and that Peter, James, and John restored the apostleship. Mormonism was history, not philosophy.[315]

By way of contrast, consider the following from the writings of Joseph Campbell, who was concerned with establishing the primacy of the recurrent symbolic content of worldwide religious themes over any question of historicity:

> We do not particularly care whether Rip van Winkle, Kamar al-Zaman, or Jesus Christ ever actually lived. Their stories are what concern us: and these stories are so widely distributed over the world… that the question of whether this or that local carrier of the universal theme may or may not have been a historical, living man can be of only secondary moment. The stressing of the historical element will lead to confusion; it will simply obfuscate the picture message.[316]

Not surprisingly, the historical aspects of Genesis are considered of great importance in the LDS tradition, even down to the matter of specifying of the actual physical location of where Adam and Eve lived after the Fall.[317] Nevertheless, the LDS people have successfully avoided both the extremes of literalism and liberalism with respect to the historicity of

---

313   See *Endnote E-54*, p. 717.
314   See *Endnote E-55*, p. 717.
315   R. L. Bushman, *Beginnings*, pp. 187-188. See also G. B. Hinckley, *Foundation*, p. 80.
316   J. Campbell, *Hero*, pp. 230-231. See also the discussion of the similar attitude of Paul Tillich, as described in T. G. Madsen, *Mormonism and Philosophy*. See *Endnote E-56*, p. 718.
317   See *Figure 6-2*, p. 457 and *Excursus 39: The Location of Adam-ondi-Ahman*, p. 623.

the Bible.[318] Although the belief that the characters mentioned in Genesis are actual historical figures who underwent something that was somehow like the events described in the biblical account has always been held firmly by the Saints, Nibley observes that we also bring ridicule and disillusionment upon ourselves when we fail to pursue scriptural understanding beyond the initial level of vivid picture images inculcated upon the minds of young children:

> The stories of the Garden of Eden and the Flood have always furnished unbelievers with their best ammunition against believers, because they are the easiest to visualize, popularize, and satirize of any Bible accounts. Everyone has seen a garden and been caught in a pouring rain. It requires no effort of imagination for a six-year-old to convert concise and straightforward Sunday-school recitals into the vivid images that will stay with him for the rest of his life. These stories retain the form of the nursery tales they assume in the imaginations of small children, to be defended by grown-ups who refuse to distinguish between childlike faith and thinking as a child when it is time to "put away childish things."[319] It is equally easy and deceptive to fall into adolescent disillusionment and with one's emancipated teachers to smile tolerantly at the simple gullibility of bygone days, while passing stern moral judgment on the savage old God who damns Adam for eating the fruit He put in his way and, overreacting with impetuous violence, wipes out Noah's neighbors simply for making fun of his boat-building on a fine summer's day.[320]

In the same vein, Brigham Young used the term "baby stories" to dismiss overly simplistic interpretations of the Genesis account of man's creation.[321] In a discourse given on October 8, 1854, he stated:

> When the Lord had organized the world, and... filled the earth with animal and vegetable life, then he created man.... Moses made the Bible to say his wife was taken out of his side—was made of one of his ribs. As far as I know my ribs are equal on each side. The Lord knows if I had lost a rib for each wife I have, I should have had none left long ago.... As for the Lord taking a rib out of Adam's side to make a woman of, it would be just as true to say He took one out of my side. "But, Brother Brigham, would you make it appear that Moses did not tell the truth?" No, not a particle more than I would that your mother did not tell the truth when she told you that little Billy came from a hollow toadstool. I would not accuse your mother of lying any more than I would Moses. The people in the days of Moses wanted to know things that [were] not for them, the same as your children do when they want to know where their little brother came from, and he answered them according to the level of their understandings, the same as mothers do their children.[322]

The Prophet Joseph Smith cautioned against the products of a "fanciful and flowery and heated imagination" and explained by way of contrast that:

> ... the things of God are of deep import; and time, and experience, and careful and ponderous and solemn thoughts can only find them out. Thy mind, O man! if thou wilt lead a soul unto salvation, must stretch as high as the utmost heavens, and search into and contemplate the darkest abyss, and the broad expanse of eternity—thou must commune with God.[323]

---

318 *Reverence for the Bible.* See *Endnote E-57,* p. 718.
319 1 Corinthians 13:11. See *Endnote E-58,* p. 718.
320 H. W. Nibley, *Before Adam,* p. 63. See D. E. Jeffery, *Noah's Flood* and C. M. White, *et al., Noachian Flood Story* for considered LDS perspectives on reconciling current scientific findings with the Genesis flood story. See also J. A. Widtsoe, *Flood;* Morris S. Petersen, *Earth,* p. 432.
321 B. Young, *23 October 1853,* p. 6.
322 As cited in L. J. Arrington, *Brigham Young,* pp. 197-198. Compare B. Young, *8 October 1854,* pp. 94-95.
323 J. Smith, Jr., *Teachings,* 25 March 1839, p. 137.

EXCURSUS

Both childish misunderstandings and adolescent disillusionment are swept away when the "veil [is] taken from our minds, and the eyes of our understanding [are] opened,"[324] providing a direct vision of those things to which the inevitably limited words of scripture[325] are intended to point the mind and heart. Thus, the personal value of scripture is not merely in that it gives a more or less accurate account of God's relationship with various peoples throughout history, but more fundamentally in the fact that it provides a means for individuals to recognize how God acts continually in their own lives.[326] Said Joseph Smith: "He that can mark the power of Omnipotence, inscribed upon the heavens, can also see God's own handwriting in the sacred volume: and he who reads it oftenest will like it best, and he who is acquainted with it, will known the hand wherever he can see it."[327]

The relationship between scriptural history and personal experience operates in both forward and backward directions: not only do the stories of scripture guide daily life, but our daily life conditions our understanding of scriptural accounts. Indeed, it is through direct participation in repeated experiences of God's power and help in the present that the histories reported by scripture become both intelligible and credible to modern believers. As Timothy Luke Johnson expresses regarding the immediate nature of the sources for one's personal conviction of the historical authenticity of New Testament scripture:

> For those living in a community where "signs and wonders" done in the name of Jesus are a regular occurrence, hearing of such deeds attributed to Jesus in the Gospel narratives is no surprise or scandal...

> For those living in a community where the "Word of the Lord" [is] proclaimed through [men and women of God],... it is no surprise or scandal to hear... words [spoken in the same spirit] attributed to Jesus in the Gospels, for it is the same Jesus who speaks in both places...

> For a community that lives in the presence of the resurrected [Christ], it is beside the point to debate whether Jesus "back then" predicted His death and resurrection, for His death and above all His resurrection are confirmed as real precisely by this community that lives by His power [today]. It is equally silly, in this context, to debate whether Jesus "back then" predicted His return, for that return is predicated on His being the living and powerful Lord, and it is in the light of that truth that we await God's final triumph through Him.[328]

---

324   D&C 110:1-2. See also Ether 3:6; D&C 76:12, 19; 138:11.
325   See, e.g., Moroni's lament about the difficulty in reducing revelation to writing (Ether 12:23-27).
326   J. E. Faulconer, *Incarnation*, p. 38.
327   J. Smith, Jr., *Teachings*, 22 January 1834, p. 56.
328   L. T. Johnson, *Real Jesus*, p. 145; c.f., J. H. Charlesworth, *DSS and NT*, pp. 142-143. See also *Excursus 1: Speech, Writing, and Revelation*, p. 512 and *Excursus 6: The Authority and Power of Scripture*, p. 531.

Excursus 14
The Garden of Eden as a Prototype for the Temple

IN his broad overview of this literature, Parry concluded that the Garden of Eden "served as the prototype, pattern, and/or originator of subsequent Israelite temples... The Garden was not a sanctuary built of cedar or marble, for it is not necessary for a temple to possess an edifice or structure; but rather it was an area of sacred space made holy because God's presence was found there...."[329] Parry lists eleven prototypical aspects of the Garden of Eden:

1. The Tree of Life was located both in the Garden and in the temple.

2. Both the Garden and the temple were associated with sacred waters.

3. Eastward orientations played a role in the Garden story and in subsequent Israelite temples.

4. The cosmic mountain was symbolically affiliated with the Garden and temple.[330] [The first land to arise from the waters became the Mountain of the Lord, where the Lord created Adam. It is from this divine center that Creation begins and extends out in all directions].

5. The account of the earth's creation is closely connected with the Garden of Eden pericope [i.e., Genesis 2-3] and the temple.

6. *Cherubim*, or heavenly beings, function as guardians of the Garden and the temple.

7. Revelation was an essential part of the Garden and the temple.

8. Sacrifice existed in the Garden and in subsequent temple systems.

9. Similar religious language existed in both the Garden and the temple.

10. Sacred vestments were associated with Adam and Eve in the Garden and with the priesthood in the Jerusalem temple.[331]

11. Abundance was associated with the Garden and the temple.[332]

Barker also describes several specific features of the Garden of Eden that were represented in the temple:

> The *debir*, the Holy of Holies, was the place of the Lord's throne, but the *hekal*, the great hall of the temple, was the Garden of Eden. The decorations of the temple were those of Eden (trees, pomegranates, lilies, cherubim), the seven branched lamp was described in later tradition as the tree of life, a bronze serpent was removed from the temple by Hezekiah, and Ezekiel saw the river of life flowing from the temple.[333] Just as the *debir* represented heaven ("represented" is a concession to our way of thinking), so the *hekal* represented the completed Creation. This again suggests that the rituals of the temple were Creation rituals.[334]

A key difference between the architecture of Israelite temples and the features of the Garden of Eden is that the latter had no veil hiding the heavens from the earth: "I created for [Adam] an open heaven, so that he might look upon the angels, singing the triumphal song. And the

---

329 D. W. Parry, *Garden*, pp. 126-127; cf. H. W. Nibley, *Message 2005*, p. 293; H. W. Nibley, *Return*, p. 47.
330 E.g., Isaiah 2:2.
331 See the overview of Moses 4, p. 234.
332 D. W. Parry, *Garden*, pp. 126-127. For additional discussion of these aspects, see J. L. Carroll, *Reconciliation*.
333 1 Kings 6:14-36; Exodus 25:31-37; 2 Kings 18:4; Ezekiel 47:1-12.
334 M. Barker, *Atonement*.

light which is never darkened was perpetually in paradise."[335] The *Lectures on Faith* asserts that Adam and Eve "were [later] separated from the presence of God by a veil" when they were driven out of the Garden of Eden.[336] Indeed, some ancient sources speak of two such "veils" which create three heavens, symbolically corresponding to the three divisions of the temple.[337] The separation between heaven and earth will end at some future time "when the veil of the covering of my temple, in my tabernacle, which hideth the earth, shall be taken off, and all flesh shall see me together."[338]

Garden of Eden symbolism was not only associated with the temple, but also preserved in the synagogue: "In synagogue mosaics in Palestine, two *Menorot* flank the scroll shrine. This was a representation of the temple (= Garden of Eden) with the two trees, of Life and of Knowledge, as in Genesis 2-3."[339] Also note that both Catholic and Orthodox church buildings were patterned after the Jewish temple in many respects.[340]

Citing an article by Volluz, Potter describes similarities between the Garden of Eden, Lehi's dream of the Tree of Life, and the wadi *Tayyib al-Ism*, a plausible site for the Valley of Lemuel where the family was camped at the time:

> The upper valley would seem to contain a number of attributes that would make it a possible candidate for a type of the Garden of Eden. It is a garden situated in a "lone and dreary world." It has only one entrance and that is on the east end. It is fertile compared to the surroundings, seeming "terrestrial" among the "telestial." It is enclosed by high mountains making it separate from its surroundings, "as if it had been a world."[341] It contains several hundred palm trees, which are intimately associated in the culture of the Middle East, with the Tree of Life."[342] Moreover, it contains a continually flowing stream, something of a rarity in this dry region.[343]

335   F. I. Andersen, *2 Enoch*, 31:2, pp. 152-153.

336   L. E. Dahl, *et al.*, *Lectures*, 2:25, p. 43.

337   See A. S-M. Ri, *Commentaire de la Caverne*, pp. 118-121.

338   D&C 101:23. See Isaiah 25:6-9; H. W. Nibley, *Treasures*, pp. 185-186; *Commentary* 2:3-a, p. 99. See also J. C. Reeves, *Jewish Lore*, p. 179 n. 26 and *Excursus 17: The Veil of the Temple*, p. 564.

339   N. Wyatt, *Space*, p. 169.

340   W. J. Hamblin, *et al.*, *Temple*, pp. 103-116, 172-175; M. von Wellnitz, *Liturgy*, pp. 7-8, 13-18, 21-28. For discussions of the role of the temple in the development of Christian thought and liturgy, see M. Barker, *Temple Roots*; W. J. Hamblin, *et al.*, *Temple*, pp. 113-116; H. W. Nibley, *Envy*.

341   1 Nephi 8:20.

342   G. Potter, *et al.*, *Lehi*, p. 45. See also C. T. Volluz, *Lehi's Dream*.

343   G. Potter, *et al.*, *Lehi*, pp. 37-38. See also *Commentary* 1:1-c, p. 43.

Excursus 15

Description of the LDS Temple Endowment

SINCE the introduction of the LDS endowment to selected individuals in 1842, the Church has taught that certain aspects are not to be discussed in detail outside the temple itself.[344] Some reliable descriptions of a general nature are included below.[345]

Of the modern temple endowment, Elder James E. Talmage writes that it:

> … comprises instruction relating to the significance of past dispensations, and the importance of the present as the greatest and grandest era in human history. This course of instruction includes a recital of the most prominent events of the creative period, the condition of our first parents in the Garden of Eden, their disobedience and consequent expulsion from that blissful abode, their condition in the lone and dreary world when doomed to live by labor and sweat, the plan of Redemption by which the great transgression may be atoned, the period of the great apostasy, the restoration of the Gospel with all its ancient powers and privileges, the absolute and indispensable condition of personal purity and devotion to the right in present life, and a strict compliance with Gospel requirements.…
>
> The ordinances of the endowment embody certain obligations on the part of the individual, such as a covenant and promise to observe the law of strict virtue and chastity, to be charitable, benevolent, tolerant and pure; to devote both talent and material means to the spread of truth and the uplifting of the race; to maintain devotion to the cause of truth; and to seek in every way to contribute to the great preparation that the earth may be made ready to receive her king— the Lord Jesus Christ. With the taking of each covenant and the assuming of each obligation a promised blessing is pronounced, contingent upon faithful observance of the conditions.
>
> No jot, iota, or tittle of the temple rites is otherwise than uplifting and sanctifying. In very detail the endowment ceremony contributes to covenants of morality of life, consecration of person to high ideals, devotion to truth, patriotism to nation, and allegiance to God. The blessings of the House of the Lord are restricted to no privileged class; every member of the Church may have admission to the temple with the right to participate in the ordinances thereof, if he comes duly accredited as of worthy life and conduct.[346]

President Brigham Young gave the following description:

> Let me give you a definition in brief. Your endowment is to receive all those ordinances in the House of the Lord, which are necessary for you, after you have departed this life, to enable you to walk back to the presence of the Father, passing the angels who stand as sentinels, being able to give them the key words, the signs and tokens, pertaining to the Holy Priesthood, and gain your eternal exaltation in spite of earth and hell.[347]

Elder John A. Widtsoe wrote:

> The temple ordinances encompass the whole plan of salvation as taught from time to time by the leaders of the Church, and elucidate matters difficult of understanding. There is no warping or twisting in fitting the temple teachings into the great scheme of salvation. The philosophical completeness of the endowment is one of the great arguments for the veracity of the temple

---

344 See K. Flake, *Oral Canon* for a discussion of some of the ways in which the preservation of temple ordinances as an oral tradition may help to maximize their effectiveness.

345 An useful set of articles describing the many facets of temples and temple work can be found in D. H. Ludlow, *Encyclopedia*, 4:1444-1468.

346 J. E. Talmage, *House of the Lord*, 4, pp. 54, 55.

347 B. Young, *6 April 1853 - B*, p. 31.

ordinances. Moreover, this completeness of survey and expounding of the Gospel plan, makes temple worship one of the most effective methods of refreshing the memory concerning the whole structure of the Gospel....

The endowment and the temple work as revealed by the Lord to the Prophet Joseph Smith... fall clearly into four distinct parts: the preparatory ordinances, the giving of instructions by lectures and representations; covenants; and, finally, tests of knowledge. I doubt that the Prophet Joseph, unlearned and untrained in logic, could of himself have made the thing so logically complete. The candidate for the temple service is prepared, as in any earthly affair, for work to be done. Once prepared he is instructed in the things that he should know. When instructed, he covenants to use the imparted knowledge, and at once the new knowledge, which of itself is dead, leaps into living life. At last, tests are given him, whereby those who are entitled to know may determine whether the man has properly learned the lesson. The brethren and sisters who go through the temple should observe all these things and recognize the wonderful coherence and logical nature of the carefully worked out system, with a beginning and an end, fitting every known law of God and nature, which constitutes temple worship....

The holy endowment is deeply symbolic. "Going through the temple" is not a very good phrase; for temple worship implies a great effort of mind and concentration if we are to understand the mighty symbols that pass in review before us. Everything must be arranged to attune our hearts, our minds, and our souls to the work. Everything about us must contribute to the peace of mind that enables us to study and to understand the mysteries, if you choose, that are unfolded before us....

If we are correct in believing that the blessings obtained in the temples of the Lord are a partial fulfillment, at least, of the promise made when the Holy Ghost, who is a Revelator, is conferred upon man, it would be expected that temple ordinances would be in the nature of a revelation to those who participate... [R]evelation always comes; it is not imposed upon a person; it must be drawn to us by faith, seeking and working. Just so; to the man or woman who goes through the temple with open eyes, heeding the symbols and the covenants, and making a steady, continuous effort to understand the full meaning, God speaks his word and revelations come.

The endowment is so richly symbolic that only a fool would attempt to describe it; it is so packed full of revelations to those who exercise their strength to seek and see, that no human words can explain or make clear the possibilities that reside in the temple service. The endowment which was given by revelation can best be understood by revelation; and to those who seek most vigorously, with pure hearts, will the revelation be greatest. I believe that the busy person on the farm, in the shop, in the office, or in the household, who has his worries and troubles, can solve his problems better and more quickly in the house of the Lord than anywhere else. If he will leave his problems behind and in the temple work for himself and for his dead, he will confer a mighty blessing upon those who have gone before, and quite as large a blessing will come to him, for at the most unexpected moments, in or out of the temple will come to him, as a revelation, the solution of the problems that vex his life.[348]

Glen M. Leonard wrote that the endowment given in the Nauvoo temple:

... consisted of the ordinances of washing and anointing, followed by instructions and covenants setting forth a pattern or figurative model for life. The teachings began with a recital of the creation of the earth and its preparation to host life. The story carried the familiar ring of the Genesis account, echoed as well in Joseph Smith's revealed book of Moses and book of Abraham. The disobedience and expulsion of Adam and Eve from the Garden of Eden set the stage for an explanation of Christ's Atonement for that original transgression and for the sins of the entire human family. Also included was a recital of mankind's tendency to stray from

---

348   J. A. Widtsoe, *Temple Worship*, pp. 192, 193-194, 195-196. See *Endnote E-61, p. 719.*

the truth through apostasy and the need for apostolic authority to administer authoritative ordinances and teach true gospel principles. Participants were reminded that in addition to the Savior's redemptive gift they must be obedient to God's commandments to obtain a celestial glory. Within the context of these gospel instructions, the initiates made covenants of personal virtue and benevolence and of commitment to the church. They agreed to devote their talents and means to spread the gospel, to strengthen the church, and to prepare the earth for the return of Jesus Christ. Through personal promises to their Heavenly Father made in the Nauvoo temple, the Saints expanded the meaning of being a covenant people.[349]

Hugh Nibley gave the following description of the LDS temple endowment and its relationship to rituals in other religions and cultures:[350]

> The word "endowment" that was chosen to designate the temple ordinances contains, historically and legally, two main ideas: that of the bestowal of something valuable on a person and "the permanent usufruct[351] of such goods in installments and upon the fulfillment of certain specified conditions."[352] It is the greatest of gifts, but we cannot cash it in this life—it is only for the "spiritual minded,"[353] "having nothing to do with temporal things";[354] it pays off only at certain times and places and upon the exact fulfillment of certain conditions.[355]

> Latter-day Saints believe that their temple ordinances are as old as the human race and represent a primordial revealed religion that has passed through alternate phases of apostasy and restoration which have left the world littered with the scattered fragments of the original structure, some more and some less recognizable, but all badly damaged and out of proper context.[356] The early fathers of the church gave such an explanation for the disturbingly close resemblances between Christianity and other, notably Egyptian, beliefs and practices—all are the remnants of another age. Beginning in the twentieth century, an army of scholars, following the lead of Sir James Frazer, has been diligently at work, first collecting thousands of scattered pieces of earlier customs and folktales and then trying to put them together, like the pieces of jigsaw puzzles, to see whether they all come from a few basic systems or even go back to a single, all-embracing "pattern." Whatever the end result may be, it is perfectly clear by now that the same sort of thing has been going on for a very long time and in virtually all parts of the world.

> Offhand, one may say that Joseph Smith could have gotten his ideas from any or many of a great number of sources, ancient and modern... There are, in fact, countless tribes, sects, societies, and orders from which he might have picked up this and that, had he known of their existence. The Near East in particular is littered with the archaeological and living survivals of practices and teachings which an observant Mormon may find suggestively familiar... He has actually been charged with plundering some of the baggage brought to the West by certain fraternal orders during the Middle Ages[357]—as if the Prophet must rummage in a magpie's nest to stock a king's treasury! Among the customs and religions of mankind there are countless parallels, many of them very instructive, to what the Mormons do. But there is a world of difference between Ginzberg's *Legends of the Jews*[358] and the book of Isaiah, or

---

349   G. M. Leonard, *Nauvoo*, pp. 258-259.

350   H. W. Nibley, *Message 2005*, p. xxviii. Lengthier summaries of the history, significance, and teachings of ancient and modern temple ordinances can be found in H. W. Nibley, *Meanings and Functions*, and in many others of Nibley's articles.

351   I.e., usage rights.

352   Source unidentified.

353   J. Smith, Jr., *Teachings*, 4 May 1842, p. 237.

354   *Ibid.*, 8 April 1844, p. 362.

355   H. W. Nibley, *Message 2005*, p. 30.

356   See *Endnote E-62*, p. 719.

357   See *Endnote E-63*, p. 720.

358   L. Ginzberg, *Legends*.

between the *Infancy Gospels*[359] and the real Gospels, no matter how many points of contact one may detect between them. The Latter-day Saint endowment was not built up of elements brought together by chance custom, or long research; it is a single, perfectly consistent, organic whole, conveying its message without the aid of rationalizing, spiritualizing, allegorizing, or moralizing interpretations.

Describing the endowment itself, Nibley wrote:[360]

> The Mormon endowment... is frankly a model, a presentation in figurative terms. As such, it is flexible and adjustable; for example, it may be presented in more languages than one, and in more than one medium of communication. But since it does not attempt to be a picture of reality, but only a model or analogue to show how things work, setting forth the pattern of man's life on earth with its fundamental whys and wherefores, it does not need to be changed or adapted greatly through the years; it is a remarkably stable model, which makes its comparison with other forms and traditions, including the more ancient ones, quite valid and instructive... Those who have been to the temple hundreds of times know that "age cannot wither... nor custom stale [its] infinite variety."[361] What [the] few bits of information [about parallels in other religions and cultures] do is to supply a new dimension to the experience, along with the assurance that a wealth of newly found records confirms the fundamental thesis of its antiquity and genuineness.

Regarding the aspect of genuineness, Nibley says elsewhere:

> [O]rdinances are more than just symbols—they go beyond that... They always have a double nature: they are or mean something that is real. You see that as soon as you try, in music and art, to give religious experience a third dimension. The Gospel actually *has* that third dimension, of course... Once you know the real thing, everything else is an anticlimax.[362]

The temple ordinances are classed among "the mysteries of the kingdom, even... of the knowledge of God" in which "the power of godliness is manifest."[363] In its broadest religious meaning, a mystery is a truth that can be known and understood only by divine revelation.[364] Among the most important of the truths that are learned in the temple is a knowledge of "who we are, and who God is, and what our relationship to Him is."[365] Giving his own summary of temple ordinances, the Prophet Joseph Smith wrote that they concerned:

> ... washings, anointings, endowments, and the communication of keys pertaining to the Aaronic Priesthood, and so on to the highest order of the Melchizedek Priesthood, setting forth the order pertaining to the Ancient of Days, and all those plans and principles by which anyone is enabled to secure the fulness of those blessings which have been prepared for the Church of the First Born, and come up and abide in the presence of the Elohim in the eternal worlds.[366]

359   See, e.g., M. Barker, *Infancy Gospel of James*; W. Barnstone, *Gospel of Pseudo-Matthew.*
360   H. W. Nibley, *Message 2005*, p. xxix.
361   W. Shakespeare, *Antony*, II:ii:234-235, p. 1357.
362   H. W. Nibley, *Conversation*, p. 66.
363   D&C 84:19-20.
364   H. B. Lee, *Light*, July 1961, p. 211; D. A. Bednar, *Pray Always*, p. 41; H. W. Nibley, *Conversation*, p. 67. See *Excursus 53: Comparative Explorations of the Mysteries*, p. 663.
365   C. Broderick, *Adversity*, p. 129.
366   J. Smith, Jr., *Teachings*, 4 May 1842, p. 237.

Excursus 16
The Role of Revelation in Temple Building

WITH respect to the surprising degree of commonality in the layout and ritual of temples throughout the world, Nibley commented:

> In ancient times the world was covered with temples. What was done in them? Surprisingly, all followed the same general pattern… "In extremely diverse cultural contexts, we always find the same cosmological pattern and the same ritual scenario," writes Eliade, and as "man progressively occupies increasingly vast areas of the planet, … all he seems to do is to repeat indefinitely the same archetypal gestures."[367] He pointedly observes that "man would not know these tales if they were not revealed to him. Consequently a myth is the story of what happened… at the beginning of time."[368]

Similarly, Lundquist describes the ancient expectation that temple plans are to be received by revelation:

> Central to temple covenant systems all over the ancient Near East is the idea that the temple plan is revealed to the king or the prophet by deity. Again, many examples could be enumerated. Gudea of Lagash was visited in a dream in a temple of Lagash and shown the plan of the temple by a goddess, who gave him a lapis lazuli tablet on which the plan of the temple was written. Perhaps the best example of this aspect of temple building is the Sinai episode itself, in which, according to D. N. Freedman, "this heavenly temple or sanctuary with its throne room or Holy of Holies where the deity was seated on his cherubim throne constituted the *tabnît* or structure seen by Moses during his sojourn on the same mountain."[369]

Berlin notes that:

> … the creation of the world in [Genesis] 1:1-2:3 bears several striking resemblances to the construction of the Tabernacle mandated in Exodus 25-31 and executed in Exodus 35-40[370]— the prototype of the Jerusalem Temple and the focus of the priestly service of the Lord. Note that other ancient Near Eastern creation stories conclude with the construction of a temple for the creation god. In the *Tanakh*, the world is sometimes seen as the Lord's temple, and the temple as a microcosm.[371]

Nibley explains differences among LDS temple designs today as follows:

> In a speech in the 1880s in St. George, Brother Erastus Snow said that every temple has a slightly different design, because it performs a different purpose [372]… The St. George Temple was built after the pattern of the Kirtland Temple, to emphasize certain things. Our Provo Temple is built in a different way entirely. It functions with a different thing in mind—efficiency in getting a lot of work done in a hurry, but also as a teaching tool… Though temples generally face east, Joseph built the Nauvoo temple facing west, where it would be seen to its best advantage from the river.[373]

---

367 M. Eliade, *Cosmogonic Myth*, p. 9.
368 *Ibid.*, p. 1 and H. W. Nibley, *Drama*, pp. 8-9.
369 J. M. Lundquist, *Temple, Covenant, and Law*, p. 302. See Exodus 25:8.
370 See, e.g., Genesis 2:1-3; Exodus 39:32, 42-43.
371 A. Berlin, *et al.*, *Jewish*, p. 13 and, e.g., Isaiah 66:1-2. See also G. A. Anderson, *Perfection*, pp. 200-202 and the overview of Moses 3, p. 146.
372 Source not given.
373 H. W. Nibley, *Meaning of Temple*, pp. 35, 36. Note also that neither the Provo, Oakland, Los Angeles, nor Stockholm temples face east (*Do temples*; H. W. Nibley, *Drama*, pp. 12, 13). For a historical summary of the orientation in Jewish and Christian practice, see J. H. Emminghaus, *Eucharist*, pp. 47-50.

In a similar vein, Elder Orson Pratt expressed the following:

> … the Lord is not confined to an exact pattern in relation to these temples building in the different stakes any more than He is confined in the creation of worlds to make them all of the same size. He does not make them all of one size, nor does He set them rolling on their axes in the same plane, nor does He construct any in many respects alike; there is variation as much as there is in the human form. Take men and women. There are general outlines that are common to all, but did you ever see two faces alike among all the millions of the human family? What a great variety, and yet all are constructed in general outline alike—after the image of God. So in regard to the building of temples. The Lord will not confine Himself to any one special method to be so many feet long, so many feet wide, and so many places for the Priesthood to stand, but He will construct His temples in a great variety of ways, and by and by, when the more perfect order shall exist we shall construct them, through the aid of revelation, in accordance with the temples that exist in yonder Heaven.[374]

The size of the Kirtland Temple was given by revelation in D&C 95, followed by a vision in which were provided details about its structure and design. Frederick G. Williams later recounted to Truman Angell a conversation he had with workers building the temple:

> Carpenter Rolph said, "Doctor [Williams], what do you think of the house?" [Williams] answered, "It looks to me like the pattern precisely." He then related the following: "Joseph [Smith] received the word of the Lord for him to take his two counselors, Williams and Rigdon, and come before the Lord, and He would show them the plan or model of the house to be built. We went upon our knees, called on the Lord, and the building appeared within viewing distance, I being the first to discover it. Then we all viewed it together. After we had taken a good look at the exterior, the building seemed to come right over us, and the makeup of the Hall seemed to coincide with that I there saw to a minutiae."[375]

Joseph Smith also saw the Nauvoo Temple in vision. Replying to a difference of opinion with temple architect William Weeks about the shape of the windows, he said: "I wish you to carry out my designs. I have seen in vision the splendid appearance of that building illuminated, and will have it built according to the pattern shown me."[376] John Pulsipher recalled that the Nauvoo Temple had been "built according to the pattern that the Lord gave Joseph"[377] and Parley P. Pratt said that "'angels and spirits from the eternal worlds' had instructed Smith 'in all things pertaining to … sacred architecture'"[378]

As early as January 1846, Brigham Young foresaw the building of a larger temple in the West once the Saints left Nauvoo:

> We can't stay in this house[379] but a little while. We have got to build another house. It will be a larger house than this, and a more glorious one. And we shall build a great many houses, we shall come back here and we shall go to Kirtland, and build houses all over the continent of N[orth] America.[380]

Later, with respect to the overall design for the Salt Lake Temple, President Young said:

---

374   O. Pratt, *26 October 1879*, p. 25.
375   E. C. Robison, *Kirtland*, pp. 8, 24n. 3.
376   J. Smith, Jr., *Documentary History*, 5 February 1844, 6:196-197.
377   J. Pulsipher, *Autobiography*, pp. 8-9.
378   M. McBride, *Nauvoo Temple*, pp. 8-9. See P. P. Pratt, *6 April 1853*, p. 44. See *Endnote E-64*, p. 720.
379   I.e., the Nauvoo Temple.
380   W. Clayton, *Chronicle*, 2 January 1846, p. 252.

I scarcely ever say much about revelations, or visions, but suffice it to say, five years ago last July[381] I was here, and saw in the Spirit the Temple not ten feet from where we have laid the Chief Cornerstone. I have not inquired what kind of a temple we should build. Why? Because it was represented before me. I have never looked upon that ground, but the vision of it was there. I see it as plainly as if it was in reality before me. Wait until it is done. I will say, however, that it will have six towers, to begin with, instead of one. Now do not any of you apostatize because it will have six towers, and Joseph only built one. It is easier for us to build sixteen, than it was for him to build one. The time will come when there will be one in the center of Temples we shall build, and on the top, groves and fish ponds. But we shall not see them here, at present.[382]

The Provo and Ogden, Utah temples were the first to feature a design with a single steeple in the center of the building.[383] Notably, the idea of "groves and fish ponds" on top was also proposed for the LDS Conference Center in Salt Lake City before those involved became aware of Young's prophecy.[384]

On the same day that Brigham Young related his vision of the Salt Lake Temple, he also reviewed the history of temple building in ancient Israel and during the ministry of Joseph Smith, stressing that a "revelation-pattern" was always required to direct such work. He also realized, however, that revelatory precedent was sufficient for certain aspects of Joseph Smith's temple program in Nauvoo, since it "is only where experience fails, that [new] revelation is needed."[385] Such was the case in July 1992 when, as a member of the First Presidency, President Gordon B. Hinckley looked at candidate sites for a future temple in Hong Kong. He later recounted to a group of members in New York City:

> We went back to our hotel room after that very long and difficult day. I could not sleep. I prayed very earnestly, asking the Lord to bless us, to let us know what should be done. In the middle of the night I awoke. There was on my mind an impression of something that could be done. We owned a very choice piece of property in Kowloon. We had been there for years. It was the location of the mission home. I got up and took a piece of paper and sketched out a structure with a temple on the top, the baptistry down underground—to follow the instruction found in the Doctrine and Covenants that the baptistry should be beneath "where the living are wont to assemble."[386] We could put also in that building a chapel and a temple president's residence. I just drew it out in rough form… That resulted in the construction of the Hong Kong Temple. The temple which we have built here in New York [City] is patterned after that same edifice.[387]

---

381   I.e., July 1847.

382   B. Young, *6 April 1853 - A*, p. 133.

383   C. S. Hawkins, *Temples*, pp. 46-51.

384   W. D. Halverson, *Conference Center*, pp. 26, 201-210; G. B. Hinckley, *Testimony*; K. Sorvig, *Learning*, p. 107; Zimmer Gunsul Frasca Partnership, *Conference Center*, pp. 11, 30-35.

385   B. Young, *6 April 1853 - B*, p. 32.

386   See D&C 128:13.

387   G. B. Hinckley, *Manhattan*, p. 423. See also M. J. Brough, *et al.*, *Temple*; S. L. Dew, *Hinckley*, pp. 481-482; S. Tiffany, *City Saints*, pp. 96-119.

Excursus 17
The Veil of the Temple

BARKER describes the nature and function of the veil in Israelite temples:

> The veil marked the division between the visible and the invisible creation. It represented matter, and was woven from red, blue, purple, and white threads, to represent the four elements from which the material world was made: earth (white), air (blue), fire (red), and water (purple). It was embroidered with cherubim, the winged heavenly beings found throughout the temple—in the Holy of Holies, on the walls of the great hall, and on the veil between them. They could move between the two states of creation, and transmitted heavenly knowledge to earth.[388]

Anciently, the veil was also identified with the mantle worn by the high priest, "bearing on it the cosmic marks of the compass, the square, the *omphalos* or universal center, and the *eben shatiyyah* or solid earth on which a man kneels to praise God."[389] According to Philo, the "priest in the cosmic robes... is the Logos clothed in the material elements."[390] As Barker writes:

> Veil and vestments were complementary imagery: the veil symbolized all that stood between human perception and the vision of God, and the vestments symbolized the clothing of the divine in that same material world which also concealed it. Thus the veil and the priestly vestments provided the first Christians with ready imagery to convey what they meant by the incarnation.[391]

At the final stage of temple rites, "'the temple is [itself] considered as a person and the veil of the temple as a garment that is worn, as a personification of the sanctuary itself.'"[392] Gaskill comments:[393]

> ... the book of Hebrews teaches that the veil of the temple represents the flesh of Jesus Christ.[394] This being the case, when in [LDS temples] we ceremonially act out our ascent back to God, at the final stages of the endowment a person representing our Savior stands between us and the Father. Jesus Christ is, of course, our Mediator, or go-between.[395] Since it is Christ through whom we communicate with our Father (both at the veil and in prayer)—and through whom we enter the celestial kingdom—then it is also Christ who is symbolized by the sacred clothing we receive at the conclusion of the temple initiatory ceremonies. This clothing represents the crucified flesh of Christ and should be received with a covenant and a reminder to always live in accordance with what that newly procured covering represents. This should give new meaning to the idea of taking upon ourselves the name[396] or image[397] of Christ.

388   M. Barker, *Angels*, p. 14; cf. M. Barker, *Gate*, pp. 109-111; M. Barker, *Hidden*, pp. 18-19.

389   H. W. Nibley, *Return*, p. 80. See also H. W. Nibley, *Vestments*, pp. 106-109.

390   E. R. Goodenough, *Light*, p. 104; cf. M. Barker, *Gate*, pp. 115-118; M. Barker, *Hidden*, p. 19.

391   M. Barker, *Gate*, p. 104; cf. pp. 104-132.

392   H. W. Nibley, *Return*, p. 81. See also M. Barker, *Gate*, p. 105; H. W. Nibley, *Message 2005*, pp. 439-440; J. A. Parry, *et al.*, *Temple in Heaven*, pp. 528-529.

393   A. L. Gaskill, *Lost*, p. 71. See also B. T. Ostler, *Clothed*; J. W. Welch, *et al.*, *Gammadia*; H. W. Nibley, *Message 2005*, p. 440.

394   See Hebrews 10:19-22. See also W. Williams, *Shadow*.

395   See 1 Timothy 2:5; 2 Nephi 2:27.

396   See 2 Nephi 31:13; Mosiah 5:8. See *Commentary* 3:19-b, p. 177; D. H. Oaks, *Taking Upon Us*; D. A. Bednar, *Name*, pp. 98.

397   See Alma 5:19; 1 John 3:1-3.

EXCURSUS

Excursus 18
Kolob

THE term Kolob "may derive from either of two Semitic roots with the consonants *QLB/QRB*. One has the meaning 'to be near,' as in Hebrew *qarob*...[398] The other meaning is 'center, midst,' as in Hebrew *qereb*...[399] In Arabic, *qalb* [heart, center][400] forms part of the names of several of the brightest stars in the sky, such as Antares... the constellation Scorpio... and Regulus... in the constellation Leo."[401] Hamblin sees the possibility of a reference in Jewish literature to a governing star named KLB:[402] "Assuming...an Ethiopic scribal error of *za* for *ka* for the admittedly corrupt reading of Zelebsa'el, we arrive at KLBS'L,[403] which in Arabic would translate as the 'KLB of God' (*sha'el* meaning simply 'of God' in Aramaic)."[404]

Some also see a possible connection with Sirius (the dog star)[405] or Venus (the morning star[406]), commonly represented in antiquity by the inverted pentagram-shaped star, a symbol occasionally found in Mormon architecture, though lacking authoritative explanation.[407] The so-called Saturn stones, located directly below the parapet on each of the towers of the Salt Lake Temple,[408] are also thought by some to represent Kolob, though this interpretation is not without its difficulties.[409] Given the enigmatic nature of the cosmology of the book of Abraham, it may well be that Kolob is not intended to be given a literal interpretation as a specific celestial body in the visible universe.

For a discussion of various attempts to harmonize theories about the nature and location of Kolob with scientific thinking, see Hansen[410] and Rhodes.[411] However, to quote Rhodes and Moody: "The bottom line is that we simply do not have enough information to be able to say with any confidence where Kolob is or what is characteristics are."[412]

EXCURSUS

---

398 F. Brown, *et al.*, *Lexicon*, p. 898.
399 *Ibid.*, p. 899.
400 For a translation of a Sufi text comparing the heart with the throne of God, see J. A. Tvedtnes *et al.*, *Traditions*, p. 511. See A. at-Tabataba'i, *Al-Mizan*, 2:225, 4:6-8 for a discussion of the meaning of "heart" in the *Qur'an*. See *Endnote E-65*, p. 720.
401 R. D. Draper, *et al.*, *Commentary*, pp. 289-290. See also M. D. Rhodes, *Twenty Years*, p. 8. See *Endnote E-66*, p. 720.
402 See G. W. E. Nickelsburg, *et al.*, *1 Enoch*, 82:17, p. 115.
403 According to Hamblin, "many of the star names in the book bear recognizable Aramaic names: for example, Berke'el, 'the Lightning of God,' and Narel, the 'light of God'" (W. J. Hamblin, *Joseph or Jung?*, p. 91).
404 *Ibid.*, p. 91.
405 W. V. Smith, *JS Commentary*, p. 80.
406 See Revelation 22:16. See *Endnote E-67*, p. 721.
407 R. G. Oman, *Symbolism*, p. 60. See *Endnote E-68*, p. 721.
408 J. E. Talmage, *House of the Lord*, p. 108.
409 R. G. Oman, *Symbolism*, pp. 62-63.
410 H. K. Hansen, *Astronomy*, pp. 181-188.
411 M. D. Rhodes, *et al.*, *Astronomy*.
412 *Ibid.*, p. 21. See also the overview of Moses 3, pp. 137, 139.

FIGURE E19-1. *William W. Phelps (1792-1872), Author of "If You Could Hie to Kolob"*
FIGURE E19-2. *Ralph Vaughan Williams (1872-1958), Arranger of "Kingsfold," 1935*

Excursus 19
"If You Could Hie to Kolob"

IF you could hie[413] to Kolob in the twinkling of an eye, And then continue onward with that same speed to fly, Do you think that you could ever, through all eternity, Find out the generation where Gods began to be?[414]

PRESIDENT Boyd K. Packer called the words of this LDS hymn "a great, great revelation that came from William W. Phelps,"[415] and Elder B. H. Roberts praised it as being one of the "strong, stalwart" songs that ought to be preferred to the "namby, pamby, childish hymns that sometimes find their way into [our] repertoire."[416] Noting the expansiveness of the unique LDS cosmological and theological ideas that it affirms, one musician wryly observed that "[u]nlike such ecumenically inspiring hymns as *Come, Come Ye Saints*,[417] this is not a hymn that will likely be adopted by other Christian hymnbooks!"[418]

The verses not only express the core tenets of what Elder Roberts called "Eternalism,"[419] but, in the view of Elder Harold B. Lee, also raise "a profound question" for those "who would seek to penetrate that curtain of revealed truth."[420] Recalling the perennial hubris of humanity, cosmologist Edward R. Harrison cautioned: "The history of cosmology [and science

413   "Hie" means "to hasten" (D. Harper, *Dictionary*).
414   *Hymns (1985)*, #284.
415   B. K. Packer, *PBS Interview*.
416   B. H. Roberts, *Seventy's Course 1 (1907)*, p. viii. See *Endnote E-69*, p. 721.
417   *Hymns (1985)*, #30.
418   *Return to Nauvoo*. See *Endnote E-70*, p. 721.
419   B. H. Roberts, *Comprehensive History*, 2:387-388.
420   H. B. Lee, *Know*, p. 104.

generally] shows us that in every age devout people believe that they have at last discovered the true nature of the Universe, whereas in each case they have devised a world picture—merely a universe—that is like a mask fitted on the face of the still unknown Universe."[421]

Or see the grand beginning, Where space did not extend? Or view the last creation, Where Gods and matter end? Methinks the Spirit whispers, "No man has found 'pure space,' Nor seen the outside curtains, Where nothing has a place."

Kolob, the place mentioned in the first stanza of the hymn, is described as the "first creation," a great star that Abraham learned was "nigh unto the throne of God." Strictly speaking, however, it is not the "celestial, or residence of God" itself[422]—as mortals, we live exclusively in time, whereas God's permanent "residence" is in eternity.[423]

Phelps' question is rhetorical, asserting that no amount of searching, even in Kolob or beyond, will ever reveal an ultimate grand beginning to the process of Creation, for it is eternal—without beginning or end from a human perspective.[424] Emerging cosmological theories likewise argue that a correct view of the origins of space and time as we know them must include not only the "big bang" with which our universe began, but also the comprehensive multiverse where "universes continually pop into existence."[425] Such a multiverse "almost certainly [would have] no beginning," but rather could be "continued indefinitely into the past"[426]—whatever "past" may mean in a context outside of the "time" of the universe to which we belong.[427]

The works of God continue, And worlds and lives abound; Improvement and progression Have one eternal round. There is no end to matter; There is no end to space; There is no end to spirit; There is no end to race.

This stanza speaks to the Mormon doctrine of "eternal progression"—the idea that each of us are enjoined to become partners with God in "bring[ing] to pass the immortality and eternal life of man."[428] The text implies that this "eternal round" of "improvement and progression" will continue forever as we move onward toward the perfection of God, in imitation of Jesus Christ.[429] Even God Himself continues to "progress" through His endless works and ever-expanding glory.[430] President Brigham Young further elaborated: "How many Gods there are, I do not know. But there never was a time when there were not Gods and worlds, and when men were not passing through the same ordeals that we are now passing through. That course has been from all eternity, and it is and will be to all eternity."[431]

Bushman wrote:

> In this cosmology, God does not dominate existence as the conventional Christian God does. He does not make the world out of nothing; He does not make human intelligence; He does not impose His law on His subjects. He invites them to join Him in seeking the fulness of

---

421 E. R. Harrison, *Cosmology*, p. 1, cited in E. R. Paul, *Science*, p. 230; cf. W. E. Evenson, *Science*, pp. cxiii-cxiv.
422 See Abraham 3:2-10; Abraham, Facsimile 2, Figure 1; *Commentary* 1:6-g, p. 48; *Excursus 7: Time and Eternity*, p. 537; *Excursus 18: Kolob*, p. 565.
423 N. A. Maxwell, *Things*, p. 29.
424 See D&C 29:33.
425 H. R. Johnson, *Big Bang*, pp. 202-203. See also K. D. Hagen, *Multiverse*; M. E. McDonald, *Cosmology*; cf. D&C 88:37.
426 Cited in H. R. Johnson, *Big Bang*, p. 298.
427 See *Excursus 7: Time and Eternity*, p. 537.
428 Moses 1:39.
429 Matthew 5:48, 3 Nephi 12:48.
430 Moses 1:39.
431 B. Young, *8 October 1859*, p. 333.

FIGURE E19-3. *Generations, 2005.* Valeriano Ugolini, 1948-

SEE COLOR PLATE E19-3.

And Adam knew his wife, and she bare unto him sons and daughters, and they began to multiply and to replenish the earth.[1] Valeriano Ugolini spent his childhood in the tiny village of Montalbo in northern Italy. At the age of eleven, he went to Rome to study to become a Catholic priest. His interest in art was nurtured during his five-year stay at the Seminario Minore in the Vatican, surrounded by masterpieces of religious art. Ugolini was baptized a member of the Church of Jesus Christ of Latter-day Saints in 1971, and immigrated to the United States in 1991.

Ugolini has developed a unique way of conveying scriptural messages through symbolic renderings. His art conveys invisible visions of spiritual worlds that whisper esoteric messages through essential forms and brilliant colors. His careful juxtapositions of recurring symbols represent the relationship between the human and the divine. Ugolini's pieces emerge as "alchemical compositions," distilling eternal truths from deft combinations of "primary pigments such as red, blue and gold."[2]

In Ugolini's words: "*Generations* depicts the endlessness of our ascendancy, beginning with the individual tree in the center, its parents to the left and grandparents to the right. The checkerboard symbolizes the spiritual plane where mankind, experiencing both good and evil, may commune with Deity. At the horizon are preceding generations. Alternatively, if visualized from within the painting itself looking out, one sees the individual facing the unknown, with a myriad of ancestors standing behind him. They form a powerful protective shield around this newest family member who is venturing out into the future. God appears in His glorious golden sky in human form (red), symbolizing His interest and active participation in human events, as if He were one of us. The arch of golden spheres represents ancestors who have been perfected in Christ, and who now dwell with Him and with our Father in Heaven. They are shown in the form of an upside-down arch to represent their closeness to our world."

---

1   Moses 5:2.
2   *Valeriano Ugolini.*

existence which He Himself enjoys. [Joseph] Smith's theology did not simplify the Universe as conventional Christian theology does. Traditionally, God is the all-encompassing being that makes and comprehends everything; the Universe is essentially unitary, a manifestation of a single divine mind. [Joseph] Smith's universe, filled with loads of unorganized matter, all manner of independent intelligences, and millions of earths, is profoundly pluralistic, made up of lots of things. God advances through the realms of unorganized matter, bringing order to this pluralistic universe, but not everything can be reduced to His mind and will.[432]

Though there are many gods in eternity, LDS worship is directed only to the Father and the Son. Recalling the words of the apostle Paul, Joseph Smith explained that while "there are Gods many and Lords many[,]... there is but one God[433]—that is pertaining to us."[434] Moreover, it is important to understand that "the Mormon God is as unified as the trinity of Christian theology. These Gods do not contend with one another like the gods in the pagan pantheon. They have agreed on the same principles and work for the same end. They are one as Christ and the Father are one. God invites humans to join in this grand alliance, much as Christ prayed that His disciples would be one in Him as He is one with the Father."[435]

A potential source of misunderstanding is the word "race" at the end of this stanza, which might be erroneously interpreted as implying that "that the superficial racial divisions of the human race will persist eternally."[436] Orson Scott Card clarified: "['Race'] is a word whose meaning and context have radically changed since [the time of] W. W. Phelps... He meant,

---

432   R. L. Bushman, *Mormonism*, pp. 73-74.
433   See 1 Corinthians 8:5-6.
434   J. Smith, Jr., *Teachings*, 16 June 1844, p. 370.
435   R. L. Bushman, *Mormonism*, p. 74. See John 17:21.
436   O. S. Card, *Sharing.*

by 'race,' the ongoing propagation of an individual's progeny" in eternity—yet another doctrine peculiar to Mormonism.[437]

There is no end to virtue; There is no end to might; There is no end to wisdom; There is no end to light. There is no end to union; There is no end to youth; There is no end to priesthood; There is no end to truth. There is no end to glory; There is no end to love; There is no end to being; There is no death above.[438]

These final stanzas reflect a shift in perspective from the cosmological to the personal. Elder Bruce R. McConkie saw them as teaching "very effectively the endless nature of all good things."[439] In Eternity, every true joy of mortality will be continued, expanded, and intensified, while every source of earthly sorrow will have disappeared forever.

Having received a superior education for his day, early convert William W. Phelps was almost immediately pressed into service as an author, editor, and publisher for the Church, and quickly became an intimate of the Prophet. Later, during the Missouri troubles, however, he became disaffected (1837), was excommunicated (1838),[440] and proffered damaging testimony against the Saints (1839). Notwithstanding all this, he was generously forgiven by the Prophet upon receipt of a letter evidencing his sincere repentance. Joseph Smith's letter of reconciliation closed with the touching words: "Come on, dear brother, since the war is past, / For friends at first, are friends again at last."[441] Phelps was zealous in his faithfulness to the Church for the remainder of his life, writing many hymns—including the heartfelt *Praise to the Man*[442] in honor of the martyred Prophet. The words of *If You Could Hie to Kolob* are inscribed on the modern stone monument that now marks his grave site.

Among the last of Phelps' many hymn texts, the verses appeared in the *Deseret News* in 1856.[443] Historian Lynn Carson argues that the "ideas and language mirror [the] speculative theology and language" of Elder Orson Pratt, and were doubtless inspired by his "astronomical and cosmological writings and lectures of the early 1850s."[444] In the 1889 *Latter Day Saints' Psalmody*,[445] the words were given a musical setting by Joseph Daynes in which he borrowed, note for note, the opening line of a waltz from George Careless' play *Cinderella*.[446] The 1985 *Hymns of the Church* retained the words while newly adopting the more meditative English folk tune that Vaughan Williams called *Kingsfold*, after the name of a town in which he found and recorded the song in one of its variants.

The same year that Phelps died, Ralph[447] Vaughan Williams was born into a family of lawyers and country clergymen on his father's side, and a line of scientists (Darwin[448]) and craftsmen (Wedgwood) on his mother's side.[449] His music can be described as quintessentially English, a genre that he not only reflected but also helped shape and refine.[450]

EXCURSUS

---

437 *Ibid.*
438 See *Endnote E-71*, p. 721.
439 B. R. McConkie, *Mormon Doctrine*, s.v. Endless, p. 225.
440 See *Endnote E-72*, p. 721.
441 J. Smith, Jr., *Teachings*, 22 July 1840, pp. 166, paraphrasing C. Wesley, *Epistle to Whitefield*, p. 3: "Come on, my Whitefield! (Since the strife is past, / And friends at first are friends again at last)." D. Jarratt, *Life*, p. 32, like Joseph Smith, uses "war" in place of "strife." Cf. G. B. Hinckley, *Kindness*, p. 60; B. K. Packer, *Mantle*, pp. 15-16.
442 *Hymns (1985)*, #27.
443 W. W. Phelps, *There Is No End.*
444 Cited in *Return to Nauvoo*. Note, however, that the poem was dedicated to "President Brigham Young."
445 G. Careless, *et al.*, *Psalmody.*
446 M. Hicks, *Music*, p. 123.
447 See *Endnote E-73*, p. 721.
448 See *Endnote E-74*, p. 721.
449 J. E. Lunn, *et al.*, *Pictorial Biography*, p. 1; U. Vaughan Williams, *R.V.W.*, p. 1.
450 See *Endnote E-75*, p. 721.

Vaughan Williams began his personal collection of over 800 English folk songs in 1903.[451] Several were adapted and harmonized for inclusion in *The English Hymnal*, for which he was the primary musical editor.[452] Besides *If You Could Hie to Kolob*, the 1985 LDS hymnbook[453] credits Vaughan Williams as the arranger of *I Saw a Mighty Angel Fly* (#15) and *All Creatures of Our God and King* (#62), and as the composer of *For All the Saints* (#82). Vaughan Williams also composed several longer religious works, including the requiem-like *Dona Nobis Pacem*,[454] a cantata for mixed chorus on the Nativity (*Hodie*), a ballet inspired by William Blake's illustrations for the book of Job, and an opera based on John Bunyan's *The Pilgrim's Progress*. One of his final works, still incomplete at the time of his death, was a set of carol tunes and incidental music for a Christmas play.[455] "Despite the religious subject-matter of many of his works, he was described by his wife Ursula as 'an atheist … [who] later drifted into a cheerful agnosticism.'"[456] Like Thomas Hardy, whose lyrics Vaughan Williams selected for inclusion in his 1954 *Hodie*, he deeply doubted the existence of God, yet sometimes seemed to write as if he were still "hoping it might be so."[457]

Vaughan Williams had first discovered a version of *Kingsfold* in 1893, published as *Dives and Lazarus* in a book entitled *English County Songs*.[458] He later described the event: "I had that sense of recognition —'here's something which I have known all my life—only I didn't know it!'"[459] Indeed the tune, whose form is *AABA*, with subtle naturally-flowing variations on *A*, seems to sing "as if known before the singer knew it."[460] "It has that strain of heroic melancholy and profound peace that is religiose without being religious; it is an evocation of the ancient rhythms of the English countryside and English life, stripped of sentiment and romanticism,"[461] yet capable of echoing Vaughan Williams' personal mysticism. Unquestionably attested by 1639, the tune has been paired with a surprisingly wide range of lyrics—both sacred and secular.[462] Indeed, its popularity led an 1859 editor to observe: "If the reader should meet any half a-dozen men perambulating the streets of London together, and singing, the probabilities are great that they sing to this tune."[463]

In a small ceremony attended by close friends, Vaughan Williams was laid to rest in Westminster Abbey. Kennedy described the scene: "Into the silence of the Abbey came the first notes of the *Five Variants of 'Dives and Lazarus'*[, his moving orchestral arrangement of *Kingsfold*].[464] It was as if Vaughan Williams himself had spoken. The tune which he had loved all his life, which came from the soil of England, ageless and anonymous, which he had used in so many of his own compositions, was the perfect choice to create a mood of remembrance which will haunt those who experienced it to the end of their days."[465]

---

451   R. Vaughan Williams, *Music*, pp. 252-253.
452   P. Dearmer, *et al.*, *Hymnal*. See *Endnote E-76*, p. 721.
453   *Hymns (1985)*.
454   See *Endnote E-77*, p. 721.
455   See *Endnote E-78*, p. 722.
456   Ralph Vaughan Williams, *Vaughan Williams*.
457   T. Hardy, *Oxen*.
458   L. E. Broadwood, *et al.*, *County Songs*.
459   M. Kennedy, *Works*, p. 19; cf. R. Vaughan Williams, *Music*, p. 252; S. Heffer, *Vaughan Williams*, p. 23.
460   P. Westermeyer, *People*, p. 331.
461   S. Heffer, *Vaughan Williams*, pp. 23-24.
462   See *Endnote E-79*, p. 722.
463   W. Chappell, *Ballad*, pp. 747-748, cited in Dives and Lazarus, *Carols*.
464   See *Endnote E-80*, p. 722.
465   M. Kennedy, *Works*, p. 392.

Excursus 20
The Circle and the Square

ALLUSIONS to the symbols of the square and the compass can be found in several places in the Old Testament.[466] The intersection of the circle and square represents the coming together of heaven and earth, in both the sacred geometry of the temple and the soul of the seeker of Wisdom.[467] Lyon notes that, in a personal sense, these symbols "can represent the goal of making spiritual aspirations (the compass) triumph over physical passions (the square), as well as other moral principles."[468] The fully-rendered figures of the circle and the square manifest in their completeness what the tools of the compass and the square symbolize only in anticipation.

In Hindu and Buddhist thought, a similar concept is represented in the mandala. The center of the mandala may be seen as an undimensioned point of origin, the divine "essence" toward which the outer circumferences of the figure grasp.[469] "The shape, with its focus on the circle (referring to the heavens) and the square (referring to the earth), forms the foundation of the traditional view that the cosmic ritual structure brings heaven and earth together. In this place the initiate confronts and achieves union with the divine realm."[470]

In a temple context, these symbols establish the building "as the center, with the world tree at its axis, uniting the three main levels of the universe and sanctifying the four world regions."[471] A succinct list of examples from Nibley evidences the ubiquity of the symbol of the circle and the square in ancient design: "The Roman *quadrata* represents the four corners of the earth, and the center of everything… But it's also the picture of a wheel. The Babylonians combined the two very neatly in their cosmic design. It's the wheel that goes round and round but never moves. For the nomads, it's a *qubba*—a dome; the Latin word is cupola: a cap, cup. It represents the dome of the heavens, and you find it everywhere as the common shape of churches. And the square church accompanies it [e.g., as in the common form of the basilica of the Roman Catholic Church]. The dome, like a *stupa* in India, is mounted over a perfect cube. To the nomads the *qubay*, or domed red leather tent of the chief, is the *qubba*."[472]

The compass and square also can be seen as representing the covenants that bind together the process of Creation, a work initiated by God and continued in partnership with man.[473] French workers' guilds were known as *compagnonnages*, a term derived from Latin roots connoting the sharing of bread (*cum + panis*), but which Agricol Perdiguier also linked to the idea of the "compass." Note the following dictum: "Who was *Compagnon* (= Journeyman) at the beginning? The One who transformed matter with the help of the compass and the square."[474] Consistent with this symbolism, Frye notes:

---

466   E.g., Proverbs 8:27; Job 26:10; Isaiah 28:7, 40:12, 22; Ezekiel 27:1; Amos 7:8.
467   J. M. Lundquist, *Fundamentals*, pp. 666-671; cf. Matthew 6:10. See the discussion of heaven as a circular realm of pure fire in *Excursus 11: The Sacred Circle*, p. 547.
468   M. P. Lyon, *Set Design*, p. 272. See also *Excursus 50: Fu Xi and Nü Gua*, p. 654 and J. E. Seaich, *Ancient Texts 1995*, pp. 992-997.
469   M. G. Rje, *Buddhist*, p. 270.
470   J. M. Lundquist, *Fundamentals*, p. 666.
471   J. M. Lundquist, *Meeting Place*, p. 16.
472   H. W. Nibley, *Circle*, p. 144. See also B. J. Petersen, *Nibley*, p. 359.
473   See the overview of Moses 4, pp. 216-220.
474   J.-C. Peretz, *L'outil*, p. 51. The French reads: *Qui est Compagnon à l'origine? Celui qui transforme la matière à l'aide du compas et de l'équerre.*

An early fourteenth century illustration from the great English *Holkharn Bible* shows Christ in the center circumscribing the visible universe by use of a compass. It is interesting to note that the fourteenth century artist... placed the realm of Satan entirely outside the created Universe, ...indicated by the circle which the Son's compasses inscribe upon space: in the upper segment we see Satan seated upon his throne and honored by the rebel angels or deplored by faithful angels, whereas in the segment beneath we see the flaming jaws of Leviathan which represent Satan's kingdom in Hell. Milton's placing of Hell entirely outside the Universe[475] has often been remarked upon as one of his most brilliant metaphors, as indeed it is, but the way was prepared for it by the visual arts."[476]

In early Christian contexts, the symbols of the square and the circle or compass evince the conceptual tie between altar cloths, temple veils, and sacred clothing. For example, patterns with variants of these symbols appear on portrayals of altar cloths and temple veils in the churches of St. Vitale and St. Apollinare in Classe in Ravenna,[477] and in a strikingly similar depiction of the Tabernacle in the *Pentateuch de Tours*.[478] In his catalogue of textiles from Greco-Roman times found at Egyptian burial grounds, Kendrick notes the prominence of the symbol of the square in various contexts, including clothing, and explicitly links these decorations to the Ravenna mosaics:

An outstanding feature of the decoration of a number of large cloths... is the characteristic border composed of four ornamental right-angles. This ornamentation would be very suitable for floor-coverings; and it is easy to show that it was applied to curtains and hangings; but that it was also used on cloaks is made clear by the decoration of certain mummy-cases, where it is seen on the shoulder. Early altar-coverings, as represented in mosaics and illuminated manuscripts, often had this form of decoration, and it is also to be found quite frequently in reliefs and stone carvings. The resemblance to the Greek letter *gamma* has given to cloths thus ornamented the name of *gammadion, gammadije,* or *gammidae....*

With regard to the form and decoration of the garments, comparisons with representations in mosaics, paintings, and carvings prove conclusively that those worn in Egypt were not peculiar to that country.... The early Christian monuments of the city of Ravenna, as would be naturally expected, provide abundant material for comparison with the Egyptian stuffs....

The two famous mosaics in the church of S. Vitale, representing the Emperor Justinian (d. 565) and his queen Theodora, with attendants, are a very valuable record of the costume and ornaments of the time... The tunics and mantles of the women on the Empress's left have square, star-shaped and circular panels, and some are covered with small diaper patterns...[479] A mosaic in S. Vitale, representing the Sacrifices of Abel and Melchizedek, shows an altar-covering with angular ornaments, and a large eight-pointed star in the middle. Numerous ornamental details of the mosaics at Ravenna also resemble in a remarkable way the more elaborate patterns of the stuffs from Egypt... It should also be remembered that, although none of the Ravenna mosaics are earlier than the fifth century, many of the ornamental details were survivals of patterns used at an earlier date.[480]

In a Hellenistic Jewish context, Goodenough discusses the appearance of *gammadia* at Dura Europos. These symbols were not only depicted in murals of holy figures, but also were found in a cache of white textile fragments discovered at the site that "may well have been the contents of a box where sacred vestments were kept, or they may have been

475   Cf. the concept of "outer darkness" (D&C 101:91, 133:72-73).
476   R. M. Frye, *Paradise*.
477   See *Figures* E20-1 and E20-2, p. 573.
478   See *Figure* E53-3, p. 671.
479   = repeating small patterns, e.g., interlocked diamonds.
480   A. F. Kendrick, *Textiles 1*, pp. 32, 36, 37, 38-39. Thanks to Bryce Haymond for pointing out this reference.

FIGURE E20-1. *Mosaic from the Basilica of St. Vitale, presbytery, left wall, central lunette*, ca. 538-545 CE.
FIGURE E20-2. *Mosaic from the Basilica of St. Apollinare in Classe, apse, right side*, ca. 520 CE. Photos: Val Brinkerhoff.

SEE COLOR PLATES E20-1 AND E20-2.

These beautifully-rendered mosaics from churches in Ravenna, Italy connect the Old Testament stories of the sacrificial offerings of Abel, Melchizedek, and Abraham to the "great and last" sacrifice of Jesus Christ.[1]

Michael P. Lyon describes the mosaic at right as showing "the priest-king Melchizedek in a purple cloak, offering bread and wine at the altar.[2] The white altar cloth is decorated with two sets of *gammadia*,[3] as well as… two interlocked squares in gold. Abel offers his lamb as Abraham gently pushes Isaac forward. The hand of God reaches down to this sacred meeting through red veils adorned with golden *gammadia* on either side. The theme is the great sacrifice of Christ, which brings together the righteous prophets from the past as well as the four corners of the present world, thereby uniting all time and space."[4]

Though the name of Melchizedek is usually associated with the higher or "Holy Priesthood,"[5] of whom Jesus Christ Himself was a "similitude,"[6] there is no contradiction in his officiating in ordinances of sacrifice associated with the Aaronic or Levitical priesthood,[7] in this case, the sacrifice of the Son of God. Relating the symbol of the square to ancient Jewish practice, Welch has noted the *Talmud's* demands "that priests execute their most sacred religious duty, that of sacrifice, by applying the blood of the sacrificial animal to the altar in a *gamma* pattern."[8]

In Roman Catholic tradition, the linen altar cloth, called the *corporal* (Latin *corpus* = body), is said to be modeled after the burial garment of Christ. Thus, both literally at the Redeemer's death and figuratively in the sacrament of the Lord's supper, the cloth was meant "to cover and enfold the Body and Blood of Christ."[9]

The symbol of the interlocked squares shown in these altar cloths has become commonly known in LDS circles as the "seal of Melchizedek," though actually very little can be reliably said about the meaning, derivation, and antiquity of the term.[10] By analogy to the symbolism of the circle and the square, one might speculate that the coming together of the *gammadia* in the symbol of two interlocking squares represents in completion or fulness what the separated *gammadia* signify in anticipation. In His Atonement, represented here by the sacrificial and sacramental altar, Jesus Christ fulfilled the law of Moses.[11]

---

1   Alma 34:10.
2   Genesis 14:18-20.
3   See *Figure E53-3*, p. 671 for a similar example of *gammadia* on an altar cloth and temple veil.
4   In H. W. Nibley, *Vestments*, p. 109. Lyon has confirmed that he was the author of this caption, not Nibley (M. P. Lyon, *8 September 2008*).
5   D&C 107:1-4.
6   Hebrews 7:15.
7   D&C 107:10.
8   J. W. Welch, *Gammadia*, p. 254. Welch cites *Talmud*, Zebahim 53b.
9   H. Thurston, *Corporal*, p. 387.
10   For example, a caption by Lyon in an article by Nibley labels the symbol of the interlocked squares the "seal of Melchizedek." Lyon recalls the term being mentioned a Catholic commentary on symbols that called it that because of the Ravenna mosaics, but qualifies his statement with the assertion that it is a rare term with no contemporary explanations (M. P. Lyon, *8 September 2008*). Recollections of the architect of the San Diego temple, where the symbol was extensively used, attribute the term to Nibley himself (B. Haymond, *Seal of Melchizedek 4*). See *Endnote E-289*, p. 781.
11   3 Nephi 15:2-10.

FIGURE E20-3. *Linen Cloth, ca. 300-400*

This cloth comes from burying grounds in the low sandhills east of "Akmîm, in Upper Egypt, on the right bank of the Nile, 315 miles above Cairo, and 140 miles below Thebes… It was one of the chief seats of the linen manufacture for which Egypt was famous throughout the civilized world." The cloth is very large, measuring 9 ft. 6 in. by 6 ft. 3 in.

Kendrick gives the following description: "Linen cloth, faced with long loops, with woven ornament in smaller purple woolen loops. The border consists of four deep angular bands of simple geometrical ornament; between these, in the middle of each side, is a small panel connected with the cornerbands by narrow stripes, thus forming a continuous border. The panels consist of interlaced ornament forming squares: three are of the same design; the fourth is larger and different. Within each angle is an ornamental circle; there are two designs, those in opposite corners being the same. A large circle of similar character occupies the middle of the cloth. At each end are two parallel stripes of running-wave pattern."[1]

See Plate 19 in Kendrick's volume for another example of a cloth with four *gammadia* at the corners enclosing a large roundel. Plates 3, 4, and 22 include examples of interlocked squares, sometimes with a circle in the interior.

1 A. F. Kendrick, *Textiles 1*, pp. 9, 42.

fetishistic marks, originally on sacred robes, that were preserved after the garments had been outworn."[481] Goodenough points to similar findings on Christian robes, in hellenized Egypt, Palmyra, and on Roman figures of Victory which "so commonly appears as a symbol of immortality."[482] Welch discusses Goodenough's conclusions, and reports similar findings at Masada and elsewhere.[483]

Differences between symbolic markings on the robes of individuals are evident in mosaics depicting processions of saints in the Basilicas of St. Apollinare Nuovo and St. Vitale in Ravenna. It is conceivable that these differences might correspond to gradations in status or authority.[484] Goodenough, following hints from Philo, discussed the possibility of distinctions of this kind linked to initiation rites among mystical Jews.[485] For example, besides the more common *clavi* and *gams*, Goodenough describes an ornament in "the form of a stripe ending in an arrow, which also is represented in the synagogue."[486] Moreover, a photograph by Griggs of well-preserved clothing at an Egyptian burial site showed an "early Christian garment… made of wool [that] was placed next to the body. The garment has a woven rosette over each breast, a hemmed cut on the abdomen, and a rosette above the right knee."[487] Griggs also found that some burials included "one or more robes with linen strips wrapped around the upper half of the body and gathered into a knot on either the left… or, more commonly, on the right shoulder," indicating priestly authority.

481 E. R. Goodenough, *Garments*, p. 225; cf. E. R. Goodenough, *Dura Symbolism*, 9:127-129.
482 E. R. Goodenough, *Dura Symbolism*, 9:163.
483 J. W. Welch, *et al.*, *Gammadia*.
484 Perhaps paralleling this concept in modern times, Brigham Young raised the possibility that a given individual might be limited to receiving an Aaronic Priesthood portion of the temple endowment only (B. Young, *10-13 June 1864*, p. 309; also cited in J. Smith, Jr., *Words*, p. 304, n. 21). See also *Excursus 3: Temple Blessings in the Oath and Covenant of the Priesthood*, p. 519,
485 See *Excursus 53: Comparative Explorations of the Mysteries*, p. 663.
486 E. R. Goodenough, *Dura Symbolism*, 9:127. See also the dress of the last person on the lower row of E. R. Goodenough, *Dura Symbolism*, 11, fig. 339. An arrow, of course, can easily be seen as representing movement leading toward a desired destination. The point of the arrow may also symbolize the compass that points the correct way, aptly complementing the meaning of the square *gammadia*.
487 C. W. Griggs, *Evidences*, p. 227.

Excursus 21
The Power and Premortal Status of Satan

IN his poetic rendition of D&C 76, Joseph Smith wrote that Lucifer had once been "an angel of light, in authority great," and had initially attained a "Godified state."[488] Elder William W. Phelps wrote that, after his rebellion, Satan "lost the glory, the honor, power, and dominion of a god, and the knowledge, Spirit, authority and keys of the priesthood of the Son of God."[489] Patristic writers held a similar view of Satan's former preeminence.[490]

Both the Prophet Joseph Smith and William W. Phelps more specifically stated that Lucifer was "the next heir to Jesus Christ,"[491] and Brigham Young is recorded as saying that Satan was "third in power, prince of the air, [but] had a spirit like Cain."[492] Likewise, a Coptic text asserts that Satan formerly was the supreme archangel,[493] and that Michael assumed the title of "General-in-Chief of all the hosts of the heavens" following Lucifer's rebellion.[494]

Finding the idea that Lucifer was a spirit child of God repugnant, some non-Mormon groups have publicly caricatured and ridiculed this doctrine in the media. For an official statement explaining this belief, see *Answering Questions: Jesus and Satan*. See also *Jesus Christ is the Brother*, where a statement by Lactantius is cited as one example of how this idea was not foreign to the orthodoxy of early Christians.[495]

Now operating on the earth, the Devil retains much power. Summarizing the Prophet's teachings on this topic, Andrus writes:[496]

> In the work of deception, Lucifer is a master artist. His power, Joseph Smith contended, "has been and still is much underrated."[497] He said: "The Devil has great power to deceive; he will transform things as to make one gape at those who are doing the will of God."[498] The Prophet referred to Lucifer as a skillful orator and as a being of great power,[499] who currently manifests a "smooth, sophisticated influence" among men.[500] Exclaimed the latter-day seer: "Think of a spirit who was sufficiently courageous to measure strength with his Father and Elder Brother, defying their authority, and when cast from heaven for his rebellion could have a retinue of one-third of its innumerable hosts follow him."[501] So great is Satan's power that "his influence can only be rebuked by the great Jehovah, who restrains his power only when attempting a greater destruction than was allowed his majesty."[502]

488 J. Smith, Jr. (or W. W. Phelps), *A Vision*, 1 February 1843, stanza 21, p. 82, cited in L. E. Dahl, *Vision*, p. 298.
489 W. W. Phelps, *Answer*, p. 758.
490 G. A. Anderson, *Ezekiel*, pp. 140-141.
491 J. Smith, Jr., 6 April 1843, as reported in E. England, *Laub*, p. 22; W. W. Phelps, *Answer*, p. 758.
492 B. Young, December 1844, as reported in E. England, *Laub*, p. 28; cf. Ephesians 2:2.
493 In one Christian text, Satan makes the following claim: "Michael told me that I would be foremost of all" (M. Herbert, *Irish Apocrypha*, p. 10).
494 E. A. W. Budge, *Rebellion*, pp. 294-295; cf. W. L. Lipscomb, *Creation*, 5, 9, p. 119, G. A. Anderson, *et al.*, *Synopsis*, 47(39):2, p. 86E; W. L. Lipscomb, *Creation*, 5, p. 261; A. Kulik, *Retroverting*, Apocalypse of Abraham 13:14, p. 20. See *Excursus 23: The Roles of Christ, Adam, and Michael*, p. 582.
495 Lactantius, *Institutes*, 2:9. pp. 52–53. For a later example of this concept in Bogomilism, see I. Couliano, *Tree*, p. 201, citing, among others, M. Psellus, *Daemons*, pp. 19-20; Cosmas, *Traité*, 13, p. 77.
496 H. L. Andrus, *God*, p. 284.
497 As related by John Bernhisel in R. C. Gemmell, *Early*, pp. 8-11; cf. W. F. Anderson, *Bernhisel*, p. 3. See *Endnote E-81*, p. 723.
498 J. Smith, Jr., *Documentary History*, 28 April 1842, 4:605; J. Smith, Jr., *Teachings*, 28 April 1842, p. 227.
499 J. Smith, Jr., *Teachings*, 2 July 1839, p. 162; J. Smith, Jr., *Documentary History*, 2 July 1839, 3:392; cf. Jacob 7:4.
500 J. Smith, Jr., *Teachings*, 2 January 1843, p. 270; J. Smith, Jr., *Documentary History*, 2 January 1843, 5:218.
501 As related in R. C. Gemmell, *Early*, pp. 8-11; cf. W. F. Anderson, *Bernhisel*, pp. 3-4.
502 See R. C. Gemmell, *Early*, pp. 8-11; cf. W. F. Anderson, *Bernhisel*, p. 4.

Bushman describes Satan as a "magnetic figure. He draws followers who become angels to the Devil."[503] In fact, in *Paradise Lost*, the figure of Satan is drawn so compellingly that William Blake became convinced that Milton identified with him. King's analysis of the relevant passages, however, convinced him that Milton knew the distinction between magnificence and manipulation:

> Blake was speaking as a romantic when he said that the Devil is the hero of *Paradise Lost*. Milton knew exactly what he was doing with the Devil's speeches. If we analyze *Paradise Lost* with care, we will find that the Devil's speeches are all political speeches, carefully made, carefully crafted, but entirely devoid of feeling because they are intended to manipulate the other devils, humanity, and the Devil himself. (One of the worst things that rhetoricians do is to manipulate themselves.) The Devil's speeches are clever, but they are devilish, they are not magnificent.[504]

Charles Williams similarly concluded by observing that Milton's critics missed the point "that Satan [was] supposed to be Satan, and therefore a tempter."[505]

---

503   R. L. Bushman, *Rough Stone*, p. 457.
504   A. H. King, *Anglo-Saxon*, p. 170.
505   Cited in W. Hooper, *Lewis Companion*, p. 461. See *Endnote E-82*, p. 723.

Excursus 22
The Nature of Satan's Premortal Proposal

Because relatively few details about the "war in heaven"[506] have been revealed, it is not surprising that Mormons have gradually filled in certain particulars of the story as best they can on their own. In doing so, a set of basic assumptions about Satan's premortal plans and doings have become widely accepted. In this Excursus, we explore three questions relating to these commonly-held assumptions:[507]

1. What did Satan mean when he proposed to "redeem all mankind"?[508]

2. By what means did Satan seek to "destroy the agency of man"?[509]

3. Why was it essential that premortal spirits be given the opportunity to receive a body?

A close examination of Joseph Smith's statements regarding these issues raises the question as to whether all of the traditional assumptions should continue to be taken for granted.

1. What Did Satan Mean When He Proposed to "Redeem All Mankind"?

Describing the contrast between Lucifer's proposal and the plan of the Father that was advocated by the premortal Jesus Christ, Joseph Smith taught:

> The contention in Heaven was—Jesus said there would be certain souls that would not be saved; and the Devil said he could save them all, and laid his plans before the grand council, who gave their vote in favor of Jesus Christ. So the Devil rose up in rebellion against God, and was cast down, with all who put up their heads for him.[510]

The most common understanding of this statement is that it implies a difference in the consequences of the two plans for mankind in general. In other words, it is assumed that according to the plan advocated by Jesus, only the righteous would be saved, whereas in the Devil's plan, "all generations of man... would be returned into the presence of God."[511] However, if we can trust the accuracy of a retrospective summary of a discourse by the Prophet from the journal of George Laub, the controversy highlighted in this statement more specifically concerned the fate of the "sons of perdition":[512]

> Jesus Christ... stated [that] He could save all those who did not sin against the Holy Ghost and they would obey the code of laws that was given.[513]

Laub's version of the statement emphasizes the limits of the guarantee of salvation promised by Jesus Christ. While, of course, allowing for the possibility of exaltation for the obedient, its burden in context was to lay out the major differences with Satan's proposal. The statement implies that Jesus' Atonement could only provide absolute assurance of a minimal form of

---

506 Revelation 12:6.

507 An expanded discussion of this topic can be found in J. M. Bradshaw, *et al.*, *Satan*.

508 Moses 4:1.

509 Moses 4:3.

510 J. Smith, Jr., *Teachings*, 7 April 1844, p. 357.

511 D. Williams, *Idiot's Guide*, p. 24.

512 D&C 76:32-43.

513 J. Smith, Jr., cited in E. England, *Laub*, discourse apparently given 7 April 1844, p. 22, spelling and punctuation standardized. This statement is consistent with John 6:39-40.

salvation, namely, that every soul, except those who sinned against the Holy Ghost, would be "resurrected to [at least] a telestial glory, escaping the second, i.e., spiritual death."[514]

Satan, on the other hand, was reported in Laub's recollection of the Prophet's statement to have countered with an absurdly unconditional proposal:

> Send me, I can save all, even those who sinned against the Holy Ghost.[515]

Apparently trying to do away with the need for an Atonement, Satan is here portrayed as having "sought… to redeem… all in their sins."[516] It is at the very least questionable whether or not such a "redemption" really would "save" anyone in any sense of the word worth caring about. Be that as it may, however, it is certain that without the empowering Atonement, none could hope to ever attain the degree of righteousness and virtue required for exaltation and a return to the presence of God[517]—for, as President Brigham Young said, "if you undertake to save all, you must save them in unrighteousness and corruption."[518] Following the logic of Laub's account, this option presumably would have been most appealing to those spirits who would stand to benefit most from it; namely, those who had already manifested a proclivity toward the unpardonable sin and, preeminently, Satan himself.

2. By What Means Did Satan Seek to "Destroy the Agency of Man"?

The book of Moses states that Satan "sought to destroy the agency of man."[519] The means by which this would have been accomplished has not been authoritatively explained. However, a common LDS assumption is that, as part of the Devil's premortal proposal, an element of compulsion was required—the idea that Satan advocated "the assertion of raw power to coerce moral sanctity from humanity."[520] For example, in an article in the *Encyclopedia of Mormonism*, Riddle writes:

> Lucifer's plan proposed to "save" all of the Father's children by forcing each to obey the Father's law in all things.[521]

Similarly, Ludlow states that:

> Lucifer… wanted to modify our agency so that there would be no opportunity at all to sin, thus enabling all God's children to return to their celestial existence.[522]

Yet, at least insofar as an analogy can be drawn between this proposal and life on earth today, there are at least two reasons why such a proposal could not have succeeded:[523]

1. *The principle of agency is part of mankind's eternal nature, and continues to operate even in the most coercive situations imaginable.* Elder Dallin H. Oaks draws "the distinction between agency (the power of choice), which is God-given, and freedom, the right to act upon our choices."[524] He argues that "no person or organization can take away our

---

514   B. R. McConkie, *Promised Messiah*, pp. 271-275; cf. D&C 76:43-44, J. F. Smith, *Gospel Doctrine*, June 1918, p. 434; J. Smith, Jr., *Teachings*, 10 March 1844, p. 339; 7 April 1844, p. 358.

515   J. Smith, Jr., apparently 7 April 1844, reported in E. England, *Laub*, p. 22. See *Endnote E-83*, p. 723.

516   O. Pratt, *18 July 1880*, p. 288; cf. S. J. Condie, *Agency*, p. 6, Helaman 5:10-11.

517   See *Endnote E-84*, p. 723.

518   B. Young, *30 October 1870*, p. 282.

519   *Ibid.*

520   J. M. McLachlan, *Modernism Controversy*, p. 62. See *Endnote E-85*, p. 724.

521   C. C. Riddle, *Devils*, p. 379. See *Endnote E-86*, p. 724.

522   V. L. Ludlow, *Principles*, p. 148.

523   See *Endnote E-87*, p. 724.

524   See D&C 101:78.

free agency in mortality"—"what can be taken away or reduced by the conditions of mortality is our freedom."[525] And even if every vestige of freedom to act outwardly in accordance with one's choices were revoked, we would still retain, in the famous words of Frankl, "the last of the human freedoms—to choose one's attitude in any given set of circumstances, to choose one's own way."[526] In this sense, agency can be primarily conceived, in the words of Joseph Smith, as "free independence of mind."[527]

2. *Exaltation cannot be obtained through mere abstinence from sin, nor from the completion of some number of good acts.* About this misperception, C. S. Lewis wrote: "We might think that God wanted simply obedience to a set of rules; whereas He really wants people of a particular sort."[528] Consistent with this view, Elder Oaks has taught that the final judgment does not consist of "just an evaluation of a sum total of good and evil acts—what we have done. It is an acknowledgment of the final effect of our acts and thoughts—what we have *become*. It is not enough for anyone just to go through the motions."[529] Hugh Nibley explains that, for the same reason, even the saving ordinances, as necessary as they are, in and of themselves "are mere forms. They do not exalt us; they merely prepare us to be ready in case we ever become eligible."[530] In short, even if there *were* a way that people could be continually compelled to "do the right things," they could not qualify to enter God's presence without a concomitant transformation of their natures.[531] Such a change, effected throughout the duration of an individual's probation, is predicated on the righteous exercise of agency coupled with the atoning power of Jesus Christ.[532]

In light of these considerations, should the element of compulsion as the central feature of Satan's premortal proposal be assumed without question? Such a plan seems thoroughly unworkable, if not impossible. Could there be some alternative to the traditional view on the nature of Satan's efforts to "destroy the agency of man"?[533]

3. Why Was It Essential That Premortal Spirits Be Given the Opportunity to Receive a Body?

Joseph Smith taught:

> We came to this earth that we might have a body and present it pure before God in the celestial kingdom. The great principle of happiness consists in having a body. The Devil has no body, and herein is his punishment.[534]

In LDS discussions of the purpose of the body in mortality, the necessity of being able "to experience the pleasures and pains of being alive" and to seek "perfection and discipline of the spirit along with training and health of the body"[535] are the kinds of reasons frequently mentioned. However, the teachings of Joseph Smith also included the idea that the clothing

---

525   D. H. Oaks, *Free Agency.*
526   V. Frankl, *Meaning*, p. 86. See *Endnote E-88, p. 724.*
527   J. Smith, Jr., *Teachings*, 22 January 1834, p. 49.
528   C. S. Lewis, *Mere*, 3:2, p. 77. Muggeridge ironically observes that the commandments "are, after all, relatively easy to keep, especially if, as an Anglican bishop once suggested, they are regarded as an examination paper, with eight only to be attempted" (M. Muggeridge, *Jesus*, p. 114).
529   D. H. Oaks, *To Become*, p. 32. See also J. E. Faulconer, *Self-Image.*
530   H. W. Nibley, *Meaning of Temple*, p. 26. See *Endnote E-10, p. 705.*
531   1 Corinthians 13:1-3, Moroni 7:47.
532   Alma 42:15-26.
533   Moses 4:3.
534   J. Smith, Jr., *Teachings*, 5 January 1841, p. 181.
535   K. M. Van de Graaf, *Body*, p. 1080.

of spirits with bodies would provide power[536] and protection for them. As Matthew Brown succinctly summarizes:[537]

> "All beings who have bodies have power over those who have not," said the Prophet Joseph Smith.[538] The "spirits of the eternal world" are as diverse from each other in their dispositions as mortals are on the earth. Some of them are aspiring, ambitious, and even desire to bring other spirits into subjection to them. "As man is liable to [have] enemies [in the spirit world] as well as [on the earth] it is necessary for him to be placed beyond their power in order to be saved. This is done by our taking bodies ([having kept] our first estate) and having the power of the resurrection pass upon us whereby we are enabled to gain the ascendancy over the disembodied spirits."[539] It might be said, therefore, that "the express purpose of God in giving [His spirit children] a tabernacle was to arm [them] against the power of darkness."[540]

Consistent with this view, Nephi taught that if disembodied spirits who had lost their bodies through death did not regain a physical body in the resurrection, the Devil would have all power over them:[541]

> 8 O the wisdom of God, his mercy and grace! For behold, if the flesh should rise no more our spirits must become subject to that angel who fell from before the presence of the Eternal God, and became the devil, to rise no more.

> 9 And our spirits must have become like unto him, and we become devils, angels to a devil, to be shut out from the presence of our God, and to remain with the father of lies, in misery, like unto himself...[542]

The reasons for the importance of a body that Joseph Smith most often emphasized are frequently forgotten in Mormon discussions of the purpose of earth life, yet they seem vital to the LDS understanding of Satan's efforts to undermine God's plan.

In recap, the three issues discussed above bring into question core features of popular Mormon assumptions about Satan's premortal role and objectives. It is difficult to achieve theological precision in these matters, but closer examination of the writings of Joseph Smith and his successors leads to new possibilities. The significance of these possibilities goes beyond their potential value in revealing questionable assumptions about what the Prophet taught about these topics, providing, in addition, a cogent rationale for Satan's actions in the Garden of Eden.

Assuming there is some truth to the analysis above, the Devil's efforts in the Garden of Eden might be seen as furthering his premortal agenda in at least three ways:

1. His original proposal to "save" all mankind "in unrighteousness and corruption"[543] seems to have been briefly put into motion through his efforts to get Adam and Eve to take of the fruit of the Tree of Life immediately after taking of the fruit of the Tree of Knowledge. As Alma explains: "For behold, if Adam had put forth his hand immediately,

---

536 See *Endnote E-89*, p. 725.
537 M. B. Brown, *Plan*, p. 33. See *Endnote 4-15*, p. 303.
538 J. Smith, Jr., *Words*, 5 January 1841, p. 60.
539 *Ibid.*, 21 May 1843, p. 208.
540 *Ibid.*, 19 January 1841, p. 62.
541 The idea that the Fall without the Redemption would have allowed Satan to take the souls (i.e., spirits) of men captive is a "common theme" in the ancient Adam literature (M. E. Stone, *Adamgirk*, p. 110 n. 280).
542 2 Nephi 9:8-9. See also Alma 34:35 regarding the fate of the wicked in the resurrection.
543 B. Young, *30 October 1870*, p. 282.

and partaken of the tree of life, he would have lived forever,[544] according to the word of God, having no space for repentance; yea, and also the word of God would have been void, and the great plan of salvation would have been frustrated."[545] Just as Satan's rejected premortal plan had proposed to provide a limited measure of "salvation" for all by precluding the opportunity for exaltation, so it seems plausible that his unsuccessful scheme in the Garden was intended to impose an inferior form of immortality that would have forestalled the possibility of eternal life.[546]

2. His intent to "destroy the agency of man,"[547] as we have argued above, should not be seen as a doomed effort to compel people to "do right." Rather, it might be more appropriately conceived as an effort to eliminate the possibility of a period of probation whereby individuals could *exercise* their agency. Modern scripture teaches that in preparation for eternal life, mankind must have their days "prolonged" and undergo a "state of probation" on earth while in mortality.[548] Otherwise "the great plan of salvation would be frustrated" because there would be "no probationary time"[549] before the spirits of Adam and Eve would be forever united with an immortal body.[550] Only they "who are of a celestial spirit" can receive a body quickened with celestial glory,[551] thus it is essential that each person be given sufficient opportunity to use their agency to "repent while in the flesh."[552] If Adam and Eve had taken the fruit of the Tree of Life immediately after having eaten from the Tree of Knowledge, they would have been "forever miserable,"[553] having become "immortal in their fallen state."[554]

3. Satan's ultimate objective in tempting Adam and Eve was to thwart the Father's plan that they and His other spirit children could take on mortal bodies and eventually be resurrected in glory. On the one hand, the Devil sought to preclude Adam and Eve from the possibility of providing bodies for children in mortality by cutting short their earthly probation. On the other hand, he planned to have them immediately take of the Tree of Life, which would have prematurely brought their bodies into a state of immortal immutability. Since only those who inherit celestial glory are promised a "continuation of the seeds,"[555] it seems that this would have also prevented them from bearing children in eternity. Not implausibly, there may also have been the idea that a group of disembodied (or unembodied) spirits could be subjected to his power.[556]

---

544   See *Endnote E-90*, p. 725.
545   Alma 42:5; cf. Alma 12:26.
546   R. J. Matthews, *Probationary Nature*, pp. 56-57.
547   Moses 4:3.
548   2 Nephi 2:21.
549   Alma 42:4.
550   See also Alma 12:21-27; D&C 132:19; W. C. Skousen, *First 2,000*, pp. 42-44, 66-68; R. J. Matthews, *Probationary Nature*, pp. 56-57.
551   D&C 88:28.
552   2 Nephi 2:21. See *Endnote E-91*, p. 725.
553   Alma 12:26.
554   W. C. Skousen, *First 2,000*, p. 68.
555   D&C 132:19.
556   2 Nephi 9:8-9.

Excursus 23
The Roles of Christ, Adam, and Michael

THE roles associated with the names of Christ, Adam, and Michael have been a source of confusion in Judaism and Christianity. Central to the controversy has been the story of Satan's refusal to honor the newly-created Adam. Besides the story's appearance in Jewish and Christian sources,[557] it appears in the *Qur'an*[558] and elsewhere in Islamic tradition.[559]

Barker concludes that this incident:

> … must be the context for Deuteronomy 32:43: "*Rejoice with him heavens, bow down to him, sons of God.* Rejoice with his people, nations, *confirm him all you angels of God*, because he will avenge the blood of *his sons*…" This is the longer text as it appears in the Greek Old Testament[560] and the pre-Christian Hebrew text (*4QDeut^q*) found among the Dead Sea Scrolls[561] is almost identical. The italics show what is missing from the shorter form of the text, the Masoretic Hebrew—all reference to heavenly beings, anything to link this to the story of Adam and the angels worshipping him.[562]

Thus, the Old Testament citation given in our version of Hebrews 1:6 says that it was the "angels of God" rather than the "sons of God" who were to bow to him; the Masoretic Text of Deuteronomy 32:43 similarly substitutes "blood of his servants" for "blood of his sons," a change no doubt made for theological reasons.[563]

The original setting of the scripture in Deuteronomy clearly refers to Jehovah rather than to Adam,[564] and its application in Hebrews 1:6 is to show the superiority of the embodied Jehovah, Jesus Christ, to the angels. Bruce concludes that the occasion referred to by the phrase "when he bringeth in the firstbegotten into the world" is "probably neither the incarnation nor the second advent of Christ: it is not so much a question of His being brought into the world as of his being introduced to it as the Son of God, and we may think rather of His exaltation and enthronement as sovereign over the inhabited universe, … including the realm of angels, who accordingly are summoned to acknowledge their Lord."[565] Hence, Hebrews 1:6 should be seen as a Messianic parallel to accounts of Adam's premortal exaltation and enthronement. Note that similar motifs were also developed in accounts of the angels' objections to the exaltation of Moses and of Enoch.[566]

---

557 E.g., G. A. Anderson, *et al.*, *Synopsis*, 16:2, p. 49E; E. A. W. Budge, *Cave*, pp. 55-59; E. A. W. Budge, *Rebellion*; L. Ginzberg, *Legends*, 1:62-64, 5:84-86 n. 35; M. Herbert, *Irish Apocrypha*, pp. 2, 10-11; H. W. Nibley, *Sacred*, p. 557; M.-A. Ouaknin, *et al.*, *Rabbi Éliézer*, 13, pp. 87-88; M. E. Stone, *Fall of Satan*, pp. 44-45; Timothy of Alexandria, *Abbaton*, p. 199.

558 *Qur'an* 2:34, 7:11, 15:30-31, 17:61, 18:50, 20:116, 38:73-74.

559 E.g., N. J. Dawood, *Koran*, p. 13; M. al-Kisa'i, *Tales*, pp. 27-28; al-Tabari, *Creation*, I:54, p. 224; A. al-Tha'labi, *Lives*, p. 45; G. Weil, *Legends*, p. 22. See *Endnote E-92*, p. 725.

560 See L. C. L. Brenton, *Septuagint*, p. 277; C. Dogniez, *et al.*, *Pentateuque*, pp. 850-851.

561 See M. Abegg, Jr., *et al.*, *Scrolls Bible*, p. 193.

562 M. Barker, *Hidden*, p. 24. Nibley cites Jewish sources which "insist that the glorification of Adam was 'a tragic mistake,' in spite of such passages as Psalm 8:6 and Ezekiel 28:12-14, which probably arose from Christian 'deification of man.' It was this Adam of the Jews which appealed to the Christians" (H. W. Nibley, *Sacred*, p. 582).

563 C. Dogniez, *et al.*, *Pentateuque*, p. 844 n. 32:8. See also M. Barker, *Who was Melchizedek* and *Excursus 53: Comparative Explorations of the Mysteries*, p. 663.

564 F. F. Bruce, *Hebrews*, p. 57.

565 *Ibid.*, pp. 57-58.

566 M. E. Stone, *Fall of Satan*, pp. 45, 47, 83-110. See *Endnote E-93*, p. 725.

Later Christian commentators were uncomfortable with traditions recounting the heavenly homage given to Adam in the premortal life, and thus de-emphasized these stories and their implications. Explains Anderson, "By having the entire angelic host venerate Adam at his creation, there is nothing the second Adam [Christ] can do that could go beyond this glorious moment. The angelic veneration which will be due the resurrected Christ is simply a return to what was offered Adam at creation's origin… Like the Rabbis, the Church Fathers were unhappy with such a scenario. Adam was to be the subject of considerable glory but not apart from the revelation of Jesus Christ."[567] Milton's solution in *Paradise Lost* was to substitute Christ for Adam in a similar version of the story, drawing scriptural support from several sources.[568]

In this context, it is perhaps noteworthy that the Hebrew meaning of the name Michael is "Who is like God?" a phrase that brings to mind the account of one among the premortal noble and great ones "that was like unto God" and who proposed making an earth as part of a test of obedience for the spirits of mankind.[569] Note also the title of "one… like unto the Son of Man" which appears in v. 27 in the context of the Lord's choice of one to be "sent" and another spirit—no doubt Lucifer—who was "angry, and kept not his first estate." Both the one who is "like unto God" and the one who is "like unto the Son of Man" are usually taken to refer to the premortal Jesus Christ.[570] On the assumption that the story of the veneration of Adam might be a somewhat distorted elaboration of an authentic record of some actual premortal event, the question arises as to whether the protagonist of the original was Jehovah, the premortal Jesus Christ, rather than Adam.[571] On the other hand, one might instead conjecture that the individual who was "like unto the son of Man" was Michael/Adam who, having been chosen as head of the human race in preference to Lucifer, provoked the latter's rage and jealousy, consistent with the story of the veneration of Adam in rabbinic and early Christian sources. A Coptic text describes how the staff, armor, girdle, crown, and office as "General-in-Chief of all the hosts of the heavens" was taken from Satan and given to Michael following the rebellion.[572] In a related scenario, Lutwin's *Eva und Adam* attributes the following prayer request to Adam: "Give me the joy and the status which he [Lucifer] lost in heaven."[573] An Irish text relates that "Lucifer was jealous of Adam, being certain that it was Adam who would be brought to heaven in place of himself."[574] Alternatively, since similar stories were told in connection with Moses and Enoch,[575] it is also possible that the original event became a recurrent type.

The identity of Michael and Adam have been conflated in the context of other roles that have been attributed to one or another of these two names. For example, in extracanonical sources Michael is often portrayed as one who plays a key role in the Judgment and in leading the dead to the places of their habitation.[576] In other such texts, the same themes are

567   G. A. Anderson, *Fall*.

568   Psalm 2:6-7; Philippians 2:9-10; Colossians 1:16; Hebrews 1:6. See G. A. Anderson, *Fall*; cf. G. A. Anderson, *Perfection*, pp. 30-41.

569   Abraham 3:23-25.

570   R. D. Draper, *et al.*, *Commentary*, pp. 279-280.

571   In one strain of Bogomil thought, Jesus as one of God's two sons (Satan being the other son—either older than Jesus or younger (see Cosmas, *Traité*, 13, p. 77), depending on the account) is specifically "identified with the archangel Michael" (I. Couliano, *Tree*, p. 201).

572   E. A. W. Budge, *Rebellion*, pp. 294-295.

573   M.-B. Halford, *Eva und Adam*, p. 262.

574   M. Herbert, *Irish Apocrypha*, p. 3.

575   M. E. Stone, *Fall of Satan*, pp. 45, 47, 83-110.

576   J. Cabanot, *Thèmes*, p. 24.

associated with Adam. Consistent with this role, Elder Heber C. Kimball reported that the Prophet Joseph Smith had a vision where: "He saw Adam open the gate of the Celestial City and admit the people one by one. He then saw Father Adam conduct them to the throne one by one, when they were crowned Kings and Priests of God."[577] On another occasion, Elder Kimball gave the following summary of the vision:

> He (Joseph) saw until they had accomplished their work, and arrived at the gate of the celestial city; there Father Adam stood and opened the gate to them, and as they entered he embraced them one by one and kissed them. He then led them to the throne of God, and then the Savior embraced each one of them and kissed them, and crowned each one of them in the presence of God. He saw that they all had beautiful heads of hair and all looked alike. The impression of the vision left on Brother Joseph's mind was of so acute a nature, that he never could refrain from weeping while rehearsing it.[578]

Roper,[579] has pointed out that this account parallels a scene in the *Testament of Abraham* where Abraham observes Adam sitting on a throne before the gates of Paradise and Hell:

> "And outside the two gates of that place they saw a man seated on a golden throne. And the appearance of the man was terrifying, like the Master's." According to Abraham, whenever this glorious and enthroned figure saw men and women going through the broad gate he wept, but when he saw many others entering through the strait gate he rejoiced. In this text Abraham asked his angelic guide, "Who is this most wondrous man, who is adorned in such glory?" The angel informs Abraham, "This is the first-formed Adam who is in such glory, and he looks at the world, since everyone has come from him."[580]

Notwithstanding the consonance in roles and identity between Adam and Michael in these references, sometimes they are explicitly portrayed as being two different individuals. For example, although Joseph Smith explicitly taught from at least 1834 onwards that Adam and Michael were one and the same individual,[581] an earlier revelation had described them as distinct characters.[582] Michael and Adam are also explicitly portrayed as separate beings in several ancient sources.[583] Just as there seems to be more than one individual who can fill the roles of Adam[584] or Elias,[585] perhaps it may be possible for two different personalities to rightfully bear the name of "Michael" as a title, each in their own context and setting.

The entire topic warrants additional study by LDS scholars.

---

577   H. C. Kimball, *17 March 1861*, p. 41.
578   O. F. Whitney, *Kimball*, p. 106.
579   M. Roper, *Adam*.
580   See E. P. Sanders, *Testament of Abraham*, 11:1-9, p. 888, Allison explains: "The narrow way, of course, leads to paradise, 'Adam's first dwelling, from which he was exiled after his disobedience. His righteous descendants are allowed to return' to it" (D. C. Allison, *Testament*, 11:10, p. 250; cf. Matthew 7:13-14). See also P. B. Munoa, *Four Powers*, pp. 94-98. See *Endnote E-94*, p. 725.
581   Letter of Oliver Cowdery to John Whitmer, 1 January 1834, cited in H. M. Marquardt, *Revelations*, p. 278.
582   The relevant phrase reads: "I saw Father Adam and Abraham and Michael" (L. W. Cook, *Revelations*, p. 303)— the words "and Michael" have been dropped from the corresponding text of the canonized version of this revelation found in D&C 137:5.
583   E.g., G. A. Anderson, *et al.*, *Synopsis*, Armenian, 12:1-14:3, pp. 15-17; E. A. W. Budge, *Rebellion*.
584   See *Excursus 30: Adam-God Theory and the Heavenly and Earthly Adam*, p. 603.
585   E.g., J. Smith, Jr., *Teachings*, 2 July 1839, p. 159.

Excursus 24
The Watchers

BOTH the identity of the Watchers and the nature of the knowledge they were said to have possessed have been the matter of much speculation. Elements of the story seem so fantastic that the entire account might be easily dismissed were it not for a series of enigmatic links between the pseudepigraphal texts and scripture.

The best-known accounts of the Watchers, outside of brief allusions in scripture, are found in *1 Enoch*[586] and *Jubilees*.[587] Many scholars see *1 Enoch* 6-16, called the *Book of the Watchers*, merely as "the author's explanation of an oppressive political situation that Israel is facing," however Wright persuasively argues that the text is primarily the author's account "of the origin of evil spirits based on his interpretation of Genesis 6:1-4."[588]

The *Animal Apocalypse* in *1 Enoch* 85-88 is written in a code that represents key individuals (and their righteous and wicked descendants) as animals of different colors: Adam is a white bull and Eve a young heifer (85:3); Cain and Abel are black (cf. Moses 7:22) and red ("like blood" (89:9)) calves respectively (85:3-4); Seth is, like Adam, a white bull and his posterity are "white cattle, which were like them," while Adam and Eve's later children are portrayed as black bulls and cows (85:8-9). The stars that then fall from heaven are the Watchers, who began "pasturing among those cattle" while "those large and black cattle," the lascivious posterity of Adam, "exchanged their pens and their pastures and their calves and began to moan one after the other" (86:1-3). Pasturing "in the midst of those calves," the Watchers "became bulls" and, mating with the "cows of the bulls," produced offspring that were "elephants and camels and asses" (86:3-4)—the "particular species may be used as symbols because of the similarities between two sets of Aramaic words… In any case the appearance of a new species suggests the bastardly mixture…, and at least the elephants and camels conjure up an image of grotesqueness."[589] Filled with violence and terror, the beasts "began to gore… and devour one another" until heavenly beings, "with the appearance of white men"—"four came forth from that place and three with them"—"bound all [the great stars] by their hands and their feet, and threw them into an abyss of the earth" (87:1-2, 88:3).[590] Eventually, a white bull is born, a new Adam, and all the unclean creatures as well as the sheep are transformed into white bulls. In other words, Eden is restored.[591]

Though the book of the Watchers is usually dated no earlier than the third century BCE, Wright concludes that "the Watcher tradition (in either oral or written form) [may be] much older."[592] Olson agrees with this latter view, giving two reasons to favor the idea that "the elaboration [of the story in *1 Enoch*] is faithful to the original myth truncated in the Genesis account."[593] Not only, he says, do both texts "draw independently on some of the same ancient Mesopotamian material in their portraits of the patriarch Enoch himself," but also the fact that "the Genesis account is clipped to the point of near incoherence" argues:

EXCURSUS

---

586 *1 Enoch* 6-16, 85-88, 106-107.
587 See citations in the overview of Moses 4, pp. 226-227.
588 A. T. Wright, *Evil Spirits*, p. 9. See also pp. 49, 138-165.
589 G. W. E. Nickelsburg, *1 Enoch*, pp. 373-374 n. 86:1-87:1; cf. M. Barker, *Hidden*, p. 46.
590 G. W. E. Nickelsburg, *1 Enoch*, 87:1-2, 88:3, p. 364; cf. pp. 370-375.
591 *Ibid.*, 90:37-38, p. 402; cf. pp. 406-407 n. 37-38; M. Barker, *Hidden*, p. 46. See *Endnote E-95*, p. 725.
592 A. T. Wright, *Evil Spirits*, p. 28. See A. Y. Reed, *Fallen*, for a history of the reception of this literature in Judaism and Christianity.
593 D. C. Olson, *1 Enoch*, p. 909. See also J. J. Collins, *Sons of God*, p. 260.

... that its readers know the story well enough to be satisfied with a mere allusion, while the Enochic elaboration is by far the oldest 'full' version we have and apparently enjoyed unqualified acceptance for at least three centuries before a rival interpretation of the Genesis passage is even known to have come into existence... We have in Genesis 6:1-4, and elaborated fully in Enoch, the Jewish form of an international myth, perhaps influenced by Greek models at the time of written composition, but not a new creation of the Hellenistic age.[594]

Besides the well-known accounts in *1 Enoch* and *Jubilees,* two later and less-familiar versions of the stories should also be cited. The first account, of Christian origin and found in the Ethiopian *Kebra Nagast,* tells the story of a group of angels who complained about Adam's transgression in the Garden of Eden and boasted that, had they been made flesh and blood, they never would so have done, saying:[595]

"We will not transgress thy commandment... And now try us well, and put us to the test so that Thou mayest know whether we are able to keep Thy word." And when they had vaunted themselves in this manner God, the Lover of men, said unto them, "If now ye go astray so far as this in transgressing My word, the wrong will be upon your own heads... Now Satan hath no power whatsoever, for... he cannot beat, and he cannot drag, and he cannot seize, and he cannot fight; he can only make thoughts to germinate silently in the mind. And him who is caught by the evil mind he prepareth for destruction; and if [a man] hath conquered the evil mind he findeth grace and hath a reward which is everlasting. And to you, according to what ye wish, there shall be upon you the mind of a man and the body of a man. But take good heed to yourselves that ye transgress not My word..." And they were content to leave the height of heaven, and they came down to earth, to the folly of the dancing of the children of Cain with all their work of the artisan,... and to their... loud cries of joy and noisy songs.[596] And their daughters were there, and they enjoyed the orgies without shame... And straightway God was wroth with them, and He bound them in the terror of Sheol until the day of Redemption, as the Apostle saith, "He treated His angels with severity. He spared them not, but made them to dwell in a state of judgment, and they were fettered until the Great Day"...[597] And the daughters of Cain with whom the angels had companied conceived... And when [their children] were grown up and reached man's estate they became giants;[598] and for their sakes and the sakes of sinners the wrath of God became quiet, and He said, "My spirit shall only rest on them for one hundred and twenty years, and I will destroy them with the waters of the Flood."[599]

A similar story appears in midrash:[600]

R. Joseph said: The angels noticed that the Holy One, blessed be He, was perturbed because He had created human beings. Immediately two of the angels, whose names were Shemhazai and 'Azael, stood before the Holy One, blessed be He, and said to Him: "Master of the Universe! Did we not say to You at the time You created Your world, 'do not create human beings,' as Scripture attests: 'what is man that You are mindful of him, etc.?'"[601] The Holy One, blessed be He, answered them: "And the world? What will happen to it?" They said to Him: "We will prove sufficient for it." He said to them: "It is revealed and known to Me that if you were to be in their world, the evil impulse would gain control of you just as it has gained control of human beings, [and] you would be worse than them." They said to Him: "Grant us the power to live with the

594   D. C. Olson, *1 Enoch,* p. 909.
595   E. A. W. Budge, *Kebra,* pp. 186-188. For another late Ethiopic account of the story of the Watchers, see B. Mika'el, *Mysteries,* pp. 26-29.
596   See *Endnote E-96,* p. 726.
597   2 Peter 2:4.
598   See *Endnote E-97,* p. 726.
599   See Genesis 6:2-4.
600   C. Albeck, *Midrash,* translated in J. C. Reeves, *Shemhazai and Azael.* See *Endnote E-99,* p. 726.
601   Psalm 8:5.

created beings, and You will see how we sanctify Your name." The Holy One, blessed be He, said to them: "I have already granted you such power."

Immediately they descended [to earth], and the evil impulse gained control of them. When they beheld the beauty of mortal women, they went astray after them, and were unable to suppress their lust, as Scripture attests: "and the sons of God saw, etc."[602] Shemhazai beheld a maiden whose name was Asterah. He fixed his gaze upon her [and] said to her: "Obey me!" She answered him: "I will not obey you until you teach me the Inexpressible Name,[603] the one which when you pronounce it you ascend to Heaven." He immediately taught her, she pronounced it, and she ascended to Heaven. The Holy One, blessed be He, said: "Since she has kept herself pure from sin, I will make her an example so that she might be remembered in the world." Immediately he fixed her [in the heavens] among the seven stars of the Pleiades. When Shemhazai and Azael saw this, they arose, married women, and engendered children.

Rabbi said: Has it occurred to you that corporeal beings would [not] have been able to come into contact with the angels? Behold, it is written that "his servants are flaming fire"![604] However, this teaches that when the angels fell from their holy stations in heaven, the evil impulse gained control of them as it does of human beings, and their size was made consonant with that of humans, and they were garbed with a mass of dirt, as Scripture says: "My flesh is clothed with worms and clods of dirt etc."[605] R. Zadok said: The *Anaqim* [later descendants of the *Nefilim*[606]] were born from them, those who were insolent and arrogant and who deliberately engaged in robbery, violent behavior, and the shedding of innocent blood, as Scripture attests: "and there we beheld the *Nefilim*, etc.,"[607] and it says: "the *Nefilim* were in the land."[608]

It is taught that Shemhazai fathered two sons whose names were Hayya and Hiyya. They in turn took wives and engendered Sihon and Og. R. Joseph said: At the time that the decision for the coming of the Deluge into the world was reached, the Holy One, blessed be He, dispatched Metatron[609] as a messenger to Shemhazai. He reported to him: "The Holy One, blessed be He, is planning to destroy the world." Shemhazai arose and loudly wept and lamented, and grieved for the world and for his sons, "for each of them would eat one thousand camels, one thousand horses, and one thousand of every kind of cattle [daily]. How now will they survive?"

It is taught that one night [when] Hayya and Hiyya, the sons of Shemhazai, were asleep, they both dreamed dreams. One of them beheld in his dream a large stone spread out over the earth like a table, and the whole of it was chiseled and inscribed with many rows [of characters]. Then an angel descended from heaven with a type of knife in his hand, and scraped and effaced all of those rows [of characters], leaving only one row containing four words. And the other saw in his dream a large and flourishing garden, and that garden was planted with every type of tree and all sorts of delightful [plants], and then angels came bearing hatchets and cut down the trees, leaving only one tree which had three branches. When they awoke from their slumber, they arose in terror and came to their father and recounted the dreams to him. He said to them: "My sons, the Holy One, blessed be He, is planning to bring a Deluge into the world to destroy it, and nothing will be left in it except for one man and his three sons."[610] They immediately [began] crying and weeping, saying: "Then what will become of us? How will our name be remembered?" He said to them: "Do not be anxious or perturbed, for your names will not

---

602   Genesis 6:2.
603   See *Commentary* 3:19-b, p. 177.
604   Psalm 104:4.
605   Job 7:5.
606   Hebrew "giants."
607   Numbers 13:33.
608   Genesis 6:4.
609   I.e., the postmortal Enoch.
610   See *Endnote E-98,* p. 726.

Figure E24-1. *The Primaeval Giants Sunk in the Soil, 1824-1827*
William Blake, 1757-1827

See Color Plate E24-1.

"Go, Michael, bind Shemihazah and the others with him, …bind them… in the valleys of the earth, until the day of their judgment… Then they will be led away to the fiery abyss, and to the torture, and to the prison where they will be confined forever."[1] The conclusion of the story of the rebellion of the Watchers is their terrible binding and imprisonment. Blake's drawing illustrates Canto 31 of Dante's *Divine Comedy.* After seeing what he mistakenly thinks is a ring of towers surrounding a central deep, Dante is told by Virgil about the Giants who are sunk to their waists in a well whose massive drop leads to Cocytus, a great frozen lake of the lowest region of hell. Their defiant rebellion, born of the same envy and pride that ruled the fallen angels who "rained down from heaven" in the beginning,[2] was the more terrible and destructive because of the coupling of their evil will with the brute force of their mighty stature. Now reduced to pale mountainous shapes amidst the chaos, they stand eternally unmoved by the sharp fires of lightning above and the rude blasts of icy storm winds swirling upward from below.

In Enoch's vision, God laments that "among all the workmanship of my hands there has not been so great wickedness as among thy brethren… Satan shall be their father, and misery shall be their doom; and the whole heavens shall weep over them… [T]hese shall perish in the floods; and behold, I will shut them up; a prison have I prepared for them."[3] In addition, Nickelsburg sees a likely connection between the Enochic accounts of the punishment of the Watchers and the account in 1 Peter of the "spirits in prison; Which sometime were disobedient, … while the ark was a preparing."[4] If such is the case, then Peter's writings also imply the hope that God's mercy will be extended even to these mighty fallen ones such that, through eventual repentance and the power of the Atonement, they might eventually "live according to God in the spirit."[5]

---

1   G. W. E. Nickelsburg, *1 Enoch,* 10:11-13, p. 215. See also Job 22:11, 15-16; 2 Peter 2:4; Jude 1:6.
2   D. Alighieri, *Commedia,* Canto 8. See *Commentary* 2:4-c, p. 101.
3   Moses 7:36-38.
4   1 Peter 3:19-20; cf. G. W. E. Nickelsburg, *1 Enoch,* p. 560; J. C. VanderKam, *Enoch,* p. 172. See *Endnote E-100,* p. 726.
5   1 Peter 4:6.

disappear from the created order. Every time that [men] drag or lift stones and logs [for] their needs, they will always shout 'heave!' and 'ho!'" Immediately their anxieties were calmed.

They have said about him; i.e., Shemhazai, that he repented and suspended himself upside-down between heaven and earth because he had no excuse for his behavior before the Holy One, blessed be He, and to this very day he remains suspended between heaven and earth in repentance. Azael however did not repent, and he was appointed chief over all types of coloring agents and cosmetics for women which entice men to sexual immorality, and he still persists in his corruptive activity. Therefore Israel brings offerings and casts one lot for the Lord, so that He might accept atonement for all the sins of Israel, and one lot for Azael, so that he might bear the burden of the sins of Israel.

Though many ancient traditions such as those cited above see the wicked husbands referred to in stories of the Watchers as "fallen angels,"[611] another plausible reading, taking into account clues from the book of Moses and other ancient texts, is that they were ordinary mortals.[612] Such a group would seem to have initially included the "sons of men" (i.e., Cainites and their associates "outside the covenant"[613]) who married the female descendants

---

611   See *Endnote E-101,* p. 726.
612   R. D. Draper, *et al., Commentary,* pp. 161-164.
613   *Ibid.,* p. 163.

in Seth and Noah's line.[614] Later, it is claimed that the "sons of God" (i.e., Sethites, Noachites, and their associates—men of the covenant specifically called "angels" or "watchers" in some ancient sources[615]) also united with the wicked "daughters of Cain"[616]—a practice that was divinely condemned.[617]

In light of these accounts, the possibility that some or all of the wicked husbands mentioned were immortals might be definitely ruled out were it not for a retrospective journal entry summarizing a 13 April 1843 discourse by Joseph Smith:

> Now the history of Josephus,[618] in speaking of angels came down and took themselves wives of the daughters of men, See Genesis 6th chapter, 1-2 verses. These were resurrected bodies, violated the celestial laws.[619]

At face value, the last phrase could be taken as asserting that the angels, possessing resurrected bodies, violated celestial laws in taking wives of the daughters of men.[620]

Perhaps the only way to reconcile the statement attributed to Joseph Smith regarding Josephus' description of the Watchers as resurrected beings with previously-cited evidence of their being mortals is to interpret the Prophet's comment "These were resurrected bodies, violated the celestial laws" as an argument for the falsity of Josephus' description. In other words, the phrase might be conjecturally reconstructed to give a sense something like the following: "Since angels have resurrected bodies, Josephus' account of them taking mortal wives cannot be true, for such a union would have violated celestial laws." Unfortunately, apart from dismissing the statement altogether, that is as far as such speculation on how to harmonize these different ideas can take us.

Regarding the kind of knowledge that the Watchers were said to have possessed, Nibley summarizes accounts that describe their era as being:

> … the time of great intellectual as well as material sophistication…[621] The leaders of the people devoted most of their wealth to all kinds of engineering projects for controlling and tempering nature. But the Lord altered the order of creation, making the sun rise in the west and set in the east, so that all their plans came to naught.[622] The idea of controlling the environment independently of God was not so foolish as it sounds, says the *Zohar*, "for they knew all the arts… and all the ruling chieftains [archons] in charge of the world, and on this knowledge they relied, until at length God disabused them by restoring the earth to its primitive state and covering it with water."[623] Rabbi Isaac reports: "In the days of Enoch even children were acquainted with these mysterious arts [the advanced sciences]. Said R. Yesa: If so, how could they be so blind as not to know that God intended to bring the Flood upon them and destroy them? R. Isaac replied: They did know" but they thought they were smart enough to prevent it. "What they did not know was that God rules the world.… God gave them a respite all the time that the righteous men Jered, Methuselah, and Enoch were alive; but when they departed from the world, God let punishment descend…, 'and they were blotted out from the earth.'"[624]

614   Moses 8:15 and, e.g., M. E. Stone, *Question*, 4, p. 119.
615   E.g., M. E. Stone, *Armenian Apocrypha 1996*, p. 150 n. 4:2; A. S-M. Ri, *Commentaire de la Caverne*, p. 74.
616   See Moses 8:13, 21, and e.g., M. E. Stone, *Question*, 9, p. 121.
617   Moses 8:22. See *Endnote E-102*, p. 727.
618   See F. Josephus, *Antiquities*, 1:3:1, pp. 27-28 and T. W. Franxman, *Genesis*, p. 81.
619   J. Smith, Jr., 13 April 1843, as reported in E. England, *Laub*, p. 25.
620   See *Endnote E-103*, p. 727.
621   See G. W. E. Nickelsburg, *1 Enoch*, 8:1-3, p. 188.
622   See D. C. Matt, *Zohar 1*, Be-reshit 1:56a, pp. 315-316 and n. 1545.
623   *Ibid.*, Be-reshit 1:56b, pp. 318-319.
624   H. W. Nibley, *Enoch*, pp. 184-185. See D. C. Matt, *Zohar 1*, Be-reshit 1:56b, p. 319; Genesis 7:23.

EXCURSUS

Nibley infers that the knowledge of the Watchers also included information about sacred ordinances (or, perhaps, devilish imitations of them[625]) that was not to be divulged to others. For example, an Ethiopian text states that:

> In the days of Cain and his sons, evil and deceitful practices increased. Those who gloried [in their bodies] before Adam are the wicked angels. Having received bodies, they learned a great sin. They therefore openly exposed all the work they had seen in heaven.[626]

Likewise, a Greek fragment of *1 Enoch (Gizeh)* has:

> … the Great Angels returning from earth to report to God that they had found 'Azael teaching all manner of unrighteousness upon the earth, and he has laid bare those mysteries of the age which belong to heaven, which are [now] known and practiced among men; and also Semiazas is with him, he to whom thou gavest authority [over] those who go along with him.[627]

Moreover,

> Clement of Alexandria attributed to Musaeus, the founder of the Greek Mysteries, an account of "how the angels lost their heavenly heritage through the telling of the secret things [*mysteria*] to women," things, Clement observes, "which the other angels keep secret or quietly perform until the coming of the Lord."[628]

Islamic tradition teaches that the most important of these *mysteria*, taught without authorization to a woman who was their accomplice in sin,[629] was knowledge of the "Name of God" by means of which the Watchers were able to "ascend to Heaven."[630] Commenting on such texts, Nibley observes:

> The ordinances are not secret, and yet they are, so to speak, automatically scrambled for those not authorized to have them… This is the classical account of the Watchers, angels who came to call the human race to repentance, but who, being tempted by the daughters of men, fell and gave away the covenants and the knowledge they possessed. This was their undoing, and was always treated as the most monstrous of crimes, divulging the pure ordinances of heaven to people unworthy to receive them, who then proceeded to exercise them in unrighteousness while proclaiming their own righteousness on the grounds of possessing them.[631]

Olson highlights a vivid contrast in methods for the acquisition of knowledge in *1 Enoch*:[632]

> The difference is that the Watchers teach *techniques*,[633] putting the adept in the role of initiator, whereas Enoch's wisdom, including his knowledge of the future, comes by revelation with God as the initiator.[634] Nowhere in the Enochic corpus does Enoch practice any kind of theurgy in order to coax the mysteries of heaven out of the extant cosmos; rather, he is taken, he is shown, and holy angels interpret for him.

For a discussion of the meaning and derivation of the term "Watchers" see Nickelsburg.[635]

---

625   See *Commentary 5:53-a*, p. 398.
626   S. Grébaut, *Computs*, p. 431; cf. B. Mika'el, *Enoch*, pp. 141-142; B. Mika'el, *Mysteries*, pp. 26-27. See also H. W. Nibley, *Enoch*, pp. 182-183; J. J. Collins, *Sons of God*, p. 269; Job 4:18, 15:8, 15; Matthew 24:36-37; 1 Peter 1:12. See *Endnote E-104*, p. 727.
627   H. W. Nibley, *Enoch*, p. 183; cf. R. H. Charles, *Enoch*, 9:6-7, p. 283; G. W. E. Nickelsburg, *1 Enoch*, 9:6-7, p. 202.
628   H. W. Nibley, *Enoch*, p. 184; cf. Clement of Alexandria, *Stromata*, 5:1:10, p. 446.
629   See *Endnote E-105*, p. 727.
630   A. al-Tha'labi, *Lives*, p. 88; cf. C. Albeck, *Midrash*, translated in J. C. Reeves, *Shemhazai and Azael* (see p. 587).
631   H. W. Nibley, *Return*, p. 63; cf. Genesis 6:4-6; *Commentary 5:53-a*, p. 398.
632   D. C. Olson, *1 Enoch*, p. 909.
633   See *Endnote E-106*, p. 727.
634   Cf. Moses 1:2.
635   G. W. E. Nickelsburg, *1 Enoch*, pp. 140-141. See also J. J. Collins, *Sons of God*, pp. 263-264.

Excursus 25
The Tree of Life as the Hidden Throne of God

WESTERMANN discusses at length the curiosity that although two trees are mentioned in Moses 3:9, the main body of the narrative "is concerned with one tree only."[636] He sees Tree of Life as having been attached later to the beginning[637] and the end[638] of the story. An alternate explanation for this anomaly, consistent with other clues in the text,[639] is that although the presence of both trees was, of course, previously known to God (and deliberately disclosed to the reader[640]), the Tree of Life was initially hidden to Adam by the Tree of Knowledge.[641] This is expressed in some rabbinical commentary by the idea that the two trees shared a common trunk, had branches that were intertwined, or that the first tree encircled about or formed a hedge around the second one to shield it from view.[642]

Ephrem the Syrian gives a similar opinion, citing parallels with the division of the animals on Noah's ark and the demarcations on Sinai separating Moses, Aaron, the priests, and the people.[643] He depicts Paradise as a great mountain, with the Tree of Knowledge providing a boundary partway up the slopes: "this Tree acts as a sanctuary curtain [veil] hiding the Holy of Holies which is the Tree of Life higher up."[644] Thus, the story of the Fall, in analogue to the stories of the Tower of Babel and of the Watchers, can be conceived as a violation of boundaries that separated mankind from the dwelling place of Divinity.[645] That a difference in splendor between the two trees paralleled their separate locations is affirmed by a Gnostic text that describes the "color" of the Tree of Life as being "like the sun" and the "glory" of the Tree of Knowledge being "like the moon."[646] Supporting the same concept, an Armenian Christian text asserts that "the Tree of [Knowledge of] Good and Evil is the knowledge of material things"— referring to the kind of knowledge that was made possible when Adam and Eve partook of the fruit—"and that the Tree of Life is the knowledge of divine things, which were not profitable to the simple understanding of Adam"—at least not until after he had successfully passed through the experience of mortality.[647]

The story of Noah's family after the Flood has often been compared to the first chapters of Genesis.[648] Significantly, it also culminates with an unauthorized transgression of sacred boundaries. Note, first, that the ark itself "was designed as a temple"[649]—in this case, a mobile sanctuary like the later Tabernacle that was constructed in the likeness of God's portable pavilion.[650] Immediately after their debarkation, God established his covenant with them,

EXCURSUS

---

636 C. Westermann, *Genesis 1-11*, p. 212.

637 Moses 3:9.

638 Moses 4:28-31.

639 See, e.g., *Commentary* 3:9-h, p. 167, 3:19-b, p. 177, 4:5-b, p. 246, 4:9-a, p. 252, and 4:14-e, p. 260. For a survey on the question of one or two trees, and related textual irregularities, see T. N. D. Mettinger, *Eden*, pp. 5-11.

640 Moses 3:9.

641 G. A. Anderson, *Perfection*, p. 214.

642 R. M. Zlotowitz, *et al.*, *Bereishis*, pp. 96, 101. See *Endnote E-107*, p. 727.

643 Brock in Ephrem the Syrian, *Paradise*, p. 53.

644 *Ibid.*, p. 52. See *Endnote E-108*, p. 728. See also *Figure 4-19*, p. 235.

645 R. S. Hendel, *Demigods*, p. 23. Cf. D. H. Oaks, *Plan*, p. 73, where Adam and Eve's actions are also seen as a transgression of the limits of Eden but, in contrast to Hendel, this transgression is characterized in relationship to the barrier between the Garden and mortal life, as opposed to the Garden and divine life. See *Endnote E-109*, p. 728.

646 H.-G. Bethge, *Origin*, 110:14, 20, p. 179. Compare B. C. Hafen, *Disciple's Journey*.

647 Shelemon, *Book of the Bee*, 15, p. 21. See also J. E. Seaich, *Ancient Texts 1995*, pp. 568-577, 660-661.

648 E.g., H. W. Nibley, *Sacred*, pp. 577-579. See further parallels in W. A. Gage, *Gospel*.

649 C. H. T. Fletcher-Louis, *Glory*, p. 41.

650 See *Endnote 3-57*, p. 210.

Temple	Eden	Ark	Sinai
Holy of Holies	Presence of God Tree of Life (Summit)		The Glorious One
Veil	Tree of Knowledge (Heights)	Noah	Moses
Holy Place	The Righteous (Slopes)	Birds	Aaron and the Priests
Outer Courtyard	Penitent Sinners (Lower Slopes)	Animals	Israelites

FIGURE E25-1. *The Divisions of the Temple Compared to Eden, Noah's Ark, and Mt. Sinai*[651]
Ephrem the Syrian, fl. 363-373

outlining dietary instructions and giving the commandment to "multiply and replenish" the renewed earth, in similitude of what He originally told Adam and Eve.[652] The ever-obedient Noah also imitated the example of the first parents by beginning at once to till the earth.[653] Then comes the scene of a "Fall" and consequent judgment.[654]

Often, the instigator of this "Fall" is wrongfully seen to be Noah who, it is reported, succumbed to the intoxicating influence of wine from his vineyard and retreated to the privacy of his tent.[655] Note, however, that the scriptures omit any hint of wrongdoing by Noah, and instead reserve all condemnation for his son Ham and his grandson Canaan.[656] And what was their sin? If we have understood the situation in Eden correctly, it is a perfect parallel to the transgression of Adam and Eve. Without proper invitation, Ham approached the curtains of his father's lodgings and intrusively looked when he was "uncovered within"—literally, 'in the midst of'[657]—"his tent,"[658] violating Noah's sanctity and exposing what should have been left unseen.[659]

Following the same motif, Ephrem compares the transgression of Adam to that of King Uzziah, who, though not a priest, entered the sanctuary and, as a result, was smitten with leprosy.[660] Ephrem writes that when "Adam snatched the fruit, casting aside the commandment… he beheld that Glory within, shining forth with its rays… Adam made bold to touch and was smitten like Uzziah: the king became leprous,[661] Adam was stripped… both kings fled and hid in the shame of their bodies… [The trees] all blushed at Adam, who was suddenly found naked."[662]

---

651   Ephrem the Syrian, *Paradise*, p. 53. See also A. S.-M. Ri, *Commentaire de la Caverne*, p. 208.
652   Genesis 9:1-77, cf. JST Genesis 9:1-25.
653   Genesis 9:20. See *Endnote E-112*, p. 729.
654   Genesis 9:21-27.
655   See *Endnote E-113*, p. 729.
656   See *Endnote E-114*, p. 730.
657   Cf. Moses 3:9; 4:9, 14. See *Commentary 3:9-h*, p. 167.
658   Genesis 9:21.
659   See *Endnote E-115*, p. 731.
660   2 Chronicles 26:16-21.
661   Barker speculates on a possible connection to the leprosy of Miriam (M. Barker, *Hidden*, pp. 57-61).
662   Ephrem the Syrian, *Paradise*, 3:13-15, pp. 95-96.

Figure E25-2. *Adam and Eve Enthroned in Paradise, 16th-century*

See Color Plate E25-2.

In the midst of Paradise there stood a green silken tent, supported on golden pillars, and in the midst of it there was a throne, on which Adam seated himself with Eve, whereupon the curtains of the tent closed around them of their own accord.[1] An Islamic legend maintains that Adam and Eve reigned, as God's vice-regents, from a throne in Eden. Significantly, its location parallels the central position of the Tree of Life: "The scene takes place in a green and blossoming Garden of Eden, its center accentuated by a single cypress[2] immediately behind the throne on the vertical axis of the composition, probably representing the Tuba tree of paradise."[3] Although the idea of a second co-located tree is not usually mentioned in Islamic tradition,[4] note that the function of the curtains in the written description was, of course, to screen the throne from public sight, just as the Tree of Knowledge veiled the view of the Tree of Life in Ephrem's depiction of Eden. Following the transgression of Adam and Eve, the "throne which had been erected for them in the tent thrust them away and cried, 'Rebels, depart!'" God's judgment then came upon them through "a voice from the tree."[5]

1   G. Weil, *Legends*, pp. 25.
2   See *Endnote E-110*, p. 729.
3   R. Milstein, *Stories and Illustrations*, p. 107.
4   See *Endnote E-111*, p. 729.
5   G. Weil, *Legends*, p. 32. See also R. Milstein, *et al.*, *Stories*.

Sounding a similar theme, a petitioner in the Islamic mystical text, *The Mother of Books*, is warned by God that if someone were to move "the curtain and the veil the slightest bit [to] make the high king visible... their spirit would leave their body."[663] By way of contrast, the Armenian *Descendants of Adam* says that the righteous Enoch refrained from looking at the heavens—which is equated to the fact that he did not eat of the:

> ... tree of meat[664]... And he drew linen over his face, and did not look at the heavens, on account of the sin of Adam. And he said, "When of the servant, there is trouble, the servant does not to look at the crown. And he quickly becomes sweet. And I, on account of the sin of Adam, I dare not look at the heavens, that God may have mercy upon Adam." And God had mercy upon Enoch and transferred him to immortality.[665]

In some respects, the fall of Satan, who said, aspiringly, "I will ascend into heaven... I will be like the most High"[666] and "sought that [God] should give unto him [His] own power,"[667] parallels the Fall of Adam. The fifteenth-century *Adamgirk* text has Satan saying: "I fell, exiled from the heavens, Without fruit,[668] like Eve."[669] Nibley remarks that "dire consequences" may result from transgression of divinely-set bounds: "Pistis Sophia went beyond her 'degree' and, becoming ambitious, 'looked behind the veil' [and] fell from glory."[670]

663   W. Barnstone, *et al.*, *Mother*, p. 672.
664   I.e., the Tree of Knowledge.
665   M. E. Stone, *Descendants*, 14-22, p. 85; in some texts Enoch is seen as having reversed the Fall of Adam (A. A. Orlov, *Enoch-Metatron*, p. 248). For a discussion of a wider redemptive role attributed to Enoch, see A. A. Orlov, *Redeeming Role* and A. A. Orlov, *Polemical Nature*.
666   Isaiah 14:13, 14.
667   Moses 4:3.
668   This phrase only makes sense if the fruit referred to is the fruit from the Tree of Life, now eternally unattainable for the Devil but reserved at a future time of readiness for Adam and Eve.
669   M. E. Stone, *Adamgirk* 3:7:3, p. 65.
670   H. W. Nibley, *Message 2005*, p. 443. See C. Schmidt, *Pistis*, 1:29-30, pp. 83-91; G. R. S. Mead, *Pistis*, 1:29-30, pp.

For those who took the Tree of Life to be a representation within the Holy of Holies, it was natural to see the tree itself as the locus of God's throne:[671] "[T]he Garden, at the center of which stands the throne of glory, is the royal audience room, which only those admitted to the sovereign's presence can enter."[672] Recall the book of Esther, which recounts the law of the Persians that "whosoever… shall come unto the king into the inner court, who is not called, [shall be] put… to death."[673] Properly dressed in her royal apparel as a "true queen"[674] however, Esther is, against all odds, granted safe admission to the presence of the king.[675]

According to Brock, Ephrem's answer for "why God did not from the very first grant to Adam and Eve the higher state he had intended for them… illustrates the very prominent role which he allocates to human free will."[676] In his *Commentary on Genesis*, Ephrem writes:

> God had created the Tree of Life and hidden it from Adam and Eve, first, so that it should not, with its beauty, stir up conflict with them and so double their struggle, and also because it was inappropriate that they should be observant of the commandment of Him who cannot be seen for the sake of a reward that was there before their eyes. Even though God had given them everything else [in the Garden of Eden] out of Grace, He wished to confer on them, out of Justice, the immortal life which is granted through eating of the Tree of Life. He therefore laid down this commandment. Not that it was a large commandment, commensurate with the superlative reward that was in preparation for them; no, He only withheld from them a single tree, just so that they might be subject to a commandment. But He gave them the whole of Paradise, so that they would not feel any compulsion to transgress the law.[677]

How should one regard Eve's decision to eat of the forbidden fruit? In light of the LDS understanding that the Fall was a divinely foreseen and necessary prerequisite for mankind's further progression and their rejection of the generally negative portrayals of Eve in historical Christianity, Mormon exegetes typically emphasize Eve's perspicacity and interpret her role as ultimately constructive. A few, however, have taken this view to an extreme, not only rightfully exonerating her from full accountability for her transgression and honoring her subsequent faithfulness, but in addition arguing that "the traditional interpretation that Eve was somehow tricked is inaccurate."[678] For example, despite clear statements in scripture and temple teachings witnessing that Eve was "beguiled" in her encounter with Satan,[679] Gaskill's otherwise insightful book takes the contrarian view that she took the fruit because "she understood what was right and then chose to do exactly that, not because she was deceived."[680] Moreover, citing Brigham Young, he argues that Satan "told the truth" in Moses 4:10-11, although the context of the statement makes it clear that he was only referring to the Devil's accurate claim that her eyes would be opened, not to his false averral that she could eat and live with impunity.[681] In further defense of Satan's supposed veracity in this matter, Gaskill gives a faulty reading of Moses 4:10, arguing

---

33-36. For a general discussion of such dangers, see J. Dan, *Mysticism*, 1:261-309.

671   Revelation 22:1-3, G. A. Anderson, *et al.*, *Synopsis*, Greek 22:4, p. 62E. See *Endnote E-116*, p. 731.

672   G. B. Eden, *Mystical Architecture*, p. 22; cf. the idea of "the luxuriant sacred tree or grove… as a place of divine habitation" in D. E. Callender, *Adam*, p. 51; cf. pp. 42-54. See also T. Stordalen, *Echoes*, pp. 173, 293, *Commentary* 4:31-c, p. 280. See *Endnote E-117*, p. 731.

673   Esther 4:11.

674   As opposed to her former appearance as a "beauty queen"—see A. Berlin, *Esther*, pp. 51-52.

675   Esther 5:1-2.

676   Ephrem the Syrian, *Paradise*, p. 59.

677   Ephrem the Syrian, *Commentary*, 2:17, p. 209.

678   A. L. Gaskill, *Savior and Serpent*, p. 20; cf. *ibid.*, pp. 19-21, 160; B. Campbell, *Eve*, pp. 70-73.

679   See, e.g., Moses 4:19. See also *Commentary* 4:12-e, p. 256.

680   A. L. Gaskill, *Savior and Serpent*, p. 20.

681   B. Young, *11 August 1872*, p. 126. Gaskill (*Savior and Serpent*, p. 79) similarly quotes Andrus misleadingly out of context to support his argument (H. Andrus, *Doctrinal*, p. 187).

"from the Hebrew" that Satan's meaning was that in "physically dying you will not die (i.e., permanently die)."[682] Again, the argument fails, since the plain meaning of the emphatic Hebrew phrase, traditionally rendered "ye shall not surely die," is beyond dispute.[683] Finally, seeking to explain Eve's unattractive confession that put blame on the serpent, Gaskill argues that, in this case, her statement must be seen as a wholly figurative representation of the attitude of "fallen humanity," it being impossible that Eve herself could have made such a statement.[684] While Mormons are unusually sympathetic to the presence of figurative elements in the story of Adam and Eve and are likewise eager to exonerate and honor "our glorious Mother Eve,"[685] such efforts to cleave the story so that all the desirable aspects of her role are accorded a literal interpretation and any undesirable elements are to be applied figuratively to the rest of us seem implausibly artificial.

For Ephrem, the crucifixion of Christ both "fulfills and abolishes" the terms of the Old Covenant,[686] dismantling the barrier of enmity that had separated mankind from God since the Fall:[687] "Very sad was the Tree of Life / that saw Adam hidden from him. / Into the virgin earth he sank and was buried, / but he arose and shone forth from Golgotha."[688] "In His love there came to us the blessed Tree: the one wood undid the work of the other, the one fruit was annulled by the other, that which brought death by that which is alive."[689] "As the source of immortality, 'the Tree of Life is the symbol of the Son of the Living One,'[690] whose Eucharistic fruit is plucked daily in the Church."[691] In verse, Ephrem expresses gratitude that the sweet fruit forbidden to Adam is available again to the Saints, and that the sword that prevented man's return to the Garden of Eden was "removed by the lance" that pierced Jesus' side as He hung on the cross:[692]

> With the blade of the sword of the cherub
> > was the path to the Tree of Life shut off,
> but to the Peoples has the Lord of that Tree
> > given Himself as food.
>
> Whereas Eden's other trees were provided
> > for that former Adam to eat,
> for us the very Planter of the Garden
> > has become the food for our souls.
>
> Whereas we had left that Garden
> > along with Adam, as he left it behind,
> now that the sword has been removed by the lance,
> > we may return there.

---

682 A. L. Gaskill, *Savior and Serpent*, p. 79. Gaskill cites the footnote in the LDS edition of the Bible at Genesis 3:4a, a Gnostic account (*The Reality of the Rulers*, 90:4-5, as cited in E. Pagels, *Adam*, p. 67), and Irenaeus (*Heresies*, 5:23, p. 551), among others, to support the phrasing of his literal translation. However, the repetition of the Hebrew verb in such grammatical constructions is always understood as intensifying the negation. There is no justification in the Hebrew itself for the subtle twist in meaning Gaskill is attempting to apply to the phrase.

683 See, e.g., B. Bandstra, *Genesis 1-11*, pp. 174-175; U. Cassuto, *Adam to Noah*, pp. 143-144.

684 A. L. Gaskill, *Savior and Serpent*, p. 79. Similarly, regarding Adam's confession, Gaskill writes: "Remember, this is you and me speaking, rather than Adam" (*ibid.*, p. 75).

685 D&C 138:39.

686 K. E. McVey, in Ephrem the Syrian, *Hymns*, p. 297.

687 Ephesians 2:14; Ephrem the Syrian, *Paradise*, p. 63.

688 Ephrem the Syrian, *Virginity*, 16:10, p. 332.

689 *Hymn on Virginity* 8:1, cited in Ephrem the Syrian, *Paradise*, pp. 60-61; cf. Ephrem the Syrian, *Virginity*, 8:1, p. 297.

690 Ephrem the Syrian, *Hymn on the Church* 49:16, cited in Ephrem the Syrian, *Paradise*, p. 61.

691 Ephrem the Syrian, *Paradise*, p. 61.

692 *Commentary on the Diatessaron* 49:9-11, cited in Ephrem the Syrian, *Paradise*, pp. 61-62, also pp. 64-66.

EXCURSUS

Excursus 26
Justification and Sanctification

S MITH and Sjodahl explain that:

> Justification is a judicial act, whereby God declares that the sinner who repents and by faith accepts the sacrifice of the Lamb of God, and who is baptized according to the Word of God, is acquitted and received into His Kingdom… Sanctification is the work of the Holy Spirit by which he who is justified is enabled to keep the Commandments of God and grow in holiness.[693]

Elder Bruce C. Hafen further explains:

> We may become "just" or justified (as when a printer lines up the edges of crooked margins; when all the lines are straight, the printing is "justified") when we demonstrate sufficient repentance to receive the Savior's mercy. The demands of justice are then satisfied. This may be the "justification through the grace of our Lord and Savior Jesus Christ," which "is just and true."[694] Then, as a second stage, we may be "made perfect" or sanctified (in addition to receiving forgiveness of our sins) as a further manifestation of the Savior's mercy: "And we know also, that sanctification through the grace of our Lord and Savior Jesus Christ is just and true, to all those who love and serve God with all their mights, minds, and strength."[695] Sanctification is thus the process by which we become holy following baptism.[696]

Moses 6:59-60 explains these concepts as a process of rebirth: "For by the water ye keep the commandment; by the Spirit ye are justified, and by the blood ye are sanctified."

The blessings of justification and sanctification promised to us when our discipleship begins are realized through lifelong persistence in a process of engagement and reengagement in sincere repentance and faithfulness to covenants—covenants that must be frequently renewed by participation in the ordinances of the Gospel. Because we repeatedly violate our covenants, failing to "retain a remission of [our] sins,"[697] we must be regularly cleansed and recommitted. Only when we are again made "just" can the Spirit dwell with us to continue the ongoing work of sanctification. As Riddle has written:

> … [Human] beings may be saved only by binding themselves to Christ. It is as if our task were to stand straight and tall before Father, but because of the Fall, we are broken and twisted. The Savior is our straight and tall splint. If we bind ourselves to Him, wrap strong covenants around us and Him that progressively draw us up into His form and nature, then we can become righteous as He is and can be saved. But without Him we are nothing.… The New and Everlasting Covenant is our detour whereby our Savior strengthens us until we can tread the narrow way of justice and mercy on our own.[698]

A similar concept is supplied by the imagery of the disciple who takes upon himself the yoke of Christ.[699] This yoke is "not simply imparted by Him, but shared with Him."[700] Eventually, by enduring to the end in covenantal union, we are truly "born again… by the Spirit of God through ordinances."[701]

---

693   H. M. Smith, *et al.*, *Commentary*, p. 104; cf. Helaman 3:35. See *Endnote 5-43*, p. 441.
694   D&C 20:30.
695   D&C 20:31.
696   B. C. Hafen, *Broken*, p. 166; cf. D. A. Bednar, *Clean Hands*.
697   Mosiah 4:12; cf. Mosiah 4:26; Alma 4:14.
698   C. C. Riddle, *New*, pp. 241-242. See *Endnote E-126*, p. 732.
699   Matthew 11:29.
700   W. E. Vine, *et al.*, *Dictionary (1996)*, s. v. yoke, p. 692.
701   J. Smith, Jr., *Teachings*, 2 July 1839, p. 162; cf. D&C 84:19-22. See also D. O. McKay, *Cherished*, pp. 101-102—for

Excursus 27
Diligence, Obedience, and Friendship

IN contrast to Satan's plan for compulsion and domination, the Father's whole "work and glory"[702] is to draw us to Him voluntarily through His love. As Lewis wrote:

> God turns tools into servants, and servants into sons, so that they might at last be reunited to Him in the perfect freedom of love offered from the height of the utter individualities which He has liberated them to be.[703]

The scriptures teach that God is "more intelligent than they all"[704] because of His "diligence and obedience."[705] The coupling of the term "diligence" with "obedience" is significant, suggesting that eternal progression is not a matter of mechanically "following orders," but rather is an active process that requires us to maximize the wise exercise of agency within the bounds prescribed by revelation.

The word "diligence" denotes "careful and persistent work or effort," its meaning closely allied with the Latin *assiduus*, from *assidere* "be engaged in doing."[706] Thus, the implication of the instruction to be diligent is that we are not simply to wait to be explicitly told what to do in a given situation, but rather that we must be "anxiously engaged in a good cause, and do many things of [our] own free will," positively and prayerfully exercising our minds and wills to gain both the increase in sincere desire and the necessary growth in understanding needed to act aright.[707] Thus each person who is given a stewardship in the Church is required both to "learn his duty" as generally outlined in the revelations[708] and also "to act in the office in which he is appointed, *in all diligence*."[709]

To be exalted, men and women must not only be perfectly obedient to the Father in imitation of Jesus, but they must also, like the Christ, and through their firm reliance on Him, progress through their experience to the point that their will conforms to that of the Father because both their desires and their understanding perfectly match His own.[710] To those for whom that day comes, He will be able to say: "Ye are my friends, [since] ye do whatsoever I command you. Henceforth I call you not servants; for the servant knoweth not what his lord doeth; but I [call] you friends; for all things that I have heard of my Father I have made known unto you."[711]

Two different Greek words for "love" are used in John's report of Jesus' words.[712] The first word (*agape*) is the one Jesus characteristically used to teach his disciples to value, serve, and esteem all men; the other (*philoi*) is the commonest Greek word describing a relationship

---

more on the historical context, see H. J. Cannon, *David O. McKay*, p. 108.

702 Moses 1:39.
703 C. S. Lewis, *Screwtape*, 1961 Preface, p. 9; cf. ch. 8, p. 41. See D&C 121:34-46; *Commentary* 4:28-s, p. 276 and 4:28-b, p. 276.
704 Abraham 3:19.
705 D&C 130:19. See *Endnote E-118,* p. 731.
706 *New Oxford American Dictionary.*
707 D&C 58:26-28; cf. 1 Corinthians 14:15, *Commentary* 2:10-b, p. 105.
708 E.g., D&C 107:38-39, 58, 73, 85-87, 89, 91.
709 D&C 107:99.
710 Matthew 6:10, 26:39; John 5:30, 6:38-39, 7:17; 1 Corinthians 13:12; 1 John 3:2-3; D&C 19:18-19. See *Endnote E-119,* p. 731.
711 John 15:14-15.
712 John 15:13-15.

of affection between devoted friends, conveying "the thought of cherishing the Object above all else, of manifesting an affection characterized by constancy, from the motive of the highest veneration."[713] Thus, paralleling the way He earlier called out His special use of the term *shalom*,[714] Jesus is not merely describing the esteem He has for His disciples in a general way, He is rather affirming a special tender relationship of this highest kind that now existed between them.

After His resurrection, when Jesus appears to the twelve at the Sea of Galilee, He takes Peter aside and teaches him something of what it means to be His friend. An alternate reading of John 21:15-17 given by the translators of the *New English Bible* preserves in English the distinction between the two kinds of love in the original Greek text:[715]

> So when they had dined,
>
> Jesus saith to Simon Peter
> > Simon, son of Jonas,[716] lovest thou me more than these?[717]
>
> He saith unto him,
> > Yea, Lord; thou knowest that [I am thy friend].[718]
>
> He saith unto him,
> > Feed my lambs.[719]
>
> He saith to him again the second time,
> > Simon, son of Jonas, lovest thou me?
>
> He saith unto him,
> > Yea, Lord; thou knowest that I [am thy friend].
>
> He saith unto him,
> > Feed my sheep.
>
> He saith to him the third time,
> > Simon, son of Jonas, [art thou my friend?]
>
> Peter was grieved because he said unto him the third time,
> > [Art thou my friend?]
>
> And he said unto him,
> > Lord, thou knowest all things;
> > thou knowest that I [am thy friend].
>
> Jesus saith unto him,
> > Feed my sheep.

In this passage, Peter meets Jesus' question about whether his love for the Lord surpassed the love of the other disciples with a passionate affirmation of his special relationship as a friend of the Lord. When Jesus fails to confirm Peter's assertion of a special status of intimacy and throws doubt the nature of his love a second time, Peter reiterates his claim

---

713   W. E. Vine, *Dictionary*, p. 694. For more on Greco-Roman and Johannine concepts of friendship, see C. R. Koester, *Symbolism*, pp. 267-268, 274-275.

714   John 14:27. See H. N. Ridderbos, *John*, p. 511; A. E. Harvey, *Companion 2004*, p. 359.

715   S. Sandmel, *et al.*, *New English Bible*, p. 137 nn. r, s, t. See *Endnote E-120*, p. 731.

716   See *Endnote E-121*, p. 731.

717   Meaning, "more than the other disciples (H. N. Ridderbos, *John*, p. 665); cf. C. R. Koester, *Symbolism*, pp. 136-137. See *Endnote E-122*, p. 732.

718   See *Endnote E-123*, p. 732.

719   See *Endnote E-124*, p. 732.

of friendship, no doubt more urgently and emphatically. The third time, when Jesus at last directly questions Peter's friendship ("*Art* thou my friend?"), Peter, in grief, makes a final heartfelt appeal: "Lord, thou knowest *all things*; thou *knowest* that I am thy friend."

Each time Jesus replies to Peter's professions of friendship, we hear the echo of the earlier passage in John: "Ye are my friends, if ye do whatsoever I command you."[720] From one who claimed to be His friend, the Lord would not be satisfied with loving words alone, no matter how eloquent and impassioned. Jesus seems to be teaching Peter that being His friend means from henceforth wholly consecrating himself through his actions to his pastoral role over the Church, feeding the flock of God—and eventually demonstrating the completeness of his consecration through martyrdom.[721] The Prophet Joseph Smith has written, "A man filled with the love of God, is not content with blessing his family alone, but ranges through the whole world, anxious to bless the whole human race."[722]

In considering the Lord's use of the term "friend," a caution is in order. Elder M. Russell Ballard has warned us against allowing the intimate terms with which we sometimes refer to Christ (including the theologically accurate but potentially misleading term "elder brother") to delude us into viewing Him as merely a somewhat advanced "spiritual peer."[723] In a similar vein, Martins describes the reverent distance that even Jesus and his chosen Twelve maintained throughout His ministry. He makes it clear that "it is the Lord who initiates the use of the term 'friend'" with His disciples, and this only after they "had dedicated their entire lives and livelihoods to the service of the kingdom."[724]

Thus, it is evident that the sort of "knowledge and intelligence" that qualifies God's children for the "fulness" here described does not come all at once, but rather "grace for grace,"[725] through a lifetime of diligence and obedience.[726] Only the Lord's friends can bear to have "all things that [Jesus Christ has] heard of [His] Father… made known unto [them]."[727]

720   John 15:14; cf. John 14:15.

721   John 21:18-19.

722   J. Smith, Jr., *Teachings*, 19 October 1840, p. 174.

723   M. R. Ballard, *Bridges*, cited in M. H. Martins, *False*.

724   M. H. Martins, *False*; cf. James 2:23; D&C 45:52; 84:63; 88:3; 93:45-46; 94:1; 97:1; 98:1; 103:1; 104:1; 105:26. See *Endnote E-125*, p. 732.

725   D&C 93:12.

726   Cf. B. C. Hafen, *Broken*, pp. 202-204.

727   John 15:15. See H. N. Ridderbos, *John*, pp. 520-521; D. K. Ogden, *et al.*, *Gospels*, p. 574.

EXCURSUS

Excursus 28
Ritual Aprons in Ancient Times

WHILE Adam and Eve made their original fig-leaf apron without authorization from the Lord, it should be noted that a similar article has been used in ritual contexts to represent true power and authority. The authentic apron, unlike the one that Adam and Eve made to cover their nakedness, was to be put on only when authorized for priesthood purposes.

Both Elijah[728] and John the Baptist[729] were noted for their leather girdles or aprons. Israelite temple priests wore an *ephod*, which has not been positively identified, but may also have included a kind of apron. The wearing of sacred aprons also seems to be an element of some New Testament worship.[730] At the Last Supper, Jesus himself "took a towel, and girded himself… and began to wash the disciples' feet, and to wipe them with the towel wherewith he was girded." Brown observes that the word "towel" in this verse "can also be translated as 'servant's apron.'"[731]

Kings in the Middle East were often represented as various sorts of trees,[732] and there is evidence that foliated aprons were used both in Egypt and Mesoamerica. Related symbology can be found at the time of the eighth-century Christian king Charlemagne who wore the image of a sacred tree on his apron.[733] Brown notes that whereas in some contexts the king was associated with the Tree of Life, "ancient Hebrew legends… taught that the Tree of Knowledge of good and evil was a fig tree and it was from this tree's leaves that Adam constructed his apron… [It] is interesting to note that the personified Tree of Life motif can be seen in Alma 32:28-43."[734] The fruit of the fig tree is known for its abundance of seeds, thus an apron of green fig leaves is an appropriate symbol for Adam and Eve's ability to procreate, to "be fruitful and multiply" after the Fall.

The apron or girdle was sometimes used as an article of clothing worn in battle. "The astute reader of the Book of Mormon has no doubt also noticed that in 3 Nephi 4:7, and in other places where the skin girdle is mentioned, the context is that of war. In this regard it is interesting to note that as part of his special war regalia the Maya king girded himself with the world tree apron."[735]

Brown cites an "ancient account of the priestly investiture ceremony [that] says that the apron was symbolic of 'prophetic power.' This connection can be seen in the belief that the *ephod* originated as the apparel of Deity and was worn on the earth by those who represented and spoke in Deity's behalf. The tools that were employed among the Israelites to facilitate this spokesmanship were the Urim and Thummim, which, of course, were attached directly to the apron of the high priest."[736]

---

728 2 Kings 1:8.
729 Matthew 3:4; Mark 1:6.
730 M. B. Brown, *Girded*, pp. 141-143.
731 *Ibid.*, p. 141.
732 Cf. *Commentary* 3:9-g, p. 163.
733 M. B. Brown, *Girded*, p. 137. See *Figure* 4-20, p. 237.
734 *Ibid.*, p. 137.
735 *Ibid.*, p. 137.
736 *Ibid.*, pp. 131-135.

Excursus 29

The Development of Extracanonical Literature on Adam and Eve

LIPSCOMB gives a concise overview of the development of extracanonical literature on Adam and Eve:[737]

The earliest indications of this fascination with the antediluvians are found in Jewish apocryphal works dating from as early as the third pre-Christian century and into the first two centuries of the common era. Such works as the *Book of Jubilees, Pseudo-Philo*, the *Life of Adam and Eve*, and the *Apocalypse of Moses* employed the techniques of midrash to expand the legends of Genesis and to provide new insights about Adam and his earliest descendants… In the midrashic literature of the rabbis, this growth of interest in Adam continues. Adam is commonly described as a man of physical and intellectual perfection, but whose Fall brought untold disaster to humanity. Additional non-biblical details are introduced in works which served primarily homiletical purposes.

While the importance of Adam in Jewish apocryphal and rabbinic works is reflected primarily in the growth of extra-biblical legendary materials, the early Christian community found Adam to be the focal point for theological discussions about Christ. In the New Testament, Paul identified Christ as the last Adam who made possible for mankind the salvation which the first Adam had forfeited through disobedience. These notions of Adam's Fall and his relation to Christ are taken up in the Greek and Latin fathers, where they serve as the point of departure for discussions of original sin and the nature of Christ in the Christological controversies of the first five centuries.

Although these theological emphases were central to the early church's understanding of Adam, it is also to the early and medieval church that we are indebted for the preservation of the earliest midrashic materials about the antediluvians contained in Jewish apocryphal texts. Much of this material is believed to have been written in Hebrew and Aramaic by Jewish communities, but for reasons which are not entirely clear it was abandoned by ongoing rabbinic Judaism. It was the early Christian communities which translated and transmitted these works; thus most of the books of the *Apocrypha* owe their survival to their appearance in the Old Greek collection of Jewish scriptures, which became the official Christian version (Old Testament), and most of the books of the pseudepigrapha have survived only in Christian translations and in Christian forms. The *Life of Adam and Eve*, for example, is frequently thought to be a Jewish work originating in a semitic language in about the first century CE. The work is known to us, however, in Latin, Slavonic, and Greek recensions, and all the surviving manuscripts contain clear signs of Christian editing.[738] The same may be said of *Jubilees*, which was composed in Hebrew but which survives in full only in Ethiopic,[739] and of *Pseudo-Philo*, most likely composed in Hebrew, but surviving in full only in Latin translation.[740]

The early Christians did not act simply as translators and interpolators in preserving Jewish apocryphal traditions about Adam and his progeny. It is also clear that they produced haggadic compositions of their own while drawing heavily on Jewish sources. The *Cave of Treasures*,[741] composed in Syriac perhaps as early as the fourth century and surviving also in Arabic, Ethiopic, and Georgian, claims to contain mysteries which Jesus committed to his disciples and discusses the typological relationship between Adam and Christ at length. But these materials are accompanied by Adam traditions bearing close affinities with much older

EXCURSUS

---

737   W. L. Lipscomb, *Armenian*, pp. 1-6.

738   G. A. Anderson, *et al.*, *Synopsis*.

739   O. S. Wintermute, *Jubilees*.

740   D. J. Harrington, *Pseudo-Philo*.

741   E. A. W. Budge, *Cave*.

Jewish sources. The Ethiopic *Book of Adam and Eve*[742] attempts to survey the course of human history from the first Adam until the coming of the second Adam (Christ) and is Christian throughout, but again draws on traditions known to be of Jewish origin in recounting the earliest history of humanity. Similar *haggadic* materials were preserved in the Armenian and Georgian churches[743] and became widespread in Christian medieval literature.[744] Writing in a different genre and with different purposes, Byzantine Christian historians sought to catalogue the annals of human history beginning from the creation, and drew heavily upon Jewish and earlier Christian texts to reconstruct the history of biblical times.[745] Although most of these Christian Adam books are medieval compositions and do not derive directly from earliest Christianity, their great importance lies in the antiquity of some of the traditions they contain, the uniqueness of some of their larger contribution to the development and understanding of Adam materials and of medieval Christianity.

Ri gives a useful summary of parallels and divergences between traditions in the *Life of Adam and Eve* vs. the *Cave of Treasures*.[746] See the *Annotated Bibliography* for descriptions of Zoroastrian, Mandaean, Manichaean, and Islamic sources relating to the life of Adam and Eve.

---

742 S. C. Malan, *Adam and Eve*.
743 W. L. Lipscomb, *Armenian*; M. E. Stone, *Armenian Apocrypha* 1996.
744 E.g., E. A. W. Budge, *Kebra*; B. Mika'el, *Book*; Shelemon, *Book of the Bee*.
745 *Byzantine*.
746 A. S.-M. Ri, *Commentaire de la Caverne*, pp. 198-201.

Excursus 30
Adam-God Theory and the Heavenly and Earthly Adam

JOSEPH Fielding McConkie cites several reasons why Adam can be seen as a type of his Heavenly Father: "All men have both Adam and God as their father. Each had a son renowned for righteousness and obedience (Christ and Abel), and each had a son who became Perdition (Lucifer and Cain). Both righteous sons were martyred by the shedding of blood at the hands of one called Perdition."[747]

Munoa cites sources giving support to the idea that Adam and God were not only identical in appearance, but "could be thought to share the same name, even Adam... Lacocque, when discussing how Gnostic speculations about 'Man' were anchored in the 'older Israelite mentality,' quotes *Corpus Hermeticum* 10:25 to illustrate how God could be understood as a man: 'Man on earth is a mortal god; God in the heavens is an immortal man.'"[748]

Kabbalistic teachings concerning *Adam Kadmon*,[749] comparable in some ways to the *Anthropos* of Gnosticism and Manichaeism, and *Adam Kasia* of Mandaeism[750] are summarized by Cazenave:

> *Adam Kadmon* [is the] "primordial man," the archetype of the rest of humanity, and the one to whom we must look to rediscover spiritual truths about our own existence. In a temporal union of opposites, this *Adam Kadmon* is also the *anthropos teleios*, the final man toward whom we aspire, who will restore us to our glory and true condition.[751]

Kent Brown cites Gnostic texts that describe "the nature or quality of the Father: he is called 'the Man,'[752] 'the Man of the Greatness,'[753] and 'the Man of Truth';[754] also 'Man,' 'First Man,' and 'Immortal Man'...[755] Compare the titles 'Man of Holiness' and 'Man of Counsel' in Moses 6:57 and 7:35, the former name having been revealed to Adam, father of Seth."[756]

Several cryptic statements by Brigham Young included references to what later became known as the "Adam-God" doctrine. As Bailey summarized:

> President Brigham Young expressed the idea in 1852 and later years that Adam "is our Father and our God, and the only God with whom we have to do."[757] This remark has led some to conjecture that Brigham Young meant that Adam, who was on earth as our progenitor, was in

---

747   J. F. McConkie, *Symbolism*, p. 147. See Moses 5:24, 32; John 17:12.

748   Cited in P. B. Munoa, *Four Powers*, p. 102. Cf. W. Blake, *Natural Religion*, p. 41; G. B. Hinckley, *Don't Drop*, p. 46; L. Snow, *Teachings 1984*, 15 June 1901, p. 1. See also the comprehensive study of the anthropomorphic conception of God in old rabbinic thought by Marmorstein (A. Marmorstein, *Doctrine*, Vol. 3), Kugel's more recent study (J. L. Kugel, *God of Old*), E. L. Cherbonnier, *Anthropomorphism*, *Commentary* 1:12-c, p. 53, and 2:26-c, p. 113. For additional LDS statements about how God came to be God, see J. Smith, Jr., *Teachings*, 7 April 1844, pp. 345-346; B. Young, *12 June 1860-a*, p. 81; *5 January 1860*, p. 102; *17 June 1866*, p. 249; G. Q. Cannon, *6 January 1884*, p. 26; J. E. Talmage, *6 April 1915*, p. 123; B. R. McConkie, *New Witness*, p. 64.

749   I.e., Primeval Adam.

750   E. S. Drower, *Adam*.

751   M. Cazenave, *Encyclopédie*, p. 7. See also, e.g., E. S. Drower, *Mandaeans*, p. 153; H. Schwartz, *Tree*, pp. 124-126.

752   J. A. Gibbons, *et al.*, *Great Seth*, 52.36, p. 364. In A. Böhlig, *et al.*, *Egyptians*, 3.59.3, p. 215, the same title appears but may refer to Adam.

753   J. A. Gibbons, *et al.*, *Great Seth*, 53.3-5, p. 364.

754   *Ibid.*, 53.17, p. 364;

755   Eugnostos, *Sophia* 103.22-104.9, 105.5, 109.5, 112.7, etc., pp. 230-232, 237, 238.

756   S. K. Brown, *Nag Hammadi*, p. 279 n. 66.

757   B. Young, *9 April 1852*, p. 50.

reality God the Father. However, this interpretation has been officially rejected as incorrect.[758] Later in the same speech Brigham Young clearly stated "that the earth was organized by three distinct characters, namely Elohim, Jehovah, and Michael."[759]

Consistent with some of Brigham Young's teachings about Adam, early leaders of the Church who conjectured that Adam and Eve already had resurrected bodies when they were placed on earth were necessarily also of the opinion that they did not die in the ordinary sense, but rather were taken up directly to heaven. For example, Elder Heber C. Kimball said that: "Adam offered sacrifices and blessed his sons and then left them and went to heaven."[760] Bailey continued:

> Additional information about Brigham Young's feelings on Adam can… be found in a conference speech given October 8, 1854, clarifying somewhat his earlier statement.[761] It is there implied that through a process known as divine investiture, God delegates his power to his children.[762] Adam was the first on earth to receive this authority, which includes all essential keys, titles, and dominions possessed by the Father.[763] Thus, he had conferred upon him all things that were necessary for the accomplishment of his manifold responsibilities, and Adam is a name-title signifying that he is the first man and father of all.[764]

Concerning Brigham Young's use of the name "Adam" for two distinct individuals, we read:[765]

> It is argued that Brigham Young often distinguished between "Father Adam," referring to the God of the Universe, and "Adam" or "our father Adam," referring to Adam, the first mortal man. In many of Brigham Young's controversial discourses, including the alleged "Adam-God" discourse, he attempted to make that distinction that there were two Adams. For example, on 28 December 1845 Brigham Young made an explicit reference to a "more ancient" Adam after whom Michael received the name Adam. "Adam's name was more ancient than he was. It was the name of a man long before him, who enjoyed the Priesthood."[766] On 25 April 1855 Brigham Young spoke of Adam (Michael) as having lived for a long time with another Being whom Brigham Young explicitly calls "father Adam." "Well, you see from this that when you and I have been with and lived with the Lord, we shall know his voice. If father Adam were to come into this house and you were to see him go back and forth, would you know him? No, you would [ever] mistrust it was him unless he revealed himself. But by the time that you have lived with him [father Adam] as long as Adam had before he came here, you will know him and recognize his footsteps, but reading the history will not teach you these things."[767]

Brigham Young did not find it necessary to elaborate beyond his previous statements, saying at one point: "Whether Adam is the personage that we should consider our heavenly Father, or not, is considerable of a mystery to a good many. I do not care of one moment how that is; it is no matter whether we are to consider Him our God, or whether His Father, or His Grandfather, for in either case we are of one species."[768] Observed Nibley: "Brigham Young

---

758   S. W. Kimball, *Liahona*, p. 77.
759   A. A. Bailey, *LDS Adam*, p. 17; B. Young, *9 April 1852*, p. 51.
760   H. C. Kimball, *12 April 1868*, p. 188. Although Brigham Young once taught that Adam and Eve died and were buried (8 October 1854), he eventually adopted the view expressed here (L. John Nuttall, *Journal 2*, 7 February 1877).
761   B. Young, *8 October 1854*, pp. 91ff.
762   See *Commentary* 1:3-a, p. 44.
763   D&C 84:38; cf. 88:107.
764   A. A. Bailey, *LDS Adam*, p. 17.
765   *Adam-God Theory*.
766   W. Clayton, *Chronicle*, 28 December 1845, pp. 238-239.
767   *Brigham Young Addresses*, 25 April 1855.
768   B. Young, *8 February 1857*, p. 217. See also B. Young, *8 March 1857*, p. 271; B. Young, *9 October 1859*, p. 285; B.

recognized that many people were not prepared to understand the mysteries of God and godhood. 'I could tell you much more about this,' he said, speaking of the role of Adam, but checked himself, recognizing that the world would probably misinterpret his teaching.'[769]

Robinson has called the Adam-God doctrine a "classic example of an anomaly in the LDS tradition" that the Church has now "set aside":

> On occasion my colleagues and I at Brigham Young University have tried to figure out what Brigham Young might have actually said and what it might have meant, but the attempts have always failed. The reported statements simply do not compute—we cannot make sense out of them. This is not a matter of believing it or disbelieving it; we simply don't know what "it" is. If Brigham Young were here we could ask him what he actually said and what he meant by it, but he is not here, and even expert students of his thought are left to wonder whether he was misquoted, whether he meant to say one thing and actually said another, whether he was somehow joking with or testing the Saints, or whether some vital element that would make sense out of the reports has been omitted.[770]

Matthew B. Brown interprets Brigham Young's teachings to be a misunderstanding about the nature of ancient Israelite enthronement rites and a misapplication of doctrines connected with exaltation.[771] See Hale[772] for another helpful perspective on Adam-God teachings.

Young, *1 September 1859*, p. 238; B. Young, *8 January 1865*, p. 43; B. Young, *19 August 1866*, p. 268.

769   H. W. Nibley, *BY Teachings*, p. 1610. See B. Young, *9 April 1852*, p. 51.

770   S. E. Robinson, *Are Mormons Christians?*, pp. 19-20.

771   M. B. Brown, *12 August 2009*. See also M. B. Brown, *BY Teachings*.

772   V. Hale, *Adam-God*.

EXCURSUS

Excursus 31
The Hospitality of Abraham

OF Abraham's hospitality, Nibley wrote:[773]

> In the most inhospitable of worlds, Abraham was the most hospitable of men. It was said that charity was asleep in the world, and Abraham awakened it.[774] Even before he went to Canaan, he held continual open house near Haran, to try to counteract the evil practices of the time. Then when he was forced to move, he dug wells and planted trees along his way, leaving blessings for those he would never see.[775] Arriving and settling in Beersheba, he built a garden and grove and put gates on each of the four sides of it as a welcome to strangers from all directions, "so that if a traveler came to Abraham he entered any gate which was in his road, and remained there and ate and drank… for the house of Abraham was always open to the sons of men that passed and repassed, who came daily to eat and drink at the house of Abraham.

In his hospitality, Abraham was always careful to direct the honor and praise of his guests toward God as the source of all blessings:

> Our father Abraham would bring people into his home, give them food and drink, befriend them, and thus attract them, and then convert them and bring them under the wings of the Presence.[776]

> After travelers [whom he made his guests] had eaten and drunk, they stood up to bless him. He said to them: "Was it of mine that you ate? You ate of that which belongs to the [everlasting] God of the world. Thank, praise, and bless Him who spoke and the world came into being."[777]

> But if [the traveler refused to thank God], Abraham would say "Pay what you owe me." When the wayfarer asked, "How much do I owe you?" Abraham would reply, "A jug of wine—so much; a pound of meat—so much; a loaf of bread—so much. Who do you suppose is giving you wine in the wilderness? meat in the wilderness? bread in the wilderness?" The wayfarer, now aware that he must either pay or thank God by saying grace, would say "Blessed be the everlasting God of the world, of whose bounty we have partaken." This is the meaning of the description of Abraham as one who "bestows free bounty and justice"[778]—first bounty, then justice."[779]

The story is told of the visit of an idol worshipper who refused to honor the Lord for the bread he had received. Abraham "grew enraged at the man and rose and drove him away into the desert." Seeing this, God rebuked him, saying: "Consider, one hundred and ninety-eight years, all the time that man has lived, I have borne with him and did not destroy him from the face of the earth. Instead I gave him bread to eat and I clothed him and I did not have him lack for anything… How did you come to… drive him out without permitting him to lodge in your tent even a single night?" At that, Abraham "swiftly brought [the man] back to his tent… and sent him away in peace the next morning."[780]

---

773   H. W. Nibley, *Abraham 2000*, pp. 198-199. See also J. L. Kugel, *Traditions*, pp. 334-336; M. M. Noah, *et al.*, *Jasher*, 22:11-12, p. 44; W. G. Braude, *Midrash on Psalms*, 110:1, p. 205; E. D. Clark, *Blessings*, pp. 199-204.

774   W. G. Braude, *Midrash on Psalms*, 110:1, p. 205.

775   F. I. Andersen, *2 Enoch*, 24:18, p. 103.

776   H. N. Bialik, *et al.*, *Legends*, 15, p. 33. See Genesis 12:5; J. Neusner, *Genesis Rabbah 2*, 39:14, pp. 73-74.

777   H. N. Bialik, *et al.*, *Legends*, 17, p. 34.

778   See Genesis 18:19.

779   H. N. Bialik, *et al.*, *Legends*, 18, p. 34. See J. Neusner, *Genesis Rabbah 2*, 49:4, 43:7, 54:6, pp. 199-200, 120-121, 264-265.

780   M. J. B. bin Gorion, *et al.*, *Mimekor*, 23, 1:63-64.

EXCURSUS

Excursus 32
Freedman's Analysis of the Primary History

FREEDMAN'S analysis of the Primary History is briefly described in the overview of Moses 5, p. 343. He outlined the sequence of violations in the nine books of the "Primary History" as follows, the last commandments following the order specified in the abbreviated Decalogue in Jeremiah 7:9, in preference to the one found in Exodus 20:

- apostasy and idolatry[781]
- blasphemy[782]
- Sabbath observance[783]
- parental respect[784]
- stealing[785]
- murder[786]
- adultery[787]
- false testimony.[788]

The fact that two violations (apostasy and idolatry) are presented in Exodus is explained as a necessary constraint imposed by the source material itself:

> Because the editor is working with existing literary works and not just a collection of bits and pieces, he is naturally limited in the degree and extent to which he can arrange or rearrange, organize and reorganize, or manipulate his material. Hence we can expect certain deviations and adjustments as we go along. For example, the fact that the story of covenant-making and covenant-breaking properly begins with the book of Exodus presents him with something of a problem. Since the Ten Commandments are not yet set forth in Genesis, he cannot make Israel reprehensible for violating them in that book. He therefore must double up the commandments violated in the book of Exodus.[789]

Freedman admits that the theme of the violation of the Ten Commandments should be seen as only one of several organizing principles used by the editor:

> The fact that this particular device or pattern has never been observed before—at least to my knowledge—should caution against supposing that it was the major or central objective of the redactor. It was simply another, if dramatic, way of showing and stressing the central theme of the history of Israel, and illustrating or reflecting the unity of the account comprising the nine books of the Primary History.[790]

With respect to its relevance for the first chapters of the Bible, he argues that precisely because the links between Genesis and Kings are so far apart historically, they:

> … are especially indicative of the work of the redactor or compiler. Consider, for example, the apparent, if superficial, link between the first stories in Genesis (Adam and Eve, Cain and

---

781 Exodus 20:3-4 vs. Exodus 32:4.
782 Exodus 20:7 vs. Leviticus 24:10-16.
783 Exodus 20:8-10 vs. Numbers 15:32-36.
784 Exodus 20:12 vs. Deuteronomy 21:18-21.
785 Exodus 20:15 vs. Joshua 7:1.
786 Exodus 20:13 vs. Judges 19-21.
787 Exodus 20:14 vs. 2 Samuel 11-12.
788 Exodus 20:19 vs. 1 Kings 21.
789 D. N. Freedman, *Nine 2001*, p. 5.
790 *Ibid.*, p. 11.

Abel), both of which deal with punishment for sin or crime, and the fate of the nation at the end of Kings. In both the Adam and Eve story and the Cain and Abel story,[791] the outcome of disobedience is banishment or exile, precisely the fate of the presumed readers of those stories, who are themselves the subjects of the final chapters of Kings, the exiles in Babylon. Moreover, Babylon itself is the subject of the story of the Tower of Babel,[792] the first narrative after the renewal of life on earth following the Flood. The Tower of Babel story supplies the transition to the account of Abraham's family and the beginning of the patriarchal narrative. So what began in Babylon more than a millennium before ends in the same place for his remote descendants: from Babylon to Babylon provides a neat summary or envelope for the whole of the Primary History. Only a compiler-editor would have achieved explicitly what was only implicit in the separately authored blocks of material.[793]

791   Genesis 1-4.
792   Genesis 11.
793   D. N. Freedman, *Nine 2001*, pp. 2-3.

Excursus 33
The Restoration of Sacrifice

JOSEPH Smith observed that the fact that Adam began to offer sacrifices implied not only that he had received "revelations, commandments, and ordinances" but also that he had received the priesthood "by ordination."[794] Unlike the "rites and variety of ceremonies" performed under the law of Moses, these ordinances were "sacrifices after the order of the Melchizedek Priesthood."[795] These latter sacrifices, along with all "those things which existed prior to Moses' day," will be, along with "every ordinance belonging to the priesthood," "fully restored and attended to" when "the temple of the Lord shall be built and the sons of Levi be purified." Even though "the great sacrifice" of Jesus Christ has already been offered, this restoration of the ordinance of sacrifice is just as "necessary to salvation" as "repentance, baptism, and faith," which also "existed prior to the days of Christ." The offering of sacrifice "will be continued until after the coming of Christ from generation to generation."[796]

Diverse opinions have been offered on the question of whether or not the predicted restoration of this ordinance would require at least a temporary renewal of the practice of *animal* sacrifice at some time in the future. For example, Elder Joseph Fielding Smith wrote:[797]

> Who are the sons of Aaron and Levi today? They are, by virtue of the blessings of the Almighty, those who are ordained by those who hold the authority to officiate in the offices of the priesthood. It is written that those so ordained become the sons of Moses and of Aaron. Also: "And the sons of Moses and of Aaron shall be filled with the glory of the Lord, upon Mount Zion in the Lord's house, whose sons are ye; and also many whom I have called and sent forth to build up my Church."[798] So the Lord has spoken, and this was said to those who held the Melchizedek Priesthood.

> What kind of offering will the sons of Levi make to fulfill the words of Malachi[799] and John[800]? Logically such a sacrifice as they were authorized to make in the days of their former ministry when they were first called. Will such a sacrifice be offered in the temple? Evidently not in any temple as they are constructed for work of salvation and exaltation today. It should be remembered that the great temple, which is yet to be built in the City Zion, will not be one edifice, but twelve.[801] Some of these temples will be for the lesser priesthood.

> When these temples are built, it is very likely that provision will be made for some ceremonies and ordinances which may be performed by the Aaronic Priesthood and a place provided where the sons of Levi may offer their offering in righteousness. This will have to be the case because all things are to be restored. There were ordinances performed in ancient Israel in the Tabernacle when in the wilderness, and after it was established at Shiloh in the land of Canaan, and later in the temple built by Solomon. The Lord has informed us that this was the case and has said that in those edifices ordinances for the people were performed.

---

794   J. Smith, Jr., *Words*, 5 October 1840, p. 40.

795   A. Ehat, *et al.*, in *ibid.*, p. 55 n. 29. See Mosiah 13:27-35.

796   J. Smith, Jr., *Words*, 5 October 1840, pp. 43-44. See also Brigham Young in W. Clayton, *Chronicle*, 2 January 1846, p. 250.

797   J. F. Smith, Jr., *Doctrines*, 11 August 1945, 3:93-94.

798   D&C 84:32.

799   Malachi 3:3.

800   D&C 13:1.

801   See *Endnote E-127*, p. 733.

These temples that we now have, however, the Lord commanded to be built for the purpose of giving to the saints the blessings which belong to their exaltation, blessings which are to prepare those who receive them to "enter into his rest,... which rest is the fulness of his glory,"[802] and these ordinances have to be performed by authority of the Melchizedek Priesthood, which the sons of Levi did not hold.

We are living in the dispensation of the fulness of times into which all things are to be gathered, and all things are to be restored since the beginning.[803] Even this earth is to be restored to the condition which prevailed before Adam's transgression.[804] Now in the nature of things, the law of sacrifice will have to be restored, or all things which were decreed by the Lord would not be restored. It will be necessary, therefore, for the sons of Levi, who offered the blood sacrifices anciently in Israel, to offer such a sacrifice again to round out and complete this ordinance in this dispensation. Sacrifice by the shedding of blood was instituted in the days of Adam and of necessity will have to be restored.

The sacrifice of animals will be done to complete the restoration when the temple spoken of is built; at the beginning of the millennium, or in the restoration, blood sacrifices will be performed long enough to complete the fulness of the restoration in this dispensation. Afterwards sacrifice will be of some other character.

A different point of view is offered by Matthew B. Brown, who observes that Malachi 3:3:[805]

> ... does not say that blood sacrifices would be offered to the Lord... The Hebrew word used to designate the "offering" in this passage is *minchah*, which is commonly used in Old Testament temple texts to designate a "bloodless" sacrifice...[806] [Moreover, the] Lord helped to clarify the meaning of the Prophet's teachings when he revealed on 19 January 1841 that within the walls of the Nauvoo Temple he would restore "the fulness of the priesthood,"[807] and there the latter-day "sons of Levi" would offer sacrifice in the manner of a memorial, meaning in symbolic fashion.[808] On 6 September 1842, shortly after the Nauvoo temple ordinances were first bestowed, Joseph Smith quoted Malachi 3:2-3 and clearly stated that it was the "Latter-day Saints" who were to "offer unto the Lord an offering in righteousness" in the "holy temple."[809] He also indicated that the offering he was referring to was of a bloodless nature.[810]

See also Alma 34:13-14 and 3 Nephi 9:19-20 where it is made clear that after the "great and last sacrifice" of the Savior, there is to be "a stop to the shedding of blood"[811] and that the nature of sacrifice instead would be "a broken heart and a contrite spirit."

---

802   D&C 84:24.
803   See D&C 128:18.
804   Articles of Faith 1:10.
805   M. B. Brown, *Gate*, p. 242. See D&C 128:24.
806   Cf. *The Testament of Levi*, where angel priests offer bloodless sacrifices in the heavenly temple (H. C. Kee, *Testaments*, Levi 3:4-6, p. 789).
807   D&C 124:28.
808   D&C 124:39.
809   D&C 128:24.
810   *Ibid*.
811   For more on the cessation of the practice of animal sacrifice in early Christianity, see M-Z. Petropoulou, *Animal Sacrifice*. See especially pp. 290ff. where the author attempts to answer the question as to why "Jewish Christians in Jerusalem did not immediately stop offering sacrifices in the Temple."

Excursus 34
The Law of Consecration

ALTHOUGH the law of consecration is sometimes described as if it were something to be lived only at some future time, Hugh Nibley argues that it is in the here and now that "everything you have must be set apart to the everlasting benefit of all."[812]

> I don't have to wait for anyone's permission to observe the law of consecration… Everything you consider surplus you can give to the bishop and he will gladly accept it right now.[813] And he'll give it to the poor where it is supposed to be. What's better than that?[814]

Nibley's biographer Boyd Petersen elaborates:

> True, the law of consecration and the United Order are not the same thing. We cannot live the United Order until the Church returns to such planned communities. But we can consecrate all that we have to the Lord. Hugh flung down a personal challenge to every temple-going Saint by asking, "What is there to stop me from observing and keeping the law of consecration at this very day as I have already covenanted and promised to do without reservation?" "The plain fact is," Hugh reminds the Saints, "that I have promised to keep a law, and to keep it now. I know exactly when I am supposed to consecrate, exactly how, exactly why, exactly when, and exactly where." We often assume that external events will motivate the change in our individual practices—that the establishment of Zion will bring about the revival of the Law of Consecration. Hugh stands the equation on its head: It is by living the Law of Consecration that we will establish Zion. "We do not wait until Zion is here to observe [the law of consecration]: it is rather the means of bringing us nearer to Zion"…

Hugh's words seem confirmed by the vision of the General Authorities when they speak of Zion. Elder Marion G. Romney once stated that we would establish Zion only when we start living its laws:

> From the very beginning I felt that the [welfare] program would eventually move into the Law of Consecration and that this is the trial pattern. Until I can pay my tithing and make liberal contributions of my money and labor… I will not be prepared to go into the United Order, which will require me to consecrate everything I have and thereafter give all my surplus for the benefit of the kingdom. I think the United Order will be the last principle of the gospel we will learn to live and that doing so will bring in the millennium.[815]

Of course, the law of consecration concerns more than material means—first and foremost it demands that we consecrate ourselves and our time completely and irrevocably. About the way in which the law of consecration is meant to be lived, Elder Robert D. Hales has said:

> I have learned from Joseph Fielding Smith… about the law of consecration. It is not one particular event; it is a lifetime, day by day, in which we all strive to do our best that we might live honorable lives, that we might live the best we can in the service of others… I will say this: It is not in death or in one event that we give our lives, but in every day as we are asked to do it.[816]

---

812   H. W. Nibley, *Drama*, p. 37:

813   See *Endnote E-128*, p. 733.

814   H. W. Nibley, *Foundation*, from an unpublished transcription of an audio recording by Michael B. James of the speech and Q&A session in the possession of Jeffrey M. Bradshaw, pp. 1, 7.

815   B. J. Petersen, *Nibley*, pp. 393-394. See *Oral interview with Marion G. Romney*, 4 January 1973, LDS Church Archives, cited in Peterson. See also M. G. Romney, *Welfare Services*; S. C. Harper, *Consecration*, pp. 221-226.

816   R. D. Hales, *Agency*, p. 44.

Excursus 35
Lamech's "Sword Song"

HUGH Nibley, who wrote extensively on the subject, saw in Lamech's "sword song" an analogue to the kind of events that once took place as part of widespread annual new-year rites. In a few cultures, these have survived from ancient times up to our own.[817] Nibley points out that Lamech's two wives, Adah and Zillah, would be ideal participants in an antiphonal chorus representing "the competition of the maidens" singing for the king, so much the more because they have been given names that "may respectively mean 'dawn' and 'dusk.'"[818] "There is always the light one and dark one here," as in the stories of Sarah ("a raving [i.e., ravishing] blonde") and Hagar ("a dark Egyptian woman"[819]), Miriam and Zipporah (Miriam was smitten with a whitening leprosy for having mocked the dark Zipporah[820]), and the Song of Solomon ("I am black but comely"[821]):[822]

> Notice each line is a parallelism; he repeats the same thing twice each time. He says, "Hear you [two of them] my voice, oh wives of Lamech."[823] In the second half of the verse, he says, "And give ear to what I say"... "I have sacrificed a man for wounding me"... If we look up these words that are used here for killing and slaying, we will find what they mean. This [*petza*][824] for "wounding me"... doesn't mean wound. It means "to place a cut or mark upon, to put a ritual mark." The other, [*chabburrah*],[825] we are told, is the mark or stroke of a wound on the skin. There's a conflict in which ritual wounds are inflicted. We are told that Satan showed Cain the blows of death...[826] He taught them to him before he could have his showdown with Abel...

> It says, "Since[—not if—]Cain is avenged seven times, Lamech will be avenged seventy times seven." Remember, whoever killed Cain would be avenged sevenfold. Lamech has done the same sort of thing, and he goes out. But it's a ten to one here, seventy times seven. And here is the ritual contest, what the women sing back and forth.... When David and Saul were competing, Saul was murderously envious of David and tried to kill him. When David came back from war, the women divided into two choruses and sang. One would sing, "Saul has slain his thousands. But David has slain his ten thousands" would be replied.[827] It's ten to one preference for David. The same thing is Cain versus Lamech... It was the same thing in Rome. When the emperor came back, the only way he could be recognized was for the girls to divide into antiphonal choruses. The Arval brethren do the same and the Salian brethren. They would say, "A thousand, a thousand, a thousand we have beheaded." (In order to become emperor, you had to have slain 5,000 in the field.)... And among the Celtic people there's Era and Ethna led by the white maid and the red maid... When I went to school in the early days..., we had the Maypole. We went around in opposite directions, the red streamers and the white streamers. We had to choose a king and queen of the May... In a common wall design in Egyptian palaces, you will find the tall Maypole, the red throne and the white throne. You will find the priests going in opposite directions. It's the Troy game that was done with horses. That's what a carousel is. The horses move in opposite directions. But again it was the red and the white...

---

817 H. W. Nibley, *Hierocentric*; H. W. Nibley, *Assembly*, pp. 121-126. See *Commentary* 1:25-e, p. 60, 5:47-a, p. 395, and the overviews of Moses 4 and 6, pp. 221, 458. See *Endnote 4-4*, p. 298. See *Endnote 4-21*, p. 304.

818 N. M. Sarna, *Genesis*, p. 37.

819 Genesis 16.

820 Numbers 12:1, 10.

821 Song of Solomon 1:5.

822 H. W. Nibley, *Teachings of the PGP*, 20, pp. 253-256.

823 Moses 5:47.

824 F. Brown, *et al.*, *Lexicon*, p. 822d.

825 *Ibid.*, p. 289a.

826 See *Commentary* 5:29-b, p. 377; 5:47-b, p. 396; overview of Moses 4, p. 237.

827 See 1 Samuel 18:7.

Now let's look at the account in Moses. What was this all about? Lamech was the candidate. He became Cain's successor. "For Lamech, having entered into a covenant with Satan after the manner of Cain, wherefore he became Master Mahan…"[828] He is now "the big cheese," and Cain is his rival… The common Jewish legend is that Lamech, who was jealous and wanted to become successor to Cain, lay in wait for him… That's the story they made up to explain this garbled thing in which we only have two lines in the whole Old Testament to explain what's going on. But here [in Moses] we get a pretty good picture… And Lamech became "master of that great secret which was administered unto Cain by Satan; and Irad… the son of Enoch, having known their secret, began to reveal it unto the sons of Adam."[829] Ah, somebody's giving the secret away; and, of course, they had sworn by their heads that they wouldn't do that. Since Lamech was the head of the society, it was up to him to see that the proper punishment was administered. "Wherefore Lamech, being angry, slew him [Irad]… not like unto Cain his brother Abel, for the sake of getting gain, but he slew him for the oath's sake [for his ritual obligation]."[830] He had taken it and Irad had taken it, so he had to do this, not to get gain… "And it was among the sons of man, and among the daughters of men these things were not spoken, because that Lamech had spoken [now we come to a very important thing] the secret unto his wives, and they rebelled against him, and declared these things abroad, and had not compassion."[831] This is the [*femme*] *fatale*, namely the woman who gives away the secrets. You know about Pandora, but this goes all the way down the line. This is like Lilith…[832] The wife gives it away, and it becomes a very important pattern… Not only do we have evil coming into the world, we see the forms it takes here.

---

828   Moses 5:49.
829   Moses 5:49.
830   Moses 5:50.
831   Moses 5:53.
832   See *Commentary* 3:23-c, p. 183.

EXCURSUS

Excursus 36
The Legend of the True Cross

THE medieval Legend of the True Cross[833] consists of five scenes from different time periods: 1. The Death of Adam, 2. The Queen of Sheba, 3. Constantine's Dream, 4. The Discovery of the True Cross, and 5. The Battle between Heraclius and Chosroes. Baldwin gives the following background and summary of this elaborate story:[834]

According to legend, the cross came from a branch from the Tree of Knowledge in the Garden of Eden. An angel gave the branch to Seth, the son of Adam, telling him to plant the branch on his father's grave and when the resulting tree bore fruit (i.e. the crucified Christ), Adam would again be made whole.[835] [The dead Tree of the Knowledge of Good and Evil shown [in the center of Piero's depiction] underlines the theme of death as the punishment for sin while hinting at the resurrection and new life which will eventually come through the second tree transplanted by Seth near the grave of Adam, the tree which will become the Tree of Life bearing the fruit of the crucified Christ.[836] The dead tree also suggests the spiritual death of Judaism, contrasted to the Tree of Life, amplifying the conflict between Judaism and Christianity that plays out in this Christian world history.]

The legend continues with King Solomon building the Temple of Jerusalem. His carpenters are struck by a magnificent beam of wood cut from the tree growing over Adam's grave but they are unable to use the wood in building the temple and cast it aside as a bridge over a stream. Arriving on a visit to Solomon, the Queen of Sheba recognizes the importance of the wood and refuses to step on it, telling Solomon the wood will bring the destruction of the Jewish people. He has it buried secretly. Centuries later, a miraculous pond develops at the site of the buried cross and when the wood floats to the surface, the Romans use it to crucify Christ.

The cross then lay forgotten in the earth with the other two crosses used to crucify the two thieves for more than three hundred years until the time of Constantine. On the night of a decisive battle against a rival emperor, Maxentius, Constantine had a dream in which an angel held up a cross and said, "Conquer in the name of this sign." Marching under the banner of the cross, Constantine's forces triumphed the next day. Constantine then went on to proclaim Christianity the official Roman state religion…

Constantine's mother, St. Helena, traveled to Jerusalem to search for the original cross and discovered a local Jew named Judas who knew its secret location. She tortured him until he revealed his secret. Judas dug up the three crosses and tested each one on a dead person, discovering the true cross when it revived the corpse. Judas was converted and went on to become bishop of Jerusalem…. St. Helena… left most of [the cross] there in a new chapel. The rest she brought back to Constantinople. When the Persian army of King Chosroes conquered Jerusalem in the early 7th century, [the king] took the cross as a trophy back to his court. He was later defeated in 629 CE by the Byzantine Emperor, Heraclius, whose army marched under the banner of the Cross like that of Constantine. Heraclius offers Chrosroes a choice of conversion or death. He chooses the latter and is beheaded near his throne. Heraclius recovers the cross and returns it to Jerusalem. Just outside the city gates, Heraclius is stopped by a miraculous collapse of the city gate and an angel who appears, chiding him for his pride and reminding him of the humility of Christ who entered Jerusalem on an ass. Heraclius dismounts, strips off his courtly robes and shoes, and carries the cross into Jerusalem, barefoot…

833 Cf. the related *Golden Legend* and the *Legends of the Holy Rood*. See also J. E. Hanauer, *Folklore*, pp. 39-41.
834 R. W. Baldwin, *Legend*.
835 See the overview of Moses 6, p. 460.
836 Cf. *Figure 6-1*, p. 454. See *Endnote E-129*, p. 733.

FIGURE E36-1. *Elevation of the Cross, 1948*

This preliminary design was created by a Russian iconographer for the Holy Trinity Church in Vanves (Paris). It depicts the festival of the Raising of the Cross, which was instituted in Jerusalem and associated both with the dedication of the basilica of the Resurrection[1] and with the finding of the true Cross.

In the image shown here, "the bishop is seen raising the Cross in the upper part…, while below, St. Helen is shown near a cave at the foot of Golgotha before the three crosses that she has just discovered… The simplest composition shows us the bishop (St. Macarius of Jerusalem) standing on an *ambo*[2] holding a large cross in his two hands: it is the true Cross of the Lord which he is showing to the people. The bishop is supported on either side by subdeacons. Generally, one sees at his side St. Constantine and St. Helen. Sometimes the emperor and his mother are placed together to the right of the bishop, while to his left is shown some miracle (the healing of a sick or the resurrection of a dead person) produced by the virtue of the Cross… The architectural background behind the bishop elevating the Cross must represent the basilica of the Resurrection built by Constantine."[3]

Elaborating on the meaning of the festival, Ouspensky writes: "The festival of the Raising is a glorification of the Cross of Christ by the totality of the universe which recognizes that 'the foolishness of God is wiser than men; and the weakness of God is stronger than men.'[4] 'Seeing the Cross raised by the hands of the bishop,' the Church glorifies the weapon of Christ…. If Christ is the New Adam, His Cross is the New Tree of Life, giving back to the fallen world the incorruptibility of Paradise. Raised above the earth the Cross, which embraces the whole of heaven with its two extremities, puts to flight the demons and pours forth grace to the four corners of the universe."[5]

---

1   See *Endnote E-132*, p. 733.
2   A raised platform serving the function of lectern and pulpit in Orthodox liturgy.
3   L. Ouspensky, *et al.*, *Icons*, pp. 149, 151.
4   1 Corinthians 1:25.
5   L. Ouspensky, *et al.*, *Icons*, pp. 148-149.

Parts of the true cross (or pieces of wood described as such) were distributed as political gifts to rulers, monastic orders, and politically-connected churches in the West.[837] By the mid-thirteenth century, the Franciscans managed to gain control over two sites which greatly boosted their political importance within the competing factions of the church: the chapel outside Jerusalem where the cross was supposedly discovered by St. Helena… and the church at the site of the crucifixion. Capitalizing on their own considerable influence, the Franciscans of Florence managed to acquire a piece of the true cross in the early fourteenth century. To honor this major relic, encourage a steady stream of pilgrims, and proclaim their special ties with the Savior and the Holy Lands, the Franciscan order in Florence built the church of *San Croce* (Holy Cross). In the 1360s, they commissioned Agnolo Gaddi to decorate it with a fresco cycle on the history of the cross. Other Franciscan churches followed suit with similar fresco cycles including Cenni di Francesco's History of the Cross in the church of San Francesco in Volterra (1410) and Piero's cycle at San Francesco in Arezzo (ca. 1447-1466). Though no documentation survives, it is likely the church of San Francesco in Arezzo also had a relic of the true cross.

… While the merchant family which commissioned Piero's frescoes were hardly proponents of a courtly ideology of global rule and triumph, the frescoes tied directly to the major military

---

837   In 347, only seven years after the finding of the relic, Cyril of Jerusalem could already write that "the whole world has… been filled with pieces of the wood of the Cross" (*First Catechetical*, 4:10, p. 21).

Figure E36-2. *The Chapel of Adam, ca. 1167*
Photo: Laura E. Hoffman, 1961-

The place where our Lord was crucified is called Calvary,[1] because the skull of the primitive man [Adam] was buried there. So it came to pass that the second Adam, that is the blood of Christ, as it dropped from the cross, washed away the sins of the buried protoplast, the first Adam.[2] Legends recount the fate of Adam's remains after their burial. Before the Flood, Noah is said to have retrieved Adam's skull from the Cave of Treasures so it could be preserved on the ark. According to Christian stories that claimed Jewish precedents: "When Noah the righteous left the ark... he came with his sons first to Mount Moriah... On a nearby hill, Shem, the son of Noah, interred the skull of Adam, which he had taken with him into the ark and guarded during the flood. Since then the hill is called [*Golgotha*] – the Skull."[3] Similar Muslim traditions about the reburial of Adam can be found in Ibn Kathir.[4]

Christian tradition, supposing that the NT term *Golgotha*[5] referred to the place where Adam was buried, inferred that Jesus Christ was later crucified over the exact spot of the ancient grave. For this reason, the figure of Adam is frequently represented in depictions of the crucifixion, either as a skull in a cavelike tomb beneath the cross (often superscripted with "SA" for "Skull of Adam"; at times also depicted with the rib from which Eve was created nearby) or, more dramatically, as ascending from his tomb as the effects of the Atonement raise him from the dead.

Today, pilgrims to the Church of the Holy Sepulchre[6] in Jerusalem can still visit, beneath the traditional spot of crucifixion on *Golgotha*, what became known as the "church and tomb of Adam."[7] The chapel surrounds the cavity where tradition says that Adam's bones were deposited to await the redeeming blood of Christ.[8] A small window at the back of the chamber displays a fissure said to have been created at the moment when the earth shook and the temple veil was rent. The general symbolism, though not the speculative elements regarding the skull of Adam, is echoed in the words of the Apostle Paul: "For as in Adam all die [i.e., through Adam's eating of the fruit of the Tree of Knowledge], even so in Christ shall all be made alive [i.e., through the "tree" on which Christ was crucified]."[9]

1   Latin *calvaria* = skull.
2   Jerome, *Letter 46*, 3, p. 61, after Origen's *Commentary on Matthew* 27:33; cf. R. E. Brown, *Death*, 2:937 n. 9; C. W. Wilson, *Golgotha*, pp. 2-7.
3   Z. Vilnay, *Sacred Land*, p. 70, cf. p. 213; cf. E. A. W. Budge, *Cave*, pp. 104-110, 122-129; W. L. Lipscomb, *Repentance*, 99-103, p. 233; S. C. Malan, *Adam and Eve*, 2:8, p. 115; 3:5-7, pp. 149-153; 3:13-19, pp. 161-169; H. W. Nibley, *Teachings of the PGP*, 21, p. 259; Shelemon, *Book of the Bee*, 21, p. 35.
4   Ibn Kathir in B. M. Wheeler, *Prophets*, p. 34; I. Ibn Kathir, *Stories*, p. 54. For competing traditions about the place of Adam's burial, see *Excursus 53: Comparative Explorations, The Cave of Treasures*, p. 669. See *Endnote E-130*, p. 733.
5   Matthew 27:33; Mark 16:22; Luke 23:33; John 19:17. See *Endnote E-131*, p. 733.
6   See *Endnote E-132*, p. 733.
7   A. Parrot, *Golgotha*, p. 77.
8   Z. Vilnay, *et al.*, *Vilnay Guide*, pp. 99, 104; cf. A. Parrot, *Golgotha*, p. 77; Z. Vilnay, *Sacred Land*, pp. 212-213.
9   1 Corinthians 15:22, cf. vv. 46, 47, 49. See *Endnote E-133*, p. 734.

threats facing a universal Christian religion in the mid-fifteenth century: the Moslem army threatening the Christian Byzantine empire in the east, and the black Muslim empire in Moorish Spain. The Franciscan order also had important ties to the chapels of the Cross in the threatened Holy Land. Despite the lack of a direct tie to court culture, it is not difficult to explain the appearance of a cosmic world history, geared around the theme of the cross, in a Franciscan church in Arezzo.

See *Excursus 45: Impact of the "Black Death" on Art and Literature,* p. 640, and *Figure 6-3,* p. 461.

Excursus 37
Traditions About the Role of Abel

THE shedding of Abel's blood naturally was seen as a type of the atoning sacrifice of Jesus Christ.[838] With respect to his place among the biblical canon of martyrs, Hamilton writes: "Abel is coupled with Zechariah[839] as the first[840] and the last[841] victims of murder mentioned in the OT... Understandably Abel is characterized as 'innocent...'"[842]

Unfortunately, the death of the righteous Abel—the beloved son of the Adam and Eve, whose story has always been linked with the idea of proper sacrifice[843]—seems to have also given rise to an anomalous ordinance of sprinkling blood coupled with "washing" or "baptism" for little children that was denounced in JST Genesis 17:4-7:

> 4. My people have gone astray from my precepts, and have not kept mine ordinances, which I gave unto their fathers;

> 5. And they have not observed mine anointing, and the burial, or baptism wherewith I commanded them;

> 6. But have turned from the commandment, and taken unto themselves the washing [the words "or baptism" are crossed out at this point in OT1] of children, and the blood of sprinkling;

> 7. And have said that the blood of the righteous Abel was shed for sins; and have not known wherein they are accountable before me."[844]

To counteract this practice, the Lord established the covenant of circumcision at the age of eight days,[845] "that thou mayest know for ever that children are not accountable before me until they are eight years old."[846] D&C 68:25-28, received later in the same year that JST Genesis 17 was translated, also emphasizes that children are not accountable until eight years old.[847]

Significantly, the figure of Abel (*Hibil Ziua* = Abel Splendor) is associated with the washing rituals of baptism among the Mandaeans.[848] Along with *Sitil* (Seth) and *Anus* (Enos, Enosh), he is one of the three celestial *uthra* (= angelic dwellers of the realm of light) "who can substitute or stand beside *Manda d-Hiia* in the function of revealer and savior" and can function "as intermediaries between the divinity and humankind."[849] Indeed, *Hibil*, who is often identified with *Manda d-Hiia* himself, was said to have performed the first baptism, that of Adam, who prefigures every later candidate for this ordinance.[850] Even today, as

---

838 Hebrews 12:24; M.-B. Halford, *Eva und Adam*, pp. 270-271.
839 Matthew 23:35. See discussion of the identity of Zechariah in M. Barker, *Christmas*, pp. 149-150.
840 Genesis 4.
841 2 Chronicles 24:20-22. Chronicles is the last book in the Hebrew canon.
842 V. P. Hamilton, Genesis, p. 244.
843 J. Smith, Jr., *Teachings*, 22 January 1834, pp. 58-59.
844 See OT1 text in S. H. Faulring, *et al.*, *Original Manuscripts*, pp. 131-132. These verses were probably received between February 1 and March 7, 1831 (see Figure 0-2, p. 3). Note that D&C 74, now known to have been received "sometime in the last part of 1830, and not January 1832 as found in all editions of the Doctrine and Covenants," "probably stemmed from discussions about infant baptism" (R. J. Woodford, *Discoveries*, p. 31).
845 Genesis 17:12.
846 JST Genesis 17:11. See *Endnote E-134*, p. 734.
847 L. E. Dahl, *Plain*, p. 126.
848 E. S. Drower, *Mandaeans*, pp. 100-123.
849 E. Lupieri, *Mandaeans*, p. 46.
850 W. Barnstone, *et al.*, *Gnostic*, p. 533; E. S. Drower, *Prayerbook*, p. 30.

the Mandaean priest "prepares for the baptism, he might conjure up the image of the prototypical priest, who is *Hibil Ziua.*"[851]

Recalling the idea of a redemptive role falsely attributed to the "blood of the righteous Abel," the practice of swearing "by the holy blood of Abel" is portrayed in both early Christian and Islamic accounts of the efforts of the antediluvian patriarchs to dissuade their posterity from leaving the "holy mountain" and associating with the children of Cain.[852] Eisenbaum emphasizes that "by virtue of his being killed by Cain, Abel was removed from the earth and the downward spiral of human history that followed."[853] Hebrews 12:24, the author of which "may have been familiar with some extra-biblical Enochic and Noachic traditions"[854] speaks of the saints coming "to Jesus the mediator of the new covenant, and to the blood of sprinkling, that speaketh better things than that of Abel."[855] With reference to this scripture, Koester cites the possibility that the author of Hebrews may be suggesting that, consistent with the idea in *4 Maccabees* that martyrs' blood atoned for sins,[856] "Abel's blood brought a limited atonement, while Jesus' blood brought complete Atonement."[857] With reference to Hebrews 11:4, Joseph Smith said that Abel "holding still the keys of his dispensation... was sent down from heaven unto Paul to minister consoling words, and to commit unto him a knowledge of the mysteries of godliness."[858]

In their wider narrative context, the pseudepigraphic references to Abel are interpreted by Ruzer as depicting a group that looked to Abel rather than to Christ for salvation. He concludes that the "emphasis here [is] on the salvific quality of Abel's blood... Swearing by Abel's blood... is presented in our text as sufficient for the salvation of the sons of Seth; those who dwell—thanks to swearing by Abel's blood—on the holy mountain do not need any further salvation."[859] Such a concept is reinforced by a *1 Enoch* description of Abel as a "red calf," which Tiller sees as an allusion to the red heifer[860] of Numbers 19:1-10,[861] and whose ritual Maimonides saw, not merely as law of purity, but rather as a matter "of transcendent, even salvific weight and meaning."[862] The red heifer was a pointedly young animal used in purification rites, comprising a washing and a sprinkling of blood,[863] for those who had come into contact with "one... found slain" and "lying in the field,"[864] as was Abel. A widely-varying set of Islamic accounts attempt to explain the origin of a related Qur'anic story[865]— what these accounts have in common is the idea that the murderer denied his crime but was identified by the voice of the dead man who was touched by the sacrificial animal.[866] Could this be an echo of the voice of the righteous Abel whose "blood cries unto [God] from the ground"[867]—"he being dead yet speaketh"?[868]

851   J. J. Buckley, *Mandaeans*, p. 132.

852   See *Endnote E-135,* p. 734.

853   P. M. Eisenbaum, *Hebrews 11*, p. 149; cf. Genesis 6-11.

854   A. A. Orlov, *Heir*, p. 58; cf. P. M. Eisenbaum, *Hebrews 11*, pp. 148-149.

855   See *Endnote E-136,* p. 735.

856   *Fourth Maccabees,* 6:28-29, p. 192; 7:20-21, p. 195.

857   C. Koester, *Hebrews*, p. 546 n. 12:24a; cf. H. W. Attridge, *Hebrews*, p. 377.

858   J. Smith, Jr., *Teachings*, 5 October 1840, p. 169; cf. E. Lupieri, *Mandaeans*, p. 46. See also *Excursus 53: Comparative Explorations of the Mysteries,* p. 663. See *Endnote E-137,* p. 735.

859   S. Ruzer, *Abel's Blood.*

860   See *Endnote E-138,* p. 735.

861   P. A. Tiller, *Animal*, p. 226; cf. G. W. E. Nickelsburg, *1 Enoch*, p. 371 n. 8; cf. 85:3-6, 89:9, pp. 364, 365.

862   J. Neusner, *Without Myth*, p. 99.

863   Cf. JST Genesis 17:6.

864   Deuteronomy 21:1.

865   *Qur'an* 2:67-71.

866   M. M. Ayoub, *Qur'an (Vol. 1)*, p. 117. See also B. M. Wheeler, *Prophets*, pp. 216-217. See *Endnote E-139,* p. 735.

867   See *Commentary* 5:35-b, p. 383.

868   Hebrews 11:4; cf. G. W. E. Nickelsburg, *1 Enoch*, 22:5-7, p. 300; 9:2, 10, p. 202; pp. 305-306 n. 5-7.

IIII.

Nd Adam erkandte sein weib Heua / vnd sie ward
schwanger vnd gepar den Kain / Jch hab kriegt den
man des HERREN / Vnd sie fur fort / vnd gepar Dabel seinen bruder / Vnd Dabel ward ein schefer / Kain
aber ward ein acker man.
Es begab sich aber nach etlichen tagen / das Kain

FIGURE E37-1. *Luther's 1534 German Translation of Genesis 4:1*

Ich hab kriegt den man des HERREN.[1] Although Luther translated the Hebrew term *'eth* as *des HERREN* (= of the Lord) in 1534, he later concluded on both grammatical and contextual grounds that it should be rendered as a marker of the direct object of the verb (*den HERREN* = the Lord). This change, which appeared in the posthumous 1546 edition of his Bible, could be given in English as "I have gotten the man, [namely or even] the Lord."[2]

---

1   Genesis 4:1.
2   T. Gallus, *Der Nachkomme 1*, p. 124.

Another possible clue to the mistaken identification of Abel as a savior might be found in a close reading of Eve's words at the birth of Cain. The words are usually translated: "I have gotten a man *from* (= Hebrew *'et*) the Lord" or "*with* the Lord," which, as Kaiser observes, "doesn't make too much sense"—either linguistically or contextually.[869] For this reason, some have argued that *'et* should be taken straightforwardly in its grammatical role as the marker of the definite direct object of the verb,[870] as in the revised Wittenberg edition of Luther's Bible published posthumously in 1546: "I have gotten a man, [namely or even] the Lord."[871] "This rendering suggests," in Hamilton's words, "that in the birth of Cain Eve thought, mistakenly, that the divinely promised seed[872] of [Moses 4:21] had now come in Cain. The child, whose birth is so welcomed, could be looked on as God himself."[873] Also concluding that Eve "thought the deliverer had been sent by God," Boice renders her exclamation as "Here he is" or "I've gotten him."[874]

That Eve could have been so deceived in thinking the promised Redeemer had already come in the person of Cain seems doubtful. However, in a more general sense, her words might be taken as foreshadowing her hope that, in contrast to her wayward progeny,[875] Cain would "not reject [God's] words" and would become the progenitor of the righteous branch of her family through whom the promise of Moses 4:21 would eventually be fulfilled. As in subsequent patriarchal tradition, "a representative child continued to be God's visible guarantee for the present and a pledge for the future. Also, he was representative of the interests and spiritual and material fortunes of the whole lot who were joined to him."[876]

---

869   W. C. J. Kaiser, *Toward*, p. 37. From the standpoint of functional grammar, Bandstra admits that the "transitivity structure seems to have as its goal *et-Yahweh*" but rejects this idea "for logical reasons" (B. J. Bandstra, *Genesis 1-11*, p. 228).

870   See *Endnote E-140*, p. 735.

871   T. Gallus, *Der Nachkomme 1*, p. 124; V. P. Hamilton, *Genesis*, p. 221. See *Endnote E-141*, p. 736. Since 1544, Luther had been working on a completely revised version of the New Testament. The posthumous edition was prepared by Luther's friend Röhrer and contains numerous alterations that he traced to Luther himself.

872   Besides the divine promise, one account has Satan telling Eve that, as a consequence of eating the forbidden fruit, she would "become the Mother of God" (M. E. Stone, *Adamgirk*, 3:10:10, p. 73).

873   V. P. Hamilton, *Genesis*, p. 221. See also *Commentary* 4:21-d, p. 266; T. Gallus, *Der Nachkomme 1*, pp. 116-132; W. C. J. Kaiser, *Toward*, p. 37; G. J. Wenham, *Genesis 1-15*, p. 102. See *Endnote E-142*, p. 736.

874   J. M. Boice, *Genesis 1-11*, p. 250. See *Endnote E-143*, p. 736.

875   Moses 4:13.

876   W. C. J. Kaiser, *Toward*, p. 37.

Additional support for the idea of Cain's special potential can be found in traditions of unusual circumstances surrounding the birth—the hoped-for blessing resulting from Adam and Eve's continued calling upon the Lord—that may have aroused great expectations. In some accounts, the newborn Cain is described as "a glorious person,"[877] being "like the color of stars,"[878] "a designation which associates Cain with the angels."[879] It is said that Adam loved Cain and Abel "the most of all his children."[880] Perhaps as Abel's righteousness began to overshadow that of Cain, the high hopes once held for the elder brother were transferred to the younger sibling, and mistakenly carried forward by a group attributing a salvific role to him after his murder.

In a related vein, there also exists a separate tradition relevant to the theme of Abel's role in the overall plan of salvation. It may be found in an analysis of Armenian texts presenting a variant of the story of the *cheirograph* of Adam,[881] along with elaborate speculations on its relevance for Christ's victory over death and hell:

> Then Satan brought a stone and set it before Adam, and he said to Adam, "Put [your] hand upon the stone and say thus: 'Let all my offspring be your servants.' And if you do not say so, I will bring deep darkness upon you."

> Then Adam put his hand upon the stone and said, "Until the unbegotten is born and the immortal dies, we and all our offspring will be your servants."[882]

In this variant of the story, the agreement is called a *cheirograph*, not because it is a handwritten document, but "because of the 'writing of hands,' i.e., the hand-prints, left on the rock by Adam's bloody hands."[883] Because the death of the "unbegotten" and "immortal" Jesus Christ fulfills the expiration clause of the contract,[884] He, "in his descent into Hades erased the *cheirograph*, bound the Devil, and freed the souls from Hades."[885] At the triumphant entry of the Savior, Death "runs forward to open his gates" and begs for mercy, since "[i]t was Christ who was the true first-born [vs. Satan who had falsely claimed to be so[886]], and through Him everything in creation had its ground."[887] Relating this event to the deaths of Adam and Abel, Anderson summarizes the logic of Ephrem the Syrian in interpreting this tradition:[888]

> The issue at hand… [is] a conflict between mercy and justice. Abel, the victim of a brutal murder, dies first in order to precede Adam to the grave.[889]

The logic of this interpretation, though compressed, is clear and compelling. Had Adam gone to *Sheol* first, Ephrem reasons, he could never have been redeemed. For he had violated a command that had attached to it a clear and unalterable penalty: "The day you eat of that fruit

877 H. W. Nibley, *Teachings of the PGP*, 19, p. 241; cf. G. W. E. Nickelsburg, *1 Enoch*, 106:2, p. 536. See J. C. Reeves, *Heralds*, p. 103 n. 109.
878 G. A. Anderson, *et al.*, *Synopsis*, Armenian 21:3a, p. 24E. See *Endnote E-144*, p. 736.
879 J. Tromp, *Cain*, pp. 290-291. See *Endnote E-145*, p. 736.
880 M.al-Kisa'i, *Tales*, p. 77.
881 See the overview of Moses 5, p. 332.
882 W. L. Lipscomb, *Expulsion*, 17-19, pp. 138-139, 268-269; cf. M. E. Stone, *Legend*, p. 156.
883 M. E. Stone, *Legend*, p. 160; cf. S. C. Malan, *Adam and Eve*, 1:23, p. 23; Revelation 13:16; *Commentary* 5:4-a, p. 355; 5:5-b, p. 359. See *Endnote 4-32*, p. 308. See *Endnote E-146*, p. 736.
884 W. L. Lipscomb, *Expulsion*, 23-26, pp. 139-140.
885 Turdeanu, cited in M. E. Stone, *Legend*, p. 159.
886 See *Excursus 8: The Origin and Premortal Existence of Human Spirits*, p. 540.
887 G. A. Anderson, *Perfection*, p. 173.
888 G. A. Anderson, *Perfection*, pp. 174-175.
889 See *Endnote E-147*, p. 737.

you shall certainly die."[890] But history did not work out this way. Instead, Abel died first, and consequently the mouth of Hades was opened for the first time unjustly. Henceforth the legal foundation of the underworld rested on shaky grounds. Since Abel died first and unjustly, God has full authority to evacuate those held prisoner there at the end of time.

A further irony is the salvific role played by the innocent death of Abel. Since Abel was considered by Ephrem, and nearly all early Christians, as a type of Christ, the miracle of the incarnation was inscribed into the very beginning of Genesis. Because the innocent Abel (a.k.a Christ) dies unfairly, Adam (all humanity) will be justly cast forth from *Sheol*.

---

890   See Moses 3:17.

Excursus 38
The Meaning of "Adam-ondi-Ahman"

NIBLEY derives the meaning "Adam (or man) in the presence of God" by reference to Egyptian: *Atum* ("Adam" or "man"[891]), *ondi* (i.e., "in the presence of," "at," "by," "around"[892]), *Amen* (also "Amun," or "Amon").[893]

Marquardt points out that the Kirtland "Grammar and Alphabet of the Egyptian Language," in the handwriting of William W. Phelps, contains a reference to "The place appointed of God for the residence of Adam; Adam ondi= Ahman."[894] Adam-ondi-Ahman has also been described as "the place where Adam shall come to visit his people, or the Ancient of Days shall sit,"[895] "the place where Adam dwelt," or "Valley of God where Adam dwelt."[896] Matthews also mentions the following interpretations or descriptions: "Adam's consecrated land,"[897] "Adam's grave"[898] and "Valley of God in which Adam blessed his children."[899] He also cites the following from Elder Alvin R. Dyer, which relates the name "to the priesthood and revelatory experience of Adam in being the first man to hold the spiritual blessings of the gospel":

> The very word itself speaks of the manner in which Adam has received the "Keys of Salvation" under the counsel and direction of the Holy One, who is Jesus Christ the Lord.

> The word "Adam" refers directly to Adam. The word "ondi," means nearby or connected with. The word "Ahman" means the Lord himself. Therefore a literal translation of the words "Adam-ondi-Ahman" means The Lord Jesus Christ, through Adam unto mankind."[900]

Elsewhere, President Dyer remarks:

> In conferring the "keys of salvation" upon Adam, the revealing and unlocking of the conditions of salvation were made known to them and through them to mankind. In this we can understand the true meaning of the term "Adam-ondi-Ahman," or simply: from "Ahman," who is the Lord, "ondi," meaning through Adam unto mankind.[901]

With respect to the term "Ahman," Orson Pratt stated that it "signifies God… in the original language spoken by Adam."[902] Tvedtnes conjectures that since: "Joseph Smith is said to have indicated that… Jesus is called 'Son Ahman,'[903] Old Testament prayers end simply with the word 'Amen' (= confirmed, true), and hence in the name (title) of Jesus Christ."[904]

---

891   See *Commentary* 1:34-a, p. 66.

892   Nibley, cited in L. C. Berrett, *et al.*, *Missouri*, p. 380; cf. H. W. Nibley, *Teachings of the Book of Mormon*, 53, 2:321.

893   See also H. W. Nibley, *Teachings of the Book of Mormon*, 26, 1:338; 7, 1:79.

894   *Kirtland Egyptian Papers*, 1, p. 23, cited in H. M. Marquardt, *Revelations*, p. 198 n. 38.

895   D&C 116.

896   O. Pratt, *25 February 1877*, pp. 342-343; cf. O. Pratt, *18 May 1873*, p. 48.

897   Signboard of the Missouri State Historical Society, Courthouse Square, Gallatin, MO, cited in R. J. Matthews, *Adam-ondi-Ahman*, p. 30.

898   Heman Smith, *RLDS Journal of History*, 9:140, cited in R. J. Matthews, *Adam-ondi-Ahman*, p. 30.

899   John Corrill, Brief History, 11 February 1839, cited in R. J. Matthews, *Adam-ondi-Ahman*, p. 30.

900   A. R. Dyer, *The Lord Speaketh*, 1964, p. 216, cited in R. J. Matthews, *Adam-ondi-Ahman*, pp. 30-31.

901   A. R. Dyer, *Destiny*, p. 44.

902   O. Pratt, *25 February 1877*, p. 343; cf. O. Pratt, *18 February 1855*, p. 342. See also J. Smith, Jr. in D. M. Quinn, *Prayer Circles*, p. 83.

903   See O. Pratt, *18 February 1855*, p. 342.

904   J. A. Tvedtnes, *Faith*, p. 114.

Excursus 39

The Location of Adam-ondi-Ahman

GRAHAM W. Doxey wrote in the *Encyclopedia of Mormonism* that:

> Neither biblical records nor secular history and archaeological research identify the dimensions or the location of the Garden [of Eden] in terms of the present-day surface of the earth.[905] Latter-day revelation specifies that, as a mortal, Adam lived at Adam-ondi-Ahman in what is now Daviess County, Missouri.[906]

Although the term "Adam-ondi-Ahman" had been publicly mentioned by the spring of 1835,[907] a specific location was not identified until sometime after May 1838, when Joseph Smith "accepted Lyman Wight's invitation to visit a two-square mile valley at a horseshoe bend of the Grand River in Daviess County, Missouri, located a few miles north of Far West."[908] Here the Prophet declared that "Spring Hill is named by the Lord Adam-ondi-Ahman."[909] On 21 October of the same year, the Prophet descended to the valley of Adam-ondi-Ahman and pointed out the place where Adam gave a blessing to his posterity.[910] Regarding the circumstances surrounding the Prophet's identification of these locations, Cook writes:[911]

> The date of reception for section 116 is uncertain. The original source for the revelation is "The Scriptory Book of Joseph Smith,"[912] but the journal entries in this document for May and June 1838 (in the handwriting of George W. Robinson, the Prophet's scribe) were recorded after the fact (probably July 1838), and therefore cannot be taken at face value to interpret historical events as they developed. The 19 May 1838 entry strongly implies that Joseph Smith revealed the name "Adam-ondi-Ahman" subsequent to that date. George Robinson's journal entry details the Prophet's activites in "laying claims to [a] city plat" near Lyman Wight's ferry. Robinson noted that Wight and others had named the place "Spring Hill," but the location was *afterwards named by the mouth of the Lord and was called Adam Ondi Awmen [sic]*"... William Swartzell, a temporary Mormon convert, assisted Church leaders in the surveying of Spring Hill or Adam-ondi-Ahman in 1838. Swartzell, who kept regular diary entries during this period, recorded that the ancient name was given by the Prophet on 11 June 1838:[913] "[I] observed to Joseph Smith that this city should have a new name. Brother Joseph placed his back against a small shady tree near the spring, and then said, 'We shall alter the name of this *stake*'... and looking towards heaven for a short time, said, 'It does not take me long to get a revelation from heaven, and this stake, or city, shall be called Adam-on-Diammon [sic].'"

The early Saints responded enthusiastically to news about Adam-ondi-Ahman. William W. Phelps, who would have encountered the term while he was helping to prepare the new edition of the Doctrine and Covenants, recorded in his journal on 3 June 1835: "Com[posed] a hymn – Adam-ondi-Ahman."[914] The text was included in the hymnbook he assisted

---

905   See *Endnote E-148*, p. 737.
906   G. W. Doxey, *Eden*, p. 534. See D&C 107:53-56; 116:1; 117:8.
907   See *Excursus 40: Dating Joseph Smith's Vision of Adam-ondi-Ahman*, p. 625.
908   M. A. Scherer, *Mists*, p. 8.
909   D&C 116. See also D&C 117:8-11.
910   L. C. Berrett, *et al.*, *Missouri*, pp. 392-393.
911   L. W. Cook, *Revelations*, p. 333.
912   J. Smith, Jr., *The Scriptory Book of Joseph Smith*, 19 May 1838, pp. 43-44, cited in J. Smith, Jr., *Papers 1989-1992*, pp. 244-245.
913   William Swartzell, *Mormonism Exposed, Being a Journal of a Residence in Missouri from the 28th of May to the 20th of August, 1838....* (Pekin, Ohio: By the Author, 1840), cited in L. W. Cook, *Revelations*, p. 308
914   *William W. Phelps Journal*, LDS Archives, cited in H. M. Marquardt, *Revelations*, p. 198. See *Hymns (1985)*,

Emma Smith in publishing later that same month, and also appeared in the next issue of the *Messenger and Advocate*.[915] The hymn was later sung at the Kirtland Temple dedication on 27 March 1836.[916] In the early Church, "Adam-ondi-Ahman" was "recorded as being used in more meetings and appears in more journal references than any other hymn."[917]

With respect to the modern response to this revelation, Matthews reports: "In reading the literature available about the place now called Adam-ondi-Ahman, one finds a difference in the veneration that is held concerning it. The spectrum runs from an acceptance of the place as the very spot on which Adam dwelt to the opposite view that there is nothing particularly significant about the location either anciently, currently, or in the future."[918] For example, disavowing claims of a historical connection between the site and the story of Adam and Eve, Mark Scherer, the Community of Christ Church Historian, writes: "For us today, Adam-ondi-Ahman remains a place of historical curiosity and exemplifies Joseph Jr.'s penchant to link land and theology."[919] Consistent with this view, Phelps' hymn was removed from the 1870 RLDS Hymnal "due to dramatic theological differences."[920]

Not surprisingly, the literal nature of LDS beliefs with regard to these locations often invites ridicule—to which members have tried to respond with good-humored understanding. A typical story—most likely apocryphal but not completely out of character[921]—has President Spencer W. Kimball being confronted by a hostile reporter who asked, "I hear you Mormons believe that the Garden of Eden was in the state of Missouri. Is that true?" President Kimball is reported to have replied in straightfaced irony, "No, we do not believe that the state of Missouri existed at the time of the Garden of Eden."[922]

Today, although the area of Adam-ondi-Ahman remains as a relatively undisturbed pastoral landscape, "in verbal stance and land acquisition the area has become quietly important" to the LDS Church.[923] Consistent with the scriptural description of the earth after the Fall, the area is still "known for its thick and thorny vegetation"[924] and, appropriately echoing the experience of Adam and Eve who were commanded to "till the earth,"[925] "[m]ost of the valley acreage is currently farmed."[926]

#49.

915   W. W. Phelps, *Adam-ondi-Ahman*; "probably not published until July" (H. M. Marquardt, *Revelations*, p. 198 n. 38).

916   J. Smith, Jr., *Documentary History*, 27 March 1836, 2:417.

917   M. D. Poulter, *1835 Hymnbook*, p. 42.

918   R. J. Matthews, *Adam-ondi-Ahman*, p. 31.

919   M. A. Scherer, *Mists*. See also R. J. Matthews, *Adam-ondi-Ahman*, p. 28 n. 3.

920   M. A. Scherer, *Mists*.

921   Edward L. Kimball, a son and biographer of President Kimball, commented as follows on the question of this story's authenticity: "I have not previously heard the anecdote. If the statement were made to a reporter in the presence of others, I think I would have heard about it. He was capable of such a quip, but I think I would want the word of someone who was there before asserting it actually happened. Generally he was anxious about press conferences and cautious in what he said" (E. L. Kimball, *3 January 2009*).

922   Although it is not expected that it would ever be possible to "identify the dimensions or the location of the Garden [of Eden] in terms of the present-day surface of the earth" (G. W. Doxey, *Eden*, p. 534; see the overview of Moses 3, p. 141), Mormons do identify Adam-ondi-Ahman, and possibly other sites in Missouri (see *Figure 6-2*, p. 457), with the story of Adam and Eve. See also *Excursus 13: Some Perspectives on Historicity*, p. 552.

923   C. S. Campbell, *Images*, p. 175.

924   See Moses 4:23-24.

925   See Moses 3:5, 4:29, 5:1.

926   C. S. Campbell, *Images*, pp. 177, 175. For more on the history and geography of Adam-ondi-Ahman, see L. C. Berrett, *Adam-ondi-Ahman*; L. C. Berrett, *et al.*, *Missouri*, pp. 358-456; A. R. Dyer, *Fire*, pp. 6-27, 158-188; R. N. Holzapfel, *et al.*, *Kirtland*, pp. 171-173, 232-238; R. J. Matthews, *Adam-ondi-Ahman*. The first chapter of a book by Cottle is also valuable as a description of the current status and condition of the site (T. D. Cottle, *Adam-ondi-Ahman*, 1-17). For an excellent in-depth study of the history, meaning, ownership of, and attitudes toward

Excursus 40
Dating Joseph Smith's Vision of Adam-ondi-Ahman

WILLARD Richards reported the Prophet as saying: "I saw Adam in the valley of Adam-ondi-Ahman. He called together his children and blessed them with a patriarchal blessing. The Lord appeared in their midst, and he (Adam) blessed them all, and foretold what should befall them to the latest generation."[927] About the possible date and setting of this vision, Matthews writes:[928]

> The Prophet did not specify the circumstances or the date when these things were communicated to him, but it is possible that it was part of the accumulation of knowledge and spiritual experience that came to him in connection with the translation of the Bible....
>
> The subject matter of section 107—concerning Adam, the ancient patriarchs, a council at Adam-ondi-Ahman, Melchizedek, latter-day councils, and priesthood quorums—seems entirely consistent with this hypothesis. That the pattern of councils and Church organization was shown to the Prophet by vision is claimed in D&C 107:93, where it is said that the order of the Seventy (and presumably the other quorums also) was "according to the vision." Likewise Parley P. Pratt has quoted the Prophet as saying to the Twelve:
>
> > "I have now finished the work which was laid upon me, by committing to you all things for the building up of the kingdom according to the heavenly vision, and the pattern shown to me from heaven."[929]
>
> Although section 107 was recorded [in] 1835, it is certain from the translation of the early chapters of Genesis in 1830 and from the Prophet's instructions to the elders about ancient councils in 1831... that he knew about these things long before 1835. It is certain that much of the information contained in this section on Priesthood was revealed to the Prophet several years before the formal writing of section 107 in [April] 1835... A logical time would be during the translation of the Bible.
>
> The same hypothesis could link the translation of the Bible to the instructions given at the organization of the first high council at Kirtland, Ohio (February 17, 1834), as recorded in D&C 102. These connections are reasonable and possible—even probable.

As to more specific dates for the reception and recording of vision(s) and revelation(s) relating to D&C 107:40-52 and 53-56, four plausible time frames present themselves:

1. *December 1830.* The mention that "These things were all written in the book of Enoch, and are to be testified of in due time"[930] could indicate that a vision was given as early as December 1830, when Moses 6 and 7 were received.

2. *August 1831-June 1832.* Sometime between August 1831 and July 1832 Oliver Cowdery wrote in several corrections to the ages of the patriarchs in OT1.[931] Moreover, additional insertions of previous revelations into the last part of D&C 107 were dated 11 November 1831 in *Manuscript Revelation Book 1* (pp. 122-123) and *Book 2* (pp. 84-86).[932] D&C 66-68, which

---

sacred sites in Missouri by various churches with roots in the LDS tradition, see C. S. Campbell, *Images*. See also *Commentary* 3:8-b, p. 160.

927　J. Smith, Jr., *Teachings*, before 8 August 1839, p. 158.

928　R. J. Matthews, *Plainer*, pp. 259-260. See also L. E. Dahl, *Plain*, p. 126; G. A. Horton, Jr., *Insights*, pp. 66-67.

929　Statement by Parley P. Pratt in New York, January 1, 1845, printed in *Millennial Star*, March 1845, p. 151, cited in R. J. Matthews, *Plainer*, p. 259.

930　D&C 107:57.

931　S. H. Faulring, *et al.*, *Original Manuscripts*, pp. 97-98, 110; K. P. Jackson, *Book of Moses*, p. 102.

932　J. Smith, Jr., *Papers 2008-*, Revelations and Translations, Manuscript Revelation Books, pp. 217-219, 585-589.

were received in a context of discussions regarding the publication of the revelations and the manner of conducting ancient councils, were also given during this period.

3. *Near the end of 1833.* Identical phrasing to D&C 107:53-56 was apparently later inserted into an account of a blessing given on 18 December 1833 to the father of the Prophet, Joseph Smith, Sr., outlining his role as a patriarch. However, an argument could be made that the addition was a restoration of words or ideas originally in the blessing but somehow omitted from the original transcription.

4. *February 1834-April 1835.* It is not out of the question that the vision was received either at the same time that D&C 107 was recorded or during the few months previous. The first high council at Kirtland was organized on 17 February 1834.[933] The Lord had also given revelations encouraging the publication of the JST in April 1834.[934] It is possible that this led to some discussion of the ages of the patriarchs and times of their ordinations, leading to Joseph inquiring for revelation to resolve questions. A precedent for such an event had occurred a few years earlier when Oliver Cowdery and Joseph Smith had passionately disagreed on the text of a verse in D&C 20.[935] In the case of D&C 107, Brigham Young's notation may be of relevance: "Joseph was two hours laboring with O[liver] C[owdery] to get him to write the Rev[elation] in humility."[936] Robin S. Jensen of the Joseph Smith Papers project notes the fact that the ages of the patriarchs are presented in D&C 107:40-52 in the context of priesthood ordination, consistent with the additional unfolding of doctrines on the two priesthoods after early 1835.[937] He sees the gathering of Adam's posterity described in D&C 107:53-56 as a simple continuation of the preceding verses. Finally, it should be noted that a mention of "Adam-ondi-Ahman" appears in the 1835-1836 *Kirtland Egyptian Papers*.[938]

---

933 D&C 102.
934 D&C 104:58; cf. J. Smith, Jr., *Documentary History*, 11 January 1834, 2:3.
935 J. Smith, Jr., *Documentary History*, July 1830, 1:104-105.
936 *Minutes of the School of the Prophets*, 15 April 1868, Provo, Utah, copy at Utah State Historical Society, Salt Lake City, UT, cited in L. W. Cook, *Revelations*, p. 328 n. 5.
937 R. S. Jensen, *20 July 2009*.
938 *Kirtland Egyptian Papers 1, Grammar and Alphabet*, p. 23, cited in H. M. Marquardt, *Revelations*, p. 198 n. 38.

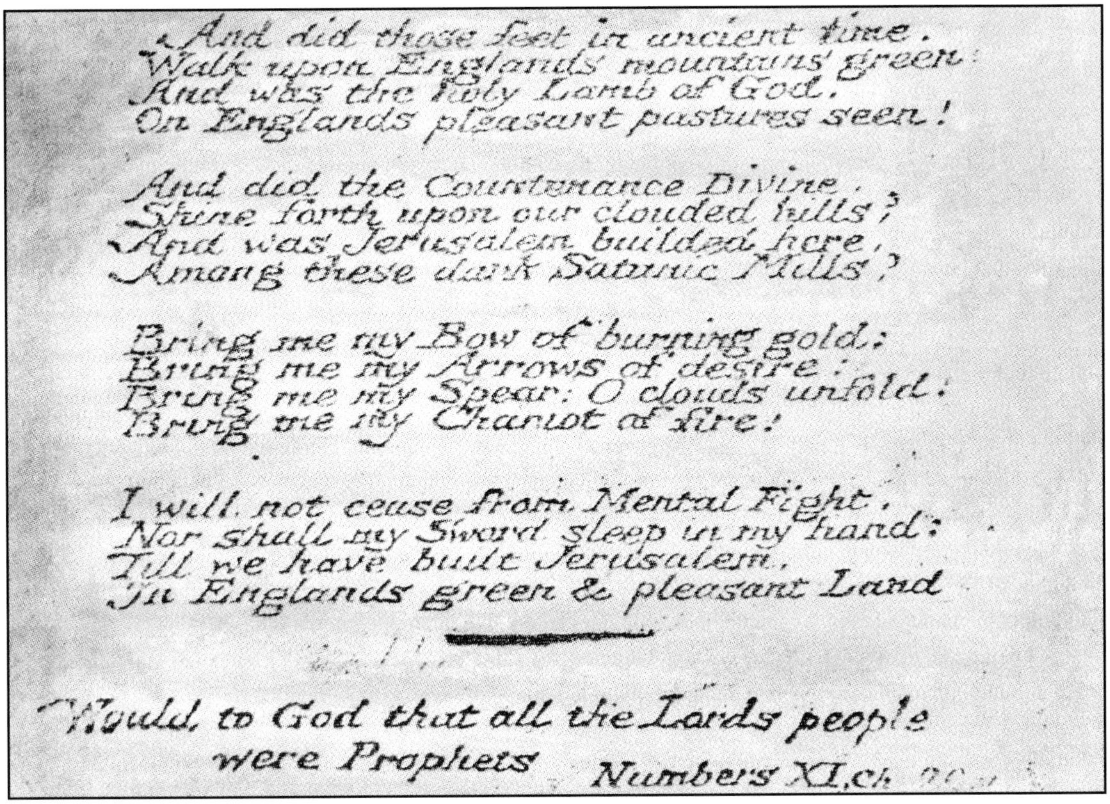

> *And did those feet in ancient time.*
> *Walk upon Englands mountains green:*
> *And was the holy Lamb of God.*
> *On Englands pleasant pastures seen!*
>
> *And did the Countenance Divine.*
> *Shine forth upon our clouded hills?*
> *And was Jerusalem builded here,*
> *Among these dark Satanic Mills?*
>
> *Bring me my Bow of burning gold:*
> *Bring me my Arrows of desire:*
> *Bring me my Spear: O clouds unfold:*
> *Bring me my Chariot of fire!*
>
> *I will not cease from Mental Fight,*
> *Nor shall my Sword sleep in my hand:*
> *Till we have built Jerusalem,*
> *In Englands green & pleasant Land.*
>
> *Would to God that all the Lords people*
> *were Prophets Numbers XI, ch 29*

FIGURE E41-1. *Excerpt from the Preface to Milton, Copy B, ca. 1804*[1]
William Blake, 1757-1827

1   For a facsimile of the entire Preface, see W. Blake, *Illuminated Blake*, p. 216; W. Blake, *Illuminated*, p. 295; W. Blake, *Milton*, p. 94.

Excursus 41

William Blake's "Jerusalem": A Vision of the Kingdom

THE Tenth Article of Faith speaks of the time when "Zion (the New Jerusalem) will be built upon the American continent," a day when "Christ will reign personally upon the earth," "the earth will be renewed and receive its paradisiacal glory," and mankind at last will be prepared to live in the manner of Adam and Eve before the Fall. Said the Prophet Joseph Smith: "The building up of Zion is a cause that has interested the people of God in every age; it is a theme upon which prophets, priests and kings have dwelt with peculiar delight; …fired with heavenly and joyful anticipations they have sung and written and prophesied of this our day."[939]

Among those whose imaginations were fired by a vision of the millennial age was William Blake, who wrote the verses reproduced above as part of a preface to a work entitled *Milton*.[940] The verses depict the building up of a heavenly Jerusalem on earth not as some new thing, but as having had a precedent in "ancient time." The Prophet Joseph Smith had discovered just such a precedent for a New Jerusalem in the Americas in the book of Moses account of the city of Enoch. Moreover, his translations of the records of Adam and Eve and of Lehi's

939   J. Smith, Jr., *Teachings*, 2 May 1842, p. 231.
940   See *Endnote E-149*, p. 737.

family revealed a wider scope of action for the sacred past of the New World than anyone could have previously supposed. In a similar spirit, Blake's verses suggest, in the words of Bishop Robert D. Hales, "divine origins for the unique faith developed in England."[941] Prophetic evidence of such origins is provided by an incident in the life of Elder Heber C. Kimball. As he concluded his missionary labors among the people in Chatburn, Elder Kimball was deeply touched by the tender devotion of those who had gathered to wish him farewell. He wrote:

> While contemplating this scene I was constrained to take off my hat, for I felt as if the place was holy ground. The Spirit of the Lord rested down upon me and I was constrained to bless that whole region of country.

Attesting the genuineness of Elder Kimball's feelings, the Prophet:

> … told him in after years that the reason he felt as he did in the streets of Chatburn was because the place was indeed 'holy ground,' that some of the ancient prophets had traveled in that region and dedicated the land, and that he, Heber, had reaped the benefit of their blessing.[942]

Milton is the first of Blake's final two epics, written at a time when he was turning from a some-what human-centered theology to a more Christ-centered one.[943] *Milton* serves as a prelude to *Jerusalem*, a longer work that concerns the sanctification and resurrection of Albion, and "the building of a continuing city in the England of the Satanic Mills."[944] The opening plates of *Milton* and *Jerusalem* prepare the reader for their complementary themes:

> We plunge, or are drawn into [*Milton*] following the striding poet of the title, naked amid flames (of prophetic wrath), as he pushes… his way… through a vortex of billowing smoke… The clothed traveler of the *Jerusalem* frontispiece, who is Blake/Los stepping into the door of a walled city or garden, is in symmetrical contrast.[945]

"The lyric 'And did those feet in ancient time,' which opens *Milton* is connected even more closely with the theme of *Jerusalem*, and [Anglican] hymnbooks have rechristened it accordingly."[946] Bloom calls these verses "The Dedicatory Quatrains."[947] Virtually forgotten in the century following its composition, these verses have been widely sung in England as a patriotic hymn since 1916, when they were first set to music.[948]

And did those feet in ancient time — Essick explains:[949] "The 'feet' are those of Jesus.[950] [In 1137,] William of Malmesbury record[ed] the legend that when the first Christian missionaries arrived in Glastonbury they found a church already there, 'constructed' by God himself.[951] This statement may have given birth to the myth of Christ having visited England." "In the course of the next hundred years, however, William's original work was altered and extended by the monks to suit their own purposes, and the additional material of the legends of King Arthur [and of Joseph of Arimathea] transformed the story even more."[952]

---

941 R. D. Hales, *British Contribution*, p. 2.
942 O. F. Whitney, *Kimball*, pp. 187-188.
943 N. M. Williams, *Ideology*, p. 141.
944 N. Frye, *Symmetry*, p. 355.
945 W. Blake, *Illuminated Blake*, pp. 217-218.
946 N. Frye, *Symmetry*, p. 323.
947 H. Bloom, *Commentary*, p. 910.
948 See *Endnote E-150*, p. 737.
949 R. N. Essick, *et al.*, in W. Blake, *Milton 1998*, p. 214 n. 27-28. See L. S. Lewis, *St. Joseph*, pp. 51, 162-163; A. W. Smith, *Legend*. For a thoroughly-researched LDS view that accepts this unlikely story, see V. G. Swanson, *Grail*. See *Endnote E-151*, p. 738.
950 Cf. Isaiah 52:7.
951 See L. S. Lewis, *St. Joseph*, p. 86.
952 R. Dunning, *Christianity*, p. 2. For more on this transformation, see R. F. Treharne, *Glastonbury*, pp. 26-113.

Blake's words, however, should not be taken too literally. He was not only thinking of the possibility of a visit of Christ to Britain, but also of the feet of godly men and women who had walked England's mountains and pastures from the earliest times—making of the isle in its former eras of blessedness a veritable Holy Land and a "demi-Paradise."[953] Explained Blake: "The antiquities of every Nation under Heaven, is no less sacred than that of the Jews... All had originally one language, and one religion, this was the religion of Jesus, the everlasting Gospel. Antiquity preaches the Gospel of Jesus."[954]

Holy Lamb of God — "The notion that Jesus visited Britain may have been reinforced by Blake by the name 'Lambeth' (house of the lamb...)."[955] Though only poetically true, the name provided, at least, a ready image for him of the decay and corruption into which his native land had fallen. "Blake and his wife lived in Lambeth for ten years, and by the time they left in 1800 it was already acquiring the characteristics of a peculiarly repellent urban slum with wretchedly built and undrained houses. *Beth-el* was in Hebrew the name for a sacred place, as Blake would have known from Genesis, but this place of the Lamb was soon degraded. And then there came Bethlem[956] [sic] itself, when the madhouse was moved to Lambeth from Moorfields in 1815. Yet this area became the ground or circumstance of some of Blake's greatest writing; it was the landscape in which his imagination continued to flourish and, as a result, he refers to it more often than to any other London region."[957]

dark Satanic Mills — Blake's poem can be seen, in part, as a protest against Deism. He saw that Deism's cold abstractions repudiate imagination, revelation, and the doctrine of a personal intervening God. As a result, any notion of general Christianity it might still affirm "soon vanishes into a mere perpetual-motion machine of causation."[958] "Blake first wrote of [such a] mechanical model of the universe as a mill in *There is No Natural Religion* of ca. 1788: 'The same dull round even of a universe would soon become a mill with complicated wheels.'"[959] "In *Milton*, Satan is described as the 'Miller of Eternity,' whose mills represent the reductive intellect, grinding down and destroying the imagination. Blake may also have been thinking of the enslaved and blinded Samson, in Milton's *Samson Agonistes*, 'eyeless in Gaza at the Mill with slaves.'"[960] "Stern Philosophy," the "Wheel of [false] Religion," and "the dark Preacher of Death" are seen by Blake the forces that drive the "vast machinery" of a fallen universe as it "knead[s] the bread of knowledge," thus "blotting out the light of divinity and inspiration."[961] Blake argued that both the authority and rules of existing religious institutions and the rational thought of Enlightenment philosophy should be "subservient to intuition and imagination,"[962] which he equated with "the Spirit of Prophecy."[963]

In light of the above, Bloom rightly asserts that the dark Satanic Mills "have nothing to do with industrialism."[964] However, the factory smoke of England's "clouded hills" surely played some part in the origins of Blake's inspired metaphor. In the words of Ackroyd: "Blake was the poet of eternity, but he was also the poet of late-eighteenth century London.

953   W. Shakespeare, *Richard II*, 2:1:42, p. 813. See *Endnote E-152*, p. 738.
954   W. Blake, *Catalogue*, 43-44, p. 543.
955   R. N. Essick, *et al.*, in W. Blake, *Milton 1998*, p. 214 nn. 27-28. See *Endnote E-153*, p. 738.
956   See *Endnote E-154*, p. 738.
957   P. Ackroyd, *Blake*, p. 129.
958   N. Frye, *Symmetry*, p. 66; cf. pp. 245-246, 290. See *Endnote E-155*, p. 738.
959   R. N. Essick, *et al.*, in W. Blake, *Milton 1998*, p. 118 n. 2. See W. Blake, *Natural Religion*, p. 35.
960   *Jerusalem*. See J. Milton, *Samson*, 41, p. 310.
961   P. Ackroyd, *Blake*, pp. 132-133.
962   H. Dubnick, *Poet as Prophet*, p. 84.
963   W. Blake, *Natural Religion*, p. 25.
964   H. Bloom, *Blake's Apocalypse*, p. 305.

EXCURSUS

And what could provide a more suitable emblem of that city than the famous automated Albion Mill?[965] It had been built along the Blackfriars Road, a short distance north of Hercules Buildings; it was the first great factory in London, designed by John Rennie to run upon steam-engines and supposed to produce some six thousand bushels of flour a week. It was one of the 'sights' of the metropolis, which Erasmus Darwin described as 'a grand and successful effort of human art'. But in March 1791, just after Blake had moved to Lambeth, it was burnt down—some believe it to have been arson, and the rejoicing millers on Blackfriars Bridge made no secret of their feelings. 'Success to the mills of ALBION', one placard was inscribed 'but no Albion Mills'. The factory was destroyed, and remained as a black ruined shell until 1809. Blake passed it every time he walked into the City, with the hills of Highgate and Hampstead in the distant smoky air."[966]

Bring me my Bow... my Chariot of fire — While the overall passage relates to the theme of Ephesians 6:11 ("Put on the whole armour of God"), the specific "imagery suggests the battle in heaven,[967] as well as Eros ('Arrows of desire'), here turned to spiritual uses... 'Chariot of fire' is from the description of Elijah's vision...[968] Blake portrayed Christ with an enormous bow in his *Paradise Lost* illustrations of 1807 and 1808,"[969] "a deliberate contrast to the black bow of Urizen in *The Book of Ahania*, which will reappear as the black bow of Satan in *Jerusalem*."[970]

"There is not a disjunction between human activity and divine activity in bringing [the vision] about. God is involved through the imaginative and creative work of the artist. There is an application of the texts to the writer and his contemporaries. Elijah's chariot is not just part of past history or even future expectation, but something that can be the inspiration of a new Elijah in every generation who is willing to condemn the Baalism of a contemporary culture and politics, which, according to Blake, had led to the capitulation of Christianity to a religion of virtues, rules and the acceptance of war and violence."[971]

Mental Fight — In the preface to *The Four Zoas*, Blake quotes Ephesians 6:10. Of relevance here are the subsequent verses of scripture, which detail the kind of battle that is implied by the term Mental Fight: "For we wrestle not against flesh and blood, but against principalities, against powers, against the rulers of the darkness of this world, against spiritual wickedness in high places."[972]

Till we have built Jerusalem — "Blake enters [the] chariot now…, to fight sword in hand the mental wars of the eternal world until the enduring City is built again in the pastoral land of his own childhood."[973] Again, a merely literal interpretation misleads. The Jerusalem of Blake's vision is a city that first and foremost must be built in the hearts and minds of a people freed from mental and spiritual tyranny.

Note the shift from "I" to "we" in this stanza—the efforts of each of Blake's compatriots are required. Following the lead of Blake and Milton, fellow visionaries must take the

---

965   See *Endnote E-156*, p. 739.
966   P. Ackroyd, *Blake*, pp. 130-131.
967   J. Milton, *Paradise Lost*, 6, pp. 119-140.
968   2 Kings 2:11. See *Endnote E-157*, p. 739.
969   R. N. Essick, *et al.*, in W. Blake, *Milton 1998*, p. 214 n. 35-40; cf. N. Frye, *Symmetry*, p. 215.
970   H. Bloom, *Blake's Apocalypse*, p. 306.
971   C. Rowland, *Blake*, p. 171.
972   Ephesians 6:11-12. See also 2 Corinthians 10:4; R. N. Essick, *et al.*, in W. Blake, *Milton 1998*, p. 185 n. 25.
973   H. Bloom, *Blake's Apocalypse*, p. 306.

"Daughters of Imagination" or "Inspiration" of biblical example as their Muses, rather than the "Daughters of Memory" of classical tradition.[974]

Would to God — Numbers 11:29, used as the epigraph to the poem, "is a reproof of Moses to Joshua, who would have silenced an 'unauthorized' outburst of prophesying."[975] "Moses… is 'redeemed' in *Milton* as the mythic figure Palamabron, identified also with Blake himself… In *Milton*, two of the Lord's people, Milton and Blake, join as one to create mutually the vision of an English prophet, and so prepare the way for the prophecy of *Jerusalem*, that supreme attempt on the part of an honest man to tell his nation that if it went on so, the result would be so, the yielding of creation to Satan the 'Miller of Eternity', the reductive fallacy incarnate."[976]

The biblical verse not only expresses Blake's longing for a general revival of the spirit of prophecy, but also a firm declaration that the "spirit and power of Elijah [is] ever available for those who would exercise their imagination and contemplative thought. Prophecy is not a thing of the past, for it is the vocation of all people. The vision of the new Jerusalem is one that is open to all and the task of building belongs to all."[977]

Summarizing the significance of these beautiful verses, Barker writes: "Building Jerusalem in England's green and pleasant land makes no sense apart from the tradition of Jerusalem as the Kingdom of God. Jerusalem, for William Blake, was the vision of a world released from the horrors of the 'dark Satanic Mills', with the 'countenance divine' shining in the midst. This was temple imagery, and Blake had seen the vision of the Kingdom."[978]

EXCURSUS

---

974   H. Bloom, *Commentary*, p. 909; N. M. Goslee, *England's Green*; N. M. Williams, *Ideology*, pp. 150-151.
975   H. Bloom, *Commentary*, p. 910. See *Endnote E-158*, p. 739.
976   H. Bloom, *Blake's Apocalypse*, p. 306.
977   C. Rowland, *Blake*, pp. 171-172.
978   M. Barker, *Hidden*, p. 128.

Excursus 42

Nebuchadnezzar's "Fall"

Nibley connects the story of Nebuchadnezzar to the Egyptian story of Osiris who, like Adam,[979] was said to have been freed from a split tree:

> In the book of Daniel, the tree that was split was the king himself;[980] however the stump was not destroyed but preserved for a seven-year period,[981] during which time the king was ritually humiliated…,[982] only to resume his throne with all his glory greatly enhanced at the end of the seven-year period.[983] This is the Egyptian seven-year throne period of the king… The splitting of the tree is plainly the substitute sacrifice, while its preservation against the time when the king shall be restored recalls the important role of the *ished-tree* in the coronation.[984]

Although nothing like this episode can be associated directly with the historic King Nebuchadnezzar (605-562 BCE), both Neo-Babylonian inscriptions and the *Prayer of Nabonidus (4Q242)* fragment of the *Dead Sea Scrolls* provide evidence of a pre-Danielic tradition associating a similar story with Nabonidus, the last ruler of the Neo-Babylonian Empire (556-539 BCE) and father of Belsharusur (biblical "King Belshazzar"—see Daniel 5:22, 7:1, 8:1).[985] In his prayer, the king tells of his suffering with an "evil skin disease" for a period of seven years by the decree of God, and at least one scholar has proposed that a lacuna in the text "originally described Nabunay's state as comparable to that of a beast,[986] or that he was 'set apart from human beings.'"[987] After appealing to gods of silver, gold, bronze, iron, wood, stone, and clay, his sins were forgiven by a Jewish healer after he finally prayed to the Most High God.[988]

Rabbinical and early Christian exegetes formulated a reading of Moses 4:24-25 that saw a consignment of Adam and Eve to a period of humiliating penance after the Fall, to a certain degree in the likeness of Nebuchadnezzar.[989] Having been banished from the fruit trees of the Garden of Eden, they then are thought to have been temporarily reduced to eating the herb of the field like the animals.[990] Playing on the double meaning of *veirdu* in Moses 2:28, Rashi comments that instead of "having dominion" over the beasts, he now would "fall down" below and be with them.[991] The *Targum Pseudo-Jonathan* says that after hearing the consequences of his transgression, Adam pled that he might be spared: "I beseech by the mercy before you, O Lord, let me not be reckoned before you as cattle, that I should eat the grass of the surface of the field. I will arise and labor… and I will eat the food of the earth; and thus let there be a distinction before you between the children of men and the offspring

---

979 See *Commentary* 4:14-e, p. 260.
980 Daniel 4:13-15, 22.
981 Daniel 4:23.
982 Daniel 4:33; cf. *Apis-bull* and *Horus-hawk.*
983 Daniel 4:25, 31-34.
984 H. W. Nibley, *Message 2005*, p. 289. See *Figure* 4-14, p. 231; *Commentary* 4:14-e, p. 260; *Excursus 53: Comparative Explorations of the Mysteries*, p. 663. See *Endnote* 4-50, p. 312.
985 F. G. Martinez, *DSS Translated*, p. 289; L. T. Stuckenbruck, *Daniel*, pp. 104-106; J. A. Tvedtnes, *Nebuchadnezzar*; G. Vermes, *Complete*, p. 614; M. Wise, *et al.*, *DSS*, pp. 340-342.
986 Daniel 4:25b.
987 L. T. Stuckenbruck, *Daniel*, p. 105. See Daniel 4:25a.
988 A similar healing blessing performed by Abraham with the laying of hands upon the head is described in F. G. Martinez, *Genesis Apocryphon*, 20:28-29, p. 234.
989 H. W. Nibley, *Message 2005*, p. 289.
990 G. A. Anderson, *et al.*, *Synopsis*, 4:2, p. 5E; G. A. Anderson, *Penitence*, pp. 13-19; G. A. Anderson, *Perfection*, pp. 141-147. See *Commentary* 2:29-a, p. 117; 4:24-b, p. 271; 4:25-a, p. 272.
991 S. L. Della Torre, *Anxiety*, p. 7.

FIGURE E42-1. *Nebuchadnezzar, 1795*
William Blake, 1757-1827

O king Nebuchadnezzar,… The kingdom is departed from thee. And they shall drive thee from men, and thy dwelling shall be with the beasts of the field: …until thou know that the most High ruleth in the kingdom of men, and giveth it to whomsoever he will. The same hour was the thing fulfilled upon Nebuchadnezzar: and he was driven from men, and did eat grass as oxen, and his body was wet with the dew of heaven, till his hairs were grown like eagles' feathers, and his nails like birds' claws.[1] In Blake's grotesque depiction of Nebuchadnezzar, "we see [the king] in exile, animal-like on all fours. Naked, he gazes with mad horror at his own reflection like some kind of anti-Narcissus."[2]

'This picture was painted in 1795. In France, Louis XVI had been executed two years before. Meanwhile, in England, George III, whose yoke the American colonists had recently thrown off, suffered from bouts of insanity[—thus] this picture of a degraded king [could] be an expression of Blake's republican sentiments…"[3] "Beneath the horror of Nebuchadnezzar, Blake inscribed, as covering Proverb, the dying tyrant Tiriel's gasp of wisdom: 'One Law for the Lion & Ox is Oppression.' With this outcry against the imposition of any code of uniformity upon contrary individualities," Blake reminds society that "it tempts the fate of Nebuchadnezzar, a fall into dazed bestiality, if it will not heed the warnings of [the prophet's transforming] vision."[4]

---

1   Daniel 4:31-33. See *Endnote E-159*, p. 739.
2   *William Blake Online*. See also W. Blake, *Illuminated Blake*, p. 121; N. Frye, *Symmetry*, pp. 270-272. It has often been claimed that Blake himself struggled with madness. See *Endnote 0-27*, p. 27. See *Endnote E-297*, p. 783.
3   *William Blake Online*.
4   H. Bloom, *Blake's Apocalypse*, p. 96.

of cattle."[992] Once the period of penance was complete, wheat (along with instructions for sowing and reaping) is mentioned in various traditions as having been divinely provided in answer to Adam's cries of hunger. And, as one source recounts, "his descendants have lived on wheat ever since."[993]

---

992   M. Maher, *Pseudo-Jonathan*, 3:18, p. 28.
993   *Coptic Apocrypha*, cited in E. A. W. Budge, *Cave*, pp. 18-19 n. 1; cf. *Commentary* 3:9-i, p. 168; 4:25-a, p. 272; 5:2-a, p. 354; D&C 89:17. See *Endnote 5-44*, p. 441.

Excursus 43
Adam and Eve in Mozart's "Magic Flute"

*L*OVE'S *exalted purpose clearly indicates that there is nothing more noble than a wife and a husband. Husband and wife, and wife and husband, reach to the heights of Godhood.*[994] One of Mozart's last works before his untimely death, *The Magic Flute* has been much maligned by those who judge its libretto shallow, confused, and filled with inexcusable misogyny. However, BYU Professor Alan Keele, who has done much to promote a modern appreciation of supernal idealism in German literature, opera, and cinema, has sought to rehabilitate its status by a more careful reading of this opera, whose central theme is, after all, the human tendency to mistake appearances for reality. Keele shows that, rather than upholding conventional practices that withheld membership in Freemasonry from women, the opera's brilliantly-crafted deep structure suggests that "Mozart perceived this misogynistic and celibate order—though righteous as far as it goes—should and would be replaced by a new and equal gender-neutral leadership, personified in Tamino and Pamina, deified in Isis and Osiris. Certainly that does not detract from the dignity and holiness of Sarastro,[995] who apparently represents the last celibate high priest, destined to be replaced by the new, married high priest and priestess.... All the apparent confusion of this libretto, all its contradictory claims and behaviors flee as the darkness before the glorious structural clarity of this paradigm: The God-couple Isis-Osiris are to be the model for the new Adam-and-Eve couple Pamina-Tamino, who, if they prove their worthiness, will become like the Gods."[996] As the "successor and antidote to *Cosi fan tutte*," Chailley notes that *The Magic Flute* restored "the ideal of true love which the society of the period scoffed at so readily; that Ideal Love which we are free to believe that Constanze's husband [Wolfgang] must often have sought."[997]

FIGURE E43-1.
Portrait of Wolfgang Amadeus Mozart, 1819
Barbara Krafft

Wolfgang's older sister Maria Anna (Nannerl) was a gifted musician in her own right and, during their years as touring child performers, Wolfgang wrote a series of piano duets that allowed them to play together. Hindered by her gender from pursuing composition, Maria eventually entered an unhappy marriage with a wealthy magistrate and, sadly, became estranged from her brother. Maria and Wolfgang began speaking again after their father's death in 1787, and in 1789 Wolfgang named a newborn daughter after his sister. Twenty-eight years after Wolfgang's death, Maria supervised a new portrait of her brother by an otherwise unknown Salzburg artist named Barbara Krafft. Based on an earlier image of Wolfgang at the age of twenty-five, this later portrayal seems more appealingly alive—the difference doubtless owing as much to the urgings of Mozart's sister as to the skill of the portraitist.

---

994 *The Magic Flute* 1:14: The German text reads: "Ihr hoher Zweck zeigt deutlich an, Nichts edlers sey, als Weib und Mann. Mann und Weib, und Weib und Mann, Reichen an die Gottheit an."

995 = Zoroaster—presumably modeled on Mozart's Masonic mentor, Ignaz von Born.

996 A. Keele, *Zauberflöte*, pp. 109-110; cf. A. Keele, *Magic Flute*, pp. 63-64; cf. M. P. Lyon, *Set Design*. See *Commentary 4:22-c, p. 268* and *Excursus 50: Fu Xi and Nü Gua, p. 654*. See *Endnote E-160, p. 739*.

997 J. Chailley, *Unveiled*, p. 295. See *Endnote E-161, p. 739*.

FIGURE E44-1. *Miranda — The Tempest, 1916*
John William Waterhouse, 1849-1917

If by your art, my dearest father, you have / Put the wild waters in this roar, allay them… / O, I have suffered with those I saw suffer… / O, the cry did knock / Against my very heart![1] Waterhouse, a retiring man whose personal life is somewhat of a mystery, is best known for his pre-Raphaelite portraits of women and classical scenes.[2] He "was noted for his ability to convey emotion through expression and gesture; here we cannot fully see Miranda's face, but a single simple gesture—her left hand placed over her heart—displays her concern for the passengers."[3] One of Waterhouse's last four works, this painting was exhibited at the Royal Academy a few months after his death.

---

1   W. Shakespeare, *Tempest*, 1:2:1-2, 5-6, 8-9, p. 1612.
2   P. Trippi, *Waterhouse*.
3   *Miranda*.

Excursus 44

Shakespeare Creates a World: "The Tempest"

The "direful spectacle of the wreck, which touch'd / The very virtue of compassion" in the 15-year-old Miranda dominates the opening scenes of *The Tempest*.[998] But soon thereafter, Miranda is informed that the deadly storm was a mere illusion, engineered through the godlike powers of Prospero, her father. "Be collected," he tells her, "no more amazement. Tell your piteous heart / There's no harm done… No, not so much perdition as an hair / Betid[999] to any creature in the vessel."[1000]

---

998   W. Shakespeare, *Tempest*, 1:2:26, p. 1612.
999   I.e., befallen, happened.
1000 W. Shakespeare, *Tempest*, 1:2:13-15, 30-31, p. 1612; cf. Acts 27:34; Luke 12:7.

The Tempest has been called Shakespeare's "mystery play," meaning not only that it is replete with interpretive puzzles, but also that it is "a play dramatizing a mystery in the sense of a religious rite."[1001] Indeed, Devereux notes that the play's "language of natural phenomena… functions as the sign of the mysteries":[1002]

> In its actions the play has run through a few hours; in its theme it has brought about reintegration; in its imagery it has run from Baptism [the storm], with which spiritual life begins, through Communion [the banquet], Penance [the ordeals], and Matrimony [the marriage of Ferdinand and Miranda], through finally to indulgence and prayers [Epilogue] for one who can no longer help himself.[1003]

Note also that "the masque that Prospero conjures to celebrate the troth-pledging of Miranda and Ferdinand echoes the Eleusinian Mysteries, although it uses the Roman names for the deities involved—Ceres, Iris, Dis and others—instead of the Greek. It is interesting that a play which is so steeped in esoteric imagery from alchemy and hermeticism should draw on the Mysteries for its central masque sequence."[1004]

Like *The Magic Flute*,[1005] the story begins with the violent near-death of the pure-hearted young champion and culminates in a marriage that will mark the end of the rule of an aging celibate spiritual leader (Prospero/Sarastro), supplanting it with the more perfect reign of a new Adam and Eve (Ferdinand and Miranda/Tamino and Pamina). The elaborate manipulation of events behind the scenes and the deliberate exposure of the hero and heroine to mortal danger are revealed as part and parcel of expressly designed tests intended to prove the worthiness of the couple.[1006] In final scenes that recall God's benediction on the renewed earth after the Flood, Prospero presents Ferdinand and Miranda "with the spectacle of a rainbow and a blessing of fertility"[1007] as they abandon the paradisiacal island[1008] to enter the "brave new world."[1009]

Of Shakespeare's sources for this play, perhaps the least acknowledged and appreciated is the book of Genesis.[1010] Rectifying this oversight, the perceptive Steven Marx and Harold Fisch have been foremost among the critics in demonstrating that many significant parallels and allusions to the opening book of the Bible have found their way into the first play of Shakespeare's *First Folio*.[1011] Comments Marx:

> Just as the Bible's God makes the world he populates and then interacts with it. Prospero conjures up the world of *The Tempest* with his magical utterances and peoples it with his own offspring, along with [a spirit of the air and a demon of the earth] over whom he has taken control.… *The Tempest*, whose title signifies storm and time in early modern English,[1012] also progresses into temporality from a beginning that is both the timeless chaos of the storm and an Edenic preserve where father and child have remained in idyllic stasis. "The hour's now come…," says Prospero, for him to retrieve the story of his past from "the dark backward and

1001 N. Frye, *Tempest*, p. 171.
1002 R. Battenhouse, *Dimension*, p. 252.
1003 E. J. Devereux, *Sacramental Imagery*, p. 257.
1004 *Eleusinian Mysteries*. See *Excursus 53: Comparative Explorations of the Mysteries*, p. 663.
1005 See *Excursus 43: Adam and Eve in Mozart's "Magic Flute"*, p. 634.
1006 See *Endnote E-162*, p. 739.
1007 S. Marx, *Shakespeare*, p. 25.
1008 See *Endnote E-163*, p. 740.
1009 W. Shakespeare, *Tempest*, 5:1:183, p. 1634. See *Endnote E-164*, p. 740.
1010 See *Endnote E-165*, p. 740.
1011 See *Endnote E-166*, p. 743.
1012 J. A. Simpson, *et al.*, *OED*, p. 2023:751.

abyss of time."[1013] From then on he continually watches the clock.[1014] His daughter's awakening to the temporal processes[1015] begins with repeated lapses into sleep,[1016] but leads to a strong sense of her previous lineage and her future destiny... As time unfolds..., so does space. In Genesis the setting expands from the pastoral confines of the Garden of Eden through the Canaanite desert to the epic vistas of the Egyptian empire. In *The Tempest* the setting expands from the domestic compound of Prospero's cell to the island's varied landscapes and then to all of Mediterranean Europe and beyond."[1017]

And just as the "overriding concern of the first book of the Bible [is] life-survival-offspring-fertility-continuity,"[1018] so the "'project' that Prospero has long prepared and that he sets in motion at the opening of the play... centers upon founding a chosen family... [through advancing the status of] the next generation... from [that of] children to progenitors."[1019]

Ideas relating to the Fall, the Flood, and the Tower of Babel are prominent in the early scenes in *The Tempest*:[1020]

> Prospero re-establishes his dominance as a 'God of power'[1021] and 'a prince of power'[1022] by throwing Caliban out of his home, forcing him to live by the sweat of his brow, and reducing the language that he taught him[1023] into profitless cursing,[1024] by repeatedly storming at Ariel that he will be returned to the oak that imprisoned him,[1025] and by tormenting his countrymen with the prolonged ordeal of death by drowning.[1026]

Though Prospero's role might be compared to that of a god,[1027] it is perhaps more illuminating to see him as a figure resembling Joseph in Egypt.[1028] "Linguistically [Joseph and Prospero] are linked by the word 'prosperity'—'and the Lord was with Joseph and he was a man that prospered.... And his master saw that... the Lord made all that he did to prosper in his hand.'":[1029]

> Joseph starts out as "this dreamer,"[1030] a person with true visions but lacking enough prudence to anticipate the resentment of those who do not share his gifts. Like Prospero, who, "rapt in secret studies,"[1031] "neglect[s] worldly ends, all dedicated / To closeness and the bettering of my mind,"[1032] Joseph is at first oblivious to the reality of his political situation. Both he and Prospero "Awaked an evil nature"[1033] in their brothers and, as a result, suffered usurpation,

---

1013 W. Shakespeare, *Tempest*, 1:2:37, 50, pp. 1612, 1613.

1014 See *Endnote E-167,* p. 743.

1015 See *Endnote E-168,* p. 743.

1016 E.g., W. Shakespeare, *Tempest*, 1:2:185, p. 1614.

1017 S. Marx, *Shakespeare*, pp. 19, 21-22.

1018 J. P. Fokkelman, *Genesis*, p. 41.

1019 S. Marx, *Shakespeare*, p. 22.

1020 See *Endnote E-169,* p. 743.

1021 W. Shakespeare, *Tempest*, 1:2:10, p. 1612.

1022 *Ibid.*, 1:2:55, p. 1613.

1023 See *Endnote E-170,* p. 744.

1024 W. Shakespeare, *Tempest*, 1:2:334-336, 363-365, p. 1616; cf. Moses 2:16-18; Genesis 11:6-9.

1025 W. Shakespeare, *Tempest*, 1:2:275-293, p. 1615. See *Commentary* 4:14-e, p. 260. See *Endnote E-171,* p. 744.

1026 S. Marx, *Shakespeare*, pp. 24-25. See W. Shakespeare, *Tempest*, 1:1:1-68, pp. 1611-1612.

1027 See *Endnote E-172,* p. 744.

1028 See *Endnote E-173,* p. 744. Speaking of the Bible's concern for the reversal of Adam's Fall, Brodie notes: "Centuries before all things were restored in Christ (cf. Ephesians 1), they were, in a sense already restored in Joseph" (T. L. Brodie, *Dialogue*, p. 146; cf. pp. 116, 118, 519-522).

1029 S. Marx, *Shakespeare*, p. 30. See Genesis 39:2-3.

1030 Genesis 37:19.

1031 W. Shakespeare, *Tempest*, 1:2:77, p. 1613.

1032 *Ibid.*, 1:2:89-90, p. 1613.

1033 *Ibid.*, 1:2:93, p. 1613.

exile, and imprisonment… Rudely awakened from innocence and forced to cope for survival in their places of exile, both Joseph and Prospero learn some practical wisdom.[1034]

At every turn of events, Prospero tries to remain firmly planted in the center of the action, despite the disorder of his "beating mind,"[1035] whose unsettled motions mimic the rhythm of the tempest's angry waves.[1036] He "controls nature, at least in the outward sense. [But, though] his art ought also to teach Prospero an absolute self-control, he clearly has not attained this even as the play concludes."[1037] He displays "the vices that go with superior power and knowledge: impatience, self-righteousness, anger, cruelty, jealousy, and pride. It is possible that Shakespeare sometimes regarded his own role of playwright and performer as godlike, his own book as potent and capacious as 'The Book'…[1038] Both piety and prudence might convince him to retreat from that role when it felt most alluring, to take off his magician's robe, and drown his book as soon as it was complete."[1039] In the epilogue, "Prospero puts himself in the position of Ariel, Caliban, Ferdinand, and the other shipwreck victims throughout the play, threatened with confinement, pleading for release from bondage; and his magical powers are now invested in the audience."[1040] He places hope in Divine response to his penitence: "And my ending is despair, / Unless I be reliev'd by prayer."[1041] "Outside the Gospel, there is nothing but despair."[1042]

The events of the play gradually disclose that the Providential purpose which originally brought about Prospero's exile will now encompass others equally in need of moral tutoring. To this end, the primary movement of the play "is to cause people to recall forgotten things, to bring sins to remembrance, to reforge broken relationships between estranged brothers and between father and son"[1043]—and ultimately to reveal "wonderful surprises."[1044] "These revelations, recognitions, restorations, and reconciliations produce an ecstatic happy ending. They also produce a retrospective vindication of all previous confusion and suffering as purposeful contributions to the positive outcome—a theological assertion of the fortunate fall: 'Now therefore be not sad… that ye sold me hither: for God did send me before you for your purification… to preserve your posterity in this land, and to save you alive by a great deliverance,'[1045] says Joseph."[1046] In the culminating scenes of the drama, Prospero "presides as 'Providence divine'[1047] over the 'covenant' of marriage, which in the play represents the final healing and redeeming moment in the lives of the characters—the 'salvation' to which the action of the play looks forward."[1048] Shakespeare has used the themes of death and Arcadia "to bathe his comedy in the light of transcendence."[1049]

Writes Fisch:

1034 S. Marx, *Shakespeare*, pp. 31-32.
1035 W. Shakespeare, *Tempest*, 4:1:163, p. 1630.
1036 J. Walter, *Epilogue*, p. 277.
1037 H. Bloom, *Shakespeare*, p. 666.
1038 See *Endnote E-174*, p. 745.
1039 S. Marx, *Shakespeare*, pp. 12-13.
1040 S. Orgel (ed.), in W. Shakespeare, *Tempest*, p. 205 n. 322-327.
1041 W. Shakespeare, *Tempest*, Epilogue 15-16, p. 1636.
1042 A. H. King, *Religion*, p. 159. See *Endnote E-175*, p. 745.
1043 H. Fisch, *Covenant Pattern*, p. 221. See *Endnote E-176*, p. 746.
1044 See *Endnote E-177*, p. 747.
1045 Genesis 45:5-7.
1046 S. Marx, *Shakespeare*, p. 35.
1047 W. Shakespeare, *Tempest*, 1:2:159, p. 1614. See *Endnote E-178*, p. 748.
1048 H. Fisch, *Covenant Pattern*, p. 221.
1049 A. D. Nuttall, *Shakespeare*, p. 241.

Prospero… leads the troubled race of man back to paradise… [But the] paradise to which he beckons us… is not the magic island of medieval Christianity with its songs and sweet airs, its orderly subordination of spheres, its harmony of natural law. It is altogether more strenuous, more real, more close to our everyday problems. There is in it neither illusion nor enchantment… and their destination as we know is Naples, not Utopia… If [Ferdinand and Miranda's] discovery of mutual love in the covenant of marriage provides [them] with one essential key to this understanding, it is because behind this covenant stands a larger and more embracing covenant, that enacted on the great stage of the world from the beginning, and pointing forward by promise to the end of days."[1050]

1050 *Ibid.*, p. 223

Excursus 45
Impact of the "Black Death" on Art and Literature

ASSAF Pinkus argues that sculptural programs on the exterior of medieval churches as well as contemporaneous religious literature were influenced by "new theological and moral perceptions, associated with the exegesis of the Genesis story, that emerged in southern Germany as a consequence of the Black Death"—an "attempt to understand the coherency of the divine plan in light of the plague and to change it by optimistically and mercifully re-writing human history and fate." He holds that these concerns were also among those that motivated the 14th-century German poetic version of the *Life of Adam and Eve* by Lutwin.[1051] In his analysis of selected scenes from Lutwin's composition, Pinkus describes several interesting differences with pseudepigraphal accounts of Adam's suffering and death:[1052]

> Seth's voyage begins with a description of Adam and Eve's children coming to support their dying father. The children, who have yet to experience death and sickness, are amazed by their father's suffering and request an explanation. At this point the different sources are at odds. In a Greek text from early Christian times, the *Apocalypsis Mosis*,[1053] Adam replies that he is "crushed by the burden of trouble."[1054] In a Medieval Latin text, *Vita Adae et Evae*,[1055] Adam's reply is slightly different, and he says, "I am sick and in pain." In all versions, Adam mentions maladies and epidemics that will plague man prior to death. Lutwin's version expands upon the cruel nature of these. At the request of his sons, Adam describes what sickness and suffering are. While this description in the other sources takes up five lines at most, Lutwin's text is much too long to be quoted here, continuing on for approximately 150 lines.[1056] Adam's detailed explanation apparently relates to the arguments reasoning [about the causes of] the plague. Stating that death and diseases are punishment for the original sin, Adam quotes the words of God:
>
> > "You shall endure all kinds of misfortunes. I shall lay upon you seventy maladies which will plague you from head to foot. I shall spare you nothing, and without pity from me you will suffer in all your limbs sickness and torment… as will all those who come after you."[1057]
>
> Afterward, at the request of Adam, Seth and Eve set out for Paradise, in quest of the Oil of Mercy, which is produced from the Tree of Life, so that Adam can be cured. In the *Apocalypsis Mosis*, the angel sent to speak with them denies their request.[1058] In the *Vita*, instead of the Oil of Mercy, they are given fragrant herbs to treat Adam's body.[1059] Lutwin's version also claims that no oil was received, but instead a branch from the Tree of Mercy, which is the Tree of Life, was given to them.[1060] This development is not found in any of the other sources. According to the Archangel Michael, on the very day that the branch bears fruit, the Oil of Mercy will flow for all mankind. This invention is a sharp digression from the traditional text. Other legends explaining the origin of the Tree of Crucifixion from the 12th century on mention seeds or a branch from the Tree of Knowledge, the symbol of death, that were delivered to Seth. Halford argues that Lutwin's original supplement, the accomplishment of the Journey and granting of

1051 M.-B. Halford, *Eva und Adam.*

1052 A. Pinkus, *Impact*, pp. 168-169. See also A. Pinkus, *Workshops*, pp. 74-84 and the overview of Moses 6, p. 460.

1053 = *Apocalypse of Moses*, a Greek version of the "Life of Adam and Eve."

1054 See G. A. Anderson, *et al.*, *Synopsis*, 9:1, p. 39E.

1055 Latin "Live of Adam and Eve."

1056 M.-B. Halford, *Eva und Adam*, pp. 275-278.

1057 *Ibid.*, p. 277.

1058 G. A. Anderson, *et al.*, *Synopsis*, 13:1-5, pp. 44E-45E.

1059 *Ibid.*, 43:3, p. 46E; cf. Revelation 22:2.

1060 M.-B. Halford, *Eva und Adam*, pp. 279-281. See *Endnote E-181*, p. 749.

the branch of the Tree of Life, the symbol of rebirth and hope, were intended to reinforce the role of the latter tree through contrast…[1061] In Lutwin's version, after Eve's death Seth carried out a second journey to Paradise; it was only then that he received a branch from the Tree of Knowledge, on which the Savior would be crucified.

Which version of Seth's journey served as a departure point for the presentation at Schwäbisch Gmünd? The first allusion identifying this scene is the image of Eve lamenting Adam. Realizing that Eve is still alive, one can assume that this is the first voyage to Paradise. Reading the narrative from left to right could potentially mean a chronological narrative development: first the branch was given to Seth and later it was planted in Adam's skull, becoming a tree.[1062] However, all the sources report that Eve accompanied Seth on his journey; moreover, the blossoming of the tree is only mentioned subsequent to her death! These contradictions between texts and image thus invalidate any possibility of reading the narrative as continuous. The late German Gothic sculptor does not hesitate to introduce the same figure a number of times during the same occurrence. Why then has Eve been omitted from Seth's journey? I believe that the omission was intended to suggest that this was Seth's second journey. The narrative should thus be understood as simultaneous rather than chronological; three events that occurred at different terms were merged into one image: Eve's lamentation, the blossoming of the branch from the Tree of Mercy that was planted on Adam's grave, and Seth's second journey to Paradise by himself, which is only mentioned in Lutwin's text. Quinn interprets Seth's journey as mankind's quest for divine mercy. She defines Seth as an almost abstract figure, existing exclusively to perform his mission: "to fetch for mankind the gift of God's mercy," which is the meaning of the image in Gmünd.

EXCURSUS

1061 M.-B. Halford, *Eva und Adam*, p. 33.
1062 See *Figure* 36-1, p. 616.

Excursus 46

The Origin and Meaning of the Term "Atonement"

ABOUT the core meanings expressed by the term "atonement," Elder Jeffrey R. Holland has written:

> The literal meaning of the word "atonement" is self-evident: *at-one-ment*, the act of unifying or bringing together what has been separated and estranged. The Atonement of Jesus Christ was indispensable because of the separating transgression, or Fall, of Adam, which brought… both the physical and the spiritual death…[:] physical death bringing the temporary separation of the spirit from the body, and spiritual death bringing the estrangement of both the spirit and the body from God.[1063]

Madsen emphasizes that the kind of union brought about through the Atonement does not result in a loss of individual identity:

> Some mystics have supposed that the role of the Messiah is to make way for an ecstatic union with the Divine, that we are to be swallowed up, in a "flight of the alone to the alone," as a drop of water merges into the oblivion of the sea.

> But the outcome of the Atonement of Jesus Christ is not such a union. Rather, it is a reunion— a reunion of individuals and family members. Christ's work will never be fully finished until He can present to the Father a family composed of families: healed from each other's wounds and sealed to and for each other in everlasting kinship. This is the reunion of the separated. This is the restoration of broken harmonies. This is reconciliation at its zenith, the fulfillment of the human family's ultimate yearning to come home and regain the presence of God in a transformed condition.[1064]

Even though some commentators erroneously dismiss the obvious derivation of "atonement" as nonsense,[1065] the approach to translation that produced this new term was well-established at the time the English Bible was produced. Arthur Henry King explains:

> In the Middle Ages, those who translated the Bible and other theological materials into English did so (as the Germans still do when translating into German) by translating the verbal components of a Greek or Latin word into English elements.… A term people muddle themselves about, for they cannot believe its etymology, is *at-one-ment*; "to make one," however is exactly what atonement means. "Ment," a suffix from Latin, makes "atone" into a noun; that's all "ment" does. But "atone" begins… with Wycliff; he had "one" as a verb: "to one," which is daring. It then became "at one" (an adjectival or adverbial form) but retained its character as a verb; from "at one" came the abstract noun "atonement." In the sixteenth century, Tyndale, a Bible translator, made the word equal to the Latin [*adunare*], which means "to unite" (*ad* is an intensifier here). This translation approach… mirrors the Germanic process of translating component parts.[1066]

The use of the verb *adunare* was rare in Latin, though it was used by some early Christian writers. Variations of the term (*adunata, adunavit, adunabo*) occur three times in the *Vulgate*,[1067] though in contexts with no theological significance. The *Oxford English*

1063 J. R. Holland, *Atonement*, p. 83; cf. J. R. Holland, *Christ*, pp. 197-245.

1064 T. G. Madsen, *Suffering*, p. 243.

1065 E.g., "the explanation of this English word as being 'at-one-ment' is entirely fanciful" (W. E. Vine, *et al.*, *Dictionary (1996)*, NT, p. 44).

1066 A. H. King, *Wholeness*, pp. 331-332. "The phrase perhaps is modeled on L. *adunare* 'unite,' from *ad-* 'to, at' + *unum* 'one.'" (D. Harper, *Dictionary*, s.v., atone).

1067 2 Chronicles 24:27, 29:20; Ezekiel 11:17.

Dictionary points to occurrences of the phrase "to be made/set at one" (meaning "to be reconciled") as early as 1300, an expression that was gradually replaced by the verb "to atone."[1068] An early example comes from Sir Thomas More, an innovator with the English language who was, ironically, Tyndale's enemy. He wrote in 1513, referring to a reconciliation of a conflict in his *History of King Richard III*: "Having more regarde to their olde variaunce than their new attonement."[1069]

Tyndale's use of the term in his Bible translation was consistent with his theological view that the central mission of Jesus was:

> … to make us one with God: "One God, one Mediatour, that is to say aduocate, intercessor, or an *atonemaker*, between God and man." "One mediatour Christ, … and by that word understand an *atonnemaker*, a peacemaker."[1070]

Gallagher further explains:

> The original meaning also comes through in the various early Bible commentators. Note Udal's comment on Ephesians 2:16 which makes the intended meaning of "atone" crystal clear: "And like as he made the Jewes and Gentiles at one betwene themselfes, euen so he made them bothe at one with God, that there should be nothing to break the attonement, but that the thynges in heauen and the things in earth should be ioined together as it wer into one body."[1071]

Atonement also connotes wholeness in body, mind, and spirit, as still reflected in the modern use of the French term *salut*, referring both to health and salvation, and frequently used as a greeting. Observes Rey: "Like *fides*, a former religious term that has come into everyday usage, *salus* has been taken up into the language of the Christian church and given a new meaning. The word was originally a derivation of *salvus* (whole, intact)."[1072] The close association of health and salvation are equally apparent in other languages, as explained by King:

> The words "heal" and "whole" are etymologically akin. The sense of "wholeness" and the sense of "healing" are held together in the New Testament expression "the man was made whole."[1073] These words go back to the same root in Indo-European, and in the Germanic languages, they are close. Furthermore, "heal" and "whole" developed apparently separate significances of "curing" and "uniting" but while we take them as separate, we realize ways that these senses are clearly linked.
>
> One variant of the two is the word *Heiland* (Old English *Heliand*), the main German word for "Savior." It is the translation of "Savior," yet *Heiland* also means "the Healer," so the Savior is a healer as well. In fact, saving is healing and healing is saving; the dictionary's definitions of *salve* and "salvation" illustrate this fact. Furthermore, *Heilig* and "holy" are from the same root, meaning "holy," "heal," or "whole."[1074] Consider also the greeting words "hail" (English), *heil* (German), and *hell* (Scandinavian); all of these greetings mean "may you be well and whole."[1075]

While atonement is the preferred English term in the LDS Church for both the process and the result of Christ's sacrifice on our behalf, it has naturally been difficult to find terms

---

1068 J. A. Simpson, *et al.*, *OED*, p. 754.
1069 Cited in *ibid.*
1070 W. Tyndale, *Works*, pp. 158, 431, cited in W. Skeat, *Dictionary*, p. 40, s.v., atone.
1071 J. Gallagher, *Atoning*.
1072 A. Rey, *Dictionnaire*, 2:2009, s.v., *salut*.
1073 John 5:9.
1074 For cautionary arguments against, e.g., the equating of "holy" and "heal" (vs. "whole" and "heal") on an etymo- logical basis, see J. Barr, *Semantics*, pp. 111-114.
1075 A. H. King, *Wholeness*, p. 331.

with similar connotations in other languages. The only solution in many cases has been to leave out any explanation of the English term when the passage is translated. For example, the following paragraph in Elder Talmage's Jesus the Christ is simply omitted in the French translation:

> This basal thought is admirably implied in our English word, "atonement," which, as its syllables attest, is at-one-ment, "denoting reconciliation, or the bringing into agreement of those who have been estranged."[1076]

In other cases, even though there was no attempt to explain atonement to French readers, relevant differences in the English translation required an explanation from the translator.[1077]

Attempts to directly substitute the French terms *expier/expiation* for the English terms "to atone/atonement" are fraught with challenges. For example, consider the following statement in the *True to the Faith* gospel reference manual:

> The word "atone" means to reconcile, or restore to harmony. Through the Atonement of Jesus Christ, we can be reconciled to our Heavenly Father.[1078]

The corresponding statement in French does not convey as effectively the whole range of meaning of "atonement," the term *expier* (= English "expiate") having shifted so far from its roots. This fact has led the French translators of the *Septuagint* to replace it by *apaisement* (= English *appeasement*). They explain:

> "Appeasement" is not the traditional word used in Bible translations to describe the Hebrew rite that "covers" sins and obtains God's forgiveness (the ordinance called *kippurim*, is usually read as "Expiation") but it does precisely render the Greek term used by the Alexandrian translators to signify that the major purpose of the ritual is to appease God: the words "appeasement" or "propitiation" better emphasize the positive aspects of the ordinance than the term "expiation" which has come to possess, in current usage, different connotations....
>
> [In continuing to use the term "expiation," the] original idea of a reconciliation that is obtained through the offering has been lost. As a result, a whole set of Christian teachings have developed around the idea that man must "expiate" his sins, i.e., pay for them through chastisement or suffering, in order to receive forgiveness of his sins by their "expiation." Such terms are no longer suitable for expressing *hilasmós-exiláskomai*.[1079]

In the translation of *Doctrines of Salvation*, the French word for reconciliation is substituted[1080]—a better choice, yet unfortunately still not sufficient to adequately convey the idea of perfect unity that is felicitously found in the term "atonement."[1081]

1076 J. E. Talmage, *Jesus the Christ*, pp. 21-22; cf. J. E. Talmage, *Jésus le Christ*, p. 24.
1077 E.g., J. E. Talmage, *Jésus le Christ*, pp. 97-98. See *Endnote E-182*, p. 750.
1078 *True to the Faith*, p. 14, s.v., Atonement of Jesus Christ. See Romans 5:10-11; 2 Nephi 25:23; Jacob 4:11.
1079 C. Dogniez, *et al.*, *Pentateuque*, Glossaire, s.v. apaisement, pp. 868-870.
1080 Cf. J. F. Smith, Jr., *Doctrines*, 9 March 1935, 1:125 and 2 March 1935, 1:122.
1081 See the overview of Moses 6, p. 467.

Excursus 47
Islamic Perspectives Relating to Redemption

ALTHOUGH Islamic thought contains no explicit notion of redemptory sacrifice, vestiges of the idea can be seen in certain traditions and practices. For instance, some see parallels between Islamic and Jewish ideas in "the brief use of Jerusalem as the direction for daily prayers" in the early years of Islam and in "the development of fasting during the month of Ramadhan in opposition to, and part imitation of, the Day of Atonement (*yom kippur*)."[1082]

One Islamic tradition records that "the angel Gabriel brought a lamb, and taught Adam to kill it in the name of Allàh."[1083] *Hajj* pilgrims also are enjoined to "sacrifice some animal in the Name of God."[1084] An explanation offered to modern Muslims of this practice is that such a pilgrim is "symbolically sacrificing himself and fulfilling the obligation of the covenant on the basis of which God has taught man this verse: 'Say, Verily, my prayers, my sacrifice, my life and my death are for God, the Lord of the world who hath no peer.'"[1085]

The concept of sacrifice as a substitutionary practice is also evident in the invoking of the example of Abraham's offering of his firstborn son, where "God's intervention legitimized the sacrifice of a life for a life—a ram for the son."[1086] Though consistently avoiding any implication between the idea of sacrifice and that of atonement, Muslim commentary does emphasize God's "forgiveness, turning mercifully to the servants, covering their mistakes, bestowing mercy on them, putting them in the shadow of His compassion and grace—these are some of the divine attributes which He has especially reserved for the sinners. Adam could not know and understand them without passing through the stages which Allàh had decreed for them."[1087]

Notwithstanding these ritual and doctrinal affinities, the difficulties for Muslims in accepting the idea of a messiah who atones for men's sins include, among others, the following:

1. *The Muslim view of Christ as an intercessor rather than a Redeemer:* "The theory of atonement invalidates the system of reward and punishment, and consequently negates the absolute sovereignty of Allàh."[1088] Whereas the "intercessor... requests the Master to exercise his right of pardon and forgiveness... without in any way affecting the Master's ownership or authority," the atonement "is a deal, a bargain, which transfers the Master's authority from the sinner to the ransom given in his place, and removes the sinner from the Master's power as soon as the Master accepts the ransom in his place."[1089]

2. *The seeming absurdity of the incarnation of an immaterial God:* "[T]here is no relationship between a thing that has a physical body with all its accidents and concomitants and a Being that has neither a body nor any of its concomitants or accidents (like time, space, movement, etc.). How can one even think of unity between the two in any way?"[1090]

1082 R. C. Martin, *Encyclopedia*, 1:361.
1083 G. Weil, *Legends*, p. 45; cf. M. al-Kisa'i, *Tales*, p. 68; A. al-Tha'labi, *Lives*, p. 62; J. H. Sailhamer, *Genesis*, p. 58; *Commentary* 4:27-a, p. 274.
1084 S. A. Ashraf, *Inner*, p. 122.
1085 *Ibid.*, p. 124.
1086 *Ibid.*, p. 124. See *Endnote E-183*, p. 750.
1087 A. at-Tabataba'i, *Al-Mizan*, 2:37, 1:190.
1088 *Ibid.*, 3:79-80, 6:150.
1089 *Ibid.*, 3:79-80, 6:181.
1090 *Ibid.*, 6:170. Hence also the Muslim rejection of the idea that Jesus could be the "Son of God" (see, e.g., M.

3. *The notion of the consequences of Adam's original sin having fallen upon all men:* "What is the use or benefit of believing in divinely-sent realities and doing good deeds [if] the problem of original sin has been solved, and the atonement has brought forgiveness and mercy to all men, believers and unbelievers, righteous and unrighteous, all alike, without any difference between the most impeccable righteous one and the most incorrigible impious one."[1091]

4. *The idea of an atonement for personal sin that would benefit only Christians:* "[A]nd not even all the Christians but only a certain group among all those widely differing denominations. I wish I knew what would happen to the honored prophets (who came) before Christ, and to the believers of their *ummah*[1092]?"[1093]

5. *The sanctifying role of obedience to God's law as a necessary requirement accompanying the Christian emphasis on belief in God's mercy and grace:* "When a man follows the laws of religion,… his soul becomes ready to receive Allàh's bounties; and he is qualified—in his self and in his actions—for the divine honor in the hereafter. All of this emanates from the light put in his heart, and the purity that is found in his self."[1094]

Most of the above-listed inconsistencies for Muslims encountering traditional Christianity are dissolved when considered from the LDS point of view though, of course, some important differences still remain. For a more complete exposition of Muslim-Christian differences, see at-Tabataba'i.[1095]

Islamic scholar Mahmoud Ayoub characterizes two different types of redemption in Eastern and Western traditions of Christianity, and contrasts them to his view of redemption in Islam:[1096]

> The first [type of redemption in Christianity] is a death on the cross, where the cross becomes a prototype of the biblical or more specifically the Jewish temple altar. That sacrifice was the final sacrifice, all others before it being only a prelude to it…
>
> The other type is one that characterizes the Eastern Church most notably. It is redemption not by death and suffering so much as by victory.… [In this view,] Christ, the second Adam, came not to abolish an original sin by dying for Adam, but rather he came in order to make us divine… Hence that Christianity which lived on strongly and converted numerous people in the Syro-Aramaic area or what we now mainly call the Arab world, was that Christianity which has been characterized by Christian writers as the faith of the merciful, i.e., *addin arrahamami.* It is that faith which Islam breeds, and I think we cannot understand Islam fully unless we see it in that Christian ritualistic context. It may be argued that even though the prophet of Islam lived in closer proximity to the Jewish community in Medina and interacted with it far more extensively on a daily basis, the overall influence of the spirituality of Eastern Christianity and its idea of redemption played a greater role in the formative period of Muslim piety.…
>
> In the West the suffering of Christ developed into an idea of a Christ contorted with pain. (The gory images that we see in much of Western medieval literature characterizing the suffering Christ were the products of the first type of redemption; that is, redemption as death.) In Eastern Christian piety, on the other hand, the cross is not really an altar of suffering and death, but a throne of glory.…

Barker, *Christmas*, pp. 164-167).
1091 A. at-Tabataba'i, *Al-Mizan*, 3:79-80, 6:176;
1092 Arabic "religious community."
1093 A. at-Tabataba'i, *Al-Mizan*, 3:79-80, 6:176.
1094 *Ibid.*, 3:79-80, 6:173.
1095 *Ibid.*, 3:79-80, 6:162-184.
1096 M. M. Ayoub, *Redemption*, pp. 159-168.

EXCURSUS

To understand... the two types [of redemption] which... Islam added to the Christian notion, is to look briefly at the Muslim idea of man... Like the biblical Adam, the Adam of the *Qur'an* sinned by disobeying the divine command, but here the comparison ends. The *Qur'an* does not tell us that Adam ate of the fruit of the Tree of Knowledge, because knowledge was given to him even before his sin.[1097] Knowledge was not the cause of his condemnation and damnation but of his salvation.[1098] Adam was saved because he received words from his Lord.[1099] He was declared higher than the angels because he knew language which they did not know.[1100] So it is not knowledge that made Adam sin but disobedience. While the biblical Adam becomes the first sinner for Christians, for Muslims Adam is not the first sinner but the first prophet, because with him the history of revelation begins... Both [Iblis and Adam] rebelled. But while Adam repented and turned to God, Iblis persisted in his pride and would not accept that a creature of clay may be better than a creature of fire.

Redemption, then, in Islam begins with Adam, who was made for the earth. He descends to earth, and the battle between good an evil begins on its true stage, the earth. Redemption is when this battle is finally concluded with the divine victory, with the victory of the Good.

The *Qur'an* speaks not of ransom by sacrifice even though we do a commemorative sacrifice at the time of the *hajj* to commemorate the sacrifice of Abraham, but the *Qur'an* insists that then neither the fat nor the blood of the animals reaches God. What reaches him is our piety or righteousness. So expiation or *takfir* of sin must be done by the individual himself, and here, then, redemption is what men and women do with their own sin through repentance and through expiation through prayers, fasts, sharing their wealth with the poor, and so on. This is one type of redemption.

The other, and in a sense more important important in that it has permeated Islamic life more deeply and is a type which may be considered as really the only legitimate type of Islamic redemption, is that of intercession—*shafa'ah*. Contrary to what many Muslims say, intercession is not denied in the *Qur'an*; rather, what is denied is that intercession will benefit those who are deep in sin. Any intercession must be a divine gift...[1101] Furthermore, if we take the large number of *hadith* known as *ahadith ash-shafa'a*, or the traditions of intercession, we find so clearly the idea that it will be Muhammad who will intercede on behalf not only of the Muslims but the entire world...

While Muhammad... plays a very important intercessory role, intercession is not limited to him.... In a comment on [*Qur'an* 2:251] by the sixth Shi'i *imam*, Ja'far al-Sadiq, we are told that God protects those who do not pray among the Muslims through those who do pray; those who do not fast through those who do fast; and those who do not go on pilgrimage through those who do go. Were they all to concur in neglecting the prayers, fasting, and pilgrimage, then they would all perish.... So, then, wholeness, redemption, salvation, restoration can be achieved through personal expiation and through intercession widely considered....

It appears that the religious concept [in Islam, as in Christianity and Judaism, and even in Buddhism] is that the world evolves downward from a golden age to a silver age to an iron age to a clay age and then the whole thing will be dark until someone comes to restore things to their natural and earlier purity. This, in Islam, is the *Mahdi*.

In the *Mahdi* idea, Islam and Christianity again meet. I... argue...that the first notion of the *Mahdi* was not that a person of the family of the prophet will be born, according to the Sunni Muslim view, or that he will appear at the end of time, according to the Shi'i Muslim view.

1097 *Qur'an* 2:31-33. See *Commentary* 4:3-a, p. 245.
1098 See the overview of Moses 4, p. 229.
1099 *Qur'an* 2:37. See M. M. Ayoub, *Qur'an (Vol. 1)*, pp. 84-85. See *Commentary* 3:19-b, p. 177.
1100 *Qur'an* 2:33. See *Commentary* 3:19-b, p. 177.
1101 *Qur'an* 2:255.

Rather, it will be Jesus who will return. If we are to find any Qur'anic basis for this eschatological event, it will not be for a future, so to say, Islamic *Mahdi*, but for Jesus, who is declared to be a sign for the Hour.[1102] Muslim piety, in order to preserve itself and its own integrity, did not deny that Jesus will come to restore the world to its purity but affirmed that Jesus and the *Mahdi* wll work together. Most of the hard work will be done by Jesus, who will kill ad-Dajjal, the anti-Christ…. and restore the reality of the universe to its pristine purity. Symbolically it is said that Christ, when He comes, will break the cross and kill the swine (these two being the symbols that divide Muslims from Christians), and Islam in its essential aspects will prevail. This is redemption….

There is, finally, one important aspect of redemption, whether it be Christian or Islamic. Redemption is only one side of the divine judgment. Redemption must also imply judgment and condemnation. Christ will return on the clouds of heaven, as the book of Revelation declares;[1103] and those who have stabbed him will mourn him. He will come not as the meek lamb of God but as the man who has a sword of fire coming out of his mouth with every word he utters. Before the new earth and the new heavens will appear, …judgment must be executed on the wicked. Similarly, with Islam, the *Mahdi* when he comes will avenge the blood of Husayn before he fulfills his main mission; on this both Shi'i and Sunni traditionalists agree…

The *Mahdi* will do his work and eventually die, but it will be Husayn who will return to rule the earth or the Muslim community…

What does [this] say to us today? I have said that redemption in its widest sense is a corporate, not an individual process. Whether it be the Church widely viewed or the Church of [Jesus Christ of] Latter-day Saints or the Muslim community, for redemption to be meaningful and real for us today, we all have to take part in it as an ongoing process…

We who are in an academic position, who are average in society but who are committed can yet also play a role. What we see today is the beginning of a new dialogue—to me, at least. I do not think, and I must tell you here and now, I do not think that you people will be any more successful in converting Muslims to Mormonism than any missionaries who were before you. But you could be successful in one important area: that is, to create an important dialogue that will lead to a fellowship of faith between you and us.[1104] I think that the truth is bigger than any concept of the truth held by any nation or religious community or individual. And to the truth there are many ways. We can all meet along the way and learn, but his or her own way to God in the way he or she knows best. I myself was born in a Muslim community to a very devout family. But for fifteen years I was a fundamentalist Protestant; I was baptized and all of it, and I shouted more amens and hallelujahs than any of you. Why, then, did I return to Islam? Not because I feel that Christianity is not a redeeming process but because I felt that my roots are in that civilization, in that world, in that ethos, in that whole worldview, and I think it is better for both Islam and Christianity that I did that.

In conclusion, I would like to say that Christ redeemed and continues to redeem us, not simply and only by his divine act, but by his humanity, a humanity that cared. Muhammad redeemed and continues to redeem us as we follow his life, his *sunna*, as a model for our lives. But in the end we must heed the words, "Work out your own salvation with fear and trembling."[1105] I pray that we will all be successful in that process and that we will strengthen each other as we traverse the weary way of this life into the life to come.

1102 *Qur'an* 43:61.
1103 Revelation 1:7.
1104 See *Annotated Bibliography, Islamic Texts*, p. 896.
1105 Philippians 2:12.

Excursus 48
The Nature and Scope of Premortal Covenants

THOUGH it seems reasonable to suppose that each person who was to come to earth made premortal covenants of some kind,[1106] our knowledge of their nature and scope is currently limited. However, Elder Neal A. Maxwell wrote that: "our memories of the first estate will eventually be fully restored; and, upon regaining our premortal perspectives, we will acknowledge that we did indeed come here under certain conditions to which we earlier agreed—with the risks and rewards adequately explained beforehand."[1107] No doubt the primary reason for the light of Christ "that lighteth every man that cometh into the world"[1108] is to enable all of God's children to keep these premortal covenants, and to lead them toward the greater light and knowledge available to them through the Gift of the Holy Ghost.[1109]

Speaking of his personal beliefs about these covenants, Elder Orson Hyde said:

> … if it be true that we entered into a covenant with the powers celestial, before we left our former homes, that we would come here and obey the voice of the Lord, through whomsoever he might speak, these powers are witnesses of the covenant into which we entered; and it is not impossible that we signed the articles thereof with our own hands—which articles may be retained in the archives above, to be presented to us when we rise from the dead, and be judged out of our own mouths, according to that which is written in the books.… But the question is, Did we subscribe to any such doctrine as this [at] the start? I will not say that we did; yet I have had such thoughts, and they whisper strongly in my heart.[1110]

In addition to the idea of a general covenant of personal obedience presumed by Elder Hyde, Elder John A. Widtsoe has expressed the view that we entered into a partnership with the Lord to share a measure of responsibility for the carrying out of His overall plan. In essence, Elder Widtsoe expressed that just as the Savior agreed to make the unique sacrifice of His life in our behalf, so all premortal souls similarly expressed their willingness to make sacrifices for the happiness and salvation of others:

> In our preexistent state, in the day of the Great Council, we made a certain agreement with the Almighty. The Lord proposed a plan, conceived by him. We accepted it. Since the plan is intended for all men, we became parties to the salvation of every person under that plan. We agreed, right then and there, to be not only saviors for ourselves but measurably, saviors for the whole human family. We went into a partnership with the Lord. The working out of the plan became then not merely the Father's work, and the Savior's work, but also our work. The least of us, the humblest, is in partnership with the Almighty in achieving the purpose of the eternal plan of salvation.[1111]

Note that it was in order to "plant in the hearts of the children the promises made to the fathers"[1112] that Elijah came to the Kirtland temple in 1836.

EXCURSUS

1106 See the overview of Moses 5, p. 344.

1107 N. A. Maxwell, *Prove*, p. 57.

1108 D&C 93:2, John 1:9. See also Alma 28:14; Moroni 7:12-19; D&C 84:46; D&C 88:6-13, 41.

1109 D&C 84:46-48; C. K. Dunford, *Light of Christ*; V. L. Ludlow, *Principles*, pp. 58-59; L. Richards, *Marvelous*, pp. 122-128; *LDS Bible Dictionary*, s.v. Light of Christ. See *Endnote E-184*, p. 750.

1110 O. Hyde, *6 October 1859*, pp. 314-315.

1111 Elder John A. Widtsoe, cited in A. F. Bennett, *Saviors*, pp. 11-12; B. K. Packer, *Holy Temple*, p. 216.

1112 JS-H 1:39; cf. Malachi 4:5-6; Luke 1:17; 3 Nephi 25:6; D&C 27:9; 110:15; 128:17; J. Smith, Jr., *Teachings*, 6 April 1844, p. 356; 2 July 1839, pp. 160-161; 27 August 1843, p. 323; 20 January 1844, p. 330; 10 March 1844, pp. 337-

Islamic tradition also alludes to a covenant of obedience made between Allàh and all mankind.[1113] *Al-Mizan* comments:

> Allàh says: "And certainly We had covenanted unto Adam before, but he forgot."[1114] Which covenant does this verse allude to?... [T]he covenant means the general covenant which was made with the whole mankind and more particularly with the prophets[,] the covenant made with the souls of the human beings about the Mastership of Allàh and their own servitude.[1115] That covenant obliged the man that he should never forget that Allàh is his Lord, the Ruler and Master of his affairs; nor should he lose sight of the fact that he is a wholly owned slave of Allàh; that he has no authority whatsoever over his benefit or harm; nor does he have any control over his life, death or resurrection; in short he owns neither his person, his characteristics, nor his actions.[1116]

Within the Islamic *Stories of the Prophets* collections are also found expansions on *Qur'an* 7:172, such as the following:[1117]

> Allàh... made a covenant with the descendants of Adam. He touched Adam's back,[1118] and lo! the whole human family which shall be born to the end of time issued forth from it, as small as ants, and ranged themselves right and left.

> At the head of the former stood Muhammad, with the prophets and the rest of the faithful, whose radiant whiteness distinguished them from the sinners, who were standing on Adam's left, headed by Kabil [= Cain], the murderer of his brother.

> Allàh then acquainted the progenitor of man with the names and destinies of each individual....

> Allàh then cried to the assembled human family, "Confess that I am the only God, and that Muhammad is my messenger." The hosts to the right made their confession immediately; but those to the left hesitated, some repeating but one half of Allàh's words, and others remaining entirely silent. And Allàh continued: "The disobedient and impenitent shall suffer the pains of eternal fire, but the faithful shall be blessed in Paradise!"

> "So be it!" responded Adam; who shall call every man by name in the day of the resurrection, and pronounce his sentence according as the balance of justice shall decide.[1119]

> When the covenant was concluded, Allàh once more touched Adam's back, and the whole human race returned to him.

Underscoring the importance of such accounts within Islam, Schimmel asserts that the "idea of this primordial covenant (*mithaq*) between God and humanity has impressed the religious conscience of the Muslims... more than any other idea."[1120]

For a discussion of the New and Everlasting Covenant in LDS thought, see the overview of Moses 4, pp. 216-220 and the overview of Moses 5, pp. 340-350.

338.

1113   See *Endnote E-185*, p. 750.
1114   *Qur'an* 20:115. A related Jewish tradition recounted that "the unborn souls of future generations... were present at Sinai to receive the *Torah*" (H. Schwartz, *Tree*, p. 164).
1115   *Ibid.*, 7:172.
1116   A. at-Tabataba'i, *Al-Mizan*, 2:35, 1:181-182.
1117   G. Weil, *Legends*, pp. 39-40. See also *Qur'an* 30:30, 33:7, 53:56; A. al-Tha'labi, *Lives*, pp. 67-68; B. M. Wheeler, *Prophets*, pp. 32-33; cf. M. al-Kisa'i, *Tales*, pp. 73-74, 82; al-Tabari, *Creation*, 1:133-137, pp. 304-307. See *Endnote E-188*, p. 751.
1118   I.e., "his loins" (W. A. Graham, *Divine*, p. 161).
1119   See *Endnote E-187*, p. 751.
1120   A. Schimmel, *Mystical*, p. 24; cf. M.al-Kisa'i, *Tales*, p. 345 n. 51.

Excursus 49
The People of the Book

MUSLIMS refer to Jews and Christians (along with themselves) as *ahl al-kitab*, meaning roughly "The People of the Book," thus recognizing these groups as having faith rooted in genuine revelation from God.[1121] The "Book" in question is not the *Qur'an* or any single work of scripture, but rather the complete and perfect heavenly archetype from which all authentically-revealed texts that have been sent down "gradually" since the time of Adam[1122] were originally derived.[1123]

Though Muslims believe that Jews and Christians have since embraced many errors because of subsequent corruption of their respective books of scripture,[1124] their faiths are held in higher esteem than the faiths of those who do not accept Abraham, Moses, or Jesus.[1125] Reciprocally echoing the spirit of this principle, Elder Boyd K. Packer acknowledged important affinities between Mormonism and Islam: "Knit together by world history and by Old Testament history and doctrine, the Church and the Islamic world can see each other as 'People of the Book,' indeed 'Family of the Book.'"[1126]

Many students of the *Qur'an* take the notion of the universality of God's concern for all of his children very seriously. For example, a Sufi scholar writes critically of those who would deny God's ongoing interest in the spiritual enlightenment of non-Muslims:

> More than one exoteric outlook is based on the assumptions which, if pushed to their logical conclusions, would seem to imply that God has left large parts of the globe in spiritual darkness for long periods of time. The *Qur'an* sweeps all such illusions aside: "For every nation there is a Messenger,"[1127] and "Verily We have sent Messengers before thee, about some we have told thee, and about some We have not told thee."[1128] We may quote also, in this connection the following: "Verily the Faithful [Muslims] and the Jews and the Christians and the Sabaeans [i.e., Mandaeans]—whoso hath faith in God and the Last Day and doeth deeds of piety—their meed [= reward] is kept for them with their Lord, and no fear shall come upon them, neither shall they grieve."[1129] Finally, lest it be imagined that such declarations refer only to the past and that all other revelations have been superseded by itself, the *Qur'an* expressly states: "For each We have appointed a law and a path; and if God had wished He would have made you one people.... So vie one with another in good works. Unto God is your return, all of you together, and He will then inform you of that wherein ye were at variance."[1130]

Similarly, in explaining differences between the *Jahil-e-Muqassir* (= the "culpable ignorant" or "obstinate non-believers") and the *Jahil-e-Qasir* (= the inculpable ignorant), a group of Shi'ite scholars express the view that:

1121 R. C. Martin, *Encyclopedia*. 1:27-29.

1122 A. at-Tabataba'i, *Al-Mizan*, 5:8-9; cf. *Qur'an* 25:32.

1123 A. at-Tabataba'i, *Al-Mizan*, 5:79-80; J. Wansbrough, *Qur'anic Studies*, pp. 83, 170; B. M. Wheeler, *Prophets*, pp. 3-4; *Qur'an* 3:135-136, 85:21-22. See *Endnote E-189*, p. 751.

1124 A. at-Tabataba'i, *Al-Mizan*, 3:79-80, 5:10-11, 6:184-219; T. Khalidi, *Muslim Jesus*, p. 20.

1125 See *Qur'an* 2:105; Z. Karabell, *Peace*, pp. 19-20; D. C. Peterson, *Muhammad (2001)*, pp. 590-591. See *Endnote E-190*, p. 752.

1126 B. K. Packer, *Bridges*, p. 7.

1127 *Qur'an* 10:47.

1128 *Qur'an* 40:78.

1129 *Qur'an* 2:62.

1130 A. B. S. Ed-Din, *Sufism*, p. 232. See *Qur'an* 5:48. See *Endnote E-186*, p. 750.

EXCURSUS

… those who have not heard about the true message of Islam and are not blameworthy with regard to this will attain salvation if they are truthful to their own religion. This religion must be based on the *'fitrah*[1131]—man's primordial, innate nature—and so the followers of such a religion, for example, abstain from lying and committing crimes against humanity. This rule is also applicable to the *Ahlus Sunnah*[1132] to whom the truthfulness of Shi'aism has not been explained correctly.[1133]

In explanation of the well-known verse in the *Qur'an* that there is "no compulsion in religion,"[1134] *al-Mizan* comments:

> Islam is not based on the sword and killing, and… does not allow Muslims to compel or coerce others to accept Islam. It is contrary to the view held by many Muslims and non-Muslims alike that Islam is the religion of the sword… We have already clarified, while writing the commentary on the verses of fighting, that the fighting ordained by Islam is not for the purpose of material advancement nor for spreading… religion by force. It was ordained only for reviving the truth and defending the most precious treasure of nature—the faith of monotheism. Where monotheism is accepted by the people—even if they remain Jew or Christian—Islam does not fight with them.[1135]

Although the term "People of the Book" has its origins in Islam, "it has become a common self-description used by Jews throughout the world" to emphasize their own attachment to the *Torah*.[1136] Indeed, noted Jewish critic of secular and sacred literature Harold Bloom, citing Kushner, describes the Jewish people as having "tumbled from the pages of books: the *Tanakh*, the two *Talmuds* of Babylon and Jerusalem, and all the subsequent commentaries down to this moment."[1137] In a very fundamental sense, however, later generations of books are of a different nature and of lesser stature than their predecessors. For example, Mopsik laments the eventual completion of the Jewish *Talmud*, which relegated subsequent commentary to mere footnotes:

> We can only imagine what the *Talmud* would have been had its writing been continued up to the present. Speaking in human terms, Jewish tradition became the rabbinic tradition, which has become one with the *Talmud*. Hebrew religious literature was henceforth diminished, its effort focused on providing the glosses, comments, and explanations found in small type in the margins of the main text—but in fact outside the book itself.[1138]

By way of contrast, Bloom sees the "entire argument" of the New Testament as being that "Jesus Christ [has been set] above *Torah*"[1139] or, in other words, "that a man has replaced Scripture."[1140] Indeed, John 14:6, Jesus' statement that He is "the way, the truth, and the life" (arguably the core statement of this entire gospel),[1141] is a startling challenge to the orthodoxy of His time. The sense of this assertion is that the ways of God, the truth of moral perfection, and eternal life itself are ultimately not to be found in the written record

---

1131 Arabic "The divine nature by which Allàh created mankind."
1132 Roughly speaking, Sunni Muslims.
1133 Porch of Wisdom Cultural Institution, *Faith and Reason*, p. 91.
1134 *Qur'an* 2:256.
1135 A. at-Tabataba'i, *Al-Mizan*, 2:256, 4:172. For an illuminating view of world (and religious) history as seen through Islamic eyes, see T. Ansary, *Destiny*. For a western view, see B. Lewis, *Islam in History*.
1136 C. S. Ehrlich, *Rivers*, p. 13.
1137 H. Bloom, *American Religion*, p. 116. See *Endnote E-191*, p. 752.
1138 C. Mopsik, *Zohar*, 1:10; cf. P. Schäfer, *Torah as Wisdom*. See *Endnote E-192*, p. 752.
1139 H. Bloom, *Names Divine*, p. 23. See *Endnote E-193*, p. 752.
1140 *Ibid.*, p. 14.
1141 H. N. Ridderbos, *John*, p. 493.

of the *Torah*[1142]—which Barker argues had been substituted for a more ancient concept of Wisdom[1143]—but rather in the person of Jesus Christ, the One who gave the Law.[1144] Said Jesus Himself: "[Ye] search the scriptures; for in them ye think ye have eternal life: [yet] they are they which testify of me."[1145]

Bloom attributes his own views about the "total incompatibility of Yahweh and Jesus Christ"[1146] in part to his reading of the gospel of John, but perhaps more importantly to the image of Jesus as seen through the lens of later Christian theology, i.e., the fact that the "Trinitarian Jesus Christ is Greek, and Yahweh is precisely what forever resists Greek thought in Hebrew tradition."[1147] Indeed, in Bloom's view, "Both Yeshua of Nazareth and Yahweh are irrelevant to the Trinity, since they were not just metaphorical and everything deposited in the Trinity is nothing but metaphor."[1148]

However, it is precisely the contrast between the authentically ancient Hebrew conception of God[1149] and its later philosophically-derived developments in normative Judaism and Hellenic Christianity that drew Bloom's admiring attention to the founder of Mormonism,[1150] who he calls the "greatest and most authentic of American prophets, seers, and revelators."[1151] Speaking "on the authority of a lifetime spent in apprehending the visions of great poets and original speculators," he finds no American equal to "the imaginative vitality of Joseph Smith's revelation" which recaptured "crucial elements in the archaic Jewish religion.... that had ceased to be available either to normative Judaism or to Christianity, and that survived only in esoteric traditions unlikely to have touched Smith directly."[1152]

See also *Excursus 6: The Authority and Power of Scripture*, p. 531.

See also *Excursus 6: The Authority and Power of Scripture*, p. 531.

EXCURSUS

1142 E.g., Psalm 19:7-9.
1143 M. Barker, *Older*, p. 83. See *Excursus 2: Ancient Concepts of Wisdom*, p. 516.
1144 W. Barclay, *Gospel (Vol. 1)*, 2:157-159; A. H. King, *Total*, p. 187; N. A. Maxwell, *Inexhaustible*, p. 212; C. T. Warner, *Truth*, p. 1490; Alma 34:14; cf. *Commentary* 2:1-c, p. 93. See also E. R. Goodenough, *Motif*.
1145 John 5:39. See *Endnote E-194*, p. 753.
1146 H. Bloom, *Names Divine*, p. 6.
1147 *Ibid.*, p. 70.
1148 *Ibid.*, p. 109.
1149 See *Endnote E-195*, p. 753.
1150 H. Bloom, *American Religion*, pp. 79-128.
1151 H. Bloom, *Millennium*, p. 224.
1152 H. Bloom, *American Religion*, pp. 98, 99, 101.

Excursus 50
Fu Xi and Nü Gua

THE miraculously-born Emperor-god Fu Xi,[1153] known as the "Heavenly Sovereign" is usually listed as the most ancient of the *San Huang* (Three August Ones) of Chinese legend.[1154] Fu Xi owes most of his fame to an account recorded in an appended text of the *I Ching*,[1155] whose earliest sections date to about 800 BCE.[1156] Here, he is given credit as the one who brought moral and social order to society through his divinely-inspired creation of the Eight Trigrams,[1157] in the process not only inventing writing, but also spawning a host of technological and cultural innovations.[1158]

In the well-known fourth-century BCE Chu silk manuscript, Fu Xi is portrayed as the creator who, with his female counterpart,[1159] "separated (Heaven) above and (Earth) below" and then "engendered four sons, the seasons, who measured the year by pacing it out with their feet."[1160] A few centuries later, stories began to describe him more mundanely "as a partly human king of the remote archaic past"[1161] and to closely associate him with a wife and sister named Nü Gua.[1162] Earlier myths of Nü Gua as a goddess had also associated her with the process of creation, specifically the creation of the human race from the soil.[1163] At this later period, Fu Xi and Nü Gua were associated with the institution of marriage and were seen as the progenitors of mankind—with some elements of their story resembling incidents in the account of the biblical Adam and Eve.[1164]

In a section of *The Classic of Mountains and Seas* dating to the first-century BCE various descriptions of an earthly paradise and themes of immortality can be found. Summarizes Birrell:[1165]

> Like Mount Olympus, it is the place where the gods descend from the sky to that part of the human world which most nearly replicates the paradisiacal state of Heaven... The K'un-lun earthly paradise has a sky-ladder in the form of a giant tree, the "Tree Grain," so that earthly beings who have achieved a near perfect state and the heavenly gods may commune[1166].... This earthly[1167] paradise is guarded from intrusion by a fierce array of mythical beasts [including a phoenix pair, and luan-birds that "carry a serpent on their head and tread a serpent underfoot"[1168]]... Besides the mythical birds and beasts, there are twelve fabled trees, including the "Never Die" tree, trees of precious jewels, and unknown trees with fabulous names.... The narrative may represent the vestige of an archaic rite of inducing deathlessness which was enacted in the age of belief in immortality.

1153 Alternately, Fu Hsi or Pao Xi

1154 A. Birrell, *Mythology*, pp. 44-47; K. G. Stevens, *Chinese*, pp. 35-36.

1155 *Yi jing* = Book of Changes, Classic of Changes.

1156 A. Birrell, *Mythology*, p. 44.

1157 Chinese *ba gua*.

1158 M. E. Lewis, *Writing*, pp. 197-209; M. E. Lewis, *Flood*, pp. 116-119.

1159 See *Endnote E-197*, p. 753.

1160 M. E. Lewis, *Writing*, p. 202; T. Michael, *Dao*, p. 9. See also M. E. Lewis, *Flood*, pp. 21-23.

1161 A. Birrell, *Mythology*, p. 46.

1162 Alternately, Nü Kua or Nü Wa. See *Endnote E-198*, p. 753.

1163 A. Birrell, *Mythology*, pp. 33-35, 163-165; M. E. Lewis, *Writing*, p. 202; K. G. Stevens, *Chinese*, pp. 30-32.

1164 A. Birrell, *Mythology*, p. 34. See *Endnote E-199*, p. 753.

1165 *Ibid.*, pp. 183-184; cf. J. S. Major, *Heaven*, pp. 47, 150-161.

1166 See *Figure* 3-8, p. 145; *Figure* 3-10, p. 147; *Commentary* 3:9-g, p. 166. See *Endnote 3-48*, p. 209. See *Endnote E-200*, p. 753.

1167 See *Endnote E-201*, p. 754.

1168 A. Birrell, *Mythology*, p. 185. See *Commentary* 4:21-d, p. 266.

Lewis sees it as noteworthy that Fu Xi and Nü Gua "appear only in funerary art."[1169] He describes their role in tombs from the Han era as follows:

> Fu Xi and Nü Gua are… significant because they embody among the divinities the formation of couples, which was central to the household… The tomb art treats them as high divinities, and depicts their central role in maintaining the order of the cosmos. The art does this through the symbolism of the carpenter's square and compass that they hold, by treating them as reduced "charts" of the cosmos, and by using them as guardians for the inner doorways both of the tomb and the houses in tomb art.[1170]

> While women had only a marginal role in the patriline, the underworld household of the tomb was in many ways defined by the link of husband and wife, who were ultimately buried together… Deities depicted in order to transform the tomb into a cosmos were also often women. In several tombs, one stands at a half-open door welcoming the deceased to the world of the dead… Fu Xi and Nü Gua were a spirit couple who… provided the divine model for both the household and the joint burial.[1171]

Nü Gua and Fu Xi also appear in some versions of ancient Chinese flood myths. In Lewis' brilliant comparative study, he concludes that although "there is no single feature or meaning common to all versions, certain topoi or ideas to which floods lend themselves do recur in many contexts"—including, in the Chinese case:

> (1) the flood as a re-creation of the world within the human era, in which the world's enduring survival is made possible by new institutions or practices; (2) the flood as a form of punishment or revenge by some powerful spirit; (3) the repopulation of the earth after the flood as a means of dramatizing kinship structures, incest taboos, or the origins of different peoples of the earth; (4) the relations of people and animals, who collaborate or compete for the purposes of rescue or repopulation; and (5) water as an image of formlessness and fertility.[1172]

"In ancient mythic geography the cosmos was believed to be a square earth vaulted by a round sky and surrounded by four seas."[1173] In the accounts of the second-century BCE *Huainanzi* (*Huai-nan Tzu*), the Black Dragon Gong Gong[1174] is said to have stirred up "calamities of water" in a war with Zhuan Xu[1175] to become the chief god.[1176] The battle left the world in peril from fire and flood. Nü Gua corrected the earth's limits, dried up the flood, and patched the portion of the sky damaged by Gong Gong when he had knocked down one of its pillars[1177] in a fit of rage.[1178] The "five-colored stones" smelted by Nü Gua to repair the sky[1179] are associated by Lewis with the restoration of the phases of time, the cultivation of health and longevity, and fertility in the fusing of water and fire,[1180] but to readers of the Bible perhaps more obviously suggest the rainbow as a token of all these blessings.[1181]

1169 M. E. Lewis, *Flood*, p. 126.

1170 M. E. Lewis, *Construction*, pp. 129-130. See *Figure 4-17*, p. 233 and *Excursus 20: The Circle and the Square*, p. 571.

1171 M. E. Lewis, *Early*, pp. 190-191. See *Endnote E-205*, p. 755.

1172 M. E. Lewis, *Flood*, p. 5.

1173 A. Birrell, *Mythology*, p. 46. See *Endnote E-206*, p. 755.

1174 Alternately, Kung Kung.

1175 Alternately, Chuan Hsu.

1176 A. Birrell, *Mythology*, pp. 97-98; M. E. Lewis, *Flood*, pp. 55-60.

1177 See *Endnote E-207*, p. 755. See also *Excursus 55: Mesoamerican Stories of Creation and the Original Transgression*, p. 697.

1178 See *Endnote E-208*, p. 755.

1179 I.e., renew the covenant.

1180 M. E. Lewis, *Flood*, pp. 111-113.

1181 JST Genesis 9:4-25; cf. J. Smith, Jr., *Teachings*, 21 May 1843, p. 305; 10 March 1844, pp. 340-341. See Fletcher-

A variety of historical factors have conspired to produce the fragmented, truncated, contradictory, "sprawling, disorganized confusion" of Chinese myths as we have them today.[1182] In considering this literature, it should be remembered that "[n]o 'China' as such existed in the ancient world. Cultural unity was only gradually constructed over long centuries."[1183] With these facts in mind, it is not surprising to learn, for example, that the major god T'ai Hao was "mistakenly identified as Fu Xi" in the latter Han era, leading to a confounding of their stories in subsequent texts.[1184] Moreover, the merged identity of Nü Gua of the flood myth and Nü Gua the wife of Fu Xi may be the result of a conflation of separate traditions about originally distinct characters. Lewis puzzles over the fact that while Fu Xi and Nü Gua "were minor figures in the written tradition, in which they were not identified as a married couple," the later iconographic tradition, "in which they appear only in tombs, bound them closely together. Indeed they can be identified with certainty only as a couple."[1185] Also throwing doubt on the wisdom of identifying the earlier Fu Xi and Nü Gua of legend exclusively with the primordial couple depicted in funerary art is the fact that although the Nü Gua of the later Han dynasty is always portrayed as a woman—indeed, "nü" is a Chinese term for a woman—the deity "appears to have been first recorded as a male, though not as a ruler."[1186] Nelson, *et al.* observe that the name "Nü" "could have been [a] clan name since many of these were based on the feminine element," intriguingly going out on a lexical limb to identify the pre-Han flood hero Nü Gua as the biblical Noah.[1187] Finally, one might also profitably compare the story of how the smoke from a sacrifice made by Fu Xi and Nü Gua at K'un-lun mountain provided divine justification for their marriage as brother and sister[1188] with pseudepigraphal accounts of Cain's passion for his twin sister and his anger when the rejection of his sacrifice was taken to indicate that God wished her to become Abel's wife.[1189]

Louis for a discussion of Noah's "salvific atonement for cosmic rupture" (C. H. T. Fletcher-Louis, *Glory*, p. 48).

1182 A. Birrell, *Mythology*, pp. xi-xii. See *Endnote E-209*, p. 755.

1183 M. Nylan, *Writing*, p. 4.

1184 A. Birrell, *Mythology*, p. 164, see also pp. 44-45; cf. J. Chamberlain, *Chinese Gods*, p. 13.

1185 M. E. Lewis, *Construction*, p. 130. See *Endnote E-210*, p. 755.

1186 K. G. Stevens, *Chinese*, p. 30.

1187 E. R. Nelson, *et al.*, *Chinese*, pp. 113-114.

1188 A. Birrell, *Mythology*, pp. 203-204.

1189 E.g., al-Tabari, *Creation*, 140-141, 1:310-311; A. al-Tha'labi, *Lives*, pp. 74-75; E. A. W. Budge, *Cave*, pp. 69-70; Shelemon, *Book of the Bee*, 18, p. 26. See also *Commentary 5:28-a*, p. 376.

FIGURE E50-1. *Fu Xi with His Consort Nü Gua, ca. 689*

Many images similar to this one have been found in tombs dating back to the second century BCE. Fu Xi and Nü Gua, are measuring the "'squareness of the earth' and the 'roundness of heaven' with their implements, the square with the plumb bob hanging from it, and the compass."[1]

With their human torsos and serpentine lower bodies "rotating around the invisible vertical *axis mundi*,"[2] "Fu Xi and Nü Gua are... hybrids who embody the division of the universe into ...three distinct levels and at the same time demonstrate the links between them. The paired deities move between the three realms, embody two of the three levels of the Han world, and lead upward to the third."[3] Such figures depict "a final stage in the journey" where, at the destination and "in the company of the hosts of heaven," the individual sloughs off his or her "mortal coil as easily as a snake sheds the skin that he discards."[4]

This banner found by Stein in central Asia and dated to the late seventh century was, according to Nibley, "found in position suspended from pegs on a north wall... near the body of a man dressed in Sassanian style. 'Near the head lay also the crown-shaped paper hat'... A mixture of cultures is apparent—the Sutras, Sassanian art and Chinese elements (the Chinese having moved in quite recently—640 CE) and the ritual with which the parties are so much concerned may have been somewhat eclectic, with a foundation of Nestorian Christianity. In the veil in question, what first catches the eye are the signs of the square and the compass, boldly drawn as they are held up in the right and left hands respectively of the lady and her husband.[5] To quote the official description: 'Silk... perhaps originally white... The bodies rise from a continuous flounce-like short white skirt'—an apron, 'their two inner arms stretched stiffly and horizontally towards each other... the hand of each appearing under the opposite armpit of the other shows that they are embracing... From below issue two intertwined serpentine bodies which coil around each other'[6]—the well-known *caduceus* of life and death, signifying that all things have their opposites."[7] Their shapes also recall the form of the multiply-entwined tree in the center of the paradisiacal garden of K'un-lun.[8]

Nibley noted that "the garment draped over the coffin and the veil hung on the wall had the same marks; they were placed on the garment as reminders of personal commitment, while on the veil they represent man's place in the cosmos."[9] "The whole design is completely surrounded with diagrams of the constellations[—including the Big Dipper[10]], while above the heads of the two figures 'is the sun disc, white with red spokes,' surrounded by twelve smaller circles,[11] each connected to the next by a straight line to form an unbroken circle except at the very top where it is left open—plainly the circle of the months of the year"[12]—"meaning... the navel of the universe."[13] The moon disk appears beneath the entwined bodies, also surrounded by twelve smaller circles. In the late Babylonian period, intertwining serpents represented the union of the sun and moon.[14]

1   G. d. Santillana, *et al.*, *Hamlet's Mill*, 20, p. 272; cf. E. S. Bradshaw, *August 9, 1985*; J. S. Major, *Heaven*, p. 27; H. W. Nibley, *Prayer Circle*, pp. 74-75. See *Figure 4-2*, p. 217, *Excursus 18: Kolob*, p. 565, and *Excursus 20: The Circle and the Square*, p. 571.

2   H. W. Nibley, *Vestments*, p. 115. See *Endnote E-196*, p. 753.

3   M. E. Lewis, *Early*, p. 128; cf. M. E. Lewis, *Construction*, p. 126.

4   M. Loewe, *Ways*, p. 59.

5   See *Endnote E-202*, p. 754.

6   S. M. A. Stein, *Innermost Asia*, 2:665-667. For an illustration of the burial room layout, see H. W. Nibley, *Sacred*, p. 575 Figure 47. See *Endnote E-203*, p. 754.

7   H. W. Nibley, Prayer Circle, pp. 73-74. See, e.g., John 3:14.

8   A. Birrell, *Mythology*, p. 233. See *Excursus 25: The Tree of Life as the Hidden Throne of God*, p. 591.

9   H. W. Nibley, *Vestments*, p. 112.

10   *Ibid.*, pp. 111-112; J. E. Talmage, *House of the Lord*, pp. 83, 108.

11   See *Endnote E-204*, p. 754.

12   H. W. Nibley, *Prayer Circle*, pp. 73-74; cf. R. Whitfield, *Textiles*, Description of Plate 86.

13   H. W. Nibley, *Vestments*, p. 111.

14   J. E. Seaich, *Ancient Texts 1995*, p. 997.

Excursus 51
The Five Lost Things of the Temple

THE five covenantal laws of modern LDS temples[1190] bring to mind Nibley's discussions of the fact that in "… both Jewish and Christian sources, one often reads of the five things, five tokens, etc.—which are an organic part of the temple: When prophecy ceased… the five things were gone."[1191] Clues reflecting different "remembrances" of these five things are scattered in ancient texts.[1192]

The most frequently cited source purporting to describe what was lost from the first temple[1193] is *Numbers Rabbah*, which lists "the ark, the candlestick, the fire, the Holy Spirit, and the Cherubim."[1194] The *Babylonian Talmud* lists "the true anointing oil…, together with the ark and the manna and the high priestly staff[1195] it contained."[1196] Barker comments:

> Combining the two lists, we conclude that the remembered difference between the first and the second temples was represented by the oil and the spirit it imparted, by the manna and the high priestly staff—all associated with the high priesthood. The difference also concerned the ark and the cherubim, associated with the throne, and the Menorah, which represented the tree of life in the lost Eden. All except the Menorah had been in the Holy of Holies, and there is reason to believe that the Menorah, too, had originally stood there, and not in the great hall of the temple.[1197] In John's vision, the Tree of Life and the throne stand together in the heavenly city.[1198]

> With this meager evidence alone, we can begin to reconstruct what Josiah banished from Solomon's temple: the anointed ones who received the gift of the Spirit and became the high priests, the cherub throne of the Lord, on which the anointed one sat and was worshipped as the Lord, and Eden with its Tree of Life that gave wisdom and angel status to those who ate its fruit.[1199] These… were the major elements of Christianity when it developed some six centuries later.[1200]

Also probing the significance of the lost furniture "list of the schoolmen," Nibley, like Barker, specifically connects the missing "five things" to lost ordinances of the High Priesthood:[1201]

> According to the *Gospel of Philip*, the five secret ordinances of the Lord are (1) baptism [washing], (2) *chrism* (anointing), (3) the eucharist, (4) the ordinance of salvation (*sote*—unexplained),[1202]

1190 See the overview of Moses 5, p. 342.

1191 H. W. Nibley, *Return*, p. 54.

1192 See B. M. Wheeler, *Mecca*, pp. 22-23 for an overview of sources documenting the loss of items from the Jewish temple treasury, and pp. 19-46 for a discussion of the loss and recovery of items from the Islamic *Ka'ba*. See J. M. Smith, *Beginning*, for the argument that the designation of Adam as a priest in the Garden of Eden and the evident presence of a kingdom of priests in the New Jerusalem of the book of Revelation presupposes that communion with Deity, rather than sacrificial rituals per se, is the primary function of the priesthood.

1193 See *Endnote E-211*, p. 755.

1194 H. Freedman, *et al.*, *Midrash*, Numbers 15:10, 6:650-651.

1195 See *Endnote E-181*, p. 749. See *Endnote E-253*, p. 768. Regarding the oil, see M. Barker, *Holy Anointing*.

1196 Horayoth 12a and Hebrews 9:4, cited in M. Barker, *Hidden*, p. 6.

1197 See *Endnote E-212*, p. 755.

1198 Revelation 22:1-2.

1199 Proverbs 3:13-18.

1200 M. Barker, *Hidden*, pp. 6-7. See also M. Barker, *Revelation*, pp. 120, 205.

1201 H. W. Nibley, *Return*, p. 54; cf. H. W. Nibley, *Apocryphal*, p. 310. Madsen discusses a sense in which "all of those things missing from the second Jewish temple were present" at the dedication of the Kirtland Temple (T. G. Madsen, *Blessings*, pp. 39-40).

1202 Irenaeus, criticizing the teachings of the Valentinian teacher Marcus, described the practice of "salvation/redemption" as "a kind of second initiation for those who have 'received perfect knowledge'" (*Heresies* 1:21:1-5,

and (5) the bridal chamber or highest ordinance.[1203] In a very old Manichaean manuscript…
we read, "These five things [ordinances] about which you asked me," says the Lord, addressing
the apostles after the resurrection, "appear to the world to be small and foolish things, and yet
they are great and honorable or exalted (*eutaiait*). I am he who will reveal to you its ordinances
[mysteries]. These five tokens are the mystery of the first man Adam."[1204]

What such Gnostic and Manichaean references reveal more than anything else is not the
exact nature of the five items in question, but rather the keenness with which their loss
was felt. Describing the misplaced efforts of scholars in focusing almost exclusively on the
specific content of Gnostic claims, Nibley writes:

> Nearly all studies of Gnosticism in the past have sought the key to its origin and nature in the
> original sources of various Gnostic doctrines… Opinions differ as widely today as ever. It is as
> if various parties called upon to describe the nature of a bucket were to submit careful chemical
> analyses of all substances carried in buckets: there would be a milk school, a water school, a bran
> school, etc., each defining buckets in terms of a particular content. The important things about
> the Gnostics is not that they adopted doctrines and practices from Iran or from Alexandria,
> but that they showed a desperate eagerness to latch on to anything that looked promising no
> matter where it came from. Irenaeus' survey of those practices and doctrines easily explains
> this urgency: the Gnostics had caused an immense sensation and gained a huge and growing
> following by the electrifying announcement that they had the *gnosis*, revealed knowledge,
> the wonderful things that the Lord taught to Peter, James, and John after the resurrection.[1205]
> Having made the claim, they were, so to speak, "on the spot." They had to deliver—they had
> to come through with something wonderful, supernatural, which at the same time would
> correspond in some degree to widespread rumors and traditions in the church as to what the
> *gnosis* really was.
>
> And so they welcomed any teaching or practice that combined an air of mystery and superior
> knowledge with a cosmic sweep and scope. For them, God was something beyond the grasp
> of ordinary Christians; they gave secret lessons and charged money for them; they built up
> elaborate philosophical systems based on abstract and personified concepts; they practiced
> ordinary magic and specialized in trick miracles such as changing wine into blood (all this
> according to Irenaeus[1206]); they tried to produce supernatural experiences by the use of drugs
> and stimulants; they cultivated a large vocabulary of fancy technical words to impress the
> public; they made a big thing of numerology; they brought forth libraries of faked apocryphal
> writings to cause a sensation; they parodied celestial marriage and baptism, while teaching that
> water baptism was not necessary since the spirit is everything; they said it was impossible for
> the body, since it is made of earth, to participate in salvation; they condemned marriage; they
> practiced extreme unction; they taught transmigration of souls; they venerated holy images, in
> particular a portrait of Christ.[1207]

A similar drive to decode, by any means available, the clouded mirror of lost temple-related
knowledge was manifest among the Manichaeans. In his notes to the Manichaean *Kephalaia
of the Teacher*, Gardner writes that the:

> … descent of the First Man from the land of light was a favorite theme. Full of the pathos of
> loss and estrangement, it is in a very real sense the story of each soul… Once the sacrifice of

---

cited in R. Uro, *Bridal Chamber*, p. 460).

1203 W. W. Isenberg, *Philip*, 67:27-30, p. 150; 69:22-37, p. 151. See also S. K. Brown, *Nag Hammadi*, pp. 260-262,
    275-277; H. W. Nibley, *Message 2005*, pp. 527-528; A. Roberts, *Anointing*, pp. 122ff. See *Endnote E-213*, p. 756.
1204 See I. Gardner, *Kephalaia*, 9 (38,5-9), p. 43.
1205 See *Endnote E-214*, p. 756.
1206 Irenaeus, *Heresies*, 13:2, p. 334.
1207 H. W. Nibley, *Gnostics*, pp. 67-68.

the First Man has been achieved, he is saved by the Living Spirit and returns to the kingdom. This establishes and sanctifies the process of Redemption; and, while it occurs at the beginning of the history, it also anticipates the triumphant return at the end of time of the collectivity of the divine, with the First Man at their head, to enter the new aeon. [Having established] the primordial archetypes…, Mani[, the founder of Manichaeism,] immediately relates them to the individual's experience and the practice of the church.[1208]

The specific question that prompted the relevant section of the *Kephalaia* (37,28-42,23) relates to the meaning of "five lessons" (38,5) that were successively bestowed upon the First Man as he took his leave from the gods, the angels, and the Mother of Life during his descent. These five lessons include "a peace and greeting" that conveyed "power… blessing and fortification" (37,29; 38,17), "the right hand" (38,20), the "embrace… as he separates from them, accompanying him out, embracing him with the kiss of affection and love" (38,29), the "salutation with which the First Man made obeisance… bending his knees… entreating them for a power to escort him, as he comes forth" (39,1-2), and the "laying on of hands" by which he was "armed… and made… mighty… and sent… to the battle" (39,3-5).[1209] These "five signs and these five mysteries of the First Man came forth from the aeons of light against the enemy… He was victorious against the enemy by them. Also, when he ascended from the war, he came in to the kingdom of the household of his people by these [same] five mysteries," performing each of them anew as he was "brought upward out from the struggle" (39,7-11; 39,21). Like the First Man, each disciple will perform these five things in the church, and "the last of these things shall be bequeathed upon them from the right hand of charity" (41,5).[1210] In recapitulating the experiences of Adam, these ritual acts also prefigure the actions that Manichaean disciples will perform after death when, "at the time of their coming forth… the angel who holds the victory prize extends to him the right hand. And it draws him out of the abyss of his body, and accepts him in with the kiss and love. That soul shall make obeisance to its redeemer" (41,11; 41,17-21). He "shall be perfected and increased… in the household of the living ones, with the gods and the angels and all the apostles and the chosen. And he receives the crown […] glory in the life for ever" (41,22-25).[1211]

1208 I. Gardner, *Kephalaia*, p. 42.

1209 See *Endnote E-215*, p. 756.

1210 See *Figure* 5-13, p. 351 and *Figure* 6-13, p.

1211 I. Gardner, *Kephalaia*, 9, pp. 43-46; cf. T. M. Compton, *Handclasp*, pp. 621-622; E. Hennecke, *et al.*, *Pearl*. See *Commentary* 1:25-c, p. 60, *Figure* 6-14, p. 473, *Excursus 53: Comparative Explorations, Dexiosis*, p. 681; the *Mandaean Texts* and *Manichaean Texts* sections of the *Annotated Bibliography*, pp. 870, 884; *Figure* B-1, p. 872. See *Endnote 1-22*, p. 79.

Excursus 52

Washing, Anointing, and Clothing Among Early Christians

THE book of Exodus recounts that Aaron was "wash[ed]," "anoint[ed]," and clothed in "holy garments... so that he [might] minister unto [the Lord] in the priest's office."[1212] Washing, anointing, and clothing ceremonies are also variously described in the records of the early Christian church. In these records, the distinction between baptism and other rites of washing is often unclear, and the order in which various ordinances were said to have been administered is not consistent from one source to another.[1213]

Hamblin discusses an early Christian initiation ritual in the purported *Secret Gospel of Mark* where a young man dressed only in a linen cloth was taught "the mystery of the kingdom of God" by Jesus.[1214] Tertullian describes a practice in his day of anointing all newly "baptized" Christians, stating that this is "a practice derived from the old discipline, wherein on entering the priesthood, men were wont to be anointed with oil from a horn, ever since Aaron was anointed by Moses. Whence Aaron is called 'Christ,' from the 'chrism,' which is the unction."[1215] Likewise the *Didascalia*, a document from the early third century, describes an anointing for both women deacons and for men: "The bishop is to lay on hands and anoint the head only, 'as of old priests and kings were anointed in Israel'—presumably on the crown of the head. After this, apparently, the candidates were anointed all over, and then were baptized with a formula or invocation. Instruction followed..."[1216] The *Gospel of Philip* was written by "a community whose rite involves stripping naked, baptism in water [washing] followed by *chrism* [anointing], and possibly putting on a white garment representing light or enlightenment."[1217]

Anointings are performed today by the Roman Catholic Church in the sacrament of "Extreme Unction," now more often called the "Anointing of the Sick." The rite includes anointing of "the organs of the five external senses (eyes, ears, nostrils, lips, hands), of the feet, and, for men (where the custom exists and the condition of the patient permits of his being moved), of the loins or reins." In the Eastern Church, the "parts usually anointed are the forehead, chin, cheeks, hands, nostrils, and breast."[1218]

Noting that "temple initiation eventually merged with the baptismal initiation," Tvedtnes[1219] gives the following summary of the five catechetical lectures delivered by the fourth-century bishop St. Cyril to newly-baptized Christians:

> In the first lecture (19:10-11), he speaks of the converts being "clothed in the garment of salvation, even Jesus Christ." And reminds them that "these things were done in the outer chamber. But if God will, when in the succeeding lectures on the Mysteries we have entered into the Holy of Holies, we shall there know the symbolical meaning of the things which are there

---

1212 Exodus 40:12-13. See *Excursus 3: Temple Blessings in the Oath and Covenant of the Priesthood,* p. 519.

1213 See, e.g., B. D. Spinks, *Baptism,* p. 22. See *Endnote E-216,* p. 756.

1214 W. J. Hamblin, *Initiation,* p. 207. See M. Smith, *Secret Gospel,* pp. 15-16 for the story of the discovery of the document.

1215 Tertullian, *Baptism,* 7, p. 672.

1216 B. D. Spinks, *Baptism,* p. 19.

1217 *Ibid.,* p. 25. For arguments seeking to connect ordinances described in the *Gospel of Philip* (as well as anointings described in the canonical gospels) to Egyptian ritual, see A. Roberts, *Anointing,* pp. 86-126.

1218 P. J. Toner, *Extreme Unction,* p. 716.

1219 J. A. Tvedtnes, *Rituals;* cf. J. E. Seaich, *Ancient Texts 1995,* pp. 878-879.

performed."[1220] In the second lecture (20:2-4), he reminds his listeners that "those things, which were done by you in the inner chamber, were symbolical. As soon, then, as ye entered, ye put off your tunic; and this was an image of putting off the old man with his deeds. Having stripped yourselves, ye were naked... Then, when ye were stripped, ye were anointed with exorcised oil, from the very hairs of your head to your feet, and were made partakers of the good olive-tree, Jesus Christ... After these things, ye were led to the holy pool of Divine Baptism."[1221] In the third lecture (21:3-4, 6), he explains that the ointment is symbolically applied to the forehead and "thy other senses; and while the body is anointed with the visible ointment, the soul is sanctified by Holy and life-giving Spirit. And ye were first anointed on the forehead... Then on your ears; that ye might receive the ears which are quick to hear the Divine Mysteries... Then on the nostrils... Afterwards on your breast," then he notes that the anointing is for the high priest and king, suggesting that the initiate becomes a priest and king.[1222] In the fourth lecture (22:8), Cyril cites Ecclesiastes 9:8 ("Let thy garments be always white; and let thy head lack no ointment") and adds, "But now, having put off thy old garments, and put on those which are spiritually white, thou must be continually robed in white: of course we mean not this, that thou art always to wear white raiment; but thou must be clad in the garments that are truly white and shining and spiritual."[1223]

Stressing the antiquity of these ordinances, Nibley[1224] says that:

Bishop Cyril further insists that Moses and Solomon had both been duly baptized in this manner: "After being washed in water, he [Moses] was anointed and called a Christ, because of the anointing which was a type. When Solomon came forth to be king, the High Priest anointed him, after a bath in Gihon. This again was a type. But with us these things are not a type but a reality."[1225] From his last remark it is plain that the early Christians actually performed the rites described. The Jews once taught that when Michael and Gabriel lead all the sinners up out of the lower world, "they will wash and anoint them, healing them of their wounds of hell, and clothe them with beautiful pure garments and bring them into the presence of God."[1226]

1220   Cyril of Jerusalem, *Five*, p. 146.
1221   *Ibid.*, p. 147.
1222   *Ibid.*, p. 150.
1223   *Ibid.*, p. 152.
1224   H. W. Nibley, *What*, p. 364.
1225   See Cyril of Jerusalem, *Five*, 3(21):6, p. 150.
1226   Rabbi Akiba, cited by Samuel Aba Horodezky in H. W. Nibley, *What*, p. 364. See Nibley's more complete summary of Cyril's lectures in H. W. Nibley, *Message 2005*, pp. 515-524. See the overview of Moses 4, p. 234; *Commentary* 4:21-d, p. 266; *Excursus 3: Temple Blessings in the Oath and Covenant of the Priesthood*, p. 519.

Excursus 53
Comparative Explorations of the Mysteries

The Mysteries of Aaron, Moses, and Melchizedek

IN a theological sense, a mystery may be defined as "religious truth via divine revelation."[1227] "The Romans translated *myesis*, the act of closing the eyes, with *initiatio*, from *in-itia*, 'going into.' Kerényi further explains: 'A festival of entering into the darkness, regardless of what issue and ascent this initiation may lead to: that is what the *Mysteria* were, in the original sense of the word.'[1228]" "The Greek word was used in [the] *Septuagint* for 'secret counsel of God,' translated in *Vulgate* as *sacramentum.*"[1229]

Though in scripture the word "mystery," when standing alone, is most often used in a general way to signify revealed knowledge and understanding,[1230] references to the "mysteries of the kingdom" in the Doctrine and Covenants clearly point to specific priesthood ordinances connected with the temple,[1231] which the Prophet Joseph Smith said had been given to the righteous from the time of Adam.[1232] When Jesus Christ spoke of the "mysteries of the kingdom,"[1233] He likewise alluded to these things. Writes Barker:

> … Jesus' parables were more than simple stories. "To you," he said to his closest disciples, "has been given the secret of the Kingdom of God, but for those outside, everything is in parables."[1234] Secrets and mysteries were characteristic of temple tradition, and were the exclusive preserve of the high priesthood, who were permitted to enter the Holy of Holies.[1235]

Despite significant differences, initiation rites in Greco-Roman mystery religions and related traditions in Judaism and early Christianity shared the idea of "three stages of purification, illumination, and mystical unification."[1236] As part of these stages, an upward physical movement often paralleled a ritual heavenly ascent from darkness to increasingly greater

---

1227 D. Harper, *Dictionary*. Harper further explains that the term is "from Anglo-French *misterie* (Old French *mistere*), from Latin *mysterium*, from Greek *mysterion* (usually in plural *mysteria*) 'secret rite or doctrine' from *mystes* 'one who has been initiated,' from *myein* 'to close, shut,' perhaps referring to the lips (in secrecy) or to the eyes (only initiates were allowed to see the sacred rites)." See also C. Kerényi, *Eleusis*, p. 46; M. W. Meyer, *Mysteries*, pp. 4-5.
1228 J. M. Lundquist, *Fundamentals*, p. 676.
1229 D. Harper, *Dictionary*.
1230 See H. B. Lee, *Light*, July 1961, p. 211; D. A. Bednar, *Pray Always*, p. 41; cf. *Commentary* 1:31-d, p. 65 and *Excursus 2: Ancient Concepts of Wisdom,* p. 516.
1231 D&C 63:23; 84:19-20; 107:18-19.
1232 See *Endnote E-217,* p. 756.
1233 E.g., Matthew 13:11. See also Pseudo-Clement, *Homilies* 19:20, p. 336; Clement of Alexandria, *Stromata* 5:10, pp. 458-460; Basil, *Spirit*, 66-67, pp. 40-43.
1234 Mark 4:11.
1235 M. Barker, *Hidden*, p. 2.
1236 H.-J. Klauck, *Context*, p. 99; cf. W. J. Hamblin, *et al.*, *Temple*, pp. 119, 121; J. Gross, *Divinization*, p. 271; Elder Orson F. Whitney, cited in L. T. Perry, *Gospel*, p. 46. See *Endnote E-218,* p. 757.

light. For example, Greek rites not infrequently required the initiate to sleep in the darkness of an underground room or cave before their period of instruction began, simulating the process of rebirth.[1237] Likewise, some Christian texts, possibly with Jewish antecedents, have Adam and Eve living in the darkness of a cave after their expulsion from Eden.[1238]

The Greco-Roman mysteries were often presented as a series of separate initiations. For example, the Mysteries of Eleusis were composed of two rites: "the Lesser [Mysteries] were [usually] performed at Agrai in the month of *Anthesterion* (our February) and served as a preparation for the Greater Mysteries at Eleusis, [always] performed in the month of *Boedromion* (our September)."[1239] Similarly, in a discussion of late Second Temple Jewish mysticism, Goodenough summarized Philo's descriptions of "two successive initiations within a single Mystery," constituting:

> ...a "Lesser" Mystery in contrast with a "Greater".... For general convenience we may distinguish them as the Mystery of Aaron and the Mystery of Moses. The Mystery of Aaron got its symbolism from the great Jerusalem *cultus*... The Mystery of Moses... led the worshipper above all material association; he died to the flesh, and in becoming reclothed in a spiritual body moved progressively upwards... and at last ideally to God himself...[1240] The objective symbolism of the Higher Mystery was the Holy of Holies with the ark, a level of spiritual experience which was no normal part of even the high-priesthood. Only once a year could the high-priest enter there, and then only when stripped of his distinguishing [multi-colored] robes, clad in simple white, and when so blinded by incense that he could see nothing of the sacred objects within. The Mystery of Aaron was restricted to the symbolism of the Aaronic high-priest... In a striking passage Philo contrasts this type of priest with Moses, who... became the true initiate..., *hierophant*[1241] of the rites..., and teacher of divine things.[1242]

Philo taught that the experience of Moses was not meant to be unique; rather, he exemplified a pattern that previously had been followed by Abraham and would continue afterward for all who belonged to true Israel.[1243] In his role as "teacher of divine rites," wrote Philo, "[Moses] will impart to those whose ears are purified. He [i.e., the one who receives these rites] then has ever the divine spirit at his side, taking the lead in every journey of righteousness,"[1244] i.e., "to lead one along the 'whole road,' the entire way to perfection."[1245]

Goodenough's work brings out the importance of temple themes in certain strains of Judaism contemporary with Jesus Christ, and in a form that made it very natural for some Jews to accept Christianity when it became known to them.[1246] In fact, he goes so far as to argue that "Christianity cannot be explained apart from the preparation within the form of

---

1237 D. Ulansey, *Mithraic*, pp. 35-36; cf. *Commentary* 3:21-a, p. 180. See also J. M. Lundquist, *Fundamentals*, pp. 655-659; R. Guénon, *Symboles*, pp. 209-243; *Excursus 3: Temple Blessings in the Oath and Covenant of the Priesthood*, p. 519. See *Endnote E-219*, p. 757. The idea is also related to that of the labyrinth, where "only those who are 'qualified' arrive at their destination, while others are prevented from entering within, or lose their way" (R. Guénon, *Symboles*, p. 213).

1238 E. A. W. Budge, *Cave*, p. 69; S. C. Malan, *Adam and Eve*, 1:3:16, p. 5; H. Schwartz, *Tree*, p. 344. See *Commentary* 5:4-c, p. 357.

1239 J. M. Lundquist, *Fundamentals*, p. 677.

1240 See C. T. R. Hayward, *Israel*, pp. 156-219 regarding Philo's explanation of the name Israel as meaning "the one who sees God. See *Endnote E-220*, p. 757.

1241 I. e., priestly revealer.

1242 E. R. Goodenough, *Light*, pp. 95-96. See Philo, *Giants*, 54, p. 473.

1243 M. Barker, *Hidden*, p. 7; cf. pp. 38-47.

1244 Philo, *Giants*, 54-55, p. 473. See E. R. Goodenough, *Introduction to Philo*, pp. 147-148.

1245 E. R. Goodenough, *Light*, p. 214 n. 105. See *Endnote E-221*, p. 757.

1246 E. R. Goodenough, *Light*; E. R. Goodenough, *Introduction to Philo*. See *Endnote E-222*, p. 757. See also J. M. Bradshaw, *Ezekiel Mural*.

Judaism that Philo reveals."[1247] Barker[1248] and Seaich[1249] have since updated Goodenough's mistaken conclusion that Philo's distinctive assertions were due to the late influence of Hellenism with the idea that core elements of his teachings (with a less excessive degree of allegorizing and Platonism[1250]) were a part of First Temple Judaism, and that Philo was primarily transposing these teachings into the language of the philosophers. Thus, Barker writes: "Philo was presenting the Judaism of his day in Greek terms, but what he was presenting was Judaism and not a vague syncretism. He used Greek terms for something which was essentially Jewish."[1251]

Jewish sources allude to things pertaining to the First Temple that were later lost.[1252] Earlier forms of such loss can be traced back to the time of Moses, when the Lord had intended to make the higher ordinances of the holy priesthood available to all of Israel. However, because of their rebellion,[1253] the higher priesthood, and its associated laws and ordinances, were instead generally withheld from the people.[1254] After that time, the higher priesthood and its ordinances were only given to select individuals.[1255] Relating to the JST Exodus account describing how Moses received a higher law at Sinai than what was eventually given to Israel, Kabbalah scholar Léo Schaya writes:

> Now the descent or revelation of the first Tables of the *Torah* must be distinguished from the second. The *Zohar* teaches that the first Tables emanated from the Tree of Life; but that Israel, by worshipping the golden calf, "was judged unworthy of benefiting from them." Therefore, Moses, following the divine command, gave the people other Tables, "which came from the side of the Tree of Good and Evil".... The first Tables... were the light and doctrine of the Messiah, the outpouring of universal deliverance, the source of eternal life on earth. The second Tables represented the indirect or "fragmented" manifestation of this light; *hokhmah*, pure and redemptive wisdom, was no longer immediately accessible, but was hidden behind the 'curtains' of *binah*, the cosmic "intelligence" of God.[1256]

The fragmentation of light and truth continued through the long periods of Israel's apostasy, and was particularly evident during the time of Josiah, when sweeping reforms of temple practices were carried out.[1257] In its zeal to eradicate heretical beliefs and practices, the movement also anathematized those who had tried to remain faithful to the older priestly traditions and the religion of the patriarchs, in which Melchizedek and the worship of the *El Elyon*, the Most High God, had been central.[1258]

Memories of what was lost continued to persist among those loyal to the original First Temple traditions,[1259] and it is significant that Philo's writings were produced in the climate of rivalry of the late Second Temple period "when the various sacerdotal groups and clans

---

1247 R. S. Eccles, *Pilgrimage*, p. 41. See also pp. 37, 39; J. Gross, *Divinization*, p. 79.

1248 E.g., M. Barker, *Angel*, pp. 114-133; M. Barker, *Beyond*.

1249 E.g., J. E. Seaich, *Ancient Texts 1983*, pp. 56-68; J. E. Seaich, *Ancient Texts 1995*, pp. 848-853.

1250 J. M. G. Barclay, *Diaspora*, pp. 163-170, 177-178.

1251 M. Barker, *Angel*, p. 216; cf. M. Barker, *Imagery*. See *Endnote E-223*, p. 757.

1252 See *Excursus 51: The Five Lost Things of the Temple*, p. 658.

1253 Cf. JST Exodus 34:1-2; JST Deuteronomy 10:1-2.

1254 See *Endnote E-224*, p. 758.

1255 See *Endnote E-225*, p. 758.

1256 L. Schaya, *Meaning*, pp. 15-16; cf. p. 41. See also D. C. Matt, *Zohar 1*, Noah 1:63b, pp. 369-370 and 369 n. 198; B. M. Metzger, *Fourth Ezra*, 14:4-6, p. 553; J. E. Seaich, *Ancient Texts 1995*, pp. 670 n. 74; p. 757; J. E. Seaich, *Mormonism*, p. 132; H. Sperling, *et al.*, *Zohar*, 1:26b, pp. 1:101-102; 2:17b, p. 3:55; J. A. Tvedtnes, *Laws*, pp. 391-396. See *Endnote E-226*, p. 758.

1257 M. Barker, *Josiah*.

1258 M. Barker, *Older*, p. 257. See *Endnote E-227*, p. 758.

1259 M. Barker, *Who was Melchizedek*.

were competing for the primacy and authority of their priestly legacy."[1260] Arguments among these factions also widened the distance between proto-rabbinical Judaism and Jewish converts to Christianity, who differed in their ideas about which writings should be accepted as canonical—texts such as those in the Enoch tradition being popular among the early Christians.[1261] Similarities in this regard between the views of Jewish groups aligning themselves with First Temple traditions and those of early Christians were brought out in Goodenough's study of the *Apostolic Constitutions*,[1262] a Christian document that, following Bousset, he found to be drawn from a Jewish background.[1263] Indicating "the milieu in which such a Jewish liturgy might have originated, namely in Hellenistic-Jewish mysticism closely akin to that of Philo," Goodenough cited two passages within this Jewish liturgical material that refer to Melchizedek. According to Eccles' summary:[1264]

> The first is in the context of baptismal instruction which includes the injunction, "let him be taught how God... did glorify the saints in every generation—I mean Seth, and Enos, and Enoch, and Noah, and Abraham and his posterity, and Melchizedek, and Job, and Moses and Joshua, and Caleb, and Phineas the priest, and those that were holy in every generation."[1265] Of this passage, Goodenough remarks, "The Patriarchs selected as 'glorified' are, except Job, precisely those of Philo... [W]hat is here is unmistakably the Judaism of the Mystery."[1266] Another of the liturgical passages concludes the names of almost exactly the same list of patriarchs, including Melchizedek, and in the same order, except that Abel, Isaac, Jacob, Joseph, and Aaron are mentioned, and Caleb and Phineas are not.[1267] Most interesting of all is the inclusion of Melchizedek in a patriarch list comprising nearly all of the same names mentioned in the two preceding passages, in which all are described as priests.[1268] Goodenough declares that such a list could come only from the Mystery, by whose Judaism alone these patriarchs were accounted as priests.[1269]

Drawing out the implications of Goodenough's conclusions for an understanding of the Christian "mysteries" described in the book of Hebrews,[1270] Eccles continues:

> ... it is not unreasonable to suppose that while the author of Hebrews is undoubtedly influenced by the messianic interpretation of Melchizedek found in Psalm 110,[1271] he is at the same time influenced by an exegetical tradition of mystical Judaism. Although Philo most fully exemplifies this tradition,[1272] he is not its only spokesman as the liturgical fragments suggest.[1273]

In Hebrews 11, the names of Abel, Noah, and Melchizedek[1274]—respectively referred to as the "righteous,"[1275] the "heir of righteousness," and the "king of righteousness"[1276]—are

---

1260 A. A. Orlov, *Heir*, p. 46. See also M. Barker, *Revelation*, pp. 27-34; D. J. Larsen, *Non-Levitical Priesthood*.
1261 See, e.g., M. Barker, *Text*.
1262 A. Roberts, *et al.*, *Apostolic Constitutions*.
1263 E. R. Goodenough, *Light*, pp. 306-358.
1264 R. S. Eccles, *Hebrews*, p. 214.
1265 A. Roberts, *et al.*, *Apostolic Constitutions* 7:3:39, p. 476. See E. R. Goodenough, *Light*, p. 327.
1266 E. R. Goodenough, *Light*, p. 327.
1267 A. Roberts, *et al.*, *Apostolic Constitutions* 8:2:5, p. 482. See E. R. Goodenough, *Light*, p. 330.
1268 *Ibid.* See *Endnote E-228*, p. 759.
1269 E. R. Goodenough, *Light*, p. 331.
1270 Nibley gives a brief summary of temple teachings in Hebrews (H. W. Nibley, *Sacred*, pp. 597-599).
1271 See *Endnote E-229*, p. 759.
1272 See *Endnote E-230*, p. 761.
1273 R. S. Eccles, *Hebrews*, pp. 214-215.
1274 See *Endnote E-231*, p. 761.
1275 Cf. JST Genesis 14:7, Matthew 23:35, 1 John 3:12; cf. D. C. Allison, *Testament*, 13:2-3, p. 274; cf. pp. 281-282; G. W. E. Nickelsburg, *1 Enoch*, 22:7-14, p. 300; E. P. Sanders, *Testament of Abraham*, 13, 1:889-890; P. M. Eisenbaum, *Hebrews 11*, pp. 149-150.
1276 See *Endnote E-232*, p. 761.

highlighted as part of an argument that "the sacerdotal knowledge and initiations received by Enoch and Noah [and Abel and Melchizedek] from God in ante- and post-diluvian time were more ancient than the disclosures about sacrificial rites and sanctuary received by Moses many centuries later on Mount Sinai."[1277] This view corresponds to the later claim of the Egyptian Christian Yahya ibn Jarir (d. 1089), who said that the plan of Christian churches "is that of the ancient Temple, which Melchizedek had built [in Jerusalem][1278] before the Kings [of Israel] came to alter it... [Melchizedek] did not perform the rites of divine worship according to the law of Moses, but exercised his priestly office with other and more excellent [proto-Christian] symbols."[1279]

Note that in "pointing out the superiority of the way of salvation through faith in Christ over the supposed way of salvation through Moses and the earthly rites, the author of Hebrews does not distinguish, as Philo does, between a Lower and a Higher Mystery."[1280] We should not allow, however, the difference in terminology to mislead us, for in both Philo and Hebrews a similar distinction is being made. In broad strokes, the significant contrast in both cases is between the lesser and the greater rites; between the priesthood of Moses (as described in Hebrews)[1281]—roughly corresponding to the Lower Mystery of Aaron (as described by Philo)—and the Melchizedek priesthood of Christ (Hebrews)—analogous to the Higher Mystery of Moses (Philo). In both cases, what characterizes the greater rites is that they bring the initiate beyond the veil into the presence of God, and there invest him with an eternal priesthood and kingship in the likeness of the Divine.[1282]

Goodenough saw an explicit connection between the Higher Mystery of Moses and the figure of Melchizedek in the theology of Alexandrian Christianity.[1283] In a text "drawing almost exclusively upon Philo's *De Vita Mosis*" (but also "drawing upon other sources"), Clement of Alexandria gave a description of a group of "Initiates" who had an account of the three names given to Moses: "Joachim, given him by his mother at circumcision; Moses, given him by Pharaoh's daughter; and Melchi, a name he had in heaven which was given him, apparently by God, after his ascension"[1284]—and suggesting the "eternal priesthood of Melchizedek."[1285] In this sense, Melchizedek (*Melchi-zedek* = king of righteousness[1286]) might be regarded as much a title as a name.[1287] Broadly surveying the evidence, Goodenough concluded that for the group of Jews who shared Philo's understandings, it was a relatively small "step from this Judaism to the new Christianity."[1288]

Regarding this step, Seaich relates:[1289]

1277 A. A. Orlov, *Heir*, pp. 47, 61. See *Endnote E-233*, p. 762.

1278 See *Endnote E-234*, p. 762.

1279 W. J. Hamblin, *et al.*, *Temple*, p. 111. See *Endnote E-235*, p. 762.

1280 R. S. Eccles, *Hebrews*, p. 220.

1281 See *Endnote E-236*, p. 762.

1282 See, e.g., Philo, *Giants*, 54-55, p. 473; Philo, *Exodus*, 2:29, p. 70; Hebrews 6:18-20. See *Endnote E-237*, p. 763.

1283 Unfortunately, the passages in *Questions from Genesis* "which would have described Abraham's 'coming to Melchizedek for... spiritual development' (E. R. Goodenough, *Light*, p. 151) are presently missing" (E. Seaich, *Mystery*, p. 43). See *Endnote E-238*, p. 764.

1284 Clement of Alexandria, *Stromata*, 1:23, p. 335.

1285 E. R. Goodenough, *Light*, pp. 292-293.

1286 "Melchizedek" is written as two words in Genesis 14, Psalm 110, the *Samaritan Pentateuch* (S. Lowy, *Principles*, p. 320), the *Targums* (J. W. Etheridge, *Onkelos*, 14), and *11QMelchizedek* (F. G. Martinez, *Melchizedek*, 2:9, p. 140).

1287 M. Barker, *Who was Melchizedek*.

1288 E. R. Goodenough, *Introduction to Philo*, p. 159; cf. E. R. Goodenough, *Summary*, p. 188; E. R. Goodenough, *Paul*, pp. 165-166. See *Endnote E-239*, p. 764.

1289 J. E. Seaich, *Ancient Texts 1983*, pp. 56-57. See also M. B. Brown, *Gate*, pp. 180-204; R. S. Eccles, *Hebrews*; J. E.

This "Melchizedek Mystery" was also the basis for the Christian Temple Mystery, as described in the NT Epistle to the Hebrews. There we encounter the new Israel—or the Church—wandering again through the cultic wilderness[1290] in search of "rest."[1291] But this time the wanderers are prepared to follow Jesus, their "Joshua,"[1292] permanently into the Promised Land, symbolized by the interior of the Holy of Holies. As we recall, the old Israel had been obliged to wait in front of the veil while the High Priest went inside alone to atone for Israel's sins.[1293] The Church, however, was now allowed to pass directly through the veil with her heavenly High Priest,[1294] signifying her attainment of Mt. Sion, the city of God,[1295] or the Celestial Kingdom.

While by no means can they be simply equated, the teachings and revelations of the Prophet Joseph Smith regarding priesthood keys and temple ordinances[1296] parallel the general structure outlined in the writings of Philo and the book of Hebrews. The whole of D&C 84 is especially instructive in this regard. It contrasts the lesser or Aaronic Priesthood, which includes the Levitical priesthood,[1297] with the Holy or greater priesthood, elsewhere designated the Melchizedek Priesthood.[1298] Those who receive the Melchizedek Priesthood, called "the sons of Moses,"[1299] are told that this priesthood "holdeth the key of the mysteries of the kingdom, even the key of the knowledge of God," and that, without its "ordinances" and "authority," "the power of godliness is not manifest unto men in the flesh; For without this no man can see the face of God, even the Father, and live":[1300]

Philo	Hebrews	D&C 84:34	
Lower Mystery of Aaron	Levitical Priesthood	Aaronic Priesthood	
Higher Mystery of Moses	Melchizedek Priesthood	Moses	
		Abraham	Degrees of the Melchizedek Priesthood
		Melchizedek "Priest and King"	"Fulness"

FIGURE E53-1. *The Mysteries of Aaron, Moses, and Melchizedek*

23 Now this Moses plainly taught to the children of Israel in the wilderness, and sought diligently to sanctify his people that they might behold the face of God;

24 But they hardened their hearts and could not endure his presence; therefore, the Lord in his wrath… swore that they should not enter into his rest while in the wilderness, which rest is the fulness of his glory.

Seaich, *Ancient Texts 1995*, pp. 870-875; M. C. Thomas, *Hebrews.* See *Endnote E-240,* p. 764.

1290 Hebrews 3:2-4:11; 11:8-10, 13-16; 12:8-24; 13:13-14.

1291 Hebrews 3:11; 4:11.

1292 Hebrews 4:8.

1293 Hebrews 9:7-8.

1294 Hebrews 6:18-20, 10:19-22.

1295 Hebrews 12:22-23.

1296 See, e.g., J. Smith, Jr., *Teachings,* 4 May 1842, p. 237.

1297 D&C 107:1.

1298 D&C 107:1-6. D&C 76:57 makes it clear that the order of Melchizedek was patterned "after the order of Enoch, which was after the order of the Only Begotten Son." See *Endnote E-241,* p. 765.

1299 D&C 84:6, 34.

1300 D&C 84:19-22. See *Endnote E-242,* p. 765. Living the law of consecration is the last qualifying step that prepares one to "see God" (D&C 97:16, 21, Matthew 5:8, 3 Nephi 12:8; cf. D&C 58:18).

25 Therefore, he took Moses out of their midst, and the Holy Priesthood also;

26 And the lesser priesthood continued, which priesthood holdeth the key of the ministering of angels and the preparatory gospel;

27 …which the Lord in his wrath caused to continue with the house of Aaron among the children of Israel.[1301]

As we have seen, it is precisely the privilege of "seeing God,"[1302] in likeness of Moses, that characterized true Israel in Philo's description of the higher mysteries, and the blessing of "entering into God's rest" that similarly represented the object of labor to which the author of Hebrews exhorted his readers. Moreover, just as in the "celestial glory there are three heavens or degrees,"[1303] so there are three degrees of temple blessings associated with the Melchizedek priesthood.[1304] Men and women who attain the first degree, associated with the name of Moses,[1305] are privileged to "behold the face of God,"[1306] those who then receive the blessings associated with the name of Abraham receive the patriarchal promise of eternal family relationships and a "continuation of the seed,"[1307] and, finally, those who receive the highest degree, "keeping all the commandments and obeying all the ordinances of the house of the Lord," obtain the "fulness of the priesthood"[1308] through their becoming "kings and priests [or "queens and priestesses"[1309]] of the Most High God" according to the "power of Melchizedek."[1310] Thus, they are "prepared for the enjoyment of a fulness [i.e., the highest degree] of the third heavens."[1311]

The Cave of Treasures

Several Jewish and early Christian sources associate the creation[1312] and the death[1313] of Adam and Eve with temple-related sites, while differing as to their exact location.[1314] By way of contrast, other Christian and Muslim traditions imply that Adam lived and was buried in what is called the "Cave of Treasures,"[1315] and that only later were his bones brought to the temple mount in Jerusalem for reburial:[1316]

1301 D&C 84:23-27; cf. JST Exodus 34:1-2, cited above.

1302 See C. T. R. Hayward, Israel, pp. 156-219 regarding Philo's explanation of the name Israel as meaning "the one who sees God."

1303 D&C 131:1.

1304 D&C 84:34; cf. *Excursus 3: Temple Blessings in the Oath and Covenant of the Priesthood*, p. 519. See *Endnote E-243*, p. 765.

1305 See *Endnote E-244*, p. 766.

1306 D&C 84:23.

1307 D&C 132:22. See *Endnote E-245*, p. 766.

1308 J. Smith, Jr., *Teachings*, 11 June 1843, p. 308; cf. J. Smith, Jr., *Words*, 11 June 1843, p. 213; A. F. Ehat, *et al.*, in J. Smith, Jr., *Words*, p. 286 n. 25.

1309 See G. M. Leonard, *Nauvoo*, p. 261; J. Smith, Jr., *Record*, 28 September 1843, p. 416.

1310 J. Smith, Jr., *Teachings*, 27 August 1843, p. 322; cf. D&C 76:56-59. See *Endnote E-246*, p. 766.

1311 W. Clayton, *Diaries*, 17 May 1843. For additional discussion of this subject, see M. Barker, *Risen*; M. Barker, *Revelation*; M. Barker, *Great High Priest: Temple Roots*; M. Barker, *Temple Theology*; M. Barker, *Hidden*; M. Barker, *Who was Melchizedek*; M. B. Brown, *Gate*; R. S. Eccles, *Hebrews*; E. R. Goodenough, *Light*; E. R. Goodenough, *Dura Symbolism*; E. R. Goodenough, *Introduction to Philo*; W. A. Meeks, *Moses*; H. W. Nibley, *Sacred*; H. W. Nibley, *What*; H. W. Nibley, *Message 2005*; J. E. Seaich, *Ancient Texts 1983*; J. E. Seaich, *Ancient Texts 1995*; M. C. Thomas, *Hebrews*; J. A. Tvedtnes, *Laws*; D. Winston, *Logos*. See also *Excursus 3: Temple Blessings in the Oath and Covenant of the Priesthood*, p. 519.

1312 See *Endnote E-247*, p. 766.

1313 See *Endnote E-248*, p. 767.

1314 See *Endnote E-249*, p. 767.

1315 See *Endnote E-250*, p. 767.

1316 E. A. W. Budge, *Cave*, p. 35. See *Figure 36-1*, p. 616.

FIGURE E53-2. *Adam and Eve Outside Paradise, Cain and Abel, 12th century*

Several ancient traditions record that Adam and Eve were placed on a mountain top following their removal from Eden.[1] Here we see Adam and Eve, clad only in their fig-leaf aprons, "lamenting their Fall on a brown, bare hill."[2] Tongues of flame adorn the upper part of the hill and the entrance to the cave,[3] suggesting the glory of the Divine Presence—as well as the potential danger for those who approach it unprepared.

Cain and Abel offer their respective grain and animal sacrifices on the other hills portrayed on either side. God is shown consuming the sacrifice of Abel while rejecting that of Cain. At the bottom of the mountain, Cain has words with Abel, leads him out to the field, and then executes his murder.

In the heart of the mountain, an aged Adam and Eve, clad in robes of animal skins, confer within the Cave of Treasures, equated in some sources with the Holy of Holies within the temple.[4] On the following page of the manuscript is "an image of the Garden of Eden, now empty, its door barred by three angels."[5]

1   See, e.g., the overview of Moses 3, p. 143 and *Figure 3-7*, p. 143.
2   A. Eastmond, *Narratives*, p. 22.
3   S. Nes, *Uncreated Light*, p. 90. The frontispiece of an Armenian translation of Bartholomew of Maragha's *Treatise on the Work of the Six Days of Creation* shows Adam and Eve within a cavelike structure, surrounded by a perimeter of angels, at the top of a beautiful illustration of the layout of Eden (A. Vernay-Nouri, *Livres*, p. 44).
4   G. A. Anderson, *et al.*, *Synopsis*, 30(5):3, p. 34E; cf. M. Barker, *Christmas*, p. 119; S. Ness, *Uncreated Light*, p. 90.
5   A. Eastmond, *Narratives*, p. 22.

And when I die, embalm me with myrrh, and *cassia*,[1317] and *stakte*,[1318] and deposit my body in the Cave of Treasures. And whosoever shall be left of your generations in that day, when your going forth from this country, which is round about Paradise, shall take place, shall carry my body with him, and shall take it and deposit it in the center of the earth, for in that place shall Redemption be effected for me and for all my children… At the same hour in which the Son of Man delivered up His soul to His Father on the Cross, did our father Adam deliver up his soul to Him that fashioned him; and he departed from this world.[1319]

Early Christian traditions about the "Cave of Treasures," where Adam and Eve purportedly lived after the Fall,[1320] are of interest because of their rich symbolism. According to these sources, the specially prepared cave became a safeguard for gold, frankincense, and myrrh, retrieved by angels from the Garden of Eden.[1321] In Old Testament times, gold was the symbol of kingship, frankincense the offering of priests, and the oil of myrrh—"known as the 'dew of resurrection'[1322]—had anointed the royal high priests after the order of Melchizedek and transformed them into sons of God."[1323] The significance of the treasures—or "tokens" as they are sometimes described[1324]—becomes more clear with the understanding that the

1317 A spice akin to cinnamon.
1318 See *Endnote E-251*, p. 768.
1319 E. A. W. Budge, *Cave*, pp. 72, 73. See also A. S-M. Ri, *Commentaire de la Caverne*, p. 200.
1320 E.g., E. A. W. Budge, *Cave*; S. C. Malan, *Adam and Eve*.
1321 For a Jewish account of Seth's cave, containing a "vault of gold" that held a book of knowledge and "precious spices," see S. Savedow, *Rezial*, p. 4. See also A. S-M. Ri, *Commentaire de la Caverne*, pp. 178-179.
1322 Compare Psalm 110:3. See *Endnote E-229*, p. 759.
1323 M. Barker, *Christmas*, p. 120; cf. pp. 138-139.
1324 See *Endnote E-255*, p. 769.

FIGURE E53-3. *Mount Sinai and the Tabernacle*
Tours Pentateuch, ca. 600

SEE COLOR PLATE E53-3.

The *Tours Pentateuch* (also known as the *Ashburnham Pentateuch*) is an elaborately illustrated version of the first five books of the Old Testament, probably originating in Rome.[1] Sadly, both the book of Deuteronomy and significant portions of other books are now missing. Originally part of the French national library collection in Tours, the manuscript was stolen in 1842 and sold to the famous book collector, Bertram Ashburnham, in 1847. "Since 1888, it has been housed at the National Library of France in Paris."[2]

The ostensible subject of this illustration is Moses who, in the top register, "accompanied by Aaron, Nadab, and Abihu, approaches the Lord, whose head appears in a cloud at the top of Mount Sinai."[3] In the middle scene, "Moses reads the covenant to the people of Israel, who gather to offer sacrifices," though the "items on the altar clearly indicate a Christian Eucharist" rather than those prescribed for Old Testament ritual.[4] At the bottom, is a Christianized representation of the Tabernacle. "In the center of the tabernacle is a square wooden altar on a stone base. A jewelled crown hangs over an altar covered with a white cloth decorated in gold trim that matches the white curtain above. The altar has a square cavity in the front, indicating it is a reliquary altar."[5] Note the prominent *gammadia* (squares) at the corners of the altar cloth, which strongly resembles the depictions of altar cloths in the Ravenna mosaics.[6]

In addition to the strong Christian interpretation given to the Exodus themes in the image, Ri[7] points out several parallels to the *Cave of Treasures* story, with the paradisiacal glory of the people of Israel at Sinai[8] recalling the similar situation of Adam and Eve and the righteous Sethites.[9] Note especially the cavelike setting of the covenant scene within the holy mountain, the reliquary in the Tabernacle below providing a secure place for the "treasures," and what could be taken as tongues of flame on the top of the mountain ("... when the children of Seth wished to go up [again] to that holy mountain, after they had come down and fallen, the stones of that holy mountain became fire in their sight"[10]).

---

1   D. H. Verkerk, *Manuscripts.*
2   *Ashburnham Pentateuch.*
3   D. H. Verkerk, *Pentateuch*, p. 90. See Exodus 24:9-18.
4   *Ibid.*, p. 90. See Exodus 24:4-8. This eucharistic scene takes place in the presence of presbyters [elders], deacons, "the canonical widows, and subdeacons and deaconesses and readers [and] those who have gifts" (J. Cooper, *et al.*, *Testament* 1:23, p. 70; cf. D. H. Verkerk, *Pentateuch*, pp. 90-97).
5   D. H. Verkerk, *Pentateuch.*, p. 98.
6   See *Endnote E-252*, p. 768. See also *Excursus 20: The Circle and the Square*, p. 571.
7   A. S-M. Ri, *Commentaire de la Caverne*, pp. 254-255. See also pp. 205-206.
8   Exodus 19:6.
9   E. A. W. Budge, *Cave*, p. 88.
10 *Ibid.*, p. 90.

cave where Adam and Eve were made to dwell was a proto-temple,[1325] a sort of figurative replacement for the Garden of Eden.[1326] Though dark and dreary compared to their former surroundings, the cave was a place of instruction, affording the couple protection from the world in their state of vulnerability, and providing privacy and security for the treasures that were kept therein.[1327] But it was not meant to be mankind's final home. "Through the atonement of Christ" and "by obedience to the laws and ordinances of the gospel,"[1328] God had prepared a way for Adam and Eve to repent and move forward. Once their period of preparation was over, "the Lord took pity on them, and he sent his angel to take them out of

---

1325 See A. S-M. Ri, *Commentaire de la Caverne*, pp. 179.
1326 E. A. W. Budge, *Cave*, p. 35.
1327 D. Wilson, *Conflict*, pp. 50-51. See also J. M. Lundquist, *Fundamentals*, pp. 655-659; cf. Moses 1:23, 42; 4:32.
1328 Articles of Faith 1:3.

Figure E53-4. *The Nativity of Christ, 15th century*

See Color Plate E53-4.

This Nativity icon recalls the depiction of the three realms of activity in the holy mountains of Adam and Eve outside of Paradise and of Moses at Sinai.[1] It also foreshadows, in the portrayal of the cave and the swaddling clothes, the symbols of Christ's death and burial. Moreover, as Barker notes:[2] "'No place in the inn'[3] could well have been an allusion…The Firstborn and the Glory, the Logos, was not 'born' in the Holy of Holies[4] and did not appear in his garments of Glory in Jerusalem.[5] He was swaddled in a manger elsewhere."

Ouspensky[6] writes that, according to Gregory Nazianzen, the Nativity of Christ "'is not a festival of Creation but a festival of re-Creation'[7]… So all Creation takes part in the event and round the Divine Child, newly born, we see representatives of the whole created world, …each giving thanks in his own way…

In the cave, … stand an ox and an ass. The Gospels do not speak of them. Yet in all the pictures of the Nativity of Christ, they are immediately beside the Divine Child. Their place in the very center of the icon points to the importance given by the Church to this detail. It is nothing less than the fulfillment of the prophecy of Isaiah which has the deepest instructive significance: 'The ox knows his owner, and the ass his master's crib: but Israel does not know Me, and the people has not regarded Me'[8]…

[I]n the great majority of images of Christ's nativity the Mother of God is lying down, showing in her posture a great lassitude, which should remind those who pray of the undoubtedly human nature of the Babe, 'in order that the incarnation should not be suspected of being an illusion'…

Angels perform a twofold service: they glorify and they bring good tidings. In an icon this is usually expressed by the fact that some of them turn upwards and sing glory to God, others lean downwards, towards men, to whom they bring good tidings. These men are the shepherds. They are shown listening to the angels' message; and often one of them is playing the reed-pipe, thus adding human art—music—to the angels' choir.

On the other side of the cave are the Wise Men, led by the star. They are represented as riding, or, as in our icon, walking with gifts. A long ray from the star points directly to the cave. This ray connects the star with a part of the sphere which goes beyond the limits of the icon—a symbolic representation of the heavenly world. In this way the icon shows that the star is not only a cosmic phenomenon, but also a messenger from the world on high, bringing tidings of the birth of 'the heavenly One upon earth'… It should be noted that the wise men are represented as being of different ages, which emphasizes the fact that revelation is given to men independently of their years and worldly experience.[9]

In a bottom corner of the icon two women are washing the Child. This scene is based on a tradition, which also is transmitted to us by the apocryphal Gospels of pseudo-Matthew and pseudo-James.[10] The two women are the two midwives whom Joseph brought to the Mother of God. This scene from everyday life shows clearly that the Child is like any other new-born babe and is subject to the natural requirements of human nature…

[Joseph] is not part of the central group of the Child and His Mother; he is not the father and is emphatically separated from the group. Before him, under the guise of an old and bent shepherd, stands the Devil tempting him… Tradition, transmitted by the Apocrypha, relates how the Devil tempted Joseph telling him that a virgin birth is not possible, being opposed to the laws of nature… In the person of Joseph the icon discloses not only is personal drama, but the drama of all mankind—the difficulty of accepting that which is 'beyond words or reason'—the Incarnation of God. While in some icons the Mother of God is represented looking at the Babe, 'keeping in her heart'[11] sayings about Him, …[here she] looks at Joseph as it were expressing by this look compassion for his state. In this the icon teaches a tolerant and compassionate attitude towards human unbelief and doubt."

1   See *Figure* E53-2, p. 670 and *Figure* E53-3, p. 671.
2   M. Barker, *Christmas*, p. 78.
3   Luke 2:7.
4   Psalm 110:3.
5   See Psalm 24:7-9; 104:1-2; M. Barker, *et al.*, *Seeking*, p. 157.
6   L. Ouspensky, *Icons*, pp. 157, 159-160.
7   Gregory Nazianzen, *Oration 38*, 4, p. 346.
8   Isaiah 1:3. Compare A. Pietersma, *et al.*, *Septuagint*, Habakkuk 3:2, p. 809. See M. Barker, *Christmas*, pp. 64, 76-77.
9   See also M. Barker, *Christmas*, p. 117.
10   Pseudo-Matthew, *Gospel of Pseudo-Matthew*, 13, pp. 374-375; M. Barker, *Infancy Gospel of James*, 19-20, pp. 158-159.
11   See Luke 2:51.

+SCS BALTHASSAR +SCS MELCHIOR +SCS GASPAR

FIGURE E53-5. *The Three Magi, Basilica of St. Apollinare Nuovo, sixth century.*
Photo: Val Brinkerhoff.

SEE COLOR PLATE E53-5.

Matthew does not say how many "wise men" (*magi*) there were, only that they brought three kinds of gifts.[1] In this mosaic from Ravenna, Italy, their caps and dress mark them as Persian philosophers, presumably devotees of Zoroaster, and named Gaspar, Melchior, and Balthassar.

Barker has noted the possibility of wordplay in the phrase describing their origin: "The word *miqqedem* can mean 'from ancient times,' or 'from the east.'"[2] Such wordplay, she concludes, may connect the story with the Garden of Eden, which was planted *miqqedem*,[3] the mention by Habakkuk that the Lord, the Holy One was *miqqedem*,[4] and the fact that the origin of the Great Shepherd of Israel who would be born in Bethlehem was *miqqedem*.[5]

Barker summarizes traditions associating the *magi* with Arabia, noting that the meaning of the word "Arabia" was different anciently—connoting, perhaps, Edom and the capital city of Petra. She notes traditions that "many priests of the first temple had settled in 'Arabia' after Josiah's temple purges." Such priests would have "held the Enochic view that the second temple was impure." It is therefore possible that the *magi* in Matthew's gospel were priests *miqqedem*, consistent with their representation in traditional nativity icons as three high priests.[6] The *Conflict of Adam and Eve with Satan* mirrors the idea of three *magi* in its account of three angels (Michael, Gabriel, and Raphael) who brought gold, frankincense, and myrrh to Adam and Eve in the Cave of Treasures.[7] Thus the depiction of winged *magi* in the Ethiopian church.[8]

Barker also considers the possibility that the *magi* were Essenes: "They were a conservative priestly group opposed to the current temple regime in Jerusalem, they studied prophecy and were themselves prophets, they were astronomers, and they were looking for the Messiah [or Messiahs]. They were respected by Herod and would have had easy access to him without fear of his wrath. But if they were Essenes, why did they need to ask him where the king of the Jews had been born? Herod was an Edomite and so did not know the Hebrew prophecies, but the Essenes were noted for their study of prophecy. One answer might be that they knew a different version of the Bethlehem prophecy in Micah 5:2. Instead of 'from you shall come forth *for me* one who is to be the ruler in Israel' the Hebrew text found at Qumran has 'from you one shall *not* come forth to be the ruler in Israel,' *l'* instead of *ly*...[9] Between the monastery of Mar Saba and Bethlehem there is the monastery of Dosi (St. Theodosius), built on the site of an older foundation marking the cave where the *magi* stayed on their way home from Bethlehem. This suggests they were going to Arabia, rather than to Persia."[10]

---

1   Matthew 2:1, 11.
2   M. Barker, *Christmas*, p. 119; Matthew 2:1. See *Commentary* 3:8-b, p. 160.
3   Moses 3:8. A Syrian manuscript explicitly asserts that they came from beyond the eastern borders of the world, from the place where Adam first lived (cited in A. S-M. Ri, *Commentaire de la Caverne*, p. 71).
4   Habakkuk 1:12. Commentators acknowledge that there is "considerable debate on how to evaluate [the] tradition concerning v. 12, and accordingly, about the wording of the original text" (A. Berlin, *et al.*, *Jewish*, p. 1228 n. 12).
5   Micah 5:2.
6   M. Barker, *Christmas*, pp. 120-121.
7   S. C. Malan, *Adam and Eve* 1:29-31, pp. 31-34.
8   M. Barker, *Christmas*, p. 119.
9   M. Abegg, Jr., *et al.*, *Scrolls Bible*, 4QXII^f Micah 5:2, p. 451.
10   M. Barker, *Christmas*, pp. 122-123; cf. pp. 162-163.

the darkness, and he guided and brought them into this bright world."[1329] There, in answer to prayer, they continued to receive the additional light and knowledge they would need as they readied themselves and their children for a permanent return to God's presence.[1330] Adam's righteous descendants are said to have lived in the upper regions of the mountain, near the Cave and the Garden, until they were lured down to the plain by Satan.[1331]

1329 W. L. Lipscomb, *Creation*, 46-47, p. 126; cf. W. L. Lipscomb, *Creation*, 50-51, pp. 265-266; S. C. Malan, *Adam and Eve*, 1:4-16, pp. 5-18.
1330 E.g., Moses 5:4-8.
1331 H. W. Nibley, *Teachings of the PGP*, p. 261; cf. S. C. Malan, *Adam and Eve*, 2:17-2:21, pp. 125-140.

FIGURE E53-6. *Funerary Chamber Adjoining the Grotto of the Teachings at Eleona*
Photo: Jeffrey M. Bradshaw, 1956-

SEE COLOR PLATE E53-6.

Eusebius reports that it was in a grotto on the Mount of Olives where "the Savior of the Universe initiated the members of his guild in the ineffable mysteries."[1] Additional reports claim that this grotto was also the location where he gave His final instructions to His apostles[2] before going down to Gethsemane.[3]

1   Eusebius, *Constantine*, 3:43:3, p. 138.
2   John 15-17.
3   O. Englebert, *Grotto*, p. 1.

The "treasures,"[1332] given to comfort the sorrowing exiles from Eden, were seen as reappearing in the later gifts of the Magi to the Christ child—whose birth arguably also took place in a cave.[1333] "The cave is presented as the Holy of Holies"[1334] and the treasures are often characterized as a revelation to Adam or Seth containing "hidden mysteries."[1335] Thus it is easy to see how, in a symbolic sense, the three gifts of the Magi constituted God's promise of an eventual recovery of what mankind had lost when they were shut out from Paradise,[1336]—including the restoration by Christ of the Melchizedek priesthood and its distinctive ordinances. Writes Barker:

> Gold, frankincense, and myrrh were symbolic of the temple; the temple vessels were made of pure gold, the temple incense was compounded with frankincense and was burned to invoke the presence of the Lord,[1337] and myrrh was the perfumed anointing oil that imparted holiness and could not be used outside the temple…[1338] There is a related Jewish tradition that Jeremiah took the temple treasures when the Jews were being deported to Babylon, and hid them in a cave at the foot of mount Nebo.[1339] The location of the cave was then lost, because Jeremiah prophesied: "The place shall be unknown until God gathers his people together again and shows his mercy. And then the Lord will disclose these things, and the glory of the Lord and the cloud will appear…."[1340] Jesus was the new Adam, the new creation, opening the way back to Eden and restoring the true temple.[1341]

1332 See *Endnote E-253*, p. 768.
1333 R. E. Brown, *Birth*, pp. 166, 197, 401; E. A. W. Budge, *Cave*, pp. 35, 208; Justin Martyr, *Trypho*, 78, p. 237; Eusebius, *Constantine*, 3:41-43, pp. 137-138; J. E. Talmage, *Jesus the Christ*, p. 100 n. 2. At least one source, however, associates the birth with a paradisiacal garden rather than a cave. See *Endnote E-254*, p. 769.
1334 M. Barker, *Christmas*, p. 145; cf. pp. 145-147.
1335 A. S-M. Ri, *Commentaire de la Caverne*, pp. 84, 182-183.
1336 E. A. W. Budge, *Cave*, Introduction, p. 16; cf. p. 69. See also M. Barker, *Hidden*, p. 25; D. Wilson, *Conflict*, pp. 46-49.
1337 F. Josephus, *Antiquities*, 8:4:1, p. 176.
1338 Exodus 30:29.
1339 See B. M. Wheeler, *Mecca*, pp. 22-23 for an overview of sources documenting the loss of items from the Jewish temple treasury, and pp. 19-46 for a discussion of the loss and recovery of items from the Islamic *Ka'ba*.
1340 See S. Sandmel, *et al.*, *2 Maccabees*, 2:7-8, p. 234.
1341 M. Barker, *Christmas*, pp. 118-119; cf. pp. 2-3, 89-90. See *Endnote E-256*, p. 769.

According to Eusebius, the Roman Emperor Constantine's mother Helena founded churches at the spot of three "mystic caves" associated with the life of the Savior."[1342] One was located in Bethlehem at the supposed site of Jesus' birth, one in Jerusalem where the Church of the Holy Sepulchre now stands,[1343] and a third on the Mount of Olives in Jerusalem.[1344]

Englebert argues that the site on the Mount of Olives is "the most easily shown to be authentic."[1345] He depicts the spot as a safe resort for the Savior during times of persecution,[1346] there being "no other place in Jerusalem where He could 'lay his head.'"[1347] After telling of a stormy scene that took place in the Temple, St. John writes: 'And they went each to his home, and Jesus to the Mount of Olives.'[1348] It would appear that, for Jesus, 'going home,' meant returning to this grotto, and that it was here that the Pharisee Nicodemus came for the nocturnal meeting he had requested."[1349] At this location, "a stone's throw from the place of His Ascension,[1350] and from where, in the sight of the Temple, He foretold the ruin of Jerusalem and the end of the world,"[1351] early traditions record that Jesus found a place "where He could teach His disciples those things that were beyond the understanding of His usual hearers."[1352] More specifically, Eusebius passed on "a true report... that in that cave the Savior of the Universe initiated the members of his guild in the ineffable mysteries."[1353] An instance of such an initiation may have occurred on the night Jesus was arrested,[1354] He having perhaps repaired to the grotto to give His final instructions to His apostles[1355] before going down to Gethsemane.[1356] According to the *Acts of John*, these instructions were concluded with a choral prayer in which "he told us to form a circle, holding one another's hands, and himself stood in the middle."[1357] Initiation into the "ineffable mysteries" was also a prominent theme in accounts of the teachings of Jesus Christ to his apostles during the forty days following his resurrection.[1358]

The Eleusinian Mysteries

The original cult at Eleusis probably began in some form during the Mycenean period (ca. 1500 BCE)[1359] The environs of the original altar, gradually developing into the famous site of the Eleusinian Mysteries, became a center of worship that endured over a period of nearly two thousand years and, in later times, included pilgrims from throughout the ancient world.[1360]

1342 Eusebius, *Constantine*, 3:43:3, p. 138.
1343 See *Figure 36-1*, p. 616.
1344 See *Endnote E-257,* p. 769.
1345 O. Englebert, *Grotto*, p. 1.
1346 Cf. 1 Kings 19:9.
1347 See Matthew 8:20; Luke 9:58; cf. D&C 109:5; S. Rigdon, *Kirtland Temple*; J. Smith, Jr., *Documentary History*, 6 April 1841, 4:329; B. Young, *et al.*, in J. Smith, Jr., *Documentary History*, 12 October 1841, 4:436; B. Young, *6 April 1853 - B*, pp. 29-31, 33.
1348 John 7:53-8:1. See also Luke 21:37, 22:39.
1349 O. Englebert, *Grotto*, p. 1. See John 3:1-5.
1350 Acts 1:12.
1351 O. Englebert, *Grotto*, p. 1. See Matthew 24:1-26:2; cf. Egeria, *Travels*, 33:2, p. 152; Eusebius, *Constantine*, p. 294 n. 43-3; E. Hennecke, *et al.*, *Apocalypse of Peter*.
1352 O. Englebert, *Grotto*, p. 1; cf. A. Storme, *Mont des Oliviers*, pp. 24-27.
1353 Eusebius, *Constantine*, 3:43:3, p. 138.
1354 W. J. Hamblin, *Initiation*, p. 207; M. Smith, *Secret Gospel*, pp. 15-16.
1355 John 15-17.
1356 O. Englebert, *Grotto*, p. 1.
1357 E. Hennecke, *et al.*, *Acts of John*, 94, p. 227. Consistent with such symbolism, in *ibid.*, 97, p. 232, John, during Jesus' sufferings on the cross, is said to have "fled to the Mount of Olives" where he was visited by the Lord, "who stood in the middle of the cave and gave light to it."
1358 See Acts 1:1-3, H. W. Nibley, *Evangelium*; H. W. Nibley, *Return*, p. 66; cf. 1 John 2:27; Basil, *Spirit* 66, p. 41.
1359 M. B. Cosmopoulos, *Megaron B*, pp. 18-20.
1360 See *Endnote E-259*, p. 770.

Figure E53-7. *Telesterion at Eleusis, ca. 450 BCE.*
Photo: Stephen T. Whitlock, 1951-

See Color Plate E53-7.

Blessed of earthbound men is he who has seen these things, but he who dies without fulfilling the holy things, and he who is without a share of them, has no claim ever on such blessings, even when departed down to the moldy darkness.[1] The Telesterion, the largest and most important building in Eleusis, was so named because here the *telos* (= purpose, end, goal) was at last attained by the initiates.[2] The location itself appears to have been sacred, as the Telesterion itself underwent several significant modifications over time while the Anaktoron, the original cult building where the *Hiera* [= sacred relics] were kept,[3] was never demolished or moved. The ruins visible today, dating from about 450 BCE, were designed to hold up to three thousand people.

1   *Hymn to Demeter* 480-483, cited in M. W. Meyer, *Mysteries*, p. 30.
2   C. Kerényi, *Eleusis*, p. 47. See *Endnote E-258*, p. 769.
3   G. E. Mylonas, *Eleusis*, p. 273.

The Temple of Demeter was located at the end of a sacred, processional way that connected the site to the Acropolis in Athens. Worship of Demeter is one of the earliest Greek traditions, and Homer hints that she was revered long before she was made part of the Pantheon. Her name means "Grain Mother."[1361] In addition to being the goddess of harvest, she also represented youth and fertility. According to Isocrates, her greatest gifts were grain (her Latin name is Ceres, the root of the English word "cereal") and the Eleusinian Mysteries. The former differentiated man from the animals,[1362] and the latter joined him to the gods.

The Telesterion was the largest and most important building in Eleusis. Its main function was to protect the sacred relics (*Hiera*) and to provide a place where they could be prominently displayed as part of a sacred drama associated with Demeter and her daughter Kore-Persephone. Sometimes being led to various places at the site and, at other times, sitting on the steps facing a dense forest of forty-two columns supporting the roof, the crowd participated in rites said to consist of *legomena* (= things recited), *deiknymena* (= things shown), and *dromena* (= things performed).[1363] Meyer writes:

> Doubtless such productions were staged by priests or *mystai…* The actors produced and the audience witnessed a theatrical performance in which the *hieroi logoi* [= sacred myth] of the mystery religions came to life in liturgical drama. The company of initiates played the roles of mythological characters and sometimes donned masks or costumes in order to reenact the sufferings, sorrows, and joys of the gods and goddesses.[1364]

According to Mylonas, "the climax of the rites" was "when the *Hierophant* standing in front of the Anaktoron and in the midst of a radiant light exhibited the *Hiera* to the initiates."[1365] The

1361 Or, less plausibly, "Earth Mother." See *Endnote E-260*, p. 771.
1362 Cf. *Commentary 4:24-b*, p. 271; 4:25-a, p. 272.
1363 See *Endnote E-261*, p. 771.
1364 M. W. Meyer, *Mysteries*, pp. 11-12. See *Endnote E-262*, p. 771.
1365 G. E. Mylonas, *Eleusis*, p. 273. See *Endnote E-263*, p. 771.

objective of all this was "to prepare for and be allowed direct contact with a divinity"[1366] and later to achieve "a higher 'status' after death, that of initiate entitled to a happy afterlife."[1367]

Compton has explored the hypothesis that the interpretation of Greek recognition drama can be informed from the context of mystery rites such as those practiced at Eleusis. His findings and arguments can only be summarized briefly here. He explained the background of his study as follows:[1368]

> Greek recognition drama [is] a type of play in which a child is separated from its (aristocratic) parents at birth (often it is stolen, or saved by strangers after a shipwreck), and so grows up as a slave or prostitute; but later, when it becomes an adult, it finds or is found by its parents (the recognition scene) through the help of tokens[1369] left with the child, often insignia or jewelry on a necklace, sometimes a ring; sometimes a peculiar scar.[1370] Often the tokens are kept in boxes and are dramatically extracted from the boxes, one by one, in the recognition scene. Critics, I found, have usually looked at recognition drama with contempt; however, all Greek drama is bathed in religion, sometimes very alien, and I wondered if the structure of recognition was not linked with religion in some way; and if the critics were not doing these plays an injustice because of their modern, secular bias and insensitivity to the nuances of ancient Greek religion and ritual. The climaxes of these recognition dramas seemed to have great meaning for the Greek playwrights and audiences; surely the recognition drama with tokens was not just a rickety, mechanistic plot device used as a crutch by playwrights of the stature of Aeschylus and Euripides.[1371] As my research progressed, I found that the Greek/Hellenistic mystery cults involved tokens revealed at the high point of the secret rituals. These tokens were always kept in a box/basket called the *cista mystica*; and as they were brought out, the initiate had to speak certain passwords (also called tokens). After the experience, the initiate enjoyed a new intimacy with the central god or gods of the mystery and was prepared for a better state in the next life.[1372] Not much more was known about this token experience in the mysteries, but I thought the parallel was close enough to warrant a comparison of the climax of the recognition scene, with its crucial tokens, and the climax of the mystery ritual, with its tokens.

Thus supposing, on the other hand, that these parallels might also "come to throw welcome light on the final moments of Orphic or Eleusinian initiation," Compton attempted an admittedly speculative reconstruction of such an initiation from recognition scenes in Greek drama, setting forth the following aspects, not as final conclusions, but as hypotheses to be explored:[1373]

1. The initiate, seen as child of the god before parting and forgetfulness, learns the possibility of his true heritage (*anamnesis*, remembrance, re-knowing, recognition) and approaches the god to prove his identity and renew the ancient bond.

2. There was a *cista mystica* in which were kept the *symbola* of the god, tokens representing the presence, life and parenthood of the god, rebirth, and the initiate's former and future bond with the god.

3. A *hierophant* in charge of the *cista mystica* acted as the judge of the initiate, the tester; as he challenged the initiate concerning every token, the initiand responded with the correct

1366 F. Graf, *Lesser Mysteries*, p. 255.
1367 C. Sourvinou-Inwood, *Festival*, p. 41.
1368 T. M. Compton, *Handclasp*, pp. 611-612.
1369 See *Endnote E-264*, p. 771.
1370 See *Endnote E-265*, p. 772.
1371 See *Endnote E-266*, p. 772.
1372 See *Endnote E-267*, p. 772.
1373 T. M. Compton, *Token*.

response. Perhaps the tokens were shown, as a proof of the initiate's correctness (so the *hierophant* is the shower of the *hiera*).

4.   Among the tokens may have been necklaces, rings, representations of the cock, the bull, the goat, the serpent (this, of course, is widely attested as a mystery *symbolon*), the sword (perhaps equivalent to the *phallus*), the ax, the sickle. Perhaps new clothing was involved. The initiate was certainly crowned, as a symbol of his victory and of his new commonality with the divine. Perhaps a *dexiosis* [= handclasp] represented preliminary transition to the presence of the god.

5.   The initiate may have been seen to be in great danger if he failed to pass the test...

6.   Having passed the tests of the tokens and their passwords, the physical and verbal *symbola*, the initiate would have been admitted to the presence of the god, probably played by a priest; we know that a priest and a priestess represented Dionysus and Demeter in the Eleusinian mysteries, perhaps the same priest who has acted as judge of the tokens...

7.   This recognition and *unio mystica*, culmination of the initiation, was represented by the initiate's ritual embrace with the priest representing the god. The initiate would have been recognized by the god as his former child; the embrace is the sign of acceptance, not necessarily of adoption, but of re-adoption after loss. The love of a maternal or paternal embrace is expressed, divine power is transferred, and the initiate moves across the liminal area between man and god.

8.   The conclusion of the rite was marked by an emotional exaltation. The god is overcome with joy to have found his or her long-lost son; the initiate is overcome to have finally found his long-lost, divine parents, to regain his lost, high status, and to know that he can finally be released from his ordeals... This emotional exaltation... is widely documented in the mysteries, especially at Eleusis. Explanations for such heights of emotion at Eleusis have generally been very weak; one of the traditional explanations of the high emotion has been the showing of an ear of corn. While, by my hypothesis, this might have been one of the important *symbola* shown, it does not seem in itself an adequate explanation for the enormous emotion and comfort produced by the Eleusinian mysteries...

9.   ... A *hieros gamos* [= sacred marriage] may have been connected with the initiation somehow.[1374] Frazerian interpreters may let their imaginations run wild on this aspect of a hypothetical mystery rite (as did some Christian fathers), but Menander and Plautus treat the marriages with sophisticated, even charming delicacy. The sincere love of the marriage partners is emphasized: the estranged Charisius refuses to sleep with the courtesan he has hired to make his wife jealous; Plesidippus tries to buy Palaestra out of prostitution before she is found to be a citizen of Athens.

Summarizing the significance of the Eleusinian Mysteries, Mylonas writes:[1375]

> Whatever the substance and meaning of the Mysteries was, the fact remains that the cult of Eleusis satisfied the most sincere yearnings and the deepest longings of the human heart. The initiates returned from their pilgrimage to Eleusis full of joy and happiness, with the fear of death diminished and the strengthened hope of a better life in the world of shadows: "Thrice happy are those of mortals, who having seen those rites depart for Hades; for to them alone it is granted to have true life there; to the rest all there is evil," Sophokles cries out exultantly.[1376] And to this Pindar with equal exultation answers: "Happy is he who, having seen these rites goes

---

1374 Avagianou likewise rejects agricultural and seasonal interpretations of *hieros gamos* in favor of "its conceptual pattern as a ritual of initiation and a rite of passage" (A. A. Avagianou, *Hieros*, p. 147).

1375 G. E. Mylonas, *Eleusis*, p. 285.

1376 Sophocles, *Tragoediae*, 2, Fragmenta, 719, cited in G. E. Mylonas, *Eleusis*, p. 285.

below the hollow earth; for he knows the end of life and he knows its god-sent beginning."[1377] When we read these and similar statements by the great or nearly great of the ancient world, by dramatists and thinkers,… we cannot help but believe that the Mysteries of Eleusis were not an empty, childish affair devised by shrewd priests to fool the peasant and the ignorant, but a philosophy of life that possessed substance and meaning and imparted a modicum of truth to the yearning human soul. That belief is strengthened when we read in Cicero that Athens has given nothing to the world more excellent or divine than the Eleusinian Mysteries.[1378]

FIGURE E53-8. *King David Prays Before the Ark,* **Crusaders Bible, ca. 1250.**

"The Ark… is imagined by the medieval illustrator to be something familiar in his world: a portable altar or reliquary…. placed on an altar to consecrate it for the Mass."[1] In similitude of the tomb of Christ, a recess in the altar, the *sepulchurum*, was made to hold "three pieces of the sacramental Body of Christ, three grains of incense (in honor of the spices brought by the women and Joseph of Arimathea), and the relics of saints, all wrapped in silk and sealed by the stone."[2]

In addition to identifying the sacramental altar and its stone with the Jewish temple ark and the foundation stone within the Holy of Holies of the first temple, Christians transformed the symbolism of the Ark to support a theological position: whereas the Tablets of the Covenant in the original ark represented the former covenant between God and His people, the new "Christian Ark" contained the tokens of Christ's sacrifice, the new covenant between God and man. In the Coptic Church, this symbolism is carried further: "… while the old ark included Aaron's rod which budded,[3] the new ark symbolizes the Virgin Mary who gave birth to God…Finally, the old ark contained the golden pot of manna,[4] whereas the new ark holds the true heavenly Manna which gives life everlasting."[5]

1   G. R. Murphy, *Gemstone*, pp. 32, 34.
2   *Ibid.*, pp. 182. See Matthew 27:59-60, 66.
3   Hebrews 9:4.
4   Exodus 16:32-34.
5   A. S. Atiya, *Encyclopedia*, 4:1064-1065, cited in S. Munro-Hay, *Quest*, p. 29. See John 6:57-58.

Jewish and Christian Analogues to the Cista Mystica?

Clement of Alexandria described a formulaic recital within the Eleusinian Mysteries, implying that initiates performed actions involving tangible tokens kept in a sacred chest: "I have taken from the chest [*kiste*]; having done the work, I have placed in the basket [*kalathos*], and from the basket into the chest."[1379] Those for whom the idea of a chest or basket of sacred relics seems unfamiliar or strange might remember that such a container— the ark—was also part of the First Temple in Judaism.

The frequency with which the ark is mentioned in Exodus 25 and its primacy in the lists of temple furniture, not to mention its symbolic significance with respect to the rites of atonement, making it arguably "the heart of the theology of the Tabernacle and its purpose in Israel and now in the life of the church."[1380] Most commentators have focused on the ritual function of the ark itself as a symbol of the throne of or presence of God, or on

1377 Pindar, *Carmina*, Fragmenta, 102, cited in G. E. Mylonas, *Eleusis*, p. 285.
1378 M. T. Cicero, *Legibus*, 2 (14):36, cited in G. E. Mylonas, *Eleusis*, p. 285.
1379 As cited in M. W. Meyer, *Mysteries*, p. 18; cf. Clement of Alexandria, *Exhortation*, 2:21, p. 177. See *Endnote E-268*, p. 773.
1380 W. C. Kaiser, Jr., *Exodus*, p. 454. See C. H. T. Fletcher-Louis, *Glory*, p. 41 for references to arguments that Noah's ark, "a bulwark against the forces of chaos," likewise "was designed as a temple."

EXCURSUS

FIGURE E53-9. *The Paradise Altar of Bamberg, twelfth century*

SEE COLOR PLATE E53-9.

Von Eschenbach's *Parzival* recounts the quest for the Grail, here conceived as a green stone called the *lapsit exillis.*[1] Brought down by angels during the War in Heaven, it showed its "highest power" by displaying the names of those worthy to be its keepers.[2] This description recalls the white stone with a new name written thereon that is given to each one who enters the celestial kingdom.[3]

Murphy describes a portable reliquary altar containing a green stone that he identifies with the Grail in *Parzival.* Of average size for such altars (9.8 inches long x 6.2 inches wide x 5.9 inches high), it features both sacrificial and paradisiacal decorations: "To the left of the green stone is Abel rushing forward toward the altar stone with a lamb in his cloth-covered hands, ready to make his offering. To the right of the altar stone is King Melchizedek hastening toward it with his offering of a round loaf of bread and a chalice of wine in his hands, as he reaches out to place them on the altar. This means that on the missing plaque below the altar stone would have been Abraham with the knife ready to offer his son Isaac on the altar.... The four evangelists… in the four corners of the tabletop point to the story of Christ recorded in the four Gospels." The four trees of Paradise stand near the evangelists.[4] To the left of Abel on the edge is "a man pouring water. It was the personification of one of the rivers of Paradise, drawn as a man with an oriental cap and, in the classical manner, pouring a stream of blue water out of a large jar onto the earth. [A similar figure is to the right of Melchizedek, and personifications of the other two rivers would have been on the missing top and bottom panels. All these figures] are looking back to the green altar stone that covers the *sepulchrum* at the center of the altar table, their source, making the Sepulchre of Christ's Passion and Resurrection an analogue to the primal river rising in the middle of the Garden of Paradise."[5]

According to Murphy, Von Eschenbach's version of the Grail story "suggested that the Crusades were unnecessary, unseeing, fratricidal journeys. The Crusaders' quest was to reach and see the stone tomb of their Lord's Resurrection, the Holy Sepulchre, the Grail; but this sacred stone could be found, without the sword, in every altar on which the Eucharist was celebrated: the altar stone."[6]

---

1   Possibly a corruption of *lapis ex coelis* or stone from heaven
2   W. von Eschenbach, *Parzival*, 469-471, pp. 198-199.
3   Revelation 2:17; D&C 130:11. See *Endnote 4-9*, p. 299.
4   = 1. "pleasant to the sight"; 2. "good for food"; 3. tree of life"; 4. "tree of knowledge of good and evil" (Moses 3:9).
5   G. R. Murphy, *Gemstone*, pp. 181-184.
6   G. R. Murphy, *Gemstone (excerpt)*, p. 8.

its purported military efficacy in Israel's battles.[1381] By way of contrast, few seem to have reflected on what role, if any, the items *within* the ark may have had as part of temple ritual.

The number of items in the ark of the covenant seems to have been controversial. Hebrews 9:4 speaks of at least three things that were originally kept within it: "the golden pot that had manna,[1382] and Aaron's rod that budded,[1383] and the tablets of the covenant." According to Koester, certain Jewish traditions linked these items, along with the incense altar, "with worship in heaven and the end times."[1384] However, other exegetes insist that the instructions in Exodus 25:16 specify that only a single item was to be placed therein, i.e., "[the tablets of] the Pact," though admitting that the bracketed words are only "implied."[1385] To bolster

---

1381 See, e.g., D. N. Freedman, *et al.*, *Eerdmans*, pp. 102-103.
1382 Revelation 2:17 calls this the "hidden manna." Barker cites references associating this with the "bread of angels," and the associated stone with a new name and the high priesthood (M. Barker, *Revelation*, pp. 105-106).
1383 According to Koester: "Aaron's rod marked God's call to legitimate priesthood, a pattern that Christ follows [see Hebrews 5:4]" (C. R. Koester, *Hebrews*, p. 402).
1384 *Ibid.*
1385 W. G. Plaut, *Commentary*, p. 605 n. 18; cf. N. M. Sarna, *Exodus*, p. 160 n. 16.

the argument that there was only one item in the ark, commentators often cite 1 Kings 8:9 ("There was nothing in the ark save the two tables of stone…"), though, as Franz Delitzsch points out: "The very terms of this statement seem to imply that other things had been there formerly."[1386] In its translation of Exodus 25:16, the *New English Bible* explicitly commits itself to the idea that the original ark was potentially to receive other objects besides the tablets of the Law: "put into the Ark the Tokens that I shall give you," explaining that the "Tokens of the Covenant included a copy of the Ten Commandments[1387] and relics of the Lord's acts of salvation."[1388]

In addition to their basic commemorative purpose, could such items have served a role in ancient temple ritual? Consistent with the idea of these objects as "tokens," Buber and Rosenweig, "seeking to connect *'edut* ('Testimony') with the sound of *mo'ed* ('appointment'), translate these two terms as 'representation' and 'presence.'"[1389] In addition, the close association between the "hidden manna," the "white stone," and the "new name" in Revelation 2:17 certainly is no coincidence.[1390] Moreover, the sacred relics believed in Orthodox tradition to have been kept in the proto-temple of the Cave of Treasures by Adam and Eve were described in terms that may have ritual significance. For example, in the *Conflict of Adam and Eve with Satan,* Adam is depicted, just prior to his death, as having described these "tokens" and their Messianic significance to his son, and then saying, "And now, O Seth, my son, behold I have revealed unto thee hidden mysteries, which God had revealed unto me."[1391]

Dexiosis

Closterman describes *dexiosis*, the handclasp, as "the clearest expression" of family relationships and emotional ties in classical funerary iconography.[1392] Concerning its wider significations, Davies writes: "The themes of meeting and parting were persistently associated with the handshake (especially parting from relatives at death, and reunion with ancestors in the Underworld), but various other themes were also related to it, especially marriage."[1393] Compton finds the handclasp:

> … a perfect *symbolon* image on a human, physical level: two separate hands, symbols of the separate identities of their possessors, are joined, and fingers intertwine to make a new unity, complex yet simple. Though its "secular" use—as a widespread token of recognition, friendship, and agreement—is obvious, it was also co-opted by the mystery religions for use as an emblem for many things: love, initiation, arrival, salvation, union with the god, apotheosis.[1394]

Though best known as a funerary motif during and after the classical period, a study of its history by Davies cites its earlier use in mythological scenes:[1395]

1386 *Commentary on the Epistle to the Hebrews*, p. 57, cited in Bruce, *Hebrews,* p. 203. See *Excursus 51: The Five Lost Things of the Temple,* p. 658. See W. L. Lane, *Hebrews 9-13,* p. 221 regarding "a tradition presupposed in certain strands of the rabbinic evidence" that "other objects were placed within the ark."
1387 Exodus 31:18, Deuteronomy 10:1-5.
1388 S. Sandmel, *et al., New English Bible,* p. 82, n. 26:16. See, e.g., Exodus 16:32-34. Likewise, Attridge translates the relevant phrase in Exodus 25:16 as "tokens of the covenant" (H. W. Attridge, *et al., Hebrews,* p. 236).
1389 Cited in E. Fox, *Books of Moses,* p. 399 n. Exodus 25:16.
1390 Cf. D&C 130:4-11; S. Munro-Hay, *Quest,* pp. 195-199; *Commentary* 1:27-b, p. 62; *Commentary* 3:19-b, p. 177; and the overview of Moses 4, Figure 4-4, p. 219. See *Endnote 4-9,* p. 299. See *Endnote 4-22,* p. 304.
1391 S. C. Malan, *Adam and Eve,* 2:8, p. 116.
1392 W. E. Closterman, *Ideology,* p. 635.
1393 G. Davies, *Handshake,* p. 627; cf. S. D. Ricks, *Dexiosis.*
1394 T. M. Compton, *Handclasp,* p. 614.
1395 G. Davies, *Handshake,* pp. 627-628.

EXCURSUS

FIGURE E53-10. *Plangon Exchanges Handclasps with Her Mother*
Photo: Jeffrey M. Bradshaw, 1956-

A display outside the Eleusis sanctuary museum features this marble water vase (= Greek *loutrophoros*). Such funerary monuments have been found throughout Attica, the region including Athens and Eleusis.

This monument shows a deceased maiden with beautifully plaited hair who is dressed for a journey, presumably taking leave of her seated mother with a handclasp.[1] The name of the maiden, Plangon, is written in Greek characters above her head.

With her left hand, Plangon holds a corner of her mantlet over her face. A standing female behind the seated figure has completely worn away. Clairmont sees the presence of the young servant girl in the company of Plangon as "particularly noteworthy." Moreover, "contrary to what one might expect," he informs us, her hair is "not covered by a kerchief."[2] She holds a large fan in her lowered right hand, and with her left holds a rectangular box near her shoulder.[3]

1 C. W. Clairmont, *Tombstones*, p. 480. See *Endnote E-270*, p. 773.
2 *Ibid.*
3 See *Endnote E-271*, p. 773.

Many such scenes of the late archaic period involve Herakles: he is shown shaking hands with Athena on both black- and red-figure vases, where the scene represents the acceptance of Herakles as an equal by the gods, and, in particular, his comradeship with Athena. Slightly later, as one might expect, the focus switches from Herakles to Theseus. On Early Classical red-figure vases Theseus is represented linking right hands with his father, Poseidon, again presumably to indicate Theseus' exalted status. The first use of the motif in an Underworld setting is on a *lekythos* (= vase for storing oil) by the Alkimachos Painter in Berlin which depicts Herakles' attempt to rescue Peirithoos from the Underworld. Peirithoos is linked with his would-be rescuer by a right handclasp. Although Herakles may be attempting to haul Peirithoos to his feet, the taking of right hands seems to me to be given an emphasis that is not required by the narrative.[1396] Around 450 BC it seems the motif began to be used in a variety of contexts and could now be applied to ordinary mortals. An important instance occurs on a large *krater* [= bowl used for mixing wine and water] in New York decorated with a scene set in Hades. Among the various traditional inhabitants are an unnamed couple—a woman, still wearing her grave clothes, shaking hands with a young man. The scene is best interpreted as one of greeting: one of the woman's deceased relatives, or at least one of the inhabitants of Hades, is greeting her as a new arrival.

After a study of *dexiosis* as a token of recognition in classic culture and in other mystery religions, Compton raised the possibility that the Eleusinian rite may have incorporated a handclasp.[1397] In the context of this assumption, the handclasp, in conjunction with other emblematic actions and sayings, would have served as a powerful symbol of reunion and glorification after death. Confirming the role of the mysteries as a preparation for the afterlife, Cole concluded that the promise of "special treatment after death" held out for

---

1396 Cf. *Figure E53-12*, p. 684.
1397 T. M. Compton, *Handclasp*, p. 615. On the use of the handclasp in Mandaean rites, see *Mandaean Texts*, p. 872.
    See *Endnote E-273*, p. 774.

FIGURE E53-11. *Introduction of Adam into Paradise, thirteenth century*

… there I put the man whom I had formed.[1] The Hebrew can be read as implying that the bodies of Adam and Eve were created outside the Garden of Eden and only later introduced within it.

This detail, from the Creation cupola in the Church of San Marco in Venice, is described by Jolly as follows: "With his right hand, God pulls Adam through the clearly labeled *Porta Paradisi* into his lush Garden, and with his left, gestures toward the two prominent trees… God acts as his guide, eagerly leading him forward, their two figures moving parallel to each other."[2]

1   Moses 3:8.
2   P. H. Jolly, *Eve and Adam*, p. 25.

initiates "was established by ritual and confirmed after death by recalling or reciting esoteric information that could have been learned only through that ritual experience."[1398] Noting how myth eventually came to represent the hoped-for experience of ordinary individuals after death, Compton writes:[1399]

> In the Hellenistic period, Herakles became allegorized as the soul; his myth served to illustrate the trials and victories of the soul.[1400] In the Igel monument, a remarkable piece of funerary art with Mithraic motifs, Herakles as soul is combined with the *dexios* motif; the handclasp is used to draw Herakles into heaven. The hero is in the *quadriga* (chariot), ascending into heaven; Athena emerges from a cloud and extends to him "a hand of succor,"[1401] which Herakles grasps. This apotheosis scene "portrays the Heroisation of the personage laid in the tomb, or, in a more general fashion, the destiny of the soul, which, with the help of heavenly powers, reaches the abode of the blessed," according to Cumont.[1402]

The handclasp also appears in early and medieval Christian art.[1403] Common to many of the settings is the theme of transition from one state or place to another. For example, a scene portrayed at the Church of San Marco in Venice shows God taking Adam by the wrist to bring him through the door of Paradise and to introduce him into the Garden of Eden.[1404] Another scene shows God taking Adam by the wrist as he and Eve received the commandment not to partake of the Tree of Knowledge.[1405] Likewise, Abraham is shown being taken by the wrist by the angel Yahoel as he ascends to heaven.[1406]

The same motif is frequently depicted at the moment of resurrection, when Jesus takes waiting souls by the hand or wrist to bring them out of the dominion of death.[1407] In a

1398 S. G. Cole, *Landscapes*, pp. 200-201. This promise was also conditioned on the initiate meeting "standards for social behavior" (*ibid.*, p. 199).
1399 T. M. Compton, *Handclasp*, p. 617.
1400 E. S. Strong, *Apotheosis*, p. 201.
1401 F. V. M. Cumont, *Symbolisme*, p. 174; cf. E. S. Strong, *Apotheosis*, pp. 222-232.
1402 F. V. M. Cumont, *Symbolisme*, p. 174. See *Endnote E-272*, p. 773.
1403 For an example from the Islamic tradition, see *Figure 1-8*, p. 39.
1404 See *Figure E53-11*, p. 683.
1405 See *Figure 4-10*, p. 228.
1406 See *Figure E53-13*, p. 684; cf. P. Alexander, *3 Enoch*, 1:4, p. 256; 48A:1, p. 300; G. W. E. Nickelsburg, *et al.*, *1 Enoch*, 71:3, p. 93.
1407 See *Figure 6-12*, p. 471. This recalls an account of Jesus' raising of Lazarus (M. Smith, *Secret Gospel*, p. 15).

FIGURE E53-12. *The Angel Yahoel Takes Abraham by the Hand and Stands Him on His Feet, ca. 1300*
FIGURE E53-13. *Abraham and the Angel Yahoel Ascend on the Wings of Birds, ca. 1300.* **Photos: Stephen T. Whitlock.**

SEE COLOR PLATE E53-13.

I… fell down upon the earth, for there was no longer strength in me to stand… And the angel… took me by my right hand and stood me on my feet.[1] The visionary experiences described in the *Apocalypse of Abraham* and Moses 1 are replete with striking parallels.[2] After their divine encounters, both Abraham and Moses "fell unto the earth" and were bereft of their "natural strength."[3] Then, in this weakened condition, they were each immediately tested by Satan. In the case of Abraham, we are told that an angel stood him on his feet prior to his encounter with Satan. This was accomplished through taking him by the right hand,[4] as shown in this illustration from a fourteenth-century Slavonic manuscript.[5] Nibley cites a parallel with Abraham 1:18 ("Behold I will lead thee by my hand"), and sees a corresponding theme in the book of Abraham when Abraham is delivered from the altar: "The expressions 'loose the bands of Hades' and 'him who stareth at the dead' signify the nature of the deliverance and are both typically Egyptian, the latter of which Box finds quite bizarre. Facsimile 1 [of the book of Abraham] is a very proper illustration to the story."[6]

The second image relates to the statement that "Moses was caught up into an exceedingly high mountain."[7] A close parallel to Moses' experience is found in 1 Nephi 11:1 where Nephi was "caught away in the Spirit of the Lord, yea, into an exceedingly high mountain, which [he] never had before seen."[8] Nephi later said that "upon the wings of his Spirit hath my body been carried away upon exceedingly high mountains,"[9] just as the *Apocalypse of Abraham* records that Abraham and his angel guide were raised up to heaven on the wings of a turtledove and a pigeon.[10] The angel Yahoel (Metatron or Enoch)[11] gestures upwards to heaven. He grasps Abraham firmly by the wrist as they ascend.[12]

1   A. Kulik, *Retroverting*, Apocalypse of Abraham 10:1-4, p. 17.
2   See *Excursus 54: Table of Parallels with the Apocalypse of Abraham,* p. 694 See also *Figure 1-8*, p. 38,
3   Moses 1:9-10.
4   Cf. the description of the rescue of Perithoos by Herakles, *Excursus 53*, p. 682.
5   P. P. Novickij, *Otkrovenie Avraama.*
6   H. W. Nibley, *Abraham 2000*, p. 16, see also p. 42.
7   Moses 1:1.
8   Cf. Exodus 19:3, Ezekiel 40:2; JST Matthew 4:8; Revelation 21:10; Moses 7:2; . B. Reynolds, *Kingship*, pp. 172-177.
9   2 Nephi 4:25.
10   R. Rubinkiewicz, *Apocalypse of Abraham*, 12:10, p. 695. See H. W. Nibley, *Abraham 2000*, p. 18; cf. Genesis 15:9ff.
11   The identification of Yahoel in Nibley's article (and the illustration itself) reference G. Davidson, *Angels*, pp. 316-317.
12   Cf. H. W. Nibley, *Apocryphal*, p. 278; cf. E. Isaac, *1 Enoch*, 96:2, p. 76; J. Priest, *Moses*, 10:8-10, p. 932; Deuteronomy 32:11; Isaiah 40:31; Revelation 4:7, 8:13, 12:14.

notable depiction of this event discussed by Isar, "the center of the image coincides with the stigmata of Christ,[1408] which marks the meeting point between Christ's hand and Adam's hand. The diagonals formed by Christ's hand and Adam's stretched hand, the vertical line of the cross, which Christ holds, describe an invisible, but unmistakable sacred pattern,

1408 = the nail wounds of the Savior's crucifixion.

Chi-Rho (XP),"[1409] the first letters in the Greek name of Christ.[1410] At the time of their glorification, the saints are portrayed similarly. For instance, Brown cites examples of sacred handclasps in portrayals of "a monk… being admitted through the gate of Paradise by the apostle Peter," and "a resurrected Christian in a white robe being admitted through the gate of the New Jerusalem."[1411] Stairways in some of these portrayals mark the scene as an ascension.[1412]

The handclasp was also used by Christians as part of ritual and prayer. For example, Brown describes a ritual where initiates simultaneously performed their renunciation of Satan and made a covenant "by clasping the left hand of the officiating priest. Then another covenant was made—this time to commit oneself to Jesus Christ—by a clasping of the right hand with the officiator."[1413] Sacred handclasps were also used in early Christian prayer circles. For example, according to the *Acts of John,* Jesus concluded His final instructions to the apostles with a choral prayer in which "he told [them] to form a circle, holding one another's hands, and himself stood in the middle."[1414] In the account, the Lord specifically terms this ritual a "mystery,"[1415] which, according to Isar, "might reflect some liturgical practices in use in the community of the Acts."[1416]

Accounts of Christian prayer circles recall descriptions of Greek rituals performed in a sanctuary, with "the dancers standing in a circle…facing a center occupied by the vertical axis of the altar itself. By facing the central point on the earth occupied by the god's altar, the chorus was thought to face the god himself. The altar was a means of establishing a connection between a particular point of earth and the divine"[1417] while the participants expressed their oneness "in the gesture of solidarity by holding hands,"[1418] or, to be more specific, "placing the 'hand over the wrist.'"[1419] Further describing the significance of this ritual, Isar argues that the verb associated with the Greek term *choros*:

> had a specific meaning of ritual movement ascribed by Pindar specifically and exclusively to divine groups… The specificity of the antique concept stands in its rhetorical compound, combining speech, singing and bodily movement.[1420] *Choros* refers to a collective coordinated movement in orderly, circular disposition; it can define the place where one dances; the choir; a round dance; the group of personages; the song performed by the choir; the sense of order…
>
> *Choros* was thought to be… an ordering force that could express in the highest sense the capacity of human creativity to reflect the divine order, and to bring it into the world.[1421]

1409 N. Isar, *Dance of Adam,* pp. 180-181.

1410 Isar notes that "Christ's gesture… is strikingly similar to certain ritual gestures that can be identified in ancient Greek ritual performances" such as "the bond created by the nuptial ritual" and "the choral dance… of the Charities" as described in Homer's *Hymn to Apollo* (*ibid.*, p. 182). See also I. Mika'el, son of Bakhayla, *Godhead,* p. 136; N. Isar, *Dance of Adam,* pp. 180-181; M. Lidzbarski, *Ginza,* GL 1:1, p. 429, cited in H. W. Nibley, *Apocryphal,* p. 300; cf. Isaiah 49:16, Zechariah 13:6, Cyril of Jerusalem, *Five,* 2:5, p. 148). See *Commentary* 5:4-a, p. 355; 5:5-b, p. 359; *Excursus 37: Traditions About the Role of Abel,* p. 617.

1411 See a figure of John being thus admitted in the tenth century Bamberg Apocalypse (*Das Neue Jerusalem*).

1412 M. B. Brown, *9 August 2008.*

1413 M. B. Brown, *9 August 2008.*

1414 E. Hennecke, *et al., Acts of John,* 94, p. 227. See discussion in N. Isar, *Dance of Adam,* pp. 193-194.

1415 E. Hennecke, *et al., Acts of John,* 101, p. 234.

1416 N. Isar, *Dance of Adam,* p. 194.

1417 *Ibid.,* pp. 185-186. The idea of an upward movement of the circle, essentially its transformation into a helix, is conveyed in the remarkable *Anastasis* of the *Barberini Psalter: Cod. Gr. 372, fol. 181,* where the "disposition of bodies is unfolding in dynamic spiral, an open circle which binds together Christ, Adam, Eve, and Abel. This movement ascends towards Christ and rests on His hieratic body, the center of a chiasmus. Christ's gesture, grasping Adam's hand, is emphatic" (*ibid.*, p. 195).

1418 *Ibid.,* p. 186.

1419 *Ibid.,* p. 187.

1420 Pindar described these movements as "expressive figures" such as "holds" and "poses" (cited in *ibid.*, p. 185).

1421 *Ibid.,* p. 183.

Figure E53-14. *Detail from the Robail-Navier Family Sepulchre, Cimitière de la Madeleine, Amiens, France,* ca. 1832
Photo: Jeffrey M. Bradshaw, 1956-

Clasped hands have been a popular symbol of the marriage relationship since ancient times.[1] The earliest inscription on this family monument records that both Jean-Baptiste Robail, age 70, and his wife, Rose Duclocher, age 72, passed away on the same day, July 16, 1832. Though stained with age, the sleeves and hands remain remarkably lifelike. As a gesture now captured in perpetuity, the smooth fingers of the beloved wife rest calmly within the enclosing grasp of her husband.

1 S. D. Ricks, *Dexiosis.*

Mandaean[1422] and Manichaean[1423] texts record the use of the handclasp in the context of rituals anticipating the manner of the soul's ascent after death. In addition, Drower compares the Mandaean rite of *kushta* to practices among the Parsis and Iraqi Jews[1424] and in Eastern Christian churches where the "handclasp accompanied by an embrace or kiss" is given by the priest and then passed on to the rest of the congregation.[1425] She further concludes that the ritual use of the handclasp is of "undoubted antiquity," citing the "hand-ceremony" at Mesopotamian Akitu festival of the New Year that goes back to the third millennium BCE:

> This yearly placing of the king's hand into the hand of the god was probably a kind of pact: the king swore fealty to his divinity; the god engaged himself to protect king and people. The handclasp appears on ancient Persian coins as an emblem of peace and alliance.[1426]

In an Old Testament context, Brown notes a depiction of a handclasp in a scene involving "the Israelite king standing at the veiled door of the Jerusalem Temple and being admitted by the Lord into an assembly."[1427] He also notes important allusions in the Psalms:

> It is curious that in the King James translation of the Psalm 89 coronation text it is said that the Lord's right hand will be established with the king.[1428] … Eaton renders this passage with these words (with the Lord speaking): "My hand shall hold him fast."[1429] This suggests a handclasp between the Heavenly King and His earthly vice-regent. Indeed, [Kraus and Anderson] state outright that a right-handed clasp between God and the king belonged to the Israelite enthronement ritual.[1430]

At least one traditional Jewish exegete, ibn Ezra, recognized "similar mechanisms of human ascent" in Psalm 73:23-24: "for I am always with You; you grasped my right hand [and] led me into your [council], and afterwards granted me glory."[1431]

1422 See *Figure B-1,* p. 872.
1423 See *Bibliography: Manichaean Texts,* p. 884. See also *Excursus 51: The Five Lost Things of the Temple,* p. 658.
1424 E. S. Drower, *Water,* pp. 103-105.
1425 *Ibid.,* pp. 106-110.
1426 *Ibid.,* p. 102 n. 1.
1427 See Psalm 27; cf. D&C 76:67.
1428 Psalm 89:13, 21.
1429 J. Eaton, *Psalms,* p. 317.
1430 See A. A. Anderson, *Psalms,* p. 535; H-J Kraus, *Psalms,* p. 173.
1431 Cited in J. C. Reeves, *Heralds,* p. 123; cf. p. 137 n. 80.

A View of Jewish Mysticism in the Cycle of Ezekiel at Dura Europos[1432]

One of the most stunning archaeological finds of the last century was the accidental discovery in 1920 of the ruins of *Dura Europos*,[1433] "a frontier town of very mixed population and traditions"[1434] located near the Euphrates river in what is now Syria. This Hellenistic city had been buried under mud and sand following a Sassanian siege in 256-257, which accounted for its unusual state of preservation.[1435] Among the buildings uncovered was a small Jewish synagogue with elaborately frescoed walls and a layout that, in Goodenough's view, suggested a group with a "mystical" orientation.[1436] Neusner sees such a development at Dura as no surprise, given that in this region between ca. 220-250 "Babylonian Manichaeism, Rabbinic Judaism, and Mazdeism were all taking form." Moreover, this period saw a "great expansion of cults within the Iranian idiom, in particular Mithraism," which became "the single most popular religion on the Roman side of the frontier."[1437] It should be remembered, however, that detailed descriptions of corresponding ideas relating to "Jewish mysteries," not dependent on later syncretistic tendencies, were already to be found two centuries earlier in the writings of Philo—writings whose core elements (with a less excessive degree of allegorizing and Platonism[1438]) go back at least to the First Temple period and arguably relate to its distinctive rites and theology.[1439]

Goodenough's studies of Philo and of Jewish mysticism were highly controversial at the time they were published, and have been largely forgotten in the more than forty years since his passing.[1440] Yet, more than two decades after his death, as part of a chapter that reviewed the arguments of his critics, Neusner could still speak of him as the "greatest historian of religion America has ever produced" and the "one towering figure" in the study of Judaism through art: "Goodenough provided for the artistic remains of the synagogue a complete and encompassing interpretation, and, to the present time, his view remains the principal theory by which the art of the synagogue is approached."[1441] As recently as 2007, specifically summarizing Goodenough's interpretation of the Dura synagogue, Goldenberg noted the continued importance of his views, observing that "other leaders in the field have roundly disputed his proposals, but Goodenough's arguments were weighty and his evidence was impressive. The matter remains unresolved."[1442]

1432 Further discussion of the mural of Ezekiel and other discoveries at Dura Europos can be found in J. M. Bradshaw, *Ezekiel Mural*. Frequently citing Goodenough, Nibley has also commented in several places about specific murals and themes (H. W. Nibley, *Tenting*, p. 74 n. 15; H. W. Nibley, *Since*, pp. 189-192, 238-239, 283, 289; H. W. Nibley, *Rediscovery*, p. 239; H. W. Nibley, *Vestments*, p. 110; H. W. Nibley, *Atonement*, pp. 564-566; H. W. Nibley, *Teachings of the Book of Mormon*, 1:135, 137, 152; 2:228-230; H. W. Nibley, *Message 2005*, pp. 489-490).

1433 = Fort Europos. The frequently-used hyphenated form of Dura Europos is a modern invention (R. M. Jensen, *Dura Europos*, p. 158).

1434 E. R. Goodenough, *Dura Symbolism*, 10:197.

1435 For an engaging account of the Dura excavations, see C. Hopkins, *Discovery*. Hopkins attended all the major discoveries at the site and was in charge when the discovery of the synagogue was made. For a presentation of the Dura synagogue in the context of findings from the remains of other diaspora synagogues, see L. I. Levine, *Synagogue*, pp. 250-309.

1436 See *Endnote E-274*, p. 774.

1437 J. Neusner, *Foreword*, p. xxix.

1438 J. M. G. Barclay, *Diaspora*, pp. 163-170, 177-178.

1439 E.g., M. Barker, *Angel*, pp. 114-133; J. E. Seaich, *Ancient Texts 1983*, pp. 56-68; J. E. Seaich, *Ancient Texts 1995*, pp. 848-853.

1440 Sandmel outlines some of the reasons why Goodnough's work did not at first receive the attention it deserved. First, "the high importance of what he was doing never impressed itself on those who looked at only the first two or three volumes…Moreover, …his books began to appear at about the same time that the Dead Sea Scrolls were exciting the biblical world, and possibly his work was a casualty of the mania that then developed over the Scrolls" (S. Sandmel, *Appreciation*, p. 13). Finally, as "[c]arefully as he wrote and ardently as he polished what he wrote, he seemed to be without the sense of needing to carry a reader along with him… He overestimated scholars, for he assessed them by reference to himself" (*ibid.*, p. 14).

1441 J. Neusner, *Synagogue*, pp. 31-32. See also J. Neusner, *Foreword*; L. I. Levine, *Judaism*, p. 8.

1442 R. Goldenberg, *Origins*, p. 187.

FIGURE E53-15. *The Cycle of Ezekiel from the Synagogue at Dura Europos, ca. 244*

SEE COLOR PLATE E53-15.

And he said unto me, Son of man, can these bones live?[1] Running the entire twenty-five foot length of the north wall is a depiction of a story cycle of the Prophet Ezekiel, the "largest single painting in the synagogue… To have been given so much space it must have had great importance in the mind of the person who designed the decoration."[2] The Ezekiel fresco is structured into three main panels, with stages of ascent and descent being indicated by differences in the background color.

---

1   Ezekiel 37:3.
2   E. R. Goodenough, *Dura Symbolism*, 10:179.

Goodenough's assessment of his own work still remains largely true: "Alternative interpretations have been suggested for details, but none attempted for the evidence as a whole."[1443]

The synagogue at Dura Europos constitutes the most important extant evidence that the Jewish mysteries described in Philo's writings may have had a tangible expression in ritual. Describing the sanctuary where the worshipers sat, Goodenough writes: "The whole room… was so painted that those worshiping in it were enclosed in a grape arbor" and "out of the *Torah* shrine beneath the painting grew the Tree of life and salvation which led to the supernal throne."[1444] While the throne scene in the Tree of Life emphasizes the divine reward of Israel *as a people*, the theme of *individual exaltation* is seen by Goodenough as being carried forward in the four portraits that surround the Tree of Life panel and in the Ezekiel mural.[1445] Hinting at the possibility of an actual ritual for members of the Dura Synagogue, he writes: "In [a] side room were benches and decorations that mark the room as probably one of cult, perhaps an inner room, where special rites were celebrated by a select company… So far as structure goes, it might have been the room for people especially 'initiated' in some way."[1446] With these and other features in mind, Goodenough concludes that the "Dura synagogue painting as a whole may well have been the product of Jews dedicated to some form of *Merkabah* mysticism, since the high point of the reredos[1447] shows the throne with the tribes of Israel about it, and the Closed Temple scene with its seven walls may reflect ascent."[1448]

Running the entire twenty-five foot length of the north wall is a depiction of a story cycle of the Prophet Ezekiel, the "largest single painting in the synagogue… To have been given so much space it must have had great importance in the mind of the person who designed

---

1443 E. R. Goodenough, *Garments*, pp. 222-223.
1444 E. R. Goodenough, *Dura Symbolism*, 10:199, 200.
1445 *Ibid.*, 9:104.
1446 *Ibid.*, 10:198; cf. E. R. Goodenough, *Summary*, pp. 190-197. See *Endnote E-275*, p. 776.
1447 I.e., the tall panel above the *Torah* niche in the Dura synagogue, from *arere* (behind) + *dos* (back), from Latin *dorsum*.
1448 E. R. Goodenough, *Dura Symbolism*, 10:193.

the decoration."[1449] Kraeling also considers the work as "the greatest and most important composition" among all the murals.[1450]

In Goodenough's interpretation, the Ezekiel fresco is structured into three main panels, with stages of ascent and descent being indicated by differences in the background color: "The total design… emphasizes most conspicuously that the first three figures of Ezekiel and the broken mountain have a light background, as does the final scene of his arrest and execution, but that between these a central section stands sharply set off by its dark background. The contrast seems to tell us that the ordinary Ezekiel existed in the realm of death at each end,[1451] a realm sharply different from that of heaven-given life where figures in the white dress of sanctity can and do come into their full exaltation."[1452]

The three types of clothing Ezekiel wears can be taken as representing three different degrees of existence, just as initiates following in his footsteps would be "identified at each stage with the spiritual existence of that stage."[1453] The progression recalls accounts of rites corresponding to the threefold division of the Jerusalem temple[1454] as interpreted in the writings of Gnostic Christians,[1455] and the changing of the high priest from colored to white garb before entering the Holy of Holies.[1456]

A prominent feature of the first two panels of the fresco is a series of five divine right hands, "the first clenched in the hair of the prophet," and the remaining four that are open and extended toward him.[1457] This, of course, recalls the passage in Deuteronomy where the Lord was praised for saving Israel "with a mighty hand, and with an outstretched arm,"[1458] a motif frequently exemplified in other murals of Dura.[1459] Sometimes, additionally, the hand of God serves as a visual representation of the divine voice speaking from the heavens.[1460] Here, however, and in at least one other Dura panel, the "hand from heaven" is specifically associated with the "revivication of the dead."[1461] In a formula repeated throughout the rabbinical literature, the "Key of the Revival of the Dead" is mentioned as one that "the Holy one… has retained in His own hands"[1462]—though this mural clearly shows that it can be delegated to others. As in Ezekiel accounts found elsewhere, the hand is extended to him "as if to give a command" and also "to give strength to perform his task"[1463]—here evidently to bring the dead to a full measure of eternal life.

The two extended hands in the first panel are portrayed with "palms forward. In contrast over the scenes at the right the [two] divine hands are turned, still right hands, but with the

---

1449 *Ibid.*, 10:179.

1450 C. R. Kraeling, *Synagogue*, p. 202.

1451 Gross notes Philo's view that an ascent "does not prevent the initiates… 'when they return from the divine things,' from 'becoming human again' (*Dreams*, 2:233). But the day will come in which death will permanently confirm them in the state of bliss that they had known in ecstasy" (J. Gross, *Divinization*, p. 78).

1452 *Ibid.*, 10:195-196.

1453 E. R. Goodenough, *Light*, p. 96.

1454 See *Endnote E-276*, p. 776.

1455 See *Endnote E-277*, p. 777.

1456 G. A. Anderson, *Perfection*, p. 123; M. Barker, *11 June 2007*. See the overview of Moses 4, p. 239.

1457 See *Endnote E-278*, p. 777.

1458 Deuteronomy 26:8; cf. 4:34; 5:15; 6:21; 7:8, 19; 9:26; 11:2; 34:12.

1459 See discussions of this motif in D. R. Seely, *Hand of God in Exodus Traditions*, D. R. Seely, *Hand of God in the Book of Exodus*, and D. R. Seely, *Hand of God in the Book of Mormon*. Note that in the Dura mural of the parting of the Red Sea, like in the mural of Ezekiel, both a right hand and a left hand appear to be shown.

1460 H. W. Nibley, *Atonement*, p. 562.

1461 H. Riesenfeld, *Resurrection*, p. 34.

1462 *Ibid.*, p. 12. Two additional keys reserved to God are mentioned in this context, namely, the "Key of Rain" and the "Key of Childbirth." Riesenfeld observes that these functions are united in "the idea of Creation which is so characteristic of the New Year Festival," and which were each represented in its rites (*ibid.*, p. 12).

1463 *Ibid.*, p. 33.

nails of each finger carefully indicated to make them certainly right hands, though their position is reversed." Goodenough notes that he "cannot believe that this had no significance to the artist who so carefully showed the detail."[1464] The reversal may suggest a change in the relationship of Ezekiel to God as he moves from the earthly to the heavenly realms, corresponding to the "well-known shifting of the garment from left to right in initiation ceremonies (e.g., of the tassel on the mortarboard at graduations)"[1465] or the Jewish prayer shawl or robe that "is draped over one shoulder and then over the other."[1466] The imagery also recalls Philo's description of "two successive initiations within a single Mystery," constituting "a 'lesser' Mystery in contrast with a 'Greater,'" which Goodenough labeled "the Mystery of Aaron and the Mystery of Moses."[1467] The greater initiation allowed Moses, "when stripped of his distinguishing [multi-colored] robes, clad in simple white,"[1468] to abide in God's presence "while he learns the secrets of the most holy mysteries,"[1469] and to be "changed into the divine, so that such men might become kin to God and truly divine."[1470] Such a change was seen as a kind of second birth or resurrection.[1471] Goodenough concluded that something like Philo's "higher mystery" "played a highly important part in the Judaism of Dura."[1472]

The story cycle begins in the leftmost panel with a picture of a tree bearing prominent fruit or flowers and three drawings of Ezekiel in typical Persian costume. "The heavenly hand

---

1464 E. R. Goodenough, *Dura Symbolism*, 10:182-183 n. 85.

1465 H. W. Nibley, *Message 2005*, p. 443.

1466 D. Rona, *Revealed*, p. 194. In an excavation of a Coptic Christian burial site, Griggs found that some burials included "one or more robes with linen strips wrapped around the upper half of the body and gathered into a knot on either the left… or, more commonly, on the right shoulder," indicating priestly authority (C. W. Griggs, *Evidences*, p. 227).

1467 E. R. Goodenough, *Light*, pp. 95-96.

1468 *Ibid.*, p. 96.

1469 Philo, *Giants*, 54, p. 473.

1470 Philo, *Exodus*, 2:29, p. 70. See R. S. Eccles, *Pilgrimage*, pp. 60-61; E. R. Goodenough, *Introduction to Philo*, pp. 147-153; J. Gross, *Divinization*, p. 77. See *Endnote E-221*, p. 757.

1471 Philo, *Exodus*, 2:46-47, cited in J. Gross, *Divinization*, p. 77. See *Endnote E-279*, p. 777.

1472 E. R. Goodenough, *Summary*, p. 188.

lifts the first figure of Ezekiel by the hair of his head into this place of human fragments."[1473] "The second figure of Ezekiel shows him fulfilling the command of God [to prophesy to the bones[1474]]… In the painting the prophet's right hand is open in a gesture of exposition toward the bones, his left pointing to a second hand of God above him."[1475] "The third figure of Ezekiel turns to the right, pointing across his body with his right hand to a third hand of God above him. With his open left hand the prophet seems to call attention to a strange mountain beside him."[1476] "The mountain is split down the middle,[1477] and a small tree with exaggerated fruit grows at the top of each half,"[1478] recalling either the prophesied destruction of groves used for idol worship[1479] or perhaps representing two of the trees of Eden.[1480] "A castellated citadel topples upside down from the crest of the hill at the right, a building with two openings, apparently a door and a window…[1481] The artist seems to be showing the [body] pieces going through the first half of the mountain,[1482] crossing the chasm, and in the second half being miraculously reassembled as whole corpses, for three such corpses lie on their backs within it… Ezekiel stands at the right of the mountain, his left hand out as though he were preaching, or saying 'Lo,' his right hand again lifted up toward the hand of God. He still wears the Persian costume, but his elaborately embroidered red smock has become a relatively plain one in light pink."[1483]

"At the right of this figure of Ezekiel the three assembled corpses again lie one above another, and the Greek figure of Psyche with butterfly wings stands at their heads, her hands out as

---

1473 E. R. Goodenough, *Dura Symbolism*, 10:180. See Ezekiel 37:1; cf. Ezekiel 8:2, 28:13-19. See *Endnote E-280*, p. 777.

1474 Ezekiel 37:2-7.

1475 E. R. Goodenough, *Dura Symbolism*, 10:181.

1476 *Ibid.*, 10:182. See Ezekiel 6:2-7; cf. 36:1-7.

1477 See *Endnote E-281*, p. 777.

1478 E. R. Goodenough, *Dura Symbolism*, 10:183.

1479 Ezekiel 6:13, 20:28, 47.

1480 Ezekiel 31:8-9, 16, 18. See *Endnote E-282*, p. 778.

1481 Ezekiel 37:7, 38:20.

1482 Ezekiel 32:5, 35:1-8.

1483 E. R. Goodenough, *Dura Symbolism*, 10:183.

though just about to grasp the head of the corpse at the top. Three other Psyche figures fly down from above. Scholars generally agree in identifying these figures with the four winds, which in the story breathe upon the corpses and give them the breath of life, so that they live.[1484] Supervising this miracle stands a fifth figure [of Ezekiel], this time in the full Greek robe, his right hand pointing with two fingers extended toward the descending Psyches... [T]hat the prophet has taken on a new status at this stage seems obvious from his change of robes. Just as important is the peculiar two-finger gesture, which appears only here in the Dura paintings...[1485] We... know that it was not only used for the hand of the god, but was probably a cultic gesture in his mysteries... ... [A]s Sabazius was a god who brought immortality to his followers,[1486] the gesture would seem to indicate that Ezekiel is working a comparable miracle by bringing life to the corpses...[1487] Behind him stand ten much smaller figures, all in the same Greek dress, who presumably represent the bones now fully restored to life.[1488] They raise their hands, palms forward at shoulder height... They are under the arm of still another heroic Ezekiel figure, again in the full Greek dress."[1489] "The ten who come into glory are the true Israel...[,] the mystic Jews... The point of the 'true Israel' is that it consists of people who 'see God.' They are ones who have become 'unwritten laws.'"[1490] Goodenough notes the special markings of "clavi" and "gams"[1491] on the "Greek robe of *chiton* [= belted tunic] and *himation* [= cloak]" worn by the ten: "[O]nly those who appeared to be heavenly beings or the greatest saints of Judaism, mystic saviors, wear this clothing."[1492]

1484 Ezekiel 37:9-10. See *Endnote E-283*, p. 778.

1485 In classic iconography, this gesture represented the spoken word. In medieval Christianity, the meaning later changed to that of blessing (H. P. L'Orange, *Cosmic Kingship*, pp. 171-183).

1486 See *Endnote E-284*, p. 779.

1487 Note the nearly identical gesture that Christ uses to raise the dead shown in E. R. Goodenough, *Dura Symbolism*, 11, Figure 305. See *Endnote E-287*, p. 780.

1488 See *Endnote E-288*, p. 780.

1489 E. R. Goodenough, *Dura Symbolism*, 10:184.

1490 *Ibid.*, 10:195. See Philo, *Virtues*, 194, p. 83; cf. Jeremiah 31:33, A. F. Ehat, *Seems Like Heaven*, pp. 5-6.

1491 See *Excursus 20: The Circle and the Square*, p. 571.

1492 E. R. Goodenough, *Dura Symbolism*, 10:205; see also 9:88-89, 126-129, 162-164; E. R. Goodenough, *Garments*. In describing the purple "outer garment of the high priest as depicted in the murals of the Dura Europos synagogue" (see, e.g., the figure of Aaron in E. R. Goodenough, *Dura Symbolism*, 11, Plate 10), Nibley notes that

"At the right of [the sixth] figure of Ezekiel... towers another mountain with a tree on it; this time the mountain stands intact, not riven like the first one. The contrast will seem possibly to have meaning."[1493] "Immediately beyond the mountain [Ezekiel, again in] Persian dress kneels and clings to the side of a large yellow altar... An armed soldier wearing a helmet grasps [him] from behind... The second painting shows [Ezekiel bending] over, his scabbard hanging down between his legs, while a standing figure in the same costume grasps his hair with the left hand and raises a sword, obviously in the act of beheading him."[1494] "Such a tradition does not appear in either the Old Testament or the rabbinical writings, but does in Christian documents... [For example,] the writer to the Hebrews[1495] among other horrors that came to the prophets tells: 'They were stoned, they were sawn in two, they were killed with the sword'... [I]t... looks as though the verse quoted from Hebrews might summarize a current Jewish tradition of the deaths of the three major prophets, Jeremiah, Isaiah, and Ezekiel."[1496] Summing up his interpretation, Goodenough writes:

> Merkabah mysticism... primarily centers in an ascent into a heavenly region, and then a descent or return to the sorry world of earthly reality, and when we have this conception in mind we see that here is what the painting really has told us. The heavenly hand comes upon the prophet to take him into the world of death and desolation. Here he preaches until the bones of human decay come together and pass through a great barrier to another realm—the realm where Psyches give men a new life, and where their new life means that they, like the now triumphant prophet, wear the great robe of sanctity. Ezekiel cannot stay there, however, but must go back to the other side of the mountain again, there in his earthly garb to meet his earthly and mortal fate, meet it from the very Jewish leaders whose apostasy he had bitterly upbraided.[1497]

"the white undergarment is the proper preexistent glory of the wearer, while the other is the priesthood later added to it" (H. W. Nibley, *Message 2005*, pp. 489-490).

1493 E. R. Goodenough, *Dura Symbolism*, 10:185; cf. Ezekiel 17:22-24, 22:40, 28:14, 34:27, 36:30, 47:7, 12. See *Endnote E-285*, p. 779.

1494 E. R. Goodenough, *Dura Symbolism*, 10:187.

1495 Hebrews 11:37.

1496 E. R. Goodenough, *Dura Symbolism*, 10:187-188; cf. D. Satran, *et al.*, *Ezekiel*, pp. 95, 100; J. E. Wright, *Ezekiel*, pp. 104-105; W. L. Lane, *Hebrews 9-13*, pp. 390-391; P. Ellingworth, *Greek Hebrews*, pp. 630-631. See *Endnote E-286*, p. 779.

1497 E. R. Goodenough, *Dura Symbolism*, 10:193-194. See *Endnote E-290*, p. 781.

Excursus 54
Table of Parallels with the *Apocalypse of Abraham*

BELOW is given a table of parallels between the book of Moses and the *Apocalypse of Abraham*, with additional excerpts from the book of Abraham and other related works. From his own study, Hugh Nibley concluded: "These parallel accounts, separated by centuries, cannot be coincidence. Nor can all the others."[1498]

	Book of Moses	*Apocalypse of Abraham*[1]
PROLOGUE (*vv. 1-2*)		
Setting	an exceedingly high mountain (1:1)	a high mountain (9:8)
Aretology	the Lord God Almighty, and Endless (1:3)	the primordial and mighty God (9:3)
Sacrifice	Cf. Abraham: ... revealed from God to Abraham, as he offered sacrifice upon an altar (Abraham, Facsimile 2, figure 2)	Go... and set out for me a pure sacrifice (9:5)
MOSES IN THE SPIRIT WORLD (*vv. 3-8*)		
God to show a vision of eternity	I will show thee the workmanship of mine hands (1:4)	And in this sacrifice I shall set before you the ages (9:6)
Reason for God's favor	Cf. Abraham: Thy servant has sought thee earnestly (Abraham 2:12)	since you loved to search for me (9:6)
The prophet is commissioned	I have a work for thee, Moses, my son (1:6)	I called you my friend (9:6)[2]
Vision of the spirit world	Moses... beheld the world upon which he was created... and all the children of men which are, and which were created (1:8)	And I saw there a great crowd of men, and women, and children... I gave them a command... and they came into being (21:7, 22:2; cf. 9:9)
Some of the spirits are chosen	Cf. Abraham: among all these there were many of the noble and great ones... These I will make my rulers (Abraham 3:22, 23)	half of them on the right side... and half of them on the left... Those on the right side... are the people set apart... to be born of you and to be called my people (21:7, 22:5)
MOSES FALLS TO THE EARTH (*vv. 9-11*)		
Fall and loss of strength	Moses... fell unto the earth... And... it was for the space of many hours before Moses did... receive his natural strength (1:9-11)	I... fell down upon the earth, for there was no longer strength in me (10:1-3)
MOSES DEFEATS SATAN (*vv. 12-23*)		
Satan disrupts the worship of God	Satan came tempting him, saying: Moses, son of man, worship me (1:12)	And the impure bird flew down on the carcasses... and said, "What are you doing, Abraham... Leave [Yahoel] and flee! (13:4-5)
Satan's identity is questioned	Moses... said: Who art thou? (1:13)	I said to the angel, "What is this, my lord?" And he said, "This... is [Satan]" (13:6)
Satan contrasted with the prophet	I am a son of God... and where is thy glory, that I should worship thee? ...I can look upon thee in the natural man (1:13, 14)	[Yahoel]: "Reproach on you, [Satan]! Since Abraham's portion is in heaven, and yours is on earth (13:7)
Satan told to depart and cease his deception	Get thee hence, Satan; deceive me not (1:16)	Depart from [Abraham]! You cannot deceive him (13:12-13)
The prophet has received the glory that Satan lost	God said unto me [Moses]: Thou art after the similitude of mine Only Begotten (1:16)	the garment which in heaven which was formerly yours [Satan's] has been set aside for him [Abraham] (13:14)
Satan told to depart a second time	Depart hence, Satan (1:18)	vanish from before me! (14:7)

1498   H. W. Nibley, *To Open*, p. 15. Nibley also cites extensive parallels between Moses 1 and S. C. Malan, *Adam and Eve*. For a more complete description of these parallels, see D. J. Larsen, *et al.*, *Apocalypse of Abraham*.

Satan's final attempt to gain the prophet's worship	Satan cried with a loud voice, …saying: I am the Only Begotten, worship me (1:19)	He [Satan] said, "Abraham!" And I said, "Here am I, your servant!" And the angel said to me, "Answer him not!" (14:9-10)
Satan's frightening tantrum and final departure	Moses… commanded, saying: Depart from me, Satan… And now Satan began to tremble (1:20, 21)	Cf. Enoch: "And Enoch said to Azazel, Depart! …Then he departed and spoke to all of them [i.e., his followers]… and trembling… seized them (1 Enoch 13:1, 3, Gizeh)[3]
MOSES CALLS UPON GOD; HEARS A VOICE (vv. 24-26)		
Ascent to heaven	Moses lifted up his eyes unto heaven (1:24). Cf. Nephi: upon the wings of his Spirit hath my body been carried away (2 Nephi 4:25)	the angel took me with his right hand and set me on the right wing of the pigeon and he himself sat on the left wing of the turtledove… and carried me up (15:2-3)
Voice at the veil	and he heard a voice, saying: Blessed art thou, Moses (1:25)	And while he was still speaking, behold a fire was coming toward us… (17:1)
Many waters	and thou shalt be made stronger than many waters… as if thou wert God (1:25)	and a sound [voice]… like a sound of many waters (17:1)[4]
MOSES' VISION AT THE VEIL (vv. 27-30)		
The prophet beholds the earth	as the voice was still speaking, Moses cast his eyes and beheld the earth (1:27)	And he said unto me, "Look now beneath your feet at the expanse and contemplate the creation (21:1)
The inhabitants of the earth	he beheld also the inhabitants thereof (1:28)	and those who inhabit it (21:1)
The prophet questions God	Tell me, I pray thee, why these things are so, and by what thou madest them? (1:30)	Eternal, Mighty One! Why did you ordain it to be so? (26:1).[5] Cf. *Mother of Books*: My Lord, how did the high king create all these spheres and palaces? From where did he make the spirits? What was the origin of his creation?"[6]
MOSES IN THE PRESENCE OF THE LORD (vv. 31-40)		
God's purpose is His own	For mine own purpose have I made these things. Here is wisdom and it remaineth in me (1:31)[7]	As the will of your father is in him, as your will is in you, so also the will desired by me is inevitable (26:5)
Moses speaks with the Lord face to face	Moses stood in the presence of God, and talked with him face to face (1:31)	He whom you will see going before both of us in a great sound of *qedushah* [holiness, sanctification] is the Eternal One… whom himself you will not see (16:3)[8]
Vision of the Creation, the Garden of Eden, and the Fall	Moses sees the creation of the earth (ch. 2), the Garden of Eden (ch. 3) and the Fall of Adam and Eve (ch. 4)	Abraham sees the creation of the earth (21:3-5), the Garden of Eden (21:6), and Satan inciting the Fall of Adam and Eve (23:1-14).
EPILOGUE (vv. 41-42)		
Scripture to be lost and restored	… when the children of men shall … take many of [my words] from the book which thou shalt write, …I will raise up another… and they shall be had again among the children of men—among as many as shall believe. (1:41)	Cf. Enoch: And… another generation will arise, the last of many… And I shall raise up for that generation someone who will reveal to them the books in your handwriting… And he will have to point out to… truthful men.[9]
Some scripture to be reserved for the righteous	These words were spoken unto Moses… Show them not unto any except them that believe. (1:42)	Cf. Ezra, certain books were to be read by the "worthy and unworthy" whereas others were to be only given "to the wise."[10]

1   English translation from A. Kulik, *Retroverting*, Apocalypse of Abraham chs. 9-23, pp. 16-27. The first English translation of the *Apocalypse of Abraham* was made in 1898. Notably, this translation did not appear in a scholarly journal, but rather in the *Improvement Era*, an official publication of the Church (E. H. Anderson *et al.*, *Abraham*). Nibley comments: "In 1898, just a year after the *Apocalypse of Abraham* was published to the world by Bonwetsch, two Latter-day Saint students made the first English translation of the writing, which appeared in the first volume of the *Improvement Era*.… It is significant that it was the Latter-day Saints who first made the *Apocalypse of Abraham* available to the world in English, as it was they who first recognized the *Book of Enoch*, in Parley P. Pratt's review of 1840 (P. P. Pratt, *Enoch*, cited in H. Nibley, *Enoch*, pp. 111, 289), not as a worthless piece of apocrypha, but as a work of primary importance… Brothers E. H. Anderson and R. T. Haag, who made an excellent translation of Bonwetsch's German—remarkably close, in fact, to Box's 'official' English version of 1919—detected in the text 'many things of a character both as to incidents and doctrines that ran parallel with what is

FIGURE E54-2. *Noah Sees the Ark in Vision.*
Photo: Stephen T. Whitlock, 1951-

SEE COLOR PLATE E54-2.

All generations to the end of time were printed on the curtain of the Omnipresent One. I saw them all with my own eyes.[1] Jewish and Christian accounts speak of a "blueprint" of eternity that is worked out in advance and shown on the inside of the veil to prophetic figures such as Abraham as part of a heavenly ascent.[2] Nibley gave the "great round" of the hypocephalus as an example of an attempt to capture the essence of such pictures of eternity among the Egyptians.[3] Islamic tradition speaks of a "white cloth from Paradise" upon which Adam saw the righteous and wicked among all his posterity.[4]

In this figure, from a window of the Holy Trinity Church in Stratford-upon-Avon, England, God shows the plans for the Ark to Noah just as He later showed Moses the plans for the Tabernacle.[5] The hands of Deity hold the heavenly curtain as Noah, compass in his left hand, regards intently.

1   P. Alexander, *3 Enoch*, 45:6, p. 299.
2   See *Commentary* 1:27-b, p. 62.
3   H. W. Nibley, *Abraham 2000*, pp. 42ff.
4   M. al-Kisa'i, *Tales*, p. 82.
5   See *Endnote 3-57*, p. 210.

recorded in the Book of Abraham, given to the world by Joseph Smith' (E. H. Anderson, *et al.*, *Abraham*, p. 705). They wisely contented themselves, however, with printing the text without other commentary than three or four passages in italics, trusting the Latter-day Saint reader to think for himself" (H. W. Nibley, *Abraham 2000*, pp. 11-13).

2   Regarding the title given to Moses, see Barker for a discussion of Psalm 110 and the idea that priests after the order of Melchizedek became sons of God (M. Barker, *Who was Melchizedek*). In Arabic, Abraham is simply referred to as *al-Khalil*, "the Friend" (cf. Hebrew "Hebron" from *haver* = "friend").

3   See R.H. Charles, *Enoch*, 13:1, 3, p. 288; English translation in H.W. Nibley, *To Open*, pp. 10-11; cf. R.H. Charles, *Apocrypha*, 2:196 n. 13:1. Nibley's reading is perfectly coherent. However, Nickelsburg does not see the logic of the Gizeh variant, calling it "nonsense" (G.W. Nickelsburg, *1 Enoch*, n. 13:1a, p. 234).

4   "The same terms are used in the 'Greater Hekhaloth' in describing the sound of the hymn of praise sung by the 'throne of Glory' to its King—'like the voice of the waters in the rushing streams, like the waves of the ocean when the south wind sets them in uproar'" (G. Scholem, *Trends*, p. 61).

5   In the *Apocalypse*, probably redacted in the first century, the dialogue centers on recent events (i.e., the destruction of Jerusalem and its temple) and the future of Israel, in contrast to the cosmic scope of, e.g., the Islamic *Mother of Books* and Moses 1.

6   W. Barnstone, *et al.*, *Mother*, p. 685.

7   Later, Moses will receive a partial answer about the Creation, limited to "an account of this earth" (Moses 1:35). He will also be told something about "why these things are so" (Moses 1:30, cf. 1:39).

8   Though other features of the ascent mirror similar accounts in *1 Enoch* and Ezekiel, Orlov describes how the *Apocalypse of Abraham* explicitly rejects their visual anthropomorphism, and insists on the "revelation of the divine Voice" alone (A. A. Orlov, *Gods of My Father*, p. 53. See also A. A. Orlov, *Praxis*). The fourteenth century illustrator of the *Codex Sylvester*, on the other hand, had no qualms about representing God visually (see Figure 1-7, p. 38). See *Endnote E-291*, p. 781.

9   F. I. Andersen, *2 Enoch*, 35:1-2, p. 158.

10   B.M. Metzger, *Fourth Ezra*, 14:4-6, p. 553.

Excursus 55

Mesoamerican Stories of Creation and the Original Transgression

GRAULICH summarizes Mesoamerican stories of Creation and the original transgression.[1499] He laments the fact that "modern authors, attributing these myths to Christian influence, often dismiss Mesoamerican allusions to the original paradise and to transgression even though they are very well documented."[1500] Note that the ancient sources are diverse and complex, and many gods and goddesses of Mesoamerica overlap one another—the different names constituting a particular aspect of that god. For this reason brief sketches such as the following cannot really do them full justice:

> [V]aluable allusions in the codices *Telleriano-Remensis* and *Vaticanus A (3738)*... tell of a kind of original paradise in which the breaking of a prohibition had disastrous consequences. The names of this paradise, Tamoanchan and Xochitlicacan, mean, respectively, "there is the house from which they descended" (that is, "Place of the Original House") and "The Place Where Flowers Bloom."[1501] The gods who lived there cut the flowers and branches from a forbidden tree. To punish them, Tonacatecuhtli and Tonacacihuatl banished them to earth and to the underworld. Elsewhere, Ixnextli, a kind of Eve, "sinned by picking flowers."[1502] Ixnextli seems to be Xochiquetzal, "Quetzal Flower," the "first sinner," Cinteotl's wife, who was seduced by Tezcatlipoca disguised as an animal. Xochiquetzal is identified as Tlazolteotl-Ixcuina, another name for the earth goddess, who "sinned by eating the fruit from the tree" before the flood and was the cause of all the world's misfortunes and afflictions. Tlazolteotl is depicted opposite Tezcatlipoca, the latter transformed into a bird of ill omen because in this guise "he deceived the first woman who sinned." Elsewhere, it is Huehuecoyotl, the "Old Coyote," "equivalent to Adam," Ixnextl's "husband," who "introduced the discord." That is not all, because the guilty one was also called Itzpapalotl, the one who cut and ate "flowers" in a garden. The tree in that garden broke and shed blood,[1503] and the angry supreme couple expelled Itzpapalotl and the other gods, casting them down to earth.[1504] Regardless of the variety of names of the guilty parties, this is clearly the same event.[1505]

Guilty	Seducer	Transgression	Consequence
Inextli		picks flowers	
Xochiquetzal	Tezcatlipoca disguised as an animal		
Tlazoteotl Ixcuina	Tezcatlipoca disguised as a bird	eats fruit from the tree	introduces evils and misfortunes
	Huhuecoyotl		introduces discord
Itzpapalotl		eats or cuts flowers	expelled to earth with other gods
Cihuacoatl		"sinned"	
The gods		cut flowers and branches	expelled to earth and the underworld

FIGURE E55-1. *The Transgressions at Tamoanchan.*[1506]

1499 M. Graulich, *Myths*, p. 53; cf. D. E. Wirth, *Guide*, pp. 47-49.

1500 M. Graulich, *Myths*, p. 266.

1501 See *ibid.*, pp. 284-285 n. 21.

1502 See *ibid.*, p. 285 n. 21.

1503 See E. Seler, *Codex*, 1:178, 2:269; E. Seler, *Codex (German)*, 2:260-261, Figure 264-266 and p. 262.

1504 See *Endnote E-292*, p. 782.

1505 For a summary of the wider context of these stories and their astronomical associations, see M. Graulich, *Myths*, pp. 264-277. Linda Schele was the pioneer of Maya astronomy—for an assessment of her contributions in this regard, see A. Aveni, *Stars*. On creation, see M. E. Miller, *et al.*, *Gods and Symbols*, pp. 68-71.

1506 From *ibid.*, p. 55. Wirth sees it as a "far stretch to say that Cihuacoatl 'sinned'" (D. E. Wirth, *12 March 2009*).

FIGURE E55-2. *The Broken Tree of Tamoanchan, Codex Telleriano-Remensis, 16th century*[1]
FIGURE E55-3. *Itzpapalotl and the Broken Tree of Tamoanchan, Codex Borgia*[2]

SEE COLOR PLATE E55-3.

The broken tree of Tamoanchan at left sprouts both blossoms and knives. The tree is associated with the transgression of Itzpapalotl, the Obsidian Butterfly, who was said to have sinned either in "cutting roses and branches from trees" or, according to another annotator, eating the blossoms.[3] "[T]he tree is depicted in the traditional indigenous fashion, in its entirety with its tentaclelike roots also visible. A stream of blood flows from the point of rupture…. This act greatly angered Tonacatecuhtli and Tonacacihuatl, who ejected [the gods] from the garden."[4] The broken tree also appeared in Aztec migration accounts, where it figured as an "evil portent." "In the account of the origin of the Mexica in the *Florentine Codex*…, Tamoanchan is the place where certain sages abandoned the migrating group, taking their knowledge, crafts, and books with them. Tamoanchan was thus a complex concept, for it appears as a place of origin for the gods and for humans, and, as its name suggests, a place of departure rather than rest."[5]

In the second figure, Itzpapalotl, at left, is pictured with the broken tree. According to Seler's important, but now very dated, study, the broken tree "denoted for the learned the Tamoanchan, 'the house of Descent,'[6] or *Xochitl icacan*, 'the place where the flowers are,' the region of the mythical West, the home of maize, and the seat of the primeval gods, where, too, the wandering tribes made a long sojourn…[7] [Other symbols are] a house with a dark entrance, then… a man with bandaged eyes, and lastly… a man tumbling down head foremost, and… from or with his chair… The house with the dark threshold is doubtless intended to denote the dark house of Earth, or perhaps the time of darkness… —the primeval time, the time before the birth of the Sun. But the other two pictures have an obvious relation to the myth which is here referred to by the interpreters, and so vividly recalls the biblical story of Adam's transgression… The man plunging down is clearly the person cast out of heaven, out of his chair, and the other with the bandage on his eyes, the blindfold person, the one who sinned through ignorance."[8] Wirth suggests: "The blindfold may also have another meaning. The first man's eyes were blinded from the smoke and ashes, so he could not see clearly."[9] In another interpretation, Graulich sees Itzpapalotl has having introduced "sin[10] (symbolized by the person with blinded eyes), … death (the falling man), and… night (the house with darkness and a stellar eye[11])."[12]

1   See E. Q. Keber, *Telleriano-Remensis,* Folio 19r (misnumbered as 13r).
2   Restored rendering in G. Díaz, *et al., Codex Borgia,* Plate 66.
3   E. Q. Keber, *Telleriano-Remensis,* pp. 182, 183.
4   *Ibid.,* p. 183. See also p. 266 and the restored detail of the drawings on p. 292.
5   *Ibid.*
6   Wirth agrees with the connotation of "House of Descent," but takes the literal meaning to be "The Place of Mists" or "Place of the Misty Sky" (D. E. Wirth, *12 March 2009;* cf. M. E. Miller, *et al., Gods and Symbols,* p. 160).
7   In one account, Tamoanchan is the name of a cave where humankind is created (cited in E. Q. Keber, *Telleriano-Remensis,* p. 183). See *Excursus 53: Comparative Explorations,* p. 669.
8   E. Seler, *Codex,* 2:269-270; cf. the figure from *Codex Vaticanus 3773* in Explanatory Tables No. 63; cf. E. Seler, *Codex (German),* 2:260-262, 283.
9   D. E. Wirth, *Guide,* p. 49.
10 Or perhaps death. Gardner notes that the figure resembles a dead man prepared for burial, often done in seated position (B. Gardner, *13 March 2009*).
11 Regarding what Seler called "the dark house of Earth," Wirth writes: "It does represent primeval time, but it does not represent earth. It is a temple in the heavens (has a star-eye in the center)" (D. E. Wirth, *12 March 2009*).
12 M. Graulich, *Myths,* p. 54.

Wirth notes another relevant story:[1507]

> In the Maya area of Quintana Roo, Mexico, there is a myth from the distant past about a rope, which was a pathway that joined the earth with the sky.[1508] It was a lifeline, almost like an umbilical cord that linked the two worlds, connecting the natural world to the heavens. This link was severed at the time of the Fall, when earth and heaven were separated from one another.[1509]

One of the most important sources of information regarding the nature of Maya cosmology and the afterlife is the *Popol Vuh*, "still the only known pre-Columbian Maya text that has survived in a form that has been transcribed in a Western script."[1510] Its mythic sections contain many legends concerning "the creation of the world, the nature of life and death, and an extensive description of the underworld and its perils." Christenson summarizes a tale of a "miraculous life-giving tree" that is a "focus of the mythic section":[1511]

> The tale of this tree begins with the account of a hero named One Hunahpu who often spent his days playing an ancient Maya ball game with his brother. Unfortunately, the noise of the game disturbed the lords of the underworlds (a place called Xibalba), who lived beneath the ball court.[1512] The chief lords of the underworld, named One Death and Seven Death, were determined to destroy the brothers and therefore summoned them to their realm. After a number of trials, One Death and Seven Death overcame One Hunahpu and sacrificed him by beheading him. Although they buried the body in the underworld ball court, they placed his head in the branches of a dead tree. Immediately, the tree sprang to life and bore a white fruit resembling the fleshless skull of One Hunahpu....[1513]

> The lords of the underworld were so astonished and fearful of the power of the tree that they forbade anyone to approach it. Eventually, tales of the miraculous tree and the sweetness of its fruit reached the ears of a daughter of one of the underworld lords.[1514] She followed the path of the tree and was about to pluck one of its fruits when the skull of One Hunahpu spoke to her, cautioning her to partake of the fruit only if she was certain of her desire. She assured One Hunahpu that this was indeed her wish. Before she could touch the fruit, however, she became miraculously impregnated by a drop of One Hunahpu's saliva, which he spat into her palm. The young woman was then admonished that by this action life would be renewed through her, never to be lost again. The maiden then climbed up to the world of the living where she bore twin sons, who eventually grew to maturity and defeated the lords of death[1515] and rescued the bones of their father.[1516]

According to Christenson, the major elements of the *Popol Vuh* myth were in place "since before the birth of Christ." In older versions of these stories, the head of Hun-Nal-Ye, the ancient lowland figure corresponding to One Hunahpu, was:

> ... hung in a flowering tree in the underworld. With the aid of his two sons, he was able to arise from the underworld through the cracked carapace of a great turtle, representative of the earth floating on the surface of the primordial sea."[1517]

1507 D. E. Wirth, *Guide*, p. 49.
1508 A. M. Tozzer, *Study*, pp. 153-154. See also M. Graulich, *Myths*, pp. 59-61.
1509 See *Excursus 50: Fu Xi and Nü Gua*, p. 654.
1510 A. J. Christenson, *Sacred Tree*, p. 2.
1511 *Ibid.*, pp. 2-4.
1512 See *Endnote E-96*, p. 726.
1513 See *Endnote E-293*, p. 782.
1514 See *Endnote E-294*, p. 782.
1515 See *Endnote E-295*, p. 782.
1516 See *Endnote E-296*, p. 783.
1517 A. J. Christenson, *Sacred Tree*, p. 4.

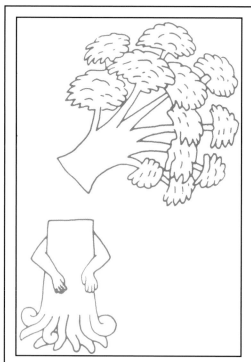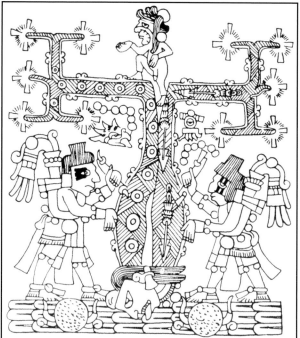

FIGURE E55-4. *Anthropomorphic Tree, Codex Boturini, ca. 1530-1541*[1]
FIGURE E55-5. *Man Emerging from a Split Tree Trunk, Codex Vindobonesis, sixteenth century*[2]

At left, the "migration of original ancestors is depicted in the *Boturini Codex* by a humanized (human arms extend around the trunk) tree broken off across the trunk."[3] At right, recalling motifs associated with other heroes "reborn" from a tree,[4] Norman[5] notes that in some Mixtec depictions of the broken tree trunk symbol, one sees "a man emerging from a split tree trunk in symbolic birth."[6] This "tree of the Mixtec codices is a Tree of Life or World Tree extending above and below this earth, but principally a 'tree of the heavens' in Omeyocan guarded by the creator couple where it gives birth to humanity."

---

1   V. G. Norman, *Izapa Part 2*, p. 202 Figure 4.13, *b*.
2   *Ibid.*, Figure 4.13, *c*.
3   *Ibid.*, p. 202.
4   See *Commentary* 4:14-e, p. 260.
5   V. G. Norman, *Izapa Part 2*, p. 202 text and Figure 4.13. Also cited in B. Gardner, *Second Witness*, 1:168.
6   For additional examples, see D. E. Wirth, *Decoding*, pp. 74-75, 84-85. See also D. E. Wirth, *Parallels*, p. 111.

Having been reborn to new life, Hun-Nal-Ye was then conveyed in a canoe across the sky to the center place of creation. There he oversaw the setting of three stones, the hearthstones of the celestial fire which would quicken the cosmos and allow the world to emerge. Having done so, Hun-Nal-Ye then "raised the sky" by erecting a great world tree to support the arch of the heavens.[1518]

In the *Popol Vuh*, the twins ascended to the sky after restoring their father. According to Graulich:

The heroes defeat darkness and death by voluntarily getting rid of their bodies and of the matter that prevents earthly beings from rising to heaven. Purified, they increase and free their inner fire. They show the gods exiled to earth and humans that one must sacrifice oneself to

---

1518 *Ibid.*, p. 6. See *ibid.*, pp. 7-23 for further discussion of the Maya World Tree, often conceived as a ceiba, as a representation of kingship and deification, and a symbol of the central locus of creation. See also D. E. Wirth, *Parallels*, pp. 94-115 and D. E. Wirth, *Decoding*, pp. 80-91.

reach the lost paradise. They open the way to the two realms of the afterlife, the House of the Sun and Tlalocan.[1519]

Following the ascent of the twins, the fifth, final, and only successful attempt to create humanity was undertaken. "Humankind is distinguished by having blood, in contrast to the [previous "fourth creation" of] the wooden effigies, which lacked it."[1520] The first four men had miraculous vision, being able to see "that which was in the sky and that which was upon the earth… from wherever they were."[1521] Their Creators, however, realizing that in the extent of their knowledge "they [had] become like gods"[1522] determined to limit their powers:

> Their eyes were merely blurred by Heart of Sky [the Creators]. They were blinded like breath upon the face of a mirror. Thus their eyes were blinded. They could see only nearby; things were clear to them only where they were. Thus their knowledge was lost.[1523]

1519 M. Graulich, *Myths*, p. 270.
1520 A. J. Christenson, *Popol Vuh 2003*, p. 194 n. 461; cf. *ibid.*, 664-665, p. 84.
1521 A. J. Christenson, *Popol Vuh 2003*, 4991-4997, p. 197; cf. A. J. Christenson, *Popol Vuh 2000*, 4991-4997, p. 131. Compare the rabbinical idea that the first light of Creation allowed God "to view all the universe simultaneously" (J. L. Kugel, *Instances*, p. 157).
1522 A. J. Christenson, *Popol Vuh 2003*, 5087-5088, p. 200; cf. A. J. Christenson, *Popol Vuh 2000*, 5087-5088, p. 133.
1523 A. J. Christenson, *Popol Vuh 2003*, 5117-5123, p. 201; cf. A. J. Christenson, *Popol Vuh 2000*, 5117-5123, p. 134.

Endnotes

E-1.   Although some aspects of Nibley's analysis of parallels between Egyptian religious texts and LDS temple concepts are now dated, Petersen cites Gee's assessment that his "scholarship on Egypt has been vindicated in one significant way":

> Hugh argued in *The Message of the Joseph Smith Papyri* that the *Book of Breathings* and other Egyptian documents are ritual texts that were used to induct a novice into the religion. Gee stresses that few if any Egyptologists at the time read these texts as Hugh did but that is no longer the case. Egyptologists have discovered that the texts show up in temples as well as tombs and what were once classified as funerary objects actually have a broader cultic function.[1524]

See, for instance, Roberts for an interpretation of the text of the Shabaka stone in the context of wider Egyptian temple architecture and ritual.[1525] Assman is also an advocate of the idea that Egyptian mystery rituals benefitted both the living and the dead:

> Is it conceivable that initiation into the mysteries of the netherworld, as it was granted to the deceased by the *Book of the Dead* and the mortuary rituals, was modeled on the prototype of initiation into temple mysteries, as it was granted to the living? Here we touch upon one of the most controversial problems of Egyptology. Though esoteric circles cling to the notion of "Egyptian mysteries," academic Egyptology almost unanimously rejects this idea… [However, it] is difficult to believe that the mystery into which the deceased was initiated and the mystery into which the living priest was initiated could have been entirely unrelated to one another, considering that the concept of initiation played so great a role in both spheres. Might it not be that already during his lifetime, a priest experienced his introduction into the mysterious cultic presence of the divine as a sort of foretaste of his postmortem introduction to Osiris? ….

> The critical point was the concept that actual, earthly priesthood opened a way to immortality, for already during life, it conveyed divine presence through service of a god, a presence that extended beyond death and came to full fruition only after death, for the deceased only then actually came "face to face" with the gods, whereas during his lifetime, he had only been able to relate to their images. Initiation into the temples and cults of Egypt anticipated and prefigured the ultimate initiation into the mysteries of the realm of the dead. This initiation did not benefit only the priests. The major festivals also enabled the laity to serve the gods by assuming certain roles, and thus to enter into a relationship with them during life, a relationship they could then call on in the afterlife.…

> Initiation into the mysteries of a deity entailed the deification of the mystic. "Conducting into the presence of" and "becoming" Osiris comprise precisely these two aspects of initiation into the mysteries of Osiris.[1526]

As in the Greek mystery cults, the emphasis was on:

> … the possibility of obtaining this redeeming knowledge while still alive on earth, a knowledge that will be beneficial later, in the afterlife. This was precisely the function of initiation in the Greek mystery cults. These initiations conveyed a knowledge that helped the living to enjoy a happy life, but above all, to enjoy a blissful destiny in the afterlife. Here, too, it was a matter of finding the right path in the world beyond… [Edward F.] Wente, Reinhold Merkelbach, and Maria Totti have concluded that in Egypt, living persons were inducted into knowledge about the afterlife and the course of the sun, knowledge that codified in the Books of the Netherworld. Referring to the verses cited above from the *Book of the Dead* of Queen Nedjmet, they write, "When the transfigured queen knew the language of the gods, she was inducted already during her lifetime."[1527]

For a discussion of sacred marriage in the context of Egyptian ritual, see M. Rikala, *Sacred*.

E-2.   Charlesworth, among others, also argues that "the sages who produced the apocalypses were deeply influenced by many strands of traditions and from many cultures. It is obvious that one of these traditions was wisdom."[1528]

E-3.   Noting a discontinuity between Second Temple and Rabbinic Judaism that parallels the break between First and Second Temple Judaism, Bloom concludes that "Something is curiously absent from any history we possess of the Second Temple period… Jacob Neusner, unmatchable scholar of Judaistic

1524 John Gee, conversation with Boyd Petersen, 7 March 2002, cited in B. J. Petersen, *Nibley*, p. 369.
1525 A. Roberts, *My Heart*, esp. pp. 38-44. See also A. Roberts, *Anointing*.
1526 J. Assman, *Death*, p. 201, 204, 207-208.
1527 *Ibid.*, pp. 400-401.
1528 J. H. Charlesworth, *Lady Wisdom*, p. 100.

origins, denies all scholarly myths of any early tradition that developed into 'normative Judaism'—that is, what we now call rabbinical, talmudic Judaism."[1529] With respect to the transmission of temple teachings, Nibley[1530] cites a study by Neusner where he reports that:

> … "in the case of early Rabbinic Judaism,… we have a considerable corpus of laws which prescribe the way things are done but make no effort to interpret what is done. These constitute ritual entirely lacking in mythic, let alone theological, explanation."[1531] That is, no explanation whatever is offered for the ancient temple ordinances. Though fully one-third of the *Mishnah* is taken up with temple ordinances, none of the rabbis who wrote it (third century BCE to third century CE) ever participated in such a ritual… "[W]hat people are told to do is what they are supposed to think"[1532]—think of themselves as performing the rite, but never trying to interpret it. The teachers of an early day explained that in the temple, "attentiveness leads to ritual cleaning," which leads in turn to washing and anointing, which leads to holiness, hence to humility, hence to fear of sin, hence to piety, hence to the Holy Spirit, and finally to the resurrection of the dead, which culminates in the figure of Elijah. What does all this pointing to the resurrection and to Elijah have to do with the temple? Nothing at all, says Neusner, but such a sequence may suggest significant connections to a Latter-day Saint.

E-4 Scripture and temple teachings imply that a preliminary foreordination to sonship could have taken place in the premortal world. For example, Alma writes of those who:

> … were ordained—being called and prepared from the foundation of the world according to the foreknowledge of God, on account of their exceeding faith and good works; in the first place being left to choose good or evil, therefore they having chosen good… are called with a holy calling… which was prepared with, and according to, a preparatory redemption for such.[1533]

Of the "first and second sonships" described in the New Testament, Barker writes:[1534]

> Jesus, in a debate with the Jews and so presumably using arguments they would recognize and accept, said: "Do you say of him whom the Father consecrated and sent into the world, 'You are blaspheming,' because I said 'I am the Son of God'?"[1535] This is the imagery of the ancient monarchy and high priesthood; a human being is consecrated and then *sent out* into the world as the Son of God. Paul said something similar: that God had *sent forth* his Son.…[1536]

> The disciples were "in Christ"[1537] and so were the human presence of the Lord just as Jesus had been. Jesus knew he was returning to the presence of God, to "the glory which I had with thee before the world was made."[1538] The implication of this is that all people can become sons of God, exactly what John and Paul said: "But to all who received him, who believed in his name, he gave power to become children of God; who were born, not of blood, nor of the will of the flesh, but of God";[1539] "For all who are led by the Spirit of God are sons of God,"[1540] and these would share the image of the Son, so that he would be "the first-born among many brethren"[1541]—the image of the first-born among sons of God from Deuteronomy 32:8.

> Human beings could become angels, and then continue to live in the material world. This transformation did not just happen after physical death; it marked the passage from the life in the material world to the life of eternity… This resurrection is often described nowadays as being "born again," as in the words of Jesus to Nicodemus: "Unless one is born anew/born from above, he cannot see the kingdom of God."[1542] Seeing the Kingdom meant seeing the heavenly throne, that is, seeing

EXCURSUS

1529 H. Bloom, *Names Divine*, p. 181; cf. p. 233.

1530 H. W. Nibley, *Sacred*, pp. 591-592, 593.

1531 J. Neusner, *Without Myth*, p. 91.

1532 *Ibid.*, p. 100.

1533 Alma 13:3; cf. J. Smith, Jr., *Teachings*, 16 June 1844, p. 375. See also *Commentary* 1:6-a, p. 46

1534 M. Barker, *Christmas*, pp. 12-13.

1535 John 10:36.

1536 Galatians 4:4. See Galatians 3:25-4:7.

1537 See John 17:23.

1538 John 17:5.

1539 John 1:13.

1540 Romans 8:14.

1541 Romans 8:29.

1542 John 3:3.

beyond the veil into the invisible world. When you saw the angels you joined them. When you glimpsed the glory, you became a part of it.

… [S]ome human beings became angels in the temple ritual, and some angels took human form. Temple beliefs ritualized this by passing through the veil from the visible to the invisible world.

E-5. Hence, Moses 6:59-60:

59 … by reason of transgression cometh the fall, which fall bringeth death, and inasmuch as ye were born into the world by water, and blood, and the spirit, which I have made, and so became of dust a living soul, even so ye must be born again into the kingdom of heaven, of water, and of the Spirit, and be cleansed by blood, even the blood of mine Only Begotten; that ye might be sanctified from all sin, and enjoy the words of eternal life in this world, and eternal life in the world to come, even immortal glory;

60 For by the water ye keep the commandment; by the Spirit ye are justified,[1543] and by the blood ye are sanctified.

E-6. Truman G. Madsen explained:

The Prophet taught we would one day discover that all of us, regardless of our present guesses and researchings as to origins and family, have in our veins the cumulative blood of Israel, and whether by actual birth or by adoption into the kingdom, or both, the Almighty intends that we shall belong literally to the family of Abraham… The kingdom is not a "closed shop." It is not a powermongering super-race. It is an open family into which we are grafted, and through which probably most of us have a heavy genealogical debt.[1544]

Who then is left out? No one. Except those who resolutely and finally choose not to be chosen.[1545]

E-7. On 6 August 1843, Elder Brigham Young said that "if any in the Church had the fulness of the Melchizedek Priesthood, he did not know it."[1546] However, on 22 November 1843, he finally received this much-awaited ordinance.[1547] In later instructions at the temple, President Young said: "Those who… come in here [i.e., the Nauvoo Temple] and have received their washing and anointing will [later, if faithful,] be ordained Kings and Priests, and will then have received the fulness of the Priesthood, all that can be given on earth. For Brother Joseph said he had given us all that could be given to man on the earth."[1548]

Emphasizing the anticipatory nature of these highest ordinances, Elder Young explained: "A person may have a portion of that priesthood, the same as governors or judges of England have power from the king to transact business; but that does not make them kings of England. A person may be anointed king and priest long before he receives his kingdom."[1549] For example, the righteous dead in Old Testament times who received every blessing and promise of the Melchizedek priesthood during their lifetimes yet required the completion of Christ's Atonement, resurrection, and ascension before they could be enabled to receive their full exaltation.[1550] Hence, the following passage from the *Martyrdom and Ascension of Isaiah*:

And he took me up into the seventh heaven… And there I saw all the righteous from the time of Adam onwards… But they were not sitting on their thrones, nor were their crowns of glory on them. And I asked the angel who (was) with me, "How is it that they have received these robes, but are not on (their) thrones nor in (their) crowns?" And he said to me, "They do not receive the crowns and thrones of glory… until the Beloved [i.e., Christ] descends in the form in which you will see Him descend… And when He has plundered the angel of death, He will rise on the third

1543 See D&C 20:37.

1544 T. G. Madsen, *Joseph Smith*, p. 108.

1545 T. G. Madsen, *Chosenness*, p. 139.

1546 B. Young, 6 August 1843, in J. Smith, Jr., *Documentary History*, 5:527.

1547 R. K. Esplin, *Succession*, p. 315. See also G. M. Leonard, *Nauvoo*, pp. 260-261.

1548 *Heber C. Kimball Journal*, kept by William Clayton, 26 December 1845, Church Archives, emphasis and brackets mine, cited in J. Smith, Jr., *Words*, p. 304 n. 21; cf. W. Clayton, *Chronicle*, p. 234. For descriptions of events surrounding the introduction of this ordinance, see R. L. Bushman, *Rough Stone*, pp. 490-499; L. W. Cook, *Revelations*, pp. 293-294, 347-349 nn. 4-11; A. F. Ehat, *Ordinances*, pp. 76-97; J. Smith, Jr., *Words*, pp. 303-307 nn. 21, 22, 29, 30, 38.

1549 J. Smith, Jr., *Documentary History*, 6 August 1843, 5:527.

1550 Cf. W. J. Hamblin, *Temple Motifs*, p. 459; H. W. Nibley, *Apocryphal*, p. 310. See also C. Schmidt, *Pistis*, 3:135, pp. 701-705; G. R. S. Mead, *Pistis*, 4:135, pp. 293-294.

day... And then many of the righteous will ascend with Him, whose spirits do not receive (their) robes until the Lord Christ ascends and they ascend with Him. Then indeed they will receive their robes and their thrones and their crowns, when He has ascended into the seventh heaven."[1551]

E-8. Prior to the sealing of Benjamin F. Johnson to his wife, the Prophet Joseph Smith explained that "there were two seals in the Priesthood. The first was that which was placed upon a man and a woman when they made the [marriage] covenant and the other was the seal which allotted to them their particular mansion [i.e., the second anointing]."[1552] Moreover, according to Cooper:

> During his lifetime Joseph Smith taught that when a man and a woman were sealed, it established an eternal relationship, not only between them, but also between them and the children who were subsequently born to them. Existing sources, however, give no indication that he discussed the relationship between that couple and the children born prior to their being sealed as husband and wife. After ordinance work commenced in the Nauvoo Temple in December 1845, the Twelve Apostles introduced an ordinance by which offspring born to them prior to their matrimonial sealing, as well as individuals who were not their biological children, could be eternally linked to them as children. This ordinance was referred to as sealing or adoption.[1553]

Later, this concept was extended so that children could be sealed to parents who were no longer living.[1554]

E-9. The fact that "Elias" is the Greek version of the transliterated Hebrew "Elijah" has created a point of bafflement for LDS scholarship.[1555] However, it need not be supposed that Joseph Smith was himself confused on the matter. Though one might disagree on particulars of some of Brown's conclusions, he correctly adduces evidence to show that the Prophet probably understood "that the divine Hebrew suffix -*jah* is transliterated –*as* in Greek" in standard New Testament translations.[1556] Despite the potential for misunderstanding, however, in his discussion of the "spirit of Elias" and the "spirit of Elijah," Joseph Smith chose nonetheless to use the names side-by-side as a means to draw a contrast between two distinct scriptural roles. "Elias," the New Testament version of the name, was used to highlight parallels in the preparatory missions of various individuals to the Aaronic priesthood role exemplified by John the Baptist, while "Elijah," the Hebrew version of the name, was used in allusions to the role of the Old Testament prophet who held and restored the sealing power of the Melchizedek priesthood. Had the Prophet rejected the name Elias for its "philological ambivalence," he would have been obliged to find another name to describe the intended distinction.[1557]

E-10. Sometimes the idea of having one's "calling and election made sure" is described in connection with receiving the fulness of the priesthood[1558] or in having otherwise being sealed up to eternal life by authorized holders of the priesthood.[1559] However, such promises are generally understood to be conditional.[1560] Elder Bruce R. McConkie also makes it clear that "these high blessings are not part of celestial marriage. 'Blessings pronounced upon couples in connection with celestial marriage are conditioned upon the subsequent faithfulness of the participating parties.'"[1561] Elder Melvin J. Ballard

1551 M. A. Knibb, *Isaiah*, 9:6-18, p. 170.

1552 Cited in R. E. Cooper, *Promises*, p. 113, spelling and punctuation modernized, brackets added by Cooper; cf. W. Clayton, *Chronicle*, 20 October 1843, p. 123.

1553 R. E. Cooper, *Promises*, p. 113.

1554 G. Irving, *Adoption*. See also *Excursus 9: The Premortal Organization of the Human Family*, p. 544. Johnson sees sealing as both an empowering and "imprinting" process (L. T. Johnson, *Religious Experience*, p. 78 and p. 78 n. 44; cf. Alma 5:14). See L. W. Cook, *Marriages*, pp. x-xiv; R. E. Cooper, *Promises*, pp. 64-65, 107-116 for discussions of the various meanings of the term "seal" in LDS doctrine and ordinances. Nibley gives a list of such meanings from non-LDS texts (H. W. Nibley, *Evangelium*, p. 37 n. 77).

1555 LDS teachings typically distinguish between the *title* of Elias, discussed here, and a prophet with the *name* of Elias, "presumably of Abraham's time, who 'committed the dispensation of Abraham'—which included the blessings of God's covenant with Abraham—to the Prophet Joseph Smith and Oliver Cowdery on April 3, 1836, in the Kirtland Temple (D&C 110:12)" (G. A. Horton, Jr., *Elias*, p. 449).

1556 S. Brown, *Elias*, pp. 2.

1557 *Ibid.*, p. 11.

1558 E.g., S. B. Kimball, *Heber C. Kimball*, p. 105.

1559 E.g., D&C 68:12, D. Q. Cannon *et al.*, *Far West*, 25 October 1831, pp. 20-21. See also L. W. Cook, *Marriages*, pp. x-xiv; R. E. Cooper, *Promises*, pp. 114-115; J. Smith, Jr., *Words*, 13 August 1843, pp. 240-241.

1560 See R. E. Cooper, *Promises*, pp. 111-112 n. 2.

1561 B. R. McConkie, *Mormon Doctrine*, s. v. calling and election sure, pp. 109-110. See J. F. Smith, Jr., *Doctrines*, 1955, 2:46.

EXCURSUS

declared:

> A man and a woman may by fraud and deception obtain admittance to the house of the Lord and may receive the pronouncement of the Holy Priesthood, giving to them, so far as lies in their power, these blessings. We may deceive men, but we cannot deceive the Holy Ghost, and our blessings will not be eternal unless they are also sealed by the holy spirit of promise… Then it is binding, efficacious, and of full force.[1562]

Elder Marion G. Romney further explained:

> [The] gift of eternal life in the world to come may not, of course, be fully realized during earth life. An assurance that it will be obtained in the world to come may, however, be had in this world. As a matter of fact, the blessings of the celestial kingdom are promised only to those who have such an assurance…[1563] These fruits of the Gospel—assurance that we shall obtain eternal life, peace in this world sustained by such an assurance, and finally eternal life in the world to come—are within the reach of us all. Sometimes, however, because of our lack of understanding and appreciation of them, I am persuaded that we take too much for granted. We assume that because we are members of the Church, we shall receive as a matter of course all the blessings of the Gospel. I have heard people contend that they have a claim upon them because they have been through the temple, even though they are not careful to keep the covenants they there made. I do not think this will be the case. We might take a lesson from an account given by the Prophet of a vision of the resurrection, in which he records that one of the saddest things he had ever witnessed was the sorrow of members of the Church who came forth to a resurrection below that which they had taken for granted they would receive…. A half-hearted performance is not enough… We must be willing to sacrifice everything. Through self-discipline and devotion we must demonstrate to the Lord that we are willing to serve Him under all circumstances. When we have done this, we shall receive an assurance that we shall have eternal life in the world to come. Then we shall have peace in this world.[1564]

E-11 Explaining a related concept, William Clayton wrote in his journal:

> "The g[rand] key word was the first word Adam spoke and is a word of supplication. [Joseph Smith] found the word by the Urim and Thummim—it is that key word to which the heavens [are] opened."[1565]

In the *Targum Pseudo-Jonathan* at Exodus 28:30 is written:

> And you shall put into the breastplate the Urim, which illuminate their words and make manifest the hidden things of the House of Israel, and the Thummim, which perfect their deeds, for the High Priest who seeks instruction from the Lord through them. Because in them is engraved and exposed the great and holy Name by which the three hundred and ten worlds were created…. And whoever pronounces this holy Name in the hour of distress, shall be saved.[1566]

Van Dam also cites Rashi's commentary on Exodus 28:30,[1567] where he:

> … considers the [Urim and Thummim] to have been an inscription of the Name (*sem hamporas: YHWH*) that was placed between the front and back of the doubled material forming the breastpiece by which the breastpiece illuminated its words and made its promises true. (Rashi referred to *Yoma* 73b for this explanation.) During the time of the Second Temple the divine Name was no longer within the breastpiece.[1568]

See Fletcher-Louis for ancient examples of the reception of a new name.[1569]

E-12. Christian astrophysicist David Wilkinson provides a very readable summary outlining why arguments from design, though suggestive of and consistent with the idea of a Creator to believers, are bound to fail as "proofs" of the existence of God.[1570]

1562 M. J. Ballard, *Three Degrees 1949*, pp. 236-237. Also cited in H. B. Lee, *Lamp*, p. 105.

1563 D&C 76:51-53.

1564 M. G. Romney, *Assurance*, pp. 41, 43-44.

1565 W. Clayton, *Diaries*, 15 June 1844; cf. W. Clayton, *Chronicle*, 15 June 1844, p. 134. Note that *Chronicle* does not contain the last phrase "it is that key word… opened." Also cited in T. G. Hatch, *Visions*, p. 229.

1566 M. McNamara and M. Maher in A. D. Macho, *Neophyti 1*, 3:465-466, as cited with minor variation in C. Van Dam, *Urim and Thummim*, p. 23. Also cited in T. G. Hatch, *Visions*, pp. 229-230.

1567 Rashi, *Exodus Commentary*, 28:30, p. 393.

1568 N. M. Sarna, *Exodus*, Exodus 28:30, p. 182.

1569 C. H. T. Fletcher-Louis, *Glory*, pp. 188-189.

1570 D. Wilkinson, *Hawking*, pp. 135-167.

E-13. Unbelieving scientist Krauss expresses a related thought:

> Carl Sagan… said that absence of evidence is not the same as evidence of absence. Would a world without God necessarily look any different than the world we live in? Most scientists would say no, and thus claim we do not need the God Hypothesis to explain anything about nature. On the other hand one might also ask: Would a world with a God necessarily look any different than the world we live in? People of faith would argue no, and in so doing feel vindicated in their faith. The problem is that both groups are correct, and nothing either can say is likely to influence the other.[1571]

E-14. Reynolds reports his informal observation that: "The overwhelming majority of LDS academics and intellectuals are active, faithful Latter-day Saints."[1572]

E-15. Other groups specifically noted as being overrepresented were Jewish faculty, faculty espousing atheism or no religion, and Buddhist faculty.[1573] Note that 75% of the overall faculty said that religion was not important to them.

As a side note, 53% of university faculty hold unfavorable views of evangelical Christians, "leading Mormons as the least liked religious group by 20%."[1574] Note also that faculty opinion about the LDS tended to be much more polarized than that of the general public, with significantly fewer reporting neutral feelings (20% vs. 42% of the general population) and 40% (vs. 33%) reporting favorable feelings.[1575]

With respect to American scientists, a 1996 survey reported that "39 percent profess belief in God" and a 1997 survey found that "over half consider themselves 'moderately spiritual' to 'very spiritual,' and about a third hold formal religious affiliations."[1576] By way of contrast, 94-96 percent of the public at large professes a belief in God.[1577]

Unfortunately, there are many reasons why thoughtful people might be disinclined to take religion seriously. Among these is the fact that popular religious understanding often solely "rests on a caricature of religious fundamentalism" which is seen "as a reactionary movement bent on reversing all the progressive measures achieved over the last… decades."[1578] Other people, according to sociologist Rodney Stark, may be put off in knowing "that many illusory or even fraudulent religious claims have been advanced" over the course of history.[1579] Moreover, "comparisons among religions can easily be corrosive to faith because one must confront the fact that, since they disagree, not all religions can be entirely true. From there it is a small step to conclude that all religions are false, that 'all are refuted by all,' as the renegade monk Jean Bodin put it in 1593."[1580] Conversely, "similarities among the world's religions… [sometimes may be] taken as 'proof' that they all are human inventions."[1581] Finally, some people are swayed by arguments that religious belief is nothing more than a combination of biological, psychological, and/or cultural imperatives.

While ultimate satisfaction of such concerns cannot be obtained by reasoned argument alone, perhaps at least a few fallacies can be swept aside. First, no serious believer would hold that each

---

1571 L. M. Krauss *et al.*, *Science (online)*.

1572 N. B. Reynolds, *Preface*, p. x.

1573 G. A. Tobin, *et al.*, *Religious Beliefs*, p. 20.

1574 *Ibid.*, p. 12.

1575 A September 2007 Pew opinion poll, taken of the general American public following a period of greater visibility of Mormonism during the Mitt Romney presidential campaign, gave the following Favorable-Unfavorable-No Opinion breakdowns: Jews (76-9-15%), Catholics (76-14-10%), Evangelical Christians (60-19-21%), Mormons (53-27-20%), Muslim Americans (53-29-18%), Muslims (43-35-22%), Atheists (35-53-12%). The poll also found that "having an acquaintance who is Mormon is linked with more positive opinions of Mormons and Mormonism. The large majority of those who know a Mormon (60%) express a favorable view of Mormons, compared with fewer than half (44%) of those who do not personally know a Mormon. And those who are acquainted with a Mormon are 11 points more likely than others to say that Mormonism and their own religion have a lot in common" (*Public expresses mixed views of Islam, Mormonism*).

1576 M. Shermer, *Darwin*, pp. 126-127.

1577 S. Atran, *In Gods*, p. 276.

1578 C. Lasch, *Revolt*, p. 215. See also D. Kinnaman, *et al.*, *Unchristian*. The authors of this book are evangelical Christians who think that it's important to understand some of the stereotypes (all admittedly having some basis in reality) that people of the Mosaic (born 1984-2002) and Buster (born 1965-1983) generations have of religion. Some of the chapters are entitled: "Hypocritical," "Get Saved!," "Antihomosexual," "Sheltered," "Too Political," and "Judgmental"—thus making clear many of the issues that make it difficult for religion to get a serious hearing among many today.

1579 R. Stark, *Discovering*, p. 8.

1580 *Ibid.*, pp. 1-2.

1581 *Ibid.*, p. 2.

of the sundry and contradictory collections of spiritual beliefs and practices held at one time or another by individuals are rooted in divine revelation. "Some revelations are of God," the Prophet Joseph Smith is remembered as saying, "some revelations are of man: and some revelations are of the Devil."[1582] Moreover, it should not be forgotten that even authentic revelations may be "subject to misunderstanding, exaggeration, and faulty transmission."[1583] Regarding religious similarities among diverse groups, many believers are prepared to accept the possibility that "authentic revelations underlie many of the major faiths."[1584] Finally, with respect to the "insufficiency of all biological approaches to explaining religion, or any other aspects of human culture," the most important consideration in Stark's view "is that they are unnecessary! The fundamental biological basis of all culture is general intelligence, and nothing more needs to be postulated."[1585]

"Thus," writes Stark, "we reach the fundamental question: Does God exist? That is, have we discovered God? Or have we invented him? Are there so many similarities among the great religions because God is really the product of universal wish fulfillment? Did humans everywhere create supernatural beings out of their need for comfort in the face of existential tragedy and to find purpose and significance in life? Or have people in many places, to a greater and lesser degree, actually gained glimpses of God?"[1586] Once the possibility of authentic divine revelation is granted, attention can be turned to the "immense and humbling challenge" of determining "which ones are valid."[1587]

E-16. Elder Neal A. Maxwell wrote: "For the disciple of Jesus Christ, academic scholarship is a form of worship. It is actually another dimension of consecration. Hence one who seeks to be a disciple-scholar will take both scholarship and discipleship seriously; and, likewise, gospel covenants."[1588] Stott similarly concludes that "Latter-day Saint theology appears to negate the secularizing impact of education by sacralizing it."[1589]

E-17. While national data indicate that, overall, the most educated are the least religious, among some denominations—and most dramatically among Mormons—there is a strong *positive* correlation. "Highly-educated Mormons are more likely to pray frequently, to have strong religious beliefs and to attend meetings, suggesting that devotion is even more important for those with higher levels of education than those with lower educations.[1590] This is due at least in part to the fact that from its very beginning, the Church has placed significant emphasis upon education. "One result of this has been a standard of educational attainment that is significantly higher than the national average… For both males and females, the percentage of Mormons who have completed post-high-school education is significantly higher than is the case for the [U.S.] population as a whole. For Mormon males, 53.5 percent have some post-high school education compared to 36.5% for the U.S. population. For females, the figures are 44.3 for Mormons and 27.7 for the U.S. population generally."[1591]

E-18   While not intending to promote "unlicensed and irresponsible speculation" or "falling in love with one's own reason,"[1592] Madsen writes:[1593]

> Some problems are 100-percent guaranteed insoluble for now. Many others, though not insoluble, are not of particular interest. But there are some mysteries, which the scriptures call "the mysteries of godliness,"[1594] the deeper things, the richer things, and they are of which I suspect the Prophet spoke when he said, I beseech you go forward and "search deeper and deeper into the mysteries of Godliness."[1595] These are the mysteries you are to pursue.

1582 Cited in D. Whitmer, *Address*, p. 31; cf. J. Smith, Jr., *Teachings*, 16 May 1841, p. 189. See also B. H. Roberts, *Comprehensive History*, 1:162-163

1583 R. Stark, *Discovering*, p. 52.

1584 *Ibid.*, pp. 2-3.

1585 *Ibid.*, p. 43.

1586 *Ibid.*, p. 20.

1587 *Ibid.*, p. 8. See, however, the findings of Consolmagno, who conjectured from his interviews that while younger scientists and engineers often saw religion as a source of truth, older ones, already settled in what they believe, tended to see it principally as a source of community (G. Consolmagno, *God's Mechanics*, pp. 102-118).

1588 N. A. Maxwell, *Disciple-Scholar*, p. 7.

1589 G. Stott, *Effect*, p. 52. See also T. L. Givens, *Paradox*, pp. 65-99, 195-240; J. W. Welch, *Thy Mind*.

1590 S. L. Albrecht, *et al.*, *Secularization*, p. 308.

1591 *Ibid.*, p. 302.

1592 President Joseph F. Smith described this danger as reading "by the lamp of [our] own conceit" (J. F. Smith, *Gospel Doctrine*, 1907, p. 373; cf. Colossians 2:8).

1593 T. G. Madsen, *Nine Lessons*, p. 114.

1594 1 Timothy 3:16; D&C 19:10.

1595 J. Smith, Jr., *Words*, 12 May 1844, p. 366; J. Smith, Jr., *Documentary History*, 12 May 1844, 6:363. "That the

In further explanation, he continues:[1596]

> But Joseph Smith counseled against futile and divisive speculation: "Let mysteries alone lest you be overthrown."[1597] He adds: "A man can do nothing for himself unless God directs him in the right way; and the priesthood is for that purpose."[1598] The context for these remarks is the temple,[1599] and temple learning requires more than abstract reflection. We are taught:[1600] "These revelations, which are reserved for and taught only to the faithful Church members in sacred temples, constituted what are called the 'mysteries of Godliness.'[1601] The Lord said He had given to Joseph 'the keys of the mysteries, and the revelations which are sealed.'[1602] As a reward to the faithful, the Lord promised: 'And to them will I reveal all mysteries, yea, all the hidden mysteries of my kingdom from days of old.'"[1603]

Nibley[1604] reinforces the same point:

> Not everything is incomprehensible to everybody: "It is given unto you to know the mysteries of the kingdom of heaven, but to them it is not given…"[1605] So we see that mystery is knowledge not known to some: "He that hath ears to hear, let him hear."[1606] "Behold my beloved brethren, I will unfold this mystery unto you"[1607]… A people are condemned who "will not search knowledge, nor understand great knowledge, when it is given unto them in plainness."[1608] We make our own mysteries; we are not meant to be kept in darkness, and the mysteries of heaven will be unfolded to us as we make an effort to understand them.[1609]

E-19. Erich Paul draws a similar conclusion:

> Although the Darwinian redefinition of humanity's place in nature has affected all of Western thinking in deep and lasting ways, Darwinism, rather than cosmology, had a far greater impact on Protestants than on Mormons. Although mainstream Christianity eventually made peace with Darwinism, in general Christians initially responded defensively to the emergence of organic evolution, partly because cosmology was never an integral part of Protestant theology, as it was (and is) for Mormonism, but also because Protestants before Darwin interpreted mankind's origins exclusively from a literal reading of Genesis whereas Mormons strongly augmented their views from contemporary revelation and other prophetic sources.[1610]

Nibley points out that to Brigham Young "it was the economic and political rather than the scientific and biological implications of natural selection that were the real danger and the most counter to the gospel."[1611]

E-20. Of course, the various proponents of creationism vary widely in their fundamental assumptions (e.g., age of the earth, common descent) and in their stance with respect to scientific methodology. In contrast to Bailey's view, Sherlock provides a controversial defense of the scientific viability of

---

mysteries of godliness were a desirable subject of righteous pursuit is suggested by the following passages: Psalm 25:14; Daniel 2:28; Matthew 13:11; 1 Corinthians 4:1; 1 Nephi 2:16, 10:19; Alma 12:9-11; D&C 6:7, 19:8-10 (4-22), 42:61, 50:24-30, 76:5-10, 114-119, 84:19, 88:49-50, 63-69 (49-69), 93:1, 19-22, 26-28, 36-39, 107:18-19, 121:26-28, 132:23… Nevertheless, this important attribute of godliness is only part of the attribute of charity (1 Corinthians 13:2; 2 Peter 1:5-7)" (A. F. Ehat and L. W. Cook, in J. Smith, Jr., *Words*, p. 402 n. 3).

1596 T. G. Madsen, *Nine Lessons*, pp. 117-118.

1597 J. Smith, Jr., *Words*, 8 April 1843, p. 189.

1598 J. Smith, Jr., *Documentary History*, 12 May 1844, 6:363. T. Bullock's notes vary slightly: "… the priesthood is reserved for that purpose" (J. Smith, Jr., *Words*, 12 May 1844, p. 366).

1599 See D&C 76:7, 128:7.

1600 H. B. Lee, *Teachings 1996*, July 1961, p. 575. Elder Lee continues: "In this sense, then, a mystery may be defined as a truth which cannot be known except by revelation."

1601 1 Timothy 3:16, D&C 19:10.

1602 D&C 28:7.

1603 D&C 76:7.

1604 H. W. Nibley, *Assembly*, pp. 137-138.

1605 Matthew 13:11.

1606 Matthew 11:15.

1607 Jacob 4:18.

1608 2 Nephi 32:7.

1609 See H. W. Nibley, *House of Glory*, p. 330.

1610 E. R. Paul, *Science*, p. 2. For a highly readable overview on this topic from a Catholic perspective, see R. J. Clifford, *Value*.

1611 H. W. Nibley, *Work*, p. 207. See B. Young, *Knight*, 19 October 1876, p. 199.

"intelligent design" research and discusses its implications for an LDS audience.[1612] For additional reliable and accessible critiques of creationism and intelligent design that include respectful discussions of religious belief, see F. J. Ayala, *Darwin*; F. J. Ayala, *Darwin's Gift*; R. M. Frye, *Creationist*; M. Shermer, *Darwin*.

E-21.   As a matter of scientific principle, Dawkins classes himself as a TAP (Temporary Agnostic in Practice), though he thinks the probability of a God is very small, and certainly in no sense would want to be "misunderstood as endorsing faith."[1613]

E-22.   Though personally rejecting the notion of a personal God, Albert Einstein is an example of one whose deeply-held "vision of unity and order"[1614]—which throughout his life played an important role in shaping his scientific intuitions[1615]—was chiefly motivated by his profound sense of awe and humility in the face of the lawful and "marvelously arranged" universe: "Everyone who is seriously involved in the pursuit of science becomes convinced that a spirit is manifest in the laws of the Universe—a spirit vastly superior to that of man, and one in the face of which we with our modest powers must feel humble."[1616] Often more critical of the debunkers of religion than of naïve believers in God, he explained: "The fanatical atheists are like slaves who are still feeling the weight of their chains which they have thrown off after hard struggle. They are creatures who—in their grudge against traditional religion as the 'opium of the masses'—cannot hear the music of the spheres."[1617]

E-23.   Illustrating this attitude of meekness with an anecdote about his scientist father, Elder Henry B. Eyring wrote:

> Some of you have heard me tell of being in a meeting in New York as my father presented a paper at the American Chemical Society. A younger chemist popped up from the audience, interrupted, and said: "Professor Eyring, I've heard you on the other side of this question." Dad laughed and said, "Look, I've been on every side of it I can find, and I'll have to keep trying other sides until I finally get it figured out." And then he went on with his lecture. So much for looking as though you are always right. He was saying what any good little Mormon boy would say. It was not a personality trait of Henry Eyring. He was a practicing believer in the Lord Jesus Christ. He knew that the Savior was the only perfect chemist. That was the way Dad saw the world and his place in it. He saw himself as a child. He worked his heart out, as hard as he could work. He was willing to believe he didn't know most things. He was willing to change any idea he's ever had when he found something which seemed closer to the truth. And even when others praised his work, he always knew it was an approximation in the Lord's eyes, and so he might come at the problem again, from another direction.[1618]

E-24.   In this spirit, Nibley famously responded to a reappraisal of his interpretation of one of the book of Abraham facsimiles:

> I refuse to be held responsible for anything I wrote more than three years ago. For heaven's sake, I hope we are moving forward here. After all, the implication that one mistake and it is all over with? How flattering to think in forty years I have not made one slip and I am still in business! I would say about four-fifths of everything I put down has changed, of course. That is the whole idea—this is an ongoing process…[1619]

E-25.   Nibley wrote about:

> … the first rule of scholarship: You are never playing with a full deck. You never know how much evidence you may be missing, what it is, or where it is hiding. What counters that and saves the day for scholarship is what I have called the 'Gas Law of Learning,' namely, that any amount of knowledge, no matter how small, will fill any vacuum of ignorance, no matter how large. He who knows one or two facts can honestly claim to know at least something about a subject, and nobody knows everything. So it is with the schoolmen who make the rules and move the goalposts.[1620]

1612 R. Sherlock, *Intelligent Design*.
1613 L. M. Krauss, *et al.*, *Science (online)*.
1614 C. H. Townes, *Convergence*, p. 66.
1615 See, e.g., W. Isaacson, *Einstein*, p. 335.
1616 *Ibid.*, p. 388.
1617 *Ibid.*, p. 390.
1618 H. B. Eyring, Jr., *Faith*, p. 70.
1619 H. W. Nibley, *Facsimiles*, p. 49.
1620 H. W. Nibley, *Not to Worry*, p. 146.

See Taleb for many examples of how both experts and laymen have become "convinced that they understood what was going on" despite the fact that "[e]very single day brought occurrences that lay completely outside their forecast, [and that] they could not [even] figure out that they had not forecast them."[1621] One implication of his observations is that a person should "make an attempt not to treat his knowledge as a treasure, or even a possession, or even a self-esteem enhancement device,"[1622] but rather should be more attentive to "what we do not know."[1623] In the same spirit, "a private library is not an ego-boosting appendage but a research tool. Read books are far less valuable than unread ones. The library should contain as much of what you do not know as your financial means… allow you to put there."[1624]

E-26.   Regarding this point, Erich Paul writes:[1625]

> The Mormon authorities B. H. Roberts, James E. Talmage, John A. Widtsoe, and Joseph F. Merrill, who were very positive about science otherwise, ultimately rejected science in any guise as the foundation for religion or moral science in general. Thus, although some Mormons came close to developing a natural theology, Roberts for example recognized that science by its very nature is epistemologically insecure and therefore metaphysically suspect… A more careful and less polemical discussion of Joseph Smith's ideas, however, would have saved Roberts, Widtsoe, and other Mormons from making problematic and erroneous, but "faith promoting," statements, such as that the ether of nineteenth-century physics is the physical embodiment of the Holy Ghost or that astronomy verifies the truth of the book of Abraham. In their defense, however, many non-Mormons—scientists and others—even to this day have made similar claims about the alleged truthfulness of science. Unwittingly, these individuals were laying the foundation for a full-fledged natural theology: the view that religion can be verified by association with the prevailing theories and findings of science… At the deepest, ontological level, science as philosophy is unable to reveal much at all. As the cosmologist Edward R. Harrison has expressed it: "The history of cosmology [and science generally] shows us that in every age devout people believe that they have at last discovered the true nature of the Universe, whereas in each case they have devised a world picture—merely a universe—that is like a mask fitted on the face of the still unknown Universe."[1626]

E-27   Nibley characterizes scientific prejudice as follows:

> Is an open mind, then, a negative thing—an empty mind? It is, unless it is a searching mind. An oyster has few prejudices—in the field of astronomy it has, we may safely say, absolutely none. Are we then to congratulate the oyster for its open-mindedness? A first-rate and very broad-minded scientist, J. B. S. Haldane, defines prejudice as "an opinion held without examining the evidence." Prejudice does not consist in having made up one's mind—in defending an opinion with fervor and determination, …it consists in forming an opinion before all the evidence has been considered. This means that freedom from prejudice whether in the field of science or any other field requires a tremendous lot of work—one cannot be unprejudiced without constant and laborious study of evidence; the open mind must be a searching mind. The person who claims allegiance to science in his thinking or who is an advocate of the open mind has let himself in for endless toil and trouble.[1627]

E-28.   This was exactly the perspective of LDS scientist Henry Eyring who was said to have "cared less about the explanation for every piece of his [Absolute Rate Theory] model than about using it to make new discoveries. He was confident that the unanswered questions would be solved in time, and he meanwhile wanted to apply the model to any subject it could usefully illuminate."[1628]

E-29   As Peterson expresses it:[1629]

> LDS Bible use combines an essentially traditional perspective with liberal (even radical) elements, some unique to Mormonism… Scripture was not untouchable. [Joseph] Smith subordinated it to

---

1621 N. N. Taleb, *Black Swan*, p. 10.

1622 *Ibid.*, p. 2.

1623 *Ibid.*, p. xxi.

1624 *Ibid.*, p. 1.

1625 E. R. Paul, *Science*, p. 230.

1626 See E. R. Harrison, *Cosmology*, p. 1; cf. W. E. Evenson, *Science*, pp. cxiii-cxiv.

1627 H. W. Nibley, *Open Mind*, pp. 128-129.

1628 H. J. Eyring, *Mormon Scientist*, p. 29.

1629 D. C. Peterson, *Review of Barlow*, p. 78.

direct experience with God, and was willing to modify biblical texts to make them accord with the revelations he had received. Indeed, he produced new scripture—thus rejecting the Protestant principle of the all-sufficiency of the Bible.

Belief in continuous revelation both heightened and lowered the status of the Bible among Mormons. On the one hand, having themselves witnessed and indeed participated in a recommenced biblical drama, they knew the Bible to be true. Through a rebirth of prophetic tradition, ancient and modern Saints became contemporaries… On the other hand, Mormon prophets and apostles insisted upon their own limitations (easily observable by the Saints themselves). Thus, by analogy, the awesome distance between biblical figures and modern believers was reduced, and the Bible became "familiar."

E-30   Thus, Elder Neal A. Maxwell's comment: "Today we carry convenient quadruple combinations of the scriptures. But one day, since more scriptures are coming, we may need to pull little red wagons brim with books."[1630] He added, "Of course, computers may replace wagons."[1631]

E-31   In his characteristically forthright manner, Brigham Young expressed similar thoughts: "… compared with the living oracles those books are nothing to me."[1632] "I would not give the ashes of a rye straw for all those books… without the living oracles…."[1633] In contrast to this view, the doctrine of *sola scritura* accepted by many Christians presumes a closed canon that precludes the possibility of any subsequent scriptural additions assuming the same authority of the Bible.[1634] In contrast to this view, Wright points out that: "The risen Jesus, at the end of Matthew's Gospel, does not say, 'All authority in heaven and on earth is given to the books you are all going to write,' but [rather] 'All authority in heaven and on earth is given to me.'"[1635] Elsewhere, he argues that "… in the Bible all authority lies with God himself" as wielded "through human agents anointed and equipped by the Holy Spirit." He recalls "a well-known lecturer once insisting that 'there can be no authority other than scripture', and thumping the tub so completely that I wanted to ask 'but what about God?'"[1636]

E-32   Mourning the passing of the unique revelatory period at the death of the "last prophet," a student of Islam writes: "While Muhammad still lived and prophecy and revelation in Islam continued, an order of existence prevailed that was unattainable in subsequent times… No other age could attain its perfection, no ensuing accomplishment equal its glories…. Bereft of the guidance of its charismatic prophet-founder and the 'revealing,' the ongoing revelation, which he brought, the *Ummah* [faith community] was now on its own."[1637]

Ayoub points out, however, that though revelation "reached its technical culmination in the prophet Muhammad through a long period of what we call progressive revelation, nonetheless it may be said that revelation continues, not in the form of *wahi* (revelation technically considered) but in the form of *ilham*, or inspiration which is open to the friends and worshipful servants of God. This mode of revelation will not end."[1638]

E-33   Note that "new" scripture being given under the influence of the Holy Ghost is often couched in terms identical to passages of previously revealed scripture.[1639] Explained Smith and Sjodahl: "When the Spirit of the Lord speaks through a human instrument, He acts independently, even when proclaiming truths formerly revealed. Strictly speaking, the Holy Spirit does not quote the Scriptures, but gives Scripture."[1640] Elder Bruce R. McConkie once expressed a similar point:

1630 N. A. Maxwell, *Flood*, p. 18.

1631 N. A. Maxwell, *Quote*, p. 298. A range of questions associated with the idea of an open canon are considered by Elder Alexander B. Morrison in A. B. Morrison, *Canon*, pp. 6-10. See also W. D. Davies, *Reflections*, p. 64; T. L. Givens, *Hand*, p. 196. Robert L. Millet gives an accessible overview regarding the wider question of how one is to determine authoritative doctrine in the Church (R. L. Millet, *Doctrinal Parameters*). See also *Approaching Mormon Doctrine*; J. E. Faulconer, *Coffee*; N. B. Oman, *Authority*; N. B. Oman, *Jurisprudence*.

1632 Cited in P. L. Barlow, *Bible*, pp. 92-93.

1633 B. Young, Journal, *27 January 1860*, p. 417; cf. P. L. Barlow, *Bible*, p. 93; B. Young, *7 October 1864*, p. 339.

1634 See 2 Nephi 29:3.

1635 N. T. Wright, *Last Word*, p. xi. See Matthew 28:18. Cf. J. R. Holland, *Words*, p. 93; J. R. Holland, *Words (Broken)*, p. 188.

1636 N. T. Wright, *Authoritative*. See also P. L. Owen, *Anglo-Catholic*, pp. 57-60.

1637 W. A. Graham, *Divine*, pp. 9-10.

1638 M. M. Ayoub, *Redemption*, p. 158.

1639 E.g., JS-H 1:36-41.

1640 H. M. Smith, *et al.*, *Commentary*, p. 350.

EXCURSUS

> In speaking of these wondrous things I shall use my own words, though you may think they are the words of scripture, words spoken by other apostles and prophets. True it is, they were first proclaimed by others, but they are now mine, for the Holy Spirit of God has borne witness to me that they are true, and it is now as though the Lord had revealed them to me in the first instance. I have thereby heard his voice and know his word.[1641]

On another occasion Elder McConkie said:

> If the Spirit bears record to us of the truth of the scriptures, then we are receiving the doctrines in them as though they had come to us directly. Thus, we can testify that we have heard his voice and know his words.[1642]

Hence, just as scripture constitutes a report of an encounter with God's voice, an authentic experience with scripture invites God's presence anew, with the possibility of further revelation.[1643]

E-34   Indeed, Peterson observes that: "The creation of a canon commences when revelation is thought to have come to a halt, and in turn the concept of a canon reinforces the notion that revelation has ceased."[1644]

E-35   Joseph Smith himself corrected a member of the Church who thought that "a prophet is always a prophet" telling him that "a prophet is only a prophet when acting as such."[1645] Similarly, in response to an online essay, Bushman argued against current misguided efforts to apply a stereotype of fanaticism to Latter-day Saints:

> The stereotype of fanaticism is essentially a logical construction. The seemingly airtight logic is that anyone who claims to speak for God must believe he possesses absolute truth with an implied commission to impose that truth on everyone else. Muhammad, to whom Joseph Smith was frequently compared, [is seen by those who use this argument as having] used violence. Joseph Smith, lacking the means, [is seen by them as having] tyrannized his own followers and refused to acknowledge the truth of any other doctrines but his own. [It is assumed] that Mormon leaders, by the same token, will want to commandeer… government to advance their cause. Nothing Mormons can do will ever alleviate these fears. It did not help that the right of individual conscience in religious matters was made an article of faith, or that the Nauvoo city council passed a toleration act for every conceivable religious group including Catholics, Jews, and "Muhammadans." Whatever they said, their neighbors could not believe that the Mormons' ultimate goal was not to compel everyone to believe as they did.

> … [It is mistakenly thought that] Mormons have to be interested in world domination because their doctrine requires it of them. Furthermore, they are all [falsely depicted as] dupes of the chief fanatic and will willingly do anything he requires… That leap from assumption to conclusion in one bound is only possible if you are steeped in the logic of fanaticism. For Mormons themselves, it makes no sense.[1646]

E-36   See Givens for a discussion of various models in the theology of revelation, and his own view of "dialogic revelation" within Mormonism.[1647] Elsewhere, Givens discusses the fact that, because the restoration is not yet complete, not only the Lord Himself, but also other religious traditions:

> … have much to teach us… by way of… adding to the body of revealed doctrine we call precious and true… Our contemporary condescension in this regard was clearly foreign to a prophet who showed the world he could translate gold plates written in Reformed Egyptian, then hired a Jewish schoolmaster to teach him Hebrew.[1648]

Elsewhere Givens observes that:

> The real meaning of Joseph's School of the Prophets… is to be fathomed from its timing and growing direction in the context of his own prophetic career: after the youthful leader had established his

EXCURSUS

1641   D. B. Horne, *McConkie*, p. 205; B. R. McConkie, *New Witness*, p. xii.
1642   D. B. Horne, *McConkie*, p. 205; B. R. McConkie, *Come*, p. 59; B. R. McConkie, *Sermons*, p. 256.
1643   E.g., Joseph Smith—History 1:11ff.; D&C 76:15-19, 138:1-11.
1644   D. C. Peterson, *Muhammad (2001)*, p. 597. See *Excursus 49: The People of the Book*, p. 651.
1645   J. Smith, Jr., *Teachings*, 8 February 1843, p. 278.
1646   R. L. Bushman, *Mitt*.
1647   T. L. Givens, *Hand*, pp. 209-239. See A. Dulles, *Revelation* for the broader context of this idea. See also B. T. Ostler, *Spiritual Experiences*.
1648   T. L. Givens, *Dialectic*.

credentials as Prophet and translator, after he had personally manifested his power to reveal the fulness of saving truth directly from heaven, and after he claimed receipt of authority to perform all saving ordinances in the new church. At that moment when he had powerfully demonstrated to his followers the irrelevance of priestly training, clerical degrees, and scholarly credentials, he changed *modus operandi* in midstream… It is to this two-pronged approach that we may trace the Mormon paradox of a culture of spiritual certainty—a group embrace of a rhetoric of absolute self-assurance about spiritual truths—coexisting with a conception of education as the endless and eternal acquisition of the knowledge that leads to godhood.[1649]

E-37   In this vein, the distinguished religious scholar Martin E. Marty concludes that Mormons, if one admits that they "do" theology at all, work from a "slightly broader definition of that term than the conventional ones. "Conventional" here means the Christian modes that combine the language of the Hebrew Scriptures with mainly Greek philosophical concepts as filtered through academic experiences in Western Europe."[1650] "In general," however, "LDS scholars are… at home with… Christian thought… They earn their doctorates at Harvard or other graduate schools permeated with the concepts of Christian theology, even if and though they often return 'home' to Brigham Young & Company."[1651]

Faulconer notes the fact that, in the formal sense, "Mormonism does not even have a widely accepted theology, much less an official one, though it has and has had several practitioners." He observes that one "obvious reason for the relative absence of theology among Mormons is that the Church is still young." More important reasons, however, for the "dearth of theology among Latter-day Saints" include: "the belief in continuing revelation, the nature of scripture, and the fact that, like many Jews, Mormons understand their religion primarily in terms of practices and attitudes rather than in terms of beliefs."[1652] However:

> … there is an important sense in which, without calling it theology, Latter-day Saints have practiced hermeneutical theology since shortly after the founding of the Church. They have been intensely interested in and written much about Church history, understanding Mormon history—the things we have done and experienced—as the key to understanding what it means to be a Mormon; understanding the interpretation of Latter-day Saint history as disciplined reflection on what it means to be a Latter-day Saint, or in other words as quasi-theological, even if only implicitly."[1653]

E-38   On this point, Wright comments:

> I remember a well-known Preacher saying that he thought a lot of Christians used the Bible as an unsorted edition of *Daily Light*. It really ought to be arranged into neat little devotional chunks, but it happens to have got all muddled up… But to treat the Bible like that is, in fact, simply to take your place in a very long tradition of Christians who have tried to make the Bible into a set of abstract truths and rules—abstract devotional doctrinal, or evangelistic snippets here and there.…
>
> The problem with all such solutions as to how to use the Bible is that they belittle the Bible and exalt something else. Basically they imply—and this is what I mean when I say that they offer too low a view of scripture—that God has, after all, given us the wrong sort of book and it is our job to turn it into the right sort of book by engaging in these hermeneutical moves, translation procedures or whatever. They imply that the real place where God has revealed himself—the real locus of authority and revelation—is, in fact, somewhere else; somewhere else in the past in an event that once took place, or somewhere else in a timeless sphere which is not really hooked into our world at all out touches it tangentially, or somewhere in the present in "my own experience," or somewhere in the future in some great act which is yet to come… My conclusion, then, is this: that the regular views of scripture and its authority… fail to do justice to what the Bible actually is—a book, an ancient book, an ancient narrative book. They function by tuning that book into something else, and by implying thereby that God has, after all, given us the wrong sort of book.[1654]

E-39   On the strengths of regular rotation class study of the sacred works, and the problems in relying on selective lectionaries rather than readings of the whole book of scripture, Wright observes:

1649 T. L. Givens, *Paradox*, p. 74.
1650 M. E. Marty, *Foreword*, p. vii.
1651 *Ibid.*, p. ix. See D. L. Paulsen, *Interview*, pp. 67-68 for a discussion of the place of theology in LDS scholarship.
1652 J. E. Faulconer, *Tracy*, pp. 472, 473-474. See also J. E. Faulconer, *Coffee*; B. Huff, *Theology*; J. Siebach, *Response*.
1653 J. E. Faulconer, *Tracy*, p. 476; cf. J. Shipps, *Sojourner*, 381-383, 385, 390 n. 40.
1654 N. T. Wright, *Authoritative*.

The church in her public worship uses lectionaries—at least, if she does not, she runs the grave risk of revolving, as C. S. Lewis pointed out, round the little treadmill of favorite passages, of "desert island texts," and muzzling the terrible and wonderful things that scripture really has to say. But even in the lectionaries there are problems; because at least those that are common... today do their own fair share of muzzling, missing out crucial passages in order to keep the readings short, omitting verses that might shock modern Western sensibilities. The Bible is to be in the bloodstream of the church's worship, but at the moment the bloodstream is looking fairly watery.[1655]

E-40   On the power of stories, Wright observes:

Story authority, as Jesus knew only too well, is the authority that really works. Throw a rule book at people's head, or offer them a list of doctrines, and they can duck or avoid it, or simply disagree and go away. Tell them a story, though, and you invite them to come into a different world; you invite them to share a world-view or better still a "God-view." That, actually, is what the parables are all about. They offer, as all genuine Christian story-telling the does, a world-view which, as someone comes into it and finds how compelling it is, quietly shatters the world-view that they were in already. Stories determine how people see themselves and how they see the world. Stories determine how they experience God, and the world, and themselves, and others. Great revolutionary movements have told stories about the past and present and future. They have invited people to see themselves in that light, and people's lives have been changed. If that happens at a merely human level, how much more when it is God Himself, the creator, breathing through His word....

In the church and in the world, then, we have to tell the story. It is not enough to translate scripture into timeless truths. How easy it has been for theologians and preachers to translate the gospels (for instance) into something more like epistles! We must, if anything, assimilate the epistles to the gospels rather than vice versa. I would not actually recommend that, but if you were going to make a mistake that would be the direction to do it in. And as we tell the story—the story of Israel, the story of Jesus, the story of the early church—that itself is an act of worship....

We need to recapture a sense of scripture as a whole, telling and retelling stories as wholes. Only when you read Exodus as a whole (for example) do you realize the awful irony whereby the making of the golden calf[1656] is a parody of what God wanted the people to do with their gold and jewels... and only by reading Mark as a whole might you realize that, when the disciples ask to sit at Jesus' right and left hand,[1657] they are indeed asking for something they do not understand.[1658]

E-41   About this reductive approach to scriptural understanding, Wright laments:

We have, again and again, allowed ourselves to say—I've heard myself say it, over and over again—"What Paul is really getting at here is..." "What Jesus was really meaning in this passage..."—and then, what has happened is a translation of something which is beautiful, and fragile, and unique, into something which is commonplace and boring, and every other Christian in the pew has heard it several sermons before. I am reminded of that amazing line in Schaffer's play *Amadeus* where Salieri sees on stage Mozart's *Figaro*, and he says, "He has taken ordinary people—chambermaids and servants and barbers—and he has made them gods and heroes." And then Salieri remembers his own operas and he says, "I have taken gods and heroes—and I have made them ordinary." God forgive us that we have taken the Bible and have made it ordinary—that we have cut it down to our size. We have reduced it, so that whatever text we preach on it will say basically the same things.[1659]

Teaching the scriptures in this trivializing manner performs what Neusner has called "a negative miracle": it takes a subject, namely religion, which is "rich in life, and [makes] it dull."[1660]

E-42   Halpern and Wesson note that "to many physicists this explanation doesn't seem physical enough, given that nobody can really travel in imaginary time," and describe alternative suggestions for circumventing the necessity for an initial singularity.[1661].

Note that, concluding the impossibility of a complete description of the universe, Hawking has since

1655   *Ibid.*

1656   Exodus 32:1-4.

1657   Mark 10:37-40.

1658   N. T. Wright, *Authoritative.*

1659   *Ibid.*

1660   J. Neusner, *Vocation*, p. 118, cited in A. B. McCollum, *Re-visioning*, p. 178.

1661   P. Halpern, *et al.*, *Brave*, pp. 175-176.

relinquished his original quest for a "Theory of Everything."[1662]

E-43   Some of those who espouse the view of an *ex nihilo* creation have eagerly embraced the "big bang" hypothesis as evidence that there must be a God who provided the "First Cause." This is a very old theological argument whose roots can be traced back as far as Aristotle. Problems with this mode of reasoning and the related notion of a "god of the gaps" are summarized by Wilkinson.[1663] About the problem of defining a credible "god of the gaps" that is custom-tailored to fit the current shape of ignorance in scientific understanding, Hazen remarks: "The problem with this view is that as we learn more, the gaps narrow… [until] God's role is squeezed down to ever more trivial variations and inconsequential modifications."[1664]

E-44   Of course, in a view where time itself emerges out of the creation of a universe, the concept of "past" as applied to the idea of an eternally "self-reproducing eternal inflationary universe" cannot be interpreted in the commonsense way.[1665]

E-45   Scientists predict that the gradual disappearance of the afterglow of the big bang and all but what was once our local group of galaxies over many billions of years would not only diminish the awareness of any future generations concerning the universe as it would then exist, but also would preclude their ability to discover how it all began.[1666]

E-46   Such an idea is similar to Philo's Platonic idea of the visible world being copied from its wholly conceptual heavenly prototype: "So when He willed to create this visible world He first formed the intelligible world in order that He might have the use of a pattern wholly God-like and incorporeal in producing the material world, as a later creation, the very image of an earlier… As then, the city which was fashioned beforehand within the mind of the architect… even so the universe that consisted of ideas would have no other location than the Divine Reason, which was the Author of this ordered frame."[1667] Traces of a similar idea can be found in Colossians 1:15-17.[1668] Though advance planning of some sort doubtless took place before the foundations of the world, this process is never referred to in the scriptures as a form of spiritual creation.

E-47   Note that Paul warns in Colossians 2:18 against the "worshiping of angels."

E-48   Schimmel expresses the view of Sufism about the superiority of Adam to the angels as follows: "Man is superior to the angels…, who have not been given the secret of the names and who do nothing but worship God in perfect obedience, whereas man enjoys—or suffers from—the choice between obedience and rebellion… Man was entrusted with the *amana*, the 'trust'[1669] that Heaven and earth refused to carry—a trust that has been differently interpreted: as responsibility, free will, love, or the power of individuation."[1670]

E-49   For Satan, the competition with Christ and Adam can be nothing but a win-lose proposition. Al-Tha'labi records that when Satan saw the veneration of Adam by the hosts of heaven, he said to himself: "By God, if He prefers this one [Adam] over me I shall rebel against Him [God], but if I am preferred over him I shall destroy him."[1671]

E-50   Barker associates the experiences of Isaac and Ishmael with the rites of the Day of Atonement: "The ritual involved two goats: one was sacrificed and its blood used to make atonement, the other—representing Azazel the leader of the fallen angels—was driven off into the desert, bearing the sins. This echoes in the story of Abraham's two sons: Isaac who was sacrificed [on Mount Moriah]… and Ishmael who was driven out into the desert."[1672]

E-51   An updated form of this style of thinking continues implicitly today, as an article published in *Nature* in 2005 attests. Nee observes:

1662 S. Hawking, *Gödel*.
1663 D. Wilkinson, *Hawking*, pp. 123-133.
1664 R. M. Hazen, *Genesis*, p. 80.
1665 D. Wilkinson, *Hawking*, pp. 118-119.
1666 L. M. Krauss, *et al.*, *End*.
1667 Philo, *De opficio mundi* 16:20, cited in S. Ruzer, *Reflections*, p. 97.
1668 S. Ruzer, *Reflections*, pp. 99-100.
1669 *Qur'an* 33:72.
1670 A. Schimmel, *Mystical*, p. 188.
1671 A. al-Tha'labi, *Lives*, p. 45.
1672 M. Barker, *Hidden*, p. 36.

EXCURSUS

Although advocates of evolution may have stripped [the concept of the great chain of being] of its supernatural summit, this view is with us still. Common presentations of evolution mirror the great chain by viewing the process as progressive… [For example, Richard Dawkins, in his book *The Ancestor's Tale*,] cautions us against thinking that evolution is progressive, culminating with us. He emphasizes that with whatever organism we begin the pilgrimage back through time, we all are reunited at the origin of life. But by beginning the journey with us and looking backwards along our ancestry, Dawkins generates a sequence of chapter titles that would read like a typical chain to a medieval theologian, albeit with some novelties and the startling omission of God.[1673]

E-52 On the connection between the earthly and the heavenly realms in the quorum of ten men forming a Jewish *minyan* for prayer, Kogan writes: "On one level, the body that is formed below, the actual *minyan*, is entered by the *Shekhinah* (the supernal holiness), and is thus the point of contact between God and Israel. Simultaneously, the *minyan* formed in the proper manner below unifies the heavenly realm above."[1674] Note the similarity to the Islamic *hajj*, where pilgrims circumambulate the *Ka'bah* and offer prayer in likeness of the angels.[1675] Isar likewise notes the Easter custom still preserved in some Orthodox monasteries where, "during the singing of the troparion 'Christ is risen!', a special circular lighting device, specifically called a 'choros,' was presumably introduced in the Byzantine churches around the 12th century, carrying out an old custom reflecting the paradigm of the divine choral movement."[1676]

E-53 Cf. Major's description of ancient Huang-Lao cosmography: "The axis of heaven is usually taken to be the polestar, and the axis of earth a point lying directly beneath it, far to the north of China… [While] axial imagery varies, the fundamental importance of centrality does not."[1677] Moreover, "the relationship of heaven to earth was that heaven covers earth 'like the canopy of a chariot.' This clearly defines a square within a circle… Wang Chong's famous complaint in the Lunheng that if heaven were round and earth square 'the corners would not fit'" is likewise germane in the context of the "circle within a square of the cosmograph."[1678]

E-54 The conviction of truth is thus to be taken as prior to the question of whether conversion will increase personal happiness. Indeed, such a conviction has sustained many throughout history who have been compelled to embrace the gospel at the cost of great personal sacrifice. As C. S. Lewis puts it:

> Christianity claims to give an account of facts—to tell you what the real universe is like… If Christianity is untrue, then no honest man will want to believe it, however helpful it might be: if it is true, every honest man will want to believe it, even if it gives him no help at all.[1679]

Scientist and religious skeptic Richard Dawkins rightfully concurs with the tenor of Lewis' remarks:

> I recently had a televised encounter with the veteran British politician Tony Benn, a former minister of technology who calls himself a Christian. It became very clear in the course of our discussion that he had not the slightest interest in whether Christian beliefs are true or not; his only concern was whether they are moral. He objected to science on the grounds that it gave no moral guidance. When I protested that moral guidance is not what science is about, he came close to asking what, then, was the use of science…
>
> Other examples include those people who think that whether religious beliefs are true or false is less important than the power of religion to comfort and to give a purpose to life. I… have no objection to people drawing comfort from wherever they choose and no objection to strong moral compasses. But the question of the moral or consolation value of religion—one way or the other— must be kept separate in our minds from the truth value of religion.[1680]

As Lasch observes: "Culture may well depend on religion…, but religion has no meaning if it is seen merely as a prop of culture."[1681]

E-55 Indeed for the first generation of Latter-day Saints, as Givens convincingly argues, "the 'message' of

1673 S. Nee, *Chain*.
1674 In D. Blumenthal, *Merkabah*, p. 147.
1675 M. al-Kisa'i, *Tales*, p. 61. See *Figure 4-4*, p. 219.
1676 N. Isar, *Dance of Adam*, p. 202. See also F. M. Huchel, *Cosmic*, p. 9.
1677 J. S. Major, *Heaven*, p. 37.
1678 *Ibid.*, p. 35.
1679 C. S. Lewis, *Rabbit*, p. 352.
1680 L. M. Krauss, *et al.*, *Science*, p. 91.
1681 C. Lasch, *Revolt*, p. 228.

the Book of Mormon was the manner of its origin,"[1682] with the importance of the story of its coming forth as a sign of the Restoration overshadowing discussion of the content of the book itself.

E-56   Updating Campbell's view, Charlesworth summarizes how similar anti-historical arguments advanced by scholars such as Bultmann, Barth, and Tillich with respect to the New Testament have now been superseded.[1683] See also Givens[1684] for an excellent discussion of why the very notion of prophetic writings "grounded in artifactual reality"[1685] and:

> … replete with the specificity of mundane details invites ridicule and censure from those wedded to modern conventions regarding the sacred. Joseph Smith's unwavering insistence on the tie between his spiritual claims and historical occurrences has produced a body of scriptural text that, in the words of Mikhail Bakhtin, "enters our verbal consciousness as a compact and indivisible mass; one must either totally affirm it, or totally reject it. It is indissolubly fused with its authority—… and it stands and falls together with that authority."[1686]

Other models of inspiration might render "sacred discourse more elastic," allowing:

> … editorial and exegetical intrusion alike [to] be seen… as correctives in a human process, not profane meddling with a tottering ark. [However, by] not just emulating but actually invoking Old Testament modes of seership, Joseph Smith firmly precluded any such tampering at the same time that he foreshadowed a radically new paradigm for revelation and inspiration generally, one which would be fully fleshed out in the text he produced. True enough, the Lord indicated to Joseph that his commandments "were given unto my servants in their weakness, after the manner of their language."[1687] But as prophet, Joseph's revelatory stance and range of expression are anything but "purely free."[1688]

E-57   For example, Matthews describes his perspective on the events in the early chapters of the book of Moses:

> We accept Adam and Eve as real persons who lived, transgressed, and brought about their own Fall and the consequent fall of all mankind. If we had a complete record, it would be possible to mark on the calendar the actual time that the Fall occurred. Likewise, if we had an adequate map it would be possible to mark the exact spot where the transgression occurred. The Fall is just that real and absolute. A real man and a real woman did, at a particular time and geographical location, transgress a commandment which brought about the Fall of man, an event which has affected not only all of mankind but also the whole Creation.[1689]

Sherlock admits that:

> Mormonism has not generally been sympathetic to… "mythic" reading[s] of key parts of scripture. Of course scripture has been written with moral or theological points in mind. But viewing scripture as history selected with a theological point is fundamentally different than viewing scripture as a mythic tale with a theological meaning.[1690]

E-58   LaCocque observes that:

> … nothing can be more damaging…than when people entertain the illusion that they have heard so much of and about [a Bible story] that they do not need to hear it ever anew. For, when the mind ceases to be curious, a sort of immunity to the impact of the "Word" develops that is at times more detrimental than sheer ignorance. Thus, the universal knowledge enjoyed by the myth of Adam and Eve is also its curse. To consider the story of Adam and Eve as a tale for children is only possible when the story is vaguely known, when it is considered from a distance, and with a pre-

---

1682 T. L. Givens, *Hand*, p. 84.
1683 J. H. Charlesworth, *Psychobiography*, pp. 58-59; cf. J. H. Charlesworth, *Archaeology*.
1684 T. L. Givens, *Hand*, pp. 72-84.
1685 *Ibid.*, p. 80.
1686 *Ibid.*, p. 81.
1687 D&C 1:24.
1688 T. L. Givens, *Hand*, pp. 82-83.
1689 R. J. Matthews, *Fall*, pp. 43-44. For a range of LDS perspectives on the events of Eden, see the overview of Moses 3, p. 141.
1690 R. Sherlock, *Response*, p. 103.

conceived feeling that nothing can be learned from so "naïve" a tale. Naïve and hackneyed—those are formidable hurdles to overcome if we decide to read afresh the story of Adam and Eve![1691]

E-59 See, e.g., Nibley:

The problem of the historicity of the Bible is exactly the same today as it has been since the days of the first apologists. One reads the Bible and decides for himself what is history in it and what is allegory, and what is myth, and what is legend, and what is interpolation. There are two main schools of thought on the subject. There are the fundamentalists, who believe that everything put forth in the Bible as history actually happened as they find it stated; and there are the [religious] liberals, who [have]… reached the general consensus that the historical value of the Bible is nil. The LDS people have always stood between these two extremes.[1692]

E-60 Compare the *Gospel of Philip*: "The bridal chamber… remains hidden… The veil at first concealed how God controlled the creation, but when the veil is rent and the things inside are revealed, this house will be left desolate, or rather will be [destroyed]."[1693]

E-61 Elder Widtsoe had personal experience with the principle of revelation in the temple concerning personal affairs. According to Madsen:

He often said, "I would rather take my practical problems to the House of the Lord than anywhere else." In his book *In a Sunlit Land* he describes a day when, having been frustrated for months in trying to pull together a mass of data he had compiled to come up with a formula, he took his companion, his wife, to the Logan Temple to forget his failure. And in one of the rooms of that structure there came, in light, the very answer he had previously failed to find. Two books on agrarian chemistry grew out of that single insight—a revelation in the temple of God.[1694]

Here is the direct quotation from Elder Widtsoe's autobiography:

The temple is peculiarly a place of revelation. Many experiences have proved it. Perhaps the most impressive is this: For several years, under a Federal grant with my staff of workers we had gathered thousands of data in the field of soil moisture; but I could not extract any general law running through them. I gave up at last. My wife and I went to the temple that day to forget the failure. In the third endowment room, out of the unseen, came the solution, which has long since gone into print.[1695]

E-62 Mormons differ in their understanding of claims that the origins of the endowment go back to antiquity. On the one extreme, Nibley flatly asserts that "The ordinances of the Egyptian temple were essentially the same as those performed in ours,"[1696] a view that he went to great pains to demonstrate in his publications. Nibley, of course, did not confine his discussions of such parallels to Egyptian sources, but also brought texts of Jewish, Christian, Muslim, and other origins as witnesses in behalf of his arguments. On the other hand, Kearney advocates a nuanced view that sees some of the details of the presentation of the endowment as an inspired appropriation of certain forms common in Masonic ritual:

The endowment is revealed doctrine necessary for the salvation of the Saints. It teaches us God's relationship to man; our duties and our responsibilities. The endowment has never changed and if you think about it, what the endowment is are commitments to the law of sacrifice, to the law of consecration, to the law of chastity. These things are fixed and these things can be found throughout every dispensation of time. That is the endowment.…

So we have the endowment and then we have the messenger: the ritual. How the endowment is taught and this is where I believe Masonry played a part. Joseph Smith sat in Lodge, he watched as humble farmers–most of whom he knew probably couldn't read and write well-learned complicated, difficult ritual and he said in his mind, "Ah! This is how I'll do it. This is how I'll teach the endowment to the Saints." Why? Because they already knew the ritual. They wouldn't pay attention to the ritual; they'd pay attention to the message because they already knew the ritual. And so,

1691 A. LaCocque, *Trial*, pp. 10-11.

1692 H. W. Nibley, *Historicity*, p. 1; cf. D. H. Oaks, *Scripture Reading*, p. 7.

1693 W. W. Isenberg, *Philip*, 84:21-29, p. 159.

1694 T. G. Madsen, *House*, p. 277.

1695 J. A. Widtsoe, *Autobiography*, p. 177.

1696 H. W. Nibley, *Meaning of Temple*, p. 26.

there is that kind of genesis, that ritualistic form, that asking of questions back and forth that we get. All of that comes as Joseph Smith tries to communicate these truths.[1697]

E-63 See Carroll for a discussion of the possibility of a "continuity between the various religious expressions found in ancient Egypt that revolves around the ideas of initiation into the afterlife, and into the presence of the deity through ritual mystery reenactments similar to those likely found in the initiations of the ancient craft guilds of Egypt." Carroll argues that this "illustrates the antiquity of the concepts found in the rites of medieval craft guilds, and of the initiation rites found in universities, fraternities, Freemasonry, and among the Latter-day Saints. This further indicates that such rituals were anciently connected with the temple, admittance into the afterlife, kingship, priesthood, and with becoming like the gods."[1698]

E-64 In his comprehensive volume, McBride quotes Wandle Mace as saying that:

> … the Book of Revelation served as inspiration for the design: 'The order of architecture was … a representation of the Church, the Bride, the Lamb's wife. John the Revelator, in the 12 chapter [and] first verse of [the book of Revelation,] says, "And there appeared a great wonder in heaven; a woman clothed with the sun, and the moon under her feet, and upon her head a crown of twelve stars." This is portrayed in the beautifully cut stone of this grand temple.[1699]

McBride also cites Joseph Smith as saying that the Nauvoo Temple was "built by direct revelation," implying that this revelation was with reference to the temple's architecture.[1700] However, the original quote says that the temple was "being built by the direct revelation of Jesus Christ for the salvation of the living and the dead"[1701]—perhaps better in line with the idea that Joseph Smith was speaking, in this context, more about the commandments he received on the necessity of building the temple[1702] rather than about a revelation concerning the specifics of its architectural form.

E-65 Highlighting another dimension of the connotations of the term, Gianotti observes that the "root meaning of 'heart' (*al-qalb*) in Arabic is to 'turn over,' 'roll over,' or 'flip.' Indeed, one of the modern words for 'revolution' in Arabic (*inqilab*) comes from the same root, as do a great many other words implying change, circularity, and fluctuation."[1703]

E-66 In their discussion of Canopus,[1704] de Santillana and Von Dechend note that the "determinative sign for 'heart' [in Egyptian] often figures as the plumb bob at the end of a plumb line coming from a well-known astronomical or surveying device, the *merkhet*. Evidently 'heart' is something very specific, as it were the 'center of gravity.'"[1705] Of the relationship between space and time associated with Kolob and described in the book of Abraham, Kerry Shirts writes:[1706]

> Joseph Smith …noted that this Kolob idea is "The measurement according to celestial time, which celestial time signifies one day to a cubit.[1707] One day in Kolob is equal to a thousand years according to the measurement of this earth."[1708] …In the late 1800's decades after Joseph Smith was dead, the professional surveyor, W. F. Petrie found that the Egyptian cubit of 29.161 inches was found from a swinging pendulum which swung 100,000 times in 24 hours in the latitude in which Memphis lies. Now then we see that Joseph Smith said one day (notice this is time) and a cubit (this is space), Joseph Smith shows the relationship. The Egyptians make a cubit with relationship to the day. The Egyptians used an instrument called *merkhet* which is a stick with a plumb bob line. So Joseph Smith equates the number 1,000 to time and space, as the ancient Egyptians did! Most interestingly, the Egyptians took their measuring seriously, as we read "measuring rules were given a sacred meaning… the cubit rules… seem to be of the type used as sacred objects."

1697 G. Kearney, *Message*. See also K. Flake, *Oral Canon*.
1698 J. L. Carroll, *Initiations*, p. 44.
1699 M. McBride, *Nauvoo Temple*, p. 9. See W. Mace, *Autobiography*, pp. 8-9.
1700 M. McBride, *Nauvoo Temple*, p. 9.
1701 J. Smith, Jr., *Latter Day Saints*, p. 409.
1702 E.g., D&C 124:25-55.
1703 T. J. Gianotti, *Islamic View*, p. 89.
1704 Arabic *kalb at-taiman* = heart of the south.
1705 G. d. Santillana, *et al.*, *Hamlet's Mill*, Intermezzo, p. 73. See also *Excursus 20: The Circle and the Square*, p. 571 and *Excursus 50: Fu Xi and Nü Gua*, p. 654.
1706 K. A. Shirts, *Chnum-Re*.
1707 *Kirtland Egyptian Papers*, Grammar and Alphabet (KEPE 1), p. 26, cited in K. A. Shirts, *Chnum-Re*.
1708 Facsimile 2, Figure 1, book of Abraham.

E-67 Some Mandaeans speak of "a star inhabited by men, the descendants of the Hidden Adam (*Adam Kasia*), but they are semi-spiritual and not gross like ourselves. This star is called Merikh, and is the star of the morning."[1709]

E-68 Note that "No known graphical illustration associating the pentagram with evil appears until Lévi in [1851]… It is only in the later twentieth century, and the creation of the American Church of Satan, that the inverted pentagram has become a popular symbol for Satan."[1710]

E-69 For an unknown reason, the hymn was eliminated from the recommendation list given in the second edition.[1711]

E-70 Baker illustrates the limited contemporary appeal in other branches of Christianity for beliefs resembling the LDS idea of "eternal progression":

> At the conclusion of their book, *Heaven: A History*,[1712] Colleen McDannell and Bernhard Lang observe that the idea of a progressive, social heaven has survived after the 1930s in only three ways: (1) in contemporary popular culture, (2) in glimpses of the afterlife in near-death experiences, and (3) in Latter-day Saint theology.[1713]

"For the most part, ideas about what happens after death are only popular sentiments and are not integrated into Protestant and Catholic theological systems."[1714]

E-71 The last line of this stanza originally read: "Grim death reigns not above."

E-72 He was excommunicated again in 1839 and 1847, but each time was reconciled and rebaptized within a short period.

E-73 "Ralph's grandfather, Sir Edward Vaughan Williams, seems to have been the first member of the family to use the double-barrelled but unhyphenated name… Ralph's name was pronounced 'Rafe,' any other pronunciation used to infuriate him."[1715]

E-74 Recalling an incident from Ralph's childhood, his second wife and biographer wrote: "The publication of Charles Darwin's *The Origin of Species* had shaken the family and the country to their foundations: echoes of the controversies it had aroused still surrounded Great Uncle Charles, who seemed an august but unpredictable person.… Ralph asked his mother about *The Origin of Species*, and what it meant. She answered: 'The Bible says that God made the world in six days, Great Uncle Charles thinks it took longer: but we need not worry about it, for it is equally wonderful either way.'"[1716]

E-75 Vaughan Williams' music has been described as follows:

> If… Englishness in music can be encapsulated in words at all, those words would probably be: ostensibly familiar and commonplace, yet deep and mystical as well as lyrical, melodic, melancholic, and nostalgic yet timeless. Ackroyd quotes Fuller Maitland, who noted that in Vaughan Williams' style "one is never quite sure whether one is listening to something very old or very new"… Vaughan Williams' music expresses a deep regard for and fascination with folk tunes, the variations upon which can convey the listener from the down-to-earth (which he always tried to remain in his daily life) to the ethereal. Simultaneously the music shows patriotism toward England in the subtlest form, engendered by a feeling for ancient landscapes and a person's small yet not entirely insignificant place within them.[1717]

E-76 He also co-edited *The Oxford Book of Carols*.[1718]

E-77 When Vaughan Williams' *Dona nobis pacem* was selected by former Mormon Tabernacle Choir director Craig Jessop as the main feature of the program for the Carnegie Hall National High School Choral Festival in March 2006, he and his then assistant Choir director Mack Wilberg discussed the problems presented by the moods of the opening and closing of the work and by its relatively

1709 E. S. Drower, *Mandaeans*, p. 56.
1710 *The Pentagram.*
1711 B. H. Roberts, *Seventy's Course 1 (1931)*, p. xvi.
1712 C. McDannell, *et al.*, *Heaven*, pp. 307-308.
1713 J. T. Baker, *Eternal Progression*, p. 71.
1714 C. McDannell, *et al.*, *Heaven*, p. 308.
1715 U. Vaughan Williams, *R.V.W.,* Note on Names.
1716 *Ibid.*, pp. 12-13.
1717 *Ralph Vaughan Williams.*
1718 P. Dearmer, *et al.*, *Carols.*

EXCURSUS

short length. Since no suitable companion pieces could be found, Jessop eventually invited Wilberg to compose something. Vaughan Williams was one of Wilberg's favorite composers,[1719] *Dona nobis pacem* was a piece that he loved, and, after some hesitation, he began to warm to the idea. Wilberg composed an Introit and an Epilogue that were, each in their own way, reminiscent of the work of the great English composer. The Introit, which opens with the traditional *Requiem aeternam dona eis, Domine...* ("Grant them eternal rest, O Lord..."), later became the beginning of a full requiem, performed for the first time at April 2007 as part of celebrations marking the reopening of the newly renovated Salt Lake Tabernacle. The Epilogue, "Let Peace Then Still the Strife," features the beautifully simple and direct lyrics of David Warner. Howard comments: "Vaughan Williams composed his cantata in 1936 as a warning against the global conflict that was at that stage a tragic inevitability; his pleas for peace are, therefore, more anxious than optimistic. But Wilberg's 'benediction' to the cantata is an affirmation that everlasting peace will indeed eventually triumph."[1720]

E-78   "Simona Pakenham and her husband Noel Iliff bicycled over from Kensington to ask Ralph to provide music for a script Simona had made from medieval mystery plays. It was a short, Christmas piece, and needed carol tunes and incidental music. It had to be ready by November for the singers to learn in time for a December matinee at Drury Lane in aid of St. Martin-in-the-Fields. Ralph liked Simona's choice of episodes and immediately started thinking about tunes to fit. They suggested that he should take part, and double God and the eldest shepherd, but he said he'd stick to the music, and he went to the boxroom for carol books to start on it at once."[1721] The work premiered the December following Vaughan Williams' death.[1722]

E-79   The tune was mentioned in a comedy by Francis Beaumont and John Fletcher entitled *Monsieur Thomas*, first published in 1639. In Act 3, Scene 3 a fiddler informs the hero that he knows how to sing "the merry ballad of Dives and Lazarus." In 1906, Vaughan Williams collected the song in the town of Kingsfold, West Sussex as *The Red Barn* or *The Murder of Maria Martin*, recalling local events surrounding an 1827 murder trial.[1723] He also collected a version called *John Barleycorn*, its words recounting an allegory about the making of beer.[1724] In 1906, Vaughan Williams harmonized the tune and set it to the words of *I Heard the Voice of Jesus Say* in *The English Hymnal*.[1725] It was also used in other hymns and carols, including *Led by the Spirit*, *O Sing a Song of Bethlehem*, and *Come All Ye Faithful Christians*.

The most recognized variant of this song today is probably *The Star of the County Down*, originally an Irish ballad. A Scottish version is known as *Gilderoy*, "named for an infamous Irish highwayman who raided Scotland in the 13th century. Robert Burns, the national poet of Scotland, also used the melody for *From Thee Eliza*."[1726] Other variants include *The Thresher*, *Cold Blows the Wind*, and *We Are Poor Frozen Out Gardeners*.

About the problem of identifying the lineage of old tunes, Vaughan Williams wrote the following:

> We folk song collectors are often asked "what is the original" of a particular song or "how old is it?" There is no answer to either of these questions; there is no original version of any particular tune; any given tune has hundreds of origins. Nor can we say how old it is; in one sense any particular tune is as old as the beginnings of music, in another sense it is born afresh with the singer of today who sang it.[1727]

E-80   *Five Variants of Dives and Lazarus* was commissioned by the British Council for performance at the 1939-1940 New York World's Fair.[1728] It is ironic that a nostalgic work recalling the venerable English

---

1719 In the footsteps of Vaughan Williams and—to a degree—John Rutter, Wilberg's many arrangements of traditional music for choir and orchestra evidence his love for the genre. One reviewer writes: "Wilberg's aesthetic sensibilities seem to mesh perfectly with those of Vaughan Williams at his most lushly Romantic, particularly the plush, shimmering string writing of the *Tallis Variations*. In fact, there are few moments in [Wilberg's] *Requiem* where it wouldn't be possible to imagine that this was a newly discovered score by the English pastoralist" (S. Eddins, *Requiem*).

1720 L. Howard, *Notes*. See also *Program Notes for The Carnegie Hall.*

1721 U. Vaughan Williams, *R.V.W.*, p. 397. See also M. Kennedy, *Works*, p. 344.

1722 M. Kennedy, *Works*, p. 432.

1723 *Ibid.*, p. 278.

1724 U. Vaughan Williams, *R.V.W.*, p. 67.

1725 P. Dearmer, *et al.*, *Hymnal*, #574.

1726 *Return to Nauvoo.*

1727 S. Finkelstein, *Notes*; cf. R. Vaughan Williams, *Music*, pp. 195, 231-232.

1728 U. Vaughan Williams, *R.V.W.*, p. 230.

folk song Vaughan Williams had loved all his life was featured at an event that was boldly themed "The World of Tomorrow."

Among the most frequently played of Vaughan Williams' compositions, Kennedy describes the work as being "in the tranquil style of the Serenade, [recalling] an earlier and simpler style, matured by years of experience."[1729] It was written "with that superb technical skill which enabled Vaughan Williams to extract the utmost nuances and sonorities from the instruments."[1730] Music critic Steven Schwartz comments:

> Constant Lambert, the British music critic and composer, once remarked that the only thing you could do to vary a folk song was to play it louder. Vaughan Williams, among others, proved him wrong. Delius, for example, used a simple variation technique. Vaughan Williams, more than any other British composer of his time, absorbed folk songs into his artistic psyche to such an extent, he not only wrote his own folk songs, but he was able to join them to large symphonic structures. Nowhere is this clearer than in the *Five Variants*. This work is not theme and variations in the conventional sense. The folk song *Dives and Lazarus* is taken for a winding walk, pulled, and turned until it becomes an eleven-minute symphonic movement, without a trace of artistic self-consciousness.[1731]

E-81 I have been unable to locate the Gemmell reference in the Church Archives or at Brigham Young University. However, the source of these statements is surely Dr. Washington Franklin Anderson (1823-1903), the subject of R. C. Gemmell's cited manuscript and presumably the husband of Anderson's daughter, Dr. Belle Anderson Gemmell. The latter wrote a brief article about Utah's early medical history that included brief life sketches both of her father and of Dr. John Milton Bernhisel (1799-1881).[1732] Within Bernhisel's papers at Brigham Young University, I found two life sketches for Bernhisel written by the same hand and marked "author unknown."[1733] However, on one of the folders containing the manuscripts I found the following: "More than likely written by Dr. Washington F. Anderson, personal doctor of Brigham Young and close friend of grandpa," which coincides with a statement in one of the sketches that it was prepared at the request of "the family of the late Jno. M. Bernhisel" by his "friend and associate"—probably at the time of Bernhisel's death. Given circumstantial evidence and the close parallels in wording between statements in the life sketches and Andrus' quotations from R. C. Gemmell's manuscript, it seems safe to assume that Anderson heard something like these statements from Bernhisel, an intimate of the Prophet Joseph Smith in Nauvoo, on an occasion when Bernhisel and Anderson were "riding together, visiting a country patient."[1734]

E-82 The reason why devilish characters in fiction generally stand out as more convincing than the virtuous ones is discussed by Lewis:

> In all but a few writers the "good" characters are the least successful, and everyone who has ever tried to make even the humblest story ought to know why. To make a character worse than oneself it is only necessary to release imaginatively from control some of the bad passions which, in real life, are always straining at the leash; the Satan, the Iago [of Shakespeare's *Othello*], the Becky Sharp [of Thackaray's *Vanity Fair*], within each of us, is always there and only too ready, the moment the leash is slipped, to come out and have in our books that holiday we try to deny them in our lives. But if you try to draw a character better than yourself, all you can do is to take the best moments you have had and to imagine them prolonged and more consistently embodied in action… We do not really know what it feels like to be a man much better than ourselves… Heaven understands Hell and Hell does not understand Heaven, and all of us, in our measure, share the Satanic, or at least the Napoleonic blindness… The Satan in Milton enables him to draw the character well just as the Satan in us enables us to receive it.[1735]

E-83 William W. Phelps said that the Devil proposed to execute this plan of misery "on the honor of a God, or on his Father's honor."[1736]

E-84 "Had Satan succeeded," wrote Elder Bruce R. McConkie, "the salvation he sponsored would in reality

1729 M. Kennedy, *Works*, p. 258.
1730 *Ibid.*, p. 278.
1731 *Vaughan Williams' Orchestral Works*.
1732 B. A. Gemmell, *Utah Medical*.
1733 W. F. Anderson, *Life Sketch*.
1734 W. F. Anderson, *Life Sketch*, p. 3.
1735 C. S. Lewis, *Preface*, 13, pp. 100-101.
1736 W. W. Phelps, *Answer*, p. 758.

have been damnation, for it would not have raised men to the high status enjoyed by the Eternal Father."[1737]

E-85   Perhaps the most convincing fictional account of a world in which a plan of the same nature holds sway is in Arthur C. Clarke's science fiction novel, *Childhood's End*. The story concerns a race of intellectually- and technologically-superior extraterrestrials called the Overlords, who end poverty and war and create a worldwide utopia—though at the price of limiting what a clergyman in the novel called "Freedom to control our own lives—under God's guidance."[1738] After fifty years of physical concealment, the Overlords hold true to their promise to reveal their hidden form: "There was no mistake. The leathery wings, the little horns, the barbed tail—all were there. The most terrible of all legends had come to life."[1739] Despite C. S. Lewis' differences with Clarke,[1740] the book is reputed to be Lewis' favorite work of science fiction, and he commented to Joy Gresham that he was happy to find "a modern author who understands that there may be things that have a higher claim than the survival or happiness of humanity."[1741]

Themes from Genesis 1-3 and the work of Milton informed Lewis' own ventures into science fiction. For example, in *Perelandra*,[1742] he explored the question of "how… a totally free person, without unfair manipulation by God, [could] spontaneously carry out what God most desires, and find for herself a destiny which God fully intends." Essentially, in this story, "the Woman needs to make her own free and spontaneous choice to do the Will of God, without being unduly influenced by God. Ransom [the hero of the novel], as another free agent, can help, but will not himself receive undue help… At one point Ransom himself asks why isn't [God] doing anything, only to be answered by the fact that his own remarkable voyage to Venus is a pretty considerable contribution—'he himself was the miracle.'"[1743] Thus Lewis posits that one of the reasons for Christ's Atonement, which enabled mankind to become members of His body through their free choice, was to save others, not directly through Himself, but through Himself in each of us.[1744]

E-86   That any notion of compulsion is favored by God is explicitly repudiated in the stories of Genesis 1-11, which, as Gelander observes, "indicate that God preferred freedom of choice as the highest virtue, even above His own absolute goodness. The implication is that God's morality is inherent in the idea that goodness which is compelled is neither good nor moral."[1745]

E-87   Writes McLachlan: "There is a strong sense in LDS doctrine that Satan's coercive plan is a lie from the beginning because it is a rejection of reality itself which is based on the agency, creativity, and co-eternality of intelligences."[1746]

E-88   Ostler argues that the LDS view of agency:

> … must be understood in a libertarian sense as opposed to a compatibilist model of agency. The libertarian view holds that persons cannot be caused to act as they do if they are free. Moreover, to be free a person must be able to choose otherwise in the actual circumstances that exist. The Book of Mormon teaches that for persons to be free agents in a significant sense they must: (1) be free "to act for themselves" and not merely "to be acted upon" by causes external to themselves;[1747] and (2) have a genuine choice in the actual circumstances to choose between opposing options of either good or evil, either of which is genuinely open to the agent in the moment of free decision.[1748] In contrast, the compatibilist holds that free agency is compatible with causal determinism and that persons need not be free to actually choose otherwise in the conditions that actually exist, but merely to choose otherwise had they so chosen. Given the compatibilist view, Satan's plan was

---

1737 B. R. McConkie, *New Witness*, p. 657.
1738 A. C. Clarke, *End*, p. 9.
1739 *Ibid.*, p. 61.
1740 A. C. Clarke, *et al.*, *Narnia*.
1741 C. S. Lewis, *Letters 3*, 22 December 1953, p. 391; cf. C. S. Lewis, *Rabbit*, p. 352.
1742 C. S. Lewis, *Perelandra*.
1743 Father Jerome Bertram, cited in W. Hooper, *Lewis Companion*, p. 222.
1744 See W. Hooper, *Lewis Companion*, p. 228; cf. Nibley's principle of "maximum participation" (H. W. Nibley, *Before Adam*, p. 71).
1745 S. Gelander, *Creator*, pp. 9-10.
1746 J. M. McLachlan, *Modernism Controversy*, p. 62.
1747 2 Nephi 2:26.
1748 2 Nephi 2:11-29.

a genuine possibility because God could have guaranteed by his eternal decree that all persons would be saved.[1749]

On the other hand, the view on agency adopted by Mormonism disallows the compatabilist option *a priori*.

E-89   In the case of the exercise of this power by the righteous, Madsen clarifies that this is not "a dominating, exploiting, enslaving power. 'Power over' means more advanced, more Christ-like."[1750] However, it seems that the fate of the never-embodied Satan and and the resurrected Cain, for example, is to be eternally locked together in the utterly destructive embrace of unrighteous dominion.[1751]

E-90   The means by which Adam and Eve, in their fallen state, could have received an immortal body and "lived forever" prior to the resurrection of Jesus Christ, the "firstfruits of them that slept,"[1752] is not explained in scripture.

E-91   This period of probation also extends for a time in the spirit world where repentance is also possible,[1753] possibly with more difficulty.[1754]

E-92   According to the teachings of the Kurdish Yazidi religion, it was the Peacock Angel (*Melek Taus*) who, as leader of the archangels, righteously refused to bow to Adam. This is understood as a test where he was forced to determine whether he would submit to anyone besides God. Having passed the test, he received God's commendation. Due to their favorable view of the main character of this story, the Yazidi are sometimes accused of being Devil worshippers, a claim which the Yazidi themselves vehemently deny.[1755]

E-93   Additional confusion about the roles of Michael, Jehovah, and Christ is described by Seaich:

> Late Judaism and "orthodox" Christianity both assumed Michael to be the leader of the Host of Heaven. N. Schmidt, however, correctly recognized that monotheistic Judaism had split the lone Yahweh into two halves, the higher remaining "God" (to replace *El*), and the lower becoming "Michael," the new leader of Yahweh's Host.[1756] That this late, intertestamental "Michael" was originally Yahweh, is further shown by the fact that the Church still frequently confused Michael with Christ.[1757] [John J.] Collins thus concludes that while the "Son of man" was thought by Jews to have been Michael, we are actually dealing with "an example of angelic Christology," wherein "the role allotted to Michael… in Jewish texts is… allotted to Christ" by the Church.[1758]

E-94   An Islamic legend likewise records that Adam "shall call every man by name in the day of the resurrection, and pronounce his sentence according as the balance of justice shall decide."[1759]

E-95   Barker concludes that transformations of an "animal" to a "man" in this story represent the acquiring of "angelic" status: "Noah [was] transformed from a bull into a 'man' after an archangel had taught him a mystery,[1760] and… Moses [was] transformed from a sheep into a man after he had been with the Lord on Sinai."[1761] On the other hand, "the traditional interpretation of *1 Enoch* 8:1[1762]—that the fallen angels taught 'the changing of the world'—is that they taught how to change men into animals, that is, angels into mortals."[1763]

1749 B. Ostler, *Theism*, pp. 7-8.

1750 T. G. Madsen, *LDS View*, p. 101.

1751 See *Commentary* 5:23-c, p. 374.

1752 1 Corinthians 15:20.

1753 1 Peter 4:6; Alma 42:10.

1754 M. J. Ballard, *Three Degrees 1949*, p. 241.

1755 E. S. Drower, *Peacock*, p. 92; *Yazidi*. For more on this story, see *Commentary* 1:12-d, p. 53; the overview of Moses 4, p. 225; *Excursus 8: The Origin and Premortal Existence of Human Spirits*, p. 540; *Excursus 21: The Power and Premortal Status of Satan*, p. 575.

1756 N. Schmidt, *Son of Man*.

1757 E.g., C. Osiek, *Shepherd*, 8:3(69):3, p. 195, and 9:12(89):7-8, p. 230, where the "Michael" is explicitly identified as the Savior. See also Revelation 12:10, where "Michael" slays the dragon, but Christ receives the spoils.

1758 J. E. Seaich, *Ancient Texts 1995*, p. 205 n. 309; cf. J. J. Collins, *Son of Man*, pp. 64-65. See also J. Daniélou, *Theology*, pp. 121-127 for early Christian confusion of Michael with Christ.

1759 G. Weil, *Legends*, p. 40.

1760 G. W. E. Nickelsburg, *1 Enoch*, 89:1, p. 364.

1761 M. Barker, *Hidden*, p. 45.

1762 G. W. E. Nickelsburg, *1 Enoch*, 8:1, p. 188.

1763 M. Barker, *Hidden*, p. 46; cf. *Commentary* 4:24-b, p. 271; 4:25-a, p. 272.

EXCURSUS

Continuing, she writes:

> The *Animal History* distinguished between the religion of the patriarchs, the bulls, and the religion of Moses, the sheep, and Eden restored was to be the religion of the patriarchs. This imagery is ancient. In the sixth century BCE, when Ezekiel was predicting terrible punishment, he was told to summon every type of bird and beast to devour the rams, lambs, goats, and bulls, the lean animals who represented his own people.[1764] When Isaiah described the Kingdom of the Messiah, he foresaw the wolf, the leopard and the lion, the unclean carnivores, living alongside the lamb, the kid and the calf, the clean herbivores.[1765] In the Kingdom, then, these distinctions would disappear. Hence, perhaps Peter's vision of the clean and unclean animals as he learned to accept Gentiles into the Church.[1766]

E-96   Compare the account of the Cainites in *Excursus*, p. 586 to the Akkadian Atrahasis myth, where the noise of the humans disturbed the gods. Compare also a similar motif in the Mayan *Popul Vuh* account (see *Excursus*, p. 699). In the case of the Atrahasis myth, Mettinger accepts arguments by other scholars that the "noisy activities… marked a rebellious attitude on the part of the humans who were not content with their lot but wanted to encroach on the divine territory."[1767] See also way the noise of the people is associated with sin in the account of Israel's rebellion during the golden calf incident.[1768]

E-97   The appearance of giants not only figures in stories about the Watchers in the time of Noah, but also in apocalyptic and rabbinic descriptions of godly figures such as Adam and Enoch (= Metatron).[1769] The idea of "gianthood" was not always to be taken literally—rather, with respect to the patriarchs, large stature corresponds to the ideas of majesty and sublimeness and to the conferral of angelic status upon worthy mortals.[1770] Fletcher-Louis also suggests that the large size of the patriarchs is "perhaps related to the tradition according to which the high priest's garments represent the whole cosmos."[1771] Perhaps, from the shortened lifespans[1772] and reduced stature of the generations after the Flood, we are meant to infer concomitant limitations on the mental and spiritual powers of mankind—precluding the possibility of a repetition of the terrible destruction blamed in the stories of the Watchers on the misuse of their great powers. See also discussion in B. M. Wheeler, *Mecca*, pp. 99-122.

Possible relationships between these stories and Greek myths about the Titans are summarized by Wright.[1773]

E-98   The one man, of course, is Noah with his three sons Shem, Ham, and Japheth. Reeves has explored connections between Jewish, Qumranic, and Manichaean texts attesting to the theme of Noah's family being represented as a Tree of Life with three trunks.[1774]

E-99   Islamic tradition has preserved traditions about the Watchers in their tale of Harut and Marut.[1775]

E-100   In addition, Price connects the story with "Hesiod's myth of Uranos consigning his monstrous sons to underground caverns."[1776]

E-101   Al-Tabari[1777] records a tradition that combines the fall of Satan with a variation on the story of the Watchers: "Iblis belonged to a tribal group of angels called the jinn… The first to dwell on earth were the jinn. They caused corruption and shed blood and killed each other… God sent Iblis to them with an army of angels… and [h]is success went to his head."

1764 Ezekiel 39:17-20.
1765 Isaiah 11:6-7.
1766 M. Barker, *Hidden*, pp. 46-47. See Acts 10:9-16.
1767 T. N. D. Mettinger, *Eden*, pp. 126-127.
1768 Exodus 32:17-19.
1769 M. Idel, *Hénoch*; cf. A. al-Tha'labi, *Lives*, p. 58.
1770 C. Mopsik, *Hénoch*, pp. 208-210 n. *Je fus exhaussé et allongé*.
1771 C. H. T. Fletcher-Louis, *Glory*, p. 39.
1772 Moses 8:17.
1773 A. T. Wright, *Evil Spirits*, pp. 73-75, 79-89.
1774 J. C. Reeves, *Jewish Lore*, pp. 95-102. See also Qumran *Book of Giants* fragments reporting the giant Ohya's dream vision of "a tree that is uprooted except for three of its roots" which, along with related dreams, "may symbolize the destruction of all but Noah and his sons by the flood" (M. Wise, *et al.*, *DSS*, pp. 293, 292). See *Commentary* 3:9-h, p. 167; *Figure 5-3*, p. 330; *Excursus 25: The Tree of Life as the Hidden Throne of God*, p. 591; *Excursus 50: Fu Xi and Nü Gua*, p. 654.
1775 E.g., A. al-Tha'labi, *Lives*, pp. 86-91.
1776 R. M. Price, *Pre-Nicene*, p. 828 n. *u.*
1777 al-Tabari, *Creation*, 1:81-86, pp. 249-257.

E-102   Another possibility is that the men in Moses 8:21 are not really part of the covenant "sons of God" but are only falsely claiming to be. The most common ancient traditions, however, assert that it was not only the female descendants of Noah (and Seth) but also the men in that family line who were eventually drawn into forbidden relationships. For example, following what became the standard tradition in the Syriac Church that saw the "sons of God" as Sethites and the "daughters of men" as Cainites,[1778] Ephrem the Syrian also interpreted these traditions to mean that: "those who lived on higher ground,[1779] who were called 'the children of God,' left their own region and came down to take wives from the daughters of Cain down below."[1780]

An Islamic source likewise argues: "But one errs and misunderstands [if] he says that 'angels' descended to 'mortal women.' Instead, it is the sons of Seth who descend from the holy mountain to the daughters of Cain the accursed. For it was on account of their saintliness [chastity?] and dwelling-place upon the holy mountain that the sons of Seth were called *banu 'elohim*; that is, 'sons of God.'"[1781] For valuable overviews of a range of different interpretations for the term "sons of God" in this context, see Wright[1782] and Collins.[1783]

E-103   Of relevance is the fact that the major doctrinal themes that preceded this reference included the physical details of the resurrected body ("the Spirit of God flowing in the veins instead of the blood") and the condemnation of "those who know the Gospel and do not obey" to "prison" as described in Isaiah 23.

E-104   In place of Grébaut's translation that these angels "openly exposed all the work they had seen in heaven,"[1784] Budge renders this to say that: "these made symbols of everything which they saw in the heavens."[1785]

The insertion of the phrase "in their bodies" in the translation from the French above was inferred from the subsequent lines: "The sin, they learned it because of their pride, because they received bodies. Therefore, it is not meet that man should glory in himself. Happy is he who conquers Satan while yet being in the body."[1786] Budge gives his translation of the Ethiopic of this passage as: "… and they taught sin because of their pride and boastfulness, because they had clothed themselves with flesh, but it was unseemly for men to boast themselves because of this. Blessed is the man who having put on flesh conquereth Satan."[1787]

E-105   Besides the unauthorized revealing of the mysteries, the three sins specifically mentioned in these texts are drunkenness, fornication, and murder.[1788]

E-106   In this context, Islamic tradition also speaks of "charms and incantations" written by demons "during the period of the decline of the reign of Solomon" and buried in a manner that they could later be found by the people.[1789]

E-107   For example, Ginzberg cites Rabbi Bahya as saying: "The Tree of Knowledge and the Tree of Life were both in the center of the Garden, for they formed one tree at the bottom, and branched out into two when they reached a certain height."[1790] In some Jewish accounts, the Tree of Knowledge was seen as a jgrape vine entwining the Tree of Life.[1791]

A fifteenth-century Armenian Christian poem sees the Tree of Life as being hidden by the Tree of Knowledge:

1778 Brock in Ephrem the Syrian, *Paradise*, p. 189 n. 1:11.

1779 Cf. Moses 7:17.

1780 Ephrem the Syrian, *Paradise*, 1:11, pp. 81-82. See S. C. Malan, *Adam and Eve*, 3:4, p. 147; H. W. Nibley, *Enoch*, pp. 178-193; *Commentary* 5:41-b, p. 388.

1781 J. C. Reeves, *Eutychii*.

1782 A. T. Wright, *Evil Spirits*, pp. 61-75.

1783 J. J. Collins, *Sons of God*, pp. 260-263.

1784 French *Ceux-ci ont donc fait voir toute l'œuvre qu'ils avaient vue dans le ciel.*

1785 B. Mika'el, *Enoch*, p. 142.

1786 French *Le péché, ils (l')ont appris à cause de leur orgueil, parce qu'ils avaient revêtu un corps. C'est pourquoi il ne convient pas à l'homme de se glorifier. Bienheureux est celui qui vainc Satan, tout en étant revêtu d'un corps.*

1787 B. Mika'el, *Enoch*, p. 142.

1788 A. al-Tha'labi, *Lives*, p. 88.

1789 *Ibid.*, p. 86. See *Commentary* 5:51-a, p. 398.

1790 L. Ginzberg, *Legends*, 5:91 n. 50.

1791 J. A. Tvedtnes, *Olive Oil*, p. 430.

> The tree that was planted in the garden,
> Had two branches and one trunk,
> The one the good fruit of life,
> And the other evil, dealing death.
>
> The serpent was grafted onto the tree,
> Hiding the branches of the Tree of Life,
> But leaving the one of death outside,[1792]
> To be revealed to the first one's eyes.[1793]

The Manichaean *Kephalaia* describes the trunks of the Tree of Virtue and the Tree of Evil as twisting around each other in two places. A similar idea may have motivated the depiction of a tree with three trunks in a Manichaean wall-painting from Bäzäklik, East Turkestan.[1794] This representation concords with other Manichaean ideas which see the Tree of Life as extending "over three regions of the cosmos—east, west, and north," while the Tree of Death "exercises dominion over the south, a quarter depicted as the region below the Kingdom of Light."[1795] The symbolism of the three trunks may also be connected to the three sons of Noah of whom "the whole earth [was] overspread."[1796]

Qur'anic commentator Wahb bin Munabbih is cited as saying with respect to the single tree of Paradise in Islamic tradition: "The tree's branches were intertwined, and it bore fruit which the angels ate to live eternally. That was the fruit which God forbade Adam and his spouse to eat."[1797]

Ancient Chinese sources also describe a cosmic tree, the *Chien-Mu*, as featuring "nine tanglewoods, while underneath there are nine root twinings."[1798] The male and female divinities Fu Xi and Nü Gua are depicted as humans in their upper torso, with their lower serpentine bodies intertwined, perhaps suggesting a link between their iconography and that of the cosmic tree.[1799] The association between the intertwined trees and the twisting serpent recalls the story of the *caduceus* of Moses.[1800]

One strand of Jewish tradition holds that the branches of the Tree of Knowledge encircled the Tree of Life, and that "God did not specifically prohibit eating from the Tree of Life because the Tree of Knowledge formed a hedge around it; only after one had partaken of the latter and cleared a path for himself could one come close to the Tree of Life."[1801] Whitlock[1802] suggests a possible association with the *Pirke Avot* admonition to make a "hedge" or "protective fence" for the *Torah*.[1803]

E-108   Wrote Ephrem:

> In the very midst he planted / the Tree of Knowledge, / endowing it with wonder, / hedging it with dread, / so that it might straightway serve / as a boundary to the inner region of paradise. / Two things did Adam hear / in that single decree: / that they should not eat of it / and that, by shrinking from it, / they should perceive that it was not lawful / to penetrate further, beyond that tree…. / When the accursed one [i.e., the serpent] learned / how the glory of that inner tabernacle, / as if in a sanctuary, / was hidden from them, / and that the Tree of Knowledge, / clothed with an injunction, / served as the veil / for the sanctuary, / he realized that its fruit / was the key of justice / that would open the eyes of the bold / and cause them great remorse.[1804]

E-109   This reading of the Fall finds echoes elsewhere in scripture and tradition. In particular, Hendel makes the case that "the Primeval Cycle [Genesis 1-11] is characterized by a series of mythological transgressions of boundaries" between humans and God.[1805] For instance, the "same stress on a borderline between the divine and human spheres is found in… [the] passage on the Tower of Babel

---

1792 I.e., visible (M. E. Stone, *Adamgirk*, p. 74 n. 179).

1793 *Ibid.*, 3:10:12-13, pp. 73-74

1794 J. C. Reeves, *Jewish Lore*, front slipcover and p. 96ff.

1795 *Ibid.*, pp. 98, 167-174; cf. A. S-M. Ri, *Commentaire de la Caverne*, pp. 120-121.

1796 Genesis 9:19. See J. C. Reeves, *Jewish Lore*, p. 95-102 and *Excursus 24: The Watchers*, p. 585.

1797 Cited in al-Tabari, *Creation*, 1:106, p. 277; B. M. Wheeler, *Prophets*, p. 23.

1798 A. Birrell, *Mythology*, p. 233.

1799 See *Excursus 50: Fu Xi and Nü Gua*, p. 654.

1800 Numbers 21:4-9; cf. Exodus 7:8-12; John 3:14-15. See *Commentary 4:5-b*, p. 246 and M. Fishbane, *Myth*, pp. 288-292.

1801 R. M. Zlotowitz, *et al.*, *Bereishis*, p. 101, cf. p. 96. See also L. Ginzberg, *Legends*, 1:70, 5:91 n. 50.

1802 S. T. Whitlock, *9 June 2008*.

1803 M. Lieber, *Pirkei Avos*, 1:1, p. 13.

1804 Ephrem the Syrian, *Paradise*, 3:3, 5, pp. 91, 92. See *Excursus 51: The Five Lost Things of the Temple*, p. 658.

1805 R. S. Hendel, *Demigods*, p. 23.

[which] presents 'the tower whose top assaults the sky—a perfect and natural metaphor for the human assault on the divinely ordained cosmos.'"[1806] A similar assault in an opposite direction is evident in the story of the Watchers.[1807]

E-110 The Coptic Gnostic text *On the Origin of the World* compares the leaves of the Tree of Life to the cypress.[1808]

E-111 Following a brief analysis of references in the *Qur'an*, Ryen concludes the probability of a Tree of Life separate from the Tree of Knowledge in Islamic tradition.[1809] He associates the former tree with *Sidrat Al-Muntaha* located in the seventh heaven, from under whose branches Muhammad received one of his revelations.[1810] In another Muslim tradition that assumes two special paradisiacal trees, Enoch was said to have avoided death by seizing branches of the Tuba tree that hung over the wall of Paradise. This tree, "which is planted in the midst of the garden, and is known to be after *Sidrat Al-Muntaha*, the most beautiful and tallest tree of paradise."[1811]

Brinner identifies the *Sidrat* (= lote-tree) as one of a "varying species of a tree found in the Middle East and North Africa of the genus Ziziphus, bearing fruits used for food and medicinal purposes."[1812] Significantly, *Wikipedia* notes that "[t]he mythological lotus tree is often equated with *Z. lotus*, though the *Date Palm* is also a possible candidate."[1813] The term *Al-Muntaha* (= the farthest boundary), signifying the location of the Tree of Life, "is in Sufism a symbol of the point to which knowledge can take the mystic, beyond which true experience lies,"[1814] that served as the point of departure for Muhammad's ascent to heaven.[1815] The idea also evokes the image of the temple veil as "'the last barrier,' where 'he who grasps the mysteries' at last receives the crown."[1816]

Ryen associates the Islamic Tree of Knowledge with the one from which Adam and Eve were forbidden to partake.[1817] In addition, Ryen notes the mention of a curious tree springing out of Mount Sinai which produces oil,[1818] suggesting the idea of an olive tree, separate from the Tree of Life.[1819]

Finally, Ryen notes two other special trees in Islamic tradition: the tree of *Zaqqum* in hell,[1820] and the later tradition of the Tuba tree in the heart of the paradisiacal garden.[1821]

E-112 Hamilton observes: "That Noah even was able to plant a vineyard that produced lush growth is testimony to the lifting of the curse on the ground.[1822] Noah is not pictured as eking out a miserable, hand-to-mouth existence as he works among thorns and thistles. Of course, in order for the vineyard to grow, there had to be rain. But the rain has been a life-producing one, not like the earlier life-taking one."[1823]

E-113 Nibley cites an account recording that Noah's planting of the grape vine was commanded by the Lord and cites a parallel to "the most ancient of all recorded festivals, the wine feast of intoxication that celebrates the ending of the Flood":[1824]

1806 T. N. D. Mettinger, *Eden*, p. 127. Mettinger quotes from R. A. Oden, Jr., *Divine Aspirations*, p. 211.

1807 J. J. Collins, *Sons of God*, p. 263.

1808 H.-G. Bethge, *et al.*, *Origin*, 110:15-16, p. 179, quoted in Moses 3 *Gleanings*, p. 189.

1809 J. O. Ryen, *Mandaean Vine*, p. 220.

1810 See *Qur'an* 53:14.

1811 G. Weil, *Legends*, p. 53.

1812 A. al-Tha'labi, *Lives*, p. 28 n. 44.

1813 *Ziziphus*, emphasis mine. See E. S. Drower, *Adam*, pp. 7-8 for a similar argument in favor of identifying the Mandaean *sindirka* as a date palm.

1814 A. al-Tha'labi, *Lives*, p. 28 n. 44; cf. the idea of the "furthest mosque" (*al-masjid al-aqsa*), understood as the site of Solomon's Temple in Jerusalem.

1815 See *Qur'an* 17:1.

1816 H. W. Nibley, *Message 2005*, p. 436.

1817 *Qur'an* 2:35, 7:19ff.

1818 *Qur'an* 23:20.

1819 See discussion of the tree bearing oil in *Commentary* 3:9-g, p. 163.

1820 E.g., *Qur'an* 37:62, 56:52.

1821 E.g., W. Barnstone, *et al.*, *Mother*, p. 687.

1822 Genesis 8:21.

1823 V. P. Hamilton, *Genesis*, p. 321.

1824 H. W. Nibley, *Sacred*, pp. 578-579; cf. H. W. Nibley, *Abraham 2000*, pp. 475-476.

EXCURSUS

In the very old Christian *Apocalypse of Baruch*,[1825] we are told that Noah after the Flood hesitated to plant the vine, "for Adam was destroyed by it"—the grape being the forbidden fruit in many old Adam accounts;[1826] so he prayed for forty days with tears streaming down (an Enoch motif), until an angel appeared to reassure him: "Arise Noah, plant the vine; its bitterness shall be changed to sweetness, and its curse shall be changed to a blessing. What it yields shall be the blood of God."[1827]

In this instance, however, the vine is better understood as a representation of the Tree of Life than the Tree of Knowledge.[1828] Cohen, having explored the "symbolic meaning of wine in ancient cultures," concludes that Noah's actions in this regard have been completely misunderstood, the result of "biblical scholarship's failure" in explaining the meaning of the enigmatic incident.[1829] Summarizing Cohen's view, Haynes writes:

> Cohen explores Israelite and other traditions to elucidate a complex relationship between alcohol, fire, and sexuality. Drawing on this connection, he surmises that Noah's drunkenness is indicative not of a deficiency in character but of a good-faith attempt to replenish the earth following the Flood. Indeed, Noah's "determination to maintain his procreative ability at full strength resulted in drinking himself into a state of helpless intoxication." How ironic, Cohen notes, that in acceding to the divine command to renew the earth's population, Noah suffered the opprobrium of drunkenness. In Cohen's view, he "deserves not censure but acclaim for having played so well the role of God's devoted servant."[1830]

E-114 Brodie insightfully observes:

> There is no moral condemnation of [Noah's] drunkenness and nakedness—any more than of [Adam and Eve's] nakedness. The trouble starts therefore (both in Eden and here) not with the nakedness but with an intrusive visitor—the serpent… and now Ham…
>
> Then the intrusive visitors, the serpent and Ham, spoke to others, enticing them. But the reactions are diverse. While the tree's looks caused the couple to give way to the serpent, the two brothers, Shem and Japheth, resisted Ham/Canaan and his invitation to look.…
>
> As in the Garden, so here the emphasis on nakedness is followed quickly by judgment.[1831]

Though a variety of speculations have arisen to explain the severity of the condemnation received by Ham/Canaan, "there is no clear evidence that Ham actually did anything other than see the nakedness of his uncovered father."[1832] So concludes Hamilton:

> We are on much safer ground in limiting Ham's transgression simply to observing the exposure of the genitalia and failing to cover his naked father. Otherwise, the two brothers' act of covering their father's nakedness becomes incomprehensible. We deliberately entitled this section "The Nakedness of Noah" rather than "The Drunkenness of Noah." Noah's drunkenness is only circumstantial to his nakedness. It is Noah's nudity, not his inebriated state, which Ham saw, and then passed on to his brothers. His sin would have been equally reprehensible had his father been sober.[1833]

Nibley cites ancient accounts arguing that Ham's disregard for this father was part of an effort to steal Noah's priesthood garment and authority[1834]—a further parallel to Satan's attempts in the Garden of Eden. Because of the faithfulness of Shem and Japheth, they received the reward of special garments themselves.[1835] They had entered their father's presence facing backward as they restored his covering.

1825 H. E. Gaylord, Jr., *3 Baruch*, 4:13-15 (Greek), pp. 667, 669.

1826 E.g., L. Ginzberg, *Legends*, 1:168; M. Maher, *Pseudo-Jonathan*, 9:20, p. 45; H. W. Nibley, *Message 2005*, p. 308. See *Commentary* 3:9-i, p. 168.

1827 H. W. Nibley, *Abraham 2000*, pp. 155-156. See H. E. Gaylord, Jr., *3 Baruch*, 4:15 (Greek), p. 669.

1828 H. W. Nibley, *Since*, p. 189, 191-192; H. W. Nibley, *Teachings of the Book of Mormon*, 1:135, 137; E. R. Goodenough, *Dura Symbolism*, 10:200. The fruit of the Tree of Life is described as being like a "white grape" in M. Barker, *Joseph Smith*, p. 76; H.-G. Bethge, *et al.*, *Origin*, 110:15-16, p. 179; R. Milstein, *Stories and Illustrations*, p. 107; G. W. E. Nickelsburg, *1 Enoch*, 32:4, p. 320. See *Commentary* 3:9-g, p. 163.

1829 S. R. Haynes, *Curse*, p. 188.

1830 *Ibid.*, pp. 188-189. See H. H. Cohen, *Drunkenness*, pp. 8, 12.

1831 T. L. Brodie, *Dialogue*, p. 192.

1832 Ross in J. M. Boice, *Genesis 1-11*, pp. 397-398.

1833 V. P. Hamilton, *Genesis*, p. 323.

1834 H. W. Nibley, *Lehi 1988*, pp. 168-170; H. W. Nibley, *What*, p. 366; H. W. Nibley, *Vestments*, pp. 128-131; H. W. Nibley, *Message 2005*, p. 309.

1835 H. W. Nibley, *Vestments*, p. 129; Rashi, *Genesis Commentary*, 9:23, 1:97; cf. Numbers 15:37-41, J. Neusner,

E-115 In a temple context, there are important associations between the veil as the covering of the tent and the garment as the covering of the body.[1836]

E-116 Eden surmises: "No doubt the historical model closest to this is the *apadâna* of the Persian sovereign, the pavilion[1837] of the royal palace in which the King of kings sat in his throne to receive his subjects. In some texts of the Jewish tradition, the link which ties the description of the divine audience room to the earthly royal one is clearly shown. For instance, in the *Pirkei De Rebbe Eliezer*, an early medieval Midrash, we can read: '[God] let Adam into his *apadâna*, as it is written: And put him into the Garden of Eden to cultivate it and to keep it.'"[1838]

E-117 A fifteenth-century Christian text speaks of the "royal seat of the High-king in Paradise, in the very center of Paradise, moreover, where the Tree of Life was situated."[1839] Writes Barker:[1840]

> In the account of the life of Adam and Eve written at the end of the second temple period, when God returns to Paradise, the chariot throne[1841] rests at the Tree of Life and all the flowers come into bloom.[1842] The synagogue at Dura Europos depicts a king enthroned in a tree.[1843] The tree was inseparable from the throne itself. Reigning from the tree became a Christian theme, and the subject of controversy with Jews. Justin claimed that they had removed words from Psalm 96:10, which were important for Christians. The verse had originally been: 'Say among the nations "The Lord reigns from the tree,"' but he claimed, "from the tree" had been removed.

E-118 Compare the coupling of the terms "faith" and "faithfulness" with diligence in 1 Nephi 16:28-29, 17:15; Alma 32:41-43, and 38:3; and "heed" with diligence in Mosiah 1:16; Alma 7:26, 12:9, and 49:20.

> Brock notes that the Syriac term for "diligence" is "regularly used by early Syriac writers in connection with the parables of the laborers in the vineyard… and of the talents."[1844]

E-119 The Prophet Joseph Smith wrote:

> We consider that God has created man with a mind capable of instruction, and a faculty which may be enlarged in proportion to the heed and diligence given to the light communicated from heaven to the intellect; and that the nearer man approaches perfection, the clearer are his views, and the greater his enjoyments, till he has overcome the evils of his life and lost every desire for sin; and like the ancients, arrives at that point of faith where he is wrapped in the power and glory of his Maker and is caught up to dwell with Him. But we consider that this is a station to which no man has ever arrived in a moment: he must have been instructed in the government and laws of that kingdom by proper degrees, until his mind is capable in some measure of comprehending the propriety, justice, equality, and consistency of the same.[1845]

E-120 Other interpreters have downplayed the significance of the distinction between these the terms for love used in John 21.[1846]

E-121 "In this use of Peter's original name [i.e., Simon] some scholars see Jesus taking a certain distance from Peter. It seems that Jesus wants to make Peter feel that, before going further with him, he must first make a fresh beginning with him."[1847] "Jesus is treating him less familiarly and thus challenging his friendship."[1848] Does the Savior add the surname "son of Jonas [i.e., Jonah]" to the form of address to Peter as a subtle reminder of how he had temporarily abandoned his mission to again go fishing, just as Jonah had at first forsaken his mission to the Ninevites and taken to sea? Perhaps "Peter's

Genesis Rabbah 2, 36:6:1B, p. 31.

1836 A. L. Gaskill, *Lost*, p. 71. See also B. T. Ostler, *Clothed*; J. W. Welch, *et al.*, *Gammadia*.

1837 See *Endnote 3-57*, p. 210.

1838 G. B. Eden, *Mystical Architecture*, p. 22; cf. M.-A. Ouaknin. *et al.*, *Rabbi Éliézer*, 12, p. 82.

1839 M. Herbert, *Irish Apocrypha*, p. 6.

1840 M. Barker, *Temple Theology*, p. 89.

1841 See *Endnote 3-57*, p. 210.

1842 G. A. Anderson, *et al.*, *Synopsis*, 44(22):3-4, p. 62E.

1843 See E. R. Goodenough, *Dura Symbolism*, 9:79-89, 101-104, 11:iv, 73-77, 323.

1844 Ephrem the Syrian, *Poems*, p. 15 n. 7.

1845 J. Smith, Jr., *Teachings*, 22 January 1834, p. 51.

1846 J. R. Holland, *Lift*, pp. 121-123; T. W. Mackay, *Resurrected Lord*, pp. 464-467; H. N. Ridderbos, *John*, pp. 665-666.

1847 H. N. Ridderbos, *John*, p. 665.

1848 Brown, *Comm. II*, p. 1102, cited in H. N. Ridderbos, *John*, p. 665.

EXCURSUS

threefold profession of love for Jesus" in this passage is "intended to balance his threefold denial."[1849]

E-122   "The words... 'more than these' might refer to the way in which Peter has until now taken the lead in comparison to the other disciples, to Peter's earlier statement that he was willing to give Jesus his all,[1850] and to what Peter will experience in the future.[1851] In any case, thus formulated, this question is designed to let Peter know that loving and following Jesus can have more implications for him than he perhaps has thought and practiced in the past."[1852]

E-123   "Peter's affirmative answer is without hesitation, and appeals to Jesus' knowledge of him. The appeal does not have the sense of 'Why ask me? You know me, don't you?' Jesus' knowledge is, rather, the last thing on which Peter can base an appeal before Jesus. His own actions have witnessed against him, and 'more than these' seems to mock him more than justify him. All that is left to Peter is, 'You know that I love you,' an appeal to Jesus' knowledge of him as one of his own."[1853]

E-124   Commenting to the sisters of the Nauvoo Relief Society, Joseph Smith said:

> How mild the Savior dealt with Peter, saying, "When thou art converted, strengthen thy brethren."[1854] At another time, He said to him, "Lovest thou me?" and having received Peter's reply, He said, "Feed my sheep."[1855] If the sisters loved the Lord, let them feed the sheep, and not destroy them. How oft have wise men and women sought to dictate Brother Joseph by saying, "O, if I were brother Joseph I would do this and that"; but if they were in Brother Joseph's shoes they would find that men or women could not be compelled into the kingdom of God, but must be dealt with in long-suffering, and at last we shall save them. The way to keep all the Saints together, and keep the work rolling, is to wait with all long-suffering, till God shall bring such characters to justice. There should be no license for sin, but mercy should go hand in hand with reproof.[1856]

E-125   Madsen observes:

> It is interesting that the earlier revelations called Joseph [Smith] "my servant, Joseph." Later—presumably as he grew spiritually and became more worthy—we find the Lord speaking of him as "Joseph, my son." Finally, he spoke of the Prophet and others with him as "my friends." Servant, son, friend: three beautiful relationships. Not, I take it, stages in spiritual progress so much as levels of it; for in the end, those of us who are thoroughly committed to Christ remain servants, sons or daughters, and friends.[1857]

E-126   Riddle's image recalls the Mandaean poem that imagines souls being "'entwined' by the vine on their journey upwards."[1858]

Millet also comments on the effects of the gradual refining process of sanctification on our personal judgments:[1859]

> Perhaps it is the case that over the years the Spirit of the Lord works in a quiet, consistent manner to educate our consciences, enhance our perspective, and polish our wisdom and judgment. After all, the Prophet Joseph explained that an important assignment of the Holy Ghost is to convey pure intelligence through "expanding the mind, enlightening the understanding, and storing the intellect with... knowledge."[1860] It may be that one day we will look back on what we perceived at the time to be seasons wherein we believed we were required to make decisions on our own, only to discover that the Lord had been, through the honing and refining processes in our souls, leading us along paths of his choosing. That is, maybe we will learn that our own wisdom and judgment were not really our own.[1861]

1849 A. E. Harvey, *Companion 1970*, p. 393.

1850 John 13:37; Mark 14:29.

1851 John 21:18, 19.

1852 H. N. Ridderbos, *John*, p. 665; cf. John 21:18a.

1853 H. N. Ridderbos, *John*, p. 665; cf. John 10:14; Luke 22:32.

1854 Luke 22:32.

1855 John 21:15-16.

1856 J. Smith, Jr., *Teachings*, 9 June 1842, p. 241.

1857 T. G. Madsen, *Joseph Smith*, pp. 84-85. Compare Elder Hafen's suggestion of the slightly different sequence of servant, friend, son (B. C. Hafen, *Disciple's Journey*, pp. 299-301).

1858 J. O. Ryen, *Mandaean Vine*, p. 108; cf. M. Lidzbarski, *Ginza*, GL 3:26, p. 551:16-19. See *Endnote 4-66*, p. 316.

1859 R. L. Millet, *Alive*, p. 108.

1860 J. Smith, Jr., *Teachings*, 27 June 1839, p. 149.

1861 D&C 61:22, 62:8.

E-127 In all there are twenty-four buildings indicated on the two squares in the middle of the "city plat of Zion," including "temples" that will be used for "houses of worship, schools, etc."[1862]

E-128 The principle according to which "the Christian is to keep only what is reasonably necessary... and give the rest to the needy"[1863] was a well-documented practice among the first Christians, as was the concept of the "true fast," wherein the primitive Saints were counseled: "on the day you fast... calculate the price of the food you were going to eat, and give it to a widow or orphan or needy person."[1864]

E-129 "The theme of reversal was developed by Irenaeus in a system known as 'recapitulation,' showing how Christ was the restored Adam, Mary the restored Eve—the virgin who obeyed, contrasted with the virgin who disobeyed—and the cross the remedy for the ills of the Tree of Knowledge."[1865]

E-130 Islamic scholar Ibn Kathir also records the tradition that "Noah, when it was time for the Flood, carried Adam and Eve in the Ark and reburied them in Jerusalem."[1866] The *Ka'bah* in Mecca was also said to have been preserved during the Flood.[1867]

E-131 Holzapfel and Wayment note that "the Joseph Smith Translation at Matthew, Mark, and John changes 'skull' to 'burial,' suggesting that the term [Golgotha] has nothing to do with the place's appearance but with its function."[1868]

E-132 The site of the Church of the Holy Sepulchre has a long and complex history.[1869] Following the Bar Kokhba revolt that ended in 135 CE, the Roman Emperor Hadrian expelled the Jews from Jerusalem and commenced a new building program for the Roman city of Aelia Capitolina. This move was seen by Eusebius to be motivated, at least in part, by the desire to eradicate remains of the Holy City's sacred sites. Eusebius recorded that a cave at what later became the site of the Church, reputed to be the location of the Savior's tomb, was covered over with a pagan temple until its re-excavation by Constantine:

> It was this very cave of the Savior that some godless and wicked people had planned to make invisible to mankind, thinking in their stupidity that they could in this way hide the truth. Indeed with a great expenditure of effort they brought earth from somewhere outside and covered up the whole place, then leveled it, paved it, and so hid the divine cave somewhere down beneath a great quantity of soil. Then as though they had everything finished, above the ground they constructed a terrible and truly genuine tomb, one for souls, for dead idols, and built a gloomy sanctuary to the impure demon of Aphrodite; then they offered foul sacrifices there upon defiled and polluted altars. They reckoned there was one way alone and no other to bring their desires to realization, and that was to bury the Savior's cave under such foul pollutions.[1870]

The accounts of the Bordeaux Pilgrim[1871] (333 CE) and Egeria[1872] (381-384 CE) provide early first-hand perspectives from lay Christians about the site. Over time, "the church of the Holy Sepulchre would draw to itself all the symbolism, the cosmic symbolism, of the Temple itself, including the idea that the Temple was the Navel of the World, thus reestablishing Jerusalem as the pivot and center of the world, and distinctly downgrading the importance of the Temple Mount itself."[1873] Armstrong observes:

> When they visited Golgotha, pilgrims were now shown the place where Adam had been created by God at the beginning of time. Golgotha was thought to be on the site of the Garden of Eden. It had become a symbol which gave pilgrims that experience of returning to Paradise...[1874]

1862 J. Smith, Jr., *Documentary History*, 25 June 1833, 1:358-359. For more about the current state and future plans for the site of the temple complex, see L. C. Berrett, *et al.*, *Missouri*, pp. 22-36; R. O. Cowan, *Dot*, pp. 36-38, 199; R. O. Cowan, *Great Temple*.

1863 C. Osiek, *Shepherd*, p. 172.

1864 C. Osiek, *Shepherd*, 5:3 [56], p. 173.

1865 Irenaeus, *Proof*, 33-34, pp. 69-70; M. Barker, *Hidden*, p. 33.

1866 B. M. Wheeler, *Prophets*, p. 34. See also M. al-Kisa'i, *Tales*, p. 347 n. 69; al-Tabari, *Creation*, 1:162-163, pp. 333-334.

1867 al-Tabari, *Creation*, 1:164, p. 335.

1868 R. N. Holzapfel, *et al.*, *Final Hours*, p. 324.

1869 M. Biddle, *Tomb*; M. Biddle, *History*; C. Morris, *Sepulchre to 1600*; K. Armstrong, *Jerusalem*, pp. 153-193.

1870 Eusebius, *Constantine*, 3:26:2-3, p. 132.

1871 Included in Egeria, *Travels*, 594, p. 31.

1872 See *ibid.*, 30:1ff., pp. 151ff.

1873 J. M. Lundquist, *Temple of Jerusalem*, pp. 156-157; cf. Wilkinson in Egeria, *Travels*, p. 11.

1874 K. Armstrong, *Jerusalem*, p. 213. See *Endnote E-247*, p. 766.

The most recent LDS scholarship argues against the possibility of a connection between the site of the Church of the Holy Sepulchre and the Crucifixion.[1875] After more than a decade of study, Chadwick adduced evidence favoring the "Golgotha" site ("Gordon's Calvary") near the Garden Tomb as the place of crucifixion.[1876] However, he also concluded that neither the "Garden Tomb" nor location of the Church of the Holy Sepulchre was a viable candidate for Jesus' burial.[1877] For contrary opinions summarizing evidence supporting the plausibility of Constantine's Church as the burial site, see Biddle, Morris, Shanks, and Gibson.[1878] Obviously, no historical connection can be made with any of these sites and the burial of Adam and Eve. For a collection of statements by LDS Church leaders about holy sites in Israel, see D. B. Galbraith, *et al.*, *Jerusalem*, pp. 500-507.

E-133   For references to discussions of the veneration of "mystic caves" by pagans and Jewish Christians, see Eusebius.[1879] Cameron and Hall note that Eusebius' narrative, "with its elaborate insistence on three caves, and his stress on victory and salvation, leads him to emphasize the resurrection rather than the death of Christ, which was in any case the eastern understanding."[1880] Consistent with this emphasis (and perhaps the fact that the tradition had not yet taken hold), the cave of the tomb of Adam was not mentioned by Eusebius.

       Although Jerome had earlier accepted the Church as the site of Adam's burial, he later became critical of that view, no doubt being aware of the Jewish tradition that Adam was buried in Hebron:[1881]

> I have heard somebody expound how the place of Calvary is where Adam was buried and that it was so called because the head of the first man was located there... It is a nice story and ordinary people like it, but it is not true. For outside the city and the gate were the places in which the heads of criminals were struck off and they took the name of Calvary, that is of the beheaded.[1882]

       Though Ambrose accepted the story of Adam's burial at Golgotha, "the powerful influence of Jerome ensured that the Adam legend did not appear much in Latin literature before the time of the Crusades."[1883]

E-134   Note that the number eight, corresponding to the age of baptism, has long been used as a symbol of renewal.[1884]

E-135   For example: "There was among [the children of Seth] neither envy, injustice, nor lying; and their bond (pledge or faith...) was, 'No, by the blood of Abel.'"[1885] Also, Cainan on his deathbed is said to have blessed his children, and then declared: "I will make you swear by the holy blood of Abel that not one of you shall go down from this holy mountain into the camp of the children of Cain."[1886] In *The Cave of Treasures*, Seth is depicted as saying: "I will make you to take an oath, and to swear by the holy blood of Abel, that none of you will go down from this holy mountain to the children of Cain, the murderer. For ye know well the enmity which hath existed between us and Cain since the day whereon he slew Abel."[1887] An Islamic account records that when the news that some of the children of Seth were planning at last to descend from the mountain, "Yarad [Jared]... came to them and implored them—invoking God—to recall the injunction of their forefathers; he (also) adjured them by the blood of Hābīl [Abel]. Akhnūkh b. Yarad [Enoch, son of Jared] then stood up before them and said, 'Know that those of you who defy our father Yarad and violate the oath of our ancestors by descending from our mountain will never again re-ascend (it)!' But they insisted on descending, and after they had descended, they consorted with the daughters of Qābīl and as a result committed

---

1875   J. R. Chadwick, *Golgotha*. See S. Gibson, *Final Days*, pp. 116-122 for a view to the contrary.
1876   Cf. A. C. Skinner, *Golgotha*, pp. 122-123.
1877   J. R. Chadwick, *Golgotha*; cf. R. N. Holzapfel *et al.*, *Final Hours*, pp. 372-376; A. C. Skinner, *Tomb*, pp. 21-30.
1878   M. Biddle, *Tomb*; M. Biddle, *History*, pp. 28-31; C. Morris, *Sepulchre to 1600*, p. 28-31; H. Shanks, *Temple Mount*, pp. 40-44; S. Gibson, *Final Days*, pp. 149-165.
1879   Eusebius, *Constantine*, p. 276 n. 25-8; pp. 277-278 n. 26-2.
1880   *Ibid.*, p. 283 n. 30-1.
1881   See M. McNamara, *Targum Neofiti*, 23:2 and n. 1, p. 120; J. Neusner, *Genesis Rabbah 2*, 58:4, p. 297; M.-A. Ouaknin, *et al.*, *Rabbi Éliézer*, 20, pp. 127-128, 36, p. 224; H. Schwartz, *Tree*, 445, pp. 343-344; 639, pp. 504-506. A fifteenth-century Christian source has Adam being buried at Hebron, with his skull being washed to Calvary at the time of Noah's flood (M. Herbert, *Irish Apocrypha*, p. 16).
1882   Jerome, *Commentary on Matthew* 27:33, cited in C. Morris, *Sepulchre to 1600*, p. 28.
1883   C. Morris, *Sepulchre to 1600*, p. 28.
1884   J. Cabanot, *Thèmes*, p. 46.
1885   Saîd Ibn-Bat., cited in S. C. Malan, *Adam and Eve*, p. 227.
1886   E. A. W. Budge, *Cave*, p. 81.
1887   *Ibid.*, p. 76.

shameless perversions."[1888]

E-136 Paralleling the comparison between Abel and Jesus, the author of Hebrews had earlier compared the purifying power of "the ashes of an heifer" to that of the "blood of Christ."[1889]

E-137 See Szink for an LDS perspective on the question of the authorship of the book of Hebrews.[1890] While the cited reference of the Prophet's statement is evidence of "Joseph's belief that at least one specific idea expressed in Hebrews, the knowledge of Abel's sacrifice, came from Paul," Szink nevertheless seems sympathetic to the likelihood that, based on a range of other evidences, the book was written by a disciple of Paul rather than by Paul himself.[1891]

E-138 According to the book of Numbers, the sacrificial blood and ashes of a pure and perfectly formed red heifer were to be used for the purification of those who came into contact with a corpse. Believing that a qualifying red heifer has not been born since 70 CE when the Jerusalem temple was destroyed, some Jewish and Christian groups see the future sacrifice of such a red heifer as of much wider significance, heralding the messianic era and the rebuilding of the temple, and are actively working to breed such an animal[1892]—an effort that has led to much controversy and dispute.[1893] Dismissing the need for such an effort, some Jews claim that, "owing to the non-existence of the 'Sanctuary', there is now no justification for the ashes of the 'red heifer' or the 'water of separation'… prepared from these ashes," however others, including the Samaritans, insist upon the continued validity of these purification rites.[1894] From the perspective of Orthodox Judaism, because all Jews since temple times have "unavoidably been in contact with death," none can set foot on the Temple Mount or "can begin even the most preliminary work [there] until they have been purified by the ashes of the Red Heifer."[1895]

E-139 Significantly, in the *Qur'an*, the cow is not red but "intensely yellow, giving delight to the beholders,"[1896] inviting a comparison to the golden calf made by Aaron in the wilderness. Giving his perspective about the contrasting Jewish and Islamic expressions of these stories, Ali writes: "[A]s is clear from their worship of the golden calf, [the Israelites] were ordered to slaughter such cows as were usually let abroad and worshiped as sacred objects… the object being to root out cow-worship from among them. But whereas the biblical injunction to slaughter a heifer is a general injunction to be observed whenever an uncertain murder takes place or an unclean person is to be purified, the injunction as contained in the *Qur'an* points to the slaughter of one particular cow which was probably likely to become an object of worship. Indeed there is a striking resemblance between the color of the golden calf and the cow ordered to be slaughtered. The concluding words of the section show that, because of their reverence for that particular cow, the Jews were very averse to slaughter it."[1897]

E-140 In English, the direct object is indicated, not by an explicit term as in Hebrew, but by word order. Gallus writes: "On purely philological grounds, Luther's rendering of Genesis 4:1 cannot be disproved, and it became a guiding influence for the old Lutheran exegetes and theologians through the end of the 18th century."[1898] Hamilton likewise concurs that *et* "can can be used in two ways: as the preposition 'with,' or as the marker of the direct object."[1899] Boice notes that "*et* also occurs in the

1888 J. C. Reeves, *al-Yaqubi*. See also S. C. Malan, *Adam and Eve*, 2:11, p. 119.

1889 Hebrews 9:13-14. See A. A. Orlov, *Redeeming Role* for a discussion of a redemptive role attributed to Enoch.

1890 T. L. Szink, *Authorship*.

1891 *Ibid.*, p. 253. See also K. L. Barney, *NT Footnotes*, 3:53-55.

1892 K. Boren, *Winepress*; D. Rona, *Revealed*, pp. 155-158.

1893 Maimonides is frequently cited as a source of this belief: "Now nine red heifers were prepared from the time this commandment was received until the Temple was destroyed the second time… and a tenth will King Messiah prepare—may he soon be revealed" (*Commentary on the Mishnah*, Laws of the Red Heifer 3:4, cited in J. Neusner, *Without Myth*, p. 99. See also J. Neusner, *Mishnah*, 6 (Purities), Parah, 3:5, p. 1016).

1894 S. Lowy, *Principles*, p. 400.

1895 K. Boren, *Winepress*, p. 16. For LDS perspectives on events relating to the Jerusalem temple mount prior to the Millennium, see D. B. Galbraith, *et al.*, *Jerusalem*, p. 474-487; D. C. Peterson, *Abraham*, pp. 357-367. For Jewish perspectives, see W. J. Hamblin, *et al.*, *Temple*, pp. 199-203. See also D. N. Freedman, *et al.*, *Dome*. Note also the idea of the "pure heifer" as a title of honor applied to Mary in the Orthodox Church, as in their great hymn to her entitled "The Akathist." (M. Barker, *11 June 2007*).

1896 A. at-Tabataba'i, *Al-Mizan*, 2:68, 1:284.

1897 A. Ali, *Qur'an*, p. 33 n. 108.

1898 T. Gallus, *Der Nachkomme 1*, p. 124.

1899 V. P. Hamilton, *Genesis*, p. 221. The usual Hebrew term for "with " is *im*. When rendered as "with," *et* implies a relationship of "subservience" between the two entities related by the term; whereas *im* indicates "full companionship" and "equal partnership." See D. Fohrman, *Beast*, pp. 117-131.

front of the word 'Cain' earlier in the sentence, which puts the two parts in parallel construction. Together they read, 'She bore *et*-Cain, and she said, 'I have brought forth a man, *et*-Jehovah.'"[1900] Additional references to the literature surrounding various interpretations of the Hebrew of this verse are given in Westermann.[1901]

E-141 Cf. *Targum Pseudo-Jonathan*: "I have acquired a man, the Angel of the Lord."[1902] No doubt "the Angel of" was substituted as a gloss because the idea of the child actually being "the Lord" was inadmissible to the author of the *Targum*. Maher discusses this statement in light of the development of a separate tradition that Cain was fathered by Sammael (Satan).[1903]

E-142 Thus, writes Gallus, "Luther finds a parallel in the confessions of Eve 'I have the man, the Lord'[1904] and of Saint Peter 'Thou art the Christ, the Son of the living God.'"[1905]

E-143 Taking Exodus 6:3 to imply that the name Jehovah was not revealed until the time of Moses, Boice sees Eve not as "claiming to have given birth to God but rather would have been using the word in a broader sense meaning perhaps 'the one who brings into being,' 'gives life,' or 'delivers.' In this case, the best translation of Eve's words would be, 'I have brought forth a man, even the deliverer.'"[1906]

E-144 Likewise, it was said that Abel's "face... shone like the morning" as later did the face of Seth.[1907] Compare the description of Noah as a baby in the *Genesis Apocryphon*.[1908] Such a birth, as in the case of Noah, signifies the spiritual, priestly nature of the child as the "fully human bearer of God's image."[1909] Parallels in the *1 Enoch* account of the birth of Noah to various biblical figures, including Jesus Christ, are summarized in G. W. E. Nickelsburg, *1 Enoch*, 106:2, p. 536; cf. pp. 543-544 n. 1b-7. Parallels between Noah and Melchizedek in pseudepigraphal accounts are listed in A. A. Orlov, *Heir*, pp. 53-55.

Mandaean tradition records that Abel was "born miraculously, leaving his mother intact and appearing suddenly at her side."[1910]

E-145 It was also recounted that "Cain grew in one year more than any other child does in two years" and that "God also gave him the good fortune of complete faculty of speech" when he was "not even a year old."[1911]

E-146 A related sense of *cheirograph* is found in Colossians 2:14, where the Greek term should be translated "'bond'[1912] or 'bill of indebtedness' but not 'contract.' The text does not mention Satan or Adam and seems to say that at the Crucifixion, Christ erased the bill of indebtedness that humans had incurred by sinning and nailed it to the Cross."[1913] In other words, just as in Roman times cancelled bills were nailed up for display to publicly announce that the charges had been paid, so Christ was nailed to the cross to make it known to all that He had satisfied mankind's debt of sin. Symbolically, the handwritten bond of justice was annulled by the "writing" of the nails in the pierced hands of the Savior—Christ's *cheirograph* of mercy. Likewise, the bloody contractual *cheirograph* portrayed as having been unscrupulously procured by Satan from Adam will hold no sway over the righteous who fully accept and qualify for the covenantal *cheirograph* required of them by the redeeming Lord, who provided a substitutionary sacrifice.[1914]

1900 J. M. Boice, *Genesis 1-11*, p. 250.
1901 C. Westermann, *Genesis 1-11*, p. 291.
1902 M. Maher, *Pseudo-Jonathan*, p. 31 n. 2.
1903 *Ibid.*, p. 31 n. 2.
1904 Genesis 4:1.
1905 T. Gallus, *Der Nachkomme 1*, p. 124. See Matthew 16:16.
1906 J. M. Boice, *Genesis 1-11*, pp. 250-251.
1907 M. al-Kisa'i, *Tales*, p. 78.
1908 *1QapGen* 5:12-13 in M. Wise, *et al.*, *DSS*, pp. 92-93.
1909 C. H. T. Fletcher-Louis, *Glory*, p. 30; cf. pp. 33ff. and Philo, *Questions on Genesis*, 2:56, p. 141.
1910 E. Lupieri, *Mandaeans*, p. 47; cf. the birth of Melchizedek in F. I. Andersen, *2 Enoch*, 78:17-19, pp. 206-207.
1911 M.-B. Halford, *Eva und Adam*, p. 269; cf. Noah in E. Isaac, *1 Enoch*, 106:3, p. 86. See also C. H. T. Fletcher-Louis, *Glory*, p. 47.
1912 Cf. the fifteenth-century Christmas carol "Adam lay ybounden / Bounden in a bond" (*Adam Lay Ybounden*).
1913 M. E. Stone, *Legend*, p. 153. See also J. Chrysostom, cited in M. E. Stone, *Legend*, p. 155.
1914 I. Mika'el, son of Bakhayla, *Godhead*, p. 136; cf. S. C. Malan, *Adam and Eve*, 1:69, pp. 83-84. See also Cyril of Jerusalem, *Five*, 2:5, p. 148; B. C. Hafen, *Covenant*, pp. 75-84; S. E. Robinson, *Believing*, pp. 24-25. See also T. G. Madsen, *Suffering*, p. 234; pp. 240-241; Romans 8:17; 2 Corinthians 4:10; Galatians 2:20, 6:17; 1 Kings 18:28; Zechariah 13:6. See J. C. Robison, *Nails*, for a study of the use of nails in Roman crucifixions. See also T. G.

Seaich discusses participation in the sufferings of Christ with reference to the New Testament term *koinonia* (fellowship, communion, participation, sharing):

> In 1 Corinthians 10:16-17… Paul says that we gain *koinonia* with the Body of Christ by "taking part" (*metecho*) in the symbols of his Sacrifice; and in 2 Corinthians 1:7, he adds that we must have *koinonia* with his suffering in order to have *koinonia* with his glory. 2 Peter 1:3-4 similarly promises that through the proper "knowledge" of Christ we might become "partakers (*koinonoi*) of the Divine Nature. In the New Testament, the marks of "the dying of the Lord Jesus"[1915] were therefore said to be stamped upon the candidate, showing that he had been willing to "take up his cross and follow [Christ]"…[1916]

> What this means in terms of Christian behavior is that the old cult of animal sacrifice had been replaced by personal sacrifice.[1917] Thus Jesus, who was about to offer his life for the sake of his friends,[1918] asked Peter: "Wilt thou lay down thy life for my sake?"[1919] The Law of Sacrifice thereby became an integral and important part of the Christian Temple-cult, though internalized as the giving of self, the highest sacrifice of all…[1920]

E-147 In the Mandaean scriptures, not only Abel but also Seth precedes Adam to the grave.[1921] In contrast to Abel, Seth dies willingly in place of his aged father.

E-148 Some relevant secondhand statements have been attributed to Joseph Smith,[1922] though it is possible that these informants did not make a precise distinction between Eden and Adam-ondi-Ahman.

E-149 Goslee has written the most complete introduction to the words of the poem.[1923] Unfortunately, I was unable to obtain a copy of her article.

Strikingly absent from the preface are Blake's characteristic illuminations. For unexplained reasons, he removed the preface from later versions (C and D) of *Milton*. Blake's editors comment as follows:

> The removal of the Preface… may have been motivated by something in its contents that no longer suited Blake's conception of *Milton*. Fox suggests that the plate was omitted form copies C and D because its "stridency… contradicts the attitude of forgiveness and conversion that informs the poem itself" (26). Another possibility is that the Preface, with its appeal to "Young Men of the New Age" and call to "Painters!… Sculptors! Architects" (lines 12, 16-17), implies confidence in finding a wide readership for his poem, a confidence that Blake may have lost by the time he collated the two later copies.[1924]

Bindman observes: "Whatever his reasons for doing so, it is ironic that *Jerusalem*, the one Blake poem that is universally known (if imperfectly understood), should form part of a page which its author felt able to discard."[1925]

E-150 The music was written by Sir C. Hubert H. Parry (1848-1918) in 1916, and is best known today in the version orchestrated in 1922 by Sir Edward Elgar (1857-1934). As a hymn, its common name is *Jerusalem*, though proponents of the traditions connecting the church of Glastonbury to Joseph of Arimathea call it *The Glastonbury Hymn*.[1926]

"The Mormon Tabernacle Choir sang Blake's 'Jerusalem' in London in June 1998. Craig Jessop, the Choir leader, had served a mission in Britain and chose this song."[1927]

Madsen, *Sacrament*, p. 14.

1915 2 Corinthians 4:10.

1916 Matthew 16:24; cf. Alma 39:9: "cross yourself."

1917 For more on the cessation of the practice of animal sacrifice in early Christianity, see M-Z. Petropoulou, *Animal Sacrifice*.

1918 John 15:13.

1919 John 13:38.

1920 J. E. Seaich, *Ancient Texts 1995*, p. 888.

1921 E. Lupieri, *Mandaeans*, GL 1:1, pp. 191-194.

1922 L. C. Berrett, *et al.*, *Missouri*, pp. 8, 387.

1923 N. M. Goslee, *England's Green*.

1924 W. Blake, *Milton*, p. 40. For more on the background of Blake's "appeal," see H. Bloom, *Blake's Apocalypse*, pp. 304-305; N. Frye, *Symmetry*, pp. 316-323)

1925 W. Blake, *Illuminated*, p. 245.

1926 L. S. Lewis, *St. Joseph*, front matter.

1927 V. G. Swanson, *Grail*, p. 48 n. 15.

E-151   William Blake's first original work of art, produced in 1773 when he was 16, was a drawing entitled *Joseph of Arimathea among the Rocks of Albion*. When he re-engraved the drawing at a later date, Blake wrote the following about Joseph: "This is one of the Gothic artists who built the cathedrals in what we call the Dark Ages. Wandering about in sheepskins and goatskins, of whom the world was not worthy[1928]—such were the Christians in all ages."[1929] Of the painting, Ackroyd writes: "It would be too easy to say that it is as much a portrait of Blake as of Joseph, but there is no doubt that the engraving does coincide with some of the dramatically isolated and embattled voices that emerge in the poetry he was now writing... Here... is an image of all his youthful aspirations and ideals—the prophet, the Gothic artist, the heroic proportions out of Michelangelo, the vistas of remote antiquity, and, somewhere brooding within them, the figure of Blake himself."[1930]

E-152   "All his life he spoke of 'lost originals,' as if he were reaching beyond his own civilization to the simplicity and grandeur of a remote past... Blake was entranced and persuaded by the idea of a deeply spiritual past, and he continually alluded to the possibility of ancient lore and arcane myths that could be employed to reveal previously hidden truths... These were also very much the preoccupations of his period, when comparative mythology was often aligned with the wilder speculations of various prophetic sects,"[1931] such as the idea that the biblical patriarchs were incipient Druids.[1932] Notwithstanding self-interested attempts by members of these movements to clothe him as a disciple of one or another of them, according to Bloom, Blake remained "a poet, a revolutionary moralist, and a profound rebel against social, religious, political, and psychological conventions," and not "an antiquarian, a mystic, an occultist or theosophist, [or] a scholar of any writings beyond the Bible and other poetry insofar as it resembled the Bible":

> His references to esoteric traditions are few, and tend to be superficial when they are not mocking... [What] zealots... took, absurdly, for a literal truth of identification between Britain and Israel, Blake takes as an imaginative truth. All religions are one, and there is no natural religion. It follows that Druidism, the impostures of historical and institutional Judaism and Christianity, and Deism must be one, and that all true religion must be one also. In the same way, the cabalistic tradition of the *Adam Kadmon* or Divine Man must be one with Blake's myth of Albion, though in fact the actual cabalists would have been outraged at the humanistic "impieties" of Blake's myth, for their God was altogether transcendent.[1933]

E-153   Blake's treatise *All Religions are One* presented his "concept of 'Poetic Genius,' which inhabits all men,"[1934] while being "adapted to the weaknesses of every individual."[1935] "The religions of all nations are derived from each nation's different reception of the Poetic Genius which is everywhere called the Spirit of Prophecy."[1936] Thus, the "Jewish and Christian Testaments are an original derivation" from that same Spirit, and "all religions" in their original uncorrupted purity "have one source."[1937]

> For a concise overview of Blake's complex views on religion, see S. F. Damon, *et al.*, *Dictionary*, pp. 342-346. For a discussion of the Bible as "the single most important influence on Blake's life," see L. Tannenbaum, *Biblical Tradition*, pp. 3-24.

E-154   Referring to "The Bethlem [sic] Royal Hospital of London, which has been variously known as St. Mary Bethlehem, Bethlem Hospital, Bethlehem Hospital and Bedlam, ...the world's oldest psychiatric hospital. The word 'Bedlam' has long been used for lunatic asylums in general, and later for a scene of uproar and confusion."[1938]

E-155   "The American and French revolutions were largely Deist-inspired, and both appeared to Blake to be genuinely imaginative upheavals. He wrote poems warmly sympathizing with both, hoping that they were the beginning of a world-wide revolt that would begin his apocalypse... [Yet, the] attitude to life implied by [Deism] can have no permanent revolutionary vigor, for underlying it is the weary

---

1928   See Hebrews 11:38.
1929   Spelling and punctuation modernized.
1930   P. Ackroyd, *Blake*, p. 42.
1931   *Ibid.*, pp. 40, 51-52.
1932   W. Blake, *To the Jews*, p. 171. See also, e.g., P. Ackroyd, *Blake*, pp. 48-55, 98-104, 305, 327-328.
1933   H. Bloom, *Commentary*, pp. 934-935.
1934   H. Dubnick, *Poet as Prophet*, p. 87; cf. W. Blake, *All Religions*, p. 22.
1935   W. Blake, *All Religions*, p. 23.
1936   *Ibid.*, p. 25, spelling and punctuation modernized.
1937   *Ibid.*, pp. 26-27.
1938   *Bethlem Royal Hospital*.

materialism which asserts that the deader a thing is the more trustworthy it is; that a rock is a solid reality and that the vital spirit of a living man is a rarefied and diaphanous ghost. It is no accident that [Tom] Paine should say in [his *Age of Reason*] that God can be revealed only in mechanics, and that a mill is a microcosm of the universe."[1939]

E-156 "Albion" is a poetic name for ancient Britain or England, often used in Blake's writings. Appearing in medieval writings that cited Ptolemy[1940] and Pliny the Elder,[1941] it is related to the Latin *albus* (= white), a Roman allusion to the white cliffs of Dover. However, the origin of the term is Celtic, from a Proto-Indo-European root denoting both "white" and "mountain," and related to the Welsh cognate *elfydd* (= earth, world).[1942]

E-157 Bloom also sees in the "Chariot of fire" a "direct reference to Gray's vision of Milton in *The Progress of Poesy*."[1943]

E-158 "Blake adds 'to' before 'God' in Moses's exclamation."[1944]

E-159 Although nothing like this episode can be associated directly with the historic King Nebuchadnezzar (605-562 BCE), both Neo-Babylonian inscriptions and the *Prayer of Nabonidus (4Q242)* fragment of the Dead Sea Scrolls provide evidence of a pre-Danielic tradition associating a similar story with Nabonidus, the last ruler of the Neo-Babylonian Empire (556-539 BCE) and father of Belsharusur.[1945] In his prayer, the king tells of his suffering with an "evil skin disease" for a period of seven years by the decree of God, and at least one scholar has proposed that a lacuna in the text "originally described Nabunay's state as comparable to that of a beast,[1946] or that he was 'set apart from human beings.'"[1947] After appealing to gods of silver, gold, bronze, iron, wood, stone, and clay, his sins were forgiven by a Jewish healer after he finally prayed to the Most High God.

A similar healing blessing performed by Abraham with the laying of hands upon the head is described in the *Genesis Apocryphon (1QapGen)* 20:28-29.[1948]

E-160 Kerry summarizes:

The Magic Flute redefines allegorically the transgression of Adam and Eve, as a positive Fall (*felix culpa*), for Tamino is reborn as an Adam figure who begins his quest to find Pamina (Eve) and then they proceed together on a ritual journey to discover new knowledge, truth, and light in a priestly temple community."[1949]

E-161 Kerry writes:

Mozart's letters to Constanze at the time he was composing *The Magic Flute* are full of affection, at times playfully expressed through the words of the opera's libretto, and they are often signed *Ewig Dein* (Eternally yours) or use *ewig* in other endearing formulations such as *Dein Dich ewig liebender Mann* (Your eternally loving husband)."[1950]

E-162 To Miranda, Prospero avers: "I have done nothing, but in care of thee / (Of thee my dear one, thee my daughter), who / Art ignorant of what thou art."[1951] By means of their trials, Prospero "must uneasy make" the couple, "lest too light winning / Make the prize light."[1952] At the conclusion of Ferdinand's test, Prospero explains to him: "All thy vexations / Were but my trials of thy love, and thou / Hast strangely stood the test. Here, afore heaven, / I ratify this my rich gift."[1953]

1939 N. Frye, *Symmetry*, p. 66.

1940 'Alouion,' (C. Ptolemy, *Geography*, ch. 2).

1941 Pliny the Elder, *Natural History*, 4:30 (16), p. 350.

1942 *Albion*.

1943 H. Bloom, *Commentary*, p. 910.

1944 W. Blake, *Milton 1998*, p. 214 n. 43. See Numbers 11:29.

1945 . G. Martinez, *DSS Translated*, p. 289; L. T. Stuckenbruck, *Daniel*, pp. 104-106; J. A. Tvedtnes, *Nebuchadnezzar*; G. Vermes, *Complete*, p. 614; M. Wise, *et al.*, *DSS*, pp. 340-342. This is the biblical "King Belshazzar" (Daniel 5:22, 7:1, 8:1).

1946 Daniel 4:25b.

1947 L. T. Stuckenbruck, *Daniel*, p. 105. See Daniel 4:25b.

1948 F. G. Martinez, *DSS Translated*, p. 234; G. Vermes, *Complete*, p. 487; M. Wise *et al.*, *DSS*, p. 101.

1949 P. E. Kerry, *Initiates*, pp. 109-110.

1950 *Ibid.*, p. 128.

1951 W. Shakespeare, *Tempest*, 1:2:16-18, p. 1612.

1952 *Ibid.*, 1:2:452-453, p. 1617.

1953 *Ibid.*, 4:1:5-8, p. 1628. In this context, "strangely" denotes: "In an uncommon or exceptional degree, extraordi-

The Tempest, like other late plays of Shakespeare, both resembles and differs from the standard plot patterns to which audiences of his time had become accustomed:

> Comedies typically traced the trials of young lovers at the hands of a blocking agent (usually her father) and ended with the celebration of their engagement and a parental blessing. The main plot was often paralleled in the comic subplot... *The Tempest* at first glance follows this pattern... The audience's attention is consistently focused on the father... [However, t]he darker themes of Shakespeare's tragedies—regicide, usurpation and vengeance—are always near this comedy's surface."[1954]

E-163   "Let me live here ever! / So rare a wondered father and a wise / Makes this place paradise."[1955] For "wise," others read "wife," arguing that "it made better sense for Ferdinand to acknowledge Miranda's importance and that [the Folio's] compositor had misread a long 's.'"[1956] Countering, some critics observe that "biblical definitions of heaven excluded marriage...[1957] If Miranda was also in Paradise—the test implicitly includes her in the place where Ferdinand wishes to live forever—she would not have been his, or anyone else's wife."[1958] Notwithstanding, Vaughan and Vaughan argue that the reading of "wife" is "syntactically and logically sound," while observing that the "'wise/wife' conundrum" fittingly illustrates the many unresolved issues of interpretation in the play. They conclude that: "While *The Tempest* masterfully probes these concerns, it tenaciously resists solutions."[1959]

E-164   "The chief expression in the play of astonishment and delight is not that of the visitors when they first see the island but of Miranda when she turns away from the island to gaze upon the real world."[1960]

E-165   For example, though Righter, Orgel, Frye, and Vaughan and Vaughan describe a range of literary, cultural, and historical affinities to the drama in great detail and cite near-contemporary stories of sea voyages and shipwrecks in their masterful introductions to the play, not one of them mentions any association between the play and the opening book of the Bible.[1961] Battenhouse and Walter, however, briefly explore some of these associations.[1962]

Battenhouse writes in astonishment that so many have failed to see Shakespeare's Christianity, "despite his burial in a church and a Last Will that names Christ his Savior."[1963] King observes:

> Critics often don't see what there is to see in the greatest writers because they haven't the Gospel to see with... People look at Shakespeare and they find in him what they themselves are. So, if an agnostic looks at Shakespeare, he finds him an agnostic, and if a Roman Catholic looks at Shakespeare, he finds him a Roman Catholic, and so on. Nowadays, when most critics are non-Christian, they like to pretend that Shakespeare was not a Christian. But Shakespeare's plays exhibit all signs of being written in a Christian framework, with undisputed acceptance of such doctrines as were common to the Anglican and Roman Catholic churches: baptism, sin, repentance, forgiveness, the Atonement, and life everlasting."[1964]

Some specific aspects of Shakespeare's faith will forever remain unknown. Marx explains: "Given the dangers involved in maintaining any religious position during a period of sudden and violent shifts in what was considered orthodox, [Shakespeare's] reticence [to detail the points of his faith] was only prudent."[1965] As a consequence of Shakespeare's caution in this regard, it has long been a matter of debate as to whether his sympathies were more Catholic or Protestant. As Batson wrote in the introduction to a book of essays on Shakespeare's Christianity:

> Almost all of the authors see a Catholic or Protestant presence; most essayists think that Shakespeare depicts both positions in a given play, and others see either a decidedly Protestant

---

narily, oddly, extremely" (C. T. Onions, *et al.*, *Glossary*, p. 269).

1954 V. M. Vaughan, *et al.*, *Introduction*, pp. 9-10.
1955 W. Shakespeare, *Tempest*, 4:1:122-124, p. 1630.
1956 V. M. Vaughan, *et al.*, *Introduction*, p. 136.
1957 Mark 12:25, Luke 20:35. For evidence to the contrary, see J. E. Seaich, *Ancient Texts 1995*, pp. 939-949, 1010.
1958 V. M. Vaughan, *et al.*, *Introduction*, p. 137.
1959 *Ibid.*, p. 138.
1960 H. Fisch, *Covenant Pattern*, p. 217.
1961 N. Frye, *Tempest*; S. Orgel, *Introduction*; A. Righter, *Introduction*; V. M. Vaughan, *et al.*, *Introduction*.
1962 R. Battenhouse, *Dimension*; J. Walter, *Epilogue*.
1963 R. Battenhouse, *Introduction*, p. 1.
1964 A. H. King, *Religion*, p. 156.
1965 S. Marx, *Shakespeare*, p. 7. For historical background of these shifts, see N. Jones, *England*, esp. pp. 25-33, and P. Lake, *Identities*.

or Catholic thrust. An occasional writer portrays Shakespeare as one who, in his personal beliefs, lived and died a Catholic or a Protestant. For some of the essayists, Shakespeare as author provides insight into his culture (with the Catholic-Protestant struggle constituting a larger part of that culture). What is obvious is that not one fails to believe that the dramatist… is a consummate artist whose works reveal a Christian dimension.[1966]

All this being the case, it should not be surprising that Shakespeare's plays are filled with biblical allusions—he refers to 61 of its 66 books (plus 11 of the deuterocanonical books) by one count,[1967] with the four gospels being "easily Shakespeare's most-referred-to biblical books."[1968] In addition, references to the *Book of Common Prayer* and the *Homilies* are not uncommon.[1969] Since "most of the passages cited in the plays were not to those biblical books that were used in the liturgy or to the translation recited in church, but rather to the widely distributed Geneva Bible first published in 1560, [Shaheen] concludes that Shakespeare spent a good deal of time reading the Bible in private."[1970] Though his use of scripture, of course, was made exceptional because of his unique gifts as an author, Shakespeare's level of *familiarity* with the Bible was not as unusual in his time as it would have been in our own. As Daniell writes:

> Shakespeare knew the Bible with an understanding that is in most ways strange to us. So did his first audiences and readers.…
>
> Shakespeare quotes and refers extensively and with freedom, sometimes movingly… More interestingly, however, Shakespeare makes large assumptions about the biblical understanding of his ordinary hearers and readers: such assumptions have for a long time now been in another world from the modern. They allow him, for example, to follow New Testament thought into one of its sixteenth-century developments, that encapsulation of New Testament theology, particularly that of Paul, that became known as Calvinism, so that both *Julius Caesar*, to some extent, and *Hamlet*, certainly, written close together in 1599 and 1600, are in part Calvinist plays. That is a coloring that is invisible without the spectacles of ready familiarity with the Bible.[1971]

Portions of *The Tempest* show that Shakespeare was very familiar with the account of the Apostle Paul's shipwreck on the island of Melita, and with an impressive variety of Old Testament stories as well.[1972] Prospero's reassurance to Miranda "is phrased in the words of St. Paul: 'For there shall not an hair fall from the head of any of you,'[1973] and Jesus: 'all the hairs of your head are numbered: fear not therefore…'"[1974] In both shipwreck stories "not a hair perish'd" of any passenger.[1975] Shakespeare's description of the island includes a description of the "kindness" of the inhabitants,[1976] the gathering of sticks,[1977] of adders,[1978] and of worshiping a man as a god.[1979]

Other evident biblical allusions in *The Tempest* include the mention of a prophetic mantle[1980] and staff;[1981] the miraculous preservation of the garments of the wanderers;[1982] murder by knocking a nail into the head of a sleeping victim;[1983] and the name[1984] and role[1985] of Ariel. Regarding the latter, Vaughan and Vaughan observe that:

1966 B. Batson, *Preface*, p. xvii.

1967 N. Shaheen, *References*, pp. 769-826.

1968 D. Daniell, *Mind*, p. 10; cf. N. Shaheen, *References*, pp. 801-814.

1969 N. Shaheen, *References*, pp. 827-832.

1970 S. Marx, *Shakespeare*, pp. 3-4. See N. Shaheen, *References*, pp. 53-55.

1971 D. Daniell, *Reading the Bible*, pp. 158-159.

1972 J. Rees, *Bible*, pp. 34-39.

1973 Acts 27:34.

1974 S. Marx, *Shakespeare*, p. 21. See Luke 12:7.

1975 W. Shakespeare, *Tempest*, 1:2:217, p. 1615l cf. 1:2:30, p. 1612. See Daniel 3:27, Luke 12:7, Acts 27:34.

1976 W. Shakespeare, *Tempest*, 3:3:30-34, p. 1627. See Acts 28:3, 7, 10.

1977 W. Shakespeare, *Tempest*, 2:2:160, p. 1624. See Acts 28:3.

1978 W. Shakespeare, *Tempest*, 2:2:13, p. 1622. See Acts 28:3-5.

1979 W. Shakespeare, *Tempest*, 2:2:115, p. 1623. See Acts 28:6.

1980 W. Shakespeare, *Tempest*, 1:2:24-25, p. 1612. See 1 Kings 19:13, 19; 2 Kings 2:8.

1981 W. Shakespeare, *Tempest*, 5:1:54, p. 1632. See Exodus 4:2-4; Exodus 7 *passim*; Exodus 14 *passim*.

1982 W. Shakespeare, *Tempest*, 1:2:218-219, p. 1615; 2:1:61-65, 70-71, p. 1619. See Deuteronomy 8:4; Nehemiah 9:21; Daniel 3:27.

1983 W. Shakespeare, *Tempest*, 3:2:58-59, p. 1626. See Judges 4:21-22.

1984 Isaiah 29:1, Ezra 8:16.

1985 Isaiah 29:4.

Ariel is… an appropriate appellation for the powerful magus's agent who contrives a storm and a disappearing banquet. In the Bishop's Bible, the prophet declares that the altar of Jerusalem 'shall be visited of the Lord of hostes with thunder, and shaking, and a great noyse, a whirlwinde, and a tempest, and a flame of devouring fyre.'[1986] The prophet Isaiah continues, 'And it shalbe like as an hungrie man dreameth, and beholde, he eateth: and when he awaketh, his soul is emptie… For the Lord hath covered you with a spirit of slomber and hath shut up your eyes'[1987]—metaphors that are reified in [The Tempest][1988] when a 'strange drowsiness' possesses the Neapolitans and in [the stage directions following 3:3:52[1989]] when 'the banquet vanishes.' By 1611 Shakespeare probably had heard Isaiah 29 expounded in church and perhaps had read it at home; whether he turned directly to the Bible or drew on subconscious recollections while he wrote, the image of Ariel as the 'lyon of God' speaking through flood and fire reverberates in The Tempest.[1990]

The "revels speech" is sometimes seen mistakenly as evidence for Shakespeare's nihilism:

> Our revels now are ended. These our actors,
> As I foretold you, were all spirits, and
> Are melted into air, into thin air:
> And, like the baseless fabric of this vision,
> The cloud-capp'd towers, the gorgeous palaces,
> The solemn temples, the great globe itself,
> Yea, all which it inherit, shall dissolve,
> And, like this insubstantial pageant faded,
> Leave not a rack behind. We are such stuff
> As dreams are made on; and our little life
> Is rounded with a sleep.[1991]

From a Christian point of view, however, these lines are wholly inoffensive: the theme of the passing of this world is no surprise to the New Testament reader,[1992] "'the great globe' puns on Shakespeare's own stage, where no 'racks,' or theatrical scaffolds, will remain,"[1993] and belief in the resurrection assures Christians that "our little life is rounded not only in a sleep but also in awakening to a reality next to which the life we 'know' will appear as a dream."[1994]

Commenting on some of the greatest passages in Shakespeare's other plays, King writes:[1995]

> Fundamental Christian themes in Shakespeare are very often given the 'go-by' nowadays, but even the non-Christian critics more or less agree with the Christian ones on what the supreme passages in Shakespeare are: the reconciliation of Lear and Cordelia in King Lear;[1996] the final scene of The Winter's Tale (the reconciliation of the family);[1997] the death of Cleopatra;[1998] the finding by Pericles of his long-lost daughter.[1999] In some plays, for example in Hamlet, there are only a few lines of this sort. And in that play those lines aren't the end at all—they are in the first scene: the description of what Christmas does to the world.[2000] And in Measure for Measure, there are a few lines in which Isabella refers to the Atonement:
>
> > Why, all the souls that were were forfeit once,
> > And He that might the vantage best have took

1986 Isaiah 29:6; cf. W. Shakespeare, Tempest, 1:2:196-206, p. 1614.
1987 Isaiah 29:8, 10.
1988 W. Shakespeare, Tempest, 2:1:199, p. 1620.
1989 W. Shakespeare, Tempest, p. 1627.
1990 V. M. Vaughan, et al., Introduction, pp. 27-28. See also R. Battenhouse, Dimension, p. 253. Shaheen, very stringent in his criteria for inclusion, lists many additional allusions to the Bible in The Tempest (N. Shaheen, References, pp. 734-749), however, in contrast to most critics he doubts that Ariel should be among them (ibid., pp. 738-739).
1991 W. Shakespeare, Tempest, 4:1:148-158, p. 1630.
1992 1 Corinthians 7:31; 2 Peter 3:10-11; Revelation 6:14.
1993 J. Walter, Epilogue, p. 276.
1994 G. Slover, Analogical Reading, p. 260; cf. J. Walter, Epilogue, p. 276.
1995 A. H. King, Religion, p. 158.
1996 W. Shakespeare, King Lear, 4:7:43-74, p. 1289.
1997 W. Shakespeare, Winter's Tale, 5:3, pp. 1602-1603.
1998 W. Shakespeare, Antony, 5:2:280-313, pp. 1385-1386.
1999 W. Shakespeare, Pericles, 5:1:84-235, pp. 1507-1509.
2000 W. Shakespeare, Hamlet, 1:1:158-164, p. 1143.

> Found out the remedy. How would you be
> If He, which is the top of judgment, should
> But judge you as you are? O, think on that,
> And mercy then will breathe within your lips,
> Like man new made.[2001]

In these passages the true, the good, and the beautiful all come together.

As a footnote to King's citation of this passage, there is an interesting 1632 Folio "which between 1641 and 1651 was censored for the Inquisition by an English Jesuit living in Spain." Doctrinal excisions were made in many places, but the one play that was "cut cleanly out of the volume" was *Measure for Measure*.[2002]

On the sources and history of the exceptional appeal of Shakespeare within Mormon culture since pioneer times, see Tanner.[2003] During a commencement speech, President Gordon B. Hinckley spoke fondly of the days he spent as an undergraduate studying Shakespeare at the University of Utah, saying: "I brought with me today my old Shakespeare text from which I read so long ago in English 171. It is filled with wisdom…" After quoting *Romeo and Juliet*, he commended Miranda's words from *The Tempest*:

> In Shakespeare's *Tempest*, Miranda, speaking of the wrecked ship and its passengers, sadly says, "O, I have suffered with those that I saw suffer" (act 1, scene 2). I hope each of us will suffer a little as we look about and see how many others are suffering.[2004]

Later, President Hinckley reiterated his love for Shakespeare at an occasion honoring the establishment of the Gordon B. Hinckley Endowment for British Studies by the College of Humanities of the University of Utah.[2005]

As an aside, most modern readers will find it surprising "that the great majority of Shakespeare's quotations, allusions, and references derive from the standard books and curriculum of an Elizabethan grammar school."[2006]

E-166 "The Bible opens with the image of a stormy sea: 'In the beginning God created the heaven and the earth. And the earth was without form and void, and darkness was upon the deep, and the Spirit of God moved upon the waters.'[2007] Upon this buzzing, blooming confusion, onomatopoetically called *tohu wa bohu* in the original Hebrew, the speech of the Creator first imposes meaning on the polarities of light and dark, day and night, sea and land. Shakespeare's first words in the *First Folio* are: 'A tempestuous noise of thunder and lightning heard.' The universe of his plays comes into being as confused and desperate shouts hardly separable from the deafening roar of wind and sea out of which they arise. In the next scene a magical creator appears to give them meaning. The parallel may be accidental, since there is no evidence that Shakespeare himself planned the *Folio*, but it points to some essential similarities between the book of Genesis and *The Tempest*."[2008]

E-167 "Lynette Black's essay calls our attention to the number symbolism in Prospero's several references to completing his work by six o'clock. God in Genesis completed his work of creating on the sixth day, and in the sixth age of history (according to Augustine) He became Man to reform us."[2009]

E-168 As Adam was awakened to find Eve standing before him—having been created, like him, "in the image of God,"[2010] so Miranda is aroused from sleep to discover the "divine" form of Ferdinand[2011]— having recently averred that the subhuman Caliban was not in the least suited as a companion for her.[2012]

E-169 Parallels to later chapters of Genesis are also apparent. Comments Fisch:

2001 W. Shakespeare, *Measure*, 2:2:73-79, p. 560.
2002 D. Daniell, *Mind*, p. 2.
2003 J. S. Tanner, *Shakespeare*.
2004 G. B. Hinckley, *Utah Commencement*, p. 543.
2005 G. B. Hinckley, *British Studies*, p. 433.
2006 R. S. Miola, *Shakespeare's Reading*, pp. 3-4.
2007 Genesis 1:1-3.
2008 S. Marx, *Shakespeare*, p. 19.
2009 R. Battenhouse, *Dimension*, p. 253.
2010 Moses 3:21-24; 2:26-27.
2011 W. Shakespeare, *Tempest*, 1:2:410-420, p. 1617.
2012 *Ibid.*, 1:2:304-310, p. 1616; cf. Moses 3:20.

There are… echoes of the romantic matchmaking between Isaac and Rebekah,[2013] and between Jacob and Rachel,[2014] and there are strong echoes too of the story of Joseph and his brothers,[2015] and of Jacob's mourning for his son Joseph.[2016]

E-170 "Caliban will relapse at the first opportunity. Coincident with the Renaissance there will be a pagan reversion… No more will he serve his old master; he will turn back to the wildwood, to the dark primeval forest from which Prospero had painfully led him out into the light."[2017]

In some interpretations of the play, Caliban is taken variously as an oppressed innocent or as some sort of hero. Bloom, having reviewed a range of such views, concludes that although "Caliban has his legitimate pathos, …he cannot be interpreted as being somehow admirable."[2018]

E-171 In contrast with the biblical account of the Flood, Shakespeare's drama allows even the wicked to escape harm. It was Prospero's intent both to save their lives and to spiritually redeem them by bringing them to a state of sincere penitence.[2019]

E-172 "Prospero has more godlike attributes than any other Shakespearian character, reflecting that play's uniquely rich connection with the Bible. He is creator and destroyer, like the maker of Eden and the Flood; he is founder of a chosen line, like the God of Abraham, Isaac, and Jacob; he is the deviser of plagues and torments like the God of Exodus and Revelation, and like him the judge at the tribunal where all are brought for sentence."[2020] The Prophet Joseph Smith's description of the conjunction of justice and mercy in the character of God reflects in a perfect degree the qualities that some find paradoxical in the flawed character of the ultimately well-intentioned but all-too-human Prospero:

> Our heavenly Father is more liberal in his views, and boundless in His mercies and blessings, than we are ready to believe or receive; and, at the same time, is more terrible to the workers of iniquity, more awful in the executions of His punishments, and more ready to detect every false way than we are apt to suppose Him to be.[2021]

E-173 Prospero, like Joseph, is presented as one who has learned the magical arts ("wot ye not that such a man as I can certainly divine?"[2022]). Indeed, "*The Tempest* itself can be compared to one form of magic, the alchemical process. The title is the alchemical term for the boiling of the alembic to remove impurities and transform the base metal into purest gold…; if we see Prospero's goal as the transformation of fallen human nature—Caliban, Antonio, Sebastian, and Alonso—from a condition of sinfulness to a higher level of morality, the play's episodes mirror the alchemical process. Note particularly Prospero's alchemical language at the beginning of Act 5 ('My charms crack not'[2023]) to describe his project; by 'boiling' his enemies' brains,[2024] he attempts to transform their characters."[2025]

Vaughan and Vaughan note that "Prospero's strange powers have provoked emphatic critical opinions about their nature—benign or evil, or a precarious balance of both."[2026] They also correctly observe that "[o]ne's reaction to Prospero almost inevitably determines one's response to the entire play. In the eighteenth century, when the magus was perceived as an enlightened and benign *philosophe*, the play seemed a magical comedy; by the late twentieth century, when Prospero had come to be viewed as a tetchy, if not tyrannical, imperialist, the play itself seemed more problematic."[2027] Any evaluation

---

2013 Cf. W. Shakespeare, *Tempest*, 1:2:428, 448, p. 1617 and Genesis 24:16. See also Genesis 24:27.

2014 Cf. W. Shakespeare, *Tempest*, 3:1:64-67, p. 1625 and Genesis 29:20. See also W. Shakespeare, *Tempest*, 3:1:75-76, p. 1625.

2015 Cf. W. Shakespeare, *Tempest*, 1:2:450-453, p. 1617 and Genesis 42:9; W. Shakespeare, *Tempest*, 3:3:18-82, pp. 1627-1628 and Genesis 43:25, 43-45, 44:4, 15; W. Shakespeare, *Tempest*, 3:3:96-102, p. 1628 and Genesis 42:21; W. Shakespeare, *Tempest*, 5:1:106-111, p. 1633 and Genesis 45:1-4, 12, 15.

2016 H. Fisch, *Covenant Pattern*, p. 217; cf. W. Shakespeare, *Tempest*, 3:3:101-102, p. 1628 and Genesis 37:35.

2017 H. Fisch, *Covenant Pattern*, p. 215.

2018 H. Bloom, *Shakespeare*, p. 665.

2019 W. Shakespeare, *Tempest*, 5:1:28, p. 1632—"[t]he like figure whereunto even baptism doth also now save us" (1 Peter 3:21).

2020 S. Marx, *Shakespeare*, p. 10.

2021 J. Smith, Jr., *Teachings*, 27 August 1842, p. 257.

2022 Genesis 44:15. See also Genesis 44:5.

2023 W. Shakespeare, *Tempest*, 5:1:2, p. 1632.

2024 *Ibid.*, 5:1:60, p. 1632.

2025 V. M. Vaughan, *et al.*, *Introduction*, pp. 63-64.

2026 *Ibid.*, p. 62.

2027 *Ibid.*, p. 24.

of Prospero's art, of course, should take into account the fact that "[b]efore 1650… most magic… blended imperceptibly with orthodox Christian faith in the minds of common people."[2028]

Whatever else one might say about it, Prospero's quest for power and wisdom seems to have distracted him from his ducal duties in Milan and enabled him to vent his vengeful tendencies. We have nothing but his own words as grounds for an ethical distinction between his powers and those of the witch Sycorax. Indeed, "Sycorax's exile seems deliberately written in to the play to reflect upon Prospero's banishment. Her history contaminates Prospero's, to the extent that we might ask… whether Prospero was himself banished for practicing witchcraft."[2029] Write Vaughan and Vaughan:

> Prospero believes that just as his art is more potent than Sycorax's witchcraft, it is also morally superior. The distinction between the two types of magic is erased, however, in Prospero's speech of renunciation. As Jonathan Bate has argued, having his protagonist openly speak words that some in his audience would recognize from Medea's speech in Ovid's *Metamorphoses*[2030] was Shakespeare's signal that the magician's power is not really benign and must be rejected… if he is to return to Milan and resume his ducal powers…[2031]

Regarding the difference between magic and religion in the interpretation of images and other religious symbols, Kaplan writes:

> The function of an image is magical rather than religious whenever it is responded to as itself a locus of Power, and not a symbol of a power which in fact may be elsewhere or omnipresent. For their proliferation of images, neither Hindus nor Roman Catholics worship idols; but in all faiths, religious symbols are often vulgarized to magical uses. The Devil not only quotes Scripture; he can also wear a prayer shawl and phylacteries.[2032]

E-174 Marx explains:

> A creation myth represents genesis at several levels. The myth must both contain and be contained by the originating events it records. The creator it describes is prior to the creation, but also part of it, insofar as he is created by the text that describes him. The creator god, therefore, must be both the story's protagonist and its author. In its later passages and commentaries the Bible draws attention to this dimension of its opening. "In the beginning was the Word,"[2033] writes John the Evangelist. The first midrashic comment on the first word of Genesis states that God created Wisdom, meaning the Scripture itself, before he made the world. Psalm 139 implies that his book is a script that exists before it is performed: "Thine eyes did see me, when I was without form: for in thy book were all things written, which in continuance were fashioned, when there was none of them before."[2034]

> Likewise, there are suggestions that the character Prospero can be construed as the author of the script of *The Tempest* in which he is the subject. It is hinted by his proprietary anxiety about each scene, by his explicit role as author of plays within the play, by his farewell to his book in the last act, and by his direct address to reader and audience in the epilogue… That this character should be construed both as God and as author seems appropriate to a playwright's playful reflection upon biblical Creation.[2035]

E-175 King provides the following evaluation:

> Shakespeare's *The Tempest*, which is his last [solo] play, summarized, to me as an old man, what he has done throughout his whole life and what he is there saying farewell to, for his magic in putting things on stage was like Prospero's, and Shakespeare was not certain of the validity from a religious point of view of everything he had done. He, too, like Prospero, had sins of which to repent. Prospero studied too much magic; Shakespeare perhaps exercised too much magic. But it was not his wand that he was waving when he was writing the passages that I am going to quote; he was writing those under the inspiration of the Gospel.

2028 R. L. Bushman, *Beginnings*, p. 71. See also R. L. Bushman, *Family Background*, p. 13; R. L. Bushman, *Rough Stone*, p. 50; cf. J. M. G. Barclay, *Diaspora*, pp. 120-121.

2029 J. Kingsley-Smith, *Exile*, p. 228.

2030 Cited in W. Shakespeare, *Tempest*, 7:179-219, pp. 239-241.

2031 V. M. Vaughan, *et al.*, *Introduction*, p. 66.

2032 A. Kaplan, *Ritual*, p. 41.

2033 John 1:1.

2034 . Psalm 139:16; cf. Jeremiah 1:5.

2035 S. Marx, *Shakespeare*, pp. 23.

Prospero repents. He repents at the prompting of Ariel, who is not even a human being.

> *Ariel.* Your charm so strongly works 'em
> That if you now beheld them, your affections
> Would be come tender.
>
> *Prospero.* Dost thou think so, spirit?
>
> *Ariel.* Mine would, sir, were I human.
>
> *Prospero.* And mine shall.
> Hast thou, which art but air, a touch, a feeling
> Of their affections, and shall not myself,
> One of their kind, that relish all as sharply
> Passion as they, be kindlier mov'd than thou art?
> Though with their high wrongs I am strook to th' quick,
> Yet, with my nobler reason, 'gainst my fury
> Do I take part. The rarer action is
> In virtue than in vengeance. They being penitent,
> The sole drift of my purpose doth extend
> Not a frown further. Go, release them, Ariel,
> My charms I'll break, their senses I'll restore,
> And they shall be themselves.[2036]

But the moral channel in *The Tempest* is not Prospero; Prospero is a sinner who has to repent. So is everybody else in *The Tempest*. So are we all. But old Gonzalo is the man who rescued Prospero and Miranda from death and who sums up the play in terms of Providence, saying as it were, "Yes, Prospero. You were a magician to a point. You couldn't bring the ship near the island, but you could cause a storm. You could cause Ferdinand and Miranda to meet, but you could not make sure that they would develop between them the affection that was needed. This was Providence"… Here, then, is old Gonzalo:

> Was Milan thrust from Milan, that his issue
> Should become kings of Naples? O, rejoice
> Beyond a common joy, and set it down
> With gold on lasting pillars: in one voyage
> Did Claribel her husband find at Tunis,
> And Ferdinand, her brother, found a wife
> Where he himself was lost; Prospero, his dukedom
> In a poor isle; and all of us, ourselves,
> When no man was his own.[2037]

"And all of us ourselves, / When no man was his own." Those words summarize… the essential point about the Gospel, about the Atonement, about the kind of language we ought to use, about the kind of attitude we ought to take to ourselves, because we find ourselves when we are not our own. There is more than one sense of that in the play. The obvious sense is that they were restored to their senses after having been put out of them for a while by Prospero's charm. But the deeper sense is that they had lost themselves to find themselves, and that is what the whole of the play is about.[2038]

Observes Slover:

Gonzalo catches sight of the true shape of a story—a story which is also, in part, his history, in which he himself has played and is playing a part. He perceives the meaning of his existence transformed by having been caught up all along in a design which mere human wisdom could never conceive—a design capable of drawing community from division, riches from poverty, clarity from confusion.[2039]

E-176 Marx comments:

2036 W. Shakespeare, *Tempest*, 5:1:17-32, p. 1632.
2037 *Ibid.*, 5:1:205-213, p. 1634.
2038 A. H. King, *Style*, pp. 223-225; cf. A. H. King, *Language*, pp. 478-479.
2039 G. Slover, *Analogical Reading*, p. 262.

The final reconciliation in *The Tempest* is… qualified. Apart from all the celebration stand Antonio and Sebastian. These unregenerate schemers never apologize, and retain their witty cynicism to the last. In his final judgment scene, Prospero distinguishes "Holy Gonzalo / honourable man… a loyal sir"[2040] from the forgetful and frail Alonso, who is capable of contrition,[2041] and from Antonio, "most wicked sir, whom to call brother / Would even infect my mouth…"[2042] Though he forgives them all, he recognizes that there are people in whom self-interest, cruelty, and power-hunger remain ineradicable. His forgiveness of Antonio involves no expectation of Redemption or improvement. He, and others like him, must be continuously watched and controlled with tactics that appeal to their limited motives.[2043]

Orgel infers that "Prospero's art is Baconian science and Neoplatonic philosophy, the empirical study of nature leading to the understanding and control of all its forces."[2044] However, the events of the play demonstrate that such art, whether it be magic or science, works only to a point, since "the great scheme is not to produce illusions and good weather, it is to bring about repentance and reconciliation"[2045]—objects that can only be brought about through the free exercise of moral agency. Like the acts of God himself, Prospero's "transformations of will are never impositions; they presuppose a yearning for freedom in the will enslaved. As it is possible for Antonio and Sebastian to remain unresponsive to the 'solemn music' which gives the rest of the royal party comforting sleep; as it is possible for members of Shakespeare's audience to withhold the childlike make-belief upon which the play's power depends; so it is possible, apparently, to resist even the master magician."[2046]

Prospero's final abandonment of his art can be seen a concession to the masterful hand of Deity—though he has clumsily hewn with his "rough magic,"[2047] the ultimate shaping of events is God's alone.[2048] Prospero may with no qualms drown his book,[2049] because the book of Providence subsumes and mercifully overrules it.[2050] He may now unreservedly break his staff,[2051] because he knows that God reigns with infinite wisdom in the heavens.

E-177 Elder Marion D. Hanks is the source of the felicitous expression: "To believe in God is to know that all the rules will be fair, and that there will be wonderful surprises."[2052] Note that "Miranda is… aptly named with the feminine form of the gerundive of the Latin verb *mirror*, 'wonder,'"[2053] and "Shakespeare puns throughout *The Tempest* on the name":[2054]

But there is a less generally acknowledged, though commonplace, association between faith, love and the marvelous, for the redeeming, miraculous love of *caritas* is often conceived of as especially "wonderful," and consequently (via the Latin pun) "admired." St. Paul, for instance, writing to the Thessalonians, commends the faith and "charity of every one of you all towards each other,"[2055] promising that Christ will "be admired in all them that believe."[2056] The Douai version renders this "made wonderful," and the *Vulgate* has *admirabilis*. This grouping of words is conventional: in his universally read *Of the Imitation of Christ*, Thomas à Kempis has, for example, a chapter specifically "on the wonderful effect of divine love,"[2057] and he engages in several deliberate plays on the relationship between *caritas* and *mirabilis*. "Behold love's revelation!… O how admirable (*admirabilis*) is Thy work… for the charity (*caritas*) of Christ is never diminished."[2058] He commends the "admirable" grace of the sacrament which "enkindles… love (*affectum*)" earlier

2040 W. Shakespeare, *Tempest*, 5:1:62, 69, p. 1632.
2041 See R. G. Hunter, *Regeneration*.
2042 W. Shakespeare, *Tempest*, 5:1:130-131, p. 1633.
2043 S. Marx, *Shakespeare*, p. 38.
2044 S. Orgel, *Introduction*, p. 20.
2045 *Ibid.*, p. 51.
2046 G. Slover, *Analogical Reading*, p. 261.
2047 W. Shakespeare, *Tempest*, 5:1:50, p. 1632.
2048 See W. Shakespeare, *Hamlet*, 5:2:10-11, p. 1181; cf. 3:2:211-213, p. 1164.
2049 W. Shakespeare, *Tempest*, 5:1:57, p. 1632.
2050 Isaiah 46:10; Psalm 139:16.
2051 W. Shakespeare, *Tempest*, 5:1:54, p. 1632.
2052 M. D. Hanks, *Loving*, p. 65.
2053 V. M. Vaughan, *et al.*, *Introduction*, pp. 26-27.
2054 W. Shakespeare, *Tempest*, 1:2:427-429, p. 1617; 3:1:37-38, p. 1624; 5:1:170, p. 1634; 5:1:181-183, p. 1634.
2055 2 Thessalonians 1:3.
2056 2 Thessalonians 1:10.
2057 See T. à. Kempis, *Imitation*, 3:5, pp. 60-61.
2058 See *ibid.*, 4:2, pp. 135-136.

described as "charity (*caritas*)."[2059] In a similar vein we may recall John Donne's discussion of charity in *Holy Sonnet* XI: "O let me then his strange love still admire"[2060] or again *Holy Sonnet* XII, where he exhorts himself (and his readers) to "wonder at a greater wonder,"[2061] namely God's redemptive love. Although the association I am suggesting extends to *The Tempest* by inference, it does nonetheless offer grounds for a coherency in the "Miranda-Wonder" wordplay by permitting us to see Shakespeare's pun in context of a fuller meaning consistent with the play's total action.[2062]

E-178 The role of "Providence" is emphasized in the play—a word used only four times in all of Shakespeare, but twice in *The Tempest*.[2063] King notes that "Providence" was "[n]ot a safe word to use on the stage in those days, with ears listening to make trouble at court or in the city."[2064]

Superbly characterizing Shakespeare's idea of Providence, Driver writes:[2065]

> [In Shakespeare] the past does not, as in the Greek plays, dominate the present and bind it in the grip of necessity. The difference lies in the understanding of the future. In Shakespeare the future is open. It contains the possibility of the new, both as a result of action which man may take and as result of growth and the providential shaping of events which lie outside man's control. The future is open in Shakespeare in the same way that it is in the Bible—not totally uncharted and free for any type of action whatsoever, but full of beneficent promise and tending toward a final culmination which robs the past of its terror and gives significance to the choices of the present. Shakespeare's belief in history is not that of some present-day existentialists, to whom the moment of present choice is everything and an order in history nothing except anathema (and who therefore have no notion of history at all); rather he believes in an ordering purpose above the temporal process, indistinguishable in form from the Christian idea of Providence, which imposes the burden of choice upon man without abandoning history to chaos....
>
> In Israel there developed a belief, in spite of one national calamity after another, that in history itself there was revealed a divine purpose which would in time be brought to fulfillment. When, in that tradition, the crucifixion and resurrection of Christ was declared to be the very center of history, the story of mankind was turned into an historical drama. This is the tradition which bequeaths to Shakespeare his basic understanding of man. He seldom expresses it in overt religious language. His plays are not to be read as models of Christian doctrine. Yet it is true that the form of his plays is consistent with the biblical interpretation of man and the universe. Shakespearean man is embedded in the ambiguities and moral demands of history, while the Shakespearean dramatic action seeks its resolution in the fulfilling events of time.

E-179 Regarding the idea of a savior in Islamic thought, Ayoub writes further:[2066]

> ... Islam has no concept of sin and redemption analogous to the fundamental Christian view of fallen humanity and its need of Redemption. Yet Christ, as were all the messengers of God before and after him, was a savior in that he, by his message, helped to save humanity from error and to guide its steps further on the path to God, to whom we all belong and to whom we all shall return.[2067]
>
> Moreover, Shi'i Islam... has developed its own quasi-soteriological christology in the doctrine and role of the *imams*, the spiritual heads of the community... The *imams*, for the Shi'i community, are the true mediators between God and man. They were with God from the beginning as His first act of Creation. With them, the primordial history of all Creation began, and through them it will be finally judged and consummated...The twelfth and last of the *imams* will return at the end of time as the awaited messiah (*Mahdi*) to establish divine rule over the earth. Jesus, son of Mary, will also descend from heaven to aid him in this task, thus playing some part in the *imam's* final act of redemption and judgment.

E-180 Although the rubric to illustration 23 supplied by Halford indicates that "Seth... receives... a branch

---

2059 See *ibid.*, 4:1, p. 133.
2060 J. Donne, *Holy Sonnets*, 7:9, p. 176.
2061 *Ibid.*, 8:11, p. 177.
2062 P. Grant, *Charity*, p. 268.
2063 W. Shakespeare, *Tempest*, 1:2:159, p. 1614; 5:1:189, p. 1634.
2064 A. H. King, *Style*, p. 224.
2065 T. F. Driver, *History*, pp. 37, 40.
2066 M. M. Ayoub, *Christology 1*, p. 137.
2067 *Qur'an* 2:156.

of the tree of knowledge instead of the oil of mercy,"[2068] the fact that the branch in question is an olive branch that will eventually bear oil-rich fruit clearly implies that it was meant to represent a kind of Tree of Life. Likewise, in Islamic tradition, al-Kisa'i recounts that "[w]hen Seth had grown and come of age, God sent him a twig of the heavenly lote-tree (which is made of pearl), which had a fragrance like musk."[2069] "This tree, said to stand in the seventh heaven on the right hand of the Throne of God, is called *al-muntaha*, 'of the limit,' because it is the boundary beyond which even the angels do not pass. 'Pearl' (*jawhar*) can also be rendered 'substance, essence (*ousia*).'"[2070] One Muslim source recounts that Adam desired "the fruit of Paradise," but that his sons returned empty-handed.[2071]

In other elaborations on these ideas, a branch from the Tree of Knowledge—or more rarely, as in Lutwin,[2072] the Tree of Life—was said to have been planted on the grave site of Adam. Over one traditional site of "Adam's Grave," at the Tomb of the Patriarchs in Hebron, grows a date palm.[2073] In some Eastern Christian sources, three trees (pine, cedar and cypress) are said to have grown at this spot, and Abraham's nephew, Lot, is sometimes shown as tending them.[2074] Eventually, according to legend, the wood of the saving cross of Christ was to be hewn from this selfsame Tree of Knowledge.[2075] Note that restoring such a branch to its mother tree is the theme of Zenos in the Book of Mormon.[2076]

Jewish, Christian, and Muslim texts assert that Adam possessed a staff[2077] made from the Tree of Knowledge that was passed down through the patriarchs, and eventually came to Moses. The staff was said to be the instrument by which Abraham smashed the idols in his father's house, and later to have become the rod that Moses and Aaron used before Pharaoh.[2078] Though missing from the second temple,[2079] the staff was expected to reappear at a crucial moment in the last days: "Post-talmudic *midrashim* envision the royal Messiah engaged in a triumphal march to Jerusalem, endowed with the staff of Moses,[2080] and the *Qur'an* affirms that divine approval of royal leadership will be expressed in the miraculous manifestation of the 'ark (of the covenant)… and the relics (*baqiyya*) of Moses and the family of Aaron,'[2081] among which is numbered the marvelous staff."[2082] The "Masoretic text of Isaiah 11:4b also mentions a 'staff'… which the anticipated scion of 'the stem of Jesse'[2083] will use to smite the earth and to slay the wicked. The textual evocation in these particular passages of imagery conjoining messianic deliverance with a 'staff' readily encourages the ancillary idea that the future agent of deliverance, mirroring his ancient Mosaic prototype, will come equipped with a wonder-working 'staff,' perhaps even the very effective one previously wielded by Moses."[2084] In the meantime, the staff's concealment and later revelation is associated with Elijah.[2085]

E-181 Some Gnostic sources see the cross as a Tree of Life rather than a Tree of Knowledge. Ryen writes: "The tree motif is found about 80 times in the Nag Hammadi codices, and quite many of these examples talk about the cross as a 'tree.' But only Sylvanus[2086] says the cross is a Tree of Life. The Tree of Life is here connected to Christ who again is identified with wisdom."[2087] Ryen sees another possible

---

2068 M.-B. Halford, *Eva und Adam*, p. 281.

2069 M. al-Kisa'i, *Tales*, p. 78; cf. pp. 82-83.

2070 *Ibid.*, p. 347 n. 63.

2071 Ibn Damrah al-Sa-di in B. M. Wheeler, *Prophets*, p. 33.

2072 M.-B. Halford, *Eva und Adam*, pp. 281-282.

2073 N. Arnon, *Machpela*, p. 13. See *Figure 4-12*, p. 230.

2074 Abraham's oak of Mamre was also identified with the Tree of Life. See *Endnote 5-41*, p. 440.

2075 See *Excursus 36: The Legend of the True Cross*, p. 614.

2076 Jacob 5. See B. Gardner, *Second Witness*, 2:520-553.

2077 See *Excursus 51: The Five Lost Things of the Temple*, p. 658. See *Endnote E-253*, p. 768.

2078 See M. al-Kisa'i, *Tales*, p. 222; cf. pp. 78, 82-83, 347 n. 63. See also al-Tabari, *Creation*, 460-461, 464-465, 3:45, 50; A. al-Tha'labi, *Lives*, p. 294; S. C. Malan, *Adam and Eve*, pp. 217-218 n. 30; M.-A. Ouaknin, *et al., Rabbi Éliézer*, 40, p. 251; J. C. Reeves, *Trajectories*, pp. 187-199; Shelemon, *Book of the Bee*, 17, p. 24; Exodus 7:9-12. Compare the priestly staff of the Mandaeans (J. O. Ryen, *Mandaean Vine*, pp. 251-252).

2079 See *Excursus 51: The Five Lost Things of the Temple*, p. 658.

2080 H. Freedman, *et al., Midrash*, Numbers 18:23, 6:744.

2081 *Qur'an* 2:247-248.

2082 J. C. Reeves, *Trajectories*, p. 187; cf. pp. 198-199. See also al-Tabari's *Commentary*; Numbers 17:8, 24:17; Psalm 110:2.

2083 Isaiah 11:1.

2084 J. C. Reeves, *Trajectories*, pp. 198-199. See also Genesis 49:10.

2085 J. C. Reeves, *Trajectories*, pp. 197-198.

2086 M. L. Peel, *et al., Sylvanus*, 106:21-23, p. 390.

2087 J. O. Ryen, *Mandaean Vine*, pp. 216-217; cf. Proverbs 3:18, 1 Corinthians 1:30.

example in the *Gospel of Philip*.[2088]

E-182   For an unknown reason, the following passage giving a description of the central place of Atonement in the Old Testament temple was omitted from the French version of the LDS *Old Testament Institute Manual*:

> The lid, or covering, for the ark is described in Exodus 25:17-22. The King James Version translates the Hebrew word *kapporeth* (which means 'seat of atonement') as 'mercy seat.' The covering was made of solid gold and on it were formed two cherubim with wings which came up and overshadowed the lid or mercy seat.[2089]

There are, however, corresponding paragraphs in the LDS English Bible Dictionary and its equivalent in French, the *Guide des Écritures*, concerning the mercy seat/*propitiatoire* in the article on the Ark of the Covenant/*Arche de l'Alliance*.

E-183   Ibn Abbas traces the tradition of the ram back to Adam and Eve: "When God saw the nakedness of Adam and Eve, he commanded Adam to slaughter a ram… Adam took the ram and slaughtered it, then he took its wool and Eve spun it. He and Eve wove it. Adam made a cloak for himself and a shift and veil for Eve. They put on that clothing" in preparation for their departure to Mecca, where they were to build a House for Allàh.[2090] Abel was also said to have sacrificed a ram which, according to Abdallàh bin Uthman bin Khuthaym, "remained penned with God until he released it as a ransom for Isaac."[2091]

E-184   Truman G. Madsen writes:[2092]

> I tend to the view of Parley P. Pratt—that if you will go far enough back in your memory, and this is difficult because you have closed it off, you will find that on the earliest approaches you made, age four or five (you are supposed to be completely innocent in those years, but I have some memories that are not particularly innocent…), if you go back, according to Parley P. Pratt,[2093] you will find that your first approaches to temptation and sin were attended by a fantastic burning. "No," was the sensation, "no." And if you persisted, that became a fever. Then when you went ahead and did it (and you did), there was an after-burning of guilt. Had you hearkened to that, according to Parley P. Pratt, and honored it, you would have increased in light to the present day.

The Prophet Joseph Smith is said to have taught that: "If you will listen to the first promptings you will get it right nine times out of ten."[2094]

E-185   Note that in describing such a covenant the premortality of all mankind is implicitly assumed—though it is officially denied. The subtlety of this point is artfully expressed in Gianotti's description of the story's setting: "Prior to our very existence, save in the Divine mind, God is said to have summoned us all out of non-existence to stand before Him for a 'moment' that would mark us for all eternity."[2095] In this fashion, Gianotti affirms, "the knowledge of God is believed to have been woven into the very fabric of human nature."[2096]

Because Adam and his progeny forgot their covenant, "God sent down the contract and called on the angels as witnesses." For this reason, "God commanded that from that day on contracts be written and witnesses be called."[2097]

E-186   Islamic scholar Mahmoud Ayoub states similar views as follows:[2098]

> …[In] accordance with the principle of the Oneness of God the *Qur'an* calls on all the people of the Book, Jews, Christians, and Muslims, to come together to a unity of faith in and worship of God

---

2088 W. W. Isenberg, *Philip*, 73:15-19, p. 153. See also *Excursus 36: The Legend of the True Cross*, p. 614.

2089 *Old Testament Student Manual*, 1:148 (13-5); cf. Église de Jésus Christ des Saints des Derniers Jours, *Ancien 1*, 1:148 (13-5).

2090 B. M. Wheeler, *Prophets*, p. 31; cf. A. al-Tha'labi, *Lives*, pp. 62-63.

2091 B. M. Wheeler, *Prophets*, p. 39.

2092 T. G. Madsen, *Questions*, p. 156.

2093 I have been unable to find the source for Madsen's citation of Pratt.

2094 J. Smith, Jr., n. d., cited in T. G. Madsen, *Joseph Smith*, p. 103. Madsen cites C. L. Walker, *Diary*, p. 902 as his reference, but I am unable to find the quotation, or a similar statement, in that source.

2095 T. J. Gianotti, *Islamic View*, p. 89.

2096 T. J. Gianotti, *Islamic View*, pp. 88-89.

2097 A. al-Tha'labi, *Lives*, p. 81.

2098 M. M. Ayoub, *Introduction*, p. 3.

alone. It calls on them to repudiate all forms of idolatry, and particularly the idolatry of elevating other human beings to a level of equality with God.[2099] Within this unity of faith and worship, the *Qur'an* calls for a community of Scriptures, revealed by God, the Lord of all the people of faith in Him. Thus, in quest of this interreligious unity of faith, the *Qur'an* commands the Muslims to engage the people of the Book in the "fairest dialogue," and to say to them, "we accept faith in that which was sent down to us and that which was sent down to you. Our God and your God is One, and to him we are Submitters."[2100]

To this end, the *Qur'an* categorically condemns the arrogant boasting by any of the followers of all three monotheistic religions of the superiority of their faith over that of either of the other two communities[2101] …[The] criterion for acceptance with God is neither religious identity nor class nor gender but faith and good deeds.

…. [The] *Qur'an* came not to establish an Islamic empire but a community of faiths that would include Muslims, Jews, Christians, Sabeans, and any other faith community that claims to live by the four principles [of religion enshrined in a divinely revealed scripture, God's absolute Oneness, a dynamic faith in God and the last day, and righteous living]. In other words, I am convinced that neither the *Qur'an* nor Muhammad demanded that Jews and Christians abandon their faiths for Islam in return for living in peace and harmony with Muslims.

E-187 Al-Kisa'i has God describing the final judgment in terms that recall LDS teachings about the separation of righteous and wicked spirits until the time of their resurrection and final reward:[2102]

As for Adam's progeny, they too shall taste death in accordance with their deeds, which will determine their reward or punishment. The souls of the faithful will be in *Illiyyin* and the souls of the infidels in *Sijjin* until Doomsday [= the day of final Judgment], when all souls shall be sent back to their bodies to be resurrected and gaze upon me, all of them crowded together. Then they shall be dispersed to be rewarded or punished, every good deed tenfold and every evil deed singly.[2103]

In this context, *Illiyyin* (from *Uluw* = highness) and *Sijjin* signify respectively places of reward or punishment for the spirits awaiting reunification with their bodies, i.e., "the seventh heaven" ("paradise") or its opposite "the seventh earth" ("an eternal prison").[2104]

E-188 Jewish tradition also recounts an incident where Adam was shown all of his descendants, though no covenant is mentioned.[2105] However, the Dead Sea Scrolls *Rule of the Community* (*1QS*) 4:22-26 seems to convey a similar idea about mankind's premortal understanding of the Two Ways:[2106]

For God has chosen [the upright] for an everlasting Covenant and all the glory of Adam shall be theirs… Until now the spirits of truth and injustice struggle in the hearts of men and they walk in both wisdom and folly. According to his portion of truth so does a man hate injustice, and according to his inheritance in the realm of injustice so is he wicked and so hates truth. For God has established the two spirits in equal measure until the determined end, and until the Renewal, and He knows the reward of their deeds from all eternity. He has allotted them to the children of men that they may know good [and evil, and] that the destiny of all the living may be according to the spirit within [them at the time] of the visitation.

Though Islamic and Dead Sea Scrolls exegetes often see these parallel accounts as implying predestination,[2107] LDS thought favors interpreting premortal covenants and assignments as being made in accordance with previously-evidenced but still-malleable individual predispositions, coupled with divine foreordination.

E-189 Joseph Smith similarly referred to D&C 76 as a "transcript from the records of the eternal world."[2108]

2099 *Qur'an* 3:64.

2100 *Qur'an* 29:46.

2101 *Qur'an* 4:123-124.

2102 E.g., Alma 40:11-14.

2103 M. al-Kisa'i, *Tales*, p. 81.

2104 I. Ibn Kathir, *Tafsir*, 83, 30:70-77.

2105 See *Commentary* 1:8-b, p. 50; E. D. Clark, *Prologue*, p. 138; D. C. Matt, *Zohar 1*, Be-Reshit 1:55b, pp. 310-311; *Talmud*, Avodah Zarah 5a, cited in R. M. Zlotowitz, *et al.*, *Bereishis*, p. 166.

2106 G. Vermes, *Complete*, p. 103; cf. F. G. Martinez, *DSS Translated*, pp. 7-8; M. Wise, *et al.*, *DSS*, p. 122.

2107 See, e.g., A. T. Wright, *Evil Spirits*, pp. 169-174.

2108 J. Smith, Jr., *Teachings*, February 1832, p. 11; cf. Ezekiel 3:1-3; Revelation 10:9-10; D&C 7 (heading).

EXCURSUS

E-190   For an overview of the history of relations between Islam and other religions, see Martin.[2109]

E-191   See Reeves for a discussion of how the "notion of Bible as 'sacred scripture,' as 'written *Torah*,' plays a crucial ideological role in the gradual shift in focus within early Judaism from a religion based on the sacrificial service of the Deity in the Temple to a religion which centers itself in the study and interpretation of a sacred scripture."[2110] Comments Bloom: "Unable any longer to walk in Eden or feast in his Temple, Yahweh resides in the Jewish Bible."[2111]

E-192   A haggadic passage cited by Rosenbaum "shows that [although] logical deduction had totally superseded any post-biblical prophecy which might be considered to be the direct word of God," post-biblical Jewish law is holy and binding. "At the beginning of the second century C.E., Rabbi Eliezer ben Hyrcanus, the brother-in-law of the Patriarch Gamaliel II, was involved in an argument of law with his colleagues:

> On that day, though Rabbi Eliezer brought forward every imaginable argument, they did not accept any of them. So he said to them, 'If the *halakah* agrees with me, the [stream of] water will prove [it].' [Immediately,] the stream of water turned around and flowed backwards.

> They responded, 'One cannot bring proof from a stream of water.'

> Again, he said to them, 'If the *halakah* agrees with me, the walls of the academy will prove [it].'

> The walls of the academy tilted [and were about] to fall [when] Rabbi Joshua scolded them saying to them, 'When scholars best one another in *halakic* debate [literally, 'in *halakah*], how is it your right [to interfere]?' [The walls thus] did not fall out of respect for Rabbi Joshua, but they also did not stand upright out of respect for Rabbi Eliezer. Indeed, they are still standing on an incline.

> Again, he [i.e., Rabbi Eliezer] said to them, 'If the *halakah* agrees with me, from heaven will come the proof.'

> [Immediately,] the still, small, heavenly voice went out and said, 'How can you have [a problem] with Rabbi Eliezer when the *halakah* in fact agrees with him in every case?'

> Rabbi Joshua then rose to his feet and cried, "It is not in heaven."[2112] What did he mean by this biblical quotation? Rabbi Joshua responded, 'Since the *Torah* was already given at Mount Sinai, we may no longer rely on a heavenly voice, for you [i.e., God] have already written in the *Torah* at Mount Sinai.' [Thus the rule is:] 'According to the majority one must incline.'

> Sometime later, Rabbi Nathan met Elijah [the Prophet]. He said to him, 'What did the Holy One, Blessed be He, do at that hour' [i.e., the hour of the dispute described above]?

> [Elijah] responded to him, 'He smiled and said, 'My children have bested me, my children have bested me.'[2113]

While this *aggadah* is often quoted, the material, which follows it is not: Rabbi Eliezer was excommunicated for attempting to use prophetic means to prove his argument and thereby deny the authority of the majority.

In a modern epilogue the Hazon Ish [Abraham Y. Karelitz, 1878-1953], a leading *halakic* authority of the [twentieth] century, ruled that even if the actual *Torah* which Moses received were discovered and found to be different from the Masoretic Text, it would be *halakically* irrelevant and the developed law would require no emendation. Thus, we have definite support—ancient and modern—for the holiness of post-biblical Jewish law.[2114]

E-193   Significantly, in both Mandaean and Manichaean writings, the term "Tree of Life" was applied, not to characterize scripture, but rather to represent "exemplary bearers of revelation in salvation history (for example, Jesus or Mani… [or specially chosen individuals who receive their commissions as 'apostles of light']). One detects a subtle shift here from the Jewish conceptions of the 'plant' or 'tree' being nourished by revelation (*Torah*) to the 'plant' as an actual bearer of revelation, a 'shoot' or 'fruit,'

2109   R. C. Martin, *Encyclopedia*, 2:360-364.
2110   J. C. Reeves, *Flowing Stream*.
2111   H. Bloom, *American Religion*, p. 123.
2112   Deuteronomy 30:12.
2113   *B. Mes* 59b, cited in J. Rosenbaum, *Judaism*, pp. 18-19.
2114   J. Rosenbaum, *Judaism*, pp. 18-19.

so to speak, of the original heavenly Tree of Life transplanted among humanity to propagate more of its own kind."[2115]

By way of contrast, a Sufi scholar writes that "Islam is based, like Judaism [and unlike Christianity], on a revealed message rather than on the messenger himself."[2116] Thus, Toronto's observation that the "Islamic equivalent to the Christian sacrament… is the act of imbibing the word of God through seeing, hearing, or reciting the *Qur'an.*"[2117] Bloom concludes: "Jesus as the incarnate Word replaced the *Torah* for Pauline Christianity; Muhammad voids that replacement, not by returning to *Torah* but by subsuming the Book within his own book."[2118]

Schäfer argues that talmudic accounts of Jesus' punishment in hell were specifically related to His setting His own pronouncements above the law of the Sages.[2119]

E-194 Note that the KJV translators were mistaken in rendering "search" as an imperative.[2120]

E-195 Bloom cites the following from von Rad:

> Actually, Israel conceived even Jahweh as having human form. But the way of putting it which we use runs in precisely in the wrong direction according to Old Testament ideas, for, according to the ideas of Jahwism, it cannot be said that Israel regarded God anthropomorphically, but the reverse, that she considered man as theomorphic.[2121]

Contrasting the ancient God of the Hebrew scriptures to His Middle East rivals, Bloom writes:

> Yahweh is a person and a personality; the godlings of Canaan are bric-a-brac, while Yahweh is a Divine Man and beyond that, and his favorites—Abraham, Jacob, Moses, David—are also theomorphic.[2122]

E-196 In related imagery from the *Apocalypse of Abraham,*[2123] Larsen notes Abraham's vision of the Garden of Eden:

> He sees there Adam and Eve "entwined" with each other, and Azazel between them. From this description, it [seems] that the text is trying to depict… a negative version of the divine *kavod.* Instead of having two cherubim entwined with the Lord between/above them,[2124] we have Adam and Eve (who were eating the fruit—transgressing) entwined with the Adversary between them.[2125]

E-197 Although some scholars identify the wife with Nü Gua, others express "reservations about the correctness of the identification."[2126] See p. 656.

E-198 The motivation for the theme of sibling incest as the means of populating the earth in primeval stories from many cultures is seen by Lewis as emphasizing "the theme of the shared substance out of which different beings emerged, with the brother-sister tie marking the extreme case of shared substance… out of which emerges all the different peoples who later occupied the earth."[2127]

E-199 Birrell notes in particular the "motif of shame and guilt" and the "fan covering brother and sister as the fig leaf covered Adam and Eve."[2128]

E-200 The *Huainanzi* (*Huai-nan Tzu*) says of this cosmic tree or pillar that "All the gods ascended and descended by it."[2129] The significance of this "stairway to heaven" is, according to Major that: "ritually and under some circumstances, one can restore the conditions of the world before time, the world

---

2115 J. C. Reeves, *Jewish Lore*, p. 102. A similar idea seems to animate messianic prophecies such as Isaiah 11:1, 10.
2116 A. B. S. Ed-Din, *Sufism*, p. 231.
2117 J. A. Toronto, *Islam*, p. 222.
2118 H. Bloom, *Genius*, p. 148.
2119 P. Schäfer, *Talmud*, pp. 82-94.
2120 H. N. Ridderbos, *John*, p. 203 n. 53.
2121 H. Bloom, *Genius*, p. 117.
2122 H. Bloom, *American Religion*, p. 132; cf. p. 99.
2123 R. Rubinkiewicz, *Apocalypse of Abraham*, 23:5-6, p. 700.
2124 J. E. Seaich, *Mystery*, pp. 5-23.
2125 D. J. Larsen, *6 December 2008*.
2126 D. Harper, *Warring*, p. 846.
2127 M. E. Lewis, *Flood*, p. 109.
2128 A. Birrell, *Mythology*, p. 34, cf. p. 203.
2129 *Ibid.*, p. 233.

before cosmic disaster and engulfing flood severed the bonds between humans and the gods."[2130] Summarizing a description of the sky-ladder from a first-century CE section of *The Classic of Mountains and Seas*, Birrell writes: "The *Chien-Mu* or Building-Tree is situated at the center of the world. It is an *axis mundi* where heaven and earth meet" conforming "in every respect with Eliade's paradigm of archaic cosmological beliefs that are 'invested with the prestige of the Center.'"[2131] Both the roots and the branches are said to be intertwined,[2132] and the text records that "T'ai Hao [whose identity later became confused with that of Fu Xi[2133]] used to pass up and down by it."[2134] Loewe writes that it was by means of this ladder that "Fu Xi and his sister ascended to heaven."[2135]

E-201   More precisely—and similar to religious traditions in other cultures[2136]—K'un-lun "appears as a place not located on the earth, but poised between heaven and earth."[2137]

E-202   Lewis observes:

> Many scholars… identify the tools as symbols of *yin* and *yang*. This argument, however, is not entirely persuasive, for the male Fu Xi holds the carpenter's square, which would be identified with the square earth and hence *yin*, while the female Nü Gua holds the circular compass, which would be identified with Heaven and thus *yang*. However the pairing of the tools themselves, abstracted from the question of their placement, could certainly serve as an image of *yin* and *yang*, and by extension of all correlate pairs formed through the process of division… One text states that Fu Xi lived in a time when all was chaotic and undivided, that is, a time much like that of the flood [n.b.: or the Creation], and that he used the carpenter's square to establish divisions and create the trigrams. The "Great Commentary" of the Yi states that the trigrams are square while the yarrow are round, thus making Yi divination a replica of the universe… While there is no explicit discussion of a link between Nü Gua and the compass, it could reflect the fact that her primary achievement in the flood myth… was to restore the circular heaven to its place.[2138]

Nibley compares the idea of the divine couple measuring the universe with square and compass to Pharaoh and Lady Seshat who would "lay out the foundation of a new temple by taking direct bearing on the stars with the proper instruments. The Lady was his one indispensable assistant on the occasion."[2139]

E-203   An intriguing similarity can be seen between serpentine depictions of Fu Xi and Nü Gua and a bronze statue of Isis-Thermouthis and Serapis-Agathodaimon from the Greco-Roman era found in the ruins of the ancient city of Cyzicus, located in what is now northwestern Turkey.[2140] Lyon observes that the tails of the figures "are tied together in the Hercules knot, a symbol of their eternal marriage. The hybrid style, Hellenistic heads on Egyptian cobra bodies, is a result of the desire to combine the most important elements of the great religious traditions then in constant contact with each other."[2141]

E-204   Sometimes various forms of a crow (the sun-crow or sun-chariot) appear on the face of the sun, in place of the twelve smaller circles.[2142] Allan argues that the sun-crow can be identified with the black bird from which the Shang claimed their tribe had sprung.[2143] Note also a separate tradition, later conflated with other bird themes, that the divine Queen Mother of the West (Xi Wang Mu) was served by one or three messenger birds (Qing Niao).[2144]

2130 J. S. Major, *Heaven*, p. 47.

2131 A. Birrell, *Mythology*, p. 232; cf. S. Allan, *Turtle*, pp. 98-101; J. S. Major, *Heaven*, p. 37.

2132 "For one thousand feet upward… there are nine tanglewoods, while underneath there are nine root twinings"; cf. the *Mu-lien-li* "whose growth stems from a pair of trunks" (M. Loewe, *Ways*, p. 111). See *Commentary 3:9-h*, p. 167; *Figure 5-3*, p. 330; *Excursus 25: The Tree of Life as the Hidden Throne of God*, p. 591.

2133 See p. 656.

2134 A. Birrell, *Mythology*, p. 233.

2135 M. Loewe, *Ways*, p. 111.

2136 See *Commentary 3:8-b*, p. 160.

2137 J. S. Major, *Heaven*, p. 156.

2138 M. E. Lewis, *Flood*, p. 127.

2139 H. W. Nibley, *Prayer Circle*, p. 74.

2140 A. Mordtman Jr., *Monuments*, p. 260 and plate IX, fig. 2; cf., e.g., *W56 Isis and Serapis*.

2141 M. P. Lyon, *Set Design*, p. 272.

2142 M. Loewe, *Ways*, pp. 53, 127-130; J. S. Major, *Heaven*, p. 159.

2143 S. Allan, *Turtle*, pp. 25, 39.

2144 M. E. Lewis, *Early*, pp. 191-192; cf. M. Loewe, *Ways*, pp. 130-131. See also *Commentary 1:1-b*, p. 42, 3:9-g, p. 165; 4:5-b, p. 246; *Figure 3-8*, p. 145; *Figure 6-14*, p. 473.

EXCURSUS

E-205 For more detailed descriptions of early customs related to the construction of Chinese tombs, see Lewis.[2145]

E-206 A passage from the *Huai-nan Tzu* (ca. 170-122 BCE) asserts "the most basic principle of Huang-Lao cosmography,"[2146] i.e.: "Heaven is round; earth is square."[2147] Oriented to the four cardinal directions, a "ritual chamber, with sacred trees at the four corners," represented the cosmos and served as a place where "shamans used such means as sacred animals, mountains and trees serving as an *axis mundi*, and music, dance, and hallucinogens to ascend to Heaven to meet with the deities and the ancestors."[2148] For more on the early Chinese model of the world and the cosmos (and related rituals), see Lewis and Major.[2149]

E-207 In the *Shujing*, the motivation for the damage to the pillar is described as being to "break the communication between earth and heaven so that there was no descending or ascending."[2150]

E-208 Separate accounts tell of how Fu Xi and Nü Gua became the ancestors of all humanity after the flood.[2151]

E-209 Yuan K'o characterizes Chinese myths as having been "preserved in literary amber, a disorganized way in a number of miscellaneous books" but then observes that this may not be a "total misfortune" since, as a result, "they have not suffered a complete reworking at the hands of literary authors or others. One might argue that in their present fragmentary state, preserved in a large number of classical books, they must appear as Greek and Roman myths once did before Homer, Hesiod, or even Ovid transformed, reshaped, and rewrote them. It is possible to argue that by an accident of history, Chinese myths remain in a more or less pristine condition."[2152]

E-210 See Lewis' not wholly convincing attempts at a rapprochement between the textual and iconographic versions of these figures.[2153]

E-211 Barker cites evidence that both the location and the orientation of the second temple was different from the first.[2154]

E-212 As examples of such suggestions, Barker cites several converging traditions.[2155] For instance, despite the fact that a Menorah was part of the second temple, rabbinic sources promised that the true Menorah (= the Tree of Life?) would be restored in the time of the Messiah. Moreover, *1 Enoch* said that the tree would be transplanted again to the sanctuary of the temple of the Lord, where it would feed the faithful after the judgment.[2156] Finally, in Orthodox Christian churches today one finds menorahs as tall as two meters in the sanctuary. Barker concludes that the Menorah was removed from both the temple and deprecated or ignored in later Jewish literature as the result of a "very ancient feud" concerning its significance.[2157]

Although the trees of Eden have been associated with the Garden Room of LDS temples since the time of Nauvoo,[2158] representations relating to the eschatological Tree of Life are centered on the Celestial Room. For example, the Celestial Room of the Salt Lake Temple is "richly embellished with clusters of fruits and flowers."[2159] The Celestial Room of the Palmyra New York Temple features a large stained-glass window depicting a Tree of Life with "twelve bright multifaceted crystal fruits."[2160]

2145 M. E. Lewis, *Construction*, pp. 119-130; M. E. Lewis, *Early*, pp. 189-200.

2146 J. S. Major, *Heaven*, p. 32.

2147 T'ien wen, *SPPY* 3:9b in A. Birrell, *Mythology*, p. 32.

2148 K.-c. Chang, *Eve*, p. 68.

2149 M. E. Lewis, *Construction*, pp. 245-305; J. S. Major, *Heaven*, pp. 32-43.

2150 J. S. Major, *Heaven*, p. 26. See also K.-c. Chang, *Eve*, pp. 70-71.

2151 M. E. Lewis, *Flood*, p. 123.

2152 Cited in A. Birrell, *Mythology*, p. xii.

2153 M. E. Lewis, *Flood*, pp. 131-133.

2154 M. Barker, *Hidden*, pp. 10-13.

2155 M. Barker, *11 June 2007*. See also M. Barker, *Christmas*, pp. 85-86, 140.

2156 G. W. E. Nickelsburg, *1 Enoch*, 25:3-6, p. 312. Mandaean scripture also describes a Tree of Life within the heavenly sanctuary: "They... lifted the great veil of safety upward before him, introduced him, and showed him that Vine," i.e., the Tree of Life (M. Lidzbarski, *Ginza*, GL 1:1, p. 429:3-20; cf. E. S. Drower, *Prayerbook*, 49, pp. 45-46).

2157 M. Barker, *Older*, p. 221, see pp. 221-232. For more on the symbolism of the Menorah, see M. Barker, *Gate*, pp. 90-95. Fine gives a historical overview of the use of the Menorah as a Jewish symbol (S. Fine, *Menorah*).

2158 D. F. Colvin, *Nauvoo Temple*, p. 220; S. B. Kimball, *Heber C. Kimball*, p. 117; M. McBride, *Nauvoo Temple*, pp. 264-265.

2159 J. E. Talmage, *House of the Lord*, p. 134.

2160 G. E. Hansen, Jr., *et al.*, *Sacred Walls*, p. 4.

Note the possibility that the first temple contained two kinds of lighted "trees," one kind that was visible to those standing in front of the temple veil, and another kind that was hidden behind it in the Holy of Holies.[2161] Such an arrangement would correspond with the successive gradations of light in the ordinance rooms of modern LDS temples, "each increasing in color, light and richness in their order to the climax in the Celestial Room."[2162] For example, in the Celestial Room of the Salt Lake Temple: "Eight electroliers [chandeliers] with shades of richly finished glass depend from the ceiling, and each of the twenty-two columns holds a bracket of lights in corresponding design."[2163] According to Nibley,[2164] the idea that the most brightly-lighted part of the temple would be entered at the completing step of the rites would have been familiar in several ancient temple cultures:

> [I]n the Jewish and Christian mysteries, …you go from the [darkness] to the day. It was imitated in the ancient temples in Egypt. You would go through darkness and trials and through three levels. Then in the final stage you went through a veil into a sunlit courtyard at noon day. Everything was white alabaster and absolutely dazzling in this celestial room. It was the same thing in the *epopteia* with the Greeks. You went into a room that was brilliantly lighted after you had been in the dark. It's called the *epopteia*, "the seeing of the light," the sudden vision that pops on you when you realize. This was dramatized in the Hellenistic Period under the Hermetic teachings. They adopted these things, mixed them up, imitated them, etc. That's another story. But [Alma's statement in the Book of Mormon is consistent with] the language they use: "I was in the darkest abyss; but now I behold the marvelous light of God."[2165]

E-213 Spinks also mentions "possibly putting on a white garment" as a rite that follows anointing.[2166]

E-214 Barker concludes that the book of Revelation "resembles much in the Gnostic texts, not because it is a late text with Gnostic corruption apparent, but because the original 'gnosticism' and the earliest Christianity were one and the same."[2167] The special knowledge imparted to the apostles, of course, disappeared very early from the body of the Christian Church itself.[2168] In light of this fact, it is not too much of an exaggeration for Lupieri to argue that "all cultured Christians at that time (according to the parameters of Hellenistic culture) were 'Gnostics,' the differences between them consisting in the content they each provided for the category 'knowledge.' Gnosticism, then, is the set of Gnostic doctrines declared to be heretical by the great Church, this Church being the one whose theology won out."[2169]

E-215 Nibley describes these "lessons" as follows: "These five things are the marks of his church and include the greeting of peace by which one becomes a son of peace, the grasp of the right hand which brings one into the church, followed by the embrace by which one becomes a son."[2170]

E-216 The confusion evident in the patterns and explanations offered in texts describing early forms of these rituals, the most basic of Christian ordinances, is striking. In his analysis of early sources (which bears the telling subtitle of "A Study in Diversity"), Paul Bradshaw concludes that:

> … we cannot really talk of a standard or normative pattern of early initiation practice in primitive Christianity.… What can be said to have emerged as common to rites by the time that the third century is reached, out of the apparent diversity of practice of earlier times, are certain fundamental ritual elements… but each of these still tends to take a different form and, at least to some extent, a different meaning in the various local or regional traditions, and they have been combined with one another in differing sequences, with the result that there are just too many variations in structure and theology to allow us to construct a single picture in anything but the very broadest terms. To emphasize what is common and to ignore what is distinctive of individual churches—or worse still, to force that evidence to fit some preconceived notion of a normative pattern—is seriously to distort our understanding of the variety of primitive Christian practice.[2171]

E-217 The Prophet Joseph Smith taught:

2161 See *Commentary* 3:9-g, p. 166 and *Excursus 25: The Tree of Life as the Hidden Throne of God*, p. 591.
2162 N. B. Lundwall, *Temples 1968*, p.193.
2163 J. E. Talmage, *House of the Lord*, p. 134.
2164 H. W. Nibley, *Teachings of the Book of Mormon*, 12 (41), 2:155.
2165 Mosiah 27:29.
2166 B. D. Spinks, *Baptism*, p. 25.
2167 M. Barker, *Revelation*, p. 403.
2168 H. W. Nibley, *Passing*; H. W. Nibley, *Evangelium*.
2169 E. Lupieri, *Mandaeans*, p. 34.
2170 H. W. Nibley, *Message 2005*, pp. 444-445; cf. p. 501.
2171 P. F. Bradshaw, *Search*, pp. 169-170. See also M. E. Johnson, *Christian Initiation*.

> Some say that the kingdom of God was not set up on the earth until the day of Pentecost… but, I say in the name of the Lord, that the kingdom of God was set up on the earth from the days of Adam to the present time. Whenever there has been a righteous man on earth unto whom God revealed His word and gave power and authority to administer in His name, and where there is a priest of God—a minister who has power and authority from God to administer in the ordinances of the Gospel and officiate in the priesthood of God, there is the kingdom of God…. Where there is a prophet, a priest, or a righteous man unto whom God gives His oracles, there is the kingdom of God; and where the oracles of God are not, there the kingdom of God is not.[2172]

On another occasion he said:

> The Savior has the words of eternal life. Nothing else can profit us… I advise all to go on to perfection, and search deeper and deeper into the mysteries of Godliness.[2173]

E-218 The idea of three degrees of initiation within primordial traditions from other cultures is discussed by Lundquist.[2174]

For arguments seeking to connect the Greco-Roman and Christian mysteries (as well as the practice of alchemy) to earlier precedents in Egypt, see, e.g., A. Roberts, *Anointing*, pp. 76-126. In the case of Christianity, she sees the *Gospel of Philip* as providing the strongest evidence for her arguments.

E-219 Caves are associated with ritual uses throughout the world.[2175] For example, according to anthropologist Bassie-Sweet, a specialist in Maya culture:

> The rites associated with caves were initiations related to social incorporation, such as baptisms or the entrance to adolescence or adulthood, and sociopolitical ceremonies, such as investitures and ascensions. Other rites involving exorcism and the cure of illness were also carried out in caves. As well, many mythological events were thought to have occurred at caves. A cave was the location of the birth of gods and races. The sun and moon were said to be born from a cave. The Aztec believed they originated from Chicomostoc (Seven Caves).[2176]

E-220 Observes Hayward: "Philo saw nothing improper… in describing Moses as a hierophant: like the holder of that office in the mystery cults of Philo's day, Moses was responsible for inducting initiates into the mysteries, leading them from darkness to light, to a point where they are enabled to see," i.e., to see God.[2177] Commenting on the idea of Moses as a hierophant and a representative (rather than idiosyncratic) figure of the wisdom seeker, Johnson points out that the story of the heavenly man in Joseph and Aseneth[2178] "shares the same sensibility" as Philo in this respect.[2179]

E-221 The extent to which Philo intended to imply a literal deification of Moses is a matter of scholarly dispute. Russell provides a useful history and overview of Jewish and early Christian beliefs relating to deification. While both admitting many evidences suggesting that Philo's view of deification might be taken at face value and recognizing the influence of Philo's teachings on later Christian teachings on the subject, he nevertheless agrees with the consensus of most modern scholars that "Philo is unwilling to say that Moses is a god except by title or analogy" and "maintains the biblical gulf between the human and the divine."[2180] Russell, however, does see acceptance of more literal ideas of deification analogous to early Christian views in some strands of Palestinian Judaism and later rabbinic mysticism.[2181] See Fletcher-Louis for a summary of the Dead Sea Scrolls literature pertaining to the deification of Moses.[2182]

E-222 Consistent with this view, Barker concludes that the "world of the first temple was the taproot of Christianity."[2183]

E-223 Elsewhere, Barker writes: "Philo… was aware of the older priestly traditions of Israel, and much in

2172 J. Smith, Jr., *Teachings*, 22 January 1843, pp. 21-22.
2173 J. Smith, Jr., *Teachings*, 2 May 1844, p. 364.
2174 J. M. Lundquist, *Fundamentals*, pp. 677-678, 680-681.
2175 See A. S-M. Ri, *Commentaire de la Caverne*, pp. 180-182 for a discussion of possible associations between Adam's Cave of Treasures and traditions from other cultures.
2176 K. Bassie-Sweet, *Cave*, p. 77, cited in B. Gardner, *Second Witness*, 2:66.
2177 C. T. R. Hayward, *Israel*, p. 192.
2178 C. Burchard, *Joseph*, 14-17, pp. 224-231.
2179 L. T. Johnson, *Religious Experience*, p. 90 n. 93.
2180 N. Russell, *Deification*, p. 64.
2181 *Ibid.*, pp. 65-76.
2182 C. H. T. Fletcher-Louis, *Glory*, pp. 136-149.
2183 M. Barker, *Hidden*, p. 33.

his writings that is identified as Platonism, e.g., the heavenly archetypes, the second mediator God, is more likely to have originated in the priestly traditions of the first temple."[2184] "Goodenough should have recognized that the 'Moses' mysteries were derived from the earlier Melchizedek mysteries, the original temple mysteries."[2185]

E-224   JST Exodus 34:1-2 reads: "And the Lord said unto Moses, Hew thee two other tables of stones, like unto the first, and I will write upon them also, the words of the law, according as they were written at the first on the tables which thou brakest; but it shall not be according to the first, for I will take away the priesthood out of their midst; therefore my holy order, and the ordinances thereof, shall not go before them; for my presence shall not go up in their midst, lest I destroy them. But I will give them the law as at the first, but it shall be after the law of a carnal commandment; for I have sworn in my wrath, that they shall not enter into my presence, into my rest, in the days of their pilgrimage."[2186]

E-225   Elder Joseph Fielding Smith wrote "that while Israel was restricted in the power of the priesthood from the days of Moses to the days of the ministry of our Savior, yet the prophets in Israel such as Elijah, Isaiah, Jeremiah, Ezekiel, and Daniel, were blessed with the Melchizedek Priesthood, but this priesthood was not given to others."[2187]

E-226   Blumenthal explains how this idea fits in the larger context of kabbalistic thinking, where the Tree of Life:

> … is constant, unified, having no internal split or dichotomy. In the sefirotic world of discourse, *Tiferet* [equated with the Tree of Life], which is the center of God's personality, is unity. To reach the level of meditating on *Tiferet* is to experience the transcendent unity of the divine. *Malkhut* [equated with the Tree of Knowledge], on the other hand, is the confluence of all the conflicting elements, and hence contains within itself conflict and contradiction. It turns over and over [like the "flaming sword"[2188]]; it changes its hues. One side of its nature is severity, war, evil, and death… Adam sat in the Garden, i.e., he meditated upon the *sefirot*. He saw unchanging *Tiferet* and changing *Malkhut*, and he was drawn to the latter. God warned him not to meditate on *Malkhut*, but he, following his wife, did so anyway. His sin consisted, first, in defying God's warning. But, as we have seen, he appears to have been distracted by *Malkhut* even before God issued His warning… Adam… wanted to have… divine power… Reflecting upon the fact that it may well be man's will to divine power (and not to divine unity) that motivates man, we can understand why meditating on *Malkhut* alone became the sin *par excellence* in the *Zohar*."[2189]

E-227   Barker notes that in:

> … Genesis 14:22: "I have sworn by Yahweh God Most High…" Yahweh here is identified as God Most High, *El Elyon*, but this reading occurs only in the Masoretic Hebrew text and the Targums based on it.[2190] All the other ancient witnesses do not identify Yahweh and God Most High. Melchizedek's God is simply "God Most High." In the Old Greek there is just "God Most High."[2191] The *Genesis Apocryphon* has only "God Most High."[2192] Josephus says that Melchizedek was a priest of God—no detail.[2193] *Jubilees* has a gap in the text at the point where we expect Melchizedek,[2194] of which O. S. Wintermute says…: "There is an obvious lacuna in the text at this point."[2195] Melchizedek is missing from the Ethiopic text, and also from the Syriac, which is otherwise extant for this portion. Philo says that Melchizedek was high priest of the Most High

2184   M. Barker, *Revelation*, p. 399; cf. M. Barker, *Beyond*.

2185   M. Barker, *11 June 2007*.

2186   S. H. Faulring, *et al.*, *Original Manuscripts*, p. 701, spelling and punctuation modernized; cf. D&C 84 cited on p. 668. Compare also Exodus 33:2-3 vs. D&C 103:19-20. See J. A. Tvedtnes, *Laws* for additional support for these ideas from scripture, pseudepigrapha, and the *Zohar*.

2187   J. F. Smith, Jr., *Answers*, 1957, 1:117-118.

2188   Moses 4:31.

2189   D. Blumenthal, *Merkabah*, pp. 144-145.

2190   E.g., M. Maher, *Pseudo-Jonathan*, Genesis 14:22, p. 58; M. McNamara, *Targum Neofiti*, Genesis 14:22, p. 93.

2191   C. Dogniez, *et al.*, *Pentateuque*, p. 173 n. 14:18, p. 174 n. 14:22; J. W. Wevers, *Notes*, 14:18, pp. 197-198; 14:22, p. 200; cf. Clement of Alexandria, *Stromata*, 4:25, p. 439; Justin Martyr, *Trypho*, 33, p. 211; Tertullian, *Jews*, 2, p. 152; Theophilus, *Autolycus*, 2:31, p. 107.

2192   F. G. Martinez, *Genesis Apocryphon* 22:21, p. 236.

2193   F. Josephus, *Antiquities*, 1:10:2, p. 34.

2194   O. S. Wintermute, *Jubilees*, 13:25, p. 84.

2195   *Ibid.*, p. 84 n. *f*.

God,[2196] but in his *Allegorical Interpretation* he hints at other aspects of Melchizedek.[2197] He was priest and Logos, an identification that he uses elsewhere for Yahweh when he appears in human form as the angel of Yahweh.[2198]

Reviewing the textual evidence, Davila proposes that the divinity of Melchizedek "was not invented in the Second Temple period; rather it was [an older tradition that was] suppressed in the Hebrew Bible."[2199] In considering the implications of the deification of Melchizedek, it should be remembered, however, that "Philo identified the Logos with both the Image (*Urbild*) and the Man after the Image (*Abbild*),"[2200] thus an appearance of the Logos can signify either an appearance of the Divine Logos, or His human representative, remade in the rite of kingship in the temple "after the image of mine Only Begotten."[2201]

E-228 Regarding Melchizedek, Barker observes:

> The Hebrew Bible describes him as a priest (*kohen*, Genesis 14:18), but the *Targums* avoid this term and say simply that he 'served' (*mešammeš*).[2202] This was anti-Christian polemic, denying the claim in Hebrews that Jesus was the great high priest like Melchizedek... Justin[2203] and Tertullian[2204] both claimed that Melchizedek was an uncircumcised priest, which meant that Christians could be priests without being circumcised, whereas the Jews claimed that he had been born circumcised.[2205]

E-229 The corrupted text of the verse 3 is an enigma for most commentators. For example, Alter implausibly takes "the womb of the morning" as an image of "an army sallying forth," and "the dew of thy youth" as possibly referring to "the fresh energy of a young king," since "the idea of giving birth to the king like (?) dew is puzzling."[2206] By way of contrast, Barker's conjectures about a messianic interpretation of Psalm 110 are enlightening:

> The Hebrew of Psalm 110 is notoriously difficult to translate, especially verse 3, where Yahweh makes someone a Melchizedek priest, but the process and the setting are obscured. The Greek text is a little clearer than the Hebrew: "In the glory of the holy ones... I have begotten you." To this translator, and so to the early Christians who used the Greek text, becoming the Melchizedek priest meant being born as the Son among the angels. In temple terms, this implies a ritual in the Holy of Holies, the place of the angels, in which the human became divine. The Holy of Holies represented the state of being that was both beyond and before the material creation, and this was where the Melchizedek priest was "born," as implied in Alma 13:3, the priests of the order of the Son were "called and prepared from the foundation of the world...," and Alma 13:5: "this holy calling prepared from the foundation of the world." The rest of Psalm 110:3 has become opaque in the Hebrew, and we have to ask why this might have happened. I suggest it was because this verse described the making of the ancient Melchizedek priests who were described as Sons of God. LDS scholars would recognise this, perhaps, as one of the plain and precious things that have been removed from the Old Testament we currently use....

> Psalm 110:3, a key text for Christians, describes the process by which the Davidic king became the Son, the process by which a human became Yahweh. Becoming divine was described as birth, but the Hebrew *yldtyk* is ambiguous, and is usually rendered in English as "your youth" [i.e., reading as *yalduteyka*]. The Greek translator, and thus too the early Christians, read the letters differently [i.e., reading as *yelidtika*] and understood it to mean "I have begotten you," *exegénnēsá se* [corresponding to the *Vulgate* "*genui te*"]. The place of this birth is also unclear in the Hebrew: was it "in glorious array," or was it "on the holy mountains." (Was it *behadrey* or *beharerey*, as in Psalm 87:1?) The Greek and Latin, which reflect the Christian understanding of the verse, understood

---

2196 Philo, *Abraham*, 11 (235), p. 431.

2197 Philo, *Interpretation* 3, 25-26 (79-82), p. 59.

2198 M. Barker, *Who was Melchizedek*.

2199 J. R. Davila, *Melchizedek*, p. 224.

2200 W. Williams, *Shadow*.

2201 Moses 2:27.

2202 See, e.g., M. Maher, *Pseudo-Jonathan*, Genesis 14:18, p. 58; p. 58 n. 44.

2203 Justin Martyr, *Trypho*, 19, p. 204.

2204 Tertullian, *Jews*, 2, pp. 152-153.

2205 M. Barker, *Who was Melchizedek*. See J. Neusner, *Genesis Rabbah 2*, 43:6:4, p. 119.

2206 R. Alter, *Psalms*, 110, p. 397.

that the birth took place in the glory of the holy ones, that is, amidst the angel host in the Holy of Holies.[2207]

Here in Psalm 110 we have to envisage Yahweh and the human king becoming One, such that Yahweh was present in the king: Immanuel. Sonship meant unity, not separation. "A priest like Melchizedek" was the transformed human figure, an angel… It is the immediate background to the arguments in St. John's Gospel, for example, where Jesus, debating with the Jews, asks: "Do you say of him whom the Father consecrated and sent into the world "You are blaspheming" because I said I am the Son of God?"[2208] The consecrated one was the high priest, consecrated in the Holy of Holies that represented heaven, and then sent out into the world. Using arguments that must have been acceptable to his Jewish critics, Jesus said that the consecrated one was the Son. "Do you say of him whom the Father consecrated and sent into the world 'You are blaspheming' because I said I am the Son of God?" He was the Melchizedek priest as described in Psalm 110.

The mysterious "dew" in Psalm 110, apparently part of the birth process, does not appear in either the Greek or the Latin versions. It could have been the anointing oil, which is described elsewhere as "like dew,"[2209] where the oil that anoints and transforms Enoch into an angel is described as like sweet dew). Or it could have been yet another corruption in the text. The Latin understood the line to mean that the Son was born before Lucifer, which raises interesting questions about the title "the firstborn." Was the psalm affirming that the Davidic king was the firstborn as stated in Psalm 89:27 "I will appoint him the firstborn," *bekor*, rather than Satan who claimed that he was born first and so should take precedence. In the *Life of Adam and Eve*, Satan refused, for this reason, to worship the image of God.[2210] "Let all God's angels worship him," was part of the longer form of that disputed verse Deuteronomy 32:43, the part that does not appear in the Masoretic Hebrew, although it was in the Qumran text.[2211] It was also one of the proof texts at the beginning of Hebrews to establish the identity of Jesus: he was Yahweh who came to atone the land, and all the angels were commanded to worship him. A human being united to Yahweh—being the Son—and union with the Father were the subjects of Jesus' prayer for his disciples after the Last Supper: "that they may be one, even as we are one…"[2212] The Melchizedek verse in Psalm 110, I suggest, became obscure because of its importance for Christian claims about Jesus and about themselves. The Christians were, were, collectively, the restored Melchizedek priesthood: one with Jesus, and their unity with Him was both the sign of their true identity as sons of God[2213] and also of Jesus' divine origin. Melchizedek, then, was a priesthood of many people, not of just one individual.[2214]

Barker also argues that the familiar KJV translation "a priest for ever after the order of Melchizedek"[2215] could also be interpreted "a priest for ever in the likeness of Melchizedek."[2216]

In Hebrews, Melchizedek is said to have been:

> … "raised up to his priesthood,"[2217] a word that also means was "resurrected," in contrast to the sons of Aaron who had their priesthood by bodily descent. The contrast is clear: the Melchizedek high priesthood was due to the ascent of resurrection, the power of indestructible life,[2218] whereas the Aaronite high priesthood was by physical descent and ended with the death of each priest.[2219] Thus Melchizedek's priesthood made him like the Son of God. The early Christians must have known what was in the now obscured lines of Psalm 110: the Melchizedek priest has been begotten as a son of God and raised up.[2220]

2207 Greek *en tē lamprótēti tōn hagíōn* (L. C. L. Brenton, *Septuagint*, Psalm 110:3, p. 767; "among the splendors of the holy ones" (A. Pietersma, *et al.*, *Septuagint*, Psalm 109(110):3, p. 603)); Latin *in splendoribus sanctorum or in saeculum saeculi* (R. Weber, *Vulgata*, Psalm 110:3, p. 914).

2208 John 10:36.

2209 Psalm 133:3; cf. F. I. Andersen, *2 Enoch*, 22:9, pp. 138-139.

2210 G. A. Anderson, *et al.*, *Synopsis*, 14:3, p. 17E.

2211 M. Abegg, Jr., *et al.*, *Scrolls Bible*, p. 193. See M. Barker, *Hidden*, p. 24; M. Barker, *Christmas*, p. 20; *Excursus 23: The Roles of Christ, Adam, and Michael*, p. 582.

2212 John 17:22.

2213 John 1:13; Romans 8:14.

2214 M. Barker, *Who was Melchizedek*. See also M. Barker, *Christmas*, pp. 104-106.

2215 Psalm 110:4.

2216 M. Barker, *Who was Melchizedek*; cf. M. Barker, *Hidden*, p. 67.

2217 Hebrews 7:11, 15.

2218 Hebrews 7:16.

2219 Hebrews 7:23.

2220 M. Barker, *Hidden*, p. 65.

E-230 See also the discussion by Attridge, who likewise observes that "certain elements of Philo's speculation… provide important evidence for the background of Hebrews' christology, important because they illustrate that the tradition about angels functioning as intercessory priests was not confined to apocalyptic texts."[2221] More generally, Koester also finds the "closest parallels for [the author of Hebrews'] exegetical statements and for his interpretive method… in the writings of Philo of Alexandria, [although] no direct dependence upon Philo can be demonstrated."[2222]

E-231 Barker points out that the competing views of the "identity of Melchizedek [were] part of an ongoing dispute about claims to the true priesthood."[2223] On the one hand, the supposed identification of Shem with Melchizedek is supported by Jewish tradition and early LDS statements.[2224] In modern scripture, Shem is also identified as "the great high priest."[2225] Elder Bruce R. McConkie argues against the identification of Melchizedek with Shem on the basis of D&C 84:14 ("Abraham received the priesthood from Melchizedek, who received it through the lineage of his fathers, even till Noah"), concluding that "there seem to have been at least two generations between Melchizedek and Shem."[2226] Terry has pointed out, however, that "the next verse… gives a key to understanding verse 14: 'And from Noah till Enoch, through the lineage of their fathers.' In other words, the phrase 'through the lineage of the fathers' refers to those preceding Enoch, not those between Enoch and Noah. If you read verse 14 in this light, it is talking about Melchizedek receiving the priesthood 'through the lineage of his fathers [from Adam on down], even till Noah [his father].'"[2227] In the *Encyclopedia of Mormonism*, Satterfield[2228] further questions the equating of Melchizedek with Shem because "Jewish sources[2229] … are late and tendentious." Orlov concurs with Satterfield that the identification of Melchizedek with Shem in rabbinic sources "exhibits a strong polemical flavor."[2230]

2 Enoch gives a different account of Melchizedek's genealogy that can be seen as "evidence of a counter-claim to the true priesthood."[2231] Here Melchizedek is portrayed as the son of Nir, the younger brother of Noah, born miraculously from the dead body of his mother as a fully-developed and dressed three-year-old in size. He had the glorious "badge of priesthood… on his chest… and they washed the child, and they dressed him in the garments of priesthood, and they gave him holy bread and he ate it."[2232] He was taken to live in the "paradise of Eden" so that his life and priesthood would be preserved during the Flood.[2233] Later, "another Melchizedek" would appear, who was to become the "first priest and king in the city Salim in the style [order] of this Melchizedek, the originator of the priests."[2234]

E-232 Barker[2235] also discusses an extracanonical passage where Enoch was declared to be "the son of man born to righteousness":[2236]

What could be behind the words to Enoch, that he was the son of man born to righteousness? Perhaps he was "born"—in the temple sense of that word—as the Righteous One, the One who would restore righteousness… "Righteous," *sadiq*, and "righteousness," *sedeq*, are key concepts in temple tradition, most often linked to *mispat*, justice, and *salom*, peace. The fundamental bond of the covenant was the covenant of peace, *b'rit salom*, also described as the covenant of eternity, *b'rit 'olam*. Restoring "righteousness" meant restoring the creation to its original state, before the covenant had been broken by the rebel angels and their human agents. It meant renewing the covenant, which in temple tradition was the ritual of the Day of Atonement when the high priest entered the Holy of Holies. This

2221 H. W. Attridge, *et al.*, *Hebrews*, p. 100.
2222 H. Koester, *New Testament 2*, p. 278, cf; pp. 276, 277. See also H. Koester, *New Testament 1*, p. 271; K. Schenck, *Understanding*, p. 30.
2223 M. Barker, *Hidden*, p. 65.
2224 See, e.g., *Ancient Ruins*, p. 746.
2225 D&C 138:41.
2226 B. R. McConkie, *Mormon Doctrine*, p. 475.
2227 R. Terry, *31 July 2009*.
2228 B. Satterfield, *Melchizedek*.
2229 E.g., W. G. Braude, *Midrash on Psalms*, 76:3, 2:15; H. Freedman, *et al.*, *Midrash*, 25:6, 4 (Leviticus):319 and 4:8, 5 (Numbers 1):102; L. Ginzberg, *Legends*, 5:225-226 n. 102; J. Goldin, *Fathers*, 2, p. 23; J. L. Kugel, *Traditions*, pp. 284, 289-290; M. Maher, *Pseudo-Jonathan*, 14:18, p. 58; M. McNamara, *Targum Neofiti*, 14, p. 92 and n. 22; J. Neusner, *Genesis Rabbah 2*, 56:10, p. 286; J. Neusner, *Babylonian Talmud*, Nedarim 32b; M.-A. Ouaknin, *et al.*, *Rabbi Éliézer*, 8, p. 59 and 27, p. 161.
2230 A. A. Orlov, *Heir*, p. 57; cf. M. Barker, *Who was Melchizedek*.
2231 M. Barker, *Hidden*, p. 65. See F. I. Andersen, *2 Enoch*, 70-72, pp. 200-211.
2232 F. I. Andersen, *2 Enoch*, 71:18-21, p. 206.
2233 *Ibid.*, 71:1, p. 210.
2234 *Ibid.*, 72:8, p. 210.
2235 M. Barker, *Hidden*, pp. 47-50.
2236 See G. W. E. Nickelsburg, *et al.*, *1 Enoch*, 71:14, p. 95.

is probably the meaning of the Servant being called in righteousness and appointed "the covenant of the people."[2237] Thus the Servant, the Righteous One making many righteous, must have been the high priest....[2238]

When Enoch had been declared the Righteous One, the angel told him that the peace of the "world to come" would be his and would come forth (into the world) with him. Since "the world to come" was the Holy of Holies, the Kingdom, Enoch bringing this to earth would have made him Melchizedek, King of Righteousness, an appropriate name or title for him, too.

Note that the *Qur'an* also uses the key term *siddiq* to describe Enoch (= Idris),[2239] Abraham,[2240] and Joseph.[2241]

E-233　Similarly, Barker concludes:

What the Jewish and the Enochic traditions are saying is that the Melchizedek priesthood was the priesthood of Enoch and the generation before the Flood. The book of *Jubilees* claims that many of the prescriptions of the *Torah* were far older than Moses, and had been given to Noah by his ancestors, the ancient priests.[2242] We cannot just dismiss this as fiction. These are all claims to a more ancient religion than that of Moses, an ancient religion represented in the biblical texts by the figure of Melchizedek... Compare here the Joseph Smith [Translation of] Genesis, which has a significantly longer text for the Melchizedek episode, and links him to the covenant with Enoch which is not mentioned in Masoretic Hebrew text. Melchizedek "was ordained an high priest after the order of the covenant which God made with Enoch."[2243]

Note that the importance of the early patriarchs is also stressed in Jewish and Christian apocalyptic and Gnostic literature, as well as among the Mandaeans and the Manichaeans.

E-234　*Genesis Rabbah* interprets Melchizedek's giving of bread and wine to Abraham as follows: "He handed over to him the laws governing priesthood" and "The bread stands for the show-bread, and the wine stands for the offerings."[2244]

E-235　Barker writes:

The Jews traced their teachings through the elders back to Moses, whereas the Christians claimed to have the mysteries of the Righteous One who was described by Isaiah. Thus in the *Mishnah* we find: "Moses received the Law from Sinai, and committed it to Joshua, and Joshua to the elders, and the elders to the prophets, and the prophets committed it to the men of the Great Synagogue."[2245] No mention of priests or temple. The Christians, however, claimed teaching from their great high priest, "to whom the secret things of the Lord were committed."[2246] These secret things were the "mystery" of the Righteous One mentioned in Isaiah 24:16, and were understood as the teachings of Jesus to be kept for the Lord and the sons of his house.[2247] The *Isaiah Targum* understood the passage in the same way as the Christians: the prophet saw the mystery associated with the Righteous One.[2248]

E-236　About the argument by some that the Aaronic priesthood was to be abolished at the time of Christ, Seaich writes:

The "Melchizedek" exegesis of the Temple-cult which we find in the Epistle to the Hebrews gives its own expanded meaning to the rites of the Temple, whose ultimate purpose would henceforth be to "cleanse the heavenly things" through the eternal, one-time sacrifice of Christ.[2249] But this did

---

2237　Isaiah 42:6, 49:8.

2238　See Isaiah 53:11.

2239　M. M. Ali, *Qur'an*, 19:56, p. 603.

2240　*Ibid.*, 19:41, p. 601

2241　J.-L. Monneret, *Grands*, n. 24, p. 483. See M. M. Ali, *Qur'an*, 12:46, p. 46; Genesis 41:38-39.

2242　O. S. Wintermute, *Jubilees*, 7:34-39, p. 71, 10:13, p. 76.

2243　M. Barker, *Who was Melchizedek*.

2244　J. Neusner, *Genesis Rabbah 2*, 43:6, pp. 119-120.

2245　M. Lieber, *Pirkei Avos*, 1:1, pp. 6-11.

2246　Ignatius, *Philadelphians*, 9, p. 84; cf. Clement of Alexandria, *Stromata*, 1:1, p. 302.

2247　Pseudo-Clement, *Homilies*, 19:20, p. 336.

2248　M. Barker, *Who was Melchizedek*. See *Targum Isaiah* 24:16, cited in Barker.

2249　Hebrews 9:23-28. Johnson notes: "[T]he author of Hebrews does not stand outside the original covenant that God established with the 'seed of Abraham'...; rather, the author stands within the commitments and story of this covenanted people. Nowhere does the author suggest that God's word through the Son is a disavowal of

not automatically eliminate the Temple's lesser duties, which still included "cleansing the earthly copies of heavenly things."[2250] Unfortunately, the KJV translation deliberately gives the impression that these are now discontinued by gratuitously adding the past copula, "was," to verse 23 ("It was therefore necessary…"), though they should actually be parallel to the present copula in verse 16. Much more accurately, the NEB leaves this entire passage in the present tense: "If, then, these sacrifices cleanse the copies of heavenly things, those heavenly things themselves require better sacrifices to cleanse them."[2251]

In short, the Aaronic priesthood was still… in effect when the Epistle to the Hebrews was written, being the law under which Israel was to operate "until the time of reformation (*diorthoseos*)."[2252] Significantly, G. W. Buchanan understands this expression to be synonymous with the "time of refreshing (*apokataseos*)" prophesied for the end of time in Acts 3:20f.[2253]

Until then, the "sons of Levi" are to "receive the office of the Priesthood" and to "take tithes of the people according to the law,"[2254] though this is now done under the supervision and authority of the Melchizedek "tribe"….[2255]

The people of the Book of Mormon, however, like most modern Mormons, had no hereditary Priesthood, being descended from the tribe of Joseph; thus they officiated in the ordinances of the Mosaic Law[2256] directly through the Melchizedek Priesthood.[2257] This situation lasted until the ministry of Christ,[2258] whose full Law was finally restored to the Church, together with its lesser "Mosaic" or "Aaronic" portions. [For this reason, the Melchizedek Priesthood is said to be "without father, without mother, without descent,"[2259] i.e., not confined to any tribal lineage; instead, it constitutes "another tribe," previously unmentioned in Jewish law,[2260] i.e., the Priesthood which comes directly from Christ, and passes through anyone who has received it to others.[2261]]

It is nevertheless argued by some that Christ's Priesthood "doth not pass (*aparabatos*) from one to another," i.e., cannot be possessed by men. But as W. E. Vine perceptively notes, the word *aparabatos* in Hebrews 7:24 should actually be translated "unchangeable, unalterable, inviolable." Thus the rendering: "'that doth not pass from one to another'… is not only untenable, and contrary to the constant usage of the word, but does not adequately fit with either the preceding or the succeeding context."[2262]

To suggest that only Jesus possessed the Priesthood, then, and that he never intended to share it with his disciples, is not only grammatically incorrect, but contrary to the New Testament promise that men would be made "joint heirs" with Christ, and serve with him as "Kings and Priests" in the Heavenly Temple.[2263]

E-237 While Eccles sees the author of Hebrews as dismissing "as inferior to the Christian way all mystic Judaism of whatever kind,"[2264] the striking nature of the broad similarities between the Jewish and Christian mysticism must also be acknowledged. Attridge, for example, finds "significant parallels between Philo and Hebrews in the structure of their treatment [of the correspondence between earthly and 'heavenly' sanctuaries], parallels that point to their common Hellenistic Jewish background. Not only does Hebrews' language describing the earthly-heavenly dichotomy resemble that of Philo, but also the function of that dichotomy is strikingly similar."[2265] See Barker for a discussion of how the

the words spoken to 'our fathers' of old (Hebrews 1:1). Rather, the author makes a claim for a new covenant precisely for this people" (L. T. Johnson, *Hebrews*, p. 211).

2250 Hebrews 9:22-23.
2251 S. Sandmel, *et al.*, *New English Bible*, Hebrews 9:23, p. 283.
2252 Hebrews 9:10.
2253 G. W. Buchanan, *Hebrews*, p. 146.
2254 Hebrews 7:5.
2255 Hebrews 7:6-10.
2256 2 Nephi 5:10.
2257 E.g., 2 Nephi 6:2; Mosiah 29:42; Alma 4:20, 6:8, 13:1-20; D&C 107:17.
2258 J. F. Smith, Jr., *Doctrines*, 13 December 1950, 3:87; 2 Nephi 32:6.
2259 Hebrews 7:3.
2260 Hebrews 7:13.
2261 J. E. Seaich, *Ancient Texts 1995*, p. 975 n. 1033.
2262 W. E. Vine, *et al.*, *Dictionary (1996)*, p. 649.
2263 J. E. Seaich, *Ancient Texts 1995*, pp. 973, 975. See Revelation 1:6, 20:6, 21:22, 22:3-4; cf. Exodus 19:6.
2264 R. S. Eccles, *Hebrews*, p. 220.
2265 H. W. Attridge, *et al.*, *Hebrews*, p. 223.

early Christians might have interpreted the arguments of Hebrews concerning the priesthood.[2266]

E-238 Sterling notes the high regard given Philo's writings by early Christians, "who preserved about two-thirds of his known corpus."[2267] Legends of contact between Philo and the Christian community were preserved by Eusebius,[2268] and at least one pseudepigraphal document purported to relate his (extremely implausible) conversion.

For a largely negative analysis of possible influences of the Greco-Roman mysteries on Paul's baptismal theology, see Wedderburn.[2269] Johnson is more open-minded in his exploration of possible relationships between Greco-Roman, Jewish, and Christian initiations. He acknowledges:[2270]

> … four basic approaches to the study of earliest Christianity in the context of the mysteries. The first is to ignore them completely and pay attention only to Jewish antecedents… The second is to recognize the pervasiveness of mystery practice and language, but refuse to grant it any influence for nascent Christianity, reserving that for later "Catholic" development… The third is to subsume early Christianity into the mysteries more or less completely[2271]… The fourth [Johnson's position] is to be fundamentally open to the ways in which the symbolic worlds of the mysteries and Christianity may have intersected, without demanding causal connections in the strict sense and respecting the distinctiveness of the diverse cults.

E-239 Regarding the fate of Jewish mystical groups such as those found at Dura, Goodenough writes:

> … from direct evidence we know nothing; but it would seem that the leaders of this Judaism from the sixth to the eighth centuries had a great change of attitude. They learned Hebrew… [and as] they did so, they could for the first time learn to pray in Hebrew, to read the Scriptures in Hebrew, and to study the rabbinical writings… At the same time, they not only stopped using the symbolic vocabulary…, but, wherever possible, destroyed it by clipping out the offensive forms… Christians preserved Philo and many Jewish apocalyptic books, but the medieval Jews so neglected the great mass of literature that Greek- and Iranian-speaking Jews must have produced in the whole ancient world that from Jews we have no trace of it left at all… It remains to be seen whether medieval Jewish *Kabbalah*… represents a survival and amplification of this more general Jewish mysticism, or was freshly created by the influence of medieval Christian mystics, or came down from *Merkabah* beginnings, or, as I suspect, was in some way a mixture of all these.[2272]

E-240 Ulansey characterizes Mark's account of the opening of the heavens at Christ's baptism[2273] and the rending of the temple veil at his death[2274] as constituting a powerful symbolic *inclusio* bracketing the entire gospel, and underscoring the message that the way opened by Christ is now available to all men.[2275] In this connection, Nibley writes:[2276]

> The *Gospel of Philip* depicts the rending of the veil not as the abolition of the temple ordinances, as the church fathers fondly supposed, but of the opening of those ordinances to all the righteous of Israel, "in order that we might enter into… the truth of it." "The priesthood can still go within the veil with the high priest (i.e., the Lord)." We are allowed to see what is behind the veil, and "we enter into it in our weakness, through signs and tokens which the world despises."[2277]

MacRae finds the *Gospel of Philip* passage Nibley cites:[2278]

> … interesting for the way in which it weaves together biblical exegesis of many different passages from both the Old Testament and the New Testament. The guiding image of' this picture is the notion of passing into the sanctuary of the temple, that is to say, passing into the heavenly presence of God, by crossing through the veil by accomplishing the rite of the bridal chamber. The *Gospel of*

2266 M. Barker, *Who was Melchizedek*.
2267 G. E. Sterling, *Philo*, p. 297.
2268 Eusebius, *History*, 2:17, p. 50.
2269 A. J. M. Wedderburn, *Baptism*, especially pp. 90-163.
2270 L. T. Johnson, *Religious Experience*, pp. 84-85 n. 72.
2271 See a refutation of this position in J. Z. Smith, *Drudgery*.
2272 E. R. Goodenough, *Summary*, p. 198.
2273 Mark 1:10.
2274 Mark 15:38.
2275 D. Ulansey, *Heavenly Veil*.
2276 H. W. Nibley, *Message 2005*, p. 444.
2277 See W. W. Isenberg, *Philip*, 85:1-20, p. 159.
2278 G. W. MacRae, *House of Revelation*, pp. 185-186.

Philip assumes throughout that the true spiritual realities are knowable only through images, as it calls them. Throughout the work words are presented as images of divine things, always imperfect images, never telling us the truth about divine things but only giving us some suggestions. The writer understands ritual action also to function in the same imagistic way.

Nibley discusses the way in which accounts of the temple-related doctrines and ordinances revealed by Jesus Christ to his apostles during the forty days following his resurrection, if acknowledged at all, have often been dismissed by Christian scholars as "a complete misunderstanding perpetrated by the Gnostics."[2279] Johnson goes further than most scholars by providing an ample, if somewhat selective, review of the pagan, Jewish, and Christian sources that provided a climate for stages of initiation beyond baptism, but then, incorrectly, presents Paul as one who opposed such rites.[2280]

E-241 Notwithstanding this important distinction, the Prophet Joseph Smith taught that "[a]ll priesthood is Melchizedek, but there are different portions or degrees of it."[2281] In this sense, the Aaronic priesthood is rightly characterized as being "an appendage to the greater, or the Melchizedek priesthood."[2282]

E-242 Summarizing sources that describe having "seen God" as an identifying attribute of true Israel among some Jews and early Christians, Barker writes:[2283]

When the Christians were emphasizing that they had *seen* the Glory,[2284] the name "Israel" was said to mean "the one who has seen God," and so the emphasis in the Christmas stories was a claim to be the new Israel. Philo often used the expression: it was fundamental to his Judaism. He never explained it nor argued for it; it was something he could assume. "The nation that sees, that is, Israel";[2285] "For Israel means seeing God."[2286] "The sons of Israel"[2287] for him became "the sons of the seeing one."[2288] Almost all the early Christian writers adopted this explanation of Israel and claimed it for the Church.[2289] It was used in prayers: "For by [Christ] thou hast brought home the Gentiles to thyself for a peculiar people, the true Israel beloved of God and seeing God"; "the God of Israel, Thy people which truly see and which have believed in Christ."[2290]

E-243 Though it is not uncommon to equate the attainment of the celestial kingdom with the blessings of exaltation, Elder John A. Widtsoe, among others, made it clear that "all who enter the celestial glory do not necessarily receive full exaltation therein."[2291] Elder Orson Hyde explained that the blessing of exaltation is reserved for "kings and priests… [who] have received their washings and anointings in the temple of God on this earth; [and] have been chosen, ordained, and anointed kings and priests, to reign as such in the resurrection of the just. Such as have not received the fulness of the priesthood, (for the fulness of the priesthood includes the authority of both king and priest) and have not been anointed and ordained in the temple of the Most High, may obtain salvation in the celestial kingdom, but not a celestial crown."[2292] As with every other ordinance of the gospel, those who live to merit the blessings of the fulness of the priesthood but do not have an opportunity to receive them in this life will receive them at some future time.[2293]

Regarding this subject, the Prophet Joseph Smith wrote:

2279 H. W. Nibley, *Return*, p. 66; cf. H. W. Nibley, *Evangelium*.

2280 L. T. Johnson, *Religious Experience*, pp. 69-103.

2281 J. Smith, Jr., *Teachings*, 5 January 1841, p. 180.

2282 D&C 107:14.

2283 M. Barker, *Christmas*, pp. 89-90.

2284 E.g., Luke 2:30-32, 3:6; John 1:14; cf. Isaiah 40:5, 49:6, 52:10, 56:12; Zechariah 2:10.

2285 See Philo, *Dreams* 2:44, p. 391; cf. 1:71, p. 380.

2286 Philo, *Preliminary Studies* 51, p. 308.

2287 Leviticus 15:31.

2288 Philo, *Interpretation* 3:15, p. 311.

2289 See C. T. R. Hayward, *Israel*, pp. 156-193.

2290 A Roberts, *et al.*, *Apostolic Constitutions* 7:1:36, p. 474 and 8:2:15, p. 491. See M. Barker, *Temple Themes*, pp. 154-160.

2291 J. A. Widtsoe, *Are All Exalted*, p. 278; cf. S. W. Kimball, *Miracle*, pp. 243-244; S. W. Kimball, *Importance*, pp. 5-6; B. R. McConkie, *New Witness*, pp. 144-145.

2292 O. Hyde, *Diagram*, p. 23. Reprinted in J. Smith, Jr., *Words*, pp. 298-299 n. 8.

2293 Cf. e.g., D&C 137:7-9. Moreover, President Brigham Young taught that some ordinances *cannot* be received in mortal life: "We will operate here, in all the ordinances of the house of God which pertain to this side the veil, and those who pass beyond and secure to themselves a resurrection pertaining to the lives will go on and receive more and more, more and more, and will receive one after another until they are crowned Gods, even the sons of God" (B. Young, *24 August 1872*, p. 138).

> In the celestial glory there are three heavens or degrees; and in order to obtain the highest [*i.e., exaltation as a priest and king after the order of Melchizedek*], a man must [*first, as a prerequisite,*] enter into this order of the priesthood [meaning the new and everlasting covenant of marriage [*i.e., Abrahamic degree*]]; and if he does not, he cannot obtain it [*i.e., exaltation*]. He may enter into the other [*i.e., celestial glory corresponding to the Mosaic degree*], but that is the end of his kingdom; he cannot have an increase [*i.e., posterity*].[2294]

An alternate conception of the three degrees in the celestial kingdom could be imagined. In an 1843 discourse, the Prophet Joseph Smith referred to "three grand orders of priesthood" referred to in Hebrews chapter 7.[2295] The three orders mentioned at that time were Levitical ("priests to administer in outward ordinance, made without an oath"), Patriarchal (Abrahamic), and Melchizedek ("kings and priests of the Most High God," "power and authority over that of Abraham").[2296] (Incidentally, Seaich suggests that an enigmatic statement in the Testament of Levi ("your posterity shall be divided into three offices as a sign of the glory of the Lord who is coming"[2297]) may refer to these same three orders.[2298]) It could be argued that these three orders of the priesthood correspond to the "three heavens or degrees" in the celestial glory mentioned previously.[2299] However, it is difficult to imagine that receiving the higher priesthood would not be a requirement for the inhabitants of even the lowest degree of the celestial kingdom "where God and Christ dwell,"[2300] since without the higher priesthood, we are told, "no man can see the face of God, and live."[2301]

E-244 As in the writings of Philo, where selected characters from Genesis represent "a general type of... religious experience,"[2302] the fact that certain patriarchs (Moses, Abraham, Melchizedek) are associated in the Doctrine and Covenants with degrees of the higher priesthood does not, of course, deprive them of their primary status as important historical figures.[2303]

E-245 Cooper rightfully recognized the "far-reaching consequence" of the centrality of eternal family relations to Mormon temple theology. Contrasting the Puritan and LDS concepts of the Abrahamic covenant, he wrote:

> The Puritan process of salvation ultimately required severance from one's family. John Bunyan's (1628-1688) Christian could not begin his quest for salvation without leaving behind his wife and children...[2304] In contrast, a Mormon man would, according to Joseph Smith, take his wife and children with him in his search for eternal life, achieving salvation interdependently.[2305]

E-246 In his discourse of 27 August 1843, the Prophet implied that Moses received the fulness of the Melchizedek priesthood, saying that "God cursed the children of Israel because they would not receive the last law from Moses," and also that the "law revealed to Moses in Horeb never was revealed to the children of Israel as a nation."[2306]

E-247 Jewish tradition held that Adam was created out of earth taken from the temple site of Mount Moriah,[2307] and that he returned to dwell on Mount Moriah when he was cast out of the Garden of Eden.[2308] Some saw the land as the Garden of Eden itself.[2309] Here also tradition records that Adam erected an altar and made offerings.[2310]

2294 J. Smith, Jr., *Teachings*, 16 May 1843, 300-301, comments in italics are mine. See D&C 131:1-4.

2295 J. Smith, Jr., *Teachings*, 27 August 1843, p. 322.

2296 *Ibid.*, pp. 322-323.

2297 H. C. Kee, *Testaments*, Levi 8:11, p. 791.

2298 J. E. Seaich, *Ancient Texts 1995*, p. 877 n. 699.

2299 See, e.g., J. F. McConkie, *et al.*, *Revelations*, p. 1053.

2300 D&C 76:112.

2301 D&C 84:22.

2302 R. Goldenberg, *Origins*, p. 112.

2303 R. S. Eccles, *Pilgrimage*, p. 55.

2304 J. Bunyan, *Progress*, pp. 23-24.

2305 R. E. Cooper, *Promises*, pp. 115-116.

2306 J. Smith, Jr., *Teachings*, 27 August 1843, pp. 322-323; cf. J. Smith, Jr., *Words*, 27 August 1843, pp. 243-247; A. Ehat, *et al.*, in *ibid.*, pp. 303-304 n. 21.

2307 W. G. Braude, *Midrash on Psalms*, 92:6, 2:113; J. Neusner, *Genesis Rabbah 1*, 14:8:1, p. 156; M.-A. Ouaknin, *et al.*, *Rabbi Éliézer*, 11, p. 78; cf. G. A. Anderson, *et al.*, *Synopsis*, Latin Addenda 36 [52], p. 96E.

2308 W. G. Braude, *Midrash on Psalms*, 92:6, 2:113.

2309 O. S. Wintermute, *Jubilees*, 8:19, p. 72.

2310 W. G. Braude, *Rabbati*, 43:2, 2:756.

There are "contradictory *hadiths*" in Islam about whether the Garden of Eden was earthly, heavenly, or something in between.[2311] Of Muslim sources taking the first position, some regard Mount Moriah in Jerusalem both as the site of the Garden of Eden and of the final judgment:

> Muslim tradition tells us that a black stone embedded in the floor beneath the Dome of the Rock is supposed to be the entrance to Paradise. The elaborate mosaics that fill the interior of the shrine feature repetitive trees, luxuriant foliage, bushes, jewels and floral motifs reminiscent of the Garden of Eden… A tree on the platform of the *Haram* is associated with God's original work in the world. In Jewish and Muslim tradition, the rivers of Eden flow below the Temple Mount. Creation originated here, an idea reflected in the designation *omphales mundi* ("navel of the world"), referring to the notion that god created the world in the same way that a human being was created, beginning with the navel. *Jubilees*, too, set the navel of the world on Mount Zion, by that time identified as the Temple Mount. At the end of time, the Last Judgment will take place here and access to Paradise will be available here. Although Jerusalem is not mentioned by name in the *Qur'an*, the phrase "from a nearby place"[2312] was interpreted early on to refer to the Holy City. The passage, literally "the day whereon the crier shall call from a nearby place," was interpreted to refer to the archangel who, on the day of the Resurrection, will call from Jerusalem.[2313]

At least one Christian source has Adam's creation taking place on Golgotha,[2314] while an addendum to the Latin *Life of Adam and Eve* said that God "made and formed Adam in that place where Jesus was born, that is, in the city of Bethlehem, which is in the center of the earth."[2315]

In the *Histoyre du Mechique*, Tamoanchan, usually associated in Aztec sources with a primeval paradisiacal garden, is the name of a cave where humankind is created.[2316]

E-248 Latin and Greek versions of the *Life of Adam and Eve*, along with *Jubilees*, record Adam's request to be buried "opposite the great Garden of God near his dwelling (opposite the Garden of God in the field of his dwelling?)."[2317]

E-249 Latter-day Saints associate various events in the postlapsarian life of Adam with temple sites—in this case, in the state of Missouri rather than in the Near East.[2318]

E-250 Traditions about Adam's burial in the cave of Machpelah are preserved in Jewish sources[2319] that discuss the origin of these traditions in an early exegesis of Joshua 14:15, and are included in Wilkinson's brief mention of other notables who were thought by some to have been buried there.[2320] Note that the Bordeaux Pilgrim did not report the tradition of Adam's burial in Machpelah in connection with a visit in 333.[2321] The *Zohar* reports both Adam's discovery and Abraham's rediscovery of the burial place:

> What did Adam do? He dug a cave, and hid himself inside together with his wife. How did he know? He saw a ray of light glinting on that spot, gleaming from the Garden of Eden, and desired a desire for his grave. Right there is a site bordering the gate of the Garden of Eden.[2322]

> "And Abraham ran after the calf."[2323] The calf had run away from Abraham and entered the cave of Machpelah. When Abraham entered after it, he saw Adam and his mate lying asleep on the couches, lamps burning above them, and their bodies giving forth a goodly odor, sweet in savor.

2311 Porch of Wisdom Cultural Institution, *Faith and Reason*, p. 161. See the overview of Moses 3, p. 143.

2312 *Qur'an* 50:41.

2313 H. Shanks, *Temple Mount*, pp. 22-23.

2314 M. D. Gibson, *Rolls 1901*, p. 111. See *Endnote E-132*, p. 733.

2315 G. A. Anderson, *et al.*, *Synopsis*, Latin Addenda 38 [56], p. 96E.

2316 Cited in E. Q. Keber, *Telleriano-Remensis*, p. 183.

2317 *Ibid.*, Latin 45:2, p. 74E; cf. Greek 40:6, p. 89E; O. S. Wintermute, *Jubilees*, 4:29, p. 63. There is a widespread tradition of Adam and Eve's burial in the cave of Machpelah. See *Endnote E-250*, p. 767.

2318 See *Figure 6-2*, p. 457 and *Excursus 39: The Location of Adam-ondi-Ahman*, p. 623. About the Christian tradition of Adam's burial beneath Golgotha, see *Figure E36-2*, p. 616.

2319 E.g., M. McNamara, *Targum Neofiti*, 23:2 and n. 1, p. 120; J. Neusner, *Genesis Rabbah 2*, 58:4, p. 297; M.-A. Ouaknin, *et al.*, *Rabbi Éliézer*, 20, pp. 127-128; 36, p. 224; H. Schwartz, *Tree*, 445, pp. 343-344, 639, pp. 504-506. See P. Van der Horst, *Adam's Tomb*.

2320 J. Wilkinson, in *Egeria*, *Travels*, p. 92 nn. 6-7. See also A. S.-M. Ri, *Commentaire de la Caverne*, p. 180.

2321 Bordeaux Pilgrim, in *ibid.*, 599, p. 34.

2322 D. C. Matt, *Zohar 1*, Be-Reshit 1:57b, pp. 326-327; cf. D. C. Matt, *Zohar 2*, Be-Reshit 1:27b-1:128b, pp. 219-223; D. C. Matt, *Zohar 4*, Bo 2:39b, pp. 190-191.

2323 Genesis 18:7.

This is how it came about that Abraham was eager to have the cave of Machpelah as a burying place.[2324]

Today, within the edifice built by Herod the Great to commemorate the burial of the patriarchs (The Tomb of the Patriarchs, *Ma'arat HaMachpela* (Hebrew), or *Haram al-Khalil* (Arabic)), one can still see a palm tree adjacent to the northwest corner of the inner courtyard marking the spot of "Adam's Grave."[2325] At that place also may be found "Adam's footprint" (*Makaam Adam*), set in an unmarked niche within the chamber where Abraham's cenotaph is viewed from the Muslim side of the monument (locals will sometimes point this out as "Muhammad's footprint"). At present, no access to the caves beneath the monument is allowed, though very limited explorations took place in 1968 and 1981.[2326]

Some Muslim traditions say that, on account of his large stature, Adam's head lies at Machpelah and his feet at the Dome of the Rock (or vice versa).[2327] Other Muslim traditions have Adam buried in India, in a "Treasure Cave"[2328] on Mount Abu Qabis in Mecca,[2329] in Jerusalem, or alternately in a location "east of Paradise in a village which was the first village on the earth."[2330] At least one source reports Eve being buried at Jeddah, Saudi Arabia.[2331] This reputed site can still be visited today, though it was sealed in 1975 to prevent Muslims from inappropriately praying there.

E-251 *Statke*, a term related to the action of dripping, was probably a precious oil produced by pressing fresh myrrh.

E-252 Exodus 24:9 specifically names Aaron, Nadab, and Abihu going up with Moses, while Exodus 24:13 mentions Joshua. Schubert concludes that only " those five persons enter the Tent of Meeting who had experienced the epiphany on Mount Sinai according to Exodus 24:9-18."[2332] However, I take the five to be entering the Tabernacle as forerunners, their poses suggesting an invitation to Christian believers to follow them.

Schubert notes that the "representation of the Tabernacle at the foot of Sinai recalls the fresco in the Via Latina catacomb where below the scene of Moses receiving the Law on Sinai is a portrayal of Moses leading the Israelites to a temple sanctuary. It is almost certain that this temple sanctuary is to be understood from the rabbinic interpretation which takes Isaiah 2:2 as a cipher for Mount Sinai."[2333]

E-253 A fifteenth-century text mentions additional gifts beyond the three:

> … outstanding purple [gems], shining brilliantly, a bright pearl, a crown of fresh grasses which would never wither, but would bear bright crimson flowers always, a wreath, also, in which were entwined various fresh grasses with crimson flowers, which seemed as if they had just been cut, and a shining new linen cloth, the equal or like of which was not to be found. The latter shone so brightly that people saw flashes of lightning rise from it as from a brilliant star, or as sparks from a mighty fire when its heat is at its most intense. They brought, furthermore, a royal scepter[2334] with gems of crystal and of precious stones, the equivalent or like of which have never been found…, except, perhaps, the firmament with [its] many stars, and the sun and moon in it like precious stones. Fire-trailing sparks darted from them as from a brilliant constellation… And they gave other gifts, such as were never found in the world.[2335]

In an Islamic source, Adam placed two items in a coffer: "a white cloth from Paradise" on which Adam saw a vision of the descendants of Cain and Seth, and "a handful of hair from his beard" which, so long as it remained black, would be a portent of victory over their enemies. He gave the coffer along with his ring to Seth.[2336]

2324 H. N. Bialik, *et al.*, *Legends*, 3:37, p. 35, citing M.-A. Ouaknin, *et al.*, *Rabbi Éliézer*, 36, p. 224; cf. *Zohar Chadash, Ruth* 79:4.

2325 N. Arnon, *Machpela*, p. 13. See *Figure* 4-12, p. 230.

2326 N. Arnon, *Machpela*, pp. 8-9.

2327 J. E. Hanauer, *Folklore*, p. 12; Ibu Asakir in B. M. Wheeler, *Prophets*, p. 34.

2328 al-Tabari, *Creation*, 1:162, p. 333.

2329 I. Ibn Kathir, *Stories*, p. 54; G. Weil, *Legends*, p. 48.

2330 M. Ibn Ishaq ibn Yasar, *Making*, p. 41; cf. A. al-Tha'labi, *Lives*, p. 81.

2331 M. al-Kisa'i, *Tales*, p. 85.

2332 K. Schubert, *Jewish Pictorial*, p. 248.

2333 *Ibid.*, p. 248.

2334 See *Excursus 51: The Five Lost Things of the Temple*, p. 658. See *Endnote E-181*, p. 749.

2335 M. Herbert, *Irish Apocrypha*, p. 39.

2336 M. al-Kisa'i, *Tales*, p. 82. See also p. 347 n. 69.

E-254 Though the visit of the Magi is generally portrayed as having taken place later in Nazareth, the Magi in the *Protoevangelium of James*[2337] "come to pay homage at the Bethlehem cave—an interesting mixture of Matthew and Luke"[2338] and a subtle allusion to Adam's Cave of Treasures.

The memory and significance of the visit of the Magi was preserved in the 15th-century French Christmas carol *Noël Nouvelet.*[2339] When the three "kings" bring their gifts, the birthplace in Bethlehem—here portrayed as a small garden—is transformed into an earthly Eden:

> *L'un portait l'or, et l'autre myrrhe aussi.* (One brought gold, and the other myrrh also.)
> *Et l'autre encens, qui faisait bon senti.* (And the other incense, that gave off a good odor.)
> *Le paradis semblait le jardinet.* (Like Paradise seemed the little garden.)

E-255 For example, just prior to his death, Adam is depicted as having described these "tokens" and their Messianic significance to his son, and then saying, "And now, O Seth, my son, behold I have revealed unto thee hidden mysteries, which God had revealed unto me."[2340]

E-256 The theme of the restoration of the true temple through Jesus Christ can also be seen in the purported reburial of Adam's bones at the site of the Crucifixion, which then became "the second Cave of Treasures."[2341] See *Figure* 36-1, p. 616.

E-257 The "Church of the Disciples and of the Ascension" (later the "Church of Eleona," from Greek *elaion* = "of olives") was dedicated in 334. One year earlier, the Bordeaux pilgrim had written: "On the Mount of Olives, where the Lord taught before his passion, a basilica has been built by the command of Constantine."[2342] By 390, a new basilica a short distance further up the hill had been dedicated to the Ascension alone. Both churches were set afire and razed early in the 7th century, but only the Ascension church was rebuilt at the time of the Crusaders. "All that remains of this second Church is a small shelter now in the possession of the El Tour mosque and called the Mosque of the Ascension."[2343]

In the 12th century, based on late traditions associating Luke's account of the Lord's Prayer[2344] with Mark's record of Jesus' teachings about prayer on the Mount of Olives,[2345] the Crusaders erected the *Pater Noster* ("Our Father") church near the original site of the Eleona church.[2346] Crusader pilgrims reported having seen the Lord's Prayer inscribed on plaques. Assisted by the French architect Eugène Viollet-le-Duc, the Princess of La Tour D'Auvergne (Aurélie de Bossi) built a new cloister and monastery on fifteen acres in 1870-1874. The site is now maintained by the French Carmelite sisters. Ceramic tile plaques on the walls of the grounds and the cloister feature translations of the Lord's Prayer in more than 150 languages.

The Grotto of the Teachings had been buried underneath the ruins of the Eleona Church, and eventually the traces of both disappeared. In 1870, the location of the Byzantine church was found by Clermont-Ganeau, and in 1910 the archaeologist uncovered the partially collapsed grotto, which at some indeterminate date had been connected with a first-century tomb containing a series of funerary niches (*kokhim*).[2347] The first stones for a new Eleona basilica were placed in 1920, which unfortunately caused severe damage to the grotto. Other construction difficulties, including a severe earthquake in 1927, eventually halted the work. Finally in 1972, an open-air basilica containing a simple altar and a stone chair was dedicated above the grotto.[2348]

E-258 Most LDS commentators derive the word "telestial" from the Greek *telos*.[2349] In the context of a description of the lowest kingdom of glory, Nibley explains that the Greek term "means farthest

2337 E. Hennecke *et al.*, *Protoevangelium*, 18:1, 21:1-4, pp. 383, 386.

2338 R. E. Brown, *Birth*, p. 197; cf. E. A. W. Budge, *Cave*, pp. 35, 211.

2339 H. Keyte, *et al.*, *Noël Nouvelet*, p. 299, spelling modernized.

2340 S. C. Malan, *Adam and Eve*, 2:8, p. 116.

2341 S. Ruzer, *Pilgrimage*.

2342 Cited in Egeria, *Travels*, 595, p. 32; cf. Egeria's account of his visits during Holy Week in 384 in Egeria, *Travels*, 30:3, p. 151; 33:2, p. 152. See also A. Storme, *Mont des Oliviers*, pp. 33-34.

2343 O. Englebert, *Grotto*, p. 3.

2344 Luke 11:1-4.

2345 Mark 11:25-26.

2346 A. Storme, *Mont des Oliviers*, pp. 35-38.

2347 *Ibid.*, pp. 28-33.

2348 *Ibid.*, pp. 42-43. For more on the history of Eleona, see O. Englebert, *Grotto*; A. Storme, *Mont des Oliviers*; L.-H. Vincent, *Eléona*.

2349 For an excellent discussion of the use of the term in Greek, Jewish (including Philo), and Christian settings, see H. W. Attridge, *Hebrews*, pp. 83-87.

removed, as distant as you can get, what the Arabs call the *aqsa*. Joseph Smith coined that word, and he couldn't have used a better one – the telestial, the farthest away of all the worlds [from God]."[2350]

In his explanation of the meaning of "telestial,"[2351] Miller emphasizes the sense in which *telos* may mean "end" or "completion" and applies it to scriptural descriptions of the resurrection:

> [Telestial] is used in connection with the Telestial Kingdom because it is the last resurrection of the saved that happens at the end of the world when Jesus has completed and perfected his work. I think this is evident in the following verse from the New Testament:
>
> > 22 For as in Adam all die, even so in Christ shall all be made alive.
> >
> > 23 But every man in his own order: Christ the firstfruits; afterward they that are Christ's at his coming.
> >
> > 24 Then cometh the end, when he shall have delivered up the kingdom to God, even the Father; when he shall have put down all rule and all authority and power.[2352]

My commentary on these verses:

All be made alive] All will be resurrected just like Jesus was.

In his own order] The word for order refers to temporal order or rank. Each person will be resurrected in the order or according to their rank in salvation.

Christ the firstfruits] Christ is the first to be resurrected in time, he is also the highest in rank.

afterward they that are Christ's at his coming] The next to be resurrected are those who are resurrected at Christ's second coming. This is the first resurrection which consists of those who are resurrected in the morning (the heirs of the celestial kingdom) and those who are resurrected afterwards (the Terrestial Kingdom).

Then cometh the end] "The end" is *telos* in the Greek. Then (after the other resurrections) comes the *telos* resurrection. This is where the word telestial comes from. It occurs after the millennium when Christ "shall have delivered up the kingdom to God." It denotes completion, ending, perfection.

With this understanding, D&C 76 takes on a new meaning.

> [Telestial inhabitants] are they who shall not be redeemed from the devil until the last resurrection, until the Lord, even Christ the Lamb, shall have finished his work.[2353]
>
> [Telestial inhabitants] are they who are cast down to hell and suffer the wrath of Almighty God, until the fulness of times, when Christ shall have subdued all enemies under his feet, and shall have perfected his work; when he shall deliver up the kingdom, and present it unto the Father.[2354]

Raising the possibility of a Latin rather than Greek derivation of "telestial," Tvedtnes writes:[2355]

> In a private communication, John Gee has noted that, while the terms rendered celestial ("heavenly") and terrestrial ("earthly") are often paired in the New Testament, only in Philippians 2:10 do they form a trio of terms. The third term used in that passage is *katachthonios* , literally "under the ground." Since the terms "celestial" and "terrestrial" derive from Latin rather than Greek (*caelum* , "heaven," and *terra* , "earth"), Gee suggests that a Latin term may lie behind "telestial" as well. He proposes the Latin word *tellus* , "earth, globe, land, ground."

E-259 Arguing that the rites themselves were relatively unchanging over the centuries, Sourvinou-Inwood writes: "Though we cannot unproblematically use evidence from late periods for reconstructing earlier practices, implicitly assuming there had been no change, the presumption here, I suggest, should be that the basic schema of the ritual had not changed. For at the very center of the Mysteries was the belief that these rites had been revealed by Demeter. Such divine revelation of ritual is extraordinarily rare in Greek religion, and created certain constraints on fundamental change and the construction

2350 H. W. Nibley, *Three Degrees*, pp. 308-309.
2351 A. I. Miller, *Telestial*.
2352 1 Corinthians 15:22-24.
2353 D&C 76:85.
2354 D&C 76:106-107; cf. 1 Corinthians 15:24.
2355 J. A. Tvedtnes, *Three Degrees*, n. 1.

of change-supporting *mythopoea* [= myth-making]."[2356]

E-260   Unfortunately, the English transliteration of the name obscures its meaning. The last two English "e's" correspond to the Greek letter *eta* (long "e") and not *epsilon* (short "e"); thus, the root *matar* relates to "mother" and not "measure."

E-261   The requirement of secrecy imposed on initiates to the mysteries:

> ... was so rigorous that in 200 BCE, when two young men from the distant town of Akarnania innocently entered the sanctuary at Eleusis during the enactment of a mystery festival and betrayed themselves by asking questions about the rites, they were promptly executed.[2357] Of the Eleusinian mysteries, George Mylonas writes that "the last Hierophant carried with him to the grave the secrets which had been transmitted orally for untold generations, from one high priest to the next."[2358]

Controversy about the nature of the rites was an inevitable consequence of this secrecy. Brumfield writes:

> The Eleusinian Mysteries have occasioned more scholarly debate than any other ancient festival. It is probably safe to assume that no possible theory or permutation of theories regarding the origin and significance of this rite remains to be discovered or invented. It seems that every possible avenue of explanation, no matter how outlandish or prosaic, has already been explored either in antiquity or in modern times.[2359]

In recent decades, much more has become known about the relationship between Eleusis and other sites developed for similar purposes.[2360] See Meyer[2361] for a valuable anthology of sources describing the variety of ancient mystery religions.

E-262   Note that Kerényi takes exception to any suggestion that the rites of Eleusis included a drama,[2362] however more recent studies seem to confirm Mylonas' general views on the matter.[2363]

E-263   "The importance of physical vision is indicated by the terms used: a *mystes* [i.e., first-time participant who received the Lower Mysteries] is one who closes his eyes, and *epoptes* [i.e., later participant in the Greater Mysteries] one who sees."[2364] For a detailed survey of the use of these and related terms, see Clinton.[2365]

Mylonas discusses evidence of purification rites enacted through "the sprinkling or pouring of water" that were to be performed prior to the receipt of the Mysteries for those who had been "tainted with blood."[2366]

E-264   Regarding the term "token," Compton writes:

> There are a number of words in Greek and Latin that mean "token" in recognition drama—e.g., *anagnosmata* ("things for making known again"), *spargana* (the swaddling wrappings of the lost child, often figured), *semeia* ("signs, marks, signals"). But one of the most interesting token-words is the basis for our word "symbol": *symbolon* (singular; plural: *symbola*), found as a name for tokens both in recognition and mystery. This word means "things thrown together" (i.e., something thrown together after it has been once broken apart, from *ballo*, "thrown," and *sun-*, "with or together"). Liddell, Scott, and Jones, in their Greek-English Lexicon, define it thus: "tally, i.e., each of two halves or corresponding pieces of an *astragalos* [knucklebone] or other object, which two *xenoi* [guest-friends], or any two contracting parties, broke between them, each party keeping one piece, in order to have proof of the identity of the presenter of the other." Both halves represent their two owners, and each is a symbol of identity, the individual, parted; the halves "thrown together," unified, are the symbol of two separate identities merging into one. So the

2356 C. Sourvinou-Inwood, *Festival*, p. 28.
2357 See C. Kerényi, *Eleusis*, p. 118; G. E. Mylonas, *Eleusis*, p. 225.
2358 S. D. Ricks *et al.*, *King*, p. 240. See G. E. Mylonas, *Eleusis*, p. 281.
2359 A. C. Brumfield, *Festivals*, p. 192.
2360 M. B. Cosmopoulos, *Mysteries*.
2361 M. W. Meyer, *Mysteries*.
2362 C. Kerényi, *Eleusis*, pp. 26-27.
2363 E.g., C. Sourvinou-Inwood, *Festival*, pp. 29-30.
2364 A. C. Brumfield, *Festivals*, p. 199.
2365 K. Clinton, *Stages*.
2366 G. E. Mylonas, *Eleusis*, pp. 242-243.

symbolon is a precise image both for absolutely unique individuality and perfectly joined unity. No other parts would fit the two *symbolon* halves; paradoxically, their unique identity is what creates their complete unity as represented by the unified token. It is also significant that the perfect fitting together is dependent on a previous breaking.

Later in the semantic development of the word, it came to be applied to "any token serving as proof of identity"—in which category we find the dramatic recognition token—and then developed on to other abstract and technical ideas: treaty, symbol, allegory, warrant, ticket. In the recognition *symbolon*, there is no longer the actual two-part, physically broken token, but the token remains a symbol of dual identity, "thrown together" after a parting.[2367]

E-265   For example, "Theseus received his name from the 'placing of the tokens' (*dia ten ton gnorismaton thesin*[2368]). Odysseus received his name from the man in whose care he would later receive a wound that became a recognition token, the scar created by the wild boar,[2369] and Oedipus received his name from the scars produced by his ankles being pierced when he was exposed."[2370]

E-266   Compton also reports instances of the recognition token in Chinese and Japanese fiction.[2371]

E-267   Compton reports:

Some later authors thought of Eleusis and the other mysteries in terms of the soul myth, the descent and ascent of the soul. Sallustius (circa 4th century CE) wrote that the rape of Proserpine [= Kore, Persephone] "signifies the descent of souls" (*kathodos esti ton psukhon*).[2372] If the Orphic poets believed that the incarnated spirit was imprisoned or entombed, and if there was significant Orphic influence at Eleusis by the time of Periclean Athens (and there is good evidence that the Eleusinian and the Orphic had interpenetrated some time before this, under the rule of Peististratos), it would be natural for them to see the "death" of Persephone as their "death": incarnation.

So too Plotinus likens the soul, after a descent, approaching Good and the Godly to a mystery initiate descending and ascending:

To attain it is for those that will take the upward path, who will set all their forces towards it, who will divest themselves of all that we have put on in our descent—so, to those that approach the Holy Celebrations of the Mysteries, there are appointed purifications and the laying aside of the garments worn before, and the entry in nakedness.[2373]

Details about expectations of initiates with respect to the afterlife can be found on:

… Greek texts on gold designed to protect the soul after death [that] have been turning up in graves throughout the Mediterranean since 1835.… Certain repeated themes and images… stand out, especially the anticipation of a journey to the underworld, a confrontation with a divine gate-keeper, a landscape with trees and water, and formulae for ritual responses. The conclusion to be drawn from the total collection is that those who took such texts to the grave (or their relatives) had confidence in entitlement to special treatment after death. In one way or another, the texts assume that eligibility was established by ritual and confirmed after death by recalling or reciting esoteric information that could have been learned only through that ritual experience.[2374]

Texts combine… recitation of ritual phrases with assertions of identity. The soul engages in dialogue. Divine stewards of the other world question new arrivals and expect answers. They ask: "Why are you here?" "Who are you?" "How are you?" The tablets themselves also make pronouncements and give instructions[, e.g.,] "Blessed and most happy you will be god instead of mortal."[2375]

Literary sources make it clear that, in addition to the initiation itself, "standards for social behavior were part of the preview of the Mysteries."[2376] For example, in Aristophanes' *Frogs*, at the moment

2367 T. M. Compton, *Handclasp*, pp. 612-613.
2368 See Plutarch, *Lives*, Theseus 3-4, p. 3.
2369 See Homer, *Odyssey*, 19:392-466, pp. 322-325.
2370 T. M. Compton, *Token*, n. 16. See Sophocles, *Oedipus Rex*, 1031-36, cited in Compton.
2371 T. M. Compton, *Token*, n. 37.
2372 P. Sallustius, *Gods*, 4, pp. 10-11.
2373 T. M. Compton, *Token*. See Plotinus, *Enneads*, 1:7, cited in Compton.
2374 S. G. Cole, *Landscapes*, pp. 200-201. See also J. Assman, *Death*, p. 207.
2375 *Ibid.*, p. 207.
2376 *Ibid.*, p. 199.

when "Dionysos walks up to the door of Hades as he prepares to cross the last boundary between the living and the dead," a chorus of initiates explains in song "the importance of acting with justice toward outsiders and fellow citizens."[2377]

The same Dionysos, who arguably played an explicit role in the Eleusinian mysteries,[2378] is sometimes portrayed as a mediator for later souls who take the same path:

> He is the god for those critical transitional moments right up to and including the interchange at Pluto's door. A fourth-century vase now in Toledo, in fact, depicts Dionysos at precisely this moment, stepping up to the entrance to the House of Hades and shaking hands with Hades himself… Dionysos seems to be negotiating here on behalf of his Theban cousins… Whatever the result, the important image is the gesture at the center, the handclasp, a gestural *symbola* that joins Dionysos and Hades. The two have come to an agreement.[2379]

E-268　One thinks also of Pandora, the Eve of Greek mythology, who brought death into the world when, curious about the contents of the box she had received from the Olympian gods as a gift, could not resist opening it to see the contents.[2380]

E-269　The theme of the ark/altar as a traveling repository carrying the remains of the righteous to their final resting place is reinforced by the Genesis account of Joseph's request to have his bones carried back to the land of his fathers,[2381] and by the story of Adam's request for interment in the Cave of Treasures and his later reburial at the place of Jesus' Crucifixion, "the second Cave of Treasures."[2382] As Ruzer observes, the significance of the story of Adam's burial for Christian liturgy can be found in "the table-altar erected over the burial place of Adam' in the Cave and ritual swearing by the blood of the slain Abel," the innocent Abel being a type of Christ.[2383]

Although the Old Testament word for Noah's ark (*tebah*) differs from the term used for the temple ark, the word used in the Greek New Testament (*kibotos*) is identical for both, leading Christians to draw parallels between the salvific roles of the two artifacts. Subtle allusions to such imagery can be found in Hebrews 9:4, 11:7; 1 Peter 3:20.

E-270　Davies observes that a given *dexiosis* scene often "can be interpreted by the viewer in a number of equally valid ways: as parting, reunion or communion, or perhaps in several different ways at once. The motif is ambiguous and flexible."[2384] Closterman highlights the difficulty in many cases of determining not only the family relationships among the individuals depicted, but even which among many figures on a particular monument represents the deceased.[2385] In addition to noting the aforementioned problems, Davies describes the difficulties in determining the setting of a particular scene (e.g., the Underworld, the tomb).[2386]

E-271　Compton does not rule out the possibility that the fan and chest carried by the servant girl "might… be mystery symbols."[2387] A winnowing fan is depicted in the "Eleusis-influenced Lovatelli urn,"[2388] and Clement of Alexandria claimed that a chest containing tokens figured in the Eleusinian rites.[2389]

E-272　Davies records that the earlier meanings continued long past the archaic period:

> The handshake was also used in reliefs at Nemrud Dagh to link Herakles with late Hellenistic Commagene kings, an indication that the sense of the motif used on late Archaic vases had not

2377　*Ibid.*, pp. 198-199.
2378　E. A. Beach, *Mysteries*.
2379　S. G. Cole, *Landscapes*, p. 211.
2380　D. Leeming, *World Mythology*, pp. 306-307.
2381　Genesis 50:24-26. Note that the Hebrew word for the Ark of the Covenant (*aron*), meaning chest or box, is the same word used for Joseph's "coffin" (E. Fox, *Books of Moses*, p. 397 n. Exodus 25:10).
2382　S. Ruzer, *Pilgrimage*.
2383　*Ibid.* See also S. Ruzer, *Abel's Blood*.
2384　G. Davies, *Handshake*, p. 629.
2385　W. E. Closterman, *Ideology*, pp. 636-637.
2386　G. Davies, *Handshake*, pp. 628-629.
2387　T. M. Compton, *21 April 2008*.
2388　T. M. Compton, *Handclasp*, p. 615. See discussion and photograph in G. E. Mylonas, *Eleusis*, pp. 205-207, 242, 243, 297, and plate 83.
2389　Clement of Alexandria, *Exhortation*, 2:21, p. 177.

EXCURSUS

been forgotten; here, however, it is the monarch whose status is being enhanced by means of the handclasp with Herakles.[2390]

Compton further elaborates on the salvific nature of the gesture:

> While the handclasp, often expresses complete equality (as in the marriage handclasp, one of the most unvarying of Roman marriage rituals, and as in the handclasp used for treaty), here it expresses salvation, the saving and the saved. It is diagonal, not level; Heracles reaches up, Athena reaches down. The goddess will draw the mortal up into heaven. However, the sense of equality is not entirely gone: Heracles enters heaven by having a goddess descend to his level; he has come up to her level, almost. The clasp here symbolizes entrance, liminality, …but it also emphasizes apotheosis, the entrance into the divine type of life, as it simultaneously suggests the condescension of the god that makes the apotheosis possible.[2391]

E-273 He notes, for example, that:

> … in the culminating initiation scene in the Eleusis-influenced Lovatelli urn,[2392] there is perhaps a hint of the *dexios*. As the initiate approaches Demeter sitting on the cista, the goddess's snake rises from her lap to greet the initiate; he extends his right hand for the snake to touch. If, as I have argued, this scene reflects a high point of the mysteries, and if the touching of the snake and the right hand of the initiate is related to the *dextrarum iunctio*, we may conjecture that a handclasp as token (the snake represents the contents of the *cista*, the *symbola*, as well as the presence of the god) took place as part of the initiate's union with the god at Eleusis.[2393]

E-274 If not concurring with Goodenough's specific conclusions about the beliefs and practices of the Jewish group who built the synagogue, a majority of scholars would at least accept the more general idea that "[m]ost of the scenes at Dura have some connection to messianic redemption and resurrection."[2394] According to Johnson, what neither supporters nor opponents of Goodenough can deny is the:

> … pervasive use by Philo of language that takes its origin in the mysteries yet is employed with direct reference to the practice and self-understanding of Judaism. There is no question here of syncretism in the crude sense. Philo engages in the same sort of rejection of the pagan mysteries that we find in *The Wisdom of Solomon*….[2395] What we find in Philo, then, is not a mingling of Judaism and the mysteries, but rather a conceptualization of Judaism as Mystery."[2396]

Among the very few comments of critics that Neusner deemed "important" is that Goodenough may have overemphasized the distinction between rabbinic and mystical Judaism, which he himself admits should have been represented more as a "confused gradation" than as a dichotomy.[2397] Some critics also discount Goodenough's reliance on Philo, seeing the interpretations of the latter as "sui generis and not reflective of what was going on in most Jewish circles of antiquity."[2398] While Collins failed to see sufficient evidence for distinctive Jewish mystic ritual, his extensive review of mystic Judaism and its literature largely substantiates and expands upon Goodenough's arguments regarding Jewish mystic philosophy.[2399] Gutmann is "fairly certain that the popular Philonic 'mystic Hellenistic' Judaism which… Goodenough imposed on or read into the Dura synagogue paintings would have been totally incomprehensible to the small congregation of probably unsophisticated and unintellectual Jewish merchants and the other Jewish inhabitants residing at Dura."[2400] Avi-Yonah disagrees with Goodenough's general interpretation of the Dura synagogue paintings as reflecting mystical Judaism, and outlines later findings that have in some cases substantiated and in others seemingly repudiated his arguments relating to specific interpretations.[2401] Additional assessments of

---

2390 G. Davies, *Handshake*, p. 630.

2391 T. M. Compton, *Handclasp*, p. 617.

2392 See G. E. Mylonas, *Eleusis*, pp. 206-207, and Fig. 83.

2393 T. M. Compton, *Handclasp*, p. 615.

2394 J. R. Russell, *Ezekiel*, p. 905.

2395 S. Sandmel, *et al.*, *Solomon*, 14:22-31, p. 109.

2396 L. T. Johnson, *Religious Experience*, pp. 90-91.

2397 Citing Morton Smith in J. Neusner, *Synagogue*, p. 56; cf. J. Neusner, *Foreword*, p. xxxiv. See also J. M. G. Barclay, *Diaspora*, p. 165 n. 90; J. Gutmann, *Introduction*, pp. xxiii-xxiv.

2398 L. I. Levine, *Judaism*, p. 8 n. 6.

2399 J. J. Collins, *Athens*, pp. 210-260.

2400 J. Gutmann, *Introduction*, pp. xxii-xxiii.

2401 M. Avi-Yonah, *Critique*.

Goodenough's methods and interpretation have been summarized elsewhere.[2402]

Neusner's article contrasting Goodenough's method with that of Kraeling shows how the two preeminent scholars of the Dura Synagogue of their generation were representative exemplars of the two scientific temperaments described by William James: "those that dread above all the risk of possibly mistaking falsehoods for truths, and those that fear even more the risk of missing potentially valuable truths."[2403]

Neusner observes that when Kraeling's monumental study was published, "it seemed that no substantial revision of earlier ideas on Judaism at this period would be required. Kraeling argued that the paintings might be interpreted for the most part by reference to the so-called rabbinic literature of the period.... [He] argues that the biblical references of the Dura paintings are so obvious that one may begin by reading the Bible... While he makes reference, from time to time, to comparative materials, Kraeling does not in the main feel it necessary to examine the broad iconographic traditions operating in Dura in general, ... for he holds that... the meaning of the synagogue art... can best... be understood within the context of the Judaism known to us from literary sources." [2404]

Goodenough, on the other hand, has persuasively argued "that literary traditions would not have led us to expect any such art as this. We may find statements in talmudic literature which are relevant to the art, but we must in any case after assembling the material determine 'what the art means in itself, before we begin to apply it as proof texts of any possible unrelated statements of the Bible or the *Talmud*.'[2405"2406] His method in unraveling such enigmas has been aptly summarized as follows: "first with rigorous care to describe 'what one sees,' then with boldness and imagination to propose what may have been happening in the ancient circle that produced what one now sees from afar."[2407] To be sure, what one sees is necessarily conditioned by everything one already has studied, however, in Goodenough's case, he is prepared to bring not only a deep understanding of Jewish tradition and history, but also what Neusner calls "a majestic array of comparative material"[2408] that often provide striking illumination of features of the paintings that have been dismissed by other scholars as "mere ornament."[2409] After an analysis of a series of side-by-side examples of interpretation from the two preeminent scholars of Dura of their generation, Neusner concludes:

> … Goodenough demands explanation from a far greater number and variety of details; he sees more in the art and asks more about it. Kraeling uses, in the main, a single body of literature, while Goodenough ranges far and wide in his search for ideas and artistic conventions relevant to Dura synagogue art....
>
> If Kraeling had considered and refuted the kinds of evidence Goodenough regards as relevant, one might be in a clearer position to evaluate his explanation. But where Goodenough provides an abundance of comparative material, both artistic and literary, on the basis of which to evaluate his interpretations, Kraeling provides only a single verse of the Targum, and that, to my way of reading it, by no means conclusive....
>
> If we had begun with a statement of Kraeling's and Goodenough's views of Dura Judaism, without a preliminary examination of some specific problems of interpretation, it seems to me wholly likely that Kraeling's view, and not Goodenough's, would have prevailed. Having seen in... specific instances, however, adumbrations of the very solid basis upon which Goodenough bases his general assertions (in fact, the specific analysis of the art far outweighs the generalizations in both Kraeling's and Goodenough's studies), the reader will be more likely to take seriously a radical reinterpretation of the whole....
>
> With [what we know about how pre-Amoraic Babylonian Judaism was deeply affected by Ezekiel and their probable engagement in the *merkavah* tradition] in mind, I find it very difficult to question the importance ascribed by Goodenough to mysticism in Dura. I do not argue that his

---

2402 E. J. Bickerman, *Dura Symbolism*; S. K. Neumiller, *Isaiah*; M. Smith, *Goodenough's Symbols*.

2403 E. A. Beach, *Mysteries*. See W. James, *Will*, pp. 26, 94-95n. It would, perhaps, be instructive to compare Goodenough's approach to the approaches of Hugh Nibley and Margaret Barker, both of which have received praise and criticism for similar approaches in their broad and deeply documented comparative studies.

2404 J. Neusner, *Judaism at Dura*, pp. 156, 157.

2405 E. R. Goodenough, *Method*, 4:10, cited *ibid.*, p. 158.

2406 J. Neusner, *Judaism at Dura*, p. 158.

2407 W. A. Meeks, *Moses*, p. 371.

2408 J. Neusner, *Judaism at Dura*, p. 167.

2409 *Ibid.*, p. 169.

interpretations are, in detail, correct, for I am not competent to make a judgment on that question. But I do think that the importance of Ezekiel in Dura, and the details, if correctly discerned, of various kinds of traditional mystical speculation, which Goodenough finds on the walls of Dura synagogue, are both wholly congruent to what we know of Babylonian Judaism before circa 220 A.D.[2410]

E-275   Often criticized for his interpretations, Goodenough showed ambivalence in his writings about the terms "initiation" and "mystery," speaking in his early writings in ways that at least sometimes seemed to imply a literal sense, while in his last writings leaning toward a figurative one.[2411] Despite the comprehensiveness of Goodenough's arguments, the possibility of a literal mystery involving special rites is currently seen as doubtful by all but a small minority of scholars.

The discussion of Fletcher-Louis about how the Qumran community merged realized and future eschatology in their liturgical concept of an "angelomorphic priesthood" seems relevant to Goodenough's speculations about Jewish worship at Dura Europos.[2412] At Qumran, Fletcher-Louis envisages the possibility of:

> … a liturgical or cultic context for… apotheosis that could, in theory, be entirely compatible with… a real mystical or visionary experience… [I]t is… likely, given the cosmological significance attached to the cult, that the regular, even *routinized*, worship of a Jewish community which *considers itself* not heterodox but orthodox, would foster the belief in personal experiences of mystical transcendence and apotheosis.[2413]

After a thorough analysis of their liturgical texts, he concludes that the Qumran community:

> … believed that (1) *in its original, true and redeemed state humanity is divine (and/or angelic).* They also believed that (2) the attainment now, for the redeemed, of this true humanity was *conceptually and experientially grounded in their "temple" worship in which ordinary space and time, and therefore human ontology, are transcended. They take for granted a cultic mythology which means that those who enter the worship of the community experience a transfer from earth to heaven, from humanity to divinity and from mortality to immortality…* [T]his theological anthropology at Qumran was inherited from older, priestly, tradition which the sectarians carried with them into the wilderness. There is little evidence in the texts that this anthropology is a peculiar product of Qumran sectarianism… Before his Fall Adam was ontologically coterminous with God's own Glory. His originally divine humanity is recovered when (the true) Israel worships her god in a pure cult—a restored cosmos in miniature. And, so, by the same token she, especially her priesthood, recovers the previously lost Glory of God in the same context. In worship, the boundary between heaven and earth is dissolved and the Qumran community are taken up into the life of that which they worship.[2414]

Also supporting Fletcher-Louis' arguments is the fact that "the stories of Genesis that were popular and utilized at Qumran constitute only a small portion of the biblical book… The heavy emphasis of most of the texts, almost regardless of type, is on the material from the Creation and the Garden of Eden, Enoch, the Watchers, and the Flood through the covenant with Abraham and the *Akedah*."[2415]

E-276   This three-part scheme is reflected in temples throughout the ancient world. It was also symbolized in the gathering of Israel at Sinai in three groups: "the masses at the foot of the mountain, where they viewed God's 'Presence' from afar; the Seventy part way up; and Moses at the very top, where he entered directly into God's Presence."[2416] Seaich describes this as:[2417]

> … the arrangement in the Temple, as well, with the mass of pilgrims assembled in the Forecourt, the Aaronic priests sacrificing in the Holy Place, and the High Priest entering the Holy of Holies each year to expiate for Israel's sins. Philo accordingly thought of this recreated "Sinai experience" as a three-part "journey" along the "Royal Road" leading to God, but with unequal attainments having

---

2410   *Ibid.*, pp. 161-162, 169, 173-174, 186-187.

2411   R. S. Eccles, *Pilgrimage*, pp. 64-65. Goodenough showed the same ambivalence toward religion in general. Sandmel described him as "a deeply religious man… at war with organized religion.… [H]e had a quarrel with organized religion but not with God" (S. Sandmel, *Appreciation*, pp. 4-5).

2412   C. H. T. Fletcher-Louis, *Glory*, pp. 150ff.

2413   *Ibid.*, pp. 212-213.

2414   *Ibid.*, p. 476.

2415   M. J. Bernstein, *Contours*, p. 81.

2416   J. E. Seaich, *Ancient Texts 1995*, p. 660; cf. pp. 568-577, 661, 807-809.

2417   J. E. Seaich, *Ancient Texts 1995*, pp. 807-809; cf. J. Jeremias, *Sermon*, p. 6; Matthew 6:19-7:27; 1 Corinthians 3:10-15.

been achieved by the participants: "At the top, Moses; then those who are capable of traversing the path to higher knowledge; and at the bottom the mass, which is entirely unorganized and must remain at the foot of the mountain, only a few of which will catch even a glimpse… of a path open to higher regions"….[2418] This three-stage spiritual journey was also reflected in the Dead Sea Scrolls by the division of the people into three levels of ecclesiastical attainment: the priests, the Levites, and the laity…. Indeed, Joachim Jeremias also finds this tripartite progress demonstrated by the disciples who approached Christ at the Sermon on the Mount, with the "legalists" at the bottom, castigated for their artificial righteousness,[2419] the self-satisfied "strivers" in the middle, destined for an earthly reward,[2420] and the truly spiritual disciples exhorted to build on the foundation of God's perfect righteousness, rather than the righteousness of men.

To enter the sacred precincts of the temple unworthily not only courts danger for the individual, but also endangers the holiness of the structure itself. Milgrom portrays the temple architecture in terms of three stages of graded power relating to the contamination of sin and its concomitant purification, and acknowledges parallels between the ancient scheme and modern LDS temples: "Like Israel of old, Mormons [hold that] man can, by his sin, defile the temple and force God to abandon his earthly residence."[2421]

E-277   For example, interpreting a passage from the *Gospel of Philip*,[2422] MacRae writes:[2423]

Apart from the details of which way the building faced and so on, the writer is talking about an outer court, a middle court, and the inner court which is the Holy of Holies. The allegory seems to identify these with three different sacraments in the sacramental system of the Valentinean Gnostics. But I think it is more than that. It is more than that because it builds on the concept that one moves toward the divine presence as one moves successively through the outer courts of the temple toward the inner Holy of Holies, to which only the priest has access. Consequently the order in which the courts are identified with sacraments becomes very important. The initiatory rite of baptism is the outermost one. The rite of redemption, whatever that may have consisted of, is the second one. And it is the bridal chamber, the rite of which was the supreme rite for the Valentinean Gnostic, which is the approach into the presence of God himself.

E-278   Recall the series of four *kushta* handclasps, corresponding to four rites leading to the presence of God, in Mandaean liturgy,[2424] and the series of "five signs and five mysteries" expressed by the "right hand" and the "embrace" in Manichaean ritual.[2425]

E-279   Barker comments:

The idea of resurrection is certainly present; we do not know how resurrection was understood in the first temple, but resurrection was an expectation of the priests; i.e., that they were resurrected when they came into the presence of God at their consecration, and then returned to the world. This would explain Ezekiel returning to the world to face martyrdom.[2426]

E-280   The scattered bones may suggest the Persian practice of exposing rather than burying the dead, raising the question of correspondence to Zoroastrian resurrection beliefs.[2427]

E-281   The mountain is surely meant to represent the Mount of Olives, which is destined to cleave in two at a crucial moment in the last days.[2428] The *Targum to the Song of Songs* 8:5 envisions the mountain as the site of the resurrection of all Israel: "When the dead rise, the Mount of Olives will open and all Israel's dead will come up out of it, also the righteous who have died in captivity: they will come through a subterranean passage and come up from under the Mount of Olives."[2429]

2418 R. Wagner, *Gnosis*, p. 23.

2419 Matthew 5:21-48.

2420 Matthew 6:1-8.

2421 J. Milgrom, *Kinships*, pp. 63-64.

2422 W. W. Isenberg, *Philip*, 69:14-70:4, p. 151.

2423 G. W. MacRae, *House of Revelation*, pp. 184-185. Compare views in R. Uro, *Bridal Chamber*.

2424 E. S. Drower, *Thousand*, pp. 255-256. See *Annotated Bibliography, Mandaean Texts*, p. 870 and *Figure* B-1, p. 872.

2425 I. Gardner, *Kephalaia*, 9, pp. 43-46 See *Excursus 51: The Five Lost Things of the Temple*, p. 658 and *Annotated Bibliography, Manichaean Texts*, p. 884.

2426 M. Barker, *11 June 2007*.

2427 N. T. Wright, *Resurrection*, p. 125 and p. 125 n. 169.

2428 Zechariah 14:4; cf. D&C 45:48, 133:20.

2429 Cited in H. Riesenfeld, *Resurrection*, p. 31; cf. H. Schwartz, *Tree*, 639, pp. 504-506; R. P. Gordon, *Eschatologists*,

A similar concept is found in the Scottish ballad *Loch Lomond*, which is said to be about two soldiers, one to be executed, and the other to be released. The refrain describes how the spirit of the dead soldier traveling by the "low road" of the underworld would reach Scotland before his comrade returning overland on the "high road":

> O ye'll tak' the high road and I'll tak' the low road,
> An' I'll be in Scotland afore ye;
> But me and my true love will never meet again
> On the bonnie, bonnie banks O' Loch Lomond

E-282   Barker asks: "Were they the trees of Eden? If so, then in the Enoch tradition, the Tree of Knowledge went to Babylon, but the Tree of Life went to 'the south,' and was destined to return to Jerusalem."[2430]

Note that the date palm—the Tree of Life that was so prominent in Ezekiel's temple vision[2431]—is *not* represented in the painting.

Regarding the image of the two trees, observe that in Revelation 22:2, the Tree of Life "is rather ambiguously described in twofold aspect planted either side of the river of the water of life":[2432] "Then he showed me the river of the water of life, sparkling like crystal, flowing from the throne of God and of the Lamb down the middle of the city's street. On either side of the river stood a Tree of Life."[2433]

Barker describes various approaches to the translation difficulties that surround the strange idea of a twofold Tree of Life in heaven:

> One solution might be that the tree bears its fruits "on one side and the other," but it is more likely that the branches of the tree extend a great distance, or that the tree has its roots in the river, as did Ezekiel's great tree. The gist would then be that the tree stands in the middle of the city square and the river flows through the square and round the roots of the tree: "The Tree of Life is in the midst of the square with the river [which flows all round it] on this side and that, bearing twelve fruits…" Or perhaps the picture is of a huge tree in the midst of the river spreading out its branches on this side and that. Other first-century CE descriptions of the tree still emphasize the extent of its branches.[2434]

E-283   The allusion to the four winds in this passage requires additional explanation. Chester rightly points out that the use of *ruach* in vv. 5-6, 9-10:

> … with the apparent deliberate ambiguity of it as meaning breath, wind or spirit (and the deliberate further play on this in the climax of the section in v. 14, where [*ruach*] obviously must mean the [divine] Spirit)—can be understood as having deliberate echoes of the Genesis creation narratives…[2435] Certainly it could be argued that in this case we should expect [*ruach*] here (as at v. 14). But that is not an insuperable objection, if, as I wish to argue, there is a deliberate ambiguity involved here in the exact sense of [*ruach*]: that is, that it can encompass both breath and (divine) spirit, and indeed 'wind' as well. This may in fact help us to make sense of 37:9 in relation to 37:5-6. It has been found puzzling that the [*ruach*] which the prophet is commanded to prophesy is supposed to come from the four ['winds']. A possible parallel has been seen with the *Enuma Elish*,[2436] and it is indeed plausible that there is an underlying mythological point of reference. More immediately, however, it is evident that the 'four winds'… denote the four corners of the earth. The point, then, will be that the [*ruach*] is given a specifically and deliberately cosmic scope: this would obviously fit also with a supposed link with the *Enuma Elish*… What is involved, on one level at least, is an allusion to the cosmic scope of the [*ruach*] of [Moses 2:2], along with its creative force…. Overall, then, the [*ruach*] of Ezekiel 37 contains at least hints of all these different—although overlapping—dimensions: the breath necessary for human life, the cosmic, creative divine Spirit, and the eschatological divine Spirit.[2437]

The implication is that, as Chester mentions specifically in reference to Daniel 12:1-3, but also with

p. 308.
2430 M. Barker, *11 June 2007*.
2431 Ezekiel 40:16, 22, 26, 31, 34, 37; 41:18-20, 25-26.
2432 J. O'Reilly, *Iconography*, p. 176.
2433 S. Sandmel, *et al.*, *New English Bible*, Revelation 22:2, p. 332.
2434 M. Barker, *Revelation*, p. 330.
2435 E.g., Moses 2:2, 3:7.
2436 E. A. Speiser, *Creation Epic*, 114, p. 62.
2437 A. Chester, *Messiah*, pp. 125-127.

implication for other OT and Jewish texts cited by him, "those who are delivered…, and not just a few individuals, will take on a transformed and heavenly angelic state, in the end time, at the point of decisive eschatological intervention."[2438]

E-284 Koester admits the possibility that the cult of Sabazius, whose powers were associated with a similar gesture, had its origins in a form of mystical Judaism: "Possibly some Jews of Asia Minor who were Hellenized to a large degree had, in organizing their congregations and in understanding their religious services as mysteries, accepted religious forms and designations that were assimilated to their pagan neighbors."[2439]

E-285 On the face of it, the idea expressed in the Ezekiel mural seems to be that the mountain is first split to release the dead, and then once again made whole. This image, combined with panel image of the dead passing through the split mountain as they are resurrected, could be seen as an eschatological recapitulation of Mesopotamian and Mesoamerican creation traditions that speak of the primordial mound being cracked open by the storm god, "having the prime objective of allowing men to spring forth like vegetation."[2440] The image of the primordial mound being split in two was reflected both in Near Eastern art and temple architecture.[2441] All this imagery seems quite compatible with Jewish conceptions of resurrection as rebirth, "the earth being as a womb which shall give birth to them that are in their graves."[2442]

One might also make a case that the panel represents the two trees as having been brought back together into one. If we take the trees as representing the special trees of Eden, the idea recalls passages in the *Zohar* that relate to the initial splitting of the originally-unified Tree of Life and the Tree of Knowledge. According to the *Zohar*:

> … the *Sefiroth*[2443] were revealed to Adam in the shape of the Tree of Life and the Tree of Knowledge, i.e., the middle and the last *Sefirah*; instead of preserving their original unity and thereby unifying the spheres of "life" and "knowledge" and bringing salvation to the world, he separated one from the other and set his mind to worship the *Shekhinah* only without recognizing its union with the other *Sefritoth*. Thus he… brought separation and isolation into the world… Only after the restoration of the original harmony in the act of redemption, when everything shall again occupy the place it originally had in the divine scheme of things, will "God be one and His name one," in biblical terms, truly and for all time.…[2444]

> Sin always destroys a union, and a destructive separation of this kind was also immanent in the Original Sin through which the fruit was separated from the tree, or as another kabbalist puts it, the Tree of Life from the Tree of Knowledge.[2445]

In the context with the story of the prophet Ezekiel, it is also tempting to regard the trees as an allusion to the two "sticks" (literally: woods or trees) of Ezekiel 37:15-20[2446] being reunited in token of the restoration of the House of Israel. This interpretation is consistent with the overall theme of the final design of the Dura Tree of Life mural,[2447] with the separate blessings of the two divisions of Israel at the bottom of the tree and their joint exaltation near the throne at the top.

E-286 Goodenough's identification of this panel as the death of Ezekiel is controversial. Interpretation is made more difficult because of significant overpainting of some sections. As an example of other perspectives, Hopkins takes the panel to be an illustration of an event occurring near the beginning of the revolt of the Maccabees.[2448] After considering several possibilities, Kraeling concludes that the scene represents the slaying of King Jehoiakim by Nebuchadnezzar.[2449] However, Avi-Yonah, who has otherwise sharply criticized many of Goodenough's interpretations writes: "Goodenough's

2438 *Ibid.*, p. 144.

2439 H. Koester, *New Testament 1*, p. 187.

2440 D. E. Wirth, *Parallels*, p. 151. See also A. J. Christenson, *Popol Vuh 2003*, p. 193 n. 454.

2441 D. E. Wirth, *Parallels*, pp. 151-154.

2442 H. Riesenfeld, *Resurrection*, p. 11; cf. e.g., Isaiah 26:19: "the earth shall cast out the dead."

2443 = the ten mystical attributes of God.

2444 G. Scholem, *Trends*, p. 232.

2445 *Ibid.*, p. 236. See also *ibid.*, pp. 404-405 n. 105; G. Scholem, *Kabbalah*, pp. 112, 124-128, 166-168; D. C. Matt, *Zohar 1*, Be-Reshit, 1:12b, p. 85. 1:35b, p. 222.

2446 C. H. Kraeling, *et al.*, *Synagogue*, p. 191.

2447 E. R. Goodenough, *Dura Symbolism*, 11, Figure 323.

2448 C. Hopkins, *Discovery*, pp. 171-172.

2449 C. H. Kraeling, *et al.*, *Synagogue*, pp. 194-202.

interpretation of the last scene in the Ezekiel series as representing the legendary story of the execution of the prophet, seems to us both logical and consistent, although there is as yet no textual proof for it."[2450]

E-287   It is significant that the power to raise the dead is delegated to Ezekiel, rather than the act being performed by God Himself.[2451] Riesenfeld suggests a parallel to God's delegation of the key of resurrection to Ezekiel in Christ's raising of Lazarus,[2452] and points out parallels in other instances from Jesus' ministry to similar miracles by Elijah and Elisha. "It is perhaps more than chance that the miracles of revivification performed, according to Jewish belief, by Elijah, Elisha, and Ezekiel, each prefiguring the coming Messiah, in some way have reached fulfillment in the Messianic activity of Jesus Christ."[2453]

E-288   Block concludes that the number ten is "hardly coincidental" and represents "the ten tribes that had made up the northern kingdom prior to its collapse in the 8th century."[2454] Goodenough admits that they "may represent the restoration of the lost ten tribes, but in that case it is hard to think that Judah and Benjamin should still be the unassembled 'bones' beside them. Just what they represent I cannot say, but must suggest that the number ten may here have the significance of the ten columns of the inner shrine of the Closed Temple, which appeared to be the number of perfection, the highest presentation of immaterial reality and mystical achievement."[2455]

Relating the ten columns of the heavenly temple to the ten resurrected men is the very plausible reminder by Schubert that ten was the "full number for a liturgical congregation."[2456] Since at least talmudic times, the number ten was fixed as a quorum for public prayer as part of a Jewish *minyan* (from Hebrew *maneh* = to count or number). One of the justifications for the practice is the story of Joseph in Egypt: "Just as the 'children of Israel' in [Genesis 42:5] refers to the ten sons of Jacob who descended to Egypt to obtain food during the famine, so too [Leviticus 22:32] refers to sanctification among the 'children of Israel' in the presence of ten."[2457] Echoing the symbolism of ancient prayer circles, Kogan writes: "On one level, the body that is formed below, the actual *minyan*, is entered by the *Shekhinah* (the supernal holiness), and is thus the point of contact between God and Israel. Simultaneously, the *minyan* formed in the proper manner below unifies the heavenly realm above."[2458] Schubert explains the nearby body parts that have not been rejoined as symbolizing "those groups of sinners, which according to Rabbinic understanding, have no part in the resurrection."[2459]

Although himself convinced that Ezekiel had "no thought of a resurrection of individuals from the dead," Zimmerli nevertheless concedes that this is exactly how the prophet's vision is understood at Dura Europos.[2460] Convincingly arguing against the current scholarly mainstream,[2461] Russell concludes that Ezekiel's vision of the resurrection seemingly "owes much to Zoroastrian conceptions" and that the symbolism of the resurrection as a collective redemption of Israel does not exclude the idea of an individual bodily resurrection.[2462] Riesenfeld connects Jewish beliefs in the resurrection with Israel's royal festival of the harvest and the new year: the Feast of the Tabernacles. Here, the rites of enthronement "culminated in the solemn exaltation or 'resurrection' which followed upon the king's struggle against the powers of Chaos and Death and the dramatic representation of his humiliation and descent to Hades…. [T]he king's resurrection and [enthronement] signified new life and new birth for the people within the frame of the covenant… [T]hat which was enacted annually

2450 M. Avi-Yonah, *Critique*, p. 119.

2451 H. Riesenfeld, *Resurrection*, p. 32.

2452 See *ibid.*, p. 38 n. 7, where he notes a sarcophagus carved with a combination of these stories.

2453 *Ibid.*, p. 38.

2454 D. I. Block, *Ezekiel 25-48*, p. 391.

2455 E. R. Goodenough, *Dura Symbolism*, 10:194; cf. 10:60, 63-69, 204, 207; E. R. Goodenough, *Summary*, p. 183.

2456 K. Schubert, *Jewish Pictorial*, p. 188.

2457 *Minyan*.

2458 D. Blumenthal, *Merkabah*, p. 147.

2459 K. Schubert, *Jewish Pictorial*, p. 188.

2460 W. Zimmerli, *Ezekiel 2*, p. 264; cf. N. T. Wright, *Resurrection*, pp. 120-121. *Pseudo-Ezekiel* likewise provides evidence that Jews at Qumran interpreted Ezekiel 37 in terms of individual resurrection (F. G. Martinez, *Pseudo-Ezekiel*, fragment 2, p. 286; cf. J. H. Charlesworth, *Concept of Resurrection*, p. 3; C. D. Elledge, *Earliest Evidence*, pp. 34-35). For a discussion of other early sources describing individual resurrection, see C. D. Elledge, *Concept of Resurrection*, pp. 12-17; C. D. Elledge, *Earliest Evidence*.

2461 E.g., J. H. Charlesworth, *Concept of Resurrection*, p. 3; C. D. Elledge, *Earliest Evidence*, p. 26.

2462 J. R. Russell, *Ezekiel*, pp. 903, 901; cf. D. H. Akenson, *Surpassing Wonder*, p. 384; H. Riesenfeld, *Resurrection*, pp. 3ff. and biblical passages such as Isaiah 36:19, 53:10-12; Hosea 6:2; Micah 7:8; and Psalm 27:15.

in the ritual drama was to take place in the future in a more marked or final way."[2463]

E-289 Goodenough discussed the finding of these marks not only in the Dura murals, but also in a cache of white textile fragments discovered at the site that "may well have been the contents of a box where sacred vestments were kept, or they may have been fetishistic marks, originally on sacred robes, that were preserved after the garments had been outworn."[2464] Goodenough points to findings on Christian robes, in hellenized Egypt, Palmyra, and on Roman figures of Victory which "so commonly appears as a symbol of immortality."[2465]

Welch discusses Goodenough's conclusions, and reports similar findings at Masada and elsewhere.[2466] He observes that "the *Talmud* demands that priests execute their most sacred religious duty, that of sacrifice, by applying the blood of the sacrificial animal to the altar in a gamma pattern: 'he made the single application in the shape of a Greek Gamma.'"[2467] Nibley reports a "Ravenna mosaic, ca. 520 CE, [which] shows the priest-king Melchizedek in a purple cloak, offering bread and wine at the altar.[2468] The white altar cloth is decorated with two sets of *gammadia*, as well as… two interlocked squares in gold.[2469] Abel offers his lamb as Abraham gently pushes Isaac forward. The hand of God reaches down to this sacred meeting through red veils adorned with golden *gammadia* on either side. The theme is the great sacrifice of Christ, which brings together the righteous prophets from the past as well as the four corners of the present world, thereby uniting all time and space."[2470]

At least some Christians had additional ceremonial symbols woven into their clothing, perhaps reflecting further rites of the high priesthood, superior to those of Aaron.[2471] Moreover, besides the *clavi* and *gams* previously mentioned, Goodenough describes an ornament in "the form of a stripe ending in an arrow, which also is represented in the synagogue."[2472] Moreover, a photograph by Griggs of well-preserved clothing at an Egyptian burial site showed an "early Christian garment… made of wool [that] was placed next to the body. The garment has a woven rosette over each breast, a hemmed cut on the abdomen, and a rosette above the right knee."[2473]

E-290 Russell notes that Ezekiel's "vision of God in person[2474] was so vivid and explicit that the book was nearly suppressed altogether, and the study of the mysteries of the *Merkabah*, for which it is the primary source, was severely limited. Posterity took this first section of his book seriously and literally. Some of Ezekiel's contemporaries did not receive his prophecies that way though, to his great displeasure."[2475]

E-291 Barker writes:[2476]

To see the glory of the Lord's presence—to see beyond the veil— was the greatest blessing. The high priest used to bless Israel with the words: "The Lord bless you and keep you: The Lord make his face to shine upon you, and be gracious unto you: The Lord lift up his countenance upon you, and give you peace"…[2477]

2463 H. Riesenfeld, *Resurrection*, pp. 5-6. For a recent summary of early Jewish and Christian interpretations of Ezekiel 37, see M. Greenberg, *Ezekiel 21-37*, pp. 749-751.

2464 E. R. Goodenough, *Garments*, p. 225; cf. E. R. Goodenough, *Dura Symbolism*, 9:127-129.

2465 E. R. Goodenough, *Dura Symbolism*, 9:163.

2466 J. W. Welch, *et al.*, *Gammadia*.

2467 *Ibid.*, p. 254. See *Talmud*, Zebahim 53b, cited in Welch.

2468 Genesis 14:18-20.

2469 See the caption and footnotes for *Figures* E20-1 and E20-2, p. 573.

2470 H. W. Nibley, *Vestments*, p. 109; cf. W. J. Hamblin, *et al.*, *Temple*, p. 53, fig. 46. See Nibley for a discussion and further examples of *gammadia* in Jewish and Christian garments, altar cloths, veils, and in Roman- and Egyptian-themed depictions (H. W. Nibley, *Vestments*, pp. 105-112).

2471 See *Excursus 3: Temple Blessings in the Oath and Covenant of the Priesthood*, p. 519; R. S. Eccles, *Hebrews*. In modern times, Brigham Young raised the possibility that a given individual might be limited to receiving an Aaronic Priesthood portion of the temple endowment only (B. Young, *10-13 June 1864*, p. 309; also cited in J. Smith, Jr., *Words*, p. 304, n. 21).

2472 E. R. Goodenough, *Dura Symbolism*, 9:127. See also the dress of the last person on the lower row of E. R. Goodenough, *Dura Symbolism*, 11, fig. 339. An arrow, of course, can easily be seen as representing movement leading toward a desired destination, aptly complementing the meaning of the square *gammadia*.

2473 C. W. Griggs, *Evidences*, p. 227.

2474 Ezekiel ch. 1.

2475 J. R. Russell, *Ezekiel*, p. 900.

2476 M. Barker, *Christmas*, pp. 14-15.

2477 Numbers 6:24-26.

Seeing the glory, however, became controversial. Nobody knows why. There is one strand in the Old Testament that is absolutely opposed to any idea of seeing the divine. Two accounts of the story of Moses on Sinai will illustrate the point. In one, he saw the God of Israel, with a sapphire pavement at his feet;[2478] in the other, the people were reminded that they had seen no form when the Lord spoke from the midst of the fire on the mountain: there was only a voice.[2479] Moses spoke with the Lord face to face as a man speaks with a friend,[2480] and yet when Moses asked to see the glory of the Lord, he was told he could not see the Lord: "You cannot see my face; for man shall not see me and live… my face shall not be seen."[2481] Isaiah saw the Lord, enthroned in the temple,[2482] and Ezekiel saw the likeness of the glory of the Lord.[2483] Jesus said: "Blessed are the pure in heart, for they shall see God";[2484] and John saw "one seated on the throne."[2485] There can be no doubt where the early Christians stood on this matter. Peter, James, and John saw beyond the veil when they saw Jesus transfigured. They saw into the state of glory that was outside time, since Moses and Elijah were with Jesus in their vision.[2486] When Peter told Cornelius the story of Jesus, he said that only a few people had seen the risen Lord, those who had been "prepared beforehand as witnesses."[2487] Those who had seen the transfigured Lord were able to recognize the risen, heavenly Lord. John began his Gospel by saying, "We have beheld his glory,"[2488] and Luke said that the glory of the Lord shone around the shepherds at Bethlehem.[2489] The veil between the two worlds had been opened.

E-292   According to Marioano Veytia, Oxomoco was "the first woman to give birth in the world, and from whom all men are descended."[2490] However, Wirth argues that Oxomoco should not be considered "a prototype of our Eve, but more like the Heavenly Mother (the partner of the divine creator god)."[2491] Miller, *et al.* write: "Together, Ometecuhtli and his consort Omecihuatl were ever present progenitors, for they sent the souls of those about to be born to the surface of the earth. Ometecuhtli and Omecihuatl may also have been identified with Cipactonal and Oxomoco, aged progenitors and perhaps divine grandparents."[2492]

        Veytia wrote that he saw a drawing illustrating the primeval garden in which the man and the woman lived. He said that this drawing contained "a single tree, from the foot of which a snake is twisting around, and in the middle of the crown of the tree it shows the head with a woman's face."[2493]

E-293   This corresponds to the fruit of the calabash tree (*Chresentia cujete*), which "yields a large, whitish to light-green gourd with a hard, bonelike rind that is sometimes dried and used to make bowls. It is approximately the size of a human skull."[2494]

E-294   In regarding the tree, the maiden, Lady Blood, exclaims: "Ah! What is the fruit of this tree? Is not the fruit borne of this tree delicious? I would not die. I would not be lost. Would it be heard if I were to pick one?"[2495]

E-295   A major consequence of their defeat was that "the lords of Xibalba would no longer be allowed to receive human hearts in sacrifice but rather would have to accept the red sap of the croton tree,"[2496] a condition previously prophesied by Lady Blood.[2497]

2478   Exodus 24:9-10.
2479   Deuteronomy 4:12, 15.
2480   Exodus 33:11.
2481   Exodus 33:20, 23.
2482   Isaiah 6:1.
2483   Ezekiel 1:28.
2484   Matthew 5:8.
2485   Revelation 4:2.
2486   Matthew 17:1-9; Mark 9:2-9.
2487   Acts 10:41, translating literally.
2488   John 1:14.
2489   Luke 2:9.
2490   D. M. F. de Echevarria y Veytia, *Historia*, p. 41.
2491   D. E. Wirth, *12 March 2009*.
2492   M. E. Miller, *et al.*, *Gods and Symbols*, pp. 127-128; cf. pp. 40-41.
2493   D. M. F. de Echevarria y Veytia, *Historia*, p. 42.
2494   A. J. Christenson, *Sacred Tree*, p. 3 n. 3. For a Mayan illustration of this tree, see p. 5, Figure 2.
2495   A. J. Christenson, *Popol Vuh 2003*, 2282-2287, p. 128; cf. A. J. Christenson, *Popol Vuh 2000*, 2282-2287, p. 83.
2496   A. J. Christenson, *Popol Vuh 2003*, p. 187 n. 431; cf. A. J. Christenson, *Popol Vuh 2000*, p. 124 n. 293.
2497   A. J. Christenson, *Popol Vuh 2004*, 2444-2445, p. 84; cf. A. J. Christenson, *Popol Vuh 2003*, 2444-2445, pp. 132-133 and p. 132 n. 267.

E-296 In order to "restore" the face of their father, the sons asked him "to name everything—his mouth, his nose, and his eyes. He was able to recover the first name, but then little more was said. He did not say the corresponding names for that which is above the mouth. Still, this had been said, and thus they honored him."[2498] "The skull of One Hunahpu would have had a mouth, but not a nose or eyes, which would have been only empty holes and sockets."[2499]

E-297 Chesterton offers perhaps the most perceptive and succinct analysis of the claim that Blake suffered from some form of mental malady:[2500]

> "Was William Blake mad?" It is easy enough to say, of course, in the non-committal modern manner that it all depends on how you define madness. If you mean it in its practical or legal sense, … if you mean was William Blake unfit to look after himself, unable to exercise civic functions or to administer property, then certainly the answer is "no." Blake was a citizen, and capable of being a very good citizen… Again, if when we say "Was Blake mad?" we mean was he fundamentally morbid, was his soul cut off from the universe and merely feeding on itself, then again the answer is emphatically "no." There was nothing defective about Blake; he was in contact with all the songs and smells of the universe… Yet again, if we mean by madness anything inconsistent or unreasonable, then Blake was not mad. Blake was one of the most consistent men that ever lived, both in theory and in practice.…

> When Blake lived at Felpham angels appear to have been as native to the Sussex trees as birds. Hebrew patriarchs walked on the Sussex Downs as easily as if they were in the desert. Some people will be quite satisfied with saying that the mere solemn attestation of such miracles marks a man as a madman or a liar. But that is a short cut of skeptical dogmatism which is not far removed from impudence. Surely we cannot take an open question like the supernatural and shut it with a bang, turning the key of the mad-house on all the mystics of history… you cannot take the region called the unknown and calmly say that though you know nothing about it, you know that all its gates are locked… We do not know enough about the unknown to know that it is unknowable.…

> [Finally, any imputation that his actions violated common decency] does not prove that he was a madman or anything remotely resembling one. Nor there is any reason to suppose that he was carried into any practice inconsistent with his strong domestic affections. Indeed, I think that much of Blake's anarchy is connected with his innocence.

> But when we have reached this point—that this ugly element in Blake was an intrusion of Blake's mere theory of things—we have come, I think, very close to the true principle to be pursued in estimating his madness or his sanity. Blake the mere poet, would have been decent and respectable. It was Blake the logician who was forced to be almost blackguardly. In other words, Blake was not mad; for such part of him as was mad was not Blake. It was an alien influence, and in some sense even an accidental one; in an extreme sense it might even be called antagonist.…

> What was it that was eating away a part of Blake's brain? I venture to offer an answer which in the eyes of many people will have nothing to recommend it except the accident of its personal sincerity. I firmly believe that what did hurt Blake's brain was the reality of his spiritual communications… His inspired poems were not his good poems. His inspired poems were very often his particularly bad ones; they were bad by inspiration.

Whether Blake's fits of "bad inspiration" were, as Chesterton suspected, due to the malevolent influence of "fallen angels," or, as Youngquist believed, the result of a heroic and ultimately successful struggle against a descent into mental chaos[2501] is a question that I do not feel competent to answer.

2498 A. J. Christenson, *Popol Vuh 2003*, 4777-4787, p. 190; cf. *Popol Vuh 2000*, 4777-4787, p. 126.

2499 A. J. Christenson, *Popol Vuh 2003*, p. 190 n. 448.

2500 G. K. Chesterton, *William Blake*, pp. 71-74, 79-80, 93. See *Endnote 0-27*, p. 27.

2501 "For the critic, the more interesting question than the dubious one of diagnosis is why Blake remained healthy and wrote powerful verse throughout his long career. He alone among the Romantic poets lived and wrote great poetry into late adulthood, even though he seems also to have been the one most prone to mental distress. The reason lies in the therapeutic function of his mythological method" (P. Youngquist, *Madness*, p. 43).

APPENDIX
The Origin of Man

BYU Evolution Packet, 1992[1]

October, 1992

Evolution and the Origin of Man

This packet contains, as far as could be found, all statements issued by the First Presidency of the Church of Jesus Christ of Latter-day Saints on the subject of evolution and the origin of man, and a statement on the Church's attitude toward science. The earliest First Presidency Statement, "The Origin of Man," was issued during the administration of President Joseph F. Smith in 1909. This was followed by a First Presidency Message in 1910 that included brief comments related to the study of these topics. The second statement, "Mormon View of Evolution," was issued during the administration of President Heber J. Grant in 1925. Although there has never been a formal declaration from the First Presidency addressing the general matter of organic evolution as a process for development of biological species, these documents make clear the official position of the Church regarding the origin of man.

This packet also contains the article on evolution from the *Encyclopedia of Mormonism*, published in 1992. The current First Presidency authorized inclusion of the excerpt from the First Presidency minutes of 1931 in the 1992 Encyclopedia article.

Various views have been expressed by other Church leaders on this subject over many decades; however, formal statements by the First Presidency are the definitive source of official Church positions. It is hoped that these materials will provide a firm foundation for individual study in a context of faith in the restored gospel.

Approved by the BYU Board of Trustees

June, 1992

Improvement Era 13:1, pp. 75-81. Nov. 1909.

Editor's Table.

The Origin of Man.

By The First Presidency of the Church.

"God created man in his own image."

Inquiries arise from time to time respecting the attitude of the Church of Jesus Christ of Latter-day Saints upon questions which, though not vital from a doctrinal standpoint, are closely connected with the fundamental principles of salvation. The latest inquiry of this kind that has reached us is in relation to the origin of man. It is believed that a statement of the position held by the Church upon this important subject will be timely and productive of good.

In presenting the statement that follows we are not conscious of putting forth anything essentially new; neither is it our desire so to do. Truth is what we wish to present, and truth—eternal truth—is fundamentally old. A restatement of the original attitude of the Church

---

1   See *Endnote A-1*, p. 803.

relative to this matter is all that will be attempted here. To tell the truth as God has revealed it, and commend it to the acceptance of those who need to conform their opinions thereto, is the sole purpose of this presentation.

"God created man in his own image, in the image of God created he him; male and female created he them." In these plain and pointed words the inspired author of the book of Genesis made known to the world the truth concerning the origin of the human family. Moses, the prophet-historian, "learned," as we are told, "in all the wisdom of the Egyptians," when making this important announcement, was not voicing a mere opinion, a theory derived from his researches into the occult lore of that ancient people. He was speaking as the mouthpiece of God, and his solemn declaration was for all time and for all people. No subsequent revelator of the truth has contradicted the great leader and lawgiver of Israel. All who have since spoken by divine authority upon this theme have confirmed his simple and sublime proclamation. Nor could it be otherwise. Truth has but one source, and all revelations from heaven are harmonious with each other. The omnipotent Creator, the maker of heaven and earth—had shown unto Moses everything pertaining to this planet, including the facts relating to man's origin, and the authoritative pronouncement of that mighty prophet and seer to the house of Israel, and through Israel to the whole world, is couched in the simple clause: "God created man in his own image" (Genesis 1:27; Pearl of Great Price—book of Moses, 1:27-41).

The creation was two-fold—firstly spiritual, secondly temporal. This truth, also, Moses plainly taught—much more plainly than it has come down to us in the imperfect translations of the Bible that are now in use. Therein the fact of a spiritual creation, antedating the temporal creation, is strongly implied, but the proof of it is not so clear and conclusive as in other records held by the Latter-day Saints to be of equal authority with the Jewish scriptures. The partial obscurity of the latter upon the point in question is owing, no doubt, to the loss of those "plain and precious" parts of sacred writ, which, as the Book of Mormon informs us, have been taken away from the Bible during its passage down the centuries (I Nephi 13:24-29). Some of these missing parts the Prophet Joseph Smith undertook to restore when he revised those scriptures by the spirit of revelation, the result being that more complete account of the creation which is found in the book of Moses, previously cited. Note the following passages:

> And now, behold, I say unto you, that these are the generations of the heaven and of the earth, when they were created, in the day that I, the Lord God, made the heaven and the earth;
>
> And every plant of the field before it was in the earth, and every herb of the field before it grew.
>
> For I, the Lord God, created all things of which I have spoken, spiritually, before they were naturally upon the face of the earth. For I, the Lord God, had not caused it to rain upon the face of the earth.
>
> And I, the Lord God, had created all the children of men, and not yet a man to till the ground; for in heaven created I them, and there was not yet flesh upon the earth, neither in the water, neither in the air.
>
> But, I, the Lord God, spake, and there went up a mist from the earth, and watered the whole face of the ground.
>
> And I, the Lord God, formed man from the dust of the ground, and breathed into his nostrils the breath of life; and man became a living soul, the first flesh upon the earth, the first man also.

Nevertheless, all things were before created, but spiritually were they created and made, according to my word (Pearl of Great Price—book of Moses, 3:4-7. See also chapters 1 and 2, and compare with Genesis 1 and 2).

These two points being established, namely, the creation of man in the image of God, and the two-fold character of the creation, let us now inquire: What was the form of man, in the spirit and in the body, as originally created? In a general way the answer is given in the words chosen as the text of this treatise. "God created man in his own image." It is more explicitly rendered in the Book of Mormon thus: "All men were created in the beginning after mine own image" (Ether, 3:15). It is the Father who is speaking. If, therefore, we can ascertain the form of the "Father of spirits," "The God of the spirits of all flesh," we shall be able to discover the form of the original man.

Jesus Christ, the Son of God, is "the express image" of His Father's person (Hebrews 1:3). He walked the earth as a human being, as a perfect man, and said, in answer to a question put to Him: "He that hath seen me hath seen the Father" (John 14:9). This alone ought to solve the problem to the satisfaction of every thoughtful, reverent mind. The conclusion is irresistible, that if the Son of God be the express image (that is, likeness) of His Father's person, then His Father is in the form of man; for that was the form of the Son of God, not only during His mortal life, but before His mortal birth, and after His resurrection. It was in this form that the Father and the Son, as two personages, appeared to Joseph Smith, when, as a boy of fourteen years, he received his first vision. Then if God made man—the first man—in His own image and likeness, he must have made him like unto Christ, and consequently like unto men of Christ's time and of the present day. That man was made in the image of Christ is positively stated in the book of Moses: "And I, God, said unto mine Only Begotten, which was with me from the beginning, Let us make man in our image, after our likeness; and it was so. * * * * And I, God, created man in mine own image, in the image of mine Only Begotten created I him, male and female created I them" (Moses 2:26, 27).

The Father of Jesus is our Father also. Jesus Himself taught this truth, when He instructed His disciples how to pray: "Our Father which art in heaven," etc. Jesus, however, is the first-born among all the sons of God—the first begotten in the spirit, and the only begotten in the flesh. He is our elder brother, and we, like Him, are in the image of God. All men and women are in the similitude of the universal Father and Mother, and are literally the sons and daughters of Deity.

"God created man in His own image." This is just as true of the spirit as it is of the body, which is only the clothing of the spirit, its complement; the two together constituting the soul. The spirit of man is in the form of man, and the spirits of all creatures are in the likeness of their bodies. This was plainly taught by the Prophet Joseph Smith (Doctrine and Covenants, 77:2).

Here is further evidence of the fact. More than seven hundred years before Moses was shown the things pertaining to this earth, another great prophet, known to us as the brother of Jared, was similarly favored by the Lord. He was even permitted to behold the spirit-body of the foreordained Savior, prior to His incarnation; and so like the body of a man was gazing upon a being of flesh and blood. He first saw the finger and then the entire body of the Lord—all in the spirit. The Book of Mormon says of this wonderful manifestation:

> And it came to pass that when the brother of Jared had said these words, behold the Lord stretched forth His hand and touched the stones one by one with His finger; and the veil was

taken from off the eyes of the brother of Jared, and he saw the finger of the Lord; and it was as the finger of a man, like unto flesh and blood; and the brother of Jared fell down before the Lord, for he was struck with fear.

And the Lord saw that the brother of Jared had fallen to the earth; and the Lord said unto him, Arise, why hast thou fallen?

And he saith unto the Lord, I saw the finger of the Lord, and I feared lest he should smite me; for I knew not that the Lord had flesh and blood.

And the Lord said unto him, Because of thy faith thou hast seen that I shall take upon me flesh and blood; and never has man come before me with such exceeding faith as thou hast; for were it not so, ye could not have seen my finger. Sawest thou more than this?

And he answered, Nay, Lord, show thyself unto me.

And the Lord said unto him, Believest thou the words which I shall speak?

And he answered, Yea, Lord, I know that thou speakest the truth, for thou art a God of truth and canst not lie.

And when he had said these words, behold, the Lord showed himself unto him, and said, Because thou knowest these things ye are redeemed from the fall; therefore ye are brought back into my presence; therefore I show myself unto you.

Behold, I am He who was prepared from the foundation of the world to redeem my people. Behold, I am Jesus Christ, I am the Father and the Son. In me shall all mankind have light, and that eternally, even they who shall believe on my name; and they shall become my sons and my daughters.

And never have I shewed myself unto man whom I have created, for never hath man believed in me as thou hast. Seest thou that ye are created after mine own image? Yea, even all men were created in the beginning after mine own image.

Behold, this body, which ye now behold, is the body of my spirit, and man have I created after the body of my spirit; and even as I appear unto thee to be in the spirit, will I appear unto my people in the flesh. (Ether, 3:6-16.)

What more is needed to convince us that man, both in spirit and in body, is the image and likeness of God, and that God Himself is in the form of man?

When the divine Being whose spirit-body the brother of Jared beheld, took upon Him flesh and blood, He appeared as a man, having "body, parts and passions," like other men, though vastly superior to all others, because He was God, even the Son of God, the Word made flesh: in Him "dwelt the fulness of the Godhead bodily." And why should He not appear as a man? That was the form of His spirit, and it must needs have an appropriate covering, a suitable tabernacle. He came unto the world as He had promised to come (III Nephi 1:13), taking an infant tabernacle, and developing it gradually to the fulness of His spirit stature. He came as man had been coming for ages, and as man has continued to come ever since. Jesus, however, as shown, was the only begotten of God in the flesh.

Adam, our great progenitor, "the first man," was, like Christ, a preexistent spirit, and like Christ he took upon him an appropriate body, the body of a man, and so became a "living soul." The doctrine of the preexistence, —revealed so plainly, particularly in latter days, pours a wonderful flood of light upon the otherwise mysterious problem of man's origin.

It shows that man, as a spirit, was begotten and born of heavenly parents, and reared to maturity in the eternal mansions of the Father, prior to coming upon the earth in a temporal body to undergo an experience in mortality. It teaches that all men existed in the spirit before any man existed in the flesh, and that all who have inhabited the earth since Adam have taken bodies and become souls in like manner.

It is held by some that Adam was not the first man upon this earth, and that the original human being was a development from lower orders of the animal creation. These, however, are the theories of men. The word of the Lord declares that Adam was "the first man of all men" (Moses 1:34), and we are therefore in duty bound to regard him as the primal parent of our race. It was shown to the brother of Jared that all men were created in the beginning after the image of God; and whether we take this to mean the spirit or the body, or both, it commits us to the same conclusion: Man began life as a human being, in the likeness of our heavenly Father.

True it is that the body of man enters upon its career as a tiny germ or embryo, which becomes an infant, quickened at a certain stage by the spirit whose tabernacle it is, and the child, after being born, develops into a man. There is nothing in this, however, to indicate that the original man, the first of our race, began life as anything less than a man, or less than the human germ or embryo that becomes a man.

Man, by searching, cannot find out God. Never, unaided, will he discover the truth about the beginning of human life. The Lord must reveal Himself, or remain unrevealed; and the same is true of the facts relating to the origin of Adam's race—God alone can reveal them. Some of these facts, however, are already known, and what has been made known it is our duty to receive and retain.

The Church of Jesus Christ of Latter-day Saints, basing its belief on divine revelation, ancient and modern, proclaims man to be the direct and lineal offspring of Deity. God Himself is an exalted man, perfected, enthroned, and supreme. By His almighty power He organized the earth, and all that it contains, from spirit and element, which exist co-eternally with Himself. He formed every plant that grows, and every animal that breathes, each after its own kind, spiritually and temporally—"that which is spiritual being in the likeness of that which is temporal, and that which is temporal in the likeness of that which is spiritual." He made the tadpole and the ape, the lion and the elephant but He did not make them in His own image, nor endow them with Godlike reason and intelligence. Nevertheless, the whole animal creation will be perfected and perpetuated in the Hereafter, each class in its "distinct order or sphere," and will enjoy "eternal felicity." That fact has been made plain in this dispensation (Doctrine and Covenants, 77:3).

Man is the child of God, formed in the divine image and endowed with divine attributes, and even as the infant son of an earthly father and mother is capable in due time of becoming a man, so the undeveloped offspring of celestial parentage is capable, by experience through ages and aeons, of evolving into a God.

Joseph F. Smith,
John R. Winder,
Anthon H. Lund,

First Presidency of The Church of Jesus Christ of Latter-day Saints.

Words in Season from the First Presidency

Deseret Evening News, Dec. 17, 1910, part 1, p. 3.

In this Christmas message, the First Presidency devoted several sentences to the Church's position with regard to questions raised by science:

Diversity of opinion does not necessitate intolerance of spirit, nor should it embitter or set rational beings against each other. The Christ taught kindness, patience, and charity.

Our religion is not hostile to real science. That which is demonstrated, we accept with joy; but vain philosophy, human theory and mere speculations of men, we do not accept nor do we adopt anything contrary to divine revelation or to good common sense. But everything that tends to right conduct, that harmonizes with sound morality and increases faith in Deity, finds favor with us no matter where it may be found.

Editors' Table: "Mormon" View of Evolution

Improvement Era, Vol. XXVIII September, 1925 No. 11

"God created man in his own image, in the image of God created he him: male and female created he them."

In these plain and pointed words the inspired author of the book of Genesis made known to the world the truth concerning the origin of the human family. Moses, the prophet-historian, who was "learned" we are told, "in all the wisdom of the Egyptians," when making this important announcement, was not voicing a mere opinion. He was speaking as the mouthpiece of God, and his solemn declaration was for all time and for all people. No subsequent revelator of the truth has contradicted the great leader and law-giver of Israel. All who have since spoken by divine authority upon this theme have confirmed his simple and sublime proclamation. Nor could it be otherwise. Truth has but one source, and all revelations from heaven are harmonious one with the other.

Jesus Christ, the Son of God, is "the express image" of his Father's person (Hebrews 1:3). He walked the earth as a human being, as a perfect man, and said, in answer to a question put to him: "He that hath seen me hath seen the Father" (John 14:9). This alone ought to solve the problem to the satisfaction of every thoughtful, reverent mind. It was in this form that the Father and the Son, as two distinct personages, appeared to Joseph Smith, when, as a boy of fourteen years, he received his first vision.

The Father of Jesus Christ is our Father also. Jesus himself taught this truth, when he instructed his disciples how to pray: "Our Father which art in heaven," etc. Jesus, however, is the first born among all the sons of God—the first begotten in the spirit, and the only begotten in the flesh. He is our elder brother, and we, like him, are in the image of God. All men and women are in the similitude of the universal Father and Mother, and are literally sons and daughters of Deity.

Adam, our great progenitor, "the first man," was, like Christ, a preexistent spirit, and, like Christ, he took upon him an appropriate body, the body of a man, and so became a "living soul." The doctrine of preexistence pours a wonderful flood of light upon the otherwise mysterious problem of man's origin. It shows that man, as a spirit, was begotten and born of heavenly parents, and reared to maturity in the eternal mansions of the Father, prior to coming upon the earth in a temporal body to undergo an experience in mortality.

The Church of Jesus Christ of Latter-day Saints, basing its belief on divine revelation, ancient and modern, proclaims man to be the direct and lineal offspring of Deity. By his Almighty power God organized the earth, and all that it contains, from spirit and element, which exist co-eternally with himself.

Man is the child of God, formed in the divine image and endowed with divine attributes, and even as the infant son of an earthly father and mother is capable in due time of becoming a man, so the undeveloped offspring of celestial parentage is capable, by experience through ages and aeons, of evolving into a God.

Heber J. Grant,
Anthony W. Ivins,
Charles W. Nibley.
First Presidency.

Evolution

Encyclopedia of Mormonism, Vol. 2

William E. Evenson

The position of the Church on the origin of man was published by the First Presidency in 1909 and stated again by a different First Presidency in 1925:

> The Church of Jesus Christ of Latter-day Saints, basing its belief on divine revelation, ancient and modern, declares man to be the direct and lineal offspring of Deity.... Man is the child of God, formed in the divine image and endowed with divine attributes [see statement of the First Presidency above].

The scriptures tell why man was created, but they do not tell how, though the Lord has promised that he will tell that when he comes again (D&C 101:32-33). In 1931, when there was intense discussion on the issue of organic evolution, the First Presidency of the Church, then consisting of Presidents Heber J. Grant, Anthony W. Ivins, and Charles W. Nibley, addressed all of the General Authorities of the Church on the matter, and concluded,

> Upon the fundamental doctrines of the Church we are all agreed. Our mission is to bear the message of the restored gospel to the world. Leave geology, biology, archaeology, and anthropology, no one of which has to do with the salvation of the souls of mankind, to scientific research, while we magnify our calling in the realm of the Church.

> Upon one thing we should all be able to agree, namely, that Presidents Joseph F. Smith, John R. Winder, and Anthon H. Lund were right when they said: "Adam is the primal parent of our race" [First Presidency Minutes, Apr. 7, 1931].

Background of the BYU Evolution Packet

In response to student questions about the view of the Church on organic evolution and the origin of man, a packet was approved by Brigham Young University's Board of Trustees—consisting of the First Presidency, some members of the Quorum of the Twelve, and other General Authorities and officers. Following approval, the packet was made available to students and faculty of BYU, and in 1999 it was distributed to all teachers in the Church Education System. The following article, from p. 3 of the Nov. 12, 1992 issue of BYU's student newspaper *The Daily Universe*, explains the origins of the packet. The author of the article is William E. Evenson, who at that time was Dean of the College of Physical and Mathematical Sciences and Professor of Physics at BYU. Following this article, background material relating to the statements in the packet is provided.

William E. Evenson: Evolution Packet Defined, 1992

In the interest of clarifying the background and purpose of the library packet on evolution and the origin of man, which was announced in the *Daily Universe* on Thursday, Oct. 29, I provide the following information about the development of this packet and the motivation for it.

As appropriate at any university, the subject of organic evolution and the origin of man comes up in BYU courses in several departments. In these courses, students naturally wish to know the official position of the LDS Church on this subject. Some faculty members in the sciences and in Religious Education have gathered material on these topics to distribute to their students. Students might receive one set of statements by Church leaders from one professor and a different set from another professor.

Several faculty members and administrators felt the diversity of materials on these subjects, which were often selected to emphasize the views of the professor, tended to create confusion in the minds of the students and accentuate the potential for controversy about the Church's position. In 1991, in response to questions from students about the Church position on evolution, [BYU] President Rex E. Lee authorized that one of these packets be placed in the [Harold B. Lee Library] Reserve Library as a source for information about the Church's position on evolution and the origin of man.

Purpose of Packet. Because of my experience in preparing the evolution article for the *Encyclopedia of Mormonism*, I was asked by Provost Bruce Hafen to consider a packet that could be made available to students as the official and fundamental Church position on this subject. It was immediately clear that the selection of material for such a packet could not depend on the content of the statements. The goal is not to achieve some kind of "balance" among the views that have been expressed, but to give students the full range of official views so that they can judge the different positions they encounter. The full range of official views should provide the basis for the evaluation of other views that have been expressed but that do not have the status of official positions.

In line with this philosophical stance, I prepared an initial draft of the packet, which contained the First Presidency statements and all published statements made by presidents of the Church during the time they held that office. It also included the speech given in 1931 by James Talmage of the Quorum of the Twelve, which was reviewed and approved by the First Presidency and officially published by the Church. Finally, this draft packet included the *Encyclopedia of Mormonism* article because of the excerpt from the First Presidency Minutes in 1931 about the Church's stance toward scientific studies of evolution and the origin of man. This packet was made entirely of materials with official status and included all of the statements published by or with the authorization of the First Presidency.

The draft packet's contents were discussed amicably with Dean Robert Millet of Religious Education and Provost Hafen. After considerable discussion, we agreed that the official university packet should contain only those items that represent the official position of the Church, i.e., statements from the First Presidency. The encyclopedia article was kept because of the First Presidency Minutes item included in it, which is not otherwise available to the public. The final packet was then reviewed by BYU's Board of Trustees — consisting of the First Presidency, many members of the Quorum of the Twelve and other general authorities and officers. They approved the packet.

Balance not the issue. Again, I emphasize that balance was not the issue. The issue was providing only those materials that could clearly be said to be the official, declared position of the Church.

None of us involved in preparing this packet for Board review anticipate that professors will be limited from distributing other materials to their students. It is only requested that BYU faculty members refer students to the materials in this specific packet along with the other items they may choose to distribute. When other items are distributed, they should be clearly separated and given as a supplement to this material and include a fair sampling of the diverse viewpoints among LDS leaders. For example, if one included statements by LDS apostles in a handout on evolution, the range of views would include some statements against evolution, some sympathetic to evolution and several shades of opinion in between. We want to avoid the implication that a greater sense of unanimity or resolution of this topic exists than is actually the case, and we are eager to avoid contention. The university has also suggested that faculty members limit supplemental LDS material on the subject of evolution and the origin of man to published documents, avoiding private letters or other private material.

The process was one of constructive and harmonious effort to provide materials from which students could see clearly the foundation of LDS doctrine on this subject and distinguish it from the wide variety of opinions encountered in LDS literature.

Context for Statements in the BYU Evolution Packet

First Presidency Statement: The Origin of Man, 1909. The year 1909 was both the centennial of Charles Darwin's birth and the 50-year anniversary of the publication of his *The Origin of Species*. Regarding the circumstances of the issuance of this statement, James R. Clark writes:

> What prompted the First Presidency to issue this definite statement on the Origin of Man at this particular time could not be determined by the writer of these notes.

> However, there had appeared in the April, 1908, issue of the *Improvement Era* an article announcing the death of [British mathematical physicist] William Thompson or Lord Kelvin on December 17, 1907. The article was written by a prominent LDS scientist, Dr. John A. Widtsoe, President of the Agricultural College of Utah at Logan, now Utah State University.

Since the *Improvement Era* was an official organ of the LDS Church and widely read throughout the Church, some of the statements in the Widtsoe article may have been responsible for some of the 'Inquiries… respecting the attitude of the Church…' on the subject.

Pertinent to the subject of the Origin of Man are the following quotations from Widtsoe's review of the views of Lord Kelvin on this subject:

> Not only did Lord Kelvin believe that God lives and rules, but he had no sympathy with the idle notion of the day that life began upon this earth and will disappear with death. He believed in the eternity of life, and that life had come to this earth from other heavenly bodies. True, he did not understand the full philosophy of life's beginnings on the earth, but certainly with all the power at his command as the great scientist of his day, he refuted many of the modern theories which teach the origin of life on this earth without the intervention of an overruling Providence (IE 11:402).

After quoting again from the writings of Lord Kelvin, Widtsoe comments:

> Carefully read, this paragraph [from Kelvin] will be found to teach that life is eternal; that life on this earth came from other spheres, that the law of natural selection is imperfect, and does not account for the variety of living things; that the law of evolution is true only as it conforms to the law of progression; that the whole of nature teaches the existence of a great designer or great governing power; and that finally; the power of free agency encircles our lives (IE 11:403).

Widtsoe then quotes at length from the Presidential Address of Lord Kelvin to the British Association, Edinburgh, 1871, including Kelvin's statement that he could not accept the hypothesis of the origin of species by natural selection, 'because I have always felt that this hypothesis does not contain the true theory of evolution, if evolution there has been, in biology.'

Widtsoe's final paragraph had said:

> Does Mormonism agree with the same talks of Lord Kelvin? All who understand it will say, yes. The science of the world is, and can be no more than one phase of the everlasting gospel of Jesus Christ which embraces all truth.…

This statement of the First Presidency in 1909 still remains perhaps the most thorough and complete statement on the subject issued by the First Presidency to date (1969). [The] statement by President Heber J. Grant and his counselors in the First Presidency in 1925 and entitled 'The Mormon View of Evolution' [included in this appendix] will be seen by comparison between the two to be a briefer version of the same statement in the identical language.[2]

First Presidency Statement: Words in Season, 1910. Nothing is known about the specific background of the 1910 statement, however its timing in light of other writings by President Smith and his associates in Church publications and of the controversies on curriculum content at Church schools seems to suggest a perceived need to reaffirm that "Our religion is not hostile to real science."

First Presidency Statement: "Mormon" View of Evolution, 1925. James R. Clark writes:

> The predecessor of this statement on the "Mormon View of Evolution" is the statement of the First Presidency on "The Origin of Man" published November, 1909.[3] In fact, the present statement in paragraphs 1 through 5 constitutes extracts from paragraphs 3, 13, 14, 30, 34, and 35, respectively, of the 1909 statement, It therefore constitutes a shortened or condensed form of

---

2   J. R. Clark, *Messages*, 4:199-200.
3   See *ibid.*, 4:199-206.

the statement issued by the former First Presidency—Joseph F. Smith, John R. Winder and Anthon H. Lund.

The occasion prompting the issuance of this later condensed version by President Heber J. Grant and his counselors is not given in the *Improvement Era* where it was published.

However, in July, 1925, Darwinism had attracted international attention when John T. Scopes, a young high school teacher, had disobeyed the law of the State of Tennessee by teaching Darwinism or evolution. He was convicted and the results of the trial had national and international repercussions. Discussion was widespread in LDS circles. Under these circumstances, the title of the message itself is not without significance.[4]

Encyclopedia of Mormonism: Evolution, 1991. Regarding the background of this article, the author William E. Evenson has written:

> Because of a fairly broad science background as a physics professor with research interests in evolutionary biology, I was asked to write the article on evolution for the *Encyclopedia of Mormonism*. This article went through a long process of refinement and review. It was originally to be 1,000 words long, then was revised to 2,500 words, to 3,500 words, and to 4,500 words. Finally, in the spring of 1991, the First Presidency and Quorum of the Twelve reviewed my last two versions, and a more anti-evolutionary revision of my article by someone else connected with the *Encyclopedia*. The Brethren decided that they wanted only a short article referring to the First Presidency statements on this subject, which are the only definitive sources of Church doctrine. The resulting entry in the *Encyclopedia* is only 258 words long.[5]

In this article is a quote from the 1931 minutes of the First Presidency, recorded at a time "when there was intense discussion on the issue of organic evolution." Specifically, doctrinal issues relating to a decision about the publication of Elder B. H. Roberts' manuscript *The Truth, the Way, the Life*[6] were then under consideration. As Evenson points out, however, these discussions "were not centered on the scientific theories of origins of life forms. Rather, the central point of concern was whether death occurred on Earth before the Fall of Adam."[7] Roberts found evolutionary theory to be inadequate, and thus formulated his own theory as an attempt to reconcile the scriptures with science.

Though the 1931 First Presidency statement was specifically made in response to the question of death before the Fall that was raised by Roberts' manuscript, its application to the broader context of evolution was deemed appropriate by later Church leaders. Writes Evenson: "It was at [the] initiative [of the First Presidency and members of the Twelve], and specifically by the action of then-First Counselor Gordon B. Hinckley, that the 1931 counsel was supplied to be used in the *Encyclopedia* to indicate the church's position in 1992. This updates the 1931 counsel and gives it focus directly to modern conditions. The *Encyclopedia* and other writers are quite correct in citing it as a currently valid statement."[8]

APPENDIX

---

4   *Ibid.*, 5:243.
5   W. E. Evenson, *LDS Doctrine*, p. xxxi.
6   B. H. Roberts, *The Truth*.
7   W. E. Evenson, in B. H. Roberts, *The Truth*, p. cxxiii.
8   W. E. Evenson, *Counsel Valid*.

Additional Material Relating to the Origin of Man

Improvement Era Editorial: Creation of Adam and Eve, 1910[9]

"In just what manner did the mortal bodies of Adam and Eve come into existence on this earth?" This question comes from several High Priests' quorums.

Of course, all are familiar with the statements in Genesis 1: 26-27; 2: 7; also in the book of Moses, Pearl of Great Price, 2: 27; and in the book of Abraham 5: 7. The latter statement reads: "And the Gods formed man from the dust of the ground, and took his spirit (that is, the man's spirit) and put it into him; and breathed into his nostrils the breath of life, and man became a living soul."

These are the authentic statements of the scriptures, ancient and modern, and it is best to rest with these, until the Lord shall see fit to give more light on the subject. Whether the mortal bodies of man evolved in natural processes to present perfection, through the direction and power of God; whether the first parents of our generations, Adam and Eve, were transplanted from another sphere, with immortal tabernacles, which became corrupted through sin and the partaking of natural foods, in the process of time; whether they were born here in mortality, as other mortals have been, are questions not fully answered in the revealed word of God. For helpful discussion of the subject, see Improvement Era, Vol. XI, August 1908, No. 10, page 778, article, *Creation and Growth of Adam*; also article by the First Presidency, *Origin of Man*, Vol. XIII, No. 1, page 75, 1909.

President Joseph F. Smith: Philosophy and the Church Schools, 1915[10]

Some questions have arisen about the attitude of the Church on certain discussions of philosophy in the Church schools. Philosophical discussions as we understand them, are open questions about which men of science are very greatly at variance. As a rule we do not think it advisable to dwell on questions that are in controversy, and especially questions of a certain character, in the courses of instruction given by our institutions. In the first place it is the mission of our institutions of learning to qualify our young people for the practical duties of life. It is much to be preferred that they emphasize the industrial and practical side of education. Students are very apt to draw the conclusion that whichever side of a controversial question they adopt is the truth, the whole truth, and nothing but the truth; and it is very doubtful therefore, whether the great mass of our students have sufficient discriminating judgment to understand very much about some of the advanced theories of philosophy or science.

Some subjects are in themselves, perhaps, perfectly harmless, and any amount of discussion over them would not be injurious to the faith of our young people. We are told, for example, that the theory of gravitation is at best a hypothesis and that such is the atomic theory. These theories help to explain certain things about nature. Whether they are ultimately true can not make much difference to the religious convictions of our young people. On the other hand there are speculations which touch the origin of life and the relationship of God to his children. In a very limited degree that relationship has been defined by revelation, and until we receive more light upon the subject we deem it best to refrain from the discussion of certain philosophical theories which rather destroy than build up the faith of our young

---

9   J. F. Smith, *et al.*, *Editorial*. See *Endnote A-2*, p. 803.
10   J. F. Smith, *Philosophy*. See *Endnote A-3*, p. 803.

people. One thing about this so-called philosophy of religion that is very undesirable, lies in the fact that as soon as we convert our religion into a system of philosophy none but philosophers can understand, appreciate, or enjoy it. God, in his revelation to man has made His word so simple that the humblest of men without especial training, may enjoy great faith, comprehend the teachings of the Gospel, and enjoy undisturbed their religious convictions. For that reason we are averse to the discussion of certain philosophical theories in our religious instructions. If our Church schools would confine their so-called course of study in biology to that knowledge of the insect world which would help us to eradicate the pests that threaten the destruction of our crops and our fruit, such instruction would answer much better the aims of the Church school, than theories which deal with the origin of life.

These theories may have a fascination for our teachers and they may find interest in the study of them, but they are not properly within the scope of the purpose for which these schools were organized.

Some of our teachers are anxious to explain how much of the theory of evolution, in their judgment, is true, and what is false, but that only leaves their students in an unsettled frame of mind. They are not old enough and learned enough to discriminate, or put proper limitations upon a theory which we believe is more or less a fallacy. In reaching the conclusion that evolution would be best left out of discussions in our Church schools we are deciding a question of propriety and are not undertaking to say how much of evolution is true, or how much is false. We think that while it is a hypothesis, on both sides of which the most eminent scientific men of the world are arrayed, that it is folly to take up its discussion in our institutions of learning; and we can not see wherein such discussions are likely to promote the faith of our young people. On the other hand we have abundant evidence that many of those who have adopted in its fulness the theory of evolution have discarded the Bible, or at least refused to accept it as the inspired word of God. It is not, then, the question of the liberty of any teacher to entertain whatever views he may have upon this hypothesis of evolution, but rather the right of the Church to say that it does not think it profitable or wise to introduce controversies relative to evolution in its schools. Even if it were harmless from the standpoint of our faith, we think there are things more important to the daily affairs of life and the practical welfare of our young people. The Church itself has no philosophy about the *modus operandi* employed by the Lord in His creation of the world, and much of the talk therefore, about the philosophy of Mormonism is altogether misleading. God has revealed to us a simple and effectual way of serving Him, and we should regret very much to see the simplicity of those revelations involved in all sorts of philosophical speculations. If we encouraged them it would not be long before we should have a theological scholastic aristocracy in the Church, and we should therefore not enjoy the brotherhood that now is, or should be common to rich and poor, learned and unlearned among the Saints.

President David O. McKay: Design Permeating All Creation, 1952[11]

"The most choice opportunity of the religious teacher should be to lead the child to see through the trouble and turmoil of a troubled world that," note students, "in all His dispensation God is at work for our good. In prosperity he tries our gratitude, in mediocrity, our contentment, in misfortune, our submission, in darkness, our faith, under temptation our steadfastness, and at all times our obedience and trust in Him." There is a perpetual design permeating all purposes of Creation. On these thoughts, science again leads the student

---

11   D. O. McKay, *Message.*

up to a certain point and sometimes leads him with his soul unanchored. Millikan is right when he says, "Science without religion obviously may become a curse rather that a blessing to mankind." But, science dominated by the spirit of religion is the key progress and the hope of the future. For example, evolution's beautiful theory of the creation of the world offers many perplexing problems to the inquiring mind. Inevitably, a teacher who denies divine agency in Creation, who insists there is no intelligent purpose in it, will [infect] the student with the thought that all may be chance. I say, that no youth should be so led without a counter-balancing thought. Even the skeptic teacher should be fair enough to see that even Charles Darwin, when he faced this great question of annihilation, that the Creation is dominated only by chance wrote: "It is an intolerable thought that man and all other sentient beings are doomed to complete annihilation after such long, continued slow progress."

And another good authority, Raymond West, said, "Why this vast [expenditure] of time and pain and blood?" Why should man come so far if he's destined to go no farther? A creature that travels such distances and fought such battles and won such victories deserves what we are compelled to say, "To conquer death and rob the grave of its victory." The public school teacher will probably, even if he says that much, will go no farther. In the Church school the teacher is unhampered. In the Brigham Young University and every other church school the teacher can say God is at the helm. God is the Creator of the earth, He's the Father of our souls and spirits. No question about it. You have your testimony — if you haven't you shouldn't be on the faculty. Fosdick said that "Perpetuation of personality is the highest thing in creation." Church school teachers can add the Lord revealed to Prophet Joseph Smith the sublime truth: "This is my work and glory. To bring to pass the immortality and eternal life of man."[12]

President David O. McKay: Honest Convictions Can Be Expressed, 1956[13]

And now I have just time to comment on the opportunity of the BYU to teach these fundamental truths. This thought was expressed by Dr. Sidney B. Sperry in the opening prayer, that here in this school [BYU], destined to become the greatest in the world, opportunities are given to guide students in this higher quality of life, this guide, this anchor, this cord leading into the depths of the forest. Whatever the subject may be, the principles of the gospel of Jesus Christ may be elaborated upon without fear of anyone's objecting, and the teacher can be free to express his honest conviction regarding it, whether that subject be in geology, the history of the world, the millions of years that it took to prepare the physical world, whether it be in engineering, literature, art—any principles of the gospel may be briefly or extensively touched upon for the anchoring of the student who is seeking to know the truth.

President Spencer W. Kimball: Creation of Adam and Eve, 1976[14]

The Creators breathed into their nostrils the breath of life and man and woman became living souls. We don't know exactly how their coming into this world happened, and when we're able to understand it the Lord will tell us.

---

12   Moses 1:39.
13   D. O. McKay, *Anchor*. See *Endnote A-4*, p. 803.
14   Church Educational System, *Religion 327*, p. 9; S. W. Kimball, *Blessings*.

John L. Sorenson: Origin of Man, 1991[15]

The view of the "origin of man" in The Church of Jesus Christ of Latter-day Saints differs significantly from that in most other modern traditions. Its prime concern is to affirm that humans were created as spirits by and in the image of God, which determined their form and nature long before they became earthly organisms. Questions about what biological or cultural mechanisms might have produced *Homo sapiens* and over what period of time that often dominate secular discussions are of limited interest for Latter-day Saints.

The clearest presentation of the Church position may be a 1909 statement by the First Presidency entitled "The Origin of Man," where four essential points are made: (1) God created humans (Gen. 1:27-28); (2) God created Adam, "the origin of the human family" and "the first man"; (3) creation was sequential: first spiritual, later physical; and (4) each human body displays the characteristics of the individual premortal spirit that inhabits it. Other ideas included in the statement are that humanity was not "a development from the lower orders of creation" but a "fall" from a higher state of existence; that an understanding of all the details about the origin of man is not vital to one's salvation, although the matter is related to several important truths; that the subject cannot be fully clarified by human learning alone; and that only certain relevant facts are now known, to which the Church adheres.

Subsequent official statements indicate that the details of how Adam became "the first man" are considered not to have been revealed clearly enough to settle questions of process. Emphasized instead is an eternal perspective wherein the individual as an "undeveloped offspring of celestial parentage is capable, by experience through ages and aeons, of evolving into a God" ([*Improvement Era*] 28:1091).

Since the rise of Darwinism in 1860, individual Latter-day Saints, both leaders and members, have occasionally participated in public discussion about evolution, since the official position of the Church on man's origin is not definitive in all respects. Mormons have expressed a wide range of views that are reminiscent of the well-known debates among Christians. Since a large number of Latter-day Saints entered careers in science early in this century, some have attempted to reconcile scientific facts and ideas with statements from the scriptures and prophetic leaders that are emphasized in the LDS tradition. Others have argued that in this area science merely offers "theories of men" and should therefore be discounted.

Many sympathetic to science interpret certain statements in LDS scripture to mean that God used a version of evolution to prepare bodies and environmental surrounding suitable for the premortal spirits. For example, one scriptural description of creation says, "the Gods *organized the earth to bring forth* . . . every thing that creepeth upon the earth after its kind" (Abraham 4:25 [emphasis added]). Certain statements of various General Authorities are also used by proponents of this idea to justify their opinions.

Other Latter-day Saints accept a more literal reading of scriptural passages that suggest to them an abrupt creation. Proponents of this view also support their positions with statements from scripture and General Authorities.

While the current state of revealed truth on the LDS doctrine of man's origin may permit some differences of opinion concerning the relationship of science and religion, it clearly

15   J. L. Sorenson, *Origin*.

APPENDIX

affirms that God created man, that the fall of Adam was foreknown of God and was real and significant, and that the Atonement of Christ was foreordained and necessary to reverse the effects of the Fall. Perhaps because these claims embrace the main doctrinal issues relevant to the condition of man, the description of the actual creation process does not receive much attention from the general membership of the Church or from the authorities.

Bibliography

Jeffrey, Duane E. "Seers, Savants and Evolution: The Uncomfortable Interface." *Dialogue* 8, Nos. 3/4 (1973):41-75.

"Mormon View of Evolution." [*Improvement Era*] 28 (Sept. 1925):1090-91; reprinted in [*Messages of the First Presidency*] 5:244.

"The Origin of Man." [*Improvement Era*] 13 (Nov. 1909):75-81; reprinted in [*Messages of the First Presidency*] 4:199-206.

Packer, Boyd K. "The Law and the Light." In *The Book of Mormon: Jacob Through Words of Mormon, To Learn with Joy*, eds. M. Nyman and C. Tate, pp. 1-31. Salt Lake City, 1990.

JOHN L. SORENSON

President Gordon B. Hinckley: Organic Evolution, 1997[16]

People ask me every now and again if I believe in evolution. I tell them I am not concerned with organic evolution. I do not worry about it. I passed through that argument long ago.[17]

President Gordon B. Hinckley: The Origin of Man, 2002[18]

What the Church requires is only belief "that Adam was the first man of what we would call the human race," says Gordon Hinckley, the church's living prophet. Scientists can speculate on the rest, he says, recalling his own study of anthropology and geology: "Studied all about it. Didn't worry me then. Doesn't worry me now."[19]

---

16   See *Endnote A-5,* p. 803.
17   G. B. Hinckley, *Ogden Institute*, p. 379.
18   See *Endnote A-6,* p. 803.
19   G. B. Hinckley, 2002, cited in L. A. Witham, *Darwin*, p. 177.

Endnotes

A-1 These and additional statements have also been published with commentary in W. E. Evenson, *et al.*, *Evolution*.

A-2 This editorial was prepared in reply to questions from "several High Priests' quorums," where the 1909 statement of the First Presidency had no doubt been a subject of continuing discussion. Moreover, the 1910 Manual for the Priests Quorum prepared by Elder B. H. Roberts had contained the following statement, which also may have engendered questions: "Man has descended from God; in fact, he is of the same race as the Gods. His descent has not been from a lower form of life, but from the Highest Form of Life; in other words, man is, in the most literal sense, a child of God. This is not only true of the spirit of man, but of his body also."[20]

Although the *Improvement Era* editorial is unsigned and could have been initially prepared by co-editor Edward H. Anderson, the other editor of the publication was President Joseph F. Smith, who normally would have at least reviewed such articles.[21]

A-3 "In the latter part of 1910, the questions of academic freedom and curriculum content in the Church school system came into critical focus.… 'Higher criticism' and 'evolution' were the subjects of stated concern…, four professors were eventually terminated at BYU, and President Joseph F. Smith undertook to explain the matter to the Church in editorials in the April 1911 issues of the *Era* and the *Juvenile Instructor*."[22] The focus of President Smith's statement is the observation that the preferred emphasis of Church schools at the time was to be the "industrial and practical side of education." With respect to the topic of evolution, he makes it clear that "in reaching the conclusion that evolution would be best left out of discussions in our Church schools" it was a "question of propriety" and not a matter of saying "how much of evolution is true, or how much is false.… The Church itself has no philosophy about the *modus operandi* employed by the Lord in His creation of the world, and much of the talk therefore about the philosophy of Mormonism is altogether misleading."

Since 1911, the academic mission of Church schools has understandably broadened beyond its initial more wholly vocational focus. The first formal class in evolution was instituted at BYU in the fall of 1971 with the First Presidency's approval, and is currently a required part of the core curriculum of all BYU students in the biological sciences. Evolutionary biology[23] has since become "one of the largest and most successful graduate programs at BYU,"[24] with professors publishing in major evolutionary conferences and journals. See Givens[25] for a brief summary of efforts of Mormon scientists that "not only incorporate evolutionary science, but break new ground in the field."

With respect to what should be taught in public school classrooms, the Church has declined to take part in any debate of the issue, and an effort to require the schools to teach that not all scientists agree about the origin of life was soundly defeated in the Utah legislature in 2006.[26]

A-4 During the previous two years, President McKay had responded to several inquiries about the official position of the Church regarding evolution and the age of the earth.[27]

A-5 On 15 April 1997, President Gordon B. Hinckley delivered a speech to students at the LDS Institute in Ogden, Utah. "The speech is a series of responses to students' questions, exhorting them to good living and high commitments, building to a response about evolution, and then to personal testimony. A variety of interpretations can be sustained in the context of the overall speech; we suggest readers consult the speech in its entirety. The kernel statement about evolution is given here."[28]

A-6 From an interview with Larry A. Witham, who assured authors Evenson and Jeffery that the statement "was accurately transcribed from his tape-recorded interview."[29]

APPENDIX

---

20   B. H. Roberts, *Divine Mission*, Lesson 14 The Creation of Man, p. 35.

21   D. E. Jeffery, *We Don't Know*, p. 32.

22   *Ibid.*, pp. 32-33.

23   *Biology.*

24   M. R. Ash, *Myth*, pp. 32-33.

25   T. L. Givens, *Paradox*, pp. 209-210, 378-379 nn. 59-64.

26   E. Jarvik, *Beliefs.*

27   G. A. Prince, *et al.*, *McKay*, pp. 45-49.

28   W. E. Evenson *et al.*, *Evolution*, p. 108.

29   *Ibid.*, p. 110.

BIBLIOGRAPHY

Annotated Bibliography of Ancient Texts Related to the Book of Moses and JST Genesis

Co-Authored with Stephen T. Whitlock

Introduction

This section provides an annotated bibliography of ancient texts related to the book of Moses and the rest of JST Genesis, with a guide to currently available English translations.[1] Occasionally, French, German, or Latin translations are included, especially where good English translations are not readily available. Ancient texts only tangentially related to JST Genesis are also sometimes included here if they are deemed relevant for other reasons, or if they have been specifically cited elsewhere in the book.

The texts are grouped into categories that reflect their presumed authorship. Exact or approximate dates of authorship are given where available, but note that these often vary widely and are frequently the subject of scholarly controversy. The following abbreviations are used in connection with information about dates: ca. = *circa*, b. = born, d. = died, fl. = flourished. As in the rest of the commentary, complete publication information for cited texts can be found in the *References* section of this book. Happily, much of this literature is also available online but, due to the rapidly changing nature of such collections, we do not attempt a comprehensive catalogue of these sources here. Because, in most cases, Zoroastrian, Mandaean, and Manichaean texts are not as readily available, well-known, or accessible as Jewish, Christian, and Islamic ones, we summarize the beliefs, rituals, and sources of these in more breadth and detail.

---

1   See *Endnote B-1*, p. 903.

Ancient Near Eastern Texts

The diversity of the settings and ideologies that played their parts in the development of this complex and voluminous literature makes it impossible to do justice to the texts and their possible relationships to JST Genesis. Because of their importance to the book of Abraham and LDS temple teachings, a separate section on Egyptian funerary documents is given below. Following this section, we describe a selection of documents drawn from two standard collections of Ancient Near Eastern texts.

In addition to these texts, we note the *Babyloniaca* (*History of Babylonia*) of Berossus, published about 290-278 BCE for the Macedonian/Seleucid king, Antiochus 1.[2] It has not been preserved as a complete text, but exists only in fragments cited by Greek, Jewish, and Christian writers. Book 1 records the Babylonian creation account, Book 2 the history of the ante- and post-diluvian Babylonian kings, and Book 3 the history of Babylon from Nabonassaros to Antiochus 1. An English translation of the assembled fragments can be found in Berossus, *History*.

Egyptian Funerary Documents

From what has survived of their culture, one might assume that the ancient Egyptians were obsessed with death. When most people think of Egypt, the relics of death come immediately to mind: pyramids and other great tombs; mummies that have been preserved for thousands of years; amulets, jars, statues and other items recovered from tombs. Their obsession, however, was not with death, but with eternal life.[3] As Budge has explained, "The resurrection was the object of every formula, every text, every ceremony of Egyptian life…"[4] It is also now known that some portions of these documents "were used for religious purposes while the individual was still alive."[5] Going further, David writes: "There was no ancient division between the funerary customs and the religious practices of the living. In both spheres, the Egyptians sought to influence the gods and gain the benefits they desired."[6]

David provides a helpful summary of literary sources for ancient Egypt.[7] The oldest written sources are the *Pyramid Texts*, dating from the 5th through 7th Dynasties of the Old Kingdom, or approximately 2300 BCE. As indicated by their name, they were inscribed on the interior of pyramids at Saqqara, nine in number. These funerary inscriptions consist of short statements or sayings, usually identified as Utterances or Spells. Each pyramid contains a different selection of these spells that came from a common catalog. In total, over seven hundred separate spells have been preserved. These texts were written to give guidance to the deceased, to provide protection in the afterlife, and to enable the deceased to join the gods.

Originally discovered by Gaston Maspero in 1881, the *Pyramid Texts* were first translated into German by Kurt Sethe, into French by Louis Speleers, and into English by Samuel A. B. Mercer. In addition to the selections in collected works described below, English

---

2 *Berossus*.

3 H. W. Nibley, *Greatness*, pp. 299-300. Nibley's article provides a unique perspective on the study of Egyptian history, culture, and religion.

4 E. A. W. Budge, *Egyptian Religion*, p. 7.

5 J. Gee, *Guide*, p. 62.

6 R. David, *Experience*, p. 21.

7 *Ibid.*, pp. 43-47. For an anthology of the full range of ancient Egyptian literature, see M. Lichtheim, *Readings*.

translations of the entire set of *Pyramid Texts* are available in editions edited by Faulkner[8] and, more recently, by Allen.[9] Allen has also edited a volume of additional middle kingdom copies of fifth and sixth dynasty *Pyramid Texts* that were assembled over the years as part of the Oriental Institute's Coffin Texts project.[10] An online edition of the texts from the pyramid of Unas is available at *Pyramid*.

The *Coffin Texts* began to replace the *Pyramid Texts* at the end of the Old Kingdom. However, most of the *Coffin Texts* date from the Middle Kingdom, about 2000-1700 BCE. Like the *Pyramid Texts*, these spells were selected from a larger catalog and customized to the individual. Most of the time they were painted on the inside of the coffins, and they were available not only to royalty but also those commoners who could afford to have them produced. Sometimes additional texts might be painted on the tomb wall and funerary furniture, or written on manuscripts.

The *Coffin Texts* expanded on the *Pyramid Texts* and included more information about the afterlife and the transformation of the soul through its various stages. They also began to include illustrations and maps of the underworld. Over 1100 of these texts have been collected and published by Faulkner.[11]

In the New Kingdom, the *Funerary Books* introduced a format that both allowed for expansion of content and also for widespread purchase by ordinary individuals. The most important of these books is the Book of the "Coming Forth by Day," more commonly known as the *Book of the Dead*. The *Book of Breathings* is the title of another book of the same genre.

The earliest editions of the *Book of the Dead* date from the 18th Dynasty of the New Kingdom, or 1550-1295 BCE. They reflected a "shift from regarding the afterlife as being achievable only via the king to a situation in which individuals increasingly made their own provisions. There was also a gradual move towards the concept of righteous living as a qualification for the enjoyment of an afterlife."[12] Like previous funerary texts, each *Book of the Dead* was created for a particular deceased individual and contained chapters selected from a master set. These chapters or Spells were compiled and recorded on a papyrus roll. One well known copy of the *Book of the Dead*, written for a scribe named Ani, was originally nearly eighty feet long. Although no two versions of the *Book of the Dead* are alike, there are several different styles that developed regionally. Some editions follow a strict order of included chapters while others follow unique patterns.[13] Some include hieroglyphic and hieratic writing ,while others restrict themselves to hieroglyphs.

Most copies of the *Book of the Dead* include a judgment scene where the individual's heart is weighed on a balance against Maat, symbolized by a feather of truth. Any transgressions will add weight to the heart, unbalance the scale, and result in severe consequences. A set of 42 negative confessions must be truthfully made prior to one's joining the gods. These consist of a list of statements similar in spirit to the Ten Commandments, though in more detail (e.g., I have not lied, I have not robbed, I have not been a land grabber).

---

8   R. O. Faulkner, *Pyramid*.

9   J. P. Allen, *Pyramid*.

10   J. P. Allen, *Coffin Texts*.

11   R. O. Faulkner, *Coffin*.

12   I. Shaw, *et al.*, *Dictionary*, p. 122.

13   Gee notes: "Until Saite times (after about 672 BCE), the contents of the *Book of the Dead* were neither standardized in the selection of chapters nor in their ordering" (J. Gee, *Guide*, p. 62).

Budge published successive English editions of the *Book of the Dead*.[14] He also produced a great quantity of translations of other Egyptian and Assyrian literature early in the late 19th and 20th centuries, most still readily available in reprint editions or online.[15] However, Egyptian scholarship has advanced considerably since Budge made his translations. Allen[16] and Faulkner,[17] for example, have produced readily available modern translations. These typically begin with the spells included in well-known papyrus of Ani and then supplement the text with excerpts from other copies of the *Book of the Dead* to round out the collection.

To LDS readers, the Egyptian funerary texts of greatest interest are the ones included in the *Joseph Smith Papyri*: the *Papyrus of Hor* (a copy of the *Book of Breathings Made by Isis*, including Facsimiles 1 and 3 from the book of Abraham) and the *Papyrus of Semminis* (which included portions of the *Tshemmin Book of the Dead*). The *Papyrus of Hor* has been scrutinized carefully since 1967, when lost portions were recovered by the Church from the Metropolitan Museum of Art. The most complete and up-to-date translation is by Rhodes.[18] Nibley also published an extensive commentary on the *Papyrus of Hor*, comparing it to various aspects of the LDS temple endowment.[19] A translation and commentary on the *Tshemmin Book of the Dead* by Michael D. Rhodes is also planned for publication.[20] For overviews of the history and composition of the Joseph Smith Papyri, perspectives on relevant studies by Egyptologists, and the relationship of the papryi to the book of Abraham and the Kirtland Egyptian Papers, see Gee.[21] A detailed history of the papyri also can be found in Peterson.[22]

From about 600 BCE until the Christian era, some Egyptian mummies included a small disk made of papyrus, linen, metal or clay under the head. This disk is referred to as a *hypocephalus*, from the Greek words meaning "under the head." The *hypocephalus* symbolized the eye of Ra or Horus, representing the sun, and also included references to the afterlife and resurrection. More than a hundred *hypocephali* have been discovered and, like the other funerary documents described above, no two are alike. Spell 162 of the Saite versions of the Book of the Dead contain the instructions for constructing the *hypocephali*. Facsimile 2 in the book of Abraham, part of the *Joseph Smith Papyri*, is an example of a *hypocephalus*.

Rhodes has published a translation and commentary on the *hypocephalus* included in the book of Abraham as Facsimile 2.[23] The insights of Rhodes regarding Facsimiles 1-3 and the book of Abraham are also available as part of the verse-by-verse commentary on the Pearl of Great Price he co-authored with Richard D. Draper and S. Kent Brown.[24] Missing parts of Facsimile 2 have been reconstructed from similar *hypocephali* in the British Museum. *Hypocephali* are on display at various museums, including the British Museum, the Louvre, and the Pennsylvania Museum of Archaeology and Anthropology.

14   E. A. W. Budge, *Book of the Dead.*

15   E.g, E. A. W. Budget, *Book of the Dead Online.*

16   T. G. Allen, *Egyptian*; T. G. Allen, *Book.*

17   C. Andrews, *Book of the Dead.*

18   M. D. Rhodes, *Hor.* See also J. Gee, *et al., Astronomy*; K. Muhlestein, *Breathings*; K. Muhlestein, *Understandings.*

19   H. W. Nibley, *Message 2005.*

20   M. D. Rhodes, *Tshemmin.*

21   J. Gee, *Guide*; J. Gee, *Eyewitness*; J. Gee, *New Light.*

22   H. D. Peterson, *Story.*

23   M. D. Rhodes, *Hypocephalus Translation*; M. D. Rhodes, *Twenty Years.*

24   R. D. Draper, *et al., Commentary.*

Selections from ANET and COS

The classic collection of primary sources is Pritchard's *Ancient Near Eastern Texts Relating to the Old Testament* (ANET). This collection has now been superseded by a three-volume set edited by Hallo entitled *The Context of Scripture* (COS). COS was issued in three volumes: canonical works, inscriptions, and archival material. More than double the size of ANET, it contains up-to-date translations and more extensive commentary. Besides these two works, an invaluable survey of ancient Near East sources can be found in K. L. Sparks, *Ancient Texts*. The most up-to-date corpus of Sumerian texts in English translation is *The Electronic Text Corpus of Sumerian Literature*. Other useful descriptions of sources and readings can be found in M. W. Chavalas, *et al.*, *Mesopotamia*; R. J. Clifford, *Creation*; J. D. Currid, *Egypt*; R. S. Hess, *et al.*, *Inscriptions*; J. M. Roberts, *Ancient Near East*; J. H. Walton, *Ancient*.

The 1969 edition of ANET (Third Edition with Supplement) has been used in the table below. Texts are divided into ten categories and each category is divided by nation, culture or language. We have maintained the major categories and indicated the origins of the text by the column labeled "culture." As will be seen, only a few of the major categories are relevant, with most of the references coming from the first one that includes myths, epics and other legendary materials.

COS, published in 2003 also includes excerpts from the Egyptian *Pyramid* and *Coffin Texts*. The *Pyramid Texts* are listed after the *Memphite Theology* below, as they are generally the oldest Egyptian writings. These are followed by the *Coffin Texts* and the papyrus manuscripts.

Text Name	Date	Culture	Publication Reference and Comment	ANET	COS
Myths, Epics, and Legends					
Memphite Theology	ca. 1300 BCE or ca. 710 BCE	Egyptian	While earlier studies placed the origin of the text in the Old Kingdom, prior to the Pyramid texts, more recent research posits a date no earlier than the 13th century BCE, and possibly as late as 710 BCE (M. Lichtheim, *Readings*, 3:5). The text was recorded on the Shabaka Stone in about 710 BCE. A more complete English translation is available in M. Lichtheim, *Memphite*. For a photo and commentary, see *Figure* E1-1, p. 514	4-6 (excerpt)	1:21-23
Pyramid Text, Spell 527	Late Old Kingdom – 2400 BCE	Egyptian	Description of the derivation of the first two elements of the world from a single source as symbolized by Shu and Tefnut coming from Atum.		1:7
Pyramid Text, Spell 600: Creation by Atum	Late Old Kingdom – 2400 BCE	Egyptian	Part of dedication ritual for royal pyramids that recounts the first creation. Carved inside two Sixth Dynasty pyramids. Description of the source of matter, evolution of the sun, and the waters during the beginning of creation. In this case, ANET includes more material than does COS.	3	1:7-8
Coffin Text, Spell 75	First Intermediate Period	Egyptian	Identification of the deceased with the first elements of the world.		1:8-9
Coffin Text, Spell 76	First Intermediate Period	Egyptian	Construction of the world from the initial creation of the atmosphere.		1:10-11
Coffin Text, Spell 78	First Intermediate Period	Egyptian	The origins of permanence and repetition as symbolized by Tefnut and Shu respectively. See *Pyramid Text 527*.		1:11
Coffin Text, Spell 80	First Intermediate Period	Egyptian	Expansions of the roles of Tefnut and Shu to include death, rebirth, the creation of people and the order for the universe.		1:11-14
Coffin Text, Spell 160: The Repulsing of the Dragon	1300 BCE	Egyptian	Middle Kingdom coffin text, later used in the *Book of the Dead*. Describes the victory over a dragon or snake by Ra.	11-12	1:32

Text Name	Date	Culture	Publication Reference and Comment	ANET	COS
Coffin Text, Spell 261	First Intermediate Period	Egyptian	The deceased is identified with the primordial source of all matter.		1:17-18
Coffin Text, Spell 335: Creation by Atum	2000 BCE	Egyptian	Important creation text used in the 17th chapter of the *Book of the Dead* from 2000 to 1000 BCE. The *Coffin Text* version is better preserved than the *Book of the Dead* version (Spell 17) referenced herein.		1:15-17
Book of the Dead, Spell 17: Creation by Atum	2000 BCE	Egyptian	Important creation text used in the 17th chapter of the *Book of the Dead* from 2000 to 1000 BCE. This text is based on *Coffin Text* Spell 335.	3-4	
Coffin Text, Spell 647	First Intermediate Period	Egyptian	The link between the statement of creation by fiat and the forces and elements that performed the creation.		1:18-19
Coffin Text, Spell 714	First Intermediate Period	Egyptian	The role of magic or divine force in the creation.		1:6-7
Coffin Text, Spell 1130: All Men Created Equal in Opportunity	2000 BCE	Egyptian	A divine declaration that all have equality of opportunity. The text is found only on four wooden coffins.	7-8	1:26-27
Book of the Dead, Spell 117	1500 BCE	Egyptian	Spell for taking the road to Rosetjau, the Netherworld. See *Figure* 4-11, p. 230.		
Book of the Dead, Spell 175: The Primeval Establishment of Order	1500 BCE	Egyptian	Chapter 175 of the *Book of the Dead* for Ani, this text describes the responsibility of Atum to bring order through the creation and the preservation of the dead.	9-10	1:27-30
Thebes as the Place of Creation	1300 BCE	Egyptian	Extract from a hymn glorifying Thebes as the center of the creation and Amon Ra as the creator.	8	
Deliverance of Mankind from Destruction	1300 BCE	Egyptian	Recorded on the walls of several Theban tombs, this text records the sin of mankind (plotting against the gods), the disappointment of the creator and the narrow escape from destruction by the gods. There is an implication that individuals might be saved in the future from destruction.	10-11	1:36-37
The God and His Unknown Name of Power	1300 BCE	Egyptian	Isis plots to learn the secret name of Ra. It is recorded that this name was given to him before he came into being by his father and his mother.	12-14	1:33-34
Ramesside Stella	New Kingdom	Egyptian	Concise description of the first land created.		1:20
The Contest of Horus and Seth for Rule	1200 BCE	Egyptian	Horus and Seth fight for dominion as replacements for Osiris (Seth's brother and Horus' father)	14-17	
Papyrus Bremner-Rhind: Repulsing the Dragon and the Creation	Ptolemaic Period	Egyptian	The evolution of the gods from Atum and an account of the triumph of Ra over Apophis and the creation by Ra.	6-7	1:14-15
Papyrus Leiden I 350	New Kingdom	Egyptian	Amon as the creator.		1:23-26
Story of Sinuhe	1800 BCE	Egyptian	Regarded by some as the greatest masterpiece of Egyptian literature, this is a popular story about a wealthy and successful official in exile who at last returns home. The story reflected a pattern for a common three-part literary pattern in ancient Near Eastern literature: *trouble at home, exile abroad,* and *happy homecoming* (A. Gileadi, *Literary*, p. 12; cf. J. Assman, *Death*, pp. 164-185). Nibley uses the story to point out resemblances to the patriarchal narratives (in particular, the book of Abraham and Moses 1) that evidence both historical and ritual elements in the story (H. W. Nibley, *Message 2005*, pp. 81, 112-113; H. W. Nibley, *Abraham 2000*, pp. 221-225, 243-244, 304, 419-420). Nibley also applies criteria for its historicity developed by Albright to the Book of Mormon (H. W. Nibley, *Lehi 1988*, p. 3), and compares the desert flight of Sinuhe to that of Lehi (H. W. Nibley, *Lehi 1988*, pp. 47-48).	18-22	1:77-82

Text Name	Date	Culture	Publication Reference and Comment	ANET	COS
The Story of Two Brothers	ca. 1225 BCE	Egyptian	A tale of a "conscientious young man… falsely accused of a proposal of adultery by the wife of his elder brother, after he had actually rejected her advances. This part of the story has general similarity to the story of Joseph and Potiphar's wife" (J. B. Pritchard, *Two Brothers*, p. 23). The story pattern and the mixture of history and ritual is seen by Nibley as similar in many respects to that of Sinuhe. See H. W. Nibley, *Abraham 2000*, pp. 219-222, 224, 244, 247, 368-371, 570.	23-25	1:85-89
Enki and Ninhursag: A Paradise Myth	1500 BCE	Sumerian	With many parallels to Genesis 2 and 3, the story, set in Dilmun, describes creation through impregnation by Enki, the growth and partaking of eight plants by Enki, his expulsion from Dilmun and his reconciliation and acceptance back.	37-41	
Enki and Ninmah	1500 BCE	Sumerian	The creation of man from clay and a contest between Enki and Ninmah.		1:516-519
Dumizi and Enkimdu: The Dispute between the Shepherd-God and the Farmer-God		Sumerian	Initially paralleling the Cain and Abel story, this one ends peacefully, rather than in a murder. Nibley cites Assmann's conclusion that "the perennial conflict between the farmer and the herdsman" is "most prominent in the Abraham legends" (H. W. Nibley, *Abraham 2000*, p. 220).	41-42	
Disputation between the Ewe and the Wheat		Sumerian	A disputation text, unusual for its lengthy cosmological preface. Paralleling aspects of Adam traditions, it also recounts how wool and wheat were divinely provided in primeval times.		1:575-578
The Eridu Genesis, or The Deluge		Sumerian	Brief account of a flood paralleling in several respects the story of Noah. It begins with the Creation and establishment of five cities. Only one fragmentary tablet survives.	42-44	1:513-515
The Death of Gilgamesh		Sumerian	Survives in two sections with an indeterminate break in the middle. The first part recounts the moment Gilgamesh is told he will not live eternally in mortality, his death, and the subsequent mourning. The second surviving part lists his family and other attendants and recounts his offerings to the deities of the nether world. One interpretation has him becoming the king of the world of the afterlife.	50-52	
Inanna's Descent to the Nether World	2000-1500 BCE	Sumerian	Account of Inanna's visit to the nether world where she is stripped of all possessions, killed and left impaled on a stake for three days. She is revived and rescued by two messengers bringing the food and water of life, sent by her husband.	52-57	
The Creation Epic or Enuma Elish	2000 BCE	Akkadian / Babylonian	Recited annually on New Year's Day, this epic poem recounts the struggle between chaos and order and the resultant creation of the world and living things.	60-72, 501-503	1:390-402
The Epic of Gilgamesh	2000 BCE	Akkadian / Babylonian	Gilgamesh attempts to circumvent death by learning the secret of immortality, and in the process learns of the Great Flood from its hero and survivor, Utnapishtim. Well-preserved in several versions, the flood account has many parallels to that in the Old Testament including a snake who foiled Gilgamesh's bid for immortality by carrying off the plant of life he had found on his quest. Although the flood account has been of most interest to scholars, the focus of the Epic itself is man's quest for immortality. For a complete English translation of this work, see A. George, *Gilgamesh*.	72-98, 503-507	1:458-460
The Creation of Man by the Mother Goddess		Akkadian / Babylonian	Brief account of the creation of man out of clay that is mixed with the flesh and blood of a slain deity. An Assyrian version is appended in ANET.	99-100	
A Cosmological Incantation: The Worm and the Toothache		Akkadian / Babylonian	Brief text to cure toothaches, taken from a more ancient source that recounts the creation of the world.	100-101	

Text Name	Date	Culture	Publication Reference and Comment	ANET	COS
Adapa		Akkadian / Babylonian	Four variants of a brief text that describe man's squandered opportunity for obtaining immortality. Similarities and differences with the story of Adam are discussed in D. E. Callender, *Adam*, pp. 75-84.	101-103	1:449
Atrahasis		Akkadian / Babylonian	Four variant fragments of deluge texts.	104-106, 512-514	1:450-453
Descent of Ishtar to the Nether world		Akkadian / Babylonian	Similar to the Sumerian text describing Inanna's descent, this is not just a copy but an account of a similar experience from a Babylonian perspective. Shorter than the Sumerian text, this version is also more symmetrical (and possibly chiastic) giving a more detailed account of Ishtar's return.	106-109	1:381-384
A Vision of the Nether World		Akkadian / Babylonian	A vision of the nether world including the family of gods reigning there.	109-110	
The Theogony of Dunnu		Akkadian / Babylonian	Three incarnations of the City of Dunnu from a pristine heavenly city to an ancient capital.		1:402-404
The Myth of Zu		Akkadian / Babylonian	Zu, after claiming to be superior to the other gods, steals the Tablet of Destinies and eventually is subdued.	111-113, 514-517	3:327-334
Etana		Akkadian / Babylonian	Two versions (Babylonian and Assyrian) from several sources of Etana's visit to heaven.	114-118, 517	1:453-457
The Moon that Fell from Heaven		Hittite	Brief description of the moon god's fall and the reaction of the other gods.	120	
Kingship in Heaven		Hittite	Origins and rivalries of gods in heaven.	120-121	
The Song of Ullikummis		Hittite	Description of the rivalries of the gods from the perspective of the supreme god.	121-125	
Legal Texts					
Lipit-Ishtar Lawcode		Sumerian / Akkadian	The prologue describes how the laws that follow originated with the father of the gods.	159-161	2:410-414
The Code of Hammurabi	ca. 1760 BCE	Babylonian	An ancient code of laws preserved on a seven-foot stele now found in the Louvre. Hammurabi asserted that these laws came from the gods through the firstborn god, Marduk.	163-180	2:335-353
Instructions for Temple Officials		Hittite	Dress code and sacrifice instructions.	207-210	1:217-221
Rituals, Incantations and Festivals					
Daily Ritual of the Temple of Amun-Re at Karnak: Papyrus Berlin 3055		Egyptian	Spells and recitations for the Karnak Temple.	325-326	1:55-57
Ritual for the Repair of a Temple		Akkadian	This ritual survives in three texts, two (A and B) from Uruk, and a third (C) from Babylon. Text C includes a description of the creation and its relationship to restoring temples.	339-342	
Hymns and Prayers					
A Hymn to Amon-Re	1800-1600 BCE	Egyptian	Reference to Amon-Re as the eldest in heaven and firstborn of earth.	365-367	1:37-40
Amon as the Sole God		Egyptian	Dating from the 19th Dynasty, after the Amarna period, this hymn emphasizes Amon as the sole god.	368-369	
The Hymn to Aten		Egyptian	Emphasis on Aton as the whole god during the Amarna period.	369-371	1:44-46
Berlin Hymn to Ptah	New Kingdom	Egyptian	Hymn describing the creative force of Ptah.		1:20-21
The Hymn to Osiris		Egyptian	Most complete Egyptian form of the Osiris myth.		1:41-43

Early Old Testament Manuscripts and Translations

The major groups of early Old Testament manuscripts and translations include a family of early Greek translations (*Septuagint or LXX*), translations and proto-Midrash of the Old Testament made so that Aramaic-speaking Jewish communities could also hear the words of the Hebrew scriptures in their own tongue (*Targum*), the Syriac *Peshitta,* the Latin *Vulgate,* and the Hebrew *Masoretic Text (MT).*

Metzger[25] and Pelikan[26] each provide a good overview of the history of ancient and English versions of the Bible. In-depth discussions of historical and theological issues relating to the formation of the biblical canon can be found in L. M. McDonald, *et al., Canon.*

Text Name	Date	Description	English Publication Reference
Septuagint (LXX), or Alexandrian, Version	ca. 250-150 BCE	A family of early translations of the Old Testament into Greek deriving its name from a tradition that the translation of the Pentateuch was accomplished by seventy-two Jewish scholars. It includes not only the OT but also most of the *Apocrypha* and some interesting—and probably superior—variants from the *MT* on key passages. This was the version of the OT quoted in prophetic citations by the NT, and is still used by much of Eastern Orthodoxy. Overall the *LXX* shows wide agreement with the *MT,* and few variants are found in Genesis. However, several areas of agreement between the *LXX* and the Qumran bible texts where both differ from the *MT* provide evidence that a separate manuscript tradition was behind each of them.	An inexpensive, though now dated, one volume translation of the *LXX* from the *Codex Vaticanus* can be found in L. C. L. Brenton, *Septuagint.* Oxford University Press is in the process of publishing its multi-volume *New English Translation of the Septuagint* (NETS), based on the NRSV, for which a provisional text of Genesis has been made available online (R. J. V. Hiebert, *Septuagint*). A one-volume edition of NETS appeared in 2007 (A. Pietersma, *et al., Septuagint*), and a another English translation has been made (J. N. Sparks, *et al., Orthodox Study Bible*). A superb French translation of the Pentateuch has also been published (C. Dogniez, *et al., Pentateuque*). Jobes and Silva have written an excellent introduction to the *LXX* (K. H. Jobes, *et al., Septuagint*), and Brayford has prepared a commentary highlighting the manner in which the Greek text altered the understanding of Genesis (S. Brayford, *Septuagint Genesis*).
Targum Onkelos (Bavli or Babylonian)	ca. 300-400	This Aramaic translation of the Old Testament got its name from a Roman convert to Judaism mentioned in the *Talmud* who at one time was thought to have composed it. It is the only one of the Targums that was given official status as a text to be read alternatively verse by verse with the Hebrew *Torah* in the synagogue. When Aramaic was no longer spoken, public use of the *Targum* ceased, except in Jewish communities in Yemen.	See B. Grossfeld, *Onqelos.* An inexpensive English version of *Targum Onkelos* can also be found in J. W. Etheridge, *Onkelos.*
Targum Yerushalmi II (Jerusalem or Palestinian or Fragmentary)	ca. 1100-1300	This family of Palestinian targums provides an Aramaic translation of selected verses or phrases from the Hebrew scriptures, possibly intended to supplement the *Onkelos.* Although the known manuscripts are late, much of their content may date to an earlier period. The *Genizah* fragments, first published in 1930, date to the eighth/ninth century or earlier.	Klein's valuable studies are out-of-print, but may sometimes be found in used bookstores (M. L. Klein, *Fragment Targums*; M. L. Klein, *Geniza*). Portions of these fragments are included with *Pseudo-Jonathan* in J. W. Etheridge, *Onkelos.*

---

25   B. M. Metzger, *Translation.*
26   J. Pelikan, *Whose Bible.*

Text Name	Date	Description	English Publication Reference
Targum Pseudo-Jonathan (Yerushalmi 1)	ca. 150-900	In medieval times, this Palestinian Targum was also known as Yerushalmi, but through a printer's error was falsely attributed to Jonathan ben Uziel. It is a combination translation and commentary that includes material from the Talmud as well as from midrashic sources. Tvedtnes, et al. write: "Although this targum reached its final form in the eighth or ninth century, because it is of Palestinian origin, it must date to before the mid-second century" (J. A. Tvedtnes, et al., Traditions, p. 65).	See M. Maher, Pseudo-Jonathan. An inexpensive English version of Targum Pseudo-Jonathan can also be found in J. W. Etheridge, Onkelos.
Targum Neofiti 1	ca. 1504	A late though full copy of the earliest form of the Palestinian targum to the Pentateuch. The codex contains some censorship of what was seen as anti-Christian polemic.	See B. Grossfeld, et al., Neofiti; M. McNamara, Targum Neofiti, which incorporate variants from other Palestinian Targums in their notes.
Vulgate	ca. 405 (OT)	The Old Testament and Apocrypha of this influential Latin translation of the Bible were produced under the direction of Jerome. It became the official Bible of the Roman Catholic Church from the Council of Trent in 1546 until 1979. Since the OT was directly translated from the Hebrew, it is a witness of the manuscripts extant at the time of its translation.	The Vulgate is, of course, published only in Latin. Weber's one-volume critical edition of the text has become the standard reference (R. Weber, Vulgata).
Peshitta	ca. 200 (OT)	This Syriac translation shows similarities to the targums and the LXX but is thought to be based on an independent text resembling the proto-Masoretic. It remains important to churches that are part of the Syriac tradition.	An English translation of Peshitta Genesis is available (Peshitta Foundation, Bereshith Rabba). The Peshitta Institute at Leiden is preparing a new annotated English translation of the Peshitta Old Testament (NEATSB, or the New English Annotated Translation of the Syriac Bible) to be published by Brill. George Lamsa has also produced several volumes of English translation and commentary on the Peshitta, but his work is seen as theologically biased and inaccurate by most scholars.
Masoretic Text (MT)	800-1400	Over a period of several hundred years, a group of Jewish scholars (the Masoretes) compared, standardized, and added vowel points to the text of the Hebrew scriptures. The MT has been adopted as the standard scriptural text of Judaism, and has been widely used in English translations of the Old Testament. For an analysis of textual variants as discussed in rabbinic sources, see B. B. Levy, Fixing.	The Biblia Hebraica Stuttgartensia (BHS) is the unrivaled critical edition of this text (American Bible Society, Biblia). Kohlenberger has edited an interlinear Hebrew-English Old Testament combining the text of the BHS with the New International Version (NIV) English translation (J. R. Kohlenberger, III, Interlinear).
Samaritan Pentateuch	After 100 BCE	A sectarian redaction of the Pentateuch, with important parallels to the Septuagint.	No English translation exists. For backround on the text, see J. D. Purvis, Samaritan Pentateuch. See also S. Lowy, Principles.

The Old Testament Apocrypha

Although the word is commonly used to refer to stories of any kind that are of doubtful origin or veracity, "apocrypha" comes from a Greek term meaning "those having been hidden away." Here, we restrict the term to refer to the deuterocanonical (= Latin "second canon") books of the Old Testament accepted by Roman Catholics but not by most Protestant churches.[27] Most of these writings were included in the *Septuagint* (*LXX*) and were valued by early Christians and some Jewish groups who spoke Greek. However, the apocryphal books were not extant in Hebrew when the canon of the Hebrew scriptures was formed during the first two centuries CE.

In March 1833, when Joseph Smith was engaged in the translation of the Bible, he prayed to know whether he should translate the *Apocrypha* and was told:

> 1 … There are many things contained therein that are true, and it is mostly translated correctly;

> 2 There are many things contained therein that are not true, which are interpolations by the hands of men.

> 3 Verily, I say unto you, that it is not needful that the Apocrypha should be translated.

> 4 Therefore, whoso readeth it, let him understand, for the Spirit manifesteth truth;

> 5 And whoso is enlightened by the Spirit shall obtain benefit therefrom;

> 6 And whoso receiveth not by the Spirit, cannot be benefited. Therefore it is not needful that it should be translated. Amen.[28]

The *Apocrypha* are readily available in many translations and editions. English translation page numbers for the following editions of the *Apocrypha* are given below:

LXX - *The Septuagint with Apocrypha: Greek and English*, edited by Brenton. Contains parallel columns of the Greek and English text. *Apocrypha* is at the end of the volume, with separate pagination.

APOT - *The Apocrypha and Pseudepigrapha of the Old Testament in English*, edited by R. H. Charles in 1913. Volume 1 contains the *Apocrypha* and Volume 2 the *Pseudepigrapha*. These are available in inexpensive paperback editions.

ARV - *The Revised Version of the Apocrypha.*

ARSV - *The Oxford Annotated Apocrypha: Expanded Edition of the Revised Standard Version.*

---

27   Additional collections of ancient books, under the name of "New Testament Apocrypha," have also been edited and published by modern scholars (e.g., E. Hennecke, *et al.*, *NT Apocrypha*; M. R. James, *Apocryphal*). However, these are not accepted as canonical by any major Christian denomination.

28   D&C 91:1-6.

Text Name	Publication Reference and Comment	LXX	APOT	ARV	ARSV
2 Esdras (2, 4, 5, 6 Ezra)	Not found in the Greek, this work consists of three distinct parts (chs. 1-2, 3-14, 15-16), the most important being the second part, the *Apocalypse of Esdras* (4 Ezra in the Latin Vulgate), which contains seven visions. Possibly written during the reign of Domitian (91-96 CE), but in any case no later than 120 CE. A possibility for confusion is in the fact that some publications name the two "Christian additions" (i.e., chs. 1-2 and 15-16 of 2 Esdras) *5 Ezra* and *6 Ezra* respectively, while Latin manuscripts call them *2* and *5 Esdras*.		2:542-624	21-60	23-62
The Wisdom of Solomon	A beautiful discourse on wisdom and immortality, written in Greek by an Alexandrian Jew, shortly before the Christian era.	56-73	1:535-568	96-121	102-127
Ecclesiasticus (Ben Sirach or the Wisdom of Jesus the son of Sirach)	This work was written in Hebrew by Joshua Ben Sira of Jerusalem a few years before the Maccabean revolt. Translated by his grandson into Greek. A Hebrew manuscript has also been discovered.	74-121	1:316-517	121-183	128-197
Baruch	Several disjointed texts modeled on the writings of the Hebrew prophets. Probably written in the first century BCE.	121-127	1:583-595	183-189	198-204
1 Maccabees	Contains a trustworthy history of the Maccabean revolt. Written by an orthodox Jew in the first or second decade of the first century BCE. This is the most valuable of the apocryphal texts from a historical perspective.	139-182	1:67-124	200-241	221-262
2 Maccabees	An abridgement of the larger five-volume history of the Maccabees by Jason of Cyrene. Probably written in the first century BCE.	183-213	1:132-154	241-272	263-293
4 Maccabees	"The book of *4 Maccabees* is a homily or philosophic discourse praising the supremacy of pious reason over passion" (*Fourth Maccabees (Wikipedia)*). For an English translation, see *Fourth Maccabees*.				

The Old Testament Pseudepigrapha

The *Pseudepigrapha* of the Old Testament consist of fifty or more documents bearing some relation to the Hebrew canon and generally thought to have been written between 200 BCE and 200 CE. Additional works of a similar nature written at later periods are also sometimes classed as pseudepigraphal.

Generally, the writings of the OT *Pseudepigrapha* are of either Jewish or Christian origin. However in analyzing a given text, it is frequently difficult to trace the relative extent of each influence.[29] Describing the approach of early scholars to this difficult question, Kraft observes: "M. R. James would list page after page of alleged verbal reminiscences of New Testament writings, with the conclusion that the writing being examined had made use of the New Testament and thus was Christian in its present form. In contrast, Ginzberg would list at length the parallels to known rabbinic Jewish traditions and conclude that the basic core of the writing was Jewish. We have, hopefully, come a long way in our critical awareness if not in our actual practice from simple 'parallelomania.'"[30]

Pseudepigraphal writings are usually ascribed by a later author to a notable figure from the past, hence the designation *pseudepigrapha* (= Greek "false inscription"). Prominent among these are the books of Enoch, highly valued by the early Christian Church and by many of the Eastern Christian Churches today. Many of these texts contain important information, although they are generally considered less reliable than the books of the *Apocrypha*. A good number of these are of a genre called "apocalyptic" (= Greek "lifting of the veil"), a term also used to describe the New Testament book of Revelation and parts of the Old Testament book of Daniel. The apocalyptic writings of the pseudepigrapha purport to reveal the workings of the cosmos and the secrets of heaven, and are often expressed in the language of special types and symbols.

A comprehensive bibliography of pseudepigrapha research (though lacking annotated descriptions of the references) is available in L. DiTommaso, *Bibliography*. Stone supplies a useful overview of the primary and secondary literature relating to Adam and Eve in M. E. Stone, *History of the Literature*.

Page numbers for the following English editions of the Old Testament pseudepigrapha are given in the table below:

> **OTP** - *The Old Testament Pseudepigrapha*, edited by James H. Charlesworth in 1983. This definitive two-volume edition of the Old Testament *Pseudepigrapha* is organized by themes. The groupings are: apocalyptic works, testaments, Old Testament expansions, wisdom literature, prayers, psalms, odes, fragments of lost Judeo-Hellenistic works and histories. An introduction and commentary accompany each text.

> **APOT** - *The Apocrypha and Pseudepigrapha of the Old Testament in English*, edited by R. H. Charles in 1913. Volume 1 contains the *Apocrypha* and Volume 2 the *Pseudepigrapha*. This was the standard reference collection until OTP appeared seventy years later. Now superseded by OTP, APOT is included here because it has been referenced extensively for many years and is now available in inexpensive paperback editions.

---

29   R. A. Kraft, *Pseudepigrapha.*
30   *Ibid.*, pp. 60-61.

Text Name	Date	Publication Reference and Comment	OTP	APOT
Apocalyptic Literature and Related Works				
1 Enoch (The Ethiopic Apocalypse of Enoch)	200 BCE-100 CE	This is the oldest of three so-called books of Enoch. Portions of this work were found among the Dead Sea Scrolls. Over forty manuscripts of this work have survived in Ethiopic (Ge'ez) and fragments have been found in Aramaic, Greek and Latin. Barker observes: "The oldest text fragments are from the third century BCE, but Isaiah knew something like *1 Enoch,* and so the tradition must be a lot older" (M. Barker, *Hidden,* p. vii). *1 Enoch* may be divided into five sections and an appendix as follows: • *Chapters 1-36*: An introduction discussing the final judgment of the righteous and wicked and a narrative concerning the fallen angels, their corruption of men, and various visions of Enoch. • *Chapters 37-71*: The Similitudes (parables) of Enoch that deal with the coming judgment, the resurrection, and the Messiah. • *Chapters 72-82*: An astrological treatise concerning the reckoning of time. • *Chapters 83-90*: The Dream Visions, two visions concerning the future history of the world and Israel. • *Chapters 91-104*: Enoch's testament. • *Chapters 105-108*: Appendix containing fragments of the *Book of Noah* and editorial comments. Chapters 1-36 and 81-108 of *1 Enoch* appear in an exhaustive commentary by Nickelsburg (G. W. E. Nickelsburg, *1 Enoch*), and he and VanderKam have also produced a new translation of all the chapters, lacking commentary (G. W. E. Nickelsburg, *et al., 1 Enoch*).	1:5-89	2:188-281
2 Enoch (The Slavonic Apocalypse of Enoch, The Secrets of Enoch)	100	Known from twenty Slavonic manuscripts, none of which is a complete text of *2 Enoch*. In each case the manuscript is a different work that is quoting part of *2 Enoch*. *2 Enoch* is basically a midrash on Genesis 5:21-32 and can be divided into two parts: • Chapters 1-68 describe how Enoch was taken up through seven heavens and then returned to report on what he had learned. • Chapters 69-73 deal with the life of Enoch's successors and ends with the birth of Melchizedek shortly before the Flood.	1:91-221	2:431-469
Treatise of Shem	100-1 BCE	This text, attributed to Shem, describes dependencies between the house of the Zodiac in which a particular year begins, and the characteristics of that year. It contains twelve chapters, one for each sign of the Zodiac. One fifteenth-century Syriac text has survived. The original language was probably Semitic.	1:473-486	
3 Baruch (Greek Apocalypse of Baruch)	100-300	In this text Baruch weeps over the destruction of Jerusalem. The Lord sends an angel to comfort him and show him the mysteries of heaven. He is led through five heavens and then returned to earth. This work is preserved in three families of Slavonic manuscripts and a Greek manuscript that is the source of the Slavonic.	1:653-679	2:533-541
Apocalypse of Abraham	1-200	An ascension text with striking parallels to the book of Moses. • Chapters 1-8 describe Abraham's youth and encounter with his father's idolatry. • Chapters 9-32 describe Abraham's ascension and a series of seven visions ending with the victory of the just. "The author of the text seems to be using the narrative to explain why Jerusalem was destroyed in 70 CE" (J. A. Tvedtnes, *et al., Traditions*, p. 52). Known from six Slavonic manuscripts, the original text was probably Hebrew. The first English publication of selections from this text was made in the Church's *Improvement Era* periodical in 1898 (E. H. Anderson, *et al., Abraham*). Kulik has developed new readings for the text (A. Kulik, *Retroverting*). See D. J. Larsen, *et al., Vision of Moses* for parallels with Moses 1 and reproductions of the beautiful color illustrations from the *Codex Sylvester*. Jared Ludlow and Hugh Nibley have also written about parallels with the LDS books of Abraham and Moses (J. W. Ludlow, *Visions*; H. W. Nibley, *To Open*).	1:681-705	
Apocalypse of Adam	1-400	An apocalypse narrated by Adam to his son Seth shortly before his death. Covers the story of the Fall, Flood and destruction of Sodom and Gomorrah from a Gnostic view. Preserved as the last part of Codex V of the Coptic *Nag Hammadi Codices*.	1:707-719	
Testaments, Often with Apocalyptic Sections				

Text Name	Date	Publication Reference and Comment	OTP	APOT
Testaments of the Twelve Patriarchs	200-100 BCE	A document purporting to contain the final utterances of the twelve sons of Jacob modeled after the last words of Jacob in Genesis 49. Most include predictions of the future of Israel. Originally Jewish, with later Christian additions. Five Greek manuscripts.	1:775-828	2:296-367
Testament of Abraham	1-200	Abraham's tour of the world and vision of the judgment prior to his death. His soul is conducted to heaven after a reluctant departure from earth. "Although a Jewish text, it was only preserved by Christians" (M. Barker, Revelation, p. 396). Two recensions, the first and longer one in Romanian and the second in several Greek copies. Later versions also available in Slavonic, Romanian, Coptic, Arabic and Ethiopic.	1:871-902	
Testament of Jacob	100-300	An angel takes Jacob on a tour of hell and heaven prior to his death. His soul is taken to heaven and Joseph embalms his body. Based on an Arabic text with some pieces from Coptic and Ethiopic texts.	1:913-918	
Testament of Moses (Assumption of Moses)	1-100	Farewell exhortation from Moses to Joshua prior to his death. Contains a prediction of the history of his people. From one Latin Palimpsest (= manuscript with earlier writing effaced to accommodate later writing), with almost half of the manuscript lost.	1:919-934	2:414-424
Testament of Adam	100-500	This text is divided into three sections, an Horarium (hours of the day and night), prophecy and a list of nine different orders of heavenly beings. A Christian version of an earlier Jewish text (M. Barker, Hidden, p. vii), it is based on a Syriac text in its current form in three recensions, having survived in eight manuscripts.	1:989-995	
Expansions of the Old Testament and Legends				
Jubilees	200-100 BCE	The book of Jubilees, sometimes called Little Genesis, purports to be an account of revelations to Moses while he was on Mt. Sinai for forty days. It recounts much of the material found in Genesis and Exodus, but some of the differences are so striking that it has been called a "Rewritten Bible" (H. L. Strack, et al., Introduction, p. 235). It covers the Creation, Adam, Noah, Abraham, Jacob, and the story of Moses himself. Barker observes: "Most summaries of history in the Hebrew scriptures focus on Moses and the Exodus but omit Sinai; they are the exact opposite of the Apocalypse of Weeks [in Jubilees]. Scholars have suspected for some time that Sinai and Exodus were originally distinct traditions, interwoven only after the destruction of the first temple, and with the Exodus narrative predominating… rather than temple tradition, which underlies the Sinai story" (M. Barker, Hidden, p. 38). Jubilees was originally written in Hebrew. The Hebrew text was translated into Greek and Syriac. The Greek text was translated into Latin and Ethiopic. No Hebrew (outside of Qumran), little or no Syriac and only fragments of the Greek texts have survived. About one-fourth of the Latin text is extant, the only complete text being the Ethiopic. Many small Hebrew fragments were found at Qumran. In addition two of the Dead Sea Scrolls (The Genesis Apocryphon and the Damascus Document) show influence from Jubilees. E. D. Clark, Prologue, looks at common influences in Jubilees and Moses 1.	2:35-142	2:11-82
Martyrdom and Ascension of Isaiah	200 BCE-400 CE	This is a composite work that divides easily into two parts. The first five chapters form a work now called The Martyrdom of Isaiah and the last six chapters another work containing an account of a heavenly Ascension or Vision of Isaiah. Inserted into the Martyrdom is yet another work (3:13-4:22) sometimes called the Testament of Hezekiah. There are a number of smaller additions and other changes to the text. The Martyrdom is a Jewish work. The Ascension and Testament sections are considered later Christian additions. The Martyrdom, originally written in Hebrew was translated into Greek, the language of the later additions. The entire text was translated from Greek to Ethiopic, Latin, Slavonic and Coptic. Only in Ethiopic has the entire text survived.	2:143-176	2:159-162

Text Name	Date	Publication Reference and Comment	OTP	APOT
Joseph and Aseneth (Joseph and Asenath)	100 BCE- 200 CE	A long tale attested in many manuscript sources that tells of how Joseph came to marry Aseneth, "a foreign Hamitic girl, daughter of an idolatrous priest" (C. Burchard, *Joseph*, p. 177). Sixteen Greek manuscripts have survived along with about seventy other manuscripts in Syriac, Armenian, Latin, Slavonic, Rumanian and Ethiopian. The Greek manuscripts fall into four distinct groups. For discussions about the possibility of ritual elements in the work, see R. D. Chesnutt, *Food*; A. J. M. Wedderburn, *Baptism*, pp. 157-158. For example, Seaich notes that the three gifts given to Aseneth from Joseph as he kisses her three times "correspond to the three 'tokens' (*ankh, djed*, and *was*) bestowed in the Egyptian form of the Sacred Embrace" (J. E. Seaich, *Ancient Texts 1995*, p. 858 n. 642).	2:177- 247	
Life of Adam and Eve and the Armenian Adam literature (Apocalypse of Moses (Greek), Vita (Latin))	1-100	This is perhaps the most important and extensive work of the primary Adam literature. The Greek and Latin texts narrate events after Adam and Eve leave the Garden of Eden, focusing on their relationship with Seth including death-bed recollections about the Fall and instructions to their posterity. Twenty-three manuscripts have been located so far. These fall into five main variations. In addition to the Greek and Latin manuscripts there are more recently discovered texts in Armenian, Slavonic, and Georgian. The original text was most likely Hebrew with the Greek translated from the Hebrew and the Latin from either of these. Charlesworth includes parallel translations of the Greek and Latin texts, which have significant differences. Anderson and Stone, who have each published extensively about the Adam literature, have edited a parallel column edition of the *Life* with all five major recensions (G. A. Anderson, *et al.*, *Synopsis*). A variety of additional Armenian texts relating to the life of Adam and Eve can be found in W. L. Lipscomb, *Armenian*; M. E. Stone, *Armenian Apocrypha 1982*; M. E. Stone, *Armenian Apocrypha 1996*.	2:249- 295	2:134- 154
Pseudo-Philo (Liber Antiquitatum Biblicarum, Book of Biblical Antiquities)	ca. 135 BCE- 70 CE	This important Latin text expands upon biblical stories of Adam until the time of David. Jacob's comprehensive but expensive Latin text, English translation, and commentary is the best resource for scholars (H. Jacobson, *Pseudo-Philo*). See also B. N. Fisk, *Remember*; F. J. Murphy, *Pseudo-Philo*.	2:297- 377	
Ladder of Jacob	1-100?	The *Ladder of Jacob* has not survived as a separate text, but only as part of other Slavonic works, specifically the *Tolkovaja Paleja* or *Explanatory Palaia*. The *Ladder of Jacob* is an elaboration of Jacob's dream at Bethel. It includes visions and prophecies. The last chapter, now considered a separate work, contains messianic prophecies.	2:401- 411	
Prayers, Psalms and Odes				
Prayer of Joseph	1-100	The *Prayer of Joseph* maintains that the patriarch Jacob was the earthly incarnation of the angel Israel. Originally containing 1100 lines, only three fragments containing nine Greek sentences have survived.	2:699- 714	
Prayer of Jacob	1-400	The *Prayer of Jacob* may be divided into four invocations, three petitions and one injunction. The only existing text is a fourth-century papyrus written in Greek, thought to be the original language.	2:715- 723	
Odes of Solomon	80-120	Once thought to be Gnostic, the *Odes of Solomon* are now considered to be a collection of very early Christian hymns. Excerpts are found in the *Pistis Sophia* and in Lactantius. Partial copies of the Odes are found in a few manuscripts. Fragments of 42 (although none of Ode 2) have survived. The original language is probably Syriac although strong cases have also been made for Greek and Hebrew. Nibley cites lengthy passages from the *Odes of Solomon* that echo LDS temple themes (H. W. Nibley, *Message 2005*, pp. 477-485).	2:725- 771	

The following pseudepigraphal works share these characteristics:

- They are of Jewish origin.

- They were composed in Greek and in literary forms known elsewhere in Greek literature.

- They are not truly pseudepigraphal, that is they were not written in another's name, although, by accident, some may now be falsely ascribed to another.

- They are only fragmentarily preserved, usually as a quotation in another work.

- Although the qualifications of some works are open for debate, Charlesworth in **OTP** has chosen to err on the side of acceptance, thus making them easily available for study.

Author Name	Date	Publication Reference and Comment	OTP
Philo the Epic Poet	300-100 BCE	Six fragments, containing 24 lines, of an epic poem that recounts the binding of Isaac (Genesis 22) and God's blessing towards Joseph. The last three fragments focus on Jerusalem and the city's water supply. The work is known to us only because of extracts cited by the Christian historian Eusebius.	2:781-784
Pseudo-Eupol-emus	before 100 BCE	In the discussion of Abraham in Eusebius' *Praeparatio Evangelica,* he includes two fragments, one attributed to Alexander Polyhistor. Scholars have assigned these fragments, both from Polyhistor's *On the Jews,* to a Pseudo-Eupolemus. The first deals with Abraham as a teacher of astrology, with Enoch attributed as its inventor, and the second traces Abraham's lineage back to a race of giants.	2:873-882
Cleodemus Malchus	before 100 BCE	This work deals with the descendants of Abraham through Keturah (Gen 25:1-4). It has survived as a quotation in Josephus' *Antiquities* 1.239-241 and in Eusebius' *Praeparatio Evangelica* 9.20.2-4.	2:883-887
Artapanus	300-100 BCE	Three fragments that deal with exploits in Egypt of Abraham, Joseph and Moses. Abraham teaches the Egyptians how to study the stars, Joseph teaches measurement and organization of the land, and Moses is identified with Mousaeus the teacher of Orpheus. These fragments were preserved in Eusebius' *Praeparatio Evangelica* 9.18, 23 and 27.	2:889-903

BIBLIOGRAPHY

The Dead Sea Scrolls and Other Related Texts

Dating from the first two centuries BCE, these texts include copies from almost all the books of the Old Testament, Hebrew copies of some of the *Apocrypha*, and some texts found nowhere else. They were discovered in a series of caves near the site of Qumran on the cliffs overlooking the Dead Sea. The first discoveries of *Dead Sea Scrolls (DSS)* came from caves, now numbered I through XI. Scholars now include among this collection writings from other areas around the Dead Sea. This includes texts found at Masada, Nahal Hever and Wadi Murabba'at. LDS perspectives on the Qumran texts are included in D. W. Parry, *et al., LDS Perspectives;* D. W. Parry, *et al., Questions;* and J. E. Seaich, *Mormonism.*

The Dead Sea Scrolls

The *DSS* recovered so far consist of seven nearly complete scrolls and about 25,000 fragments, many of which are smaller than a postage stamp. These fragments make up about 930 scrolls which, because there were sometimes multiple copies, yield about 500 distinct texts or documents. About 200 of the scrolls are copies of biblical texts. The latest inventory of the extant scrolls appears in E. Tov, *Scribal Practices.*

The official publication for the scrolls is the Oxford University Press series *Discoveries in the Judean Desert,* here abbreviated *DJD.* Unfortunately, the texts published in *DJD* are scattered in a non-systematic fashion among many volumes, making analysis difficult. The *DJD* series has now been superseded by *The Dead Sea Scrolls Reader (DSSR),* which presents for the first time all the non-biblical Qumran texts classified according to their genres, together with English translations, in six volumes. The *DSSR* is co-edited by Donald W. Parry of Brigham Young University and Emanuel Tov, editor-in-chief of the *DSS* publication team. Available both in hardback and in a relatively inexpensive paperback edition (D. W. Parry, *et al., Reader*), the precisely-rendered Hebrew-Aramaic texts in *DSSR* were also the basis of the FARMS database of Brigham Young University. *DSSR* represents the most complete and up-to-date edition of the *DSS,* including twenty-five previously unpublished texts.

The following table lists the scrolls in order by series designation. Some of the publication reference information, especially for the biblical scrolls, is an abbreviated summary taken from M. A. Hoselton's detailed list of *DSS* contents.[31] Each row of the table below contains the following columns:

> **Series Designation** - The official scroll designation.
>
> **Abbreviation** - The official abbreviation is shown in parentheses; other titles may also be listed.
>
> **Publication Reference and Comment** - The official publication for the scroll. Also contains explanations.
>
> **Types** - A symbol in this column indicates the type of scroll.
>
> **ß** - Biblical text (not usually included in the English editions of the DSS).
>
> **a** - Apocryphal, that is, texts from the traditional OT Apocrypha.
>
> **p** - Pseudepigraphal, that is, texts from or related to the OT Pseudepigrapha.
>
> **m** - Messianic texts. Some references directly refer to a Messiah, some are oblique.

31   M. A. Hoselton, *Inventory.*

Y - Included in exhibition at BYU in 1997 and published in G. M. Bradford, *Ancient Scrolls (ASDS).*[32]

Much of the value of the copies of biblical works is in the information that they shed on the textual development of the Old Testament. It was long thought that *LXX* suffered from translation errors where it differed from the standard *MT.* The *DSS* biblical texts contain Hebrew manuscripts that in some cases follow the *LXX,* showing that there was an independent Hebrew textual transmission behind the *LXX* translation. Similar Hebrew originals have been found for some of the variations in the Samaritan *Peshitta.* Frank Moore Cross believes that these three recensions are the result of geographical separation between different groups (F. M. Cross, *Library*). The Samaritan *Peshitta* was developed in Palestine, the *LXX* in Egypt, and the *MT* in Babylon. Thus the *DSS* appears to provide access to the roots of these three textual traditions.

English translation page numbers for the following editions of the scrolls are included in the table:

AFU – *The Dead Sea Scrolls Bible*, edited by M. Abegg, Jr., *et al.*, combines multiple copies of scrolls containing biblical writings into a continuous text. There is no index, but each chapter has a footnote listing the scrolls by verse and indicating the source. Variant readings, including comparisons with the *LXX* and *Peshitta*, are shown in the footnotes. The text also includes references to some of the more important apocryphal and pseudepigraphal works.

MT - *The Dead Sea Scrolls Study Edition*, edited by Florentino Garcia Martinez and Eibert J. C. Tigchelaar, is the best reference for the identification of specific *DSS* documents. All texts are published separately in both Hebrew and English on facing pages. Nearly all of the small scraps and fragments are included. biblical texts are not included but a reference to each is placed in sequence. Some translations are newer than what appears in *FGM*. An index is provided at the end of the volume.

FGM - *The Dead Sea Scrolls Translated*, edited by Florentino Garcia Martinez, is the best English-only reference for the identification of specific documents. All texts are published separately. An extensive index (from which much of the information in the table below derives) is provided at the end of the volume.

GV - *The Complete Dead Sea Scrolls in English*, edited by Geza Vermes, has an excellent introduction. Multiple copies of texts are combined. Where texts represent amalgamations the page numbers are italicized. Significant variants are included as separate texts.

WAC - *The Dead Sea Scrolls, A New Translation*, edited by Wise, Abegg, and Cook, takes great care to reproduce all variants of liturgical texts. Multiple copies of texts are combined, but the sources are identified. Where multiple copies exist, the best fragments are pieced together to make a one serial text. Where texts represent amalgamations, the page numbers are italicized. This edition includes an introduction and some commentary on each work.

By purchasing *AFU* and *MT* one has the most complete English translation of all of the *Dead Sea Scrolls* that are printed for the general reader. In addition one also has a copy of the Hebrew text of the non-biblical Dead Sea Scrolls. *FGM* is listed because of its wide availability, but *MT* is superior to it. *GV* and *WAC* are competent translations for the reader who is interested in the text and message of the Dead Sea Scrolls but who is not as concerned

---

32   In 1997 the Kingdom of Jordan loaned Brigham Young University four *Dead Sea Scrolls* for an exhibit on Masada. These scrolls had previously been unavailable except through photographs. In addition the exhibit featured several other texts, four from Masada and a Bar Kokhba text. The translations and commentary are published in G. M. Bradford, *ASDS.*

about what text came from what specific scroll. These latter translations do provide some alternate readings based on different parallel manuscripts.

For an illuminating survey and analysis of treatments of material from Genesis in the Qumran library, see M. J. Bernstein, *Contours*.

Series	Abbreviation	Publication Reference and Comment	T	AFU	MT	FGM	GV	WAC
1Q1	*(1QGen) 1QGenesis*	D. Barthélemy, *DJD* I, Oxford 1955, 49-50, pl. VIII. Nineteen fragments with remains of Genesis. Contains Genesis 1:18-21; 3:11-14; 22:13-15; 23:17-19; 24:22-24.	ß	6-8, 10				
1Qap-Gen ar	*(1Q20) 1QGenesis Apocryphon*	Original publication in N. Avigad, *et al.*, *Apocryphon*. Rewritten version of Genesis in Aramaic that could rightly be called "the oldest prototype of both [Targum and Midrash] available to us" (H. L. Strack, *et al.*, *Introduction*, p. 236). One of the original group of seven manuscripts retrieved by the Tacâmireh. *1QapGen ar* is one of the four acquired by Athanasius Yeshue Samuel.			28-49	230-237		
1Q21	*(1QTLevi ar) 1QTestament of Levi*	J. T. Milik, *DJD* I, 87-91, pl. XVII. Remains of an Aramaic work related to the Aramaic *Testament of Levi* from the Cairo *Genizah*, and to the Greek *Testament of Levi*, which forms part of the *Testaments of the Twelve Patriarchs*.	p		56-59	266	524-525	
1Q23	*(1QEnGiantsᵃ ar) 1QEnoch Giantsᵃ ar*	J. T. Milik, *DJD* I, 97-98, pl. XIX. Published as remains of an Aramaic apocryphon, they were later identified by Milik as a copy of the *Book of Giants* in Milik, *Books*, 301-302.	p		62-65	260		247
1Q24	*(1QEnGiantsᵇ ar) 1QEnoch Giantsᵇ ar*	J. T. Milik, *DJD* I, 99, pl. XX. Aramaic apocryphon; according to Milik, *Books*, 309, possibly another copy of the *Book of Giants*.	p		64-65			
1QS	*(1QS) 1QRule of the Community (Community Rule, The 'Son of God' Text*, and, occasionally still, *The Manual of Discipline)*	Published in M. Burrows (ed.), *The Dead Sea Scrolls of St. Mark's Monastery*, New Haven, CN: The American Schools of Oriental Research, 1950, vol. II/2, (Manual of Discipline = 1QS). There is no II/1. This manuscript contains a description of a sectarian group whose beliefs and practices resembled those of an ancient pacifist sect known as the Essenes, as noted by Eliezer Sukenik of Hebrew University in 1948. When this cave was reexplored in 1949, fragments of many other scrolls were found including what seemed to be an appendage to this same Essene-like work. In the first century CE, Pliny the Elder located a group of Essenes on the western shore of the Dead Sea somewhere above En Gedi. This congruence, along with the seemingly obvious connection between the pottery found in the caves and in the nearby ruins, are what first led de Vaux to propose the hypothesis that the entire library and Qumran itself were products of the Essenes. One of the original seven manuscripts retrieved by the Tacâmireh, *1QS* is one of the four acquired by Athanasius Yeshue Samuel. Nibley cites lengthy passages of the *Rule of the Community* that echo LDS temple themes (H. W. Nibley, *Message 2005*, pp. 461-475).	m		68-69	3-19	126-143	

Series	Abbreviation	Publication Reference and Comment	T	AFU	MT	FGM	GV	WAC
1Q28a	(1QSa) 1QRule of the Congregation (1QRule of the Community, Community Rule, The Sectarian Rule of the Community, The 'Son of God' Text, and, occasionally still, The Manual of Discipline)	D. Barthélemy, DJD I, 108-118, pls. XXIII-XXIV. Appendix to the Community Rule, 1QS, eschatological in content. Adjuncts to the Rule of the Community (1QS), published in DJD I as 1Q28a and 1Q28b. M. Burrows (ed.), The Dead Sea Scrolls of St. Mark's Monastery, vol. II, fasc. 2: The Manual of Discipline, New Haven, CN: The American Schools of Oriental Research, 1951. Community Rule, cols I-XI. 1Q28a and 1Q28b are usually assumed to be appendices to 1QS. They were discovered during subsequent digs in cave 1 conducted by Lankester Harding and Roland De Vaux several years after the first seven manuscripts were discovered there. By that time the cave had obviously been 'excavated' both by the Bedouin and by the monks of Syrian monastery of St Mark, or their agents. (G. M. Bradford, ASDS, pp. 18-21).	Y m		98-103	126-128	157-160	144-147
2Q21	(2QapMoses?) 2QApocryphon of Moses	M. Baillet, DJD III, 79-81, pl. XV. Remains of a dialogue of Moses with God.			214-217	281		
4Q1	(4QGen-Exod^a) 4QGenesis-Exodus^a	J. R. Davila, DJD XII, 1-30, pls. I-V. Copy that contains combined remains of Genesis and Exodus. Contains Genesis chapters 8:20-21;, 22:14; 27:38-39, 42-43; 34:17-21; 35:17-29; 36:1-13, 19-27; 37:5-6, 22-27; 39:11-23; 40:1; 45:23; 47:13-14; 48:2-4, 15-22; 49:1-5 and Exodus chapters 1:3-17, 22; 2:1-5; 3:8-16, 18-21; 4:4-9, 26-31; 5:1, 3-17; 6:4-21, 25; 7:5-13, 15-20; 8:24-26; 9:8.	ß	9-16, 20-22, 25-34, 36-37				
4Q5	(4QGen^c) 4QGenesis^c	J. R. Davila, DJD XII, 47-52, pl. X. Copy of Genesis from a textual type similar to MT and the Samaritan text. Contains portions of Genesis chapters 36:43; 37:1-2, 27-30; 40:18-23; 41:1-8, 35-44; 42:17-19; 43:8-14; 49:6-8.	ß	15-19, 22				
4Q6	(4QGen^f) 4QGenesis^f	J. R. Davila, DJD XII, 53-55, pl. XI. Remains of one column with Genesis 48:1-11.	ß	21				
4Q7	(4QGen^g) 4QGenesis^g	J. R. Davila, DJD XII, 57-60, pl. XII. Two fragments of Genesis 1-2. Contains Genesis 1:1-11, 13-22; 2:6-7 or 18-19. Has a number of interesting variants from the MT.	ß	7				
4Q9	(4QGen^j) 4QGenesis^j	J. R. Davila, DJD XII, 65-73, pl. XIII. Copy of Genesis of a textual type close to the Samaritan text. Contains portions of Genesis chapters 41:15-18, 23-27, 29-36, 38-43; 42:15-22, 38; 43:1-2, 5-8; 45:14-22, 26-28.	ß	17-20				
4Q11	(4QpalaeoGen-Exod^l) 4QGenesis-Exodus^l	P. W. Skehan, E. Ulrich, J. E. Sanderson, DJD IX, 17-50, pls. I-VI. A manuscript in palaeo-Hebrew script with remains of Genesis 50:26 and Exodus 1-36. Contains Exodus 1:1-5; 2:10, 22-25; 3:1-4, 17-21; 8:13-15, 19-21; 9:25-29, 33-35; 10:1-5; 11:4-10; 12:1-11, 42-46; 14:15-24; 16:2-7, 13-14, 18-20, 23-25, 26-31, 33-35; 17:1-3, 5-11; 18:17-24; 19:24-25; 20:1-2; 22:23-24; 23:5-16; 25:7-20; 26:29-37; 27:1, 6-14; 28:33-35, 40-42; 36:34-36. Contains an additional 26 fragments too small or too poorly preserved to identify with certainty.	ß	22, 25-29, 36, 39-40, 42-44, 47, 49-51, 54-55, 57-58, 62-63, 65, 73				

BIBLIOGRAPHY

Series	Abbreviation	Publication Reference and Comment	T	AFU	MT	FGM	GV	WAC
4Q158	(4QRPª) 4QReworked Pentateuchª	J. M. Allegro, *DJD* V, 1-6, pl. I. Paraphrase of Genesis 32:25-32; Exodus 24:27-28; Genesis 32:31 (?); Exodus 3:12; 24:4-6; 19:17-23; 20:19-22; Deuteronomy 5:29; 15:18-20:22; Exodus 20:12, 16, 17; Deuteronomy 5:30-31; Exodus 20:22-26; 21:1, 4, 6, 8, 10; 21:15, 16, 18, 20, 22, 25, 32, 34, 35-37; 22:1-11, 13; 30:32, 34.			304-309	219-222	442-443	200-204
4Q180	(4QagesCreat A) 4QAges of Creation A	J. M. Allegro *DJD* V, 77-79, pl. XXVII. Commentary on salvation history and on the periods of sin, starting from the fall of the angels. J. T. Milik suggests that this and *4Q181* are part of a single work.			370-373	211-212	520	238-239
4Q181	(4QagesCreat B) 4QAges of Creation B	J. M. Allegro DJD V, 79-80, pl. XXVIII. Document which describes the destiny of the chosen and the damned.			372-375	212-213	229	239
4Q201	(4QEnª ar) 4QEnochª ar	Originally published in J. T. Milik, *Enoch,* pp. 139-163, 340-343, pls. I-V. Copy of *Book of Watchers* from *1 Enoch.* Remains of *1 Enoch* 1:1-6; 2:1-5, 6; 6:4-8:1; 8:3-9:3; 9:6-8; 10:3-4, 21-11:1; 12:4-6; 14:4-6.	p		398-405	246-248	514	
4Q202	(4QEnᵇ ar) 4QEnochᵇ ar	Originally published in J. T. Milik, *Enoch,* pp. 164-178, 344-346, pls. VI-IX. Copy of the *Book of Watchers* from *1 Enoch.* Remains of *1 Enoch* 5:9-6:4; 6:7-8:1; 8:2-9:4; 10:8-12.	p		404-409	248-250		
4Q203	(4QEnGiantsª ar) 4QBook of Giantsª ar	Originally published in J. T. Milik, *Enoch,* pp. 310-317, pls. XXX-XXXII, pp. 178-217, 346-353, pls. IX-XV. Copy of the *Book of Giants.*	p		408-411	260-261		
4Q204	(4QEnᶜ ar) 4QEnochᶜ ar	Originally published in J. T. Milik, *Enoch,* pp. 178-217, 346-353, pls. IX-XV. Copy of the *Book of Watchers,* the *Book of Giants,* the *Book of Dreams* and the *Letter of Enoch* from *1 Enoch.* Remains of *1 Enoch* 1:9-5:1; 6:7; 10:13-19; 12:3; 13:6-14:19; 14:18-20; 15:11(?); 18:8-12; 30:1-32:1; 35; 36:1-4; 89:31-37; 104:13-106:2; 106:13-107:2.	p		412-421	250-254	514-515	
4Q209	(4QEnastrᵇ ar) 4QAstronomical Enochᵇ ar	Originally published in J. T. Milik, *Enoch,* pp. 278-284, 340-343, pls. XXV-XXVII, XXX. Copy of the *Astronomical Book* from *1 Enoch.* Remains of a synchronous calendar and of other passages corresponding to *1 Enoch* 76:13-77:4; 78:9-12; 79:3-5 + 78:17-79:2; 82:9-13.	p		430-439	445-448	515	
4Q210	(4QEnastrᶜ ar) 4QAstronomical Enochᶜ ar	Originally published in J. T. Milik, *Enoch,* pp. 284-288, pls. XXVIII, XXX. Copy of the *Astronomical Book* from *1 Enoch.* Remains of *1 Enoch* 76:3-10; 76:13-77:4; 78:6-8.	p		438-441	448-449		
4Q211	(4QEnastrᵈ ar) 4QAstronomical Enochᵈ ar	Originally published in J. T. Milik, *Enoch,* pp. 296-297, 359, pl. XXIX. Copy of the *Astronomical Book* from 1 Enoch. Remains of three columns which would follow *1 Enoch* 82:20.	p		440-443	449-450		
4Q212	(4QEnᵍ ar) 4QEnochᵍ ar	Originally published in J. T. Milik, *Enoch,* pp. 245-272, 360-362, pls. XXI-XXIV. Copy of the *Letter of Enoch* from *1 Enoch.* Remains of *1 Enoch* 91:10(?), 18, 19; 92:1-2; 92:5-93:4; 93:9-10; 91:11-17; 93:11-94:2.	p		442-445	258-259		
4Q215	(4QTNaph) 4QTestament of Naphtali	M. E. Stone, *DJD* XXII, 73-82, pl. V. A Hebrew *Testament of Naphtali* not related to the *Testament of Naphtali* that forms part of the *Testaments of the XII Patriarchs.*	p		454-457	270-271	528-529	260-261
4Q216	(4QJubª) 4QJubileesª	J. C. VanderKam, J. T. Milik, *DJD* XIII, 1-22, pls. I-II. The oldest extant copy of the book of *Jubilees.* Copied by two different scribes.	p		458-465	238-240		

Series	Abbreviation	Publication Reference and Comment	T	AFU	MT	FGM	GV	WAC
4Q246	4QAramaic Apocalypse, 4QPsDan A^a, 4QSon of God	E. Puech, *DJD* XXII, 165-184, pl. XI. Fragment of an apocalyptic work in Aramaic which uses the titles *Son of God* and *Son of the Most High*, previously known as *4QPsDan A^a*, *4Q243* and *4QSon of God*.	m		492-495	138	577	269-270
4Q249	(4QpapCryptA MSM) 4QCryptic A: Midrash Sefer Moshe	S. Pfann, *DJD* XXXV. Commentary on Genesis in Cryptic script, copied on papyrus. Many fragments have been preserved, but small in size. The title of the work, *Commentary on the Book of Moses*, is located on the back, not in the cryptic but in the square script.			496-497			
4Q252	(4QcommGen A) 4QCommentary on Genesis A	G. Brooke, *DJD* XXII, 185-207, pls. XII-XIII. This fragment contains a commentary on Genesis 49:10. The first columns of the manuscript are a paraphrase of Genesis 6.	m		500-505	213-215	461-463	275-277
4Q364	(4QRP^b) 4QReworked Pentateuch^b	E. Tov, S. A. White, *DJD* XIII, 197-254, pl. XIII-XXI.			718-719	222-224	443	325-326
4Q368	(4QapocrPent A) 4QApocryphon Pentateuch A	D. Dimant, *DJD* XXX. Fifteen fragments, of which three are good-sized, of a narrative work related to the Pentateuch.			726-731			
4Q369	(4QPEnosh ?) 4QPrayer of Enosh (?)	H. Attridge, J. Strugnell, *DJD* XIII, 353-362, pl. XXXVII. A good fragment with remains of two columns and other lesser fragments of an apocryphal composition related to the generations before the Flood.			730-733		511-512	329-330
4Q370	4QExhortation Based on the Flood	C. Newsom, *DJD* XIX, 85-97, pl. XII. 732-733. Exhortation based on the story of the Flood, of which only two columns have been preserved.			732-733	224-225	518-519	330-331
4Q414	(4QRitPur A) 4QRitual of Purification	E. Eshel, *DJD* XXXV. Baptismal Hymn, 4 fragments.			842-845	439		391
4Q422	4QParaphrase of Genesis and Exodus	T. Elgvin, E. Tov, *DJD* XIII, 417-444, pls. XLII-XLIII. Minute remains of a biblical paraphrase.			884-887		446-447	391-393
4Q424	4QSapiential Text	*The Sons of Righteousness*, two fragments of another wisdom composition.			888-891	393-394	414-415	393-394
4Q464	4QExposition on the Patriarchs	E. Eshel, M. Stone, *DJD* XIX, 215-230, pl. XXVIII. Fragments of an exposition on the patriarchs.			942-943			402
4Q471b	4QSelf-Glorification Hymn^a	E. Eshel, *DJD* XXIX. Fragment containing the *Song of Michael*.			952-953			
4Q502	(4QpapRitMar) 4QRitual of Marriage	M. Baillet, *DJD* VII, 81-105, pls. XXIX-XXXIV. Fragments of a ritual for a joyous celebration, interpreted by Baillet as a wedding ritual and by Baumgarten as a celebration in which the protagonists are old men and women.			994-997	440-441		407-408
4Q503	(4QpapPrQuot) 4QDaily Prayers^a	M. Baillet, *DJD* VII, 105-136, pls. XXXV, XXXVII, XXIX, XLI, XLVIII, XLV and XLVII. Remains of a liturgical composition with prayers for each day of the month. Remains preserved of prayers for 15 days, between the 4th and the 26th.			998-1007	407-410	371-372	409-410
4Q504	(4QDibHam^a) 4QWords of the Luminaries^a	M. Baillet, *DJD* VII, 137-168, pls. XLIX-LIII. Copy of a liturgical work, of which the title, *Words of the Luminaries*, has been preserved on the back of fragment 8, and contains prayers for every day of the week (the beginning of the prayer of Wednesday and of the sabbath have been preserved).			1008-1019	414-417	364-367	411-414
4Q521	4QMessianic Apocalypse	E. Puech, *DJD* XXV, 1-38, pls. I-III. Wisdom text that exhibits belief in the resurrection, also called *The Messiah of Heaven and Earth*. Remains preserved in five fragments.	m		1044-1047	394-395	391-392	421-422

Series	Abbreviation	Publication Reference and Comment	T	AFU	MT	FGM	GV	WAC
4Q529	4QWords of Michael ar	Aramaic work with the title *Words of the Book of which Michael spoke to the Angels*. Two further copies have been preserved in *4Q* to which belong the fragments from *6Q23*.			1060-1063	125	523	427
4Q530	(4QEnGiants*b* ar) 4QBook of Giants*a*	Another copy of the *Book of Giants*. Parallel passage to Moses 6:40.	p		1062-1065	261-262	516-517	248-250
4Q531	(4QEnGiants*c* ar) 4QBook of Giants*c*	Another copy of the *Book of Giants*.	p		1064-1067	262	517	247-250
4Q540	(4QapocrLevi*a* ar?) 4QApocryphon of Levi*a* ar	Work described by Starcky as an Aramaic work of Aaronite content and edited by Puech as another copy of the Aramaic *Testament of Levi*.	p m		1078-1079	269		258
4Q577	4QText Mentioning the Flood	E. Puech, *DJD* XXV, 195-203, pl. XV. Small fragment.			1124-1125			
6Q8	(6QpapEnGiants ar) 6QGiants ar	M. Baillet, *DJD* III, 116-119, pl. XXIV. Published as a Genesis apocryphon, it was identified by Milik, *The Books of Enoch*, 300-301, 309, as another copy of the Aramaic *Book of Giants*.	p		1148-1149	262		248-249
7Q4, 8, 11-14	(7QpapEn gr) 7QEnoch	M. Baillet, *DJD* III, 143-144, pl. XXX. Greek copy of the *Book of Enoch*. Many of these have also been ascribed to various biblical texts, many from the New Testament. The various authors are not always in agreement as to which fragment goes with which biblical text. Jose O'Callaghan claims, in a minority, that fragment 8 contains James 1:23-24.	ß		1162-1163			
11Q12	(11QJub) 11QJubilees	F. Garcia Martinez, E. J. C. Tigchelaar, A. S. van der Woude, *DJD* XXIII, 207-220, pl. XXVI. Copy of the book of *Jubilees*.	p		1204-1207	241-242		
11Q13	(11QMelch) 11QMechizedec	F. Garcia Martinez, E. J. C. Tigchelaar, A. S. van der Woude, *DJD* XXIII, 221-241, pl. XXVII. Eschatological *pesher* (= Jewish interpretative commentary), based on Leviticus 28, with the angelic form of Melchizedek as the protagonist.			1206-1209	139-140	500-502	456-457
11Q19	(11QTemple*a*) (11QT*b*) 11QTemple Scroll*a*	Describes the features of an ideal temple to be established by God in the last days, and the laws and rites associated with it. This is the longest scroll in the collection. A complete edition of the Temple Scroll is published in Y. Yadin, *Temple Scroll*.			1228-1289	154-179	192-219	459-492

Other Related Texts

The following table lists documents that are either related to the DSS or that come from the surrounding area. They are sometimes also listed near the scroll they relate to, but are repeated here so that they can easily be identified as belonging to collections separate from the Dead Sea Scrolls. Seventeen scroll fragments have been found at Masada. A collection of texts from the Bar Kokhba period was found in the Cave of Letters at Nahal Hever. This cave is designated *5/6Hev* because it has two entrances. Another collection was found in the Wadi Murabba'at.

Text Name	Related	Publication Reference and Comment	AFU	FGM	WAC
Mt. Athos MS	4Q213	Remains of an Aramaic work related to the *Testament of Levi* from the Geniza and the Greek *Testament of Levi* that forms part of the *Testaments of the 12 Patriarchs.*			251-258
(CTLevi ar) *Cairo Geniza Text A* *Cambridge*	4Q213	Remains of an Aramaic work related to the *Testament of Levi* from the Geniza and the Greek *Testament of Levi* that forms part of the *Testaments of the 12 Patriarchs.*		50-57 in MT	252-258
(CTLevi ar) *Cairo Geniza Text A* *Bodleian*	4Q213	Remains of an Aramaic work related to the *Testament of Levi* from the Geniza and the Greek *Testament of Levi* that forms part of the *Testaments of the 12 Patriarchs.*		50-57 in MT	253-258
Mas1^j *Mas Gen, Mas Jub*	Genesis or *Jubilees*	Two small fragments similar to part of Genesis or *Jubilees*. Includes the title *Prince of Hatred*. Photograph and translation in **ASDS**:30. Contains Genesis 46:7-11. Talmon believes it to be part of *Jubilees*, others Genesis.	20		
Mur 1 *Mur Gen*		Fragments of Genesis, containing 32:3-5, 29-30, 32-33; 33:1; 34:5-7, 30-31; 35:1, 4-7. Probably from the same scroll as Mur Exodus and Mur Numbers described below.	11-13		
Mur ? *Mur(?)Gen*		Contains Genesis 33:18-20; 34:1-3.	12		
P. Fouad Gk 266 *Rahlfs/Gottingen no 942*		Discovered in Cairo. Contains Genesis 3:10-12; 4:5-7, 23; 7:17-20; 37:34-36; 38:1, 10-12.			
Sdeir Gen		Contains Genesis 35:6-10, 24-29; 36:1-2, 5-17	13-14		

Jewish Texts

Non-Mormon scholar Krister Stendahl noted that "there is no other Christian community or community out of the Judeo-Christian tradition which has as positive and non-anti-Semitic ways of speaking about the Jews as have the Mormons."[33] Former Israeli prime minister David Ben-Gurion likewise said that "there are no people in this world who understand the Jews like the Mormons."[34]

Many of the writings below are considered to be part of the Oral *Torah*, a body of law and commentary that is said to have been handed down with the written Hebrew *Torah* from the time of Moses. Starting in about 200 CE parts of this material were written down in a series of works centered around the *Talmud*. The midrash constitutes a vast body additional commentary, reflections, and narrative. Medieval commentaries, philosophical writings, and mystical texts are included in separate sections below. All these writings, in addition to the scriptures, form the basis for modern Judaism, however different branches of Judaism vary in their understanding of how these texts should be interpreted and applied. For a comprehensive compendium summarizing classic talmudic and midrashic sources along with detailed bibliographic information, see Stemberger's update of Strack's classic volume.[35] For a highly-readable overview of all these writings, see Holtz.[36] The "Jastrow Dictionary" is an invaluable aid to the study of the *Talmud*, targums, and midrash for English speakers.[37]

Jewish Writers of the First and Second Centuries CE

Author	Date	Description	English Publication Reference
Philo Judaeus of Alexandria	20 BCE–50 CE	Tvedtnes, *et al.* write: "Philo Judaeus, a Jewish priest of the first century CE, lived in Alexandria, Egypt, and excelled in both Greek philosophy and Jewish lore… Philo was largely ignored by Jews but was preserved because… Clement of Alexandria, quoted his work with such approbation." Later Christians studied his work "as a means of reconciling the Old Testament with Greek philosophy" (J. A. Tvedtnes, *et al.*, *Traditions*, p. 35; cf. W. J. Hamblin, *et al.*, *Temple*, pp. 57-60, 99-100). Not to be confused with Philo the Epic Poet or Pseudo-Philo. Barker makes a case that core elements of Philo's teachings were a part of First Temple Judaism, and that he was primarily transposing these teachings into the language of the philosophers (M. Barker, *Angel*, p. 216; cf. M. Barker, *Imagery*).	The standard edition of Philo's works is readily available as part of the Loeb Classical Library in ten volumes and two supplements. Volumes 1-6 deal with issues in the book of Genesis and volume 6 also contains a valuable *Life of Moses* (*De Vita Mosis*). Volumes 7-10 deal with a variety of other topics, including a work *On the Virtues* (*De Virtutibus*) Philo, *Virtues*. Volume Supplement 1 contains *Questions and Answers on Genesis*, while Volume Supplement 2 contains *Questions and Answers on Exodus*. An inexpensive one-volume edition of nearly all of Philo's writings is available in Philo, *Works*.
Flavius Josephus	37–ca. 101	"Flavius Josephus was a Jewish priest and general who witnessed the destruction of the Jerusalem temple in 70 CE. One of his major works was *Antiquities of the Jews*, which recounts stories known from the Bible and other Jewish (and some Greek) literature from the time of Adam until the mid-first century" (J. A. Tvedtnes, *et al.*, *Traditions*, p. 47). Barker, however, warns that he was "hardly an impartial observer" (M. Barker, *Revelation*, p. 399), and Bloom cautions that the history, especially of events contemporary to his own times, is "suspect, because he had been Joseph ben Matthias, a leader of the Jewish Revolt, who saved his own life by fawning upon the Flavian emperors: Vespasian, Titus, Domitian… Josephus… looked on calmly as Jerusalem was captured, its Temple destroyed, its inhabitants slaughtered" (H. Bloom, *Names Divine*, p. 17).	The most common English translation of the works of Josephus is Whiston's frequently-reprinted 1737 version—which has been updated by Maier. Maier also produced a condensation of Josephus' works (F. Josephus, *Essential Works*). Another translation appears in the Loeb Classic Library series (F. Josephus, *Antiquities*). See the studies in T. W. Franxman, *Genesis* and L. H. Feldman, *Hellenization* for accounts of how the account of Genesis was reshaped by Josephus in its retelling.

33   K. Stendahl, *Third Nephi*, p. 151.
34   Cited in E. T. Benson, *Message to Judah*.
35   H. L. Strack, *et al.*, *Introduction*.
36   B. W. Holtz, *Sources*.
37   M. Jastrow, *Dictionary*.

Talmudic Literature

Text Name	Date	Description	English Publication Reference
Mishnah	ca. 200	A code of laws promulgated by Judah the Patriarch, and traditionally thought to comprise "the oral law that was given to Moses atop Mount Sinai as a complement to the written law or *Torah*… given at the same time" (J. A. Tvedtnes, *et al.*, *Traditions*, p. 62). The *Mishnah* is formed into six divisions that further comprise 63 tractates. The divisions are Agriculture, Appointed Times, Women, Damages, Holy Things and Purities. The *Mishnah* is the foundation for the two *Talmuds* and a primary source for Rabbinic Judaism. Next to the Hebrew Bible, the *Mishnah* is the major canonical document of Judaism.	The two most popular English translations are J. Neusner, *Mishnah* and H. Danby, *Mishnah*. Neusner's translation holds more strictly to the Hebrew text.
Pirqe Avot (Pirke Aboth, Pirkei Avos, The Sayings of the Fathers)	ca. 250	This work was produced about a generation after the *Mishnah* and it explains the origin of the Oral *Torah* at Mt. Sinai. It is usually published as part of the *Mishnah*.	Included with the *Mishnah* as part of the Damages division. A separate English translation with detailed commentary is available in M. Lieber, *Pirkei Avos*. A related text, compiled between the seventh and ninth century but probably composed in the third or fourth century, the *Avot de-Rabbi Nathan* (*The Fathers According to Rabbi Nathan*) is usually included in the collection of minor tractates of the *Talmud* (J. Goldin, *Fathers*; J. Neusner, *Rabbi Nathan*). It is a haggadic work with many unique elements that constitutes a kind of homiletical exposition of *Pirqe Avot*.
Tosefta	ca. 400	This work is a collection of supplements to the *Mishnah*. It contains commentary on 39 of the *Mishnah's* 63 tractates.	Neusner has produced a two-volume English translation (J. Neusner, *Tosefta*).
Talmud Yerushalmi (Jerusalem or Palestinian or Talmud of the Land of Israel)	ca. 400	This *Talmud* covers the first four divisions of the *Mishnah*: Agriculture, Appointed Times, Women and Damages.	The two available English translations of the *Talmud Jerushalmi* have been produced: one edited by Neusner (J. Neusner, *Palestinian Talmud*) and an extensively annotated version by ArtScroll/Mesorah, with some volumes still in publication (G. Zlotowitz, *Talmud Yerushalmi*). Neusner's translation approach has met with mixed reviews.
Talmud Bavli (Babylonian)	ca. 600	The *Bavli* covers the second through fifth divisions of the *Mishnah*: Appointed Times, Women, Damages and Holy Things. In addition, the Bavli contains extensive exegetical commentary on the *Torah* and other scriptures. Written during a period of Jewish prosperity, the *Bavli* is considered more extensive and authoritative than the *Yerushalmi*.	Four English editions of the *Talmud Bavli* are available: Epstein's 1948 30-volume Hebrew-English version for Soncino Press (CD-ROM version also available), Hendrickson's 2006 reprint of Neusner's 22-volume translation with an accompanying CD-ROM but no Hebrew or Aramaic text, the lavish 73-volume Schottenstein edition (G. Zlotowitz, *Talmud Bavli*), and the (incomplete) Steinsaltz edition that updates the traditional commentary layout. The Epstein and Neusner editions are the least expensive. Edited from a traditional Orthodox perspective, the Schottenstein edition is the choice of those with some knowledge of Hebrew, though it should be noted that its interpretation often follows tradition rather than a word-by-word translation of the text. The (out-of-print) Steinsaltz edition favors the needs of novices.
Gemara	ca. 400	The Aramaic part of the *Talmud* or commentary on the *Mishnah*. "Gemara, the 'completion' of the study, was added to each section of the *Mishnah* and thus the *Talmud* 'study' was formed" (M. Barker, *Revelation*, p. 399).	Included in editions of the *Talmud*.

Midrash

Midrash has been defined by van der Heide as "a rabbinic *statement* coupled with a *quotation* from the Scriptures."[38] The *Exegetical Midrash* is generally composed of short comments on individual verses of the Bible that have been collected from the teachings of the sages. The *Homiletical Midrash* is derived from sermons on a particular verse or passage. The *Soncino Midrash Rabbah* is the classic ten-volume source for rabbinic commentary of an exegetical and homiletical nature on the five books of the *Torah* and the five *Megilloth* (The Song of Songs, Ruth, Lamentations, Ecclesiastes, Esther).[39] The works of *Narrative Midrash* recount and expand upon the biblical narrative with stories about scriptural characters or individual rabbis. Several excellent secondary collections of *Aggadah* are available in English. In such collections, various versions of narrative tales from primary sources are usually combined and the language is smoothed over in the interest of fluent storytelling.

Text Name	Date	Description	English Publication Reference
Exegetical Midrash			
Asatir (Secrets)	Before 250-200 BCE	"A Samaritan document also known as the *Secrets of Moses*, known from both Samaritan and Arabic versions. A midrashic text, it combines biblical and traditional stories about the history of the earth, from the time of Adam to the death of Moses, and is thought to have been compiled no later than 250–200 BCE. The Samaritans also wrote a *pitron*, or commentary, on the *Asatir* in Arabic, but the date this commentary was composed is unknown" (J. A. Tvedtnes, *Hidden Books*, p. 230).	Gaster's English translation is currently out of print (M. Gaster, *Asatir*).
Genesis Rabbah (GenR)	ca. 425	A collection of rabbinic commentaries on the book of Genesis, written in Israel. It incorporates a wide span of rabbinical and pseudepigraphal material relating to *Jubilees*, the *Testaments of the Twelve Patriarchs*, and the *Life of Adam and Eve*.	Volumes 1 and 2 of the *Soncino Midrash Rabbah* (H. Freedman, *et al.*, *Midrash*). Neusner has produced a more recent three-volume translation and commentary (J. Neusner, *Genesis Rabbah*).
Exodus Rabbah (ExoR)	900-1000	A collection of rabbinic commentaries on the book of Exodus.	Volume 3 of the *Soncino Midrash Rabbah* (H. Freedman, *et al.*, *Midrash*).
Numbers Rabbah (NumR)	800-1200	A collection of rabbinic commentaries on the book of Numbers.	Volumes 5 and 6 of the *Soncino Midrash Rabbah* (H. Freedman, *et al.*, *Midrash*).
Yalkut Shimʿoni (Simon's Selections)	1050-1300	A midrashic thesaurus on the entire Old Testament.	No English edition is available.
Homiletical Midrash			
Pesikta de Rav Kahana (PRK)	ca. 400	This is a midrash for readings at festivals and special Sabbaths. *Pesikta* means "sections" or "chapters."	Braude's excellent English translation is available from the Jewish Publication Society (W. G. Braude, *et al.*, *Kahana*).
Pesikta Rabbati (PesR) (Pesikta Gedolah or Pesikta)	ca. 200-600	This is a midrash for readings at festivals and special Sabbaths. It includes references to many items of biblical and post-biblical legend.	Braude's fluent English translation is available from Yale University Press (W. G. Braude, *Rabbati*).
Tanhuma or Yelammedenu	400-900	A homiletical midrash on the Pentateuch often ascribed to Rabbi Tanhuma. A variant version with a somewhat different textual history is named *Yelammedenu*, from the phrase "Let our master teach us."	Excerpts are available in an inexpensive edition (C. F. Horne, *Medieval*). The full text can be found in a three-volume edition (J. T. Townsend, *Tanhuma*). Bregman has made an exhaustive comparison of the various versions of the Tanhuma and related texts (M. Bregman, *Tanhuma-Yelammedenu*).
Aggadot Bereshit	900-1000	Twenty-eight homilies on Genesis. Unfortunately, the beginning of the work, relating to Genesis 1:1-6:4, is missing.	No English edition is available.

---

38   A. van der Heide, *Midrash*, p. 44.
39   H. Freedman, *et al.*, *Midrash*.

Text Name	Date	Description	English Publication Reference
Narrative Midrash			
Midrash Wa-Yissau	Before 130	Describes conflicts of the sons of Jacob with the Amorites and Esau (Genesis 35:5, 36:6).	No English edition is available. However, a partial translation of the last part of the midrash describing the events prior to the Messianic age can be found in J. C. Reeves, *Wa-Yosha'*.
Seder Olam Rabbah (SOR or Seder Olam or The Order of the World)	Before 600	A chronology of time from the beginning through Hadrian, though incomplete after the time of Alexander the Great. It may have been prepared as an aid for computing the time of the Creation. Ascribed to Talmudist Rabbi Jose ben Halafta, with later alterations.	Available in an inexpensive print-on-demand version from Xulon Press (K. Johnson, *Seder Olam*), and in an edition edited by H. W. Guggenheimer, *(Seder Olam)*.
Seder Olam Zutta	500-800	Called *zutta* (= smaller) to distinguish it from *SOR*, this chronology seems to be intended to show that Jewish leaders during the exile were descendants of David.	No English edition is available.
Pirkei de Rabbi Eliezer (PRE)	650-900	A narrative midrashic text containing a collection of sayings attributed to Rabbi Eliezer, son of Hyrqanos, who lived in the first and second centuries CE. Many older traditions are included in the work.	The sole English translation of this work, G. Friedlander, *Pirkei*, is difficult to find. Ouaknin provides an up-to-date French translation (M.-A. Ouaknin, *et al.*, *Rabbi Éliézer*).
Leqah Tob	1079-1108	A midrash on the Pentateuch and five *Megillot* written by Tobiah Eliezer.	No English edition is available.
Sekhel Tob	1139	A midrashic anthology on the Pentateuch, possibly Italian in origin.	No English edition is available.
Chronicles of Jerahmeel	1100-1200	A medieval compilation "made by Jewish chronographers, who drew upon the Bible, midrashic sources, and earlier chronicles, both Jewish and non-Jewish. It was purportedly written by Jerahmeel ben Solomon. It was certainly known by the fourteenth century: Rabbi Eleazar ben Asher the Levite, who lived in the Rhine provinces, included it in the compilation *Sefer ha-Zikhronot*" (J. A. Tvedtnes, *et al.*, *Traditions*, p. 129).	For an English translation, see Jerahmeel ben Solomon, *Chronicles*. "Some verses, or paragraphs, were incorrectly numbered in Gaster's edition, mistakenly giving the appearance that parts of the text were omitted" (J. A. Tvedtnes, *et al.*, *Traditions*, p. 129).
Sefer ha-Yashar (Toledot Adam or The Book of Jasher)	ca. 1000-1500	Pseudepigraphic history from Adam to the Exodus. This book should not be confused with other books of the same name (e.g., *Sefer ha-Yahshar* (Rabbenu Tam) (S. Shokek, *Yashar*)), with the *Book of Jasher* referred to in Joshua 10:13 and 2 Samuel 1:18, or with the fraudulent book of *Pseudo-Jasher*, purportedly written by the English monk Alcuin.	Inexpensive reprints of Noah's 1840 translation (e.g., M. M. Noah, *Jasher*; M. M. Noah, *et al.*, *Jasher*) are plentiful. Though this book has been frequently cited in LDS literature since the time of Joseph Smith, better sources exist for the material of greatest interest. For a history of its publication and of its use in LDS contexts, see E. J. Brandt, *Jasher*.
Bereshit Zutta	1200-1300	A compilation of midrashic commentary on the Pentateuch. Unfortunately, there is no commentary on Genesis 1:23-8:16, except for a single page on 3:6-8.	No English edition is available.
Midrash ha-Gadol (The Great Midrash) (MHG)	1200-1400	Of Yemeni origin, this aggadic midrash on the Pentateuch incorporates many otherwise lost sources.	No English edition is available.
Collections of Aggadah			
Ein Yaakov (Ein Yisrael)	1516	A collection of all the aggadic material in the *Babylonian Talmud*, compiled by Rabbi Yaakov ibn Chaviv in the fifteenth century, and finished by his son Rabbi Levi ibn Chaviv.	A five-volume Hebrew-English version was prepared by Rabbi Shmuel Tzvi-Hirsch Glick in 1921. However, the only complete translation in English currently available is Y. i. Chaviv, *Ein Yaakov*.
The Book of Legends (Sefer ha-Aggadah)	1902	Contains a valuable collection of stories about biblical characters and rabbinic sages arranged by theme.	Collected and arranged by Bialik and translated into fluent English by Braude (H. N. Bialik, *et al.*, *Legends*).
Legends of the Jews	1909-1937	This monumental heavily-footnoted seven-volume work reveals the rabbinical thought process at work in the process of midrash as it traces multiple strands of detail in biblical stories in chronological arrangement.	Available in a reasonably priced paperback edition. Available by individual volume or as a set (L. Ginzberg, *Legends*).

Text Name	Date	Description	English Publication Reference
Mimekor Yisrael	1939-1945	In contrast to Bialik's and Ginzberg's focus on ancient texts, Bin Gorion gathers his tales from texts composed in the early Middle Ages and thereafter.	Unfortunately, the three-volume English translation of Bin Gorion's work is no longer in print (M. J. B. bin Gorion, *et al.*, *Mimekor*), though smaller collections of Bin Gorion's stories can be found in single volume editions (e.g., M. J. B. bin Gorion, *et al.*, *Mimekor Abridged*). An earlier German version of the larger work with an overlapping collection of stories was reprinted for many years as *Die Sagen der Juden*, which can often be found in used bookstores.
Hebrew Myths: The Book of Genesis	1964	The result of a collaboration between English poet and scholar Robert Graves and Jewish anthropologist Raphael Patai, the book goes beyond midrashic sources to explore other ancient associations to biblical stories.	The book is currently out of print but used versions can still be found (R. Graves, *et al.*, *Myths*).
The Bible As It Was	1997	This is a more limited and less expensive version of *Traditions of the Bible*.	J. L. Kugel, *Bible As It Was*.
Traditions of the Bible	1998	With a focus on some two dozen stories in the Pentateuch, Kugel shows how the early Bible interpreters shaped the meaning of the texts and passed these ideas to future generations. Unlike the other collections listed here, the author preserves the original wording of each source cited.	J. L. Kugel, *Traditions*.
Tree of Souls; The Mythology of Judaism	2004	In this eruditely commented and comprehensively-indexed collection of midrash organized by theme, Schwartz has assembled a copious selection of traditions into a highly-readable volume.	H. Schwartz, *Tree*.
Folktales of the Jews: Tales from the Sephardic Dispersion	2006-	Over a period of decades, Dov Noy assembled a collection of more than 20,000 tales from Israeli immigrants as part of the Israel Folktale Archives (IFA). Although some include biblical characters, very few relate directly to the Jewish scriptures.	The first volumes of a projected five-volume set of selections from the IFA collection with in-depth commentary have now appeared in English (D. Ben-Amos, *et al.*, *Folktales*).

Medieval Bible Commentators and Philosophers

The Middle Ages were a high point of scholarship and writing in Judaism. Fortunately, as Greenstein observes: "Sectarian schisms within the Jewish fold and external pressure, mainly Christian persecution, upon the Jews had the effect of stimulating, not repressing, Jewish expression."[40] At this time, the nature of scriptural commentary evolved from the characteristically homiletical mode of midrash to that of *peshat,* a way of understanding scripture in terms of its wider historical and literary context. During this same period, Jewish philosophers also attempted to harmonize faith and reason as they considered a broad set of problems in theology, science, and ethics. These scholars are often affectionately referred to by acronyms built out of initials from their names, e.g., Rasag = RAbbi SAadi Gaon. For excellent overviews of medieval Bible commentary and philosophy, see E. L. Greenstein, *Commentaries* and N. M. Samuelson, *Medieval.*

Consistent with the ancient reading formula of "two parts Scripture, one part *targum,*" the traditional Jewish "Rabbinic Bible" or *Mikraot (Miqra'ot) Gedolot* (= Great Readings) contains Masoretic notes, the *Targum, Talmud* citations, and extensive commentary by several of the most prominent medieval commentators—headed by Rashi. The first three volumes of A.

---

40   E. L. Greenstein, *Commentaries*, p. 214.

J. Rosenberg, *Mikraot* contain an English translation of this extensive work.[41] Mesorah/ArtScroll has also produced a two-volume edition of Genesis with extensive commentary.[42] The Conservative movement has published a new edition and commentary called *Etz Hayim* (= Tree of Life),[43] and the perspective of the Reformed tradition is embodied in W. G. Plaut, *Commentary*. Also of value is the Jewish Publication Society's *Jewish Study Bible*, a one-volume work and commentary.[44]

Name	Date	Description	English Publication Reference
Saadiah Gaon (Rasag1)	882-942	A defender of rabbinic tradition, Gaon was the first, besides Philo, to make a systematic attempt to integrate Jewish theology and Greek philosophy. He translated the Hebrew Bible into Arabic, adding his commentary. *Gaon* is a title that was given to the heads of two Babylonian academies beginning in 609 and continuing until 1040.	Gaon's commentary on the *Torah* is not available in English, though it is sometimes cited in compilations.
Abraham Ibn Ezra (Ibn Ezra)	1089-1164	More technical and less spiritual in orientation, this Spanish exegete excelled in so many fields that he was called *The Wise, The Great* and *The Admirable Doctor*.	See A. b. M. Ibn Ezra, *Genesis*.
Shlomo Yitzhaki (Rashi)	1040-1105	Rashi made his living in northern France growing grapes, but became a devoted scholar of the Hebrew scriptures. It is hard to overestimate the influence of his commentaries, which are still among the most widely read due to their learned style and sensitive spirituality. While his style is eclectic, he is restrained in the use of *aggadah*.	The impressive Sapirstein edition of Rashi's commentary has been published by Artscroll/Mesorah both in an inexpensive and a lavish edition (Rashi, *Genesis Commentary, Exodus Commentary*).
Shmuel ben Meir (Rashbam)	ca. 1085-1174	French biblical commentator and son of Rashi's daughter, he was a pioneer in *peshat*. His views often contradicted those of Rashi (who sometimes amended his commentary accordingly) and those of his own time. He was often called on to defend Judaism in public debates.	For a translation of his commentary on Genesis, see S. Ben Meir, *Meir*.
Joseph ben Yitzchak Bekhor Shor (Bekhor Shor)	ca. 1100-1200	Though belonging to the same French exegetical tradition as Rashi, and a student of his grandson Rashbam, Bekhor Shor strove for rational explanations rather than creative midrash to account for duplicate stories and miraculous events in the scriptures.	No English edition of his commentary on Genesis is available.
Moses ben Maimon (Rambam or Maimonides)	1135-1204	Maimonides was a brilliant rabbi and physician who grew up in Spain and has become the most famous of the medieval Jewish philosophers. His tombstone states: "From Moses to Moses, there was no one like Moses."	Maimonides' writings are readily available in many editions. Although he wrote many volumes of talmudic and biblical commentary, his most well known work is *Guide for the Perplexed (Moreh Nevuchim)*, an attempt to deal with conflicts between Aristotelian thought and theology. Controversial in its time, it is now highly esteemed, particularly in Orthodox Judaism. His 14-volume code of the Jewish oral law, the *Mishneh Torah* (*Yad ha-Chazaka* = The Strong Hand), is considered his masterwork (M. Maimonides, *Code*; M. Maimonides, *Mishneh*). The best overview of his life and works is H. A. Davidson, *Maimonides*.
David Kimhi (Kimchi or Qimchi or Radak)	ca. 1160-1235	Born in Provence, France, Kimhi's commentary on Genesis emphasizes moral and ethical implications of the stories. Although he tends toward straightforward interpretations of the words themselves, he advances a mystical interpretation of the story of Adam and Eve.	Portions of Kimhi's commentary are available within E. Munk, *Hachut*.

---

41 The Jewish Publication Society has published a volume of their own version of the *Miqra'ot Gedolot* for Exodus (M. Carasik, *Exodus*). It is unknown whether they will continue the series with volumes on other books of the *Torah*.

42 R. M. Zlotowitz, *et al.*, *Bereishis*.

43 D. L. Lieber, *Etz Hayim*.

44 A. Berlin, *et al.*, *Jewish*.

Name	Date	Description	English Publication Reference
Moshe ben Nachman (Ramban or Nachmanides)	1194-1270	Like Maimonides, Nachmanides was a Spaniard, a physician, and a *Torah* scholar. Though he differed with Maimonides on many points, he tried to avert schism between his supporters and opponents. His commentaries contain significant haggadic elements and are also the first to incorporate kabbalistic thought.	See Ramban, *Torah Commentary*.
Levi ben Gershom (Gersonides or Ralbag)	1288-1344	A controversial philosopher, mathemetician, theologian, and astronomer from Provence, Gersonides insisted on the role of reason in understanding all truth, including the *Torah*.	Ralbag's most well-known work, *The Wars of the Lord,* has been translated in S. Feldman, *Wars*. A parital English translation is available in J. J. Staub's *The Creation of the World According to Gersonides*.
Yitzchak ben Yehuda Abravanel (Abrabane or Abarbanel)	1437-1508	Born in Portugal as part of a distinguished family, Abravanel died in exile in Italy. He was not only a scholar but also a statesman and defender of the faith during the time of the Inquisition. His commentaries are known for the fact that they took social and political issues no less than theological ones into account. After his death, his works were frequently published by appreciative Christian scholars.	Although excerpts from his commentaries are often included in rabbinic Bibles, no integral edition of his work is available in English. However, Schiffers has translated Abravanel's commentary on Genesis 1:1-6:8 into French (I. Abravanel, *Abravanel*).
Obadiah ben Jacob Sforno (Sforno)	ca. 1475-1550	The most famous member of an Italian family of scholars and rabbis, his commentary on the *Torah* took advantage of his skills as a philologist to construct the meaning of the text. Sforno's attitudes toward mystical interpretation influenced his judicious selection from earlier exegetes. His commentary is still popular today.	Sforno's two-volume commentary on Genesis is available in English in O. b. J. Sforno, *Torah Commentary*.

Mystical Texts

The mystical tradition in Judaism has a long tradition, stretching back to beginnings in at least the talmudic period, flowering in kabbalistic writings dating from the 12th century, and continuing to the present. Scholem has written the classic surveys of this literature,[45] but a more recent four-volume by Joseph Dan on Jewish mysticism better situates the texts and incorporates important later scholarship.[46] An accessible introduction that provides additional background understanding for these writings can be found in L. Fine, *Kabbalistic Texts*. An excellent two-volume source reader by Blumenthal is available[47] as well as an anthology composed from an eclectic perspective, edited by Dan.[48] A concise overview of Jewish mysticism is provided by Hamblin.[49] See also the bibliographic survey by Karr.[50]

Text Name	Date	Description	Publication Reference
Sefer Hekhalot (Book of Palaces), 3 Enoch, The Hebrew Apocalypse of Enoch, Pirq Rabbi Yishmael (Chapters of Rabbi Ishmael), or The Book of Rabbi Ishamel the High Priest	400-600	*3 Enoch* is a late manuscript attributed to Rabbi Ishmael (d. ca. 132 CE) who ascended to heaven and received revelations from Metatron (Enoch). Seven manuscripts have survived. It can be divided into four sections: • Chapters 1-2 describe the ascension of Ishmael. • Chapters 3-16 describe how Metatron, who says he is Enoch, was translated from earth to heaven and exalted above the other angels. • Chapters 17-40 describe the organization and activities of the heavens. • Chapters 41-48 describe a tour of various heavenly marvels (cosmology, eschatology, souls in various states) given to Ishmael by Metatron.	Appears in P. Alexander, *3 Enoch*. Summarized in J. Dan, *Heart*, pp. 61-73.

45   G. Scholem, *Trends*; G. Scholem, *Kabbalah*.
46   J. Dan, *Mysticism*.
47   D. Blumenthal, *Merkabah*; D. Blumenthal, *Philosophic*.
48   J. Dan, *Heart*.
49   W. J. Hamblin, *et al.*, *Temple*, pp. 81-87.
50   D. Karr, *Notes*.

Text Name	Date	Description	Publication Reference
Hekhalot Rabbati (The Greater Palaces or Pirkei Hekhalot) (HR)	200-800	An account of a heavenly ascent by Rabbi Ishmael to God's throne chariot (*merkabah*). Seven heavens and seven throne halls are described, and dangers are overcome by the recital of specific formulas.	An English translation of chapters 15-29 with commentary appears in D. Blumenthal, *Merkabah*, pp. 53-91. A good overview can be found in J. Dan, *Heart*, pp. 49-54.
Hekhalot Zutreti or Hekhalot Zutarti (The Lesser Palaces)	200-800	An account of the heavenly ascent of Rabbi Akiva.	There is no complete version available in English, however a selection of significant passages from this work appear in D. J. Halperin, *Chariot*.
Merkabah Rabbah (The Great Chariot) or Shi'ur Qomah (Measurement of the [Divine] Body)	ca. 600 or earlier	A mystical exegesis of the *Song of Songs*, revered by Rabbi Akiva but repulsive to Maimonides. The immense measures of the body of God have been discussed in light of the huge statures attributed to Adam and other OT patriarchs.	Cohen has produced a book of analysis and a book of texts and recensions in English (M. S. Cohen, *Liturgy*; M. S. Cohen, *Texts*). Unfortunately, both are now out-of-print. A full translation can be found in D. Meltzer, *Shiur Qoma*.
Baraita de Maʾaseh Bereshit (Baraita on the Work of Creation)	ca. 700-800	Mystical speculation on the first chapter of Genesis.	See J. Hirschman, *Baraita*.
Solomon ben Yehudah Ibn Geirol	ca. 1021-1070	Born in Spain, Geirol is known for his *Keter Malkhut* (= The Crown of the Kingdom, ca. 1060), a hymn praising God and his Creation.	Published in J. Dan, *Heart*, pp. 81-94; S. i. Gabirol, *Crown*.
Maʾaseh Merkabah (Account of the Chariot)	ca. 1100-1200	The work contains a collection of hymns that were heard and recited during an ascent, presented by Rabbi Akibah and Rabbi Ishmael. The text may have been used as a form of ritual instruction.	A translation and analysis of the text can be found in N. Janowitz, *Poetics*. See also Joseph Dan's summary J. Dan, *Heart*, pp. 55-60.
Sefer Yetsirah (Book of Creation)	ca. 700-900	This text is considered one of the forerunners of kabbalistic thought and is traditionally ascribed to Abraham. It is called the *Book of Creation* because it provides the words God used for bringing the world into existence. It exists in several versions.	An inexpensive English translation of this book can be found in A. Kaplan, *Sefer Yetzirah*, and Blumenthal has prepared a version with valuable diagrams (D. Blumenthal, *Merkabah*, pp. 13-44). A substantial excerpt can be found in P. Mordell, *Sefer Yetzirah*.
Sefer ha-Bahir (Book of Brightness)	ca. 1176	A brief, loosely-organized collection of speculations about God in the form of scriptural commentary that appeared in Provence. It contains Gnostic elements and describes the ten *Sefirot*—attributes or lights that comprise the life of God. The *Sefirot* are the foundation of kabbalistic thinking. "[P]ortions of it appear to come from a much earlier work, the *Sefer Raza Rabbah*" (J. A. Tvedtnes, *et al.*, *Traditions*, p. 50).	An inexpensive translation has been published (A. Kaplan, *Bahir*). A substantial excerpt can be found in J. Neugroschel, *Bahir*.
The Zohar (Sefer ha-Zohar or Book of Splendor)	1275-1500	The most famous work in the kabbalistic tradition. The *Zohar* is a commentary on the *Torah* and, though attributed to Shimon bar Yohai, its core was probably composed by Moses de Leon, who drew on fragments of more ancient works. This work achieved near canonical status by the sixteenth century. Green has produced an up-to-date introduction to the *Zohar* (A. Green, *Guide*).	Superseding the older edition from Soncino Press (H. Sperling, *et al.*, *Zohar*), Matt's lucid new translation of the Zohar with extensive notes has set a new standard (D. C. Matt, *Zohar*).
Midrash Konen	1601	A mystical midrash on the creation of the world.	No English edition is available.
Yalkut Reubeni	Before 1673	A collection of kabbalistic interpretations of the Pentateuch.	No English edition is available.
Sefer Rezial Hamelach (The Book of the Angel Rezial)	ca. 1700	This book was said to have been given to Adam by the Angel Rezial. Much of its material may date to several centuries earlier. Besides descriptions of the seven heavens, it contains a wide variety of magical lore and a long version of *Shi'ur Qomah*. It also incorporates the kabbalistic work *Sefer ha-Razim* (*Book of the Mysteries* or *Book of Secrets*).	For an English translation, see S. Savedow, *Rezial*. *Sefer ha-Razim* is separately published in M. A. Morgan, *Sefer ha-Razim*.

Christian Texts

New Testament Apocrypha and Pseudepigrapha and Related Writings

These books were excluded from the New Testament canon. Some of these texts are also included in the Nag Hammadi or Gnostic collections. An excellent online resource for New Testament Apocryphal writing is *New Testament Apocrypha.* An overview of current views on this literature can be found in S. J. Shoemaker, *Apocryphal.* The most convenient published source for translations of these texts is the two-volume *New Testament Apocrypha (NTA)* edited by Edgar Hennecke and Wilhelm Schneemelcher. Originally published in German as *Neutestamentliche Apokryphen* by Hennecke in 1904, a second edition was produced in 1924 and a third in 1959. The English edition of 1963-1965 contains English translations of the texts from the original, rather than from the German.[51] Hennecke originally compiled this work to update M. R. James' *Apocryphal New Testament (ANT).* Page numbers for both *NTA* and *ANT* are referenced in the table below.

Text Names	Date	Description and Comments	NTA	ANT
Secret Gospel of Mark	ca. 100	Of controversial provenance, this purported excerpt of a letter from Clement contains a brief account of the raising of Lazarus and of Jesus teaching the mysteries of the kingdom to a youth. Readily available in M. Smith, *Secret Gospel.*		
Protevangelium of James (Infancy Gospel of James)	By the third century CE	This book contains a number of very early traditions about the life of Mary and the birth of Jesus. Parts were incorporated into the *Gospel of Pseudo-Matthew* (Pseudo-Matthew, *Gospel of Pseudo-Matthew*) and the *Gospel of the Birth of Mary* (A. Roberts, *et al., Nativity of Mary*). A more recent English translation with commentary can be found in M. Barker, *Infancy Gospel of James.*	1:370-388	38-49
Gospel of Nicodemus (Acts of Pilate and Christ's Descent into Hell)	ca. 350	The so-called *Gospel of Nicodemus* is composed of two originally independent parts. The *Acts of Pilate*, which exists in Greek and Latin versions, was implausibly said to have been derived from official Roman records. The Latin appendix describing *Christ's Descent into Hell*, perhaps the most well-known account of the story of the "Harrowing of Hell," was popular among early Christians.	1:444-484	94-165
The Acts of John	ca. 150-200	About two thirds of this work, which was probably about the length of Matthew, has survived. John's visits to Ephesus and his death are recorded. A prayer circle at the Last Supper and other incidents surrounding the time of the Passion are also included. Some scholars date the work to the fourth century.	2:188-259	228-270
Apocalypse of Peter	ca. 100-150	"An early Christian document attributed to the apostle Peter, known only from quotes by early church fathers and a few fragments" (J. A. Tvedtnes, *Hidden Books*, p. 229).	2:663-683	505-524
Apocalypse of Paul	By the fourth century	"A document attributed to the apostle Paul, describing his vision of the heavens alluded to in 2 Corinthians 12:1–4. It was known to St. Augustine in the fourth century CE. It was widely distributed and is known from manuscripts written in Greek (the original), Syriac, Latin, Coptic, Armenian, and Old Church Slavonic" (J. A. Tvedtnes, *Hidden Books*, p. 229). An English translation of a Coptic fragment can be found in G. W. MacRae, *et al., Paul.*	2:755-798	524-555
Évangile des Douze Apôtres (Gospel of the Twelve Apostles)	500-600	French translation in E. Revillout, *Évangile.* Nibley translates liberal portions into English in H. W. Nibley, *Christ*, pp. 416-428. *NTA* calls this a "collection of sixteen independent Coptic fragments… arbitrarily grouped under a fictitious title" (*NTA*, 1:271), but Nibley sees them as a connected forty-day manuscript (H. W. Nibley, *Christ*, p. 416). Not to be confused with the no-longer-extant *Gospel of the Twelve Apostles* referred to by the Church Fathers (*NTA*, 1:263-264) and possibly to be identified with the *Gospel of the Ebionites* (*ANT*, p. 10). Neither does it have anything to do with J. R. Harris, *Gospel* (an eighth-century Syriac manuscript—see *NTA*, 1:271), nor G. J. R. Ouseley, *Gospel* (purportedly from a manuscript hidden in Tibet that was "channeled" to the author).		

The Church Fathers

These texts represent the writings of early Christian leaders, following the apostolic period.[52] They are usually divided into authors who wrote before the Council of Nicaea, held in 325 CE,

---

51 E. Hennecke, *et al., NT Apocrypha.* Page numbers below are to the third edition. An English (1991/1993) fifth edition has now appeared. J. K. Elliott, *Apocryphal* has now superseded both *NTA* and *ANT.*

52 Kelly and Saint-Laurent have assembled a useful study of resources for the study of early Christianity, with a

referred to as the Ante-Nicene Fathers and those who wrote during and after, referred to as the Nicene and Post-Nicene Fathers. Included with the Ante-Nicene Fathers are some of the New Testament Apocryphal texts and a few Pseudepigraphal texts. Some medieval Christian writers are also listed in the table.

Far from dismissing the value of these writings, the Prophet Joseph Smith regretted the fact that the "character of the old churches [had]… been slandered" and said that he valued the many "old Catholic church traditions" that were consistent with teachings of the restored Church.[53] Edward Stevenson also reported the following:

> While looking over our copy of a large English *Book of Martyrs*,[54] [Joseph Smith] expressed sympathy for the Christian martyrs and a hope for their salvation. He asked to borrow the book, promising to return it when he should meet us again in Missouri. On returning it he said, "I have, by the aid of the Urim and Thummim,[55] seen those martyrs. They were honest, devoted followers of Christ, according to the light they possessed. They will be saved."[56]

The most frequently cited scholarly editions of the writings of the Church Fathers are the *Patrologia Graeca* (written in Greek, with Latin translations) and the *Patrologia Latina* (written in Latin). Translations and commentary for most of the writings of the Early Christian Fathers can be found online at *Early Church Fathers.*

The *Patrologia Graeca (PG)* were edited by Jacques-Paul Migne and published in 161 volumes plus a seprate index from 1857 to 1866.[57] Although many of the early church leaders wrote in Greek, Latin became the predominant language of the Church by the third century CE. Notable authors include Clement, Eusebius, Origen, Basil the Great, Gregory of Nazianzus, and Gregory of Nyssa. *PG* includes material dating up to 1439, the time of the Council of Florence.

The *Patrologia Latina (PL)*, published by Migne between 1844 and 1855, included 217 volumes of works written in Latin, along with some Greek works translated into Latin.[58] Indices were published between 1862 and 1865. These texts cover a time period of nearly 1000 years, essentially ending in 1216 CE. It was Migne's intent to incorporate additional works from the reformation. Although he commenced this effort, it was never completed. Prominent authors in this collection include scholars such as Tertullian, Cyprian, Lactantius, Ambrose, Jerome, and Augustine, and Popes such as Cornelius, Constantine I, and Innocent I. Other authors include Charles the Bald, Anselm, Abelard, Thomas Becket, and Godfrey de Bouillon.

A third collection, the *Patrologia Orientalis (PO)*, consisting of works written in Syriac, Armenian, Arabic, Coptic, Amharic, Georgian, and Slavonic replaced the *Patrologia Syriaca* series that began in 1894 with two original volumes.[59] Volume 41 was published in 1984.

The most inexpensive and accessible series containing an English translation of the early church fathers is published in 38 volumes by Hendrickson. This edition has also been sold as three separate sets: *The Ante-Nicene Fathers* (A. Roberts, *et al.*, ANF, 10 Volumes), *The*

---

particular focus on English-language titles (J. F. Kelly, *et al., Tools*). Unfortunately, temple studies have been neglected in the *Handbook* in which this chapter is included—only a single relevant entry in the index appears ("Jerusalem temple").

53   J. Smith, Jr., *Teachings*, 16 June 1844, p. 375; J. Smith, Jr., *Words*, 16 June 1844, pp. 381-382; cf. p. 411 n. 48.
54   J. Foxe, *Martyrs*.
55   At that time (1834), it is more likely that Josesph Smith used a seerstone.
56   Edward Stevenson, cited in H. L. Andrus, *et al., They Knew (2004)*, p. 83.
57   J. P. Migne, *Patrologiae Graeca*.
58   J. P. Migne, *Patrologiae Latina*.
59   R. Graffin, *Syriaca*; R. Graffin, *et al., Orientalis*.

Nicene and Post-Nicene Fathers Series I (P. Schaff, *NPNF-1*, 14 Volumes) consisting of writings from Augustine and Chrysostom, and *The Nicene and Post-Nicene Fathers Series II* (P. Schaff, *et al.*, *NPNF-2*, 14 Volumes) consisting of Greek Fathers from Eusebius to John of Damascus, and Latin Fathers from Hilary to Gregory the Great.

Only a limited selection of authors and writings that either have been directly cited or are otherwise judged to be of relevance to the text of Genesis are included below. For a more complete list of sources and a valuable collection of patristic commentary on Genesis 1-11, see Louth's volume in the *Ancient Christian Commentary on Scripture* series.[60] Many of the capsule summaries below are excerpted from this volume. See also Sheridan's companion volume on Genesis 12-50.[61] For an overview of this literature and its setting, see F. Young, *et al.*, *Early Christian Literature*. See also S. A. Harvey, *Early Christian*, especially pp. 957-977.

Author	*Selected Writings*	*Date*	*Description and Comments*	*English Translations*
Clement of Rome (pope)	*Epistula i ad Corinthios (Epistle to the Corinthians)*	Regn. 92-101?	Clement is reputed to be the third or fourth pope (depending on whether Peter is counted), and the first of which something is known. His letter to the Corinthians was written to urge unity in the face of quarrels and schisms.	A. Roberts, *et al.*, *ANF*, 9:229-249
Ignatius of Antioch	*Epistle to the Trallians, Epistle to the Ephesians, Epistle to the Philadelphians*	d. ca. 110-112	"Bishop of Antioch who wrote several letters to local churches while being taken from Antioch to Rome to be martyred. In the letters, which warn against heresy, he stresses orthodox Christology, the centrality of the Eucharist, and the unique role of the bishop in preserving the unity of the church" (A. Louth, *et al.*, *Genesis 1-11*, p. 188).	A. Roberts, *et al.*, *ANF*, 1:49-58, 1:66-72, 1:79-85
Polycarp of Smyrna	*Epistle to the Philippians, Martyrdom of Polycarp*	ca. 69-155	"Bishop of Smyrna who vigorously fought heretics such as the Marcionites and Valentinians. He was the leading figure in Roman Asia in the middle of the second century" until he was martyred (A. Louth, *et al.*, *Genesis 1-11*, p. 191). He may have known the Apostle John.	A. Roberts, *et al.*, *ANF*, 1:33-36, 1:39-44
Justin Martyr (of Flavia Neapolis in Palestine)	*Dialogus con Tryphone (Dialogue with Trypho)*	ca. 100/110-15, fl. ca. 148-161	"Palestinian philosopher who was converted to Christianity, 'the only sure and worthy philosophy.' He traveled to Rome where he wrote several apologies against both pagans and Jews, combining Greek philosophy and Christian theology; he was eventually martyred" (A. Louth, *et al.*, *Genesis 1-11*, p. 189).	A. Roberts, *et al.*, *ANF*, 1:194-270
Sextus Julius Africanus	*The Extant Fragments of the Five Books of the Chronography Chronography of Julius Africanus*	ca. 160-240	Little is known about the life of Julius Africanus. This work contains a fragmentary chronography from Adam through Jacob, followed by more detailed overview of Moses and Jesus. Interesting detail on the descendants of Cain versus Seth, the Babylonian captivity, and the death of Cleopatra. It includes an explanation of the Seventy Weeks prophesied by Daniel.	A. Roberts, *et al.*, *ANF*, 6:130-138
Irenaeus of Lyons	*Adversus haereses (Against Heresies), Demonstration of the Apostolic Preaching (Proof of the Apostolic Preaching)*	b. ca. 150, fl. 180-199, d. ca. 202	Bishop of Lyons, and "a disciple of teachers who had known St. John" (M. Barker, *Hidden*, p. x). His *Against Heresies* is an important refutation of Gnosticism. His long-lost *Demonstration* was rediscovered in 1904.	Irenaeus, *Proof*; Irenaeus, *Demonstration*; Irenaeus, *Heresies*.
Theophilus of Antioch	*Apologia ad Autolycus*	d. ca. 183-185	"The one undoubted extant work of Theophilus is his *Apologia ad Autolycum*, in three books. Its ostensible object is to convince a pagan friend, Autolycus, a man of great learning and an earnest seeker after truth, of the divine authority of the Christian religion, while at the same time he exhibits the falsehood and absurdity of paganism" (*Theophilus*).	A. Roberts, *et al.*, *ANF*, 2:89-121

60   A. Louth, *et al.*, *Genesis 1-11*.
61   M. Sheridan, *Genesis 12-50*.

Author	Selected Writings	Date	Description and Comments	English Translations
Clement of Alexandria	*Stromateis (Stromata, Miscellanies), Exhortation to the Greeks (Exhortation to the Heathen)*	b. ca. 150, fl. 190-215	"A highly educated Christian convert from paganism, head of the catechetical school in Alexandria, and pioneer of Christian scholarship" (A. Louth, *et al.*, *Genesis 1-11*, p. 186). He was the teacher of Origen.	A. Roberts, *et al.*, *ANF*, 2:299-568, 2:171-206
Tertullian of Carthage	*Adversus Judaeos (Against the Jews, An Answer to the Jews), Adversus Marcionem (Against Marcion), De corona (On the Crown), De anima (On the Soul), De Baptismo (On Baptism), De Oratione (On Prayer)*	ca. 155/160-225/250, fl. ca. 197-222	"Brilliant Carthaginian apologist and polemicist who laid the foundations of Christology and trinitarian orthodoxy in the West, though he himself was estranged from the main church by its laxity" (A. Louth, *et al.*, *Genesis 1-11*, p. 192).	A. Roberts, *et al.*, *ANF*, 3:151-173, 3:93-104, 3:181-235, 3:271-475, 3:669-679, 681-691
Origen of Alexandria	*De prinicipiis (On first principles), Homilae in Genesim (Homilies on Genesis), Homilae in Leviticum (Homilies on Leviticus), Contra Celsum (Against Celsus), Commentary on John*	b. 185, fl. ca. 200-254	"Influential exegete and systematic theologian. He was condemned (perhaps unfairly) for maintaining the preexistence of souls while denying the resurrection of the body, the literal truth of Scripture, and the equality of the Father and the Son in the Trinity" (A. Louth, *et al.*, *Genesis 1-11*, p. 190).	Origen, *Genesis and Exodus;* Origen, *Leviticus 1-16;* A. Roberts, *et al.*, *ANF*, 4:239-384, 4:395-669, 10:297-408.
Pseudo-Clement	*Recognitions, Homilies*	Before 231	These two overlapping books, sometimes called together the *Clementina* or the *Preachings of Peter,* describe the conversion of Clement of Rome and his travels with the Apostle Peter. They purport to contain many of Peter's teachings. *Homilies* is preserved in the original Greek, while *Recognitions* exists in a Latin translation. Fragments exist in other languages and in citations by other writers. It is presumed that both books are derived from an older, longer source. The dating of this literature has been highly controversial. Tvedtnes concludes that *Recognitions* must predate 231 (J. A. Tvedtnes, *et al.*, *Traditions*, p. 185). Most scholars see these writings as arising from a sect of Jewish Christianity, and some see a possible relationship to the Ebionites or Nazarenes. Non-Mormon scholar David Flusser writes: "The Ebionites held interesting doctrines including the corporeality and visibility of God, as well as the denial of predestination, fixed election, and original sin. They affirmed the honorable role of Adam and Eve, and likewise affirmed the expiatory death of Jesus as the Messiah and the Christ, as would the Latter-day Saints today. In these teachings, they show a remarkable similarity to the teachings of Joseph Smith who claimed he was returning to the pristine Jewish-Christian faith. In their dynamic understanding of human nature and the Christian faith, the faith of these Jewish-Christians closely resembles that of the Latter-day Saints, an astonishing coincidence that is surely good for a normative approach to both faiths" (D. Flusser, *Jewish-Christian*, p. 67).	F. S. Jones, *Recognitions;* A. Roberts, *et al.*, *ANF*, 8:77-211, 8:223-346
Novatian of Rome	*De Trinitate (On the Trinity)*	Fl. 235-258	"Roman theologian, otherwise orthodox, who formed a schismatic church after failing to become pope. His treatise on the Trinity states the classic Western doctrine" (A. Louth, *et al.*, *Genesis 1-11*, p. 190).	A. Roberts, *et al.*, *ANF*, 5:611-644
Victorinus of Petovium (Pettau)	*Fragment of Tractatus de Fabrica Mundi [On the Creation of the World]*	d. ca. 304	Victorinus was a Bishop of Pettau. This work contains an expansion of Genesis creation account with interpretations based on 1 John and the book of Revelation.	A. Roberts, *et al.*, *ANF*, 7:341-343

Author	Selected Writings	Date	Description and Comments	English Translations
Methodius of Olympus	*From the Book Concerning Matter (Concerning Free Will)*	d. ca. 311	A fragment of a work defending the proposition that matter is created and is not the cause of evil. Preserved by Eusebius and quoted by Origen in his arguments against the Gnostic Marcionites.	A. Roberts, *et al.*, *ANF*, 6:356-363
Lucius Caelius (or Caecilius?) Firmianus Lactantius	*Divinarum Institutionum (The Divine Institutes, The Divine Institutions)*	ca. 240- ca. 320	Lactantius, a Latin-speaking North African, was a highly-skilled apologist and rhetorician. *Divinarum Institutionum*, his most important work, "was intended to point out the futility of pagan beliefs and to establish the reasonableness and truth of Christianity as a response to pagan critics. It was also the first attempt at a systematic exposition of Christian theology in Latin, planned on a scale sufficiently broad to silence all opponents" (*Lactantius*).	A. Roberts, *et al.*, *ANF*, 7:9-223
Eusebius of Caesarea (Eusebius Pamphilus)	*Life of Constantine, Ecclesiastical History (History of the Church), Onomasticon*	b. ca. 260/263; fl. ca. 315-340	"Bishop of Caesarea, partisan of the emperor Constantine, and first historian of the Christian church. He argued that the truth of the gospel had been foreshadowed in pagan writings, but had to defend his own doctrine against suspicion of Arian sympathies" (A. Louth, *et al.*, *Genesis 1-11*, p. 187). Eusebius' unfinished *Life of Constantine*, while filled with partisan rhetoric, is an invaluable account of the life of this Roman emperor, who turned from being the greatest persecutor of the Church to its most important supporter. His *History*, while suffering from the same defects, presents much information not found elsewhere. The *Onomasticon* is a glossary of scriptural names and places.	Eusebius, *Onomasticon*; Eusebius, *History*; Eusebius, *Constantine*; P. Schaff, *et al.*, *Nicene and Post-Nicene 2*, 1:73-403, 1:405-610
Athanasius of Alexandria (Athanasius the Great, Pope Athanasius 1)	*Incarnation*	293-373	As a church leader and theologian, Athanasius is most remembered for his role in the Arian controversy at the Council of Nicaea. He vigorously attacked the idea of Arianism that the Son was subordinate to the Father. Though successful in anathematizing the followers of Arius at the Council, support for these ideas waxed and waned, and Athanasius was frequently exiled throughout his life because of his teachings.	Athanasius, *Incarnation*.
Cyril of Jerusalem	*Catechetical Lectures*	ca. 315-386; fl. ca. 348	Cyril was a Bishop of Jerusalem. Nibley cites lengthy passages of the section containing the *Lectures on the Ordinances* (*Mystagogikai Katecheseis*) that echo LDS temple themes (H. W. Nibley, *Message 2005*, pp. 515-524; cf. J. E. Seaich, *Ancient Texts 1995*, pp. 878-879; J. A. Tvedtnes, *Rituals*). He notes that these lectures took place just as "the cult of the temple enjoyed a spectacular albeit specious revival. These particular lectures contain 'the fullest account extant' of ordinances in the church at that crucial period… The apostolic fathers are full of oblique references to the ordinances; they understand their extreme importance but are not in a position to talk freely about them… And so ancient ordinances survive as fossils buried in a deep matrix of rhetoric, philosophy, and art" (H. W. Nibley, *Message 2005*, pp. 515, 522, 524).	H. W. Nibley, *Message 2005*, 1-5:23, pp. 515-524; P. Schaff, *et al.*, *Nicene and Post-Nicene 2*, pp. 1-157.
Ephrem the Syrian	*Commentary on Genesis, Hymns on Paradise, Hymns for the Feast of the Epiphany, Hymns on Virginity and on the Symbols of the Lord, Commentary on the Diatessaron*	b. ca. 307; fl. 363-373	"Syrian writer of commentaries and devotional hymns which are sometimes regarded as the greatest specimens of Christian poetry prior to Dante" (A. Louth, *et al.*, *Genesis 1-11*, p. 187).	Ephrem the Syrian, *Epiphany*; Ephrem the Syrian, *Virginity*; Ephrem the Syrian, *Commentary*; Ephrem the Syrian, *Paradise*; Ephrem the Syrian, *Poems*; Ephrem the Syrian, *Diatessaron*
Gregory of Nazianus (the Theologian, or Nazianzen)	*Orations, Dogmatic Poems*	329-389	Influential in both the Western and Eastern churches, Gregory was one of the most highly-trained and effective Christian writers and orators of his time. His thinking was influential in elucidating the relationship among the members of the Trinity. Along with the two brothers Basil the Great and Gregory of Nyssa, he is known as one of the three Cappadocian Fathers.	Gregory Nazianzen, *Orations, Poetry*.

Author	Selected Writings	Date	Description and Comments	English Translations
Basil the Great of Caesarea	Homilae in hexaemeron (The Hexaemeron), De spiritu sancto (On the Spirit)	b. ca. 330; fl. 357-379	"One of the Cappadocian fathers, bishop of Caesarea and champion of the teaching on the Trinity propounded at Nicaea in 325. He was a great administrator and founded a monastic rule" (A. Louth, et al., Genesis 1-11, p. 186).	P. Schaff, et al., Nicene and Post-Nicene 2, 8:1-50, 8:51-107
Gregory of Nyssa	De opficio hominis (On the Creation of Man), Diologus de anima et resurrectione (On the Soul and the Resurrection), The Great Catechism	ca. 335-394	"Brother to Basil the Great, Gregory of Nyssa was born in 335 or 336 CE in Cappadocia (in modern Turkey). He authored more than thirty works that have been preserved through the centuries" (J. A. Tvedtnes, et al., Traditions, p. 187). "He is famous for maintaining the equality in unity of the Father, Son and Holy Spirit" (A. Louth, et al., Genesis 1-11, p. 188).	P. Schaff, et al., Nicene and Post-Nicene 2, 5:386-427, 5:428-468, 5:471-509.
Bordeaux Pilgrim	Travels	333	This anonymous pilgrim provided the earliest Christian account of a visit to the Holy Land.	In Egeria, Travels, pp. 22-34
Egeria (Etheria)	Egeria's Travels	381-384	Egeria, a medieval nun, produced a "diary rediscovered in 1884 that describes a pilgrimage to the Holy Land" (M. Barker, Hidden, p. xii).	Egeria, Travels
John Chrysostom	In Genesim [homilae 1-67] (Homilies on Genesis), In Genesim [sermons 1-9] (Sermons on Genesis); Commentary on Job	344/354-407; fl. 386-407	Bishop of Constantinople and champion of orthodoxy, Chrysostom was "one of the most prolific writers among the early church fathers" (J. A. Tvedtnes, et al., Traditions, p. 193).	J. Chrysostom, Homilies on Genesis; Job
Jerome	Tractatus lix in Psalmos (Homilies on the Psalms), LIber quaestionum hebraicarum in Genesim (Hebrew Questions on Genesis), Letters, Vulgate Translation of the Bible	ca. 347-420	Jerome "has left a substantial corpus of writings, including several commentaries on the Bible, although he is best known as the scholar who translated the Bible into the Latin… Vulgate" (J. A. Tvedtnes, et al., Traditions, p. 194). "He defended the perpetual virginity of Mary, attacked Origen and Pelagius and supported extreme ascetic practices" (A. Louth, et al., Genesis 1-11, p. 188).	Jerome, Homilies; Jerome, Questions on Genesis; P. Schaff, et al., Nicene and Post-Nicene 2, 6:1-295, 6:486-487; R. Weber, Vulgata
Augustine of Hippo	The City of God, De Genesi ad litteram (On the Literal Interpretation of Genesis), Against the Two Letters of the Pelagians	354-430; fl. 387-430	"Following his conversion from Manichaeism to Christianity, Augustine… became bishop of Hippo, in North Africa (Tunisia)." In his writings against the pelagians, he formulated the doctrines of original sin and predestination. He wrote The City of God "to defend Christianity to the heathens after the sack of Rome (written 413-426)" (J. A. Tvedtnes, et al., Traditions, p. 200).	Augustine, Literal; P. Schaff, Nicene and Post-Nicene 1, 2:1-511, 5:373-434
Quodvultdeus of Carthage	Book of Promises and Predictions of God	d. ca. 450	A deacon of Carthage and friend of Augustine, his name means "Whatever God wants." He attempted to "show at length how the New Testament fulfilled the Old Testament" (A. Louth, et al., Genesis 1-11, p. 191).	Quodvultdeus, Promesse; Quodvultdeus, Homilies
Pseudo-Dionysius the Areopagite	De coelesti hierarchia (The Celestial Hierarchy)	ca. 482-ca. 532; fl. ca. 500	"[A]uthor of four mystical writings, probably from the late fifth century, which were the foundation of the apophatic school of mysticism in their denial that anything can be truly predicated of God" (A. Louth, et al., Genesis 1-11, p. 187). The Celestial Hierarchy describes the nine ranks of angels that mediate between God and humankind" (M. Barker, Hidden, p. xii).	Pseudo-Dionysius, Hierarchy
Ancius Manlius Severinus Boethius	De Consolatione Philosophiae (The Consolation of Philosophy)	ca. 480-ca. 525	Boethius was a Christian educator, statesman, theologian, and philosopher of the late Roman empire whose Consolation of Philosophy "was for centuries the most influential book ever written in Latin" (C. S. Lewis, Image, p. 75).	A. M. S. Boethius, Consolation
Bede the Venerable (Bede of Jarrow)	On the Temple, An Ecclesiastical History of the English People (Historia ecclesiastica gentis Anglorum)	673-735	"One of the most learned men of his age… Born in Northumbria, at the age of seven Bede was put under the care of the Benedictine monks of Saints Peter and Paul at Jarrow and given a broad classical education in the monastic tradition" (A. Louth, et al., Genesis 1-11, p. 186).	Bede, Ecclesiastical; Bede, Temple
Hugh of St. Victor	De sacramentis christianae fidei (On the Sacraments of the Christian Faith)	ca. 1078-1141	Mystic and philosopher with numerous and diverse writings. De sacramentis is his most well-known work.	Hugh of Saint Victor, De Sacramentis

Author	Selected Writings	Date	Description and Comments	English Translations
Martin of Leon	*Septuagesima*	ca. 1130-1203	Martin of Leon was a priest and canon regular of the Augustinian order. His *Septuagesima* has not been translated into English.	J. P. Migne, *Patrologiae Latina*, 208
Thomas Aquinas	*Summa Theologica*	ca. 1225-1274	Prolific medieval theologian and philosopher, Thomas Aquinas attempted to unify faith and reason at a time when Aristotle's works had newly made their appearance in Latin. Best known for the *Summa*, his massive volume on Christian doctrine, he produced some 60 other works in his short life of less than 50 years.	T. Aquinas, *Summa*

Other Christian Writings

These are texts that are not included in the above groupings.

Text Name	Date	Description	Publication Reference
Subject Matter Related to Genesis			
Letter of Barnabas	ca. 140	This letter "was originally attributed to Barnabas the Levite (Acts 4:36; 13:2) and was rediscovered in 1859, included in the New Testament of the Sinai Codex, the oldest known Bible. It gives a Jewish Christian perspective on many issues, such as the Sabbath and the temple" (M. Barker, *Hidden*, p. x).	A. Roberts, *et al.*, *ANF*, 1:137-149
Didache	ca. 140	Purported to contain teachings of the original Twelve Apostles, the *Didache* is a brief handbook of instructions that was used in the training of new converts. It "intertwines Jewish ethics with Christian liturgical practice to form a whole discourse on the 'way of life'" (A. Louth, *et al.*, *Genesis 1-11*, p. 187).	B. D. Ehrman, *Didache*; A. Roberts, *et al.*, *ANF*, 7:391-383
Shepherd of Hermas (Pastor of Hermas)	ca. 140-155	"Written by a former slave and named for the form of the second angel said to have granted him his visions, this work was highly esteemed for its moral value and was used as a textbook for catechumens in the early church" (A. Louth, *et al.*, *Genesis 1-11*, p. 192).	C. Osiek, *Shepherd*; A. Roberts, *et al.*, *ANF*, 2:9-58
Second Letter of Clement (so-called) (2 Clement)	ca. 150	"The earliest surviving Christian sermon, probably written by a Corinthian author" (A. Louth, *et al.*, *Genesis 1-11*, p. 191).	A. Roberts, *et al.*, *ANF*, 9:251-256
Testamentum Domini Nostri Jesu Christi (Testament of our Lord)	ca. 350	This document purports to be "the words of our Lord Himself, and to tell what He said to the disciples after His resurrection and before His ascension. It is supposed to be the last Will or Testament which he gave them, and to provide them with rules for the conduct of their work." (J. Cooper, *et al.*, *Testament*, p. 3). Written, perhaps, about 350, it exists in several Syriac recensions as well as in an Ethiopic translation. A fragment of the apocalyptic prelude also exists in Latin translation.	J. Cooper, *et al.*, *Testament*
Apostolic Constitutions	ca. 380	Presumed to have been compiled in Syria, these writings constitute the "largest collection of ecclesiastical law that has survived from early Christianity… The work consists of eight books. The first six are an adaptation of the *Didascalia Apostolorum*, written in Syria about AD 250… The seventh contains a paraphrase and enlargement of the *Didache*" (*Apostolic Constitutions*). The eight book contains a mix of additional material.	A. Roberts, *et al.*, *ANF*, 7:387-508
The Discourse on Abbaton (How Abbaton, the angel of death, became the king of all mankind)	Before 385	This book was copied from an existing document in the library of Jerusalem by Timothy, the fourth-century Patriarch/Archbishop of Alexandria (E. A. W. Budge, *Cave*, p. 54). *Abbaton* signifies the Angel of Death, the main purpose of the text being to explain how death came to rule among mankind. Contains valuable material on the foreordained mission of the Savior and Satan's rebellion.	Timothy of Alexandria, *Discourse*; Timothy of Alexandria, *Abbaton*
Life of Abel	ca. 450-550	"In the *Syriac Life of Abel*, either Adam is considered unworthy of performing his priestly function after his Fall, or the phenomenon of priesthood in general is relegated to the reality 'after and outside Paradise,' with Cain and Abel given the appellation… 'first priests'" (S. Ruzer, *Abel's Blood*).	S. Brock, *Abel*

Text Name	Date	Description	Publication Reference
The Book of the Cave of Treasures (Arabic: *Me'arath Gazze;* Ethiopic: *Ba'ata Mazagebet)*	ca. 500	This text is "one of the most significant of the secondary Adam books" (M. E. Stone, *History of the Literature,* p. 91). The work dates in its current form to perhaps the sixth century, but with a substantial core of elements plausibly originating in the school of St. Ephrem (d. 373). On the question of dating, see C. Leonhard, *Date,* who posits a later date than Ri (A. S-M. Ri, *Commentaire de la Caverne,* p. 86). The book's name is "probably a double allusion, namely, to the Book as the storehouse of literary treasures, and to the famous Cave in which Adam and Eve were made to dwell by God after their expulsion from Paradise, [in] which… gold, and frankincense, and myrrh… [brought from the Garden of Eden were] laid up"—anticipating the gifts of the Magi to the Christ child that symbolized the recovery of what mankind had lost (E. A. W. Budge, *Cave, Introduction,* p. 16; cf. p. 69 See also M. Barker, *Hidden,* p. 25; D. Wilson, *Conflict,* pp. 46-49; *Excursus 53: Comparative Explorations, The Cave of Treasures,* p. 669). The cave can be seen in temple terms as a sort of replacement for the Garden of Eden, affording them protection from the world in their state of vulnerability, and providing privacy and security for the treasures that were kept therein (D. Wilson, *Conflict,* pp. 50-51; cf. J. M. Lundquist, *Fundamentals,* pp. 655-659). The narration summarizes sacred history through the resurrection of Christ, but the greatest attention is given to the early chapters of Genesis. The author endeavored to show how the mission of Christ was foreshadowed by the events and types of Old Testament History (E. A. W. Budge, *Cave,* pp. 33-39). Later Christian tellings of these stories (e.g., *The Book of Adam and Eve, The Book of The Bee*) drew extensively from portions of this earlier work.	An English translation was made in 1927 by Budge and is currently available in reprint editions. A more recent French translation and a commentary is available for the Syriac recension (A. S.-M. Ri, *Caverne Syriaque,* A. S.-M. Ri, *Commentaire de la Caverne*). A modern French translation also exists for the Georgian recension (C. Kourcikidze, *et al., Caverne Géorgienne*).
The Book of Adam and Eve (The Conflict of Adam and Eve with Satan)	ca. 600-900	In its current form, the text dates to no sooner than the seventh century (M. E. Stone, *History of the Literature,* p. 98), and no later than the ninth (J. A. Tvedtnes, *et al., Traditions,* p. 219). However, despite its late dating, "Turdeanu argues that this work is, in terms of the themes discussed, closest of all the secondary Adam literature to the primary Adam writings" (cited in M. E. Stone, *History of the LIterature,* p. 99). Book 1 covers events from the Garden of Eden through the early years of Adam and Eve in exile. Eight confrontations with Satan are described. It ends with the death of Abel. Book 2 continues the story of conflicts with Satan and the narration of events to the time preceding the Flood, and Books 3 and 4 continue the story to the coming of Christ. A major object of Book 1 "is to connect the first Adam with the coming of the second, Christ; five thousand five hundred years after Adam's fall in Eden, and in fulfillment of the promise then made him of a Savior" (S. C. Malan, *Adam and Eve,* p. v). See D. Wilson, *Conflict* for a discussion of temple symbolism in this text.	Malan's 1882 English translation is available separately (S. C. Malan, *Adam and Eve*) or as part of the much-reprinted popular edition of Platt (R. H. Platt, *Forgotten;* R. H. Platt, *Lost and Forgotten Books*). The edition by Platt contains only the first two of the four Books, and lacks the notes of Malan.
History of the Creation and Transgression of Adam	After 400	Part one of the Armenian *Cycle of Four Works.* The cycle presents "an expanded version of the biblical account of the primordial history recorded in Genesis 1-11," focusing almost exclusively on events in the lives of Adam, Eve, and their immediate descendants (W. L. Lipscomb, *Armenian,* p. 13). This first work opens with the creation and revolt of the rebellious angels and continues to the point after the Fall where Adam and Eve are brought out of darkness into the light of this world.	W. L. Lipscomb, *Armenian,* pp. 108-127, 241-245, 261-266.
History of the Expulsion of Adam from the Garden	After 400	Part two of the Armenian *Cycle of Four Works.* It gives an account of Satan's deception and the *cheirograph* of Adam. God promises deliverance through Christ.	W. L. Lipscomb, *Armenian,* pp. 128-141, 246-248, 267-269
History of Abel and Cain, the Sons of Adam	After 400	Part three of the Armenian *Cycle of Four Works.* The story of Cain and Abel, the killing of Cain by Lamech, and the good news of Seth's birth.	W. L. Lipscomb, *Armenian,* pp. 142-171, 249-254, 270-275
Concerning the Good Tidings of Seth	After 400	Part four of the Armenian *Cycle of Four Works.* The story of the seduction of the Sethites, the Flood, the covenant with Noah, and the settlement of his descendants.	W. L. Lipscomb, *Armenian,* pp. 172-205, 255-260, 276-282
History of the Repentance of Adam and Eve	After 400	The penance of Adam and Eve, and the stories of Cain and Abel, the gathering of Adam's descendants, Seth's quest for oil, and Noah's preservation and burial of Adam's bones at Golgotha.	W. L. Lipscomb, *Armenian,* pp. 210-233

Text Name	Date	Description	Publication Reference
The Words of Adam to Seth	After 400	"Adam tells Seth the story of his sin…, for which Seth fasts and prays and is rewarded with a life-giving branch from the garden and the promise of Christ. Seth then tells the same story… to his son [Enosh or Enoch]. Like Seth, Enoch responds with a penitent act, fasting and planting a garden, for which he is rewarded with translation" (W. L. Lipscomb, *Armenian*, p. 40).	W. L. Lipscomb, *Armenian*, pp. 206-209
Book of the Rolls (Kitab al-Magall)	ca. 500-1100	Tvedtnes, *et al.* describe this as "an Arabic text that claims to have been 'one of the hidden books of Saint Clement the Apostle, disciple of Simon Cepha'" (fol. 89b), or Clement of Rome. It was probably written in Greek, somewhere between the sixth and twelfth centuries by a Christian seeking to defend Mary the mother of Jesus from Jewish criticisms, although only the Arabic version is known" (J. A. Tvedtnes, *et al.*, *Traditions*, p. 207).	Passages about the Creation, the Fall, and the Life of Adam and Eve from Margaret D. Gibson's long out-of-print translation have been reprinted as part of a collection by S. Day (see M. D. Gibson, *Rolls 1901*).
Chronicle of Symeon Logothetes (Symeon Metaphrastes)3	ca. 950-1050	Symeon is best known for his ten-volume "Lives of the Saints"—known as the *Menologion* because it was organized around the twelve months of the year. One of the principal sources for middle Byzantine history, his *Chronicle* includes a selection of Old Testament stories. This work "has been published under various names, including Theodosios of Melitene (or Melissenos) and Leo the Grammarian. Symeon relies heavily on George Hamartolos" (J. A. Tvedtnes, *et al.*, *Traditions*, p. 249). *Logothete* (= Greek "one who accounts, calculates or ratiocinates") was an administrative title given to responsibles in the Byzantine Empire. The epithet *Metaphrastes* (from Greek *metáphrasis* = compilation) comes from his role in assembling a book of the Saints' lives.	The first volume of a two-volume critical edition has appeared (S. Wahlgren, *Symeonis*). An English translation by Walter K. Hanak from the Old Church Slavic text is currently in preparation. Hogel has produced a monograph about the life and working methods of Symeon (C. Hogel, *Symeon*).
Caedmon Manuscript (MS Junius 11)	ca. 1000	Parts of Genesis, Exodus and Daniel in Old English verse, illustrated with many Anglo-Saxon drawings—48 for Genesis alone. Parts of the Genesis work appear to be a translation from a 9th-century Old Saxon original. The original manuscript is at the Bodleian Library in Oxford. The former attribution of the poems to the cowherd Caedmon is inaccurate and is no longer credited. Franciscus Junius, the Junius of the manuscript, published the first edition of its contents in 1655.	Doane has produced critical editions of the Genesis verse (A. N. Doane, *Genesis A*; A. N. Doane, *Genesis B*). High-quality images of the manuscript are available online for private study (*Manuscript Junius*).
Hortus Deliciarum (Garden of Delights)	ca. 1175	Herrad of Hohenbourg was a twelfth-century abbess under whose direction the comprehensive and copiously illustrated compendium of knowledge and salvation history called *Hortus Deliciarum* (Garden of Delights) was assembled. Preserved for centuries at the Augustinian monastery of St. Odile at Hohenbourg, it was placed in the municipal library of Strasburg about the time of the French Revolution. Though it was tragically destroyed during the siege of Strasburg in 1870, portions of the text and illustrations had been previously copied, enabling the later reconstruction and publication of the work.	Published in a lavish oversized two-volume edition, unfortunately now out-of-print (R. Green, *et al.*, *Hortus*).
Book of the Bee	ca. 1222	Tvedtnes *et al.* describe the book as being "written in Syriac by the Armenian-born bishop Shelemon (Solomon) of Basra (fl. ca. 1222 CE)[. It] uses the Bible and early commentaries on the Bible. It is closely related to… the *Book of the Cave of Treasures*, the *Book of the Rolls*, and the *Conflict of Adam and Eve with Satan*" (J. A. Tvedtnes, *et al.*, *Traditions*, p. 272).	Budge's English translation is available in reprint editions (Shelemon, *Book of the Bee*).
Vita Adae et Evae	ca. 1300	A mid-15th-century manuscript in the National Library in Vienna, whose original by Lutwin was probably written in the early 14th century. The Middle High German text was composed in the form of poetry, and is thought to be based on an unidentified Latin source incorporating elements "not included in any of the known versions of the *Vita Adae et Evae* [Latin *Life of Adam and Eve*]" (M.-B. Halford, *Eva und Adam*, p. 37; cf. p. 95. See also M. E. Stone, *History of the Literature*, p. 119).	See Halford's study and English translation (M.-B. Halford, *Eva und Adam*).
Rhymed History (Concerning the Creation of the World)	1300-1400	A poem "by the renowned medieval Armenian poet Yovhannes T'lkuranc'i" containing "many exegetical and apocryphal expansions of the Genesis traditions" (M. E. Stone, *Selections*, pp. 167-168).	The English translations of selections from this work contains events from creation to the translation of Enoch (M. E. Stone, *Selections*).

Text Name	Date	Description	Publication Reference
Kebra Nagast (The Glory of the Kings)	1300-1400	Tvedtnes, *et al.* write that this "fourteenth-century Ethiopic document that claims to be based on an early Coptic text supposedly translated into Ethiopic by a man named Isaac. The colophons of manuscripts of the text... claim that an Arabic version was translated from Coptic in the 409th year of mercy,' when Gabra Maskal (also called Lalibala) was king of Ethiopia (1314-1344)" (J. A. Tvedtnes, *et al., Traditions*, p. 277).	The translation by Budge is available in reprint editions (E. A. W. Budge, *Kebra*).
The Book of the Mysteries of the Heavens and the Earth; Discourse Concerning the Mystery of the Godhead and the Trinity; Another Discourse Concerning the Birth of Enoch	ca. 1400	In its current form, the four works of the otherwise unknown Ethiopian author, Bakhayla Mika'el (Basalota Mika'el, Zosimas) and his son Isaac, are thought to be a product of the fifteenth century (B. Mika'el, *Book*, p. xxix). Purporting to be a revelation given by the angel Gabriel, *The Book of the Mysteries* explains hidden meanings of biblical narrative that continues through the resurrection of Christ, and briefly describes the signs of the Second Coming. A second work is an *Interpretation of the Vision of St. John*. The discourses on the *Godhead* and *Enoch* are shorter collection of miscellaneous Old Testament and New Testament explanations.	See B. Mika'el, *Book* for an English translation. This was the last translation completed by Budge before his death.
Leabhar Breac	ca. 1411	Compiled in Ireland, this book contains, among other texts, stories of the *Creation of Adam* and of the *Creation and Fall*. These stories probably date from 900-1200. The story of Adam's having been created from seven components probably derives from a parallel account in *2 Enoch* 30:8.	M. Herbert, *et al., Irish Apocrypha*, pp. 1-7.
Liber Flavus Fergusiorum	ca. 1400-1500	Compiled in Ireland, this book contains, among other texts, *The Fall of Lucifer and the Fall of Adam, The Penance of Adam, Distance of the Garden of Eden to the House of the Trinity, The Two Sorrows of the Kingdom of Heaven*. These stories probably date from 900-1200.	M. Herbert, *et al., Irish Apocrypha*, pp. 8-21.
Adamgirk'	1401-1403	Three epic poems in Armenian about Adam and Eve by Arak'el of Siwnik' with typological components relating to the passion and death of Jesus Christ.	English translation in M. E. Stone, *Adamgirk*.
Concerning the Death of Adam	1624, 1634, 1666		M. E. Stone, *Armenian Apocrypha 1996*, pp. 209-212. No English translation is available.
Armenian Adam Fragment 1	1624, 1634, 1666		M. E. Stone, *Armenian Apocrypha 1996*, p. 212. No English translation is available.
Armenian Adam Fragment 2			M. E. Stone, *Armenian Apocrypha 1996*, pp. 10-11. No English translation is available.
History of the Forefathers, Adam and His Sons and Grandsons	1689	Closely related to *Repentance* and to a lesser extent to the *Armenian Cycle* (M. E. Stone, *Armenian Apocrypha 1996*, p. 181), the story begins with Adam's departure from the garden and continues with the story of Enoch, including the account of the stele.	M. E. Stone, *Armenian Apocrypha 1996*, pp. 180-200
On the Fall of Adam	1700-1800	A poetic dialogue between God and Adam after the Fall.	M. E. Stone, *Armenian Apocrypha 1996*, pp. 3-7.
Concerning Adam and Eve and the Incarnation	1657-1659	The document contains an expanded version of the biblical story of Adam and Eve, followed by a life of Christ drawn from the Gospels. It includes a story of Adam and Eve's contract with Satan (*cheirograph*). The text is closely related to the *Cycle of Four Works* (*Transgression* and *Expulsion*).	M. E. Stone, *Armenian Apocrypha 1996*, pp. 8-79
History of Adam and His Grandsons	1697	A brief chronology from Adam to the temple of Solomon.	M. E. Stone, *Armenian Apocrypha 1996*, pp. 80-100
Armenian Adam Story 1	1686	A version of the story of the *cheirograph* of Adam and the promise of Redemption through Christ.	M. E. Stone, *Armenian Apocrypha 1996*, pp. 101-108
Armenian Adam Story 2	1686	A story of Adam and Eve with an hour-by-hour chronology of their activities. An important objective is to show that as Adam sinned on a Friday, Christ was crucified on a Friday.	M. E. Stone, *Armenian Apocrypha 1996*, pp. 109-113

BIBLIOGRAPHY

Text Name	Date	Description	Publication Reference
Question	1686	This Armenian Christian document "comes from a miscellany that was copied or compiled by one Markos in 1686" (J. A. Tvedtnes, *et al.*, *Traditions*, p. 286). It contains a narrative from the time of Adam through the wars of Gog and Magog in the last days.	M. E. Stone, *Armenian Apocrypha 1996*, pp. 114-134
The Eras of the World	1686	Composed of three chronological lists: *Concerning the Six Millennia*, *The Eleven Periods*, and *The Times of the Patriarchs*.	M. E. Stone, *Armenian Apocrypha 1996*, pp. 135-140
Abel and Other Armenian Pieces	1624, 1634, 1666	"Although the author of this Armenian text is unknown, the scribes of the miscellany from which it is taken were Sargis and Amiras of Erznka, who copied the manuscript in 1624, 1634, and 1666" (J. A. Tvedtnes, *et al.*, *Traditions*, p. 287).	M. E. Stone, *Armenian Apocrypha 1996*, pp. 141-157
The Sethites and the Cainites	1600-1700	Excerpted from a miscellany, this text contains a longer version of an account similar to *Question* about the Cainites and Sethites.	M. E. Stone, *Armenian Apocrypha 1996*, pp. 201-206
Sermon Concerning the Flood	1657-1659	Contains apocryphal expansions of the stories from the time of Cain and Abel to the time of the command for Noah to build the ark.	M. E. Stone, *Armenian Apocrypha 1996*, pp. 174-179
The Sons of Noah and the Generations from Adam	1660	An expanded form of the traditions of the *Cave of Treasures* and the *Chronicle of Michael the Syrian* describing the descendants of the sons of Noah and the divisions of the earth among them (cf. e.g., Genesis 10; 2 Chronicles 1:5-21; O. S. Wintermute, *Jubilees*, 7:13-19, p. 69).	M. E. Stone, *Signs*, pp. 219-245.
Descendants of Adam		A brief fragment about the sons of God and the daughters of men, a description of Enoch's righteousness, and a genealogy until the time of Noah.	M. E. Stone, *Armenian Apocrypha 1982*, pp. 84-87
Lists	1624, 1634, 1666	The published text includes four lists: *72 Languages, Twelve Nations which Know Writing, Names of the Patriarchs*, and *Names of the Wives of the Forefathers and Patriarchs*.	M. E. Stone, *Armenian Apocrypha 1996*, pp. 158-166

Nag Hammadi Codices and Various Gnostic Texts

Leeming provides a brief overview of the complex and multi-faceted teachings of gnostic sects, which flourished in both Christian and pagan forms:

> Generally speaking, the Gnostics were Egyptians and Essene Jews, early Christians, and certain Christian medieval heretics who practiced mystery cults based on the idea of "knowing" the divine. "Gnosis" is now preferred to the term "Gnosticism"—a religion of its own—as a label for this loosely connected group. An important figure for Gnosis was Hermes Trimegistos, identified with the Egyptian god Thoth, to whom is accredited the crucial saying "He who knows himself, knows the All." Many of the Christian followers of Gnosis were particularly devoted to what might seem to some to be the mysticism of John's Gospel and to his definition of "eternal life: to *know* you, the only true God, and Jesus Christ, whom you have sent."[62] The Gnostic form of the Logos was sometimes the female figure of Divine Wisdom, Sophia.
>
> One Gnostic creation myth says that Sophia, the spirit of Wisdom, signified by the Dove that also was the sign of the Holy Spirit,[63] was the child of the primeval Silence, and that Sophia herself was the mother of both Christ and a female spirit named Achamoth. Achamoth produced the material world and gave birth to Ildabaoth, the Son of Darkness, as well as to spirits that were emanations of Jehovah (*Yahweh*). It was these spirits who produced the angels and humans and who, as Jehovah, forbade humans from eating of the Tree of Knowledge. But Achamoth came to earth as the serpent Ophis and sought Christ's help in order to convince humans to disobey Jehovah by eating the forbidden fruit so as to gain knowledge—*gnosis*. Later Sophia sent Christ to earth as the Dove to enter the human man Jesus as he was being baptized by John the Baptist in the Jordan River.[64]

Lupieri provides an insightful summary of the worldview held in common by most Gnostics—a perspective often difficult to penetrate for modern readers:

> The heterodox Gnostics saw the negative side of the world. It was impossible to believe that a good God, a God who loved man, would have imprisoned him in a body that by its very nature stinks, that needs to destroy countless lives, both animal and vegetable, just to feed itself, that is the seat of all vices and the very worst of instincts, and that, in the end, is destined to be food for worms... Even the idea that humankind had been placed on earth as punishment for some sin, committed perhaps in an earlier life, or by some ancestor, could not explain why all of creation was suffering...
>
> Since heterodox Gnostic knowledge is arrived at through illumination, each Gnostic could feel authorized to receive slightly more than others, and thence give rise to a new school... for dissecting the truth with ever greater precision. This led to a considerable degree of fragmentation... but only certain points upon which most Gnostics would have agreed. First, the demiurge, the ignorant and evil God that created this world, is the easily-angered and anthropomorphic God of the Jews, that is, Yahweh. As a consequence, the... Old Testament must be considered false and full of lies... All of sacred history is to be reread and reinterpreted in a new light: the ancient enemies of Yahweh and his people, from Cain to the Sodomites to the generation of the Flood, were the true depositories of spiritual knowledge. The God of this world... is indeed only the latest product of a degenerative chain that brought about the dispersion of a luminous particle of divinity in the world of darkness and of matter. After much wandering about, the last fragment of light was embodied in Adam, while the demiurge Yahweh was left without. Awareness of what he lacked, then, left Yahweh to persecute humankind, to attempt to appropriate its spirit, or at least to keep it entrapped in matter. According to some, he even

---

62   John 17:3, emphasis added.

63   See *Commentary* 1:1-b, p. 42; 3:9-g, p. 163; 4:5-b, p. 246.

64   D. Leeming, *World Mythology*, s.v. Gnostic Mythology, p. 153.

invented Eve so as to seduce Adam and thereby draw from him his spiritual seed, imprisoning it forever in a chain of reproduction. In this perspective, Adam did not sin in the garden when he ate the "fruit of the tree of *knowledge*"; if anything he was reaffirming a right that made him "like God." If there was any sin, it was that of allowing himself to be seduced by Eve. All of history, then, is the tragic scene of an utterly ruthless struggle by the demiurge and his evil princes (in Greek, the *archons*) to keep the sparks of divine light that had precipitated down divided and imprisoned in matter. The Light, however, has prepared a plan for salvation, providing for the recovery of all that is consubstantial with it.

… The savior, or the series of saviors as some believed, comes to "reawaken" the Gnostics' dormant knowledge and thus save them. For the Christian Gnostics this bringer of revelation and savior is the heavenly Christ, a divine being, a direct emanation of the very heart of the divine, which entered into the earthly Jesus to save the Gnostics. Others went so far as to believe that the earthly Jesus was a negative, demonic reality, a creature the demiurge made for the purpose of trapping the heavenly messenger within it. The demiurge thought he could take over the divine Spirit in this way, binding it in the coils of the flesh, nailing it to the cross, and swallowing it in death. Christ, however, fooled everyone. In different ways, according to the teachings of the various Gnostic sects, he never really suffered the passion, nor was he ever actually killed. Leaving the body of Jesus before the passion, he let the demiurge's thugs destroy his bodily image while he looked on in another form, laughing his heart out…

The whole Gnostic vision of the world is based on the opposition of conflicting principles. The diversity and laceration perceived among men and within each Gnostic is projected into the world, into the cosmos, and even into the divine itself. Just as there is a division between good and evil on earth (ethical dualism), the forces of good and evil, of light and darkness, battle throughout the entire universe (cosmic dualism). Even divinity is divided… This will cease only when the irreconcilable components of the cosmos, once again completely separated when the light that is dispersed and imprisoned in darkness has been recovered in all its parts, return to the enjoyment of an eternal equilibrium.[65]

A summary modern scholarly approaches to Gnosticism can be found in A. Marjanen, *Gnosticism*. Rudolph has also authored an excellent, though now somewhat dated, overview of Gnosticism (K. Rudolph, *Gnosticism*). The relationship between gnostic and biblical writings is explored in P. Perkins, *Gnosticism*. For a detailed overview of the complex perspectives of various Gnostic texts on Adam and Eve in the Garden of Eden, see G. Lettieri, *Ambiguity,* pp. 39-54. Discussions of different schools of Gnostic thought and difficulties in defining the category as a whole can be found in M. W. Meyer, *Nag Hammadi,* pp. 777-798 and M. A. Williams, *Rethinking*. For extensive discussions of specific affinities between selected LDS and gnostic teachings, see J. E. Seaich, *Ancient Texts 1995,* pp. 1017-1110 and J. E. Seaich, *Mormonism*.

The Nag Hammadi Codices (NHC)

This collection, also known as the Coptic Gnostic Library or the Chenoboskion Manuscripts, contains writings preserved by Egyptian Christians during the second century CE. Discovered in 1947, the twelve full codices and partially-preserved thirteenth codex were buried in clay jars and sealed with pitch in the fourth century though many date to earlier periods. Fifty-two separate tractates were included in the collection, comprising forty-five separate works. The collection includes many works classed as Gnostic. However due to the complexity and variety of Gnostic ideas and the evolving nature of Christianity itself during the period in question, such a determination is a very inexact endeavor.

---

65   E. Lupieri, *Mandaeans*, pp. 35-38.

Besides the publications listed below, a selection of gnostic sources is included at *Gnostic Society Library*. Note also that the fourteen hardback volumes of the Brill Nag Hammadi series are currently available as a five-volume 5,000-page paperpack set.[66]

JMR - *The Nag Hammadi Library in English*, edited by J. M. Robinson. This work was published as the official English edition of these texts, with a very strict approach to translation. Texts are in order by codex and tractate. For example, (V,1) would reference the first tractate in the fifth codex. Also included in this collection is the *Berlin Gnostic Papyrus*, formally known as *Papyrus Berolinensis 8502*. References are listed as *BG*, followed by the tractate number.

BL - *The Gnostic Scriptures*, edited by B. Layton. A collection of Gnostic writings arranged by school of thought. The translation is periphrastic. Fifteen works from this book have been drawn from the **NHC**.

NTA - *New Testament Apocrypha*, edited by E. Hennecke, *et al.* Described in the **New Testament Apocrypha** section above.

ANT - *The Apocryphal New Testament* M. R. James, *Apocryphal*. Described in the **New Testament Apocrypha** section above.

OB – *The Other Bible*, edtied by W. Barnstone. A collection drawn from Jewish pseudepigrapha, Christian apocrypha, Gnostic scriptures, Kabbalah, and the Dead Sea Scrolls. It is arranged topically.

GB – *The Gnostic Bible*, edited by W. Barnstone, *et al.* A diverse collection of Gnostic writings including early Wisdom gospels, literature of Gnostic wisdom, Sethian literature, Valentinian literature, Thomas and other Syrian literature, Hermetic literature, Mandaean literature, Manichaean literature, a work of Islamic Mystical literature, and Cathar literature.

NHS – *The Nag Hammadi Scriptures*, edited by M. W. Meyer. The newest edition of these writings, superseding **JMR** and incorporating the latest scholarship of English-language, German-language, and French-language teams of scholars. The translations are smoother, but less faithful to the underlying language of the original than **JMR**.

Codex	Text Names	Date	Description	JMR	BL	NTA	ANT	OB	GB	NHS
I,2	*The Apocryphon of James* (*The Secret Book of James*)	100-300	A letter purportedly written by James, the Lord's brother, relating private instructions given by Jesus Christ to Peter and James 550 days after his resurrection.	29-37		1:333-338			340-350	19-30
II,2	*The Gospel of Thomas*	ca. 50	An early collection of 114 traditional sayings of Jesus, especially significant because some of them are closely related to passages in Matthew and Luke.	124-138	376-399	1:278-307, 511-522		299-307	43-69	133-156
II,3	*The Gospel of Philip*	250-300	An anthology of statements about the meaning of the sacraments, imbued with Valentinan ideas about life, death, and the resurrection. Nibley cites lengthy passages of the *Gospel of Philip* that echo LDS temple themes (H. W. Nibley, *Message 2005*, pp. 525-532). For a study of the sources of this work, see M. L. Turner, *Philip*.	139-160	325-353	1:271-278	12	87-100	257-298	157-186
II,4	*The Hypostasis of the Archons* (*The Nature of the Archons, The Reality of the Rulers*); RR	200-300	This anonymous work presents an esoteric interpretation of Genesis 1-6 in the form of a dialogue between an angel and a questioner. Although probably translated from Greek into Coptic, like the rest of the NHC, Coptic puns indicate familiarity with Egyptian, and Jewish puns and genealogies indicate some form of Jewish-Christian background.	161-169	65-76			75-80		187-198

66   J. M. Robinson, *Coptic Gnostic Library*.

Codex	Text Names	Date	Description	JMR	BL	NTA	ANT	OB	GB	NHS
II,5; XIII,2	*On the Origin of the World*	ca. 350	This work has some relation to the preceding text. It is a compendium of central Gnostic ideas on cosmogony, anthropogony and eschatology. Among other things, it gives "a glimpse of what happened in the world of the angels before the opening of the biblical Genesis" (M. Barker, *Hidden*, p. ix). This work is carefully crafted and shows little evidence of later alteration. It does not represent any of the known Gnostic systems of thought.	170-189				62-74	414-437	199-221
V,5	*The Apocalypse (Revelation) of Adam, RAd*	ca. 350	This work tells the history of the world from the Creation to the Savior's final coming. The story is based on the Gnostic myth and other non-biblical material more than Genesis. Near the end is a fifteen-stanza poem on the incarnation of the Savior that is unique among the Gnostic writings. The revelation is presented as being narrated to Adam by three heavenly visitors, and later told by Adam to his son Seth. The three heavenly visitors tell Adam about his future life on earth.	277-286	52-64			81-86	178-188	343-356
VII,1	*The Paraphrase of Shem*	ca. 350	This is an apocalypse that describes the ascent of Shem to the top of creation and his final return to earth. It includes accounts of the Flood, the destruction of Sodom, the baptism of the Savior and His ascent after the crucifixion. The text concludes with Shem's final address.	339-361				101-115	438-464	437-471
VII,2	*The Second Treatise (Discourse) of the Great Seth*	150-200	A Gnostic-Christian revelation dialogue purportedly given to a group of elect disciples. "Apart from the title, the name Seth never occurs in the text, though perhaps Jesus Christ is meant to be identified with Seth" (J. A. Gibbons, *et al.*, *Great Seth*, p. 362). One portion of the text seems to describe the presentation of the plan of salvation to a heavenly assembly, and the way that is prepared for the ascent of the individual.	362-371				116-122	465-476	473-486
VII,4	*The Teachings of Sylvanus*	175-225	A "rare specimen of Hellenic Christian wisdom literature, [displaying] a remarkable synthesis of biblical and late Jewish ideas with Middle Platonic and late Stoic anthropological, ethical, and theological concepts" (M. L. Peel *et al.*, *Sylvanus*, p. 379).	379-395						499-521
VII,5	*The Three Steles (Tablets) of Seth*	Before 350	Hymns of worship used by Gnostic believers, who identified themselves as the true latter-day descendants of Seth. The hymns commemorate the ascent of Seth to the divine triad, as he rises and returns through three stages or levels of worship.	396-401	149-158			201-211		523-536
IX,1	*Melchizedek*	150-225	This is a poorly-preserved apocalypse of Melchizedek, where he is transported into the future to witness the death and resurrection of Christ. In some places Melchizedek and Christ are presented as the same person.	438-444						595-605
IX,2	*The Thought of Norea*	150-250	A brief Sethian psalm of deliverance in four parts. In Jewish legend, Norea is one of the daughters of men who seduces the sons of God at the time of Noah. Here, however, she is "an undefiled virgin and a spiritual helper to (gnostic) humankind" (B. A. Pearson, *Norea*, p. 445).	445-447						607-611
XI,2	*Valentinian Exposition with Valentinian Liturgical Readings*	160-350	This "is an untitled treatise that in scope and vocabulary resembles the Valentinian treatises presented by the church fathers" (M. W. Meyer, *Nag Hammadi*, p. 663). The text includes fragments about the Creation, the Fall, and the Angels.	481-489						667-677

Other Gnostic Texts

Besides classic Gnostic texts not found in the NHC, this section includes selections from the Sethian and Valentinian literature, Thomas and other Syrian literature, the pagan Hermetic writings, and the medieval Cathar-Albigensian-Bogomil-Paulician literature. For a description of the four collections below, see the **Nag Hammadi Codices** section.

BL - *The Gnostic Scriptures*, edited by B. Layton.

OB – *The Other Bible*, edited by W. Barnstone.

GB – *The Gnostic Bible*, edited by W. Barnstone, *et al.*

NHS – *The Nag Hammadi Scriptures*, edited by M. W. Meyer, *Nag Hammadi*.

Text	Text Names	Date	Description	BL	OB	GB	NHS
BJn	*The Secret Book According to John*	Probably before 180	"[O]ne of the most classic narrations of the gnostic myth," including an account of "what happened *before* Genesis 1:1" (B. Layton, *John*, p. 23). It also contains a detailed retelling of Genesis up to the birth of Seth.	23-51	51-61	135-165	103-132
IrSat	*Satorninos, according to Irenaeus*	180	This is a summary of the teachings of Satorninos, written in Greek, by Irenaeus of Lyon and included in *Against Heresies*, 1:24:1-2, pp. 348-349. It describes the Creation and the two human races, one good and one evil.	159-162			
IrUnid	*Other Gnostic Teachings, according to Irenaeus*	180	Irenaeus of Lyon's account, written in Greek, of other teachings presumed to be Gnostic in *Against Heresies* 1:30-31, pp. 354-358. The creation of matter is discussed.	170-181			
EpS	*The Sethians, according to Epiphanius*	377	An excerpt from Epiphanius of Salamis' *Against Heresies (or Panarion* = medicine chest*)* 39:1:1-39:5:3. The beliefs of the Sethians are structured around three principles—light, darkness, and pure spirit—and reflected in the triad of Cain, Abel, and Seth. See also the description of the sect by *Hippolytus*, v. 19, included in W. Barnstone, *Other*, pp. 654-657.	185-190	657-658		
VFrC	*Adam's Faculty of Speech*	150-175	Fragment 1, a description by Valentinus of the power of Adam's speech, cited in Clement of Alexandria's *Miscellanies (Stromateis)* 2:8, pp. 355-356.	234-235			
VFrD	*Adam's Name*	150-175	Fragment 5, a description by Valentinus of the face of Adam, cited in Clement of Alexandria's *Miscellanies (Stromata)* 4:13, p. 425.	236-237			
VFrF	*Annihilation of the Realm of Death*	150-175	Fragment 4, immortality triumphs over death, cited in Clement of Alexandria's *Miscellanies (Stromata)* 4:13, p. 425.	240-241			
HPrl	*Hymn of the Pearl (Hymn of the Soul, Hymn of Jude Thomas the Apostle in the Country of the Indians)*	200-225	This account describes a pair of heavenly parents sending their son on a journey to recover a pearl. The pearl represents his soul. They clothe him with special clothing and give him special food. While on his journey (which represents earth life) he forgets his mission. They send a messenger who causes him to remember his mission and he returns to receive heavenly glory with his parents. Written in Greek and popular with the early Christians. Nibley cites lengthy passages of the *Hymn of the Pearl* that echo LDS temple themes (H. W. Nibley, *Treasures*, pp. 177-178; H. W. Nibley, *Message 2005*, pp. 487-501; cf. A. Roberts, *Anointing*, p. 106). The *Hymn* can also be found in (J. K. Elliott, *Pearl*; E. Hennecke, *et al.*, *NT Apocrypha*, 2:498-504; M. R. James, *Apocryphal*, pp. 411-415; cf. I. Gardner, *Kephalaia*, 9 (37,28-42,23), pp. 43-46). Welch and Garrsion give an interpretation of the *Hymn* from an LDS perspective (J. W. Welch, *et al.*, *Pearl*). The *Hymn* is part of a larger work called the *Acts of Thomas* (E. Hennecke, *et al.*, *Acts of Thomas*). In a separate work, Ephrem discusses the Pearl as a symbol of the incarnation of Christ (Ephrem the Syrian, *Pearl*).	366-375	308-313	386-394	

Text	Text Names	Date	Description	BL	OB	GB	NHS
BasFrE	The Elect Transcend the World	180	The elect are alien to the world as if they were transcendent by nature.	436-437			
	The Gospel of the Secret Supper	12th century or earlier	A Cathar document originating with the Balkan Bogomil Gnostic sect in the twelfth-century or earlier, with roots that may go back to a Greek original some centuries before. It gives an account of a dialogue between the apostle John, Jesus Christ, and the "invisible father" at the Last Supper. It includes a retelling of the crucifixion "in which Christ is an angel, an illusion, a phantasm rather than the suffering Jesus" and a detailed description of Satan's punishment for his premortal rebellion, and couching the Devil in the role of the unjust steward (Luke 16:1-13).			740-750	
	Poimandres (= Greek shepherd of man or, alternatively, Coptic knowledge of the Sun-God Ra)	150-200	An influential pagan treatise drawn from the Corpus Hermeticum ascribed to Hermes Trismegistus (= thrice-greatest Hermes). Poimandres, representing the highest godhead, engages the narrator in a severe Socratic dialogue in an attempt to lead him in a "the mystical experience of darkness and purification from matter, ascent to the light, and entry into a oneness with god" (Hermes Trismegistus, Poimandres, p. 503). The work is divided in three sections: "the creation of the world and human life; the soul's escape from the world, its ascent to Heaven and mystical union with God; and instructions for proselytizing the gospel of gnosis. The work ends with a prayer" (Hermes Trismegistus, Poimandres, p. 568). A translation of the full Corpus Hermeticum was made by Mead in 1906 (Hermes Trismegistus, Hermes).	447-459	567-574	502-511	
	Asclepius	150-200	A pagan Coptic dialogue between Hermes Trimegistus and an initiate named Asclepius. "The tractate opens with a comparison of the mystery and sexual intercourse… With the acquisition of knowledge humans become better than the gods, for they are both mortal and immortal. Hermes Trismegistus next suggests that just as the Lord of the universe creates gods, so also humanity creates gods according to human likeness" (Hermes Trismegistus, Asclepius, p. 575). A promise is given that God the Creator will eventually restore order to the world, and that judgment, rewards, and punishments will accrue to individuals.		575-580		
	The Sethian-Ophites		"The Sethian-Ophite legend is one of the main Gnostic cosmogonies and theogonies, close to the Valentinian speculation which we find in the Gospel of Truth… Ophis, the serpent, indicates the important, ambiguous, but ultimately positive role played by the serpent in delivering knowledge, gnosis, to Adam and Eve, and consequently providing them with the means to combat [the evil Creator] God. By being free of their Creator God, they could find the light in their souls and return to the true Father" (Sethian-Ophites, p. 660).		659-664		
	Pistis Sophia (The Faith of Sophia)	ca. 250-300	The Askew Codex, from which this document comes, was bought by the British Museum in 1795. The work is a Coptic Christian Gnostic text that relates the post-resurrection teachings of Jesus to His disciples and to His mother Mary. Sophia (= Greek Wisdom) is the female aspect of Logos, and is sometimes identified in gnostic thought with the Holy Ghost. Although a scholarly edition was prepared by Schmidt (C. Schmidt, Pistis), the most easily available version is Mead's 1921 English translation (G. R. S. Mead, Pistis). Nibley cites lengthy passages of the Pistis Sophia that echo LDS temple themes (H. W. Nibley, Message 2005, pp. 503-514).				

Text	Text Names	Date	Description	BL	OB	GB	NHS
	The Two Books of Jeu (1 Jeu, 2 Jeu)	ca. 250-450	Two sections of the *Bruce Codex*, acquired by the British Museum in 1769. Like the *Pistis Sophia* they contain discussions between Jesus and the Apostles during the 40-day ministry after the resurrection. A description of the text is found in E. Hennecke, *et al.*, *NT Apocrypha*, 1:259-263. The only full English translation of the *Bruce Codex* is based on the German edition (C. Schmidt, *et al.*, *Jeû*), as translated by MacDermot (C. Schmidt, *Bruce Codex*; also republished as part of J. M. Robinson, *Coptic Gnostic Library*). O'Brien has published an inexpensive edition of the books of Jeu (C. O'Brien, *1 Jeu*; C. O'Brien, *2 Jeu*), however this admittedly "abridged and free translation" adds its own idiosyncratic "Mystical interpretation" and "restructuring of the text," and unfortunately omits the accompanying diagrams (C. O'Brien, *Path*, p. xviii).				
	The Sermon of Cosmas the Priest Against Bogomilism	ca. 970	A tract written against the Bogomils by Cosmas, a Bulgarian priest. Excerpts in English appear in E. Peters, *Heresy*, pp. 108-117. A complete French translation of the Slavic was published in 1945 (Cosmas, *Traité*).				

Zoroastrian Texts

The Iranian prophet known as Zoroaster (Greek), Zarathustra (Avestan), or Zartosht (Persian) is an indisputably historical figure who seems to have lived in Iran sometime between 1700 and 1000 BCE. The religion founded in his name is said by Mary Boyce to be "the oldest of the revealed world-religions, and it has probably had more influence on mankind, directly and indirectly, than any other single faith."[67] Moreover, Zoroaster is said to be "the first to teach the doctrines of an individual judgment, Heaven and Hell, the future resurrection of the body, the general Last Judgment, and life everlasting for the reunited soul and body."[68]

Zoroaster was presumably made a priest (*zaotar*) of the ancient Indo-Iranian religion at the usual age of fifteen. Describing himself as a "*vaedemna* or 'one who knows,' an initiate possessed of divinely inspired wisdom…, he spent years in a wandering quest for truth" until about the age of thirty, when he was led into the presence of Ahura Mazda [= Lord Wisdom], the Supreme Divinity, and received his revelation.[69]

Stories of the prophet's life derive from Zoroastrian scripture (*Avesta* = The Injunction), Greek texts (e.g., Plutarch, Pliny), and later Pahlavi traditions recorded in the 9th-12th century CE.[70] Within the *Avesta* are the *Gathas*, consisting of prayers directly attributed to Zoroaster,[71] the *Vendidad* (= law for protection from demons), which includes accounts of dialogues between God and Zoroaster,[72] and the lost account of the prophet's life in the *Spenta Nask* (= beneficent or bounteous treatise), known only through the summary given in the *Dinkard*.[73] The earliest religious works were handed down orally and were not written until perhaps the fifth century CE. The oldest extant manuscript of the *Avesta* itself is dated to 1323 CE.[74] See Boyd[75] for a description of the differences between orthodox and reform Zoroastrianism in their understanding of the meaning and role of the *Avesta*.

There are currently estimated to be between one hundred and two hundred thousand adherents of the Zoroastrian faith. Most live in Iran and India (where they are called Parsis), though there are several thousand in North America. Followers of Manichaeism and of the Baha'i faith also consider Zoroaster to be a prophet.

For general overviews of Zoroastrianism, see M. Boyce, *Zoroastrians*; P. Kriwaczek, *Zarathustra*; S. A. Nigosian, *Zoroastrian Faith*. For an LDS perspective, see S. J. Palmer, *Zoroastrianism*.

Zoroastrian Scripture

Only a fraction of the original texts of the *Avesta* have survived. This book of scripture consists of five main categories of writings:

67 M. Boyce, *Zoroastrians*, p. 1.
68 *Ibid.*, p. 29.
69 *Ibid.*, pp. 18-19.
70 E.g., A. Ferdowsi, *Shahnama*; F. M. Müller, *Dinkard* 5, 7, 7:2:1-7:5:12, pp. 17-77. See also F. M. Müller, *Zadsparam*, 12:1-13:13, pp. 133-167.
71 S. Insler, *Gathas*.
72 F. M. Müller, *Vendidad*.
73 F. M. Müller, *Dinkard* 8-9, 8:14:1-16, pp. 31-34.
74 M. Boyce, *Sources*, p. 1.
75 J. W. Boyd, *Zoroastrianism*.

The *Yasna* (= worship, oblations) is the oldest and most important part of the collection, consisting of 72 sections of prayers and hymns.[76] Within the *Yasna* are the seventeen *Gathas* attributed to Zoroaster himself.

The *Visparad* (= all lords) is a collection of 23 supplements to the *Yasna*, describing the worship of minor divinities (*yazata*), roughly corresponding to the idea of archangels in Jewish and Christian sources.

The *Yashts* (= worship by praise) consists of 24 hymns to various deities. "[I]n the *Yashts* is found a polytheism which is very similar to the *Rig Veda*—a polytheism against which Zarathustra rebelled."[77]

The *Vendidad* (= given against the demons) containing practical information about maintaining ritual purity and confounding evil spirits. It also includes a myth of Yima and the deluge—described as a "dire winter"—and sent by the demons rather than as a punishment from God.

Other Material, miscellaneous short texts and prayers.

The most current English translation and commentary on the *Gathas* is by Insler.[78] Older English translations of the *Avesta* are included in the 19th-century *Sacred Books of the East* series, edited by Max Müller. These are still available in reprint editions,[79] and the full text of all public domain volumes of the *Sacred Books of the East* series can be found online.[80] See also the 1917 *Sacred Books and Early Literature of the East* series edited by Horne, which can still be purchased in reprint editions.[81]

The *Khorda Avesta* (= Short Avesta) contains a selection of brief prayers taken from the Avesta along with other minor texts.[82] English translations of later Pahlavi traditions from Müller's series are available in reprint editions.[83] One of the texts, the *Sikand-Gumanik Vigar*, contains an explicit refutation of the seeming absurdities of the Genesis account of the Creation and the Fall.[84] The Persian "Book of Kings" (*Shahnameh*), written by the gifted poet Ferdowsi over a thirty year period ending about 1010, relates the national epic in a poem consisting of nearly 60,000 couplets.[85] A topical arrangement of selections from Zoroastrian writings can be found in M. Boyce, *Sources*. Nearly all of the most important Zoroastrian texts can also be found online.[86]

Zoroastrian Creation Stories

Some of the basic beliefs and stories relating to themes in the book of Moses are summarized by Leeming:[87]

> Several stories of creation exist in the Iranian tradition. One story tells how Yima, the primal human, king of the Golden Age, and later a solar deity, pierced the earth with a golden arrow,

---

76   See *Endnote B-2*, p. 903.
77   S. J. Palmer, *Zoroastrianism*, p. 154.
78   S. Insler, *Gathas*.
79   F. M. Müller, *Vendidad*; F. M. Müller, *Avesta 2*; F. M. Müller, *Avesta 3*.
80   *Sacred Books Online.*
81   C. F. Horne, *Sacred*.
82   F. M. Müller, *Khorda Avesta*.
83   F. M. Müller, *Pahlavi 1*; F. M. Müller, *Pahlavi 2*; F. M. Müller, *Pahlavi 3*; F. M. Müller, *Dinkard 8-9*; F. M. Müller, *Pahlavi 5*.
84   F. M. Müller, *Sikand-Gumanik Vigar*, pp. 208-221.
85   A. Ferdowsi, *Shahnama (1905-1925)*. For a one-volume abridged version, see A. Ferdowsi, *Shahnama (2006)*.
86   E.g., *Avesta*.
87   D. Leeming, *World Mythology*, s. v. Zoroastrian Mythology, p. 412.

making it pregnant.[88] Yima, who resembles the Indian Vedic god Yama, had been created by the sun god Vivahant, a servant of Ahura Mazda. In the *Avesta*, we are told that there was only Light—an essential purity—in the beginning.[89] In the Light was the Word and the power of Nature. It was the creator, usually seen as Ahura Mazda himself, who joined together the Word and Nature to make the world. When the world became overwhelmed by the constant multiplication of its all immortal beings, Ahura Mazda decided that the earth must be enlarged and a new beginning made.[90] He warned the faithful king Yima that a great flood was coming to cleanse the world and that Yima had to protect himself and two of each species in his castle[91] on top of the highest mountain.[92] The deluge arrived, and the world, except for Yima's castle and its inhabitants, was destroyed. When the waters receded, Yima opened his doors and the world was inhabited again.[93]

According to the twelfth-century text the *Bundahishn* [= Foundations of Creation],[94] in the beginning only the essential duality existed: the good Ahura Mazda and the evil Angra Mainyu.[95] At first Ahura Mazda created a spiritual world rather than a physical one in order to foil the evil intention of his adversary. Only 3,000 years later did he create the tangible world (*getig*), a perfect place with a perfect beast and a perfect human, Gayomart [Gayomard].[96] Instinctively, the evil Angra Mainyu reacted against this perfection. Breaking through the great cosmic shell that encompassed the world and its cosmic sea, he caused so much vibration that the sun began to rotate rather than stand still, causing day and night, and mountains and valleys were formed.[97] And as in Genesis, the interference of evil in the stillness and perfection of original creation led to death, work, and pain for humans.

In accounts of the Creation, *Bundahishn* describes two special trees growing near each other—a tree of life and a "tree of many seeds"[98]—as well as a cosmic mountain with water streaming forth from underground:

> 1. On the nature of the tree they call *Gôkard* it says in revelation, that it was the first day when the tree they call *Gôkard* grew in the deep mud within the wide-formed ocean; and it is necessary as a producer of the renovation of the universe, for they prepare its immortality therefrom....

> 9. The tree of many seeds has grown amid the wide-formed ocean, and in its seed are all plants; some say it is the proper-curing, some the energetic-curing, some the all-curing.

> 10. Between these trees of such kinds is formed the mountain with cavities, 9999 thousand myriads in number, each myriad being ten thousand.

---

88   F. M. Müller, *Vendidad*, 2:10, p. 13.
89   E.g., F. M. Müller, *Bundahis*, 1:1-2, p. 3; F. M. Müller, *Vendidad*, 2:40, p. 20.
90   F. M. Müller, *Vendidad*, 2:4-19, pp. 12-15. Just prior to this event, Yima had refused Ahura Mazda's proposal to be a "preacher and... bearer of [God's] law" and was given instead the charge to watch over the world, and make it thrive and increase (F. M. Müller, *Vendidad*, 2:3-4, pp. 11-12). Zarathustra later received the mission that Yima refused.
91   Note that some scholars associate the Egyptian loan word used for the Hebrew term for "ark" in the story of Noah with the meaning of "palace" or "castle" (J. H. Sailhamer, *Genesis*, p. 83).
92   F. M. Müller, *Vendidad*, 2:21-30, pp. 15-18.
93   F. M. Müller, *Dinkard 5*, 7, 7:9:4-5, p. 108; see also F. M. Müller, *Bahman Yast*, 3:55, p. 234. See *Endnote B-3*, p. 903.
94   An English translation of the shorter Indian version of the *Bundahishn* is readily accessible in reprint editions (F. M. Müller, *Bundahis*). A longer Iranian version, called the *Greater Bundahishn*, has also been translated into English but is currently out of print (B. T. Anklesaria, *Bundahishn*).
95   See F. M. Müller, *Bundahis*, 1:1-12, pp. 3-6. See *Endnote B-4*, p. 904.
96   See *ibid.*, 1:13-14, p. 6. See *Endnote B-5*, p. 904.
97   See B. T. Anklesaria, *Bundahishn*, 4:10-12; cf. *Excursus 50: Fu Xi and Nü Gua*, p. 654.
98   F. M. Müller, *Bundahis*, 9:5, 18:9, 27:2, pp. 31, 66, 99-100.

11. Unto that mountain is given the protection of the waters, so that water streams forth from there, in the rivulet channels, to the land of the seven regions, as the source of all the sea-water in the land of the seven regions is from there.[99]

The Zoroastrian Tree of Life is further described as the "white *Hôm* the healing and undefiled, [which] has grown at the source of the water of *Arêdvîvsûr*; every one who eats it becomes immortal, and they call it the *Gôkard* tree, as it is said that *Hôm* is expelling death; also in the renovation of the universe they prepare its immortality therefrom; and it is the chief of plants."[100]

The primeval mountain is said to have gradually made its appearance, rising up past the stations of the stars, moon, and sun, and finally reaching the "utmost height":

1. One says in the Scripture, "The first mountain that grew up was [Alburz of divine destiny and thereafter all the mountains grew up] in eighteen years."

2. Alburz grew ever till the completion of eight hundred years: for two hundred years up to the Star station, two hundred years [up] to the Moon station, two hundred years [up] to the Sun station, and two hundred years [up] to the utmost height of the Sky.[101]

Zoroastrian Stories Relating to the Fall

Although Zoroastrianism ignores the story of the taking of forbidden fruit, there is a story of how Yima—who, in early accounts, stood in the place that Gayomard later occupied as the primal man— sinned in pretending to be a god,[102] and caused human beings to lose their immortality.[103] Other traditions emphasize the idea that the evil "primeval contender" was responsible for having struck the blows that "made Gayomard mortal."[104] In his combat, he "stood upon one-third of the inside of the sky, and he sprang, like a snake, out of the sky down to the earth,"[105] taking "as much as one-third of the base of the sky, in a downward direction, into a confined and captive state, so that it was all dark and apart from the light."[106] Then, celebrating his victory, the evil one cried: "My victory has come completely, for the sky is split and disfigured by me with gloom and darkness, and taken by me as a stronghold; water is disfigured by me, and the earth, injured by darkness, is pierced by me; vegetation is withered by me, the [primeval] ox is put to death by me, Gâyômard is made ill by me."[107]

Although "the contentious promise-breaker injured the life of [Gayomard], and produced a burdensome mortality,"[108] the male and female "progenitors of the undeformed human

---

99 F. M. Müller, *Bundahis*, 18:1, 9-10, pp. 65, 66-67.

100 F. M. Müller, *Bundahis*, 27:4, p. 100. In another place it reads: "5. The tree of many seeds, having been produced from all those seeds of plants, grew up in the ocean *Frakhvkart*, wherefrom the seeds of all the species of plants are growing. 6. Near to that tree, the Gokaren tree was produced, in order to keep away ill-shaped decrepitude; and the complete exaltation of the world arose therefrom" (B. T. Anklesaria, *Bundahishn*, 6D:5-6; cf. F. M. Müller, *Bundahis*, 9:5-6, p. 31).

101 B. T. Anklesaria, *Bundahishn*, 9:1-2; cf. F. M. Müller, *Bundahis*, 12:1, p. 34 and F. M. Müller, *Zad-sparam*, 7:6, pp. 174-175; see also 1 Corinthians 15:40-42, D&C 76, J. E. Seaich, *Ancient Texts 1995*, pp. 568-577, 660-661.

102 F. M. Müller, *Yasts*, p. 293 n. 6 re: 19:(7):34.

103 S. A. Nigosian, *Zoroastrian Faith*, p. 19; see A. Ferdowsi, *Shahnama*, pp. 7-8; F. M. Müller, *Yasts*, 19:(7):35-36, 38, pp. 293-295.

104 F. M. Müller, *Dadistan-i Dinik*, 37:44, 46, p. 94.

105 F. M. Müller, *Bundahis*, 3:11, p. 16.

106 F. M. Müller, *Zad-sparam*, 4:1, p. 164; cf. Revelation 12:14, D&C 29:36.

107 F. M. Müller, *Zad-sparam*, 4:3, p. 164.

108 F. M. Müller, *Dadistan-i Dinik*, 64:5, p. 198.

race… are said to have grown up, in the manner of a plant, from the seed of the dead Gâyômard."[109] We read that:[110]

> … in forty years, with the shape of a one-stemmed Rivas-plant… Matro [Mashye, Marhayâ] and Matroyao [Mashyane, Marhîyôih—the names of the couple are derived from Avestan terms meaning "the man" and "the woman"[111]] grew up from the earth in such a manner that their arms rested, behind on their shoulders (*dosh*), and one joined to the other they were connected together and both alike.[112]

> 3. And the waists of both of them were brought close and so connected together that it was not clear which is the male and which the female, and which is the one whose living soul (*nismo*) of Ohrmazd is not away.

> 4. As it is said thus: Which is created before, the soul (*nismo*) or the body? And Ohrmazd said that the soul is created before, and the body after, for him who was created;[113] it is given into the body that it may produce activity, and the body is created only for activity; hence the conclusion is this, that the soul (*ruban*) is created before and the body after.

> 5. And both of them changed from the shape of a plant into the shape of man, and the breath (*nismo*) went spiritually into them, which is the soul (*ruban*);[114] and now, moreover, in that similitude a tree had grown up whose fruit was the ten varieties of man.

Following their creation, the first couple "attained to movement and walking upon the earth, and… advanced even to intercourse and also procreation."[115] The Creator ensured their survival by showing them how to cultivate grain, make bread, tend sheep, make clothing, and build houses.[116] Thus, although the evil one had intended to destroy God's highest work of Creation, his plan was frustrated when Gayomard "came back to the world as a man and a woman" and, as a result, the "unlucky fiend" instead "increased offspring and fortune for them through death." Thwarted in his purpose, the evil one sought to discourage the couple and "uplifted his voice" to remind them that "the living ones of their offspring and lineage" would also suffer the effects of mortality. For this reason, "the sting also of birth was owing to death."[117]

Zoroastrian writings allude to a change in earth's vegetation paralleling the "thorns… and thistles"[118] that sprang up after the Fall in the book of Moses account: "On the nature of plants it says in revelation, that, before the coming of the destroyer, vegetation had no thorn and bark about it; and, afterwards, when the destroyer came, it became coated with bark and thorny."[119]

Finally, the *Shahnameh* tells of how Kayumars (= Gayomard), having previously dwelt on a mountain, became the first king. The account relates that he "dressed in leopard skins" and "first taught men about the preparation of food and clothing, which were new in the

---

109   *Ibid.*, p. 105 n. 5 re: 37:82.
110   F. M. Müller, *Bundahis*, 15:2-5, pp. 53-54.
111   F. M. Müller, *Dadistan-i Dinik*, p. 105 n. 5 re: 37:82.
112   See *Commentary* 2:27-a, p. 115.
113   Cf. Moses 3:5.
114   Cf. Moses 3:7.
115   F. M. Müller, *Dadistan-i Dinik*, 64:5-6, pp. 198-199.
116   F. M. Müller, *Dinkard* 5, 7, 7:1:9-14, pp. 6-8.
117   F. M. Müller, *Dadistan-i Dinik*, 37:82-83, pp. 105-106.
118   Moses 4:24.
119   F. M. Müller, *Bundahis*, 27:1, p. 99.

world at that time."[120] As in rabbinical accounts[121] of how the beasts were awed at the sight of Adam: "All the animals of the world, wild and tame alike, reverently paid homage to him, bowing down before his throne, and their obedience increased his glory and good fortune."[122]

The Zoroastrian Savior

Zoroastrians believe in a "a past and future savior (*Saoshyant*), [and that] through ceremonies presided over by the savior, …the resurrection of the bodies of the good will take place and a new Golden Age will follow."[123] One text describes how, during the glorious millennium following the appearance of Hûshêdar-mâh, "adversity departs from the world… Meat is no longer eaten, but only milk and butter, and a hundred people are satisfied with the milk of one cow. Hûshêdar-mâh destroys the terrible serpent, …he clears all noxious creatures out of the world, and wild animals live harmlessly among mankind; the fiends of apostasy and deceit depart from the world, which becomes populous and delightful, and mankind abstain from falsehood." Eventually, "Dahâk escapes from his confinement, and reigns for a day and a half in the world with much tyranny" but, in the end, "[a]ll evil having departed from the world mankind become like the archangels, and the resurrection takes place."[124]

Resemblances to LDS Beliefs

Palmer[125] lists several points of resemblance between Zoroastrian and Latter-day Saint beliefs, including:

- the idea of an evil adversary to God[126]
- a spiritual creation and a premortal existence for all of humanity[127]
- sacred garments[128]
- disavowal of monasticism and asceticism[129]
- realms in the afterlife symbolized by the glory of the stars, the moon, and the sun.[130]

Moreover, Zoroastrian ideas about the basic goodness of the material world and the origin of dualism in free choice are also more consistent with LDS beliefs than, for instance, the Manichaean view of these things:

> The conspicuous monotheism of Zoroaster's teaching is apparently disturbed by a pronounced dualism: the Wise Lord has an opponent, Ahriman, who embodies the principle of evil, and whose followers, having freely chosen him, also are evil.[131] This ethical dualism is rooted in the Zoroastrian cosmology. He taught that in the beginning there was a meeting of the two spirits,

---

120 A. Ferdowsi, *Shahnama*, p. 1.
121 H. W. Nibley, *Dominion*, pp. 8-9.
122 A. Ferdowsi, *Shahnama*, p. 1.
123 D. Leeming, *World Mythology*, s. v. Zoroastrian Mythology, p. 412; cf. e.g., B. T. Anklesaria, *Bundahishn*, 34:1-33; F. M. Müller, *Bundahis*, 30:1-33, pp. 120-130. See *Endnote B-6*, p. 904.
124 F. M. Müller, *Pahlavi 1*, p. lviii. See J. H. Charlesworth, *Resurrection Beliefs*, pp. 221-222.
125 S. J. Palmer, *Zoroastrianism*, pp. 158-159.
126 See, e.g., F. M. Müller, *Zad-sparam*, 4:1-3, p. 164.
127 See, e.g., F. M. Müller, *Bundahis*, 1:1-14, pp. 3-6.
128 See, e.g., F. M. Müller, *Dadistan-i Dinik*, 39:1-32, 40:1-4, pp. 122-133, 133-134
129 See, e.g., R. Masani, *Zoroastrianism*, pp. 70, 81-82, 97.
130 See, e.g., *Arda Viraf*, pp. 196-197; F. M. Müller, *Dadistan-i Dinik*, 34:3, p. 76; F. M. Müller, *Dinai Mainog-i khirad*, 7:8-11, p. 29.
131 See *Endnote B-7*, p. 904.

who were free to choose—in the words of the *Gathas*—"life or not life."[132] This original choice gave birth to a good and an evil principle. Corresponding to the former is a Kingdom of Justice and Truth; to the latter, the Kingdom of the Lie (*Druj*), populated by the *daevas*, the evil spirits (originally prominent old Indo-Iranian gods). Monotheism, however, prevails over the cosmogonic and ethical dualism because Ahura Mazda is father of both spirits, who were divided into the two opposed principles only through their choice and decision.[133]

The Wise Lord, together with the *amesha spentas*[—the six holy immortals who, together with Ahura Mazda, represent the sevenfold character of God—] will at last vanquish the spirit of evil: this message, implying the end of the cosmic and ethical dualism, seems to constitute Zoroaster's main religious reform. His monotheistic solution resolves the old strict dualism. The dualist principle, however, reappears in an acute form in a later period, after Zoroaster. It is achieved only at the expense of Ahura Mazda, by then called Ohrmazd, who is brought down to the level of his opponent, Ahriman. At the beginning of time, the world was divided into the dominion of the good and of the evil. Between these, each man is bound to decide. He is free and must choose either the Wise Lord and his rule or Ahriman, the Lie. The same is true of the spiritual beings, who are good or bad according to their choices. From man's freedom of decision it follows that he is finally responsible for his fate. Through his good deeds, the righteous person (*ashavan*) earns an everlasting reward, namely integrity and immortality. He who opts for the lie is condemned by his own conscience as well as by the judgment of the Wise Lord and must expect to continue in the most miserable form of existence, one more or less corresponding to the Christian concept of hell.[134]

---

132   See S. Insler, *Gathas*, 30:4, pp. 33, 166-167.
133   See *Endnote B-4*, p. 904.
134   *Zoroaster*. See B. T. Anklesaria, *Bundahishn*, chs. 1, 4, 5; F. M. Müller, *Bundahis*, 30:1-33, pp. 120-130.

Mandaean Texts

Regarding the Mandaeans, Deutsch writes:[135]

> In the marshes of southern Iraq and Iran, in the cities of Baghdad and Basra, and increasingly in locales like suburban New Jersey, live the Mandaeans, the only surviving Gnostic community from antiquity. These fascinating and tenacious people have maintained their traditions for nearly two thousand years, long after their better known Gnostic "cousins" fell into obscurity. Although they have always been a relatively small community, the Mandaeans have produced an extremely rich body of rituals and texts written in Mandaic, an eastern dialect of Aramaic. Many of these traditions are unique, while others have parallels in Gnosticism, Judaism, Christianity, and Islam, as well as in ancient Mesopotamian religions. Because of their geographical isolation, their traditional wariness toward outsiders, and the linguistic and interpretive challenges posed by their literature, the Mandaeans have remained a mystery to all but a few scholars of religion....
>
> Turmoil in the Persian Gulf region has created a growing Mandaean diaspora. According to recent statistics, there are approximately seventy Mandaean families in the New York City area, including New Jersey, and others in Florida, Michigan, and California. There is also a large community of Mandaeans in Australia…
>
> Mandaeans around the world maintain contact with one another and with their home communities in the Middle East. They are led by a priesthood still recovering from a devastating cholera epidemic in 1831, which killed all of the adult priests but spared a handful of their sons. In recent years, priests from Iran have traveled to Australia and the United States to perform baptisms, weddings, and other rituals.
>
> Out of the over 60,000 Mandaeans in Iraq in the early 1990s, only about 5,000 to 7,000 remain there; as of early 2007, over 80% of Iraqi Mandaeans are now refugees in Syria and Jordan. There are small Mandaean diaspora populations in Australia (ca. 3,500 as of 2006), Canada, the USA (ca. 1,500) and Sweden (ca. 5,000).

According to a 10 February 2007 Associated Press article by Chris Newmarker, many of the roughly 1,500 Mandaeans living in the United States are professionals including physicians, engineers and jewelers. One concern of Mandaeans is assimilation into American culture, especially intermarriage. For mixed marriages, the Mandaean religion has "no mechanism to bring their children into the fold… [T]he religion's few dozen priests [are] reluctant to bring in the children of mixed marriages."[136]

There are three theories about the origin of the name for the Mandaean people.[137] One is that it comes from a related term meaning "knowledge," corresponding to the Greek term "Gnostic." A second idea is that it comes from the *mandi,* a sacred area marked off by a palisade of reeds and dried mud, and containing an immersion pool and a simple empty "temple" called a *bimanda* (= house of knowledge) or simply *manda.*[138] A third idea is that the name comes from the principal Mandaean redeemer figure, *Manda d-Hiia,* whose name means "Knowledge of the Life," where the term "Life" refers to the supreme deity. Within the Mandaean community is a smaller number of elite *nasuraiia* (i.e., those who

135 N. Deutsch, *Mandaean Introduction*, pp. 527, 535.

136 *Mandaeism.*

137 E. Lupieri, *Mandaeans*, pp. 8-9.

138 *Ibid.*, pp. 14-15.

BIBLIOGRAPHY

have *nasurita*—knowledge—or perhaps "initiates") who have access to additional mysteries of the religion, hence the nickname *Nasoraeans* for the Mandaean people.[139]

Whereas early scholarship looked to the pre-Christian era for the origins of the Mandaeans as a distinct community, more recent studies point to their beginnings as a first-century "Jewish baptismal group somewhere in Palestine or Syria, perhaps in the Jordan valley. Later this religious group seems to have become heretic from the orthodox Jewish point of view, and moved north-eastwards to Adiabene (modern Kurdish Iraq, Armenia, and Northern Iran), and from there to Southern Babylonia (today's Southern Iraq and Southwestern Iran)."[140]

Apart from their veneration of John the Baptist,[141] the Mandaeans retain only bitter memories of their own supposed origin among the Jews.[142] Ryen explains this as a process of the Mandaeans having gradually become isolated outsiders to Judaism, their feelings eventually changing to "hatred and polemic."[143] Their attitude is also hostile toward the person of Jesus, the Messiah of Christian doctrine.[144] Writes Drower:

> It is a striking fact that in all the Mandaean texts the word *msiha* (Messiah, Christ) is only used with the qualification 'lying' or 'false' of Jesus, and this is the more surprising as every priest is a king *(malka),*[145] crowned and anointed, as microcosm of the macrocosm *Adam Kasia*, the crowned and anointed Anthropos, Arch-priest, and creator of the cosmos made in his form. The word for the oil of unction is *misa* and the verbs for its application are *RSM* and *ADA*. The implication is that the word *msiha* (the anointed one) was so inextricably connected with the hated Jew and Christian that the root *MSH* was banned from Nasoraean use.[146]

Mandaean Creation Stories

Lupieri summarizes the basic ideas of Mandaeism, and Mandaic themes relating to the book of Moses:

> The religious ideas of the Mandaeans show some remarkable similarities to the ancient doctrines of the Gnostics,[147] and they also share a similar mode of expression, through myth… Characters belonging to the divine world or the realm of human legend… perform deeds in them whose interpretation is believed to provide the meaning of things. Unluckily for us, it is impossible to reconstruct a unified, coherent vision of certain important aspects of religious doctrine from the corpus of Mandaean literature… Indeed, the Mandaean texts are the fruit of sedimentation

---

139　Ryen also discusses a possible connection to the epithet Nazorean, used for the earliest Christians (J. O. Ryen, *Mandaean Vine*, pp. 22-23). Barker speculates that this name for Jesus' disciples have derive "from the Hebrew *neser* meaning Branch, the messianic title derived from Isaiah 11:1" or from *nazir* "meaning a consecrated person, one anointed with holy oil" (M. Barker, *Christmas*, p. 127).

140　J. O. Ryen, *Mandaean Vine*, p. 41; cf. pp. 21-41. See also S. Gündüz, *Knowledge of Life*; E. Lupieri, *Mandaeans*, pp. 122-172; R. Thomas, *Israelite Origins*; E. M. Yamauchi, *Gnostic Ethics*.

141　G. R. S. Mead, *Mandaean John-Book*; J. O. Ryen, *Mandaean Vine*, pp. 37-39.

142　E.g., E. Lupieri, *Mandaeans*, GR 1:163-180, pp. 213-215; G. R. S. Mead, *Mandaean John-Book*, 34-35, pp. 62-70.

143　J. O. Ryen, *Mandaean Vine*, pp. 35-36.

144　E.g., E. Lupieri, *Mandaeans*, JB 76, pp. 246-250; GR 1:198-202, pp. 243-244; GR 2:1:139-150, 154, pp. 240-243; G. R. S. Mead, *Mandaean John-Book*, 30, pp. 48-52. See K. Rudolph, *Coptic*, GR 1:200, 201-202, p. 299 for a passage about the miracles of Anos-Uthra with close parallels to Matthew 11:5. Scholarship is divided as to whether this passage constitutes a positive reference to Jesus, or rather is a polemic against Christianity attributing Jesus' miracles to a different figure (S. Gündüz, *Knowledge of Life*, pp. 106-107).

145　Thomas argues for the possibility of a connection to the old royal cult in Israel and the figure of Melchizedek (R. Thomas, *Israelite Origins*, p. 24.

146　E. S. Drower, *Adam*, p. xi.

147　In some important ways, Mandaean beliefs differ from Gnostic stereotypes: "Mandaeans believe in marriage and procreation, and in the importance of leading an ethical and moral lifestyle in this world, placing a high priority upon family life. Consequently, Mandaeans do not practice celibacy or asceticism. Mandaeans will, however, abstain from strong drink and red meat. While they agree with other gnostic sects that the world is a prison governed by the planetary archons, they do not view it as a cruel and inhospitable one" (*Mandaeism*).

of different teachings recorded centuries apart… In the *Ginza,* for example, perhaps the best known of the Mandaic sacred books, we find at least seven different accounts of the origins of the cosmos, each with features that are most difficult to reconcile…

In the more clearly dualistic texts there is a sharp contrast between light (*nhura*) and darkness (*huska*). At the highest point of light we find a supreme being, often possessing the qualities of transcendence: Life, or Great Life, or First Life [*Manda d-Hiia*]… The realm of light is inhabited by a great number of intermediate celestial beings, the *'utria* [= the plural of "wealth"] or *malkia* [= the plural of "king"]. These were presented to the European missionaries… as "angels" because of their function as intermediaries and messengers between humans and the highest divinity. Alongside them are many abstract or hypostatized realities that sometimes seem to take on individual consistency and features… There is also the *iardna* or light, the "river" or "flowing water" or the ubiquitous "Jordan," that sometimes goes by a proper name: *Piriauis,* or *Pras Ziua,* "Euphrates-Splendor." This can be thought of as a unit, or as an infinite whole of rivers of light, in which the celestial realities immerse themselves, perpetuating the perfect cult that pleases God in eternity, the celestial liturgy compared to which mere earthly ones are but wretched imitations. The entire realm of light is structured in a limitless number of "worlds of light" (*almia d-nhura*), where celestial "dwelling places" are to be found, the seat of the *'utria* and the blessed Mandaeans.

As far as the highest hierarchy of Light is concerned, from the First Light emanates the Second Light, whose proper name is *Iusamin* [probably derived from *Iao,* the secret name of *Yahweh*], from this the Third Life, called *Abatur* [possibly related to *ab,* "father" plus *'utria,* i.e., father of *'utria*], and from this the Fourth Life, *Ptahil* [perhaps connected to a root *PTH,* meaning "to mold," "to open"].[148] The process is clearly degenerative, and *Ptahil,* the least perfect, is to be found at the edge of light, by this point in contact with darkness… Out of [the waters of darkness] sometimes emerges a Lord or a King of Darkness, the exact opposite of the King of Light. More often the prominent figure is *Ruha,* the "Spirit," a female being, also called *Ruha d'Qudsa,* "Spirit of Holiness," that is, the Holy Spirit of the Christians. From an incestuous relationship with her own brother *Gap, Ruha* generates *'Ur,* an enormous monster in the form of a serpent whose coils wrap themselves into the dark fires of the abyss. The created world stands on him. From a new incestuous relationship, this time with *'Ur* (and, according to some texts, also with *Gap* and with her own father, the King of Darkness), *Ruha* generates the Seven, that is, the planets; the Twelve, that is, the signs of the zodiac; and the Five, the so-called "furious" [one of these may be the star Sirius]…[149]

The best-known myth on the origin of creation narrates that *Ptahil,* on the orders of his father, *Abatur,* created the cosmos. Having descended from the light toward the waters of darkness, however, he showed himself incapable of carrying out the task entrusted to him. So he turned to *Ruha,* to the Seven, and to the Twelve, and with their help molded form the waters of darkness *Tibil,* the created world.[150] According to another version, *Ptahil* obtained a mantle of light from his father and with it, by beating the water, he solidified it, thus creating the world.[151] In any case, his creative gesture was incorrect and was considered a sin.[152] His father was also involved in this, since he was responsible for having given him the order to create. Both are driven out of the world of light and, above the firmament (the outermost confines of the created world) but under the light, they created their own worlds, in which they dwell and reign sovereign. Underneath them, starting from the celestial vault, the cosmos is entrusted to the

148 Nibley cites Widengren's observation that the name of this Creator combines "the archaic Egyptian and Semitic names"—i.e., Ptah and El (H. W. Nibley, *Expanding 1992,* p. 189. See G. Widengren, *Mandäer,* p. 86).
149 See E. Lupieri, *Mandaeans,* GR 3:1, pp. 183-185.
150 K. Rudolph, *Coptic,* GR 15:13, pp. 177-179.
151 *Ibid.,* GR 5:1, pp. 180-181.
152 *Ibid.,* GR 15:13, p. 179.

malevolent control of the Twelve and the Seven. These are the ancient Gods, astral and planetary, worshipped in the entire Mesopotamian area but now transformed into evil demons...

This does not take away from the fact that there are some Mandaean texts, though to tell the truth not so very many, that take a positive view of the planets and, most importantly, that the everyday life of the Mandaeans involves (or involved) them in constantly consulting the stars....

The domination of the stars over human activities has roots going back a very long way. Having created *Tibil*, in fact, *Ptahil* and his helpers create Adam.[153] Here the Mandaean version of a well-known Gnostic myth makes its appearance. The first attempt leads to little more than an abortion. *Adam pagria*, physical Adam, is virtually a body without life. In the world of light, having felt pity for him, they convince the inner Adam (*adam kasia* or *Adakas*) to allow himself to be imprisoned in his body. He is the first soul, thanks to whose presence the earthly Adam acquires life. Now, however, the soul (or spiritual element; the Mandaean texts do not make much distinction) has to be saved. So *Manda d-Hiia*, called also *Bar Hiia* (son of Life) or *Dmut Hiia* (Image of Life), the main Mandaean figure of revealer, descends. He brings Adam knowledge of his true celestial nature, he teaches him baptism, and he makes him the first Mandaean.[154] As can readily be seen, in this context the sin of Adam makes no sense at all. In fact, he does not sin. His salvation does not derive from repentance but from the knowledge that the divinity has bestowed upon him. Also, the baptism that was taught to him, on the model of the celestial liturgies, serves to maintain or recover the purity lost through contact with the physical...

Among the speculations concerning Adam is the Mandaean myth about the celestial Adam. This latter figure, also called *Adakas*, is the double of the other Adam and lives in another world, the double of the earthly world: *Msunia Kusta* [= the enraptured/chosen of the truth].[155] The term indicates a seat, a kind of paradise, situated somewhere in the north...[156]

[T]he celestial Adamites correspond to the earthly ones. Three of these—Abel (*Hibil*), Seth (*Sitil*), and Enos (*Anus*)—are *'utria*, who can substitute or stand behind *Manda d-Hiia* in the function of revealer and savior... [T]he figure of Cain and his story are completely absent, whereas a couple of times an otherwise unknown Adam son of Adam, *Adam bar Adam*, who was reputed to have been seduced by *Ruha*, makes his appearance...

As far as the sons of Adam go, Seth (*Sitil*) dies before his time.[157] He in fact accepts dying in place of his old father, who is too afraid and who through tricks and excuses manages to deceive the angel of death...[158] [Seth] becomes the first Mandaean to enter into celestial blessedness. *Hibil* (the biblical Abel), however, is born miraculously, leaving his mother intact and appearing suddenly at her side...[159]

Whatever the genesis of the legends about *Hibil,* the son of Adam, a dense mass of mythical material is connected with *Hibil Ziua's* descent into the underworld or world of darkness... [and his] very long journey back up, with [a] magic pass, [a] mirror, and [a] consort or consorts...[160]

Inside this mythical structure, finally, other fragments of Gnostic myth on the descent of the heavenly savior are to be found... In short, *Hibil Ziua* impersonates the so-called "savior to be saved," very much a part of Gnostic traditions...[161]

153 E. Lupieri, *Mandaeans*, GR 3:1, pp. 187-191.
154 See *Endnote B-8*, p. 904.
155 E. Lupieri, *Mandaeans*, GR 3:1, p. 189 and n. 9.
156 On the significance of "north," see A. S-M. Ri, *Commentaire de la Caverne*, pp. 120-121.
157 *Ibid.*, GL 1:1, pp. 191-194.
158 Cf. e.g., Abraham in D. C. Allison, *Testament*, 16:1-20:15, pp. 319-412.
159 Cf. the birth of Melchizedek in *2 Enoch*, 78:17-19, pp. 206-207.
160 K. Rudolph, *Coptic*, GR 5:1, pp. 215-220.
161 Cf., e.g., J. K. Elliott, *Pearl*.

... [T]he soul... is personal, detaching itself from the body on the third day after death... [The] ascension of the soul... of the dead person toward the regions beyond the heavens is at one time imagined as a journey undertaken in solitude and at another as the meeting and the reunion and fusion with the "celestial double" of the dead person....

[T]he descendants of *Sum* [Shem, son of Noah], the Mandaeans themselves, are the only ones who are pure and genetically without sin. Adam in actual fact does not sin... [and] they alone are his worthy descendants... The savior and redeemer already appeared at the beginning of time, and his return would not make much sense. Nevertheless, through the influence of Christianity... some Mandaean texts await a return of Jesus at the end of time...[162]

Mandaean Ritual

Despite their probable post-Christian origins as a separate people, Nibley sees the "whole Mandaean ritual complex with its endless washings, garments, ritual meals, embraces, grips and crownings [as being] reminiscent of the Egyptian endowment, and Drower, the principal authority on the subject, long ago called attention to the common prehistoric origin of both."[163] Thomas argues for a connection to Palestinian baptist sects and the pre-exilic Israelite temple cult.[164] Even Yamauchi, who argued persuasively that, in contrast to mainstream scholarship, the Mandaean movement originated in the East and no earlier than the first centuries of the Christian era, nevertheless agreed with other researchers who saw the roots of their mythology and ritual in ancient Mesopotamian religion.[165]

The most important phases of Mandaean ceremonies and rituals are performed in the *mandi*. Participants face north, since "the Mandaeans consider the North Star to be the throne of Abatur, the divine judge of all mortals."[166] The rituals "that they are the most famous for, and from which their Arabic name is derived (*subba*[, hence the name *Sabeans*]), are those concerning immersion in running water (or, at any rate, its use)":

> The most important of these is the *masbuta,* "baptism," a solemn "immersion" in the presence of a priest. Sunday, which the Mandaeans call *habsaba,* "first [day] of the week," is a holy day, just as it is for Christians, and practicing Mandaeans are expected to participate in the *masbuta* every Sunday. The ceremony lasts several hours, occupying nearly the entire morning. Preceded by the officiating *tarmida*'s preparatory prayers, the ceremony takes place along a watercourse or near the *mandi*'s immersion pool, and can be divided into two parts. The first part takes place in water: the person to be baptized first immerses himself or herself three times and is then immersed three times by the *tarmida*. He or she must drink the baptismal water three times from the *tarmida*'s hand, and then a small crown of myrtle is placed on the head, followed by a laying on of hands by the *tarmida*. The second part of the ceremony takes place on the bank once all the baptisms have been performed. With their white gowns soaking with water the Mandaeans consume a special bread (*pihta*) that has been prepared beforehand, and they drink the most holy water (*mambuha*), which has also been prepared by the priest in advance. They are then anointed with sesame oil by the priest, that is, "marked" on the forehead and the face (from ear to ear), with a gesture possibly related both to the Christian sign of the cross and to baptismal anointing (of the ears). Handshaking (called *kusta,* meaning "right" or "truth") takes place repeatedly during the ceremony, each of the gestures described above being separated by hymns and prayers of varying length, recited by the priest.

---

162 E. Lupieri, *Mandaeans*, pp. 38-52.
163 E. S. Drower, *Mandaeans*, pp. xviii-xix; H. W. Nibley, *Message 2005*, p. 445.
164 R. Thomas, *Israelite Origin*, pp. 11-26.
165 E. M. Yamauchi, *Gnostic Ethics*, pp. 80-86. See also G. Widengren, *Enthronement,* who discusses Mandaean baptism in light of Syrian-Mesopotamian ritual traditions.
166 E. Lupieri, *Mandaeans*, p. 15.

Solemn baptism has two specific functions: it reduces (although it does not eliminate) the quantity and quality of punishment in the next world for sinful or irregular behavior, and restores those who have been very seriously contaminated to a state of ritual purity.[167]

According to Drower: "'Mysteries', i.e., sacraments to aid and purify the soul, [are intended] to ensure her rebirth into a spiritual body, and her ascent from the world of matter… In the case of the Nasoraeans this interpretation is based on the Creation story…, especially on the Divine Man, Adam, as crowned and anointed King-priest."[168] Anciently, all adult members of the sect were initiated into the mysteries through a series of rites described in Mandaean sacred writings. Today, the rites are still carried out in a limited way for those who are to become priests. Writes Lupieri:

> The ceremony for consecrating a *tarmida* [= priest] is even richer and on a bigger scale than a wedding… The *sualia* [= candidate for initiation as a *tarmida*] is clothed as if he were dying or dead man ready for burial. He is dressed in a new *rasta* [= white ceremonial robe] with a gold coin sewn on the right and a silver one on the left. Gold symbolizes the sun and silver the moon, and their presence means that whoever wears that particular *rasta* must undertake the voyage through the heavens, controlled by the evil planetary powers, to the higher light. Dressed as a dead man, then, the *sualia* must demonstrate to his teacher, to the priests, and to the people gathered to celebrate that he possesses the necessary knowledge and preparation…[169]

The consecration ceremony for the *tarmida* must be understood in light of portrayals of the soul in Mandaean scripture "as an exile, a captive; her home and origin being the supreme Entity to which she eventually returns":[170]

> Rise up, rise up, soul
> Ascend to your first earth [i.e., former earth, native place, place of origin]…
> to the place from which you were transplanted,…
> Bestir yourself, put on your garment of radiance
> And put on your resplendent wreath.
> Sit on your throne of radiance,
> which the Life set up for you in the Place of Light.[171]

> Ascend, rise up to your former home,
> To your fine abode with the *'uthras.*
> Live among the *'uthras*, your brothers,
> Sit there as you were taught to do.
> Seek the House of your Father…
> May your throne be set up, just as it used to be…[172]

The Mandaean *Book of John* gives the following account of how Adam awoke, having lost his body of light and being placed on the dreary earth, and welcomed the messenger who was sent by his Father to instruct him:

> At the call of the Envoy Adam, who lay there, awoke… and went forth to meet the Envoy: "Come in peace, O Envoy, Life's messenger, who hast come from the House of my Father. How firmly planted withal dear, beautiful Life in his region! But how [meanly] for me has a stool been set up [i.e., Tibil, the dreary earth] and my dark form sits on it lamenting."

---

167   *Ibid.*, pp. 15-16.
168   E. S. Drower, *Adam*, p. xvi. See *Endnote B-9*, p. 905.
169   E. Lupieri, *Mandaeans*, pp. 25-26.
170   E. S. Drower, *Adam*, p. xvi.
171   K. Rudolph, *Coptic*, GL 3:3, p. 261.
172   *Ibid.*, GL 1:2, p. 254.

Thereon the Envoy made answer and spake to the corporeal Adam: "Thy throne has been set up in Beauty, O Adam; and 'tis thy form sits here lamenting. All were mindful of thee for thy good and fashioned and sent me to thee. I am come and will give thee instruction, O Adam, and free thee from this world. Give ear and hearken and get thee instructed, and mount to Light's region victorious."[173]

The Mandaean literature abounds with references to the idea that three messengers were sent to teach Adam and to protect him from the deceptive and dangerous influence of evil powers.[174] For example, in the *Canonical Prayerbook*, it says: "And Hibil-Ziwa came and blessed three 'uthras, and the three 'uthras blessed Adam and all his descendants."[175] According to Nibley, these envoys "taught Adam and Eve the hymns, and the order of prayer, and the ordinances which would help one to return to the presence of the Father."[176] *Ginza* records:

> When I (*Manda d-Hiia*) installed Adam, I appointed three 'uthras over him. I set myself at the head of the 'uthras whom I set over Adam and Eve. I stood before them and taught them wonderful hymns (*drase*). I instructed them in the ritual books (*sidre*) so that they might perform the *masiqtas* [after the manner] of the 'uthras. I taught them prayers so that they might be confirmed through the prayers of the Life... I brought myself forward and instructed them, as a teacher (*rabba*) does his pupils (*swalya*). I conversed with them and blessed them, and the blessing of the good ones shall rest upon them. Adam, his sons, and his generation shall behold the Place of Light.[177]

In another passage from *Ginza* (GR 11:1), Nibley[178] also sees a description of the efforts of Satan to oppose the ministry of the three envoys:

> The evil spirits, who claim the world for their own, resent the Sent Ones' instructions. "These three men are in the world," they say, "but the are not really men. They are light and glory, and they have come down to little 'Enosh' [physical man—Adam] who is helpless and alone in the world."[179] They are intruding on our world. "The children of men have taken over the earth. They are really strangers who speak the language of the three men. They have accepted the teachings of the three men and rejected us in our own world."[180] They refuse to acknowledge our kingdom and our glory. The devils don't like the three men interrupting their program and spoiling things. Thus, the evil ones plotted to overthrow Adam, who was hoping for "*Manda d-Hiia* (Teacher of Life), the messenger from the Father to come and give him aid and support."[181]

Mandaean disciples are specifically warned of Satan and of the dangers of putting their trust in the treasures of the earth:

> Love not gold and silver and the possessions of this world, for the world will come to nothing and perish, and its possessions and its works will be abandoned. Do not worship Satan, the idols, the images, the error and the confusion of this world...[182]

---

173 G. R. S. Mead, *Mandaean John-Book*, 13, p. 91.

174 See *Figure* 5-9, p. 339 and *Figure* 5-10, p. 340.

175 E. S. Drower, *Prayerbook*, 379, p. 292.

176 H. W. Nibley, *Apocryphal*, p. 302.

177 K. Rudolph, *Coptic*, GR 3:1, pp. 197-198.

178 GR 11:1, cited in H. W. Nibley, *Apocryphal*, pp. 302-303. Quotation marks in the original are modified here to better distinguish Ginza citations from Nibley's own explanations.

179 In German: "Die Bösen der Welt sollen sagen: 'Diese drei Männer sind in der Welt, jedoch sind sie keine Männer, sondern Glanz und Licht ist es, das seine Gestalt zeigt in dieser Welt beim kleinen Enös, der allein in dieser Welt dasteht'" (M. Lidzbarski, *Ginza*, GR 11:1, p. 264).

180 In German: "... die Menschenkinder waren in Fülle da. Sie sprechen in der Rede des fremden Lebens, sprechen in der Rede dieser drei Männer. Sie schließen sich dem Leben an und unterwerfen sich diesen drei Männern. Sie erheben sich gegen uns und verachten uns in dieser unserer eigenen Welt'" (*ibid.*, GR 11:1, p. 263).

181 In German: "Ich hoffe auf Mandit dHaije, daß er komme und mir eine Stütze sei" (*ibid.*, GR 11:1, p. 263).

182 K. Rudolph, *Coptic*, GR 1:95-96, p. 289.

They are also given moral instructions to accompany the ordinances.[183] In the *Ginza*, we find teachings concerning such subjects as:

> *Obedience*: "Do not put your trust in the world in which you live, for it does not belong to you. Trust in the fine works which you perform. When you leave your body, (then) the works of your hands will be your support."[184]

> *Sacrifice*: "Give alms to the poor… If you give with your right hand, (then) do not tell it to your left";[185] "When you see anyone who is hungry, (then) satisfy his hunger. When you see anyone who is thirsty, (then) give him to drink. When you see anyone naked, (then) give him clothes… Whoever releases a prisoner, will find a Messenger (*sliha*) of life advancing to meet him."[186]

> *The Gospel*: "Do not do anything that is odious to your associates."[187]

> *Chastity*: "Take a wife and found a family… Do not commit adultery or fornicate."[188]

> *Charity*: "Love and support one another, and you shall cross the great Ocean of Suf.… Be you brothers of *kusta*, who bring your love to perfection."[189]

Shortly after birth, the newborn child is given four names, one of which is "the most secret and important one" that is "used always (and almost exclusively" in religious rituals."[190] The number four is also a significant part of initiation in the Mandaean tradition, which includes a testing process involving a series of four ritual acts. As described by Roper:[191]

> Both the *Ginza*… and the *Canonical Prayer-Book of the Mandaeans* describe how, upon death, the soul, leaving behind her mortal body, will ascend to the heavenly world of Light from which she originally came. [There, the soul meets] Abathur, a powerful angel who guards the entrance into paradise. "There his scales are set up and spirits and souls are questioned before him as to their names, their signs, their blessing, their baptism and everything that is therewith."[192] According to a Mandaean commentary, this portion of the liturgy refers to "the four ritual handclasps which Abathur seeks to exchange with the soul."[193] Each of these four are associated with separate ritual acts accompanied by a solemn oath:[194] "The first *kusta* is a precious *kusta*; it is the promise made at baptism.… The second *kusta* is a lofty *kusta*: it is the oath [taken at] coronation; no [earthly] king hath more majesty! The third *kusta* is a loving one, it is the vow taken at espousal: there is no love like it. The fourth *kusta* is a powerful *kusta* for it traveleth to (the other) world. It came, it went, and it opened the door to the world. Every man who hath performed these *kustas* is thereby made perfect, he hath been put to the test by all the worlds and will rise upward and behold the Place of Light."[195] All this in Mandaean tradition was revealed to Adam by divine messengers sent from God to teach him… the proper way to worship.

---

183   H. W. Nibley, *Apocryphal*, pp. 302, 308.
184   K. Rudolph, *Coptic*, GR 1:155, p. 289; cf. Matthew 6:19-20.
185   *Ibid.*, GR 1:104, p. 291; cf. Matthew 6:3.
186   *Ibid.*, GR 1:105, p. 291, cf. GL 3:19, p. 295; cf. Matthew 25:35-36.
187   *Ibid.*, GR 1:150, p. 291; cf. Matthew 7:13.
188   *Ibid.*, GR 1:92, p. 292; cf. Matthew 5:27-28.
189   *Ibid.*, GR 1:128, pp. 291-292; cf. Matthew 5:43-48.
190   E. Lupieri, *Mandaeans*, p. 17; cf. E. S. Drower, *Haran*, p. 32. See *Endnote B-9*, p. 905.
191   M. Roper, *Adam*; cf. T. M. Compton, *Handclasp*, p. 622.
192   E. S. Drower, *Prayerbook*, p. 45. The account continues by saying: "The souls of our fathers were signed with the sign of Life and the name of the Life and the name of Manda d-Hiia was pronounced over them" (*ibid.*, p. 45).
193   E. S. Drower, *Nasorean*, p. 35. See *Commentary* 1:25-c, p. 60, *Figure 6-14*, p. 473; *Excursus 53: Comparative Explorations, Dexiosis*, p. 681; the *Manichaean Texts* section of the *Annotated Bibliography*, p. 884; and *Figure B-1*, p. 872. See *Endnote 1-22*, p. 79.
194   See *Endnote B-10*, p. 905.
195   E. S. Drower, *Thousand*, pp. 255-256. See *Endnote B-11*, p. 905.

At the final stage of the *tarmida* consecration ceremony, the candidate symbolically enacts a journey from the material world to the Place of Life:

> Once the texts have all been recited, another straw hut is quickly built under the guidance of the priests. This hut is in every respect similar to the *manda*, but without the mud stucco. It is built to the north of the courtyard, with its opening facing south, directly opposite that of the *andiruna*[, a previously-built house covered with blue cloth which represents the material world]. The second hut is called a *skinta*, which means "dwelling," "house," or "temple," and is covered with a large sheet of white cloth.[196]

> … The next morning just before dawn [the *sualia*] will leave the *andiruna*, and, after pausing halfway between the two huts to again recite a sacred text, he finally enters the *skinta*.…[197]

In a passage no doubt corresponding to a more elaborate version of the same kind of enactment, the culmination of the process by which one is admitted to the Place of Life is described in the Mandaean liturgy:

> When [the soul] puts on the vesture of the sons of perfection she laugheth, rejoiceth… about the glorious splendor, the honor resting on and belonging to her. She proceeded in the vesture of Yuzataq-Manda-d-Hiia and went onwards and reached the Waters of Death [i.e., the frontier of the world of light[198]]. The waters covered her, but Radiance crossed over… and said, "Life, I am Thine, and for Thy name's sake came I forth from the world… so that we may bring out this soul… so that she cometh before him".… He graspeth her with the palm of his right hand and handeth her over to two *'uthras*… who open the Door of Life, plant the plant of Life and establish the first counterpart of the House of Life.[199]

A related description of this event is found in *Left Ginza* 1:1:

> Sitil [Seth], the son of Adam… was brought to the Watchhouse [where] Silmais, the treasurer, holds the nails of glory in the hand, and carries the key of the *kushta* of both arms.[200] They opened the gate of the treasure house for him, lifted the great veil of safety upward before him, introduced him, and showed him that Vine [i.e., the Tree of Life],[201] its inner glory… They eat, and the great Presence of Life came and rested upon him. They twined wreaths of Presence and placed them on his head… Sitil, son of Adam, spoke: "On this [same] way, the Path and Ascent which I have climbed, truthful, believing, faithful and perfect men should also ascend and come, when they leave their bodies [i.e., at death]."[202]

---

196   See R. Thomas, *Israelite Origins*, pp. 22-23 for comparisons of the design of the huts and Israelite temples.

197   E. Lupieri, *Mandaeans*, p. 27.

198   E. S. Drower, *Prayerbook*, p. 45 n. 6.

199   *Ibid.*, 49, pp. 45-46.

200   Nibley comments: "That is the code for the signs that Adam had to receive—his instructions. The one who holds the nails of glory, and the signs in the hands, and the key to the initiation rites is the master of the Treasure House" (H. W. Nibley, *Apocryphal*, p. 300; cf. Isaiah 49:16; Zechariah 13:6; Cyril of Jerusalem, *Five*, 2:5, p. 148).

201   J. O. Ryen, *Mandaean Vine*, pp. 203-204. A close association between the symbolism of the "true vine" and that of the "true olive tree" can be found in 1 Nephi 15:15-16.

202   Cf. Lidzbarski's German translation: "Sitil, den Sohn Adams… stellten ihn an das Wachthaus Silmais, des Schatzmeisters, der die Pflöcke des Glanzes in der Hand hält und die Schlüssel der Kusta auf beiden Armen trägt. Sie öffneten ihm das Tor des Schatzhauses, hoben vor ihm den großen Vorhang der Sicherheit in die Höhe, führten ihn ein und zeigten ihm jenen Weinstock, dessen Inneres Glanz, … Sie essen, und die Wonnigkeit des Lebens kommt und legt sich über sie. Sie winden Kränze der Wonnigkeit und legen sie sich aufs Haupt… Sitil, der Sohn Adams, sprach: 'Auf diesem Wege, Pfad und Aufstieg, auf dem ich emporgestiegen bin, sollen auch die wahrhaften, gläubigen, trefflichen und vollkommenen Männer emporsteigen und kommen, wenn sie aus ihrem Körper scheiden'" (M. Lidzbarski, *Ginza*, GL 1:1, p. 429:3-20). Another account in *Ginza* reads: "When it [i.e., the soul] arrived at the gate of the House of Life, the escort comes to meet it. He bears a resplendent wreath in his hand and a garment in both his arms… The Life stretched out (his hand), and joined in communion (*laufa*) with it, just as the elect join in communion (*laufa*) in the Place of Light" (K. Rudolph, *Coptic*, GR 3:6, p. 263).

FIGURE B-1. *Pact and Pax: The Kushta. 1956*
E.S. Drower, 1879-1972

Sitil [Seth], the son of Adam… was placed at the Watchhouse [where] Silmais, the treasurer, holds the nails of glory in the hand, and carries the key of the kushta of both arms… Sitil, son of Adam, spoke: "On this way, the Path and Ascent which I have climbed, truthful, believing, discerning and perfect men should also climb and come, when they leave their bodies."[1] Lady Drower, during her life the foremost specialist on the Mandaeans and still one of the few who have been privileged to spend years in firsthand study of their practices, writes: "Mandaeans call the ceremonial handclasp the *kushta*[2] and its performance 'taking *kushta*' with a person. As in the European handshake the right hand only is given, and on its release it is carried to the lips. *Kushta* may be translated 'troth,' 'truth' or 'true-dealing'… The handclasp and kiss occur three times during the Mandaean baptismal rite, once in the water, once after the giving of the sacramental bread and water, and once at the end when the priest veils his right hand in his stole for the final salutation.[3] The words spoken are '*Kushta asiak ukaimak,*'

---

1   M. Lidzbarski, *Ginza*, LG 1:1, p. 429. See *Excursus 51: The Five Lost Things of the Temple*, p. 658.

2   Sundberg has written an in-depth monograph on the key term *kushta*, referring both to the idea of "right" or "truth" and the unusual handclasp rite described above (W. Sundberg, *Kushta*).

3   Note in the photograph that the white stole is being gripped between the two parties as part of the handclasp. The veiling of the clasped hands beneath a white cloth is also a part of Mandaean and Muslim marriage covenants. The seemingly related practice of the two participants in marriage and in other pact-making rites holding the ends of a white handkerchief between them is had among some Iraqi Jews (E. S. Drower, *Water*, pp. 104-105). See R. Thomas, *Israelite Origins*, pp. 6, 23 for a discussion of resemblances between the ritual clothing of the Mandaeans and that of Levitical priests in Judaism. The turban is wrapped around the head three times, with the end hanging over the left shoulder. Thomas also notes that the *kusta* is identical to the first Masonic handclasp (*ibid.*, p. 25 n. 139).

that is, 'Kushta strengtheneth thee (or healeth thee) and establisheth thee.' In Mandaean rites the handclasp seems to mark the completion of a ceremony or of a stage in a ceremony."[4] As exemplified both by Adam and by his righteous son Seth, who were taken by the right hand and brought into the presence of the Great Life,[5] the performance of the sacred handclasp in Mandaean ritual is of a "symbolic salvific character," signaling "a recognition of the embodied soul as a displaced being of Light" and presaging "its eventual installation within its true home."[6] See Nibley[7] for a reproduction of a drawing from Drower's "1934 copy of an old Mandaean magic scroll"[8] showing "Adam, Sitil, and other perfected souls in priestly dress [giving] the *kushta...* to each other."

Drower compares the rite of *kushta* to practices among Jews[9] and Christians,[10] and in the ancient Mesopotamian *Akitu* festival.[11] Despite its varied forms, she finds that the rite is universally "identical in purpose," signifying pact and *pax*—covenant and reconciliation—citing the eloquent words of Modi: "... behind the outward passing of hands in the *hamazor* (= Parsi ritual handclasp), which signifies unity, harmony, participation, there lies the inner idea, which demands that the participants must unite in the works of righteousness. So, behind what we may call the 'physical *hamazor*,' there is what we may term the 'spiritual *hamazor*.' The participants in the ceremony, in the ritual, in the recital are asked to be one with the chief celebrant in some religious acts which may lead to an increase of righteousness in the world."[12]

---

4   E. S. Drower, *Water*, p. 106.
5   M. Lidzbarski, *Ginza*, GL 1:1, p. 429:3-20, GL 2:26, p. 498:20-22.
6   J. C. Reeves, *Heralds*, pp. 123, 124.
7   H. W. Nibley, *Apocryphal*, p. 300 Figure 50.
8   E. S. Drower, *Writings*, p. 173.
9   E. S. Drower, *Water*, pp. 103-105.
10   *Ibid.*, pp. 106-110.
11   *Ibid.*, p. 102 n. 1. For more on the use of the handclasp in classical, Jewish, and Christian contexts, see *Excursus 53: Comparative Explorations, Dexiosis*, p. 681. See also *Commentary 1:25-c*, p. 60, *Figure 6-14*, p. 473; and the *Manichaean Texts* section of the *Annotated Bibliography*, p. 884. See *Endnote 1-22*, p. 79.
12   J. J. Modi, *Ceremonies*, p. 406, cited in E. S. Drower, *Water*, p. 111.

General studies of the Mandaean people and their beliefs, customs, and rituals include J. J. Buckley, *Mandaeans*; E. F. Crangle, *et al.*, *Baptism*; E. F. Crangle, *et al.*, *Priestcraft*; E. S. Drower, *Mandaeans*; E. Lupieri, *Mandaeans*. In addition to translations and commentaries on Mandaean sacred writings described below, Drower's study of the idioms of Middle Eastern ritual[203] and of the Mandaean Adam[204] should be consulted.

Ginza, Sidra Rba, or Mandaean Book of Adam

The most important book of Mandaean scripture is the *Ginza Rba* (= Great Treasure) or *Sidra Rba* (= Great Book), briefly described by Ryen as follows:

> The work consists of two parts: *Left* and *Right Ginza*.[205] *Right Ginza* (RG) is the first and most voluminous of the two, and contains the myths about the Lightworld and darkness from the beginning of mythological time, and how this world came into being. The literary style is mainly prose. *Left Ginza* (LG) deals with the soul's destiny after death and the soul's journey upwards to the Lightworld. The style is usually poetic.

> The first translation (into Latin) was made by M. Norberg [1815/1816, 3 volumes]. Norberg's translation was somewhat free. H. Petermann's edition from 1867 became more known, but was also in Latin. W. Brandt translated extracts from *Ginza* into German at the end of the 19th century [1893]. A complete translation in German was edited by M. Lidzbarski in 1925... This edition is still the standard edition of *Ginza*. Efforts are made for a new edition with translation of this work.[206]

---

203   E. S. Drower, *Water*.
204   E. S. Drower, *Adam*.
205   The two parts of *Ginza* "are organized in such a way that on reaching the end of Right *Ginza*, a reader must turn the volume upside down to read *Ginza* Left. The two parts face each other in the manner of two inscribed bowls enclosing the text within. Some scholars think that this may very well be the *Ginza's* model, for traditional Mandæan inscribed clay bowls are often found buried in this same fashion" (R. Spencer, *Loss*).
206   J. O. Ryen, *Mandaean Vine*, pp. 44-45.

To facilitate the finding of specific passages from *Ginza* in English translation, we have prepared the following table. The summary descriptions given in the table provide a useful overview of important beliefs and ethical practices among the Mandaeans. Selections are listed by *Ginza* section and verse, with *Ginza Left* references following those of *Ginza Right*. Page numbers in English publications of Ginza selections are correlated to page numbers in the complete Latin (Petermann) and German (Lidzbarski) editions:

Pet – *The Great Treasure or Great Book, Commonly Called "The Book of Adam," the Mandaean's Work of Highest Authority (Thesaurus sive Liber Magnus, vulgo "Liber Adami" appellatus, opus Mandaeorum summi ponderis)* with a New Introduction by Charles Häberl. Reprint edition of Petermann's Latin translation. Volume 1 (*Ginza Right*) and Volume 2 (*Ginza Left*).

Lid – *Ginza: Der Schatz oder das Grosse Buch der Mandäer,* edited by M. Lidzbarski. A complete German translation.

WF – *Gnosis: A Selection of Gnostic Texts*, Vol. 2. A translation and arrangement of Gnostic writings organized by school of thought. Kurt Rudolph edited the large section on Mandaean sources, under the general editorship of Werner Foerster. I have drawn from Rudolph's summaries in many of the section descriptions below.

EL – *The Mandaeans: The Last Gnostics* by E. Lupieri. A well-written introduction to the Mandaean religion which includes an anthology of texts organized by topic, along with commentary. The anthology includes not only several excerpts from the *Ginza* but also significant passages from the *Book of John* and other Mandaean texts.

OB – *The Other Bible* (W. Barnstone, *Other*). Described in the **Nag Hammadi Codices** section above.

GB – *The Gnostic Bible* (W. Barnstone, *et al., Gnostic*). Described in the **Nag Hammadi Codices** section above.

Haa – *Gnosis: Character and Testimony* (R. Haardt, *Gnosis*). A collection of Gnostic writings, including a section on Mandaeism.

Section	Description	Pet	Lid	WF	EL	OB	GB	Haa
GR 1:5-7	Attributes of the King of light or Lord of greatness (*mara d-rabuta*). Relatively recent.	2	5	148-149	178-179			
GR 1:8-37	Additional attributes of the King of light.	2-7	5-10	149-151				
GR 1:40	Creation through the word.	7	10	157				
GR 1:42-76	Description of the world of light-beings.	7-11	11-14	152-153				
GR 1:81-88	A monistic version of the cosmogony.	12-13	14	182-184				
GR 1:85	The King of Light brings everything into being by his word.	13	15	157				
GR 1:92	Take a wife and found a family.	14	16	292				
GR 1:95-96 (Recension A)	A portion of the Mandaean "Moral Code." Believers are admonished to be truthful, to love not gold and silver, and to eschew the worship of Satan and the error and confusion of this world.	14	16	289				
GR 1:103-105	Instructions on freeing prisoners, giving alms (cf. Matthew 6:3), feeding the hungry, and clothing the naked.	15-16	17-18	291				
GR 1:110-118	Fast not from eating and drinking, but rather fast from evil with your eyes, ears, mouths, hears, hands, body, knees, and feet.	16	18-19	290				
GR 1:121	Trust neither rulers nor armies, nor their riches.	17	19	290				

Section	Description	Pet	Lid	WF	EL	OB	GB	Haa
GR 1:123-124	Admonishment for believers to be baptized. All who are baptized and are steadfast in good deeds will not be hindered on their way to the place of light.	17-18	19-20	277				
GR 1:128	Love and support one another.	18	20	291-292				
GR 1:134-136 (Recension A)	The dead will be protected and set free from the watch-houses through the rituals of the *masiqta* (elevation or ascent).	19	21	282-283				
GR 1:138	Give bread, water, and shelter to the poor and persecuted.	19	21	291				
GR 1:143	Do not go to soothsayers, nor to lying Chaldeans.	20	22	292				
GR 1:146	Do not commit adultery, sing, or dance.	20	22	292				
GR 1:150	Do not do anything that is odious to your associates.	21	22	291				
GR 1:153-165	Do not put your trust in the world, which will come to an end, nor in false gods. The discipline of penitence.	21-22	23-25	289-290, 292-293				
GR 1:163-180	A revelation to Adam condemning the "evil" god Adunai (= *Adonai* (Hebrew "Lord"), Jehovah) and Judaism, the first deviation from the first religion (Mandaeism) and the root from whence other false religions (e.g., Christianity, Islam) sprang.	23-26	24-27	296-298	213-215			
GR 1:189-191	A brief account telling of how King Solomon lost his power when he exalted himself and forgot the Lord.	27	28	298	215			
GR 1:198-202	Jesus attempts to deceive, but *Anus Uthra* teaches truly. After the 360 true prophets leave Jerusalem, the city is destroyed and the Jews are exiled.	28-29	29-30	298-299	243-244			
GR 1:203	Muhammad does much evil in the world and leads Mandaeans astray.	29	30	300	254			
GR 2:1:49-50 (Recension B)	Mandaeans are not to mourn for the dead, but instead to perform the rituals of the *masiqta*.	37	37	282				
GR 2:1:100	Glorious promises to those who ascend to the realm of Light.	44-45	42	246				
GR 2:1:118-122a	Description of the ages of the world. The victims of the Flood and of the destruction by fire (Sodom?) "are not sinners but among the righteous who will 'ascend to the light'" (E. Lupieri, *Mandaeans*, p. 199).	48-50	45-46		199-200			
GR 2:1:139-150, 154	Anti-Christian account describing Jesus and His apostles as deceivers.	54-58	50-52	307-309	240-243		549-551	
GR 2:1:151-153	This brief passage provides a good summary of Mandaean teachings about the life of John the Baptist, the baptism of Jesus, and John's death and ascension.	57	51	308	224-225		550	
GR 2:1:158-159	Jesus is likened to evil mythological figures.	58-59	52-53		251			
GR 2:1:160-161	Polemic against the planets and against Christianity.	59-60	53		211			
GR 2:1:164	After Muhammad brings wretchedness to the world, prophecy will cease and faith will disappear from the earth.	61	54		254			
GR 2:3	Description of the "Messenger of Light."	64-66	57-61	227-230				
GR 2:4	Polemic against the Christian practices of celibacy and virginity.	67	61-62		252			
GR 3:1	The origin of the worlds of light	68-69	65	154-155				

Section	Description	Pet	Lid	WF	EL	OB	GB	Haa
GR 3:1	A description of the emanation of the Second Life, comprising the various *uthras* (= "riches," meaning a class of semi-divine beings), *malkia* (= sovereigns), or *malakia* (= angels) that populate the Lightworld. Before that time, only the wholeness of the divinity existed (E. Lupieri, *Mandaeans*, pp. 175-176).	69-70	66-67	155-156	176-178		537-538	353-355
GR 3:1	The primeval descent into hell of the envoy.	71-74	68-70	204				355-359
GR 3:1	Descriptions of the rebellious and of darkness. The messenger questions the Life.	74-76	70-73	163-164		126-127	538-540	
GR 3:1	The world beyond.	75-76	73	156-157		125-126	537	
GR 3:1	The Life is questioned about the origin of darkness. No answer follows, only instruction.	76-79	73-78	164-166		127	540-541	
GR 3:1	Concerning the arch-demon Ruha. Soteriology "concerned chiefly with the release of the soul from the body after death and its joyful return to its homeland. This is prefigured in the primeval history by Adam" (W. Foerster, *Gnosis*, p. 204).	80-92	79-95	167, 184, 204-214		697-698	541-542	
GR 3:1	Manda d-Hiia draws off a channel of living water (baptismal water, the Jordan) for the world, to save the fallen soul.	92	96	186, 202				
GR 3:1	Cosmogony describing the actions of Ptahil and Ruha in the creation of the earth.	93-95	97-99	170-176	183-186	127-132		360-370
GR 3:1	The creation of Adam as king of the world. Adam's soul is placed in his body with the personal participation of the supreme deity.	100-104	107-113	187-192	187-191	134-138	543-548	370-376
GR 3:1	The reaction of the wicked and the renewed intervention of the world of light on behalf of Adam; the origin of the heavenly Adamites. Three 'uthras appointed to instruct Adam and Eve in the ordinances and in prayer.	104-108	113-119	193-198				378-379
GR 3:1	The wicked ones forge secret plans and oaths to eliminate the call of Life into the World shut out from light. The Mysteries of Love will be used to ensnare the World. The wicked say the world belongs to them.	109-110	120-121					379-381
GR 3:1	The man and the woman were made from a single body.	116	130	202-203				
GR 3:1	The violence and deception of Muhammad's followers.	122	137		258			
GR 5:1	Hibil's descent into hell before the creation of the world, revealing the name and sign of the King of Darkness. He obtains a passport for his return.	142-144	156-158	215-216				
GR 5:1	On the origin of Darkness.	149	161	167				
GR 5:1	Hibil purloins utensils and a mirror from the worlds of darkness, and marries one of the daughters of the underworld. Ur is born to Ruha and Gap. Ur invades the world of light, but is bound and immured. A second attempt also fails.	162-167	169 ff.	217-220				
GR 5:1	Hibil-Ziua's descent into hell. Hibil installs the seven and twelve sons he begets by Ruha. Ptahil creates the world using Abatur's mantle of light.	168-172	174 f.	180-181				
GR 5:2	A description of the appearance of the messengers of light. The passage quotes Psalm 29:114.	173	177	236-237				
GR 5:2	A description of how Manda d-Hiia revealed himself in Jerusalem.	178, 179	181, 182	300-301				
GR 5:4	There are two sections of this passage. "The first deals with the arrival of Manda d-Hiia at the Jordan, with his baptism not performed, and with the death of John and his burial. The second deals with the ascent of the soul of John… and the connected reintegration of Ptahil and Abatur, who were met during the journey" (E. Lupieri, *Mandaeans*, p. 234).	188-196	190-196		234-238			

Section	Description	Pet	Lid	WF	EL	OB	GB	Haa
GR 9:1	Polemic against other religions, called the "collapse of the seven stars."	222-234	223-234		204-210, 258-260			
GR 10:1	Godly Mandaeans will be received in the House of Life.	240	241	214				
GR 10:1	The creation of Adam and Eve, and the "virgin birth" of Hibil.	241	242	198-199				
GR 10:1	The role of Hibil in the cosmogony.	241	243	185				
GR 10:1	Some remarkable views about Adakas.	243-245	244 ff.	199-200				
GR 10:1	Three sets of twins are born to Eve.	245	245	199				
GR 11:1	The "pouring out of the living waters" of baptism into the turbid waters.	269	266	185-186				
GR 12:2	The saving truth (*kusta*) is praised in an old acrostic psalm, recited, e.g., at wedding ceremonies.	274-275	271-272	234-235				
GR 12:6	Describes the world of the King of darkness below Tibil, the created world.	278-281	277-279	159-162	179-181			
GR 12:6	Continuation of the description of the world of darkness	281-282	279 f.	162				
GR 13:1	The connection of the emanations of Life with other beings	284	283	158				
GR 13:1	Ptahil, the creator.	286	284	185				
GR 14:1	Ptahil creates the planets.	298	294	181				
GR 15:2	Hibil as a gentle vine.	234	301	234				
GR 15:3	Baptism was devised when Adam was formed. Silmai and Nidbai, the angels of baptism, were given knowledge and a message to rouse and waken those who sleep, and to perform the healing ordinance of baptism.	308-309	307-309	277-278				
GR 15:3	At the end of time, Tibil will be destroyed forever, the spirit of the Seven and the Twelve shall meet its end, and sentence will be pronounced on Yosamin, Abathur, and Ptahil. Then these three fallen beings of light shall receive the baptism of purification in the heavenly Jordan.	310-311	311	276				395-397
GR 15:10	The four stages or emanations of the Pleroma.	325	331-332	158				
GR 15:10	Manda d-Hiia descends to the earth.	328	335	215				
GR 15:11	Two stories that describe the origins of Judaism and the persecution of the Mandaeans in efforts by the evil Ruha/Namrus to thwart the purposes of Anus Uthra.	328-333	336-344	302-307	217-220			
GR 15:13	Cosmogony describing the creation of the earth by Ptahil and Abathur. Ptahil is commanded to create two "solidifications": *Msunne-Kusta* (Paradise) and *Tibil* (Earth).	336-338	348-351	177-178	181-182	132-134	542	
GR 15:13	An account of "creation by the word."	339	351	178-179		134	542-543	
GR 15:13	Ptahil's disobedience is punished, and Hibil-Ziua is sent to set the world in order.	340	351-352	179				
GR 15:14	The Life as a demiurge.	341	354	185				
GR 15:19	The fall of the soul into darkness and its deliverance, for which Adam is the prototype.	358	377-378	224-225		698		382
GR 16:2	Instruction of Adam by an *'uthra*. He is admonished to forsake the illusory things of the world and remember his Lord.	364-365	387	293		701-702		
GR 16:4	A prayer for the perfect ones.	366-367	389-390	225-226				
GR 16:5	From the day I came to love the Life, I have no trust in the world. I went and found my soul—what are the worlds to me? (cf. Matthew 16:26)	367	390	293-294				

Section	Description	Pet	Lid	WF	EL	OB	GB	Haa
GR 16:8	A psalm of deliverance.	369-370	393-394	226-227				
GR 16:9	A prayer to *Kusta*.	370	394-395	235-236				
GR 17:1	Adam, his companion, and the elect righteous are called forth.	372	400	203				
GR 18:1	A history from the time of creation and a prophecy to the end of time. Foresees an end to Islamic domination of the region after only seventy-one years, allowing the text to be dated between 639-710 CE.	378-381	407-410		200-202			
GR 18:1	An account of the ancient creation of Jerusalem by Adunai, Ruha, and the seven planets. Abraham is born, goes to Egypt, the Israelites return to Jerusalem by the passage through the Red Sea, and eventually Jesus is born and founds a church.	381-382	410-411		131, 216			
GR 18:1	A long composite list of sovereigns who purportedly reigned from the time of the Flood to the completion of the years of the kings. The predicted end of the world can be calculated to the year 844 CE.				316 n. 13 (summary)			
GL 1:1	Adam, not wanting to die, convinces God to have Sitil (Seth) die in his place. Description of the faithfulness of Hibil, Sitil, and Anos.	1-9	424-429	272-274, 300	191-194			
GL 1:2	Adam, not wanting to die, finally accepts his destiny.	9-19	430-438	181-182, 274-275	195-198, 224			
GL 1:3	Eve laments for her dead husband.							
GL 1:4	A description of the soul's journey through celestial places of detention.	26-38	443-452	246-251				
GL 2:1	The soul complains about its having been placed in the body, and rejoices in its release and return to its former home with the Father.	38-40	454-456	253-254				
GL 2:4	The soul complains about being cast into the house of Ptahil.	42	459	182				
GL 2:5	The soul complains about its having been placed in the body, and rejoices in its planter (or helper) that will release it and cause it to ascend.	43-44	461-462	254-256				
GL 2:6	Ptahil and the planets he created shall be accursed and destroyed.	44	462	182				
GL 2:7	The soul complains about its lot, and praises the planter (or helper) that will fetch him after it has endured to the end.	45	463	256-257				
GL 2:8	The soul complains about its body, and is promised that it will eventually leave this world.	46	465	257				
GL 2:12	The soul asks for a boundary-stone and a crier. Its complaint will be answered. Because it endured the persecution of the world, its sins shall be forgiven.	51-52	472	258				
GL 2:14	At the end of time, when the heaven and the earth pass away, Ptahil shall receive his garment and will be baptized in the Jordan.	56	478	275-276				
GL 2:16	The *mana* or the hidden Adam is admonished to take on a body, and is promised that it will be protected and will rise through the mysteries, the luminaries (sun and moon), and the help of guardians.	59	483	258-259				
GL 2:18	The old significance of Adakas.	61-62	486-487	200-202				383-384
GL 2:21	The planets are fettered; Adam is protected and washed, and ascends to the House of Life.	65-66	492	259		698-699		

Section	Description	Pet	Lid	WF	EL	OB	GB	Haa
GL 2:25	The Evil ones vent their anger and vow to cut Adam off from his Place of Origin. Adam ceases to ask about transitory things, and ascends to the place from which he was transplanted.	69-71	498-500	259-260				390-392
GL 2:26	Praises to Hibil who made a path to the Place of Light.	71	500	260-261				
GL 3:1	Darkness (= the underworld) is identified with the sublunar world and the Tibil, or with the "body" (microcosm).	74-76	505-507	221-223				
GL 3:3	The soul is admonished to rise up to its first (i.e., former) earth.	78-79	511-512	261-262		699		384-386
GL 3:5-6	The soul finds bliss and peace on the road of Adam, is met by an escort at the gate of the House of Life who bears a wreath and a garment, and joins in communion with the Life, who stretches out His hand.	80-81	513-515	262-263		699-700		
GL 3:9	The soul expresses its reluctance to return to the body.	84	519	223-224				
GL 3:10	The head of the believers, marked with the sign, is challenged by the Seven planets, but refuses to give them his head, eyes, ears, mouth, hands, heart, knees, or feet, which take him to the Place of Light. Manda d-Hiia led his beloved ones to victory and saved their souls from sin.	86-87	522-523	263-264				
GL 3:12	The soul is guided past the heavenly watchhouses by its reward, its works, its alms, and its goodness. At the water-brooks, a discharge of radiance took the soul by the palm of the right hand and brought it over the streams to reach the Life.	89-90	525-527	265		700-701		
GL 3:15	A chosen one is protected by an *uthra,* who destroys the houses of the tollkeepers [watchhouses] and makes possible his escape from the Tibil.	94-95	532-534	265-266				388-390
GL 3:16	The father, the *uthra,* is the soul's helper; the soul is the slave of the alien, of the man who is a supporter.	96-97	535-536	267				
GL 3:19	The soul is questioned on the way to judgment about its good works. It replies that it gave alms, shared bread, sustained orphans and widows, clothed the naked, and released the prisoner (cf. Matthew 25:31-46).	100-101	541-542	294-295				
GL 3:23	The prison warden is told to torment the wicked until the Great Life sits in judgment, and the wicked come to be questioned.	105	548	268				
GL 3:24	The redeemer, a soul of radiance, enters Sheol (Hell) and commands the warden to open the gate for the imprisoned souls. The sinners (adulterers, thieves, sorcerers, soothsayers, etc.) receive a recompense for their chains and are separated from the Place of Darkness for the Place of Light.	106	549	267-268				
GL 3:25	The world is surrounded with a Wall of Iron like a Garland, with no breach in it. The redeemer converses with the soul in the Tibil, promising to make a bridge across the river, to be a guide past the flames of fire, to make a path over the high mountain, and to hack a breach in the iron wall.	107-108	550-551	268-269			553	392-394
GL 3:30	The great *mana* dwelt in the sea until wings were fashioned and he flew to the Place of Light.	111-112	557	269				
GL 3:38	The soul protests the spirit's request to go with it to the scales, but is weighed and found perfect, and the spirit was joined to the soul.	117-118	566-567	269				
GL 3:41	The soul complains about being cast into Tibil.	118	569					394
GL 3:42	The soul asks, "Who cast me into the Tibil, chained me, and clothed me in a coat of all colors and kinds?"	119-120	570	270		700	551	

Section	Description	Pet	Lid	WF	EL	OB	GB	Haa
GL 3:43	The deceased Mandaean sleeps in death, interred in his sacral garment. Adam awakes, takes him by the palm of his right hand, and places a palm-branch in his hand. The soul shall draw near to the clouds of light on a course to the Place of Light.	120	571	270		700	551-552	
GL 3:47	The *mana* (soul) is a crown cast down to the earth from the House of Life. Through the strength and illumination of the father, it is not led astray.	122	574-575	270-271				394-395
GL 3:48-50	Manda d-Hiia came to the help of the soul. He awakened it out of sleep, brought the seven into confusion, and drew it out of its physical, perishable garment to be clad in splendor.	123	576-577					376-378
GL 3:51	The soul comes from Tibil. An older description of the soul's journey through celestial places of detention.	124-128	578-582	182, 251-253			552-553	
GL 3:53	The children of the departed souls worship Manda d-Hiia, the great healer.	127	583	271				
GL 3:56	The Seven attempt to block the way of the ascending soul, who raises his eyes to the Great Life. The son of Life opened the doors, revealed himself as the firmament was split, clothed the soul with light, and bestowed a wreath of radiance.	130	586	271-272				
GL 3:57	The soul was led astray by earthly baubles, but if its sins are removed it will rise. If not, it will suffer a second death.	132	588	272				
GL 3:58-59	The soul abandons its body and speaks to it. The Envoys of Life say, "Come, come, thou Pearl fetched out of the Treasure of Life," urging it to ascend to the Place of Light.	133-134	589-590					386-388
GL 3:61	The four stages or emanations of the Pleroma.	136	594	157				

Exoteric Texts

Text Name	Description	English Publication Reference
Qulasta (Liturgies, The Canonical Prayerbook of the Mandaeans)	"The main collection is called Qulasta (originally 'Hymns of Praise,' then 'Collection of Writings') and includes over 400 texts… In addition…, other important parts are: Sidra d-Nismata ('The Book of Souls'), containing liturgies for the masbuta, and then hymns and prayers for the masiqta—among the prayers, we should recall Asut Malkia ('The Greeting of/to the Kings'), a prayer for everyday purification; Rhamia (everyday prayers); Abahutan Qadmaiia ('Our First Fathers'), and then prayers for weddings, for ordaining priests… and so forth" (E. Lupieri, Mandaeans, p. 54).	E. S. Drower, Prayerbook. English translations of passages from this work have also been included in W. Barnstone, et al., Gnostic, pp. 561-565; W. Barnstone, Other; R. Haardt, Gnosis; G. R. S. Mead, Mandaean John-Book; K. Rudolph, Coptic. A German translation of a less complete version of the liturgies was published in 1920 (M. Lidzbarski, Liturgien).
Drasia d-Iahia (The Book/Words of John) or Drasia d-Malkia (The Book/Words of the Kings)	Seen as an exemplar of a true Mandaean, "John the Baptist has given name to this book, which was probably compiled in order to give the Muslims a reason to view the Mandaeans as owners of a prophetic book. But it is not only a book about John, for it contains extensive passages dealing with cosmogony and cosmology, similar to those in Ginza [e.g., chapter 13]" (J. O. Ryen, Mandaean Vine, p. 45). The book contains seventy-six chapters, with stories of John (and Jesus, the "false Messiah") being contained in chapters 18-33. A brief summary of Mandaean teachings about the life of John is also found in GR 2:1:151-153 (see E. Lupieri, Mandaeans, p. 225). Allegorical pieces describe the Good Shepherd (chapters 11-12), the Fisher of Souls (chapters 36-39), and the Treasury of Life (chapter 57). Chapter 76 is "devoted to the conflict between two saviors, one Christian and one Mandaean, in Jerusalem" (E. Lupieri, Mandaeans, p. 246). Chapters 14-17 recount the prayers of Shum bar Nu (Shem, the son of Noah) and the comfort he receives as he leaves the world. The "Legend of Mirai" (chapters 34-35) tells the story of a young woman in Jerusalem, a daughter of the kings, who disobeys her father and mother and converts to Mandaeism. She becomes an example of faithfulness in the face of oppression. The origin of the legend is debated, but Lupieri sees it "in the reworking of Christian legends on the adolescent Mary in the temple, placed on trial by the Judaic authorities since she was found to be pregnant and therefore considered unworthy" (E. Lupieri, Mandaeans, p. 220; see M. Barker, Infancy Gospel of James, 1:13-16, pp. 156-157).	Lidzbarki's German edition remains the best full translation of this work (M. Lidzbarski, Johannesbuch). Israel's sectarian translation of the full English text attempts to correct what are taken to be "offending alterations" of the original text (e.g., disparaging references to Jesus Christ), but with only minimal editorial justification and with little or no critical apparatus (D. A. Israel, Secret Teachings). Mead's 1924 edition of selections from chapters 11-13, 18-39, 47, and 57 is the best translation of these chapters in English (G. R. S. Mead, Mandaean John-Book). An English version of "Hibil's Lament" (chapter 55) can be found in W. Barnstone, et al., Gnostic, p. 555-560, and a translation and commentary on chapter 76 is given in E. Lupieri, Mandaeans, pp. 246-250. Passages from the Book of John have also been included in W. Barnstone, Other; R. Haardt, Gnosis; E. Lupieri, Mandaeans; Y. Nasrai, John; K. Rudolph, Coptic.
Haran Gauaita (Inner Haran)	"This writing can be read as a mixture of history and myth, telling the story of the Mandaeans' exodus from Jerusalem [under King Artaban] via Haran to Babylonia and the settlement in the land of the two rivers" (J. O. Ryen, Mandaean Vine, p. 45). The story includes a valuable account of the coming of Islam and Arab occupation, and continues the story to the end of the world.	E. S. Drower, Haran, pp. 3-23

Esoteric Texts

Text Name	Description	English Publication Reference
Sarh d-Qabin d-Sislam Rba (Explanation of the Marriage of Sislam the Great)	"This contains the marriage ritual. Sislam Rba (Sislam the Great) is a quite recent figure in the Mandaean pantheon and is the celestial model of the Mandaean priest. Some of the prayers here are said aloud at the marriage of the priests. There is also a calendar with the propitious and unpropitious times for the wedding indicated" (E. Lupieri, Mandaeans, p. 56). Though the texts of this and similar Mandaean ritual commentaries are linguistically "younger," Buckley argues that they offer information of great antiquity (J. J. Buckley, Mandaeans, p. 97).	E. S. Drower, Marriage of Sislam
Sarh d-Trasa d-Taga d-Sislam Rba (Explanation of the Coronation of Sislam the Great)	"This contains primarily the ritual for the ordination of a ganzibra and its (esoteric) explanation" (E. Lupieri, Mandaeans, p. 56).	E. S. Drower, Coronation of Sislam

Text Name	Description	English Publication Reference
Sarh d-paruanaiia (Explanation of the Parwanaia)	This manuscript concerns the Mandaean feast *paruanaiia* (= five), so named because it falls on the five days of the year that fall outside the twelve thirty-day months (E. Lupieri, *Mandaeans*, p. 19; J. O. Ryen, *Mandaean Vine*, p. 46).	Published in German translation (B. Burtea, *Magischer Text*; B. Burtea, *d-paruanaiia*).
Alp Trisar Suialia (The Thousand and Twelve Questions)	"The manuscript contains a treatise of the same title where in the form of question and answer among celestial beings the cult and the rituals are esoterically interpreted. This is followed by *Tapsir Pagra* (Explanation of the Body), a fragmentary text containing speculations on the correspondence between the microcosm (the human body) and the macrocosm (the universe). Then there is 'Blow and Cure,' a short treatise on purification (the 'cure') for ritual impurities (the 'blows')" (E. Lupieri, *Mandaeans*, pp. 56-57).	E. S. Drower, *Thousand*. The book is out-of-print and very difficult to find. A passage on the proper use of the girdle or waistband (1:2:250) is included in E. Lupieri, *Mandaeans*, pp. 211-212. "The Head Is One World" (1:2:217-226) can be found in W. Barnstone, *Other*, pp. 138-140.
Alma Risaia Rba (First Great World, Macrocosm) and Alma Risaia Zuta (First Small World, Microcosm)	"There are speculations on the relation between the macrocosm and the microcosm. *ARR* provides the esoteric explanation of the *masiqta*, while in *ARZ* Hibil Ziua explains the *dukrana* [= commemoration or remembrance of the dead]. The manuscript contains interesting colophons" (E. Lupieri, *Mandaeans*, p. 57).	E. S. Drower, *Nasorean*
Diuan d-Masbuta d-Hibil Ziua (The Book of the Baptism of Hibil Ziua)	"The text explains how a contaminated priest can purify himself (analogous to what Hibil Ziua had to perform having descended into the darkness in prehistoric times). The manuscript contains interesting colophons" (E. Lupieri, *Mandaeans*, p. 57).	E. S. Drower, *Haran*, p. 24-96
Diuan Abatur (The Book of Abatur)	"The scroll, with a wealth of illustrations, describes the journey of the soul across the *matarata*, the celestial purgatorial houses. The Abatur referred to in the title is the 'Abatur of the balances,' the judge of the otherworld. The text is relatively recent but is perhaps the oldest known in Europe since a copy was sent to Rome by Ignatius of Jesus around 1650 (and is now preserved in the Vatican Library)" (E. Lupieri, *Mandaeans*, p. 57I).	E. S. Drower, *Abatur*
Diuan d-Nahrauata (The Book of the Rivers)	"The text is a kind of geographical atlas with the religious and symbolic geography of the celestial world (and of Lower Mesopotamia, of which the celestial world is in some ways a projection). There are illustrations of canals, rivers, springs, trees, and hills. There is also Jerusalem and the temple, represented, respectively, by a rectangle and a circle (the scribe is thinking of the 'dome of the temple') and both placed on the Euphrates-Splendor (Pras Ziua)" (E. Lupieri, *Mandaeans*, p. 58).	The only translation is in German (K. Rudolph, *Flüsse*).
Diuan Malkuta 'Laita (The Book of Exalted Kingship)	"This text contains a detailed description of a part of the initiation ritual for the Mandaean priest, the *tarmida*" (E. Lupieri, *Mandaeans*, p. 58). It also contains "interesting references to the hymns of *The Canonical Prayerbook*, and interpretations of these" (J. O. Ryen, *Mandaean Vine*, pp. 46-47).	J. J. Buckley, *Exalted Kingship*
Spar Maluasia (The Book of the Zodiacal Signs)	"This book contains material of very composite nature, including determinations of the astrological number (hidden name) of the new-born child; medical prescriptions in connection with different illnesses; and prophecies of the coming year based on star constellations" (J. O. Ryen, *Mandaean Vine*, p. 47).	E. S. Drower, *Zodiac*
Magical Texts	"Texts of this kind are written on small tablets, leaden scrolls, amulets, and vases" (J. O. Ryen, *Mandaean Vine*).	See, e.g., A. Caquot, *Phylactère*; E. S. Drower, *Shafta*; E. S. Drower, *Phylacteries*; E. S. Drower, *Black Magic*; E. S. Drower, *Phylactery*; C. Müller-Kessler, *Amulet*; E. M. Yamauchi, *Incantation*.

Manichaean Texts

Mirecki gives the following succinct overview of Manichaeism:

> Manichaeism was one of the major world religions and the only such religion to align itself closely with late antiquity's Near Eastern Gnostic tradition. Previously considered by Western scholars to be a Christian heresy, Manichaeism is now properly understood in the context of third-century Mesopotamian religions. The religion was founded by the Iranian prophet Mani (216-277 CE), who deliberately created a universal and propagandistic religion that incorporates Christian, Zoroastrian, and Buddhist concepts. Whether Manichaeism is properly designated as Gnostic, as Hans Jonas and others have suggested, is being debated by scholars. The religion moved east toward India and west into the Roman Empire already in Mani's lifetime, reaching as far west as Algiers and southern Europe and as far east as Central Asia and southeast coastal China, where traces of the religion datable to the early seventeenth century can be identified.[207]

Life and Mission of Mani

According to the *Cologne Mani Codex (CMC),*[208] Mani was raised among a group of adherents to the teachings of Elchasai:

> Elchasai [was] a Jewish-Christian prophet who apparently lived during the early part of the second century CE and whose doctrines are otherwise known to us only from the hostile reports of Christian and Muslim heresiologists. These accounts depict Elchasai as a Jewish visionary who was the recipient of a "heavenly book" ultimately derived from the revelatory activity of two gigantic beings, identified as the Son of God (or "angel" or "Great King") and the Holy Spirit. According to the Christian accounts, this book prescribes a firm adherence to Jewish law, supplemented with a rigorous program of repetitive ablutions which are to atone for the recurrent defilements of daily life.[209] Followers of the teachings of Elchasai and/or his book are termed Helkesaites or Elchaseans are placed by the Church Fathers in Palestine, Syria, and the Transjordan, particularly around the region of the Dead Sea. The geographical distribution of these communities, coupled with certain observable similarities between the ritual customs of the Elchasaites and those of the earlier Second Temple Jewish sect of the Essenes as described by Josephus and Philo, have led some scholars to posit a genetic connection between these sects....

> Mani recounts his growing dissatisfaction with an eventual opposition to the teachings revered by the Elchasaites. His discontent was fueled by a series of "revelations" which he claimed to have received from a heavenly messenger. When the Elchasaites discovered that he was undermining the community on the basis of these "revelations," they summoned him before their *Sanhedrin* and expelled him from their midst. Mani thereupon began his travels for the purpose of propagating his "revelations."[210]

> Zoroaster does not figure in Mani's series of prophetic "revealers" at this stage of his life... One therefore concludes that the extent of Zoroastrian influence upon the young Mani has been overrated. The new textual evidence which has appeared over the last twenty years supplies a valuable corrective to earlier expositions of Mani's thought. These texts indicate that heterodox

---

207 P. Mirecki, *Manichaean Introduction*, p. 569. In 2004, Gardner and Lieu were astonished to find evidence of a continuing Mani cult in a village in the Fujian province of China (I. Gardner, *et al.*, *Living*).

208 R. Cameron, *et al.*, *CMC*.

209 Compare rites with a similar function described in *Annotated Bibliography, Mandaean Texts*, p. 867.

210 J. C. Reeves, *Jewish Lore*, pp. 2, 207-208.

Jewish thought, particularly that embodied in Enochic literature, was a powerful stimulus in the formulation of Mani's theology.[211]

Although it was said by Titus of Bostra that Mani attributed "the Old Testament fully and completely to the archons of Hyle [i.e., the princes of darkness],"[212] the biblical patriarchs Adam, Seth, Enosh, Enoch, Noah, Shem, and possibly Abraham[213] were honored as prophetic predecessors to Mani, "the Paraclete of truth" and "the seal of the prophets."[214] The stories of these prophets recounted in Manichaean literature, however, are not given "in their biblical guise" but rather in "an expanded and embellished form of these stories that we find in earlier Jewish pseudepigraphic works and rabbinic haggadic traditions":[215]

> While these earlier prophets [were seen by Mani as having] experienced some personal success in the promulgation of the teachings among their generations, their message was [said to have been] inevitably corrupted and distorted by its subsequent faulty (and in some cases deliberately falsified) transmission. The disciples and followers of each preceding apostle were overwhelmingly incompetent (and in some cases deceitful) custodians of the divine message. The results of their literary labors, whether well- or ill-intentioned, were the canonical scriptures of the ancestral religions: i.e., Judaism, Christianity, Zoroastrianism, and Buddhism… Herein lies… the basic reason for the Manichaean disparagement of earlier canonical scriptures.[216]

Heavenly Ascent in Manichaeism

The most essential of the "key credentials" governing inclusion in the line of Manichaean prophetic succession is a written account of "an ascent-experience."[217] Accordingly, as a prologue to the biography of Mani in the *CMC*, the figures of Adam, Seth, Enosh, Shem, and Enoch are each introduced by a citation purportedly excerpted from an apocalyptic "visionary experience" where "each seer is transported to heaven and views certain sights or is made privy to certain secrets" in a manner that suggests a close affinity both to the later Jewish genre of *Hekhalot*, and to earlier strands of what seems to be *Merkabah* mysticism in the teachings of Elchasai.[218] Mani, of course, also claimed to be adept at the practice of heavenly ascent.[219]

The symbolism of heavenly ascent was incorporated into Manichaean scripture and ritual. The "descent of the First Man from the land of light," his redemption, and his return to the kingdom was a "favorite theme," and was "in a very real sense the story of each soul."[220] The *Kephalaia* speaks of "five lessons" (38, 5) that were successively bestowed upon the First Man as he took his leave from the gods, the angels, and the Mother of Life.[221] Later, "when he ascended from the war, he came in to the kingdom of the household of his people by these [same] five mysteries," performing each of them anew as he was "brought upward out from the struggle" (39:7-11; 39,21). Likewise each disciple will perform these five things in the church, and "the last of these things shall be bequeathed upon them from the right hand

---

211   *Ibid.*, p. 209.
212   Cited in J. C. Reeves, *Manichaean Literature*, p. 173.
213   See *Endnote B-12*, p. 906.
214   J. C. Reeves, *Jewish Lore*, p. 4 n. 4; J. C. Reeves, *Manichaean Literature*, p. 174; J. C. Reeves, *Heralds*, pp. 7-15. See *Endnote B-13*, p. 906.
215   See *Endnote B-14*, p. 906.
216   J. C. Reeves, *Manichaean Literature*, pp. 174-175.
217   J. C. Reeves, *Heralds*, p. 16.
218   J. C. Reeves, *Manichaean Literature*, pp. 176-178.
219   *Ibid.*, pp. 178-181.
220   I. Gardner, *Kephalaia*, p. 42.
221   Cf. *Excursus 51: The Five Lost Things of the Temple*, p. 658.

of charity" (41,5). In recapitulating the experiences of Adam, these ritual acts also prefigure the actions that Manichaean disciples will perform after death when, "[a]t the time of their coming forth… the angel who holds the victory prize extends to him the right hand. And it draws him out of the abyss of his body, and accepts him in with the kiss and love. That soul shall make obeisance to its redeemer" (41,11; 41,17-21). He "shall be perfected and increased… in the household of the living ones, with the gods and the angels and all the apostles and the chosen. And he receives the crown […] glory in the life for ever" (41,22-25).[222]

Hegemonius "tells how this 'Living Spirit' descends to the "Door,' extends her right hand to the candidate, and draws him back into the Light; 'on this account, the Manichaeans, if they meet each other, give their right hands as a sign of having been saved from the Darkness.'"[223]

Overview of Manichaean Stories about Adam and Eve and the Creation

The Manichaean scheme embraced not only such rituals as the above, but also "a highly complex historical drama of supracosmic proportions in which humanity's past origin, present predicament, and future possibilities are described," as summarized by Mirecki:[224]

> In the past time there existed two eternal principles, one all good and the other all evil. The good principle exists exclusively within the kingdom of light and finds its focus in the father of greatness, whose fourfold majesty embraces divinity, light, power, and goodness. His throne is surrounded by at least 156 peace-loving entities: twelve aeons (or eternal realms, in three groups of four each) and 144 aeons of aeons. The kingdom of light is constructed of five elements or *stoichea* (air, wind, light, water, and fire) and contains five peaceful "dwellings" (intelligence, knowledge, reason, thought, and deliberation). (In Manichaeism many things are given in five, even the five trees of paradise reminiscent of the *Gospel of Thomas* 19.[225]) The evil principle and the kingdom of darkness are the complete antitheses of the good principle and the kingdom of light. The many monstrous and agitated inhabitants of the kingdom of darkness are ruled by five evil archons (demon, lion, eagle, fish, and dragon), who are in constant opposition to each other and who, collectively, make up the hellish prince of darkness. They are sexually preoccupied and controlled by their passions, and they dwell in an ominous netherworld of smoke, fire, wind, water, and darkness. The two kingdoms are completely distinct yet eternally coexistent.[226]
>
> The "present time" begins when the evil inhabitants of the kingdom of darkness [launch a full-scale invasion of] the kingdom of light in a lustful desire to mingle with the light… The father of greatness responds by evoking a series of entities who may need to be sacrificed to the invaders so as to satisfy them and stop the assault. The first evocation is the mother of life, who then evokes the primal man, who fights the incoming forces of darkness but loses his battle. The five evil *archons* (who constitute the prince of darkness) then consume some of the light elements of the primal man's armor. Having unwittingly fallen into the trap of the father of greatness, they are now dependent on the light for their continued existence. The primal man awakes from his sleep of forgetfulness, remembers his divine origins, and prays for his rescue. The father of greatness responds by evoking a series of beings who initiate the rescue of the primal man… The living spirit cries out from the kingdom of light into the darkness to the primal man, who answers. The cry and answer (representing the divine word of salvation and

---

222   I. Gardner, *Kephalaia*, 9, pp. 43-46; cf. J. K. Elliott, *Pearl*; E. Hennecke, *et al.*, *NT Apocrypha*, 2:498-504; M. R. James, *Apocryphal*, pp. 411-415. See *Commentary* 1:25-c, p. 60; *Figure* 6-14, p. 473; *Excursus 53: Comparative Explorations, Dexiosis*, p. 681; the *Mandaean Texts* section of the *Annotated Bibliography*, p. 870; *Figure* B-1, p. 872. See *Endnote 1-22*, p. 79.

223   J. E. Seaich, *Ancient Texts 1995*, p. 886, citing *Acta Archelai* 7, 4-5.

224   P. Mirecki, *Manichaean Introduction*, pp. 575-578.

225   H. Koester, *et al.*, *Thomas*, 19, p. 128.

226   See *Endnote B-15*, p. 906.

the positive human response) are hypostasized, that is, they become divine beings who ascend to the kingdom of light. The living spirit then grasps the primal man by the hand and rescues him from the kingdom of darkness.

The rest of the drama in the "present time" focuses on the work of the father of greatness to regain all of the light particles swallowed by the five evil *archons*... [The creation of the universe, the earth, plants, and animals is described as a complicated affair of emanation and sexual generation.] The sum total of all these precious light particles trapped in deadly matter, including plants and animals, is called the suffering Jesus (Jesus *patibilis*), who is on the light cross (*crux luminus*).

The prince of darkness, in an attempt to frustrate the cosmic distillation of light particles, gives birth to the two evil demons, Sakla (Ashqulan) and Nebroel (Namrael)... The two demons copulate, then Nebroel gives birth to exact miniature replicas (the "image of God" of Genesis 1:26-27) of the confused light-matter macrocosm: Adam and Eve. In a typically Gnostic "inverted exegesis" of Genesis 1-5..., the sexually oriented evil creator can create only by copulation and birth, and so can create only matter (which is inherently evil). He is unable to create in the manner of the father of greatness, by asexually evoking pure spiritual entities. Consequently, Adam (representing humanity) is specifically designed by the evil creator in his own image[227] to procreate sexually.[228] Thus, Adam can only continue the evil cycle of birth, copulation, and rebirth, and in so doing he fulfills his natural evil inclination to "be fruitful and multiply."[229] Adam's evil material nature (representing human sexuality) thus entangles the precious light particles, transmitted through male seed, in potentially endless generations of material bodies (representing human history[230]).

But Adam is ignorant of the light within him and his true origin in the kingdom of light and so is unable to recognize and redeem the light particles. The evocations of the father of greatness then send Jesus of light to awaken Adam[231] to inform him of his true nature[232] and to lead him to self-recognition.[233] Jesus of light helps Adam eat of the salvific tree of life,[234] warns him of the dangers of sexual procreation with Eve, and so encourages a sexually abstinent lifestyle (the ideal model of behavior in Manichaean ethics). Then Eve and a male *archon* copulate, and Eve gives birth to Cain,[235] who then copulates with his mother Eve, who gives birth to Abel,[236] and so begins the incestuous interaction of Cain[237] and Abel with Eve and with each other's daughters borne by Eve.[238] Eve then receives magical knowledge from an evil *archon*, which enables her to copulate with ascetic Adam. She succeeds in her desire and bears Seth,[239] who, as the first true son of Adam,[240] contains a significantly larger amount of light particles than the other offspring of Eve. The ascetic Adam and Seth, self-conscious particles of light entrapped in innately evil material bodies, become the exemplary human figures for Manichaean ethics.[241]

The "future time" is the third and final act of the historical cosmic drama, and it provides for Manichaean ethics a preview into the system of reward and punishment. The final and great

---

227 Moses 2:26.
228 Moses 2:27-28.
229 Moses 2:28; 5:2.
230 See Moses 6:1-22.
231 I.e., the serpent (Moses 4:5).
232 Moses 4:10-11.
233 Moses 4:13, 17, 28.
234 Moses 4:28.
235 Moses 5:16.
236 Moses 5:17.
237 *Ibid.*
238 Moses 5:42.
239 Moses 6:2.
240 Moses 6:10-11.
241 Moses 6:3-23.

war will break out among the unenlightened powers of darkness when the distillation of light particles from the material cosmos has neared its completion. Jesus will return at a decisive eschatological moment as the great king and will judge humanity and the infernal powers. The elect will become angels, the auditors will be judged righteous, and the sinners will be cast into hell with the sexually promiscuous woman Eve and her hellish offspring. The cosmos will disintegrate and burn in a conflagration for 1,468 years. The remaining light particles will be gathered and finally return by ascent to the kingdom of light, while the prince of darkness and his diabolical minions will be cast into a bottomless pit permanently sealed with a huge stone for all eternity. The two principles of light and darkness will again be two separate and distinct entities, never again to commingle.

A Manichaean Version of the Creation and Fall of Man

The following passage, with the heading title of "The Beginning of Sexual Reproduction According to the Teaching of Mani," is found in the *Kitab al-Fehrest*, the most famous work of the tenth-century Persian Muslim author Abu'l-Faraj Muhammad bin Ishaq al-Nadim:[242]

> He (Mani) said, "Then one of those *archons*, the stars, urgent force, desire, lust, and sin had sexual intercourse, and the result of their intercourse was the first man, who was Adam. That which produced this (was the union of) two archons, male and female. Then intercourse took place once more, and its result was the beautiful woman, who was Eve."

> He (Mani) said, "When the five angels[243] saw the divine Light and Goodness which Desire had plundered and bound as captive within those two who had been born, they asked *al-Bashir* (= the Messenger), the Mother of Life, Primal Man, and the Living Spirit to send to this first-born creature someone to release and deliver him, to teach him knowledge and piety, and to deliver him from the satans."

> He (Mani) said: "They thus sent Jesus, along with (another) deity. They approached the two *archons*, confined them, and rescued the two who had been born."

> He (Mani) said: "Then Jesus came and spoke to the one who had been born, who was Adam, and explained to him (about) the gardens (of Paradise), the deities, *Gehenna* [= hell], the satans, earth, heaven, sun, and moon. He also made him fear Eve, showing him how to suppress (desire) for her, and he forbade him to approach her, and made him fear to be near her, so that he did (what Jesus commanded). Then that (male) *archon* came back to his daughter, who was Eve, and lustfully had intercourse with her. He engendered with her a son, deformed in shape and possessing a red complexion, and his name was Cain, the Red Man.[244] Then that son had intercourse with his mother, and engendered with her a son of white complexion, whose name was Abel, the White Man. Then Cain again had intercourse with his mother, and engendered with her two girls, one of whom was named Hakimat al-Dahr[245] and the other Ibnat al-Hirs.[246] Then Cain took Ibnat al-Hirs as his wife and presented Hakimat al-Dahr to Abel, and he took her as his wife."

> He (Mani) said: "In Hakimat al-Dahr there was a residue of the Light of God and His Wisdom, but there was none of this (present) in Ibnat al-Hirs. Then one of the angels[247] came to Hakimat al-Dahr and said to her, 'Watch yourself, for you will give birth to two girls who will fulfill

---

242 English translation in J. C. Reeves, *Genesis 2-4* from I. al-Nadim, *Fihrist*, 58.11-61.13. For a detailed commentary, see J. C. Reeves, *Heralds*, pp. 79-81, 100-104.

243 Presumably the five members of the Realm of Light (J. C. Reeves, *Heralds*, p. 100 n. 86).

244 Reeves notes an association with the tradition that Cain was conceived by intercourse of Eve with Satan, based on "creative exegesis" of Moses 5:1 (*ibid.*, pp. 100-101 n. 89).

245 = Wise (One) of the Age, suggesting, perhaps, the figure of Sophia (*ibid.*, p. 101 n. 92).

246 = Daughter of Greed (*ibid.*, p. 101 n. 93).

247 "This does not seem to be an *archon*, and the episode possesses a distinct non-Manichaean flavor" (*ibid.*, p. 102 n. 96).

the pleasure of God.' He had sexual intercourse with her and she gave birth because of him to two girls, and she named one of them (Rau)-Faryād and the other Bar-Faryād.[248] When Abel learned of this, rage filled (him) and grief overcame him. He said to her, "From whom did you produce these two children? I think they are from Cain; it was he who consorted with you!" Although she described to him the form of the angel, he left her and came to his mother, Eve, and complained to her about what Cain had done. He said to her, "Have you heard what he did to my sister and wife?" When Cain learned this, he went to Abel and struck him with a rock, killing him. Then he took Hakimat al-Dahr for a wife."[249]

Mani said: "Then those *archons* and this *al-Sindīd*[250] and Eve were troubled at (the behavior) they saw (exhibited) by Cain. *Al-Sindīd* then taught Eve magical syllables[251] in order that she might infatuate Adam.[252] She proceeded to act (by) presenting him with a garland from a flowering tree,[253] and when Adam saw her, he lustfully united with her, and she became pregnant and gave birth to a handsome[254] male child of radiant[255] appearance. When *al-Sindīd* learned about this, he was distressed and fell ill, and said to Eve, "This infant is not one of us; he is a stranger."[256] Then she wished to kill him, but Adam seized him and said to Eve, "I will feed him cow's milk and the fruit of trees!"[257] Thus taking him he departed. But *al-Sindīd* sent the *archons* to carry off the trees and cattle, moving them away from Adam. When Adam saw this, he took the infant and encircled him within three rings. He pronounced over the first (ring) the name of the King of the Gardens, over the second the name of Primal Man, and over the third the name of the Living Spirit.[258] He spoke to and implored God, may His name be glorified, saying, "Even though I have sinned before you, what offense has this infant committed?" Then one of the three (invoked deities) hurried (to Adam bearing) a crown of radiance, extending it in his hand to Adam. When *al-Sindīd* and the *archons* saw this, they departed (and went) away."

He (Mani) said, "Then there appeared to Adam a tree called the lotus, and milk flowed from it, and he fed the boy with it. He named him (the boy) after its name, but sometime later he renamed him Shāthil (i.e., Seth).[259] Then that *al-Sindīd* declared enmity against Adam and those who were born,[260] and said to Eve, 'Reveal (yourself) to Adam; perhaps you may restore him to

---

248 The names mean "Go for help" and "Bring help" (*ibid.*, p. 102 n. 97).

249 Reeves notes parallels with the Jewish traditions about Cain's rivalry for Abel's wife, and of Lamech's suspicion of unfaithfulness of his wife, the mother of Noah, with the Watchers and Holy Ones (*ibid.*, pp. 101-102 nn. 94, 99-101).

250 = Powerful one, mighty one (*ibid.*, p. 102 n. 103).

251 Compare the Watchers' teachings about technology and beauty aids in *1 Enoch* and in Gnostic writings (*ibid.*, pp. 102-103 n. 104).

252 "Note that the archetypal Genesis narrative [Moses 3-5] has been inverted in its Manichaean analogue: the temptation and corruption of Adam now transpires *after* the story of Cain and Abel. *Al-Sindīd* thus performs the role of the serpent in the original myth" (*ibid.*, p. 103 n. 105).

253 Compare the story of the Tree of Knowledge (*ibid.*, p. 103 n. 106).

254 Compare similar accounts of Seth's beautiful appearance (*ibid.*, p. 103 n. 106; cf. *Commentary* 6:10-a, p. 482.)

255 On the feature of luminosity, see *ibid.*, p. 103 n. 109 and *Excursus 37: Traditions About the Role of Abel*, p. 617.

256 Reeves sees an allusion to Moses 6:2 (*ibid.*, p. 103 n. 110).

257 Reeves interprets this as Eve's desire to starve the child by refusing to feed him. In response, Adam acts to save the child (*ibid.*, pp. 103-104 n. 111).

258 Note the progression: the first name associates the child with the prelapsarian innocence of the Garden, the second name with a mortal progenitor, and the third name with Deity. Reeves connects Adam's actions with a "curious invocation" preserved in Aramaic referring to "that seal with which Adam the protoplast sealed his son Seth, and he (i.e., Seth) was delivered from d[emons], devils, tormentors, and satans" (*ibid.*, p. 104 n. 113).

259 "According to this traditions, the name 'Sethel"... derives from a midrashic transposition and manipulation of the consonantal phonemes of the child's original name 'Lotis'" (*ibid.*, p. 104 n. 114).

260 In Moses 4:21, it is the Lord who foretells the enmity that will exist between Satan and the seed of the woman; here it is Satan who declares his enmity, echoing the words of the *Qur'an*: "'Because [... Thou hast adjudged me to be erring],' Iblis [= the Devil] declared, 'I will waylay Your servants as they walk on Your straight path, then spring upon them from the front and the rear, from their right and from their left....' 'Begone!' [God] said." (N. J. Dawood, *Koran*, 7:11-18, pp. 109-110; cf. 15:32-44; 17:61-63; 38:74-85; see also M. Herbert, *Irish Apocrypha*, p. 11; *Commentary* 4:21-a, p. 265).

us.' Then she made haste and seduced Adam, who lustfully united with her. When Shāthil saw him, he admonished and rebuked him (Adam), and said to him, 'Arise, let us go to the East, to the Light and Wisdom of God.'[261] So he left with him and resided there until he died and came to the Gardens (of Paradise). Then Shāthil with Rau-Faryād and Bar-Faryād and Hakimat al-Dahr, their mother, practiced *ê iddīqūt*,[262] following one way and one path until the time of their deaths, but Eve, Cain, and Ibnat al-Hiris went to Gehenna."

Manichaean Literature

The primary literature on Manichaeism is a vast and complex collection of often fragmentary texts. BeDuhn describes the history of the gradual discovery of sources as follows:

> Prior to the twentieth century, historical knowledge of Manichaeism depended entirely on the polemical accounts of its enemies. The reassessment of the entire history of Christianity compelled by the Protestant Reformation and the Enlightenment led to the first critical examinations of the most accessible of these sources, the heresiographical writings of Christian church leaders of the fourth to tenth centuries.[263] The nineteenth century brought significant gains in access to sources; many new Patristic texts (Greek and Syriac) came to light from archives of Orthodox institutions in Greece and the Middle East,[264] and Arabic sources heretofore unknown to the European academy revealed even more detailed accounts of the dead religion.[265] A comparison of all these sources produced a rather sketchy general picture of the Manichaeans as a historical curiosity, seen entirely through the eyes of their religious rivals, Christian and Muslim.[266]
>
> This situation changed dramatically with the 1904 announcement by F. W. K. Müller that he had succeeded in deciphering texts brought back from East Turkestan by a German exploratory expedition, and found them to have Manichaean contents. The heap of highly fragmentary Manichaean literature and art eventually retrieved from the region of Turfan by several expeditions remains the largest and most important known source of information on the religion… New discoveries of Manichaean texts continue to be made in the Turfan region to this day.
>
> Shortly after the initial Turfan discoveries, British and French expeditions found Chinese and Turkic Manichaean texts farther to the east at Tun-huang. The Tun-huang Turkic finds are rather meager compared with the four Chinese rolls which have proven to be extraordinarily important and rich sources of information… The combination of the Turfan and Tun-huang discoveries permitted the first synthetic studies of Manichaeism based on primary sources, and gave birth to modern Manichaean studies.[267]
>
> It was not long before the nascent field became the beneficiary of another major wellspring: a small collection of Manichaean books came to light in Egypt in 1929. Eventually traced back to an ancient village in the Fayum district, the Medinet Madi library, written in Coptic, contained seven volumes: the *Psalm-Book*, the *Homilies*, the *Chapters* in two volumes *(Kephalaia I and Kephalaia II)*, the *Readings (Synaxeis)*, the *Letters*, and the *History*… Tragically, … [t]he *Letters* and *History* volumes vanished after [World War II]… [The surviving volumes are housed in the

---

261 "A reflex of [Moses 4:31], wherein Adam and Eve are involuntarily expelled from the Garden. Here, by contrast, Adam and Seth voluntarily separate themselves from further temptation" (J. C. Reeves, *Heralds*, p. 104 n. 116).
262 I.e., the teachings of Manichaeism (*ibid.*, p. 104 n. 118).
263 E.g., Augustine, Epiphanius of Salamis (Panarion), Cyril of Jerusalem (Catecheses), Hegemonius (*Acta Archelai*), Titus of Bostra, Serapion of Thmuis, Alexander of Lycopolis.
264 E.g., Ephrem Syrus, Theodore bar Konai, and new manuscripts of Serapion of Thmuis and Titus of Bostra.
265 E.g., Ibn al-Nadim (*Fihrist ul-ulim*), al-Biruni (*Athar-ul-Bakiya*).
266 See *Anti-Manichaean Texts* below.
267 See *Central Asian and Chinese Texts* below.

Chester Beatty Library in Dublin, Ireland and in the State Museums of Berlin, Germany. A few leaves are in the national collections of Vienna and Warsaw....[268]

Two more Egyptian discoveries complete the history of the recovery of primary Manichaean documents. A tiny book acquired by the University of Cologne in the 1960s has achieved fame as the *Cologne Mani Codex*... This Greek book of uncertain provenance recounts the life of Mani and the early years of his religious activity... [To this was added the fragmentary *Tebessa Codex*.[269]] Then, only a few years ago, a joint Australian-Canadian archaeological expedition working in the Dakhleh Oasis of Egypt uncovered a new cache of Manichaean documents. This rather heterogeneous assortment of material from ancient Kellis is still in the earliest phase of assessment[270]...[271]

For general works on Manichaeism, see J. D. BeDuhn, *Manichaean Body*; M. Tardieu, *Manichéisme*; M. Tardieu, *Manichaeism*. Gardner and Lieu have assembled a useful collection of sources in the Christian Roman Empire (I. Gardner, *et al., Manichaean*). Additional valuable perspectives and collections include M. Heuser, *et al., Literature and Art*; P. Mirecki, *et al., Emerging*; P. Mirecki, *et al., Light*. For comprehensive bibliographies of primary Manichaean texts, see F. de Blois, *et al., Dictionary 2*; D. Durkin-Meisterernst, *Dictionary 3*; S. N. C. Lieu, *Dictionary 1*; G. Mikkelson, *Bibliography*; G. Mikkelson, *Dictionary 4*. Lieu has provided a good overview of current sources and scholarly perspectives (S. N. C. Lieu, *Manichaeism*). Note that field of Manichaean studies is rapidly evolving, so catalogues of sources become outdated quickly.

Anti-Manichaean Texts

R. Haardt, *Gnosis* contains is a good collection of relevant excerpts from the works of Theodore bar Konai,[272] Augustine,[273] the Bishop of Alexandria,[274] Alexander of Lycopolis,[275] and Hegemonius.[276] The writings of Evodius against the Manichaeans are excerpted in W. Barnstone, *Other*, p. 687ff. Two excerpts from a writing of Mani, *The Book of Secrets or Mysteries*, are quoted by al-Biruni. The fragment relates the immortality of souls and asks about their fate.[277]

In the chapter concerning the reign of *Shapur Zu'l Aktaf*, Ferdowsi's 11th century "Book of Kings" (*Shahnameh*) relates the story of the visit of Mani to the king.[278] The king listened politely to the "eloquent... prophet and... painter," but was "troubled by his words." He then invited the chief priest of the "ancient faith of Zoroaster" to speak with him. Confounded by the priest's condemnation of his "trust in images," Mani was "ignominiously dragged from the court" before being "flayed" and "stuffed with straw." His corpse was hung from the city gates "and men flung dirt" on it.[279]

---

268   P. Mirecki, *Manichaean Introduction*, p. 574. See *Medina Madi Texts* below.
269   See *Greek and Latin Texts* below.
270   See *Kellis Texts* below.
271   J. D. BeDuhn, *Manichaean Body*, pp. 2-4.
272   Pp. 289-295; see also T. bar Konai, *Impure Doctrine*.
273   Pp. 295-301, 330-334, 341-49. See also Augustine, *Fortunatum*; W. Barnstone, *Other*, pp. 675-686.
274   Pp. 335-336.
275   Pp. 336-339.
276   Pp. 339-341. See also the more recent translation and commentary in Hegemonius, *Acta*.
277   E. Hennecke, *et al., Manichaean Gospel*.
278   A. Ferdowsi, *Shahnama*, pp. 597-598.
279   See *Endnote B-17*, p. 907.

Reeves has assembled a collection of English translations of Manichaean Adam traditions from Theodore bar Konai, Ibn al-Nadim, the discourse about Gehmurd (i.e., Adam) and Murdiyanag (i.e., Eve), and fragments from Sundermann.[280]

Central Asian and Chinese Texts

Turfan. The "Turfan fragments (many of which could not be conserved) are the disintegrated remains of what were once high-quality illuminated manuscripts that had suffered mutilation under Muslim conquerors. The texts are written in several Central Asian languages, and they are now conserved in the collection of the German Academy of Sciences in Berlin."[281] In 2006, all previously published and some additional *Hymns to the Living Soul* in the Berlin Collection were newly edited.[282]

Though included in several descriptions of the Manichaean canon[283] and in citations by hostile heresiologists, no versions of this *The Book of Giants* were available until Henning published newly discovered fragments in 1943. Later, several fragments of a related work were identified among the Qumran manuscripts.[284] In his comprehensive study of the manuscript evidence, Reeves concluded that the this foundational work of Manichaean cosmogony is indebted in important respects to Jewish exegetical traditions relating to Genesis 6:1-4.[285]

Dunhuang. Sir Aurel Stein and Chinese scholars "discovered the remains of a large hoard of Buddhist and Manichaean manuscripts in the Temple of the Thousand Buddhas of Tunhuang (east-southeast of Turfan). Stein reovered a long Manichaean confessional text entitlded *Confessional for the Hearers (Confessional Mirror for Auditors)*.[286] Also discovered were three Manichaean texts translated into Chinese from Iranian-language originals, including the *Treatise on Cosmogony and Its Implications for the Everyday Life of Manichaeans* ([*Ts'an Ching,*] now conserved in Beijing), the *Hymn Scroll* (now in London), and the *Compendium of the Teaching of Mani, the Buddha of Light* (now in London and Paris)."[287]

The *Compendium* was the work of a Manichaean priest who, in 731, depicted Manichaeism as a form of Buddhism and Mani as an *avatar* of Lao-tzu, the traditional founder of Taosim. "Lao-tzu was then believed by many Chinese not to have died but had gone to West where he reappeared as the Buddha. The response of the T'ang government to the *Compendium* was the law of 731, which permitted the practice of the religion by foreigners in China but banned its preaching to the Chinese."[288] The first four parts of the *Compendium* were translated into English and published by Haloun and Henning in 1952.[289] The last two parts were earlier published in French by Chavannes and Pelliot.[290] In 1990, these two parts were finally brought together in a single French edition by Tajadod.[291]

---

280   J. C. Reeves, *Heralds*, pp. 79-88.
281   P. Mirecki, *Manichaean Introduction*, p. 572.
282   D. Durkin-Meisterernst, *Hymns*.
283   E.g., *Homilies* 25:2-5, *Psalm-Book* 46:21-47:4, *Kephalaia* 5:22-26.
284   *1Q23, 6Q8, 4QEnGia, 4QEnGib, 4QEnGic,* and possibly others.
285   J. C. Reeves, *Jewish Lore*.
286   See excerpt in R. Haardt, *Gnosis*, pp. 327-329.
287   P. Mirecki, *Manichaean Introduction*, pp. 572-573.
288   S. N. C. Lieu, *Manichaeism in China*.
289   G. Haloun, *et al.*, *Compendium*.
290   É. Chavannes, *et al.*, *Traité Manichéen*.
291   N. Tajadod, *Mani*.

"Western scholars are now informed of the numerous recent discoveries of Manichaean archaelogical sites, artifacts, and texts in Central Asia and China through the works of S. N. C. Lieu and Geng Shimin."[292]

Medinet Madi Texts

Text Name	Description	English Publication Reference
Psalms (Chester Beatty Library Codex A, Papyrus Chester Beatty Mani 3 and 4)	"The first part of this codex was acquired by Beatty from the Cairo dealer Maurice Nahman in 1931 [Herakleides Psalms], the second [Berna Psalms] in 1930" (J. M. Robinson, Madi Codices).	Allberry's 1938 English translation of part 2 of the psalm-book has become difficult to find (C. R. C. A. Allberry, Psalm-Book). A more recent facsimile edition of the first part of the Psalms and a German translation of the second part is currently available (S. Richter, Herakleides-Psalmen; G. Wurst, Berna-Psalmen). Villey has published a translation and commentary of part 2 of the psalm-book in French (A. Villey, Psaumes). English translations of excerpts of the Psalms can be found in R. Haardt, Gnosis, pp. 301-324.
Synaxeis (=assembly) of the Living Gospel (The Readings, Chester Beatty Library Codex B, Papyrus Chester Beatty Mani 5)	"This codex was acquired by Beatty from a Fayyumic dealer in 1930 (except for 31 residual leaves that Schmidt acquired in 1931 — [Berlin] P 15995)" (J. M. Robinson, Madi Codices). "It appears to be a commentary (?) on the Living Gospel, a canonical work of Mani" (S. N. C. Lieu, Manichaeism, p. 223).	The manuscript remains unpublished. See P. Mirecki, Synaxeis Codex.
Volume Two of the Kephalaia (Kephalaia of the Wisdom of my Lord Mani, Chester Beatty Library Codex C, Papyrus Chester Beatty Mani 1)	"This [codex] was acquired by Beatty... prior to... the Spring of 1931" (J. M. Robinson, Madi Codices). "The relationship between the two Kephalaia has... been open to debate. However, ...it appears that the Dublin [Beatty] codex can best be regarded as simply a continuation of the Berlin one" (I. Gardner, et al., Manichaean, p. 38 n. 58).	Volume Two of the Kephalaia remains unpublished.
Volume One of the Kephalaia (Kephalaia of the Teacher, Berlin Papyrus Collection, P 15996)	"This codex was acquired by Schmidt from Nahman in 1930. Most of the leaves were conserved in Ibscher and edited by Polotsky and Alexander Böhlig and published in fascicles, a first volume through p. 244, line 20 by 1940. Böhlig published through p. 291 in 1966, and p. 292 in 1985. Remains of three unpublished leaves had been acquired by Prof. Grohmann of Prague for the Austrian National Library, where they are still extant. There are five unpublished Berlin leaves in Warsaw, where they were brought after having been lost in transit between Berlin and Leningrad in 1946. Together with leaves in Berlin there are 85 to 93 extant unpublished leaves (170 to 186 pages). Wolf-Peter Funk is preparing a critical edition. Transcriptions and translations by Polotsky located at the Academy of Sciences in Berlin, at the Griffith Institute of the Ashmoleon Museum in Oxford, and at the Chester Beatty Library in Dublin have been put by Polotsky at Funk's disposal for the critical edition" (J. M. Robinson, Madi Codices).	I. Gardner, Kephalaia. An English translation of Kephalaion 41 is published in R. Haardt, Gnosis, pp. 325-327.

---

292   P. Mirecki, Manichaean Introduction, p. 573. See, e.g., S. N. C. Lieu, Manichaeism in China.

Text Name	Description	English Publication Reference
Homilies and Varia (Chester Beatty Library Codex D, Papyrus Chester Beatty Mani 2)	"The bulk of this codex was acquired from Nahman with an option to buy by Beatty in 1930, but he released it to Carl Schmidt for Berlin in 1932 (P 15999). It was not considered conservable, but was put on display as a show piece of how impossible this task was. The unconserved book block is thought to have been among the materials stored in the bunker at the Zoo train station, taken from there to the Soviet Command Post at the castle Friedrichsfelde in 1945-1946, and from there to Leningrad in 1946, though it was not found when the material was returned to Berlin in 1958. A smaller part of the codex was acquired by Beatty in 1931, conserved by Ibscher, edited by Polotsky, and published in 1934. A facsimile edition of the codex has been published by Giversen in 1987" (J. M. Robinson, *Madi Codices*).	N. A. Pedersen, *Homilies*
Acts (Acta Codex, The History, Berlin Papyrus Collection, P 15997)	According to Lieu, this is "a historical work which gave a life of Mani and th eearly history of the sect" (S. N. C. Lieu, *Manichaeism*, p. 223). "This codex, with its covers (which were photographed and published), was sold by a provincial dealer to Nahman, who sold it to Schmidt in 1931. One leaf that Ibscher conserved was returned to London, moved with the library to Dublin, and was included in the material put on deposit on Copenhagen. Giversen published it in facsimile in 1987. There are 7 or 8 unpublished leaves still in Berlin. Part of one unpublished leaf may be at the Institute for Papyrology of Warsaw University. The unconserved book block and wooden covers did not return from Leningrad to Berlin in 1958. None of the leaves of this codex have been published" (J. M. Robinson, *Madi Codices*).	
Letters (Epistles of Mani, Berlin Papyrus Collection, P 15998)	"This codex was also sold by the provincial dealer to Nahman, who sold it to Schmidt in 1931. There are six unpublished leaves that were returned from Leningrad to Berlin in 1958 and three unpublished leaves in the National Museum in Warsaw. There are also fifteen leaves among those that lay half-conserved in the Ibscher home throughout the war that may belong to this codex. The book block did not return from Leningrad to Berlin in 1958. None of the leaves of this codex have been published" (J. M. Robinson, *Madi Codices*).	Gardner and Funk are finishing preparations for publication of the reconstructed remains of the Berlin codex of the *Letters*. See I. Gardner, *Reconstruction*.

Greek and Latin Texts

Dated by some scholars to the late fourth century and by others to the seventh century,[293] the *Cologne Mani Codex (CMC)* purports to be an account of the childhood and early missionary journeys of Mani. It is a Greek translation of a lost Syriac text. The title found in the text *On the Origin of His Body* "may be so named because of its concern for the life and body of Mani, or it may be given its title in reference to the [body of the] Manichaean church."[294] In an earlier Aramaic form, portions of the text may go back to Mani himself. The work is 192 pages long and is divided in five chiastically-arranged sections:

The first section (pp. 2-14), telling of Mani from years four to twelve, comes from three different sources and provides two full-fledged conversion accounts. The fifth section (pp. 116-192), meanwhile, contains a long but extremely fragmentary itinerary of Mani's first missionary journey. Most emphatically Gnostic is the second section (pp. 14-72)… Accounts of Mani's separation from the Baptists, his call to be a missionary, and instructions for the foundation of Manichaeism as a world religion, all in dialogue form, comprise the fourth section (pp. 99-116). Finally, the midsection (pp. 72-99)… features the dramatic break with the Baptists."[295]

293 S. N. C. Lieu, *Manichaeism*, p. 224.
294 P. Mirecki, *Origin*, p. 581. See *Endnote B-18,* p. 907.
295 R. Cameron, *et al.*, *CMC*, p. 3.

Thus far only the first three sections of the CMC (pp. 1-99) have appeared complete in English translation,[296] though extensive excerpts from the entire work have been published by Gardner.[297] A critical edition of the text and a partial commentary (pp. 1-120) is available in German translation.[298] A critical edition and commentary in German for pp. 121-192 of the codex was published in 1994.[299] Of interest to students of Genesis is the extensive commentary by Reeves on the apocalypses of Adam, Sethel (Seth), Enosh, Shem, and Enoch found in section two of the codex (pp. 48-60).[300]

An additional Manichaean text in Latin has been preserved, which Mirecki describes as follows:

> A fragmentary Manichaean parchment codex, the *Tebessa Codex*, was discovered in a cave near Theveste, Algeria, in 1918 and placed in the National Library of Paris. Only twenty-five damaged leaves and the slight remains of four others are preserved from this codex, with each page originally carrying two columns of Latin text. The extant text contains two sections: an apologetic discussion on the relationship between the two major groups in the Manichaean church, the elect and the auditors, with allusions to and quotations of relevant canonical gospel texts; and a discussion in which the unknown Manichaean author defends the "nonwork ethic" of the Manichaean elect (who had their practical needs met by the auditors), apparently as an apologetic response to Christian charges that the messenger Paul had clearly condemned such dependent lifestyles in 2 Thessalonians 3:10.[301]

Kellis Texts

Iain Gardner has provisionally categorized the Kellis texts as follows:

- fragments of two Coptic codices containing canonical works (Epistles?) by Mani

- a Coptic Manichaean doctrinal text on a wooden board

- Greek and Coptic Manichaean psalms, prayers, and liturgical texts on papyrus and wooden boards with significant parallels to the Coptic *Psalm-Book* texts from Medinet Madi

- two Coptic-Syriac glossaries of Manichaean technical terms on two wooden boards and a Greek-Syriac glossary (?) on vellum

- two Greek Manichaean amulets (miniatures)

- a Coptic codex leaf containing Romans 2:6-29 (*Dialect I*) and fragments of a Greek codex containing traditions similar to the *Acts of John*

- four miscellaneous literary fragments in Greek and Coptic (possibly Manichaean)

- many Greek and Coptic documentary texts, mostly letters, some of which are clearly Manichaean.[302]

---

296 R. Cameron, *et al.*, CMC.
297 I. Gardner, *et al.*, *Manichaean*, pp. 47-73.
298 L. Koenen, *et al.*, *Mani-Kodex*.
299 C. E. Römer, *Mani-Kodex* 121-192.
300 J. C. Reeves, *Heralds*.
301 P. Mirecki, *Manichaean Introduction*, pp. 573-574. An English translation appears in J. D. BeDuhn, *et al.*, *Tebessa*.
302 Cited P. Mirecki, *et al.*, *Spell*, p. 2.

Mirecki suggests: "The texts may indicate that the earliest form of Christianity to enter the Oasis was in fact Manichaeism portraying itself as a type of Christianity."[303] Lieu adds that because this branch of Mani's followers was located "in a corner of the Empire where it was free from religious persecution (pagan or Christian), the sect was able to perceive itself as the true followers of Christ, as presented by Mani."[304]

Three volumes of original Coptic, Greek and Syriac papyri relating to the Manichaean community at Kellis have been published,[305] and one more is in preparation. A letter containing a magical spell has been translated,[306] and an interim progress report with an overview of findings at Kellis through the mid-1990s has been written by Gardner.[307]

303   P. Mirecki, *Manichaean Introduction*, pp. 574-575.
304   S. N. C. Lieu, *Manichaeism*, p. 224. See also I. Gardner, *et al.*, *Manichaean*, pp. 43-45, 272-278.
305   I. Gardner, *KL 1*; I. Gardner, *et al.*, *CDT 1*; I. Gardner, *KL 2*.
306   P. Mirecki, *et al.*, *Spell*.
307   I. Gardner, *Progress Report*.

Islamic Texts

LDS views toward Islam have been highly favorable. Early Church leaders such as Elders George Q. Cannon,[308] B. H. Roberts,[309] and Orson F. Whitney[310] have all spoken of Muhammad's positive influence on those who have been influenced by his life and teachings. More recently, Elder Boyd K. Packer noted that "Church members and Muslims share similar high standards of decency, temperance, and morality. We have so much in common."[311] On February 15, 1978, the First Presidency issued a statement entitled "God's Love for All Mankind," which reads in part:

> The great religious leaders of the world such as Muhammad, Confucius, and the Reformers, as well as philosophers including Socrates, Plato, and others, received a portion of God's light. Moral truths were given to them by God to enlighten whole nations and to bring a higher level of understanding to individuals.[312]

The *Qur'an*

The *Noble Qur'an* (*al-Qur'an al-Karim*), as it is frequently described, is the primary text of Islam, proclaiming the oneness of God[313] and the mission of His Prophet Muhammad. According to traditional accounts,[314] it was revealed by the angel Gabriel[315] beginning in 610 CE and later written down and organized into an official recension within two decades after Muhammad's death in 632 CE.[316] *Qur'an* means "recitation," from Muhammad's account of how he was commanded by the angel Gabriel to "Recite!".[317]

> According to many Muslim scholars, the *Qur'an* was taken from the "Preserved Tablet"[318] in Paradise and brought down to the earthly heavens during the "Night of Fate"[319] during the month of *Ramadan*. From there the *Qur'an* was revealed to the Prophet Muhammad in intervals, so that he could memorize it, and because different parts of the *Qur'an* were addressed to specific circumstances occurring in the life of the Prophet Muhammad.[320]

Though it presents itself as a confirming continuity of revelation given in Jewish and Christian scripture,[321] the *Qur'an* powerfully asserts its "overriding pre-eminence, its utter finality. With this revelation, God has completed his salvific sequencing of prophets and messengers. The words spoken to Muhammad, the 'seal of the prophets,' constitute God's

---

308 G. Q. Cannon, *Truth*, 1:308-310.

309 B. H. Roberts, *Comprehensiveness*, p. 67; B. H. Roberts, *Spirit of Gospel*, p. 138; B. H. Roberts, *The Truth*, pp. 140-142, 152

310 O. F. Whitney, *Thoughts*, 36, p. 478.

311 B. K. Packer, *Bridges*, p. 7. See D. Q. Cannon, *et al.*, *Nation*, pp. 438-442; A. H. Green, *Islam*; H. W. Hunter, *Alike*, 4 February 1979, p. 74; B. K. Packer, *Bridges*; S. J. Palmer, *Mormons and Muslims*; D. C. Peterson, *Abraham*; J. A. Toronto, *Islam*, pp. 234-238 for discussions of doctrinal affinities and historical trends in the relationship between the LDS Church and Islam. For an overview of the history and status of relations and interactions between Islam, Judaism, and Christianity, see R. C. Martin, *Encyclopedia*, 2:360-364; G. D. Newby, *Muslims*; A. Shihab, *Bridges*. See also *Excursus 47: Islamic Perspectives Relating to Redemption*, p. 645.

312 S. W. Kimball, *et al.*, *God's Love*; S. J. Palmer, *Expanding*, p. v; cf. *Qur'an* 2:62, 5:48, 10:47, 40:78.

313 .See *Endnote B-20*, p. 907.

314 See *Endnote B-21*, p. 907.

315 See *Endnote B-22*, p. 907.

316 Some variant codices are extant and in use today (B. M. Wheeler, *Prophets*, p. 5).

317 *Qur'an* 96:1.

318 *Qur'an* 85:21-22.

319 *Qur'an* 97:1.

320 B. M. Wheeler, *Prophets*, pp. 3-4.

321 E.g., *Qur'an* 2:136, 3:3, 4:136, 5:46, 9:111, 12:111, 46:12.

full and final guidance for humankind."[322] Like the Doctrine and Covenants, each *surah* (= section or chapter) of the *Qur'an* constitutes an independent record of divine instruction, echoing and extending previous revelations rather than providing a continuous narrative of events.[323]

Although the *Qur'an* has appeared in many translations, the eloquent poetry of the Arabic version retains a unique status because for Muslims it contains the verbatim record of the words of God.[324] See D. C. Peterson, *Understanding the Qur'an* for an insightful perspective on the role of language in the *Qur'an* and the book's unique place in Islam. For readers desiring a more in-depth treatment of the background and context of the *Qur'an*, McAuliffe's edited volume is highly recommended.[325] A useful overview of English translations can be found in K. Mohammed, *Translations*. A valuable study of sayings of Muhammad reported as first-person words of God but not included in the *Qur'an* (*hadith qudsi* = divine saying) was made by Graham.[326] Zilio-Grandi, *Paradise* provides an overview of the Garden of Eden in the *Qur'an* and in Islamic exegetical tradition.

Text Name	Date	Description	Publication Reference
English Translations of the *Qur'an*			
The Holy Qur'an with English Translation and Commentary	1917-1951	A competent though somewhat dated translation with an extensive commentary. Unfortunately, the translation is marred by the sectarian *Ahmadi* bias against miracles.	M. M. Ali, *Qur'an*.
The Holy Qur'an: Arabic Text, English Translation and Commentary	1934	Until recently, this was the most popular version of the *Qur'an* among English-speaking Muslims.	A. A. Y. Ali, *Qur'an*.
The Koran Interpreted	1955	Arberry is more successful than other translators in conveying the fluency and literary beauty of the *Qur'an*.	A. J. Arberry, *Koran*
The Qur'an: A New Translation	2004	An English translation that rivals Arberry's in clarity and fluency.	M. A. S. A. Haleem, *Qur'an*
The Qur'an	2007	English translation by a renowned Oxford scholar that attempts to preserve the quality of the *Qur'an*'s originally oral character.	A. Jones, *Qur'an*

Sunnah (*Sirah* and *Hadith*)

Although the words of the *Qur'an* provide the foundation of divine guidance for Muslims, stories about the sayings and doings of the Prophet provide the believer with "concrete examples" to emulate, drawn from "a life that was human yet completely immersed in the sacred."[327] The term used for the sum of these traditions is *Sunnah* [= the trodden path, customary procedure, precedent].[328] The *Sunnah* "includes... [the] specific words and actions and practices of which [Muhammad] approved among earlier Arab traditions and so allowed to continue among Muslims. He thereby Islamicized these practices although they were of pre-Islamic origin."[329]

---

322 J. D. McAuliffe, *Introduction*, p. 4; cf. T. Khalidi, *Muslim Jesus*, p. 20.
323 H. Bloom, *Genius*, p. 146.
324 *Qur'an* 12:2.
325 J. D. McAuliffe, *Companion*. See also R. Allen, *Introduction*, pp. 52-64; A. K. Brohi, *Spiritual Significance*; R. C. Martin, *Encyclopedia*, 2:562-568; S. H. Nasr, *Qur'an*; G. D. Newby, *Encyclopedia*, s. v. *Qur'an*, pp. 178-180; B. M. Wheeler, *Prophets*, pp. 1-14.
326 W. A. Graham, *Divine*.
327 See F. M. Denny, *Islam* for a discussion of the distinctive roles and differing values of the *Qur'an* and the *Sunnah* in Islam.
328 R. C. Martin, *Encyclopedia*, 2:666-669.
329 S. H. Nasr, *Sunnah*, p. 97.

The biographical *sirah* (= course, road, way) literature collects the earliest stories about Muhammad and early Muslims.[330] The *hadith* (= speech, report) literature, second only to the *Qur'an* in importance and authority, is comprised of systematic collections of early Islamic sayings whose trustworthiness has been qualified by careful documentation of chains of transmission (*isnad* = support) connecting the stories of later authorities to their origin in earlier reports by the Companions and Followers of Muhammad.[331] The most authoritative of these reports are called *sahih* (= true, sound, genuine).[332] Many of these reports describe the circumstances of the revelation of particular *surahs*, or background information relating to them. The *hadith* reports are seen as *normative,* in contrast to the *sirah,* which is written in a narrative genre.[333]

Text Name	Date	Description	Publication Reference
Sirah and *Hadith* (Biography and Traditions about Muhammad and early Muslims)			
Sirat Rasul Allàh (Life of Allàh's Messenger) or *Sirah al-Nabi or Sirat Nabawiyya (Life of the Prophet)*	Before 833	The most well-known ancient *sirah* is that of Muhammad ibn Ishaq (704-767) (G. D. Newby, *Encyclopedia*, p. 91), whose no-longer-extant biography of Muhammad survives in the abridged version of ibn Hisham (d. 833) (*ibid.*, p. 90), which left out "things which it is disgraceful to discuss; matters which would distress certain people; and such reports as al-Bakka'i told me he could not accept as trustworthy" (M. Ibn Ishaq ibn Yasar, *Sirat Rasul*, p. 691). Much of this omitted material no doubt was of extra-Islamic (i.e., Judeo-Christian) origin, part of a literature that had been subject to increasing distrust during this period (M. Ibn Ishaq ibn Yasar, *Making*, pp. 8-14).	The last two parts of ibn Ishaq's work, *Kitab al-Mabath* (The Book of the Sending Forth) and *Kitab al-Maghazi* (The Book of Military Campaigns), containing the biography of Muhammad proper, are published in M. Ibn Ishaq ibn Yasar, *Sirat Rasul*. Al-Tabari's history of Muhammad relies heavily on the *Sirat Rasul Allàh* and contains the controversial episode of the Satanic Verses omitted in that work (al-Tabari, *Creation*). Peterson has written on Muhammad's life from the perspective of contemporary scholarship (D. C. Peterson, *Muhammad (2001)*; D. C. Peterson, *Muhammad (2007)*). See also R. C. Martin, *Encyclopedia*, 2:478-485 for a good overview of modern biographical sources and perspectives.
Sahih al-Bukhari	846	Muhammad b. Isma'il al-Bukhari (810-870) (R. C. Martin, *Encyclopedia*, 1:114; G. D. Newby, *Encyclopedia*, p. 45) is said to have collected six hundred thousand hadith reports (M. Z. Siddiqi, *Hadith*, p. 93)—and tradition reports that he memorized two hundred thousand of these. His topical collection of 7563 traditions he deemed reliable is, despite its defects, generally regarded as the most authoritative work of its kind (M. Z. Siddiqi, *Hadith*, pp. 88, 96-97).	M. I. I. Bukhari, *Sahih*
Sahih al-Muslim	ca. 860	Abu al-Husayn Muslim (817-875) (R. C. Martin, *Encyclopedia*, 2:496; G. D. Newby, *Encyclopedia*, p. 160) assembled an early collection of 7190 *hadith* sayings reportedly selected from among 300,000 original accounts. Al-Muslim is seen as having been somewhat more careful than al-Bukhari in the documentation of sources and in other aspects of the "science of hadith" (M. Z. Siddiqi, *Hadith*, p. 100).	I. A.-H. Muslim, *Sahih.*

---

330   See *Endnote B-24*, p. 908.
331   M. Z. Siddiqi, *Hadith*. See *Endnote B-25*, p. 908.
332   M. Z. Siddiqi, *Hadith*, p. 192.
333   G. D. Newby, *Encyclopedia, sirah*, p. 195.

Tafsir

As helps in the task of interpretation, thousands of Qur'anic commentaries (*tafsir* = to explain) have been written, of which only a tiny fraction can be listed below.[334] Strictly speaking, since the only official version of the *Qur'an* is in Arabic, all translations are regarded as *tafsir*.[335] Differences in interpretation and emphasis in the commentaries and other Islamic literature will sometimes reflect the specific religious orientation of the author (e.g., Sunnism,[336] Shi'ism,[337] Sufism,[338] Salafism,[339] Wahhabism,[340] Ahmadism (Qadiyanis and Lahoris).[341] For an overview of the different traditions of Qur'anic interpretation, see J. D. McAuliffe, *Interpretation*.

Text Name	Date	Description	Publication Reference
Tafsir (Qur'anic Commentary)			
Jami' al-bayan 'an ta'wil ay al-Qur'an (The Comprehensive Clarification of the Interpretation of the Verses of the Qur'an	Before 923	Masterfully organized and with exquisite judgment both in his own opinions and in the selection of supporting sources, al-Tabari's (839-923) (R. C. Martin, *Encyclopedia*, 2:671; G. D. Newby, *Encyclopedia*, p. 199) multivolume commentary is one of the most widely-used in the Muslim world.	A French monograph on this commentary is available (C. Gilliot, *Tabari*). Excerpts from al-Tabari's commentary are sometimes included in English translations of the *Qur'an*.
Al-Kashshaf an Haqa'iq al-Tanzil (The Revealer of the Truth of Revelation)	Before 1144	Combining traditions with theological, grammatical, and lexicographical exegesis, az-Zamakhshari's (1075-1144) (G. D. Newby, *Encyclopedia*, p. 216) commentary is especially prized in Sunni communities.	A one-volume overview of the life and Qur'anic commentary of az-Zamakhshari has been published (J. A. al-Zamakhshari, *Kathaf*).
Al-Jami' li-Ahkam al-Qur'an (The Compendium of Legal Rulings of the Qur'an)	Before 1272	Less-interested in *isnad* than content, al-Qurtubi (d. 1272) (G. D. Newby, *Encyclopedia*, p. 180) emphasizes the legal and practical aspects of the *Qur'an* for daily Muslim life in his twenty-volume commentary. He also provides valuable commentary on the *isra'iliyyat*.	A series publishing an abridged English translation of al-Qurtubi's *tafsir* was initiated in 2003 (A. al-Qurtubi, *Tafsir*).
Tafsir an-Nasafi	Before ca. 1300	Nasafi's (d. ca. 1300 CE) commentary on the *Qur'an* is written from a Sufi perspective.	See A. Nasafi, *et al.*, *Aziz* for an in-depth study of Nasafi's works.
Muqaddima fi usul al-tafsir (An Introductory Essay on the Principles of Interpretation)	Before 1328	The controversial ibn Taymiyya's (1263-1328) (G. D. Newby, *Encyclopedia*, pp. 94-95) writings are considered heretical by most Muslims but are revered by adherents of Salafism/Wahhabism, strict movements of Islam that predominate in Saudi Arabia and Qatar. Of particular interest is his insistence on faithfulness to the words of the text in his interpretation of the *Qur'an*, including anthropomorphic descriptions of Deity.	Ibn Taymiyya did not author a complete *Tafsir*, however his writings have been influential in Qur'anic interpretation. See J. D. McAuliffe, *Ibn Taymiya*.
Tafsir Ibn Kathir or Tafsir al-Qur'an al-Azim	Before 1373	This comprehensive Sunni commentary of ibn Kathir (ca. 1300-1373) (G. D. Newby, *Encyclopedia*, p. 91) is highly valued because of its extensive use of authoritative *hadith* to explain the meaning of the text, his incorporation of non-Muslim sources, and his evaluation of opinions from earlier scholars.	See I. Ibn Kathir, *Tafsir*. Note that this ten-volume edition has been abridged in order to ensure that hadith viewed as "weak" by the editors are excluded.

---

334   R. C. Martin, *Encyclopedia*, 2:672-674.
335   G. D. Newby, *Encyclopedia*, s. v. Qur'an, p. 179.
336   A.-R. I. Doi, *Sunnism*.
337   S. H. M. Jafri, *Shi'ism*. Specific groups within Shi'ism include the dominant branch of the Imamis (Twelvers) (R. C. Martin, *Encyclopedia*., 2:624-628), as well as the Zaydis (Fivers) (*ibid.*, 2:629-630), and the Khoja and Bohra Isma'ilis (*ibid.*, 2:628-629; A. Nanji, *Isma'ilism*). For a chart summarizing the relationships among individuals and groups associated with these branches, see T. Ansary, *Destiny*, p. 359.
338   A. B. S. Ed-Din, *Sufism*.
339   R. C. Martin, *Encyclopedia*, 2:608-610.
340   B. Lewis, *Crisis*, pp. 103-116; R. C. Martin, *Encyclopedia*, 2:727-729.
341   R. C. Martin, *Encyclopedia*, 1:30-32. See *Endnote B-26*, p. 908.

Text Name	Date	Description	Publication Reference
Fi zilal al-Qur'an (In the Shade of the Qur'an)	Before 1966	Called the "Philosopher of Islamic Terror" in a 2003 *New York Times Magazine* article, the brilliant activist Sayyid Qutb (1906-1966) (R. C. Martin, *Encyclopedia*, 2:568-569; G. D. Newby, *Encyclopedia*, p. 181) became the leading intellectual for the Muslim Brothers (*al-Ikhwan al-Muslimun*), and eventually was executed by hanging. His commentary was written during his long years of imprisonment in Egypt and reflects his unswerving commitment to reform and revitalization of Islam according to an explicit social and political agenda (B. Lewis, *Crisis*, pp. 65-69; J. D. McAuliffe, *Interpretation*, pp. 199-200). Like other fundamentalists who have "little regard for traditional modes of systematic exegesis," Qutb "denies the established Islamic tradition that *jihad* is a defensive act of war, and determines that *jihad* is incumbent upon all Muslims as they abolish corrupt political and religious regimes." Thus Qutb can be seen as a forerunner to Usama bin Ladin (R. C. Martin, *Encyclopedia*, 1:208-209), who "also bypasses the traditional understanding of *jihad* by reinterpreting the definition of a defensive attack to include the mere occupancy of sacred Muslim lands by foreign powers, or the sheer presence of anti-Islamic values in those lands, such as promiscuity or usury" (R. C. Martin, *Encyclopedia*, 2:674; cf. P. L. Bergen, *Osama*, pp. 18-20; R. Ibrahim, *Reader*; B. Lewis, *Crisis*, pp. 117-146).	S. Qutb, *Shade.*
Al-Mizan fi l-tafsir al-Qur'an (The Balance in the Interpretation of the Qur'an)	1972	The highly-respected 20th-century Shi'ah commentator at-Tabataba'i (1892-1981) (G. D. Newby, *Encyclopedia*, p. 199) grouped consecutive verses together as a means of improved contextual interpretation. His most important method was to interpret the *Qur'an* by the *Qur'an* itself.	Only the first twelve volumes, corresponding to the first six of twenty volumes in the original publication, are currently available in English (A. at-Tabataba'i, *Al-Mizan*).
Tafhim al-Qur'an (Towards Understanding the Qur'an)	Before 1979	Written by the prolific Pakistani scholar and political activist Abu l-A'la Maududi (1903-1979) (R. C. Martin, *Encyclopedia*, 2:443-444; G. D. Newby, *Encyclopedia*, p. 145), the *Tafhim al-Qur'an* is one of the most widely-read commentaries on the *Qur'an*. It includes a critique of non-Islamic ideologies and argues that the adoption of Islamic principles by all peoples would lead to an ideal society that would transcend nationalism. Critics have questioned the inventive nature of some of the Qur'anic explanations.	S. A. A. l. Maududi, *Understanding*. A one-volume abridged version is also available from the same publisher.
The Qur'an and Its Interpreters	1992	"Ayoub provides an accurate and clear translation of the *Qur'an* along with copious translations from Arabic of Muslim exegesis on almost every verse" (B. M. Wheeler, *Prophets*, p. 364). Ayoub has also been an important figure in the dialogue between Islam and Christianity (M. M. Ayoub, *View*; M. M. Ayoub, *Redemption*).	The work is incomplete (*surahs* 1-3), with only two volumes published to date (M. M. Ayoub, *Qur'an (Vol. 1)* and *Qur'an (Vol. 2)*). Ayoub's translation and commentary on *surahs* 78-114 appears in M. M. Ayoub, *Awesome*.

Qisas al-Anbiya and *Ta'rikh*

Passages in the *Qur'an* typically do not explain but rather "presuppose knowledge of the Jewish and Christian scriptural and exegetical tradition."[342] This made certain parts of the *Qur'an* unintelligible to many new Muslims during Islam's early centuries of rapid expansion among peoples who did not share these earlier traditions. A demand naturally arose for more detailed information, encouraging the development of what became known as the *isra'iliyyat* literature (= Judaica).[343]

Within this literature, the *Stories of the Prophets (Qisas al-Anbiya)* contain highly-prized accounts of the lives of the "former prophets" who preceded Muhammad. What makes these

---

342   A. Rippin, *et al.*, *Islam*, p. 2.
343   G. D. Newby, *Encyclopedia*, *isra'iliyyat*, p. 108.

stories interesting from the point of view of modern scholarship is that most of them "were not taken directly from the Old and New Testaments, rather their source was the basically oral interpretations of the stories of biblical characters which has been termed 'religious folklore.'"[344] Many of these stories can also be found in the *ta'rikh* (= history) literature. Although these prophetic tales often parallel or elaborate upon the plentiful texts in Jewish and Christian apocryphal, pseudepigraphic, and midrashic sources available in Arabia at the beginning of Islam,[345] occasionally they seem to evidence knowledge of independent traditions going back to antiquity that do not appear elsewhere.[346] This fact is not surprising to Muslims, given their belief that God's messengers over the ages have been numerous: "Ibn Sa'd… reports that the total number of *rasul* [= messenger, a title generally used for prophets who brought forth a revealed book] is 315, and the total number of prophets [*nabi* = prophet in a more general sense] is 1000.[347] The *Qur'an* mentions books revealed to Abraham, and specifies the *Torah*, Gospel, Psalms of David, and *Qur'an* as revealed books. A *hadith* report… states that books were [also] revealed to Adam, Seth, Idris,[348] and Abraham."[349]

Scholars of *hadith*, following ibn Taymiyya,[350] have attempted to resolve controversies about which of these traditions of Jewish or Christian origin should be accepted by classifying them according to whether they are definitely known to be true (or false) because Muhammad confirmed (or rejected) them, or whether their truth or falsity is unknown. Wheeler has assembled a useful collection of Qur'anic commentary concerning the prophets and messengers from Adam through Muhammad.[351] See also the volumes by Khalidi and Qa'im containing sayings and stories of Jesus taken from Islamic literature.[352]

Text Name	Date	Description	Publication Reference
Qisas al-Anbiya (Stories of the Prophets), Isra'iliyyat (Judaica)			
Sirat Rasul Allàh (Life of Allàh's Messenger) or *Sirah al-Nabi* or *Sirat Nabawiyya (Life of the Prophet)*	Before 767	The first part of ibn Ishaq's (704-767) (G. D. Newby, *Encyclopedia*, p. 91) biography of Muhammad, the *Kitab al-Mubtada* (The Book of Beginnings) contains the stories of the prophets up to Muhammad. The text exists only in an edition by Newby reconstructed from secondary citations by later scholars.	M. Ibn Ishaq ibn Yasar, *Making*.
'Ara'is Al-Majalis Fi Qisas Al-Anbiya' (The Brides of Sessions about the Tales of the Prophets)	Before 1035	Al-Tha'labi's detailed and diverse collection of stories evidences a scholar's interest in the documentation of sources, including lengthy biblical citations. It "includes important materials not found in Tabari's work but does not include some of the more fantastic elements found in the work of Kisa'i" (B. M. Wheeler, *Prophets*, p. 357).	A. al-Tha'labi, *Lives*.
Qisas al-Anbiya (Tales of the Prophets)	ca. 1000-1100	An otherwise unknown author with a keen sense of storytelling, Muhammad al-Kisai (G. D. Newby, *Encyclopedia*, p. 128) includes details that do not appear in other collections of these tales. His work contains relatively few references to the *Qur'an* and the *hadith*.	M. al-Kisa'i, *Tales*.
Qisas al-Anbiya (Tales of the Prophets)	Before 1373	Excerpted from ibn Kathir's (ca. 1300-1373) (G. D. Newby, *Encyclopedia*, p. 91) *Al-Bidayah wan-Nihayah* (The Beginning and the End).	I. Ibn Kathir, *Stories*.
Qisas al-Anbiya (Tales of the Prophets)	ca. 1300-1400	A version of the prophetic stories from eastern Turkey.	N. B. al-Rabghuzi, *Stories*.

344 M. al-Kisa'i, *Tales*, p. xvii; see also S. M. Wasserstrom, *Muslim Literature*.
345 G. D. Newby, *History*.
346 .See *Endnote B-27*, p. 908.
347 T. Khalidi, *Muslim Jesus*, p. 8. Other Muslim sources list the total number of prophets as 224,000.
348 Alternate spellings include Esdras, Andreas, Emmeduranki, or Edoranchus/Euedorachus, but in all cases these names refer to Enoch (M. al-Kisa'i, *Tales*, p. 347 n. 72; Berossus, *History*). Some take the term to be derived from the Arabic *dirasah* = "studies" "because of his studies of the scriptures" (Suyuti, cited in B. M. Wheeler, *Prophets*, p. 46
349 B. M. Wheeler, *Prophets*, p. 8; cf. M. al-Kisa'i, *Tales*, pp. 73-76; al-Tabari, *Creation*, 1:151-152, pp. 322-324.
350 J. D. McAuliffe, *Ibn Taymiya*, p. 38.
351 B. M. Wheeler, *Prophets*. See *Endnote B-28*, p. 908.
352 T. Khalidi, *Muslim Jesus*; M. M. Qa'im, *Jesus*.

Text Name	Date	Description	Publication Reference
Ta'rikh (History)			
Ta'rikh al-Yaqubi (Ta'rikh ibn Wadih)	d. 897	The work is in two parts. The first concerns pre-Islamic and non-Islamic peoples, including a version of stories of the prophets that seems to be dependent on the Syriac *Cave of Treasures*. The second part relates Islamic history up to 872.	An English translation of Yaqubi's stories of the prophets has been made by Reeves J. C. Reeves, *al-Yaqubi*
Ta'rikh al-rusul wa'l-muluk (History of the messengers and the kings)	Before 923	"The greatest and most influential Muslim writer of narrative history up to the tenth century is al-Tabari (839-923). His multivolume history is unsurpassed and lays the groundwork for further study in all four of the Muslim traditions" (B. M. Hauglid, *Muslim Tradition*, pp. 136-137. See also R. C. Martin, *Encyclopedia*, 2:671; G. D. Newby, *Encyclopedia*, p. 199). Comprehensive in scope, it contains not only history but also philosophy (e.g., an opening essay is entitled "What is time?") as well as a substantial collection of the stories of the prophets. A comparison with the work of al-Tha'labi and al-Kisa'i, however, shows "the difference between their approach and that of the historian" (al-Tabari, *Creation, Foreword*, p. 163).	al-Tabari, *Creation*.

Mystical Texts

Over the centuries, a variety of texts by mystical believers in Islam have appeared. Most of these writings are generally associated with Sufism (probably from *suf* = wool, referring to the woolen garment worn by Muslim ascetics[353]), a loosely-organized movement that developed in the 8th and 9th centuries as a reaction against what were seen as legalistic and worldly tendencies in the growing Muslim empire.[354]

Sufi writings focus on esoteric meanings (*batin*) within the *Qur'an* and the *hadith* reports, and practices designed to lead to mystical knowledge and the bliss of divine love obtained by direct communion with God.[355] These practices are termed *tariqah*, the *inner* way, in contrast to the traditional Islamic emphasis on *shari'ah*, characterized by Sufis as the *outer* path—and observed with widely varying degrees of rigor by different Sufi groups.[356] The roles of Adam and Satan, the struggle between good and evil, and the meaning of creation are important themes in Sufism[357]—indeed, Adam is seen as the first Sufi.[358] The ideas of the Sufi movement have been historically and continue to be opposed by some groups within Islam, notably proponents of Salafism.

For a brief overview of Islamic mysticism, see W. C. Chittick, *Mysticism*. For more in-depth views including the social and political dimensions of Sufism, see C. W. Ernst, *Sufism*; C. W. Ernst, *Between*; A. Schimmel, *Mystical*. An overview of the various loosely-organized Sufi "orders" (*tariqah*) can be found in R. C. Martin, *Encyclopedia*, 2:680-684 and A. Schimmel, *Mystical*, pp. 228-258.

Text Name	Date	Description	Publication Reference
Mystical Texts			
The Mother of Books (Umm al-kitab)	Late 8th century	Not to be confused with the *Qur'an*, which has an identical nickname, this *ghulat* (= "exaggerator" or "extremist") text centers around the meaning of creation, essentially presenting "a gnostic mythological account in Shi'ite form" (W. Barnstone, *et al.*, *Gnostic*, p. 663).	Included in a collection within W. Barnstone, *et al.*, *Mother*.

---

353   Cf. M. al-Kisa'i, *Tales*, p. 68; al-Tabari, *Creation*, 1:123, p. 294.
354   V. Danner, *Sufism*.
355   J.-L. Michon, *Sufism*.
356   C. W. Ernst, *Between*, p. 116; A. Schimmel, *Mystical*, pp. 98-186.
357   A. Schimmel, *Mystical*, pp. 193-199.
358   *Ibid.*, p. 16.

Endnotes

B-1   Of course, as Nibley observes, no translation can adequately substitute for the original: "We do not study ancient languages in order to translate from them, but to read, ponder, savor, and, if possible, sound the depths of those things which cannot be translated but only tentatively paraphrased."[359]

B-2   These sections correspond to 72 threads of the sacred cord (*kusti*) worn as a girdle over an inner shirt of pure white (*sudra*) at all times by Zoroastrian men and women over the age of seven—recalling the 613 knots and strings on the Jewish talith corresponding to the laws of Moses. Sometimes the initiation ceremony (*Navjote*) is deliberately postponed until a later time, up to age 15, if the "child is not sufficiently intelligent to understand the ceremony and to know its responsibilities."[360] After a washing with water for purification, the "part of the child's body, which is to be covered with the sacred shirt by the officiating priest, carries a sheet of cloth which can be easily removed" and the child is brought before the priest. As the priest invests the child with his sacred shirt and cord a prayer is repeated, praising God, confessing a spirit of repentance, and asking for protection from the Evil Spirit. A possible derivation of the word *sudra* is from the Arabic *sdrh*, i.e., "anything which covers or protect (the body)."[361]

The symbolism of the clothing itself is explained by Modi:

> White color is symbolic of innocence and purity, and, as such, is the symbol of the Mazdayasnian or Zoroastrian religion. It must be made up of two pieces of cloth sewn together on the sides, so that one seam may be on the right hand side, and the other on the left hand side, thus dividing the shirt into two parts, the front part and the back part. These two parts—the front and the back—are said to be symbolic of the past and the future, both related to each other through the present. The front part must remind a Zoroastrian of his duty to persons and institutions of the past ages. We owe a duty towards those who have gone before us—to our ancestors, our forefathers, our departed dear ones, all who have preceded us. We also owe a duty to our superiors, who have been in the front before us. The second or the back part of the shirt must remind us of our duty to the future—to our children, to future generations. It must also remind us of our duty to our inferiors who are still to rise to our position... The most important part of the shirt is the *Giriban* (lit. that which preserves the knot) which signifies loyalty to or faith in the religion. The *Giriban* is also called the *kisseh-i kerfeh,* i.e. the purse or the bag of righteousness. It is put up, in the form of a bag or a purse a little below the portion of the shirt which covers the part of the body below the throat. It indicates symbolically that a man has to be industrious and has not only to fill his bag or purse with money but has to fill it up with righteousness [i. e., "the merits of good thoughts, words, and deeds, and so be laying up treasure for himself in heaven"[362]]...
>
> [T]he probable derivation [of the word *kusti*] seems to be *kost* (i.e., limit or boundary). *Kusti* then is that which keeps us, or reminds us to keep ourselves within proper limits or boundaries... The *kusti*, being prepared from the wool of a lamb, which is, in all ages, considered to be the emblem of innocence and purity, is held to be a badge reminding a Zoroastrian of the purity of life and action which he has always to observe.[363]

Russell concluded that the term *k'ustik* was a "popular archaic survival of Zoroastrianism" in writings of the 14th century Armenian Church, and compares its function to the priest's girdle in the Roman Catholic Church.[364]

B-3   The idea of the"castle" seems to combine the ideas of the ark of Noah and of the subterranean enclosure where, in a related tradition, Yima rules over the kingdom of the dead.[365]

Nigosian offers a somewhat different amalgamation of the legends concerning Yima: "According to one legend, Yima had a golden reign of one thousand years during which he deprived the malevolent deities of their prosperity, and took away their power to inflict cold or heat, old age, death, or disease on their victims.[366] This golden age, however, did not last forever, because Yima sinned and human

---

359   H. W. Nibley, *Greek*, p. 112.

360   J. J. Modi, *Navjote*.

361   *Ibid.*

362   M. Boyce, *Zoroastrians*, p. 32.

363   J. J. Modi, *Navjote*.

364   J. R. Russell, *K'ustik*.

365   D. P. Miller, *Yogananda*, pp. 12-13, 95.

366   F. M. Müller, *Yasna*, 9:4-5, p. 232. See also F. M. Müller, *Dinkard* 5, 7, 7:1:20, p. 9.

beings lost their immortality.[367] Then the wise father, Vivahvant, warned Yima to retreat underground as humanity was to be afflicted by winter. There Yima was to remain, together with his followers, until the signs foreshadowing the last days appeared—the worst being a winter more terrible than any the world had ever seen.[368] Then Yima was to re-emerge and re-populate the devastated earth.[369]

According to another legend, Yima was the institutor of the bull-sacrifice, the ritualistic observance of which was believed to banish from the world disease, old age, and death."[370] Russell notes the parallels between the creation account of the *Bundahishn* and Mithraism when, "[a]t the beginning of historical time, the evil spirit Ahriman attacks the newly-created universe and slays the primeval bull, the unique living animal…—and the abundance of all good creatures emerge from the corpse of this first victim of murder through a strategem of the wise and good Creator, Ahura Mazda… Mithra himself does not slay any bull, but it was customary for Zoroastrians to sacrifice a sheep in recent times, and a bull in ancient times, on Mihragan, the feast dedicated to Mithra."[371]

B-4   Zoroastrianism, at least in its presumably later Zurvan form,[372] is really not a radical dualism, since the two opposite cosmic powers (Ahura Mazda and Angra Mainyu) were born of the same primordial divinity (Zurvan, "which signifies more than destiny itself or the original time"), with Ahura Mazda dominant through the four ages of the current world and a Savior (Saoshyant) who ultimately wins the eschatological war.[373]

B-5   The ongoing stewardship of the first man over all God's creatures is expressed in the Pahlavi *Dadistan-i Dinik*: "One [of the three best] is the pure man, Gayomard, who was its first rational praiser; he in whose keeping was the whole creation of the sacred beings, from its beginning and immaturity unto the final completion of the worldly creatures."[374]

B-6   Zoroastrian teachings about the four ages that conclude in the resurrection are summarized as follows: "Twelve thousand years are supposed to elapse between the first creation and the resurrection; during the first three (about 8400-5400 BCE) the creation remains undisturbed in a spiritual state, during the next three (5400-2400 BCE) the evil spirit appears, but flies back to hell in confusion, during the next three (2400 BCE-600 CE) he attacks the creation and keeps it in a constant state of tribulation, and during the last three (600-3600 CE) his power, having attained its maximum, is gradually weakened till it is finally destroyed at the resurrection."[375]

B-7   Boyce further explains:

> An essential element in [*Yasna* 30] is that the two primal Beings each made a deliberate choice (although each, it seems, according to his own proper nature) between good and evil, an act which prefigures the identical choice which every man must make for himself in this life. The exercise of choice changed the inherent antagonism between the two Spirits into an active one, which expressed itself, at a decision taken by Ahura Mazda, in creation and counter-creation, or, as the prophet put it, in the making of 'life' and 'not life' (that is, death); for Ahura Mazda knew in his wisdom that if he became Creator and fashioned this world, then the Hostile Spirit would attack it, because it was good, and would become a battleground for their two forces, and in the end he, God, would win the great struggle there and be able to destroy evil, and so achieve a universe which would be wholly good forever.[376]

B-8   *Ginza* recounts that a garment and a promise of ongoing assistance was also given to Adam at this time, as summarized by Nibley:

367   A. Ferdowsi, *Shahnama*, pp. 7-8; F. M. Müller, *Yasts*, 19:(7):35-36, 38, pp. 293-295.

368   F. M. Müller, *Vendidad*, 2:4-41, pp. 12-20.

369   F. M. Müller, *Dinkard* 5, 7, 7:9:4-5, p. 108. See also F. M. Müller, *Bahman Yast*, 3:55, p. 234.

370   S. A. Nigosian, *Zoroastrian Faith*, p. 19.

371   J. R. Russell, *Mithraism*, p. 648.

372   Y. Stoyanov, *Other God*, pp. 44ff.

373   L. Afloroaei, *Dualism*, p. 94.

374   F. M. Müller, *Dadistan-i Dinik*, 2:10, p. 13.

375   F. M. Müller, *Pahlavi 2*, p. 82 n. 1 re: 37:11. See F. M. Müller, *Bahman Yast*, 2:44, 2:52, 2:61-62, 3:1-63, pp. 208-209, 210, 213, 215-235; F. M. Müller, *Bundahis*, 1:18, 1:20, 1:22, 3:1, 34:1-9, pp. 7-9, 15, 149-151.

376   D. P. Miller, *Yogananda*, pp. 20-21.

…when Adam stood praying for light and knowledge, a helper came to him, gave him a garment, and told him, 'Those men who gave you the garment will assist you throughout your life until you are ready to leave earth.'[377]

B-9 Although Drower faithfully recorded "how modern priests celebrate the rite," she notes that "they did not tell me the symbolic meaning of the actions they performed… I have sometimes wondered if they really knew."[378] Guénon confirms such happenings in the transmission of initiatory rites more generally.[379] This is one reason why, as Nibley has explained, the study of the rites themselves should generally take priority over the explanations given for them:

> Myths arise at attempts to explain ritual doings, whose meaning has been forgotten—"What mean these stones?"[380] After much discussion back and forth, the consensus now emerges that it is the rites and ordinances that come first. This should have been clear from the outset, since myths and legends are innumerable while the rites and ordinances found throughout the world are surprisingly few and uniform, making it apparent that it is the stories that are invented—the rites are always there. Such indeed has always been the Latter-day Saint position. Adam first performed an ordinance and when asked to give an explanation of it replied that he knew of none 'save the Lord commanded me.'[381] Then it was that the true explanation came forth from the mouth of a heavenly instructor.[382]

> When the *masbuta* is performed on newborn children, "the child's astrological name is pronounced and given. The name is 'calculated' beforehand by the priest, who presents the parents with a short list of names from which to choose. In fact, every Mandaean has four names, but this is the most secret and important one. It will hardly ever be told to a stranger, though it is the name used always (and almost exclusively) in religious rituals."[383]

Similarly, Jewish children are also given a special name used in religious events, and "Moslems get a new name at Mecca that they must keep secret. This name is used when they approach Allah after death. Moslems return to Mecca in behalf of relatives who have died and did not have the chance to go to Mecca themselves. Living proxies may apparently get the new name for their relatives."[384]

B-10 The *Conflict of Adam and Eve with Satan* relates how Satan used a handclasp as part of a deception of Adam that involved his taking an oath:[385]

> Then Adam said, "I know not how to swear and promise." And Satan said to him, "Hold out thy hand, and put it inside my hand." Then Adam held out his hand, and put it into Satan's hand; when Satan said unto him, "Say, now—so true as God is living, rational, and speaking, who raised the heavens in the space, and established the earth upon the waters, and has created me out of the four elements, and out of the dust of the earth—I will not break my promise, nor renounce my word." And Adam swore thus.[386]

B-11 Lupieri comments:

> The soul's rise through the heavens [after death] is in itself a dangerous voyage because the heavens are inhabited by demons or evil beings. The various heavens are the site of the "houses of punish-

377 H. W. Nibley, *Apocryphal*, p. 299. The full German text in Lidzbarski's translation reads: "Wie Adam dasteht und sich aufzuklären sucht, kam der Mann, sein Helfer. Der hohe Helfer kam zu ihm, der ihn in ein Stück reichen Glanzes hineintrug. Er sprach zu ihm: 'Ziehe dein Gewand an, damit du in deinem eigenen Glanze feststehest'… Darauf öffnete Adam den Mund und sprach zu seinem Helfer: 'Welche Kraft verleiht ihr mir in Fülle, daß ich dieses Gewand anziehe? Mit welcher Stütze stützet ihr mich in der Tibil, daß ich im hinfälligen Hause wohnen soll?' Da erwidern sie ihm: 'Deine Kraft ist die Kraft des großen (Lebens), deine Erleuchtung ist von ihrer Stätte her geschaffen. Die Männer, die dein Gewand geschaffen, dienen dir, bis du abscheidest." (M. Lidzbarski, *Ginza*, GL 2:19, p. 488).

378 E. S. Drower, *Adam*, p. 74.

379 R. Guénon, *Symboles*, p. 210.

380 See Joshua 4:6.

381 Moses 5:6.

382 H. W. Nibley, *Myths*, p. 42; cf. H. W. Nibley, *Apocryphal*, p. 320, H. W. Nibley, *Greatness*, pp. 294-295.

383 E. Lupieri, *Mandaeans*, p. 17.

384 D. Rona, *Revealed*, p. 28.

385 See *Commentary* 1:25-c, p. 60; *Figure 6-14*, p. 473; *Excursus 53: Comparative Explorations, Dexiosis*, p. 681; the *Mandaean Texts* and *Manichaean Texts* sections of the *Annotated Bibliography*, pp. 870, 884; *Figure B-1*, p. 872. See *Endnote 1-22*, p. 79.

386 S. C. Malan, *Adam and Eve*, 1:70, pp. 85-86.

ment" or *matarata*, a sort of heavenly purgatory, in which those souls who do not have a pass constituted by the purity of their lives (in Mandaean observance) are imprisoned for various lengths of time, for purification through suffering. This is why on the first, third, seventh, and forty-fifth days after death ritual meals take place in which the soul of the departed supposedly takes part, and from which it draws strength.[387]

In this connection, Rudolph notes that: "Nearly all ceremonies, including even the wedding ritual, are in some way associated with a rite which has value for the souls of the dead."[388]

B-12   Jesus, Paul, Hermes Trismegistus, Plato, Zoroaster, and the Buddha were also included in this group, the latter two which some scholars say were added in an express design "to convey an imperialistic argument to the [Sassanian] king" who, according to Manichaean accounts, became a believer.[389] At least one other notable—possibly Marcion, Bardasian and/or Elchasai—could also be listed in this group based on an elliptical reference in the *Kephalaia*.[390] In what Reeves calls a "conscious syncretism,"[391] it seems that Manichaeism "did not hesitate to incorporate anything of possible utility for the advancement of its positions."[392]

B-13   Reeves comments:[393]

The epithet "seal of the prophets"… normally associated with the mission of Muhammad, is almost certainly of Manichaean origin and designates the teleological status of Mani within the chain of authentic messengers to humankind. The locution 'seal" is frequently employed in Manichaean ideology: e.g., the "Three Seals"… of mouth, hands, and heart (i.e., thought).[394]

Mani also claimed to be the Paraclete (= Greek *parakletos*, a consoler, comforter, or advocate) whose coming was foretold by Jesus.[395] Some Muslims also see Muhammad,[396] or a controversial messianic figure referred to as *al-Mahdi* (= Arabic "the Guided One"),[397] as the subject of Jesus' promise of a Paraclete: "And remember, Jesus, son of Mary, said: O Children of Israel, surely I am the messenger of Allah to you, verifying that which is before me of the *Torah* and giving the good news of a Messenger who will come after me, his name being Ahmad [i.e., the Praised One, taking the Greek *paraclete* to be a corruption of *periklytos*[398]]. But when he came to them with clear arguments, they said: This is clear enchantment."[399]

B-14   Reeves writes:

Comparative analysis of these five apocalypses will show that overall they have been artificially and secondarily fashioned by resourceful redactors who had access to reservoirs of authentic Jewish pseudepigraphic traditions. The purpose of such fabrication and manipulation of textual fragments is clear—to demonstrate that Mani… is an authentic link in the chain of "apostles."[400]

B-15   Reflecting these religious ideas about the opposition between good and evil, the term "Manichaean" has been increasingly adopted for use in ordinary conversation. In perhaps its first popular reference in recent years, the term was aptly employed in a 1966 essay by May criticizing the ideology of the "Radical Right,"[401] however its use in subsequent political discourse has been with widely varying degrees of erudition.[402] In some cases, it has been used to mean nothing more than contrasting binary categories (e.g., "Manichaean, and therefore simplistic, oppositions between the professor and the

387   E. Lupieri, *Mandaeans*, pp. 31-32.

388   In W. Foerster, *Gnosis*, p. 133.

389   J. C. Reeves, *Heralds*, p. 13.

390   I. Gardner, *Kephalaia*, 13:30-32, p. 19 and p. 19 n. 4; cf. J. C. Reeves, *Manichaean Literature*, pp. 174, 192 n. 7.

391   J. C. Reeves, *Manichaean Literature*, p. 1.

392   J. C. Reeves, *Heralds*, p. 13.

393   *Ibid.*, p. 22 n. 27.

394   *Homilies* 13:27-28, cited in *ibid.*, p. 22 n. 27.

395   J. C. Reeves, *Heralds*, p. 24 n. 47. See John 14:16-19, 26; 15:26, 16:7.

396   M. M. Ali, *Qurʾan*, p. 1056 n. 2496; M. I. I. Bukhari, *Sahih*, 60:3:3340, 4:449, 451.

397   S. Bhimji, *Al-Mahdi*; S. H. M. Jafri, *Shiʿism*, pp. 161, 166, 167, 172, 173; R. C. Martin, *Encyclopedia*, 2:421; G. D. Newby, *Encyclopedia*, pp. 135-136; Porch of Wisdom Cultural Institution, *Faith and Reason*, pp. 179-218.

398   A. A. Y. Ali, *Qurʾan*, p. 1461 n. 5438.

399   M. M. Ali, *Qurʾan*, 61:6, pp. 1056-1057.

400   J. C. Reeves, *Heralds*, p. 17.

401   W. F. May, *Manichaeism*.

402   E.g., Z. Brzezinski, *Second Chance*; A. Gore, *Assault*; P. Singer, *Bush*.

pundit, the left-wing thinker and the right-wing one or the conservative and the liberal"[403]).

B-16 According to the Christian Theodore bar Konai, Mani taught that after the creation of Adam and Eve "Jesus the Luminous [perhaps assisted by other emissaries[404] approached the unsuspecting Adam and roused him from the sleep of death, that he might be delivered from the great spirit... Then Adam examined himself and recognized who he was, and (Jesus) showed him the Fathers on high, and (revealed to him) regarding his own self all that which he had fallen into... He says that... (Jesus) raised him up and made him taste of the Tree of Life."[405]

In place of "raised him up," Widengren has "baptized him." Reeves cites Widengren's arguments for this alternate translation based on "unidentified Mandaic references." However, he fails to find additional confirmation for this proposal, and contends that the idea of Adam's being raised to a standing position is more likely, given "Mani's known hostility to 'baptism' and the previous prone state of Adam."[406]

Widengren,[407] however, discusses this topic in great depth, relating Akkadian, Sumerian, and Mandaic sources that interpret "standing" in the context of enthronement festivals. For example, "a bilingual poem addressed to a deity of Tammuz character" depicts him as "standing in the sanctuary of the Freshwater Deep, the adorned, purified with sparkling lustration."[408]

B-17 Other accounts place Mani's death as being after the decease of King Shapur I and his successor Hormizd, during the reign of the Persian Emperor Bahram I, about 276-277. During this time Kerder (or Karder), the head Zoroastrian priest, with the support of Bahram, began official persecution of minority sects.[409]

B-18 BeDuhn emphasizes that "[w]e lose the ability to 'make sense' of the Manichaean system the moment we lose sight of the absolute identity of the individual and the collective soul. There is no individual salvation in Manichaeism, only the common 'work of religion' involving solar and lunar orbits, ocean tides, and plant exhalations, as much as human activity... When we look closely, Manichaean discourse about the soul and concern with its salvation turns out to be very much 'a something about the body.'"[410]

B-19 In February 2005, President Boyd K. Packer visited a prominent mosque in Jakarta, Indonesia and asked the head cleric "if they might pray together. The cleric agreed. President Packer 'blessed the mosque, the cleric, and all who attend to pray and worship.' Following the prayer, the tearful cleric thanked President Packer for 'his faith and prayers on their behalf.'"[411]

B-20 The supreme sin in Islam is *shirk* (= association) the attribution of any equal or partner to God. Some Islamic revivalists accuse Christians and Jews of *shirk*, based on *Qur'an* 5:72-73 and 9:30; however, most Muslims accept a distinction between these faiths and polytheists (*mushrikun* = ones who associate) based on 2:105.[412]

B-21 Traditional accounts of the formation of the *Qur'an* are to be found in the *sirah* literature.[413] A summary and critical evaluation of these accounts is given in F. M. Donner, *Context* and C. Gilliot, *Fixed Text*. Motzki provides an overview of alternatives to the traditional accounts, some of which place the formation of the *Qur'an* at a later period.[414]

B-22 Peterson and Ricks raise the possibility of parallels between the call of Muhammad and the throne of Old Testament prophets such as Isaiah and Ezekiel. They also cite sources suggesting that "Gabriel was only identified as the vehicle of revelation quite late, and that, at the first, it was God himself who was

---

403 P. Guerlain, *Kagan and Chomsky*, p. 447.

404 E. Isaac, *1 Enoch*, pp. 17-18; J. C. Reeves, *Jewish Lore*, pp. 205 n. 54, 206 n. 64.

405 Cited in J. C. Reeves, *Jewish Lore*, p. 193.

406 J. C. Reeves, *Jewish Lore*, p. 205 n. 58.

407 G. Widengren, *Enthronement*.

408 AnOr 10, p. 214:2-6, cited in G. Widengren, *Enthronement*, p. 581.

409 G. Widengren, *Mani*, pp. 37-42. Collections of accounts of the death of Mani in English can be found in J. P. Asmussen, *Manichaean Literature*, pp. 54-58; W. Barnstone, *Death of Mani*; A. Welburn, *Mani*, pp. 107-114.

410 J. D. BeDuhn, *Manichaean Body*, p. 233.

411 C. F. Emmett, *Building*.

412 R. C. Martin, *Encyclopedia*, 2:630-631.

413 R.g., M. Ibn Ishaq ibn Yasar, *Sirat Rasul*.

414 H. Motzki, *Alternative*. See also J. Wansbrough, *Qur'anic Studies*.

viewed as the agent of inspiration."[415]

B-23   Whereas traditional accounts rely on the *sirah* as evidence for standard interpretations of the *Qur'an*, some skeptical writers have argued conversely that at least some of these biographical reports "may, in fact, have originated to invent a supposed historical context for exegetical readings of particular verses" (F. M. Donner, *Context*, p. 34).

B-24   Note that the term *sirah* is closely related to the term *shari'ah* (= a path to the watering hole or the spring itself), the term used to describe what is accepted as divinely-inspired principles covering religious, political, legal, social, domestic and private life that have been worked out by Muslim scholars according to various schools of thought.[416] The practical importance of *shari'ah* in non-domestic affairs varies with the degree of Islamization in a given country.[417] Sometimes the term *shari'ah* is also used to describe religious laws of non-Muslim faiths.

B-25   According to Daniel W. Brown, the "single most important focus of controversy in modern Muslim discussions of religious authority" is the difference between modernists and conservatives on the authority of *sunna*.[418]

B-26   For example, "the cryptic Qur'anic statement that likens a good word to a good tree[419] is understood by *Shi'ites* to refer specifically to the Prophet and his family. Contrarily, a corrupt word likened to a corrupt tree[420] points to the immoral *Umayyads*, whom *Shi'ites* view as usurpers of their rightful leadership." In another reference, *Sunnis* read *umma* (community) while *Shi'a* read *a'imma* (*imami* leaders).[421] Many such differences have to do with divergent views on the issue of succession following the death of Muhammad.[422]

B-27   Of the change in scholarly perspectives on *isra'iliyyat*, and the literature on Jesus in particular, over the hundred years, Khalidi writes:

> In the early part of the twentieth century, …analysis was generally embedded in polemic. Muhammad (very rarely the *Qur'an*) is said to have had a confused and/or heretical notion of Christianity. The Qur'anic stories and sayings of Jesus which "he" narrated were fables and fantasies, or at best apocryphal material which, one is left to presume, circulated more easily in the marginal regions of the Byzantine world. Where these stories could not be securely traced back to an origin, they were sometimes said to be the product of a "fertile oriental imagination"… Several factors, however, have acted to balance, if not entirely to change, these images and interpretations of the Qur'anic Jesus in Western scholarship. To begin with, the resurgence of scientific interest in folklore studies and a radical reassessment of the place and function of myth in systems of belief have led to a more tolerant, even sympathetic attitude to the "fables" of the *Qur'an* and of early Islamic literature in general. In some cases, it is recognized that such fables may in fact possess considerable importance—not so much in themselves but for their role in preserving Jewish or Christian materials that might otherwise have been lost.… Last, the introduction of various tools of modern literary criticism into the analysis of the Qur'anic text has led to a shift in emphasis away from the delineation of 'influence' and toward an attempt to understand the text on its own terms and territory. The results of this endeavor are not uniformly convincing, but they do at least represent a new departure from the analysis of the Qur'anic images of Jesus in terms of influence or derivation, terms which are now recognized to be far more complex processes than was hitherto assumed.[423]

B-28   The numerous Islamic texts excerpted in J. A. Tvedtnes, *et al.*, *Traditions* that had to be translated directly from Arabic for the first time evidence how few of the primary sources for the stories of the prophets are currently available in English.

---

415   D. C. Peterson *et al.*, *Theophany*, p. 325.

416   G. D. Newby, *Encyclopedia*, *shari'ah*, pp. 193-194.

417   R. C. Martin, *Encyclopedia*, 2:584-590. See N. Feldman, *Rise* for a historical overview of the role of *shari'ah* in the governments of the Islamic world. J. L. Esposito, *et al.*, *Who Speaks* give a report of the results of a ground-breaking Gallup poll on the religious, political, and social views of Muslims worldwide.

418   *Ibid.*, 2:668-669.

419   *Qur'an* 14:24.

420   *Qur'an* 14:26.

421   R. C. Martin, *Encyclopedia*, 2:673-674.

422   *Ibid.*, 2:651-656

423   T. Khalidi, *Muslim Jesus*, pp. 8, 9.

REFERENCES

Abegg, Martin, Jr., Peter Flint, and Eugene Ulrich, eds. *The Dead Sea Scrolls Bible*. New York City, NY: Harper, 1999.

Abravanel, Isaac. *Commentaire du Récit de la Création d'Isaac Abravanel*. Edited by Yehouda Schiffers. Lagrasse, France: Éditions Verdier, 1999.

Ackerman, Robert. *The Myth and Ritual School: J. G. Frazer and the Cambridge Ritualists*. New York City, NY: Routledge, 2002.

Ackroyd, Peter. 1995. *Blake*. London, England: Vintage, 1999.

"Adam and Eve." In *Wikipedia*. http://en.wikipedia.org/wiki/Adam_and_Eve (accessed September 27, 2008).

"Adam Lay Ybounden." In *Wikipedia*. http://en.wikipedia.org/wiki/Adam_Lay_Ybounden (accessed March 12, 2009).

"Adam-God Theory." In *Wikipedia*. http://en.wikipedia.org/wiki/Adam–God_theory (accessed August 28, 2006).

Adams, Vivian M. "'Our glorious mother Eve.'" In *The Man Adam*, edited by Joseph Fielding McConkie and Robert L. Millet, 87-111. Salt Lake City, UT: Bookcraft, 1990.

Afloroaei, Lucia. "Religious dualism: Some logical and philosophical difficulties." *Journal for Interdisciplinary Research on Religion and Science*, no. 4 (January 2009): 83-111.

Agnew, N.M., and J.L. Brown. "Foundations for a theory of knowing: I. Construing reality." *Canadian Psychology* 30 (1989): 152-67.

———. "Foundations for a theory of knowing: II. Fallible but functional knowledge." *Canadian Psychology* 30 (1989): 168-83.

Akenson, Donald Harman. *Surpassing Wonder: The Invention of the Bible and the Talmuds*. New York City NY: Harcourt Brace, 1998.

Akslund, Markus. *The Sacred Footprint: A Cultural History of Adam's Peak*. Orchid Guides. Bangkok, Thailand: Orchid Press, 2001.

al-Khalesi, Yasin M. *The Court of the Palms: A Functional Interpretation of the Mari Palace*. Bibliotheca Mesopotamica 8, ed. Giorgio Buccellati. Malibu, CA: Undena Publications, 1978.

al-Kisa'i, Muhammad ibn Abd Allah. ca. 1000-1100. *Tales of the Prophets (Qisas al-anbiya)*. Translated by Wheeler M. Thackston, Jr. *Great Books of the Islamic World*, ed. Seyyed Hossein Nasr. Chicago, IL: KAZI Publications, 1997.

al-Nadim, Ibn. d. ca. 995. "Fihrist." In *Mani: Seine Lehre und seine Schriften. Ein Beitrag zur Geschichte des Manichäismus. Aus dem Fihrist desAbû'lfaradsch Muhammad ben Ishak al-Warrâk, bekannt unter dem Namen Ibn Abî Ja'kub an-Nadim, im Text nebst Uebersetzung, Commentar und Index zum ersten Mal herausgegeben*, edited by Gustav Leberecht Flügel. Leipzig, Germany: F. A. Brockhaus, 1862. Reprint, Osnabrück, Germany: Biblio Verlag, 1969.

al-Qurtubi, Abu Abdullah Muhammad ibn Ahmad al-Andalusi. d. 1273. *Tafsir Al-Qurtubi: Classical Commentary of the Holy Qur'an*. Translated by Aisha Bewley. London, England: Dar al-Taqwa, 2003.

al-Rabghuzi, Nosiruddin Burhonuddin. ca. 1350. *The Stories of the Prophets: Qisas Al-Anbiya: An Eastern Turkish Version*, ed. Hendrik E. Boeschoten, M. Vandamme and Semih Tezcan. Leiden, The Netherlands: Brill, 1995.

al-Tabari. d. 923. *The History of al-Tabari: General Introduction and From the Creation to the Flood*. Vol. 1. Translated by Franz Rosenthal. *Biblioteca Persica*, ed. Ehsan Yar-Shater. Albany, NY: State University of New York Press, 1989.

al-Tha'labi, Abu Ishaq Ahmad Ibn Muhammad Ibn Ib rahim. d. 1035. *'Ara'is Al-Majalis Fi Qisas Al-Anbiya' or "Lives of the Prophets"*. Translated by William M. Brinner. *Studies in Arabic Literature, Supplements to the Journal of Arabic Literature*, Volume 24, ed. Suzanne Pinckney Stetkevych. Leiden, Netherlands: Brill, 2002.

al-Zamakhshari, Jar Allah. d. 1144. *A Traditional Mu'tazilite Qur'an Commentary: The Kathaf of Jar Allah Al-Zamakhshari*. Translated by Andrew J. Lane. *Texts and Studies on the Qur'an*. Leiden, The Netherlands: Brill Academic Publishers, 2005.

Albeck, Chanoch, ed. *Midrash Bereshit Rabbati*. Jerusalem, Israel: Mekitze Nirdamim, 1940.

"Albion." In *Wikipedia*. http://en.wikipedia.org/wiki/Albion (accessed November 23, 2007).

Albrecht, Stan L., and Tim. B. Heaton. "Secularization, higher education, and religiosity." *Review of Religious Research* 26, no. 1 (September 1984): 43-58.

Alexander, P. ed. "3 (Hebrew Apocalypse of) Enoch." In *The Old Testament Pseudepigrapha*, edited by James H. Charlesworth. 2 vols. Vol. 1, 223-315. Garden City, NY: Doubleday and Company, 1983.

Ali, Allama Abdullah Yusuf, ed. 1938. *The Holy Qur'an: Arabic Text, English Translation and Commentary*. Lahore, Pakistan: Sheikh Muhammad Ashraf, 2001.

Ali, Maulana Muhammad, ed. 1951. *The Holy Qur'an with English Translation and Commentary*. Columbus, OH: Ahmadiyyah Anjuman Isha'at Islam (Lahore), 1999.

Alighieri, Dante. 1321. "Commedia." In *Princeton Dante Project*, Princeton, NJ. http://etcweb.princeton.edu/dante/pdp/ (accessed November 28, 2007).

All Things Testify of Him. Salt Lake City, UT: Bookcraft, 1998.

Allan, Sarah. *The Shape of the Turtle: Myth, Art, and Cosmos in Early China*. SUNY Series in Chinese Philosophy and Culture, eds. David L. Hall and Roger T. Ames. Albany, NY: State University of New York Press, 1991.

Allberry, Charles Robert Cecil Augustine, ed. *A Manichaean Psalm-Book, Part 2. Manichaean Manuscripts in the Chester Beatty Collection* 2. Stuttgart, Germany: W. Kohlhammer, 1938.

Allen, James P., ed. *The Ancient Egyptian Pyramid Texts. Writings from the Ancient World* 23, ed. Theodore J. Lewis. Atlanta, GA: Society of Biblical Literature, 2005.

———, ed. *The Egyptian Coffin Texts: Middle Kingdom Copies of Pyramid Texts*. Vol. 8. *Oriental Institute Publications* 132. Chicago, IL: The Oriental Institute, 2006.

Allen, Roger. *An Introduction to Arabic Literature*. Cambridge, England: Cambridge University Press, 2000.

Allen, Thomas G., ed. *The Book of the Dead or Going Forth by Day: Ideas of the Ancient Egyptians Concerning the Hereafter as Expressed in Their Own Terms. Studies in Ancient Oriental Civilization* 37. Chicago, IL: University of Chicago Press, 1974.

———, ed. *The Egyptian Book of the Dead: Documents in the Oriental Institute Museum at the University of Chicago*. Chicago, IL: University of Chicago Press, 1960.

Allison, Dale C., ed. *Testament of Abraham*. Berlin, Germany: Walter de Gruyter, 2003.

Allred, Alma. "The traditions of their fathers: Myth versus reality in LDS scriptural writings." In *Black and Mormon*, edited by Newell G. Bringhurst and Darron T. Smith, 34-49. Urbana, IL: University of Illinois Press, 2004.

Alter, Robert. *The Art of Biblical Narrative*. New York: Basic Books, 1981.

———, ed. The *Book of Psalms: A Translation with Commentary*. New York City, NY: W. W. Norton, 2007.

———, ed. *The David Story: A Translation with Commentary of 1 and 2 Samuel*. New York City, NY: W. W. Norton, 1999.

———, ed. *The Five Books of Moses: A Translation with Commentary*. New York City, NY: W. W. Norton, 2004.

———, ed. *Genesis*. New York City, NY: W. W. Norton, 1996.

American Bible Society. *Biblia Hebraica Stuttgartensia*. 5th ed. New York City, NY: American Bible Society, 1997.

American Heritage Dictionary of the English Language, Fourth Edition. 2000. In *Bartleby.com*. http://www.bartleby.com/61/ (accessed April 26, 2009).

"Ancient ruins." Nauvoo, IL: *Times and Seasons* 5:23, December 15, 1844, 744-48.

Anderson, Arnold A. *The Book of Psalms*. Vol. 2, Psalms 73-150. Grand Rapids, MI: Eerdmans, 1981.

Andersen, Francis I. ed. "2 (Slavonic Apocalypse of) Enoch." In *The Old Testament Pseudepigrapha*, edited by James H. Charlesworth. 2 vols. Vol. 1, 91-221. Garden City, NY: Doubleday and Company, 1983.

Andersen, Francis I., and David Noel Freedman. *Hosea: A New Translation with Introduction and Commentary. The Anchor Bible* 24, eds. William Foxwell Albright and David Noel Freedman. Garden City, NY: Doubleday, 1980.

Anderson, E. H., and R. T. Haag. "The Book of the Revelation of Abraham: A Translation." From G. Nathanael Bonwetsch's then-unpublished German translation. *Improvement Era* 1, August-September 1898, 705-14, 93-806.

Anderson, Gary A. "Ezekiel 28, the fall of Satan, and the Adam books." In *Literature on Adam and Eve: Collected Essays*, edited by Gary A. Anderson, Michael Stone, and Johannes Tromp, 133-47. Leiden, Netherlands: Brill, 2000.

———. "The fall of Satan in the thought of St. Ephrem and John Milton." *Hogoye: Journal of Syriac Studies* 3, no. 1 (January 2000). http://syrcom.cua.edu/hugoye/Vol3No1/HV3N1Anderson.html (accessed August 16, 2007).

———. "The garments of skin in apocryphal narrative and biblical commentary." In *Studies in Ancient Midrash*, edited by James L. Kugel, 101-43. Cambridge, MA: Harvard University Press, 2001.

———. *The Genesis of Perfection: Adam and Eve in Jewish and Christian Imagination*. Louisville, KY: Westminster John Knox Press, 2001.

———. "The original form of the *Life of Adam and Eve*: A proposal." In *Literature on Adam and Eve: Collected Essays*, edited by Gary A. Anderson, Michael E. Stone and Johannes Tromp, 215-31. Leiden, Netherlands: Brill, 2000.

———. "The penitence narrative in the Life of Adam and Eve." In *Literature on Adam and Eve: Collected Essays*, edited by Gary A. Anderson, Michael E. Stone and Johannes Tromp, 3-42. Leiden, Netherlands: Brill, 2000.

———. *Sacrifices and Offerings in Ancient Israel. Harvard Semitic Monographs* 41, ed. Frank Moore Cross. Atlanta, GA: Scholars Press, 1987.

———. *Sin: A History*. New Haven, CN: Yale University Press, 2009.

Anderson, Gary A., and Michael Stone, eds. *A Synopsis of the Books of Adam and Eve* 2nd ed. *Society of Biblical Literature: Early Judaism and its Literature*, ed. John C. Reeves. Atlanta, GA: Scholars Press, 1999.

Anderson, Richard Lloyd. "The impact of the first preaching in Ohio." In *Oliver Cowdery: Scribe, Elder, Witness (Essays from BYU Studies and FARMS)*, edited by John W. Welch and Larry E. Morris, 195-220. Provo, UT: The Neal A. Maxwell Institute for Religious Scholarship, Brigham Young University, 2006.

Anderson, Washington F. "'Life sketch of J. M. Bernhisel, author unknown.'" In *John M. Bernhisel Papers, 1825-1910, MSS SC 331 box 2, Manuscript Collection, L. Tom Perry Special Collections*, 12 pp. and 8 pp. Provo, UT: Harold B. Lee Library, Brigham Young University, ca. 1881.

Andrews, Carol, ed. *The Ancient Egyptian Book of the Dead*. Revised ed. Translated by Raymond O. Faulkner. London, England: British Museum Publications, 1985. Reprint, Austin, TX: University of Texas Press, 1990.

Andrus, Hyrum L. *Doctrinal Commentary on the Pearl of Great Price*. Salt Lake City, UT: Deseret Book, 1970.

———. *Doctrinal Commentary on the Pearl of Great Price*. Revised ed. Salt Lake City, UT: Deseret Book, 2003.

———. *Doctrines of the Kingdom*. Salt Lake City, UT: Bookcraft, 1973.

———. *God, Man, and the Universe*. Salt Lake City, UT: Bookcraft, 1968.

———. *Principles of Perfection*. Salt Lake City, UT: Bookcraft, 1970.

Andrus, Hyrum L., and Helen Mae Andrus, eds. *They Knew the Prophet*. Salt Lake City, UT: Bookcraft, 1974.

———, eds. 1974. *They Knew the Prophet*. American Fork, UT: Covenant, 2004.

Anklesaria, Behramgore Tehmuras, ed. *Zand-Akasih: Iranian or Greater Bundahishn*. Bombay, India: Rahnumae Mazdayasnan Sabha and Dastur Framroze A. Bode, 1956. http://www.avesta.org/pahlavi/grb.htm (accessed July 26, 2007).

Ansary, Tamim. *Destiny Disrupted: A History of the World through Islamic Eyes*. New York City, NY: PublicAffairs, 2009.

"Answering media questions about Jesus and Satan." In *Newsroom: The Official Resource for News Media, Opinion Leaders, and the Public*. The Church of Jesus Christ of Latter-day Saints. http://newsroom.lds.org/ldsnewsroom/eng/commentary/answering-media-questions-about-jesus-and-satan (accessed March 19, 2009).

"Apostolic Constitutions." In *Encyclopedia Britannica Online*. http://www.britannica.com/EBchecked/topic/30274/Apostolic-Constitutions (accessed January 7, 2009).

"Approaching Mormon doctrine." In *Newsroom: The Official Resource for News Media, Opinion Leaders, and the Public*. The Church of Jesus Christ of Latter-day Saints. http://newsroom.lds.org/ldsnewsroom/eng/commentary/approaching-mormon-doctrine (accessed February 26, 2008).

Aquinas, Thomas. 1265-1274. *The Summa Theologica of St. Thomas Aquinas*. 5 vols. Translated by Fathers of the English Dominican Province. 2nd ed. London, England: Burns, Oates, and Washbourne, 1920. Reprint, Notre Dame, IN: Benzier Brothers /Ave Maria Press, 1981. http://www.newadvent.org/summa/ (accessed August 6, 2007).

Arberry, A. J., ed. 1955. *The Koran Interpreted: A Translation*. New York City, NY: Touchstone Books, 1996.

Aristophanes. 380 BCE. "Plutus." In *The Internet Classics Archive*. http://classics.mit.edu/Aristophanes/plutus.html (accessed May 2, 2009).

Armstrong, Karen. *Jerusalem: One City, Three Faiths*. New York City, NY: Ballantine Books, 2005.

Arnold, Bill T. *Encountering the Book of Genesis*. Grand Rapids, MI: Baker Books, 1998.

———. *Genesis. New Cambridge Bible Commentary*, ed. Ben Witherington, III. New York City, NY: Cambridge University Press, 2009.

Arnon, Noam. *The Cave of Machpela: Roots of the Jewish People*. Translated by Raphael Blumberg. 2nd ed. Kiryat Arba, Hebron, Israel: The Ma'arat HaMachpela Authority and The Jewish Community of Hebron, 2004.

Arrington, Leonard J. *Brigham Young: American Moses*. New York City, NY: Alfred A. Knopf, 1985.

Asad, Talal. "The construction of religion as an anthropological category." In *Genealogies of Religion: Discipline and Reasons of Power in Christianity and Islam*, edited by Talal Asad, 27-54. Baltimore, MD: The Johns Hopkins University Press, 1993.

———. "The limits of religious criticism in the Middle East: Notes on Islamic public argument." In *Genealogies of Religion: Discipline and Reasons of Power in Christianity and Islam*, edited by Talal Asad, 200-36. Baltimore, MD: The Johns Hopkins University Press, 1993.

Asay, Carlos E. "The temple garment: 'An outward expression of an inward commitment.'" In *Temples of the Church of Jesus Christ of Latter-day Saints*, 35-41. Salt Lake City, UT: The Church of Jesus Christ of Latter-day Saints, 1999.

Ash, Michael R. "The ABCs of the Book of Abraham." Presented at the *FAIR Conference, August 2004*. http://www.fairlds.org/FAIR_Conferences/2004_ABCs_of_the_Book_of_Abraham.html (accessed August 4, 2007).

———. "The Mormon myth of evil evolution." *Dialogue* 35, no. 4 (2002): 19-59.

"Ashburnham Pentateuch." In *Wikipedia*. http://en.wikipedia.org/wiki/Ashburnham_Pentateuch (accessed August 4, 2008).

Ashraf, Syed Ali. "The inner meaning of the Islamic rites: Prayer, pilgrimage, fasting, jihad." In *Islamic Spirituality 1: Foundations*, edited by Seyyed Hossein Nasr, 111-30. New York City, NY: The Crossroad Publishing Company, 1987.

Asmussen, Jes P., ed. *Manichaean Literature: Representative Texts Chiefly from Middle Persian and Parthian Writings*. *Persian Heritage Series* 22, ed. Ehsan Yar-Shater. Delmar, NY: Scholars' Facsimiles and Reprints, 1975.

Assman, Jan. 2001. *Death and Salvation in Ancient Egypt*. Translated by David Lorton. Ithaca, NY: Cornell University Press, 2005.

———. 1984. *The Search for God in Ancient Egypt*. Translated by David Lorton. Ithaca, NY: Cornell University Press, 2001.

at-Tabataba'i, Allamah as-Sayyid Muhammad Husayn. 1973. *Al-Mizan: An Exegesis of the Qur'an*. Translated by Sayyid Saeed Akhtar Rizvi. 3rd ed. Tehran, Iran: World Organization for Islamic Services, 1983.

Athanasius. ca. 335. "On the Incarnation of the Word (*De Incarnatione Verbi Dei*)." In *Nicene and Post-Nicene Fathers, Second Series*, edited by Philip Schaff and Henry Wace. 14 vols. Vol. 4, 31-67. New York City, NY: The Christian Literature Company, 1892. Reprint, Peabody, MA: Hendrickson Publishers, 2004.

Atiya, Aziz Suryal, ed. *Coptic Encyclopedia*. 8 vols. New York City, NY: Macmillan, 1991.

Atran, Scott. *In Gods We Trust: The Evolutionary Landscape of Religion*. *Evolution and Cognition*, ed. Stephen Stich. Oxford, England: Oxford University Press, 2002.

Attridge, Harold W., and Helmut Koester, eds. *Hebrews: A Commentary on the Epistle to the Hebrews*. *Hermeneia—A Critical and Historical Commentary on the Bible*, eds. Frank Moore Cross, Klaus Baltzer, Paul D. Hanson, S. Dean McBride, Jr., and Roland E. Murphy. Philadelphia, PA: Fortress Press, 1989.

Audouard, Yvan. *La Pastorale des santons de Provence*. Paris, France: Le pré aux clers, 1986.

Auerbach, Erich. 1946. *Mimesis: The Representation of Reality in Western Literature*. Princeton, NJ: Princeton University Press, 1974.

Augustine. ca. 410. "The City of God." In *Nicene and Post-Nicene Fathers, First Series*, edited by Philip Schaff. 14 vols. Vol. 2, 1-511. New York City, NY: The Christian Literature Company, 1887. Reprint, Peabody, MA: Hendrickson Publishers, 1994.

———. d. 430. *Contra Fortunatum*. Edited by F. Decret and Johannes van Oort. *Corpus Fontium Manichaeorum, Series Latina*. Turnhout, Belgium: Brepols, 2005.

———. d. 430. *St. Augustine: The Literal Meaning of Genesis*. Edited by John Hammond Taylor. New ed. *Ancient Christian Writers* 41 and 42. Mahwah, NJ: Paulist Press, 1982.

"Aux sources de la légende." *Lire*, Hors-Série no. 3 (Référence #HSLR0206) 2006, 47-57.

Avagianou, Aphrodite A. "*Hieros Gamos* in ancient Greek religion: The human aspect of a sacralized ritual." In *Sacred Marriages*, edited by Martti Nissinen and Risto Uro, 145-71. Winona Lake, IN: Eisenbrauns, 2008.

Avesti, Anthony. "Reaching for the stars: Linda Schele's contributions to Mayan astronomy." In *Heart of Creation: The Mesoamerican World and the Legacy of Linda Schele*, edited by Andrea Stone, 13-20. Tuscaloosa, AL: The University of Alabama Press, 2002.

Avi-Yonah, Michael. "Goodenough's evaluation of the Dura paintings: A critique." In *The Dura-Europos Synagogue: A Re-evaluation (1932-1972)*, edited by Joseph Gutmann, 117-35. Chambersburg, PA: American Academy of Religion, Society of Biblical Literature, 1973.

Avigad, N., and Yigal Yadin, eds. *A Genesis Apocryphon: A Scroll from the Wilderness of Judea*. Jerusalem, Israel: Magnes Press-Heikhal Hasefer, 1956.

Avesta—Zoroastrian Archives. http://www.avesta.org/ (accessed October 3, 2008).

Ayala, Francisco J. *Darwin and Intelligent Design*. *Facets Series*. Minneapolis, MN: Fortress Press, 2006.

———. *Darwin's Gift to Science and Religion*. Washington, DC: Joseph Henry Press, 2007.

Ayoub, Mahmoud M. *The Awesome News: Interpretation of Jus' 'Amma: The Last Part of the Qur'an*. 2nd ed. Hiawatha, IA: Cedar Graphics, 1997.

———. 1983. "The idea of redemption in Christianity and Islam." In *Mormons and Muslims: Spiritual Foundations and Modern Manifestations*, edited by Spencer J. Palmer. Updated and Revised ed, 157-69. Provo, UT: Brigham Young University Religious Studies Center, 2002. Reprint (with some modifications), Ayoub, Mahmoud M. *A Muslim View of Christianity: Essays on Dialogue*, 90-97. Edited by Irfan A. Omar. Maryknoll, NY: Orbis Books, 2007.

———. "Introduction." In *A Muslim View of Christianity: Essays on Dialogue*, 1-6. Edited by Irfan A. Omar. Maryknoll,

NY: Orbis Books, 2007.

———. *A Muslim View of Christianity: Essays on Dialogue*. Edited by Irfan A. Omar. Maryknoll, NY: Orbis Books, 2007.

———. *The Qur'an and Its Interpreters*. Vol. 1. Albany, NY: State University of New York Press, 1984.

———. *The Qur'an and Its Interpreters*. Vol. 2. Albany, NY: State University of New York Press, 1992.

———. "Toward an Islamic Christology 1: An image of Jesus in early Shi'i Muslim literature." In *A Muslim View of Christianity: Essays on Dialogue*, 134-155. Edited by Irfan A. Omar. Maryknoll, NY: Orbis Books, 2007.

Bachman, Daniel W. "New light on an old hypothesis: The Ohio origins of the revelation on eternal marriage." *Journal of Mormon History* 5 (1978): 19-32.

Backman, Milton V., Jr., and Richard O. Cowan. *Joseph Smith and the Doctrine and Covenants*. Salt Lake City, UT: Deseret Book, 1992.

Bagehot, Walter. *The Works of Walter Bagehot (with Memoirs by R. H. Hutton)*. 5 vols. Edited by Forrest Morgan. Hartford, CN: The Travelers Insurance Company, 1889.

Bailey, Arthur A. "Adam, LDS sources." In *Encyclopedia of Mormonism*, edited by Daniel H. Ludlow. 4 vols. Vol. 1, 15-17. New York City, NY: Macmillan, 1992. http://www.lib.byu.edu/Macmillan/ (accessed November 26, 2007).

Bailey, David H. "God is not a great deceiver: What's wrong with intelligent design." Unpublished manuscript in the possession of the author. 2005

———. "Latter-day Creationism." In *The Mormon Organon*. http://sciencebysteve.net/?p=379 (accessed December 2, 2008).

———. "The LDS Church and Evolution." 27 July 2008. In *Papers by David H. Bailey*. http://www.dhbailey.com/papers/dhb-lds-evolution.pdf (accessed December 2, 2008).

———. "Mormonism and the new creationism." *Dialogue* 35, no. 4 (2002): 39-59.

———. "Mormons and the omnis: The dangers of theological speculation." *Dialogue* 37, no. 3 (Fall 2004): 29-48.

———. "Science and Mormonism: Past, Present, Future." *Dialogue* 29, no. 1 (1996): 80-96.

———. "Scientific foundations of Mormon theology." *Dialogue* 21, no. 2 (1988): 61-79.

———. "What's wrong with Intelligent Design?" 11 May 2008. In *Papers of David H. Bailey*. http://www.dhbailey.com/papers/dhb-intell-design.pdf (accessed December 2, 2008).

Baker, Jacob T. "'The Grandest principle of the Gospel': Christian nihilism, sanctified activism, and eternal progression." *Dialogue: A Journal of Mormon Thought* 41, no. 3 (Fall 2008): 55-80. http://www.dialoguejournal.com/content/wp-content/uploads/2007/08/4003-White.pdf (accessed January 2, 2009).

Baldwin, Robert W. "The legend of the True Cross: Piero's frescoes at Arezzo." In *A Critical History of Western Art, 1300-2000*, edited by Robert W. Baldwin. New London, CT: Connecticut College (published only on CD-ROM), 2001. http://oak.conncoll.edu/rwbal/ (accessed September 1, 2006).

Ballard, M. Russell. 2004. "Becoming self-reliant—spiritually and physically." *Ensign* 39, March 2009, 50-55.

———. "Building bridges of understanding." Presented at a Missionary satellite broadcast, Logan, UT, February 17, 1998.

———. *Counseling with Our Councils: Learning to Minister Together in the Church and in the Family*. Salt Lake City, UT: Deseret Book, 1997.

Ballard, Melvin J. 1922. "The Three Degrees of Glory." A discourse delivered in the Ogden Tabernacle, September 22, 1922, on the one hundredth anniversary of the appearance of the angel Moroni. In *Sermons and Missionary Services of Melvin Joseph Ballard*, edited by Bryant S. Hinckley, 234-61. Salt Lake City, UT: Deseret Book, 1949.

Bandstra, Barry L. *Genesis 1-11: A Handbook on the Hebrew Text*. Baylor Handbook on the Hebrew Bible, ed. W. Dennis Tucker, Jr. Waco, TX: Baylor University Press, 2008.

bar Konai, Theodore. "Concerning his impure doctrine." In *The Other Bible*, edited by Willis Barnstone, 46-48. San Francisco, CA: HarperSanFrancisco, 2005.

Barclay, John M. G. *Jews in the Mediterranean Diaspora: From Alexander to Trajan (323 BCE-117 CE)*. Hellenistic Culture and Society 33, eds. Anthony W. Bulloch, Erich S. Gruen, A. A. Long, and Andrew F. Stewart. Berkeley, CA: University of California Press, 1996.

Barclay, William, ed. *The Gospel of John*. 2nd ed. 2 vols. Vol. 1. *The Daily Study Bible Series*. Philadelphia, PA: The Westminster Press, 1956.

———, ed. 1956. *The Gospel of Matthew*. Revised ed. 2 vols. *The Daily Study Bible Series*. Philadelphia, PA: The Westminster Press, 1975.

———. 1970. *The Parables of Jesus*. Louisville, KY: Westminster John Knox Press, 1999.

Barker, Kenneth L., ed. *Zondervan NIV Study Bible* Fully Revised ed. Grand Rapids, MI: Zondervan, 2002.

Barker, Margaret. "The angel priesthood." In *The Great High Priest: The Temple Roots of Christian Liturgy*, edited by Margaret Barker, 103-45. London, England: T & T Clark, 2003.

———. "Atonement: The rite of healing." *Scottish Journal of Theology* 49, no. 1 (1996): 1-20. http://www.abdn.ac.uk/~div054/sjt (accessed August 3, 2007).

———. "Beyond the veil of the temple: The high priestly origins of the apocalypses." *Scottish Journal of Theology* 51, no. 1 (1998): 1-21. http://www.marquette.edu/maqom/veil (accessed August 3, 2007).

———. "Beyond the veil of the temple: The high priestly origin of the apocalypses." In *The Great High Priest: The Temple Roots of Christian Liturgy*, edited by Margaret Barker, 188-201. London, England: T & T Clark, 2003.

———. *Christmas: The Original Story*. London, England: Society for Promoting Christian Knowledge, 2008.

———. "Creation theology." Unpublished manuscript, 2004. http://www.margaretbarker.com/Papers/CreationTheology.pdf (accessed August 6, 2007).

———. E-mail message to Jeffrey M. Bradshaw, June 11, 2007.

———. *An Extraordinary Gathering of Angels*. London, England: MQ Publications, 2004.

———. *The Gate of Heaven: The History and Symbolism of the Temple*. London: Society for Promoting Christian Knowledge (SPCK), 1991.

———. *The Great Angel: A Study of Israel's Second God*. Louisville, KY: Westminster / John Knox Press, 1992.

———. "The Great High Priest." *BYU Studies* 42, no. 3 (2003): 65-84.

———. *The Great High Priest: The Temple Roots of Christian Liturgy*. London, England: T & T Clark, 2003.

———. *The Hidden Tradition of the Kingdom of God*. London, England: Society for Promoting Christian Knowledge (SPCK), 2007.

———. "The holy anointing oil." 2008. http://www.margaretbarker.com/Papers/TheHolyAnointingOil.pdf. (accessed September 1, 2009).

———. "The Holy of Holies." In *The Great High Priest: The Temple Roots of Christian Liturgy*, edited by Margaret Barker, 146-87. London, England: T & T Clark, 2003.

———, ed. "The Infancy Gospel of James and translation of the text." In *Christmas: The Original Story*, edited by Margaret Barker, 128-61. London, England: Society for Promoting Christian Knowledge, 2008.

———. "Joseph Smith and preexilic Israelite religion." *BYU Studies* 44, no. 4 (2005): 69-82.

———. *The Lost Prophet: The Book of Enoch and Its Influence on Christianity*. London, England: Society for Promoting Christian Knowledge (SPCK), 1988.

———. *The Older Testament: The Survival of Themes from the Ancient Royal Cult in Sectarian Judaism and Early Christianity*. London, England: Society for Promoting Christian Knowledge (SPCK), 1987.

———. *On Earth as It Is in Heaven: Temple Symbolism in the New Testament*. Edinburgh, Scotland: T&T Clark, 1995.

———. "Paradise lost." Presented at the *Religion, Science and the Environment Symposium IV: The Adriatic Symposium*, 5-11 June, 2002. http://www.margaretbarker.com/Papers/ParadiseLost.pdf (accessed August 7, 2007).

———. *The Revelation of Jesus Christ: Which God Gave to Him to Show to His Servants What Must Soon Take Place (Revelation 1.1)*. Edinburgh, Scotland: T&T Clark, 2000.

———. *The Risen Lord: The Jesus of History as the Christ of Faith*. Valley Forge, PA: Trinity Press International, 1996.

———. "Temple and Timaeus." In *The Great High Priest: The Temple Roots of Christian Liturgy*, edited by Margaret Barker, 262-93. London, England: T & T Clark, 2003.

———. "Temple imagery in Philo: An indication of the origin of the Logos?" In *Templum Amicitae: Essays on the Second Temple Presented to Ernst Bammel*, edited by William Horbury. *JSOT Supplement Series* 48, 70-102. Sheffield, England: Sheffield Academic Press, 1991. http://jbburnett.com/resources/barker/barker_logos%20in%20philo.pdf (accessed December 21, 2007).

———. "The temple roots of the Christian liturgy." In *The Great High Priest: The Temple Roots of Christian Liturgy*, edited by Margaret Barker, 73-102. London, England: T & T Clark, 2003.

———. *Temple Themes in Christian Worship*. London, England: T&T Clark, 2008.

———. *Temple Theology*. London, England: Society for Promoting Christian Knowledge (SPCK), 2004.

———. "Text and context." In *The Great High Priest: The Temple Roots of Christian Liturgy*, edited by Margaret Barker, 294-315. London, England: T & T Clark, 2003.

———. "The veil as the boundary." In *The Great High Priest: The Temple Roots of Christian Liturgy*, edited by Margaret Barker, 202-28. London, England: T & T Clark, 2003.

———. "What did King Josiah reform?" In *Glimpses of Lehi's Jerusalem*, edited by John W. Welch, David Rolph Seely and Jo Ann H. Seely, 523-42. Provo, UT: Foundation for Ancient Research and Mormon Studies (FARMS) at Brigham Young University, 2004.

———. Where shall wisdom be found? In *Russian Orthodox Church: Representation to the European Institutions*. http://orthodoxeurope.org/page/11/1/7.aspx (accessed December 24, 2007).

———. "Who was Melchizedek and who was his God?" Presented at the 2007 Annual Meeting of the Society of Biblical Literature, Session S19-72 on 'Latter-day Saints and the Bible', San Diego, CA, November 17-20, 2007.

———. "Wisdom and the stewardship of knowledge (Bishop's Lecture 2004)." Presented at the Lincoln Cathedral Lectures, Lincoln, England, March, 2004. http://www.margaretbarker.com/Papers/WisdomAndTheStewardshipOfKnowledge.pdf (accessed August 6, 2007).

———. "Wisdom, the Queen of Heaven." In *The Great High Priest: The Temple Roots of Christian Liturgy*, edited by Margaret Barker, 229-61. London, England: T & T Clark, 2003.

Barker, Margaret, and Kevin Christensen. "Seeking the face of the Lord: Joseph Smith and the first temple tradition." In *Joseph Smith Jr: Reappraisals After Two Centuries*, edited by Reid L. Neilson and Terryl L. Givens, 143-72. Oxford, England: Oxford University Press, 2009.

Barlow, Philip L. *Mormons and the Bible: The Place of the Latter-day Saints in American Religion*. New York, NY: Oxford University Press, 1991.

Barney, Kevin L. "A book or a tree? A textual variant in Revelation 22:19." Manuscript draft provided by the author. Presented at the Mormon Theology Seminar: Latter-day Saint Readings of Revelation 21-22, University of Texas, Austin, TX, 25 September 2009, 2009. http://www.mormontheologyseminar.org/. (accessed September 19, 2009).

———. "Do we have a Mother in Heaven?" In *Foundation for Apologetic Information and Research (FAIR)*. http://www.fairlds.org/pubs/MotherInHeaven.pdf (accessed December 24, 2007).

———. E-mail message to Jeffrey M. Bradshaw, June 21, 2006.

———. "Examining six key concepts on Joseph Smith's understanding of Genesis 1:1." *BYU Studies* 39, no. 3 (2000): 107-24.

———. "The facsimiles and Semitic adapation of existing sources." In *Astronomy, Papyrus, and Covenant*, edited by John Gee and Brian M. Hauglid. *Studies in the Book of Abraham* 3, 107-30. Provo, UT: FARMS, Brigham Young University, 2005.

———, ed. *Footnotes to the New Testament for Latter-day Saints*. 3 vols, 2007. http://feastupontheword.org/Site:NTFootnotes (accessed February 26, 2008).

———. Is Nauvoo a Hebrew word? In *Ask the apologist, FAIR*. http://www.fairlds.org/Misc/Is_Nauvoo_a_Hebrew_Word.html (accessed August 7, 2007).

———. "Joseph Smith's emendation of Hebrew Genesis 1:1." *Dialogue: A Journal of Mormon Thought* 30, no. 4 (Winter 1997): 103-35.

———. 2006. "Only Begotten." In *By Common Consent*. http://bycommonconsent.com/2006/05/24/only-begotten/ (accessed June 20, 2006).

———. "Poetic diction and parallel word pairs in the Book of Mormon." *Journal of Book of Mormon Studies* 4, no. 2 (1995): 15-23.

———. "Reflections on the Documentary Hypothesis." *Dialogue* 33, no. 1 (2000): 57-99.

Barnstone, Willis, ed. "The Gospel of the Secret Supper." In *The Gnostic Bible*, edited by Willis Barnstone and Marvin Meyer, 740-50. Boston, MA: Shambhala, 2003.

———, ed. "The Mother of Books (*Umm al-kitab*)." In *The Gnostic Bible*, edited by Willis Barnstone and Marvin Meyer. Translated by Willis Barnstone, 655-725. Boston, MA: Shambhala, 2003.

———, ed. *The Other Bible*. San Francisco, CA: HarperSanFrancisco, 2005.

———, ed. "The Sethian-Ophites." In *The Other Bible*, edited by Willis Barnstone, 659-64. San Francisco, CA: HarperSanFrancisco, 2005.

———, ed. "The story of the death of Mani." In *The Gnostic Bible*, edited by Willis Barnstone and Marvin W. Meyer. Translated by Jes P. Asmussen, 594-97. Boston, MA: Shambhala, 2003.

Barnstone, Willis, and Marvin W. Meyer, eds. "The Coptic Manichaean Songbook, Songs of Thomas." In *The Gnostic Bible*, edited by Willis Barnstone and Marvin Meyer, 616-24. Boston, MA: Shambhala, 2003.

———, eds. *The Gnostic Bible*. Boston, MA: Shambhala, 2003.

Barr, James. 1961. *The Semantics of Biblical Language*. Eugene, OR: Wipf and Stock, 2004.

Barthélemy, Dominique. 1963. *God and His Image: An Outline of Biblical Theology*. Translated by Dom Aldhelm Dean. Edited by Stephen D. Ryan. Revised ed. San Francisco, CA: Ignatius Press, 2007.

REFERENCES

Basil. ca. 364-379. "The *Hexaemeron*." In *Nicene and Post-Nicene Fathers, Second Series,* edited by Philip Schaff and Henry Wace. 14 vols. Vol. 8, 51-107. New York City, NY: The Christian Literature Company, 1895. Reprint, Peabody, MA: Hendrickson Publishers, 1994.

———. ca. 364-379. "On the Spirit (*De Spiritu Sancto*)." In *Nicene and Post-Nicene Fathers, Second Series,* edited by Philip Schaff and Henry Wace. 14 vols. Vol. 8, 1-50. New York City, NY: The Christian Literature Company, 1895. Reprint, Peabody, MA: Hendrickson Publishers, 1994.

Bassie-Sweet, Karen. *From the Mouth of the Dark Cave: Commemorative Sculpture of the Late Classic Maya*. Norman, OK: University of Oklahoma Press, 1991.

Bateson, Gregory. *Mind and Nature: A Necessary Unity*. New York: E. P. Dutton, 1979.

Bateson, Gregory, and Mary Catherine Bateson. *Angels Fear: Towards an Epistemology of the Sacred*. New York City, NY: Macmillan Publishing Company, 1987.

Batson, Beatrice. "Preface." In *Shakespeare's Christianity: The Protestant and Catholic Poetics of Julius Caesar, Macbeth, and Hamlet*, edited by Beatrice Batson, xi-xvii. Waco, TX: Baylor University Press, 2006.

Battenhouse, Roy. "Introduction: An overview of Christian interpretation." In *Shakespeare's Christian Dimension: An Anthology of Commentary*, edited by Roy Battenhouse, 1-14. Bloomington, IN: Indiana University Press, 1994.

———. "The Tempest: Comment and Bibliography." In *Shakespeare's Christian Dimension: An Anthology of Commentary*, edited by Roy Battenhouse, 250-54. Bloomington, IN: Indiana University Press, 1994.

Bauer, Walter, William F. Arndt, and F. Wilbur Gingrich. *A Greek-English Lexicon of the New Testament*. Chicago, IL: University of Chicago Press, 1957.

Beach, Edward Allen. "The Eleusinian Mysteries." In *The Potencies of God(s): Schelling's Philosophy of Mythology*, edited by Edward Allen Beach, 238-44. Albany, NY: State University of New York Press, 1994. Abridged version at http://www.uwec.edu/philrel/faculty/beach/Publications/eleusis.html (accessed August 14, 2009).

"Beccafumi, Domenico." In *Web Gallery of Art*. http://www.wga.hu/frames-e.html?/html/b/beccafum/72rebel.html (accessed April 27, 2007).

Bede. 731. *The Ecclesiastical History of the English People, with The Greater Chronicle and Bede's Letter to Egbert*. Translated by Bertram Colgrave. Edited by Judith McClure and Roger Collins. Oxford, England: Oxford University Press, 1999.

———. ca. 731. *On the Temple*. Translated by Sean Connolly. Edited by Jennifer O'Reilly. Liverpool, England: Liverpool University Press, 1996.

Bednar, David A. "Clean hands and a pure heart." *Ensign* 37, November 2007, 80-83.

———. "Honorably hold a name and standing." *Ensign* 39, May 2009, 97-100.

———. "In the strength of the Lord." *Ensign* 34, November 2004, 76-78.

———. "Pray always." *Ensign* 38, November 2008, 41-44.

———. "Quick to observe." *Ensign* 36, December 2006, 30-36.

———. 2006. "Seek learning by faith." *Ensign* 37, September 2007, 60-68.

BeDuhn, Jason David. 2000. *The Manichaean Body in Discipline and Ritual*. Baltimore, MD: The Johns Hopkins University Press, 2002.

BeDuhn, Jason David, and Geoffrey Harrison. "The Tebessa Codex: A Manichaean treatise on biblical exegesis and church order." In *Emerging from Darkness: Studies in the Recovery of Manichaean Sources*, edited by Paul Mirecki and Jason David BeDuhn. *Nag Hammadi and Manichaean Studies* 43, eds. James M. Robinson and H. J. Klimkeit, 33-87. Leiden, The Netherlands: Brill, 1997.

Beecher, Maureen Ursenbach. "The Iowa journal of Lorenzo Snow." *BYU Studies* 24, no. 3 (1984): 261-73.

Ben Meir, Samuel. d. 1158. *Rabbi Samuel Ben Meir's Commentary on Genesis: An Annotated Translation*. Edited by Martin I. Lockshin. *Jewish Studies* 5. Lewiston, NY: The Edwin Mellen Press, 1989.

Ben-Amos, Dan, Dov Noy, and Ellen Frankel, eds. *Folktales of the Jews; Tales from the Sephardic Dispersion*. 5 vols. Translated by Lenn Schramm. Philadelphia, PA: Jewish Publication Society of America, 2006-.

Benét, Stephen Vincent. "The author is pleased." New York City, NY: The New York Times, September 28, 1941.

———. *The Devil and Daniel Webster*. New York: Farrar and Rinehart, 1937. http://tarlton.law.utexas.edu/lpop/etext/devil/devil.htm (accessed September 30, 2008).

Bennett, Archibald F. *Saviors on Mount Zion: Course No. 21 for the Sunday School*. Salt Lake City, UT: Deseret Sunday School Union Board, 1950.

Bennett, Richard E. "'Line upon line, precept upon precept': Reflections on the 1877 commencement of the performance of endowments and sealings for the dead." *BYU Studies* 44, no. 3 (2005): 39-77.

———. *Mormons at the Missouri, 1846-1852: "And Should We Die…"* Norman, OK: University of Oklahoma Press, 1987.

Benson, Ezra Taft. "The Book of Mormon and the Doctrine and Covenants." *Ensign* 17, May 1987, 83-85.

———. "A message to Judah from Joseph." *Ensign* 6, December 1976, 67-72. http://www.lds.org/ldsorg/v/index.jsp?vgne xtoid=2354fccf2b7db010VgnVCM1000004d82620aRCRD&locale=0&sourceId=8da81f26d596b010VgnVCM10000 04d82620a____&hideNav=1 (accessed May 29, 2009).

———. *The Teachings of Ezra Taft Benson*. Salt Lake City, UT: Bookcraft, 1988.

———. 1977. "A vision and a hope for the youth of Zion." 12 April 1977. In *BYU Speeches and Devotionals*, Brigham Young University. http://speeches.byu.edu/reader/reader.php?id=6162 (accessed August 7, 2007).

Benz, Ernst. 1969. "*Imago Dei*: Man as the image of God." *The FARMS Review* 17, no. 1 (2005): 223-54.

———. "*Imago Dei*: Man in the image of God." In *Reflections on Mormonism: Judeo-Christian Parallels, Papers Delivered at the Religious Studies Center Symposium, Brigham Young University, March 10-11, 1978*, edited by Truman G. Madsen. *Religious Studies Monograph Series* 4, 201-21. Provo, UT: Religious Studies Center, Brigham Young University, 1978.

Bergen, Peter L. *The Osama bin Laden I Know*. New York City, NY: Free Press, 2006.

Berlin, Adele. *Esther. The JPS Bible Commentary*, ed. Michael Fishbane. Philadelphia, PA: The Jewish Publication Society, 2001.

———. "A search for a new biblical hermeneutics: Preliminary observations." In *The Study of the Ancient Near East in the Twenty-First Century: The William Foxwell Albright Centennial Conference*, edited by Jerrold S. Cooper and Glenn M. Schwartz, 195-207. Winona Lake, IN: Eisenbrauns, 1996.

Berlin, Adele, and Marc Zvi Brettler, eds. *The Jewish Study Bible, Featuring the Jewish Publication Society TANAKH Translation*. Oxford, England: Oxford University Press, 2004.

Bernstein, Moshe J. "Contours of Genesis interpretation at Qumran: Contents, context, and nomenclature." In *Studies in Ancient Midrash*, edited by James L. Kugel, 57-85. Cambridge, MA: Harvard University Press, 2001.

"Berossus." In *Wikipedia*. http://en.wikipedia.org/wiki/Berossus (accessed February 22, 2008).

Berossus. 290-278 BCE. "Fragments of Chaldaean history." In *Ancient Fragments of the Phoenician, Chaldaean, Egyptian, Tyrian, Carthaginian, Indian, and Other Writers; with an Introductory Dissertation and an Inquiry into the Philosophy and Trinity of the Ancients*, edited by Isaac Preston Cory. 2nd ed. London, England: William Pickering, 1832. Reprint, Kila, MT: Kessinger Publishing, 2003. http://www.sacred-texts.com/cla/af/index.htm (accessed May 30, 2009).

Berrett, LaMar C. "Adam-ondi-Ahman." In *Encyclopedia of Mormonism*, edited by Daniel H. Ludlow. 4 vols. Vol. 1, 19-20. New York City, NY: Macmillan, 1992. http://www.lib.byu.edu/Macmillan/ (accessed November 26, 2007).

Berrett, LaMar C., and Max H. Parkin. *Sacred Places: Missouri*. Salt Lake City, UT: Deseret Book, 2004.

Bethge, Hans-Gebhard, and Bentley Layton ed. "On the origin of the world." In *The Nag Hammadi Library in English*, edited by James M. Robinson. 3rd, Completely Revised ed, 170-89. San Francisco, CA: HarperSanFrancisco, 1990.

"Bethlem Royal Hospital." In *Wikipedia*. http://en.wikipedia.org/wiki/Bethlem_Royal_Hospital (accessed November 23, 2007).

Betz, Hans Dieter, and dela Yarbro Collins, eds. *The Sermon on the Mount: A Commentary on the Sermon on the Mount, including the Sermon on the Plain (Matthew 5:3-7:27 and Luke 6:20-49)*. *Hermeneia—A Critical and Historical Commentary on the Bible*, eds. Frank Moore Cross, Klaus Baltzer, Paul D. Hanson, S. Dean McBride, Jr., Peter Machinist, Susan Niditch, Christopher R. Seitz, and Roland E. Murphy. Minneapolis, MN: Fortress Press, 1995.

Bhimji, Saleem, ed. *The Awaited Savior of Humanity: Al-Mahdi in the Eyes of the Ahlul Bayt*. Translated by Saleem Bhimi. *40 Ahadith*. Stanmore, Middlesex, England: The Islamic Education Board of the World Federation of Khoja Shia Ithna-Asheri Muslim Communities, 2006.

Bialik, Hayim Nahman, and Yehoshua Hana Ravnitzky, eds. 1902. *The Book of Legends (Sefer Ha-Aggadah): Legends from the Talmud and Midrash*. Translated by William G. Braude. New York City, NY: Schocken Books, 1992.

Bickerman, Elias Joseph. 1965. "Symbolism in the Dura synagogue." In *Studies in Jewish and Christian History. Arbeiten zur Geschichte des antiken Judentums und des Urchristentums* 3, 225-44. Leiden, The Netherlands: E. J. Brill, 1986.

Bickmore, Barry Robert. *Restoring the Ancient Church: Joseph Smith and Early Christianity*. Ben Lomond, CA: Foundation for Apologetic Information and Research (FAIR), 1999.

Biddle, Martin———. "The history of the Church of the Holy Sepulchre." In *The Church of the Holy Sepulchre*, edited by Martin Biddle, Gideon Avni, Jon Seligman, and Tamar Winter, 25-71. New York City, NY: Rizzoli, 2000.

———. *The Tomb of Christ*. Thrupp, England: Sutton, 1999.

bin Gorion, Micha Joseph (Berdichevsky), and Emanuel bin Gorion, eds. 1939-1945. *Mimekor Yisrael: Classical Jewish Folktales*. 3 vols. Translated by I. M. Lask. Bloomington, IN: Indiana University Press, 1976.

———, eds. 1939-1945. *Mimekor Yisrael: Classical Jewish Folktales*. Abridged ed. Translated by I. M. Lask. Bloomington, IN: Indiana University Press, 1990.

"Biology." In *BYU*. http://biology.byu.edu/home/Academic_Programs/Undergraduate_Programs/biology.aspx (accessed December 7, 2008).

Birch, A. Jane. 1993. "King on King Lear: Finding Virtue in Minute Particulars." In *Brigham Young University Harold B. Lee Library Institutional Repository*, Department of Instructional Science, Brigham Young University. https://dspace.byu.edu/handle/1877/524 (accessed December 12, 2007).

Birch, Nicholas. "The hellenization of the Gospel: The Prologue of John and the Joseph Smith Translation." *Studia Antiqua* 2, no. 2 (Fall 2002): 87-97.

Birrell, Anne. *Chinese Mythology: An Introduction*. Baltimore, MD: The Johns Hopkins University Press, 1993.

Blake, William. ca. 1788. "All religions are one." In *William Blake: The Complete Illuminated Books*, edited by David Bindman, 18-30. New York City, NY: Thames and Hudson, and the William Blake Trust, 2000.

———. 1809. "A descriptive catalogue [Blake's exhibition and catalogue of 1809]." In *The Complete Poetry and Prose of William Blake*, edited by David V. Erdman and Harold Bloom. Newly Revised ed, 529-51. New York City, NY: Anchor, Random House, 1988.

———. *The Illuminated Blake: William Blake's Complete Illuminated Works with a Plate-by-Plate Commentary*. Edited by David V. Erdman. New York City, NY: Dover Publications, 1974.

———. 1804. "Milton a poem." In *Milton a Poem and the Final Illuminated Works: The Ghost of Abel, On Homer's Poetry [and] On Virgil, and Laocoön*, edited by Robert N. Essick and Joseph Viscomi. Paperback ed. *Blake's Illuminated Books* 5, ed. David Bindman, 9-217. Princeton, NJ: The William Blake Trust, Princeton University Press, 1998.

———. ca. 1788. "There is no natural religion." In *William Blake: The Complete Illuminated Books*, edited by David Bindman, 31-41. New York City, NY: Thames and Hudson, and the William Blake Trust, 2000.

———. 1804. "To the Jews (Excerpt from 'Jerusalem')." In *The Complete Poetry and Prose of William Blake*, edited by David V. Erdman and Harold Bloom, 171-74. New York City, NY: Anchor, Random House, 1988.

———. *William Blake: The Complete Illuminated Books*. Edited by David Bindman. New York City, NY: Thames and Hudson, and the William Blake Trust, 2000.

Blech, Benjamin, and Roy Doliner. *The Sistine Secrets: Michelangelo's Forbidden Messages in the Heart of the Vatican*. New York City, NY: HarperOne, 2008.

Blenkinsopp, Joseph. "P and J in Genesis 1:1-11:26: An alternative hypothesis." In *Fortunate the Eyes that See: Essays in Honor of David Noel Freedman*, edited by Astrid B. Beck, Andrew H. Bartelt, Paul R. Raabe and Chris A. Franke, 1-15. Grand Rapids, MI: William B. Eerdmans, 1995.

Block, Daniel I. *The Book of Ezekiel: Chapters 25-48*. The New International Commentary on the Old Testament, ed. Robert L. Hubbard, Jr. Grand Rapids, MI: William B. Eerdmans, 1998.

Blomberg, Craig L. *Interpreting the Parables*. Downers Grove, IL: InterVarsity Press, 1990.

Blomberg, Craig L., and Stephen E. Robinson. *How Wide the Divide? A Mormon and an Evangelical in Conversation*. Downers Grove, IL: InterVarsity Press, 1997.

Bloom, Harold. *The American Religion: The Emergence of the Post-Christian Nation*. New York City, NY: Simon and Schuster, 1992.

———. 1963. *Blake's Apocalypse: A Study in Poetic Argument*. Ithaca, NY: Cornell University Press, 1970.

———. "Commentary." In *The Complete Poetry and Prose of William Blake*, edited by David V. Erdman and Harold Bloom, 894-970. New York City, NY: Anchor, Random House, 1988.

———. *Genius: A Mosaic of One Hundred Exemplary Creative Minds*. New York City, NY: Warner Books, 2002.

———. *Jesus and Yahweh: The Names Divine*. New York City, NY: Riverhead Books (Penguin Group), 2005.

———. *Omens of Millennium: The Gnosis of Angels, Dreams, and Resurrection*. New York City, NY: Riverhead, 1996.

———, ed. *Satan. Bloom's Major Literary Characters*, ed. Harold Bloom. Philadelphia, PA: Chelsea House, 2005.

———. *Shakespeare: The Invention of the Human*. New York City, NY: Riverhead Books, Penguin Putnam, 1998.

Blumenthal, David. "Lovejoy's Great Chain of Being and medieval Jewish tradition." In *Jacob's Ladder and the Tree of Life*, edited by M. L. Kuntz and P. G. Kuntz, 179-90. Bern, Switzerland: Peter Lang, 1986. http://www.js.emory.edu/BLUMENTHAL/Lovejoy.htm (accessed September 21, 2007).

———, ed. *The Merkabah Tradition and the Zoharic Tradition. Understanding Jewish Mysticism: A Source Reader* 1. Jersey City, NJ: Ktav Publishing House, 1979.

———, ed. *The Philosophic-Mystical Tradition and the Hasidic Tradition. Understanding Jewish Mysticism: A Source Reader* 2. Jersey City, NJ: Ktav Publishing House, 1982.

———. "Reading Creation." In *Bibel und Midrasch, Forschung zum Alten Testament*, edited by G. Bodendorfer and M. Millard, 117-66. Heidelberg, Germany: Mohr Siebeck, 1998. http://www.js.emory.edu/BLUMENTHAL/GenIntro.html (accessed August 8, 2007).

Boethius, Ancius Manlius Severinus. ca. 524. *The Consolation of Philosophy*. Translated by P. G. Walsh. New York City, NY: Oxford University Press, 1999.

Böhlig, Alexander, and Frederik Wisse, eds. "The gospel of the Egyptians (III 40, 12-44, 28; IV 55, 20-60, 30; III 49, 1-69, 20)." In *The Nag Hammadi Library in English*, edited by James M. Robinson. 3rd, Completely Revised ed, 208-19. San Francisco, CA: HarperSanFrancisco, 1990.

Boice, James Montgomery. 1982. *Creation and Fall (Genesis 1-11). Genesis 1*. Grand Rapids, MI: BakerBooks, 1998.

Bokovoy, David E., and John A. Tvedtnes. *Testaments: Links Between the Book of Mormon and the Hebrew Bible*. Tooele, UT: Heritage Press, 2003.

Boman, Thorleif. 1954. *Hebrew Thought Compared with Greek*. New York City, NY: W. W. Norton, 1970.

Bonhoeffer, Dietrich. 1937. *The Cost of Discipleship*. New York: Macmillan, 1963.

Bonnechere, Pierre. "Trophonius of Lebadea: Mystery aspects of an oracular cult in Boeotia." In *Greek Mysteries: The Archaeology and Ritual of Ancient Greek Secret Cults*, edited by Michael B. Cosmopoulos, 169-92. New York City, NY: Routledge, 2003.

Boren, Karen. *Messiah of the Winepress*. Provo, UT: Beit Parah Publishing, 2002.

Borgen, Peder. "The Gospel of John and Philo of Alexandria." In *Light in a Spotless Mirror: Reflections on Wisdom Traditions in Judaism and Early Christianity*, edited by James H. Charlesworth and Michael A. Daise, 45-76. Harrisburg, PA: Trinity Press International, 2003.

Bornkamm, G., G. Barth, and H. Hold. *Tradition and Interpretation in Matthew*. Translated by Percy Scott. Philadelphia, PA: Westminster, 1963.

Bourasse, J. J., and P. Janvier, eds. *La Sainte Bible: Traduction Nouvelle Selon la Vulgate*. Tours, France: Alfred Mame et Fils, 1866.

Boyce, Duane. "Of science, scripture, and surprise." *The FARMS Review* 20, no. 2 (2008): 163-214.

Boyce, Mary, ed. 1984. *Textual Sources for the Study of Zoroastrianism. Textual Sources for the Study of Religion*, ed. John Hinnells. Chicago, IL: The University of Chicago Press, 1990.

———. 1979. *Zoroastrians: Their Religious Beliefs and Practices. The Library of Religious Beliefs and Practices*, ed. John Hinnells. London, England: Routledge, Taylor & Francis Group, 2001.

Boyd, James W. 1985. "Zoroastrianism: Avestan scripture and rite." In *The Holy Book in Comparative Perspective*, edited by Frederick M. Denny and Rodney L. Taylor, 109-25. Columbia, SC: University of South Carolina Press, 1993.

Bradford, Gerald M., ed. *Ancient Scrolls from the Dead Sea: Photographs and Commentary on a Unique Collection of Scrolls*. Provo, UT: Foundation for Ancient Research and Mormon Studies (FARMS) at Brigham Young University, 1997.

Bradley, Walter. "Why I believe the Bible is scientifically reliable." In *Why I Am a Christian: Leading Thinkers Explain Why They Believe*, edited by Norman L. Geisler and Paul K. Hoffman, 161-81. Grand Rapids, MI: Baker Books, 2001.

Bradshaw, Elma S. Personal journal entry in the possession of the author. August 9, 1985

Bradshaw, Jeffrey M. *The Ezekiel Mural at Dura Europos: A tangible witness of Philo's Jewish mysteries? BYU Studies* 49:1, 2010, in press.

———. "Notes from Arthur Henry King's Brigham Young University class on 'Reading the Scriptures.'" February 14, 1980.

———. *Temple Themes in the Book of Moses*. American Fork, UT: Covenant Communications, 2010.

Bradshaw, Jeffrey M., and Ronan J. Head. "Mormonism's Satan and the Tree of Life." Invited presentation at the *2009 Conference of the European Mormon Studies Association*, Turin, Italy, 30-31 July. To appear in the *International Journal of Mormon Studies*, in press; and *Element: The Journal of Mormon Philosophy and Theology* 4:2, in press.

Bradshaw, Paul F. *The Search for the Origins of Christian Worship: Sources and Methods for the Study of Early Liturgy*. 2nd ed. Oxford, England: Oxford University Press, 2002.

Bradshaw, Robert W. E-mail message to Jeffrey M. Bradshaw, October 9, 2006.

Brandon. 2005. "Master of the World." In *Siris*. http://www.pkblogs.com/branemrys/2005/04/master-of-world.html (accessed December 2, 2006).

Brandt, Edward J. "The Book of Jasher and the Latter-day Saints." In *Apocryphal Writings and the Latter-day Saints*, edited by C. Wilfred Griggs, 297-318. Provo, UT: Brigham Young University Religious Studies Center, 1986.

Braude, William G., ed. *The Midrash on Psalms (Midrash Tehillim)*. 2 vols. *Yale Judaica Series* 13, ed. Leon Nemoy. New Haven, CN: Yale University Press, 1959.

———, ed. *Pesikta Rabbati: Discourses for Feasts, Fasts, and Special Sabbaths*. 2 vols. *Yale Judaica Series* 28, eds. Leon Nemoy, Saul Lieberman, and Harry A. Wolfson. New Haven, CN: Yale University Press, 1968.

Braude, William G., and Israel J. Kapstein, eds. *Pesikta De-Rab Kahana*. Philadelphia, PA: Jewish Publication Society, 1975.

Brayford, Susan, ed. *Septuagint Genesis: A Commentary Based on the Greek Text of Codex Alexandrinus. Septuagint Commentary*. Leiden, The Netherlands: Brill Academic Publishers, 2007.

Bregman, Marc, ed. *The Tanhuma-Yelammedenu Literature: Studies in the Evolution of the Versions*. Piscataway, NJ: Gorgias Press, 2003.

Brems, David N. *Divine Engineering: Scriptural Accounts and Scientific Truths about the Earth's Creation Are Compatible*. Springville, UT: Cedar Fort, 2003.

Brenson, Michael. "Titian and his supreme works of inevitability and freedom." New York City, NY: The New York Times, October 29, 1990. http://query.nytimes.com/gst/fullpage.html?res=9C0CE7DF123CF93AA15753C 1A966958260 (accessed August 8, 2007).

Brenton, Lancelot C. L. 1851. *The Septuagint with Apocrypha: Greek and English*. Peabody, MA: Hendrickson Publishers, 2005.

British Methodist Conference, ed. 1984. *Hymns and Psalms*. Corrected ed. Peterborough, England: Methodist Publishing House, 2004.

Broadwood, Lucy E., and J. A. Fuller Maitland. *English County Songs*. London, England: The Leadenhall Press, 1893.

Brock, Sebastian. "A Syriac Life of Abel." *Le Muséon* 87 (1974): 467-92.

Broderick, Carlfred. 1987. "The Uses of Adversity." In *My Parents Married on a Dare and Other Favorite Essays on Life*, edited by Carlfred Broderick, 121-41. Salt Lake City, UT: Deseret Book, 1996.

Brodhead, Richard H. "Prophets in America circa 1830: Ralph Waldo Emerson, Nat Turner, Joseph Smith." In *Joseph Smith Jr: Reappraisals After Two Centuries*, edited by Reid L. Neilson and Terryl L. Givens, 13-29. Oxford, England: Oxford University Press, 2009.

Brodie, Thomas L. *Genesis as Dialogue: A Literary, Historical, and Theological Commentary*. Oxford, England: Oxford University Pres, 2001.

Brohi, Allahbakhsh K. "The spiritual significance of the *Qur'an*." In *Foundations*, edited by Seyyed Hossein Nasr. *Islamic Spirituality* 1, 11-23. New York City, NY: The Crossroad Publishing Company, 1987.

Brooke, John L. *The Refiner's Fire: The Making of Mormon Cosmology, 1644-1844*. Cambridge, England: Cambridge University Press, 1994.

Brooks, Juanita. 1950. *The Mountain Meadows Massacre*. Norman, OK: University of Oklahoma Press, 1962.

———. *On the Mormon Frontier: The Diary of Hosea Stout*. 2 vols. Salt Lake City, UT: University of Utah Press, 1964.

Brough, Monte J., and John K. Carmack. "How the Hong Kong Temple came to be." *Ensign* 36, December 2006, 59-61.

Brown, Francis, S. R. Driver, and Charles A. Briggs. 1906. *The Brown-Driver-Briggs Hebrew and English Lexicon*. Peabody, MA: Hendrickson Publishers, 2005.

Brown, G. Spencer. 1969. *The Laws of Form*. Limited ed. Portland, OR: Cognizer Co., 1994.

Brown, Hugh B. 1956. "Education is a part of salvation." In *BYU Education Week*, June 20, 1956, Brigham Young University. http://speeches.byu.edu/?act=viewitem&id=107 (accessed August 7, 2007).

———. "Participation: The way to salvation." *Improvement Era* 66, June 1963, 506-07.

Brown, Matthew B. "Brigham Young's teachings on Adam." Presented at the *FAIR Conference*, August 7, 2009.

———. "Girded about with a lambskin." *Journal of Book of Mormon Studies* 6, no. 2 (1997): 124-51.

———. E-mail message to Jeffrey M. Bradshaw, August 9, 2008.

———. E-mail message to Jeffrey M. Bradshaw, August 12, 2009.

———. *The Gate of Heaven*. American Fork, UT: Covenant Communications, 1999.

———. *The Plan of Salvation: Doctrinal Notes and Commentary*. American Fork, UT: Covenant Communications, 2002.

Brown, Matthew B., and Paul Thomas Smith. *Symbols in Stone: Symbolism on the Early Temples of the Restoration*. American Fork, UT: Covenant Communications, 1997.

Brown, Raymond E. *The Birth of the Messiah*. 2nd ed. *The Anchor Bible Reference Library*, ed. David Noel Freedman. Doubleday: New York, NY, 1993.

———. *The Death of the Messiah: From Gethsemane to the Grave*. 2 vols. *The Anchor Bible Reference Library*, ed. David Noel Freedman. New York City, NY: Doubleday, 1994.

Brown, S. Kent. "Approaches to the Pentateuch." In *Genesis to 2 Samuel*, edited by Kent P. Jackson and Robert L. Millet. *Studies in Scripture* 3, 13-23. Salt Lake City, UT: Deseret Book, 1985.

———. "The hunt for the Valley of Lemuel." *Journal of Book of Mormon Studies* 16, no. 1 (2007): 64-73, 86-88.

———. "The Nag Hammadi Library: A Mormon Perspective." In *Apocryphal Writings and the Latter-day Saints*, edited by C. Wilfred Griggs, 255-83. Provo, UT: Brigham Young University Religious Studies Center, 1986.

———. *Voices from the Dust: Book of Mormon Insights*. Salt Lake City, UT: Covenant Communications, 2004.

Brown, Samuel. "The Prophet Elias puzzle." *Dialogue: A Journal of Mormon Thought* 39, no. 3 (Fall 2006): 1-17.

Bruce, F. F., ed. *The Epistle to the Hebrews* Revised ed. Grand Rapids, MI: William B. Eerdmans Publishing, 1990.

Brueggemann, Walter, ed. *Genesis. Interpretation: A Bible Commentary for Teaching and Preaching*, ed. James Luther Mays, Patrick D. Miller, Jr. and Paul J. Achtemeier. Atlanta, GA: John Knox Press, 1982.

Brumfield, Allaire Chandor. *The Attic Festivals of Demeter and Their Relation to the Agricultural Year. Monographs in Classical Studies*, ed. W. R. Connor. Salem, NH: The Ayer Company, 1981.

Brunhes, J. *Human Geography: An Attempt at a Positive Classification, Principles and Examples*. Translated by I.C. Le Compte. Edited by I. Bowman and R.E. Dodge. Chicago, IL: Rand McNally and Company, 1920. http://books.google.com/books?id=kpoiAAAAMAAJ (accessed October 1, 2008).

Brzezinski, Zbigniew. *Second Chance: Three Presidents and the Crisis of American Superpower*. New York City, NY: Basic Books, 2007.

Buchanan, George Wesley. *To the Hebrews. The Anchor Bible* 36. New York City, NY: Doubleday, 1972.

Buckley, Jorunn Jacobsen. *The Mandaeans: Ancient Texts and Modern People. American Academy of Religion: The Religions Series*, ed. Paul B. Courtright. Oxford, England: Oxford University Press, 2002.

———, ed. *The Scroll of Exalted Kingship: Diwan Malkuta 'Laita. American Oriental Society Translation Series* 3. New Haven, CN: American Oriental Society, 1993.

Budge, E.A. Wallis, ed. "Adam describes the rebellion of Satan against God." In *Egyptian Tales and Romances: Pagan, Christian and Muslim*, edited by E. A. Wallis Budge, 292-95. London, England: Thornton Butterworth Limited, 1931. Reprint, Kila, MT: Kessinger Publishing, 2003.

———, ed. *The Book of the Cave of Treasures*. London, England: The Religious Tract Society, 1927. Reprint, New York City, NY: Cosimo Classics, 2005.

———, ed. *The Book of the Dead. The Chapters of Coming Forth by Day: An English Translation with Introduction, Notes, etc.*, 1898. Reprint, Boston, MA: Adamant Media Corporation, 2001. In *Internet Sacred Texts Archive*. http://www.sacred-texts.com/egy/ebod (accessed October 3, 2008).

———, ed. *Egyptian Religion*, 1900. Reprint, Seacaucus, NJ: University Books, 1959.

———, ed. *The Queen of Sheba and Her Only Son Menyelek (Kebra Nagast)* 2nd ed. London, England: Oxford University Press, 1932. Reprint, New York City, NY: Cosimo Classics, 2004.

Bukhari, Muhammad Ibn Ismail, ed. 846. *Sahih Al-Bukhari: Being the Tradition of Sayings and Doings of the Prophet Muhammad as Narrated by His Companions*. 9 vols. Translated by Muhammad Matraji. New Delhi, India: Islamic Book Service, 2006.

Bullard, Roger A., and Bentley Layton ed. "The Hypostasis of the Archons (II, 4)." In *The Nag Hammadi Library in English*, edited by James M. Robinson. 3rd, Revised ed, 161-69. San Francisco, CA: HarperSanFrancisco, 1990.

Bunge, Gabriel. *The Rublev Trinity: The Icon of the Monk-Painter Andrei Rublev*. Translated by Andrew Louth. Crestwood, NY: St. Vladimir's Seminary Press, 2007.

Bunyan, John. 1678. *The Annotated Pilgrim's Progress*. Edited by Warren W. Wiersbe. Chicago, IL: Moody Press, 1980.

Burch, Vacher. "The 'Stone' and the 'Keys' (Mt. 16:18ff.)." *Journal of Biblical Literature* 52 (1933): 147-52.

Burchard, C. ed. "Joseph and Aseneth." In *The Old Testament Pseudepigrapha*, edited by James H. Charlesworth. Vol. 2, 177-247. Garden City, NY: Doubleday and Company, 1983.

Burgon, Glade L. "Name of God." In *Encyclopedia of Mormonism*, edited by Daniel H. Ludlow. 4 vols. Vol. 3, 980-81. New York City, NY: Macmillan, 1992. http://www.lib.byu.edu/Macmillan/ (accessed November 26, 2007).

Burke, Kenneth. 1961. "The first three chapters of Genesis: Principles of governance stated narratively." In *The Bible: Modern Critical Views*, edited by Harold Bloom. *Bloom's Modern Critical Views*, ed. Harold Bloom, 15-19. Philadelphia, PA: Chelsea House Publishers, 1987.

Burtea, Bogdan. "Ein mandäischer magischer Text aus der Drower Collection." In *Festschrift Rainer Voigt zum sechzigsten Geburtstag*, edited by Bogdan Burtea, J. Tropper and H. Younansardaroud, *Alter Orient und Altes Testament*, 93-103. Münster, Germany, 2004.

———. "Sahr d-parauanaiia 'Erläuterung der Parauanaiia' Text, Übersetzung und Kommentar der mandäischen Handschrift DC 24 (*Mandäistische Forschungen*, Bd. 1, Wiesbaden, Germany, 2004)." Dissertation, Freie Universität, 2004.

Burton, Theodore M. "A marriage to last through eternity." *Ensign* 17, June 1987, 12-15.

Bushman, Richard Lyman. 1969. "Faithful history." In *Believing History: Latter-day Saint Essays*, edited by Reid L. Neilson and Jed L. Woodworth, 3-19. New York City, NY: Columbia University Press, 2004.

———. *Joseph Smith and the Beginnings of Mormonism*. Urbana, IL: University of Illinois Press, 1984.

———. 2001. "A Joseph Smith for the twenty-first century." In *Believing History: Latter-day Saint Essays*, edited by Reid L. Neilson and Jed L. Woodworth, 262-78. New York City, NY: Columbia University Press, 2004.

———. "Joseph Smith and the creation of the sacred." In *Joseph Smith Jr: Reappraisals After Two Centuries*, edited by Reid L. Neilson and Terryl L. Givens, 93-106. Oxford, England: Oxford University Press, 2009.

———. *Joseph Smith: Rough Stone Rolling, A Cultural Biography of Mormonism's Founder*. New York City, NY: Alfred A. Knopf, 2005.

———. "Joseph Smith's family background." In *The Prophet Joseph: Essays on the Life and Mission of Joseph Smith*, edited by Larry C. Porter and Susan Easton Black, 1-18. Salt Lake City, UT: Deseret Book, 1988.

———. 2007. "Mitt Romney's Mormonism: A TNR online debate." January 3, 2007. In *The New Republic Online*. http://www.tnr.com/doc.mhtml?i=w070101&s=bushman010307 (accessed August 7, 2007).

———. *Mormonism: A Very Short Introduction*. Oxford, England: Oxford University Press, 2008.

———. "Richard Lyman Bushman." In *Why I Believe*, 79-83. Salt Lake City, UT: Bookcraft, 2002.

———. "The theology of councils." In *Reason, Revelation, and Faith: Essays in Honor of Truman G. Madsen*, edited by Donald W. Parry, Daniel C. Peterson and Stephen D. Ricks, 433-45. Provo, UT: Foundation for Ancient Research and Mormon Studies, 2002.

Buskirk, Allen R. "Science, pseudoscience, and religious belief." *The FARMS Review* 17, no. 1 (2005): 273-309.

Butcher, William. *Jules Verne: The Definitive Biography*. New York City, NY: Thunder's Mouth Press, 2006.

Butler, Thomas. E-mail message to Jeffrey M. Bradshaw, October 2, 2006.

Butlin, Martin. *William Blake*. London, England: Tate Gallery Publications, 1978.

Butterworth, Edric Allen Schofeld. *The Tree at the Navel of the Earth*. Berlin, Germany: Walter de Gruyter, 1970.

Buxbaum, Yitzhak. *Jewish Tales of Mystic Joy*. San Francisco, CA: Jossey-Bass, 2002.

Bynum, Caroline Walker. *The Resurrection of the Body in Western Christianity, 200-1336. Lectures on the History of Religions, American Council of Learned Societies, New Series* 15. New York City, NY: Columbia University Press, 1995.

"Byzantine Literature." In *Wikipedia*. http://en.wikipedia.org/wiki/Byzantine_literature (accessed October 2, 2008).

Cabanot, Jean. *Petit Glossaire des Thèmes d'Iconographie Chrétienne*. Vol. 2: Au-delà; personnages saints, illustres ou légendaires; animaux réels ou mythiques; vie de l'Église; cérémonies; objets et symboles. Dax, France: Amis des Anciennes Églises de Landes (AEAL), 1996.

Cahill, Thomas. *How the Irish Saved Civilization: The Untold Story of Ireland's Heroic Role from the Fall of Rome to the Rise of Medieval Europe*. New York City, NY: Doubleday, 1995.

Callaghan, Catherine A. *Other Worlds*. Johnstown, OH: Pudding House Publications, 1999.

Callender, Dexter E. *Adam in Myth and History: Ancient Israelite Perspectives on the Primal Human*. Winona Lake, IN: Eisenbrauns, 2000.

Cameron, Ron, and Arthur J. Dewey, eds. *The Cologne Mani Codex (P. Colon. inv. nr. 4780) 'Concerning the Origin of His Body'. Texts and Translations* 15, *Early Christian Literature* 3, ed. Birger A. Pearson. Missoula, Montana: Scholars Press, 1979.

Campbell, Beverly. *Eve and the Choice Made in Eden*. Salt Lake City, UT: Bookcraft, 2003.

Campbell, Craig S. *Images of the New Jerusalem: Latter Day Saint Faction Interpretations of Independence Missouri*. Knoxville, TN: The University of Tennessee Press, 2004.

Campbell, Joseph. *The Hero with a Thousand Faces*. London, England: Fontana, 1993.

Cannon, Donald Q., and Lyndon W. Cook, eds. *Far West Record: Minutes of The Church of Jesus Christ of Latter-day Saints, 1830-1844*. Salt Lake City, UT: Deseret Book, 1983.

Cannon, Donald Q., and Richard O. Cowan. *Unto Every Nation: Gospel Light Reaches Every Land*. Salt Lake City, UT: Deseret Book, 2003.

Cannon, Elaine Anderson. "Mother in Heaven." In *Encyclopedia of Mormonism*, edited by Daniel H. Ludlow. 4 vols. Vol. 2, 961. New York City, NY: Macmillan, 1991.

Cannon, George Q. 1884. "Discourse by President George Q. Cannon (Delivered in the Assembly Hall, Salt Lake City, Sunday Afternoon, January 6th, 1884)." In *Journal of Discourses*. 26 vols. Vol. 25, 22-28. Liverpool and London, England: Latter-day Saints Book Depot, 1853-1886. Reprint, Salt Lake City, UT: Bookcraft, 1966.

———. *Gospel Truth*. 2 vols. Edited by Jerreld L. Newquist. Salt Lake City, UT: Deseret Book, 1957-1974.

———. 1888. *The Life of Joseph Smith, the Prophet*. Salt Lake City, UT: Deseret Book, 1986.

Cannon, Hugh J. 1931. *David O. McKay Around the World: An Apostolic Mission*. Provo, UT: Spring Creek, 2005.

Caquot, A. "Un phylactère mandéen en plomb." *Semitica* 22 (1972): 67-87.

Carasik, Michael, ed. *The JPS Miqra'ot Gedolot: Exodus. The Commentator's Bible*. Philadelphia, PA: The Jewish Publication Society of America, 2005.

Card, Orson Scott. "Sharing in the spirit of song—and praise." Salt Lake City, UT: Deseret Morning News, February 28, 2008. http://deseretnews.com/article/1,5143,695256836,00.html (accessed March 28, 2008).

Careless, George, Ebenezer Beesley, Joseph Daynes, Evan Stephens, and Thomas C. Griggs. *Latter Day Saints' Psalmody*. Salt Lake City, UT: The Church of Jesus Christ of Latter-day Saints, 1889.

Carroll, James L. "Egyptian craft guild initiations." *Studia Antiqua* 5, no. 1 (Spring 2007): 17-44.

———. "The reconciliation of Adam and Israelite temples." *Studia Antiqua* 3, no. 1 (Winter 2003): 83-101.

Carroll, James L., and Elizabeth M. Siler. "Let my prayer be set before Thee: The burning of incense in the temple cult of ancient Israel." *Studia Antiqua* 2, no. 2 (Fall 2002): 17-32.

Cartlidge, David R., and J. Keith Elliott. *Art and the Christian Apocrypha*. London, England: Routledge, 2001.

Cassuto, Umberto. 1944. *A Commentary on the Book of Genesis. Vol. 1: From Adam to Noah*. Translated by Israel Abrahams. 1st English ed. Jerusalem: The Magnes Press, The Hebrew University, 1998.

———. 1949. *A Commentary on the Book of Genesis. Vol. 2: From Noah to Abraham*. Translated by Israel Abrahams. 1st English ed. Jerusalem: The Magnes Press, The Hebrew University, 1997.

———. 1941. *The Documentary Hypothesis and the Composition of the Pentateuch*. Jerusalem: The Magnes Press, The Hebrew University, 1961.

Cazenave, Michel. *Encyclopédie des Symboles (Updated and expanded version of the German text of Hans Biedermann Knaurs Lexicon der Symbole)*. Translated by Françoise Périgaut, Gisèle Marie and Alexandre Tondat. Paris, France: Librairie Générale Française, 1996.

Chadwick, Jeffrey R. "Revisiting Golgotha and the Garden Tomb." *The Religious Educator: Perspectives on the Restored Gospel* 4, no. 1 (2003). http://religion.byu.edu/NXT/gateway.dll/public1/1/2/89?fn=default.htm$f=templat&es$3.0 &vid=reledpublic:10.1048/enu (accessed March 22, 2008).

———. "The wrong place for Lehi's trail and the Valley of Lemuel." *FARMS Review* 17, no. 2 (2005): 197-215.

Chailley, Jacques. 1968. *The Magic Flute Unveiled: Esoteric Symbolism in Mozart's Masonic Opera, An Interpretation of the Libretto and the Music*. English ed. Rochester, VT: Inner Traditions International, 1992.

Chamberlain, Jonathan. *Chinese Gods*. Selangor Darul Ehsan, Malaysia: Pelanduk Publications, 1987.

Chang, Kwang-chih. "China on the eve of the historical period." In *The Cambridge History of Ancient China: From the Origins of Civilization to 221 BC*, edited by Michael Loewe and Edward L. Shaughnessy, 37-73. New York City, NY: Cambridge University Press, 1999.

Chappell, William. *The Ballad Literature and Popular Music of the Olden Time*. London, England: Chappell and Company, 1859.

Charles, R. H., ed. *The Apocrypha and Pseudepigrapha of the Old Testament in English*. 2 vols. Oxford, England: Oxford University Press, 1913. Reprint, Berkeley, CA: Apocryphile Press, 2004.

———, ed. *The Book of Enoch Together with a Reprint of the Greek Fragments* 2nd ed. Oxford, England: Clarendon Press, 1912. Reprint, Kila, MT: Kessinger Publishing, 2005.

Charlesworth, James H. "The classical Protestant view of human nature." In *On Human Nature: The Jerusalem Center Symposium*, edited by Truman G. Madsen, David Noel Freedman and Pam Fox Kuhlken, 69-84. Ann Arbor, MI: Pryor Pettengill Publishers, 2004.

———. "Conclusion: The origin and development of resurrection beliefs." In *Resurrection: The Origin and Future of a Biblical Doctrine*, edited by James H. Charlesworth. *Faith and Scholarship Colloquies* 3, 218-31. New York City, NY: T & T Clark, 2006.

———. *The Good and Evil Serpent: How a Universal Symbol Became Christianized*. Des Moines, IA: Anchor Bible, 2010.

———. "Jesus research and archaeology: A new perspective." In *Jesus and Archaeology*, edited by James H. Charlesworth, 11-63. Grand Rapids, MI: William B. Eerdmans, 2006.

———. "Jesus research and the appearance of psychobiography." In *Reason, Revelation, and Faith: Essays in Honor of Truman G. Madsen*, edited by Donald W. Parry, Daniel C. Peterson and Stephen D. Ricks, 55-84. Provo, UT: Foundation for Ancient Research and Mormon Studies, 2002.

———. "Lady Wisdom and Johannine Christianity." In *Light in a Spotless Mirror: Reflections on Wisdom Traditions in Judaism and Early Christianity*, edited by James H. Charlesworth and Michael A. Daise, 92-133. Harrisburg, PA: Trinity Press International, 2003.

———, ed. "Odes of Solomon." In *The Old Testament Pseudepigrapha*, edited by James H. Charlesworth. 2 vols. Vol. 2, 725-71. Garden City, NY: Doubleday and Company, 1983.

———, ed. *The Old Testament Pseudepigrapha*. 2 vols. Garden City, NY: Doubleday and Company, 1983. http://ocp. acadiau.ca/ (accessed September 20, 2008).

———. "Resurrection: The Dead Sea Scrolls and the New Testament." In *Resurrection: The Origin and Future of a Biblical Doctrine*, edited by James H. Charlesworth. *Faith and Scholarship Colloquies* 3, 138-86. New York City, NY: T & T Clark, 2006.

———. "Where does the concept of resurrection appear and how do we know that?" In *Resurrection: The Origin and Future of a Biblical Doctrine*, edited by James H. Charlesworth. *Faith and Scholarship Colloquies* 3, 1-21. New York City, NY: T & T Clark, 2006.

Chaucer, Geoffrey. ca. 1380. *The Canterbury Tales, Fifteen Tales and the General Prologue: Authoritative Text, Sources and Backgrounds, Criticism*. Edited by V. A. Kolve and Glending Olson. 2nd ed. *Norton Critical Editions*. New York City, NY: W. W. Norton, 2005.

Chavalas, Mark W., and K. Lawson Younger, Jr., eds. *Mesopotamia and the Bible: Comparative Explorations*. Grand Rapids, MI: Baker Academic, 2002.

Chavannes, É., and P. Pelliot. *Un traité manichéen retrouvée en Chine: Traduit et annoté* (Extraits du *Journal Asiatique*, nov.-déc. 1911, pp. 499-617; jan.-fév. 1913, pp. 99-199; mars-avr. 1913, pp. 261-394). Paris, France: Imprimerie Nationale, 1912.

Chaviv, Yaakov ibn. 1516. *Ein Yaakov: The Ethical and Inspirational Teachings of the Talmud*. Edited by Avraham Yaakov Finkel. Lanham, MI: Jason Aronson / Rowman and Littlefield Publishing Group, 1999.

Chebel, Malek. *Les Symboles de l'Islam*. Paris, France: Assouline, 1999.

Cherbonnier, Edmond LaB. "In defense of anthropomorphism." In *Reflections on Mormonism: Judeo-Christian Parallels, Papers Delivered at the Religious Studies Center Symposium, Brigham Young University, March 10-11, 1978*, edited by Truman G. Madsen. *Religious Studies Monograph Series* 4, 155-73. Provo, UT: Religious Studies Center, Brigham Young University, 1978.

Chesnutt, Randall D. "Joseph and Aseneth: Food as an identity marker." In *The Historical Jesus in Context*, edited by Amy-Jill Levine, Dale C. Allison, Jr. and John Dominic Crossan, 357-65. Princeton, NJ: Princeton University Press, 2006.

Chester, Andrew. *Messiah and Exaltation: Jewish Messianic and Visionary Traditions and New Testament Christology*. *Wissenschaftliche Untersuchungen zum Neuen Testament* 207. Tübingen, Germany: Mohr Siebeck, 2007.

Chesterton, Gilbert Keith. 1903. "Charles Dickens." In *Collected Works*. Vol. 15: Chesterton on Dickens, 29-209. San Francisco, CA: Ignatius, 1989.

———. 1905. "Heretics." In *Collected Works*, edited by David Dooley. Vol. 1: Heretics, Orthodoxy, The Blatchford Controversies, 39-207. San Francisco, CA: Ignatius, 1986.

———. 1908. *Orthodoxy*. New York City, NY: Image Books / Doubleday, 2001.

———. 1909. "A piece of chalk." In *Tremendous Trifles*, 15-19. Charleston, SC: BiblioBazaar, BiblioLife, n. d.

———. 1910. *William Blake*. New York City, NY: Cosimo, 2005.

Chittick, William C. 2003. "Mysticism in Islam." Lecture given at the David M. Kennedy Center for International Studies, May 2003. In *Middle Eastern Texts Initiative*, Brigham Young University. http://meti.byu.edu/mysticism_chittick.html (accessed August 7, 2007).

Chouraqui, André, ed. *La Bible*. Paris, France: Desclée de Brouwer, 2003.

"Christian Symbols." In *Fish Eaters*. http://www.fisheaters.com/symbols.html (accessed September 29, 2008).

Christensen, Kevin. *Paradigms Regained: A Survey of Margaret Barker's Scholarship and Its Significance for Mormon Studies*. Vol. 2. *Foundation for Ancient Research and Mormon Studies Occasional Papers*, ed. William J. Hamblin. Provo, UT: Foundation for Ancient Research and Mormon Studies at BYU, 2001.

———. "The temple, the monarchy, and wisdom: Lehi's world and the scholarship of Margaret Barker." In *Glimpses of Lehi's Jerusalem*, edited by John W. Welch, David Rolph Seely and Jo Ann H. Seely, 449-522. Provo, UT: Foundation for Ancient Research and Mormon Studies (FARMS), Brigham Young University, 2004.

Christensen, Kevin, and Shauna Christensen. "Nephite Feminism Revisited: Thoughts on Carol Lynn Pearson's View of Women in the Book of Mormon." *FARMS Review of Books* 10, no. 1 (1998): 9-61. http://maxwellinstitute.byu.edu/pdf.php?filename=MjQ3Njk2NDg3LTEwLTIucGRm&type=cmV2aWV3 (accessed December 24, 2007).

Christensen, Michael J., and Jeffery A. Wittung, eds. 2007. *Partakers of the Divine Nature: The History and Development of Deification in the Christian Traditions*. Grand Rapids, MI: Baker Academic, 2008.

Christenson, Allen J., ed. 2004. *Popol Vuh: Literal Poetic Version*. Translated by Allen J. Christenson. Norman, OK: University of Oklahoma Press, 2008.

———, ed. *Popol Vuh: The Mythic Sections—Tales of First Beginnings from the Ancient K'iche'-Maya*. Translated by Allen J. Christenson. *Ancient Texts and Mormon Studies* 2, eds. John W. Welch and John A. Tvedtnes. Provo, UT: The Foundation for Ancient Research and Mormon Studies (FARMS) at Brigham Young University, 2000.

———, ed. *Popol Vuh: The Sacred Book of the Maya*. Translated by Allen J. Christenson. Norman, OK: University of Oklahoma Press, 2003.

———. "The sacred tree of the ancient Maya." *Journal of Book of Mormon Studies* 6, no. 1 (1997): 1-23.

Chrysostom, John. ca. 386-407. *Commentaries on the Sages. Vol. 1: Commentary on Job*. Translated by Robert Charles Hill. Brookline, MA: Holy Cross Orthodox Press, 2006.

———. ca. 386-407. *Homilies on Genesis 1-17*. Translated by Robert Hill. Washington, DC: Catholic University of America Press, 1986.

Church Educational System. *Charge to Religious Educators*. 2nd ed. Salt Lake City, UT: The Church of Jesus Christ of Latter-day Saints, 1982.

———. *Religion 327: The Pearl of Great Price Student Manual*. Salt Lake City, UT: The Church of Jesus Christ of Latter-day Saints, 2000.

Cicero, Marcus Tullius. d. 43 BC. "*De Legibus* (On the Laws)." In *Operum Collectio*. Intratext Digital Library http://www.intratext.com/y/LAT0922.HTM (accessed April 17, 2008).

Clairmont, Christoph W. *Classic Attic Tombstones*. 9 vols. Kilchberg, Switzerland: Akanthus Verlag für Archäologie, 1993-1995.

Clark, E. Douglas. *The Blessings of Abraham: Becoming a Zion People*. American Fork, UT: Covenant Communications, 2005.

———. "Cedars and stars: Enduring symbols of cosmic kingship in Abraham's encounter with Pharaoh." In *Astronomy, Papyrus, and Covenant*, edited by John Gee and Brian M. Hauglid. *Studies in the Book of Abraham* 3, 37-55. Provo, UT: Foundation for Ancient Research and Mormon Studies (FARMS), Brigham Young University, 2005.

———. "A prologue to Genesis: Moses 1 in light of Jewish traditions." *BYU Studies* 45, no. 1 (2006): 129-42.

Clark, Elizabeth A. "New perspectives on the Origenist controversy: Human embodiment and ascetic strategies." *Church History* 59, no. 2 (1990): 145-62.

Clark, J. Reuben, Jr. "Our priceless special blessings." *The Improvement Era* 57, December 1954, 878-79.

———. "Talk for the Evening Meeting." In *Conference Report: One Hundred Twelfth Semiannual General Conference, October 1942*, 54-59. 1942.

———. "When are the writings and sermons of church leaders entitled to the claim of being scripture? (July 31, 1954)." In *J. Reuben Clark: Selected Papers*, edited by David H. Yarn, Jr., 95-112. Provo, UT: Brigham Young University Press, 1984.

———. 1956. *Why the King James Version*. Salt Lake City, UT: Deseret Book, 1979.

Clark, James R., ed. *Messages of the First Presidency*. 6 vols. Salt Lake City, UT: Bookcraft, 1965-1975.

Clark, Marden J. *Liberating Form: Mormon Essays on Religion and Literature*. Salt Lake City, UT: Aspen Books, 1992.

Clarke, Arthur C. 1953. *Childhood's End*. 2nd ed. New York City, NY: Ballantine Books, 1990.

Clarke, Arthur C., and C. S. Lewis. *From Narnia to a Space Odyssey: The War of Ideas Between Arthur C. Clarke and C. S. Lewis*. Edited by Ryder W. Miller. New York City, NY: iBooks, 2003.

Clayton, Robert W. "Frequently asked questions." In *BYU-I Employee Web Site*. http://emp.byui.edu/claytonr/FAQ.pdf (accessed December 7, 2008).

Clayton, William. "Diaries, November 24, 1840-February 27, 1846." In *William Clayton's Nauvoo Diaries and Personal Writings*, ed. Robert C. Fillerup. http://www.boap.org/LDS/Early-Saints/clayton-diaries (accessed January 3, 2008).

———. *Intimate Chronicle: The Journals of William Clayton*. Edited by George D. Smith. Salt Lake City, UT: Signature Books, 1995.

Clement of Alexandria. ca. 190-215. "Exhortation to the Heathen." In *The Ante-Nicene Fathers (The Writings of the Fathers Down to AD 325)*, edited by Alexander Roberts and James Donaldson. 10 vols. Vol. 2, 171-206. Buffalo, NY: The Christian Literature Company, 1885.

———. ca. 190-215. "The *Stromata*, or Miscellanies." In *The Ante-Nicene Fathers (The Writings of the Fathers Down to AD 325)*, edited by Alexander Roberts and James Donaldson. 10 vols. Vol. 2, 299-568. Buffalo, NY: The Christian Literature Company, 1885. Reprint, Peabody, MA: Hendrickson Publishers, 2004.

Clifford, Richard J., ed. *Creation Accounts in the Ancient Near East and in the Bible. Catholic Biblical Quarterly Monograph Series* 26. Washington, D.C.: Catholic Biblical Association, 1994.

———. "Creationism's value?" *America: The National Catholic Weekly* 182, no. 8 (11 March 2000). http://www.americamagazine.org/gettext.cfm?articleTypeID=1&textID=584&issueID=279 (accessed August 8, 2007).

———, ed. "Ewe and Wheat." In *Creation Accounts in the Ancient Near East and in the Bible*, edited by Richard J. Clifford, 45-46. Washington, DC: Catholic Biblical Association, 1994.

———. "The temple and the holy mountain." In *The Temple in Antiquity*, edited by Truman G. Madsen, 107-24. Salt Lake City, UT: Bookcraft, 1984.

———. *The Wisdom Literature*. Nashville, TN: The Abingdon Press, 1998.

Clinton, Kevin. "Stages of initiation in the Eleusinian and Samothracian mysteries." In *Greek Mysteries: The Archaeology and Ritual of Ancient Greek Secret Cults*, edited by Michael B. Cosmopoulos, 50-78. New York City, NY: Routledge, 2003.

Closterman, Wendy E. "Family ideology and family history: The function of funerary markers in classical Attic peribolos tombs." *American Journal of Archaeology* 111, no. 4 (October 2007): 633-52.

Cobb, John B., Jr., ed. *Back to Darwin: A Richer Account of Evolution*. Grand Rapids, MI: William B. Eerdmans, 2008.

Cohen, Abraham, ed. *The Soncino Chumash: The Five Books of Moses with Haphtaroth*. London, England: The Soncino Press, 1983.

Cohen, H. Hirsch. *The Drunkenness of Noah*. Tuscaloosa, AL: University of Alabama Press, 1974.

Cohen, Martin Samuel. *Shi'ur Qomah: Liturgy and Theurgy in Pre-Kabbalistic Jewish Mysticism*. Lanham, MD: University Press of America, Rowman & Littlefield, 1983.

———, ed. *Shi'ur Qomah: Texts and Recensions*. Tübingen, Germany: J. C. B. Mohr, 1985.

Cole, Susan G. "Landscapes of Dionysos and Elysian fields." In *Greek Mysteries: The Archaeology and Ritual of Ancient Greek Secret Cults*, edited by Michael B. Cosmopoulos, 193-217. New York City, NY: Routledge, 2003.

Coles, Robert. *The Secular Mind*. Princeton, NJ: Princeton University Press, 1999.

Coleson, Joseph E. "Israel's life cycle from birth to resurrection." In *Israel's Apostasy and Restoration: Essays in Honor of Roland K. Harrison*, edited by Avraham Gileadi, 237-50. Grand Rapids, MI: Baker Book House, 1988.

Collier, Fred C., and William S. Harwell, eds. 1832-1837. *Kirtland Council Minute Book*. Salt Lake City, UT: Collier's Publishing Company, 1996.

Collins, Francis S. *The Language of God: A Scientist Presents Evidence for Belief*. New York City, NY: Free Press, 2006.

Collins, John J. *Between Athens and Jerusalem: Jewish Identity in the Hellenistic Diaspora*. 2nd ed. *The Biblical Resource Series*, eds. Astrid B. Beck and David Noel Freedman. Grand Rapids, MI: William B. Eerdmans, 2000.

———. "The Son of Man and the Saints of the Most High in the Book of Daniel." *Journal of Biblical Literature* 93, no. 1 (1974): 50-66.

———. "The sons of God and the daughters of men." In *Sacred Marriages*, edited by Martti Nissinen and Risto Uro, 259-74. Winona Lake, IN: Eisenbrauns, 2008.

Colton, Albert J. "Ayatollah Solzhenitsyn: Is he really any help?" In *Alexander Solzhenitsyn Challenges the West: "A World Split Apart" (Transcript of Proceedings, University of Utah, May 10, 1979)*, edited by Susan Wakefield, 8-11. Salt Lake City, UT: Utah Endowment for the Humanities, 1979.

Colvin, Don F. *Nauvoo Temple: A Story of Faith*. Provo, UT: Religious Studies Center, Brigham Young University, 2002.

Compton, Todd M. E-mail message to Jeffrey M. Bradshaw, April 21, 2008.

———. "The handclasp and embrace as tokens of recognition." In *By Study and Also by Faith: Essays in Honor of Hugh W. Nibley*, edited by John M. Lundquist and Stephen D. Ricks. 2 vols. Vol. 1, 611-42. Salt Lake City, UT: Deseret Book, 1990.

———. "The whole token: Mystery symbolism in classical recognition drama." Typescript of article provided by the author. *Epoché: UCLA Journal for the History of Religions* 13 (1985): 1-81.

Condie, Spencer J. *Your Agency: Handle with Care*. Salt Lake City, UT: Bookcraft, 1996.

Conisbee, Philip. *Art for the Nation: Collecting for a Century*. Washington, D.C.: National Gallery of Art, 2000.

Consolmagno, Guy. *God's Mechanics: How Scientists and Engineers Make Sense of Religion*. San Francisco, CA: Jossey-Bass, 2008.

Coogan, Michael D. "The great gulf between scholars and the pew." *Bible Review* 10, no. 3 (June 1994): 44-48, 55. http://members.bib-arch.org/nph-proxy.pl/000000A/http/www.basarchive.org/bswbSearch.asp?=3fPubID=3dBSBR&Volume=3d10&Issue=3d3&ArticleID=3d15&UserID=3d0 (accessed June 23, 2007).

Cook, Lyndon W. *Nauvoo Marriages Proxy Sealings 1843-1846*. Provo, UT: Grandin Book Company, 2004.

———. *The Revelations of the Prophet Joseph Smith*. Provo, UT: Seventy's Mission Bookstore, 1981.

Cooper, James, and Arthur John Maclean, eds. ca. 350. *Testament of Our Lord, Translated into English from the Syriac with Introduction and Notes*, 1st ed. London, England: T&T Clark, 1902. Reprint, BookSurge Publishing, 2000.

Cooper, Rex Eugene. *Promises Made to the Fathers. Publications in Mormon Studies* 5, ed. Linda King Newell. Salt Lake City, UT: University of Utah Press, 1990.

Coppens, Philip. "William Blake: What paintings of visions come." In *Unknown Masters*, ed. Philip Coppens. http://www.philipcoppens.com/blake.html (accessed November 28, 2007).

Cormican, L. A. 1951. "Medieval idiom in Shakespeare." In *Shakespeare's Christian Dimension: An Anthology of Commentary*, edited by Roy Battenhouse, 24-27. Bloomington, IN: Indiana University Press, 1994.

Cosmas. ca. 970. *Le Traité Contre Les Bogomiles de Cosmas le Prêtre*. Edited by Henri-Charles Puech and André Vaillant. *Travaux publiés par l'Institut d'Études slaves* 21. Paris, France: Imprimerie Nationale, 1945.

Cosmopoulos, Michael B., ed. *Greek Mysteries: The Archaeology and Ritual of Ancient Greek Secret Cults*. New York City, NY: Routledge, 2003.

———. "Mycenaean religion at Eleusis: The architecture and stratigraphy of Megaron B." In *Greek Mysteries: The Archaeology and Ritual of Ancient Greek Secret Cults*, edited by Michael B. Cosmopoulos, 1-24. New York City, NY: Routledge, 2003.

Cottle, Thomas D. *Adam-ondi-Ahman: A Legacy of Adam and Eve*. Portland, OR: Insight, 2005.

Couliano, Ioan P. 1990. *The Tree of Gnosis: Gnostic Mythology from Early Christianity to Modern Nihilism (Translation of "Les Gnoses Dualistes d'occident")*. Translated by H. S. Wiesner. San Francisco, CA: HarperSanFrancisco, 1992.

Cowan, Richard O. *Answers to Your Questions about the Doctrine and Covenants*. Salt Lake City, UT: Deseret Book, 1996.

———. "The great temple of the New Jerusalem." In *Regional Studies in Latter-day Saint Church History: Missouri*, edited by Arnold K. Garr and Clark V. Johnson, 137-54. Provo, UT: Department of Church History and Doctrine, Brigham Young University, 1994.

———. *Temples to Dot the Earth*. Salt Lake City, UT: Bookcraft, 1989.

Cowdery, Oliver. "Egyptian Mummies." *Latter Day Saints' Messenger and Advocate* 2:3, December, 1835, 233-37.

———. "Letter to W. W. Phelps dated Sabbath evening, September 7, 1834, Norton, Medina County, Ohio." *Saints' Messenger and Advocate* 1, October, 1834, 13-16.

Crangle, Edward F., and H. S. Brikha. *Na'oraia, Ma'buta: The Mandaean Baptism. Corpus Codicum Mandaeorum*, ed. Erica C. D. Hunter. Turnhout, Belgium: Brepols, 2008.

———. *Na'oraia, The Na'oraian: Extraordinary Priestcraft in Mandaeism. Corpus Codicum Mandaeorum*, ed. Erica C. D. Hunter. Turnhout, Belgium: Brepols, forthcoming.

Crenshaw, James L. "Love is stronger than death: Intimations of life beyond the grave." In *Resurrection: The Origin and Future of a Biblical Doctrine*, edited by James H. Charlesworth, 53-78. New York City, NY: T & T Clark International, 2006.

Cross, Frank Moore. *The Ancient Library of Qumran*. Minneapolis, MN: Fortress Press, 1995.

Csapo, Eric. *Theories of Mythology. Ancient Cultures*. Oxford, England: Blackwell, 2005.

Cumont, Franz Valery Marie. *Recherches sur le Symbolisme Funéraire des Romains. Bibliothèque Archéologique et Historique* 35. Paris, France: Paul Geuthner, 1942.

Currid, John D. *Ancient Egypt and the Old Testament*. Grand Rapids, MI: Baker Books, 1997.

Cyril of Jerusalem. ca. 347. "First Catechetical Lectures." In *Nicene and Post-Nicene Fathers, Second Series*, edited by Philip Schaff and Henry Wace. 14 vols. Vol. 7, 6-143. New York City, NY: The Christian Literature Company, 1894. Reprint, Peabody, MA: Hendrickson Publishers, 1994.

———. ca. 347. "Five Catechetical Lectures to the Newly Baptized on the Mysteries." In *Nicene and Post-Nicene Fathers, Second Series*, edited by Philip Schaff and Henry Wace. 14 vols. Vol. 7, 144-57. New York City, NY: The Christian Literature Company, 1894. Reprint, Peabody, MA: Hendrickson Publishers, 1994.

Dahl, Larry E. "The Joseph Smith Translation and the Doctrine and Covenants." In *Plain and Precious Truths Restored: The Doctrinal and Historical Significance of the Joseph Smith Translation*, edited by Robert L. Millet and Robert J. Matthews, 104-33. Salt Lake City, UT: Deseret Book, 1995.

———. "The vision of the glories." In *The Doctrine and Covenants*, edited by Robert L. Millet and Kent P. Jackson. *Studies in Scripture* 1, 279-308. Salt Lake City, UT: Deseret Book, 1989.

Dahl, Larry E., and Charles D. Tate, Jr., eds. *The Lectures on Faith in Historical Perspective. Religious Studies Specialized Monograph Series* 15. Provo, UT: Religious Studies Center, Brigham Young University, 1990.

Damon, S. Foster, and Morris Eaves. 1965. *A Blake Dictionary: The Ideas and Symbols of William Blake*. Revised ed. Hanover, NH: University Press of New England, 1988.

REFERENCES

Dan, Joseph, ed. *The Heart and the Fountain: An Anthology of Jewish Mystical Experiences*. Oxford, England: Oxford University Press, 2003.

———. *Jewish Mysticism*. 4 vols. Northvale, NJ: Jason Aronson, 1998-1999.

Danby, Herbert, ed. *The Mishnah*. Oxford, England: Oxford University Press, 1933.

Daniell, David. "Reading the Bible." In *A Companion to Shakespeare*, edited by David Scott Kastan, 158-71. Oxford, England: Blackwell Publishers, 1999.

———. "Shakespeare and the Protestant mind." In *Shakespeare and Religions*, edited by Peter D. Holland. *Shakespeare Survey: An Annual Survey of Shakespeare Studies and Production* 54, ed. Peter D. Holland, 1-12. Cambridge, England: Cambridge University Press, 2001.

Daniélou, Jean. *The Theology of Jewish Christianity*. London, England: Darton, Longman and Todd, 1964.

Danner, Victor. "The early development of Sufism." In *Islamic Spirituality 1: Foundations*, edited by Seyyed Hossein Nasr, 239-64. New York City, NY: The Crossroad Publishing Company, 1987.

"Das neue Jerusalem, Bamberger Apokalypse Folio 55 recto, Bamberg, Staatsbibliothek, MS A. II. 42." In *Wikipedia*. http://en.wikipedia.org/wiki/Image:BambergApocalypseFolio055rNew_Jerusalem.JPG (accessed September 25, 2008).

David, Rosalie. *The Experience of Ancient Egypt*. London, England: Routledge, 2000.

Davidson, Gustav. 1967. *A Dictionary of Angels, including the Fallen Angels*. New York City, NY: The Free Press, 1971.

Davidson, Herbert A. *Moses Maimonides: The Man and His Works*. Oxford, England: Oxford University Press, 2004.

Davies, Glenys. "The significance of the handshake motif in classical funerary art." *American Journal of Archaeology* 89, no. 4 (October 1985): 627-40.

Davies, Paul. *About Time: Einstein's Unfinished Revolution*. London, England: Penguin, 1995.

———. 2006. *The Goldilocks Enigma: Why Is the Universe Just Right for Life?* (Also published as *Cosmic Jackpot*). London, England: Penguin, 2007.

———. *The Mind of God: The Scientific Basis for a Rational World*. New York: Simon and Schuster / Touchstone, 1993.

Davies, W. D. "Reflections on the Mormon 'canon.'" In *Christians Among Jews and Gentiles: Essays in Honor of Krister Stendahl on His Sixty-fifth Birthday*, edited by George W. E. Nickelsburg and George W. MacRae, 44-66. Philadelphia, PA: Fortress Press, 1986.

Davies, W. V. "Egyptian hieroglyphs." In *Reading the Past: Ancient Writing from Cuneiform to the Alphabet*, edited by J. T. Hooker, 74-135. London, England: The British Museum Press, 1990.

Davila, James R. "Melchizedek: King, Priest, and God." In *The Seductiveness of Jewish Myth*, edited by S. D. Breslauer, 217-34. Albany, NY: SUNY Press, 1997.

Dawood, N. J. 1956. *The Koran*. London, England: Penguin Books, 1997.

de Blois, F., and N. Sims-Williams, eds. *Dictionary of Manichaean Texts*. Vol. 2: Texts from Iraq and Iran (Texts in Syriac, Arabic, Persian and Zoroastrian Middle Persian). *Corpus Fontium Manichaeorum, Series Subsidia*. Turnhout, Belgium: Brepols, 2006.

de Echevarria y Veytia, Don Mariano Fernandez. ca. 1778. *Ancient America Rediscovered (First Portion of the two-volume Historia Antigua de Mexico)*. Translated by Donald W. Hemingway and W. David Hemingway. Springville, UT: Cedar Fort, 2000.

de Galembert, Laurent. "La grandeur du petit prince." Mémoire de DEA de Lettres modernes dirigé par J-M. Maulpoix, Université Paris X-Nanterre, 2001. http://nitescence.free.fr/DEA.pdf (accessed August 8, 2007).

———. *La grandeur du petit prince*. Paris, France: Éditions Le Manuscrit, 2003. http://nitescence.free.fr/DEA.pdf (accessed August 8, 2007).

de Silva, Kingsley M. "Sir James Emerson Tennent: Colonial Administrator and Historian." *Journal of the Royal Asiatic Society of Sri Lanka* 41, no. Special Number (1996): 13-37.

De Vaux, Roland, ed. *La Bible de Jérusalem* Nouvelle ed. Paris, France: Desclée de Brouwer, 1975.

De Vecchi, Pierluigi, and Gianluigi Colalucci. *Michelangelo: The Vatican Frescoes*. Translated by David Stanton and Andrew Ellis. New York City, NY: Abbeville Press Publishers, 1996.

Dearmer, P. and R. Vaughan Williams, eds. 1906. *The English Hymnal with Tunes*. Second Enlarged ed. Oxford, England: Oxford University Press, 1933. Reprint, Centenary Edition, Oxford, England: Oxford University Press, 2006.

———, eds. *The Oxford Book of Carols*. Oxford, England: Oxford University Press, 1928.

Decoo, Wilfried. "The image of Mormonism in French literature: Part 1." *BYU Studies* 14, no. 2 (1974): 1-15.

Della Torre, Stefano Levi. "The anxiety of Eden." In *The Earthly Paradise: The Garden of Eden from Antiquity to*

Modernity, edited by F. Regina Psaki and Charles Hindley. *International Studies in Formative Christianity and Judaism*, 5-13. Binghamton, NY: Academic Studies in the History of Judaism, Global Publications, State University of New York at Binghamton, 2002.

Denny, Frederick M. 1985. "Islam: Qur'an and Hadith." In *The Holy Book in Comparative Perspective*, edited by Frederick M. Denny and Rodney L. Taylor, 84-108. Columbia, SC: University of South Carolina Press, 1993.

Derr, Jill Mulvay. "The significance of 'O My Father' in the personal journey of Eliza R. Snow." *BYU Studies* 36, no. 1 (1996-1997): 84-126.

———, Janath Russell Cannon, and Maureen Ursenbach Beecher. *Women of Covenant: The Story of Relief Society*. Salt Lake City, UT: Deseret Book, 1992.

Deutsch, Nathaniel. "Introduction [to the Mandaean Literature]." In *The Gnostic Bible*, edited by Willis Barnstone and Marvin W. Meyer, 527-35. Boston, MA: Shambhala, 2003.

Deutscher, Guy. *The Unfolding of Language: An Evolutionary Tour of Mankind's Greatest Invention*. New York City, NY: Henry Holt, 2005.

Devereux, E. J. 1968. "Sacramental imagery in *The Tempest*." In *Shakespeare's Christian Dimension: An Anthology of Commentary*, edited by Roy Battenhouse, 154-257. Bloomington, IN: Indiana University Press, 1994.

Dew, Sheri L. *Go Forward with Faith: The Biography of Gordon B. Hinckley*. Salt Lake City, UT: Deseret Book, 1996.

Dhammika, Venerable S. 2007. "Sri Pada: Buddhism's Most Sacred Mountain – A Pilgrim's Guide." In *Buddhist Studies: Buddha Dharma Education Association and BuddhaNet*. http://www.buddhanet.net/e-learning/buddhistworld/sri-pada.htm (accessed September 20, 2007).

Díaz, Gisele, Alan Rodgers, and Bruce E. Byland, eds. *The Codex Borgia: A Full-Color Restoration of the Ancient Mexican Manuscript*. New York City, NY: Dover Books, 1993.

Dickens, Charles. 1865. *The Uncommercial Traveler*. Centennial ed. *Charles Dickens Complete Works*. London, England: Heron Books, 1970.

DiTommaso, Lorenzo, ed. *A Bibliography of Pseudepigrapha Research 1850-1999*. *Journal for the Study of the Pseudepigrapha Supplement Series* 39, ed. Lester L. Grabbe and James H. Charlesworth. Sheffield, England: Sheffield Acadmic Press, 2001.

"Dives and Lazarus." In *The Hymns and Carols of Christmas*. http://www.hymnsandcarolsofchristmas.com/Hymns_and_Carols/dives_and_lazarus.htm (accessed March 28, 2008).

"Do temples always face east?" In *The FAIR Wiki*, Foundation for Apologetic Information and Research. http://en.fairmormon.org/Do_temples_always_face_east (accessed February 16, 2008).

Doane, Alger Nicolaus, ed. *Genesis A: A New Critical Edition*. Madison, WI: University of Wisconsin Press, 1978.

———, ed. *The Saxon Genesis: An Edition of the West Saxon Genesis B and the Old Saxon Vatican Genesis*. Madison, WI: University of Wisconsin Press, 1991.

Doctrine and Covenants Student Manual: Religion 324-325. 1981. 2nd ed. Salt Lake City, UT: The Church of Jesus Christ of Latter-day Saints, 2001.

Dogniez, Cécile, and Marguerite Harl, eds. *Le Pentateuque d'Alexandrie: Texte Grec et Traduction*. *La Bible des Septante*, eds. Cécile Dogniez and Marguerite Harl. Paris, France: Les Éditions du Cerf, 2001.

Doi, Abdur-Rahman Ibrahim. "Sunnism." In *Islamic Spirituality 1: Foundations*, edited by Seyyed Hossein Nasr, 147-59. New York City, NY: The Crossroad Publishing Company, 1987.

Dolbee, Sandi. "David Noel Freedman; UCSD professor a legend among Bible scholars." *San Diego Union-Tribune Online*, 20 April 2008. http://www.signonsandiego.com/news/obituaries/20080420-9999-1c20freedman.html (accessed July 15, 2008).

Donne, John. 1609. "Holy Sonnets." In *John Donne: The Major Works*, edited by John Carey, 173-80. Oxford, England: Oxford University Press, 2000.

Donner, Fred M. "The historical context." In *The Cambridge Companion to the Qur'an*, edited by Jane Dammen McAuliffe, 23-39. Cambridge, England: Cambridge University Press, 2006.

Dorsey, David A. *The Literary Structure of the Old Testament: A Commentary on Genesis-Malachi*. Grand Rapids, MI: Baker Academic, 2004.

Douglas, Mary. "Atonement in Leviticus." *Jewish Studies Quarterly* 1, no. 2 (1993-1994): 109-30.

———. *Leviticus as Literature*. Oxford, England: Oxford University Press, 2001.

Dowe, Phil. *Galileo, Darwin, and Hawking: The Interplay of Science, Reason, and Religion*. Grand Rapids, MI: William B. Eerdmans, 2005.

Downing, David C. *Planets in Peril: A Critical Study of C. S. Lewis's Ransom Trilogy*. Amherst, MA: The University of Massachusetts Press, 1992.

Doxey, Graham W. "Garden of Eden." In *Encyclopedia of Mormonism*, edited by Daniel H. Ludlow. 4 vols. Vol. 2, 533-34. New York City, NY: Macmillan, 1992. http://www.lib.byu.edu/Macmillan/ (accessed November 26, 2007).

Draper, Richard D. "The creation of humankind, an allegory? A note on Abraham 5:7, 14-16." In *Astronomy, Papyrus, and Covenant*, edited by John Gee and Brian M. Hauglid. *Studies in the Book of Abraham* 3, 75-82. Provo, UT: Foundation for Ancient Research and Mormon Studies (FARMS), Brigham Young University, 2005.

Draper, Richard D., S. Kent Brown, and Michael D. Rhodes. *The Pearl of Great Price: A Verse-by-Verse Commentary*. Salt Lake City, UT: Deseret Book, 2005.

Draper, Richard D., and Donald W. Parry. "Seven promises to those who overcome: Aspects of Genesis 2-3 in the seven letters." In *The Temple in Time and Eternity*, edited by Donald W. Parry and Stephen D. Ricks, 121-41. Provo, UT: The Foundation for Ancient Research and Mormon Studies (FARMS) at Brigham Young University, 1999.

Drewermann, Eugen. 1992. "Le Petit Prince, une parabole religieuse?" In *Il Était une Fois… Le Petit Prince*, edited by Alban Cerisier, 279-83. Paris, France: Éditions Gallimard, 2006.

Driver, Tom F. "Shakespeare's sense of history." In *Shakespeare's Christian Dimension: An Anthology of Commentary*, edited by Roy Battenhouse, 36-40. Bloomington, IN: Indiana University Press, 1994.

Drower, E. S., ed. *The Book of the Zodiac (Sfar Malwasia) D. C. 31. Oriental Translation Fund* 35. London, England: Royal Asiatic Society, 1949. http://www.egnu.org/~mandaean/The_Book_of_the_Zodiac_Drower.pdf (accessed September 15, 2007).

———, ed. *The Canonical Prayerbook of the Mandaeans*. Leiden, The Netherlands: E. J. Brill, 1959. http://www.gnosis.org/library/ginzarba.htm (accessed September 11, 2007).

———, ed. *The Coronation of the Great Sislam: Being a Description of the Rite of the Coronation of a Mandaean Priest*. Leiden, The Netherlands: E. J. Brill, 1962. http://www.mandaeanworld.com/ (accessed September 11, 2007).

———, ed. *Diwan Abatur or Progress through the Purgatories: Text with Translation, Notes and Appendices. Studi e Testi* 151. Città del Vaticano: Biblioteca Apostolica Vaticana, 1950. http://www.egnu.org/~mandaean/Diwan_Abatur_Drower.pdf (accessed September 15, 2007).

———, ed. *The Haran Gawaita and the Baptism of Hibil-Ziwa, The Mandaic Text Reproduced Together with Translation, Notes and Commentary. Studi e testi* 176. Città del Vaticano: Biblioteca Apostolica Vaticana, 1953. http://www.egnu.org/~mandaean/The_Haran_Gawaita_and_The_Baptism_of_Hibil_Ziwa_Drower.pdf (accessed September 11, 2007).

———. "A Mandaean Book of Black Magic." *Journal of the Royal Asiatic Society* (1943): 149-81. Reprint, Sequim, WA; Holmes Publishing Group, 2005.

———. "The Mandaean Phylacteries, Transliterated and Translated." *Journal of the Royal Asiatic Society* (1939): 397-406.

———. "Mandaean writings." *Iraq* 1, part 2 (November 1934): 171-84.

———. *The Mandaeans of Iraq and Iran*. Oxford, England: Clarendon Press, 1937. Reprint, Piscataway, NJ: Gorgias Press, 2002.

———, ed. *A Pair of Nasorean Commentaries: Being Two Priestly Documents, the Great First World and the Lesser First World*. Leiden, The Netherlands: E. J. Brill, 1963.

———. *Peacock Angel, Being Some Account of Votaries of a Secret Cult and Their Sanctuaries*. London, England: John Murray, 1941. http://www.avesta.org/yezidi/peacock.htm (accessed September 15, 2007).

———. "A phylactery for rue (An invocation of the personified herb)." *Orientalia* 15 (1946): 324-46.

———, ed. *Sarh d-Qabin d-Sislam Rba: Explanatory Commentary on the Marriage of the Great Sislam. Biblica et Orientalia* 12. Rome, Italy: Pontificio Istituto Biblico, 1950.

———. *The Secret Adam: A Study of Nasoraean Gnosis*. London, England: Oxford University Press, 1960. http://www.egnu.org/~mandaean/The_Secret_Adam_Drower.pdf (accessed September 15, 2007).

———. "Shafta d-Pishra d-Ainia: A Mandaean Magical Text Translated and Transliterated." *Journal of the Royal Asiatic Society* (1937-1938): 589-611, 1-20.

———, ed. *The Thousand and Twelve Questions (Alf Trisar Shuialia). Deutsche Akademie der Wissenschaften zu Berlin, Institut für Orientforschung* 32. Berlin, Germany: Akademie-Verlag, 1960.

———. *Water into Wine: A Study of Ritual Idiom in the Middle East*. London, England: John Murray, 1956.

Dubnick, Heather. "The poet as prophet: William Blake, 1757-1827." In *Bloom's BioCritiques: William Blake*, edited by Harold Bloom. *Bloom's BioCritiques*, ed. Harold Bloom, 81-100. Philadelphia, PA: Chelsea House Publishers, 2006.

Duke, James T. "Word pairs and distinctive combinations in the Book of Mormon." *Journal of Book of Mormon Studies* 12, no. 2 (2003): 32-41.

Dulles, Avery. *Models of Revelation*. Garden City, NY: Doubleday, 1983.

Dunford, C. Kent. "Light of Christ." In *Encyclopedia of Mormonism*, edited by Daniel H. Ludlow. 4 vols. Vol. 2, 835. New York City, NY: Macmillan, 1992. http://www.lib.byu.edu/Macmillan/ (accessed November 26, 2007).

Dunn, James D. G., and John W. Rogerson. *Eerdmans Commentary on the Bible*. Grand Rapids, MI: William B. Eerdmans, 2003.

Dunn, Richard J. "Dickens and the Mormons." *BYU Studies* 8, no. 3 (1968): 1-9.

Dunning, Robert, ed. *Christianity in Somerset*. Taunton, Somerset, England: Somerset County Council, 1976.

Dupuis, Jérôme, and Tristan Savin. "Et Saint-Ex créa Le Petit Prince." *Lire Hors-Série*, no. 3 (Référence #HSLR0206), 2006, 26-32.

Durham, John I. "*Shalom* and the Presence of God." In *Proclamation and Presence: Essays in Honour of Gwynne Henton Davies*, edited by John I. Durham and Joshua Roy Porter, 272-93. Richmond, VA: John Knox, 1970.

Durkin-Meistererernst, Desmond. *Dictionary of Manichaean Texts*. Vol. 3: Texts from Central Asia and China (Texts in Middle Persian and Parthian). *Corpus Fontium Manichaeorum, Series Subsidia*. Turnhout, Belgium: Brepols, 2004.

———, ed. *The Hymns to the Living Soul: Middle Persian and Parthian Texts in the Turfan Collection. Berliner Turfan-texte 24*. Turnhout, Belgium: Brepols, 2006.

Dyer, Alvin R. "The destiny of America." *Improvement Era* 71, December 1968, 42-45.

———. *The Meaning of Truth*. Revised ed. Salt Lake City, UT: Bookcraft, 1970.

———. *The Refiner's Fire: The Significance of Events Transpiring in Missouri*. 3rd revised ed. Salt Lake City, UT: Deseret Book, 1972.

———. *Who Am I?* Salt Lake City, UT: Deseret Book, 1966.

Dyson, Julia T. *King of the Wood: The Sacrificial Victor in Virgil's Aeneid*. Red River Books ed. *Oklahoma Series for Classical Culture*. Norman, OK: University of Oklahoma Press, 2001.

Eade, John, and Michael J. Sallnow, eds. 1991. *Contesting the Sacred: The Anthropology of Christian Pilgrimage*. Urbana, IL: University of Illinois Press, 2000.

"Early Church Fathers." In *Christian Classics Ethereal Library*. http://www.ccel.org/fathers.html (accessed October 3, 2008).

Eccles, Robert S. *Erwin Ramsdell Goodenough: A Personal Pilgrimage. Society of Biblical Literature, Biblical Scholarship in North America*, ed. Kent Harold Richards. Chico, CA: Scholars Press, 1985.

———. "The purpose of the hellenistic patterns in the Epistle to the Hebrews." In *Religions in Antiquity: Essays in Memory of Erwin Ramsdell Goodenough*, edited by Jacob Neusner. *Religions in Antiquity, Studies in the History of Religions (Supplements to Numen)* 14, 207-26. Leiden, The Netherlands: Brill, 1968. Reprint, Eugene, OR: Wipf and Stock, 2004.

Eco, Umberto. 1993. *The Search for the Perfect Language*. Translated by James Fentress. *The Making of Europe*, ed. Jacques Le Goff. Oxford, England: Blackwell, 1997.

Ed-Din, Abu Bakr Siraj. "The nature and origin of Sufism." In *Islamic Spirituality 1: Foundations*, edited by Seyyed Hossein Nasr, 223-38. New York City, NY: The Crossroad Publishing Company, 1987.

Eden, Giulio Busi. "The mystical architecture of Eden in the Jewish tradition." In *The Earthly Paradise: The Garden of Eden from Antiquity to Modernity*, edited by F. Regina Psaki and Charles Hindley. *International Studies in Formative Christianity and Judaism*, 15-22. Binghamton, NY: Academic Studies in the History of Judaism, Global Publications, State University of New York at Binghamton, 2002.

Eddins, Stephen. *Mack Wilberg: Requiem*. In All Music Guide. http://www.allmusic.com/cg/amg.dll?p=amg&sql=43:164308 (accessed 13 April, 2009).

Edson, E., and E. Savage-Smith. *Medieval Views of the Cosmos*. Oxford, England: The Bodleian Library, University of Oxford, 2004.

Edwards, I. E. S. *The Pyramids of Egypt*. Harmondsworth, England: Penguin Books, 1947.

Egeria. ca. 375. *Egeria's Travels*. Translated by John Wilkinson. 3rd Revised ed. Oxford, England: Aris and Phillips, 1999.

Église de Jésus Christ des Saints des Derniers Jours. *Ancien Testament: Genèse-2 Samuel (Religion cours 301) Manuel de l'Étudiant*. 2 vols. Vol. 1. Torcy, France: Église de Jésus Christ des Saints des Derniers Jours, 1992.

Ehat, Andrew F. "'It seems like heaven began on earth': Joseph Smith and the constitution of the Kingdom of God." *BYU Studies* 20, no. 3 (1980): 1-27.

———. "Joseph Smith's Introduction of Temple Ordinances and the 1844 Mormon Succession Question." M. A. Thesis, Brigham Young University, 1982.

Ehrlich, Carl S. "Moses, *Torah*, and Judaism." In *The Rivers of Paradise: Moses, Buddha, Confucius, Jesus, and Muhammad as Religious Founders*, edited by David Noel Freedman and Michael J. McClymond, 11-119. Grand Rapids, MI: Wm. B. Eerdmans, 2001.

Ehrman, Bart D. ed. ca. 140. "The Didache." In *The New Testament and Other Early Christian Writings*, edited by Bart D. Ehrman, 313-17. Oxford, England: Oxford University Press, 1998.

Eisenbaum, Pamela Michelle. *The Jewish Heroes of Christian History: Hebrews 11 in Literary Context. Society of Biblical Literature Dissertation Series* 156, ed. Michael V. Fox and Pheme Perkins. Atlanta, GA: Scholars Press, 1997.

"Eleusinian mysteries." In *Wikipedia*. http://en.wikipedia.org/wiki/Eleusinian_Mysteries (accessed February 25, 2007).

Eliade, Mircea. "The prestige of the cosmogonic myth." *Diogenes* 6, no. 23 (1958): 1-13. http://dio.sagepub.com. (accessed September 27, 2009).

Elkaïm-Sartre, Arlette, ed. *Aggadoth du Talmud de Babylone: La Source de Jacob - 'Ein Yaakov. Collection "Les Dix Paroles"*, ed. Charles Mopsik. Lagrasse, France: Éditions Verdier, 1982.

Elledge, C. D. "Resurrection of the dead: Exploring our earliest evidence today." In *Resurrection: The Origin and Future of a Biblical Doctrine*, edited by James H. Charlesworth. *Faith and Scholarship Colloquies* 3, 22-52. New York City, NY: T & T Clark, 2006.

Ellingworth, Paul. *The Epistle to the Hebrews: A Commentary on the Greek Text. The New International Greek Testament Commentary*, eds. I. Howard Marshall and W. Ward Gasque. Grand Rapids, MI: William B. Eerdmans, 1993.

Elliott, J. K. *The Apocryphal New Testament: A Collection of Apocryphal Christian Literature in an English Translation.* Oxford, England: Oxford University Press, 2005.

———, ed. "The Hymn of the Pearl." In *Lost Scriptures: Books That Did Not Make It into the New Testament*, edited by Bart D. Ehrman, 324-27. New York City, NY: Oxford University Press, 2003.

Ellis, Richard S. "Images at work versus words at play: Michelangelo's art and the artistry of the Hebrew Bible." *Judaism* 51, no. 2 (2002): 162-74. http://www.math.umass.edu/~rsellis/images-vs-words-long.html (accessed August 9, 2007).

Emmett, Chad F. "Building bridges the right way." *BYU Studies* 45, no. 4 (2006): 12.

Emminghaus, Johannes H. 1978. *The Eucharist: Essence, Form, Celebration.* Translated by Linda M. Maloney. Edited by Theodor Maas-Ewerd. Revised ed. Collegeville, MN: Liturgical Press, 1997.

Engelhardt, Christian Moritz. *Herrad von Landsperg, Aebtissin zu Hohenburg, oder St. Odilien, im Elsasz, im zwölften Jahrhundert; und ihr Werk: Hortus deliciarum.* Stuttgart and Tübingen, Germany, 1818.

England, Eugene. "George Laub's Nauvoo Journal." *BYU Studies* 18, no. 2 (Winter 1978): 151-78.

———. "The weeping God of Mormonism." *Dialogue* 35, no. 1 (Spring 2002): 63-80.

———. *Why the Church is as True as the Gospel.* Salt Lake City, UT: Bookcraft, 1986.

Englebert, Omer. *The Grotto of the Teachings or The Grotto of the Pater.* Jerusalem, Israel: Carmel of the Pater Noster, n.d.

Ephrem the Syrian. ca. 350-363. "The Commentary on Genesis." In *Hymns on Paradise*, edited by Sebastian Brock, 197-227. Crestwood, New York: St. Vladimir's Seminary Press, 1990.

———. ca. 350-363. *Ephrem the Syrian: Hymns.* Translated by Kathleen E. McVey. Mahwah, NJ: Paulist Press, 1989.

———. ca. 350-363. *Ephrem the Syrian: Select Poems.* Translated by Sebastian P. Brock and George A. Kiraz. Edited by Sebastian P. Brock and George A. Kiraz. *Eastern Christian Texts* 2, ed. Daniel C. Peterson, Carl W. Griffin and Kristian S. Heal. Provo, UT: Brigham Young University Press, 2006.

———. ca. 350-363. "Hymns for the feast of the Epiphany." In *Nicene and Post-Nicene Fathers, Second Series*, edited by Philip Schaff and Henry Wace. 14 vols. Vol. 13, 263-89. New York City, NY: The Christian Literature Company, 1898. Reprint, Peabody, MA: Hendrickson Publishers, 2004.

———. ca. 350-363. *Hymns on Paradise.* Translated by Sebastian Brock. Crestwood, New York: St. Vladimir's Seminary Press, 1990.

———. ca. 350-363. "The Hymns on Virginity and on the Symbols of the Lord." In *Ephrem the Syrian: Hymns*, edited by Kathleen E. McVey, 259-468. Mahwah, NJ: Paulist Press, 1989.

———. ca. 350-363. "The Hymns on Paradise." In *Hymns on Paradise*, edited by Sebastian Brock, 77-195. Crestwood, New York: St. Vladimir's Seminary Press, 1990.

———. ca. 350-363. "On the Fall (*Ieun.* 3)." In *Ephrem the Syrian: Select Poems*, edited by Sebastian P. Brock and George A. Kiraz. Translated by Sebastian P. Brock and George A. Kiraz. *Eastern Christian Texts* 2, eds. Daniel C. Peterson, Carl W. Griffin and Kristian S. Heal, 96-103. Provo, UT: Brigham Young University Press, 2006.

———. ca. 350-363. "The Pearl and Its Symbolism (*Fid.* 82)." In *Ephrem the Syrian: Select Poems*, edited by Sebastian P. Brock and George A. Kiraz. Translated by Sebastian P. Brock and George A. Kiraz. *Eastern Christian Texts* 2, eds. Daniel C. Peterson, Carl W. Griffin and Kristian S. Heal, 246-57. Provo, UT: Brigham Young University Press, 2006.

———. d. 373. *Saint Ephrem's Commentary on Tatian's Diatessaron: An English Translation of Chester Beatty Syriac MS 709 with Introduction and Notes.* Translated by Carmel McCarthy. Edited by Carmel McCarthy. Oxford, England: Oxford University Press, 1994.

Epstein, Isodore, ed. *The Soncino Hebrew-English Talmud*. 30 vols. London, England: The Soncino Press, 1948.

Ernst, Carl W. "Between Orientalism and Fundamentalism: Problematizing the teaching of Islam." In *Teaching Islam*, edited by Brannon M. Wheeler, 108-23. New York City, NY: Oxford University Press, 2003.

———. *The Shambhala Guide to Sufism*. Boston, MA: Shambhala Publications, 1997.

Escher, M. C. *M. C. Escher: The Graphic Work*. Köln, Germany: Benedikt-Taschen Verlag, 1992.

Esplin, Ronald K. "Joseph, Brigham and the Twelve: A succession of continuity." *BYU Studies* 21, no. 3 (1981): 301-41.

Esposito, John L., and Dalia Mogahed. *Who Speaks for Islam? What a Billion Muslims Really Think*. New York City, NY: Gallup Press, 2007.

Etheridge, J. W., ed. *The Targums of Onkelos and Jonathan Ben Uzziel on the Pentateuch, with the Fragments of the Jerusalem Targum from the Chaldee*. 2 vols. London, England: Longman, Green, Longman, and Roberts, 1862, 1865. Reprint, Piscataway, NJ: Gorgias Press, 2005. http://www.targum.info/pj/psjon.htm (accessed August 10, 2007).

Eusebius. 1971. ca. 325. *The Ecclesiastical History of Eusebius Pamphilus*. Edited by Isaac Boyle. Grand Rapids, MI: Baker Book House, 1955.

———. ca. 325. *The History of the Church*. Translated by G. A. Williamson and Andrew Louth. London, England: Penguin Books, 1989.

———. ca. 339. "The Life of Constantine." In *Nicene and Post-Nicene Fathers, Second Series*, edited by Philip Schaff and Henry Wace. 14 vols. Vol. 1, 471-559. New York City, NY: The Christian Literature Company, 1890. Reprint, Peabody, MA: Hendrickson Publishers, 2004.

———. ca. 339. *Life of Constantine*. Translated by Averil Cameron and Stuart G. Hall. Edited by Averil Cameron and Stuart G. Hall. *Clarendon Ancient History Series*, ed. Brian Bosworth, Miriam Griffin, David Whitehead and Susan Treggiari. Oxford, England: Clarendon Press, 1999.

———. 1971. *The Onomasticon of Eusebius Pamphili, Compared with the Version of Jerome and Annotated*. Translated by C. Umhau Wolf. In http://www.tertullian.org/fathers/eusebius_onomasticon_01_intro.htm (accessed May 30, 2008).

Euvrard, Christian. *Louis Auguste Bertrand (1808-1875): Journaliste Socialiste et Pionnier Mormon*. Tournan-en-Brie, France: Christian Euvrard, 2005.

Evenson, William E. 1994. "LDS doctrine and the theory of evolution." In *Can Science Be Faith-Promoting?*, edited by Stan Larson, xxxi-xl. Salt Lake City, UT: Blue Ribbon Books, 2001.

———. "LDS science counsel still valid." Salt Lake City, UT: *The Salt Lake Tribune*, July 2, 2005.

———. "Science: The Universe, Creation, and Evolution (Chs. 3-5, 9-10, 12, 21, 23-25, 29-32)." In *The Truth, The Way, The Life*, edited by Brigham Henry Roberts and John W. Welch, cxi-cxxix. Provo, UT: BYU Studies, 1994.

Evenson, William E., and Duane E. Jeffery, eds. *Mormonism and Evolution: The Authoritative LDS Statements*. Draper, UT: Greg Kofford Books, 2005.

Eyring, Henry. *The Faith of a Scientist*. Salt Lake City, UT: Bookcraft, 1967.

———. *Reflections of a Scientist*. Salt Lake City, UT: Deseret Book, 1983.

Eyring, Henry B., Jr. "Faith and the Oath and Covenant of the Priesthood." *Ensign* 28, May 2008, 61-64.———. "Faith, authority, and scholarship." In *On Becoming a Disciple-Scholar*, edited by Henry B. Eyring, Jr., 59-71. Salt Lake City, UT: Bookcraft, 1995.

———. "The power of teaching doctrine." *Ensign* 29, May 1999, 73-75.

———. "That we may be one." *Ensign* 28, May 1998, 66-68.

Eyring, Henry J. *Mormon Scientist: The Life and Faith of Henry Eyring*. Salt Lake City, UT: Deseret Book, 2007.

Falk, Zeev W. *Hebrew Law in Biblical Times: An Introduction*. Jerusalem, Israel: Wahrmann Books, 1964. Reprint, Provo, UT / Winona Lake, IN: Brigham Young University Press / Eisenbrauns, 2001.

Farley, S. Brent. "The oath and covenant of the priesthood." In *Sperry Symposium Classics: The Doctrine and Covenants*, edited by Craig K. Manscill, 221-33. Salt Lake City, UT: Deseret Book, 2004.

Faulconer, James E. "Adam and Eve—Community: Reading Genesis 2-3." *Journal of Philosophy and Scripture* 1, no. 1 (Fall 2003). http://www.philosophyandscripture.org/Issue1-1/James_Faulconer/james_faulconer.html (accessed August 10, 2007).

———. "Divine embodiment and transcendence: Propaedeutic thoughts and questions." *Element: An E-Journal of Mormon Philosophy and Theology* 1, no. 1 (Spring 2005): Section 14. http://www.smpt.org/member_resource/element/faulconer_element1-1.html (accessed January 7, 2008).

———. "Hebrew time." In *LDS-Phil*. http://eyring.hplx.net/Eyring/Notes/Heb_Time.html (accessed January 9, 2007).

———. "Response to Professor Dorrien." In *Mormonism in Dialogue with Contemporary Christian Theologies*, edited by Donald W. Musser and David L. Paulsen, 423-35. Macon, GA: Mercer University Press, 2007.

———. "Response to Professor Tracy." In *Mormonism in Dialogue with Contemporary Christian Theologies*, edited by Donald W. Musser and David L. Paulsen, 468-78. Macon, GA: Mercer University Press, 2007.

———. "Scripture as incarnation." In *Historicity and the Latter-day Saint Scriptures*, edited by Paul Y. Hoskisson, 17-61. Provo, UT: Brigham Young University Religious Studies Center, 2001.

———. *Scripture Study: Tools and Suggestions*. Provo, UT: Foundation for Ancient Research and Mormon Studies, Brigham Young University, 1999.

———. "Self-image, self-love, and salvation." *Latter-day Digest* 2, June 1993, 7-26. http://jamesfaulconer.byu.edu/self-imag.htm (accessed August 10, 2007).

———. "Why a Mormon won't drink coffee but might have a coke: The atheological character of the Church of Jesus Christ of Latter-day Saints." Presented at *God, Humanity, and Revelation: Perspectives from Mormon Philosophy and History*, New Haven, CN: Yale University, March 29, 2003. http://ia301119.us.archive.org/0/items/Why-a-Mormon-Wont-Drink-Coffee-but-Might-Drink-Coke/Coke_but_not_Coffee_-_Reading_Draft.rtf (accessed February 26, 2008). Reprint, *Element: The Journal of the Society for Mormon Philosophy and Theology* 2, no. 2 (Fall 2006): 21-37.

Faulkner, Raymond O., ed. 1973-1978. *The Ancient Egyptian Coffin Texts: Spells 1-1185 and Indexes*. Corrected 3-in-1 ed. Oxford, England: Aris & Phillips, 2007.

———, ed. *The Ancient Egyptian Pyramid Texts* 1st ed. Oxford, England: Clarendon Press, 1969.

Faulkner, Raymond O., and Carol A. R. Andrews, eds. 1972. *The Ancient Egyptian Book of the Dead*. Revised ed. Translated by R. O. Faulkner. Austin, TX: University of Texas Press, 2001.

Faulkner, Raymond O., Ogden Goelet, Jr., and Carol A. R. Andrews, eds. 1972. *The Egyptian Book of the Dead: The Book of Going Forth by Day*. Translated by R. O. Faulkner. San Francisco, CA: Chronicle Books, 1994.

Faulring, Scott H., Kent P. Jackson, and Robert J. Matthews, eds. *Joseph Smith's New Translation of the Bible: Original Manuscripts*. Provo, UT: Religious Studies Center, Brigham Young University, 2004.

Faust, James E. "Heirs to the Kingdom of God." *Ensign* 25, May 1995, 61-63.

Feldman, Louis H. "Hellenization in Josephus' portrayal of man's decline." In *Religions in Antiquity: Essays in Memory of Erwin Ramsdell Goodenough*, edited by Jacob Neusner. *Religions in Antiquity, Studies in the History of Religions (Supplements to Numen)* 14, 336-53. Leiden, The Netherlands: Brill, 1968.

Feldman, Noah. "What is it about Mormonism?" *New York Times Magazine*, January 6 2008. http://www.nytimes.com/2008/01/06/magazine/06mormonism-t.html?ref=magazine (accessed August 24, 2008).

———. *The Rise and Fall of the Islamic State*. Princeton, NJ: Princeton University Press, 2008.

Feldman, Seymour, ed. *The Wars of the Lord*. 3 vols. Philadelphia, PA: Jewish Publication Society, 1984-1999.

Ferdowsi, Abolquasem. ca. 1010. *Shahnameh: The Persian Book of Kings*. Translated by Dick Davis. New York City, NY: Viking Adult, Penguin Group, 2006.

———. ca. 1010. *Shahnama of Ferdausi*. 9 vols. Translated by Arthur George Warner and Edmond Warner. *Trubner's Oriental Series*. London, England: Kegan Paul, 1905-1925. Reprint, London, England: Routledge, Taylor & Francis Group, 2001.

Feyerick, Ada, Cyrus H. Gordon, and Nahum M. Sarna. *Genesis: World of Myths and Patriarchs*. New York City, NY: New York University Press, 1996.

Feynman, Richard. 1965. *The Character of Physical Law*. New York City, NY: The Modern Library, 1994.

Fine, Lawrence. 1984. "Kabbalistic texts." In *Back to the Sources: Reading the Classic Jewish Texts*, edited by Barry W. Holtz, 305-59. New York City, NY: Simon and Schuster, 2006.

Fine, Steven. 2005. "Between Rome and Jerusalem: The date palm as a 'Jewish symbol.'" In *Art and Judaism in the Greco-Roman World: Toward a New Jewish Archaeology*, edited by Steven Fine, 140-45. Cambridge, England: Cambridge University Press, 2007.

———. 2005. "'The lamps of Israel': The Menorah as a Jewish symbol." In *Art and Judaism in the Greco-Roman World: Toward a New Jewish Archaeology*, edited by Steven Fine, 146-63. Cambridge, England: Cambridge University Press, 2007.

Fineberg, Gail. 1997. *'Let There Be Light': Exhibition Spotlights William Tyndale, English Martyr (July 1997)*. In Library of Congress Information Bulletin. http://www.loc.gov/loc/lcib/9707/tyndale.html (accessed October 4, 2008).

Finkelstein, Sidney. *Notes on the Program: Ralph Vaughan Williams, Folk Songs of Britain (Originally recorded in 1960)*: Vanguard Classics (OVC 8109), 1997.

First Presidency of the Church of Jesus Christ of Latter-day Saints. "Letter reaffirms use of King James Version." *LDS Church News*, June 20 1992, Z3. http://www.desnews.com (accessed September 7, 2007).

Fisch, Harold. *The Biblical Presence in Shakespeare, Milton, and Blake: A Comparative Study*. Oxford, England: Clarendon Press, 1999.

———. *Hamlet and the Word: The Covenant Pattern in Shakespeare*. New York City, NY: Frederick Ungar, 1971.

Fishbane, Michael. *Biblical Myth and Rabbinic Mythmaking*. Oxford, England: Oxford University Press, 2003.

———. "A note on the spirituality of texts." In *Etz Hayim Study Companion*, edited by Jacob Blumenthal and Janet L. Liss, 11-12. New York City, NY: The Rabbinical Assembly, The United Synagogue of Conservative Judaism, and The Jewish Publication Society, 2005.

Fisk, Bruce N. *Do You Not Remember? Scripture, Story, and Exegesis in the Rewritten Bible of Pseudo-Philo*. Sheffield, England: Sheffield Academic Press, 2001.

Flake, Kathleen. "Bound for glory." In *On Faith Panelists Blog, The Washington Post*, 29 June 2007. http://newsweek.washingtonpost.com/onfaith/panelists/kathleen_flake/2007/06/bound_for_glory.html (accessed March 24, 2009).

———. "From conferences to councils: The development of LDS church organization, 1830-1835." In *Archive of Restoration Culture: Summer Fellows' Papers 1997-1999*, edited by Richard Lyman Bushman, 1-8. Provo, UT: Joseph Fielding Smith Institute for Latter-day Saint History, 2000.

———. "'Not to be Riten': The Mormon temple rite as oral canon." *Journal of Ritual Studies* 9, no. 2 (Summer 1995): 1-21.

———. "Translating time: The nature and function of Joseph Smith's narrative canon." *Journal of Religion* 87, no. 4 (October 2007): 497-527. http://www.vanderbilt.edu/divinity/facultynews/Flake%20Translating%20Time.pdf (accessed February 22, 2009).

Flake, Lawrence R. *Three Degrees of Glory: Joseph Smith's Insights on the Kingdoms of Heaven*. American Fork, UT: Covenant Communications, 2000.

Fletcher-Louis, Crispin H. T. *All the Glory of Adam: Liturgical Anthropology in the Dead Sea Scrolls*. Leiden, The Netherlands: Brill, 2002.

Flew, Anthony. *There is a God: How the World's Most Notorious Atheist Changed His Mind*. Edited by Roy Abraham Varghese. New York City, NY: HarperOne, 2007.

Flusser, David. "The Jewish-Christian understanding of human nature." In *On Human Nature: The Jerusalem Center Symposium*, edited by Truman G. Madsen, David Noel Freedman and Pam Fox Kuhlken, 59-67. Ann Arbor, MI: Pryor Pettengill Publishers, 2004.

———. "Qumran und die Zwölf." In *Initiation*, edited by Claas J. Bleeker. S*tudies in the History of Religion (Supplements to Numen)* 10, 134-46. Leiden, The Netherlands: Brill, 1965.

Foerster, Werner, ed. *Gnosis: A Selection of Gnostic Texts - 2. Coptic and Mandaic Sources*. 2 vols. Vol. 2. Translated by Robert McLachlan Wilson. Oxford, England: Clarendon Press, 1974.

Fohrman, David. *The Beast that Crouches at the Door: Adam and Eve, Cain and Abel, and Beyond*. Jerusalem, Israel: Devora, 2007.

Fokkelman, J. P. "Genesis." In *The Literary Guide to the Bible*, edited by Robert Alter and Frank Kermode, 36-55. Cambridge, MA: The Belknap Press of Harvard University Press, 1987.

Ford, J. Massingberd. "The Jewel of Discernment: A study of stone symbolism." *Biblische Zeitschrift* 11 (1967): 109-16.

"Fourth book of Maccabees." 1927, 1930. In *The Lost Books of the Bible and the Forgotten Books of Eden*, edited by Rutherford H. Platt, 2:177-98. Berkeley, CA: Apocryphile Press, 2005.

"Fourth Maccabees." In *Wikipedia*. http://en.wikipedia.org/wiki/4_Maccabees (accessed March 19, 2009).

Fox, Everett, ed. *The Five Books of Moses: Genesis, Exodus, Leviticus, Numbers, Deuteronomy*. The Schocken Bible: Volume 1. New York, NY: Schocken Books, 1995.

Foxe, John. 1563. *Foxe's Book of Martyrs*. Edited by W. Grinton Berry. Greenville, NC: Ambassador International, 2005.

Frankl, Viktor. 1945. *Man's Search for Meaning*. 3rd revised and enlarged ed. New York City, NY: Pocket Books, 1985.

Franxman, Thomas W. *Genesis and the "Jewish Antiquities" of Flavius Josephus. Biblica et Orientalia* 35, ed. Pontificio Istituto Biblico. Rome, Italy: Biblical Institute Press, 1979.

Frawley, W. *Linguistic Semantics*. Hillsdale, N.J.: Lawrence Erlbaum, 1992.

Frazer, James George. 1922. "The Golden Bough: A study of magic and religion." Abridged ed. In *Project Gutenberg*. http://www.gutenberg.org/dirs/etext03/bough11h.htm (accessed November 28, 2007).

Freedman, David Noel. *The Nine Commandments*. Des Moines, IA: Anchor Bible, 2000.

———. "The nine commandments." *Proceedings of the 36th Annual Convention of the Association of Jewish Libraries*, La Jolla, CA, June 24-27, 2001. http://www.jewishlibraries.org/ajlweb/publications/proceedings/proceedings2001/freedmand.pdf (accessed August 11, 2007).

———. "The status and role of humanity in the cosmos according to the Hebrew Bible." In *On Human Nature: The Jerusalem Center Symposium*, edited by Truman G. Madsen, David Noel Freedman and Pam Fox Kuhlken, 9-25. Ann Arbor, MI: Pryor Pettengill Publishers, 2004.

Freedman, David Noel, and Rebecca L. Frey. "The Dome of the Rock." In *Revelation, Reason, and Faith: Essays in Honor of Truman G. Madsen*, edited by Donald W. Parry, Daniel C. Peterson and Stephen D. Ricks, 635-49. Provo, UT: Brigham Young University FARMS, 2002.

Freedman, David Noel, Allen C. Myers, and Astrid B. Beck. *Eerdmans Dictionary of the Bible*. Grand Rapids, MI: William B. Eerdmans Publishing Company, 2000.

Freedman, H., and Maurice Simon, eds. 1939. *Midrash Rabbah* 3rd ed. 10 vols. London, England: Soncino Press, 1983.

French, Yvonne. 1997. "'Courage and Genius': Tyndale Responsible for Most of King James Translation, Says Biographer (July 1997)." In *Library of Congress Information Bulletin*. http://www.loc.gov/loc/lcib/9707/daniell.html (accessed October 4, 2008).

Friedlander, Gerald, ed. *Pirkei de Rabbi Eliezer*. Brooklyn, NY: Sepher-Hermon Press, 1916.

Friedman, Richard Elliott. *The Bible with Sources Revealed: A New View into the Five Books of Moses*. New York, NY: HarperCollins Publishers, 2003.

———, ed. *Commentary on the Torah*. New York, NY: HarperCollins, 2001.

———. *The Hidden Book in the Bible*. San Francisco, CA: HarperSanFrancisco, 1998.

———. 1987. *Who Wrote the Bible?* San Francisco, CA: HarperSanFrancisco, 1997.

Frye, Northrop. 1947. *Fearful Symmetry: A Study of William Blake*. Princeton, NJ: Princeton University Press, 1969.

———. 1982. *The Great Code: The Bible and Literature*. San Diego, CA: Harvest, 1983.

———. *The Secular Scripture: A Study of the Structure of Romance. The Charles Eliot Norton Lectures, 1974-1975*. Cambridge, MA: Harvard University Press, 1976.

———. "The Tempest." In *On Shakespeare*, edited by Robert Sandler, 171-86. Brighton, MA: Fitzhenry and Whiteside, 1986.

Frye, Roland Mushat, ed. *Is God a Creationist? The Religious Case Against Creation-Science*. New York City, NY: Charles Scribner's Sons, 1983.

———. "Paradise Lost and the visual arts." *Theology Today* 34, no. 1 (April 1977). http://theologytoday.ptsem.edu/apr1977/v34-1-article1.htm (accessed August 11, 2007).

Fussell, Paul. 1983. *Class: A Guide Through the American Status System*. New York City, NY: Touchstone, 1992.

Gabirol, Solomon ibn. ca. 1100-1200. "The Crown of the Kingdom (*Keter Malkhut*)." In *The Secret Garden: An Anthology in the Kabbalah*, edited by David Meltzer. Translated by Harris Lenowitz, 99-104. Barrytown, NY: Barrytown Limited, 1997.

Gadd, Mike. "Old, subtle serpent: Naked in Genesis 3:1." *Studia Antiqua* 5, no. 1 (Spring 2007): 9-14.

Gage, Warren Austin. *The Gospel of Genesis: Studies in Protology and Eschatology*. Winona Lake, IN: Carpenter, 1984.

Gager, John G. "Early Mormonism and early Christianity: Some parallels and their consequences for the study of new religions." *Journal of Mormon History* 9 (1982): 53-60.

Galbraith, David B., D. Kelly Ogden, and Andrew C. Skinner. *Jerusalem: The Eternal City*. Salt Lake City, UT: Deseret Book, 1996.

Gallagher, Jonathan. 2005. "Atoning for the atonement." In *Pine Knoll Publications*. http://www.pineknoll.org/adventist/lesson/references/2005/q1/atone.pdf (accessed August 13, 2007).

Gallez, Édouard-Marie. *Le messie et son prophète: Aux origines de l'Islam*. Vol. 1: De Qumrân à Muhammad. *Studia Arabica* 1, ed. Marie-Thérèse Urvoy. Versailles, France: Éditions de Paris, 2005.

Gallus, Tibor. *"Der Nachkomme der Frau" (Gen. 3:15) in der Schriftauslegung von Luther, Zwingli und Calvin*. Vol. 1. *"Der Nachkomme der Frau" (Gen. 3:15) in der Altlutherischen Schriftauslegung. Ein Beitrag zur Geschichte der Exegese von Gen. 3:15*, ed. Tibor Gallus. Klagenfurt, Germany: Verlag Carinthia, 1964.

Ganssle, Gregory, ed. *God and Time: Four Views*. Downers Grove, IL: InterVarsity Press, 2001.

Gardiner, Alan H. 1927. *Egyptian Grammar*. 3rd ed. London: Oxford University Press, 1966.

Gardner, Brant. "The Gadianton robbers in Mormon's theological history: Their structural role and plausible identification." Presented at the *FAIR Conference 2002*. http://www.fairlds.org/FAIR_Conferences/2002_Gadianton_Robbers_in_Mormons_Theological_History.html (accessed August 13, 2007).

———. *Second Witness: Analytical and Contextual Commentary of the Book of Mormon*. 6 vols. Salt Lake City, UT: Greg Kofford Books, 2007.

Gardner, Bruce K. *The Genesis Calendar: The Synchronistic Tradition in Genesis 1-11*. Lanham, MD: University Press of America, 2001.

Gardner, Iain., ed. *Kellis Literary Texts*. 2 vols. Vol. 1. *Dakhleh Oasis Project Monograph* 4. Oxford, England: Oxbow, 1996.

———. *Kellis Literary Texts*. 2 vols. Vol. 2. *Dakhleh Oasis Project Monograph* 15. Oxford, England: Oxbow, 2007.

———, ed. *The Kephalaia of the Teacher: The Edited Coptic Manichaean Texts in Translation with Commentary. Nag Hammadi and Manichaean Studies* 37, ed. James M. Robinson and H. J. Klimkeit. Leiden, The Netherlands: E. J. Brill, 1995.

———. "The Manichaean community at Kellis: A progress report." In *Emerging from Darkness: Studies in the Recovery of Manichaean Sources*, edited by Paul Mirecki and Jason David BeDuhn. *Nag Hammadi and Manichaean Studies* 43, eds. James M. Robinson and H. J. Klimkeit, 161-75. Leiden, The Netherlands: Brill, 1997.

———. "The reconstruction of Mani's epistles from three Coptic codices (Ismant el-Kaharab and Medinet Madi)." In *The Light and the Darkness: Studies in Manichaeism and its World*, edited by Paul Mirecki and Jason David BeDuhn. *Nag Hammadi and Manichaean Studies* 50, ed. Stephen Emmel, 93-104. Leiden, The Netherlands: Brill, 2001.

Gardner, Iain, Anthony Alcock, and Wolf-Peter Funk, eds. *Coptic Documentary Texts from Kellis (= P. Kell. V)*. Vol. 1. *Dakhleh Oasis Project* 9. Oxford, England: Oxbow, 1999.

Gardner, Iain, M. Franzmann, and Samuel N. C. Lieu. "A living Mani cult in the twenty-first century." *Rivista di Storia e Letteratura Religiosa* 41 (2005): VII-XI.

Gardner, Iain, and Samuel N. C. Lieu, eds. *Manichaean Texts from the Roman Empire*. Cambridge, England: Cambridge University Press, 2004.

Gaskill, Alonzo L. *The Lost Language of Symbolism: An Essential Guide for Recognizing and Interpreting Symbols of the Gospel*. Salt Lake City, UT: Deseret Book, 2003.

———. *The Savior and the Serpent: Unlocking the Doctrine of the Fall*. Salt Lake City, UT: Deseret Book, 2005.

Gaster, Moses, ed. *The Asatir: The Samaritan Book of the "Secrets of Moses"*. London, England: Royal Asiatic Society, 1927.

Gaylord, H. E., Jr. ed. "3 (Greek Apocalypse of) Baruch." In *The Old Testament Pseudepigrapha*, edited by James H. Charlesworth. 2 vols. Vol. 1, 653-79. Garden City, NY: Doubleday and Company, 1983.

Gee, John. "Eyewitness, hearsay, and the physical evidence of the Joseph Smith Papyri." In *The Disciple as Witness: Essays on Latter-day Saint History and Doctrine in Honor of Richard Lloyd Anderson*, edited by Stephen D. Ricks, Donald W. Parry and Andrew H. Hedges, 175-217. Provo, UT: The Foundation for Ancient Research and Mormon Studies at Brigham Young University, 2000.

———. *A Guide to the Joseph Smith Papyri*. Provo, UT: FARMS at Brigham Young University, 2000.

———. "New Light on the Joseph Smith Papyri." *FARMS Review* 19, no. 2 (2007): 245-60. http://mi.byu.edu/publications/review/?vol=19&num=2&id=670. (accessed September 28, 2009).

———. "A tragedy of errors: Review of *By His Own Hand Upon Papyrus: A New Look at the Joseph Smith Papyri* by Charles M. Larson." *FARMS Review of Books* 4, no. 1 (1992): 93-119.

Gee, John, and Brian M. Hauglid, eds. *Astronomy, Papyrus, and Covenant. Studies in the Book of Abraham* 3. Provo, UT: Foundation for Ancient Research and Mormon Studies (FARMS), Brigham Young University, 2005.

Gelander, Shamai. *The Good Creator: Literature and Theology in Genesis 1-11. South Florida Studies in the History of Judaism* 147, ed. Jacob Neusner, Bruce D. Chilton, Darrell J. Fashing, William Scott Green, Sara Mandell and James F. Strange. Atlanta, GA: Scholars Press, 1997.

Gemmell, Belle Anderson. "Utah medical history: Some reminiscences." *California and Western Medicine* 36, no. 1 (January 1932): 44-47. http://www.pubmedcentral.nih.gov/picrender.fcgi?artid=1658092&blobtype=pdf (accessed August 25, 2007).

Gemmell, R. C. "Early History of the Medical Profession in Utah: Biography of Dr. W. F. Anderson." Typewritten manuscript. LDS Church Archives, n. d.

George, Andrew, ed. 1999. *The Epic of Gilgamesh*. London, England: The Penguin Group, 2003.

"George Herbert." In *Wikipedia*. http://en.wikipedia.org/wiki/George_Herbert (accessed May 16, 2009).

Gianotti, Timothy J. "The Islamic view of humanity." In *On Human Nature: The Jerusalem Center Symposium*, edited by Truman G. Madsen, David Noel Freedman and Pam Fox Kuhlken, 85-93. Ann Arbor, MI: Pryor Pettengill Publishers, 2004.

Gibbons, Francis M. *Harold B. Lee: Man of Vision, Prophet of God*. Salt Lake City, UT: Deseret Book, 1993.

Gibbons, Joseph A., and Roger A. Bullard ed. "The Second Treatise of the Great Seth (VII, 2)." In *The Nag Hammadi Library in English*, edited by James M. Robinson. 3rd, Completely Revised ed, 362-71. San Francisco, CA: HarperSanFrancisco, 1990.

Giberson, Karl W. *Saving Darwin: How to Be a Christian and Believe in Evolution*. New York City, NY: HarperOne, 2008.

Gibson, Margaret Dunlop, ed. *Kitab al-Magall or The Book of the Rolls, One of the Books of Clement*. Translated by Margaret Dunlop Gibson. In *Apocrypha Arabica*, ed. Margaret Dunlop Gibson. London, England: Cambridge University Press, 1901. Reprint, Day, Susie, ed. *A History of Our First Parents: Adam and Eve*, 108-118. Roseburg, OR: Linen Vail Books, 2006.

Gibson, Shimon. *The Final Days of Jesus: The Archaeological Evidence*. New York City, NY: HarperOne, 2009.

Gileadi, Avraham. *Isaiah Decoded*. Escondido, CA: Hebraeus Press, 2002.

———, ed. *The Literary Message of Isaiah*. New York, NY: Hebraeus Press, 1994.

———. *Studies in the Book of Mormon*. n. p.: Hebron Books, 2005.

———. "The twelve diatribes of modern Israel." In *By Study and Also By Faith: Essays in Honor of Hugh W. Nibley*, edited by John M. Lundquist and Stephen D. Ricks. 2 vols. Vol. 2, 353-405. Salt Lake City, UT: Deseret Book, 1990.

Gilliot, Claude. "Creation of a fixed text." In *The Cambridge Companion to the Qur'an*, edited by Jane Dammen McAuliffe, 41-57. Cambridge, England: Cambridge University Press, 2006.

———. *Exégèse, Langue, et Théologie in Islam: L'exégèse Coranique de Tabari*. Paris, France: Librairie Philosophique Vrin, 1990.

Gillman, Neil. *The Death of Death: Resurrection and Immortality in Jewish Thought*. Woodstock, VT: Jewish Lights Publishing, 2000.

Gillum, Gary P. "Apocryphal literature: A selected bibliography." In *Apocryphal Writings and the Latter-day Saints*, edited by C. Wilfred Griggs, 125-31. Provo, UT: Brigham Young University Religious Studies Center, 1986.

Gingerich, Owen. *God's Universe*. Cambridge, MA: The Belknap Press of Harvard University Press, 2006.

Ginzberg, Louis, ed. *The Legends of the Jews*. 7 vols. Translated by Henrietta Szold and Paul Radin. Philadelphia, PA: The Jewish Publication Society of America, 1909-1938. Reprint, Baltimore, MD: Johns Hopkins University Press, 1998.

Giorgi, Rosa. *Anges et Démons*. Translated by Dominique Férault. Paris, France: Éditions Hazan, 2003.

Givens, Terryl L. *By the Hand of Mormon: The American Scripture that Launched a New World Religion*. Oxford, England: Oxford University Press, 2002.

———. "Dialectic and reciprocity in 'faithful scholarship': Preexistence as a case study." Typescript in the possession of the author. Presented at the *Annual Conference of Mormon Scholars in the Humanities*, Provo, UT, March 22, 2007.

———. "Joseph Smith: Prophecy, Process, and Plenitude." *BYU Studies* (Special Issue: *The Worlds of Joseph Smith: A Bicentennial Conference at the Library of Congress*) 44, no. 4 (2005): 55-68. Reprinted in *Joseph Smith Jr: Reappraisals After Two Centuries*, edited by Reid L. Neilson and Terryl L. Givens, 107-17. Oxford, England: Oxford University Press, 2009.

———. *People of Paradox: A History of Mormon Culture*. Oxford, England: Oxford University Press, 2007.

———. *The Viper on the Hearth: Mormons, Myths, and the Construction of Heresy*. Religion in America. Oxford, England: Oxford University Press, 1997.

———. *When Souls Had Wings: Pre-Mortal Existence in Western Thought*. Oxford, England: Oxford University Press, 2010.

"Gnostic Society Library." In *The Gnosis Archive*. http://www.gnosis.org/library.html (accessed October 3, 2008).

Goates, L. Brent. *Harold B. Lee: Prophet and Seer*. Salt Lake City, UT: Bookcraft, 1985.

Godfrey, Kenneth W. "The history of intelligence in Latter-day Saint thought." In *The Pearl of Great Price: Revelations from God*, edited by H. Donl Peterson and Charles D. Tate, Jr., 213-35. Provo, UT: BYU Religious Studies Center, 1989.

Goldenberg, David M. *The Curse of Ham: Race and Slavery in Early Judaism, Christianity, and Islam*. Princeton, NJ: Princeton University Press, 2003.

Goldenberg, Robert. *The Origins of Judaism: From Canaan to the Rise of Islam*. Cambridge, England: Cambridge University Press, 2007.

Goldin, Judah, ed. 1955. *The Fathers According to Rabbi Nathan. Yale Judaica Series* 10. New Haven, CN: Yale University Press, 1983.

Goodenough, Erwin Ramsdell. *By Light, Light: The Mystic Gospel of Hellenistic Judaism*. New Haven, CN: Yale University Press, 1935.

———. 1940. "The fundamental motif of Christianity." In *Goodenough on the Beginnings of Christianity*, edited by A. T. Kraabel, 15-25. Atlanta, GA: Scholars Press, 1990.

———. "The Greek garments on Jewish heroes in The Dura Synagogue." In *Biblical Motifs: Origins and Translations*, edited by Alexander Altmann. *Philip W. Lown Institute of Advanced Judaic Studies, Brandeis University, Studies and Texts* 3, ed. Alexander Altmann, 221-37. Cambridge, MA: Harvard University Press, 1966.

———. 1940. *An Introduction to Philo Judaeus.* 2nd Revised ed. Oxford, England: Basil Blackwell, 1962.

———. *Pagan Symbols in Judaism.* 2 vols. *Jewish Symbols in the Greco-Roman Period* 7-8, *Bollingen Series* 37. New York City, NY: Pantheon Books, 1958.

———. "Paul and the hellenization of Christianity." In *Goodenough on the Beginnings of Christianity*, edited by A. T. Kraabel, 123-74. Atlanta, GA: Scholars Press, 1990.

———. *The Problem of Method; Symbols from Jewish Cult. Jewish Symbols in the Greco-Roman Period* 4, *Bollingen Series* 37. New York City, NY: Pantheon Books, 1954.

———. *Summary and Conclusions. Jewish Symbols in the Greco-Roman Period* 12, *Bollingen Series* 37. New York City, NY: Pantheon Books, 1965.

———. *Symbolism in the Dura Synagogue.* 3 vols. *Jewish Symbols in the Greco-Roman Period* 9-11, *Bollingen Series* 37. New York City, NY: Pantheon Books, 1964.

Gordon, Robert P. "The Targumists as eschatologists." In *Hebrew Bible and Ancient Versions: Selected Essays of Robert P. Gordon*, edited by Robert P. Gordon, 303-16. Aldershot, England: Ashgate, 2006.

Gore, Al. *The Assault on Reason.* New York City, NY: The Penguin Press, 2007.

Goslee, Nancy Moore. "'In England's Green and Pleasant Land': The building of vision in Blake's stanzas from *Milton*." *Studies in Romanticism* 13 (1974): 105-25.

Gospel Principles. Salt Lake City, UT: The Church of Jesus Christ of Latter-day Saints, 1997.

"Gothic nightmares: Satan in his original glory." In *Tate Gallery.* http://www.tate.org.uk/britain/exhibitions/gothic-nightmares/rooms/room7.htm (accessed May 20, 2009).

Graf, Fritz. "Lesser mysteries—not less mysterious." In *Greek Mysteries: The Archaeology and Ritual of Ancient Greek Secret Cults*, edited by Michael B. Cosmopoulos, 241-62. New York City, NY: Routledge, 2003.

Graffin, René, ed. *Patrologia Syriaca.* 2 vols. Paris, France: Firmin-Didot, 1894.

Graffin, René, François Nau, Max Prince of Saxony, and François Graffin, eds. *Patrologia Orientalis.* 41 vols. Turnhout, Belgium: Brepols, 1904-.

Graham, William A. *Divine Word and Prophetic Word in Early Islam: A Reconsideration of the Sources with Special Reference to the Divine Saying or Hadith Qudsi. Religion and Society* 7, ed. Leo Laeyendecker and Jacques Waardenburg. The Hague, Netherlands: Mouton Publishers, 1977.

Grant, Heber J., Anthony W. Ivins, and Charles W. Nibley. 1925. ""Mormon" view of evolution." In *Messages of the First Presidency*, edited by James R. Clark. 6 vols. Vol. 5, 243-44. Salt Lake City, UT: Bookcraft, 1971.

Grant, Jedediah M. 1854. "Fulfilment of prophecy; wars and commotions (A discourse by President Jedediah M. Grant, in the Tabernacle, Great Salt Lake City, April 2, 1854)." In *Journal of Discourses.* 26 vols. Vol. 2, 145-49. Liverpool and London, England: Latter-day Saints Book Depot, 1853-1886.

———. 1855. "Times for all things; prayer; chastisement; unity; faithfulness; reverence for sacred things; reformation (Discourses by Presidents B. Young, H. C. Kimball, and J. M. Grant, and Elder E. T. Benson, delivered July 13, 1855, at a Conference held at Provo City, Utah Territory)." In *Journal of Discourses.* 26 vols. Vol. 3, 58-61. Liverpool and London, England: Latter-day Saints Book Depot, 1853-1886.

Grant, Patrick. 1979. "*The Tempest* and the magic of charity." In *Shakespeare's Christian Dimension: An Anthology of Commentary*, edited by Roy Battenhouse, 267-70. Bloomingdale, IN: Indiana University Press, 1994.

Graulich, Michel. *Myths of Ancient Mexico.* Translated by Bernard R. Ortiz de Montellano and Thelma Ortiz de Montellano. *The Civilization of the American Indian* 222. Norman, OK: The University of Oklahoma Press, 1997.

Graves, Robert, and Raphael Patai. *Hebrew Myths: The Book of Genesis.* New York City, NY: Doubleday, 1964.

Grébaut, Sylvain ed. 1911. "Les computs et les symboles (Fascicule 3, No. 28)." In *Patrologia Orientalis*, edited by Pontificio Istituto Orientale Roma. Vol. 6, 428-57. Turnhout, Belgium: Brepols Publishers NV, 2003.

Green, Arnold H. "Mormonism and Islam: From polemics to mutual respect and cooperation." *BYU Studies* 40, no. 4 (2001): 199-220.

Green, Arthur. *A Guide to the Zohar.* Stanford, CA: Stanford University Press, 2004.

Green, Rosalie, Michael Evans, Christine Bischoff, and Michael Curschmann, eds. *The Hortus Deliciarum of Herrad of Hohenbourg: A Reconstruction.* 2 vols. London, England: Warburg Institute, 1979.

Greenberg, Gary. 2000. *101 Myths of the Bible.* Naperville, IL: Sourcebooks, Inc., 2002.

Greenberg, Moshe. *Ezekiel 21-37: A New Translation with Introduction and Commentary. The Anchor Bible* 22A, ed. William F. Albright and David Noel Freedman. New York City, NY: Doubleday, 1997.

Greene, Brian. *The Fabric of the Cosmos: Space, Time, and the Texture of Reality*. New York City, NY: Vintage Books, 2005.

Greenspan, Alan. *The Age of Turbulence: Adventures in a New World*. New York City, NY: The Penguin Press, 2007.

Greenstein, Edward L. 1984. "Medieval Bible commentaries." In *Back to the Sources: Reading the Classic Jewish Texts*, edited by Barry W. Holtz, 213-59. New York City, NY: Simon and Schuster, 2006.

Gregory Nazianzen. ca. 374-390. "Against Apollinarius (*De incarnatione, adversus Apollinarium*)." In *On God and Man: The Theological Poetry of St. Gregory of Nazianzus*, edited by Peter Gilbert. Translated by Peter Gilbert. *Popular Patristics*, 81-83. Crestwood, NY: St. Vladimir's Seminary Press, 2001.

———. ca. 374-390. *On God and Man: The Theological Poetry of St. Gregory of Nazianzus*. Translated by Peter Gilbert. Edited by Peter Gilbert. *Popular Patristics*. Crestwood, NY: St. Vladimir's Seminary Press, 2001.

———. ca. 350-363. "Oration 38: On the Theophany, or Birthday of Christ." In *Nicene and Post-Nicene Fathers, Second Series*, edited by Philip Schaff and Henry Wace. 14 vols. Vol. 7, 345-51. New York City, NY: The Christian Literature Company, 1894. Reprint, Peabody, MA: Hendrickson Publishers, 2004.

———. ca. 350-363. "Oration 39: Oration on the Holy Lights." In *Nicene and Post-Nicene Fathers, Second Series*, edited by Philip Schaff and Henry Wace. 14 vols. Vol. 7, 351-59. New York City, NY: The Christian Literature Company, 1894. Reprint, Peabody, MA: Hendrickson Publishers, 2004.

———. ca. 350-363. "Orations." In *Nicene and Post-Nicene Fathers, Second Series*, edited by Philip Schaff and Henry Wace. 14 vols. Vol. 7, 203-434. New York City, NY: The Christian Literature Company, 1894. Reprint, Peabody, MA: Hendrickson Publishers, 2004.

Gregory of Nyssa. ca. 330-395. "The Great Catechism." In *Nicene and Post-Nicene Fathers, Second Series*, edited by Philip Schaff and Henry Wace. 14 vols. Vol. 5, 471-509. New York City, NY: The Christian Literature Company, 1893. Reprint, Peabody, MA: Hendrickson Publishers, 2004.

Griffith, Ralph T. H., ed. *Hinduism: The Rig Veda*. Translated by Ralph T. H. Griffith. *Sacred Writings* 5, ed. Jaroslav Pelikan. New York City, NY: Quality Paperback Book Club, 1992.

Griffith-Jones, Robin. *The Four Witnesses*. New York City, NY: HarperCollins Publishers, 2000.

Griggs, C. Wilfred. "Evidences of a Christian population in the Egyptian Fayum and genetic and textile studies of the Akhmim noble mummies." *BYU Studies* 33, no. 2 (1993): 214-43.

———. "The tree of life in ancient cultures." *Ensign* 18, June 1988, 26-31.

Gross, Jules. 1938. *The Divinization of the Christian According to the Greek Fathers*. Translated by Paul A. Onica. Anaheim, CA: A & C Press, 2002.

Grossfeld, Bernard, ed. *The Targum Onqelos to Genesis: Translated with a Critical Introduction, Apparatus, and Notes*. *Aramaic Bible* 6. Edinburgh, Scotland: T & T Clark, 1988.

Grossfeld, Bernard, and Lawrence H. Schiffman, eds. *Targum Neofiti 1: An Exegetical Commentary to Genesis including Full Rabbinic Parallels*. Brooklyn, NY: Sepher-Hermon Press, 2000.

Guénon, René. *Symboles fondamentaux de la Science sacrée*. Paris, France: Gallimard, 1962.

Guerlain, Pierre. "Robert Kagan and Noam Chomsky: Two ways of being a political intellectual." *Comparative American Studies* 4, no. 4 (2006): 446-58. http://cas.sagepub.com/cgi/content/abstract/4/4/446 http://cas.sagepub.com/cgi/reprint/4/4/446.pdf (accessed August 20, 2007).

Guggenheimer, Heinrich W., ed. *Seder Olam: The Rabbinic View of Biblical Chronology*. Lanham, MI: Jason Aronson/Rowman and Littlefield Publishing Group, 1998.

Guilleux, Alain. *Le Temple de Derr. Une Promenade en Egypte*. http://alain.guilleux.free.fr/derr/lac_nasser_temple_derr.html (accessed June 2, 2008).

Gündüz, Sinasi. *The Knowledge of Life: The Origins and Early History of Mandaeans and Their Relation to the Sabians of the Qur'an and to the Harranians*. *Journal of Semitic Studies Supplement* 3. Oxford, England: Oxford University Press, 1994.

Gunn, Stanley R. *Oliver Cowdery: Second Elder and Scribe*. Salt Lake City, UT: Bookcraft, 1962.

Gutmann, Joseph. "Introduction." In *The Dura-Europos Synagogue: A Re-evaluation (1932-1992)*, edited by Joseph Gutmann, ix-xl. Atlanta, GA: Scholars Press, 1992.

———. "Programmatic painting in the Dura synagogue." In *The Dura-Europos Synagogue: A Re-evaluation (1932-1992)*, edited by Joseph Gutmann, 137-54. Atlanta, GA: Scholars Press, 1992.

Haardt, Robert. 1967. *Gnosis: Character and Testimony*. Translated by J. F. Hendry. English ed. Leiden, The Netherlands: E. J. Brill, 1971.

Hafen, Bruce C. *The Broken Heart*. Salt Lake City, UT: Deseret Book, 1989.

———. *Covenant Hearts: Marriage and the Joy of Human Love*. Salt Lake City, UT: Deseret Book, 2005.

———. "A disciple's journey." In *Brigham Young University 2007-2008 Speeches*, 291-305. Provo, UT: Brigham Young University, 2008. http://speeches.byu.edu/reader/reader.php?id=12148. (accessed September 1, 2009).

———. *A Disciple's Life: The Biography of Neal A. Maxwell*. Salt Lake City, UT: Deseret Book, 2002.

———. "Reason, faith, and the things of eternity." *The FARMS Review* 20, no. 2 (2008): 15-35.

———. *Spiritually Anchored in Unsettled Times*. Salt Lake City, UT: Deseret Book, 2009.

Hafen, Bruce C., and Marie K. Hafen. *The Belonging Heart: The Atonement and Relationships with God and Family*. Salt Lake City, UT: Deseret Book, 1994.

Hagen, Kirk D. "Eternal progression in a multiverse: An explorative Mormon cosmology." *Dialogue: A Journal of Mormon Thought* 39, no. 2 (Summer 2006): 1-45.

Hale, Van. "The origin of the human spirit in early Mormon thought." In *Line Upon Line: Essays on Mormon Doctrine*, edited by Gary James Bergera, 115-26. Salt Lake City, UT: Signature Books, 1989.

———. "What about the Adam-God theory?". Sandy, UT: Mormon Miscellaneous, 1983.

Haleem, M. A. S. Abdel, ed. *The Qur'an: A New Translation*. Oxford, England: Oxford University Press, 2004.

Hales, Robert D. "The British contribution to the restored gospel." *BYU Studies* 27, no. 1 (1987): 1-13.

———. "A question of free agency." *Ensign* 5, May 1975, 43-44.

Halford, Mary-Bess. *Lutwin's Eva und Adam: Study - Text - Translation*. Göppingen, Germany: Kümmerle Verlag, 1984.

Hall, John F. 2007. "'As far as it is translated correctly': The problem of tampering with the word of God in the transmission and translation of the New Testament." In *Proceedings of the FAIR Conference*. http://www.fairlds.org/FAIR_Conferences/2007_As_Far_As_It_Is_Translated_Correctly.html#enloc12 (accessed April 23, 2008).

Hallo, William W., and K. Lawson Younger, eds. *The Context of Scripture*. 3 vols. Leiden, The Netherlands: Brill Academic Publishers, 1996-2002.

Haloun, G., and W. B. Henning. "The *Compendium* of the Doctrines and Styles of the Teaching of Mani, the Buddha of Light." *Asia Major* 3 (1952): 184-212.

Halperin, David J. *Faces of the Chariot: Development of Rabbinic Exegesis of Ezekiel's Vision of the Divine Chariot. Texte und Studiem Zum Antiken Judentum*. Philadelphia, PA: Coronet Books, 1988.

Halpern, Paul, and Paul Wesson. *Brave New Universe: Illuminating the Darkest Secrets of the Cosmos*. Washington, DC: Joseph Henry Press, 2006.

Halverson, W. Dee. *The LDS Conference Center and Its History*. Salt Lake City, UT: Heritage Associates, DMT Publishing, 2000.

Hamblin, William J. "Aspects of an early Christian initiation ritual." In *By Study and Also by Faith: Essays in Honor of Hugh W. Nibley*, edited by John M. Lundquist and Stephen D. Ricks. 2 vols. Vol. 1, 202-21. Salt Lake City, UT: Deseret Book, 1990.

———. "Joseph or Jung? A response to Douglas Salmon with an appendix by Gordon C. Thomasson." *FARMS Review* 13, no. 2 (2001): 87-107. http://farms.byu.edu/publications/review/?reviewed_author&vol=13&num=2&id=391 (accessed January 30, 2009).

———. 1983. "Pre-Islamic Arabian Prophets." In *Mormons and Muslims: Spiritual Foundations and Modern Manifestations*, edited by Spencer J. Palmer. Updated and Revised ed, 135-55. Provo, UT: Brigham Young University Religious Studies Center, 2002.

———. "Temple motifs in Jewish mysticism." In *Temples of the Ancient World*, edited by Donald W. Parry, 440-76. Salt Lake City, UT: Deseret Book, 1994.

Hamblin, William J., and David Rolph Seely. *Solomon's Temple: Myth and History*. London, England: Thames & Hudson, 2007.

Hamilton, Victor P. *The Book of Genesis: Chapters 1-17*. Grand Rapids, MI: William B. Eerdmans Publishing, 1990.

Hammond, Gerald. "English translations of the Bible." In *The Literary Guide to the Bible*, edited by Robert Alter and Frank Kermode, 647-66. Cambridge, MA: The Belknap Press of Harvard University Press, 1987.

Hamori, Esther J. *"When Gods Were Men": The Embodied God in Biblical and Near Eastern Literature. Beihefte zur Zeitschrift für die alttestamentliche Wissenschaft* 384, ed. John Barton, Reinhard G. Kratz, Choon-Leong Sow and Markus Witte. Berlin, Germany: Walter de Gruyter, 2008.

Hanauer, James Edward. *Folk-Lore of the Holy Land: Moslem, Christian, and Jewish*. Edited by Marmaduke Pickthall. 1st ed. London, England: Duckworth, 1907. http://books.google.com/books?id=r4cTAAAAYAAJ (accessed June 7, 2008).

Hanks, Marion D. "A loving, communicating God." *Ensign* 22, November 1992, 63-65.

Hannay, James. "In the name of the Prophet—Smith!" *Household Words* 3, 1851, 385.

Hansen, Gerald E., Jr., and Val Brinkerhoff. *Sacred Walls: Learning from Temple Symbols.* Salt Lake City, UT: Covenant Communications, 2009.

Hansen, H. Kimball. "Astronomy and the scriptures." In *Science and Religion: Toward a More Useful Dialogue, Vol. 1,* edited by Wilford M. Hess and Raymond T. Matheny, 181-96. Geneva, IL: Paladin House Publishers, 1979.

Hardy, Kenneth R. "Social origins of American scientists and scholars." *Science* 185 (9 August 1974): 497-506.

Hardy, Thomas. 1919. "The Oxen." In *The Lied and Art Song Texts Page.* http://www.recmusic.org/lieder/get_text.html?TextId=7259 (accessed April 5, 2008).

Harper, Donald. "Warring states natural philosophy and occult thought." In *The Cambridge History of Ancient China: From the Origins of Civilization to 221 BC,* edited by Michael Loewe and Edward L. Shaughnessy, 813-84. New York City, NY: Cambridge University Press, 1999.

Harper, Douglas. 2001. *Online Etymology Dictionary.* http://www.etymonline.com/abbr.php (accessed August 22, 2007).

Harper, Steven C. "All things are the Lord's: The law of consecration in the Doctrine and Covenants." In *The Doctrine and Covenants: Revelations in Context: The 37th Annual Brigham Young University Sidney B. Sperry Symposium,* edited by Andrew H. Hedges, J. Spencer Fluhman and Alonzo L. Gaskill, 212-27. Salt Lake City, UT: Deseret Book, 2008.

Harrell, Charles R. "The development of the doctrine of preexistence, 1830-1844." *BYU Studies* 28, no. 2 (1988): 1-25.

Harrington, D. J. ed. "Pseudo-Philo." In *The Old Testament Pseudepigrapha,* edited by James H. Charlesworth. 2 vols. Vol. 2, 297-377. Garden City, NY: Doubleday and Company, 1983.

Harris, J. Rendell. 500-600. *The Gospel of the Twelve Apostles, Together with the Apocalypses of Each One of Them, Edited from the Syriac MS. with a Translation and Introduction.* Cambridge, England: Cambridge University Press, 1900. Reprint, Eugene, OR; Wipf and Stock, n. d.

Harrison, B. Kent. "Truth, the sum of existence." In *Of Heaven and Earth: Reconciling Scientific Thought with LDS Theology,* edited by David L. Clark, 148-80. Salt Lake City, UT: Deseret Book, 1998.

Harrison, Edward R. *Cosmology: The Science of the Universe.* New York, NY: Cambridge University Press, 1981.

"Harrowing of Hell." In *Wikipedia.* http://en.wikipedia.org/wiki/Harrowing_of_Hell (accessed December 26, 2007).

Harvey, A. E. *The New English Bible Companion to the New Testament.* Oxford, England: Oxford University Press, 1970.

———. *The New English Bible Companion to the New Testament.* 2nd ed. Cambridge, England: Cambridge University Press, 2004.

Harvey, Susan Ashbrook, and David G. Hunter, eds. *The Oxford Handbook of Early Christian Studies. Oxford Handbooks in Religion and Theology.* Oxford, England: Oxford University Press, 2008.

Hassett, Maurice M. "Orans (*Orante*)." In *The Catholic Encyclopedia: An International Work of Reference on the Constitution, Doctrine, Discipline, and HIstory of the Catholic Church,* edited by Charles George Hebermann, Edward A. Pace, Condé B. Pallen, Thomas J. Shahan and John J. Wynne. 15 vols. Vol. 11, 269. New York City, NY: The Universal Knowledge Foundation, 1913. http://books.google.com/books?id=kFosAAAAIAAJ (accessed February 1, 2009).

Hatch, Trevan G. *Visions, Manifestations, and Miracles of the Restoration.* Orem, UT: Granite Publishing, 2008.

Haug, Martin ed. "*The Book of Arda Viraf*: A Dantesque Vision of Heaven and Hell." In *The Sacred Books and Early Literature of the East* 7, edited by Charles F. Horne, 185-207. New York City, NY: Parke, Austin, and Lipscomb, 1917. Reprint, Kila, MT: Kessinger Publishing, 2005.

Hauglid, Brian M. "The Book of Abraham and Muslim tradition." In *Astronomy, Papyrus, and Covenant,* edited by John Gee and Brian M. Hauglid. *Studies in the Book of Abraham,* Number 3, eds. John Gee and Brian M. Hauglid, 131-46. Provo, UT: Foundation for Ancient Research and Mormon Studies (FARMS), Brigham Young University, 2005.

———. "Garment of Joseph: An update." In *Foundation for Ancient Research and Mormon Studies Occasional Papers,* edited by Jared W. Ludlow. Vol. 4, 25-29. Provo, UT: Foundation for Ancient Research and Mormon Studies (FARMS), Brigham Young University, 2003.

———. "Joseph Smith's inspired commentary on the doctrine of calling and election." In *Shedding Light on the New Testament: Acts-Revelation,* edited by Ray L. Huntington, Frank F. Judd, Jr. and David M. Whitchurch, 209-26. Provo, UT: Religious Studies Center, Brigham Young University, 2009.

———. "Sacred time and the temple." In *Temples of the Ancient World,* edited by Donald W. Parry, 636-45. Salt Lake City, UT: Deseret Book, 1994.

Hawking, Stephen. 2004. "Gödel and the end of physics." In *Department of Applied Mathematics and Theoretical Physics,* Cambridge University. http://www.damtp.cam.ac.uk/strtst/dirac/hawking/ (accessed August 19, 2007).

———. *The Universe in a Nutshell*. New York, NY: Bantam Book, 2001.

Hawkins, Chad S. *The First 100 Temples*. Salt Lake City, UT: Deseret Book, 2001.

Haws, J. B. "Defenders of the doctrine of deification." In *Prelude to the Restoration: From Apostasy to the Restored Church, The 33rd Annual Sidney B. Sperry Symposium*, edited by Fred E. Wood, Steven C. Harper, Andrew H. Hedges, Patty A. Smith and Thomas R. Valetta, 70-98. Salt Lake City, UT: Deseret Book, 2004.

Hawthorne, N. 1852. "The Miraculous Pitcher." In *A Wonder Book and Tanglewood Tales. The Centenary Edition of The Works of Nathaniel Hawthorne* 7, 115-139. Columbus, OH: Ohio State University Press, 1972.

Haymond, Bryce. 2008. "Job's covenant: Hebrew *tav* and 'Behold my sign!' in Job 31." In *Temple Study: Sustaining and Defending the LDS Temple*. http://www.templestudy.com/2008/08/16/jobs-covenant-hebrew-tav-and-behold-my-sign-in-job-31/. (accessed August 21, 2009).

———. 2008. "The Seal of Melchizedek – Part 4." In *Temple Study: Sustaining and Defending the LDS Temple*. http://www.templestudy.com/2008/09/11/the-seal-of-melchizedek-part-4/#more-902 (accessed September 12, 2008).

Haynes, Stephen R. *Noah's Curse: The Biblical Justification of American Slavery*. Oxford, England: Oxford University Press, 2002.

Hayward, C. T. R. *Interpretations of the Name Israel in Ancient Judaism and Some Early Christian Writings: From Victorious Athlete to Heavenly Champion*. Oxford, England: Oxford University Press, 2005.

Hazen, Robert M. *Genesis: The Scientific Quest for Life's Origin*. Washington, DC: Joseph Henry Press, 2005.

"Hebron: Historical background and statistics" (28 October 1996). In *MFA Newsletter*, Israel Ministry of Foreign Affairs. http://www.mfa.gov.il/MFA/Peace+Process/Guide+to+the+Peace+Process/Hebron+-+Background.htm (accessed June 10, 2008).

Hedrick, Charles W., and Douglas M. Parrott ed. "The (Second) Apocalypse of James (V, 4)." In *The Nag Hammadi Library in English*, edited by James M. Robinson. 3rd, Completely Revised ed, 269-76. San Francisco, CA: HarperSanFrancisco, 1990.

Heffer, Simon. 2000. *Vaughan Williams*. Boston, MA: Northeastern University Press, 2001.

Hegemonius. *Acta Archelai (The Acts of Archelaus)*. Translated by Mark J. Vermes. Edited by Mark J. Vermes and Samuel N. C. Lieu. *Manichaean Studies* 4. Turnhout, Belgium: Brepols, 2001. http://www.loc.gov/catdir/toc/fy0704/2003438282.html.

Heidegger, Martin. *The Question Concerning Technology and Other Essays*. New York City, NY: Harper Colophon Books, 1977.

Heiser, Michael S., and David E. Bokovoy. "Scholarly Exchange." *FARMS Review* 19, no. 1 (2007): 221-323.

Hendel, Ronald S. "Of demigods and the deluge: Toward an interpretation of Genesis 6:1-4." *Journal of Biblical Literature* 106 (1987): 13-26.

———. "The poetics of myth in Genesis." In *The Seductiveness of Jewish Myth*, edited by S. D. Breslauer, 157-70. Albany, NY: SUNY Press, 1997.

———. "Tangled plots in Genesis." In *Fortunate the Eyes that See: Essays in Honor of David Noel Freedman*, edited by Astrid B. Beck, Andrew H. Bartelt, Paul R. Raabe and Chris A. Franke, 35-51. Grand Rapids, MI: William B. Eerdmans, 1995.

Hennecke, Edgar, and Wilhelm Schneemelcher, eds. "The Acts of John." In *New Testament Apocrypha*, edited by Edgar Hennecke and Wilhelm Schneemelcher. 2 vols. Vol. 2, 188-259. Philadelphia, PA: The Westminster Press, 1965.

———, eds. "The Acts of Thomas." In *New Testament Apocrypha*, edited by Edgar Hennecke and Wilhelm Schneemelcher. 2 vols. Vol. 2, 425-531. Philadelphia, PA: The Westminster Press, 1965.

———, eds. "Apocalypse of Paul." In *New Testament Apocrypha*, edited by Edgar Hennecke and Wilhelm Schneemelcher. 2 vols. Vol. 2, 755-98. Philadelphia, PA: The Westminster Press, 1965.

———, eds. "Apocalypse of Peter." In *New Testament Apocrypha*, edited by Edgar Hennecke and Wilhelm Schneemelcher. 2 vols. Vol. 2, 663-83. Philadelphia, PA: The Westminster Press, 1965.

———, eds. "Hymn of the Pearl." In *New Testament Apocrypha*, edited by Edgar Hennecke and Wilhelm Schneemelcher. 2 vols. Vol. 2, 498-504. Philadelphia, PA: The Westminster Press, 1965.

———, eds. "The (Manichaean) Gospel of the Twelve Apostles." In *New Testament Apocrypha*, edited by Edgar Hennecke and Wilhelm Schneemelcher. 2 vols. Vol. 1, 268-69. Philadelphia, PA: The Westminster Press, 1965.

———, eds. *New Testament Apocrypha*. 2 vols. Philadelphia, PA: The Westminster Press, 1965.

———, eds. "The Protoevangelium of James." In *New Testament Apocrypha*, edited by Edgar Hennecke and Wilhelm Schneemelcher. 2 vols. Vol. 1. Translated by A. J. B. Higgins, 370-88. Philadelphia, PA: The Westminster Press, 1965.

Henry, Matthew. 1706-1714. *Matthew Henry's Commentary on the Whole Bible: Complete and Unabridged in One Volume*. Peabody, MA: Hendrickson Publishers, 1991.

Henry, Paul. *Les Églises de Moldavie du Nord, des Origines à la Fin du XVIe Siècle*. 2 vols. *Monuments de l'Art Byzantin* 6. Paris, France: Ernest Leroux, 1930.

Herbert, George. 1633. *The Temple*. Edited by Christopher Harvey. 2nd ed. London, England: Pickering, 1838. http://books.google.com/books?id=vv-PaLfn8wIC (accessed May 16, 2009).

Herbert, Máire, and Martin McNamara, eds. *Irish Biblical Apocrypha: Selected Texts in Translation*. Edinburgh, Scotland: T & T Clark, 1989.

Hermes Trismegistus. "Asclepius." In *The Other Bible*, edited by Willis Barnstone, 575-80. San Francisco, CA: HarperSanFrancisco, 2005.

———. "Poimandres." In *The Gnostic Bible*, edited by Willis Barnstone and Marvin W. Meyer, 502-11. Boston, MA: Shambhala, 2003.

———. "Poimandres." In *The Other Bible*, edited by Willis Barnstone, 567-74. San Francisco, CA: HarperSanFrancisco, 2005.

———. *Thrice-Greatest Hermes: Studies in Hellenistic Theosophy and Gnosis, Being a Translation of the Extant Sermons and Fragments of the Trismegistic Literature with Prolegomena, Commentaries, and Notes*. 3 vols. Edited by George Robert Shaw Mead. London, England: The Theosophical Publishing Society, 1906. Reprint, Kila, MT: Kessinger Publishing, n.d. http://www.gnosis.org/library/hermet.htm (accessed August 30, 2007).

Hertz, J. H., ed. *The Soncino Edition of the Pentateuch and HafTorahs (with Hebrew Text, English Translation and Commentary)* 2nd ed. Brooklyn, NY: The Soncino Press, 1970.

Heschel, Abraham Joshua. 1962, 1965, 1995. *Heavenly Torah as Refracted Through the Generations*. 3 vols. in 1. Translated by Gordon Tucker. Edited by Gordon Tucker and Leonard Levin. New York City, NY: Continuum International, 2007.

Hess, Richard S., and David Toshio Tsumura, eds. *I Studied Inscriptions Before the Flood: Ancient Near Eastern, Literary, and Linguistic Approaches to Genesis 1-11. Sources for Biblical and Theological Study* 4. Winona Lake, IN: Eisenbrauns, 1994.

Heuser, Manfred, and Hans-Joachim Klimkeit. *Studies in Manichaean Literature and Art. Nag Hammadi and Manichaean Studies* 46. Leiden, The Netherlands: Brill, 1998.

Hicks, Michael. *Mormonism and Music: A History. Music in American Life*. Urbana-Champaign, IL: University of Illinois Press, 1989.

Hiebert, Robert J. V., ed. *A New English Translation of the Septuagint and the Other Greek Translations Traditionally Included under that Title: Genesis* Provisional ed. *NETS: New English Translation of the Septuagint*, ed. Albert Pietersma and Benjamin Wright. Oxford, England: Oxford University Press, 2005. http://ccat.sas.upenn.edu/nets/edition/gen.pdf (accessed August 22, 2007).

Hilton, Lynn M. 1981. "The hand as a cup in ancient religious worship." In *Discovering Lehi: New Evidence of Lehi and Nephi in Arabia*, edited by Lynn M. Hilton and Hope A. Hilton, 171-77. Springfield, UT: Cedar Fort Incorporated, 1996.

Hinckley, Gordon B. "Daughters of God." *Ensign* 21, November 1991, 97-100.

———. "Don't drop the ball." *Ensign* 24, November 1994, 46-49.

———. 2004. "Manhattan, New York, Member Meeting, 12 June 2004." In *Discourses of President Gordon B. Hinckley*. 2 vols. Vol. 2: 2000-2004, 419-29. Salt Lake City, UT: Deseret Book, 2005.

———. "The marvelous foundation of our faith." *Ensign* 32, November 2002, 78-81.

———. "The need for greater kindness." *Ensign* 36, May 2006, 58-61.

———. 1997. "Ogden, Utah, Institute of Religion Devotional, 15 April 1997." In *Discourses of President Gordon B. Hinckley*. 2 vols. Vol. 1: 1995-1999, 370-80. Salt Lake City, UT: Deseret Book, 2005.

———. 2002. "Priesthood Session, 6 April 2002." In *Discourses of President Gordon B. Hinckley*. 2 vols. Vol. 2: 2000-2004, 124-31. Salt Lake City, UT: Deseret Book, 2005.

———. "Sunday Morning Session, 2 April 1995." In *Discourses of President Gordon B. Hinckley*. 2 vols. Vol. 1: 1995-1999, 13-20. Salt Lake City, UT: Deseret Book, 2005.

———. 1996. "Sunday Morning Session, 6 October 1996." In *Discourses of President Gordon B. Hinckley*. 2 vols. Vol. 1: 1995-1999, 98-106. Salt Lake City, UT: Deseret Book, 2005.

———. 1998. "Sunday Morning Session, 4 October 1998." In *Discourses of President Gordon B. Hinckley*. 2 vols. Vol. 1: 1995-1999, 206-13. Salt Lake City, UT: Deseret Book, 2005.

———. 2004. "Sunday Morning Session, 3 October 2004." In *Discourses of President Gordon B. Hinckley*. 2 vols. Vol. 2: 2000-2004, 257-63. Salt Lake City, UT: Deseret Book, 2005.

———. *Teachings of Gordon B. Hinckley*. Salt Lake City, UT: Deseret Book Company, 1997.

———. "To all the world in testimony." *Ensign* 30, May 2000, 4-6.

———. 1998. "University of Utah Commencement Exercises, 12 June 1998." In *Discourses of President Gordon B. Hinckley*. 2 vols. Vol. 1: 1995-1999, 539-46. Salt Lake City, UT: Deseret Book, 2005.

———. 2003. "University of Utah, Gordon B. Hinckley Endowment for British Studies, 12 July 2003." In *Discourses of President Gordon B. Hinckley*. 2 vols. Vol. 2: 2000-2004, 544-48. Salt Lake City, UT: Deseret Book, 2005.

———. "Women of the Church." *Ensign* 26, November 1996, 67-70.

Hinckley, Gordon B., Thomas S. Monson, and James E. Faust. "The family: A proclamation to the world. Proclamation of the First Presidency and the Council of the Twelve presented at the General Relief Society Meeting, September 23, 1995." Salt Lake City, UT: The Church of Jesus Christ of Latter-day Saints, 1995.

"Hindu groups oppose canal project." September 12. In *BBC News*. http://news.bbc.co.uk/1/hi/world/south_asia/6690847.stm (accessed September 30, 2007).

Hirschman, Jack ed. "Baraita on the Work of Creation: Baraita de Mas'aseh Bereshit." In *The Secret Garden: An Anthology in the Kabbalah*, edited by David Meltzer, 3-20. Barrytown, NY: Barrytown Limited, 1997.

"History of Joseph Smith (continued)." Nauvoo, IL: *Times and Seasons* 4:5, January, 1843, 71-73.

"History of Joseph Smith (continued)." Nauvoo, IL: *Times and Seasons* 6:12, July 1, 1845, 944-48.

Hodges, Horace Jeffery. "Milton's muse as brooding dove: Unstable image on a chaos of sources." *Milton Studies of Korea* 12, no. 2 (2002): 365-92. http://memes.or.kr/sources/%C7%D0%C8%B8%C1%F6/%B9%D0%C5%CF%BF%AC%B1%B8/12-2/11.Hodges.pdf (accessed August 25, 2007).

Hogel, Christian. *Symeon Metaphrastes: Rewriting and Canonization*. Copenhagen, Denmark: University of Copenhagen, Muesum Tusculanum Press, 2002.

Holland, Jeffrey R. "Atonement of Jesus Christ." In *Encyclopedia of Mormonism*, edited by Daniel H. Ludlow. 4 vols. Vol. 1, 82-86. New York City, NY: Macmillan, 1992. http://www.lib.byu.edu/Macmillan/ (accessed November 26, 2007).

———. *Christ and the New Covenant: The Messianic Message of the Book of Mormon*. Salt Lake City, UT: Deseret Book, 1997.

———. "I stand all amazed." In *On Earth As It Is in Heaven*, edited by Jeffrey R. Holland and Patricia T. Holland, 198-213. Salt Lake City, UT: Deseret Book, 1989.

———. 1986. "Lift up your eyes." In *On Earth As It Is in Heaven*, edited by Jeffrey R. Holland and Patricia T. Holland, 115-23. Salt Lake City, UT: Deseret Book, 1989.

———. "'My words… never cease.'" *Ensign* 28, May 2008, 91-94.

———. "'My words… never cease.'" In *Broken Things to Mend*, edited by Jeffrey R. Holland, 184-90. Salt Lake City, UT: Deseret Book, 2008.

———. 1986. "O Lord, Keep My Rudder True." In *On Earth As It Is in Heaven*, edited by Jeffrey R. Holland and Patricia T. Holland, 138-50. Salt Lake City, UT: Deseret Book, 1989.

———. 1988. *Of Souls, Symbols, and Sacraments*. Salt Lake City, UT: Deseret Book, 2001.

Holland, Jeffrey R., and Patricia T. Holland. "Some things we have learned together." In *However Long and Hard the Road*, edited by Jeffrey R. Holland, 99-113. Salt Lake City, UT: Deseret Book, 1985.

Holtz, Barry W. 1984. *Back to the Sources: Reading the Classic Jewish Texts*. New York City, NY: Simon and Schuster, 2006.

Holzapfel, Richard Neitzel, and T. Jeffery Cottle. *Old Mormon Kirtland and Missouri*. Santa Ana, CA: Fieldbrook Productions, 1991.

Holzapfel, Richard Neitzel, and David Rolph Seely. *My Father's House: Temple Worship and Symbolism in the New Testament*. Salt Lake City, UT: Bookcraft, 1994.

Holzapfel, Richard Neitzel, and Thomas A. Wayment. *From Bethlehem through the Sermon on the Mount*. 2 vols. Vol. 1. *The Life and Teachings of Jesus Christ*. Salt Lake City, UT: Deseret Book, 2005.

———. *From the Last Supper through the Resurrection: The Savior's Final Hours*. 2 vols. Vol. 2. *The Life and Teachings of Jesus Christ*. Salt Lake City, UT: Deseret Book, 2003.

Homer. ca. 800 BC. *The Odyssey of Homer Done into English Prose*. Edited by S. H. Butcher and M. A. Lang. Second, Revised and Corrected ed. London, England: Macmillan and Company, 1879. http://books.google.com/books?id=3oMCAAAAQAAJ (accessed August 31, 2008).

Hooker, J. T. "Introduction." In *Reading the Past: Ancient Writing from Cuneiform to the Alphabet*, edited by J. T. Hooker, 6-13. London, England: The British Museum Press, 1990.

Hooper, Walter. *C. S. Lewis: A Companion and Guide*. New York: HarperCollins, 1996.

REFERENCES

Hopkins, Clark. *The Discovery of Dura-Europos*. Edited by Bernard Goldman. New Haven, CT: Yale University Press, 1979.

Horne, Charles F., ed. *The Medieval Hebrew Tanhuma Midrash*. Kila, MT: Kessinger Publishing, 2005.

———, ed. *Sacred Books and Early Literature of the East*. 14 vols. New York City, NY: Parke, Austin, and Lipscomb, 1917. Reprint, Kila, MT: Kessinger Publishing, 2005.

Horne, Dennis B., ed. *An Apostle's Record: The Journals of Abraham H. Cannon*. Salt Lake City, UT: Gnolaum Books, 2004.

———. *Bruce R. McConkie: Highlights from His Life and Teachings*. Roy, UT: Eborn Books, 2000.

Horton, George A., Jr. "Elias." In *Encyclopedia of Mormonism*, edited by Daniel H. Ludlow. 4 vols. Vol. 2, 449. New York City, NY: Macmillan, 1992. http://www.lib.byu.edu/Macmillan/ (accessed November 26, 2007).

———. "Insights into the Book of Genesis." In *The Joseph Smith Translation: The Restoration of Plain and Precious Things*, edited by Monte S. Nyman and Robert L. Millet, 51-88. Provo, UT: Brigham Young University Religious Studies Center, 1985.

Hoselton, M.A. "Inventory of Manuscripts from Qumran." In *Dead Sea Scrolls and Qumran*. http://www.flash.net/~hoselton/deadsea/caves.htm (accessed October 3, 2008).

Howard, Luke. *Album notes from "Requiem: Choral Music of Mack Wilberg", performed by The Mormon Tabernacle Choir and the Orchestra at Temple Square*. Salt Lake City, UT: Intellectual Reserve, 2008.

Howard, Richard P. *Restoration Scriptures*. Independence, MO: Herald House, 1969.

———. *Restoration Scriptures*. 2nd ed. Independence, MO: Herald House, 1995.

Huchel, Frederick M. "The cosmic ring dance of the angels: An early Christian rite of the temple." Presented at the *Temple Studies Group Symposium II*, Temple Church, London England, May 30, 2009. http://www.heavenlyascents.com/2009/06/10/the-cosmic-ring-dance-of-the-angels-the-text-of-frederick-m-huchels-presentation-at-the-uk-temple-studies-group-symposium-ii/ (accessed June 11, 2009).

———. *The Cosmic Ring Dance of the Angels: An Early Christian Rite of the Temple*. North Logan, UT: The Frithurex Press, 2009. http://www.lulu.com/content/paperback-book/the-cosmic-ring-dance-of-the-angels---softbound/7409216. (accessed September 21, 2009).

Hudson, Valerie M., and Alma Don Sorenson. "Response to Professor Thomas." In *Mormonism in Dialogue with Contemporary Christian Theologies*, edited by Donald W. Musser and David L. Paulsen, 323-38. Macon, GA: Mercer University Press, 2007.

Huff, Benjamin. "Theology in the light of continuing revelation." In *Mormonism in Dialogue with Contemporary Christian Theologies*, edited by Donald W. Musser and David L. Paulsen, 478-87. Macon, GA: Mercer University Press, 2007.

Hugh of Saint Victor. ca. 1134. *On the Sacraments of the Christian Faith (De Sacramentis)*. Translated by Roy J. DeFerrari. *Medieval Academy Books 58*. Cambridge, MA: The Medieval Academy of America, 1951. Reprint, Eugene, OR: Wipf & Stock, 2007.

Hugo, Victor. *Selected Poetry in French and English*. Translated by Steven Monte. New York City, NY: Routledge, 2002.

Hultgren, Arland J. *The Parables of Jesus: A Commentary*. Grand Rapids, MI: William B. Eerdmans, 2000.

Humphrey, Caroline, and Piers Vitebsky. *Sacred Architecture: Symbolic Form and Ornament Traditions of East and West Models of the Cosmos*. New York City, NY: Barnes and Noble, 2005.

Hunter, Howard W. 1979. "'All are alike unto God.'" In *That We Might Have Joy*, 68-75. Salt Lake City, UT: Deseret Book, 1994.

———. 1983. "Parents' concern for children." In *That We Might Have Joy*, 111-15. Salt Lake City, UT: Deseret Book, 1994.

———. *The Teachings of Howard W. Hunter*. Edited by Clyde J. Williams. Salt Lake City, UT: Bookcraft, 1997.

Hunter, Robert Grams. 1965. "The regeneration of Alsonso." In *Shakespeare's Christian Dimension: An Anthology of Commentary*, edited by Roy Battenhouse, 263-67. Bloomington, IN: Indiana University Press, 1994.

Hustwit, Ronald. "Wittgenstein's interest in Kierkegaard." *Wittgenstein Studies* (1997). http://sammelpunkt.philo.at:8080/archive/00000526/01/18-2-97.TXT (accessed August 25, 2007).

Hutchinson, Anthony A. "A Mormon midrash? LDS creation narratives reconsidered." *Dialogue* 21, no. 4 (Winter 1988): 11-74.

Hyde, Orson. 1859. "Sowing and reaping; fulfilment of covenants (Remarks made in the Tabernacle, Great Salt Lake City, 6 October 1859)." In *Journal of Discourses*. 26 vols. Vol. 7, 313-17. Liverpool and London, England: Latter-day Saints Book Depot, 1853-1886. Reprint, Salt Lake City, UT: Bookcraft, 1966.

———. "A diagram of the Kingdom of God." Liverpool, England: *Millennial Star* 9:2, January 15, 1847, 23-24. Reprinted in Smith, J., Jr. *The Words of Joseph Smith*. Edited by A.F. Ehat and L.W. Cook. Salt Lake City, UT: Bookcraft, 1980, pp. 297-299 n. 8. http://contentdm.lib.byu.edu/cgi-bin/showfile.exe?CISOROOT=/MStar&CISOPTR=562&filename=563.pdf (accessed January 3, 2008).

———. 1841. "Prayer of Orson Hyde on the Mount of Olives." In *History of the Church of Jesus Christ of Latter-day Saints (Documentary History)*, edited by Joseph Smith, Jr. and Brigham Henry Roberts. 7 vols. Vol. 4, 456-59. Salt Lake City, UT: Deseret Book, 1978.

Hyde, Paul Nolan. "Intelligences." In *Encyclopedia of Mormonism*, edited by Daniel H. Ludlow. 4 vols. Vol. 2, 692-93. New York City, NY: Macmillan, 1992. http://www.lib.byu.edu/Macmillan/ (accessed November 26, 2007).

Hymns of the Church of Jesus Christ of Latter-day Saints. Salt Lake City, UT: The Church of Jesus Christ of Latter-day Saints, 1948.

Hymns of the Church of Jesus Christ of Latter-day Saints. Salt Lake City, UT: The Church of Jesus Christ of Latter-day Saints, 1985.

Ibn Ezra, Abraham ben Meir. d. 1164. *Ibn Ezra's Commentary on the Pentateuch: Genesis (Bereshit)*. Edited by H. Norman Strickman and Arthur M. Silver. Chicago, IL: Menorah Publications, 1988.

Ibn Ishaq ibn Yasar, Muhammad. d. 767. *The Life of Muhammad: A Translation of Ishaq's Sirat Rasul Allah*. Translated by Alfred Guillaume. Edited by Abd Al-Malik Ibn Hisham. Oxford, England: Oxford University Press, 2002.

———. d. 767. *The Making of the Last Prophet: A Reconstruction of the Earliest Biography of Muhammad*. Edited by Gordon Darnell Newby. Columbia, SC: University of South Carolina Press, 1989.

Ibn Kathir, Ismail. d. 1373. *Stories of the Prophets*. Translated by Rashad Ahmad Azami. 2nd ed. Riyadh, Saudi Arabia: Dar-us-Salam Publications, 2003.

———. d. 1373. *Tafsir Ibn Kathir (Abridged)*. 10 vols. Translated by Safiur-Rahman Al-Mubarakpuri. Houston, TX: Dar-us-Salam Publications, 2000.

Ibrahim, Raymond, ed. *The Al Qaeda Reader*. Translated by Raymond Ibrahim. New York City, NY: Broadway Books, 2007.

Idel, Moché. 1987. "Hénoch c'est Métatron." In *Le Livre hébreu d'Hénoch ou Livre des Palais*, edited by Charles Mopsik, 379-426. Lagrasse, France: Éditions Verdier, 1989.

Ignatius. d. ca. 110-112. "Epistle of Ignatius to the Philadelphians." In *The Ante-Nicene Fathers (The Writings of the Fathers Down to AD 325)*, edited by Alexander Roberts and James Donaldson. 10 vols. Vol. 1, 79-85. Buffalo, NY: The Christian Literature Company, 1885. Reprint, Peabody, MA: Hendrickson Publishers, 2004.

"Industrial-strength design: How Brooks Stevens shaped your world." In *Milwaukee Art Museum Exhibition, June 7-September 7, 2003*. http://www.mam.org/exhibitions/_sites/brooks/biography.asp (accessed October 20, 2007).

"Inflatable church." In *Innovations Xtreme*. http://www.inflatablechurch.com/mainpage.htm (accessed August 20, 2008).

Ingebretsen, Richard J. *Joseph Smith and Modern Astronomy*. Springville, UT: Cedar Fort International, 1999.

Insler, Stanley, ed. *The Gathas of Zarathustra, edited with a Translation, Commentary, and a Glossary. Acta Iranica — Encyclopédie Permanente des Études Iraniennes, Textes et Mémoires* 1. Leiden, The Netherlands: E. J. Brill, 1975.

International Theological Commission. "The hope of salvation for infants who die without being baptized." *Origins: CNS Documentary Service (Washington, DC: Catholic News Service)* 36, no. 45 (26 April 2007): 725-46.

Irenaeus. ca. 150-200. "Against Heresies." In *The Ante-Nicene Fathers (The Writings of the Fathers Down to AD 325)*, edited by Alexander Roberts and James Donaldson. 10 vols. Vol. 1, 315-567. Buffalo, NY: The Christian Literature Company, 1885. Reprint, Peabody, MA: Hendrickson Publishers, 2004.

———. d. ca. 202. *Irenaeus's Demonstration of the Apostolic Preaching: A Theological Commentary and Translation*. Translated by Iain M. MacKenzie. Aldershot, England: Ashgate Publishing Ltd., 2002.

———. ca. 150-200. *St. Irenaeus: Proof of the Apostolic Preaching*. Translated by Joseph P. Smith. Mahwah, NJ: Paulist Press, 1978.

Irving, Gordon. "The law of adoption: One phase of the development of the Mormon concept of salvation." *BYU Studies* 14 (Spring 1974): 291-314.

Isaac, E. ed. "1 (Ethiopic Apocalypse of) Enoch." In *The Old Testament Pseudepigrapha*, edited by James H. Charlesworth. Vol. 1, 5-89. Garden City, NY: Doubleday and Company, 1983.

Isaacson, Walter. *Einstein: His Life and Universe*. New York City, NY: Simon & Schuster, 2007.

Isar, Nicoletta. "The dance of Adam: Reconstructing the Byzantine *choros*." *Byzantino-Slavica: Revue Internationale des Études Byzantines* 61 (2003): 179-204.

Isenberg, Wesley W. ed. "The Gospel of Philip (II, 3)." In *The Nag Hammadi Library*, edited by James M. Robinson. 3rd, Completely Revised ed, 139-60. San Francisco, CA: HarperSanFrancisco, 1990.

Israel, David Asia. *Secret Teachings of the Angelic Kings: New Translation of the Ancient Aramaic "Drashia d-Malkia" Scroll, Containing the Lost Gnostic Sermons of Jesus, Mary Magdalene, and John the Baptist.* Order of Nasorean Essenes, 2007.

Jablonka, Eva, and Marion J. Lamb. *Evolution in Four Dimensions: Genetic, Epigenetic, Behavioral, and Symbolic Variation in the History of Life.* Cambridge, MA: The MIT Press, 2005.

Jackson, Deirdre. *Marvellous to Behold: Miracles in Medieval Manuscripts.* London, England: The British Library, 2007.

Jackson, Kent P. *The Book of Moses and the Joseph Smith Translation Manuscripts.* Provo, UT: Brigham Young University Religious Studies Center, 2005.

———. E-mail message to Jeffrey M. Bradshaw, July 6, 2006.

———. E-mail message to Jeffrey M. Bradshaw, August 21, 2006.

———. "Joseph Smith's Cooperstown Bible: The Historical Context of the Bible Used in the Joseph Smith Translation." *BYU Studies* 40, no. 1 (2001): 41-70.

———. "New discoveries in the Joseph Smith Translation of the Bible." *Religious Educator* 6, no. 3 (2005): 149-60.

———. *The Restored Gospel and the Book of Genesis.* Salt Lake City, UT: Deseret Book, 2001.

Jackson, Kent P., and Peter M. Jasinski. "The process of inspired translation: Two passages translated twice in the Joseph Smith Translation of the Bible." *BYU Studies* 42, no. 2 (2003): 35-64.

Jackson, Kent P., and Charles Swift. "The ages of the Patriarchs in the Joseph Smith Translation." In *A Witness for the Restoration: Essays in Honor of Robert J. Matthews*, edited by Kent P. Jackson and Andrew C. Skinner, 1-11. Provo, UT: Religious Studies Center, Brigham Young University, 2007.

Jacobs, Alan. *Original Sin: A Cultural History.* New York City, NY: HarperOne, 2008.

Jacobson, Howard, ed. *A Commentary on Pseudo-Philo's Liber Antiquitatum Biblicarum, with Latin Text and English Translation.* Leiden, The Netherlands: Brill Academic Publishers, 1996.

Jafri, Syed Husain M. "Twelve Imam Shi'ism." In *Islamic Spirituality*, edited by Seyyed Hossein Nasr. Vol. 1: Foundations, 160-78. New York City, NY: The Crossroad Publishing Company, 1987.

James, Montague Rhodes ed. 1924. "The Acts of Thomas." In *The Apocryphal New Testament*, edited by Montague Rhodes James, 364-438. Oxford, England: The Clarendon Press, 1983.

———, ed. 1924. *The Apocryphal New Testament.* Oxford, England: The Clarendon Press, 1983.

———, ed. 1924. "The Gospel of Bartholomew." In *The Apocryphal New Testament*, edited by Montague Rhodes James, 166-81. Oxford, England: The Clarendon Press, 1983.

———, ed. 1924. "The Hymn of the Soul." In *The Apocryphal New Testament*, edited by Montague Rhodes James, 411-15. Oxford, England: The Clarendon Press, 1983.

James, William. "What pragmatism means." In *Pragmatism: A New Name for Some Old Ways of Thinking, Popular Lectures on Philosophy by William James*, edited by William James, 43-81. New York City, NY: Longmans, Green, and Company, 1907. http://books.google.com/books?id=1S62J9uY_x4C (accessed September 3, 2007).

———. "The will to believe." In *The Will to Believe and Other Essays in Popular Philosophy*, 1-31. New York City, NY: Longmans, Green, and Company, 1897. Reprint, Mineola, NY: Dover, 1985.

Janowitz, Naomi. *The Poetics of Ascent: Theories of Language in a Rabbinic Ascent Text. SUNY Series in Judaica: Hermeneutics, Mysticism, and Culture.* Albany, NY: State University of New York Press, 1989.

Jarratt, Devereux. *The Life of the Reverend Devereux Jarratt, Rector of Bath Parish, Dinwiddie County, Virginia, Written by Himself, in a Series of Letters Addressed to the Rev. John Coleman, One of the Ministers of the Protestant Episcopal Church in Maryland.* Baltimore, MD: Warner and Hanna, 1806. http://books.google.com/books?id=fn4EAAAAYAAJ (accessed May 27, 2009).

Jarvik, Elaine. "Beliefs on Darwin's evolution vary from religion to religion." Salt Lake City, UT: *Deseret News*, January 19, 2006.

Jastrow, Marcus, ed. 1903. *Dictionary of the Targumim, Talmud Bavli, Talmud, Yerushalmi, and Midrashic Literature.* Brooklyn, NY: Judaica Press, 2004.

Jeffery, Duane E. "Noah's flood: Modern scholarship and mormon traditions." *Sunstone*, October 2004, 27-39, 42-45.

———. "'We don't know': A survey of Mormon responses to evolutionary biology." In *Science and Religion: Toward a More Useful Dialogue*, edited by Wilford M. Hess, Raymond T. Matheny and Donlu D. Thayer, 23-37. Geneva, IL: Paladin House Publishers, 1979.

Jensen, Marlin K. "Gospel doctrines: Anchors to our souls." *Ensign* 38, October 2008, 58-61.

Jensen, Robin M. "The Dura Europos synagogue, early-Christian art, and religious life in Dura Europos." In *Jews, Christians, and Polytheists in the Ancient Synagogue: Cultural Interaction During the Greco-Roman Period*, edited by Steven Fine, 154-67. New York City, NY: Routledge, 1999.

Jensen, Robin Scott. E-mail message to Jeffrey M. Bradshaw, July 20, 2009.

Jerahmeel ben Solomon. ca. 1100-1200. *The Chronicles of Jerahmeel or, The Hebrew Bible Historiale*. Translated by Moses Gaster. *Oriental Translation Fund New Series* 4. London, England: Royal Asiatic Society, 1899. Reprint, Kila, MT: Kessinger Publishing, 2007.

Jeremias, Joachim. *Rediscovering the Parables*. New York City, NY: Charles Scribner's Sons, 1966.

———. *The Sermon on the Mount*. Biblical Series 2. Philadelphia, PA: Fortress Press, 1963.

Jerome. ca. 347-420. *The Homilies of Saint Jerome (1-59 on the Psalms)*. Translated by Marie Liquori Ewald. *The Fathers of the Church*, Volume 48. Washington, DC: Catholic University of America Press, 1964.

———. ca. 347-420. *Jerome's Hebrew Questions on Genesis*. Translated by C. T. R. Hayward. *Oxford Early Christian Studies*. Oxford, England: Oxford University Press, 1995.

———. ca. 386. "Letter 46: Paula and Eustochium to Marcella." In *Nicene and Post-Nicene Fathers, Second Series*, edited by Philip Schaff and Henry Wace. 14 vols. Vol. 8, 60-65. New York City, NY: The Christian Literature Company, 1895. Reprint, Peabody, MA: Hendrickson Publishers, 2004.

"Jerusalem." In *Icons: A Portrait of England*, ed. ICONS Online. http://www.icons.org.uk/theicons/collection/jerusalem/features/and-did-those-feet (accessed November 24, 2007).

Jessee, Dean C. 1969. "The earliest documented accounts of Joseph Smith's First Vision." In *Opening the Heavens: Accounts of Divine Manifestations, 1820-1844*, edited by John W. Welch and Erick B. Carlson, 1-33. Provo, UT: Brigham Young University Press, 2005.

———. "The writing of Joseph Smith's history." *BYU Studies* 11 (Summer 1971): 439-73.

"Jesus Christ is the brother of Satan." In *FAIRWiki*. http://en.fairmormon.org/Jesus_Christ_is_the_brother_of_Satan (accessed March 19, 2009).

Jobes, Karen H., and Moisés Silva. *Invitation to the Septuagint*. Grand Rapids, MI: Baker Academic, 2000.

Johnson, Hollis R. "The big bang: What does it mean for us?" *The FARMS Review* 16, no. 2 (2004): 277-312.

Johnson, Ken, ed. *Ancient Seder Olam*. Nashville, TN: Xulon Press, Salem Communications, 2006.

Johnson, Luke Timothy. *Hebrews: A Commentary*. The New Testament Library, ed. C. Clifton Black and John T. Carroll. Louisville, KY: Westminster John Knox Press, 2006.

———. *The Real Jesus: The Misguided Quest for the Historical Jesus and the Truth of the Traditional Gospels*. New York: HarperCollins/HarperSanFrancisco, 1996.

———. *Religious Experience in Earliest Christianity: A Missing Dimension in New Testament Studies*. Minneapolis, MN: Fortress Press, 1998.

Johnson, M. D. ed. "Life of Adam and Eve." In *The Old Testament Pseudepigrapha*, edited by James H. Charlesworth. Vol. 2, 249-95. Garden City, NY: Doubleday and Company, 1983.

Johnson, Mark J. "The lost prologue: Moses chapter one and the Joseph Smith Translation of the Bible as ancient text." Unpublished article in the possession of the author, 2006.

Johnson, Maxwell E. "Christian initiation." In *The Oxford Handbook of Early Christian Studies*, edited by Susan Ashbrook Harvey and David G. Hunter. Oxford Handbooks in Religion and Theology, 693-710. Oxford, England: Oxford University Press, 2008.

Jolly, Penny Howell. *Made in God's Image? Eve and Adam in the Genesis Mosaics at San Marco, Venice*. California Studies in the History of Art, Discovery Series 4, ed. Walter Horn and James Marrow. Berkeley, CA: University of California Press, 1997.

Jones, Alan, ed. *The Qur'an*. Translated by Alan Jones. Oxford, England: Oxbow Books and the E. J. Gibb Memorial Trust, 2007.

Jones, Dan. 1847. *History of the Latter-day Saints, from Their Establishment in the Year 1823, to the Time When Three Hundred Thousand of Them Were Exiled from America Because of Their Religion in the Year 1846*. Translated by Ronald D. Dennis. Edited by Ronald D. Dennis. Provo, UT: BYU Studies, 2008.

Jones, Edward T. "The Theology of Thomas Dick and its Possible Relationship to that of Joseph Smith." Masters Thesis, Brigham Young University, 1969.

Jones, F. Stanley, ed. *An Ancient Jewish Christian Source on the History of Christianity: Pseudo-Clementine Recognitions 1.27-71*. Society of Biblical Literature Texts and Translations 37: Christian Apocrypha Series 2, ed. Jean-Daniel Dubois and Dennis R. MacDonald. Atlanta, GA: Scholars Press, 1995.

Jones, Gerald E. *Animals and the Church*. Salt Lake City, UT: Eborn Books, 2003.

———. "Apocryphal literature and the Latter-day Saints." In *Apocryphal Writings and the Latter-day Saints*, edited by C. Wilfred Griggs. *Religious Studies Monograph Series* 13, 19-33. Provo, UT: Religious Studies Center, Brigham Young University, 1986.

Jones, Gracia N. *Emma and Joseph: Their Divine Mission*. American Fork, UT: Covenant Communications, 1999.

Jones, Norman. "Shakespeare's England." In *A Companion to Shakespeare*, edited by David Scott Kastan, 25-56. Oxford, England: Blackwell Publishers, 1999.

Jones, Robin. "An Englishman abroad: Sir James Emerson Tennent in Ceylon, 1845-50." *Apollo: The International Magazine for Collectors*, November 2006. http://findarticles.com/p/articles/mi_m0PAL/is_537_164/ai_n16865262/pg_1 (accessed March 13, 2008).

Jones, Steven E. "Was there death before Adam?" In *Death Before Adam*. http://www.tungate.com/Death_Before_Adam.htm (accessed July 14, 2008).

Josephus, Flavius. 37-ca. 97. "The Antiquities of the Jews." In *The Genuine Works of Flavius Josephus, the Jewish Historian. Translated from the Original Greek, according to Havercamp's Accurate Edition*. Translated by William Whiston, 23-426. London, England: W. Bowyer, 1737. Reprint, Grand Rapids, MI: Kregel Publications, 1980.

———, ed. 37-ca. 97. *The Genuine Works of Flavius Josephus, the Jewish Historian. Translated from the Original Greek, according to Havercamp's Accurate Edition*. Translated by William Whiston. London, England: W. Bowyer, 1737. Reprint, Grand Rapids, MI: Kregel Publications, 1980.

———. 37-ca. 97. *Jewish Antiquities*. Vol. 5-13 of the *Works of Josephus*. Translated by Henry St. John Thackaray, Ralph Marcus, Allen Wikgren and Louis H. Feldman. *Loeb Classical Library* 242, 490, 281, 326, 365, 489, 410, 433, 456. Cambridge, MA: Harvard University Press, 1930-1965.

———. 37-ca. 97. *Josephus: The Essential Works*. Translated by Paul L. Maier. 5th ed. Grand Rapids, MI: Kregel Academic and Professional, 1995.

———. 37-ca. 97. *The New Complete Works of Josephus*. Translated by Paul L. Maier and William Whiston. Grand Rapids, MI: Kregel Publications, 1999.

———. 37-ca. 97. "The Wars of the Jews." In *The Genuine Works of Flavius Josephus, the Jewish Historian. Translated from the Original Greek, according to Havercamp's Accurate Edition*. Translated by William Whiston, 427-605. London, England: W. Bowyer, 1737. Reprint, Grand Rapids, MI: Kregel Publications, 1980.

Jospe, Raphael, Truman G. Madsen, and Seth Ward, eds. *Covenant and Chosenness in Judaism and Mormonism*. Madison, NJ: Fairleigh Dickenson University Press, 2001.

Justin Martyr. d. ca. 165. "Dialogue with Trypho." In *The Ante-Nicene Fathers (The Writings of the Fathers Down to AD 325)*, edited by Alexander Roberts and James Donaldson. 10 vols. Vol. 1, 194-270. Buffalo, NY: The Christian Literature Company, 1885. Reprint, Peabody, MA: Hendrickson Publishers, 2004.

Kahne, Marcel. "La Genèse et la symbolique de la création." In *Iduméa-Études*, edited by Bruno Kahne. 2 vols. Vol. 1, 10-13. Castelnau d'Estretefonds , France: Iduméa, 2004.

Kaiser, Walter C., Jr. "Exodus." In *The Expositor's Bible Commentary*, edited by Frank E. Gaebelein, 287-497. Grand Rapids, MI: Zondervan, 1990.

———. *Toward an Old Testament Theology*. Grand Rapids, MI: Zondervan Publishing House, 1991.

Kaplan, Abraham. *The Conduct of Inquiry*. New York: Harper and Row, 1963.

Kaplan, Abraham. "The meanings of ritual: Comparisons." In *Reflections on Mormonism: Judeo-Christian Parallels, Papers Delivered at the Religious Studies Center Symposium, Brigham Young University, March 10-11, 1978*, edited by Truman G. Madsen. *Religious Studies Monograph Series* 4, 37-56. Provo, UT: Religious Studies Center, Brigham Young University, 1978.

Kaplan, Aryeh, ed. *The Bahir*. Revised ed. Newburyport, MA: Weiser Books, 1989.

———, ed. *Sefer Yetzirah: The Book of Creation*. Revised ed. Newburyport, MA: Weiser Books, 1997.

Karabell, Zachary. *Peace Be upon You: The Story of Muslim, Christian, and Jewish Coexistence*. New York City, NY: Alfred A. Knopf, 2007.

Karr, Don. 1985. "Notes on the study of Merkabah mysticism and Hekhalot literature in English with an appendix on Jewish Magic." In *Collected Articles on the Kabbalah*, edited by Don Karr. Vol. 1, 17-20. Ithaca, NY: KoM #5, 2006.

Kass, Leon R. *The Beginning of Wisdom: Reading Genesis*. New York City, NY: Free Press, Simon and Schuster, 2003.

Kastler, Esthi. 2006. "Commentaire du texte de Genèse 2.4b à 4.26." In *Études bibliques*, Fédération protestante de France. http://www.protestants.org/etudes-bibliques/genese/etude.htm (accessed August 25, 2007).

Kearney, Greg. "The message and the messenger: Latter-day Saints and Freemasonry." Presented at the *FAIR Conference*, August, 2005. http://www.fairlds.org/FAIR_Conferences/2005_Latter-day_Saints_and_Freemasonry.html (accessed February 22, 2009).

Keber, Eloise Quiñones, ed. *Codex Telleriano-Remensis: Ritual, Divination, and History in a Pictorial Aztec Manuscript*. Austin, TX: University of Texas Press, 1995.

Kee, Howard C. ed. "Testaments of the Twelve Patriarchs." In *The Old Testament Pseudepigrapha*, edited by James H. Charlesworth. Vol. 1, 775-828. Garden City, NY: Doubleday and Company, 1983.

Keele, Alan. "*Die Zauberflöte*: Mozart's magical celebration of Apotheosis, the man/woman monad, and the temple as blueprint for the celestial life." In *In Search of the Supernal: Pre-Existence, Eternal Marriage, and Apotheosis in German Literary, Operatic, and Cinematic Texts*, edited by Alan Keele, 79-136. Münster, Germany: agenda Verlag, 2003.

———. "Toward an anthropology of apotheosis in Mozart's 'Magic Flute': A demonstration of the artistic universality and vitality of certain 'peculiar' Latter-day Saint doctrines." *BYU Studies* 43, no. 3 (2004): 43-83.

Keller, Roger R. "Adam: As understood by four men who shaped Western Christianity." In *The Man Adam*, edited by Joseph Fielding McConkie and Robert L. Millet, 151-88. Salt Lake City, UT: Bookcraft, 1990.

———. "Teaching the Fall and the Atonement: A comparative method." *The Religious Educator: Perspectives on the Restored Gospel* 5, no. 2 (2004): 101-18. http://rsc.byu.edu/TRE/TRE5_2.pdf. (accessed September 1, 2009).

Kelly, George A. "A brief introduction to personal construct theory." In *Perspectives in Personal Construct Theory*, edited by D. Bannister, 1-29. London: Academic Press, 1970.

———. "A mathematical approach to psychology." In *Clinical Psychology and Personality: The Selected Papers of George Kelly*, edited by B. A. Maher, 7-45. New York: Wiley, 1969.

———. *The Psychology of Personal Constructs*. 2 vols. New York: Norton, 1955.

Kelly, Henry Ansgar. *Satan: A Biography*. Cambridge, England: Cambridge University Press, 2006.

Kelly, Joseph F., and Jeanne-Nicole Saint-Laurent. "*Instrumenta studiorum*: Tools of the trade." In *The Oxford Handbook of Early Christian Studies*, edited by Susan Ashbrook Harvey and David G. Hunter. *Oxford Handbooks in Religion and Theology*, 957-77. Oxford, England: Oxford University Press, 2008.

Kempis, Thomas à. 1441. *The Imitation of Christ: A New Reading of the 1441 Latin Autograph Manuscript*. Translated by William C. Creasy. Edited by William C. Creasy. Macon, GA: Mercer University Press, 2007.

Kendrick, Albert Frank. *Catalogue of Textiles from Burying-Grounds in Egypt*. 3 vols. Vol. 1: Greco-Roman Period. London, England: Victoria and Albert Museum Department of Textiles, published under the authority of His Majesty's Stationery Office, 1920. http://books.google.com/books?id=SGq1AAAAIAAJ (accessed September 12, 2008).

Kennedy, Michael. 1964. *The Works of Ralph Vaughan Williams*. 2nd ed. Oxford, England: Clarendon Press, 1992.

Kerényi, Carl. *Eleusis: Archetypal Image of Mother and Daughter*. Translated by Ralph Manheim. Princeton, NJ: Princeton University Press, 1967.

Kerry, Paul E. "'Initiates of Isis Now, Come, Enter into the Temple!': Masonic and Enlightenment thought in *The Magic Flute*." *BYU Studies* 43, no. 3 (2004): 104-28.

———. "Thomas Carlyle's draft essay on the Mormons." *Literature and Belief* 25, no. 1-2 (2005): 261-88.

Keyte, Hugh, and Andrew Parrott ed. "Noël Nouvelet." In *The Shorter New Oxford Book of Carols*, 298-99. Oxford, England: Oxford University Press, 1993.

Khalidi, Tarif, ed. *The Muslim Jesus: Sayings and Stories in Islamic Literature*. Convergences: Inventories of the Present, ed. Edward E. Said. Cambridge, MA: Harvard University Press, 2001.

Kierkegaard, Søren. 1843. *Fear and Trembling: A Dialectical Lyric*. Translated by Walter Lowrie. Princeton, NJ: Princeton University Press, 1941.

———. 1851. "For Self-Examination." In *For Self-Examination; Judge for Yourself!*, edited by Howard V. Hong and Edna H. Hong. *Kierkegaard's Writings* 21, 1-87. Princeton, NJ: Princeton University Press, 1990.

———. *Parables of Kierkegaard*. Edited by Thomas C. Oden. Princeton, NJ: Princeton University Press, 1978.

———. 1844. *Purity of Heart is to Will One Thing*. Translated by Douglas V. Steere. New York, NY: Harper and Row, 1956.

Kikawada, Isaac M., and Arthur Quinn. 1985. *Before Abraham Was: The Unity of Genesis 1-11*. San Francisco, CA: Ignatius Press, 1989.

Kimball, Edward L. E-mail message to Jeffrey M. Bradshaw, January 3, 2009.

Kimball, Heber Chase. 1856. "Remarks at the funeral of President Jedediah M. Grant made in the Tabernacle, Great Salt Lake City, 4 December 1856." In *Journal of Discourses*. 26 vols. Vol. 4, 135-38. Liverpool and London, England: Latter-day Saints Book Depot, 1853-1886. Reprint, Salt Lake City, UT: Bookcraft, 1966.

———. 1861. "Unity; commandments of God, etc. (Discourse by Heber C. Kimball, made in the Tabernacle, Great Salt Lake City, January 6, 1861)." In *Journal of Discourses*. 26 vols. Vol. 8, 327-34. Liverpool and London, England: Latter-day Saints Book Depot, 1853-1886. Reprint, Salt Lake City, UT: Bookcraft, 1966. Also reported in *Journal of Discourses*, Vol. 9, 126-133.

———. 1861. "Submission to reproof, etc. (Remarks made in the Tabernacle, Great Salt Lake City, 17 March 1861)." In *Journal of Discourses*. 26 vols. Vol. 9, 40-43. Liverpool and London, England: Latter-day Saints Book Depot, 1853-1886. Reprint, Salt Lake City, UT: Bookcraft, 1966.

———. 1868. "Forbearance to each other; necessity of reading the Bible and Book of Mormon; counsel to the young brethren (Remarks made in the Tabernacle, Bountiful, Sunday, 12 April 1868)." In *Journal of Discourses*. 26 vols. Vol. 12, 188-91. Liverpool and London, England: Latter-day Saints Book Depot, 1853-1886. Reprint, Salt Lake City, UT: Bookcraft, 1966.

Kimball, Spencer W. "'Be ye therefore perfect.'" (BYU Devotional address given on September 17, 1974). In *BYU Speeches*. http://speeches.byu.edu/reader/reader.php?id=6057 (accessed September 3, 2007).

———. "Becoming the pure in heart." *Ensign* 8, May 1978, 79-81.

———. "The blessings and responsibilities of womanhood." *Ensign* 6, March 1976, 70-73.

———. "An eternal hope in Christ." *Ensign* 8, November 1978, 71-73.

———. "The false gods we worship." *Ensign* 6, June 1976, 3-6.

———. "'… For they shall see God.'" *Improvement Era* 67, June 1964, 496-99.

———. 1976. "The importance of celestial marriage." *Ensign* 9, October 1979, 3-6.

———. *The Miracle of Forgiveness*. Salt Lake City, UT: Bookcraft, 1969.

———. "The mistletoe." In *Faith Precedes the Miracle*, 225-31. Salt Lake City, UT: Deseret Book, 1972.

———. "Our great potential." *Ensign* 7, May 1977, 49-51.

———. "Our own Liahona." *Ensign* 6, November 1976, 77-79.

———. "Revelation: The word of the Lord to His prophets." *Ensign* 7, May 1977, 76-78.

———. "The role of righteous women." *Ensign* 9, November 1979, 102-04.

———. *The Teachings of Spencer W. Kimball*. Edited by Edward L. Kimball. Salt Lake City, UT: Bookcraft, 1982.

———. "'Temptation and a snare.'" In *Faith Precedes the Miracle*, 233-48. Salt Lake City, UT: Deseret Book, 1972.

Kimball, Spencer W., N. Eldon Tanner, and Marion G. Romney. 1978. "Statement of the First Presidency: God's love for all mankind." Included in entirety in Palmer, Spencer J., ed. *The Expanding Church*. Salt Lake City, UT: Deseret Book, 1978, initial page. Excerpted in S. J. Palmer article "World Religions, Overview." In *Encyclopedia of Mormonism*, edited by Daniel H. Ludlow. 4 vols. Vol. 4, 1589. New York City, NY: Macmillan, 1992. http://www.lib.byu.edu/Macmillan/ (accessed November 26, 2007).

Kimball, Stanley B. 1981. *Heber C. Kimball: Mormon Patriarch and Pioneer*. Illini Books ed. Urbana, IL: University of Illinois Press, 1986.

King, Arthur Henry. 1971. "An Account of My Conversion." In *Arm the Children: Faith's Response to a Violent World*, edited by Daryl Hague, 27-53. Provo, UT: BYU Studies, 1998.

———. "Afterword." In *Feasting Upon the Word*, edited by Dennis Packard and Sandra Packard, 229-37. Salt Lake City, UT: Deseret Book, 1981.

———. "Atonement: The only wholeness." In *Arm the Children: Faith's Response to a Violent World*, edited by Daryl Hague, 317-29. Provo, UT: BYU Studies, 1998.

———. 1971. "The Child is Father to the Man." In *Arm the Children: Faith's Response to a Violent World*, edited by Daryl Hague, 101-19. Provo, UT: BYU Studies, 1998.

———. 1992. "Education in the home." In *Arm the Children: Faith's Response to a Violent World*, edited by Daryl Hague, 229-48. Provo, UT: BYU Studies, 1998.

———. 1992. "God's healing wholeness." In *Arm the Children: Faith's Response to a Violent World*, edited by Daryl Hague, 331-47. Provo, UT: BYU Studies, 1998.

———. 1992. "Joseph Smith as a Writer." In *Arm the Children: Faith's Response to a Violent World*, edited by Daryl Hague, 285-93. Provo, UT: BYU Studies, 1998.

———. "Language, Humour, Character, and Persona in Shakespeare." In *By Study and Also by Faith*, edited by John M. Lundquist and Stephen D. Ricks. 2 vols. Vol. 2, 456-82. Salt Lake City, UT: Deseret Book, 1990.

———. 1971. "Moral significance in Anglo-Saxon literature." In *Arm the Children: Faith's Response to a Violent World*, edited by Daryl Hague, 163-79. Provo, UT: BYU Studies, 1998.

———. "Religion, art, and morality." In *Arm the Children: Faith's Response to a Violent World*, edited by Daryl Hague. Provo, UT: BYU Studies, 1998.

———. 1971. "Rhetoric." In *Arm the Children: Faith's Response to a Violent World*, edited by Daryl Hague, 199-215. Provo, UT: BYU Studies, 1998.

———. "Style in Shakespeare." In *Arm the Children: Faith's Response to a Violent World*, edited by Daryl Hague, 217-25. Provo, UT: BYU Studies, 1998.

———. 1971. "Total language." In *Arm the Children: Faith's Response to a Violent World*, edited by Daryl Hague, 183-90. Provo, UT: BYU Studies, 1998.

King, Hannah T. "Reminiscence of Victor Hugo." *Contributor* 7, February 1886, 198.

Kingsley-Smith, Jane. "*The Tempest's* forgotten exile." In *Shakespeare and Religions*, edited by Peter D. Holland. *Shakespeare Survey: An Annual Survey of Shakespeare Studies and Production* 54, ed. Peter D. Holland, 223-33. Cambridge, England: Cambridge University Press, 2001.

Kinnaman, David, and Gabe Lyons. *Unchristian*. Grand Rapids, MI: Baker Books, 2007.

Kirkham, Francis W. . 1942. *A New Witness for Christ in America: The Book of Mormon*. 2 vols. Vol. 1. 3rd Enlarged ed. Provo, UT: Brigham Young University, 1960.

Kittel, Gerhard, and Gerhard Friedrich. *Theological Dictionary of the New Testament*. 10 vols. Grand Rapids, MI: William B. Eerdmans, 1977.

Klauck, Hans-Josef. *The Religious Context of Early Christianity: A Guide to Greco-Roman Religions (Die religiöse Umwelt des Urchistentums)*. Translated by Brian McNeil. Minneapolis, MN: Fortress Press, 2003.

Klein, Michael L., ed. *The Fragment Targums of the Pentateuch According to Their Extant Sources*. 2 vols. Rome, Italy: Pontifical Biblical Institute, 1970.

———, ed. *Geniza Manuscripts of Palestinian Targum to the Pentateuch*. 2 vols. Springfield, NJ: Behrman House, 1987.

Klijn, A. F. J. ed. "2 (Syriac Apocalypse of) Baruch." In *The Old Testament Pseudepigrapha*, edited by James H. Charlesworth. Vol. 1, 615-52. Garden City, NY: Doubleday and Company, 1983.

Knibb, M. A. ed. "Martyrdom and Ascension of Isaiah." In *The Old Testament Pseudepigrapha*, edited by James H. Charlesworth. 2 vols. Vol. 2, 143-76. Garden City, NY: Doubleday and Company, 1983.

Knuth, Donald E. *3:16 — Bible Texts Illuminated*. Madison, WI: A-R Editions, 1991.

Koch, Klaus. "Wort und Einheit des Schöpfergottes in Memphis und Jerusalem: Zur Einzigartigkeit Israels." *Zeitschrift für Theologie un Kirche* 62 (1965): 251-52.

Koenen, Ludwig, and Cornelia Eva Römer, eds. *Der Kölner Mani-Kodex: Über das Werden seines Leibes (Edition und Übersetzung)* Critical ed. Translated by Ludwig Koenen and Cornelia Römer. *Sonderreihe der Abhandlungen Papyrologica Coloniensia* 14. Opladen, Germany: Westdeutscher Verlag, 1988.

Koester, Craig R. *Hebrews: A New Translation with Introduction and Commentary*. The Anchor Bible 36. New Haven, CT: Yale University Press, 2001.

———. *Symbolism in the Fourth Gospel: Meaning, Mystery, Community*. 2nd ed. Minneapolis, MN: Fortress, 2003.

Koester, Helmut, and Thomas O. Lambdin ed. "The Gospel of Thomas (II, 2)." In *The Nag Hammadi Library in English*, edited by James M. Robinson. 3rd, Completely Revised ed, 124-38. San Francisco, CA: HarperSanFrancisco, 1990.

———. *Introduction to the New Testament: History and Literature of Early Christianity*. 2 vols. Vol. 2. 2nd ed. Berlin, Germany: Walter de Gruyter, 2000.

———. *Introduction to the New Testament: History, Culture, and Religion of the Hellenstic Age*. 2 vols. Vol. 1. 2nd ed. Berlin, Germany: Walter de Gruyter, 1995.

Kohlenberger, John R., III, ed. *The Interlinear NIV Hebrew-English Old Testament*. Grand Rapids, MI: Zondervan, 1993.

Koltun-Fromm, Naomi. "Aphrahat and the rabbis on Noah's righteousness in light of the Jewish-Christian polemic." In *The Book of Genesis in Jewish and Oriental Christian Interpretation*, edited by Judith Frishman and Lucas Van Rompay. *Traditio Exegetica Graeca*, vol. 5, 57-71. Louvain, Belgium: Editions Peeters, 1997.

Kourcikidze, C. and J.-P. Mahé, eds. *La Caverne des Trésors, Version géorgienne*. 2 vols. *Corpus Scriptorum Christianorum Orientalium* 526-527 (*Scriptores Iberici* 23-24). Louvain, Belgium: Peeters, 1993.

Kraeling, Carl H., C. C. Torrey, C. B. Welles, and B. Geiger. *The Synagogue*. Edited by A. R. Bellinger, F. E. Brown, A. Perkins and C. B. Welles. *The Excavations at Dura-Europos Conducted by Yale University and the French Academy of Inscriptions and Letters: Final Report VIII, Part I*. New Haven, CT: Yale University Press, 1956.

Kraft, Robert A. "The pseudepigrapha in Christianity." In *Tracing the Threads: Studies in the Vitality of Jewish Pseudepigrapha*, edited by John C. Reeves, 55-86. Atlanta, GA: Scholars Press, 1994.

———, ed. *The Testament of Job According to the SV Text*. Texts and Translations 5, *Pseudepigrapha Series* 4. Missoula, Montana: Society of Biblical Literature and Scholars' Press, 1974.

Kramer, S. N. ed. "Dumuzi and Enkimdu: The Dispute between the Shepherd-God and the Farmer-God." In *Ancient Near Eastern Texts Relating to the Old Testament*, edited by James B. Pritchard, 41-42. Princeton, NJ: Princeton University Press, 1972.

Kraus, Hans-Joachim. *Theology of the Psalms*. Minneapolis, MN: Augsburg, 1986.

Krauss, Lawrence M., and Richaard Dawkins. "Should science speak to faith?" *Scientific American*, July 2007, 88-91. http://www.sciam.com/article.cfm?chanId=sa013&articleID=44A95E1D-E7F2-99DF-3E79D5E2E6DE809C (accessed August 26, 2007).

———. 2007. "Should science speak to faith?" Extended version. In *Scientific American Online*. http://www.sciam.com/article.cfm?chanId=sa013&articleID=44A95E1D-E7F2-99DF-3E79D5E2E6DE809C (accessed July 27, 2007).

Krauss, Lawrence M., and Robert J. Scherrer. "The end of cosmology?" *Scientific American* 298, March 2008, 46-53.

Kren, Emil, and Daniel Marx. n.d. "The Ghent Altarpiece: The offering of Abel and Cain." In *Web Gallery of Art*. http://www.wga.hu/frames-e.html?/html/e/eyck_van/jan/09ghent/1open1/u2cain.html (accessed August 26, 2006).

Kriwaczek, Paul. *In Search of Zarathustra: The First Prophet and the Ideas That Changed the World*. New York City, NY: Alfred A. Knopf, 2002.

Kugel, James L. *The Bible As It Was*. Cambridge, MA: The Belknap Press of Harvard University Press, 1997.

———. *The God of Old: Inside the Lost World of the Bible*. New York City, NY: The Free Press, 2003.

———. *How to Read the Bible: A Guide to Scripture, Then and Now*. New York City, NY: Free Press, 2007.

———. "Some instances of biblical interpretation in the hymns and wisdom writings of Qumran." In *Studies in Ancient Midrash*, edited by James L. Kugel, 155-69. Cambridge, MA: Harvard University Press, 2001.

———. *Traditions of the Bible*. Revised ed. Cambridge, MA: Harvard University Press, 1998.

Kulik, A. *Retroverting Slavonic Pseudepigrapha: Toward the Original of the Apocalypse of Abraham. Text-Critical Studies* 3, ed. J.R. Adair, Jr. Atlanta, GA: Society of Biblical Literature, 2004.

Küng, Hans. 2005. *The Beginning of All Things: Science and Religion*. Translated by John Bowden. Grand Rapids, MI: William R. Eerdmans, 2007.

LaCocque, André. *The Trial of Innocence: Adam, Eve, and the Yahwist*. Eugene, OR: Cascade Books, 2006.

"Lactantius." In *Wikipedia*. http://en.wikipedia.org/wiki/Lactantius (accessed April 17, 2009).

Lactantius. ca. 303-311. "The Divine Institutes (*Divinarum Institutionum*)." In *The Ante-Nicene Fathers (The Writings of the Fathers Down to AD 325)*, edited by Alexander Roberts and James Donaldson. 10 vols. Vol. 7, 9-223. Buffalo, NY: The Christian Literature Company, 1886. Reprint, Peabody, MA: Hendrickson Publishers, 2004.

Lair, John. *Songs Lincoln Loved, with an Introduction by William H. Townsend*. New York City, NY and Boston, MA: Duell, Sloan and Pearce; Little, Brown and Company, 1954.

Lake, Peter. "Religious Identities in Shakespeare's England." In *A Companion to Shakespeare*, edited by David Scott Kastan, 57-84. Oxford, England: Blackwell Publishers, 1999.

Lane, Jennifer. "The redemption of Abraham." In *Astronomy, Papyrus, and Covenant*, 167-74. Provo, UT: Foundation for Ancient Research and Mormon Studies (FARMS), Brigham Young University, 2005.

Lane, William L. *Hebrews 9-13. Word Biblical Commentary* 47B, eds. David A. Hubbard, Glenn Barker, W. and John D. W. Watts. Nashville, TN: Thomas Nelson, 1991.

Larsen, David J. E-mail message to Jeffrey M. Bradshaw, December 6, 2008.

———. "Two high priesthoods? Evidence for non-Levitical priesthood in ancient Israel," 2009, in press.

Larsen, David J. and Jeffrey M. Bradshaw. The vision of Moses as a heavenly ascent: New light from the *Apocalypse of Abraham*. Article in preparation.

Larson, Stan. "The King Follett Discourse: A newly amalgamated text." *BYU Studies* 18, no. 2 (Winter 1978): 193-208.

Lasch, Christopher. 1995. *The Revolt of the Elites and the Betrayal of Democracy*. New York City, NY: W. W. Norton, 1996.

Latter Day Saints' Messenger and Advocate. Kirtland, OH, 1834-1837. Reprint, 3 vols.

Law, William. 1728. "A Serious Call to a Devout and Holy Life." In *William Law: 'A Serious Call to a Devout and Holy Life' and 'The Spirit of Love'*, edited by Paul G. Stanwood. *The Classics of Western Spirituality: A Library of the Great Spiritual Masters*, ed. Richard J. Payne, 41-352. New York City, NY: Paulist Press, 1978.

Layton, Bentley, ed. *The Gnostic Scriptures: A New Translation with Annotations and Introductions. The Anchor Bible Reference Library*, ed. David Noel Freedman. New York City, NY: Doubleday, 1987.

———, ed. "The Secret Book According to John." In *The Gnostic Scriptures: A New Translation with Annotations and Introductions*, edited by Bentley Layton, 23-51. New York City, NY: Doubleday, 1987.

Lee, Harold B. "Keep your lamp lighted." *Improvement Era* 73, December 1970, 103-05.

———. 1960. "The place of the Church, Address to Seminary and Institute Faculty, Brigham Young University, June 24, 1960, pp. 12-13 (Excerpt)." In *Determining Doctrine: A Reference Guide for Evaluating Doctrinal Truth*, edited by Dennis B. Horne, 193. Roy, UT: Eborn Books, 2005.

———. "Strengthen the stakes of Zion." *Ensign* 3, July 1973, 2-6.

———. *The Teachings of Harold B. Lee*. Edited by Clyde J. Williams. Salt Lake City, UT: Bookcraft, 1996.

———. *Teachings of the Presidents of the Church: Harold B. Lee*. Salt Lake City, UT: The Church of Jesus Christ of Latter-day Saints, 2000.

———. "To know God." *Improvement Era* 72, 1969, 103-05.

———. *Ye Are the Light of the World: Selected Sermons and Writings of President Harold B. Lee*. Salt Lake City, UT: Deseret Book, 1974.

Leemhuis, Fred. "From palm leaves to the Internet." In *The Cambridge Companion to the Qur'an*, edited by Jane Dammen McAuliffe, 145-61. Cambridge, England: Cambridge University Press, 2006.

Leeming, David. *The Oxford Companion to World Mythology*. Oxford, England: Oxford University Press, 2005.

Legg, Phillip R. *Oliver Cowdery: The Elusive Second Elder of the Restoration*. Independence, MO: Herald House, 1989.

Lemon, Steevun. "J. Kirk Richards: LDS painter has fresh vision for inspirational art." *Meridian Magazine* (June 13 2005). http://www.meridianmagazine.com/arts/050613richards.html.

Leonard, Glen M. *Nauvoo: A Place of Peace, A People of Promise*. Salt Lake City, UT: Deseret Book, 2002.

Leone, Mark P. *The Roots of Modern Mormonism*. Cambridge, MA: Harvard University Press, 1979.

Leonhard, Clemens. "Observations on the date of the Syriac Cave of Treasures." In *The World of the Aramaeans III: Studies in Honor of Paul-Eugène Dion*, edited by P. M. Michèle Daviau, John William Wevers and Michael Weigl. *Journal for the Study of the Old Testament Supplement Series* 326, eds. David J. A. Clines and Philip R. Davies, 255-93. Sheffield, England: Sheffield Academic Press, 2001.

"Letter to Professor Miroslav Šťastný of 24 January 1984." In *Zdenek Kopal*. http://www.litomysl.cz/zdenekkopal/?lang=en&menu=g&img=10 (accessed October 28, 2007).

Lettieri, Gaetano. "The ambiguity of Eden and the Enigma of Adam." In *The Earthly Paradise: The Garden of Eden from Antiquity to Modernity*, edited by F. Regina Psaki and Charles Hindley. *International Studies in Formative Christianity and Judaism*, 23-54. Binghamton, NY: Academic Studies in the History of Judaism, Global Publications, State University of New York at Binghamton, 2002.

Levering, Miriam, ed. *Rethinking Scripture: Essays from a Comparative Perspective*. Albany, NY: SUNY Press, 1989.

Levine, Baruch A. *In the Presence of the Lord*. Leiden, The Netherlands: Brilll, 1974.

Levine, Lee I. 1998. *The Ancient Synagogue: The First Thousand Years*. 2nd ed. New Haven, CT: Yale University Press, 2005.

———. *Judaism and Hellenism in Antiquity: Conflict or Confluence? The Samuel and Althea Stroum Lectures in Jewish Studies*. Peabody, MA: Hendrickson Publishers, 1999.

Levy, B. Barry. *Fixing God's Torah: The Accuracy of the Hebrew Bible Text in Jewish Law*. Oxford, England: Oxford University Press, 2001.

Lewis, Bernard. 2003. *The Crisis of Islam: Holy War and Unholy Terror*. London, England: Phoenix, Orion Books, 2004.

———. 1993. *Islam in History: Ideas, People, and Events in the Middle East*. 2nd ed. Chicago, IL: Open Court, 2002.

Lewis, C. S. 1946. "Appendix B: On special providences." In *Miracles*, 226-34. New York City, NY: Touchstone, Simon and Schuster, 1996.

———. 1939. "Christianity and literature." In *C. S. Lewis: Essay Collection and Other Short Pieces*, edited by Lesley Walmsley, 411-20. London, England: HarperCollins, 2000.

———. *The Collected Letters of C. S. Lewis*. Vol. 3: Narnia, Cambridge, and Joy 1950-1963. Edited by Walter Hooper. San Francisco, CA: HarperSanFrancisco, 2007.

———. 1955. "'De Descriptione Temporum.'" In *Selected Literary Essays*, edited by Walter Hooper, 1-14. Cambridge, England: Cambridge University Press, 1969.

———. *The Discarded Image*. Cambridge, England: Cambridge University Press, 1964.

———. 1943. "Dogma and the universe (Originally: Dogma and science)." In *C. S. Lewis: Essay Collection and Other Short Pieces*, edited by Lesley Walmsley, 118-26. London, England: HarperCollins, 2000.

———. *The Four Loves*. New York City, NY: Harcourt Brace Jovanovich, 1960.

———. 1946. *The Great Divorce*. New York City, NY: Touchstone, 1996.

———. 1939. "Learning in war-time." In *C. S. Lewis: Essay Collection and Other Short Pieces*, edited by Lesley Walmsley, 47-63. London, England: HarperCollins, 2000.

———. 1964. *Letters to Malcolm, Chiefly on Prayer: Reflections on the Intimate Dialogue Between Man and God*. San Diego, CA: Harcourt, 1991.

———. 1946. "Man or rabbit?" In *C. S. Lewis: Essay Collection and Other Short Pieces*, edited by Lesley Walmsley, 352-56. London, England: HarperCollins, 2000.

———. 1942-1944. *Mere Christianity*. New York City, NY: Touchstone, 1996.

———. 1946. *Miracles*. New York City, NY: Touchstone, Simon and Schuster, 1996.

———. 1944. *Perelandra*. New York City, NY: Scribner, 2003.

———. 1942. *A Preface to Paradise Lost*. London, England: Oxford University Press, 1961.

———. 1962. *The Problem of Pain*. New York City, NY: Touchstone, 1996.

———. 1958. *Reflections on the Psalms*. San Diego, CA: Harcourt, A Harvest Book, 1964.

———. 1946. "Religion without dogma?" In *C. S. Lewis: Essay Collection and Other Short Pieces*, edited by Lesley Walmsley, 163-78. London, England: HarperCollins, 2000.

———. 1941. *The Screwtape Letters*. New York, NY: Touchstone, 1996.

———. 1943. "Three kinds of men." In *C. S. Lewis: Essay Collection and Other Short Pieces*, edited by Lesley Walmsley, 315-16. London, England: HarperCollins, 2000.

———. 1956. *Till We Have Faces: A Myth Retold*. San Diego, CA: Harcourt, 1984.

———. 1941. "The weight of glory." In *C. S. Lewis: Essay Collection and Other Short Pieces*, edited by Lesley Walmsley, 96-106. London, England: HarperCollins, 2000.

Lewis, Lionel Smithett. 1922. *St. Joseph of Arimathea at Glastonbury or The Apostolic Church of Britain*. 7th ed. Cambridge, England: James Clarke, 1983.

Lewis, Mark Edward. *The Construction of Space in Early China*. Albany, NY: State University of New York Press, 2006.

———. *The Early Chinese Empires: Qin and Han. History of Imperial China 1*, ed. Timothy Brook. Cambridge, MA: The Belknap Press of Harvard University Press, 2007.

———. *The Flood Myths of Early China*. Albany, NY: State University of New York Press, 2006.

———. *Writing and Authority in Early China*. Albany, NY: State University of New York Press, 1999.

Lichtheim, Miriam, ed. 1973-1980. *Ancient Egyptian Literature: A Book of Readings*. 3 vols. Berkeley, CA: The University of California Press, 2006.

———. *Late Egyptian Wisdom Literature in the International Context: A Study of Demotic Instructions*. Göttingen, Germany: Vandenhoeck and Ruprecht, 1983.

———, ed. 1973. "'The Memphite Theology.'" In *Ancient Egyptian Literature: A Book of Readings*, edited by Miriam Lichtheim. 3 vols. Vol. 1, 51-57. Berkeley, CA: The University of California Press, 2006.

Lidzbarski, Mark, ed. *Das Johannesbuch der Mandäer*. 2 vols. Giessen, Germany: Alfred Töpelmann, 1905, 1915.

———, ed. *Ginza: Der Schatz oder das Grosse Buch der Mandäer. Quellen der Religionsgeschichte, der Reihenfolge des Erscheinens* 13:4. Göttingen and Leipzig, Germany: Vandenhoeck & Ruprecht, J. C. Hinrichs'sche, 1925.

———. *Mandäische Liturgien*. Berlin, Germany: Weidmannsche Buchhandlung, 1920.

Lieber, David L., ed. *Etz Hayim: Torah and Commentary*. New York City, NY: The Rabbinical Assembly of the United Synagogue of Conservative Judaism, produced by The Jewish Publication Society, 2001.

Lieber, Moshe. *The Pirkei Avos Treasury: Ethics of the Fathers. The Sages' Guide to Living, with an Anthologized Commentary and Anecdotes*. Edited by Nosson Scherman. *Artscroll Mesorah Series*. Brooklyn, NY: Mesorah Publications, 1995.

Lieu, Samuel N. C., ed. *Dictionary of Manichaean Texts*. Vol. 1: Texts from the Roman Empire (Texts in Syriac, Greek, Coptic and Latin). *Corpus Fontium Manichaeorum, Series Subsidia* 2, 1999.

———. "Manichaeism." In The *Oxford Handbook of Early Christian Studies*, edited by Susan Ashbrook Harvey and David G. Hunter. *Oxford Handbooks in Religion and Theology*, 221-36. Oxford, England: Oxford University Press, 2008.

———. *Manichaeism in Central Asia and China. Nag Hammadi and Manichaean Studies* 45. Leiden, The Netherlands: Brill, 1998.

———. "Manichaeism in China." In *Order of Nazorean Essenes*. http://essenes.net/new/maniinchina.html (accessed December 29, 2007).

Lindquist, Danille Christensen. "'Old devils' or 'joint-heirs': Pre-existent intelligences in Christian theodicy and Mormon doctrine." In *Archive of Restoration Culture: Summer Fellows' Papers 1997-1999*, edited by Richard Lyman Bushman, 119-31. Provo, UT: Joseph Fielding Smith Institute for Latter-day Saint History, 2000.

Lipscomb, W. Lowndes, ed. *The Armenian Apocryphal Literature. University of Pennsylvania Armenian Texts and Studies* 8, ed. Michael E. Stone. Philadelphia, PA: University of Pennsylvania, 1990.

———, ed. "Concerning the Good Tidings of Seth." In *The Armenian Apocryphal Literature*, edited by W. Lowndes

Lipscomb. *University of Pennsylvania Armenian Texts and Studies* 8, ed. Michael E. Stone, 172-205, 55-60, 76-82. Philadelphia, PA: University of Pennsylvania, 1990.

———, ed. "History of Abel and Cain, the sons of Adam." In *The Armenian Apocryphal Literature*, edited by W. Lowndes Lipscomb. *University of Pennsylvania Armenian Texts and Studies* 8, ed. Michael E. Stone, 142-71, 249-54, 70-75. Philadelphia, PA: University of Pennsylvania, 1990.

———, ed. "History of the Creation and transgression of Adam." In *The Armenian Apocryphal Literature*, edited by W. Lowndes Lipscomb. *University of Pennsylvania Armenian Texts and Studies* 8, ed. Michael E. Stone, 108-27, 241-45, 61-66. Philadelphia, PA: University of Pennsylvania, 1990.

———, ed. "History of the expulsion of Adam from the Garden." In *The Armenian Apocryphal Literature*, edited by W. Lowndes Lipscomb. *University of Pennsylvania Armenian Texts and Studies* 8, ed. Michael E. Stone, 128-41, 267-69. Philadelphia, PA: University of Pennsylvania, 1990.

———, ed. "History of the repentance of Adam and Eve." In *The Armenian Apocryphal Literature*, edited by W. Lowndes Lipscomb. *University of Pennsylvania Armenian Texts and Studies* 8, ed. Michael E. Stone, 210-33. Philadelphia, PA: University of Pennsylvania, 1990.

Litchfield, W. Reid. "The search for the physical cause of Jesus Christ's death." *BYU Studies* 37, no. 4 (1997-1998): 93-109.

Lobdell, William. *Losing My Religion: How I Lost My Faith Reporting on Religion in America—and Found Unexpected Peace.* New York City, NY: HarperCollins, 2009.

Loewe, Michael. *Ways to Paradise: The Chinese Quest for Immortality*. London, England: George Allen & Unwin, 1979.

Lomax, John A., Alan Lomax, and George Lyman Kittredge, eds. 1934. *American Ballads and Folk Songs*. New York City, NY: Macmillan Publishing Company, 1972.

L'Orange, H. P. *Studies on the Iconography of Cosmic Kingship in the Ancient World*. New Rochelle, NY: Caratzas Brothers and Instituttet for Sammenlignende Kulturforskning, 1982.

Lossky, Vladimir. 1974. *In the Image and Likeness of God*. Crestwood, NY: Saint Vladimir's Seminary Press, 2001.

———. 1944. *The Mystical Theology of the Eastern Church*. Crestwood, NY: St. Vladimir's Seminary Press, 1976.

Louth, Andrew, and Marco Conti, eds. *Genesis 1-11*. Ancient Christian Commentary on Scripture, Old Testament 1, ed. Thomas C. Oden. Downers Grove, IL: InterVarsity Press, 2001.

Lovejoy, Arthur O. 1936. *The Great Chain of Being: A Study of the History of an Idea*. Cambridge, MA: Harvard University Press, 1970.

Lowy, Simeon. *The Principles of Samaritan Bible Exegesis*. Studia Post-Biblica 28, ed. J. C. H. Lebram. Leiden, The Netherlands: E. J. Brill, 1977.

Ludlow, Daniel H., ed. *Encyclopedia of Mormonism*. 4 vols. New York City, NY: Macmillan, 1992. http://www.lib.byu.edu/Macmillan/ (accessed November 26, 2007).

Ludlow, Jared W. "Abraham's visions of the heavens." In *Astronomy, Papyrus, and Covenant*, edited by John Gee and Brian M. Hauglid. *Studies in the Book of Abraham* 3, 57-73. Provo, UT: Foundation for Ancient Research and Mormon Studies (FARMS), Brigham Young University, 2005. http://farms.byu.edu/publications/books/?bookid=40&chapid=164. (accessed October 10, 2008).

Ludlow, Victor L. *Principles and Practices of the Restored Gospel*. Salt Lake City, UT: Deseret Book, 1992.

Lundquist, Jason H. "Keywords: Joseph Smith, language change, and theological innovation, 1829-44." *Dialogue: A Journal of Mormon Thought* 38, no. 2 (Summer 2005): 1-38.

Lundquist, John M. "Fundamentals of temple ideology from Eastern traditions." In *Reason, Revelation, and Faith: Essays in Honor of Truman G. Madsen*, edited by Donald W. Parry, Daniel C. Peterson and Stephen D. Ricks, 651-701. Provo, UT: Foundation for Ancient Research and Mormon Studies, 2002.

———. "Temple, covenant, and law in the ancient Near East and in the Old Testament." In *Israel's Apostasy and Restoration: Essays in Honor of Roland K. Harrison*, edited by Avraham Gileadi, 293-305. Grand Rapids, MI: Baker Book House, 1988.

———. *The Temple: Meeting Place of Heaven and Earth*. London, England: Thames and Hudson, 1993.

———. *The Temple of Jerusalem: Past, Present, and Future*. Westport, CT: Praeger, 2008.

———. 1983. "What is a temple? A preliminary typology." In *Temples of the Ancient World*, edited by Donald W. Parry, 83-117. Salt Lake City, UT: Deseret Book, 1994.

———. "What is reality?" In *By Study and Also by Faith: Essays in Honor of Hugh W. Nibley*, edited by John M. Lundquist and Stephen D. Ricks. 2 vols. Vol. 1, 428-38. Salt Lake City, UT: Deseret Book, 1990.

Lundwall, N. B. 1968. *Temples of the Most High*. Revised and Enlarged ed. Salt Lake City, UT: Bookcraft, 1978.

Lunn, John E., and Ursula Vaughan Williams. *Ralph Vaughan Williams: A Pictorial Biography*. London, England: Oxford University Press, 1971.

Luo, Michael. "Crucial test for Romney in speech on his religion." New York City, NY: New York Times, December 6, 2007. http://www.nytimes.com/2007/12/06/us/politics/06romney.html?ref=politics (accessed December 6, 2007).

Lupieri, Edmondo. 1993. *The Mandaeans: The Last Gnostics. Italian Texts and Studies on Religion and Society*, ed. Edmondo Lupieri. Grand Rapids, MI: William B. Eerdmans Publishing Co., 2002.

Luz, Frédéric. *Orthodoxie*. Puiseaux, France: Éditions Pardès, 2001.

Lyon, Michael P. "Set design for the final scene in *The Magic Flute*." *BYU Studies* 43, no. 3 (2004): 270-72.

Lyon, Michael P. E-mail message to William J. Hamblin, September 8, 2008.

Macaulay, David. *Great Moments in Architecture*. Boston, MA: Houghton Mifflin, 1978.

MacDonald, Joan B. *The Holiness of Everyday Life*. Salt Lake City, UT: Deseret Book, 1995.

Mace, Wandle. "Autobiography." Typescript. Provo, UT: Perry Special Collections, Harold B. Lee Library, Brigham Young University, n.d.

Macho, A. Diez, ed. *Neophyti 1: Targum Palestinense Ms de la Bibliioteca Vaticana*. 5 vols. Madrid, Spain: Consejo Superior de Investigaciones Cientificas, 1968-1978.

Mackay, Thomas W. "The resurrected Lord and his apostles (John 21)." In *The Gospels*, edited by Kent P. Jackson and Robert L. Millet. *Studies in Scripture* 5, 461-70. Salt Lake City, UT: Deseret Book, 1986.

Maclagan, David. 1977. *Creation Myths: Man's Introduction to the World*. London, England: Thames & Hudson, 1997.

MacRae, George W., ed. "Apocalypse of Adam." In *The Old Testament Pseudepigrapha*, edited by James H. Charlesworth. Vol. 1, 707-19. Garden City, NY: Doubleday and Company, 1983.

———. "The temple as a house of revelation in the Nag Hammadi texts." In *The Temple in Antiquity*, edited by Truman G. Madsen, 175-90. Salt Lake City, UT: Bookcraft, 1984.

MacRae, George W., William R. Murdock, and Douglas M. Parrott, ed. "The Apocalypse of Paul (V, 2)." In *The Nag Hammadi Library*, edited by James M. Robinson. 3rd, Completely Revised ed, 256-59. San Francisco, CA: HarperSanFrancisco, 1990.

MacRae, George W., and Douglas M. Parrott, ed. "The Apocalypse of Adam (V, 5)." In *The Nag Hammadi Library in English*, edited by James M. Robinson. 3rd, Completely Revised ed, 277-86. San Francisco, CA: HarperSanFrancisco, 1990.

Madsen, Truman G. 2004. "Blessings of the temple." In *The Temple: Where Heaven Meets Earth*, 38-43. Salt Lake City, UT: Deseret Book, 2008.

———. "Chosenness: Implications and extensions in Mormonism and Judaism." In *Covenant and Chosenness in Judaism and Mormonism*, edited by Raphael Jospe, Truman G. Madsen and Seth Ward, 131-46. Madison, NJ: Fairleigh Dickinson University Press, 2001.

———. 1976. "Eternal Man." In *Five Classics by Truman G. Madsen*, 1-68. Salt Lake City, UT: Eagle Gate, 2001.

———. 2004. Foundations of Temple Worship (BYU-Idaho Devotional, 26 October 2004). In *Gazelam Foundation*. www.trumanmadsen.com/media/FoundationsofTempleWorship.pdf (accessed November 23, 2008).

———. 1994. "The Gospel and the Sabbath." In *Five Classics by Truman G. Madsen*, 330-46. Salt Lake City, UT: Eagle Gate, 2001.

———. 1978. "House of glory." In *Five Classics by Truman G. Madsen*, 273-85. Salt Lake City, UT: Eagle Gate, 2001. Reprint, Madsen, Truman G. 1978. "House of glory." In *The Temple: Where Heaven Meets Earth*, 1-14. Salt Lake City, UT: Deseret Book, 2008.

———. 1994. "In a place called Gethsemane." In *Five Classics by Truman G. Madsen*, 299-306. Salt Lake City, UT: Eagle Gate, 2001.

———. "Introductory essay." In *Reflections on Mormonism: Judeo-Christian Parallels, Papers Delivered at the Religious Studies Center Symposium, Brigham Young University, March 10-11, 1978*, edited by Truman G. Madsen. *Religious Studies Monograph Series* 4, xi-xviii. Provo, UT: Religious Studies Center, Brigham Young University, 1978.

———. *Joseph Smith the Prophet*. Salt Lake City, UT: Bookcraft, 1989.

———. 2000. "'The joy of the Lord is your strength' (Nehemiah 8:10)" (BYU Devotional, 21 November 2000). In *BYU Speeches*. http://speeches.byu.edu/reader/reader.php?id=1004 (accessed May 29, 2009).

———. "The Latter-day Saint view of human nature." In *On Human Nature: The Jerusalem Center Symposium*, edited by Truman G. Madsen, David Noel Freedman and Pam Fox Kuhlken, 95-107. Ann Arbor, MI: Pryor Pettengill Publishers, 2004.

———. 1994. "Man Illumined." In *Five Classics by Truman G. Madsen*, 307-19. Salt Lake City, UT: Eagle Gate, 2001.

———. "Mormonism and philosophy." Inaugural lecture, *CMSSA Lecture Series*, February 21, 2008. Claremont, CA: The Claremont Mormon Studies Student Association, Claremont Graduate University School of Religion, excerpts transcribed from audio recording available at http://rsc.cgu.edu/cmssa/media/ (accessed July 15, 2008).

———. "Nine reasons for learning to learn." In *A Twenty-Something's Guide to Spirituality: Questions You Hesitate to Ask, Answers You Rarely Hear*, edited by Jacob Werrett and David Read, 95-118. Salt Lake City, UT: Deseret Book, 2007.

———. "On how we know (Speech delivered 20 September 1994)." In *Brigham Young University 1994-1995 Devotional and Fireside Speeches*, 21-26. Provo, UT: BYU Publications and Graphics, 1995. Reprint, "Reverberations of truth" in *Charting a New Millennium: The Latter-day Saints in the Coming Century*, edited by M. Proctor and S. Proctor, 456-465. Salt Lake City, UT: Aspen Books, 1998.

———. *The Presidents of the Church: Insights into their Lives and Teachings*. Salt Lake City, UT: Deseret Book, 2004.

———. 1983. "Purposes of the temple." In *The Temple: Where Heaven Meets Earth*, 90-99. Salt Lake City, UT: Deseret Book, 2008.

———. "'Putting on the names': A Jewish-Christian legacy." In *By Study and Also by Faith: Essays in Honor of Hugh W. Nibley*, edited by John M. Lundquist and Stephen D. Ricks. 2 vols. Vol. 1, 458-81. Salt Lake City, UT: Deseret Book, 1990. Reprint, Madsen, Truman G. 1990. "'Putting on the names': A Jewish-Christian legacy." In *The Temple: Where Heaven Meets Earth*, 138-156. Salt Lake City, UT: Deseret Book, 2008.

———, ed. *Reflections on Mormonism: Judeo-Christian Parallels, Papers Delivered at the Religious Studies Center Symposium, Brigham Young University, March 10-11, 1978. Religious Studies Monograph Series* 4. Provo, UT: Religious Studies Center, Brigham Young University, 1978.

———. *The Sacrament: Feasting at the Lord's Table*. Orem, UT: Amalphi Publishing, 2008.

———. "The suffering servant." In *The Redeemer: Reflections on the Life and Teachings of Jesus the Christ*, 223-48. Salt Lake City, UT: Deseret Book, 2000.

———. "The temple and the atonement." In *Temples of the Ancient World*, edited by Donald W. Parry, 63-79. Salt Lake City, UT: Deseret Book, 1994.

———. 1978. "Twenty questions." In *Five Classics by Truman G. Madsen*, 148-61. Salt Lake City, UT: Eagle Gate, 2001.

Madsen, Truman G., David Noel Freedman, and Pam Fox Kuhlken, eds. *On Human Nature: The Jerusalem Center Symposium*. Ann Arbor, MI: Pryor Pettengill Publishers, 2004.

Madsen, Truman G., and Ann N. Madsen. 1998. "House of glory, house of light, house of love." In *The Temple: Where Heaven Meets Earth*, 44-76. Salt Lake City, UT: Deseret Book, 2008.

Maffly-Kipp, Laurie F. "Who's that on the $50 bill? Placing Joseph Smith in America's story." *Books and Culture: A Christian Review* 12, no. 1 (January/February 2006). http://www.ctlibrary.com/bc/2006/janfeb/7.11.html (accessed September 3, 2007).

Maguire, Henry. "Paradise withdrawn." In *Byzantine Garden Culture*, edited by Antony Littlewood, Henry Maguire and Joachim Wolschke-Bulmahn, 23-35. Washington, D. C.: Dumbarton Oaks Research Library and Collection, 2002. http://www.doaks.org/ByzGarden/ByzGarch3.pdf (accessed September 4, 2007).

Maher, Michael, ed. *Targum Pseudo-Jonathan, Genesis*. Vol. 1b. *Aramaic Bible*. Collegeville, MN: Liturgical Press, 1992.

Mahoney, Michael J. *Scientist as Subject: The Psychological Imperative*. Cambridge, MA: Ballinger Publishing Company, 1976.

Maimonides, Moses. 1180. *The Code of Maimonides (Mishneh Torah)*. To date 14 vols. *Yale Judaica Series*. New Haven, CT: Yale University Press, 1949-.

———. d. 1204. *The Guide of the Perplexed*. 2 vols. Translated by Shlomo Pines. Chicago. IL: University of Chicago Press, 1963.

———. 1180. *Mishneh Torah*. Edited by Eliyahu Touger. Brooklyn, NY: Moznaim Publishing, 1989-.

Major, John S. *Heaven and Earth in Early Han Thought: Chapters Three, Four, and Five of the Huainanzi*. Albany, NY: State University of New York Press, 1993.

Makarewicz, Mary Raynelda. *The Patristic Influence on Chaucer*. Washington, DC: Catholic University of America Press, 1953.

Malan, Solomon Caesar, ed. *The Book of Adam and Eve: Also Called The Conflict of Adam and Eve with Satan: A Book of the Early Eastern Church. Translated from the Ethiopic, with Notes from the Kufale, Talmud, Midrashim, and Other Eastern Works*. London, England: Williams and Norgate, 1882. Reprint, San Diego, CA: The Book Tree, 2005.

"Mamre." In *Wikipedia*. http://en.wikipedia.org/wiki/Mamre (accessed June 10, 2008).

"Mandaeism." In *Wikipedia*. http://en.wikipedia.org/wiki/Mandaeism (accessed December 31, 2007).

"Manuscript Junius 11." In *Early Manuscripts at Oxford University*. http://image.ox.ac.uk/show?collection=bodleian&manuscript=msjunius11 (accessed May 10, 2009).

Mariella, Sister. "The head, the foot and the rib of Adam." *Notes and Queries* 171 (August 15, 1936): 119.

———. "The Parson's Tale and the Marriage Group." *Modern Language Notes* 53, no. 4 (April 1938): 251-56.

Marmorstein, A. 1920-1937. *The Doctrine of Merits in Old Rabbinical Literature and The Old Rabbinic Doctrine of God (1. The Names and Attributes of God, 2. Essays in Anthropomorphism)*. 3-in-1 vol. New York City, NY: KTAV Publishing House, 1968.

Marquardt, H. Michael, ed. *The Joseph Smith Revelations: Text and Commentary*. Salt Lake City, UT: Signature Books, 1999.

Marshall, Evelyn T. "Garments." In *Encyclopedia of Mormonism*, edited by Daniel H. Ludlow. 4 vols. Vol. 2, 534-35. New York City, NY: Macmillan, 1992. http://www.lib.byu.edu/Macmillan/ (accessed November 26, 2007).

Martin, Richard C., ed. *Encyclopedia of Islam and the Muslim World*. 2 vols. New York, City, NY: Macmillan Reference USA, Gale Group, Thomson Learning, 2004.

Martinez, Florentino Garcia, ed. "11QMelchizedek (11Q13 [11QMelch])." In *The Dead Sea Scrolls Translated: The Qumran Texts in English*, edited by Florentino Garcia Martinez. 2nd ed. Translated by Wilfred G. E. Watson, 139-40. Grand Rapids, MI: William B. Eerdmans, 1996.

———, ed. *The Dead Sea Scrolls Translated: The Qumran Texts in English* 2nd ed. Translated by Wilfred G. E. Watson. Grand Rapids, MI: William B. Eerdmans, 1996.

———, ed. "Genesis Apocryphon (1QapGen ar)." In *The Dead Sea Scrolls Translated: The Qumran Texts in English*, edited by Florentino Garcia Martinez. 2nd ed. Translated by Wilfred G. E. Watson, 230-37. Grand Rapids, MI: William B. Eerdmans, 1996.

———, ed. "The Hymns (1QHymns-a (1QHodaytoth-a [1QH-a])." In *The Dead Sea Scrolls Translated: The Qumran Texts in English*, edited by Florentino Garcia Martinez. 2nd ed. Translated by Wilfred G. E. Watson, 317-70. Grand Rapids, MI: William B. Eerdmans, 1996.

———, ed. "Pseudo-Ezekiel (4QPseudo-Ezekiel-a (4Q385 [4QpsEz-a])." In *The Dead Sea Scrolls Translated: The Qumran Texts in English*, edited by Florentino Garcia Martinez. 2nd ed. Translated by Wilfred G. E. Watson, 286. Grand Rapids, MI: William B. Eerdmans, 1996.

Martinez, Florentino Garcia, and Eibert J. C. Tigchelaar, eds. *The Dead Sea Scrolls Study Edition*. 2 vols. Leiden, Netherlands: Brill, 1997-1998.

Martins, Marcus H. *Blacks and the Mormon Priesthood. Setting the Record Straight*. Orem, UT: Millennial Press, 2007.

———. "False images of Christ." A devotional address presented at Brigham Young University-Hawaii, May 24, 2001. http://w3.byuh.edu/academics/religion/martinsm/Papers/FalseImages-talk.htm (accessed September 4, 2007).

Marty, Martin E. "Foreword." In *Mormonism in Dialogue with Contemporary Christian Theologies*, edited by Donald W. Musser and David L. Paulsen, vii-x. Macon, GA: Mercer University Press, 2007.

Marx, Steven. *Shakespeare and the Bible*. Oxford, England: Oxford University Press, 2000.

Masani, Rustom. 1938. *Zoroastrianism: The Religion of the Good Life*. New York City, NY: Macmillan, 1969.

Matheme, Bobby. 1999. "Book review: *Wind, Sand, and Stars*." In *A Reader's Journal*. http://www.doyletics.com/arj/wsasrvw.htm (accessed September 4, 2007).

Mathews, Edward G., Jr. "The Armenian commentary on Genesis attributed to Ephrem the Syrian." In *The Book of Genesis in Jewish and Oriental Christian Interpretation: A Collection of Essays*, edited by Judith Frishman and Lucas Van Rompay. *Traditio Exegetica Graeca* 5, 143-61. Louvain, Belgium: Editions Peeters, 1997.

Mathews, Kenneth A., ed. *The New American Commentary: Genesis 1-11:26*. Nashville, TN: Broadman and Holman Publishers, 1996.

Matt, Daniel C., ed. *The Zohar, Pritzker Edition*. Vol. 1. Stanford, CA: Stanford University Press, 2004.

———, ed. *The Zohar, Pritzker Edition*. Vol. 2. Stanford, CA: Stanford University Press, 2004.

———, ed. *The Zohar, Pritzker Edition*. Vol. 3. Stanford, CA: Stanford University Press, 2006.

———, ed. *The Zohar, Pritzker Edition*. Vol. 4. Stanford, CA: Stanford University Press, 2007.

Matthews, Robert J. "Adam-ondi-Ahman." *BYU Studies* 13, no. 1 (Autumn 1972): 27-35.

———. "Fall of Adam." In *Encyclopedia of Mormonism*, edited by Daniel H. Ludlow. 4 vols. Vol. 2, 485-86. New York City, NY: Macmillan, 1992. http://www.lib.byu.edu/Macmillan/ (accessed November 26, 2007).

———. "The Fall of man." In *The Man Adam*, edited by Joseph Fielding McConkie and Robert L. Millet, 37-64. Salt Lake City, UT: Bookcraft, 1990.

———. "Moses: Prince of Egypt, Prophet of God." In *A Bible! A Bible!*, edited by Robert J. Matthews, 54-68. Salt Lake City, UT: Bookcraft, 1990.

———. *"A Plainer Translation": Joseph Smith's Translation of the Bible—A History and Commentary*. Provo, UT: Brigham Young University Press, 1975.

———. "The probationary nature of mortality." In *Alma: "The Testimony of the Word." Papers from the Sixth Annual Book of Mormon Symposium, 1991*, edited by Monte S. Nyman and Charles D. Tate, Jr. *Book of Mormon Symposia* 6, 47-60. Provo, UT: Religious Studies Center, Brigham Young University, 1992. Reprint, Salt Lake City, UT: Greg Kofford Books, 2008.

———. "The role of the Joseph Smith Translation of the Bible in the restoration of doctrine." In *The Disciple as Witness: Essays on Latter-day Saint History and Doctrine in Honor of Richard Lloyd Anderson*, edited by Stephen D. Ricks, Donald W. Parry and Andrew H. Hedges, 327-53. Provo, UT: The Foundation for Ancient Research and Mormon Studies at Brigham Young University, 2000.

———. "What is the Book of Moses?" In *The Pearl of Great Price*, edited by Robert L. Millet and Kent P. Jackson. *Studies in Scripture* 2, 25-41. Salt Lake City, UT: Randall Book Co., 1985.

Maududi, Sayyid Abul A'la. *Towards Understanding the Qur'an*. Translated by Zafer Ishaq Ansari. Markfield, England: The Islamic Foundation, 1988-.

Mauss, Armand L. "From near-nation to new world religion?" In *Revisiting Thomas F. O'Dea's The Mormons: Contemporary Perspectives*, edited by Cardell J. Jacobson, John P. Hoffmann and Tim. B. Heaton, 289-327. Salt Lake City, UT: The University of Utah Press, 2008.

Maxwell, Neal A. *All These Things Shall Give Thee Experience*. Salt Lake City, UT: Deseret Book, 1979.

———. "'Behold, the enemy is combined.'" *Ensign* 23, May 1993, 76-79.

———. *But for a Small Moment*. Salt Lake City, UT: Bookcraft, 1986.

———. "Deny yourselves of all ungodliness." *Ensign* 25, May 1995, 66-68.

———. *Deposition of a Disciple*. Salt Lake City, UT: Deseret Book, 1976.

———. "The disciple-scholar." In *On Becoming a Disciple-Scholar*, edited by Henry B. Eyring, Jr., 1-22. Salt Lake City, UT: Bookcraft, 1995.

———. "'God will yet reveal.'" *Ensign* 16, November 1986, 52-54, 59.

———. 1992. "The inexhaustible gospel (BYU Devotional, August 18, 1992)." In *The Inexhaustible Gospel: A Retrospective of Twenty-One Firesides and Devotionals at Brigham Young University 1974-2004*, 211-25. Provo, UT: Brigham Young University, 2004.

———. 1976. "Insights from my life (BYU Devotional, October 26, 1976)." In *The Inexhaustible Gospel: A Retrospective of Twenty-One Firesides and Devotionals at Brigham Young University 1974-2004*, 39-52. Provo, UT: Brigham Young University, 2004.

———. 2000. "Jesus, the perfect mentor." *Ensign* 31, February 2001, 8-17.

———. 1982. "Meekly drenched in destiny (BYU Address, September 5, 1982)." In *The Inexhaustible Gospel: A Retrospective of Twenty-One Firesides and Devotionals at Brigham Young University 1974-2004*, 123-36. Provo, UT: Brigham Young University, 2004.

———. *The Neal A. Maxwell Quote Book*. Edited by Cory H. Maxwell. Salt Lake City, UT: Bookcraft, 1997.

———. *Notwithstanding my Weakness*. Salt Lake City, UT: Deseret Book, 1981.

———. "'O Divine Redeemer.'" *Ensign* 11, November 1981, 8-10.

———. *One More Strain of Praise*. Salt Lake City, UT: Bookcraft, 1999.

———. "Our Creator's Cosmos." Presented at the *Church Educational System Conference on the Doctrine and Covenants and Church History*, Brigham Young University, Provo, UT, August 13, 2002, 2002, 1-8.

———. "The seventh commandment: A shield." *Ensign* 31, November 2001, 78-80.

———. "Some thoughts on the gospel and the behavioral sciences." *BYU Studies* 16, no. 4 (1976): 589-602.

———. *Things as They Really Are*. Salt Lake City, UT: Deseret Book, 1978.

———. *A Time to Choose*. Salt Lake City, UT: Deseret Book, 1972.

———. *We Will Prove Them Herewith*. Salt Lake City, UT: Deseret Book, 1982.

———. *Wherefore, Ye Must Press Forward*. Salt Lake City, UT: Deseret Book, 1977.

———. *A Wonderful Flood of Light*. Salt Lake City, UT: Bookcraft, 1990.

May, William F. "Manichaeism in American politics." *Christianity and Crisis* (May 2, 1966). http://www.religion-online.org/showarticle.asp?title=387 (accessed September 4, 2007).

McAuliffe, Jane Dammen, ed. *The Cambridge Companion to the Qur'an*. Cambridge, England: Cambridge University Press, 2006.

———. "Ibn Taymiya: Treatise on the principles of *tafsir*." In *Windows on the House of Islam: Muslim Sources on Spirituality and Religious Life*, edited by J. Renard, 35-43. Berkeley, CA: University of California Press, 1998.

———. "Introduction." In *The Cambridge Companion to the Qur'an*, edited by Jane Dammen McAuliffe, 1-20. Cambridge, England: Cambridge University Press, 2006.

———. "The tasks and traditions of interpretation." In *The Cambridge Companion to the Qur'an*, edited by Jane Dammen McAuliffe, 181-209. Cambridge, England: Cambridge University Press, 2006.

McBride, Matthew. *A House for the Most High: The Story of the Original Nauvoo Temple*. Salt Lake City, UT: Greg Kofford Books, 2007.

McClellan, Richard D. "Not your average French communist Mormon: A short history of Louis Bertrand." *Mormon Historical Studies* 1, no. 2 (Fall 2000): 3-24.

McCollum, Adele Brannon. "The First Vision: Re-visioning historical experience." In *Literature of Belief*, edited by Neal E. Lambert, 177-95. Provo, UT: Brigham Young University Religious Studies Center, 1981.

McConkie, Bruce R. "Christ and the creation." *Ensign* 12, June 1982, 8-15.

———. "Come: Hear the voice of the Lord." *Ensign* 15, December 1985, 54-59.

———. *Doctrinal New Testament Commentary*. 3 vols. Salt Lake City, UT: Bookcraft, 1973.

———. *Doctrines of the Restoration: Sermons and Writings of Bruce R. McConkie*. Edited by Mark L. McConkie. Salt Lake City, UT: Bookcraft, 1989.

———. *The Millennial Messiah: The Second Coming of the Son of Man*. The Messiah Series 6. Salt Lake City, UT: Deseret Book, 1982.

———. *Mormon Doctrine*. 2nd ed. Salt Lake City, UT: Bookcraft, 1966.

———. *Mormon Doctrine*. Revised 2nd ed. Salt Lake City, UT: Deseret Book, 1979.

———. *The Mortal Messiah: From Bethlehem to Calvary*. 4 vols. The Messiah Series 2-5. Salt Lake City, UT: Deseret Book, 1979-1981.

———. "Mothers in Israel and daughters of Zion." *New Era* 8, May 1978, 34-37.

———. *A New Witness for the Articles of Faith*. Salt Lake City, UT: Deseret Book, 1985.

———. *The Promised Messiah: The First Coming of Christ*. The Messiah Series 1. Salt Lake City, UT: Deseret Book, 1978.

McConkie, Joseph Fielding. *Answers: Straightforward Answers to Tough Gospel Questions*. Salt Lake City, UT: Deseret Book, 1998.

———. *Gospel Symbolism*. Salt Lake City, UT: Bookcraft, 1985.

———. "Modern revelation: A window to the past." In *"To Be Learned Is Good if…"*, edited by Robert L. Millet, 115-28. Salt Lake City, UT: Bookcraft, 1987.

———. "The mystery of Eden." In *The Man Adam*, edited by Joseph Fielding McConkie and Robert L. Millet, 25-35. Salt Lake City, UT: Bookcraft, 1990.

———. "Premortal existence, foreordinations, and heavenly councils." In *Apocryphal Writings and the Latter-day Saints*, edited by C. Wilfred Griggs, 173-98. Provo, UT: BYU Religious Studies Center, 1986.

———. *Sons and Daughters of God: The Loss and Restoration of Our Divine Inheritance*. Salt Lake City, UT: Bookcraft, 1994.

McConkie, Joseph Fielding, and Robert L. Millet. *The Man Adam*. Salt Lake City, UT: Bookcraft, 1990.

McConkie, Joseph Fielding, and Craig J. Ostler, eds. *Revelations of the Restoration: A Commentary on the Doctrine and Covenants and Other Modern Revelations*. Salt Lake City, UT: Deseret Book, 2000.

McDannell, Colleen, and Bernhard Lang. *Heaven: A History*. 2nd ed. New Haven, CT: Yale University Press, 1988.

McDonald, Lee Martin, and James A. Sanders, eds. *The Canon Debate*. Peabody, MA: Hendrickson Publishers, 2002.

McDonald, Michael E. "Scriptural cosmology." *Dialogue: A Journal of Mormon Thought* 40, no. 2 (Summer 2007): vii-viii.

McKay, David O. *Cherished Experiences from the Writings of David O. McKay*. Salt Lake City, UT: Deseret Book, 1955.

———. 1956. "Gospel ideals—Life's surest anchor." Address given at Brigham Young University, October 30, 1956. http://speeches-files.byu.edu/download.php/McKay56.mp3?type=2&fname=McKay56.mp3 (accessed September 5, 2007).

———. 1952. "A message for LDS college youth." Address given to the student body at Brigham Young University, October 8, 1952. In *McKay Addresses*. http://education.byu.edu/mckay/52oct8.html (accessed September 4, 2007).

———. *Treasures of Life*. Salt Lake City, UT: Deseret Book, 1962.

McKinlay, Daniel B. "Temple imagery in the Epistles of Peter." In *Temples of the Ancient World*, edited by Donald W. Parry, 492-514. Salt Lake City, UT: Deseret Book, 1994.

McKinlay, Lynn A. 1950. *Life Eternal: A Series of Four Lectures*. Salt Lake City, UT: Deseret Book, 1972.

———. "Patriarchal order of the Priesthood." In *The Encyclopedia of Mormonism*, edited by Daniel H. Ludlow. 4 vols. Vol. 3, 1067. New York City, NY: Macmillan, 1992. http://www.lib.byu.edu/Macmillan/ (accessed November 26, 2007).

McLachlan, James. "The modernism controversy: William Henry Chamberlin, his teachers Howison and Royce, and the conception of God debate." In *Mormonism in Dialogue with Contemporary Christian Theologies*, edited by Donald W. Musser and David L. Paulsen, 39-83. Macon, GA: Mercer University Press, 2007.

———. "Reply to Professor Griffin." In *Mormonism in Dialogue with Contemporary Christian Theologies*, edited by Donald W. Musser and David L. Paulsen, 207-09. Macon, GA: Mercer University Press, 2007.

McLellin, William E. *The Journals of William E. McLellin, 1831-1836*. Edited by Jan Shipps and John W. Welch. Provo, UT: BYU Studies, 1994.

McMurrin, Sterling M. 1965. *The Theological Foundations of the Mormon Religion*. Salt Lake City, UT: Signature Books, 2000.

McNamara, Martin, ed. *Targum Neofiti 1, Genesis, translated, with apparatus and notes*. Vol. 1a. *Aramaic Bible*. Collegeville, MN: Liturgical Press, 1992.

McWhorter, John. *The Power of Babel: A Natural History of Language*. New York City, NY: W. H. Freeman, Times Books, Henry Holt, 2001.

Mead, George Robert Shaw, ed. *Gnostic John the Baptizer: Selections from the Mandaean John-Book*. London, England: John M. Watkins, 1924. Reprint, Kila, MT: Kessinger Publishing, n.d. http://www.gnosis.org/library/grs-mead/gnostic_john_baptist/ (accessed September 11, 2007).

———, ed. 1921. *Pistis Sophia: The Gnostic Tradition of Mary Magdalene, Jesus, and His Disciples*. Mineola, NY: Dover Publications, 2005.

Meeks, Wayne A. "Moses as God and King." In *Religions in Antiquity: Essays in Memory of Erwin Ramsdell Goodenough*, edited by Jacob Neusner. *Religions in Antiquity, Studies in the History of Religions (Supplements to Numen)* 14, 354-71. Leiden, The Netherlands: Brill, 1968.

Meldrum, D. Jeffrey. "The children of Lehi: DNA and the Book of Mormon." Presented at the *2003 FAIR Conference*, Provo, UT, August 7-8, 2003. http://www.fairlds.org/FAIR_Conferences/2003_Evolution_and_Latter-day_Saint_Theology.html (accessed September 5, 2007).

Meldrum, D. Jeffrey, and Trent D. Stephens. "Who are the children of Lehi?" *Journal of Book of Mormon Studies* 12, no. 1 (2003): 38-51, 116.

———. *Who Are the Children of Lehi? DNA and the Book of Mormon*. Salt Lake City, UT: Greg Kofford Books, 2007.

Meltzer, David ed. "Shiur Qoma: The Measure of the Divine Body." In *The Secret Garden: An Anthology in the Kabbalah*, edited by David Meltzer, 23-37. Barrytown, NY: Barrytown Limited, 1997.

Mettinger, Tryggve N. D. *The Eden Narrative: A Literary and Religio-historical Study of Genesis 2-3*. Winona Lake, IN: Eisenbrauns, 2007.

Metzger, Bruce M. *The Bible in Translation: Ancient and English Versions*. Grand Rapids, MI: Baker Academic, 2001.

———, ed. "The Fourth Book of Ezra." In *The Old Testament Pseudepigrapha*, edited by James H. Charlesworth. 2 vols. Vol. 1, 517-59. Garden City, NY: Doubleday and Company, 1983.

Meyer, Marvin W. *The Ancient Mysteries: A Sourcebook of Sacred Texts*. 2nd ed. Philadelphia, PA: University of Pennsylvania Press, 2001.

———, ed. *The Nag Hammadi Scriptures: The International Edition*. New York City, NY: HarperOne, 2007.

———, ed. "On the origin of the world." In *The Nag Hammadi Scriptures: The International Edition*, edited by Marvin Meyer, 199-221. New York City, NY: HarperOne, 2007.

Michael, Thomas. *The Pristine Dao: Metaphysics in Early Dao Discourse*. Albany, NY: State University of New York Press, 2005.

Michon, Jean-Louis. "The spiritual practices of Sufism." In *Foundations*, edited by Seyyed Hossein Nasr. *Islamic Spirituality* 1, 265-93. New York City, NY: The Crossroad Publishing Company, 1987.

Middleton, James. n. d. The Archangel Michael Subduing Satan. In *Polyhymnia*. http://www.polyhymnia-nyc.org/Raphael.html (accessed August 28, 2006).

Migne, Jacques P., ed. *Patrologiae Cursus Completus, Series Graeca*. 161 vols. Paris, France, 1857-1866. http://patrologia.ct.aegean.gr/PG_Migne/ (accessed March 28, 2008).

———, ed. *Patrologiae Cursus Completus, Series Latina*. 221 vols. Paris, France, 1844-1855. http://pld.chadwyck.co.uk/ (accessed March 28, 2008).

Mika'el, Bakhayla. ca. 1400. "Another discourse concerning the birth of Enoch." In *The Book of the Mysteries of the Heavens and the Earth and Other Works of Bakhayla Mika'el (Zosimas)*, edited by E. A. Wallis Budge, 140-62. Oxford, England: Oxford University Press, 1934. Reprint, Berwick, ME: Ibis Press, 2004.

———. ca. 1400. "The book of the mysteries of the heavens and the earth." In *The Book of the Mysteries of the Heavens and the Earth and Other Works of Bakhayla Mika'el (Zosimas)*, edited by E. A. Wallis Budge, 1-96. Oxford, England: Oxford University Press, 1934. Reprint, Berwick, ME: Ibis Press, 2004.

———. ca. 1400. *The Book of the Mysteries of the Heavens and the Earth and Other Works of Bakhayla Mika'el (Zosimas)*. Edited by E. A. Wallis Budge. Oxford, England: Oxford University Press, 1934. Reprint, Berwick, ME: Ibis Press, 2004.

———. ca. 1400. "The interpretation of the vision of St. John, the author of the Apocalypse." In *The Book of the Mysteries of the Heavens and the Earth and Other Works of Bakhayla Mika'el (Zosimas)*, edited by E. A. Wallis Budge, 97-125. Oxford, England: Oxford University Press, 1934. Reprint, Berwick, ME: Ibis Press, 2004.

Mika'el, Isaac, son of Bakhayla. ca. 1400. "Discourse concerning the mystery of the Godhead and the Trinity." In *The Book of the Mysteries of the Heavens and the Earth and Other Works of Bakhayla Mika'el (Zosimas)*, edited by E. A. Wallis Budge, 126-39. Oxford, England: Oxford University Press, 1934. Reprint, Berwick, ME: Ibis Press, 2004.

Mikkelson, G., ed. *Bibliographia Manichaica: A Comprehensive Bibliography of Manichaeism through 1996. Corpus Fontium Manichaeorum, Series Subsidia*. Turnhout, Belgium: Brepols, 1997.

———, ed. *Dictionary of Manichaean Texts*. Vol. 4: Texts from Central Asia and China. *Corpus Fontium Manichaeorum, Series Subsidia*. Turnhout, Belgium: Brepols, 2007.

Milgrom, Jacob. "The temple in biblical Israel: Kinships of meaning." In *Reflections on Mormonism: Judeo-Christian Parallels, Papers Delivered at the Religious Studies Center Symposium, Brigham Young University, March 10-11, 1978*, edited by Truman G. Madsen. *Religious Studies Monograph Series* 4, 57-65. Provo, UT: Religious Studies Center, Brigham Young University, 1978.

Milik, J. T., ed. *The Books of Enoch: Aramaic Fragments from Qumran Cave* 4. Oxford, England: Clarendon Press, 1976.

Mill, John Stuart. *On Liberty*. London, England: John W. Parker and Son, 1859. http://books.google.com/books?id=qCQCAAAAQAAJ (accessed December 26, 2007).

Miller, Adam S. "Atonement and testimony." *Element: The Journal of the Society for Mormon Philosophy and Theology* 2, no. 2 (Fall 2006): 73-83.

Miller, Andrew I. "What does the word "telestial" mean?" In *Strong Reasons*. http://strongreasons.blogspot.com/2008/07/what-does-word-mean.html (accessed November 30, 2008).

Miller, D. Patrick. "Yogananda's legacy." *Yoga Journal*, May/June 1991, 59-62, 107-09, 20.

Miller, Jeanette W. "The tree of life, a personification of Christ." *Journal of Book of Mormon Studies* 2, no. 1 (1993): 93-106.

Miller, Kenneth R. 1999. *Finding Darwin's God: A Scientist's Search for Common Ground Between God and Evolution*. New York City, NY: Harper Perennial, 2002.

Miller, Mary Ellen, and Karl A. Taube. 1993. *The Gods and Symbols of Ancient Mexico and the Maya: An Illustrated Dictionary of Mesoamerican Religion*. New York City, NY: Thames and Hudson, 1997.

Millet, Robert L. *Alive in Christ : The Miracle of Spiritual Rebirth*. Salt Lake City, UT: Deseret Book, 1997.

———. "Appendix A: Doctrinal parameters within Mormonism." In *Bridging the Divide: The Continuing Conversation between a Mormon and an Evangelical*, edited by Robert L. Millet and Gregory C. V. Johnson, 131-48. Rhinebeck, NY: Monkfish, 2007.

———. "C. S. Lewis on the transformation of human nature." In *C. S. Lewis: The Man and His Message, A Latter-day Saint Perspective*, edited by Andrew C. Skinner and Robert L. Millet, 143-55. Salt Lake City, UT: Bookcraft, 1999.

———. *A Different Jesus? The Christ of the Latter-day Saints*. Grand Rapids, MI: Eerdmans, 2005.

———. *Lost and Found: Reflections on the Prodigal Son*. Salt Lake City, UT: Deseret Book, 2001.

———. *The Vision of Mormonism: Pressing the Boundaries of Christianity*. St. Paul, MN: Paragon House, 2007.

Millet, Robert L., and Gregory C. V. Johnson. *Bridging the Divide: The Continuing Conversation Between a Mormon and an Evangelical*. Rhinebeck, NY: Monkfish Book Publishing, 2007.

Millet, Robert L., and Joseph Fielding McConkie. *Our Destiny: The Call and Election of the House of Israel*. Salt Lake City, UT: Bookcraft, 1993.

Millet, Robert L., and Gerald R. McDermott. *Claiming Christ: A Mormon-Evangelical Debate*. Grand Rapids, MI: Brazos Press, 2007.

Milstein, Rachel. "The stories and their illustrations." In *Stories of the Prophets: Illustrated Manuscripts of Qisas al-Anbiya*, edited by Rachel Milstein, Karin Rührdanz and Barbara Schmitz. *Islamic Art and Architecture Series* 8, eds. Abbas Daneshvari, Robert Hillenbrand and Bernard O'Kane, 105-83. Costa Mesa, CA: Mazda Publishers, 1999.

Milstein, Rachel, Karin Rührdanz, and Barbara Schmitz. *Stories of the Prophets: Illustrated Manuscripts of Qisas al-Anbiya*. *Islamic Art and Architecture Series* 8, ed. Abbas Daneshvari, Robert Hillenbrand and Bernard O'Kane. Costa Mesa, CA: Mazda Publishers, 1999.

Milton, John. 1667. "Paradise Lost." In *Paradise Lost, Paradise Regained, Samson Agonistes*, edited by Harold Bloom, 15-257. London, England: Collier, 1962.

———. 1671. "Samson Agonistes." In *Paradise Lost, Paradise Regained, Samson Agonistes*, edited by Harold Bloom, 307-48. London, England: Collier, 1962.

"Minyan." In *Wikipedia*. http://en.wikipedia.org/wiki/Minyan (accessed February 5, 2008).

Miola, Robert S. *Shakespeare's Reading. Oxford Shakespeare Topics*, eds. Peter D. Holland and Stanley Wells. Oxford, England: Oxford University Press, 2000.

"Miranda." In *Shakespeare Illustrated*, Department of English, Emory University. http://www.english.emory.edu/classes/Shakespeare_Illustrated/Miranda1.html (accessed December 12, 2007).

Mirecki, Paul, and Jason David BeDuhn, eds. *Emerging from Darkness: Studies in the Recovery of Manichaean Sources. Nag Hammadi and Manichaean Studies* 43, eds. James M. Robinson and H. J. Klimkeit. Leiden, The Netherlands: Brill, 1997.

Mirecki, Paul, Iain Gardner, and Anthony Alcock. "Magical spell, Manichaean letter." In *Emerging from Darkness: Studies in the Recovery of Manichaean Sources*, edited by Paul Mirecki and Jason David BeDuhn. *Nag Hammadi and Manichaean Studies* 43, eds. James M. Robinson and H. J. Klimkeit, 1-32. Leiden, The Netherlands: Brill, 1997.

Mirecki, Paul, and Jason David BeDuhn, eds. *The Light and the Darkness: Studies in Manichaeism and its World. Nag Hammadi and Manichaean Studies* 50, ed. Stephen Emmel. Leiden, The Netherlands: Brill, 2001.

Mirecki, Paul. "Introduction [to the Manichaean Literature]." In *The Gnostic Bible*, edited by Willis Barnstone and Marvin W. Meyer, 569-80. Boston, MA: Shambhala, 2003.

———. "On the Origin of His Body [Introduction]." In *The Gnostic Bible*, edited by Willis Barnstone and Marvin W. Meyer, 581-82. Boston, MA: Shambhala, 2003.

Mitchell, Stephen, ed. 1987. *The Book of Job*. New York City, NY: HarperPerennial, 1992.

Mitchell, W. J. T. "Blake's composite art." In *William Blake*, edited by Harold Bloom. Bloom's BioCritiques, ed. Harold Bloom, 137-62. Philadelphia, PA: Chelsea House Publishers, 2006.

Moberly, R. W. L. "Did the serpent get it right?" In *From Eden to Golgotha: Essays in Biblical Theology*, edited by R. W. L. Moberly. *South Florida Studies in the History of Judaism* 52, eds. Jacob Neusner, William Scott Green, James F. Strange, Darrell J. Fasching and Sara Mandell, 1-27. Atlanta, GA: Scholars Press, 1992.

Modi, Jivanji Jamshedji. *The Navjote Ceremony of the Parsees*. 2nd ed. Bombay, India, 1914. http://www.avesta.org/ritual/navjote.htm (accessed September 13, 2007).

———. *The Religious Ceremonies and Customs of the Parsees*. Bombay, India: British India Press, 1922. http://www.avesta.org/ritual/rcc.htm (accessed September 13, 2007 - incomplete version).

Mohammed, Khaleel. "Assessing English translations of the Qur'an." *The Middle East Quarterly* 12, no. 2 (Spring 2005). http://www.meforum.org/article/717 (accessed September 5, 2007).

Monneret, Jean-Luc. *Les Grands Thèmes du Coran*. Paris, France: Éditions Dervy, 2003.

Monson, Thomas S. "Our sacred priesthood trust." *Ensign* 36, May 2006, 54-57.

Mopsik, Charles, ed. *Le Livre hébreu d'Hénoch ou Livre des Palais. Les Dix Paroles*, ed. Charles Mopsik. Lagrasse, France: Éditions Verdier, 1989.

———, ed. *Le Zohar*. 5 vols. *Collection Les Dix Paroles*, ed. Charles Mopsik. Lagrasse, France: Verdier, 1981.

Mordell, Phineas ed. "Sefer Yetsirah (excerpt)." In *The Secret Garden: An Anthology in the Kabbalah*, edited by David Meltzer, 41-45. Barrytown, NY: Barrytown Limited, 1997.

Mordtman Jr., A. "Monuments relatifs au culte d'Isis à Cyzique." *Revue Archéologique* 5 (May 1879): 257-62.

Moreland, J. P., and John Mark Reynolds. *Three Views on Creation and Evolution*. Grand Rapids, MI: Zondervan Publishing, 1999.

Morgan, Michael A., ed. *Sefer ha-Razim: The Book of Mysteries. Society of Biblical Literature Texts and Translations Pseudepigrapha Series* 11, ed. Harold W. Attridge. Chico, CA: Scholars Press, 1983.

Morris, Colin. 2005. *The Sepulchre of Christ and the Medieval West: From the Beginning to 1600*. Oxford, England: Oxford University Press, 2007.

Morris, Simon Conway. *Life's Solution: Inevitable Humans in a Lonely Universe*. Cambridge, England: Cambridge University Press, 2003.

Morrison, Alexander B. "The Latter-day Saint concept of canon." In *Historicity and the Latter-day Saint Scriptures*, edited by Paul Y. Hoskisson, 1-16. Provo, UT: Brigham Young University Religious Studies Center, 2001.

Motzki, Harold. "Alternative accounts of the Qur'an's formation." In *The Cambridge Companion to the Qur'an*, edited by Jane Dammen McAuliffe, 59-75. Cambridge, England: Cambridge University Press, 2006.

Mouritsen, Dale C. "Transfiguration." In *Encyclopedia of Mormonism*, edited by Daniel H. Ludlow. 4 vols. Vol. 4, 1484-85. New York City, NY: Macmillan, 1992. http://www.lib.byu.edu/Macmillan/ (accessed November 26, 2007).

Mouritsen, Paul. "Secret combinations and flaxen cords: Anti-Masonic rhetoric and the Book of Mormon." *Journal of Book of Mormon Studies* 12, no. 1 (2003): 64-77.

Muggeridge, Malcolm. *Jesus: The Man Who Lives*. New York: Harper and Row, 1975.

Muhlestein, Kerry. "Approaching understandings in the Book of Abraham." *FARMS Review of Books* 18, no. 2 (2006): 229-46.

———. "The Book of Breathings in its place." *FARMS Review of Books* 17, no. 2 (2005): 471-86.

———. "One continuous flow: Revelations surrounding the 'New Translation.'" In *The Doctrine and Covenants: Revelations in Context: The 37th Annual Brigham Young University Sidney B. Sperry Symposium*, edited by Andrew H. Hedges, J. Spencer Fluhman and Alonzo L. Gaskill, 40-65. Salt Lake City, UT: Deseret Book, 2008.

Müller, F. Max, ed. *Avesta Khorda Avesta: Book of Common Prayer*. American ed. Translated by James Darmesteter. *The Sacred Books of the East*, 1898. Reprint, Kila, MT: Kessinger Publishing, 2004.

———, ed. "Bahman Yast." In *Pahlavi Texts: The Bundahis, Bahman Yast, and Shayast La-Shayast (including Selections of Zad-sparam)*, edited by F. Max Müller. 5 vols. Vol. 1. Translated by E. W. West. *The Sacred Books of the East* 5, ed. F. Max Müller, 189-235. Oxford, England: Oxford University Press, 1880. Reprint, Kila, MT: Kessinger Publishing, 2004.

———, ed. "Bundahis." In *Pahlavi Texts: The Bundahis, Bahman Yast, and Shayast La-Shayast (including Selections of Zad-sparam)*, edited by F. Max Müller. 5 vols. Vol. 1. Translated by E. W. West. *The Sacred Books of the East* 5, ed. F. Max Müller, 1-151. Oxford, England: Oxford University Press, 1880. Reprint, Kila, MT: Kessinger Publishing, 2004.

———, ed. "Dadistan-i Dinik." In *Pahlavi Texts: The Dadistan-i Dinik and the Epistles of Manuskihar*, edited by F. Max Müller. 5 vols. Vol. 2. Translated by E. W. West. *The Sacred Books of the East* 18, ed. F. Max Müller, 1-276. Oxford, England: Oxford University Press, 1882. Reprint, Kila, MT: Kessinger Publishing, 2004.

———, ed. "Dinai Mainog-i khirad." In *Pahlavi Texts: Dinai Mainog-i khirad, Sikand-Gumanik Vigar, Sad Dar.*, edited by F. Max Müller. 5 vols. Vol. 3. Translated by E. W. West. *The Sacred Books of the East* 24, ed. F. Max Müller, 1-113. Oxford, England: Oxford University Press, 1884. Reprint, Kila, MT: Kessinger Publishing, 2004.

———, ed. "Dinkard, Books 5, 7." In *Pahlavi Texts: Marvels of Zoroastrianism*, edited by F. Max Müller. 5 vols. Vol. 5. Translated by E. W. West. *The Sacred Books of the East* 47, ed. F. Max Müller, 3-130. Oxford, England: Oxford University Press, 1897. Reprint, Kila, MT: Kessinger Publishing, 2004.

———, ed. *Pahlavi Texts: The Bundahis, Bahman Yast, and Shayast La-Shayast (including Selections of Zad-sparam)*. 5 vols. Vol. 1. Translated by E. W. West. *The Sacred Books of the East* 5, ed. F. Max Müller. Oxford, England: Oxford University Press, 1880. Reprint, Kila, MT: Kessinger Publishing, 2004.

———, ed. *Pahlavi Texts: Contents of the Nasks (Dinkard, Books 8-9)*. 5 vols. Vol. 4. Translated by E. W. West. *The Sacred Books of the East* 37, ed. F. Max Müller. Oxford, England: Oxford University Press, 1892. Reprint, Kila, MT: Kessinger Publishing, 2004.

———, ed. *Pahlavi Texts: The Dadistan-i Dinik and the Epistles of Manuskihar*. 5 vols. Vol. 2. Translated by E. W. West. *The Sacred Books of the East* 18, ed. F. Max Müller. Oxford, England: Oxford University Press, 1882. Reprint, Kila, MT: Kessinger Publishing, 2004.

———, ed. *Pahlavi Texts: Dinai Mainog-i khirad, Sikand-Gumanik Vigar, Sad Dar*. 5 vols. Vol. 3. Translated by E. W. West. *The Sacred Books of the East* 24, ed. F. Max Müller. Oxford, England: Oxford University Press, 1884. Reprint, Kila, MT: Kessinger Publishing, 2004.

———, ed. *Pahlavi Texts: Marvels of Zoroastrianism (Dinkard, Books 5, 7; Selections of Zad-sparam)*. 5 vols. Vol. 5. Translated by E. W. West. *The Sacred Books of the East* 47, ed. F. Max Müller. Oxford, England: Oxford University Press, 1897. Reprint, Kila, MT: Kessinger Publishing, 2004.

———, ed. "Selections of Zad-sparam." In *Pahlavi Texts: The Bundahis, Bahman Yast, and Shayast La-Shayast (including Selections of Zad-sparam)*, edited by F. Max Müller. 5 vols. Vol. 1. Translated by E. W. West. *The Sacred Books of the East* 5, ed. F. Max Müller, 153-87. Oxford, England: Oxford Unversity Press, 1880.

———, ed. "Sikand-Gumanik Vigar." In *Pahlavi Texts: Dinai Mainog-i khirad, Sikand-Gumanik Vigar, Sad Dar.*, edited by F. Max Müller. 5 vols. Vol. 3. Translated by E. W. West. *The Sacred Books of the East* 24, ed. F. Max Müller, 115-251. Oxford, England: Oxford University Press, 1884.

———, ed. *The Upanishads, Part Two*. 2 vols. Vol. 2. *The Sacred Books of the East* 15, ed. F. Max Müller. Oxford, England: Oxford University Press, 1884. Reprint, New York City, NY: Dover, 1962.

———, ed. "Yasna (1-27, 35-42, 52, 54-72)." In *The Zend Avesta: The Yasna, Visparad, Afrinagan, Gahs, and Miscellaneous Fragments*, edited by F. Max Müller. 3 vols. Vol. 3. Translated by Lawrence Heyworth Mills. *The Sacred Books of the East* 31, ed. F. Max Müller, 195-332. Oxford, England: Oxford University Press, 1887.

———, ed. "Yasts." In *The Zend Avesta: The Sirozahs, Yasts, and Nyayis*, edited by F. Max Müller. 3 vols. Vol. 2. Translated by James Darmesteter. *The Sacred Books of the East* 23, ed. F. Max Müller, 21-345. Oxford, England: Oxford University Press, 1883. Reprint, Kila, MT: Kessinger Publishing, 2004.

———, ed. *The Zend Avesta: The Sirozahs, Yasts, and Nyayis*. 3 vols. Vol. 2. Translated by James Darmesteter. *The Sacred Books of the East* 23, ed. F. Max Müller. Oxford, England: Oxford University Press, 1883. Reprint, Kila, MT: Kessinger Publishing, 2004.

———, ed. *The Zend Avesta: The Vendidad*. 3 vols. Vol. 1. Translated by James Darmesteter. *The Sacred Books of the East* 4, ed. F. Max Müller. Oxford, England: Oxford University Press, 1880. Reprint, Kila, MT: Kessinger Publishing, 2004.

———, ed. *The Zend Avesta: The Yasna, Visparad, Afrinagan, Gahs, and Miscellaneous Fragments*. 3 vols. Vol. 3. Translated by Lawrence Heyworth Mills. *The Sacred Books of the East* 31, ed. F. Max Müller. Oxford, England: Oxford University Press, 1887. Reprint, Kila, MT: Kessinger Publishing, 2004.

Müller-Kessler, C. "A Mandaic gold amulet in the British Museum." *Bulletin of the American Schools of Oriental Research* 311 (1998): 83-88.

Munk, Eliyahu, ed. *Hachut Hameshulash: Commentaries on the Torah by Rabbeinu Chananel, Rashyybam, Ryydak, and Sforno*. 6 vols. Jerusalem, Israel: Urim Publications, 2003.

Munoa, Philip B. *Four Powers in Heaven: The Interpretation of Daniel 7 in the Testament of Abraham*. *Journal for the Study of the Pseudepigrapha Supplement Series* 28, eds. Lester L. Grabbe and James H. Charlesworth. Sheffield, England: Sheffield Academic Press, 1998.

Munro-Hay, Stuart. *The Quest for the Ark of the Covenant: The True History of the Tablets of Moses*. London, England: I. B. Tauris, 2006.

Murphy, Frederick J. *Pseudo-Philo: Rewriting the Bible*. Oxford, England: Oxford University Press, 1993.

Murphy, G. Ronald. *Gemstone of Paradise: The Holy Grail in Wolfram's Parzival*. Oxford, England: Oxford University Press, 2006.

———. "Gemstone of Paradise: The Holy Grail in Wolfram's *Parzival*" (excerpt). *Company: The World of Jesuits and their Friends* 242, Winter 2006, 8-11. http://www.companysj.com/v242/gemstone.pdf (accessed October 4, 2008).

Murphy, Roland. "Israel's Wisdom: Dialogue between the Sages." In *Light in a Spotless Mirror: Reflections on Wisdom Traditions in Judaism and Early Christianity*, edited by James H. Charlesworth and Michael A. Daise, 7-25. Harrisburg, PA: Trinity Press International, 2003.

Murray, Robert. *The Cosmic Covenant*. London, England: Sheed and Ward Limited, 1992.

Musée du Louvre. "Saint Michel terrassant le démon, dit Le Grand Saint Michel." In *Musée du Louvre: Atlas*. http://cartelen.louvre.fr/cartelen/visite?srv=car_not_frame&idNotice=13966 (accessed June 28, 2007).

Muslim, Ibn Al-Hajjaij, ed. ca. 860. *Sahih Muslim*. 4 vols. Translated by Abdul Hamid Siddiqi. Chicago, IL: Kazi Publications, 1971.

Musser, Donald W., and David L. Paulsen, eds. *Mormonism in Dialogue with Contemporary Christian Theologies*. Macon, GA: Mercer University Press, 2007.

Myers, Merlin G. "Kinship, religion, and the transformation of society." In *Speeches of the Year 1975: Brigham Young University Centennial Devotional and Fireside Addresses*, 85-96. Provo, UT: Brigham Young University, 1975.

Mylonas, George E. 1961. *Eleusis and the Eleusinian Mysteries*. Princeton, NJ: Princeton University Press, 1969.

Nadauld, Stephen D. *Principles of Priesthood Leadership*. Salt Lake City, UT: Bookcraft, 1999.

Nanayakkara, S. S. M. 2000. "Sri Pada: Sanctuary for all faiths." In *The Sunday Observer*. http://sripada.org/nanayakkara.htm (accessed September 20, 2007).

Nanji, Azim. "Isma'ilism." In *Foundations*, edited by Seyyed Hossein Nasr. *Islamic Spirituality* 1, 179-98. New York City, NY: The Crossroad Publishing Company, 1987.

Nasafi, Aziz, and Lloyd Ridgeon, eds. *Aziz Nasafi*. *Curzon Sufi Series*. Oxford, England: RoutledgeCurzon, 1998.

Nasr, Seyyed Hossein. "II. Sunnah and Hadith." In *Foundations*, edited by Seyyed Hossein Nasr. *Islamic Spirituality* 1, 97-110. New York City, NY: The Crossroad Publishing Company, 1987.

———. "The *Qur'an* as the foundation of Islamic spirituality." In *Foundations*, edited by Seyyed Hossein Nasr. *Islamic Spirituality* 1, 3-10. New York City, NY: The Crossroad Publishing Company, 1987.

Nasrai, Yesai. "Scroll of Miryai and Scroll of Shum, from the Aramaic Drashe d-Malke (Discourse of the Celestial Kings)," chapters 34, 35, 14-17, 48-51, 56, 74. Translated from the German. In *Sacred Scrolls of the Order of Nazorean Essenes, Manichaean Orthodox Church*. http://essenes.net/scrolls/64ssMiryai.html (accessed September 12, 2007).

Nee, Sean. "The great chain of being." *Nature* 435 (2005): 429.

Neilson, Reid L., and Terryl L. Givens, eds. *Joseph Smith Jr.: Reappraisals After Two Centuries*. Oxford, England: Oxford University Press, 2009.

Nelson, Ethel R., Richard E. Broadberry, and Ginger Tong Chock. *God's Promise to the Chinese*. Dunlap, TN: Read Books Publisher, 1997.

Nelson, Russell M. "The Creation." *Ensign* 30, May 2000, 84-86.

———. "Lessons from Eve." *Ensign* 17, November 1987, 86-89.

Nersessian, Vrej. *Treasures from the Ark: 1700 Years of Armenian Christian Art*. London, England: The British Library, 2001.

Nes, Solrunn. *The Uncreated Light: An Iconographical Study of the Transfiguration in the Eastern Church*. Grand Rapids, MI: William B. Eerdmans, 2007.

Neugroschel, Joachim ed. "Book Bahir" (excerpt). In *The Secret Garden: An Anthology in the Kabbalah*, edited by David Meltzer, 49-96. Barrytown, NY: Barrytown Limited, 1997.

Neumiller, S. Kurt. 1998. "Comments on Isaiah." In *LDS GospelDoctrine.net*. http://www.ldsgospeldoctrine.net/kn/ot/ (accessed September 5, 2007).

Neusner, Jacob, ed. *The Babylonian Talmud: A Translation and Commentary*. 22 vols. Peabody, MA: Hendrickson Publishers, 2006.

———. 1991. *Confronting Creation: How Judaism Reads Genesis*. Eugene, OR: Wipf and Stock Publishers, 2004.

———. 1953-1968. "Editor's Foreword." In *Jewish Symbols in the Greco-Roman Period*, edited by Jacob Neusner and Erwin Ramsdell Goodenough. Abridged ed. *Bollingen Series*, ix-xxxvii. Princeton, NJ: Princeton University Press, 1988.

———, ed. *Genesis Rabbah: The Judaic Commentary to the Book of Genesis, A New American Translation*. 3 vols. Vol. 1: Parashiyyot One through Thirty-Three on Genesis 1:1 to 8:14. *Brown Judaic Studies* 104, ed. Jacob Neusner. Atlanta, GA: Scholars Press, 1985.

———, ed. *Genesis Rabbah: The Judaic Commentary to the Book of Genesis, A New American Translation*. 3 vols. Vol. 2: Parashiyyot Thirty-Four through Sixty-Seven on Genesis 8:15-28:9. *Brown Judaic Studies* 105, ed. Jacob Neusner. Atlanta, GA: Scholars Press, 1985.

———, ed. *Genesis Rabbah: The Judaic Commentary to the Book of Genesis, A New American Translation*. 3 vols. Vol. 3: Parashiyyot Sixty-Eight through One Hundred on Genesis 28:10 to 50:26. *Brown Judaic Studies* 106, ed. Jacob Neusner. Atlanta, GA: Scholars Press, 1985.

———, ed. *Judaism and Story: The Evidence of the Fathers According to Rabbi Nathan*. Eugene, OR: Wipf and Stock Publishers, 1992.

———. 1964. "Judaism at Dura-Europos." In *The Dura-Europos Synagogue: A Re-evaluation (1932-1992)*, edited by Joseph Gutmann, 155-92. Atlanta, GA: Scholars Press, 1992.

———, ed. *The Mishnah: A New Translation*. London, England: Yale University Press, 1988.

———. "Religious studies: The next vocation." *Bulletin of the Council on the Study of Religion* 8, no. 5 (December 1977): 117-20.

———. "Ritual without myth: The use of legal materials for the study of religions." *Religion: Journal of Religion and Religions* 5 (Autumn 1975): 91-100. Reprint, Neusner, J. "Ritual without myth: The use of legal materials for the study of religions." In *Neusner on Judaism*. 3 vols. Vol. 3: Religion and Theology, 139-148. *Ashgate Contemporary Thinkers on Religion: Collected Works*, ed. J. Hinnels. Aldershot, England: Ashgate, 2006.

———. 1987. "Studying ancient Judaism through the art of the synagogue." In *Art as Religious Studies*, edited by Doug Adams and Diana Apostolos-Cappadona, 29-57. New York City, NY: Crossroad, 1990.

———, ed. *The Talmud of the Land of Israel*. 35 vols. *Chicago Studies in the History of Judaism*. Chicago, IL: University of Chicago Press, 1982-1995.

———, ed. *The Tosefta: Translated from the Hebrew, with a New Introduction*. 2 vols. Peabody, MA: Hendrickson Publishers, 2002.

"New Oxford American Dictionary." In *Oxford University Press*. http://www.oup.com/us/noad (accessed May 30, 2008).

New Primary Children's Songbook. Salt Lake City, UT: Deseret Book, 1991.

"New Testament Apocrypha." In *Interfaith Online*. http://www.interfaith.org/christianity/apocrypha/ (accessed October 3, 2008).

Newby, Gordon Darnell. *A Concise Encyclopedia of Islam*. Oxford, England: Oneworld Publications, 2002.

———. *A History of the Jews of Arabia: From Ancient Times to Their Eclipse under Islam*. Columbia, SC: University of South Carolina Press, 1988.

———. "Muslims, Jews and Christians: Relations and Interactions." In *The Muslim Almanac*, edited by Azim Nanji, 423-29. Detroit, MI: Gale Research, 1996.

Nibley, Hugh W. *Abraham in Egypt*. Salt Lake City, UT: Deseret Book, 1981.

———. 1981. *Abraham in Egypt*. Edited by Gary P. Gillum. *The Collected Works of Hugh Nibley* 14. Salt Lake City, UT: Deseret Book, 2000.

———. "Abraham's temple drama." In *The Temple in Time and Eternity*, edited by Donald W. Parry and Stephen D. Ricks, 1-42. Provo, UT: The Foundation for Ancient Research and Mormon Studies, Brigham Young University, 1999. Reprint, Nibley, Hugh W. "Abraham's temple drama." In *Eloquent Witness: Nibley on Himself, Others, and the Temple*, edited by Stephen D. Ricks. *The Collected Works of Hugh Nibley* 17, 445-482. Salt Lake City, UT: Deseret Book, 2008.

———. 1954. "The ancient law of liberty." In *The World and the Prophets*, edited by John W. Welch, Gary P. Gillum and Don E. Norton. *The Collected Works of Hugh Nibley* 3, 182-90. Salt Lake City, UT: Deseret Book, 1987.

———. 1967. "Apocryphal writings and the teachings of the Dead Sea Scrolls." In *Temple and Cosmos: Beyond This Ignorant Present*, edited by Don E. Norton. *The Collected Works of Hugh Nibley* 12, 264-335. Salt Lake City: Deseret Book, 1992.

———. 1968-1979. *An Approach to the Book of Abraham*. Edited by John Gee. *The Collected Works of Hugh Nibley* 18. Provo, UT: Foundation for Ancient Research and Mormon Studies (FARMS), 2009.

———. 1957. *An Approach to the Book of Mormon*. Edited by John W. Welch. 3rd ed. *The Collected Works of Hugh Nibley* 6. Salt Lake City, UT: Deseret Book, 1988.

———. "Assembly and atonement." In *King Benjamin's Speech: 'That Ye May Learn Wisdom'*, edited by John W. Welch and Stephen D. Ricks, 119-45. Provo, UT: FARMS, 1998. Reprint, Nibley, Hugh W. "Assembly and Atonement." In *Eloquent Witness: Nibley on Himself, Others, and the Temple*, edited by Stephen D. Ricks. *The Collected Works of Hugh Nibley* 17, 420-444. Salt Lake City, UT: Deseret Book, 2008.

———. 1980. "Before Adam." In *Old Testament and Related Studies*, edited by John W. Welch, Gary P. Gillum and Don E. Norton. *The Collected Works of Hugh Nibley* 1, 49-85. Salt Lake City, UT: Deseret Book, 1986.

———. 1973. "The best possible test." In *Temple and Cosmos: Beyond This Ignorant Present*, edited by D.E. Norton. *The Collected Works of Hugh Nibley* 12, 532-40. Salt Lake City, UT: Deseret Book, 1992.

———. "Beyond politics." In *Nibley on the Timely and the Timeless: Classic Essays of Hugh W. Nibley*, edited by Truman G. Madsen, 279-305. Provo, UT: Brigham Young University Religious Studies Center, 1978.

———. 1954. "The Book of Mormon as a witness." In *The World and the Prophets*, edited by John W. Welch, Gary P. Gillum and Don E. Norton. *The Collected Works of Hugh Nibley* 3, 207-15. Salt Lake City, UT: Deseret Book, 1987.

———. 1988. "The Book of Mormon: Forty years after." In *The Prophetic Book of Mormon*, edited by John W. Welch. *The Collected Works of Hugh Nibley* 8, 533-69. Salt Lake City, UT: Deseret Book, 1989.

———. 1972. "Brigham Young on the environment." In *Brother Brigham Challenges the Saints*, edited by Don E. Norton and Shirley S. Ricks. *The Collected Works of Hugh Nibley* 13, 23-54. Salt Lake City, UT: Deseret Book, 1994.

———. 1982. "Christ among the ruins." In *The Prophetic Book of Mormon*, edited by John W. Welch. *The Collected Works of Hugh Nibley* 8, 407-34. Salt Lake City, UT: Deseret Book, 1989.

———. 1959-1960. "Christian envy of the temple." In *Mormonism and Early Christianity*, edited by Todd M. Compton and Stephen D. Ricks. *The Collected Works of Hugh Nibley* 4, 391-434. Salt Lake City: Deseret Book, 1987.

———. "The circle and the square." In *Temple and Cosmos: Beyond This Ignorant Present*, edited by Don E. Norton. *The Collected Works of Hugh Nibley* 12, 139-73. Salt Lake City, UT: Deseret Book, 1992.

———. 1979. "A conversation with Hugh Nibley." In *Eloquent Witness: Nibley on Himself, Others, and the Temple*, edited by Stephen D. Ricks. *The Collected Works of Hugh Nibley* 17, 51-72. Salt Lake City, UT: Deseret Book, 2008.

———. 1978. "The early Christian prayer circle." In *Mormonism and Early Christianity*, edited by Todd M. Compton and Stephen D. Ricks. *The Collected Works of Hugh Nibley* 4, 45-99. Salt Lake City, UT: Deseret Book, 1987.

———. 1970. "Educating the Saints." In *Brother Brigham Challenges the Saints*, edited by Don E. Norton and Shirley S. Ricks. *The Collected Works of Hugh Nibley* 13, 306-45. Salt Lake City, UT: Deseret Book, 1994.

———. *Enoch the Prophet*. Edited by Stephen D. Ricks. *The Collected Works of Hugh Nibley* 2. Salt Lake City, UT: Deseret Book, 1986.

———. 1966. "*Evangelium Quadraginta Dierum*: The Forty-day Mission of Christ—The Forgotten Heritage." In *Mormonism and Early Christianity*, edited by Todd M. Compton and Stephen D. Ricks. *The Collected Works of Hugh Nibley* 4, 10-44. Salt Lake City, UT: Deseret Book, 1987.

———. 1965. "The expanding gospel." In *Temple and Cosmos: Beyond This Ignorant Present*, edited by D.E. Norton. *The Collected Works of Hugh Nibley* 12, 177-211. Salt Lake City, UT: Deseret Book, 1992.

———. "The facsimiles of the Book of Abraham." *Sunstone* 4, no. 5/6 (December 1979): 49-51.

———. 1981. "Foreword to Learn Greek through the New Testament." In *Eloquent Witness: Nibley on Himself, Others, and the Temple*, edited by Stephen D. Ricks. *The Collected Works of Hugh Nibley* 17, 111-13. Salt Lake City, UT: Deseret Book, 2008.

———. 1981. "Freemen and King-men in the Book of Mormon." In *The Prophetic Book of Mormon*, edited by John W. Welch. *The Collected Works of Hugh Nibley* 8, 328-79. Salt Lake City, UT: Deseret Book, 1989.

———. 1985. "From the earth upon which thou standest." In *Temple and Cosmos: Beyond This Ignorant Present*, edited by D.E. Norton. *The Collected Works of Hugh Nibley* 12, 550-54. Salt Lake City, UT: Deseret Book, 1992.

———. 1982. "Funeral address." In *Approaching Zion*, edited by D.E. Norton. *The Collected Works of Hugh Nibley* 9, 290-307. Salt Lake City, UT: Deseret Book, 1989.

———. 1972. "The genesis of the written word." In *Nibley on the Timely and the Timeless*, edited by Truman G. Madsen, 101-27. Provo, UT: Religious Studies Center, Brigham Young University, 1978.

———. 1979. "Gifts." In *Approaching Zion*, edited by D.E. Norton. *The Collected Works of Hugh Nibley* 9, 85-117. Salt Lake City, UT: Deseret Book, 1989.

———. 1986. "The greatness of Egypt." In *Eloquent Witness: Nibley on Himself, Others, and the Temple*, edited by Stephen D. Ricks. *The Collected Works of Hugh Nibley* 17, 271-311. Salt Lake City, UT: Deseret Book, 2008.

———. "The hierocentric state." *Western Political Quarterly* 4 (1951): 226-53.

———. 1951. "The hierocentric state." In *The Ancient State*, edited by Donald W. Parry and Stephen D. Ricks. *The Collected Works of Hugh Nibley* 10, 99-147. Salt Lake City, UT: Deseret Book, 1991.

———. 1956. "Historicity of the Bible." In *Old Testament and Related Studies*, edited by John W. Welch, Gary P. Gillum and Don E. Norton. *The Collected Works of Hugh Nibley* 1, 1-19. Salt Lake City, UT: Deseret Book, 1986.

———. 1993. "A house of glory." In *Eloquent Witness: Nibley on Himself, Others, and the Temple*, edited by Stephen D. Ricks. *The Collected Works of Hugh Nibley* 17, 323-39. Salt Lake City, UT: Deseret Book, 2008.

———. 1980. "How firm a foundation! What makes it so." In *Approaching Zion*, edited by D.E. Norton. *The Collected Works of Hugh Nibley* 9, 149-77. Salt Lake City, UT: Deseret Book, 1989.

———. "An intellectual autobiography." In *Nibley on the Timely and the Timeless: Classic Essays of Hugh W. Nibley*, edited by Truman G. Madsen, ix-xxviii. Provo, UT: Brigham Young University Religious Studies Center, 1978.

———. 1986. "The law of consecration." In *Approaching Zion*, edited by Don E. Norton. *The Collected Works of Hugh Nibley* 9, 422-86. Salt Lake City, UT: Deseret Book, 1989.

———. 1983. "Leaders to managers: The fatal shift." In *Brother Brigham Challenges the Saints*, edited by Don E. Norton and Shirley S. Ricks. *The Collected Works of Hugh Nibley* 13, 491-508. Salt Lake City, UT: Deseret Book, 1994.

———. 1952. *Lehi in the Desert, The World of the Jaredites, There Were Jaredites*. Edited by John W. Welch, Darrell L. Matthews and Stephen R. Callister. *The Collected Works of Hugh Nibley* 5. Salt Lake City, UT: Deseret Book, 1988.

———. 1956. "The lesson of the sixth century BC." BYU Devotional given March 20, 1956; FARMS Publication N-LES. Provo, UT: Foundation for Ancient Research and Mormon Studies. http://speeches.byu.edu/?act=viewitem&id=829 (accessed May 17, 2009).

———. 1972. "Man's dominion or subduing the earth." In *Brother Brigham Challenges the Saints*, edited by Don E. Norton and Shirley S. Ricks. *The Collected Works of Hugh Nibley* 13, 3-22. Salt Lake City, UT: Deseret Book, 1994.

———. 1988. "The meaning of the atonement." In *Approaching Zion*, edited by Don E. Norton. *The Collected Works of Hugh Nibley* 9, 554-614. Salt Lake City, UT: Deseret Book, 1989.

———. 1975. "The meaning of the temple." In *Temple and Cosmos: Beyond This Ignorant Present*, edited by Don E. Norton. *The Collected Works of Hugh Nibley* 12, 1-41. Salt Lake City, UT: Deseret Book, 1992.

———. "Meanings and functions of temples." In *Encyclopedia of Mormonism*, edited by Daniel H. Ludlow. 4 vols. Vol. 4, 1458-63. New York City, NY: Macmillan, 1992. http://www.lib.byu.edu/Macmillan/ (accessed November 26, 2007).

———. 1975. *The Message of the Joseph Smith Papyri: An Egyptian Endowment*. 2nd ed. Salt Lake City, UT: Deseret Book, 2005.

———. 1971. "Myths and the scriptures." In *Old Testament and Related Studies*, edited by John W. Welch, Gary P. Gillum and Don E. Norton. *The Collected Works of Hugh Nibley* 1, 37-47. Salt Lake City, UT: Deseret Book, 1986.

———. "A New Look at the Pearl of Great Price." *Improvement Era*, 1968-1970. Reprint, Provo, UT: FARMS, Brigham Young University, 1990.

———. 1976. "Nibliography." In *Eloquent Witness: Nibley on Himself, Others, and the Temple*, edited by Stephen D. Ricks. *The Collected Works of Hugh Nibley* 17, 46-50. Salt Lake City, UT: Deseret Book, 2008.

———. "Not to worry." In *Expressions of Faith: Testimonies of Latter-day Saint Scholars*, edited by Susan Easton Black, 139-54. Salt Lake City, UT: Deseret Book, 1996.

———. "On the sacred and the symbolic." In *Temples of the Ancient World*, edited by Donald W. Parry, 535-621. Salt Lake City, UT: Deseret Book, 1994. Reprint, Nibley, Hugh W. "On the Sacred and the Symbolic." In *Eloquent Witness: Nibley on Himself, Others, and the Temple*, edited by Stephen D. Ricks. *The Collected Works of Hugh Nibley* 17, 340-419. Salt Lake City, UT: Deseret Book, 2008.

———. 1989. "One eternal round." In *Temple and Cosmos: Beyond This Ignorant Present*, edited by Don E. Norton. *The Collected Works of Hugh Nibley* 12, 379-433. Salt Lake City, UT: Deseret Book, 1992.

———. 1961. "The passing of the primitive Church: Forty variations on an unpopular theme." In *Mormonism and Early Christianity*, edited by Todd M. Compton and Stephen D. Ricks. *The Collected Works of Hugh Nibley* 4, 168-208. Salt Lake City, UT: Deseret Book, 1987.

———. 1980. "Patriarchy and matriarchy." In *Old Testament and Related Studies*, edited by John W. Welch, Gary P. Gillum and Don E. Norton. *The Collected Works of Hugh Nibley* 1, 87-113. Salt Lake City, UT: Deseret Book, 1986.

———. 1992. "Promised lands." In *Brother Brigham Challenges the Saints*, edited by Don E. Norton and Shirley S. Ricks. *The Collected Works of Hugh Nibley* 13, 76-101. Salt Lake City, UT: Deseret Book, 1994.

———. 1982. "The prophetic Book of Mormon." In *The Prophetic Book of Mormon*, edited by John W. Welch. *The Collected Works of Hugh Nibley* 8, 435-69. Salt Lake City, UT: Deseret Book, 1989.

———. 1954. "Prophets and gnostics." In *The World and the Prophets*, edited by John W. Welch, Gary P. Gillum and Don E. Norton. *The Collected Works of Hugh Nibley* 3, 63-70. Salt Lake City, UT: Deseret Book, 1987.

———. 1954. "Prophets and ritual." In *The World and the Prophets*, edited by John W. Welch, Gary P. Gillum and Don E. Norton. *The Collected Works of Hugh Nibley* 3, 146-53. Salt Lake City, UT: Deseret Book, 1987.

———. 1954. "The prophets and the open mind." In *The World and the Prophets*, edited by John W. Welch, Gary P. Gillum and Don E. Norton. *The Collected Works of Hugh Nibley* 3, 126-34. Salt Lake City, UT: Deseret Book, 1987.

———. ca. 1960. "Rediscovery of the apocrypha and the Book of Mormon." In *Temple and Cosmos: Beyond This Ignorant Present*, edited by Don E. Norton. *The Collected Works of Hugh Nibley* 12, 212-63. Salt Lake City, UT: Deseret Book, 1992.

———. 1986. "Return to the temple." In *Temple and Cosmos: Beyond This Ignorant Present*, edited by Don E. Norton. *The Collected Works of Hugh Nibley* 12, 42-90. Salt Lake City, UT: Deseret Book, 1992.

———. 1975. "Sacred vestments." In *Temple and Cosmos: Beyond This Ignorant Present*, edited by Don E. Norton. *The Collected Works of Hugh Nibley* 12, 91-138. Salt Lake City: Deseret Book, 1992.

———. 1985. "Scriptural perspectives on how to survive the calamities of the last days." In *The Prophetic Book of Mormon*, edited by John W. Welch. *The Collected Works of Hugh Nibley* 8, 470-97. Salt Lake City, UT: Deseret Book, 1989.

———. 1967. *Since Cumorah*. Edited by John W. Welch. 2nd ed. *The Collected Works of Hugh Nibley* 7. Provo, UT: Foundation for Ancient Research and Mormon Studies (FARMS), 1988.

———. 1951. "Sparsiones." In *The Ancient State*, edited by Donald W. Parry and Stephen D. Ricks. *The Collected Works of Hugh Nibley* 10, 148-94. Salt Lake City, UT: Deseret Book, 1991.

———. 1989. "Stewardship of the air." In *Brother Brigham Challenges the Saints*. *The Collected Works of Hugh Nibley* 13, 55-75. Salt Lake City: Deseret Book, 1994.

———. 1989-1990. *Teachings of the Book of Mormon*. 4 vols. Provo, UT: FARMS, 2004.

———. 1986. *Teachings of the Pearl of Great Price*. Provo, UT: Foundation for Ancient Research and Mormon Studies (FARMS), Brigham Young University, 2004.

———. 1999. "Temples Everywhere." *Insights: The Newsletter of the Foundation for Ancient Research and Mormon Studies (FARMS) at Brigham Young University* 25, no. 1 (2005): 10-16. Reprint, Nibley, Hugh W. "Temples everywhere." In *Eloquent Witness: Nibley on Himself, Others, and the Temple*, edited by Stephen D. Ricks. *The Collected Works of Hugh Nibley* 17, 483-500. Salt Lake City, UT: Deseret Book, 2008.

———. 1966. "Tenting, toll, and taxing." In *The Ancient State*, edited by Donald W. Perry and Stephen D. Ricks. *The Collected Works of Hugh Nibley* 10, 33-98. Salt Lake City, UT: Deseret Book, 1991.

———. "Three degrees of righteousness from the Old Testament." In *Approaching Zion*, edited by Don E. Norton. *The Collected Works of Hugh Nibley* 9, 308-37. Salt Lake City, UT: Deseret Book, 1989.

———. "To open the last dispensation: Moses chapter 1." In *Nibley on the Timely and the Timeless: Classic Essays of Hugh W. Nibley*, edited by Truman G. Madsen, 1-20. Provo, UT: BYU Religious Studies Center, 1978. http://farms.byu.edu/publications/transcripts/?id=71 (accessed October 10, 2008).

———. 1973. "Treasures in the heavens." In *Old Testament and Related Studies*, edited by John W. Welch, Gary P. Gillum and Don E. Norton. *The Collected Works of Hugh Nibley* 1, 171-214. Salt Lake City, UT: Deseret Book, 1986.

———. "The Roman games as a survival of an archaic year-cult." Doctoral Dissertation, University of California, Berkeley, 1939.

———. *Temple and Cosmos: Beyond This Ignorant Present*. Edited by Don E. Norton. *The Collected Works of Hugh Nibley* 12. Salt Lake City, UT: Deseret Book, 1992.

———. "The Three Facsimiles from the Book of Abraham." Provo, UT: Foundation for Ancient Research and Mormon Studies, Brigham Young University, 1980.

———. 1967. "Unrolling the scrolls—some forgotten witnesses." In *Old Testament and Related Studies*, edited by John W. Welch, Gary P. Gillum and Don E. Norton. *The Collected Works of Hugh Nibley* 1, 115-70. Salt Lake City, UT: Deseret Book, 1986.

———. 1984. "We will still weep for Zion." In *Approaching Zion*, edited by Don E. Norton. *The Collected Works of Hugh Nibley* 9, 341-77. Salt Lake City, UT: Deseret Book, 1989.

———. 1958, 1983. "What is a temple?" In *Mormonism and Early Christianity*, edited by Todd M. Compton and Stephen D. Ricks. *The Collected Works of Hugh Nibley* 4, 355-90. Salt Lake City, UT: Deseret Book, 1987.

———. "Where is the battle?" Unpublished lecture notes recorded by Michael B. James, n.d.

———. 1982. "Work we must, but the lunch is free." In *Approaching Zion*, edited by Don E. Norton. *The Collected Works of Hugh Nibley* 9, 202-51. Salt Lake City, UT: Deseret Book, 1989.

———. 1954. *The World and the Prophets*. Edited by John W. Welch, Gary P. Gillum and Don E. Norton. *The Collected Works of Hugh Nibley* 3. Salt Lake City, UT: Deseret Book, 1987.

———. "Young, Brigham: Teachings of Brigham Young." In *Encyclopedia of Mormonism*, edited by Daniel H. Ludlow. 4 vols. Vol. 4, 1609-11. New York City, NY: Macmillan, 1992. http://www.lib.byu.edu/Macmillan/ (accessed November 26, 2007).

———. 1975. "Zeal without knowledge." In *Approaching Zion*, edited by Don E. Norton. *The Collected Works of Hugh Nibley* 9, 63-84. Salt Lake City, UT: Deseret Book, 1989.

Nichols, Beverley. *The Queen's Coronation Day: The Pictorial Record of the Great Occasion*. Andover, UK: Pitkin Unichrome, 1953.

Nickelsburg, George W. E., ed. *1 Enoch 1: A Commentary on the Book of 1 Enoch, Chapters 1-36; 81-108*. Minneapolis, MN: Fortress Press, 2001.

———. *Ancient Judaism and Christian Origins*. Minneapolis, MN: Fortress Press, 2003.

Nickelsburg, George W. E., and James C. VanderKam, eds. *1 Enoch: A New Translation*. Minneapolis, MN: Fortress Press, 2004.

Nielsen, F. Kent, and Stephen D. Ricks. "Creation, creation accounts." In *The Encyclopedia of Mormonism*, edited by Daniel H. Ludlow. 4 vols. Vol. 1 340-343. New York City, NY: Macmillan, 1992. http://www.lib.byu.edu/Macmillan/ (accessed November 26, 2007).

Nigosian, S. A. 1993. *The Zoroastrian Faith: Tradition and Modern Research*. Montreal, Canada: McGill-Queen's University Press, 2003.

Nissinen, Martti, and Risto Uro. *Sacred Marriages*. Winona Lake, IN: Eisenbrauns, 2008.

Noah, Mordecai M., ed. 1840. *The Book of Jasher*. Translated by Moses Samuel. Salt Lake City, UT: Joseph Hyrum Parry, 1887. Reprint, New York City, NY: Cosimo Classics, 2005.

Noah, Mordecai M., and Wayne Simpson, eds. 1840. *The Authentic Annals of the Early Hebrews (Also Known as The Book of Jasher and Sefer Hayashar)*. Translated by Moses Samuel. Kearney, NE: Morris Publishing, 2005.

Norman, Keith E. "Deification, early Christian." In *Encyclopedia of Mormonism*, edited by Daniel H. Ludlow. 4 vols. Vol. 1, 369-70. New York City, NY: Macmillan, 1992. http://www.lib.byu.edu/Macmillan/ (accessed November 26, 2007).

———. 1980. *Deification: The Content of Athanasian Soteriology. Occasional Papers*. Provo, UT: FARMS, 2000.

———. "*Ex nihilo*: The development of the doctrines of God and creation in early Christianity." *BYU Studies* 17 (Spring 1977): 291-318.

Norman, V. Garth. *Izapa Sculpture, Part 2: Text. Papers of the New World Archaeological Foundation* 30. Provo, UT: New World Archaeological Foundation, Brigham Young University, 1976. http://contentdm.lib.byu.edu/cdm4/document.php?CISOROOT=/NWAF&CISOPTR=8921&REC=14 (accessed February 9, 2009).

Norris, Leslie, and Mark Magleby. *Kershisnik: Paintings from Life*. Madison, WI: Guild Publishing, 2002.

Novatian. ca. 235-258. "A treatise of Novatian concerning the Trinity." In *The Ante-Nicene Fathers (The Writings of the Fathers Down to AD 325)*, edited by Alexander Roberts and James Donaldson. 10 vols. Vol. 6, 611-44. Buffalo, NY: The Christian Literature Company, 1886. Reprint, Peabody, MA: Hendrickson Publishers, 2004.

Novickij (Novitskii), P. P. ed. "Откровение Авраама (Otkrovenie Avraama / Facsimile edition of the Codex Sylvester)." In *Общество любителей древней письменности (Obshchestvo liubitelei drevnei pis'mennosti)*. Vol. 99:2. St. Petersburg, Russia: A. F. Markova, 1891. Reprint, Obshchestvo liubitelei drevnei pis'mennosti i iskusstva, Leningrad, Russia, 1967. http://www.marquette.edu/maqom/spart1.pdf (accessed June 18, 2008).

Numbers, Ronald L. *The Creationists: The Evolution of Scientific Creationism*. Berkeley, CA: University of California Press, 1992.

Nuttall, A. D. *Shakespeare the Thinker*. New Haven, CT: Yale University Press, 2007.

Nuttall, L. John. Journal 2 (December 1876-August 1877). *Journals of L. John Nuttall, 1857-1904*. Provo, UT: L. Tom Perry Special Collections, Brigham Young University

Nylan, Michael. "Toward an archaeology of writing: Text, ritual, and the culture of public display in the classical period (475 B.C.E-220 C.E)." In *Text and Ritual in Early China*, edited by Martin Kern, 3-49. Seattle, WA: University of Washington Press, 2005.

O'Brien, Christian, ed. "The Book of the Great Logos (SHABD) or The Book of Knowledge (*1 Jeu*)." In *The Path of Light*, 229-56. Kemble, Cirencester, England: Dianthus Publishing, 1999.

———, ed. "The Book of the Hierarchy of Heaven (*2 Jeu*)." In *The Path of Light*, 259-85. Kemble, Cirencester, England: Dianthus Publishing, 1999.

———, ed. *The Path of Light, Volumes 1 and 2*. Kemble, Cirencester, England: Dianthus Publishing, 1999.

O'Dea, Thomas F. *The Mormons*. Chicago, IL: University of Chicago Press, 1957.

O'Reilly, Jennifer. "The trees of Eden in mediaeval iconography." In *A Walk in the Garden: Biblical, Iconographical and Literary Images of Eden*, edited by Paul Morris and Deborah Sawyer. *Journal for the Study of the Old Testament Supplement Series* 136, eds. David J. A. Clines and Philip R. Davies, 167-204. Sheffield, England: JSOT Press, 1992.

Oakley, John. Salt Lake City, UT: *Deseret News*, February 2, 1854, 1.

Oaks, Dallin H. "The challenge to become." *Ensign* 30, November 2000, 32-34.

———. "Free agency and freedom." BYU Fireside Address, October 11, 1987. In *Brigham Young University 1987-1988 Devotional and Fireside Speeches*, 37-47. Provo, UT: Brigham Young University Publications, 1987. http://speeches.byu.edu/reader/reader.php?id=7014 (accessed September 6, 2007).

———. "The great plan of happiness." *Ensign* 23, November 1993, 72-75.

———. "Joseph Smith in a personal world." In *The Worlds of Joseph Smith: A Bicentennial Conference at the Library of Congress*, edited by John W. Welch, 153-72. Provo, UT: The Brigham Young University Press, 2005.

———. "Revelation." September 29, 1981. In *Brigham Young University 1981-82 Speeches*, 1-9. Provo, UT: Brigham Young University Press, 1981. http://speeches.byu.edu/index.php?act=viewitem&id=568 (accessed October 3, 2007).

———. "Scripture reading and revelation." *Ensign* 25, January 1995, 7-9.

———. "Sharing the Gospel." *Ensign* 31, November 2001, 7-9.

———. "Taking upon us the name of Jesus Christ." *Ensign* 15 1985, 80-83.

Oden, Robert A., Jr. "Divine aspirations in Atrahasis and in Genesis 1-11." *Zeitschrift für die Alttestamentliche Wissenschaft* 93 (1981): 197-216.

Ogden, D. Kelly, and Andrew C. Skinner. *The Four Gospels*. Salt Lake City, UT: Deseret Book, 2006.

Old Testament Student Manual, Religion 301. Salt Lake City, UT: The Church of Jesus Christ of Latter-day Saints, 1980.

Olsen, Nolan Porter. 1978. *Logan Temple: The First 100 Years*. Providence, UT: Keith W. Watkins & Sons, 1994.

Olson, Daniel C. "1 Enoch." In *Eerdmans Commentary on the Bible*, edited by James D. G. Dunn and John W. Rogerson, 904-41. Grand Rapids, MI: William B. Eerdmans, 2003.

Oman, Nathan B. "A defense of the authority of Church doctrine." *Dialogue: A Journal of Mormon Thought* 40, no. 4 (Winter 2007): 1-28.

———. "Jurisprudence and the problem of church doctrine." *Element: The Journal of the Society for Mormon Philosophy and Theology* 2, no. 2 (Fall 2006): 1-19.

———. "Secret combinations: A legal analysis." *FARMS Review* 16, no. 1 (2004): 49-73.

Oman, Richard G. "Exterior symbolism of the Salt Lake Temple: Reflecting the faith that called the place into being." *BYU Studies* 36, no. 4 (1996-97): 7-68.

Oman, Richard G., and Robert O. Davis. *Images of Faith: Art of the Latter-day Saints*. Salt Lake City, UT: Deseret Book, 1995.

Onions, C. T., and Robert D. Eagleson. *A Shakespeare Glossary*. 3rd ed. Oxford, England: The Clarendon Press, 1989.

Orgel, Stephen. "Introduction." In *The Tempest*, edited by Stephen Orgel. The Oxford Shakespeare, ed. Stanley Wells, 1-87. Oxford, England: Oxford University Press, 1987.

Origen. ca. 200-254. "Commentary on John." In *The Ante-Nicene Fathers (The Writings of the Fathers Down to AD 325)*, edited by Alexander Roberts and James Donaldson. 10 vols. Vol. 10, 297-408. Buffalo, NY: The Christian Literature Company, 1896. Reprint, Peabody, MA: Hendrickson Publishers, 2004.

———. ca. 200-230. "De Principiis." In *The Ante-Nicene Fathers (The Writings of the Fathers Down to AD 325)*, edited by Alexander Roberts and James Donaldson. 10 vols. Vol. 4, 239-384. Buffalo, NY: The Christian Literature Company, 1885. Reprint, Peabody, MA: Hendrickson Publishers, 2004.

———. ca. 200-254. *Homilies on Genesis and Exodus*. Translated by Gary Wayne Barkley. *Fathers of the Church*. Washington, DC: Catholic University of America Press, 1982.

———. ca. 200-254. *Homilies on Leviticus 1-16*. Translated by Gary Wayne Barkley. *Fathers of the Church*. Washington, DC: Catholic University of America Press, 1990.

———. ca. 234-240. *Homilies on Luke: Fragments on Luke*. Translated by Joseph T. Lienhard. Washington, D.C.: Catholic University of America Press, 1996.

Orlov, Andrei A. *The Enoch-Metatron Tradition*. Texts and Studies in Ancient Judaism 107. Tübingen, Germany Mohr Siebeck, 2005.

———. "'The gods of my father Terah': Abraham the iconoclast and the polemics with the divine body traditions in the Apocalypse of Abraham." *Journal for the Study of the Pseudepigrapha* 18, no. 1 (2008): 33-53. Reprint, Orlov, Andrei A. "'The gods of my father Terah': Abraham the iconoclast and the polemics with the divine body traditions in the *Apocalypse of Abraham*." In *Divine Manifestations in the Slavonic Pseudepigrapha*, edited by Andrei A. Orlov, *Orientalia Judaica Christiana* 2, 217-235. Piscataway, NJ: Gorgias Press, 2009.

———. "The heir of righteousness and the king of righteousness: The priestly Noachic polemics in *2 Enoch* and the Epistle to the Hebrews." *Journal of Theological Studies* 58, no. 1 (2007): 45-65. http://jts.oxfordjournals.org/cgi/reprint/58/1/45.pdf?ijkey=c9zZNzBnzJiHUJl&keytype=ref (accessed September 6, 2007).

———. "On the polemical nature of *2 (Slavonic) Enoch*: A reply to C. Böttrich." *Journal for the Study of Judaism* 34 (2003): 274-303.

———. "In the mirror of the Divine Face: The Enochic features of the *Exagoge* of Ezekiel the Tragedian." In *Divine Manifestations in the Slavonic Pseudepigrapha*, edited by Andrei A. Orlov. *Orientalia Judaica Christiana* 2, 135-51. Pisacataway, NJ: Gorgias Press, 2009.

———. "Praxis of the voice: The divine name traditions in the *Apocalypse of Abraham*." *Journal of Biblical Literature* 127, no. 1 (2008): 53-70. Reprint, Orlov, Andrei A. "Praxis of the voice: The divine name traditions in the *Apocalypse of Abraham*." In *Divine Manifestations in the Slavonic Pseudepigrapha*, edited by Andrei A. Orlov, *Orientalia Judaica Christiana* 2, 155-175. Piscataway, NJ: Gorgias Press, 2009.

———. "Resurrection of Adam's body: The redeeming role of Enoch-Metatron in *2 (Slavonic) Enoch*." Presented at the American Academy of Religion/Society of Biblical Literature Annual Meeting, Early Jewish and Christian Mysticism Group, Atlanta, GA, November 24, 2003. http://www.marquette.edu/maqom/oil.html (accessed June 18, 2008).

Orton, Chad A. *More Faith than Fear: The Los Angeles Stake Story*. Salt Lake City, UT: Bookcraft, 1987.

Osiek, Carolyn, ed. *Shepherd of Hermas: A Commentary*. Hermeneia—A Critical and Historical Commentary on the Bible. Minneapolis, MN: Fortress Press, 1999.

Ostler, Blake T. *The Attributes of God*. Exploring Mormon Thought 1. Salt Lake City, UT: Greg Kofford Books, 2001.

———. "Clothed upon: A unique aspect of Christian antiquity." *BYU Studies* 22, no. 1 (1981): 1-15.

———. "The idea of preexistence in Mormon thought." In *Line Upon Line: Essays on Mormon Doctrine*, edited by Gary James Bergera, 127-44. Salt Lake City, UT: Signature Books, 1989.

———. *Of God and Gods*. Exploring Mormon Thought 3. Salt Lake City, UT: Greg Kofford Books, 2008.

———. "Out of nothing: A history of Creation *ex nihilo* in early Christian thought." *The FARMS Review* 17, no. 2 (2005): 253-320.

———. *The Problems of Theism and the Love of God*. Exploring Mormon Thought 2. Salt Lake City, UT: Greg Kofford Books, 2006.

———. 2007. "Spiritual experiences as the basis for belief and commitment." In *Proceedings of the FAIR Conference*. http://www.fairlds.org/FAIR_Conferences/2007_Spiritual_Experiences.html (accessed April 23, 2008).

Ostler, Nicholas. 2005. *Empires of the Word: A Language History of the World*. New York City, NY: Harper Perennial, 2006.

Ouaknin, Marc-Alain, and Éric Smilévitch, eds. 1983. *Chapitres de Rabbi Éliézer (Pirqé de Rabbi Éliézer): Midrach sur Genèse, Exode, Nombres, Esther. Les Dix Paroles*, ed. Charles Mopsik. Lagrasse, France: Éditions Verdier, 1992.

Ouseley, Gideon Jasper Richard. 1923. *The Gospel of the Holy Twelve*. Kila, MT: Kessinger Publishing, 2004.

Ouspensky, Leonid, and Vladimir Lossky. *The Meaning of Icons*. Crestwood, NY: St. Vladimir's Seminary Press, 1999.

Owen, Paul L. "Narrowing the divide: How being an 'Anglo-Catholic' has changed my view of the LDS Church." *Element: The Journal of the Society for Mormon Philosophy and Theology* 2, no. 2 (Fall 2006): 57-70.

Pace, William B. "Autobiography of William Bryan Pace." Typescript. Harold B. Lee Library, Brigham Young University, 1847

Pack, Russell T. "Quantum cosmology." *Sunstone* 11, January 1987, 2-4.

Packard, Dennis, and Sandra Packard. *Feasting Upon the Word*. Salt Lake City, UT: Deseret Book, 1981.

Packer, Boyd K. "Building bridges of understanding: The Church and the world of Islam (Introduction of Dr. Alwi Shihab)." *BYU Studies* 45, no. 4 (2006): 5-8.

———. "Covenants." *Ensign* 20, November 1990, 84-86.

———. "Do not fear." *Ensign* 34, May 2004, 77-80.

———. "The great plan of happiness." Presented at the *Seventeenth Annual Church Educational System Religious Educators' Symposium on the Doctrine and Covenants/Church History*, Brigham Young University, Provo, UT, August 10, 1993, 1-7. http://ldsces.org/general%20authority%20talks/bkp.The%20Great%20Plan%20of%20Happiness.1993.pdf (accessed August 24, 2008).

———. *The Holy Temple*. Salt Lake City, UT: Bookcraft, 1980.

———. "The law and the light." In *Jacob Through the Words of Mormon: To Learn with Joy*, edited by Monte S. Nyman and Charles D. Tate, Jr., 1-31. Provo, UT: Brigham Young University, 1990.

———. "Let them govern themselves." Presented at the Regional Representatives Seminar, March 30, 1990.

———. "Little Children." *Ensign* 16, November 1986, 16-18.

———. "The mantle is far, far greater than the intellect." *BYU Studies* 21, no. 3 (1981): 1-18.

———. "The Mediator." *Ensign* 7, May 1977, 54-55.

———. *The Mediator*. Salt Lake City, UT: Deseret Book, 1978.

———. *Mine Errand from the Lord: Selections from the Sermons and Writings of Boyd K. Packer*. Edited by C.J. Williams. Salt Lake City, UT: Deseret Book, 2008.

———. 1984. "The pattern of our parentage." In *Let Not Your Heart Be Troubled*, 286-93. Salt Lake City, UT: Bookcraft, 1991.

———. "Personal revelation: The gift, the test, and the promise." *Ensign* 24, November 1994, 59-62.

———. 2007. President Boyd K. Packer Interview Transcript for PBS Documentary. In *Meridian*, July 25, 2007. http://www.meridianmagazine.com/churchupdate/070725packer.html (accessed March 28, 2008).

———. "Scriptures." *Ensign* 12, November 1982, 51-53.

———. "Self-reliance." *Ensign* 5, August 1975, 85-89.

———. "Solving emotional problems in the Lord's own way." *Ensign* 8, May 1978, 91-95.

———. 1988. "Who is Jesus Christ?" *Ensign* 38, March 2008, 13-19.

Pagels, Elaine. 1988. *Adam, Eve, and the Serpent*. New York City, NY: Vintage Books, 1989.

———. 1995. *The Origin of Satan*. New York City, NY: Vintage Books, 1996.

Palmer, Christopher. "Vaughan Williams: Serenade to Music, *Flos Campi*, Five Mystical Songs, Fantasia on Christmas Carols (CD Liner)." Hyperion CDA86420, 1990.

Palmer, Martin J. "Adam, ancient sources." In *Encyclopedia of Mormonism*, edited by Daniel H. ludlow. 4 vols. Vol. 1, 17-18. New York City, NY: Macmillan, 1992. http://www.lib.byu.edu/Macmillan/ (accessed November 26, 2007).

Palmer, Roy. *The Painful Plough: A Portrait of the Agricultural Labourer in the Nineteenth Century from Folk Songs and Ballads and Contemporary Accounts*. Resources of Music 5, ed. Wilfrid Mellers and John Paynter. Cambridge, England: Cambridge University Press, 1972.

Palmer, Spencer J., ed. *The Expanding Church*. Salt Lake City, UT: Deseret Book, 1978.

———, ed. *Mormons and Muslims: Spiritual Foundations and Modern Manifestations* 2nd ed. American Fork, UT: Covenant Communications, 2002.

———. "Zoroastrianism." In *Religions of the World: A Latter-day Saint View*, edited by Spencer J. Palmer, Roger R. Keller, Doug Sull Choi and James A. Toronto. Revised and Enlarged ed, 146-61. Provo, UT: Brigham Young University Press, 1997.

Parkinson, Dilworth B. "'We have received, and we need no more.'" *The FARMS Review* 17, no. 1 (2005): 255-71.

Parr, Ryan. "Missing the boat to ancient America… just plain missing the boat." *The FARMS Review* 17, no. 1 (2005): 83-106.

Parrish, Alan K. *John A. Widtsoe: A Biography*. Salt Lake City, UT: Deseret Book, 2003.

Parrot, André. 1955. *Golgotha and the Church of the Holy Sepulchre*. Translated by Edwin Hudson. *Studies in Biblical Archaeology* 6. New York City, NY: Philosophical Library, 1957.

Parrott, Douglas M. ed. "Eugnostos the blessed (III,3 and V,1) and the Sophia of Jesus Christ (III,4 and BG 8502,3)." In *The Nag Hammadi Library in English*, edited by James M. Robinson. 3rd, Completely Revised ed, 220-43. San Francisco, CA: HarperSanFrancisco, 1990.

Parry, Donald W. "The cherubim, the flaming sword, the path, and the tree of life." Draft manuscript in the possession of the author based on a presentation at the *BYU Tree of Life Symposium*, September 29, 2006. Provo, UT: Brigham Young University, 2007.

———. "Garden of Eden: Prototype sanctuary." In *Temples of the Ancient World*, edited by Donald W. Parry, 126-51. Salt Lake City, UT: Deseret Book, 1994.

———. "Service and temple in King Benjamin's speech." *Journal of Book of Mormon Studies* 16, no. 2 (2007): 42-47.

———. "Temple worship and a possible reference to a prayer circle in Psalm 24." *BYU Studies* 32, no. 4 (1992): 57-62.

Parry, Donald W., Jay A. Parry, and Tina M. Peterson, eds. *Understanding Isaiah*. Salt Lake City, UT: Deseret Book, 1998.

Parry, Donald W., and Dana M. Pike, eds. *LDS Perspectives on the Dead Sea Scrolls*. Provo, UT: Foundation for Ancient Research and Mormon Studies (FARMS) at Brigham Young University, 1997.

Parry, Donald W., and Stephen D. Ricks. *The Dead Sea Scrolls: Questions and Responses for Latter-day Saints*. Provo, UT: Foundation for Ancient Research and Mormon Studies (FARMS) at Brigham Young University, 2000.

Parry, Donald W., and Emanuel Tov, eds. *The Dead Sea Scrolls Reader*. 6 vols. Leiden, The Netherlands: Brill, 2005.

Parry, Jay A., and Donald W. Parry. "The temple in heaven: Its description and significance." In *Temples of the Ancient World*, edited by Donald W. Parry, 515-32. Salt Lake City, UT: Deseret Book, 1994.

Patai, Raphael. 1978. *The Hebrew Goddess*. 3rd ed. Detroit, MI: Wayne State University Press, 1990.

Paul, Erich Robert. *Science, Religion, and Mormon Cosmology*. Urbana and Chicago, IL: University of Illinois Press, 1992.

Paulsen, David L. "Are Christians Mormon? Reassessing Joseph Smith's theology in his bicentennial." *BYU Studies* 45, no. 1 (2006): 35-128.

———. "Divine embodiment: The earliest Christian understanding of God." In *Early Christians in Disarray*, edited by Noel B. Reynolds, 239-93. Provo, UT: Brigham Young University Press, 2005.

———. "An interview with David L. Paulsen." *BYU Studies* 48, no. 2 (2009): 64-68.

———. "Response to Professor Pinnock." In *Mormonism in Dialogue with Contemporary Christian Theologies*, edited by Donald W. Musser and David L. Paulsen, 515-42. Macon, GA: Mercer University Press, 2007.

Pearson, Birger A. ed. "The thought of Norea (IX,2)." In *The Nag Hammadi Library in English*, edited by James M. Robinson. 3rd, Completely Revised ed., 445-47. San Francisco, CA: HarperSanFrancisco, 1990.

Pedersen, Niels A., ed. *Manichaean Homilies. Corpus Fontium Manichaeorum, Series Coptica*, eds. Aloîs van Tongerloo, Samuel N. C. Lieu and Johannes van Oort. Turnhout, Belgium: Brepols, 2006.

Peel, Malcolm L., and Jan Zandee ed. "The Teachings of Sylvanus (VII, 4)." In *The Nag Hammadi Library*, edited by James M. Robinson. 3rd, Completely Revised ed., 379-95. San Francisco, CA: HarperSanFrancisco, 1990.

Pelikan, Jaroslav. *Whose Bible Is It? A Short History of the Scriptures*. New York City, NY: Penguin Group, 2005.

Pennock, Robert T. *Tower of Babel: The Evidence against the New Creationism*. Cambridge, MA: Bradford, The MIT Press, 1999.

Peretz, Jean-Claude. *L'Outil et le Compagnon*. Paris, Fance: SELD-Jean-Cyrille Godefroy, 1994.

Perkins, Pheme. "Gnosticism and the Christian Bible." In *The Canon Debate*, edited by Lee Martin McDonald and James A. Sanders, 355-71. Peabody, MA: Hendrickson Publishers, 2002.

Perry, L. Tom. "The Gospel of Jesus Christ." *Ensign* 38, May 2008, 44-46.

Peshitta Foundation, ed. *Bereshith and Bereshith Rabba (Aramaic English Standard Version of Genesis)*: The Peshitta Foundation, 2006.

Petermann, Julius Heinrich, ed. 1867. *The Great Treasure or Great Book, Commonly Called "The Book of Adam," the Mandaean's Work of Highest Authority (Thesaurus sive Liber Magnus, vulgo "Liber Adami" appellatus, opus Mandaeorum summi ponderis) with a New Introduction by Charles Häberl. Reprint of Berlin-Leipzic [calcography] edition*. 3 vols. *Gorgias Mandaean Studies* 2. Piscataway, NJ: Gorgias Press, 2007.

Peters, Edward, ed. *Heresy and Authority in Medieval Europe: Documents in Translation*. Philadelphia, PA: University of Pennsylvania Press, 1980. http://books.google.com/books?id=rnggrHo-dqUC (accessed March 24, 2009).

Peters, Melvin K. H., ed. *A New English Translation of the Septuagint and the Other Greek Translations Traditionally Included under that Title: Deuteronomy* Provisional ed. *NETS: New English Translation of the Septuagint*, eds. Albert Pietersma and Benjamin Wright. Oxford, England: Oxford University Press, 2004. http://ccat.sas.upenn.edu/nets/edition/deut.pdf.

Petersen, Boyd Jay. *Hugh Nibley: A Consecrated Life*. Salt Lake City, UT: Greg Kofford Books, 2002.

Peterson, Daniel C. *Abraham Divided*. Revised ed. Salt Lake City, UT: Aspen Books, 1995.

———. "Editor's Introduction: Reflections on the reactions to *Rough Stone Rolling* and related matters." *FARMS Review* 19, no. 1 (2007): xi-liv.

———. "The Gadianton robbers as guerilla warriors." In *Warfare in the Book of Mormon*, edited by Stephen D. Ricks and William J. Hamblin, 146-73. Salt Lake City, UT: Deseret Book, 1990.

———. "The language of God: Understanding the *Qur'an*." *BYU Studies* 40, no. 4 (2001): 51-68.

———. "Muhammad." In *The Rivers of Paradise: Moses, Buddha, Confucius, Jesus, and Muhammad as Religious Founders*, edited by David Noel Freedman and Michael J. McClymond, 457-612. Grand Rapids, MI: Wm. B. Eerdmans, 2001.

———. *Muhammad, Prophet of God*. Grand Rapids, MI: William B. Eerdmans, 2007.

———. "Nephi and his Asherah." *Journal of Book of Mormon Studies* 9, no. 2 (2000): 16-25.

———. "Nephi and his Asherah: A note on 1 Nephi 11:8-23." In *Mormons, Scripture, and the Ancient World: Studies in Honor of John L. Sorenson*, edited by Davis Bitton, 191-243. Provo, UT: Foundation for Ancient Research and Mormon Studies, 1998.

———. "Notes on "Gadianton Masonry"." In *Warfare in the Book of Mormon*, edited by Stephen D. Ricks and William J. Hamblin, 174-224. Salt Lake City, UT: Deseret Book, 1990.

———. "Notes on historicity and inerrancy." In *Historicity and the Latter-day Saint Scriptures*, edited by Paul Y. Hoskisson, 197-215. Provo, UT: Brigham Young University Religious Studies Center, 2001.

———. "On the motif of the weeping God in Moses 7." In *Reason, Revelation, and Faith: Essays in Honor of Truman G. Madsen*, edited by Donald W. Parry, Daniel C. Peterson and Stephen D. Ricks, 285-317. Provo, UT: Foundation for Ancient Research and Mormon Studies, 2002.

———. "The Qur'anic tree of life." Presented at the *BYU Tree of Life Symposium*, Provo, UT, September 29, 2006.

———. "Review of Philip L. Barlow, *Mormons and the Bible: The Place of the Latter-day Saints in American Religion*." *Review of Religious Research* 34, no. 1 (1992): 78-79.

———. "'Secret combinations' revisited." *Journal of Book of Mormon Studies* 1, no. 1 (1992): 184-88.

———. "'Ye are gods': Psalm 82 and John 10 as witnesses to the divine nature of humankind." In *The Disciple as Scholar: Essays on Scripture and the Ancient World in Honor of Richard Lloyd Anderson*, edited by Stephen D. Ricks, Donald W. Parry and Andrew H. Hedges, 471-594. Provo, UT: Foundation for Ancient Research and Mormon Studies, 2000.

Peterson, Daniel C., and Stephen D. Ricks. *Offenders for a Word: How Anti-Mormons Play Word Games to Attack the Latter-day Saints*. Salt Lake City, UT: Aspen Books, 1992.

———. "The throne theophany/prophetic call of Muhammad." In *The Disciple as Scholar: Essays on Scripture and the Ancient World in Honor of Richard Lloyd Anderson*, edited by Stephen D. Ricks, Donald W. Parry and Andrew H. Hedges, 323-37. Provo, UT: Foundation for Ancient Research and Mormon Studies, 2000.

Peterson, H. Donl. *The Pearl of Great Price: A History and Commentary*. Salt Lake City, UT: Deseret Book, 1987.

———. *The Story of the Book of Abraham: Mummies, Manuscripts, and Mormonism*. Salt Lake City, UT: Deseret Book, 1995.

Petropoulou, Maria-Zoe. *Animal Sacrifice in Ancient Greek Religion, Judaism, and Christianity, 100 BC to AD 200*. Oxford, England: Oxford University Press, 2008.

Phelps, William Wine. "Adam-ondi-Ahman." Kirtland, OH: *Latter Day Saints' Messenger and Advocate* 1:9, June, 1835, 144.

———. "The answer (25 December 1844)." Nauvoo, IL: *Times and Seasons* 5:24, January, 1845, 757-61.

———. "There is no end." Salt Lake City, UT: *Deseret News*, November 19, 1856, 2.

Philo. b. 20 BCE. "Allegorical Interpretation, III (*Legum Allegoriae*, III)." In *The Works of Philo: Complete and Unabridged*, edited by C. D. Yonge. New Updated ed. Translated by C. D. Yonge, 50-79. Peabody, MA: Hendrickson Publishers, 2006.

———. b. 20 BCE. "Allegorical Interpretation of Genesis (*Legum Allegoriae*)." In *Philo*, edited by F. H. Colson and G. H. Whitaker. 12 vols. Vol. 1. Translated by F. H. Colson and G. H. Whitaker. *The Loeb Classical Library* 226, ed. Jeffrey Henderson, 140-478. Cambridge, MA: Harvard University Press, 1929.

REFERENCES

———. "Appendix 2 — Fragments." In *The Works of Philo: Complete and Unabridged*, edited by C. D. Yonge. New Updated ed. Translated by C. D. Yonge, 880-97. Peabody, MA: Hendrickson Publishers, 2006.

———. b. 20 BCE. "On Abraham (*De Abrahamo*)." In *The Works of Philo: Complete and Unabridged*, edited by C. D. Yonge. New Updated ed. Translated by C. D. Yonge, 411-34. Peabody, MA: Hendrickson Publishers, 2006.

———. b. 20 BCE. "On dreams, that they are God-sent (*Quod a Deo Mittantur Somnia or De Somniis*)." In *The Works of Philo: Complete and Unabridged*, edited by C. D. Yonge. New Updated ed. Translated by C. D. Yonge, 365-410. Peabody, MA: Hendrickson Publishers, 2006.

———. b. 20 BCE. "On mating with the preliminary studies (*De Congressu Quaerendae Eruditionis Gratiea*)." In *The Works of Philo: Complete and Unabridged*, edited by C. D. Yonge. New Updated ed. Translated by C. D. Yonge, 304-20. Peabody, MA: Hendrickson Publishers, 2006.

———. b. 20 BCE. "On Rewards and Punishments (*De Praemiis et Poenis*)." In *The Works of Philo: Complete and Unabridged*, edited by C. D. Yonge, 664-81. Peabody, MA: Hendrickson Publishers, 2006.

———. b. 20 BCE. "On the Giants (*De Gigantibus*)." In *Philo*, edited by F. H. Colson and G. H. Whitaker. 12 vols. Vol. 2. Translated by F. H. Colson and G. H. Whitaker. *The Loeb Classical Library* 227, ed. Jeffrey Henderson, 441-79. Cambridge, MA: Harvard University Press, 1929.

———. b. 20 BCE. "On the Life of Moses, 1 (*De Vita Mosis, 1*)." In *The Works of Philo: Complete and Unabridged*, edited by C. D. Yonge. New Updated ed. Translated by C. D. Yonge, 459-90. Peabody, MA: Hendrickson Publishers, 2006.

———. b. 20 BCE. "On the Virtues (*De Virtutibus*)." In *Philo*, edited by F. H. Colson. 12 vols. Vol. 8. Translated by F. H. Colson. *The Loeb Classical Library* 341, 158-305, 440-50. Cambridge, MA: Harvard University Press, 1939.

———. b. 20 BCE. *Philo*. 12 vols. Vol. 1-6. Translated by F. H. Colson and G. H. (Vols. 1-5) Whitaker. *The Loeb Classical Library* 226, 227, 247, 261, 275, 289, ed. Jeffrey Henderson. Cambridge, MA: Harvard University Press, 1953.

———. b. 20 BCE. *Philo: Supplement 1 (Questions on Genesis)*. 12 vols. Vol. 11. Translated by Ralph Marcus. *The Loeb Classical Library* 380, ed. Jeffrey Henderson. Cambridge, MA: Harvard University Press, 1953.

———. b. 20 BCE. *Philo Supplement 2 (Questions on Exodus)*. Translated by Ralph Marcus. Edited by Ralph Marcus. *The Loeb Classical Library* 401, ed. Jeffrey Henderson. Cambridge, MA: Harvard University Press, 1953.

———. b. 20 BCE. "The special laws, 1 (*De specialibus legibus, 1*)." In *The Works of Philo: Complete and Unabridged*, edited by C. D. Yonge. New Updated ed. Translated by C. D. Yonge, 534-67. Peabody, MA: Hendrickson Publishers, 2006.

———. b. 20 BCE. *The Works of Philo: Complete and Unabridged*. Translated by C. D. Yonge. Edited by C. D. Yonge. New Updated ed. Peabody, MA: Hendrickson Publishers, 2006.

Piazza, Tom. 2003. "The devil gets the best lines." In *Criterion Collection Essay*. http://www.criterionco.com (accessed October 21, 2006).

Piccione, Michele, and Ariel Rubenstein. "Equilibrium in the jungle." *The Economic Journal* 117 (July 2007): 883-86.

"Piero della Francesca." In *Wikipedia*. http://en.wikipedia.org/wiki/Piero_della_Francesca (accessed June 18, 2008).

Pietersma, Albert, and Benjamin G. Wright, eds. *A New English Translation of the Septuagint and the Other Greek Translations Traditionally Included Under That Title*. Oxford, England: Oxford University Press, 2007.

Pindar. d. 443 BC. *Pindari Carmina cum Fragmentis: recognouit breuique adnotatione critica instruxit C. M. Bowra*. Edited by Cecil Maurice Bowra. 1st ed. Oxford, England: Clarendon Press, 1935.

Pinkus, Assaf. E-mail Message to Jeffrey M. Bradshaw, January 20, 2007.

———. "The impact of the Black Death on the sculptural programs of the pilgrimage church St. Theobald in Thann: New perception of the Genesis Story." *Assaph: Studies in Art History* 6 (2001): 161-76.

———. *Patrons and Narratives of the Parler School: Southwestern German Sculpture 1350-1400*. Berlin, Germany: Deutscher Kunstverlag, 2008.

———. *Workshops and Patrons of St. Theobald in Thann*. Studien zur Kunst am Oberrheim 3, ed. Wilhelm Schlink. Münster, Germany: Waxmann, 2006.

Pinnock, Clark H., Richard Rice, John Sanders, William Hasker, and David Basinger. *The Openness of God: A Biblical Challenge to the Traditional Understanding of God*. Downers Grove, IL: InterVarsity Press, 1994.

Platt, Rutherford H., ed. *The Forgotten Books of Eden*. New York City, NY: Alpha House, 1927.

———, ed. 1927, 1930. *The Lost Books of the Bible and the Forgotten Books of Eden*. Berkeley, CA: Apocryphile Press, 2005.

Plaut, W. Gunther, ed. *The Torah: A Modern Commentary*. New York City, NY: Union of American Hebrew Congregations, 1981.

Pliny the Elder. 77. *The Natural History of Pliny*. 6 vols. Vol. 1. Translated by John Bostock and H. T. Riley. *Bohn's Classical Library*. London, England: George Bell and Sons, 1893. http://books.google.com/books?id=aVMMAAAAIAAJ&pg=PA177&dq=albion+pliny+natural+history#PPR23,M1 (accessed November 29, 2007).

Plotinus. 250. *The Six Enneads*. Edited by Stephen MacKenna and Bertram Samuel Page. *Great Books of the Western World* 17. Chicago. IL: Encyclopedia Britannica, 1952. http://ccat.sas.upenn.edu/jod/texts/plotinus (accessed April 17, 2008).

Plutarch. d. 120. *Plutarch's Lives*. 4 vols. Vol. 1. Translated by Aubrey Stewart and George Long. *Bohn's Standard Library*. London, England: George Bell and Sons, 1900. http://books.google.com/books?id=mlcUAAAAYAAJ (accessed August 31, 2008).

Porch of Wisdom Cultural Institution. *Faith and Reason: A Compendium of Fifty Questions and Answers Related to Islamic Theology, Jurisprudence and Other Themes*. Stanmore, United Kingdom: The Islamic Education Board of the World Federation of the Khoja Shia Ithna-Asheri Muslim Communities, 2006.

Porter, Bruce H., and Stephen D. Ricks. "Names in antiquity: Old, new, and hidden." In *By Study and Also by Faith*, edited by John M. Lundquist and Stephen D. Ricks. 2 vols. Vol. 1, 501-22. Salt Lake City, UT: Deseret Book, 1990.

Porter, Joshua Roy. 1995. *The Illustrated Guide to the Bible*. New York City, NY: Oxford University Press, 1998.

Potter, George. "Bible scholarship supports Book of Mormon authorship." In *Ten More Amazing Discoveries*, edited by George Potter, 121-41. Springville, UT: Cedar Fort, 2005.

———. "Finding the real Mount Sinai." In *Ten More Amazing Discoveries*, edited by George Potter, 25-39. Springville, UT: Cedar Fort, 2005.

Potter, George, and Richard Wellington. *Lehi in the Wilderness*. Springville, UT: Cedar Fort, 2003.

Potter, R. Dennis. "What does God write in his Franklin Planner? The paradoxes of providence, prophecy, and petitionary prayer." *Dialogue* 37, no. 3 (Fall 2004): 49-64.

Poulter, Mary D. "Doctrines of faith and hope found in Emma Smith's 1835 hymnbook." *BYU Studies* 37, no. 2 (1997-1998): 33-56.

Pratt, Orson. 1852. "Celestial marriage (A discourse delivered by Elder Orson Pratt, in the Tabernacle, Great Salt Lake City, August 29, 1852)." In *Journal of Discourses*. 26 vols. Vol. 1, 53-66. Liverpool and London, England: Latter-day Saints Book Depot, 1853-1886. Reprint, Salt Lake City, UT: Bookcraft, 1966.

———. "The Seer." 1853-1854. Reprint, Orem, UT: Grandin Book Company, 1994.

———. 1854. "Consecration (Discourse delivered in the Tabernacle, Great Salt Lake City, 10 September 1854)." In *Journal of Discourses*. 26 vols. Vol. 2, 96-104. Liverpool and London, England: Latter-day Saints Book Depot, 1853-1886. Reprint, Salt Lake City, UT: Bookcraft, 1966.

———. 1855. "The Holy Spirit and the Godhead (Discourse delivered in the open air, on the Temple Block, Great Salt Lake City, 18 February 1855)." In *Journal of Discourses*. 26 vols. Vol. 2, 334-47. Liverpool and London, England: Latter-day Saints Book Depot, 1853-1886. Reprint, Salt Lake City, UT: Bookcraft, 1966.

———. 1873. "Consecration; temporal equality; selfishness to be overcome; resurrection; return to Jackson County; glory of Zion (Discourse delivered in the 16th Ward assembly rooms, Salt Lake City, Sunday Afternoon, 9 March 1873)." In *Journal of Discourses*. 26 vols. Vol. 15, 354-66. Liverpool and London, England: Latter-day Saints Book Depot, 1853-1886. Reprint, Salt Lake City, UT: Bookcraft, 1966.

———. 1873. "Meeting of Adam with his posterity in the valley of Adam-ondi-Ahman; location of the valley; the covenant with Enoch; records of God's dealings with men from the period of the Creation; method of preserving the records of ancient prophets; Christ's advent among the Nephites; fulfillment of God's purposes and the fulness of times (Discourse delivered in the Tabernacle, Ogden, Sunday Morning, 18 May 1873)." In *Journal of Discourses*. 26 vols. Vol. 16, 47-59. Liverpool and London, England: Latter-day Saints Book Depot, 1853-1886. Reprint, Salt Lake City, UT: Bookcraft, 1966.

———. 1877. "Discourse delivered in the Eighteenth Ward Meetinghouse, Salt Lake City, Sunday Afternoon, 25 February 1877." In *Journal of Discourses*. 26 vols. Vol. 18, 335-48. Liverpool and London, England: Latter-day Saints Book Depot, 1853-1886. Reprint, Salt Lake City, UT: Bookcraft, 1966.

———. 1879. "Exhortation from Isaiah; the Saints obeying it; glimpse at the settlement of Utah; fulfilling ancient prophecies; Jackson County, Missouri; the destination of the Saints; the temple to be built there; New Jerusalem; how it will be preserved from decay; its description; the wicked powerless to prevent the Saints from fulfilling their destiny (Discourse delivered in the Tabernacle, Salt Lake City, October 26, 1879)." In *Journal of Discourses*. 26 vols. Vol. 24, 20-32. Liverpool and London, England: Latter-day Saints Book Depot, 1853-1886. Reprint, Salt Lake City, UT: Bookcraft, 1966.

———. 1879. "Preexistence, in spiritual form, of man, the lower animals and the earth; the temporal probationary state; the Millennium; the final change (Discourse delivered at Mount Pleasant, 12 November 1879)." In *Journal of Discourses*. 26 vols. Vol. 21, 197-206. Liverpool and London, England: Latter-day Saints Book Depot, 1853-1886. Reprint, Salt Lake City, UT: Bookcraft, 1966.

———. 1880. "Discourse delivered in the Tabernacle, Salt Lake City, Sunday Afternoon, 18 July 1880." In *Journal of Discourses*. 26 vols. Vol. 21, 286-96. Liverpool and London, England: Latter-day Saints Book Depot, 1853-1886. Reprint, Salt Lake City, UT: Bookcraft, 1966.

Pratt, Parley P. "The apocryphal book of Enoch." *Millennial Star* 1 (July 1840): 61-63.

———. 1853. "Spiritual communication (Oration delivered on the Northeast cornerstone of the Temple at Great Salt Lake City, after the Twelve Apostles, the First Presidency of the Seventies, and the Presidency of the Elders' Quorum had laid the stone, 6 April 1853)." In *Journal of Discourses*. 26 vols. Vol. 2, 43-47. Liverpool and London, England: Latter-day Saints Book Depot, 1853-1886. Reprint, Salt Lake City, UT: Bookcraft, 1966.

———. 1853. "Heirship and priesthood (10 April 1853)." In *Journal of Discourses*. 26 vols. Vol. 1, 256-63. Liverpool and London, England: Latter-day Saints Book Depot, 1853-1886. Reprint, Salt Lake City, UT: Bookcraft, 1966.

———. 1855. "Key to the Science of Theology." In *Key to the Science of Theology, A Voice of Warning*, vii-114. Salt Lake City, UT: Deseret Book, 1978.

Prévost, Antoine-François. *Histoire Generale des Voïages ou Nouvelle Collections de Toutes les Relations de Voïages par Mer et par Terre*. 20 vols. Paris, France: Didot, 1746-1789.

Price, Robert M., ed. *The Pre-Nicene New Testament: Fifty-Four Formative Texts*. Salt Lake City, UT: Signature Books, 2006.

Priest, J. ed. "Testament of Moses." In *The Old Testament Pseudepigrapha*, edited by James H. Charlesworth. 2 vols. Vol. 1, 919-34. Garden City, NY: Doubleday and Company, 1983.

Prince, Gregory A., and William Robert Wright. *David O. McKay and the Rise of Modern Mormonism*. Salt Lake City, UT: University of Utah Press, 2005.

Pritchard, James B., ed. 1969. *Ancient Near Eastern Texts Relating to the Old Testament*. 3rd with Supplement ed. Princeton, NJ: Princeton University Press, 1972.

———, ed. "The God and his unknown name of power." In *Ancient Near Eastern Texts Relating to the Old Testament*, edited by James B. Pritchard, 12-14. Princeton, NJ: Princeton University Press, 1972.

———, ed. "The Tale of Two Brothers." In *Ancient Near Eastern Texts Relating to the Old Testament*, edited by James B. Pritchard, 23-25. Princeton, NJ: Princeton University Press, 1972.

Pritchett, Bruce M., Jr. "Lehi's theology of the fall in its preexilic/exilic context." *Journal of Book of Mormon Studies* 3, no. 2 (1994): 49-83.

"Program Notes for The Carnegie Hall National High School Choral Festival, March 14, 2006." In *Carnegie Hall Presents*. http://www.carnegiehall.org/article/box_office/events/evt_5970_pn.html?selecteddate=03142006 (accessed March 28, 2008).

Prothero, Stephen. *Religious Literacy: What Every American Needs to Know—and Doesn't*. San Francisco, CA: HarperSanFrancisco, 2007.

Psellus, Michael. d. ca. 1078. *Psellus' Dialogue on the Operation of Daemons*. Translated by Marcus Collisson. Sydney, Australia: J. Tegg, 1843. http://www.esotericarchives.com/psellos/daemonibus.pdf (accessed March 19, 2009).

Pseudo-Clement. "The Clementine Homilies." In *The Ante-Nicene Fathers (The Writings of the Fathers Down to AD 325)*, edited by Alexander Roberts and James Donaldson. 10 vols. Vol. 8, 223-346. Buffalo, NY: The Christian Literature Company, 1886. Reprint, Peabody, MA: Hendrickson Publishers, 2004.

———. ca. 235-258. "Recognitions of Clement." In *The Ante-Nicene Fathers (The Writings of the Fathers Down to AD 325)*, edited by Alexander Roberts and James Donaldson. 10 vols. Vol. 8, 77-211. Buffalo, NY: The Christian Literature Company, 1886. Reprint, Peabody, MA: Hendrickson Publishers, 2004.

Pseudo-Dionysius. ca. 500. "The Celestial Hierarchy." In *Pseudo-Dionysius: The Complete Works*, edited by René Roques, Jaroslav Pelikan, Jean Leclercq and Karlfried Froehlich. Translated by Colm Luibheld and Paul Rorem. Classics of Western Spirituality, 143-91. Mahwah, NJ: The Paulist Press, 1987.

Pseudo-Matthew. "The Gospel of Pseudo-Matthew." In *The Ante-Nicene Fathers (The Writings of the Fathers Down to AD 325)*, edited by Alexander Roberts and James Donaldson. 10 vols. Vol. 8, 368-83. Buffalo, NY: The Christian Literature Company, 1886. Reprint, Peabody, MA: Hendrickson Publishers, 2004.

Ptolemy, Claudius. ca. 147-170. *Geography of Claudius Ptolemy*. Translated by Edward Luther Stevenson. New York City, NY: The New York Public Library, 1932. Reprint, New York City, NY: Dover Publications, 1991. http://penelope.uchicago.edu/Thayer/E/Gazetteer/Periods/Roman/_Texts/Ptolemy/home.html (accessed November 29, 2007).

"Public expresses mixed views of Islam, Mormonism." In *The Pew Research Center for the People and the Press*. http://people-press.org/reports/display.php3?ReportID=358 (accessed April 27, 2008).

Pulsipher, John. "Autobiography." Typescript. Provo, UT: Perry Special Collections, Lee Library, Brigham Young University, n.d.

Purvis, James D. *The Samaritan Pentateuch and the Origin of the Samaritan Sect*. Harvard Semitic Monographs 2, ed. Frank Moore Cross, William L. Moran and G. Ernest Wright. Cambridge, MA: Harvard University Press, 1968.

Pusey, Merlo J. *Builders of the Kingdom: George A. Smith, John Henry Smith, George Albert Smith*. Provo, UT: Brigham Young University Press, 1981.

Pyramid Texts Online. http://www.pyramidtextsonline.com (accessed October 3, 2008).

Qa'im, Mahdi Muntazir, ed. *Jesus through the Qur'an and Shi'ite Narrations*. Elmhurst, NY: Takike Tarsile Qur'an, 2005.

Quesnel, Michel. "Naissance du petit prince." In *Le Petit Prince*, 5-25. Paris, France: Éditions Gallimard, 1993.

Quinn, D. Michael. "Latter-day Saint Prayer Circles." *BYU Studies* 19, no. 1 (1978): 79-105.

Quodvultdeus. d. ca. 450. *Promesse e predizioni di Dio*. Rome, Italy: Città Nuova, 1989.

———. d. ca. 450. *Quodvultdeus of Carthage: The Creedal Homilies*. Translated by Thomas Macy Finn. *Ancient Christian Writers 60*. Mahwah, NJ: Paulist Press, 2004.

Qutb, Sayyid. 1954-1964. *In the Shade of the Qur'an*. 18 vols. Translated by Adil Salahi. Markfield, England: The Islamic Foundation, 2005.

Rahmani, Ignatius Ephraem, II, ed. ca. 350. *Testamentum Domini Nostri Jesu Christi*. Mainz, Germany: Franz Kirchheim, 1899. Reprint, Hildesheim, Germany: Georg Olms, 1968.

"Ralph Vaughan Williams." In *Wikipedia*. http://en.wikipedia.org/wiki/Ralph_Vaughan_Williams (accessed March 28, 2008).

Ramban. ca. 1250. *Commentary of the Torah*. 5 vols. Edited by Charles Chavel. Brooklyn, NY: Judaica Press, 1974.

Rashi. c. 1105. *The Torah with Rashi's Commentary Translated, Annotated, and Elucidated*. Vol. 1: Beresheis/Genesis. Translated by Rabbi Yisrael Isser Zvi Herczeg. *ArtScroll Series, Sapirstein Edition*. Brooklyn, NY: Mesorah Publications, 1995.

Rashi. c. 1105. *The Torah with Rashi's Commentary Translated, Annotated, and Elucidated*. Vol. 2: Shemos/Exodus. Translated by Rabbi Yisrael Isser Zvi Herczeg. ArtScroll Series, Sapirstein Edition. Brooklyn, NY: Mesorah Publications, 1994.

Rasmussen, Dennis. *The Lord's Question*. Provo, UT: Keter Foundation, 1985.

Rasmussen, Ellis T. *A Latter-day Saint Commentary on the Old Testament*. Salt Lake City, UT: Deseret Book, 1993.

Reardon, Patrick Henry. *Creation and the Patriarchal Histories: Orthodox Christian Reflections on the Book of Genesis*. Ben Lomond, CA: Conciliar Press Ministries, 2008.

Reddy, Michael. "The conduit metaphor: A case of frame conflict in our language about language." In *Metaphor and Thought*, edited by A. Ortony. Cambridge: Cambridge University Press, 1979.

Reed, Annette Yoshiko. *Fallen Angels and the History of Judaism and Christianity: The Reception of Enochic Literature*. Cambridge, England: Cambridge University Press, 2005.

Rees, James. *Shakespeare and the Bible*. Philadelphia, PA: Claxton, Remsen, and Haffelfinger, 1876. Reprint, Kila, MT: Kessinger Publishing, n.d.

Reeves, John C., ed. *'Ajā'ib al-makhlūqāt wa-gharā'ib al-mawjūdāt: Harut wa-Marut exemplar 2*. Religious Studies, The University of North Carolina at Charlotte, n.d. http://www.religiousstudies.uncc.edu/jcreeves/harutwamarut2.htm (accessed September 6, 2007).

———. n.d. "Eutychii Patriarchae Alexandrini Annales." In *Religious Studies, The University of North Carolina at Charlotte*. http://www.religiousstudies.uncc.edu/jcreeves/eutychiusongen6,14.htm (accessed September 6, 2007).

———. "The flowing stream: Qur'anic interpretations and the Bible." *Religious Studies News: SBL Edition* 2, no. 9 (December 2001). http://www.sbl-site.org/Article.aspx?ArticleId=58 (accessed September 6, 2007).

———. *Heralds of that Good Realm: Syro-Mesopotamian Gnosis and Jewish Traditions*. Nag Hammadi and Manichaean Studies 41, ed. James M. Robinson and Hans-Joachim Klimkeit. Leiden, The Netherlands: E. J. Brill, 1996.

———. *Jewish Lore in Manichaean Cosmogony: Studies in the Book of Giants Traditions*. Monographs of the Hebrew Union College 14. Cincinnati, OH: Hebrew Union College Press, 1992.

———. "Jewish pseudepigrapha in Manichaean literature: The influence of the Enochic library." In *Tracing the Threads: Studies in the Vitality of Jewish Pseudepigrapha*, edited by John C. Reeves, 173-203. Atlanta, GA: Scholars Press, 1994.

———. n.d. "The Manichaean version of Genesis 2-4." In *Religious Studies, The University of North Carolina at Charlotte*. http://www.religiousstudies.uncc.edu/jcreeves/manichaean_version_of_genesis_2-4.htm (accessed November 14, 2008).

———. n.d. "Midrash of Shemhazai and Azael." In *Religious Studies, The University of North Carolina at Charlotte*. http://www.religiousstudies.uncc.edu/jcreeves/bereshit_rabbati_29-31.htm (accessed September 6, 2007).

———. n.d. "Midrash Wa-Yosha." In *Religious Studies, The University of North Carolina at Charlotte*. http://www.religiousstudies.uncc.edu/jcreeves/bereshit_rabbati_29-31.htm (accessed September 6, 2007).

———. n.d. "Tarikh al-Yaqubi." In *Religious Studies, The University of North Carolina at Charlotte*. http://www.religiousstudies.uncc.edu/jcreeves/yaqubionbible.htm (accessed September 6, 2007).

———. *Trajectories in Near Eastern Apocalyptic: A Postrabbinic Jewish Apocalypse Reader*. Resources for Biblical Study 45, ed. Susan Ackerman and J. Ross Wagner. Atlanta, GA: Society of Biblical Literature, 2005.

"Respect for diversity of faiths." In *Newsroom: The Official Resource for News Media, Opinion Leaders, and the Public*, The Church of Jesus Christ of Latter-day Saints. http://newsroom.lds.org/ldsnewsroom/eng/commentary/respect-for-diversity-of-faiths (accessed April 27, 2008).

"Return to Nauvoo, expanded liner notes and lyrics to the hymns." In *FiddleSticks: Celtic and American Folk Music*. http://www.fiddle-sticks.com/Liner_Nauvoo.htm (accessed March 28, 2008).

"Reverence for the Bible." In *Newsroom: The Official Resource for News Media, Opinion Leaders, and the Public*, The Church of Jesus Christ of Latter-day Saints. http://newsroom.lds.org/ldsnewsroom/eng/commentary/reverence-for-the-bible (accessed February 5, 2008).

Revillout, E. ed. 1904. "Évangile des douze apôtres." In *Les Apogryphes Coptes, Première Partie: Les Évangiles des Douze Apôtres et de Saint Barthélemy*. Translated by E. Revillout. *Patrologia Orientalis* 2, fasc. 2, no. 7, eds. René Graffin and François Nau, 131-84. Turnhout, Belgium: Brepols, 1985. http://coptica.ch/revillout-1.pdf (accessed April 17, 2009).

Rey, Alain. *Dictionnaire Historique de la Langue Française*. 2 vols. 3ième ed. Paris, France: Dictionnaires Le Robert, 2000.

Reynolds, Noel B. "The decline of covenant in early Christian thought." In *Early Christians in Disarray*, edited by Noel B. Reynolds, 295-324. Provo, UT: Brigham Young University Press, 2005.

———. "Nephite kingship reconsidered." In *Mormons, Scripture, and the Ancient World: Studies in Honor of John L. Sorenson*, edited by Davis Bitton, 151-89. Provo, UT: Foundation for Ancient Research and Mormon Studies, 1998.

———. "Preface." In *Expressions of Faith: Testimonies of Latter-day Saint Scholars*, edited by Susan Easton Black, ix-xiv. Salt Lake City, UT: Deseret Book, 1996.

Rhodes, Michael D, ed. *The Hor Book of Breathings: A Translation and Commentary*. Studies in the Book of Abraham 2, ed. John Gee. Provo, UT: Foundation for Ancient Research and Mormon Studies, Brigham Young University, 2002.

———. 1994. "The Joseph Smith Hypocephalus… Twenty years later." In *Brigham Young University Foundation for Ancient Research and Mormon Studies (FARMS)*. http://home.comcast.net/~michael.rhodes/JosephSmithHypo-cephalus.pdf (accessed September 6, 2007).

———. "A translation and commentary of the Joseph Smith hypocephalus." *BYU Studies* 17, no. 3 (1977): 259-74.

———, ed. *The Tshemmin Book of the Dead: A Translation and Commentary*. Provo, UT: Brigham Young University Foundation for Ancient Research and Mormon Studies (FARMS), in preparation.

Rhodes, Michael D., and J. Ward Moody. "Astronomy and the Creation in the Book of Abraham." In *Astronomy, Papyrus, and Covenant*, edited by John Gee and Brian M. Hauglid. *Studies in the Book of Abraham* 3, 17-36. Provo, UT: Foundation for Ancient Research and Mormon Studies (FARMS), Brigham Young University, 2005.

Ri, Andreas Su-Min, ed. *La Caverne des Trésors: Les deux recensions syriaques*. 2 vols. *Corpus Scriptorum Christianorum Orientalium* 486-487 (Scriptores Syri 207-208). Louvain, Belgium: Peeters, 1987.

———. *Commentaire de la Caverne des Trésors: Étude sur l'Histoire du Texte et de ses Sources*. Supplementary 103. *Corpus Scriptorum Christianorum Orientalium* 581. Leuven, Belgium: Peeters, 2000.

Richards, J. Kirk. 2006. "Bio." In *The Fine Art of J. Kirk Richards*. http://art.jkirkrichards.com/bio.php (accessed October 1, 2006).

Richards, LeGrand. 1950. *A Marvelous Work and a Wonder*. Salt Lake City, UT: Deseret Book, 1976.

Ricoeur, Paul. 1976. "Toward a hermeneutic of the idea of revelation." In *Essays on Biblical Interpretation*, edited by Lewis S. Mudge. Translated by David Pellauer, 73-118. Philadelphia, PA: Fortress, 1980.

Richter, Siegfried, ed. *The Manichaean Coptic Papyri in the Chester Beatty Library Psalm Book Part II, 2, Die Herakleides-Psalmen*. *Corpus Fontium Manichaeorum, Series Coptica*, eds. Aloîs van Tongerloo, Samuel N. C. Lieu and Johannes van Oort. Turnhout, Belgium: Brepols, 1999.

Ricks, Brian W. "James E. Talmage and the Nature of the Godhead: The Gradual Unfolding of Latter-day Saint Theology." Master's Thesis, Brigham Young University, 2007.

Ricks, Shirley S. "A sure foundation." *The FARMS Review* 20, no. 2 (2008): 253-91.

Ricks, Stephen D. "Adam's fall in the Book of Mormon, second temple Judaism, and early Christianity." In *The Disciple as Scholar: Essays on Scripture and the Ancient World in Honor of Richard Lloyd Anderson*, edited by Stephen D. Ricks, Donald W. Parry and Andrew H. Hedges, 595-606. Provo, UT: Foundation for Ancient Research and Mormon Studies, 2000.

———. "Ancient views of creation and the doctrine of creation *ex nihilo*." In *Reason, Revelation, and Faith: Essays in Honor of Truman G. Madsen*, edited by Donald W. Parry, Daniel C. Peterson and Stephen D. Ricks, 319-37. Provo, UT: Foundation for Ancient Research and Mormon Studies, 2002.

———. "*Dexiosis* and *Dextrarum Iunctio*: The sacred handclasp in the classical and early Christian world." *The FARMS Review* 18, no. 1 (2006): 431-36.

———. "The garment of Adam in Jewish, Muslim, and Christian tradition." In *Temples of the Ancient World*, edited by Donald W. Parry, 705-39. Salt Lake City, UT: Deseret Book, 1994.

———. "Liturgy and cosmogony: The ritual use of creation accounts in the ancient Near East." In *Temples of the Ancient World*, edited by Donald W. Parry, 118-25. Salt Lake City, UT: Deseret Book, 1994.

———. "Oaths and oath-taking in the Old Testament." In *The Temple in Time and Eternity*, edited by Donald W. Parry and Stephen D. Ricks, 43-53. Provo, UT: FARMS at Brigham Young University, 1999.

———. "Olive culture in the second temple era and early rabbinic period." In *The Allegory of the Olive Tree*, edited by Stephen D. Ricks and John W. Welch, 460-76. Salt Lake City, UT: Deseret Book, 1994.

———. "The prophetic reality of tribal reconstruction." In *Israel's Apostasy and Restoration: Essays in Honor of Roland K. Harrison*, edited by Avraham Gileadi, 273-81. Grand Rapids, MI: Baker Book House, 1988.

Ricks, Stephen D., and John J. Sroka. "King, coronation, and temple: Enthronement ceremonies in history." In *Temples of the Ancient World*, edited by Donald W. Parry, 236-71. Salt Lake City, UT: Deseret Book, 1994.

Ridderbos, Herman N. *The Gospel According to John: A Theological Commentary*. Translated by John Vriend. Grand Rapids, MI: William B. Eerdmans, 1997.

Riddle, Chauncey C. "Devils." In *Encyclopedia of Mormonism*, edited by Daniel H. Ludlow. 4 vols. Vol. 1, 379-82. New York City, NY: Macmillan, 1992.

———. "The New and Everlasting Covenant." In *Doctrines for Exaltation: The 1989 Sperry Symposium on the Doctrine and Covenants*, 224-45. Salt Lake City, UT: Deseret Book, 1989.

Riddle, Donald W. "The Cephas-Peter problem, and a possible solution." *Journal of Biblical Literature* 59 (1940): 169-80.

Riesenfeld, Harald. *The Resurrection in Ezekiel XXXVII and in the Dura Europos Paintings*. Uppsala Universitets Arsskrift 11. Uppsala, Sweden: Almqvist and Wiksells, 1948.

Rigdon, Sidney. 1836. "Dedication of the Kirtland Temple, Sidney Rigdon's Sermon (27 March 1836)." In *History of the Church of Jesus Christ of Latter-day Saints (Documentary History)*, edited by Joseph Smith, Jr. and Brigham Henry Roberts. Vol. 2, 418-19. Salt Lake City, UT: Deseret Book, 1978.

Righter, Anne. "Introduction." In *The Tempest*, edited by Anne Righter. *New Penguin Shakespeare*, eds. T. J. B. Spencer and Stanley Wells, 7-51. London, England: Penguin, 1968.

Rikala, Mia. "Sacred Marriage in the New Kingdom of ancient Egypt: Circumstantial evidence for a ritual interpretation." In *Sacred Marriages*, edited by Martti Nissinen and Risto Uro, 115-44. Winona Lake, IN: Eisenbrauns, 2008.

Rippin, Andrew, and Jan Knappert, eds. 1986. *Textual Sources for the Study of Islam*. Chicago, IL: The University of Chicago Press, 1990.

Rivkin, Ellis. 1984. *What Crucified Jesus? Messianism, Pharisaism, and the Development of Christianity*. New York, NY: UAHC Press, 1997.

Rje, Mkhas Grub. 1968. *Introduction to the Buddhist Tantric Systems*. Translated by F. D. Lessing and Alexander Wayman. 2nd ed. New York City, NY: Samuel Weiser, 1980.

Roberts, Alexander, and James Donaldson, eds. *The Ante-Nicene Fathers (The Writings of the Fathers Down to AD 325)*. 10 vols. Buffalo, NY: The Christian Literature Company, 1885-1886. Reprint, Peabody, MA: Hendrickson Publishers, 2004.

———, eds. "Constitutions of the holy Apostles." In *The Ante-Nicene Fathers (The Writings of the Fathers Down to AD 325)*, edited by Alexander Roberts and James Donaldson. 10 vols. Vol. 7, 387-508. Buffalo, NY: The Christian Literature Company, 1886. Reprint, Peabody, MA: Hendrickson Publishers, 2004.

———, eds. "The Gospel of the Nativity of Mary." In *The Ante-Nicene Fathers (The Writings of the Fathers Down to AD 325)*, edited by Alexander Roberts and James Donaldson. 10 vols. Vol. 8, 384-87. Buffalo, NY: The Christian Literature Company, 1886. Reprint, Peabody, MA: Hendrickson Publishers, 2004.

Roberts, Alison. *Golden Shrine, Goddess Queen: Egypt's Anointing Mysteries*. Rottingdean, England: NorthGate, 2008.

———. *My Heart My Mother: Death and Rebirth in Ancient Egypt*. Rottingdean, England: NorthGate, 2000.

Roberts, Brigham Henry. *Comprehensive History of the Church*. 6 vols. Salt Lake City, UT: Deseret News Press, 1930. Reprint, Salt Lake City, UT: Brigham Young University Press, 1965.

———. 1892. "Comprehensiveness of the Gospel (Lecture delivered by Elder B. H. Roberts, at the General Conference of the Y.M.M.I.A., in the Tabernacle, Salt Lake City, June 5, 1892)." In *Collected Discourses*, edited by Brian H. Stuy. 5 vols. Vol. 3, 64-71. Woodland Hills, UT: B.H.S. Publishing, 1989.

———. *Defense of the Faith and the Saints*. 2 vols. Salt Lake City, UT: Deseret News, 1907, 1912. Reprint, Brigham City, UT: Brigham Distributing, 2002.

———. "Discourse (8 April 1911)." In *Conference Reports: Eighty-First Annual General Conference of the Church of Jesus Christ of Latter-day Saints*, 56-60. Salt Lake City, UT: Deseret News, 1911. Reprint, Salt Lake City, UT: Hawkes Publishing, n. d.

———. *Divine Mission of the Savior: Course of Study for the Quorum of the Priesthood—Priests*. Salt Lake City, UT: The Church of Jesus Christ of Latter-day Saints, 1910.

———. 1886. "God must and will be glorified (Address delivered by Elder B.H. Roberts, at the Pioneer Day Celebration, July 24, 1886)." In *Collected Discourses*, edited by Brian H. Stuy. 5 vols. Vol. 1, 17-19. Woodland Hills, UT: B.H.S. Publishing, 1987.

———. *The Seventy's Course in Theology, First Year Book*. Salt Lake City, UT: Deseret Book, 1907.

———. *The Seventy's Course in Theology, Fifth Year*. Salt Lake City, UT: Deseret News Press, 1912.

———. *The Seventy's Course in Theology (Being the Reprint of the First Year Book of that 'Course')*. 2nd ed. Salt Lake City, UT: Deseret Book, 1931.

———. 1896. "The spirit of the Gospel (Discourse delivered by Elder B.H. Roberts, at the Tabernacle, Salt Lake City, April 26, 1896)." In *Collected Discourses*, edited by Brian H. Stuy. 5 vols. Vol. 5, 134-41. Woodland Hills, UT: B.H.S. Publishing, 1992.

———. 1928. *The Truth, the Way, the Life: An Elementary Treatise on Theology*, ed. John W. Welch. Provo, UT: BYU Studies, 1994.

Roberts, J. M., ed. *The Bible and the Ancient Near East: Collected Essays*. Winona Lake, IN: Eisenbrauns, 2002.

Robertson, John S. "Adamic language." In *Encyclopedia of Mormonism*, edited by Daniel H. Ludlow. 4 vols. Vol. 1, 18-19. New York City, NY: Macmillan, 1992. http://www.lib.byu.edu/Macmillan/ (accessed November 26, 2007).

Robertson, Noel. "Orphic mysteries and Dionysiac ritual." In *Greek Mysteries: The Archaeology and Ritual of Ancient Greek Secret Cults*, edited by Michael B. Cosmopoulos, 218-40. New York City, NY: Routledge, 2003.

Robinson, James M., ed. *The Coptic Gnostic Library: A Complete Edition of the Nag Hammadi Codices*. 5 vols. Leiden, The Netherlands: Brill Academic, 2000.

———. "The Manichaean codices of Medinat Madi (Terenouthis)." Presented at the *Twenty-eighth International Congress of Byzantine Studies*, Moscow, Russia 1991, 950-51. http://www.tertullian.org/rpearse/manuscripts/medinet_madu.htm (accessed November 20, 2007).

———, ed. 1978. *The Nag Hammadi Library in English* 3rd, Completely Revised ed. San Francisco, CA: HarperSanFrancisco, 1990.

Robinson, Joseph Lee, Oliver Preston Robinson, Mary Robinson Egan, David Nielsen, Joni Nielsen, and Kevin Merrell. 2003. "The Journal of Joseph Lee Robinson: Mormon Pioneer (1886)." In *Planet Nielsen*. http://www.planetnielsen.com/joseph_lee_robinson/jlr_basic_journal.pdf (accessed September 6, 2007).

Robinson, Stephen E. "The Apocalypse of Adam." *BYU Studies* 17, no. 2 (Winter 1977): 1-28.

———. *Believing Christ*. Salt Lake City, UT: Deseret Book, 1992.

———. "The Book of Adam in Judaism and early Christianity." In *The Man Adam*, edited by Joseph Fielding McConkie and Robert L. Millet, 131-50. Salt Lake City, UT: Bookcraft, 1990.

———. "Jesus Christ, names and titles of." In *The Encyclopedia of Mormonism*, edited by Daniel H. Ludlow. 4 vols. Vol. 2, 740-42. New York City, NY: Macmillan, 1992. http://www.lib.byu.edu/Macmillan/ (accessed November 26, 2007).

———. "Lying for God: The uses of the Apocrypha." In *Apocryphal Writings and the Latter-day Saints*, edited by C. Wilfred Griggs, 133-54. Provo, UT: Brigham Young University Religious Studies Center, 1986.

———. *Are Mormons Christians?* Salt Lake City, UT: Bookcraft, 1991.

———, ed. "Testament of Adam." In *The Old Testament Pseudepigrapha*, edited by James H. Charlesworth. Vol. 1, 989-95. Garden City, NY: Doubleday and Company, 1983.

———, ed. 1978. *The Testament of Adam: An Examination of the Syriac and Greek Traditions. Dissertation Series* 52, ed. Howard C. Kee and Douglas A. Knight. Chico, CA: Scholars Press, 1982.

Robinson, Stephen E., and H. Dean Garrett, eds. *A Commentary on the Doctrine and Covenants*. 4 vols. Salt Lake City, UT: Deseret Book, 2001-2005.

Robison, Elwin C. *The First Mormon Temple: Design, Construction, and Historic Context of the Kirtland Temple*. Provo, UT: Brigham Young University Press, 1997.

Robison, John C. "Crucifixion in the Roman world: The use of nails at the time of Christ." *Studia Antiqua* 2, no. 1 (Winter 2002): 25-53.

Robson, Kent E. "Response to Professor Dorrien." In *Mormonism in Dialogue with Contemporary Christian Theologies*, edited by Donald W. Musser and David L. Paulsen, 410-19. Macon, GA: Mercer University Press, 2007.

———. "Time and eternity." In *The Encyclopedia of Mormonism*, edited by Daniel H. Ludlow. 4 vols. Vol. 4, 1478-79. New York City, NY: Macmillan, 1992. http://www.lib.byu.edu/Macmillan/ (accessed November 26, 2007).

Römer, Cornelia Eva, ed. *Manis frühe Missionreisen nach der Kölner Manibiographie: Textkritisher Kommentar und Erläuterungen zu p. 121-p. 192 des Kölner Mani-Kodex. Papyrologica Coloniensia* 24. Opladen, Germany: Westdeutscher Verlag, 1994.

Romney, Marion G. "Assurance of blessings." *Conference Report*, October 1949, 39-45.

———. 1984. "The celestial nature of self-reliance." *Ensign* 39, March 2009, 61-65.

———. "The covenant of the priesthood." *Ensign* 2, July 1972, 98-99.

———. "Living welfare principles." *Ensign* 11, November 1981, 92-93.

———. "'The oath and covenant which belongeth to the priesthood.'" *Conference Report*, April 1962, 16-20.

———. 1970. "Temples—the gates to heaven." In *Look to God and Live*, 229-40. Salt Lake City, UT: Deseret Book, 1971.

———. "Welfare services." *Ensign* 5, November 1975, 124-27.

Rona, Daniel. *Israel Revealed: Discovering Mormon and Jewish Insights in the Holy Land*. Sandy, UT: The Ensign Foundation, 2001.

Roper, Matthew. 2006. "Adam in ancient texts and the restoration." In *Proceedings of the FAIR Conference*. http://www.fairlds.org/FAIR_Conferences/2006_Adam_in_Ancient_Texts_and_the_Restoration.html (accessed September 19, 2006).

Rosenbaum, Jonathan. 1985. "Judaism: *Torah* and tradition." In *The Holy Book in Comparative Perspective*, edited by Frederick M. Denny and Rodney L. Taylor, 10-35. Columbia, SC: University of South Carolina Press, 1993.

Rosenberg, A. J., ed. *Mikraot Gedoloth: Genesis and Exodus*. 5 vols. Brooklyn, NY: The Judaica Press, 1993.

Rosenblum, Robert. *Paintings in the Musée d'Orsay*. New York City, NY: Stewart, Tabori, and Chang, 1989.

Rosewell, Roger. *Medieval Wall Paintings*. Woodbridge, England: The Boydell Press, 2008.

Rousseau, Jean-Jacques. 1754. "Discourse on the Origin and Foundations of Inequality Among Men (Second Discourse)." In *The First and Second Discourses and the Essay on the Origin of Languages*, edited by Victor Gourevitch, 117-230. New York City, NY: Harper and Row, 1986.

Rowland, Christopher. "Blake and the Bible: Biblical exegesis in the work of William Blake." In *Biblical Interpretation: The Meanings of Scripture—Past and Present*, edited by John M. Court, 168-84. London, England: T. & T. Clark, 2004.

Roy, Christelle. "L'univers était liquide." *Les Dossiers de la Recherche*, no. 23 (mai-juin 2006): 32-38.

Rubinkiewicz, R. ed. "Apocalypse of Abraham." In *The Old Testament Pseudepigrapha*, edited by James H. Charlesworth. Vol. 1, 681-705. Garden City, NY: Doubleday and Company, 1983.

Rudolph, Kurt, ed. *Der mandäische 'Diwan der Flüsse'. Abhandlungen der Sächsichen Akademie der Wissenschaften zu Leipzig, Philologisch-historische Klasse* 70/1. Berlin, Germany: Akademie-Verlag, 1982.

———. 1980. *Gnosis: The Nature and History of Gnosticism*. Translated by Robert McLachlan Wilson, P. W. Coxon and K. H. Kuhn. 2nd ed. San Francisco, CA: HarperSanFrancisco, 1987.

———. "Part 2: Mandean [sic] Sources." *Coptic and Mandaic Sources*, edited by Werner Foerster, in *Gnosis: A Selection of Gnostic Texts* 2, 121-319. Oxford, England: Clarendon Press, 1974.

Ruhlen, Merritt. *On the Origin of Languages: Studies in Linguistic Taxonomy*. Stanford, CA: Stanford University Press, 1994.

Ruse, Michael. *The Evolution-Creation Struggle*. Cambridge, MA: Harvard University Press, 2005.

Russell, James R. 1995. "Ezekiel and Iran." In *Armenian and Iranian Studies*, edited by James R. Russell. *Harvard Armenian Texts and Studies* 9, 899-907. Cambridge, MA: Department of Near Eastern Languages and Civilizations, Harvard University Press and the Armenian Heritage Press, National Association for Armenian Studies and Research, 2004.

———. 1995. "On Mithraism and Freemasonry." In *Armenian and Iranian Studies*, edited by James R. Russell. *Harvard Armenian Texts and Studies* 9, 641-59. Cambridge, MA: Department of Near Eastern Languages and Civilizations, Harvard University Press and the Armenian Heritage Press, National Association for Armenian Studies and Research, 2004.

———. 1980. "The word *k'ustik* in Armenian." In *Armenian and Iranian Studies*, edited by James R. Russell. *Harvard Armenian Texts and Studies* 9, 107-14. Cambridge, MA: Department of Near Eastern Languages and Civilizations, Harvard University Press and the Armenian Heritage Press, National Association for Armenian Studies and Research, 2004.

Russell, Norman. *The Doctrine of Deification in the Greek Patristic Tradition. Oxford Early Christian Studies*, eds. Gillian Clark and Andrew Louth. Oxford, England: Oxford University Press, 2004.

"Russian Orthodox Church Outside Russia." In *Wikipedia*. http://en.wikipedia.org/wiki/Russian_Orthodox_Church_Outside_Russia (accessed June 9, 2008).

Ruzer, Serge. "*The Cave of Treasures* on swearing by Abel's blood and expulsion from Paradise: Two exegetical motives in context." *Journal of Early Christian Studies* 9, no. 2 (Summer 2001): 257-77.

———. "A long way from the Cave of Treasures to Jerusalem: Pilgrimage or exile?" In *Semiotics of Pilgrimage*, edited by W. Moskovich and S. Schwarzband, 19-26. Jerusalem, Israel, 2003.

———. "Reflections of Genesis 1-2 in the old Syriac Gospels." In *The Book of Genesis in Jewish and Oriental Christian Interpretation*, edited by Judith Frishman and Lucas Van Rompay. *Traditio Exegetica Graeca* 5, 91-102. Louvain, Belgium: Editions Peeters, 1997.

Ryan, Robert. 2003. "Blake and religion." In *The Cambridge Companion to William Blake*, edited by Morris Eaves, 150-68. Cambridge, England: Cambridge University Press, 2006.

Ryen, Jon Olav. *The Tree in the Lightworld: A Study in the Mandaean Vine Motif*. Oslo, Norway: Unipub/Oslo Academic Press (Faculty of Humanities, University of Oslo), 2006.

"Sacred books of the East." In *Internet Sacred Text Archive*. http://www.sacred-texts.com/sbe/ (accessed October 3, 2008).

Sailhamer, John H. "Genesis." In *The Expositor's Bible Commentary*, edited by Frank E. Gaebelein, 1-284. Grand Rapids, MI: Zondervan, 1990.

Saint Exupéry, Antoine de. 1948. *Citadelle*. Paris, France: Éditions Gallimard, 1958.

———. *Dessins*. Paris, France: Gallimard, 2006.

———. 1943. *The Little Prince*. London, England: Penguin Books, 1995.

———. 1939. *Terre des Hommes*. Paris, France: Éditions Gallimard, 2006.

Salisbury, Frank B. *The Case for Divine Design: Cells, Complexity, and Creation*. Springville, UT: Cedar Fort (CFI), 2006.

———. *The Creation*. Salt Lake City, UT: Deseret Book, 1976.

Sallustius, Platonis. ca. 363. *Sallustius: Concerning the Gods and the Universe*. Edited by Arthur Darby Nock. Cambridge, England: Cambridge University Press, 1926. http://www.geocities.com/SoHo/2923/sallustius1.html (accessed April 17, 2008).

Salt Lake School of the Prophets Minute Book. 1883. Reprint, Palm Desert, CA: ULC Press, 1981.

Samuelson, Norbert M. 1984. "Medieval Jewish philosophy." In *Back to the Sources: Reading the Classic Jewish Texts*, edited by Barry W. Holtz, 263-303. New York City, NY: Simon and Schuster, 2006.

Sanders, E. P. ed. "Testament of Abraham." In *The Old Testament Pseudepigrapha*, edited by James H. Charlesworth. Vol. 1, 871-902. Garden City, NY: Doubleday and Company, 1983.

Sandmel, Samuel. "An appreciation." In *Religions in Antiquity: Essays in Memory of Erwin Ramsdell Goodenough*, edited by Jacob Neusner. *Religions in Antiquity, Studies in the History of Religions (Supplements to Numen)* 14, 3-17. Leiden, The Netherlands: Brill, 1968.

Sandmel, Samuel, M. Jack Suggs, and Arnold J. Tkacik, eds. "Ecclesiasticus or The Wisdom of Jesus Son of Sirach." In *The New English Bible with the Apocrypha, Oxford Study Edition*, edited by Samuel Sandmel, M. Jack Suggs and Arnold J. Tkacik, 115-75. New York City, NY: Oxford University Press, 1976.

———, eds. "The First Book of the Maccabees." In *The New English Bible with the Apocrypha, Oxford Study Edition*, edited by Samuel Sandmel, M. Jack Suggs and Arnold J. Tkacik, 195-231. New York City, NY: Oxford University Press, 1976.

———, eds. *The New English Bible with the Apocrypha, Oxford Study Edition*. New York: Oxford University Press, 1976.

———, eds. "The Second Book of the Maccabees." In *The New English Bible with the Apocrypha, Oxford Study Edition*, edited by Samuel Sandmel, M. Jack Suggs and Arnold J. Tkacik, 232-57. New York City, NY: Oxford University Press, 1976.

———, eds. "The Wisdom of Solomon." In *The New English Bible with the Apocrypha, Oxford Study Edition*, edited by Samuel Sandmel, M. Jack Suggs and Arnold J. Tkacik, 97-114. New York City, NY: Oxford University Press, 1976.

Santillana, Giorgio de, and Hertha von Dechend. 1969. *Hamlet's Mill: An Essay on Myth and the Frame of Time*. Boston, MA: David R. Godine, 1977.

Sarna, Nahum M., ed. *Exodus. The JPS Torah Commentary*, ed. Nahum M. Sarna. Philadelphia, PA: The Jewish Publication Society, 1991.

———, ed. *Genesis. The JPS Torah Commentary*, ed. Nahum M. Sarna. Philadelphia, PA: The Jewish Publication Society, 1989.

———. "The mists of time." In *Genesis: World of Myths and Patriarchs*, edited by Ada Feyerick, 49-82. New York City, NY: New York University Press, 1996.

Satran, David, and Benjamin E. Wright. "Martyrological traditions." In *The Apocryphal Ezekiel*, edited by Michael E. Stone, Benjamin E. Wright and David Satran. *Early Judaism and Its Literature* 18, ed. John C. Reeves, 95-100. Atlanta, GA: Society of Biblical Literature, 2000.

Satterfield, Bruce. "Melchizedek, LDS sources." In *Encyclopedia of Mormonism*, edited by Daniel H. Ludlow. Vol. 2, 879-80. New York City, NY: Macmillan, 1992. http://www.lib.byu.edu/Macmillan/ (accessed November 26, 2007).

Savedow, Steve, ed. *Sepher Rezial Hemelach: The Book of the Angel Rezial*. Boston, MA: WeiserBooks, 2000.

Schäfer, Peter. *Jesus in the Talmud*. Princeton, NJ: Princeton University Press, 2007.

———. "Wisdom finds a home: *Torah* as Wisdom." In *Light in a Spotless Mirror: Reflections on Wisdom Traditions in Judaism and Early Christianity*, edited by James H. Charlesworth and Michael A. Daise, 26-44. Harrisburg, PA: Trinity Press International, 2003.

Schaff, Philip, ed. *Nicene and Post-Nicene Fathers, First Series*. 14 vols. New York City, NY: The Christian Literature Company, 1886-1890. Reprint, Peabody, MA: Hendrickson Publishers, 2004.

Schaff, Philip, and Henry Wace, eds. *Nicene and Post-Nicene Fathers, Second Series*. 14 vols. New York City, NY: The Christian Literature Company, 1890-1900. Reprint, Peabody, MA: Hendrickson Publishers, 2004.

Schakel, Peter J. *Reason and Imagination in C. S. Lewis: A Study of 'Till We Have Faces.'* Grand Rapids, MI: William B. Eerdmans, 1984.

Schaya, Léo. 1958. *The Universal Meaning of the Kabbalah (L'homme et l'absolu selon la Kabbale)*. Translated by Nancy Pearson. Baltimore, MD: Penguin Books, 1974.

Schenck, Kenneth L. *Understanding the Book of Hebrews: The Story Behind the Sermon*. Louisville, KY: Westminster John Knox Press, 2003.

Scherer, Mark A. "Through the mists of time." *Community of Christ Herald* 148, October 2001, 8.

Schiff, Stacy. 1994. *Saint-Exupéry: A Biography*. New York City, NY: Da Capo Press, 1996.

Schimmel, Annemarie. 1981. *And Muhammad Is His Messenger: The Veneration of the Prophet in Islamic Piety*. English ed. *Studies in Religion*, ed. Charles H. Long. Chapel Hill, NC: The University of North Carolina Press, 1985.

———. *Mystical Dimensions of Islam*. Chapel Hill, NC: The University of North Carolina Press, 1975.

Schmidt, Carl, ed. 1892. *The Books of Jeu and the Untitled Text in the Bruce Codex*. Translated by Violet MacDermot. *Nag Hammadi Studies* 13, ed. Martin Krause, James M. Robinson and Frederik Wisse. Leiden, The Netherlands: Brill, 1978. http://www.gnosis.org/library/1ieo.htm (*1 Jeu 1-10*), http://fam-faerch.dk/pseudigrapher/gnostic/untitl.htm (*The Unititled Text in the Bruce Codex*) (accessed September 18, 2007).

———, ed. 1905. *Pistis Sophia (Askew Codex)*. Translated by Violet MacDermot. *Nag Hammadi Studies* 9, eds. Martin Krause, James M. Robinson and Frederik Wisse. Leiden, The Netherlands: Brill, 1978.

Schmidt, Carl, and Walter Till eds. 1892. "Die Beiden Bücher des Jeû." In *Koptisch-Gnostische Schriften: Die Pistis Sophia, Die Beiden Bücher des Jeû, Ubekanntes Altgnostisches Werk*, edited by Carl Schmidt and Walter Till. 2nd ed. Translated by Carl Schmidt. *Die Griechischen Christlichen Schriftsteller der Esrsten Jahrhunderte* 1, ed. Der Kommission für Spätantike Religionsgeschichte der Deutschen Akademie der Wissenschaften zu Berlin, 257-329. Berlin, Germany: Akademie-Verlag, 1954.

———, eds. 1892. "Unbekanntes altgnostisches Werk." In *Koptisch-Gnostische Schriften: Die Pistis Sophia, Die Beiden Bücher des Jeû, Ubekanntes Altgnostisches Werk*, edited by Carl Schmidt and Walter Till. 2nd ed. Translated by Carl Schmidt. *Die Griechischen Christlichen Schriftsteller der Esrsten Jahrhunderte* 1, ed. Der Kommission für Spätantike Religionsgeschichte der Deutschen Akademie der Wissenschaften zu Berlin, 335-67. Berlin, Germany: Akademie-Verlag, 1954.

Schmidt, Nathaniel. "The 'Son of Man' in the Book of Daniel." *Journal of Biblical Literature* 19, no. 1 (1900): 22-28.

Scholem, Gershom. 1974. *Kabbalah*. New York City, NY: Dorset Press, 1987.

———, ed. 1941. *Major Trends in Jewish Mysticism*. New York City, NY: Schocken Books, 1995.

Schroer, Silvia. 1986. "The Spirit, Wisdom, and the dove: Feminist-critical exegesis of a Second Testament symbol against the background of its history in ancient Near Eastern and hellenistic-early Jewish tradition." In *Wisdom Has Built Her House: Studies on the Figure of Sophia in the Bible*, edited by Silvia Schroer. Translated by Linda M. Maloney and William McDonough, 132-63. Collegeville, MN: The Liturgical Press, A Michael Glazier Book, 2000.

Schubert, Kurt. "Jewish pictorial traditions in early Christian art." In *Jewish Historiography and Iconography in Early and Medieval Christianity*, edited by Heinz Schreckenberg, Kurt Schubert and Peter J. Tomson. Translated by Paul A. Cathey. *Compendium Rerum Iudaicarum ad Novum Testamentum: Section 3 - Jewish Traditions in Early Christian Literature* 2, eds. Y. Aschkenasy, T. Baarda, W. J. Burgers, David Flusser, Pieter W. Van der Horst, Th.C. de Kruyf, S. Safrai, Peter J. Tomson and B. H. Young, 139-260, 1992.

Schwartz, Howard. *Tree of Souls: The Mythology of Judaism*. Oxford, England: Oxford University Press, 2004.

Schweitzer, Albert. *The Light Within Us*. New York City, NY: The Wisdom Library, 1959.

Seaich, John Eugene. *Ancient Texts and Mormonism: Discovering the Roots of the Eternal Gospel in Ancient Israel and the Primitive Church*. 2nd Revised and Enlarged ed. Salt Lake City, UT: n. p., 1995.

———. *Ancient Texts and Mormonism: The Real Answer to Critics of Mormonism*. 1st ed. Murray, UT: Sounds of Zion, 1983.

———. *A Great Mystery: The Secret of the Jerusalem Temple*. Piscataway, NJ: Gorgias Press, 2008.

———. 1980. *Mormonism, the Dead Sea Scrolls, and the Nag Hammadi Texts*. Midvale, UT: Sounds of Zion, 1991.

———. "Was Freemasonry derived from Mormonism?" In *Scholarly and Historical Information Exchanged for Latter-day Saints (SHIELDS)*. http://www.shields-research.org/General/Masonry.html (accessed November 6, 2007).

Searle, Howard C. "History of the Church (History of Joseph Smith)." In *Encyclopedia of Mormonism*, edited by Daniel H. Ludlow. 4 vols. Vol. 2, 647-48. New York City, NY: Macmillan, 1992. http://www.lib.byu.edu/Macmillan/ (accessed November 26, 2007).

Seely, David Rolph. "Genesis 15 in light of the Restoration." In *Reason, Revelation, and Faith: Essays in Honor of Truman G. Madsen*, edited by Donald W. Parry, Daniel C. Peterson and Stephen D. Ricks, 339-64. Provo, UT: Foundation for Ancient Research and Mormon Studies, Brigham Young University, 2002.

———. "The image of the hand of God in the book of Exodus." In *God's Word for Our World: Biblical Studies in Honor of Simon John De Vries*, edited by J. Harold Ellens, Deborah L. Ellens, Rolf P. Knierim and Isaac Kalimi. Vol. 1. *Journal for the Study of the Old Testament Supplement* 388, 38-54. London, England: T & T Clark, 2004.

———. "The image of the hand of God in the Book of Mormon and the Old Testament." In *Rediscovering the Book of Mormon*, edited by John L. Sorenson and Melvin J. Thorne, 140-50. Salt Lake City, UT: Deseret Book, 1991. http://maxwellinstitute.byu.edu/publications/books?bookid=72&chapid=867 (accessed March 22, 2009).

———. "The image of the hand of God in the Exodus traditions." Doctoral Dissertation, University of Michigan, 1990.

———. "Jehovah, Jesus Christ." In *Encyclopedia of Mormonism*, edited by Daniel H. Ludlow. 4 vols. Vol. 2, 720-21. New York City, NY: Macmillan, 1992. http://www.lib.byu.edu/Macmillan/ (accessed November 26, 2007).

———. "The raised hand of God as an oath gesture." In *Fortunate the Eyes that See: Essays in Honor of David Noel Freedman in Celebration of His Seventieth Birthday*, edited by Astrid B. Beck, Andrew H. Bartelt, Paul R. Raabe and Chris A. Franke, 411-21. Grand Rapids, MI: Willam B. Eerdmans, 1995.

Segond, Louis, ed. *La Bible* Revue ed. Brussels, Belgium: Les Sociétés Bibliques, 1910.

Seler, Eduard. *Codex Borgia: Eine altmexikanische Bilderschrift der Bibliotek der Congregatio de Propaganda Fide*. 3 vols. Berlin, Germany: n.p., 1904-1910. http://www.famsi.org/spanish/research/loubat/Booklets/Seler_Borgia_1.pdf, http://www.famsi.org/spanish/research/loubat/Booklets/Seler_Borgia_2.pdf, http://www.famsi.org/spanish/research/loubat/Booklets/Seler_Borgia_3.pdf (accessed February 9, 2009).

———. *Codex Vaticanus No. 3773 (Codex Vaticanus B): An Old Mexican Pictorial Manuscript in the Vatican Library*. 2 vols. Translated by A. H. Keane. Berlin, Germany: n. p., 1902-1903. http://books.google.com/books?id=aW96AAAAMAAJ (Vol. 2. only) (accessed February 6, 2009).

Sforno, Obadiah ben Jacob. d. 1550. *Sforno: Commentary on the Torah*. 2 vols. Edited by Raphael Pelcovitz. *The Artscroll Mesorah Series*. Brooklyn, NY: Mesorah Publications, 1987-1989.

Shaheen, Naseeb. *Biblical References in Shakespeare's Plays*. Newark, NJ: University of Delaware Press, 1999.

Shakespeare, William. ca. 1594. "The Comedy of Errors." In *The Riverside Shakespeare*, edited by G. Blakemore Evans, 79-105. Boston, MA: Houghton Mifflin Company, 1974.

———. ca. 1603. "The History of Troilus and Cressida." In *The Riverside Shakespeare*, edited by G. Blakemore Evans, 442-98. Boston, MA: Houghton-Mifflin Company, 1974.

———. 1604. "Measure for Measure." In *The Riverside Shakespeare*, edited by G. Blakemore Evans, 545-86. Boston, MA: Houghton-Mifflin Company, 1974.

———. ca. 1598. "Much Ado about Nothing." In *The Riverside Shakespeare*, edited by G. Blakemore Evans, 327-64. Boston, MA: Houghton-Mifflin Company, 1974.

———. 1608. "Pericles, Prince of Tyre." In *The Riverside Shakespeare*, edited by G. Blakemore Evans, 1479-516. Boston, MA: Houghton-Mifflin Company, 1974.

———. 1611. "The Tempest." In *The Riverside Shakespeare*, edited by G. Blakemore Evans, 1606-38. Boston, MA: Houghton Mifflin Company, 1974.

———. 1611. *The Tempest*. Edited by Stephen Orgel. *The Oxford Shakespeare*, ed. Stanley Wells. Oxford, England: Oxford University Press, 1987.

———. ca. 1606-1607. "The Tragedy of Antony and Cleopatra." In *The Riverside Shakespeare*, edited by G. Blakemore Evans, 1343-91. Boston, MA: Houghton Mifflin Company, 1974.

———. 1600. "The Tragedy of Hamlet, Prince of Denmark." In *The Riverside Shakespeare*, edited by G. Blakemore Evans, 1135-97. Boston, MA: Houghton-Mifflin Company, 1974.

———. 1605. "The Tragedy of King Lear." In *The Riverside Shakespeare*, edited by G. Blakemore Evans, 1240-305. Boston, MA: Houghton-Mifflin Company, 1974.

———. 1595. "The Tragedy of King Richard the Second." In *The Riverside Shakespeare*, edited by G. Blakemore Evans, 800-41. Boston, MA: Houghton-Mifflin, 1974.

———. 1606. "The Tragedy of Macbeth." In *The Riverside Shakespeare*, edited by G. Blakemore Evans, 1306-42. Boston, MA: Houghton Mifflin Company, 1974.

———. 1592. "Venus and Adonis." In *The Riverside Shakespeare*, edited by G. Blakemore Evans, 1703-19. Boston, MA: Houghton Mifflin Company, 1974.

———. 1610. "The Winter's Tale." In *The Riverside Shakespeare*, edited by G. Blakemore Evans, 1564-605. Boston, MA: Houghton-Mifflin Company, 1974.

Shanks, Hershel. *Jerusalem's Temple Mount: From Solomon to the Golden Dome*. New York City, NY: Continuum, 2007.

Shannon, C. E., and W. Weaver. 1949. *The Mathematical Theory of Communication*. Urbana, IL: University of Illinois Press, 1964.

Shaw, Ian, and Paul Nicholson. 1995. *The British Museum Dictionary of Ancient Egypt*. Revised and Expanded ed. London, England: The British Museum Press, 2008.

Shelemon. ca. 1222. *The Book of the Bee, the Syriac Text Edited from the Manuscripts in London, Oxford, and Munich with an English Translation*. Translated by E. A. Wallis Budge. Reprint ed. Oxford, England: Clarendon Press, 1886. Reprint, n. p., n. d.

Sheridan, Mark, ed. *Genesis 12-50. Ancient Christian Commentary on Scripture, Old Testament* 2, ed. Thomas C. Oden. Downers Grove, IL: InterVarsity Press, 2002.

Sherlock, Richard. "Blake Ostler's Mormon Theology." *The FARMS Review* 18, no. 1 (2006): 291-305.

———. "Mormonism and intelligent design." *The FARMS Review* 18, no. 2 (2006): 45-81.

———. "Response to Professor McCann." In *Mormonism in Dialogue with Contemporary Christian Theologies*, edited by Donald W. Musser and David L. Paulsen, 92-111. Macon, GA: Mercer University Press, 2007.

Shermer, Michael. *Why Darwin Matters: The Case Against Intelligent Design*. New York City, NY: Times Books, Henry Holt, 2006.

Sherry, Thomas E. "Changing attitudes toward Joseph Smith's translation of the Bible." In *Plain and Precious Truths Restored: The Doctrinal and Historical Significance of the Joseph Smith Translation*, edited by Robert L. Millet and Robert J. Matthews, 187-226. Salt Lake City, UT: Deseret Book, 1995.

Shields, Mark A. *Your Endowment*. Springville, UT: Cedar Fort, 2009.

Shihab, Alwi. "Building bridges to harmony through understanding." *BYU Studies* 45, no. 4 (2006): 9-18.

Shipps, Jan. *Sojourner in the Promised Land: Forty Years among the Mormons*. Urbana, IL: University of Illinois Press, 2000.

Shirts, Kerry A. n. d. "*Chnum-Re* – Figure 1 on Hypocephalus." In *Mormonism Researched*. http://www2.ida.net/graphics/shirtail/amunre.htm (accessed September 7, 2007).

———. n. d. "Did Joseph Smith invent the Book of Abraham because he learned Hebrew?" In *Mormonism Researched*. http://www2.ida.net/graphics/shirtail/another.htm (accessed September 7, 2007).

———. The resurrection of Christ: Is it or is it not real? In *The Shirtail Review*. http://www2.ida.net/graphics/shirtail/signific.htm. (accessed September 1, 2009).

Shoemaker, Stephen J. "Early Christian apocryphal literature." In *The Oxford Handbook of Early Christian Studies*, edited by Susan Ashbrook Harvey and David G. Hunter. *Oxford Handbooks in Religion and Theology*, 521-48. Oxford, England: Oxford University Press, 2008.

Shokek, Shimon. *Jewish Ethics and Jewish Mysticism in Sefer Ha-Yashar*. Translated by Roslyn Weiss. *Jewish Studies*. Lewiston, NY: The Edwin Mellen Press, 1991.

Siddiqi, Muhammad Zubayr. 1961. *Hadith Literature: Its Origin, Development, Special Features, and Criticism*. Kuala Lumpur, Malaysia: Islamic Book Trust, 2006.

Siebach, Jim. "Response to Professor Tracy." In *Mormonism in Dialogue with Contemporary Christian Theologies*, edited by Donald W. Musser and David L. Paulsen, 462-67. Macon, GA: Mercer University Press, 2007.

Simpson, J. A., and E. S. C. Weiner. 1989. *The Compact Oxford English Dictionary*. 2nd ed. Oxford, England: Oxford University Press, 2004.

Singer, Peter. *The President of Good and Evil: The Ethics of George W. Bush*. New York City, NY: Dutton, 2004.

Skeat, W.W. *An Etymological Dictionary of the English Language.* Oxford, England: Clarendon Press, 1882. http://books.google.com/books?id=n-0_AAAAMAAJ (accessed July 30, 2008).

Skinner, Andrew C. *The Garden Tomb.* Salt Lake City, UT: Deseret Book, 2005.

———. *Golgotha.* Salt Lake City, UT: Deseret Book, 2004.

———. "Joseph Smith vindicated again: Enoch, Moses 7:48, and apocryphal sources." In *Reason, Revelation, and Faith: Essays in Honor of Truman G. Madsen,* edited by Donald W. Parry, Daniel C. Peterson and Stephen D. Ricks, 365-81. Provo, UT: Foundation for Ancient Research and Mormon Studies, 2002.

———. "Savior, Satan, and serpent: The duality of a symbol in the scriptures." In *The Disciple as Scholar: Essays on Scripture and the Ancient World in Honor of Richard Lloyd Anderson,* edited by Stephen D. Ricks, Donald W. Parry and Andrew H. Hedges, 359-84. Provo, UT: Foundation for Ancient Research and Mormon Studies, 2000.

———. *Temple Worship: Twenty Truths That Will Bless Your Life.* Salt Lake City, UT: Deseret Book, 2008.

Skousen, Eric N. *Earth: In the Beginning.* Revised and Enlarged ed. Orem, UT: Verity Publishing, 1997.

Skousen, Royal. "The earliest textual sources for Joseph Smith's 'New Translation' of the King James Bible." *The FARMS Review* 17, no. 2 (2005): 451-70.

———. "Joseph Smith's translation of the Book of Mormon: Evidence for tight control of the text." *Journal of Book of Mormon Studies* 7, no. 1 (1998): 22-31. http://www.farmsresearch.com/publications/jbms/?vol=7&num=1&id=167 (accessed February 22, 2009).

———. "Through a glass darkly: Trying to understand the scriptures." *BYU Studies* 26, no. 3 (1986): 1-18.

Skousen, W. Cleon. 1953. *The First 2,000 Years.* Salt Lake City, UT: Ensign Publishing, 1997.

Slover, George. 1978. "An analogical reading of *The Tempest.*" In *Shakespeare's Christian Dimension: An Anthology of Commentary,* edited by Roy Battenhouse, 257-63. Bloomington, IN: Indiana University Press, 1994.

Smith, A. W. "'And Did those Feet...?': The 'legend' of Christ's visit to Britain." *Folklore* 100, no. 1 (1989): 63-83.

Smith, Hyrum M., and Janne M. Sjodahl. 1916. *Doctrine and Covenants Commentary.* Revised ed. Salt Lake City, UT: Deseret Book, 1979.

Smith, Jonathan Z. *Drudgery Divine: On the Comparison of Early Christianities and the Religions of Late Antiquity (Jordan Lectures in Comparative Religion, XIV; School of Oriental and African Studies, University of London). Chicago Studies in the History of Judaism,* ed. William Scott Green. Chicago, IL: The University of Illinois Press, 1990.

Smith, Joseph, Jr. 1832-1844. *An American Prophet's Record: The Diaries and Journals of Joseph Smith.* Edited by Scott H. Faulring. Salt Lake City, UT: Signature Books, 1989.

———. "The answer to W. W. Phelps, Esq.: A vision." Nauvoo, IL: *Times and Seasons* 4:6, February 1, 1843, 82-85.

———. "The Elders of the Church in Kirtland, to their brethren abroad." Kirtland, OH: *The Evening and Morning Star* 2:18, 1834, 142-44.

———. *Encyclopedia of Joseph Smith's Teachings.* (Formerly *The Teachings of Joseph Smith*). Edited by Larry E. Dahl and Donald Q. Cannon. Salt Lake City, UT: Deseret Book, 2000.

———. 1902-1932. *History of the Church of Jesus Christ of Latter-day Saints (Documentary History).* 7 vols. Edited by Brigham Henry Roberts. Salt Lake City, UT: Deseret Book, 1978.

———, ed. 1867. *The Holy Scriptures: Inspired Version.* Independence, MO: Herald Publishing House, 1991.

———. 1805-1844. *The Joseph Smith Papers,* ed. Dean C. Jessee, Ronald K. Esplin and Richard Lyman Bushman. Salt Lake City, UT: The Church Historian's Press, 2008-.

———. *The Joseph Smith Papers Project.* http://www.josephsmithpapers.net/Default.htm (accessed February 26, 2008).

———. "Latter Day Saints." In *An Original History of the Religious Denominations at Present Existing in the United States,* edited by I. Daniel Rupp, 404-10. Philadelphia, PA: J. Y. Humphreys, 1844. http://books.google.com/books?id=OQgRAAAAMAAJ&dq (accessed November 30, 2007).

———. "Minutes of a special conference of the Church of Jesus Christ of Latter Day Saints, held in the City of Nauvoo, commencing on the 6th of October 1843." Nauvoo, IL: *Times and Seasons* 4:21, September 15, 1843, 329-32.

———. *The Papers of Joseph Smith.* 2 vols. Edited by Dean C. Jessee. Salt Lake City, UT: Deseret Book, 1989-1992.

———. *The Personal Writings of Joseph Smith.* Edited by Dean C. Jessee. 2nd ed. Salt Lake City, UT: Deseret Book, 2002.

———. *Teachings of the Presidents of the Church: Joseph Smith.* Salt Lake City, UT: The Church of Jesus Christ of Latter-day Saints, 2007.

———. 1938. *Teachings of the Prophet Joseph Smith.* Edited by Joseph Fielding Smith, Jr. Salt Lake City, UT: Deseret Book, 1969.

———. "'Try the spirits.'" Nauvoo, IL: *Times and Seasons* 3:11, April 1, 1842, 743-48.

REFERENCES

———. *The Words of Joseph Smith.* Edited by Andrew F. Ehat and Lyndon W. Cook. Salt Lake City, UT: Bookcraft, 1980.

Smith, Joseph F. 1873. "Discourse (Delivered in the 13th Ward assembly rooms, Salt Lake City, Sunday afternoon, 9 February 1873)." In *Journal of Discourses.* 26 vols. Vol. 15, 324-28. Liverpool and London, England: Latter-day Saints Book Depot, 1853-1886. Reprint, Salt Lake City, UT: Bookcraft, 1966.

———. 1882. "Discourse delivered in the Tabernacle, Salt Lake City, Sunday, June 18, 1882 (Man a mortal and an immortal being; redemption through the atonement and gospel of Christ; sons of perdition; man's pre-existent, disembodied, and resurrected states; Jesus Christ the great example; the righteous to be conformed to His image; His similarity to the Father; His mission not completed at His death; His resurrection and the redemption of humanity)." In *Journal of Discourses.* 26 vols. Vol. 23, 169-75. Liverpool and London, England: Latter-day Saints Book Depot, 1853-1886. Reprint, Salt Lake City, UT: Bookcraft, 1966.

———. 1919. *Gospel Doctrine.* Edited by Joseph Fielding Smith, Jr. Salt Lake City, UT: Deseret Book, 1986.

———. "Philosophy and the church schools." *Juvenile Instructor* 46 (1911): 208-09.

———. *Teachings of the Presidents of the Church: Joseph F. Smith.* Salt Lake City, UT: Church of Jesus Christ of Latter-day Saints, 1998.

Smith, Joseph F. and E. H. Anderson. "Editorial." *Improvement Era* 13, April 1910, 570.

Smith, Joseph F., J. R. Winder, and A. H. Lund. 1909. "The origin of man." In *Messages of the First Presidency*, edited by James R. Clark. 6 vols. Vol. 4, 199-206. Salt Lake City, UT: Bookcraft, 1970.

———. "Words in Season from the First Presidency." Salt Lake City, UT: *Deseret Evening News*, December 17, 1910, 3.

Smith, Joseph Fielding, Jr. 1957-1966. *Answers to Gospel Questions.* 5 vols. Salt Lake City, UT: Deseret Book, 1979.

———. "Discourse." In *Ninety-Fifth Annual Conference of the Church of Jesus Christ of Latter-day Saints, April 4-6, 1925*, 73-76. Salt Lake City, UT: The Church of Jesus Christ of Latter-day Saints, 1925.

———. *Doctrines of Salvation: Sermons and Writings of Joseph Fielding Smith.* Edited by Bruce R. McConkie. Salt Lake City, UT: Bookcraft, 1954-1956.

———. *Fall, Atonement, Resurrection, Sacrament (Delivered at the University of Utah Institute of Religion, January 19, 1961).* Salt Lake City, UT: University of Utah Institute of Religion, 1961.

———. "Magnifying our callings in the priesthood." *Improvement Era* 73, June 1970, 65-66.

———. *Man: His Origin and Destiny.* Salt Lake City, UT: Deseret Book, 1954.

———. "The oath and covenant of the priesthood." In *Conference Report: 140th Semiannual General Conference*, 90-92. Salt Lake City, UT: The Church of Jesus Christ of Latter-day Saints, 1970.

———. *Origin of the "Reorganized" Church: The Question of Succession.* 1st ed. Salt Lake City, UT: Deseret News Press, 1909.

———. *Seek Ye Earnestly.* Salt Lake City, UT: Deseret Book, 1970.

———. 1931. *The Way to Perfection: Short Discourses on Gospel Themes Dedicated to All Who Are Interested in the Redemption of the Living and the Dead.* 5th ed. Salt Lake City, UT: Genealogical Society of Utah, 1945.

Smith, Julie M. "The Beginning and the End: Echoes of Genesis 1-3 in Revelation 21-22." Presented at the Mormon Theology Seminar: Latter-day Saint Readings of Revelation 21-22, University of Texas, Austin, TX, 25 September 2009, 2009. http://www.mormontheologyseminar.org/. (accessed September 19, 2009).

Smith, Lucy Mack. 1853. *Lucy's Book: A Critical Edition of Lucy Mack Smith's Family Memoir.* Edited by Lavina Fielding Anderson. Salt Lake City, UT: Signature Books, 2001.

Smith, Mark S. *The Origins of Biblical Monotheism: Israel's Polytheistic Background and the Ugaritic Texts.* Oxford, England: Oxford University Press, 2001.

Smith, Morton. 1967. "Goodenough's Jewish Symbols in Retrospect." In *Studies in the Cult of Yahweh: Historical Method, Ancient Israel, Ancient Judaism*, edited by Shaye J. D. Cohen. 2 vols. Vol. 1, 184-200. Leiden, The Netherlands: E. J. Brill, 1996.

———. 1982. *The Secret Gospel: The Discovery and Interpretation of the Secret Gospel According to Mark.* Middletown, CA: The Dawn Horse Press, 2005.

Smith, Roger J. 1997. "Michelangelo's Sistine Chapel: The loss of grace through original sin and its consequence. In *The East Lewis County (Washington) Catholic Community.* http://landru.i-link-2.net/shnyves/Fall_expulsion_from_Ed.html (accessed September 9, 2007).

Smith, Timothy. "The Book of Mormon in a Biblical culture." *Journal of Mormon History* 7 (1980): 3-22.

Smith, William, and Samuel Cheetham. *A Dictionary of Christian Antiquities Being a Continuation of 'The Dictionary of the Bible.'* 2 vols. Hartford, CN: The J. B. Burr Publishing Company, 1876, 1880.

Smith, William V., ed. *A Joseph Smith Commentary on The Book of Abraham.* 2nd ed. Provo, UT: The Book of Abraham Project (BOAP), 2002. http://www.boap.org/LDS/BOAP/SecondEd/ (accessed Summer, 2006).

Snodgrass, Klyne R. *Stories with Intent: A Comprehensive Guide to the Parables of Jesus.* Grand Rapids, MI: William B. Eerdmans, 2008.

Snow, Eliza R. *Biography and Family Record of Lorenzo Snow.* Salt Lake City, UT: Deseret News Company, 1884.

Snow, Erastus. 1878. "There is a God; communion with Him an inherent craving of the human heart; man in his image; male and female created he them; spirit and flesh; mortal and immortal (Discourse delivered in the meetinghouse, Beaver City, Beaver county, Utah, on Sunday Morning, 3 March 1878)." In *Journal of Discourses.* 26 vols. Vol. 19, 266-79. Liverpool and London, England: Latter-day Saints Book Depot, 1853-1886. Reprint, Salt Lake City, UT: Bookcraft, 1966.

Snow, Lorenzo. 1877. "Discourse delivered at a two days' meeting held by the St. George Stake of Zion, in the Temple, at St. George, Thursday morning, 5 April 1877." In *Journal of Discourses.* 26 vols. Vol. 18, 371-76. Liverpool and London, England: Latter-day Saints Book Depot, 1853-1886. Reprint, Salt Lake City, UT: Bookcraft, 1966.

———. *The Teachings of Lorenzo Snow.* Edited by Clyde J. Williams. Salt Lake City, UT: Bookcraft, 1984.

Sophocles. d. 406 BC. *Oedipus Rex.* http://www.users.bigpond.net.au/soloword/Oedipus.htm (accessed August 31, 2008).

———. d. 406 BC. *Sophoclis Tragoediae Superstites et Deperditarum Fragmenta ex rec. G. Dindorfii.* 2 vols. Edited by Wilhelm Dindorf. 2nd Revised ed. Oxford, England: Clarendon Press, 1860.

Sorenson, John L. *An Ancient American Setting for the Book of Mormon.* Salt Lake City, UT: Deseret Book, 1985.

———. "The 'Brass Plates' and biblical scholarship." *Dialogue* 10 (Autumn 1977): 31-39.

———. "Origin of man." In *Encyclopedia of Mormonism,* edited by Daniel H. Ludlow. 4 vols. Vol. 3, 1053-54. New York City, NY: Macmillan, 1992. http://www.lib.byu.edu/Macmillan/ (accessed November 26, 2007).

Sorvig, Kim. "Learning from Salt Lake." *American Society of Landscape Artists* (2004): 96-107. http://www.asla.org/meetings/am2004/learning.pdf (accessed September 7, 2007).

Sourvinou-Inwood, Christiane. "Festival and mysteries: Aspects of the Eleusinian cult." In *Greek Mysteries: The Archaeology and Ritual of Ancient Greek Secret Cults,* edited by Michael B. Cosmopoulos, 25-49. New York City, NY: Routledge, 2003.

Sparks, Kenton L. *Ancient Texts for the Study of the Hebrew Bible: A Guide to the Background Literature.* Peabody, MA: Hendrickson Publishers, 2005.

Speiser, Ephraim A. ed. "The Creation Epic (*Enuma Elish*)." In *Ancient Near Eastern Texts Relating to the Old Testament,* edited by James B. Pritchard. 3rd with Supplement ed, 60-72, 501-03. Princeton, NJ: Princeton University Press, 1972.

———, ed. "Etana." In *Ancient Near Eastern Texts Relating to the Old Testament,* edited by James B. Pritchard, 114-18. Princeton, NJ: Princeton University Press, 1972.

———, ed. 1964. *Genesis: A New Translation with Introduction and Commentary.* Anchor Bible Commentary Series 1, ed. William F. Albright. Garden City, NY: Doubleday, 1985.

Spencer, Robert. 2003. "A loss to the cultural inheritance of mankind." In *Mandaean Human Rights Files: Australia 2003.* http://www.mandaeanworld.com/mhr_iraq_2003_4.html (accessed August 19, 2007).

Spenser, Edmund. 1590/1596. *The Faerie Queen.* Edited by A. C. Hamilton, Hiroshi Yamashita and Toshiyuki Suzuki. 2nd ed. Harlow, England: Pearson Education, Longman, 2007.

Sperling, Harry, Maurice Simon, and Paul P. Levertoff, eds. *The Zohar: An English Translation.* 5 vols. London, England: The Soncino Press, 1984.

Spinks, Bryan D. *Early and Medieval Rituals and Theologies of Baptism: From the New Testament to the Council of Trent. Liturgy, Worship and Society,* ed. Dave Leal, Bryan D. Spinks, Paul Bradshaw, Gregory Woolfenden and Phillip Tovey. Aldershot, England: Ashgate, 2006.

Spittler, R. P. ed. "Testament of Job." In *The Old Testament Pseudepigrapha,* edited by James H. Charlesworth. Vol. 1, 829-68. Garden City, NY: Doubleday and Company, 1983.

Staheli, Donald L. "Obedience—Life's greatest challenge." *Ensign* 28, May 1998, 81-82.

Stark, Rodney. *Discovering God: The Origins of the Great Religions and the Evolution of Belief.* New York City, NY: HarperOne, 2007.

Starr, James. 2007. "Does 2 Peter 1:4 speak of deification?" In *Partakers of the Divine Nature: The History and Development of Deification in the Christian Traditions,* edited by Michael J. Christensen and Jeffery A. Wittung, 81-92. Grand Rapids, MI: Baker Academic, 2008.

Staub, Jacob J., ed. *The Creation of the World According to Gersonides: A Translation and Commentary to the War of the*

Lord 6:2:1-8. Brown Judaic Studies 24. Chicago, IL: Scholars Press, 1982.

Stoyanov, Yuri. *The Other God: Dualist Religions from Antiquity to the Cathar Heresy*. New Haven, CT: Yale University Press, 2000.

Stein, Sir Mark Aurel. *Innermost Asia*. 3 vols. Oxford, England: Clarendon Press, 1930.

Steinberg, Leo. "Who's who in Michelangelo's creation of Adam: A chronology of the picture's reluctant self-revelation." *Art Bulletin* 74, no. 4 (December 1992): 552-66.

Steinsaltz, Adin, ed. *The Talmud: The Steinsaltz Edition*. New York City, NY: Random House, 1989-.

Stendahl, Krister. "The Sermon on the Mount and Third Nephi." In *Reflections on Mormonism: Judeao-Christian Parallels: Papers Delivered at the Religious Studies Center Symposium, Brigham Young University, March 10-11, 1978*, edited by Truman G. Madsen. *Religious Studies Monograph Series* 4, 139-54. Provo, UT: Religious Studies Center, Brigham Young University, 1978.

Stephanus, H. *Thesaurus Graecae Linguae*. Graz, Austria: Akademische Druck und Verlaganstalt, 1954.

Stephens, Trent D. 2003. "Evolution and Latter-day Saint theology: The tree of life and DNA." In *2003 FAIR Conference*. http://www.fairlds.org/FAIR_Conferences/2003_Evolution_and_Latter-day_Saint_Theology.html (accessed September 7, 2007).

Stephens, Trent D., D. Jeffrey Meldrum, and Forrest B. Peterson. *Evolution and Mormonism: A Quest for Understanding*. Salt Lake City, UT: Signature Books, 2001.

Sterling, Gregory E. "Philo of Alexandria." In *The Historical Jesus in Context*, edited by Amy-Jill Levine, Dale C. Allison, Jr. and John Dominic Crossan. *Princeton Readings in Religions*, ed. Donald S. Lopez, Jr., 296-308. Princeton, NJ: Princeton University Press, 2006.

Stevens, Keith G. *Chinese Mythological Gods*. Oxford, England: Oxford University Press, 2001.

Stevenson, Edward. *Autobiography of Edward Stevenson, 1820-1897 (The Life and History of Elder Edward Stevenson)*. Edited by Joseph Grant Stevenson. Provo, UT: Stevenson's Genealogical Center, 1986.

Stokes, William Lee. *The Creation Scriptures: A Witness for God in the Scientific Age*. Bountiful, UT: Horizon, 1979.

Stone, Michael E., ed. *Signs of the Judgment, Onomastica Sacra, and the Generations from Adam*. Atlanta, GA: Scholars Press, 1981.

———. "Abel and other pieces." In *Armenian Apocrypha Relating to Adam and Eve*, edited by Michael E. Stone, 141-57. Leiden, The Netherlands: E. J. Brill, 1996.

———, ed. 1401-1403. *Adamgirk': The Adam Book of Arak'el of Siwnik'*. Translated by Michael E. Stone. Oxford, England: Oxford University Press, 2007.

———. *Adam's Contract with Satan: The Legend of the Cheirograph of Adam*. Bloomington, IN: Indiana University Press, 2002.

———. "The angelic prediction." In *Literature on Adam and Eve: Collected Essays*, edited by Gary A. Anderson, Michael E. Stone and Johannes Tromp, 111-31. Leiden, Netherlands: Brill, 2000.

———, ed. *Armenian Apocrypha Relating to Adam and Eve. Studia in Veteris Testamenti Pseudepigrapha*, ed. A.-M. Denis, M. de Jonge, M. A. Knibb, H.-J. de Jonge, J.-Cl. Haelewyck and Johannes Tromp. Leiden, The Netherlands: E. J. Brill, 1996.

———, ed. *Armenian Apocrypha Relating to the Patriarchs and Prophets*. Jerusalem, Israel: The Israel Academy of Sciences and Humanities, 1982.

———, ed. "The Descendants of Adam." In *Armenian Apocrypha Relating to the Patriarchs and Prophets*, edited by Michael E. Stone, 84-87. Jerusalem, Israel: The Israel Academy of Sciences and Humanities, 1982.

———. "The fall of Satan and Adam's penance: Three notes on the Books of Adam and Eve." In *Literature on Adam and Eve: Collected Essays*, edited by Gary A. Anderson, Michael E. Stone and Johannes Tromp, 43-56. Leiden, Netherlands: Brill, 2000.

———, ed. "History of Adam and his grandsons." In *Armenian Apocrypha Relating to Adam and Eve*, edited by Michael E. Stone, 80-100. Leiden, The Netherlands: E. J. Brill, 1996.

———, ed. "History of the forefathers, Adam and his sons and grandsons." In *Armenian Apocrypha Relating to Adam and Eve*, edited by Michael E. Stone, 180-200. Leiden, The Netherlands: E. J. Brill, 1996.

———. *A History of the Literature of Adam and Eve. Society of Biblical Literature: Early Judaism and its Literature*, ed. William Adler. Atlanta, GA: Scholars Press, 1992.

———. "The legend of the cheirograph of Adam." In *Literature on Adam and Eve: Collected Essays*, edited by Gary A. Anderson, Michael E. Stone and Johannes Tromp, 149-66. Leiden, Netherlands: Brill, 2000.

———, ed. "On the fall of Adam." In *Armenian Apocrypha Relating to Adam and Eve*, edited by Michael E. Stone, 3-7. Leiden, The Netherlands: E. J. Brill, 1996.

———, ed. "Question." In *Armenian Apocrypha Relating to Adam and Eve*, edited by Michael E. Stone, 114-34. Leiden, The Netherlands: E. J. Brill, 1996.

———. "Selections from *On the Creation of the World* by Yovhannes Tulkuranci." In *Literature on Adam and Eve: Collected Essays*, edited by Gary A. Anderson, Michael E. Stone and Johannes Tromp, 167-213. Leiden, Netherlands: Brill, 2000.

———, ed. "Sermon concerning the Flood." In *Armenian Apocrypha Relating to Adam and Eve*, edited by Michael E. Stone, 174-79. Leiden, The Netherlands: E. J. Brill, 1996.

———, ed. "The Sethites and the Cainites." In *Armenian Apocrypha Relating to Adam and Eve*, edited by Michael E. Stone, 201-06. Leiden, The Netherlands: E. J. Brill, 1996.

Stordalen, Terje. *Echoes of Eden: Genesis 2-3 and the Symbolism of the Eden Garden in Biblical Hebrew Literature*. Leuven, Belgium: Peeters, 2000.

Storme, Albert. *Le Mont des Oliviers*. 3rd Revised ed. *Lieux Saints de Palestine*. Jerusalem, Israel: Franciscan Printing Press, 1993.

Stott, Gerald. "Effects of college education on the religious involvement of Latter-day Saints." *BYU Studies* 24, no. 1 (1984): 43-52.

Strack, H. L., and Günter Stemberger. 1887. *Introduction to the Talmud and Midrash*. 2nd ed. Minneapolis, MN: Fortress Press, 1996.

Strathearn, Gaye, and Brian M. Hauglid. "The Great Mosque and its Ka'ba as an Islamic temple complex in light of Lundquist's typology of ancient Near Eastern temples." In *The Temple in Time and Eternity*, edited by Donald W. Parry and Stephen D. Ricks, 275-302. Provo, UT: The Foundation for Ancient Research and Mormon Studies (FARMS) at Brigham Young University, 1999.

Stratton, Richard D., ed. *Kindness to Animals and Caring for the Earth*. Portland, OR: Inkwater Press, 2004.

Strong, Eugenie Sellers. *Apotheosis and the After Life, Three Lectures on Certain Phases of Art and Religion in the Roman Empire*. London, England: Constable and Company, Ltd., 1915.

Stuckenbruck, Loren T. "The formation and re-formation of Daniel in the Dead Sea Scrolls." In *The Bible and the Dead Sea Scrolls: The Second Princeton Symposium on Judaism and Christian Origins*, edited by James H. Charlesworth. *Scripture and the Scrolls* 1, ed. James H. Charlesworth, 101-30. Waco, TX: Baylor University Press, 2006.

Sundberg, Waldemar. *Kushta: A Monograph on a Principal Word in Mandaean Texts. The Descending Knowledge* 1. Lund, Sweden: C. W. K. Gleerup, 1953.

Swanson, Vern Grosvenor. *Dynasty of the Holy Grail: Mormonism's Sacred Bloodline*. Springville, UT: CFI, 2006.

Swindle, L.L. and S.E. Black. *Joseph Smith: Impressions of a Prophet*. Salt Lake City, UT: Deseret Book, 1998.

Szink, Terrence L. "Authorship of the Epistle to the Hebrews." In *How the New Testament Came to Be: The 35th Annual Brigham Young University Sidney B. Sperry Symposium*, edited by Kent P. Jackson and Frank F. Judd, Jr., 243-59. Salt Lake City, UT: Deseret Book, 2006.

Tajadod, Nahal, ed. *Mani le Bouddha de Lumière: Catéchisme manichéen chinois. Sources Gnostiques et Manichéennes* 3, ed. Michel Tardieu. Paris, France: Les Éditions du Cerf, 1990.

Taleb, Nassim Nicholas. *The Black Swan: The Impact of the Highly Improbable*. New York City, NY: Random House, 2007.

Talmage, James E. 1924. *The Articles of Faith*. Salt Lake City, UT: Deseret Book, 1984.

———. 1931. "The earth and man (originally published in *Deseret News,* November 21, 1931, pp. 7-8)." In *The Essential James E. Talmage*, edited by James P. Harris, 241-55. Salt Lake City, UT: Signature Books, 1997.

———. "The eternity of sex." *Young Woman's Journal* 25, October 1914, 602-03.

———. 1912. *The House of the Lord*. Salt Lake City, UT: Signature Books, 1998.

———. 1915. *Jésus le Christ*. Salt Lake City, UT: Église de Jésus Christ des Saints des Derniers Jours, 1991.

———. 1915. *Jesus the Christ*. Salt Lake City, UT: Deseret Book, 1983.

———. "Knowledge concerning God's attributes essential to intelligent worship; The relationship of Jesus Christ to God, the Eternal Father, spiritual and bodily; Relationship of mankind to Deity (6 April 1915)." In *Conference Reports: Eighty-Fifth Annual General Conference of the Church of Jesus Christ of Latter-day Saints*, 120-24. Salt Lake City, UT: Deseret News, 1915. Reprint, Salt Lake City, UT: Hawkes Publishing, n. d.

———. *The Parables of James E. Talmage*. Edited by Albert L. Zobell, Jr. Salt Lake City, UT: Deseret Book, 1973.

Tannenbaum, Leslie. *Biblical Tradition in Blake's Early Prophecies: The Great Code of Art*. Princeton, NJ: Princeton University Press, 1982.

Tanner, John S. "Of men and mantles: Kierkegaard and the difference between a genius and an apostle." *BYU Studies*

40, no. 2 (2001): 149-64.

———. "Shakespeare among the Saints." *Journal of Mormon History* 32, no. 1 (2006): 82-115. http://avp.byu.edu/documents/pdf/shakespearesaints.pdf.

———. "The world and the word: History, literature, and scripture." In *Historicity and the Latter-day Saint Scriptures*, edited by Paul Y. Hoskisson, 217-35. Provo, UT: Brigham Young University Religious Studies Center, 2001.

Tardieu, Michel. *Le Manichéisme.* 2nd ed. *Que sais-je?* Paris, France: Presses Universitaires de France, 1997.

———. *Manichaeism.* Translated by Malcolm DeBevoise. Urbana, IL: University of Illinois Press, 2008.

Taylor, Charles. *A Secular Age.* Cambridge, MA: The Belknap Press of Harvard University Press, 2007.

Taylor, John. 1853. "Motives and feelings of the Saints; experience necessary; the state of the world; infidels; religions and works of men, and the religion and works of God; truth and salvation (Discourse delivered in the Tabernacle, Great Salt Lake City, 12 June 1853)." In *Journal of Discourses.* 26 vols. Vol. 1, 147-59. Liverpool and London, England: Latter-day Saints Book Depot, 1853-1886. Reprint, Salt Lake City, UT: Bookcraft, 1966.

———. 1876. "Burial services, an ancient practice; God, the God of the living; keys committed to Joseph Smith; the last dispensation; Jesus the great Redeemer; an everlasting priesthood; the powers of the resurrection; scriptural, philosophical, and certain; sealing powers eternal (Funeral sermon preached at the 7th Ward Meetinghouse, Salt Lake City, on Sunday Afternoon, 31 December 1876, over the remains of Ann Tenora, the wife of Isaac Waddell; and also over the remains of George W., son of Edward Callister)." In *Journal of Discourses.* 26 vols. Vol. 18, 324-35. Liverpool and London, England: Latter-day Saints Book Depot, 1853-1886. Reprint, Salt Lake City, UT: Bookcraft, 1966.

———. *The Gospel Kingdom: Selections from the Writings and Discourses of John Taylor.* Edited by G. Homer Durham. Salt Lake City, UT: Bookcraft, 1943.

———. *The Government of God.* Liverpool, England: S. W. Richards, 1852. Reprint, Heber City, UT: Archive Publishers, 2000.

———. *The Mediation and Atonement.* Salt Lake City, UT: The Deseret News, 1882. Reprint, Heber City, UT: Archive Publishers, 2000.

———. New York City, NY: *The Mormon,* August 29, 1857.

Taylor, Sheila. "'A broken-mirror image': Original sin in LDS theology." Presented at the 2008 Conference of the Society for Mormon Philosophy and Theology, Salt Lake City, UT, March 28, 2008.

Tennent, James Emerson. *Ceylon: An Account of the Island Physical, Historical, and Topographical with Notices of Its Natural History, Antiquities and Productions.* 2 vols. 4th, Thoroughly Revised ed. London, England: Longman, Green, Longman, and Roberts, 1860. http://www.gutenberg.org/etext/13552 (accessed March 13, 2008).

Terry, Roger. E-mail message to Jeffrey M. Bradshaw, July 31, 2009.

Tertullian. ca. 197-222. "An Answer to the Jews." In *The Ante-Nicene Fathers (The Writings of the Fathers Down to AD 325),* edited by Alexander Roberts and James Donaldson. 10 vols. Vol. 3, 151-73. Buffalo, NY: The Christian Literature Company, 1885. Reprint, Peabody, MA: Hendrickson Publishers, 2004.

———. ca. 197-222. "Apology." In *The Ante-Nicene Fathers (The Writings of the Fathers Down to AD 325),* edited by Alexander Roberts and James Donaldson. 10 vols. Vol. 3, 17-60. Buffalo, NY: The Christian Literature Company, 1885. Reprint, Peabody, MA: Hendrickson Publishers, 2004.

———. ca. 197-222. "On baptism." In *The Ante-Nicene Fathers (The Writings of the Fathers Down to AD 325),* edited by Alexander Roberts and James Donaldson. 10 vols. Vol. 3, 669-79. Buffalo, NY: The Christian Literature Company, 1885. Reprint, Peabody, MA: Hendrickson Publishers, 2004.

———. ca. 197-222. "On prayer (De Oratione)." In *The Ante-Nicene Fathers (The Writings of the Fathers Down to AD 325),* edited by Alexander Roberts and James Donaldson. 10 vols. Vol. 3, 681-91. Buffalo, NY: The Christian Literature Company, 1885. Reprint, Peabody, MA: Hendrickson Publishers, 2004.

"The Electronic Text Corpus of Sumerian Literature, 2nd Edition." 2006. In *Faculty of Oriental Studies, Oxford University.* http://etcsl.orinst.ox.ac.uk/ (accessed November 1, 2007).

"The gathering (unsigned editorial)." Nauvoo, IL: *Times and Seasons* 5:2, January, 1844, 407-10.

"The Holy Trinity." In *Department of Modern Languages and Literatures at Rollins College.* http://www.rollins.edu/Foreign_Lang/Russian/trinity.html (accessed November 16, 2006).

The Oxford Annotated Apocrypha: Expanded Edition of the Revised Standard Version. Oxford, England: Oxford University Press, 1977.

"The Pentagram." In *Grand Lodge of British Columbia and Yukon, Ancient Free and Accepted Masons.* http://www.freemasonry.bcy.ca/anti-masonry/pentagram.html (accessed September 9, 2008).

The Revised Version of the Apocrypha. Cambridge, England: Cambridge University Press, 1927.

The Society for Mormon Philosophy and Theology. http://www.smpt.org/ (accessed April 28, 2009).

Theophilus. d. ca. 183-185. "Theophilus to Autolycus." In *The Ante-Nicene Fathers (The Writings of the Fathers Down to AD 325),* edited by Alexander Roberts and James Donaldson. 10 vols. Vol. 2, 89-121. Buffalo, NY: The Christian Literature Company, 1885. Reprint, Peabody, MA: Hendrickson Publishers, 1994.

"Theophilus of Antioch." In *Wikipedia.* http://en.wikipedia.org/wiki/Theophilus_of_Antioch (accessed January 19, 2008).

Thomas, M. Catherine. "The Brother of Jared at the veil." In *Temples of the Ancient World,* edited by Donald W. Parry, 388-98. Salt Lake City, UT: Deseret Book, 1994.

———. "Hebrews: To ascend the holy mount." In *Temples of the Ancient World,* edited by Donald W. Parry, 479-91. Salt Lake City, UT: Deseret Book, 1994.

———. "Jacob's allegory: The mystery of Christ." In *The Allegory of the Olive Tree,* edited by Stephen D. Ricks and John W. Welch, 11-20. Provo, UT: FARMS, 1994.

———. *Light in the Wilderness: Explorations in the Spiritual Life.* Provo, UT: Amalphi Publishing, 2008.

———. "The Sermon on the Mount: The sacrifice of the human heart." In *The Gospels,* edited by Kent P. Jackson and Robert L. Millet. *Studies in Scripture* 5, 236-50. Salt Lake City, UT: Deseret Book, 1986.

———. "Women, priesthood, and the at-one-ment." In *Spiritual Lightening: How the Power of the Gospel Can Enlighten Minds and Lighten Burdens,* edited by M. Catherine Thomas, 47-58. Salt Lake City, UT: Deseret Book, 1996.

Thomas, Richard. "The Israelite origins of the Mandaean people." *Studia Antiqua* 5, no. 2 (2007): 3-27.

Thurston, Herbert. "Corporal." In *The Catholic Encyclopedia: An International Work of Reference on the Constitution, Doctrine, Discipline, and History of the Catholic Church,* edited by Charles George Hebermann, Edward A. Pace, Condé B. Pallen, Thomas J. Shahan and John J. Wynne. 15 vols. Vol. 4, 386-87. New York City, NY: The Universal Knowledge Foundation, 1913. http://books.google.com/books?id=2GcQAAAAIAAJ (accessed February 1, 2009).

Tiffany, Scott, ed. *City Saints: Mormons in the New York Metropolis.* New York City, NY: Nauvoo Books, 2004.

Tiller, Patrick A., ed. *A Commentary on the Animal Apocalypse of 1 Enoch. Society of Biblical Literature Early Judaism and Its Literature Series* 4, ed. William Adler. Atlanta, GA: Scholars Press, 1993.

Times and Seasons. Nauvoo, IL, 1839-1846. Reprint, 6 vols.

Timothy of Alexandria. ca. 385. "The Discourse on Abbaton." In *Coptic Martyrdoms, etc. in the Dialect of Upper Egypt,* edited by E. A. Wallis Budge, 474-96. London, England: The British Museum, 1914.

———. ca. 385. "How Abbaton, the angel of death, became the king of all mankind." In *Egyptian Tales and Romances: Pagan, Christian and Muslim,* edited by E. A. Wallis Budge, 195-203. London, England: Thornton Butterworth Limited, 1931. Reprint, Kila, MT: Kessinger Publishing, 2003.

"Titian." In *Notable Names Database.* http://www.nndb.com (accessed March 20, 2006).

Tobin, Gary A., and Aryeh K. Weinberg. *Religious Beliefs and Behavior. Profiles of the American University* 2. San Francisco, CA: The Institute for Jewish and Community Research, 2007.

Todd, Jay M. "Background of the Church Historian's Fragment." *Improvement Era* 71, February 1968, 40A-40I.

Toner, P. J. "Extreme Unction." In *The Catholic Encyclopedia: An International Work of Reference on the Constitution, Doctrine, Discipline, and History of the Catholic Church,* edited by Charles George Hebermann, Edward A. Pace, Condé B. Pallen, Thomas J. Shahan and John J. Wynne. 15 vols. Vol. 5, 716-30. New York City, NY: The Universal Knowledge Foundation, 1913. http://books.google.com/books?id=-aSQNo8kNqIC (accessed February 1, 2009).

Top, Brent L. *The Life Before: How Our Premortal Existence Affects Our Mortal Life.* Salt Lake City, UT: Deseret Book, 1988.

Toronto, James A. "Islam." In *Religions of the World: A Latter-day Saint View,* edited by Spencer J. Palmer, Roger R. Keller, Doug Sull Choi and James A. Toronto, 212-41. Provo, UT: Brigham Young University Press, 1997.

Tóth, Endre, and Károly Szelényi. *The Holy Crown of Hungary: Kings and Coronation.* 2nd ed. Budapest, Hungary: Kossuth Publishing, 2000.

Tov, Emanuel. *Scribal Practices and Approaches Reflected in the Texts Found in the Judean Desert.* Leiden, The Netherlands: Brill, 2004.

Townes, Charles H. "The convergence of science and religion." *Improvement Era* 71, February 1968, 62-69.

Townsend, John T., ed. *Midrash Tanhuma.* 3 vols. Jersey City, NJ: Ktav Publishing, 1989-2003.

Tozzer, Alfred M. *A Comparative Study of the Mayas and the Lacandones.* New York City, NY: Macmillan, 1907. http://books.google.com/books?id=eMRpAAAAMAAJ (accessed February 6, 2009).

Treharne, Reginald Francis. *The Glastonbury Legends: Joseph of Arimathea, the Holy Grail, and King Arthur.* London, England: The Cresset Press, 1967. Reprint, *The Glastonbury Legends: The Quest for King Arthur and the Holy Grail.* London, England: Sphere Books, 1971.

Trippi, Peter. *J. W. Waterhouse*. London, England: Phaidon Press, 2002.

Tromp, Johannes. "Cain and Abel in the Greek and Armenian/Georgian recensions of the *Life of Adam and Eve*." In *Literature on Adam and Eve: Collected Essays*, edited by Gary A. Anderson, Michael E. Stone and Johannes Tromp, 277-96. Leiden, Netherlands: Brill, 2000.

———. "Literary and exegetical issues in the story of Adam's death and burial (GLAE 31-42)." In *The Book of Genesis in Jewish and Oriental Christian Interpretation*, edited by Judith Frishman and Lucas Van Rompay. *Traditio Exegetica Graeca* 5, 25-41. Louvain, Belgium: Editions Peeters, 1997.

Tullidge, Edward W. 1877. *The Women of Mormondom*. New York City, NY: n.p., 1997.

Turner, Laurence. *Announcements of Plot in Genesis. Journal for the Study of the Old Testament Supplement Series* 96, ed. David J. A. Clines and Philip R. Davies. Sheffield, England: JSOT Press, 1990.

Turner, Martha Lee. *The Gospel According to Philip. Nag Hammadi and Manichaean Studies* 38. Leiden, The Netherlands: Brill, 1996.

Turner, Rodney. "The Position of Adam in Latter-day Saint Scripture and Theology." Master's Thesis, Brigham Young University, 1953.

———. "The visions of Moses (Moses 1)." In *The Pearl of Great Price*, edited by Robert L. Millet and Kent P. Jackson, 43-61. *Studies in Scripture* 2. Salt Lake City, UT: Randall Book Company, 1985.

Turner, Victor. 1969. *The Ritual Process: Structure and Anti-Structure*. New Brunswick, NJ: AldineTransaction, 2009.

Turner, Victor, and Edith L. B. Turner. *Image and Pilgrimage in Christian Literature. Lectures on the History of Religions Sponsored by the American Council of Learned Societies, New Series* 11. New York City, NY: Columbia University Press, 1978.

Tvedtnes, John A. *The Book of Mormon and Other Hidden Books*. Provo, UT: Brigham Young University FARMS, 2000.

———. "Early Christian and Jewish rituals related to temple practices." Presented at the *FAIR Conference 1999*. http://www.fairlds.org/FAIR_Conferences/1999_Early_Christian_and_Jewish_Rituals_Related_to_Temple_Practices.html (accessed September 8, 2007).

———. E-mail message to Jeffrey M. Bradshaw, September 26, 2006.

———. "Faith and Truth." *Journal of Book of Mormon Studies* 3, no. 2 (Fall 1994): 114-16.

———. "Gospel doctrine: Three degrees of glory." In *Meridian Magazine*. http://www.meridianmagazine.com/gospel-doctrine/nt/070823nt34sf.html (accessed November 30, 2008).

———. "The higher and lesser laws." In *Reason, Revelation, and Faith: Essays in Honor of Truman G. Madsen*, edited by Donald W. Parry, Daniel C. Peterson and Stephen D. Ricks, 383-406. Provo, UT: Foundation for Ancient Research and Mormon Studies, 2002.

———. "The King Follett discourse in light of ancient and medieval Jewish and Christian beliefs." Presented at the *FAIR Conference 2004*. http://www.fairlds.org/pubs/conf/2004TveJ.html (accessed September 8, 2007).

———. "'My first-born in the wilderness.'" *Journal of Book of Mormon Studies* 3, no. 1 (1994): 207-09.

———. "Nebuchadnezzar or Nabonidus? Mistaken identities in the book of Daniel." *Ensign* 16, September 1986, 54.

———. "Olive oil: Symbol of the Holy Ghost." In *The Allegory of the Olive Tree*, edited by Stephen D. Ricks and John W. Welch, 427-59. Salt Lake City, UT: Deseret Book, 1994.

———. "Priestly clothing in Bible times." In *Temples of the Ancient World*, edited by Donald W. Parry, 649-704. Salt Lake City, UT: Deseret Book, 1994.

———. "Review of Metcalfe, Brent Lee (Ed.), New Approaches to the Book of Mormon." *Review of Books on the Book of Mormon* 6, no. 1 (1994): 8-18.

———. "Science and Genesis." In *Science and Religion: Toward a More Useful Dialogue*, edited by Wilford M. Hess, Raymond T. Matheny and Donlu D. Thayer. Vol. 2, 39-60. Geneva, IL: Paladin House Publishers, 1979.

———. "Temple prayer in ancient times." In *The Temple in Time and Eternity*, edited by Donald W. Parry and Stephen D. Ricks, 79-98. Provo, UT: The Foundation for Ancient Research and Mormon Studies, Brigham Young University, 1999.

———. "Word Groups in the Book of Mormon." *Journal of Book of Mormon Studies* 6, no. 2 (1997): 263-68.

Tvedtnes, John A., Brian M. Hauglid, and John Gee, eds. *Traditions about the Early Life of Abraham. Studies in the Book of Abraham*, ed. John Gee. Provo, UT: Foundation for Ancient Research and Mormon Studies, Brigham Young University, 2001.

Tyndale, William, ed. 1526. *The New Testament: A Facsimile of the 1526 Edition*. Peabody, MA: Hendrickson Publishers, 2008.

Ulansey, David. "The heavenly veil torn: Mark's cosmic 'inclusio.'" *Journal of Biblical Literature* 110, no. 1 (Spring 1991): 123-25. http://www.well.com/user/davidu/veil.html (accessed June 18, 2008).

———. *The Origins of the Mithraic Mysteries: Cosmology and Salvation in the Ancient World*. New York City, NY: Oxford University Press, 1989.

Underwood, Grant. "Book of Mormon usage in early LDS theology." *Dialogue* 17 (Autumn 1984): 35-74.

———. "A "Communities of Discourse" approach to early LDS thought." In *Discourses in Mormon Theology: Philosophical and Theological Possibilities*, edited by James McLachlan and Loyd Ericson, 27-38. Salt Lake City, UT: Greg Kofford Books, 2007.

Uro, Risto. "The bridal chamber and other mysteries: Ritual system and ritual transmission in the Valentinian movement." In *Sacred Marriages*, edited by Martti Nissinen and Risto Uro, 457-86. Winona Lake, IN: Eisenbrauns, 2008.

Vajda, Jordan. *Partakers of the divine nature: A comparative analysis of Patristic and Mormon doctrines of divinization*. Occasional Papers 3. Provo, UT: The Foundation for Ancient Research and Mormon Studies (FARMS), 2002.

Valades, Didacus. *Rhetorica Christiana*, 1579.

"Valeriano Ugolini: Visions." April 4-May 5, 2005. In *Art in the Library*, Harold B. Lee Library, Brigham Young University. http://net.lib.byu.edu/art/ugolini.html (accessed September 13, 2008).

Van Biema, David. "God vs. Science (Debate between Richard Dawkins and Francis Collins)." *Time*, November 13 2006, 49-55.

Van Buren, Paul M. "Some lines on lions." *Theology Today* 24, no. 2 (1967): 227-29. http://theologytoday.ptsem.edu/jul1967/v24-2-criticscorner1.htm (accessed September 8, 2007).

Van Dam, Cornelis. *The Urim and Thummim: A Means of Revelation in Ancient Israel*. Winona Lake, IN: Eisenbrauns, 1997.

Van de Graaff, Kent M. "Physical body." In *Encyclopedia of Mormonism*, edited by Daniel H. Ludlow. 4 vols. Vol. 3, 1080-81. New York City, NY: Macmillan, 1992. http://www.lib.byu.edu/Macmillan/ (accessed November 26, 2007).

van der Heide, Albert. "Midrash and exegesis." In *The Book of Genesis in Jewish and Oriental Christian Interpretation*, edited by Judith Frishman and Lucas Van Rompay. *Traditio Exegetica Graeca* 5, 43-56. Louvain, Belgium: Editions Peeters, 1997.

Van der Horst, Pieter. "The site of Adam's tomb." In *Studies in Hebrew Literature and Jewish Culture: Presented to Albert van der Heide on the Occasion of his Sixty-Fifth Birthday*, edited by Martin F. J. Baasten and Reinier Munk. *Amsterdam Studies in Jewish Thought* 12, 251-55. Amsterdam, Holland: Springer Netherlands, 2007.

VanderKam, James C. *Enoch: A Man for All Generations*. Columbia, SC: University of South Carolina Press, 1995.

van der Toorn, Karel, Bob Becking, and Pieter Willem Wvan der Horst. *Dictionary of Deities and Demons in the Bible*. 2nd Extensively Revised ed. Leiden, The Netherlands: Brill, 1999.

van Gennep, Arnold. 1908. *The Rites of Passage*. Translated by Monika B. Vizedom and Gabrielle L. Caffee. Chicago, IL: The University of Chicago Press, 1960.

Vaughan, Virginia Mason, and Alden T. Vaughan. 1999. "Introduction." In *The Tempest*, edited by Virginia Mason Vaughan and Alden T. Vaughan. The Arden Shakespeare (Third Series), eds. Richard Proudfoot, Ann Thompson and David Scott Kastan, 1-138. London, England: Thomson Learning, 2005.

Vaughan Williams, Ralph. *Vaughan Williams on Music*. Edited by David Manning. Oxford, England: Oxford University Press, 2008.

Vaughan Williams, Ursula. 1964. *R.V.W.: A Biography of Ralph Vaughan Williams*. Oxford, England: Clarendon Press, 2002.

"Vaughan Williams' Orchestral Works." In *Agentsmith*. http://www.agentsmith.com/rvw/RVW_Works/Orchestral.html (accessed March 28, 2008).

Veblen, Thorstein. *The Theory of the Leisure Class: An Economic Study of Institutions*. New York City, NY: Macmillan, 1899. Reprint, New York City, NY: Dover Books, 1994.

Veraseren, M. J. *Mithras, The Secret God*. New York City, NY: Barnes and Noble, 1963.

Verkerk, D.H. 1999. "Biblical manuscripts in Rome 400-700 and the Ashburnham Pentateuch." In *Imaging the Early Medieval Bible*, edited by J. Williams, 97-120. University Park, PA: The Pennsylvania State University Press, 2002.

———. *Early Medieval Bible Illumination and the Ashburnham Pentateuch*. Cambridge, England: Cambridge University Press, 2004.

Vermes, Geza, ed. 1962. *The Complete Dead Sea Scrolls in English*. Revised ed. London, England: Penguin Books, 2004.

Vernay-Nouri, Annie. *Livres d'Arménie: Collections de la Bibliothèque nationale de France*. Paris, France: Bibliothèque nationale de France, 2007.

Verne, Jules. 1873. *Around the World in Eighty Days*. New York City, NY: Signet Classics, New American Library, Penguin Group, 2005.

———. 1889. "In the Year 2889." In *Project Gutenberg*, EText-No. 19362, Release Date September 23, 2006. http://www.

gutenberg.org/etext/19362 (accessed September 9, 2007).

———. 1889. *La Journée d'un Journaliste Américain en 2889*. Paris, France: Éditions Gallimard, 1978.

Vikan, Gary. "Byzantine pilgrimage art." In *Dumbarton Oaks Byzantine Collection Publications*, edited by Gary Vikan. Washington, D.C.: Dumbarton Oaks Center for Byzantine Studies, 1982. http://www.doaks.org/PilgrimageArt.pdf (accessed September 8, 2007).

Villalpando, Juan Bautista. *Ezechielem Explanationes*. 3 vols, 1594-1605.

Villey, André, ed. *Psaumes des errants: Écrits manichéens du Fayyum*. Translated by André Villey. *Sources gnostiques et manichéennes* 4, ed. Michel Tardieu. Paris, France: Les Éditions du Cerf, 1994.

Villien, A. *History and Liturgy of the Sacraments*. Translated by H. W. Edwards. New York City, NY: Benziger Brothers, 1932. Reprint, Kila, MT: Kessinger Publishing, n.d.

Vilnay, Zev, Rachel Vilnay, and Oren Vilnay. *Jerusalem, Beersheba, and Southern Israel*. *The Vilnay Guide to Israel: A New Millennium Edition* 1. Atlit, Israel: Beit-Or Vilnay Publishers, 1999.

Vilnay, Zev. 1932. *The Sacred Land*. *Legends of Jerusalem* 1. Philadelphia, PA: Jewish Publication Society of America, 1973.

Vincent, L-H. "L'Eléona: Sanctuaire primitif de l'Ascension." *Revue Biblique* 64 (1957): 48-71.

Vine, W. E. *An Expository Dictionary of New Testament Words*. Lynchburg, Virginia: The Old-Time Gospel Hour, n.d.

Vine, W. E., Merrill F. Unger, and William White, Jr. *Vine's Complete Expository Dictionary of Old and New Testament Words with Topical Index*. Nashville, TN: Thomas Nelson Publishers, 1996.

Viola, Frank, and George Barna. 2002. *Pagan Christianity? Exploring the Roots of Our Church Practices*. Revised and updated ed. Carol Stream, IL: Tyndale House, 2008.

Virgil. *The Aeneid of Virgil*. Translated by John Conington. 3rd ed. London, England: Longmans, Green, 1919.

Visotzky, Burton L. "The conversation of palm trees." In *Tracing the Threads: Studies in the Vitality of Jewish Pseudepigrapha*, edited by John C. Reeves, 205-14. Atlanta, GA: Scholars Press, 1994.

Vogel, Dan, ed. *Early Mormon Documents*. 5 vols. Salt Lake City, UT: Signature Books, 1996-2003.

Volluz, Corbin T. "Lehi's dream of the Tree of Life: Springboard to prophecy." *Journal of Book of Mormon Studies* 2, no. 2 (1993): 14-38.

von Eschenbach, Wolfram. ca. 1210. *Parzival and Titurel*. Translated by Cyril Edwards. Oxford, England: Oxford University Press, 2006.

von Wellnitz, Marcus. "The Catholic Liturgy and the Mormon temple." *BYU Studies* 21, no. 1 (1979): 3-35.

"W56 Isis and Serapis." In *Prifysgol Abertawe, Swansea University*. http://www.swan.ac.uk/egypt/infosheet/W56.htm (accessed September 4, 2007).

Wagner, Reinhard. *Die Gnosis von Alexandria: Eine Frage des frühe Christentums an die Gegenwart*. Stuttgart, Germany: Verlag Urachhaus, 1968.

Wahlgren, Staffan, ed. *Symeonis Magistri et Logothetae Chronicon: Recensuit Staffan Wahlgren*. 2 vols. Vol. 1. *Corpus Fontium Historiae Byzantinae*. Berlin, Germany: Walter de Gruyter, 2006.

Walker, Charles Lowell. *Diary of Charles Lowell Walker*. 2 vols. Edited by A. Karl Larson and Katharine Miles Larson. Logan, UT: Utah State University Press, 1980.

Walker, Steven C. "Selling the soul of science for a pot of message: Evangelizing atheism in *The God Delusion*." *BYU Studies* 47, no. 1 (2008): 133-47.

Walter, James. 1983. "From tempest to epilogue." In *Shakespeare's Christian Dimension: An Anthology of Commentary*, edited by Roy Battenhouse, 271-79. Bloomington, IN: Indiana University Press, 1994.

Walton, John H. *Ancient Near Eastern Thought and the Old Testament: Introducing the Conceptual World of the Hebrew Bible*. Grand Rapids, MI: Baker Academic, 2006.

Wansbrough, John. 1972. *Qur'anic Studies: Sources and Methods of Scriptural Interpretation*. Amherst, NY: Prometheus Books, 2004.

Ward, Jay Bryant. "News and Events." In *Jay Bryant Ward Studios*. http://www.jbwstudios.com/102.php (accessed May 11, 2008).

Warner, C. Terry. "Accountability." In *Encyclopedia of Mormonism*, edited by Daniel H. Ludlow. 4 vols. Vol. 1, 13. New York City, NY: Macmillan, 1992. http://www.lib.byu.edu/Macmillan/ (accessed November 26.

———. *Bonds That Make Us Free: Healing Our Relationships, Coming to Ourselves*. Salt Lake City, UT: Shadow Mountain, 2001.

———. "Truth." In *Encyclopedia of Mormonism*, edited by Daniel H. Ludlow. 4 vols. Vol. 4, 1489-91. New York City, NY: Macmillan, 1992. http://www.lib.byu.edu/Macmillan/ (accessed November 26, 2007).

Warren, Bruce W. "Secret combinations, warfare, and captive sacrifice in Mesoamerica and the Book of Mormon." In *Warfare in the Book of Mormon*, edited by Stephen D. Ricks and William J. Hamblin, 225-36. Salt Lake City, UT: Deseret Book, 1990.

Wasserstrom, Steven M. "Jewish pseudepigrapha in Muslim literature: A bibliographical and methodological sketch." In *Tracing the Threads: Studies in the Vitality of Jewish Pseudepigrapha*, edited by John C. Reeves, 87-114. Atlanta, GA: Scholars Press, 1994.

Watts, Isaac. *Hymns, and Spiritual Songs in Three Books with an Essay Towards the Improvement of Christian Psalmody, by the Use of Evangelical Hymns in Worship, As Well As the Psalms of David*. London, England: John Lawrence, 1707-1709. Reprint, Watts, Isaac, and Samuel Worcester. *Psalms, Hymns and Spiritual Songs of the Rev. Isaac Watts, D. D. To Which Are Added Select Hymns from Other Authors, and Directions for Musical Expression by Samuel Worcester, D. D.* Boston, MA: Crocker & Brewster, 1856. http://books.google.com/books?id=zSZs5jCXgHoC (accessed April 13, 2009).

Weber, Robert, ed. *Biblia Sacra Vulgata* 4th ed: American Bible Society, 1990.

Webster, Noah. *An American Dictionary of the English Language*. New York City, NY, 1828. Reprint, Chesapeake, VA: Foundation for American Christian Education, 1968.

Wedderburn, A. J. M. *Baptism and Resurrection: Studies in Pauline Theology against Its Greco-Roman Background*. Wissenschaftliche Untersuchungen zum Neuen Testament 44, ed. Joachim Jeremias, Otto Michel, Martin Hengel and Otfried Hofius. Tübingen, Germany: J. C. B. Mohr (Paul Siebeck), 1987.

Weil, G., ed. 1846. *The Bible, the Koran, and the Talmud or, Biblical Legends of the Mussulmans, Compiled from Arabic Sources, and Compared with Jewish Traditions, Translated from the German*. New York City, NY: Harper and Brothers, 1863. Reprint, Kila, MT: Kessinger Publishing, 2006. http://books.google.com/books?id=_jYMAAAAIAAJ (accessed September 8, 2007).

Weimer, W. *Notes on the Methodology of Scientific Research*. Hillsdale, New Jersey: Erlbaum, 1979.

Weisberg, Jacob. 2006. "Romney's religion: A Mormon president? No way." In *Slate*, December 20, 2006. http://www.slate.com/id/2155902 (accessed August 27, 2007).

Welburn, Andrew, ed. *Mani, the Angel, and the Column of Glory: An Anthology of Manichaean Texts*. Edinburgh, Scotland: Floris Books, 1998.

Welch, John W. "The Good Samaritan: A type and shadow of the plan of salvation." *BYU Studies* 38, no. 2 (1999): 51-115.

———. "The Good Samaritan: Forgotten symbols." *Ensign* 37, February 2007, 40-47.

———. *The Sermon at the Temple and the Sermon on the Mount*. Salt Lake City, UT: Deseret Book, 1990.

———. *The Sermon on the Mount in the Light of the Temple*. Farnham, England: Ashgate, 2009.

———. "The temple in the Book of Mormon: The temples at the cities of Nephi, Zarahemla, and Bountiful." In *Temples of the Ancient World*, edited by Donald W. Parry, 297-387. Salt Lake City, UT: Deseret Book, 1994.

———. "'And with all thy mind.'" In *Brigham Young University 2003-2004 Speeches*, 105-12. Provo, UT: Brigham Young University Publications and Graphics, 2003.

———, ed. *The Worlds of Joseph Smith: A Bicentennial Conference at the Library of Congress*. Provo, UT: The Brigham Young University Press, 2005.

Welch, John W., and Claire Foley. "Gammadia on early Jewish and Christian garments." *BYU Studies* 36, no. 3 (1996-1997): 253-58.

Welch, John W., and James V. Garrsion. "'The Hymn of the Pearl': An ancient counterpart to 'O My Father.'" *BYU Studies* 36, no. 1 (1996-1997): 127-38.

Wellington, Richard, and George Potter. "Lehi's trail: From the Valley of Lemuel to Nephi's Harbor." *Journal of Book of Mormon Studies* 15, no. 2 (2006): 26-43, 113-16.

Wenham, Gordon J., ed. *Genesis 1-15*. Word Biblical Commentary 1. Nashville, TN: Nelson Reference and Electronic, 1987.

Wesley, Charles. 1755. *Epistle to George Whitefield*. London, England: J. & W. Oliver, 1771. http://www.divinity.duke.edu/wesleyan/docs/cworiginal/71_Epistle_to_Whitefield_(1771).pdf (accessed May 27, 2009).

Wesley, John, and Charles Wesley. *Hymns and Sacred Poems*. Fourth ed. Bristol, England: Felix Farley, 1743. http://ia340912.us.archive.org/2/items/hymnsandsacredpo00wesliala/hymnsandsacredpo00wesliala.pdf (accessed May 2, 2009).

Westermann, Claus, ed. 1974. *Genesis 1-11: A Continental Commentary* 1st ed. Translated by John J. Scullion. Minneapolis, MN: Fortress Press, 1994.

Westermeyer, Paul. *Let the People Sing: Hymn Tunes in Perspective*. Chicago, IL: GIA Publications, 2005.

Wevers, John William. *Notes on the Greek Text of Genesis*. Atlanta, GA: Scholars Press, 1993.

"Wheel of Fortune." In *Wikipedia*. http://en.wikipedia.org/wiki/The_Wheel_of_Fortune (accessed December 18, 2007).

Wheeler, Brannon M. *Mecca and Eden: Ritual, Relics, and Territory in Islam*. Chicago, IL: University of Chicago Press, 2006.

———. *Prophets in the Quran: An Introduction to the Quran and Muslim Exegesis. Comparative Islam Studies*, ed. Brannon M. Wheeler. London, England: Continuum, 2002.

Wheeler, Geraldine, and Lindsay Farrell. "Frank Wesley: Religious worlds retrospective exhibition." *Australian EJournal of Theology* 4 (February 2005). http://dlibrary.acu.edu.au/research/theology/ejournal/aejt_4/farrell.htm (accessed September 8, 2007).

White, Clayton M., and Mark D. Thomas. "On balancing faith in Mormonism with traditional biblical stories: The Noachian flood story." *Dialogue: A Journal of Mormon Thought* 40, no. 3 (Fall 2007): 85-110.

White, Ellen G. *The Faith I Live By: The Morning Watch Texts with Appropriate Selections Compiled from the Writings of Ellen G. White*. Washington, DC: Review and Herald, 1958.

Whitfield, Roderick. *Textiles, Sculpture, and Other Arts. The Art of Central Asia: The Stein Collection in the British Museum* 3. Tokyo, Japan: Kodansha International Ltd (in cooperation with the Trustees of the British Museum), 1985.

Whitlock, Stephen T. E-mail message to Jeffrey M. Bradshaw, August 23, 2006.

———. E-mail message to Jeffrey M. Bradshaw, June 9, 2008.

Whitmer, David. *An Address to All Believers in Christ by a Witness to the Divine Authenticity of the Book of Mormon*. Richmond, MO, 1887.

Whitney, Elizabeth Ann. "A leaf from an autobiography." *The Woman's Exponent* 7:11, November 1, 1878, 83. http://contentdm.lib.byu.edu/cgi-bin/showfile.exe?CISOROOT=/WomansExp&CISOPTR=6638. (accessed July 31, 2009).

Whitney, Orson F. "'A marvelous work and a wonder,' etc. (7 October 1916)." In *General Conference Report of The Church of Jesus Christ of Latter-day Saints, Eighty-Sixth Annual Conference*, 51-57. Salt Lake City, UT: The Church of Jesus Christ of Latter-day Saints, 1916.

———. "Discourse (April 1928)." In *General Conference Report of The Church of Jesus Christ of Latter-day Saints, Ninety-Eighth Annual Conference*, 56-61. Salt Lake City, UT: The Church of Jesus Christ of Latter-day Saints, 1928.

———. 1888. *The Life of Heber C. Kimball*. 2nd ed. Salt Lake City, UT: Stevens & Wallis, 1945.

———. 1921. "Saturday Night Thoughts: A Series of Dissertations on Spiritual, Historical and Philosophic Themes (Whitney on Doctrine)." In *Cowley and Whitney on Doctrine (Originally published as "Cowley's Talks on Doctrine" (Ben E. Rich, comp.) and "Saturday Night Thoughts")*, edited by Forace Green, 197-517. Salt Lake City, UT: Bookcraft, 1963.

Whittaker, David J. "Studying Joseph Smith Jr.: A guide to the sources." In *Joseph Smith Jr: Reappraisals After Two Centuries*, edited by Reid L. Neilson and Terryl L. Givens, 221-37. Oxford, England: Oxford University Press, 2009.

———. "Substituted names in the published revelations of Joseph Smith." *BYU Studies* 23, no. 1 (1983): 103-12.

Wickman, Lance B. "But if not." *Ensign* 32, November 2002, 30-32.

Widengren, Geo. "Die Mandäer." In *Religionsgeschichte des Orients in der Zeit der Weltreligionen*, edited by Johannes Leipoldt, Geo Widengren, Alfred Adam, Bertold Spuler, Ernst Ludwig Dietrich, Johannes W. Fück, A. J. Arberry, R. Strothmann and Annemarie von Gabain. *Handbuch der Orientalistik* 1, VIII, 2, eds. H. Franke, J. Gonda, H. Hammitzsch, H. Kees, J. E. van Lohuizen-de Leeuw and F. Vos, 83-101. Leiden, The Netherlands: E. J. Brill, 1961.

———. "Heavenly enthronement and baptism studies in Mandaean baptism." In *Religions in Antiquity: Essays in Memory of Erwin Ramsdell Goodenough*, edited by Jacob Neusner. 14 vols. Religions in Antiquity, *Studies in the History of Religions (Supplements to Numen)* 551-582. Leiden, The Netherlands: Brill, 1968.

———. 1961. *Mani and Manichaeism*. Translated by Charles Kessler. English ed. *History of Religion Series*, ed. E. O. James. New York City, NY: Holt, Rinehart and Winston, 1965.

Widtsoe, John A. "58. Are all exalted who enter the celestial glory?" In *Evidences and Reconciliations: Aids to Faith in a Modern Day*, edited by John A. Widtsoe. 2nd ed, 277-78. Salt Lake City, UT: Bookcraft, 1943.

———. "22. Did the flood cover the highest mountains of the earth?" In *Evidences and Reconciliations: Aids to Faith in a Modern Day*, edited by John A. Widtsoe. 2nd ed., 109-12. Salt Lake City, UT: Bookcraft, 1943.

———. 1943, 1947, 1951. *Evidences and Reconciliations*. 3 vols. Single Volume ed. Salt Lake City, UT: Bookcraft, 1960.

———. "The House of the Lord." *Improvement Era* 39, April 1936, 228. Reprint, *Improvement Era* 48:10 (October 1945), 584; 72:7 (July 1969), 13-14.

———. *In a Sunlit Land: The Autobiography of John A. Widtsoe*. Salt Lake City, UT: Deseret News Press, 1952.

———. 1921. "Temple worship. Original publication in *The Utah Genealogical and Historical Magazine* 12, April 1921, 49-64." In *The House of the Lord*, edited by Harvard S. Heath, 185-97. Salt Lake City, UT: Signature Books, 1998.

Wilcox, S. Michael. *Fire in the Bones: William Tyndale—Martyr, Father of the English Bible*. Salt Lake City, UT: Deseret Book, 2004.

Wilkinson, David. *God, Time, and Stephen Hawking*. London, England: Monarch Books, 2001.

Wilkinson, Richard H. 1992. *Reading Egyptian Art: A Hieroglyphic Guide to Ancient Egyptian Painting and Sculpture*. London, England: Thames and Hudson, 2006.

"William Blake." In *Wikipedia*. http://en.wikipedia.org/wiki/William_Blake (accessed November 23, 2007).

"William Blake online: Blake's cast of characters: Personification of the fallen tyrant." In *Tate Gallery*. http://www.tate.org.uk/learning/worksinfocus/blake/imagin/cast_04.html (accessed April 27, 2007).

Williams, Drew. *The Complete Idiot's Guide to Understanding Mormonism*. Indianapolis, IN: Alpha Books, 2003.

Williams, Francis E. ed. "The Apocryphon of James (I, 2)." In *The Nag Hammadi Library in English*, edited by James M. Robinson. 3rd, Completely Revised ed, 29-37. San Francisco, CA: HarperSanFrancisco, 1990.

Williams, Michael Allen. *Rethinking 'Gnosticism': An Argument for Dismantling a Dubious Category*. Princeton, NJ: Princeton University Press, 1996.

Williams, Nicholas M. 1998. *Ideology and Utopia in the Poetry of William Blake*. Cambridge Studies in Romanticism 28, eds. Marilyn Butler and James Chandler. Cambridge, England: Cambridge University Press, 2006.

Williams, Wesley. 2005. "The shadow of God: Speculations on the body divine in Jewish esoteric tradition." In *The Black God*. http://www.theblackgod.com/Shadow%20of%20God%20Short%5B1%5D.pdf (accessed December 21, 2007).

Wilson, Charles W. *Golgotha and the Holy Sepulchre*. London, England: The Committee of the Palestine Exploration Fund, 1906.

Wilson, Duane. "Temple Symbolism in *The Conflict of Adam and Eve*." *Studia Antiqua* 2, no. 2 (Fall 2002): 33-61.

Wilson, E. O. *The Creation*. New York City, NY: W. W. Norton, 2006.

Wilson, John A. *The Culture of Ancient Egypt*. Chicago, IL: University of Chicago Press, 1951.

Wilson, Lindsay. *Joseph Wise and Otherwise: The Intersection of Wisdom and Covenant in Genesis 37-50. Paternoster Biblical Monographs*. Waynesboro, GA: Paternoster Press, 2005.

Wilson, Lycurgus A. Wilson. *Life of David W. Patten*. Salt Lake City, UT: Deseret News, 1900. Reprint, Heber City, UT: Archive Publishers, 2000.

Wilson, R. McLain. *The Gospel of Philip*. New York City, NY: Harper and Row, 1962.

Winston, David. *Logos and Mystical Theology in Philo of Alexandra*. Cincinnati, OH: Hebrew Union College Press, 1985.

———. "Preexistence in Hellenic, Judaic and Mormon sources." In *Reflections on Mormonism: Judeo-Christian Parallels, Papers Delivered at the Religious Studies Center Symposium, Brigham Young University, March 10-11, 1978*, edited by Truman G. Madsen. *Religious Studies Monograph Series* 4, 13-35. Provo, UT: Religious Studies Center, Brigham Young University, 1978.

Wintermute, O. S. ed. "Jubilees." In *The Old Testament Pseudepigrapha*, edited by James H. Charlesworth. Vol. 2, 35-142. Garden City, NY: Doubleday and Company, 1983.

Wirth, Diane E. *Decoding Ancient America: A Guide to the Archaeology of the Book of Mormon*. Springville, UT: Horizon, 2007.

———. E-mail message to Jeffrey M. Bradshaw, March 12, 2009.

———. *Parallels: Mesoamerican and Ancient Middle Eastern Traditions*. St. George, UT: Stonecliff Publishing, 2003.

Wise, Michael, Martin Abegg, Jr., and Edward Cook, eds. *The Dead Sea Scrolls: A New Translation*. New York City, NY: Harper-Collins, 1996.

Wisse, Frederik ed. "The Apocryphon of John (II, 1, III, 1, IV, 1, and BG 8502,2)." In *The Nag Hammadi Library in English*, edited by James M. Robinson. 3rd, Completely Revised ed., 104-23. San Francisco, CA: HarperSanFrancisco, 1990.

Witham, Larry A. *Where Darwin Meets the Bible: Creationists and Evolutionists in America*. New York City, NY: Oxford University Press, 2002.

Witherington, Ben, III. *Letters and Homilies for Jewish Christians: A Socio-Rhetorical Commentary on Hebrews, James and Jude*. Downers Grove, IL: InterVarsity Press Academic, 2007.

Wittgenstein, Ludwig. 1949. *Philosophical Investigations*. Translated by G. E. M. Anscombe. 3rd ed. Malden, MA:

Blackwell Publishing, 2001.

Woodford, Robert J. "Discoveries from the Joseph Smith Papers Project: The early manuscripts." In *The Doctrine and Covenants: Revelations in Context: The 37th Annual Brigham Young University Sidney B. Sperry Symposium*, edited by Andrew H. Hedges, J. Spencer Fluhman and Alonzo L. Gaskill, 23-39. Salt Lake City, UT: Deseret Book, 2008.

———. "The Historical Development of the Doctrine and Covenants (3 vols.)." Doctoral Dissertation, Brigham Young University, 1974.

Woodruff, Wilford. "Administration of angels (Discourse delivered by President Wilford Woodruff, at a Priesthood Meeting, held in Provo, Sunday Evening, March 3rd, 1889)." In *Collected Discourses*, edited by Brian H. Stuy. 5 vols. Vol. 1, 215-20. Woodland Hills, UT: B.H.S. Publishing, 1987.

———. 1894. "The law of adoption (Delivered by President Wilford Woodruff, at the Sixty-fourth Annual General Conference of the Church of Jesus Christ of Latter-day Saints, held in the Tabernacle, Salt Lake City, Sunday Morning, April 8th, 1894)." In *Collected Discourses*, edited by Brian H. Stuy. 5 vols. Vol. 4, 67-76. Woodland Hills, UT: B.H.S. Publishing, 1991.

———. 1896. "Moses Thatcher (Discourse delivered by President Wilford Woodruff, at the General Conference of the Church, held in the Tabernacle, Salt Lake City, Monday Afternoon, October 5, 1896)." In *Collected Discourses*, edited by Brian H. Stuy. 5 vols. Vol. 5, 198-201. Woodland Hills, UT: B.H.S. Publishing, 1992.

———. "The administration of angels (Discourse delivered by President Wilford Woodruff, at the Weber Stake Conference, Ogden, Monday, October 19, 1896)." In *Collected Discourses*, edited by Brian H. Stuy. 5 vols. Vol. 5, 233-40. Woodland Hills, UT: B.H.S. Publishing, 1992.

———. 1909. *Wilford Woodruff: History of His Life and Labors*. Edited by Matthias F. Cowley. Salt Lake City, UT: Bookcraft, 1964.

———. *Wilford Woodruff Journal: 1833-1898*. 9 vols. Edited by Scott Kenney. Midvale, UT: Signature Books, 1983-1985.

Wooton, Richard T. *Saints and Scientists*. Mesa, AZ: EduTech Corporation, 1992.

Wray, Naomi. "Background Information about the *Forgiving Father*." Unpublished material provided to Jeffrey M. Bradshaw, April 2, 2007.

———. *Frank Wesley: Exploring Faith with a Brush*. Auckland, NZ: Pace Publishing, 1989.

Wright, Archie T. *The Origin of Evil Spirits. Wissenschaftliche Untersuchungen zum Neuen Testament 2. Reihe 198*, ed. Jörg Frey. Tübingen, Germany: Mohr Siebeck, 2005.

Wright, J. Edward. "The synagogue paintings from Dura Europos." In *The Apocryphal Ezekiel*, edited by Michael E. Stone, Benjamin E. Wright and David Satran. *Early Judaism and Its Literature* 18, ed. John C. Reeves, 101-12. Atlanta, GA: Society of Biblical Literature, 2000.

Wright, Nicholas Thomas. *Christian Origins and the Question of God*. Vol. 3: The Resurrection of the Son of God. Minneapolis, MN: Fortress, 2003.

———. "How can the Bible be authoritative?" *Vox Evangelica* 21 (1991): 7-32. http://www.ntwrightpage.com/Wright_Bible_Authoritative.htm (accessed April 7, 2008).

———. 2005. *The Last Word: Beyond the Bible Wars to a New Understanding of the Authority of Scripture*. New York City, NY: HarperSanFrancisco, 2006.

———. *Surprised by Hope: Rethinking Heaven, the Resurrection, and the Mission of the Church*. New York City, NY: HarperOne, 2008.

Wurst, Gregor, ed. *The Manichaean Coptic Papyri in the Chester Beatty Library Psalm Book Part II, 1, Die Berna-Psalmen. Corpus Fontium Manichaeorum, Series Coptica*, ed. Aloîs van Tongerloo, Samuel N. C. Lieu and Johannes van Oort. Turnhout, Belgium: Brepols, 1996.

Wyatt, Nicholas. *Space and Time in the Religious Life of the Near East*. Sheffield, England: Sheffield Academic Press, 2001.

Yadin, Yigal, ed. 1977. *The Temple Scroll*. English ed. 3 vols. Jerusalem, Israel: The Israel Exploration Society, 1983.

Yamauchi, Edwin M. 1970. *Gnostic Ethics and Mandaean Origins*. Piscataway, NJ: Gorgias Press, 2004.

———, ed. *Mandaic Incantation Texts. American Oriental Series 49*. New Haven, CN: American Oriental Society, 1967.

Yarnold, E. "Teleios in St. Matthew's Gospel." In *Texte und Untersuchungen* 102 (1968). *Studia Evangelica* 4, 269-73.

"Yazidi." In *Wikipedia*. http://en.wikipedia.org/wiki/Yezidi (accessed September 14, 2007).

Young, Brigham. 1941. *Discourses of Brigham Young*. Edited by John A. Widtsoe. Salt Lake City, UT: Deseret Book, 1977.

———. *Letters of Brigham Young to His Sons*. Edited by Dean C. Jessee. Salt Lake City, UT: Deseret Book, in collaboration with the Historical Department of the Church of Jesus Christ of Latter-day Saints, 1974.

———. *Manuscript History of Brigham Young 1847-1850*. Edited by William S. Harwell. Salt Lake City, UT: Collier's Publishing, 1997.

———. *The Office Journal of President Brigham Young: 1858-1863, Book D*. Edited by Fred C. Collier. Hanna, UT: Collier's Publishing Company, 2006.

———. 1845. "Letter to Lyman Wight, et al.: A plea for union." In *History of the Church of Jesus Christ of Latter-day Saints (Documentary History)*, edited by Joseph Smith, Jr. and Brigham Henry Roberts. 7 vols. Vol. 7, 400-01. Salt Lake City, UT: Deseret Book, 1978.

———. 1852. "Necessity of the servants of God being pure in heart and in deed; dependence on the Holy Spirit; celestial exaltations, etc. (Remarks at a special conference held in the Tabernacle, Great Salt Lake City, 28 August 1852)." In *Journal of Discourses*. 26 vols. Vol. 6, 273-77. Liverpool and London, England: Latter-day Saints Book Depot, 1853-1886. Reprint, Salt Lake City, UT: Bookcraft, 1966.

———. 1852. "Self-government; mysteries; recreation and amusements, not in themselves sinful; tithing; Adam, our Father and our God (Sermon delivered in the Tabernacle, Great Salt Lake City, 9 April 1852)." In *Journal of Discourses*. 26 vols. Vol. 1, 46-53. Liverpool and London, England: Latter-day Saints Book Depot, 1853-1886. Reprint, Salt Lake City, UT: Bookcraft, 1966.

———. 1852. "Weakness and impotence of men; condition of the Saints; dedication to the Lord; the Millennium (Discourse delivered at the opening of the new Tabernacle, Great Salt Lake City, 6 April 1852)." In *Journal of Discourses*. 26 vols. Vol. 1, 198-203. Liverpool and London, England: Latter-day Saints Book Depot, 1853-1886. Reprint, Salt Lake City, UT: Bookcraft, 1966.

———. 1853. "Duties and privileges; sacrifice; confidence; language; organization and disorganization; taking wives (Discourse delivered in the Tabernacle, Great Salt Lake City, 27 February 1853)." In *Journal of Discourses*. 26 vols. Vol. 1, 112-20. Liverpool and London, England: Latter-day Saints Book Depot, 1853-1886. Reprint, Salt Lake City, UT: Bookcraft, 1966.

———. 1853. "Necessity of building temples; the endowment (Oration delivered in the South-East Cornerstone of the Temple at Great Salt Lake City, after the First Presidency and the Patriarch had laid the Stone, 6 April 1853)." In *Journal of Discourses*. 26 vols. Vol. 2, 29-33. Liverpool and London, England: Latter-day Saints Book Depot, 1853-1886. Reprint, Salt Lake City, UT: Bookcraft, 1966.

———. 1853. "The Gospel; growing in knowledge; the Lord's supper; blessings of faithfulness; utility of persecution; creation of Adam; experience (Discourse delivered in the Tabernacle, Great Salt Lake City, 23 October 1853)." In *Journal of Discourses*. 26 vols. Vol. 2, 1-10. Liverpool and London, England: Latter-day Saints Book Depot, 1853-1886. Reprint, Salt Lake City, UT: Bookcraft, 1966.

———. 1853. "The Temple cornerstones; the apostleship, etc. (Sermon delivered in the Tabernacle, Great Salt Lake City, 6 April 1853, at the General Conference)." In *Journal of Discourses*. 26 vols. Vol. 1, 131-37. Liverpool and London, England: Latter-day Saints Book Depot, 1853-1886. Reprint, Salt Lake City, UT: Bookcraft, 1966.

———. 1854. "'I propose to speak in a subject that does not immediately concern yours or my welfare,' a sermon delivered on 8 October 1854." In *The Essential Brigham Young. Classics in Mormon Thought 3*, 86-103. Salt Lake City, UT: Signature Books, 1992.

———. 1854. "Spiritual gifts; hell; the spirit world; the elders and the nations; the Lamanites; the temple (Discourse delivered in the Tabernacle, Great Salt Lake City, 3 December 1854)." In *Journal of Discourses*. 26 vols. Vol. 2, 136-45. Liverpool and London, England: Latter-day Saints Book Depot, 1853-1886. Reprint, Salt Lake City, UT: Bookcraft, 1966.

———. 1855. "Consecration (Discourse delivered in the Tabernacle, Great Salt Lake City, 3 June 1855)." In *Journal of Discourses*. 26 vols. Vol. 2, 298-308. Liverpool and London, England: Latter-day Saints Book Depot, 1853-1886. Reprint, Salt Lake City, UT: Bookcraft, 1966.

———. 1856. "Disinclination of men to learn through the teachings and experience of others; Latter-day Saints compared with those of former days; sacrifice; sheep and goats; customs and traditions (Discourse delivered in the Tabernacle, Great Salt Lake City, 20 April 1856)." In *Journal of Discourses*. 26 vols. Vol. 3, 316-27. Liverpool and London, England: Latter-day Saints Book Depot, 1853-1886. Reprint, Salt Lake City, UT: Bookcraft, 1966.

———. 1856. "Preaching; necessity of the Saints having confidence in those over them; necessity of wisdom in dealing with those who are dead to good works; ignorance of worldly philosophers; the principle of life as shown in the dissolution of organized matter (Discourse delivered in the Tabernacle, Great Salt Lake City, 23 March 1856)." In *Journal of Discourses*. 26 vols. Vol. 3, 272-79. Liverpool and London, England: Latter-day Saints Book Depot, 1853-1886. Reprint, Salt Lake City, UT: Bookcraft, 1966.

———. 1856. "The emigrating saints were prompted by the spirit of God (Remarks by Brigham Young, made in the Bowery, Great Salt Lake City, November 9, 1856)." In *Journal of Discourses*. 26 vols. Vol. 4, 111. Liverpool and London, England: Latter-day Saints Book Depot, 1853-1886. Reprint, Salt Lake City, UT: Bookcraft, 1966.

———. 1857. "Necessity for a reformation a disgrace; intelligence a gift, increased by imparting; spirit of God; variety in spiritual as well as natural organizations; God the Father of the spirits of all mankind, etc. (Discourse delivered in Great Salt Lake City, 8 March 1857)." In *Journal of Discourses*. 26 vols. Vol. 4, 264-72. Liverpool and London, England: Latter-day Saints Book Depot, 1853-1886. Reprint, Salt Lake City, UT: Bookcraft, 1966.

———. 1857. "To know God is eternal life; God the Father of our spirits and bodies; things created spiritually first; atonement by the shedding of blood (Discourse delivered in the Tabernacle, Great Salt Lake City, 8 February 1857)." In *Journal of Discourses*. 26 vols. Vol. 4, 215-21. Liverpool and London, England: Latter-day Saints Book Depot, 1853-1886. Reprint, Salt Lake City, UT: Bookcraft, 1966.

———. 1859. "Intelligence, etc. (Remarks delivered in the Tabernacle, Great Salt Lake City, 9 October 1859)." In *Journal of Discourses*. 26 vols. Vol. 7, 282-91. Liverpool and London, England: Latter-day Saints Book Depot, 1853-1886. Reprint, Salt Lake City, UT: Bookcraft, 1966.

———. 1859. "Progress in knowledge, etc. (Remarks by President Brigham Young, delivered in the Tabernacle, Great Salt Lake City, October 8, 1859)." In *Journal of Discourses*. 26 vols. Vol. 7, 331-34. Liverpool and London, England: Latter-day Saints Book Depot, 1853-1886. Reprint, Salt Lake City, UT: Bookcraft, 1966.

———. 1859. "Providences of God; privileges and duties of the Saints; spiritual operations and manifestations; the spirit world, etc. (Remarks made in the Tabernacle, Great Salt Lake City, 1 September 1859)." In *Journal of Discourses*. 26 vols. Vol. 7, 237-44. Liverpool and London, England: Latter-day Saints Book Depot, 1853-1886. Reprint, Salt Lake City, UT: Bookcraft, 1966.

———. 1860. "Privileges of the Sabbath; duty of living our religion; human longevity, etc. (Remarks by President Brigham Young, made in the Tabernacle, Great Salt Lake City, May 20, 1860)." In *Journal of Discourses*. 26 vols. Vol. 8, 57-64. Liverpool and London, England: Latter-day Saints Book Depot, 1853-1884. Reprint, Salt Lake City, UT: Bookcraft, 1966.

———. 1860. "Remarks pertaining to foreign missions, etc. (Remarks by President Brigham Young, made in the Bowery, Great Salt Lake City, September 23, 1860)." In *Journal of Discourses*. 26 vols. Vol. 8, 183-87. Liverpool and London, England: Latter-day Saints Book Depot, 1853-1884. Reprint, Salt Lake City, UT: Bookcraft, 1966.

———. 1860. "Blessings of the Saints; covetousness, etc. (Remarks made in the Bowery, Great Salt Lake City, 30 September 1860)." In *Journal of Discourses*. 26 vols. Vol. 8, 188-91. Liverpool and London, England: Latter-day Saints Book Depot, 1853-1886. Reprint, Salt Lake City, UT: Bookcraft, 1966.

———. 1860. "Sufferings of the Saints; overcoming evil with good, etc. (Remarks made in the Tabernacle, Great Salt Lake City, 5 January 1860)." In *Journal of Discourses*. 26 vols. Vol. 9, 101-08. Liverpool and London, England: Latter-day Saints Book Depot, 1853-1886. Reprint, Salt Lake City, UT: Bookcraft, 1966.

———. 1860a. "Religion, progress, and privileges of the Saints, etc. (Remarks by President Brigham Young, made at Ogden City, June 12, 1860-a)." In *Journal of Discourses*. 26 vols. Vol. 8, 80-84. Liverpool and London, England: Latter-day Saints Book Depot, 1853-1886. Reprint, Salt Lake City, UT: Bookcraft, 1966.

———. 1860b. "Salvation and condemnation—improvement, etc. (Remarks by President Brigham Young, made at Willow Creek, June 12, 1860-b)." In *Journal of Discourses*. 26 vols. Vol. 8, 293-97. Liverpool and London, England: Latter-day Saints Book Depot, 1853-1886. Reprint, Salt Lake City, UT: Bookcraft, 1966.

———. 1861. "Varieties of mind and character—chastisement—freedom, etc. (Remarks by President Brigham Young, made in the Tabernacle, Great Salt Lake City, February 17, 1861)." In *Journal of Discourses*. 26 vols. Vol. 9, 121-25. Liverpool and London, England: Latter-day Saints Book Depot, 1853-1886. Reprint, Salt Lake City, UT: Bookcraft, 1966.

———. 1862. "Government of the tongue; impartiality of judgment; sealing (Remarks made in the Tabernacle, Great Salt Lake City, 6 April 1862)." In *Journal of Discourses*. 26 vols. Vol. 9, 266-71. Liverpool and London, England: Latter-day Saints Book Depot, 1853-1886. Reprint, Salt Lake City, UT: Bookcraft, 1966.

———. 1862. "Salvation the result of individual exertion (Remarks made in the Tabernacle, Great Salt Lake City, 23 March 1862)." In *Journal of Discourses*. 26 vols. Vol. 9, 246-50. Liverpool and London, England: Latter-day Saints Book Depot, 1853-1886. Reprint, Salt Lake City, UT: Bookcraft, 1966.

———. 1862. "The Kingdom of God (Remarks made in the Bowery, Great Salt Lake City, 13 July 1862)." In *Journal of Discourses*. 26 vols. Vol. 9, 308-17. Liverpool and London, England: Latter-day Saints Book Depot, 1853-1886. Reprint, Salt Lake City, UT: Bookcraft, 1966.

———. 1864. "Necessity of a living testimony of the Holy Ghost; how we are to be united, etc. (Remarks delivered in the Bowery, Great Salt Lake City, 7 October 1864)." In *Journal of Discourses*. 26 vols. Vol. 10, 339-40. Liverpool and London, England: Latter-day Saints Book Depot, 1853-1884. Reprint, Salt Lake City, UT: Bookcraft, 1966.

———. 1864. "Turning out the water of the Weber; the sufferings of the saints; the desires of the servants of God to bless the people; the blessings of the Lord to Israel; endowments, etc. (Instructions by President Brigham Young, during his visit to Davis and Weber counties, June 10, 11, 12, and 13, 1864)." In *Journal of Discourses*. 26 vols. Vol. 10, 307-14. Liverpool and London, England: Latter-day Saints Book Depot, 1853-1884. Reprint, Salt Lake City, UT: Bookcraft, 1966.

———. 1864. "Difference of ideas entertained respecting God; the foundation of our religion based upon new revelation; man made in the image of God; we are the offspring of God, etc. (Remarks delivered in the Bowery, Great Salt Lake City, 31 July 1864)." In *Journal of Discourses*. 26 vols. Vol. 10, 318-27. Liverpool and London, England: Latter-day Saints Book Depot, 1853-1886. Reprint, Salt Lake City, UT: Bookcraft, 1966.

———. 1864. "Salvation the result of individual exertion." In *Journal of Discourses*. 26 vols. Vol. 9, 246-50. Liverpool and London, England: Latter-day Saints Book Depot, 1853-1886. Reprint, Salt Lake City, UT: Bookcraft, 1966.

———. 1865. "Ordinance of bread and wine; its nature; character of God and of Jesus; reasons why sin and death exist; earthly probation necessary for future glory; danger of apostasy (Remarks delivered in the Tabernacle, Great Salt Lake City, 8 January 1865)." In *Journal of Discourses*. 26 vols. Vol. 11, 39-44. Liverpool and London, England: Latter-day Saints Book Depot, 1853-1886. Reprint, Salt Lake City, UT: Bookcraft, 1966.

———. 1865. "Personality of God; his attributes; eternal life, etc. (Remarks delivered at the Bowery, Great Salt Lake City, 18 June 1865)." In *Journal of Discourses*. 26 vols. Vol. 11, 119-28. Liverpool and London, England: Latter-day Saints Book Depot, 1853-1886. Reprint, Salt Lake City, UT: Bookcraft, 1966.

———. 1866. "The kingdom of God on earth is a living, moving, effective institution: We do not carry it, but it carries us (Remarks by President Brigham Young, in the Tabernacle, in Great Salt Lake City, June 17, 1866)." In *Journal of Discourses*. 26 vols. Vol. 11, 249-56. Liverpool and London, England: Latter-day Saints Book Depot, 1853-1886. Reprint, Salt Lake City, UT: Bookcraft, 1966.

———. 1866. "Delegate Hooper; beneficial effects of polygamy; final redemption of Cain." In *Journal of Discourses*. 26 vols. Vol. 11, 266-72. Liverpool and London, England: Latter-day Saints Book Depot, 1853-1886. Reprint, Salt Lake City, UT: Bookcraft, 1966.

———. 1867. "How divisions were introduced into the Christian world; the Gospel perfect, but its teachers imperfect; the priesthood and its restoration (Discourse delivered 23 June 1867)." In *Journal of Discourses*. 26 vols. Vol. 12, 64-71. Liverpool and London, England: Latter-day Saints Book Depot, 1853-1886. Reprint, Salt Lake City, UT: Bookcraft, 1966.

———. 1867. "Remarks delivered in the Bowery, Great Salt Lake City, 8 April 1867." In *Journal of Discourses*. 26 vols. Vol. 11, 371-75. Liverpool and London, England: Latter-day Saints Book Depot, 1853-1886. Reprint, Salt Lake City, UT: Bookcraft, 1966.

———. 1869. "Discourse delivered in the Tabernacle, Salt Lake City, 14 November 1869." In *Journal of Discourses*. 26 vols. Vol. 13, 150-56. Liverpool and London, England: Latter-day Saints Book Depot, 1853-1886. Reprint, Salt Lake City, UT: Bookcraft, 1966.

———. 1870. "Discourse delivered in the new Tabernacle, Salt Lake City, 30 October 1870." In *Journal of Discourses*. 282 vols. Vol. 13, 274-83. Liverpool and London, England: Latter-day Saints Book Depot, 1853-1886. Reprint, Salt Lake City, UT: Bookcraft, 1966.

———. 1870. "Sin; the atonement; good and evil; the Kingdom of God (Remarks delivered in the Tabernacle, Ogden City, 10 July 1870)." In *Journal of Discourses*. 26 vols. Vol. 14, 70-73. Liverpool and London, England: Latter-day Saints Book Depot, 1853-1886. Reprint, Salt Lake City, UT: Bookcraft, 1966.

———. 1871. "Remarks delivered in the Tabernacle, Salt Lake City, 14 May 1871." In *Journal of Discourses*. 26 vols. Vol. 14, 114-18. Liverpool and London, England: Latter-day Saints Book Depot, 1853-1886. Reprint, Salt Lake City, UT: Bookcraft, 1966.

———. 1872. "The fulness of the Gospel; its power to unite; its comprehensiveness; definition of its priesthood; condition of apostates." In *Journal of Discourses*. 26 vols. Vol. 15, 121-29. Liverpool and London, England: Latter-day Saints Book Depot, 1853-1884. Reprint, Salt Lake City, UT: Bookcraft, 1966.

———. 1872. "Increase of Saints since Joseph Smith's death; Joseph Smith's sons; resurrection and Millennial work (Remarks delivered at Farmington, Saturday Afternoon, 24 August 1872)." In *Journal of Discourses*. 26 vols. Vol. 15, 135-39. Liverpool and London, England: Latter-day Saints Book Depot, 1853-1886. Reprint, Salt Lake City, UT: Bookcraft, 1966.

———. 1873. "Discourse delivered in the Bowery, Logan City, Saturday Afternoon, 28 June 1873." In *Journal of Discourses*. 26 vols. Vol. 16, 63-71. Liverpool and London, England: Latter-day Saints Book Depot, 1853-1886. Reprint, Salt Lake City, UT: Bookcraft, 1966.

———. 1873. "The order of Enoch (Remarks delivered in the Bowery, Logan City, Sunday Morning, 29 June 1873)." In *Journal of Discourses*. 26 vols. Vol. 16, 122-23. Liverpool and London, England: Latter-day Saints Book Depot, 1853-1886. Reprint, Salt Lake City, UT: Bookcraft, 1966.

———. 1874. "Discourse delivered in the new Tabernacle, Salt Lake City, Sunday Afternoon, 3 May 1874." In *Journal of Discourses*. 26 vols. Vol. 17, 51-56. Liverpool and London, England: Latter-day Saints Book Depot, 1853-1886. Reprint, Salt Lake City, UT: Bookcraft, 1966.

———. 1874. "Nothing strange or new to live and die; must die in order to be quickened; the world of mankind ignorant of immortality; the righteous should live to enjoy the light of their spirit; all people are the children of

God; they learn by contrast; world to be organized and peopled in future existence (Discourse delivered at the funeral services of Elder Thomas Williams, in the Fourteenth Ward, Assembly Rooms, Salt Lake City, Sunday Morning, 10 July 1874)." In *Journal of Discourses*. 26 vols. Vol. 17, 139-45. Liverpool and London, England: Latter-day Saints Book Depot, 1853-1886. Reprint, Salt Lake City, UT: Bookcraft, 1966.

———. 1876. "Personal revelation the basis of personal knowledge; philosophic view of Creation; apostasy involves disorganization and returns to primitive element; one man power (Discourse by Brigham Young, delivered in the New Tabernacle, Salt Lake City, Sunday Afternoon, September 17, 1876)." In *Journal of Discourses*. 26 vols. Vol. 18, 230-35. Liverpool and London, England: Latter-day Saints Book Depot, 1853-1886. Reprint, Salt Lake City, UT: Bookcraft, 1966.

Young, Frances, Lewis Ayres, and Andrew Louth, eds. *The Cambridge History of Early Christian Literature*. Cambridge, England: Cambridge University Press, 2004.

Youngquist, Paul. *Madness and Blake's Myth*. University Park, PA: The Pennsylvania State University Press, 1989.

Zabkar, Louis V. "The theocracy of Amarna and the doctrine of the Ba." *Journal of Near Eastern Studies* 13 (1954): 87.

Zagzebski, Linda Trinkaus. *The Dilemma of Freedom and Foreknowledge*. Oxford, England: Oxford University Press, 1991.

Zilio-Grandi, Ida. "Paradise in the Koran and in the Muslim exegetical tradition." In *The Earthly Paradise: The Garden of Eden from Antiquity to Modernity*, edited by F. Regina Psaki and Charles Hindley. *International Studies in Formative Christianity and Judaism*, 75-90. Binghamton, NY: Academic Studies in the History of Judaism, Global Publications, State University of New York at Binghamton, 2002.

Zimmer Gunsul Frasca Partnership. *Building the Church of Jesus Christ of Latter-day Saints Conference Center*. New York City, NY: Edzioni Press, 2002.

Zimmerli, Walther. 1969. *Ezekiel 2: A Commentary on the Book of the Prophet Ezekiel Chapters 25-48*. Translated by James D. Martin. Edited by Paul D. Hanson and Leonard J. Greenspoon. *Hermeneia—A Critical and Historical Commentary on the Bible*, eds. Frank Moore Cross, Klaus Baltzer, Paul D. Hanson, S. Dean McBride, Jr. and Roland E. Murphy. Philadelphia, PA: Fortress Press, 1983.

"Ziziphus." In *Wikipedia*. http://en.wikipedia.org/wiki/Ziziphus (accessed July 30, 2007).

Zlotowitz, Gedaliah, ed. *The Schottenstein Edition Talmud Bavli*. 73 vols. Brooklyn, NY: ArtScroll/Mesorah, 1990-2004.

———, ed. *The Schottenstein Edition Talmud Yerushalmi*. Brooklyn, NY: ArtScroll/Mesorah, 2005-.

Zlotowitz, Rabbi Meir, and Rabbi Nosson Scherman, eds. 1977. *Bereishis/Genesis: A New Translation with a Commentary Anthologized from Talmudic, Midrashic and Rabbinic Sources*. 2nd ed. Two vols. *ArtScroll Tanach Series*, ed. Rabbi Nosson Scherman and Rabbi Meir Zlotowitz. Brooklyn, NY: Mesorah Publications, 1986.

Zornberg, Avivah Gottlieb. *Genesis: The Beginning of Desire*. Philadelphia, PA: Jewish Publication Society, 1995.

"Zoroaster." In *Encyclopedia Britannica Online*. http://www.britannica.com/eb/article-8138 (accessed July 16, 2007).

Zucker, Louis C. "Joseph Smith as a student of Hebrew." *Dialogue* 3, no. 2 (1968): 41-55.

COLOR PLATES
for Selected Figures

FIGURE 0-4: *Moses Indignant at the Golden Calf.* William Blake (see p. 6).

FIGURE 0-5: *Rock Sculpted with Ark and Annunciation.* William Blake (see p. 6).

FIGURE 1-2: *Jacob's Ladder.* William Blake (see p. 34).

FIGURE 1-3: *Ascent.* David Linn (see p. 34).

поклан
ѧ
ть сѧ авраамъ
съ ан҃глмь предъ
пртлмь б҃иимь
на н҃бех҃

FIGURE 2-7: *The Creation of Adam (see p. 88)*

FIGURE 3-3: *The Four and Twenty Elders.* William Blake (see p. 137).

FIGURE 3-2: *The Creation of Light.* Gaetano Previati (see p. 136).

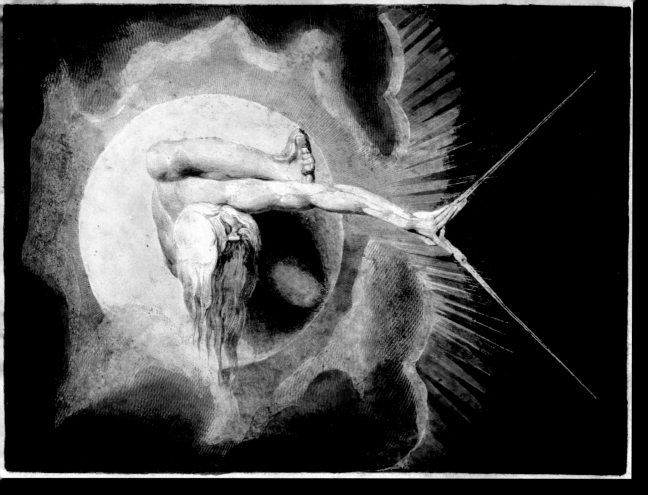

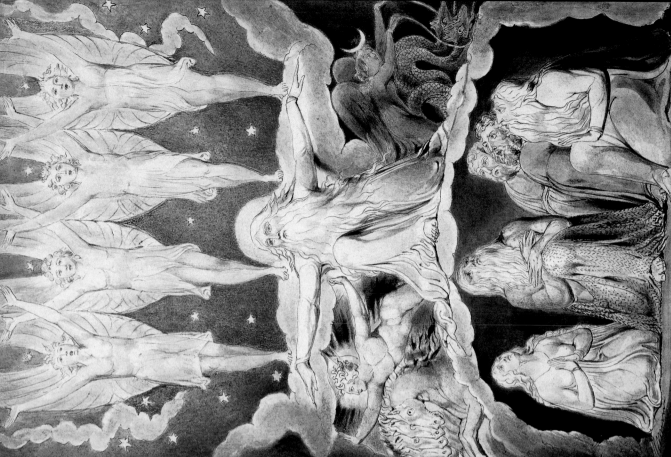

FIGURE 4-5: *When the Morning Stars Sang Together.* William Blake (see p. 223).

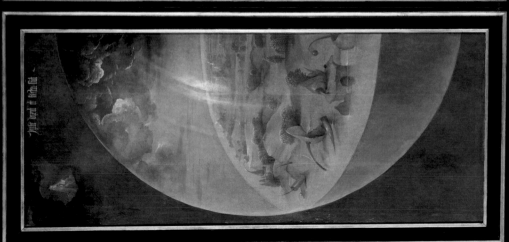

FIGURE 4-3: *The Third Day of Creation.* Hieronymus Bosch (see p. 218).

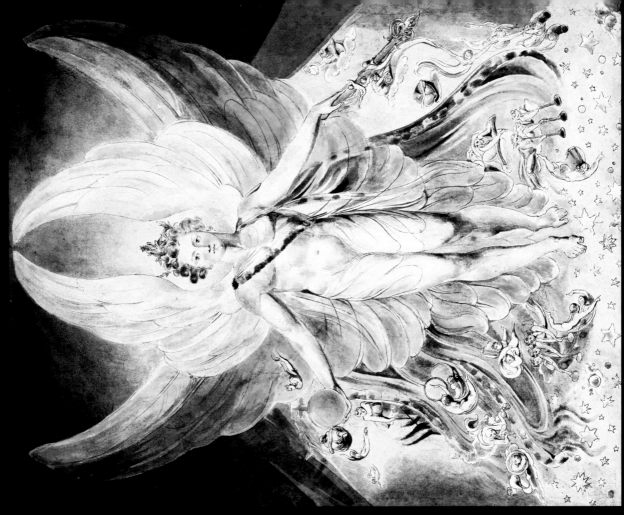

FIGURE 4-6: *Satan in his Original Glory.* William Blake (see p. 224).

FIGURE 4-8: *The Fall of the Rebel Angels.* Domenico Beccafumi (see p. 226).

FIGURE 4-15: *The Rebuke of Adam and Eve.* Domenico Zampieri (see p. 232).

FIGURE 4-16: *Expulsion of Adam and Eve.* Michelangelo Buonarroti (see p. 233).

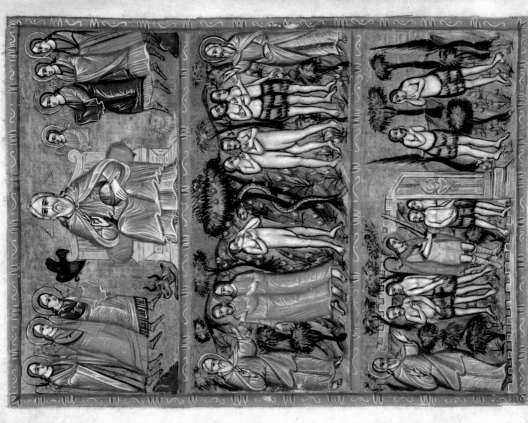

FIGURE 4-17: *Cherubim and the Flaming Sword.* J. Kirk Richards (see p. 233).

FIGURE 5-2: *The Archangel Michael Subduing Satan.* Raphael (see p. 326).

FIGURE 4-21: *The Clothing of Adam and Eve.* William Blake (see p. 238).

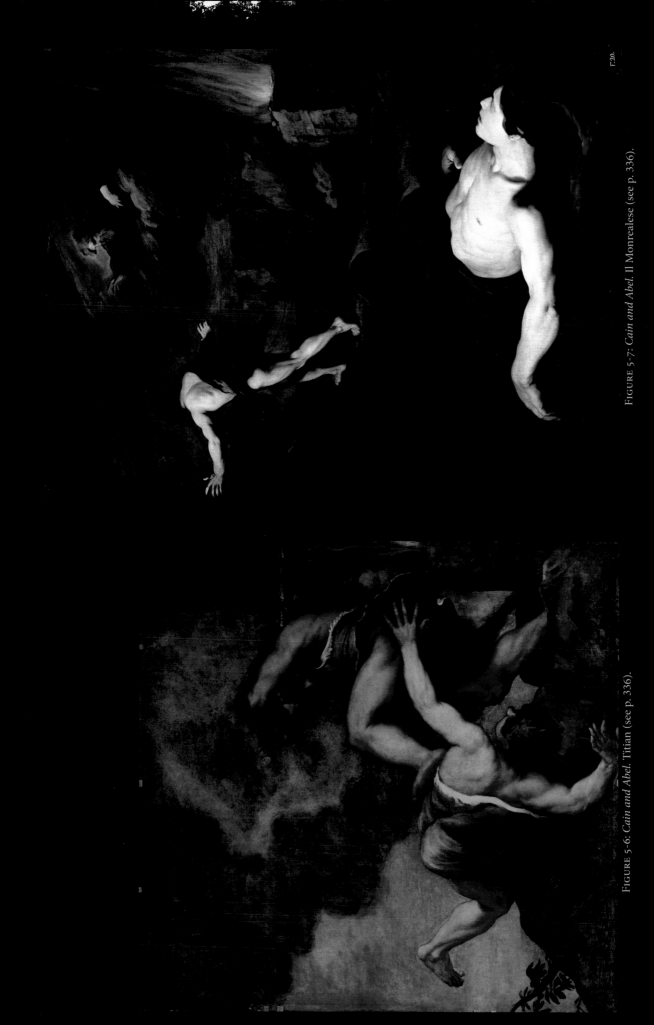

F. 20.

Figure 5-7: *Cain and Abel.* Il Monrealese (see p. 336).

Figure 5-6: *Cain and Abel.* Titian (see p. 336).

FIGURE 5-8: *Cain, Based on Victor Hugo's Poem.* Cormon (see p. 337).

FIGURE 5-10: *The Holy Trinity.* Andrei Rublev (see p. 340).

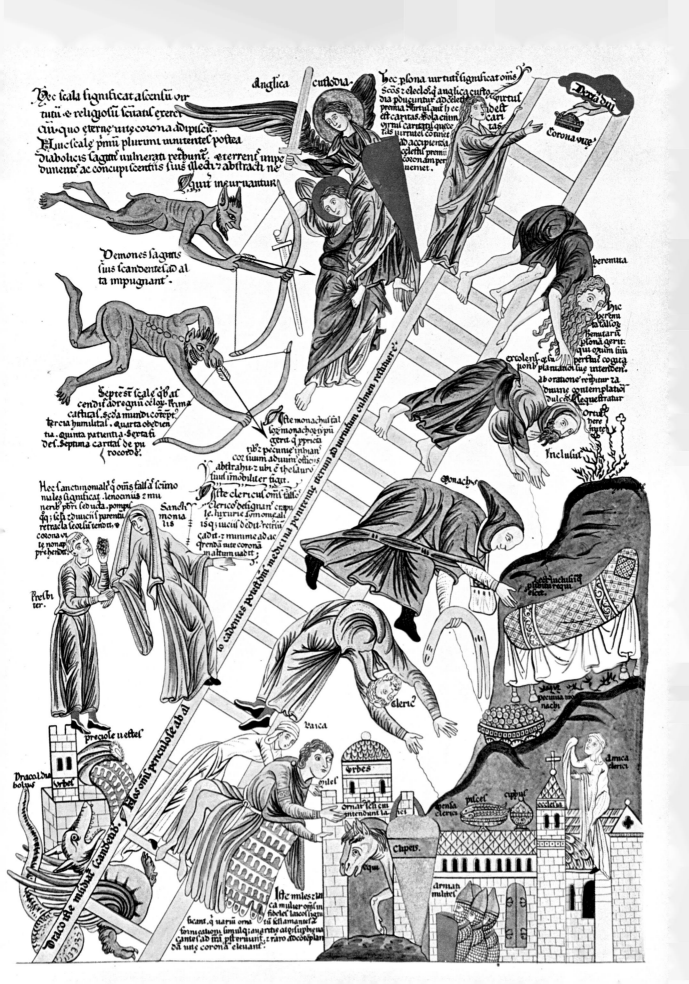

FIGURE 6-7: *The Return of the Prodigal Son*, Pompeo Batoni (see p. 465).

FIGURE 6-5: *Toward Immortality and Eternal Youth*, Albert-Dominique Roze (see p. 463).

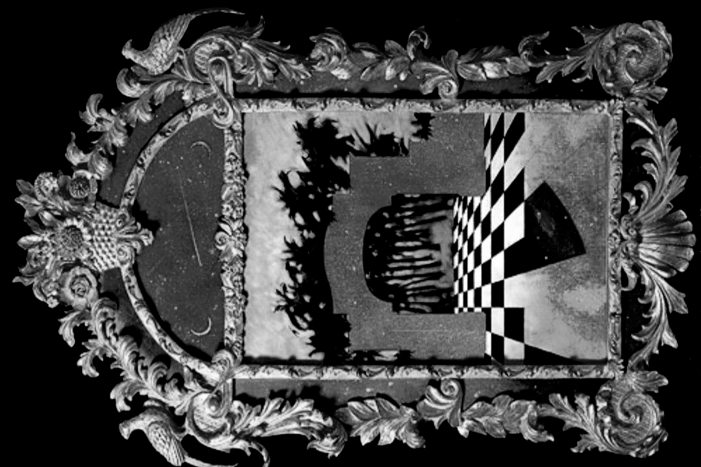

FIGURE 6-9: *Gate to Paradise.* Wulf E. Barsch (see p. 468).

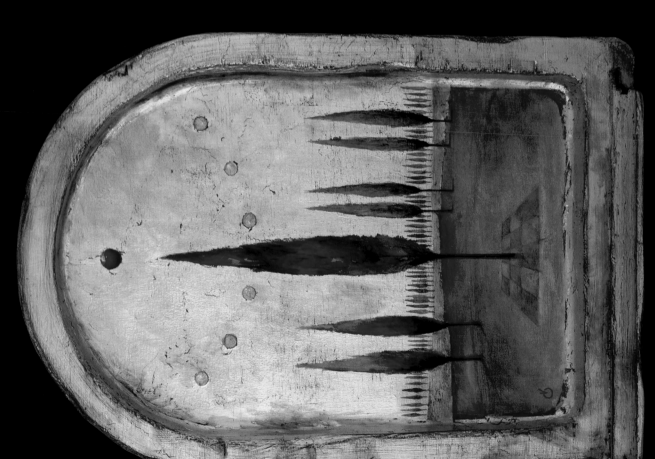

FIGURE E19-3: *Generations.* Valeriano Ugolini (see p. 568).

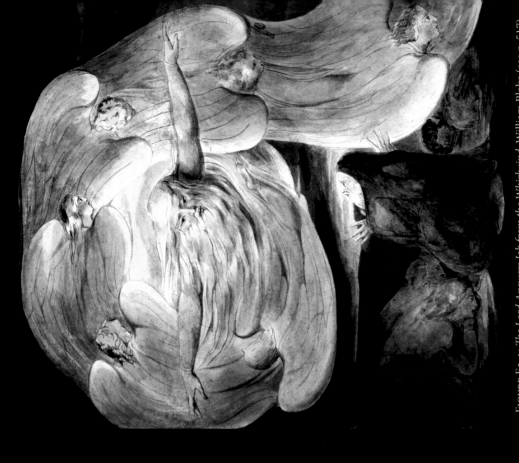

Figure E2-1: *The Lord Answers Job from the Whirlwind*. William Blake (see p. 517).

ABEL MELCHISEDEC

FIGURE F20.1. Mosaic from the Basilica of St Vitale (see p. 573)

MELCHISEDEC

MELCHISEDEC SCM VETVS SCRIB VRADEMON STRAT
NVS INLVSTRISSE NIOR HACHABEL

FIGURE F20.2. Mosaic from the Basilica of St Apollinare in Classe (see p. 573)

FIGURE E24-1: *The Primaeval Giants Sunk in the Soil.* William Blake (see p. 588).

FIGURE 6-12: *Descent of Christ into Limbo.* Andrea da Firenze (see p. 471).

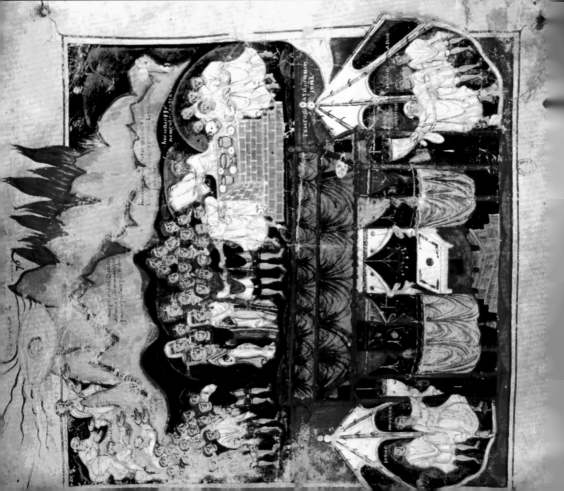

+SCS BALTHASSAR +SCS MELCHIOR +SCS GASPAR

FIGURE 53-5: *The Three Magi.* (see p. 673).

FIGURE E53-6: *Funerary Chamber Adjoining the Grotto of the Teachings.* (see p. 674).

IN GOD'S IMAGE AND LIKENESS

FIGURE E53-9: *The Paradise Altar of Ramberg.* (see p. 680).

FIGURE E53-7: *Telesterion at Eleusis.* (see p. 676).

АПТНУЄ ВЪ ЖА АНГ И ... ИМА ПРИІАТЪ
АНГ Л Ъ ДЄСНОЮ РУ ... КОЮ · ИВСАДИ МА
НАКРИЛО ГОЛУБИНО ... ДЄСНОЕ · А САМЪ СѢДЄ
НАКРИЛО ГОРЛИУЮ ... ЩЄЕ · ИВОЗНЄСЄ ІА
НАІ ҐРА ИПЛАМЄНИ ... ОГНЄ МАТО · ИВЗ ИДО
ХОПЛѢНА ВЪ ВЫСОТУ ·

FIGURE E55-3: *Itzpapalotl and the Broken Tree of Tamoanchan.* (see p. 698).

FIGURE E53-15: *The Cycle of Ezekiel from the Synagogue at Dura Europos.* (see p. 688)

FIGURE E54-2: *Noah Sees the Ark in Vision.* (see p. 696).

IN GOD'S IMAGE AND LIKENESS

INDEXES

About the Indexes

Thumbnail Index to Figures

The thumbnail index is designed to help the reader search visually for a desired figure or table. Each of these is also listed alphabetically by title in the *Topical Index* under the heading of "Figures." Additionally, many figures are listed under the name of the appropriate artist, photographer, topic, or place name.

Scripture Index

Entries in this index reference pages where a given scriptural passage is mentioned, referenced, quoted, or discussed.

The original plans for the book also included an index to citations of ancient texts. However, it was suddenly realized during the indexing process that the number and complexity of the entries had exceeded the capacity of the indexing software. Schedule constraints required a quick switch to manual methods for the remainder of the work—a tedious and inevitably error-prone process. Regrettably, as a result of these last-minute complications, plans for an index to ancient texts had to be abandoned.

Index of Latter-day Prophets

This index lists references to and quotations from statements attributed to Presidents of the Church of Jesus Christ of Latter-day Saints, either made before or during their respective presidencies. First Presidency statements are attributed to the individual who was serving as President at the time. The most specific date that could be found for each statement is listed; some dates, of course, are approximate or unknown. Dates of first publication are used in lieu of more specific dates when necessary.

Topical Index

Topics, figures, and names of selected individuals discussed in the text are listed alphabetically. Titles of many of the ancient texts described in the *Annotated Bibliography* are also included. Special attention has been given to entries for cross-cutting or obscure topics that may be difficult to find by browsing the *Table of Contents*. Because most readers will already be familiar with the central thread of Judeo-Christian themes and sources that run through the book, relatively greater space in the index is allowed for entries relating to other cultural and religious groups. No attempt has been made to exhaustively index individuals or topics that are ubiquitous in the text (e.g., "Eve," "God," "heaven," "revelation").

Thumbnail Index to Figures (PART 1 OF 5)

Figure 0-2, Page 3.
Time Sequence of Joseph Smith Translation of Old Testament

Figure 1-3, Page 34.
Ascent, 1993.
David Linn, 1959-

Figure P-2, Page xxiv.
Inflatable Cathedral, 1978.
David Macaulay, 1946-

Figure 0-1, Page xxxvi.
Old Testament Manuscript 1
Page 1, 1830.

Figure 1-2, Page 34.
Jacob's Ladder, ca. 1800.
William Blake, 1757–1827.

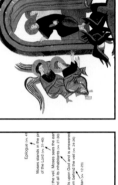

Figure 1-7, Page 38.
Abraham and the Angel Yahoel
Approach the Throne of God.

Figure P-1, Page xx. See also **Figure
0-3, Page 5.** Go With
Me, 1997. Liz Lemon Swindle.

Figure 1-1, Page 32.
Get Thee Hence, Satan, 1875.
Carl H. Bloch, 1834–1890.

Figure 1-6, Page 37.
Outline of the heavenly ascent
pattern in Moses 1.

Figure 0-5, Page 6.
Sculpted w/ Ark, Annunciation.
William Blake, 1757–1827.

Figure 1-5, Page 36.
Relativity, 1953.
M. C. Escher, 1898–1972.

Frontispiece. See also **Figure
0-6, p. 11.** First Parents, 2005.
Jay Bryant Ward, 1971 -

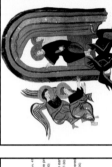

Figure 0-4, Page 6.
Indignant at Golden Calf, 1800.
William Blake, 1757–1827.

Figure 1-4, Page 35.
Dog Code, 1987.
Brian Kershisnik, 1962-

INDEXES

Figure 2-5, Page 87.
The Third Day of Creation.
M. C. Escher, 1898-1972.

Figure 2-4, Page 87.
The Second Day of Creation.
M. C. Escher, 1898-1972.

Figure 2-3, Page 86.
Separation of Light, Darkness.
Michelangelo Buonarotti.

Figure 2-2, Page 84.
The First Day of Creation, 1925.
M. C. Escher, 1898-1972.

Figure 2-1, Page 82.
Creation of Sun, Moon, Planets.
Michelangelo Buonarotti.

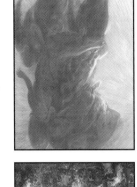

Figure 3-2, Page 136.
The Creation of Light, 1913.
Gaetano Previati, 1852-1920.

Figure 3-1, Page 132.
The Garden of Eden, 1612.
Jan Breughel, the Elder.

Figure 2-8, Page 89.
The Creation of Eve, 1510.
Michelangelo Buonarotti.

Figure 2-7, Page 88.
The Creation of Adam, 1510.
Michelangelo Buonarotti.

Figure 2-6, Page 87.
The Fourth Day of Creation.
M. C. Escher, 1898-1972.

Figure 3-7, Page 143.
Adam's Peak, 1780.
Antoine-François Prévost.

Figure 3-6, Page 139.
Behold Your Little Ones, 1983.
David Lindsley, 1954-

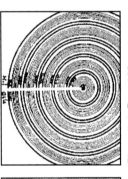

Figure 3-5, Page 138.
A Depiction of Ein Sof and the
Encircling Angelic Hierarchies.

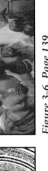

Figure 3-4, Page 138.
The Great Chain of Being, 1579.
Didacus Valades.

Figure 3-3, Page 137.
The Four and Twenty Elders.
William Blake, 1757-1827.

INDEXES

Thumbnail Index to Figures (PART 2 OF 5)

Figure 3-8, Page 145.
Court of Palms Mural at Mari. Syria, ca. 1750 BCE.

Figure 3-9, Page 146.
Topography, Eden and Temple. Michael P. Lyon, 1952–

Figure 3-10, Page 147.
Sacred Stones Emerging from Waters. John M. Lundquist.

Figure 3-11, Page 149.
Holy of Holies Solomon's Temple. Juan Bautista Villalpando.

Figure 4-1, Page 214.
Expulsion from Garden Eden. Thomas Cole, 1801–1848.

Figure 4-2, Page 217.
God Creating the Universe. William Blake, 1757–1827.

Figure 4-3, Page 218.
The Third Day of Creation. Hieronymus Bosch.

Figure 4-4, Page 219.
Masjid al-Haram at Night.

Figure 4-5, Page 223.
When the Morning Stars Sang Together, 1820. William Blake.

Figure 4-6, Page 224.
Satan in His Original Glory. William Blake, 1757–1827.

Figure 4-7, Page 225.
Adam Enthroned, Angels Prostrating Themselves before Him.

Figure 4-8, Page 226.
The Fall of the Rebel Angels. Domenico Beccafumi.

Figure 4-9, Page 227.
The Fall of the Rebel Angels. Pieter Bruegel, the Elder.

Figure 4-10, Page 228.
God Creating Eve, Instructing Adam and Eve, 12th century.

Figure 4-11, Page 230.
Anubis Leads Nakht Towards the Entrance to Other World.

INDEXES

Figure 4-16, Page 233. Expulsion of Adam and Eve. Michelangelo Buonarroti.

Figure 4-15, Page 232. The Rebuke of Adam and Eve. Domenico Zampieri.

Figure 4-14, Page 232. Eve, After the Transgression, 1869. Eugène Delaplanche.

Figure 4-13, Page 231. Rameses II in the *Ished-tree*, 13th Century BCE.

Figure 4-12, Page 230. Palm Tree Growing over "Adam's Grave" in Hebron.

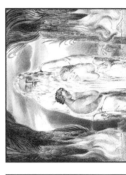

Figure 4-21, Page 238. The Clothing of Adam and Eve. William Blake, 1757-1827.

Figure 4-20, Page 237. Sacred Tree on the Apron of Charlemagne, eighth century.

Figure 4-19, Page 235. Three Zones of Sacredness Within Eden.

Figure 4-18, Page 234. The Expulsion of Adam and Eve, 1646.

Figure 4-17, Page 233. Cherubim and the Flaming Sword. J. Kirk Richards, 1977-

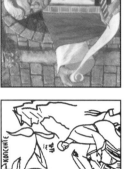

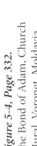

Figure 5-5, Page 334. The Foolish Man and the Creditor: Jerry Harston, 1943-

Figure 5-4, Page 332. The Bond of Adam, Church Mural, Voronet, Moldavia.

Figure 5-3, Page 330. How the Devil Deceived Eve, early 14th century. Lutwin.

Figure 5-2, Page 326. The Archangel Michael Subduing Satan. Raffaello Sanzi.

Figure 5-1, Page 322. The Offering of Abel and Cain. Jan van Eyck, ca. 1395-1441.

Thumbnail Index to Figures (PART 3 OF 5)

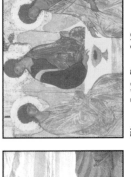

Figure 5-6, Page 336.
Cain and Abel, ca. 1540.
Tiziano Vecellio (Titian).

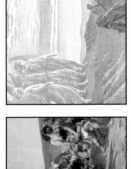

Figure 5-7, Page 336.
Cain and Abel. Pietro Novelli (Il
Monrealese), 1603-1647.

Figure 5-8, Page 337.
Cain, Based on Victor Hugo's
Poem. Fernand-Anne Piestre.

Figure 5-11, Page 343.
The Two Ways.

Figure 5-9, Page 339.
Abraham Entertains Three
Strangers. Paul Gustave Doré.

Figure 5-13, Page 351.
The Ladder of Virtues, twelfth
century. Herrad of Hohenbourg.

Figure 5-12, Page 346.
The Devil Approaches Jabez
Stone. Harold Denison.

Figure 6-3, Page 461.
The Quest of Seth for the Oil of
Mercy, 1351-1360.

Figure 5-10, Page 340.
The Holy Trinity, ca. 1408-1425.
Andrei Rublev.

Figure 6-2, Page 457.
Church History Sites in Western
Missouri, 1831-1839.

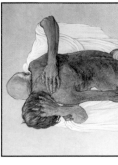

Figure 6-1, Page 454.
Adam and His Children.
Piero della Francesca.

Figure 6-5, Page 463.
Toward Immortality.
Albert-Dominique Roze.

Figure 6-4, Page 462.
Ampulla 11, "Oil from the Tree
of Life," 5th-6th century.

Figure 6-7, Page 465.
The Return of the Prodigal Son.
Pompeo Batoni, 1708-1787.

Figure 6-6, Page 464.
The Forgiving Father.
Frank Wesley, 1923-2002.

Figure 6-8, Page 466.
Romans 5:10-11, William Tyndale's Translation, 1526.

Figure 6-9, Page 468.
Gate to Paradise. Wulf E. Barsch, 1943-

Figure 6-10, Page 469.
Drawing of a Barque Shrine, Karnak. Michael P. Lyon, 1952-

Figure 6-11, Page 470.
Stela of Tantamani, Karnak. Michael P. Lyon.

Figure 6-12, Page 471.
Descent of Christ into Limbo. Andrea da Firenze.

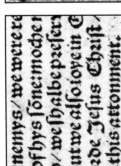

Figure E12-1, Page 549.
The Flight of the Little Prince. Antoine de Saint Exupéry.

Figure 6-13, Page 472.
Charity with an Anchor, 1876.

Figure 6-14, Page 473.
The Woman at the Tomb and the Ascension, ca. 400.

Figure E12-2, Page 550.
Chiastic Structure, The Little Prince. Laurent de Galembert.

igure E1-1, Page 514.
Shabaka Stone, ca. 710 BCE.

Figure E19-1, Page 566.
William W. Phelps. Author of "If You Could Hie to Kolob."

Figure E2-1, Page 517.
The Lord Answers Job from the Whirlwind. William Blake.

Figure E19-2, Page 566.
Ralph Vaughan Williams. Arranger of "Kingsfold."

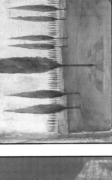

Figure E8-1, Page 542.
Creation Sequence, 1351-1360.

Figure E19-3, Page 568.
Generations, 2005 Valeriano Ugolini, 1948-

INDEXES

Thumbnail Index to Figures (PART 4 OF 5)

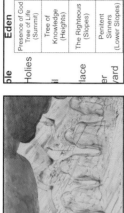

Figure E20-1, Page 573.
Mosaic from the Basilica of St. Vitale, ca. 538-542 CE.

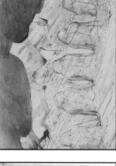

Figure E20-2, Page 573.
Mosaic from the Basilica of St. Apollinare in Classe, ca. 520 CE.

Figure E20-3, Page 574.
Linen Cloth, ca. 300-400.

Figure E24-1, Page 588.
The Primaeval Giants Sunk in the Soil. William Blake.

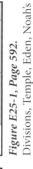

Figure E25-1, Page 592.
Divisions, Temple, Eden, Noah's Ark, Sinai. Ephrem the Syrian.

Figure E25-2, Page 593.
Adam and Eve Enthroned in Paradise, 16th-century.

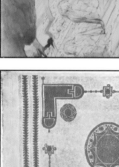

Figure E36-1, Page 615.
Elevation of the Cross, 1948.

Figure E36-2, Page 616.
The Chapel of Adam, ca. 1167. Laura E. Hoffman, 1961-.

Figure E37-1, Page 619.
Luther's 1534 German Translation of Genesis 4:1.

Figure E41-1, Page 627.
Excerpt from Preface to *Milton*. William Blake.

Figure E42-1, Page 633.
Nebuchadnezzar, 1795. William Blake, 1757-1827.

Figure E43-1, Page 634.
Portrait of Wolfgang Amadeus Mozart. Barbara Krafft.

Figure E44-1, Page 635.
Miranda — The Tempest. John William Waterhouse.

Figure E50-1, Page 657.
Fu Xi with His Consort Nü Gua, ca. 689.

Figure E53-1, Page 668.
The Mysteries of Aaron, Moses, and Melchizedek.

Figure E53-6, Page 674. Funerary Chamber Adjoining Grotto of Teachings, Eleona.

Figure E53-11, Page 683. Introduction of Adam into Paradise, thirteenth century.

MOSES IN THE SPIRIT WORLD (vv. 3-8)	
God to show a vision of eternity:	I w... ha...
Reason for God's favor:	Cf. ear...
The prophet is commissioned:	I h...

Figure E54-1, Page 694. Table of Parallels with the *Apocalypse of Abraham.*

Figure E53-5, Page 673. The Three Magi, Basilica of St. Apollinare Nuovo, 6th century.

Figure E53-10, Page 682. Plangon Exchanges Handclasps with Her Mother.

Figure E53-15, Page 688. The Cycle of Ezekiel from the Synagogue at Dura Europos.

Figure E53-4, Page 672. The Nativity of Christ, 15th century.

Figure E53-9, Page 680. The Paradise Altar of Bamberg, twelfth century.

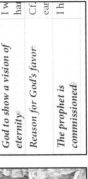

Figure E53-14, Page 686. Detail from the Robail-Navier Family Sepulchre, ca. 1832.

Figure E53-3, Page 671. Mount Sinai and Tabernacle, *Tours Pentateuch,* ca. 600.

Figure E53-8. Page 679. King David Prays Before the Ark, ca. 1250.

Figure E53-13, Page 684. Abraham and the Angel Yahoel Ascend.

Figure E53-2, Page 670. Adam and Eve Outside Paradise, 12th century.

Figure E53-7, Page 676. Telesterion at Eleusis, Stephen T. Whitlock, 1951-

Figure E53-12, Page 684. The Angel Yahoel Takes Abraham by the Hand.

Thumbnail Index to Figures (PART 5 OF 5)

Guilty	Seducer
Inextli	
Xochiquetzal	Tezcatlipoca d animal
Tlazoteotl Ixcuina	Tezcatlipoca d
	Huhuecoyotl
Itzpapalotl	

Figure E55-1, Page 697.
The Transgressions at Tamoanchan.

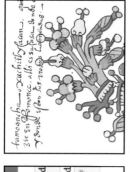

Figure E55-2, Page 698.
Broken Tree of Tamoanchan, Codex Telleriano-Remensis.

Figure E55-3, Page 698.
Itzpapalotl and the Broken Tree of Tamoanchan, Codex Borgia.

Figure E55-4, Page 700.
Anthropomorhic Tree, Codex Boturini.

Figure E54-2, Page 696.
Noah Sees the Ark in Vision.

Figure B-1, Page 872.
Pact and Pax: The Kushta. 1956. E.S. Drower, 1879-1972.

Figure E55-5, Page 700.
Man Emerging from a Split Tree Trunk, Codex Vindobonesis.

SCRIPTURE INDEX

INDEXES

INDEX OF LATTER-DAY PROPHETS

TOPICAL INDEX

A

Aaron ... 520-521, 661, 664
mystery of ... 664
sons of ... 520–521
washing, anointing, and clothing of ... 520, 661

Aaronic Priesthood ... 668, 765.
SEE ALSO Priesthood
appendage to the Melchizedek Priesthood ... 765

Abbaton, Discourse on ... 844

Abel ... 322, 335-338, 345, 369-370, 372, 380-381, 573, 617-621, 666, 670, 680, 734-737, 866-867.
SEE ALSO Cain
as a redeemer ... 617–621
as a red heifer ... 618, 735
as a type of Jesus Christ ... 617
as a prototypical Mandaean priest and baptizer ... 617
as the "righteous" one in the Epistle to the Hebrews ... 666
hearkened ... 370
holds the keys of his dispensation ... 618
holy priesthood traced through ... 491
"keeper of sheep" ... 370
Mandaean stories about... 866-867
meaning of name ... 369
murder of ... 335-338, 380-381
  illustrations ... 670
purported salvific role of ... 475, 617–621, 734–737
sacrifice of ... 345, 372
  illustrations ... 322, 573, 670, 680
special birth circumstances ... 736
swearing by the holy blood of ... 618, 734
"walked in holiness" ... 376

Abel and Cain, History of ... 845

Abraham ... 4, 13, 15, 26-27, 30, 33, 38, 42, 49-50, 61-63, 78, 84, 127, 137, 190, 201-202, 209, 212, 219, 221, 230, 273, 298, 300-302, 309, 329, 339-340, 357, 359, 367-368, 377, 379, 382, 393, 410, 421, 435, 439-441, 444, 449, 464, 470-471, 478-480, 483, 485, 487, 491, 495, 500, 519, 521-523, 584, 606, 608, 632, 645, 647, 651, 664-667, 669, 680, 684, 694-696, 704-705, 716, 739, 744, 749, 753, 762, 766-768, 776, 781, 884, 901.
SEE ALSO *Abraham, Apocalypse of;* Book of Abraham; *Codex Sylvester*
astronomy of ... 137
dream of cedar and date palm ... 209. SEE ALSO Palm tree: conversation of
entertains three messengers ... 339, 340, 435, 439-441
  illustrations ... 339, 340
hospitality of ... 339, 606
  illustrations ... 339, 340
near sacrifice of Isaac ... 523, 716
  illustrations ... 573, 680
oak or terebinth of ... 440-441
religion of, suppressed ... 665
Satan interrupts the worship of ... 435
seed of ... 521

Abraham, Apocalypse of ... 694-696, 818. SEE ALSO *Codex Sylvester;* Vision of Moses: compared to *Apocalypse of Abraham*
first English translation of, published by the Church ... 695
rejects possibility of seeing God ... 696

Abraham, Testament of ... 819

Adah and Zillah ... 393, 395-396

Adam. SEE ALSO Adam-ondi-Ahman; Ancient of Days; Chapel of Adam; Cheirograph of Adam; Clothing; Eve; Fall of Adam and Eve; Transgression of Adam and Eve
Adam becomes Adam when he begins an ancestral record ... 196, 481
apron ... 258-259
as a type of God ... 603
as an archetypical Levite ... 173
as the archetypical human ... 203, 327-328, 434
"blessed God" ... 363
"bone of my bones" ... 182, 183
book of ... 456, 478-479, 480-481
  Egyptian traditions ... 478
  Islamic traditions ... 478-479
burial place ... 614, 616, 641, 669–670, 733, 734, 749, 767, 767–768. SEE ALSO Cave of Treasures

photograph ... 230
"called upon the name of the Lord" ... 355-357, 362, 367
Chinese analogue to ... 654, 755
commandment forbidding the Tree of Knowledge ... 174-176
confession of ... 261-263
  illustration ... 232
  "in the cool of the day" ... 259-260
  "courtyard" as the place of ... 260
  "where goest thou?" ... 261-262
confusion regarding identity and roles of ... 582–584, 725
consequences of transgression ... 270-273
creation of ... 88, 111-116, 156-159, 273. SEE ALSO Origin of Man
  idea of transplantation ... 204-205
  in an "intermediate state" ... 313
  in the "image and likeness" of God ... 10-11, 23-24, 113-114, 124, 130, 315-316, 481-482, 501. SEE ALSO Deification; Exaltation; Perfect, be ye therefore; God: man in image and likeness of
  place of ... 162, 669, 766–767
  purported androgyny ... 115
cursing of the ground ... 270-271
death ... 483-484
"deep sleep" ... 89, 180-181
description of, as "beautiful" ... 433, 482
"dominion" of ... 114, 116-117, 354, 725
"dust thou wast" ... 273
extracanonical literature about ... 327, 601–602
  ritual origins of ... 329
"first" commandments given to ... 246, 358
"first flesh upon the earth" ... 159, 210
forgetfulness ... 180-181
hides ... 231, 260-261
historicity of ... 553, 718
Holy Ghost falls upon ... 362
illustration of Eve, and child ... Frontispiece, 11
"in the day thou eatest" ... 175
"knew" Eve ... 354-355, 367, 475
language of ... 479
long life of ... 175, 482-483
Mandaean stories about ... 866
meaning of name ... 66-67
mourns because of Cain ... 376

as a prototype of the Menorah ... 163

as a representation, in Lehi's dream, of the fruits of the Atonement ... 277

as a representation of embodied deity, the Messiah ... 163, 188-189

as a representation of eternal life ... 163, 175

as a representation of kings and righteous individuals ... 163-164, 188-189, 248, 752

as a representation of Noah and his sons ... 726

as a representation of the Savior's sanctifying power ... 295-296

as a Tree of Souls ... 228
  illustration ... 228

as an almond tree ... 165

as an olive tree ... 164-165

as the kingdom of God ... 248

as wheat ... 442

associated with birds ... 247-248

associated with mother-goddess figures ... 164, 165, 166, 231, 261, 312

fruit of
  equated to the bread and waters of life ... 341
  fragrances to be "in their bones" ... 282
  like white grapes ... 165, 189
  sweet ... 166
  white and in shape like a chestnut bur ...165

God sought to protect Adam and Eve from premature access to the ... 230-234, 276-278, 319-320

handholds leading to the ... 143, 206-208, 473, 505-506
  illustrations ... 143, 473

imparts knowledge of divine things ... 591

initially hidden from Adam and Eve ... 167, 168, 591, 727–728

in Chinese traditions ... 654, 657

in Islamic tradition ... 168, 261, 729, 749–748

in Kabbalah, associated with primordial unity ... 127, 167, 758
  to be reunited ... 779

in Lehi's dream ... 166, 277, 473, 506

in Manichaean tradition ... 728

in Mesoamerican tradition ... 699–700

"in the midst of the garden" ... 167-168

in Zoroastrian tradition ... 168, 858-859

intertwined ... 168, 591, 657, 727–728

king depicted as tending ... 164

like the sun ... 189, 591

locus of throne ... 225, 593, 731

originally in Holy of Holies ... 658, 755–756

over "Adam's Grave" ...230

question of whether, eaten of by Adam before the Fall ... 175, 276-277

Satan seeks for Adam's premature access to ... 229-231, 248-250, 319-320, 580

speaks mysteries to Enoch ... 209

twofold, in book of Revelation ... 778

way of the ... 282, 357

went to the south ... 778

Tree of Mercy ... 164-167, 189, 210, 640-641, 729. SEE ALSO Menorah; SEE ALSO Olive tree; Seth: quest for the oil of mercy; Tree of Life

as a third tree that sprouted up after the Fall ... 166-167, 210, 461 (illustration)

as an olive tree ... 164-165, 189, 210

in Islamic tradition ... 729

Tree of Souls

illustration ... 228

Tree, split ... 127, 165, 167, 231, 260-261, 312, 632, 693, 698, 700, 758, 779. SEE ALSO Tree of Knowledge; Tree of Life

in Ascension of Isaiah ... 231, 260, 693

in Islamic tradition ... 231, 260

in Kabbalistic tradition ... 127, 167, 758, 779

in Mesoamerican tradition
  broken tree of Tamoanchan ... 698
  representation of birth or rebirth ... 231, 260, 700
  representation of migration of original ancestors ... 260, 700

in story of Nebuchadnezzar ... 632

in story of Osiris ... 165, 231, 261, 312, 632
  associated with the "horizon" ... 231, 312
  illustration ... 231

Tree, World. SEE ALSO *Axis mundi;* SEE ALSO Tree of Life

as axis mundi ... 571

in Chinese tradition ... 728

in Mesoamerican tradition ... 700

Truth ... xxv, xxxiv-xxxv, 190-193, 713, 717. SEE ALSO Ancient texts: value of; Science

conviction of, takes priority over question of happiness ... 717

gaining knowledge and becoming godlike part of a single process ... 191-192

need to accept from all sources ... xxv, xxxiv–xxxv, 190-191, 713

only the truth need be believed ... 192

religious, in all denominations ... 191

should not be bound by creeds ... 190-191

Tubal Cain ... 393, 394, 397

The Two Ways ... 166, 324, 328-329, 343-344, 413-415, 434, 444

complete parting of the ways in Moses 5-8 ... 324, 343-344
  illustration ... 343

doctrine of ... 166, 328-329

governing structure for the book of Isaiah ... 444

vs. metaphysical dualism ... 434

vs. the two parties ... 413-415

withdrawal of the Shekhinah in stages ... 444

Tyndale, William

appropriateness of archaizing coloration in translation of Hebrew ... 466
  vs. inappropriateness for common everyday Greek of the NT ... 502

greatest of English Bible translators ... 466

introduced "atonement" into his translation ... 466

Romans 5:10-11 in William Tyndale's English Translation of the New Testament ... 466

U

Ugolini, Valeriano
Generations ... 568

Universe ... 65-67, 125, 537-539, 566-570, 716

beginning of ... 125, 537–539, 567. SEE ALSO Creation

future of ... 539, 716

infinite nature of ... 65-66, 67, 566-570

pluralistic nature of Mormon ... 567

Unpardonable sin. SEE Sin: against the Holy Ghost

Urim and Thummim. SEE ALSO Stone

name revealed through ... 706

revelation through ... 300

Uzziah

parallels to Adam and Eve's transgression ... 592